# The
# CHELSEA HOUSE LIBRARY
## *of* LITERARY CRITICISM

_The_

# CHELSEA HOUSE LIBRARY
# _of_ LITERARY CRITICISM

# TWENTIETH-CENTURY
# AMERICAN LITERATURE

_Volume 4_

_General Editor_

## HAROLD BLOOM

1986
CHELSEA HOUSE PUBLISHERS
New York
New Haven      Philadelphia

MANAGING EDITOR
S. T. Joshi

ASSOCIATE EDITORS
Patrick Nielsen Hayden
Teresa Nielsen Hayden
Larson Powell
Daniel Carmi Sherer
Anna Williams

EDITORIAL COORDINATOR
Karyn Gullen Browne

EDITORIAL STAFF
Marie Claire Cebrian
Richard Fumosa
Susan B. Hamburger
Perry King

RESEARCH
Anthony C. Coulter

BIOGRAPHER
Jack Bishop

PICTURE RESEARCH
Emily Miller

DESIGN
Susan Lusk

Printed and bound in the United States of
America.

Library of Congress Cataloging in Publication
Data

Twentieth-century American literature.
(The Chelsea House library of literary
criticism)
Includes bibliographies and indexes.
1. American literature—20th century—
History and criticism—Collected works.
2. Authors, American—20th century—
Biography—Dictionaries. I. Bloom, Harold.
I. Series.
PS221.T834    1986        810'.9'005
84-27430
ISBN 0-87754-804-8 (v. 4)

CHELSEA HOUSE PUBLISHERS

133 Christopher Street, New York, NY 10014
345 Whitney Avenue, New Haven, CT 06510
5014 West Chester Pike, Edgemont, PA 19028

Acknowledgments for selections used in this
volume commence on page 2553.

# CONTENTS

Abbreviations .............................................. vi
Illustrations .............................................. vii
Chester Himes .............................................. 1903
Daniel Hoffman ............................................. 1907
John Hollander ............................................. 1913
Richard Howard ............................................. 1928
Langston Hughes ............................................ 1934
Zora Neale Hurston ......................................... 1950
David Ignatow .............................................. 1974
William Inge ............................................... 1982
John Irving ................................................ 1989
Shirley Jackson ............................................ 1994
Randall Jarrell ............................................ 2005
Robinson Jeffers ........................................... 2020
James Jones ................................................ 2031
June Jordan ................................................ 2038
George S. Kaufman .......................................... 2043
William Kennedy ............................................ 2050
X. J. Kennedy .............................................. 2060
Jack Kerouac ............................................... 2065
Ken Kesey .................................................. 2079
Galway Kinnell ............................................. 2092
Carolyn Kizer .............................................. 2103
John Knowles ............................................... 2108
Kenneth Koch ............................................... 2116
Jerzy Kosinski ............................................. 2124
Maxine Kumin ............................................... 2136
Oliver La Farge ............................................ 2142
Ring Lardner ............................................... 2148
Irving Layton .............................................. 2160
Stephen Leacock ............................................ 2165
Ursula K. Le Guin .......................................... 2177
Denise Levertov ............................................ 2203
Philip Levine .............................................. 2217
Sinclair Lewis ............................................. 2229
Vachel Lindsay ............................................. 2259
John Logan ................................................. 2270
Jack London ................................................ 2280
H. P. Lovecraft ............................................ 2296
Amy Lowell ................................................. 2318
Robert Lowell .............................................. 2323
Mina Loy ................................................... 2349
Alison Lurie ............................................... 2355
Mary McCarthy .............................................. 2361
Carson McCullers ........................................... 2371
Claude McKay ............................................... 2387
Archibald MacLeish ......................................... 2392
Hugh MacLennan ............................................. 2404
Norman Mailer .............................................. 2411
Clarence Major ............................................. 2436
Bernard Malamud ............................................ 2441
David Mamet ................................................ 2466
William March (W. E. M. Campbell) .......................... 2474
Edwin Markham .............................................. 2479
John P. Marquand ........................................... 2485
Don Marquis ................................................ 2496
Edgar Lee Masters .......................................... 2503
William Maxwell ............................................ 2513
H. L. Mencken .............................................. 2518
William Meredith ........................................... 2538

Additional Reading ......................................... 2544
Acknowledgments ............................................ 2553

The Index to this series, *Twentieth-Century American Literature*, appears in Volume 7.

# ABBREVIATIONS

| | | | |
|---|---|---|---|
| Am | AMERICA | MPS | MODERN POETRY STUDIES |
| AM | AMERICAN MERCURY | NALF | NEGRO AMERICAN LITERATURE FORUM |
| AmSt | AMERICAN STUDIES | ND | NEGRO DIGEST |
| AnR | ANTIOCH REVIEW | NEQ | NEW ENGLAND QUARTERLY |
| APR | AMERICAN POETRY REVIEW | NL | NEW LEADER |
| AS | AMERICAN SCHOLAR | NM | NEW MASSES |
| At | ATLANTIC | NR | NEW REPUBLIC |
| BALF | BLACK AMERICAN LITERATURE FORUM | NS | NEW STATESMAN |
| Bkm | BOOKMAN (NEW YORK) | NWR | NORTHWEST REVIEW |
| BlS | BLACK SCHOLAR | NY | NEW YORKER |
| BlW | BLACK WORLD | NYRB | NEW YORK REVIEW OF BOOKS |
| BMR | BLACK MOUNTAIN REVIEW | NYTBR | NEW YORK TIMES BOOK REVIEW |
| CL | CANADIAN LITERATURE | Opy | OPPORTUNITY |
| CLAJ | CLA JOURNAL | PR | PARTISAN REVIEW |
| Cmty | COMMENTARY | PRev | PARIS REVIEW |
| CoL | CONTEMPORARY LITERATURE | QQ | QUEEN'S QUARTERLY |
| Com | COMMONWEAL | Rep | REPORTER |
| Ctrice | COCKATRICE | RIH | RHODE ISLAND HISTORY |
| ETJ | EDUCATIONAL THEATRE JOURNAL | Salm | SALMAGUNDI |
| Expl | THE EXPLICATOR | SAQ | SOUTH ATLANTIC QUARTERLY |
| GIT | GREAT IDEAS TODAY | Scy | SCRUTINY |
| GR | GEORGIA REVIEW | SEP | SATURDAY EVENING POST |
| HB | HARPER'S BAZAAR | Shen | SHENANDOAH |
| HC | HOLLINS CRITIC | Spec | SPECTATOR |
| HdR | HUDSON REVIEW | SR | SATURDAY REVIEW |
| IR | IOWA REVIEW | SSF | STUDIES IN SHORT FICTION |
| JCan | JOURNAL OF CANADIAN STUDIES | SWR | SOUTHWEST REVIEW |
| KQ | KANSAS QUARTERLY | TLS | TIMES LITERARY SUPPLEMENT |
| KR | KENYON REVIEW | VQR | VIRGINIA QUARTERLY REVIEW |
| LT | LISTENER | WPBW | WASHINGTON POST BOOK WORLD |
| MFS | MODERN FICTION STUDIES | YR | YALE REVIEW |

# ILLUSTRATIONS

Chester Himes        *facing* page 1934
John Hollander
Richard Howard
Langston Hughes

Zora Neale Hurston   *facing* page 1935
William Inge
John Irving
Shirley Jackson

Randall Jarrell      *facing* page 2042
Robinson Jeffers
James Jones
George S. Kaufman

William Kennedy      *facing* page 2043
X. J. Kennedy
Jack Kerouac
Ken Kesey

Galway Kinnell       *facing* page 2108
Carolyn Kizer
John Knowles
Kenneth Koch

Jerzy Kosinski       *facing* page 2109
Maxine Kumin
Oliver La Farge
Ring Lardner

Irving Layton        *facing* page 2202
Stephen Leacock
Ursula K. Le Guin
Denise Levertov

Philip Levine        *facing* page 2203
Sinclair Lewis
Vachel Lindsay
John Logan

Jack London          *facing* page 2354
H. P. Lovecraft
Amy Lowell
Robert Lowell

Alison Lurie         *facing* page 2355
Mary McCarthy
Carson McCullers
Archibald MacLeish

Norman Mailer        *facing* page 2502
Clarence Major
Bernard Malamud
David Mamet

John P. Marquand     *facing* page 2503
Don Marquis
Edgar Lee Masters
H. L. Mencken

# CHESTER HIMES

## 1909–1984

Chester Boman Himes was born in Jefferson City, Missouri, July 29, 1909. His parents, Joseph and Estelle Boman Himes, were both black teachers. The family lived in several cities in the south-central and midwestern United States, and settled in Ohio. Himes went to high school in Cleveland, and studied for a year at Ohio State University. At the age of nineteen he was convicted of armed robbery and sentenced to twenty years in Ohio State Penitentiary. He served seven years' time. During his incarceration Himes wrote an account of a tragic fire which broke out in the prison and killed three hundred men. He began publishing prison stories in various magazines. On his release he joined a WPA writers' project, and went on to become a feature writer for the Cleveland *Daily News*. Himes was involved with the labor movement and the Communist party. He married Jean Johnson in 1937. During the Second World War Himes worked as a shipfitter and riveter in California. His experiences shaped his first novel, *If He Hollers Let Him Go* (1945). Himes's early novels were explosive studies of the situation of the black man in a racist society. They enjoyed only moderate success in America, but in Europe Himes was lauded as a powerful voice of social criticism. He moved to Spain in 1954, and spent the rest of his life there and in Paris.

In Europe Himes wrote his famous Harlem thrillers, such as *For Love of Imabelle* (1957), *The Real Cool Killers* (1959), and *The Heat's On* (1966). He also published fiction and non-fiction in the protest vein of his early works—including *The Primitive* (1955), *Pinktoes* (1961), and his two volumes of autobiography, *The Quality of Hurt* (1972) and *My Life of Absurdity* (1976).

Himes was awarded the French Grand Prix de Littérature Policière. He died of Parkinson's disease in Moraira, Spain, on November 12, 1984.

Chester Himes had the immense advantage, for our purpose, of writing about Negroes from the inside, from their side of the fence. ⟨. . .⟩ The important thing ⟨about *If He Hollers Let Him Go*⟩ is that the character of Bob is sincerely and solidly drawn, and that his character, his state of moral being, is a function of his social situation. He is a black man without place in a world of hostile whites. They are hostile in the sense of denying him recognition or any of the means by which he might realize his nature. This book has not the power and sweep, the subtlety and depth, of *Native Son*. But in its lesser way it is an impressive performance. It will have done a great service to us all if it tends to promote a sympathetic understanding of the simple fact which lies at the heart of the Negro problem. This fact is the Negro's sense of being excluded from our community and thereby in effect deprived of the very bread of life.—Joseph Warren Beach, "The Dilemma of a Black Man in a White World," *NYTBR*, Dec. 2, 1945, p. 7

*If He Hollers Let Him Go* is the story of Bob Jones, a young Negro from Ohio who works as a leaderman in a West Coast shipyard during the war. Bob has a natural sense of dignity, which brings him into conflict with the Southern whites on the job, and with anti-Negro prejudice in general. To begin with merits, I liked particularly Mr. Himes's inclusion of sexual equality among the Negroes' demands for justice, and the use he makes of this theme in depicting the relationship between his hero and one of the workers, Madge, a Southern bitch, who teases him, taunts him and finally frames him on a charge of rape. It is regarded as a well established fact of sociology that sexual equality is last on the list of Negroes' demands and also least in importance to them. But the moral that Mr. Himes seems to draw is that a free man does not count his rights in order of importance, but feels himself entitled to enjoy them simultaneously, the great with the small. Which is correct as well as courageous. Accordingly, the scenes in which Madge and Bob are together are the best in the book; the author is on his surest ground, and his conviction gives free play to his insight. He also makes good use of various language patterns,

jive, bourgeois stuffiness and social workers' terminology, representing the social classes that come within his range.

⟨. . .⟩ *If He Hollers Let Him Go* is well sustained in action, but sacrifices too much to the melodramatic uses of violence. When Mr. Himes writes in his own person, abandoning the rhythms of jive or professionalism, he loses rhythm altogether; his style is a compact thing, known to the trade as "hard-hitting," acceptable because it is free of the major irritants of journalese, but lacking in real literary distinction. Moreover, his book fails as a work of serious reflection on the Negro problem through a basic irresoluteness. Bob is shown to have but two alternatives: to accept the values of his light-skinned fiancée, Alice the social worker, who wants him to study law, make the most of his limited opportunities as a Negro and climb as high as he can, socially and professionally; or to take the practically suicidal risk of his militancy, which will satisfy his sense of human dignity but leave him frustrated in every other respect. At one point in the novel Bob appears to have repudiated Alice and the compromises that she stands for (the characterization of Alice has been directed toward this end). But there is a sudden shift in the final section and instead Bob repudiates his militancy, his pride and violence and plans to marry Alice, which leaves the novel with no real conclusion; for the principle of his original rejection of Alice's world is not revoked by his coming to terms with that world. The dénouement, furthermore, in which Madge brings a charge of rape against him (the charge, patently false, is dropped when he agrees to enter the Army), does not really prove that Bob was wrong to compromise with the white world by way of his engagement to Alice, for the frame-up is not a consequence of his engagement, and the moral—that it is useless to expect justice from the whites—was obviously known to him when he decided to take a chance on bourgeois success. Compromise is shown to be a calculated risk rather than an enlightening error.—Isaac Rosenfeld, "With the Best Intentions," *NR*, Dec. 31, 1945, pp. 909–10

A generation or so ago the new immigrant and his struggles to overcome obstacles and prejudice formed an important element in American writing. Today two top fiction best-sellers deal with racial problems, the one with anti-Semitism, the other with anti-Negroism.

Chester Himes's ⟨Lonely Crusade⟩ is a study of the American Negro, a brave and courageous probing into the Negro psyche. His diagnosis reveals a racial malady for which there is no immediate remedy. The cure, as he sees it, is centuries of equality and miscegenation. And in the beginning simple equality is not enough. Equality to the Negro means special privileges.

Mr. Himes's hero, Lee Gordon, is indeed a lonely crusader, seeking justice in a white ocean of prejudice and discimination. A college graduate, a sensitive Negro of basic honesty and integrity, he comes up against the usual barriers. His college degree cannot get him a white-collar job, and since he refuses to take menial work, he and his devoted wife live in poverty, with the result that Lee Gordon's sense of manhood and fitness is gradually corroded, and his wife loses faith in him, though not her love for him. This tragedy Lee Gordon blames on the white man.

Lee Gordon's real troubles begin in the spring of 1943 when, at the age of thirty-one, he gets a job as union organizer of an aircraft plant in Los Angeles. The job is given to him not because he is a professional union organizer—he is not even a member of the union—but because the union needs a Negro organizer. And Lee Gordon takes the job because it is a white-collar job. The next fifty days are a nightmare. His honest efforts are thwarted at every turn, by the plant management and its deputy sheriffs and by the Communist Party, which tries to gain control of the new union. Lee Gordon refuses to sell out to either, and in the end is destroyed by both.

Mr. Himes's story, for all its hard realism and able writing, reads like a melodrama, with the Communist Party the real villain and the deputy sheriffs the actual murderers. His story also suffers from a form of elephantiasis. He tries to embrace too much and his themes cross and get mixed up, so that in the end Lee Gordon's tragedy could just as well have been that of a white man. This overzealousness led Mr. Himes into long generalizations and oversimplifications. The usual racial prejudices and discriminations against the Negro are merely catalogued, with the result that large segments of his book read not like a novel but like excerpts from extended social studies.

Mr. Himes has touched upon every phase of the Negro problem and has mercilessly vivisected the American Negro's personality. We have here clinical revelations of the Negro's homicidal mania, of his lust for white women, of his pathetic sense of inferiority, of his paradoxical anti-Semitism, of his arrogance and his incurable Uncle Tomism. At times it seems that Mr. Himes is trying to convince us that the whole Negro race in America, as a result of centuries of brutal oppression, is sick at soul.

Hatred reeks through his pages like yellow bile. The Negro hates the Jew and the Gentile and he hates his own Negroness; the Jew hates the Negro and the Gentile and his own Jewishness. The pure Marxist Rosenberg, who hates nobody except the capitalists, is expelled from the Communist Party because of his goodness.

The strict Party-line Communists will not like Mr. Himes's book and will no doubt denounce it. The Trotskyites will probably take it to their bosoms, as certainly will all those who believe in unions free of Communist control. As for the Negro problem, it occasionally finds momentary resolution in oversexed white women mixing up Marxism with Negro macrogenitalism.—STOYAN CHRISTOWE, *At*, Oct. 1947, p. 138

Himes feels the trunk and roots of American society are so corrupted as to make normal growth and development impossible. His concern is not primarily with social protest, as has so often been alleged, for protest implies some hope of appropriate reform, and Himes, one suspects, regards the American scene as beyond redemption. His principal subject is the human consequences of a distorted and diseased civilization. His characters, on the other hand, prefer to interpret their warped and maddened psyches in terms of the society that has conditioned them. Being Negroes, they are more attuned to social abuse, and being middle-class and intellectual, they are all the more aware of their frustrations since their aspirations, though similar to those of the white bourgeoisie, are blocked by their color. "Successful" professional Negroes are more frequently more embittered than persons of lower socioeconomic strata, whose expectations are not nearly so great. And it is men like Himes who are often the bitterest enemies of their own social class for having compromised their values in submission to caste mores.

Somewhere James Baldwin has written that Chester Himes is the only Negro writer who has described male-female relationships in other than violent terms. This is not altogether accurate, since Jessie Fauset and Nella Larsen probed along these lines in the 1920's, as have some latter-day novelists, notably Kristen Hunter and Paule Marshall. Nor is Himes's treatment of love without its elements of sadism and self-laceration. But it is undoubtedly true that Himes, in each of his major works, has focused much of his attention on lovers, and has attempted to track down the vagaries and nuances of their emotions. He has, in addition, an unabashed eye for the physical and sensual. It is true as well that he appears to be devoting more and more of his work to material hitherto regarded as taboo—interracial love. Perhaps Himes feels, like so many other Negro authors and intellectuals, that underlying the structure of American society is an unresolved residue of erotic guilt that manifests itself, among other ways, as "the Negro problem."—EDWARD MARGOLIES, "Race and Sex: The Novels of Chester Himes," *Native Sons*, 1968, p. 89

---

## ROBERT BONE
From "The Contemporary Negro Novel"
*The Negro Novel in America*
1958, pp. 173–76

Chester Himes' *If He Hollers Let Him Go* (1946) is an impressive failure—with accent on the adjective. It takes the novel of pure race consciousness to its utmost limit, where it strangles to death in its own contradictions. The novel is Wrightian to the core, which is hardly surprising in view of the author's background and experience. Himes, like Wright, is a product of the Great Depression, of association with the Labor movement, the Federal Writers' Project, and the Communist party. A kind of Yerby in reverse, he began his writing career with popular fiction but veered sharply in the direction of protest. He has published short stories in *Esquire* and *Coronet*, as well as in *Crisis* and *Opportunity*, and as of 1952 was the author of three full-length novels of which the present work is the most important.

The novel is no mere catalogue of grievances, though these are amply provided, within the context of a wartime California shipyard. Racial oppression is a *donnée*; Himes is interested in the personal adjustment of a sensitive Negro to the bitter fact of caste. For the most part, the conflict is successfully internalized, as the protagonist is forced to choose between revenge and moderation—a theme first treated in Negro fiction by Sutton Griggs and Charles Chesnutt. The alternatives are given concrete dramatic expression through the rebellious protagonist and his accommodationist fiancée.

As a psychological study of a man who is obsessed by race, the novel has power and authority. The protagonist lives on the verge of violence, one minute rebelling, the next conforming; one hating, the next loving; now despondent, now exhilarated by his girl or simply by driving his car—battered from emotional pillar to post by external pressures which he can't control. To render this innner agony, Himes has borrowed freely from the visceral style of Richard Wright: "I started drawing in my emotions, tying them, whittling them off, nailing them down. I was so tight inside, I was like wood. My breath wouldn't go any deeper than my throat and I didn't know whether I could talk at all. I had to get ready to die before I could get out of the house."

This characteristic hyperbole is perhaps appropriate, since the whole plan of the novel rests upon magnifying normal emotions to pathological intensity. It has the disadvantage, however, of all overstatement: the reader builds up a gradual immunity. Somewhat more successful is the dream device through which Himes gives us occasional glimpses of his protagonist's subconscious. Here—through a freely symbolic medium—his naked hatred of whites, his violent oscillation between energy and impotence, and his corrosive feelings of rejection, fear, and shame are vividly conveyed.

The problem with case-study fiction is to generalize successfully. Himes solves it by developing Bob Jones as a symbol of will-lessness. By thematic repetition of key phrases ("beyond my control," "I didn't have a chance"), he conveys the feeling of helpless frustration which ensues whenever one surrenders control of his destiny to others. It is a feeling which every slave, every convict, every conscripted soldier knows intimately. Bob Jones knows it in those areas of his life where he is deprived of will by the whites: "I don't have anything at all to say about what's happening to me. I'm just like some sort of machine being run by white people pushing buttons."

It is in these terms that the main tension of the novel is resolved. "To accept being black as a condition over which you have no control" seems in the eyes of the protagonist an ignominious surrender. For most of the novel he resists, but experience convinces him that personal defiance is suicidal: "I knew with the white folks sitting on my brain, controlling my every thought, action, and emotion, making life one crisis after another, day and night, asleep and awake, conscious and unconscious, I couldn't make it. I knew that unless I found my niche and crawled into it, unless I stopped hating white folks and learned to take them as they came, I couldn't live in America." The crowning irony is that Jones' decision to conform is—disallowed. He makes his truce, but the white world will not respect it: he is framed on a rape charge and nearly sent to jail for thirty years. By a quirk of fate he is set "free," providing he is willing to "volunteer" for the Army. As a result, he loses both his girl and his dream of manhood.

In its denouement the novel reveals a fatal structural flaw. Here is a black nationalist, hypersensitive, neurotic, unable to mobilize his energies for anything but the race war, driven by his obsession to the brink of murder. The whole novel moves inexorably toward the opposing view that some kind of accommodation is the price of sanity. The protagonist chooses;

he is born again; but suddenly we are confronted with a chain of events whose logic seems to justify his former view of reality.

Earlier in the novel, Himes has argued convincingly that in every human being there is an inner world which lies within his power to control. Is it now his thesis that in all crucial matters concerning a Negro's fate, the will of society is decisive? If so, we feel put upon, for we have been following Jones' inner conflict as if it mattered. Suddenly it is revealed as meaningless—no matter what Jones decides, society will dispose of his future. Such a thesis requires that the tensions of the novel be resolved on a sociological plane; the very basis of a psychological novel is destroyed.

At bottom the trouble is ideological: neither revenge nor accommodation is acceptable to Himes, and as a result, the novel flounders to an inconclusive finish. Earl Conrad writes of _If He Hollers Let Him Go_: "the book is at war with itself, as is Jones, as is Himes, as is the American Negro." The novel suffers ultimately from a one-to-one correlation between form and content: in portraying a divided personality, Himes has written a divided novel. But formless and chaotic is precisely what art cannot afford to be.

## EDWARD MARGOLIES
### From "Race and Sex: The Novels of Chester Himes"
#### Native Sons
##### 1968, pp. 97–99

The title of the novel, _The Primitive_ ⟨1955⟩, of course refers to the role Jesse plays in his affair with Kriss. From the world's viewpoint Jesse lives up to this image by murdering Kriss. But the irony lies in the fact that, far from being primitive, Jesse kills because he is overcivilized. His sensibilities have been stretched to the breaking point, and it is precisely because he feels his individual humanity is never recognized that he finds his existence unbearable. In killing Kriss, Jesse strikes back at the primitivism of "civilized" whites who deny him his dignity. His "primitive" act of violence thus makes him civilized in their eyes. When he realizes he has murdered Kriss, he muses sardonically to himself that he can now join the human race.

Himes's point is basically that anything that dehumanizes is primitive, and the racial attitudes of American society are symptoms of a dehumanized culture. The India Institute, where Kriss works, is a case in point. Kriss's colleagues are passionless and petty, and although the Institute is presumably dedicated to humanitarian ends, none of the employees appears to find his work meaningful. The dehumanized lives of all Americans, from the exploited poor to the characterless sophisticates of Kriss's circle, torment Jesse in drunken dreams. Perhaps most symbolic of all is the prophetic monkey forecasting the news. It is as if this nonhuman, precivilized creature really expresses the nature of American life.

It is in the area of sexual relationships that the theme of the novel makes its greatest impact. Kriss and Jesse perceive one another in primitive images—not as individuals but as projections of their own inchoate impulses, desires, and terrors. For Kriss, Jesse is at once a symbol of sexual power, a whipping boy for all her self-loathing and frustration, and an instrument to taunt the sensibilities of white men who have rejected her in the past. But Kriss, by a strange twist of logic, tends subconsciously to blame Negros for the failure of her marriage. In taking a Negro lover, she can also direct her anger toward Negro men generally. For her, an act of love is as much an act of hostility as anything else. Jesse, in turn, is motivated by certain primitive and dangerous elements in his nature.

When he first sees Kriss he feels himself utterly defeated; in a way he is already spiritually dead. Prior to their meeting he says he *needs a white woman*. Without acknowledging it to himself, Jesse is seeking out his physical destruction, but just as significantly he is seeking out the cause of his destruction. For him Kriss represents the white world that has crushed him, and, unconsciously, Jesse decides to kill her. Kriss knows of Jesse's intentions; she watches him sadistically as he writhes in his sleep, muttering to himself, "Kill you!" Yet she does not flee, for she seeks her own death. It would be her final act of vengeance on all the men who have drained her.

It is difficult to do justice to this novel. Parts are extremely well-written and Himes's cast of characters is authentically conceived. Jesse is especially interesting. His self-pity—of which he has plenty—is seldom irritating, and this is a remarkable feat for any author. Himes laces Jesse's gloom with a kind of dry wit, a sad intellectual humor that saves him from sentimentality.

> No more worrying about what's right and what's wrong. Just what's expedient. You're human now. Went in the back door of the Alchemy Company of America a primitive, filled with things called principles, integrity, honor, conscience, faith, love, hope, charity and such, and came out the front door a human being, completely purged. End of a primitive; beginning of a human. Good title for a book but won't sell in America with the word *human* in it. Americans sensitive about that word. Don't want to know they're human. Don't blame them, though. Poses the only problem they've never been able to solve with all their gadgets—the human problem. But they'll know damn well you're human. Be in all the newspapers: *Black man kills white woman*. Not only natural, plausible, logical, inevitable, psychiatrically compulsive and sociologically conclusive behavior of a human being, but mathematically accurate and politically correct as well. Black man has got to have some means of joining the human race. Old Shakespeare knew. Suppose he'd had Othello kiss the bitch and make up. Would have dehumanized him.

This is Himes's most pessimistic work. He has lost faith in the human capacity to reason its way out of its dilemmas. Jesse and Kriss, two intelligent human beings, are as muddled and distressed about their own identities as the worst racists. But here lies the trouble. Himes has, in a curious way, written two books—one about Jesse and Kriss, and one about racist America—and the two do not quite mesh, because Jesse and Kriss are too atypical and too idiosyncratic. Himes's ideas require a novel with a wider scope than one shabby Harlem tenement, one Gramercy Park apartment, and a few decadent intellectuals. Whether or not he will succceed in writing such a novel remains to be seen.

## EDWARD MARGOLIES
### "America's Dark Pessimism"

*Saturday Review*, March 22, 1969, pp. 59, 64–65

For some years the expatriate Negro novelist Chester Himes has been writing thrillers about a couple of black Harlem police detectives, Coffin Ed Johnson and Grave Digger Jones, who plow their way through the layers of sin, venality and official corruption in their community in order to get their man—and often enough their woman. Ostensibly these books

are potboilers. Himes seems to have written them off the top of his head—their construction is loose, their narrative swift with occasional strands of plot not quite in place as the story ends, and there is always plenty of gore, as well as sex to the lively accompaniment of much bawdy satirical humor. Himes's crime fiction sells rather well in France, where presumably it whets and sates an appetite for erotica-exotica (violent and passionate jungle-black Harlemites); perhaps it also narcotizes French readers about their own race problems. Although from time to time an occasional piece will appear in a French journal declaring that Himes has plumbed the savage-sick essence of America, learned allusions have not yet harmed Himes's reputation with his mass French readership—and they have scarcely been expressed (in print) over here.

Himes's very minor American reputation rests on an elongated interracial sex novel, *Pinktoes* (1965), and five "major" works, the first of which was published nearly a quarter of a century ago. Two worth exhuming are *Cast the First Stone* (1952), a prison novel dealing in part with the strange, tender love relationship of two convicts (white), and *The Primitive* (1955), a taut, spare, intense work narrating the love-hate affair in New York of a soured black intellectual and his sophisticated and alienated white mistress. Himes's other three novels, though not without interest, remain for the time being, at least, better off interred.

His thrillers are something else again. It is not simply that they say something about the core of racism that underlies the rottenness of American institutions. Other detective stories have implied the disintegration of society—their cynical, lonely, battle-scarred private eyes relentlessly pursuing truth through a morass of decay and betrayal. And occasionally the best of these tales transcend genre; one thinks immediately of Dashiell Hammett and Raymond Chandler, whose themes express a kind of terrifying deracinated isolation. The point about Himes is that he does not transcend genre; indeed he seemingly insists on maintaining a kind of pop-campy dime-detective format—despite the ever widening chaos each of his books describes. It is as if Himes in the course of writing potboilers inadvertently discovered that not only had he freed himself from the "art" of the novel (he need no longer be serious about being serious; he could now allow his imagination far freer play), but that the kind of detective fiction he chose to write—implying, as it does, the comic, the violent, and above all the absurd—exactly suited his vision. In a peculiar fashion, for Himes the genre *is* the message.

*Blind Man with a Pistol* is the ninth of his crime stories, and in certain ways it follows the pattern of the others. The reader is introduced chapter by chapter to Himes's usual gallery of low life—in this instance, petty thieves, pimps, prostitutes, pederasts, lesbians, con men, quacks, vice lords, hopheads, narcotics peddlers, white teeny boppers, Black Power charlatans, Black Jesus charlatans, and others, each doing his hustling, each from time to time engaging racist cops and Himes's tough, cynical and embittered black detective heroes. As in his other works, all members of Himes's demimonde are linked in one way or another to some rather picturesque crimes, but it would be fruitless to rehearse the plot of this novel, partially because so many fragments are unresolved, partially because the very issue of the book is their irresolution. In their investigation Coffin Ed and Grave Digger are ultimately frustrated by police superiors, who are obviously bowing to political pressures in order to protect the lucrative Harlem rackets. To attempt to discover justice in an unjust racist system is therefore an absurdity—just as the system itself is absurd and chaotic. The novel's conclusion is, therefore, altogether appropriate.

Himes is especially good at producing images of chaos. Indeed there is something of the feeling of a Brueghel canvas in all the anarchic, bustling activities of his swarms of participants. Somewhere near the middle of the novel he describes the convergence from different directions of three parades on 135th Street and Seventh Avenue. It is Nat Turner Day, and each of the groupings represents opposing ideologies: Brotherly Love, Black Power, and Black Jesus. The first, a mob of white and black marchers mindlessly gripping hands, is led by a simple-minded black youth and his dumpy middle-aged Swedish mistress, while the latter two parades are headed by unprincipled black phonies.

At a critical juncture all the marchers fling themselves madly on one another whereupon the confusion is compounded by an invasion of police. Himes conveys the scene in broad comic strokes, but below the surface lies utter revulsion at the simplistic slogans and cure-alls that aggravate the sicknesses of the black community. For, as Himes shows, the violence of blacks is more frequently directed at one another than at whites, and the exploitation of the ghetto by the white peripheral city is mirrored in minuscule by false black leaders and blck racketeers and businessmen who gull the poor and ignorant of their own community.

All of which suggests Hime's rather ambivalent feelings about Harlem and its residents. These are most obviously revealed in his heroes who, if they do not always speak for their author, do manage to communicate by their actions certain curious attitudes. For all their expressed compassion for slum dwellers, their idealism in pursuing wrong-doers, their cynicism and bitterness about a system that renders their efforts futile, when Grave Digger and Coffin Ed do go into action, they somehow always employ excessive force on persons (generally black) whom they suspect. How much of their sadism is related to understandable anger, how much to the popular view that black cops are harder on their own than white cops, how much to the hallowed American convention that hard-boiled dicks must beat up people, and how much to Himes's own possible pent-up fury at black people, the reader can only guess.

But something in the very tone and imagery of the book raises the same questions. On the one hand Himes's Harlemites are terribly sophisticated. They recognize in their sad comic way that life is a jungle and that in order to survive anything goes. They recognize as well that they must pretend otherwise, and their ingenuity in balancing themselves between appearance and reality wins grudging admiration from the two detectives and their author. Here, for example, is an exchange at a diner between a black counterman and a white pederast who wants to procure a "sissie."

> I know what you want.
> How you know that?
> Just lookin at you.
> Cause I'm white?
> Tain't that. I got the eye.
> You think I'm looking for a girl.
> Chops is your dish.
> Not pork.
> Naw.
> Not overdone.
> Naw. Just right.

But there are other occasions when Himes images his blacks in such minstrel-like caricature (At night, from the black squares of tenement windows, "crescent-shaped whites of eyes and quarter moons of yellow teeth bloomed like Halloween pumpkins."), such Amos 'n' Andy dialogue ("I helps the old and the sick," Doctor Mubuta jawed. "I rejuvenates the disrejuvenated.") that it sounds as if he were telling a "nigger joke." And perhaps he is, but it is not just on his blacks; the joke is on his whites as well—all caught up in the absurdity of racism, the meanness of violence that reduces their humanity to cartoon dimensions. Thus Himes, fifteen years away from America, apart from brief visits, has written an exceedingly American book, a book whose very Americanness constitutes its author's darkest pessimism.

# DANIEL HOFFMAN

## 1923–

Daniel Gerard Hoffman was born in New York City on April 3, 1923. His parents, Daniel and Frances Beck Hoffman, had one other child, a girl. Hoffman grew up in Larchmont and New Rochelle, and attended local schools. He went to Columbia College in 1940, but his studies were interrupted by the war. Hoffman was a serviceman from 1943 to 1946, editing the Army Air Force *Technical Data Digest*. He received his B.A. from Columbia in 1947 and his Ph.D. in 1956 from the same institution.

Hoffman began writing poetry as an adolescent. He wrote throughout his period of study, and in 1954 his first book of verse, *An Armada of Thirty Whales*, was selected by W. H. Auden for the Yale Series of Younger Poets. Later volumes of poetry include *A Little Geste and Other Poems* (1960), *Broken Laws* (1970), and *Brotherly Love* (1981).

Throughout his career Hoffman has deftly managed to balance his three concerns: poetry, criticism, and teaching. He is one of the rare scholar-poets who have abandoned neither creative nor analytical efforts. He has taught at Columbia, Swarthmore, and the University of Pennsylvania. Hoffman married Elizabeth McFarland in 1948. They have two children.

## Works

### POETRY

A poet today, particularly perhaps if he is an American like Mr. Hoffman, who sets out to take his themes from Nature is in a very different and much more difficult situation than a Romantic poet like, say, Wordsworth. By the end of the eighteenth century the Newtonian cosmology had destroyed the ancient beliefs in Nature as the abode of actual spirits good or bad, so that the continued use in poetry of Greek mythology had degenerated into genteel periphrasis. At the same time, life was still rural enough for men to feel instinctively that Nature was numinous. Wordsworth's achievement in poetry, parallel to that of Kant in philosophy, was to preserve the validity of this feeling by describing it, not in the traditional mythological terms, but in terms of the psychology of his time. But the poet today is faced not only with the question of contemporary expression but also with the task of recovering the feeling which he and the public have largely lost, that Nature is numinous. He has to make a much more conscious and deliberate effort. At this point I hear the Accuser adopt his "honest Iago" voice: "This is sentimental rubbish. You don't feel that Nature is holy and as a modern man you never can. Genuine art is the mirror of genuine feelings, and the only real feelings you have are of self-pity at your alienation. So be frank, be modern. Express your pity for your self in the rhythmless language really used by metropolitan man." The only way to counter this lie is to realize its half-truth, namely, that our conception of Nature cannot be that of some prescientific magician, nor our modes of poetic expression those of some agricultural community without a written literature.

Mr. Hoffman has not been led astray by the Accuser. While admitting the pains and tragedies of life, he can find joy in life and say so. Nor, on the other hand, does he try to pretend to a Wordsworthian intimacy with Nature. He knows that, for any member of our urban culture, such intimacy is not given but is a prize slowly and patiently to be won: we all start as outsiders. Sometimes, as in *"An Armada of Thirty Whales,"* he uses natural objects as heraldic symbols, but more often starts with direct observation and description. Such an approach produces, I feel, more interesting results. There is always a danger of becoming whimsical in using some animal as a symbol when you have no personal experience of it as an animal.

A number of Mr. Hoffman's poems are concerned with the same kind of place, the frontier between earth and water, and with the creatures associated with it, and they are written in the same kind of meter, a loose couplet, stopped between the lines and sometimes employing internal rhymes in lieu of end rhymes; e.g.:

> All shrinks in the rage of the sun
>> save the courage of clams, and their faith:
> Sacrificing the water they breathe
> seems to urge the tall moon from her orbit;
> she tugs ocean, cubit by cubit
> over killdeer's kingdom
> and ends parched freedom.
>> Moon, with sky-arching shell
> and bright snout nine thousand miles long
> and anemones in her kelp hair
> that gleam in the heaven around her,
>> responds with the wave of their prayers
> or sucks the sea unawares.
>
> ("The Clams")

The skeptical caution of the last line seems to me right, but so does the analogy Mr. Hoffman perceives between the clams and human ritual. Indeed if such analogies are not valid, no art is possible. As Malcolm de Chazal has written: "Symbolism was born when Adam, wishing to tell Eve with a single gesture of the immensity of his love for her, pointed with his hand to the disk of the sun."—W. H. AUDEN, "Foreword" to *An Armada of Thirty Whales*, 1954

Too bad that a poet's audience cannot respond like a tenor's, for the only satisfactory comment on the second volume by Daniel Hoffman, *A Little Geste and Other Poems*, would be a roll of applause and a crackle of bravos. This is poetry, no doubt about that. It is learned, ingenious, and technically sophisticated, of course; but also—and by no means of course—it sings, it shocks, it stirs, it raises the old, infallible goose flesh on your arms.

There are some lapses, to be sure, among the "Other Poems" of the book: leftovers, odds and ends, and exercises in abstraction such as "Scholiast Iconoclast" [the title tells all], which might better have been left to the gnomists. Hoffman's business is with the other kind of gnomes, or at least with wizards, new-born gods, lightning ("a zaggedy white trombone of lightshot"), "a hoof-deep pool," "fingers, rippling on the lute like minnows," "wakeless water." He invokes

> the instinctual wisdom of the hawk's wing,
> the dumb cow's long-tongued patience, the seals'
> handwebbed finesse in motion indivisible
>
> from the cold seas', joyous in their submitting
> to the tide's seasons and turn, leaving my heels'
> prints on the shore, visible or invisible.

He is a poet of the visible and palpable, a subtle rhymer, a minter of metaphors, and a praiser of instinct and blood-knowledge.

His title poem, or sequence, is a bold piece of myth-making which rescues Robin Hood from his shrunken state of "democratic thief" and restores him to a Dionysian, Druidic, Laurentian godhood. Every character of the old geste is charged with mythic power (Marian rises like Aphrodite from the fecund sea; Submagus Tuck chants a fire-hymn; Robin is metamorphosed into robin with bloodstained breast), and ancient alliterative and ballad forms are adapted with stunning success to the demands of a modern poetic idiom. That's a poem, as M. H. L. Gay would put it, that's a poem and a half.—JOSEPH SLATKIN, "Wizards and New-Born Gods," *SR*, Jan. 7, 1961, pp. 28–29

Perhaps the best thing that can be said for the American poetry of the past decade is that it is wildly catholic. The reader can choose between the most desiccated of academic verse; passionate political statement blossoming in the vernacular or in full-blown rhetoric; arcane adventures in self-expression; the undigested distress of the mournful emotions; one or two major voices; and a handful of poets whose wit and intelligence have served, instead of overridden, their poetry. Daniel Hoffman belongs to the last group. *The Center of Attention* is a very good collection of poems.

Hoffman brings to his poetry what he has learned from his prose books such as *Barbarous Knowledge* and *Poe Poe Poe Poe Poe Poe Poe*. He demonstrates not only a considerable psychological insight and sense of drama, but more important, a sense of all the nuances of pace. Some of the poems, such as "The Center of Attention," "The Princess Cassimassima" or "Tolerance" are story-poems; but others, which are poems of intensified insight, like "Old Photo in an Old Life," or "Boar," also move in every syllable.

Reading the entire Hoffman poetic oeuvre, one is aware of

three major strands that knit into a strong texture: myth, history and the immediate experience, personal and colloquial. It's a rich fusion; one thinks immediately of other poets wedded more or less faithfully to one of the three. Hoffman's polygamy works well. He never writes without that sense of the dead which was so precious to Auden; he has as thorough a response to myth as Muir himself, and he can write of a personal shock or rage with total directness. What he once wrote of Robert Graves is true of his own work. Both combine "a Dionysian compulsion to belief with an Apollonian clarity of presentation."

And see, there kneels the executioner

Wiping his scimitar upon a torso's ripped
Sash. At ease, the victors smoke. A gash
Of throats darkens the river. 1900, The Boxer
Rebellion. Everyone there is dead now.
What was it those unbodied mouths were saying?
Something of relevance to this morning.

"The Boar" talks about a hunt, a cornered boar whose

clumsy bulk
Dances on murderous hooves in sudden lunges
And the scimitar tusks drip red.

But the scene connects with a wider and darker energy: the dogs'

ardor
Is chilled by an ancient ardor that stays the blood.
If the hunters with trumpets and guns dare stop
within range
Of those hooves and tusks they will know the single
purpose
Of which the boar is steward.

Hoffman's boar is cousin to Roethke's pike and killer-birds on the wing. In *The White Goddess*, "The boar is the beast of death and the 'fall' of the year begins in the month of the boar."

But then in "Vows," perhaps the book's most impressive poem, Hoffman steps straight from his other persona into a direct and extremely moving poem of personal emotion. It could easily belong to that most embarrassing of all genres, the o-would-I-were-other lament; but by energy and control it frees itself into a dignified discreteness.

In an early book, *An Armada of Whales*, there is a poem in which the poet's child stares across a rough sea, uncertain as to the terms that will create what she sees.

the world without description
is vast and wild as death

the word the tongue has spoken
creates the world and truth.

Scrupulously attentive, Hoffman continues to name: qualities, situations, legacies; he conquers resistant nameless territory foot by foot. He has decided that for his purpose, his prosody will be highly flexible, its ear versed in, but not subservient to rules. The techniques are as varied as the poems, but there is a great deal of tough skill which at its happiest has the ease of an acrobat's control, the smooth sum of a dozen hidden efforts.

When he wishes to be grim, Hoffman commands a bland toughness, more effective than any number of head-on blasts. Delivered in the dead-pan tone of a practical recipe, "Rats" says more of the desperation of greed than a dozen social treatises.

Some of the poems in the book's last section are less successful as individual poems, being occasionally not much more than skillful and sensitive description, though never purely of surfaces; but by some curious element of balance they strengthen the book as a whole, altering the intensity of the pressure and inviting us to admit pauses. And even in this

section, lulled, one comes upon "Runner," or "The Poem," and learns not to relax expectancy.—JOSEPHINE JACOBSEN, "A Rich Fusion," NR, April 6, 1974, p. 30

A national epic is hardly a topic for serious consideration nowadays in literary and academic circles. The Bicentennial came and went without a major poet even attempting something so ambitious. Daniel Hoffman's poem, *Brotherly Love*, has all the makings of an epic: the founding of a new land, a hero of stature, his odyssey and struggle toward self-fulfillment and identity, an invocation to the muse (in this case, Clio), and a divine purpose made manifest in changing events.

The poem celebrates the founding of Pennsylvania as an image of the origin of our country, from its first contacts with the Indians to the configurations of all its cultures in the nation as it is today. Pennsylvania could not have been a happier choice. Before William Penn landed in 1682, settlers were already there, waiting for an identity of their own. Even today, Pennsylvania "Dutch" refers not to natives of Holland but to the descendants of German and Swiss immigrants. A more typical melting pot could not be found.

Hoffman investigates these European roots in the war between the English and Dutch in which Admiral William Penn, the founder's father, played an important role. The poet shows how the son turned inward, how a consciousness of destiny unfolded through his religious experiences, how his suffering of injustices brought him to respect civil laws, and how his biblical sense of history led him to plan a heavenly city for earthly men. When Penn set foot in America he came armed with laws, contracts, plans and ideas; he began to carry them out with amazing alacrity and grace.

His famous pact with the Delaware Indians provides the material for the opening section of the poem which is in three parts: "Treating with Indians," "An Opening of Joy" and "The Structure of Reality." There are a total of 61 poems, documents, adaptations and three illustrations from paintings that act as key images for each of the three main divisions.

The central theme, "the motion of the Lord/upon the soul," can be seen in the Benjamin West re-creation of the treaty with the Indians, in the portrait of Penn as as young man and in Edward Hick's version of "The Peaceable Kingdom" which depicts the Christ Child extending a branch of peace while the treaty is signed in the distance. Poem 8 describes the union of the two peoples, white and red man, when "The destinations of two journeys meet." The moment is sacred for "Behind the clouds," an unseen witness participates: "Great Manito, the Lord, whose will is done." Both the biblical and Indian names of God sanction the event as a holy covenant between brothers.

The last part of the poem recounts the sad breakdown of trust between peoples, the ruin of the Delaware by murder, exile, poverty and disease. Yet they keep the memory of Penn untarnished—more than we can say of his followers—and the Indians increase in dignity with their absolute resignation to the Spirit. Through their example and Penn's integrity, the poet tells us we can still gain "in our life in time/an intimation of that Light" which "God causes to glow/in every soul."

*Brotherly Love* is a true epic waiting to be explored and absorbed. Like the landscape around us, it is a reminder that cities, fields and hills summon us to fresh discoveries of ourselves, of our coming hither and our going hence: "In the Lord's love for each person/is his revelation/Perpetual and unending,/And they shall come together in a city." Hoffman has no illusions about the "wrangling" city that Philadelphia has become, but he affirms "a spirit in this place" and sees "possibilities of grace" in the soil that first received the seeds of brotherly love. His book is one way of letting the seed grow again on good ground and bring forth fruit. What more can we want of a poem?—JAMES FINN COTTER, *Am*, July 25, 1981, pp. 37–38

### CRITICISM

Daniel Hoffman, attempting to synthesize and to further the work of Constance Rourke, F. O. Matthiessen, and Richard Chase, argues ⟨in *Form and Fable in American Fiction*⟩ that the romance-writer is distinguished from the novelist by the former's "structural and thematic concern . . . with folklore, myth, and ritual." Analyzing the fabulous in our literature, Hoffman redefines the forms and contents of such American classics as *The Scarlet Letter, Moby-Dick,* and *Huckleberry Finn.* He contends that American writers have used "the detritus of the pagan past" and appropriated from myth and folklore the "archetypal themes of journey, quest, and initiation." They have done so because the tragic resolution and the Christian resolution have both appeared false to life as they knew it. Our literature is further complicated by the "opposition of the New World to the Old." In a startling metaphor, Hoffman—a poet as well as a critic—imagines "the heroes of native folk experience" in a "cultural tug-of-war" with the "heroes of the European tradition": on the one end of the rope, Ben Franklin, the Kentucky Screamer, and Johnny Appleseed; on the other, Adonis, Prometheus, and Christ.

After an acrobatic set of chapters in which the witches of Matherdom jostle Mike Fink, Davy Crockett, and the cockalorum braggarts of frontier humor, Hoffman shows that Irving's "Legend of Sleepy Hollow" is a "prefiguration" of the romances of Hawthorne, Melville, and Mark Twain. The remainder of the book is given to an extensive discussion of these major figures. Tracing the allegorical and the preternatural in *The Scarlet Letter,* the Edenic and the mesmeric in *The Blithedale Romance,* the "Myth, Magic, and Metaphor" of *Moby-Dick,* the folkloric and metamorphic in *The Confidence Man,* the white and black magic of *Huckleberry Finn,* Hoffman illuminates the canonic books. The prose is sometimes gnarled: "In his protean and hydra-headed versatility the metamorphic Franklin seemed a moral chameleon." More often, it is clear and conclusive: "Young Goodman Brown, like his own fathers, like Goody Cloyse and all of Salem, like Hawthorne's distinguished ancestors too, really believed in witches, rather than in men. And so he joylessly became one." (The analyses of Hawthorne's stories are the best I have ever read.) Hoffman set forth to "discover certain themes which have profoundly influenced the early masters of American fiction," and his quest is—by and large—successful.

The qualification above is forced upon me by Hoffman's set quotations, unexplained omissions, and occasional misreadings. Chapter One begins with Hawthorne's Preface to *The House of the Seven Gables* and moves to Henry James's enumeration of "the items of high civilization . . . absent from the texture of American life." Tocqueville appears immediately thereafter; Crèvecoeur on "the American, this new man," is delayed. Hoffman quotes Mark Twain's monitory Preface to *Huckleberry Finn* and follows it with a three-page commentary on the critics' transgressions; I had rather have less of this—and none of the dubious link between Davy Crockett and the late Senator McCarthy—and more on the early Melville or, to name a book omitted altogether, *The Marble Faun.* More serious, in this book on the mythic and folkloric, is the omission of Natty Bumppo. Surely Leatherstocking and his historical prototypes are as important as Colonel Crockett and Nimrod Wildfire. Hoffman writes of the Adamic theme, of

the contrast between Nature and Civilization, and of the pastoral mode; his comments are weakened by his failure to profit by the critical insights of such writers as R. W. B. Lewis, Henry Nash Smith, and Leo Marx. Finally, there are occasional misreadings, the worst of which is of *The House of the Seven Gables.* Hoffman says that "there is no single controlling symbol" to unify the disparate elements of the action. But the title of the tale is, like that of *The Scarlet Letter,* an obvious clue to the controlling symbol. Hoffman might have seen this if, in quoting Holgrave's passionate speech against dead men's books and dead men's jokes, he had included Holgrave's peroration against "dead men's houses."

Such plaints as those above are signs of ingratitude. Hoffman reconciles whole schools of criticism and reintegrates books torn apart—Hoffman's hyperbole is catching—by literary factions. Considering his book's very great contributions *and* its shortcomings, one can say emphatically that it should have been twice as long as it is.—ALLEN GUTTMANN, *NEQ*, March 1962, pp. 115–17

Daniel Hoffman is both a poet and a scholar of American literature, and if his effusively entitled book ⟨*Poe Poe Poe Poe Poe Poe Poe*⟩ is responsive to a wide and profound grasp of all the historical, biographical and critical material on Poe that his academic colleagues have accumulated over the years, it is nevertheless resolute in its refusal to be shaped by its scholarship. The work of a poet and scholar, *Poe Poe Poe* ⟨. . .⟩ is determined, without any bows to modish French critical methods, to be that of a reader. Personal, aggressively casual in diction and tone, sometimes annoyingly flip, often pungent in the way of its great prototype, D. H. Lawrence's *Studies in Classic American Literature* (that living rebuke to so much of the work of professional "Americanists"), Hoffman's book works hard to avoid being merely Hoffman's book.

Often autobiographical by way of detailing the history of his own reading of Poe from boyhood on, as if both to recapitulate the phylogeny of Poe criticism's own history, and to contrast strongly with it, Hoffman employs reverie, allusion, invective, and even such 19th-century bellelettristic devices as anecdotal accounts of first encounters with particular tales and poems in particular editions. These devices are all enlisted in aid of a struggle against inauthenticity; Hoffman chooses to speak out of the almost cranky privacy of the poet's encounter with his forebear, and while his tone frequently suggests the haranguing of the autodidact who cannot believe in intellectual sophistication, his knowledge and his arguments are informed and subtle.

What emerges is a very exciting reading of Poe, truly serious and liberated from many traditional critical and scholarly solemnities. The poems, tales and critical essays are treated as part of a disunified but organic *oeuvre,* a total text, parts of which are used to shed light on other parts even when they seem most disparate. Thus, the detective stories and "The Gold-Bug," for example, are read as modes of quest romance, and the pre-Dostoevskian figure of the Double in "William Wilson" is shown to be frighteningly ubiquitous. The relation between puzzle and myth he shows to be a central one, and far from trivial—to this extent, we have a post-Borgesian reading of Poe.

In commenting on "The Murders in the Rue Morgue," Hoffman observes that "the only condition, for Poe, approaching that of terror and grief in the stimulation of ecstasy is *the ratiocinative control of the mind aware of the operation of its own powers.*" The understanding of the peculiar relation, in Poe, between the engines of fancy and the larger imaginative power allows Hoffman's reading to penetrate even the demonic evasions of literary triviality, to see in parody and literary satire many instances of what he calls "pure fiction cast as a send-up," and to deal in a convincing way (for the first time, for me) with the rhetoric and intention of Poe's essay on "The Raven," "The Philosophy of Composition," like Scripture, so diversely read and applied.

Hoffman is illuminating and convincing, too, on the subject of Poe's more palpable romantic fictions, and he is able not to condescend to the poems even when they are very bad because of sympathy with their predicament and a kind of generosity accompanying real skill in the analysis of their failure. His long, attentive reading of *Eureka* is also most unusual, and we must conclude from his presentation of it that Poe's essay in visionary cosmology belongs in its limited way to the same genre as those other modern compendia of mythologies, *Finnegans Wake*, *The White Goddess*, and *A Vision*. In general, this book seems most unusually responsive to the realm in Poe's art governed by his lack of what Keats called "negative capability."—JOHN HOLLANDER, *NYTBR*, Feb. 13, 1972, pp. 7, 18

⟨*Poe Poe Poe Poe Poe Poe Poe*⟩ is the most refreshing and original volume of literary study to appear for a long time. One may even hope that it will set a new style in literary criticism, particularly as it deals with American subjects—although there cannot be many critics around who combine Daniel Hoffman's discernment, controlled quirkiness, poetic eloquence, and sense of the intellectual value of laughter.

The title invokes Poe's name seven times: partly, one supposes, because the word "bells" was repeated seven times in Poe's poem about them, and Poe was an iterative fellow; but partly to point to the numerous dimensions of Poe's achievement. Mr. Hoffman, often piling up clashing adjectives seven at a time, explores that achievement seriatim: the poems; the critical theory; the detective stories; the social and political commentary (who remembers that Poe wrote so many sketches in this area?); a goodly number of the tales; *Arthur Gordon Pym*; the philosophical prose poem *Eureka*; and climactically "The Fall of the House of Usher."

The book is at every turn uncommonly engrossing, with constant changes of tone and pace, and a number of rhetorical devices aimed at keeping the reader awake, and at getting into still another facet of Poe's writing. The style is essentially conversational, sometimes exclamatory, and it is salted with colloquialisms: Poe, Mr. Hoffman remembers from his youth, is a writer "who can frighten a boy out of his pajamas"; and after quoting Roderick Usher's screech to the narrator, as Madeline totters back from her tomb, "*Madman! I tell you that she now stands without the door,*" Mr. Hoffman instantly lowers the pitch by commenting: "Most readers think it odd that Usher, who is as crazy as a bedbug, should call Narrator a madman," and goes on to offer a sound explanation for that phenomenon.

There are lively little dialogues with the reader: "What! You seriously propose that . . .? Well, yes I do." There are Joycean tricks with Poe's name: Edgarpoe, Edgar Élan Poet, Hoaxipoe (the author of the spoof stories), Idgar Poe. There are head-shaking apostrophes to Poe, and pauses while the author seems to mop his brow at some new Poeian extravagance and cries, "Whew!"

Above all there is the steady expression of Daniel Hoffman's lifelong personal involvement with the writings of E. A. Poe—from childhood through a year as Fulbright lecturer at Dijon where Professor Hoffman tried to persuade the French idolaters of Po*eh* that their hero was an imperfect versifier, to recent years and a total reimmersion in the *oeuvre*.

In the course of all this, the analytic sobrieties of the New Criticism are no so much cast aside as absorbed, made excellent use of, and gone far beyond. Admirable, admirable.

These devices, approaches and postures are, I am convinced, entirely relevant and necessary to Mr. Hoffman's deeply serious purpose, which is to give an account of Poe that is faithful to the highly mixed experience of reading him. It is an account that wants to be faithful both to that larger part of Poe that in James Russell Lowell's words was genius and to the smaller part that was "sheer fudge." And it wants to disclose the genius that often shines agonizedly beneath the fudged surfaces of individual poems or tales: beneath the appalling rhymes, the inflated prose, the preposterous interior decors of the protagonists' apartments.

Poe, as Mr. Hoffman roundly views him, sought to express the inexpressible—certain basic hideosities of human impulse, and phenomena detached from time, earth, sanity and the body—and in this he was more successful in the tales than in the poems. Mr. Hoffman draws a little upon the psychoanalyzing Marie Bonaparte (yes, Ligeia *is* to a degree Poe's defecting mother Elizabeth Arnold), and a great deal more on Richard Wilbur, the most illuminating student of Poe before Mr. Hoffman himself; but if the latter's suggestions are not always wholly original, there is something arrestingly fresh about every major reading.—R. W. B. LEWIS, "Genius and Sheer Fudge," *AS*, Autumn 1972, pp. 680–82

---

JOHN ALEXANDER ALLEN
From "Another Country:
The Poetry of Daniel Hoffman"
*Hollins Critic*, October 1978, pp. 3–18

## II

Inasmuch as a sense of being exiled from another life has, from the beginning, been the keynote of Hoffman's poetry, this survey of his achievement can usefully begin by glancing at three of his early poems that have this theme in common. It will be readily apparent to the reader that the style and technique of these poems differs markedly from that of "A Visitation," which appeared in Hoffman's fourth collection. Other recent poems on the theme of exile will be the subject of comment in Section V and elsewhere. ⟨. . .⟩

Like any well-schooled young poet, Hoffman began his career in print with poems that rather ingenuously cast about for objective correlatives of his inner feelings. *An Armada of Thirty Whales* contains a number of poems in which creatures—whales, seals, clams—serve as surrogates for the poet himself. The whales of the title poem have, in the unaccountable fashion of their species, grounded themselves on a Florida beach. That much is fact. But Hoffman challenges the reader's belief by saying that the whales, in their predicament, "declare / their element henceforth air." As the unfortunate mammals, "who won't swim and can't stand / lie mired in mud and in sand," the poet may well identify their putative desire for a new life with his own very real one. The trouble is that whales do not in fact possess such a desire, and it is no good telling us, however whimsically, that they do. Again, in "The Clams," the poet uses the title bivalves as a basis for presenting the reader with a series of even less plausible non-facts. Left high and drying in the sand of the Bay of Fundy at low tide, they are praised for the "desperate hope" they allegedly display by erecting "valved snouts" and squirting out quantities of their remaining supply of moisture. "All shrinks in the rage of the sun," the poet declares, "save the courage of clams, and their faith." It is surely one of the less persuasive analogies for the unyielding spirit of the exiled poet.

'The Seals in Penobscot Bay" is a more successful poem than either of the foregoing. Here, the poet is perforce engaging in a trial run on a naval destroyer, and the seals are not endowed with any emotions or aspirations but are plausibly said simply not to hear the poet's shouted warning concerning the atom bomb. It is the poet who must live with the knowledge of this danger, while he not unnaturally envies the playful sea creatures their apparent immunity to fear and their freedom to "plunge, bubbling, into the brine, / and couple & laugh in the troughs . . ." Here, the only dubious touch is that word "laugh." Hoffman's emphasis on the joyful coupling of the seals is in keeping with a strong, and generally sanguine, though sometimes ambiguous, emphasis upon sexuality that has persisted in his work. His poems are seldom explicitly sexual (though see "In Cytherea" —*A Little Geste*), but a number of his best love poems—all of which are securely domestic—successfully use sexual fulfillment to figure forth the sense of perfect union that is one quality of the "other world" the poet seeks.

"The Seals" doubles the notion of the poet's exile by bringing in reference to Odysseus' "sweet agony" at the sirens' song as a contrast to what the naval captive must hear as the destroyer's guns "punched dark holes in the sky." Song—more often that of birds than of sirens—is regularly associated in Hoffman's poems with the world from which the poet is exiled. Hoffman is, in fact, ear-oriented. Music, for him, is thought, the "true ground / The ordained cadences" of which may be as apparently inconsequential as "vestigial / Bird's whistle" or "wailed / Snatch on boy's harmonica" ("The Sounds").

In a much more recent poem, "Ten Thousand Dreaming Seamen Proven Wrong" (*Broken Laws*), Hoffman's strong emotional response to the sirens' song appears delightfully in the form of ironic glee. This is one of the poet's rare truly funny poems. He is amused to the point of chuckling out loud by the report of "Researchers" that seamen, in spinning their traditional yarns, have not *lied* about seeing mermaids but have simply been honestly mistaken. What they actually saw, as Hoffman reports, trying to keep a straight face, was

> the bearded manatee
> That pouts and floats, fat lady-like, along
> Southern lagoons; further, it pleased their fancy
> To strum the snoutish snorts of that dugong
> On memory's lyre.

He rounds the sonnet out by imagining contemporary sailors lining the rail to gaze ashore, where "girls as sleek as seals sun on the beach." With one such mermaid, "whose molten eyes beseech," he leaves the question, "can the seafarer / Turn from your proffered love, or not be lost?" Hoffman has a dependably fine scorn for the products of intellect (Researchers) unalloyed by passion and imagination. After all, he has been a sailor himself. When the wind is right, he is incapable of mistaking a mermaid for a dugong, or vice versa: and this alone, in my view, is sufficient reason for reading his work with respectful attention. ⟨. . .⟩

## IV

A substantial number of Hoffman's poems deal with the big questions of his trade: What is the poet's purpose in writing, and How does a poem succeed in communicating what he wishes to say? Poems on these subjects can be tedious—mere shop talk or a kind of narcissism. On the other hand, such poems are always justified when the poet is not just taking you through his workshop but is pointing out that his problem as poet is everyman's problem: that of staying alive imaginatively and establishing the possibility of meaningful communication

between the inner man (his emotions, his imaginative vision) and the world outside himself. Hoffman's poems about poetry are of this kind.

From various early poems by Hoffman, one gets the impression of an earnest, idealistic young man who tries to believe that the voice of the bard will collar passers-by and impose enlightenment upon them. In "A Black-Letter Broadside" (*L.G.*), he tells his reader that

> You, in tumultuous nets of voices
> Borne by that unrelenting throng,
> Cannot escape what blaze rejoices
> Me, nor disavow my song.

This is surely a sentiment that invites dissent. But time passes, with its attrition. Hoffman is not about to give up his faith in the imagination, but he finds that the spawn of unreason and power require that faculty, "great with rage," to

> Turn . . . and conceive
> On days like dragons' teeth.

to

> Retell, in the leaping of exultant breath,
> In the blood that sighs,
> What knowledge in the bone this side of death
> Death makes us prize.
> ("Reading the Times," —*The City of
> Satisfactions*)

Hoffman's tone has again altered by the time that he faces "A New Notebook" in the last poem of *Broken Laws*. Here the emphasis is not on mantic authority nor on rage and imaginative frenzy but on redemptive vision and power analogous to that of love. He hopes to "incise" upon the empty pages "images / the soul has seized / out of confusion . . . ,"

> redeemed from dark and changed
> from accustomed sight
> as though by love's altering
> . . .
> to what like love's
> imperial behests
> cannot be disbelieved.

The case has altered once again in *The Center of Attention*, where the emphasis falls on waiting time out, paying attention, having patience: "What awaits us we / Can know only / By our deliverance" ("East"). Finally, in the last poem of the same volume ("The Poem"), Hoffman conceives of his art as itself an exile seeking deliverance. It remains faithful in adversity, and, with luck, may just have strength to deliver its message to the well-disposed reader (I quote in full):

> Arriving at last,
> It has stumbled across the harsh
> Stones, the black marshes.
> True to itself, by what craft
> And strength it has, it has come
> As a sole survivor returns
> From the steep pass.
> Carved on memory's staff
> The legend is nearly decipherable.
> It has lived up to its vows
> If it endures
> The journey through the dark places
> To bear witness,
> Casting its message
> In a sort of singing.

Other readers may react differently, but I find this ragged wreck of a poem, just making it home, simply irresistible. I vow to listen faithfully to its nearly decipherable message, to rejoice quite voluntarily in its sort of singing—even to celebrate its heroism, according to my lights, in word and deed. . . .

## VIII

Every poet writes his own epitaph, not once but many times, and changes it, from time to time, as he himself—and with him, his art—changes with the years. If I were to choose such a poem from *The Center of Attention*, it would be "Shell," which I will quote in full:

I would have left the me that was then
Clinging to a crack in the bark of the tree,
Stiffened in wind, the light translucent,
A brittle shell that had the shape of me;
And down the back a split through which had burst

A new creature, from mean appearance free,
Swaying now where the topmost boughs of the tree
    sway
At the center of the sound that's at the center of the
    day.

To be sure, there has never been anything mean about Daniel Hoffman or about the poems he has given us. But every good person and good poet should be allowed his divine discontent. May the angelic Hoffman step from his split shell the just image of all he could wish to be, and may the exile live forever in the country of his choice.

# JOHN HOLLANDER

## 1929–

On October 28, 1929, John Hollander was born in New York City. His mother, Muriel Kornfeld Hollander, was a high school teacher. His father, Franklin Hollander, was a physiologist. Hollander attended Hunter Model School, The Bronx High School of Science, and Columbia College. He received his B.A. in 1950 and his M.A. two years later. He went to Indiana University the following year and married Anne Helen Loesser. Hollander's first poems were published around this time, in magazines.

He left Indiana to take a fellowship at Harvard before completing his dissertation. From 1954 to 1957 he devoted much of his time to writing. His first volume of poetry was published in 1958 by the Yale Younger Poets Series; it was entitled *A Crackling of Thorns*. Subsequent volumes of verse include *Types of Shape* (1969), *The Night Mirror* (1971), *Selected Poems* (1972), *Spectral Emanations* (1978), and *Blue Wine* (1979).

Hollander has taught on the English faculties of Connecticut College, Yale University, and Hunter College. At present he is the Director of Graduate Studies of the Department of English, Yale University. Hollander has two daughters by his first marriage, which ended in divorce. He now lives in Connecticut with his second wife, who is a sculptor.

### General

*J.D. McClatchy:* First, what's drawn *you* to syllabics? They've not attracted many modern poets (I can think of Auden, Marianne Moore, Richard Howard), perhaps because, even more than conventional metrics, they violated modernism's sense of "the musical phrase." Even Dr. Johnson seemed aware of this when he spoke of "such verses as stood the trial of the finger better than of the ear."

*John Hollander:* I know. My own ear always used to demand something accentual sounding through whatever other kind of pattern there was, or wasn't. When we were undergraduates together at Columbia, Richard Howard was already writing in pure syllabics from time to time, but I never did. The difference between a strictly decasyllabic line (like "A Line with ten syllables you can't hear/Without using your fingers to count them") and an accentual-syllabic pentameter with ten syllables ("One with five downbeats clearly sounding out") was central for me. It was only in 1969–70, in some poems in *The Night Mirror*, that I fell into syllabics; it was for some dark, intense extended epigrams—"Power Failure," "Another Firefly," "As the Sparks Fly Upward"—that I used seven- and eight-syllabled lines, instead of accentual tetrameters. Syllabics have been more flexible for me than other kinds of line, and I can move in and out of whatever rhythm the "sentence sound," as Frost called it, beats out. Speech sound, and the so-called "music" of variously drawn-out terminations, are still there. ⟨. . .⟩

*JDMcC:* Let me look back now. Several of your earlier collections are centered by a long poem, and they've succeeded one another in complexity and ambition—from "Upon Apthorp House" (1962) to *Visions from the Ramble* (1965), to "The Head of the Bed" (1972), and on to your spy poem *Reflections on Espionage* (1976). The grandest and most daunting of them, I think, has been "Spectral Emanations," the glory of your *Selected Poems* (1978). Is *it* a culmination of a kind of poem you had been writing or the achievement of a kind of poem you'd wanted to write?

*JH:* That's interesting. Of course it's easy to say: both! But first of all, I should say that "Spectral Emanations" is more like *Visions from the Ramble* in having a plan or scheme—in having parts I knew from the very beginning I'd have to write—than it's like the spy poem or "Apthorp House."

"Upon Apthorp House" I would treat now as a kind of verse essay, like my poem called "New York." Although it was full of all the concerns I had for and in writing poetry at the moment, it was when I still had a different sense of the requirements of poetry from the one I do now. I asked, I think, less of it. I asked a good deal of myself. It was something very hard for me to do, and something I had to live with for a long time—rather than a poem I would live with while composing for perhaps a week but no more, and then continue with in the process of revision. But that long poem was like living with part of one's own life that one had lived before, not just coping with the consequences of an act. Living with a very long poem was a different matter. It had to have a beginning, a middle, and an end; and middles I've noticed, are the hardest parts of poems to write. And so it extended and extended, and I began to cope with the history of—well, finally, of my own life.

*JDMcC:* Then, *Visions from the Ramble* seems the same sort of autobiographical intention, but assumes a romantic rather than a neo-classical mode.

*JH:* Exactly. I was asking a little more of myself by that time. I was asking *too* much, I was asking what I couldn't deliver. I *thought* I was asking for myself something as organized as Hart Crane's *The Bridge*. It was to be a poem about New York, rather than fragments of poems that took place in New York. And, of course, I wasn't up to it; partially because, among other reasons, I didn't understand *The Bridge* yet. I thought *The Bridge* was a long poem-with-parts, not realizing that it was much more complicated than that. I was still thinking of a poem as what I would now think of as "good writing," as a well-organized piece of rhetoric. I don't think I had begun to touch yet on the ways in which a poem is itself a metaphor, and which—had I even sufficiently understood *The Bridge*—I wouldn't have tried to do at the time. It was not within my resources. Instead, *Visions from the Ramble* has I think a great deal of very good rhetoric.

*JDMcC:* Then, on the way toward "Spectral Emanations" your method becomes more visionary in "The Head of the Bed," and there's a kind of textuality to the vision in *Reflection on Espionage*.

*JH:* Very much so. "The Head of the Bed" in particular. It's the second poem I wrote that I didn't fully understand (the first one was "The Night Mirror"). I knew that the poem had to be the way it was. I didn't know why. I didn't know what it meant.

*JDMcC:* For a man of your temperament, it seems that would have been a bother to you, that you didn't understand.

*JH:* At first, it was. I wrote it and a few people admired it very much and it annoyed me that they thought that and I didn't know why. Since then I don't "understand" a lot of what I write at first but it doesn't bother me—I expect not to. I figure I must be doing something right. And things I wrote earlier which were over-comprehended were perhaps under-determined, and poems which were over-determined were perhaps under-comprehended. Perhaps that's the heart of the matter—I want my poems to be wiser than I am, to know more about themselves than I do. "The Head of the Bed" really came that way. I didn't know what I was doing. I produced a few of the sections—just the opening ones at the beginning—almost in order. I didn't really know where they were going: there was a lot of material about sleeping and waking, a lot of poetry of the Horizontal Life that had not been written by me, but was part of what I felt.

*JDMcC:* What was the momentum, then, if you didn't know what those first stanzas were in service to or where they might be heading?

*JH:* That's very interesting. I had to discover that I started with these and then I knew that *they* were starting something. I'd chosen the form obviously with some kind of Stevensian triad in mind, but that was *only* a formal thing. There is, I'm afraid, a lot of Stevens in it, but put at least to some useful purpose—not just for rhetorical show but as part of the world through which the quester of the poem moves. I think it's partially a matter of moving through certain kinds of language and coming out to other things. By about the third or fourth section, I realized there was going to have to be a sequence, it was going to have to go somewhere. And I think if you follow

the poem through, you see that it picks up motion, that the narrative action is of sleeping, waking, going back to sleep again, waking up after that, going back to sleep yet again; it's the interstices that become very complicated. The poem isn't sure whether waking moments are interstices in sleeping, or sleeping moments are interstices in waking. So it isn't really a matter of dream. It's something else. About halfway through writing it, I did have the dream, in fact, which is the prose epigraph—that of the Trumpeter—a literal transcription of a dream I had, a very short one, involving that trumpeter, hearing him. I actually woke up hearing that call. And the gloss on it—about the border between two countries, about not knowing whether the trumpeter was theirs or ours, is simply a declaration of some kind of political buffer-zone to be uncommitted to the state of dream or not-dream. ⟨. . .⟩

*JH:* I recently published a book which is all prose, called *In Place*. It could be considered as a group of prose poems—I really think of it as a sequence of meditations on fiction, on the replacement of things by other things, on standing-for—but almost every one of them starts out so that you think it's going to be a particular kind of short story. And then the story stops—the telling gets lost in itself, and in poetry.

*JDMcC:* But the character of your voice is not as insistent there as it is in many of the poems.

*JH:* Well, that's quite right.

*JDMcC:* There's a sense in which your prose is more "poetic." It's almost as if the schemes of verse allowed you a more varied or natural tone.

*JH:* That's quite possible. The tone of the prose pieces is quite contrived, and a lot of it is, in a sense, parodic. And even when it drifts off and away from that, it wanders off still following the ground rules set by the parody of other kinds of talk. My verses all generate their own voice. That's what form is for, to elicit and amplify voice. I think some people think form is for constraint of voice. I don't, and I never found that so whatever the level of form. Structures, patterns and games all conjure up voice and intensify it. That doesn't mean that something you do merely for the sake of rhyme is going to be good. Something you do for the sake of rhyme alone is probably *not* going to be good. But something you do for the sake of rhythm may very often be remarkable. You may discover something you didn't know in an effort to get the cadence right; you may bring to the surface a word you'd hidden from yourself. But in general I find that when a particular formal decision has been made, or I feel has been made for me, it does release the voice.

*JDMcC:* Let me ask about your *Selected Poems*. You arranged them in reverse chronology. Someone could say there are diminishing returns with that method of arrangement. Or do you want the recent work to guide the reader through the earlier, to influence his perception of persistent themes or recurring concerns?

*JH:* Put it this way: from my first book I include only those poems which I would really save in this company; I mean, that I don't think I was really writing many *poems* until *The Night Mirror*. A lot of it was verse-essay, epigram-literature—

*JDMcC:* What kind of poet was the poet of *A Crackling of Thorns* and *Movie-Going*? Who was he?

*JH:* Oh, he was a modernist of the 1950s, a creature not only of New Criticism but, I suppose you might say, of the literary culture of New York of the '40s and '50s. Somebody who was interested in celebrating, as well as could be celebrated, the avoidance of certain risks. Somebody who was willing to put a hedge of wit around certain terrors, and who was interested in exploring the avenues of his taste.

*JDMcC:* Well, what kind of poet is the one now who characterizes the earlier poet?

*JH:* I don't know. A sadder one. I hope a wiser one. I think I demand more of a poem, and of what a poem *is.*—JOHN HOLLANDER, Interview by J.D.McClatchy, APR, Sept.–Oct. 1982, pp. 23–26

## Works

### POETRY

John Hollander's A *Crackling of Thorns,* which Mr. Auden has chosen for this year's publication in the Yale Series of Younger Poets, is in point of technique the best first book of poems I have read in a good many years. By technique I mean not only the arrangement of stanzas, the selection of rhymes, the control of diction and rhythm, though these are skills which Mr. Hollander possesses in an enviable degree, but also the methods of manipulating poetic thought and feeling which have been established in the progress of the fashionable and "metaphysical" tradition of modern American verse. The tradition, it seems, comes to its ultimate flowering in poems like Mr. Hollander's; they gleam with jewel-like brilliancy as perfect formal specimens. What further can be done? Here is an impression of the minutest clarity in each formal detail, a rococo elegance—not inimical to sturdiness—which seems the very apex of the baroque development.

Mr. Hollander's ability makes his poems eminently enjoyable and readable. His songs especially, songs in literature being the utmost of artifice, are delightful. Here is a young poet who rejoices in a positively Apollonian mastery of feminine rhymes, for he bends them marvelously to his will. Again, his way of pointing a sentence within the line-structure—thought within feeling—is exquisitely economical. The longer poems are more excursive and some are rather involved. They expand in an ornamentation of word-play, allusion, foreign languages, etc. Mr. Hollanders is, as he himself says of one of his characters, a "dialectical cat". This is the stylish breed of tom, excruciatingly erudite, waggishly moral or sometimes morally waggish, above all amorous. He possesses as profound a capacity for seduction as for philosophy, and given time all is possible. But of course there isn't time; ergo a number of poems are devoted to time itself, the accepted metaphysical enigma.

What I have been trying to say is that Mr. Hollander's poems are very fine, very much to be admired and liked by anyone who is aware of the difficulties of writing verse, and that probably they are representative of the best writing now being done by young Americans, if writing is considered solely in terms of the formal skills. What I have been trying to intimate is that something else is lacking. In assimilating the fashionable voice so entirely Mr. Hollander has run the risk of losing his own. This is, after all, a first book, and perhaps a certain indeterminateness is to be expected. But I think Mr. Hollander must put his great skills to the service of a more personal insight if he is to produce work of any appreciable durability. A high proportion of his poems, for instance, spring from purely literary sources, and are equipped with the appropriate apparatus of titles, epigraphs, and dedications to signify their origins. Now this is an approved method of writing, it has produced good poems which we all know and love, but it comes more and more often as our era wanes to be an intimation of the poem's masked remove from experienced reality, and this, I'm afraid, is the impression given by some of Mr. Hollander's work. There is a kind of bombast, not of the word, but of the idea, to which metaphysical poets fall victim if

they are not careful, a kind of witful scrollwork applied in the pure joy of intellectual excess. Such a poem as Mr. Hollander's "By the Sea," which is elaborately built up in long syntactical units and a circuitous progression of imagery, is likely to collapse in a heap if one looks too hard at the slight conception upon which it rests. It seems to have been written for the sake of the method, not for the sake of the poem itself. The songs are better; most good songs occur in a dramatic context, the popular tradition, even in love songs, being for a public emotion, or at least an emotion belonging to somebody else. But the personal lyric (quite distinct from the song) and the meditative lyric—the two mainstays of the lyric tradition—exist solely by virtue of the individual poet's authority and require an individual voice, an achieved style which can only be appropriated from the common style to the extent that the individual struggle tends in the common direction. At this point the reviewer hesitates; to go on here may be to presume on the poet himself. Can we let Paul Valéry speak on our behalf? "A work demands love, meditation, obedience to your finest thoughts, the invention of laws by your soul, and many other things that it draws miraculously from your own self, which did not suspect that it possessed them"—a notion we ought to recall from time to time, I think, now that our rules of practice begin to stiffen so noticeably.—HAYDEN CARRUTH, *Poetry,* Nov. 1958, pp. 107–9

For more than a decade poets have been dismantling the old traditions. They have experimented with surreal images and new subject matters. They have burrowed deep into their personal anguish, and deeper into the calamities of American public life. It seemed that some new and permanent shape had arisen in American letters in the work of poets as different as Allen Ginsberg, John Ashbery, W. S. Merwin, Gary Snyder. But experiments and moral anguish are exhausting. The recent nostalgia that everyone is talking about, for the graceful, private, paranoid and white years of the fifties, has not left poetry untouched. Lately voices have been heard—James Merrill, Richard Howard, Daryl Hine—making a claim again for rhyme and iambic pentameter; for poems about traveling in Italy; for lengthy elegant phrases, raising life out of the crude realities into a saraband of sunlit forms and airy monologues.

John Hollander's new book, *The Night Mirror,* belongs with a vengeance to the poetry of the new nostalgia. In a sense, it is a brave book, ignoring just about all of the changes that poetic language has undergone in America since Ezra Pound first convinced everybody that they should "make it new." Hollander's motto instead is, make it old. The book is so full of selected echoes that the effect must be intentional. Hollander's use of "turbulence" for example ("Away we turn, awakening/A long memorial turbulence") to describe the experience of mystical insight, recalls Yeats's use of the word in "The Magi" ("Being by Calvary's turbulence unsatisfied"). In another poem, the lines "We took to the clear water/Writing our names in the book," recall Keats's famous epitaph: "Here lies a man whose name is writ in water." These are only some of the ghosts which haunt *The Night Mirror.*

Hollander is at his best among the generalities of the high style, which he manages with a sort of brilliance. At times a genuine rhapsodic sweep lifts his language, as in this poem entitled "In Fog, Tacit, outside Cherbourg":

> Stretching ahead from the afterrail,
> This wash, this prophecy,
> Leads the eye out of vision, where I see
> Even now, the moon's broad track
> Golden and treacherous, along
> Wide swells, extending toward its source

> But leading only into black,
> Lost waters, like lunacies of hope
> At night.

The language is antiquated, but the extended swell of the lines is managed with skill and suppleness. The best poems in *The Night Mirror* have a similar quality of old-fashioned brilliance. A few of them are frankly imitations, like the elegy for Andrew Chiappe, entitled "Damoetas," which echoes Milton's *Lycidas*. Reading "Damoetas" is like entering a museum. All the paraphernalia of the pastoral elegy are present: the swans, the stone bridges over brooks in green meadows, the mourning of the seasons, the pastoral pseudonym. To resuscitate these old forms verges on eccentricity, but the poem has genuinely moving moments:

> This was too heavy a spring, the April
> Vacant, the conditional May
> Shattered with cold, and now old
> Damoetas dead: and suddenly thereby
> Our dying has commenced, and dry
> Languages of mourning hold
> Fast in their unfilled beds.

Hollander's language here is simple and deliberate, using the traditional mood of elegy to strengthen its emotion.

Readers who enjoy this sort of high language will find a great deal to please them in *The Night Mirror*. All too often, however, I found myself admiring the performance, while I wondered why it was being given. In many of his poems, Hollander is like a virtuoso without a subject matter. The language soars in complicated trills, but in the end it becomes clear that no secrets are being told. Here is an example:

> O my Best Bear who stands
> And, not by reason of light
> But by fiat of fur, commands
> The height, the essential shore, the mere,
> The dryness outreaching into an icy, rich sea.
>
> The lord of our landless pole
> Is white, is white, and he hides
> On stretches of chlorous ice; the pale aurora,
> Rising behind him, thunders across the night.
> *But I am too wise now and fat*
> *To acknowledge a lesser one, here, than His Black-*
> ness.

Where is the shagginess of the beast in these lines? The vast loneliness of ice? What are we supposed to feel about "His Blackness" after we have made a few dull symbolic connections with the devil, or the blackness of evil? What we have here is simply run-on eloquence, and there is a lot of it in *The Night Mirror*.

Often Hollander attempts to anchor his lofty language in contemporary scenes: a couple groping at each other in a parked car; a trip on the IRT; a power blackout. But the poem registers a serious failure here, because these gritty urban images cannot be digested by Hollander's rhetoric. They stand out clumsily, or else they become curiously unsubstantial:

> Far beyond us, bluer
> Than a warm bulb's ripe light, of a colder color
> Than my white radiant calyx lets me pluck
> Or showers across my desk: Star, hanging between
> High, light-flecked peaks downtown, far yellower
> Than what the icy color of vapor streetlights
> Will yet yield up.

This might be New York City, or it might be some romantic setting in a castle filled with fairies. Hollander makes sideswipes at the real world, but in the end it eludes him. The worst poem in the book is a three liner about Noam Chomsky:

> Curiously deep, the slumber of crimson thoughts:
> While breathless, in stodgy viridian,
> Colorless green ideas sleep furiously.

I cannot even guess what these obtuse images have to do with Chomsky the political moralist or the linguist; in fact, with any human being.

By guiding his language into such glittering generalities Hollander sets himself an insoluble problem, for the life of the emotions will not enter here. That is a shame, because there are moments of real strength in *The Night Mirror*; these lines, for example, from the opening poem in the book:

> On the Memorial Building's
> Terrace the sun has been buzzing
> Unbearably, all the while
> The white baking happens
> To the shadow of the table's
> White-painted iron. It darkens,
> Meaning that the sun is stronger,
> That I am invisibly darkening
> Too, the while I whiten.

The images are crisp and strong, creating a felt connection between the inward and outward worlds. If *The Night Mirror* had answered the promise of lines like these, it would have been a different, and a far more moving book.—PAUL ZWEIG, *NYTBR*, Oct. 17, 1971, pp. 4, 20

"Light Verse" brings back the fifties when somebody's volume of the stuff was always getting reviewed. But with the exception of James Merrill (in a poem like "The Summer People") I don't know an American poet better at turning out sophisticated, hard-nosed (but good-hearted too) social verse than John Hollander, and it ends up not feeling "light," like light whiskey, at all. This volume ⟨*Town and Country Matters*⟩, published in 1972 in a handsome edition by David R. Godine, is made up of Erotica and Satirica, "translations and fresh creation" of "a world of classical urbanity" says the blurb. John Hollander's dirty mind is excellently displayed throughout, and Anne Hollander has provided appropriately feelthy and not so feelthy pictures as illustrations. The idea of setting out to be dirty and daring is a depressing one, but in fact these poems don't let themselves get locked into lubricious points. For me the best things in a never less than interesting collection are eighteen "Sonnets for Roseblush"—this sort of thing:

> I thought of turning you into a boy
> So that my queer friends, too, might feel the quick
> Of my longing when they read this, and the joy
> Of my having. But it's much too hard a trick
> Just as it is, to keep you breathing fast,
> Moving beneath me on this bed of paper.
> My lady is too volatile to last;
> How can I risk her substance to reshape her?
> Yes, that means you, sweet, I can feel you twist
> Against me still and freeze in a brief cry,
> My true deep secret that does not exist:
> Why should I break you out into a lie?
> No. Ed and Fred and Ted and Ike and Mike
> Will just have to imagine what it's like.

*Liber Amorem Liberat*, and there is a drawing of the lovers reading and writing while in other ways satisfactorily engaged. But the gem of the volume, and I would claim the best poem Hollander has ever written, is a long one called "New York," spun off from Juvenal, the friend "Rus" leaving town for good because living in the city has grown impossible, the poet staying behind to reflect on the meaning of living there. Written in strong couplets the verse twists and moves rapidly through the junk and glories of urban life. "Rus" sees through the whole thing as a sell:

> Across the park, the other Met is ill:
> You can find pots and pictures in it still
> I guess, among the crowds who are lured in
> Not by the touching bronze-age safety pin,
> The Dirck Bouts, or the Hellenistic head,
> Beauties and truths of the unending dead.
> But by the price-tag on the latest purchase
> While guards now eye us warily, and search us
> For razors, car antennae, pots of grease
> With which mobs humanize a masterpiece,
> The Mammon of attendance figures stands,
> Rubbing his failing directorial hands.
> Dear Hoving! let him repossess with love
> Those parks he was a good commissioner of!

Hoving as seen through Dr. Johnson seeing through Juvenal ("In full-blown dignity see Wolsey stand") or Pope ("In office here fair Cloacina stands,/And ministers to Jove with purest hands")—the poem is filled with eighteenth-century lines. Other institutions are similarly seen through and dispensed with by the exile. But after he leaves, the poet has his own fling at seeing through life in the country ("Dilapidated walls in cold Vermont") and eventually comes to a moving account of why he (Hollander in no disguise) will stay put to "see the ending out from where we should":

> With nothing working, services gone slack,
> Mushrooms on the abandoned subway track,
> Telephones silent between twelve and two,
> Thousands of cats reclaim an empty zoo.

He moves on to a lovely elegiac passage:

> West in Manhattan where the sun has set
> The elevator rises calmly yet
> In my dark tower, against the tower-dimmed sky
> Whose wide, old windows yield my narrower eye
> Images no revision can defeat: . . .
> Calm steam rising from manholes in the dark;
> Clean asphalt of an avenue; the spark
> Of gold in every mica window high
> On westward faces of the peaks

and concludes wonderfully:

> Gardens? Lead me not home to them: a plain
> Of rooftops, gleaming after April rain
> In later sunlight, shines with Ceres' gold
> Sprung up, not ripped, from earth; gained as of old.
> Our losses are of gardens. We create
> A dense, sad city for our final state.

I have not come across any better lines than these recently. To take back my earlier words, "New York" is neither a speciality nor a sport, just an admirable piece of work.—WILLIAM H. PRITCHARD, "Poetry Matters," *HdR*, Autumn 1973, pp. 590–92

⟨. . .⟩ John Hollander writes poems that are all mostly panoplied, at their best not at their most hermetic ("The Head of the Bed," reprinted here ⟨*Tales Told of the Fathers*⟩, breathes too much the exhalations of Stevens) but rather at their most graceful, in the poetry of compliment, like the poem given with a gold chain:

> Finite, but unended,
> Too narrow, like all our circles,
> To seem an eternal one. . . .
> Gold, like the touch of hands
> Clasping, but unchained.

Something apparently momentous but too often unintelligible is presumed in these poems—portents, allegories, hints. A

sequence of uneven poems, "Something about It," contains the poem I liked best on rereading, a poem about a man (called "It") contemplating his own writing:

> It sat gazing through the heat of Manhattan
>   Not at that heat but beyond
> At Its own dim pages, from which gray words dripped
>   Not unlike tears, or dried to
> Unsuspicious stains, ghosts of ghosts of scribbles.

There is an elegy for Auden (written in fact for his 65th birthday) in which, in a courtly bow to convention, Hollander turns the dead into a constellation:

> And now the constellation . . .
> Rises: *Der Dichter*—if not seasonal, then all the more
> Present continuingly, and *Alpha Poetae*, the brightest
> Star, the one whose name everyone always recalls,
> Burns away knowingly.

It is an elegy stylized and stylish, fulfilling Milton's command to poets, that they should "with lucky words favor [each other's] destined Urn,/And bid fair peace be to [the] sable shroud." In this elegy and the one for Mark Van Doren, Hollander shows how his gifts, too easily veering by themselves into complication for complication's sake, can be saved by a given occasion.—HELEN VENDLER, *NYTBR*, April 6, 1975, pp. 29–30

⟨. . .⟩ John Hollander's *Reflections on Espionage* is an extended metaphorical treatment of a special sort of conspiracy—"Us," the milieu of art, vision, understanding, the "altogether inconvenient little republic" of letters, against "Them," the philistines. Beginning with this neat analogy for the marginal state of contemporary poets, Hollander's long poem establishes several more equivalences: the verse is presented as a series of encoded messages, identified by month and day, and transmitted to other agents or to a "control" (who may be understood as a sympathetic critic). The "Work" undertaken by Hollander's group of master-spies is nothing less than the writing of the poetry of our own day; and it is all done under the direction of a topflight commander styled "Lyrebird," viz., Apollo or the Muse.

The poem's agent-narrator, code name "Cupcake," is, I assume, based on Hollander himself, and I believe "real life" prototypes for most of the other agents could be found. (The temptation is to guess who these might be; but, apart from the danger of putting one's foot in one's mouth, there is, again, the consideration that poems should be judged primarily as imaginative fictions.)

What Cupcake and his creator have in common is that they both seem to know everything. John Hollander holds, surely, the Monsieur Teste chair in American letters. His earlier poetry and criticism frequently and usefully allude to many kinds of learning—scientific, historical, musical—when these might throw light on the issues under consideration. *Vision and Resonance*, his study of poetry as a sonic and visual entity, is the most informative and infectiously interesting treatise to date on that subject. And Hollander's learning serves him well in his poetry, both as stimulus and substance. So often when we read poetry we feel we are sharing the life of perhaps heartening but elementary minds; I always welcome any occasion to listen to poetry that is rich in verifiable truths as well as in vatic ones—especially when, as in Hollander's case, it's all done with agility and good humor.

Amusement will probably be most readers' first reaction to Hollander's parodic spy-thriller, but I doubt it will be the last. The humor and wit so apparent in these pages suggest that the poet is dealing with matters too important to be presented with unrelieved earnestness, too urgent to risk leaving the reader in the detachment of pity or polite toleration. Cupcake's modest, jaunty transmissions, his simple faith in the Work, and his quietly stated doubts about his own value to it, or its overall significance, activate our sympathies without exacting them:

> I ask for nothing
> More than to do the work, to be able
> To work. It is not given us to complete
> It; neither are we free to desist from it.
>                                                    (9/13)

For nine months we observe Cupcake at the Work, listen to his characterization of other agents, and weigh his own ratiocinative or imaginative meditations, all of them cast in hendecasyllabic lines (or code "grids") as in the above sample. Some of Cupcake's most interesting reflections turn around the relationship between espionage (poetry) and the agent's "cover" (his ostensible profession), since in our day most poets must make their living by doing something besides writing poetry (teaching, for example, as in Hollander's case.) Cupcake raises, and wisely does not settle, many pointed questions on this subject. There are, besides, other issues to confront. During the nine-month period recorded, something seems to be gestating; this proves to be Cupcake's death or rather his "Termination," the order for it coming down from Lyrebird. No definite reason for the "termination" is given—but it is implicit. When Hollander's Muse stops being stimulated by the persona of "Cupcake," it's time to drop him and for the book to end. Of course, there may be more to it than that, for *Reflections on Espionage* is a richly textured work, multilayered, and evocative of meanings leading in several directions.

Among Cupcake's concerns some can be deciphered as visionary; and the terms he uses in talking about them remind us of Mallarmé and Stevens. Anyone who knows modern poetry will almost reflexively decode Cupcake's aspirations toward a Final Cipher as the Supreme Fiction Stevens made notes toward, or, again, as the final book Mallarmé asserted the world was destined to become. Mallarmé appears to be Hollander's most telling precursor in French (though possibly the same could be said for any American poet who has read him; Mallarmé is, I think, the quintessential modern poet.) In his poem "Aristotle to Phyllis" (from *Movie-Going*) there are, as Hollander has pointed out, several lines from Mallarmé's "Brise marine" buried in the text as English sonic approximations—the *mots d'heures gousse rames* word-game, but in reverse. Again, in Section V of his *Visions from the Ramble*, Hollander rings changes on the famous "Ces nymphes, je les veux perpétuer," which opens *L'Après-Midi d'un faune*: "These nymphs the winter would perpetuate, / Secure in their twigs. . . ."

In the present volume, the theme of the night-long poetic vigil at the heart of "Brise marine" and "Don du poème" is rendered by Cupcake in his 4/18 transmission to agent Image as follows: "long stretches of intensity / Without the quickening excitement which comes / With decipherment, and then nausea at dawn. . . . / It is as if one had been drained of something / Like light." And the Mallarméan (or Stevensian) longing for a final fusion of world and text takes this form in Hollander:

> To come upon the final Cipher,
> . . .
>           one would come to discern
> The world—even the innocent, unworking
> World—in it, would somehow walk in its rhythms
> Of transposition, in its modes of shifting.
>
> . . .
> A poem whose form was of the world itself.
>                                                    (5/10)

(Notice here that when Cupcake needs a metaphor for his

cipher, he arrives at "poem," much as a mirror image, reflected again, restores left to left and right to right. Reflections indeed.)

Cupcake then, among recent American voices, seems to have the clearest sense of the Mallarméan imagination. And Mallarmé's notion of the *azur* he seems very much at home with. The most characteristic Hollander moment has always seemed to be one captured in an environment at high altitudes and low temperatures, with cloudless, ultramarine skies. Canto X from *The Head of the Bed* and "Mount Blank" from *Tales Told of the Fathers* spring to mind as examples. In such an atmosphere, the clear-eyed intellect of a "Cupcake" sees what it is best skilled to describe:

> The weather
> Is dry and very cold, and the reception
> Should be better in this clear, cornflower-blue
> Evening sky, low winds humming through icy
> Wires above clusters of starlings crackling—
>                                                    (1/18)

Among English poets probably the most important for Hollander is Ben Jonson. Certainly Jonson has had few critics as sympathetic as Hollander. The two are alike in their complete possession of poetic tradition; and Hollander also seems to share Jonson's healthy attitude toward the classics, which the English poet termed "Guides, not Commanders." It may be, too, that the whole encoding conceit in *Reflections* is an allusion to Jonson's notoriously reasonable method of composition: poems were written "first in prose, for so his master Cambden had Learned him." Or, as Cupcake puts it, "a pressing message / Remains, uncoded in its naked plain on / The desk by one's left hand. . . ." I single out one more hidden allusion in the book's footnote to transmission 1/27: "These 'refrains' were enciphered simply as 'turn' after the first one." This may remind the reader of Jonson's *Ode* to Cary and Morison, with its strophes labeled "The Turne," "The Counterturne," and "The Stand," a poem Hollander has written about with great affection. The three labels already figured in a line from the lovely poem "The Sundial," collected in Hollander's first book.

In the twentieth century the poet most resembling Jonson is Auden; and some of the typical concerns of both—reasonableness, loyalty, and an interest in writing in many different poetic genres—have been inherited by Hollander. The association between Hollander and Auden was personal as well as literary, of course; and here I will quote the first but one of Cupcake's transmissions, which details the death of "Steampump," an agent unquestionably based on Auden:

> Steampump is gone. He died quietly in his
> Hotel room and his sleep. His cover people
> Attended to everything. What had to
> Be burned was burned. He taught me, as you surely
> Know, all that I know;
>                                                    (1/15)

I hazard that one of the germinating impulses for *Reflections* was a desire to present, in code, a portrait of what remains of Auden's influence in American poetry. The "covers" that I can identify all seem to have at least a tenuous relationship to Auden, either as poets he chose for the Yale Series, or as his friends, his disciples, or disciples of his disciples. This group, *mutatis mutandis*, is a fair equivalent for the celebrated Tribe of Ben that accounts for most of the important early seventeenth-century poetry in England after Jonson's death. Perhaps this parallel struck Hollander. Certainly it seems to be the case that, with the passing of Auden, we lack any figure of international stature in poetry. Greatness in the poetry of this moment is probably best judged as a joint achievement, the sum of a group effort.

The assertion of a real—though not pious—sense of community in Hollander's rendering of the present milieu of poetry is one of the book's most attractive features. He allows us to see how poets, at least some of them, must view each other's work and careers—not as a mad, competitive scramble, but as a kind of teamwork (see, for example, Cupcake's enthusiastic reaction to agent Image's "Project Alphabet"). The world limned out in this book has broader implications than its immediate reference, of course. It could serve as a model for an imaginative community on any scale, one whose members were all respectfully conscious of the others' lives, work, and "signifying" capacity. In such a utopia, citizens specifically designated as poets might vanish. Cupcake seems to be aware of the possibility: "as if the whole world perhaps were/ At the work? What then? Why then there would be no/ Need of it." But we are far away from that, I think. A book like *Reflections on Espionage* is still very necessary, nor could anyone but a poet have written it.—ALFRED CORN, GR, Summer 1977, pp. 536–41

"Spectral Emanations," the extraordinarily brilliant and ambitious work in poetry and prose which leads off this collection of John Hollander's new and selected poems (*Spectral Emanations*), is prompted in part by a passage, quoted in the volume's epigraph, in which Hilda of Hawthorne's *The Marble Faun* talks about the menorah, the golden lamp of seven branches brought to Rome in A.D. 70 from the Second Temple in Jerusalem and now presumably lying under the Tiber's mud. In *The Marble Faun*, Hilda proposes a parable in which the lamp will be recovered and its seven branches kindled, each with a different color, until the world is illumined by "the white light of truth."

"It will," she says, "be a seven-branched allegory, full of poetry, art, philosophy, and religion," and she goes on, in a passage not quoted by Hollander, to say that she will propose such a project—a project by which the imagination will create a poem in lieu of a lamp—to seven poets.

In effect, Hollander is these seven poets in one, and in *Spectral Emanations* he has written a poem in seven parts, one for each color, each of which is, to a different degree, political because it provokes the doubt that any one mode of consciousness or state of being or "color band" can be exclusive of any other.

This is a matter central to all of Hollander's work, and is responsible for his now being, to my mind, the most intellectually daring, poignant, and thrilling poet writing in the Emersonian tradition of our poetry. He is passionately absorbed in the transitional, what Emerson called the "vehicular" nature of substantial things. In the American mythos, things are "double" at the very least—a New World that is textualized by the Old, a new American personage (Whitman's dream) who is also an ancient. As constituted within this situation, the self is at the same time visionary and haunted, tentative and brave, and committed, almost of necessity, to a style best described by that noble Emersonian William James: "We ought to say a feeling of *and*, a feeling of *if*, a feeling of *but*, and a feeling of *by*, quite as readily as we say a feeling of blue. . . Yet we do not; so inveterate has our habit become of recognizing the existence of the substantive parts alone, that language almost refuses to lend itself to any other uses. . . . It is, the reader will see, the reinstatement of the vague and inarticulate to its proper place in our mental life which I am so anxious to press on the attention."

With its sense of the transitional, of crossed boundaries,

Hollander's poetry never indulges in the contemporary taste for fragmentation. As his critical writings alone would suggest, he is a master of classical and English forms; he can do a poem like "Fireworks" in strict Pindaric triads or a book length sequence like *Reflections on Espionage*, the unflaggingly brilliant and haunting book that preceded this one, in the hendecasyllabics favored by Catullus. He is forever playful about forms. There are included here six pieces from *Types of Shape*—one in the form of a car key, another of a light bulb—which are a delight to eye and ear. He is a formalist but a decidedly witty one. The changes that can be worked within form are made incumbent upon the discovery that any form is implicitly a substitute for or an interpretation of some other. Any form exists in the shadow of some other, and is on the verge sometimes of eliding into it; and the more you are aware—as Hollander asks you to be—of the form even of particular words, the more they are on the brink of those puns into which he sometimes lets them drop.

It is also crucial to any appreciation of Hollander's demonstrably major achievement that his sense of losses, deprivations, and transformations is never satiric in a distancing or disdainful way. His satiric manner is meditative, affectionate, and, above all, self-questioning. His is, in fact, a more radical self-questioning than any found in the confessional poetry, so called, of these times. Hollander escapes the limits of confessional poetry because he will not imagine the self—his or any other—in isolation, as a "substantive," to recall James, deprived of the relational and blurring effects of "and" and "if," of "but" and "by."

He suffers as true poets often do, not because he centralizes himself, as a confessional poet would, but because he does not and will not. Instead he finds himself, culpably, in everything, including the responsibilities for loss. Thereby we are given the extraordinarily moving conclusion to the new "Collected Novels," in which the speaker has been going over, with the woman he loves, some imaginary novels that might have been written while they were together:

> The last one, in press, being *Some Natural*
> *Tears*, which we were to have read together, hand
> In hand. You may perhaps now guess its subject—
> The old story we all know and can never
> Comprehend, its fierce transfers of elation
> Across the bound of loss, its presentiments
> Of endings, departures in the evening
> Shade of sky and distant horizontal woods

Form in Hollander is inextricable from visionary experience, from seeing things within a mode that can be shared because it is in part inherited and in part the result of some common pursuit, some corporate enterprise. The price is a necessary pain of complicity in the labors of composition, whether in the making of love or the making of poetry. Things are "safe for the heart because unenvisioned," he writes in "From the Ramble," and it is his human and poetic accomplishment, one of the very highest order, not to be satisfied with that kind of safety.—RICHARD POIRIER, "Crossing Poetic Boundaries," WPBW, Dec. 17, 1978, p. 5

## CRITICISM

There is hardly a writer in whom there is not some jealousy of music. Music can accomplish certain things that language strives for without ever quite succeeding. It can conjure up mood and atmosphere in an instant. It can generate simultaneously different and even contradictory impressions and meanings; what the poet aims at laboriously when he tries to suggest a plurality of feeling, through pun, ambiguity, or paradox, the musician can achieve at once through polyphony. When music is performed, its audience is intimately a part of the act of creation; but in literature, the reader or theatrical spectator is always an outsider. The poet sings to him, not with him.

Above all, music seems to offer the composer a miracle of constant renewal, whereas language, even in the hands of a master, bears upon it the stamp of long historical usage. Mallarmé and Ezra Pound, two of the modern poets most steeped in music, declared that it is the prime task of a great writer "to make words new." But this is immensely difficult. Being the current coin of life, words depreciate. The musical sound, which is by definition subject to limitless manipulation and variance, can be a totally new idiom to each composer. Indeed, Schönberg did what no writer, not even a James Joyce, could possibly hope to do: he invented a new alphabet.

The very image and emblems of poetry betray the persistent nostalgia for music. When we identify the act of poetry with Orpheus, when we depict the poet and the poet's Muse holding a lyre (not a pen!), when we divide epics into "songs" and "cantos," when we speak of the "harmony," "cadence," or "voice" of a literary style—in each instance we pay unconscious tribute to the role of music in the self-awareness, in the mirror image, of literature. So does T. S. Eliot when he entitles his most solemn poetry *Four Quartets*, or Joyce, with more ribaldry, when he calls his short poems *Chamber Music*. In fact, a lyric poem could be defined as a text in search of music as yet uncomposed.

Thus when poetry speaks of and about music, it is speaking, in a complex and often uneasy way, about itself. A poem about the nature and performance of music is a kind of inward dialogue. What John Hollander has set out to do in this massive, difficult, yet fascinating book ⟨*The Untuning of the Sky*⟩ is to record and examine this inward dialogue in English poetry in the period of the Renaissance and the baroque. So far as English is considered, 1500–1700 is the decisive period, for in it English poetry and English music achieved their richest coexistence. After that, the two voices of the imagination draw apart.

But Mr. Hollander, who is himself both poet and musicologist, begins much earlier. He explores the twilit regions of late antiquity and the early Middle Ages in order to show how Greek theories and practices of music were transmitted through Roman and medieval hands. Neoplatonized commentaries on Macrobius, Cicero's scale of seven tones, Judaeo-Arabic modal systems, and the problem of how King Alfred rendered Boethius are matters of sufficient perplexity. They are made no less forbidding by Mr. Hollander's style, which reads at times like a malicious translation of some Prussian musicologist, by his Carlylean predilection for capital letters, and by his decision to quote all texts in their most archaic and scholarly version.

Still, the reader should persevere. For it is in these opening sections that Mr. Hollander explains a distinction which dominates musical-poetic thought from the time of Chaucer to that of Dryden. It is the distinction between *musica speculativa* and practical music. "Speculative music" is an entrancing domain: it deals with numerology, with the attempt to discover concordances between the proportions of the universe and the divisions of the scale; it includes lore concerning the fabled effects of music on beasts and men, ancient doctrines of the power of music to madden or heal; above all, it concerns itself with the "music of the spheres," the notion still vital in Kepler, that the planets produce musical sounds concordant with the mathematics of their motion and

distance ("intervals") from the sun. It is the physiological lore of *musica speculativa*, not some vague metaphor of harmony, that makes Shakespeare assert that he "that hath no music in himself . . . Is fit for treasons, stratagems, and spoils."

Practical music, in contrast, deals with instruments, techniques of singing, improvements in notation, and most of what is included in the modern definition of musical theory. Mr. Hollander traces poetic accounts of the performance of music from the Old English *Phoenix* (ninth century) to the close of the seventeenth century. With massive erudition, he demonstrates that many a literary conceit thought to be fantastical or vague describes some technical musical usage. For example, he shows how the musical allusion in Donne's "Second Anniversary"—

> Think thyself labouring now with broken breath,
> And think those broken and soft notes to be
> Division, and thy happiest harmony—

depends on an exact knowledge of technical terms: "Breaking," in seventeenth-century music, is the process of figuration, of elaboration of the line of a particular melody with rapid figures and passages; sets of figures, variations improvised on a particular melody, were called "divisions." The broken, strained breathing, even the death rattle itself, is turned, because it announces the blessed state of death, into "division," sweet music. And behind the entire conceit lies the ancient image of the human body as a viol upon which the soul plays.

Applied to the use of musical terms and metaphors in Shakespeare, Donne, Marvell, and Milton, Mr. Hollander's knowledge of *musica speculativa* and practical music yields brilliant insights. No one before him had seen the full coherence and virtuosity of Dryden's cantatas, the "Song for St. Cecelia's Day," and "Alexander's Feast."

Coleridge would have savored this book. It is like a rich, faintly exotic banquet. One feels churlish, therefore, in asking for more. Yet I wished that Mr. Hollander had broached what seems to me a vital and puzzling question: Why has the English language drifted away from music? What happened after 1700 to disrupt the intimate alliance between verse and song that made possible the glory of the Elizabethan lyric and the splendor of English seventeenth-century vocal writing? Why the long, gray gap between Purcell and Benjamin Britten? There have scarcely been any English lieder in modern times, and until recently the thought of opera in English seemed somehow illicit. Why?

Perhaps Puritanism was at fault. Perhaps the language rhythms that molded modern English—iambic pentameter, the prose of the Authorized Version and of the Augustans—proved intractable to music. I don't know. But I should like to hear Mr. Hollander's guess. And if this means another book, all the better!—George Steiner, "The Lyre and the Pen," *Rep*, Feb. 16, 1961, pp. 58–60

*Vision and Resonance*, John Hollander's first critical book since *The Untuning of the Sky* (1961), proves to have been well worth waiting for. The earlier work was a comprehensive study of ideas about music, and the interrelation between music and poetry, in English verse of the 16th and 17th centuries. The shifting dialectic of attitudes toward music and verse is still very much part of Hollander's subject in his new book, but now he moves beyond literary history to a general analysis of how sound in poetry interacts with syntax, generic convention, and the visually scanned shape of the printed poem, to produce the complexities of poetic statement.

*Vision and Resonance* is the most subtle, convincing account I have seen of the operation of accentual syllabic verse in English. Hollander is meticulous in the use of concepts and terms where others have variously perpetuated a centuries-old legacy of vagueness, and the key distinctions he develops—such as between meter and rhythm, or between performative and descriptive scansion—seem not only precise but demonstrably valuable as he applies them. This enormously learned, technical study is a model of lucidity and, often, even of witty liveliness. The analysis of a variety of poetic texts from Donne to Blake to William Carlos Williams not only illustrates the general observations being made about English prosody, but also demonstrates how a discriminating approach through prosody can illuminate difficult or semantically dense poems. Hollander's readings of brief passages from Donne, Milton, and Blake have an Empsonian brilliance, without Empson's abrasive quirkiness: they impress one not as exercises in ingenuity but as fuller perceptions than previous readers have enjoyed.

The discussions of contrastive stress in English, and of the career of English enjambment (with special attention to Milton), are especially rich in such perceptions. In his account of Milton, Hollander finds the complex meanings of *Paradise Lost* in the interplay between metrical line and large rhythm, between printed word-placement and unfolding syntax, between the poem seen and the poem heard: "These two impulses—the one toward systematic, static pattern, the other toward periodic flux and articulated paragraphing—are the warp and the weft of the verse fabric of *Paradise Lost*." And in his final chapter, Hollander suggests that any poem must be located along the two axes of the eye and the ear, the former locked into meter, generic indentity, tradition, collective literary experience, the latter associated with rhythm, the particular objects of representation, individual talent, the intuition of the moment. "The ear responds to the dimension of natural experience, the eye to that of convention." The distinction is so sweeping and simple that at first one suspects it cannot be altogether true, but it is surprising how sturdily the generalization holds up under scrutiny, as Hollander's own abundant illustrations from a variety of poetic texts make clear.

This way of conceiving two intersecting axes of poetry has one important consequence for literary ideology: in even the most radically iconoclastic poetry, tradition and convention remain an ineluctable dimension of the poem. Modern poets may wilfully ignore the old boundary lines of poetic genre, but none can escape from the convention-bound axis of the eye. The seeming metrical chaos in Blake, as Hollander shows, is actually a refashioning of an older, discarded English tradition of seven-stress lines. Walt Whitman may have dreamed of a wholly organic, non-conventional prosody, "claiming to have made a metrical principle out of the unique shapes of rhythm," but in fact what he did was to introduce a new metrical convention, based on clearly end-stopped lines, the coincidence between complete syntactical units and linearity being a strict rule of his ostensibly spontaneous, oracular verse. More recent American free-verse experiments, in analogous ways, either generated their own metrical conventions, or "engage certain prior conventions . . . to form a new tradition, discontinuous in some ways as it may be," and the flaunted metrical freedom of the verse frequently proves, upon analysis, to relate quite directly to Milton's innovative prosody in the burden of meaning carried by nuances of enjambment.

In elucidating Ben Jonson's constant invocation of classical models in his poetry, Hollander stresses what he calls "the modality of verse"; a poetry which avowedly elects long-established forms of expression works toward "creating discourse in an ideal community, within which the literary dialect would be as speech." Modern poets have often rejected all notions of the modality of verse, breaking down genre and decorum in the effort to forge a uniquely personal, purely *expressive* style. Some, however, like W. H. Auden, have actually reaffirmed modality, adopting from the tradition a variety of forms and styles through which they implicitly assert a public realm of literary discourse more durable than the transitory idiom of individual experience.—ROBERT ALTER, "The Critic as Poet," *Cmty*, Sept. 1975, pp. 94–95

---

## W. H. AUDEN
### "Foreword"
### A *Crackling of Thorns*
1958, pp. vii–xiv

Every poem, be it big or small, simple or complex, is recognizably a world. What we call *the* world we infer to be a world, but no individual can perceive it as such; for each of us it is broken into fragments, some of which he knows quite well, some a little, some not at all, and even of those he knows best he can never truthfully say "I know what it is" but only "I know what it was."

In a poetic world, however, these obstacles to knowledge are eliminated: in a poem there are no strangers—every inhabitant is related to every other and the relationship is known; there are no secrets—a reader may notice something on a second reading which he missed on the first, but it was never concealed; there is no chance—the series of cause and effect is without any hiatus; and there is no time but the present—nothing can grow, die, or change.

There is among poetic worlds, however, an element of physical diversity which is lacking in the worlds, for instance, of painting and music; though the inhabitants of all poetic worlds are made of a verbal substance, this has developed into different linguistic strains which rarely permit of intermarriage. English is a more mongrel tongue than most and, for this reason, is perhaps the least prejudiced against words of another color; but even in English successful assimilation is rare and cannot be hurried.

So far as the practical and political life of the world is concerned, what happened at the Tower of Babel must, no doubt, be regarded as a curse but for poetry I can imagine no greater blessing. Indeed, at a time when so many of the forces making for world unity are so dangerous and disagreeable, the defiantly parochial character of poetry may even have an extra-artistic moral value. One can imagine a future world in which everybody on earth believes the same dogmas, obeys the same authorities, and is nourished on the same diet; but one cannot imagine a world in which Hungarian poetry, let us say, would be indistinguishable from Finnish.

It is just and proper that literary criticism should concern itself primarily with those problems and values which are common to all poetry, the nature of image and metaphor, the boundaries between the poetic and the nonpoetic, etc.; but it should also keep a place for the consideration of that which is peculiar to the poetry of a particular tongue, of those elements in a poem which are a priori untranslatable. Thus, while metaphors are usually, at least in theory, translatable, it is obvious that puns are not.

When Mr. Hollander writes:

> The question was whether to live like trees or towers,
> Evolving from the bare hills like conifers,
> Pretending ignorance of the changes of winter,
> Or standing bare as sorrow in the snow,

Striped red and green to show one's parentage
In the colored rocks of the hills he's quarried from.
Was memory to be the philogeny of towers
Or the languages of trees? A Past, that honors
Bright spears and perils held surely to the canter,
Or a History, with garlands at the brow
Of verdure and all her silent heritage?
The branch, or the eternal stone to come?

for all the complexity of this passage, one can imagine a translation of it into another tongue which would be intelligible so long as, in the culture which spoke that tongue, towers, trees, and time had the same kind of significance that they have in our English-speaking culture. But when he writes:

Europe, Europe is over, but they lie here still,
While the wind, increasing,
Sands teeth, sands eyes, sands taste, sands every-
              thing.

one cannot imagine any translation which would at once give the overt meaning and recall the line from Jaques' speech. (The operative word in this case reminds me of a line by Humbert Wolfe which I cannot resist quoting. "'Sugar,' he said, and pointed to the sand.")

Puns are, of course, a minor matter, but the linguistic idiosyncrasy of which they are an extreme case is exhibited in every aspect of poetry that is concerned with forms.

Many of Mr. Hollander's most successful poems are songs or, at least, "words for music perhaps." The song—the lyric is not quite the same thing—is, of all kinds of poetry, the one in which the formal verbal elements play the greatest role and are, indeed, the main source of interest. In the world of the song, one might say, the important relationship between the inhabitants is not any community of concern or action so much as family kinship. The satisfaction I get from reading a poem by Campion, for example, is similar to the satisfaction I get from studying a well worked out genealogical tree. (A wet afternoon could be pleasantly spent developing this analogy. Starting with the notion that masculine rhymes represent brothers, feminine rhymes sisters, refrains identical twins, one could ask what verbal relationship would be equivalent to a second cousin once removed. From there one could go on to consider what discords correspond to marriage within the prohibited degrees, e.g., to marrying one's deceased wife's sister.)

English is a language to which the most natural measured rhythm is accentual iambic; it has many common monosyllables, the metrical value of which depends not upon their intrinsic quantity but upon their position in the line; and it has, relatively, few rhymes, in particular few noncomic feminine rhymes. The criteria, therefore, by which one judges a song writer are firstly, his ability, by the use of equivalence and substitution of feet, to avoid rhythmical monotony without falling into rhythmical anarchy; secondly, his ability to vary the line length within a stanza in a way that sounds natural to what is said; and lastly, his skill in the finding of rhymes which sound neither forced nor cliché and in the placing of them so that the stanza is made an indivisible whole.

To my ear Mr. Hollander passes all these tests with ease.

Advocate the cause of cloth,
Though it's absurd;
And tender a suit against the moth;
Question him, and watch his sloth
To speak a word.
The furry silence that he keeps
Can be shown to be
    Like the one that creeps
  From quiet Roseblush as she sleeps
As silent as the moth, but not with me;
Softly in a bush, but not with me.

The use of masculine rhymes throughout preserves the iambic ground, but the omission of the first syllable in lines one, four, and eleven suggests a trochaic counterpoint; in lines seven and eight there is a felicitous hint of the anapaest, which is, however, kept within bounds since it is possible to scan these lines either as three feet or as two. The lines vary in length from five feet to two, and it will be noticed how Mr. Hollander keeps his stanza together by his placing of the rhymes in relation to this variation; sometimes rhyme and line length coincide, sometimes they run in contrast.

He is particularly skillful in his handling of feminine rhymes. The following two examples show what a difference the placing of such rhymes can make to the whole movement of a stanza.

Save one who, with a pair
Of emeralds at her ear,
    Felt for her shining toys
      And nestled to their nearness,
    Making a tiny noise,
    Idolatrous and bald.
      This was unenvying queerness.
    The boys were quite enthralled.

. . .

Living with men has made me
A dialectical cat;
Ergo, I argued that
Her course was to upbraid me:
She refused and she spat
(She claimed no punishment
But held that I'd repent).
    All this was repaid me
When, at the end of the quarrel,
I had her over a barrel.

They also show how, in a song, the thought and emotion, what the words *mean*, are inseparable from the form, the way in which the words move. It is impossible to imagine the one without the other: both are two aspects of a single imaginative act which, like all acts of the imagination, is a marriage of the given to the calculated.

In longer, nonlyrical, discursive poems, the element of conscious calculation is likely to be greater, and greater the danger, therefore, of a form which seems arbitrarily imposed upon the subject matter.

The test in such cases is, I believe, the opposite of what it is in a song. In a song the reader should be immediately aware of the formal structure, but in a discursive poem the latter should be unobtrusive so that he does not perceive it unless he deliberately looks for it.

In several poems Mr. Hollander has set himself the formidable task of constructing a fourteen-line stanza.

Feeling that it is vaguely undignified
To win someone else's bet for him by choosing
The quiet girl in the corner, not refusing
But simply not preferring the other one;
Abashed by having it known that we decide
To save the icing on the chocolate bun
Until the last, that we prefer to ride
Next to the window always; more than afraid
Of knowing that They know what sends us screaming
Out of the movie; even shocked by the dreaming
Our friends do about us, we vainly hope
That certain predictions never can be made,
That the mind can never spin the Golden Rope
By which we feel bound, determined, and betrayed.

Beyond noticing that all the lines are five-foot iambic and that there are rhymes, one's attention at first reading is concentrated upon what is being said, and one will never be obliged to see the structure unless one is curious about such matters. But if one investigates one will see that, in its rhyme structure, the stanza divides into two symmetrical halves rhymed abbcaca, the b's being feminine.

To prevent the stanza simply breaking in two Mr. Hollander allows no pause in sense at the end of the seventh line and generally, indeed, allows such pauses only in the middle of lines; thus the main pause comes in the middle of line eleven with subsidiary pauses in the middle of lines three, seven, eight, and ten. Further, there is no full stop until the end of the final line.

If in "The Fear of Trembling" and "The Great Bear," which are also written in fourteen-line stanzas, though differently constructed, the form seems more obtrusive than it ought to be, one of the reasons is that Mr. Hollander runs the sentences on from one stanza to the next so that the choice of fourteen lines seems a bit arbitrary.

In the pleasure he takes in begetting closely knit verbal clans, Mr. Hollander is a traditionalist, but he also shows a desire, characteristic of our own time, for the maximum amount of physical diversity. Like many modern poets, one of the questions he puts to himself is: "How many oddities, dwarfs, giants, albinos and the like can I credibly make my family breed? What variety of costume and haircut can I make socially tolerable?" This search for diversity is apt to breed a family of Bohemian eccentrics; that is to say, it is usually more successful when the poem is intended to be comic or seriocomic.

> I should rather
> Not involve her father,
> Nor did some bumbling fool
> Push her into the pool
> Without design;
> And we are all far subtler
> Than to accuse The Butler.
> Waly O how rotten
> That she was never mine.

In a serious poem there is a greater risk.

> For then, with the sun upon us, we remember
> That old prayers were extrapolations, fears
> Held in the cold were no mere casual guesses

It was sporting of Mr. Hollander to try to get in "extrapolations," but the result, I'm afraid, is a miscarriage.

I suppose Mr. Hollander must be called a "literary" poet in the sense that the inhabitants of his poems know more about poetry, particularly poetry of the seventeenth century, than they know about, say, gardening or cooking; and one has the impression that, on returning from a walk, they could tell one more of what they had worried about than of what they had seen. But, after all, why shouldn't they? Parnassus is a free country. Besides, when the worrier does manage to look at something, he may see what the naturalist would miss.

> No wind we know can stir
> This olive blackness that surrounds us when
> It becomes the boundary of what we know
> By limiting the edge of what we see.
> When sunlight shows several spruces in a row,
> To know the green of a particular tree
> Means disbelief in darkness; and the lack
> Of a singular green is what we mean by black.

## HAROLD BLOOM
## From "The White Light of Trope:
## An Essay on John Hollander's *Spectral Emanations*"

*Kenyon Review*, Winter 1979, pp. 90–115

Interpretation, like philosophy, begins in wonder, but otherwise unlike philosophy it pursues that course which Angus Fletcher has called "lateral fall," or wandering. The wonderful difficulty of John Hollander's "Spectral Emanations" has already proved a stumbling-block to some reviewers who have been concerned to treat the volume of *Spectral Emanations: New and Selected Poems*, in which it appears, as the work of the very witty neoclassical lyricist and verse-essayist he was twenty years ago, but has remained only occasionally, and with the work of his left hand, as it were, since 1965. His new long poem comes to us at the head of an important group of new poems including among others the somewhat Borgesian "Collected Novels," a poetic replacement for an oeuvre scattered along a road not taken; "Nocturne" and "The Lady of the Castle," two different modes of fearful confrontation with a female *daimon*; and "On the Calendar." This last is a sequence of short, prophetic scenarios falling on the thirty-one days of an imaginary month, each foreseeing a different way of death for the speaker, avoiding pointedly that form of execution on a gallows which would too literally have manifested the poem's *Galgenhumor*. This new group and, indeed, the whole volume of selections from all the poet's prior work save for *Reflections on Espionage*, and including some helpful and rather poignant notes and glosses, provides a useful context for the title poem. The whole volume, however, I have reviewed elsewhere, and should like in these pages to attend to the difficulties and the splendid achievement of Hollander's "Poem in Seven Branches in Lieu of a Lamp," as it is subtitled.

"Spectral Emanations" is manifestly a sequence of seven poems, each one named by one of the seven spectral colors, and each followed by a prose section of varying length and character. The whole is prefaced by a prologue called "The Way to the Throne Room," a parable of what looks like a kind of bardic ordeal in which are manifested the dangers that lie even in that trope of questing in which the poet, in search of a late sublimity linking form and subject, is always engaged. The narrator answers correctly seven questions apparently about the preparation and lighting of an oil lamp, the answers consisting in the identification of a number of angelic figures: "*Who trimmed the wick? Gananiel*, I confessed, *the lopper of branches, the one who limits that the many may flourish. Surely he did it.*" "*Who struck a light? Bhel*, I reconstructed, *the starred one, that we may see, that we may write our poor books, white fire on black fire.*" The name "Gananiel" would suggest, from the Hebrew root, a gardening angel, and that of "Bhel" is the Indo-European base (often prefaced by an asterisk because it is a reconstructed and not attested form, glossed by Calvert Watkins as "To shine, flash, burn; shining white and various bright colors; fire"). "Bhel" is treated with mythological playfulness in an episode in Hollander's recent poem, "Blue Wine."[1]

Having answered these questions, the quester moves through a series of seven antechambers, each of which constitutes a trap for some part of the company of all the lost adventurers, his peers, who are not to reach the throne room, or what we might read as the seat of vision in the *merkubah* or throne-chariot of Ezekiel. Unlike the two younger brothers in Hollander's mixed verse and prose romance for children, *The Quest of the Gole*, who fail to complete a sublime quest by succeeding so well at a lower one, these candidates lapse in variously intense ways:

> On the way to the fourth chamber, strange pictures
>     hung: a
> glass of green fur, an open apple, a house of loss;
>     and
> portraits of the Baron of Grass, the Count of
>     Nought.
> Those who approached to read the titles had to go
>     all the
> way back.
> On the way to the fifth chamber, all was smooth and
>     slate, as
> if beauty were a disease of surface, an encroach-
>     ment of
> depth. Many fell asleep, and had to be removed.

It will be seen that the progression from the surrealistic sportiveness of the fourth anteroom ("un verre de vair vert"? Having to "go all the / way back" sounds suspiciously like the children's game of "Giant Steps") to the Tennysonian swoon of the fifth is like a shift of phase in a romance of mythological island-hopping.

It is enough to say here that the narrator himself fails in the last antechamber, responding inappropriately to the glimmering of marble slabs there: "They / dazzled mine eyes, and it was not at my own tears that I / cried out *O water! Water!* Thus I was never to enter." It is clear that the text of "Spectral Emanations," a self-proclaimed replacement for an irrecoverable Jewish lamp, is to attempt sublimity only in an awareness of how its own route of ascent must by nature stop short of it. The solar spectrum itself, an image whose magic has been long since eradicated, could not, as I shall shortly show, provide a form for organized imagining, and it is by means of a reentry into a height of abstraction and visual arc previously identified with sublimity—a reentry through an almost fanciful intermediate trope—that a sequence of colors becomes a major myth. ⟨. . .⟩

The seven sections of "Spectral Emanations" depend for their form and scale on the seven-branched quality of the menorah itself, evoking not so much the traditional calendrical and mystical significances of the number seven as an importance totally ad hoc to the myth of the poem. There are exactly 504 lines in the whole poem, or 7! ÷ 10, divided into sections 72 lines long. The lines are syllabic, starting with six ("Red") and proceeding by augmentation to eight ("Orange"), ten ("Yellow"), twelve ("Green"), then down again by twos to six ("Violet"). These lines are grouped differently in each poem, from the epical twelves of the stanzas of "Red" to the sparkling tercets of "Violet." In a note we are told that Philo of Alexandria had associated a different planet with each branch of the temple menorah. Hollander follows his Hellenistic precursor in his use of planetary allusions in each section, save that, as he says in a note, "Saturn and Mars have had to exchange their places"—"bloodied Saturn" appearing in "Red," and a statue of Mars in "Yellow." (He grimly comments later that the confusion of these "is always more than a matter of the mechanics of vision.") Thus we have the displacement of Saturn by Mars at the left-hand, westernmost and, here, red first branch of the menorah; the whole array goes as follows: Mars (R), Jupiter (O), Saturn (Y), Sun (G), Mercury (B), Venus (I), Moon (V).

"Red" is certainly Mars's poem. The first of the sequence, it is a representation of redness as primitive, both creatively (the Adamic earth) and destructively (the blood of warfare, or the crude heroic). The poem was composed, we are told, during the 1973 Arab-Israeli war, and concerns the death of a soldier in a desert battle. The soldier is known only as J; he is both the soldier and the prophet Jonah (like him, J is "exceedingly glad" of a gourd-shaped shadow which affords him some shade). The poet connects the destroyed soldier and the reluctant prophet of destruction by reference to the fact that the Book of Jonah is read on the afternoon, in Jewish liturgy, of the Day of Atonement (on which the 1973 war broke out). The poem is spectacular and violent, but before the protagonist's destruction by "the fiery worm" of a rocket, a vision links the battle of "Red" to all the fables of desert warfare everywhere in Western history. The "unwilling prophet of / His past" sees "screaming / Seals ripped open" and echoes of Mycenae ("Bronze / Spears smash grayware pitchers"). Gideon's battles in the Bible ("Torches splash fear near tents"), classical, medieval, and romantic warfare all emerge:

> as can by
> Opened can the film of
> The ages runs in coils
> Across his mind's sky.

This celebration of the "wide realm of the red" is followed by perhaps the most beautiful of the prose "commentaries," and certainly the most pure prose-poem of them all, a meditation on the primitiveness of red starting out with the hieroglyph of its name in Semitic: an ox, a door, some water (the aleph, daleth, mem of the word "adom" were originally pictograms for these). It ends with a vision of an epic bard (one of the seven poets suggested by Hilda, perhaps):

> The red singer sits looking back toward the violet
> becoming black. His songs are capable of the opened
> and the spilled; only for them the wind sings in his
> hair. He stands outside the door; his shadow falls
> across it. Blown dust makes a false threshold.

"Orange" follows, a rather brassy poem which moves from an evocation of morning awakening, rising orange-colored sun, and breakfast, "the rising hemisphere of / Huge Florida orange," to metallic gold, the brutish version of value or worth which follows upon the primitive grandeur of battle. Its mythological figures are Midas, whose golden touch here turns even an erotic partner into a lump of gold; and Jupiter, coming to Danaë in a shower of gold coins, imbruting himself thereby. Here, the only heroic diction in "Orange" is flung up in criticism:

> Not with the juice of sunlight
> Streaming with magnificence does
> The crude chrysomorph enter her,
> But like light interred in the hard
> Shining that dazzles poor eyes with
> Mere models of the immortal.

Gold as the travesty of fruitful goldenness, Jupiter as the usurper of the milder harvester, Saturn, is the subject of "Orange." A glimpse of a way back to the Saturnian gold appears in a mention of a reality principle, "the living dullard / Of daylight"; he reappears in the prose commentary as the poem's clown, Roy G Biv, the traditional mnemonic acronym of the color-names whom Hollander associates with lead because of a Hebrew pun on the word *Biv* ("sewer pipe"). Biv mocks the systems of tropes by which gold is made noble, or by which colors can be mixed; he is what we might call an Idiot Answerer who smashes the myths of gold in order to move us on to the realm of what Milton calls the "vegetable gold" of Paradise, the region of Yellow:

> Dirty gold sublimed from the black earth up
> In bright air: these are the awaited stalks,
> The ripeness possible to imagine
> Even among mezzotints of winter,

And to remember having imagined
Oddly amid the late spring's lackadaisies
And all of the earlier primulas.

With this opening, the powerful poem of "Yellow" asserts its own aspirations to sublimity, even as its opening words have become transformed by the time the colon in the second line has been reached. "Yellow," save possibly only for "Violet," is the strongest verse section of the whole poem, a romantic crisis-ode of great beauty. The floral yellow of the opening stanza modulates through a moment of self-representation:

the attentive images of
Jonquils peering out at themselves along
The wide bank

to the yellow of candle-flames burning in sunlight, among golden grain, "the bright fruit / Of what we after all have"— fruit, flame, eye and flower. This modulation follows the first of the three poetic crossings (Election, Solipsism, Identification) which I have elsewhere mapped as the structure of the poem of crisis. The Crossing of Election from irony to synecdoche covers the gulf of doubt: "Am I truly a poet?" Here, the reflections of the jonquils, the last trope on one side of the crossing, are followed by the turn away toward a new source of figuration:

Which would be no fulfillment
In any event, of early pallor:
It would remain an interpretation
Of the flimsy text, half remembered,
Dimming evermore and diminishing.

The second eighteen-line stanza performs the two tasks of celebrating the myth of yellow, now totally free of even a tincture of its prior neighbor, orange, and of confirming the poetic voice of the propounder of true fictions. Its climax starts with an echo of a Jewish prayer made at annual festivals, said in thanks for having been sustained and preserved and enabled to experience the present moment, and proceeds through to a gentle but still energetic revision of the hard, ironic images of entrepreneurial awakening in "Orange":

To have been kept, to have reached this season,
Is to have eternized, for a moment,
The time when promise and fulfillment feed
Upon each other, when the living gold
Of sunlight struck from the amazing corn
Seems one with its cold, unending token,
The warm time when both seem reflections from
The bright eyes of the Queen of the Peaceful
Day being welcomed with these twin burnings,
These prophetic seeds of the Ripener,
Brightness rising and getting on with things.

Yellow has redeemed even orange, the goldenness of American corn (maize) has reversed the traditional trope and declared metallic gold only to be an image of itself; the presiding figure who in fact emanates both of these is Hollander's version of the Sabbath Queen, celebrated in the liturgical imagery of normative rabbinic Judaism, but associated Kabbalistically, as he may have learned from Scholem, with the eros of symbolic marriage.

In any event, the second Crossing of Solipsism, as I have called it—the realization in figure of the will's question, "Am I able to love?"—occurs with the startling opening of the next stanza. The opening word, "*Or*," is both the name of gold in romance languages and the poet's figurative gold of word-hoard; Hollander must be consciously or unconsciously echoing the rhetorically complex "or" by which Milton moves from simile to simile, classical comparison to comparison, a move which, if it implies that the reader is to take his pick, is lying.

"*Or*" is followed by a strange metrical effect, a compression into the pure syllabic lines of the jingle of minor romantic song, such as Thomas Moore's:

In the air there is a soft *gleaming*
As of fair light in certain *hair,* and wind
Through the pale curtains *streaming* like moonlight
In the dark *air.*

(Italics mine, to mark the rhymes of the hidden verse.) But this mode of evocation is rejected in a turn, with the italics here the poet's own, toward keener sounds of evocation: "*This has been all of silver,*" he says, and then proceeds to describe the birth of the true erotic and poetic counterpart, as "the man of earth inhales a girl of air," bringing with her a "return of everlastingness" and leaving even the creator-lover's emptied arms "with light beyond seeming," the sublimed trope of worth beyond counting.

The final crossing, that of Identification, occurs in the middle of the final stanza at a point of transumptive vision,

When the world's yellow is of burning sands
Leading down to the penultimate blue
Of, say, the Ionian sea,

and where the blue of the clearest of water ("penultimate" both in relation to violet in the larger scheme, and in relation to the trope of death) reveals the final meaning of the blessedness of yellow to the swimmers, whose golden bodies are "in their purest / And most revealing element at last." The adventures of "Orange" were a travesty of pathos, as well as of worth; the arioso of "Yellow" has redeemed them both.

The prose of "Yellow," like that of the "Indigo" section, is the most explicit commentary on a transition from one color region to another. It starts with what is surely a rhymed quatrain printed as italicized prose and ascribed to a mythical French Jewish poet, but proceeds through two anecdotes to gloss the creative and imaginative progress from the orange-gold to the yellow-golden. The first describes an imaginary painting that might have been done by the American Romantic, Thomas Cole, one of his visionary "The Course of Empire" series. (Hollander had written an interpretive essay about it some years earlier.) It is seen from the point of view of a spectator, perhaps a traveller from some other antique land, at Cole's huge scenes of "Fulfillment" (with its crowds of worshippers, in form somewhere between John Martin and Cecil B De Mille) and "Destruction." "Their famous chryselephantine Saturn," he says, has loomed up behind them as they watch triumphal parades. "But it would only be after that lowering crimson, rhymed in the red fires of the Conquerors come that same evening," he continues, that they should discover the statue, about to fall into ruins, "to have been one of Mars, sword curved in the same flat crescent as scythe, gatherer of red rather than of yellow." The whole first sequence from red to yellow, including the Saturn-Jupiter-Mars displacement, is here summed up.

The second anecdote is a parable of transumptive figuration, of copying as *copia,* of incorporation and originality: "Hilda laid on the gold leaf. The copy she was making of 'The Miracle of the Field' flourished and sprouted under her shining care. . . ." Hawthorne had himself implied that Hilda's copies were more authentic works of art than the original paintings of others (and in this, Hilda may be also the muse of that remarkable prose romance, *The Recognitions* of William Gaddis); the painting Hollander has invented for her is of a myth of imaginative transformation, a field of golden grain, probably, and evolving from the fields in such of his relatively recent poems as "Rotation of Crops" and "Being Alone in the Field." The anecdote concludes with an assurance that "This was true plenty."

"Green" is a vision of summer and love. At the midpoint of the sequence, its expansive, long lines and its high rhetoric have a relaxed quality that starts with the opening chant of a summer evening, whose darkening will bring green to black, with the poem's own hope of "some hushed / Nocturnal verdant." The delimitation of green from the blue that borders it is not handled in the quizzical parodies of argument that the author's earlier poems employ, but rather by an embodiment in a *locus amoenus*, a paradisal landscape:

> In the high day, clear at the viridian noon,
> Blue water, enisled in the broad grass singing hot
> Choruses of summer, lies still; and far away
> Half-gesturing lakes surrounded by dense, quiet
> Spruces recall the silence that we are told lies
> As a green hedge around blue wisdom. At the edge
> Of things here and now, soft-looking cedars, waving
> Away at azure, keep the sky at a distance.

There may be an echo here of a Talmudic saying to the effect that silence is a hedge around wisdom. The movement of the poem's green going brings it past a stanza of love being made on a lawn, and another of a poetic wanderer, a Whitmanian "nomad among the verdures" who partakes of the intensity of this central, high greenness. Hollander quotes from Goethe's *Theory of Color*, one of his precursor texts for a mythology of hue: "*Man will nicht weiter, und man kann nicht weiter*" (one neither desires, nor is capable of, anything beyond green), and in a final stanza he specifically rejects a series of prior readings of the meaning of green ("no flag of what state one is in" is clearly a turn, albeit somewhat uneasy, against Whitman's unfurling of the trope of grass: "I guess it is the flag of my disposition").

Hollander's hymn to green is followed by a prose section which is less like incantation than any of the others. The procession through the first, or "warm," half of the spectrum from heroic through ironic to meditative lyric has been paralleled by a counterprogression in the prose pieces, from lyric (in "Red") to the narrative romance of the 12-page "Leaves from a Roman Journal" (in "Green"). This quirky and poignant story of a caper—the rescuing of the historical menorah from the Tiber's bed and the transporting of it secretly to Jerusalem—shares some tonal and parabolic elements with *Reflections on Espionage*; its unnamed narrator, one of a group of seven conspirators (their names are those of the colors in various languages, and the narrator must be the missing indigo), sometimes sounds like a prosy Cupcake, Hollander's pastoral poet-spy. "Leaves from a Roman Journal" has all the trappings of a romance novella, including a mock table of contents of the story of what is happening, should it be written up; however, this section is darkened by the true grimness of a preceding personal confession, allusive of the narrative prayer (a reminder of the history of providence) in the Passover service, whose refrain is "*Dayenu*"—"it would have been sufficient." There is also a good deal of anxiety expressed by the conspirators about unearthing and destroying various false simulacra of the Lamp (as it is called throughout). I shall only observe here that the playful and the literal version of "The Recovery of the Sacred Candlestick," as Hilda called it, constitute an exorcism of the various spectres of reductiveness, of failed figuration, which might turn the poem's own poetic quest awry. It is protected in the poem by its dreamy occurrence in the region of summer night, amidst

> The patience of the deep that black has when green
> ends
> The still unquenchable absorption of its gaze.
> It will not be, can never be a mere return.

"Blue" I must confess to liking the least of the seven. It may be here only that scheme has blocked high eloquence, and it is not irrelevant that this was the first of the seven verse sections to be written. The language of the four strophes, two of four quatrains and two of five, is most palpably Stevensian, as are some of the versions of the trope of blue itself. Its fables and their ordering cleave perhaps too closely to the line of *Notes toward a Supreme Fiction*, and its mythopoeia of tinctures of *l'azur*—two moons, "two modes of night," sea-blue and sky-blue—may be, despite an elegant and exuberantly pleasurable rhetoric, less fully realized than we might hope for a region following upon green. Mercury's assigned appearance in the poem is as a kind of sad prankster substitute for Venus as an evening star:

> Mercury leered out of the bold cobalt
> He was returning to, remembering
> Azure anterior to this night's share.

But he returns, far more effectively, as the liquid metal bearing his name in the prose following "Blue," an Ashberyan instruction manual for building a contraption for creating a poetic self. It is a mysterious machine whose structure seems more important than what it does (which remains undisclosed until the end). Akin to Elizabeth Bishop's monument, to the machine in Kafka's penal colony and, perhaps ultimately, to the allegory of the decay of the body in *Ecclesiastes* with its breaking of golden skull and loosing of silver spinal cord, the manual warns against too open an acceptance of its own tropes:

> Do not make the mistake of sentimentalizing the mechanical parts: for the flywheel, archaic and precise with its gleaming spokes, is a horror of solemnity, going berserk at the insinuations of jiggle—the twin moons of the governor are a cramp on exuberance—the pistons slide joylessly in their cold oil—the shining brass gauges were unwisely calibrated in a time of hope.

Activity, whether athletic, artistic, sexual or moral, will suffer by being represented in reduced—here, mechanical—terms. It emerges only at the end of the commentary that the machine is a system for the deconstruction—and here I employ the word in a sense far less figurative than that of Derrida and de Man—of all "those to be dealt with," the "despots," finally identified in the last paragraph: "If you get it to work properly, it will put an end to them, your predecessors." The element of destructiveness in blue, which had not arisen in the verse, is revealed in the baroque wit of the prose to be a crucial element of imaginative creativity, even as the Kabbalah reminds us of how vessels must be broken that light may re-emanate.

"Departed Indigo" pauses for a moment, on the way toward the ultimate darkenings of violet, to propound a lovely fiction of beneficent night. It starts out from what would, in the poet's earlier work, have been a more philosophical exercise, perhaps a pseudo-Wittgensteinian questioning of the meaning for nature of the contraction of the conventional spectral colors from seven to six, as they are taught in schools today. But this poem turns to fable instead, and supposes an Astraea-like lady (although no virgin) departing the fallen world at a recent time, but inhabiting the color of the night sky in among the stars:

> the rich, hopeful darkness seems
> Deepened by her presence, under
> Which we live and, hushed, still breathe the
> Night air's perfume of discernment.

Along with "Red," the hymn to indigo is more immediately accessible out of context than some of the others. Its prose I have already touched upon; aside from recapitulating the system of songs of the entire work, it moves to a close with a charming and domestic version of the rising of nighttime's blue from our own midst, with perhaps a reminiscence of the rising of the kite at the beautiful ending of Beckett's *Murphy*:

> And so at the end of the day, the sky deepening as we
> walked back from the Prater, or home from the zoo,
> or along the river away from the fun-fair, the
> youngest child's balloon, the dark one, escaped from
> a fist tired at last, vanishing into its own element of
> the color between day and night.

"Violet" is the region of endings, of color on the verge of its own cancellation in blackness. Its relation to red, the other liminal domain, is made clear at the outset:

> At the song's beginning
> Even as our voices
> Rise we know the last words
> And what it will sound like
> To sing them at the end
> Of the final burden.

This opening figure, drawn from the experience of actual singing, reappears throughout "Violet" in associations of text and song, even of musical notation. But this last incantation of a region past even belatedness, "this chamber of codas," is also linked to the genesis of "Red" by being "The epic of whispers." The central trope here is as manifestly Judaic as the scene of the opening, but it is drawn from the tragic, marginal realm of the Marranos, the Jews of Spain and Portugal forced into Christian conversion but who often practiced Judaism in secret and sometimes reconverted in such havens of toleration as Amsterdam and Turkey. (Beatrice de Luna, a heroine of Marranism in the sixteenth century, enters the musings of the narrator of the romance of "Green.") The image is of a candle "set / Down inside a pitcher," carried out into a dark field. Its illumination, a metaleptic treatment as it may be of the "ironic points of light" in Auden's poem of the onset of World War II, is that of true poetry itself:

> Like a star reflected
> In a cup of water,
> It will light up no path:
> Neither will it go out.

At this point, "Violet" becomes quite explicitly Kabbalistic in some of its references, but Keatsian as well, in its acknowledgments of light giving way to sound at the end of the Autumn ode, in a "wailful choir of / Natural small songs." That the emanations of the colors are themselves to be identified at some level with the seven lower *Sefirot*, or images of the transcendent, is made clear in the prose of "Violet" which, of all the prose "commentaries," seems most intimately connected to, and most directly to follow from, its verses. Toward the end, the prose moves toward the free-verse cadences of the prologue: "It will be only his old man's dream of dawn that unrobes the violet, allows the early rose to take her morning dip." This is followed by the counsels of closure: "He remembers this, and thinks not to quest among the regions of black for what lies beyond violet, But would stay to hum his hymn of the hedges, where truth is one letter away from death, and will ever so be emended." The allusion here is, I believe, to a story translated by Gershom Scholem about the construction of a *golem* or Frankensteinian replacement for man, who had, like Adam, the Hebrew word *emeth* ("truth") inscribed on his forehead, but who asked that, like Adam, he be allowed to die by having the initial letter erased so that the word would read *meth* ("dead"). And hence, I believe, Hollander's fearful pun on "M-ended" and *"emeth,"* at the moment of destruction, by completion, of his own golem, or poem.

The conclusion of "Violet" and its black prose coda

expresses a final ambivalence about the transcendence of metaphor, moving beyond the cautions about "what lies beyond violet"—in electromagnetic radiation, the realm of the harmful, in trope, the regions of silent darkness—to a series of ritual blessings for the gift of poetic language itself: "Blessed be he who has crushed the olive for the oil. Blessed be he who has cracked the oil for the light. Blessed be he who has buried the light for the three tones beyond. . . ." Whether these "three tones beyond" are an allusion to the higher *Sefirot* of the Kabbalah or to hues which have emerged from visibility into audible tonality and have become images of voice, the sense of this poem's ending is clear, and its closure the kind of trope of death which has always allowed figures of life beyond life to follow. ⟨. . .⟩

In earlier poems like "At the New Year," Hollander had brooded over the ghostly demarcations which mark the phases of our natural and human cycles and, in an actual emblem poem from *Types of Shape*, had meditated upon the significance of the *Magen David*, the shield-of-David-as-hexagram, "of no great antiquity," as he correctly observes in a subtitle, as a "liturgical symbol." "Graven Image" (*Spectral Emanations*, p. 143) acknowledges, by its title, the aniconic strain in Judaism; for the belated diasporic poet, the forbidden images are not those of stone idols, but rather *eidola*, mythological images of poetry. "Craving the rich dark icons ever denied us," the poet goes on to explore, by the very act of producing the typographical form, the significances lurking in the six-pointed star, commencing with the "momentary finial" of the upper triangle:

> A
> bit
> of an
> image a
> hint only

and ending with an ultimate commitment to a dark, pre-Judaic reading of the sign as the interpenetration of male and female genital forms:

> Let there be only
> this final sign
> this triangle
> of the dark
> about thy
> opening
> loves
> own
> V

The poem ends on its own omega, the capital letter whose form is synecdochic for that of half the image itself. On the way "down" the poem, the reading touches on the antithetical Nazi and Zionist uses of the emblem ("unshielding be it in blue or yellow"), but resolves to substitute its own misprision of the sign, the poem itself. The star, the poet says, "with the broad menorahs feathered wings was all / the symbol we were permitted"; it remained for his major poem of a decade later to reinterpret the menorah on a far grander scale, associating it with a tree (as it is in an incised carving on the Hellenistic synagogue in Sardis) and, specifically, in "Violet," with a substitute for the locus of the Divine Voice:

> —A tree of light. A bush
> Unconsumed by its fire.
> Branches of flame given
> 
> Sevenfold tongue that there
> Might be recompounded
> Out of the smashed vessels

Of oil, of blood and stain,
Wine of grass and juice of
Violet, a final
White.

This grand trope, at once a fresh Breaking of the Vessels and a superb *Tikkun* or restitution, is the inevitable apogee of Hollander's poem, which I do not hesitate to proclaim as one of the central achievements of his generation, matching the long poems of Merrill, Ashbery, and Ammons.

*Notes*

1. This serio-comic suite of explanations—mock rabbinic *midrashim,* or interpretations—of what blue wine might be appears in the

current issue of *The Kenyon Review.* It was apparently occasioned by Hollander's having seen his friend Saul Steinberg's parodic wine-labels, pasted on bottles filled with a blue fluid, in the artist's apartment one day. The episode in question, a Homeric fantasy, intrudes upon its Tennysonian voyaging a local myth of the dispersal of *Bhel* by *Kel* (the Indo-European base for "cover, conceal") into various kinds of light, all named in words descending from *bhel. Steinberg's first language was Rumanian, which may account for the *"vin albastru"* ("blue wine") in the final, explanatory episode. I suspect that the whole poem may have resulted from Hollander's own uneasiness, whether conscious or not, about the "Blue" section of "Spectral Emanations," the completion of all of which enabled him to write more freely of azure matters.

# RICHARD HOWARD

## 1929–

Richard Howard was born on October 13, 1929, in Cleveland, Ohio. He received his B.A. in 1951 and his M.A. in 1952, both from Columbia University. Howard served as editor for the *Columbia Review.* He studied for a year at the Sorbonne, and then worked for four years as a lexicographer. In 1958 he committed himself to the profession of writing, and he has been a prolific poet, translator, and critic ever since.

Howard's first book of poems, *Quantities,* appeared in 1962. Critics praised the poet's technical skills, but faulted his thematic and narrative disjointedness. Later works were better received, and Howard's *Untitled Subjects* (1969) was awarded the Pulitzer Prize in 1970. Other collections of verse include *The Damages* (1967), *Findings* (1971), and *Fellow Feelings* (1976).

Howard published a critical study of forty-one poets, *Alone with America,* simultaneously with his Pulitzer Prize–winning volume of poetry. It was also highly praised. As a translator Howard has made significant contributions. He was among the first to introduce the French *nouveau roman* to the American audience. He translated Robbe-Grillet's *The Voyeur* (1958), *Jealousy,* and *In the Labyrinth* (1960); Breton's *Nadja* (1961); Gide's *The Immoralist* (1970); and Barthes's *Critical Essays* (1972), among many others.

Howard has also worked as an editor and anthologist.

Richard Howard is a poet of substantial gifts who has in addition most of the negative virtues; he is not prolix, not overdecorated, not pseudo-referent, not bardic, not otherwise affected. *Quantities,* if all of it maintained the level of its first poem, would be an impressive achievement indeed. "Advice from the Cocoon" sets a high standard.

Here is a grub
Of summer, modest in its public state
But growing by a private appetite
To prouder life . . .
The larva, not quite wool, but not yet will,
Is wrapped up well between his other lives.

Would you, like him, survive at any cost?
Then seal yourself in layers of yourself

Mr. Howard knows the diction of conversation may become poetry, but the rhythm of it cannot. Most of his collection is in strict meter, and, as in the passage quoted, rises to a strength no accidental measure can. The moral is obvious: if conversation is what you want, converse.

In "De Manus Fabrica" he is still impressive, but shows a characteristic fault.

Take a living hand; learn from it how
Upon love's skeleton, within
The protocol of bones unwavering

And white, some red imperfect
Self must keep us wet and keep us warm.

The mannerism is that of ending a line on the weakest possible word. Here and elsewhere it is too consistently held not to be deliberate. Occasionally it makes a striking effect:

can I do
Else in the wrong
Weather but look up and
Label it spring?
("September Twenty-
ninth")

but in the long run it is deleterious:

Later, when you were so
Warmly obliged to give
Away your old fancies
Was it not difficult
To face the hard choices,
Hating as you did to
Abandon the legend
("The Shepherd Corydon")

Of this one can say only, if an actor throws away every other line, he ends by throwing away the performance.

However, downbeat in the manner may be inherent in the matter. Howard is poet of the limited commitment, the negligent action.

Intercede
for us: we shall lose our hair. Comfort us
with stomachs: we shall be unhappy.
("Petition")
—TURNER CASSITY, *Poetry*, Dec. 1963, pp. 192–94

In Richard Howard's new book, *The Damages*, nearly every poem achieves a level of excellence not far below the peak moments in the best poems—the book is characterized by more evenness of performance than any of the other books considered in this review. If we can depend upon Howard never to fall short of a rigorous competency in any poem, we can also rely on him to be more predictable—to surprise and uplift us less with moments of genius—than an apocalyptic poet like W. S. Merwin. I hope that these remarks will not be misconstrued as a way of patronizing the artistic dependability of the solid craftsman, or of disparaging him by damning with faint praise. A few thoroughgoing technicians like Richard Howard are desperately needed to provide an esthetic backbone for any generation of poets. No poet writing in America today is a more exquisite—a more fastidiously deliberate—esthetician than Howard. His poetry is always lavishly textured, though the components of texture vary extensively from poem to poem. He is never without stylistic finesse, measure, proportion; however, in reading many of his poems at once, I find myself wishing, occasionally, to be outraged by an unseemly disproportion—an idea, or image, that in its crudity or excess may overpower its context. If only he were less determined to be flawless, and more willing to take risks. Howard is perhaps the only contemporary poet in whom unfailing artistic tastefulness may seem to become, at times, a vice.

The most abiding quality of Howard's new poetry is surface brilliance. Though most of the poems are without what is called psychological depth, they contain extraordinary quantities of topographical depth. If we can regard depth in art—unlike philosophy—as being a by-product of denseness and intensity of sensory data, then depth in Howard's poetry is to be sought less in the quality of the author's thought than in the superior elegance of his form. The best poems in *The Damages* are fortresses of poetic structure. The massive architecture of "The Encounter," "The Author of 'Christine'," and "Bonnard: A Novel"—to my mind, the three most distinguished poems Howard has written—seems to be capable of sustaining limitless amplification without losing the essential rhythm of experience that is set in motion at the start of each poem. Above all, this is a poetry of architectonics. Every line is consciously structured, and is felt to be an integral unit in the superstructure of the poem's surface.

If at first reading, structure appears to dominate subject in these poems, repeated readings may reveal that the true subject of this poetry is the structure itself; each poem being an adventure in which the structure is a persona, if you will, in the act of discovering and evolving itself; all the components of structure, then—the phrases, images, ideas, story—by a peculiar reversal of the usual priorities, may be viewed as vehicles for the enlargement of structure. It is no accident that the most successful poems are the ones in which structure is all-of-a-piece, rather than being deployed as a sequence of stanzas. To illustrate, let us consider the function of one element of structure—ideas—in the poem "Bonnard: A Novel." I will excise a random chunk of the poem for inspection:

Sophie, damp, dashes in
dishevelled from the forest, dumping out a great bag of morels
on the table: the white
cloth will surely be spoiled,
but the mushrooms look iridescent, like newly opened oysters
in the raindark air, blue

by this light. Calling it
accidental is only declaring that it exists. Then tea
downstairs, Jean opening
the round pantry window:
the smell of wet soil and strawberries with our cinnamon toast: all
perception is a kind
of sorting out, one green
from another, parting leaf from leaf, but in the afternoon rain
signs and shadows only,
the separate life renounced,
until that resignation comes, in which all selfhood surrenders.
Upstairs, more Scriabin
and the perfect gestures
of Sophie and Jean playing ball with the dog. All the cats are deaf.

Characteristically, this passage presents ideas as sensuous materials, fragments flowing in and out of the narration, with no more logic of arrangement than the logic of emotional associations—those intuitive stopgaps that connect colors in a painting, musical notes in a chord harmony. Not that the ideas are chosen arbitrarily or inconsequentially, but ideas are consequential in a new way: they act as just one of many portions in the sensuous amalgam of the poem's dazzling surface. Significantly, the ideas do not function autonomously, nor do they occur on a separate level of mind—or of the poetic medium—from elements of description, or events of narration. A reader unfamiliar with Howard's esthetics may suspect him of intellectual frivolity—why, one wonders, are the ideas in the poem not held more seriously in the mind of the poet? To fully apprehend Howard's technique, we must acquaint ourselves with a new posture of seriousness in the handling of ideas in art.—LAURENCE LIEBERMAN, *YR*, Summer 1968, pp. 604–6

Richard Howard's *Alone with America* is at once a philosophic, an imperative, and a descriptive work of literary criticism and so is, at the outset, an awesomely ambitious book. It is, further, a personal book—as Howard tells us in the Foreword, "If I intended to go on writing my own poetry . . . there was a choice of coming to terms with my contemporaries . . . or having no terms of my own to come to." Quoting Shaw on belief in one's own age, Howard then says: "This is the rescuing anatomy of such a belief; the construction, piece by piece, of a *credendum*—articles of faith." The book, in other words, is in the mode of the diary or personal journal, in which one uses the public language of empirical description to construct a private belief and so satisfy personal needs. Unlike the critic, the diarist is free to mingle modes, to speak in philosophic accents and to issue imperatives, precisely to the extent his audience senses the continuing presence and force of his personality. Once the diarist absents himself, and the rhetorical relation with his audience is lost, his search for a *credo* vanishes and the entire effort becomes literally purposeless and therefore worthless. Unlike much contemporary criticism, then, *Alone with America* seeks its coherence primarily through an anatomy of private belief and finds its purpose in the personality needing that belief. As a result, the book has—and needs—no other internal organization than the alphabet (forty-one chapters, from A. R. Ammons to James Wright) and no other general argument than a scant suggestion about the myth of King Midas. And since its purpose and coherence are personal, the book succeeds or fails on the grounds of its rhetorical relation: that is, on the most public of grounds.

Every rhetorician must assume his audience exists and is inclined to accept him at face value to the extent that they will listen comprehendingly—such are the barest starting points of the endeavor. And it is here, where matters must be simple and certain, that Howard's task seems so complicated and tentative.

For instance, very few who *count* these days would understand, let alone assent—as I believe Howard would—to Leopardi's deeply perceptive statement about the nature of translation: "When a language, generally speaking (that is, not in one or two sentences, in this or that particular nicety, but in general), is incapable of rendering in translation the subtleties of another language, that is certain proof that the nation into whose language one is translating has a shallower culture than the first." (Nabokov alone as a translator who "counts" seems to know this, but even truth from his lips sounds like a Mandarin irony and so is regarded as a trick.) Howard knows Leopardi's truth and his long experience is translating French prose has given him what few "imitators" of foreign verse ever approach: a love for one's subject which does not destroy that subject by altering it into a mirror of oneself. This sort of love informs the criticism of *Alone with America*, and behind it, serving as its ground of motive and final cause, is what Leopardi rightly calls culture, just as its absence and opposite is surely *lo spirito men coltivato*. Culture in this sense is thus the means whereby one is freed to love and serve things other than oneself as well as the sphere where it occurs, while barbarism is the bondage to self-regard and self-serving. Culture, moreover, permits and even encourages the personal in a way the absence of it cannot, for within a culture the appearance of the personal becomes evidence of one's literary seriousness, while in a barbaric context it merely enacts one's literary doom. *Alone with America* presupposes and embodies this sense of culture and therefore requires it as a public fact in order for its proper rhetorical relation to be sustained. I do not think the required culture exists and its absence has crucial effects upon the book.

One major result is Howard's sense of his subject. He sees recent American poetry as an existential drama about the search for self—a drama played out when no culture exists. This drama is at once for him the joy and despair of the art, and he captures in each essay its paradoxical effects: "There is, certainly, a loves-of-Jupiter aspect to all Dickey's late work, an erotic mastery of metamorphosis by which he reconstitutes, in a narrative utterly without ritual, the very mythology he has been at such pains to disintegrate in his figures, his meters." Howard's attention is supreme and so the general paradox becomes in every instance new and *specific*, not only within each essay but in the different aspects of each poet's art. In this sense, Howard's success with his subject is undisputed: he can sustain nearly six hundred pages of very specific commentary without becoming discrete because he is constantly demonstrating—and not simply asserting—both the coherence and the co-inherence of the general drama and the specific art. All forty-one poets he chooses are necessary to this demonstration, and he properly omits those whose poetry, since it is derivative, adds nothing. Howard's taste thus merges perfectly into his subject and so gives him the ability (not often seen in recent criticism) to quote perceptively and usefully. In this fashion, then, the absence of the proper public dimension gives Howard his subject and contributes to his success with it.

Where the absence is damaging, I think, is in the prose style. Since the audience is not there, Howard transforms rhetorical relation into verbal rhetoric:

> Hieratically disposed, but with a characteristic invitation for that very reason to pillage, to *profanation*, the works of John Hollander, monuments indeed, shapely at times to the point of a glassy impenetration stand before us in an alluring perspective worthy of Poussin for its rhythmic passage of saliences and recessions, its fair *attitudes*; and though I intend to violate these marbles as relentlessly as Lord Elgin looted his, for it seems to me that Hollander is

precisely the poet of an obsessive, overpoweringly confessional necessity, I think it is only justice to pause first and marvel a little at their presence among us as *completions*.

One suspects that such a sentence began life with a simple syntax and that the elaborations were then painstakingly *added*. Its complexity, in other words, is not central but additive and linear, and the whole is thus not a unity but an eccentricity. Outside of perverse whimsy, the only serious explanation I can see for such a style is that it is intended to serve in place of the absent audience—as if the endlessly changing modulations of a single voice within an elaborate style could somehow substitute for the variety of voices in an actual culture. In this light, the style stands condemned by the very assumptions that created the context for the attempt: it is in its effects a self-regarding and therefore barbarous style.

The book is, in the best sense, unfinished, in that the construction of belief is an open-ended, lifelong affair. The quality and content of Howard's belief seem to me deeply significant because, acting as the motives for extended and useful description, they also serve to help Howard articulate that permanent need for poetry and (as Mallarmé's swan did not) *chanté la région où vivre*. Where the belief betrays Howard is where its construction becomes simply syntactic and the required relationships only verbal rhetoric—a trap surely as chilling as the swan's *exil inutile*. In *Alone with America*, then, Howard is a rarity among critics: he not only demonstrates his view of his subject simply by describing it, he exhibits that subject's deepest, most despairing nature.—DONALD SHEEHAN, "Numquam Minus Solus Quam Solus," *Poetry*, Jan. 1971, pp. 258–61

I am puzzled by the inaptness of Richard Howard's title for his new book, *Findings*. Of course one may find something at the end of the most labored exploration, and presumably this is the sense he intends to convey, since nothing in his poems suggests the luck of unexpected discovery. Instead we have conscious artifice, the most elaborate "literary" poems. Clearly Howard does not fall under my strictures respecting lack of verbal tension in the common style; he has done everything to avoid the common. Or almost everything: for his originality, nearly unique today, is still based on the example of a famous forebear, Robert Browning. Howard has made his reputation, which is now considerable, from his Browningesque dramatic monologues, and it is fitting that the longest in his new book, fourteen pages in length, should be given to the *maestro*, speaking on his last day. Howard's monologues are almost flawlessly written: voice and manner acutely toned; smooth, careless, erudite to the point of acknowledged ironic pedantry, aristocratic: *suave* is the word, I think. Everything permitted for the sake of texture. Yet though I have read them with a certain fascination, as I might read the speeches of Harry Truman if his ghostwriter had been William Faulkner, I cannot quite accept them. Why? I ask myself if I can still accept Browning, and I turn back to my favorites, "Andrea," "Fra Lippo," "How It Strikes a Contemporary."

> I am grown peaceful as old age to-night.
> I regret little, I would change still less.
> Since there my past life lies, why alter it?
> The very wrong to Francis!—it is true
> I took his coin, was tempted and complied,
> And built this house and sinned, and all is said.
> My father and my mother died of want.
> Well, had I riches of my own? you see
> How one gets rich! Let each one bear his lot.

They were born poor, lived poor, and poor they died:
    And I have laboured somewhat in my time
    And not been paid profusely.

Did anyone ever talk like that? No, of course not; yet a serious
melancholy man, God knows, a man given to fear, sin,
poverty, given to art and the degradation of age, might wish to
speak so.

There is always another, one more,
    one *last* Grand Hotel: far-fetched, far-flung,
but built to last. At least penultimate, surely,
    Rimini's Grand Hotel du Miroir
    stares down its methodical rivals,
modest interlopers on the English Parade
    where all the pretty kiosks pointed
    once as a matter of course to this
thermal term, this nearly pearly, nougat-textured,
    art-nouveau pavilion.

Would anyone wish, really wish, to speak like this, anyone but
a *poseur* and Jack-a-dandy? Browning was a poet; which is to
say, a maker, a creator, not an artificer. He was serious about
what he was doing. And the first test of seriousness in poetry is a
willingness to resist the temptations of poetry. Howard has
resisted nothing; every verbal ornament goes in, every alliteration, assonance, bouncing rhythm, and wicked epithet; and
frankly, when I come to "this thermal term, this nearly pearly,
nougat-textured, art-nouveau pavilion," I gag. Yet the difference, evident as it is to our senses, is not easy to track to its
origin. Both Browning and Howard are conspicuous in their
poems; they can't be mistaken. Perhaps it is a matter of
positioning. Browning in his best work seems subservient to his
lines, while Howard, like the Master of the Hunt, whips his
pack along.—HAYDEN CARRUTH, *HdR*, Summer 1971, pp.
329–30

In 1911, confident at last in the fusion of music and movement
and meaning, Hugo von Hofmannsthal wrote to a friend about
the final rehearsals for the premiere of *Der Rosenkavalier*,
marveling at "Reinhardt quietly moving here and there, and
everything slowly and steadily taking on greater reality and
shape, becoming ever more elegant, more subdued and finally
more human." The sense of that sequence—from elegance to
humanity—is one which a majority of our poets and their
readers seem either to have abandoned or to mistrust. But
fortunately, a few of our best artists have guarded grace as a
condition of their verse and vision—the kind of grace that, as
Pascal says, gives what it imposes, that allows the affirmations
of form and the intuitions of a cultured memory to reveal our
human mysteries and to redeem them.

With his fifth collection, *Two-Part Inventions*, Richard
Howard has graced us again with what seems, at first, his
familiar and elegant concern: to explore the last-century
personality through the voices of its most fascinating artists.
And the six long poems in this book deal generally with the
generation that turned the century: Hölderlin, the old Whitman, Ibsen, Edith Wharton, Rodin, and an imaginary
architect named Alessandro di Fiore, who seems to combine
Gordon Craig, Antonio Gaudi, Louis Tiffany, and echoes of
Ezra Pound ("an ancient man who looked / exhausted by his
own head of hair")—the type of the aged artist who has
survived his art. But these new poems are not cast as the
dramatic monologues that earlier won for Howard a Pulitzer
Prize and the acclaim of critics as the heir to Robert Browning.
By releasing the implication of his form in *Untitled Subjects*—
the other presence, the secret sharer—he has made each poem
an invented encounter, epistolary or conversational, in which
the dialogue between the artist and his ironic correspondent

stretches toward a recognition scene which at once transforms
and confirms identities. The personalities, thus split and
gestured in intricately versed confrontations, and supported by
the completed rhetoric and polite formalities of an age past,
achieve a unique dramatic force which fulfills Howard's
experiments to combine the structural intimacies of voice with
the elaborate situations of speech. Perhaps it is the poet's own
discovery of the possibilities of his form that, in turn, allows us
to discover the true figure for comparison—granted that all
comparisons are merely figures. For by inflecting these
civilized conversations to show that, as one of its characters
remarks, "Knowledge is / not what you have but what you are,"
*Two-Part Inventions* recalls not Browning's dynamics of will
but Henry James's moral drama of understanding. Like James,
the intention of Howard's art and all the work of his craft has
been to dramatize the human heart and intelligence at their
most difficult, their most lucid, their most *telling* points of
convergence. Each of these enacted poems—these expenses of
energy, both exhausting and costly—moves toward what we
have learned to call a Jamesian acceptance, a state of
consciousness that Howard has taught us again is "that final /
act which enables us to see clearly."

The framing poems, on Hölderlin ("After the Facts") and
Fiore ("A Natural Death"), are epistolary and seem the earliest
composed—perhaps when Howard was first calculating his
converted ambition—and are, paradoxically, the most studied
and visionary. A correspondence, initiated by curiosity and
answered with caution, between a French matron and a
German doctor, follows long after the facts of a childhood
memory: a Stranger, to himself and the estate, madly wandering among the marbled gods around a moonlit pool, proclaiming the earth's divinity. Posed against that resonant image is the
resulting condition: the hospitalized poet, once the "Master of
our German Muse" and now "the witless Scardanelli,"
babbling in broken Italian that can no longer "recover itself
into poetry." This meditation on the Romantic sensibility is
resumed in what is probably the volume's most virtuosic poem,
"A Natural Death," set in 1947 as a graduate student's report of
her research into and eventual meeting with another "poor lost
*Maestro*," Fiore. The innocent, industrious Cynthia tramps
across the Continent to track down her subject's objects, only to
discover those masterworks all "made too late to last," ruined
by time's neglect or men's malice. And when, having learned
how much of art is loss, she meets the old man in Paris and
transcribes, in the italics of shorthand, his last words, that loss
is transfigured: *"the end of art   it is the recovery of paradise."*
The news she brings him comes like death to enable this
resignation:

it is only when you have   given everything
that you can give more   that you have more to
give   it is inadmissible for a man to leave
the trace of his passage upon earth   give it
all back   the elements   the compassionate sea
and the fire and the ground   and the growing
air   as you described it   we must survive
what we have made   it is not ours

The losses that necessitate art, and the acts of atonement
an artist fashions of the life he destroys, focus the other four
poems as well. "A Phenomenon of Nature" brilliantly
reimagines *When We Dead Awaken* back to its inspiration,
exchanging the high Norwegian mountains for the cliffs of
Capri, the deathly model Irene for an early romance whom the
poet names Sophie. Ibsen's insistent theme—the betrayal of
love—is here traced to the playwright's own vision on his art,
just as, in "The Lesson of the Master," Edith Wharton admits

that "whatever we manage to do is merely / a modification / of what we have failed to do." The word that recurs in these titles is the cue: to discover the nature of things—for an art, for a life or death—is finally the purpose and force of Howard's book, and authorizes its expansive, inclusive, *novelistic* dimensions: "Not fact but *finding* / is why I must write." The *ficelles* in all these poems are either women or homosexuals: sensual, submissive, haunting, predatory, *natural*—the attraction of earth and impulse that shapes art's attempted escapes. And the tension thus drawn out between them—at lengths that make quotation difficult—is the kind of delaying action that dominates Howard's meanings and manner. For his poems are, in their largest sense, elaborate, even evasive, surrenders to silence, to the wordless void which is held distant by gorgeous gestures of redefinition and rhetoric, by fencing with idiom and identity, by a temporizing verse. During those delays it is the privilege of Howard's art and of our understanding to learn: to learn how "the passionate dead act within us," how an earth left godless by design is made divine by desire, how "pleasure rises to the pitch of vision," how we must surrender what we cannot lose. They are the lessons we expect of the old humane novels, whose absorbing sweep alone seems able to bring so much diverse life to light, but which Howard has allowed to verse whose lyric mode is only strengthened by its dramatic encounters. They are the lessons of a master.—J. D. McCLATCHY, YR, Spring 1975, pp. 422–25

In *Two-Part Inventions* Richard Howard has pursued a hint from Bach: "to play clearly in two voices and . . . to arrive at a singing style and at the same time to acquire a strong foretaste of composition." The dialogues that result are an elaboration of the careless-careful method of Mr. Howard's earlier book, *Untitled Subjects*, where an interlocutor might be implied but never introduced. Though Mr. Howard's speakers do tend to go on and on, with a garrulous drone more crafty and insinuating than could be dreamt of in Mr. Snyder's philosophy, the splendid achievement of much of his volume deserves first notice. The poem about Hölderlin, an exchange of letters between a neutral (but very anxious and very feminine) chance observer of the poet and his physician (firm, condescending, and resigned—in a pun Mr. Howard would cherish—simply to patience), is a gorgeous piece of writing, as it is also the most sympathetic and detached observation of the poetry in madness that I can recall having read. Hölderlin, at liberty, in despair and madness, on a strange estate, has been asked his name, and here is what Mr. Howard makes of the possibility:

> Thereupon the man fell again to his knees,
>     his face in his hands
> (which I had occasion then to remark: thin,
> pale for all the dirt, and curving at the tips
> as if they would scoop the darkness hovering
>     round the blue pupils)
> and promised to tell us . . . the next day! "It is
> difficult for me, remembering my name.
> To escape a city is one thing, to choose
>     a road, another."
> These were his last words, for with them, as if
> summoned *by* them, one of our peacocks appeared,
> crest trembling like a lyre, coral claws oddly
>     *raw* upon the moss,
> and with the hollow clash of an opening
> parasol, spread his perfect fan before me,
> white quills quivering, each one an inducement
>     to admiration.
> Faced with this . . . rival, the Stranger turned
>     away,
> and I never saw him again. Nor have I

forgotten what I *heard:* that night I wakened
    to a horrid scream,
never explained, from the servants' hall, a scream
like the peacocks' (though they do not cry at night).

Hölderlin with his hands "thin, / pale for all the dirt, and curving at the tips / as if they would scoop the darkness hovering round the blue pupils"; the abrupt scream from an unexpected animal singer; the last sorrowful reiteration, which remarks simply, wonderingly, yet with a subdued and perfect pathos, "a scream / like the peacocks' (though they do not cry at night)": these incidental touches, like the exquisite movement of the poem as a whole, have a vividness that comes to most poets once in a lifetime. (It has come to Mr. Howard several times already, notably in "November, 1889" and "A Pre-Raphaelite Ending, London.") Certainly, he is the oddest truly original poet since Elizabeth Bishop and indeed, in the calculated, witty jaggedness of his descriptive power, appears to owe something to her style.

According to Mr. Howard, it was Robert Browning who gave first impulse to the Howard dramatic monologue and dialogue. To my mind the connection with Browning is rather thin: these two poets go about their business to different ends. With Mr. Howard the dramatic setting is there chiefly not to unleash but to refine and limit poetic energy. He is, for better and worse, utterly outside the thrall of that religious fury which is displaced into comedy in a poem like "Soliloquy of the Spanish Cloister," and can be seen under the phantasmagoric surface of "Childe Roland" as well. The final or isolate state of Browning's artist-questers is lunacy, whereas Mr. Howard's characters move toward a boundary of intoxicating and, to the reader, insufferable aestheticism. Rather than derange the world with excess of imagination, Mr. Howard employs himself by rearranging.

Is there another contemporary poet who lives and breathes the medium of his own verse quite as freely as Mr. Howard? He is himself what he calls Ibsen, "a phenomenon of nature." Given the brightness and facility of his accomplishment, it is a pity that many readers should be acquainted with him only or mainly through his prose, a grotesque late-Jamesian pastiche that is more than faintly reminiscent of Auden's "Caliban to the Audience." But Mr. Howard is, to some extent, conscious of himself as a public figure, a philanthropic editor and administrator to whom other poets are rightly grateful, and the occasional too-palpable awareness of his station that works so disastrously upon his criticism has just begun to enter his verse: one hopes it will stop. In three of the inventions, which treat Whitman, Rodin, and Edith Wharton to their respective last epiphanies, an interlocutor uncomfortably associated with Mr. Howard is allowed too naggingly to score points off the artist he fancies. There is a threshold, insouciantly crossed in some of these poems, beyond which mere coyness becomes positively cloying: Mr. Howard should have known better than to fix Edith Wharton with a line like "manqué see manqué do."

Yet these complaints are irrelevant to the colloquial rightness, the large and tender humanity, which predominate in *Two-Part Inventions*. The last poem in the book, composed of letters from an art student visiting Italy to her professor in America, is nearly in a class with that on Hölderlin, and prompts the thought that there is hardly a critic writing on art whom one could prefer to Mr. Howard in his poetry. And his loveliest prose *is* in his poetry. I have seen reviewers notice the circumstance and arm themselves with it as an accusation. Pope was once a "classic of our prose"—may Mr. Howard enjoy the company. I will quote once more, from the Hölderlin poem, a passage in which the physician laments the fallen splendor of the soul he attends, who is now asking to be called Scardanelli:

> Alas, earth is no more than an old sun
> and the moon a dead earth. Many a time
> I have shown to Signor Scardanelli
> (as he must be called) manuscripts of his,
> written at twenty. At twenty, Madame,
> the Poet is always right. At sixty,
> the Doctor is never wrong, and to these
> confrontations his response is one blaze
> of invariable babble, the rough
> scratching of filthy talons on the page,
> and then the poor creature begins to sing.

Mr. Howard's gentle gravity is neither borrowed from other poets nor shared with them. His example affirms for anyone who needs to know that it is no use choosing between this or that poetics. There are only poets.—DAVID BROMWICH, GR, Fall 1975, pp. 740–41

Richard Howard is unlike any other contemporary poet I know in that while he writes a critical prose (usually about other poets) of needless opacity and boundless pretentions, he has developed into a poet who though without any particular accent that characterizes The Howard Style, is nonetheless almost always lucid and interesting to read. Interesting, that is, if you like gossip, literary anecdote, jokes (usually nice, not malicious) and the more or less continuous hovering of Howard's elders and betters, the great dead and some of the quick on whom he depends for the substance of his poems. Depends on them to the extent that they must make personal appearances; for example, in a poem written at the time of Auden's death, I note within two pages Cocteau, Stravinsky, Piaf, MacNeice, Roethke, Magnani, Neruda, Rod McKuen, plus Donnas Anna and Elvira, Santa Maria sopra Minerva and a couple of Harvard freshmen just thrown in. What distinguishes this volume (*Fellow Feelings*) from Howard's earlier impersonations of nineteenth-century artistic and literary figures doing their acts (in *Untitled Subjects* and *Two-Part Inventions*) is that, in the title of one of the new poems, "Howard's Way" is now in the picture. Poems to Proust, Auden, Hart Crane—it's clear what some of the fellow feelings are which move Howard to utterance. But even confessing to the love that dare not speak its name is done with verve and the resolve not to be a bore about it. Speaking to Crane, and with Whitman in mind, the poet says ". . . Take my hand / as you gave yours to him. We suffer from / the same fabled disease, and only the hope / of dying of it keeps a man alive. Keeps!" And in a slightly different tone, Howard's musing about whether Auden failed, as one obituary said about him, to make his way inside "a world of emotion," leads to this:

> But my *personal* knowledge is odd, my evidence
>     suspect even:
> on a club-car up to Cambridge, two freshmen
>     scribbled a note—
> "Are you Carl Sandburg?" "You've ruined," you
>     wrote back, "mother's day."
> Was that emotion? Was this—the time backstage at
>     the Y
> when impatient to read to the rustling thousands out
>     front, you asked
> (possessing no small talk—and with you I possessed
>     no large)
> why it was I no longer endured a difficult mutual
>     friend.
> "Because he calls everyone *else* either a kike or a
>     cocksucker,
> and since, Wystan, both he and I are . . . well,
>     both of them . . ."

> "My *dear*," you broke in, and I think you were
>     genuinely excited,
> "I never knew you were Jewish!" No, not a world of
>     emotion—
> say, for the time being, as you said, the emotion of a
>     world.

This seems to me quite marvelous. It is a curious poetry that depends so little on typography, meter, even rhythm—and no doubt Howard would find rhyme merely an impediment to lucidity; but one often finds oneself reading along simply to find out what happens next, and this virtue is a rare one in contemporary poetry.—WILLIAM H. PRITCHARD, "More Poetry Matters," *HdR*, Autumn 1976, pp. 459–60

The term "man of letters" may have become defunct, the species survives. Richard Howard, for one, embodies the term. It is more than an obsession. As Mr. Howard writes of Guiseppe Verdi in *Lining Up*,

> we don't accuse
> oysters of insincerity for making
> their disease into a pearl.

"Disease" seems too strong. Yet the very epithet "man of letters" does suggest a personality unfitted to survive without constant literary and artistic dialysis.

Mr. Howard is eager to display such a personality. He pores over photographs by the 19th-century portraitist Nadar of Berlioz, Delacroix, Michelet, Corot, lingers at the monument to Pierre Louÿs in the Jardin du Luxembourg in Paris or looks into R. W. Chapman's critical bibliography of Jane Austen. Again and again he pays homage or does a variety of "impersonations":

> I go round on the back of that other life
>     my reading relinquishes
> like the little Egyptian heron that lives
> on the backs of cows. The shoe fits perfectly.

His is donnish poetry, then—witty, discursive, learned, engaging—whose personal glimpses reveal little more than the making of the embryo man of letters.

> Your name meant a row of red books, properly
>     voluminous although not
> Anatolian as far as I could determine

begins a poem entitled "Anatole France." He cannot resist a pun (ogling the reader "with a wild surmise, silent on a pique") or imparting information (on etymology or the uses of photography). But when in this profusion of monologues can we leave the museum? Where can we meet real-life citizens and not another recount of Rodin's sculpture "The Burghers of Calais"?

Mr. Howard is good company as he moves with Alexandrian wit through the museums of the world. One is delighted to hear his annotations and be tugged along in the wake of his allusions. But what lies beyond the Palace of Art? How can we survive without Leda or Lewis Carroll to conciliate our desires? When contemporary life percolates through the encrustation, it is revealed partly in a bath-house and partly in a backroom bar. At this point the fun is not nearly heady enough. When the emotions are fully engaged, the intellectual reflex becomes almost trite. "On Hearing Your Lover Is Going to the Baths Tonight" merely gathers itself into a Proustian sigh:

> two mouths
> have never drunk twice from the same chimera.
> What he does with you is you; with others, them;
>     "he" remains a mystery—
> you personify only what you are not,
>     and you are not there.

It is not for such wisdom that one turns to Mr. Howard
—not to be out on the town with Ken, Leagros, Larry and
others.

> Ken lives in hell and likes it; Larry runs
> past, his days a color and his night a sport;
>      Scott entertains a downward
> appetite to mix with mud . . . Surely ours is
> a longing once held to be impossible
>            and now inevitable,

the craving to create what is there and not
         merely to contemplate it.

That "surely" is a desperate cry against the wind, and Mr.
Howard knows it. His poetry lingers precisely between "the
craving to create" and mere contemplation. That is both its
strength and weakness. Like the figures on his "Attic Red-
Figure Calyx," he circles around "an undisturbed absence at
the center / of which we may never speak."—HAROLD BEAVER,
"Snapshots and Artworks," *NYTBR*, March 18, 1984, p. 30

# LANGSTON HUGHES

## 1902–1967

James Langston Hughes was born in Joplin, Missouri, on February 1, 1902. His mother, Carrie
Langston Hughes, had been a schoolteacher; his father, James Nathaniel Hughes, was a
storekeeper. James Hughes left for Mexico while his son was still an infant, and the latter was raised
mostly by his grandmother, Mary Langston. Hughes lived for a time in Illinois with his mother,
who remarried, and went to high school in Cleveland. He spent a year in Mexico with his father,
then entered Columbia University.

After a year of schooling, Hughes took on various jobs in New York, on trans-Atlantic ships,
and in Paris. He returned to America, and while working as a busboy in Washington he slipped
three poems beside Vachel Lindsay's plate. Lindsay was impressed, and began promoting the young
poet. In 1925 Hughes won a black literary contest in *Opportunity*, and his writing career was
launched. His first collection of poems, *The Weary Blues*, was published in 1926. Another volume,
*Fine Clothes to the Jew*, came out the next year. A benefactor sent Hughes to Lincoln University,
from which he received a B.A. in 1929. After that Hughes supported himself as a poet, novelist, and
writer of stories, screenplays, articles, children's books, and songs. A first novel, *Not without
Laughter*, appeared in 1930. The first stories were collected in *The Ways of White Folks* in 1934. In
the fifties and sixties, Hughes gained popularity through the recurring protagonist of his stories, Jesse
B. "Simple" Semple.

Hughes also translated the works of Mexican, Cuban, and Haitian authors. He received the
*Palms* Intercollegiate Poetry Award in 1927, the Harmond Gold Medal for Literature in 1931, and a
Guggenheim fellowship in 1935. Lincoln University granted him a Litt.D. in 1943, and he
received an American Academy of Arts and Letter grant in 1947. Hughes never married. He died of
congestive heart failure in New York City on May 22, 1967.

## General

Hughes is one of the lasting fruits of the ⟨Harlem⟩ Renaissance,
and we forget that a movement is finally measured by a few
men who persist and realize its potentialities. Hughes's complexity is even more difficult to suggest in a few lines than that
of Claude McKay. He gave folk and cultural tradition a greater
rendering power than it had had before in self-conscious
literature. His use of blues form and jazz rhythms was the
major innovation in black poetry of the Harlem Renaissance,
and his alliance with free verse provided him with the benefit of
a form known for flexibility and freedom from rigid implications and limitations of the more restricted verse. Hughes has
cumulative impact, and if read with a sure sense of the
implications of folk culture in mind, reveals discoveries not yet
domesticated by the public. To illustrate: his novel *Not without
Laughter*, though flawed, attempts to embody, separately and
then combined, the blues and spirituals traditions; and his
short play *Soul Gone Home* reaches into religious and
supernaturalist sources.

Hughes's main limitation is that, for whatever reason, he
remained too close to the folk forms and did not take the liberty
to force upon them as much signification as they could be

made to bear.—GEORGE E. KENT, "Patterns of the Harlem
Renaissance," *The Harlem Renaissance Remembered*, ed. Arna
Bontemps, 1972, pp. 40–41

## Works

### POETRY

Here is a poet with whom to reckon, to experience, and here
and there, with that apologetic feeling of presumption that
should companion all criticism, to quarrel.

What has always struck me most forcibly in reading Mr.
Hughes' poems has been their utter spontaneity and expression
of a unique personality. This feeling is intensified with the
appearance of his work in concert between the covers of a book.
It must be acknowledged at the outset that these poems ⟨*The
Weary Blues*⟩ are peculiarly Mr. Hughes' and no one's else. I
cannot imagine his work as that of any other poet, not even of
any poet of that particular group of which Mr. Hughes is a
member. Of course, a microscopic assiduity might reveal
derivation and influences, but these are weak undercurrents in
the flow of Mr. Hughes' own talent. This poet represents a
transcendently emancipated spirit among a class of young

CHESTER HIMES

JOHN HOLLANDER

RICHARD HOWARD

LANGSTON HUGHES

ZORA NEALE HURSTON

JOHN IRVING

SHIRLEY JACKSON

WILLIAM INGE

writers whose particular battle-cry is freedom. With the enthusiasm of a zealot, he pursues his way, scornful, in subject matter, in photography, and rhythmical treatment, of whatever obstructions time and tradition have placed before him. To him it is essential that he be himself. Essential and commendable surely; yet the thought persists that some of these poems would have been better had Mr. Hughes held himself a bit in check. In his admirable introduction to the book, Carl Van Vechten says the poems have a *highly deceptive air of spontaneous improvisation*. I do not feel that the air is deceptive.

If I have the least powers of prediction, the first section of this book, *The Weary Blues*, will be most admired, even if less from intrinsic poetical worth than because of its dissociation from the traditionally poetic. Never having been one to think all subjects and forms proper for poetic consideration, I regard these jazz poems as interlopers in the company of the truly beautiful poems in other sections of the book. They move along with the frenzy and electric heat of a Methodist or Baptist revival meeting, and affect me in much the same manner. The revival meeting excites me, cooling and flushing me with alternate chills and fevers of emotion; so do these poems. But when the storm is over, I wonder if the quiet way of communing is not more spiritual for the God-seeking heart; and in the light of reflection I wonder if jazz poems really belong to that dignified company, that select and austere circle of high literary expression which we call poetry. Surely, when in *Negro Dancers* Mr. Hughes says

> Me an' ma baby's
> Got two mo' ways,
> Two mo' ways to do de buck!

he voices, in lyrical, thumb-at-nose fashion the happy careless attitude, akin to poetry, that is found in certain types. And certainly he achieves one of his loveliest lyrics in "Young Singer." Thus I find myself straddling a fence. It needs only "The Cat and the Saxophone," however, to knock me over completely on the side of bewilderment, and incredulity. This creation is a *tour de force* of its kind, but is it a poem:

> EVERYBODY
> Half-pint,—
> Gin?
> No, make it
> LOVES MY BABY
> corn. You like
> don't you, honey?
> BUT MY BABY

In the face of accomplished fact, I cannot say *This will never do*, but I feel that it ought never to have been done.

But Mr. Hughes can be as fine and as polished as you like, etching his work in calm, quiet lyrics that linger and repeat themselves. Witness "Sea Calm":

> How still,
> How strangely still
> The water is today.
> It is not good
> For water
> To be so still that way.

Or take "Suicide's Note":

> The Calm,
> Cool face of the river
> Asked me for a kiss.

Then crown your admiration with "Fantasy in Purple", this imperial swan-song that sounds like the requiem of a dying people:

> Beat the drums of tragedy for me,
> Beat the drums of tragedy and death.
> And let the choir sing a stormy song
> To drown the rattle of my dying breath.
> Beat the drums of tragedy for me,
> And let the white violins whir thin and slow,
> But blow one blaring trumpet note of sun
> To go with me to the darkness where I go.

Mr. Hughes is a remarkable poet of the colorful; through all his verses the rainbow riots and dazzles, yet never wearies the eye, although at times it intrigues the brain into astonishment and exaggerated admiration when reading, say something like "Caribbean Sunset":

> God having a hemorrhage,
> Blood coughed across the sky,
> Staining the dark sea red:
> That is sunset in the Caribbean.

Taken as a group the selections in this book seem onesided to me. They tend to hurl this poet into the gaping pit that lies before all Negro writers, in the confines of which they become racial artists instead of artists pure and simple. There is too much emphasis here on strictly Negro themes; and this is probably an added reason for my coldness toward the jazz poems—they seem to set a too definite limit upon an already limited field.

Dull books cause no schisms, raise no dissensions, create no parties. Much will be said of *The Weary Blues* because it is a definite achievement, and because Mr. Hughes, in his own way, with a first book that cannot be dismissed as merely *promising*, has arrived.—COUNTEE CULLEN, "Poet on Poet," *Opy*, Feb. 1926, 73–74

The title of this little book of verse 〈*Montage of a Dream Deferred*〉 tells a good deal about it. The language is that of the work-a-day urban world whose pleasures are sometimes drearier than its pains. The scene is the particular part of the Waste Land that belongs to Harlem. The singer is steeped in the bitter knowledge that fills the blues. Sometimes his verse invites approval, but again it lapses into a facile sentimentality that stifles real feeling as with cheap scent. As he bandies about the word "dream," he introduces a whiff of the nineteenth century that casts a slight mustiness on the liveliest context.

Langston Hughes can write pages that throb with the abrupt rhythms of popular music. He can draw thumbnail sketches of Harlem lives and deaths that etch themselves harshly in the memory. Yet the book as a whole leaves one less responsive to the poet's achievement than conscious of the limitations of folk art. These limitations are particularly plain in the work of a man who is a popular singer because he has elected to remain one. His verse suffers from a kind of contrived naïveté, or from a will to shock the reader, who is apt to respond coldly to such obvious devices.

It is a pity that a poet of undeniable gifts has not been more rigorous in his use of them. There are several contemporaries, especially among the French, whose subject matter and whose method are not too different from his, but who, being more sensitive artists, are also more powerful. Mr. Hughes would do well to emulate them.—BABETTE DEUTSCH, "Waste Land of Harlem," *NYTBR*, May 6, 1951, p. 23

Every time I read Langston Hughes I am amazed all over again by his genuine gifts—and depressed that he has done so little with them. A real discussion of his work demands more space than I have here, but this book 〈*Selected Poems of Langston Hughes*〉 contains a great deal which a more disciplined poet would have thrown into the waste-basket (almost all of the last section, for example).

There are the poems which almost succeed but which do not succeed, poems which take refuge, finally, in a fake simplicity in order to avoid the very difficult simplicity of the experience! And one sometimes has the impression, as in a poem like "Third Degree"—which is about the beating up of a Negro boy in a police station—that Hughes has had to hold the experience outside him in order to be able to write at all. And certainly this is understandable. Nevertheless, the poetic trick, so to speak, is to be within the experience and outside it at the same time—and the poem fails.

Mr. Hughes is at his best in brief, sardonic asides, or in lyrics like "Mother to Son," and "The Negro Speaks of Rivers." Or "Dream Variations":

> To fling my arms wide
> In some place of the sun,
> To whirl and to dance
> Till the white day is done.
> Then rest at cool evening
> Beneath a tall tree
> While night comes on gently,
> 　Dark like me—
> That is my dream!
>
> To fling my arms wide
> In the face of the sun,
> Dance! Whirl! Whirl!
> Till the quick day is done.
> Rest at pale evening . . .
> A tall, slim tree . . .
> Night coming tenderly
> Black like me.

I do not like all of *The Weary Blues*, which copies, rather than exploits, the cadence of the blues, but it comes to a remarkable end. And I am also very fond of "Island," which begins "Wave of sorrow/Do not drown me now."

Hughes, in his sermons, blues and prayers, has working for him the power and the beat of Negro speech and Negro music. Negro speech is vivid largely because it is private. It is a kind of emotional shorthand—or sleight-of-hand—by means of which Negroes express, not only their relationship to each other, but their judgment of the white world. And, as the white world takes over this vocabulary—without the faintest notion of what it really means—the vocabulary is forced to change. The same thing is true of Negro music, which has had to become more and more complex in order to continue to express any of the private or collective experience.

Hughes knows the bitter truth behind these hieroglyphics: what they are designed to protect, what they are designed to convey. But he has not forced them into the realm of art where their meaning would become clear and overwhelming. "Hey, pop!/ Re-bop!/ Mop!" conveys much more on Lenox Avenue than it does in this book, which is not the way it ought to be.

Hughes is an American Negro poet and has no choice but to be acutely aware of it. He is not the first American Negro to find the war between his social and artistic responsibilities all but irreconcilable.—JAMES BALDWIN, "Sermons and Blues," *NYTBR*, March 29, 1959, p. 6

## PROSE AND DRAMA

The importance of Hughes as a literary figure far transcends that of his only novel, *Not without Laughter* (1930). Primarily a poet, his verse was influenced thematically by the social realism of Lindsay, Masters, and Sandburg, and technically by the rhythms of jazz. His first two volumes of poems, *The Weary Blues* (1926) and *Fine Clothes to the Jew* (1927), provoked a

fierce controversy because of their forthright and sympathetic treatment of lower-class Negro life. Hughes, perhaps more than any other author, knows and loves the Negro masses. His newspaper sketches of Jess B. Semple, an unlettered but philosophical Harlemite (just be simple), are among his finest literary creations. ⟨. . .⟩

Laughter is the central symbol of ⟨*Not without Laughter*⟩—the complex, ironic laughter which is the Negro's saving response to racial oppression. The characters cluster around the poles of laughter and not-laughter. Jimboy and Harriet, with their low-down blues and comical dances, are the hub of laughter in Aunt Hager's household. Anjee, too, must be near laughter (Jimboy), at whatever cost. Hager and Tempy, for different reasons, represent the forces of sobriety. Hager's religion requires her to regard laughter as sinful, while for Tempy, laughter is an inexcusable digression from the serious business of accumulating property. Unfortunately, Sandy disrupts the symbolic unity of the novel. Presumably torn by the conflicting forces which divide the family, his inner struggle fails to materialize. There is no laughter in his life, but only an altogether commendable determination to be a credit to the race. At this point, the novel bogs down in hopeless ideological confusion.

The author sets out to make a defense of laughter. To those like Tempy who claim that Negroes remain poor because of their dancing and singing and easy laughter, Hughes replies: "The other way 'round would be better; dancers because of their poverty; singers because they suffered; laughing all the time because they must forget." Such a view of laughter rests on the assumption that "achievement," at least for the Negro masses, is largely illusory, and that some form of compensatory self-expression is therefore necessary. But it is precisely on this point that Hughes is most ambivalent. If he defends laughter, he also defends achievement: "I wants you to be a great man, son." "I won't disappoint you, Aunt Hager." At the end of the novel, Sandy returns to school to fulfill his grandmother's dream.

In short, Hughes tried to reject the Protestant ethic (joy is wrong), while retaining the success drive on which it is based. It is an untenable halfway house, which Claude McKay and Jessie Fauset would equally scorn to occupy. In any event, Hughes' ideological ambivalence has disastrous aesthetic consequences. The novel and its main character simply part company. Instead of supporting the defense-of-laughter theme, Sandy emerges as a symbol of racial advancement, which is hardly a laughing matter. Given his main theme of suffering and self-expression, Hughes might better have written the novel around Harriet, who emerges from a life of prostitution to become "Princess of the Blues."

*Not without Laughter* has been compared in some quarters to the first book of the *Studs Lonigan* trilogy. No service is rendered either to American literature or to Hughes by this exaggerated claim. A mediocre novel, *Not without Laughter* was undertaken before its author was prepared to meet the rigorous requirements of the genre. Ideologically confused and structurally defective, the novel gives a final impression of sprawling formlessness. The author, to his credit, is fully aware of these shortcomings, if some of his friendly critics are not. In his autobiography, *The Big Sea* (1940), Hughes makes a courageous apology to the characters of his early novel: "I went to Far Rockaway that summer and felt bad, because I had wanted their novel to be better than the published one I had given them; I hated to let them down." —ROBERT BONE, "Harlem Renaissance," *The Negro Novel in America*, 1958, pp. 75–77

It is highly probable that Langston Hughes reached his most appreciative, as well as his widest, audience with a character whom he named, eponymously and with obvious relish, Jesse B. Semple. The *Jesse*, not too incidentally, clearly invited an abbreviation to Jess.

Simple made his bow to the world in the columns of the *Chicago Defender*, the Negro weekly which, in its heyday from early in World War I through the whole of World War II, circulated into virtually every nook and cranny of Negro America and, indeed, functioned as a sort of bible to many Negroes in every walk of Negro life. Via the columns of the *Defender*, then, Hughes addressed not so much the Negro elite, cultural or otherwise. Rather, thus he spoke, powerfully and directly, to the very Negro of whom Simple was supposed to constitute an almost perfect replica. He spoke, that is, in great part to the black rank and file of our industrial Babylon, who may not be nearly so illiterate as their slave forebears, but who even now are still a far cry in their rapport with the world of books from the proverbial Harvard graduate.

Illiterate or not, however, these Negroes, a twentieth-century equivalent of Chaucer's fair field full of folk, seem to have taken Simple to their hearts. They followed Simple week after week in the columns of the *Defender*. They gossiped about him with their associates of their own kind. They found Simple understandable and comfortably convincing. True, they had not created Simple from an impulse originating in their own minds, nor made him what he became through arts which they had learned to practice, as, for instance, an earlier epoch of folk Negroes had created, and then, in effect, composed the Negro spiritual. In these senses, but only in these senses, Simple lacks the full authenticity of folk material. He was an adopted child, not a native son. Yet the attitude of his foster parents, the often so-called "common, ordinary" Negroes, toward him, their ready identification with him, suggests a special status of importance for his significance. Whether or not he is truly like most ordinary Negroes, he is certainly, in both form and substance, what many ordinary Negroes were at least once prepared to concede without rancor they thought they were. At least, to that extent, Simple must be accounted a folk Negro's concept of the folk Negro. Thus, too, he must be seriously considered a valuable specimen of Americana. ⟨. . .⟩

What ⟨. . .⟩ are Negroes really like? This is the question which Langston Hughes seems to ask with his portrait of Simple. And his reply seems to be altogether different from many of the chilling responses to that same question provided by the apostles of a belief in the Negro *manqué*. Thus, in Hughes' warm and sane definition of an average Negro, Simple is no freak of any kind. He adores Jackie Robinson and respects Ralph Bunche, but he is no superman like either of them. Simple is an ordinary person who happens to be a Negro. He has an understandable distaste for white people who abuse him merely because he is a Negro or who commit acts which contribute to the system that exists solely to perpetuate a continuing series of such abuses. On the other hand, he takes also a dim view of the nastiness often observable in Negroes. His landlady, he has noted, is no angel of sweetness and light and, indeed, he scathes a Negro girl who is clerking in a white chain store for her rudeness and incompetence quite as much as he does President Eisenhower for spending so much time playing segregated golf in segregated Georgia.

To Simple, quite obviously, the millennium is far, far in a distant future. His vision of the good life is a modest conception only remotely related to the heady doctrine of the perfectability of man, as articulated, let us say, by such an evangelist of a New Order as a Shelley or a Fourier. It is based upon a soberly realistic acceptance of human society in which due allowance is made for man's limitations as well as his potential for self-improvement. Nor is Simple unique in the art of Langston Hughes. Rather he is representative. He belongs to the same world as the Negro characters, more memorable for their ordinariness than anything else, in Hughes' one novel, *Not without Laughter*. For Hughes never succumbed to the monstrous error of arguing that, because race prejudice is itself monstrous, it has made Negroes monsters.

⟨. . .⟩ Black and white ⟨. . . people⟩ will be like Simple. Thus, they will justify, as they demonstrate, Langston Hughes' faith in human nature and illustrate the soundness of his affirmations about Negroes, America and humanity in general. These future Americans, that is, will join the Negro readers whom, when Simple did appear in the *Defender*, rallied round him in such a manner as to indicate their conviction of his reality. They will give further incontrovertible proof, in their sentiments as well as their conduct, of the validity of Hughes' judgments on his chosen subject, the true character of the Negro Everyman. They will vindicate, in fact, the basic implications of our political and social creeds in America which argue that governments and communities exist not for the priviliged few, but in the interest of everyone—even, and indeed most, for the Simples of this earth.—BLYDEN JACKSON, "A Word about Simple," *CLAJ*, June 1968, pp. 310–18

---

### ARTHUR P. DAVIS
#### From "Langston Hughes: Cool Poet"
##### *CLA Journal*, June 1968, pp. 282–88

Harlem is the predominating theme in the poetry of Mr. Hughes. Either stated or implied, used as subject or background or protagonist, and on occasion even as a symbol for Negroes everywhere, Harlem has been a constantly recurring theme in Langston Hughes' poetry. Fascinated by the Black Metropolis and its colorful inhabitants, he never tired of delineating the endlessly changing moods of that ghetto. Speaking of the people of Harlem, Hughes once wrote: "I love the color of their language; and, being a Harlemite myself, their problems and interests are my problems and interests." On another occasion, the author, speaking through a character in *Simple*, has this to say: "I didn't come here to Harlem to get away from my people. I came here because there's more of 'em. . . . I love my people." In every major poetical publication except one, from *The Weary Blues*, published in 1926, down to *The Panther and the Lash*, published in 1967, there are references to Harlem—many and diverse references to the Black Ghetto.

It is intriguing to note how the picture of Harlem changes over the years. In 1926, the Harlem of *The Weary Blues* is generally the swinging, Joyous Harlem of the New Negro Renaissance. A night-time Harlem, it is "Jazzonia," an exciting never-never land in which "sleek black boys" blow their hearts out on silver trumpets while "shameless gals" "strut and wiggle" in a "whirling cabaret." But even in this first publication one finds Hughes' customary two-fold vision. The joyousness of "Jazzonia" is not unmixed. "The rhythm of life / Is a jazz rhythm" for this cabaret world, but it brings eventually "The broken heart of love / The weary, weary heart of pain." Even as a young man living in the excitement of the New Negro Renaissance, Langston Hughes saw that Harlem in spite of surface appearance was a sad and not a gay place.

In subsequent pictures of Harlem, the moods become darker. By the time of *One Way Ticket* (1949) Harlem has gone through the Depression, has had its riot, and now a thoroughly disillusioned city, it has become the "edge of hell;" and yet characteristically it could still be, as it is in "Negro Servant," a refuge for the black folks who worked down-town and had to bow and scrape to white folks all day. Hughes was always aware that there are many Harlems, not just one.

Moreover, he was always quick to discover the humor even in so-called serious incidents. For example, his reaction to a certain near-riot in Harlem is given in the "Ballad of Margie Polite," who

> Kept the Mayor
> And Walter White
> And everybody
> Up all night.
> When the PD car
> Taken Margie away—
> It wasn't Mother's
> Nor Fathers—
>     It were
> Margie Day.

The fullest and most penetrating treatment of this many-sided black city appears in *Montage of a Dream Deferred* (1951). Actually one long poem of seventy-five pages, this work employs a "jam session" technique (which is explained below) that allows the poet to make use of a host of varied, blending and constrasting vignettes to paint a full picture of Harlem's frustrations. The whole work asks one all-powerful question about Harlem and its people:

> What happens to a dream deferred?
> Does it dry up
> like a raisin in the sun?
> Or fester like a sore—
> And then run?
> Does it stink like rotten meat?
> Or crust and sugar over—
> like a syrupy sweet?
> Maybe it just sags
> like a heavy load.
> *Or does it explode?*

Very few cities have received the in-depth analysis that Harlem receives in this volume. Many critics believe that *Montage of a Dream Deferred* is Hughes' best work. If so, it is most fitting that his finest production should be on the Harlem theme. In a real sense, Hughes is the poet-laureate of Harlem.

Hughes' treatment of the African theme, like that of Harlem, changed and matured over the years. Like other New Negro poets, he features in his early works the alien-and-exile theme. Made famous by Countee Cullen's "Heritage," this attitude was an effort on the part of American Negro writers to make Africa a literary homeland for the creative artist. In all probability, it was influenced by the Garvey Movement of the period. As it appeared in New Negro poetry, the alien-and-exile tradition portrayed the American Negro as an alien, perpetually estranged, and deeply nostalgic over the loss of his beautiful sundrenched home.

In Hughes, the theme was never important, but it did color his early poems. He stated or implied the superiority of black beauty and black wisdom to the pale, washed-out looks and the foolishness of the whites. He also, from time to time, spoke of "jungle joys," and he imagines that the "night-dark girl of the swaying hips," who dances in a cabaret has slept beneath jungle trees bathed in the splendor of a tropical "star-white moon." In the "Lament for Dark Peoples," the speaker protests his being taken from the African motherland and "caged in the circus of civilization." In another poem called "Afraid," the speaker moans:

> We cry among the skyscrapers
> As our ancestors
> Cried among the palms in Africa
> Because we are alone

At its best, the alien-and-exile movement was an attempt on the part of New Negro poets to find productive traditional roots. At its worst, it was a phony and unconvincing kind of literary black nationalism—phony and unconvincing because it dealt, not with the real Africa but an Africa of fantasy. The African poems in Hughes' first publication appear almost childish when compared with those in his last work. In one, he is writing about a world that never existed on land or sea; in the other, he writes about the world of Lumumba and Kenyatta, the real world of an emerging embittered Africa for whom

> The past has been a mint
> Of blood and sorrow.
> That must not be
> True of tomorrow.

This concern with Africa brings to mind Mr. Hughes' connection with *négritude*—a word as popular now and as indefinable as that other popular and indefinable term, *black power*. In recent years, Leopold Senghor, the high priest of *négritude*, and other African and West Indian writers, have insisted that Langston Hughes is one of the fathers of the *Négritude* Movement. During a visit to Washington in the fall of 1966, Senghor had a talk with a few friends which was taped and subsequently printed in the May, 1967, issue of *Negro Digest*.

Senghor was asked the question: "In which poems of our, American, literature [do] you find evidence of Negritude?" His reply was:

> Ah, in Langston Hughes; Langston Hughes is the most spontaneous as a poet and the blackest in expression. For me, it is Langston Hughes and also the popular poems of Sterling Brown. You see? It appears to me that Langston Hughes and Sterling Brown are the most Negro. I do not say that theirs are the best poems on an artistic level. Take for instance, Countee Cullen. . . . He has beauty, but the songs of Langston Hughes are pure, spontaneous and simple.

I am not sure I know what *négritude* is. The term obviously has a wide range of meaning and no two critics I have read agree on a definition. I am convinced, however, that for the West African poets, the word has mystical and philosophical connotations which may not be applicable to our Afro-American *négritude*. And I am also convinced that Langston Hughes, characteristically, had more than one attitude towards *négritude*. In an article entitled, "The Twenties: Harlem and Its Négritude" (*African Forum*, Spring, 1966), he tends to use the term very loosely. "To us," he wrote, "negritude was an unknown word, but certainly pride of heritage and consciousness of race was ingrained in us." At the Dakar Festival, however, he was much more specific. As reported by the New York *Times* (April 24, 1966), he states, "As I understand it, . . . negritude has its roots deep in the beauty of the black people—in what younger American writers and musicians call *soul*." Mr. Hughes then defined *soul* as "the essence of Negro folk art redistilled—particularly the old music and its flavor, the ancient basic beat out of Africa, the folk rhymes and Ashanti stories—all expressed in contemporary ways so emotionally colored with the old that it gives a distinctly Negro flavor to today's music, painting or writing." In short, he is saying "soul is contemporary Harlem's negritude."

Hughes, as one would expect, had more than one type of

négritude poem. For example, in "Note on Commercial Theatre," he has what I would call *négritude*, Afro-American style—the kind which simply shows a consciousness *of*, and a pride *in*, the American Negro's unique contribution to world culture. It also urges the Negro to make greater artistic use of his gifts.

> You've taken my blues and gone—
> You sing 'em on Broadway . . .
> And you fixed 'em
> So they don't sound like me.
> Yep, you done taken my blues and gone.
> You also took my spirituals and gone. . . .
>
> But someday somebody'll
> Stand up and talk about me,
> And write about me—
> Black and beautiful—
> And sing about me,
> And put on plays about me!
> I reckon it'll be
> Me myself!
> Yes, it'll be me.

But one finds another kind of *négritude* in the following lines, one whose tone is closer to that mystical emphasis on blackness which the West Africans have in their poetry:

> Body out of Africa
> Strong and black
> As iron
> First smelted in
> Africa
> Song
> Out of Africa
> Deep and mellow song
> Rich as the black earth
> Strong as black iron . . .
> My song
> From the dark lips
> Of Africa.

The protest-and-social commentary theme like the Harlem theme runs through the whole body of Mr. Hughes' poetry, but in his early works the stream is just a trickle. In *The Weary Blues* and *Fine Clothes to the Jew*, there are few poems of this type, but by the time of *One Way Ticket* in 1949 the stream is flowing fully. Like other New Negro poets, he used lynching as the major symbol of American injustice to the Negro, and in *One Way Ticket* Hughes devotes a whole section of the work ("Silhouette") to lynching poems. From this work on down to his last, protest and social commentary became increasingly important in the publications of Mr. Hughes. He never stopped needling America. He wrote or commented on particular incidents such as "Roland Hayes Beaten" or "Restrictive Covenants"; he also commented on our general failures as a "Democracy."

It is interesting to compare Hughes' attitude toward protest poetry with that of Countee Cullen. During his later years, Cullen used to agonize over being a *Negro poet*. "To make a poet black and bid him sing," Cullen thought a peculiar kind of malevolence on the part of God. Hughes, on the other hand, seemed to accept and to glory in his mission as a Negro writer. The word *mission* may be too strong, but I sincerely believe Langston Hughes looked upon his protest poetry as a weapon in the arsenal of American democracy.

## JAMES A. EMMANUEL
### From "The Literary Experiments of Langston Hughes"
*CLA Journal*, June 1968, pp. 336–44

Technical experimentation in the author's short fiction ⟨. . .⟩ becomes inseparable from personal style as the reader grows accustomed to Hughes's interspersed songs, parenthetical tableaus, and recurrent, racially significant images. Some unusual passages, however, are clearly experimental. Chief among them are his uses of interior monologue, limited to "Red-Headed Baby" and "Blessed Assurance." The rarity of stream-of-consciousness writing in Hughes's fiction rouses speculation about the occurrence of it even in those two stories, published twenty-eight years apart. A brief inspection of the contexts in which these passages of interior monologue appear may throw light on the problem of craftsmanship which they were meant to resolve. ⟨. . .⟩

After the midpoint of ⟨"Red-Headed Baby"⟩, told almost completely through the fragmented thoughts of the predatory white sailor, Clarence takes on his lap the girl who three years before was a church-going teetotaler, but who now drinks liquor "strong enough to knock a mule down." He thinks:

> Soft heavy hips. Hot and browner than the moon—good licker. Drinking it down in little nigger house Florida coast palm fronds scratching roof hum mosquitoes night bugs flies ain't loud enough to keep a man named Clarence girl named Betsy old woman named Auntie from talking and drinking in a little nigger house on Florida coast dead warm night with the licker browner and more fiery than the moon.

Near the end of the story, the sailor, thoroughly startled by the features of the child ("over two years old," says Betsy's mother, "and can't even say, 'Da!'"), vigorously insists on the baby's removal from the room:

> A red-headed baby. Moonlight-gone baby. No kind of yellow-white bow-legged goggled-eyed County Fair baseball baby. Get him the hell out of here pulling at my legs looking like me at me like me at myself like me red-headed as me.

The third and final passage, on the last page of the story, reveals the sailor's thoughts as he stumbles out of the shack:

> Knocking over glasses by the oil lamp on the table where the night flies flutter where skeleton houses left over from boom sand in the road and no lights in the nigger section across the railroad's knocking over glasses at edge of town where a moon-colored girl's got a red-headed baby deaf as a post like the dolls you wham at three shots for a quarter in the County Fair half full of licker and can't hit nothing.

In this story—a favorite of Hughes's—why does the author forsake standard exposition in these three passages? He is expert with dialogue, whether it is spoken by one of the Negro characters ("That chile near 'bout worries de soul-case out o' me. Betsy spiles him, that's why") or by the sailor ("Hey! Take your hands off my legs, you lousy little bastard!"). And expository sentence fragments elsewhere effectively convey the careless but sentient rush of the sailor's movements. The probable answer credits Hughes with an artistic deliberation that has seldom been recognized, linked with a humanity that, on the contrary, is widely acknowledged. Hughes must get inside the mind of Clarence, now slightly muddled with liquor but nevertheless—and perhaps for that very reason—keenly aware on a nonverbal level of its meandering fusions of personal and racial responses. The knowledge that he is white and that he is a father—and that he momentarily is both these things under the wrong conditions and in the face of the wrong consequences—unsettles him with a shock that defines a predicament of twentieth-century white America.

Hughes catches all the meaning, none of which would be as effective if rendered in coherent, rational prose. In the first passage, one senses the rough comforts of a sailor ashore; voluptuousness; brown skin turned into brown liquor; humming sounds that ward off a "scratching" world and unite three people with names instead of races in a carousal subconsciously ritualistic with its "Auntie" and "nigger" setting. The disruptive truth appears and controls the second passage, which appropriately begins with hints of ambivalent paternal pride and masculine sternness. In the middle of that natural response obtrudes awareness of race ("looking like me at me like me"), which is the signal for racial unreason and its stylistic counterpart, syntactical incoherence. That incoherence properly dominates the final passage. One should estimate Hughes's feeling for the sailor—as a father, not as a white man—in the complex of sensations and ideas blurred in the paragraph: blind, almost fearful, escape; perception of economic and political injustice; and guilt-ridden violence accentuated by a sense of failure (the failure of bawdy virility fathering only a "baby deaf as a post," a "baseball baby" whose rollicking sire in his sexual life "can't hit nothing"). Asked whether the stream-of-consciousness style was deliberately chosen as a necessary effect in "Red-Headed Baby," Hughes wrote to me in July, 1961, "Yes—like what goes through the characters' minds in the room." ⟨. . .⟩

As in "Red-Headed Baby," three passages of interior monologue detail the protagonist's crucial bewilderment ⟨in "Blessed Assurance"⟩. The first one offers a glimpse of the thoughts of John, the father, when his seventeen-year-old son chooses spectacles with exaggerated rims: "'At least he didn't get rhinestone rims,' thought John half-thought didn't think felt faint and aloud said nothing." The second passage pictures John wondering about Delmar after the boy starts to grow a beard in imitation of certain beatniks he has seen in Greenwich Village:

> "God, don't let him put an earing in his ear like some," John prayed. He wondered vaguely with a sick feeling in his stomach should he think it through then then think it through right then through should he try then and think it through should without blacking through think blacking out then and there think it through.

Instead of thinking it through, John ponders Delmar's remark that he would like to study at the Sorbonne in Paris—not at Morgan, the Negro university that is his own alma mater. After the embarrassment at the Spring Concert, John wonders about the Sorbonne: "Does it have dormitories, a campus? In Paris he had heard they didn't care about such things. Care about such what things didn't care about what?"

Again, why does Hughes not employ standard exposition? Dealing this time with a Negro father and son whose race is essentially irrelevant to their dilemma—rather than with a white sailor whose race exacerbates his predicament—the author must again illuminate a perversion of feeling by reaching psychological depths where the whirl of things remembered and feared constitute a disorder frightfully coherent to the unsteady mind but resistant to the shaping powers of traditional syntax. John's thinking and not thinking—that is, his thinking about his son and half-thinking or not thinking about himself—are captured in the first passage with an economy not available to ordinary prose. In the second passage, interior monologue makes almost kaleidoscopic the

changing patterns of the father's unstated past failures and his present weakness—the patterns of causation and time, as modified by doubts about the laws of heredity, being strictly controlled by the juxtapositions "then then" and "then and there." In the third passage, the knuckle-rapping self-administered by the father sharply opposes consciousness and conscience in this man struggling to be honest with himself. That struggle, according to a letter that Hughes wrote to me on September 19, 1961, represents to the author the plight of "one afraid to fully face realities." (And the dilemma of Clarence in "Red-Headed Baby," the same letter indicates, is meant to show that white people "are human, too.")

The relatively unknown experimental techniques that add interest to many of Hughes's poems are too numerous to record in a brief essay. Yet, their categories can be fairly represented, some by example and others by descriptive reference. Examples are necessary in the case of Hughes's topographical and emblematic experiments—forms having antecedents in seventeenth-century England and America, and ultimately related to the acrostic verse of early Greek and Latin poets. His "Angels Wings" is a good example:

> The angels wings is white as snow,
>     O, white as snow,
>         White
>             as
>                 snow.
> The angels wings is white as snow,
>     But I drug ma wings
>     In the dirty mire.
>     O, I drug ma wings
>     All through the fire.
> But the angels wings is white as snow,
>     White
>         as
>             snow.

The grammar of the first line brings the poem into the domain of Jesse B. Semple; and the zest and imagery of the Negro folk sermon possessively move through what would otherwise seem an emblematic verse by the pious English rector, George Herbert, shaped like the angel's wings that it praises.

Another kind of experimental thrust by Hughes is represented by "Jitney," a poem topographical in conception, intended to convey the reader almost physically on the jumpseat of a jitney cab making two round trips up and down South Parkway in Chicago. The first half of the poem follows:

> Corners
> Of South Parkway:
> Eeeoooooo!
> Cab!
> 31st,
> 35th,
> 39th,
> 43rd,
> Girl, ain't you heard?
> *No, Martha, I ain't heard.*
> I got a Chinese boy-friend
> Down on 43rd.
> 47th,
> 51st,
> 55th,
> 63rd,
> Martha's got a Japanese!
> Child, ain't you heard?
> 51st,
> 47th,
> Here's your fare!
> Lemme out!

I'm going to the Regal,
See what this week's jive is all about:
The Duke is mellow!
Hibbler's giving out!
43rd,
39th,
Night school!
Gotta get my teaching!
35th,
31st,
Bless God!
Tonight there's preaching!
*31st! All out!*
Hey, Mister, wait!
I want to get over to State.
*I don't turn, Madam!*
*Understand?*
*Take a street car*
*Over to the Grand.*

The form itself is meant to capture the single-street route, endlessly turning back upon itself; the numbers indicate the bouncing speed; and the distortions of rumor—realistically introduced after the 43rd Street intersection and continued only after Martha has left the cab—are thoughtfully mixed with references to educational ambition as well as entertainment among South Side Negroes.

An additional type of poem expressing the innovative bent of Hughes at work on total form is exemplified by "The Cat and the Saxaphone/ (2 A.M.)," which merges a swinging Negro lyric with a traditional but Harlem-toned dramatic dialogue. The first half reads as follows:

EVERYBODY
Half-pint,—
Gin?
No, make it
LOVES MY BABY
corn. You like
liquor,
don't you, honey?
BUT MY BABY
Sure. Kiss me,
DON'T LOVE NOBODY
daddy.
BUT ME.

Hughes's modernity in 1926 (when this poem appeared in *The Weary Blues*), evident in the advanced form as well as in the typography of the title and the final line of the poem (consisting of a single exclamation point), anticipates modes common to poets of the 1960's. The flow of meaning between the phrases of the lyric and the contiguous dialogue ably accentuates the poet's ingenuity.

A number of stylistic ventures in other poems merit attention. The use of folk diction and of urban slang from the milieu of jazz and be-bop, like certain characteristics of his short stories, so often informs Hughes's poetic style that familiarity wears down the reader's surprise, if not his satisfaction. Phrases like "birthing is hard" in "Advice," and "put de miz on me" in "Brief Encounter," and "don't ig me" in "Midnight Chippie's Lament," all poems from the 1940's, are examples. In his work of the 1950's, when the dawn "bops bright" in "Chord," when a "cool bop daddy" goes by in "Dead in There," and when boys are "copping a thrill" in "Up-Beat," the innovative language is still part of the life style of Hughes's Harlem models.

Other experimental devices found in the poet's work owe less to racial sources, although Hughes adapts them to his racial materials. The kind of stylistic freedom widespread among American poets in the 1920's and strengthening among writers of fiction is particularly apparent in such poems of Hughes's as "Ballad of the Landlord," which uses newspaper captions as lines of verse. A related technique, employed almost twenty years later in "Neon Signs" (in *Montage of a Dream Deferred*, 1951), yields a poem almost totally comprised of the names of Harlem bars and night clubs. As if toying with a concept of medley and miscellany, Hughes writes "Deferred" a few years later, using twelve voices besides his own. In the same decade, his "Good Morning" and "In Explanation of Our Times" use unpunctuated series of geographical and personal names to bring new fluidity into his images and to make phrasal units out of groups that sociologically or economically are bound together. This same technique is practiced with greater virtuosity in the later *Ask Your Mama*.

Hughes's final book of poems, *The Panther and the Lash* (1967)—distinguished partly for its reprinting of that passionately brave and artful poem of 1931 that nearly caused a riot at the University of North Carolina, "Christ in Alabama"—contains three poems relevant to this sketch of Hughes as innovator. "Elderly Leaders," "Go Slow," and "Stokely Malcolm Me" all elaborate upon a technique forecast forty years earlier in "The Cat and the Saxaphone/ (2. A.M.)." The final lines of each poem appear on the page as follows:

| "ELDERLY LEADERS" | "GO SLOW" |
|---|---|
| $$$$$ | ???? |
| $$$$ | ??? |
| $$$ | ?? |
| $$ | ? |
| $ | |

"STOKELY MALCOLM ME"
???
??
?

The structural authenticity of the ending of each of the first two poems can be estimated by its obvious summation of the meaning discernible even in the title. The ending of the third poem is emphatic, but less functional.

These last poems connect Hughes the stylist with LeRoi Jones and other young poets who are reaching in many directions for style strong enough to control the fervor of their substance. Every reader of poetry, in perusing the work of Hughes, connects solidly with him many times, in the plain truth of his utterance, in the warmth or gaiety of the life that he pictures, or in the freshness of his style. It is the responsibility of the critics to sift among Hughes's poems, stories, and other productions to preserve his best art, to strengthen in his countrymen what the novelist Joyce Cary has called "the bridge between souls."

## WILLIAM MILES

### "Isolation in Langston Hughes' *Soul Gone Home*"
*Five Black Writers*, ed. Donald B. Gibson

1970, pp. 178–82

F ew writers have been as prolific in their attempt to describe and interpret Negro American life as Langston Hughes. Poet, novelist, short story writer, and dramatist, "he writes to express those truths he feels need expressing about characters he believes need to be recognized."[1] One such truth is the forced isolation of the majority of black people by the culture within which they are forced by circumstance to exist. The intensity and repressiveness of such isolation alienates the black person not only from the culture at large, but frequently from his own brothers as well.[2] This is the theme of Hughes' powerful one-act play, *Soul Gone Home*. In less than four pages of text he presents a tragic and poignant picture of a people so isolated from each other that the establishment of meaningful emotional relationship is no longer possible.

The theme of isolation is not, of course, original with Hughes. What is original in *Soul Gone Home*, however, is the manner in which this theme is treated. The play is a fantasy in both situation and structure. Reality as we commonly experience it is replaced by the unreal, the dreamlike; the usual physical laws governing life and death are suspended. Yet the emphasis of the play is clearly on things as they exist in actuality. The play is about a situation resulting from the condition of black people in America. The immediate situation explored within the fantastic world of the play is itself unreal: a conflict between an uncaring mother and the ghost of her dead son in which the latter condemns his mother ("You been a hell of a mama! . . . I say you been a no-good mama.")[3] because she failed to provide him with the necessities of life, food, clothing, "manners and morals."

This internal conflict in the realm of fantasy forms the center of the drama, but the structural limits are defined by reality. *Soul Gone Home* begins with the mother grieving over her son's body and concludes with his removal by the ambulance drivers. However, Hughes has constructed even these two apparently real incidents in such a way as to render them unreal. For example, the opening stage direction informs us that the mother is "loudly simulating grief" (p. 39) and the play ends on the same note with her again feigning grief in the presence of the indifferent ambulance drivers.

The importance of both this underlying structure and the unreality of the situation is that they immediately establish the fact of the isolated condition of the mother and son. The boy is, of course, apart from the real world in the sense that he is dead, and, likewise, the mother is removed by the very fact that she can openly converse with him. Indeed, the mother is actually doubly removed: her "real" life, or what glimpses we get of it, is characterized by a sense of unreality. Symbolically, therefore, she is not a part of the reality defined by the general society, and her being outside in large part is the result of her race. To emphasize this fact, Hughes underlines the isolated condition of both mother and son through their lack of relatedness to the white ambulance drivers.[4] Both are completely oblivious and indifferent to the dead boy and the tears of the "grieving" mother, and their lack of responsiveness to the situation is a measure of the vast gulf separating black and white.

Structurally, therefore, fantasy functions to establish the complete physical isolation of the two main characters from the real world. The focal point of the play, the inability of mother and son to relate on the emotional level, exists in a cause-and-effect relationship with their isolation from the society: forced and repressive physical isolation of one group by another results in severe emotional alienation among members of the persecuted group. In developing and emphasizing this emotional element, Hughes superimposes upon his fantasy clear implications of stark reality. Thus the total effect of *Soul Gone Home* is realism, and while the central conflict may be internal, the implied commentary relates wholly to the external world.[5]

The conflict itself takes place in appropriate surroundings: it is night and the scene is "a tenement room, bare, ugly and dirty." (p. 39) Such a setting is explicitly illustrative of the type of life which the dead boy was forced to live and with keen insight into his once human condition, he attacks his mother

for her lack of concern. Always in need of food, he had grown up "all bowlegged and stunted from undernourishment," and had died at sixteen of tuberculosis brought on by a lack of "milk and eggs" in his diet. Furthermore, he has come to realize that his "home" totally lacked an atmosphere of love and failed to provide him with examples of proper "manners and morals." Sickly and treated as nothing more than a burdensome bastard, he was forced out on the streets to grub out whatever money he could find. However, refusing to recognize her existence for what it really is, the mother sadly defends her actions and is quick to point out that the boy *was* nothing more than a burden to her. As this argument is developed, one can easily see that the gulf between white and black is as great and unbridgeable as the one existing between this mother and son.

Hughes does not explicitly explore the causes of such a situation nor the reasons it is permitted to persist. Why should a sixteen-year-old boy have to die from the lack of necessary foods; why should a mother be forced to view her child in terms of how much monetary help he can be; and, indeed, why should a mother herself be forced to turn to prostitution in order to scratch out an existence? Such questions are left unanswered, but Hughes does indicate responsibility. All the implications of *Soul Gone Home* point directly to the white world as the source of the problems of the majority of Negro Americans. Two incidents in the play illustrate this fact: the complete indifference of the white ambulance drivers, and the mother's symbolic whitening of her face before she goes out to prostitute her body.

It is interesting to note that the son, ironically, gains his great insight into the essential condition of life and his true relationship with his mother only upon dying. When the mother demands to know where he learned "all them big words" such as "manners and morals," he replies, "I learn't 'em just now in the spirit world." "But you ain't been dead no more'n an hour," the mother counters. "That's long enough to learn a lot," he says. (p. 40) In less than an hour of death the son has learned more about life than he did in sixteen years of real existence on earth. This new insight into and knowledge of what his and his mother's life has been is symbolically represented by the throwing off of the pennies (the material world) which cover his eyes.

> *Son:* I'm dead now—and I can say what I want to say.
> *(Stirring)* You done called on me to talk, ain't you? Lemme take these pennies off my eyes so I can see. (p. 39)

Hughes' implicit comment that only death (or some type of escape from existing conditions) can provide true insight into the human condition of the black American in a closed white society is closely paralleled in the work of Richard Wright. When Bigger Thomas commits the accidental murder of Mary Dalton in *Native Son*,

> he blossoms into full consciousness as a personality. He is at once free of the society in which he lives. He can now analyze the relationship between the Negro and white world. He can probe into his own personality reactions and those of the people around him. For the first time in his life he lives as a whole human being.[6]

Likewise, the son in the play is able truly to see and assess his situation only when he is free from the constraints of the white-dominated physical and material world; only then can he "see" and "talk." Only in death has he found a home and a "real" life; he is a "soul gone home."

It is also an ironical but poignant consequence of the conflict between the mother and son that the mother utterly fails to comprehend what her son is talking about. Always on the defensive, she not only justifies her own position and actions, but even attempts to shift the blame for them to the boy.

> Mother: (*Proudly*) Sure, I could of let you die, but I
> didn't. Naw, I kept you with me—off and on.
> And I lost the chance to marry many a good
> man, too—if it weren't for you. No man wants
> to take care o' nobody else's child. (*Self-
> pityingly*) You been a burden to me, Randolph.
> Son: (*Angrily*) What did you have me for then, in the
> first place?
> Mother: How could I help havin' you, you little
> bastard? Your father ruint me—and you's the
> result. And I been worried with you for sixteen
> years. (*Disgustedly*) Now, just when you get big
> enough to work and do me some good, you have
> to go and die. (p. 41)

The mother's complete isolation from her son is firmly implanted in the minds of the audience by her final gestures. She again feigns grief over the loss of her son; she smooths out the bed where he lay, thus seemingly blotting out any signs of his former existence; and she makes a final statement which indicates that her love for her son is less than complete.

> Mother: Tomorrow, Randolph, I'll buy you some
> flowers—if I can pick up a dollar tonight. You
> was a hell of a no-good son, I swear! (p. 42)

Through the skillful combination of situation, structure, character and symbol, Hughes has produced a compact and powerful play of a people so isolated that even the ordinarily secure relationship between mother and son is impossible. And while this thematic consideration is immediately relevant to the Negro American, *Soul Gone Home* does achieve a sense of universality in that its social commentary relates to any oppressed minority. Furthermore, the play also fulfills the criteria for "high art" laid down by LeRoi Jones.

> High art, first of all, must reflect the experience, the
> emotional predicament of the man, as he exists, in
> the defined world of his being. It must be produced
> from the legitimate emotional resources of the soul
> in the world. It can *never* be produced by evading
> these resources or pretending that they do not exist. It
> can never be produced by appropriating the withered
> emotional responses of some strictly social idea of
> humanity. It must issue from *real* categories of
> human activity, *truthful* accounts of human life, and
> not fancied accounts of the attainment of cultural
> privilege by some willingly preposterous apologists
> for one social "order" or another.[7]

As Jones would have it, *Soul Gone Home* "tells it like it is," but in such a way as to create an impact and effect not soon nor easily forgotten.

### Notes

1. *Langston Hughes: Five Plays*, edited with an introduction by Webster Smalley (Bloomington: Indiana University Press, 1963), p. vii.
2. This phenomenon is explored at length and in great depth by Richard Wright in *Black Boy*. There it is made explicitly clear that the relationships within the author's family are directly determined by the condition of the black person in the society.
3. Hughes, p. 39. All subsequent quotations from the play will be taken from this edition and noted directly within the text of the essay.
4. We are never told directly that the drivers are white, but we must assume them to be if simply because the mother thinks they are.
5. At this point I should like to make it clear that the interpretation of

the play as a study of what happens emotionally to victims of a white culture which has isolated them depends wholly upon implications which abound in the work. As Smalley points out, "That which is unsaid becomes almost more important than that which is put into the dialogue." Certainly one could interpret the boy's death as resulting simply from the character of an irresponsible mother, but even a cursory reading of Hughes' work reveals an almost total concern for and awareness of the social implications of themes and characters.

6. Constance Webb, "What Next for Richard Wright?" *Phylon*, X (1949), 161.
7. "Problems of the Negro Writer," *Saturday Review*, XLVI (April 20, 1963), 20.

## ONWUCHEKWA JEMIE
### From *Langston Hughes: An Introduction to the Poetry*
1973, pp. 24–32, 194–99

The characteristic quality of Hughes's poetry is simplicity, and one of its strategic ingredients is humor. His poems are stark, unadorned, crystal-clear surfaces through which may be glimpsed tremendous depths and significant human drama. In "The Negro Artist and the Racial Mountain" he spoke of his efforts to capture and express the ironic humor of the blues. (In his Marxist pronouncement he seemed to consider humor out of place—unless it was the laughter of a triumphant proletariat—and the two Marxist-influenced works are uncharacteristically humorless.) Hughes never seemed to take himself too seriously, was rarely in too deadly earnest to be able to laugh. However tragic or serious his subject matter, he usually manages to see the humorous and ironic side—which is precisely what the blues artist does. Commenting on black life and its relations to the problems of democracy is a serious matter; but still, Jim Crow is so "desperately and grotesquely funny"[1] that the comedy often outweighs the tragedy. He criticizes the "serious colored magazines" like *The Crisis* and *Phylon* which "evidently think the race problem is too deep for comic relief." But most black people do not think so; it is the ability of the black masses to see the funny side that has helped them survive oppression.

> Colored people are always laughing at some wry Jim
> Crow incident or absurd nuance of the color line. If
> Negroes took all the white world's daily boorishness
> to heart and wept over it as profoundly as our serious
> writers do, we would have been dead long ago.[2]

But of course Jim Crow is not always funny. "The race problem in America is serious business, I admit. But must it *always* be written about seriously?"[3] To Hughes, lack of humor is unnatural, something akin to lack of humanity. And he speculates that there might be a connection between humorlessness and rabid racism and brutality.

> Personally, I know that not all white Americans
> practice Jim Crow at home and preach democracy
> abroad. But what puzzles me about those who do is
> their utter lack of humor concerning their own
> absurdities.
>     I have read that Hitler had no sense of humor
> either. Certainly, among Hitler's hunting trophies
> today are thousands of human heads, scattered across
> the world in the bloody mud of battle. I suppose the
> greatest killers cannot afford to laugh. Those most
> determined to Jim Crow me are grimly killing
> America.

Afro-American humor represents a profound criticism of America, a sane antidote to an insane circumstance. And if Jim

Crow humor is sometimes macabre, it is a quality inherent in the situation, certainly not the fault of the victims. Following the example of the black masses and of the blues, Hughes seeks to capture, in all its density and complexity, that humor that is "too deep for fun."[5]

Hughes's people are the lower classes, the urban folk: porters, bell boys, elevator boys, shoe shine boys, cooks, waiters, nurse maids, rounders, gamblers, drunks, piano players, cabaret singers, chorus girls, prostitutes, pimps, and ordinary, decent, hard-working men and women. These are the "low-down folks, the so-called common element,"[6] the ones who crowd the street corners, stoops, bars, beauty shops and barber shops and churches, hot rented rooms and stuffy apartments all over the black sections of cities. They are the dwellers on Beale Street, State Street and Seventh Street, Central Avenue and Lenox Avenue. They are the ones who made Chicago's South Side and New York's Harlem both famous and infamous. Hughes has himself listed them in "Laughers."[7] His treatment of them is stark and unsentimental, capturing at once the wretchedness and beauty of their lives. As Charles S. Johnson has pointed out, there is in Hughes's depiction of them "no pleading for sympathy, or moralizing; there is a moment's blinding perception of a life being lived fiercely beneath the drunken blare of trombones, or in blank weariness of the Georgia roads."[8]

Hughes's particular world is the inner city and, specifically, Harlem. The "colored middle class" or "black bourgeoisie" rarely appear, and when they do they are "'buked and scorned." The disrespect was mutual: the "black bourgeoisie" and their spokesmen denounced his work vehemently. Critic Allison Davis called Hughes's poems "vulgar," "sordid" and "sensational."[9] Benjamin Brawley, whom Hughes has described as "our most respectable critic," wrote of *Fine Clothes to the Jew* that "it would have been just as well, perhaps better, if the book had never been published. No other ever issued reflects more fully the abandon and vulgarity of its age."[10] To them and the many who thought like them, Hughes's answer is a shrug of the shoulders: "I have never pretended to be keeping a literary grazing pasture with food to suit all breeds of cattle."[11] The "respectable" people hated his preference for blues and jazz and the cabaret and its habitués over the middle class (white) arts and places and people. Hughes's supreme creation, Jesse B. Semple, and his exemplary urban domain, for instance, were to the "black bourgeoisie" no more than reminders of a heritage they were struggling to leave behind in their "progress forward and upward." To Hughes, however, it is the Simples that are the soul of the race and that most deserve to be expressed in black art. It is the *simple* folk, their life style, their dreams, their stupidities, and their deep wisdom that Hughes immortalizes in his work.

Hughes's speech on accepting the Spingarn Medal in 1960[12] is an homage to these simple folk, an expression of profound gratitude for the things they gave him. They are, he says, the source and substance of his poems and stories, plays and songs. It was their singing in the little churches of his childhood that opened his ears to "the lyric beauty of living poetry not of books." It was a blind guitar player on a Kansas City street corner singing, "Going down to the railroad, lay my head on the track—but if I see the train a-coming, I'll jerk it back," that opened his eyes to the laughter and sadness of the blues which was to become a part of his own poetry. It was the old folks recounting their memories of slavery that made possible his great heritage poems such as "The Negro Speaks of Rivers," "Aunt Sue's Stories," "Mother to Son," and "The Negro Mother." And it was the endless stories, tall tales, jokes,

comments, and complaints, which he assiduously listened to in black communities across the nation, that enabled him to create the irrepressible, lifelike figure of Jesse B. Semple and the cycle of Simple tales. Hughes' relentless mining of this literary black gold is in keeping with his prescription in "Racial Mountain" and a lesson for all black writers.

Hughes entertained no doubts as to the sufficiency and greatness of the molds provided by black music, nor of black life as subject matter. On the question of whether such black matter and manner could attain "universality," Hughes in his Spingarn Speech issued a definitive answer:

> There is so much richness in Negro humor, so much beauty in black dreams, so much dignity in our struggle, and so much universality in our problems, in us—in each living human being of color—that I do not understand the tendency today that some American Negro artists have of seeking to run away from themselves, of running away from us, of being afraid to sing our own songs, paint our own pictures, write about ourselves—when it is our music that has given America its greatest music, our humor that has enriched its entertainment media, our rhythm that has guided its dancing feet from plantation days to the Charleston, the Lindy Hop, and currently the Madison. . . .
>
> Could you possibly be afraid that the rest of the world will not accept it? Our spirituals are sung and loved in the great concert halls of the whole world. Our blues are played from Topeka to Tokyo. Harlem's jive talk delights Hong Kong. Those of our writers who have concerned themselves with our very special problems are translated and read around the world. The local, the regional can—and does— become universal. Sean O'Casey's Irishmen are an example. So I would say to young Negro writers, do not be afraid of yourselves. You are the world.[13]

Hughes' confidence in blackness is a major part of his legacy, for the questions he had to answer have had to be answered over again by subsequent generations of black artists. Black culture is still embattled; and Hughes provides a model for answering the questions and making the choices. Whether they say so or not, those who, like Cullen and Braithwaite, plead the need to be "universal" as an excuse for avoiding racial material, or for treating such material from perspectives rooted in alien sensibilities, invariably equate "white" or "Western" with "universal," and "black" or "non-Western" with its opposite, forgetting that the truly universal—that is, the foundation elements of human experience, the circumstances attending birth, growth, decline, and death, the emotions of joy and grief, love and hate, fear and guilt, anger and pain— are common to all humanity. The multiplicity of nations and cultures in the world makes it inevitable that the details and particulars of human experience will vary according to time, place, and circumstance, and it follows that the majority of writers will dramatize and interpret human life according to the usages of their particular nation and epoch. Indeed, the question whether a writer's work is universal or not rarely arises when that writer is European or white American. It arises so frequently in discussions of black writers for no other reason than that the long-standing myth of white superiority and black inferiority has led so many to believe that in literature, and in other areas of life as well, the black particular of universal human experience is less appropriate than the white particular.

The question of universality, in the terms in which it has invariably been raised, usually by hostile critics of black literature, is a false issue. The real issue is whether the drama is lively, whether the portrait is vivid and memorable, whether the interpretation is perceptive and accurate; in short, whether the work is well done. But of course, to be able to judge whether the work is well done, one must have standards of judgment derived from the nation, epoch, and milieu from which the work itself derives. One cannot judge a European sonnet and a Japanese haiku by exactly the same criteria; nor a German lieder and an Afro blues; nor a Beethoven symphony and a Coltrane set; nor Wordsworth's "Intimations of Immortality" and Hughes's "Mother to Son." The cultures are that distinct, each autonomous, governed by its own laws. Which brings us to the central issue involved in the idea of a black esthetic, namely, the extrapolation of standards for judging black art from within the culture-sensibility.

Whatever the technical excellences of a work of imaginative literature by a black writer, if it is rooted in an alien sensibility it cannot be central or important to blacks. On the other hand, mere fidelity to the culture-sensibility is not enough: what is required is a happy marriage of technical excellence and sensibility. Langston Hughes is a great poet because, among other things, he combines *to an unusual degree* such poetic virtues as economy, lucidity, evocativeness of imagery, and mellifluousness of movement, with a deep-rooted fidelity to the Afro-American sensibility. He is therefore a proper source for extracting some of the governing principles of black art, some of the standards by which black literature, and in particular black poetry, is to be judged. These principles are implicit in his work, as follows:

(1) His central concern is the central concern of the Afro-American people, namely, their struggle for freedom. His is, from first to last, a socially committed literature, ulilizing, for a brief period of time at least, a Marxist ideological frame. Whether he says it in these terms or not, one of the aims and ultimate effects of his work is the raising of our consciousness, the strengthening of black people in their struggle in America and elsewhere. Starting with black America, he expands into the pan-African world in his later years, especially in *Ask Your Mama* and *The Panther and the Lash.*

(2) Hughes has anchored his work in Afro-American oral tradition, thereby serving the vital function of cultural transmission. His utilization of black musical forms—jazz, blues, spirituals, gospel, sermons—is the most comprehensive and profound in the history of Afro-American literature. Blues appears in various guises: in the strict, classic, three-line verse form; in a variety of modified verse forms paralleling the infinite variety of folk blues which do not conform to the classic verse pattern; and in the blues spirit and world view incorporated into non-blues poems and into his prose fiction and drama. His jazz poems are appropriately cast in free verse and often in black idiom, and they approximate the bouncy rhythms and light-hearted exuberance of the music. Much of his poetry is in Afro-American idiom, usually Northern urban, sometimes unalloyed, sometimes modified with standard English usage. In addition, he employs the forms and techniques of contemporary "street poetry"—rapping, signifying, toasting, and playing the dozens (ranking, screaming, sounding, louding, woofing). The effect of his choice of forms, and his ease and smoothness in handling them, is to situate his works brilliantly and unequivocally in the black world.

(3) Finally, Hughes's black characters are authentic and memorable, the greatest of them being Jesse B. Semple, Madam Alberta K. Johnson of "Madam to You," and the Black Madonnas of "Mother to Son" and "The Negro Mother." Hughes is essentially *a dramatic poet.* He speaks in a multiplicity of voices, through a multitude of personas, each of them the purveyor of authentic black attitudes—attitudes, views, and life-styles that are as heterogeneous as the Afro-American population.

The matter of greatness in art extends beyond the narrow limits of formal esthetics into the realm of politics. However well written, it is unlikely that a pro-Nazi novel would be well received at this time in Western Europe or America, or in Israel. If blacks had greater power in America, it would have been impossible, for instance, for William Styron to receive a national award for his novel, *The Confessions of Nat Turner* (1968), which turns history upside down, slanders the Afro-American people and their heroes, and mocks black suffering. In short, the question of an autonomous black esthetic is centrally involved with politics, as all questions of esthetics, which is itself a branch of ethics, ultimately are. When therefore I speak of the qualities that make for greatness in Hughes's work, I speak with awareness of the political existence of black people in America as a suppressed nation within a nation. If it were not for oppression, the matter of commitment to liberation and raising of consciousness might not arise. But it is from the standpoint of the distinctive character and needs of a long oppressed people that the conservation and transmission of the folk heritage, of which Hughes is so smooth a vehicle, becomes not merely and indifferently "desirable," but *essential* to cultural coherence and group survival.

Charles S. Johnson, a perceptive contemporary observer and interpreter of the arts of the Harlem Renaissance, wrote of the new racial poetry of which Hughes's was a leading example:

> The new racial poetry of the Negro is the expression of something more than experimentation in a new technique. It marks the birth of a new racial consciousness and self conception. It is a first frank acceptance of race, and the recognition of difference without the usual implications of disparity. It lacks apology, the wearying appeals to pity, and the conscious philosophy of defense. In being itself it reveals its greatest charm. In accepting this life it invests it with a new meaning. . . . Who would know something of the core and limitations of this life should go to the Blues. In them is the curious story of disillusionment without a saving philosophy and yet without defeat.[14]

Hughes had forecast that perhaps the common people, the folk whose lives formed the axis on which the new poetry revolved, "will give to the world its truly great Negro artist, the one who is not afraid to be himself." Hughes is himself the fulfillment of that dream. His work stands as a Great Pyramid against which all other monuments in the Valley of Afro-American Poetry will have to be measured.

### Conclusion

⟨. . .⟩ Hughes's social and philosophical universe is no more circumscribed or parochial than the universes of Aeschylus, Aristophanes, Dante, Shakespeare, Milton, Wordsworth, Keats, Whitman, Dostoevsky, Hopkins, Joyce, Pound, Eliot, Gide, or Sartre. His philosophical system, the hidden infrastructure of ideas and procedures over and around and onto which his art is molded, is as firm, complete, autonomous, and vaild as theirs. Entry into the particular world of any of these writers, Hughes included, is accomplished only by an effort of the imagination. The black life experiences which Hughes soul-mirrors may indeed be foreign and distant to white readers; but how close or familiar to black readers is the spiritual dessication and emotional emptiness of the white middle and upper classes which Eliot repeatedly mourns in his poetry, or the details of European history, mythology, literature, and art which Pound so copiously copies into his? It is only by an effort of the imagination—by projection of the self into an alien environment, by deliberate assumption of alien perspectives, by sympathetic identification—that a 20th-century reader in any part of the black world could comfortably enter into the world of the *Divina Commedia, Hamlet, Paradise Lost, Ulysses, The Waste Land,* or *L'Immoraliste.* Hughes's *Montage of a Dream Deferred,* or his *Ask Your Mama,* or any other black work of magnitude, exacts an equivalent white effort.

A well-worded rebuke to the excessive devotion to formal complexity, which characterizes the modernist sensibility and which is largely responsible for the low esteem of Hughes's poetry among the critics, is now and always in order. Regardless what the elitist, antidemocratic, modernist school-men think and teach, poetic value is not commensurate with difficulty of comprehension, nor with erudition exhibited in masses of esoterica and obscure allusions, nor with the paucity of the audience to whom a poet chooses to address his work. Hughes did not choose to address his work to little circles of "experts," nor to members of some secret society of "Art." His aim, to borrow the happy phrase of the younger generation, was to unite the academy and the street—to write in such a way that both the minimally educated and the maximally schooled would find themselves maximally rewarded in reading his work. And his poetry is evidence, if evidence were needed, that even in the 20th century lucidity of surface and depth of meaning are not mutually exclusive.

As Margaret Larkin noted in an early review, Hughes's work represents a contribution to the effort in the early part of this century to free poetry "from the stiff conventions which Anglo-Saxon prosody inflicted upon it."[15] What Pound and Eliot, taking their cue from Whitman, did for poetry using standard English, Hughes, taking his cue from Dunbar, Sandburg, and Lindsay, did for it using black English. Hughes participated in the task of exploding the old boundaries of poetry in English by infusing it with a black sensibility independent of the received stereotypes, by expanding it to accommodate the black experience and language and style. This is his particular achievement as a prosodist, that in spite of the nay-sayers, white and black, he succeeded in bringing into the overall poetic arena, away from the locus of side-shows, such forms as the jazz poem, the blues poem, the sermon, the gospel shout, and the exhortatory call-and-response of black theatre. By so doing, Hughes helped pave the way for the Beat movement of the 50s, for the Black Arts revolution of the 60s and 70s whose impact on white American poetry and drama is yet to be measured, and for the burgeoning Ethnopoetics movement of the 70s. The ethnopoets, led by Jerome Rothenberg,[16] are successors to the Beats and fellow-laborers with the black poets in the same vast vineyard, in a universe of poetry whose substance and example is all of the primal word-deeds of the world's vast variety of cultures. Their emphasis, both as translators and as original poets, is on the oral act, on performance, on the poem as numenal sound rather than as written letter. In these movements which Hughes preceded and influenced, the unification of written with oral poetry is for the first time a realistic possibility.

Hughes's poetry exhibits many of the characteristics of oral poetry the world over.[17] It is marked by an economy of means, by an almost ruthless exclusion of extraneous embellishments, resulting in a lean, spare, uncluttered style, and in efficient structure and logistics that permit no tedious or unnecessary diversions. Its commitment to the auditory, which in oral poetry is primary and definitive, and to a popular mass audience, makes indispensable a lucidity of surface, normal syntax, a contemporary and colloquial rather than archaic or learned idiom, and vivid, concrete, and evocative imagery—in short, felicitous speech and mellifluous motion. Hughes's poetry is to be commended both for its fidelity to traditional forms and themes and for its transposition, manipulation, and adaptation of them.

Hughes's technically efficient poetic machinery, modeled on and assembled with parts borrowed from the oral tradition, is in the service of a sweeping social vision, is a vehicle for moving matters that are of importance to the poet's community. Hughes is very much aware of his historical placement, of the imperatives of his *race, moment, milieu;* and he makes his art respond to those imperatives, which include the raising of consciousness among an oppressed people, the affirmation, conservation, and onward transmission of their culture, and the battling of injustice through exposition and protest. The black artist's mission, as Hughes originally defined it for himself and his contemporaries in "The Negro Artist and the Racial Mountain," calls for depth of vision, breadth of sympathies, passion, and courage. Hughes's passion and courage are obvious from the tenacity of his views and methods, but the intensity of his anger is not, mainly because he usually holds it at a distance, controlled and barricaded behind the sardonic humor of the blues, wrapped in irony, satire, wit and a general playfulness:

> This mornin' for breakfast
> I chawed de mornin' air.
> This mornin' for breakfast
> Chawed de mornin' air.
> But this evenin' for supper
> I got evenin' air to spare.[18]

> Great names for crowns and garlands!
>     Yeah!
> I love Ralph Bunche—
> But I can't eat him for lunch.[19]

Hughes wears a genial mask that fits so well it is possible to mistake it for his face. But a careful second glance, even without a visit to the backstage dressing room, is enough to reveal a man burning with a rage as absolute as the fiery furnaces of LeRoi Jones or Sonia Sanchez. Indeed, we miss Hughes's rage only if we wilfully elect to concentrate on his humor. Usually he manages to mold his anger into the porcelain of his poetry—but without blunting its sharp and bitter edges; on the contrary, the jagged edges stand out even more fiercely against the smoothness:

> I could tell you,
> If I wanted to,
> What makes me
> What I am.

> But I don't
> Really want to—
> And you don't
> Give a damn.[20]

I said before that Hughes's work is swept by the two positive compulsions or radical energies which may be said to dominate Afro-American literature—in its impulse toward the oral tradition and toward a literature of social struggle. Much of Afro-American literature of any consequence utilizes and projects black folk culture to a greater or lesser degree, and handles its matter in a way that would enhance the black struggle. In a sense the two propositions are one or can become one: some works hold the two impulses in equilibrium, give them more or less equal play, or fuse and compel them to function as an undifferentiated whole. This is the case with

Hughes. In his work these dual energies are not only greatly visible, prolonged, and relentless in their operation, but they are held in balance and quite often fused, so that the form becomes the function, the instrument the purpose, the medium the message. In Hughes, black folk culture is the weapon, black social and economic sufficiency the prize fought for. By utilizing the black heritage so fully in his work, Hughes preserves and transmits that heritage and thereby aids the survival of Afro-Americans as a distinct people. One of the far-reaching effects of his esthetic, and of its elaborations and extensions by others, is to compel us, in evaluating a black writer, to take into account his attitude to himself and his people and heritage, and what use he makes or fails to make of that heritage. In other words, we must consider the presence, balance, and power of the positive compulsions in his work. Perhaps more than any other writer of his generation, Hughes permits these positive energies the most uninhibited, prolonged and unified play.

### Notes

1. Hughes, "White Folks Do the Funniest Things," *Negro Digest*, February 1944, p. 34.
2. Hughes, "Humor and the Negro Press," address at the Windy City Press Club Banquet, Chicago, Illinois, January 10, 1957. Hughes Archive, Schomburg Collection, New York Public Library.
3. Ibid.
4. Hughes, "Laughing at White Folks," *Chicago Defender*, National Edition, September 8, 1945, p. 12.
5. Hughes's Spingarn Medal Acceptance Speech, NAACP Convention, St. Paul, Minnesota, June 26, 1960. Hughes Archive, Schomburg Collection.
6. Hughes, "The Negro Artist and the Racial Mountain," *The Nation*, June 23, 1926, pp. 692–94.
7. Hughes, "Laughers," *Fine Clothes to the Jew* (New York, Knopf, 1927), pp. 77–78.
8. Charles S. Johnson, "Jazz Poetry and Blues," *The Carolina Magazine*, May 1928, pp. 16–20.
9. Allison Davis, "Our Negro 'Intellectuals,'" *The Crisis*, 35, No. 8 (August 1928), pp. 268–69 ff.
10. Benjamin Brawley, *The Negro Genius* (New York, Dodd, Mead, 1937), p. 248; Hughes, *Big Sea* (New York, Knopf, 1940), p. 266.
11. Hughes, Letter to the Editor, *The Crisis*, 35, No. 9 (September 1928), p. 302.
12. See n. 5.
13. Ibid.
14. Charles S. Johnson, "Jazz Poetry and Blues."
15. Margaret Larkin, "A Poet of the People," *Opportunity*, March 1927, p. 84.
16. See Jerome Rothenberg, *Technicians of the Sacred* (New York, Doubleday, 1968), and *Shaking the Pumpkin* (New York, Doubleday, 1972); Jerome Rothenberg and George Quasha, *America: A Prophecy* (New York, Random House, 1973). See also *Alcheringa: Ethnopoetics*, "A First Magazine of the World's Tribal Poetries," founded in 1970 by Jerome Rothenberg and Dennis Tedlock.
17. The passage that follows is adapted from Onweuchekwa Jemie, Chinweizu, and Ihechukwu Madubuike, "Towards the Decolonization of African Literature," *Okike*, No. 7, April 1975, pp. 80–81; *Transition*, No. 48, April 1975, p. 56.
18. Hughes, "Evenin' Air Blues," *Shakespeare in Harlem* (New York, Knopf, 1942), p. 38.
19. Hughes, "Crowns and Garlands," *Panther and the Lash* (New York, Knopf, 1967), p. 6.
20. Hughes, "Impasse," ibid., p. 85.

### LLOYD W. BROWN
### "The Portrait of the Artist as a Black American in the Poetry of Langston Hughes"

*Studies in Black Literature*, Winter 1974, pp. 24–27

During the Harlem Renaissance of the twenties the young Langston Hughes offered a self-description which has since become a manifesto in the contemporary Black aesthetic movement: "Most of my own poems are racial in theme and treatment, derived from the life I know . . . We younger Negro artists who create now intend to express our individual dark-skinned selves without fear or shame."[1] Hughes' ideal of the Black artist as a committed spokesman is obviously consonant with the primary criteria of the current Black arts movement—particularly in the writings of LeRoi Jones. But in emphasizing the relationship, in Hughes' essay, between the Black community and the Black artist, some critics have tended to minimize or obscure another crucial implication of his declaration. For, quite apart from the controversial pros and cons of the Black aesthetic as such, Hughes' statement is of special interest because it sheds light on a significant area of his own work—specifically, on the symbolic role of the artist as archetype. Of course this role is always implicit in any political or aesthetic description of the artist as spokesman and representative. Such an implication is clear enough when Hughes makes his emphasis on the ethnic mission of the Black writer in terms of a self-portrait: the desired racial themes and objectives are "derived" from his personal experiences; and the ethnic responsibilities of Black artists in general are a kind of collective self-expression. In Hughes' poetry this implied self-portrait has a complex, exploratory function that goes beyond the immediate context of a Black aesthetic manifesto: the Black artist is a recurring archetype whose personality is conceived as a paradigm of tensions and self-conflicts within the Black American's situation, and whose art is conceived as a perceptual and expressive process. In other words, the distinctive features of each art form are integrated, symbolically, with Hughes' poetic art, and in the process, with that Black American experience which is the burden of Hughes' themes.

Broadly speaking, the thematic significance of Black American art forms is not peculiar to Langston Hughes' poetry. The blues, in particular, has frequently been traced in the themes of a major-writer like Richard Wright.[2] But Hughes' poetry is specially noteworthy in this regard for two reasons. First, the artist-archetype is not limited to the blues motif but includes the dancer and poet as well as the musician; and in this regard, Hughes frequently emphasizes the relationship between the art forms, and artists (poet-musician, musician-dancer, composer-poet, and so forth) at the same time that he demonstrates intrinsic connections between the respective art forms and the artist's ethnic experience. Secondly, Hughes' thematic interest in art is distinguished by his concern, not only with a mode of perception, but also with specific techniques and generic structures which characterize the selected art forms. Hence the blues, for example, would interest Hughes not only as a philosophical concept, or as a pattern of experience, such as has been noted in, say, Ralph Ellison's *Invisible Man*.[3] More to the point, Hughes has also concentrated on characteristic techniques in the composition of certain musical forms, then archetypally exploits the artist and the artist's techniques. And this is generally true of other art forms in his poetry,[4] especially those poems which project the expectations/disillusionments in the tradition of the Black American dream for social fulfillment, and which apply this dream motif to the ambiguities and tensions in the Black American's identity.

In "Afro-American Fragment" these ambiguities are simultaneously explored and dramatized by the duality of the Black musician and poet, and by their respective art forms:

> So long
> So far away
> Is Africa.
> Not even memories alive
> Save those that history books create,
> Save those that songs
> Beat back into the blood—
> Beat out of blood with words sad-sung
> In strange un-Negro tongue.

In effect the Black American's African heritage is really experienced as a creative process—to be distinguished from the creations (i.e. fabrications) of history books. And the creative process of Black American music is a microcosm of this larger cultural experience. For that music typifies the duality and tensions of the Black American identity in its fusion of an ethno-musical heritage: an African "beat" or rhythm is combined with (a) the history of slavery and oppression ("beat out of blood") and (b) the non-African language and culture of a Western heritage ("strange un-Negro tongue"). In forging a new, hybrid art form, the Black musician is therefore an archetypal symbol of an historical process through which the transported African created an "Afro-American" identity from the fragments of an African past, the Western present, and the distinctive experience of being Black in White America. And, in turn, the musician's re-creation of the "Afro-American" experience has now been implicitly duplicated by the poet.

"Daybreak In Alabama" returns to the musical imagination and to that duality which is as characteristic of the Black American's dream / aspiration as it is of the hybrid Afro-American personality. Thus the composer-persona conceives of his song (about daybreak in Alabama) as an imaginative blending of all the discrete groupings of American society. And this musical apotheosis of the melting-pot ideal is presented as the dream-motive of the composer's own ethnic group:

> I'm gonna put some tall tall trees in it . . .
> And long red necks
> And poppy colored faces
> And big brown arms
> And the field daisy eyes
> Of black and white black white black people
> And I'm gonna put white hands
> And black hands and brown and yellow hands
> And red clay earth hands in it
> Touching everybody with kind fingers.

What Hughes' musician-persona has done has been to apply to his American situation the distinctively harmonious, and harmonizing, role of music in particular, and art in general. Thus the opening line of the poem ("When I get to be a composer") simultaneously announces the specific imaginative activity of the musician as artist and the social ideal which Hughes attributes to the Black American as a kind of artist-archetype—that is, the Black American as one whose experience of disharmony and hatred gives him a special interest in dreams of a harmoniously composed society founded on universal goodwill. And in this poem, too, the poet's own art is linked with the musician-persona's archetypal role. The harmonic symbolism of music as an imaginative composition is integrated with the *transforming* powers of the poet's imaginative manipulation of verbal forms, and all with the effect of enforcing the vision of a harmonious, integrated society. Hence the negative racial connotations of "red necks,"

"white," and "black" are deliberately invoked and simultaneously transformed into distinctive but compatible patterns in Nature (pine needles, red clay, red necks etc.) and in society (colored faces, brown arms, white hands, yellow hands, "everybody"). Once again, the distinctive modes of the artist-persona and his art are (1) a microcosm of the actual Black-White ambiguities, or tensions, in Black America, and (2) a symbolic process in which the Black American as artist-archetype envisions the transmutation of social and racial tensions into a harmonious whole.

This is the kind of progression, from a perception of conflict to a vision of harmony, that Hughes also explores through the modes of another artist-persona—the dancer, In "As I Grew Older," for example, the movements of dance and the light-dark variations of the dancer's stage-craft are all absorbed into the poet's metaphoric rendition of ethnic "movements," or growth, and Black-White relationships:

> I lie down in the shadow.
> No longer the light of my dream before me,
> Above me.
> Only the thick wall.
> Only the shadow.
> My hands!
> My darkhands!
> Break through the wall!
> Find my dream!
> Help me to shatter this darkness,
> To smash this night,
> To break this shadow
> Into a thousand lights of sun,
> Into a thousand whirling dreams
> Of sun!

The spotlight-sun symbol through which the poet-dancer celebrates the Black American's dream also appears in "Dream Variations" where the dance motif is even more explicit:

> To fling my arms wide
> In some place of the sun
> To whirl and to dance
> Till the white day is done.

As in "I Grew Older" the dancer's art represents a progressive movement from a stark light-dark (sunlight) antithesis to a whirling vision of both sun and darkness in positive and creative terms. And, simultaneously, these referents of the dancer's art provide a verbal framework for the poem's metaphoric structure. Thus "place of the sun" and "white day" are finely balanced by a poetic sense of ironic ambiguities: each phrase is poised between the pejorative ("place of the sun" as the tropical "savage's" domain, and "white" day as the racist's milieu) and the ideal ("sun" as the vital, life-giving source of both the Blacks' experience and the Whites' "day"). Moreover, the progression of the dance to an unequivocal celebration of both night and day is duplicated by the poet's unambiguous vision of ethnic pride within a wider context of social harmony:

> Dance! Whirl! Whirl!
> Till the quick day is done.
> Rest at pale evening . . .
> A tall, slim tree . . .
> Night coming tenderly
> Black like me.

Finally, the dancer-persona of each poem is comparable with Hughes' poet and musician archetypes in that the dance form does not merely describe the tensions, ambiguities of the Black American's identity, and the harmonious certitudes of the Black American dream. The dance form is also a microcosm of its subject area. In these poems Hughes had modelled his archetypal artist on a blend of contemporary Western dance (complete with the stage-craft of spotlighting and light-dark settings) and the visual evocation of an Afro-American motif—without blurring the distinctive traits of either tradition. And, particularly during the triumphant dream-climax of each poem, this choreographic fusion of Black and White dance traditions is analogous to that social harmony, or synthesis, which lies at the heart of the dream itself. Once again, then, Hughes projects a Black American dream motif, envisioning a socially integrated and ethnically harmonious society; and he does so through art forms (dance, poetry, musical composition, and song) which both represent the tensions in their cultural and ethnic sources and exemplify a transcendental fusion of those sources in the Black American dream—especially the kind of "Afro-American" fusion which accentuates distinctive "fragments" ("Afro" and "Western") within a harmonious whole. Indeed, from this point of view one may detect a certain kind of subtlety even in a poem like "Danse Africaine" which some critics have dismissed as an example of "phony . . . black nationalism" based on Hughes' alleged "fantasy" about Africa.[5] For the initial impression of a simplistically overwhelming African presence—due to the insistent beating of the tom-toms behind the dancer—is balanced by the pivotal halfway lines of the poem:

> Dance!
> A night-veiled girl
>     Whirl softly into a
>     Circle of light.

Here too the dancer image combines the symbolism of the spotlight ("White" and a product of Western technology) with the suggestive blackness of the dancer's color and/or costume. ("A night-veiled girl"). It is therefore appropriate that this image occurs at the halfway point in the poem because its metaphoric celebration of a cultural synthesis literally becomes a central pivot for the insistent, and more obtrusive, tom-tom images: the total structure of the poem therefore presents the African tom-tom, not as the "escape fantasy" of some "phony" Black nationalism, but as an active cultural memory that continues to beat even as it becomes a part of a non-African world.

Conversely, Hughes prefers those art forms, especially in music and dance, which are more distinctively Black American whenever he deals with the frustration of the dream ideal and with the Black American's subsequent disillusionment. In such poems the emphasis on the blues-singer's art, the boogie-woogie, or the be-bop, has the effect of heightening the sense of a *separate* as well as distinctive identity—one which is both proud of its distinctiveness and embittered by its exclusion from the American Dream:

> What's written down
> for white folks
> ain't for us a-tall:
> "Liberty and Justice—
> Huh—For All."
>     Oop—pop—a—da!
>     Skee! Daddle—de—do!
>     Be-Bop!

The be-bop rhythms of "Children's Rhymes" are comparable with the boogie-woogie design of "Dream Boogie" where an abrasive sarcasm underscores both the pride and the bitterness of the outsider:

> Good morning, daddy!
> Ain't you heard
> The boogie-woogie rumble
> Of a dream deferred?
> Listen closely!
> You'll hear their feet
> Beating out and beating out . . .
>     Hey, pop!
>     Mop!
>     Y-e-a-h!

In both poems the ethnic dance forms are emphasized as distinctive modes that are less integrated with structures of the majority culture. And this distinctiveness of the art form complements the singer-dancer's emphasis on an outsider identity.

In the final analysis, then, Hughes' artist-archetypes represent a coherent view of the Black artist and the artist's techniques: the art form is not merely structure as structure (or "art for art's sake") but design as an expression of the artist's ethno-social experience. And, by extension, the poet's choice of art forms and artist archetypes is dictated by the mode of perception, or patterns of experience, which motivates his own art, and which seems intrinsic to each chosen form. In fact, this aspect of Hughes' poetry seems to be determined by these criteria rather than by chronology: there appears to be no significant variation in the *nature* of his thematic choices, in this regard, over the years. In turn, the poet's varied choices, and the variety of ideas and emotions which these represent, imply a rather selfconscious emphasis by Hughes on the dual relationship between the poet and society, and society and art. In this regard, the art forms and artist-archetypes serve the poet as modes of self-perception and self-expression: the symbolic values which they derive from their social sources reflect the poet's own duality, his dreams and disillusionment, the aspiration towards social integration, and an ambiguous sense of separateness. In effect, Hughes' poet and his other artists are not conceived in the relatively simple terms of all-knowing seers and moral leaders. Their individual experiences and their notions of their own selfhoods—complete with all the inherent conflicts and vicissitudes—are really a microcosm of the Black American's shifting, and ambiguous patterns of self-perception.

*Notes*

1. Langston Hughes, "The Negro Artist and the Racial Mountain," reprinted in *Black Expression: Essays by and about Black Americans in the Creative Arts*, ed. Addison Gayle, Jr. (New York, 1969), pp. 258–263.

2. Ralph Ellison, "Richard Wright's Blues," in *Shadow and Act*, Signet ed. (New York, 1966), pp. 89–104.

3. Edward Margolies, "History as Blues: Ralph Ellison's *Invisible Man*," in *Native Sons: A Critical Study of Twentieth Century Negro American Authors*, Paperback ed. (Philadelphia, 1968), pp. 127–148.

4. All poems discussed here are cited from *Selected Poems of Langston Hughes* (New York, 1959).

5. See, for example, Arthur P. Davis, "Langston Hughes: Cool Poet," *College Language Association Journal*, XI (1967–1968), 285.

# ZORA NEALE HURSTON

## c. 1901–1960

Zora Neale Hurston was born probably on January 7, 1901, in America's first all-black incorporated town, Eatonville, Florida. In her teens, five years after the death of her mother, Hurston left Eatonville to work as a maid for a traveling Gilbert and Sullivan troupe. She studied at Morgan College in Baltimore and at Howard University, where her first short story appeared in the college literary magazine. She later won a scholarship to Barnard College to study with the eminent anthropologist Franz Boas.

While living in New York Hurston worked as a secretary to the popular novelist Fannie Hurst. Hurston is considered a major force in the Harlem Renaissance of the 1920s and 1930s. She collaborated on several plays with various writers, including *Mule Bone: A Comedy of Negro Life in Three Acts* (1931), written with Langston Hughes. Boas arranged a fellowship for Hurston which allowed her to travel throughout the South and collect folklore. The result of these travels was the publication of a collection of black folk tales, *Mules and Men* (1935). Hurston is thought to be the first black American to have collected and published Afro-American folklore. In later years her interest in anthropology took her to several Latin American countries, including Jamaica, Haiti, and Honduras.

Hurston's first novel, *Jonah's Gourd Vine* (1934), is loosely based on the lives of her parents in Eatonville. Probably her best known work is the novel *Their Eyes Were Watching God* (1937), which focuses on a middle-aged woman's quest for fulfillment in an oppressive society. In addition to her life as a writer, Hurston worked temporarily as a teacher, a librarian at an Air Force base, a staff writer at Paramount Studios, and as a reporter for the *Fort Pierce* (Florida) *Chronicle*.

Hurston published two collections of black folklore which are thought by many writers to be an excellent source for myths and legends about black culture. Her autobiography, *Dust Tracks on a Road*, won the 1943 Annisfield Award. Her final novel, *Seraph on the Suwanee*, appeared in 1948. Hurston's other honors include Guggenheim Fellowships in 1936 and 1938. She died on January 28, 1960, in Fort Pierce, Florida.

## Personal

Well, that is the way things stand up to now. I can look back and see sharp shadows, high lights, and smudgy inbetweens. I have been in Sorrow's kitchen and licked out all the pots. Then I have stood on the peaky mountain wrappen in rainbows, with a harp and a sword in my hands.

What I had to swallow in the kitchen has not made me less glad to have lived, nor made me want to low-rate the human race, nor any whole sections of it. I take no refuge from myself in bitterness. To me, bitterness is the under-arm odor of wishful weakness. It is the graceless acknowledgment of defeat. I have no urge to make any concessions like that to the world as yet. I might be like that some day, but I doubt it. I am in the struggle with the sword in my hands, and I don't intend to run until you run me. So why give off the smell of something dead under the house while I am still in there tussling with my sword in my hand?

If tough breaks have not soured me, neither have my glory-moments caused me to build any altars to myself where I can burn incense before God's best job of work. My sense of humor will always stand in the way of my seeing myself, my family, my race or my nation as the whole intent of the universe. When I see what we really are like, I know that God is too great an artist for we folks on my side of the creek to be all of His best works. Some of His finest touches are among us, without doubt, but some more of His masterpieces are among those folks who live over the creek.

So looking back and forth in history and around the temporary scene, I do not visualize the moon dripping down in blood, nor the sun batting his fiery eyes and laying down in the cradle of eternity to rock himself into sleep and slumber at instances of human self-bias. I know that the sun and the moon must be used to sights like that by now. I too yearn for universal justice, but how to bring it about is another thing. It is such a complicated thing, for justice, like beauty, is in the eye of the beholder. There is universal agreement on the principle, but the application brings on the fight. Oh, for some disinterested party to pass on things! Somebody will hurry to tell me that we voted God to the bench for that. But the lawyers who interpret His opinions, make His decisions sound just like they made them up themselves. Being an idealist, I too wish that the world was better than I am. Like all the rest of my fellow men, I don't want to live around people with no more principles than I have. My inner fineness is continually outraged at finding that the world is a whole family of Hurstons.

Seeing these things, I have come to the point by trying to make the day at hand a positive thing, and realizing the uselessness of gloominess.

Therefore, I see nothing but futility in looking back over my shoulder in rebuke at the grave of some white man who has been dead too long to talk about. That is just what I would be doing in trying to fix the blame for the dark days of slavery and the Reconstruction. From what I can learn, it was sad. Certainly. But my ancestors who lived and died in it are dead. The white men who profited by their labor and lives are dead also. I have no personal memory of those times, and no responsibility for them. Neither has the grandson of the man who held my folks. So I see no need in button-holing that grandson like the Ancient Mariner did the wedding guest and calling for the High Sheriff to put him under arrest.

I am not so stupid as to think that I would be bringing this descendant of a slave-owner any news. He has heard just as much about the thing as I have. I am not so humorless as to visualize this grandson falling out on the sidewalk before me, and throwing an acre of fits in remorse because his old folks held slaves. No, indeed! If it happened to be a fine day and he had had a nice breakfast, he might stop and answer me like this:

"In the first place, I was not able to get any better view of social conditions from my grandmother's womb than you could from your grandmother's. Let us say for the sake of argument that I detest the institution of slavery and all that it implied, just as much as you do. You must admit that I had no more power to do anything about it in my unborn state than you had in yours. Why fix your eyes on me? I respectfully refer you to my ancestors, and bid you a good day."

If I still lingered before him, he might answer me further by asking questions like this:

"Are you so simple as to assume that the Big Surrender (Southerners, both black and white speak of Lee's surrender to Grant as the Big Surrender) banished the concept of human slavery from the earth? What is the principle of slavery? Only the literal buying and selling of human flesh on the block? That was only an outside symbol. Real slavery is couched in the desire and the efforts of any man or community to live and advance their interests at the expense of the lives and interests of others. All of the outward signs come out of that. Do you not realize that the power, prestige and prosperity of the greatest nations on earth rests on colonies and sources of raw materials? Why else are great wars waged? If you have not thought, then why waste up time with your vapid accusations? If you have, then why single *me* out?" And like Pilate, he will light a cigar, and stroll on off without waiting for an answer.

Anticipating such an answer, I have no intention of wasting my time beating on old graves with a club. I know that I cannot pry aloose the clutching hand of Time, so I will turn all my thoughts and energies on the present. I will settle for from now on.

And why not? For me to pretend that I am Old Black Joe and waste my time on his problems, would be just as ridiculous as for the government of Winston Churchill to bill the Duke of Normandy the first of every month, or for the Jews to hang around the pyramids trying to picket Old Pharaoh. While I have a handkerchief over my eyes crying over the landing of the first slaves in 1619, I might miss something swell that is going on in 1942. Furthermore, if somebody were to consider my grandmother's ungranted wishes, and give *me* what *she* wanted, I would be too put out for words.

What do I want, then? I will tell you in a parable. A Negro deacon was down on his knees praying at a wake held for a sister who had died that day. He had his eyes closed and was going great guns, when he noticed that he was not getting any more "amens" from the rest. He opened his eyes and saw that everybody else was gone except himself and the dead woman. Then he saw the reason. The supposedly dead woman was trying to sit up. He bolted for the door himself, but it slammed shut so quickly that it caught his flying coat-tails and held him sort of static. "Oh, no, Gabriel!" the deacon shouted, "dat aint no way for you to do. I can do my own running, but you got to 'low me the same chance as the rest."

I don't know any more about the future than you do. I hope that it will be full of work, because I have come to know by experience that work is the nearest thing to happiness that I can find. No matter what else I have among the things that humans want, I go to pieces in a short while if I do not work. What all my work shall be, I don't know that either, every hour being a stranger to you until you live it. I want a busy life, a just mind and a timely death.

But if I should live to be very old, I have laid plans for that so that it will not be too tiresome. So far, I have never used coffee, liquor, nor any form of stimulant. When I get old, and my joints and bones tell me about it, I can sit around and write for myself, if for nobody else, and read slowly and carefully the mysticism of the East, and re-read Spinoza with love and care. All the while my days can be a succession of coffee cups. Then when the sleeplessness of old age attacks me, I can have a likker bottle snug in my pantry and sip away and sleep. Get mellow and think kindly of the world. I think I can be like that because I have known the joy and pain of deep friendship. I have served and been served. I have made some good enemies for which I am not a bit sorry. I have loved unselfishly, and I have fondled hatred with the red-hot tongs of Hell. That's living.

I have no race prejudice of any kind. My kinfolks, and my "skin-folks" are dearly loved. My own circumference of everyday life is there. But I see their same virtues and vices everywhere I look. So I give you all my right hand of fellowship and love, and hope for the same from you. In my eyesight, you lose nothing by not looking just like me. I will remember you all in my good thoughts, and I ask you kindly to do the same for me. Not only just me. You, who play the zig-zag lightning of power over the world, with the grumbling thunder in your wake, think kindly of those who walk in the dust. And you who walk in humble places, think kindly too, of others. There has been no proof in the world so far that you would be less arrogant if you held the lever of power in your hands. Let us all be kissing-friends. Consider that with tolerance and patience, we godly demons may breed a noble world in a few hundred generations or so. Maybe all of us who do not have the good fortune to meet, or meet again, in this world, will meet at a barbecue.—ZORA NEALE HURSTON, "Looking Things Over," *Dust Tracks on a Road* (1942), 1970, pp. 280–86

Of these "niggerati," Zora Neale Hurston was certainly the most amusing. Only to reach a wider audience, need she ever write books—because she is a perfect book of entertainment in herself. In her youth she was always getting scholarships and things from wealthy white people, some of whom simply paid her just to sit around and represent the Negro race for them, she did it in such a racy fashion. She was full of side-splitting anecdotes, humorous tales, and tragicomic stories, remembered out of her life in the South as a daughter of a travelling minister of God. She could make you laugh one minute and cry the next. To many of her white friends, no doubt, she was a perfect "darkie," in the nice meaning they give the term—that is a naïve, childlike, sweet, humorous, and highly colored Negro.

But Miss Hurston was clever, too—a student who didn't let college give her a broad *a* and who had great scorn for all pretensions, academic or otherwise. That is why she was such a fine folk-lore collector, able to go among the people and never act as if she had been to school at all. Almost nobody else could stop the average Harlemite on Lenox Avenue and measure his head with a strange-looking, anthropological device and not get bawled out for the attempt, except Zora, who used to stop anyone whose head looked interesting, and measure it.

When Miss Hurston graduated from Barnard she took an apartment in West 66th Street near the park, in that row of Negro houses there. She moved in with no furniture at all and no money, but in a few days friends had given her everything, from decorative silver birds, perched atop the linen cabinet, down to a footstool. And on Saturday night, to christen the place, she had a *hand*-chicken dinner, since she had forgotten to say she needed forks.

She seemed to know almost everybody in New York. She had been a secretary to Fannie Hurst, and had met dozens of celebrities whose friendship she retained. Yet she was always having terrific ups-and-downs about money. She tells this story on herself, about needing a nickel to go downtown one day and wondering where on earth she would get it. As she approached the subway, she was stopped by a blind beggar holding out his cup.

"Please help the blind! Help the blind! A nickel for the blind!"

"I need money worse than you today," said Miss Hurston, taking five cents out of his cup. "Lend me this! Next time, I'll give it back." And she went on downtown.—LANGSTON HUGHES, "Harlem Literati," *The Big Sea*, 1940, pp. 238–40

"What is your name?" I ask the woman who has climbed into the back seat.

"Rosalee," she says. She has a rough, pleasant voice, as if she is a singer who also smokes a lot. She is homely, and has an air of ready indifference.

"Another woman came by here wanting to see the grave," she says, lighting up a cigarette. "She was a little short, dumpty white lady from one of these Florida schools. Orlando or Daytona. But let me tell you something before we gets started. All I know is where the cemetery is. I don't know one thing about the grave. You better go back in and ask her to draw you a map."

A few moments later, with Mrs. Patterson's diagram of where the grave is, we head for the cemetery.

We drive past blocks of small, pastel-colored houses and turn right onto 17th Street. At the very end, we reach a tall curving gate, with the words "Garden of the Heavenly Rest," fading into the stone. I expected, from Mrs. Patterson's small drawing, to find a small circle—which would have placed Zora's grave five or ten paces from the road. But the "circle" is over an acre large and looks more like an abandoned field. Tall weeds choke the dirt road and scrape against the sides of the car. It doesn't help either that I step out into an active anthill.

"I don't know about y'all," I say, "but I don't even believe this." I am used to the haphazard cemetery-keeping that is traditional in most Southern black communities, but this neglect is staggering. As far as I can see there is nothing but bushes and weeds, some as tall as my waist. One grave is near the road, and Charlotte elects to investigate it. It is fairly clean, and belongs to someone who died in 1963.

Rosalee and I plunge into the weeds; I pull my long dress up to my hips. The weeds scratch my knees, and the insects have a feast. Looking back, I see Charlotte standing resolutely near the road.

"Aren't you coming?" I call.

"No," she calls back. "I'm from these parts and I know what's out there." She means snakes.

"Shit," I say, my whole life and the people I love flashing melodramatically before my eyes. Rosalee is a few yards to my right.

"How're you going to find anything out here?" she asks. And I stand still a few seconds, looking at the weeds. Some of them are quite pretty, with tiny yellow flowers. They are thick and healthy, but dead weeds under them have formed a thick gray carpet on the ground. A snake could be lying six inches from my big toe and I wouldn't see it. We move slowly, very slowly, our eyes alert, our legs trembly. It is hard to tell where the center of the circle is since the circle is not really round, but more like half of something round. There are things crackling and hissing in the grass. Sandspurs are sticking to the inside of my skirt. Sand and ants cover my feet. I look toward the road and notice that there are, indeed *two* large curving stones, making an entrance and exit to the cemetery. I take my bearings from them and try to navigate to exact center. But the

center of anything can be very large, and a grave is not a pinpoint. Finding the grave seems positively hopeless. There is only one thing to do:

"Zora!" I yell, as loud as I can (causing Rosalee to jump), "are you out here?"

"If she is, I sho hope she don't answer you. If she do, I'm gone."

"Zora!" I call again. "I'm here. Are you?"

"If she is," grumbles Rosalee, "I hope she'll keep it to herself."

"Zora!" Then I start fussing with her. "I hope you don't think I'm going to stand out here all day, with these snakes watching me and these ants having a field day. In fact, I'm going to call you just one or two more times." On a clump of dried grass, near a small bushy tree, my eye falls on one of the largest bugs I have ever seen. It is on its back, and is as large as three of my fingers. I walk toward it, and yell "Zo-ra!" and my foot sinks into a hole. I look down. I am standing in a sunken rectangle that is about six feet long and about three or four feet wide. I look up to see where the two gates are.

"Well," I say, "this is the center, or approximately anyhow. It's also the only sunken spot we've found. Doesn't this look like a grave to you?"

"For the sake of not going no farther through these bushes," Rosalee growls, "yes, it do."

"Wait a minute," I say, "I have to look around some more to be sure this is the only spot that resembles a grave. But you don't have to come."

Rosalee smiles—a grin, really—beautiful and tough.

"Naw," she says, "I feels sorry for you. If one of these snakes got ahold of you out here by yourself I'd feel *real* bad." She laughs. "I done come this far, I'll go on with you."

"Thank you, Rosalee," I say. "Zora thanks you too."

"Just as long as she don't try to tell me in person," she says, and together we walk down the field.—ALICE WALKER, "In Search of Zora Neale Hurston," *Ms.*, March 1975, pp. 79, 85

## Works

### JONAH'S GOURD VINE

*Jonah's Gourd Vine* can be called without fear of exaggeration the most vital and original novel about the American Negro that has yet been written by a member of the Negro race. Miss Hurston, who is a graduate of Barnard College and a student of anthropology, has made the study of Negro folklore her special province. This may very well account for the brilliantly authentic flavor of her novel and for her excellent rendition of Negro dialect. Unlike the dialect in most novels about the American Negro, this does not seem to be merely the speech of white men with the spelling distorted. Its essence lies rather in the rhythm and balance of the sentences, in the warm artlessness of the phrasing.

No amount of special knowledge of her subject, however, could have made *Jonah's Gourd Vine* other than a mediocre novel if it were not for Miss Hurston's notable talents as a story-teller. In John, the big yellow Negro preacher, and in Lucy Potts, his tiny brown wife, she has created two characters who are intensely real and human and whose outlines will remain in the reader's memory long after the book has been laid aside. They are part and parcel of the tradition of their race, which is as different from ours as night from day; yet Miss Hurston has delineated them with such warmth and sympathy that they appeal to us first of all as human beings, confronting a complex of human problems with whatever grace and humor, intelligence and steadfastness they can muster.

John was a "yaller nigger," hated by his dusky foster-father because of the white blood in his veins. "His mamma named him Two-Eye John after a preacher she heered, but dey called him John Buddy for short." When he was too big to be beaten or bullied the share-cropping Ned Crittenden turned him off the farm. John got a job on Mr. Alf Pearson's place, and created with his big young body and his rich voice a great stir among the brown maidens in Mr. Pearson's service, and fell in love with Lucy Potts, a bright-eyed little girl who could run faster and recite longer pieces than anybody else in school. In the interests of his ardent courtship, John learned to read, and when Lucy attained her fifteenth birthday they were married.

John really loved Lucy and intended to be true to her, but he was totally unable to resist the open and insistent blandishments of other women. Even after he felt a "call" to the ministry he was always mixed up with some woman or other, frequently to the point of an open breach with his horrified and interested congregation. John's long and futile struggle with his lusty appetites, Lucy's cleverness and devotion in protecting him from the consequences, his entanglement after Lucy's death with the magic-making Hattie, his public ruin and public regeneration all make an extraordinarily absorbing and credible tale.

Not the least charm of the book, however, is its language—rich, expressive and lacking in self-conscious artifice. From the rolling and dignified rhythms of John's last sermon to the humorous aptness of such a word as "shickalacked," to express the noise and motion of a locomotive, there will be much in it to delight the reader. It is to be hoped that Miss Hurston will give us other novels in the same colorful idiom.— Margaret Wallace, "Real Negro People," *NYTBR*, May 6, 1934, pp. 6–7

*Jonah's Gourd Vine* (1934), her first novel, is based on the lives of her parents. Written after she had collected the folktales subsequently published in *Mules and Men* (1935), the novel exemplifies both her strengths and her weaknesses.

The protagonist is John Buddy, upon whom all major actions depend—or more appropriately, upon whom all actions are perpetrated. Passive except when angered, John Buddy does not create situations intentionally. Instead, he reacts to fortune's winds, which most often emanate from the gusty pantings of lustful women.

John Buddy, an illegitimate child born during slavery, lives on the wrong side of the creek. He and his family sharecrop for a white farmer who cheats them. When John Buddy leaves home to escape his abusive stepfather, he goes to his mother's former home at the Pearson plantation on the other side of the creek. While living there, he discovers his dangerous attractiveness to women; but, knowing that he actually loves only Lucy Potts, he marries her despite the objections of her mother, who had hoped for a more prosperous son-in-law. Even Lucy cannot curb his philandering, which consumes the little income he provides. Forced to leave town to escape imprisonment for stealing a hog and attacking Lucy's brother, he wanders South to the recently established all-Negro town of Eatonville, Florida. There, his carpentry and his ministry earn him a position of respect which he continually endangers by his promiscuity. After his wife dies, he marries Hattie, who estranges him from his children. When he is persuaded that she has placed a voodoo curse on him, he divorces her; but, by pleading the injustice of his actions, she wins the sympathy of the townspeople who, refusing either to hire him or to pay what they owe, force him to leave Eatonville. Drifting to Jacksonville, he marries a wealthy woman who helps him reestablish himself as a prosperous preacher. Returning to Eatonville to flaunt his new possessions, however, he is debauched by a young girl. Blinded by shame, he drives in front of a train and is killed.

Because it derives its movement from the action of John-Buddy, the plot is logically structured until the second marriage. At that point, desiring to provide poetic justice for her father vicariously, Miss Hurston resorted to melodrama, most apparent in the discovery of the voodoo symbols which motivated John Buddy to divorce his second wife and in the restoration of his fortune.

Although Miss Hurston delineated her protagonists credibly, she exaggerated minor figures. Because she hated her stepmother, Miss Hurston caricatured Hattie, John Buddy's second wife, as a vituperative, ignorant, immoral, vindictive monster. Miss Hurston designed a black girl, Mehaley, as a comic foil for Lucy. Whereas Lucy is intelligent, educated, affectionate, and relatively obedient to her mother's rigid morality, Mehaley is slothful, sensual, and amoral. The contrast reaches a farcical climax in the difference between Lucy's marriage and Mehaley's. Lucy marries John Buddy in a simple, decorous ritual performed with the reverence customary for a sacrament of the church. Mehaley's wedding is delayed first by the tardiness of the bridegroom. It is further delayed by her father, a self-appointed preacher, who refuses to permit an ordained minister to perform the ceremony. After the father prevails and after the bridegroom again imprisons his aching feet in his new shoes, the marriage vows are recited by the illiterate father, who pretends to read the words from a book which he believes to be the Bible but which is actually an almanac. That evening, the bride postpones consummating the marriage until she has satisfied her craving for snuff.

Miss Hurston's predilection for farcical statement frequently distorts the tone of the novel. For instance, while Ned and Amy Crittenden are arguing about the merits of mulattoes, Amy rebukes Ned's argument that Negroes cannot faint:

> "Dass awright. Niggers gwine faint too. May not come in yo' time and it may not come in mine, but way after while, us people is gwine faint jus lak white folks."

The statement ceases to amuse when one realizes that, by attributing it to ex-slaves, Miss Hurston, for the sake of a laugh, denied the existence of slaves who fainted from exhaustion, hunger, and pain.

Exploitation of the exotic weakens the dialogue, which constitutes both the major strength and the major weakness of the novel. Effectively, Miss Hurston created a dialect, or dialects, which, if not authentic, nevertheless suggest a particular level of speech without ridiculing the speaker. The language also exhibits the rural Southern blacks' imaginative, vivid use of metaphor, simile, and invective:

> God was grumbling his thunder and playing the zig-zag lighting thru his fingers.
>
> "De chickens is cacklin' in de rice and dey say 'Come git it whilst iss fitten' cause t'morrer it may be frost-bitten!'"
>
> "Seben years ain't too long fuh uh coudar tuh wear uh ruffled bosom shirt."
>
> "Ah means to beat her 'til she rope lak okra, and den agin Ah'll stomp her 'til she slack lak line."

The verisimilitude of the language is intensified not merely by the dialect and idiom but even by words, such as "lies," "jook," "piney wood rooters," which require definition in the glossary.

But exploiting the appeal of this language, she piled up metaphorical invective to a height difficult for any mortal to attain:

"And you, you old battle-hammed, slew foot, box-ankled nubbin, you! You ain't nothin' and ain't got nothin' but whut God give uh billy-goat, and then round tryin' tuh hell-hack folks! . . . if you wants tuh fight,—dat's de very corn Ah wants tuh grind. You come grab me now and Ah bet you Ah'll stop *you* from suckin' eggs. . . . Bet Ah'll break uh egg in you! Youse all parts of uh pig! You done got me jus' ez hot ez July jam, and Ah ain't no mo use fuh yuh than Ah is for mah baby shirt. Youse mah race but you sho ain't mah taste. . . .

"Ah'm jus' lak uh old shoe—soft when yuh rain on me and cool me off, and hard when yuh shine on me and git me hot. . . . Ah'm goin tuh Zar, and dat's on de other side of far. . . ."

Each idiom attributed to John Buddy undoubtedly is authentic, but the ratio of metaphors to nonmetaphorical phrases is incredible.

Even less artistically, Miss Hurston sacrificed mood to metaphor in a quarrel between Lucy and John at a tense moment:

"Ah wouldn't be no man a tall tuh let you' brother uh nobody else snatch uh bed out from under you, mo' special in yo' condition."

"John dat's goin' tuh cause trouble and double, Bud hate you and now you done hit 'im he ain't goin' tuh let his shirt tail touch 'im til he tell it tuh de white folks. . . ."

"Ah ain't goin' tuh no chain-gang. If dey ever git in behind me, Ah'll tip on cross de good Lawd's green. Ah'll give mah case tuh Miss Bush and let Mother Green stand mah bond."

"Dey liable tuh grab yuh, 'fo' yuh know it."

"Aw les' squat dat rabbit and jump uh 'nother one. You act lack you done cut loose."

"Naw, Ah ain't cut loose but look lak wese tied tuhgether by uh long cord string and youse at end and Ahm at de other. Way off."

"You kin take in some de slack."

"Don't look lak it."

"Aw, lemme see de caboose uh dat. Less eat dis hog meat and hoe-cake. Jus' 'cause women folks ain't got no big muscled arm and fistes lak jugs, folks claims they's weak vessels, but dass uh lie. Dat piece uh red flannel she got hun 'tween her jaws is equal tuh all de fistes God ever made and man ever seen."

The self-conscious use of metaphor in each utterance weakens the verisimilitude of the otherwise realistic situation.

Miss Hurston's attitude toward interracial relationships in the South seems curiously ambivalent if a reader does not know her social philosophy. On the "poor" side of the creek, John's mother, Amy Crittenden, bitterly denounces slavery, sharecropping, and abusive, unjust white "trash." On the other side of the river, however, John and even Lucy unquestioningly accept Alf Peterson's paternalism. Thus, Miss Hurston imputes all abuses of blacks to lower-class Southern masters, a sentiment which is commercially expedient but false. Except for these opening scenes in Alabama, however, the action of *Jonah's Gourd Vine* is confined to Eatonville, Florida, where the black inhabitants are unaffected by the white people of neighboring communities.

In the novel, Miss Hurston experimented with symbols with varying degrees of success. The image of "Jonah's gourd vine" does not seem to represent John effectively because no Jonah exists. The fact that John Buddy is created by God and is smitten by God furnishes merely a strained analogy. Miss Hurston, however, used a railroad train more effectively. One of the first objects which John sees after he had crossed the creek, the railroad locomotive impresses him as the most powerful, potentially dangerous force he has ever known. More than a machine or even an agent for transportation, however, it symbolizes his sexual awareness. Coming into his consciousness when he first enters a world of heterosexual relationships, it dominates his thoughts and finally destroys him.—DARWIN S. TURNER, "Zora Neale Hurston: The Wandering Minstrel," *In a Minor Chord*, 1971, pp. 100–105

### THEIR EYES WERE WATCHING GOD

*Their Eyes Were Watching God* is the story of Zora Neale Hurston's Janie who, at sixteen, married a grubbing farmer at the anxious instigation of her slave-born grandmother. The romantic Janie, in the highly charged language of Miss Hurston, longed to be a pear tree in blossom and have a "dust-bearing bee sink into the sanctum of a bloom; the thousand sister-calyxes arch to meet the love-embrace." Restless, she fled from her farmer husband and married Jody, an up-and-coming Negro business man who, in the end, proved to be no better than her first husband. After twenty years of clerking for the self-made Jody, Janie found herself a frustrated widow of forty with a small fortune on her hands. Tea Cake, "from in and through Georgia," drifted along, and, despite his youth, Janie took him. For more than two years they lived happily; but Tea Cake was bitten by a dog and infected with rabies. One night in a canine rage Tea Cake tried to murder Janie, thereby forcing her to shoot the only man she had ever loved.

Miss Hurston can write; but her prose is cloaked in that facile sensuality that has dogged Negro expression since the days of Phillis Wheatley. Her dialogue manages to catch the psychological movements of the Negro folk-mind in their pure simplicity, but that's as far as it goes.

Miss Hurston *voluntarily* continues in her novel the tradition which was *forced* upon the Negro in the theater, that is, the minstrel technique that makes the "white folks" laugh. Her characters eat and laugh and cry and work and kill; they swing like a pendulum eternally in that safe and narrow orbit in which American likes to see the Negro live: between laughter and tears.

[Waters] Turpin's faults as a writer are those of an honest man trying desperately to say something; but Zora Neale Hurston lacks even that excuse. The sensory sweep of her novel carries no theme, no message, no thought. In the main, her novel is not addressed to the Negro, but to a white audience whose chauvinistic tastes she knows how to satisfy. She exploits that phase of Negro life which is "quaint," the phase which evokes a piteous smile on the lips of the "superior" race.—RICHARD WRIGHT, "Between Tears and Laughter," *NM*, Oct. 5, 1937, p. 25.

The genesis of a work of art may be of no moment to literary criticism but it is sometimes crucial in literary history. It may, for example, account for the rare occasion when an author outclasses himself. *Their Eyes Were Watching God* (1937) is a case in point. The novel was written in Haiti in just seven weeks, under the emotional pressure of a recent love affair. "The plot was far from the circumstances," Miss Hurston writes in her autobiography, "but I tried to embalm all the tenderness of my passion for him in *Their Eyes Were Watching God*." Ordinarily the prognosis for such a novel would be dismal enough. One might expect immediacy and intensity, but not distance, or control, or universality. Yet oddly, or perhaps not so oddly, it is Miss Hurston's best novel, and possibly the best novel of the period, excepting *Native Son*.

The opening paragraph of *Their Eyes Were Watching God*

encompasses the whole of the novel's meaning: "Ships at a distance have every man's wish on board. For some they come in with the tide. For others they sail forever on the horizon, never out of sight, never landing, until the Watcher turns his eyes away in resignation, his dreams mocked to death by Time. That is the life of man." For women, the author continues, the dream is the sole reality. "So the beginning of this was a woman, and she had come back from burying the dead."

Janie has been gone for almost two years as the action of the novel commences. The townspeople know only that she left home in the company of a lover much younger than herself, and that she departed in fine clothes, but has returned in overalls. Heads nod; tongues wag; and the consensus is that she has played the fool. Toward the gossiping women who, from the safety of a small-town porch "pass nations through their mouths," Janie feels only contempt and irritation: "If God don't think no mo' 'bout 'em than Ah do, they's a lost ball in de high grass." To Pheoby, her kissing-friend, she tells the story of her love for Tea-Cake, which together with its antecedents comprises the main body of the novel.

Janie's dream begins during her adolescence, when she is stirred by strange wonderings as she watches a pear tree blossom. No sooner is her dream born, however, than it is desecrated by her grandmother. Nanny, who has witnessed her share of the sexual exploitation of Negro women, declares firmly: "[Neither] de menfolks white or black is makin' a spit cup outa you." Seeking to protect Janie from the vicissitudes of adolescent love, she puts her up on the auction block of marriage. To Nanny, being married is being like white folks: "You got yo' lawful husband same as Mis' Washburn or anybody else." Against her better judgment, therefore, Janie acquiesces in an early marriage with Logan Killicks, a hard-working farmer considerably older than herself.

"There are years that ask questions and years that answer: Did marriage compel love like the sun the day?" Janie soon realizes her mistake. She aspires to more than sixty acres and an organ in the parlor, and refuses to barter her fulfillment as a woman in exchange for property rights: "Ah ain't takin' dat ole land tuh heart neither. Ah could throw ten acres of it over de fence every day and never look back to see where it fell." Affairs reach a crisis with the appearance of Jody Starks, a younger man who offers Janie a fresh start in a neighboring county. "Janie pulled back a long time because he did not represent sun-up and pollen and blooming trees, but he spoke for far horizon." Her first dream dead, she runs off with Jody to the all-Nergo town of Eatonville.

Janie's second dream scarcely fares better than the first. Although her husband becomes "a big voice," a property owner, and eventually mayor of the town, Janie remains restless, unfulfilled. Asked by Jody how she likes being "Mrs. Mayor," she replies: "It keeps us in some way we ain't natural wid one 'nother. Youse always off talkin' and fixin' things, and Ah feels lak Ah'm jus' markin' time." A widening rift develops in the marriage as a fundamental clash of values becomes apparent. Janie can no more reconcile herself to Jody's store than to Logan Killicks' sixty acres: "The store itself was a pleasant place if only she didn't have to sell things." On one occasion, when the townsfolk playfully take off from work for the mock funeral of a dead mule, Jody remarks, "Ah wish mah people would git mo' business in 'em and not spend so much time on foolishness." Janie's reply is caustic: "Everybody can't be lak you, Jody. Somebody is bound tuh want tuh laugh and play."

By this time, the wider meaning of the novel has begun to emerge. A dramatic tension has arisen between the sound business instincts of Janie's two husbands and her own striving toward a full life, which is later to take on flesh in the person of Tea-Cake. At first glance, what seems to be taking shape in the dramatic structure of the novel is the familiar cultural dualism of the Negro Renaissance. Although this Renaissance pattern is definitely present, Miss Hurston pitches her theme in a higher key. Janie rejects the Nanny-Killicks-Jody way of life because of its cramped quarters and narrow gauge: "Nanny belonged to that other kind that loved to deal in scraps." It is Janie's urge to touch the horizon which causes her to repudiate respectability.

Meanwhile, Janie's second marriage moves toward a culmination in Jody's illness and death. For many years their relationship has been purely perfunctory: "The spirit of the marriage left the bedroom and took to living in the parlor." Only on his deathbed does Janie confront her husband with the bitter knowledge of an inner life which she has been unable to share with him: "You done lived wid me for twenty years and you don't half know me atall." Taking stock after Jody's death, Janie senses in this repressed phase of her life an unconscious preparation for her great adventure: "She was saving up feelings for some man she had never seen."

If the first half of the novel deals with the prose of Janie's life, the latter half deals with its poetry. Not long after Jody's death, Tea-Cake walks into her life. First off, he laughs; next he teaches her how to play checkers. One afternoon he urges her to close up shop and come with him to a baseball game. The next night, after midnight, he invites her on a fishing expedition. Their relationship is full of play, of impulsiveness, of informality, and of imagination. Easy-going, careless of money, living for the moment, Tea-Cake is an incarnation of the folk culture. After a whirlwind courtship, he persuades Janie to leave Eatonville and to try his way.

On a deeper level, Tea-Cake represents intensity and experience. As Janie puts it in summing up her two years with him: "Ah been a delegate to de big 'ssociation of life." Their new life begins with a trip to Jacksonville, "and to a lot of things she wanted to see and know." In the big city, Tea-Cake deserts Janie for several days, while she suffers the torments and anxieties of a middle-aged lover. Upon his return she learns that he had won a large sum in a crap game and had immediately given a barbecue for his friends, in order to find out how it feels to be rich. When she protests at being left out, he asks with amusement, "So you aims tuh partake wid everything, hunh?" From that moment, their life together becomes an unlimited partnership.

From Jacksonville, Janie and Tea-Cake move "down on the muck" of the Florida Everglades for the bean-picking season. Janie goes to work in the fields in order to be with Tea-Cake during the long working day. They share the hard work and the hard play of the folk, laughing together at the "dickty" Negroes who think that "us oughta class off." In this milieu of primitive Bahaman dances, of "blues made and used right on the spot," and of "romping and playing . . . behind the boss's back," Janie at last finds happiness. In true Renaissance spirit, it is the folk culture, through Tea-Cake, which provides the means of her spiritual fulfillment.

One night, "the palm and banana trees began that long-distance talk with rain." As the winds over Lake Okechobee mount to hurricane force, the novel moves to a swift climax. Janie and Tea-Cake find themselves swept along with a crowd of refugees, amid awesome scenes of destruction and sudden death. In the midst of their nightmarish flight, Tea-Cake is bitten by a dog and unknowingly contracts rabies. Some weeks later, suffering horribly, he loses his senses and attacks Janie when she refuses him a drink of water. In the ensuing melee,

Janie is compelled to shoot Tea-Cake to protect her own life. "It was the meanest moment of eternity." Not merely that her lover dies, but that she herself is the instrument—this is the price which Janie pays for her brief months of happiness. Her trial and acquittal seem unreal to her; without Tea-Cake she can only return to Eatonville to "live by comparisons."

As the reader tries to assimilate Janie's experience and assess its central meaning, he cannot avoid returning to a key passage which foreshadows the climax of the novel: "All gods dispense suffering without reason. Otherwise they would not be worshipped. Through indiscriminate suffering men know fear, and fear is the most divine emotion. It is the stones for altars and the beginning of wisdom. Half gods are worshipped in wine and flowers. Real gods require blood." Through Tea-Cake's death, Janie experiences the divine emotion, for her highest dream—to return to the opening paragraph of the novel—has been "mocked to death by Time." Like all men, she can only watch in resignation, with an overpowering sense of her own helplessness.

Yet if mankind's highest dreams are ultimately unattainable, it is still better to live on the far horizon than to grub around on shore. Janie does not regret her life with Tea-Cake, or the price which is exacted in the end: "We been tuhgether round two years. If you kin see de light at daybreak, you don't keer if you die at dusk. It's so many people never seen de light at all. Ah wuz fumblin' round and God opened de door." As the novel closes, the scene returns to Janie and her friend in Eatonville. Pheoby's reaction to the story she has heard is a clinching statement of the theme of the novel: "Ah done growed ten feet higher from jus' listenin' tuh you, Janie. Ah ain't satisfied with mahself no mo'."—ROBERT BONE, "Aspects of the Racial Past," *The Negro Novel in America*, 1958, pp. 127–32

In Black literature, we have lost many jewels to the glare of white, mass-media manipulation: According to whitepower, Ralph Ellison was the only Black novelist writing in this country while his star was allowed to shine. Later, the media "gave" us James Baldwin—evidently all by himself. And then there was *only* Eldridge Cleaver. (Remember him?)

Towering before and above these media-isolated giants, there was always Richard Wright. He has been presented as a solitary figure on the literary landscape of his period. But, right along with him, and six years his senior, there was Zora Neale Hurston. The fact is, we almost lost Zora to the choose-between games played with Black Art. Until recently, no one had ever heard of her; certainly, no one read her books. And yet, anyone who has dipped into her work, even once, will tell you: the long-term obscurity of her joy and wisdom is an appalling matter of record. So we would do well to carefully reconsider these two, Hurston and Wright: perhaps that will let us understand the cleavage in their public reception and prevent such inequity and virtual erasure from taking place, again.

Each of them achieved unprecedented, powerful and extremely important depths of Black vision and commitment in their lifework; according to the usual criteria, they were both Great Writers. Yet, while Richard Wright spawned many, many followers, and enjoyed the rewards of well-earned fame, Zora Neale Hurston suffered through devastating, critical and popular neglect, inspired no imitators, and finally died, penniless, with no marker to identify her grave. Why did this happen?

I believe we were misled into the notion that *only one kind* of writing—protest writing—and that *only one kind* of protest writing deserves our support and study.

A few years back, Hoyt Fuller posed the primary functions of Protest and Affirmation as basic to an appreciation of Black Art. Wright's *Native Son* is widely recognized as the prototypical Black protest novel. By comparison, Hurston's novel, *Their Eyes Were Watching God*, seems to suit, perfectly, the obvious connotations of Black affirmation.

I would add that the functions of protest and affirmation are not, ultimately, distinct: that, for instance, affirmation of Black values and lifestyle within the American context is, indeed, an act of protest. Therefore, Hurston's affirmative work is profoundly defiant, just as Wright's protest unmistakably asserts our need for an alternative, benign environment. We have been misled to discount the one in order to revere the other. But we have been misled in other ways. Several factors help to explain the undue contrast between the careers of Wright and Hurston.⟨. . .⟩

Zora Neal Hurston was born and raised in an all-Black Florida town. In other words, she was born into a supportive, nourishing environment. And without exception, her work—as novelist, as anthropologist/diligent collector and preservor of Black folktale and myth—reflects this early and late, all-Black universe that was her actual as well as her creative world.

You see her immovable, all-Black orientation in *Their Eyes Were Watching God*: whites do not figure in this story of Black love; white anything or anybody is not important. What matters is the Black woman and the Black man who come together in a believable, contagious, full Blacklove that makes you want to go and seek and find, likewise, soon as you finish the book.

Since white America lies outside the Hurston universe, both in fact and in her fiction, you do not run up on the man/the enemy. Protest, narrowly conceived, is therefore beside the point; rhythm or tones of outrage or desperate flight would be wholly inappropriate in her text. Instead, you slip into a total, Black reality where Black people do not represent issues: they represent their own, particular selves in a Family/Community setting that permits relaxation from hunted/warrior postures, and that fosters the natural, person-postures of courting, jealousy, ambition, dream, sex, work, partying, sorrow, bitterness, celebration, and fellowship.

Unquestionably, *Their Eyes Were Watching God* is the prototypical Black novel of affirmation; it is the most successful, convincing, and exemplary novel of Blacklove that we have. Period. But the book gives us more: the story unrolls a fabulous, written-film of Blacklife freed from the constraints of oppression; here we may learn Black possibilities of ourselves if we could ever escape the hateful and alien context that has so deeply disturbed and mutilated our rightful efflorescence—*as people.* Consequently, this novel centers itself on Blacklove—even as *Native Son* rivets itself upon white hatred.

But: because Zora Neale Hurston was a woman, and because we have been misled into devaluating the functions of Black affirmation, her work has been derogated as romantic/the natural purview of a woman (*i.e.*, unimportant), "personal" (not serious) in its scope, and assessed as *sui generis*, or idiosyncratic accomplishment of no lasting reverberation or usefulness.

All such derogation derives from ignorance and/or callow thinking we cannot afford to continue. Although few of us have known the happiness of an all-Black town/universe, every single one of us is the torn-away descendant of a completely Black/African world; today, increasing numbers of us deem an all-Black circumstance/nation as our necessary, overriding goal. Accordingly, the Sister has given us the substance of an exceptional, but imperative vision, since her focus is both a historical truth and a contemporary aim.

As for the derision of love as less important, somehow, than war or violence, that is plain craziness, plain *white* craziness we do not need even to discuss.

And, is it true that *Native Son* represents you and me more than Hurston's heroine, Janie Starks? Both of them bespeak our hurt, our wished-for fulfillment and, at various times, the nature and the level of our adjustment to complete fulfillment or, on the other hand, complete frustration.

I do not accept that Wright and Hurston should be perceived, properly, as antipathetic in the wellsprings of their work: Bigger Thomas, the whole living and dying creation of him, teaches as much about the necessity of love, of being able to love without being, therefore, destroyed, as Hurston's Janie Starks. Their address to this subject—this agonizingly central need—differs, perhaps, as men and women have been taught to cope with human existence, differently. Moreover, I submit that *Their Eyes* . . . treats with a want and a hope and a tragic adjustment that is at least as reverberating, as "universal"— namely, positive (loving) self-fulfillment—as the material of *Native Son*, which emphasizes the negative trajectories of that same want, hope and confrontation.

But, rightly, we should not choose between Bigger Thomas and Janie Starks; our lives are as big and as manifold and as pained and as happy as the two of them put together. We should equally value and equally emulate Black Protest and Black Affirmation, for we require both; one without the other is dangerous, and will leave us vulnerable to extinction of the body or the spirit.

We should take care so that we will lose none of the jewels of our soul. We must begin, now, to reject the white, either/or system of dividing the world into unnecessary conflict. It is both tragic and ridiculous to choose between Malcolm X and Dr. King: each of them hurled himself against quite different aspects of our predicament, and each, literally, gave his life to our ongoing struggle.

We need everybody and all that we are. We need to know and make known the complete, constantly unfolding, complicated heritage that is our Black experience. We should absolutely resist the superstar, one-at-a-time mentality that threatens the varied and resilient, flexible wealth of our Black future, even as it shrinks and obliterates incalculable segments of our history.—June Jordan, "On Richard Wright and Zora Neale Hurston: Toward a Balancing of Love and Hatred," *BlW*, August 1974, pp. 4–8

### DUST TRACKS ON A ROAD

Zora Neale Hurston is a paradox among American black autobiographers. To begin with, she is, politically, something of an establishment black writer, and like those who yearn for the establishment she gives up militancy and denies any racial conflict within herself. Yet she goes beyond a conservative like George Schuyler, whose autobiography is entitled *Black and Conservative*, by innovating within the form of black autobiography through the independence, not of her politics, but of her style. Because she is free in a personal way, she is willing to take liberties with autobiographical form that others have not. Because of her willingness to be colloquial, she becomes the sophisticated person who uses style for a deliberate effect. And because she is one autobiographer who is willing to allow the folklore of her race to influence her work, it has a broader sense of cultural vision, language, and idiom than the works of her— mostly male—contemporaries. As a result of her attitudes and influences, then, Hurston's autobiographical style leads away

from that of the traditional self-written accounts of a life reviewed at the end of a successful career and toward the "as-told-to" oral narration of contemporary black autobiographers like Malcolm X. Since she can use all three stages of class language—colloquial, informal, and formal, although she shies away from the latter—using the differences without making invidious distinctions, she adds to the genre a sense of assimilation, a stylistic sense that says, "One is what he is." Hurston proves that there is no longer any need for painstakingly concentrating on being formally "literate." Consequently, where a McKay or a Hughes autobiographically (in *A Long Way from Home* and *The Big Sea*) emphasizes the independent flair in his lifestyle, Hurston reinforces our sense of her personal uniqueness not only through action and narration, but also through prose style.

Hurston avoids as stumbling blocks the issues of politics and race in her fiction, and she minimizes their affect on her life in her autobiography. Perhaps naively, she ends *Dust Tracks on a Road* by saying, "I have no race prejudice of any kind." Going on to deny the existence of a problem, she writes:

My kinfolks, and my "skin-folks" are dearly loved. My own circumference of everyday life is there. But I see their same virtues and vices everywhere I look. So I give you all my right hand of fellowship and love, and hope for the same from you. In my eyesight, you lose nothing by not looking just like me. I will remember you all in my good thoughts, and I ask you kindly to do the same for me. Not only just me. You, who play the zig-zag lightning of power over the world, with the grumbling thunder in your wake, think kindly of those who walk in the dust. And you who walk in humble places, think kindly too, of others. There has been no proof in the world so far that you would be less arrogant if you held the level of power in your hands. Let us all be kissing-friends. Consider that with tolerance and patience, we godly demons may breed a noble world in a few hundred generations or so. Maybe all of us who do not have the good fortune to meet, or meet again, in this world, will meet at a barbecue.

Said any other way, a comment like this would elicit considerable hostility from friends and foes alike. But Hurston is such a "character" herself that her style comes off as being both naively ridiculous and camp in a finely ironic self-parody. Through style alone she can get away with saying things for which a straight conservative like Schuyler could never be forgiven.

By beginning the study of Zora Hurston at the end of her own story, one can immediately intuit her spirit and the form its expression takes; both influence the "truth" of her telling. In a foreword to her book Darwin T. Turner remarks, "as someone once said, *Dust Tracks* may be the best fiction Zora Neale Hurston ever wrote."—Ann Rayson, "*Dust Tracks on a Road*: Zora Neale Hurston and the Form of Black Autobiography," *NALF*, Summer 1973, pp. 39–40

If much of *Dust Tracks* confuses or compromises racial militance to an ideal of racial harmony or turns out to be less than frank about Hurston's life, at least one major part of the book never disappoints—Hurston's style. The style dazzles, capturing the subtlety, energy, and rhythm of southern black idiom. Subtlety becomes "hitting a straight lick with a crooked stick." There is no more to poor white trash "than the stuffings out of a zero." Her mother's method of shaping her father is to "bareknuckle him from brogans to broadcloth." Motivation is a "rod of complement . . . laid to my back." Rewriting becomes "rubbing a paragraph with a soft cloth."

Hurston's style, rich and expressive, is a natural by-product of her attempt to represent the oral voice in written narrative, a process that marks the only times that public and private personae come together in the *Dust Tracks* text. Yet even at such moments the famous writer and the young Eatonville girl usually coexist rather than fuse, demonstrating the dual perspective that characterized so much of Hurston's experience.

When her mother, during courting, asked her family about John Hurston's parents, she found that the Hurstons were "niggers from over de creek. . . . Regular hand-to-mouth folks. Didn't own pots to pee in, nor beds to push em under. . . . The inference was that Lucy Potts had asked about nothing and had been told." The idiom is southern black, the language Zora grew into from birth—rough, earthy, and effective. But "inference" sticks out in the sentence like a sore thumb. Essential to its meaning, but not its imagery, inference is the language of the Eatonville ethnographer who feels compelled to interpret for her audience; she explains the communication process meant to instruct young Lucy Potts in the courting practices appropriate to her class and status. "Inference"—the anthropologist's word—announces the voice of authority that will contextualize the stream of colorful invective; this apparently simple communicative exchange is part of a large context of class bias, courtship custom, and generational transfer. What appears to be simply expressive language, full of pithy humor, is really a complex product of an author who sees through two sets of eyes simultaneously.

The passage suggests that Hurston never found a voice that could unify the dualistic vision of *Dust Tracks*. Her style, rich in sensory imagery, always searches for the right image for the expressed emotion, but her voice never quite builds beyond imagery to idea. Grown people who grow impatient at a child's insistent "Why?" have a "pigeon hole way of life." Poverty is "dead dreams dropping off the heart like leaves in a dry season and rotting around the feet. . . . People can be slave ships in shoes." When she struggled with her feelings as a young person, "I would cry inside and be depressed for days, until I learned how to mash down on my feelings and numb them for a spell." When she is initiated into a hoodoo cult, she strides "across the heavens with lightning flashing from under my feet, and grumbling thunder following in my wake." In short, one *sees* Hurston's prose. One also hears it, smells it, and touches it, but primarily one sees it. As she put it, "I am so visual minded that all the other senses induce pictures in me."

Interestingly enough, this admission comes when she is describing her reaction to first reading Samuel Taylor Coleridge's *Kubla Khan*. The adult writer, a professional woman of words, describes the process whereby literature creates its personal effects for the Eatonville novice. If Hurston has a fault in *Dust Tracks*, it may be that she overestimated the power of the image and underestimated her audience's curiosity about what is behind the image.

Hurston's account of men enamored of their own sexuality is visually hilarious: "I may be thinking of turnip greens with dumplings, or more royalty checks, [and] there is a man who visualizes me on a divan sending the world up in smoke." If a lover persists after her momentary ardor has cooled, calling up to remind her of "every silly thing I said," then "it is the third presentation of turkey hash after Christmas. It is asking me to be a seven-sided liar." The image begs for another dimension, for the sources of Hurston's sexual independence, for the trials of chauvinism that she had faced. But we are left only with the image, and the mystery of the woman who can so easily visualize her own amorous exploits as warmed-over turkey hash.

Emphasizing the process of Hurston's vision leads to the twelve visions meant to structure her life for her autobiography. Although intended to explain Hurston's life, these visions do not successfully shape the book. She even forgets about them after a while, so that the twelve visions, each "like clearcut stereopticon slides" that flashed before her as a young girl, end with vision nine in the text.

However, the visions do suggest Hurston's literary dilemma in the autobiography. A conscious literary device, the visions were intended to explain how an imaginative young girl could travel from Eatonville to the horizon, discovering fame and fortune as a nationally known author. But the visions also beg the question of how she got there, a black writer in a white world, a woman who refused the roles men imposed, a southern agrarian who learned her way around the city. The private Zora Neale Hurston of Eatonville, a mischievous child who "used to take a seat on top of the gate post and watch the world go by," never actually becomes one with the famous black novelist and anthropologist whose life story is of sufficient interest to merit an autobiographical statement. How did the transformation take place? Hurston never really explains the inner workings of the metamorphosis. As she admitted about *Dust Tracks*, "I have the feeling of disappointment about it. I don't think that I achieved all that I set out to do. I thought that in this book I would achieve my ideal, but it seems that I have not yet reached it . . . it still doesn't say all that I want it to say."

The paradox of the public and private Zora Neale Hurston, the enigma of a personality who could be culturally nationalistic and politically accommodationist, is never fully explained or explored in the picturesque prose of *Dust Tracks*. In the end, style in *Dust Tracks* becomes a kind of camouflage, an escape from articulating the paradoxes of her personality. Hurston used her talent for visual imagery as a snapshot photographer, not as a serious painter. Her style deflects high seriousness and implies that life is simpler than it is. Finally, though, the style does not deflect enough, and serious questions multiply. As Mary Helen Washington has argued, the chapters on her adult life become a "study in the art of subterfuge."

*Dust Tracks* fails as autobiography because it is a text deliberately less than its author's talents, a text diminished by her refusal to provide a second or third dimension to the flat surfaces of her adult image. Hurston avoided any exploration of the private motives that led to her public success. Where is the author of *Their Eyes Were Watching God?* One is never sure in *Dust Tracks*, even as we know that the mystery behind the question—who is Zora Neale Hurston?—will continually send us back to the *Dust Tracks* text for whatever clues might be wrestled from its enigmatic author.—ROBERT HEMENWAY, "Introduction" to *Dust Tracks on a Road*, 1984, pp. xxxiv–xxxix

---

ROBERT HEMENWAY
"Zora Neale Hurston and
the Eatonville Anthropology"
*The Harlem Renaissance Remembered*
ed. Arna Bontemps
1972, pp. 190–214

Z ora Neale Hurston is one of the most significant unread authors in America, the author of two minor classics and four other major books. What follows is openly intended to stimulate further interest in her art, and is part of a more extensive study of her life and work now in progress. My purpose here is not to provide a comprehensive account of her association with the Harlem Renaissance, but to articulate one intellectual problem facing her during that period. It should be acknowledged from the start that it is a white man's reconstruction of the intellectual process in a black woman's mind. That is not an irrelevant fact, either sexually or racially; people falsely impressed with the mythical "objectivity" of criticism and the presumed "universality" of literature will claim that it is. They are wrong. All men possess an anthropology which is less their own creation than a special burden of value and idea culturally imposed. Inevitably this anthropology—this view of man as he is—affects analytic efforts, but it is not a fact the critic can or should apologize for. A published author belongs in a special way to the world of culture—he is subject to the inquiry of any reader who would seek his example and learn his truth. When this process of inquiry is shared with others, it becomes criticism, and the success of criticism depends directly on the critic's ability to distinguish the parts of his cultural burden which can be responsibly shouldered from the parts to be shucked away forever because they limit his humanity. The existential irony making criticism frustrating is that one's acceptance or rejection of such burdens is a process of self-discovery, a condition of becoming. This leaves the critic in the same tentative position as the artist: he creates offerings. That is all the following essay presumes to be.

On January 16, 1959, Zora Neale Hurston, suffering from the effects of a stroke and writing painfully in longhand, composed a letter to the "editorial department" of Harper & Brothers inquiring if they would be interested in seeing "the book I am laboring upon at present—a life of Herod the Great."[1] One year and twelve days later, Zora Neale Hurston died without funds to provide for her burial, a resident of the St. Lucie County, Florida, Welfare Home. She lies today in an unmarked grave in a segregated cemetery in Ft. Pierce, Florida, a resting place generally symbolic of the black writer's fate in America. The letter to Harper's does not expose a publisher's rejection of an unknown masterpiece, but it does reveal how the bright promise of the Harlem Renaissance deteriorated for many of the writers who shared in its exuberance. It also indicates the personal tragedy of Zora Neale Hurston: Barnard graduate, author of four novels, two books of folklore, one volume of autobiography, the most important collector of Afro-American folklore in America, reduced by poverty and circumstance to seek a publisher by unsolicited mail. The letter makes the survival of three hundred pages of the "Herod the Great" manuscript all the more poignant; its posthumous destruction by county custodians was halted when a deputy sheriff extinguished its flame with a garden hose.

*Herod the Great* is a good beginning for understanding Hurston's role in the Harlem Renaissance, because it is unlike any of her Renaissance work. It is a straightforward, standard English, historical narrative of the ruler of Galilee from 40 to 4 B.C., the father of the Herod to whom Christ was sent for trial by Pontius Pilate. Hurston spent most of her energy over the last seven years of her life in the attempt to write this story, and yet even the most sympathetic reader concludes that the manuscript is not a major achievement, that it lacks the force, style, and significance of her other work. I think it fails because it illustrates how far Hurston had retreated from the unique sources of her esthetic: the music and speech, energy and wisdom, dignity and humor, of the black rural South. Her achievements during the Renaissance increase or diminish in direct proportion to her use of the folk environment which she had grown up in and would later return to analyze.

*I*

Zora Neale Hurston was born in 1903 in Eatonville, Florida,[2] an all-black town in central Orange County which claims to be the first incorporated totally black city in America. This fact of birth makes Hurston unique among black writers, and it was the major shaping force in her life. Growing up in Eatonville meant that Zora Hurston could reach the age of ten before she would realize that she had been labeled a "Negro" and restricted from certain social possibilities by chance of race. It meant that from early childhood she would hear the "lying sessions" on Major Joe Clark's storefront porch, the men "straining against each other in telling folks tales. God, Devil, Brer Rabbit, Brer Fox, Sis Cat, Brer Bear, Lion, Tiger, Buzzard and all the wood folk walked and talked like natural men."[3] It meant that the Saturday night music and the Sunday morning praying, the singing, working, loving, and fighting of black rural life would become the fecund source for her adult imagination.

The strong daughter of strong parents, Hurston was graced by the evangelical Christianity of her father's preaching and the permanent truths of her mother's rustic wisdom. Her parents and their neighbors had little formal education. They lived lives of rural poverty in a society of white racism, and they contributed to that elaborate mechanism of survival which makes Afro-American folklore one of the most remarkable products of ingenuity and intelligence in the human species. Hurston left the familial environment at fifteen, after her mother had died, working variously as a maid in a traveling Gilbert and Sullivan troupe, a manicurist in a barbershop catering to congressmen, and a servant for prominent black Washingtonians. She also finished high school and managed two years of credit at Howard University (where she studied under Alain Locke), before Charles S. Johnson, the editor of *Opportunity*, solicited her fiction and suggested she come to New York sometime. She arrived in January 1925 with "$1.50, no job, no friends, and a lot of hope."[4]

If one accepts the geography in the label, Zora Hurston's physical presence during the Harlem Renaissance could be overemphasized. She did not arrive on the scene until fairly late, and in February 1927 she left for four years of more or less continuous folklore collecting. Yet she was an important contributor to the Renaissance spirit, as any survivor of the age will confirm. She very quickly became one of the most dazzling émigrés of the influx of young black artists. A brilliant raconteur, a delightful if sometimes eccentric companion, she fit in well with the "Roaring Twenties"—both black and white divisions. Shortly after her arrival she was employed as Fannie Hurst's private secretary; she quickly became a favorite of the black intelligentsia and the recipient of a scholarship specially arranged for by a Barnard trustee. Her wit was legendary; she called Negro uplifters "Negrotarians," and Carl Van Vechten claimed she combined Negro and literati into one of the famous ironic labels of the period: "Niggerati." Much of her personal success was built around her storytelling, which more often than not emphasized the Eatonville milieu. She could become a living representative of the Southern folk-idiom and she never failed to entertain with the material. Her stories, of course, were not unknown to Harlem, for black immigrants of the "great migration" could tell similar tales from neighborhood stoops. William Wells Brown, Arthur Huff Fauset, and other blacks had reported folklore sympathetically; Joel Chandler Harris's Uncle Remus stories had been popular among whites in the late nineteenth century.

But the folk materials seldom had been dramatized for the black artists and intellectuals of Hurston's acquaintance, and almost never for the white folks so often in attendance on the "New Negro." In fact, few of the literary participants in the Renaissance knew intimately the rural South; Hughes arrived from Cleveland and Washington, Bontemps from California, Thurman from Utah and Los Angeles; Cullen was from New York City, Toomer from Washington; the list can go on, but the point is obvious. Zora Neale Hurston represented a known, but unexperienced segment of black life in America. Although it is impossible to gauge such matters, there seems little question that she helped to remind the Renaissance—especially its more bourgeois members—of the richness in the racial heritage; she also added new dimensions to the interest in exotic primitivism that was one of the most ambiguous products of the age.

Yet the brilliance of her personality should not obscure her personal development. Hurston in New York was initially a country girl, wide-eyed, and if not altogether innocent, at least capable of being often impressed. She is still remembered at Howard by fellow students and retired faculty as merely a bright working girl, very rough about the edges. In the midst of her duties as Hurst's secretary, she could take time out to send a friend some matches shared one night by "Fannie Hurst, Stefansson (the explorer), Charles Norris and Zora Neale Hurston," adding that "Irvin S. Cobb was there also but he used another pack with Jessie Lasky and Margaret Anglin."[5] Later she would write the same friend about all there is to see in New York, admitting, "I won't try to pretend that I am not thrilled at the chance to see and do what I am. I love it!"[6] The sending of used matchbooks hardly constitutes jaded sophistication, and although Hurston could frequently hide behind masks, the youthful excitement here seems genuine. Her emotions are also the social analogs to her intellectual experience at Barnard.

Hurston came to New York in 1925 as a writer but left Barnard two years later as a serious social scientist, and although these are not incompatible vocations, they can imply different uses for personal experience. She had the relatively rare opportunity to confront her culture both emotionally and analytically, both as subject and object. She lived Afro-American folklore before she knew that such a thing existed as a scientific concept, or had special value as the product of the adaptive creativity of a unique subculture. This is extraordinary knowledge for one to learn about oneself, and Zora Hurston found it a fascinating and frustrating acquisition. Even before coming to New York there had begun to build within her a distance between the facts of her Eatonville existence and the esthetic uses she would make of it. Barnard conceptualized that distance between 1925 and 1927, the years of her most active participation in the cultural uprisings of Harlem.

The Barnard experience is seldom discussed when dealing with Hurston, but I believe it is central to understanding her role in the Renaissance and her subsequent career. She entered Barnard as a young, earnest scholar, feeling "highly privileged and determined to make the most of it." She was particularly impressed with her own admission—"not everyone who cries 'Lord! Lord!' can enter those sacred iron gates"—and with Barnard's "high scholastic standards, equipment, the quality of her student body and graduates." She quickly came under the influence of anthropologists Ruth Benedict, Gladys Reichard, and Franz Boas. By far the most important of these was Boas, one of the leading American scientists of the early twentieth century and a man of great personal magnetism. Boas recognized Hurston's genius almost immediately and urged her to begin training as a professional anthropologist. One can grasp how important Boas became to Hurston by reading her autobiography, *Dust Tracks on a Road* (1942).[7] Boas was "the greatest anthropologist alive," the "king of kings," and yet she was permitted to call him "Papa Franz." She admittedly "idolized" him. Perhaps the conclusive example of Hurston's serious commitment to Boas's training lies in her willingness to be equipped with a set of calipers and sent to Harlem to measure skulls—an act which many contemporaries feel only Zora Hurston could have gotten away with, and which only a dedicated student would be likely to attempt. Finally, in February 1927, after she had completed the requirements for her B.A. degree, Boas arranged, through Carter Woodson's Association for the Study of Negro Life and History, to finance her on a folklore collecting trip to the South.

Going back was a difficult experience, one she describes with some anguish:

> My first six months were disappointing. I found out later that it was not because I had no talents for research, but because I did not have the right approach. The glamor of Barnard College was still upon me. I dwelt in marble halls. I knew where the material was all right. But, when I went about asking, in carefully accented Barnardese, 'Pardon me, but do you know any folk-tales or folk-songs?' The men and women who had whole treasuries of material just seeping through their pores looked at me and shook their heads. No, they had never heard of anything like that around there. Maybe it was over in the next county. Why didn't I try over there? I did, and got the selfsame answer. Oh, I got a few little items. But compared with what I did later, not enough to make a flea a waltzing jacket. Considering the mood of my going South, I went back to New York with my heart beneath my knees and my knees in some lonesome valley.
>
> I stood before Papa Franz and cried salty tears.[8]

The causes of her initial failure were varied, but at least one of them was philosophical. She was not returning to the South as a local girl home from college, but as a young, serious intellectual equipped with the analytic tools of anthropological theory and a desire to further the cause of science. In her experience with Boas she had tried to emulate what she called his "genius for pure objectivity,"[9] but her academic training did not suffice once she was in the field. The problem went beyond techniques of collecting. Hurston had acquired a conceptualization for her experience. The Eatonville folk were no longer simply good storytellers, admirable in their lifestyles, remarkable in their superstitions, the creators of profound humor, the matrix for a vital, local-color fiction. Now they were a part of cultural anthropology; scientific objects who could and should be studied for their academic value. These are not irreconcilable positions, but for one who has previously conceived of such experience esthetically, it is a definite skewing of perception. Where before Eatonville had been considered a totally unique body of material known only to Zora Hurston (even her black fellow artists in the Renaissance knew little about it), now the town and her experience in it were abstracted to the level of science—a subculture created and maintained by adaptive techniques of survival, many of which had scientific labels and theoretical significance. The altered perception created in Hurston a dual consciousness.

A tension, perhaps latent since her removal from the Eatonville scene, became manifest between the subjective folk experience and the abstract knowledge of the meaning of that experience, and it was complicated by the stress on objectivity intrinsic to the Boas training. First in New York, and then in the South as a collector, Zora Hurston sought a scientific explanation for why her own experience in the black rural South, despite all her education, remained the most vital part of her life, and further, why the black folk-experience generally was such a source of vitality in literature. Moving between art and science, fiction and anthropology, she searched for an expressive instrument, an intellectual formula, that could accommodate the poetry of Eatonville, the theories of Morningside Heights, and the esthetic ferment she had known in Harlem.

This was a unique intellectual tension complicated by the personal factors of sex, race, and nationality, that whole complex of ambiguous identifications American culture imposes on its members. Hurston struggled with it during the Renaissance, and to some extent throughout her life. It is reflected in her unsuccessful attempt to return to Columbia for a Ph.D. in 1934—she told Boas, "You don't know how I have longed for a chance to stay at Columbia and study"[10]—her handling of her collected folklore in *Mules and Men* (1935) and *Tell My Horse* (1938); the attempts at esthetic resolution in her novels of the thirties (*Jonah's Gourd Vine*, 1934; *Their Eyes Were Watching God*, 1937; *Moses, Man of the Mountain*, 1939); and her final retreat from the issue entirely. Bitter over the rejection of her folklore's value, especially in the black community, frustrated by what she felt was her failure to convert the Afro-American world view into the forms of prose fiction, Hurston finally gave up. Her unsuccessful 1948 novel, *Seraph on the Suwanee*, is about white people; her later research interests were the Mayan Indian cultures of Central America; she spent the final seven years of her life writing a "nonracial" biography of Herod the Great.

## II

Hurston's writing during the Renaissance years comes generally from the pre-Barnard or early Barnard period. After she became a serious Boas student, most of her energies were turned to the problems of folklore collecting. As a student at Howard she had been a striving English major, capable of such lyrics as "O Night":

> O Night, calm Night,
> Creep down and close my burning eyes,
> Blot out this day of heavy sighs,
>     O Night.
> Dam up my tears and hide my face,
> Efface from mind this time and place,
> O Night, black Night.[11]

"John Redding Goes to Sea," in Howard's *Stylus* for 1921 (later reprinted in *Opportunity*), is a sentimental story—the account of a rustic dreamer who achieves his wish of going to sea only after a heavy rain sends an errant log downstream with his corpse. Yet Hurston also realized early the rich possibilities of the Eatonville material, even if she did not quite understand her personal relationship to it. The first story sent in response to Charles S. Johnson's request was "Drenched in Light," published in *Opportunity* in December 1924, a month before her arrival in New York. It is a day in the life of Isie Watts, a "little Brown figure perched upon the gate post" in front of her Eatonville home. "Everybody in the country," knows "Isie Watts, the joyful," and how she likes to laugh and play, how she lives to the fullest every minute of her young life. Isie gets into various scrapes, including an attempt to shave her sleeping grandmother, and eventually is given a ride by a passing white motorist, despite her grandmother's disapproval. The point appears to be that Isie, poor and black, is far from tragic: rather, she is "drenched in light," a condition which endears her to everyone and presents her grandmother with a discipline problem. Isie is persistently happy, and the implication is that

whites suffer from an absence of such joy; Isie's white benefactor ends the story, "I want a little of her sunshine to soak into my soul. I need it."

Hurston is probably manipulating white stereotypes of black people here, but it is not a simple matter of satire. She remembered Eatonville as a place of great happiness, and "Drenched in Light" is clearly autobiographical. To realize how much so, one has only to read her autobiography, or her May 1928 article in *The World Tomorrow*, "How It Feels to be Colored Me." In this essay Hurston admits "My favorite place was atop the gate-post. Proscenium box for a born first-nighter. Not only did I enjoy the show, but I didn't mind the actors knowing that I liked it." She, too, used to take rides from white motorists if her family was not watching, and she admits to liking to perform for the white folks:

> They liked to hear me "speak pieces" and sing and wanted to see me dance the parse-me-la, and gave me generously of their small silver for doing these things, which seemed strange to me for I wanted to do them so much that I needed bribing to stop. Only they didn't know it.

There is an element of satire in both pieces, but it seems useful to place the emphasis on the Eatonville memory. The whole point to "How It Feels to Be Colored Me" is that

> I am not tragically colored. There is no great sorrow dammed up in my soul, nor lurking behind my eyes. I do not mind at all. I do not belong to the sobbing school of Negrohood who hold that nature somehow has given them a lowdown dirty deal and whose feelings are all hurt about it . . . No, I do not weep at the world—I am too busy sharpening my oyster knife.

This is hardly a satiric tone, and Hurston is making a serious point: she is proud to be black, proud to be the product of a culture which endows her with a special response to the jazz of the "New World Cabaret." When the band starts playing she "follows them exultingly" and is amazed that "the great blobs of purple and red emotion" have not touched her white companion.

Hurston was as vulnerable as anyone to the cult of primitivism in the twenties, and some of the vulnerability is illustrated in the *World Tomorrow* article. Still, even before coming to New York, as the autobiographical "Drenched in Light" indicates, Hurston was trying to define her own special relationship to Eatonville, its folklore, the pastoral idyll that she associated with her first ten years there, and the implications of all of this for her art.

Hurston's use of Eatonville is also seen in her prize-winning story in the 1925 *Opportunity* contest, "Spunk." Spunk takes another man's wife, kills the cuckolded husband, and then rides to his death on the log at the saw mill—apparently the victim of the dead husband's return for vengeance. Eatonville is not exactly idyllic, although the violence just below the town's surface admittedly does not appear ominous. It is a place where superstition and "conjure" are everyday facts of life, and where existence has a continuity that transcends the moment. As the story ends: "The woman ate heartily of the funeral baked meats and wondered who would be Lena's next. The men whispered coarse conjectures between guzzles of whiskey."

Not all of Hurston's writing during the Renaissance years deals with Eatonville, but certainly the best of it does. Her attempt to illustrate the Eatonville novice newly arrived on the Harlem cabaret scene, "Muttsy" (*Opportunity*, August 1926), is poorly plotted but provides a nice ironic touch to the *Pamela* motif; the girl preserves her innocence in capturing the worldly Muttsy, but the story ends with him going back to his gambling ways: "What man can't keep one li'l wife an' two li'l bones?" Her play "Color Struck," the second-prize winner in the 1926 *Opportunity* contest and later reprinted in *Fire*,[12] is sentimental, a somewhat unconvincing account of color consciousness within the black community, but its cakewalk setting has considerable vitality. Another play, "The First One," also submitted to the *Opportunity* contests and later printed in Charles S. Johnson's *Ebony and Topaz*, is a biblical account of the Ham legend, comic in its presentation of Ham's curse being a product of shrewishness in Shem's and Arrafat's wives; Ham is presented as a lover of dancing and music, a man of joy contrasted with his brothers' materialism.

More representative of Hurston's talent during this period is "Sweat," published in *Fire*'s single issue, and the "Eatonville Anthology," published serially in *The Messenger* between September and November 1926. The "Anthology" is a series of thirteen brief sketches told with great economy and humor. "Sweat" is probably Hurston's finest short story of the decade, remarkably complex at both narrative and symbolic levels. The account of a Christian woman learning how to hate in spite of herself, a story of marital cruelty, an allegory of good and evil, it illustrates the unlimited potential in the Eatonville material. The story centers on Delia and her husband Sykes. Sykes hates his wife, beats her, and lives with another woman; he finds excuses to be cruel. And yet Hurston sees through even such a distasteful character; one reason Sykes hates his wife is that she emasculates him by earning their living washing white men's clothes. His resultant behavior is perceptively analyzed by Joe Clark: "There's plenty men dat takes a wife lak dey do a joint uh sugar-cane. It's round, juicy an' sweet when dey gits it. But dey squeeze an' grind, squeeze an' grind an' wring tell dey wring every drop uh pleasure dat's in em out. When dey's satisfied dat dey is wrung dry, dey treats em jes lak de do a cane-chew. Dey throws em away. Dey knows whut dey is doin' while dey is at it, an' hates theirselves fuh it but they keeps on hangin' after huh tell she's empty. Den dey hates huh fuh bein' a cane-chew an' in de way." Sykes eventually tries to drive Delia from her own house by penning a rattlesnake near her back door, and then attempts murder by moving it to her clothes hamper. When the released rattler kills Sykes instead, even though Delia could have saved him, we understand how high Delia's "spiritual earthworks" of Old Testament vengeance have been built against Sykes; she truly hates him "like a suck-egg dog." But this makes the story Delia's tragedy, too, and when Sykes dies at Delia's feet with "his horribly swollen neck and his one open eye shining with hope," a burden is not lifted but newly imposed. Her situation testifies to the prevalence of evil in a world we shape with our own needs.

What these early Eatonville stories illustrate is that by 1925–26, Zora Hurston had taken the irrevocable step of the artist who must remove himself from his experience in order to give it form and meaning. The step was both physical—she had removed herself to Washington and New York, she had entered college—and mental: she was analyzing her experience for its esthetic possibility. When this removal was placed in an academic setting, the process of assigning meaning to her experience became transferred from the esthetic to the scientific, and the next four years of Hurston's life exhibit the ascendency of a scientific impulse toward the systematic collecting of folklore for serious academic purposes.

"Sweat" and the "Eatonville Anthology" were published during her last semester at Barnard, the time in which she became most closely associated with Boas and advanced anthropological study. Significantly, Hurston does not return again to Eatonville as a source for fiction until "The Gilded Six-bits," published in *Story* in 1933, an account of marital infidelity that led in 1934 to a contract for her first novel, *Jonah's Gourd Vine*. What happened to her in the intervening period is largely an untold or misunderstood story.

### III

Hurston's 1927 collecting expedition lasted for six months, from February to October. Neither Woodson nor Boas was overly impressed. Woodson printed her article on Cudjo Lewis, a survivor of the last slave ship to America, in the *Journal of Negro History*,[13] but he apparently also used her as a common research hack. At one point she was copying legal documents from the Jacksonville, Florida, court records about a black-owned traction company of 1909. The folk material sent to Boas did not please, for it was similar to material collected by others, and her report to Boas on the conclusions of the expedition took only three double-spaced pages. Hurston had now, however, largely given up the writing of fiction to pursue a career as a scientist. Even though her field trip had not been a success, she is dedicated to anthropology, convinced of the need to collect her people's folklore before it is obliterated by the encroachments of modern civilization. In her report to Boas she stresses that material is slowly slipping away: "The bulk of the population now spends its leisure in the motion picture theatres or with the phonograph."[14] One cannot overemphasize the extent of her commitment. It was so great that her marriage in the spring of 1927 to Herbert Sheen was short-lived. Although divorce did not come officially until 1931, the two separated amicably after only a few months, Hurston to continue her collecting, Sheen to attend Medical School. Hurston never married again.

Hurston's return to her folklore collecting in December of 1927 was made possible by Mrs. R. Osgood Mason, an elderly white patron of the arts, who at various times also helped Langston Hughes, Alain Locke, Richmond Barthé, and Miguel Covarrubias. Hurston apparently came to her attention through the intercession of Locke, who frequently served as a kind of liaison between young black talent and Mrs. Mason. The entire relationship between this woman and the Harlem Renaissance deserves extended study, for it represents much of the ambiguity involved in white patronage of black artists. All her artists were instructed to call her "Godmother"; there was a decided emphasis on the "primitive" aspects of black culture, apparently a holdover from Mrs. Mason's interest in the Plains Indians. In Hurston's case there were special restrictions imposed by her patron: although she was to be paid a handsome salary for her folklore collecting, she was to limit her correspondence and publish nothing of her research without prior approval.

Hurston was financed by Mrs. Mason for an initial two-year period, from December 1927 to December 1929, and then was given an extension to March 31 of 1931. Although she spent time in the West Indies, most of her effort was in the South, and she collected a body of material which she would draw on for the rest of her life. Her correspondence during these years is remarkable for its enthusiasm. She feels that she is getting to the core of Afro-American culture, seeing it as an illustration of man's most basic impulses. She wants to present the material unadorned, letting it speak for itself as eloquent testimony for black creativity. She is impressed with the inherent beauty of the folklore itself, the way preaching is poetry, the way folk singing is more alive than classical music. She frequently rails against white distortions of this material, especially against Howard Odum and Guy Johnson, early white collectors in the field. In one letter she asks Boas point-blank if these men can be "serious scientists."[15] She also thought analytically about the material, formulating general principles to guide her study. She wrote Langston Hughes about theories of dialect: "Some laws in dialect. The same form is not always used. Some syllables and words are long before or after certain words and short in the same position. Example: you as subject gets full value but is shortened to yuh as an object. Him in certain positions and 'im in others depending on consonant preceding. Several laws of aspirate H."[16] In letter after letter Hurston emphasizes the uniqueness of black culture. She stresses the "basic drama" of black life, the ingenuity and wit in black dialect, the "asymmetry" of black art, the "dynamism" of black dancing, the originality of the entire Afro-American subculture.[17]

A measure of her sense of discovery and scientific commitment to it is the absence of her own creative effort between the fall of 1927 and the spring of 1930; even then she only began work with Langston Hughes on an ill-fated play, *Mule Bone*, itself a drama constructed out of a folktale. Hurston had previously used the Eatonville setting and its rural folklore as the stuff of fiction; now she is given to the collecting of songs, dances, games, conjure ceremonies, or anything else that can contribute to her body of information. As she told Hughes, "I am truly dedicated to the work at hand and so I am not even writing."[18] Her reports of her research are basically academic, apparently mainly by choice, although it was also a form approved by Locke and Mrs. Mason. She completed two pieces for the *Journal of American Folklore*, "Dance Songs and Tales of the Bahamas"[19] and the 110-page monograph, "Hoodoo in America."[20] She consulted with Boas and Benedict about her efforts and asked Boas's advice about the theories she was formulating—many of which were eventually published in a most unscientific volume, Nancy Cunard's *Negro* (1934). At one point she had planned seven books from her materials: "One volume of stories. One children's games. One dance and the Negro. One 'Mules and Men' a volume of work songs with guitar accompaniment. One on religion, One on words and meanings. One volume of love letters with an introduction on Negro love."[21] She was also interested in presenting on stage the true folk experience, eventually putting together a group of actors, singers, and dancers, and with Mrs. Mason's help producing an authentic folk concert at the John Golden Theatre on January 10, 1932: Extremely proud of her admission to the American Folklore Society, the American Ethnological Society, and the American Anthropological Society, she made sure that any news stories about her contained mention of these professional memberships. The Howard English major and the short-story writer of the Harlem Renaissance had apparently become a Barnard anthropologist, a folklore collector of considerable zeal and importance.

That transformation never fully took place, however, and although Hurston would continue to collect and use folklore for most of her career, establishing herself as the most important collector in the field, she grew away from the scientific view of her material. She came to doubt the efficacy of scholarly publication, pointing out to the Rosenwald Fund in 1934 that "it is almost useless to collect material to lie upon the shelves of scientific societies."[22] My own opinion is that she never became a professional, academic anthropologist, because such a vocation was alien to her exuberant sense of self, her admittedly artistic and sometimes erratic temperament. A good argument can be made for Hurston's never completely realizing this herself, but if there is a single theme which emerges from her creative effort during the thirties—her five books, her fiction, her essays—it is that eventually immediate experience

takes precedence over analysis, emotion over reason, the self over society, the personal over the theoretical. She learned that scientific objectivity is not enough for a black writer in America, and she went on to expose the excessive rationality behind the materialism of American life, the inadequacy of a sterile reason to deal with the phenomena of living. She forcefully affirmed the humanistic values of black life, contrasting them to the rationalized inhumanity of white society, and she asserted early arguments for black cultural nationalism. Beginning with *Jonah's Gourd Vine* (1934), her writing exhibits a studied antiscientific approach, and in her nonfiction even the most technical data are personalized. Her rejection of the scholarly bias and the scientific form was a process instead of a revelation, forming a chapter in her personal history too complex to detail here. Its cultural context is relevant, however, for Hurston's intellectual experience is in some ways a paradigm for the much debated "Crisis" of the black creative intellectual of the Harlem Renaissance.

I think Hurston was predisposed in favor of an anthropological conception of Eatonville simply because she was a creative writer. Although that sounds paradoxical, it is actually a logical product of the environment of ideas surrounding her. The black writer is especially vulnerable to the prescriptions which an idolatry of western European "high culture" imposes on American artists. He is urged to aspire toward a "raceless ideal" of literature, which technically interpreted has meant that he should not write about race, that he should not create "Negroes" but "human beings"—as if they were mutually exclusive categories. Above all he must never stoop to "propaganda." Such prescriptions were constantly offered during the Harlem Renaissance, and many of its participants aided and abetted such dubious aims. In fact, prior to the revolution in consciousness attending the current Black Arts Revolution, all black writers were badgered with such advice, the writer's success occurring in direct proportion to his ability to reject it. The attitude which invites the act of this prescribing, as well as the substance of the prescription, is a conception of the black condition as something which must be "overcome," since it is somehow manifestly less than human— a habit of mind institutionalized as American racism. All black American writers confront in some way this attitude and its resultant phenomena: the condition of black people. Thus, the dynamics of the culture make it as natural as breathing for the black artist to confront the issue of race.

In such a context, the attraction of a scientific conception for black experience becomes considerable for the writer-intellectual, especially if he has taken part in the formal educational system. The educational process in America is essentially one of assigning and reinforcing class structures through the creation of an educated middle class. This acculturative process informed Hurston that black sharecroppers were peasants (a pejorative term, especially within the self-enterprise mythology of American agriculture), that superstition was a crutch of the ignorant, that her folk experience was quaintly interesting but hopelessly unsophisticated. It is to Hurston's credit that she resisted much of this sort of knowledge, as is illustrated in an article she wrote for the *Messenger* in 1925, "The Hue and Cry about Howard University." Howard's white president liked to hear his students sing, and his motives are suspect as best. When the students objected, however, they did so for the wrong reasons; they argued that the spirituals were (a) "low and degrading, being the product of slaves and slavery"; (b) "not good grammar"; (c) "they are not sung in white universities."

Hurston supported the president for the right reasons,

when she should have resisted his unconscious racism. Her prospiritual argument would later become a fight to make blacks aware of how "conservatory concepts" had corrupted native Afro-American music, and her awareness of the inadequacies in the antispiritual argument is part of her larger awareness of the black condition. For she *knew* that Joe Clarke and his Eatonville cronies were human beings of complexity and dignity, no matter what their grammar, no matter how unsophisticated their manner might be, no matter how much white society distorted them. This knowledge typifies a dilemma of the black intellectual, for knowing this fact, how does one assert its truth and assign it meaning in the midst of a country whose institutions are structured to deny it? For Zora Neale Hurston, and for others, one way has been to assert black humanity by emphasizing its anthropological confirmation, a particularly effective way of accounting for human truth in a technological society, and one which mostly sidesteps the purely esthetic issue of "universality" vs. "propaganda." Blacks can be measured, studied, and charted in the interests of proving the general equality of the races. One has only to cultivate a "genius for pure objectivity" and let the evidence prove the absurdity of racial prejudice. Moreover, because anthropology also proves the existence of particular cultural differences while simultaneously positing a basic sameness in the human condition, one can maintain the integrity of black culture without sacrificing it to the mythical American melting pot. The scientific collection of the data of black life, its folklore, comes to prove black humanity as it asserts the beauty of the culture; meanwhile the artist who affirms the same thing is accused of special pleading.

What I should like to conclude with is the hypothesis that one reason Zora Neale Hurston was attracted to the scientific conceptualization of her racial experience during the late twenties and early thirties was its *prima facie* offering of a structure for black folklore. That is, it offered a pattern of meaning for material that white racism consistently distorted into "Negro" stereotypes. A folk singer was a cultural object of considerable scientific importance to the collecting anthropologist precisely because his folk experience affirms his humanity, a fact that Hurston could know subjectively as she proved it scientifically. The scientific attraction became so strong that she was led into seriously planning a career as a professional anthropologist, and it continued to affect her writing even after she had rejected such a possibility. When she used Eatonville as fiction in *Jonah's Gourd Vine* (1934) and folklore as personal narrative in her collection, *Mules and Men* (1935), she was in the process of rejecting the scientific conceptualization, but had not yet reached the esthetic resolution in fiction that characterized her two masterpieces of the late thirties, *Their Eyes Were Watching God* (1937), and *Moses, Man of the Mountain* (1939). Hurston never denied the usefulness of the Barnard training, but she made it clear that something more was needed for the creation of art. As she once told a reporter: "I needed my Barnard education to help me see my people as they really are. But I found that it did not do to be too detached as I stepped aside to study them. I had to go back, dress as they did, talk as they did, live their life, so that I could get into my stories the world I knew as a child."23

In sum, then, Zora Neale Hurston was shaped by the Harlem Renaissance, but by Boas as well as by Thurman and Hughes, by Barnard as well as by Harlem. This should not necessarily suggest that the Boas experience was of a superior quality; in many ways it seriously hindered her development as an artist. Nor should it suggest that the esthetic excitement among the Harlem literati failed to influence her thought. It

does mean that the attraction of scientific objectivity was something Hurston had to work through to arrive at the subjective triumphs of her later books. But the ferment of the Harlem Renaissance should also not be underestimated. Hughes, in particular, showed Hurston the poetic possibilities of the folk idiom and she was continually impressed when a reading from Hughes's poems would break the ice with dock loaders, turpentine workers, and jook singers. The mutual effort involved in the creation of *Fire*, the nights at Charles S. and James Weldon Johnson's, the *Opportunity* dinners, even the teas at Jessie Fauset's helped make Zora Hurston aware of the rich block of material which was hers by chance of birth, and they stimulated her thinking about the techniques of collecting and presenting it.

Yet, even Wallace Thurman, the chief of the "Niggerati," tacitly acknowledged that anthropology was Hurston's primary concern during the Renaissance years. In his 1934 novel, *Infants of the Spring*, a scarcely disguised account of the Harlem Renaissance, Thurman's Sweetie May Carr is transparent reportage of Zora Neale Hurston. Sweetie May is a storyteller from an all-black Mississippi town, "too indifferent to literary creation to transfer to paper that which she told so well." In one of his better jokes Thurman transfers Hurston's area of study and probably imposes some of his own cynicism on her character, but still suggests a preoccupation with scientific study: " 'It's like this,' [Sweetie May] told Raymond. 'I have to eat. I also wish to finish my education. Being a Negro writer these days is a racket and I'm going to make the most of it while it lasts . . . I don't know a tinker's damn about art. I care less about it. My ultimate ambition, as you know, is to become a gynecologist. And the only way I can live easily until I have the requisite training is to pose as a writer of potential ability.' "

One should be careful about accepting fictional characters as biographical evidence, but I hope the previous reconstruction suggests that Thurman was at least partially right. His insight provides a context for the study of Hurston's published books of the 1930s, a period in which she *did* give a tinker's damn, and created some of the best fiction ever written by a black American.

*Notes*

1. ALS., Zora Neale Hurston to Harper & Brothers, in the Hurston Collection, University of Florida Library. Quoted by permission of the Hurston family, Mrs. Marjorie Silver, and the University of Florida Library.
2. Hurston variously gave her birthdate as January 7, 1900, 1901, 1902, and 1903; no contemporary records were kept, but the 1903 date is the one given in a 1936 affadavit by her brother John, and the one she most often cited.
3. Zora Neale Hurston, *Dust Tracks on a Road* (New York, 1942), p. 71.
4. Ibid., p. 176.
5. ALS., Zora Neale Hurston to Constance Sheen, January 5, [1926], in the University of Florida Hurston collection. Quoted by permission of the Hurston family, the University of Florida Library, and Mrs. Marjorie Silver.
6. ALS., Zora Neale Hurston to Constance Sheen, February 2, [1926], in Florida's Hurston collection. Quoted by same permission as above.
7. All quotations in this paragraph from *Dust Tracks*, pp. 177–79.
8. Ibid., pp. 182–83.
9. Ibid., p. 182.
10. ALS., Zora Neale Hurston to Franz Boas, December 14, 1934. In The American Philosophical Society Library. Quoted by permission of the Hurston family and The American Philosophical Society.
11. *The Stylus* (Howard University), I (May 1921), p. 42.

12. *Fire's* only issue was published in either December 1926 or January 1927. Countee Cullen, writing in *Opportunity* of January 1927, welcomes it as the "outstanding birth" of the month.

13. XII (October 1927), pp. 648–63.

14. Zora Neale Hurston, "The Florida Expedition," 3 pp., typescript, signed, in The American Philosophical Society Library. Quoted by permission of the Hurston family and The American Philosophical Society.

15. ALS., Zora Neale Hurston to Franz Boas, October 20, 1929, in The American Philosophical Society Library. Quoted by permission of the Hurston family and The American Philosophical Society.

16. ALS., Zora Neale Hurston to Langston Hughes, April 12, 1928, in the James Weldon Johnson Memorial Collection of Yale University's Beinecke Library. Quoted by permission of the Hurston family and Yale.

17. Ibid. Quoted with same permissions as above.

18. ALS., Zora Neale Hurston to Langston Hughes, March 8, 1928, in James Weldon Johnson Memorial Collection of Yale University's Beinecke Library. Quoted by permission of the Hurston family and Yale.

19. XLIII (July-October 1930), pp. 294–312.

20. XLIV (October-December 1931), pp. 317–417.

21. ALS., Zora Neale Hurston to Langston Hughes, August 6, 1928, in James Weldon Johnson Memorial Collection at Yale University's Beinecke Library. Quoted by permission of the Hurston family and Yale.

22. Application for Rosenwald Fellowship, December 14, 1934, in Fisk University Library's Rosenwald Collection.

23. "Author Plans to Upbraid Own Race," *New York World Telegram*, February 6, 1935.

## ELLEASE SOUTHERLAND

### "Zora Neale Hurston:
### The Novelist-Anthropologist's Life/Works"

*Black World*, August 1974, pp. 20–30

In 1932, Zora Neale Hurston introduced Bahamian songs and dances to a New York audience at the John Golden Theater. Hall Johnson's "Run Li'l Chillun" was built around Miss Hurston's concert, "From Sun to Sin." She collected over 100 Bahamian tunes and corrected Broadway's misconception of Black rituals, pointing out that Black men have never been moon-worshippers. She was invited to join the American Folklore Society, the American Ethnological Society and the American Anthropological Society. She collected Indian lore. She studied under two-headed doctors in New Orleans and in Haiti and collected her works in two books, *Mules and Men* and *Tell My Horse*. A Guggenheim fellow, she authored four novels, two folklore collections, an autobiography, several short stories, two plays and many essays and articles. All her major works bring together a religion of opposites, and when these opposites are made to coincide, there is the power of new life. Each work vibrates with her powerful imagination. The accuracy of her words builds heat for the sun, gives body to thought. Zora Neale Hurston: a beautiful writer, the most prolific Black female writer in America.

Miss Hurston was born January 7, 1901. It was hog-killing time in the all-Black town of Eatonville. Her father, John Hurston—preacher, mayor, carpenter, and a mulatto—was away at the time of her birth. He already had one daughter and wasn't ready for another, especially one with brash manners and uppity ways. It was Zora's mother, Lucy Ann Potts, a small, dark-skinned woman, who protected Zora from her father's rage. Her father, gray-green eyes, sandy hair, felt that this child who looked more like him than his other children was getting protection from the mother because of these looks.

His resentment showed in the frequent threats to "whip" this child. The strong color conflict is the subject of Miss Hurston's first novel, *Jonah's Gourd Vine*. Perhaps her mother did understand her better. Her childhood fantasies were sometimes listened to, sometimes ignored by a busy mother, but they were never discouraged. Zora's father and maternal grandmother, on the other hand, heard her tales of a talking tree, talking lake, as bald-faced lies and would have punished her if the mother hadn't intervened. All her novels show that nature did indeed speak to her.

Then Zora's mother died when she was nine years old. With the death came hard times. The family of eight children was broken up. Within three months, the father remarried. The new wife somehow provoked bad relationships between father and children. At age 10, Zora, a student at a boarding school in Jacksonville, was forced to scrub stairs when her father was not able to send the necessary money. That was her last year of formal education for several years. At 14, tired of life from relative to relative, she tried supporting herself, working as a maid. She had many jobs, since she was often found reading when she should have been dusting.

At 17, a minor change in jobs: she became lady's maid to an actress and came in touch with the theater. While the theater offered new experience and a chance to travel, there was a negative side. Zora was not always paid for her work. And sleeping on a cot in the actresses' room left her without privacy. After this job, Zora returned to school. At night. From there she went to Morgan Academy, to Howard University and to Barnard College, graduating in 1928. During her period at Howard, she met Alain Locke. At Barnard she wrote a term paper which earned the attention of Franz Boas, the famed anthropologist who arranged a fellowship so that she could study folklore. This was the beginning.

Miss Hurston's insights as a student of folklore influenced the form of all her works, even her autobiography, *Dust Tracks on a Road*. This work describes techniques of the folklorist, as well as some very real dangers encountered in collecting her matieral. In Polk County, place of sun, sand, sweat and sawdust, place where the blues are born, place where they dance the scronch and the belly-rub and tell great stories, she was almost knifed to death. In explaining how laughter and death work so closely together, Miss Hurston says, "primitive minds are quick to sunshine and quick to anger."[1] So on the evening she partied at the jook, enjoying the music, dancing and drinking, the music came to a sudden halt and a woman, jealous of Zora, faced her with a knife. Zora had no knife and didn't know how to use one anyway. If a friend, Big Sweet, had not interfered, it would have meant certain death for the writer. In the general fighting that broke out, blood already had spilled on the floor and many people with open switch-blades already had joined the fight when a friend told Zora to run, shoved her toward the door. And she says she ran all the way from Polk County to New Orleans.

In New Orleans, there were other dangers, not physical this time. Mind and spirit had to be spent as Miss Hurston studied under all the famous two-headed doctors in order to bring us new and important information on Hoodoo in America. This information is not available to outsiders. One must be initiated. One must learn the ceremonies, herbs, formulas. Miss Hurston did all these things; she fulfilled the most demanding ceremony, calling for a three-day fast during which she was to lie on her stomach, naked, with her navel in touch with a snake skin. During this ceremony, she had five psychic experiences which she said seemed real for weeks. This was under the two-headed doctor, Luke Turner, nephew to the famous Marie Leveau. Her work with him lasted five months.

Despite the stress and the dangers, Miss Hurston's autobiography is filled with the laughter so characteristic of the oral tradition. What is known as "the dozens" in New York is call "playing" in a family situation, "reading," "specifying" or "putting the foot up" in Polk County. Miss Hurston records her friend, Big Sweet, "putting her foot up" on a particular man's stoop and proceeding to tell him that his pa was a "double-humpted camel and his ma was a grass-gut cow, but even so, he tore her wide open in the act of getting born, and so on and so forth. He was a bitch's baby out of a buzzard egg."[2]

The tales and jokes bring a gentler humor. They give new life to Bible passages, slave narratives. In discussing *Mules and Men*, attention will be drawn to some of the tales and jokes.

Three closing chapters of the autobiography deal with love, race and religion. Of race, Miss Hurston says, "Personal benefits run counter to race lines too often for it to hold. . . . Since the race line has never held any other group in America, why expect it to be effective with us?" This was the kind of comment that brought criticism. It led to ideas of Miss Hurston as lacking serious race consciousness. If the statement brings criticism, then her works should correct that criticism; her folklore collections show her love, respect and appreciation for Black art.

Of love, Miss Hurston is careful to say that she is no expert. She was married in 1934, but the marriage was unhappy; she more or less eased away. She loved again, but her suitor insisted that she give up her career. She felt she could not. It was this love that gave strength to her best novel *Their Eyes Were Watching God*.

In commenting on religion, Miss Hurston, preacher's daughter, states that she does not pray. Prayer for her is "a cry of weakness, and an attempt to avoid, by trickery, the rules of the game as laid down."[3] But at the same time, she feels that any form of worship is valid if it is a positive force for the worshipper. For herself, "The springing of the yellow line of morning out of the misty deep of dawn, is glory enough."[4]

The autobiography, coming after three novels and two folklore collections, has a unique form. It is strangely silent in showing Miss Hurston's relationship with her sisters and brothers before her mother's death. After all, she was one of eight children. We don't sense their nearness as the story begins. Perhaps their early separation and the mother's death created this loneliness that blocked out the pleasant times common with big families. And the emphasis on education is, at times, uneven. But it is impressive that a woman whose life had been so disordered gathered herself together enough to bring important findings to the American public.

During the Harlem Renaissance, time of rebirth of Black literature, when Black writers and Black artists were "in," when every white party had to have its Black partygoers, and Blacks around the world looked to Harlem as their cultural capital, Zora Neale Hurston and Richard Wright wrote the best novels of the period—her work, *Their Eyes Were Watching God*. But 1948 was a fateful year in her life. The woman whose spirit made parties, whose classmates and teachers invited her to dinner and gave her gifts, found herself faced with enemies. There were false charges of indecent behavior brought against her, supposedly involving two demented minors and one adult. Zora was not even in the country when the crime was to have taken place. The charges were dropped, but not before the Black press played up the scandal enough to break Zora's spirit. This scandal coincides with Zora's literary silence. After 1948,

she wrote a few articles and essays. She died January 28, 1960, in Florida, working as a maid.

Written in 1932 and published in 1935, *Mules and Men*, Zora's first work, is packed every inch with the most accurate humor, primarily because she presents the folk material in a unique way that makes no separation between the teller and the tale. When a mannerism contributes to the story, it is included. The entire setting is naturally Black. So that when stories are told about the woodpecker on the ark or how the possom lost the hair on his tail, the speaker's personality adds to the story. The group settings stimulate the storyteller, who must often face real arguments over an invented tale. Once a wife calls a story-teller to come home and do some chores; he ignores his wife.

The stories often came naturally, that is, when no formal lying contest was held. Zora's ear was always ready. On a Friday afternoon, someone remarked that it was unusually silent, that no birds were singing. This occasioned an explanation of where the birds go on Fridays. It seems that they visit hell, each with a grain of sand in its beak, to assist a man who befriended it. Story begets story, until we have the full, entertaining collection in *Mules and Men*. The images are freely taken from all aspects of life. No subject is too serious, too whimsical to be worked through the imagination of the story-tellers. Religion, slavery, Black men as a race, the white man, women, Adam and Eve are common subjects. And of course all the animals, entitled Brer, come into play.

Most of the laughter and jokes are left to the first part of the book. The second part, dealing with Hoodoo in New Orleans, is quiet. Serious. The party crowd of the first half is reduced to a few people, often the two-headed doctor and Zora, sometimes Zora very much alone. She learned formulas for making and breaking marriages, killing by remote control, silencing juries. Of course, she paid a price for this information: the initiation ceremonies. She learned that each doctor had different methods and would use different methods for different people. Zora learned herbs: when to pick them, that some must be picked with ceremony, while others, more potent, could only be handled by the doctor himself.

In addition to recounting her experiences, she provides an excellent glossary, an appendix of Negro songs with music, lists Hoodoo formulas used by doctors and prescriptions of root doctors. A very complete work, sensitively written.

It might first seem natural for a preacher's daughter to meet up with emotional difficulties when moving from Christianity to African-derived Hoodoo. Not so. The Christians in Zora's hometown were no strangers to Hoodoo. One of the characters in *Jonah's Gourd Vine* says that the Bible is the greatest Hoodoo book. And Zora, who saw the Bible used on many occasions by Hoodoo doctors, cites Moses as the greatest Hoodoo man.

*Jonah's Gourd Vine*, published in 1934, even takes its title from the Bible. The main character is a preacher, with many characteristics of Zora's own father. The mother, a small Black woman, resembles Zora's mother. Many incidents parallel Zora's life, and perhaps the laughter of children, so conspicuously absent in the autobiography, had already been written here. There are children's games, the dozens, work songs, and a 12-page sermon packed with images powerful enough to make an atheist preach. The sermon is so impressive that one white critic claimed no unlettered Black preacher could speak in such a manner. Zora, naturally upset by the comment, wrote James Weldon Johnson that he or she could hear such sermons several times in a week.

Another strong point of this novel is the preacher's marriage to a woman who worked Hoodoo in order to get him. We feel the Hoodoo's power to make a man do what he doesn't want to do. And when he discovers the trick, we sense the wife's fear when she returns home one day, sees the hole at the gate and at the front steps, finds the mattress torn. She knows that her root-work had been discovered and that there will be prices to pay.

Again, at the close of the Christian novel, the African drums sound: "Not Kata-kumba, the drum of triumph, that speaks of great ancestors and glorious wars. Not the little drum of kid-skin, for that is to dance with joy and to call to mind birth and creation, but O-go-doe, the voice of Death—that promises nothing, that speaks with tears only, and of the past."[5] This African drum ceremony is at the funeral of a preacher. Zora includes a glossary in this book too.

Zora's second novel, *Their Eyes Were Watching God* (1937), is most widely read in universities, in Black Studies classes. A work of joy and love, its positive vibrations are a relief from the grim, death-ridden themes that weigh so many novels. Yet it does not ignore realities. It involves death: the main character, Janie Woods, is forced to kill the man she loves. There is a terrible flood, and the slave narrative of a Black woman abused by a white master. But life still dominates this work. Its total impression rests with Zora, whose quick wit and imagination create beautiful passages. This is the first novel of a Black woman in search of joy, love, happiness. In search of people, rather than things. A young Black woman with her eyes on the horizon.

*Their Eyes Were Watching God* begins with Janie's marriage to a middle-aged man. The grandmother arranging the marriage had been a slave and wanted worldly comfort for her granddaughter. But life as Mrs. Killicks is not enough for sixteen-year-old Janie. The 60 acres of land and the house do not in themselves bring happiness. She leaves her husband to live with Jody Starks, who becomes the first mayor of an all-Black town, builds a store and a post office. His ambition is powerful enough, but his love short-sighted. He does not allow his wife to participate in vulgar pleasures. She is not to join in the joking and storytelling that take place on the store porch. Neither is she allowed to come to the mock funeral held for a dead mule. The bitterness builds. Finally, after 20 years, when Jody is dying, Janie explains to him the causes for their unhappy marriage. She says, "Mah mind had tuh be squeezed and crowded out tuh make room for yours in me."[6]

There were occasions when Janie spoke her mind, especially after hearing men discuss the stupidities of women. Janie told the group, "Sometimes God gits familiar wid us womenfolks too and talks His inside business. He told me how surprised He was 'bout yall turning out so smart after Him makin' yuh different."[7] Janie surprised the men, most of all her husband, who thought he fully understood her and never expected her to voice an opinion.

Janie's third marriage is very complete indeed. Tea Cake teaches her to play checkers, takes her fishing. They work side by side picking beans in the muck of the Everglades. And while Tea Cake cannot offer the security or ambition of the first husbands, he brings her joy in many simple ways.

Tragic irony works so that Janie is forced to kill the man she loves. However, as the novel comes to a close, Janie is an inspiration to her friend, Phoeby. Janie's strength gives power to the novel, so that, in spite of the hard times and the death, the novel speaks for life.

*Their Eyes Were Watching God* is not Zora's only work giving thoughtful consideration to the lives of women. In her book on Voodoo in Jamaica and in Haiti, Zora devotes a chapter to women of the Caribbean. She states that Black, poor women are used as mules and can be seen carrying heavy loads up and down the mountains. The woman's honor is readily sacrificed for a man's. And it is a law that no woman may accuse a man of fathering her child unless he is her husband.[8] Zora points out that a woman's chance for better treatment is increasing if she is mulatto and rich.

Zora was frequently questioned by men, who did not understand why she should write and think; they felt those were a man's preoccupations. This idea of women as mindless beings is dealt with in many of Zora's novels. In *Seraph on the Suwanee*, her last published novel, Jim, the main character, says, "Women folks don't have no mind to make up nohow. They wasn't made for that. Lady folks were just made to laugh and act loving and kind and have a good man to do for them all he's able and have him so happy that he's willing to work and fetch in every dad-blamed thing that his wife thinks she would like to have. That's what women are made for."[9] A similar comment is made in *Their Eyes Were Watching God* when Jody Starks retorts, "Somebody got to think for women and chillun and chickens and cows, I god, they sho don't think none theirselves."[10] These and similar statements recur in Zora's works, and their frequency emphasizes the author's point of view.

Zora's novel *Moses, Man of the Mountain* (1939) works well when under the full control of her imagination, but too frequently it follows the Bible story much too closely. There are, however, many nice touches, many quotable lines. First, it is understood that Moses is an excellent Vodoo man. He is associated with the Voodoo god Damballah.

It was Moses who lifted up the serpent in the wilderness, when all who looked upon it were healed. The serpent is Damballah's signature. Damballah's day is Wednesday. So Moses, in his many threats against Pharoah, promises to be back next Wednesday. Also, in presenting himself to Pharoah, Moses salutes the cardinal points as the *houngan* salutes the points in a Voodoo ceremony. It is through possession of the black cat bone that Moses controls the battle when he holds up his arms. Many details of Voodoo are thus uncovered in the Christian text and through her imagination, and Zora reduces the distance and time until we feel the very human qualities of the people: the petty bickerings, Aaron and Miriam wanting more recognition, the people complaining about the food and water, Moses getting tired of the complaints—all hold an air of humor, especially since the dialect is southern Black.

For all her works, Zora wrote the most beautiful endings. *Moses, Man of the Mountain* is no exception. It closes: "The moon in its reddest mood became to him a standing place for his feet and the sky ran down so close to gaze on Moses that the seven great suns of the Universe went wheeling around his head. He stood in the boom of thunder. . . . Moses stood in the midst of it and said 'Farewell.' Then he turned with a firm tread and descended the other side of mountain and headed back over the years."[11]

In a sense, *Moses, Man of the Mountain*, can be viewed as a folk tale, elaborately related. The telling is certainly very much in the oral tradition.

Zora's study of Jamaican and Haitian voodoo, *Tell My Horse* (1938), begins with the terms and takes us to the ceremonies. We are introduced to the gods, their days, colors, ceremonies and their attributes. She tells us that Damballah is the supreme god whose signature is the serpent. His day is Wednesday afternoon, his sacrifice a pair of white chickens—a hen and a cock. He is offered flowers and perfume, sweet wine. He is fourth in order of service. Erzulie is the goddess of love. Thursday and Saturday are her days. She is served with sweets and perfume. "Erzulie Nin Nin Oh" is Haiti's favorite folk song. The title takes its name from the person said to be mounted by the god. The person possessed is the horse.

*Tell My Horse* is a book libraries have trouble keeping. More often than not it is missing, possibly because of the excellent photographs. Zora states that she was the first person to photograph a zombie, pointing out emphatically that zombies do exist. She explains that people who become zombies die in a similar way, after a two-day sickness. Apparently the person has been drugged in a way that arrests the vital signs and destroys speech and memory. They are used as slaves by the same person who drugged them, then broke into the grave and revitalized them. The families who discover a relative abused as a zombie are too intimidated to seek court action. And even if they were brave enough, they wouldn't know who to blame. The formulas of the drugs are very secret. So the only protection a family can give a "dead" person is to make sure that he is really dead by driving a knife or stake through his heart. This is necessary, since bodies are not usually embalmed in Haiti.

The study is careful in its reporting. Add to the spiritual strength word-power, and we get a valuable report encompassing politics and religion, demonstrating their relationship. There are many strange stories in this book, some very terrifying, especially the stories of cannibalistic societies hiding under the Voodoo religion. There is much that is so personal and so unusual that a novice would have stumbled in working with such material.

A selection from the chapter entitled: "Night Song After Death" attests to her skill. "It was asymmetric dancing that yet had balance and beauty. It certainly was most compelling. There was a big movement and a little movement. The big movement was like a sunset in its scope and color. The little movement had the almost imperceptible ripple of a serpent's back. It was a cameo in dancing."[12] Again, in the scene about the funeral of a poor man:

> We were a sort of sightless, soundless, shapeless, stillness there in the dark, wishing for life. At last a way-off whisper began to put on flesh. In the space of a dozen breaths the keening harmony was lapping our ears. Somebody among us struck matches and our naked lights flared. The shapeless crowd-mass became individuals.[13]

Where some other author might have made distinctions, Zora showed connections, all done with a positive feeling for life.

Zora Neale Hurston: woman who stood on a table in Polk County and sang two verses of John Henry, who went to California to write *Dust Tracks on a Road* and traveled to Haiti to write *Their Eyes Were Watching God*; preacher's daughter who studied under all the famous two-headed doctors of New Orleans; who gathered her scattered childhood and went to work with an exciting imagination and an outrageous sense of humor, brought new songs and correct religious ideas to the reading public. In all her works, Zora shows the power and life of the oral tradition—African culture that survived slavery and Americanization. We are beginning to read her books. It's about time.

*Notes*

1. *Dust Tracks on a Road*, page 178.
2. Ibid. page 187.
3. Ibid. page 278.
4. Ibid. page 279.
5. *Jonah's Gourd Vine*, page 312.
6. *Their Eyes Were Watching God*, page 74.
7. Ibid. page 65.
8. *Tell My Horse*, page 80.
9. *Seraph on the Suwanee*, page 32.
10. *Their Eyes Were Watching God*, page 62.
11. *Moses, Man of the Mountain*, page 351.
12. *Tell My Horse*, page 74.
13. Ibid. page 73.

## S. JAY WALKER
### "Zora Neale Hurston's *Their Eyes Were Watching God*: Black Novel of Sexism"

*Modern Fiction Studies*, Winter 1974–75, pp. 519–27

The primary goals of the major American Liberation movements, Black Lib, Women's Lib, and Gay Lib, are in such affinity that it seems on the surface almost incredible that the three should not long since have formed an effective working alliance. In general terms, each demands, essentially, three things: definition of self, ending of oppression, and acceptance by society of the group's own goals and standards regarding itself.

Yet it is obvious that this alliance neither exists, nor is, beyond *pro forma* expressions of mutual sympathy, likely to exist. For whereas the generalized goals may be similar, the priorities and the applications of priority are different. The immediate practical goal of Black Lib is seizure of the political and economic levers which will provide decent schooling, decent housing, decent jobs. Women's Lib seeks first day-care centers, salary equity, and access to the higher levels of professional life. And Gay Lib demands an immediate end to police entrapment and legalized harrassment.

Each, inevitably, will scratch first where he or she itches; it was precisely this difference in priorities that shattered the Abolitionist/Woman's Suffrage coalition in the nineteenth century.

There have been mutual interchanges of concern and regard: Huey Newton has publicly acknowledged Gay and Women's groups as part of the general liberation struggle, whereas John Murray and Gloria Steinem have recognized that while racism remains pervasive in society there can be no real freedom for anyone. Yet Gay Lib and Women's Lib remain primarily white, middle-class organizations, and Black Lib remains virtually totally black.

In the Black Lib/Women's Lib crossover there are, of course, notable exceptions, particularly that most remarkable of women of any shade, Representative Shirley Chisholm. Yet Ms. Chisholm's widely-quoted comment that she has suffered more from being a woman than from being a black seems to find little response among the rank and file of black women.

A 1971 *Ebony* article reported the majority of its black female respondents at best indifferent and at worst hostile to Women's Lib, with opinions ranging from the idea that the struggle with racism is enough for any black's energies to the belief that the last thing needed by black men at this time is being put down by black women, ("We should stand behind our men, not against them"),[1] to the assertion that Women's Lib is a game being played by bored middle-class white women whose toilets are being cleaned by working-class, black women: you have to be in a Doll's House to want to get out of one.

The thrust of the Black Nationalist organizations, too, taken largely, one feels, from the leadership of the Black Muslims, is heavily male-oriented. It is seldom expressed with the brutality of Stokeley Carmichael's reported response to the question of what should be the "proper position" of women in the struggle—"Prone," he said. Yet it is clear that Carmichael is a lot closer to grass roots than Chisholm. Black Liberation makes a point of respecting, even revering, black women, but they are respected or revered *in their place*, a place perhaps best defined by Amina Baraka (a.k.a. Mrs. LeRoi Jones). The duty of black women, she writes, is "to inspire our men, educate our children, and participate in the social development of our nation."[2] The accepted role, then, is clearly that of an auxiliary.

Thus it comes as something of a shock to discover that Zora Neale Hurston's neglected 1937 masterpiece, *Their Eyes Were Watching God*, deals far more extensively with sexism, the struggle of a woman to be regarded as a person in a male-dominated society, than racism, the struggle of blacks to be regarded as persons in a white-dominated society. It is a treatment virtually unique in the annals of black fiction, and in her handling of it, Ms. Hurston not only shows an aching awareness of the stifling effects of sexism, but also indicates why the feminist movement has failed, by and large, to grasp the imaginations of black womanhood.

Janie Killicks Starks Woods, the heroine of the novel, is followed through three marriages, the first of which brings her safety, the second wealth and prestige, and the third love. On the surface, it sounds indistinguishable from the women's-magazine fiction which has been denounced as the most insidious form of sexism. Yet a great deal goes on beneath the surface of Hurston's novel, leading to a final interpretation of love that denies not sexuality but sex-role stereotypes. The love that completes the novel is one that the previous marriages had lacked because it is a relationship between acknowledged equals. Janie and "Tea Cake," her husband, share resources, work, decisions, dangers, and not merely the marriage bed.

It is something less than a primer of romanticized love. At one point, Tea Cake, jealous of a suspected rival, beats Janie; at another, Janie, having the same suspicion, beats Tea Cake. Each has weaknesses, fears; but in the final analysis each respects the other as a person, and it is that respect that allows them to challenge the world's conventions and to find each other, and themselves.

Hurston has a technical problem in maintaining this intensely personal vision during the desperate period, 1883–1923, in which the novel is set, without betraying herself into a Catfish Row fantasy of black life. She solves it by the simplest of devices: for the major exploration of the sexist theme, the second marriage, she removes her characters from the white world, establishing them in Eatonville, Florida, an all-black village (and one in which the author herself grew up) in which Janie's husband, Starks, is Mayor and owner of the general store, thus freeing them from contact with or economic dependence upon the white world.

It is within this society, secure both in person and prestige, that Janie ruminates to her crony, Pheoby Watson, on her personal desires as opposed to those of the grandmother who had reared her, and on the limitations of security and prestige:

> She [the grandmother] was borned in slavery times when folks, dat is black folks, didn't sit down anytime dey felt lak it. So sittin' on porches lak de white madam looked lak uh mighty fine thing tuh her. Dat's whut she wanted fuh me—don't keer whut it cost. Git up on uh high chair and sit dere. She didn't have time tuh think whut tuh do after you got up on de stool of do nothin'. . . . So Ah got up on de high stool lak she told me, but Pheoby, Ah done nearly languished tuh death up dere. Ah feel lak de

world wuz cryin' extry and Ah ain't read de common news yet.[3]

And Pheoby answers, "Maybe so, Janie. Still and all Ah'd love to experience it for just one year. It look lak heben tuh me from where Ah'm at" (p.96).

The distinction here is clearly drawn. Janie is the mayor's wife, but Pheoby is a worker, one of those Eatonsville citizens described as becoming human only when "the sun and the bossman were gone." Her life is dominated almost entirely by the struggle to survive, and her tedious round between field and kitchen makes Janie's "stool of do nothing" appear a throne.

A *Black Scholar* article, "The Black Movement and Women's Liberation," by Linda La Rue sums up the ordinary class/race distinction between blacks and whites in a single question: "Is there any logical comparison between the oppression of the black woman on welfare who has difficulty feeding her children and the discontent of the suburban woman who has the luxury to protest the washing of the dishes on which her family's full meal has been consumed?"[4]

This is the dichotomy—class, not race—which Hurston explores. Janie seeks to expand her experience, her understanding, her personality. Pheoby replies for all the black women who have never been admitted to the Doll's House. And who are not flocking into Women's Lib.

The path to that dissatisfied eminence has been a long one for Janie. It began with her grandmother, feeling that she was soon to die, seeking safety for the sixteen-year-old girl, threatening her with the dangers awaiting the unprotected black woman and ending with a plea: "Ah didn't want tuh be used for a work-ox and a brood-sow and Ah didn't want mah daughter used dat way neither. . . . Ah can't die easy thinkin' maybe de menfolks white or black is makin' a spitcup outa you" (pp. 18, 21).

The safety envisioned by the grandmother is marriage to Logan Killicks, an elderly man who is "prosperous" in that he owns a sixty-acre farm. But the grandmother warns even against Killicks. ". . . de white man throw down de load and tell de nigger man tuh pick it up. He pick it up because he have to, but he don't tote it. He hand it to his womenfolks. De nigger woman is de mule of de world so fur as Ah can see" (p. 16).

One of the few favorable responses to the *Ebony* article echoed this "we are the slaves of slaves" sentiment: "It is not enough for black men to be free—black women cannot afford to wait . . . to deal with our oppression as women."[5]

Janie's response to this warning is, in fact, to establish firmly the sex-oriented roles in their marriage. When her husband calls to her to come to assist him in the barn, she calls back from the kitchen, "You don't need no help out dere, Logan. Youse in yo' place and Ah'm in mine" (p. 29). And when Killicks grumbles that she might at least carry the firewood into the kitchen, pointing out that his first wife had even chopped it, Janie hurls at him the essential *kinder, küche, und kirche* put-down: "Ah'm just as stiff as you is stout. If you can stand not to chop and tote wood Ah reckon you can stand not to get no dinner. 'Scuse my freezolity, Mist' Killicks, but Ah don't mean to chop de first chip" (p. 25).

Killicks doesn't give up easily; he makes plans to buy a second mule, one that a woman can handle. Nor does Janie. She is preparing to fight for her place in the kitchen rather than behind the plow when she realizes that, even winning that fight, she will lose. For whereas Killicks can give her safety and respectability and a modicum of comfort, he cannot give her love.

Love seems to be offered by Joe Starks, the ambitious, debonnaire stranger who passes en route to Eatonville and who stays to court her with a new vision of what life can be: "A pretty doll-baby lak you is made to sit on de front porch and rock and fan yo'se'f" (p. 27).

She thinks over his words for several days, and then one morning, while quarreling with Killicks and cooking his breakfast, she walks out of the house and, with a fine symbolic gesture, unties her apron, flings it over a low bush, and runs away with Starks. (It is also perhaps symbolic of the identification of form with respectability that she and Starks marry the same evening, without either considering the matter of divorce.)

If the marriage to Killicks constitutes the "kitchen" era of Janie's existence, the marriage to Starks constitutes the "porch" era. Arrived in Eatonville, Starks takes charge of the growing community. He buys additional land and increases the settlers. He builds the store; he establishes the post office; he erects the first street-light; he arranges for the village's incorporation, and, inevitably, he becomes Mayor Starks.

Janie is "Mrs. Mayor Starks," and she finds the experience somehow disquieting. She tells Starks:

> "Youse always off talkin' and fixin' things and Ah feels lak Ah'm just markin' time. Hope it soon gits over." "Over, Janie?" [he replies.] . . . "Ah ain't even started good. Ah told you in de very first beginnin' dat Ah aimed tuh be a big voice. You oughta be glad, 'cause dat makes uh big woman outa you." . . . A feeling of coldness and fear took hold of her. She felt far away from things and lonely. (p. 41)

It is at this point that Hurston begins to develop her theme. Clearly it is not enough for Janie to be made a big woman by her husband's being a big man. Sitting on the porch and fanning herself, watching the endless checker games of the village men and listening to their conversations, in neither of which she is expected to participate, Janie is merely "marking time." What is more, the "place" for which she had so doggedly fought Killicks now seems stultifying. Starks' "pretty doll-baby" is just that: his toy, his possession; and he emphasizes his ownership by insisting that Janie wear a turban, a "head-rag," in public, so that the sight of her beautiful hair can be enjoyed by no one other than himself. The device oddly foreshadows that Black Muslim women's costume of the 1950's and 1960's.

But perhaps even more galling than the possessiveness of Starks is his demand that Janie leave every decision to him. When she is invited to make a speech at one of the village celebrations, Starks replies for her:

> ". . . mah wife don't know nuthin' 'bout no speech-makin'. Ah never married her for nothin' lak dat. She's uh woman and her place is in de home."
>
> Janie made her face laugh after a small pause, but it wasn't too easy. She had never thought of making a speech and didn't know if she cared to make one at all. It must have been the way Joe spoke out without giving her a chance to say anything one way or another that took the bloom off things. (p. 39)

Starks also insists that she maintain her caste, above and separate from the common people of Eatonville: "He didn't want her talking [with] . . . trashy people. 'You're Mrs. Mayor Starks, Janie. . . . Ah can't see what uh woman uh yo' [class] would want tuh be treasurin' all dat gum-grease from folks dat don't even own de houses dey sleeps in'" (p. 47).

Essentially, what Janie is deprived of is the company of other women, of the sisterhood of those with common experiences and common problems, and she begins to fight a lonely battle against Starks', and man's, definition of women:

> *Starks:* "Somebody got to think for women and chillun and chickens and cows. . . . they sho' don't think none themselves."
> *Janie:* "Ah knows a few things, and womenfolks thinks sometimes, too!"
> *Starks:* "Ah naw they don't. They just think they thinkin'. When Ah sees one thing Ah understands ten. You see ten things and don't understand one." (p. 62)

The attitude is a red flag waved before Janie's eyes, and she becomes, almost unwillingly, the Eatonville spokesman, if not for women's liberation, at least for women's dignity. It is an unwilling decision because she, too, is trapped into a pattern of thinking which makes her status dependent upon her husband's. "'Maybe he ain't nuthin','  she cautioned herself, 'but he is somethin' in my mouth. He's got tuh be else Ah ain't got nuthin' tuh live for. Ah'll lie and say he is'" (p. 66).

But even lying, maintaining the façade of Mrs. Mayor Starks, she bursts out again and again at the casually disparaging remarks of her husband and his cronies:

> "Sometimes God git familiar with us womenfolks too and talks His inside business. He told me how surprised He was 'bout y'all turnin' out so smart after Him makin' yuh different; and how surprised y'all is agoin' tuh be if you ever find out you don't know half as much 'bout us as you think you do. It's so easy to make yo'self out God Almight when you ain't got nothin' tuh strain against but women and chickens."
>
> "You gettin' too moufy, Janie," Starks told her. "Go fetch me de checker board *and* de checkers." (p. 65)

The marriage is at an end, even though it drags on for years, and it is only when Starks is on his deathbed that Janie is able to force him to listen to her assessment of the emptiness of her life:

> Ah ain't here tuh blame nobody. Ah'm just tryin' tuh make you know what kind a person Ah is befo' it's too late. . . . You wasn't satisfied wid me de way Ah wuz. Nah! Mah own mind had tuh be squeezed and crowded out tuh make room for yours in me. . . . All dis bowin' down, all dis obedience under yo' voice—dat ain't whut Ah rushed off down de road tuh find out about you." (pp. 73, 75)

Starks dies, and Janie makes another symbolic gesture. Just as she had untied her apron and "flung it on a low bush" when leaving Killicks, now, "before she slept that night she burnt up every one of her head-rags and went about the house next morning with her hair in one thick braid swinging well below her waist" (p. 76).

It is another step, and the penultimate one, towards emancipation. She has left Killicks; she has defied and finally outlived Starks. Now she must combat both society and conventional wisdom. Janie is forty years of age, and when "Tea Cake" Woods, twelve years her junior, comes to court her, both the village and a deep caution within herself warn that he can be after nothing except her money. The village has a "suitable" third husband selected for her: a middle-aged undertaker with money, and whereas Janie quickly rejects that association with death, she cannot easily accept the association with life that Tea Cake offers to her.

It is simply too foreign to her experiences, and yet its foreignness is delightful. The checkerboard, that symbol of masculine exclusiveness and dominance, becomes an early indicant of what Tea Cake is to mean. He invites her to play and, when she confesses ignorance of the game, offers to teach her. "She found herself glowing inside. Somebody wanted her to play. Somebody thought it natural for her to play" (p. 81).

And from there they move through a series of small but significant challenges to the-way-things-ought-to-be. They dig worms at midnight and fish until dawn; they rent an automobile and drive to the nearest city to watch baseball games. Because Tea Cake likes her in it, Janie wears blue satin, though Eatonsville considers it inappropriate to her age and station. And finally, against the advice of friends, legends of the sad fates of others, and her own forebodings, she agrees to follow Tea Cake to Jacksonville and marry him there. It is for her the ultimate expression of her thoughts after Starks' death:

> She had been getting ready for her great journey to the horizons in search of *people*; it was important to all the world that she find them and they find her. But she had been whipped like a cur dog, and run off down a back road after *things*. (p. 77)

It is important to note that in one respect Hurston diverges here from the radical feminists of the 1970's. Janie's search for *people* can only be accomplished through a *person*, a man. In this sense of an individual being incomplete without an individual, personal love, Hurston returns, in effect, to the romantic tradition of reciprocal passion, a tradition as old as Charlotte Brontë and George Eliot, and it is in terms of that tradition that finally she views the relationship between Tea Cake and Janie. Janie herself recognizes that personal love is the cement of her life, and is uncaring that the world will not understand or approve it:

> Dey gointuh make 'miration 'cause mah love didn't work lak they love, if dey ever had any. Then you must tell 'em dat love ain't somethin' lak uh grindstone dat's de same thing everywhere and do de same thing tuh everything it touch. Love is lak de sea. It's uh movin' thing, but still and all, it takes its shape from de shore it meets, and it's different with every shore. (p.158)

And certainly her love and Tea Cake's is "different." If the apron was symbolic of her life with Killicks and the head-rag of her life with Starks, overalls are the symbol of her life with Tea Cake, for she dons them and goes into the fields to work side by side with him as a migrant laborer in the Everglades.

It may seem a strange "liberation," particularly for the girl who didn't "mean to chop de first chip" for Killicks, but it *is* a liberation; it grows neither out of need nor greed but simply of the desire of Janie and Tea Cake to be together, to share all their experiences, "to partake wid everything," as Tea Cake puts it. And the sharing is genuine: after their day in the fields, Tea Cake helps to get supper. There is no longer the "youse in yo' place and Ah'm in mine" because there are no longer separate places, and it is that blurring of "places," essentially the blurring of sex-role stereotypes within an intensely sexual relationship, that constitutes the liberation and happiness of Janie Killicks Starks Woods.

It is significant that only in this portion of the novel does Hurston shift into what is ordinarily the primary theme of the black novelist: the exploration of racism and black reactions to it. The experiences of racism, as they occur here, are experiences that Janie and Tea Cake can meet and master because they meet them side by side.

As they await the onslaught of the hurricane which is, indirectly, to kill Tea Cake, he questions her about their life: "Ah reckon you wish now you had of stayed in yo' big house 'way from such as dis, don't yuh?" And she replies,

> Naw. We been tuhgether round two years. If you kin see de light at daybreak, you don't keer if you die at dusk. It's so many people never seen de light at all. Ah wuz fumblin' round and God opened de door. (pp. 130–131)

Following Tea Cake's death, Janie returns to Eatonsville, still wearing her overalls, to live out her life as she sees fit and to tell her story to her friend Pheoby. There is an ironic indication in the final pages of the novel that Janie, in her own liberation, has become a subversive influence, one that the village arbiters will be hard-pressed to cope with. For, as she concludes her story to Pheoby, her friend, who little more than two years earlier had been one of the strongest backers of the "respectable undertaker" marriage, breathes out shock and admiration:

> Lawd! Ah done growed ten feet higher from jus' listenin' tuh you, Janie. *Ah ain't satisfied wid mahself no mo'*. Ah means tuh make Sam take me fishin' wid him after this. (p. 158, Italics mine.)

Women's Lib has come to Eatonsville, Florida, and Sam Watson, Pheoby's husband, and the other men, will probably find that it takes a little getting used to, just as the world of 1975 finds that the various Liberation groups take a little getting used to.

But in the final analysis, they will probably make it, for as Zora Neale Hurston recognized, the real enemy of progress is not hostility; it is mental inertia, masquerading as hostility or ridicule.

Joe Starks' initial plan for a post office in Eatonsville, for instance,

> irritated Hicks and he didn't know why. He was the average mortal. It troubled him to get used to the world one way and then suddenly have it turn different. He wasn't ready to think of colored people in post offices yet. He laughed boisterously. (p. 35)

Yet the laughter notwithstanding, Eatonsville got its post office, and the world, and even Hicks, were none the worse for it.

*Notes*

1. Helen M. King, "The Black Woman and Women's Lib.," *Ebony*, March 1971, p. 68.
2. King, p. 75.
3. Zora Neale Hurston, *Their Eyes Were Watching God* (New York: Fawcett World Library, 1969), p. 96. Hereafter cited in the text.
4. Linda La Rue, "The Black Movement and Women's Liberation," *The Black Scholar*, May 1970, p. 36.
5. "Letter to the Editor," *Ebony*, May 1971, p. 20.

## HENRY LOUIS GATES, JR.
### "A Negro Way of Saying"

*New York Times Book Review*, April 21, 1985, pp. 1, 43–45

Zora Neale Hurston's last encounter with her dying mother, as described in *Dust Tracks on a Road* (1942), is one of the most moving passages in autobiography. "As I crowded in, they lifted up the bed and turned it around so that Mama's eyes would face east," Hurston writes. "I thought that she looked to me as the head of the bed reversed. Her mouth was slightly open, but her breathing took up so much of her strength that she could not talk. But she looked up at me, or so I felt, to speak for her. She depended on me for a voice." We can begin to understand the rhetorical distance that separated Hurston from her fellow writers if we compare this passage to a similar scene depicted just three years later by Richard Wright, who was dominant among Hurston's black male contemporaries and her chief rival. In *Black Boy*, a memoir of his childhood, Wright wrote: "Once, in the night, my mother called me to her bed and told me that she could not endure the pain, and she wanted to die. I held her hand and begged her to be quiet. That night I ceased to react to my mother; my feelings were frozen."

Hurston represents her final moments with her mother as a search for a voice. Wright attributes to a similar experience a certain "somberness of spirit that I was never to lose," one that "grew into a symbol in my mind, gathering to itself . . . the poverty, the ignorance, the helplessness." Few authors in the black tradition are more dissimilar than these two. Wright reigned as one of the predominant authors of the 1940's; Hurston's fame reached its zenith in 1942 with a cover story in the *Saturday Review of Literature* proclaiming the success of *Dust Tracks on a Road*. In 1950 she was discovered working as a maid in a fashionable section of Miami; in 1960 she died penniless in a welfare home in St. Lucie County, Fla.

How was Hurston—the recipient of two Guggenheim Fellowships and the author of four novels, a dozen short stories, two musicals, two books on black mythology, dozens of essays and a prizewinning autobiography—lost from all but her most loyal followers for two full decades? There is no easy answer to this question. It is clear, however, that the enthusiastic responses Hurston's work engenders today were not shared by several of her black male contemporaries. In reviews of *Mules and Men* (1935), *Their Eyes Were Watching God* (1937) and *Moses: Man of the Mountain* (1939), Sterling A. Brown, Richard Wright and Ralph Ellison condemned her work as "socially unconscious" and derided her "minstrel technique." Of *Moses*, Ellison concluded, "for Negro fiction, it did nothing." Hurston's mythic realism, lush and dense with a lyrical black idiom, was regarded as counterrevolutionary by the proponents of social realism, and she competed with Wright, Ellison and Brown for the right to determine the ideal fictional mode for representing Negro life. She lost the battle but may yet win the war.

In a marvelous example of what Freud might call the return of the repressed, Hurston has been rediscovered in a manner unprecedented in the black literary tradition. Several black women writers, among them some of the most accomplished in America today, are repeating, imitating or revising her narrative strategies. In the same way that Leon Forrest, James Alan McPherson, Ernest Gaines, Ishmael Reed, John Wideman and David Bradley are literary heirs of Ralph Ellison, so Alice Walker, Toni Morrison, Toni Cade Bambara, Gloria Naylor and Jamaica Kincaid, among others, seem to have grounded their fictions in the works of Zora Neale Hurston. While black male writers have ardently denied a connection to those who came before them, Hurston's daughters acknowledge her influence. They are a tradition within the tradition—voices that are black and women's.

Alice Walker's choice of diction and character development in *The Color Purple*, published in 1982, extends potentials Hurston registered in her 1937 novel *Their Eyes Were Watching God*. Since 1975, when Miss Walker published "In Search of Zora Neale Hurston," a moving account of her search for and discovery of her own literary lineage and Hurston's grave, contemporary readers have been treated to a feast of the formerly forgotten writer's words in re-edited versions of her works and in two sustained literary biographies. Of these publications, none are more important to reassessing Hurston's standing than Robert Hemenway's new edition of

*Dust Tracks on a Road* and Blyden Jackson's edition of her third novel, *Moses: Man of the Mountain*.

Mr. Hemenway, a professor of English at the University of Kentucky and the author of a superb Hurston biography, has restored three chapters that were either heavily revised for or deleted from the autobiography when it was first published. In these chapters Hurston gives us, among other things, her full critique of racial chauvinism, imperialism, neocolonialism and economic exploitation.

Even Hurston's most devoted readers have had difficulty understanding some conservative aspects of her politics—particularly her disapproval of the United States Supreme Court decision outlawing racial segregation in public schools. However, the restored version of the chapter entitled "Seeing the World as It Is" reveals that Hurston questioned "race consciousness"—"It is a deadly explosive on the tongues of men"—because she viewed it as being on a continuum with Nazism. She also argued that Hitler's transgression in subjugating neighboring countries was that he treated Europeans just as Europeans had treated their colonial subjects in Africa, Asia and Latin America. She devotes much of this chapter to a critique of neocolonialism: "One hand in somebody else's pocket and one on your gun, and you are highly civilized. Your heart is where it belongs—in your pocketbook. . . . Democracy, like religion, never was designed to make our profits less." Virtually overnight Hurston's politics have become so much more complex and curious. One wonders what Wright would have thought had he read this restored material.

Not only was Hurston more "political" than we believed, but—according to this edition—she was a decade older as well. When she enrolled in Howard University in 1918, she was not 17 years old; she was 27. And when she died broken in spirit and health in 1960, she not only looked to be a women of 69, she *was*. These two facts are certain to generate all sorts of reconsiderations of Hurston's place in the black literary tradition, most, I would imagine, to her benefit.

Mr. Hemenway, in an introduction that is much too brief, explains that *Dust Tracks* is full of lacunas, silences and political compromises that are at odds with sentiments expressed in Hurston's private correspondence and elsewhere. Hurston, he maintains, dons a mask of style that "dazzles, capturing the subtlety, energy, and rhythm of southern black idiom." But even her capacity to capture the black vernacular voice in her writing fails, Mr. Hemenway argues, because "style . . . becomes a kind of camouflage, an escape from articulating the paradoxes of her personality." In Mr. Hemenway's opinion, the book fails as an autobiography because "the private Zora Neale Hurston . . . never actually becomes one with the famous black novelist and anthropologist" and "because it is a text deliberately less than its author's talents, a text diminished by her refusal to provide a second or third dimension to the flat surfaces of her adult images."

Rereading Hurston, I was struck by how *conscious* her choices were. The explicit and the implicit, the background and the foreground, what she states and what she keeps to herself—these, it seems to me, reflect Hurston's reaction to traditional black male autobiographies (in which, "in the space where sex should be," as one critic says, we find white racism) and to a potentially hostile readership. As Lyndall Gordon says of Virginia Woolf, "the unlovable woman was always the woman who used words to effect. She was caricatured as a tattle, a scold, a shrew, a witch." Hurston, who had few peers as a wordsmith, was often caricatured by black male writers as frivolous, as the fool who "cut the monkey" for voyeurs and pandered to the rich white women who were her patrons. I believe that for protection, she made up significant parts of herself, like a masquerader putting on a disguise for the ball, like a character in her fictions. Hurston *wrote* herself just as she sought in her works to rewrite the "self" of "the race." She revealed her imagination as it sought to mold and interpret her environment. She censored all that her readership could draw upon to pigeonhole or define her life as a synecdoche of "the race problem."

Hurston's achievement in *Dust Tracks* is twofold. First, she gives us a *writer's* life—rather than an account of "the Negro problem"—in a language as "dazzling" as Mr. Hemenway says it is. So many events in the book were shaped by the author's growing mastery of books and language, but she employs both the linguistic rituals of the dominant culture and those of the black vernacular tradition. These two speech communities are the sources of inspiration for Hurston's novels and autobiography. This double voice unreconciled—a verbal analogue of her double experiences as a woman in a male-dominated world and as a black person in a non-black world—strikes me as her second great achievement.

Many writers act as if no other author influenced them, but Hurston freely describes her encounter with books, from Xenophon in the Greek through Milton to Kipling. Chapter titles and the organization of the chapters themselves reflect this urge to testify to the marvelous process by which the writer's life has been shaped by words. "The Inside Search" and "Figure and Fancy" reveal the workings of the youthful Hurston's mind as she invented fictional worlds, struggled to find the words for her developing emotions and learned to love reading. "School Again," "Research" and "Books and Things" recount her formal education, while "My People! My People!"—printed in its original form for the first time—unveils social and verbal race rituals and customs with a candor that shocks even today. Hurston clearly saw herself as a black woman writer and thinker first and as a specimen of Negro progress last. What's more, she structured her autobiography to make such a reading inevitable.

Here is an example of the verdant language and the twin voices that complement each other throughout *Dust Tracks*: "There is something about poverty that smells like death. Dead dreams dropping off the heart like leaves in a dry season and rotting around the feet; impulses smothered too long in the fetid air of underground caves. The soul lives in a sickly air. People can be slave-ships in shoes," Elsewhere she analyzes idioms used by a culture "raised on simile and invective. They know how to call names," she concludes, then lists "'gator-faced," "box-ankled," "puzzle-gutted," "shovel-footed." "It is an everyday affair," she writes, to hear someone described as having "eyes looking like skint-ginny nuts, and mouth looking like a dish-pan full of broke-up crockery!"

Immediately after the passage about her mother's death, she writes: "The Master-Maker in His Making had made Old Death. Made him with big, soft feet and square toes. Made him with a face that reflects the face of all things, but neither changes itself, nor is mirrored anywhere. Made the body of death out of infinite hunger. Made a weapon of his hand to satisfy his needs. This was the morning of the day of the beginning of things."

Language in these passages is not merely "adornment," which Hurston called a key black linguistic practice; rather, sense and sound are perfectly balanced. She says the thing in

the most meaningful manner without being cute or pandering to a condescending white readership, as Wright thought. She is "naming" emotions, as she says, in a private, if culturally black, language.

The unresolved tension between Hurston's two voices suggests that she fully understood the principles of modernism. Hers is a narrative strategy of self-division, the literary analogue of the hyphen in "Afro-American," the famous twoness W. E. B. Du Bois said was characteristic of the black experience. Hurston uses the two voices to celebrate both the psychological fragmentation of modernity and the black American. Hurston—the "real" Zora Neale Hurston whom we long to locate in this book—dwells in the silence that separates these two voices: she is both and neither, bilingual and mute. This brilliant strategy, I believe, helps explain why so many contemporary critics and writers can turn to her works again and again and be repeatedly startled at her artistry.

I wrote at the outset that Hurston's works have served as models that a new generation of black women writers have revised. Who in the black tradition did Hurston revise? Who were her formal influences? Blyden Jackson's insightful introduction to *Moses: Man of the Mountain* not only restores to us this important allegorical novel but helps us understand much about Hurston's influences.

The novel translates the Moses myth into the black tradition, creating a Moses who is an accomplished hoodoo man. Though allegorical, the novel is also a satire of, as Mr. Jackson writes, the "regrettably wide and deep division in loyalties among [the black] upper class, its black bourgeoisie, and the Negro masses from whom [Hurston's] folklore came." Mr. Jackson, a professor of English at the University of North Carolina, writes that *Moses* is unique in the black tradition because mythology not only informs the structure of the novel but assumes that structure as well. In other words, Hurston creates, or re-creates, a myth, the myth of a black Moses. She *signifies* on the Moses legends—she parodies and revises them, making them at once black and an allegory of black history in the West. The myth and allegory in *Moses* protect her tale from reduction to propaganda, just as her disguise in *Dust* shields her life from the same fate. These tactics would later change the direction of the black literary tradition.

Ralph Ellison wrote of *Moses* that *Green Pastures*, the melodramatic, widely popular play that depicted an all-black heaven, had challenged Hurston to do for Moses what it had done for Jehovah. But Hurston did it artistically rather than melodramatically. Mr. Hemenway reminds us that Freud published two controversial essays on Moses' Egyptian origins a year before Hurston wrote her *Moses*. Perhaps these shaped her writing. I believe, however, that Hurston's ultimate source was another black woman writer, Frances E. W. Harper, who published her own account in *Moses: A Story of the Nile* in 1869. Both works are allegories, both stress Moses' identity as a conjurer, and both utilize multiple voices.

If a generation of splendid writers has turned to Hurston for their voices, it is fitting that she herself quite probably turned to a black female literary ancestor. But Hurston's lasting and most original contribution is that she always found, as she put it, "a Negro way of saying" a thing and appropriated the English language and Western literary forms to create the black and female perspectives that her texts so splendidly embody. The publication of Hurston's complete uncollected works is what we actually need. But with the republication of these two books, we will not lose Hurston again.

# DAVID IGNATOW

## 1914–

The son of Jewish immigrants, David Ignatow was born in Brooklyn, New York, on February 7, 1914. When he was a child his father often read the stories of the great Russian writers to him. After graduating in 1932 from New Utrecht High School in Brooklyn, Ignatow attended Brooklyn College for two months before leaving to work in his father's bindery firm. He was very unhappy at his father's business and left in 1934 to take a job as a WPA reporter on the Newspaper Project. Later he worked at odd jobs, including positions as a shipyard handyman, a hospital night admitting clerk, and eventually as the editor of various publications. From 1949 to 1959 he was co-editor of the *Beloit Poetry Journal* and from 1962 to 1963 he was poetry editor of *The Nation*. Ignatow married Rose Graubart, an artist and writer, in 1937. They have two children. Ignatow has taught at the New School for Social Research (1964–65), University of Kentucky at Lexington (1965–66), University of Kansas at Lawrence (1966–67), Vassar College (1967–68), York College, CUNY (1969–76), and Columbia University (1969–75).

Ignatow's first collection of poetry, *Poems* (1948), shows the influence of William Carlos Williams, with whom the younger poet was friendly. Other volumes of poetry include *The Gentle Weight Lifter* (1955), *Say Pardon* (1961), *Figures of the Human* (1964), *Rescue the Dead* (1968), *Earth Hard* (1968), *Facing the Tree* (1975), *The Animal in the Bush: Poems on Poetry* (1977), *Tread the Dark* (1978), *Sunlight: A Sequence for My Daughter* (1979), *Whisper to the Earth* (1981), and *Leaving the Door Open* (1984). In addition to Williams, Ignatow cites Walt Whitman as a major influence on his writings. In 1973 he published *The Notebooks of David Ignatow*, which provide a close look at his life and the forces which motivate him to write. In 1954 he was forced to return to his father's business, which he ran until 1962, when he sold the firm. In 1980 *Open Between Us* was published; the book contains a collection of interviews with the poet with several critical works, including essays on William Carlos Williams. Although critical acclaim has been slow in coming, Ignatow has received numerous honors and awards, including in 1977 both the Bollingen Prize and the Wallace Stevens Fellowship. Ignatow resides in New York.

David Ignatow's poems are quiet, observant, matter-of-fact comments on ordinary urban life—or, more surprisingly, on Oedipus and Odysseus and Bathsheba and such—made by a man who seems individually sensitive and morally imaginative yet also, in a rather favorable sense, the man in the street. William Carlos Williams calls him "a first-rate poet . . . to whom language is like his skin," but really he's an unratable poet to whom language is like William Carlos Williams' skin. His methods are simple Williams, and his language—not at all rhetorical, close to an easy natural prose, but not prosaic—is that of a loving disciple. His temperament, unfortunately, lacks the heights and depths of Williams'. One respects and likes this poet, but one reads the poems with a mild blurred feeling of seeing them and not seeing them, a clear daze like water or late evening air; one isn't sure, sometimes, whether one is reading a new poem or rereading an old—one isn't even sure that one cares. The poems are sand that has almost been fused into glass; one feels, always, the lack of some last heat or pressure, concentration and individualization, that would have turned a photograph into a painting, a just observation into a poem. There is something humble and matter-of-course about the poems' methods: they are content, always, with an honest penny; and after a while the reader sees, rather in dismay, that it's bills he's interested in.—RANDALL JARRELL, *YR*, Sept. 1955, pp. 123–24

The world of David Ignatow's poetry is remarkable for the particularity of its detail. His attitude toward his art is summed up in "The Escapade," which must inevitably be quoted in discussing this book ⟨*Say Pardon*⟩:

> Poet and gangster reach in the dark,
> blind flashes reveal them.
> The dead collapse and the living scatter

for cover. Alone now, they think the street
is theirs and swiftly make their getaway,
in the left hand the haul, in the right
jammed in the driver's back the weapon
as they careen; and at the hideout set up
to repel the law—coming nearly as swift
sirening. In the inferno, started by both sides,
riddled, still seeking to shoot,
they sink to their deaths,
the haul beside them still theirs.

The idea of a poem as loot is particularly appropriate when applied to Ignatow's work, and it does not necessarily involve flirtation with the figure of the *poète maudit*. His poetry is grabbed from the everyday, particularly from the urban everyday, and from dream or fantasy. Such is the abruptness, the completeness of his snatch—as if he were scooping up the white and yolk of a broken egg in one swift movement—that the poems of fantasy are as clearly realized as his poems of fact.

In the simplicity of his language and the sureness of his movement he is reminiscent of William Carlos Williams, who in fact shares half the book's dedication. Now imitators of Williams are two a penny these days, and practically all imitate him at his most slapdash and indefensible. And yet he is one of the few poets of this century from whom there *are* still useful lessons to be learned: the lessons of how to find value in the actual and ordinary, of how to speak of it with lucidity, and of how to present it as one unhurried but continuous act of perception. Ignatow is the only poet I have come across who has absorbed these lessons, and the last of them is the one he has learnt the best. His poems are accurate records undelayed by any elements outside of the original perception. His perception is careful and modest, and his control over the movements prevents the language from becoming flat. Here is the poem called "Errand Boy II":

It was the way he went to pick up the carton
fallen to the gutter from his handtruck,
his arms outstretched, his body stooping
to the ground. I wondered at the smile,
weary and amused and so gentle withal,
as if this was what he had expected,
not for the first time and not
for the last time either.

The smile is inescapably there, loot from experience. At the same time one may note that though it is an impression certainly worth preserving, it is fragile in itself, and would have been no more than a detail in a poem like Williams' nineteenth in *Spring and All*, the one about the errand boys. Ignatow's publishers are being less than helpful when they claim that his poetry creates "a grand and tragic vision": the point is, surely, that his poetry does not even *set out* to be grand or tragic, but accomplishes something very different and probably of equal value within certain clearly defined limits. With accomplishment and consistency it documents an attitude of tenderness and care for the human world.—THOM GUNN, "Outside Faction," YR, June 1961, pp. 593–95

From his previous Wesleyan collection *Say Pardon*, I had decided that David Ignatow's poems were, as he called them there, "poems to tiredness / and disillusion, and to hope pinnacled / upon receding towers". There were no personations in that bleak urban landscape, no opposing selves—the poet spoke always in his own patient voice, save once as Walt Whitman in the Civil War hospitals, and then the good gray tone merely enforced Ignatow's own version of poetry as a maieutic enterprise: sapless, moralizing, necrological. This new volume ⟨*Figures of the Human*⟩ includes many poems—about half the book—from Ignatow's first two collections, though most of the historical or mythological pieces in the Cavafy mode have been dropped in favor of the tired businessman's reflections on social injustice and violence as a means of self-expression:

Whatever we do, whether we light
strangers' cigarettes—it may turn out
to be a detective wanting to know who is free
with a light on a lonely street nights—
or whether we turn away and get a knife
planted between our shoulders for our discourtesy . . .

But the new poems, while they continue the mixture as before—direct, even abrupt notations, paranoiac psychanda (seventeen of the twenty-nine pieces are concerned with violence, generally an attack from behind, in the shadows, by Someone with a Knife)—have reduced, to use the sauce-cook's word, this poet's meager means and major message to an obsessive *roux*. Their debt to William Carlos Williams is of a moral rather than a technical nature: it is evident from the complacency of this low style that the older poet afforded Ignatow a release rather than an influence. The imitation of action by the rhythms of speech, the concern to get it down as it happened, unmediated by formal devices, by rhetoric, produces, of course, its own rhetoric, a pseudo-speech with its own "literary" overtones:

No theory will stand up to a chicken's guts
being cleaned out, a hand rammed up
to pull the wriggling entrails,
the green bile and the bloody liver;
no theory that does not grow sick
at the odor escaping.

Here the tough-guy approach to the event obscures for the poet—and for the reader, it must be granted—the fallacy of the statement; the violent verbs and the subtle rhythm of that last line (I have quoted the poem entire) are so effective in presenting the action that we are almost convinced, until we realize that it is precisely theory, *only* theory, which will "stand up to" such operations, as the events of human history have proved in the last twenty-five years. If we ignore "theory"—by which I take Ignatow to mean the life of the mind, its methods and monsters—we are doomed to be destroyed by it. Thus Ignatow assumes his habitual nightmare of unprovoked and lethal assault as his own guilt, remote from ideas, from intellection.

You [the murderer] know comradeship
in our shared knowledge
in the anger that I feel towards you
and towards myself.

He is not really concerned, as he claims, with the events of human history, or even the history of chickens, for he does not regard events as part of a history, but as dreadful unitary devices, meaningless and mostly vicious, rising from the chaos within the self, exhibiting no design and allowing none to be imposed upon them:

A photo is taken of the family
enjoying the sunshine
and that night someone sneaks up
from behind in your flat
as you sit reading the papers
and clobbers you. You never
find out why or who, you just
lean back and die.
The sunshine is gone too,
the photograph gets into the news.
You bring up a family in three small rooms,
this crazy man comes along
to finish it off.

—RICHARD HOWARD, *Poetry*, July 1965, pp. 298–99

"All small things," as Gaston Bachelard's *The Poetics of Space* (1958) proposes, "must evolve slowly, and certainly a long period of leisure, in a quiet room, was needed to miniature the world. Also one must love space to describe it as minutely as though there were world molecules, to enclose an entire spectacle in a molecule of drawing." Bachelard sees the inclination to miniature as the opposite of intuitional perception which takes everything in at one glance, for "in looking at a miniature, unflagging attention is required to integrate all the detail." This "unflagging attention" forces the detachment of the artist from the normal world so that he resists his dissolving into surrounding atmosphere. In the case of Ignatow's miniatures, one critic is willing to posit their origin in a corollary to the love of space—the love of time—and in a proverbial motto of business that "time is money." Victor Contoski's "Time and Money" (1968) shows how Ignatow's awareness of time forms the subject of a number of poems and characterizes the style of the pieces as "short and to the point, like business letters. Contoski also indicates the presence in the work of something approximating Anderson's "imperial self," resulting perhaps from the detachment that must be part of an "unflagging attention." Contoski envisions Ignatow as wanting to play God: "He sees everything from the point of view of eternity, a mysterious eternity that offers him no consolation for his suffering."

Reviewers like Robert Bly and Louis Simpson, on the other hand, have noted the need for unusual concentration on the part of a reader if he is to respond to Ignatow's work, and Hayden Carruth's reviews of both *Figures of the Human*

(1964) and *Rescue the Dead* (1968) have called for an understanding of the dynamics of the small poem as a prerequisite to an appreciation of Ignatow's skills. Bly's sense of the situation is part of a larger complaint that readers generally do not know how to read poetry unless the ideas of the poem have been denuded enough and presented "under stark enough light" so that they can be grasped. While admitting an element of snobbery may have prompted a resistance to Ignatow's early work, Simpson describes the effect of the poems as an uncomfortable but necessary "drilling through asphalt." The reader is required to look at the collections of detail not as part of a superficial or sentimental cataloguing of ephemera that may include designs of Coca Cola bottles as well as histories of motion picture actors, but as something that shows these phenomena as affecting deeply the psyche of Americans, often as something that may substitute for or obscure the perception of real danger. Thus, Carruth's suggestion that for a proper appreciation of the poetry a reader begin with an understanding of the dynamics of small poems seems especially wise. In many ways, Ignatow's reinterpretation of the small, flat poem of Williams ideally illustrates both his peculiar world view and a pivotal change in the shift in sensibility from the post-modernism represented by Jarrell to that typified by the generation after.

By redirecting the emphasis of Williams' small poem away from marriage and into matters of succession and reinterpreting its scope to include urban and political matters, Ignatow touches on the principal concerns of both generations: how to succeed poets like Ezra Pound, T. S. Eliot, and William Carlos Williams; and how to achieve identity without undergoing dehumanization in a society that has gotten progressively urban, conformist, and impersonal. Bly's "Slipping toward the Instincts" (1968) somewhat deceptively notes that, although of the generation of John Berryman, Robert Lowell, and Karl Shapiro, none of these poets has defended his work. True, but Jarrell and William Meredith have both praised Ignatow's poetry, and Winfield Townley Scott was among the first to see the positive effects of concentration in the poems. William Carlos Williams even proposed that "the best of them . . . be printed on pulp and offered at Woolworth's, a dime a copy." Thus, when Bly contends that "it is men younger than Ignatow who have insisted that his poetry be reviewed and published," he ignores for polemical considerations what is common to Ignatow and his generation: the acceptance, as Jarrell calls it, of "Darwin, Marx, Freud and Co.," the importance of history, and the restatement of philosophical problems as psychological states. Bly misses thereby what may be the real attraction of readers to the small poem structure in addition to those stresses on daily recurrence and continuity that Ruskin, Pearce, and Ignatow have each maintained.

Critics have often asserted that smallness is part of the appeal of Emily Dickinson's poetry and, at the onset of his discussion of miniatures, Bachelard discourages a view that the tendency to smallness be thought of as geometric, "exactly the same thing in two similar figures, drawn to different scale." Such a "simple relativism of large and small," he maintains, belies the unequal conviction with which the imagination approaches the objects. Thus, a reader should not think of small poems as shrunken large poems or, as Ignatow's publisher had once, of their necessarily being parts in the creation of "a grand and tragic vision." Thom Gunn's review of *Say Pardon* (1961) rightly affirms, "the point is, surely, that [the] poetry does not even *set out* to be grand or tragic." Still, in regard to Ignatow's work, one would be as wrong to accept without qualification Bachelard's dismissal of the view that "the tiny

things we imagine simply take us back to childhood, to familiarity with toys and *the reality of toys*." There is in Ignatow's miniatures, as in Dickinson's, a tendency to oppose authority, to equate it and largeness—those "aristocrats of Greek society" that one accepts in childhood—but not quite to enter those encapsulations from ordinary life that one associates with toys and sometimes feels with miniatures.

In Ignatow's case, there is instead an open-endedness that Carruth's review of *Figures of the Human* describes as producing a "certain abruptness" when the poem ends just as "the reader is beginning to get interested." Carruth wisely questions "that going back over the poem again, even a dozen times, will make up for the foreshortening," but he does not suggest that the abruptness may be similar to that gnomic quality one gets from Miss Dickinson's poetry where, by having to resort to interpretation, the particulars of the poem are rendered universal and yet personal. Nor does he suggest that sense Ruskin writes of in regard to Gothic architecture when, at the moment the eye leaves one part of the structure, it lights upon another as interesting and where abruptness works to liberate the viewer into his next observation. Rather, despite a call for understanding the dynamics of small poems, Carruth's own manner of dealing with the situation is a "geometric" scaling down: "When I examine them closely to see what is missing— beginning, middle, or end—I find that I cannot make up my mind." He goes on to imagine the poems not as parts of some ongoing vision but as "complete in embryo; or, as Ignatow would no doubt prefer to say, in essence." The approach presupposes with no apparent explanation that the deliberately limited techniques and subject of an Ignatow poem may be extended at will with no appreciable loss of interest.—JEROME MAZZARO, "Circumscriptions : The Poetry of David Ignatow," *Salm*, Spring–Summer 1973, pp. 167–70

---

## ALFRED KAZIN
### "The Esthetic of Humility"

*American Poetry Review*, April–May 1974, pp. 14–15

> What is the price of Experience? do men buy it for a
>     song?
> Or wisdom for a dance in the street? No, it is bought
>     with the price
> Of all that a man hath, his house, his wife, his
>     children.
> Wisdom is sold in the desolate market where none
>     come to buy,
> And in the wither'd field where the farmer plows for
>     bread in vain.
>
>                                       (Blake: *The Four Zoas*)

In some ways it seems presumptuous to "review" the notebooks of David Ignatow. The book represents, it *is*, a man's whole life, with every kind of trouble this man has fought through—contentious immigrant parents, a disordered son, the struggle of a businessman maddened by anxiety, but struggling to keep erect and somehow to find the energy for writing poetry. The peculiar capacity of Jews for internalizing their long unhappy history, the peculiar ability of poets to locate the secret of their vocation in their private grief and terror, the forebodings of the depression generation about all the bloody history that has continued straight out of the crisis of the 1930s! Taken together, compounded by the anxiety that seems more and more necessary so that men can keep running against each other in the American system, nerve-torn by the grittiness of New York, the pages add up to a cruelly exemplary life, to a Book of Lamentations. A Poet And His Life, cry woe and woe again! There is so much unhappiness, frustration, emotional starvation, literary uncertainty reiterated in the book that at first, certainly, I found it unbearable. The *cri de coeur* not only reached me; it deafened me, at first, to the singularity of Ignatow's achievement.

My first thought was indeed that Ignatow has no humor, no associates outside business and his family, no subject matter in the actual world outside this anxious round, no magic, no fantasy. And Ignatow is indeed all too strikingly a man of feeling, living in a world of feeling. The burden of so much "feeling"—by which I also mean the generality and conventionality of many emotional reactions to his hard life—the problem (and so one to us) of a man living in what is too often exclusively a *world* of feeling—this can be overwhelming in its reiteration, and Ignatow certainly relies upon reiteration in order to make himself heard—by God, by the reader, by anyone out there in the silent dark that often surrounds him.

The trouble with having so much self-inflicted feeling, the trouble with *any* mental world too much pressed down with conscious "feeling," is that in our tightly organized mental hierarchy feeling seems to have no "solution," as indeed Ignatow is the first to complain in these pages. If "poetry makes nothing happen," as a much cooler customer than Ignatow said, too often the emotion that goes into poetry is not *happening*. It is just there, stuck on the page like a man's academic credentials. And when the emotions *are* happening, as in Ignatow's notebooks and better still in his poetry, the reader minds getting caught up, shaken up. Too vulnerable oneself, afraid of the assault, I found myself at first recoiling not so much from "emotion" as from the sometimes numbing consistency of Ignatow's writing, the repeated unrelieved quality that he brings to his notebook.

This consistency, this unrelievedness . . . amazing how rarely he spares himself or can divert himself. Page after page the same lament, the same sometimes whimsical bitterness, the attempt to recoil without seceding from one pitiless claim on him after another . . . All this becomes more graphic, ironically enough, since these are public "selections" from a private notebook and surely not as rough on us as the whole record would be. So all this presents an amazingly tight, rigorously severe and punishing picture of a man just held in thrall, of a man who feels that his life is not his own, of a classic compulsive, tragically internalized Jew. Ignatow is beset even by efforts that seem to present no redemption, and unlike so many with his problems, he does not even have conventional intellectual access to these problems. Neither Marx nor Freud nor any other messiah of intellect comes into this record with a helping hand.

Yet *The Notebooks of David Ignatow* become, after the first shock of much unrelieved suffering, a fascinating, even haunting book. These are not "brilliant" *cahiers*, in the French sense; although there are some wonderful insights (characteristically, they end up some passage that itself just teeters on the edge of the maudlin), the book has no intellectual originality or poet's wisdom in the style of Auden's criticism. And, despite the wealth of emotion in response to a harried New York life, Ignatow does not give us any "realistic," "novelistic" pictures of the desperately commonplace life that he has led as a businessman, father, husband. There are many shattering moments in these notebooks, but few actual portraits. He is terribly bound up in himself. One feels the blow after blow directed against Ignatow by "life," but the circumstances themselves are never illuminated. The fact is that Ignatow has been too closed in by his experience to force it to yield up what

another diarist would have done with this overwhelming experience.

Yet this sense of the overwhelming makes the book remarkable, very much as Ignatow's poetry does. Many of the passages are clearly arguments for a poem, a poem seems to get itself secretly written in the course of many a notebook entry, and the passages succeed each other, as Ignatow's poems regularly do, by falling into the same cadence, manner, issue. This desperate sincerity, this sometimes unbelievable humility of manner, is Ignatow's witting or unwitting way of making something of his life. Largely, I would guess, on the basis of what Santayana called "animal faith," or the sheer intuition that can present itself to a writer by the nature of his experience: that the experience alone will bring him home to the form he needs in order to redeem his experience in the form of art.

Ignatow's life, he says it over and over, has been bitter to an extreme. He feels himself to have been a victim. Yet if we ask why the notebooks, like the poems of which they are the worldly shells (and with which they are connected in ways far more intimate than poets' prose usually does), do succeed as a valuable and even stirring continuum of experience, the answer is that Ignatow is not only a slave to his humility but writes out of it. His good faith is complete. His sincerity is primitive to a degree. Because of the frightening poverty of spiritual life that surrounds him, Ignatow has stumbled, as only a lower-class American can, on the belief that the insistency of his experience, the untranscendable violations that hold it back, are actually enough to carry the lines into passages and the passages into poetry.

The esthetic of humility, which relies on the sufficiency of one's experience but also sees that experience as the only power-force or divinity around, is in the American tradition. Whitman first found it; Dreiser mastered it in the crushing irresistible rhythms of his narratives; Williams (who was more observer of the lower-class world than participant) *imitated* it. This esthetic (which one writer can never learn from another) relies on the idea that there is a rhythm to *your* experience (not just your conscious subject matter), a pattern donated to you by the motion you can detect within your experience.

One form of humility is not having many writers to talk to. Ignatow's prose style is sometimes immigrant-genteel, often self-consciously lofty. The sum of his self-educated literary manners is sometimes happily preposterous, idiosyncratic. It takes you over by its very faults. It forces itself upon you by its terrifying openness. I want! I want! So again and again the reader finds himself falling in with Ignatow's cadences, empathizing with him past sense, certainly past his own faint aversion from so much unrelieved suffering. Yet as Ignatow says, explaining the hold his "troubles" have on him, and so, grindingly, on us:

> That is what really bothers you, having troubles and
> troubles and troubles with nothing to show for them.
> You're against that and you rebel and that is what
> writing means to you, to get all those troubles on
> paper to show how worthwhile they've been when
> they can bring such words that take in so much and
> sound so full of life that people begin to fall in love
> with their troubles all over again . . .

Or this, where the awkwardness is genuine enough to make us start, and where the impact of the man's emotions on himself is actually far more interesting than what he says, as concept or "deliverance," *about* himself:

> I'm beginning to think that the something equivocal
> in my character is the cause of my obscure fate in
> poetry. The inability to make a strong stand. I'm just

happy to get along and suffer for myself until I get a poem I can call good, usually about my suffering. It's a small, intense, self-circuited world. At least I'm sure it's mine and that's all, man making himself suffer in order to write and writing about it. Important. Yes, for the reason that there doesn't seem to be any other way of getting the poem done except through and by suffering. Depleting oneself of energy in order to put it all into a poem. The act of depleting oneself is one of suffering, the drawing out of the energy, the tension between the reluctant body and the stubborn will coupled to an excited mind in order to say we have produced something unusual.

What impresses me there is not the "self-knowledge," which is correct enough so far as it goes within the conventional psychology (even though Ignatow draws so sharply on his own resources). It is the fact that with passage after passage of such homely, sometimes touchingly unreal, attempts to reason his "suffering" out, the important thing is the spell his life has on him and so on the journal-like continuum of moods, laments, startled observations, accidents and near-catastrophes that has put his life into his poetry. In Ignatow's *Poems 1934–1969* we really get a *book*, put together from single poems, rather than a selection of poems. The poems in this book are amazingly uniform in quality, but they make a book, they become a successful long poem that could have been called *New York*, and is indeed a better long poem than *Paterson*. Precisely because of Ignatow's docility, the modest, the sometimes unbearable self-denial, of the city poet who has come out of so much suffering, and is so much up against it still that line after line is really an attempt to propitiate the Gods.

Ignatow is not cursed, as so many flashier poets are today, by a feeling of the *sacredness* of his experience. Unlike Ginsberg, say, Ignatow has never identified his life itself with sex, least of all with the party-line omnipresence of one kind of sex. Instead, unbelievable man, terribly correct man, he writes a poem called "Poem,"

> I am tired of you
> as I am tired of myself.
> There is a mountain I am climbing
> in the dark,
> and when I reach its top
> the dark will be there.

Poem after poem of this "climbing," and we get a book, a real long poem! When Poe said that a long poem is impossible, he really meant (knowing that EAP could write either about his damnation or professionally weave spells) that a long poem called for too much guile, too much professional manner, and above all too much palaver about the divine mission of poetry, very good fill-in for a poet like Pound, obsessed by "History," but too literary to describe anything real in it.

Ignatow lacks guile. He lacks, from any contemporary point of view, cleverness . . . and a passionate beat. He lacks knowledge of the world of power, of objective political relations, of the "big world." He is too careful in his lines, too worried, too obedient even as a poet—though his only freedom has been in tracing into form the twists and turns of his own experience. He is a slave not just to his own family but to the myth of necessary suffering. He has literary "dreams" of becoming something he is not, and he sometimes gets maudlin about this. As when he says:

> What is the secret of my heart? An absolute despair of myself ever becoming what I dream is my rightful role, the national poet of America, the central voice, the one who speaks for the millions and who speaks to the person, who makes listening a must by the soul

of his voice, the voice that brings men to alleviate one after another of their misery, in bondage to one another, that soothes the difficult life and opens a way to freedom. The slaves among us are familiar. They are us. The main and only theme of our times is man's enslavement to man, man's necessary bondage to man. To write about this is to be angry and tragic, filled with futility and tears and utter loss of self, for the self is bound over to the other self, the one that obeys and serves and is cheerful doing it. There can be no other choice but to be cheerful or else the loss is complete. There is no way out of this cheerful drek except this writing in a book.

The ideas are commonplace, the writing is threadbare to the point of vulgarity (*who makes listening a must by the sound of his voice*), yet by the testimony and accumulation of his book, Ignatow is right. This is a life itself. To paraphrase what Blake said in *Jerusalem* to the Jews—"If Humility is Christianity, you, o Ignatow, are a true believer—and artist."

## RICHARD LAVENSTEIN
### From "A Man with a Small Song"

*Parnassus: Poetry in Review*, Fall–Winter 1975, pp. 211–22

Over thirty years ago David Ignatow proclaimed himself "a man with a small song." Now, many years and several books of poetry later, it remains a slogan of accurate description, a motto of modesty which, even as a banner (and how our poets love them), bespeaks a man nervous and uncertain, worried about the dynamics of lyric rather than length, asking finally to be judged gently by individual acts of poetic effort and their inevitable by-product, sheer accumulation. And so for several decades David Ignatow has tenaciously continued to sing, building up that storehouse of songs which every poet hopes will rescue his single works from the relative obscurity of improbably titled magazines like *Shankpainter Ten, Mouth*, and *Unmuzzled Ox*. Several collections of Ignatow's work, and particularly the substantial volume with the tersely informative rubric *Poems: 1934–1969*, have helped to rescue his reputation from the icy fringes of literary disregard and to make him if not a commanding presence, certainly a recognizable landmark in an often bewilderingly amorphous landscape. ⟨. . .⟩

*The Notebooks of David Ignatow*, which appears to be a companion piece to *Poems: 1934–1969*, or to its reduced and revised version, *Selected Poems*, is a logical starting place, allowing us an intimate look into the growth of the poet's mind and craft. Covering the years between 1934 and 1971, with two gaps between 1934 and 1950, the *Notebooks* gives us the raw material—a dense collection of private deliberations, tormented poetic musings, and nearly endless anecdotes of gloom, misery, and madness—which have often inspired Ignatow's poems. While its 375 pages have been reduced and readied for the public from a thirteen-hundred-page manuscript, it is still a very long book. Diary readers, devotees of shrewd or irreverent *cahiers* in the manner of Gide, Valéry or even saturnine Camus, will probably be disappointed, however. Others, who may remember and admire the subtleties of Henry James's notebooks, Virginia Woolf's diary, or Edmund Wilson's copious memories and confessions (at their undisputed best in the masterful *Upstate*), may respond to Ignatow's notebooks with dismay. Gone is an attempt at narrative organization or pointed observation. Except for the author, no "characters" or personalities stand out about whom we know much; nor are we offered highbrow gossip, brilliant *aperçus*, scurrilous and mordant insight into the state of letters, or sexual revelations by which we discover that everyone was at one time or other in bed with everyone else. What we have instead, all under Ralph Mills's editorial tutelage, are Ignatow's rambling descriptions of business life, overstuffed theorizings on aesthetics, frequent exclamations of suffering counterpointed by lamentations on the human condition, and confessions about the poet's relationship with parents, wife, and children. Into this austerely alembicated scrapbook a few unclassifiable diversions manage to slip in; one complete entry reads, "A pear is sliced in half."

But for the greater part of its bulk, *The Notebooks of David Ignatow* gives us the history of a working man who is also a poet, one determined against odds to preserve a Whitmanesque variousness and integrity in his desperate life and work that will give eloquent proof to the expression, "My life and poetry are one." As with many poets, that oracular statement exists as credo—a particularly necessary one for a man whose days have been divided between the business world he hated yet was forced to participate in and the creative life which is his real sustenance. Like many of Ignatow's epigrammatic remarks, it is also a statement of self-defense, guardedly asking us to tread lightly, remembering that his poems are won by blood, sweat, and many tears. The unrelievedly stark prose of the *Notebooks* attempts to explore the conundrum, or what appears more like the suppurating wound, between Art and Life. Asked to approve yet forbidden to judge these public-private documents, the reader is set at once on a treadmill of apologias: the life is an excuse for the poetry, the poetry an excuse for the life, and at the end we're left in an aesthetic and metaphysical lurch. At best the *Notebooks* urge our commiserations to go out to Ignatow for years of hardship, suffering, stifled desires. At worst we become overwhelmed and even deadened by these same sorrows, by a life that often seems more drab than tragic. Holding on to our lapels or shaking us by the collar, insisting, as Nigel Dennis once said, that "the whole fun of pain is in the sharing of it," Ignatow exhibits a dangerous disregard for pleasure and posterity—that which, according to Chamfort, "judges men of letters by their works alone, without considering the positions they have held. The principle seems to be 'what they have done, not what they have been.'"

But what Ignatow has been, and here he reminds us of Whitman and Williams, is at the heart of his poetry and therefore his journals. His version of the poetry of humanity stems from a life spent not among intellectuals (or academics, whom he treats with contempt) but among factories, laborers, noisy machines, cranky salesmen, and the oppressively grim squalor of New York City. As it emerges in the *Notebooks* the story begins with Ignatow's early difficulties with domineering parents who, while trying to push him into his father's small bindery business, conspired to thwart his literary ambitions. Along with this ordeal went a burden of financial struggle, a life split between scrambling for the elusive dollar and trying to find time to write, publish, and become renowned:

> It would be a pleasure now to sleep but I would feel guilty of neglecting my career as a poet. It bothers me like something false, this idea of a career. I have wanted my writing to come to me not from outside pressure but it seems inevitable that the fear of being forgotten as a poet, my name not appearing in magazines, etc., is one stimulus to writing, while the most important one of all, the one by which I should guide myself, the poem shaping itself in my thoughts, is made subordinate to my ambition as a poet.

The cost of this ambition was high. As Ignatow openly admits in his journal, his preoccupation with literary success made his behavior irascible and erratic, eventually aiding the onset of his young son's mental illness. Already knowing the answer, Ignatow asks himself:

> Was poetry worth this child's decline into madness? He found relief from me, me a poet raging day and night, filled with hatreds and alarms and suspicious thoughts to kill, maim, abandon, seduce, lose or frighten into bondage others to my use for my advancement hand in hand with conscious scruples and further rages of regret that it must be this way.

This passage and others like it, despite florid and clumsy prose, provide the most memorable reflections in Ignatow's journals. They record the authentic voice of anguish probing mercilessly into the price of our dreams and demonstrate that a life lived in the service of art is not necessarily benign. Like their poetry, the evils poets do live after them.

Ambition versus family, first as the struggle develops between the young poet and his parents, and then in its ironic reappearance between Ignatow and his son is a theme running through the *Notebooks* with depressing constancy. Ultimately it is stupefying. What Ignatow proclaims as high tragedy— "Nothing is true to me but tragedy. As I look back on my life, it is the perfect example of a tragic existence"—loses its force because of incessant repetition. In the end we have an idle, high flown rhetoric, a litany of grumblings:

> I'm just a battered piece of junk, if that is what the world looks like to most people. I've had so many things happen to me that I can't recall what I was supposed to be doing in the first place and why. I'm just full of holes, dents, cuts, and scrapings. . . .
> I have learned one thing: nobody wants to see you crying for long.
> In New York to make love is to stick your cock in a meat grinder with your face grimacing in pain that is called joy.
> My breath stinks, my armpits smell, my stomach aches. I am not what I thought I was.

And so on. These journal entries soon begin to sound like the meditations of a man who has had a lifetime of bad days at the office. Unfortunately, made uncomfortably public, they gratuitously affront the reader under the protective aegis of "confession," that modern day license which allows everyone to spout blather as long as it looks like honest blather. Meanwhile, we are left with a dull book with no reticences left to exploit, a cornucopia of despair justified by the shrill cry of "Truth!" But it is the kind of truth that once prompted Oscar Wilde's wise quip, "Telling the truth makes us burn with the desire to convince our audience, whereas telling a lie affords ample leisure to study the results."

An awful truth aside, the ostensible purpose of Ignatow's journals, and the cause for which Ralph Mills most vigorously argues in his Introduction, is the insight we get into the poetry. As I read this interminable book I tried to remember Mills's promise, believing, or at least hoping, that insight was just around the corner. Instead I found only laborious reflections on our contemporary Grub Street lecturer's perennial topic, "the creative process." If all this sounds ungenerous, consider, for example, the way a long and semi-mystical rumination on darkness and light and darkness visible turns into a poem of equally inscrutable austerities:

> Climbing pitifully, climbing in the dark this world, bent, exhausted, sweating and nearly dead, but climbing as long as strength exists to move an arm, leg muscle, for to stand still is to believe darkness is everywhere, that darkness is the world, that we are dark and are born to die in dark, so that the spirit that

knows better grows bitter and dies and man shrivels up and blows away as a cinder. Nothing can make man believe in this. He and the spirit are one. They are one and the source . . . so that man may sing, feeling free in the dark, giving himself the fruits of it, his joy in himself, and the dark is what casts the light upon himself and he may see and give out the radiance of his joy by which he lights his way, and there is no more darkness but the way and the way is the salvation of his spirit that has been suffering up till now.

Now for the poem that follows:

> I think that when the yellow pillow
> is thrown against the blue wall
> God is in the room, for I know
> there can be no ultimate evil—
> when as an argument ensues
> yellow is shown in glowing contrast
> to deep blue.
>
> ("Consolation")

A total of twenty-four poems are written this way, though I am not certain "poem" is the proper term for these odd ditties. As for that lofty prose, it seems a sure cure for insomnia.

Vehemently asserting Ignatow's importance, one of the blurbs on the jacket of *Selected Poems* demands, "He must be read." The outside of the book bullies us like a threatening mother telling her son to eat his vegetables, while the contents, arranged by editor Robert Bly, promise the variety and surprises of a box of chocolates. In an effort to show Ignatow's inclusive range Bly catalogues the poems according to ill-defined and noxiously titled sections, among them: "What Clings like the Odor of a Goat," "The Struggle between the Statistical Mentality and Eros," and "A New Theme." The last one perplexes even the editor who created it: "I don't understand the theme very well . . . I can't describe the theme very well either, only allude to its edges." These frank remarks are subsequently proven. The other introductory sections, which do some elaborate if unsatisfactory explaining, commit more banalities than seems possible in such short space. With a wonderfully constant tone of low-keyed hysteria Bly notes that "A man watching television gets to know the television personalities, but they do not know him." "We know that behind every civilized person a primitive man is standing with his arms out. . . ." "It's clear that in our society, the demonic is generally repressed. . . ." "Doing violence is a way of proving that you can still affect others. . . ." Besides this Cliff's Notes version of civilization and its discontents, other recondite musings tease us with the semblance of meaning: "If the psyche insists that we shall all be friends, that we are friends, immediately cemetaries must be laid out for all those who will die soon of murder, rape and insanity."

For the reader of Ignatow's poetry Bly's comments are no more foolish than his arbitrary principles of selection. Because most of Section II ("Working for a Living") and Section V ("Living in the City") could be collapsed under the heading of Section IV ("The Struggle between the Statistical Mentality and Eros"), many of the poems break the promise of variety, doing little service to the poet. Thus "Pricing," a splendid poem of stern subtleties about Ignatow's father buying a gravestone for his (dead) wife, is lost in the dismal shuffle of "Living in the City," a section of consummately uninteresting work. "Pricing" has nothing to do with living in the city. Its themes are the difficulty of expression and an old man's fear and stifled familial affection, both of which are subjected to circumspect reflection:

> . . . an old man who has lost his wife,
> his only companion, and himself soon to go,
> alone now, living among strangers,
> though they were his kin.

"Pricing" ends neatly with the father reduced to "saying something hackneyed," then taking refuge in the material solace of tangible measurement: ". . . until at home / finally with his daughter he discussed / the price and the stone's color / and its width." That last word "width" is, for a grave marker, the perfect dimension on which to dwell (too narrow and cramped for that last resting place? sufficiently wide enough for two plots?) and summarizes the latent terrors that stir the poem's life.

"Pricing," with its unaffected correspondence between event and language, fulfills the poetic aims Ignatow sets for himself and which he inherits from William Carlos Williams. Like Williams, Ignatow in his poetry shuns the exotic to concentrate on the readily observable details of our daily lives. It is an attempt at turning the common into something magically ingratiating and vivid. Rushing for a bus, watching the evening news, talking to salesmen, shouting at business associates, offering consolation to a friend—all are little situations meant to strike us with the force of heightened *déjà vu*. In some of the best lyrics in *Selected Poems*, "Nice Guy," "A Guided Tour through the Zoo," "The Business Life," "In Place of Love," "For My Daughter" (the last a tangential exploration to "Pricing") the reader tags along as a fellow participant, sympathetic, his thoughts turned toward familiar yet renovated perceptions. The collective dream of the poetry, distilled in "The Errand Boy I," is to "lie down in a sleep that is a dream / of completion," which is not necessarily to catch the bus as it is driving away but to stop running after it, to simply turn the eyes "upwards to all things."

But sometimes, with his eyes fixed on the sky Ignatow forgets to look where he is going. Such poems as "I Want," "I See a Truck," "With the Door Open," and "The Derelict" remain inert, annoyingly smug grotesqueries which only full quotation can do justice to:

> You were rotten
> and I sliced you into pieces
> looking for a wholesome part,
> then threw you into the street.
> You were eaten by a horse,
> dipping his head to nibble
> gently at the skin.
> I heard later he became violently ill,
> died and was shipped off
> to be processed. I think about it
> and write of the good in you.
>
> ("To an Apple")

In "The Bagel," a poor imitation in reverse of Williams' "The Term," Ignatow writes a poem that wishes to express exuberance yet delivers only aborted gestures of ludicrous self-satisfaction: "Like a bagel, and strangely happy with myself." Beginning in chagrin and attempting to move toward joy ("I stopped to pick up the bagel / rolling away in the wind, / annoyed with myself / for having dropped it / . . . and I found myself doubled over / rolling down the street / head over heels. . . ."), Ignatow gets lost in the triviality of his few images. Besides, is it possible to write a poem about a bagel and not be writing comedy, regardless of intent? It reminds me of the numerous "unpoetical" subjects Dr. Johnson railed against during the eighteenth century and his deflating query about Grainger's "The Sugar-Cane, A Poem": "What could he make of a sugar cane? One might as well write 'The Parsley-Bed, A Poem.'"

Other lyrics present other problems. "While I Live" sins by that already archaic bathos which sprang up in great abundance during the sixties, only to be mercifully dismissed: "I want my trees to love me / and my grass to reach up to the porch / where I am no one but the end of time, / as I stand waiting for renewal in my brain." I'm not certain about nature but poetry abhors a vacuum. Here the problem is not "no ideas but in things" but simply no ideas. *Selected Poems* suffers too much from this sort of intellectual slackness, which gets worse as the poems become increasingly ambitious, or, to use that maligned word, "philosophical." Too bad there are not more poems like "East Bronx" in the collection, a surprising little lyric which turns nightmare ("in the street two children sharpen knives against the curb. . . .") into dream ("two tortoises on an island in the Pacific- / always alone and always / the sun shining. . . .") through an almost miraculous recording of image and imagination / ("Parents leaning out the window / above gaze and think and smoke. . . .")

In Ignatow's latest volume, *Facing the Tree*, the faults most damaging to the poet's work recur in plentiful supply. Seeking to approximate a mood of somnambulistic calm (in his journals Ignatow is always in a hurry, and therefore always wanting sleep), too many of the poems, particularly in their last lines, dwindle into hazy non-conclusion. Not open-endedness but entropy makes them go flaccid, as in "Autumn I," where the poet concedes that "Having nowhere to go, / nothing in particular to do, / I keep marching." So does the poem. Characteristically, one poem is entitled "Sh, This Poem Wants to Say Something" (I forget what) while an untitled poem turns out to be signified with proper accuracy:

> Once there was a woman smiled at me
> from her open door. I wanted her
> at once and sat through a political
> meeting in her house, thinking
> of just that.

If the above looks and sounds suspiciously like prose, *Facing the Tree* contains even prosier examples which strike me as neither words in the best order nor the best words in the best order. Mostly there are just words:

> I give you a little stick, you give me
> a tiny pebble. We're exciting each other to
> think differently of ourselves, and we can
> see an opening in each other that will lead
> to music and to dance. I probe with the stick
> you press with the pebble against my flesh.
> It hurts, but it's meaningful and we're in love.

What is worse than that is the really gory stuff he dishes out with such abandon:

> You can find me in my bed, bleeding but
> strong. I am afloat in my blood. It has
> become my bed. I lie back upon a pillow of
> coagulated blood and from there I observe
> the steady trickling of my wound. . . .
> ("I Showed Him My Wound")

Prose poems are a tricky genre, uneasy and often pretentious hybrids which can lose their proper sense of direction. If Ignatow's attempts were dropped from his new volume, they would not be missed.

Many of the poems in *Facing the Tree* tacitly demand or, as in "Backyard," explicitly state, "I want / an explanation of the world." This desire is mostly frustrated, which is just as

well. Who wants to give up that mystery—as if, indeed, we were really able to—imaged in a recent poem by Richard Eberhart as "a sky so high / Nothing in it will die, / Or be fully known"? Beyond his grumblings, Ignatow knows this, and even delightedly admits it in some of his better, less claustrophobic poems. In "For Marianne Moore" he realizes that "In her garden were flowers / she had not yet named" because to name them would be "to lose their life / in words." And like a distant paraphrase of Williams' "The Red Wheelbarrow," Ignatow's "Birds in Winter" with lovely clarity makes tentative forays into several themes—the succession of generations, the inevitability of nature's design, fear of departures and hope of arrivals—without attempting an answer beyond that bittersweet, hopelessly sufficient explanation: because that is the way things are.

The best moments in *Facing the Tree* acknowledge this mystery and our curious debt to it, to wisdoms which may be intuited but not explained or explained away. In "The Future" Ignatow tells his daughter, "I give you this / worth more than money, / more than a tip on the market: / keep strong; / prepare to live without me / as I am prepared." It is solemn, courageous advice about the unknown.

This new book's worst fault is, in a sense, not of the poet's own devising, but rather, inherited from Whitman and Williams who can be the sort of poetic models that, paraphrasing Eliot, lead to some untidy lives. It is most clearly expressed by Ignatow in one of his typically saturnine boasts: "My idea of being a moral leader is to point out the terrible deficiencies in man." Oh my. For Whitman, whose norm was, as Hugh Kenner recently wrote, an "easy inclusiveness," this may have been a possibility; for Ignatow it is not. Though he aspires to the sentiments of *alle menschen werden Brüder*, Ignatow more commonly assesses his fellow man as embarrassingly bovine. Worse still, his political vision, molded into dreadful parable, has the sort of outraged earnestness which we might expect of someone who has just been told that elections are often fixed, public officials are crooks, and so forth. This is nothing to be sanguine about, but it is also a good idea to remember the example of Horace, Dryden, Pope, Swift—those cooler customers who understood the value of derisive satire rather than aimless hysteria.

From Whitman Ignatow takes a pose; the language, which is everything, gets left behind. *Facing the Tree* suffers from a style which is cumbrous, flat, and wooden. Ignatow's vocabulary gets in the way like a stammer. Quite simply, there are just not enough interesting words, and little sense of the expansiveness of language. Thus the emotion behind the poem may be furious, but the expression remains tepid, stymied, and strained.

After reading these three volumes I remain unconvinced by Ralph Mills's claim that the poetry "clearly stakes an irrevocable claim for David Ignatow as one of the best, most memorable writers of his generation, a generation which also numbers Theodore Roethke, Charles Olson, John Berryman, Richard Eberhart, Karl Shapiro and Robert Lowell among its poets." The significance, unintended I think, of this drolly miscellaneous list is that all these poets are quite unlike Ignatow and quite unlike each other. This attempt at sainthood by association (and always the same damn saints, too) only reminds us that Ignatow is pitted against poets of amplitude, of large poetic gestures, while he remains that man with a small song, too often singing in the wrong key.

# WILLIAM INGE

## 1913–1973

William Inge was born in Independence, Kansas, on May 3, 1913. His father was a traveling salesman, often absent from home, and Inge's childhood was spent in the company of his mother. He graduated from high school in 1930, entering the University of Kansas at Lawrence in the same year. He graduated with a degree in Speech and Drama in 1935, but being unsure of his acting abilities decided to forego a stage career, instead entering a graduate program at George Peabody Teachers College in Nashville. Frustrated with his studies, in 1936 Inge left school and returned to Independence, where he worked for two years first as a highway laborer and later as a radio announcer, before completing his studies in Nashville. He taught for several years, then in 1943 became the arts critic for the St. Louis *Star-Times*. He relinquished this job in 1946 when his predecessor returned from serving in World War II, and took a teaching position at Washington University.

During his years as a drama critic, Inge met Tennessee Williams who encouraged his writing career. In 1947 Inge's *Farther Off from Heaven* was performed in Dallas. The Broadway production of *Come Back, Little Sheba* in 1950 received critical acclaim and was a commercial success as well, and Inge proceeded to score a series of similar hits with *Picnic* (1953), *Bus Stop* (1955), and *The Dark at the Top of the Stairs* (1957). *Picnic* won the 1953 Pulitzer Prize for drama, and was named best new American play of the 1952–53 season by the New York Drama Critics' Circle. Inge continued to write plays, but starting with *A Loss of Roses* in 1959 managed only a succession of flops; the sole exception was his screenplay for the movie *Splendor in the Grass*, for which he won an Academy Award in 1961. Plagued by alcoholism and unable to reconcile himself to his homosexuality, Inge committed suicide in Los Angeles on June 10, 1973.

## Personal

*Picnic*, the theatrical hit whose major theme is the unsettling effect a highly masculine no-good has on the ladies, young and old, of a small Kansas town upon which he meteorically descends, is the second Broadway success of its author, William Inge, the first being *Come Back, Little Sheba*, produced a few years ago. We descended upon Mr. Inge at the Dakota, on Central Park West, last week, and found him a serious, low-voiced bachelor of thirty-nine, a seasoned student of the second sex. "I was born in Independence, Kansas," he said. "As a child, I was struck by the fact that the women there were always protesting, while men pursued. I got the idea that women hated men. I later came to the conclusion that this was an act—that there was a certain artificiality in their attitude. Some women love so passionately that they're embarrassed about it, because it makes them dependent on men. In *Picnic*, the schoolteacher protests at first, then humbly begs the man to marry her. You feel her deep loneliness. I've tried, in it, to catch a variety of female reactions to men. I get interested in the characters to begin with, and then find a theme if I can."

Mr. Inge, who was wearing gray flannels, a gray sports shirt, and black moccasins at the time of our talk, is the son of a travelling salesman, now retired. "One of my grandmothers was a Booth," he said. "She told me she was related to the acting Booths, but I've never checked up on it." He also had an uncle whom he described as a frustrated actor. He himself became a frustrated actor after some years of theatricals in high school and at the University of Kansas. "I toured Kansas with a tent show, as the juvenile, for a couple of summers while I was in college," he said. "I lived on peanut-butter sandwiches and milk. I hoped to come to New York in the fall of 1936, but I couldn't get together enough money. The George Peabody College for Teachers, in Nashville, Tennessee, offered me a scholarship, and it seemed the sensible thing to accept. I gave up acting, but with no inner contentment. I became morose." He next taught English, morosely, at a high school in

Columbus, Kansas, and then, less morosely, joined Maude Adams as a member of the drama department of Stephens College for Women, in Columbia, Missouri. Beginning in 1943, he spent six years in St. Louis—first as drama and music critic of the *Star-Times*, then as an English instructor at Washington University. "I wrote my first play, *Farther Off from Heaven*, while I was on the *Star-Times*," he said. "It was produced in Dallas—a family-portrait sort of thing. It didn't have much story or action. I regard it as a first draft. I'm thinking of rewriting it."—UNSIGNED, "The Talk of the Town," NY, April 4, 1953, pp. 24–25

## Works

For the purposes of this department, I define a good play as one that embodies a true experience of life in an honest and absorbing manner. Sometimes the author's main contribution is the honesty, while the "absorbing manner" is provided by the players, the director and the other craftsmen who have made the production. It may be of critical value to distinguish which artist has contributed what particular element to our enjoyment, but from a purely theatrical standpoint what we see on the stage as a whole is *the play*. On this basis, *Come Back, Little Sheba* is a good play.

It is true Americana of a kind that has become rather rare on the stage for the past ten years or more. In the days when a few playwrights tried to translate a feeling about American lower-middle-class life to the stage in the manner of such American novelists as Sherwood Anderson or—in a slightly different mood—Josephine Herbst, there were many more plays like this one by William Inge. But the reticence, humbleness and lack of spectacular theatrics in *Come Back, Little Sheba*, together with its unhappy core, make it bitter medicine for playgoers who require their realism "hyped up."

The play is a picture of little, repressed people living, with all their inhibitions, moral confusion, awry ideals and profound isolation, in a kind of Middletown heartbreak house.

The drab spiritual desert that forms the atmosphere for these people would justify our calling *Come Back, Little Sheba* a form of suicide literature were it not for an element of tenderness that sweetens it. The author manages to introduce this softer touch into his unyielding portrait not through any process of poetic ennoblement or social interpretation, but by a human sympathy, which is sounder than tolerance.—HAROLD CLURMAN, "A Good Play," *NR*, March 13, 1950, p. 23

As in *Come Back, Little Sheba*, it is a half-undressed young male who upsets the emotional defenses of the characters in Inge's next play, the Pulitzer-prize winning *Picnic* (1953). In this play, however, it is an exclusively feminine world, protective and serene on the surface. Wrote Inge, "I was fascinated to find how . . . the women seemed to have created a world of their own, a world in which they seemed to be pretending men did not exist. It was a world that had to be destroyed, at least for dramatic values." The male who arrives to do this is Hal Carter, a vagabond with a muscular physique and little else; he is the rooster that manages to arouse this whole barnyard colony of hens. Handled as romantic comedy with a Chekhovian orchestration of the various characters' frustrated lives, *Picnic* is an intimate and powerful handling of the emotional needs of a group of women in a small, monotonous Kansas town.

The dumpy, middle-aged lady, Mrs. Potts, who is burdened with her senile mother (who once forced her to annul her marriage), takes in the penniless young Hal and gives him breakfast, lets him do chores for her and finds her outlet in mothering him. In the house adjacent lives a widow with two daughters: Millie at sixteen is a wiry adolescent who seems to have stepped right out of the work of Carson McCullers, whose *Ballad of the Sad Café* Millie is currently reading. She swears and dresses like a boy, and, as does the girl in *Climate of Eden*, fiercely resents her sister, Madge, for her beauty and success with boys. Madge, who works in a dime store, takes her beauty for granted, finds it less satisfying than a train whistle which suggests wonderful faraway places, and is often embarrassed by her good looks, lamenting, "What good is it to be pretty?" Her wealthy fiancé, Alan, respectfully hero-worships her and his kisses leave her unaroused; not overly bright, she is ill at ease with Alan's wealthy friends. She is thus more than ready for Hal. Also boarding with the widow and her daughters is an old-maid school-teacher, Rosemary, whose defense mechanism is to reiterate that although men want to marry her, "I don't have time for any of 'em when they start gettin' serious on me."

Hal, who has been in reform school, suffers extreme inferiority feelings: his father died in jail from alcoholism, his mother attempted to declare him insane to get his property, and his fraternity brothers in college lorded it over him for his crudity. He tells Alan of his having been picked up by two girls, taken to a motel and held as prisoner until both had been satiated. The only thing Hal has is his frank virility, reinforced by such little devices as boots. The women all become conscious of Hal working around the yard with his shirt off, and are both repelled and intrigued by his brash male braggadocio. The Labor Day picnic provides the occasion for the eruption of the awakened sexuality of the women. Hal's whisky breaks down Rosemary's inhibitions and she screams at a piece of garden hose, fearing it is a snake—or a phallic symbol. Hal and Madge finally come together in a dance which ". . . has something of the nature of a primitive rite that would mate the two young people." Rosemary wants to dance that way too, but must settle for a middle-aged store-keeper, while Millie, who wears her first feminine frock, gets nauseated from Hal's liquor. Instead of going on the

picnic, Hal and Madge find each other in a powerful surge of desire after Rosemary had fiercely upbraided him for his rottenness. The aftermath of the picnic for Rosemary is intimacy with Howard, the store-keeper, after which they return, drained and weary. But Rosemary becomes hysterically insistent and in a tremendous scene, not fully realized in the production, she browbeats him into a promise of marriage. Hal and Madge return too, ashamed and trying to fight their desires for Alan's sake. Hal must flee town because Alan has reported his car stolen when they stayed out all night, but he wants Madge to come to Tulsa and meet him. Her mother, who sees a repetition of her own marital failure, tries valiantly to keep Madge from going to Tulsa; but it is clear that she must go—her deepest emotional needs have been answered by Hal with his combination of aggressive virility and small-boy self-pity; Hal, too, has found compassion and tenderness for the first time. Though the ending is painful from the mother's point of view, Inge seems to suggest that the marriage of Hal and Madge has a fighting chance, for it is based upon a deep-level satisfaction of mutual needs. Perhaps all of the vagabond, maladjusted, delinquent Hals need only to find themselves through being loved.

*Picnic* illustrates the most mature level of the American drama in the fifties, able to draw upon Freudian insights without succumbing to the obvious or the trite, able to extract ever fresh and original patterns of human relationship from contemporary life and to view with psychological as well as aesthetic perception the life around us. Inge ably summarized his own approach to psychoanalytic drama in his questionnaire:

> I'll put it briefly—Freud has deepened and expanded man's own awareness of himself. Any writer, inwardly involved with his own time, can not help but reflect the feelings and viewpoints that Freud has exposed in us. Yet, I cannot point out any specific plays (of my own or of other playwrights) that intentionally serve to illustrate Freud. Rather I feel that the understanding and sympathy expressed for human character in such plays as *The Glass Menagerie, All My Sons, Golden Boy, A Streetcar Named Desire, The Shrike, Skin of Our Teeth, Death of a Salesman* come about as the result of Freud's discoveries, even though the authors of these plays may not have read Freud, or any of the psychoanalytic writers since.

Inge's two naturalistic dramas have quickly found their way to the company of these plays he mentions and have earned him a conspicuous place among the new playwrights.—W. DAVID SIEVERS, "New Freudian Blood," *Freud on Broadway*, 1955, pp. 354–56

Mr. Inge is, of course, the apostle of the domestic; one must admit his positive genius for contracting life to the prosy arena of back porch or parlor or stranded prairie cafe. His modesty gives always a little stir of pleasure, it is publicly well thought of; the very refusal of *The Dark at the Top of the Stairs* to move beyond the cautious immediate, to look remotely like anything conceivable as art ("all that junk jewelry and paint and giving herself airs: who does she think she is!")—this mousy charm has ironically won the play its accolade as Mr. Inge's "best." It is full of the pleasures of recognition: the set a solid horror of delight (period Harding), detailed with imaginative witty love; the sentimental glimpses acute—Miss Eileen Heckart swinging on her halter of iridescent beads, a flapper tugging her foot in curdled glee. Of course, there are deeper ripples: with Mr. Inge, there always are. A husband is riled and a wife slapped; any number of people do not Feel Wanted, and there are echoes of suicide and intimacy ("Do you know I'm frigid?"), deceptively innocuous bits about swords—Symbolism and All That—and sibilant Freudian whispers from the Vienna Woods (I'm Oedipus, who are you?). At the end, Mr. Inge invokes the wise forgiveness of let-us-all-understand-one-another and, charmingly, it works. One never doubted that it would. It has before.—RICHARD HAYES, "A Question of Reality," *Com*, March 14, 1958, pp. 615–16

The recent discovery of *A Loss of Roses*, a mid-twentieth-century playscript attributed to one William Inge, represents a notable, if slightly dull, contribution to Freudian archeology. Many of its pages proved, on inspection, to have been defaced by scribbled comments and emendations of a scurrilous nature, probably indicating that the owner of the volume was a precocious rebel against the cult of Freudian infallibility. These "revisions," however, have been chemically erased, and the text now stands revealed as a ritual drama of semi-magical character, designed as a conventional act of homage to the memory of Freud, whose spirit is alleged in the course of the entertainment to have been immanent even in the rural districts of Kansas as long ago as 1933. The play, or interlude, thus takes its place, albeit a lowly one, in the cycle of Freudian Mysteries that formed the religious core of the winter theatre festivals held annually on the island of Manhattan for the benefit of the United Hospital Fund. Founded on the Freudian myth concerning the mischievous behavior of the mind deity called Oedipus, or Funny Foot, the narrative (which may be no more than a fragment; certainly something appears to be missing) is composed in a halting, nondescript style that affords solid confirmation of the theory that most of the lesser plays in the cycle are the work of one hand, possibly that of a priest.

If we accept this hypothesis, internal evidence suggests that *A Loss of Roses* was written either very early or very late in the career of its industrious author. The plot, which deals with latent incestuous impulses in the relationship between a middle-aged widow and her twenty-one-year-old son, is dutifully Freud-centered—one might even say Freud-fearing—in conception, but the execution is tentative and halfhearted throughout, as if the author had not quite decided what he wanted to say, or whether, indeed, he wanted to say anything. Was this because he was a tyro, unversed in the techniques of religious drama? Or must we see him as an aging propagandist whose faith had dimmed and who felt disillusioned and Freud-forsaken? We cannot be sure. What we do know is that the action of the play is minimal and that it tells us almost nothing about the First Great Depression, during which it is supposed to unfold. These facts, unfortunately, are of little help to us in ascertaining the author's age at the time of composition. From first to last, monolithic Freudianism subjected all its captive artists to a process of brainwashing that taught them to equate "introspection" with "action" and to regard the phrase "social environment" as meaningless at best and dangerously heretical at worst. My own hunch, unscientific though it may be, is to plump for teen-age authorship of *A Loss of Roses*. I picture a pink-faced acolyte with literary ambitions singling out the much-loved Funny Foot legend as the one most likely to win him preferment. Boldly, he submits his play to the festival, in competition with established dramatists like Williams, Mac-Leish, and Kazan. His inexperience betrays him; the notorious Tribunal of Seven turns thumbs down, and he is consigned to the dreaded Doghouse—from which, as we know, he later emerged to write the series of gnomic texts that are among our richest sources of information about the short-lived epoch during which Freudianism held despotic sway over what used to be called "the Western world," though it has since come to

be known as the Middle East. The texts to which I refer include, among many others, *A Clearing in the Woods*, *The Silver Cord*, *Cue for Passion*, *Oh, Men! Oh, Women!*, *Masquerade*, and *The Dark at the Top of the Stairs*, all of which derive from the doctrinaire school of Freudian drama that was founded by Barrie with *Peter Pan*. Despite the restrictions imposed on the self-styled Inge by his creed, archeology owes a great debt to the dedicated scribe, whose . . .

In other words, if I may parachute down from this bumpy flight of fancy, the new William Inge play at the Eugene O'Neill Theatre is a mess. Mother (Betty Field, far below her best) shares a bungalow outside Kansas City with her son (Warren Beatty), who works at a gas station. For reasons that are unspoken but unquestionably erotic, he cannot bring himself to abandon her and take a better job elsewhere. She feels much the same way about him, but has found outlets for her emotions in good works and religion. Into this uneasy ménage there irrupts an old friend of the family, who turns out to be a catalyst in disguise. This is Carol Haney, playing a brassy, pathetic actress-*cum*-hoofer temporarily unemployed and in need of shelter. Swiftly sizing her up as a member of the age group—forty and upward—that attracts him most, the boy makes a drunken pass at her. His first attempt fails, but before long he contrives to seduce the woman, a substitute mother if ever I saw one. This sexual triumph enables him at last to leave home. Miss Haney, shattered, attempts to commit suicide by slashing her wrists, but eventually departs on the arm of a brutish ex-lover to make blue movies in Kansas City. We are meant to infer from her experience that reality is pitiless and unchangeably hostile. "It's like the depression," she says wanly. "You've got to make the best of it." Yet the depression, unless my memory has run mad, was lifted by organized human effort; reality was changed, by a transfusion of practical pity.

Miss Haney tends to overplay, performing every scene in the same vein of corrosive urgency, but Mr. Beatty, sensual around the lips and pensive around the brow, is excellent as the boy, and there is nothing wrong with Daniel Mann's direction that a stronger script could not have remedied. The main fault of the piece lies elsewhere, and deeper. The truth is that you cannot write a first-rate play about the Oedipus complex alone. (*Oedipus Rex* is about a city that is languishing under a curse, and its hero does not suffer from an Oedipus complex.) A serious dramatist who analyzes personal problems without analyzing the social problems that encircle and partly create them is neglecting a good half of his job, though if he is writing at high pressure, with the fullest kind of insight, he may succeed in persuading us to forget about the other half. In *A Loss of Roses*, Mr. Inge displays no such persuasive power. I commend to his attention what an English critic, the late Christopher Caudwell, once said about the limitations of an exclusively Freudian approach to human behavior:

> It is as if a man, seeing a row of trees bent in various ways by the prevailing winds, were without studying the relation between growth and environment to deduce that a mysterious complex in trees caused them always to lean as the result of a death instinct attracting them to the ground, while eternal Eros bade them spring up vertically.

There is more to trees, and much more to us, than that. —KENNETH TYNAN, "Roses and Thorns," *NY*, Dec. 12, 1959, pp. 99–100

GERALD WEALES
From "The New Pineros"
*American Drama since World War II*
1962, pp. 41–49

Until the appearance of A *Loss of Roses* (1959), Inge had a reputation as a playwright whose work did not fail. Following the modest success of *Come Back, Little Sheba* (1950), Inge's next three plays, *Picnic* (1953), *Bus Stop* (1955), and *The Dark at the Top of the Stairs* (1957), established him as one of Broadway's most successful playwrights; because of our strange belief in the corollary relationship between income and reputation, Inge also came to be accepted as one of America's leading dramatists. His own ambiguous sense of his position is made clear in the Foreword to *4 Plays* in which he dwells on his longing for both big success ("but none of them has brought me the kind of joy, the hilarity, I had craved as a boy") and artistic success, a feeling of having contributed something to the theater.

If the self-image that Inge projects in that Foreword—the playwright who went into analysis after the first hint of success with *Sheba*—tags him as a representative American (intellectual, artistic variation) of the fifties, it is not surprising that his plays should embody the theatrical commonplaces of the decade. *The Dark at the Top of the Stairs* is almost a casebook of clichés for our time. It has, in Reenie, a sensitive adolescent girl who takes refuge in her music ("All you do is *pity* yourself at the piano") or in books, a kind of Laura Wingfield without a limp; in the early version of the play, *Farther Off from Heaven*, which was produced at Margo Jones's theater in Dallas in 1947, Reenie has, at least, a broken front tooth. Another Inge adolescent, Millie in *Picnic*, sits around reading Carson McCullers, so she is more Frankie Addams than Laura, but funnily sad or shiveringly sad the lonely adolescents, male and female, have been as busy on the stage in the past fifteen years as they have been in novels. The basic pattern in these plays is to confront the child with a situation that must push him or her toward maturity (see Moss Hart's *The Climate of Eden*, Julian Funt's *The Magic and the Loss*, Robert Anderson's *All Summer Long*, above all McCullers' *The Member of the Wedding*). In *Dark*, Reenie has to discover, through the off-stage suicide of Sammy, that her fear is a kind of selfishness. Her little brother has his lesson to learn, too. A ten-year-old with a passion for collecting photographs of movie stars, Sonny does a relentlessly specific Oedipal double with his mother ("For a moment, mother and son lie together in each other's arms") until, at the beginning of Act III, she takes him aside and explains that he is too big to share her bed any longer. *Dear Dr. Franzblau: My son is ten years old and all he does is lie around looking at movie star pictures and the other boys tease him and . . .*

Act II, the therapy and diagnosis act, is particularly rich in bromide. In the first half, Sammy arrives to escort Reenie to a party. Presumably because he is a Jew and the neglected son of a much-married movie bit player, he is able to understand Reenie, with whom he is politely shy, and Sonny, whom he stops in mid-tantrum. The off-stage anti-Catholicism of Lottie are atypical of the fifties, an echo of the immediate postwar period, the years of Laurents' *Home of the Brave* and N. Richard Nash's *The Young and the Fair*, when playwrights mistook a healthy social conscience for healthy theater.[1] Although there is something a little old-fashioned in Sammy's presence on the stage in 1957, he is contemporary enough to be more a tortured adolescent than a victim of bigotry.

Once the children are sent off to their party, the stage is cleared for the long confessional scene in which Cora, the play's heroine, listens to her bawdy-talking sister Lottie explain the failure of her marriage, her own frigidity ("I never did enjoy it the way some women . . . say they do") and the accompanying emasculation, spiritual and sexual, of her husband. The old problem of character development has been solved here and in much of the theatrical writing of the last decade by allowing characters to indulge in the favorite contemporary sport of analysis, self and other. The articulate self-awareness that Inge and most of his contemporaries give to their characters disposes of the virtue of revelation through dramatic action, through the conflict of personality, through the interaction of one man's life on another. Walter Kerr likes to blame the leadenness of so much of the talk that goes on in contemporary drama on the ghosts of Ibsen and Chekhov, but the audience at an Ibsen or Chekhov play has to be alert to keep from being taken in by any one person's speeches because the characters in their plays, like most of us, have a way of lying to themselves and to others. Speeches, such as those of Lottie's, are hardly Chekhovian revelation; they are much more like the show-and-tell period at the neighborhood kindergarten. Behind Lottie's self-definition and those of Sammy in *Dark*, Hal and Rosemary in *Picnic*, Dr. Lyman in *Bus Stop*, and Doc and Lola in *Sheba* (these last two are not always conscious of what they are saying as their brother confessors are) lies the remnants of a first-year course in psychology or an incompletely digested analysis. At least, Inge, in his psychologizing, avoids the kind of jargon that some of his fellow playwrights use. The line that most incredibly typifies this tendency in contemporary plays is that of the young girl in Paddy Chayefsky's *The Tenth Man*: "I'm a little paranoid and hallucinate a great deal and have very little sense of reality, except for brief interludes like this, and I might slip off any minute in the middle of a sentence into some incoherency." She does not quite follow this with "Now tell me about yourself," but she does not have to because the author and the audience know that nothing could keep the young man from offering a reciprocal self-diagnosis.

Although Inge's characters spend a good part of their time explaining their motivations (in *Picnic*, for instance, although one good scene between the two sisters would make everything clear, Millie must indicate frequently that she resents Madge's beauty and Madge must have a speech in which she complains that beauty is not enough), they still have to go through the regular expositional hoops to give the audience the past out of which the dramatic present has grown. Some of the less conservative playwrights have tried to find technical ways to escape the awkwardness of such exposition. Arthur Miller has made the past and present contemporaneous in Willy's brain in *Death of a Salesman* and Arthur Laurents has used the expressionism of *A Clearing in the Woods* to let his heroine exist simultaneously at four different ages; Tennessee Williams, in *Sweet Bird of Youth*, has simply dropped any pretense at realism and lets his characters speak directly to the audience. Inge, who is far too wedded to naturalism to try anything unusual, falls back on a trick of characterization by making Lottie in *Dark* and Lola in *Sheba* uncontrollably garrulous women. "Did I ever tell you about the first time she met Rubin?" Lottie asks her husband; although he answers, "Yes, honey," she plows on into a long narrative, prefaced by "I did not!" Although the postman and the milkman in *Sheba* give every indication that they have heard the story before, Lola reminds them and tells us about Doc's alcoholism. The clumsiest exposition in the early Inge plays comes in *Bus Stop* in which Elma Duckworth, another of the adolescent yearners, wanders from character to character, gathering information as though she were a researcher for *Current Biography*. The logical end product of Inge's tendency toward explanation is *A Loss of Roses*, in which practically nothing happens except in the narrated past.

One of the recurring criticisms of American drama in the last fifteen years is that in it action has given way to talk. There is a kind of validity in that position, but since good talk in the theater is often a kind of action, the difficulty lies not in the fact of but the quality of the talk. The naturalistic tradition seems to have spawned a host of dull people who are bromidic and repetitive, inarticulate except at those moments of high whine when they grind out their tales of woe; Inge's plays have their quota of such characters. My generalized carping about the people who walk our stage today does not mask an implicit longing for the tragic tradition that supposedly demands that heroes be kings; I would as happily spend the afternoon with Prince Hal hanging around a tavern in Eastcheap as eavesdrop on King Henry's guilty musings. It is not status I yearn for, it is interest. I could throw a handful of paper clips out of the window of the third-floor walk-up in which I am now writing and hit a half-dozen ordinary people who have more life, more vitality, more originality, and more serious problems than the lonely, longing people who infest the Inge plays. My disapproval is too blanket, of course. There are characters in the early Inge plays, particularly Lola in *Sheba*, who are strong enough, in their pathos or comedy, to insist that their ties to life are stronger than their ties to soap opera. Inge, who has an ear for Midwestern speech, apparently built Lola consciously out of the clichés of common usage, but they are only the vehicle of her expression; she transcends them—and not simply in Shirley Booth's performance of the role—because Inge can allow himself a certain comic indulgence that would be impossible with Doc, whose pretensions really demand a satirist. The result is that Lola is more endearing and more unpleasant than Doc; she is, in short, a realized character in a way that Doc never is. Rosemary, in *Picnic*, has some of Lola's virtues as a character; although she is solidly based on the stereotype of the old-maid schoolteacher, Inge's conception of her as comic allows him more easily to bring the submerged pathos into the open, makes her more touching than the romanticized Hal and Madge. There is a kind of tough funniness about Cherie and a certain charm about the bumptiousness of Bo in *Bus Stop* that makes that out-and-out comic couple more theatrically palatable than many of Inge's other characters.

By *The Dark at the Top of the Stairs*, in which everyone is something and no one is, the casebook had triumphed over characterization. This is nowhere more evident than in *A Loss of Roses*, in which Lila turns up with the remnants of the dramatic company with which she has been touring. What the play needs at this point, having just passed through the dinner scene between Helen and Kenny, one of the dullest passages in the Inge canon, is some big, boozy theatrical caricatures that might wake up the play. What we get are thin suggestions of the *grande dame* manager, the aging homosexual juvenile, the company cocksman. ⟨. . .⟩ Inge, who after all once traveled with a Toby company himself, should have provided Lila with associates as interesting as Cherie, but *Loss*, like *Dark*, talks itself to death, not to life.

Of all the clichés that keep *Dark* afloat, the most blatant is the ending, when, having got the children off to the movies, Cora mounts the stairs to join Rubin who stands (we just see his feet) where the dark once lurked, waiting to take her to bed. In one sense, this is the ending to all of the plays except *A Loss of Roses* and, even in that play, Lila goes off with Ricky to keep

from being completely alone. In *Sheba*, Doc and Lola agree on their mutual need; in *Picnic*, Madge follows Hal and Rosemary traps Howard; in *Bus Stop*, Cherie goes off with Bo, and Grace settles for the momentary comfort of Carl. Inge's recurrent theme, as Robert Brustein has pointed out (*Harper's*, November 1958), is that man finds his "salvation from fear, need, and insecurity only through fulfillment of domestic love." He qualifies this theme as surface and finds "a psychological substatement to the effect that marriage demands, in return for its spiritual consolations, a sacrifice of the hero's image (which is the American folk image) of maleness." Brustein points out that each of the plays has a scene in which the hero pleads his weakness to win the heroine's love, although that scene in *A Loss of Roses*, which came after his analysis of Inge, is simply a technique of seduction. Although Brustein's description of Inge's work is a convincing one, I am less interested in and less annoyed by the substructure—after all, serious drama, unless it ends catastrophically, is almost always about what a man must give up of himself for the consolations of home, state, church—than the surface solution. Broadway's prevailing belief that love conquers all ⟨. . .⟩ is as fatuous a solution to dramatic problems as an age is likely to come up with. *Bus Stop* is after all a romantic comedy, so it is proper that Cherie and Bo exit together for a Montana ranch where, according to the conventions of the theater, they will live happily ever after. Unhappily, Inge, like so many of his fellow playwrights, has transferred the romantic-comedy ending to all of his plays. He has done so diffidently, as though he were unsure that the evidence at the box office really proved the validity of the sentimental fade-out. In the original version of *Picnic*, Madge did not follow Hal, and in *Sheba*, still his best play, the joining of Doc and Lola at the end is more of a truce than an embrace. Even so, the prevailing message of the plays is that love is a solution to all social, economic, and psychological problems.

The final scene of *Dark* is not only an example of the love-panacea ending, it is representative of a popular variation within the general type—the sex-as-salvation conclusion. The dramatic purpose of Lottie's detailed analysis of her marriage, in so far as it has any, is that it convinces Cora that she is happy with Rubin. Although Inge takes the trouble to indicate that the couple have radically different ideas about social and personal goals, although the father and his children have lost any ability to communicate with one another, and although the family is faced with a genuine economic crisis, the suggestion is that sexual compatibility will carry the day. This kind of phallic romanticism is also evident in *Picnic* in which Hal, who has been a kind of "Male at Stud," to use Val's phrase from *Orpheus Descending*, suggests that his future is likely to be rosier than his past after one night of love with Madge: "Not like last night, baby. Last night was . . . *(Gropes for the word) inspired.*" Tennessee Williams and *A Streetcar Named Desire* are almost certainly responsible for the currency of this dramatic myth. Stanley and Stella overcome all differences of taste, erase all evidences of personal history, when they get "them colored lights going!" Stella's words to Blanche are almost a slogan for the new movement: "But there are things that happen between a man and a woman in the dark—that sort of make everything else seem—unimportant." It was Speed Lamkin who finally carried the whole idea of sexual sufficiency to its ridiculous end. In *Comes a Day* (1958), a play ostensibly about whether or not a young girl should marry for love or money, he not only made the poor boy sexually capable, he made the rich one a psychopathic sadist; you see what happens, the play seems to say, if you are not good in bed, as likely as not you will break down, foaming at the mouth, and chew up an expensive set. Inge is not so silly about the whole thing as Lamkin is; even so, the *Dark* is gross enough, particularly if it is played smirkingly as it was in the Elia Kazan production on Broadway. All joy to Cora and Rubin, but, when the curtain comes down, the harness business is still on the rocks.

There is, also, still dark at the top of the stairs. Inge's titular metaphor for every man's fear of the uncertain future is indicative of an intrusive symbolism that he had not used since *Sheba.* In that play, the missing dog, so insistently equated with Lola's lost youth, stands out incongruously in a simple naturalistic play that has no need of it. There is the same kind of obviousness in the symbolic use of Turk's javelin and the excessive explicitness of Lola's dreams. It may well have been *The Glass Menagerie,* which, as Inge has admitted, brought him to the writing of plays, that caused him to sprinkle *Sheba* with symbols that do not grow out of the drama, but are grafted onto it. In any case, such devices are not evident in *Picnic* and *Bus Stop.*[2] With *Dark,* Inge reverted to his earlier practice. Too much is made in terms of set, lighting, and action of the area at the head of the stairs. If we must have an Inge symbol, I prefer Sammy's sword in Act II, which is introduced, does its work, and then is forgotten. Sammy, who is in the uniform of the military school he attends, answers Sonny's question: "I wear a sword to protect myself! . . . To kill off all the villains in the world!" Sonny then borrows the sword and does a mock-suicide. Both gestures of childish reaction to the real or imagined oppressions of the world, they tell us all we need really know about Sammy and Sonny and render a good part of Sammy's exposition unnecessary.

By trying to reach Inge's work through *The Dark at the Top of the Stairs,* which for me is one of his least attractive plays, I have perhaps been unfair to the playwright. He has (or had in the early plays) a genuine talent for small, touching effects; this is a real theatrical virtue. Still, *Dark* is a play that received both critical and popular approbation, and it is certainly typical of his work. One of the difficulties with Inge and with other playwrights who ponder heavily over the same concerns is that Paul Osborn's *Morning's at Seven* makes it almost impossible to take them seriously. This play, which was first presented unsuccessfully in 1939, jumbles together enough clichés of situation and language to provide Inge with material for four or five plays; Osborn, however, although he occasionally reaches for a pathetic moment, presents the whole thing as wry comedy, almost a parody of the idea of lonely lostness in the Midwestern backyard. It is a kind of judgment on Inge that Eileen Heckart, who was Rosemary in *Picnic* and Lottie in *Dark,* could play Myrtle Brown in the Play of the Week production of *Morning's at Seven* with very little broadening of the mannerisms she used in the two Inge plays. In his Foreword to *4 Plays,* Inge wrote: "I deal with surfaces in my plays, and let whatever depths there are in my material emerge unexpectedly so that they bring something of the suddenness and shock which accompany the discovery of truths in actuality." He might well have stopped at the end of the first clause.

*Notes*

1. The social effectiveness of such direct propagandizing is as doubtful as its dramatic validity. I still remember the woman who sat behind me at *Lost in the Stars,* crying copiously as the stiff-necked South African white man walked across the stage to shake hands with the Negro preacher after both men had lost their sons; in her unmistakably Southern voice, choked with tears, she told her neighbor: "Of course, I'd never shake his hand."

2. *Bus Stop* is loaded with significant names, a kind of symbolism. The drunken professor is Dr. Lyman; the forceful sheriff, Will Masters; the cowboy who sends Bo and Cherie off with his love,

Virgil Blessing; even Cherie, as the lines indicate, is a comic play on *cherry.* It was a student in one of my classes who first pointed out Inge's use of significant names in this play; he was intent on proving that Elma was a satirical figure because her last name is Duckworth. That way lies exegesis.

## WALTER KERR
### From "As We Were: Conventional Theater"
*The Theater in Spite of Itself*
1963, pp. 238–44

#### Mr. Inge

Inge has been with us and not with us, warmly with us in *The Dark at the Top of the Stairs,* remote and troubled in *A Loss of Roses.*

The former is a touching example of one of our commonest theater experiences: the memory play. In performance almost the first thing you noticed about designer Ben Edwards' long, rambling, old-fashioned Oklahoma living room was the alcoves: the dim recess where a swinging door opened and closed silently, the tiny back parlor where the player piano lurked behind fringed drapes, the empty space that surrounded the front screen door and seemed to lead off to nowhere. There was also, to be sure, a wildly steep staircase that shot bolt upright to the dark at the top of it, but it was the private nooks and crannies that counted most.

For this was to be the kind of play that a child might have overheard as he passed, hastily or idly, through the corners of his parents' lives. Whenever a youngster with a mop of yellow hair sprawled over his forehead and a lower lip set in a stubborn indifference barged swiftly in or out of his elders' universe, all inflections changed.

Eileen Heckart, as an aunt with bobbed hair and jade earrings that rattled as rapidly as her tongue, might very well have been whispering a fast, scandalous confidence to the boy's broken-hearted mother. But the entrance of the child became a warning for skyrockets to go up, for Miss Heckart's scratched-slate voice to strip gears violently and bellow open into whooping affection. This child, like all of us, heard one tone at the threshold, another as he was sighted, still another as he vanished again through the portieres.

And it was the remembered, mysteriously rising and falling, heard and not-heard universe of oddly behaved adults that Mr. Inge and his director, Elia Kazan, had caught with such accuracy in the half-light. Not that the children's roles were dominant; they were simply ears that listened, legs that shuffled perplexedly, eyes that stared in incomprehension and occasional hysterical defiance as a mother and father fought over a party dress, as an aunt painfully refused to take the family into her own household, as lonely voices in the kitchen cried out during an all-night rain.

Thus the loss of a later play by Mr. Inge was not to be taken lightly. We had come to expect from the playwright a friendly sympathy for likable slatterns, a feeling for the fears that badger quite recognizable families, even a mildly poetic awareness of the dreams that torment tough-minded people who spend their lives thumbing rides on the roadside. If Mr. Inge's mood had most often been rueful, it had always been warm. If the voices overheard in parlors and bars had always had a commonplace twang to them, their very commonness and familiarity had helped to stir our affection.

But *A Loss of Roses,* the author's fifth play and first failure, was neither familiar in spirit nor touching in effect, and its difficulties stemmed, I think, not from any momentary fatigue on the playwright's part but from a growing tendency in the conventional theater. The tendency, which is also a temptation, is for the dramatist to work in an ever narrower range, and with an ever softer and more indulgent touch.

The softness of A *Loss of Roses* may have derived from a conviction that the satisfactions of the flesh are sufficient. The play dealt with a son's unnatural attachment for his mother, and with his temporary transfer of that attachment to a blowzy, not quite bright, tent-show actress who was old enough to serve as a mother-image while remaining a legitimate object of sexual desire.

If the edgy and secretive guerrilla warfare that went on between these three small-town people did not interest us for very long, it was probably because Mr. Inge had nowhere suggested that anything more powerful was at work than an aberration of the senses.

When the son moved impulsively toward his mother for a good-night kiss or bolted rebelliously away from her rigid refusal of warmth, the confused drive inside him was wholly physical; it was perfectly plain that neither her revival-meeting character nor her dinner-table conversation had inspired any part of the strangled affection he felt. The issue was not at all psychological; it was steadfastly, and simply, sensual.

The mother, unfailingly alert to every gesture that disturbed the tranquillity of a fatherless home, responded in kind: nothing passed between these two to suggest any tangling of minds over the long, lonely years; only an unlucky proximity and a physical resemblance between dead father and demanding son lay at the root of the contest.

When the actress-interloper bustled about the Kansas living room in cascades of tight black fringe and then succumbed in astonishment to the lad's importunities, the flare of passion that overtook them, and the disillusionment that followed, were both crises of nerves, mutual cries for comfort. The drama was skin-deep.

That the sting of the flesh is a powerful force in any man's life, or in any man's play, is surely not to be denied. That it should be thought to constitute a spectrum broad enough and varied enough to sustain an entire evening at fierce dramatic pitch is perhaps another matter. A surge of sensuality takes on genuine importance and complexity in the theater when it begins to engage, and challenge, the total personality, when the mind and will are pressed into the struggle, when the dramatist lays open not one layer of surface response but cuts resolutely into human tissue until a cross-section has been exposed. A *Loss of Roses* seemed to attempt no such penetration; it halted, rather, at the actress' straightforward but dramatically inadequate warning that she was "emotionally immature"; and the preoccupation with immaturity made us squirm rather than sympathize.

Mr. Inge's play faltered further in its symptomatic confinement to a narrow and clinical range of observation. "I never heard of such people," murmured the mother in mild protest as she listened, more or less placidly, to an account of the lively and indiscriminate sexual activities of an acting troupe. The point of the line, of course, was that she had indeed heard of them and had chosen to ignore their existence. The line was also meant to remind the rest of us that the things that were taking place in A *Loss of Roses* do happen, perhaps more frequently than we like to think.

But even as we acknowledged the truth of the inference, we were restive: if the twilight world of the seriously abnormal is real, it is also restricted. It is restricted emotionally, because of the emotional paralysis of its figures. It is restricted intellectually, because development has, in one way or another, been arrested. We may be quick to grant that such imprisonments of personality take place, and that otherwise attractive people suffer for them; but we are slower to concede that they occupy quite so impressive a place in the scheme of things as they have just now usurped on the stage.

In our own busy and complicated world we have come to enjoy a somewhat busier and more complicated field of vision: we are bound to the foolish, sinful, nearly normal people we know as we cannot become bound to these honorably drawn but palely loitering wraiths of the half-world. I suppose it must always be remembered that the so-called disturbed personality is not more complex than its presumably healthy opposite, but simpler. It is simpler because the obsession that deforms it tends to become self-centered and single-minded.

As a result, one's experience of a merely clinical play is always a little like navigating a bleak and endless alley in the company of people who deserve and rather querulously demand assistance but do not become the more winning for their crying over odd compulsions. We feel, as we watch, that what is truly pathological requires treatment and understanding, but not necessarily our presence during the therapy.

### The Mirror

There is a distinction to be made, however, between what is neurotic or immature and what is violent or ugly, just as there is a distinction to be made between the merely fashionable posture of self-pity and the fact that savage pressures exist.

Too often the lines that may be drawn between these things are blurred, all troubled visions are lumped together under the single epithet "depressing," and a great hue and cry is raised against dramatists generally for failing to report the first crocus.

Contemporary playwrighting tends to view the human condition as though it were entirely scrofulous, the outraged insist, and isn't it time for a brighter-eyed craftsman to say a kind word about our nobler traits? Nobler traits do exist, surely, even in New York City, and wouldn't it simply be playing fair to devote an evening or two to rounding out the picture?

The complaint is understandable enough. It isn't much fun—nor is it profoundly moving in the tragic sense—to stumble night after night into a nest of badly reared vipers, there to be told almost without interruption that the situation is hopeless, hopeless. An enormous number of our most successful plays do wear a morose, as some wear a twisted, countenance. The playgoer who has done his best from nine to five, and who goes right on trying to construct a decent world from five till bedtime, may well be forgiven his impatience and his disbelief as he is forced to look at intricate patterns of corruption each time he visits Broadway.

Score one for the complainers. I am myself obviously somewhat impatient with the drama of neurosis, not so much because I am looking for uplift and light, but because it seems to me—almost in the nature of things—to be minor drama. The true neurotic is generally a victim of forces he does not understand and therefore cannot subdue or even do intelligent battle against. Barring a god from the machine who will rescue him, whether that god wear a psychiatric beard or some other life-saving symbol, he is a tormented and baffled victim of circumstances quite beyond his personal control.

Since he is also, by definition, ill just now, he tends to remove himself to the observation ward. By this I mean that because he has effectively isolated himself from the rest of us, who fancy that we enjoy a sort of minimum health, he has made any real interplay between us impossible. We can watch him behind glass; but because he is imprisoned in a snarl of nerves, inhibitions, and impulses that is unique rather than common, we no longer share with him a common tongue or a common pattern of memories and drives. We can try to understand what has happened to him, and we can be perfectly well aware that it might happen to us; but until his private knot is undone, we cannot really communicate with him, nor he with us. "Universality" is an easy word to toss around. But it does have a meaning, and the plays we cherish most are cherished precisely because they speak so intimately to so many.

# JOHN IRVING

## 1942–

John Irving was born in Exeter, New Hampshire, on March 2, 1942. Irving attended Exeter Academy, where his father taught Russian history. At school Irving developed two passions, writing and wrestling, which would continue to be central forces in his life for many years. In 1961 Irving went to the University of Pittsburgh because of its reputation for excellent collegiate wrestling. Unable to dominate his competitors as he had done in high school, Irving returned to study at the University of New Hampshire. He traveled to Vienna in 1963 where he studied at the Institute of European Studies for one year. There he married Shyla Leary, an artist he had met earlier in the United States. Irving received a B.A. from the University of New Hampshire in 1965. He spent the next two years at the University of Iowa Writers Workshop, studying with Vance Bourjaily and Kurt Vonnegut, Jr. Irving later taught at Iowa from 1972 to 1975. From 1975 to 1978 he was an assistant professor of English at Mount Holyoke College.

Irving's first novel, *Setting Free the Bears* (1969), was praised by the critics and sold moderately well. Irving went to Vienna in 1969 to begin work on a film version of his first book, but returned to the United States in 1971 when the project was abandoned. Irving was not pleased with the efforts of his publisher, Random House, on his next two books, *The Water-Method Man* (1972) and *The 158-Pound Marriage* (1974). He decided to move to Dutton, where *The World According to Garp* was published in 1978. *Garp* sold over three million copies and won the American Book Award in 1979 for best paperback novel. Irving published two more successful novels, *The Hotel New Hampshire* (1981) and *The Cider House Rules* (1985). Irving lives in Putney, Vermont, with his wife and two sons.

## Personal

Q: In your books you seem fascinated by turn, counter-turn, coincidence—the sequence of events we call "plot," or used to before it got a bad reputation.

A: I care very much about plot, yes. When I was a child, plot was the first thing that made me admire novels and made me want to be a writer. Before I understood what was true to life about the good novels, or what was energizing and moving about the great characters in fiction—before that was plot. Simply: was it a good story? I believe that's one of the novelist's responsibilities: to tell a good story. That's one of the burdens we must put on our imaginations. You're cheating a reader out of something a reader has a right to expect from a good novel if you don't make up a good story. I put aside a lot of well-written, intelligent novels about true-to-life characters simply because I know the writer isn't interested in telling me a good story, or can't. I'm willing to admit that—at least in this respect—I still read a novel with the expectations of a child. I want the novelist to tell his story so skillfully that I can't wait to find out what happens next.

Q: Who are the contemporary writers you admire?

A: I admire you—you're so hard on the people you write about, yet you love them and forgive them for how badly they behave. I admire all human storytelling of that truthful kind. I like Gail Godwin for this reason, too. And Cheever, who always writes about people who matter; he writes about people who are caught in the act of being lost, or at least they're confused by the values of everyone around them—whether the people are in prison or in the suburbs. I like Vonnegut, for his kindness, but also for his absolute and insistent originality. It's not easy to write straightforward, easy-to-read sentences, although a lot of very hard-to-read stuff has given people the idea that easy-to-read writing is easy to write. It's always easier, for a writer, to be hard to understand than to be clear. I like Heller; he knows what he means—he doesn't grope. And to come back with a different sort of writer: I admire John Hawkes, also for his absolute originality. To some people Hawkes and Vonnegut may seem to be strange bedfellows, but they share an important insistence. They insist on the world according to them. I like their arrogance; I like how right they are to claim that the world is how they see it. And I like Heinrich Böll and Günter Grass, for their morality, their solid storytelling, their good instincts for human behavior and, especially in the case of Grass, for the imagination.

Q: Do you consider yourself "up" on contemporary fiction?

A: I don't really read that much contemporary fiction. I missed so many books when I was being educated, I keep going back to read those writers I never got around to reading. And I do a lot of rereading of the books I greatly admire. I love Conrad—all that morality! I love Virginia Woolf for her language and her absolutely truthful observations of people as they are, and how little we know them. I love Hardy for his stern judgments and his crankiness. And Lawrence—like Hawkes and Vonnegut—for his originality. I read Dickens a lot just to be in touch with that energy, that investing of everything with life. Stanley Elkin really excites me with that same quality Dickens had: Elkin can make everything wriggle and leap; he can make you laugh out loud, yet with the uncomfortable knowledge that you might be made to squirm over the very next sentence.

Q: I'm aware that any fiction writer feels it's beside the point to be asked that inevitable question: How much is Garp—or the heroes of any of your novels—you? How much of what you write is autobiographical? And I know you've said that you loathe most autobiographical fiction. Still, it's a question most people want to ask. Personally, when I'm asked that question I mumble a lot. But Garp is your age, he grew up in a New England prep-school town, he's been educated partly in Europe, he's a wrestler, he has a wife and two sons, and he's a writer of fiction. All that is true of you, yet you say you're not an autobiographical writer.

A: I'm not. I make up all the important things. I've had a very uninteresting life. I had a happy childhood. I'm grateful for how ordinary my life is because I'm not ever tempted to think that something that happened to me is important simply because it happened to me. I have no personal axes to grind; I'm free, therefore, to imagine the best possible ax to grind—and I really mean that: that's a significant freedom from the tyranny and self-importance of autobiography in fiction. The only suffering in my childhood occurred when I was 15 or 16 and I knew I wanted to be a writer. How lonely that was! There was nothing like majoring in French or going to law school or medical school to look forward to; I had a terrible sense of how different I was from all my friends, and I didn't want to be different at all. No kid wants to be different. We learn to cultivate and make use of how "different" we are as we get older. When I was younger, too, I kept wishing that I'd suffered more significantly. I remember hearing a Chilean writer, José Donoso, talk about American writers: Donoso said that the problem with us was that we hadn't suffered enough. I was young enough at the time to believe this, and Donoso was (and is) very impressive to me; I became deeply worried about the lack of suffering in my life. That was more than 10 years ago; since then, I've been able to convince myself that Donoso was wrong. To suffer adequately—in order to write truly about suffering, I suppose—it is only necessary to have two things: a firm and early belief that death is, as I've said, horrible and final and frequently premature; and a good imagination. It's not necessary to be tortured in childhood or to live in a political climate where one's toes are only inches from the hot coals. In fact, we've all read any number of bad books by people who've suffered profoundly. And in many cases, it seems to me, their suffering has proved too much for them. It's distracted them from writing well.

Q: What about short stories? You've written very few short stories. Is the short story a form you feel uncomfortable in?

A: Exactly. I honestly never want to write a short story again. I haven't written as many as half a dozen, ever. And only a couple of them are any good; the best one is part of *The World According to Garp*. I just want to write novels.

Q: Long novels?

A: Well, broad novels—I want to be broad. And probably pretty long, although I hope not as long as *The World According to Garp*, at least not for another book or two. But I want to write novels that tell about someone's whole life: how a person grows up and ends up. That necessitates a certain breadth, and probably some length, too.

Q: How about nonfiction? Articles or reviews?

A: No, never. Just novels. Maybe an interview with another novelist—like you're doing. This has been fun for me. But I'm a novelist, and all I want to write right now is another novel. And then another and another, for the time remaining.—JOHN IRVING, Interview by Thomas Williams, *NYTBR*, April 23, 1978, pp. 26–27

## Works

### THE WORLD ACCORDING TO GARP

"It's everywhere" is an appropriate sentiment for *The World According to Garp*, except that there the phrase would refer not to a changed historical situation but to something like the condition of the universe, a place of casual overkill and uncanny bad luck. Injury time is a fairly relevant notion too, since John Irving's impressive score is three rapes, two assassinations, two accidental deaths, the loss of an eye, the loss of an arm, a penis bitten off, and a whole society of women with amputated tongues. Irving is very deft at moving from grotesque, even cruel, humor to amiable realism and back, and his novel is consistently intelligent and amusing, has an appealing equanimity in the midst of apparent awfulness. Yet the book feels rather tame in the end, in spite of its violence and timeliness, its response to the turbulences set off by the women's movement. ⟨. . .⟩

There are fine set pieces in the novel: Garp's conception in the hospital where his mother worked, his father a terminal case just alive enough to do the necessary deed (Garp's mother was determined to manage without men in her life as far as possible); Garp's attending his mother's funeral in drag because no men were to be allowed in, and his discovery there by his future assassin ("Hi!" he writes on a pad, thinking he has hit upon a way of concealing his gruff voice, "I'm an Ellen Jamesian." "Like hell you are," the girl replies. "You're T. S. Garp"); Garp's sudden death in the wrestling room at the Steering Academy. And Irving is very persuasive about what Garp sees as the "leer of the world," an expression first found on the face of a rapist caught by Garp and the police and released almost immediately because "nobody proved nothing." Garp's publisher thinks that the writer's death, "in its random, stupid, and unnecessary qualities—comic, and ugly, and bizarre—underlined everything Garp had ever written about how the world works." "It was a death scene," the publisher thinks, "that only Garp could have written." This is a nice touch since Irving has written it, while Garp only played it, but we may also glimpse here a reason for the tameness of this accomplished novel.

There is really no gap between the way the world works and the way Garp thinks it works, no resistance to his attention, only gruesome confirmation of it. I don't mean there is no gap between Irving and Garp. Indeed, Irving works at this very problem, invents characters he says Garp could not have invented, has Garp himself think of writers as "observers" and "imitators" of human behavior; has him see writing as a kind of hopeless salvage operation: "A novelist is a doctor who sees only terminal cases."

At one point Irving dramatizes the question memorably, when Garp invites an interviewer to tell him anything that had ever happened to her. "I can improve upon the story," Garp says, "I can make the details better than they were." The interviewer is a divorcée with four young children, one of whom is dying of cancer. But Irving really does present reality as something to be transcended or worked over rather than be reported on or understood, and Garp's central difficulty is that he is so caught up in his life that he can't *imagine* anything, and therefore can't get back to being a writer. This neat antagonism between the real world and the writer's world, this romantic conception of the creative imagination, insure the insulation of literature, however much reality may be pillaged as a source. The imagination wins all such matches because it makes up all the rules: and a novelist who sees only terminal cases is too sure of the world he sees, and sees too little of the world.—MICHAEL WOOD, "Nothing Sacred," *NYRB*, April 20, 1978, pp. 9–10

John Irving writes so wittily about the misapprehensions of reviewers that it takes some courage to embark on an account of his latest novel, *The World According to Garp*—though I am comforted a little by the fact that he clearly has friends in both camps, and that his novel is in a sense a review of itself, and of his own literary pilgrimage. But it is not merely a book about writing a book: in the first chapters, his defensive, distancing techniques strike more than the reality of the subject matter; it is only gradually that the meaning is released. This is just as well, for the book contains almost intolerable pain. It is a bloody package, and if he had flung this in front of us we would have backed away in horror. As it is, we read on, at first entertained, then puzzled, then trapped, wanting to look away, but by this time unable to avert our eyes . . . or at least, this is what happened to me. ⟨. . .⟩

It is a baffling book in many ways. Beneath the surface lies a solid, suburban, everyday life, where men worry about their children, are mildly unfaithful to their wives, crack up when their wives are unfaithful to them; an ordinary life of cooking and jogging in the park and cinemas and students, the kind of life with which John Irving at his college in Vermont (if he is still there) is doubtless familiar. Garp's perceptions of his children, his anxious protective love, his rebellion against and acceptance of this deadly anxiety, are beautifully done: there is a fine scene where, worried about the fecklessness of the mother who has invited his son to stay for the night, he creeps around to spy at one o'clock in the morning, and sees through a window in the lethal rays of the television

> crammed against the sagging couch the casual bodies of Duncan and Ralph, half in their sleeping bags, asleep (of course), but looking as if the television has murdered them. In the sickly TV light their faces look drained of blood.

This sense of death round the corner grows in the novel, and finally dominates it; the Garp family calls it the Under Toad, after a misapprehension of Garp's baby Walt about warnings against the undertow in the ocean. Every anxious parent knows the Under Toad, and I am not sure if anxious parents should be recommended to read this book, for the way in which the Toad gets Walt is really too much to bear, even dressed up as it is in such a macabre array of horror.

The macabre elaboration is, I imagine, designed to diminish rather than to intensify the book's message about the violent insecurity of the world we are forced to inhabit. But Irving's fantasies are so near the bone that three-quarters of the way through the novel I began to wonder whether perhaps there really *was* an American feminist society called the Ellen Jamesians, named after a child rape victim named Ellen James whose tongue had been cut out by her attackers. Lost tongues, lost ears, severed penises, blinded eyes, broken bones, Gothic nightmares, Jacobean melodramas, tasteless jokes about disability: it all sounds like a self-indulgent fantasy, the kind of clever creative-writing-school trick writing that one would go a long way to avoid. But it isn't that, at all.

For one thing, it does have a good deal to say about feminist movements and the changing roles of husbands and wives. Garp is a good housewife, happy with the supper and the shopping, and it is no accident that one of the most

sympathetic characters is a transsexual. More important, to me, was the novel's commentary on what I have to call the creative process, pretentious though those words always sound. Irving has some sharp comments on reviewers who look for autobiography in fiction, and the quarrels of Garp's biographers after his death ought to make one pause, but they don't. It is obvious that Garp/Irving is commenting in the novel on Irving's own literary career: his first novel, *Setting Free the Bears*, was set in Vienna and featured bears and the Vienna Zoo, as does Garp's first imaginative effort, "The Pension Grillparzer." The second novels of both remain unknown to me, though I was pleased to note a chapter heading, "Second Children, Second Novels, Second Love," that seemed to imply a natural coincidence of these three events, a coincidence I have noted in women writers before, but not in men, or not at least confessed by men. The worlds of Bensenhaver and Garp and Irving are the worlds of the mid-thirties, of mid-career, when a crushing awareness of an accumulating store of memory, most of it unpleasant, threatens to warp and inhibit the imagination. Irving's account of this process is particularly interesting. Unlike poets, most novelists seem to look forward to middle age, and to the fund of experience and observation upon which the older writer can draw: after all, many major writers didn't even start until they were older than Irving now is. Moreover, most novelists tend to look upon personal tragedy as something that can eventually be made useful, turned into grist for the mill; the more the writer suffers, the more he has to write about.

Irving challenges this assumption. His protagonist looks back to the days of visionary gleam, when he could write purely, happily, from out of the air, not from out of himself. These days have gone. Garp, struck down by the death of his son, for which he bears terrible responsibility, looks back to the first sentence of his first book, and says:

> Where had it come from? He tried to think of sentences like it. What he got was a sentence like this: "The boy was five years old; he had a cough that seemed deeper than his small, bony chest." What he got was memory, and that made muck. He had no pure imagination any more.

This is finely said, though luckily untrue, for the novel itself contains muck, memory, and imagination, and the muck gives it a weight that *Setting Free the Bears* lacked. The zaniness has been replaced by stoicism, and the jokes are now black. But there are also tenderness, respect, humanity. I particularly liked publisher John Wolf, surely one of the most appreciative portraits ever drawn by a writer; he smokes himself to death, for his "deep restlessness and unrelieved pessimism could only be numbed by smoking three packs of unfiltered cigarettes per day." Forget the bears: the wolves will do fine.—MARGARET DRABBLE, "Muck, Memory, and Imagination," *Harper's*, July 1978, pp. 82–84

### THE HOTEL NEW HAMPSHIRE

⟨. . .⟩ *The Hotel New Hampshire*, regardless of what its author tells *Publishers Weekly* and *Time*, is very much like *The World According to Garp*. First there is the subject matter, which will be familiar to anybody who has read *any* of Irving's previous work: seedy New England prep schools, fears both real and imaginary, Vienna, weight lifting and physical fitness generally, rape, violent death, mutilation, and very odd families. Of the ten major characters in the book—eight of whom belong to the first-person narrator's family—five die, two are raped and one is blinded before the story ends. Of those deaths only one is what policemen and newspaper reporters call "natural," and it is curious: Grandad, an aging football coach, drops dead of a heart attack while lifting weights and coming face to face unexpectedly with the family's recently deceased Labrador retriever, stuffed and mounted in an "attack" pose by the homosexual brother whose hobby is taxidermy. The dog's name is Sorrow. Sorrow, as readers have sad occasion to learn later, also floats; it is one of the novel's recurring themes. In life, though, the dog had been notoriously flatulent. Neither the animal nor the emotion can be alluded to later on without the narrator's reminiscing about the "old farter."

Yet whatever one's ultimate response to Irving's customary mix of vulgarity and portentousness—using those words for the moment as nonjudgmentally as one can—there is no denying that he has at least one thing in common with ⟨. . .⟩ Twain and Dickens: he can tell stories. Things *happen* in *The Hotel New Hampshire*; if one admired Irving for nothing else, one would have to admit that he can keep as many narrative balls in the air without dropping them as anyone in America now writing fiction. Whether or not his books instruct and delight as we critics are supposed to think they should, they are full of characters and events, and suffused with details, surprises, digressions, subplots and asides. They are very much *written* too, which is to say they are literary constructs as opposed to screenplay outlines in disguise. For all of that, they move; most readers will not fail, having begun *The Hotel New Hampshire*, to read all the way to the last sad death.

Speaking personally, I cared for only one of the book's many characters, a small boy recognizably doomed and killed off fairly early on. (Despite his penchant for dispatching them, one quality I like in Irving is his ability to create children who act like children.) After the child's demise, for reasons I shall expand upon presently, my heart went out of the book. But I kept going because I wanted to see what would happen. Readers should perhaps be warned, however, that this reviewer once knocked off sixteen John D. MacDonald mystery novels in one month. In MacDonald's books, the reader knows that the love interest is going to get it sooner or later, if not towards the end of *The Empty Copper Sea*, then in the opening of *The Green Ripper*; Travis McGee is a loner, you see, and very much into sentimental revenge. What Irving is into is something else again. It is the beloved and the innocent who get it in his books too, but there is nobody to blame except the god of Irony. And in *The Hotel New Hampshire* that deity, I fear, is a sophomore. ⟨. . .⟩

*The Hotel New Hampshire* has absolutely nothing to do with the hotel business, about which Irving knows less, I would wager, than the night clerk at a Holiday Inn. Well, so what? Kafka was not an entomologist; *The Metamorphosis* is not a reliable source of beetle lore. But where Kafka penetrates the grotesque, Irving takes the reader water-skiing. The novel is all surfaces, all situations. Brother Frank is a homosexual and a taxidermist. He is also a pessimist. But that is *all* one knows about Frank. We meet none of his lovers, learn literally nothing about how and when he discovered his inclination, what he thinks or feels about it, what he wears, how he walks, talks, relates to heterosexuals . . . nothing. Here's Frank. He's a homo who stuffs Labrador retrievers. Can you believe it? (Turn up the laugh track.) And here's little sister Lilly. She's so little she's a dwarf. I mean, can you believe this family? See Lilly dance "stoically, with one of Father and Mother's friends, Mr. Matson, an unfortunately tall man—although if he had been short, he couldn't have been short enough for Lilly. They looked like an awkward, perhaps unmentionable animal act." (Chuckles.) That's it for Mr. Matson, whom Irving invents just to dance with the dwarf. Lilly pretty much disappears from the

book until she writes *Trying to Grow*, her best seller. As far as we know it's about her crazy family, like the book we are reading. Then she kills herself. Why? Who cares? We've got a story to keep moving here, an Imagination to show off. Even incest—which could very well be the pop-lit sexual theme of the Reagan years—gets a sketchy treatment. "When you're in love with your sister," the narrator tells us in one of Irving's better lines, "you lose a lot of perspective on the real world." Yet an all-day and half-the-night session with Franny affects our boy no more than a head cold. Once it's done we hardly hear about it again. Whether Franny tells Junior Jones we are not informed. But then Junior wouldn't be at all perturbed, one guesses. He's your basic big, black Teddy Bear, and changes not a jot from prep school to law school, college and pro career notwithstanding. I kept waiting for him to start hollering "less filling," or "tastes great."

Imagination-land is like most theme parks. The grown-ups will enjoy it once a lot more than they'll admit, but unlike the children, they'll never want to go back. John Irving ought to quit wasting his time there too; he's frittering away his narrative gift on nonsense.—GENE LYONS, "Something New in Theme Parks," *Nation*, Sept. 26, 1981, pp. 277–80

Family dailiness—traditional sitcom material—is in nearly constant view throughout the novel. Father and mother tell stories about their youth to their children. Grandfather teaches grandson his special athletic skills. Mother intercedes when older siblings try to force their juniors into premature knowing-ness. Mothers speaks out against slovenliness. ("Your room, Lilly," Mother said. "What am I going to say about your room?") Children tease each other ferociously, engage in fistfights, learn to work together in the family business, learn to drive cars, learn forbearance, find their affection for one another strengthening over time. And toward the end, children are seen taking up parental roles, caring for the elders whose hour as nurturers and protectors has begun to fade. Four of the eight family members with whom this book begins are gone at the end, but the survivors are close-knit, and a new Berry baby is on the way, assuring the continuity of the generations.

Simple, unsadistic stuff. But, as I've hinted, it's conjoined with matter remote from everyday, and the combination creates surprising narrative rhythms and a sharply distinctive tone. *The Hotel New Hampshire* is structured as a succession of shrewdly prepared explosions of violence, each of which blends the hideous and the comic, and projects a fresh length of story line that hisses forward into the next blowup almost before the dust of the last has settled. A typical sequence runs as follows: Franny Berry is gang-raped by members of a prep school football team on Hallowe'en; on the same day, her father, Win Berry, takes the family pet, an ancient Labrador named Sorrow who is dear to Franny but troublingly afflicted with flatulence, to the local vet to be put to sleep. Conscious of his fearfully violated younger sister's need for the comfort of her pet, Frank Berry races to the animal hospital in hope of saving the beast. He's too late, but he does recover Sorrow's body, and, having earlier learned taxidermy in a biology course, resolves to stuff the dog and offer it to his sister as a gift. New narrative fuse lit and burning, obviously, and explosion is imminent. It occurs a chapter later, on Christmas Day. Stuffed and mounted in an "attack" pose, hidden in an upstairs closet, Sorrow suddenly springs out at Grandfather Berry when the latter, working out with weights in his room, accidentally knocks open the closet door:

> . . . before I could get my breath back and tell my grandfather that it was only a Christmas present for Franny—that it was only one of Frank's awful

projects from down at the bio lab—the old [man] slung his barbell at the savage attack dog and threw his wonderful lineman's body back against me (to protect me, no doubt; that must have been what he meant to do) . . . [and] dropped dead in my arms.

The rape-taxidermy sequence shuttles swiftly between the farcical and the pathetic. Franny Berry's anguished weeping is in our ears as we watch her brother push the stiffening dog's body into a trash bag (the vet's wife murmurs, "It's so sweet"). We jump cut from Franny's shattered effort to convince herself that her assailants haven't damaged the "*me* in me" to a series of one-liners exchanged by brothers discussing dog-stuffing. (Brother John: "I don't know if Franny will like that." Brother Frank: "It's the next-best thing to being alive.") We're never in doubt of Frank Berry's sympathy for his sister's suffering, but the gags superimposed upon this sympathy do contort it. And comparable contortions abound elsewhere in the book's action. The primary moment of catharsis occurs when the Berry children, with aides, manage to terrify the rapists' ringleader with a brilliantly staged threat that he himself will be raped by a bear. The book's narrative crisis occurs when Father Berry handily smashes (with a Louisville Slugger) a ring of terrorists in the Austrian Hotel New Hampshire who are about to blow up Vienna's opera house and take the Berry family hostage. Always, the sympathy and solidarity of the family members are in evidence—qualities placing the Berrys firmly in a world of light and affirmation. But often the visible deeds and spoken words verge upon the violently sadistic, or the black comic, or the melodramatically grotesque.

And the author's taste for incongruity affects characterization as well as action. Each of the Berrys is normal in his or her feeling for parents and siblings—loving, concerned, loyal:

> ". . . we *aren't* eccentric, we're *not* bizarre. To each other," Franny would say, "we're as common as rain." And she was right: to each other, we were as normal and nice as the smell of bread, we were just a family.

But it's a fact that the Berry kids don't invariably sound "normal and nice." On the first page of the book, one child speculates to another about the precise date when their parents "started screwing"; from then on the children's sprightly R-rated obscenities decorate virtually every paragraph. Nor can it be said that these folks are untouched by deviance. Franny Berry is, for an interval, caught in a lesbian love affair. She and John Berry are in love with each other and consummate their incestuous passion in an extended sexual bout. Frank Berry is an out-of-the-closet homosexual given to expressions of glee in his aberrancy. Lilly Berry is a suicide.

The entire family, furthermore, thrives on exposure to ills of the public world that more conventional families labor to avoid. Day in and day out in Vienna, the Berrys deal not only with a gang of terrorists (resident on one floor of their hotel) but with a sly, dirty-talking circle of prostitutes (resident on another floor of the place). They're beset both by racists and by enraged victims of racism. They're even obliged to learn how to handle the media. (Lilly Berry's fans, hyped into a condition of hysterical idolatry, are infuriated with her relatives for their unwillingness to cooperate in establishing her as a secular saint.) If, in short, the quality of the children's sense of fun and feeling for each other stands forth as "normal and nice," neither the children's environment nor their individual natures quite warrant those labels. Nightmare and sunshine simultaneously, once again.

A fair question about this pairing is: What's it for? Does juxtaposing the quotidian and the melodramatic—the norma-

tive and the eccentric, the healthy and the sadistic—offer much besides shock value? Doesn't it become merely confusing? John Irving's triumph in his last book was traceable, I believe, to the brisk ingenuity with which he dispatched these doubts. *Garp*, as will be remembered, is in part about a novelist and his audience—a novelist plagued, like most, by readers whose interest seems sometimes to derive exclusively from curiosity about whether his stories are autobiographical. The most horrible episode of rape and murder in the book is presented as a chapter of a novel written by T. S. Garp shortly after losing a beloved child in an automobile crash. As one reads the episode, one isn't merely titillated by the grisly and forbidden; one is shown, dramatically, how a writer transforms personal experience into an achieved imaginative narrative that, despite being complexly rooted, in every detail, in "real life," is remote from any set of actual happenings. Graphically depicted sexual encounter becomes, through elegant indirection, a lesson about art and its sources, a means of access to a father's inexpressible grief, and an instrument capable of reconciling totally opposite modes of feeling.

I confess I suspected that this feat—the purposeful linking of the normative and the perverse or hateful—couldn't be brought off a second time, but I was wrong. Less bloody than *Garp*, *The Hotel New Hampshire* nevertheless is rich, from start to finish, in incongruous juxtapositions, and it offers genuine pleasures. I don't pretend to know all of Mr. Irving's secrets, but I'm fairly certain about one of them. Early in the book the reader is nudged into noticing resemblances between the narrative proceedings at hand and those of a fairy tale—the only literary form that has ever satisfactorily tamed the horrible. Half-magical attachments between human and animal creatures (men and bears) hold our attention from the start. John Irving reflects time and again on dreams, wish fulfillment, happy endings. And in the touching final page, he steps forward to acknowledge that he and his reader have been living in a "fairy-tale hotel," spinning wish fulfillments: "We give ourselves a sainted mother, we make our father a hero; and someone's older brother, and someone's older sister—they become our heroes, too. We invent what we love, and what we fear. There is always a brave, lost brother—and a little lost sister, too. We dream on and on: the best hotel, the perfect family. . . ." Guided by the narrator, we intuit that this work (when the grotesque heaves into sight) is not only about the unbearable but about our instinct for refusing the unbearable—not only about the worst of life but about our capacity for willing away the worst. That intuition does much, throughout, to soothe our unease with contortions and contrarieties.

We're also soothed because a good deal of the worst in *The Hotel New Hampshire* really is willed away. A few dread events in the story—a plane crash, a blinding—are irreversible. But, as it turns out, they're exceptions to the book's rule. Brother and sister fall in love and sexually embrace—but their embrace is a means of canceling the memory of the cruel rape: before the end Franny Berry transcends her incestuous passion and her lesbian attachment, and gives herself fully to marriage, procreation, health. Frank Berry, self-absorbed homosexual, is led out of his enclosure into the sunlight of selflessly generous relationships with both siblings and elders. A young woman once so convinced of her ugliness that she went about the world in disguise is helped to discover her beauty, arrives at a positive view of herself, becomes the means through which John Berry conquers his infatuation with his sister.

And as it goes with individuals, so it goes with impersonal forces of negation. The racism and sexism that stalk the opening chapters bow in shame at the conclusion. Blacks and whites come together in harmony that is rooted in perception of their shared humanity. The brutalizing rapist Caliban who attacked Franny understands that he too must alter his ways. And—highly impressive utopian accomplishment—the terrible energy of rape comes to seem less real, less momentous, than the infinitely loving, patient process by which a rape crisis center brings about, in the abused, the rebirth of trust. We occupy, in other words, a world wherein nearly everything comes out as we should like, the formal and psychological sequences moving from tragedy to comedy, from despair to hope. And, to repeat, because we begin to feel, close to the start, the inevitability of that fairy-tale progress, the intermingling of destructive and nurturing elements just escapes the taint of arbitrariness.—BENJAMIN DEMOTT, "Domesticated Madness," *At*, Oct. 1981, pp. 102–5

Lurching glumly to the end of this joyless romp, the reviewer finds a surge of pejoratives to hand: narcissistic, ponderous, cute, brutal, relentless, self-adoring, vulgar, popular, American. . . . At which point alarm bells start to ring in the critical command centre.

It's easy to despise a certain gauche deftness, an un-Englishly energetic ambitiousness. What exactly grates? If Irving seems heartless, so does Waugh; if his characters are robotic, so are Orwell's; if he kills them off with abandon, so did Shakespeare; if he is extravagant, so was Poe; if he is obsessed, so was Melville; if he is long, so is Art; if he is untrue to real life, so is Real Life.

None of which reconciles me to the style Irving adopts here, a diction consistently ungracious, sometimes ungrammatical ("to we children"), slangy and redundant. Here a terrorist gang is about to blow up the Vienna Opera House; the narrator observes:

> On the Kärtnerstrasse across from the Opera was a sausage vendor, a man with a kind of hot-dog cart selling different kinds of *Wurst mit Senf und Bauernbrot*—a kind of sausage with mustard on rye. I didn't want one.

It would be hard to imagine anything more inessential than a description of the sort of sausage that the hero doesn't want at a critical juncture; and all those "kinds" make us less than kin. Sometimes Irving can cram a great deal of redundancy into a small compass: "The band was named either after Doris or after the mild hurricane of some years before—which was also named Doris. The band was called, naturally, Hurricane Doris." Naturally.

Irving has either chosen this style deliberately or is suffering from fatty degeneration of the prose, for he was capable of other styles: *The 158-Pound Marriage* is almost laconic, and *The Water-Method Man* has donnish wit. (My brisk jog through the *oeuvre* of Irving tested and dismissed two hypotheses: that my pleasure varied inversely with the length of the book or directly with the order of publication. The one I like the least is not the longest. The one I like the most is not the earliest.) ⟨. . .⟩

Some of Irving's best and worst jokes depend on the literal realization of metaphor. Sorrow the dog and sorrow the emotion recur—doggedly. "Sorrow floats", we are told, and the narrator's first sexual prospect finds the half-burnt canine in the bath, dead but buoyant, "while she is diaphragming herself"—an unlovely expression, if not quite as gross as "unpantsed" from *Garp*. ("If the world would stop indulging wars and famines and other perils, it would still be possible for human beings to embarrass each other to death".) The dead dog reappears in the debris of the plane crash. Questions of taste aside, if you give the name Sorrow to a farting Labrador it is quite easy to make comical references. If you choose to name a fictional character "Freud" it is surely slightly underhand to make a number of "who said that, our Freud or the other one?" jests. (In my forthcoming *Groundwork for a Structuralist Phenomenology of the Joke*, a dismissive chapter is devoted to jokes that invest a large improbable datum for a small return in amusement.)

The interchange of metaphor and fact, of real and mock—especially real and mock sex, real and mock violence—seems to be Irving's chief concern. The joke revolutionaries can kill; and Screaming Annie's fake orgasms, which arouse (or at least awaken) the whole hotel, turn out to be real after all. Mockery can heal—Franny exorcizes her rape by subjecting the chief rapist to a ludicrously sinister masquerade in which the whole family joins. But it can also kill—in one of the few passages written with real passion, the narrator speaks of the terrorist as "simply another kind of pornographer. . . . The pornographer pretends he is disgusted by his work; the terrorist pretends he is uninterested in the means . . . but they are both lying."

Critics of Irving who complain that he treats his characters inhumanly, and also that his characters are lifeless simulacra, are trying to have it both ways. But so is Irving.—ERIC KORN, "Trying to Grow the Freudian Way," *TLS*, Nov. 6, 1981, p. 1302

# SHIRLEY JACKSON

## 1919–1965

Shirley Jackson was born in San Francisco on December 14, 1919. In 1933 her family moved to Rochester, New York, and Jackson soon after matriculated at the University of Rochester. Severe depression forced Jackson to leave Rochester after only one year. She later enrolled at Syracuse University, where she received a B.A. in 1940. While at Syracuse she met Stanley Edgar Hyman, an author and critic, whom she married in 1940. Together she and Hyman worked on literary magazines at Syracuse. After her graduation she moved to New York where she held a clerical job. Her years as a clerk were later recounted in the story "My Life with R. H. Macy." After the birth of her first two children (she eventually was the mother of four), Jackson moved to North Bennington, Vermont. Here she found more time to write, and in 1948 her famous short story "The Lottery" was published in *The New Yorker*. The story, which focuses on the modern reenactment of ancient scapegoat rituals, prompted more reader mail than anything previously published in *The New Yorker*.

The same year her first novel, *The Road through the Wall*, was published. Set in Burlingame, California, where she spent her childhood, this novel was followed by *Hangsaman* (1951), a novel about schizophrenia. *The Bird's Nest* (1954) also deals with schizophrenia. Jackson's other novels include *The Sundial* (1958), *The Haunting of Hill House* (1959), and *We Have Always Lived in the Castle* (1962), which describes a web of family murder and bizarre liaisons. Jackson's fiction is noted for its gothic qualities and its resemblance to Hawthorne's tales. In addition to her novels, Jackson wrote a children's book, *The Witchcraft of Salem Village* (1956), and two collections of short stories chronicling domestic life, *Life among the Savages* (1953) and *Raising Demons* (1957). Jackson won the 1961 Edgar Allan Poe Award for her story "Louisa, Please." She died unexpectedly at her Vermont home on August 8, 1965, of heart failure.

## Personal

In her short and busy life—she died peacefully of heart failure during a nap in her forty-sixth year—Shirley Jackson managed to publish quite a few short stories and twelve books: six novels, a volume of stories, two fictionalized memoirs, and three juveniles, one of them a play. At the time of her death, she was at work on a new novel, savagely comic in tone, and a fantasy book for children.

People often expressed surprise at the difference between Shirley Jackson's appearance and manner, and the violent and terrifying nature of her fiction. Thus, many of the obituaries played up the contrast between a "motherly-looking" woman, gentle and humorous, and that "chillingly horrifying short story 'The Lottery'" and similar works. When Shirley Jackson, who was my wife, published two lighthearted volumes about the spirited doings of our children, *Life among the Savages* and *Raising Demons*, it seemed to surprise people that she should be a wife and mother at all, let alone a gay and apparently happy one. This seems to me to be the most elementary misunderstanding of what a writer is and how a writer works, on the order of expecting Herman Melville to be a white whale.

Shirley Jackson wrote in a variety of forms and styles because she was, like everyone else, a complex human being, confronting the world in many different roles and moods. She tried to express as much of herself as possible in her work, and to express each aspect as fully and purely as possible. While she wanted the fullest self-expression, consistent with the limits of literary form, at the same time she wanted the widest possible audience for that self-expression; in short, she wanted a public, sales, success. For her entire adult life she regarded herself as a professional writer, one who made a living by the craft of writing, and as she did not see that vocation as incompatible with being a wife and mother, so she did not see her dedication to art as incompatible with producing art in salable forms. In this, as in other respects, she was curiously old-fashioned.

Despite a fair degree of popularity—reviews of her books were generally enthusiastic, reprints and foreign publications were numerous, and her last two novels, *The Haunting of Hill House* and *We Have Always Lived in the Castle*, became modest best sellers—her work has been very little understood. Her fierce visions of dissociation and madness, of alienation and withdrawal, of cruelty and terror, have been taken to be personal, even neurotic, fantasies. Quite the reverse: They are a sensitive and faithful anatomy of our times, fitting symbols for our distressing world of the concentration camp and The Bomb. She was always proud that the Union of South Africa banned "The Lottery," and she felt that *they*, at least, understood the story. Obituary references to her in such terms

as the "Virginia Werewolf of séance-fiction writers" show a considerable obliviousness to her meanings and purposes.

After the first years, she consistently refused to be interviewed, to explain or promote her work in any fashion, or to take public stands and be a pundit of the Sunday supplements. She believed that her books would speak for her clearly enough over the years, and I share her belief. The only exception she made to this vow of silence was a willingness, even an eagerness, to lecture about the craft of fiction at colleges and writers' conferences, where she could assume an audience with some serious interest in such matters. She was reluctant to publish those lectures, for a variety of reasons, but they include some of the few sensible and useful words I know on that impossible subject—what fiction is and how it's made.

For all her popularity, she won surprisingly little recognition. She received no awards or prizes, grants or fellowships. She saw those honors go to inferior writers—or to writers who were no writers—without bitterness, but with the wry amusement which was her habitual attitude toward her own life and career. Those few contemporary writers whose work she valued, almost without exception, knew her work and valued it, and she was content with the approbation of her fellow craftsmen. In this, as in so many other respects, she was the purest of professionals.

I think that the future will find her powerful visions of suffering and inhumanity increasingly significant and meaningful, and that Shirley Jackson's work is among that small body of literature produced in our time that seems apt to survive. That thought, too, she would have found wryly amusing.—STANLEY EDGAR HYMAN, "Shirley Jackson: 1919–1965," *SEP*, Dec. 18, 1965, p. 63

## Works

### SHORT STORIES

Many of the short stories in Shirley Jackson's *The Lottery, or The Adventures of James Harris* (1949) resemble closely the kind of new fiction written by (Paul) Bowles, and by Capote too. Where Bowles is strident and melodramatic, she manages a low-keyed and quiet nihilism which is nonetheless almost as pervasive as his. Where both men force us to look into the uncovered face of evil, she quite matter of factly assumes its presence everywhere; indeed, her healthy-looking, apparently normal children reveal a particular appetite for contemplating violence and horror. Seemingly content to deal with ordinary experience in an ordinary way, she is always aware of the other side of consciousness, of the lurking figure, real or imagined, who leads her characters out into a strange nowhere. Her unpretentious and rather colorless prose is a suitable vehicle for the laconic expression of an equation of disintegration: as the culture seems to be going to pieces in some of these stories, so does the human personality. Her fiction is created out of this play on the incongruity between the ordinariness of her manner and the unreality of the reality that she perceives. Her dedication to a pessimistic view of experience is everywhere explicit, but occasionally it is obscured by the manipulation of her paradoxes.—CHESTER E. EISINGER, "The New Fiction," *Fiction of the Forties,* 1963, pp. 288–89

"The Possibility of Evil," one of Shirley Jackson's superb stories, provides a key to much of her fiction. It contains many of the elements basic to her work, including a sensitive but narrow female protagonist, a gothic house, economy of language, intimations of something "other" or "more," a free-floating sense of depravity, experiences of dissociation, and a final turn about in events or a judgment.

At seventy-one, Miss Adela Strangeworth, the protagonist of "The Possibility of Evil," lives alone in the house on Pleasant Street built two generations earlier by her family. She is proud of her house—"with its slimness and its washed white look"—and especially proud and protective of the beautiful roses that lined the front of the house. She knows everyone in town, and she loves her town so much that she has never spent more than a day away from it her entire life. In fact, "she sometimes found herself thinking that the the town belonged to her." As she goes about her life she wonders about the behavior of her fellow townsmen, and sometimes comments, if not to them, then to herself.

For a year now Miss Strangeworth has been sending little notes to various townspeople, using common colored writing paper and writing with a dull stub pencil in a childish block print. She did not sign her name. "She was fond of doing things exactly right." The notes were cruel, gossipy, and vicious, based on half-truths or on none at all. "Miss Strangeworth never concerned herself with facts, her letters dealt with the more negotiable stuff of suspicion." She was always after the "possible evil lurking nearby," because "as long as evil existed unchecked in the world, it was Miss Strangeworth's duty to keep her town alert to it. . . . There were so many wicked people in the world and only one Strangeworth left in the town. Besides, Miss Strangeworth liked writing her letters." This is her secret contribution to keeping her town sweet and clean, her private war with the forces of evil. After her nap and dinner she takes her evening walk in order to mail the notes she had written that day. She thinks: "There was so much evil in people. Even in a charming little town like this one, there was still so much evil in people." Preoccupied, she did not notice when one of her letters fell onto the ground. But two teenagers saw it and picked it up; since Miss Strangeworth did not hear them when they called her, they decided to deliver the letter to the address; they thought: "Maybe it's good news for them." Miss Strangeworth awakes the next morning happy that three more people will receive her notes: "Harsh, perhaps, at first, but wickedness was never easily banished, and a clean heart was a scoured heart." But when she opens her own mail that morning she finds a little letter very much like the ones she sends. "She began to cry silently for the wickedness of the world when she read the words: Look Out at What Used to Be Your Roses."

Like many Jackson stories this one has a parable-like quality about it—we do not know where or when the story takes place; we are given just enough information to see the universality of the human problem involved. Even with the undercurrent of comic irony the story is reminiscent of many of Hawthorne's tales, his characters haunted by the idea of a knowledge beyond knowledge and so utterly committed to achieving it that they become perverted in the process, such as

Goodman Brown and Ethan Brand. Here, Shirley Jackson summons up one more fierce Puritan who personally takes on the forces of evil, and who thus demonstrates, in William Van O'Connor's phrase, "the evil lurking in the righteous mind." Miss Strangeworth is not aware that her own humanity is corroded by making the struggle against evil her sole reason for living. She is corrupted by her own narcissism. As Lionel Rubinoff observes: ". . . by pretending to be angels we shall surely become devils. . . . [Because] the possibility of real virtue exists only for a man who has the freedom to choose evil." This freedom Miss Strangeworth cannot and will not give, because she herself holds an evil belief: "a belief that one *cannot do wrong*," to use D. H. Lawrence's remarks about one of Hawthorne's characters. Lawrence concludes: "No men are so evil to-day as the idealists, and no women half so evil as your earnest woman, who feels herself a power for good." Paradoxically, Miss Strangeworth is doing evil in order to further good. Miss Strangeworth reveals the unscrupulosity of the devout, and the only people more unscrupulous than the devout are the frightened, and they are often the same people.

Shirley Jackson reveals a fundamental problem here, one especially crucial in American culture: the revelation of the imagination that sees evil only *out there*, and which thus must be smashed at any cost. Miss Strangeworth does not see that evil is a component within us all that can be transcended only through its recognition and acceptance. Heinrich Zimmer, writing of the meaning of an ancient tale, says:

> The function of evil is to keep in operation the dynamics of change. Cooperating with the beneficient forces, though antagonistically, those of evil thus assist in the weaving of the tapestry of life; hence the experience of evil, and to some extent this experience alone, produces maturity, real life, real command of the powers and tasks of life. The forbidden fruit—the fruit of guilt through experience, knowledge through experience—had to be swallowed in the Garden of Innocence before human history could begin. Evil had to be accepted and assimilated, not avoided.

Accordingly, Lionel Rubinoff observes: "It is the excessive rationalistic and abstract apocalyptic imagination that defines evil as an object of scorn, or as an incurable disease. The apocalyptic imagination is sober, passive, and detached. It seeks to reduce mystery to rational order. It sits in judgment, protected by certainty, and condemns." This is Miss Strangeworth before she opens her own letter of judgment which may have torn the veil of innocence from her imagination and open her to a reconsideration of "the possibility of evil."

Though she is northern and urban Shirley Jackson is here reminiscent of Flannery O'Connor, who frequently brought a "moment of truth" to her characters, though it usually arrived too late, as in her story "Greenleaf." Writing about her own work Flannery O'Connor said: "St. Cyril of Jerusalem . . . wrote: 'The dragon sits by the side of the road, watching those who pass. Beware lest he devour you. We go to the Father of Souls, but it is necessary to pass by the dragon.' No matter what form the dragon may take, it is of this mysterious passage past him, or into his jaws, that stories of any depth will always be concerned to tell." This aptly describes what Shirley Jackson is doing in her fiction. She brings many of her characters by or into the dragon, or, to change the image, she brings them to the edge of the abyss: some fall, some cling desperately to the edge, and only a few find their way to safety, but such are evil's possibilities.—JOHN G. PARKS, "The Possibility of Evil: A Key to Shirley Jackson's Fiction," *SSF,* Summer 1978, pp. 320–23

## NOVELS

*Hangsaman* does not reach the level of "The Lottery," which had a murderous impact, but it confirms the belief that Miss Jackson is an exceptional writer. In the longer form, she loses tension, and her repeated glimpses into her heroine's mind, clear and sharp though they are, give somehow the effect of taking her eye off the ball. The brilliantly objective vision at which she excels makes almost anything else seem like a loss of power. The theme of *Hangsaman* is simple and unoriginal. Natalie, seventeen-year-old daughter of a priggish but not unlikeable writer who not only thinks he understands her, but uses her as compensation for his wife's dislike, escapes from home to college. Her English tutor and his wife get on little better than her parents, she makes no real contact with the other girls, and finally becomes involved in an obscure adventure with the only girl who attracts her. The end of the book suggests that the hangman has "stayed his hand awhile," but does not tell us what will happen to Natalie; and I wanted to know.

The merits of this exciting and suggestive story stare at us from the page: the defects that blur its brilliance are less easy to analyse. Looking back to Miss Jackson's short stories, I think the answer is that her power to suggest intangible terrors derives directly from her power to see and to describe *objects*. Thus, when she analyses, there is a loss of clarity, of immediacy. The best in her writing is the enemy of the good. There is a self-consciousness about the early chapters of *Hangsaman* which was hardly ever apparent in the short stories. If Miss Jackson had not written those stories, *Hangsaman* would be a triumph. As she did, it is merely an astonishingly good first novel. —L. A. G. STRONG, *Spec*, Oct. 5, 1951, p. 452

Miss Jackson's newest ghost story ⟨*The Sundial*⟩ is laid in a luxurious New England estate inhabited by a rather choice collection of creeps. A senile old gentleman, whose nanny reads him *Robinson Crusoe*; his power-hungry mate, dreaming of ruling the estate at any cost; their asthmatic daughter-in-law, mourning for her husband who has apparently been pushed down the stairs by mommy to ensure her control; and their sweet little granddaughter, happily defacing grandma's portraits and sticking significant pins in waxen dolls. There is also Aunt Fanny, given to receiving minatory visions of her deceased father, founder of the line and builder of the mansion. The family is rounded out with a bounder supposedly cataloguing the books in the library and a sissy nursemaid.

They are all mad, of course, which makes it somewhat easier for them to accept batty Aunt Fanny's disturbing report from her father that the world is soon to come to an end. Taking the apocalyptic tidings in stride, they are modestly consoled by the revelation that the estate itself is to be spared. There follows what might be called a period of adjustment, with the domineering Mrs. Halloran deciding which guests and relatives are to be permitted to stay on, and thus be allowed to enter the new world that is to be born after the destruction of the old, and which are to be consigned to the cataclysm. Not unpredictably, some of the younger, more earthbound members of the establishment, even though they are more than half-sold on Aunt Fanny's warnings of the ineluctable, yearn for the fleshpots of the dying outer world and attempt to return to it.

The inference is obvious. Miss Jackson takes ample advantage of it, and of the entire situation, to utter a number of acerbic and sibylline comments on our world and what are laughingly known as its inhabitants. The title itself refers to the sundial of the Halloran garden, on which is inscribed WHAT IS THIS WORLD? In a sense, the novel itself can be read as

Miss Jackson's partial answer to the cosmic question, embroidered with comic embellishments.

The household expends a good deal of energy in laying in a store of supplies for the new life to come. "There was a carton of anti-histamine preparations. . . . There were cartons of plastic overshoes and rubbers, in assorted sizes, of instant coffee, of cleansing tissue and sunglasses. Suntan lotion, salted nuts in cans, paper napkins, soap, both bar and flaked, toilet paper (four cartons). . . ." Of course the logical place to store these essential ingredients of the brave new world is the library; after the books have been removed to the yard and burned, the breakfast foods and citronella seem to fit quite nicely on the shelves.

Miss Jackson does not miss too many opportunities. Negotiations are undertaken between the residents of the fortress-to-be and the leadership of a religious sect which also believes in the approaching destruction of the globe, but plans a relocation on another planet. Refugees are accepted as guests of the estate on the basis of their qualifications as seers or breeding machines. And hints are dropped from time to time that those of us who enjoy doing so may read the characters as symbols, either of the seven deadly sins or as other ectoplasm manifestations, with the emphasis on the irony of survival of the worst.

Why is it then that the book finally leaves such a small impression? For one reader it is primarily because, while Miss Jackson is an intelligent and clever writer, there rises from her pages the cold fishy gleam of a calculated and carefully expressed contempt for the human race.

Pleasure in the vilenesses that human beings can commit one upon the other soon palls, particularly it is unaccompanied by any imaginary representation of the specific moral gravity of a good human being. The result is that the figures in this literary landscape become less and less human and more and more simply the vehicles for an extended bitter joke that ends after several hundred pages by being merely tedious.—HARVEY SWADOS, "What Is This World?," *NR*, March 3, 1958, pp. 19–20

Shirley Jackson's forte, as everybody knows, is the projection of a certain kind of psycho-supernatural horror. In the remote past our legitimate fear of the evil shapes and forms in nature was matched by the fantasies of evil which man himself invented. And which was which? Is nature mad, or are we? That is the central problem in *The Haunting of Hill House*, as it was in "The Lottery," and to Miss Jackson's credit there are brilliant episodes in her new book which give you the shivers and the shakes.

The story develops slowly, however, and it is just about reaching the midway point when we get caught up by it. The opening sections may seem almost banal, or certainly very familiar, in the tradition of the Gothic novel. Hill House is haunted, surely, and Dr. Montague, a professional figure with a weakness for psychic investigation, hires three "assistants" to help him make a study of the place. Two of these assistants are women who have had earlier experiences with the "other world." The third is Luke, an engaging young scoundrel, who has been forced upon the good doctor by the absentee owners of Hill House. So far so good, or rather, so bad.

If Miss Jackson is proficient in describing the alarums and excursions of human pathology, she is correspondingly weak on the "normal" world of human relations, or even of ordinary social gossip. The two women in the story, Eleanor and Theodora, engage in a curious kind of infantile Lesbian affection that is meant to be sophisticated, but is usually embarrassing. There is too much of this whimsy in the earlier parts of the novel; eventually it turns out that both women have an eye on Luke, and that their real relation is one of love-hate. While all this goes on, the doctor lectures us intermittently on the role played by haunted houses in the annals of magic.

It is only when the monster at Hill House strikes at last (and how!) that Miss Jackson's pen becomes charmed, or rather demonic, and the supernatural activity is really chilling. Why or what is it that closes every door in this "masterpiece of architectural misdirection"; that has the smell of putrefaction, the cold breath of death; that writes on the wall, pounds at the doors, whimpers and snickers, and leaves its tracks in a substance indistinguishable from blood? Our suspicion falls in turn upon each member of the little group, and then in particular upon one of the girls, Eleanor, who has been selected, it appears, as the special "victim" of the monster.

In fairness to Miss Jackson's readers, I can say no more than this—though my own conviction is that the author is not altogether fair with us. After the crime tales of a William Roughead, or the mystery tales of Henry James himself, we are bound to expect a "rationale" of even the supernatural. Miss Jackson never deigns to offer this to us. She is concerned only with the effect of a terrifying atmosphere—which she calls "reality"—upon a mind already rather preoccupied with horrors. But in this rather restricted and peculiar medium Shirley Jackson is, I must say, very eloquent.—MAXWELL GEISMAR, "Annals of Magic," *SR*, Oct. 31, 1959, pp. 19, 31

I have always felt that some writers should be read and never reviewed. Their talent is haunting and utterly oblique; their mastery of craft seems complete. Even before reading Shirley Jackson's latest novel ⟨*We Have Always Lived in the Castle*⟩, I would have thought her case to be clear: she is of that company. And now Miss Jackson has made it even more difficult for a reviewer to seem pertinent; all he can do is bestow praise.

Yet praise can take many forms. Perhaps the best thing one can say of this author is that she offers an alternative to the canonical view of "seriousness" in literature. Like the late Isak Dinesen, she is a meticulous storyteller who can evoke the reality of the times without invoking its current, cloying clichés. Her work moves on the invisible shadow line between fantasy and verisimilitude; it also hovers between innocence and dark knowledge. Above all, her work never averts itself from the human thing, which it quickens with chilly laughter or fabulous imaginings.

*We Have Always Lived in the Castle* is not as eerie as some of Miss Jackson's other works, but it is every bit as deviate and gripping. There are three people who live in the ancestral home of the Blackwoods, up on a hill. Their life is a hermetic one, shut against the fearful and railing villagers below, and overcast by the memory of a mass murder, by arsenic, of most of the Blackwood family. The three are Constance Blackwood, who cooks and cares lovingly for the others, acquitted somehow of the murder; Uncle Julian, a survivor of that grim event, now an invalid, and Constance's younger sister, Mary Katherine, better known as "Merricat," who is still in her teens. Merricat is the shy, wild narrator of the story: the significance of that literary fact is one of the grisly discoveries that every reader must make for himself.

Yet the effect on the book does not only depend on mystery or suspense; nor on the casual intimations of evil that Miss Jackson can put in a phrase like "the falseness of spring." The effect depends rather on her ability to specify a real world which is at once more sane and more mad than the world we see. It is a feminine world—men tread lightly in it—full of bewitched or magical heirlooms, but also full of clean crockery, rhubarb jam and dandelion pies. The other side of that world is "the moon," the safe, dream space in which Merricat lives:

"On the moon we have everything," Merricat intones. "Lettuce, and pumpkin pie and *Amanita phalloides*. We have cat-furred plants and horses dancing with their wings. All the locks are solid and tight, and there are no ghosts."

The "ghosts," the intruder, is Cousin Charles, a greedy, insensitive man lured to the Blackwood mansion by rumors of a buried fortune. The havoc he wreaks, and the unsuspected dénouement of the action, bring into soft focus the human ambivalences of guilt and atonement, love and hate, health and psychosis. There is nothing illusory about these ambivalences, and also nothing final. Shirley Jackson has once again effected a marvelous elucidation of life in the ageless form of a story full of craft and full of mystery.—IHAB HASSAN, "Three Hermits on a Hill," *NYTBR*, Sept. 23, 1962, p. 5

---

## SHIRLEY JACKSON
### "Biography of a Story" (1960)
*Come Along with Me*, ed. Stanley Edgar Hyman
1968, pp. 211–24

On the morning of June 28, 1948, I walked down to the post office in our little Vermont town to pick up the mail. I was quite casual about it, as I recall—I opened the box, took out a couple of bills and a letter or two, talked to the postmaster for a few minutes, and left, never supposing that it was the last time for months that I was to pick up the mail without an active feeling of panic. By the next week I had had to change my mailbox to the largest one in the post office, and casual conversation with the postmaster was out of the question, because he wasn't speaking to me. June 28, 1948 was the day *The New Yorker* came out with a story of mine in it. It was not my first published story, nor my last, but I have been assured over and over that if it had been the only story I ever wrote or published, there would be people who would not forget my name.

I had written the story three weeks before, on a bright June morning when summer seemed to have come at last, with blue skies and warm sun and no heavenly signs to warn me that my morning's work was anything but just another story. The idea had come to me while I was pushing my daughter up the hill in her stroller—it was, as I say, a warm morning, and the hill was steep, and beside my daughter the stroller held the day's groceries—and perhaps the effort of that last fifty yards up the hill put an edge to the story; at any rate, I had the idea fairly clearly in my mind when I put my daughter in her playpen and the frozen vegetables in the refrigerator, and, writing the story, I found that it went quickly and easily, moving from beginning to end without pause. As a matter of fact, when I read it over later I decided that except for one or two minor corrections, it needed no changes, and the story I finally typed up and sent off to my agent the next day was almost word for word the original draft. This, as any writer of stories can tell you, is not a usual thing. All I know is that when I came to read the story over I felt strongly that I didn't want to fuss with it. I didn't think it was perfect, but I didn't want to fuss with it. It was, I thought, a serious, straightforward story, and I was pleased and a little surprised at the ease with which it had been written; I was reasonably proud of it, and hoped that my agent would sell it to some magazine and I would have the gratification of seeing it in print.

My agent did not care for the story, but—as she said in her

note at the time—her job was to sell it, not to like it. She sent it at once to *The New Yorker*, and about a week after the story had been written I received a telephone call from the fiction editor of *The New Yorker*; it was quite clear that he did not really care for the story, either, but *The New Yorker* was going to buy it. He asked for one change—that the date mentioned in the story be changed to coincide with the date of the issue of the magazine in which the story would appear, and I said of course. He then asked, hesitantly, if I had any particular interpretation of my own for the story; Mr. Harold Ross, then the editor of *The New Yorker*, was not altogether sure that he understood the story, and wondered if I cared to enlarge upon its meaning. I said no. Mr. Ross, he said, thought that the story might be puzzling to some people, and in case anyone telephoned the magazine, as sometimes happened, or wrote in asking about the story, was there anything in particular I wanted them to say? No, I said, nothing in particular; it was just a story I wrote.

I had no more preparation than that. I went on picking up the mail every morning, pushing my daughter up and down the hill in her stroller, anticipating pleasurably the check from *The New Yorker*, and shopping for groceries. The weather stayed nice and it looked as though it was going to be a good summer. Then, on June 28, *The New Yorker* came out with my story.

Things began mildly enough with a note from a friend at *The New Yorker*: "Your story has kicked up quite a fuss around the office," he wrote. I was flattered; it's nice to think that your friends notice what you write. Later that day there was a call from one of the magazine's editors; they had had a couple of people phone in about my story, he said, and was there anything I particularly wanted him to say if there were any more calls? No, I said, nothing particular; anything he chose to say was perfectly all right with me; it was just a story.

I was further puzzled by a cryptic note from another friend: "Heard a man talking about a story of yours on the bus this morning," she wrote. "Very exciting. I wanted to tell him I knew the author, but after I heard what he was saying I decided I'd better not."

One of the most terrifying aspects of publishing stories and books is the realization that they are going to be read, and read by strangers. I had never fully realized this before, although I had of course in my imagination dwelt lovingly upon the thought of the millions and millions of people who were going to be uplifted and enriched and delighted by the stories I wrote. It had simply never occurred to me that these millions and millions of people might be so far from being uplifted that they would sit down and write me letters I was downright scared to open; of the three-hundred-odd letters that I received that summer I can count only thirteen that spoke kindly to me, and they were mostly from friends. Even my mother scolded me: "Dad and I did not care at all for your story in *The New Yorker*," she wrote sternly; "it does seem, dear, that this gloomy kind of story is what all you young people think about these days. Why don't you write something to cheer people up?"

By mid-July I had begun to perceive that I was very lucky indeed to be safely in Vermont, where no one in our small town had ever heard of *The New Yorker*, much less read my story. Millions of people, and my mother, had taken a pronounced dislike to me.

The magazine kept no track of telephone calls, but all letters addressed to me care of the magazine were forwarded directly to me for answering, and all letters addressed to the magazine—some of them addressed to Harold Ross personally; these were the most vehement—were answered at the magazine and then the letters were sent me in great batches, along with carbons of the answers written at the magazine. I have all the letters still, and if they could be considered to give any accurate cross section of the reading public, or the reading public of *The New Yorker*, or even the reading public of one issue of *The New Yorker*, I would stop writing now.

Judging from these letters, people who read stories are gullible, rude, frequently illiterate, and horribly afraid of being laughed at. Many of the writers were positive that *The New Yorker* was going to ridicule them in print, and the most cautious letters were headed, in capital letters: NOT FOR PUBLICATION or PLEASE DO NOT PRINT THIS LETTER, or, at best, THIS LETTER MAY BE PUBLISHED AT YOUR USUAL RATES OF PAYMENT. Anonymous letters, of which there were a few, were destroyed. *The New Yorker* never published any comment of any kind about the story in the magazine, but did issue one publicity release saying that the story had received more mail than any piece of fiction they had ever published; this was after the newspapers had gotten into the act, in midsummer, with a front-page story in the San Francisco *Chronicle* begging to know what the story meant, and a series of columns in New York and Chicago papers pointing out that *New Yorker* subscriptions were being canceled right and left.

Curiously, there are three main themes which dominate the letters of that first summer—three themes which might be identified as bewilderment, speculation, and plain old-fashioned abuse. In the years since then, during which the story has been anthologized, dramatized, televised, and even—in one completely mystifying transformation—made into a ballet, the tenor of letters I receive has changed. I am addressed more politely, as a rule, and the letters largely confine themselves to questions like what does this story mean? The general tone of the early letters, however, was a kind of wide-eyed, shocked innocence. People at first were not so much concerned with what the story meant; what they wanted to know was where these lotteries were held, and whether they could go there and watch. Listen to these quotations:

(Kansas) Will you please tell me the locale and the year of the custom?
(Oregon) Where in heaven's name does there exist such barbarity as described in the story?
(New York) Do such tribunal rituals still exist and if so where?
(New York) To a reader who has only a fleeting knowledge of traditional rites in various parts of the country (I presume the plot was laid in the United States) I found the cruelty of the ceremony outrageous, if not unbelievable. It may be just a custom or ritual which I am not familiar with.
(New York) Would you please explain whether such improbable rituals occur in our Middle Western states, and what their origin and purpose are?
(Nevada) Although we recognize the story to be fiction is it possible that it is based on fact?
(Maryland) Please let me know if the custom of which you wrote actually exists.
(New York) To satisfy my curiosity would you please tell me if such rites are still practiced and if so where?
(California) If it is based on fact would you please tell me the date and place of its origin?
(Texas) What I would like to know, if you don't mind enlightening me, is in what part of the United States this organized, apparently legal lynching is practiced? Could it be that in New England or in equally enlightened regions, mass sadism is still part and parcel of the ordinary citizen's life?

(Georgia)   I'm hoping you'll find time to give me further details about the bizarre custom the story describes, where it occurs, who practices it, and why.

(Brooklyn, N.Y.)   I am interested in learning if there is any particular source or group of sources of fact or legend on which and from which the story is based? This story has caused me to be particularly disturbed by my lack of knowledge of such rites or lotteries in the United States.

(California)   If it actually occurred, it should be documented.

(New York)   We have not read about it in *In Fact*.

(New York)   Is it based on reality? Do these practices still continue in back-country England, the human sacrifice for the rich harvest? It's a frightening thought.

(Ohio)   I think your story is based on fact. Am I right? As a psychiatrist I am fascinated by the psychodynamic possibilities suggested by this anachronistic ritual.

(Mississippi)   You seem to describe a custom of which I am totally ignorant.

(California)   It seems like I remember reading somewhere a long time ago that that was the custom in a certain part of France some time ago. However I have never heard of it being practiced here in the United States. However would you please inform me where you got your information and whether or not anything of this nature has been perpetrated in modern times?

(Pennsylvania)   Are you describing a current custom?

(New York)   Is there some timeless community existing in New England where human sacrifices are made for the fertility of the crops?

(Boston)   Apparently this tale involves an English custom or tradition of which we in this country know nothing.

(Canada)   Can the lottery be some barbaric event, a hangover from the Middle Ages perhaps, which is still carried on in the States? In what part of the country does it take place?

(Los Angeles)   I have read of some queer cults in my time, but this one bothers me.

(Texas)   Was this group of people perhaps a settlement descended from early English colonists? And were they continuing a Druid rite to assure good crops?

(Quebec)   Is this a custom which is carried on somewhere in America?

(A London psychologist)   I have received requests for elucidation from English friends and patients. They would like to know if the barbarity of stoning still exists in the U.S.A. and in general what the tale is all about and where does the action take place.

(Oregon)   Is there a witchcraft hangover somewhere in these United States that we Far Westerners have missed?

(Madras, India)   We have been wondering whether the story was based on fact and if so whether the custom described therein of selecting one family by lot jointly to be stoned by the remainder of the villagers still persists anywhere in the United States. *The New Yorker* is read here in our United States information library and while we have had no inquiries about this particular article as yet, it is possible we shall have and I would be glad to be in a position to answer them.

(England)   I am sorry that I cannot find out the state in which this piece of annual propitiatory sacrifice takes place. Now I just frankly don't believe that even in the United States such things happen—at least not without being sponsored by Lynching Inc. or the All-American Morticians Group or some such high-powered organization. I was once offered a baby by a primitive tribe in the center of Laos (Indochina) which my interpreter (Chinese) informed me I had to kill so that my blood lust was satiated and I would leave the rest of the tribe alone. But NOT in the United States, PLEASE.

(Connecticut)   Other strange old things happen in the Appalachian mountain villages, I'm told.

As I say, if I thought this was a valid cross section of the reading public, I would give up writing. During this time, when I was carrying home some ten or twelve letters a day, and receiving a weekly package from *The New Yorker*, I got one letter which troubled me a good deal. It was from California, short, pleasant, and very informal. The man who wrote it clearly expected that I would recognize his name and his reputation, which I didn't. I puzzled over this letter for a day or two before I answered it, because of course it is always irritating to be on the edge of recognizing a name and have it escape you. I was pretty sure that it was someone who had written a book I had read or a book whose review I had read or a story in a recent magazine or possibly even—since I come originally from California—someone with whom I had gone to high school. Finally, since I had to answer the letter, I decided that something carefully complimentary and noncommittal would be best. One day, after I had mailed him my letter, some friends also from California stopped in and asked—as everyone was asking then—what new letters had come. I showed them the letter from my mysterious not-quite-remembered correspondent. Good heavens, they said, was this really a letter from *him*? Tell me who he is, I said desperately, just tell me who he is. Why, how could anyone forget? It had been all over the California papers for weeks, and in the New York papers, too; he had just been barely acquitted of murdering his wife with an ax. With a kind of awful realization creeping over me I went and looked up the carbon of the letter I had written him, my noncommittal letter. "Thank you very much for your kind letter about my story," I had written. "I admire *your* work, too."

The second major theme which dominates the letters is what I call speculation. These letters were from the people who sat down and figured out a meaning for the story, or a reason for writing it, and wrote in proudly to explain, or else wrote in to explain why they could not possibly believe the story had any meaning at all.

(New Jersey)   Surely it is only a bad dream the author had?

(New York)   Was it meant to be taken seriously?

(New York)   Was the sole purpose just to give the reader a nasty impact?

(California)   The main idea which has been evolved is that the author has tried to challenge the logic of our society's releasing its aggressions through the channel of minority prejudice by presenting an equally logical (or possibly more logical) method of selecting a scapegoat. The complete horror of the cold-blooded method of choosing a victim parallels our own culture's devices for handling deep-seated hostilities.

(Virginia)   I would list my questions about the story but it would be like trying to talk in an unknown language so far as I am concerned. The only thing

that occurs to me is that perhaps the author meant we should not be too hard on our presidential nominees.
(Connecticut) Is *The New Yorker* only maintaining further its policy of intellectual leg-pulling?
(New York) Is it a publicity stunt?
(New Orleans) I wish Mrs. Hutchinson had been queen for a day or something nice like that before they stoned the poor frightened creature.
(New York) Anyone who seeks to communicate with the public should be at least lucid.
(New Jersey) Please tell me if the feeling I have of having dreamed it once is just part of the hypnotic effect of the story.
(Massachusetts) I earnestly grabbed my young nephew's encyclopedia and searched under "stoning" or "punishment" for some key to the mystery; to no avail.
(California) Is it just a story? Why was it published? Is it a parable? Have you received other letters asking for some explanation?
(Illinois) If it is simply a fictitious example of man's innate cruelty, it isn't a very good one. Man, stupid and cruel as he is, has always had sense enough to imagine or invent a charge against the objects of his persecution: the Christian martyrs, the New England witches, the Jews and Negroes. But nobody had anything against Mrs. Hutchinson, and they only wanted to get through quickly so they could go home for lunch.
(California) Is it an allegory?
(California) Please tell us it was all in fun.
(Los Angeles *Daily News*) Was Tessie a witch? No, witches weren't selected by lottery. Anyway, these are present-day people. Is it the post-atomic age, in which there is insufficient food to sustain the population and one person is eliminated each year? Hardly. Is it just an old custom, difficult to break? Probably. But there is also the uncomfortable feeling that maybe the story wasn't supposed to make sense. The magazines have been straining in this direction for some time and *The New Yorker*, which we like very much, seems to have made it.
(Missouri) In this story you show the perversion of democracy.
(California) It seems obscure.
(California) I caught myself dreaming about what I would do if my wife and I were in such a predicament. I think I would back out.
(Illinois) A symbol of how village gossip destroys a victim?
(Puerto Rico) You people print any story you get, just throwing the last paragraph into the wastebasket before it appears in the magazine.
(New York) Were you saying that people will accept any evil as long as it doesn't touch them personally?
(Massachusetts) I am approaching middle age; has senility set in at this rather early age, or is it that I am not so acute mentally as I have had reason to assume?
(Canada) My only comment is what the hell?
(Maine) I suppose that about once every so often a magazine may decide to print something that hasn't any point just to get people talking.
(California) I don't know how there could be any confusion in anyone's mind as to what you were saying; nothing could possibly be clearer.
(Switzerland) What does it mean? Does it hide some subtle allegory?
(Indiana) What happened to the paragraph that tells what the devil is going on?

(California) I missed something here. Perhaps there was some facet of the victim's character which made her unpopular with the other villagers. I expected the people to evince a feeling of dread and terror, or else sadistic pleasure, but perhaps they were laconic, unemotional New Englanders.
(Ohio) A friend darkly suspects you people of having turned a bright editorial red, and that is how he construed the story. Please give me something to go on when I next try to placate my friend, who is now certain that you are tools of Stalin. If you *are* subversive, for goodness sake I don't blame you for not wanting to discuss the matter and of course you have every constitutional right in back of you. But at least please explain that damned story.
(Venezuela) I have read the story twice and from what I can gather all a man gets for his winnings are rocks in his head, which seems rather futile.
(Virginia) The printers left out three lines of type somewhere.
(Missouri) You printed it. Now give with the explanations.
(New York) To several of us there seemed to be a rather sinister symbolism in the cruelty of the people.
(Indiana) When I first read the story in my issue, I felt that there was no moral significance present, that the story was just terrifying, and that was all. However, there has to be a reason why it is so alarming to so many people. I feel that the only solution, the only reason it bothered so many people is that it shows the power of society over the individual. We saw the ease with which society can crush any single one of us. At the same time, we saw that society need have no rational reason for crushing the one, or the few, or sometimes the many.
(Connecticut) I thought that it might have been a small-scale representation of the sort of thing involved in the lottery which started the functioning of the selective-service system at the start of the last war.

Far and away the most emphatic letter writers were those who took this opportunity of indulging themselves in good old-fashioned name-calling. Since I am making no attempt whatsoever to interpret the motives of my correspondents, and would not if I could, I will not try now to say what I think of people who write nasty letters to other people who just write stories. I will only read some of their comments.

(Canada) Tell Miss Jackson to stay out of Canada.
(New York) I expect a personal apology from the author.
(Massachusetts) I think I had better switch to the *Saturday Evening Post*.
(Massachusetts) I will never buy *The New Yorker* again. I resent being tricked into reading perverted stories like "The Lottery."
(Connecticut) Who is Shirley Jackson? Cannot decide whether she is a genius or a female and more subtle version of Orson Welles.
(New York) We are fairly well educated and sophisticated people, but we feel that we have lost all faith in the truth of literature.
(Minnesota) Never in the world did I think I'd protest a story in *The New Yorker*, but really, gentlemen, "The Lottery" seems to me to be in incredibly bad taste. I read it while soaking in the tub and was tempted to put my head under water and end it all.
(California; this from a world-famous anthropologist) If the author's intent was to symbolize into

complete mystification and at the same time be gratuitously disagreeable, she certainly succeeded.
(Georgia) Couldn't the story have been a trifle esoteric, even for *The New Yorker* circulation?
(California) "The Lottery" interested some of us and made the rest plain mad.
(Michigan) It certainly is modern.
(California) I am glad that your magazine does not have the popular and foreign-language circulation of the *Reader's Digest*. Such a story might make German, Russian, and Japanese realists feel lily-white in comparison with the American. The old saying about washing dirty linen in public has gone out of fashion with us. At any rate this story has reconciled me to not receiving your magazine next year.
(Illinois) Even to be polite I can't say that I liked "The Lottery."
(Missouri) When the author sent in this story, she undoubtedly included some explanation of place or some evidence that such a situation could exist. Then isn't the reader entitled to some such evidence? Otherwise the reader has a right to indict you as editor of willfully misrepresenting the human race. Perhaps you as editor are proud of publishing a story that reached a new low in human viciousness. The burden of proof is up to you when your own preoccupation with evil leads you into such evil ways. A few more such stories and you will alienate your most devoted readers, in which class I—until now—have been included.
(New Hampshire) It was with great disappointment that I read the story "The Lottery." Stories such as this belong to *Esquire*, etc., but most assuredly not to *The New Yorker*.
(Massachusetts) The ending of this story came as quite a jolt to my wife and, as a matter of fact, she was very upset by the whole thing for a day or two after.
(New York) I read the story quite thoroughly and confess that I could make neither head nor tail out of it. The story was so horrible and gruesome in its effect that I could hardly see the point of your publishing it.

Now, a complete letter, from Illinois.

EDITOR:

Never has it been my lot to read so cunningly vicious a story as that published in your last issue for June. I tremble to think of the fate of American letters if that piece indicated the taste of the editors of a magazine I had considered distinguished. It has made me wonder what you had in mind when accepting it for publication. Certainly not the entertainment of the reader and if not entertainment, what? The strokes of genius were of course apparent in the story mentioned, but of a perverted genius whose efforts achieved a terrible malformation. You have betrayed a trust with your readers by giving them such a bestial selection. Unaware, the reader was led into a casual tale of the village folk, becoming conscious only gradually of the rising tension, till the shock of the unwholesome conclusion, skillful though it was wrought, left him with total disgust for the story and with disillusionment in the magazine publishing it.

I speak of my own reaction. If that is not the reaction of the majority of your readers I miss my guess. Ethics and uplift are apparently not in your repertoire, nor are they expected, but as editors it is

your responsibility to have a sounder and saner criterion for stories than the one which passed on "The Lottery."

Heretofore mine has been almost a stockholder's pride in *The New Yorker*. I shared my copy with my friends as I do the other possessions which I most enjoy. When your latest issue arrived, my new distaste kept me from removing the brown paper wrapping, and into the wastebasket it went. Since I can't conceive that I'll develop interest in it again, save the results of your efforts that indignity every week and cancel my subscription immediately.

Another letter, this one from Indiana.

SIR:

Thanks for letting us take a look at the nauseating and fiction-less bit of print which appeared in a recent issue. I gather that we read the literal translation.

The process of moving set us back a few weeks, but unfortunately your magazine and Miss Jackson's consistently correct spelling and punctuation caught up with us.

We are pleased to think that perhaps her story recalled happier days for you; days when you were able to hurl flat skipping stones at your aged grandmother. Not for any particular reason, of course, but because the village postmaster good-naturedly placed them in your hands, or because your chubby fingers felt good as they gripped the stone.

Our quarrel is not with Miss Jackson's amazingly clear style or reportorial observation. It is not with the strong motives exhibited by the native stone-throwers, or with the undertones and overtones which apparently we missed along the way.

It is simply that we read the piece before and not after supper. We are hammering together a few paragraphs on running the head of our kindly neighbor through the electric eggbeater, and will mail same when we have untangled her top-piece. This should give your many readers a low chuckle or at least provide the sophisticates with an inner glow. Also it might interest you to know that my wife and I are gathering up the smoothest, roundest stones in our yard and piling them up on the corner in small, neat pyramids. We're sentimentalists that way.

I have frequently wondered if this last letter is a practical joke; it is certainly not impossible, although I hope not, because it is quite my favorite letter of all "Lottery" correspondence. It was mailed to *The New Yorker*, from Los Angeles, of course, and written in pencil, on a sheet of lined paper torn from a pad; the spelling is atrocious.

DEAR SIR:

The June 26 copy of your magazine fell into my hands in the Los Angeles railroad station yesterday. Although I donnot read your magazine very often I took this copy home to my folks and they had to agree with me that you speak straitforward to your readers.

My Aunt Ellise before she became priestess of the Exalted Rollers used to tell us a story just like "The Lottery" by Shirley Jackson. I don't know if Miss Jackson is a member of the Exhalted Rollers but with her round stones sure ought to be. There is a few points in her prophecy on which Aunt Ellise and me don't agree.

The Exalted Rollers donnot believe in the ballot box but believe that the true gospel of the redeeming light will become accepted by all when the prophecy comes true. It does seem likely to me that our sins will bring us punishment though a great scouraging war with the devil's toy (the atomic bomb). I don't think we will have to sacrifice humin beings fore atonement.

Our brothers feel that Miss Jackson is a true prophet and disciple of the true gospel of the redeeming light. When will the next revelations be published?

Yours in the spirit.

Of all the questions ever asked me about "Lottery," I feel that there is only one which I can answer fearlessly and honestly, and that is the question which closes this gentleman's letter. When will the next revelations be published, he wants to know, and I answer roundly, never. I am out of the lottery business for good.

## HELEN E. NEBEKER
### From "'The Lottery': Symbolic Tour de Force"
*American Literature*, March 1974, pp. 101–7

"The Lottery" really fuses two stories and themes into one fictional vehicle. The overt, easily discovered story appears in the literal facts, wherein members of a small rural town meet to determine by lot who will be the victim of the yearly savagery. At this level one feels the horror, senses clearly the "dichotomy in all human nature,"[1] the "doubleness of the human spirit,"[2] and recoils in horror. This narrative level produces immediate emotional impact. Only after that initial shock do disturbing questions and nuances begin to assert themselves.

It is at this secondary point that the reader begins to suspect that a second story lies beneath the first and that Miss Jackson's "symbolic intentions" are not "incidental" but, indeed, paramount. Then one discovers that the author's careful structure and consistent symbolism work to present not only a symbolic summary of man's past but a prognosis for his future which is far more devastating than the mere reminder that man has savage potential. Ultimately one finds that the ritual of the lottery, beyond providing a channel to release repressed cruelties, actually serves to *generate* cruelty not rooted in man's inherent emotional needs at all. Man is not at the mercy of a murky, savage id; he is the victim of unexamined and unchanging traditions which he could easily change if he only realized their implications. Herein is horror.

The symbolic overtones which develop in this second, sub rosa story become evident as early as the fourth word of the story when the date of June 27th alerts us to the season of the summer solstice with all its overtones of ancient ritual. Carefully the scene is set—the date, the air of festivity, release, even license. The children newly freed from school play boisterously, rolling in the dust. But, ominously, Bobby Martin has already stuffed his pockets with stones and Harry Jones and Dickie Delacroix follow his example, eventually making a great pile of stones in the corner which they guard from the raids of other boys. By the end of just two paragraphs, Jackson has carefully indicated the season, time of ancient excess and sacrifice, and the stones, most ancient of sacrificial weapons. She has also hinted at larger meanings through name symbology. "Martin," Bobby's surname, derives from a Middle English word signifying ape or monkey. This, juxtaposed with "Harry Jones" (in all its commonness) and "Dickie Delacroix" (of-the-Cross), urges us to an awareness of the Hairy Ape within us all, veneered by a Christianity as perverted as

"Delacroix," vulgarized to "Dellacroy" by the villagers. Horribly, at the end of the story, it will be Mrs. Delacroix, warm and friendly in her natural state, who will select a stone "so large she had to pick it up with both hands" and will encourage her friends to follow suit. Should this name symbology seem strained, superimposed, a little later we shall return to it and discover that every major name in the story has its special significance.

Returning to the chronology of the story, the reader sees the men gather, talking of the planting and rain (the central issues of the ancient propitiatory rites), tractors and taxes (those modern additions to the concerns of man). The men are quieter, more aware, and the patriarchal order (the oldest social group of man) is quickly evidenced as the women join their husbands and call their children to them. When Bobby Martin tries to leave the group and runs laughing to the stones, he is sharply rebuked by his serious father, who knows that this is no game. Clearly this is more than the surface "idyllic" small-town life noted by Heilman;[3] the symbolic undercurrents prepare us to be drawn step by step toward the ultimate horror, where everything will fuse.

In the fourth paragraph, Mr. Summers, who ironically runs the "coal" business, arrives with the postmaster, Mr. Graves, who carries the three-legged stool and the black box. Although critics have tended to see the box as the major symbol, careful reading discloses that, while the box is referred to three times in this paragraph, the stool is emphasized four times and in such strained repetition as to be particularly obvious. Further, in the next two paragraphs it will be stressed that the box rests upon, is supported by, the *three-legged stool*. It would thus seem that the stool is at least as important as the box: in my opinion, it is the symbol which holds the key to Jackson's conclusive theme. In the interest of structure and coherence, this point must be developed later in the article.

Returning to the symbol of the box, its prehistoric origin is revealed in the mention of the "original wood color" showing along one side as well as in the belief that it has been constructed by the first people who settled down to make villages here (man in his original social group). The chips of wood, now discarded for slips of paper, suggest a preliterate origin. The present box has been made from pieces of the original (as though it were salvaged somehow) and is now blackened, faded, and stained (with blood perhaps). In this box[4] symbol, Jackson certainly suggests the body of tradition— once oral but now written—which the dead hand of the past codified in religion, mores, government, and the rest of culture, and passed from generation to generation, letting it grow ever more cumbersome, meaningless, and indefensible.

Jackson does not, however, attack ritual in and of itself. She implies that, as any anthropologist knows, ritual in its origin is integral to man's concept of his universe, that it is rooted in his need to explain, even to control the forces around him. Thus, at one time the ritual, the chant, the dance were executed precisely, with deep symbolic meaning. Those chosen for sacrifice were not victims but saviors who would propitiate the gods, enticing them to bring rebirth, renewal, and thanking them with their blood. This idea explains the significance of Mrs. Delacroix's comment to Mrs. Graves that "'there's no time at all between lotteries any more'" and her reply that "'Time sure goes fast.'" To the ancients, the ritual was a highly significant time marker: summer solstice and winter solstice, light versus dark, life versus death. These modern women only verify the meaninglessness of the present rite. Later, in a similar vein, when one of the girls whispers, "'I hope it's not Nancy,'" Mr. Warner replies, "'People ain't the way they used to be,'" implying that, anciently, honor and envy were accorded those chosen to die for the common welfare. Another neat symbolic touch tied to the meaningful ritualistic slaughter of the past is suggested by the character Clyde Dunbar. He lies at home, unable to participate in this year's lottery because of his broken leg. This reminds us that in every tradition of propitiation the purity and wholeness of the sacrifice was imperative. This "unblemished lamb" concept is epitomized in the sacrifice of Christ. In view of the interweaving of these ideas, it is difficult to see only "incidental symbolism" or to overlook the immediate and consistent "symbolic intention" of the narrative.

From the symbolic development of the box, the story moves swiftly to climax. Tessie Hutchinson hurries in, having almost forgotten the lottery in her round of normal, housewifely duties. She greets Mrs. Delacroix and moves good-humoredly into the crowd. Summers consults his list, discovers that Clyde Dunbar is missing and asks who will draw for him. When Janey Dunbar replies, "'Me, I guess,'" Summers asks, "'Don't you have a grown boy to do it for you Janey?' *although Mr. Summers and everyone else in the village knew the answer perfectly well*" (italics added). In this seemingly innocent exchange the reader is jarred into a suspicion that the mentioned "grown boy" has been a previous victim and that his father cannot face the strain of being present, raising the question whether the breaking of his leg has been accidental or deliberate. At any rate, this loss of a son will explain the unusual encouragement given Janey by the women as she goes to draw her slip of paper, her great anxiety as she awaits results with her remaining two sons—"'I wish they'd hurry. . . . I wish they'd hurry'"—and her sending her older son with the news to her husband who, we may surmise, waits in agony for the outcome.

Significantly, the name Dunbar may in itself suggest that thin gray line which separates those who have been personally marked by the horror of the lottery from those who have not. If this seems to be flagrant symbol hunting, we might remember that it is Mrs. Dunbar who, at the time of the stoning, holds back as Mrs. Delacroix urges her to action. Mrs. Dunbar, with only small stones in her hands, gasping for breath, says, "'I can't run at all. You'll have to go ahead and I'll catch up.'" But we may believe that she will not. Marked by the loss of her son, she may still be a victim but she will not be a perpetrator. Herein lies the only humane hope raised in the story.

Next, because of the sequence of details, we are brought to consider that Jack Watson is another villager touched personally by the lottery. Immediately after querying Mrs. Dunbar and making a note on his list, Mr. Summers asks, "'Watson boy drawing this year?'" Note that the name Watson does not immediately succeed Dunbar; there seems to be a special quality about those whose names are checked previous to the actual lottery when the names will be called from A to Z. When Jack replies, "'Here . . . I'm drawing for m'mother and me,'" blinking nervously and ducking his head, the crowd responds with "'Good fellow, Jack,'" and "'Glad to see your mother's got a man to do it,'" encouraging him excessively as they do Mrs. Dunbar. Later, after the drawing, they will specifically ask, "'Is it the Dunbars?'" "'Is it the Watsons?'" Surely, at least the elder Watson—and maybe others in the family—has been a previous victim of the rite.

Now the symbolic names crowd upon us: "Old Man Warner," prototype of the prophet of doom, voice of the past, foe of change, existing from everlasting to everlasting; Old Man Warner, seventy-seven (ancient magic number of indefiniteness) years old, the oldest of them all, juxtaposed with Jack Watson, the youngest patriarch, both part of the same

unchanging horror. "Steve Adams"—Adam the father of the race and Stephen the first Christian martyr. "Baxter"[5] Martin, the eldest brother of Bobby, again suggesting primitive origins changed only superficially by even the best thought of the centuries. Tessie Hutchinson, more subtle in reference but "Hutchinson" reminiscent of early American Puritan heritage, while "Tessie," diminutive for "Theresa," derives from the Greek *theizein* meaning "to reap," or, if the nickname is for "Anastasia" it will translate literally "of the resurrection." What deliberate symbolic irony that Tessie should be the victim, not of hatred or malice, or primitive fear, but of the primitive ritual itself.

Now, as Tessie stands at bay and the crowd is upon her, the symbols coalesce into full revelation. "Tessie Hutchinson," end product of two thousand years of Christian thought and ritual, Catholic and Puritan merged, faces her fellow citizens, all equally victims and persecutors. Mrs. "Of-the-Cross" lifts her heavy stone in response to ritual long forgotten and perverted. "Old Man Warner" fans the coals (not fires) of emotions long sublimated, ritualistically revived once a year. "Mr. Adams," at once progenitor and martyr in the Judeo-Christian myth of man, stands with "Mrs. Graves"—the ultimate refuge or escape of all mankind—in the forefront of the crowd.

Now we understand the significance of the three-legged stool—as old as the tripod of the Delphic oracle, as new as the Christian trinity. For that which supports the present day box of meaningless and perverted superstition is the body of unexamined tradition of at least six thousand years of man's history. Some of these traditions (one leg of the stool if you like), are as old as the memory of man and are symbolized by the season, the ritual, the original box, the wood chips, the names of Summers, Graves, Martin, Warner (all cultures have their priesthoods!). These original, even justifiable, traditions gave way to or were absorbed by later Hebraic perversions; and the narrative pursues its "scapegoat" theme in terms of the stones, the wooden box,[6] blackened and stained, Warner the Prophet, even the Judaic name of Tessie's son, David. Thus Hebraic tradition becomes a second leg or brace for the box.

Superimposed upon this remote body of tradition is one two thousand years old in its own right. But it may be supposed the most perverted and therefore least defensible of all as a tradition of supposedly enlightened man who has freed himself from the barbarities and superstitions of the past. This Christian tradition becomes the third support for the blood-stained box and all it represents. Most of the symbols of the other periods pertain here with the addition of Delacroix, Hutchinson, Baxter and Steve.

With this last symbolic intention clearly revealed, one may understand the deeper significance of Jackson's second, below-the-surface story. More than developing a theme which "deals with 'scapegoating', the human tendency to punish 'innocent' and often accidentally chosen victims for our sins"[7] or one which points out "the awful doubleness of the human spirit—a doubleness that expresses itself in blended good neighborliness and cruelty . . . ,"[8] Shirley Jackson has raised these lesser themes to one encompassing a comprehensive, compassionate, and fearful understanding of man trapped in the web spun from his own need to explain and control the incomprehensible universe around him, a need no longer answered by the web of old traditions.

Man, she says, is a victim of his unexamined and hence unchanged traditions which engender in him flames otherwise banked, subdued. Until enough men are touched strongly enough by the horror of their ritualistic, irrational actions to reject the long-perverted ritual, to destroy the box completely—or to make, if necessary, a new one reflective of their own conditions and needs of life—man will never free himself from his primitive nature and is ultimately doomed. Miss Jackson does not offer us much hope—they only talk of giving up the lottery in the north village, the Dunbars and Watsons do not actually resist, and even little Davy Hutchinson holds a few pebbles in his hands.[9]

*Notes*

1. Virgil Scott, *Studies in the Short Story*, Instructor's Manual (New York, 1968), p. 21.
2. Cleanth Brooks and Robert Warren, *Understanding Fiction*, 2nd ed. (New York, 1959), p. 76.
3. Robert B. Heilman, *Modern Short Stories: A Critical Anthology* (New York, 1959), p. 384.
4. Etymologically, the closeness of our words "box" and "book" is indicated in the O.E. derivation from words meaning "evergreen tree or shrub" and "beech tree," probably from the habit of carving runic characters on the beech. The Latin words *codex* and *liber* have the same similarities.
5. Richard Baxter was a seventeenth-century English Puritan minister and writer who postulated the doctrine of free grace.
6. The Ark of the Covenant itself is one of the earliest representations of the literal box.
7. Scott, p. 20.
8. Brooks and Warren, p. 76.
9. This paper was written under a grant from Arizona State University.

# RANDALL JARRELL

## 1914–1965

Randall Jarrell was born in Nashville, Tennessee, on May 6, 1914. Jarrell spent most of his childhood in Nashville, although he lived in California with his grandparents for several years during his parents' separation. In 1931 he graduated from Hume-Fogg High School in Nashville. The following fall Jarrell began his studies at Vanderbilt, where he received a B.A. in psychology in 1935. While at Vanderbilt he associated with the Fugitive writers, including John Crowe Ransom, Robert Penn Warren, and Allen Tate. He began work on a master's thesis at Vanderbilt, but left in 1937 to follow Ransom to Kenyon College in Gambier, Ohio, where he lived in the Ransoms' attic room with another young student, Robert Lowell. The two poets remained lifelong friends. While at Kenyon, Jarrell taught English and completed his thesis on A. E. Housman.

Jarrell's first published poem appeared in *The American Review* in 1934. In 1940 twenty of his poems were featured in John Ciardi's *Five Young American Poets*. Jarrell's first volume of poetry, *Blood for a Stranger* (1942), appeared just prior to his enlistment in the U.S. Air Force. He failed to become a pilot, so served instead as a celestial navigation tower operator. In 1945 a second volume of poetry, *Little Friend, Little Friend*, was published. The following year Jarrell moved to New York with his first wife, Mackie Langham, whom he had married in 1939. He taught at Sarah Lawrence College while he worked as the literary editor of *The Nation*; later he worked for both *Partisan Review* and the *Yale Review*. In 1947 Jarrell moved to Greensboro, North Carolina, to teach at the Women's College, a division of the University of North Carolina. Although Jarrell often lectured elsewhere, Greensboro was his home until his death.

Jarrell is remembered for his incisive and often scathing criticism as well as his own highly praised writings. Jarrell wrote one novel, *Pictures from an Institution* (1954), and numerous volumes of poetry. His *Woman at the Washington Zoo* won the 1961 National Book Award for Poetry. He also authored several children's books, including *The Gingerbread Rabbit* and *The Bat-Poet*, both illustrated by Maurice Sendak. Jarrell edited several anthologies of Kipling's stories and translated Rilke, Goethe, and Chekhov. He spent the last thirteen years of his life with Mary Eloise von Schrader, whom he married in 1952 after divorcing his first wife. After a nervous breakdown in early 1965, Jarrell was accidentally hit by a car, outside of Chapel Hill. He died immediately on October 14, 1965, and was buried in Greensboro. His semi-autobiographical verse collection, *The Lost World*, was published a few months after his death by his old friend Robert Lowell.

Randall Jarrell is our most talented poet under 40, and one whose wit, pathos and grace remind us more of Pope or Matthew Arnold than of any of his contemporaries. I don't know whether Jarrell is unappreciated or not—it's hard to imagine anyone taking him lightly. He is almost brutally serious about literature and so bewilderingly gifted that it is impossible to comment on him without the humiliating thought that he himself could do it better.

He is a man of letters in the European sense, with real verve, imagination and uniqueness. Even his dogmatism is more wild and personal than we are accustomed to, completely unspoiled by the hedging "equanimity" that weakens the style and temperament of so many of our serious writers. His murderous intuitive phrases are famous; but at the same time his mind is essentially conservative and takes as much joy in rescuing the reputation of a sleeping good writer as in chloroforming a mediocre one.

Jarrell's prose intelligence—he seems to know *everything*—gives his poetry an extraordinary advantage over, for instance, a thunderbolt like Dylan Thomas, in dealing with the present; Jarrell is able to see our whole scientific, political and spiritual situation directly and on its own terms. He is a tireless discoverer of new themes and resources, and a master technician, who moves easily from the little to the grand. Monstrously knowing and monstrously innocent—one does not know just where to find him . . . a Wordsworth with the obsessions of Lewis Carroll.

*The Seven-League Crutches* should best be read with Jarrell's three earlier volumes. *Blood for a Stranger* (1942) is a Parnassian tour-de-force in the manner of Auden; nevertheless, it has several fine poems, the beginnings of better, and enough of the author's personality for John Crowe Ransom to write in ironic astonishment that Jarrell had "the velocity of an angel." *Little Friend, Little Friend* (1945), however, contains some of the best poems on modern war, better, I think, and far more professional than those of Wilfred Owen, which, though they seem pathetically eternal to us now, are sometimes amateurish and unfinished. The determined, passive, sacrificial lives of the pilots, inwardly so harmless and outwardly so destructive, are ideal subjects for Jarrell. In *Losses* (1948) and more rangingly in *Seven-League Crutches*, new subjects appear. Using himself, children, characters from fairy stories, history and painting, he is still able to find beings that are determined, passive and sacrificial, but the experience is quiet, more complex and probably more universal. It's an odd universe, where a bruised joy or a bruised sorrow is forever commenting on itself with the gruff animal common sense and sophistication of Fontaine. Jarrell has gone far enough to be compared with his peers, the best lyric poets of the past: he has the same finesse and originality that they have, and his faults, a certain idiosyncratic willfulness and eclectic timidity, are only faults in this context.

Among the new poems, "Orient Express," a sequel, I think, to "Dover Beach," is a brilliantly expert combination of regular and irregular lines, buried rhymes, and sestina-like repeated rhymes, in which shifts in tone and rhythm are played off against the deadening roll of the train. "A Game at Salzburg" has the broken, charmed motion of someone thinking out loud. Both, in their different ways, are as skillful and lovely as any short poem I know of. "The Knight, Death, and the Devil" is a careful translation of Dürer's engraving. The description is dense; the generalizations are profound. It is one of the most remarkable word-pictures in English verse or prose, and comparable to Auden's "Musée de Beaux Arts." —ROBERT LOWELL, "With Wild Dogmatism," *NYTBR*, Oct. 7, 1951, pp. 7, 41

⟨*Poetry and the Age*⟩ is, I believe, the most original and best book on its subject since *The Double Agent* and *Primitivism and Decadence* by R. P. Blackmur. Since the other ablest American critic of modern poetry in the generation now about forty, Delmore Schwartz, has not collected his essays, we may be specially glad that Jarrell has begun to, and the book is overdue. It does not, indeed, contain his most plunging criticism so far, which will be found in his articles and reviews and lectures on Auden, whose mind Jarrell understands better than anyone ought to be allowed to understand anyone else's, especially anyone so pleasant and destructive as Jarrell; these will make another volume. But it exhibits fully the qualities that made Jarrell the most powerful reviewer of poetry active in this country for the last decade; and in its chief triumphs, the second essay on Frost and the first review of Lowell (I mean the first of the two here preserved) it exhibits more.

William Empson I suppose was Jarrell's master. An early piece on Housman, not reprinted, seems to prove this, and there are several handsome references here. His prose is not so manly as Empson's; it giggles on occasion, and nervous over-emphasis abounds; but it sounds always like a human being talking to somebody—differing in this from nine-tenths of what

other working American critics manufacture. It is cruel and amusing, undeniably well known for these qualities, which it developed so far beyond Empson's traces that that critic presents in comparison an icon of deadpan charity. But what really matter in Jarrell are a rare attention, devotion to and respect for poetry. These, with a natural taste in poetry hardly inferior to Tate's, restless incessant self-training, strong general intelligence, make up an equipment that would seem to be minimal but in fact is unique.

The second essay on Frost is nothing much but thirty pages of quoted poems and passages, with detailed comment. To see how astonishing it is, you ought first to read through a pallid assemblage called *Recognition of Robert Frost*, to the authors of which (except Edward Garnett and Mark Van Doren) the Frost that Jarrell displays would be a horrifying stranger. Perhaps nothing of this vivid sort has ever surpassed the page on "Provide Provide," unless it is the pages following on "Design."

*Lord Weary's Castle* was one of the stiffest books to review that has ever appeared. I have reason to know: Jarrell's was not only superior—far—to my own attempt: it is probably the most masterly initial review of an important poetic work, either here or in England, of this century so far. You have to compare it with wider-ranging reviews, like Eliot's of Grierson, or Dr. Johnson's of Soame Jenyns to feel its narrower but harder learning, its similar but submissive strength.

The studies of Ransom, Stevens, Marianne Moore (again especially the second piece on her), more conventional than those on Frost and Lowell, are nearly as good. A fine citation of Whitman, wittier even than usual, seems better now under a new, more modest title than it did originally, because it does not examine, as Jarrell usually does, substance or method or (save for a few remarks) style. This attention equally in him to matter and manner constitutes a development from what is called the New Criticism.

His general essays, on Obscurity and the Age of Criticism, which strike me as diffuse and making points rather familiar, will undoubtedly help many readers. At least the points made are right. A salient truth about Jarrell, for the present reader, is that he is seldom wrong. About William Carlos Williams' poetry, some of which I love too, he does, I think, exaggerate, and these papers are his weakest; even here he says much that is true, gay, and useful. One of his shrewdest, most characteristic remarks is apropos of a poet one might suppose he would not appreciate at all, the author of the beautiful "Song of the Mad Prince": "It is easy to complain that de la Mare writes about unreality; but how *can* anybody write about unreality?" One cannot but remark the healthy breadth of Jarrell's taste. Behind the writers here treated, perhaps his strongest obvious admirations are for Hardy, Rilke, and of course Eliot, and I hope he will treat them; and Proust, and I wish he dealt more with prose.

On the other hand, his neglect to theorize about poetry, and to theorize above all about criticism, is one of the most agreeable features of a prepossessing and engaging book. Criticism of criticism—at best a languid affair, as Irving Babbitt observed in the preface to one of his books about criticism—is probably best left to very young men and older men. The point is to deal with the stuff itself, and Jarrell does, nobody better. Everybody interested in modern poetry ought to be grateful to him.—JOHN BERRYMAN, "Matter and Manner," *NR*, Nov. 2, 1953, pp. 27–28

Randall Jarrell was a romanticist of the generation which came to adulthood during the miserable 1930s in a society whose most active intellectual centers were dominated by the thought and style of T. S. Eliot and, behind him, of Irving Babbitt. Jarrell reacted as did the others. He launched into a search for a way out of the social and cultural order which seemed to him, and which was, superannuated. More than this, he launched —in spite of his Southern politesse, for he was born in Nashville and graduated from Vanderbilt—with an eagerness that was virtually demoniacal. Among his romantic contemporaries, he was an especially pure example of the type—at least so I have always thought. He was what Jacques Barzun has called an *intrinsic* romanticist; that is, a figure existing outside the primary epoch of European romanticism but still exhibiting the romanticist's primary characteristics.

What these are is open to question. But leaving aside the secondary characteristics, such as the romanticist's commitments to freedom, to individualism, to irrationalism, etc., certainly one of his primary characteristics is his hang-up between man's power and man's misery, between the vision of glory and the experience of degradation. "Man is born free; and everywhere he is in chains." In his youth this was precisely the paradox that Jarrell saw in the world around him: at the top a culture oriented toward tradition and devoted to the methodical delectation of aesthetic splendor, at the bottom a society sick in every member, vitiated by pain and injustice. As the 1930s advanced—Harlan County, Abyssinia, Detroit, Spain —the realities were unmistakable. But so were Jarrell's longings. For years the commonest locution in his poems was the phrase "and yet . . ." uttered sometimes wistfully, sometimes mordantly, sometimes in hollow despair.

To surmount this impasse the romanticist seeks a faith, or at least a synthesis, which will define and accommodate both sides of the paradox. Historically speaking, few have managed it, especially among the poets. Probably the commonest way out has been through radical social action, based on Hegelian concepts of history. For poets a surer but much more difficult course has been the ascent from romantic agony to genuine tragic vision, which in turn destroys its own romantic base by imposing upon it the classical order of the tragic world. The great example, of course, is Goethe. In our own time we have the smaller but very instructive case of Theodore Roethke. He began with a verbal and mental style different from Jarrell's, granted, but with much the same poetic materials, the same view of nature and human reality; but he converted them into an at least sporadically consistent tragic vision. Roethke continued to write with more and more depth of feeling until he died, while Jarrell, almost exactly contemporary, dwindled away into fragments and exercises.

Not that Jarrell didn't try. Social action was effectively denied him, since his connection with the amorphous, self-doubting radicalism of the *Partisan Review* was doomed from the start to futility. Apparently conventional religious faith was also inaccessible to him. But he tried other means of escape, especially by pursuing romantic revulsion to its logical ends in dream and fantasy. Time and again he constructed elaborate dream visions, Germanic—not to say Gothic—in style, from within which he looked out at the "dream" of the waking world and denounced it. But the stress of actuality always supervened. Jarrell was sane, excruciatingly sane, and he could never secure his dream beyond the limits of a few separate, though quite splendid, poems.

Similarly he tried, but only half-heartedly, to commit himself to the mystique of creative impunity, to the expressionistic anti-world of style and imagination; he tried to give himself, not to the meretricious elites of Gottfried Benn and Wyndham Lewis (he was too radical for that) but to the commonalty of alienated poets—troubadours, dandies—pre-served against social, moral and metaphysical blight by the self-sustaining integrity of their creative endeavor. In a few passages he sounds surprisingly like Vachel Lindsay. But it is noteworthy that Jarrell's most consistent statement of these ideas occurs in neither his poetry nor his criticism but in a story for children, *The Bat-Poet*. He didn't believe it himself. Jarrell simply could not forgo the exquisite anguish of his dual attachment to vision and experience. In the end he was left in the wilderness of romantic nihilism with no base but sensibility.

The results are evident. In his criticism Jarrell gave us vibrant readings of individual poets, Frost, Williams and others, but no theoretical statement of importance. In the last twenty years of his poetry, although the dream poems and a few others are interesting, he fell more and more into fragmentary utterance, false starts, scraps and notes, and into set pieces— "story poems" and "character poems," updated Robert Frost— that lacked the verve of his youthful work. Then, too, there was the endless translating and retranslating of the German poets, especially Rilke. What Jarrell needed, apparently, in order to write successfully, was an occasion which gave him not only the reality of an episode and the framework in which to place it but a certain distance from the complexity of the ordinary world: and the only sustained occasion of this kind which occurred in his life was World War II. Jarrell's war poems are his best in every sense. They are the most alive poetically, the most consistent thematically.

All this is what I have thought for some years, and in reading *The Complete Poems* I find it confirmed. The book would be a melancholy monument at best. Here is Randall Jarrell complete and completed, the same Randall Jarrell who so enlivened our literary and social consciences only a short time ago: at least the time must seem short to readers of my generation. Now he is stuffed in a great fat tome, for the dusty corner of a low shelf, to be looked at once and then forgotten. Well, the poems deserve far better. Some of them are great.

The book contains all Jarrell's poems from his previous books, plus three additional sections: one for new work written between his last book and his death, a second for poems published in magazines but not previously collected, the third for earlier unpublished poems. It is, we are made to understand, complete. But curiously it is the only book of its kind that I know in which we discover no hint of the person upon whose authority we are to accept either its completeness or its other attributions; it has no editor; which accounts for the unusual form of the headnote to this review. I have given the bibliographical data as they appear on the title page, and nothing further can be learned from the book or its dust jacket.

We have, then, a considerable bulk of poetry, in which the war poems make a distinct, superior unit. They are not many, perhaps thirty or forty altogether, but even if they were fewer they would be a remarkable achievement. How anyone could write while soldiering is difficult to understand; as one who went through the war unable to write a word, I can only marvel. But Jarrell had been writing for nearly ten years before America entered the war. His early poems are sometimes mannered or imitative, and often artificially opaque; but from the first, as nearly as one can tell, he wrote with ease, and suffered none of the verbal embarrassment customary among young poets. When the war came he already possessed a developed poetic vocabulary and a mastery of forms. Under the shock of war his mannerisms fell away. He began to write with stark, compressed lucidity.

Nowadays we commonly hear critics declare that World War II produced no memorable poetry. Even a critic as acute as George Steiner has said that the poetry of 1940–45 is without "the control of remembrance achieved by Robert Graves or Sassoon" in 1914–18 (*The Death of Tragedy*). To this I can only reply that if I know what "control of remembrance" means, in my experience the poems of Jarrell have it, and they have it pre-eminently. I am certain that other readers of my age, those who were there, find in these poems of soldiers and civilians, the dead, wounded and displaced, the same truth that I do.

Warfare gave Jarrell the antagonist he needed; not fate, not history, not the state, not metaphysical doubt but all these rolled into one—The War—that brute momentous force sweeping a bewildered generation into pathos, horror and death. Today our young dissenters and resisters sometimes ask us why we didn't resist too, why we were willing to go along with the militarists. Shamefacedly and unsuccessfully, we try to explain that willingness had nothing to do with the matter. But we needn't try; it is all there in Jarrell's poems. Cannot they be republished separately—and *cheaply*—with a proper introduction and editorial notes where needed? It would be a benefaction to all concerned. The irresistibility of the war, the suffering of its victims, Americans, Germans, Japanese—Jarrell wrote it all with equal understanding, equal humane sympathy. And he wrote it then, there, at that time and in those places, with power, spontaneity and perfect conviction. Against what I have already said about his poetry, I must in basic honesty conclude with an amendment: in his powerful war poems Randall Jarrell did rise, as if in spite of himself and at the command of a classical force outside his own consciousness, to his moment of tragic vision.—HAYDEN CARRUTH, "Melancholy Monument," *Nation*, July 7, 1969, pp. 19–20

---

### JEROME MAZZARO
#### "Between Two Worlds: Randall Jarrell" (1971)
*Postmodern American Poetry*
1980, pp. 32–58

In his lifetime (1914–65) Randall Jarrell found his poetry consistently praised in reviews yet excluded from Oscar Williams's influential anthologies and, except for a National Book Award in 1961, ignored by all prize committees. As a result, his poetry never quite succeeded into popular acceptance or acclaim. The occasional recognition it did get from the *Southern* or *Sewanee Review*, the Guggenheim foundation, or *Poetry* merely reinforced the image of a poet with an intense but narrow audience. *The Complete Poems* (1969) provides a basis for discussing why this image occurred as well as for determining Jarrell's proper place among the poets of his generation. The view that Karl Shapiro expressed in 1966, shortly after Jarrell's death—that he had outpaced all of his contemporaries—seems already overgenerous. The decision that Helen Vendler offered three years later seems no more lasting. Her review of *The Complete Poems* leans heavily on Oscar Wilde's self-estimation when she asserts that Jarrell "put his genius into his criticism and his talent into his poetry." Jarrell's own sense in *A Sad Heart at the Supermarket* (1962) that all poetic audiences were falling before "the habitual readers of Instant Literature" (p. 28) indicates how he might have explained the neglect, but one has the sense, too, from essays like "The End of the Line" (1942) that with the other immediate heirs of the modernist movement, Jarrell was "wandering between two worlds, one dead, / The other powerless to be born."[1]

More accurate is the metaphor that Jarrell used about Wallace Stevens: "In a lifetime of standing out in thunder-storms," he managed to be "struck by lightning" (PA, 124) enough times to secure himself a notable but not paramount place among those poets who came into their own during and after World War II. Though individually laudable, the twenty or so outstanding poems Jarrell wrote do not allow for the "continuing," "significant consistent, and developing personality"[2] that Eliotic critics have made requisite to a major writer. Instead, like the period which prompted them, the poems stand as isolated crystalizations of a mind that may have been too various and responsive to the discrete experiences of modern life to settle them into a single overriding pattern. It is as if in giving up the assurance of the modernists, the poet could not impose his own views with any finality. Like those of his predecessors, any assurances required constant reexamination and revision until at Jarrell's death the total pattern of the vision was either incomplete or obscure. The technological advances that revolutionized transportation, communication, and living settled too many questionable options to propose a final direction. Given Jarrell's own need to excel, to go on living life to the fullest and highest reaches and aims, this judgment of the work may seem harsh; but it is one which he often made of the work of others and which in his last volume he seems to have understood about his own poetry.

More than any of his contemporaries, Jarrell took seriously Matthew Arnold's hope that the writer should see the world "'with a plainness as near, as flashing' as that with which Moses and Rebekah and the Argonauts saw it" (PA, 118). To this hope Jarrell had added Arnold's statement in "The Study of Poetry" (1880) that "more and more mankind will . . . have to turn to poetry to interpret life."[3] Arnold contended that most of what was considered religion and philosophy would be replaced by poetry. Without poetry even science would seem incomplete. This attachment in poetry of emotion to the idea and the attachment's refusal to materialize in the fact would allow poetry to realize certain psychological and rhetorical truths. Indeed one way in which Jarrell differs from the poets of the previous generation is a post-modernist's acceptance of Freud's view of the psyche. "The English in England" (1963) hypothesizes of Rudyard Kipling's late stories: "If the reality principle has pruned and clipped them into plausibility, it is the pleasure principle out of which they first rankly and satisfyingly flowered" (TBC, 282). Similarly "Stories" (1958) establishes, "the writer is, and is writing for, a doubly- or triply-natured creature, whose needs, understandings, and ideals—whether they are called id, ego, and superego, or body, mind, and soul—contradict one another." In the same essay, Jarrell asserts, "Reading stories, we cannot help remembering Groddeck's 'We have to reckon with what exists, and dreams, daydreams too are also fact; if anyone really wants to investigate realities, he cannot do better than to start with such as these. If he neglects them, he will learn little or nothing of the world of life'" (SH, 141, 140–41).

Mrs. Jarrell reports that by the end of his life *The Interpretation of Dreams* (1900) and *The Psychopathology of Everyday Life* (1904) were recommended readings for the poet's classes, friends, and family. "The volumes of [Freud's] *Collected Papers* [were] strewn with little bent page corners and [Ernest] Jones' *Life and Work* . . . smeared with lemonade and tennis sweat, . . . and the coincidence that Randall and Freud shared the same birthday was, in his word, 'astronomical.'"[4] The familiarity with Freud and Georg Groddeck may have begun as early as Jarrell's undergraduate days as a psychology major at Vanderbilt, but it was undoubtedly strengthened by the early poems of W. H. Auden into a literary possibility. Often the two analysts' separations of life into stimuli colored by subjective interpretation explain the "factitiousness" that Jarrell's writing recurs to. Particulars dissolve into rhetorical predicaments whose emotions then act as bridges to thoses emotions Arnold would attach to the unmaterialized idea. The psychological coloring of an event defines the reality of a situation by defining the character of the person undergoing the experience and the "reality" evolves into an ideal world by extending these distortions into art whose essence is "the union of a wish and a truth" or a "wish modified by a truth" (SH, 26).

The previous generation's rejection or neglect of Freud frequently left it without a means for handling the discrepancies of inner and outer experience except through the terminologies of philosophy and religion and with no language to speak of to handle the area of the age's tendencies toward self-consciousness. Stevens accordingly erred for Jarrell by "thinking of particulars as primarily illustrations of general truths, or else as aesthetic, abstracted objects, simply there to be contemplated"; he "often treats things or lives" so that they seemed "no more than generalizations of an unprecedented low order." Jarrell goes on to insist that "a poet *has* to treat the concrete as primary, as something far more than an instance, a hue to be sensed, a member of a laudable category" (PA, 127–28). Yet William Carlos Williams, who does treat particulars as primary in his early poetry, errs by neglecting the "organization, logic, narrative, generalization" of poetry, thinking it enough to present merely "*data brought back alive*" (PA, 222). Kipling's description of his writing suffers from a comparable failure in that he, according to Jarrell, "was a professional but a professional possessed by both the Daemon he tells you about, who writes some of the stories for him, and the demons he doesn't tell you about, who write others." "Nowadays," he continues, reverting to psychoanalytic terminology, "we've learned to call part of the unconscious *it* or *id*; Kipling had not, but he called this Personal Daemon of his *it*" (SH, 124). In "From the Kingdom of Necessity" (1946) Jarrell praised Robert Lowell's "detailed factuality" and the "contrary, persisting, and singular thinginess of every being in the world" which set themselves against the "elevation and rhetorical sweep of much earlier English poetry" (PA, 196).

For Jarrell the expression of all art involves a balance between emotion and idea or id and superego along lines similar to those which Arnold and Freud drew and carries in their mediation residues of both extremes. In "The Age of the Chimpanzee" (1957), for example, he presents the hands of a figure in Georges de La Tour's *St. Sebastian Mourned by St. Irene* as resembling "(as so much art resembles) the symptomatic gestures of psychoanalysis, half the expression of a wish and half the defence against the wish";[5] and Jarrell's few comments on music suggest a corresponding emphasis. Jarrell may even have believed that art was a kind of medium to make the forces of the id acceptable to the superego and that, in literature, language worked as wit or dream works in Freud to allow passage through an ontogenetic censor of what Jarrell consistently depicts as dark and phylogenetic feelings. Certainly wit and dream form several of his main stresses when dealing with poetic language. His review of Walter McElroy's translation of Tristan Corbière (1947), for instance, makes "puns, mocking half-dead metaphors, parodied clichés, antitheses, and paradoxes, idioms exploited on every level . . . the seven-league crutches on which . . . poems bound wildly forward" (PA, 147); and, as if to emphasize the connection, Jarrell entitles his own next volume of poetry *The Seven-League Crutches* (1951) and includes in it his own versions of Corbière's "La Poète contumace" and four "Rondels pour Après."

Likewise, as early as "Poetry in War and Peace" (1945), Jarrell is investing the previous generation's poetry with Freudian equivalents, dividing it along conscious and unconscious lines, and indicating of Williams that "the tough responsible doctor-half that says and does" and "the violent and delicate free-Freudian half that feels and senses" contribute to one of the "great mythological attitudes" of the country—"the truck-driver looking shyly at the flower."[6] In "The Situation of a Poet" (1952) he notes further of Williams that "he speaks for the Resistance or Underground inside each of us" (PA, 244–45), and he says of Walter de la Mare (1946) that "from his children and ghosts one learns little about children and nothing about ghosts, but one learns a great deal of the reality of which both his ghosts and his children are projections, of the wishes and lacks and love that have produced their 'unreality'" (PA, 139). Much of the discussion in his "Robert Frost's 'Home Burial'" (1962) is given over to distinguishing the characters' rational and compulsive behavior; and, in "Changes of Attitude and Rhetoric in Auden's Poetry" (1941), he cites the prehuman forms which lurk always behind Auden's individuals in the early poems and concludes: "Many of the early poems seem produced by Auden's whole being, as much unconscious as conscious, necessarily made just as they are; the best of them have shapes (just as driftwood or pebbles do) that seem the direct representation of the forces that produced them." He then generalizes on poetry that it "represents the unconscious (or whatever you want to call it) as well as the conscious, our lives as well as our thoughts; and . . . has its true source in the first and not the second" (TBC, 148, 149).

The unique character of the ontogenetic half-self assures Jarrell that its presence is the language of art without any additional mannerisms will make that art human and individual. He lauds Frost for "a verse that uses, sometimes with absolute mastery, the rhythms of actual speech" (PA, 28). In reviews of Auden's later work, Jarrell sees increased mannerisms subverting the unconscious. In "Poetry in a Dry Season" (1940) he says of *Another Time*: "Auden at the beginning was oracular (obscure, original), bad at organization, neglectful of logic, full of astonishing or magical language, intent on his own world and his own forms; he has changed continuously toward organization, plainness, accessibility, objectivity, social responsibility. . . . Now, in too many of the poems, we see not the will, but the understanding, trying to do the work of the imagination." Jarrell dismisses the volume as "moral, rational, manufactured, written by the top of the head for the top of the head." He repeats the complaint a year later in a review of *The Double Man*. "Auden's ideas once had an arbitrary effective quality, a personality value, almost like the ideas in Lawrence or Ezra Pound. They seem today less colorful but far more correct—and they are derived from, or are conscious of elements over most of the range of contemporary thought."[7] Thus, given a situation where the "thought" of Arnold's overt moral view of art conflicts with an honest resolution of life's "realities," Jarrell chooses Freud and Groddeck; and one gets the first suggestion of the two worlds which his art would wander between.

Later, when Jarrell returns to praise Auden for *The Shield of Achilles*, he does so in the *Yale Review* (1955) with statements that indicate his impatience at Auden's having let art's morality conflict with life. In an effort to keep art moral, Jarrell proposes that "perhaps Auden had always made such impossibly exacting moral demands on himself and everybody else partly because it kept him from having to worry about more ordinary, moderate demands; perhaps he had preached so loudly, made such extraordinarily sweeping gestures, in order to hide himself from himself in the commotion. But he seems, finally, to have got tired of the whole affair, to have become willing to look at himself *without doing anything about it*, not even shutting his eyes or turning his head away." Writing of the same volume in *Harper's*, Jarrel repeats his reluctance to abandon his belief that moral and artistic senses lie very close together. He attributes their separation in Auden's writing to a lack of Arnoldian high seriousness. "A few of the poems are good, and all of them are brilliant, self-indulgent, marvelously individual: if Auden sometimes loses faith with something as frivolous as poetry, he never loses it in anything as serious as Auden."[8]

This last is an illusion to *The Age of Anxiety* (1947), which Jarrell had reviewed, complaining of Auden's statement that "all art is . . . essentially frivolous." Even later in "The Old and the New Masters" (1965) he will reply to Auden's "Musée des Beaux Arts" (1939). Auden had contended in his poem that the great artists were never wrong in placing suffering "in a corner" of their work, leaving the center of someone else "eating or opening a window or just walking dully along." Jarrell, for whom suffering is a central concern of poetry, sees the Auden position as passive and asserts that "the old masters disagree." Some like La Tour and Hugo van der Goes make suffering central to their paintings as humanity is central of their meaning. In contrast, modern painters are guilty of abstractions like those of Auden's *New Year Letter*: "How hard it is to set aside / Terror, concupiscence and pride / Learn who and where and how we are, / The children of a modest star." They, too, depict the earth as "a bright spot somewhere in the corner" of canvases devoted to cosmic perspectives. Implied in Jarrell's description is his lament in "The Age of the Chimpanzee." Modern art denies the evolutionary process by equating the art of the chimpanzee to that of man. Of course, Jarrell adds, "there is an immense distance between my poor chimpanzee's dutiful, joyful paintings and those of Jackson Pollock," yet he regrets not living "in an age when painters were still interested in the world. . . . All the poet must do, Rilke said, is praise: to look at what is, and to see that it is good, and to make out of it what is at once the same and better, is to praise."[9]

Conversely "The Age of the Chimpanzee" indicates Jarrell's opposition to a complete submergence of art into the unconscious half-self where it would have at no time the redeeming factors of individuality, Freudian reality, or Arnoldian morality. "Abstract-Expressionism," he writes, "has kept one part [the unconscious] of this process, but has rejected as completely as it could the other part and all the relations that depend on the existence of this other part; it has substituted for a heterogeneous, polyphonic process a homogeneous, homophonic process." This opposition to unconscious art is expanded to include such notions of man as his being an objective uncensoring recorder. In a review of *Paterson* (1951) Jarrell complains of Williams that he should not have left so much of book 2 "real letters from a real woman. . . . What has been done to them," he asks, "to make them part of the poem *Paterson?* I can think of no answer except: 'They have been copied out on the typewriter'" (PA, 238). Trite and unexamined language comes in for similar condemnation. In "These Are Not Psalms" (1945) he objects that the work of A. M. Klein "has none of the exact immediacy, the particular reality of the language of a successful poem; it has instead the voluntary repetition of the typical mannerisms of poetry in general—mannerisms that become a generalized, lifeless, and magical ritual without the spirit of which they were once the peculiar expression."[10]

The redemption of language by this spirit prompts Jarrell to fall back on Goethe's statements concerning technical facility and risk. In "Poetry, Unlimited" (1950) Jarrell asserts: "Goethe said that the worst thing in art is technical facility accompanied by triteness. Many an artist, like God, has never needed to think twice about anything." In "The Profession of Poetry" (1950) he attacks the timidity of Howard Nemerov: "He knows very well that the poet, as Goethe says, is someone who takes risks (and today most intellectuals take no risks at all—are, from the cradle, critics); but he thinks romantic and old-fashioned, couldn't believe, or hasn't heard of something else Goethe said: that the poet is essentially naive." This naiveté, which would allow a dark-world layer into the poem, provides the basis through which Jarrell would merge Freud and Arnold so that poetry might outlast religion and philosophy. As he explains in "Ernie Pyle" (1945), "what he cared about was the facts. But the facts are only facts as we see them, as we feel them; and he knew to what a degree experience . . . is 'seeing only faintly and not wanting to see at all.' The exactly incongruous, the crazily prosaic, the finally convincing fact—that must be true because no one could have made it up . . . was his technical obsession."[11]

Jarrell's stress on naiveté—the individually unreflective as opposed to the overly refined—may have led him, as John Berryman in "Randall Jarrell" (1967) contends, to overvalue Williams considerably. "I'm very fond of Bill Williams' poetry," Berryman writes, "but not as fond as Jarrell was." Moreover the view would ally Jarrell with John Ruskin, who had written in *Modern Painters* (1855) of the soul's need "to *see* something and tell what it saw in a plain way" as "poetry, prophecy, and religion,—all in one." Jarrell in his preface to *The Best Short Stories of Rudyard Kipling* (1961) refers to Ruskin's stand on perfectibility in art: Kipling's stories "are not at all the perfect work of art we want—so perhaps Ruskin was right when he said that the person who wants perfection knows nothing about art" (SH, 121–22). A precise lack of naiveté in the overly refined, lifeless perfection of Richard Wilbur's poetry turns Jarrell against it. In "A View of Three Poets" (1952) he accuses Wilbur of being "too poetic," of letting life become an excuse for poetry and, as Ruskin would have it in the opening volume of *Modern Painters* (1843), of letting art "sink to a mere ornament" and "minister to morbid sensibilities, ticklers and fanners of the soul's sleep."[12]

The strongest indication of the role of language as a mediator between one's senses of art and life and the descending priorities which Jarrell attaches to the mediation as its impulses move progressively outward comes in a review of Rolfe Humphries's *Forbid Thy Ravens* (1948): "What Mr. Humphries's poems say is agreeable, feeling common sense, necessarily a little too easy and superficial, since it has neither the depth of the unconscious, nor that of profound thought, nor that of profound emotion, nor that of the last arbitrary abyss of fact." Under such conditions, poetry in its inmost and purest state would work as Groddeck's It or a Hegelian Geist so that a sequence of its manifestations provides proof of that motivating inner force adumbrated by psychoanalysis or a history of the highest and noblest thoughts of man similar to the imperfect picture of God that results from a Hegelian survey of history. Jarrell's view in "The Profession of Poetry" that "a poet in the true sense of the word [is] someone who has shown to us one of those worlds which, after we have been shown it, we call the real world" substantiates such an hypothesis. Jarrell proposes what critics typically hold for psychoanalysis. For them Freud "thought of the artist as an obdurate neurotic who, by his creative work, kept himself from a crack-up but also from any real cure." The artist fashioned his fantasies into a "new kind of reality" that men conceded "justification as valuable reflections of actual life."[13]

The contexts of Jarrell's view which in its desirability embraces Hegelian "highest and noblest thoughts" is the German poet Rainer Maria Rilke. "Rilke, in his wonderful 'Archaic Statue of Apollo,' ends his description of the statue, the poem itself, by saying without transition or explanation: *You must change your life*. He needs no explanation. We know from many experiences . . . we have shared the alien existences both of this world and of that different world to which the work of art alone give us access—unwillingly accuses our lives." The view also coincides with the starting point of existential philosophy, that existence precedes essence and that man knows his essence by reflection. As early as "The Dramatic Lyricism of Randall Jarrell" (1952) Parker Tyler hinted at a connection when he framed Jarrell's view of existence and knowledge to echo Jean-Paul Sartre's famous pronunciamento. Tyler wrote: "*Existence* comes before *knowledge* because it retains, even after knowledge has arrived, the unknowable that is often the unpredictable."[14]

The Sartrean position which moves beyond Groddeck's It has led to the development of an existential psychoanalysis. One difference of this psychoanalysis and Freud's is, as Rollo May in *Existence* (1960) maintains, the belief that "what an individual seeks *to become* determines what he remembers of his *has been*. In this sense, the future determines the past"; but the future makes the determination in order to change the *present*. The pattern of potentiality that the individual perceives becomes his instrument for handling the domains of past and present. As Hendrik M. Ruitenbeek writes in his introduction to *Psychoanalysis and Existential Philosophy* (1962), "unlike Freudian analysis, which deals with the *Umwelt* and the *Mitwelt*, the biological and social worlds, but almost ignores the *Eigenwelt*, existential analysis stresses the self and the mode of the patient's relationship to that self."[15] Existential psychoanalysis offers to the patient the future directedness and the choice that the Rilke poem suggests, but its Dasein—unlike Hegel's Geist or Groddeck's It—shows a conscious and willful shaping force which, like his reliance on naiveté rather than consciousness, a need for metaphysical mystery will not let Jarrell wholeheartedly accept. As he formulates the present's relation to the future in "A Sad Heart at the Supermarket" (1960), Hegel and Arnold seem most influential: "An artist's work and life presuppose continuing standards, values extended over centuries and millennia, a future that is the continuation and modification of the past, not its contradiction or irrelevant replacement. He is working for the time that wants the best that he can do: the present, he hopes—but if not that, the future" (SH, 73).

Upon the sequence of the changes brought about by one's reactions to art, the present world shapes its future along with an evolving new poetry, conceived of for such purposes and, as Arnold believes, in terms "worthily and more highly than it has been the custom to conceive of it" and "capable of higher uses, and called to higher destinies, than those which in general men have assigned to it hitherto."[16] Thus a second, more practical disjunction between future and present arises from Jarrell's efforts to fuse psychoanalysis and Arnold, and his refusal to accept the consciousness of existential psychoanalysis prevents its resolution. Throughout his criticism Jarrell can complain, on the one hand, of living in a time that is worse than Arnold's or Goethe's and, on the other, admit that he is "old-fashioned enough to believe, like Goethe, in Progress—the progress I see and the progress I wish for and do not see" (PA, 20). The blindness and optimism of this progress—since for Jarrell only

the future can judge the best of the past and that by what it has knowingly incorporated—raises certain questions about the purposefulness of the present which repeatedly, as Arnold before him, Jarrell tries to solve but which, unlike Auden, he is not willing to dismiss by disowning the seriousness of art.

The failure to collapse these visions into one suggests a schematicization of the world—an inner lens—through which one is to see darkly the darkling plain with the "plainness near and flashing" that Arnold called for. Moreover the failure seems to be built into the vision, for as Moses and Rebekah and the Argonauts had cosmic views against which to measure their daily experiences and which never dissolved into an atmosphere of complete immediacy, so, too, in Arnold and Jarrell forces outside their work dictate the choice of words. Goethe's view that the poet must be naive is at least to that extent negated; the "ignorant armies," for instance, which end Arnold's "Dover Beach" are ignorant not because of anything in the poem but because of the world view out of which the poem springs. The same may be said of the emotive language of many Jarrell poems. Delmore Schwartz registers such a complaint in "The Dream from Which No One Wakes" (1945): "In his first two books many of the poems were weakened by a thinness and abstractness of texture and reference; it was as if the poet saw his subjects through opera glasses. . . . For all the genuineness of the poems, the net result resembled the dim and ghastly negative which has to be held up to the light, and not the developed photograph full of daylight and defined objects."[17]

Jarrell's various positions on Auden demonstrate, in addition, an unwillingness to resolve the matter of these disjunctions by focusing necessarily on one persona or about the writings of a single man. This suggests another kind of disjunction hinted at by Shapiro: a yearning for and an opposition to Authority. Shapiro writes of Jarrell's opposition: "It became necessary for everyone my age to attack Auden, as sculptors must attack Mount Rushmore. Nevertheless Auden and Mount Rushmore still stand and probably always will."[18] Nor was Williams a more suitable subject. Jarrell notes of him: "He is a *very* good but *very* limited poet, particularly in vertical range" (PA, 240). Jarrell adds: "He keeps too much to that tenth of the iceberg that is above water, perhaps" (PA, 245). Jarrell is more generous toward Frost: "Frost is that rare thing, a complete or representative poet, and not one of the brilliant partial poets who do justice, far more than justice, to a portion of reality, and leave the rest of things forlorn" (PA, 61). And Jarrell says of Whitman: "Of all modern poets he has, quantitatively speaking, 'the most comprehensive soul'—and, qualitatively, a most comprehensive and comprehending one, with charities and concessions and qualifications that are rare in any time" (PA, 115). But he reduces his praise of Frost by adding: "If we compare this wisdom with, say, that of the last of the Old Ones, Goethe, we are saddened and frightened at how much the poet's scope has narrowed, at how difficult and partial and idiosyncratic the application of his intelligence has become, at what terrible sacrifices he has had to make in order to avoid making others still more terrible" (PA, 62).

As an alternative to shaping his views into a single voice, Jarrell seems at times to suggest multiple personae. He champions, for example, anthologies as an ideal critical expression and exposition of an age's taste and laments the fact that Arnold's touchstones "never evolved into an anthology" (PA, 155). He also praises individual poets like Williams, Whitman, and Frost for their abilities to get out of themselves, to suggest other voices than their own in their poetry; and he complains of Robert Lowell in "A View of Three Poets" that "you can't tell David from Bathsheba without a program: they both (like the majority of Mr. Lowell's characters) talk just like Mr. Lowell" (PA, 231). A decade earlier, "Poets: Old, New, and Aging" (1940) had noted the same of Pound: "Everything is seen as through a glass darkly, the glass being Mr. Pound: 1766 B.C. talks exactly like 1735 A.D., and both exactly like Ezra Pound. To the old complaint, 'All Chinamen look alike,' Mr. Pound makes one add, 'And talk alike, and act alike—and always did.'"[19] Jarrell repeatedly insists on dramatic monologue as the poetic vehicle, though, at times, as in the case of Elizabeth Bishop, he is willing to grant morality to description and landscape as had Ruskin.

All three suggestions—anthologies, flexible voices, and the dramatic monologue technique—seem part of a philosophical relativism which Jarrell betrays in statements like "Williams had a real and unusual dislike of, distrust in, Authority; and the Father-surrogate of the average work of art has been banished from his Eden. His ability to rest (or at least to thrash happily about) in contradictions, doubts, and general guesswork, without ever climbing aboard any of the monumental certainties that go perpetually by, perpetually on time—this ability may seem the opposite of Whitman's gift for boarding every certainty and riding off into every infinite, but the spirit behind them is the same" (PA, 220). His enlisting of readers to join him on such journeys recalls Oswald Spengler's position in *The Decline of the West* (1918). Spengler branded this philosophical relativism the modern counterpart to classical skepticism which was ahistorical and denied outright. The new skepticism which "is obliged to be historical through and through" gets its solutions "by treating everything as relative, as a historical phenomenon, and its procedure is psychological."[20] It leads to a voice in Jarrell's poetry that is consciously nonauthoritative or whose authoritative tone is undermined by the poem's context in the volume or by other tones within it. Only in his criticism was Jarrell willing to become authoritative, and this may have prompted Helen Vendler's remark that his poetry had talent but that his real genius lay in criticism.

Jarrell's treatment of the childhoods of Auden and Kipling and his poems like "A Story" (1939) indicate that there may be other personal reasons behind his dislike of Authority. The accounts in these works strangely blend into each other and, one suspects, Jarrell's own boyhood. In "Freud to Paul: The Stages of Auden's Ideology" (1945) he says of Auden's childhood and its part in the creation of "the wicked Uncle": "It is no surprise to learn, in *Letters from Iceland* and other places, that Auden's parents were unusually good ones, very much venerated by the child: Auden moralizes interminably, cannot question or reject Authority except under the aegis of this pathetically invented opposing authority, because the superego (or whatever term we wish to use for the mechanism of conscience and authority) is exceptionally strong in him." Jarrell then cites a statement by Abram Kardiner that "the superego is based on affection, not hatred" (TBC, 164). Of Kipling's boyhood Jarrell notes, "For the first six years of his life the child lived in Paradise, the inordinately loved and reasonably spoiled son of the best of parents; after that he lived in the Hell in which the best of parents put him, and paid to have him kept" (SH, 129). After six years they rescued the boy "and for the rest of their lives they continued to be the best and most loving of parents, blamed by Kipling for nothing, adored by Kipling for everything" (SH, 130). Jarrell goes on to conclude: "It is *this* that made Kipling what he was: if they had been the worst of parents, even fairly bad parents, even ordinary parents, it would have all made sense, Kipling himself could have made sense out of it. As it was, his world had been torn in two and he himself torn in two: for under the part of

him that extenuated everything, blamed for nothing, there was certainly a part that extenuated nothing, blamed for everything—a part whose existence he never admitted, most especially not to himself" (SH, 130).

Jarrell's "A Story" details the same emotions in the son of "the best of parents." The lad eventually extenuates everything and blames his parents for nothing while at the same time he extenuates nothing and blames them for everything. He arrives at the "Hell" of a boarding school whose emptiness is juxtaposed to the "good" mother's concern—even to the point of using the "right" language: "Remember to change your stockings every day— / Socks, I mean." Recollection of the concern changes to resentment as the boy's "mail-box is still empty, / Because they've all forgotten me, they love their / New friends better." The boy plots to punish his parents by disappearing. The same "concern" and "indictment" fill late poems like "Windows" (1954), in which the parents who have been accused by their son of being "indifferent" show their concern in noting "you have not slept." For Jarrell, whose parents were divorced, these "parents" are often his paternal grandparents with whom he lived for a while in Hollywood. Significantly the movement in these later poems runs ever away from indictment to forgiveness. "In Those Days" (1953) he recalls: "How poor and miserable we were. / How seldom together! / And yet after so long one thinks: / In those days everything was better." The sentiment extends to both "The Lost World" and "Thinking of the Lost World" (1963), which concludes that, having spent most of his life learning to forgive his parents for having damaged him, he is left with "nothing" as his reward. The mechanisms by which one's self has been defined, once withered away by forgiveness, leave one nothing by which to define self—a fear implicit in any real skepticism and here expressed "in happiness."

Jarrell had come to a similar conclusion twenty-three years before in "For an Emigrant" (1940), and the despair of nothingness, so much complained of by reviewers, runs through the early books. In one of his last poems, "A Man Meets a Woman in the Street" (1967), the narrator gives up identity and the human drive of imagination and contents himself with the wish of the birds that "this day / Be the same day, the day of my life." Faced with these various disjunctions, his advice in "The Obscurity of the Poet" (1951) is that "there is nothing to do different from what we already do: if poets write poems and readers read them, each as best they can—if they try to live not as soldiers or voters or intellectuals or economic men, but as human beings—they are doing all that can be done" (PA, 20). Here he falls back on the thesis of Groddeck's *The Book of the It* (1923) that at man's inception he incurs a force that shapes his destiny, and things like breathing which have much to do with the It have little to do with the will. Man may, as Jarrell indicates in "To Fill a Wilderness" (1951), find that the world imaged by poetry is "our nation's life as Yeats saw his own—as a preparation for something that never happened."[21]

"A Girl in a Library" (1951), the opening selection of *The Complete Poems*, depicts the conditions of such a perverse preparation. Centering on a girl, a "student of Home Economics and Physical Education, who has fallen asleep in the library of a Southern College," it evolves into a colloquy between the poem's speaker (the present) and Tatyana Larina (the past), who materializes out of Aleksandr Pushkin's *Eugene Onegin* (1833). Tatyana wonders at the value of a life of sleep where "the soul has no assignments, neither cooks / Nor referees; it wastes its time." Without ideas against which to shape the present, a person is no more than a "machine-part"; dream and reality are one and homogeneous like the homogeneous abstract expressionism attacked in "The Age of the Chimpanzee." Indulgent with this "machine-part," as often Jarrell's speakers are not, the narrator responds that since "the ways we miss our lives are life," it is better at death "to squawk like a chicken" and meet Death's challenge "with a last firm strange / Uncomprehending smile" and, then, to see the "blind date that you stood up; your life," than to be aware of the failure beforehand. Incorporated in this response is Jarrell's inconsistent view that, whatever the innate or obscure and expanding reaches of excellence, like Rebekah and the Argonauts, people should strive after them. As with Groddeck's patients, this striving may take the form of a self-examination to make one adjust himself to the It, but no amount of will can shape an It that is not there.

Knowledge by way of Tatyana emphasizes literature as an important source of reform. Jarrell repeats this stress in "The Intellectual in America" (1955) where he speaks of the writer again as "the man who will make us see what we haven't seen, feel what we haven't felt, understand what we haven't understood—he *is* our best friend" (SH, 15). The student's failure, like the failures of the children of "Lady Bates" (1948) and "The Black Swan" (1951) and of the pilot of "The Dead Wingman" (1945), relegates her to an unearned oblivion of "everlasting sleep." In contrast the "saved"—those whose visions help shape the future—become part of a hovering Spirit which "Burning the Letters" (1945) shows inspiring the present. But even there it must be finally abandoned in order to let new life evolve. In time, as "The Memoirs of Glückel of Hameln" (1942) asserts, "We take your place as our place will be taken." In both instances "The Knight, Death, and the Devil" (1951) maintains, man achieves his judgment not by any human design but by doing what he must. Under such non-traditional terms "The Night before the Night before Christmas" (1949) indicates that "to use God's name" (that is, to imagine him) is "to misuse His name," for what can be imagined, as "In the Ward: The Sacred Wood" (1946) makes clear, can also be unmade. "A Sick Child" (1949) depicts God as "all that I never thought of," and "Eighth Air Force" (1947) shows Christ not as divine but as a "just man" without fault, whom the speaker has tried to imitate. This imitation causes "suffering" and a final self-image as Pontius Pilate, and in "Seele im Raum" (1950), it produces the "eland," that imaginary creature of the mind which gives life to the soul and humanity to the "machine" and which in German translates as "wretched" (*elend*).

The human designs which result from this wretchedness—often dictated in terms of daydream, wish, fairy tale, make-believe, dream, myth, miracle, and masterwork—are the products, Jarrell insists, only of children and men, and men only insofar as they are childish. In no case are they as idiosyncratic as Heideggerian Daseins. Girls have them until they marry and become women. Then, as "Woman" (1964) states, they become "realists; or as a realist might say, / Naturalists," for it is "woman's nature / To want the best, and to be careless how it comes." "Cinderella" (1954) records a coy but significant conversation between a daydreaming girl and her daydream godmother (the Virgin Mary) in the absence of Prince Charming and Christ, who are out childishly imagining. It ends with God's mother inviting the girl to await inside the return of their men, which might be soon or never. "Mary" herself has taken on the aspects of the Devil's grandmother in Grimm's "The Devil with the Three Golden Hairs." In the light of man's inability to imagine correctly the Divine Will, the "wisdom" of their position is obvious, for what they do realize by becoming mothers is a role in Jarrell's almost Darwinian evolution and divinely willed preservation of the species. Here, however the individual may be disregarded, the form or species will be cherished. Yet, as Jarrell seems to say in

variations of the "Cinderella" situation such as "The End of the Rainbow" (1954), "Seele im Raum" (1950), and "The Woman at the Washington Zoo" (1959), becoming a woman is not very easy. The women of these poems are looked on by their worlds as machine-parts. Only in their imaginations do they preserve their humanity, often by dreaming of fairy-tale and animal creatures in whom to invest their love.

As in Arnold the cherishing of this species takes the form of the perfection of the state—"the nation in its collective and corporate character"—rather than of the individual. Many of the essays in A *Sad Heart at the Supermarket* are directed toward this end, which critics of Jarrell's early poetry mistook for Marxism. In such essays as "The Taste of the Age" (1958) Jarrell presents himself as a latter-day Arnold or as Arnold's favorite, Goethe. The essay opens with a negative reaction to the age: "When we look at the age in which we live—no matter what age it happens to be—it is hard for us not to be depressed by it." Jarrell then goes on to note: "We can see that Goethe's and Arnold's ages weren't as bad as Goethe and Arnold thought them: after all, they produced Goethe and Arnold" (SH, 16, 17). The rest of the essay unfolds as an attack on popular culture and an appeal for continuing to upgrade culture, as Arnold had thought to do, through education. Similarly, in recommending the second book of William Wordsworth's "The Excursion" in the *New York Times*'s "Speaking of Books" column (1955), Jarrell writes: "I feel Matthew Arnold's approving breath at my shoulder, and see out before me, smiling bewitchingly, the nations of the not-yet-born."[22] The state thus conceived becomes organic, and war in "The Range in the Desert" (1947) is looked upon as the pitting of one state against another in a struggle for survival much as the lizard of the poem survives by devouring "the shattered membranes of the fly."

Caught in a movement from greater to lesser imperfection similar to man's, the state at no time is perfect and incapable of change. Yet, as "The Night before the Night before Christmas" indicates, only a just state may triumph, for the triumph of an unjust state is an indication of an unjust God. The view of this relationship between the state and God is declared in "Kafka's Tragi-Comedy" (1941): "God is the trust, the state, all over again at the next higher level. God's justice and the world's contradict each other; and yet what is God's justice but the world's, raised to the next power, but retaining all the qualities of its original."[23] Rather than legally centered upon the protection of the many, the justice of this state is built upon "poetic justice"—the good receiving rewards and the bad, punishments. This central wellspring of art adds a vein of aestheticism which is not obvious in Arnold but which is consistent with nineteenth-century philosophy. It frequently held that the act of poetic creation was closest to the nature of God.

Such pieces as "A Sad Heart at the Supermarket" are willing to admit the aestheticism: "To say that Nature imitates Art . . . is literally true. . . . Which of us hasn't found a similar refuge in the 'real,' created world of Cézanne or Goethe or Verdi?" (SH, 78–79). But the aestheticism which existential psychoanalysis relegates to the past and present by creation of the Dasein is negated in part by Jarrell's drive toward the future. While granting, as had Wilde, "that the self-conscious aim of Life is to find expression, and that Art offers it certain beautiful forms through which it may realize that energy,"[24] Jarrell in locating the real force of art in the realm of the spirit—the phylogenetic or Groddeck's It—gives it a timelessness which transcends, as he supposed Freudian analysis might, the otherwise past-directedness of recollected childhood. In "The

State" (1945) the poet tries to make acceptable through wit a state's having killed a child's mother and drafted his sister and cat. Although the acts lead finally to the child's wish to die, they may in the realm of the spirit be ultimately right. The deranged nature of the speaker prevents any clear assurance, but Jarrell's concluding remarks in "Auden's Ideology," published in the same year, indicates a willingness to put up with some inconveniences to direct his efforts toward a larger enemy. One senses this "larger enemy" is fears like those expressed in Arthur Miller's *Situation Normal* (1944). Miller defined World War II as a struggle to maintain "the right of each individual to determine his freedom" against "the tyrannic corporate control of the minds and wills of men."[25]

"A Lullaby" (1944) had approached these fears directly. Its soldier's life is submerged to the service of the state. He "is lied to like a child, cursed like a beast," and generally so nonhumanly treated that his life "is smothered like a grave, with dirt," forgotten or "recalled in dreams or letters." "A Field Hospital" (1947) describes an injured soldier being so sedated by the state that he "neither knows" nor "remembers" but "sleeps, comforted." The volumes in which these poems appeared express the hope that the personal sacrifices and losses of the war may be offset by a willingness to create a better world afterward, based on the cost to the individual to let the past continue or to allow its recurrence. A later poem, "A Well-to-do Invalid" (1965), tells of a self-interested nurse (the individual?) who tends a self-indulgent invalid (the state?), taking to herself his care so that she feels her justification and her hope of his inheritance in his not being able to get along without her. She dies, and the poem's speaker sees the invalid "well with grief," realizing in the act how easily her vacancy will be filled. The premise of the poem echoes Jarrell's comments on Alex Comfort (1945). Recognizing "that the states themselves are at present the main danger their citizens face," Jarrell adds reluctantly: "It is we who wither away, not the state" (PA, 142–43). In the "radically-pastoral, romantically nostalgic, bittersweet idylls" that followed these war poems and caused him to begin to lose him his audience, Jarrell began to see even more conclusively that the resolve he hoped might come from the war was not forthcoming. Veterans preferred to forget their sacrifices and accept the sleep that the postwar culture offered. Meaninglessness set in.

Jarrell comes to these views slowly, and even more slowly is a reader able to put them together. Some are already formed by *The Rage for the Lost Penny* (1940), but their presence is obscured in a more conspicuous admixture of Audenesque phrases. These include "efficiently as a new virus," "the star's distention," and "the actuaries end." They later disappear, but their presence here affirms Jarrell's statement in the preface that "Auden is the only poet who has been influential very recently; and this is because, very partially and uncertainly, and often very mechanically, he represents new tendencies, a departure from modernist romanticism." One tendency was the dream poem and its mediation of subconscious and conscious levels, typified by the second poem in Auden's first collection. The poem, which was dropped in subsequent reprintings, forms one reason why Jarrell always cited the 1930 edition of *Poems*, though for convenience he tended to quote from the 1934 edition. A second tendency was Auden's millennialism rooted in "Darwin, Marx, Freud and Co., . . . all characteristically 'scientific' or 'modern' thinkers" about whom the previous generation had "concluded, regretfully: 'If they had not existed, it would not have been necessary to ignore them' (or deplore them)."[26] A third was the power of women to motivate history, as typified by the mothers of Auden's *Paid on Both Sides*. These

women keep the feud between their families alive and bloody; and their power, which occurs often in the backgrounds of these early poems, becomes more apparent as women move into the foreground of Jarrell's poetry with *Losses* (1948).

In *The Rage for the Lost Penny* are located a number of poems which belong to the child's sing-song world and whose half-lines and themes occasionally foreshadow lines and themes in Theodore Roethke's *The Lost Son* (1948). The narrator of "A Little Poem" (1940) speaks to his yet-to-be-conceived younger brother in the womb with such Roethkean expressions as "My brother was a fish" and references to the world as "this sink of time." The opening lines of "The Ways and the Peoples" (1939) add: "What does the storm say? What the trees wish" and "I am the king of the dead." This last assertion finds itself repeated in Berryman's *The Dispossessed* (1948), at the end of the second and psychologically based "Nervous Songs" ("The Song of the Demented Priest"). Jarrell's introduction to *The Golden Bird and Other Fairy Tales* (1962) makes the connection between these poems and Freud apparent: "Reading *Grimm's Tales* tells someone what we're like, inside, just as reading Freud tells him. *The Fisherman and His Wife*—which is one of the best stories anyone ever told, it seems to me—is as truthful and troubling as any newspaper headlines about the new larger-sized H-bomb and the new antimissile missile: a country is never satisfied either, but wants to be like the good Lord." Earlier Jarrell in his essay on Kafka had described *Amerika* as "a charming and often extremely funny story, a sort of Candide *à la* Hans Christian Andersen, with extraordinary overtones": "This world is hardly *judged* at all; its cruelties and barbarities elicit only the blankly anthropological interest we extend to the vagaries of savages or children. The conscientious naïveté, the more-than-scientific suspension or tentativeness of judgment of the later books, are already surprisingly well developed in *Amerika*. In its capacity for generating ambiguity and irony (reinforced in the later books by the similar possibilities of allegory), the attitude resembles that of Socrates, that of the scientist making minimal assumptions, or that of the 'humble observer': child, fairy-tale simpleton or third son, fool."[27]

In addition Jarrell knows enough about the Arnoldian future of his poetry to begin *The Rage for the Lost Penny* with "On the Railway Platform" (1939). Like the later "A Girl in a Library" it has as its theme the ideas that man travels "by the world's one way" and that his "journeys end in / No destination we meant." What man leaves, he leaves forever. "When You and I Were All" (1939) continues the Arnoldian cast with the lines: "What kiss could wake / whose world and sleep were one embrace?" The influence reappears as well in the telling question of "The Refugees" (1940): "What else are their lives but a journey to the vacant / Satisfaction of death?" "For the Madrid Road" (1940) adds the prospect of people who die to preserve their ideals and who ask continually, "But when were lives men's own? . . . Men die / . . . that men may miss / The unessential ills." Malcolm Cowley's review of *Blood for a Stranger* (1942) lists the further echoes of Wilfred Owen's "The Snow" in "The Automaton" (1937) and of Allen Tate's "Ode to the Confederate Dead" in "A Description of Some Confederate Soldiers" (1936). But the reader's task has been formed; he must reject the surface and work backward from the language of Jarrell's writing not to influences but to the conscious and unconscious impulses which fashioned the work.

Moreover the views translate into an over-all sense of a poetry which, in striving after the noblest thoughts of men and a style which might serve the higher destinies to which poetry has been called, consistently appears unreal and valueless.

Often the unreality is necessary, for, by believing that imagination must precede change, Jarrell must stress moments of imagination—daydream, fairy tale, and wish—and minimize the fact. In this he faces a problem similar to that faced by Dante and Gerard Manley Hopkins: weighing the sensuous beauty of the world which attracts the artist against the idealism which leads him to reject that world for the idea. In reviewing, Jarrell faced the problem by beginning his reviews with his most adverse statements, reversing the usual order of reviewers and prompting Berryman's comment: "Jarrell's reviews did go beyond the limit; they were unbelievably cruel." But their cruelty was often the way Jarrell had for forcing readers out of their complacency into realms where the imagination might function. Since the highest and noblest thoughts of men exclude the ugly, Jarrell tended to exclude it from his poetry or redeem it by means of sentimentalism and romanticism. In a war situation like that opening "Transient Barracks" (1949), the ugly may intrude and allow a sense of life to emerge, but this is rare, and one suspects the additional influence of Pyle. Miller's analysis of Pyle here proves relevant: "Ernie Pyle's thought *was* in his columns. His thought is people. His thought is details about people. War is about people, not ideas. You cannot see ideas bleeding."[28]

More common are the moments in Jarrell's last volume where man is located amid a gross commercialism that hawks its panaceas of Cheer and Joy and All and where things are stripped plain. At those moments, as ever where the fact and idea clash, Jarrell's wit intrudes to work, as Freud indicates all wit works, to overcome the valuelessness by letting an unaltered or nonsensical ambiguity of words and multiplicity of thought-relations appear to the consciousness at the same time senseful and admissible as jest. In "A Man Meets a Woman in the Street" Jarrell is willing to forego such ambiguity by accepting the factuality of the world, but the willingness is itself indication that the fact has not occurred. These instants when idea and fact clash are most often the occasions where the purposelessness of the present fades into the brilliance of Jarrell's lines as the concerted direction of his life lay always obscured by the veneer of an incessant instinct of expansion and a refined sensibility. This sensibility, for all its stress on modernism, relished sports cars, bucolic atmospheres, traditional art, good music, poetry, technological advances, and Russian ballet. Lowell in "Randall Jarrell" (1967) recalls: "His mind, unearthly in its quickness, was a little boyish, disembodied, and brittle. His body was a little ghostly in its immunity to soil, entanglements, and rebellion. As one sat with him in oblivious absorption at the campus bar, sucking a fifteen-cent chocolate milk shake and talking eternal things, one felt, beside him, too corrupt and companionable. He had the harsh luminosity of Shelley—like Shelley, every inch a poet, and like Shelley, imperiled perhaps by an arid, abstracting precocity."[29]

Only the imaginary protrait of the poet—akin to the Imaginary Portraits of fin-de-siècle writers—shifting among Goethe, Arnold, and Auden and formed early by Jarrell—offered him something worldly and static and positive against which to shape his life. That portrait is sketched in the allusions to these writers, the self-comparisons with them, and the appropriations of their tastes that run through all of Jarrell's work. These appropriations go hand in hand with an attack on idiosyncratic individualism which he associated in "The End of the Line" with modernism. This sense led early to a growing drift from the personal that was not reversed until *The Woman at the Washington Zoo* (1960) and *The Lost World* (1965). Here, as M. L. Rosenthal in *The New Poets* (1967) observes, "a change had begun to take place, heralded by three poems in

the former book: 'In Those Days,' 'The Elementary Scene,' and 'Windows.' These are poems of private memory—of a time in the past that seemed, often was, 'poor and miserable' (and yet 'everything was better'); of the sadness of what appears, in 'The Elementary Scene,' to have been an unsatisfactory childhood, with a last ironic allusion to the speaker's adult condition ('I, I, the future that mends everything'); and of the impossibility of recovering the dead, simple past of parents who 'have known nothing of today.'" This reversal which brings Jarrell into the confessional school, so much a part of the age, was roundly applauded by reviewers who, like Philip Booth, tended to refer to *The Lost World* as a "great new book."[30]

In fact one might chart the progress of *The Complete Poems* as a succession of efforts by Jarrell to rid himself of the "aloneness" which he felt—without resorting to the condemnations of parents which he associated with both Kipling and Auden. Repeatedly one senses what in *The Divided Self* (1960) R. D. Laing calls "ontological insecurity": "The individual in the ordinary circumstances of living may feel more unreal than real; in a literal sense, more dead than alive; precariously differentiated from the rest of the world, so that his identity and autonomy are always in question." Jarrell's personae are always involved with efforts to escape engulfment, implosion, and petrification, by demanding that they somehow be miraculously changed by life and art into people whose ontologies are psychically secure. The changes may allow them then to drop the mechanism by which in their relations they preserve themselves and to feel gratification in relatedness. Laing, who indirectly cites Kafka as a prime example of a writer of ontological insecurity, strikes close to Jarrell's own sensibility. Something there along with Rilke's Apollo or Norman O. Brown's *Love's Body* (1966) announces: "Meaning is not in things but in between; in the iridescence, the interplay; in the interconnections; at the intersections, at the crossroads."[31]

For a person with less skill, such purposelessness and such militating against the fact might be enough to make his life and poetry unwelcome. Without Williams's rhythms of descent or a comparable instrument of sacramentalization to bridge inner and outer existences, Jarrell's world remains disparate; and he must rely on language as his major means for keeping it together. This reliance runs explicitly through much of his criticism and is implicit in his poetry; yet, as he perceived in "The Taste of the Age," even language was failing him: "The more words there are, the simpler the words get. The professional users of words process their product as if it were baby food and we babies: all we have to do is open our mouths and swallow" (SH, 28). Without a complex language, a language capable of multiplicity, of the ambiguity necessary to wed conscious and unconscious realms, successful poetry would become impossible. Nevertheless a thingy liveliness might be preserved and, because the future always holds something better, hope as well. Like Arnold, who never realized his dream of some day supplanting Tennyson and Browning as the poet of the mid-nineteenth century because of the self-defeating nature of his momentary stays against the confusion of the world, Jarrell seems destined because of his overwhelming reliance on the translucency of language for a secondary role. Here the excellence and abundance of wisdom, hope, humanity, and despair that the in-between of Jarrell's poetry contain, affirm his role in bringing psychological techniques to American themes. If, as Shapiro senses, he failed in that role, all the same by his efforts he made others aware of the course poetry must take. His nostalgic laments for the passing may be perhaps not so centrally important as the celebrations of renewal by other poets of his generation, but Jarrell remains by virtue of the laments imposingly significant.

Notes

1. Karl Shapiro in *Randall Jarrell: 1914–1965*, ed. Robert Lowell, Peter Taylor, and Robert Penn Warren (New York: Farrar, Straus and Giroux, 1967), p. 201; Helen Vendler, "The Complete Poems," *New York Times Book Review*, 2 February 1969, p. 5. The following abbreviations of Jarrell's books have been adopted for internal citation: PA—*Poetry and the Age* (New York: Vintage Books, 1955); SH—*A Sad Heart at the Supermarket* (New York: Atheneum, 1962); TBC—*The Third Book of Criticism* (New York: Farrar, Straus and Giroux, 1969). The abbreviations are accompanied by page citations.
2. T. S. Eliot, *Selected Essays*, rev. ed. (London: Faber and Faber, 1951), p. 203. For Jarrell's subscription to this view, see his remarks on Theodore Roethke in *The Third Book of Criticism*, pp. 326–27.
3. Matthew Arnold, "The Study of Poetry," in *Essays in Criticism: Second Series* (London: Macmillan and Co., 1888), p. 2.
4. Mary von Schrader Jarrell, "Reflections on Jerome," *Jerome: The Biography of a Poem* (New York: Grossman, 1971), p. 13.
5. Randall Jarrell, "The Age of the Chimpanzee," *Art News* 56 (summer 1957), 34.
6. Randall Jarrell, "Poetry in War and Peace," *Partisan Review* 12 (1945): 123.
7. Randall Jarrell, "Poetry in a Dry Season," *Partisan Review* 7 (1940): 166; Jarrell, "New Year Letter," *Nation* 152 (1941): 440.
8. Randall Jarrell, "Recent Poetry," *Yale Review* 44 (1955): 607; Jarrell, "The Year in Poetry," *Harper's* 211 (October 1955): 100.
9. Randall Jarrell, "Verse Chronicle," *Nation* 165 (1947): 424; "The Age of the Chimpanzee," p. 35.
10. Randall Jarrell, "These Are Not Psalms," *Commentary* 1 (November 1955): 88.
11. Randall Jarrell, "Poetry, Unlimited," *Partisan Review* 17 (1950): 191; Jarrell, "The Profession of Poetry," *Partisan Review* 17 (1950): 726; Jarrell, "Ernie Pyle," *Nation* 160 (1945): 573.
12. John Berryman in *Randall Jarrell: 1914–1965*, p. 16; John Ruskin, *Modern Painters*. Illustrated Library Edition. 3 vols. (Boston: Aldine Book Publishing Co., 1900): 3:330–31, 1:108.
13. Randall Jarrell, "Verse Chronicle," *Nation* 166 (1948):360; "The Profession of Poetry," p. 731; René Welleck and Austin Warren, *Theory of Literature*, 3rd. ed. (New York: Harvest Books, 1962), p. 82.
14. "The Profession of Poetry," p. 728; Parker Tyler, "The Dramatic Lyricism of Randall Jarrell," *Poetry* 129 (1952): 344.
15. Rollo May, "Contributions of Existential Psychotherapy," in *Existence*, ed. Rollo May, Ernest Angel, and Henri F. Ellenberger (New York: Clarion Books, 1958), p. 69; Henrik M. Ruitenbeek, Introduction to *Psychoanalysis and Existential Philosophy* (New York: E. P. Dutton, 1962), p. xx.
16. "The Study of Poetry," p. 2.
17. Delmore Schwartz, "The Dream from Which No One Wakes," *Nation* 161 (1945): 590.
18. Shapiro, p. 225.
19. Randall Jarrell, "Poets: Old, New, and Aging," *New Republic* 103 (1940): 800.
20. Oswald Spengler, *The Decline of the West*, trans. Charles Frances Atkinson (New York: Modern Library, 1965), p. 35.
21. Randall Jarrell, "To Fill a Wilderness," *Nation* 173 (1951): 570.
22. Randall Jarrell, "Speaking of Books," *New York Times Book Review*, 24 July 1955, p. 2.
23. Randall Jarrell, "Kafka's Tragi-Comedy," *Kenyon Review* 3 (1941): 118.
24. Oscar Wilde, *The Artist as Critic*, ed. Richard Ellmann (New York: Random House, 1969), p. 320.
25. Benjamin Nelson, *Arthur Miller: Portrait of a Playwright* (New York: David McKay, 1970), p. 55.
26. Randall Jarrell, "A Note on Poetry," in *Five Young American Poets* (Norfolk, Conn.: New Directions, 1940), p. 89; "New Year Letter," p. 440.
27. Randall Jarrell, "Grimm's Tales," *The Golden Bird and Other Fairy Tales* (New York: Crowell Collier, 1962), p. v; "Kafka's Tragi-Comedy," pp. 116–17.
28. Berryman, p. 16; Arthur Miller, *Situation Normal* (New York: Reynal & Hitchcock, 1944), p. 166.
29. Robert Lowell in *Randall Jarrell: 1914–1965*, p. 102.
30. M. L. Rosenthal, *The New Poets* (New York: Oxford University Press, 1967), p. 330; Philip Booth in *Randall Jarrell: 1914–1965*, p. 22.
31. R. D. Laing, *The Divided Self* (Baltimore: Penguin Books, 1965), p. 42; Norman O. Brown, *Love's Body* (New York: Random House, 1966), p. 247.

# RUSSELL FOWLER
## From "Randall Jarrell's 'Eland':
## A Key to Motive and Technique in His Poetry"
*Iowa Review*, Spring 1974, pp. 113–26

The growing critical interest in the work of Randall Jarrell reveals two things: his reputation as one of the most perceptive and helpful literary critics of the last three decades continues to flourish, while his own poetry remains the center of intense controversy. Judgments of its overall value and place alongside the work of contemporaries like Robert Lowell and Theodore Roethke vary radically, and even his admirers seem unable to relate his poetry conclusively to any of the major critical or methodological "schools" of this century. For friend and foe alike he is the most "idiosyncratic" of modern poets, for the one consistent element in the diverse collection of strategies and subjects found in the poems from "The Rage for the Lost Penny" (1940) to *The Lost World* (1965) is an insistence on unfettered improvisation, an absolute refusal to be systematic or provide a theoretical or symbolic paradigm for his own work. This attitude is also clearly operative in his criticism, and, ironically, is chiefly responsible for its fresh and innovative approaches to writers like Whitman and Frost. Nothing like Stevens' "Supreme Fiction," Frost's characteristic idioms and landscapes, or Pound's consistent use of private sources is available to the reader of Jarrell, for the core of his work, the announced *purpose* for its existence, is emotional and quasi-mystical rather than theoretical or aesthetic.

What unifies the poems modeled after German Märchen and dreams, the dramatic monologues on war and super-markets, and the tortuous, syntactically dense considerations of life and death in the "Modern Age" is the attitude behind them, the belief that they all provide specific answers for the same vague question and sponsor recognition (not necessarily understanding) of the human condition in its primal form. Necessary manifestations of this belief in the poetry are an ongoing, painfully sympathetic tone and an overt hostility toward absolute definition of any kind or "that traumatic passion for Authority, any Authority at all, that is one of the most unpleasant things in our particular time and our particular culture."[1] Once one recognizes the fundamental character of Jarrell's sensibility and its insistence that poetry function as a "location" where the effects of experience are most dramatically presented, the common purpose behind much of Jarrell's experimentation with the dramatic monologue and the vital presentation of scenes of childhood, warfare, and modern culture becomes clearer. His characteristic use of syntactically complex stanzas, heavy with apposition and qualification, his love of paradox and his "muscular identification with his subject matter" (a phrase Jarrell used to explain his special admiration for Rilke's lyrics), are all designed to show the "real and difficult face" of human experience *and to* promote sympathy for those who suffer its effects.

Many critics have either failed to recognize the importance of this emotional nexus or dismissed it as sentimental and self-indulgent. The latter is an easy judgment often applied to the work of recent poets, but it is particularly damaging to Jarrell's since the intensity of tone and underlying plea for emotional recognition are not simply poetic devices or alternatives but recurring indications of the vague yet constant aims behind all his poetry. Stephen Spender feels, "Jarrell is very difficult to 'place' or even describe as a poet," because he "seems to complain against most of the human condition without . . . much discrimination."[2] His critique is predicated on what he sees as a lack of selectivity, of "self-control," in subject matter joined with a tedious, unchanging tone and approach. "B.," the "Opposing Self" of James Dickey's article on Jarrell, sharply dismisses his poetry on more theoretical grounds as lacking conscientious "technique" and too dependent on mere presentation of a generalized, domesticated reality.[3] Both critics quarrel as much with the intentions of Jarrell's poetry as with its aesthetics or how successfully those intentions are realized, and base their major objections on personal views of what poetry "should do." Jarrell partisans have tended to reply in kind, proclaiming how well Jarrell creates direct, moving visions of modern life free of personal prejudices and the pointless verbal gymnastics of more formal poetry.

It is my intention not to join in this general debate about the "true function" of poetry, but to define as precisely as possible that central attitude behind all of Jarrell's poems responsible for both their diversity of content and consistency of approach. One can at least gain a clearer understanding of Jarrell's real aims and accomplishments by briefly charting his development of a mature technique which he felt best expressed the basic motivations and themes behind all his work and then examining in more detail one of the finest examples of his mature verse, a dramatic monologue entitled "Seele im Raum."

Jarrell's earliest work, the poems published in "The Rage for the Lost Penny"[4] and *Blood for a Stranger* (1942), encompasses an astonishing variety of subjects, strategies, and influences. Clearly the young poet was searching among the various methods and idioms of his contemporaries for those he could best adapt to his own themes and poetic needs. The early poetry of W. H. Auden seems to have had the most dramatic effect on Jarrell's own experimentation. Early efforts like "A Little Poem" and "On the Railway Platform" adopt Auden's conversational, economical mode of address and also employ the domestic and travel imagery associated with much of Auden's best early poetry. Above all, Auden's ability to build a complex mood with a progression of concrete images, often vigorously idiomatic in nature, seems to have impressed Jarrell. He explained his special admiration for Auden's language in a critical essay on the poet:

> They [Auden's images] gain uncommon plausibility from the terse understated matter-of-factness of their treatment, the insistence (such as that found in the speech of children, in Mother Goose, in folk or savage verse, in dreams) upon the "thingness" of the words themselves.[5]

Jarrell continued to use concrete, descriptive imagery in his dramatic poetry in order to "locate" their events and themes in scenes with their own sense of dramatic immediacy and "uncommon plausibility." His development of the dramatic monologue in the war poems of *Little Friend, Little Friend* (1945) and *Losses* (1948) and his ceaseless revision of earlier poems suggest a common impulse, an insistence on poems with their own autonomous settings and internal developments, on a total elimination of the didactic authorial voice. Jarrell's subsequent rejection of his early Audenesque models

seems an outgrowth of this same basic concern, for although he first adopted Auden's brusque, declarative mode of authorial address along with his sharp, idiomatic imagery, he later abandoned it as too didactic and "omniscient" in tone and perfected a narrative approach that is more conditional, iterative, and often mildly rhetorical in its general assertions and "judgments." Auden's allegorical landscapes and his occasional tendency toward straightforward social commentary are too one-dimensional and declarative for Jarrell's purposes in his later, more investigative verse.

His rejection of the early, more assertive tone of his own poetry is clearly a factor in his personal selection of the poems to be included in the *Selected Poems* edition of 1955. Of the forty-odd poems of *Blood for a Stranger*, only ten were included, and most of those had either been revised structurally or were similar in strategy and tone to Jarrell's later poems. Perhaps the best poem from that first volume, "Children Selecting Books in a Library," is the most instructive of all in indicating the motives and effects of Jarrell's revisions. A quick comparison of the first stanzas of the original and revised versions will show what Jarrell was about:

> The little chairs and tables by a wall
> Bright with the beasts and weapons of a book
> Are properties the bent and varying heads
> Slip past unseeingly: their looks are tricked
> By our fondness and their grace into a world
> Our innocence is accustomed to find fortunate.
> Our great lives find the little blanched with dew;
> Their cries are those of crickets, dense and warmth.
> We wept so? How well we all forget!
> One taste of memory (like Fafnir's blood)
> Makes all their language sensible, one's ears
> Burn with the child's peculiar gift for pain.[6]

> With beasts and gods, above, the wall is bright.
> The child's head, bent to the book-colored shelves,
> Is slow and sidelong and food-gathering,
> Moving in blind grace . . . Yet from the mural, Care,
> The grey-eyed one, fishing the morning mist,
> Seizes the baby hero by the hair
> And whispers, in the tongue of gods and children,
> Words of a doom as ecumenical as dawn
> But blanched, like dawn, with dew. The children's cries
> Are to men the cries of crickets, dense with warmth
> —But dip a finger into Fafnir, taste it,
> And all their words are plain as chance and pain.[7]

The second version not only has a greater complexity and ease of rhythm and imagery but also transforms the comparatively stiff personal address of the original into a more lyrical, direct observation of characters who are involved in a process rather than serving as mere "illustrations" for a series of declarative, general remarks. The first line of the revision is more syntactically complex and manages to convey most of the raw information of the first two lines of the original. This movement toward more complex and condensed phrasing and syntax is perhaps the most consistent and characteristic stylistic development in all of Jarrell's poetry. As in these lines, the use of syntactical pauses and inverted phrases became a favorite device of Jarrell's, for they allow syntactical rhythms that were sonorous while remaining conversational in tone. In the words of Denis Donoghue, Jarrell had a special understanding of "the relation between silence and speech, the flow of feeling between them," and could do "wonderful things with a full stop, a colon, a question mark."[8]

But even more important for our purposes is the abrupt

change in the mode of address, for it is a sure technical clue to the motives behind Jarrell's mature style. The speaker in the original, who seems to control so insistently the "meanings" of his narration, withdraws to a greater distance in the revised version and refuses to generalize about the scene until it has worked itself out. The imagery likewise moves toward greater specificity and dramatic autonomy. The general category of "bent and varying heads" becomes "The child's head . . . / Moving in blind grace." The rather stuffy commentator disappears, and the "wordly wisdom" he supplied is expressed by another "character" involved in the drama, by the fantastic figure of "Care," who belongs to the scene itself and does not intrude upon it with extraneous generalizations. In short, Jarrell transforms a mere "example" into a self-realized and dramatically intact scene. The change partially relieves the author of his responsibilities as an omniscient interpreter, a stance Jarrell finds particularly uncomfortable. The worst examples of such awkward commentary and "public" imagery occur in the following lines and explain their total deletion from the revised poem:

> They are not learning answers but a method:
> To give up their own dilemmas for the great
> Maze Of The World—to turn in all their gold
> For the bank-notes of the one unwithering State.

Such major revisions throughout the poem show the key technical effects of Jarrell's later revolt against the relatively complacent moralizer who often narrates Auden's early poetry and much of Jarrell's own. The ever-increasing use of personae and dramatic scenes in the war poems of Jarrell's middle period and the adoption of the dramatic-monologue strategy almost exclusively in his most mature poetry seem a direct consequence of the attitudes and aims behind the extensive revision of "Children Selecting Books in a Library." Although Jarrell never overtly defined these aims in philosophical or critical terms, we have clear evidence of consistent and intense motives behind his revisions and the characteristic strategy he develops in his later poetry. His "speakers" become participants in concrete, dramatic situations—as wounded fighter pilots, tired housewives, or aging government employees—and Jarrell speaks *for* them if he speaks at all. Increasingly he expresses general themes *through* specific personae or the confusing, "unexplainable" circumstances which often entrap them. The ponderous "explanations" in early lines, like "Our great lives find the little blanched with dew," are strenuously avoided, are changed through a less declarative approach to specific subject matter.

Jarrell channels his general themes into intricate symbolic and syntactical patterns that express their "own" meanings through the interaction of characters and key phrases, producing less didactic but more subtle and complex expressions of emotional themes that are themselves often vague, intricate, and paradoxical. The more successful war poems, like "Eighth Air Force," where the moralizing speaker is inevitably drawn into his own judgment of soldiers who are both children and murderers at the same time, are those where the distinct, often bizarre scenes of World War II and its participants are allowed to sort out the paradoxical, absurd meanings of their own actions and machinations. The combatants, as unique representatives of human kind, are usually the real subjects of such poems and are always shown to be both victimizers and victims with equal cogency.

A wide reading of Jarrell's work begins to reveal a recurrent attitude behind the diverse events and scenes, the sense that explanation itself, as a pat, logical generalization about what human life "means," is the greatest absurdity of all. The

motives behind Jarrell's own movement away from the didactic voice are best explained by the constant undercutting (and often downright parodies) of the didactic, positivist approach to experience in the later poems themselves. In his best criticism, the praise of poets like Whitman and W. C. Williams for courageously *presenting* the world of human experience with all its contradictions and absurdities intact helps us understand his own attitude. Ultimately his poetry seems designed to present specific examples of the "human condition," not in general, abstract terms, but through the direct, often consciously colloquial description of individual lives. Jarrell's final development of a personal style can best be understood as an attempt to find an approach which best *allows* such presentations. In one of his finest essays, "Some Lines from Whitman," Jarrell almost certainly speaks for his own poetics as well:

> There is in him almost everything in the world, so that one responds to him, willingly or unwillingly, almost as one does to the world, that world which seems both evil beyond any rejection and wonderful beyond any acceptance. We cannot help seeing that there is something absurd about any judgment we make of its whole—for there is no "point of view" at which we can stand to make the judgment, and the moral categories that mean most to us seem no more to apply to its whole than our spatial and temporal or casual categories seem to apply to its beginning or end.[9]

Jarrell's avoidance of absolutes or "categorical judgments" in the few comments on his own poetry and his frequent dismissal of them as useless within the poems themselves is surely related to such critical praise of the same attitudes in the work of other poets. Although I have only been able to give the most cursory attention to the development of Jarrell's mature style, it is clear even from the briefest examination that the strategies related to the dramatic monologue so widely and effectively used in Jarrell's final collections, *The Seven-League Crutches* (1951), *The Woman at the Washington Zoo* (1960), and *The Lost World* (1965), are designed to permit the most direct, concrete presentation of "things and lives" as they are in the modern world *and* thereby sponsor recognition of the human predicament. The latter can only be "judged" by the sum of its parts, and the particular characters and scenes of the final volumes compose a "gallery" of unique instances which defy logical summation.

⟨. . .⟩ it is clear that Jarrell is often more interested in the emotional impact of his poems than in their formal artistry, and that this places him at odds with much of the practice of recent years. His increasing use of the dramatic monologue and straightforward, descriptive imagery in his last years seems a natural outgrowth of this demand for recognizable, accessible "portraits" of modern life in America. His developed style is clearly intended as a means to an end, and "Seele im Raum" suggests with special clarity the philosophical source of this shift in emphasis from "objective technique" and general assertion toward more subjective, impressionistic explorations of "private lives" and personal experiences. The concrete experience is primary; its aesthetic articulation is evaluated by its ability to *transmit* the physical and emotional outlines of a "single life" as directly and comprehensively as possible.

In developing a style capable of expressing such attitudes in the poems themselves, Jarrell drew on a wide variety of sources he felt shared his intense concern for non-rational, intuitive states of awareness. His poetry and criticism are filled with references to Freudian psychology, American Transcendentalism (of the "applied" Whitmanian school), German Märchen, and Proust's analysis of memory in *Remembrance of*

*Things Past*, to cite only a few examples. Jarrell's extensive allusions to such diverse and wide-ranging sources, despite their single-mindedness of purpose, are a new phenomenon and suggest more about the wide-open, cross-cultural eclecticism and the explosion of "subjective" poetic conventions and systems of the last three decades then they do about the "purer," more codified theories of the Imagists or Surrealists. But because Jarrell's emotional description of ideal human awareness demands the inclusive vision of all mystical systems and feeds on paradox and unchecked observation, it is extremely difficult to define with any precision or selectivity. I have seized upon Randall Jarrell's "eland" simply because it is a distinct manifestation of this attitude with the temerity to express it literally and in precise language.

Jarrell's "eland self," as a soul or source of being, cannot be related to the Christian conception of that entity, for the Judeo-Christian soul is involved in its own linear, temporal progress toward some finite moment of redemption and is subject to all kinds of moral and existential categories and judgments. As Jarrell's speaker tells "A Girl in a Library," "The soul has no assignments . . . / it wastes its time."[10] Its functions and value for each individual must be *recognized* rather than understood; as the woman in "Seele im Raum" explains, she had "Not seen it so that I knew I saw it." These are some of the reasons I have identified Jarrell's "Soul in Space" as essentially mystical in conception; it defines enlightenment as a state of comprehensive and intuitive awareness rather than as the complex organization of logical and empirical hypotheses. In fact, the latter are impediments to a direct and unified recognition of true self. Near the end of "Seele im Raum," the speaker can only suggest the nature of her eland by defining what it "is not." In so doing she employs the process of "negative definition" found in the writings of many mystics when they describe the character of God or the soul. In like manner, Jarrell's own refusal to provide a theoretical definition for his aesthetic or philosophical intentions should not be judged as irresponsible or self-indulgent, but as a necessary extension of the attitudes expressed in the poems themselves. Attempts to objectively define rather than simply present the "beliefs" behind such feelings are always self-defeating, like the speaker's attempt to define what he seeks in "A Sick Child": "If I can think of it, it isn't what I want."[11] But in "Bamberg," a short poem written the year of his death, Jarrell uncharacteristically employs simple religious imagery to suggest the depth of his belief in the unifying "powers of concentration":

> You'd be surprised how much, at
> The Last Judgment,
> The powers of concentration
> Of the blest and damned
> Are improved, so that
> Both smile exactly alike
> At remembering so well
> All they meant to remember
> To tell God.[12]

As Jarrell's "representative," the eland mocks the world's logical dichotomies (visible and invisible, material and spiritual, life and death) by adopting both alternatives simultaneously and timelessly; it "grazes on its own grave." It expresses the insistently emotional, anti-logical view of human life around which Jarrell's poetry must be unified. The varied interests and sources which influenced his own practice, his intense interest in Freud and the nature of dreams, his admiration for Rilke's surrealistic imagery, and his insistence on dealing with contemporary American scenes in American idioms, all relate to the subliminal nature yet concrete personal

relevance of a "state of mind" his poetry is designed to encourage. His poems are instructional without being prescriptive or undercutting the responsibility for personal recognition of one's own condition. His tone is often desperate and painfully sharp because he feels modern culture besets his enlightened personae on all sides, insisting on a lobotomy of the consciousness and fragmented, unfocused perceptions. The world defines "real knowledge" only as the accumulation of objective, impersonal data—"divides itself into facts," according to Jarrell's positivist Satan[13]—and demands that one "makes sense." Yet, as the persona of "Seele im Raum" knows, such knowledge is fundamentally *useless* in helping her live her life. It is, in fact, destructive to the soul, to the emotional, imaginative sense of being that is her birthright. In a poem called "The Lost World," one of Jarrell's last works, he makes clear his own feelings about the world's wisdom with images similar to those of "Seele im Raum":

> In my
> Talk with the world, in which it tells me what I know
> And I tell it, "I know—"how strange that I
> Know nothing, and yet it tells me what I know!—
> I appreciate the animals, who stand by
> Purring. Or else sit and pant. It's so—
> So *agreeable*.[14]

And in an essay from *Poetry and the Age* Jarrell provides an effective description of those embattled beings he wishes his poetry might encourage and protect:

> Children are playing in the vacant lots, animals are playing in the forest. Everything that the machine at the center could not attract or transform it has forced out into suburbs, the country, the wilderness, the past: out there are the fairy tales and nursery rhymes, chances and choices, dreams and sentiments and intrinsic aesthetic goods—everything that doesn't pay and doesn't care.[15]

Again, the ultimate "utility" Jarrell strives for in his verse is akin to that of the parable or the spiritual exercise. The poems of his late period, the products of endless technical experimentation and revision, are intended as psychic "catalysts," and their direct, often highly emotional approaches to their subject matter are part of their design. We, of course, are still faced with the ongoing controversy about them, yet it seems that Jarrell's critics must at least deal with those elements of his work they find excessive as integral components of an overall method. It seems too easy to react to any consistently strong emotion in modern poetry as mere lack of artistic control, and this is certainly not the case in Jarrell's practice. Sister Bernetta Quinn, in discussing Jarrell's last book, *The Lost World*, suggests the real source of the debate over Jarrell's poetry:

> There is a great tenderness here, with a willingness to present emotion without apology, unique among poets today.[16]

Perhaps, ironically, Jarrell simply worked his design too well. We must be content, like so many of his personae, to take sides. Yet it is hoped that both Jarrell's advocates and his detractors will at least know what they are fighting about. In yet another of his critical essays Jarrell probably described the best criteria for those who would judge his own poetry:

> To have the distance from the most awful and most nearly unbearable parts of the poems to the most tender, subtle, and loving parts, a distance so great; to have this whole range of being treated with so much humor and sadness and composure, with such plain truth; to see that a man can still include, connect,

and make humanly understandable so *much*—this is one of the freshest and oldest of joys.[17]

*Notes*

1. Randall Jarrell, *Poetry and the Age* (New York, 1955), p. 90.
2. Stephen Spender, "Randall Jarrell's Complaint," *New York Review of Books*, ix, No. 9 (Nov. 23, 1967), p. 28.
3. James Dickey, "Randall Jarrell," *Randall Jarrell / 1914–1965*, ed. Robert Lowell et al. (New York, 1967), pp. 33–48.
4. *Five Young American Poets* (Norfolk, Conn., 1940), pp. 81–124.
5. Randall Jarrell, *The Third Book of Criticism* (New York, 1969), p. 155.
6. Randall Jarrell, *Blood for a Stranger* (New York, 1942), p. 15.
7. Randall Jarrell, *Selected Poems* (New York, 1955), p. 97.
8. *Randall Jarrell / 1914–1965*, p. 55.
9. *Poetry and the Age*, p. 114.
10. *Selected Poems*, p. 4.
11. Ibid., p. 43.
12. Randall Jarrell, *The Complete Poems* (New York, 1969), p. 490.
13. Ibid., p. 31.
14. Ibid., p. 287.
15. *Poetry and the Age*, p. 99.
16. *Randall Jarrell / 1914–1965*, p. 147.
17. *Third Book of Criticism*, p. 302.

# ROBINSON JEFFERS

## 1887–1962

Robinson Jeffers was born on January 10, 1887, in Pittsburgh, Pennsylvania. Given the name John at birth, Robinson was descended from a long line of well-to-do Easterners of English and Irish extraction. Jeffers accompanied his father, a scholar and theologian, on several trips to Europe and the Near East. At age twelve Jeffers was sent to a Swiss boarding school, where he was nicknamed "the little Spartan" because of his fondness for hiking and swimming. In 1902 he entered the University of Western Pennsylvania, but moved with his family to California in 1903 because of his father's poor health. Jeffers received a B.A. from Occidental College in 1905, and began graduate work in literature at the University of Southern California the next fall. In 1907, however, he abandoned his literary studies and after a brief visit to Europe he returned to USC to study medicine. With no intention of becoming a doctor Jeffers left USC in 1910 and moved to Seattle with this family. There he enrolled in the School of Forestry at the University of Washington. Finally in 1913 he married Una Call, who first had to obtain a divorce from her husband. They settled in Carmel, California, in 1914, remaining there for the rest of their lives.

Jeffers's first volume of poetry, *Flagons and Apples*, was printed in 1912. A second volume, *Californians*, followed in 1916. From 1919 to 1924 Jeffers built by hand his granite home, known as Tor House, and the accompanying Hawk Tower. His wife gave birth to twins in 1916, Garth and Donnan. In 1924 his *Tamar and Other Poems* received enthusiastic reviews. *Roan Stallion* was added to the collection in 1925, and was followed by *The Woman at Point Sur* (1927), *Cawdor* (1928), and *Dear Judas* (1929). Known as the poet of the Pacific, Jeffers's favorite form was the narrative poem. Early critics compared his poetic voice to Whitman's. However, Jeffers's poetry became darker as his denunciations of Western civilization became stronger. During the late 1930s and 1940s his popularity waned as his political views set him apart from mainstream American values. His philosophy known as inhumanism called for a shift of emphasis away from the introverted human self and toward nature and the world which surrounds humankind. Jeffers's later poetic works include *The Double-Axe* (1948) and *Hungerfield and Other Poems* (1954), written after his wife's death in 1950.

In his later years Jeffers worked on dramatic adaptations of his earlier works. *The Tower Beyond Tragedy* was staged in New York in 1950. In 1946 Jeffers also wrote a successful stage version of *Medea*. In 1958 he was given a fellowship by the Academy of American Poets and in 1961 he received the Shelley Memorial Award. Jeffers died in Carmel on January 20, 1962.

## *Personal*

Meeting him for the first time, one is not readily at ease because evidently he is uncomfortable himself. This seems to be true of nearly everyone I know who has met him. He glances at one reticently, shrinking with a sort of alarm. He looks about as though seeking a way of escape or of getting rid of the intruder. His manner is intense with restraint, which one is apt to mistake for nervousness. His hand-grip is reluctant and, while firm, lacking in friendly warmth. He is like Lawrence of Arabia in his dislike of being touched, and never shakes hands voluntarily with anyone.

His mesmeric eyes, which are the color of the Pacific along the Monterey shore on a sunless day, meet your own, but just for an instant at a time; then he lowers the sensitive eyelids as though resenting your natural curiosity to know the thoughts and feelings that glow beyond them, or perhaps fearing to fascinate you too much with their metallic strangeness, of which he must be aware. One eye seems slightly out of focus, at times even different in color, and you wonder if the singular gaze of the two eyes is the result of a physical deformity or the manifestation of some mental or emotion condition of his inmost being. Sitting silently in a company of people in his house, while the charming Una Jeffers entertains them, he keeps his eyes lowered most of the time; and even when he talks with one, part of him appears to be "away" some place.

He smiles, but the quality of his smile, too, is illusive.

You wonder: does he smile because that is the thing to do? Before his wife takes charge of the visitors, he is painfully ill at ease and gives the impression that he is unsociable. He is that; but one of his best friends assures me that at the bottom of his unsociability is his extremely self-conscious sensitiveness and shyness which verge upon morbidity. To those who during the summer months pass through his gate he is polite and seems even to want to be nice to them after they are settled down in his living-room and Una is conducting the conversation, but evidently he is determined that none will affect him aside from wasting his time. He has written: "I am quits with the people."

He is uninterested in what anyone thinks of him, his verse, or anything else. He almost never talks of his work. "If I bring it into light," he explains, "it leaves me." He accepts no invitations and extends few. He never goes out of his way to meet anyone. One of his best friends, Dr. Lyman Stookey ⟨. . .⟩ he has seen but once in seventeen years, and of his other friends he would think just as much if they came near him only once in a decade. Yet there is no trace of malice or spite in him. He just doesn't care for such things.

He never speaks ill of people or imputes mean motives. Indeed, he hardly ever speaks of anyone. A number of very fine people I know consider him the most completely and consistently courteous person within their ken. He never argues with anyone about anything if he can avoid it. He is extremely reserved. Usually his attention in conversation disarms the visitors' pique at his silence. Notwithstanding the things he has written about the "apes that walk like herons" and "brainfuls of perplexed passions," he appears to have a strong feeling for essential human dignity and never violates his own or others'. He writes few letters and reads fewer criticisms of his poetry.

His voice comes in low, restrained tones which for a time make it hard to understand him. He uses the fewest words possible. Most questions and remarks he answers in monosyllables, some wordlessly with a barely perceptible shrug or a "Mona Lisa smile," which you are free to interpret as you like.

Every phrase of his personality seems to be under powerful, apparently conscious and voluntary, control. Before you are with him long, you know that he is an extraordinary character. His face is thin, a poet's face, profound, not quite of this age and place, mediaeval, with strength written all over it: pale-brown, weather-beaten, masculine, clean shaven, with a straight slim nose and sensitive nostrils, a well-formed mouth with lips of moderate thickness, a firm chin, a high smooth forehead rising from staight eyebrows, and medium-sized, handsome ears. His hair is brown, beginning to gray at the temples. There appears to be just a suggestion of asymmetry. All his senses obviously are very acute.

The occasional smile enlivens the face but little: which is also true of his gaze. Somehow, both the smile and the eyes seem to insist with their singularity that the observer consider them by themselves, apart from the face; it is they that do most to make his outward personality enigmatic, fascinating.

His physique harmonizes with the cut of the face. The slender body is above medium height, hard, sinewy, agile. My first glimpse of him was as he vaulted a fence just as I entered the young forest of cypress-trees and eucalypti he is planting on his estate. As I saw later, he had turned on the hydrant to water the seedlings and was making a dash around the building to beat the current to the nozzle of the hose on the other end of the grounds. The leap, performed with grace and a minimum of movement, testified to the fine control he has over his body. He is forty-two years of age. He is a good swimmer, summer and winter, and hikes considerably along the Monterey coast and in the hills in back of Point Lobos. He likes to toss ball,

wrestle, jump, and race with his two young sons. He has no taste for competitive sport and abhors killing animals and birds.

He wears shirts open at the throat, army breeches and leggings; in cool weather, a leather jerkin over the shirt. He disdains fine raiment and luxurious motors. He eats sparingly, and only the simplest food. A man of the out-of-doors, an athlete. His excellent physical condition may be partly due to his low pulse—forty in the morning, sixty in the afternoon. There is a cool aura about his person, which, however, does not cause shivers; rather, it endows him with a dignity I have never seen in anyone else.—LOUIS ADAMIC, *Robinson Jeffers: A Portrait*, 1929, pp. 7–12

We used to walk in the Del Monte Forest in the days when it was uninhabited. Near the place where we climbed a fence to enter the woods there was a deep ravine, bridged by the watermain that ran from the dam up the Carmel Valley to the reservoir lake back of Monterey. A wooden trestle supported the big pipe where it crossed the gorge, and this was our bridge into the farther woods; but we had to scramble carefully, for wild bees hived halfway over, in the timbers against the pipe. And it was harder coming back; I had to make two crossings then, one to carry the dog, and one with the firewood that we brought home from the forest.

This was twenty-one years ago, and I am thinking of a bitter meditation that worked in my head one day while I returned from the woods and was making my two crossings by the pipe-line. It had occurred to me that I was already a year older than Keats when he died, and I too had written many verses, but they were all worthless. I had imitated and imitated, and that was all.

I have never been ambitious, but it seemed unpleasant just the same to have accomplished nothing, but exactly nothing, along the only course that permanently interested me. There are times when one forgets for a moment that life's value is life, any further accomplishment is of very little importance comparatively. This was one of those times and I can still taste its special bitterness; I was still quite young at twenty-seven.

When I had set down the dog and went back over our bridge for the bundle of firewood my thoughts began to be more practical, not more pleasant. This originality, without which a writer of verses is only a verse-writer, is there any way to attain it? The more advanced contemporary poets were attaining it by going farther and farther along the way that perhaps Mallarmé's aging dream had shown them, divorcing poetry from reason and ideas, bringing it nearer to music, finally to astonish the world with what would look like pure nonsense and would be pure poetry. No doubt these lucky writers were imitating each other, instead of imitating Shelley and Milton as I had done . . . but no, not all of them, someone must be setting the pace, going farther than anyone had dared to go before. Ezra Pound perhaps? Whoever it was, was *original*.

Perhaps this was the means to attain originality: to make a guess which way literature is going, and go there first. Read carefully your contemporaries, chart their line of advance, then hurry and do what they are going to do next year. And if they drew their inspiration from France, I could read French as well as any of them.

(This was not all quite seriously thought, partly I was just tormenting myself. But a young man is such a fool in his meditations, at least I was; let me say for shame's sake that I have not considered "trends" since turning thirty, nor been competitive either.)

But now, as I smelled the wild honey midway the trestle and meditated the direction of modern poetry, my discouragement blackened. It seemed to me that Mallarmé and his followers, renouncing intelligibility in order to concentrate the music of poetry, had turned off the road into a narrowing lane. Their successors could only make further renunciations; ideas had gone, now meter had gone, imagery would have to go; then recognizable emotions would have to go; perhaps at last even words might have to go or give up their meaning, nothing be left but musical syllables. Every advance required the elimination of some aspect of reality, and what could it profit me to know the direction of modern poetry if I did not like the direction? It was too much like putting out your eyes to cultivate the sense of hearing, or cutting off the right hand to develop the left. These austerities were not for me; originality by amputation was too painful for me.

But—I thought—everything has been said already; there seems to be only this way to go on. Unless one should do like the Chinese with their heavy past: eliminate one's own words from the poem, use quotations from books as the elder poets used imagery from life and nature, make something new by putting together a mosaic of the old. A more promising kind of amputation; one or two noble things might be done that way, but not more, for the trick would pall on Western ears; and not by me, who never could bear the atmosphere of libraries since I escaped from my studious father's control.

I laid down the bundle of sticks and stood sadly by our bridge-head. The sea-fog was coming up the ravine, fingering through the pines, the air smelled of the sea and pine-resin and yerba buena, my girl and my dog were with me . . . and I was standing there like a poor God-forsaken man-of-letters, making my final decision not to become a "modern." I did not want to become slight and fantastic, abstract and unintelligible.

I was doomed to go on imitating dead men, unless some impossible wind should blow me emotions or ideas, or a point of view, or even mere rhythms, that had not occurred to them. There was nothing to do about it.

We climbed the fence and went home through the evening-lighted trees. I must have been a charming companion that afternoon.—ROBINSON JEFFERS, "Introduction" to *Roan Stallion, Tamar, and Other Poems*, 1935, pp. vii–x

## General

It is as difficult to conceive Robinson Jeffers in any other place than Carmel, California, as it would be to think of Shelley living in Whitechapel, Dostoievsky at Narragansett Pier or William Blake in Pittsburg. If ever a man and the Spirit of Place had conspired for a mystical union it is here.

That portion of California—its hills, sea, blue lupins, golden poppies, sea-gulls, dirt roads, pines, firs, hawks, herons and lighthouses—stretching between Point Joe and Point Lobos (roughly, about thirty miles) belongs as absolutely to Robinson Jeffers, poet of Tragic Terror, as Wessex belongs to Thomas Hardy. This place has chosen this man to tell its secret spiritual and physical tragedies to the world and to voice its bitter beauties in his long-rolling, crashing, choppy lines: the transfiguration in his sensibility of the brawling harmonies and bickering winds of the sea. His work is the colossal symphony of a mad Dante.

Jeffers,—stark, elemental, monk-like—has grown into the landscape. He is physically part of the fauna and flora. He has coupled with this sky, this earth and this sea on the iron beds of his consciousness. Unearthly, twisted, gnarled, weird, diabolically beautiful Point Lobos has whispered into his ear, as a tree once whispered into the ear of another, "Thou untold life of me!"

The wind and the sea have wrought the trees at Point Lobos and the adjacent hills to grotesque and macabre shapes.

By day unearthly, by night it is ghostly. From it stream the elemental and demoniacal psychical forces that engulf the whole coast to Monterey. It needs the genius of Poe, of Lafcadio Hearn, of Chopin, of Doré, of Baudelaire, of Jeffers to translate into art-forms the overwhelming emotion of brutal beauty and abysmal melancholy that Point Lobos inflicts upon the sensitive, receptive soul. Here damnation and the forbidden well out of the very rocks. In all the world no fitter place could have been found to conceive and give birth to the tremendous tragedies of Robinson Jeffers. His steel-muscled genius has lifted Carmel to Golgotha.

When I read Jeffers' "Tamar" and "The Coast-Range Christ" I get a feeling of vastness that I have experienced only in Aeschylus, Shakespeare, Hardy and Whitman. There is for me no vastness, for instance, in the pages of Balzac or Dostoievsky. Depth, height—yes. Vastness—no. Vastness is a quality that is psychically communicable. In Jeffers' work— even in his smallest poems—this vastness is implicit. It is the sense of the eternal and the fatalistic not, as a passing mood, injected or worked into the poem for the purpose of "artistic effect", but as something in which Jeffers, like Hardy and Whitman, perpetually lives, moves and has his being. ⟨. . .⟩

The cold tragic beauty of "Tamar", "Roan Stallion", "The Tower Beyond Tragedy", "The Coast-Range Christ" and "The Women at Point Sur" is also a perfect reflection of the man, who is cold. He burns with a white fire. He tells his story in these poems with the sublime aloofness of a being who has dismissed life as an ethical problem entirely from his consciousness—if it was ever there. Life is a play of forces, of which the dramatic values alone concern him. He records it with a brutal negligence. Those magnificent and beautiful Choroses and Antichoroses in "The Coast-Range Christ" are cold, incandescent suns that revolve above the tragedy of the boy slacker. They are as inhuman, as impersonal, as melodiously sublime as the God of Spinoza and Hardy—the Hardy of *The Dynasts*. ⟨. . .⟩

Jeffers' mysticism is the mysticism of pantheism. All is in God, God is in all things. Everything exists in the glamor of Spirit—his clouds, his herons, his sea-fogs, his characters, even Woodrow Wilson. Whatever is is poetic, mysterious, frail effigies of reality, blown bubbles of ecstatic and satanic gods. Tremendously real, vital and wide-awake in his visualized descriptions, Jeffers contrives by the magical power of his genius to make an object or a character both familiar and unfamiliar to us under the same light. Each thing is seen simultaneously under the aspect of time and eternity—a house, a tree, a nymphomaniac, an idiot, a sheriff, a sea-gull, a crazy messiah. ⟨. . .⟩

Behind every page of Jeffers stalks Fatality, tall as the stars and as serenely implacable in its trajectories and orbits. With "unhurrying feet" it overtakes its predestined victims. It moves like a murky-luminous cloud over the five tragedies of Jeffers— world-old gigantic cloud that conceals the thunderbolt forged in the bone and blood and flesh of the ancestors of all the characters. Fatality is of the essence of tragic beauty, and nowhere have I found it more completely and clearly expressed than in "Tamar". There is only one tragedy in the whole world's literature that I would rank with "Tamar" from the angle of fatality, and that is the *Oedipus Rex* of Sophocles. ⟨. . .⟩

There is nothing extraneous in Jeffers' work. It is dense, compact, a pattern woven by a man who takes every stitch with precision and who has plotted out the whole scheme and is complete master of it. There is not a superfluous line in all his poetry. It is an arterial, a ganglionic system, to remove one tiny bit of which would cause the story of the poem to bleed to death.

I know of no two more perfect works of art, as art, in the whole range of dramatic literature than "Tamar" and "The Coast-Range Christ". They are, structurally, vast and perfect cathedrals of words. His sunrises, his sunsets, his creeks and his herons, what appear superficially as his lyrical asides and divagations, are part and parcel of the unfolding drama. It is a blending of spiritual and material scenery. The dramas in the hearts of his men and women are meshed with the elements, with the slow-revolving panorama of the California year. All that is his *mise-en-scène* for the catastrophic lives of men and women on a tiny star moving *con furia* from nowhere to nowhere in the mathematical pandemonium of the spheres.

His "obscurity"—and he is "obscure" at times—is the obscurity of an unexpected individualization of language, a sudden eruption into our anemic, sleek and dutiful prose and poetry of a powerful and original genius whose expressional roots are in himself. When I have come across passages in his volume that seem to be obscure, I put it down to my own obtuseness. I should clamber up to his thought. There is no reason why he should descend to me. I have paused many times to get at the heart of words, startling flights into the star-jungles of far etymological heavens, and I have always been rewarded by dragging up from my thought and Jeffers "obscurity" amazing and dazzlingly beautiful treasures. ⟨. . .⟩

Never in all the history of prose and poetry has there been attempted such a satanic transvaluation of all earthly values as in "The Women at Point Sur". The Rev. Dr. Barclay, who moves through this longest of Jeffers' tragic poems, after fifteen years of chastity proclaims himself God on the hills of Carmel. He is God turned Anti-Christ. He is Zarathustra-Satan, an illuminated incarnation of the New Evil, a post-war immoralist and dethroner of reason magnified to cosmic proportions. Mephistopheles, Iago and Vautrin are Boy Scouts compared to this tremendous being who announces that "all is permitted"—rape, incest, murder and war—in the making of the New Race. ⟨. . .⟩

Robinson Jeffers is barely forty. He is the greatest event in American literature since Whitman. He is a Colossus, and already is an immortal—at least among those who instinctively feel the difference between the men of the hour and the men of the century.

In his work there is a wild, dishevelled, remote beauty and the music of an infernal but contained madness.—BENJAMIN DE CASSERES, "Robinson Jeffers: Tragic Terror," *Bkm*, Nov. 1927, pp. 262–66

Mr. Jeffers is theologically a kind of monist; he envisages, as did Wordsworth, Nature as Deity; but his Nature is the Nature of the physics textbook and not of the rambling botanist—Mr. Jeffers seems to have taken the terminology of modern physics more literally than it is meant by its creators. Nature, or God, is thus a kind of self-sufficient mechanism, of which man is an offshoot, but from which man is cut off by his humanity (just what gave rise to this humanity, which is absolutely severed from all connection with God, is left for others to decide): there is consequently no mode of communication between the consciousness of man and the mode of existence of God; God is praised adequately only by the screaming demons that make up the atom. Man, if he accepts this dilemma as necessary, is able to choose between two modes of action: he may renounce God and rely on his humanity, or he may renounce his humanity and rely on God.

Mr. Jeffers preaches the second choice: union with God, oblivion, the complete extinction of one's humanity, is the only good he is able to discover; and life, as such, is "incest," an insidious and destructive evil. So much, says Mr. Jeffers by

implication, for Greek and Christian ethics. Now the mysticism of, say, San Juan de la Cruz offers at least the semblance of a spiritual, a human, discipline as a preliminary to union with Divinity; but for Mr. Jeffers a simple and mechanical device lies always ready; namely, suicide, a device to which he has not resorted.

In refusing to take this logical step, however, Mr. Jeffers illustrates one of a very interesting series of romantic compromises. The romantic of the ecstatic-pantheist type denies life, yet goes on living; nearly all romantics decry the intellect and philosophy, yet they offer justifications (necessarily foggy and fragmentary) of their attitude; they deride literary "technique" (the mastery of, and development of the sensitivity to, relationships between words, so that these relationships may extend almost illimitably the vocabulary) yet they write (of necessity, carelessly, with small efficiency). Not all romantics are guilty of all of these confusions, nor, doubtless, is Mr. Jeffers; but all of these confusions are essentially romantic—they are very natural developments of moral monism. And Mr. Jeffers, having decried human life as such, and having denied the worth of the rules of the game, endeavors to write narrative and dramatic poems—poems, in other words, dealing with people who are playing the game. Jesus, the hero of "Dear Judas," speaking apparently for Mr. Jeffers, says that the secret reason for the doctrine of forgiveness is that all men are driven by the mechanism-God to act as they do, that they are entirely helpless; yet he adds in the next breath that this secret must be guarded, for if it were given out, men would run amuck, would get out of hand—*they would begin acting differently.*

"The Women at Point Sur" is a perfect laboratory of Mr. Jeffers' philosophy. Barclay, an insane divine, preaches Mr. Jeffers' religion, and his disciples, acting upon it, become emotional mechanisms, lewd and twitching conglomerations of plexi, their humanity annulled. Human experience, in these circumstances, having necessarily and according to the doctrine no meaning, there can be and is no necessary sequence of events: every act is equivalent to every other; every act is at the peak of hysteria; most of the incidents could be shuffled around into varying sequences without violating anything save, perhaps, Mr. Jeffers' private sense of their relative intensity. Since the poem is his, of course, such a private sense is legitimate enough; the point is that this is not a narrative, nor a dramatic, but a lyrical criterion. A successful lyrical poem of one hundred and seventy-five pages is unlikely, for the essence of lyrical expression is concentration; but it is at least theoretically possible. The difficulty is that the lyric achieves its effect by the generalization of emotion (that is, by the separation of the emotion from the personal history that gives rise to it in actual concrete experience) and by the concentration of expression. Narrative can survive in a measure without concentration, or intensity of detail, provided the narrative logic is detailed and compelling, as in the case of Balzac, though it is only wise to add that this occurs most often in prose. Now Mr. Jeffers, as I have pointed out, has abandoned narrative logic with the theory of ethics, and he has never achieved, in addition, a close and masterly style. His writing is loose, turgid, and careless; like most anti-intellectualists, he relies on his feelings alone and has no standard of criticism for them outside of themselves. There are occasional good flashes in his poems, and to these I shall return later, but they are very few, are very limited in their range of feeling and in their subject matter, and they are very far between. Mr. Jeffers has no remaining method of sustaining his lyric, then, other than the employment of an accidental (i.e., non-narrative) chain of anecdotes (i.e., details that are lyrically impure); his philosophical doctrine and his artistic dilemma alike decree that these shall be anecdotes of hysteria. By this method Mr. Jeffers continually *lays claim* to a high pitch of emotion which has no narrative support (that is, support of the inevitable accumulation of experience), nor lyrical support (that is, support of the intense perception of pure, or transferable, emotion), which has, in short, no support at all, and which is therefore simply unmastered and self-inflicted hysteria.

"Cawdor" alone of Mr. Jeffers' poems contains a plot that in its rough outlines might be sound, and "Cawdor" likewise contains his best poetry; the poem as a whole, and in spite of the confused treatment of the woman, is moving, and the lines describing the seals at dawn are fine, as are the two or three last lines of the apotheosis of the eagle. Most of the preceding material in the latter passage, however, like most of the material in the sections that give Mr. Jeffers' notions of the post-mortem experience of man, are turgid, repetitious, arbitrary, and unconvincing. The plot itself is blurred for lack of stylistic finish (that is, for lack of ability on the part of the poet to see every detail of sense and movement incisively down to the last preposition, the last comma, as every detail *is* seen in Racine or Shakespeare); and it remains again a fair question whether a moral monist *can* arrive at any clear conclusions about the values of a course of action, since he denies the existence of any conceivable standard of values within the strict limits of human life as such. In "The Tower Beyond Tragedy" Mr. Jeffers takes a ready-made plot, the Clytemnestra-Orestes situation, which is particularly strong dramatically, because Orestes is forced to choose between two sins, the murder of his mother and the refusal to avenge his father. But at the very last moment, in Mr. Jeffers' version, Orestes is converted to Mr. Jeffers' religion and goes off explaining (to Electra, who has just tried to seduce him) that though men may think he is fleeing before the furies he is really just drifting up to the mountains to meditate on the stars; and the preceding action is, of course, rendered morally and emotionally meaningless. ⟨. . .⟩

Self-repetition has been the inevitable effect of anti-intellectualist doctrine on all of its supporters. If life is valued, explored, subdivided, and defined, poetic themes are infinite in number; if life is denied, the only theme is the rather sterile and monotonous one of the denial. Similarly, those poets who flee from form, which is infinitely variable, since every form is a definite and an individual thing, can achieve only the uniformity of chaos; and those individuals who endeavor to escape morality, which is personal form and controlled direction, can, in the very nature of things, achieve nothing save the uniformity of mechanism. One might classify Mr. Jeffers as a "great failure" if one meant by the phrase that he had wasted unusual talents; but not if one meant that he had failed in a major effort, for his aims are badly thought-out and are essentially trivial.—YVOR WINTERS, "Robinson Jeffers," *Poetry*, Feb. 1930, pp. 279–86

In his best poetry Jeffers provides us with a world that is beautifully and sometimes terrifyingly real—or real in the sense that any artistic creation is real; the world of every artist is, of course, visionary; the degree of his success is in proportion to the reader's or viewer's or listener's being convinced that the "world" is real and, in addition, has meaning for the auditor. In his tribute in *Ave, Vale, Robinson Jeffers*, Lawrence Clark Powell wrote, "This was his genius. To summon the spirit of place. To people the countryside with personages more real than its living inhabitants. To forge poetry on the anvil of thoughtful feeling with passion and certitude, the result and reward of which is quite simply literary immortality." Certainly no other American poet has approached him in the ability to

endow character with life; his people, tormented and tormenting creatures, haunt the memory like grisly phantoms or spectral shapes rising from some atavistic depth of which we were unaware. Passing before the mind's eye, they reveal those gulfs over which we daily pass. In their strengths and weaknesses we see ourselves; they reveal to us, above all else, how slippery is our hold on reason and how tempting are the lures of irrationality in all its forms. Which is to say, Jeffers did what all great writers have done: he provided insight into the human condition.

Insight, above all else. And what insight does not stop with the human condition, but extends outward into the larger and, for Jeffers, more important natural world. No other poet of this century strove more successfully to "catch the inhuman God" in his lens. In this area, indeed, Jeffers had few peers in all of literature. The violence and extreme passion of the natural world color his lines in an unforgettable fashion. Though he protested in "Love the Wild Swan" that "this wild swan of a world is no hunter's game" and despaired of ever catching in his mirror "one color, one glinting flash, of the splendor of things," he knew that all such efforts by any poet were doomed to (relative) failure.

His failure to reproduce that beauty is attributable to the nature of things—to the primary fact that art can never be truly representative, that no attempt to reproduce or imitate can ever be totally objective. But that is a truism that, once admitted, need never stay us (it certainly never stayed Jeffers) from partaking in the sensual dance of life. Jeffers knew this, as he also knew that only death can perform the miracle of making us one with the divine substance—only at the dance's end do we become a part of what our senses imperfectly perceived and our artistry failed to reproduce. Man may and should worship the God, or divine substance, but only in a mineral sense can he become part of what he worshipped, and then he is without senses and mind to know and admire. He notes this truth again in "The Shears," one of the last poems he wrote, published posthumously in *The Beginning and the End* in 1963. There this almost painful love for the world of things, of which man is one thing only, is expressed with haunting tenderness:

> A great dawn-color rose widening the petals around
> her gold eye
> Peers day and night in the window. She watches us
> Breakfasting, lighting lamps, reading, and the chil-
> dren playing, and the dogs by the fire,
> She watches earnestly, uncomprehending,
> As we stare into the world of trees and roses
> uncomprehending,
> There is a great gulf fixed. But even while
> I gaze, and the rose at me, my little flower-greedy
> daughter-in-law
> Walks with shears, very blond and housewifely
> Through the small garden, and suddenly the rose
> finds herself rootless in-doors.
> Now she is part of the life she watched.
> —So we: death comes and plucks us: we become part
> of the living earth
> And wind and water whom we so loved. We are they.

In "My Loved Subject," from the same volume, Jeffers commented that though old age prevented him from walking the mountains as in the past, his loved subject remained unchanged:

> Mountains and ocean, rock, water and beasts and
> trees
> Are the protagonists, the human people are only
> symbolic interpreters.

The human drama, whether comic or tragic, is little more than a relief against what he called in an early poem the "divinely superfluous beauty" of the natural world. And "if the great manners of death dreamed up / In the laboratories work well" and humans do succeed in killing themselves off, that beauty will certainly remain. The poetry of Jeffers enables us better to see and understand both ourselves and the shining glory of the world.—WILLIAM H. NOLTE, "Coda," *Rock and Hawk: Robinson Jeffers and the Romantic Agony*, 1978, pp. 199–201

---

## DELMORE SCHWARTZ
### From "The Enigma of Robinson Jeffers"
*Poetry*, October 1939, pp. 30–38

At least one source ⟨of Jeffers's work⟩ is the scientific picture of the universe which was popular and "advanced" thought until a few short years ago. The versions of the implications of 19th-century science afforded by writers like Haeckel and Huxley seemed to create a picture of the world in which there was no room for most human values. The world was a wound-up machine or a whirling mass of chemical elements which stretched out without end and without purpose. No Deity assured justice or love or immortality, but the infinite emptiness reported by astronomy and the survival of the fittest of Darwinism seemed to comprise a definite and indubitable answer to human effort and belief. This is the world-view which has been the basis, in part, of the work of many other and quite different authors. It is to be found in the novels of Theodore Dreiser, in the plays of Bernard Shaw, in the criticism of H. L. Mencken (who suggests Nietzsche as an early and much more serious example), in the early philosophical writing of Bertrand Russell, in the poetry of Archibald MacLeish, and Joseph Wood Krutch's *The Modern Temper*, where it is explicitly announced that such things as love and tragedy and all other specifically human values are not possible to modern man. Russell suggests I. A. Richards, whose "sincerity ritual" to test the genuineness of a poem operates in part by envisaging the meaninglessness of the universe in the above sense, and Krutch suggests some of the best poems of Mark Van Doren, where the emptiness of the sky is the literal theme.

When Jeffers says ⟨. . .⟩ in a number of his poems that he wishes to avoid lies, what he means by lies are all beliefs which would somehow deny or ameliorate this world-view. When he speaks repeatedly of stars, atoms, energy, rocks, science, and the power of Nature, it is the Nature of 19th-century science which he has in mind and which obsesses him. For Wordsworth, but a hundred years before, Nature was an image of the highest values; for Jeffers it has become merely a huge background which proffers only one delight, annihilation, and which makes human beings seem to him puny and disgusting beasts whose history is the tiniest cosmic incident.

But Jeffers' disgust with human beings seems to have another and less intellectual source. The poems he has written about Woodrow Wilson and Clemenceau and the brutality of modern warfare suggest that the source of his obsession with human violence was the World War. Here again parallels plead to be mentioned, as if an age were an organic entity, for one remembers that other writers who came to young manhood during the war, William Faulkner, Eugene O'Neill, Ernest Hemingway, have been similarly obsessed with violence, cruelty, rape, murder, and destruction. The California coast which serves as a background for Jeffers, and to which he came, he says, by pure accident, provides a third dominant

element. "The strange, introverted, and storm-twisted beauty of Point Lobos", as Jeffers' stage-set for his narrative poems is merely another example of how birds, or perhaps one should say, hawks, of a feather flock together.

The world-picture of 19th-century science, the World War, and Jeffers' portion of the Pacific Coast are not, however, merely sources of his work, but actually, with little disguise, the substance of his poems. Of these three elements, the cosmology in question has definitely been discarded with the radical progress of science and scientific thought, and with the recognition that some of the supposed implications of 19th-century science were only the emotions of those who had lost their childhood faith or been dismayed by the bigness of the universe, as if bigness were an especially significant aspect. The World War too turns out not to have been either merely a display of human brutality or the crusade of an idealist, as Jeffers seems to take it to be when he writes of Wilson; but something quite different. And as for Point Lobos, one may very well question whether it can be accepted as a more accurate exhibit of Nature than Wordsworth's Lake Country, the state of Connecticut, or the city of New York. Such a question is to be raised only when the poet takes his landscape as being of universal significance.

The point involved is one of truth, the truth not of ultimate beliefs, but given facts. The poetry of Jeffers represents for the most part a response to the particular facts just mentioned. But if the facts are poorly envisaged, how adequate can the response be? Stated in terms of ideas, Jeffers' reponse is an ideology. Stated in terms of the emotions, his response is hysterical. Human beings are often brutal, Nature is sometimes violent, and life is indeed a mystery, but to respond as Jeffers does by rejecting humanity and saluting the peace of death is to come to a conclusion which is not only barren, a result which pleases Jeffers, but also false, and thus in the end without interest and without value.

This falsity has various consequences which define it precisely. There is no need to raise the usual and banal objections, to argue like a schoolboy over whether or not Jeffers is self-contradictory in denying human freedom and presenting characters who choose their actions, or to urge the contradiction of writing poetry which will only be read by the species which is being rejected, or to howl with facile radicalism that this tragic attitude is made possible by an income. It would be simple for the admirer of Jeffers to answer each of these accusations. But what cannot be adequately defended are the consequences in the poetry itself, both in the lyrics where we are presumably to get a representation of emotion and in the narrative poems where we ought to be getting a representation of human action.

The narrative poems constitute the major part of Jeffers' work and it is upon them that the weight of untruth is most unfortunate. In "The Tower Beyond Tragedy," for example, the alternatives presented to the hero are: either incest or a complete rupture with humanity. One needs no knowledge of the Agamemnon story to know that this is not a genuine tragic dilemma, either for Orestes or for any other human being. And again in "Roan Stallion," the two alternatives presented to the heroine, either sexual intercourse with a drunken and brutish husband or with a horse, are not mutually exhaustive of all possible choices, and the dénouement is not made more plausible when the stallion kills the man, in obedience to nothing but the doctrinal requirements of the poet. What happens in both stories and throughout the narrative writing is not only not true of human life even at its most monstrous— such untruth might conceivably be justified as an extreme use of symbols—but the untruth is essentially a matter of the contexts provided by the poet, the situations which he has furnished for his characters. Orestes' choice is unjustified by the character he has been given and the life which confronts him, and the heroine of "Roan Stallion" is untrue in the same literal sense, both characters being compelled to their acts by nothing but the emotion of the poet, an emotion utterly removed from their lives and differently motivated.

The same lack is present in the lyrics, and as in the narratives it was a narrative lack, so in the lyrics what is absent betrays itself in lyrical terms. The following poem, "Science," is worth quoting as an example to justify this judgment and also as a typical statement of doctrine:

> Man, introverted man, having crossed
> In passage and but a little with the nature of things
>        this latter century
> Has begot giants; but being taken up
> Like a maniac with self-love and inward conflicts
>        cannot manage his hybrids.
> Being used to deal with edgeless dreams,
> Now he's bred knives on nature, turns them also
>        inward: they have thirsty points though.
> His mind forbodes his own destruction;
> Actaeon who saw the goddess naked among leaves
>        and his hounds tore him.
> A little knowledge, a pebble from the shingle,
> A drop from the oceans: who would have dreamed
>        this infinitely little too much?

What is to be noted here is the number of shifts the poet finds necessary in order to state the observation which concerns him. The machines of science which man cannot manage are named as giants, hybrids, knives. The knowledge of science which makes possible these machines is successively compared to a vision of Diana, a pebble, and a drop of water. The classical allusion to Actaeon's vision of the goddess is also in abrupt disjunction with the previous metaphor, man as a dreamer who has bred knives and as an introvert who has begotten giants. There is no rule or law which makes it impossible for a poet to go from one metaphor to another even in a very short poem, but such a transit can only be justified if it accomplishes some expressive purpose. Here the shifts, however, weaken each metaphor, preventing the reader from getting a clear picture of a thing, process or condition, by means of which to grasp the notion and the emotion in question. Actaeon's vision of Diana is plainly not at all symmetrical with man as a begetter of dangerous giants. And the reason for this disorder is the desire of the poet to state an emotion about modern industrialism or armament in terms of the belief—too general to be meaningful—that knowledge is a dangerous thing for man. If the emotion were justified by a fact, then the fact would provide the emotion with adequate lyrical terms. But, to repeat, since the fact was imperfectly envisaged and the poet saw modern industrialism merely as an instance of incestuous brutality (man is introverted, self-loving, and thus incestuous for Jeffers), the emotion could not command the metaphors which would make it consistent and vivid upon the page.

The argument may seem theoretical and had better be made more evident and more lucid by comparison. Lear upon the heath with Kent and the fool represents a vision of the cruelty of the human heart which is in every sense more appalling than any equivalent desolation to be found in Jeffers. And yet the difference in literary terms is immense. The poet has managed to adhere to the formal burden of the play and of blank verse, he has provided a suitable individuation for the main characters, and he has not found it necessary to resort to continuous physical violence in order to present the emotion

he feels about the human heart. A further point to be made, probably by the open-eyed optimist, is that Kent, the faithful friend, does accompany Lear upon the heath, and Cordelia does balance the cruelty of Goneril and Regan at the plausible ratio of two-to-one. One could scarcely consider *King Lear* a play in which it is affirmed that God's in His heaven and all's well with the world. Nor could one conceivably affirm that the poet was engaged in telling comforting lies about the human species. But the play is nevertheless a representation of life which can stand as a measure of what one means by the whole truth when one is confronted by such writers as Jeffers. Two other relevant touchstones may be mentioned in passing, *Moby-Dick*, in which there is a similar regard for Nature, and the writing of Pascal in which the astronomical diminution of man is considered in its implication as to man's importance in the universe.

The mention of Shakespeare, however, may suggest a fundamental difficulty with the critical method which is being used. If the poet is examined by his ability to present the truth, and if many of his formal defects are attributed to emotions which spring from a distorted view of particular facts, then what is one to say when a ghost or witch appears in Shakespeare, or when in some respect the poet's substance is a response to beliefs about the world which the reader does not find acceptable? The problem of belief in poetry makes its inevitable re-appearance, like an unwanted cat. Without wishing to raise the whole subject, the answer here seems fairly plain. The predicament of Hamlet does not depend in the least upon the actuality of ghosts (a question about which there is no need to be dogmatic), and in general, most great poetry does not depend upon the truth of its philosophical beliefs, although it requires them as a structure and a framework. But in Jeffers the beliefs about the world and the consequent emotions are the substance of poetry, and the observations of land and sea and the narrative characters are merely the means, which reverses the relationship. In the *Inferno*, the Christian system helps to make possible a vision of human beings; in Jeffers, the human beings are there to make possible a vision of Jeffers' ideas of the world. Hence the literary critic is pressed to judge the ideas and the emotion which they occasion. It might also seem that Jeffers is being taken too literally, that his avowed rejection of humanity is "really" a subliminal disguise; and his hatred of cities might be understood as a social reaction. But in Jeffers, as opposed to other poets, it is impossible to make such a translation without ceasing to be a literary critic and becoming biographer, psychoanalyst, or sociologist. The substance of the poetry is his emotion about humanity and the wide world. The poet's business is to *see*, by means of words, and we can only judge him by what he presents as seen.

One is permitted to adopt any belief, attitude, or emotion that especially pleases one. But when one begins to act upon belief or emotion, and in particular when one begins to write poetry, a million more considerations, in addition to the few already mentioned, intrude of necessity. When one attempts to write narrative poems about human beings, the obligation of a sufficient knowledge of human beings intervenes, the necessity of a definite measure of rhythm descends upon one, and literature as an organic tradition enters upon the scene. Jeffers undoubtedly has a keen sense for the landscape and seascape he writes about and he is by no means without a knowledge of human beings. But on the basis of detesting humanity, the natural tendency is to turn away from a strict view of human beings as they actually are and to regard a concern with literature, *technically*, as being at best unnecessary, at worst a hindrance. The result is that the characters Jeffers writes about tend to become repetitive abstractions, and the long line of Jeffers' verse is corrupted repeatedly by the most gauche inconsistencies of rhythm. The causal sequence seems indubitable. The poet has decided that the emotion he feels is strong enough to justify any manipulation of characters; and the breaches of consistency in his rhythm appear to him to be merely a "literary" or formal matter:

> I say
> Humanity is the mould to break away from, the crust
>      to break through, the coal to break into fire,
> The atom to be split . . .

and the poet is breaking away from literature as well as humanity in his poems, which we are asked to accept as literature, and in which we are presumably presented with humanity.

## HORACE GREGORY
"Poet without Critics:
A Note on Robinson Jeffers" (1955)
*The Dying Gladiators and Other Essays*
1961, pp. 3–20

### I

At the moment there are good reasons for rereading the poetry of Robinson Jeffers. First of all, the poet himself is a singular figure in American letters and he occupies the rare position in this country of being a "poet" in the European sense of the word. He insists upon holding to a world view as well as his own handful of currently unpopular opinions. He has become a master of a style without nervous reference to recent fashions in literary criticism. "I can tell lies in prose," he once wrote, which means that his primary concern is with the statement of a few essential poetic truths. Today it is obvious that he is willing to leave a final judgment of what he has written to the decision of posterity.

To reread him is to step aside from the classroom discussions and shoptalk of poetry that flood the rear sections of literary quarterlies where his name is seldom mentioned at all. He is well removed from the kind of company where poetry is "taught" so as to be understood, where critics and reviewers are known to be instructors of literature in colleges and universities. But he is also at some distance from the time when his Californian narratives in verse, "Roan Stallion" and "Tamar," swept through the furnished rooms and studios of Greenwich Village with the force of an unpredicted hurricane. That was thirty years ago. Today as Jeffers is reread there is no danger of being smothered by the heavily breathing presence of a deep-throated, bare-thighed-and-breasted Jeffers–D. H. Lawrence cult, who had read Freud not wisely but with artless ardor and spent vacations in New Mexico.

Writers like Lawrence and Jeffers who are worshiped by cults, frequently inspire the more violent forms of academic snobbery. Neither came from the "right" prep school, college, or university; neither Oxford or Cambridge could claim Lawrence, nor could the Ivy League universities and colleges in the United States gather their share of glory from Jeffers' reputation. Both Lawrence and Jeffers have outlived their cults; and Lawrence, safely dead and of British origin, no longer irritates the thin, tightly stretched surface of academic temper in the United States. This phenomenon, which is not without its trace of envy, partly explains the neglect, in quarterly reviews, of Jeffers' later writings. It can be said that in recent years Jeffers has been a poet without critics, but this does not mean that his name has been forgotten, his books unread, or his plays in verse neglected on the stage. A few years ago his *Medea* had a respectable run on Broadway, and an off-Broadway theater in New York found audiences for his new play, *The Cretan Woman*.

The initial advantage of rereading Jeffers' poetry now is that it can be approached without the formulas of critical fashions ringing in one's ears. Since 1925 he has published more than fifteen books of verse—a quantity of poetry which resembles the production of his ancestors, the romantic poets of nineteenth-century Britain. Rereading his poems, one finds them falling into three divisions: the Southwestern narratives with their richness of California sea-sky-and-landscape; the shorter poems which are largely conversation pieces—for Jeffers is not a lyric poet—and a fine group of elegies, his *Descent to the Dead*, the result of a visit in 1929 to the British Isles; and the semidramatic poems inspired by Greek themes and overlaid with Nietzschean and twentieth-century philosophies.

### II

It is best to begin when and where Jeffers' earlier reputation began; the time was 1925 and the place was New York; and credit for the publication of *Roan Stallion, Tamar, and Other Poems* should be given to James Rorty, a writer who met Jeffers during a stay in California and with selfless enthusiasm persuaded New York friends to read "Tamar," to write about it, to make the presence of Jeffers known to New York publishers. Although Jeffers never shared the excitements and diversions of literary circles on the Atlantic Coast, the moment was prepared to receive his semi-Biblical, semi-Sophoclean American Southwestern narratives. Discussions of Steinach operations for restoring sexual vitality were in the air, and so were questions from Krafft-Ebing, Freud, and Jung; D. H. Lawrence's *The Rainbow* was in print as well as Sherwood Anderson's *Dark Laughter*. If a post World War I urban generation had not discovered sex, it had learned to talk loudly and almost endlessly about it. Nothing was easier than to apply cocktail conversations to Jeffers' "Tamar" and "Roan Stallion," which at first reading—and particularly to those who lived in cities—held the same attractions as an invitation to a nudist colony on the Pacific Coast.

Yet it was not without self-critical discernment that Jeffers gave first place to "Tamar" when he prepared his *Selected Poetry* in 1937. For whatever reasons his public had accepted it twelve years earlier, at a time when he had passed the age of thirty-five, the poem has all the merits of a style that he had made his own. As early as 1912 he had paid for the printing of a first book, *Flagons and Apples*; in 1916 a second book, *Californians*, had been published by Macmillan; and neither, aside from the praise of a small group of friends, had received encouragement. His friendships, which included the long-sustained devotion of his wife, Una Call, also embraced the good will of George Sterling, who had known Ambrose Bierce, Joaquin Miller, and Jack London, and who was one of the few to see promise in Jeffers' early books of poems. Like Jeffers, who had been born in Pittsburgh in 1887, Sterling, a native of New York State, had become a converted Californian. Sterling's own verse had been inspired by the pages of *The Savoy* and *The Yellow Book* as well as by readings in Oscar Wilde and Ernest Dowson. "Poetry . . . ," he said, "must . . . cherish all the past embodiments of visionary beauty, such as the beings of classical mythology." Sterling's last work, shortly before his suicide in 1926, was a pamphlet written in praise of Jeffers. No doubt Jeffers had been made aware of the presence of evil through his wide readings, but it was through the loyal patronage of Sterling that he became an heir of "Bitter" Bierce. To the general reader, however, Jeffers' first two books offered little more than glimpses of a belated debt to Dante Gabriel Rossetti in *Flagons and Apples*, and a Wordsworthian manner, which included hints of pantheism, in *Californians*.

Before Jeffers met his wife and Sterling, he had had an unusual education. He was the precocious son of a teacher of theology at Western Theological Seminary in Pittsburgh. His father taught him Greek, Latin, and Hebrew; and when the boy was five or six, took him on trips to Europe. For three years, between the ages of twelve and fifteen, his father sent him to boarding schools in Switzerland and Germany; and at fifteen, Jeffers entered the University of Western Pennsylvania. The next four years were spent in Occidental College and the Universities of Zurich and Southern California, and these years included studies in medicine and forestry. All this would be of no importance if it did not throw light on the individual ranges of Jeffers' poetry, his familiarity with Greek and Roman and Biblical themes, with German philosophy, with medical terms and semiscientific details, and—since he read French with facility—his possible knowledge of the writings of Sade. Certainly his education[1] provided reasons for an affinity with Sterling, whose idea of poetry embraces, however vaguely, "beings of classical mythology." At the very least, Jeffers is a writer whose early years had prepared him for more than a regional view of the world and its affairs.

A second reading of "Tamar" reveals it as a Biblical story in Californian undress. Characters in Jeffers' Southwestern narratives, from "Tamar" to "The Loving Shepherdess," from "Give Your Heart to the Hawks" to "Hungerfield," are often lightly clothed and are subject to the wind, sun, and rain of Californian climate. Chapter 13 of the second book of Samuel is one source of Jeffers' parable,[2] which contains the story of Amnon's love for his sister Tamar. Other associations taken from the two books of Samuel permeate the poem, for the sons of Samuel "walked not in his ways, but turned aside after lucre and took bribes, and perverted judgment," a statement which is appropriate to Jeffers' view of America and Western civilization. As a parable the poem acquires the force of a Calvinist sermon from an American pulpit, yet it also carries within it echoes of Nietzsche's speech of Silenus, "What is best of all is beyond your reach forever: not to be born, not to *be*, to be *nothing*," and behind these words Sophocles' remark, "Not to be born is best for man." In Tamar's words the echoes are clearly heard: "O God, I wish / I too had been born too soon and died with the eyes unopened. . . ." Jeffers also puts into the mouth of Tamar a remark which has its origins in the doctrines of Sade "we must keep sin pure / Or it will poison us, the grain of goodness in a sin is poison. / Old man, you have no conception / Of the freedom of purity." And as Tamar speaks she has given herself over to unchecked forces of evil. In Sade's novel *Justine*, his heroine is tortured because she fails to purge her taint of goodness; as the poem nears its end, the whipping of Tamar by her brother is the last love scene between them.

This is not to say that Jeffers by voicing echoes of Sade's doctrines had advanced them as examples of Californians to follow; it is rather that he has given the forces of evil a well-established voice of authority, but in doing so he has succeeded with such vehemence that he might be misunderstood by a careless reader. Even at this risk, he has also succeeded in giving the unleashed forces of hell refreshed reality. In his poem, the house of David, Tamar's father—and Tamar is the daughter of King David in the second book of Samuel—is destroyed by fire which in its first association creates a literal image of hell and, in its second, of the funeral pyres of the Romans.

So far I have mentioned only the principal elements of "Tamar," its Californian setting, one of the sources of its story, and a few of the concepts which are made relevant to the retelling of the story—but these do not complete the list of associations that the poem brings to mind, for "Tamar," beneath the surface of a swiftly moving plot, has a richness of detail which rivals the complex fabric of Elizabethan dramatic verse. In the Biblical story the seduction of Tamar by Amnon is scarcely more than an invitation to come to bed; in Jeffers' version the seduction scene has an Ovidian ring; a hidden stream, a pool tempts brother and sister; naked, they enter it and one recalls Ovid's stories of Narcissus and Echo, Hermaphroditus and Salmacis, and by association there is a particularly Roman touch, a glimpse of Phoebus' chariot wheel, from a window of David's house overlooking the Pacific:

> It was twilight in the room, the shiny
>     side of the wheel
> Dipping toward Asia; and the year dipping toward
>     winter encrimsoned the grave spokes of
>     sundown. . . .

It is this kind of richness that places "Tamar" among the major accomplishments in twentieth-century poetry. And what of the ghosts that haunt the house of David in "Tamar"? They are very like the images of guilt that invade the darkened walls of Macbeth's castle. An idiot sets fire to David's house, and one thinks of the line ". . . a tale told by an idiot, full of sound and fury." In this instance, an idiot hastens the end of sound and fury.[3]

How deliberate Jeffers was in making a highly individual combination of Californian locale, Biblical and Græco-Roman themes, Elizabethan richness of detail, plus Nietzschean ethics and Calvinist denouements, it is impossible to say. The great probability is that, having a deeply felt desire to warn the world of the dangers of its involvements in world wars, Jeffers brought all the resources, conscious or hidden, of his imagination into play. To Jeffers, World War I was a warning of weaknesses inherent in a civilization that permitted mass murders and a situation that approached total war. War, by example, creates a precedent for violent action; and in "Tamar" that conclusion is shown by the desire of Tamar's brother to leave his father's house to go to war, not merely to escape the consequences of evil at home, but to plunge himself into scenes of mass destruction. Private violence and public warfare are mutually influential—and the essential sin was not to walk in the ways of Samuel.

Whatever else may be said of Jeffers' beliefs and opinions as they appear with marked consistency throughout the various poems he has written, he has gone to war in the cause of peace; and it should also be said that Jeffers' emotional fervor, his honesty, and his lack of personal vanity strongly resemble the evangelical passion of his Protestant heritage: his image of Christ is always divine. His poem to America, his "Shine, Perishing Republic," has that fervor, its eloquence, its nobility, its protest against earthly tyrants:

> And boys, be in nothing so moderate as in love of
>     man, a clever servant, insufferable master.
> There is in the trap that catches noblest spirits, that
>     caught—they say—God, when he walked on
>     earth.

But before one considers the merits of Jeffers' best writings, one should spare breath for certain of their failures, for Jeffers is a poet of large flaws and no weaknesses—and the flaws are often easier to see than his larger merits. In the great army of characters that his poems present to us, one has yet to discover a wholly admirable or completely rounded human being—the nearest approach, and her virtue is one of courage, is the heroine of "Give Your Heart to the Hawks," a woman who attempts to save her husband from suicide and fails. An impatient reader of Jeffers, overwhelmed, yet half attracted, and then repelled by the scenes of overt Lesbianism in "The Women at Point Sur" and by the sight of a mother offering herself, half naked, to her son in "Such Counsels You Gave to Me," would conclude that the poet kept bad company and was himself "immoral." The same reader would also find difficulties in fully accepting Jeffers' beautiful pastoral, "The Loving Shepherdess," which may have been written with a memory of the Elizabethan John Fletcher's *The Faithful Shepherdess* in mind.[4] The witless little shepherdess, dressed in the fewest of rags, is open to all men, young and old; and it is as though she had obeyed Sade's instructions to little girls. Whenever in Jeffers' poetry one finds a possible echo of Sade's doctrines, the mind, if not the blood, runs cooler. Even Robespierre and Bonaparte, worldly men enough at the sight of blood, and who welcomed Sade as a forthright critic of elder institutions, were shocked and grew chilled when they read Sade's manifestoes in the cause of sexual freedom; they were not prudes, but they concluded that Sade's remarks were too much of a good thing. And truly enough Sade implied too much deliberation in the pursuits of his particular happiness; his logic created a law for sexual lawlessness that all institutions, ancient or modern, have been forced to reject. Jeffers' desire to deal solely with elemental passions tends to mislead the reader into the colder regions of hell which are a paradox of romantic agony: the reader is repelled.[5]

Another reader, equally impatient, finds something ridiculous in Jeffers' scenes of sexual violence; since no comic relief is given to the reader in Jeffers' Californian narratives, the reader is forced to supply that missing element in the progress of the story—and sex viewed from a point outside the scene itself always has a touch of the ridiculous in it; if it did not there would be no moments of relaxation in the stories that used to be told in smoking cars. It is almost gratuitous to say that Jeffers' characters lack humor, which is a flaw that Jeffers shares with Wordsworth; and in the progress of his more violent scenes of action, a need is felt for a drunken porter to cross the stage in *Macbeth*. This does not mean, however, that Jeffers lacks ability to write of drunkenness; few scenes in contemporary fiction can equal the vividness of the drunken party which is prelude to the story of "Give Your Heart to the Hawks"; in poetry, and in its own grim fashion, its veracity equals the mild, half-melancholy scene of E. A. Robinson's "Mr. Flood's Party." (Robinson, by the way, is one of the few elder American poets for whom Jeffers has expressed firm admiration.) "Such Counsels You Gave to Me" must be counted as one of Jeffers' more conspicuous failures: the bare bones of the "Oedipus complex" shine too brightly through it. As the story opens one knows only too well that the weak son is fated to poison his red-faced, hard-drinking father; since 1900 this situation has been the stock property of countless novels and plays; a sinister yet charming hero-villain disposes of a father who is overweight or a rich aunt who spikes her tea with whisky. But in Jeffers' case these flaws are not those of a small-minded writer or a minor poet.

### III

Jeffers' merits as a poet are less well known than the flaws which I have just enumerated. From "Roan Stallion" and "Tamar" onward, Jeffers' technical contribution to twentieth-century poetry has been the mastery of alternate ten and five stress lines in narrative verse; in some of his shorter poems and in passages of some of his dramatic sequences, he employs a five and three stress variation of his narrative line. In this particular art no living poet has equaled him, and no other poet in America, from Philip Freneau to E. A. Robinson, has developed a narrative style of greater force, brilliance, and variety than his. While reading one of Jeffers' poems one never falls asleep; although there are times when his moral fervor is overweighted and has results which seem far from his stated intentions, he has never committed the greatest of all literary crimes—dullness. Among his shorter poems, his conversation pieces have contained prophecies which at the moment of publication seemed wrongheaded, probably mad, or willfully truculent. Time has proved Jeffers right more frequently than his adverse readers had thought possible; although the poem is too long for quotation here, the thoughtful reader cannot fail to be impressed by his "Woodrow Wilson (February 1924)" today. Wilson, the nearly tragic American hero, has been and still is the most difficult of all public figures to write about, yet Jeffers has succeeded in doing so. The poem's last lines, words spoken as if from Wilson's lips, indicate, however briefly, the nature of Wilson's failure:

"This is my last
Worst pain, the bitter enlightenment that buys
       peace."

Jeffers' opinions (which are less political than colored by his hatred of war, his adaptation of Nietzschean ethics, and non-churchgoing Christianity) occasioned his publishers, in a recent book of his poems, *The Double Axe*, to disclaim responsibility for them. Jeffers had strange things to say of World War II and its aftermath, which he had predicted long before they arrived; he was much too familiar with the scene to be tactful; in another ten years he will probably be found less far from the truth than the majority of his contemporaries. There has been considerable misunderstanding of Jeffers' portrait of Hitler which he included in *Be Angry at the Sun* in 1941; his Hitler was a figure not unlike Macbeth, a Macbeth who had also become the hero of a Wagnerian opera; his doom was accurately foretold; yet at the time Jeffers' poem appeared many thought that Jeffers had praised Hitler, or at least had made him seem too powerful. There is less doubt today that Jeffers' portrait needs no retouching to give it greater veracity.

Of the shorter poems, his volume *Descent to the Dead* is among his masterpieces; it includes his lines on "Shakespeare's Grave," "In the Hill at New Grange," "Ghosts in England," "Iona: The Graves of the Kings"—all memorable poems. It is impossible for an anthologist to make a neat selection of Jeffers' poems and then bind them shrewdly between the poems written by his contemporaries. It so happens that Jeffers has never written an "anthology poem";[6] he is best represented by his *Selected Poetry* which shows the range of his narratives tempered by his elegies, self-critical comments, and occasional observations; many of them may be read as footnotes to his longer poems. Selections of his shorter poems by anthologists distort the essential qualities of his poetry.

A few quotations from Jeffers' shorter poems do show, however, how he has shocked people of rigidly fixed political opinions; from "Blind Horses" one may take the lines:

Lenin has served the revolution
Stalin presently begins to betray it. Why? For the
       sake of power, the Party's power, the state's
Power, armed power, Stalin's power, Caesarean
       power.

And these were printed in 1937 when many people throughout Europe and some in the United States thought differently or would have feared to make their opinions known at all. And from "Thebaid" the observation:

> How many turn back toward dreams and magic, how
>     many children
> Run home to Mother Church, Father State.

This is a statement which, like other elements in Jeffers' poetry, many may find easy to read but difficult to take; and yet it defines with Jeffers' insight and discernment a symptom of the times through which he has lived. Of the same temper are these lines from "Ave Caesar":

> We are easy to manage, a gregarious people,
> Full of sentiment, clever at mechanics, and we love
>     our luxuries.

Something of the force of Jeffers' sense of the past may be glimpsed at in these lines from "Ghosts in England":

>                 There was also a ghost of a king, his
>                     cheeks hollow as the brows
> Of an old horse, was paddling his hands in the reeds
>     of Dozmare Pool, in the shallow, in the rainy
>     twilight,
> Feeling for the hilt of a ruinous and rusted sword.
>     But they said
> "Be patient a little, you king of shadows,
> But only wait, they will waste like snow." Then
>     Arthur left hunting for the lost sword, he
>     grinned and stood up
> Gaunt as a wolf; but soon resumed the old labor,
>     shaking the reeds with his hands.

It is scarcely necessary to add that this image of King Arthur searching for Excalibur and his early moment of glory has the character of major verse. And the style in which it is written also reveals Jeffers' interlinear art of writing verse.

## IV

Jeffers' success in reviving Greek themes through Nietzschean and even Wagnerian interpretation has also been a source of annoyance to those who hope to read their classics in "pure" translations. The "pure" translation of Graeco-Roman classics do not and cannot exist in English; and it is a truism that absolute translations of poetry from one language into another cannot be made. The best that can be hoped for is that the translator has a more than literal understanding of the poetry he translates and that he has the genius to convert his original sources into poetry in English. Jeffers' re-creations of ancient stories, particularly the plays of Euripides into English dramatic verse, have never pretended to be more than adaptations of situations, scenes, and characters. Actually, his performances are as far removed from their original sources as Shakespeare's adaptations from Plutarch's *Lives* in *Julius Caesar* and *Antony and Cleopatra*, as far as Jeffers' "Tamar" is from the second book of Samuel in the Old Testament. In his own way he has applied to ancient writings Ezra Pound's rule, "make it new." Like W. B. Yeats, Jeffers was not "a born dramatist"; as Yeats was essentially a lyric poet, so Jeffers has been a distinguished writer of contemplative and narrative verse. As Yeats's adaptation of *Oedipus at Colonus* reflects Irish seascape in a Dublin accent, so Jeffers' adaptations from the Greek are never far from the climate of the California Pacific Coast.

If Jeffers, even more than Yeats, is not a professional dramatist and is far removed from those who can be called "men of the theater," there are times when his poetry reaches high levels of dramatic power. This has long been evident in his variation of the Orestes cycle in "The Tower Beyond Tragedy"; and its concluding statement of how Orestes "climbed the tower beyond time, consciously, and cast humanity, entered the earlier fountain" (walked then, as Nietzsche would say, beyond good and evil) places the poem among the major

accomplishments of our time. The same power enters his poem "At the Fall of an Age," with its story of the death of Helen on the island of Rhodes where she was worshiped as a tree-goddess, twenty years after the fall of Troy. The two speeches of Achilles' Myrmidons, risen from the dead, have all the accents of living yet timeless verse; the second speech runs as follows:

> Is there any stir in the house?
> Listen: or a cry?
> Farm-boys with spears, you sparrows
> Playing hawk, be silent.
> Splendid was life
> In the time of the heroes, the sun went helmeted, the
>     moon was maiden,
> When glory gathered on Troy, the picketed horses
> Neighed in the morning, and long live ships
> Ran on the wave like eagle-shadows on the slopes of
>     mountains.
> Then men were equal to things, the earth was
>     beautiful, the crests of heroes
> Waved as tall as the trees.
> Now all is decayed, all corrupted, all gone down,
> Men move like mice under the shadows of the trees,
> And the shadows of the tall dead.
> The brightness of fire is dulled,
> The heroes are gone.
> In naked shame Agamemnon
> Died of a woman.
> The sun is crusted and the moon tarnished,
> And Achilles has chosen peace.
> Tell me, you island spearmen, you plowboy warriors,
> Has anyone cried out in the dark door?
> Not yet. The earth darkens.

There is nothing in poetry written during the twentieth century that is quite like this speech; few poets have written as well and the authority of the speech is unmistakable. Jean Cocteau once wrote that a true poet writes to be believed, not praised, and in these lines Jeffers' art of persuading the reader is unquestionable. Nor is he less convincing in the writing of Aphrodite's speech in his recent play, *The Cretan Woman*, a play inspired by and not a translation of Euripides:

> . . . So I have come down to this place,
> And will work my will. I am not the least clever of
>     the powers of heaven . . .
>                 I am the goddess the Greeks
>                     call Aphrodite; and the
>                     Romans will call me
>                     Venus; the Goddess of
>                     Love. I make the
>                     orchard-trees
> Flower, and bear their sweet fruit. I make the joyful
>     birds to mate in the branches, I make the man
> Lean to the woman. I make the huge blue tides of the
>     ocean follow the moon; I make the multitude
> Of the stars in the sky to love each other, and love the
>     earth, without my saving power
> They would fly apart into the horror of the night.
>     And even the atoms of things, the hot whirling
>     atoms,
> Would split apart: the whole world would burst apart
>     into smoking dust, chaos and darkness; all life
> Would gasp and perish. But love supports and
>     preserves them: my saving power.
>     This is my altar,
> Where men worship me. Sometimes I grant the
>     prayers of those that worship me: but those who
>     reject me
> I will certainly punish.

The quality of this speech equals the speeches in the plays of the Greek dramatists, but it is also singularly modern poetry; the quality of its language is direct and unstrained—no irrelevant effort at meaning is forced into it: the poetic nature of the speech is *there*, and for its purpose cannot be said in any other way; it is evidence enough of the genius of the man who wrote it. *The Cretan Woman* is a far more successful play to read than Jeffers' *Medea*; for his *Medea* opens with a flood of emotional speeches that cannot be sustained throughout the first act, therefore the play is top-heavy, and his readers as well as his audiences are likely to be exhausted long before the final curtain falls. Jeffers' version of Euripides' *Hippolytus* reserves its strength for the last scene and agony of Theseus; and at this conclusion, one believes that Jeffers has lost none of the mastery that he acquired thirty years ago, rather he has set himself the further task of transforming his narrative genius into writing verse for the stage, or perhaps television.

Robinson Jeffers' accomplishments and the modesty of his private life, now saddened by the death of his wife, should serve as an example to the present as well as the next generation of writers. Within the last thirty years he has made no compromise with the changing fashions of the day. For some readers Jeffers' attitude, which is not unlike the positions held by William Faulkner and W. B. Yeats, has always seemed too aristocratic. Even now I can hear someone saying, "Jeffers loves nothing but rocks and stones; I love mankind." But those who love abstract mankind too feverishly deny the rights of individual distinction and all the choices between men of good and bad, and by implication they also deny the right of the artist to be himself. Jeffers has re-established the position of the poet as one of singular dignity and courage. He is neither voiceless nor without his readers; and he is not without wisdom in seeming to await the verdict of posterity.

*Notes*

1. Jeffers' education was of a kind familiar to well-to-do European gentry of the nineteenth century, but considerably less so to young Americans of the same period. Exceptions in the United States were Henry James's early travels with his father, and the continued educations after college of Longfellow, Trumbull Stickney, George

Cabot Lodge, and Henry Adams. Jeffers' development as a narrative poet also follows the precedent of many major nineteenth-century poets; Jeffers and his writings are "in the tradition."

2. For biographical information concerning Jeffers, as well as the fact that one of the sources of "Tamar" may be found in the second book of Samuel, I am indebted to Lawrence Clark Powell's *Robinson Jeffers: The Man and His Work*.

3. In Jeffers' short poem "Self-Criticism in February," there are the following lines which describe the nature of his ghosts, his romanticism, his unchurched belief in God:

> *It is certain you have loved the beauty of storm, disproportionately.*
> But the present time is not pastoral, but founded
> Of violence, pointed for more massive violence: perhaps it is not
> Perversity but need that perceives the storm-beauty.
> *Well, bite on this: your poems are too full of ghosts and demons,*
> *And people like phantoms—how often life's are—*
> . . .
>                    *you have never mistaken*
>     *Demon nor passion nor idealism for the real God.*
>     Then what is most disliked in those verses
>     Remains most true.

4. This supposition is not so fantastic as it may seem: John Fletcher's lyrical *The Faithful Shepherdess* was far too static in movement to be a successful play; it is, however, an excellent poem. Its plot closely resembles Jeffers' poem with this difference: Fletcher's shepherdess is deceived into being promiscuous through magic worked by a sullen shepherd and she is at last rescued and absolved by a river god.

5. In a footnote to the pamphlet called "Frenchmen! A further effort is needed if you would be republicans!" in his *La Philosophie dans le boudoir* (1795), Sade wrote: "The first stirring of desire that a girl feels is the moment that Nature means her to prostitute herself, and with no other consideration in mind, she should obey Nature's voice; she outrages Her laws if she resists them."

6. The perfect "anthology poem" is a showpiece of which Poe's "The Raven" and Tennyson's "May Queen" and "Crossing the Bar" were valiant examples; many minor poets seem to write for anthologies alone; and indeed, some poets like A. E. Housman are at their best when a small selection of their poems are reprinted in anthologies. With more wit and, incidentally, more truth than tact, Laura Riding and Robert Graves reviewed the practice of editing anthologies in their book, *A Pamphlet against Anthologies*.

# JAMES JONES

## 1921–1977

James Jones was born in Robinson, Illinois, on November 6, 1921. The youngest son a well-to-do midwestern family that had fallen on hard times, Jones enlisted in the armed forces after his high school graduation in 1939. He became a champion welterweight boxer while stationed at Pearl Harbor and before shipping out he took a few literature courses at the University of Hawaii. In 1943 he was wounded at the battle of Guadalcanal and received the Purple Heart and the Bronze Star for his heroic efforts. After his medical discharge in 1944, which was partially prompted by his unstable mental condition, Jones lived with Lowney and Harry Handy in Robinson. His mother was already dead and his father had committed suicide in 1942. Jones began writing under the stern guidance of Lowney Handy, who encouraged him to take writing courses at New York University. He returned to Illinois in 1946 and continued working on his first novel, *From Here to Eternity* (1951). An overwhelming success, his first novel sold over four million copies and was awarded the National Book Award in 1952. His violent, passionate writing shows the influence of his early idol, Thomas Wolfe, whose *Look Homeward, Angel* Jones had read while stationed in Hawaii.

With the money from the film rights, Jones helped the Handys establish a writers' colony in Marshall, Illinois, run more like a monastery than an artists' retreat: the writers had to follow strict dietary regulations, abstain from sexual activity, and copy the great classics word for word. Jones left the Handys and married Gloria Mosolino in 1957. They eventually moved to Paris the following year and remained there until 1974. Jones's lengthy second novel, *Some Came Running* (1957), was poorly received by the critics, but the second part of his war trilogy, *The Thin Red Line* (1962), received better reviews. Jones continued writing despite the lukewarm praise given most of his books. He returned to the U.S. in 1974 and settled in Sagaponack, Long Island, with his wife and two children. Nearing the end of his work on *Whistle*, the last installment in his war trilogy that began with *From Here to Eternity*, Jones suffered a fatal heart attack. He died on May 9, 1977, in Southampton, New York. His friend Willie Morris finished the remaining chapters of *Whistle*, working from Jones's notes and tape recordings. The novel was published in 1978.

## Personal

I had met him for the first time about ten years before, at a party for him and Gloria in New York City at Jean and William vandenHeuvals', one of the places where people met in those days.

I knew much about him from a distance. I had read almost everything he had written, and believed *From Here to Eternity*, *The Thin Red Line*, and *Some Came Running* three of the great novels in American literature. When I first encountered *From Here to Eternity* in college, I was stunned by its power. The scene at Schofield Barracks when Private Robert E. Lee Prewitt sounds "Taps" was as memorable to me in those days as young Ike McCaslin's confrontation with the bear in Faulkner's novella, or as Twain's storm on the Mississippi in *Huck Finn*. Passages in *Some Came Running*, *The Pistol*, and *The Thin Red Line* also touched me deeply. I knew then that the Army was, in truth, his Yoknapatawpha County. From book to book the names changed, but the characters remained the same, with cryptic keys to their identities. Sergeant Warden in *From Here to Eternity* became Sergeant Welsh in *The Thin Red Line* (and Sergeant Winch in *Whistle*)—and in the same way, Stark-Storm-Strange and Prewitt-Witt-Prell. As I grew older I recognized that by his hard-earned craftsmanship he had enlarged the limits of the language in America as perhaps no other writer of his time had done. Irwin Shaw later wrote: "[His work] came from a group of men who spoke plainly, without euphemisms, using words about death and sex and cowardice and chicanery and despair that before Jones had rarely been on the printed page in this country. From the stink of the battlefield and the barracks came a bracing, clear wind of truth. To use a military term, he walked point for his company." Subsequently I felt that the more hostile of the critics seemed to be assessing a writer quite different from the one I admired, as if he had committed that most unpardonable literary crime—great success too early.

I had read articles about him in *Life* and *Esquire* and other magazines. I knew he had grown up in Robinson, Illinois, the son of a father who killed himself and of a mother he hated—a tortured and lonely childhood. I knew he had made a lot of money and owned a house on the Île St. Louis, where the Americans in Paris congregated, with plenty of poker games and hard drinking. And barroom fights with cracked ribs and broken teeth to show for them, and cocktails on Boulevard St. Michel at twilight, and afternoons at the track. Despite four years of Oxford and numerous trips to the Continent, I was never part of that world, but I sometimes wished I had been—it sounded romantic, part of the writing life. I had heard about the trips to the Mediterranean, weekends in Deauville, summers in Greece, skin diving in the Caribbean. I knew about his years in a trailer camp in Indiana when he was writing under the patronage of Lowney Handy. I knew also, from mutual friends such as Rose and William Styron and

Irwin Shaw, that he was beloved by many people, and that he had one of America's most beautiful, funny, and lovable wives.

I did not know then, but he told me later, of the time he was discharged from the Army after months in hospitals, with a badly damaged ankle and not all that good in the head, when he went to the mountains around Asheville, North Carolina, because he had been absorbed by Thomas Wolfe, and rented a cabin from a farmer and drank a lot of mountain whiskey in solitude to try and get over the war. The combat had been bad enough, God knows, but he was all alone in the jungle one day when a half-starved Japanese soldier came out at him from the undergrowth, and after a struggle he had to kill him with a knife, and then found the family photographs in the dead man's wallet; for a time he refused to fight again, and they put him in the stockade and busted him to private. Nor did I know that he came to New York City after Carolina and wrote a novel, then went to the Scribner's office and demanded to see Maxwell Perkins, and that Perkins did not like the novel but was taken by a paragraph in a later letter about how his next book would deal with life in the peacetime Army, and eventually gave him a $500 option to write that one. I had always been curious to know why a man so intensely American, from the border-state America which had produced Mark Twain and Theodore Dreiser and Sherwood Anderson, a man who had written so powerfully about the beauty and rootlessness and promise of America, had chosen to live in Europe for so many years.

The jacket photographs had given me the impression of a somewhat pugnacious and snarling fellow, someone who was not to be trifled with—a fancy dresser with big rings on his fingers. Although I had more or less become part of the "literati," I will admit I was in awe of him on that first meeting.

It was a brutally hot night in the summer, and the air-conditioner was not working. After the hostess introduced us, he and I stood off to the side of the crowd—writers, publishers, theater people, politicians—talking about mutual friends, about southern Illinois and Mississippi, about the magazine business. He had a jutting jaw, piercing eyes, and his accent was almost southern in its intonations, as was the way he used the grammar. The way he talked (except for the profanity) reminded me a little of my father, who was a small-town boy from western Tennessee.

"Holy shit, it's hot," he said. He proceeded to take off his coat and roll up his sleeves. I did likewise. We were standing near the bar, and he left momentarily to talk with some new arrivals. The bartender had vanished into the kitchen. Suddenly Ted Kennedy came up to me and extended his glass. "Another Scotch and soda, please," he said. This swift motion took me by surprise. I made the drink and handed it to him. It took me a few seconds to realize he had mistaken me for the bartender. From a distance I noticed that this scene had not been lost on Jim Jones. He was laughing so hard he put his hand against the wall for support. Soon Kennedy came up to me again: "What are *you* doing there? Let me fix *you* a drink."

When he left, Jim walked over to me and said, "I told him you ain't the bartender, you're the fuckin' editor-in-chief of *Harper's Magazine*."

I was to learn over the years that beneath the rough exterior was a profoundly cultured and sophisticated man, a student of literature, history, art, and music. He loved a good time more than most, and had the craziest laugh. He had always had, too, an almost religious dedication to his work. Up until two days before he died he was talking into a tape recorder about his novel. Even with the final collapse of his body he was the sanest man I ever knew. He was, in the truest and best sense, an old-fashioned man. He could not stand fraud, or phoniness, or meanness, and often he would respond to the remark of some pompous or devious ass with the enlisted man's contemptuous "Sir?" His honesty was utterly unself-righteous, rooted in a sense of life's absurdities. He knew firsthand the terrible price exacted for civilization. Although he looked and sometimes tried to sound like a tough guy, he was in fact the most pacific of men, not at all drawn to the Hemingway macho, and the fights he had were invariably with bullies. His courage needed no proving. He was deeply loving and tender, but he did not want just anybody to know it. He never said anything merely to be smart. That was one of the reasons I always wanted to know what he thought about things.

In 1971 I went through an unhappy experience running the magazine and resigned. I had given too much of myself to someone else's property. Perhaps I had done too much too young—seen too much, or succeeded too easily, or gotten too old too soon. This shortens things. It is an American hazard. In that sense I suppose Jim and I, despite the age difference of older and younger brothers, were closer to being contemporaries.

I left the city and tried to get down to my own work. Jim Jones, too, like many writers, felt he had served his years in the city and seldom went in anymore unless he had to, and when he did he usually went to P. J. Clarke's and sat at a table in the back room and talked with the old friends who drifted through.

For awhile I was rather self-righteous about fraudulence and the petty conceits. The way people dropped you was a good lesson to learn. Yet for a time I found myself missing some of the perquisites of a position of relatively high station. Jim was not much for the ceremonial trimmings. The honesty and courage and unadorned values of the man were tempered, yet enhanced, by his simplicity. He was a man of deep moral principle. I do not believe it silly to say that he set an example for me, as he did for a lot of people. We shared a love for literature, America, the South, sitting around and telling stories—shared, too, a distrust of ideologues. He was a prop, a pillar. He knew about character because he had character.
—WILLIE MORRIS, "A Friendship: Remembering James Jones," *At*, June 1978, pp. 49–50

## General

James Jones's fictional terrain is limited to that peculiar all-male world governed by strictly masculine interests, attitudes, and values. Into this world, no female can step without immediately altering its character. The female must remain on the periphery of male life—a powerful force in male consciousness, but solely as a provocative target for that intense sexual need that has nothing to do with procreation or marriage. In civilian life, the closest approximation to this all-male world is the camp of the weekend fisherman or hunter who becomes totally absorbed in technical details about sports and sporting equipment, who enjoys the camaraderie of shared masculine interests, who competes for the distinction of being the toughest guy, the best shot, the bravest, boldest hunter, the greatest seducer. In this atmosphere, men strip themselves of the refinements of sensibility and language that they adopt in their life with women. Not intellect, nor manners, nor moral and aesthetic sensitivity, but technical skill and knowledge, physical strength and endurance, boldness and courage are the coveted virtues of this exclusively male world.

Individualism is identified, in *From Here to Eternity*, with this masculine life, as if the army were the final frontier of rugged individualism. There are two major threats to the masculine freedom of the enlisted man's existence—the bureaucracy represented by the officer class, and women. Robert E. Lee Prewitt, co-protagonist of the novel, loves not so much the army but the masculinity of barracks life. He wants to be a thirty-year-man because the raw violence, the drunken sprees, the sex without responsibility, the demands on physical endurance and technical skill express and challenge his maleness. Prewitt's war with the army is touched off by a breach of the freedom he expects in return for his loyalty and service as a soldier. The army can have no claim upon his skill at bugling and his ability in the boxing ring. These are voluntary activities, and when an inferior bugler is promoted above him, Prew chooses to transfer to an infantry outfit. A willing boxer until he inflicted a permanent injury on a sparring partner, Prew decides to keep a promise to a woman—his dying mother—not to hurt others unnecessarily, and he refuses to go out for the regimental team. At stake is Prewitt's self-defined integrity, his freedom to choose to do what he wants beyond his obligations as a soldier.

His assertion of individual rights sets into motion the juggernaut of the organization. As Jones makes clear throughout his story, Prew's quixotic struggle can only end in his destruction. Prewitt's history is an eloquent paean to a concept of individualism rapidly becoming anachronistic in an increasingly bureaucratic society. Milt Warden, the co-protagonist of the novel, embodies in his personality the masculine world of the enlisted man. He equates his integrity with the existence of the enlisted man, and when he falls in love with the company commander's wife, Karen, and finally refuses the commission which would make her permanently available to him, he preserves his integrity and his individualism. He does not sell out to the bureaucracy or to women. At the end of the novel, Prew is dead, but Warden drinks and brawls on the way to Mrs. Kipfer's brothel as the *Lurline* sails from Hawaii with Karen aboard.

Jones's second novel contains a facsimile of barracks life in the ménage of Dave and 'Bama. Like the soldiers in Schofield Barracks, the group of ex-GI's drink and gamble and brawl and whore, creating a masculine fortress in the very midst of a feminized, stifling bourgeois society. But this symbolic individualism has no chance of resisting for long the attacks of society and of women. *Some Came Running* presents the histories of a large number of characters, but though a few receive more attention than others, none emerges as a true protagonist. Jones's attitude toward his characters is also far more objective than it was in *From Here to Eternity*. It is almost impossible to feel sympathetic with any character in the entire 1,266 pages of the book. There are no loveable Maggios, nor are there any characters like the sadistic Judson whom one can hate. Jones has already discovered that "There's only a thin red line between the sane and the mad," the good and the bad.

*The Thin Red Line* has no protagonist. The story concerns an infantry company fighting in the jungles and hills of

Guadalcanal. If a single character comes into focus momentarily, he quickly recedes into the background as Jones shifts attention to another soldier. The company encompasses the individuals that make it up. It is an abstract unit with a table of organization designating a variety of positions which human beings fill. In battle, the company, made up of platoons which are made up of squads, is deployed by the battalion commander according to a pre-established plan of attack. The battalions in the regiment are deployed by the regimental commander. The regiments are deployed by the division commander; the divisions deployed by the army commander, and the armies deployed all over the globe by a staff in Washington, D. C. Within this hierarchy, which gets larger and larger as it moves up the chain and farther and farther from the battle lines, the fighting soldier is a grain of sand on a beach encircling the globe.

Jones utilizes a number of effective techniques to dramatize the insignificance of the individual soldier in this massive organization. Concentrating most of his attention upon the activities of C-for-Charlie Company, he permits the reader to become a partisan rooter for the fighting unit. Then, he widens the angle of vision to make the reader aware of companies on each flank of C Company also encountering severe hardships and fierce battles with the enemy. When C-for-Charlie reaches Boola Boola village, its final objective in the campaign, the effect of this dramatic climax is deliberately deadened: another company has already occupied the village and the fighting is about over. The over-enthusiastic C Company commander is relieved from his command because he had acted independently rather than as a unit in the organization.

Jones uses a similar technique in presenting the individual soldiers. By shifting from character to character, he gradually creates the impression that the individual is not only of little importance within the organization but he is of little importance to anyone but himself. When the men see wounded and dead for the first time they are shocked and horrified. During their first battle, they react intensely to the suffering and death of their comrades. But as the fighting continues, the dead bodies of their fellow-soldiers no longer really bother them, and they lose all compunction about killing enemy soldiers. The starving Japanese prisoners are treated inhumanly, but only because the combat situation has revealed to their captors the insignificance of the individual human life except to the being who possesses it. Dead, the grotesque uniformed figure is a piece of carrion to be buried before its stench becomes nauseating.

Jones's existential novel strips away all inherited concepts and all illusions, metaphysical or social, about man's inherent dignity and being. Atheistic or religious, brave or cowardly, these men are equally vulnerable to the indiscriminate governance of chance. Even those incalculable forces within man which make him a coward or a hero under fire are beyond the individual's control. The same men who zig zag bravely through enemy fire on an heroic mission will know soul-shaking terror a week later when, safe in a noncombat area, they hear bombs dropping miles away. Occasionally courage is psychologically explicable; most often it is not. Circumstances create values, and a man's sense of himself comes from his actions in these circumstances. Each man contains within his being the potential for every human virtue or vice, heroism and cowardice, compassion and sadism. The same men who under other conditions would show compassion for any living thing, in the feverish aura of combat are capable of murdering and torturing prisoners without the slightest qualm of conscience. No cause and effect relationship exists between virtue and

destiny. The spattering mortar fragments slash the brave and the cowardly.

The ultimate insignificance of individual man is conveyed at the end of the novel. The campaign for Guadalcanal has ended and C-for-Charlie Company begins training for the coming attack on New Georgia. The great battle is reduced to one of a series of battles. Most of the men who made up the company are dead or dispersed. The dead and the evacuated wounded are replaced to fill out the table of organization. The individual men may live or die, come or go, but the abstraction C-for-Charlie Company remains.

Jones's vision of human existence is brutal and unsentimental, and he conveys it with superb artistry. His story of battle is fast-paced, tightly structured, painfully realistic. James Jones's fictional terrain is limited, but within that limited area he has presented a frightening twentieth-century view of individual man's insignificance in society and in the universe.—EDMOND L. VOLPE, "James Jones—Norman Mailer," *Contemporary American Novelists*, ed. Harry T. Moore, 1964, pp. 108–12

Deprived of the built-in dramatic tensions of the military world, where everything conspired to violate one's virgin integrity or get one killed or wounded, his civilian characters were left to shuffle around in the peacetime malaise with nothing on their minds except sex, the one other activity besides soldiering that Jones found meaningful in human life and which so constantly preoccupied his soldiers that they were barely able to perform their professional functions of fighting wars, joyously beating one another bloody in the barracks, or getting themselves soused on beer down at the PX. Jones's civilians were actually only soldiers on permanent weekend pass. But removed from their natural habitat, they were exposed as products of an imaginative emptiness that could not be filled by even the most remarkable tumescence. All one learned from them was that in the years since he wrote *From Here to Eternity*, Jones's sexual fantasies had grown increasingly sophisticated and had evolved from straight male-female copulation to the quirkier titillations of lesbianism and female masturbation, while of course skirting with good red-blooded macho fastidiousness any hint of male homosexuality.

Military life provided Jones with a subject that exactly suited his energetic but narrow talent. Its dramatic features were obvious and did not need to be imagined, analyzed or explained. They also did not depend on elaborate motivation or character development. But perhaps the most compatible element for Jones in the army experience was that most of his perceptions of it were exactly on the level of the average, uneducated enlisted man. The limitation that handicapped him in writing about civilian life became a virtue when he wrote about soldiers. For whatever they said or thought, however bathetic or banal, rang with conviction because Jones believed just as they did. There is no discernible edge of irony anywhere in his portraits of them. When they work up the acuity, as Prewitt does in *From Here to Eternity*, to formulate such leaden insights as "When you cut with life you had to use the house deck, not your own," one can be sure it is their maker speaking. Their profundity perfectly matches his, and so does their jock-strap philosophy of life.

Fighting is what real men do, and in a perverse way enjoy doing, and women are the things they have sex with when they are not fighting. During intervals away from fighting, if women happen to be unavailable, one can relax and have one's real emotional life with the good ol' boys in the platoon or company. Thoughts on the Big Questions of existence can be exchanged with them because they have all suffered through the same experiences and come to share the same values. They believe as one in personal integrity and manly independence, pride in service and the absolute importance of never letting a buddy down.

These values—defiantly upheld in *From Here to Eternity*—continue to be at least nominally operative in *Whistle*. But the debilitating and deranging effects of prolonged combat, which were dramatized with such violence in *The Thin Red Line*, have seriously weakened their power to govern the conduct of men who once saw them as sacred. In fact, what now becomes clear is that the developing theme of the trilogy as a whole is the gradual disintegration of the knightly code of the old peacetime army under the pressures of a kind of warfare requiring for survival a radically altered mode of existence. One cannot be sure that Jones recognized this as his conscious intention. But his instinctual responses to his material everywhere provide evidence for it, even as they testify to his profoundly darkened apprehension of the meaning of the war experience.

One also cannot be sure that Jones understood the implications of another statement he makes in his "Author's Note," but it has the greatest bearing on the problem he faced in trying to form the three novels into a coherently developed trilogy. He says that he had originally intended Prewitt to be the central figure in all three, but because for dramatic reasons Prewitt had to be killed at the end of *From Here to Eternity*, there was no way short of miraculous resurrection that this intention could be fulfilled. Jones felt obliged, therefore, to create in the second and third volumes a Prewitt-like character, called in each by a slightly different name, and to rename the other characters at the same time. Prewitt thus becomes Witt, then Prell; Sergeant Warden becomes Welsh, then Winch; and Mess Sergeant Stark becomes Storm, then Strange.

On the face of it, all this seems off until one perceives that Jones's intuitions as a novelist were a great deal sounder than his thoughts on novelistic strategy. The fact was that he felt compelled to change their names because his characters, as they undergo the experiences described in *The Thin Red Line* and *Whistle*, are transformed into altogether different people. He might of course still have retained them, except for Prewitt, under their original names and shown this transformation gradually taking place within them. But that would have required a subtler psychological understanding and a better memory of his first conception of them than he possessed. Besides, he appears to have sensed that the old Prewitt, Warden and Stark had been effectively destroyed, and that their later incarnations did not and could not resemble them because nothing in their past lives had prepared them for, or was relatable to, what had happened to them on Guadalcanal and New Georgia. At the expense of his plans for a coherent trilogy, Jones was therefore required to settle for three separate novels and three different sets of characters. But he did so, whether consciously or not, because he could not violate the logic of his materials or escape the consequences of his own fidelity to their implications. He could not avoid seeing that the war had outmoded the most fundamental moral premises on which his characters had initially been drawn.

In *From Here to Eternity* the issues were concrete and clear-cut, and it was possible for one man of sufficient courage to have a decisive effect on them. The conflict was between the lone individual fighting to preserve his honor and freedom of choice and the forces of bureaucratic oppression bent on breaking his will. Prewitt refused to become a boxer for his regiment and so was persecuted outrageously. However, nothing that could be done to him weakened his determination to hold out for what he believed. But beginning with *The Thin Red Line* the individual disappears into the bureaucratic collective, and the issue becomes not honor but survival. In combat, questions of personal morality are shown to be meaningless. Courage and cowardice are wholly arbitrary responses dependent on chance and physical circumstances, the vagaries of the existential moment. Men die in combat for no reason or for absurd reasons. They fight not to win the war or kill the enemy but to keep from being killed, and to achieve this they will commit absolutely any treachery or brutality. ⟨. . .⟩

Jones may not be recognized as a literary artist of the first rank. But he was a powerful naturalistic chronicler of certain essential realities of warfare and of the responses of men at war, and he had a gift for being absolutely honest about what he felt and thought. This is a rarer gift among novelists than one might suppose, and on the evidence of ⟨*Whistle*⟩ it would seem to have been very much alive in him when he died.—JOHN W. ALDRIDGE, "The Last James Jones," *NYTBR*, March 5, 1978, pp. 1, 30–31

## Works

⟨*From Here to Eternity*⟩ is the violent saga of some violent men who belonged in that tiny proportion of our population which up to World War II was the U.S. Army, more specifically still a company stationed in Hawaii whose bitter, brawling professional soldiers live out the months leading up to the Japanese attack on Pearl Harbor. The principal figures are Private Prewitt and Sergeant Warden, and the two women they love in cynical and transient fashion. Warden's affair with his captain's wife is conventional adultery in an exotic setting, but Prewitt's passion for Lorene, née Alma Schmidt, the spoiled goddess of a Honolulu brothel, seems destined to prove the most original love story of the year. By the time the novel reaches its climax in the wild chaos of the Pearl Harbor attack the love affairs are already over. Warden, who has rejected his chance at a commission, sees the company he knew disintegrating, while Prewitt meets death after almost unbelievably sordid, tragic adventures in barrack rooms, bars, and prison stockade. ⟨. . .⟩

*From Here to Eternity* is filled with the hunger and loneliness, the confusion and despair that are Prewitt's life and longings and his search for that rarest moment when one human could find and touch the soul of another. Prewitt is a fighter who does not know what he is fighting "because the real enemy, the common enemy, was so hard to find since you did not know what it was to look for it and could not see it to get your hands on it, so you fought each other, which was easier. . . ." It is a book full of hatred—for the officer class, for women, for fools and stuffiness and authority, save that which is freely given by a man to his friend. It is also a book full of love—for the comradeship of the helpless, for the company of pain.

The background of Prewitt's experiences is saturated with the class struggle in America and the deeds of its martyrs. In that, as in his style, Jones is like Dreiser. Prewitt, like his creator, is a man of utter honesty. And Jones, like Prewitt, has been there. When we have read him we have been there, too, and have been shaken and chastened by what he has made us feel. This is proof that, in spite of imperfections, *From Here to Eternity* is a work of genius.—NED CALMER, "The Real Enemy Is Hard to Find," *SR*, Feb. 24, 1951, pp. 11–12

The predicament of the Negro is sometimes attributed to the simple fact that he is an alien in Western culture—his ancestors were not among the singing masons who raised up the spires of Chartres nor did they help Galileo invent the telescope. The condition of the Negro, however, is not irrelevant to the fate of modern man whose alienation from the proud tradition he once possessed has taken a more subtle and insidious character. This is clear, painfully so, in James Jones's first and best novel, *From Here to Eternity.*

If the whole of history, as Emerson thought, can be incarnated in the life of one man, then history can find its explanation only in the experience of each man. When the man is like Private Robert E. Lee Prewitt, son of Harlan County, Kentucky, coal miner, one-time hero on the bum turned into a U. S. Army thirty-year man, then history must be what he suffers in the Schofield Barracks Stockade. Prewitt is neither a Negro nor a Jew—his Scotch-English ancestors swarmed the hills of Kentucky before the Revolution—but he is nonetheless the perennial collector of injustices, the consecrated underdog. His only code—the simple freedom to be a *man*, as Prewitt insists—is precisely what the Army he so desperately loves must crush until, still unbroken, he dies. The "tragedy" is familiar; it is the tragedy of the man who won't "play ball," who has no "angles" on life, who insists on his individuality in the barracks as in the whorehouse. "Men are killed by being always alike, always unremembered," Prew tells his beloved prostitute, Lorene. But Prew has nothing to give that the world, let alone the Pineapple Army, can recognize as a valid token of social existence. (Proud and independent too, Warden has at least a Company to run, Stark his messhall, Malloy his quasi-mystical vision, and the inconquerable Wop, Maggio, ironic heir of the American Dream, has none of that loyalty for the Army which is Prewitt's nemesis.) A crack boxer who won't fight, an inspired bugler who won't barter his blues-drenched soul for stripes, and a prodigal lover who nevertheless can't renounce his peculiar idea of freedom, Prewitt in the last analysis is destined, is qualified, only to suffer. He suffers by a choice so free that it seems ineluctable, and he comes to know that there is a satisfaction in "having borne pain that nothing else could ever quite equal, even though the pain was philosophically pointless and never affected anything but the nervous system." Unable to commit himself wholly to the philosophy of passive resistance which Jack Malloy, the jail-king messiah, tries to teach him in the stockade, and unable also to articulate, as Malloy can, an encompassing vision of love or justice, Prewitt remains locked within the all-too-human confines of his personal integrity. Malloy may be right in saying that men cannot be hated for what they do; it is only the "system" that must be hated. But for Prewitt justice, like history, is defined by that personal sense of outrage men feel in their bones; for him the killing of a sadist like Fatso is a necessary, self-appointed task, and violence sometimes the only means by which men regain the individuality of which they are despoiled. The best "soljer" in Company G, after Warden, turns out to be Prewitt who thinks of himself as "a sort of super arch-revolutionary . . . a sort of perfect criminal type, very dangerous, a mad dog that loves underdogs." The life of our military hero is consummated in anarchy even more than protest.

It is not in the least difficult to deride in Jones's book that plainness of style of which the author seems almost proud (hardly an image, rhythm, or sentence, outside the dialogue, takes us with the surprise of discovery); or to deride the subliterary psychology which constantly intrudes itself on the relation between men and women or the groin-clutching glorification of masculinity (men "step happily" to a fight, roar in their drinks, and bull their way past the madam); or again to deride the naïve exaltation of bum and tough as true rebels (the cream of American manhood, we are told with less irony than

makes for comfort, reside in the No. 2 Ward for incorrigibles in the Schofield Stockade, patronized by the departed spirit of John Dillinger). Such offenses seem more like a parody of themselves than the result of any influence exerted by the infinitely more crafty Hemingway or more credible London.

But when all these faults have been dutifully noted in deference to our critical acumen, the novel, unlike its sequel, *Some Came Running*, remains to be reckoned with. Its anger and its compassion are not canceled by its misdeeds; its exposé of life in an army on the threshold of war discloses another war which is quietly ravaging—so well is it censored—the American soul. The social background of the action is awkwardly, unmistakably felt. There are frequent references to the Wobblies who exhausted their vision, to the "good" movies of the Thirties, starring Garfield and Cagney, which gradually yielded to the sentimental conceptions of Hollywood, and to the simple doctrine enunciated by General Slater at an army stag, that "social fear is the most tremendous single source of power in existence." But Prewitt himself is never more than vaguely aware of those "leftist" implications which the novel tries to engage. Consequently, the meanings of social and of individual protest jostle throughout the book without finding the theme or form to unite them. If the work has a focus, it is the nature of power or authority as defined by the responses of men to them—Jones's third novel, *The Pistol*, is not a very successful condensation of the same theme. In the unequal conflict between individual and society, Prewitt stands as an emblem of antipower. Recalcitrance is the badge of his heroism—and his victimization.—IHAB HASSAN, "Contemporary Scenes: The Victim with a Thousand Faces," *Radical Innocence*, 1961, pp. 83–86

⟨. . .⟩ James Jones's *From Here to Eternity* (1951) obviously owes its thorough documentation of the old prewar army to Jones's experience. It is so much a book that has been lived—centering on the army as System and Racket—that the documentation lives on in one's mind with a surly ominous bitterness. Since most of the book takes place before Pearl Harbor (and of course ends with the attack itself), everyone expects America to be at war soon, the officers in particular look forward to war as a way of getting promoted, and so everyone in the book simplemindedly predicts war as a natural, necessary, stimulating activity. This matter-of-factness (as subject) helps to establish the army as a piece of social reality. War still seems entirely "normal," war is what these men know they are in for, war helps men to get along in the world, war is just another part of the natural world.

"Naturalness" is Jones's great theme. His book brilliantly imposes itself on the reader, even when his occasional rhetoric seems as retarded as some of his characters, because he has the strictest, plainest, most functional sense of what his protagonists Warden and Prewitt think of as their "maleness." "Maleness" in Jones's book is need, need is aggressive, sexual, honorable, and indefatigable. Although "maleness" is inevitably described by Jones as tragic (it is the nature of the army—of the world—to frustrate the deepest cravings of a man), we recognize in reading *From Here to Eternity* that Jones sees the tragedy in maleness because there is nothing in his world but "maleness." Prewitt and Warden are doomed not because they seek a freedom which the system denies them, but because the world exists for them only as a way of satisfying this maleness. Of course they can never get their way. They can never see the world itself as anything but a limitation.

This is the fate of soldiers—to feel totally impoverished. But Jones's insistence on needs, his sense of their primitive importance, gives his soldiers a kind of honor, a belief in valor—even when this is only the most embittered obstinacy. Virtually alone among World War II novels, *From Here to Eternity* gives us a view from within of the old regular army, of the "thirty-year man" who enlisted because he was a Harlan County miner's son (Prewitt) who could not find work; a natural leader and organizer (Warden) who could play the game in the army; an old Wobbly (Jack Malloy), or a gutter rat (Maggio) who had nowhere else to go. These tough morsels—even the sadist, Fatso, who happily tortured prisoners in the Stockade—are ultimately a judgment on a society whose men have no real work, whose skills are the real lament of the book. Men are employed by the army, but *they* are not used. Just as their "maleness" is stated by Jones to be always in "excess," is always felt as a burden—so Prewitt's skill as a bugler and fighter, Warden's genuine thoughtfulness, Maggio's antic pride—are all in "excess" of anything they are allowed to have and to do. The regular army before December 7 is shown up as a put-on, a world of simulated busyness, routines which require no intelligence, ferocious strictness whose only purpose is to exact mechanical obedience. These regular soldiers are really boondoggling; this army is just another government work project. The West Pointers riding herd on them equally suffer from this dissimulated idleness and unconscious anomie. But since they are in authority, their fundamental vacuity expresses itself in driving their favorites to gain athletic honors for the regiment and in brutally authoritarian views of America's future role in the world.

Our sense of all this "maleness" not in use, of all this "excess" of a man over his function, is gained without much effort. There is no complexity to most of the characters, no contradiction in anyone's basic nature except the consciousness of being "repressed." When his surrogate voice, Jack Malloy in the stockade, gives us Jones's celebration of the romantic rebel in America, we feel that Jones is interrupting his own documentation; the Wobbly philosopher is as insignficant to the machine as are Prewitt's "views" when compared with Prewitt's sufferings at the hands of the army. But what Jones does capture, harrowingly, is inner desolation so total, re-gularized and systematized that these soldiers are virtually unconscious of how savage it feels. First Sergeant Milton Anthony Warden, who despises Captain Holmes but also hates this "superior" as a force he cannot do anything about, looks at Holmes walking away after making an empty show of his authority:

> Through the obscuring mist of anger in him, the stark nakedness of the rain drenched earth and muddy grass and the lonely moving figure of Holmes huddled in his topcoat made a picture in his mind of a ghost town street and a strong wind rolling along a tattered scrap of paper in the gutter to some unfore-seen and unimportant destination, moaning with the sadness of its duty.

This emptiness is Jones's achievement in *From Here to Eternity*. And just as the characters descend all too smoothly (cogs in the wheel, items in the naturalistic tale) to their various catastrophes, so Jones's own work seems to require no great imaginative effort. It is the old-fashioned product of an old-fashioned war.—ALFRED KAZIN, "The Decline of War: Mailer to Vonnegut," *Bright Book of Life*, 1973, pp. 77–81

There was a time, I suspect, when James Jones wanted to be the greatest writer who ever lived. Now, if *The Thin Red Line* is evidence of his future, he has apparently decided to settle for being a very good writer among other good writers. The faults and barbarities of his style are gone. He is no longer the worst writer of prose ever to give intimations of greatness. The language has been filed down and the phrases no longer collide like trailer trucks at a hot intersection. Yet I found myself nostalgic for the old bad prose. I never used to think it was as bad as others did, it was eloquent and communicated Jones' force to the reader. It is not that *The Thin Red Line* is dishonest or narrow; on the contrary it is so broad and true a portrait of combat that it could be used as a textbook at the Infantry School if the Army is any less chicken than it used to be. But, sign of the times, there is now something almost too workman-like about Jones. He gets almost everything in, horror, fear, fatigue, the sport of combat, the hang-ups, details, tactics; he takes an infantry company through its early days in combat on Guadalcanal and quits it a few weeks later as a veteran outfit, blooded, tough, up on morale despite the loss of half the original men, gone, dead, wounded, sick or transferred. So he performs the virtuoso feat of letting us know a little about a hundred men. One can even (while reading) remember their names. Jones' aim, after all, is not to create character but the feel of combat, the psychology of men. He is close to a master at this. Jones has a strong sense of a man's psychology and it carries quietly through his pages.

*The Thin Red Line* was of course compared to *The Naked and the Dead*, but apart from the fact that I am the next-to-last man to judge the respective merits of the two books, I didn't see them as similar. *The Naked and the Dead* is concerned more with characters than military action. By comparison it's a leisurely performance. *The Thin Red Line* is as crammed as a movie treatment. No, I think the real comparison is to *The Red Badge of Courage*, and I suspect *The Red Badge of Courage* will outlive *The Thin Red Line*. Yet I don't quite know why. *The Thin Red Line* is a more detailed book; it tells much more of combat, studies the variations in courage and fear of not one man but twenty men and gets something good about each one of them. Its knowledge of life is superior to *The Red Badge of Courage*. *The Thin Red Line* is less sentimental, its humor is dry to the finest taste, and yet . . . it is too technical. One needs ten topographical maps to trace the action. With all its variety, scrupulosity, respect for craft, one doesn't remember *The Thin Red Line* with that same nostalgia, that same sense of a fire on the horizon which comes back always from *The Red Badge of Courage*.

No, Jones' book is better remembered as satisfying, as if one had studied geology for a semester and now knew more. I suppose what was felt lacking is the curious sensuousness of combat, the soft lift of awe and pleasure that one was moving out onto the rim of the dead. If one was not too tired, there were times when a blade of grass coming out of the ground before one's nose was as significant as the finger of Jehovah in the Sistine Chapel. And this was not because a blade of grass was necessarily in itself so beautiful, or because hitting the dirt was so sweet, but because the blade seemed to be a living part of the crack of small-arms fire and the palpable flotation of all the other souls in the platoon full of turd and glory. Now, it's not that Jones is altogether ignorant of this state. The description he uses is "sexy," and one of the nicest things about Jim as a writer is his ease in moving from mystical to practical reactions with his characters. Few novelists can do this, it's the hint of greatness, but I think he steered *The Thin Red Line* away from its chance of becoming an American classic of the first rank when he kept the mystical side of his talents on bread and water, and gave his usual thoroughgoing company man's exhibition of how much he knows technically about his product. I think that is the mistake. War is as full of handbooks as engineering, but it is more of a mystery, and the mystery is what separates the great war novels from the good ones. It is an

American activity to cover the ground quickly, but I guess this is one time Jones should have written two thousand pages, not four hundred ninety-five. But then the underlying passion in this book is not to go for broke, but to promise the vested idiots of the book reviews that he can write as good as anyone who writes a book review.—NORMAN MAILER, "Some Children at the Goddess" (1963), *Cannibals and Christians*, 1966, pp. 112–13

# JUNE JORDAN

## 1936–

June Jordan was born in New York on July 9, 1936. Her parents, who were immigrants from Jamaica, wanted their daughter to be a doctor and sent her to the Northfield School, an exclusive girls' school in Massachusetts. One of the few black students in her class, Jordan graduated in 1953 and entered Barnard that fall. Two years later she married a Columbia graduate student, Michael Meyer, and abandoned her own studies to take care of their son.

After moving with her husband to Chicago, Jordan returned to Harlem around 1960 and began working on Frederick Wiseman's film about life in the ghetto, *The Cool World*. Around this same time she became interested in city planning and met Buckminster Fuller, with whom she devised plans for the revitalization of Harlem. Her marriage ended in 1965 and she continued to work as a freelance journalist, writing poetry in her spare time. A long poem titled *Who Look at Me* was published in 1969. Two years later her first novel, *His Own Where*, was nominated for a National Book Award. Her other works include a collection of poetry, *Things That I Do in the Dark* (1977), and *Civil Wars*, a book of essays written over the past twenty years. In addition to her poetry and novels, she has worked on several children's books.

Since 1969 Jordan has held various teaching positions. She is currently a professor of English at the State University of New York at Stony Brook.

I could dig knowing Kenny and Jerome. They're a couple of black teen-agers having a rap about a show they want to put on at the Center. It's called *Dry Victories*, and that means, as Jerome explains, "*nothing-like-victory* be taking place, ever, during Reconstruction days or in them other days, the days of Civil Rights."

The "skinny"—the inside information—Kenny and Jerome exchange concerns some "parallels" between the promises made to black Americans after the Civil War, and again after the Supreme Court School Desegregation Decision in 1954. "It took place on the paper, Reconstruction . . . but you notice nobody saying a thing about rights to work, rights to solid dollar bills so you can pay the rent, or like land." And then later, "Civil Rights Era full of every right but the right to eat. Right to work." The skinny is that it all went wrong: "We all freedmen. We all in the same bad box. Black and white poor still be begging for bread on the street."

There's so much right about *Dry Victories*—the two characters, who are alive, funny, bitter, cool; the magnificent selection of photographs: slaves and cotton pickers, Congressmen and civil rights leaders, police clubs and hoses at Birmingham and a bombed church, a smiling Southern President and the casket of a Northern one, the whole pictorial history of three decades of hope, anguish, despair—that it's a shame the book isn't completely successful.

The fault here is that while the problems are stated clearly, the conclusions are hazy. Miss Jordan says voting isn't "where it's at"—that civil rights are meaningless without the "economic bases of freedom." Yet nowhere does she deal with the forces that have served to maintain, or at least permit poverty. For example, Reconstruction failed, not because President Grant was "bored," but because, as John Hope Franklin wrote, the South was taken over by Northern industrial interests, destroy-

ing chances for radical alternatives such as land reform and redistribution of wealth. The Poor People's Campaign didn't collapse because President Grant was "bored." It listens intently to those interests that support Right to Work laws and call social welfare socialism.

*Dry Victories* ends with the boys hoping that "parents and them other folk" will . . . "do something." But what has obstructed that "something," or what it should or could be, is never spelled out.—JANET HARRIS, *NYTBR*, Feb. 11, 1973, p. 8

June Jordan assembles *Some Changes* out of the black experience, and she does so coherently. Her expression is developed out of, or through, a fine irony that manages to control her bitterness, even to dominate her rage against the intolerable, so that she can laugh and cry, be melancholic and scornful and so on, presenting always the familiar faces of human personality, integral personality. She adapts her poems to the occasions that they are properly, using different voices, and levels of thought and diction that are humanly germane and not disembodied rages or vengeful shadows; thus she can create her world, that is, people it for us, for she has the singer's sense of the dramatic and projects herself into a poem to express its special subject, its individuality. Of course it's always her voice, because she has the skill to use it so variously: but the imagination it needs to run through all her changes is her talent. Moreover she seems not to have rejected on principle what has been available to poets in the way of models; in other words, you can see all the white poets she has read, too. She has been assimilating their usages of phrase and stanza; she sees with her own eyes through them, speaks them with her own voice, which is another way of remarking that she is interested in poetry itself. No matter how she will use her poems, and most of them are political in thrust, she has the great good sense, or taste, not to politicize her poetry. There is a difference, even in love poetry, nature poetry, and she has some of that sort, between speaking as yourself and editorializing for others. She is both simple and strong; she is clear in the head, besides. Her compassion and suffering for others is put into lyrical statement, and not into poems which are weapons. I can't shield myself against her, and have no wish to do so, let alone feel myself forced to deliver counter-blows, forced to feel gratuitous pain, gratuitous outrage. It may be because Jordan is a woman, that even her anger and despair are kept within the bounds of the humane, where poetry is too. That is the circle I draw round myself, though it is often broken into, or broken out of, as the case may be. ⟨. . .⟩ When June Jordan goes through her changes, she does it; she doesn't talk about doing it. For us there is pleasure in that, because we can go through them with her. And that means she has poetry near her.—JESCHA KESSLER, "Trial and Error," *Poetry*, Feb. 1973, pp. 301–3

1. *The Black Poem: It has to be somewhere . . . you can get to it . . .*

I've been asked to address some Black and White questions about Black poetry: ". . . how Black and White communities may communicate with each other beyond color lines, i.e. what aspects of the Black man's life are like that of the white man's, and vice versa . . ." *(not)* "physical resemblances or obvious human things." . . . *(but)* "what each of us has to contribute to one another . . . without violating the differences. . . ."

Well, I have studied the letter presenting these questions, a number of times; each reading provokes a mixture of puzzled, angry feelings: It seems misplaced: the burden of these inquiries: For one thing, I would not presume to tell white readers what they should look for, in Black Art. Nobody has held my hand, with respect to the white poetry I read and live with, and count upon, as ordinarily as I read the news.

For another thing, the questions point to a black-and-white reality I consider quite infuriating: white people/white editors of major/nationwide magazines and publishing houses simply do not read and do not value and do not publish what I will call The Black Poem. After the compensatory, commercial flares of Black appearance under white auspices, during the middle to late sixties, traditional, white attitudes towards distinctively Black work resumed a ruling prevalence: Black poetry was cancelled out—again. And if you think I overstate the case, I challenge you to tell me how often, within even the past 15 years, for example, you have seen a Black Poem published by *The New Republic, The N.Y. Times, The New Yorker, The New York Review of Books, New American Review, Harper's, The Atlantic*, Harper & Row, Farrar, Straus & Giroux, Doubleday, etc.

Let's be specific: although *The New Republic* regards itself as a political journal, when have you seen a political Black poem published there? Or, although *The N.Y. Times* regularly presents a full page review of one book of poems by one, white poet, how often have you seen a Black poet accorded comparable space and care? For that matter, when have you seen Black poetry, *per se*, reviewed in *The N.Y. Times Book Review/N.Y. Review of Books*, etcetera.

You may plead ignorance, or allude to an allegedly declining exclusion of Black poetry from general anthologies: That will not get over. The facts are these: Distinctively Black poetry continues to be written and perfected and (obscurely) available to a stunning, efflorescent degree, across the country; there is certainly no decrease in the dazzling abundance of terrific, wonderful, necessary Black poets writing this minute up and down. (Much of the most exciting, new Black poetry

that I know, comes to me, by mail, from *un*-published manuscripts.) *Nevertheless*, my white contemporary, the poet Mark Strand, for instance, has seen fit to issue an anthology of "American" poetry that includes not a single Black poet and, moreover, the overwhelming majority of major anthologies that title themselves Anthologies of American/English Language/Living/Great (and so forth) Poetry do *not* include Black poets, at all, let alone inclusion of a representative/proportional nature. At the least, this particular outrage cheats the reading public: misleads and deprives the willing, waiting reader of Black poems.

This reminds me of a few writing faculty meetings at Sarah Lawrence College where I teach these days: Last October, every Black poet I proposed as someone to invite for a campus reading turned out to be a Black poet that none of my white colleagues had ever heard of! Now, you can't have it both ways: you can't keep us out and then ease off that hook by suddenly discovering that we are not as conveniently nearby as your nearest bookstore, or college library, or usual, literary publications.

To find us, you should check out *Black World, Essence,* Broadside Press, Emerson Hall Publishing Company, Third Press, Third World Press, Jihad Publications, Barlenmir House Press, and like that. Or, perhaps, an occasional, defiantly dogged, university press will bring you, perhaps, Michael Harper, maybe, or a wayward, white publishing house will lapse into letting out a new book of Black poetry—or, probably not that so much as a book of poetry by a Black poet, if you can dig the difference.

To catch up with The Black Poem, as things stand today, as good a means as any is the creation of or location of Black poetry readings to which you just carry pencil and paper and, afterward, take down the vital information: name/address of publisher/price of book.

Obviously, this will not do: indeed, the plight of Black poetry is disgusting and destined to defy our utmost ingenuity/obduracy, if we will survive The Big, White, No.

A last word on this point, a word that expands the compass of my complaint, as it should expand: Yesterday, my son came home, talking as usual about his current, English course, entitled *The Contemporary, American Novel:* do you believe there was not a solitary Black novel on the list? Believe it.

To summarize so far: *Black poetry can bring nothing to anyone white or Black, unless it becomes available:* in readings, journals, and books across the board, on a first class basis. At the moment, the availability of Black poetry heavily depends upon whitepower which is, evidently, indifferent, at best.

2. *The Black Poem . . . Distinctively Speaking.*

What is it? Quite apart from individual volumes of Black poetry, I have learned that I hold decidedly different expectations of a Black Anthology, as compared to any other kind. If the single poem, or if the anthology qualifies as distinctively Black, then, as compared to a "white anthology" or a "white poem," I expect the following:

*A striving for collective voice, or else its actual, happy accomplishment. Even if the poem proceeds in the 1st person singular, I expect a distinctively Black poem to speak for *me*-as-part-of-an-*us*, a bounded group that the poem self-consciously assumes as an integral, guiding factor in her/his/their individual art.

*From a reaching for collective voice, as a self-conscious value, it follows that a distinctively Black poem will be accessible to random readers, rather than "hard," or arrantly inaccessible. (This does not mean that prolonged/repeated study will not yield new comprehension. But it does mean that the first time around, which may be an only time, the poem has to "hit" and "stick," clearly, and openly, in a welcoming way.)

\*Collective voice necessarily refers to spoken language: Distinctively Black poems characteristically deal memories and possibilities of spoken language, as against literary, or written, language. This partially accounts for the comparative *directness* and force of Black poetry; it is an intentionally collective, or *inclusive*, people's art meant to be shared, heard and, therefore, spoken—meant to be as real as bread.

\*Sound patterns, rhythmic movement and change-ups often figure as importantly as specific words, or images, in distinctively Black poetry. (Even if the poet says nothing especially new, I can expect to take pleasure in the musical, textural aspects of the poem; they will be as intrinsic to the work, as the words.)

To conclude this second point: Distinctively Black poetry adheres to certain, identifiable values—political and aesthetic—that are open to adoption, enjoyment by anyone. Overriding everything else is the striving and respect for collective voice. These distinctive values also constitute the main sum of what I look for, and prize, in The Black Poem.—JUNE JORDAN, "The Black Poet Speaks of Poetry," APR, May–June 1974, pp. 49–51

In the *American Poetry Review* issue for May/June 1974 there are a number of interesting contributions, not the least of which, to my biased mind, is June Jordan's "The Black Poet Speaks of Poetry." Her thesis is that "white people/white editors, of major/nationwide magazines and publishing houses simply do not read and do not value and do not publish what I would call The Black Poem." There follow citations of who those major/nationwide magazines are and lo, *The New Republic* leads all the rest: "Although *TNR* regards itself as a political journal, when have you seen a political Black poem published there?"

You will note that the black poem, in the course of a few sentences, has transmuted itself to something called the *political* black poem. When I wrote to her to point out the notice *TNR* has taken of black poets and writers, she made this distinction: "The kind of poetry I am referring to is Distinctly Black/Political poetry." Disclaiming my citations of Alice Walker, Sterling Brown, Barbara Smith, Michael Harper, Ishmael Reed, Ivan Webster as examples of writers whom *TNR* either has published, is about to publish, or has dealt with critically, she said none of them qualified under her stringent definition, which by now had acquired a new word, "Distinctly." She accused *TNR* of "having been offered, and has steadily refused to publish Distinctly Black/Political Poetry many times in the last several years" (capital letters are all hers). My response was that I had no way of knowing for certain from the ms. that the DBP poetry *was* black, or was by a black. So it was entirely possible that, for reasons other than racist, I or my predecessor *had* returned the poetry offered to us by DBP poets. Our correspondence went on in this fashion, she accusing me of "patronizing response" that is "so apparently the nature of your immediate reaction to criticism by Black People."

This drove me not so much to anger as to June Jordan's own poetry, the only DBP poet she cited in her letter as having been rejected by us. (I am constrained to add that when I wrote telling her the names of other noted poets—*white*—whose poems I had rejected she suggested we discontinue our correspondence because she could not read my handwriting.) Her newest book is called *New Days*, published in September

of this year by Emerson Hall publishers. It contains some very admirable poems, some very angry ones (clearly what she would call Political), but an even greater number that I would call love poems, or poems of exile and return in her words in which neither the color of the poet nor her politics are apparent. For example:

### SHORTSONG FROM MY HEART

Within our love the world
looks like a reasonable easy plan
the continents the ocean
are not harder/larger than the dreams
Our dreams
so readily embrace
and time is absolute newspace
beginning where you are
the sex of family and clear
far goal at once
beginning where you are
I am beginning to belong/befree
Let me be borne into the mystery
with you
Let me come home.

There are other very good ones, some I like somewhat less, though they are not necessarily the Distinctly Black Political ones, and a few I liked not at all, convincing me that *TNR* or the other media she accuses—*NY Times, New Yorker, NY Review of Books, American Review, Harper's, Atlantic,* and a number of publishing houses—may have rejected poets for a number of reasons besides racism, among them, the private esthetic of the literary editor, the poetic value of the submitted poem, the state of things at the publishing house at the moment (some publications, like ours, are stocked for a year or more with accepted poetry) and, God help us, space limitations.—DORIS GRUMBACH, "Fine Print," NR, Nov. 9, 1974, p. 44

To be in exile & be a poet is to be turned in on oneself / more than to be free of the trauma / there is a case that the whole nation of us who are Afrikan are in exile / here in this english-speakin place / but the collections of poems by june jordan ⟨*New Days*⟩ / & joseph jarman ⟨*Black Case*⟩ steer us away from a sense of dislocation / these are exiles returned / & more ourselves than many of us who stayed durin the holocausts & frenzy of sixties / illusions grow in newark & paris / wherever we have stepped outta cycle / outside ourselves / ⟨. . .⟩ aside from confrontin the vast disarray that is the contemporary world / circlin on itself / maybe swallowin us / loosin us in the momentum / less we do as jarman chants:

can you look at your black skin
your black self if you got one
and then do itit is
time
say do it yes
go sing
the sound the music it is *fire.*

& jordan incants:

YOUR BODY IS A LONG BLACK WING
YOUR BODY IS A LONG BLACK WING

we shall twist in dispair & distortion / in conceits & wrong information same as those jarman's ODAWALLA moved through 'the people of the Sun' teachin through 'the practice of the drum and silent gong' / or jordan's "Gettin Down to Get Over":

momma momma
teach me how to kiss
the king within the kingdom
teach how to t.c.b. / to make do
an be
like you
teach me to survive my
momma
teach me how to hold a new life
momma
help me
turn the face of history
*to your face*

movin back in on ourselves / to discover all that is there / is not lovely worth holdin / but necessary to know / what is real / who we are / jordan & jarman examine mercilessly their own dilemmas / which become / all of ours / cuz these are seekers / same as legendary initiates in other times / they have become familiar with dissolution & consciously re-constructed / a person / more in touch & sense lithe / determined as jordan in 'Fragments of a Parable' to undo what is untrue in herself:

Let me more than words: I would be more than medium or limestone. I would be more than looking more than knowing more than any of these less than looking less than knowing (words) On the dirt and stones between us was my hand that lay between us like another stone. Desire has no sound . . .
I have heard the rope in your throat ready to squeeze me into the syntax of stone
The sound of my life is a name you may not remember
I am losing the touch of the world to a word
*You must have said anything to me*

o we listen so close as she / who can be reached always / how to move thousands if we cannot first move our own self / & always there is between these two / jarman & jordan / an intertwinin of themes & dynamics / so one / the woman or the man / picks up from the other where the song / began to falter / or soar / to change voices on the same note / lose not texture or validity / to be able to give / up / share / the song / in joseph's words:

as if it were the seasons
the life flows on
we must let it be its self
flow on its own
it is self protected
by the self alone
it is song
canyou love it
can you see your own
made of love
as strong as song

is work / to sing / be / the song of our own self / shatter glass / lull infants / signal the motion / jarman & jordan have returned to us / returned so fulla themselves / so fulla our lives & love / we read these poems / as texts / for discoveries of our sequential dimensions / ourselves in space / we are in time & more able to reach for ourselves / as june jordan & joseph jarman allow us to reach out to them / not for an answer / for a rhythm of livin / how we are //—NTOZAKE SHANGE, *BlS*, March 1977, pp. 53–55

Passion as defined by Webster is "Emotion as distinguished from reason . . . affection . . . suffering . . . sexual desire." June Jordan's latest book of poems ⟨*Passions*⟩ deals with all of these emotions and a few more. It is a book that hurts sometimes because passion isn't always sweet. Yet it's necessary;

as necessary as realizing the amount of violence that exists right now in so many of our communities, as necessary as humor.

June has demonstrated her creativity so well in this new book, her ability to see beyond the surface and cause us to react. In "A Poem about Intelligence for My Brothers and Sisters" June confronts us with the limitations of intelligence, makes us think about the whole issue of being a genius; like who are they beyond their area of expertise, who can tolerate them personally and how did they get on the pedestal in the first place? She's talking about Einstein who didn't remember to wear socks and ". . . Never made nobody a cup of tea in his whole brilliant life."

Violence, particularly police violence is a theme that June deals with a lot in this book. Having recently completed a play, *Issue*, about police violence in the black community, she seems committed to generating alternatives to this genocidal trend.

Tell me something
what you think would happen if
everytime they kill a black boy
then we kill a cop
everytime they kill a black man
then we kill a cop
you think the accident rate would lower subsequently?
                              ("Poem about Police Violence")

In "Poem about My Rights" a powerful statement is being made about oppressive conditions placed on us . . . by ourselves and our families sometimes but mostly by outside forces like America and its C.I.A., Exxon, South Africa = racism. Searching for identity and truth under these conditions is, in the least, a struggle. June talks about being raped by a systemic oppressive force so powerful . . . so powerful!

I am the history of the rejection of who I am
I am the history of the terrorized incarceration of my self . . .
I have been the problem everyone seeks to eliminate . . .

Then the poet gets some clarity, gathers her strength and rebels.

. . . I am not wrong: wrong is not my name
my name is my own my own my own
and I can't tell you who the hell set things up like this
but I can tell you that from now on my resistance
my simple and daily and nightly self determination
may very well cost you your life.
                              ("Poem about My Rights")

⟨. . .⟩ In the preface June celebrates a connection with Walt Whitman, calling him one of the "New World Poets", a poet who had the courage to speak out on issues not necessarily popular at the time. It is about taking risks. Something all writers are familiar with. It is what she's done in this collection of passions, taken a few risks, uncovered some fears and shared some further depths . . . of her thoughts . . . her world . . . and ours.—MILDRED THOMPSON, *BlS*, Jan. 1981, p. 96

A recent release from the National Coalition Against Censorship reported that two poems, Allen Ginsburg's *Howl!* and June Jordan's "Getting Down to Get Over," have been effaced from an anthology used in the high school of Gretna, Va. The release cited similar efforts in other communities, which is not surprising, given the mood of the country. If the Parent-Teacher Association of Gretna objected to the corrupting influence of those two poems, then the town should be warned against June Jordan's *Civil Wars*, a book of thorough and unwavering radicalism.

*Civil Wars* is a collection of essays, lectures and letters, concerned with the dramatic upheavals of the 60's and the still pressing problems of racism, sexism, police violence. Arranged chronologically, taking in two decades, the articles form a kind of autobiography of thought and feeling, the story of one individual's activism and search for community. June Jordan is a poet, a woman, a black, and these things define the issues that engage her. "In 1960, I was a very young twenty-four-year-old, interracially married, the mother of a two-year-old son, and living in the housing projects in Queens," she writes. "At the time, interracial marriage was a felony in 43 states, but in the projects, our many neighbors wondered only if my husband and I had secured parental consent for the relationship we were, evidently, carrying on." The essays are personal as well as political, though June Jordan would argue that there is no real distinction.

*Civil Wars* is the record of a strenuous, complicated journey. It includes an indictment of ghetto schools, a remembrance of writing workshop for minority teen-agers, a conversation with a young man on the Harlem set of a film ("Q. What's school like? A. Boring."), a "position paper" in favor of black studies, a discussion of the implications of the DeFurns case (the "reverse discrimination" predecessor to the Bakke case) and affirmative action, the frustrations and satisfactions of teaching, reflections on her disillusionment as a student at Barnard College. Very little is forgotten and much is forgiven as June Jordan travels from one subject to another. Themes recur inextricably linked: in the way a locomotive speedily pulls the rest of the train into view, the question of education brings forth other matters of trying to survive in a hostile society. "The white problem," she writes, "will never be solved as long as American Black life is an imagining, a TV spectacular." Whether her target is William Shockley and his theories of racial superiority or the misguided efforts of journalists or the sad malice of bigotry, Jordan is volatile in her criticism but never shrill as she contemplates the pernicious distortions of what Jacobo Timerman calls "semantic adventurers."

Many of her opinions are provocative. Her poetry and her interpretations of literary texts are informed by her experiences as a black woman. She notes the political character of Shelley's *Queen Mab*, speculates on the reasons for the obscurity of Zora Neale Hurston and the canonization of Richard Wright, reviews the poetry of the Angolan revolutionaries, Antonio Jacinto and Agostinho Neto. A blistering attack is launched on Conrad's *Heart of Darkness*. Jordan, like Chinua Achebe, thinks *Heart of Darkness* is disfigured by racist mythology. V. S. Naipaul, perhaps, would disagree. It may be that a writer cannot live outside his historical moment. June Jordan defends "Black English: "Language is political." Sentences such as "'You are forgotten you existed!'" cannot be translated into standard speech without violating a quality that is central to black culture.

June Jordan recalls vividly the nightmare of the Harlem riot of 1964: "Bullets were flying past the booth and all about me. . . . Women had begun to scream, simply scream and not move." She offers impressions of Malcolm X and Fannie Lou Hamer, is skeptical of conventional black leadership, and ponders the value of nonviolence as she records a murder in Mississippi, the attack on a black youth in a Hasidic neighborhood, the circumstances of police killings of blacks in Brooklyn. Trouble and outrage are unending; if it is not Vietnam, it is famine in Africa, until she appreciates the thorough disgust she found extolled in William Hazlitt's "The Pleasures of Hating."

"A week after the riot, my husband wrote saying he was not coming back," she writes. Miss Jordan considers at length the importance and trials of feminism for black women. She prefers to think of feminism as an inseparable part of a worldwide struggle against all forms of domination, and hence she criticizes the narrow concentration of some feminists. Throughout, she writes of her determination to resist the temptation to hate. "Is there, in fact, somebody else alive, besides each one of us? Is there some way to prove that there is somebody else alive, without violence?" she asks. She attempts to find solutions to the problems that capture her imagination, collaborating with Buckminster Fuller on a plan to redesign Harlem, developing a manual for land reform in Mississippi. Rage leads her to applaud the recent disturbances in Miami, but always she seeks to temper her anger with a measure of determined optimism and, as she calls it, love. That is a word she does not shrink from using, at the risk of seeming sentimental or propagandistic, which is valiant in an era as cynical as ours.

*Passion* is an appropriate title for this gathering of 51 new poems. Miss Jordan, in the preface, calls for a "people's poetry," hailing Walt Whitman and Pablo Neruda as notable examples. It is impossible to accept her charge that there is a "vendetta" against Whitman in America. Even before recent scholarly work that sympathetically discusses the homoerotic in Whitman's sensibility, there was Randall Jarrell's important essay. It is also difficult to understand why the quest for a "New World" poetry must entail the rejection of T. S. Eliot, Robert Lowell, Wallace Stevens or Elizabeth Bishop, four of the finest poets in the language. There is no contradiction in admiring *The Waste Land* as well as lyrics from the streets. One can learn from any tradition.

The poems in *Passion*, mostly in free verse, share many of the themes of the essays. These poems are confidently within an oral tradition, and although the oral can often mean the merely rhetorical, Miss Jordan serves the tradition well, with a sensitive ear for the vernacular, for the ironic tone,

> I remember finding you inside the laundromat
> in Ruleville
> lion spine relaxed/hell
> what's the point to courage
> when you washin clothes?

Her poems are striking in their immediacy,

> Our own shadows disappear as the feet of thousands
> by the tens of thousands pound the fallow land
> into new dust that
> rising like a marvelous pollen will be
> fertile

Sometimes there is stinging clarity,

> My name is my own my own my own
> and I can't tell you who the hell set things up like this
> but I can tell you that from now on my resistance
> my simple and daily and nightly self-determination
> may very well cost you your life

There are, of course, happier moments,

> Wanting to stomp down Eighth Avenue snow
> or no snow where you might be so we
> can takeover the evening by taxi
> by kerosene lamp by literal cups of tea

The energy and seriousness of these poems are impressive and, like the essays, they are the work of a writer of integrity and will.—DARRYL PINCKNEY, "Opinions and Poems," *NYTBR*, Aug. 9, 1981, pp. 8, 26

JAMES JONES

ROBINSON JEFFERS

RANDALL JARRELL

GEORGE S. KAUFMAN

WILLIAM KENNEDY

X. J. KENNEDY

KEN KESEY

JACK KEROUAC

# GEORGE S. KAUFMAN

## 1889–1961

George Kaufman was born on November 16, 1889, in Pittsburgh, Pennsylvania. The son of Jewish immigrants, Kaufman led a sheltered life as a child. The death of his parents' first son caused them to be overly protective with George. As a result, later in life Kaufman carried with him an enormous fear of death and a phobia about touching supposedly germ-ridden individuals. Kaufman lasted only three months at law school and afterwards took a series of odd jobs, including work with a surveying team in West Virginia, a clerical position in Pittsburgh, and a sales job with a ribbon company in New Jersey. While living in New Jersey Kaufman often contributed pieces to Franklin P. Adams's "Always in Good Humor" column. Eventually Adams procured newspaper jobs for the young Kaufman, first in Washington and then back in New York. By 1917 Kaufman was drama editor for the *New York Times*, a post he held until 1930. Kaufman's journalistic prose is noted for its short, snappy wit.

While working at the *Times* Kaufman began to associate with the Algonquin Round Table. By 1920 he was working on various Broadway productions. Kaufman collaborated with numerous playwrights, including Marc Connelly, Edna Ferber, Moss Hart, Ring Lardner, Howard Teichmann, and Alexander Woollcott. Kaufman won Pulitzer Prizes for *Of Thee I Sing* (1932), written with Morrie Ryskind, and *You Can't Take It with You* (1937), written with Moss Hart. Kaufman later won the 1951 Tony Award for Best Director for his production of *Guys and Dolls*. In total Kaufman worked on forty-five Broadway shows as well as several movies. *A Night at the Opera* (1935), which starred the Marx Brothers, was one of Kaufman's most successful Hollywood endeavors. Kaufman claimed to have modeled his wit after Mark Twain.

On June 2, 1961, Kaufman died of a heart attack in his New York apartment.

## Personal

In the bemused minds of the laity, there used to be occasional evidence of a tendency to confuse George S. Kaufman, the blissfully unconscious subject of this memoir, with S. Jay Kaufman, an erstwhile journalist at present without portfolio. It was the latter Kaufman who helpfully suggested an ingenious key to unlock the confusion. He himself could be identified as the *kind* Kaufman.

With that point nicely cleared up, there remains for the present historian only to instruct the layman how to tell the unkind Kaufman from Zoë Atkins, Eugene O'Neill, Channing Pollock, and others of his contemporaries, among the playwrights of today. Given a few hints (as you certainly will be in these brief biographical notes), you will be able to distinguish him from the others almost at a glance. Thus, it is neither Brother Pollock nor Sister Atkins who seldom writes a play without a collaborator; who, rather than let a fresh vegetable soil his lips, subsists on a severe diet of meat, bread and chocolate peppermints; who, in the laboratory work any dramatist must do, limits his studies of human nature and the American scene as far as possible to the moments when he is dummy at the New York Bridge Club; who, while walking hatless and alone a-down our avenues, talks continuously to himself in what appears to terrified passersby as a low, confidential snarl; and who, during the seven or eight years in which he has been one the most competent, fertile, and successfully productive of American playwrights, has hung on with puzzling tenacity to the same newspaper job with which he was, by a narrow margin, keeping body and soul apart when his first play was accepted for production. There is Mr. Kaufman for you in a nutshell. ⟨. . .⟩

If he has stuck to this post all these years, it was partly because it fitted in with his passionate preference for life in Times Square over all other garden spots on earth, and partly because he found it no mean social and domestic convenience to be able to rise each evening at eleven and walk out of then most tenacious situation with a plausible explanation that he had to go to the office. Then he had, it is true, gradually fixed it so the job involved practically no work at all.

As a rule, publishers and editors have all manner of difficulties as soon as any of their departmental heads becomes financially interested in the field of his department. Thus the usefulness of a Wall Street reporter is considerably impaired the moment he opens a brokerage account, and a dramatic editor with his finger in a half-dozen theatrical ventures is regarded as something of a problem. Mr. Kaufman has walked this difficult way with such unerring taste and such fanatical fairness, however, that the only considerable outcries of the wounded to reach the alert ears of the *Times* have come not from the theatrical managements in which he was not interested but from those in which he was. For instance, in the days when he was George Tyler's favorite playwright, that wrathy impresario used to complain to High Heaven and Louis Wiley that the *Times* was the only paper into which he could not squeeze any publicity of a Sunday.

Kaufman's earlier plays included *Someone in the House*, *Dulcy*, *Merton of the Movies*, *The Deep Tangled Wildwood*, *Beggar on Horseback*, and the libretto of a musical show called *Be Yourself*. The first-named was a comparative failure, repair work on which was attempted by three hands, one of them Kaufman's. The next six, four of them conspiciously successful, were written in felicitious collaboration with Marc Connelly. When these partners separated it was popularly assumed that each wished to demonstrate to the other, and more probably to himself, that he could write a play alone. Kaufman demonstrated it with The *Butter and Egg Man*, and Connelly, even more emphatically, I think, with *The Wisdom Tooth*. Also on his own Kaufman wrote the book for *The Cocoanuts*, and, with Morris Ryskind, the book for *Animal Crackers*, both of them vehicles for the Marx brothers, who, though inclined to get out of any vehicle and carry it instead, remain addicted to Kaufman as their favorite author, if they must have one. ⟨. . .⟩

About this chronic collaborator have grown up several legends. You will hear it said of him that he is almost deranged by pessimistic apprehension on his own first nights; that he is a wag of the first water; and that, while really a good and gentle creature at heart, he is curiously ungracious and snorty toward underlings such as office-boys, soda-clerks, waiters, taxi-drivers, and—God help me—telephone-girls. There is this to be said about these popular notions of Kaufman. They are all quite correct.

Taking up these points *seriatim*, let us first consider the ghastly picture of despair that Kaufman presents at the premiere of every play of his. Pale, distraught, he weaves about the balcony, and is occasionally so afflicted that angry drama-lovers have been compelled to rebuke him for getting up in the middle of a scene to take a long, frantic ramble in the aisle. On the uproarious first night of *Dulcy* in Chicago, the more rational and frankly delighted Connelly went backstage after Act Two, only to find Kaufman on the point of self-slaughter behind a bit of scenery. Then I have not often heard more genuine laughter in the theatre than that which burst the seams of the Longacre at the premiere of *The Butter and Egg Man*. In the seat next to me, Charlie Chaplin laughed so helplessly and so loudly that I was embarrassed, and tried to look as though he were a distasteful stranger who had not come with me at all. Around Gregory Kelly, after the final curtain, a great swarm of congratulatory admirers billowed and tossed. He worked his way clear at last, to find Kaufman crushed against a wall, and looking a little like the late Marie Antoinette in the tumbril. The wretched creature surrendered a chill, moist hand to Kelly.

"Well," he said, "we did our best. It isn't our fault if they didn't like it." And went home, convinced that the play was a disaster. It lived for two seasons.—ALEXANDER WOOLLCOTT, "The Deep, Tangled Kaufman," NY, May 18, 1929, pp. 26–29

He was, to me, already a legendary figure. As a high-school boy, I had been entranced by *Dulcy* and *To the Ladies*; I had made my long-suffering family take the *Morning World* instead of the *American* so that I might follow his all-too-few-and-far-between contributions to F. P. A.'s column, while the Sunday drama section of the *Times*, of which he was then editor, became a weekly religious ritual. By the time I had seen *Merton of the Movies* and *Beggar on Horseback*, I had developed one all-consuming ambition—to write plays in the Kaufman tradition.

I may say that it was while I sat in the gallery of the Broadhurst Theatre, drinking in a performance of *June Moon* that the idea of *Once in a Lifetime* struck me—if that is the word one uses for those creative occasions. As a matter of fact, I started the first act that night on my return from the theatre and three weeks later saw the play finished. I dimly realized that what it lacked in technique it perhaps made up in freshness of approach, and while I was not altogether unhopeful of its ultimate sale, I truly believe that it was basically written for the sole purpose of procuring an interview with George Kaufman. That he would like it well enough to collaborate, I don't believe ever crossed my mind. In some childlike fashion I considered it as a letter of introduction that might serve in some way to procure that precious interview. At best, I had fond hopes of some obscure position as second stage manager with a play of his, if it aroused his interest sufficiently.

When I received word that he had read the play, and not only liked it but definitely wanted to collaborate on the revisions, I suppose my excitement was a little unearthly, so that I entered the office for that first meeting wide-eyed with hero worship and drunk with my own perfume.

It was only later that I discovered he shied at the slightest display of emotion as most men flee from smallpox and when I recall that my performance that afternoon was mildly reminiscent of Lillian Gish in *The White Sister*, I can understand a little better the sharpness of his tone and the brevity of the interview. I left the office, however, mad with power, for I had not only met George S. Kaufman, but we were to start work the very next day. I recall also that my father and mother were not a little startled, on my return, to find me talking in strange, clipped accents, addressing my bewildered brother as "Mr. H.," and my shocked aunt as "The Old Lady from Dubuque." I was, of course, already talking like George Kaufman, and for some two months after that my dismayed friends and family suffered from the curious combination of what they knew to be a rank sentimentalist talking in terms of a rabid Algonquinite. It was a difficult time, I imagine, for that particular section of Brooklyn known as Flatbush.

At any rate, I reported for work the next morning, stupidly innocent and blissfully eager, and there began what I now fondly call "The Days of the Terror." Our working day consisted of ten o'clock in the morning until exhausted—somewhere, perhaps, around one or two o'clock the next morning—with perhaps fifteen minutes out for such meals as Mr. Kaufman considered necessary to keep alive. Since he cared nothing for food, I found myself, at the end of the day, not only exhausted but starved as well.

Also, to add to my growing alarm, work proceeded at what I considered a maddeningly slow pace. Two hours would be spent sometimes in shaping one short sentence into a mosaic-like correctness. A whole day would pass in merely discussing an exit. If I had had visions of an early production, I was to learn the fitness of that time-worn phrase, "Plays are not written, but rewritten." And the rewriting process under the guidance of the eagle-eyed Mr. Kaufman slowly formulated itself in my mind as a combination of the Spanish Inquisition and the bloodiest portions of the First World War.

I was to discover, also, that a series of personal idiosyncrasies on the part of Mr. Kaufman were as much a part of the actual working day as sitting at the typewriter, and I came to watch for them much as one watches a steadily falling barometer on a rough day at sea.

I was to learn, for instance, that a slow and careful picking of lint from the carpet was invariably the forerunner of the emergence of a good line. I was to learn that Mr. Kaufman's lanky form stretched full-length on the floor for long periods at a time meant trouble. And I came to know that what Mr. Kaufman needed much more than fresh air and food was the immediate necessity to remove his shoes and to pace madly before he could even think of working. Shoelaces drove him crazy and so, I discovered much later on, did my cigar smoking; but since he never complained I puffed contentedly on, not quite realizing that a major portion of his pacing was a frantic effort to elude the blue clouds of smoke with which I filled the room. Moreover, since the room we worked in didn't provide enough pacing space for two, I was the one who sat stiffly for long hours in an overstuffed chair while I watched Mr. Kaufman perform gymnastics that would make *The Man on the Flying Trapeze* turn green with envy.

With "Curtain" finally typed—we had begun in December and it was now June—I heaved a breathless sigh of relief, but the relief was short-lived. Rehearsals, to which I had looked forward with such eagerness, were a trifle marred by the fact that what had seemed so right at the typewriter seemed suddenly so wrong on the stage. And it became the regulation thing, as rehearsals proceeded, to sit up most of the night rewriting and to appear at rehearsals fresh and bright at ten o'clock the next morning.

The dress rehearsal I remember only as an unpleasant nightmare. The train ride to Atlantic City I remember not at all, and the opening I have been living down quietly ever since. I am, I suppose, notorious for the way I behave on the opening night of any play of mine, and this first play was no exception. The fact that I am unable to retain food of any kind for at least three days before an opening is unpleasant enough, but the horrible fact that I am compelled to spend most of the opening night in the men's room of the theatre, unable to witness the performance at all, has always been the sore spot in my career as a writer. I emerged long enough, however, to catch fleeting glimpses of Mr. Kaufman on the stage. He was, you may remember, Lawrence Vail, the playwright, in *Once in a Lifetime*, and the greenish pallor of his face sent me scurrying back to my retreat as fast as I could go.

It was not an auspicious opening. Mr. Kaufman had told me—I may say that I still called him Mr. Kaufman in those days—that his experience with Sam Harris had taught him that if Sam Harris liked a play, he remained for the full week of its tryout in Atlantic City. If he didn't like the play, he said nothing but quietly slipped out of town the next morning. I waited then, not so much for the reviews in the Atlantic City papers, but to see if Mr. Harris still remained in town. He didn't. I learned, to my horror, that he had not even waited until the next morning. He had left at eleven-thirty that night, leaving only a message in our box which said, "It needs work, boys," which sentence I have since had engraved as the largest understatement since the spring of 1910.

We played out the week in Atlantic City, and another week at Brighton Beach. There was obviously so much work to be done, the play was so unwieldy, so cumbersome, so filled with actors, scenery and costumes, that the only possible thing to do was to close it and get back to a typewriter as fast as we could. That was the tenth of July. There followed, then, the longest, hottest, most exhausting summer I have spent or ever hope to spend. Mr. Kaufman, in the face of disaster, seemed suddenly to come to life. If I had thought that our working sessions were tough before, it seemed to me now that I had wandered into a concentration camp, and an eraser took on all the semblance of a rubber truncheon. This time, Mr. Kaufman forgot entirely about food. He paced two rooms instead of one. There were days at a time when we never left the house. And I remember reflecting bitterly that if this were what the theatre was like, I had sooner be a good insurance agent. Because, in my dim-witted way, I began to realize that this was but the beginning. And I was right.

For the second production, rehearsals took on a new ghastliness. I was depressed by the fact that Mrs. Kaufman, for whose critical judgment I had come to have an enormous respect, liked the new third act not at all and by the time the Philadelphia opening rolled around, a numbness had crept into my bones which I thought nothing, not even the biggest hit in the world, would assuage.

There was a large contingent of New Yorkers who came down for the opening, and I remember my panic when I saw them leave in the middle of the third act. It meant only one thing to me: dire failure. I didn't realize that they *had* to leave, whether they liked it or not, to catch the midnight back to New York, and since we had only reached the middle of the third act by midnight, it will be noted by even the least theatrically wise person that our play was a shade too long.

And then came the dawn. Only we never saw the dawn, nor the day, nor the night either. For in the next six days I never left my room at the hotel. Mr. Kaufman had to leave because he was acting in the play, but his schedule, and I still cannot realize how he managed to do it, ran something like this: he returned from the theatre at eleven thirty. We worked steadily through the night until ten o'clock the next morning. He would then leave to put the new stuff into rehearsal and rehearse until two. Then, while the actors learned the new lines for the evening's performance, he would return to my room at the hotel and work until eight-thirty; then back to the theatre for the performance; then back to my room again to work all night until ten o'clock the next morning.

I may add, resentfully, that he seemed to blossom through all this; that his eyes sparkled with an unwonted brightness; that his hand holding a pencil was like a surgeon's hand holding a scalpel. I may also add that one three o'clock in the morning, strolling out for a breath of fresh air, which I insisted upon, we came upon a children's carrousel in some little public playground, and it was there I discovered the marshmallow heart. Instinctively, we both made for the carrousel, and for half an hour, in the ghostly light of a Philadelphia dawn, we swung madly around on it. Whether, by this time, I was growing less frightened of him, ⟨. . .⟩ I do not know; but his essential kindliness, his great good humor, the curious kind of nobility which he possesses more than any other man I know, had given me a fondness for him that enveloped my original timidity. And I found by the closing night in Philadelphia that while he still remained my hero, he was a hero I could talk to comfortably.

The night before the New York opening, the night of the final dress rehearsal at the Music Box, he unbent sufficiently to smile and say, "Don't worry too much. It's been swell anyway. And let's do another one." So that I didn't care particularly whether the play went well the next night or not. It had been pretty fine, at that. And as you can see by this book, we married and had several beautiful children.—Moss HART, "Men at Work," *Six Plays*, 1942

For some time now, I have suspected the existence of an organization whose scope and energies are so enormous that they stagger the imagination. I am not prepared to say with certainty that such an organization exists, but there are various recurrent phenomena in my life that can be explained only by the theory that a major plan is in operation—a plan so vast and expensive that it is almost impossible to envision it.

The organization that carries out this plan must spend millions of dollars annually to achieve its object. It has—it must have—great suites of offices, and thousands upon thousands of employees. On a guess, I would put its running cost at ten million dollars a year; if anything, the figure may be higher. With some presumption, I have christened it Annoy Kaufman, Inc., though I will admit that I cannot find that title in any lists of corporations.

But the facts are incontrovertible:

First there is the matter of going to the bank. Let us say that I have run out of money and am required to cash a small check. Now, no one knows that I am going to the bank on that particular morning. There is nothing about it in the papers. I am not immodest, and I know that, at best, such an announcement would get only a few lines on a back page: "George S. Kaufman is going to the bank this morning to cash a check. We wish him success"—something like that.

But not a word is printed. No one knows about it. As a matter of fact, I have probably not made up my mind to go until about eleven o'clock. Yet the organization is prepared. It immediately arranges that half a dozen big companies should be drawing their payroll money that morning, and that each of them should send a clerk to the bank with a list of payroll requirements—so many five-dollar bills, so many dollar bills, so many quarters, dimes, nickels, pennies. Next it is arranged that all these people should get to the tellers' windows just a few seconds ahead of me.

Now, this takes doing. Remember, the organization has not known just which morning I was planning to go to the bank, so for weeks and weeks these clerks have been held in readiness somewhere. And suppose I stop to talk to a friend and arrive five minutes later than expected. Obviously, several relays of clerks must be kept in reserve in a corner of the bank, awaiting a signal.

Moreover, these are not people who are just pretending to be cashing payrolls; the bank would never stand for that. No, they are people from real companies—companies founded by the organization and kept in business for years and years, probably at an enormous loss, just so that their representatives can get to the bank windows ahead of me. And it is not always the same people who stand in front of me; it is different ones. This, in turn, means a large number of separate companies to maintain. These companies run factories, keep books, pay income taxes, hold board meetings, advertise on television, pension their employees. Surely this side of the enterprise alone must run to a pretty figure.

My next example may sound like a simple and inexpensive thing to manage, but it isn't. It has to do with the engineer's little boy, Danny. Danny is six years old. In fact, he has been six years for the thirty-five years that I have been making overnight train journeys. (I suppose that, actually, they keep on having an engineer's little boy born every year, but even that takes planning.) Anyhow, for years and years Danny has been begging his father to let him run the locomotive some night. For years and years, his father has been saying no. Then, finally, the night comes. "Can I run the engine tonight, Daddy?" asks Danny, who is too young to know about "can" and "may." And his father says, "Yes, Danny, boy. We have just got word that Kaufman will be on the train tonight, and he is very tired and needs a good night's sleep, so you can run the engine." So Danny runs the engine, the result being the neckbreaking stops and starts that keep me awake all night.

The organization has, of course, the incidental expense of maintaining Danny in Chicago or Pittsburgh or Cleveland, as the case may be, until I am ready to make the return trip. (Danny's father obviously cannot wait over to take care of him; he must go back to running the engine properly on the nights when I am not travelling.) So the organization must keep branch offices in Chicago and Pittsburgh and Cleveland (and wherever else I may go), and provide someone else to take care of Danny, and schools for him to go to, and somebody to make sure that he doesn't practice, and so learn how to run the engine better, before I make my return trip. This seemingly small part of the business can run to fantastic sums over the years.

But the bank and Danny are, after all, relatively minor matters. Once done with, they are over till the next time. I come now to the major opus—the basic activity for which Annoy Kaufman, Inc., was founded.

Years ago, when I moved to New York, I noticed that a little man in a gray overcoat was watching me closely as I took the ferry from Jersey City to Twenty-third Street. I don't know why, but I think his name was Mr. Moffat. At all events, Mr. Moffat was the first person off the ferryboat when it docked. Hurriedly joining his pals in a midtown office, Mr. Moffat reported as follows: "Boys, he's here. We can take out

incorporation papers in Albany tomorrow and go to work. In a day or two, I'll have all the dope for you."

Now you may think it arrogant of me to claim that the entire rebuilding of New York City, at present in full bloom, came about solely as a result of my arrival here, but I can only cite the facts. No sooner did I move to a given neighborhood than the wreckers were at work on the adjoining building, generally at eight o'clock in the morning. The pneumatic asphalt-ripper, with which we are all now familiar, was first used early one morning as a weapon against the slumber of none other than myself. The first automatic rivet came into existence to be the destroyer of my sleep. (All dates and names of streets are on file in the office of my attorney.) Naturally, I kept moving to new neighborhoods in quest of peace, but the boys were always ready and waiting. Can you blame me for feeling that it was I, and I alone, who unwittingly charted the course of the city's onward sweep?

Only once, in all these years, did they slip up. Acting without sufficient research, they put up Lever House just to the south of me, unaware that my bedroom was on the other side of my apartment. Discovering their error, they, of course, bought the property to the north and went quickly to work. Well, sir, heads rolled in the office that morning, I can tell you. Mr. Moffat, I like to think, shot himself, but I suspect he was immediately succeeded by his son, and since then the organization has functioned so efficiently that I am now exactly thirty-seven years behind on sleep, with only an outside chance of making it up.

With all that on their hands, you wouldn't think they'd have time for Congressional lobbying, too, would you? This ultimate move came to light during a visit of mine to Washington a few weeks ago. Having been made suspicious, over the years, by my dealings with the Internal Revenue people, I went to the trouble of looking up the original text of the income-tax law, as filed in the Library of Congress. Sure enough, there it was—Paragraph D, Clause 18—just as I had suspected: "The taxpayer, in computing the amount of tax due to the Government, may deduct from his taxable income all legitimate expenses incurred in the course of conducting his business or profession—except," it added, "in the case of George S. Kaufman."—GEORGE S. KAUFMAN, "Annoy Kaufman, Inc.," NY, Dec. 21, 1957, pp. 25–26

Kaufman's timing was always perfect. Groucho speaks of it, Jack Benny speaks of it, as do others.

Leonora Corbett was the subject of a classic Kaufman line. The first time he saw her, following the end of a romantic interlude between them, an elevator door opened, and Miss Corbett emerged followed by her latest suitor. Before her stood Kaufman waiting to enter the elevator.

Without batting an artificial eyelash, she introduced the two gentlemen, adding, "Mr. So-and-So is in cotton."

Kaufman peered over the rims of his glasses at the gentleman who was in cotton, then turned his attention to Miss Corbett saying, "And them that plants it is soon forgotten."

The elevator door was still inviting. Kaufman stepped into the car, the door closed, and so did Miss Corbett's open mouth. ⟨. . .⟩

Oddly enough, despite all he wrote and said, he was not a talker. He was, if anything, an intense listener. What was unique about Kaufman as a wit were his great stretches of silence.

Generally, comics are compulsive. Once they get the floor, they fight furiously before giving it up. Kaufman was the direct opposite of this. He would sit and listen to those about him for half an hour or even longer. Then, when the right moment came, he would drop in a single line that would sound like a bell note in the clatter of random chatter. Or, if he did speak, it would be only a few words, just enough to set up the talk as a target. Then he would draw, aim, and fire. He would sit through an entire evening and say five sentences. Yet people would go away vowing that he was the funniest man alive.—HOWARD TEICHMANN, "The Wit," *George S. Kaufman: An Intimate Portrait*, 1972, pp. 128, 152

It was a bridge game, incidentally, which enabled Kaufman to bring forth one of his most famous lines. It occurred when he was teamed with Herman Mankiewicz, and he watched in horror as Mankiewicz played one of the dumbest games he'd ever seen in his life. He finally exploded. "I know you learned the game this afternoon," he said. "But what *time* this afternoon?"

Kaufman was equally caustic with another poor player. His partner could tell from Kaufman's glower that he was not pleased. Defensively, he said, "Okay, George, how would *you* have played that hand?" "Under an assumed name," Kaufman said.—SCOTT MEREDITH, "The Games," *George S. Kaufman and His Friends*, 1974, p. 176

## Works

George S. Kaufman and Marc Connelly, whose delectable comedies *Dulcy* and *To the Ladies* struck one more through their reserve than through any expression of ironic vision, have let themselves go at last. To keep the mood of laughter vivid at every moment, however, they have fitted their extraordinarily inclusive and biting satire of the life about them into an imaginative framework that was ready to their hand. This framework was afforded them by Paul Apel's rich and delightful work *Hans Sonnenstössers Höllenfahrt* which, being interpreted, means *Johnny Sunstormer's Trip to Hell*. In Apel's play, as in *Beggar on Horseback* (Broadhurst Theater), an idealistic young artist is tempted, in order to escape the curse of hackwork and save his creative powers, to marry into a family of the grossest Philistines. There, as here, he falls asleep and dreams that he has yielded to the temptation, and the play consists of the humorous and ironic exhausting of the resultant situation. Nothing could have been done by a direct use of Apel's text, since the German *Philister*, though own blood-brother to the American Babbitt, differs from the latter very radically in both mentality and manner. Thus Messrs. Kaufman and Connelly hit upon the happy notion of keeping Apel's scheme, imitating the scientific verisimilitude of his dream-technique, but making the satiric substance of the play entirely and perfectly American. The result is a dramatic work which, though wholly imitative in structure and method, is as wholly original in creative substance.

It is this substance that is both delightful and valuable. I doubt whether any of our professed realists of the theater have painted American life with such unerring strokes. Here, furthermore, as in *The Adding-Machine*, the technique permitted speed and concentration, so that the picture is a wonderfully inclusive one and there is hardly a species of "bunk" that is not both accurately and hilariously exhibited. The Cady family reach a kind of greatness. Of course, we are dealing with satire and the figures are stripped of all but the essentials. These essentials, however, have been selected both with satiric insight and with scientific delicacy and precision, and Mr. and Mrs. Cady are portraits not unworthy of Hogarth. On an equally high plane are the satiric inventions by which the authors illustrate the scene and ethos on which their eyes are fixed. Chief amid these inventions are the factory for the efficient mass-production of literature, poetry, music, and the

Freudian yet highly realistic dream trial scene. Throughout the delineation of these characters and the invention of these scenes the American idiom is used with a blending of actuality with symbolic driving force that is, I believe, unequaled elsewhere.

Finally I wish to praise the authors of *Beggar on Horseback* most heartily for this, that they laugh at fatuousness and gross materialism, at triviality of mind and soul, at stubborn stupidity and dishonor no longer conscious of itself, not as these qualities are contrasted with some specious moralistic idealism, but as they are contrasted with art, with the eternal creative spirit, with the quest of him who is driven despite himself to pursue that beauty which is also truth. This central motivation they found, of course, in the original of Paul Apel. But I am glad that they dared so fully and explicitly to keep it in their American version.

The production, like all the productions of Mr. Winthrop Ames, is graceful, imaginative, and exact. I am not especially impressed with the Pantomime, happily enough named and invented, the function of which is to oppose beauty to grossness and significance to triviality. It is a little slight for the purpose, and at variance with its slightness is the music of Mr. Deems Taylor which, skilful and not unimpressive, is so afraid of being less than almost of tomorrow that it will not let itself be either as lovely or as eloquent as it might well have been. But it is charming enough and the acting in the play itself, primarily of Mr. Roland Young but also of his numerous associates, is genuine and telling.

I must not neglect to mention the *Morning-Evening*, a four-page newspaper distributed to the audience during, at least, the early performances of *Beggar on Horseback*. In this quite precious travesty of a contemporary yellow sheet, prepared exclusively for morons, the mentality of both the makers and the consumers of such printed matter is exhibited and excoriated with a touch that is among the best and most promising and most wholesome things in American letters. —LUDWIG LEWISOHN, "Inferno," *Nation*, Feb. 27, 1924, pp. 238–39

To G. Seldes's for dinner, and had a merry time with his boy Timothy, and so all to the Musick Box, to see *Of Thee I Sing*, wrote by Geo. Kaufman and M. Ryskind, and the musick wrote by Geo. Gershwin and the song-words by I. Gershwin. I deemed it the most satirickall American libretto ever I saw, and the greatest step up, I think, that the stage has had in my day. As to the musick, I thought that it helped the play mighty little, and as to the songs, it was too hard to understand most of the words, either because the musick was too loud and brazen, or because the players were unable to sing them trippingly on the tongue. And I thought the chief players were not perfectly fitted to shew comedy, except Mr. Victor Moore and Mr. Florenz Ames, who I thought could not have been any better. So to J. Warburg's for a little while, and thence for a ride here and there with Betty Dietz, and we met some quiet roisterers, and exchanged banter with them, being a trifle on the exchange, and so home, my wife having got there two minutes before me.—FRANKLIN PIERCE ADAMS, *The Diary of Our Own Samuel Pepys* (entry for Dec. 26, 1931), Vol. 2, 1935, p. 1070

When Edna Ferber and George Kaufman collaborate on a play, the general public prepares to enjoy itself thoroughly. A few years ago they got together on a piece so successful that it is still mentioned with awe in managerial circles, and it was generally supposed that as soon as the promised new opus appeared, the theatrical season would escape from the routine into which it had prematurely fallen. Success was predestined and success will be enjoyed in a considerable measure. For the present, at least, the new play will be the obvious choice for theater parties, and one will have to see it if one expects to be in on the small talk of the moment. But the sad fact remains that it is not quite good enough to add very much to reputations already as high as those of Miss Ferber and Mr. Kaufman.

*Dinner at Eight* is the title of the slice of life which they have prepared for exhibition at the Music Box Theater. This title is ironically restrained, but the restraint stops at the title, for in addition to some minor blackmail and a death by heart failure promised for a moment shortly after the fall of the final curtain, the piece includes one seduction, one adultery, one bigamous marriage, one suicide by gas (very elaborate), one financial ruin, and one duel—the latter fought in the butler's pantry with a carving knife and its accompanying fork. Obviously, then, the evening is not uneventful and neither is it lacking in ingenuity. All the personages are somehow linked with one another by the fact that all are concerned in one way or another with a fashionable dinner party which collapses about the head of the hapless hostess because all the important guests are prevented from coming by one or another of the incidents mentioned above. In a way both the scheme and the intention are vaguely suggestive of *Grand Hotel*, in that *Dinner at Eight*, like the previous play, links together a number of separate stories by means of a mechanical device and then exclaims by implication, "Such, you see, are the dramas which go on just below the surface of our everyday existence," or even, as the old melodramas had it, "Such is life in a great city." But *Dinner at Eight* is less frankly melodramatic, less frankly a tour de force, and just to that extent less satisfactory as an evening of frank unreality.

I grant that the action is lively. I grant in addition a remarkable dexterity in the management of the various episodes and some flashes of smart dialogue. But if anyone should ask me what more, in God's name, I expect of a play, I should reply that I expect at least one of several other possible things—such as, for example, some evidence of an emotion really felt, some characterization deeper than that minimum required for a dramatic puppet, or, failing that, then some recognizable individuality of style. In *Dinner at Eight* I found none. With the possible exception of the aging actress played admirably by Constance Collier, every one of the characters is straight out of innumerable other plays, and each of the incidents is merely one developed with sufficient brevity to conceal a familiarity which would be boring if one were given time to recognize just how familiar it is. Buried among smarter phrases, such precious bits of dialogue as "Not after all that we have been to one another" and "This is the only decent thing I have ever done in my life" reached my incredulous ears, and they represent not unfairly the underlying substance of a play which Miss Ferber and Mr. Kaufman certainly wrote in some of their less inspired moments. Perhaps a manager besought them to supply him with a sure success. If so, then they worked conscientiously and hard at that particular task, but they did not really care about the story they were writing and were not concerned for one moment with the various hard fates of their characters. They produced their success, but if it had been presented anonymously no one could have guessed which of a half-dozen good contemporary workmen had turned this particular trick. A few lines back I called the play "a slice of life." It is really five or six slices not very freshly carved, and on second thought one is tempted to describe it as a plate of cold cuts.—Joseph Wood Krutch, "Cold Cuts," *Nation*, Nov. 9, 1932, pp. 464–65

*The Cocoanuts* got off to a roaring start at the first rehearsal. George Kaufman sat on the empty stage, under a worklight, and began to read the script. Halfway through the first scene,

Chico fell asleep. Somewhere in the second scene, I fell asleep. It wasn't that I was bored. I felt comfortable, and confident. There would be no need for Zep to rassle Kaufman and Ryskind, two shows or nothing. I had heard enough to know that they'd written no string of blackouts, but a real musical play—whatever the hell it was about.

By the time we opened in Boston, Kaufman didn't know what it was about either, we were ad libbing so much. Whenever a new bit occurred to Chico or me, we did it. Whenever a gag popped into Groucho's mind, he delivered it. The first performance ran forty minutes too long. All the critics and most of the audience had left long before the curtain finally came down.

Berlin, Kaufman and Ryskind stayed up all night trying to hack the show down to size. They cut a chorus here, a chorus there, and a couple of dance numbers. The next day we obediently rehearsed the new version. The next performance ran even longer. There was scarcely enough dough in the box office to pay the stagehands' overtime.

Berlin, Kaufman and Ryskind held an emergency meeting. Only thing to do, said Kaufman morosely, was to cut another production number, two more choruses, and two songs altogether. Irving Berlin yelped like he'd been stabbed in the back. "My God!" he said. "Any more cuts and this will be a musical without any music!"

Kaufman had a long, lugubrious brood, twisting an arm around his head and massaging an ear, and rubbing his collarbone with his chin. "Tell you what, Irving," he said. "You waive the songs and I'll waive the story."—Harpo Marx, "No Use Talking," *Harpo Speaks!*, 1961, pp. 188–189

## SCOTT MEREDITH
### "The Solo"
### *George S. Kaufman and His Friends*
#### 1974, pp. 267–74

Around the time Kaufman was putting the finishing touches on the third act of *The Butter and Egg Man*, he received a call from a producer he had known casually for a number of years. The producer, Sam H. Harris, had a proposition. He asked Kaufman, "How'd you like to write a show for the Marx Brothers?"

Kaufman respected and admired Harris, as everybody in the theatre did, but he was appalled by the proposal. "I'd as soon," he said, "write a show for the Barbary apes."

He knew, of course, he told Harris, that Groucho, Chico, Harpo, and Zeppo Marx had recently become the hottest act in show business. But he was also aware, both because it was common knowledge in the field and from personal observation of Harpo and other of the Marxes at poker games and Round Table luncheons, that they were lovable but uncontrollable lunatics who could turn a writer's life into a nightmare. It was true, he admitted, that he'd heard that, during the run of *I'll Say She Is*, the musical in which the brothers had just closed, there had been performances in which the comedians had stayed fairly close to the script. Far more often, however, they ignored the script almost completely and devoted the evening to saying or doing whatever popped into their heads, and engaging in repartee with each other or with members of the audience—all of which created great hilarity in theatregoers but undoubtedly created only thoughts of suicide or homicide in the writers of the play. He was further prepared to admit, he said, that the script for *I'll Say She Is* was a very bad one, and probably needed the Marxian ministrations it had received, but it was his strong feeling that the Marx Brothers would assassinate any script, good or bad, given to them. All this considered, he concluded pleasantly but firmly, he wanted no part whatever of Harris's proposition.

Less than two years before, the Marx Brothers had been only a moderately successful vaudeville team. They were receiving $1100 a week, which was not sensational even in its entirety since it had to be divided four ways, and was made much worse by the fact that they were also required to dip into that and pay their own transportation, commissions, and the salaries of several girls they were then using in their act. The big break came for them when, in 1924, after several producers had told them that their brand of comedy was simply not for the legitimate stage, a little-known Philadelphia entrepreneur named James P. Beury decided to take a chance and bring the quartet to Broadway in *I'll Say She Is*. The play was poor, so much so that the generally kindly Brooks Atkinson later called it "ramshackle and awful." But Atkinson, as Woollcott did shortly afterward, fell in love with the Marx Brothers themselves, and so in time did the rest of New York. *I'll Say She Is* ran for a year, mostly to jammed houses. And when it ended, the Marx Brothers had offers to do another Broadway play from such top managers as the Shuberts, Charles Dillingham, Florenz Ziegfeld, and others.

Harris understood at once, however, why Kaufman might be reluctant to work with the team; he had had much the same reaction himself when the idea had first been proposed to him. Harris was fifty-three years old when he called Kaufman that day in 1925, but he had already been in show business for thirty-six years, the last twenty-one of these as one of the most successful producers in the country. His initial response, therefore, to the suggestion that he produce a play starring the mad Marxes had been, like Kaufman's: Who needs it? ⟨. . .⟩

Harris was one of the few major producers who did not chase after the Marx Brothers following their scintillating success in *I'll Say She Is*. But, perhaps partly for this reason, the Marx Brothers decided that he was the one producer they really wanted to do their next show. Harpo asked one of the team's most fervent admirers, Irving Berlin, to talk to Harris on their behalf. Harris and Berlin were close friends and business associates; they had built the Music Box Theatre together in 1921, a theatre which was so fortunate right from the start in the plays it housed that it is still known as "the home of hits" and a lucky playhouse. It took Berlin several days to talk the producer out of his initial reluctance, and Harris finally agreed to consider the comedians only if they would come around and show him their stuff right in his own office. The comics hurried over and soon turned the Harris office into a madhouse, leaving Harris and his associates weak with laughter. But even after that, Harris said only that he would let the team know, and he spent a few additional days in deep thought before calling them in Syracuse, where they'd gone to put on a brief run of *I'll Say She Is*, and stating that he'd decided to produce their next show.

The producer described his own doubts to Kaufman, saying, "I wanted to be sure myself that I was willing to rent a room in the lunatic asylum." He went on to explain that he had decided to do the show for both artistic and commercial reasons: artistic because the Marx Brothers were clearly the freshest and brightest comedy talents to emerge on the American scene in decades, and it was as important to present them as it had been for him to present *Icebound*, a Harris production which had won a Pulitzer Prize two years before, and commercial because the Marx Brothers in a really good play would bring in a fortune. He then pressed his point home, saying he felt Kaufman should accept the assignment for the same reasons.

Kaufman became slightly less determined, but he was still not convinced. "How can you write for Harpo?" he asked. "What do you put down on paper? All you can say is 'Harpo enters,' and then he's on his own." He went on to state similar problems about the other brothers, whose styles were so different from one another, the difficulties involved in switching gears from line to line and writing Italian dialect for Chico, straight-man lines for Zeppo, and God knows what for Groucho. Harris brushed it all aside, airily. "You just write good stuff," he said. "They'll twist and turn it and fit it to their own styles." "That's what I'm worried about," Kaufman said. But he continued to listen to Harris's persuasive arguments, and, when the conversation ended a half-hour later, he had agreed to write the play.

The one thing Harris did not tell Kaufman was that he was not the first writer called in on the project. When Harris had phoned the comedians to say that he would produce their show, he told them at the same time that he was sending a blackout writer right up to do some new sketches on them. A blackout writer was the last thing in the world the Marxes wanted. They had plenty of comedy sketches and bits of their own, and, furthermore, the employment of a blackout writer sounded as though Harris was contemplating a revue, whereas they wanted a genuine, plotted play and a real playwright to write it. They decided to deal with the blackout writer in their own way.

When the man arrived, they insisted that he remove his coat, and Zeppo, who was a bodybuilding enthusiast at that time and had bulging, rippling muscles, stepped up close to him. "I'll wrestle you to a fall," Zeppo said threateningly. "You write two shows for us or none." The writer, a small man, retrieved his coat and disappeared into the night, and it was after Harris heard of this that he called Kaufman. Kaufman might have been made nervous if he had heard the story because, though much taller than the blackout writer, he was not much of a wrestler himself. But he really had nothing to worry about. He was exactly the kind of writer the Marx Brothers wanted. The comedians promised Harris sincerely that they would behave—at least within their own interpretation of the word.

*The Cocoanuts*, the play Kaufman subsequently wrote for the comedy team, is often listed in theatrical histories as Kaufman's second solo flight. This is an error, though an understandable one because Kaufman received sole credit as author of the book in the show's programs and advertisements, and in all other listings. The fact is, however, that he worked with a sort of assistant in writing the play, a man who was not a collaborator in the ordinary sense of the word because he contributed very little actual wordage to the play, but who helped with ideas for comedy situations and plot construction, and also served to fulfill Kaufman's need for someone to whom he could talk and on whom he could try out lines. The assistant was a way-station for Kaufman on his trip back to full collaboration. He had written a play by himself and had found it lonely work, and he never again, after *The Butter and Egg Man* and *The Cocoanuts*, wrote another play without a partner. (Some people regard *Hollywood Pinafore*, a pastiche of the Gilbert and Sullivan operetta which Kaufman put together in 1945, as a solo effort, since Kaufman wrote his own book and his own lyrics for the play. But in the strictest sense, he was collaborating with Sir Arthur Sullivan on that one.)

Kaufman's assistant on *The Cocoanuts* was Morrie Ryskind, who eventually became a full-fledged collaborator—Kaufman's co-author on *Animal Crackers, Of Thee I Sing*, and others. Kaufman and Ryskind knew each other because Ryskind, like Kaufman himself and so many others, was also a protégé and discovery of Frank Adams. Ryskind was born in New York on October 20, 1895, was six years younger than Kaufman, and had begun contributing material to Adams's columns while still in high school, eventually achieving enough popularity among readers so that Adams once even accepted and ran a Ryskind contribution which occupied a full column. As a regular contributor, Ryskind was invited to one of Adam's famous annual dinners, and it was there that Adams introduced him to Kaufman. Thereafter, Kaufman allowed Ryskind to visit him at the *Times* every now and then, making Ryskind feel very professional by permitting him to rewrite some of the material slated for the Sunday drama page. The two men became increasingly friendly, and Ryskind was a very obvious choice when Kaufman decided he wanted someone to assist him on *The Cocoanuts*. He was young, unattached, and eager; he was, and is, a very funny man; and he had not yet succumbed to the fervor of ultra-conservatism which eventually caused some of his friends either to begin to avoid him or make sport of him, as Ira Gershwin did by showing up at Ryskind's poker games with a copy of the *Daily Worker* protruding ostentatiously from his pocket. And when Kaufman phoned and said, "I've signed to do a show for the Marx Brothers. You want to help out?," Ryskind's acceptance was instant and joyful.

The script which Kaufman began to concoct was no masterpiece of ingenuity and complexity; it had to be kept simple and straightforward to allow room for and give full rein

to the stars' special brand of madness. But he worked as hard on the show as he had worked on more prestigious projects like *Beggar on Horseback*. As was always the case when he was deeply involved in a play, he ate very little on some days and nothing at all on others. He was never, of course, tremendously concerned about food, a fact which Beatrice once bewailed in print when she was on the staff of *PM* and wrote a guest column for the vacationing food editor, Charlotte Adams. "As a gourmand, and I hope a gourmet," Beatrice wrote, "I find the attitudes of most men toward food irritating. Their reaction to eating goes to extremes, indifference or passion, but this is, one hears, characteristic of them in other important phases of life. Into this first classification, indifference, go those men who eat only because to eat is to live, and they go through the processes of tasting, chewing and swallowing not knowing or caring what they are eating. I cannot go through the pain of discussing them any further. Unfortunately my husband has this attitude toward food. Eating is really a nuisance to him and he wishes he could take a little capsule three times a day and call the whole thing quits." But it was even worse when Kaufman was working on a play: if eating was an annoying interruption to him during leisure times, if often became an unbearable burden to be completely avoided during work periods. He much preferred to spend the time pacing the floors, lying prone on the carpets, picking up hundreds of pieces of lint, tying innumerable and permanent knots in window-curtain cords, and in general struggling over and perfecting every line and plot situation in the agonized way which once caused Woollcott to say about him, "In the throes of composition, he seems to crawl up the walls of the apartment in the manner of the late Count Dracula."

# WILLIAM KENNEDY

## 1928–

William Kennedy was born in Albany, New York, on January 16, 1928. The son of a deputy sheriff and a secretary, Kennedy came from a working-class Irish background. He attended Siena College, receiving a B.A. in 1949. After his graduation he began working for the *Post Star* of Glen Falls, New York. He served in the Army from 1950 to 1952, and afterwards was a reporter for the Albany *Times-Union*. In 1956 Kennedy moved with his wife Ana Daisy Sosa to San Juan, Puerto Rico. There he was the founding managing editor of the San Juan *Star*. In 1959 he returned to Albany to devote himself to fiction writing. From 1963 to 1970 he wrote occasionally for the *Times-Union*.

Kennedy's first novel, *The Ink Truck*, was published in 1969. Although favorably reviewed, it was not a financial success. In 1974 Kennedy began to lecture at SUNY-Albany, where he is presently a professor of English. *Legs*, the first of his trilogy of novels set in Albany during the Depression, was published in 1975. It was followed by *Billy Phelan's Greatest Game* in 1978. Kennedy's publisher, Viking, seemed reluctant to release the third book in the series, *Ironweed*. As with the other novels, the subject matter was downbeat, as Kennedy chronicled the lives of Albany's forgotten citizens. However, Kennedy's friend Saul Bellow wrote to Viking warning them of their potential error in failing to publish *Ironweed*, and the novel finally appeared in 1983 to enthusiastic reviews.

*Ironweed* won the 1984 Pulitzer Prize for fiction, catapulting Kennedy from relative obscurity into the literary limelight. In 1984 he worked with Francis Ford Coppola on the screenplay for *The Cotton Club* (1985). Kennedy also was awarded a grant from the MacArthur Foundation of $264,000, tax free, for his creative genius. In 1983 Kennedy published a collection of essays about Albany titled *O Albany! An Urban Tragedy*. In this group of essays taken from articles written mostly during the 1960s for the *Times-Union*, Kennedy again shows his sensitivity to the plight of the less fortunate residents of the Empire State's capital city. Today Kennedy lives in his hometown in a refurbished downtown house.

## Works

### O ALBANY!

In *O Albany!* William Kennedy sets out to prove his native city is "centered squarely in the American and human continuum." There is no question that he succeeds marvelously. So well, in fact, that I could have sworn at various times I was reading a chapter in an unpublished treasure I happen to possess, *The Autobiography of Frank Hague*, or a slightly modernized version of that 1903 classic by Alfred Henry Lewis, *The Boss: And How He Came to Rule New York.*

That opus contains the rules that all the bosses, including Albany's satrap, Daniel Peter O'Connell, faithfully obeyed to perpetuate their unholy reigns—"Never interfere with people's beer . . . give 'em clean streets. . . . Kape the street free of ba-ad people. The public don't object to dirt but it wants it kept in the back alleys. . . . Follow what I tell you, you can do what size ye plaze." ⟨. . .⟩

Mr. Kennedy ends his personal reminiscence of growing up in North Albany by describing how he walked out of church during "narrowback" sermons, refused to sing "Too-ra-loo-ra-loo-ral" and registered to vote as an independent. Eventually he discovered the only thing he could not shed was his Irishness, although two trips to Ireland and one visit to the Ancient Order of Hibernians' St. Patrick's Night Dance convinced him to abandon trying to write about the Emerald Isle.

This remnant of Irishness has led Mr. Kennedy into history and a fresh view of American reality. In many ways, *O Albany!* is his acceptance of the power of the past. This vision has carried him far beyond the bitter naturalism of James T. Farrell's *Studs Lonigan*, the moral anguish of Harry Sylvester's *Moon Gaffney*, the ambivalence displayed by Edwin O'Connor in his comparatively neglected but superior novel *The Edge of Sadness.* You can almost hear William Butler Yeats chanting in Mr. Kennedy's ear, "Cast a cold eye / On life, on death." Except that his eye is anything but cold. He has given a lot of thought to death; he has also noticed life's habit of dancing on graves.

For example, in *O Albany!* his recounting of the joint careers of Dan O'Connell and Erastus Corning ends with two funerals, each reported in careful detail. Francis Phelan, the drunken-bum hero of Mr. Kennedy's third novel, *Ironweed*, a man who spends a lot of time talking to the dead, would have no difficulty getting the point of this denouement of six decades of ruthless chicanery.

Another example. If he ran a public library today, Mr. Kennedy says, he would recruit a certain number of old bums and bag ladies like the ones he encountered in libraries during the Depression, when he was reading his way to spiritual independence. These losers would remind him that he was "a keeper of universal, not merely elitist verities."

With its nostalgic recollections of vanished neighborhoods bearing names like Gander Bay, Pluck Hollow and Cabbagetown, *O Albany!* also reminds us how much of life is beyond or above politics. It recalls how many incarnations Albany and the rest of America have undergone in the 370 years since a handful of Dutchmen sailed up the Hudson to open a fur trading post and ended with a city on several hills. So many flourishings, fadings, deaths and rebirths. Albany has been counted out a dozen times—with the disappearance of the fur trade, the waning of the Erie Canal, the collapse of the railroads, the evisceration of its downtown section. Each time it has returned to improbable life. Its motto could well be the last line of Mr. Kennedy's first novel, *Legs*. With three bullets

in his brain, Jack Diamond, the wildest Irish hoodlum of them all, says to the narrator, "I really don't think I'm dead."

Downtown Albany now is strutting again, thanks to a new generation that has grown weary of suburban boredom and expensive gasoline. Albany has also benefited from the manic vision of the state capital's greatest capitalist, Nelson Rockefeller, whose $1.9 billion mall has brought new skyscrapers, motels, nightclubs and tourists. Most miraculous of all, a new mayor presides in city hall, promising honesty and openness.

Mr. Kennedy freely admits that this latest resurrection may not prove durable or even genuine. But you have the feeling that another one, even more improbable, is sure to be around the corner. Maybe that is why you come away from this book's fascinating view of the American experience, the human experience, feeling hopeful. You may not like it all, but there is something here for everybody. Besides, as Martin Daugherty observed after he regained his forbearance, "It's the only cosmos in town."—THOMAS FLEMING, "A City and Its Machine," *NYTBR*, Jan. 1, 1984, pp. 11–12

For those so inclined, *O Albany!* can serve as a kind of Baedeker to the world of Kennedy's novels. Not that the one must be read in connection with the others. It need not be. This book stands on its own, its protagonist the eponymous city that like all real cities is many cities, a concatenation of ethnic neighborhoods, one often superimposed on the other, held together by the streets or horsecars or trolleys or subways running out from the heart of a commercial downtown. In many American cities the old ticker gave out long ago, done in by the malpractice of America's roadbuilders with their mania for the double and triple bypass. But in Albany things have gone a little differently. According to Kennedy they usually do. ⟨. . .⟩

As a young man, Kennedy in good Irish fashion turned his back on this parochial world of pols and prelates, shook the dust from his feet and set out to forge the unforged consciousness wherever artists do such things. And also in good Irish fashion, he remained a prisoner to the place, recognizing that he is "a person whose imagination has become fused with a single place. And in that place finds all the elements that a man needs for the life of the soul."

The Irish Irish, in the days before the English, had a name for this sort of thing, Dinnsheanchas, the poetry of place, an amalgam of history, mythology and folklore through which a person came to know the past of every piece of the landscape, to understand its associations and thereby gain control of the unseen forces that could cure or curse him.

*O Albany!* follows in that tradition, naming names, recording history, retelling the myths and stories, following the city from its origins through its myriad manifestations: frontier outpost, river town, trading post, lumber town, Gateway to the West/East (depending on which way you were going), railway center, immigrant city, Roaring-Twenties Gomorrah, an all-American city for all the wrong or right reasons (depending on which way you look at it)—greed, boundless energy, ambition, corruption, inexhaustible optimism, endless building and rebuilding, boom and bust, magnificence mixed with squalor.

Let me do an un-Irish thing and let the writer himself have the last words on what he has written: "It is the task of this and other books I have written, and hope to write, to peer into the heart of this always shifting past, to be there when it ceases to be what it was, when it becomes what it must become under scrutiny, when it turns so magically, so inevitably, from then into now."

Well, almost the last word. The late Patrick Kavanagh once wrote a poem about the doubts a writer can face when trying to tell the epic of the world's secondary places, their squabbles and struggles—doubts that haunted him in his small corner of Ireland. "Till Homer's ghost came whispering to my mind/He said: I made the Iliad from such/A local row. Gods make their own importance."

In Kennedy, Albany has found its Homer.—PETER QUINN, *Am*, March 17, 1984, pp. 190–91

### THE INK TRUCK

In the days of the *Westminster Review* and the *Edinburgh Review*, new novels were written about at considerable length—George Eliot could be damned or praised in 5,000 seemingly reasonable words. Today such a freedom exists only in esoteric backwaters where skiffs of phantom critics scull across the becalmed currents of academe. And so we invent an understandable but perhaps unjustified shorthand—X's new novel seems to me a rather poor cross between Agatha Christie and William Shakespeare—in the hope that something of a novel's tone may be communicated in a mere sixteen words.

The good novel, of course, pre-empts such brachygraphics; but there aren't, in any one week, many *good* novels. William Kennedy's *The Ink Truck* is a possible exception. It begins with a buttonholing, lapel-grabbing prose which lies ill inside the head of a reviewer whose mind is still being jogged by the implications of the phrase 'George Eliot'. But perhaps Mr Kennedy knows this, for his hero, Bailey, a charismatic and seemingly indestructible striking journalist soon assumes, despite the writer's rhetoric, genuinely heroic stature. The strike has been on for a long time, so long that only a triplet of militants remains. And if they give in, they will lose more than they possessed at the strike's outbreak. Only Bailey, a syndicated columnist, refuses to accept the inevitable.

Impressed by nothing, a printer's devil turned juggernaut, he rolls through violence and persuasion with an unshakeable belief in his own secular divinity. His progress, like the writing, is often clumsy: 'Lust crept up Bailey's pantleg and tickled him. He wondered about its cause, conjectured on Irma's stockings and her possible garter belt as catalysts . . .' Amends are made by some better thought-out exchanges: Bailey, injured, remarks to his mistress: 'The trouble with richly endowed women like yourself . . . is that they lack a sense of humour and life.' She replies: 'Shut up and quit bleeding.' Crude, but effective.

Mr Kennedy has a useful line in incantatory curses and too frequently casts it, as it were, towards our muted skiffers; the paradigmatic introduction of a collection of gipsy scabs not helping. One of these, incidentally, is a would-be Jesus figure called Smith who gives the book the allegorical undertone hinted at in the publisher's hysterical blurb. In the end, though, the author's own words are perhaps sufficient: 'It is my hope that *The Ink Truck* will stand as an analgesic inspiration to all weird men of good will and rotten luck everywhere.' —BARRY COLE, "Short-handed," *Spec*, Aug. 15, 1970, pp. 161

Albany is to this gifted writer what the city of Paterson was to William Carlos Williams, and like our great laureate of urban plenitude, he wrests from an unlikely source a special kind of lyricism. Mr. Kennedy has examined with a scholar's eye the streets and structures of his city, and with a lover's passion he has researched its myths and legends, its scandals, its celebrated aristocrats and splendid nobodies. Interweaving historical facts with the fantasies of his powerful imagination, he has created in the Albany cycle (*Legs, Billy Phelan's Greatest Game, Ironweed*) some of the most memorable fiction to appear in the last two decades.

*The Ink Truck*, a comic narrative first published in 1969 and almost immediately forgotten, has never been considered part of this cycle, though in a note for this edition Mr. Kennedy emphasizes that the book is about "Albany, N.Y., and a few of its dynamics during two centuries." Not unexpectedly, given his devotion to place and to a particular kind of macho character, the novel reveals numerous thematic links with the later books. It also reveals an energetic but as yet undisciplined artist working his way somewhat clumsily to the flexible style that would become his trademark, a style indebted to Joyce, Fitzgerald and Beckett yet very much his own.

In this novel, Bailey, a syndicated columnist in his 30's, leads a band of strikers in a series of real and surreal confrontations with a corrupt newspaper establishment. His dream is to bleed the paper's ink truck, thus "to truly mark the earth with his signature," a resonant image for a first novel. Like Legs Diamond (*Legs*) and Francis Phelan (*Ironweed*), he is a battler who courts disaster, a man who knows the debauchery of the spirit that follows intense failure yet who somehow survives, mired in hope. And like Billy Phelan, another of Mr. Kennedy's volatile protagonists, Bailey follows a sharply defined code of conduct, believing that a man has to do what he has to do.

Bailey is in love with his own integrity and also, alas, with his own voice. A barroom philosopher who has clearly kissed the Blarney stone, he does not so much talk as hold forth, and after a hundred or so pages, his self-conscious language becomes tedious. In the later books, Mr. Kennedy discovers a racy, naturalistic idiom for his gangsters, small-time hustlers and derelicts. The rhetoric of his better-educated journalist, by contrast, sounds secondhand, literary.

"I'm after mutation now," Bailey says in the course of a typical aria, "lopping off parts till the species is as slick and streamlined as a buttered bullet. Eventually I may be able to sell myself to a freak museum as the Transmogrified Man. . . . What you see before you, ladies and gentlemen, is the vile corpse. Note that it has petrified ears, vulcanized genitals and a calcified liver. Proceeds from this exhibition will go to the former owner, who has since become an anopheles mosquito." This creative outpouring is apparently meant to sound Shakespearean. A little more than a little is by much too much.

The sexual attitudes expressed by the voluble Bailey are mostly of the locker-room variety, with women seen as either nurturing goddesses or insatiable shrews. What is especially disturbing is not just that the female characters lack credibility but that they are consistently linked with decay and bestiality. One woman, for example, is likened to "rancid meat," another to "a dry carcass." A woman is accused by her husband of having given a social disease to their dog, while another, provocatively tattooed, persuades Bailey to wear the mask of a bull's head while making love to her, prompting a "long cry in basse-tones: 'Moooooo.'" Perhaps Mr. Kennedy is slyly making the point that his priapic males, through whom these images are filtered, are the embodiment of adolescent attitudes. Whatever the reason for the demeaning carnal imagery, the book leaves an unpleasant impression and raises questions about the level of the author's social consciousness at this early stage of his career.

One reason it is important for publishers to keep in print even the apprentice work of our most gifted writers is to provide a sense of esthetic and moral development. It is useful, thus, to have *The Ink Truck* back in circulation, however serious its flaws. The reappearance, moreover, of an all but forgotten book by a formerly uncelebrated author should give hope to artists with rotten luck everywhere. There are, after all, any number of American novelists who have not enjoyed the recognition they deserve. It may be reassuring to think that they too may someday blaze across the sky like the Kennedy comet.—JOEL CONARROE, "Columnist Bites Newspaper," *NYTBR*, Sept. 30, 1984, p. 11

When William Kennedy's *Ironweed* walked away with the literary prizes this year, more than *Ironweed* came into the spotlight. *Legs* and *Billy Phelan's Greatest Game*—the two earlier novels in the "Albany cycle"—suddenly started popping up in even the most standard bookstores. All at once William Kennedy's crackling, vivid prose, his gritty characters and hard-edged plots are available wherever you turn.

That's a side effect of literary prizes—sometimes a positive one, sometimes not. Certainly the Albany cycle deserves to be recalled entire to our attention; regardless of whether you happen to enjoy it, it is undeniably literature. On the other hand, his very first novel is best forgotten. But here we have it nonetheless: *The Ink Truck*, originally published in 1969, now being reissued.

The book's hero is Bailey, a newspaper columnist who has been involved for one full year in a strike against his paper. During that year 247 of the strikers have defected. Only 4 of the 18 remaining have any real commitment: Bailey himself, his friend Rosenthal, his sometimes girlfriend Irma, and Jarvis, the leader, a man "rather above average in ineptitude." Jarvis organizes "motorcades" two cars long. When he gives the strikers their signal—"Whistle While You Work"—he has to hum it because he doesn't know how to whistle. In his negotiations with management, he is reduced to arguing about whether the company should split tuxedo-rental costs for reporters covering formal functions. (By no means are dress shirts included; "reporters are notorious gravy spillers.") Current salary proposals hover somewhere around 40 percent below pre-strike level.

Plainly, to remain on this sinking ship Bailey would have to be a man obsessed—and he is. He admits it himself:

> The strike had created something so callous in him that he often thought he would make no more relationships that would last beyond the moment. Ties would bind as long as the moment lasted; an instant, or perhaps a year, but no longer. And he would not grieve when the moment ended. It was desirable to get beyond sentimental attachments, beyond trouble, beyond love, to be equal even to death. . . . His life now was almost like a sealed bottle that nothing could touch.

That passage sums up all that's wrong with the book; for although it may be possible to write a wonderful novel about someone who has reached such a state, William Kennedy was not skillful enough at the time to do it. What he gave us, instead, was a thin, brutal, wisecracking tale about a man so devoid of warmth that he can't enlist the slightest sympathy from the reader. Callous Bailey certainly is—posturing and self-centered, prone to the kind of manic joke that excludes the listener—but the strike, as presented here, is not sufficient excuse for it.

Bailey fills his column with arcane nonsense and lets his readers sink or swim. He has a repellent wife whom he ditches without a thought; he absent-mindedly fondles a smitten neighbor woman in order to gain access to her phone. His method of publicly squelching an opponent—a successful method, we're led to believe, and one that's presented as if it were funny and original—is to leap around like a gorilla, scratching his armpits and making ape sounds for reporters. He

is given to lengthy, feverish diatribes that sound like James Joyce's Bloom suddenly gone senile:

> I'm heading for new depths. No more fresh starts for Bailey. I'm after mutation now, lopping off parts till the species is as slick and streamlined as a buttered bullet. Eventually I may be able to sell myself to a freak museum as the Transmogrified Man. He cut out his vital parts and fed the birds and the sewers. He opened his veins and dribbled out his blood to thirsty pigs. And he sold his brain to raise funds for a fashionable supermarket. What you see before you, ladies and gentlemen, is the vile corpse. Note that it has petrified ears, vulcanized genitals and a calcified liver. Proceeds from this exhibition will go to the former owner, who has since become an anopheles mosquito.

Some of the book's flaws are echoed in the later Albany cycle: a wasteful excess of violence and a slapdash, run-on style that occasionally blurs the plot. (William Kennedy bears a strong resemblance to one of those brilliant cocktail party talkers—not conversationalists, mind—who keep their guests royally entertained but also a little confused.) But in the Albany cycle, those flaws are balanced by the depth of the stories being told. There's no such depth in *The Ink Truck*. People are mashed, smashed, lacerated—people we don't much care about, so we're forced to endure all this gruesomeness for no good reason. Even an orgy turns out to be gruesome—a pointless orgy anyway, made all the more so by the fact that its participants might have been rejects from a Bosch painting:

> Popkin, hairless, and Morelli, apelike with hair; one of Stanley's maids with only one breast and beside her an Old Mother Hubbard's pair hanging to the waist like overstuffed satchels; a chicken-breasted scab with a long, dangling prong, and an executive's beer-bellied vat with an almost invisible faucet under its great curve; a hump growing out of a gray-haired executive wife's back. . . . Some men had womanly sags to their chests, knobby navels, hairy backs, boils and cultured muscles. Some women had pimples, face-lift scars, stretch marks. . . . There were women with oiled skin, surgical scars, acne and Man Tan, men with scarlet splotches, warts, wens, moles, birthmarks . . .

Well, you get the general idea.

Is all this to say that there are no redeeming features in *The Ink Truck*? No, moments do flash out from time to time—inklings of the later William Kennedy. At one point, Bailey takes an accidental time trip to a nineteenth-century cholera epidemic in Albany, and this is our first sense of a real place that we can practically touch. (Albany has been the setting all along, but up till now we only knew it because we were told so in an Author's Note at the start.) At another point, Bailey visits an uncle whose life revolves about his cat; and his household with its arsenal of rubber mice and flea powders is another place that pulls us in. But as for the rest—well, call it practice. A finger exercise for the Abany cycle. And don't feel you have to rush out and buy it.—ANNE TYLER, "Albany Warm-Up," *NR*, Oct. 15, 1984, pp. 39–40

## LEGS

One of the pleasures of *Legs*, Kennedy's second novel, is that it drove me back to his first, *The Ink Truck*, now six years old. Both books have in common Kennedy's sustained verbal energy. His is a talent that has traditionally clustered on the front porches of country stores, or in taverns, or on the airwaves of special disc jockeys. It is a compulsive talent, made all the more valuable as the recent world threatens daily to leave words behind. Taking that abandonment as a challenge, Kennedy sometimes seems to show how he can, hocus pocus, weave the whole world with words. His is a spell that works. I'd like to sit down on the bar, or on the stoop, listening to this man pump his language. If Kennedy has a case of *cacoethes loquendi*, still it's compost for growth. To read him is to know how the tomato plants must feel when the nitrogen hits their roots. Yes, that's when they know the Big Boys are coming after all.

The Big Boy in *The Ink Truck* was named Bailey, a budding columnist full of baloney, himself and his words. Out on a failing strike from his paper, Bailey dreamed of a gesture that would transcend protest: "He would be done with the mortifying slouch of the timid piss ant." Timid he's not, and piss ant he's not, but what is he? He's a mouthful of style, he's jobless, he's hovering, but he's not transcendent. He's one of the noble zanies to whom the novel of the '60s fondly tended here and abroad. He's hanging just beyond credibility, but just short of myth's ozone.

As if to solve these problems, Kennedy has chosen for his next Big Boy, Mr. Jack "Legs" Diamond, the great gangster, a man who is both entirely credible in that rags-to-riches way of American history and entirely ozonic in the splendiferous way of American headlines. Kennedy's narrator calls him "Horatio Alger out of Finn McCool and Jesse James . . . a pioneer, the founder of the first truly modern gang, the dauphin of the town for years . . . a fusion of the individual life flux with the clear and violent light of American reality." At the time FDR lowered the crippling 14-count indictments against him in 1931, when Legs was 33, he'd gone from Philly's streets to Catskill stills worth $10 million in warehouse stock alone. He'd gone from city urchin to the slickest of the early gangsters and on to forced hibernation in Catskill where a local wag described him as "the biggest name we've had locally since Rip Van Winkle woke up." He was a man with gargantuan appetites and deeds; Kennedy's style would have had to invent them if they didn't exist. Legs Diamond has innate credibility. You don't believe this character is a real possibility? Well, go look him up yourself.

Legs had to retire from New York City when he shot up a customer in his own nightclub, shot him once in the forehead, twice in the temple and twice in the groin. Then he cracked the man's brother on the head with the spent revolver. On an upstate lark, Legs tried to hang a local farmer who had a private cider business. In the Catskills he ran up against a stubborn rum-running competitor, and dismembered and burned his body in a still.

*Legs* is an unflinching description of those and more: of Legs' attempts to smuggle heroin; his buying of politicians, judges and cops, his whoring, whorehouses, women and wife (who stuck by him past even the end). A lady's man and a tough's tough, Diamond had a body that shone all over with scar tissue in certain light. Women, it's said, loved to trace the scars with their fingers. An outlaw's outlaw, Legs eluded cops and courts alike; he died, finally, of three bullets from members of his own gang. Legs was the idol of America.

He also became the idol of Marcus Gorman, Kennedy's narrator and Diamond's lawyer, who is a mixture of the best qualities of Nick Carraway in *The Great Gatsby* and Jack Burden in *All the King's Men*, but he's older than his predecessors, so is more reconciled to the ways of the world than either of them. Gorman admits the murders, stills, heroin and filth, but champions the fame, fun and fantasy that were inextricably webbed in the violence and extralegal activity of his client. Marcus Gorman is no Clarence Darrow picking his clients for righteous reasons. And Legs Diamond is deadlier than either Gatsby or Willie Stark. As in all memoir novels, the ultimate interest lies in the rememberer's sensibility. *Legs* will stand on Gorman's case for his client. Or it will fall on the same, for not everyone will accept such casual cynicism embedded in lush metaphor as Gorman produces.

The pretense around which Gorman organizes the novel is that Legs never died. Indeed, Jack's alive twice over. First, he was unquestionably an ancestral paradigm for modern urban gangsters, upon whom his pioneering was obviously not lost. He left a legacy of money and guns that would dominate the American city on through the 1970s, even though his latter-day followers, such as Richard Nixon . . . lacked the white core fantasy that can give evil a mythical dimension. Second, Legs did have that "white core fantasy," a capacity for living at "the outer limit of boldness." Diamond could be religious, know the importance of the rosary, go to church, sincerely and still out-gangsterize the rest, because he made no judgments about the quality of life. He took what came and responded in kind on its own terms, transforming it in the process. At the victory party after the last trial Legs faced, Gorman raised a glass to him, saying "I toast also to his uncanny ability to bloom in hostile seasons and to survive the blasts of doom." Gorman's implicit claim is that such survival is the unrequited dream at the psychic center of modern urban life.

Speaking through Gorman, Kennedy has touched the myth of the American city's soul at the moment it began to spread toward Europe and toward the outlying parts of its own land. Kennedy's interests are clearly sociological and psychological, but he is a novelist at bottom. He wants the sort of indefinite and suggestive truth germane to fiction, hostile to statistics and finally dependent on the lode of language mined in the privacy of imagination. Kennedy says he wrote the novel obsessively over more than five years. His care and devotion are clearly repaid in *Legs*. Don't be fooled by the jacket cover's nostalgic tinge. Kennedy has looked to the compost of the past not to escape the present, not to establish a preconceived thesis, but to talk about one of the sources for our own days. Legs was one of the Big Boys of the American compost. We can thank Kennedy's green thumb that we have him alive again.—W. T. LHAMON, JR., NR, May 24, 1975, pp. 23–24

Oscar Wilde's observation that America chooses its heroes from the criminal classes was never more true than in the Twenties, when Al Capone, Dutch Schultz and Jack 'Legs' Diamond warred with each other to minister to the thirst of a generation. Through them and their gangland vendettas, Middle America acted out their frontier fantasies. Scott Fitzgerald chose Legs Diamond as his prototype for Gatsby (the novelist and gangster met on a transatlantic crossing in 1926). Fifty years on, William Kennedy, having meticulously researched the life of Legs Diamond for his novel, *Legs*, seems no less captivated by his subject: 'one of the truly American Irishmen of his day: Horatio Alger out of Finn McCool and Jesse James' is how the narrator describes him.

The unkillable Legs rips through the soft underbelly of the Jazz Age like a buzz-saw, shooting, torturing, bullying subordinates and breaking the fingers of his mistress. 'I make no case for Jack as a moderate,' muses his lawyer, attempting to explain his own ambivalence towards the gangster, 'only as a man of primal needs.' I have less sympathy for Legs Diamond then Mr Kennedy has, even in fictional form; but I found the book compulsive reading, although the hard-boiled prose sounded better when read out of the corner of the mouth.—TONY ASPLER, "Looking Tough," LT, May 6, 1976, p. 578

Forty-three years after his death the old comrades of the now legendary Jack "Legs" Diamond are reminiscing atop their barstools in a somewhat boozier than Conradian vein. Among them, her memory juiced-up by the drink, one Flossie recalls that Diamond "had a tan collie, could count to fifty-two and do subtraction", that he "could turn on the electric light sometimes just by snapping his fingers", that "he could tie both his shoes at once". But the story that's enclosed within this romanticizing frame and told us by William Kennedy's ersatz-Marlowe—a lawyer called Marcus who's paid to bail out the boys and front the mob with a clean bib and tucker—amounts to something less fantastic but considerably more gripping. Not that the narrative is consistently exciting: it does come with longueurs and detumescences, and as is the wont of stories told in flashes back it lights up only in flashes. Still, these climaxes are certainly worth waiting for, from the early shoot-out in the Hotsy Totsy Club which drives Legs to hold up in the Catskills, through the plugging and ice-picking of Billy Blue (from St Loo) while he's in complicated *flagrante* in a flophouse, and the cutting up of Charlie Northrup's cadaver ("I'll trim off the edges"), to Leg's come-uppance from a stubborn hick who will let himself go hang rather than split on his cider still's whereabouts.

Above all, though, the coherence and attraction of the novel are a matter of tonality. Acidic *mots* are jerked out of the sides of badmouthing bad guys' mouths in the best manner of 1940s movies about 1920s gangsters. Legs has met Fitzgerald; he likes Von Sternberg films; he follows the boxing careers of Jack Sharkey and Benny Shapiro. And his world is delightfully peopled with the likes of Mendel (The Ox) Feinstein, Murray (The Goose) Pucinski, Tony (The Boy) Amapola, Edward (Fats MacCarthy) Popke, and Big Frenchy De Mange.

If only all this were all, Legs would make a decently engaging read, but total enjoyment is blunted by the gangster's memorialist only allowing us to have his boss when portentously trailing the heavy festoons of a thesis. Legs Diamond is not just an attractive thug, he stands for the American Dream of shooting your way to riches and glory. As a licensed killer eventually to be cathartically slain, he ensures, we are assured, the health of the social system. He is even made the prophet of the intimate interlocking of American city politics and crookery in later decades ("he was unquestionably an ancestral paradigm for modern urban political gangsters, upon whom his pioneering and his example were obviously not lost"). Windy stuff, but then Marcus first endeared himself to Diamond with some headily threadbare philosophizing about Jolson. If it were clear that the author disconnected himself from his Marlowe all would be well (or at least better than it is). But Kennedy and his novel appear simply unperturbed by their narrating man's inevitably curious moral position as a mobsters' legal adviser: a morally and philosophically alerter fiction would certainly want more clearly to disown this narrator.—VALENTINE CUNNINGHAM, "Theoretical Thuggery," *TLS*, Aug. 20, 1976, p. 103

## BILLY PHELAN'S GREATEST GAME

I once lived in or around Albany, New York, for a stretch of almost 20 years. I thought I knew something about its history; its geography; its heavily Irish Catholic population; its patriarchal, dictatorial, and benevolent Democratic political machine, run, until his recent death, by Uncle Dan O'Connell. But after reading William Kennedy's exciting, mad, rich new novel, *Billy Phelan's Greatest Game*, I realize that I hardly knew the old place at all.

Kennedy is a born-and-bred patriot of Albany. He knows more about his special Hibernian turf than anyone else. He knows every bar, hotel, store, bowling alley, pool hall, and whorehouse that ever opened in North Albany. He knows where the Irish had their picnics and parties—and what went on at them; where their churches were; where they bet on horses, played the numbers, and gathered for poker. He can recreate with absolute accuracy the city room conversations at the Albany *Times-Union*, where his hero, Martin Daugherty, works (and where Kennedy once worked and found the material for his first novel, *The Ink Truck*, about an Albany Newspaper Guild strike).

Most important for this new book, Kennedy's pitch is perfect. His is the true comic spirit, conveyed by a tumult of fierce and wonderful language. Conversations in places frequented by his bookies and gamblers and politicians are quick-witted and often filled with unsavory, irreverent street talk and with brawling, wise guy, barroom argot. Kennedy is the unquestioned authority on the dialogue in the State Street bowling alley on that momentous night in 1938 when Billy Phelan rolls 299 against champion Scotty Strech (who "lived with his bowling ball as if it were a third testicle"). At the end of the game, Scotty falls dead. "Holy Mother of God, that was a quick decision," says Charlie McCall, an onlooker who is "the most powerful young man in town."

Charlie's subsequent kidnapping is the novel's main event. Politically and socially, the McCall family rules the city, determining the present and future of its population. Rescuing Charlie takes some days, during which minor events play themselves out. An entire *Decameron* of anecdotes, memories, and details of small lives enriches the narrative, so by the time Charlie is back home, we too are authorities on the corrupt politics and on the life of the bum; the small-time bookie; the call girl; Martin's old father and young, priesthood-bound son; Melissa (mistress at the same time of Martin and his father) doing a play in town; Billy's long-absent father; and Billy's lady friend, Angie, who wants to marry Billy and tries to pull a neat trick on him. To these, add a few non-Irish characters like Ben Berman, who was the city's best tailor; his son, Jake, the liberal lawyer who tries to run against the McCall machine; and Jake's son, Morrie, the black sheep in whom "the worthy Berman family strain had gone slightly askew."

Kennedy works them all into a rich gallimaufry, seasoned by his own unsavory language. The meat in this Irish stew is fathers, sons, uncles, and grandfathers, for Albany's Irish society is heavy on the male side and its activities take place in men-only sanctums. The other sex is present, in bed or at home, but women are usually on the minds of these men only when everything else fails or closes.

Kennedy's affection for the goings-on in Albany during the Twenties and Thirties was first manifest in *Legs*, a book he wrote a few years ago about Jack Diamond. "He [was] not merely the dude of all gangsters, the most active brain in the New York underworld, but . . . one of the truly new American Irishmen of his day: Horatio Alger out of Finn McCool and Jesse James . . . a pioneer, the founder of the first truly modern gang, the dauphin of the town for years." The same rolling prose and informed anecdote that distinguished Kennedy's first-rate, fictionalized account of Legs Diamond are present in his depiction of the McCall gang and its friends and enemies—those who make up the close and closed society of Colonie Street: "They all clustered together . . . to live among their own kind, and the solidarity became an obvious political asset." Fighting, challenging, and defending one another, profoundly Irish and equally profoundly American, the cast of *Billy Phelan* is, quite simply, a wonder—a magical bunch of thugs, lovers, and game players. No one writing in

America today (I say this with assurance, being prepared at the same time for contradiction from some quarter or other) has Kennedy's rich and fertile gift of gab; his pure, verbal energy; his love of people, and their kith and kin. Like his characters, he too is a wonder.—DORIS GRUMBACH, "Fine Print," *SR*, April 29, 1978, p. 40

### IRONWEED

William Kennedy's new novel, *Ironweed*, is also accompanied by outriders—in this case two earlier works that have been simultaneously reissued as Penguin paperbacks. These are *Legs* (1975) and *Billy Phelan's Greatest Game* (1978), both of which belong, as does *Ironweed*, to Kennedy's "Albany cycle." They are to be welcomed, for together they form an impressive body of work by an entertaining and inventive writer who is by no means as well known as he should be. Collectively—and from strikingly different angles—the three novels reconstruct a time and a place and a population: the little world of Irish-Americans living in Albany, New York, as Kennedy imagines it to have existed five and more decades ago.

*Legs* is a fictional account of the career of "Legs" Diamond, the notorious Prohibition-era gangster who was shot to death in an Albany rooming house in 1931 just after he had been acquitted (to the tumultuous cheers of his fans) of kidnapping charges. Though less centered in Albany than the other two novels, *Legs* throws its own distinctive light on the Irish-American ethos of that city through the ambivalent self-revelations of its narrator, Marcus Gorman, a rising Albany lawyer with political ambitions who, like millions of tabloid-reading Americans, allows himself to be seduced by the glamorous aura surrounding a psychopathic criminal of ability, daring, and reckless brutality. Not a profound work, *Legs* is fast moving and absorbing, expert in its documentation of the period.

In *Billy Phelan's Greatest Game*, a more thickly textured novel set in 1938, the focus is upon the interconnections of Albany's Democratic machine, run by the McCall brothers, and a colorful, low-life collection of poolroom sharks, poker players, bartenders, bookies, and assorted night crawlers who run errands for the bosses and depend upon them for handouts, protection, and patronage. Here the ethical point of view is supplied chiefly by a middle-class journalist, Martin Daugherty, while the action itself centers upon a sharply dressed and resourceful petty gambler, Billy Phelan, who has his own peculiar standards to uphold.

*Ironweed*, also set in 1938, reveals a radical shift not only in its angle of vision but also in its style. In it Kennedy largely abandons the rather breezy, quasi-journalistic narrative voice of his previous fiction and resorts to a more poetically charged, often surrealistic use of language as he re-creates the experiences and mental states of an alcoholic bum, Francis Phelan, who, after a long absence, is once again in Albany, lurching around the missions and flophouses of the city's South End. ⟨. . .⟩

The story of Francis is balanced by that of Helen, his companion in drink and homelessness during the past nine years. Outwardly, Helen is "a drunken old douchebag" with a tumor-swollen belly and spindly legs who will submit to the sexual fumbling of a fellow derelict in order to sleep in his wheelless wreck of a car; within, she is still a nice Catholic girl, musically inclined, who was well brought up by an adoring father. She is an innocent who can't be trusted to cross the street on her own, someone whom Francis loves and tries to protect even while he drunkenly reviles her at times with outbursts of pure hatred. The peregrinations of the unsteady

couple as they search for shelter on a chilly night (hoping always to avoid the fate of sleeping in the weeds of a vacant lot) form one of the movements of this musically composed novel. Another is based upon the wagon trip that Francis makes with a crusty old junk dealer, a journey that takes him through all the old neighborhoods before depositing him near the home of his long-deserted wife and grown children.

Throughout the novel Kennedy plays with the contrast between sordid event and exalted illusion, between remembered past and threadbare present, between precise description and blunt colloquialism on the one hand and on the other a style so heightened as to become rhapsodic. At times he flirts perilously with Irish sentimentality—and for the most part gets away with it. Here is the account of Helen's final moments in a fleabag hotel:

> And so when crippled Donovan knocks again at eleven o'clock and asks if Helen needs anything, she says no, no thank you, old cripple, I don't need anything or anybody anymore. . . . And after he goes away from the door she lets go of the brass and thinks of Beethoven, Ode to Joy,
> And hears the joyous multitudes advancing,
> Dah dah-dah,
> Dah dah-de-dah-dah,
> And feels her legs turning to feathers and sees that her head is floating down to meet them as her body bends under the weight of so much joy,
> Sees it floating ever so slowly
> As the white bird glides over the water until it comes to rest on the Japanese kimono
> That has fallen so quietly,
> So softly
> Onto the grass where the moonlight grows.

Thus quoted in isolation, the passage seems shameless in both its sentimentality and its poetic inflation. But in the context already established of Helen's deluded self-image, one sees that Kennedy is, so to speak, allowing her one final aria, an aria to cap the sentimental songs she had earlier sung—to imagined applause—in a sleazy skid-row saloon.

Though there is much shrewd observation of both conscious and unconscious motivation, *Ironweed* was not intended to be read as a psychologically realistic portrayal of alcoholic degradation and its causes. Did or did not Francis, the glorious ballplayer, mean to kill the strikebreaking trolley conductor? At one point he contemplates "the evil autonomy of his hands." At another he believes himself to be "a creature of unknown and unknowable qualities, a man in whom there would never be an equanimity of both impulsive and premeditated action." A few sentences later he reaches the "unutterable" conclusion that his guilt is all that he has left: "If I lose it, I have stood for nothing, been nothing, done nothing." But Kennedy never allows the issue to be closed. What he has written is a kind of fantasia on the strangeness of human destiny, on the mysterious ways in which a life can be transformed and sometimes redeemed. As such, *Ironweed* seems to me a work of unusual interest, original in its conception, full of energy and color, a splendid addition to the Albany cycle.—ROBERT TOWERS, "Violent Places," *NYRB*, March 31, 1983, pp. 11–12

### ALBANY CYCLE

William Kennedy came to fiction after a long career as a newspaperman in Albany, where he was born and where all three of his novels are set. Reissued in paperback alongside his newest book ⟨*Ironweed*⟩, *Legs* (1975) still seems the best and *Billy Phelan's Greatest Game* (1978) almost as good. They both reek of city room slang, love of fact, bottom-line bluntness, and headline speed. *Legs* is a shade more convincing, not because it dramatizes an historic figure, the infamous Jack "Legs" Diamond, but because he is created for us by a narrator, his sidekick lawyer Marcus Gorman, and because Gorman pieces the story together from memories. Twice-distanced, the speakeasies and gangsters and fast talk seem both immediate and legendary, with Irish Catholic Albany as a microcosm of the thirties. Like E. L. Doctorow, Kennedy uses an outmoded style, the sort that Dos Passos and Hammett and Harold McCoy used (expletives and sex added), but the effect snags on anachronisms and too much verbal touching-up. *Ironweed* focuses on Francis Phelan, Billy's father, who backed out of home decades ago, killed a man in a streetcar-strike riot, and has been a hobo and stumblebum ever since, he doesn't really know why. Francis makes some money digging graves and clopping about the city with old Rosskam in his junk wagon ("Raaaa-aaaaags!"), trying to stay warm and get drunk, seeing a few old friends, meeting a few ghosts, making a pathetic visit to his old home. Sadly, because Kennedy is an earnest writer who is not after flashy effects, the book fails to convince. Fine writing creeps in to overpower the colloquial rightness. The blear-eyed bum is made to think, "He was at war with himself, his private factions mutually bellicose, and if he was ever to survive, it would be with the help not of any socialistic god but with a clear head and a steady eye for the truth; for the guilt he felt was not worth the dying." Francis needs some sympathetic person to remember him for us and conjecture his feelings. Without something like that, the effect is sentimental and incredible. As the title suggests, Kennedy wants us to value his protagonist as a survivor, an archetype, a perennial: "The name refers to the toughness of the stem," runs the epigraph from the Audubon Field Guide. Kennedy harms his camera-eye authenticity, however, when these archetypes creep into the text. Here for contrast is how much more deftly Kennedy handles the archetypal Jack Diamond:

> So the newsmen, installing Jack in the same hierarchy where they placed royalty, heroes, and movie stars, created him anew as they enshrined him. They invented a version of him with each story they wrote, added to his evil luster by imagining crimes for him to commit . . . Jack had imagined his fame all his life and now it was imagining him.

This leaves Jack free to say, "Good stuff. Sounds like one of my dreams." Here's hoping that Kennedy can put down his copies of Jung and Huizenga, and go back to the city room.—DEAN FLOWER, *HdR*, Summer 1983, pp. 375–76

What holds ⟨the Albany cycle⟩ together ⟨. . .⟩ is a controlling vision of American society, or at least the Irish contribution to it, that is a curious mixture of warped idealism, mysticism, a need to create legends and heroes, and a notion of transcendental style that is contained in the concept of having "class". The chief protagonist of each book is thought of as being touched by magic. The gangster Jack Diamond, who may have been the model for his fellow Irish-American Scott Fitzgerald's Jay Gatsby, has miraculously survived a succession of ambushes that have left his body a battleground of wounds. The journalist Martin Daugherty treats Billy Phelan as an existential hero, and Daugherty's playwright father, in his day the peer of Eugene O'Neill, wrote a play about the 1901 strike called *The Car Barn* that was inspired by Francis Phelan. Diamond, Francis Phelan and his son Billy are violent, destructive men, in flight from an oppressive, guilt-ridden religion, and from that cloying domesticity created by women who see themselves as upholders of proper Catholic values. ⟨. . .⟩

Kennedy is aware of the dangers of his enterprise, and the observer of his most unlikely hero asks himself, "Martin Daugherty, why are you so obsessed with Billy Phelan? Why make a heroic *picaro* out of a simple chump?"

Daugherty is blessed with a form of double vision rather like that possessed by the extraterrestrial in Nicolas Roeg's film *The Man Who Fell to Earth*. Not only can he foresee the future but the past is so real that palpable images of it haunt him as he walks around town. Somewhat folksier is the gift of Francis Phelan. Prematurely senile at the age of fifty-eight, he has conversations with his infant son and other inhabitants of Albany Catholic cemetery. His behaviour is easily excused because the corpses talk among themselves, and we are reminded of the scene in the New England graveyards that ends Thornton Wilder's *Our Town*. There are also strong resemblances between *Ironweed* and Wilder's novel *The Eighth Day*, where a mid-western miner sets off on a lifetime's wandering exile after being the accidental agent of a man's death in 1902. It is indeed possible that Kennedy is bringing back the all-American feyness, sentimental fatalism and woozy rhetoric that made Wilder so popular some forty years ago.

So far Kennedy has written, and occasionally overwritten, some eloquent chapters of imaginative social history. His sense of place is exact, his dialogue unerring, his big heart and robust humour endearing. The three books modify and fortify each other. They do not yet, however, as Saul Bellow appears to believe, constitute a substantial *oeuvre*; but they might well be the beginning of one.—PHILIP FRENCH, *TLS*, Oct. 5, 1984, p. 1116

---

## GEORGE STADE
### From "Life on the Lam"

*New York Times Book Review*, January 23, 1983, pp. 1, 14–15

Frankly, I have a prejudice against lyrical novels, and not just because they make me think of Anaïs Nin. A lyrical novelist is less interested in his fictions than in his attitudes toward them. He dissolves his characters and events into a nimbus of sentiment. The intention of a lyrical novelist, I mean, is not to *render*, not to disappear behind the greater reality of his characters and their doings, but to flash his wounded heart, his noble soul, his soaring imagination, his golden tongue—among other indencenies. It makes me mad.

I have a double prejudice against mythifications, especially when what's being mythified is the raw material of an entertainment. A pox on Graham Greene! Who needs his wretched allegories? Give me Eric Ambler every time. Give me the real thing, anything by Max Brand or Ernest Haycox, say, rather than E. L. Doctorow's *Welcome to Hard Times*, which is a western transmogrified by the mythic commentary on itself. If you love baseball more than any idea of it, you will read mythologizing novels like Bernard Malamud's *Natural* and Philip Roth's *Great American Novel* with the indignation of a man who discovers that some one has sprayed Reddi-Wip on his spare ribs. Tell me honestly, wouldn't you rather re-dream your way through *Rebecca* than doze your way through Iris Murdoch's latest mytho-mystification? Is not the naïve *Dracula* more of a grabber than Anne Rice's sophisticated *Interview with a Vampire*? Is not the cool purity of *The Maltese Falcon* preferable to some *policier* infused with existential dread, à la Norman Mailer and a plague of Frenchmen? "An American Dream" indeed! We could use a few new primary myths, all right, but that's different from getting the old ones going around admiring themselves in reflexive prose.

The justification for this grousing is that entertainments

you can read without embarrassment are hard to come by. Good light novels, such as Mario Puzo's *Godfather* and James Dickey's *Deliverance*, are as rare as great heavyweights such as William Gaddis's *JR* and Thomas Pynchon's *Gravity's Rainbow*. Of worthy middle-serious contenders for the book awards there are more each year than anybody can read, alas. A novelist, then, who has it in him to write an entertainment but turns it into something else, a writer who arouses appetites he can satisfy but doesn't—because he has more exalted aspirations—is like a mission hall preacher who prolongs his sermon for hungry men while the macaroni–and–cheese burns.

It is prejudices like these, anyhow, that made me dislike the first of William Kennedy's Albany novels, *Legs*, when it came out in 1975. I also disliked its successor, *Billy Phelan's Greatest Game* (1978). I now like both novels very much, as I like *Ironweed*, the most recent of these interconnected novels set mostly in Albany in the 1930's. There are virtues in these novels sufficient to neutralize the most recalcitrant of prejudices, even though all three of them are built out of the raw materials of an entertainment, even though they are intermittently lyrical and self-consciously mythifying.

Take *Legs*, for example. Its hero is "Legs" Diamond, né John T. Nolan, the gangster whom other people have described as a psychopathic killer. Marcus Gorman, Diamond's lawyer and our narrator, describes his client as "one of the truly new American Irishmen of his day; Horatio Alger out of Finn McCool and Jesse James," "a singular being in a singular land, a fusion of the individual life flux with the clear and violent light of American reality." Not only has Legs Diamond met Fitzgerald and read *The Great Gatsby*, he also knows Edward Fuller, on whom Gatsby was modeled; his roadster, like his ideal conception of himself, is a "facsimile" of Gatsby's. Diamond's mythomania, and our own, finally have "the effect of taking Jack Diamond away from himself, of making him a product of the collective imagination. Jack has imagined his fame all his life and now it was imagining him." Passages such as these put my prejudices on the prowl.

They were quashed on rereading, however, by Mr. Kennedy's steady-eyed demonstration that Diamond was "a venal man of integrity, for he never ceased to renew his vulnerability to punishment, death, and damnation. It is one thing to be corrupt. It is another to behave in a psychologically responsible way toward your own evil." When at the end Marcus Gorman toasts the dead Jack Diamond for "his talent for making virtue seem unwholesome," for "his defiance, his plan not to seduce the world but to terrify it, to spit in the eye of the public which says no Moloch shall pass," we are with him.

The hero of *Billy Phelan's Greatest Game* is a pool shark and gambler who, thank God, has no conception of himself, ideal or otherwise. Martin Daugherty, a journalist from whose point of view we see much of the action, has. His function in this novel is much like Marcus Gorman's in *Legs*: to mythify his hero. "Why," Daugherty asks himself, "are you so obsessed with Billy Phelan? Why make a heroic *picaro* out of a simple chump?" A good question—which Daugherty answers when he writes an article in praise of Billy, whose unself-conscious integrity has put him in the wrong with the pols who rule Albany. "He viewed Billy as a strong man, indifferent to luck, a gamester who accepted the rules and played by them, but who also played above them," a man, in short, who shows grace under pressure. "I aspire to the condition of Billy Phelan," concludes Daugherty.

That condition is inseparable from Albany's late-Depression sporting underworld, which Mr. Kennedy resur-

rects before our inner eyes in a remarkable feat of imagination. Billy's condition is also inseparable from his relations with his father, which reflect and comment on a whole series of father-son relationships, some tragic, some comic, all murderous. Daugherty, too, knows "how it is to live in the inescapable presence of the absence of the father." His hard-earned conclusion is "that all sons are Isaac, all fathers are Abraham, and that all Isaacs become Abrahams if they work at it long enough." Billy's integrity, Albany's underworld, all those Abrahams and Isaacs—these knocked the feet from under my prejudices the second time around. ⟨. . .⟩

We soon come to value this loser ⟨Francis Phelan⟩, who loses largely because he plays by stricter rules than he sets for anyone else. Like his son, Billy Phelan, like Legs Diamond, he has a perverse kind of integrity. He only lies to himself when the truth would make things easier for him. Because we value him, the restrained scene in which he visits his faithful wife, a disappointed Penelope, and his resentful daughter—he has been avoiding them for over 20 years—is very moving. The scene in which Helen, Francis' roadmate, lays herself down for the big sleep is almost as moving. It would have been perfect, perhaps, without the echoes of Molly Bloom and Gerty McDowell from *Ulysses*, that stumbling block in the way of every Irish novelist since Joyce. At the end of *Ironweed* Francis is once more a murderer, once more in hiding.

*Ironweed* is different from its predecessors in tone and style, in the very status of its words. There is no participant-narrator, no Marcus Gorman; the words, in fact, do not feel as though they were spoken (or written) by anyone. They feel, rather, as though they somehow emanated from the events they described, as though the events were becoming conscious of themselves as they occurred. The prose is therefore as various as the events it seeps out of, hovers over, looks down on, dissolves back into, becomes. In one passage of negative lyricism, Francis has a vision of his dead parents coupling at the moment of his conception, a moment of "newly conceived death":

> Francis watched this primal pool of his own soulish body squirm into burgeoning matter, saw it change and grow with the speed of light until it was the size of an infant, saw it then yanked roughly out of the maternal cavern by his father, who straightened him, slapped him into being, and swiftly molded him into a bestial weed. The body sprouted to wildly matured growth and stood fully clad at last in the very clothes Francis was now wearing. He recognized the toothless mouth, the absent finger joints, the bump on the nose, the mortal slouch of this newborn shade, and he knew then that he would be this decayed self he had been so long in becoming, through all the endless years of his death.

But for all the rich variety of prose and event, from hallucination to bedrock realism to slapstick and to blessed quotidian peace, "Ironweed" is more austere than its predecessors. It is more fierce, but also more forgiving. On its own scale it is to its predecessors as *Oedipus at Colonus* is to *Antigone* and *Oedipus Rex*. There is no apotheosis, but there is an ironic equivalent.

In spite of my prejudices, for the last few weeks Mr. Kennedy's Irish stews, crooks, roughnecks, cons, gamblers, bums, pols and working stiffs have been moving around in my head, setting examples, giving good advice. His tough-minded and defiant humanism has left me chastened but feeling good. My guess is that it will have the same effect on many readers.

## WILLIAM H. PRITCHARD
### "The Spirits of Albany"

*New Republic*, February 14, 1983, pp. 37–38

The third of William Kennedy's "Albany novels," *Ironweed*, is also the best, and it should bring this original and invigorating novelist to the attention of many new readers, especially since it is written in a language that is vital throughout. The previous two novels, *Legs* and *Billy Phelan's Greatest Game* (both just reissued by Penguin) had excellent parts, scenes in which Mr. Kennedy's skill in the vivid rendering of speech and action works perfectly. One remembers, for example, the moment in *Legs* when Jack Diamond, the legendary gangster, gives a demonstration—to the book's nervous lawyer-narrator, Marcus Gorman—of how to shoot a gun, one midsummer Sunday afternoon at Jimmy Biondo's place in the Catskills. Or there was the day Billy Phelan bowled a near-perfect game (a score of 299) at the Downtown Health Amusement Club ("no women, no mixed leagues, please, beer on tap till 4:00 AM"), causing his opponent, Scotty Streck (from the West End German neighborhood of Cabbagetown) to fall dead of a heart attack ("it was reliably reported during his [Scotty's] lifetime that he would not give a sick whore a hairpin"). But the books as a whole are less good than their individual parts: *Legs* is too long, repetitive, episodic; *Billy Phelan's Greatest Game* feels a shade wandering, not quite focused on a significant action.

But *Ironweed* is so focused, from its strong beginning in Saint Agnes's Cemetery, where Francis Phelan—shoveling dirt on various caskets in order to earn, for a change, a day's wages—confronts in the most natural and inevitable-seeming way, the spirits of the dead. It is the eve of All Saints Day in 1938, and in a line of encounters stretching through the book, Francis begins by meeting his parents, then his son Gerald, whom as thirteen-day-old infant he let slip through his hands while changing a diaper. Gerald died instantly of a cracked neckbone, after which Francis left home and for the last twelve years has been running. He and his friend Rudy ("A little chilly," [Francis] said, "but it's gonna be a nice day." "If it don't puke," said Rudy),

> . . . and both knew intimately the etiquette, the taboos, the protocol of bums. By their talk to each other they understood that they shared a belief in the brotherhood of the desolate; yet in the scars of their eyes they confirmed that no such fraternity had ever existed; that the only brotherhood they belong to was the one that asked that enduring question: How do I get through the next twenty minutes?

As one of the novel's epigraphs informs us, tall ironweed is a member of the sunflower family with an especially tough stem. We are invited to think of Francis, the book's hero, in similar terms; for he is a fighter, can sleep the last night of October—"the unruly night when grace is always in short supply and the new dead walk abroad in this land"—in a patch of weeds, arising none the worse for it to walk another day about the streets of Albany. The spirit of place is admirably present in Kennedy's writing, and for someone like myself whose knowledge of Albany is limited to dimming memories of making bus and train connections there thirty years ago, or driving through it and occasionally stopping for spaghetti, his presentation is authoritative. Sometimes a deeper, more lyric sense of place is created, as in these sentences early in the novel when Francis pauses from his shoveling to take a look around him:

> . . . down the hill toward Broadway and over toward the hills of Rensselaer and Troy on the other side of the Hudson, the coke plant spewing palpable smoke from its great chimney at the far end of the Menands bridge. Francis decided this would be a fine place to be buried. The hill had a nice flow to it that carried you down the grass and out onto the river, and then across the water and up through the trees on the far shore to the top of the hills, all in one swoop. Being dead here would situate a man in place and time.

Against such yearnings to be "situated" in a more permanent position, as it were, is Francis's ironweed-like persistence. At one moment later in the novel, he turns on the "spooks" (or are they saints?) who have haunted him and tells them that "You ain't real and I ain't gonna be at your beck and call no more": "You're all dead, and if you ain't, you oughta be. I'm the one is livin'. I'm the one that puts you on the map." We may be reminded of Joyce's Bloom in the cemetery with his sudden recognition that he is not dead, not yet: "Let them sleep in their maggoty beds. They are not going to get me this innings. Warm beds: warm full-blooded life."

But the fullblooded life in *Ironweed* is most copiously found in the language with which Kennedy has endowed these "marginal" people so as to make them anything but marginal. Particularly Francis Phelan, who is not only a sometime baseball player but the bum-as-poet, as when he walks past Hawkins Stadium:

> He remembered when it was a pasture. Hit a ball right and it'd roll forever, right into the weeds. Bow-Wow Buckley'd be after it and he'd find it right away, a wizard. Bow-Wow kept half a dozen spare balls in the weeds for emergencies like that. Then he'd throw the runner out at third on a sure home run and he'd brag about his fielding. Honesty. Bow-Wow is dead. Worked on an ice wagon and punched his own horse and it stomped him, was that it? Nah. That's nuts. Who'd punch a horse?

Or he relates a list of bums who slept in the weeds in cold weather, to rise no more:

> There was another guy, Pocono Pete, he died in Denver, like a brick. And Poocher Felton, he bought it in Detroit, pissed his pants and froze tight to the sidewalk. And a crazy bird they called Ward Six, no other name. They found him with a red icicle growin' out of his nose. . . . Foxy Phil Tooker, a skinny little runt, he froze all scrunched up, knees under his chin.

Or he decides, with the proceeds of a day hauling rags for a ragman, to purchase a turkey and visit with his wife and children for the first time in twelve years. Asking where he can get such a bird, he manages to frighten a lady, and her husband launches into action:

> "What did you ask my wife?" he said.
> "I asked if she knew where I could get a turkey."
> "What for?"
> "Well," said Francis, and he paused, and scuffed one foot, "my duck died."
> "Just keep movin', bud."
> "Gotcha," Francis said, and he limped on.

Kennedy's comic poetry of dialogue bears comparison with another contemporary expert at this game—George V. Higgins.

Like Updike's Rabbit Angstrom, Francis runs, and his creator expresses this condition in an elevated level of diction that is another aspect of the book's style;

the running from the calumny of men and women, the running from family, from bondage, from destitution of spirit through ritualistic straightenings, the running, finally, in a quest for pure flight as a fulfilling mannerism of the spirit.

This sort of high talk could be dangerous to the book's poise, which is essentially a comic one—though with scenes of fine pathos as, most notably, in Francis's return home, turkey under his arm. On occasion I felt the writing about the hero, and about

Helen—the women for whom Francis cares and whose own tale is important here—was grandiose, perhaps too ambitious. But Kennedy is an exuberant writer who likes to try out different styles, and he succeeds so well so much of the time that I was quite won over. It is extremely satisfying to come upon a new novelist, so resourcefully assured in his command of language and place. I plan to stop in Albany next time, avoid all recent creations of Mr. Rockefeller's city, and do instead some reconstructing, with the aid of William Kennedy's novels, of what once was there.

# X. J. KENNEDY

## 1929–

Joseph Charles Kennedy was born in Dover, New Jersey, on August 21, 1929. As a teenager he was active in science fiction fandom and amateur journalism, and founded the long-running Spectator Amateur Press Association, for which he published a magazine of poetry entitled *Green Thoughts*. He graduated from Seton Hall College in South Orange, New Jersey, with a B.Sc. degree in 1950, and earned an M.A. at Columbia in 1951, after which he served in the U.S. Navy for four years. He studied at the Sorbonne for two years and then returned to the U.S. to undertake graduate studies at the University of Michigan from 1956 to 1962. He married Dorothy Mintzlaff in 1962 and took his first teaching job at the University of North Carolina in Greensboro. He joined the faculty at Tufts in 1963, where he continues to teach today.

His first volume of poetry, *Nude Descending a Staircase* (1961), was inspired by the Marcel Duchamp painting of the same name. His second collection, *Growing into Love*, did not appear until 1969. His poetry is characterized by the use of traditional meters and by an irreverent questioning of commonly held beliefs. Known as a self-deflating satirist, Kennedy supposedly adopted the initials X. J. so as to avoid confusion with the more famous Massachusetts Kennedys. He has worked for the *Paris Review* as a poetry editor and founded a literary magazine called *Counter/Measures* with his wife. He has edited several anthologies of poetry, most recently compiling *The Tygers of Wrath: Poems of Hate, Anger, and Invective* (1981). He has also devoted considerable effort to children's poetry during the last ten years. His latest book, a collected edition of his poetry entitled *Cross Ties*, appeared in 1985. The father of five, Kennedy lives with his wife and children in a suburb of Boston.

## Works

### NUDE DESCENDING A STAIRCASE

X. J. Kennedy, who won quick critical attention and the Lamont poetry prize with this first book ⟨*Nude Descending a Staircase*⟩, is already more than a promise. Technically speaking, he is not one of the revolutionary iconoclasts who try for new revelations by casting language and meter into the melting pot. His energy channels itself into restraining molds the better to achieve or retain purity. Intensity thus gained is memorable and gives the pleasure of a renewal of the old forms, the assurance of that continuity of language which makes it possible to believe in its future. It is perhaps a subtler kind of revolution, and I wouldn't be saying these things of X. J. Kennedy if his adherence to traditional patterns were a simple matter of formalistic decorum. There is of course a part of his carefully polished work which constitutes just exercise, and pieces like "On a Child Who Lived One Minute" or "At the Stoplight by the Paupers' Graves" show how well he can mimic Frost's voice if he sets his mind to it:

> My engine shudders as if about to stall
> But I've no heart to wait with them all night
> That would be long to tense here for a leap,
> Thrall to the remote decisions of the light.

But this is Kennedy's own prehistory as a poet (Frost being only one of the ancestors who compose that prehistory), and if we want to catch the actuality of his tone, we shall seek it in poems like "In Faith of Rising," "To Break a Marble Block," "Lilith," "The Sirens," "Little Elegy," "Lewis Carroll," "Nude Descending a Staircase," and certain epigrams.

Yet making this choice gets us into the trouble of defining *what* that actual, personal tone of Kennedy is. The title piece would seem to stand by itself as a pure feat of craftsmanship, a tribute Kennedy pays to Valéry and Wilbur:

> One-woman waterfall, she wears
> Her slow descent like a long cape
> And pausing, on the final stair
> Collects her motions into shape.

The "I" of the poet here appears only as an eye—an extremely curious one, to be sure, and we could wish for many more such retinas on Parnassus. But the poem is finally a witty *pièce de bravoure*, no matter how keen its pictorial and dynamic sensibility. Unlike the Frostian pieces, it certainly belongs to the maturity of Kennedy, yet it only shows what he can do with his own instrument when playing for recreation. It is a fine *étude*. Its alertness and wit, to be sure, are what make it a meaningful rather than an empty exercise, and they provide the nexus with those poems where the "I" is involved, existentially speaking, and Kennedy gives more of himself.

Perhaps the ideal transition in this sense could be found in "Lewis Carroll," the unassuming piece which sounds like an urbane joke on the pixy-like author of *Alice*, and resonates with metaphysical sadness:

> On tiptoe past intimidated primroses,
> His head ateeter on its collar wall,
> The Reverend Mr Dodgson longdivided
> God's cipher (1 goes 3 × 3)
>
> And shrinking as his Alice grew, rejected
> The little flask of love that said *Drink Me*

I think I have read this poem a dozen times, and it grows on me (without making me shrink) every time. Straight from the breezy beginning ("Click! down the whiterabbithole . . .") it moves with a swift choppiness of rhythm that seems the ideal embodiment for the Ariel-like whimsicality of our "Reverend" fabulist, mathematician and photographer. I defy anybody to write a better concise biography (though "biography" is not the point here). Humor and sadness come to unimprovable focus with the last line but one—in how many relevant senses Alice "grew" while her author "shrank"! For here the physical growth of the little girl who inspired the book is implied, along with the mythical fortune of her fictional counterpart; and again, if Carroll himself "shrank" antithetically, it isn't only because he was withering into old age and death, but because he was refining himself into that spirit of wonder which the erstwhile child had to leave forever behind in entering the world of common sense (music in the ears of Wordsworth).

When "Ariel" grieves, he writes things like "Little Elegy for a Child Who Skipped Rope":

> Here lies resting, out of breath,
> Out of turns, Elizabeth
> Whose quicksilver toes not quite
> Cleared the whirring edge of night . . .

The play on analogies, which can become mere cleverness of an academic type, attains here the result of magical astonishment, and the reader is himself left breathless.

When "Ariel" is in the mood of playing tricks on sailors, he writes "The Sirens," and weaves a sure spell:

> Roared; as the music sweetened, railed
> Against his oarsmen's bent wet slopes,
> Imprisoned in propriety
> And pagan ethic. Also ropes.
>
> Sails strummed. The keel drove tapestries
> Of distance on the sea's silk loom
> Leaving those simple girls beyond
> Woven undone rewoven foam . . .

And when he wants "to break a marble block," he does, very firmly—only to tell us that art can be black magic, and the statue a Medusa to her Michaelangelo. The insistent hammering of the sculptor's chisel is heard throughout—obsessive, incantatory repetition of the very word "stone" achieves that effect. Kennedy's humor (ranging from the subtle to the earthy) and Kennedy's earnestness make for a unique combination, seething under the surface of formal decorum to the point of breaking it. Rather than expand, he concentrates—but there is nothing sedate about him.—GLAUCO CAMBON, *CoL*, Spring–Summer 1962, pp. 111–13

Mr. Kennedy is never simply funny. His humor, wryness, and irony always enact themselves in a way that serves to open the human condition to the cognitive capacities of the mind. His wit is the source of his creativity and the auspices under which his understanding conducts itself—in short, it provides that groundwork in texture to his work that we call "style". It allows

him to go far afield for comparisons that produce insights that would not be possible in different, more serious contexts. Here, in not one of the best poems in the book, about a sailor on shore-leave at the sites of ancient Greece, see how there shows through these stanzas,

> On high from the sacked Parthenon
> A blackbird faintly warbles.
> Sellers of paperweights resell
> The Elgin marbles.
>
> Here where queen-betrayed
> Agamemnon had to don
> Wine-purple robes, boys in torn drabs
> Try my whitehat on.

the bathos, the worn triviality, and the ghostly superfices of modern life. In a poem that will last as long as men and women do, a tired floozie sings of her faded beauty and past conquests. In what conducts itself with the good-hearted cheer of a robust drinking song, the whole pattern of the psyche's involvement with sex looks out from apparently accidental allusions taken for the sake of their rhyme:

> 'All the gents used to swear that the white of my calf
> Beat the down of the swan by a length and a half.'

The fatted calf, the curse, the innocence and the corruption of society beneath the first line; the Leda and Helen myths, the destructiveness, and lascivious overtones of the second.

> 'When the horses bowed down to me that I might choose,
> I bet on them all, for I hated to lose.
> Now I'm saddled each night for my butter and eggs
> And the broken threads run down the back of my legs.'

The archetype of her whole psychology—and so much of human existence—the first two lines are a model of, that necessarily contains its own doom and failure within its very assumptions; the physical imperatives of the body's uses in love that make euphemisms of "butter" and "eggs"; the run-down life, the mad dash, and the muscular decay, with its psychological accompaniment, of the final line. And then she says to her young accomplices in this life about time, in Mr. Kennedy's incomparable mastery of pun, "You'll be hard-pressed to stop him from going too far."—THEODORE HOLMES, "Wit, Nature, and the Human Concern," *Poetry*, Aug. 1962, pp. 320–21

All the poetry in *Nude Descending a Staircase*, serious and light, displays that love of temporal displacement that has spawned a hundred *Astounding* cover paintings: those depicting feathered Indians backgrounded by a spaceship in landing cradle, or people in medieval costume fingering futuristic weapons. The group of poems titled "Inscriptions After Fact" are built largely of this science-fictional effect; one poem in the section, "Theater of Dionysus," contains little else:

> Over stones where Orestes fled
> The sonorous Furies
> Girls hawking flyspecked postcards
> Pursue the tourist. . . .

In "Where Are the Snows of Yesteryear?" we discover how the heroes and heroines of the heroic age have disappeared and become natural and mechanical effects in our own age: "Deirdre, her combustive hair / Filaments of wavelengthed air" and "Heroes struck on Homer's lyre / Strummings of the AP wire." Nature is further considered in mechanistic terms in the poem "Airport in the Grass," which describes a place where "Grasshopper copters whir" and "A red ant carts / From the fusilage of the wren that crashed / Usable parts."

All these juxtapositions of today and yesterday, nature and

machine, are fairly conventional provender for the poet, but here are redeemed by Kennedy's lively insight and phrasemaking talent. There are a number of impressive if not truly memorable poems in this collection. In addition to those already mentioned, I would name "Solitary Confinement" and "B Negative" as among the best.

But even the best of the poems in *Nude Descending a Staircase* are basically thin and disappointingly narrow in scope. Many start out from trivialities inferrable from their titles: "At the Ghostwriter's Deathbed," "Leave of Absence (for an Instructor in Composition)," and few are in earnest labor to say anything profound. These poems seem to be mere exercises, and not strenuous ones at that. If we can judge from his quatrain "Ars Poetica," X. J. has a theory of artless art:

> The goose that laid the golden egg
> Died looking up its crotch
> To find out how its sphincter worked.
> Would you lay well? Don't watch.

After such knowledge, Kennedy is inevitably at his best at his lightest, like breakfast rolls. While I am not one to sneer at an artificer who manages witty conversational and deft verse such as this, I am sorry to discover that Joe apparently lost nerve after such thundering failures as the ludicrous poem I perversely recall from *Green Thoughts*. He has the ability to succeed in efforts far more sustained and impressive than these. I wish he would be more daring.—REDD BOGGS, "Parnassus on Jets," *Ctrice*, Spring 1963, pp. 12–13

X. J. Kennedy's poetic version of Marcel Duchamp's famous cubist painting of the same title ("Nude Descending a Staircase") is occasionally anthologized but rarely discussed, despite its compact brilliance. A brief look at salient features of the poem's sound and rhythm, language and imagery should indicate the extraordinary skill with which Kennedy figures forth his vision of motion.

The poem turns on an implicit analogy between beautiful women and beautiful poems: both are composed of individually beautiful parts but their unity is dynamic. Poems, like women, move, and their shapes are to be understood as a harmony of integrally related moving parts—"poetry in motion," to borrow the popular song's metaphor for the singer's girlfriend. The corollary of this analogy is that things are seen in their most beautiful aspect precisely when they are seen at their most essential. The conception of nudity follows directly from this premise, giving special point to the fact that the woman's only clothes are the "cape" of her own descent. The fact that she has nothing "on her mind" is thus an indication not of Kennedy's male chauvinism but rather of his attempt to zero in on pure physical beauty. But the more important implication is that since the most fundamental quality of a woman and a poem is dynamism, both will appear the more beautiful as we perceive them in motion. Kennedy's task, then, is not unlike Herrick's in "Delight in Disorder": to draw a human portrait enriched but not overshadowed by the analogy with poetry.

It is in the poem's rhythms more than anywhere else that we see the analogy at work. Though there is considerable caesural subtlety and an occasional trochaic inversion, the central beat is iambic tetrameter. But in the beginning of the last stanza, we come upon a dramatic reversal: "One-woman waterfall, she wears/Her slow descent like a long cape." In addition to slowing it down by metrical means, Kennedy impedes the poem's movement by stringing together long *w* and *l* sounds. In a classic joining of sound and sense, the rhythms tell of their own "slow descent." In the next line they pause, as does the nude, and finally they collect their own

"motions into shape," returning to perfect iambic as the woman comes to the bottom of the stairs.

The waterfall is only part of a carefully constructed pattern of images ("snowing"-l.1, "sifts"-l.3, "thresh"-l.5) that have two things in common: the suggestion of downward motion and of parts or segments. The nude's descent is like the falling of snow or water, the sifting of flour, and the threshing of grain (the latter two by implication, of course): the parts separate out and collect at the bottom. But the poet's interest is in the shape of the motion itself rather than of the individual parts either in isolation or combination. Her motion is at once soft and slow, liquid and lucid. In its dimension of whiteness "snowing" combines with the implicit flour of "sifts" to suggest the purity associated with the nude—a purity that is emphasized by the images of threshing and sifting, both of which are processes that sort out the good parts, as it were. But Kennedy colors the whiteness with "sunlight" (l.3) and the "gold of lemon, root and rind" (l.2), a tactile image that eroticizes the nude by picturing the goosebumpy texture of her skin.

In order to emphasize her dynamism Kennedy uses the gerundive or present participle to describe not only her flesh ("snowing") and her motion ("pausing"-l. 11) but also the very medium she moves through ("the swinging air"-l.7). There is, however, another sense in which the medium she moves through is the poem itself, which is also in motion and which, like the air, "parts to let her parts go by" (l.8) The elaborate pun on *parts* both elaborates the analogy between the nude and the poem and underlines the larger relationship between shape and motion that the poem has been celebrating. To use the same word as noun and verb to describe a thing as well as an action is, in the context of this poem, to blur the distinction. By directing our attention to that blur, Kennedy literally embodies the notion that for poem and nude alike their most beautiful shape is their motion.—RONALD A. SHARP, *Expl*, Spring 1979, pp. 2–3

### GROWING INTO LOVE

Like Auden and Smith, Kennedy can tune the music of his forms precisely to the various attitudes of his speakers, and so can avoid, in his serious poems, the cloying cuteness which often invades the dead-pan poems of such light-verse virtuosos as Phyllis McGinley and John Updike. Even within the same poem, Kennedy can make successful shifts of tone by increasing or decreasing his dependence on light-verse techniques. In a long poem called "Reading Trip," he recounts an experience which many poets have had, but which few have seen so clearly. The poem is wildly playful in spots, as when the poet encounters, during the question-and-answer session, a young man who asks, "Don't you find riming everything a drag?"

> A drag, man? Worse than that! Between the eyes,
>   I take the blade of his outrageous stare.
> Whoever crosses him, the varlet dies,
>   Trapped Guest to his unancient Mariner:
>   "Get with it, baby, what you want to be
>   So artsy-craftsy for? Screw prosody . . ."

The trip is recounted in familiar detail, which is partly the source of the humor—Kennedy's typed characters and situations are funny because we know them. But the familiarity also imparts a wistful quality to the poem. A poet's intensity may be heightened by the experience of being a "trapped Guest," but even the intensity becomes routine after a while, as James Dickey has shown in his brilliant, often hilarious essay, "Barnstorming for Poetry." Kennedy captures the wistfulness, and the cyclical nature of the process, in his concluding stanza:

Edge out into the dusk to claim my slot
In the home-droning traffic, less and less
The bard on fire, more one now with the blot
That hoods the stars above Los Angeles,
Hard gunning, on the make for far-off nights,
Like any other pair of downcast brights.

This poem is not as slight as it may at first seem; the playfulness is part of a serious vision.

Most of the poems in ⟨Growing into Love⟩ exhibit a remarkable control, though few of them pull together so wide a range of tones. Of those which are more obviously serious, the best are in "Countrymen," the middle section of the book. Here Kennedy has assembled several character sketches and dramatic monologues; these poems best demonstrate his imagination, compassion and involvement with contemporary life.

Through all the forms and voices of his monologues, there comes Kennedy's own quite distinctive voice, which is characterized by a high degree of tension and an astonishing ability to absorb and revivify the flat rhythms and colloquialisms of contemporary American speech.—HENRY TAYLOR, "Singing to Spite This Hunger," *Nation*, Feb. 2, 1970, p. 123

At first glance, the poems of X. J. Kennedy seem free of the Romantic challenge that I have been, perhaps unjustly, urging upon Mr. Ammons. The stakes and risks of that challenge are high; superb artistic courage is needed to get beyond sensitive reporting and simple introspection into the realm in which outward observation is transformed and re-directed by its internalization. Kennedy, in any first reading, seems clearly of the order of Classical ironists: worldly, satirical, wry, astringent. His sonnet "Nothing in Heaven Functions as It Ought" wittily transposes certain conventional notions of Heaven and Hell and manages, at the same time, to bury its hatchet in the totally anaesthetic skull of computerized technology. A coolly "modern" candor pervades the poems of love and marriage. The crushingly knowledgeable "The Korean Emergency" hits hard, not through polemic but through its closeup of men on a destroyer in the Mediterranean and their behavior when they "hit the beach with fifty bucks to burn"—a comment, not so much on the men (though the realities of their world are, not very admirably, there) as on the whole situation and attitude inevitable in such circumstances. Kennedy's little witticisms in "Apocrypha" and elsewhere, too, place *Growing into Love*, like his earlier book, in the light verse tradition of what A. J. M. Smith has called "the worldly muse."

Some of Kennedy's work, though, is so passionate in its sense of life and art that, despite his surface amusement at romantic mystification and its magical symbols, he exposes himself as vulnerable and sympathetic to their magnetism after all. An interesting instance is his poem called "Poets." It is built around two epigraphs. The first comes from a letter written by D. H. Lawrence in 1923 while he was staying in Kennedy's native town, Dover, N.J. "These people," wrote Lawrence, "are . . . quenched. I mean the natives." The quotation is both simple and ambiguous. (I take it on faith, without checking, that the quotation is authentic and not a whimsical improvisation by Kennedy.) The second epigraph is Mallarmé's famous opening line—"*Le vierge, le vivace et le bel aujourd'hui*"—in his sonnet about a swan trapped by ice that has formed around him in a frozen lake.

"Poets" consists of five iambic pentameter quatrains. Its rhyme-scheme (*abba, cddc*, etc.) somewhat parallels the Petrarchan scheme of Mallarmé. Its structure is intrinsically looser, however; and the tone is superficially far lighter because each stanza makes a joke or two and because the tone appears to mock the mentality of poets and their use of swans as glamorous poetic symbols. It is easy, then, to overlook certain implications of the form and the theme. The long lines and the sustained stanza patterns make their own serious insistence. So do the themes of poet and swan although their surface treatment is disdainfully negative. When poets are young schoolboys, we are told, they are unmanly, self-conscious, squeamish, and "moody, a little dull." And swans, when caught in ice (it happened every winter in Dover) are stupid, vicious, and disgusting:

A fireman with a blowtorch had to come

Thaw the dopes loose. Sun-silvered, plumes aflap,
Weren't they grand, though?—not that you'd notice
it,
Crawling along a ladder, getting bit,
Numb to the bone, enduring all their crap.

Yet the presence of beauty, even if he says the swans are "so beautiful, so dumb," is stressed by the poet. He sees it as inseparable from the unworldliness, as it were, of these birds that let the ice form around them because they cannot focus on it "through their dreams." They are exactly like the poets when the poets were inept children—and Kennedy says the swans are "birds of their quill," kindred beings. He has, in the first half of the poem, gradually made these poet-children grave, intense beings who interest him as they might have interested Lawrence: "Quenchers of their own wicks, their eyes turned down / And smoldering."

What emerges is a view of swan and poet in Romantic perspective after all. A great deal rides on such words and phrases as "smoldering," "beautiful," "dreams," and "sun-silvered," on the sheer weight of the form despite the apparent tone, and on the evocation of Lawrence's feelings against the repression ("quenching") of psychic energies and of Mallarmé's marvelous poignancy and pride.

It is a pleasure to see Kennedy being a poet of power in this way, and using common speech and experience and humor toward such ends.—M. L. ROSENTHAL, "Poetic Power—Free the Swan!," *Shen*, Fall 1972, pp. 89–91

Kennedy exploits the concept of norm and deviation in this sonnet ("Nothing in Heaven Functions as It Ought") to deal with the nature of heaven and hell, questioning our conventional notions about each. The general strategy seems initially clear, even obvious: the description of heaven properly belongs to hell, that of hell to heaven. But closer reading reveals more complexity. The malfunctioning sonnet becomes the perfect vehicle for the poet's message as he comments on the limitations of traditional views.

The poet uses the Petrarchan form, but varies that form subtly. First he creates the expected structural and thematic division between octave and sestet and then employs a rhyme scheme approaching the conventional Petrarchan mode. But he uses slant rhyme in the octave at ll. 2, 3, 5, and 8 (abca deef) and makes the sestet peculiarly regular (ghghgh). Normally the Petrarchan sonnet displays high regularity in the octave (abba abba) and some irregularity in the sestet (cde cde / cdc dcd). Kennedy overturns the convention of the form itself to overturn the convention of our accepted values; and by disrupting or conforming to tradition, he emphasizes meaning in both sections of the poem. Nothing in heaven, or in this sonnet, functions as it ought.

The poet similarly manipulates meter. Whereas iambic pentameter, with occasional trochaic or spondaic substitutions, usually characterizes the sonnet, the meter here is chaotic in the octave, regular in the sestet, once more coinciding with the meaning of each. Lines 3, 4, 5, 7, and 8 are all hypermetric, and ll.5–6 display enjambment while caesurae appear unpredictably throughout the octave. These technical features contrast significantly with the strict iambic pentameter, end-stopped lines, and predictable rhythm in the sestet.

Finally, imagery and diction work within the pattern of established and defeated expectations in the poem. Two words are important in the first line, establishing the machine imagery to be fully aborted in the octave and fully developed in the sestet. "Nothing" and "functions" call up images of mere objects, mere things, in motion, but are followed not only by "bifocals" and "gates" but by "gangs" and "choirs" and by rich, vibrant, and seemingly disorganized, uncontrolled imagery. The personified gates "lurch" instead of swing and produce an incongruous noise that shifts our attention from the personified gates to the image of a rooster. Instead of choruses of slaughtered innocents, we have gangs of them in riotous, playful disarray, "huffing" the transfigured halo off Bede. And the angelic choir giggles and coughs, not keeping to its business. There is real delight in disorder here, and the mercurial imagery flows with the shifting sense of life and vigor that accounts for the octave's vibrant tone.

The sestet, on the other hand, turns slowly and methodically on static, uniform, mechanistic imagery with neither "freewheeling" nor extraneous part. The word "none" here complements "nothing" in the octave, and Kennedy uses it just as ironically. The pronoun usually refers to people, living beings, but the creatures in Kennedy's hell, or a more conventitonal poet's heaven, become things, parts in a machine programmed for specific action, producing a uniform sound and only on command. The "none" in l. 10 becomes the "anyone" in l. 11 and finally the universal "he" in l. 12. And the single "click" emitted from him differs considerably from the multifarious "cracking," "cackling," "hushing," "huffing," "breaking," and "coughing" of the octave. No individuals people hell; no variety adorns it. Kennedy uses imagery and diction, like form and meter, to underscore meaning and intensify the markedly ironic, Shavian tone of his ostensibly simple poem.—ROBERT E. BJORK, *Expl*, Winter 1982, pp. 6–7

## EMILY DICKINSON IN SOUTHERN CALIFORNIA

No mistaking X. J. Kennedy's meaning! The chaos and near-mythic wonderment spawned in our climatic and irrational equivalent of Asia Minor have provoked numerous barrages of satiric attack. Perhaps the target of this democracy decayed to such anarchy looms too large and vulgar, for the ridicule hurled at it frequently descends to blatant rhetoric or mere invective. ⟨In *Emily Dickinson in Southern California*⟩ Kennedy tries a more effective tack. With impish glee he borrows Emily Dickinson's epigrammatic style to debunk current follies. Insistent little pecks—measured in short phrases sepa-

rated by dashes—chip away at the bronzed and brazen images of our modern Lotus Land, home of the beach-combers, Hollywood heroes, razor-blade barons, and hapless prisoners queued for miles on what are euphemistically termed "freeways". Take, for example, the first part of the title poem:

> I called one day—on Eden's strand
> But did not find her—Home—
> Surfboarders triumphed in—in Waves—
> Archangels of the Foam—
>
> I walked a pace—I tripped across
> Browned couples—in cahoots—
> No more than Tides need shells to fill
> Did they need—bathing suits—

or the eighth section of the same:

> But gazing at the Fresno—Grape—
> Of sleek perfectioned Jaw—
> I fear the Planet should gape wide—
> Did One discern its Flaw—

This approach can get arch or coy, but it beats self-righteous condescension. In other poems Kennedy abandons the gentle mockery for disquieting realism. "Evening Tide" reveals the boring and disjointed melancholy lingering amid the comforts of suburbia. Clapboard houses occasionally plunge into the shafts of "Mining Town," where "It takes a while to learn to sleep on edge". The father in the strange and moving lullaby, "Last Child," calls the "unplanned" child a "small vampire" and himself a pimp, and with a curious mixture of resentment and tenderness he wonders, "Will yours be that last straw that breaks earth's back?"

For those who view our current overpopulation of fools and ask, Where are Dryden and Pope, now that we need them? Kennedy provides a partial answer. Though his concise couplets usually lack Augustan polish, they precisely hit the mark. Unlike his devastating mentors' Kennedy's attitude, in a series called "Japanese Beetles" is, however, more amused than outraged. To wit:

> By the cold glow that lit my husband's eye
> I could read what page eight had said to try.
>
> > ("2")
>
> On solemn asses fall plush sinecures
> So keep a straight face and sit tight on yours.
>
> > ("To a Young Poet")
>
> Who deal in early drafts and casual words
> Would starve the horse to death and prize his turds.
>
> > ("At a Sale of Manuscript")

The refreshing candor and irreverent humor continue in "Two Views of Rime and Meter," in which the latter, a thudding carpetbeater "fogging the air / with boredom / in dull time", copulates with the former, "To come at the same time."—JOSEPH PARISI, "Coming to Terms," *Poetry*, Sept. 1974, pp. 347–48

# JACK KEROUAC

## 1922–1969

Jean Louis Lebirs de Kerouac, later known as Jack Kerouac, was born in Lowell, Massachusetts, to a devoutly Catholic French-Canadian immigrant family, on March 12, 1922. He attended Lowell's Catholic grammar school, then went on to Lowell High School where he distinguished himself as a football player. This led to a year's scholarship at Horace Mann, a prestigious New York prep school, and in 1940 an athletic scholarship at Columbia University.

At Columbia Kerouac developed a strong interest in progressive jazz, but he was otherwise an erratic student and in 1942 dropped out to join the Navy. When the Navy discharged him as unfit for military service he joined the Merchant Marine, but by 1944 he was back in New York again. His relations with his father, Leo Kerouac, had been strained since dropping out of college, and worsened when his father's Lowell printshop failed. The family had had to relocate first to New Haven, Connecticut, then to Ozone Park in Queens; and Leo Kerouac had become terminally ill. This uprooting of his family, his conflicts with his father and his father's death, and his nostalgic sorrow for his vanished childhood, all became material for Kerouac's first novel, *The Town and the City* (1950). Together with *Doctor Sax* (1959), *Maggie Cassidy* (1959), *Visions of Gerard* (1960), and *Vanity of Duluoz* (1968), *The Town and the City* is one of Kerouac's "Lowell novels," and its tone of longing for lost and vanished times, and the writer's ambivalence toward the conventional society he grew up in, are re-echoed in the later works.

In the meantime Kerouac had become acquainted with Allen Ginsberg and William S. Burroughs; both were involved in the nascent New York "Beat" scene. Kerouac was drawn to it as well. After his father's death he began a series of almost random journeys back and forth across the continent, occasionally in the company of Burroughs, and frequently in company with Ginsberg. In 1947 he met Ginsberg's friend Neal Cassady, a Proust-reading speed-tripping railroad worker who became Kerouac's muse. Their travels and conversations were the basis for *On the Road* (1957); in this and its sequels, *Vision of Cody* (1959), *The Subterraneans* (1958), *The Dharma Bums* (1958), *Tristessa* (1960), and *Big Sur* (1962), all lightly fictionalized, intensely subjective accounts of the doings of Kerouac and his friends, Cassady is a central mythic image. Kerouac conceived of the Road novels as "the Legend of Duluoz" (his name in them for himself), a chronicle of his life written in "spontaneous prose," a deliberately unrevised verbal outpouring that was often composed under the influence of drugs.

With the publication of *On the Road* Kerouac became identified as the spokesman of the "Beat Generation." However, his later work reflected his growing dissatisfaction with the value of compulsive unreflective action and with the subculture that *On the Road* had helped to shape; and he turned gradually toward a solitary religious mysticism. He returned to Lowell, where his last years were marked by ill-health related to acute alcoholism and years of drug abuse. In 1969 he went to St. Petersburg, Florida, where on October 21 of that year he died.

SET-UP. The object is set before the mind, either in reality, as in sketching (before a landscape or teacup or old face) or is set in the memory wherein it becomes the sketching from memory of a definite image-object.

PROCEDURE. Time being of the essence in the purity of speech, sketching language is undisturbed flow from the mind of personal secret idea-words, *blowing* (as per jazz musician) on subject of image.

METHOD. No periods separating sentence-structures already arbitrarily riddled by false colons and timid usually needless commas—but the vigorous space dash separating rhetorical breathing (as jazz musician drawing breath between outblown phrases)—"measured pauses which are the essentials of our speech"—"divisions of the *sounds* we hear"—"time and how to note it down." (William Carlos Williams)

SCOPING. Not "selectivity" of expression but following free deviation (association) of mind into limitless blow-on-subject seas of thought, swimming in sea of English with no discipline other than rhythms of rhetorical exhalation and expostulated statement, like a fist coming down on a table with each complete utterance, bang! (the space dash)—Blow as deep as you want—write as deeply, fish as far down as you want, satisfy yourself first, then reader cannot fail to receive telepathic shock and meaning-excitement by same laws operating in his own human mind.

LAG IN PROCEDURE. No pause to think of proper word but the infantile pileup of scatalogical buildup words till satisfaction is gained, which will turn out to be a great appending rhythm to a thought and be in accordance with Great Law of timing.

TIMING. Nothing is muddy that *runs in time* and to laws of *time*—Shakespearian stress of dramatic need to speak now in own unalterable way or forever hold tongue—*no revisions* (except obvious rational mistakes, such as names or *calculated* insertions in act of not writing but *inserting*).

CENTER OF INTEREST. Begin not from preconceived idea of what to say about image but from jewel center of interest in subject of image at *moment* of writing, and write outwards swimming in sea of language to peripheral release and exhaustion—Do not afterthink except for poetic or P. S. reasons. Never afterthink to "improve" or defray impressions, as, the best writing is always the most painful personal wrung-out tossed from cradle warm protective mind—tap from yourself the song of yourself, *blow!—now!—your* way is your only way—"good"—or "bad"—always honest, ("ludicrous"), spontaneous, "confessional" interesting, because not "crafted." Craft *is* craft.

STRUCTURE OF WORK. Modern bizarre structures (science fiction, etc.) arise from language being dead, "different" themes give illusion of "new" life. Follow roughly outlines in out-fanning movement over subject, as river rock, so mindflow over jewel-center need (run your mind over it, *once*) arriving at pivot, where what was dim formed "beginning" becomes sharp-necessitating "ending" and language shortens in race to wire of time-race of work, following laws of Deep Form, to conclusion, last words, last trickle—Night is The End.

MENTAL STATE. If possible write "without consciousness" in semi-trance (as Yeats' later "trance writing") allowing subconscious to admit in own uninhibited interesting necessary and so "modern" language what conscious art would censor, and write excitely, swiftly, with writing-or-typing-cramps, in accordance (as from center to periphery) with laws of orgasm, Reich's "beclouding of consciousness." *Come* from within, out—to relaxed and said.—JACK KEROUAC, "Essentials of Spontaneous Prose," *BMR*, Autumn 1957, pp. 226–28

The despondency trailing after the American way of life has for a long time been the subject of American writers. A dream has been spoiled. Or it has turned into a nightmare. The idea that organised society is an evil in itself is perennial in American literature; one can trace the theme in Fenimore Cooper, in *Huckleberry Finn*, in Melville, Thoreau, Henry Miller, Hemingway. It changes but it is always there. Huck Finn wanted 'to light out to the territory'. The narrator of Jack Kerouac's *On the Road*—the moving spirit of the 'beat generation', the latest variant—dreams of 'going West to see the country' and he does so in the company of an hysterical minor delinquent. Once in the West he looks back and sees the wide howling spaces of American loneliness are in the East as well: there is always the 'brickwall dawn', the people looking like 'broken down movie extras, a lemon lot'. It is all 'Where go? What do? What for—sleep.' In Huck Finn's time the territory was open; now it is closed. Whether we regard it as land or a state of mind it is locked up and owned by the Squares, the good citizens with the dollars and the neutralising psychiatrists. The only territory to light out into is the inside country of the 'beat', *i.e.* of the sick, the irresponsible, the delinquent, the psychopath, the disaffiliated, who have slipped out of it and have become malingerers or casualties. Have the courage to light out into the ruthlessness of the serious neurotic, and one has freedom. One rediscovers the painful, innocent self, the 'sweet' personality with its 'sweet nauseas'—'sweet' is a favourite word—the self the totalitarian hammer has cracked. In the coming anarchy, one will at least be equipped to survive in a world made for psychopaths. For the psychopath has had to try to come to terms with the violence inside himself. ⟨. . .⟩

The 'beats' reached literary respectability in Jack Kerouac's *On the Road*. The narrator of the novel has one foot in the Square world, for he can always get 50 dollars off his aunt, he is writing a novel and shipping a script to Hollywood, and he agrees with his aunt that he will never make good if he hangs around much longer with his Bohemian friends. So the book has some air of a search for copy. But he is a clean narrative writer, pure and true in line, whose every word is as clear as a pebble. He has the American genius for restlessness and movement. He 'goes', though it is true that he merely goes on and on. He watches everyone else 'going' and, from first to last, the delight of the eye and ear never drops. The novel is entirely about a number of crazy journeys in fast cars all over the continent, in the company of a spell-binding, incoherent friend, a reform-school boy whose criminal side has been

straightened up by the analysts. Dean is a frenzied, somnambulistic ex-juvenile, living with two or three wives, 'gunning' for girls, drugging, drinking, sponging, howling, laughing, whoring, getting 'kicks' and 'digging' everything. A shocking guest and a man who will infallibly let any friend down in a jam, his spell is in his crazy behaviour and his meddling, tender seriousness as a listener. You tell him your problems and six months later he will cross the continent because he has accumulated an enormous mouthful of half-baked ejaculations bearing on the subject. That old dream you told him: well, of course, the shrouded figure in the desert was Death. He is a 'W. C. Fields mystic'. In the end we leave him on the sidewalk in New York, dirty, ragged, reduced to speechlessness by drugs, the sainted vagrant who is already a holy nuisance. The gang tear about the continent in an old Hudson at 70, with the radio playing Bop day and night. They pick up easy money in odd jobs. In any strange sense they have no adventures, though there is a good deal of comedy when they pile in on someone trying to live a quiet life. But one does get an astonishing, detailed picture of their hourly lives, their awkward love affairs, and their ecstatic sense that something is happening to them; there is the verve of preoccupied youth. Above all, any human being interests them and they are all interested deeply and personally in one another, with a sort of detached tenderness—there is a remarkable absence of hatred among the beat; even the women, always badly treated, are amenable. ⟨. . .⟩

The bitterness and disgust which marked the American attempts at the picaresque novel is the Thirties, the one-up-manship which mars Hemingway and makes him false, is absent. On the other hand, Kerouac's range of experience is very narrow and he is interminable. There is a brief idyll in New Mexico in which he ventures among an older race who know more about life than his narrator does; but outside of that he does not go. The exciting thing—at any rate to a foreign reader—is the easy, natural, felt wonder at the sight of the American continent. One smells the Mississippi, one feels the warmth of the summer after the northern winter, one has the dramatic sensation of loneliness. Impatiently concerned with themselves and their wild travelling, the group are continually knocked back by the people and things they are seeing in American landscape and life. There is intimacy without tedium and without the awful emotionalism and outpouring which wrecked the novels of Thomas Wolfe, with whom Kerouac has been recklessly compared. From *On the Road* one picks up the jargon, the rituals, and interests of the 'beats', their naivety, their basic sentimentality. It is a document which must be read together with Norman Mailer's speculations. These are not (at the time of writing) borne out by Kerouac. Whether they are depends on whether the movement is a movement, or is just one more American circus already half over. Probably not: one thing a very standardised society always produces sooner or later, is a strong pocket of anarchism. Here the State is withering away in a puff of marijuana. You wake up; the State is still there.—V. S. PRITCHETT, "The Beat Generation," *NS*, Sept. 6, 1958, pp. 292–96

Of course there is no Beat Generation, but there is an effort at refreshment at the springs of the kind of naivete of which in the long ago Booth Tarkington, say, drank deep. The rococo sensualities drop away, and there those fellows are, indeed part of a national tradition, but one proposed by Tarkington, by Eugene Field and James Whitcomb Riley. There is a freckle-faced kid who stalks through American literature, scaring the daylights out of everyone—and here he is again, and here is Kerouac again to celebrate him, his suspect naivete which is slipping constantly into real naivete. He is a young man of clean habits, for all the filth he picks up, and scrubbed mind, and he is in search of Maturity and Truth (the two are resolved into Sanskrit, in this instance), and there is something invigorating, Kerouac would say, in the spectacle of a boy briskly avoiding on his way all those pitfalls by which youth is indeed beset, the quicksands, for instance, of heterosexual sexual activity, Bohemians ("hanger-onners on the arts," parasites and phonies, not incipient he-men like us), and the commercial corruption of taste in this country ("And I'm bringing real chocolate pudding, not that instant phony stuff but good chocolate pudding that I'll bring to a boil and stir over the fire and then let it cool ice cold in the snow." "Oh boy!")— all of which, with the protagonist's lambent desire for transcendental self-extinction, would seem to be the effective content of *The Dharma Bums*. The book is about a couple of Kerouac fellows playing Zen, their sacramental fervor and their adventures by the way.

Kerouac is, of course, easy game, and it serves no purpose further to belay the ecstatic simplisms of which he is symbol, symptom, and claque, the inert drama he celebrates, and the impoverishment of idiom. It is only nostalgia for some post-World War I literary hijinks in Paris and New York that finds any real excitement in the San Francisco Renaissance. On the other hand, and despite the overt challenge, to 'look at me, I'm an American cultural phenomenon,' one needn't take the high aesthetic line. Kerouac is very funny and I think that finally it doesn't matter whether one laughs with him or at him. If one is sufficiently relaxed, behold! there he is performing some of the best deadpan rhetorical slapstick around. After all, it is only the high-minded and the liberal who are solemn before pratfalls. —MARCUS KLEIN, "Imps from Bottles, Etc.," *HdR*, Winter 1958–59, p. 620

After publishing the semi-conventional *The Town and the City* in his late twenties, Kerouac (now thirty-six) felt a dissatisfaction with the academic notion of the novel-form; he turned his back on every falsity that he felt in the made-up, "fictional" conception of the novel, carried over from the nineteenth century and embalmed in the universities, and tried to find a form that was more on a level with his actual experience. With much fumbling, he at last hit upon what his buddy Allen Ginsberg, the young howling poet, has described a little pretentiously as "spontaneous bop prosody." Broken down, this means completely spontaneous composition with none of the super-ego restraints formerly enjoined upon the writer; and also, very important to the method, *no rewriting* once the original words and the shape of sentences are first cast by the mind.

Kerouac's "bop prosody" represented a breakthrough for him as a writer which should be appreciated even if one has doubts about the method: it enabled him to express his experience with much greater accuracy and reality than if he still wore around his neck what he felt as heavy stones of "responsibility" and "literature." The bulk of highbrow young writers Kerouac's own age were strangling themselves, he believed, with grueling and ultra-sober notions of "wit," "tension," "density" and "complexity" in writing—a set of catchwords coming out of the New Criticism and the high-powered little magazines. All this seemed falsely over-intellectual and forced to Kerouac and his band of guerrillas. Writing, they thought, loses all of its value to the individual if it has to be put through such a grotesquely convoluted process. Kerouac felt he had to return to the primary reality of his experience and forget the consequences; otherwise he could never have gotten under way and reached a pitch in his faith and certainty where he could really "let go" with some of the actuality that he had undergone. Thus Kerouac's "rhythm

writing"—no censoring, no rationalizing, no tampering with the flow—was a most dramatic counterpart to the kind of statically intellectual work he felt was slowing down the literary scene. He wanted to tear open all the vents of being and let the actual thought at the moment it was conceived drop upon the page without apology.

In this Kerouac wasn't without precedent, of course. It is an ancient artistic notion, and in our time Jackson Pollock of the so-called "action painters" of the abstract expressionist group had reached comparable conclusions and John Cage done similar things in music. But in Kerouac's case, especially after the publication of *On the Road* (which was edited and cleaned up by Viking before being offered to the public) a barrage of moral criticism was leveled at him which artists like Pollock and Cage never had to cope with. Because the work of these two men is abstract, critics could wrangle about the method but the ambiguity of the content presented a challenge which had to be brooded upon. But in Kerouac's case people hardly noticed the method because the life he seemed to glorify—promiscuity, pot-smoking, the hot pursuit of speed, kicks, excitement—was so much more tangible than "art." —SEYMOUR KRIM, "King of the Beats," *Com*, Jan. 2, 1959, p. 360

Jack Kerouac, in *Desolation Angels*, describes meeting in Tangiers an American writer called Bull who has written a book called *Nude Supper* "all about shirts turning blue at hangings, castration, and lime," about whom he says:

> You may talk to me about Sinclair Lewis the great American writer, or Wolfe, or Hemingway, or Faulkner, but none of them were as honest [as Bull], unless you name . . . but it aint Thoreau either.

Honesty, then, is the criterion. Honest about what? Not about what goes on outside you, nor even about what goes on in the mind, but honest about your entrails, and honest about whatever unconsidered, uncensored, unreflecting stream of expressions comes out.

Kerouac's book is an example of the required honesty. It asks of the reader firstly that he should be Kerouac's spiritual companion on Desolation Peak in northwestern Washington. This is Kerouac at his best, alone amidst nature and pouring out prose poems partly about his surroundings, partly his reminiscences, which at their best recall Whitman. As writing, this gets a bit tedious, but since what we are asked to consider, after all, is not writing but life, or life become identical with the writing, then Kerouac translated into snowy mountains is Kerouac at his best.

After 120 pages, however, Kerouac, thinly disguised as a character called Jack Duluoz, descends from the heights to San Francisco, and now we are among the beatniks with their beards and blue jeans; their stage properties of the bed and bottle in the pad; their ritualistic parties; their cult of an incommunicable witless slang with which they wish to communicate with everybody; their resort to alcohol, drugs, and sex, which they regard as Aladdin lamps supposed, after rubbing, to produce the genie of spontaneous utterance; their pretentious anti-intellectual streams of ideas; their name-dropping acquaintance with God, Christ, Buddha; their air of superiority over everyone who is disciplined, intelligent, industrious, humble; their total incapacity to enter into any real interchange of conversation; the tendency of all their activities toward the brawl, the prayer meeting, or the sexual orgy (all and any of which they regard as interchangeable); their lives forever verging on a nonstop party where everyone is proving to everyone else (down to stripping off the last inch of clothing) how natural he is and how spontaneous. Everyone here is a genius, but no one says anything interesting. Describing a poetry reading given by a poet called Merrill Randall (learning the trick of Kerouac's witless transpositions, I assume this to be Randall Jarrell), Kerouac relates how he hears a line or two, then hurries from the room because "in it I hear the craft of his carefully arranged thoughts and not the uncontrollable involuntary thoughts themselves, dig. . . ." and it is revealing that in his clumsy attempt to parody a line of "Merrill Randall," he can produce only a line of pure Kerouac:

> "The duodenal abyss that brings me to the margin consuming my flesh."

So "uncontrollable involuntary thoughts" become the criterion by which everything is judged. This is so unreliable a standard that Kerouac's world is one in which people are totally lost, unable to do anything except try to live up to the act of self-conscious spontaneity which is the common pretense of the group. Finally, on many occasions, one does not know whether Kerouac approves or disapproves of the things done and said by his uninvented characters. We are told, for instance, that in Tangiers, "Bull goes arm swinging and swaggering like a Nazi into the first queer bar, brushing Arabs aside and looking back at me with: 'Hey what?' I cant see how he can have managed this except I learn later he's spent a whole year in the little town sitting in his room on huge overdoses of morfina and other drugs staring at the tip of his shoe too scared to take one shuddering bath in eight months. So the local Arabs remember him as a shuddering skinny ghost who's apparently recovered, and let him rant. Everybody seems to know him, boys yell 'Hi!' 'Boorows!' 'Hey!' " Reading this one has an ashamed certainty that unless there was an awareness of the American fleet at the back of the boys' minds, they would fling "Bull" or "Boorows" into the harbor.

And yet, with all this, we are assured that Kerouac is an apostle of love. "His mysticism and religious yearning are . . . finally ineradicable from his personality . . . If critics were to give grades for humanity, Kerouac would snare pure A's each time out," writes Seymour Krim in an incredible introduction. This is a world in which it is assumed that you only have to go around saying that you love everyone for it to be accepted that you are a mystic and a saint. And to point out the difficulties involved in loving anyone is regarded as square. The difficulty of the position of utter spontaneity is that it removes all basis for self-criticism.—STEPHEN SPENDER, "Literature," *GIT*, 1965, pp. 194–96

Jack Kerouac is, of course, mawkish enough for a whole literature and *Maggie Cassidy*, now reprinted after twenty years of merciful silence, is a book fatally flawed by Kerouac's singleminded devotion to his own passions. He employs that familiarly incantatory prose which has won the hearts of Eng. Lit. students everywhere, and in this story of awakening adolescence it summons up squads of emotion with code-words like "tragic," "brooding," "sad," "alone," "incredibly" to much the same purpose and with much the same effect as Pepsi glamourise their Cola.

It was a prose which worked magnificently in *The Town and the City*, a first novel which showed the depths to which Kerouac could aspire as a romantic novelist, but in *Maggie Cassidy* it is a weaker and looser thing, becoming so loose, in fact, that it connects with no 'reality' other than the wayward burst of Kerouac's sentiment. It is quite in character that the novel should be dominated by Kerouac's ulterior ego, a snivelling French Canadian known somewhat archly as Jacky Duluoz, and the narrative is much concerned with his secret passions, his sporting prowess, his first love and his delayed maturity. The titular heroine hardly gets mentioned, and

becomes yet another sacrificial victim to Kerouac's pathetic and abandoned sense of chronology.

*Maggie Cassidy* is indeed a pallid book, casting post-impressions like dried petals and capitalising hugely on the universal and sympathetic attractiveness of 'first love'. Every event is mediated through Kerouac's reverent but gaseous memory and the narrative is interesting only if you happen to find Kerouac interesting. When he forgets about his own emotions, the prose reverts to that low and montonous hum which is characteristic of generators waiting to be utilised. His occasional genius lies only in expressing the most conventional impressions with an exuberance that makes them apparently his own, but they remain stubbornly unoriginal for all that. The depths of this book's particular solipsism can be measured in the fact that large areas of dialogue are altogether pointless and unreal. The book falls apart into a number of fine and memorable phrases which I have, unfortunately, already forgotten.—PETER ACKROYD, "Mawkish Moments," *Spec*, Aug. 24, 1974, pp. 246–47

When *On the Road* first appeared, the *New York Times* heralded it with superlatives: "The most beautifully executed, the clearest and most important utterance" yet made by a young writer, likely to represent the current generation as *The Sun Also Rises* had the twenties. A few other favorable reviews appeared, including one by Ralph Gleason in the *Saturday Review*. But negative reactions soon developed and rapidly grew into a nearly united storm of disapproval with the appearance of Kerouac's subsequent books. *Time* grumbled that *On the Road* failed to show an author "anywhere near the talents of Fitzgerald, Hemingway, or Nathanael West." Herbert Gold went in for the kill, arguing that the book was "a proof of illness rather than a creation of art, a novel." Reviewing Kerouac's *The Subterraneans* for the *New Republic*, Dan Pinck recalled that *On the Road* "was populated by a chain-gang of weirds," while the later book proved that "Kerouac is simply ignorant, but a name-dropper supreme." Whipsawed by damning criticisms of his books while being lured into writing insipid travel articles for *Holiday* magazine, Kerouac lost most of his influence on American culture after 1960.

He had already published three novels which, taken together, exemplify a change of consciousness so subversive to prevailing American values and institutions and so attractive, at least within a decade, to millions of Americans that all defenders of the Establishment felt compelled to shout them out of existence. Kerouac's novels are more readily summarized than Ginsberg's poetry or the Beats' innovations in life styles, but all three manifest a rebellion against the Establishment—the goals and habits of middle-class America—which has produced all the varieties of youthful dissent appearing in the past fifteen years. "More than anything else," as Jack Newfield so succinctly put it, "the Beat Generation was a portent, the first wind of a new storm, a coded signal that America's youth was starting to gag on conformity, materialism and silence."

*On the Road*, written in 1951 concerning events of the preceding four years, superficially appears to be much as the book's cover brazenly proclaims, a "wild Odyssey of two dropouts who swing across America wrecking and rioting—making it with sex, jazz, and drink as they Make the Scene." Jack Kerouac and Neal Cassady, under the pseudonyms of Sal Paradise and Dean Moriarity, speed back and forth between New York and San Francisco with a varying mélange of friends and lovers. Sal occasionally stops long enough to work on his next novel but is soon distracted by Dean or boredom to make another trip. Each time, "We were all delighted, we all realized we were leaving confusion and nonsense behind and performing our one and noble function of the time, *move*." Sal and his friends "were like the man with the dungeon stone and the gloom, rising from the underground, the sordid hysteria of America, a new beat generation." It all seemed to be an unrestrained Whitmanesque celebration of the open road, that peculiarly American joy in moving for its own sake: "I didn't know where all this was leading," Sal once confessed: "I didn't care."

The ambiguity of the enterprise, however, crept out almost immediately and persistently reappeared throughout the book. Sal's friends "rushed down the street together, digging everything in the early way they had, which later become so much sadder and perceptive and blank." The innocent early pleasure repeatedly confronted the meaninglessness of such a life. Compulsively rushing across the continent, Sal could not avoid an impasse: "Here I was at the end of America—no more land—and now there was nowhere to go but back." The trip always turned into a bummer. The somber warning of Carlo Marx (i.e., Allen Ginsberg) kept returning to haunt them: "Now I'm not trying to take your hincty sweets from you, but it seems to me that the time has come to decide what you are and what you're going to do. . . . The days of wrath are yet to come. The balloon won't sustain you much longer. And not only that but it's an abstract balloon."—J. MEREDITH NEIL, "1955: The Beginnings of Our Own Times," *SAQ*, Autumn 1974, pp. 434–36

---

## NORMAN PODHORETZ
### From "The Know-Nothing Bohemians"
*Partisan Review*, Spring 1958, pp. 305–18

When *On the Road* appeared last year, Gilbert Milstein commemorated the event in the New York *Times* by declaring it to be "a historic occasion" comparable to the publication of *The Sun Also Rises* in the 1920's. But even before the novel was actually published, the word got around that Kerouac was the spokesman of a new group of rebels and Bohemians who called themselves the Beat Generation, and soon his photogenic countenance (unshaven, of course, and topped by an unruly crop of rich black hair falling over his forehead) was showing up in various mass-circulation magazines, he was being interviewed earnestly on television, and he was being featured in a Greenwich Village nightclub where, in San Francisco fashion, he read specimens of his spontaneous bop prosody against a background of jazz music.

Though the nightclub act reportedly flopped, *On the Road* sold well enough to hit the best-seller lists for several weeks, and it isn't hard to understand why. Americans love nothing so much as representative documents, and what could be more interesting in this Age of Sociology than a novel that speaks for the "younger generation?" (The fact that Kerouac is thirty-five or thereabouts was generously not held against him.) Beyond that, however, I think that the unveiling of the Beat Generation was greeted with a certain relief by many people who had been disturbed by the notorious respectability and "maturity" of post-war writing. This was more like it—restless, rebellious, confused youth living it up, instead of thin, balding, buttoned-down instructors of English composing ironic verses with one hand while changing the baby's diapers with the other. Bohemianism is not particularly fashionable nowadays, but the image of Bohemia still exerts a powerful fascination—nowhere more so than in the suburbs, which are filled to overflowing with men and women who uneasily think

of themselves as conformists and of Bohemianism as the heroic road. The whole point of *Marjorie Morningstar* was to assure the young marrieds of Mamaroneck that they were better off than the apparently glamorous *Luftmenschen* of Greenwich Village, and the fact that Wouk had to work so hard at making this idea seem convincing is a good indication of the strength of prevailing doubt on the matter.

On the surface, at least, the Bohemianism of *On the Road* is very attractive. Here is a group of high-spirited young men running back and forth across the country (mostly hitch-hiking, sometimes in their own second-hand cars), going to "wild" parties in New York and Denver and San Francisco, living on a shoe-string (GI educational benefits, an occasional fifty bucks from a kindly aunt, an odd job as a typist, a fruit-picker, a parking-lot attendant), talking intensely about love and God and salvation, getting high on marijuana (but never heroin or cocaine), listening feverishly to jazz in crowded little joints, and sleeping freely with beautiful girls. Now and again there is a reference to gloom and melancholy, but the characteristic note struck by Kerouac is exuberance:

> We stopped along the road for a bite to eat. The cowboy went off to have a spare tire patched, and Eddie and I sat down in a kind of homemade diner. I heard a great laugh, the greatest laugh in the world, and here came this rawhide oldtimes Nebraska farmer with a bunch of other boys into the diner; you could hear his raspy cries clear across the plains, across the whole gray world of them that day. Everybody else laughed with him. He didn't have a care in the world and had the hugest regard for everybody. I said to myself, Wham, listen to that man laugh. That's the West, here I am in the West. He came booming into the diner, calling Maw's name, and she made the sweetest cherry pie in Nebraska, and I had some with a mountainous scoop of ice cream on top. "Maw, rustle me up some grub afore I have to start eatin myself or some damn silly idee like that." And he threw himself on a stool and went hyaw hyaw hyaw hyaw. "And throw some beans in it." It was the spirit of the West sitting right next to me. I wished I knew his whole raw life and what the hell he'd been doing all these years besides laughing and yelling like that. Whooee, I told my soul, and the cowboy came back and off we went to Grand Island.

Kerouac's enthusiasm for the Nebraska farmer is part of his general readiness to find the source of all vitality and virtue in simple rural types and in the dispossessed urban groups (Negroes, bums, whores). His idea of life in New York is "millions and millions hustling forever for a buck among themselves . . . grabbing, taking, giving, sighing, dying, just so they could be buried in those awful cemetery cities beyond Long Island City," whereas the rest of America is populated almost exclusively by the true of heart. There are intimations here of a kind of know-nothing populist sentiment, but in other ways this attitude resembles Nelson Algren's belief that bums and whores and junkies are more interesting than white-collar workers or civil servants. The difference is that Algren hates middle-class respectability for moral and political reasons—the middle class exploits and persecutes—while Kerouac, who is thoroughly unpolitical, seems to feel that respectability is a sign not of moral corruption but of spiritual death. "The only people for me," says Sal Paradise, the narrator of *On the Road*, "are the mad ones, the ones who are mad to live, mad to talk, mad to be saved, desirous of everything at the same time, the ones who never yawn or say a commonplace thing, but burn,

burn, burn like fabulous yellow roman candles exploding like spiders across the stars. . . ." This tremendous emphasis on emotional intensity, this notion that to be hopped-up is the most desirable of all human conditions, lies at the heart of the Beat Generation ethos and distinguishes it radically from the Bohemianism of the past.

The Bohemianism of the 1920's represented a repudiation of the provinciality, philistinism, and moral hypocrisy of American life—a life, incidentally, which was still essentially small-town and rural in tone. Bohemia, in other words, was a movement created in the name of civilization: its ideals were intelligence, cultivation, spiritual refinement. The typical literary figure of the 1920's was a midwesterner (Hemingway, Fitzgerald, Sinclair Lewis, Eliot, Pound) who had fled from his home town to New York or Paris in search of a freer, more expansive, more enlightened way of life than was possible in Ohio or Minnesota or Michigan. The political radicalism that supplied the characteristic coloring of Bohemianism in the 1930's did nothing to alter the urban, cosmopolitan bias of the 1920's. At its best, the radicalism of the 1930's was marked by deep intellectual seriousness and aimed at a state of society in which the fruits of civilization would be more widely available—and ultimately available to all.

The Bohemianism of the 1950's is another kettle of fish altogether. It is hostile to civilization; it worships primitivism, instinct, energy, "blood." To the extent that it has intellectual interests at all, they run to mystical doctrines, irrationalist philosophies, and left-wing Reichianism. The only art the new Bohemians have any use for is jazz, mainly of the cool variety. Their predilection for bop language is a way of demonstrating solidarity with the primitive vitality and spontaneity they find in jazz and of expressing contempt for coherent, rational discourse which, being a product of the mind, is in their view a form of death. To be articulate is to admit that you have no feelings (for how can real feelings be expressed in syntactical language?), that you can't respond to anything (Kerouac responds to everything by saying "Wow!"), and that you are probably impotent.

At the one end of the spectrum, this ethos shades off into violence and criminality, main-line drug addiction and madness. Allen Ginsberg's poetry, with its lurid apocalyptic celebration of "angel-headed hipsters," speaks for the darker side of the new Bohemianism. Kerouac is milder. He shows little taste for violence, and the criminality he admires is the harmless kind. The hero of *On the Road*, Dean Moriarty, has a record: "From the age of eleven to seventeen, he was usually in reform school. His specialty was stealing cars, gunning for girls coming out of high school in the afternoon, driving them out to the mountains, making them, and coming back to sleep in any available hotel bathtub in town." But Dean's criminality, we are told, "was not something that sulked and sneered; it was a wild yea-saying overburst of American joy; it was Western, the west wind, an ode from the Plains, something new, long prophesied, long a-coming (he only stole cars for joy rides)." And, in fact, the species of Bohemian that Kerouac writes about is on the whole rather law-abiding. In *The Subterraneans*, a bunch of drunken boys steal a pushcart in the middle of the night, and when they leave it in front of a friend's apartment building, he denounces them angrily for "screwing up the security of my pad." When Sal Paradise (in *On the Road*) steals some groceries from the canteen of an itinerant workers' camp in which he has taken a temporary job as a barracks guard, he comments, "I suddenly began to realize that everybody in America is a natural-born thief"—which, of course, is a way of turning his own stealing into a bit of boyish

prankishness. Nevertheless, Kerouac is attracted to criminality, and that in itself is more significant than the fact that he personally feels constrained to put the brakes on his own destructive impulses.

Sex has always played a very important role in Bohemianism: sleeping around was the Bohemian's most dramatic demonstration of his freedom from conventional moral standards, and a defiant denial of the idea that sex was permissible only in marriage and then only for the sake of a family. At the same time, to be "promiscuous" was to assert the validity of sexual experience in and for itself. The "meaning" of Bohemian sex, then, was at once social and personal, a crucial element in the Bohemian's ideal of civilization. Here again the contrast with Beat Generation Bohemianism is sharp. On the one hand, there is a fair amount of sexual activity in *On the Road* and *The Subterraneans*. Dean Moriarity is a "new kind of American saint" at least partly because of his amazing sexual power: he can keep three women satisfied simultaneously and he can make love any time, anywhere (once he mounts a girl in the back seat of a car while poor Sal Paradise is trying to sleep in front). Sal, too, is always on the make, and though he isn't as successful as the great Dean, he does pretty well: offhand I can remember a girl in Denver, one on a bus, and another in New York, but a little research would certainly unearth a few more. The heroine of *The Subterraneans*, a Negro girl named Mardou Fox, seems to have switched from one to another member of the same gang and back again ("This has been an incestuous group in its time"), and we are given to understand that there is nothing unusual about such an arrangement. But the point of all this hustle and bustle is not freedom from ordinary social restrictions or defiance of convention (except in relation to homosexuality, which is Ginsberg's preserve: among "the best minds" of Ginsberg's generation, who were destroyed by America are those "who let themselves be ———— in the —— by saintly motorcyclists, and screamed with joy, / who blew and were blown by those human seraphim, the sailors, caresses of Atlantic and Caribbean love"). The sex in Kerouac's books goes hand in hand with a great deal of talk about forming permanent relationships ("although I have a hot feeling sexually and all that for her," says the poet Adam Moorad in *The Subterraneans*, "I really don't want to get any further into her not only for these reasons but finally, the big one, if I'm going to get involved with a girl now I want to be permanent like permanent and serious and long termed and I can't do that with her"), and a habit of getting married and then duly divorced and re-married when another girl comes along. In fact, there are as many marriages and divorces in *On the Road* as in the Hollywood movie colony (must be that California climate): "All those years I was looking for the woman I wanted to marry," Sal Paradise tells us. "I couldn't meet a girl without saying to myself, What kind of wife would she make?" Even more revealing is Kerouac's refusal to admit that any of his characters ever make love wantonly or lecherously—no matter how casual the encounter it must always entail sweet feelings toward the girl. Sal, for example, is fixed up with Rita Bettencourt in Denver, whom he has never met before. "I got her in my bedroom after a long talk in the dark of the front room. She was a nice little girl, simple and true [naturally], and tremendously frightened of sex. I told her it was beautiful. I wanted to prove this to her. She let me prove it, but I was too impatient and proved nothing. She sighed in the dark. 'What do you want out of life?' I asked, and I used to ask that all the time of girls." This is rather touching, but only because the narrator is really just as frightened of sex as that nice little girl was. He is frightened of failure and he worries about his performance. For *performance* is the point—performance and "good orgasms," which are the first duty of man and the only duty of woman. What seems to be involved here, in short, is sexual anxiety of enormous proportions—an anxiety that comes out very clearly in *The Subterraneans*, which is about a love affair between the young writer, Leo Percepied, and the Negro girl, Mardou Fox. Despite its protestations, the book is one long agony of fear and trembling over sex:

> I spend long nights and many hours making her, finally I have her, I pray for it to come, I can hear her breathing harder, I hope against hope it's time, a noise in the hall (or whoop of drunkards next door) takes her mind off and she can't make it and laughs— but when she does make it I hear her crying, whimpering, the shuddering electrical female or- gasm makes her sound like a little girl crying, moaning in the night, it lasts a good twenty seconds and when it's over she moans, "O why can't it last longer," and "O when will I when you do?"—"Soon now I bet," I say, "you're getting closer and closer"—

Very primitive, very spontaneous, very elemental, very beat.

For the new Bohemians interracial friendships and love affairs apparently play the same role of social defiance that sex used to play in older Bohemian circles. Negroes and whites associate freely on a basis of complete equality and without a trace of racial hostility. But putting it that way understates the case, for not only is there no racial hostility, there is positive adulation for the "happy, true-hearted, ecstatic Negroes of America."

> At lilac evening I walked with every muscle aching among the lights of 27th and Welton in the Denver colored section, wishing I were a Negro, feeling that the best the white world had offered was not enough ecstasy for me, not enough life, joy, kicks, darkness, music, not enough night. . . . I wished I were a Denver Mexican, or even a poor overworked Jap, anything but what I was so drearily, a "white man" disillusioned. All my life I'd had white ambitions. . . . I passed the dark porches of Mexican and Negro homes; soft voices were there, occasionally the dusky knee of some mysterious sensuous gal; and dark faces of the men behind rose arbors. Little children sat like sages in ancient rocking chairs.

It will be news to the Negroes to learn that they are so happy and ecstatic; I doubt if a more idyllic picture of Negro life has been painted since certain Southern ideologues tried to convince the world that things were just as fine as fine could be for the slaves on the old plantation. Be that as it may, Kerouac's love for Negroes and other dark-skinned groups is tied up with his worship of primitivism, not with any radical social attitudes. Ironically enough, in fact, to see the Negro as more elemental than the white man, as Ned Polsky has acutely remarked, is "an inverted form of keeping the nigger in his place." But even if it were true that American Negroes, by virtue of their position in our culture, have been able to retain a degree of primitive spontaneity, the last place you would expect to find evidence of this is among Bohemian Negroes. Bohemianism, after all, is for the Negro a means of entry into the world of the whites, and no Negro Bohemian is going to cooperate in the attempt to identify him with Harlem or Dixieland. The only major Negro character in either of Kerouac's two novels is Mardou Fox, and she is about as primitive as Wilhelm Reich himself.

The plain truth is that the primitivism of the Beat Generation serves first of all as a cover for an anti- intellectualism so bitter that it makes the ordinary American's hatred of eggheads seem positively benign. Kerouac and his friends like to think of themselves as intellectuals ("they are intellectual as hell and know all about Pound without being pretentious or talking too much about it"), but this is only a form of newspeak. Here is an example of what Kerouac considers intelligent discourse—"formal and shining and com- plete, without the tedious intellectualness":

> We passed a little kid who was throwing stones at the cars in the road. "Think of it," said Dean. "One day he'll put a stone through a man's windshield and the man will crash and die—all on account of that little kid. You see what I mean? God exists without qualms. As we roll along this way I am positive beyond doubt that everything will be taken care of for us—that even you, as you drive, fearful of the wheel . . . the thing will go along of itself and you won't go off the road and I can sleep. Furthermore we know America, we're at home; I can go anywhere in America and get what I want because it's the same in every corner, I know the people, I know what they do. We give and take and go in the incredibly complicated sweetness zigzagging every side."

You see what he means? Formal and shining and complete. No tedious intellectualness. Completely unpretentious. "There was nothing clear about the things he said but what he meant to say was somehow made pure and clear." *Somehow.* Of course. If what he wanted to say had been carefully thought out and precisely articulated, that would have been tedious and pretentious and, no doubt, *somehow* unclear and clearly impure. But so long as he utters these banalities with his tongue tied and with no comprehension of their meaning, so long as he makes noises that come out of his soul (since they couldn't possibly have come out of his mind), he passes the test of true intellectuality.

Which brings us to Kerouac's spontaneous bop prosody. This "prosody" is not to be confused with bop language itself, which has such a limited vocabulary (Basic English is a verbal treasure-house by comparison) that you couldn't write a note to the milkman in it, much less a novel. Kerouac, however, manages to remain true to the spirit of hipster slang while making forays into enemy territory (i.e., the English language) by his simple inability to express anything in words. The only method he has of describing an object is to summon up the same half-dozen adjectives over and over again: "greatest," "tremendous," "crazy," "mad," "wild," and perhaps one or two others. When it's more than just mad or crazy or wild, it becomes "really mad" or "really crazy" or "really wild." (All quantities in excess of three, incidentally, are subsumed under the rubric "innumerable," a word used innumerable times in *On the Road* but not so innumerably in *The Subterraneans*.) The same poverty of resources is apparent in those passages where Kerouac tries to handle a situation involving even slightly complicated feelings. His usual tactic is to run for cover behind cliché and vague signals to the reader. For instance: "I looked at him; my eyes were watering with embarrassment and tears. Still he stared at me. Now his eyes were blank and looking through me. . . . Something clicked in both of us. In me it was suddenly concern for a man who was years younger than I, five years, and whose fate was wound with mine across the passage of the recent years; in him it was a matter that I can ascertain only from what he did afterward." If you can ascertain what this is all about, either beforehand, during, or afterward, you are surely no square.

In keeping with its populistic bias, the style of *On the Road* is folksy and lyrical. The prose of *The Subterraneans*, on the other hand, sounds like an inept parody of Faulkner at his worst, the main difference being that Faulkner usually produces bad writing out of an impulse to inflate the commonplace while Kerouac gets into trouble by pursuing "spontaneity." Strictly speaking, spontaneity is a quality of feeling, not of writing: when we call a piece of writing spontaneous, we are registering our impression that the author hit upon the right words without sweating, that no "art" and no calculation entered into the picture, that his feelings seem to have spoken themselves, seem to have sprouted a tongue at the moment of composition. Kerouac apparently thinks that spontaneity is a matter of saying whatever comes into your head, in any order you happen to feel like saying it. It isn't the *right* words he wants (even if he knows what they might be), but the first words, or at any rate the words that most obviously announce themselves as deriving from emotion rather than cerebration, as coming from "life" rather than "literature," from the guts rather than the brain. (The brain, remember, is the angel of death.) But writing that springs easily and "spontaneously" out of strong feelings is *never* vague; it always has a quality of sharpness and precision because it is in the nature of strong feelings to be aroused by specific objects. The notion that a diffuse, generalized, and unrelenting enthusiasm is the mark of great sensitivity and responsiveness is utterly fantastic, an idea that comes from taking drunkenness or drug-addiction as the state of perfect emotional vigor. The effect of such enthusiasm is actually to wipe out the world altogether, for if a filling station will serve as well as the Rocky Mountains to arouse a sense of awe and wonder, then both the filling station and the mountains are robbed of their reality. Kerouac's conception of feeling is one that only a solipsist could believe in—and a solipsist, be it noted, is a man who does not relate to anything outside himself.

Solipsism is precisely what characterizes Kerouac's fiction. *On the Road* and *The Subterraneans* are so patently autobiographical in content that they become almost impossible to discuss as novels; if spontaneity were indeed a matter of destroying the distinction between life and literature, these books would unquestionably be It. "As we were going out to the car Babe slipped and fell flat on her face. Poor girl was overwrought. Her brother Tim and I helped her up. We got in the car; Major and Betty joined us. The sad ride back to Denver began." Babe is a girl who is mentioned a few times in the course of *On the Road*; we don't know why she is overwrought on this occasion, and even if we did it wouldn't matter, since there is no reason for her presence in the book at all. But Kerouac tells us that she fell flat on her face while walking toward a car. It is impossible to believe that Kerouac made this detail up, that his imagination was creating a world real enough to include wholly gratuitous elements; if that were the case, Babe would have come alive as a human being. But she is only a name; Kerouac never even describes her. She is in the book because the sister of one of Kerouac's friends was there when he took a trip to Central City, Colorado, and she slips in *On the Road* because she slipped that day on the way to the car. What is true of Babe who fell flat on her face is true of virtually every incident in *On the Road* and *The Subterraneans*. Nothing that happens has any dramatic reason for happening. Sal Paradise meets such-and-such people on the road whom he likes or (rarely) dislikes; they exchange a few words, they have a few beers together, they part. It is all very unremarkable and commonplace, but for Kerouac it is always the greatest, the wildest, the most. What you get in these two books is a man proclaiming that he is *alive* and offering every trivial experience he has ever had in evidence. Once I did this, once I did that (he is saying) and by God, it *meant* something! Because I

*responded!* But if it meant something, and you responded so powerfully, why can't you explain what it meant, and why do you have to insist so?

I think it is legitimate to say, then, that the Beat Generation's worship of primitivism and spontaneity is more than a cover for hostility to intelligence; it arises from a pathetic poverty of feeling as well. The hipsters and hipster-lovers of the Beat Generation are rebels, all right, but not against anything so sociological and historical as the middle class or capitalism or even respectability. This is the revolt of the spiritually underprivileged and the crippled of soul—young men who can't think straight and so hate anyone who can; young men who can't get outside the morass of self and so construct definitions of feeling that exclude all human beings who manage to live, even miserably, in a world of objects; young men who are burdened unto death with the specially poignant sexual anxiety that America—in its eternal promise of erotic glory and its spiteful withholding of actual erotic possibility—seems bent on breeding, and who therefore dream of the unattainable perfect orgasm, which excuses all sexual failures in the real world. Not long ago, Norman Mailer suggested that the rise of the hipster may represent "the first wind of a second revolution in this century, moving not forward toward action and more rational equitable distribution, but backward toward being and the secrets of human energy." To tell the truth, whenever I hear anyone talking about instinct and being and the secrets of human energy, I get nervous; next thing you know he'll be saying that violence is just fine, and then I begin wondering whether he really thinks that kicking someone in the teeth or sticking a knife between his ribs are deeds to be admired. History, after all—and especially the history of modern times—teaches that there is a close connection between ideologies of primitivistic vitalism and a willingness to look upon cruelty and blood-letting with complacency, if not downright enthusiasm. The reason I bring this up is that the spirit of hipsterism and the Beat Generation strikes me as the same spirit which animates the young savages in leather jackets who have been running amuck in the last few years with their switch-blades and zip guns. What does Mailer think of those wretched kids, I wonder? What does he think of the gang that stoned a nine-year-old boy to death in Central Park in broad daylight a few months ago, or the one that set fire to an old man drowsing on a bench near the Brooklyn waterfront one summer's day, or the one that pounced on a crippled child and orgiastically stabbed him over and over and over again even after he was good and dead? Is that what he means by the liberation of instinct and the mysteries of being? Maybe so. At least he says somewhere in this article that two eighteen-year-old hoodlums who bash in the brains of a candy-store keeper are murdering an institution, committing an act that "violates private property"—which is one of the most morally gruesome ideas I have ever come across, and which indicates where the ideology of hipsterism can lead. I happen to believe that there is a direct connection between the flabbiness of American middle-class life and the spread of juvenile crime in the 1950's, but I also believe that juvenile crime can be explained partly in terms of the same resentment against normal feeling and the attempt to cope with the world through intelligence that lies behind Kerouac and Ginsberg. Even the relatively mild ethos of Kerouac's books can spill over easily into brutality, for there is a suppressed cry in those books: Kill the intellectuals who can talk coherently, kill the people who can sit still for five minutes at a time, kill those incomprehensible characters who are capable of getting seriously involved with a woman, a job, a cause. How can anyone in his right mind pretend that this has anything to do with private property or the middle class? No. Being for or against what the Beat Generation stands for has to do with denying that incoherence is superior to precision; that ignorance is superior to knowledge; that the exercise of mind and discrimination is a form of death. It has to do with fighting the notion that sordid acts of violence are justifiable so long as they are committed in the name of "instinct." It even has to do with fighting the poisonous glorification of the adolescent in American popular culture. It has to do, in other words, with being for or against intelligence itself.

## BERNARD DUFFEY
"The Three Worlds of Jack Kerouac"
*Recent American Fiction*, ed. Joseph J. Waldmeir
1963, pp. 175–84

### I

If, in the 1960's, there is still a special something called the Beat Generation, and if it is still to be thought of as contributing to recent fiction, then one name especially, that of Jack Kerouac, must be taken as representative of its nature and work. The movement with which he has been identified is now nearly twenty years old. It has to some considerable extent merged into a broadening sea of personal restlessness. It has produced a number of poets and a widely felt area of influence in poetry, but its one distinct achievement in fiction is marked by Kerouac's work. The Beat Generation, as I shall note, has never so much been an artistic as a social phenomenon, a post-war response to post-war times, which produced some writing along the way. Kerouac himself has been clear enough in this matter, and, whatever the fate of the Beats or Kerouac's relation to them, he has identified himself with their world sufficiently to make that the first and most basic of his own three worlds.

> . . . there's nothing to get excited about. Beat comes out actually of old American whoopee, and it will only change a few dresses and pants, and make chairs useless in the living room. And pretty soon we'll have Beat Secretaries of State and there will be instituted new tinsels, in fact new reasons for malice and new reasons for virtue and new reasons for forgiveness.

But immediately following such light-heartedness, Kerouac falls into an apocalyptic turn of speech.

> But yet, but yet, woe unto those who think that the Beat Generation means crime, delinquency, immorality . . . woe unto those who attack it on the grounds that they simply don't understand history and the yearning of human souls . . . woe unto those who don't realize that America must, will, is changing now, for the better I say. Woe unto those who believe in the atom bomb, who believe in hating mothers and fathers, who deny the most important of the Ten Commandments. Woe unto those (though) who don't believe in the unbelievable sweetness of sex love, woe unto those who are the standard bearers of death, woe unto those who believe in conflict and horror and violence and fill our books and screens and living-rooms with all that crap, woe in fact unto those who make evil movies about the Beat Generation where innocent housewives are raped by beatniks! Woe unto those who are the real dreary sinners that even God finds room [*sic*] to forgive . . . woe unto those who spit on the Beat Generation, the wind'll blow it back.[1]

This neo-Freudian denunciation is far from accidental to Beat

living and thinking. It is the heart of much that is most revealing in the Beat Generation and in the fiction of Kerouac and the other writers of the school. The Beats have formed one more crest in the continuing wave of romantic American dissent—but with this difference. They came not to replace one political or moral scheme with another, but to deny all such systems in favor of apparent anarchy. Where American dissenters have often made qualified or systematic negations, the Beats have made a total and immediate sweep. And then, the work of demolition accomplished, they attempt a total affirmation. Perhaps the word demolition is badly chosen. The Beats would not so much destroy society and its values as simply disaffiliate, and, once free, begin a quest for some reality, but one governed only by individual existence. It is in this search that the fiction of Jack Kerouac makes an intelligible place for itself in recent American writing.

Kerouac himself was born into a family of French-Canadian extraction in 1922. Through high school he lived in Lowell, Massachusetts—a city, to judge by his account, of glooms and wonders dominated by dark mills and shadowy mansions, and populated largely by a polyglot working class left to its own devices for living in so alien a town. It may be noted that Kerouac, like Dreiser, belongs to that small but increasing number of American novelists who come to their trade from working class and other than English speaking origins, suggesting something of the kind of penetration which American writing must expect from our later nineteenth and early twentieth century immigration. Kerouac did some work at Columbia University but left without a degree and spent several years living like a compound of the vagabond characters in his own novels.

Even so scanty a sketch takes on importance in that, as it indicates a way of life, so does it indicate the foundation upon which Kerouac's fiction rests. Edgar Lee Masters, a member of an earlier dissenting generation, wrote in 1919 to Theodore Dreiser:

> What would you think about preparing a manifesto calling it the Artists' Manifesto, and get ten to twenty leading men and women to sign it, on the general subject of the state of the country?
> What I have in mind is that something should be done to counteract the influence and the insistent labors of these people—preachers, professors and suburban minds who are really running the country.
> . . . We could lay down a program with reference to liberty of speech and the press, marriage, ethics, art, or anything else, and all other things important. Make it forthright and direct, revolutionary if that word be applicable.[2]

Kerouac's generation, however, have found their act of negation not in manifestoes against society but in act, they vote with their behavior. How much or what kind of Existentialism may be active in so total a commitment is hard to gauge, but there are similarities between the two. Negation or affirmation is unreal until it enters into and becomes life itself. To have joined the Beat Generation is to participate in the life of the Beats. The religious overtones of certain beat writing, including Kerouac's own, is genuine, not affected. The Beat Generation would settle finally for nothing less than the whole soul: whoever is not with them is against them.

In this sense, Kerouac's novels are not only about the Beat Generation but of it. They came into existence because the Beats came into existence, and this is another fact setting them apart from the generality of American dissenters. Dissent literature, where it has most truly become literature, has grown most often from the imagination and craft of individual artists turned to a concern with individual plights without much reliance on group movements. To take some names typical of earlier vanguards, Sherwood Anderson, or Ezra Pound, or James Farrell—each one stood as spokesman for his kind of individual against what he saw as the dehumanization of the twentieth century. But when all was said and done, they could achieve little identity except that of affirmation. Even Marxism in Farrell or Christianity in Eliot have led to the ultimate assertion of individual existence. But this is the point which Kerouac takes as his starting place. For, if a philosophical point may be made about a largely unphilosophical movement, the Beat Generation may be said to have all its character compressed into the radical aseity of the formula, "I am that I am." Other movements have sought to derive personal identity from sources outside the self: deity, fate, nature, family, society, ideology, history—all these have been drawn upon to support that claim to identity that man has made his own. But the Beats, I will suggest, are the most important example in America of a movement which has spread itself broadly through western life. They are Beat precisely because none of the older sources of identity hold any promise. I do not know that their feeling is right, but, in various guises it is widely shared. Jacques Maritain describes the state of mind which he thinks gave rise in the early century to the vitalistic philosophy of Henri Bergson and which remains an admirably succinct description of the prevailing mentality.

> The whole effort of modern philosophy ended in mathematicism or universal mechanism and in that venerable mixture of materialism and scepticism called the scientific or positive outlook. . . . Thus, the absolute was unknowable, there was no other reality for us but phenomena, that is to say appearance and accident; the superior had its whole being and its whole reason in the inferior from which it sprang spontaneously; everything happened as though God did not exist, men had no soul, free will was an illusion incompatible with scientific determinism, and the world was one day to be taken apart by scientists like a big mechanical toy.[3]

Bergson's response was to construct a philosophy of intuition designed to bring a sense of life back into a dead world. But for the Beats, even his effort would be less than sufficient. What must be done is to *act out* the proposition. "Nevertheless, existence." And to dig whatever in existence may be, and, finally, is.

The Beats, it can be said, have had no program critical of the modern orthodoxy except to dub it "square," and if you don't quite dig that, the lengthiest explanation you are likely to get is a shrug of the shoulders. You have to intuit because intuiting is the one resource available in the face of all the arid tangles which immobilize modern man. Beat rejection is one forced by history rather than invented. For the Beat who attains it, the proper state is "cool." As nearly as this term can be translated, it means a poise centered in the self alone without regard to any circumstance, a total concentration in what the German existentialists have called the *Eigenwelt*, the world of one's self only. It is the self affirming itself in despair.

The cool Beat, what Kerouac has called the "subterranean," is most typically the user of narcotics, partly as an analgesic aid in preserving the stricken self and partly because narcosis is an assertive chemical act. If the self is so to be put at bay, then let the self be its own hunter and, finally, executor of its own sad triumph. In John Clellon Holmes' novel, *Go*, a drug addict riding on a bus thinks thus to himself:

> They're disgusted because they've got to save their own egos, you see. But I haven't got one, I mean I

don't care about all that anymore, so it doesn't matter to me. . . . I just accept it so as not to get hung up.

Here a man has found some kind of soul by losing it. The resemblance of this to traditional sanctity is striking in itself, and all the more so when it is compared with the reported self-denials of the less savory saints. But a great difference remains in the fact that the religious ascetic denies himself for a reality presumed to be outside himself. The Beat's final cause is himself, the recovery of existence in a world but outside an ego he has never made.

Kerouac's fiction lies short of the cool to share in what he dubs the hot, an active and ceaseless effort at affirmation still stemming from the individual will but flowing through different channels.

> . . . the "hot" today is the crazy talkative shining eyed (often innocent and open hearted) nut who runs from bar to bar, pad to pad, looking for everybody, shouting, restless, lusty, trying to "make it" with the subterranean beatniks who ignore him. Most Beat generation artists belong to the hot school, naturally since that hard gemlike flame needs a little heat. In many cases, the mixture is 50–50 . . . In 1948 the "hot hipsters" were racing around in cars like in *On The Road* looking for wild bawling jazz like Willis Jackson or Lucky Thompson (the early) or Chubby Jackson's big band while the "cool hipsters" cooled it in dead silence before formal and excellent musical groups like Lennie Tristano or Miles Davis.

Kerouac explains that he himself began hot but "finally cooled it in Buddhist meditation" and has remained a mixture of the two.

I hope I have said enough to make two or three central facts clear. The Beat Generation is characterized by a way of life which can be grasped only by living it. Its nature is ineffable. At its fullest it combines a total rejection of any life governed by conventional space, time or causality with a total affirmation of the self thus exiled. It is colored by some sense of the holy or sacred, and if this can only be found in the implacable reality of narcotics, then let it there be found. It is, in a word, a late and vehement assertion of the native romantic spirit against an obdurately unromantic American ethos.

*II*

But what of the romantic's writing in a world where the romantic ideal has diminished almost to extinction? The form to which Kerouac has committed himself is personal narrative, one scribbled down without correction and at high speed in a quest for the same spontaneity of expression in letters as in living. His is an affirmative attitude in which wonder and delight take the largest place, but a wonder and delight always in himself, his adventures, and his friends. Too often, perhaps, the result has been a collapse into literary sentiment or authorial self-indulgence carried to a tiresome length. At his worst he is a bore, and this charge has been repeated against him over and over. He writes too much about too little and is too easily enamored of his friends, his style, and his life. We get tired of his special admiration, Neil Cassaday, who, as Dean Moriarty, dominates *On the Road*, and who is given an apotheosis as Cody Pomeray in *Visions of Cody*. Whatever Cassaday's appeal may have been gets lost in the sheer bulk of Kerouac's admiration and language. Where he is strongest, as in *The Subterraneans*, *Doctor Sax*, or *Lonesome Traveler*, there is a sharper evocation of character and "feel," apparently because his "spontaneous prose" has, for the time, led him away from rhapsody and into the definition of characters through action and setting.

Rhapsody, however, is the indispensable second world of Jack Kerouac. His child-men will never have a growing-up, but they will survive in their Beatness and celebrate that which has granted them survival. They are victims, sufferers from the angular world of the squares. Their cities, like those of Eliot's *Waste Land*, are unreal. A vainglorious idealism has disposed of the sacred; science has disposed of nature; and the competitive rat race has disposed of most people. Here, I think, Kerouac takes our age at a most sensitive point—the widely felt crisis of existence—and if his work suffers from sentimental self-indulgence it perhaps springs from the same cause which puffs so many of his adverse critics into a pompous self-indulgence. The advantages of joy and wit, however, remain with the author.

Although the subject does not receive extended discussion in his work, Kerouac's fiction shares with much other modern writing a relapse into the world of subjective and qualitative time. To "dig," in Beat talk, is to allow something to fill one's time-consciousness. By this means, the whole world built on event, feeling, thought, and motive in time is replaced by a world in which all these are themselves time and are the only stuff of human apprehension and of life itself. If Kerouac is an irrationalist, it is less because he opposes reason with some other faculty than because he would feel reason, given its mechanistic concept of time, to be denying itself any chance of seeing life truly. An hour is really a cluster of events, but our time-bound apprehension mistakes mensuration for reality. The latter is in events alone, and we have no choice but to base our action on immediate apprehension or intuition of events. Other considerations are in fact irrelevant.

The result is the immediacy and unrelatedness of everything. This introduces us to a world which seems strange but which is, in fact, the world we all inhabit but have been taught to ignore. Stripped of its ordering scaffold of time, it becomes, in Beat jargon, simply "it," the unnameable which exists only in its own manner and quality. In this sense, "digging" experience is not a transcendental act but a more purely aesthetic thing where, in words older than Kerouac's, not the fruit of experience but experience itself is the end. The conventional world having been dismissed for the operative and subjective illusion it is, we are rewarded by the gift of the real world, but that is a gift which is almost too much. Along with Dean Moriarty of *On the Road*, we must live by saying, "Yes, yes, yes, yes yes," no matter what happens.

> "Oh man! man!" moaned Dean. "And it's not even the beginning of it—and now here we are at last going East together, we've never gone East together; Sal, think of it, we'll dig Denver together and see what everybody's doing, although that matters little to us, the point being that we know what IT is and we know TIME and we know that everything is really FINE." Then he whispered, clutching my sleeve, sweating: "Now you just dig them in front [the people driving the car]. They have worries, they're counting the miles, they're thinking about where to sleep tonight, how much money for gas, the weather, how they'll get there anyway, you see. But they need to worry and betray time with urgencies false and otherwise, purely anxious and whiny, their souls really won't be at peace unless they can latch on to an established and proven worry, and having once found it they assume facial expressions to fit and go with it, which is, you see, unhappiness, and all the time it all flies by them and they know it and that too worries them, no end."

The critical problem is not really one of who is right but of whether Moriarty does illuminate for the reader something of the reader himself and the world in which he lives. What seems not to be recognized is that Kerouac's desire to drive his fiction back to the strangeness of nature is in fact a continuing of the drive that has existed since romanticism began. True to the organic principle, the only one which literary romanticism can admit without committing suicide, Kerouac founds his style upon the substance of experience, that which stands under it and constitutes its reality. Like the Zen devotee he has sometimes thought himself to be, the Beat artist seeks to clear away the debris of convention, to discover anew the reality which pattern has come to obfuscate, and so recapture the living process of art itself.

### III

Where such a discovery does, in fact, occur, Kerouac fights free of the intransitive subjectivity which weakens his lesser work to carry his reader into a discovery of art as process analogous to the discovery of nature. The reader's pleasure becomes that of seeing the work grow into its natural form rather than using it as a token by which he observes the frantic doings of the Beats or strains for sympathy with a less than Ionic rhapsody. As organic time is the essence of the writer's work, so is it of his reader's. Kerouac's third world, the process of fiction, incorporates its foundations in the Beat Generation and the privately inspired rhetoric of *On the Road* or *Visions of Cody*. But it changes these from literary objects in their own right to avenues of imaginative discovery. It is here that his theory of spontaneous prose justifies itself, perhaps in serendipity or perhaps in something a little more calculated. In conventional terms, I would suggest that his achievement is that of romantic comedy, romantic in its continued embroilment in the strangeness of nature but comic in a growing power of wry detachment from the preciousness of its subject or the author's self. But "the achievement of comedy" suggests too static an accomplishment unless the sense of "achieving" as a verb is remembered. *The Subterraneans*, *Doctor Sax*, or *Lonesome Traveler* are more acts than things, and their object is the literary process itself.

They are, for example, more like Sherwood Anderson's stories than like Hemingway's. My own term, "world," is misleading since we do not walk into them as we walk into the world of the Lost Generation in *The Sun Also Rises*. Rather, we watch what happens in them and, along with the author, learn as his circumstances make learning possible. Like Anderson, Kerouac is a storyteller rather than a god who stands outside his creation paring his finger nails, and much of the interest in a story told must lie in the telling; the performance of the storyteller as it runs parallel to or counterpoints the story he is telling. Kerouac has been compared to Thomas Wolfe, but there is a great difference in that direction too. Wolfe was always overwhelmed by his subject. Kerouac is fascinated by his subject, but only as subject, not as ethos or revelation. His great temptation is mannerism, and he succumbs to it sometimes. But in the tradition to which he belongs, that of Anderson or Mark Twain, mannerism is a paradoxical risk of improvised narrative. That art, in any case, must be seen for the kind of thing it is and not as a clumsy imitation of something it was never meant to be.

In a perceptive essay on Kerouac's style, Warren Tallman has found its chief influence to be that of Bop, in which jazz fights it way free of structure. The great musicians are those, like Charlie Parker, who without losing their own kind of control make their escape from original melody and rhythm into free improvisation. The performer becomes a performer-composer, a creator of new music. The Bop musician clears away the fixity of conventional pattern to discover a new reality and so recaptures the nature of music itself. His hearer, like Kerouac's reader, listens not only to a musical object but to a musical process in action.

Spontaneous prose must justify itself through such a discovery of its own nature. The author's seemingly random gyrations eventually fall into place as being the only possible way in which his discovery can present itself to his reader as discovery. In the strict sense of a battered old term, his prose is experimental, made up of trial efforts which sometimes come off and sometimes don't. As Kerouac puts it in the "Preface" to *Visions of Cody:* "My work comprises one vast book like Proust's *Remembrance of Things Past*, except that my remembrances are written on the run instead of afterwards in a sickbed."

No doubt, there is also an art of "spontaneity," as perhaps in E. E. Cummings, where the author is not really naive but sentimental, a pretend primitive. Kerouac's work, however, gives every sign, including that of its collapses, of genuine experiment and discovery. *On the Road* and *The Dharma Bums* lead, by and large, to experience which has its being apart from the writing of the stories. They are conventional but mussed up by the author's manner, still tied to the preconceived end which goes far toward determining their structure. The character of Neil Cassaday, the discipline of Zen Buddhism do not depend on having stories told about them for their existence, and the stories emerge mainly as perfervid reports. But Kerouac's blunderingly ironic discovery of his real marriage to his writing, his "constructions," in the teeth of the rival love affair, engrossing, sad, and funny, in the *Subterraneans*, or the surprised discovery of his portentous but rather vaguely allegorical comic-book hero in *Doctor Sax* that evil, as in some kinds of comedy, does away with itself, or the several discoveries of the author in *Lonesome Traveler* of railroading, or shipping-out, or spending a hermit summer as fire-watcher—all these come through to the reader as things found. Again, the problem is not that of the philosophic rightness of Kerouac's conclusions, which, in any case, are only occasionally of philosophic breadth. Rather it is the complex clarity generated by his textual progress.

In addition, there is a second level of discovery, one different from the over-all curve of the story or sketch, which occurs in the line-by-line divagations, the associations of thought and feeling as experienced so that the detail of experience becomes the object of the author's questing.

> . . . ah, loved it all, and the first night finest night, the blood, "railroading gets in yr blood" the old hogshead is yelling at me as he bounces up and down in his seat and the wind blows his striped cap visor back and the engine, like a huge beast is lurching side to side 70 miles per hour breaking all rulebook rules, zomm, zomm, were crashing through the night and out there Carmelity is coming, Jose is making her electricities mix and interrun with his and the whole earth charged with juices turns up the organo to the flower, the unfoldment, the stars bend to it, the whole world's coming as the big engine booms and balls by with the madman of the white cap California in there flossing and wow there's just no end to all this wine—[4]

Locomotive, sex, the wild engineer, his strangely white-capped fireman who merges into the white-capped California coast, the movement of the train, of the earth, and of the universe toward whatever ends they may have, all done up in endless wine—a great jumble no doubt, but one nevertheless held in control by its own context and prevented from flying off on irrelevant historical or philosophical tangents of the kind produced in Thomas Wolfe. The specific experience itself. Kerouac leads us not into the subjectivity of his feelings finally, as does Wolfe, but into the objectivity of his writing. As the train bangs along, we hang onto our hats.

One may well argue that Jack Kerouac offers little to the philosophic future of American literature except through his identification with the disaffiliate movement. His literary contribution, however, has a distinction and a value. This may be generalized by reference to a dictum, surprisingly enough, from George Bernard Shaw: ". . . it is the business of the stage to make its figures more intelligible to themselves than they would be in real life; for by no other means can they be made intelligible to the audience." One cannot imagine Shaw and Kerouac finding much common ground for definitions of intelligibility, but both could agree to its mystical nature, as Shaw does in the preface to *St. Joan* from which his opinion is taken. For Shaw, the life is known by intelligence, its specifically generated power of knowing itself. For Kerouac it is more blindly known by accidental experience. It is tactile, felt in many bits and pieces. This kind of knowledge, like the unrationalizable knowledge one has while eating a grapefruit that one is eating a grapefruit, is Kerouac's literary medium and goal in one. It has its obvious limits, but within such limits it achieves its own literary being. This is not confined to the kind of enthusiasm which is most apparent in quotably short excerpts. It can be summed up by saying that the writer comes to a practical knowledge of himself as a writer about his experience and invites the reader to share in that particular and radical literary experience.

Leo Percepied in *The Subterraneans*, after his intense love affair, is sent away by his mistress, Mardou:

> I think you're like me—you want one love—like, men have the essence in the woman, there's an essence . . . and the man has it in his hand, but rushes off to build big constructions.

But his anguish over losing Mardou cannot blunt the rightness of her perception. He has one love. He wants "big constructions" more than he wants her and is willing to make even of their tangled and intimate passion precisely such a construction. It will become the subject of his writing and so, perhaps, be made intelligible to him.

> What'll we do? I think—now I go home, and it's all over for sure, not only now is she bored and has had enough but has pierced me with adultery of a kind, has been inconstant. . . .
>   "Baby, it's up to you," is what she's actually saying, "about how many times you want to see me and all that—but I want to be independent like I say."
>     And I go home having lost her love.
>     And I write this book.

*Notes*

1. *Playboy*, Vol. 6, No. 6 (June, 1959), p. 79.
2. Chicago, March 10, 1919. In the Theodore Dreiser Collection, University of Pennsylvania Library.
3. *Bergsonian Philosophy and Thomism* (New York, 1955), p. 120.
4. *Lonesome Traveler* (New York, 1960), p. 83.

## ALLEN GINSBERG
### From "Kerouac" (1971)
#### *Allen Verbatim*
#### 1974, pp. 151–57

Kerouac was a regular style prose writer writing in the forms of Thomas Wolfe; that is to say, long, symphonic-sentenced, heavy-voweled periods, a little with echo of Milton. Wolfe had that same Biblical Miltonic prose echo in his sentences, and in a book called *The Town and the City* written in the late forties by Kerouac there are similar lengthily constructed sentences.

So Kerouac was the first writer I ever met who heard his own writing, who listened to his own sentences as if they were musical, rhythmical constructions, and who could follow the sequence of sentences that make up the paragraph as if he were listening to a little jazz riff, a complete chorus, say of "Lady Be Good," by the then-hero of saxophone, Lester Young, or a later hero of alto, Charlie Parker. So he found a rhythmic model, listening to their rhythms, the rhythm of Lester Young's saxophone sentences or paragraphs in his choruses of "Lester Leaps In" or any one of a number of—at that time—celebrated jazz classic records (which are still very listenable, if anybody has the historic ear to know them).

And he would model sentences on the choruses, on the particular squiggly little "dadadadadadaduhdada"—"As I was goin' walkin' down to Larimer" of "Lester Leaps In" is "dadada dadadada dadada, dadadadadadada, dadada, dadadadada dada dadada, dadaadadaydyadadda." So it was a definite rhythmical squiggle that he was hearing when he was writing his prose sentences, a funny body rhythm, a breathing rhythm and a speech rhythm that he was conscious of writing when he was writing prose. So he added a dimension to prose which most prosateurs have not yet actually discovered exists or is necessary for epic or historical prose.

Kerouac got to be a great poet on that basis, 'cause he could hear American speech, and he could hear it in musical sequence. He has a book called *Mexico City Blues*— poem choruses, one page apiece, on Buddhist themes, generally, like a little subject rolling from one chorus to the next, one page to another and he would get to funny little rhythmic constructions like

> The Eagle on the Pass,
> the Wire on the Rail,
> the High Hot Iron
> of my heart,
> The Blazing Chickaball
> Whap-by
> Extry special Super
> High Job
> Ole 169 be
> floundering
> Down to Kill Roy

Kill Roy (Gilroy, California) being the end of the Southern Pacific line, where the Southern Pacific finishes in the South. "The Blazing Chickaball/Whap-by/Extry special Super/High Job/Ole 169 be/floundering/Down to Kill Roy."

And so he would write prose paragraphs and prose sentences that way, in his own speech rhythms, in chosen American speech rhythms. If you don't write your own prose out as part of your own body rhythm, some actual rhythm from real speech, as some really spoken tale as might be spoken by Homer or any old taleteller, you wind up with an impersonal prose, a prose that doesn't proceed from anybody, and thus a kind of bureaucratic prose or a fictional prose that comes from an assignment, an assignment to make money, or a publishing company, or a magazine; you wind up with an hallucination of prose, rather than an actual piece of prose as it issues from the human body.

In other words you can wind up with prose which is a lie, which doesn't represent anything you or anybody else or any human body actually thinks, but only represents a style of prose that is commercially viable or written in a marketplace of plastic political artifacts. All you have to do is look at Nixon's prose style as "prose style" to realize that it does not proceed from his physical body, but proceeds from a composite of information-serving bureaucrats—not personal, not representing any individual human spirit as manifested in a single body.

That's a digression. The main point I was trying to make was that there is a tradition of prose in America, including Thomas Wolfe and going through Kerouac, which is personal, in which the prose sentence is completely personal, comes from the writer's own person—his person defined as his body, his breathing rhythm, his actual talk. And the word *person* there I'm taking from the context of Walt Whitman, who talks about "What we need is large conscious American Persons," as distinct from objects, or citizens, or subjects, or ciphers, or nonentities, or market-research digits.

Kerouac then got more and more personal in his prose, and finally decided that he would write big books without even having a plot, but just write what was going on, without like an "impersonally" constructed plot, impersonal to his life. He would just write a book in his own persona, as if he were telling his best friend the story of what they did together in a five-year period of running around the country in automobiles.

So he wrote a long book called *On the Road* and his project was to sit down, using a single piece of paper, like a teletype roll that he got from the United Press office in New York (which is like hundreds and hundreds of feet) and sit down and type away as fast he could everything he always thought of, going chronologically, about a series of cross-country auto-mobile trips he and a couple buddies took, with all their girls, and the grass they were smokin' in '48–'49–'50 and the peyote they were eating then, and the motel traveling salesmen they met, the small-town redneck gas station attendants they stole gas from, the small-town lonely waitresses they seduced, the confusions they went through, and the visionary benzedrine hallucinations they had from driving a long time on benze-drine, several days, until they began getting visions of shrouded strangers along the road saying "Woe on America," and disappearing, flitting like phantoms.

So what he did was try to write it all out, as fast as it came to his mind, all the associations; the style being as if he were telling a tale, excitedly, all night long, staying up all night with his best friend. The prose style being modeled on two buddies telling each other their most intimate secrets excitedly, the long confessional of everything that happened, with every detail, every cunt-hair in the grass included, every tiny eyeball flick of orange neon flashed past in Chicago by the bus station included—in other words, all the back-of-the-brain imagery, which would require, then, sentences that did not necessarily follow exact classic-type syntactical order, but which allowed for interruption with dashes—allowed for the sentences to break in half, take another direction (with parentheses that might go on for paragraphs)—allowed for individual sentences that might not come to their period except after several pages of self-reminiscence, interruption and piling-on of detail, so that what you arrived at was a sort of stream of consciousness, except visioned around a specific subject (the tale of the road being told) and a specific viewpoint, a personal viewpoint, that is, two buddies talking to each other late at night—maybe high on benny or else beer, or just smokin' together—but meeting and recognizing each other like Dostoyevsky characters and telling each other the tale of their childhood or . . .

But then Kerouac finished the book, which was not published for almost a decade after it was finished, and was dissatisfied because he had tied his mind down to fixing it in strictly chronological account. He'd tied his mind down to chronology, and so he was always halting his sentences and stopping to go back to keep it chronological so that if an orange neon light from Chicago intruded on a purple martini glass in neon over a Denver bar ten years earlier, he included the purple neon Denver bar martini glass though he was still trying to keep it up chronologically and tell what happened in Chicago.

So he decided to write another book, which has never been published, his greatest book, called *Visions of Cody*,[1] which deals with the same main character in about five hundred pages. But called *Visions of Cody*, meaning instead of doing it chronologically, do it in sequence, as recollection of the most beautiful, epiphanous moments. Visionary moments being the structure of the novel—in other words each section or chapter being a specific epiphanous heartrending moment no matter where it fell in time, and then going to the center of that moment, the specific physical description of what was happening. One, in particular: two guys taking a piss next to each other in a bar in Denver and having a long conversation and one says to the other "I love you." Which was like one tender moment between them of a real frank meeting of feelings. A second moment being both of them in Mexico and one taking the car leaving the other guy sick, to get home hitchhiking, 'cause there wasn't enough money and Kerouac had to go home and see his mama. So that was the second epiphany. A third epiphany was the main hero with his wife and children in California with his wife yellin' at him, saying that he's a creep, he's always running away, like he's never at home when the wife needs him, when the children need him, that he's always bringing chicks back to fuck in the attic, and he's always smokin' grass and that all the men runnin' around together are puttin' women down, and so tearing him apart, with neighbor wife girl friends in, all of them finally attacking the guy who was originally the hero of the book. And him going out alone, totally torn down.

But then as he was trying to write out of his present consciousness about the epiphany remembered, and as the prose became more and more elongated, he found that after a while his present consciousness of language would obtrude over even the epiphany subject matter: the subject matter itself would begin disappearing, and that he would hear the babble of language in his head, sometimes associated with the epiphany, and sometimes taking off from it and going into, like, Bach fugues of language rhythm without any kind of reference, necessarily, just syllable after syllable, "ogmogaged-dablab, sabadabuv" but still maintaining the same "Whap-by/ Extry special" language, "bopgooglemop" part of it, so continuing into one pure syllabic "mop mop mop" after another. So then that novel continues with a hundred pages of pure sound as prose. Then the exact transcription of taped conversations many nights between him and hero . . . then it goes into a "heavenly imitation" of the tape, then the prose reconstructs itself and comes back to narrative form and describes a scene with the wife yelling at the husband in the end. And that goes on for two hundred pages or so, or a hundred pages, and I think at the end—I haven't read it for many years, I read it in '55—at the end, there's sumpin' that really impressed Robert Duncan, who also saw the novel in the early fifties, 'cause it ends with the hero going out alone, walking past his car by a gas station downtown San Francisco, going out for a pack of beer, I guess, and as he goes out he sees the flash on the highly polished fender of his car of a barber shop mirror, mirrored in the fender of the car, the mirror in the

barber shop window mirroring the neon light of a purple martini glass and an orange light from a supermarket across the street, plus a star I guess enters in, or a moon, curved on the fender so making it odd shapes, illusory shapes, and suddenly has like a moment of realization that all nature around him is a total illusory mirror within mirror within mirror, bent out of shape, which he's perceiving, and so Kerouac has a fifty-page description of the contents of the visual imagery on the fender of the automobile. And Duncan, when he saw that, said, like, "He must be a great genius—he's the only one I know who could write fifty pages on what a polished automobile fender looks like, and have it all make sense."

*Notes*

1. *Visions of Cody* has now been published by McGraw-Hill (1973), with introduction by Allen Ginsberg.

## ALLEN GINSBERG
### From "The Great Rememberer"
*Saturday Review*, December 2, 1972, p. 63

I'm writing this book because we're all going to die . . . my heart broke in the general despair and opened up inwards to the Lord, I made a supplication in this dream." This is the most sincere and holy writing I know of our age—at the same time for Pre-Buddhist Jack, a complete display of knowledge of Noble Truths he soon discovered in Goddard's *Buddhist Bible*.

Yet Jack had another 18 years ahead with Neal on earth, neither was dead ("Neal is Dead") except this vision book was all out effort to understand early in the midst of life, what Jack's yearning and Neal's response and both their mortal American energy was all about, was directed to—but only time could tell, & both got tired *several* times—Jack went off to write not only *Dr. Sax* but *Mexico City Blues* in the next year & then *The Subterraneans* & *Springtime Mary (Maggie Cassidy)* and more and more and more climaxed 5 years later with some fame, and the brilliant Buddhist exposition *Dharma Bums*, and also *Desolation Angels* later, to keep the perfect chronicle going—"rack my hand with labor of Nada"—and many poems—not to speak of his *Book of Dreams* and giant as-yet-unpublished *Some of the Dharma*, 1000 pages of haikus, meditations, readings, commentaries on Prajnaparamita & Diamond Sutras, brain-thinks, Samadhi notes, scholarship in the Void—reading Shakespere & Melville all the while & listening to Bach's *St. Matthew's Passion* evermore—

Saying farewell to Cody, Jack was saying farewell to the World, both of them gave up several times—But at that 1952 time both of them were at their wits' ends with the world and America—The "Beat Generation" was about that time formulated, the Vietnam War just about to be continued American bodied (as 'twas already funded American dollar'd via opium pushing France & French-Corsican Intelligence agencies)—Two years after completion of this book Neal lived in a quiet home, receptive and friendly but by then entered into a blank new insistent religiosity, "like Billy Sunday in a suit" epistled Jack, namely Edgar Cayce study—which reincarnation philosophy drove Jack to study Buddhism; a new phase not even recorded or mentioned in this vast essay on Early or Middle Neal.

I remember the sleepless epiphanies of 1948—everywhere in America brain-consciousness was waking up, from Times Square to the banks of Willamette River to Berkeley's groves of Academe; little Samadhis and appreciations of intimate spaciness that might later be explain'd and followed as the

Crazy Wisdom of Rinzai Zen or the Whispered Transmission of Red Hut, Vajrayana Path Doctrine, or Coyote's empty yell in the Sierras. Out of Burroughs' copy of Spengler Kerouac arrived at the conception of "Fellaheen Eternal Country Life"—Country Samadhi for Jack, country Ken & consciousness latent discovered in Mexico as our heroes crossed the border; immediate recognition of Biblical Patriarch Type in Mexic Fellaheen fathers: the Bible those days the only immediate American mind-entry to primeval earth-consciousness non-machine populace that inhabits 80 per cent of the world—"Jeremiacal hoboes lounge, shepherds by trade . . . I can see the hand of God. The future's in Fellaheen. At Actopan this biblical plateau begins—it's reached by the mountain of Faith only. I know that I will someday live in a land like this. I did long ago." Heartbreaking prophecy. And intelligent Neal'd said, "What they want has already crumbled in a rubbish heap—they want banks."

Jack didn't write this book for money, he wrote it for love, he *gave* it away to the worlds; not even for fame, but as an explanation and prayer to his fellow mortals, and gods—with naked motive and humble piety Search—that's what makes *Visions of Cody* a work of primitive genius that grooks next to Douanier Rousseau's visions, and sits well-libraried beside Thomas Wolfe's Time & River (which Thos. Mann from his European eminence said was the great prose of America) & sits beside Tolstoi for its *prayers*. A La La Ho!

So we see the end of the American road in the U.S. boy's conscious discovery of the eternal natural man, primitive, ancient Biblical or Josephaic Shepherd or Khartoum Mongolian Gnothic Celtic: thus the magic political formulation idiotically stark sanely presented—a quote from the mustached Vice Regent Consul of Empire next to a quote from Jackey Keracky:

"*False nonsense*"—Acheson, 1952

"*You've got to legalize the Fellaheen*"—Duluoz, 1952

And why this paean to Neal? It's a consistent panegyric to heroism of mind, to the American Person that Whitman sought to adore. And now, "The holy Coast is done, the holy Road is over." Jack thought Cody'd gone back to California Marriage, would settle down be silent & die of old age—Little he knew the Psychedelic Bus, as if *On the Road* were transported to Heav'n, would ride on the road again through America, the Great Vehicle painted rainbow colored as Mahayana illusion with its tantric Kool-aid & Celestial passengers playing their Merry Pranks "Furthur" thru the land, "A vote for Goldwater is a Vote for Fun" sign painted on busside en route to find sad drunken Jack, enthusiastic but speechless high bring him to Acid Apartment on Park Avenue crowded at midnight with 50 Prankster bus passengers all cynically expectant jester-dressed & starry eyed worshipping—The old red faced W. C. Fields Toad Guru trembling shy hungover sick potbellied Master tenderly came back to the city afraid to drink himself to death—A Park Avenue apartment the site for Great Union Reunion Kerouac Cassady Kesey & Friends all together at last once in New York under unofficial mock but real Kleig lights with microphones reverb feedback wires snaking all over th'electrified household living room floor 86th St. upper East Side—An American Flag draped over couch, on which shocked Jack refused to sit—Kesey respectful welcoming and silent, fatherly timid host, myself marveling and sad, it was all out of my hands now, History was even out of Jack's hands now, he'd already written it 15 years before, he could only watch hopelessly one of his more magically colored prophecy shows, the Hope Show of Ghost Wisdoms made modern Chemical & Mechanic, in this Kali Yuga, he knew the worser death gloom to come, already on him in his alcohol ridden trembling no longer sexually tender corpus—Anyway, O clouds over Tetons, great Rain clouds over Idaho, lowbellied cumulus over Gros Ventre rain!—the conversation in that brilliant lit apartment Manhattan 1967 was sparse halting sad disappointing yet absolutely real, & thus recorded on tape as Jack already did, as well as (new era technology 15 years later Spenglerean time) on Film! O rain spoils't thou man's toys & images? Washest Time? And then the Bright Vast Bus on the magic road went honking up to Dr. Leary's Millbrook tantric mansion, what eras're ushered in on us?

The last pages say, "All America marching to this last land." The book was a dirge for America, for its heroes' deaths too, but then who could know except in the unconscious—A dirge for the American Hope that Jack (& his hero Neal) carried so valiantly through the land after Whitman—an America of pioneers and generosity—and selfish glooms & exploitations implicit in the pioneers' entry into Foreign Indian & Moose lands—but the great betrayal of that manly America was made by the pseudo-heroic pseudo-responsible masculines of Army and Industry and Advertising and Construction and Transport and toilets and Wars.

Last pages—how tender—"Adios King!" a farewell to all the promises of America, an explanation & prayer for innocence, a tearful renunciation of victory & accomplishment, a humility in the face of "the necessary blankess of men" in hopeless America, hopeless World, in hopeless wheel of Heaven, a compassionate farewell to Love & the Companion, Adios King.

# KEN KESEY

## 1935–

Ken Kesey was born in La Junta, Colorado, on September 17, 1935. In 1946 his family of farmers and ranchers moved to Springfield, Oregon. Much of his childhood was spent outdoors working on his father's dairy farm or participating in school athletics. At the University of Oregon Kesey was an outstanding wrestler and almost made the 1960 Olympic team. In 1956 he married his childhood sweetheart, Faye Haxby, and the following year he graduated from Oregon with a degree in Speech and Communications.

Initially he wanted to pursue an acting career and he spent two summers in Hollywood working as a gopher on television and movie sets. However, by the time of his graduation from college Kesey had decided to try his hand at writing. He entered Stanford's creative writing program in 1958, studying with Malcolm Cowley. After he finished the two-year program he remained in Palo Alto, living in the famed bohemian quarter along Perry Lane. Here he began his experimentation with various drugs, including LSD. During the summer of 1960 he also was a paid volunteer for the government testing of hallucinatory drugs at a local veteran's hospital in Menlo Park. Later Kesey worked the night shift as a psychiatric aide in this VA hospital. During this time he was inspired to write his acclaimed first novel, *One Flew Over the Cuckoo's Nest* (1962), parts of which Kesey claims to have written while under the influence of drugs. Two years later he published his second novel, *Sometimes a Great Notion*. Although it received some favorable reviews, this story about a logging family in the Pacific Northwest was not nearly as popular as his first book, which by this time had achieved cult status among college-age readers.

In 1964 Kesey set out in a 1939 International Harvester school bus on a cross-country trek with a group known as the Merry Pranksters. The driver was Neal Cassady, after whom Kerouac had modeled his character Dean Moriarty. While taking psychedelic drugs and painting the bus and themselves with day-glo paints, the Merry Pranksters shot over forty hours of color film. The project, known as "The Movie," was never completed and the many reels of film remain unedited. This communal psychedelic version of *On the Road* was immortalized in Tom Wolfe's *The Electric Kool-Aid Acid Test* (1968). Kesey became a cult figure credited with bridging the gap between the Beat generation and the hippies.

In 1965 Kesey was arrested in California for possession of marijuana. He was arrested again before his appeal and in 1966 he fled to Mexico to escape imprisonment. He returned a year later and served a five-month jail sentence. At that time he seemed to renounce writing as he moved back to Oregon to live with his wife and four children on a farm in Pleasant Hill. Although he still lives on his Oregon farm, he has continued to write, but at a much slower pace. A collection of various works titled *Kesey's Garage Sale* appeared in 1973 and was followed by the publication of several short stories as well as an occasional magazine called *Spit in the Ocean*.

### TOM WOLFE
### "The Electric Suit"
### *The Electric Kool-Aid Acid Test*
#### 1968, pp. 26–33

Through the sheet of sunlight at the doorway and down the incline into the crazy gloom comes a panel truck and in the front seat is Kesey. The Chief; out on bail. I half expect the whole random carnival to well up into a fluorescent yahoo of incalculably insane proportions. In fact, everybody is quiet. It is all cool.

Kesey gets out of the truck with his eyes down. He's wearing a sport shirt, an old pair of pants, and some Western boots. He seems to see me for an instant, but there is no hello, not a glimmer of recognition. This annoys me, but then I see that he doesn't say hello to anybody. Nobody says anything. They don't all rush up or anything. It's as if . . . Kesey is back and what is there to say about it.

Then Mountain Girl booms out: "How was jail, Kesey!"

Kesey just shrugs. "Where's my shirt?" he says.

Mountain Girl fishes around in the debris over beside a bunch of theater seats and gets the shirt, a brown buckskin shirt with an open neck and red leather lacings. Kesey takes off the shirt he has on. He has huge latissimi dorsi muscles making his upper back fan out like manta-ray wings. Then he puts on the buckskin shirt and turns around.

Instead of saying anything, however, he cocks his head to one side and walks across the garage to the mass of wires, speakers, and microphones over there and makes some minute adjustment. ". . . The Nowhere Mine . . ." As if now everything is under control and the fine tuning begins.

From out of the recesses of the garage—I didn't even know they were there—here comes a woman and three children. Kesey's wife Faye, their daughter Shannon, who is six, and two boys, Zane, five, and Jed, three. Faye has long, sorrel-brown hair and is one of the prettiest, most beatific-looking women I

ever saw. She looks radiant, saintly. Kesey goes over to her and picks up each of the kids, and then Mountain Girl brings over her baby, Sunshine, and he picks up Sunshine a moment. All right—

Then Kesey loosens up and smiles, as if he just thought of something. It is as if he just heard Mountain Girl's question about how was jail. "The only thing I was worried about was this tooth," he says. He pops a dental plate out of the roof of his mouth and pushes a false front tooth out of his mouth with his tongue. "I had the awfulest feeling," he says. "I was going to be in court or talking to reporters or something, and this thing was going to fall down like this and I was going to start gumming my words," He gums the words "start gumming my words," to illustrate.

Three weeks later he was to replace it with a tooth with an orange star and green stripes on it, an enameled dens incisus lateral bearing a Prankster flag. One day at a gas station the manager, a white guy, gets interested in the tooth and calls over his helper, a colored guy, and says, "Hey, Charlie, come over here and show this fellow your tooth." So Charlie grins and bares his upper teeth, revealing a gold tooth with a heart cut out in the gold so that a white enamel heart shows through. Kesey grins back and then bares *his* tooth—the colored guy stares a moment and doesn't say anything. He doesn't even smile. He just turns away. A little while later, down the road, Kesey says very seriously, very sorrowfully, "That was wrong of me. I shouldn't have done that." "Done what?" "I outniggered him," says Kesey.

Outniggered him! Kesey has kept these countryisms, like "the awfulest feeling," all through college, graduate school, days of literary celebration . . .

"How did it happen?" says Freewheeeling Frank, meaning the tooth.

"He got in a fight with a Hell's Angel," says Mountain Girl.

"What?—" Freewheeling Frank is truly startled.

"Yeah!" says Mountain Girl. "The bastard hit him with a chain!"

"What!" says Frank. "Where? What was his name!"

Kesey gives Mountain Girl a look.

"Naw," she says.

"What was his name!" Frank says. "What did he look like!"

"Mountain Girl is shucking you," Kesey says. "I was in a wreck."

Mountain Girl looks repentant. Angels' duels no joke with Frank. Kesey breaks up . . . the vibrations. He sits down in one of the old theater seats. He is just talking in a soft, conversational tone, with his head down, just like he is having a conversation with Mountain Girl or somebody.

"It's funny," he says. "There are guys in jail who have been in jail so much, that's their whole thing. They're jail freaks. They've picked up the whole jail language—"

—everybody starts gathering around, sitting in the old theater seats or on the floor. The mysto steam begins rising—

"—only it isn't their language, it's the guards', the cops', the D.A.'s, the judge's. It's all numbers. One of them says, 'What happened to so-and-so?' And the other one says, 'Oh, he's over in 34,' which is a cellblock. 'They got him on a 211'—they have numbers for different things, just like you hear on a police radio—'they got him on a 211, but he can cop to a 213 and get three to five, one and a half with good behavior.'

"The cops like that. It makes them feel better if you play their game. They'll chase some guy and run him down and pull guns on him and they're ready to blow his head off if he moves a muscle, but then as soon as they have him in jail, one of them will come around and ask him how his wife is and he's supposed to say she's O.K., thanks, and ask him about his kids, like now that we've played the cops-and-robbers part of the game, you can go ahead and like me. And a lot of them in there go along with that, because that's all they know.

"When you're running, you're playing their game, too. I was up in Haight-Ashbury and I heard something hit the sidewalk behind me and some kid had fallen out the window. A lot of people rushed up and a woman was there crying and trying to pick him up, and I knew what I should do is go up and tell her not to move him but I didn't. I was afraid I was going to be recognized. And then up the street I saw a cop writing out parking tickets and I was going to go up and tell him to call an ambulance. But I didn't. I just kept going. And that night I was listening to the news on television and they told about a child who fell out of a window and died in the hospital."

_And that's what the cops-and-robbers game does to you._ Only it is _me_ thinking it. Figuring out parables, I look around at the faces and they are all watching Kesey and, I have not the slightest doubt, thinking: and _that's what the cops-and-robbers game does to you._ Despite the skepticism I brought here, _I_ am suddenly experiencing _their_ feeling. I am sure of it. I feel like I am in on something the outside world, the world I came from, could not possibly comprehend, and it _is_ a metaphor, the whole scene, ancient and vast, vaster than . . .

Two guys come in out of the daylight on Harriet Street, heads by the looks of them, and walk up to Kesey. One of them is young with a sweatshirt on and Indian beads with an amulet hanging from the beads—a routine acid-head look, in other words. The other one, the older one, is curiously neat, however. He had long black hair, but neat, and a slightly twirly mustache, like a cavalier, but neat, and a wildly flowered shirt, but neat and well-tailored and expensive, and a black leather jacket, only not a motorcycle jacket but tailored more like a coat, and a pair of English boots that must have set him back $25 or $30. At first he looks like something out of Late North Beach, the boho with the thousand-dollar wardrobe. But he

has a completely sincere look. He has a thin face with sharp features and a couple of eyes burning with truth oil. He says his name is Gary Goldhill and he wants to interview Kesey for the Haight-Ashbury newspaper _The Oracle_, and when could he do that—but right away it is obvious that he has something to get off his chest that can't wait.

"The thing is, Ken"—he has an English accent, but it is a middle-class accent, a pleasant sort of Midlands accent—"the thing is, Ken, a lot of people are very concerned about what you've said, or what the newspapers say you've said, about graduating from acid. A lot of people look up to you, Ken, you're one of the heroes of the psychedelic movement"—he has a kind of Midlands England way of breaking up long words into syllables, psy-che-delic move-ment—"and they want to know what you mean. A very beautiful thing is happening in Haight-Ashbury, Ken. A lot of people are opening the doors in their minds for the first time, but people like you have to help them. There are only two directions we can go, Ken. We can isolate ourselves in a monastery or we can organize a religion, along the lines of the League for Spiritual Discovery"—the League for Spi-ri-tu-al Dis-cov-er-y—"and have acid and grass legalized as sacraments, so everyone won't have to spend every day in fear waiting for the knock on the door."

"It can be worse to take it as a sacrament," Kesey says.

"You've been away for almost a year, Ken," Goldhill says. "You may not know what's been happening in Haight-Ashbury. It's growing, Ken, and thousands of people have found something very beautiful, and they're very open and loving, but the fear and the paranoia, Ken, the waiting for the knock on the door—it's causing some terrible things, Ken. It's re-spon-si-ble for a lot of bad trips. People are having bad trips, Ken, because they take acid and suddenly they feel that any moment there may be a knock on the door. We've got to band together. You've got to help us, Ken, and not work against us."

Kesey looks up, away from Goldhill, out across the gloom of the garage. Then he speaks in a soft, far-off-voice, with his eyes in the distance:

"If you don't realize that I've been helping you with every fiber in my body . . . if you don't realize that everything I've done, everything I've gone through . . ."

—it is rising and rising—

"I know, Ken, but the repression—"

"We're in a period now like St. Paul and the early Christians," Kesey says. "St. Paul said, if they shit on you in the city, move on to another city, and if they shit on you in the city, move on to another city—"

"I know, Ken, but you're telling people to stop taking acid, and they're not going to stop. They've opened up doors in their minds they never knew existed, and it's a very beautiful thing, and then they read in the papers that somebody they've looked up to is suddenly telling them to stop."

"There's a lot of things I can't tell the newspapers," says Kesey. His eyes are still focused long-range, away from Goldhill. "One night in Mexico, in Manzanillo, I took some acid and I threw the I Ching. And the I Ching—the great thing about the I Ching is, it never sends you Valentines, it slaps you in the face when you need it—and it said we had reached the end of something, we weren't going anywhere any longer, it was time for a new direction—and I went outside and there was an electrical storm, and there was lightning everywhere and I pointed to the sky and lightning flashed and all of a sudden I had a second skin, of lightning, electricity, like a suit of electricity, and I knew it was in us to be superheroes and that we could become superheroes or nothing." He lowers his eyes. "I couldn't tell this to the newspapers. How could I? I wouldn't be put back in jail, I'd be put in Pescadero."

—rising—rising—

"But most people aren't ready for that, Ken," Goldhill says. "They're just beginning to open the doors in their minds—"

"But once you've been through that door, you can't just keep going through it over and over again—"

"—and somebody's got to help them through that door—"

"Don't say stop plunging into the forest," Kesey says. "Don't say stop being a pioneer and come back here and help these people through the door. If Leary wants to do that, that's good, it's a good thing and somebody should do it. But somebody has to be the pioneer and leave the marks for others to follow." Kesey looks up again, way out into the gloom. "You've got to have some faith in what we're trying to do. It's easy to have faith as long as it goes along with what you already know. But you've got to have faith in us all the way. Somebody like Gleason—Gleason was with us this far." Kesey spreads his thumb and forefinger about two inches apart. "He was with us as long as our fantasy coincided with his. But as soon as we went on further, he didn't understand it, so he was against us. He had . . . no faith."

No faith!—bay fog turns steam, hissing in the old cranium—

Faith! Furthur! And it is an exceedingly strange feeling to be sitting here in the Day-Glo, on poor abscessed Harriet Street, and realize suddenly that in this improbable crazy ex-pie factory Warehouse garage I am in the midst of Tsong-Isha-pa and the sangha communion, Mani and the wan persecuted at The Gate, Zoroaster, Maidhyoimaongha and the five faithful before Vishtapu, Mohammed and Abu Bekr and the disciples amid the pharisaical Koreish of Mecca, Gautama and the brethren in the wilderness leaving the blood-and-kin families of their pasts for the one true family of the sangha inner circle—in short, true mystic brotherhood—only in poor old Formica polyethylene 1960s America without a grain of desert sand or a shred of palm leaf or a morsel of manna wilderness breadfruit overhead, picking up vibrations from Ampex tapes and a juggled Williams Lok-Hed sledge hammer, hooking down mathematical lab drugs, LSD-25, IT-290, DMT, instead of some water, heading out in American flag airport coveralls and an International Harvester bus—yet for real!—amid the marshmallow shiny black shoe masses—

TONY TANNER
From "Edge City"
*City of Words: American Fiction 1950–1970*
1971, pp. 373–80

**O**ne *Flew Over the Cuckoo's Nest* is about a mental hospital (Kesey worked in one while writing it). It is dominated by Big Nurse, a female of dread authority. She is the servant, or rather the high priestess, of what is referred to as the 'Combine' or 'system', another version of the notion that society is run by some secret force which controls and manipulates all its members, which is so common in contemporary American fiction. Big Nurse keeps the patients cowed and docile, either by subtle humiliations or punitive electric shock treatment. In a crude way she embodies the principles of Behaviorism, believing that people can and must be adjusted to the social norms. Into her ward comes a swaggering, apparently incorrigible character called Randle McMurphy. He is outraged to see how Big Nurse has reduced the men to puppets, mechanically obeying her rules. He tries to inculcate by example the possibilities for independent action, for the assertion of self against system. By the end Big Nurse finds an excuse to have him lobotomized, but her authority has been broken and most of the inmates break free of the institution. The opposition is intentionally stark. Big Nurse speaks for the fixed pattern, the unbreakable routine, the submission of individual will to mechanical, humourless control. McMurphy speaks an older American language of freedom, unhindered movement, self-reliance, anarchic humour and a trust in the more animal instincts. His most significant act is to persuade a group of the inmates to accompany him on a one-day sea voyage. Most of the men are frightened to venture outside at first (they are mainly self-committed to the institution). It is this fear which keeps them cowering inside Big Nurse's routines. But McMurphy persuades the men to come with him, and he duly leads them to the edge of the land—where the ocean starts. The voyage they then embark on is one of very unconcealed significance: it affords the various pleasures of sex, drink, fishing, and the authentic joy and dread of trying to cope with the immense power of the sea. McMurphy has brought them all out of the System, and into—'Reality'.

It may be objected that such a parabolic simplification of American life is excessively schematic. McMurphy is like a cliché hero in a cartoon-strip, a Captain Marvel or Superman; while Big Nurse is a cartoon horror—like Spider Lady, who drew her victims into an electrified web (cf. the electric shock treatment meted out by Big Nurse). I think this is deliberate. Comparisons with cartoons are made throughout, so Kesey is hardly unaware of his technique. Someone calls McMurphy a TV-cowboy; a girl gives him some underpants with white whales on them because '"she said I was a symbol."' He is addicted to comic-strips and TV which have in turn nourished his stances and speeches. You could say that he is acting out one of the most enduring and simple of American fantasies—the will to total freedom, total bravery, total independence. Big Nurse is a projection of the nightmare reverse to that fantasy—the dread of total control. Wolfe in *The Electric Kool-Aid Acid Test* (1968)[1] records Kesey talking about 'the comic-book Superheroes as the honest American myths', and Kesey may be defying us to distinguish comic-book clarity from mythic simplicity. In the contemporary world as he portrays it, to be a hero you have to *act* a hero (it is a discovery in his next novel that while weakness is real, strength has to be simulated: 'you can't ever fake being weak. You can only fake being strong.'). McMurphy has had to base his act on the only models he has encountered, in cartoons and movies. He is, if you like, a fake, a put-together character with all the seams showing. But, the book suggests, such fakery is absolutely necessary, unless you want to succumb to authentic weakness and the mindless routine supervised by Big Nurse. It is McMurphy's fakery and fantasy which lead others out into reality. In time, it would be Kesey's.

What makes the novel more interesting than just another cartoon, or John Wayne film, is that Kesey understands the need or compulsion to fantasize which is prior to the emergence of such apparitions as McMurphy and Big Nurse. As some of the men in the institution realize, they are really driving McMurphy to play out the role of heroic rebel. When he finally moves to attack Big Nurse, the act which gives her the excuse to have him lobotomized, the narrator recalls: 'We couldn't stop him because we were the ones making him do it. It wasn't the nurse that was forcing him, it was our need that was . . . pushing him up, rising and standing like one of those motion-picture zombies, obeying orders beamed at him from forty masters.' Fantasies of the weak converge upon him; one of the burdens McMurphy is carrying (and he is exhausted by the end) is the number of wish-fulfilment reveries which are secretly, perhaps unconsciously, projected on to him by the inmates. The clichés he acts are the clichés they dream. It is worth remembering that he was committed to the institution as a psychopath: the psychopath as hero is not a new idea in America. Robert Musil, in *The Man without Qualities*, made a profound study of the psychopath in the figure of Moosbrugger and added the suggestive comment: 'if mankind could dream collectively it would dream Moosbrugger.' The inmates of the asylum in Kesey's novel are American and as such they have a particular popular culture determining their most elementary fantasies. If they could dream collectively they would dream McMurphy. From one point of view that is exactly what they do.

We must read McMurphy, then, in two ways. In a sense he is an authentic rebel who steps to the music that he hears; yet there is a sense in which he is marching to the music of the fantasies projected on to him and, as such, in his own way a kind of 'zombie' too, a servitor of the versions imposed on him. Perhaps Kesey intends us to understand that McMurphy's heroism is in realizing this second truth, and nevertheless continuing with the imposed role. He is a singular man inasmuch as not many people would be able to support the fantasies of strength and independence projected on to him; the majority are more likely to submit to the controlling plot and imposed pictures of the Combine and step to the mechanical music of Big Nurse.

But how we react to McMurphy necessarily depends on our sense of the narrator, since his version of things is the only one to which we have access—and he is a giant, schizophrenic Indian called Bit Chief.[2] He is a rather notional Indian, a representative of the towering vitality of the original life of the American continent, now tamed to terrified impotence by all the mechanical paraphernalia of the white man's institutions. McMurphy teaches him to regain the use of his strength and at the end of the novel he is running away from the hospital and towards the country of his ancestors. This is all fairly obvious. What is unusual is the brilliant way in which Kesey has recreated the paranoid vision of a schizophrenic in the narrating voice.

Big Chief's vision of the hospital as a great nightmare of hidden machinery, wires, magnets, push-buttons, and so on, is utterly convincing. He is sure that the powers in the institution have fabricated a completely false environment: 'they' can accelerate or decelerate time, the windows are screens on which they can show whatever movie they want to impose as reality, they have fog machines which fill the air with a dense scummy medium in which Big Chief gets utterly cut off from everything and lost. They can do whatever they like with individuals because they have installed automative devices inside them (such as Indwelling Curiosity Cutout). It is a very Burroughs-like vision. This coherent paranoid fantasy extends to the world outside the hospital ward, for that world too is being 'adjusted' by Big Nurse and her like. What others would call factories and suburban housing developments, Big Chief sees as evidence of the spreading power of the Combine, which works to keep people 'jerking around in a pattern'. What the Combine is spreading is another version of entropy—all individual distinctions and differences erased and nature's variety brought down to the deadly uniformity of a mechanically repeated pattern. Some people may want to get 'out', or protest, but any such deviants are sent to the hospital where special machines can adjust them. (One interesting point is that a simple man may escape the Combine—'being simple like that put him out of the clutch of the Combine. They

weren't able to mold him into a slot.' This sense of the special value of simplicity is recognizably American, and it is related to the detectable anti-intellectualism in Kesey's work.)

For Big Chief, McMurphy is the man who demonstrates that the Combine is not all-powerful: McMurphy makes the fog go away and enables him to see things clearly; he makes the pictures imposed on the windows vanish, so that when Big Chief looks out he sees the actual world. He gives Big Chief the sense of what it is to be an individual; he restores reality to him, and restores him to reality. At one point Big Chief writes: 'I still had my own notions—how McMurphy was a giant come out of the sky to save us from the Combine that was net-working the land with copper wire and crystal.' The importance of people's 'notions' of other people, and reality, looms large for Kesey.

His second novel, *Sometimes a Great Notion* (1964), concerns a logging family in Oregon. The novel centres on the mainstay of the family, Hank Stamper, a tough and stubborn individualist cast in the same mould as McMurphy, and nourished in his childhood on the same Captain Marvel comics. He is the strongest man in the book when it comes to any physical deed of bravery, effort or endurance. He is a Paul Bunyan type, and, in holding out against the coercive group pressure of a union in a local logging dispute, Hank is asserting a kind of American individualism which Kesey clearly admires. But there are aspects of his relationships with his wife, Viv, and his brother, Lee, which suggest that he suffers from being sealed off in his heroic role. He is more at home confronting the elements, as, for instance, on the dangerous logging run down river on which he has just embarked when the book concludes.

Not that nature in this book is benevolent. There are few pastoral moments in Kesey's sombre Pacific north-west. Through a series of very powerful and evocative descriptions one is made aware of a continual background process of dissolution and erosion: the endless rains, the turbulent rivers, the changing sea, the heavy clouds, the penetrating fog, all make this particular part of America seem like a dream world of endless decay, on which man can never hope to leave any 'permanent mark'. It is a lush and fecund land, but it is also a land 'permeated with dying'. The slow death by drowning of a man trapped in a rising river, described in very poignant detail, serves to focus the more general dread of obliteration, and the absolute certainty of it, which permeates the lives of all who live there. The ubiquitous sense of all things flowing steadily away is responsible for the underlying fear which pervades the community in Kesey's account.

Since logging is the livelihood of the community, some contact with this awesomely flowing nature is inevitable. But there are degrees of removal. Lee Stamper has gone east to study at a university, and has become a neurotic intellectual (much of the plot is concerned with what happens when he returns to Oregon). The union official, Draeger, is a man who believes he has reality neatly contained in his own system of definitions and maxims. He lives in the 'dream of a labeled world', and operates in a verbal world of disputes between workers and management. Hank has little time for this world and prefers to be out in the forests doing the actual cutting. He does not sentimentalize nature. It is something which has to be fought, and fought with machines too. But the direct encounter with nature provides an experience of reality which cannot be had in the protective structures of society. Hanks is another American who prefers to move out to the edge. '"It's the part of the show I like best, this edge, where the cutting stops and the forest starts."' He likes to get to that point at which the contact with untouched nature has to be resumed. It is shown that life in this area can be very dangerous; but at least it is pure. One is beyond categories and, somehow, into the thing itself. In this connection the location of the Stamper house is very suggestive. It stands nearest to the threatening and ever-widening river from which all the other inhabitants have moved back for fear of being washed away. For all its exposed position, it has nevertheless preserved its identity longer than the other houses—'a two-story monument of wood and obstinacy that has neither retreated from the creep of erosion nor surrendered to the terrible pull of the river.' This suggests that perilous point, somewhere between the social edifice (to which the population has 'retreated') and the unselving flow of elemental natural forces, which so many recent American authors and their heroes seem to be seeking. Right at the edge, but not over it. Mailer's parapet makes an obvious comparison.

As a study of a certain mode of heroic individualism the book has surprising power and authority; but it is another aspect of the book which I want to touch on here. The book is framed by an encounter between Draeger and Viv in a bus depot. Draeger has come to ask her to explain her husband Hank to him. She in turn refers him to a photograph album she has with her, covering the family history of the Stampers. At the end Viv gets on a bus, leaving behind the photographs as she is leaving Hank and Lee and the whole area. Throughout this meeting it is raining very heavily. This juxtaposition of the photographs and the rain seems to me to point to a more profound tension in the book between fixed images and flowing forces. At bottom Kesey's novel is a meditation on themes implicit in this conjunction.

Photography can be seen as an activity which treats people as objects, a substitute for conducting a living relationship. In the novels considered in the course of this study there are many figures who find it easier to photograph other people than to try to establish relationships with them. The last words of Malamud's *A New Life* are ' "Got your picture!" '—the revealing cry of the impotent Gilley who can now only take photographs. As we have seen, the dread of being involved in some imposed film version of reality is pervasive. Photographs and films catch and 'fix' the individual, disregarding the full dimensions of his living uniqueness. This brings me back to Kesey's novel, and Viv, whose name, like her temperament, suggests just the mysterious quality of 'life' itself.

Both Hank and Lee in their differing ways 'love' Viv; at the same time Kesey makes it clear that each tries to impose his own version of her. From the start of their marriage Hank has told her how to cut her hair, what to wear, how to behave, turning her into his idea of a mate without wondering what was going on inside her. Lee's love seems to be more sympathetic and sensitive, but he gives himself away when he asks to be allowed to take away a photograph of her which is, we learn later, an early photograph of his own mother. The implication is that he has never seen the real Viv, but only the image he has projected on to her. Thus in differing ways, Viv has been made to fit into the brothers' reality pictures, while her own reality has remained unperceived and thus unloved. This is not depicted as cruelty; if anything it is one of the sad results of that loss of ability to recognize and communicate with other people's reality which more than one American novelist has portrayed.

Before she marries Hank, Viv takes one last look in her mirror and kisses her reflection goodbye. The meaning of this gesture is brought out by one of her later thoughts. 'It means this is the only way we ever see ourselves; looking out . . .' Viv is the one character who has had the ability to move

beyond narcissism and look *out* at other people and really see them, and their needs, and this is the only way that true vision—of self and others—can be reached. In some ways, Hank and Lee are still operating within the images they project. It is appropriate that at the end Viv leaves both brothers, for despite the generosity of her love she cannot devote her whole self simply to being what other people need her to be. She gets on the bus simply to move on, with no destination in mind. It is a bid to escape from the images that have been imposed on her, and leave the photographs behind. Almost her last words are—' "I'm just going." ' Just so, life itself flows away despite all attempts to hold it.

Photographs are like art and human identity in the one respect that they offer a temporary extrapolation from the flow, a holding of some fragment of the flux of nature in fixed outlines. A novelist has to work with outlines, and Kesey's own novel is the verbal equivalent of a family album. At the same time, the timeless ongoing truth of nature's flow must not be forgotten, and Kesey does what he can do to remind us of it: 'the Scenes Gone By and the Scenes to Come flow blending together in the sea-green deep while Now spreads in circles on the surface.' This is what lies behind the narrative strategy of the book which involves a dissolving of chronological time so that past and future events swim into each other, and during the fictional present we move without transitions from place to place, person to person. The intention seems to be to achieve the illusion of temporal and spatial simultaneity in which 'everything is at once'. (As in his first novel, it is possible that Kesey drew on LSD-induced sensations for his narrative strategy.)

The novel suggests that although human perception necessarily deals with particular configurations of reality, we must beware of identifying these temporary arrangements and fixities with the 'whole Truth'—whether we are thinking of reality arrested in photographs or arranged in verbal conceptual systems. We must always be willing to look round the edge of the fixed image to the flow behind it. We must also be aware, as Viv is, that, *'There are bigger forces . . . I don't know what they are but they got ours whipped sometimes.'* One chapter has as a heading a little story about a squirrel who lived in a davenport. He knew the inside so well that he could always avoid being sat on. However, the outside got worn out and it was covered with a red blanket. This confused him and undermined all his certainties about the inside. Instead of trying to incorporate this blanket 'into the scheme of his world', he moved to a drainpipe and was drowned in the next fall of rain—'probably still blaming that blanket: damn this world that just won't hold still for us!' It is a neat reminder that we must keep our schemes of reality flexible so that they can be expanded to incorporate any new phenomenon which the outside world may present. Our notions are only our notions, while the flow is more than we can ever know.

*Notes*

1. Farrar, Straus and Giroux, New York, 1968; Weidenfeld and Nicolson, London, 1969.
2. For some suggestions as to the significance of the use of the figure of the Indian in contemporary American fiction see *The Return of the Vanishing American* by Leslie Fiedler (Jonathan Cape, London, 1968).

RAYMOND M. OLDERMAN
"The Grail Knight Arrives"
*Beyond the Waste Land*
1972, pp. 35–51

Randle Patrick McMurphy sweeps into the asylum waste land of Ken Kesey's *One Flew Over the Cuckoo's Nest*[1] like April coming to T. S. Eliot's waste land: "mixing / Memory and desire, stirring / Dull roots with spring rain." He literally drags the unwilling asylum wastelanders out of the tranquillized fog that protects them—a fog that is forever "snowing down cold and white all over" (p. 7), where they try to hide "in forgetful snow, feeding / A little life with dried tubers." And, by dragging them from their retreat, he cures the Fisher King, Chief Bromden—a six-foot-eight giant from a tribe of "fish Injuns," who is wounded, like all other wastelanders, in his manhood. The cure takes hold most dramatically on a fishing trip when McMurphy supplies the Chief and eleven other disciples with drink for their thirst, a woman for their desires, stimulation for their memories, and some badly needed self-respect for their shriveled souls—and all this despite the fact that the Chief "fears death by water." ("Afraid I'd step in over my head and drown, be sucked off down the drain and clean out to sea. I used to be real brave around water when I was a kid." [p. 160]) The silent Chief's voice is restored and he becomes the prophet who narrates the tale, while the false prophet, the enemy, the Big Nurse, Madame Sosostris, who has the "movement of a tarot-card reader in a glass arcade case" (p. 188), is deprived of her voice in the last moments of the book.

The tale takes place in the ward of an insane asylum where an iron-minded, frost-hearted Nurse rules by means of one twentieth-century version of brutality—mental and spiritual debilitation. Her patients are hopeless "Chronics" and "Vegetables," or they are "Acutes" who do not, according to McMurphy, seem "any crazier than the average asshole on the street" (p. 63). McMurphy comes to the asylum from a prison work farm. He has been a logger, a war hero, a gambler, and generally a happy, heavily muscled, self-made drifter and tough guy. A contest develops between McMurphy (whose initials R. P. M. urge us to note his power) and the Big Nurse (whose name, Ratched, tips us off about her mechanical nature as well as her offensive function as a "ball-cutter"). The implications of the contest deepen; it becomes a battle pitting the individual against all those things that make up the modern waste land, for the Nurse represents singly what the institution and its rules really are. The drama of the battle is intense, and the action seesaws as McMurphy gradually discovers he must give his strength to others in order to pry loose the Big Nurse's hold on their manhood. As they gain in health, McMurphy weakens, and his ultimate victory over the Big Nurse is a mixed one. He is lobotomized, a "castration of the frontal lobes," but he gives his lifeblood to Chief Bromden who breaks free and leaves behind in the Nurse and the Institution not a destroyed power but a shrunken, silent, and temporarily short-circuited one. Beautifully structured, the novel provides us with both a brilliant version of our contemporary waste land and a successful Grail Knight, who frees the Fisher King and the human spirit for a single symbolic and transcendent moment of affirmation.

The world of this waste land is mechanically controlled from a central panel, as the narrator sees it, so that everything in it is run by tiny electrical wires or installed machinery. People are often robots or are made of electric tubing and wiring and springs, as the "adjusted" ones seem to be. The Big Nurse is only one agent of a "Combine" which rules all things including time and the heart and mind of man. *Combine*, as the word implies, is not just an organization; it is a mechanism, a machine that threshes and levels; its ends are Efficiency and Adjustment. According to Chief Bromden, the Combine had gone a long way in doing things to gain total control,

> things like, for example—a *train* stopping at a station and laying a string of full-grown men in mirrored suits and machine hats, laying them like a hatch of identical insects, half-life things coming pht-pht-pht out of the last car, then hooting its electric whistle and moving on down the spoiled land to deposit another hatch. [pp. 227–28]

Those are the adjusted ones. The ones who cannot adjust are sent to the asylum to have things installed so that the Combine can keep them in line.

> The ward is a factory for the Combine. It's for fixing up mistakes made in the neighborhoods and in the schools and the churches, the hospital is. When a completed product goes back out into society, all fixed up good as new, *better* than new sometimes, it brings joy to the Big Nurse's heart; something that came in all twisted different is now a functioning, adjusted component, a credit to the whole outfit and a marvel to behold. Watch him sliding across the land with a welded grin, fitting into some nice little neighborhood. [p. 38]

He is a "Dismissal," spiritually and morally empty, but "happy" and adjusted. If you do not fit, you are a malfunctioning machine—"machines with flaws inside that can't be repaired, flaws born in, or flaws beat in over so many years of the guy running head-on into solid things that by the time the hospital found him he was bleeding rust in some vacant lot" (p. 4). That is what is called a "Chronic." Some people do escape in a way. People like McMurphy who keep moving, and people like Peter Bancini who are just too simple, are missed by the combine, and if they are lucky, they can get hidden and stay missed.

All this is only the view of the narrator, a paranoid Indian. But there is enough evidence in the way the world around Chief Bromden runs to make his terms more and more acceptable as the novel progresses. Among the few characters on the "Outside" that Kesey takes the time to describe is one of the insulting loafers who taunt the patients while they wait to board their boat for the fishing trip. The man is described as having "purple under his eyes," the same kind of purple that appears under the eyes of all the Ward's finished, lobotomized products. There is, at least for a moment, a frightening suggestion that the Combine's inmates may truly be everywhere. For Chief Bromden it is no madman's logic—after seeing the actual persecution of his father, family, and tribe by the U.S. Department of Interior—to posit a large central organization that seeks the doom of all things different.

The waste land of the asylum is characterized not only by mechanization and efficiency but by sterility, hopelessness, fear, and guilt. The inmates are aimless, alienated, and bored; they long for escape; they "can connect / Nothing with Nothing," not even picture puzzles; they are enervated and emasculated; their dignity is reduced to something less than human. Most of all, they are run as the Asylum is run—by women; it is a "Matriarchy," and behind almost every ruined man is a grasping, castrating female whose big bosom belies her sterility but reveals a smothering momism. So, McMurphy perceives almost immediately that Big Nurse Ratched is pecking at their "everlovin' balls." But the same has been true of Harding's wife, and Chief Bromden's mother, and Billy Bibbit's mother—and these are just about the only women you see in the novel, except a couple of sweet whores named Candy and Sandy. However, what is more startling about this terrible world is its leveling sense of order and its rules. In one incident McMurphy wants to brush his teeth before the proper teeth-brushing time. He is told that the toothpaste is locked up. After questioning the Aide about what possible harm anyone could do with a tube of toothpaste, he is advised that the toothpaste is locked up because it is the rules, and rules are rules. After all, what would happen if everyone just started brushing his teeth whenever he had a mind to. Kesey's point by this time is clear; the true madness, the real dry root of the waste land is not the patient's irrationality, but the deadly order, system, and rationality of the institution. What is normal is perverted and reason becomes madness, while some small hope for salvation lies in the nonrational if not the downright irrational.

All of what the institution means and its effect on humanity come together in the single person of the Big Nurse, who causes the patients' hopelessness, their inadequacy, fear, anxiety, and alienation. She is the institution itself, the waste land personified. White and starched stiff, she suggests Melville's plunge into the dreadful ambiguity and possible evil that could live in the heart of what is white. (McMurphy wears fancy shorts with white jumping whales on them, given to him by an Oregon State co-ed who called him a "symbol.") But with the Big Nurse the ambiguity is only superficial and thrives only on the name of respectability—her real villainy is clear. She is the enemy, the "Belladonna," obstacle to the Grail Knight. She enervates her patients by playing upon their fears, guilts, and inadequacies. She and all other castrators are "people who try to make you weak so they can get you to toe the line, to follow their rules, to live like they want you to. And the best way to do this, to get you to knuckle under, is to weaken you by gettin' you where it hurts the worst" (p. 58). She is relentless in her crippling pity and capable of using any weapon in order to preserve her control. She has handpicked her aides, three shadowy and sadistic black men who are hooked to her by electrical impulses of hate. They have been twisted by white brutality, and their response is savage. As weapons in the Big Nurse's arsenal, they serve as symbols of the force of guilt which she uses to torment her patients. Guilt and the black man twine identities in the white mind to cut deeper into its already vitiated self-respect.

The Big Nurse is continually pictured in images of frost or machinery, or as a crouching swelling beast. She is described as a collection of inert materials, plastic, porcelain—any of modern America's favorite respectable synthetics. "Her face is smooth, calculated, and precision-made, like an expensive baby doll, skin like flesh-colored enamel, blend of white and cream and baby-blue eyes, small nose, pink little nostrils—everything working together except the color on her lips and fingernails, and the size of her bosom" (p. 5). She is sexless and cold enough to halt McMurphy's lecture on how a man can always win out over a woman; she is "impregnable" in almost every sense, even by so vaunted a "whambam" as McMurphy.

> What she dreams of there in the center of those wires
> is a world of precision efficiency and tidiness like a
> pocket watch with a glass back, a place where the
> schedule is unbreakable and all the patients who
> aren't Outside, obedient under her beam, are wheel-
> chair Chronics with catheter tubes run direct from
> every pant-leg to the sewer under the floor. [p. 27]

She controls clock time, has all the rules on her side, and uses insinuation like a torture rack. Fear, cowardice, and timidity

are all she sees in man. She sums up all that is debilitating to the individual about a modern world of massive institutions. In waste land terms, she is the keeper of the keys, the false prophet; for not only is she the cause of enervation and division, but she also perverts the holy words that are the key to coping with the waste land. When she gives she emasculates; when she sympathizes she reduces; and when she controls she destroys. McMurphy, the Grail Knight, the savior, not only must contest her power, but must listen to, learn how to live by, and restore the true meaning of the holy words from "What the Thunder Said": Give, Sympathize, Control.

The narrative movement of the novel is built around McMurphy's growth in knowledge and his progress toward curing Chief Bromden. As he learns to give and to sympathize, he moves toward death while the Chief moves toward rebirth, "blown-up" to full size by McMurphy's sacrifice and gift of self-control. At the beginning we are given two images foreshadowing McMurphy's fate: Ellis, the patient who stands like an empty Christ, arms outstretched in tortured crucifixion, fixed that way by an electric shock machine used as a weapon of the institution; and Ruckly, blanked of all but mindless, obscene answers and beaten by the trump card of the institution—lobotomy—beaten as a means of dealing with his rebellion. McMurphy will also be personally beaten, crucified, and lobotomized because there is no final victory over the Big Nurse and her waste land; she will continue just as Eliot's waste land continues after the rain that falls.

> She's too big to be beaten. She covers one whole side
> of the room like a Jap statue. There's no moving her
> and no help against her. She's lost a little battle here
> today, but it's a minor battle in a big war that she's
> been winning and that she'll go on winning . . .
> just like the Combine, because she has all the power
> of the Combine behind her. [p. 109]

But the little battle she loses is enough to cure the Chief and bring a little rain to a parched land.

Ironically, McMurphy enters the asylum supposedly on a request for "transfer" to get "new blood" for his poker games, but from that very entrance, as he laughs, winks, and goes around shaking limp hands, it is he that does the transferring and the giving of blood. The first foretelling of his effect on Chief Bromden comes as McMurphy seizes the Chief's hand: "That palm made a scuffing sound against my hand. I remember the fingers were thick and strong closing over mine, and my hand commenced to feel peculiar and went to swelling up out there on my stick of an arm, like he was transmitting his own blood into it. It rang with blood and power. It blowed up near as big as his" (pp. 23–24). He brings contact, the human touch, to a place sterilized of all but inverted relationships. His giving and his sacrifice are not, however, a continuous unbroken process, but are correlated to his learning. He launches into full battle with the Big Nurse and begins pulling the patients out of their tranquillized fog. His first assault reaches its peak in the contest over TV privileges.

McMurphy strengthens the other men enough to rebel in unison against the Big Nurse, and he does it by the symbolic gesture of attempting to lift a massive "control panel." It is a symbol of his resistance and willingness to keep trying even when he is going to be beaten, even when he *knows* he is going to be beaten. The strain on him is balanced by his effect on the men and on Chief Bromden in particular. The Chief asserts himself for the first time. He raises his hand to join the vote against the Big Nurse and recognizes that no external power is controlling him—he himself had lifted his own arm expressing his own decision. This first sign of self-control, inspired by

McMurphy's struggle with the control panel, leads the Chief out of his fog and out of his safety; he ceases to be the blind, impotent Tiresias and literally begins to see again. Waking up late at night, he looks out a window and sees clearly, without hallucination—something he has been unable to do since he has been in the asylum. What he sees, on another level, is that McMurphy has succeeded in being himself, that it is possible to be yourself without hiding and without the Combine getting you. But just as the Chief makes the discovery McMurphy learns what it really means to be "committed" in this asylum, and he faces the temptation that is hazard to any Grail Knight—the temptation to quit.

Learning that most of the patients are "voluntary," that he is one of the few "committed," and that the duration of his commitment is to be determined by the Big Nurse, McMurphy becomes "cagey" (an ominous word in this mechanized world). He promptly ceases giving and he ceases sympathizing. The immediate result is an assertion of the waste land—Cheswick, one of the patients dependent on McMurphy, drowns himself. Without resistance from the Grail Knight, the waste land perverts water, the symbol of fertility, into the medium of death.

But the demands made on McMurphy by the weaker inmates determine his return to battle, for the weak are driven to the waste land by "Guilt. Shame. Fear. Self-belittlement," while the strong are driven by the needs of the weak. As the Chief ultimately realizes, McMurphy is driven by the inmates, and this drive "had been making him go on for weeks, keeping him standing long after his feet and legs had given out, weeks of making him wink and grin and laugh and go on with his act long after his humor had been parched dry between two electrodes" (pp. 304–05). To signal his renewed challenge to the institution and his acceptance of commitment, McMurphy stands up at what looks like the Big Nurse's decisive victory, strides mightily across the ward, "the iron in his boot heels cracking lightning out of the tile," and runs his fist through the Big Nurse's enormous glass window, shattering her dry hold as "the glass comes apart like water splashing." McMurphy knows where his gesture will lead; he was told in the very beginning that making trouble and "breaking windows" and all like that will lead him to crucifixion on the shock table and destruction by lobotomy.

What McMurphy has learned is the secret of "What the Thunder Said," for, as one critic of Eliot's poem explained it,

> If we can learn to give of ourselves and to live in sympathetic identification with others, perhaps we may also learn the art of self-control and thereby prepare ourselves to take on the most difficult of responsibilities: that of giving directions ourselves, of controlling our destinies and perhaps those of others, as an expert helmsman controls a ship.[2]

McMurphy as helmsman leads his twelve followers, including Chief Bromden, aboard a ship and on to a fishing trip where, through his active sympathy, he gives them the gift of life so that they may gain control of their own destinies. The fishing trip—considering the fish as the traditional mystical symbol of fertility—is the central incident in McMurphy's challenge to the waste land. What he gives to the men is drained from his blood, and the path of his descent to weariness is crossed by Chief Bromden "pumped up" to full size, the cured Fisher King. And at that point, we are told "the wind was blowing a few drops of rain." "*Damyata:* The boat responded / Gaily, to the hand expert with sail and oar."

McMurphy gives the men not only self-confidence and a renewed sense of virility, but also what Kesey sees as man's only weapon against the waste land—laughter. There has been no laughter in the asylum; McMurphy notices that immediately and comments, "when you lose your laugh you lose your *footing.*" By the end of the fishing trip McMurphy has everyone laughing "because he knows you have to laugh at the things that hurt you just to keep yourself in balance, just to keep the world from running you plumb crazy" (pp. 237–38). In effect, he teaches the men to be black humorists, and it is the vision and the balance of black humor that Kesey attempts to employ as a stay against the waste land. To Kesey, being human and having control means being able to laugh, for the rational ordered world has done us in, and only an insurgence of energy from the irrational can break through the fear and sterility that have, paradoxically, made the world go mad. It is ultimately their laughter that the men cram down the Big Nurse's maw in their brief moment of victory.

In the final section of the book, McMurphy works with growing fatigue and resignation toward his inevitable sacrifice. He battles with the Nurse's Aides, gets repeated shock treatments, has a chance to capitulate to the Big Nurse and refuses, returns from the cruelty of the shock table to the ward where he is faced with the charge of mixed and ulterior motives, and finally holds his mad vigil in the upside-down world of the Chapel Perilous. But madness here is antiorder, and so a sign of health. The scene is the night of Billy Bibbit's lost virginity. McMurphy and his followers run wild, completely subverting the order of the Big Nurse's ward and violating the sanctity of all rules. Billy's entrance into manhood symbolizes their initiation into the final mysteries of life and fertility. All this is as it should be during and following a vigil in the Chapel Perilous. But, as we already know, you cannot beat the Big Nurse. She regains her power by cowing Billy with shame and forcing him to betray his deliverer. Billy, broken again, slits his throat, and the Big Nurse attempts one last time to turn guilt against McMurphy. His response is the ultimate sacrificial gesture; he rips open her dress, exposing her mountainous and smothering breasts, and chokes her—not able to kill her, but only to weaken and silence her. The contest ends in violence, the individual's last offense against the immensities that oppress him. Kesey, like John Hawkes, finds something ultimately necessary and cleansing about violence.

At McMurphy's fall "he gave a cry. At the last, falling backward, his face appearing to us for a second upside down before he was smothered on the floor by a pile of white uniforms, he let himself cry out: A sound of cornered-animal fear and hate and surrender and defiance" (p. 305). It was the only sound and the only sign that "he might be anything other than a sane willful, dogged man performing a hard duty." His madness is all the salvation the twentieth century can muster, for to give and to sympathize in our kind of waste land is itself a sign of madness. McMurphy is lobotomized, and in the final moments of the book Chief Bromden snuffs out the life of the body connected to that already dead spirit, and with his gift of life, seizes the huge "control panel" McMurphy had blown him up to lift, and spins it through the asylum window. "The glass splashed out in the moon, like a bright cold water baptizing the sleeping earth" (p. 310). The Fisher King is free. Although the waste land remains, McMurphy the redheaded Grail Knight has symbolically transcended it through his gesture of sacrifice, and at least allowed others to "Come in under the shadow of this red rock."

*One Flew Over the Cuckoo's Nest* is a modern fable pitting a fabulous kind of good against a fabulous kind of evil and making use of many ⟨. . .⟩ traditional devices of American romance ⟨. . .⟩ For example: it emphasizes plot and action (not character), and it employs myth, allegory, and symbol. There are equally obvious points of contact between the themes of this book and traditional American themes: for example, the rebellion against old orders and old hierarchies, and the need for communal effort in the face of an alien and overwhelmingly negative force. This book is more closely tied to American tradition than any other book we will deal with, and yet there is much in it that offers a paradigm for what is different about the characteristic vision in the American novel of the 1960s. It does not return to the past, gaze toward the future, or travel to the unknown to get its "romance" setting. The setting is the static institution which sums up both the preoccupation of our age with the mystery of power, and the substitution of an image of the waste land for the image of a journey between Eden and Utopia. It is shot through with the vitality of its use of the here and the now. We are constantly shocked into discovering how the book is really tied to the recognizable, not to the distant or strange, but to our very own—to technology we know of, to clichés we use, to an atmosphere possible only in the atomic tension of our times. Just as no one can confidently say who is mad and who is not in Kesey's novel, no one cay say in what sense his story is real and in what sense it is fiction. The narrator sounds a note that echoes everywhere in the sixties: "You think this is too horrible to have really happened, this is too awful to be the truth! But, please. it's still hard for me to have a clear mind thinking on it. But it's the truth even if it didn't happen" (p. 8). The romance elements in the book are not based on devices that whisk us away to some "theatre, a little removed from the highway of ordinary travel,"[3] and then whisk us back fueled up with truth. We suspect with horror that what we are seeing very possibly *is* our highway of ordinary travel, fantastic as it may seem.

The romance elements in *One Flew Over the Cuckoo's Nest* are inspired by a world vision which questions the sanity of fact. It is a cartoon and comic-strip world—where a man's muscles can be "blown-up" like Popeye's arms after a taste of spinach—"a cartoon world, where the figures are flat and outlined in black, jerking through some kind of goofy story that might be real funny if it weren't for the cartoon figures being real guys" (p. 31). Not only is this a good image of Kesey's world, but it supplies the pattern for his character development. The movement from being a cartoon figure to becoming a painfully real guy is exemplified by Billy Bibbit. His name and his personality are reminiscent of comic-strip character Billy Batson, a little crippled kid, weak and helpless, who could say "Shazam" and turn into Captain Marvel. And just when Billy Bibbit stops being a little crippled kid, after the comic book fun of his tumble with Candy, just when his "whambam" Shazam should turn him into this big, powerful, unbeatable Captain Marvel, the Big Nurse turns him into a real guy—a judas, in fact, who proceeds from betrayal to slitting his very real throat.[4] While Kesey attempts to employ the mode of black humor, and while he does see the value of laughter in coping with the waste land, one suspects that he is more pained and bittered by the "real guy" than a black humorist can afford to be. His humor often loses that fine edge between pain and laughter that we see in Elkin, Vonnegut, Barth, and Pynchon, while his "flat" portrayal of women and of Blacks is more stereotypic and uncomfortable than funny or fitting with his cartoon character pattern. It borders too much on the simplistic.

The romance elements also revolve around our new version of mystery. Though we may certainly be tempted to call it paranoia, it is definitely a part of the equipment of our times, and it is undoubtedly malevolent. The Big Nurse, The

Combine, The Asylum—all three seem to symbolize that immense power that reduces us, and that seems to be mysteriously unlocatable. Kesey is one of those writers of the sixties who explore some mystery about Fact itself that portends mostly defeat for man. This sense of mystery adds complexity to the paradoxes of what is mad and sane, real and unreal, for it drives us to seek its heart in some huge force conspiring against us. Although it arises in connection with the image of the waste land, this mystery is the antipathy of Eliot's hoped-for God. It is only a further cause of divisive fear.

The mystery is best represented, to Kesey, by the asylum itself, but he leaves us with two possible locations of the mystery's source. It could be located somewhere external to us as Chief Bromden sees it, or as McMurphy tries to explain, maybe blaming it on a Combine is "just passing the buck." It may really be our own "deep-down hang-up that's causing the gripes." Perhaps there is some big bad wolf—and then perhaps there is only us. In the past the essential shock in American fictional experience has been a character's discovery that deep down he too is capable of evil; the shock in the sixties is the character's discovery that deep down he may be a source of unrelenting insanity. Down there, perhaps, that unknowable and seemingly immense power against us comes into being and then mounts to become a world gone mad. Against that or within that the writer, the prophet, sees new paradoxes of reason and irrationality, fact and mystery, and writes his novels no longer sure of what is fact or fiction and where malevolence lies—within or without. His only rationale can be the one stated by one of Kesey's characters: "These things don't happen. . . . These things are fantasies you lie awake at night dreaming up and then are afraid to tell your analyst. You're not *really* here. That wine isn't real; *none* of this exists. Now, let's go on from there" (p. 285).

*Notes*

1. *One Flew Over the Cuckoo's Nest* (New York: Viking Press, 1962). Page numbers for citations will be included parenthetically in the text.
2. Kimon Friar and John Malcolm Brinin, eds., *Modern Poetry* (New York: Appleton-Century-Crofts, 1951), p. 472.
3. Nathaniel Hawthorne, "Preface" to *Blithedale Romance* (New York: Norton, 1958), p. 27.
4. Kesey actually refers directly to the "Captain Marvel" comic strip in a long discussion in his second novel *Sometimes a Great Notion* (New York: Viking Press, 1964), pp. 142–43.

## TERENCE MARTIN

### From "*One Flew Over the Cuckoo's Nest* and the High Cost of Living"

*Modern Fiction Studies*, Spring 1973, pp. 48–55

### III

In his essay "The Concept of Character in Fiction," William H. Gass remarks that "a character, first of all, is the noise of his name, and all the sounds and rhythms that proceed from him."[1] Even in this primary sense, McMurphy is quite a character. His name not only proclaims his paternity but suggests the brawling Irishman of fiction and fact. Moreover, the *sounds* of McMurphy pervade Kesey's novel—and we are all the more prepared to hear them because we have a narrator like Chief Bromden. As I noted earlier, the Chief hears McMurphy before he sees him, and he "sounds big." He comes into the ward laughing—"free and loud"; it is the first laugh the Chief has heard "in years." After the first Group

Meeting, McMurphy himself comments that the patients are afraid to laugh. "I haven't heard a real laugh since I came through that door. . . . Man, when you lose your laugh you lose your *footing*."[2] The next morning the sound of McMurphy singing booms out of the latrine, and "everybody's thunderstruck. They haven't heard such a thing in years, not on this ward" (p. 88).

The Big Nurse's ward has its own sounds, among them those of canned music played loudly over a speaker throughout the day. Annoyed because poker bets can hardly be heard, McMurphy objects, and if we can credit his remark we can see why: "Can't you even ease down on the volume?" he asks the Big Nurse; "It ain't like the whole state of Oregon needed to hear Lawrence Welk play 'Tea for Two' three times every hour, all day long!" (p. 102). The consequence of his objection is that he gets another room for their game; the issue of sounds has resulted in more space for McMurphy's activities.

McMurphy's laughter and singing, his tall biographical tales, and the authentic ring of his idiom at once dominate the ward and define him to the other patients. His example, of course, evokes the choked off manhood of the men on the ward and a sense of freedom they have forgotten, or not known. When, later, McMurphy organizes the fishing expedition, it is a shared adventure, exciting, fun, and noisy. During one hectic, scrambling moment on the boat, with Candy's breast bruised and bleeding and the Chief's thumb smarting red from the line, McMurphy looks on and laughs—"because he knows you have to laugh at the things that hurt you just to keep yourself in balance, just to keep the world from running you plumb crazy. He knows there's a painful side . . . ; but he won't let the pain blot out the humor no more'n he'll let the humor blot out the pain" (p. 238). Harding is laughing this time, and Scanlon, too, "at their own selves as well as at the rest of us." And Candy laughs, "and Sefelt and the doctor and all." The laughter

> started slow and pumped itself full, swelling the men bigger and bigger. I watched, part of them, laughing with them—and somehow not with them. I was off the boat, blown up off the water and skating the wind with those black birds, high above myself, and I could look down and see myself and the rest of the guys, see the boat rocking there in the middle of those diving birds, see McMurphy surrounded by his dozen people, and watch them, us, swinging a laughter that rang out on the water in ever-widening circles, farther and farther, until it crashed up on beaches all over the coast, on beaches all over all coasts, in wave after wave after wave. (p. 238)

Community laughter this, comic, aware, the signature of a deep experience, the expression of freedom—earned and shared. The fishing expedition, brilliantly handled by Kesey, accentuates the growing sense of community among the patients. It also contains the most joyous sounds in the novel. McMurphy, we know, has red hair, tattoos, and hands that bear the marks of work and combat. But his capacity for laughter is fundamental to his identity as a character—along with his ability to make us laugh. "That's clean enough," he says to the orderly watching him clean the urinals, "maybe not clean enough for some people, but myself I plan to piss in 'em, not eat lunch out of 'em" (p. 151).

The McMurphy who shakes hands with all of the men and announces himself as "bull goose looney" has much to learn about his new situation beyond the fact of matriarchal authority. He is, at first, what he has always been, the con man, the gambler in search of new territory; and he has

managed to get himself committed to avoid the regimen of the work farm. Characteristically, he seizes the opportunity to bet on his ability to outmaneuver the Big Nurse. Surprised and disappointed when the patients do not support his motion to watch the World Series on TV, McMurphy again bets on himself, this time with a new purpose: his failure to lift the steel and cement control panel, foredoomed, according to the Chief, is an example of courage not lost upon the others. The next day they attempt the impossible and, as we have seen, reach their majority, twenty-one, in a second vote on the Series. (Interestingly, one of McMurphy's favorite games is blackjack, or twenty-one. Another, fittingly, is stud poker.) That they sit watching a blank screen, courtesy of Miss Ratched, gives their gesture an added, self-contained, significance; the cowboy-hero turned home-run hitter is now in their midst. They are now, as even the Big Nurse knows, a different group from the one they were before the advent of McMurphy.

McMurphy goes through two other stages in the course of the novel, both the result of increasing awareness. From the lifeguard at the swimming pool he learns the difference between being *sentenced* and being *committed*. He realizes for the first time that he will be released only when the Big Nurse approves a release for him. The information has an immediate effect. As they are leaving the pool, a hydrocephalic patient from another ward lies helplessly on his side in the footbath, his head bobbing around in the disinfectant. Harding twice asks McMurphy to help him and Cheswick lift the boy up. "Let him lay," says McMurphy, as he walks on, "maybe he don't like deep water" (p. 163). The next morning McMurphy polishes the latrine "till it sparkled" and waxes the hall floors when asked to.

As the others recognize, McMurphy is playing the game, playing it safe—"getting cagey," the way "Papa finally did." At one time the Chief's father used to poke fun at the government men, speaking to them dead-pan like a stage Indian addressing tourists—to the great amusement of his Council. Like McMurphy, Chief Bromden's father learned to play it smart. The other patients on the ward understand about McMurphy; they are not angry or even disappointed. But there is a fearful cost to McMurphy's decision to think of Number One: Cheswick, who has achieved a certain momentum toward manhood, gets caught in the drain the next time they are at the swimming pool and drowns well before McMurphy, the lifeguard, and the orderlies can bring him to the surface.

McMurphy has one staggering fact left to learn. It astonishes him into meditative silence, then catapults him into his final role of savior. He hears from Harding that only a few of the patients on the ward, indeed, in the whole hospital, are committed. The great majority are there voluntarily, because, as Billy Bibbit says sobbingly, they don't have the guts to be Outside. The news is hardly credible to McMurphy. But his reaction to it is swift and thorough. At the ensuing Group Meeting he walks "big as a house" toward the Big Nurse, the "iron in his boot heels" cracking "lightning out of the tile," and rams his hand through the window in the front of her office as he reaches for his cigarettes. When a new glass is installed, he does it again. And when a third glass is put in, with a whitewashed X on it to make it clearly visible, Scanlon accidentally bounces a basketball through it before the whitewash is even dry.

Direct violations of the Big Nurse's private office, symbolic sexual assaults, are only the beginning. McMurphy, aware now of what *committed* means, aware, too, that the frightened men on the ward are there voluntarily, and aware, further, that he cannot defeat the Big Nurse and all that is behind her—even as he could not lift the control panel—begins to act for the others rather than for himself. Before McMurphy arrived, the patients were set against each other in the name of therapy and adjustment. Each man was a spy for the Big Nurse, eager to write down information about someone else in the log book near the Nurses' Station. In Group Therapy sessions they would peck at the victim of the day, currying favor by making one of their own miserable. McMurphy once says (apropos of the way in which Harding and his wife make each other impossible). "All I know is this: nobody's very big in the first place, and it looks to me like everybody spends their whole life tearing everybody else down" (p. 174). It is a central insight for the unsophisticated McMurphy—and one of the truest and most generally applicable statements in the novel.

During McMurphy's final stage things on the ward *begin* to change radically. Kesey, in masterful control of the fully activated materials in his novel, takes his madhouse men one last inevitable step, to an achieved sense of community. It is something he has consistently held dear: Ken Babbs's "great statement," Kesey remarked in an interview in the *Rolling Stone* (March 7, 1970), was—"We don't want a commune, we want a community" (p. 29). Kesey's "great statement," made eight years before, was to turn a bunch of rabbits into a community of men, "close-knit," as Joseph J. Waldmeir observes, and "functioning."[3] McMurphy organizes a ward basketball team, with Doctor Spivey (to Miss Ratched's amazement) approving, a team fated to lose its game against the orderlies, but a team, nevertheless, composed of people playing together in a common effort. The fishing trip deepens and enlarges the sense of community; as Raymond M. Olderman points out, it likewise evokes the idea of fertility and functions as "the central incident in McMurphy's challenge to the waste land"[4] of the hospital. And the party on the ward turns the great cast of characters into a group of Merry Pranksters, contributing, one and all, to a night of spectacular celebration.

The men on the fishing trip and at the party are a far cry from the little boys who spied on each other and tattled in the Big Nurse's log book. No longer do they *tear* each other down. Before Harding signs out and is picked up by his wife, *he* deals blackjack in the tub room and tells the silent Big Nurse on her return, "Lady, I think you're full of so much bullshit" (p. 307). The language of the novel virtually insists that we see McMurphy as a kind of Christ figure (at Shock Therapy time: "Do I get a crown of thorns?" [p. 270] and earlier: "McMurphy led the twelve of us toward the ocean" [p. 227]), doling out his life so that others may live. The action of the novel dramatizes the manner in which he makes his sacrifices, amid doubts and rejoicings on the part of his followers. And the perception of Chief Bromden, now highly sensitized to the task, prepares us at times tenderly to appreciate McMurphy's legacy—manhood, friendship suffused with affection, and, finally, love. Miss Ratched's face at the time of McMurphy's last attack displays a "terror forever ruining any other look she might ever try to use again" (p. 305). She has her revenge, lobotomy, a "castration of the frontal lobes." But Chief Bromden denies the Big Nurse her trophy. "He creeps into the bed of his friend," in the words of Leslie A. Fiedler, "for what turns out to be an embrace—for only in a caricature of the act of love can he manage to kill him."[5] It is, of course, as Mr. Fiedler signifies, a true act of love, performed with a manhood McMurphy has poured into the Chief.

In the terms of the narrative, there can be no more fog or time control. Thus, the Chief, bigger than ever before, makes his escape by picking up the control panel McMurphy could

not even budge, the epitome of all the machinery in the hospital, of all machinery that has victimized him and diminished his people ("I heard the wires and connections tearing out of the floor"), and throws it through the window. "The glass splashed out in the moon, like bright cold water baptizing [and thus perhaps awakening] the sleeping earth" (p. 310).

### IV

Despite the fact that the term Big Nurse inevitably recalls the term Big Brother and thus invokes memories of *1984* and other controlled worlds, *One Flew Over the Cuckoo's Nest* is not in its thrust and emphasis an anti-Utopian novel. The specific make-up of the Combine remains vague, as indeed it must, since the word *combine* is not simply a synonym for *organization*, since it is the Chief's protean metaphor for all that mechanizes, threshes, and levels—for all that packages human beings into "products." In this sense, the idea of a Combine contributes powerfully to the dramatic coherence of the novel. The ward, the Chief says, employing the logic of the metaphor, "is a factory for the Combine. It's for fixing up mistakes made in the neighborhoods and in the schools and in the churches" (p. 38). The metaphor is not monolithic; there are other wards in the hospital. The Japanese nurse on the Disturbed Ward is pleasant—she gives gum to the Chief (a fresh stick), a cigarette to McMurphy, and she even criticizes the Big Nurse. And there is an Outside, increasingly regulated by the Combine, as is everything else, though not so rigorously as in the factory-ward.

On the trip to the ocean Chief Bromden notices "signs of what the Combine had accomplished since I was last through this country": five thousand houses "punched out identical by a machine," five thousand identically dressed kids playing on an acre of "crushed gravel," five thousand men deposited like insects by a commuter train (p. 228). It is, recognizably, the world of our suburbs and sub-divisions, standardized, mechanized, virtually anesthetized. Coming back from the ocean, however, the Chief "noticed vaguely that I was getting so's I could see some good in the life around me. McMurphy was teaching me. I was feeling better than I remembered feeling since I was a kid, when everything was good and the land was still singing kids' poetry to me" (p. 243). Again the Chief faces a world of threshed out sameness; but he brings to it now—after the fishing trip—a sense of possibility which enlarges the dimensions of his spirit. The Combine, of course, continues to adjust things. But things may be increasingly adjusted (to pick up another idea from Mr. Olderman, who got it from McMurphy) because they are increasingly adjustable—which means, we realize with a sinking feeling of responsibility, that the Combine's power to control may exist in ratio to our willingness to forfeit manhood.

*One Flew Over the Cuckoo's Nest* directs our attention to such a point: we have surrendered a sense of self, which, for Kesey, is involved with a sense of space—and thus possibility. "The American has a sense of something that the European doesn't have," he remarked in the *Rolling Stone* interview, "and it's a sense of space. No matter how tight things get, there's more space, there's places you can go. . . . It's the most that we have to offer the world, just to communicate that sense" (p. 30). To lose the *sense* of space is to be confined (whether it be on the Outside or on the Big Nurse's ward), to contribute to the encroaching power of the Combine.

And so Kesey gives us McMurphy, the advocate of our manhood, who brings a sense of space, freedom, and largeness onto the ward as something co-existent with his life. We hear him, we see him, and once we smell him—the outdoor odor of man working. We are even treated on occasion to the splendor of his white whale shorts. Given to him by a co-ed at Oregon State who told him he was a symbol, McMurphy's shorts have, no doubt, a sexual significance. If Melville can spell "arch-bishopric" with a final "k," Kesey can surely play on the name Moby-*Dick*. Beyond that, McMurphy's shorts have already become ambiguous. Joseph J. Waldmeir, in his fine essay on Joseph Heller and Kesey, comes to see McMurphy as Captain Ahab because of his shorts.[6] And that, I believe, is an error with unfortunate implications. McMurphy may represent the indomitableness of Moby-Dick himself: as Moby-Dick cannot be vanquished by the monomaniac Ahab, so the spirit of McMurphy cannot be quenched by the Combine. Much more meaningfully, however, the leaping white whales suggest *Moby-Dick*, a novel that dramatizes with a fierceness of its own the inter-dependence of man in the face of Ahab's will to stand alone. Ahab curses the "inter-indebtedness" of man, that which binds one man to another; Ishmael sees it and accepts it, most notably, perhaps, when a literal line ties him to Queequeg in "The Monkey-Rope" chapter. And *Moby-Dick* validates Ishmael's vision of reality in the world.

The men on the Big Nurse's ward become stronger once they recognize their inter-dependence. McMurphy becomes heroic once he throws his lines out to them. And we come to appreciate the force of Kesey's novel once we see that *One Flew Over the Cuckoo's Nest* is an intense statement about the high cost of living—which we must be *big* enough to afford. That, I should think, is the "truth" the Chief speaks about at the outset. It will "burn" him to tell about it; it will "roar out" of him "like floodwaters." And it will remain true, for him and for all of us, "even though it didn't happen" (p. 8).

## Notes

1. *Fiction and the Figures of Life* (New York: Vintage Books, 1972), p. 49.
2. Ken Kesey, *One Flew Over the Cuckoo's Nest* (New York: Compass Books Edition, Viking Press, 1962), p. 68. Subsequent references to this edition will appear in the text.
3. "Two Novelists of the Absurd: Heller and Kesey," *Wisconsin Studies in Contemporary Literature*, 5 (1964), 198.
4. *Beyond the Waste Land* (New Haven and London: Yale University Press, 1972), p. 45.
5. *The Return of the Vanishing American* (New York: Stein and Day, 1968), p. 182.
6. "Two Novelists of the Absurd," p. 203.

## M. GILBERT PORTER
### From "The Ringing of Hank's Bell: Standing Tall in Wakonda"
### *The Art of Grit: Ken Kesey's Fiction*
### 1982, pp. 37–40

In his second novel Kesey reaffirms the necessity for strength and courage and the validity of human heroism, but his focus is different, for in *Cuckoo's Nest* Kesey examined what the hero owes to others; in *Sometimes a Great Notion* he examines what the hero owes to himself—and, paradoxically, how being true to the self ultimately serves the community (as Emerson and Thoreau had taught). The strength/weakness, courage/fear polarities from *Cuckoo's Nest* appear in the second novel in the conflict between Hank Stamper as self-reliant, independent logger and the collective weakness of the union, between Hank's gusto for life and Lee's fear of it. Bromden's fog of fear is paralleled by Lee's paranoiac inner voice crying "Watch Out!" Biggy Newton is a kind of residual Big Nurse, a

focal figure for combat, but without the symbolic force of Big Nurse. What McMurphy does for Bromden, Hank does for Lee, though in much different circumstances: Both are liberated from the stranglehold of bad faith, the loss of trust in the self.

Prominent characters are more complex and realistic than in *Cuckoo's Nest*. Lee is a less sympathetic figure than Bromden, Hank a less sterling hero than McMurphy. Even-write, Draeger, Gibbon, Newton, and the union are not merely the straw figures that Harding, Bibbit, Cheswick, Big Nurse, and the staff tend often to be. Old Henry is a finely drawn curmudgeon. Viv is a sensitive, haunting beauty more human than any of the women in *Cuckoo's Nest*. Joe Ben is an optimist who commands trust as Public Relation is an optimist who arouses distrust. The supporting characters from Indian Jenny to Simone to Willard Eggleston and Boney Stokes are worthy of Steinbeck, Bellow, and Malamud at their best. There is in this novel a density of texture and a realistic richness of character frequently missing in *Cuckoo's Nest*, which em-ployed different techniques for other effects.

Although Hank's self-interest denies him the adoration of the townspeople that McMurphy enjoys in the eyes of the inmates of the cuckoo's nest, the effect Hank has on the community is comparably significant. He embodies for them the qualities of strength, resourcefulness, bravery, and inde-pendence they need for survival. he demonstrates what a man can be and do and thus provides for them a standard of heroism to aspire to, however begrudgingly on both sides. These communal benefits, however, are incidental to Hank's design. He is not the altruistic figure into which McMurphy evolves, nor does he consciously seek to change anyone's values except Lee's, and he tries to help Lee as much from a sense of guilt over Myra as from a desire to improve the quality of Lee's life.

The struggle between the two brothers is a central conflict in the novel, and that struggle magnifies the parallel conflict between the union brotherhood and the maverick "brother" Hank, who eschews collectivism out of ingrained family tradition. The Stamper credo "Never give a inch" comes to Hank from old Henry as both a duty and a curse. Though it makes him strong, it isolates him and makes him the target for bitter or envious attacks: "I *always*," Hank laments, "have to be goddammit working up to *fighting* with *some*-guy-or-other!"[1] Hank's extraordinary strength functions ambivalently: It both inspires achievement and indicts weakness. Lee's plan to return home "to measure up . . . or pull him down" (66) under-lines the duality of Hank's heroism, as do Biggy Newton's repeated but unsuccessful attempts to defeat Hank in a fistfight.

The symbol for Hank's stature is appropriate for a logger: the tree, a symbol that must have originated in Tee Ah Millatoona, Bromden's father, The-Pine-That-Stands-Tallest-on-the-Mountain. Failing at first to measure up to Hank, Lee, like the members of the union, wants to cut him down, hoping to elevate himself by reducing Hank to his level. Old Henry and Joe Ben expect Hank to maintain his characteristic strength. In the middle of these opposing forces and feeling the pressure in both directions is Hank, whose independence is complicated by Viv's sympathy for the striking union members and for Lee. The plot develops from this basic placement of forces (as McMurphy was placed between the weak and the strong).

The tree symbolism is as important to this novel as synecdoche is to the first one, for the tree symbolism embodies the themes of heroism and the conflict of strength with weak-ness, and life with death, as well as the themes of time and place: "*Time overlaps itself. . . . As a shiny new ax, taking a swing at somebody's next year's split-level pinewood pad, bites all the way to the Civil War. As proposed highways break down through the stacked strata of centuries"* (191). Like the golden doubloon on the mast of the *Pequod*, the trees represent different things to different people and thus reveal collective or individual character. To the union members, the trees are simply a source of income, an inexhaustible material resource to be converted by labor into lumber in return for a paycheck. To Jonas the forest is an intimidating place of death and sinister destruction. To Viv it is a place of beauty and enchantment, a consoling presence. To Joe Ben it is a magnificent manifestation of God's unlimited bounty (but ironically the cause of his death). To Henry and Hank it is a challenging and worthy opponent, bringing out the best of their manhood and their own worthy competitors' appreciation. To Lee, the forest and the river are walls, obstacles to the future he pursues and a prison containing a childhood he must retrieve in order to get on with his life. The omniscient eye that watches over these disparate viewpoints observes with sufficient scope to encompass them all.

For where *Cuckoo's Nest* was integrated by the restricted first-person narration of Bromden, here the integrating principle is a frequently shifting though tautly controlled multiple point of view that moves skillfully from the omniscient voice of what I call the Tutelary Spirit, who provides the epigraphs to each chapter and much of the internal commentary, to conventional third-person omniscience, to the individual characters revealing their own perceptions in various persons and tenses. The effect of these multiple voices is to render the complexity of the world Kesey treats in the complexity of his technique and thus to embody his themes: the ambivalence of Nature, the conflict between the strong and the weak, the intricate way time and place and people shape character and determine destinies, and the nature and function of heroism in human events.

*Notes*

1. Ken Kesey, *Sometimes a Great Notion* (New York: Bantam, 1965), p. 314. Page numbers hereafter in parentheses in the text.

# GALWAY KINNELL

## 1927–

Galway Kinnell was born in Providence, Rhode Island, on February 1, 1927. Kinnell grew up in Pawtucket, a small mill town outside of Providence. After completing high school he served in the Navy from 1944 to 1946. Kinnell studied at Princeton, receiving a B.A. in 1948. While at Princeton Kinnell became friendly with fellow student W. S. Merwin. Kinnell did his graduate work at the University of Rochester, earning an M.A. in 1949. He held a series of teaching posts at Alfred University, University of Chicago, and later abroad in both France and Iran. During the 1960s Kinnell was active in the civil rights movement and vehemently protested against the war in Vietnam.

Kinnell's first volume of poetry, *What a Kingdom It Was*, appeared in 1960. Since then he has published over a half dozen collections of poetry, one novel, and several translations. Kinnell's only novel, *Black Light*, was published in 1966. His translations include works by René Hardy, Yves Bonnefoy, Yvan Goll, and François Villon. *Walking Down the Stairs*, a selection of interviews given by Kinnell, was published in 1978. Frequent comparisons have been made between Kinnell's and Whitman's poetry. Among his best-known works is "The Avenue Bearing the Initial of Christ into the New World." The title of the edition of his collected early verses, this poem derives its name from Avenue C, which runs through New York's Lower East Side. Another of Kinnell's highly praised poems, "The Bear," gives an account of the Eskimo method of catching bears.

Following the publication of his *Selected Poems* (1983), Kinnell was named the co-recipient of the American Book Award for Poetry as well as the winner of the 1983 Pulitzer Prize for poetry. Kinnell divides his time between New York and Sheffield, Vermont, living with his wife Inés and their two children.

GALWAY KINNELL
From an Interview by A. Poulin, Jr.,
and Stan Sanvel Rubin (1971)
*Walking Down the Stairs: Selections from Interviews*
1978, pp. 20–29

*P*oulin: ⟨. . .⟩ What kinds of impulses originally necessitated your writing poetry and under what kinds of circumstances did you start writing?

*Kinnell*: I knew, from the age of twelve on, that writing poetry was what I wanted to do, but it wasn't until I was around eighteen that I began to write what you might call seriously. As

for the impulses that set me writing, I remember I lived a kind of double life: my "public" life was everyone I knew—brother, sisters, parents, friends, and so on—and my secret life with the poems I would read late at night. I found my most intimate feelings were shared in those poems more fully than in the relationships I had in the world. I suppose I came to think that in poetry it might be possible to say the things I couldn't express in ordinary life.

*Poulin*: Do you recall what poems you were reading?

*Kinnell*: A lot of Poe. Also Dickinson, Shelley, Wordsworth, Kipling, Housman, even James Whitcomb Riley and Robert Service.

*Rubin*: Did you read Whitman early?

*Kinnell:* Yes, but I didn't understand him. It wasn't until I was in my mid-twenties that I really discovered him. Then I found him marvelous. It could be Whitman isn't a poet for young people. He's physical, but mystically physical. The young are both too down-to-earth, and too spiritual, to take to that. The teenager is almost gnostic in his dualism.

*Poulin:* Besides reading, what other kinds of events or experiences influenced your work? In his review of *What a Kingdom It Was*, James Dickey stated: "Perhaps to a degree more than is true of other poets, Kinnell's development will depend on the actual events of his life." How accurate was Dickey's prediction?

*Kinnell:* My poetry does stay fairly close to the experiences of my life. I don't usually write in others' voices. Probably this has come to be even more true in my last two books. My children, for example, appear often in *The Book of Nightmares*. I think in the book Dickey was reviewing a number of the poems were pure inventions—part of a series I wrote about how it might be to grow up on the Illinois prairie in the nineteenth century, of which "First Song" is one. So there was perhaps a certain prescience in his remark.

*Poulin:* But reading your poems one doesn't have the sense, as one does with more personal poets—Lowell, Plath, or Sexton—that this is an actual, real person speaking. There is always the sense of a kind of persona in the poem. I mean, one doesn't feel one's getting to know Galway Kinnell the private person.

*Kinnell:* That may be true, I don't know. But insofar as I use my own life in my poems I think of it as being much the same as others' lives. I change things, mostly to bring out something, but perhaps also to take away some detail that keeps it merely autobiographical.

*Rubin:* You've written that the poem comes in part out of the poet's desire to be changed, out of his struggle with his own nature. Is the death of the ego a recognizable point in a poem; is it a place you go through when you're writing a poem?

*Kinnell:* In some great poems, like *Song of Myself*, a reader is taken through one person into some greater self; there is a continual passing into the "death of the self," to use that phrase. It's one of the things that makes *Song of Myself* glorious. As we read this poem, we have to open ourselves if we are to get anything at all out of it. When we come to the lines "I was the man, I suffered, I was there," we already understand what it is to disappear into someone else. The final action of the poem, where Whitman dissolves into the air and into the ground, is for me one of the great moments of self-transcendence in poetry. In one way or another, consciously or not, all poems try to pass beyond the self. The best poems are those in which you are not this or that person, but anyone, just a person. If you could go farther, you would no longer be a person but an animal. If you went farther still you would be the grass, eventually a stone. If a stone could speak your poem would be its words.

*Rubin:* That makes me think of the topic of death which runs throughout your poetry.

*Kinnell:* Yes, as death has two aspects—the extinction, which we fear, and the flowing away into the universe, which we desire—there is a conflict within us that I want to deal with.

*Rubin:* It also seems to me that you almost feel at times that the moment of death is the moment of heightened clinging to life. I know you've written about Emily Dickinson's "I Heard a Fly Buzz When I Died."

*Kinnell:* Yes, I think that's what Emily Dickinson was doing when she wrote the poem—imagining the heightened feeling she would have for the world when she left it. The last section of *The Book of Nightmares* was written in something of that spirit.

*Rubin:* This is something then that we should be able to do continuously?

*Kinnell:* Many think we should forget about death. Much of contemporary culture is devoted to helping us do this. But I like what Hegel says: "The life of the spirit is not frightened at death and does not keep itself pure of it. It lives with death and maintains itself in it." Yves Bonnefoy uses this as the epigraph to his wonderful book, *On the Motion and Immobility of Douve*.

*Poulin:* I find myself disagreeing with both of you. My reading of *The Book of Nightmares* suggests an equal strain of transcendence of some kind. There's a profound traditional religious attitude toward death; if not life after death, then at least some form of transcendence both in the newer poems as well as in the earlier ones.

*Kinnell:* I think that about halfway through my first book I ceased to look for that traditional kind of transcendence. Certain poems in the last half of the book are explicit struggles to be rid of such a desire. But such desires run deep and perhaps the most we can do is disguise them.

*Poulin:* You said once that "the dream of every poem is to be a myth," and I wonder if any orthodox mythology is viable today, and if not, what then are the materials of a more contemporary myth.

*Kinnell:* I doubt if old myths, born at other times, in other cultures, can be very much alive for us. When I said that, I don't know if I meant myth in the usual sense. Perhaps I meant that the poem is a kind of paradigm of what the human being wants to say to the cosmos. The old myths were a bit like that. This is what John Logan has in mind when he speaks of poetry's "sacramental character."

*Rubin:* Your poem, "The Dead Shall Be Raised Incorruptible," has perhaps more of what might be termed political content, social content, than almost any of your other poems. What motivated that poem?

*Kinnell:* I wrote that poem out of the same obsessive concerns that have led almost every poet in this country to turn to political subjects. Many of the poems we wrote were terrible, but they had to be written. My own poem fails in some ways, but it did force me to try to understand certain things, such as what has become of us that we can kill on a vast scale and not even be able to say why.

*Rubin:* I asked you that because it is a kind of exception in *The Book of Nightmares*, and yet it clearly relates to the nightmare you're speaking of. It's not the way you normally write or the kind of theme you normally handle.

*Kinnell:* That's probably true, although in the previous book there is a poem called "The Last River" which is as political, and a good deal longer. You see, what I wanted to do in *The Book of Nightmares* in regard to politics, as well as in regard to other elements that come into the poem, was to bring from the central core of the poem a sort of light onto—well, I could say onto any subject whatever. I wanted it to be that any one of those ten sections could have been about anything at all. This light would bind each unconnected thing into the wholeness of the poem.

*Poulin:* What, exactly, would you say, is that central core?

*Kinnell:* I was afraid you might ask me that!

*Poulin:* Why do you think so many poets have been working on long poems and sequences recently?

*Kinnell:* The desire for a poem in which you can say everything, in which there is nothing that has to be left out.

*Poulin:* That's very close to what Ginsberg is trying to do and, of course, it recalls Whitman, doesn't it—to include the entire universe?

*Kinnell:* I suppose that Ezra Pound has had the most influence on the way the long poem has developed. For myself, while I want a poem that can include everything, I don't yet want to abandon what I think of as organic form—where the poem isn't made by accretion, by adding lines and stanzas, sections and books, and so on, indefinitely, as *Paterson* and the *Cantos* were made. I still want a long poem to be an organism: to be born, to grow, to come to a certain fullness and climax, and to end. It may be in the future I will want to write a flat poem, without boundaries, a kind of medieval wandering—I don't rule that out.

*Rubin:* While reading *The Book of Nightmares*, which I did read as one poem—I couldn't put it down because the voice was continuous and gripping—I felt that something's happened to your relationship with time. I don't know how, perhaps your children may have something to do with that.

*Kinnell:* What do you feel had happened?

*Rubin:* A sense that a particular kind of affirmation of natural life that one gets reading your earlier poems is somewhat modulated here. Even in the opening poem, "Under the Maud Moon," there is a real consciousness of time-future I think, in a way that I don't precisely sense in your earlier work. For example, the last image in the book: "see if you can find the one flea which is laughing." Somehow that's a little more tentative than, say, the poem "The Fly."

*Kinnell:* Perhaps. For myself, *The Book of Nightmares*, for all that tentative and fearful quality you correctly see in it, is as affirmative as anything I've written. I'm the last person to be able to judge such things, of course. It's true that throughout the poem there is a harping on transience. In earlier poems it's not quite so constant, and there's usually an effort to make it seem all right. There is one early poem, "Spindrift," in which the final—and seventh—section reads,

> What does he really love,
> That old man,
> His wrinkled eyes
> Tortured by smoke,
> Walking in the ungodly
> Rasp and cackle of old flesh?
>
> The swan dips her head
> And peers at the mystic
> In-life of the sea,
> The gull drifts up
> And eddies toward heaven,
> The breeze in his arms . . .
>
> Nobody likes to die
> But an old man
> Can know
> A kind of gratefulness
> Towards time that kills him,
> Everything he loved was made of it.

I like this passage; I don't disavow it in any way. But I have grown older—the poem was written about 1960—and, more crucially, there have come into my life two children, as you say. It would be nice if in a single poem one could resolve a given problem forever—come to terms with it once and for all. But each poem comes out of its own moment. In *The Book of Nightmares* I seem to face time's passing as if for the first time. It is bound up now with the twin fears that parents of small children feel, the fear of losing the children and the fear of leaving them. I hoped the flea of the last line wouldn't sound *quite* so tentative. I had been thinking, you see, that fleas on the body of a happy person would be a bit happier than other fleas.

*Poulin:* In your essay, "The Poetics of the Physical World," you spoke of the dichotomy between the "poetics of heaven" and the "poetics of the physical world." But in *The Book of Nightmares* you seem to have managed a reconciliation between them.

*Kinnell:* I came to feel very free in writing that poem. I felt I could set down the very worst, anything, no matter what. I could evoke in the poem the most revolting presences. I could do this in total faith that something was sustaining the whole poem that would not allow it to be a record of self-disgust, or hatred of nature, or fear of death, or loneliness, or defeat, but rather ultimately a restorative and healing and, if I can use the word, a happy poem.

*Poulin:* There's been a great change in the structure of your poems from *What a Kingdom It Was* to *The Book of Nightmares* and I'm rather fascinated by some of them. In "The Poetics of the Physical World," you say that for the modern poet rhyme and meter, having lost their sacred meaning and natural basis, amount to little more than mechanical aids for writing. First of all I'm intrigued by why they've lost their sacred and natural basis for the modern poet or for you.

*Kinnell:* Oh, I'm just guessing. I guess that the Elizabethans, for instance, sensed some lovely repetitiveness about existence. The rhymes in their poems are a way of acknowledging the everlasting return of things. A harmony sounded through time. The formal aspects of their poems were ways of sharing in it, perhaps of propitiating it. Most of us moderns hear nothing like that. When we listen we hear outer space telling us we're a race living for a while on a little planet that will die. As for what lies beyond, we know nothing—our brains are the wrong kind, or are too small, or something. When the astronauts looked back at the earth, what they felt most keenly was its fragility. The seasons do return, but now with poignancy, because almost nothing else does.

## RICHARD HOWARD
### From "Galway Kinnell"
*Alone with America*
1969, pp. 259–66

The poetry of Galway Kinnell ⟨. . .⟩ is an Ordeal by Fire. It is fire which he invokes to set forth his plight, to enact his ordeal, and to restore himself to reality. It is fire—in its constant transformations, its endless resurrection—which *is* reality, for Kinnell as for Heraclitus: "The world is an ever-living fire, with measures of it kindling and measures of it going out." As the American poet translates this, it becomes:

> And in the sky there burns this shifty jellyfish
> That degenerates and flashes and re-forms.

And just as the pre-Socratic had affirmed that "all things are an exchange for fire, and fire for all things," so Kinnell muses, in his broken, aphoristic way that has so many analogies with the Greek's:

> The invisible life of the thing
> Goes up in flames that are invisible
> Like cellophane buring in the sunlight.
> It burns up. Its drift is to be nothing.
> In its covertness it has a way
> Of uttering itself in place of itself . . .

Yet there is a terrible and tremendous inflection in Galway Kinnell's pyromania, which we shall trace out in a moment, that altogether transforms his impulse from the orphic pitiless-ness of Heraclitus. When the Greek says "Fire in its advance will judge and convict all things," there is awe but no tragedy in it, for there is no belief in incarnation. But when Kinnell evokes mortality as a commitment to the fire, there is an unappeasable grief in his "heart's hell": it is the grief of history, the pain of things happening once and once only, irreversibly,[1] that is the burden of Christianity, of the Incarnation:

> . . . It is true
> That only flesh dies, and spirit flowers without stop
> For men, cows, dung, for all dead things; and it is
>      good, yes—
> But an incarnation is in particular flesh
> And the dust that is swirled into a shape
> And crumbles and is swirled again had but one shape
> That was this man. When he is dead the grass
> Heals what he suffered, but he remains dead,
> And the few who loved him know this until they die.

Between Heraclitus, then, and Kinnell the agonized Believer who remarks, in *Black Light*, of his abject hero: "It was as if his virtue, his very devotion to God, were succeeding where vice had failed, in making an atheist out of him"—the proper mediator, the exegetical figure that will set us coursing over Kinnell's burning landscape in search of clues to the resurrection is, of course, Hopkins, the Hopkins who in his sonnet "That Nature is a Heraclitean Fire and of the comfort of the Resurrection" watched while "Million-fueled nature's bonfire burns on" and declared that the "world's wildfire leaves but ash / in a flash, at a trumpet's crash."[2] The agony of that knowledge—the knowledge or at least the conviction that all must be consumed in order to be reborn, must be reduced to ash in order to be redeemed—gives Galway Kinnell's poetry its astonishing resonance, the accents of a conflict beyond wisdom as it is beyond piety: "I don't know what you died of," one of the characters in his novel says, "whatever it was, that is what will bring you alive again." ⟨. . .⟩

The fire opens Kinnell's first book ⟨*What a Kingdom It Was*⟩, where it is seen benevolently enough as the vital energy of earthly things:

> Cold wind stirs, and the last green
> Climbs to all the tips of the season, like
> The last flame brightening on a wick.
> Embers drop and break in sparks . . .

The sense of the self-consuming candle as the characteristic avatar of flame is one that will remain with Kinnell to the end—as in *Black Light*, where he speaks, about to blow out the candle, of "the point of the flame, that shifting instant where the flame was turning into pure spirit." Even in this early poem, "First Communion," the fire is seen not only as vital impulse, but as the agent of transmutation, the "last flame" moving up the wick of the trees until they are burnt away to "pure spirit." Then comes the poem called "Burning," the anecdote of a man of the woods who kills the dog that has saved him from drowning, buries it, and goes back into his shack to sleep, leaving the speaker to watch:

> I saw him sleepless in the pane of glass
> Looking wild-eyed at sunset, then the glare
> Blinded the glass—only a red square
> Burning a house burning in the wilderness.

Here the notion of the universal conflagration is more subtly diffused, not only in the sunset that gives all things fire's color ("a red square burning a house burning"), but in the particulars of aberrant human conduct ("a house burning in the wil-derness")—it is the man inside, his conscience and his craziness, that are given the appropriate outer emblem by the

setting sun reflected on the glass. Between this poem and the next to rehearse Kinnell's fiery theme, intervene a pair of studies in primitivism, "The Wolves" and "Westport," where life's cautery is only obliquely touched on—shooting buffalo in the days of the great herds ("I fired . . . He looked, trotted off, and became dead"), and the look of the land after a storm ("a red streak in the west lit all the raindrops . . . and the shining grasses were bowed towards the west as if one craving had killed them"). It is of course the craving of fire, as murderous as any gunpowder, that Kinnell sees in the west; in a further poem, "Lilacs," he sees that craving not only in the sun's red decline, but in the day's very warmth:

> . . . Down the south slope
> A bitch stretched, and swaths of fierce lilacs
> Opened astonishing furnaces of scent . . .
>      . . . The blossoms climbed
> And blazed in the air . . .

The nuance of sexuality is added to the mere growth of animals and plants, and in this poem the woman subject to the "burning" lilacs, "her dry legs crackling in darkness," is drawn into the universal fire, "the hot scent of herself beating herself out of closets in the well-governed flesh." The recognition of sensual riot, "the nestfire of roses," is another emblem of destruction for Kinnell, one that will obsess him in later work. But at this point in his first book, he is concerned to come, still, to terms with his given faith: in "Easter," one of Kinnell's most successful poems in his earlier, "formal" manner, the death of a nurse, "raped, robbed, weighted, drowned," is conjugated with the Easter service, "the extensive sermon, the outcry of the inaudible prayer"; speculating on the rotting body, "trapped or working loose," and on the mystery of Christ's rising, the poet promises to crown the victim with an "Easter Fire" as the "brown water shoves [her] senselessly on past smoking cities, works of disaster"; he urges her to turn her "unwavering gaze" on "the dream you lived through":

> It is as you thought. The living burn.
> In the floating days may you discover grace.

Life is just that continuous conflagration ("the smoking cities") which it is Christianity's effort to transcend by a final "Easter Fire." The beautiful, tentative last line ("In the floating days . . .") of this carefully joined poem suggests, though, that no such glory waits for us, victims rather than victors of death this Easter. *The living burn*, and the dead, if they are lucky, merely dissolve.

That vision of burning and drowning together is extended in "Alewives Pool," which begins:

> We lay on the grass and gazed down and heard
> The world burning on the pulse of April . . .

and which ends with an eloquent vision of the possibilities of transfiguration, once the mortal flesh has been consumed away by the processes of life itself:

> In the trees even the birds are astonished
> By the fierce passion of their song. The mind
> Can only know what love has accomplished
> When love has consumed it in the burning pond.
> Now on the trembling pulse let death and birth
> Beat in the self as in the April grass—
> The sudden summer that the air flames forth
> Makes us again into its blossomers—
> Stand on the pulse and love the burning earth.

The ecstasy of knowing oneself a part of the world's *physis*, of knowing that within oneself there is the same pulse on which "the world burns," the radiant interchange between mind and love, between body and earth, between water and fire, is here registered in Kinnell's happiest key, when Being is so wrought up in its oneness of possibilities—"the air flames forth"—that a man's "days to come flood on his heart as if they were his past."

It is an easier thing, I suppose, merely to report the world in conflagration without insisting on an engagement of identity, without being rigorously *in question*. Easier or not— and in any case, the act of *seeing* the world as on fire, consuming itself away to a transfigured life, is certainly an involvement of a heroic order—some of the "nature poems" of this book have allowed Kinnell a delicacy in his art that he shrinks from when his persona is committed. "Leaping Falls," an account of a frozen cascade, reveals the diction of a poet who can, when he chooses, enact by the movement of language on the lips and in the mind the very transaction— distinct yet expanding, icy yet intense—he would rehearse in vision:

> . . . A topmost icicle came loose
> And fell, and struck another
> With a bell-like sound, and
> Another, and the falls
> Leapt at their ledges, ringing
> Down the rocks and on each other
> Like an outbreak of bells
> That rings and ceases.
> The silence turned around
> And became silence again.
> Under the falls on the snow
> A twigfire of icicles burned pale blue.

There is a wonderful play of contraries here, sound and silence, liquid and solid, heat and freezing, ice and flame—but they are resolved in a place beyond contraries, at a moment of vision, and at that moment the "fire of icicles burned pale blue." It is the ecstatic moment the surrealists were always trying for, when the conventional notions of opposites no longer stood opposed, but worked toward a transcendence where up and down, hot and cold, stillness and motion ceased to gainsay each other, and a man's existence glowed into a kind of godhead—this is what Kinnell means, or it is one of the things he means, by "burning."

Of course he is easier about it than that, sometimes; sometimes it is merely a notation of intensity he wishes to record, existence not transfigured, but merely heightened:

> . . . the duck took off,
> Skimmed the swells as it ascended,
> Brown wings burning and flashing
> In the sun as the sea it rose over
> Burned and flashed beneath it.

Yet if this is not a major instance of Kinnell's igneous reading of the world, it is significant that the conjugation of water and fire is here enlarged from the alewives pool and the frozen falls to the sea itself that is said to burn. It is as though the poet were reaching for Heraclitus' great truth, as he enlarged his focus like a burning glass: "The transformations of Fire are, first of all, the sea . . ." reads one of the Heraclitean fragments, and in Kinnell's second book (*Flower Herding on Mount Monadnock*), one of his most arresting poems—a kind of nature-log, "Tilamook Journal," in which the poet stares at "the Burn as it went out in the twilight, its crags broken, its valleys soaked in night"—comes to its triumphant conclusion: "It is only steps to the unburnable sea." Unburnable because it is the one thing that cannot be transformed, being already all transformation. Unburnable because it is always burning.

But to continue with *What a Kingdom It Was*, and Kinnell's fire sermon as he develops it, poem by poem: one of the most ambitious poems in the collection, "Seven Streams of

Nevis," memorializes seven ruined lives the poet invokes as he climbs Ben Nevis. Speaking of one of these friends, Sir Henry, Kinnell observes that he

> Decided fire brings out the best
> In things, and that anyone who
> Has cooked his eyes at the sunrise
> Of beauty, and thumbed himself blind, is wise.

Though merely a characterization, we have had enough clues from the poet to take such wisdom to heart. Especially when, on the top of the mountain, in one of those moments where contraries are resolved,

> Where merely to be still was temperate,
> Where to move was brave, where justice was a glide,
> Knowledge the dissolving of the head-hung eyes;
> There my faith lay burning, there my hope
> Lay burning on the water, there charity
> Burned like a sun.

So even the theological virtues are seen enkindled, sun and water united in the same drastic combustion: "In the heart's hell you have it; call it God's Love." And in the last and longest poem in the book, "The Avenue Bearing the Initial of Christ into the New World," where Kinnell turns on New York's Lower East Side the incandescent scrutiny of a visionary, the religious tenor of the burning is given its most explicit, almost ritual voice. After a few decorative notes, like describing the pushcart vegetables in terms of his old antinomies: "Icicle-shaped carrots that through black soil wove away like flames in the sun"—Kinnell warms to his theme:

> Children set fires in ashbarrels,
> Cats prowl the fires, scraps of fishes burn.
> A child lay in the flames.
> It was not the plan. Abraham
> Stood in terror at the duplicity.
> Isaac whom he loved lay in the flames . . .
> The children laugh.
> Isaac means *he laughs*.
> Maybe the last instant
> The dying itself, *is easier* . . .

Only the pain of such sacrifice, here in "the living streets, where instants of transcendence drift in oceans of loathing and fear," can redeem the Fallen City,

> Burning in the night, flames opening out like
> Eyelashes from the windows . . .
>                    But this evening
> The neighborhood comes out again, everything
> That may abide the fire was made to go through the fire
> And it was made clean.

From there, the poem goes on in an ecstasy of accountability, for whatever Kinnell sees—and he sees everything:

> The garbage disposal truck
> Like a huge hunched animal
> That sucks in garbage in the place
> Where other animals evacuate it
> Whines, as the cylinder in the rear
> Threshes up the trash and garbage,
> Where two men in rubber suits
> (It must be raining outside)
> Heap it in. The groaning motor
> Rises in a whine as it grinds in
> The garbage, and between-times
> Groans. It whines and groans again . . .
> If it is raining outside
> You can tell only by looking
> In puddles, under the lifted streetlamps.
> It would be the spring rain.

—has gone through that refining fire, has been *made clean*. By his ransacked, purified, literally inflamed imagination, Kinnell is able to ransom his world, having reached in his most sustained effort that place where everything which is is blessed.

*Notes*

1. Kinnell dramatizes this situation, the suffering brought about by Nature's irreversibility, in his novel *Black Light*: "He looked at the leaves again. How would it be, he thought, if one of them, even an unimportant one, should wither of its own free will and creep back into the limb?"
2. One of the opening poems in Kinnell's first book takes for its title the dedication of Hopkins' "Windhover": "To Christ Our Lord," and the poem ends with a characteristic Hopkins vision of "inscape":

    Then the Swan spread her wings, cross of the cold north,
    The pattern and mirror of the acts of earth.

## CHARLES MOLESWORTH
From "'The Rank Flavor of Blood':
The Poetry of Galway Kinnell" (1973)
*The Fierce Embrace*
1979, pp. 99–108

Kinnell's poetry of this period involves itself with a virtual rediscovery of how to view objects intensely, while continuing to avoid any prescribed system. Even as early as his long poem, "The Avenue Bearing the Initial of Christ into the New World," which falls outside the scope of the present study, though it deserves an essay of its own, Kinnell's poetry has been celebratory and inclusive in its characteristic attitude toward the world of objects. "There are more to things than things," says one modern French philosopher, and the contemporary poet instinctively agrees; but how to discover that "more" without falling into mere attitudinizing remains problematic. Pound taught his successors, who include most American poets, that no authority could replace personal testament, especially when such testament involved accurate perception and attentive apperception. But poets could still remain estranged from things; they might fall into a glorified listing of the mundane, or make the operations of the mind so dominant that the poems would lose their subjects in a welter of "impressions." Pound's influence dominated developments in American poetry so completely that poets as diverse as, say, Robert Creeley and William Meredith could easily refuse to yield to each other in their admiration for Pound's accomplishments. Kinnell took from Pound, however, only so much as could fruitfully be grafted onto the traditions of Blake and Whitman; and, though for some Pound's concern with "technique" might seem inimical to inspiration, such need not be the case. Pound's concern with objective "vision" on the physiological level corrects rather than replaces the concern with the "visionary." But Kinnell was still faced with the problem of how to bring his poetry out of the modernist cul-de-sac of irony into a postmodernist aesthetic. He did this in large measure by two actions, which may appear contradictory but are in fact complementary: self-discovery and self-destruction, the heuristic and the incendiary actions of poetry.[1] Kinnell became a shamanist, rather than a historicist of the imagination.

The first volume to contain poems Kinnell wrote in the sixties was *Flower Herding on Mount Monadnock* (1964), a book divided into two parts, the first heavily concerned with cityscapes and urban consciousness, and the second almost totally rural in its subjects and locales. The last poem of the first section, "For Robert Frost," offers a convenient transition into the second section, a transition important for the next volume, *Body Rags* (1969), filled as it is with a poetry of nature rather than of history. Such a reductive distinction can be misleading, of course, and it may help to look briefly at the poem for Frost to see in part how Kinnell views America's most famous "nature poet." The pastoralism of Frost both echoes and disjoins Kinnell's sensibility:

When we think of a man who was cursed
Neither with the mystical all-lovingness of Walt
    Whitman
Nor with Melville's anguish to know and to suffer,
And yet cursed . . . A man, what shall I say,
Vain, not fully convinced he was dying, whose
    calling
Was to set up in the wilderness of his country,
At whatever cost, a man, who would be his own
    man,
We think of you.

The qualified praise here may well bring to mind Auden's elegy for Yeats, a typically modern poem in the way it refuses to follow the ordinary "rules" for elegiac praise and insists on an honesty that threatens to dislocate the very discourse of the poem and move down to the level of verse epistle or even satire. Still, Kinnell sees Frost as "cursed," not perhaps as the same sort of *poète maudit* as Melville, but as someone tied to, perhaps bound down by, his bourgeois virtues of self-reliance and rugged individualism. The obverse of those virtues reflects the loneliness, the alienation, in Frost's life, the "desert places," against which confusion the poems offer only a "momentary stay." This surely is the side of Frost that most attracts Kinnell (as the third section of the poem makes clear), and he almost appears to be exorcising those other, civilized virtues of Frost that made him such a master ironist. When we look back on this poem from the perspective of Kinnell's two latest books, the most stringent criticism of Frost he proposes may be when he says that the older poet was "not fully convinced he was dying." Such an affirmation of life *against* death will become for Kinnell a weakness, a mark of the weak self-love, an unwillingness to accept the "last moment of increased life." As he says in "The Poetics of the Physical World,"[2] "The poetics of heaven agrees to the denigration of pain and death; the poetics of the physical world builds on these stones."

Along with death, Kinnell places pain at the base of his poetics, and pain plays a large part in the poems of *Flower Herding*. The first section of the book is concerned with pain as a subject, or at least as a surrounding condition of other subjects. Chief among these subjects, Kinnell places an awareness of time's ongoingness, an intense awareness that this particular moment, this *now* is isolate, thrown up by itself to baffle and defeat human expectations. Here is a passage from "The River That Is East," the first poem of the book:

We stand on the shore, which is mist beneath us,
And regard the onflowing river. Sometimes
It seems the river stops and the shore
Flows into the past. Nevertheless, its leaked promises
Hopping in the bloodstream, we strain for the future,
Sometimes even glimpse it, a vague, scummed thing
We dare not recognize, and peer again
At the cabled shroud out of which it came,
We who have no roots but the shifts of our pain,
No flowering but our own strange lives.

All New York poems with bridges in them, such as this one, must recall Hart Crane, though part of the success of this poem lies in how effectively it uses its poetic forebears without being strangled by them. This is true of much of Kinnell's poetry and is one of the several ways in which he resembles Theodore Roethke. The images here of mists, scum, and shrouds should remind us of how early Kinnell was involved in a poetry obsessed with death and pain, a product of a consciousness in which sharp juxtapositions and sudden changes of perspective appear endemic. The root and the flower of his experience exist without any system except what they may discover for themselves in an existential framework.

It is in section II of *Flower Herding* that we find the first seeds of Kinnell's "poetics of the physical world," as that poet concentrates on natural, as opposed to urban, objects, moments, and landscapes. Here, too, pain and death are present, almost omnipresent. But the isolate moments, the "leaked promises," of continuity, or of wholeness, become, in the rural setting, moments of ecstasy. The perspective of the future as "a vague, scummed thing/we dare not recognize" fades into a more empty perspective, perhaps; but it is that very emptiness that constitutes such promise for Kinnell. As Kinnell suggests in "The Poetics of the Physical World," death represents the last, absolute perspective; its very finality makes it a magnificent possibility, or rather, the source of magnificent possibilities.

> We may note that the desire to *be* some other thing is itself suicidal; it involves a willingness to cease to be a man. But this is not a simple wish for extinction so much as it is a desire for union with what is loved.
> And so it is a desire for more, not less, life.

Reading *Flower Herding* as part of a putative spiritual autobiography, the reader will decide that it is only when Kinnell escapes the city for the country that the possibilities of mortality become positive rather than negative. When we regard *Flower Herding* as the barometer of other, larger currents at work in American poetry in the sixties, it clearly stands with Bly's *Silence in the Snowy Fields* (1962) and Wright's *The Branch Will Not Break* (1963). These three books can be seen as developments away from the ironic mode practiced and perfected by, among others, Ransom, Tate, Nemerov, and Wilbur, and toward a poetic mode first announced by Theodore Roethke as early as 1950, but largely unheeded until ten years later. Here is Roethke characterizing the lyric poet in "Open Letter," from *On the Poet and His Craft*:

> He must scorn being "mysterious" or loosely oracular, but be willing to face up to a genuine mystery. His language must be compelling and immediate: He must create an actuality. He must be able to telescope image and symbol, if necessary, without relying on the obvious connectives: to speak in a kind of psychic shorthand . . . He works intuitively, and the final form of his poem must be imaginatively right.

Such phrases as "psychic shorthand" and "telescop[ing] image and symbol" illuminate the shifts in perspective and the imagistic density that make the typical Kinnell poem. Here are the final lines of the title poem of *Flower Herding*:

> It burns up. Its drift is to be nothing.
>
> In its covertness it has a way
> Of uttering itself in place of itself,
> Its blossoms claim to float in the Empyrean,
> A wrathful presence on the blur of the ground.
> The appeal to heaven breaks off.
> The petals begin to fall, in self-forgiveness.
> It is a flower. On this mountainside it is dying.

Heaven and the void vie with each other to be the flower's proper domain; the flower makes claims it cannot demonstrate,

and yet it forgives itself; it needs its covertness in order to survive, and yet it must utter itself, make known and articulate its "invisible life." All of these contradictory impulses suggest that we can "interpret" the flower as an image from the processes of nature and as a symbol for the act of writing the poem, or even for the psychic paradoxes of the poet himself.

Nowhere are such leaps from the imagistic to the symbolic made clear; in fact, the tone of the poem occasionally works against such leaps, especially in the last line. But the pain and the ecstasy of the consciousness that employs such telescopings tell us that aspiration and acceptance are two aspects of the same intentionality. We might even say that the dialectic between aspiration and acceptance provides the central energy of the poem and that that dialectic reveals its terms most clearly in the tone of a line such as "A wrathful presence on the blur of the ground," where overtones of an almost biblical phrasing terminate in the flatness of the final five words. But the flatness of such a termination, along with phrases like "breaks off," can't be called ironic, at least not if we use irony to mean a kind of qualifying defensiveness. If anything, the variations in texture in these lines reflect quite openly the actuality of the circumscribed transcendence in the poem, circumscribed because it sustains itself only through an acceptance of death. And the persistence of fire and death imagery throughout Kinnell's poetry forces us to disregard, or at least to minimize, the habitual expectation of ironic distance that we bring to much modern poetry. His obviously attempts to be a poetry of immersion into experience rather than of suspension above it.

Kinnell's next book after *Flower Herding* presents several difficulties; these result in part simply because several of the single poems in *Body Rags* are difficult ("The Last River" and "Testament of the Thief"), but also because the mode of expression throughout can seem half-formed, occasionally alternating between the densely remote and the flatly commonplace. At least seventeen (out of twenty-three) of the poems are constructed in "sections," and the section becomes the organizing principle of *The Book of Nightmares* as well as of the best poems in *Body Rags*: "The Poem," "The Porcupine," and "The Bear." But eight of the poems in *Body Rags* contain only two sections each, and these represent, I think, some of Kinnell's least successful poems. At the same time, the concentration of imagery and attention that they contain, along with the multiple and shifting perspectives, eventually culminates in what remains Kinnell's typical strength. Here is one poem that has some strength but finally fails to be as powerful as several others in the same format:

NIGHT IN THE FOREST

1
A woman
sleeps next to me on the earth. A strand
of hair flows
from her cocoon sleeping bag, touching
the ground hesitantly, as if thinking
to take root.
2
I can hear
a mountain brook
and somewhere blood winding
down its ancient labyrinths. And
a few feet away
charred stick-ends surround
a bit of ashes, where burnt-out, vanished flames

Postmodernist poetry insofar as it rejects or moves beyond irony, runs the risk of sentimentality on the one hand and of being "loosely oracular" on the other. Here, the "blood winding/down its ancient labyrinths" is susceptible to either charge, though perhaps especially the latter. Such resonance as the poem does have originates in the subtly controlled tone and syntax of the last few lines. But, considering the total statement of the poem as a dialectic between its two "sections" doesn't particularly increase our appreciation of it. The poem goes beyond descriptive prettiness only by hinting at emotions that would probably be mawkish if further explored. ⟨. . .⟩

Kinnell had begun *Body Rags* with a poem called "Another Night in the Ruins," which has the following terminal section:

> How many nights must it take
> one such as me to learn
> that we aren't, after all, made
> from that bird which flies out of its ashes,
> that for a man
> as he goes up in flames, his one work
> is
> to open himself, to *be*
> the flames?

The volume ends with "The Bear," a shamanistic immersion in the unknown, a "dance of solitude" that describes in great detail the hunting of the animal with "the chilly, enduring odor of bear." I think one phrase that might adequately hint at how the poem achieves its power over us is Denise Levertov's *natural allegory*. Pursued so intensely, the bear must end up "meaning something else," but only the briefest of analogical touchstones appears at the end of the poem, after the speaker has killed the bear and is watching a dam bear give birth to her cubs, "lumps of smeared fur":

> the rest of my days I spend
> wandering: wondering
> what, anyway,
> was that sticky infusion, that rank flavor of blood,
> that poetry, by which I lived?

Exploration and attentiveness provide the grounds of existence for the hunter of bear, for the poet; and those grounds are both the occasion and the subject of his most insistent questionings.

The hunter kills the bear by coiling a bone and freezing it in blubber; when the bear ingests it, the bone uncoils and pierces his inner organs. The resultant internal bleeding dominates the images of the poem, and the speaker eventually tracks down the bear, hacks "a ravine in his thigh," tears him "down his whole length," and climbs inside. Once the hunter is inside, his empathetic identification with the bear becomes literal, and the poet recapitulates by dreaming the bear's death. The final death agony of the poet-shaman-dreamer can easily be read as the moment of greatest artistic risk, when the flux of experience yields to the stasis of form.

> and now the breeze
> blows over me, blows off
> the hideous belches of ill-digested bear blood
> and rotted stomach
> and the ordinary, wretched odor of bear,
> blows across
> my sore, lolled tongue a song
> or screech, until I think I must rise up
> and dance. And I lie still.

Only by digesting the blood that leaked into his stomach, that is, only by destroying himself, could the bear have lived; and such self-transcendence, Kinnell seems to be saying, can only be achieved by someone tracking down and recording the experience. Such evidence as becomes available for this act may only be a carcass, a remnant of what has "just occurred"; but, through empathetic dream-work, through poetry, such

exploration and attentiveness can be the source of new life. Again, from "Poetry, Personality, and Death":

> The death of the self I seek, in poetry and out of poetry, is not a drying up or withering. It is a death, yes, but a death out of which one might hope to be reborn more giving, more alive, more open, more related to natural life. . . . For myself, I would like a death that would give me more loves, not fewer. And greater desire, not less.

The song may be no more than a screech, but it still expresses the organism's need to come to terms with its environment, and for Kinnell such a coming to terms involves growth.

*Notes*

1. See Richard Howard's essay in *Alone with America: The Art of Poetry in the United States since 1950* (New York, 1969), pp. 258–71, where Kinnell's use of fire imagery is discussed.
2. The essay was originally presented as a lecture at Colorado State University in 1969.

## CARY NELSON
## From "Ecclesiastical Whitman:
## Galway Kinnell's *The Book of Nightmares*"
## *Our Last First Poets*
### 1981, pp. 76–96

*T*he *Book of Nightmares* fulfills everything Kinnell attempted before it. This volume is so much the fruition of his previous poems—their language, structures, and themes—that many of them now read like its early drafts. To reread the first three books and the other early poems after *The Book of Nightmares* is to find their whole enterprise retroactively preempted. Indeed even *Mortal Acts, Mortal Words*, published in 1980, reads like it predates *The Book of Nightmares*.

In this book Kinnell's vision is a wholly verbal achievement, no longer dependent on the reader automatically granting an American poet the right to Whitmanesque prophecy. Moreover, Kinnell's poetry no longer depends on narrative anticipation for its impact. The change begun with "The Porcupine" and "The Bear" is complete; we are now primarily conscious of the poem's language. Kinnell's mystical vocabulary is not simply invoked; it is rendered into complex and singualr images that nonetheless convince the reader a common source is undergoing metamorphosis. His recurrent terms—death, emptiness, flowers, darkness, and light—are interwoven with images of blood, bone, and stone. This verbal tapestry is linked to a number of motifs introduced in the poem's separate narratives, such as the hen's death, the old man's shoes, and the births of his children. The result is a matrix of repetition and variation, in which the narratives of the ten individual sections begin to lose their identity through their relationship to the poem's larger form.

Throughout the book, the pervasive binarism of Kinnell's language is inescapable. In the first poem he writes that he learned his "only song" by climbing down to riverbands to witness the "long rustle / of being and perishing" (7). Toward the end of the book he walks out into the fields and out of himself, seeking like the very stones of the earth "to be one / with the unearthly fires kindling and dying" (66), but the fields are as much the poem's ten sections as they are any literal landscape. He describes himself as "dumped alive / and dying" (14) into his bed. Such casually paired terms for life and death are commonplace enough. Renewal and extinction are linked as always by the temporal process that extends from one to the other. In moments of change, ends and origins come together. Neither surprised nor enlightened, we are shown a familiar concept and set at ease. Yet some of the details supporting this theme are unusual: at birth, his daughter turns blue when her umbilical cord is cut, seeming to die for a moment. Her tie to the resources of the womb's darkness is severed and she begins to forget what she had been, her "limbs shaking / as the memories rush out of them" (6). That loss will always be with her, like the imprint of a void and anonymous self, a self she, like Kinnell and Roethke, would embrace again. Already her "featherless arms" are "clutching at the emptiness" (7).

From the first pages, it is apparent that Kinnell's binarism is unstable and reversible. Kinnell wants to make the opposite terms of polarities coalesce. His daughter Maud is born "clotted with celestial cheesiness' (6); she glows "with the astral violet / of the underlife." "Cheesiness" suggests both ripeness and cheesy degeneration: "celestial" renders both meanings oxymoronic. Dramatic as Kinnell's narrative is, his main emphasis is verbal. He is less interested in the experience of birth than in the changes he can ring on the words we use to describe it. His daughter's birth occurs at the outset; it establishes the verbal ground on which the rest of the book is written, the vocabulary whose first association Kinnell will both reinforce and invert.

The verb "to suck," for example, is only used a few times, but it is still given a double meaning. Maud "enters the headhold / which starts sucking her forth" (6); as she "sucks / air" and screams "her first song," she seems both to arrive and depart. The language is forceful but affirmative. Yet we soon read of "the sucked / carcass" of a hen killed by a weasel, and Kinnell later wills his twentieth-century brain to the fly, "that he may suck on it and die" (43). Nothing felicitous remains in those usages, but they are still linked with the earlier connotations. With his lover ("she who lies halved / beside me"), he watches bees "sucking / the blossom-dust / from the pear-tree" (68). In time the bees will be "burned down into flies" and thus be connected with more demonic sucking. Like lovers, the bees will only be whole when paired with their verbal opposites.

The verbal metamorphoses are often more complicated. When Maud awakens, "the green / swaddlings tear open" (5). Her consciousness begins as a ceremonial violence against substance: "a filament or vestment / tears." The sacrament of birth is a rude but celebratory opening. As Maud's "black eye / opens," so too will she someday "open / this book, even if it is the book of nightmares" (8). In the next poem, Kinnell looks into "the opened cadaver / of hen." In a mass of tiny eggs, he reaches toward "the icy pulp / of what is" (13), a cosmic point retaining only the abstract arc of the egg: "I have felt the zero / freeze itself around the finger dipped slowly in." Linked with eggs and origins, the word "open" undergoes a series of changes. He sees the Northern Lights "opening across the sky and vanishing" (13), illuminating themselves so thoroughly that they disappear. The word's ambivalent force increases with "the sweet, excremental / odor of opened cadaver" (37) and the decaying body whose "belly / opens like a poison nightflower" (44). Yet there are also visionary openings. The lovers feel their "bodies opened to the sky . . . the bodies of our hearts / opened" (59). Meanwhile he has described the "opened tail of peacock" and the opened bodies of dead birds. The resonance of the word becomes broad enough for him to write that "a way opens" into "everything I ever craved and lost" (67). Eventually, any use of the word implies all its meanings; none are exclusively positive or negative. In the final pages the openings are kaleidoscopic. A violinist puts his sorrow "into the opened

palm / of the wood" (74). Each ordinary opening is imbued with everything opened or closed. The poet feels the bones of his foot "ripple together in the communion / of the step" and "open out / in front into toes." His stride opens outward "to dissolve into the future" (73). And opening is a temporal and hierarchical nexus for a vision embodied in linguistic transformations. Among discarded rubbish on earth and simultaneously in the heavens, "in the hole torn open in the body of the Archer" (74), the dead repossess their beginning in their end. The poem also opens itself in closure; Kinnell compares it to a sky-diver "opening his arms" as he falls.

The variations on individual words are also woven together into larger patterns. Each important element of his diction, for example, is cast several times into imagery of death, imagery that occurs in each poem. The individual words are also continually aligned in new combinations. One perceives, overall, a broad vision worked into and out of the language itself. Through these interlocking images, Kinnell would demonstrate that language coheres beneath a surface of differences.

For a poet like Merwin, or for novelists like Beckett and Burroughs, that covert verbal matrix sets conclusive limits to everything we can say. Language for them is a tool whose use and function are predetermined. Moreover, we are shaped and possessed by the words we utter. The mouth, as Merwin writes, is "the door at the base of the skull where now the performers enter each with his eye fixed on the waiting instrument."[1] For those writers, submission to language occasionally prompts the kind of ecstasy Yeats associated with the experience of being taken up and used by historical destiny. More often, however, they see language as either ironic or suffocating. Language is the only form of self-consciousness; it is an index to all human action. Kinnell reacts differently to the same data; for him, as for Whitman, or for Robert Duncan, the celebration of the warp and weft of words is intrinsically liberating. Yet in Kinnell's book the interconnectedness of language sometimes becomes so pervasive that all change disappears before the obsessive reduction of each verbal difference to the same message. At that point, celebration yields to despair, and Kinnell's tone edges toward Merwin's. Yet Kinnell never follows the project to its paralyzed conclusion. His Whitmanesque democratization of language does, however, infuse a strain of melancholy into his poetry. This melancholic joy in the interrelations between words typifies the aesthetic of open forms in American poetry, and it reflects a covert awareness that America's history includes more dubious public achievements. If it willfully and optimistically reverses much that Marxist aesthetics suggests about the social pressures exerted through speech, implicitly arguing that language can overcome history by compensating for it, it also testifies fatalistically to history's inescapable determinism. Yet the dream, however often it is thwarted, persists.

For Kinnell, this dream parts from the modernist revulsion with language as the foremost evidence that human thought degenerates into materiality. Kinnell's poetic travels the same hierarchy in reverse. Like Norman O. Brown, he believes language can redeem the body by elevating it to consciousness. Language and consciousness can come into their own full power only by occupying the territory of the physical world. The mind's descent into the body, like the hunter's dream while he sleeps in the bear's carcass, is a submission to flesh that brings enlightenment:

And the brain kept blossoming
all through the body, until the bones themselves
    could think,

and the genitals sent out wave after wave of holy
    desire
until even the dead brain cells
surged and fell in god-like, androgynous fantasies—
and I understood
the unicorn's phallus could have risen, after all,
directly out of thought itself.

        (59)

When the brain blossoms through the body, consciousness enables substances to be self-aware. In the verbal connectiveness of *The Book of Nightmares* we are to see the brain blossoming through the body of language, creating a collective life that compensates for a unity the nation has never achieved. The verbal blossoming renders human thought and the materiality of language copresent to one another. Then, as in Roethke's ecstatic visions, the center of the self is everywhere; like an instinct, thought seems to originate in the senses. Inevitably, the imagination is sexualized, and thought becomes an organic origin: "The unicorn's phallus could have risen, after all, / directly out of thought itself." Everything has the potential to flower verbally. Toward the end of the book, he walks out "among the stones of the field, / each sending up its ghost-bloom / into the starlight" (66), his rebirth signaled when "an eerie blue light blooms / on all the ridges of the world" (68).

Kinnell's sense of flowering recalls Williams's dedication to that image throughout his career. For both poets, as for Roethke, flowering is an essential metaphor for unfolding form. As the image of flowering accumulates associations in *The Book of Nightmares*, it unifies what seem contradictory emotions of ecstasy and despair. It is a figure that both dramatizes and transcends its constitutive binarism. Maud awakens as a blue flower opening and grows in concert with all organic life, her hair "spouting" and her gums "budding." Yet flowering also suggests isolated, self-witnessed form: "the rose would bloom no one would see it" (13). Kinnell writes that Maud will remember, beyond the reach of consciousness, the songs she heard in infancy, not "the songs / of light . . . but a blacker / rasping flowering" (7). Later he remembers the hen's "deathsmells, / blooming again in the starlight" (30). Unwilling to accept change, Maud tells flowers not to die (49). But we are already the fruit of dead flowers. In battlefields, "the belly / opens like a poison nightflower" (44); there the only seed is the "wrung-out / blossom of caput mortuum flower" (67). For Kinnell, as for Roethke, the flower suggests a violate, emptied selfhood: "it has a way / of uttering itself in place of itself" (*FH*, 58). The invisible life of a flower "burns up. Its drift is to be nothing" (*FH*, 58). Kinnell dreams of an acre "where the kissing flower may bloom, / which kisses you so long your bones explode under its lips" (43). For Kinnell, as for Baudelaire, flowering mingles death and consummation. When a fly caught in a spider's net gives up its struggle, Kinnell says its wings "flutter out the music blooming with failure / of one who gets ready to die" (35). Then he imagines an old drunk's relief in unconsciousness: "I blacked out into oblivion by that crack in the curb where the forget-me blooms." The mind flowers into emptiness. As the self's flower opens, the germinating seed and the falling petals, origin and end, are combined in the arc of a single gesture. All flowering is secondary, derivative, but in that derivation memory and anticipation are folded together. As Kinnell wrote earlier, "The petals begin to fall, in self-forgiveness" (*FH*, 58).

This rich, obsessive intratextual play of difference and repetition has its apotheosis in a sequence of visionary landscapes. There the figure of flowering is integrated with imagery of light and stone:

I come to a field
glittering with the thousand sloughed skins
of arrowheads, stones
which shuddered and leapt forth
to give themselves into the broken hearts
of the living,
who gave themselves back, broken, to the stone.
(65)

. . .

I walk out from myself,
among the stones of the field,
each sending up its ghost-bloom
into the starlight, to float out
over the trees, seeking to be one
with the unearthly fires kindling and dying.

        (66)

These landscapes are linguistic fields of force in tension, sites of verbal transformation situated between verbal opposites. They seek to overcome a melancholic past and a fatalistic future, a history of remembered and anticipated failure, by combining them in a figural present. The landscapes call up the elemental underlife of the earth and draw near to us the movements of constellations. They are composed in a verbal territory neither exclusively internal nor external. Kinnell has said that "when you do get deep enough within yourself, deeper than the level of 'personality,' you are suddenly outside yourself, everywhere."[2] His landscapes, at once intimate and open, recall the landscapes at the end of the last three poems in Roethke's "North American Sequence." For Kinnell, they grow out of the secure rhetorical territory, the idealized American space, in which the transfigurations of "The Avenue Bearing the Initial of Christ into the New World" take place. But this terrain has now become an open, unprotected site for unpredictable verbal changes. What was a static repository is now a field in linguistic motion.

Established by elaborate verbal echoes and consummated in Kinnell's visionary landscapes, this textual field of change is also reinforced by explicit structural linkage. Kinnell has always been fond of structures that link beginnings and endings, and *The Book of Nightmares* uses them extensively. Most of the poems, for example, either repeat or rewrite their title near their conclusion.[3] Thus we expect the final poem to echo the first. In both poems a small twig-fire set on old ashes burn in the rain, and a black bear, "his fur glistening / in the rain" and his head "nodding from side / to side," sniffs blossom-smells, eats a few flowers and "trudges away."[4] Kinnell's daughter Maud is born in the first poem, and his son Fergus is born in the last. The balance amplifies the poem's multiple sense of completion and renewal. Thus the first poem is not merely repeated in the last; it is simultaneously completed and begun again. The origin (zero) and the beginning (one) recur in the number of the final poem, ten: "one / and zero / walk off together" (73). The dead, he writes in a gesture against history, "lie / empty, filled, at the beginning" (74).

The old mystical formula, "as above, so below," which Kinnell quotes (68), reaffirms the poem's converging categories of verbal opposition. Temporally—the beginning and the end, past and future, two births separated in time, become copresent; spatially—the various settings, the isolated lovers, the whole physical breadth of the narrative, are clasped together in the poem; and hierarchically—heaven and earth, mind and body, are transformed into self-regarding images of one another. With these opposing terms equated, the poet can imagine that all speech is simultaneous. The poems, we are to feel, are all equivalent; they traverse the same ground.[5] The form is the emptiness awaiting the words that fill it. ⟨. . .⟩[6]

As an accomplished form, as a purely verbal system, the book almost surmounts every obstacle to its fulfillment. Yet Kinnell, following an historical imperative, deliberately subverts the self-referential perfection of the book's formal development. In the sixth poem, near the center of *The Book of Nightmares*, he opens the book to precisely those historical circumstances it cannot undo:

> "That you Captain? Sure,
> sure I remember—I still hear you
> lecturing at me on the intercom, *Keep your guns up,*
>     *Burnsie!*
> and then screaming, *Stop shooting, for crissake,*
>     *Burnsie,*
> *those are friendlies!* But crissake, Captain,
> I'd already started, burst
> after burst, little black pajamas jumping
> and falling . . . and remember that pilot
> who'd bailed out over the North,
> how I shredded him down to catgut on his strings?
> one of his slant eyes, a piece
> of his smile, sail past me
> every night right after the sleeping pill . . .
>
> "It was only
> that I loved the *sound*
> of them, I guess I just loved
> the *feel* of them sparkin' off my hands . . ."
>                                          (41–42)[7]

Much of the rhetoric of this monologue is essentially untouched by the verbal matrix of the surrounding poem, and that is exactly the point. It testifies to the anguish that makes the poem's vision at once necessary and insufficient. Like Whitman meditating over the dead of the Civil War, Kinnell confronts those people on whom America has conferred eternal life, but unlike Whitman Kinnell realizes his poetry cannot alleviate that horror. This history, of course, is more than American, "Christian man" having "exterminated . . . Jews, Moslems, witches, mystical seekers, / black men, Asians, and . . . every one of them for his own good" (42). Yet we have our own particularly American history of genocide—"a whole continent of red men for living in unnatural community / and at the same time having relations with the land." This history did away with the very collective organic life toward which we now aspire with futility. And the compensatory myth of resurrection has its secular American version. "The Dead," we delude ourselves, "Shall be Raised Incorruptible" in America's inclusive form. "Can it ever be true," Kinnell asks, "all bodies, one body, one light / made of everyone's darkness together" (30). The ecclesiastical dream is finally wedded to its democratic realization. Moreover, the verbal interconnectedness of *The Book of Nightmares*, which is its chief accomplishment and its central aesthetic, is itself an expression of a dream of democratic relations.

The verbal interconnectedness Kinnell works into his poem is incredibly elaborate. Through it, the narratives are absolved of their individual anxiety or misery, but they are also thereby dissolved into the play of discourse. The language's interconnectedness absorbs all temporal process, seeking to replace history with its own inclusive space. Yet it cannot transform the national history it acknowledges. In accepting its American heritage, the book obliges itself to fail: our *"corpse will not stop burning"* (41). Form's transforming fire makes flesh, blood, bones, air, earth and water, light and darkness, interchangeable. Yet when this equalizing process is given a national name and an historical past, one variable but democratic substance pervades it all:

> carrion
> caput mortuum,
> orts,
> pelf,
> fenks,
> sordes,
> gurry dumped from hospital trashcans.
>                                          (41)[8]

The book's mythic, archetypal form can never wholly surmount its singular American content. "This earthward gesture / of the sky-diver" is Kinnell's American version of the myth of Christian martyrdom. The formal closure of the poem can never be complete. The first and last section is each "a torn half / whose other" it keeps "seeking across time," and the traversal across time, through history, makes the fusion of the two halves impossible. At once calm and anxious, ethereal and mundane, *The Book of Nightmares* offers us a body suspended between communal fusion and communal disintegration. Vision and history confront one another in Kinnell's major work; they are mutually causative, reactive, and finally irreconcilable. The verbal apotheosis of *The Book of Nightmares* is also its failure.

*Notes*

The following books by Galway Kinnell are abbreviated and documented internally: *FH—Flower Herding on Mount Monadnock* (Boston: Houghton Mifflin, 1964); *MM—Mortal Acts, Mortal Words* (Boston: Houghton Mifflin, 1980); *WS—Walking Down the Stairs; Selections from Interviews* (Ann Arbor: University of Michigan Press, 1978). *The Book of Nightmares* (Boston: Houghton Mifflin, 1971) is documented internally by page number only.

1. Merwin, *The Carrier of Ladders* (New York: Atheneum, 1970), p. 94.

2. "'Deeper Than Personality': A Conversation with Galway Kinnell," ed. Philip L. Gerber and Robert J. Gemmett, *Iowa Review*, 1, No. 2 (1970), 133.

   Cf. Kinnell's "Poetry, Personality, and Death," *Field*, No. 4 (Spring, 1971), pp. 65–66: "We move toward a poetry in which the poet seeks an inner liberation by going so deeply into himself—into the worst of himself as well as the best—that he suddenly finds he is everywhere."

3. In several poems a specific image occurs at the beginning and the end: a reference to "cursed bread" in the first poem, a description of being "sprawled face down" on a mattress of hen feathers in the second, an image of an old Crone foretelling the future in the third. In the sixth poem, the first and last sections end with the same exclamation: *"Lieutenant! / This corpse will not stop burning!"* Sometimes the image is altered, but the effect is comparable. The fifth poem has an image of "the gaze / from the spider's clasped forebrains" in the first section and an image of "the light / from the joined hemisphere of the spider's eyes" in the last. There are numerous other repetitions throughout the book. A few examples will suffice. In the second poem Kinnell sees "the cosmos spelling itself" when he reads the shoulder blade of a ram, a common method of discovering hidden knowledge; in the next poem, the Crone reads Kinnell's own shoulder bones. In the eighth poem, a sheriff presses the "whorls / and tented archways" of Kinnell's fingers into a police blotter; in the next poem, he finds himself "alive / in the whorled / archway of the fingerprint of all things." Sometimes the second reference is a comic inversion, a technique that builds to the healing laughter of the final poem. In the second poem, a rooster groans out *"it is the empty morning"* to signal Peter's denial of Christ. Two poems later, a deskman in a cheap hotel forgets to bang *"it is morning"* on the sheet metal door.

4. Both of the first and last poems have an image of the Archer: "the Archer lay / sucking the icy biestings of the cosmos, / in his crib of stars" (7); "the hole torn open in the body of the Archer" (74).

5. The sense of formal equivalence is reinforced by having each of the poems divided into seven sections, a division that also creates the sort of parallel structures we found in "The Procupine." Though the breaks here generally come at logical points in the narrative, they are not, however, strictly necessary. They therefore create an

almost diffident sense of reoccurrence. In "To the Roots: An Interview with Galway Kinnell," *Contemporary Poetry in America*, ed. Robert Boyers (New York: Shocken, 1974), James J. McKenzie asks "Did you have the seven-part divisions of each poem from the beginning also?" Kinnell replies: "No. But the sections seemed to be coming out that way, so I made them all come out that way. It's clear that some of the poems could have been divided into eight or six parts quite as easily" (p. 244).

6. Cf.: "that enormous emptiness / carved out of such tiny beings as we are / asks to be filled" (*MM*, 15).
7. Cf. Kinnell's comments in an interview (*WS*, 109–10), in which he describes how this passage conflates references to both the Vietnam and Korean wars.
8. Kinnell is sometimes fond of archaic diction, especially when he can show that the history of the language can be drawn out of its contemporary materiality and made co-present in the poem.

# CAROLYN KIZER

## 1925–

Carolyn Kizer was born in Spokane, Washington, on December 10, 1925. Her mother was a biologist and her father was a lawyer. She graduated from Sarah Lawrence with a B.A. in 1945. She then spent a year studying in China before returning to Seattle to study with Theodore Roethke at the University of Washington. She married Charles Stimson Bullitt in 1948 and bore three children. She divorced her husband in 1954 and five years later helped found *Poetry Northwest*. Kizer edited this Seattle-based magazine until 1964 when she traveled to Pakistan to study Urdu and Bengali poetry under the auspices of the U.S. State Department. In 1966 she took a job with the National Endowment for the Arts as the director of their literary programs. She left Washington in 1970 and taught at the University of North Carolina at Chapel Hill for four years. Since then she has been poet-in-residence at several universities. In 1975 she married John Woodbridge, an architect.

Her first book of poetry, *The Ungrateful Garden*, was published in 1961, and two other volumes followed in 1965 and 1971. Among these early collections the poem "Pro Femina" is probably best known. Written after Kizer read Simone de Beauvoir's *The Second Sex*, this poem focuses on the lives of "liberated" women writers. In 1984 she published two long-awaited books, *Yin* and *Mermaids in the Basement: Poems for Women*. Both works continue the open dialogue with feminist ideology which characterizes her earlier poetry. Both were highly acclaimed and *Yin* received the 1985 Pulitzer Prize for poetry. Although Kizer has published only five books of poetry, her reputation as a leading American poet is secure. Today she lives with her husband near Berkeley, California.

Despair is Carolyn Kizer's place ⟨in *Knock upon Silence*⟩, especially in "A Month in Summer," a sequence of notations charting the end of an affair. This poem is beautiful as some short stories are beautiful; not too little, not too much, not even too much moderation, the experience is weighed and judged with remarkable tact. What is fine is not only the words but the tact which separates them in formal groups so that they do not sprawl along the road to claim our attention. And the loneliness is given partly by bare sentences and, more than that, by the pathetic advances of the victim toward other people, her father, her children, the visit home; and then the return to a place abandoned by the household gods. This sequence adds to the store of the human by the dignity of its tone, which claims only that degree of self-pity proper to a reasonable victim in pain. Miss Kizer's new collection also includes "Pro Femina," a causerie on Woman which is likely to become famous for all the wrong reasons. In fact, it is brash, clever, and entirely pointless, a mistake: it should have been handed over to a journalist. "Pro Femina" is Miss Kizer as High Priestess, trying to out-Beauvoir Beauvoir, the Voice of American Clever Women, the State Department's Woman in Pakistan. As good luck would have it, though, it is possible to forget "Pro Femina" and concentrate on the Chinese translations—imitations, as she rightly calls them—and the versions of Tu Fu, which are full of sweet cadences.—DENIS DONOGHUE, "The Store of the Human," *HdR*, Winter 1965–66, p. 603

Carolyn Kizer's poems ⟨in *Midnight Was My Cry*⟩ often go on for too long and there is a sense of diffuseness about her new and selected volume. But also lots of intelligence, a relaxed sense of how much she can do and a less than total infatuation with her own powers. "Singing Aloud" begins with the admission that:

> We all have our faults. Mine is trying to write poems.
> New scenery, someone I like, anything sets me off!
> I hear my own voice going on, like a god or an oracle,
> That cello-tone, intuition. That bell-note of wisdom!

But the self-deprecation is never mawkish; she accepts the fact that when a new poem comes along "I no longer rush out to impose it on friendly colleagues," and ends up as a poet talking to the animals:

> When I go to the zoo, the primates and I, in communion,
> Hoot at each other, or signal with earthy gestures.
> We must move further out of town, we musical birds and animals
> Or they'll lock us up like the apes, and control us forever.

It is easy to like and take seriously the presence behind these lines:

> The moonlight on my bed keeps me awake;
> Living alone now, aware of the voices of evening,

A child weeping at nightmares, the faint love-cries of
    a woman,
Everything tinged by terror or nostalgia. . . .
This collection might well have included "Pro Femina," a
witty and effective rallying cry.

But Carolyn Kizer may be too easy to take in; she never
gets really *angry* in poems, never dips into what the excited
*Sunday Times* reviewer referred to (in connection with Diane
Wakoski) as "the hive of her anger."—WILLIAM H. PRITCHARD,
"Youngsters, Middlesters, and Some Old Boys," *HdR*, Spring
1972, pp. 124–25

It is a dangerous interval, the one somewhere between
juvenilia and senilia, when poets decide they must represent
their achievement (concilia?) at the retrospective pitch, the
abyss of "selection": the danger is one of sclerosis, for the
trouble with getting it all together, as we say now, is getting
anything, afterwards, apart. Consider Carolyn Kizer's case. To
thirty-five poems from *The Ungrateful Garden* (1961) and to
eight (less shapely, more ambitious) from *Knock upon Silence*
(1965), both books being out of print, she has added another
sixteen from the last decade, two of these poems no more than
newspaper leaders (or followers), one or two others no less than
autovoyeurism, the remainder as fine as anything she has
done, unresolved but inescapable, learned but not knowing,
fluent yet anything but easy—say, then, she has reinforced her
canon by some dozen first-rate poems, observant, solicitous,
lithe: where does the new emphasis thereby fall, the refinement
and recognition, now, of certain shared contours, of welcomed
limits? An answer is brought home to me as much by what is
left out as by what is committed to the leavings: an early
villanelle "On a Line from Julian" has given way to—or been
outdistanced by—one "On a Line from Sophocles". And the
new line is "Time, time, my friend, makes havoc everywhere"—a poetical sententia which must be earned, as it is
here, by a concrescence of experience, disastrous, wide-
ranging, amical. To forego the Apostate and his futile rebellion
against the odds of history for the all-seeing Greek, tragic in his
presentment of events but articulating so much more life in his
very acknowledgment of what happens—that is the burden
Miss Kizer so gracefully shoulders here. The additional poems
are not fractious, merely frank in their response to hopes and
horrors alike ("for women learn to be a holy show . . . but we
break out of the harem of history!"), and there is no effort
merely to will The Enemy out of the way by stamping a tiny
foot ("You failed, I failed . . . we are true neither to life nor
nature, / but perhaps to one another as we write"). Instead, the
Kizer poem "wrapt in a caul of vulnerability", weds chaos and
failure, welcomes pain and farce, "signalling, / self-amazed, its
willingness to endure", for as the poet writes to an attempted
suicide to whom she sends, with her words, white azaleas:

        . . . we live in wonder,
Blaze in a cycle of passion and apprehension
Though once we lay and waited for a death.
The effect, *en gros* and better still, in fine, of this selection is to
dispel the dangers of its program. She has submitted her figure
to her fate, has worked out of the exoticisms which once rather
specialized and so limited Carolyn Kizer—this is to say, she has
given up impersonating Mae West and Shanghai Lily and your
all-purpose Women's Libertine for the sake and the success of a
style we may recognize anywhere—in Holland, in Ohio; in
dudgeon, in delight—as consistently Carolingian, fruitfully
injured:

This bronze is mortal, gaping in defeat,
The form that wombed it split to let it be.
    —RICHARD HOWARD, "Pursuits and Followings,"
    *Poetry*, Aug. 1972, pp. 302–3

⟨. . .⟩ I was more than usually pleased to read the latest work
of two poets I have long admired, Carolyn Kizer and Robert
Watson. As always, I found its effectiveness unquestionable. I
have often heard the comment made by men and intended as a
compliment, "She doesn't write like a woman." Kizer would
find that no compliment. Hers, though, is clearly a woman's
consciousness, and the poetry that comes out of it is strong
indeed. Her third book, *Midnight Was My Cry*, is a collection
of recent verse as well as selections from her two previous
volumes. By virtue of its skill, depth, and variety, it should
establish her as one of our better poets.

I suppose what impresses me most about this book is its
mastery of different types of poems, from love poems to
narrative poems to poems in the Oriental manner, to name a
few. I especially like the latter, perhaps because they remind
me of my own earlier attachment to Oriental verse. Such
poems as "Winter Song," "The Skein" (which reminds me of
Li Ch'ing Chao's verse), "For Jan at Bar Maria," "Amusing
Our Daughters," and "Summer near the River" show how she
has adapted the Oriental tradition to suit her own voice. This is
the ending of "Summer near the River":

When you return, reeking of fish and beer,
There is salt dew in your hair. Where have you been?
Your clothes weren't that wrinkled hours ago, when
    you left.
You couldn't have loved someone else, after loving
    me!
I sulk and sigh, dawdling by the window.
Later, when you hold me in your arms
It seems, for a moment, the river ceases flowing.
Throughout we hear the echoes of those centuries-old Chinese
voices, but up-dated, made more distinctly erotic, more frankly
female.

I also like the poems about the poet's mother. They are not
sentimental; nor are they examinations of neuroticism à la
Plath or Sexton. In them Kizer's mother emerges as a strong,
admirable woman. "A Long Line of Doctors" is a good
example. It is a witty, brilliant poem and I am dazzled by the
craftsmanship and energy of it. It begins:

Mother, picked for jury duty, managed to get through
A life of Voltaire in three volumes. Anyway, she
    knew
Before she half-heard a word, the dentist was guilty.
As a seminarist whose collar is his calling
Chokes up without it, baring his naked neck,
The little, furtive dentist is led across the deck,
Mounts the plank, renders a nervous cough.
Mother frowns, turns a page, flicks a fly-speck
With her fingernail. She will push him off!
And even though the poem is rather long, it never loses its
momentum.

"The Great Blue Heron," which deals with her mother's
death, is to me the most moving poem in the collection. After
seeing a heron on the beach, the poet remembers seeing the
"spectral bird" years before and running to fetch her mother,
only to return and find the heron gone. She says "In the middle
of my loss, I realized she knew: / My mother knew what he
was." The bird becomes the symbol of loss, specifically the loss
of her mother as the poet realizes that for fifteen years the bird
has stood patiently in her mind,

Waiting upon the day
When, like gray smoke, a vapor
Floating into the sky,
A handful of paper ashes,
My mother would drift away.

This is one of her most emotional poems, but its emotion is kept under firm control. Kizer is always the good craftsman.

A few poems do not measure up to the majority. "Singing Aloud," for example, promises to be another good poem on the subject of writing poetry itself but is marred by an incongruous ending. And some of the poems dealing with classical mythology seems less strong than the others. But even these are marked by her insight and learning. I can only agree with John L'Heureux on the dust jacket that "she is a first-class poet." —KATHRYN STRIPLING BYER, GR, Spring 1973, pp. 117–18

---

## DOMINIC CHEUNG
"Carolyn Kizer and Her Chinese Imitations" (1978)
*China and the West*, eds. William Tay,
Ying-hsiung Chou, and Heh-hsiang Yuan
1980, pp. 77–84

In the acknowledgements which preface her book *Knock upon Silence*, Carolyn Kizer confesses the debt she owes to Arthur Waley's translations of Chinese poems.[1] It is from Waley's translations that Kizer derives the material for the group of her own poems which appear in the section of her book titled "Chinese Imitations." These eight poems are dedicated to Waley whose translations Kizer has read, she frankly admits, since her childhood, adding that "like so many of my contemporaries, my debt and my devotion to him is incalculable."[2]

Admittedly, it would be difficult to talk about the impact of the Chinese poems themselves on Carolyn Kizer's poems since her "imitations" are essentially imitations of Arthur Waley's translations. However, although the risks of any influence study run high, an examination of the sources available to Kizer is appropriate in order to furnish a clearer appreciation of what Kizer has undertaken.

Waley modestly assures us in the preface of his translations that his Chinese friends attest to the closeness of his translations, "closer, they have sometimes been kind enough to say, than those of any other translater."[3] Nevertheless, certain inaccuracies do exist in Waley's work; quite inexplicably, for instance, the Chinese poem "Reciting Alone in the Mountain" is translated as "Madly Singing in the Mountain."[4] Twice removed from the original, Carolyn Kizer's "Singing Aloud" is evidence of yet another stage in the metamorphosis of the poem.[5]

In another instance, Kizer claims that two of her works are derived from Arthur Waley's translation of *The Book of Songs*, a selection of ancient odes which were composed around the tenth century B.C. In actuality, Kizer's poems are based on the Waley translation of the "Tzu-yeh Songs", ballads written in the third century A.D. The confusion is compounded further by the fact that the fourth of the five "Tzu-yeh Songs" which Waley translated is in fact taken from the tenth-century A.D. "Mo-ch'ou Songs".

However, the effect of these inaccuracies on Carolyn Kizer's poems is minimal since she is engaged in the creation of imitations derived from the Chinese works rather than translating the works from the original. On the other hand, considering the conciseness of the Chinese language and the resulting ambiguities and indirectness such a language poses when employed in poetry, it is rather amazing (particularly for those versed in the Chinese poems themselves) to note that Carolyn Kizer has effectively captured the subtlest nuances of the Chinese works while often bringing latent connotations to full and precise imagistic expression.

It is never a matter of referring Kizer's pieces to the Chinese poems themselves or vice versa since Kizer's works successfully demonstrate her sensitive explorations of material available to her. What she finally voices in her own poems is no longer the solitary cry of the oriental woman, but that which belongs neither to the east nor to the west and is not confined in terms of either space or time. Three stanzas of Kizer's "Summer near the River" are modelled after the "Tzu-yeh Songs." The last stanza, which actually belongs to the "Mo-ch'ou Songs" and which Waley mistook as belonging to the "Tzu-yeh Songs" is gracefully combined with the "Tzu-yeh" verses in the form of a dramatic monologue which utilizes all the episodes inherent in the original poems.

The word "Tzu-yeh" is a somewhat meaningless title of one of the largest group of songs from the Six Dynasties in China. According to a historical treatise, one of the original songs was said to have been written by a maiden named Tzu-yeh. The treatise goes on to describe, in all seriousness, the singing of two ghosts in two households of the T'ai-yuan period (A.D. 376–396). Since the ghosts kept singing the words "Tzu-yeh," the historians concluded that Tzu-yeh must have been the creator of these songs!

Carolyn Kizer's version of the "Tzu-yeh" assumes the title of "Summer near the River." In this work, two images immediately present themselves: the image of summer and that of a flowing river. Traditionally, summer symbolizes passion, the season of ripening love. In Kizer's poem, it is a season when life forces surge strongly but are counteracted by the cold determinism of the river, a symbol of the relentless flow, the clearly defined course of life. Where summer presents a wide variation of color in nature, the river, on the other hand, suggests a certain fixedness by virtue of its defined path.

The river and summer are thus two antithetical images which Carolyn Kizer uses, tying them together through the use of internal rhymes such as "Sum*mer* n*ear* the Ri*ver*." By persistently stressing the grief which is inherent in the symbol of summer, the poet is able to extend herself into the realm of dramatic details. The first two stanzas:

> I have carried my pillow to the windowsill
> And try to sleep, with my damp arms crossed upon it
> But no breeze stirs the tepid morning.
> Only I stir . . . Come, tease me a little!
> With such cold passion, so little teasing play,
> How long can we endure our life together?
>
> No use. I put on your long dressing-gown!
> The untied sash trails over the dusty floor.
> I kneel by the window, prop up your shaving mirror
> And pluck my eyebrows.
> I don't care if the robe slides open
> Revealing a crescent of belly, a tan thigh.
> I can accuse that non-existent breeze . . .[6]

In Arthur Waley's translations of two of the "Tzu-yeh Songs" we read:

> I have brought my pillow and am lying at the
>   northern window,
> So come to me and play with me awhile.
> With so much quarreling and so few kisses
> How long do you think our love can last?
>
> I will carry my coat and not put on my belt;
> With unpainted eyebrows I will stand at the front
>   window.
> My tiresome petticoat keeps on flapping about:
> If it opens a little, I shall blame the spring wind.[7]

A word-for-word translation of the Chinese original reads:

carry—pillow-north—window—lie
you (man/boy)—come—to—me (woman/girl)—
    play/tease
little—joy—more—clashes
to pity each other—can—how long.
carry—gown—not—tie—sash
lightly—brows—out—front—window
gauze—dress—easy—wavers
little—exposure—blame/accuse—east-wind.

When compared to Waley's translation of the Chinese work, Kizer's verses are, psychologically, much richer in their depiction of the dejected woman. The opening lines "I have carried my pillow to the windowsill / And try to sleep, with my damp arms crossed upon it," direct our attention immediately to the meanings associated with the heat of summer. Physically confined to her chamber, the woman's discomfort is heightened by the oppressive warmth which, in turn, creates a sense of stasis since "no breeze stirs . . . / Only I stir." On the psychological level, there is the same sense of oppression which is manifested by physical reality. Thus when the woman moves toward the window, she is not only seeking physical relief from the "tepid" morning, but, locked in her own ego, is trying to establish contact with the outside world. By providing her own details, Kizer thus amplifies the emotional tenor of the original work without departing from the basic thrust of Waley's "I have brought my pillow and am lying at the northern window."

Although each stanza of Kizer's poem is in fact an independent poem, she has managed, by reversing the order of the original poems, to melt the disparate elements into a single unified poem. The invitation "Come, tease me a little!" followed by "With such cold passion, so little teasing play, / How long can we endure our life together?" for instance, successfully prepares us for the actions which follow in the next stanza, where the woman, having failed to engage the man in a "little teasing," rises and slips on his dressing gown. Kizer's own use of the pronoun "your" with regard to the man's dressing gown, may, at first glance, seem immaterial. Several suggestions are implied, however, by the woman's use of her companion's dressing gown. The malaise which is created by the heat in the first verse is now paralleled by an emotional lassitude: the woman does not bother to dress, but merely slips on her companion's dressing gown allowing the untied sash to trail on the floor. It might have been suggested, too, that by wearing her companion's robe, the woman subconsciously strives for the physical contact which is not in the offing from the man whose passion is "cold" and who is so little inclined toward the "little teasing play."

By having the woman wear her lover's robe, Kizer effectively sets the stage, so to speak, for the crucial closing lines in the second verse where the woman says "I don't care if the robe slides open / Revealing a crescent of belly, a tan thigh." Elsewhere in her poem "Hiding Our Love," a modification of Wu-ti's "People Hide Their Love", Kizer again uses the seemingly casual detail as a means of bringing certain facts to light without overt reference to them. In Waley's translation of Wu-ti's poem we read:

Round my waist I wear a double sash
I dream that it binds us both with a same-heart knot.[8]

In Kizer's version she says:

The sash of my dress wraps twice around my waist
I wish it bound the two of us together.[9]

In Wu-ti's poem, the sash is a symbol of platonic love, the illusory bond between two hearts. In Kizer's poem, the sash is utilized to convey two levels of meaning: a separation between lovers has affected the woman; that the sash can be wound twice around her waist suggests that her health has failed and that she has grown thin. By winding the sash around her waist, the woman, undoubtedly, is reminded of the binding power of love, hence the words "I wish it bound the two of us together."

Similarly, in "Summer near the River," the trailing sash, a seemingly small detail, is utilized to convey several levels of meaning. Where the sash in "Hiding Our Love" is a symbol of the woman's desire to be bound in love, the trailing sash in "Summer near the River" suggests a deteriorating relationship, a slackening of love on the part of the woman's companion. It is also a means of leading into the last lines of the verse where the robe slides open, blown apparently by a "nonexistent breeze" to reveal the "crescent of belly, [and] a tan thigh." The untied sash in Kizer's poem is a parallel to the fluttering gauze dress worn by the lady in the Chinese poem. In both instances, the seemingly casual dishabille is an attempt at seduction, but where the sliding robe reveals belly and thigh, the diaphanous gauze dress is allowed to flap open in the spring wind and perhaps "open a little."

The defiance in Kizer's "I don't care if the robe slides open / Revealing a crescent of belly, a tan thigh" is absent in the Chinese poem. The woman's defiance as well as the subjunctive mood in which she states that she "can accuse that nonexistent breeze" is weak because there is only the remotest possibility that a breeze would stir the "tepid morning." In the Chinese poem, whatever the "wavering" dress reveals is not mentioned and neither are reasons given as to what causes the dress to "waver" in the first place. The attention is thus drawn not to what the opening dress reveals, but rather, to why the spring wind is being used as an excuse for the dishabille and not the gauze dress or the deliberately unfastened sash.

In Kizer's poem, we learn of a waning interest on the man's part and the woman's suspicion of his infidelity later in the poem. Laying the blame on the "non-existent breeze" for the exposed belly and thigh thus lends a poignant air to the situation in the poem. For although she is aware of the "cold passion," the woman's pride is maintained sufficiently to the extent that the efforts to win back the man must appear casual and not actively sought. True desperation over an impending loss cannot be revealed, hence the feeble lie, that a wind, and a non-existent wind at that, has caused the robe to fall open.

In the third verse of "Summer near the River," the woman's pride is affirmed in the midst of her fears over her vagrant lover. She reveals that:

I am as monogamous as the North Star
But I don't want you to know it. You'd only take
    advantage.
While you are as fickle as spring sunlight.[10]

Her love and desire to hold on to her companion cannot be revealed to him, for in contrast to her steadfastness he is "as fickle as spring sunlight."

In comparing her lover to the spring sunlight, Kizer, once again, stays close to the astrological imagery used in the Chinese poem. In the "Tzu-yeh Songs," fidelity and faithlessness are described in terms of the North Star and the sun:

Where I am the dawn star of the North
Never shifting for thousands of years,
You bear the heart of the bright sun
East in the morning, west at dusk.[11]
                                    (my translation)

As an archetype, the sun is a representation of truth, righteousness and supremacy. Used in the "Tzu-yeh," the sun conceit is similar to the image employed by Donne in "A Valediction, Forbidding Mourning." In Donne's poem, lovers are bound as one by their love. As two separate entities, the poet sees himself as the active half which, when it "far doth roam," "leans and hearkens after" "the fixed foot," which "in the center sit."[12] In the "Tzu-yeh" and "Summer near the River," the path taken by the sun each day from east to west suggests not only the man's infidelity, but perhaps his natural inability to remain constant. For just as the sun may pass through northern skies at certain times of the year, it must, inevitably, move on in its established course leaving the Northern star which never shifts in a thousand years. The very inevitability of such a course in nature only heightens the harsh reality which exists in terms of the human love relationship.

It is not until the last two verses of the poem that Kizer introduces the image of the river, and where the passion associated with summer is identified with the man who is seen "striding toward the river," while the woman petulantly exclaims, "The cat means more to you than I." When he returns "reeking of fish and beer," the woman notes that:

> There is salt dew in your hair, where have you been?
> Your clothes weren't that wrinkled hours ago, when
>     you left.
> You couldn't have loved someone else, after loving
>     me.[13]

In her distress at the sight of her returning lover, all of the woman's senses are brought into play as she smells the beer and fish, notes the wrinkled clothes and salt dew in his hair.

The river is mentioned again in the closing lines of the poem when the man embraces the woman, causing her to say, "for a moment, the river ceases flowing."[14] The river, as we have previously noted, is a symbol of unrelenting fate. Specific applications of the symbol are made in turn to the man and the woman in "Summer near the River." The man, for instance, strides toward the river, and figuratively the act may be seen as the control he has over his life and fate. The woman's fate, on the other hand, rests on the man himself, her happiness and peace of mind depend on his uncertain love. Fate, like the relentless flow of the river, has already decreed a change in the relationship, but in the moment that the man embraces her, the woman feels that what is foreordained cannot possibly occur. In the light of her present ecstacy, the future without him is stalled, hence "for a moment, the river ceases flowing."

In the Chinese poem, the stilled river is placed in context of a separation between a woman and her lover. She sees him off on his journey, going "with him as far as Ch'u-shan." When he, against all social conventions, embraces her in public, she ecstatically says:

> For a moment you held me fast in your outstretched
>     arms.
> I thought the river stood still and did not flow.[15]

Here, as in "Summer near the River," a parting of the ways is in the offing, harshly determined perhaps by fate. The breach of socially accepted behavior is sufficient reason for the woman's ecstatic "I thought the river stood still and did not flow," but in terms of the river as a symbol of predetermined factors in life, it would seem that here, as in Kizer's poem, the ecstasy can, and does momentarily, halt the tide of fate. In the Chinese poem, the moment is crystallized by the illusion of the river's stillness, and the setting of mountains surrounding the embracing pair is fixed in a perfectly harmonious whole. While Carolyn Kizer's poems are not exact translations, they do utilize the substance, stylistics and subtle nuances of Chinese works. Where basically oriental allusions with no English equivalent appear, they are used as points of departure for Kizer's own personal experiences without jeopardy to the essential details of the original Chinese works. The graceful

artistry of Kizer's poems lies on the strength of the balance she has struck between her vision and that which is inherent in the Chinese poems, for her poems are never merely accurate copies of the Chinese poem, nor are they simply a vehicle.

It cannot be said that Kizer lacks originality in what she has undertaken to write, since what she has taken from the Chinese is synthesized by her own passion and sensitivity. The extent of this synthesis is seen in a comparison of her lines from "Winter Song" with those of Arthur Waley:

(1) So I go on, tediously on and on . . .
    We are separated, finally, not by death but by
    life.[16]

                                              (Kizer)

    On and on, always on and on
    Away from you, parted by a life-parting[17]
                                              (Waley)

(2) How can you and I meet face to face
    After our triumphant love?
    After our failure?[18]

                                              (Kizer)

    The way between is difficult and long,
    Face to face how shall we meet again?[19]
                                              (Waley)

In the lines quoted above, we see that Waley, like many established sinologists, has tended to present the original poem as closely as possible. With Carolyn Kizer's renditions, we sense for the first time an attempt at exploring the poems for meanings which go beyond the linguistic representations. With her lyric temperament and acute sensibilities, Kizer peels away at the different layers of metaphor, exhausting words and allusions of their ultimate meanings. Thus, although her works may be deemed interpretive, they, on occasion, exceed even the Chinese poems themselves, for the vibrancy which Kizer has infused into them.

*Notes*

1. Carolyn Kizer, *Knock upon Silence* (Seattle and London: Univ. of Washington Press, 1968). These are the words found in the beginning paragraph of her acknowledgments: "I have been reading the poetry of Arthur Waley since childhood, and, like so many of my contemporaries, my debt and my devotion to him is incalculable."

2. Ibid. In her notes following the poems, Kizer has singled out each poem's originality as follows: "The first three poems in the book are written in the style of Po Chu-I. 'Hiding Our Love' is modeled on a poem of the Emperor Wu-Ti. 'Night Sounds' and 'Summer near the River' are based on themes in the Book of Songs."

3. In preparing for an illustrated edition of his translations, Waley confidently states, "Since then [translations made over twenty years ago] my own knowledge of Chinese and the general study of it in America and Europe have made enormous progress. In arranging the poems for this illustrated edition I have corrected a certain number of mistakes. . . . There is a great deal that specialists might quarrel with; but not much, I hope, that will be definitely misleading to the general public. . . ." See Preface, in *Translations from the Chinese* by Arthur Waley (New York: Vintage, 1971). Incidentally, the earliest edition was published by Alfred A. Knopf, Inc. in 1919. Therefore, the translation made by Waley twenty years ago must have been sometime around 1900.

4. Waley, ibid., p. 197. The title of this poem has also been adopted for a posthumous volume in memory of Arthur Waley's works. See Ivan Morris, ed., *Madly Singing in the Mountains: An Appreciation of Arthur Waley* (New York: Harper & Row, 1970).

5. Kizer, pp. 4–5.

6. Kizer, p. 11.

7. Waley, p. 35.

8. Waley, p. 104. A clarification is needed here. The Wu-ti who wrote this poem is Liang Wu-ti (A.D. 464–?), or Emperor Wu of the Liang Dynasty.

9. "Hiding Our Love," Kizer, p. 8.

10. "Summer near the River," Kizer, p. 12.
11. The original Chinese poem can be found in Kuo Mou-ch'ien, ed., *Yüeh-fu shih chi* (Taipei: Shang-wu, 1968), II, 521.
12. *The Complete Poetry and Selected Prose of John Donne*, ed. Charles M. Coffin (New York: Random House, 1952), pp. 38–39. Other examples that demonstrate love triumphing over the inconstancy of the sun can be found in Donne's other poems like "The Anniversarie," and "Song: Sweetest Love, I do Not Goe."

13. Kizer, p. 12.
14. Waley, p. 35. The original poem can be found in *Yüeh-fu shih-chi*, II, 574.
15. Waley, p. 35.
16. "Winter Song," Kizer, p. 14.
17. "Seventeen Old Poems," Waley, p. 37.
18. Kizer, p. 14.
19. Waley, p. 37.

# JOHN KNOWLES

## 1926–

John Knowles was born in Fairmont, West Virginia, on September 16, 1926. After his graduation from Phillips Exeter Academy in 1945 he enlisted in the armed forces. Knowles served only eight months in the Air Force before returning to civilian life. He graduated from Yale in 1949 and spent the next three years in Connecticut working for the *Yale Alumni Magazine* and the *Hartford Courant*. He moved to New York in 1952 and worked as a freelance journalist until 1956 when he accepted an editorial position with *Holiday* magazine.

Knowles published his first novel, *A Separate Peace*, in 1959. Set at a fictitious New England prep school called the Devon School, the short, psychologically compelling story achieved instant fame. Along with Salinger's *The Catcher in the Rye* and Golding's *Lord of the Flies*, *A Separate Peace* is among the best-known adolescent classics of the postwar period. Over nine million copies of the book have been sold, providing Knowles with a steady income for the past twenty-five years. He has continued to write fiction, but his successes have been smaller in comparison. He dedicated his third novel, *Indian Summer* (1966), to his mentor, Thornton Wilder. *Peace Breaks Out*, which also is set at the Devon School, was published in 1981 as a companion to *A Separate Peace*. His most recent novel, *A Stolen Past* (1983), takes place at his alma mater. Knowles lives in Southampton, Long Island.

### JAY L. HALIO
### "John Knowles's Short Novels"

*Studies in Short Fiction*, Winter 1964, pp. 107–12

At a time when best-sellerdom has fostered many overwritten, overpublicized, and often overpraised novels like James Jones's *From Here to Eternity*, William Styron's *Set This House on Fire*, and most recently Philip Roth's *Letting Go*, the problem of how to say much and say it well—in the compass of about two hundred normal-sized pages—has become serious. It has become a challenge to the writer who wishes to go beyond the limitations of the short story in order to develop the full complexities of his theme without at the same time dissipating his art and his energies in much padded or repetitive verbiage. Among younger writers it is therefore heartening to see a few like John Knowles who, taking his cue from *The Sun Also Rises* rather than from *For Whom the Bell Tolls*, had brought back to recent fiction some of the clear craftsmanship and careful handling of form that characterizes our earlier and best fiction in this century.

It is also heartening to see that among the same writers many have shown an unremitting preoccupation with the exploration of the self—a preoccupation, too, of earlier writers, both at home and abroad, but now somewhat relieved of impinging social concerns, though not (which would be a poorer thing) totally divorced from them. The prevailing attitude seems to be that before man can be redeemed back into social life, he must first come to terms with himself, he must first—as has been said so often of American writers—discover who and what he is. That we must look inward and learn to face honestly what we see there and then move onwards or anyway outwards is necessary if in the long run we are to salvage any part of our humanity—if, indeed, humanity is in the future to have any meaning or value. This is the enterprise carried forward in contemporary literature by such novelists as Angus Wilson in England and Saul Bellow at home; and alongside their novels John Knowles has now placed two brilliant pieces of fiction, *A Separate Peace* (1960) and *Morning in Antibes* (1962; both published by Macmillan). His gift is different from theirs as theirs is different from each other, for he speaks with a voice that is at once personal and lyrical in a mode that, with the possible exception of Bellow's *The Victim*, neither of the others has as yet attempted. In his first novel, moreover, Knowles achieves a remarkable success in writing about adolescent life at a large boys' school without falling into any of the smart-wise idiom made fashionable by *The Catcher in the Rye* and ludicrously overworked by its many imitators.

*A Separate Peace* is the story of a small group of boys growing up at an old New England prep school called Devon during the early years of World War II. The principal characters are the narrator, Gene Forrester, and his roommate, Phineas, or "Finny," who has no surname. As yet but remotely aware of the war in Europe or the Pacific, the boys give themselves up during Devon's first summer session to sports and breaking school rules under the instigations of the indefatigable Finny. It is the last brief experience of carefree life they will know, for most of them will graduate the following June. But within this experience, another kind of war subtly

CAROLYN KIZER

KENNETH KOCH

GALWAY KINNELL

JOHN KNOWLES

JERZY KOSINSKI

RING LARDNER

MAXINE KUMIN

OLIVER LA FARGE

emerges, a struggle between Gene, who is a good student and an able competitor in sports, and Finny, who is the school's champion athlete but poor at studying. Believing Finny's instigations aim at ruining his chances to become valedictorian of their class—and so upset the delicate balance of their respective achievements—Gene awakens to a mistaken sense of deadly enmity between them. (Anyone who has attended such schools will immediately recognize this conflict between intellectual and athletic glory.) Impulsively, Gene causes his roommate to fall from a tree during one of their more spectacular games, and cripples him. This is the central episode of the novel, and the fear which lies behind such destructive hatred is its major theme.

How Gene eventually loses this fear, and so is able to enter that other war without hatred, without the need to kill, is the business of the succeeding episodes. Confession by Gene of deliberate viciousness is alone insufficient release; indeed, far from bringing release, it causes deeper injury to Finny and to himself because of its basic half-truth. Freedom comes only after an honest confrontation of both his own nature and that extension of it represented by Finny, whose loss at the end of the novel he must somehow accept and endure. For if, as the book shows, Finny is unfit for war, and hence unfit for a world engaged in a chronic condition of war, it is because of his fundamental innocence or idealism—his regard for the world not as it is, but as it should be—that renders him unfit. Under Finny's influence, most of the summer of 1942 was, for Gene, just such a world; and it is briefly restored during the following winter when, after convalescing, Phineas returns to Devon. But the existence of this world, and the separate peace this world provides, is doomed. In Finny's fall from the tree Gene has violated, or rather surrendered, his innocence, and he learns that any attempt to regain it, to "become a part of Phineas" (p. 72), is at best a transient experience, at worst a gesture of despair. Nor will either of the twin expedients, escape or evasion, serve him. Escape, as it presents itself to Gene after Finny's second fall, the final crisis in the novel, is rejected as "not so much criminal as meaningless, a lapse into nothing, an escape into nowhere" (p. 164). And evasion—any recourse into the various dodges of sentimentality, such as aggressive arrogance, insensitive factionalism, or self-protective vagueness, as variously portrayed by other boys at Devon— such evasion, Gene comes to realize, is only a mask behind which one does not so much seek reality, as hide from it, for it is a mask to cover fear. "Only Phineas never was afraid, only Phineas never hated anyone," the book concludes. The essential harmony of his nature could not allow such emotions, and his "choreography of peace" in a world he alone could create and sustain, as for example during Devon's first, only, and illegal "Winter Carnival," is not the dance of this world. His death, coming as it does on the eve of graduation, is, then, for Gene a kind of necessary sacrifice before he can take the next step. And his forgiveness is Gene's way of forgiving himself for what he at last recognizes is "something ignorant in the human heart" (p. 183), the impersonal, blind impulse that caused Finny's fall and that causes war. It is an acceptance, too, the acceptance (as Eliot shows in *Four Quartets*) of a reality which includes ignorance and prepares for humility, without which the next step remains frozen in mid-air.

In *Morning at Antibes*, Knowles prepares to take the next step—or to complete the first—the step that leads to the possibility of human encounter, of real and fruitful meetings with others. But before actually taking this step, he repeats much of what he has already presented in A *Separate Peace*. Perhaps this repetition is necessary for the shape of the novel,

which ostensibly is not a continuation of the first (as part of a trilogy, for example) and must tell its own story. But to readers of Knowles's first book, *Morning in Antibes* unavoidably appears as a retelling, in part, of what he has already demonstrated; and so it drags a bit, if only just slightly. The novel opens with the separation of a young couple, Nicholas and Liliane Bodine, after a brief and unhappy marriage. Nick has left Liliane in Paris for the pleasures and transparent lures of the Riviera and for the love he mistakenly hopes to find there; but his unfaithful wife, now deeply troubled and wanting to reconcile, follows him to Juan-les-Pins. It is the summer of 1958, and reflected against this portrait of impending marital dissolution is the mounting struggle of Algeria to free itself from France during the last days of the Fourth Republic: as in A *Separate Peace*, the private and the public war are clearly related. Before reconciliation is possible, however, or even desirable, both Nick and Lili must suffer an agonizing inward look, recognize their self-limitations with neither exaggeration nor minimizing, and with this knowledge of both good and evil in the human heart, discover the means and the will to forgive, and to love.

The first, futile attempt at reconciliation, pushed forward by Liliane, fails badly because it is motivated mainly by a sense of guilt that is as yet too vague to be instructive and by a self-interest that regards her husband primarily as a useful commodity rather than as a fulfilment of her being. Nick, naturally enough, is not interested, even though he allows himself at one point to be trapped into a sexual encounter—which dramatizes for him (as for the reader) the insufficiency of sex, even with so lovely a girl as Liliane, and even in so sex-centered a place as the French Riviera. After this fiasco, Liliane disappears, and a new person enters Nick's life, a young man called Jeannot, whom Nick at first distrusts implicitly: he is an Algerian and all Algerians in France are naturally suspect. But Nick's distrust gradually gives way before Jeannot's gentleness and his profound need to be treated as a human being, even though he is an unemployed Algerian in France during her most stressful period since the War. Nicholas learns a great deal from Jeannot during Liliane's absence, much of it having to do with Jeannot's love for the country which has misprised and misused him. In the midst of Algerian terrorism, which reaches even to the vacation shores of Mediterranean resort towns, Jeannot is no terrorist: like his old father in North Africa, he is forced to give funds to the F.L.N., but that is the extent of his activities. He is troubled by his failure to make good at some profession or trade in France, has left Paris because both terrorism and discrimination have made life impossible for him there, and still loving the country which tries to reject him but at the same time insists he is a part of it—a French citizen with full rights— has come to Antibes. There the French are decent to him; there he is, in his phrase, "well loved," by people who know him (p. 87). But the Riviera can scarcely help Jeannot to the kind of success that will allow him, a first-born son, to return home without disgrace. Needing a job, but somehow attracted by Nick (whose domestic problems resemble Jeannot's social and political ones), he starts to insinuate himself into Nick's scanty ménage, at one point effecting a momentary but civilized truce between Nick and Lili that is to harbinger their eventual reconciliation.

For it is through Jeannot as much as by his wife's absence—to go on a prolonged cruise with a cynical, degenerate French nobleman—that Nicholas begins to understand what love means and what it demands. Through Jeannot, Nick learns that love begins by valuing (or loving) ourselves justly; only then can we take others at their own just evaluation. Love prevents either party from imposing false valuations upon themselves. In this way Nick's relationship with Jeannot grows and flourishes. Liliane's adultery with Marc De La Croie is an open gesture to show Nick that she has learned to value herself in the way he values her; but in the final resolution of the novel both Nick and Lili realize that this valuation is wrong. Liliane is not so bad as she believes, as her proposed marriage to M. Marc would establish: she is frightened, she confesses—afraid of real love because of the terrifying exertions it repeatedly forces us to make; but in Nick's courage, perhaps, in his willingness to fight, she finds some courage of her own. All this comes out at the end of the novel in her long speech (p. 184) that may be a little too stagey, a little too artificial—as once or twice elsewhere in the novel we feel this to be true—but the essence of what she says is otherwise conveyed, and the speech serves mainly to make it explicit. Significantly, before his reconciliation with Lili occurs, Nicholas and Jeannot part company forever. Learning that the French have killed his father, Jeannot returns home—despite Nick's urgent pleas to come to America with him, to avoid what he cannot make good, what will probably result in his death, too. Graciously, and with deep gratitude, Jeannot refuses Nick's offer to escape or evasion. At the same time, he denies any real courage for what he is about to do; he is simply carrying out the dictates of his heart. "I have to do what I feel there," he says. "Everybody does, it's natural. Everybody does" (p. 181). He still loves France, the country that in its confused, possessive, sadistic way loves him, too; that has enabled him to learn, to get off the hilltop in North Africa and get on the train going somewhere (p. 179). But it is an impossible love, he sees at last, and now he must go home to help destroy it.

At the end of *Morning in Antibes*, Nick sums up his experience and contrasts it to Jeannot's: "I had come for her. I had not gone away, I had come for her. Not an act of golden courage, not like giving up your life for what lies deeply in your heart; but just a short but definite and irrevocable step. Since I had never walked that way in my life, the first step could only be a short one" (pp. 185–6). In all humility, Nick minimizes the fortitude of his act and the importance of his step. The longest journey begins, after all, with but a single step, however short. It is often the hardest one.

As a second novel, *Morning in Antibes* stands up well against *A Separate Peace*, although readers will doubtless recognize the superior achievement of Knowles's first book. Finny's fall from the tree, while it makes use of old and familiar symbolism, loses none of its power but gains instead by its complete integration within a realistic design. By contrast, Nick's skin-diving episode just before Liliane returns to Juan-les-Pins, though it draws upon equally ancient symbols, parallels too closely Jake Barnes' deep dives off San Sebastian in *The Sun Also Rises*. Here, as in other places, such as a few clipped passages of dialogue, or some detailed descriptions of French cuisine, a purely literary recollection intervenes, detracting from the reader's experience of the presentation and robbing it of some of its felt reality. Nevertheless, in his second novel Knowles retains much of the individual voice mentioned earlier; despite the occasional ventriloquism, it is still there. Moreover, he demonstrates an important development of his theme, and we may well wait for what he has to say next with aroused expectations.

## RONALD WEBER
"Narrative Method in *A Separate Peace*"

*Studies in Short Fiction*, Fall 1965, pp. 63–72

Professor Halio's recent appreciation of the two short novels of John Knowles was especially welcome.[1] Knowles's work, and in particular his fine first novel, *A Separate Peace*, has not yet received the close attention it merits. In a time that has seen high praise for fat, awkwardly-managed novels, he stands out as a precise and economical craftsman. For this alone he demands serious consideration.

Although Professor Halio calls attention to this technical achievement—Knowles, he writes, "has brought back to recent fiction some of the clear craftsmanship and careful handling of form that characterizes our earlier and best fiction in this century" (p. 107)—he is not concerned to illustrate it. He is more interested in examining what he sees as Knowles's second strong point: a thematic concern with the individual's efforts to come to terms with himself as a prior condition to his coming to terms with his society. A reversal of this emphasis—focusing on technique and the relationship of technique to theme—can, I believe, add something to an understanding of Knowles's work. Unlike Professor Halio, however, who gives equal attention to Knowles's second novel, *Morning in Antibes*, I wish to limit my remarks to *A Separate Peace*.

Since the novel deals with young boys in prep school setting, it inevitably calls to mind *The Catcher in the Rye*. Hoping to capitalize on this similarity, a paperback cover blurb declares it the "best since" *Catcher*.[2] In a different vein, Professor Halio also makes passing reference to Salinger's novel:

> In his first novel . . . Knowles achieves a remarkable success in writing about adolescent life at a large boys' school without falling into any of the smart-wise idiom made fashionable by *The Catcher in the Rye* and ludicrously overworked by its many imitators. (pp. 107–108)

Although the two novels have some obvious similarities, they are fundamentally different books—different in technique, as the quotation suggests, and different in theme. In spite of this, a comparison of *A Separate Peace* with *Catcher*—especially a comparison of the way narrative method relates to theme—offers a useful approach to Knowles's novel.

In both books the narrative is presented from a first-person point of view; both Holden Caulfield and Gene Forrester tell their own stories, stories in which they serve not only as observers but as narrator-agents who stand at the center of the action. Generally, first-person narration gives the reader a heightened sense of immediacy, a sense of close involvement with the life of the novel. This surely is one of the charms of *Catcher* and one of the reasons for its immense popularity. The reader, particularly the young reader, is easily caught up in the narrative and held fast by a voice and an emotional experience he finds intensely familiar. With Knowles's novel, however, this is not the case. While the reader may greatly admire the book, it does not engage him quite as directly or perhaps even as deeply as *Catcher*; throughout it he remains somewhat outside the action and detached from the narrator, observing the life of the novel rather than submerged in it. This difference in reader response, taking place as it does within the framework of first-person, narrator-as-protagonist telling, is, I believe, a highly-calculated effect on Knowles's part. It indicates a sharply different thematic intention, and one that is rooted in a skillful alteration of the conventional method of first-person telling.

Holden Caulfield never comes to an understanding of his experience. He never quite knows what it means; he only feels certain things about it. In the final paragraph of the novel, responding to D.B.'s question about what he now thinks of his experience, he says: "I didn't know what the hell to say. If you want to know the truth, I don't *know* what I think about it" (Little, Brown, pp. 276–277). At the end, as throughout the novel, Holden is much more aware of what he feels, in this case a broad sympathy for the people he has described. "About all I know is," he adds, "I sort of *miss* everybody I told about" (p. 277). Gene Forrester, on the other hand, arrives at a clear understanding—a deeply felt knowledge—of the experience he narrates. At the end of the novel he knows, unlike Holden, precisely what he thinks about it.

Understanding demands a measure of distance. We can seldom understand an experience, truly know it, until we are clearly removed from it—removed in time and removed in attitude. Holden achieves such distance only slightly, hence his understanding is slight at best. He tells his story at only a short remove in time from the actual experience of it. It all took place, the reader learns at the start, "around last Christmas" (p. 3). Just as there has been some lapse of time between the experience and the telling, there has also been some shift in Holden's attitude. At the end of the novel, when we again return to the opening perspective, the recuperating Holden now thinks he will apply himself when he returns to school, just as he now sort of misses the people he had told about. In both cases, however, Holden is not sufficiently separated from his experience, either in time or attitude, to admit any real mastery of it.

Holden's relation to the experience of the novel illustrates a major problem of first-person telling. Although the method, by narrowing the sense of distance separating reader, narrator, and fictional experience, gains a quality of immediacy and freshness, it tends for the same reason to prohibit insight or understanding. This latter point has been clearly noted by Brooks and Warren:

> First-person narration tends to shorten the distance between the reader and the fictional character; for instance, the character narrating his own story tends to give us the world strictly in his own terms, in his own feelings and attitudes, and he can scarcely see himself in a large context. He tends to reveal himself rather than to pass judgment upon himself, to give comments about himself, or to analyze himself. Such judgments, comments, and analyses exist in such a story, but they exist by implication, and the reader must formulate them for himself.[3]

Understanding exists in *Catcher*, but not self-understanding for Holden. Because of the intense method of narration, narrowing rather than enlarging the sense of distance in the novel, understanding exists only for the reader, and then only by implication. This situation, as we shall see, is wholly congenial to Salinger's thematic intention; Knowles, however, seeks a different end, and therefore he must somehow modify the effect of his narrative method.

Unlike Holden, Gene Forrester is separated by a broad passage of time from the experience he relates. "I went back to the Devon School not long ago," Gene says in the novel's opening sentence, "and found it looking oddly newer than when I was a student there fifteen years before" (Macmillan, p. 1). That this lapse in time between the experience and the telling has brought understanding is also established early. "Looking back now across fifteen years," Gene says a few paragraphs later, "I could see with great clarity the fear I had lived in . . ." (p. 2). Although Knowles quickly leaves the

distant perspective and turns to immediate scene, he keeps the reader aware that Gene is looking back on the experience with a mature vision. At one point, for example, the distant perspective suddenly opens up at the end of a scene when Gene says: "But in a week I had forgotten that, and I have never since forgotten the dazed look on Finny's face when he thought that on the first day of his return to Devon I was going to desert him" (p. 95). Later, beginning a chapter, Knowles reëstablishes the perspective with a long passage that again looks ahead of the present action:

> That night I made for the first time the kind of journey which later became the monotonous routine of my life: traveling through an unknown countryside from one unknown settlement to another. The next year this became the dominant activity, or rather passivity, of my army career, not fighting, not marching, but this kind of nighttime ricochet; for as it turned out I never got to the war. (p. 122)

The distant point of the narration allows a detachment that permits Gene the mastery of his experience. Even when Knowles gives over the narrative wholly to immediate scene the reader is reminded, sometimes with a phrase, at other times with an entire passage, of the perspective. The war, in addition, serves to create an increased sense of distance, a removal in attitude, within the story. Although the war touches Devon School only slightly—one of the joys of the summer session is that it seems totally removed from the world of war—it cannot be forgotten or ignored for long; it exists not only as an event that stands between the experience of the novel and Gene's telling, but as an event that, at the very moment of the experience, dominates the life of each character. "The war," Gene says in retrospect, "was and is reality for me. I still instinctively live and think in its atmosphere" (p. 31). The anticipation of war forces Gene and his companions into a slight yet significant detachment from their life at Devon—a life that, at times, seems unimportant and even unreal—and towards an unusual amount of serious, if carefully guarded, reflection. The relation between the fact of war and the atmosphere of detachment or removal in the novel—removal, again, necessary for understanding—can be seen in Phineas' disclosure that, despite his humorous disavowal of the existence of the war, he has been trying for some time to enlist:

> I'll *hate* it *everywhere* if I'm not in this war [he tells Gene]! Why do you think I kept saying there wasn't any war all winter? I was going to keep on saying it until two seconds after I got a letter from Ottawa or Chungking or some place saying, "Yes, you can enlist with us. . . ." Then there would have been a war. (pp. 172–173)

Similarly, the war serves to remove Gene from his immediate experience and to provoke serious self-scrutiny:

> To enlist [he thinks in response to a day spent freeing snowbound trains in a railroad yard as part of the war effort]. To slam the door impulsively on the past, to shed everything down to my last bit of clothing, to break the pattern of my life—that complex design I had been weaving since birth with all its dark threads, its unexplainable symbols set against a conventional background of domestic white and schoolboy blue, all those tangled strands which required the dexterity of a virtuoso to keep flowing—I yearned to take giant military shears of it, snap! bitten off in an instant, and nothing left in my hands but spools of khaki which could weave only a plain, flat, khaki design, however twisted they might be. (p. 87)

The depth of insight revealed in the passage is made

possible both by the narrator's removal in time from the experience and by the existence within the experience of the war as a focus of attention outside of him. Finally, the passage suggests how the central dramatic event of the story, Gene's involvement in the injury of Phineas, adds to the atmosphere of detachment in the novel. The injury, which occurs early in the story and underlies the bulk of the narrative, is another force thrusting Gene away from his immediate experience and towards self-scrutiny; as such, it combines with the distant point of the narration and the existence of war to create the broad quality of detachment that makes understanding both possible and plausible.

Gene comes of self-understanding only gradually through a series of dramatic episodes, as we shall see; the final extent of his understanding can, however, be indicated by a passage from the concluding chapter. "I was ready for the war," he says, thinking ahead to his entry into the army, "now that I no longer had any hatred to contribute to it. My fury was gone, I felt it gone, dried up at the course, withered and lifeless" (p. 185). This final awareness contrasts sharply with Holden Caulfield's lack of self-understanding at the end of Catcher. While Holden, looking back on his experience, thinks he may be somewhat changed, Gene is certain he is a radically different person. This differing response of the characters to the experience they relate is additionally underscored for the reader by the tone of their narration. In each case, Holden and Gene indicate their relation to their experience as much by how they speak as by what they say and when they say it. Holden's voice, uncertain at times and dogmatic at others, is always exuberant and emotional; it is a voice vividly responsive to the experience of the novel but one that suggests little mastery of it. Gene's voice, on the other hand, is dispassionate, reflective, and controlled; it is, in his own words, a voice from which fury is gone, dried up at its source long before the telling begins. If Holden's voice is that of the restless adolescent groping for an uncertain maturity, Gene's is a voice looking back on adolescence after the hard passage to maturity has been won.

It is clear that Knowles, to return to Professor Halio's phrase, does not fall into the "smart-wise idiom made fashionable" by Salinger's novel. He does not follow in Salinger's wake because of the important variation he works on the method of first-person narration used in Catcher. By attempting to maintain a sense of distance within a narrative method that naturally tends to narrow distance, he sacrifices some of the method's freshness to gain depth and insight. In Catcher the reader, with Holden, tends to respond to the experience with feeling rather than knowledge; understanding exists for him in the novel only by implication. In A Separate Peace the reader, with Gene, remains partially detached from the experience, able to examine and reflect upon it; and understanding can finally take the form of direct statement.

At this point we can begin to see some connection between Knowles's narrative method and his thematic concern. Again, comparison with Catcher is useful. Both novels, in a broad and very basic sense, are concerned with the response of the central character to an awareness of evil in the world; they are narratives in which the characters confront, during a concentrated period, part of the reality of life. In face of this reality Holden Caulfield suffers a severe physical and mental breakdown. At the end of the novel, when Holden admits he misses the people he has told about—the assorted phonies who represent the world—the reader is to understand that he now has begun to make some beginning accommodation with that world. Holden of course does not understand this change; it is, as we have said, merely a new feeling, a feeling of missing

people he previously despised. Although it is clear that some change has taken place in Holden, it is important to see that it is explained in terms of other people; what must in fact be an inner change—Holden arriving at some peace within himself—is communicated in exterior terms.

In the course of his maturing process, Gene Forrester likewise must confront the fact of evil in the world. But in this case the location of that evil is quite different. At the very beginning of the novel, in a passage quoted earlier, Gene, looking back fifteen years, says he can see with great clarity the "fear" he had lived in at Devon School and that he has succeeded in making his "escape" from. Even now, he adds, he can feel "fear's echo," and this in turn leads him back to the direct experience of the story (p. 2). The meaning of this experience is to be found in the development of the words fear and escape—in Gene's growing realization of what they mean as well as what they do not mean.

When his friend and roommate Phineas breaks a Devon swimming record and then refuses to let anyone know about it, Gene is deeply troubled:

> Was he trying to impress me or something? Not tell anybody? When he had broken a school record without a day of practice? I knew he was serious about it, so I didn't tell anybody. Perhaps for that reason his accomplishment took root in my mind and grew rapidly in the darkness where I was forced to hide it. (p. 35)

Later, during an overnight escapade on an oceanside beach, Phineas causes him another moment of uncertainty. Just before the two boys fall asleep, Phineas frankly declares that Gene is his "best pal."

> It was a courageous thing to say [Gene reflects]. Exposing a sincere emotion nakedly like that at the Devon School was the next thing to suicide. I should have told him then that he was my best friend also and rounded off what he had said. I started to; I nearly did. But something held me back. Perhaps I was stopped by that level of feeling, deeper than thought, which contains the truth. (p. 38)

Gene's troubled feelings rise to the level of thought in a following scene during which he comes to the conclusion that Phineas, the school's finest athlete, envies him his academic success. This knowledge instantly shatters any notions he has had of "affection and partnership and sticking by someone and relying on someone absolutely in the jungle of a boys' school" (p. 42). He now sees that Phineas is his rival, not his friend, and this in turn explains his failure to respond properly when Phineas broke the swimming record and when he confessed his friendship. He now sees that he has been envious of Phineas too—envious to the point of complete enmity. Out of the wreck of their friendship this dual rivalry emerges as a saving bit of knowledge:

> I found it [Gene says]. I found a single sustaining thought. The thought was, You and Phineas are even already. You are even in enmity. You are both coldly driving ahead for yourselves alone. You did hate him for breaking that school swimming record, but so what? He hated you for getting an A in every course but one last term. (p. 43)

Their mutual hatred not only explains Gene's inability to respond properly to Phineas, but it relieves him of any further anxiety:

> I felt better. Yes, I sensed it like the sweat of relief when nausea passes away; I felt better. We were even after all, even in enmity. The deadly rivalry was on both sides after all. (p. 43)

Gene's sense of relief, it turns out, is of short duration. When Phineas, in a moment of seriousness, urges him to stick with his studies rather than come along on a campus diversion, Gene suddenly sees he has been wrong—Phineas has never envied him. During a scene immediately following, in which he and Phineas perch in a tree waiting to leap into a river below, Gene is overwhelmed by the implications of this new insight:

> Any fear I had ever had of the tree was nothing beside this. It wasn't my neck, but my understanding which was menaced. He had never been jealous of me for a second. Now I knew that there never was and never could have been any rivalry between us. I was not of the same quality as he. I couldn't stand this. (pp. 48–49)

It is at this moment that he causes Phineas to fall from the tree, an "accident" that cripples him and ends his athletic career. After watching Phineas crash through the branches of the tree and hit the bank, Gene jumps confidently into the river, "every trace of my fear of this forgotten." (p. 49)

It is Phineas' innocence that Gene cannot endure. As long as he can believe Phineas shares his enmity, he can find relief; but with this assurance gone, he stands condemned before himself and must strike out against his tormentor. *Fear*, again, is the key word. Fear in this instance is the emotional response to the discovery of hate, the vast depths of enmity that exist within the human heart. Gene loses his fear and achieves his separate, personal peace only when he acknowledges this fundamental truth. It is a truth that he must first recognize and then accept; he can neither avoid it, as he tries to do in his first encounter with Phineas after the accident (p. 53), nor flee from it, as he again seeks to do when Leper charges that he always has been a "savage underneath" (p. 128). He can find escape from fear only in the acceptance of its true source and the location of that source. Gene must come to see and endure the truth, as he finally does in a climactic scene just before Phineas dies from a second fall, that his fear is the product not of rivalry nor of circumstance but of "some ignorance inside me, some crazy thing inside me, something blind." (p. 174)

None of Gene's companions at Devon could bring themselves to face this inner source of their fear. When they began to feel this "overwhelmingly hostile thing in the world with them" (p. 184), they looked beyond themselves and felt themselves violently pitted against something in the outer world. When they experienced this "fearful shock" of the "sighting of the enemy," they began an "obsessive labor of defense" and began to parry the menace they thought they saw facing them. They all

> constructed at infinite cost to themselves these Maginot Lines against this enemy they thought they saw across the frontier, this enemy who never attacked that way—if he ever attacked at all; if he was indeed the enemy. (p. 186)

The infinite cost in this case is the loss of self-knowledge. Only Phineas is an exception; only Phineas "never was afraid" because only he "never hated anyone" (p. 186). Phineas alone is free of the awareness of that hostile thing that is to be found not across any battlefield but within the fortress itself. As the archetypal innocent, he must serve as the sacrifice to Gene's maturity. "I was ready for the war," Gene says at the end, "now that I no longer had any hatred to contribute to it. My fury was gone. . . . Phineas had absorbed it and taken it with him, and I was rid of it forever." (p. 185)

Gene Forrester comes to learn that his war, the essential war, is fought out on the battlefield within. Peace comes only when he faces up to this fact. The only escape, the price of peace, is self-awareness. One finds the resolution of Holden Caulfield's war, on the other hand, beyond him, in his relation to society. As Holden flees a corrupt world he is driven increasingly in upon himself, but towards collapse rather than awareness. Salinger presents the hope that is finally raised for him not in terms of self-knowledge but in the ability to move out of himself. It is not, then, awareness that is offered for him so much as a kind of accommodation; he must somehow learn to live, as Mr. Antolini tells him, with what is sickening and corrupt in human behavior. Although this implies facing up to what is corrupt in his own nature, this is not Salinger's emphasis. He seeks to focus the novel outside Holden rather than within him; and for this the conventional method of first-person narration with its tendency to narrow and intensify the story, eliminating the sense of distance vital for the narrator's self-understanding, is admirably suited. Knowles, using a similar but skillfully altered narrative method, develops a very different theme—that awareness, to put it baldly, must precede accommodation, that to look without before having first searched within is tragically to confuse the human condition. To convey his theme Knowles modifies the first-person narrative to create for both narrator and reader an atmosphere of detachment that permits the novel to be focused within Gene, where, he shows, a basic truth of life is to be found.

While the reader may come to feel the experience of *A Separate Peace* somewhat less than that of *Catcher*, he eventually knows it more. While Salinger may give him a stronger sense of life, Knowles provides a clearer statement about life. Although the two novels work towards different ends with different means, they help finally to illustrate, in their separate ways, the close functional relation of meaning and method of telling in carefully-wrought fiction.

*Notes*

1. Jay L. Halio, "John Knowles's Short Novels," *Studies in Short Fiction*, I (Winter 1964), 107–12.
2. Dell edition, 1961.
3. Cleanth Brooks and Robert Penn Warren, *Understanding Fiction*, 2nd ed. (New York, 1959), p. 664.

## JAMES J. McDONALD
### "The Novels of John Knowles"

*Arizona Quarterly*, Winter 1967, pp. 335–42

It may be too early to attempt more than a tentative appraisal of the overall achievement of John Knowles. Certainly one can say that he ranks among the most promising young American novelists; and one can recognize the obvious fact that *A Separate Peace* (winner of the William Faulkner Foundation Award and the Rosenthal Award) has become a small classic among college students and seems likely to last for some time. His other novels, however, have only been noticed in passing: *Morning in Antibes* and *Indian Summer* have not really been analyzed and evaluated. Nor is there any substantial critical commentary on Knowles's work as a whole.

I would like to begin such a commentary; and I propose to do so by placing Knowles, as it were—by relating him to the American literary tradition which I see him working within. He is writing what Lionel Trilling has called "the novel of manners"; and it seems to me that there are affinities between his aesthetic preoccupations and those of Henry James and F. Scott Fitzgerald. An examination of his subjects, themes, and techniques should show this affinity; and I hope that it will also provide a basis for a reasonably sound estimate of Knowles's stature as a novelist.

From the beginning of his career, Knowles—like James and Fitzgerald—has written about manners, about what Trilling defines as "a culture's hum and buzz of implication . . . the whole evanescent context in which its explicit statements are made."[1] In Knowles's first novel, *A Separate Peace* (New York, 1959), the "explicit statements" are the Second World War and its moral effect on American society; the "context" is made up of the precarious situation of American prep-school students who will soon be combatants, and of the moral responses that they, their teachers, and their parents make to this situation.

As many critics have noted, *A Separate Peace* can be viewed as a war novel, drawing its title from Frederic Henry's personal declaration of personal armistice in *A Farewell to Arms*. Knowles's concern, however, is not with the direct confrontation of the obvious realities of the battlefield; rather, it is with the impact of war on the minds and sensibilities of individuals who are not, as yet, immediately involved. The novel examines the cultural upheaval created by the war, and shows how the resulting moral climate affects the thoughts, feelings, attitudes, and actions of Gene Forrester, Phineas, Leper, Brinker, and the others. The novel deals, then, with culture; and with the sensibility of the individual as it is formed by a particular culture: like James and Fitzgerald, Knowles draws the reader's attention to the individual's efforts to adjust to cultural change, and to the quality of his moral responses as he attempts to cope with the disruption of his formerly stable world.

Particularly Jamesian in this novel is Knowles's use of point of view. The narrator, the principal character, is Gene Forrester. On the surface, it appears that he is telling his story honestly, attempting to grapple with his past and forthrightly informing the reader of its significance. Yet, like the narrators of James's "The Liar" or *The Aspern Papers*, for example, Forrester frequently seems either unaware of or deliberately unwilling to acknowledge the moral nature and consequences of his attitudes and actions. There is, then, a discrepancy between Forrester's judgments and the actions and attitudes he is judging. The reader's awareness of this discrepancy is enforced by the dramatic statements of other characters in the novel, especially by the comments of Leper.

Thus the reader's judgments are not always the same as the narrator's; and so the reader is led to question the narrator's motives and interpretations. Should Forrester be taken at his own evaluation? Or is he really, as Leper charges, "a savage underneath" his pose of refined, dispassionate, reflective survivor and recounter of the ordeal? (pp. 128–129).

The complexity—or the ambiguity—of the novel is precisely here, and so is Knowles's debt to James. Neither novelist merely uses his narrator to direct the narrative. Both, instead, use the narrative as the scene and occasion of a complex, dramatic confrontation between the narrator and his past which the reader participates in. For James and Knowles, the aesthetic effect of this type of novel depends on a dramatic interplay between the narrator's judgments and the reader's; and, in this sense, the narrator *is* the story.

The locale of Knowles's second novel, *Morning in Antibes* (New York, 1962), naturally leads the reader to think of F. Scott Fitzgerald. Knowles's sleek, sparkling Riviera reminds one of the destructive playground evoked in *Tender Is the Night*. The similarity extends to the quality of observation: Dick Diver himself might have described the "very young couple" that Nick Bodine sees early in Knowles's novel:

". . . the girl angelically lovely, tanned and formed for love, the boy like a nearly naked matador" (p. 7). Knowles's concentration on manners also is akin to Fitzgerald's. Both writers keenly perceive "tone, gesture, emphasis, or rhythm . . . the arts of dress or decoration"[2] as signs of cultural trends; and they use these signs to indicate the moral implications of cultural norms and fashions:

> The French bathing suit was invented because aging women discovered that the skin in the middle of the body often remained soft, and that part of the body shapely, after the arms and legs had begun to coarsen and sag. They were all contenders, wives and mothers for twenty years or not; they were still in training for love (p. 6).

The actual situation and themes of the novel, however, are closer to those of James than to Fitzgerald's. *Morning in Antibes* offers the classic Jamesian situation of the innocent American encountering the complexities of European culture. The thematic lines of the novel follow James's typical pattern: a conflict between American innocence and European experience is drawn. The naïveté and vitality of the Americans, Nick and his wife Liliane, are juxtaposed to the worldliness and moral sterility of the Europeans Marc de la Croie and his sister Constance.

The narrative line of the novel revolves around the struggle between these two worlds for the soul of Liliane; and the struggle is drawn in terms of a sharply defined political situation: the rise of De Gaulle in opposition to French Fascism during the Algerian crisis. But the "evanescent context" of manners is all-important in this novel. Liliane's rejection of Marc de la Croie is, of course, a stand against his decadent Fascism: she realizes that he has been "dead for fifteen years," and that in him "nothing survives except the wish to kill" (p. 184). But she is also repudiating the affluent, corrupt cultural norms and attitudes that he represents. Her sarcastic denunciation of de la Croie is framed by a contrast between her natural vitality and the cultivated "atmosphere" in which he plunders:

> Her face, fragile and tanned, with a certain liquid quality about her eyes and hair, her face turned radiant then and she said suddenly: "Do you know, this has been a perfect dinner! Perfect. I can't tell you. How do you manage to achieve this atmosphere? So goodbye, Monsieur Marc. . . . and remember, De Gaulle to power! Let me stress, never has there been such a dinner!" I started with her out of the dining room (p. 185).

Politically, the novel, then, raises the question "who will rule France?" But it also asks what moral positions are involved in this struggle for power; and Knowles tries to define the cultural attitudes which are desirable and necessary if the individual is to survive and maintain his integrity. It seems to me that Knowles has advanced beyond the achievement of *A Separate Peace*. The issues are drawn more precisely; his subject has a greater range; and his evaluation of the material is much more clear than it was in his first novel.

Knowles's latest book, *Indian Summer* (New York, 1966), is his most ambitious attempt to establish himself as a novelist of genuine stature. In it, he takes up the theme which has obsessed so many major American writers—"the American Dream." And, in dealing with this theme, he seems deliberately to force the reader to think of F. Scott Fitzgerald and *The Great Gatsby*.

Certain affinities between Cleet Kinsolving, the hero of *Indian Summer*, and Fitzgerald's Nick Carraway are immediately discernible. Both encounter the world of the rich, the wealth and luxury, the success and the good life to which so many Americans aspire. Both act as stewards to the rich: Nick to Gatsby and the Buchanans, Cleet to the Reardon family. Cleet helps to oversee a party given by the Reardons; and Knowles inserts a list which, echoing the "hum and buzz" of our culture and thus presenting its implications, cannot but recall Nick's memorable list of those who came to Gatsby's parties:

> There were Mr. and Mrs. Hugh G. Harvey and their daughter Cassie; Charles Crownover, whose play *Maxine* had been a Broadway success during the wartime season, when any theatre which opened its doors had been assaulted by people desperate for a means to spend their money and forget the war; Mrs. Morgan Seelinger; Parker Evans Sharp, the retired radio singer; Fred Hatch, soccer coach at Country Day, and his wife, the librarian; the Craft girls, Ginny and Mary Eleanor; Gloria Garrison, who was very good fun and always had been; Mrs. Van Revellon; Cynthia Manning and her half brother, Clay Gingel, who always entertained at parties, she by singing "Deep Purple" and he by doing tricks; Pauline Frey; Fred and Kitty Winkler; the Jesse Gerkinses; "Red" and Phyllis McKecknie; the news commentator Greg Zahl and his girl friend; Mrs. Margaret Bitting and her daughter Ula; Georgia's mother and father; Lynn; business associates of Mr. Reardon, and so on (p. 124).[3]

The narrative of *Indian Summer* is constructed on a series of gradual discoveries about the disintegration of the American Dream. Cleet and Georgia, Neil Reardon's wife, slowly come to an understanding of the cultural and moral realities of wealth; they learn what money and privilege have done to the rich. Their discovery is remarkably close to Nick Carraway's realization that the Buchanans were "careless people" who "smashed up things and creatures and then retreated back into their money or their vast carelessness . . . and let other people clean up the mess they had made." Cleet encounters the same carelessness, the same ruthlessness. So does Georgia. She learns that the Reardons "used for their own ends emotions and deception and generosity and bribery and loyalty and ambition and philanthropy and willfulness . . ."; she realizes that the Reardons' behavior is based on "charts and . . . instruments . . . passed on from fortune to fortune as though these very rich families all belonged to some secret confraternity, with special totems and rituals and, above all, special rights" (p. 107).

It is a case of wealth hideously and dangerously misused. Success has been attained; but the Reardons, like the Buchanans, have lost the American Dream of greatness, the vision of the ideal, which inspired it:

> It was as though the energy which created the fortune burned as fiercely in the new generation as ever, but with no goal now, and where it had before pursued the next deal, it pursued a fox or a stag, the genius for investment gambling was turned to poker, the family tenacity transferred from commerce to tennis, the gift for grasping the moment's opportunity shifted from finance to tourism, the ability to organize complex situations quickly and efficiently passed from the world of business into the world of friends and picnics (pp. 165–166).

The American Dream now exists only as a memory of what once might have been. Nick Carraway thinks of the "fresh, green breast of the new world" which had once

appeared to the Dutch sailors, of something which was "for the last time in history . . . commensurate" to man's "capacity for wonder"; and he realizes that the dream has vanished with the past, "somewhere back in that vast obscurity beyond the city, where the dark fields of the republic rolled on under the night." Cleet Kinsolving and Georgia also sense this loss. The American Dream has vanished, and now, "as America started into the second half of the twentieth century," Georgia knows that there is no dream worthy of the dreamer, that "the world had become too mechanized for his [Cleet's] kind of nature, he asked too much of life. . . . What a pity, what a waste, what a tragedy. . . . He was like a beautifully armored warrior facing a tank" (p. 226). Finally, like Nick, Cleet can remember what once might have been: he imagines a magnificent square-rigger sailing down the Connecticut River, "carrying on its stem head a beautiful figure of an angel, its wings flung back against the great oak hull, gliding seraphically above the waters . . ." (p. 231).

Knowles, however, adds another dimension to Cleet Kinsolving. As Georgia realizes, Cleet is "one of the few remaining heirs to a far older tragedy" than the unfulfilled promise of the American Dream. His face, expression, and impassivity exhibit "the last vestiges and relics of his Indian blood . . . that persistent strain in his nature making him sometimes utterly bewildered by this America today . . ." Cleet is "an alien who however felt in his blood that this was and always has been home"; he is the "aboriginal American, bound and affronted" (pp. 226–227).

As such, then, Cleet is an embodiment of the "Adamic Myth" which so many critics have seen as characteristic of American literature. And, as such, he can be related to the "bound and affronted" heroes of Henry James, struggling honorably for life amidst those forces which stifle it. He stands with Christopher Newman, Isabel Archer, Adam Verver, and Milly Theale; he has taken the advice which Lambert Strether offered to little Bilham:

> ". . . don't forget that you're young—blessedly young; be glad of it . . . and live up to it. Live all you can; it's a mistake not to. It doesn't so much matter what you do in particular, so long as you have your life. If you haven't had that, what *have* you had?"

Cleet's "deepest ambition" is "simply to be a full human man, making the best of himself." His greatest fear is of being "defeated as most people in the world were . . . simply by not really living, eaten by the termites of a half life semilived." He knows that he has "to be closer to the pulse of life, to feel it pound, to be scared and ecstatic and despairing and triumphant by turns" (pp. 116–117). Cleet may not be as eloquent as Strether; but essentially his ideal, and his message, are the same:

> ". . . people can't delay their life if they've got any sense, not wait, stall, that's why they've got to make the life they want early and soon, before it's too late . . ." (p. 209).

Clearly, *Indian Summer* is another step forward for Knowles. He has dared to treat a theme which has been dealt with by some of the masters of American fiction—Cooper, Melville, Twain, James, Dreiser, Fitzgerald, and Faulkner, for example. Few contemporary novelists would be willing to risk the obvious comparisons.

It would be foolish, of course, to claim that Knowles belongs in the select company of Fitzgerald and James, to contend that *Morning in Antibes* and *Indian Summer* are comparable in quality to *Tender Is the Night* and *The Ambassadors*. But I think that he is an enormously promising novelist, and that he has already achieved a genuine stature. He has exibited the courage to tackle large subjects and significant themes; and he has treated them with taste, understanding, and considerable technical skill. He certainly deserves more attention than he has received up until now.

### Notes

1. "Manners, Morals, and the Novel," *The Liberal Imagination* (Garden City, N.Y., 1957), p. 200.
2. Trilling, p. 200.
3. There are important differences. The world of *The Great Gatsby*, as revealed by Nick's list, is one in which glamor and frivolity mask senseless violence and destruction. The world of *Indian Summer*, as the list implies, is characterized by triviality and exhaustion.

# KENNETH KOCH

## 1925–

Kenneth Koch was born in Cincinnati, Ohio, on February 27, 1925. After his graduation from high school in 1943 Koch served with the Army as a rifleman in the Pacific until 1946. He graduated from Harvard in 1948, and began graduate work at Columbia after a year in France on a Fullbright scholarship. While studying at Columbia Koch taught at Rutgers University and Brooklyn College. After his graduation in 1959 he joined the Columbia faculty and eventually became a professor of English and Comparative Literature in 1971.

Koch's literary fame rests on a substantial body of poetry. Noted for his quick wit and effective use of satire, one of Koch's best known verse collections is *Ko, or A Season on Earth* (1959). This unusual comic epic is modeled after both Byron's *Don Juan* and Ariosto's *Orlando Furioso*. Koch's only novel, *The Red Robins* (1975), was later dramatized. Koch is associated with the avant-garde New York School of poetry. As director of the Poetry Workshop at the New School for Social Research from 1958 to 1966, Koch's literary colleagues included John Ashbery and Frank O'Hara. Koch's prominence in New York's avant-garde circles brought him into contact with artist Larry Rivers, with whom he collaborated on several poetry-painting projects. Koch perhaps is best known for his love of teaching poetry. He believes poetry is for men and women of all ages. His *Wishes, Lies, and Dreams: Teaching Children to Write Poetry* (1970) and *Rose, Where Did You Get That Red?* (1973) are based on his classroom experience with fifth graders at New York's P.S. 61. In these books Koch outlines how children should be exposed to both reading and writing poetry. Koch later wrote *I Never Told Anybody: Teaching Poetry Writing in a Nursing Home* (1977).

Koch has received numerous honors, including the 1976 National Institute of Arts and Letters Award. Presently he lives in New York with his wife and daughter.

Koch's position in modern poetry is not easy to determine. It may help to begin by pairing him with a long-established elder poet to whom his relations are close enough in some respects, and distant enough in others, to be instructive. In part he is one of those "literalists of the imagination" who are commended by Marianne Moore and whose principles are exemplified in her own work. Like Miss Moore, Koch is fond of making poetry out of poetry-resistant stuff. Locks, lipsticks, business letterheads, walnuts, lunch and fudge attract him; so do examples of inept slang, silly sentiment, brutal behavior and stereotyped exotica and erotica. Whatever helps him to "exalt the imagination at the expense of its conventional appearances" (Richard Blackmur's formula for Marianne Moore) is welcome, although not to the exclusion of the sun, the sea, trees, girls and other conventional properties. But Koch rarely submits either kind of phenomenon to any Moore-like process of minute and patient scrutiny. He is an activist, eagerly participating in the realm of locks and fudge at the same time that he is observing it. And if, like Marianne Moore, he is always springing surprises, he does not spring them as if he were handling you a cup of tea. Her finely conscious demureness is not for him. For him, the element of surprise, and the excitement created by it, are primary and absolute. In short, life does not present itself to Kenneth Koch as picture or symbol or collector's item. It talks,

sighs, grunts and sings; it is a drama, largely comic, in which there are parts for everyone and everything, and all the parts are speaking parts.

> Filmed in the morning I am
> A pond. Dreamed of at night I am a silver
> Pond. Who's wading through Me? Ugh!

Those pigs! But they have their say elsewhere in the poem, called "Farm's Thoughts."

The thirty-one poems in ⟨*Thank You and Other Poems*⟩ were written during the past ten or twelve years and are very uneven in quality. Some of this unevenness may be the result of a defective sense of proportion, even a defective ear, on the poet's part. Mostly, it seems to spring from a certain abandon inherent in his whole enterprise. Koch is determined to put the reality back into Joyce's "reality of experience," to restore the newness to Pound's "Make it New," while holding ideas of poetry and of poetic composition which are essentially different from those of the classic modern writers. In his attempt to supersede—or transform—those writers, Koch seems to have drawn upon a good many far-flung sources; they range from Kafka to certain recent French poets, including Surrealists, to Whitman, Gertrude Stein, William Carlos Williams and others in the native book.

His general aims are made clear—well, *pretty* clear—in a

dialogue poem called "On the Great Atlantic Rainway" which starts the present volume off. A T. S. Eliot character is uncomfortably present at the exchange of views: "an old man in shorts, blind, who has lost his way in the filling station." A wise old Yeatsian bird, also on hand, finds occasion to remark: "And that is our modern idea of fittingness." But our poet raises these ghosts only to shoo them away. His own idea of fittingness is to shed all formulas, "to go from the sun/Into love's sweet disrepair," to await whatever forms of "unsyntactical beauty might leap up" beneath the world's rainways. In other words, he will flee the sunlight of approved poetic practice, staking his poetic chances on whatever wonders may turn up in the wet weather ("rainways") of *unapproved* poetic practice. He will talk to himself, improvise, consult his dreams, cherish the *trouvaille*, and misprize the well-wrought poem.

Such, as I make it out, is Kenneth Koch's unprogrammatic program (or a part of it), and the calamitous possibilities in it are obvious. Like the similar program of certain of the Beats, it could turn the writing of poetry into a form of hygiene. It could and does: some of Koch's efforts, like many of theirs, suggest the breathing exercises of a particularly deep-breasted individual. "Fresh Air," his most overt attack on the poetic Establishment, is half a witty skirmish, half an interminable harangue. The Unconscious dotes on clichés; and those unsyntactical beauties supposedly lurking beneath Koch's rainway sometimes turn out to be discarded umbrellas. Consulting the sybil of the unconscious, moreover, he is sometimes stuck with mere mouthfuls of images and with lines of verse that make no known kind of music. "I want spring. I want to turn like a mobile/In a new fresh air." He might start by freshening up his images. "I love you as a sheriff searches for a walnut / That will solve a murder case unsolved for years. . . ." Back to the Varsity Show with him. And if his verse is sometimes lacking in the delights of a reliable style, it also offers few of the conveniences of a consistent lucidity. To me his idiom is often a Linear B which remains to be cracked.

But having deciphered quite a lot of it, I feel hopeful that the rest will come clear in time. And for the sheriff and the mobile there are constant compensations. There is "a wind that blows from / The big blue sea, so shiny so deep and so unlike us." Marvelous. And there is the strange excitement aroused by this beginning of a poem called "Summery Weather."

> One earring's smile
> Near the drawer
> And at night we gambling
> At that night the yacht on Venice
> Glorious too, oh my heavens
> See how her blouse was starched up.

"Summery Weather" is a poem of only twenty-five lines, into which is concentrated much of the romance of travel as well as much of the banality of that romance.

There are also several poems of greater length in the volume, two of the best of them being "The Artist" and "The Railway Stationery." Both can be read as portraits of the artist, possibly as fanciful self-portraits of Koch himself in two of his many guises. The first is about a sort of mad Action Painter or Constructivist Sculptor who uses the American landscape as his canvas or showroom. A man with inexhaustible creative powers and many commissions, he consults only his sybil, coming up with a series of colossi which are neither artifacts nor art objects; and all the time he records in his journals various Gide-like reflections on the ecstasies and pangs of the creative life. "May 16th. With what an intense joy I watched the installation of the *Magician of Cincinnati* today, in the Ohio River, where it belongs, and which is so much a part of my original scheme."

The *Magician of Cincinnati* happens to render navigation on the Ohio impossible. But never mind. The Artist will soon attempt something quite different. He never repeats himself— thank God.

"The Railway Stationery" is about a sheet of company letterhead; engraved on it is a half-inch engine which, when the paper is looked at from the reverse side, seems to be backing up; and there is a railway clerk who writes on the stationery, very carefully, a letter beginning "Dear Mary." This poem, composed in blank verse as transparent as the stationery, as touchingly flat as the salutation, may be Kenneth Koch's offering to the artist (lower case) in everyone and everything. —F. W. DUPEE, "You're Welcome," *NYRB*, Vol. 1, No. 2 (1963), pp. 10–12

Speaking of parody, Kenneth Koch is a virtuoso, a marvelous literary mimic who makes high art out of it. When he jokes with operatic drama, chronicle plays or romantic theatre, he does so gently. The pleasure of his comedy is in the fun made not of but *out of* these things, and in the process they really do become interesting and lovable to us again. *Bertha, George Washington, The Construction of Boston*, and *Angelica* all employ, for example, a mock-heroic exaggeration which leaves us with honestly affectionate feelings toward their respective characters. Most of the pieces in *Bertha and Other Plays*, however, don't evoke a specific literary object—they're a blend of many types of parody, hilarious images of social, conversational, patriotic, and civic manners. And everywhere Koch's art shyly applauds the conventions it laughs at, the wonderful delicacy of his humor touches everything lightly with a halo of friendly respect and tolerance. One common type of play in the book is the surrealist skit, as in *Pericles, The Merry Stones, Without Kinship, Guinevere, The Return of Yellowmay, The Revolt of The Giant Animals, The Building of Florence*. In these works Koch writes dramatic verse with the grace and ease of a professional, a craftsmanship that's unnoticeable because the language always remains deliciously fresh, the spirit delightfully irreverent. Another kind of play, the improvisation, establishes itself as extravagantly and preposterously unproducible in traditional terms of direction and performance, and then treats you anyway to an image that smacks of the lively interaction you always expect of stage entertainment. Here's one of them, *The Lost Feed*:

> Seven actresses, impersonating hens and chickens, should, while retaining their human modesty and dignity, act out in as chicken-like a way as possible, the drama of the lost feed. The feed for the day is missing. None of the hens or chickens present is responsible for the absence of the feed, but each one suspects that some one of the others on-stage may be the culprit. Whatever the hens and chickens do, they should make no strictly *personal* remarks when they accuse one another. Their accusations should be rather flat and rather general, accusations which could be leveled at anybody about just about anything. Chicken life is not thought to be very differentiated. After the chickens and hens have been arguing for a long time, the feed should be brought in and given to them.

I think *Bertha* and *George Washington*, and a few of the *Six Improvisational Plays*, are real masterpieces, but there aren't any plays in the book I don't love! They're all wildly funny and beautifully imaginative and civilized. And somehow they manage to be very theatrical although completely fantastic, because Koch's comic sense has everything to do with people. Its witty elegance and point never become cruel or embarrassing, and this politeness is lovely.—TOM CLARK, "A Poetry Chronicle," *Poetry*, May 1967, pp. 108–9

The poems in Kenneth Koch's *Thank You and Other Poems* create a world of surreal wit, a kind of word-playground, the component parts of which are always pleasant and tasty, filled with sunlight and color, with circuses, red shimmering fish, farmyards sprinkled with yellow straw and violets, with green oceans and chugging, rusty ships. (Koch's poems are drenched in the characteristic colors of Matisse, bright, unshaded, and primary.) All of his work is theatrical, and theater has led him to write some delicious little dadaistic farces collected in *Bertha and Other Plays*.

Though he is sometimes insufferably silly, Koch is also a wit—perhaps the most polished wit writing in English, working in the discontinuous, unexpected rhythms of the Marx Brothers. The macabre is very strong in his work, but it is never even remotely depressing. On the contrary, Koch's convulsive catastrophes erupt in technicolor, but noiselessly:

> We laughed at the hollyhocks together
> and then I sprayed them with lye.
> Forgive me, I simply do not know what I am doing.
>
>         . . .
>
> Last evening we went dancing and I broke your leg.
> Forgive me. I was clumsy, and
> I wanted you here in the wards, where I am the
>         doctor!

The most noticeable fact about Koch's work is that it is never, absolutely never, about real pain. The breezy, echoing absence of any appeal to human suffering and its dignity makes his work unique in contemporary poetry, both in and out of the New York School.—STEPHEN KOCH, "The New York School of Poets: The Serious at Play," *NYTBR*, Feb. 11, 1968, p. 5

Some poets, some very good poets, like to stand on edges.

Wordsworth was always on the edge of bathos, and frequently fell over. Whitman was always about to lose his tonsils, and I can't say for sure that he didn't. What was Shakespeare in danger of?—Nothing maybe, unless he was in danger of being the writers he stole his plays from.

Kenneth Koch is always on the edge of nonsense or frivolity, or of a bottomless pit of images, fancies, words.

Take his well known early poem "Fresh Air"—it is a marvelous "fit" (as in Lewis Carroll) on the sad state of divine poesy. In it the edge he teeters on is between mock and serious, or perhaps between rational statement and yawp. The poem is a dramatic display of supermanner, with Koch trying to see how extravagantly he can gesture without dislocating his elbow.

The new book, *The Pleasures of Peace*, is an even more extravagant version of the same game, with gesture or manner displacing statement or content as thoroughly as Koch can manage. "Fresh Air" was, though tenuously, reduceable to some freshman's miserable precis—"Mr. Koch disapproves of the sterility of academic poetry and criticism"—but many of the new poems are further out. Does anybody want to interpret "O Labrador, you are the sexual Pennsylvania of our times"?

Better not try. These are anti-interpretation days. The oracle, Susan Sontag, has advised us to cultivate an erotics rather than a hermeneutics of art, and surely Koch's latest poems, like Ashbery's and many lesser gamesmen's, suggest that he agrees. His poems may be compared musically with a long jam session (oh ancient phrase) on "Ain't She Sweet" or, more tonily, with Beethoven's "Diabelli Variations" where the original waltz is merely the departure point for the concert. Koch is a master of such music. He is marvelously various and inventive. He can play the names of the forty-eight states (he hasn't got to fifty yet) as if they were the complete works of Beethoven, and do the same with sounds, faces, islands, with the phrase "sleeping with women," with erotic proper names, in short anything he finds worthy of gaming with.

Sometimes he adds a harebrained plot, as in the poem "Scales," where he follows a singer's laborious ascent of Do-Re-Mi three times, and the descent once, and then has her reach too low, hemorrhage on Fa and die.

Funny. Clever. The curse of the game. When the poems fall over the edge they are last-days-of-the-empire stuff. The reader wants to put Koch to work in a salt mine.

There are good ponderous reasons why saying something gets harder and harder in poetry, among which is the big reason that everything has been said and is being said badly and constantly. We're awash in statement. "What oft was said but ne'er so well expressed . . ." is a joke of poetic policy when practically every "what" a poet can think of has been said so oft that it has achieved the vigor of "Ain't She Sweet" before he gets to it. At least that seems to be Koch's position on truths in poetry: they are dead ducks in this age of truth overkill, unless you treat them *as* dead, in which case the deader the better.

The title poem, my favorite, takes that deadest of ducks, peace, and improvises around it. Koch presents himself as writing a poem for peace in competition with one Giorgio *Finogle* who is also doing one. Giorgio throws himself out a window for peace, which slows up his poem. Koch keeps on, meanwhile making love for peace and parodying solemn statements of lovers.

He finishes his poem and then gives us samples—for the poem still goes on—of the reviews of it: "Great, man!" "Dead, man!" "I will expect you at six!" Meanwhile, back at the world, monkeys and boats and "all the really important mountains" are for peace, and we emerge sweaty, after 16 pages, with our freshman paraphrase: Nothing is more futile than being for peace.

Over the edge? I don't know, but I think so. I had hoped something other than the usual manner would be displayed in the poem, for the poem is in part a complaint against the manner, a complaint against the wild and futile gesticulations of pacifists. I was looking for Koch to come clean, speak straight from the shoulder about peace, about anything. He didn't, and rightly or wrongly I was disappointed. The poem is so good I would have liked it to have been serious too.

Where is the future of the mode? For the unsubtle imitators of Koch—and there seem to be a lot—the future is over the edge into dada, mockery of mockery, absolute non-statement. But for Koch the future is unclear because he obviously has the capacity, if not the inclination, to be thoroughly rationalist in his verse, and to play a number of other roles than those he chooses.

Since I like Koch but don't like the nonsense world that much of his poetry edges toward, my inclination is to pray for him to come back from the edge. I'm dubious of the results of the prayer, though. Koch might reply by writing a poem about it:

> They are praying for me in
>         Andalusia—or is it
>                 the bathroom?
> They are praying and I hear them,
>         The worms,
> They are perfecting me into a
>         service station.

—REED WHITTEMORE, *NR*, Aug. 2, 1969, p. 23

Mostly Koch encouraged in his students what he calls

"unrhymed, nonmetrical, fairly unliterary poetry"; it was an easier kind for beginning students to approach. But they enjoyed hearing and occasionally trying to write a more formal and intricate language. They would, no doubt, recognize a familiar spirit at play in the pages of *The Duplications.* Their teacher has completed a long poem, somewhat arbitrarily divided in half by an autobiographical section. Using mostly rhymed octets, he sets out to abolish space, time and historical experience in order to create exuberant images that entertain, and occasionally (though with a light hand) instruct. The narrator is a rather sensuous, symbol-prone itinerant, at once rhapsodic and skeptical. He clearly sympathizes with those "Students dreaming up some pure Havanas/Where love would govern all, not francs or dollars"; but he worries that new tyrannies, announced with messianic slogans, keep replacing their predecessors—one of the "duplications" intended by his title, which more broadly refers to the cyclic rhythms of life. He is, always, very much an individual—someone who might not bother Fidel Castro, but who certainly would arouse the suspicions of his bureaucratic henchmen: "O Liberty, you are the only word at/Which the heart of man leaps automatically."

Koch has a delicious sense of ironic detachment running through his rather lyrical, if not ecstatic, celebrations of the flesh. On a Greek island, contemplating the serene beauty of the Aegean, he thinks of the life underneath: ". . . Fish are nice/In being, though we eat them, not revengeful/I think that we would probably be meaner/To those who washed us down with their retsina!" It is an observation utterly worthy of Pueblo or Hopi children, who, like Emerson or Thoreau—speaking of duplications—are not especially inclined to what in the 19th century was called "human vainglory." He is especially wry and touching when he tells of his struggles to write while living in Ireland. He had finished part of the poem, put it aside for other interests (teaching children or the elderly how to write poetry?) and had come back to himself, his mind's (the writer's) self-centeredness. Ought he to go on, "Continue my narration of the fallacy/We find by being born into this galaxy"? His answer is characteristically lacking in egoistic justifications, or sly academic boasting. He simply wants to reach others; maybe make them feel like singing, or smile in recognition of a particular vision, suggestion, anecdote. Of course, he cannot resist, occasionally, tucking into his narrative a bit of philosophical speculation or moral concern.

His is a wanderer's unyielding struggle for life: ". . . Take that, you/Dull insect Death! . . ." His is a naturalist's pantheistic, humorous advocacy: "Now turtles have on Mount Olympus landed/With numerous troops, and pistols, flags, and bells/And hostile mottoes painted on their shells/DOWN WITH OLYMPUS! WHY SHOULD WE ENDURE/AN ALIEN RULE? LET TURTLES REIGN O'ER TURTLES/AND GODS GO HOME! THE VERY AIR IS PURE/WE TURTLES BREATHE. WE DO NOT NEED MYRTLES,/THE OAK, THE BAY, THE SHINING SINE-CURE!/GIVE US OUR LIVES TO LIVE IN OUR HARD GIRDLES!" It is a point of view one can imagine the old ones in the American Nursing Home of New York's Lower East Side taking to rather heartily: their good, dear friend Kenneth Koch doing some of his marvelously entertaining and sometimes unnerving acrobatic stunts.—ROBERT COLES, "Teaching Old Folks an Art," *NYTBR,* April 10, 1977, p. 26

---

### RICHARD HOWARD
### "Kenneth Koch: 'What Was the Ecstasy, and What the Stricture?'"
*Alone with America*
1969, pp. 281–91

To be interested, we are reminded by no less an authority than Martin Heidegger, means to be among and in the midst of things, to be at the center of a thing and stay with it, though today's "interest" accepts as valid only what is *interesting*—the sort of thing that can readily be regarded as indifferent *the next moment* and be replaced by another thing. The conflict between these attitudes, the contradiction between these acceptations of a word—the psychomachia, really, between the ecstatic moment-out-of-time and the movement *of* time (resolved only if we remember that the moment *is* the movement, the smallest unit of movement being a *momentum*); between what Kenneth Koch calls "the imagination in which there is no advance, in which one is always at the peaks" and what he calls, though the chronal italics are mine, "an imagination that demands to be thrilled *at every instant*"; between "a poem in which the same thing happens on every page" and "a poem which is *continually* gorgeous and exciting"—this confrontation supplies the torque, the twist of impulse which makes us stay with this poet, "tourists / in recognition as we are," which makes us stand for the patter: the combat of delight and duration, of eternity and time, of death and life even, is merely a matter of words to Kenneth Koch, as it must be, for he is a poet, the man for whom words matter, for whom they are *material*:

>            . . . a cry
> Of joy and sorrow both, of understanding,
> That pleasure, which is ever so demanding,
> Demanded that he follow through his plan . . .
> Or else with aftermath would be alloyed
> His perfect moments.

He begins far and wide, he begins with an epic, though an epic in which "all's transformed into / one shimmering self!" Kenneth Koch's first book, published in 1959, is a comic epic (though in fact all epics are comic for they are recounted *at length,* they rest or come to rest in *duration*) called *Ko, or A Season on Earth.* By truncating his own name (one shimmering self indeed), the poet gets his Hero's, conveniently that of a Japanese baseball player,

>        Ko was more than a mere fan,
> But wished as a playing member to do a hitch
> with some great team—something to think about
> More interesting than merely Safe and Out.

And by his subtitle, with its lovely punning message—that is, a *baseball* season embracing the globe ("Meanwhile the Dodgers . . . In Athens, Do- / ris climbs the Acropolis . . . While their big barge is moving down the Thames / let's turn to Indianapolis . . . Meanwhile Ko / is pitching, pitching, pitching . . ."), and also the obverse of Rimbaud's *saison en enfer* ("by what we love / spontaneously, we gain awareness of / our freedom and the realizeable world!")—Koch defines his genre and defends his theme: this is to be a poem of secular impulse ("no matter where he is / a man is cheered to see a naked girl") and celebratory echoes ("Oh, how great is art / that brings us on a purple-rainy day / a world of sunshine, insights"), episodic, haphazard ("it's an esthetic moment. Be content"); and by its personnel (including, besides Ko, a neurotic financier who wants to control all the dogs on earth, an English Private eye, an "Action Poet . . . as calm as any man can be / whose poems do not lie in any book / and so are dead to his posterity" and some two dozen others we may find "in an airplane, forest, soap-mine, gulch or tower") as well as by its geographical accommodation, *general*. The clue to what Koch calls "the courage of his large designs" is given out even more insistently than it can be taken in by the epigraph to the entire work, a distich from Ariosto's *Orlando Furioso* I translate here because Koch supplies it only in Italian and, with that fecklessness so typical of the erudite anti-intellectual, misplaces it in the source: "Now, no more! return another time, / you who would hear the splendid tale." *Ko*, then, is to be the "other time," yet here is also a warning that the story will not be splendid, but rather splenetic, sporadic, in every sense of the word a *sport*. We recall that Ariosto's mock-epic "completed" (or at least completed the destruction of) Boiardo's chivalric romance *Orlando Innamorato*, and in its swamping size and apparently chaotic structure reflects a world apart, a world *falling* apart. The gap between the poem's decorous surface and its riotous substance, between seeming order and sensed mutability is not a rift the poet unwittingly creates or creeps into: the split is the poem's subject, and no one is more aware of this than Ariosto, or than Koch hard upon his heels:

> integrity
> Makes him, unlike most poets, actualize
> In everyday life the poem's unreality.

Countless episodes of *Ko* reveal and revel in its own shortcomings, delusions, absurdities. Koch has Byron's delight in the preposterous rhyme: "oranger" / "porringer" or, my favorite, "naturally" / "catcher will he"; he has his own disconcerting sense of simile: "remorseless as a parking meter"; he has the born storyteller's sense of convincing detail: "dachshunds swinging sideways with delight"; and he has, of course, when he wants to invoke the gorgeous, a French symbolist's appanage of correspondences:

> The city of Paris forming in the clouds
> And in that wrack of whitest whisperies.

At the whim of a rhyme, at the beck of a metaphor, things in *Ko* are never what they seem, though they often become what they might be—too much is going on, impinging, underlying, to allow any one set of standards, any one apparatus of judgment the last word, the final say: there is no *final say* here, no ultimates of any sort, only the pleasure of speaking on, and on—*la bella istoria*. The poem—even more radically in Koch's five cantos and 438 stanzas and 3,504 lines than in Ariosto's immensities—is fatally, or at least fitfully (in *fits*, as the old name for stanzas of heroic action had it) examining the poem, rejecting or *showing up* its own criteria by showing them, in order to substitute other possibilities, other *interests*. The success of this enormous poem of vignettes—and it will be the success of all Koch's projects, a prowess which marks, which *is* the borderline between accident and will, between hysteria and method—amounts to the tension between the moment of ecstasy and the movement elsewhere; to the pressure built up in the reader's mind—"in nervous patience till the glory starts"— as the result of a promise to remain at the center yet a *practice* of eccentricity. Over and over, the poet twitches the text away from us with a teasing laugh: "I leave this sportive celebration / and go to England"; which capricious topography is more than the conventional advancement of the narrative on several fronts ("Meanwhile in Tampa . . ."); rather, it is the fear that ecstasy is escaping us, leaking out of duration, that we are not always likely to be on the heights if we stay, merely, where we are. In order to bind the poem to the Interesting forever, in either the sense of instant gratification or the sense of the gratification of the *next* instant, Koch is forever searching

the natural world for new contingencies, now models of ordering, "new seeds of interest and a cure for care." What he wants is some disposition of the poem suggested, even instituted, by a perceived disposition of the Real World or the rational one—say, a poem that, being about the United States, had fifty versicles, mentioning one State in each. Take the scene in *Ko*, when all the girls in Kansas shuck off their clothes; their bodies become

> . . . almanacs to teach
> The . . . poet how to shape his lines,
> The woodsman what is lacking in the pines.

The Body Beautiful as an *ars poetica*, then. Though Koch will use, often to hilarious point ("I thought Axel's Castle was a garage"), the *données* and distractions of literary culture, about which he is wickedly informed ("the poetry / written by the men with their eyes on the myth / and the Missus and the midterms"), his own poems will not submit to the familiarities and fashions of the past except in travesty. He is, for instance, the best parodist of our time, and his Frost, Pound and Perse pieces cannot be expelled, save perhaps by his "Variations on a Theme by William Carlos Williams," which concludes:

> Last evening we went dancing and I broke your leg.
> Forgive me. I was clumsy, and
> I wanted you here in the wards, where I am the doctor!

Reversing the standard pedagogic point, Koch says, "we cannot know anything about the past unless we know about the present," and flings himself into today's loose, baggy garments with tremendous abandon: "Is there no one who feels like a pair of pants?" The heartening if equivocal discovery that art can be ransomed from its fitfulness, from its fretful discontent with the here and now ("Dear coolness of heaven, come swiftly and sit in my chairs!") by a subservience to the natural order, or at any rate to some other order not its own ("we are not / inside a bottle, thank goodness!"), is Kenneth Koch's special Eureka, the resonance ("the fur rhubarb did not please Daisy") we might elsewhere have recognized and rejected in the characteristic modern hero's daydream:

> Then the band would play a march, an amnesty
> would be declared, the Pope would agree to retire
> from Rome to Brazil; then there would be a ball for
> the whole of Italy on the shores of Lake Como at the
> Villa Borghese (the lake of Como being for that
> purpose transferred to the neighborhood of Rome);
> there would come a scene in the bushes, and so on—

We might spot this as the idiosyncratic tonality of our poet[1] if it were not that the *pleasure* of his poems is lacking in it, "the recurring and instinctive joy that is tied to speech," the joy that lets us escape the hysterical aggression in *Ko*, for example, more readily than we may duck away from the anxiety of Dostoievsky's famous invalid in *Notes from Underground* which I have cited here. The point is worth emphasizing, for it determines the absence from these poems of the negative in all its labor and labefactation as well as the presence of so much gaiety and good spirits; as Koch says in his outrageous swipe from the realm of psychological novels, indeed from the realm of psychological novelty which he calls "The Departure from Hydra";

> I can't judge vitality in any way but the way
> It gives me pleasure, for if I do not get
> Pleasure from life, of which vitality
> Is just the liquid form, then what am I
> And who cares what I say? I for one don't . . .[2]

Elsewhere Koch speaks prescriptively of "the detachment of beautiful words from traditional contexts and putting them in curious new American ones," by which we must realize that he indeed *believes in* "beautiful words," in the pleasure they will bestow, once they are put in their curious American contexts. Pleasure and beauty, aesthetic moments, are discovered as "a cure for care." But it is only when the discovery is made without the imposition of the will that Kenneth Koch succeeds in these "large designs" of his; it is only when the composition is come upon rather than compelled that his long poems do more than astonish us (they astonish as a matter of course, a matter of taking their course, "as of course they must if they are to please"). The entire Occidental program, in poetry, of *la difficulté vaincue* is in Kenneth Koch's enterprise given over or gainsaid in favor of *la facilité trouvée.* That is why, henceforth—and henceforth means the work included in two volumes of poems, *Thank You and Other Poems* (1962) and *The Pleasures of Peace* (1969) and a volume of little plays, *Bertha and Other Plays* (1966)—his poems will be written in a prosody attuned to his heart's meters, the stanzas of his breathing, the paragraphs of organs and limbs, but never in the old verse, the versions instinct with some energy of recuperation, of return, of reference to a *given:*

> Until tomorrow, then, scum floating on the surface
>     of poetry! goodbye for a moment, refuse that
>     happens to land in poetry's boundaries! . . .
> Ah, but the scum was deep! Come, let me help you!
>     and soon we pass into the clear blue water. Oh
> GOODBYE, castrati of poetry! farewell, stale
>     pale skunky pentameters (the only honest Eng-
>     lish meter, gloop gloop!) until tomorrow, hor-
>     rors! oh, farewell!
> Hello, sea! good morning, sea! hello, clarity and
>     excitement, you great expanse of green—
> O green, beneath which all of them shall drown!³

This outcry is from Koch's rhetorical manifesto *Fresh Air,* a screed which explains, or at least explodes, the fallacies of all other poets except Kenneth Koch. In it he asserts that his form must be come upon, must be *invented (benedictus qui invenit in nomine Naturae)* or risk losing interest. Hence the terrorism of many of Koch's larger, more deliberate creations which drive themselves by recipe and will to the end of their tether and of ours, a final triumph of method whereby nothing can be made of them except the stunned constatation that *they* have been made. Such poems stand or rather loom at the edges of Koch's career like barbarous temples, brightly lighted but without a congregation to distract us from the hard brilliance of the great American monosyllables—blue, girl, ugh, fun, lunch, pants—festooning every capital, every vault; and on the altar, very reverently placed, as H. G. Wells once said of Henry James' later style, lie a dead kitten, two egg-shells and a bit of string. The significance of a passage like the following from "January Nineteenth":

> The sheep tree, the lightning and thunder!
> Powder writes another novel to itself:
> Passengers, adroit pyramids, and blue triremes!
> Oh how I hate to "Gogol"! Now, baby sweater!
> The Green Cab Sighs have fallen in love.

is precisely that it is not a *passage,* a passing-through the lines, but rather a series of tiny—or immense—epiphanies, unavailing in their tug at one another save as the will decides. For all the "adroit pyramids" of syntactical maneuver, these teratomas of Koch's are made up only of "beautiful words," and fail to be interesting at length because of their willed insistence on the interest of the instant; again and again this poet affords us the enormous trapped *instances* of his genius, his unique posture in our gallery of *outrances:* the victory of moment over movement.

The late Frank O'Hara, who in 1952 (specifically in a text called "Day and Night in 1952") had already diagnosed the poet's situation shrewdly: "Kenneth continually goes away and by this device is able to remain intensely friendly if not actually intimate," suggested to Koch the following year that he undertake something monumental. "I had no clear intention," the poet confides in a note of 1964 on O'Hara, "of writing a 2400-line poem (which it turned out to be) before Frank said to me, on seeing the first 72 lines—which I regarded as a poem by itself—'Why don't you go on with it as long as you can?' " The astounding poem *When the Sun Tries to Go On*—truly, with some things by Roussel and George, one of the monster feats of all modern letters—was published in 1960 in Alfred Leslie's one-shot review *The Hasty Papers,* and its hundred 24-line stanzas, full of soft-drinks, patent medicines, candy bars and the frantic pullulation of overheard trivia, certainly compose a monument—a monument to what the will can accomplish, or if that is too honorific a verb, let us say can *accommodate,* when it articulates itself "as long as it can." Here are the closing lines of the third stanza, originally the conclusion of what the poet "regarded as a poem by itself" (which it certainly is, in one sense of that phrase):

> O hat theory
> Of the definite babies and series of spring
> Fearing the cow of day admonished tears
> That sigh, "Blue check. The tan of free councils
> Cloaks the earth is hen blonde, oh want
> The dye-bakers' coke and hilly plaza, too
> Sunny, bee when halls key tuba plaza corroboration
> Mat nickels." O tell us the correction, bay
> Ex-table, my cocoa-million dollars! Next
> To. O dare, dare-Pullman Car! The best way
> You howling confetti, is "Easter tray,
> As moat-line, promise." How teach the larks!

How indeed. Certainly there are principles of organization, or at least of control, in the work—the repetition of certain classes of nouns, certain expletives, the demands upon innocent syntax which may make any two words together generate some sort of comic effect ("jewelry sevenths," "simplex bumblebees")—but the "interest" in any extent of the thing, and here we are asked to extend our interest over a passage of two thousand four hundred such lines, is so excessively local that the poem becomes, is indeed intended as, a challenge to stay with it as well as a defiance to get a move on. Few who brave the defiance or take up the challenge will reach the end of it, the dying fall: "Gentle hiatus of sarabande cuckoo eep-lariat!"

A dilemma, then, in Koch's poems—"Is the basketball coach a homosexual lemon manufacturer? . . . Is he a lemon memnon?"—will be to hold the line, to draw it at least, and to draw it *in* at best, between the list and the lyric, between the rapture and the (mere) record:

> We must figure out a way to keep our best musicians
>     with us.
> The finest we have always melt into the light blue
>     sky!

Without the mediating tension of a form, an outline of expectation ("we're due to be dawned on, I guess"), a figure from the world of given shapes, taken signals, which is capable of modelling the poem beyond the compulsive anxieties of the poet's gift ("I love you but it's difficult to stop writing"), the poems turn in the one direction into no more than vicious catalogues:

> Messalina gave the canned roastbeef to Horace
>     Greeley
> While Robert Browning sat inside the mudpie.

A tuneful tribute to attitudes rose up
From the far stretches of the salt wampum.
The Queen of Sheba guzzled the iced salad oil like a
 veteran
And January visited the swings . . .

and into catastrophes in the other, reality "profaned or talked at like a hat," cut-ups and explosions of posture momentarily fertile at the expense of any possible continuity:

If I boiled you father
I am sorry and
St. Roch. Still, sex and scary
He wanders over the
She abides
They trade kisses in barefoot hallways
The lemon-sun shines only for them
It will burn their feet! watch out!
But no,
For them it is gentle.

One solution for this conflict between the ecstasy and the stricture, as Koch calls them, is hinted at in the plays, which exploit a tremendous variety of traditional orders to keep the premises up and the pressure down: Elizabethan chronicles, court masques, miracle-plays, No-plays, ballet and opera. Almost anything will feed "the modern idea of fittingness, / to, always in motion, lose nothing"; but the nourishment *as play* offers at least the notion of a cartilage, the connective-tissue of attention between one conniption and the next. In addition to the triumph of *Bertha*—the kind of historical pageant which makes Beerbohm's *Savonarola Brown* seem literal and listless, for Koch conjugates his imperious command of genre with the genuine lunacy of his aggression to produce tableaux of daemonic insouciance—the most significant development, for his poems, in Koch's dramatic devices is the "improvisational play," a scenario or set-piece in which the willfullness can be elided by being described rather than endured. The effect, surprisingly, is the same (we recover, I mean, as much from being *told* that two Monks try to explain the gold standard to each other for four hours as from listening to them do it), and the effort greatly reduced; the "play" element triumphs over the neurotic defense:

Eight or ten actors come on stage, being anyone they want. They speak for 30 minutes. The only requirement is that every sentence they utter must contain the phrase "coil supreme." They may distort the language in any way they wish in order to do this. They should try to generate as much excitement as possible by what they say and do, and the play should end on a note of unbearable suspense.

The great successes in Koch's collections of shorter poems incorporate, whether by flattering or flouting the tradition, some sort of dramatic outline, generally the contour of persecution, as in "Thank You" itself, a grand paranoiac fantasia on themes of disqualification and withdrawal ("and thank you for the pile of driftwood. / Am I wanted at the sea?") singular for its tonality of glee, its brain-splitting peacock laugh that comes just before the damages must be added up and paid for:

And thank you for the chance to run a small hotel
In an elephant stopover in Zambezi,
But I do not know how to take care of guests,
 certainly they would all leave soon
After seeing blue lights out the windows and rust on
 their iron beds—I'd rather own a bird-house in
 Jamaica:
Those people come in, the birds, they do not care
 how things are kept up . . .

It's true that Zambezi proprietorship would be exciting, with people getting off elephants and coming into my hotel,
But tempting as it is I cannot agree . . .

Tantrums, tears of extravagance, follies . . . The supreme achievement in all this is *The Artist*, a jolting, savagely funny account—this is not witty poetry, it is *funny* (as in funny-papers, funny-bone)—of a kind of expanding Gutzon Borglum-persona, pieced together from his journals, remarks, and newspaper clippings. The privilege of the text—it is eight pages long—is in its final propriety of form: high-voiced, light-headed, dangerous, abashing, the speaker faces Koch's own problem and solves it—what to do next, what to make now, where to turn. *The diary* is precisely that discourse which lies between the enumeration and the aria, it is the ledger of the will, and Koch can therefore inflect it between his ecstatic interests and his interests in being elsewhere. Offered in analogy to some of the artistic and social follies of our age, the text transcends satire and parody because in this cascade of nutty impositions we hear the poet's own dilemma, his own desperation voiced on its giddy spiral from interest to interest, from moment to moment, just one damned thing after another; here are three swatches from "The Artist"—at the start, in mid-career, and at his gasping, speculative end:

Cherrywood avalanche, my statue of you
Is still standing in Toledo, Ohio,
O places, summer, boredom, the static of an acrobatic blue!

And I made an amazing zinc airliner
It is standing to this day in the Minneapolis zoo . . .

Old times are not so long ago, plaster-of-paris haircut!

I just found these notes written many years ago.
How seriously I always take myself! Let it be a lesson to me.
To bring things up to date: I have just finished *Campaign*, which is a tremendous piece of charcoal.
Its shape is difficult to describe; but it is extremely large and would reach to the sixth floor of the Empire State Building. I have been very successful in the past fourteen or fifteen years.
June 3rd. It doesn't seem possible—The Pacific Ocean! I have ordered sixteen million tons of blue paint. Waiting anxiously for it to arrive. How would grass be as a substitute? cement?

Having ransacked every genre, every convention, every possibility of outrage and confiscation—"never stop revealing yourself"—Koch has in "The Artist" and in several other uproarious instances ("You Were Wearing," "Locks," "Lunch," "Down at the Docks") produced poems which are entirely *his own*. That is their limitation of course, but it is their great resource too, their great and problematic *interest*, flickering between the intolerable moment and the intolerable movement, the unendurable *now* and the unendurable *next*, an oscillation which, as the poet himself remarks, can conclude only "when Kenneth is dead"—

. . . like the sunlight at the end of the tunnel, like
 my rebirth in the poems of Kenneth Koch.

*Notes*

1. It is the parallel if not the progenitor of any random quote from Koch's "novel"—his habit, by the way, of casting a distance upon just about anything by quotation marks is as infectious as a giggle—

a kind of Raymond Roussel collage of compositional procedures called *The Red Robins*:

> The ennui became almost unbearable. Forests shook. Lynn took off her sweater and performed "semi-nude" imitations of all the Japanese prints of Hokusai. This time the country began to deliberate quite a lot about the hawsers . . .

2. The terrible trot of these prose pentameters—what else to call them?—is the march Koch has stolen on the blank-verse deliberations of a Wordsworth, a Wallace Stevens. Whenever he speaks normatively, Koch claps on a mask, a costume he accounts for thus in his text "The Postcard Collection": "There are a great many human relationships and a great many situations inside other relationships in which there is no communication without disguise and self-mockery . . . They are rarely, except at the heights of hysteria or inspiration, recognized as such."

3. The ocean, beneath the scum of forms, is of course the necessary and obdurate antagonist of the metrical norms: "nothing gives so much pleasure as the sea."

## JOHN GARDNER

*New York Times Book Review*, December 23, 1973, pp. 1, 14

It's not strictly necessary to read both of Kenneth Koch's excellent and enormously important books on children and poetry, though I strongly recommend it, if only for the pleasure both books give. Each stands on its own, implying the whole argument. But they're better together, and to anyone for whom the subject is important—parents, teachers, anyone who has the normal human delight in true poetry, or anyone who wonders how his normal human pleasure was dwarfed and twisted—the pair of books will, I think, be a revelation.

*Wishes, Lies, and Dreams*, originally published in 1970, is the record of Koch's highly successful experiment with teaching children to write poetry at P.S. 61 in Manhattan. In schools all over America, children are excited when the art teacher comes in; and a look at children's art in recent years shows that something really happens in those art classes. Why then should the art of poetry be, for children, an annoyance and a bore? Koch, himself the author of such books of poetry as "The Pleasures of Peace," "Thank You" and "Ko, or A Season on Earth" and a professor of English and comparative literature at Columbia, set out to prove—and has clearly proved—that writing poetry can be as exciting as anything in a child's experience. When he entered a classroom, his pupils (grades 1 through 6) shouted and clapped. When he left the classroom, he left children's poems that might make an adult poet envious. Poems like this:

> Snow is as white as the sun shines.
> The sky is as blue as a waterfall.
> A rose is as red as a beating of drums.
> The clouds are as white as the busting of a fire-
>     cracker.
> A tree is as green as a roaring lion.

*Wishes, Lies, and Dreams* tells how he did it and how, hopefully, anyone can do it. I can suggest here only the general approach. He began with the firm conviction that the thing could be done. He writes: "One thing that encouraged me was how playful and inventive children's talk sometimes was. They said true things in fresh and surprising ways. Another was how much they enjoyed making works of art—drawings, paintings, and collages. I was aware of the breakthrough in teaching children art some forty years ago. I had seen how my daughter and other children profited from the new ways of helping them discover and use their natural talents. That hadn't happened yet in poetry. Some children's poetry was marvelous, but most

seemed uncomfortably imitative of adult poetry or else childishly cute. It seemed restricted somehow, and it obviously lacked the happy, creative energy of children's art."

To get what he was after, he knew he must slay two ancient schoolroom dragons. One was inhibition, the child's fear of getting something wrong, proving for the thousandth time that he's stupid, unacceptable. The other was, in effect, the child's innocence of cultural tradition. However free and open a child may feel, he nevertheless has the question, "What shall I write about?"—really the difficult question, "What is a poem?"

Koch slew the first dragon by establishing a comfortable, fairly noisy classroom much like that typical of art classes; by encouraging students to write whatever they pleased, joke poems (even ornery jokes on Mr. Koch), mean poems, poems involving sex, and so on; by placing no importance on spelling, grammar, or neatness (all matters which could be attended to later); and by discouraging the use of rhyme, since rhyme tends to limit imagination and honest feeling. As for the child's question, "What shall I write?," Koch worked out a set of "Ideas for Poems"—simple, essentially formal ideas that should get things moving in any classroom. One is, *Begin every line with "I wish."* Another is, *Use a comparison in every line.* (He offers many more.) The poem I quoted earlier, "Snow is as white as the sun that shines," is a result of the comparison idea. Here is another:

> Thunder is like bowling
> Clouds are like a feather
> The sun is like a yellow balloon in the sky
> A tiger is like the beating of drums.

I quote this second poem partly to relay one of Koch's most important points. Both poems I've quoted, you'll have noticed, contained the phrase "beating of drums." A bad teacher would call that plagiarism. In fact, it's a proof of live poetic tradition in P.S. 61. Again and again, Koch's students borrowed each other's ideas, attempting to improve on them. (That's one of the things art is all about.) Koch forced this valuable process along by getting children to write in collaboration. He says, "Composing a poem together is inspiring: the timid are given courage by braver colleagues; and ideas too good to belong to any one child are transformed, elaborated on, and topped." A typical result of collaborative writing:

> I wish I was an apple
> I wish I was a steel apple
> I wish I was a steel apple so when people bit me their
>     teeth would fall out. . . .

The poems by children published in *Wishes, Lies, and Dreams* show how vital poetic tradition was at P.S. 61. Naturally, it was a somewhat limited tradition: children learned from each other and from their teacher's suggestions, but the children themselves felt a need for something more. Koch's response was to shift the experiment to "teaching great poetry to children," thus broadening the tradition available to them. And the record of this experiment and its startling results is *Rose, Where Did You Get That Red?*

In his new book Koch explains in detail how he introduced—how any good teacher might introduce—poems ranging from Blake's "The Tyger" to Rimbaud's "Voyelles." Briefly, the method went like this: Koch would pass out and read the poem, he and the children would talk about it, not worrying about every single detail but getting the feeling, the core idea. With "The Tyger," for instance, the core idea is "A person talking to an animal." As soon as the teacher senses that the children have got it—that is, they feel the awe at the heart of the poem, the shocking quality of the nightmare lines ("burning bright / In the forests of the night," or the idea of God hammering out the tiger on an anvil)—the teacher sets the children to work on poems of their own.

Look at three results. First, a poem-fragment which shows imagistic influence from Blake:

> Giraffe! Giraffe!
> What kicky, sticky legs you've got.
> What a long neck you've got. It looks
>      like a stick of fire . . .

Second, a fragment from a brilliant joke poem that shows that its young author really *did* imagine conversation with an animal:

> Glub blub, little squid. Glub blub, why blub do you glub have blub Glubbblub blub such glub inky blub stuff blubbb? I use it for a protective shield against my enemies blubbb . . .

Third, a poem I quote simply because it's terrific:

> Giraffes, how did they make Carmen? Well, you see, Carmen ate the prettiest rose in the world and then just then the great change of heaven occured and she became the prettiest girl in the world and because I love her.
> Lions, why does your mane flame like fire of the devil? Because I have the speed of the wind and the strength of the earth at my command.
> Oh Kiwi, why have you no wings? Because I have been born with the despair to walk the earth without the power of flight and am damned to do so.
> Oh bird of flight, why have you been granted the power to fly? Because I was meant to sit upon the branch and to be with the wind.
> Oh crocodile, why were you granted the power to slaughter your fellow animal? I do not answer.

Not everyone can teach children poetry as well as Kenneth Koch, a man who, as a superb poet himself, perhaps knows more about poetry than he realizes. Telling how he worked in the classroom, he says: "Sometimes a student would be stuck, unable to start his poem. I would give him a few ideas, while trying not to give him actual lines or words— 'Well, how do musical instruments sound? Why don't you write about those?' or 'What do you hear when you're on a boat?' Sometimes students would get stuck in the middle of a poem, and would do the same sort of thing. Sometimes I would be called over to approve what had been written so far, to see if it was OK. I often made such comments as 'That's good, but write some more,' or 'Yes, the first three lines in particular are terrific—what about some more like that?' or . . . 'I think maybe it's finished. What about another poem on the other side?'"

I talked with a college professor in California, a well-known literary critic, who tried teaching young children by Koch's method. The problem, he told me frankly, was that he was never absolutely sure what to praise, what to call finished, and so on. If it was hard for my friend, it may be harder yet for, say Miss Watson at East Pembroke Central.

Nevertheless, the principle is right, and not just for poets. What we have now fails almost invariably; Koch's method will work for everybody at least some of the time. His two books could—*should*—be the beginning of a great revolution. I urge you to buy them, pass them around, exert influence on schools. Help stamp out the kind of poetry children are normally forced to read and write—for example this horrible textbook piece (from "September," in *The World of Language*, Book 5, Follett Educational Corporation) which Kenneth Koch quotes:

> . . . Asters deep purple,
> A grasshopper's call,
> Today it is summer,
> Tomorrow is fall.

Koch compares, with devastating effect, a fifth-grader's poem on spring:

> Spring is sailing a boat
> Spring is a flower waking up in the morning
> Spring is like a plate falling out of a closet for joy
> Spring is like a spatter of grease. . . .

# JERZY KOSINSKI

## 1933–

Jerzy Kosinski was born on June 14, 1933, the son of Russian Jews living in Lodz, Poland. His father was a classical scholar at the University of Lodz; his mother was a pianist. The Nazi invasion of Poland in 1939 separated Kosinski from his parents; he spent the next six years wandering throughout eastern Poland. In 1945 his parents, who had miraculously survived the Holocaust, found him in a Lodz orphanage; it transpired that he had lost the power of speech following an emotional confrontation in a village whose inhabitants had refused to shelter him from the occupying German forces. However, in 1948 he was knocked unconscious in a skiing accident; when he awoke, his ability to speak had returned. Kosinski subsequently finished high school, and began his studies at the University of Lodz in 1950. By 1955 he had been awarded two M.A.s, in history and in political science; in 1957, frustrated with restrictions on free speech behind the Iron Curtain, he left Poland; the circumstances of this are unclear. It is known that shortly afterward he enrolled at Columbia University, where he did doctoral work on the sociology of literary forms and languages.

Kosinski's first two works, *The Future Is Ours, Comrade* (1960) and *No Third Path* (1962), were non-fiction analyses of life in Communist Russia and Poland. Both works received high praise; one reader who wrote her praises directly to Kosinski was Mary Weir, the young widow of the billion-dollar steel magnate Ernest Weir. Kosinski and Weir eventually met, and were married in 1962. During the next several years they lived together at her various residences in New York, Southampton, Paris, and London, and on several yachts. However, Mary died in 1968, and her wealth reverted back to her first husband's estate; but by this time Kosinski had begun to make a fortune of his own. His first novel, *The Painted Bird* (1965), an account of a lost child's wanderings in Eastern Europe during World War II, drew a tremendous response. His second novel, *Steps* (1968), won the National Book Award. Although Kosinski has published six more novels since then, most critics agree that the first two are his best to date. In 1979 and 1981, respectively, Kosinski won awards from the Writers Guild of America and from the British Academy of Film and Television Arts for his screenplay for *Being There*, adapted from his 1971 novel of the same title. In 1982 Kosinski made his screen debut as G. Zinoviev in *Reds*, Warren Beatty's film about John Reed and the Russian Revolution.

A highly controversial figure in the world of American letters, Kosinski has held teaching positions at Wesleyan, Princeton, and Yale. From 1973 to 1975 he served as president of the American Center of P.E.N. In 1982 Kosinski was embroiled in a tabloid war over allegations concerning his background and the authorship of his novels. Although nothing was proved by any of the parties to the dispute, the confusion surrounding Kosinski's person has not decreased. Largely as the result of his own efforts, much of his life remains shrouded in mystery.

One measure of Jerzy Kosinski's quality is that he arrived in the US in 1957 without a word of English and by 1968 he has written four books in English: two works of non-fiction, published under the pen-name Joseph Novak, and two novels, *The Painted Bird* (1965) and now *Steps*. A better measure of his quality is that this achievement is irrelevant. Both his novels (I haven't read the Novak books) are admirable in themselves, and the second one pushes into extraordinary inner chambers, echoing and appalling. These days any impatient juvenile can show his impatience with the traditional novel by giving us loose pages in a box or omitting description or omitting everything else. In *Steps* Kosinski breaks with the traditional novel in a traditional way: he makes his book so scorchingly personal that it is unique. It's possible to make comparisons (as I shall) because no artwork is completely new, but *Steps* is a "new" novel because it is so utterly Kosinski's, wrought in memories and understanding of himself, his own fierce fight to find breathing-space in the welter of overwhelming experience.

In a pamphlet about *The Painted Bird*, he described that book as "the author's vision of himself as a child, a *vision*, not . . . a revisitation of childhood . . . the result of the slow unfreezing of a mind long gripped by fear. . . ." It is a series of short chapters about a homeless Jewish child in Eastern Europe during the Second War whose experiences with peasants and soldiers are so icily brutal that they justify the quotation from Artaud in Kosinski's pamphlet: "Cruelty is above all lucid, a kind of rigid control and submission to necessity." The inner coil of the book slackens somewhat toward the end, but it is one of the best works of literature to come out of the European horror. The author says that *The Painted Bird* is organized "in little dramas, in spurts of experience, with the links largely omitted, as is the case with memory." In *Steps* this method is further refined, with a greater admixture of imagination to experience.

The new book, only 148 pages, consists of some 50 episodes arranged in eight unnumbered sections. Many of the episodes are linked in content; all of them are unified in vision. It would be too bald to say that *Steps* is about the boy-protagonist of *The Painted Bird* as a man. The arrangement is no longer chronological, and the settings now sometimes seem metaphorical, as does some of the action. The real relation with the first book is in the mosaic method and in the fact that *Steps* derives from the world of *The Painted Bird*.

There is no attempt here to tell a sequential story; the individual stories construct a cosmos. A few of the episodes, the only ones with dialogue, are snatches of conversation in the "present" between the narrator and his mistress. Almost all of them are stories about the narrator, self-contained but thematically cumulative. Some of them suggest Babel, some a darker Dinesen, some de Maupassant. All are touched with sexuality or violence or both, all share the quality of an author who insists on forcing one foot in front of another into the irrational maze of his life. It is a life that epitomizes in thousandfold intensity the questions and fears of most contemporary men. The author calls up his experience for examination, for *adjustment*; he is saying, "I cannot make life rational or humane, but I can record that some rational and humane men live it, knowing what they pay in reason and humaneness."

⟨. . .⟩ Sentences are generally short and direct. It is a style made of small, deceptively plain, exploding capsules. Except for the narrator, there are no characters, only figures who perform clarifying functions. The steady coolness of the book and its very brevity—which heightens the sense of tremendous distillation—add to its power. The book has a last irony. In the closing episode the viewpoint shifts to the "present" mistress and shows her as victim of the narrator. The world has done its hardening work on him.

In *The Painted Bird* I felt the author pulling himself free of his past as out of a quagmire, each page a knot on the rope by which he climbed upward. Not so here. *Steps*, a superior work, more subtly conceived, is a piercing view of that past as part of the world's present. For me, the title does not signify progress from one place to another or from one state to another but simply action about experience: steps taken to accommodate experience and continuing reality to the possibility of remaining alive.

A few of the episodes show the bones of contrivance, like one about a contest with cars to knock books off other cars' fenders. A few of them, even after a second or third reading, yield insufficient resonance. But in the main, *more* than the main, this small book is a very large achievement. Through all its smoke and fire and pain, a curious pride persists. The book says finally: "Hell. Horror. Lust. Cruelty. Ego. But *my* hell and horror and lust and cruelty and ego. Life is—just possibly—worth living if at last we are able to *see* what we do, if we can imagine it better and imagine it worse."—STANLEY KAUF-MANN, "Out of the Fires," *NR*, Oct. 26, 1968, pp. 22, 41

The dust jacket of *Being There* tells us that the author, Jerzy Kosinski, was born in Poland in 1933, and that the first of his two earlier novels, *The Painted Bird*, has been translated into thirty-two languages, and the second, *Steps*, into twenty-nine.

One wonders what the missing three are—Urdu? Korean? Arawak? *Being There*, simultaneously with its American publication, is being published in England, Holland, Germany, and France, and the flap copy, with its promise of a "modern parable" and a "quintessential anti-hero," seems to be warming up an international audience in easy Esperanto. The description of the book, however, is twelve lines shorter than the description of the author, and, bizarrely, at the end of the novel the typography suggests that Kosinski's biography is the last chapter—two pages' worth of his degrees, his fellowships, his professorships, his awards, his translations. In short, the author, not the novel, is the product being pushed. Which is shrewd, since the novel, like its hero, barely exists.

The hero is called Chance. He is an illiterate foundling kept by a rich old man known, with a simplicity too ominous, as the Old Man. Chance has two activities: he tends the Old Man's garden (Madam, I'm Adam) and watches television. After the Old Man dies, lawyers discover that Chance's existence has generated no external evidence—no driver's license, no credit cards, no tax records, not even dental records. He is cast out of the garden, and instantly encounters (hello, Eve) EE, the wife of another very rich old man, Rand. Everywhere, Chance creates an excellent impression, and he comports himself very well; gardening and television-watching seem to be at least as adequate a preparation for adult life as a college education. Though he doesn't know how to read or make love beyond the preliminaries shown on the idiot box, he can make speeches that win the heart not only of EE but of the President of the United States. As the saga ends, Chance, a total nonentity four days before, has the Vice-Presidential nomination in his pocket. No doubt there is a lot in this, from political satire (Chance = Agnew) to philosophical allegory ("being there" = Heidegger's *Dasein*). Also, there is some kind of joke on McLuhanite coolness; Chance is a walking television screen: people "began to exist, as on TV, when one turned one's eyes on them. . . . The same was true of him." The dust jacket, helpful to a fault, calls Chance "prelapsarian man" and asks, "Is Chance the technocrat of the future? . . . Or is he Rousseauesque, with a touch of natural goodness to which men respond?" Tune in next parable. Myself, I prefer to see him as the blind Chance that rules the universe, into which people touchingly read omniscience and benevolence and anthropomorphic Divinity.

The trouble is that all this symbolic superstructure, and the manipulative fun it invites, rests on a realistic base less substantial than sand. Rand has one amusing, almost lifelike speech. Chance's sensations when he appears on television, "the cameras . . . licking up the image of his body," can be felt. There is one sharp image, of "frosty sculptures," in rooms of vague furniture. Otherwise, the texture of events is thin, thin, preposterously thin. The rich and powerful may be stupid, but they would not mistake a comatose illiterate for a financial wizard. A hermit might be innocent, but his body would know how to achieve an erection. Fortune may be arbitrary in bestowing her favors, but she is not totally berserk. When a character in the book expresses incredulity at Chance's abrupt and baseless fame, he is appealing to laws of probability that have never been established. There is not enough leverage even to spring a laugh. No two things are incongruous, because hardly anything in *Being There* is *there*.

You could say that this is an immigrant's impression of America, an "other planetary perspective." But compare Nabokov; also an immigrant, from the same Slavic hemisphere as Kosinski, he assiduously put himself to school with American particulars and came up with a portrait—not only in *Lolita* but in the background of *Pnin* and in the poem *Pale Fire*—of

the United States grotesquely and tellingly acute in its details. Mr. Kosinski's portrait expresses little but the portraitist's diffident contempt for his subject—the American financial and political Establishment. He does not enough hate it to look hard at it; the result is not even a cartoon. Stylized also were the nameless villages of the Polish marsh in *The Painted Bird*, but those scenes were in Kosinski's blood, and the plausibililty gaps were filled with an experienced terror that redeemed the parade of Grand Guignol episodes from being merely sensational. In *Steps*, an adult man's erotic explorations were interwoven with these same horrific villages, and incriminated in the same sinister cruelty. Perhaps the intention of *Being There* was to transfer this sinisterness to an America befogged by media and ruled by stuffed shirts. The result is feebly pleasant—a dim and truncated television version of those old Hollywood comedies wherein a handsome bumpkin charms the world and makes good. Unlike Kosinski's other novels, *Being There* is not painful to read, which in his special case is not a virtue.—JOHN UPDIKE, "Bombs Made out of Leftovers," NY, Sept. 25, 1971, pp. 132–34

Reading *The Devil Tree* one is aware of those things that Kosinski does with consummate skill: the mode that lies somewhere between Kafka and our own sense of daily reality; the flat, underplayed, uncomprehending style; the use of a kind of narrative parataxis, all of those short, unrelated bits of narrative, much of whose force lies in the art with which they are detached from each other. "The auditorium grew silent," one such section begins, "the lights dimmed; only one bright spotlight followed the frail man who walked slowly towards the marble podium. The all-male audience sat motionless, its gaze fixed upon him. The man stumbled on one of the steep steps leading to the podium, but promptly recovered his balance. No one moved." It is a unique fictional method, so starkly inimitable that anyone who had ever read anything by Kosinksi would know who had written those lines. The narrative parataxis, moreover, is a marvelously expressive device for Kosinski's purposes in *The Devil Tree*: wishing to show the rootlessness of his central character, he is able to move him from Manhattan to Nepal without transition or modulation; wishing presumably to show the particular shallowness of his quest for sensation, he is able to show unfulfilled sex, unmotivated drug use, and unresolved encounter sessions by the rhythms and omissions of his narrative segments.

Kosinski evidently intends for his novel to embody American myth and American reality, American dreams and American limitations, which means that *The Devil Tree* aims in a somewhat different direction from *Steps*, which locates all of its scarifying brutality in no particular place, and *Being There*, which projects a fatuous extension of American power without much attempt to place that movement in the solid texture of American reality. What such a purpose requires is a certain consistency of mode. Yet the book moves among a variety of modes: at one time it is neopicaresque, the central figure a bemused invisible man in the world of petty functionaries; at other times it seems a rather unfocused and old-fashioned piece of satiric realism; and at still other times it is cut loose altogether from social fact, in a country of the mind like Kafka's *Amerika*. So it is that its import is diffuse, its ability to move the reader is intermittent, its parts are better than its whole, and its voice is greater than its vision.—PHILIP STEVICK, "Voice & Vision," PR, 1974, p. 305

There are certain great moments in fiction, when the vast mists of the world suddenly part; *Blind Date* has one of them: 'Levanter could not speak. Mute, dispirited, he started the engine. Without pausing to look back, Jaques Monod walked away. As he started to climb the steps to the house, the last rays of the setting sun wrapped him in their glow.' I haven't come across such a potent combination of effects since I last opened an American novel, but the mixture here of name-dropping, cheap romance and rather precious fictionalising succeeds mainly by being worse than anything that has come before it. *Ragtime* turned this particular tone into an industrial process. It consists of saying as little as possible in the largest possible space—while at the same time convincing the reader that he is part of an amazing and genuinely historical experience. But the flatness of the writing here is peculiarly un-American; Kosinski himself is of European origin, and so he tries hard to avoid the flashiness of his contemporaries. He provides the emptiness, but without the rhetoric.

The tone of the book is unsettling: at one moment we dive into the wide-eyed breathlessness of conventional romantic fiction (where girls are girls, and 'Levanter studied the shadows her lashes cast on her cheeks . . .'), and at the next we're in the City of the Night where Levanter, the 'hero' of the novel, cuts through the undergrowth like a chainsaw. He sleeps with his mother, with a transsexual, with a real woman, and with himself; he kills people and he tricks people; he has a conscience, and he has a heart. It is always easy to load one character with so many meretricious blessings, but it's difficult to make him interesting as a result. Characters fade in a novel unless they are comprehensible or sympathetic: Levanter is a creature of fantasy and, like all fantasies, he becomes quickly and irredeemably boring. He could climb the Eiffel Tower while balancing a poisoned orange on his nose, but he won't survive if his dialogue is flatulent and the general context is banal.

Kosinski must realise this in part, since he has divided the novel into a number of separate but unrelated episodes, so the reader can switch off at any point without actually missing very much. Levanter is a Russian expatriate, now living in America and representing something known as Investors International, who has given up a career of athletic and mental prowess in order to play a few absurd confidence tricks, fight for 'natural justice' and deluge his libido in some watery scenes. But none of it really adds up to much, and the narrative flaps and crawls along the ground as the fictional puppets are introduced alongside Charles Lindbergh, Monod, and even Svetlana Alliluyeva. Kosinski has clearly included everyone and everything he can think of, on the principle that bad writing abhors a vacuum—even when it is one of its own making. But when real figures jostle beside the fictional characters, narratives become troublesome and ambiguous; fantasies can be disastrous if the line between life and art isn't carefully measured and maintained.

In fact that line is blurred only for suspect purposes, when the imagination is not strong enough and life is not real enough. And in order to confer a solid identitiy upon Levanter, this creature of his imaginings, Kosinski has had to create a two-dimensional world which will act as a support. One dimension stretches into some fantasy of sexuality and virility, where all the usual cliches are brought into play, and the other wanders out into some half-real world where Levanter meets important people and thereby becomes important himself. It is the usual alchemy of false writing.

And so the novel founders on unreality; since Kosinski doesn't recognise, let alone acknowledge, the ambiguities that surround his central figure, Levanter simply becomes a vehicle for grey fantasies and brutally prurient acts. When a character is only a cypher, anything can happen to it. At one moment Levanter is the great lover, and at the next he is a sadistic killer: 'When the entire blade had penetrated, the corpse lay motionless. Levanter covered it with a sheet.' And then, as if Kosinski were trying to prove that life can be as banal as his art, all of this is followed by some idiotic 'realistic' posturing. 'Knowing Jaques Monod did not have much time left, Levanter decided to go to Cannes to be with him.' I don't know if Monod would care to spend his last hours on earth with a sadistic murderer, but it's certainly no fun for the reader.

Living people—that includes you and me, who have to read the stuff, let alone Monod—are diminished and cheapened by a book which treats everyone as an object of prurient fantasy. The fact that Kosinski drags in real human suffering almost as an after-thought—he deals at some length, and inexplicably, with the Sharon Tate killings—only makes his attempts at significance and 'meaning' all the more gratuitous and unpleasant. Death is the easiest merchandise for a bad writer. And *Blind Date* makes *Mein Kampf* seem like a miracle of good taste.—PETER ACKROYD, "Prurience," *Spec*, Feb. 11, 1978, p. 20

Jerzy Kosinski's fictional persona easily made the transition from victim, in *The Painted Bird*, to victimizer, in *Steps*. Throughout the four subsequent novels, the cold blooded, impervious Kosinski hero changed little; CIA operative Tarden of *Cockpit* was as cruel as freelance secret agent Levanter of *Blind Date*. *Passion Play*, however, finds the persona somewhat mellowed. In his latest reincarnation, he is an aging polo player named Fabian. He regretfully notes the sagging flesh of his face, assiduously squeezes the pus from his pores and worries over his greying pubic hairs, but fears that plucking them will metastasize a cancer. The consuming aggression of past heros has been turned inward, modulated into a neurotic self-absorbtion with the body and sickness.

⟨. . .⟩ Now it is true that Kosinski has produced one great work, *The Painted Bird*. In that first novel, he summoned through his vivid writing images of horror that no reader is likely to forget. Since then, he has done only passably well with the spare action writing of the detective novel. He doesn't have the crude power of Mickey Spillane, the finesse of Ross McDonald, or even the professionalism of any number of detective writers. But his prose is functional as a vehicle for moving something from point A to point B, and is unobjectionable as long as it remains unobtrusive.

Unfortunately, it does not often remain unobtrusive. The erotic passages, for instance, are on a par with the mechanical thumpings the editors of *Penthouse* grind out every month in their letters column. Kosinski's all-purpose euphemism for the genitals, "flesh," is particularly disagreeable, with its (probably unintended) cannibalistic connotations.

His forays into lyrical description are frankly embarrassing, too. About halfway through *Cockpit* we come upon the following: ". . . the Ruh, the wet wind from the warm lakes, swept through the region. . . . The dull glow of morning hovered over the spreading gray hills, and the raindrops, the children of the Ruh, shook themselves loose from the sky, scuttling fast. The Ruh punished them as they fled, forcing them aslant and hurling them against the ground."

*Passion Play* teems with this sort of clichéd imagery and amateurish anthropomorphism. Fall leaves cling "defiantly" to trees. And a bit later: "Like a skiff bringing up the rear, a solitary leaf, its fretted veins a lair for the sun, would scud in his wake, gliding through the dappled air." Well, is the leaf gliding or is it scudding? Overloaded with such imagery, it is surprising it doesn't drop like a brick. And dappled air?

Along with his prose, Kosinski also has been lauded by one critic for "the pure genius" of his plotting; other reviewers have been hardly less enthusiastic. They must all be minimalists. For what little plot there is in Kosinski's novels simply follows the peregrinations of the protagonists. This makes for an episodic and often disjointed narrative, particularly in *Passion Play*, perhaps Kosinski's most plotted work. In the time it takes to move from the genesis of an idea to its predictable conclusion one simply loses interest.⟨. . .⟩

The ingenious perversity and remorseless violence of Kosinski's earlier novels inspired enthusiastic readers to talk of "deeply buried fantasies" and "devastating" commentaries "on contemporary Western life." I would suspect that these fantasies, to the extent we really all do share them, are not so deeply buried: They are the effluvium of our mass-market fantasy machine, the fluff of adolescent thrillers and adventure stories. An admiring critic once described Kosinski as an "Existential Cowboy." This could be Kosinski's epitaph, for it perfectly registers his level of seriousness. Certainly he is far from being "One of the foremost psychological novelists in the world," as Gail Sheehy called him in a *Psychology Today* interview.

Kosinski's new opus will force some critical reappraisal even from his fans. From *Steps* to *Blind Date* he appeared to have dispensed entirely with sentiment as a useless hindrance. In *Passion Play*, we are flooded with teenage romanticism. This is not such a surprising evolution. In line with Hannah Arendt's argument about the banality of evil, it may be noted that Kosinski's maudlin sentimentality is the flip side of his sadomasochism. The brutality of his earlier novels and the melodrama of *Passion Play* differ only on the surface; both are a palsied caricature of life that never reaches down to stir up our truly buried fantasies.

Kosinski's protagonists are always taking pictures. As an image, photography captures his peculiar mix of alienation, volation and aggressive voyeurism. Here is Tarden, of *Cockpit*, in an uncharacteristically reflective moment, pondering photographs of himself making love to various women: "These photos were taken by cameras equipped with a delayed action mechanism. When I think about the energy expended during the last decades in picking up these women, and in taking, developing and enlarging these photographs, I am overcome by its pointlessness." Understandably so.—Joshua Gilder, "Existential Cowboy Gone Astray," *NL*, Nov. 19, 1979, pp. 19–20

---

### IRVING HOWE
### "From the Other Side of the Moon"

*Harper's*, March 1969, pp. 102–5

Jerzy Kosinski was born in Poland in 1933. He lived through the war and then the Stalinist occupation of his country; at the age of twenty-four he came to the United States. He has since published two works of social commentary and two of fiction, *The Painted Bird* (1965) and *Steps* (1968). He writes in English, and by some miracle of training, which recalls the linguistic bravado of Conrad and Nabokov, he is already a master of a pungent and disciplined English prose. Simply as a stylist, Kosinski has few equals among American novelists born to the language. And I have also become convinced, after reading *Steps*, that he is one of the most gifted new figures to appear in our literature for some years.

*Steps* is an experimental work, which is partly to say that it follows upon the "tradition of the new" that has dominated Western writing for the past century but that it also deviates sharply in tone and technique from that tradition—otherwise it could no longer be described as experimental. It is a work highly problematic in aesthetic strategy and moral implication, and even after two careful readings I do not pretend to grasp it

fully. All I hope is that I will not gloss over my puzzlement by means of an overheated "literary" rhetoric, such as overwhelmed reviewers often employ to mask their difficulties.

Kosinski's first piece of fiction, *The Painted Bird*, apart from being a brilliant work in its own right, offers some clues to his literary intentions. *The Painted Bird* is organized as an autobiographical recollection of the sufferings endured by a six-year-old boy who in the fall of 1939 was sent from a large city in Eastern Europe, "like thousands of other children, to the shelter of a distant village." Written with a rapacious intensity, *The Painted Bird* charts the boy's wanderings from village to village: hunted, beaten, starved, violated. The world of the East European peasants comes to seem a brute double of the Nazis' technological horrors, and at the very least the book should burn out all notions about noble savages and primitive creatures of earth. Kosinski's theme appears to be the spiritual interchangeability between backward and advanced civilizations, their union in hate. ("No death is granted to hate," he writes in a commentary on his novel, "it follows in the wake of life, and as the tail is part of the comet, so is hate a part of life itself.") The final effect of *The Painted Bird*, described by its author as "an attempt to peel the gloss off the world," is like that of a Bosch painting or a Buñuel film: often literally unbearable, so that one rushes to agree with Buñuel when he remarks about the book, "I had to stop a couple of times, almost terrified by some of its chapters."

About Kosinski's powers for graphic evocation there can be no doubt, but finally one wonders whether there is not in this book a numbing surplus of brutality. *The Painted Bird* comes to seem too close to that which it portrays, too much at the mercy of its nightmare. Literature is not life, and there is a question—at least there always has been—as to how much of the world's gloss can be peeled off in a book. About the possibilities for peeling in the world itself we all know.

As a self-conscious artist, Kosinski seems to have been aware of these problems and decided to free himself from expressionist detail while searching for another form, more serene in its external dress and likelier to allow for symbolic compression and ellipsis.

*Steps* is the kind of fiction a critic finds easy to evoke but difficult to describe. It communicates the deracinated atmosphere of Europe in the totalitarian age, and also, perhaps, the hallucinatory self-displacement that occurs whenever a man looks too closely at his own experience. The materials are those of terror, violence, corruption, and decadence; the tone is that of an all but "classical" lucidity. Somewhere Kafka lurks in the background, as logician of the illogical, and Camus too, as inspector of motives; but these are influences thoroughly absorbed. Kosinski writes from the other side of the moon: beyond heat, beyond protest, beyond alienation.

*Steps* is very short. It contains some two dozen miniature episodes or vignettes, among which are interspersed extremely biting fragments of conversation, printed in italic, between the voices of a man and a woman either just before or just after the sexual act. These fragments of conversation seem to occur in time present, between characters neither named nor located, while the episodes or vignettes are in time past. The latter are arranged not in the traditional time-sequence of the novel, with an integrated movement of incidents so as to form a coherent action; they appear, instead, as a group—I was about to say "a series," but that is just what remains in question—of panels or tableaux in a juxtaposed simultaneity of recollection and fantasy. The relationships among these panels of incident are apparently meant to be "spatial," that is, to be perceived as if on a flat surface and thereby freed from the obligation of incremental narrative. Sequence is broken, causality dissolved, coherence imperiled.

The figures who appear in these panels have no names: they represent a still further step in the emptying-out of life which had almost been completed in *The Painted Bird*, where the characters did, however, retain first names. Nor do the figures in *Steps* have much visible relation to one another, except insofar as they impinge on the narrator, also unnamed, an "I" who cryptically but with great force dredges up pieces of memory. I say "pieces," but Kosinski does not here indulge in what some critics call "the fallacy of imitative form," namely, that the depiction of chaos requires works that are themselves chaotic or at least partake in the chaotic. Each incident in *Steps* is beautifully complete, rendered with a polished icy discipline.

Place names too are withheld, though a few tips are given. It becomes clear that most of the incidents are set in Europe during and after the war, that the narrator lives in a country ruled by "the Party" under circumstances suggesting Communist Poland, and that he then comes to America, where he undergoes several bits of comic initiation, somewhat like the protagonist of Kafka's *Amerika*.

The first incident shows a man—"I"—traveling in a European country and picking up a girl by a display of magic: she is dazzled by his credit cards, which enable him to purchase anything he may wish. One *guesses* this incident to occur in the postwar years, and to represent a plane of time simultaneous with the incidents that come at the end.

There follow remembered incidents ranging from detached horror to the comic bizarre. A woman copulates with an animal somewhere in the countryside of Eastern Europe while peasants bet on the depth to which she can be entered. A soldier escapes from a tiresome dress parade and, caught asleep by his unit, salutes his captors with member erect. Two civilians are killed casually, almost unnoticed, in a military maneuver. A woman is discovered by the narrator in a village, locked in a cage and used for barbaric amusements; the local priest, forced to defend his silence before this ghastliness, shows no repentance. The narrator, hiding with farmers during the war, is mercilessly beaten and takes his revenge by enticing the farmers' children to swallow ground glass. Later, the same narrator watches the rape of a girl friend, and learns in consequence how to inflict upon her a range of psychic defilements. After the war he becomes a student at the University and befriends a young man who, in order to escape Party surveillance, hides himself in toilet-stalls, his "temples," until discovered and destroyed. Hiding in an abandoned factory, the narrator kills an old watchman gratuitously, simply to study the reactions of a victim. And meanwhile, during the interspersed talk with his mistress, there are suggested a range of sexual perversions.

We have here, then, the standard repertoire of modern— or if you prefer, human—horrors, but it soon becomes absolutely clear that none of this is meant merely to shock. One is at times unnerved and at other times perversely aroused; but the pain of attention is never eased. As the reader tries to mobilize his resources to perceive some order in Kosinski's materials, he does not doubt for a minute that the episodes themselves are remarkable. The prose is lean, fierce, stripped, tremendously graphic; indeed, so subject to the matter at hand it cannot be quoted with advantage.

Meanwhile the paradox of this writing, as perhaps of all such writing, is that even while Kosinski, in a comment on *Steps*, claims that it has "no plot in the Aristotelian sense" and

that its content "precludes a sequential or objective ordering of time," a major pleasure in reading the book derives from the "Aristotelian" plot of each incident, so compressed and lapidary it might be called the plot of a plot.

And a still more urgent paradox: stripped though the book is of ordinary personality or character and thereby of individual psychology, and indifferent as it appears to be to precise denotations of significance, *Steps* arouses an intense eagerness, indeed an accumulating anxiety, for the reestablishment of traditional order: that is, for taking the panels of incident and arranging them in one's mind as the coherent "Aristotelian" action Kosinski has declared inappropriate to his material.

The effect resembles that of other fictions composed in our century. If you read Virginia Woolf's *To the Lighthouse*, you struggle desperately to extract from its stream of subjective impression an articulated action; if you read a Robbe-Grillet novel, you struggle desperately to extract from his charting of pure gesture an articulated psychology. Perhaps, then, there is inherent in our way of perceiving human conduct some indestructible urge to order? Perhaps the Aristotelian principle of sequence, accumulation, and resolution is not just "another" convention like all usable literary conventions, but is rather a principle conforming to a need of our minds?

Kosinski, in his own comment on *Steps*, makes things a little too easy for himself:

> Each incident . . . is morally ambiguous. The reader is guided to an area of experience but he must digest the experience by himself. His gain is the product of his own sifting through and refining of much of the author's imagery. The reader should do this unconsciously, leaving each episode with a tingle of recognition, an intimation—no more. . . . Given these experiences . . . he will perceive the work in a form of his own devising, automatically filling in its intentionally loose construction with his own formulated experiences and fantasies.

Clever; but I do not believe it. And what is more, if I may be forgiven for falling back on authority, I doubt that the great critics of the past would have believed it, either. Kosinski does himself an injustice, since his work has a more authoritative, even commanding structure than he allows. While it is true that every reader brings to a work of fiction, or anything else, "his own formulated experiences and fantasies"—he does this even with so classically lucid a work as *Tom Jones*—it is not at all true that he will be content to leave each episode, let alone the entire work, "with a tingle of recognition, an intimation— no more." That is often the state one experiences after a first reading, but I am convinced that serious readers must go further. Whatever degree of unconscious activity may go into the composition of a novel, it must be read and evaluated through a rational consciousness. No matter how recalcitrant or obscure a work may be, one must try to discover in it principles of structural order and implications of moral life. Which does not necessarily mean that I, or anyone else, always can.

The structural problem of *Steps*, as I've already suggested, is that of the inner relationship of parts: do the steps form a staircase? The very title is provocative, since steps—even in dreams—lead somewhere: up or down, to or away from castles. There can, I suppose, even be circular staircases, provided someone like Kosinski designs them. To see if I could come up with an answer, I jotted down in outline the main incidents of the book, hoping thereby to establish some kind of sequence or pattern; but I could not find any direct line through time.

At least as an image for the breakdown of connection and cognition, all of this jumble seems possible: an author may so conceive it. But as soon as he tries to create a literary work which has *parts* and thereby internal relationship, the steps cannot be entirely "alone." To communicate the sense of "aloneness," the steps must be arranged into some kind of pattern. It's the paradox of art, the paradox making it into a discipline, that chaos can be adequately represented only through versions of coherence.

Steps, circles, spirals, whatever image or arrangement we propose: the difficulties remain and with them fundamental questions which we must not be unwilling to ask out of a fear of seeming unsophisticated. Is there any binding reason why one incident follows another? Would the symmetry and significance, the graphic vividness of *Steps* be impaired if certain incidents were reshuffled or omitted entirely? Is the twentieth incident dependent for its impact on the fact that it comes after the first nineteen? Such questions can sound foolish, and I ask them out of a conviction that it's time critics were willing to risk sounding foolish. What is more, I know the standard answers only too well, since I often use them in the classroom and in print. But either "non-Aristotelian" art will find its own Aristotle, or we may end up drifting back to Aristotle.

Steps signify some kind of journey, and here, in grappling with this book, we can feel a great deal more secure, mainly because Kosinski is so evocative a writer—indeed too good a writer merely to be content with "a tingle of recognition, an intimation." The narrator's journey comes to seem a gradual stripping or destruction of social personality as it is enforced by the pressures of social experience. In times of relative social harmony we can live out our lives more or less at peace with the roles available to us; but when society bears down too heavily, we crack inside ourselves—it's a fine touch that Kosinski's narrator, shortly after coming to America and still feeling threatened by encounters with other people, should pass himself off as a deaf-mute. Now there are people who believe, these days, that the kind of stripped self to which Kosinski's "I" has cut through, a self bared to sex and violence, is humanity's "true self," but I think they are terribly wrong and even guilty of a moral libel against whatever defines us as human. No, this "true self" is a deprived and abandoned one: deprived of those circumstances which enable us to live abandoned by God and man.

Finally, then, we reach the problem: what is Kosinski's tacit moral valuation of this stripping of self he has portrayed in *Steps*? We have no trouble in recognizing the abstracted verisimilitude of Kosinski's episodes: all of modern life and literature has prepared us for them. But there is a trouble in making out the relation between writer and narrative, between what the "I" registers and how Kosinski would have us respond. There is something extremely unnerving about the detachment, seemingly the color of water, which rules this book: it is like the distance in the Kierkegaardian scheme between an inaccessible God and helpless man.

For what are we to make of a detachment seemingly beyond judgment, beyond anger, beyond grief? In peeling off "the gloss of the world," Kosinski writes as if it were a world from which he had severed his ties, or to change the figure, as if he were an astronomer locating dead stars.

Yet even while registering this uneasiness of mine, I want to say a word in opposition to it. The evil he records is not of his making; the messenger is not to be blamed for the news; and perhaps, indeed, the stars are dead. If, as I think, there is a kind of immoralism in the stance of pure spectator, I see no reason to suppose that Kosinski does not know this. And one must also remind oneself that the kind of aesthetic discipline that goes

into a book like *Steps* is made possible only by an urgent moral passion, even if a passion for the moment unclear or invisible.

One searches for clues . . . The dedication: "To my father, a mild man." I'm not sure how much can be made of a dedication in discussing a work of fiction, but the key word here is "mild," which can be seen as a kind of opposition to all that is depicted in the book. And there is an epigraph taken from *The Bhagavad Gita:*

> For the uncontrolled there is no wisdom, nor for the uncontrolled is there the power of concentration; and for him without concentration there is no peace. And for the unpeaceful, how can there be happiness?

I assume Kosinski used this passage for reasons more urgent than to justify the enormous control with which he has written; I assume the epigraph, like the dedication, is meant as a counterpoint to what the narrator sees and discovers, step by step. But if so, we are still left with questions. Where are we to find the steps that take men from the moral universe of this novel to the moral universe suggested by the sentences from *The Bhagavad Gita*? How does the author of *Steps* return to a world in which the figures of an action can again be men with names?

## SAMUEL COALE
### "The Quest for the Elusive Self: The Fiction of Jerzy Kosinski"

*Critique*, Volume 14, Number 3 (1973), pp. 25–37

In a time when most modern writers have resorted to the techniques and concerns of accurate although "novelistic" newsreporting (one thinks of Truman Capote and Norman Mailer) in an attempt to create a more "genuine" form of realism, discovering a writer vitally concerned with the nature of the individual consciousness is refreshing and exciting. The nature of the self, not in a narrowly psychological sense but in the broader moral and ethical (perhaps even "religious") sense, has continuously fascinated many American writers from the days of the "American Adam" in the 1850's through those of E. A. Robinson's "Man Against the Sky" in the 1900's to those of Philip Roth's querilous Portnoy in our own. In the 1850's the theme primarily concerned man's attempt to overcome or assimilate nature—the externals of human experience; we have witnessed the different results in Thoreau's transcendentalism and Melville's more tragic demonism. By the 1900's the situation had reversed itself; the works of Frank Norris and Theodore Dreiser reveal how determinedly nature had come to overwhelming man. At present we have reached a stalemate, a conscious standoff between man and nature, marked both by a philosophic indifference and a continuing technocratic lust to report it all in detail. Jerzy Kosinski, an expatriate Polish writer, whose experiences uniquely parallel America's own flight from Europe and who has renounced his native tongue to write in that of his adopted homeland, embodies this ambiguous modern attitude and has engaged himself totally (as every writer must) in defining the self against such a background.

Art does not seek to define so much as it suggests multiple possibilities. Kosinski "defines" the self in his works as that individual consciousness which is opposed to and therefore different from the forms of collective behavior which he has encountered in his native Poland. That self is defined in negative terms, in terms different from the external world of the "non-self." As Kosinski writes of his protagonist in *Steps:* "to him the most meaningful and fulfilling gesture is negative; it is aimed against the collective and is a movement towards the solitude within which the self can display its reality."[1] The quest to discover that renewed reality motivates the best of Kosinski's art. His complete rejection of collectivist methods is unquestionable, although, as we shall see, these methods contribute a good deal to his theories of art as a superior and separate realm of its own.

This anti-collectivist ethic permeates his art, but his obsession with it is much the same as Hawthorne's with puritanism of an earlier era. Of the great writers of the American renaissance, Hawthorne was the least mythic. Unlike Whitman and Melville he was not concerned primarily with man's transcendence over external nature but with the transcendence over his own. Men could become brothers recognizing their common humanity, not by renouncing their separate guilts but by accepting the interrelationship of such guilts, that "dreadful sympathy." The decayed puritan ethic of the 1850's supplied Hawthorne with a dramatic framework on which to erect his allegorical examination of human sin. In much the same way Kosinski's anti-collectivist bias works as a dramatic framework and basic underpinning for his quest of the elusive self, of what being an individual in the modern age can mean. Only when secluded in his photographic darkroom in Poland did Kosinski fully comprehend instinctively the blessings and terrors of the individual consciousness. In that darkroom, complete with photographically realized scenes, much of his work develops.

Every collectivist society (Communist Poland is a prime example) defines the self in strictly external terms—political loyalties, class consciousness, and cultural blocs. For Kosinski such definition has transformed the "modern" sensibility as well, as much in America as in Poland. To attempt to experience the reality of the self in other terms becomes the primal element of Kosinski's fiction. He knows what the self is not: he is searching for what it may be. The burden of his art carries with it the weight of this endless and excruciatingly modern quest.

"Today," writes Kosinski, "the basis of horror is often the theft of the self, the fear of having one's identity overshadowed" (_Self_, 29). Kosinski's coming to America and mastering a new language illustrate his attempt to create a new self through a new life. Kosinski himself has said that the use of a new language literally demands a creation of a new self: the two are inseparable. Sounding very much like Whitman, the new Adam naming what he sees in the very act of creating it, Kosinski has a horror of the Polish years which prevents him from sharing Whitman's optimism. The hero of _Steps_ writes:

> If I could magically speak their language and change the shade of my skin, the shape of my skull, the texture of my hair, I would transform myself into one of them. This way I would drive away from me the image of what I once had been and what I might become; would drive away the fear of the law which I had learned, the idea of what failure meant, the yardstick of success; would banish the dream of possession, of things to be owned, used, and consumed, and the symbols of ownership—credentials, diplomas, deeds. This change would give me no other choice but to remain alive.[2]

The experience of Nazi collectivism permeates the whole of his work in a way that the dark, ineradicable shadows in Hawthorne's _The Scarlet Letter_ do. In its greater mythic significance, however, one ought more to compare Kosinski's gloom with Melville's sense of despair than Hawthorne's frail humanity.

Kosinski's conception of the self remains incredibly fragile when deprived of the physical realities of the external world, thus acknowledging its essentially negative and solipsistic

quality. Always the external world threatens to overwhelm the single consciousness. _The Painted Bird_ (1966) traces a boy's growth toward a belligerent and revengeful manhood transcending his environment only by reducing himself to a machine of retribution against all others who inhabit it. _Steps_ (1969) reveals the breakdown of the self when faced with an external reality so powerful it nearly overwhelms the necessary limits of art itself. In _Being There_ (1970) external reality has won out completely, confining us within the limits and structure of an intellectualized fable in which humanity has been reduced to a demented zombie named Chance, and Kosinski's art to a flattened replica of its former self. The threat of solipsism as opposed to the reality of collectivism intrudes on Kosinski's art so that the self, the narrator of _Steps_ for instance, seems to be nothing more than a disembodied voice howling in some surrealistic wilderness. The tension between the self as isolated voice and as externally controlled entity (that kind of self defined by John Watson's behavioral psychology) provides the kinetic energy of Kosinski's writing, and when that essential energy is missing, as in _Being There_ where it has been reduced to structural considerations instead of broadly thematic ones, artful indirection has been replaced by allegoric statement.

In Kosinski's work that sense of self which so clearly motivates the work of Faulkner, Proust, and Joyce is nearly non-existent. Proust's inability to appreciate and capture external reality as completely as he would have liked contrasts with Kosinski's belief that reality is all too easily captured and threatens to overwhelm him. Joyce, Faulkner, and Eliot strove to reproduce the moment of simultaneity in which all mankind and myth are illuminated. Although their themes were often desperate, documenting the processes of decay and disintegration, their spiritual center or imaginative fecundity (the "self") held. Imagination, providing its own sense of order and fulfillment, substituted for their religion. Such certainty in Kosinski's work, particularly in _Steps_, collapses, the self remaining unfixed and elusive, becoming both an artistic and a philosophic dilemma for the writer, and hinting of imminent self-destruction.

Kosinski's fiction derives in part from the "new wave" novels of Robbe-Grillet in its insistence on constructing a sense of mood and motion by the minute registration of detailed impressions. Each scene is graphically described as objectively and as fully as possible, as if Kosinski's mind were a camera recording the intimate details of the photographer's art. Each detail simulates an external reality more "real" than external nature itself and provides that surreal quality of the writings of Poe, Kafka, Nathanael West, Beckett, and Hawkes. Each of Kosinski's scenes reminds one of the naked and "stripped down" images of Stephen Crane's poetry, painful in its deliberateness and accuracy. Such scenic detail grips the reader's sensibilities, nailing him to his own violent and blatantly sexual fantasies. This undiluted presentation of savage and elemental experiences in that surreal world where fantasy and reality are interchangeable approximates the ritualistic patterns of ancient myths: the most primitive forms become the most symbolic by their very proximity to the terrible springs of life itself. On this level Kosinski generates emotional and imaginative power.

Nathan A. Scott, Jr., defines Flannery O'Connor as a radical secularist,[3] seeing in her work a seeming celebration of absolute materialism: her attention to detail is impeccable and unrelenting. Like William Carlos Williams in "Spring and All" she seems to grip down to the very roots of life and yet (as in that poem) her celebration reverses itself and turns out to be broadly religious and inherently human. Such attention to detail can result in the mechanical foppery of many of Poe's gothic tales and in many of Whitman's "negligent lists." Scott points out, however, that O'Connor, in pushing the negation of all things human far enough in her strict adherence to the minutiae of experience, had re-created genuine mythic and deeply religious moments. For her pains a sense of mystery and genuine awe, radiating as they do and must from the ordinary details of existence, had renewed itself and went on to illuminate the religious sensibility of her fiction.

In *The Painted Bird* Kosinski, without O'Connor's religious beliefs, has accomplished a similar if necessarily different thing. The mythic sense revives as Kosinski "zeroes in" on his objects. The episodes themselves, imbedded within the images of violent sex and violent death, suggest more than themselves by their very primitiveness and clarity, approximating the particularity of Jungian dreams, free from any taint of abstraction. Here, however, Kosinski is halted, as if finding these external episodes and images virtually impenetrable and essentially valueless toward human self-perception. The reality of the external world threatens to engulf his own consciousness as the collectivist realities of the modern sensibility (particularly those of his native Poland) threatened to destroy his very being. Kosinski faces an impenetrable wall, unable to break through it toward some symbolic transcendence, viewing experience as a series of cinematically graphic images and episodes which flash by his consciousness. No wonder *Steps* ends with a drowning and *Being There* ends in the peaceable realm of non-existence. Even Kosinski's painted bird mocks him—in the way Poe's raven mocked his distraught and neurotic narrator. External reality remains the impenetrable "other," destroying the artist's attempt to penetrate it, resulting in Poe's exile to dreamland and Kosinski's (hopefully temporary) surrender to tepid and colorless allegory in *Being There.*

Kosinski's fiction (as all good art perhaps) displays a tension between his formal approaches and his thematic concerns. The radical secularism of his Kafkaesque techniques precludes any attempt to view the self as a mainly subjective being. Kosinski himself has defined his art: "There is no art which is reality; rather, art is the using of symbols by which an otherwise unstateable subjective reality is made manifest."[4] The idea of a detailed impression, an essentially objective projection, is probably more accurate in a description of Kosinski's work than the word "symbol." While on the one hand he is attempting to extricate the self from the collectivist sensibilities of the modern world, on the other hand he is writing about the nature of that self in an extremely objective and collectivist form. He collects impressions which are concretely reproduced to simulate a form of external reality so well that he cannot extricate his heroes from it. The self is trapped in a world that is not so much symbolic of something else as it is symbolic of itself; although it may have mythic overtones, it is symbolic of nothing else. Its very concreteness (as in the theories of the early Imagist poets) precludes more abstract and "eternal" possibilities, such as the apprehension of human and ethical values or meaning.

The boy in *The Painted Bird* survives, not only because he cannot think to do otherwise, but also because he is learning and, therefore, moving forward. Because he is essentially innocent, he cannot weigh the philosophical possibilities of his experiences but can only report them. In *Steps* agonized self-consciousness leads to disintegration and paralysis: "I had to believe I was not myself any more and that whatever happened would be imaginary. I saw myself as someone else who felt nothing" (*Steps*, 146). The self is lost with no possibility of its being in any way regained. Like Miss Lonelyhearts, the

narrator cannot get out of the limited world (one without the connections with social reality suggested by West's satire) that his creator has made for him, and so he must succumb to it. Such close rendering of external reality has ironically produced a void from which the solipsistic and isolated self cannot return. It is left with an apocalyptic fury to destroy the detailed tapestry which Kosinski has himself created and which becomes at last transparent and non-existent:

> I would wait for the midnight storm which whips the streets and blurs all shapes, and I would hold my knife against the back of a doorman, yawning in his gold-frogged uniform, and force him to lead me up the stairs, where I would plunge my knife into his body. I would visit the rich and the comfortable and the unaware, and their last screams would suffocate in their ornate curtains, old tapestries, and priceless carpets. Their dead bodies, pinned down by broken statues, would be gazed upon by slashed family portraits. (*Steps*, 136)

*The Painted Bird* is Kosinski's first and best novel. The lost boy who is the hero of the book finds himself, in the autumn of 1939, in a primitive peasant world which Kosinski has recreated and transfigured into an evocative and terrible realm of superstition, fear, and cruelty ruled by the capricious malice of an omnipotent Mephistopheles. Not often in modern literature has original sin assumed such vivid and horrifying proportions. Within this prerational, mythic world Kosinski has illuminated the horrors of existence, that "blackness ten times black" that so entranced Melville, that "sense of the awful" which Tennessee Williams describes as "the desperate black root of nearly all significant modern art."[5] The boy realizes that his own existence can be determined only by its separation from and persecution of other selves. "If he shrank from inflicting harm on others, if he succumbed to emotions of love, friendship, and compassion, he would immediately become weaker and his own life would have to absorb the suffering and defeats that he spared others."[6] He must attack or be attacked; his sense of self is dependent totally upon his perpetrating violence on others, on nature itself:

> A person should take revenge for every wrong or humiliation. There were far too many injustices in the world to have them all weighed and judged. A man should consider every wrong he had suffered and decide on the appropriate revenge. Only the conviction that one was as strong as the enemy and that one could pay him back double, enabled people to survive. (*Bird*, 194)

Unlike Ahab, centering all his heroic revenge on one whale, the boy must strike his blows continually: revenge and retribution become the way of life. The only joy he can know is the absence of pain: "I found at the very bottom of this experience the great joy of being unhurt" (*Bird*, 198).

Such a brutally natural state produces Nazism as its natural product. The horror of the Nazi regime is not that it had created such cruelty but that it had capitalized on the existing natural cruelty of existence, streamlined it, mechanized it, and made of it an efficient organization and political reality. In *The Painted Bird* Nazism becomes the mechanized metaphor of human existence, and the boy's desperate adventures transform him into the mechanic embodiment of hate and revenge upon which the Nazi vision of the world was built. As Kosinski has written, "Maybe hate is a way of self-fulfillment? For hate takes on a mystical aura; to possess hate is to possess great power, and the wielder of that power has control of magnificent gifts" (*Notes*, 27).

The rich tapestry of the book reveals a surreal, Gothic

landscape peopled by the extraordinary creatures of an Hieronymus Bosch painting. Kosinski's radical secularism approaches the intricate reality of a terrible symbolism, although the main symbol, the painted bird, is too simply and allegorically identified with the boy himself. The boy, reduced wholly to a reactor to events (analogous to Jung's archetypal preconscious state of human consciousness, as Kosinski has pointed out), is molded by an impenetrable external reality, almost more "real" than he. As Kosinski writes, *"The Painted Bird* can be considered as fairy tales *experienced* by the child, rather than *told* to him" (*Notes*, 19); the experience, as in all fairy tales, remains horrible and terrifying. The reality of such an experience Kosinski has fully captured: the self steels itself to survive. The boy, having lost his voice and become mute (another way of making him more isolated from reality and from articulate consciousness), regains his voice at the conclusion of the novel, revealing Kosinski's most hopeful conclusion in any of his books. The questions remain: what now will he tell us? what does his experience mean in human terms?

Kosinski fully illuminates the texture of his book with moral, religious, and social concerns which seem to have eluded him in his later works. The psychology of Nazism is a case in point. Organized religion and organized party politics prove to be as faulty and as fragile as humanity itself and provide illusory sanctuaries for bigoted veterans. As for the sense of self, it remains defined in terms of its separation from others which clearly singles out the need for a scapegoat in Nazi Germany—the Jew. As Leduc replies in Miller's *Incident at Vichy*: "Part of knowing who you are is knowing we are not someone else. And Jew is only the name we give to that stranger, that agony we cannot feel, that death we look at like a cold abstraction. Each man has his Jew; it is the other" (*Notes*, 20). Kosinski's achievement has raised modern hate and horror to the semblance of that deep sense of reality experienced in only the greatest of art.

*Steps* is Kosinski's second, most complex, and most experimental novel. The book is a series of seemingly disjointed vignettes, as brutally particular as the episodes in *The Painted Bird*, interspersed with italicized sections between the narrator and his lover discussing the possibilities of love and of discovering the nature of each other's separate self. The boy in *The Painted Bird* has here been "replaced" by the reader, as the narrator becomes a transparent glass; each incident flashes before him and he retains it in an effort to put the puzzle, which has come apart, back together again, hoping that the individual steps of the separate episodes will lead to some revelation. Unfortunately the connecting link will not come. The reader experiences the frustrations and furies of the lost boy longing for a solution when there seems to be none. The quest to locate the self in terms of external reality, to define the human consciousness only as the sum of its related parts and nothing more, has come up against a stone wall. As discovered by Fellini's director in 8½, the various flotsam and jetsam of external reality will not add up to any revelation. We are left with the disembodied voice that raged in Ellison's *Invisible Man* but which could conjure up finally only its own invisibility. "The only thing that the protagonist of *Steps* is aware of, is his self, and that is ephemeral. He knows himself by hints, by allusions; he approaches and steps away from himself; he looks for himself in others, hoping that every new situation would bring forth a new 'I'" (*Self*, 16)—and of course it does not.

One can consider the various incidents which Kosinski treats in at least two ways, although the results are similar. The individual fantasies can be viewed as fragments of the memory,

called up "as a defense against spontaneity of the present moment" (*Self*, 22) in order to avoid close contact with the empty, meaningless present condition of the self. Hemingway's heroes drank, fought, and talked in order to avoid those heavy and frightening silences that conveyed to them the present void threatening to overwhelm them. Each recollected scene can be an attempt to escape the present—as Webster Scott has written about Auden, "the more structured the time the less threatening its passage."[7] As Kosinski has written, *"The Painted Bird* is rather the result of the slow unfreezing of a mind long gripped by fear, of isolated facts that have become interwoven into a tapestry" (*Notes*, 12). Thus *Steps* seems to lead nowhere but to the recognition of present impotence masquerading in a tapestry of past exploit.

Although all art is truly the creature of the memory, Kosinski's scenes grip the imagination so intimately that they convey an overwhelming sense of present execution as if we were living them at the moment. If we can conceive these episodes as a string of present realities, they become impenetrable in their unrelenting audacity. If a disintegrated memory is the key to Kosinski's art, a memory unfrozen but broken and fragmented, then *Steps* reveals the attempt of its hero to avoid the present by taking refuge in a shattered sanctuary. As in an Ibsen play, the quest of the elusive self is as much a backward journey as it is a forward one. If a disintegrated present reality is the key to Kosinski, a present fluid and distorted, then *Steps* reveals the attempt of its hero to create a self out of the bits and pieces which testify only to its inevitable loss and destruction. In either, the impenetrabililty of the fragments remains, and the last scene fulfills Eliot's warning—"Fear death by water." Nature has triumphed over man, indifference and defeat over the quest for the elusive self. The tensions of great art are like those of Keats' "cold pastoral"; here they have reached a standoff, and Kosinski's steps lead but to the grave. Still *Steps* remains Kosinski's most intricate book, and achievement of the highest order complete with the artistic perils inherent in its fragmented structure.

Kosinski's latest book, *Being There*, is essentially an intriguing and well-crafted novel of ideas, a parable of modern life, as pointed out by John Aldridge.[8] The texture here is the thinnest of Kosinski's books, stripped down, "barren of adornment,"[9] to the point almost of flat statement. As Anatole Broyard wrote, "the book has no felt characters or situations, no felicities of language or style. Reading it is like taking a pill instead of eating."[10] For Broyard only limp satire; for Aldridge the approximation of myth. In comparison with the "radical energy"[11] of Kosinski's previous books, it must be seen as a falling off. What exactly has happened?

If the hero of *Steps* was conscious of his attempts to define himself, if the quest was still one of active although desperate pursuit, in *Being There* it has been abandoned altogether. The hero Chance, a retarded "innocent," has been molded by television; it is all he knows of the world outside his apartments. As a gardener he participates in a natural ritual which has lost all significance for both him and the modern world. When he is forced out of his Candide-like existence, he is used by those he meets for their own self-deluding ends. The outside world creates him as senselessly and as coldly as Kosinski has. As the self has been diminished, so has the texture of the fiction—we are left in thin, dry soil of an arid garden populated only by abstractions and theories, all passions spent, all humanity drained from the scene. To criticize television's impact and influence is one thing; to create a book in precisely the same fashion is another.

Chance speaks of gardening, which is all he knows; it is at

once interpreted as giving advice in a clever, metaphorical way. The simple occupation is denied its mythic simplicity, for the modern world which has so divorced itself from elemental existence cannot recognize such simplicity. It weaves its own analogies, produces its own images on television to hypnotize itself. Thus Chance, produced by television, becomes a created television image himself: a trick done with mirrors. The self only observes; it no longer acts. The unfortunate thing is that Kosinski's flattened prose has taken its inspiration from its theme and thus is as transparent and as vacant as the television images it attacks. The outward thrust to restore the self in *Steps* has become the cardboard self which both Kosinski and the unenlightened outside world see here.

To escape the threat of solipsism, one of the centers of dramatic tension in his earlier work, Kosinski has taken refuge in the sanctuary of the philosophic fable, a step which could prove fatal to the wellspring of his greatest art. He has written that "the knowledge we form of ourselves is nothing but a collective image which, like ubiquitous television, engulfs us . . . we are a culture of the denial of the self."[12] Kosinski has learned all too well, denying his Chance any shred of selfhood at all. He has created a selfless character and then condemned him because he has no self. At the conclusion, again the void:

> Chance was bewildered. He reflected and saw the withered image of Chauncey Gardiner: it was cut by the stroke of a stick through a stagnant pool of rain water. His own image was gone as well.[13]

Kosinski's dramatic framework remains the struggle toward personal identity complicated by his own acceptance of a new land, a new language, and consequently a "new" self. His dramatic centers continue to be the self, that mysterious and impenetrable entity, and collectivism, that increasingly omnipresent and modern reality. The radical secularism of his art triumphs only when his sense of self is ascendent; otherwise it traps him in a kind of collective impressionism from which he cannot extricate himself. His genius lies in his ability to recreate an elemental sense of primitive and dark reality inherent in his violent and sexual images. From this dark well his art must be drawn. Yet it is a dangerous and frightful well into which to descend, for we who admire him are aware of the stark and terrible contours of his unrelenting imagination.

*Notes*

1. Jerzy Kosinski, *The Art of the Self* (New York: Scientia-Factum, 1968), p. 40; cited later as *Self*.
2. Jerzy Kosinski, *Steps* (New York: Bantam Books, 1969), pp. 134–5; cited later as *Steps*.
3. Nathan A. Scott, Jr., "Flannery O'Connor's Testimony: The Pressure of Glory," *The Added Dimension: The Art and Mind of Flannery O'Connor*, ed. Melvin J. Friedman and Lewis A. Lawson (New York: Fordham University Press, 1966).
4. Jerzy Kosinski, *Notes of the Author on* The Painted Bird (New York: Scientia-Factum, 1967), p. 11; cited later as *Notes*.
5. Tennessee Williams, "Introduction," *Reflections in a Golden Eye*, by Carson McCullers (New York: Bantam Books, 1950), pp. xiv–xv.
6. Jerzy Kosinski, *The Painted Bird* (New York: Pocket Books, 1966), p. 135; cited later as *Bird*.
7. Quoted by Alan Levy, "In the Autumn of the Age of Anxiety," *New York Times Magazine* (8 August 1971), p. 36.
8. John W. Aldridge, "The Fabrication of a Culture Hero," *Saturday Review* (24 April 1971), pp. 25–7.
9. Ibid., p. 27.
10. Anatole Broyard, "The High Price of Profundity," *New York Times* (21 April 1971), p. 45.
11. Paul Delany, "Chance Learns How from Television," *New York Times* (25 April 1971), p. 59.
12. Jerzy Kosinski, "Dead Souls on Campus," *New York Times* (13 October 1970), p. 45.
13. Jerzy Kosinski, *Being There* (New York: Harcourt Brace Jovanovich, 1970), p. 140.

# HANS KONING
## "Missions Impossible"

*Nation*, September 15, 1979, pp. 216–18

Jerzy Kosinski, author of such novels as *The Painted Bird* and *Steps* and now of *Passion Play*, has during the past fifteen years been one of our not very numerous successful, yet serious, novelists. His books, including this new novel, are highly fragmented; they are full of violence and sex (and sexual violence) and make for what some librarians call "easy reads," but there is of course more to them than that.

Kosinski is a political writer and his novels are political propaganda. So are, in my semantics, all novels: the most private love story, when taking our present society for granted, is a free enterprise/democracy propaganda message, though the author would not have had any such intentions. Kosinski, who left his native Poland in 1957, is a dissident only in that he rejects everything to do with the political and economic structure of Eastern Europe, in which he perceives absolutely nothing but institutionalized criminality. He has made it clear that he is in the United States not as an exiled foreigner but as an American writer, with English the only language he cares to think and work in. As such a writer, he fits by choice into no clear tradition or niche.

The heroes of his novels are lonely and anonymous men, outsiders, never with an everyday profession. In *Blind Date*, the hero was called Levanter; in *Passion Play*, Fabian. These men have colorless stage names and they themselves are almost indistinguishable from one another. They are usually refugees or escapees from Eastern Europe, though the rich American heir of *The Devil Tree* thinks and talks not very differently from Fabian in *Passion Play*, whose very origin has become anonymous: we are told that he was born "in one of those marginal 'old countries,' their borders and boundaries forgotten now. . . ." (Actually, I cannot think of any country to which this would apply. The Baltic republics? Their boundaries are not forgotten, not even in the U.S.S.R.)

Many authors keep such a distance from their books that it would be improper to look for a link between them and their protagonists. Not so with Kosinki. His novels are personal accusatory statements, and he clearly wants us to draw no line between his own reality and that of his fiction. In fact, it would be hard for him to hide behind the concept of "fiction," for his novels cry out, "This is how the world looks, and I am the sworn witness to the truth of it." In a new introduction he wrote to *The Painted Bird*, his first novel, his own adventures are depicted as interwoven and of a piece with those of his heroes.

*The Painted Bird*, which established his name, is different from the later novels in that its hero is the child, not the man; but the child, too, is lonely, an outsider, anonymous. Describing a childhood in German-occupied Poland, the novel builds a platform from which the later novels took off. I don't doubt that it created the stir it did because so many Americans considered it their first real insight into life in Europe during World War II. In the same way, his following novels appeared to give readers here a shockingly direct feel of life under Communism or state socialism, the more convincing since Kosinski never tried to contrast his view with pleasant images from the West. Although one of his heroes says, "I have found people to be good everywhere," he shows Americans (like the French or the Swiss) living in jungles of unmitigated greed and cruelty. The lives of old people are as vile in Poland *(Steps)* as they are in Florida *(Cockpit)*. In the United States as in Eastern Europe, Kosinski's characters move from one grotesque catastrophe to another.

Having lived under a German occupation myself, I have always been intensely uncomfortable with the images in *The Painted Bird*. In his new introduction, Kosinski writes that its critics felt it was too violent. That, assuredly, was not my objection. On the contrary, in my experience the violence was even more pervasive, but it was also less dramatic, less "American." To give an example, in *The Painted Bird* the Polish peasants perpetrate acts of the most cruel sexual sadism; it is as if the violence of the Germans conjures up a sexual violence among their victims. But in reality, the German violence was all tangled up with daily degradations and, more important, with hunger and cold. It did not engender sadism but sexlessness. Men and women, perpetually humiliated, aware of their physical being in a negative way only, had little interest in their own or others' bodies, or in any appetite but for food.

I had another crucial reservation about *The Painted Bird*. Much of its drama hinges on the hero, the dark outsider child, repeatedly being taken for a Jew. This mystery of identity, too, seemed to me an oddly American idea. In Eastern Europe, no families that weren't Jewish, except perhaps a few upper-class, Americanized ones, had their boys circumcised, and the Germans used circumcision as a shibboleth that decided between life and death. (I knew of a German Army surgeon in Amsterdam during the war who de-circumcised gentiles with a cosmetic operation.) Thus the drama of *The Painted Bird*, in real life, would have begun and ended with S.S. men and Polish peasants taking down the boy's pants.

In that same introduction, Kosinski described how a couple of Polish police toughs had come to his New York apartment to beat him up. Kosinski, training a pistol on them with one hand, took photographs of them with the other, thus intimidating them into a hasty retreat. I mention this to illustrate how the author and his heroes are birds of a feather. To point a pistol at two Communist agents while taking pictures of them seems to me a very difficult trick. I'm not questioning the author's word, but it shows an adroitness usually seen only in the movies or on television, and this is fitting because Kosinski's heroes function as faultlessly as *Mission Impossible* agents or (joyless) James Bonds, whether murdering without leaving a trace, or outwitting the bureaucracies of Eastern Europe. Their setting is not the natural world, where plans go awry and people do the unexpected, but a mechanical one where every action leads to a foreseeable reaction.

Kosinski's missions impossible are performed in the name of a general "getting even." They are of obsessive intensity even when the opponents seem unworthy of such ire: in *Passion Play* the hero dabs dog pee onto the jackets of annoying neighbors on a café terrace in order to expose them to the smelly attentions of their own dogs; in *Blind Date*, a rich man goes through an elaborate mime as a drooling idiot just to scare a French postal clerk into giving him, contrary to the rules, a tax receipt for three dozen airmail stamps. These are acts of vengeance by knights who perceive not Love but Evil behind each blade of grass.

I use the word "knights" advisedly, for that is how Kosinski would have us see his protagonists. *Passion Play* at times seems written for no other purpose but to hammer this home. Its hero

is a wandering polo player—perversely, while most Kosinski heroes are very rich, this is a poor polo player, making his living as a trainer while driving around the United States in a mobile home with a horse trailer. Again and again the fully equipped polo player on his pony, holding his mallet, is made to conjure up the knight in armor, charging with tilted lance. The enemy is less visible this time; this knight Fabian doesn't tilt at Communist bureaucracy and its minions but at what he calls "the group code," an anti-individualistic perversion of freedom that he finds in such seemingly conservative places as the stables of an Argentine playboy, whose reliance on "team mentality" loses him a duel with the lonely Fabian. Which doesn't solve a problem that Fabian, too, poses. He, like Kosinski's previous heroes, lacks one quality among his innumerable accomplishments: human kindness. He shows no trace of a knowledge of its existence. Is anger alone enough to explain knighthood?

Kosinski's view of a loveless and joyless world (the many sex acts in his novels hardly spread joy) is an essential element in his picture of Eastern Europe, which so acutely confirms the worst that Americans think of the place. With not a single idea or ideal motivating them but the thirst for power, everything the pseudo-socialists of those countries think up must become a cruel travesty. On Kosinski's pages, a mountain vacation for workmen as organized in the U.S.S.R. becomes a Bruegelian tableau of vomiting peasants falling down the mountainsides where the Party orders them to ski. But while Kosinski's anger may be an indictment of those authoritarian bureaucracies from which he fled, the actual bureaucrats are people, more human, more complicated and perhaps more pathetic. Even a Stalinist sending the poor to a mountain resort may have thought, and may have been justified in thinking, that he was doing good.

The light Kosinski throws on East or West is not a friendly one and not, I think, a true one. It distorts; it is the strobe light of an American horror movie, in which only absolutes are considered shocking enough to move the audience. In the natural world things are less stark, less mechanically acute. Mares aren't stabled with stallions (as they are in *Passion Play*). The Manson killings were not in the repertory of American revolutionaries (as in *Blind Date*), and having a woman stand in front of a plane's radar does not kill her (as it does in *Cockpit*); only radar as powerful as the Greenland anti-missile station can do that.

Another passage in *Cockpit* may illuminate the point. Its hero, thinking back to his life as a 12-year-old in the new western territories ceded by Germany to Poland after World War II, describes how he "punished" all those Polish farmers who, like his father, "had surrendered their rights by accepting resettlement." Spending his days on the telephone and pretending to be a party official, he phones the farmers, some of whom are illiterate, others recovering from a heart attack or watching over a sick child, and summons them on wild goose chases to Warsaw. None of them dare refuse, though the trip may be fatal to some. The calls almost ruin the resettlement scheme.

I have visited those new territories as a journalist and felt that there was much to admire in what the Poles were doing. The heavy hand of Russia lay on them, but Russia was also the country that had liberated them, the only power that could protect them from the *furor teutonicus*. Instead of carping in all directions, as so often in their history, they seemed set on making the best of it.

My point, though, is not that Kosinski's political view of

what was happening seems distorted and wrong to me. The point is simpler. In those days and in that area there were no functioning telephones to speak of, and a phone in a European farmhouse would then have been a most unusual item anyway.

Kosinski does not describe a real landscape, East or West, but a combination of the worst in both. He superimposes a mechanized—an "American"—model of an alienated and crime-racked individualism onto an East European society whose commonality does nothing but lay it wide open to a cannibalistic abuse of power.

In such a world we are indeed left with little to expect for humanity and little to hope for except to be left alone. To be left alone is the only Grail the polo knight, like his predecessors in the earlier novels, is pursuing.

# MAXINE KUMIN

## 1925–

Maxine Winokur was born, the daughter of Jewish parents, in Philadelphia on June 6, 1925. She grew up in a Catholic neighborhood in Philadelphia, and was involved in competitive swimming, even considering trying out for the U.S. Olympic team. Instead she decided to concentrate on her studies, attending Radcliffe and earning a B.A. in 1946 and an M.A. in 1948. She married Victor Kumin in 1946; the couple has three children.

She taught at Tufts for three years before receiving a grant for independent study from Radcliffe in 1961. That same year her first collection of poetry, *Halfway*, was published. Anne Sexton was also a scholar at Radcliffe at that time and the two poets became close friends, collaborating on several children's books and reading each other's poetry in progress. Although Kumin was associated with Robert Lowell and was a personal friend of Sexton's, her work is not generally considered to be in the confessional manner characteristic of those writers. In 1973 she won a Pulitzer Prize for *Up Country: Poems of New England* (1972). Her poetry, with its many images drawn from the New England landscape, has affinities with the work of Robert Frost. Although she was severely shaken at the time by Anne Sexton's suicide, Kumin has since then continued to write poetry as well as adult and children's fiction, and recently served as poetry consultant to the Library of Congress. She now lives with her husband on their New Hampshire farm.

## Works

### POETRY

The realizations which confront Maxine Kumin ⟨in *Halfway*⟩ are more fragile and tentative than those ⟨Ned⟩ O'Gorman requires; she herself defines her intention and accomplishment in a few lines from "The Moment Clearly":

> Write, saying this much clearly:
> Nearly all, this is nearly all,
> The small sounds of growing, the impress
> Of unarrested time, raising
> The prized moment.

The realizations are small, but they become important by reason of the care and precision with which they are expressed. Picking up her book and looking at the first poem, one might suppose that the images were going to be arbitrary. "Isosceles of knees" the poem starts, but it goes on "my boys and girls sit / cross-legged in blue July / and finger the peel / of their sun-killed skin". The images return always to a strict visual accuracy; behind the startling word lies its solid justification. Consider Miss Kumin on bats: "until the terrible mouse with wings / notched like bread knives came skittering / down the chimney next to my bed". Or on travelling northward after a spring funeral in the south: "Homeward, the spendthrift streams pursed their mouths, / the trees unfleshed, the ground locked up its ruts, / and farther, death belonged / in this place. Weeks late, the rotten ice went out."

Miss Kumin is more successful in personal poems than in those which attempt public stances, as do "Eleventh Century Doors," and "For Anne at Passover." She is wiser, too, when she avoids complex formal exercises; maybe all sestinas now have a slight lab-specimen smell. At her worst she can be trivially humorous, but she is seldom at her worst, and her humor can also show a grim sardonic force. I would be happy to have this book if only for "Fräulein Reads Instructive Rhymes"; I am happier yet to have it for "The Lunar Probe":

> Long before morning they waked me to say
> the moon was undone; had blown out, sky high,
> swelled fat as a fat pig's bladder, fit
> to burst, and then the underside had split.
>
> I had been dreaming this dream seven nights
> before it bore fruit (there is nothing so sweet
> to a prophet as forethought come true). They had
> 　　meant
> merely to prick when . . . good-bye, good intent!
>
> Dozing, I saw the sea stopper its flux,
> dogs freeze in mid-howl, women wind up their
> 　　clocks,
> lunatics everywhere sane as their keepers.
> I have not dreamed since in this nation of sleepers.

> —WILLIAM DICKEY, "Revelations and Homilies,"
> 　　*Poetry*, Nov. 1961, pp. 125–26

It's hard to know what to say about Maxine Kumin's new volume ⟨*House, Bridge, Fountain, Gate*⟩. It suffers from a disease of similes: children "naked as almonds," kisses "like polka dots," a corset spread out "like a filleted fish," someone "patient as an animal," a visit "as important as summer," chromosomes "tight as a chain gang," and genes "like innocent porters" all inhabit one poem, and the disease (one shared with Anne Sexton) becomes mortal as the book continues. The poems talk about family, about living in Kentucky, about horses; and they have a cheerful will to make the best of things, to make things grow, to save things from frost, to take lessons from nature. There is something admirable about this as an attitude, but the whimsy in Kumin gets in my way, the spunkiness of "the survival artist" finally cloys. In "A Time for the Eating of Grasses" we progress through the seasons from spring to fall (and Kumin's poems are often predictable in their structure), watching grass being eaten by geese, then lambs, then cows, and finally by the goat, "still stripping brush/after the blight of frost":

> Goat an efficient factory
> a fermentation vat
> spilling the beebee shot wastes
> out of the basket of his rectum
> goat the survival artist.

Well, is it worth surviving to be a factory and a fermentation vat and a manufacturer of organic beebee droppings? It's not clear how Kumin herself feels about this problem, but she continues her strenuous efforts nevertheless, saying in a dream (that dreariest of genres, telling other people your dreams) to a French woman poet whom she is translating,

> See here, my friend,
> my double, let us breathe
> mouth to mouth like a lifesaving class
> as chockful and as brave
> forcefeeding each other's stopped lungs
> so that at the feast of words
> there will be no corpse to carve.

There is no point in asking Kumin to be other than whimsical, because when she tries to be deadly serious she is speaking under strain and constraint. She dutifully describes, for instance, various hideous experiments performed by the Defense Department (sewing eyelids of rabbits open; giving shocks to dolphins, mice and monkeys; implanting electrodes into cats; substituting plastic hearts in calves) and then ends her poem—"Heaven as Anus"—with an embarrassing indictment of some invisible deity:

> And what is any of this to the godhead. . . .
> It all ends at the hole. No words may enter
> the house of excrement. We will meet there
> as the sphincter of the good Lord opens wide
> and He takes us all inside.

This is still comic language presumably intending a Swiftian effect, with a side glance toward something dignified with the name of "excremental vision." But Swift would not have parodied the hymnal at the end; somehow the bitterness here can't find a proper language. Kumin's less ambitious poems, like the riddling "Song for Seven Parts of the Body," are closer to her competence; here she is plausible and light, if still too girlish for some tastes:

> I have a life of my own
> he says. He is transformed
> without benefit of bone.
> I will burrow, he says
> and enters. Afterwards
> he goes slack as a slug.
> He remembers little.
> The prince is again a frog.

—HELEN VENDLER, "False Poets and Real Poets,"
*NYTBR*, Sept. 7, 1975, pp. 7–8

*House, Bridge, Fountain, Gate* (from Rilke's suggestion, *Sind wir vielleicht hier, um zu sagen—*) is an admixture, a collection of the work done since the selected New England poems of *Up Country.* The title of the present volume suggests not only the range but the essential nature of the "things" speaking through the poet as witness. The range goes from growing up in the thirties and early forties to being Jewish in Danville, Kentucky to acting as home-gardener/lover to celebrating her New Hampshire horse, Amanda. The nature of her objects, phenomenologically, is not so easy to surround. In addition to several books of poetry, Maxine Kumin has published four novels, a fact that may help account for the thoroughness with which she pursues her material. Her imagination is simply able to transfer a tremendous amount of information. Yet as stories, Kumin's poems depend less on forward-motion, on action, than on language—a language very much of the flesh, of all the senses seeing:

> This is the year that my mother stiffens.
> She undresses in the closet giving me
> her back as if I can't see
> her breasts fall down like pufferfish,
> the life gone out of their crusty eyes.

Or:

> All of those kisses like polka dots
> touched to the old man's wrinkles
> while his face jittered under our little wet mouths
> and he floated to the top of his palsy . . .

As structures, her poems depend less on cause and effect than on a kind of accretion, so that we often end up more with the numbers than with their sums. Both of these characteristics— the sexuality (the imagination as carnal knowledge) and the hierarchy (the aesthetic order as the accumulation of images)— distinguish the best of these new poems as full-bodied metaphors of detail. Kumin is probably the least abstract of her contemporaries. Her objects, her things, get themselves transformed all right, but the penetration is to deepen our awareness of the physical, diurnal, existential world, not the meta-world of ultimate causes, ultimate effects. The common denominators of reality have too much currency in her work for Kumin to be called, as she sometimes is, a transcendentalist. Her best poems are as uncompromising in vision as they are rich in texture. They make music as a first principle. "To hear the owl is the poet's prerogative"—

> In the hand-me-down of dead hours
> I hear him moving up the mountain
> tree by tree insistent as
> a paranoid calling out his one verse
> raising the break-bone alarm . . .

"The Thirties Revisited," "Life's Work," "Insomnia," and the Amanda poems, as instances, are poems of distinction. But the qualities that can bless can also blame. In much of this work, the rhythms, the language, the imagery seem to take on lives of their own, as if they were attached to no centers of gravity, only to the broad force-field itself. In "Sperm," for example, a four-pager, the iambs finally begin to sound like *Beowulf,* in alternating tetrameter/pentameter. "Living Alone with Jesus" (from the Kentucky poems) has the opposite rhythmic problems: its patronizing prose has all the imaginative depth of a crank letter ("Can it be/I am the only Jew residing in Danville, Kentucky,/looking for matzoh in the Safeway and the A&P?"). "On Digging Out Old Lilacs" offers up this gratuity:

> I stand in a clump of dead athletes.
> They have been buried upright
> in Olympic poses. One
> a discobolus clutching a bird's nest.
> One a runner trailing laces of snakeskin.
> One a boxer exploding toads of cracked leather.

This is "creative writing." Kumin herself has set the standard against which such lines fail.—STANLEY PLUMLEY, *APR,* March–April 1976, pp. 45–46

Which of her poetic peers does Maxine Kumin resemble? Unlike Sylvia Plath and Anne Sexton, she keeps her demons bridled. Unlike Elizabeth Bishop or May Swenson, she is bawdily personal. Like Adrienne Rich, she makes us pay respectful attention to images of strong female identity, yet she avoids ideology. And is there another poet who finds or invents such a sweet male alter ego?

Henry Manley, the country neighbor who is one of several recurring figures in *Our Ground Time Here Will Be Brief*, could be the most endearing animus in the business. "Last fall he dug a hole and moved his privy / and a year ago in April reamed his well out," though in his dotage. Having had a phone installed, he tramps two New England miles, "shy as a girl," to ask the poet if she'd be so kind as to call him one day. Stricken with aphasia, Manley is "as loose in his skin as a puppy" and frightened after dark. But at dawn

> he gets up, grateful once more
> for how coffee smells. Sits stiff
> at the bruised porcelain table
> saying them over, able
> to with only the slightest catch.
> *Coffee. Coffee cup. Watch.*

Typical of Maxine Kumin's art are the sensory weight, the play of alliteration and assonance sliding into the closing couplets, the perfectly expressive halting and crystallizing rhythms. In another poem Henry breaks his hip, is taken in by neighbors, loves his new role of storytelling sage. When he goes on crutches to see his old, collapsing house, presently occupied by porcupines, he says, "You can't look back."

Mirroring his creator, Henry Manley is a supervisor, a capable countryperson of multiple skills. He will die before the poet does, and he is one of her many means of studying mortality. He is also what she is not, or can be only through him: an *isolé*. He is alone, not looking back. For her, not looking back would be intolerable.

*Our Ground Time Here Will Be Brief* contains selections from Maxine Kumin's first six volumes as well as 29 new poems, all but one of them gems; the book amounts to 20 years' solid work. Her Pulitzer Prize-winning *Up Country* comes just about halfway, both in chronology and in power; rather like Frost's imagined wanderer to the edge of doom, she is not changed, only more sure—so that her poems become increasingly unforgettable, indispensable. What drives her throughout is attachment. If she had her way, no loved (or hated) human or animal would die unremembered. Thus she writes not only the usual kinfolk poems but "Sperm," a tragicomic celebration of 17 look-alike cousins.

Since dreams reinforce memory and reveal the true shape of connection, in "The Incest Dream" a sorrowing hangman brings her beloved dying brother's severed penis, "pressed as faithfully, / as a wild flower" for the poet to keep "and lie back down in my lucky shame." When the brother has died, "Retrospect in the Kitchen" tells of the 40 pounds of plums she takes from his tree and carries 3,000 miles to preserve. The making of preserves is a recurring image in these poems and a beautiful metaphor for what the poet wants to do with the whole world. Other tricks also work. People fade, but animals "retrieve" them: Ponies begging for apples equal two elderly aunts; a boy once loved, buried at sea in World War II, reappears in a yearling's gallop. To split wood is to release the soul of the beech and recall the soul of the lost friend, Anne Sexton.

Children, especially daughters, keep cropping up, growing as they go, from Mrs. Kumin's earliest work to her most recent. No poet writes more richly and more subtly of mother-daughter relations. Or, for that matter, of animal-human relations, since her attachment and attention extend to the forms and gestures, the detailed lives and deaths of mice, turtles, frogs, goats, beavers, cows and calves, sheep and lambs,

and—most powerfully—horses. Creatures surround her; she sees and touches them; she foresees their doom. At times—see "Woodchucks" or "How It Goes On"—she is their doom's guilty agent. At times—see "Thinking of Death and Dogfood" or "A Mortal Day of No Surprises"—she contemplates the uses of horseflesh and her own potential to sweeten a crop, and wishes her mare and herself good endings. I believe that Thoreau would commend her honesty, the precision of her language and her occasional moral allegory.—ALICIA OSTRIKER, "Memory and Attachment," *NYTBR*, Aug. 8, 1982, p. 10

When Kumin relaxed her idiom ⟨in *Our Ground Time Here Will Be Brief*⟩, she did so in the general direction of a laid-back low-profile modesty that can be engaging if it can manage to avoid being merely discursive and prosaic. Her "new and selected" volume shows the virtues and the shortcomings of her usual style. In a good Kumin poem, such as "Retrospect in the Kitchen" or "Seeing the Bones," some world is registered with convincing, touching, moving lineaments. In weaker poems, parts of a world make cameo appearances that are diminished or distorted by metaphor, platitude, and reflection. Too often, a Kumin poem reports its essential news and then appends a sensitive, intelligent editorial, all earnestness and sincerity. *And thought:* "I think of the last day of your life"; "I think of what drops from us"; "I think of the wolf"; "I think of how it goes on"; "I think of the sweet streets" and "I think of those summer nights"; "She thinks of him tomorrow at his desk." After a while I begin talking back to such poems: "Leave 'I think' to Joyce Kilmer. Don't think. You aren't paid to think. Be a poem, poem." For all of Kumin's excessively poised present-tense reflections, the generic epigraph could come from "This Day Will Self-Destruct": "All this takes place in the head, / you understand." I suppose I do understand. I suppose that all poetry takes place in the head. But I wish it would not keep wearing its head on its sleeve. What takes place in the head comes down to figures of thought (not "of speech") that, if radically genuine, can distinguish a poet's work as original. Kumin can be powerfully original, but the originality is much vitiated by repetition. A "selected" volume might bring out such besetting habits. Kumin's certainly does. Ball bearings, for example, are interesting things with an interesting name. In an early poem, "Quarry, Pigeon Cove," the swimmer-speaker says, "I hung on the last rung of daylight, / breathing out silver ball bearings." Later, in "How It Goes On," we encounter a "yellow horse slick with the ball-bearing / sleet," and, in "Body and Soul: A Meditation," a passage about "the little ball-bearing soul." "My job is metaphor," the poet and Consultant in Poetry says, "connotative modes of thought" (the dullest part of the book). To invoke ball bearings thrice in 130 pages without much exploitation of their possibilities, without elevating the figure to the status of refrain or motif, without doing much but observing that bubbles, sleet, and the soul all can be likened to ball bearings, sort of, more or less, is just to yield to a tempting but treacherous habit. Examples could be multiplied.—WILLIAM HARMON, "Kumin and Kinnell (and Kilmer)," *Poetry*, April 1983, pp. 50–51

## FICTION

Mrs. Kumin's powers of observation, interpretation, and phrasing ⟨in *The Passions of Uxport*⟩ are as strong as Updike's and less marred by moral perversity, excessive symbolism, and fine writing. But her novel is ⟨also⟩ preoccupied ⟨. . .⟩ with animal decay and the struggle to conquer the fear of death. And her narrative also suggests that sexual loss, though not the whole of this fear, is central to it. Hallie's mysterious stomach pain, which sends her eventually to a psychoanalyst, is the novel's dominating fact. It is called "death," but we see that it has much to do with the fact that her husband will be away a great part of this year, that his adulteries have for the first time been discovered, that her children are growing beyond her care, that her niece's predicament arouses old resentments concerning her early marriage and hysterectomy, and above all that it disappears only when she asserts her sexuality by hurting her husband with a report of her own adultery. Mrs. Kumin is unnecessarily burdened by the idea that the analysis of Hallie's motives will cancel the moral value of her acts of rescuing and mending which her husband and doctor question. In any case we can accept Hallie's identification with Christ the prophet of social justice and the protector of outcasts. Mrs. Kumin is particularly impressive in conveying the moral bond between the insane Ernie, obsessed with his private rituals, and her more or less normal, very intelligent, and earnest heroine. Hardly less impressive is the fact that she can raise the question of individual moral commitment in connection with the Nazi holocaust without making one squirm.

The one major blemish is the ambitious portrait of Dr. Zemstvov, "the last of Freud's inner circle." Mrs. Kumin is conscientious enough to describe with some success Zemstvov's private feelings and the process of treatment. But there are crudely fitting pieces that make one uncomfortably aware of the author's own vanity and spite. Zemstvov at eighty comes out of retirement, reluctantly, to take on the fascinating Hallie, spouts jargon to the point of parody, intensifies the treatment against her wishes when he learns he is going to die, almost forces her to deny her belief that a certain dream means she wants to stop treatment (he admits he behaved badly here), dies the next day assuming "a foetal position," and is heavily mourned by Hallie with no mention of any relief at being rid of him. This won't do, and it looks worse in view of the illogicality of her two principal charges against psychoanalysis itself: first, that it wrongly tries to be a substitute religion, although it is clearly the Bible-haunted Hallie who is searching for that; and, second, that it imposes on its practitioners an Olympian detachment in contrast to Hallie's belief in "total commitment," a charge which is not only inconsistent with the first but which looks weak in itself, for the instances specified (Zemstvov advising her not to help Ernie further, another analyst advising Sukey not to have a baby) are instances of intervention, not detachment. But fortunately a sympathetic attitude toward psychoanalysis is not a requisite for insight, and *The Passions of Uxport* is often a wise and satisfying book. —DAVID J. GORDON, "Some Recent Novels: Styles of Martyrdom," YR, Autumn 1968, pp. 120–21

Maxine Kumin is a woman who writes like some male writers, specifically like Erich Segal, author of the novel *Love Story*, which was an earlier and highly successful variation on Kumin's theme of love, domesticity and money (in *The Designated Heir*). Her plot is simple: Can Robin Parks, a highborn Bostonian and the "designated heir" of the title, find happiness with Jeffrey Rabinowitz, a nice Jewish boy from East 62nd Street? The answer is not absolutely certain, although a probable "yes" seems safe. After all "you don't need a yarmulka on East Sixty-second Street," as Jeffrey's mother says. . . .

Maxine Kumin uses a lot of literary devices—sections from Jeffrey's Peace Corps journal; symbol and metaphor applied like band-aids or perhaps tourniquets—to mask the essential banality of her plot. They are not enough. She is fond of words like "argufy" and "horripilate" ("she read still omnivorously, horripilated by modern fiction, yet determined to keep abreast"). She has an unerring eye for the inept simile: "from the rafters vegetables hung down as simply as shoelaces" and "the porcelain cup and saucer rode in his left hand as easily as a sailboat at its moorings," to cite two. She also likes to pass

on aphoristic wisdom, better when it comes by way of Thoreau, whom she quotes frequently, than from the author. Here are three examples of hers: "the art of capitulation is grace"; "the real primal scene is the first time you have to be a parent to your parent. The first time you have to be the forgiver"; and, "love means different things to different people." (Lest we forget, love also means never having to say you're sorry, and *pace*, Erich.) When Robin is told, "your head is a bank vault stuffed full of useless aphorisms," the reader cheers.

Such infelicities might not be so surprising in a creative writing student, but Kumin is an experienced, indeed an honored, writer. She won the Pulitzer Prize for poetry in 1973 for *Up Country: Poems of New England*, and *Poetry* magazine's Eunice Tietjens Memorial Prize the year before. Altogether she has published four books of poems and four novels. She has lectured in English at various Massachusetts colleges, and is now translating some contemporary French women poets. Clearly she is not an amateur, which is why I read this book twice, thinking, hoping that I'd missed something the first time. But no. I didn't believe it the second time either. *The Designated Heir* is a marshmallow of a book—sticky, sweet and soft in the center, and suitable for roasting.—WILLIAM McPHERSON, NR, Aug. 10–17, 1974, pp. 25–26

---

### PHILIP BOOTH
#### "Maxine Kumin's Survival"

*American Poetry Review*, November–December 1978, pp. 18–19

I know a professional critic who last year spoke his doubt of Maxine Kumin in simple imprecation: "I just wish she'd quit writing about her goddamn *horse*."

But the mare in question has just foaled, and Maxine Kumin, too, has survived: survival is what *The Retrieval System* is first of all about. And there on the dustjacket, undoubtedly assaulting my critical friend's sensibilities, is Maxine Kumin—looking casually horsey as she leans against her New Hampshire barn-door. I have never seen Maxine Kumin ride; but if Freud was right about the ascendant ego being like a little girl learning to ride a big horse, I can only imagine that Maxine Kumin rides with the high-risk grace, and experienced control, she brings to her poems. Their maturity is the uniquely lovely maturity of a woman who has never forgotten the girlhood she has long since outgrown.

The values *The Retrieval System* values (without moralizing about them) are primarily conservational. The book in no way presents itself as any kind of "breakthrough" experiment; it isn't *Life Studies* or *Ariel*, nor does it want to be. It is, rather, prime Maxine Kumin, who has simply gotten better and better at what she has always been good at: a resonant language, an autobiographical immediacy, unsystematized intelligence, and radical compassion. One does not learn compassion without having suffered, but poems like "Splitting Wood at Six Above," amply show that suffering doesn't require confession to validate pain. Maxine Kumin's mode is memorial rather than confessional: in celebrating the past, and her own part in its passing, she celebrates in herself the very capacity to survive.

Recurrence and memory steady Maxine Kumin "against the wrong turn, / the closed-ward babel of anomie." Beyond her daily milk-runs between house and barn, she often makes the connection between present and past by way of dreams. But her dreams are dreams worked-through to poems: they shape and make a music of their meanings even as they explore and report them. Jerome Bruner says somewhere that the problem of information is "not storage but retrieval;" Maxine Kumin's poems are over and over informed, and lent depth by, the individuality of *The Retrieval System* which is this book's title and its introductory poem. She deeply sees what

                    features
come up to link my lost people
with the domestic beasts of my life.

                    . . .

My elderly aunts, wearing the heads of willful
intelligent ponies, stand at the fence begging apples.
The sister who died at three has my cat's faint chin,
my cat's inscrutable squint, and cried catlike in pain.
I remember the funeral. *The Lord is my shepherd*,
we said. I don't want to brood. Fact: it is people who
                    fade,
it is animals that retrieve them. A boy
I loved once keeps galloping back as my yearling colt,
cocksure at the gallop, racing his shadow
for the hell of it. He runs merely to be.
A boy who was lost in the war thirty years ago
and buried at sea.

What other poet (saving only, perhaps, Elizabeth Bishop
or A. R. Ammons) would risk that "fact" with its colon? Few
poets would chance *following* the flat statement of memory by
the apparently equal flatness of "*The Lord is my shepherd*, / we
said." But the flatness is redeemed by how "shepherd" is
echoed by "said," "brood," "fade"; the irony of "we said"
precisely derives from how the previous line is end-stopped. To
miss as much, or as little, in reading Maxine Kumin is to
miss—in this poem—how gently the ironies reverberate within
its seeming facticity, until, in the unexcused absence of the
Lord, it is animals that shepherd our most human remembering.

Maxine Kumin is, so to speak, as full of facts as either
Bishop or Ammons, but her work is innately inclined toward
less speculation about what she feels or how she sees. In her
seemingly total recall of childhood,

          I rode to the end of the line
          in Ocean City, where the motormen's
          black lunchboxes hung open
          in the roundhouse like old
          galoshes and I stuffed thumbs
          in my ears as metal bit metal
          on the turntable . . .

or in her psychological insight,

          The doctor brings me as promised
          in his snap-jawed black leather satchel . . .

          He takes me out in sections
          fastens limbs to torso
          torso to neck stem
          pries Mama's naval open
          and inserts me, head first . . .

Maxine Kumin's book most strongly of all calls to mind the
charged facticity of Randall Jarrell's *The Lost World*.

Jarrell's lost-world urbanity knew Saks Fifth Avenue as
well as California supermarkets, ball-turrets as well as the
Washington Zoo; yet he was finally more at home in the nightmare forests of the Märchen than in anything near the
upcountry woodlot Maxine Kumin gets firewood and poems
from. Nobody who has read her fiction, or "In April, in
Princeton," here, can doubt her own urbanity. But the
distinctive nature of Maxine Kumin's present poems derives
from the primary fact that she lives in, and writes from, a world
where constant (if partial) recovery of what's "lost" is as sure as
the procession of the equinoxes, or as familiar as mucking-out the
horses' daily dung. Insofar as dung, decently spread in due season,
revives almost any garden, Maxine Kumin's not unpuritan
concern for excrement is quite literally organic to her poems:

We eat, we evacuate, survivors that we are.
I think these things each morning with shovel
and rake, drawing the risen brown buns
toward me, fresh from the horse oven. . . .

          . . .

I think of the angle of repose the manure
pile assumes, how sparrows came to pick
the redelivered grain, how inky-cap

coprinus mushrooms spring up in a downpour
I think of what drops from us and must then
be moved to make way for the next and next
However much we stain the world, spatter

it with our leavings, make stenches, defile
the great formal oceans with what leaks down,
trundling off today's last barrowful,
I honor shit for saying: We go on.

Such cyclical optimism isn't cheaply earned. When one
reaches fifty, and beyond, regeneration of any kind is hard to
come by. But the second essential fact of these poems is that
Maxine Kumin has come to the time of her lifetime when, as
poet and person, she finds it vitally necessary to outlive the
departed by surviving their present absence. Billy Graham may
try to assure her that "Angels, God's secret agents, / . . . circulate among us to tell / the living they are not alone," but the
poet's binocular vision knows better: she is familiar (in every
sense) with how one's parents depart toward death at nearly the
same time one's children leave to find lives of their own.
Inevitable as such desertions may be, their coincidence
(multiplied by a close-in suicide) is the shock which these
seismographic poems record and try to recover from.

Just as Jarrell came to identify finally not with lost
children or wounded airmen but with ageing women, so
Maxine Kumin can write a fine five-poem portrait of an old
farmer named Henry Manley. Her compassion is never
condescending; her emotions, however complex, are always
clear, even in those poems which confront the suicide of her
closest friend. *The Retrieval System* also deals strongly with the
death of her father; but Maxine Kumin is most of all moving
when she focuses on her daughters (to whom *Retrieval* is
dedicated), and the mutual "uncertainties" she shares with
them in what she wryly calls "this mothering business."

Even "Sunbathing on a Rooftop in Berkeley," half
"pretending summer is eternal," Maxine Kumin knows that
she and her lawschool daughter "bulge toward the separate
fates that await us," and that her own fate is bearing the
realization of mortality that accompanies maternity:

               the truth is
          no matter how I love her, Death
          blew up my dress that day
          when she was in the egg unconsidered.

As grown mother of a grown daughter who "moves with the
assurance of a cheetah," Maxine Kumin can coincidentally
review herself "in a checked gingham outfit," a sometime
"Sleeping Beauty" about to take "an illicit weekend in El Paso"
with the Navy man who, as she wakes up years late, becomes
the immediate target of her domestic anger.

          Was it *her* fault he took so long
          to hack his way through the brambles?
          Why didn't he carry a chainsaw
          like any sensible woodsman?
          Why, for that matter, should any
          twentieth-century woman
          have to lie down at the prick of
          a spindle, etcetera etcetera
          and he is stung to reply
          in kind and soon they are at it.

What they "are at" Maxine Kumin sees as part of life's process as surely as copulation, evacuation, and death. No more or less than the obverse of love, what they "are at" is such familiar anger as, turned on children, "turns the son into a crow / the daughter, a porcupine." The poet's "Wishing the furious wish" revivifies memory for her as surely as "seeing the bones" of another grown daughter's now defunct junior-high biology project. The poet says she is "afflicted" with the immediacy of memory; but such memory is, as she well knows, the sure vitality of these poems. Even in the tense present of "Changing the Children," or "Parting," or "Sunbathing . . ." or "Seeing the Bones," Maxine Kumin sees both ways: *back* to her now very old mother (who "had to go four times to the well / to get me . . ."), and *forward* to her hope (against death) that she may be "borne onward" in her daughters' bellies

> like those old pear-shaped Russian dolls that open
> at the middle to reveal another and another, down
> to the pea-sized irreducible minim . . .

Whether sensing the world *in utero* or *post partum*, Maxine Kumin knows that we are all "locked up in our own story"; but she equally knows that to tell each story is part of the poet's function. Whether she knows it or not, she is intuitively faithful to the sense of Isak Dinesen's "Be loyal to the story" as Hannah Arendt interprets it: "Be loyal to life . . . accept what life is giving you, show yourself worthy of whatever it may be by recollecting and pondering over it, thus repeating it in imagination; this is the way to remain alive." These poems recollect in every sense; the story for Maxine Kumin is most of all telling in how surely the laws of conservation apply to family as well as to farmstead:

> Eventually we get them back.
> Now they are grown up.
> They are much like ourselves.
> They wake mornings beyond cure,
> not a virgin among them.
> We are civil to one another.
> We stand in the kitchen
> slicing bread, drying spoons,
> and tuning in to the weather.

I marvel at those once-virgin "drying spoons" (insofar as the poet's syntax invites such reverberation). But poems as human as these, by the very definition of humanity, are bound to have some small failings. A line like "when she was in the egg unconsidered" seems to me, in context, rhythmically flat; I'm also stopped by some enjambed lines which look and sound (even within a single poem) otherwise parallel to lines which are end-punctuated. My reader's ear is repeatedly troubled that so aurally sophisticated a poet should add to modulated rhyming the sibilance that always derives from playing off what's singular against plurals ("winter"/"manners" or "save"/ "graves" etc.). But these are mostly such minor flaws as one poet often hears in another poet's work yet seldom notices in his own. What is more surely worth notice in Maxine Kumin's work is the extent to which she has individually outrun the limitations of the generation which poetically came-of-age twenty years ago. Whether burdened by convention or rebellion, the limitations of one's poems are likely to be generational: that poets come of age in the 1950's can still write poems too-clever-for-their-own-good is no more or less remarkable than the self-imitating surrealism which is the comparable tic of the 1970's. What is remarkable, I repeat, is the extent to which poets like Maxine Kumin can survive and outdistance both their peers and themselves by increasingly trusting those elements of their work which are most strongly individual. One of Maxine Kumin's strengths has always been the way in which her implied narratives combine a Frostian delight in metaphor

with Marianne Moore's insistence on being a "literalist of the imagination." There are few poets who so clearly know the names of things, or who value more deeply the eventful literalness of our language (consider, above, how "Eventually" bears on how mother and daughters tune in to their common loss of virginity). Where being a "literalist" suffices, Maxine Kumin can let language be; where she wants metaphor, her metaphors are deeply rooted in the facticity of what Jarrell called "the dailiness of life."

Nobody's poems of that "dailiness" are, this side of Frost, as strongly peopled as Jarrell's. Neither are anybody's peopled poems as strongly creaturely as those in *The Retrieval System*. The child, "terrified" at ten, who went down in cellar "darkness to lie on old carpet, / next to the incontinent puppy" has become the woman who exorcises her demons by making a poetry of horses. And not only horses, but the usual run of dogs, cats torturing chipmunks, porcupines, raccoons, chickadees, deer, fieldmice, frogs, woodchucks, pigs and lambs— the backyard familiars of rural life anywhere. I again think of Jarrell, with only the memory of a childhood rabbit to touch him, as he finally told himself into the very woods his darkest poems always dreamt of. I think of Thoreau: "One while we do not wonder that so many commit suicide, life is so barren and worthless; we only live on by an effort of the will. Suddenly our condition is ameliorated, and even the barking of a dog is a pleasure to us." Reading *The Retrieval System*, I wonder if to refuse suicide, yet be able to come to terms with a friend's killing herself, may not have much to do with the dailiness of farm life and farm death, with a poetry which comprehends how

> my pony
> filching apples, rears and catches
> his halter on a branch and hangs
> himself all afternoon. . . .

No, Maxine Kumin is not immune from anguish; but anguish becomes integrated in how the poems get written, in how the book (or the life) is composed. *The Retrieval System* is brilliantly sectioned and ordered; its poems are so much of a piece, so skilfully equal to the variety of their concern, that each reinforces the other. An organic book, a family of poems. It is not random that the book's second from final poem is "How It Goes On," a poem which identifies, as Jarrell repeatedly did, with victimized innocence:

> O lambs! The whole wolf-world sits down to eat
> and cleans its muzzle after.

But it *does* go on, the dailiness of life, in spite of the ways in which man is wolf to both lamb, wolf, and himself. The book's penultimate poem returns again to *process*, this time by way of "The Grace of Geldings in Ripe Pastures":

> they graze
> and grazing, one by one let down
> their immense, indolent penises
> to drench the everlasting grass
> with the rich nitrogen
> that repeats them.

It "goes on" every day. And every day has become for Maxine Kumin, as her final title tells, "A Mortal Day of No Surprises." The poet rests in the marginal assurance that, although "the mares's / in heat and miserable, / squirting, rubbing her tail bare. . . ," the day is as predictable as the song of a whitethroat sparrow; the poet, too, will predictably pass:

> When I'm scooped out of here
> all things animal
> an unsurprised will carry on.

And there will even be, on that predictable land renewed by another family, "someone else's mare to call / to the stallion."

As she lends "a rakish permanence to / the idea of going on," Maxine Kumin's acceptance of death as "fact" (colon) in no way reduces her tough-minded will to survive, or her capacities as surveyor of what's past but never done with. Being gifted, she knows to give form to her recollection: in the full context they provide for their emotion, in the generosity of their description, these poems clearly make a present of the present. They honor the moment by duly valuing the past that composes it; written from ground-level, they are not above caring for horses as part of the world's total poem. These poems retrieve our best instincts, our realizing that it is possible to survive grief: not without pain, but also not without joy.

# OLIVER LA FARGE

## 1901–1963

Oliver Hazard Perry La Farge was born in New York on December 19, 1901. He was the son of a prominent Roman Catholic family from Rhode Island; his father was an architect and his mother worked in a nursing school. His ancestors include Ben Franklin and Commodore Oliver Hazard Perry. La Farge received his early education at Groton and went on to study at Harvard. He was president of the editorial board of the *Advocate*, Harvard's literary magazine, and graduated with a degree in anthropology in 1924. During the summer of 1921 he traveled on his first anthropological expedition to Arizona, where he studied the Navajo Indians. La Farge continued his studies at Tulane with the eminent anthropologist Frans Blom. Together they traveled to Mexico and to Guatemala to study Mayan culture. La Farge returned to Harvard in 1928 to complete his master's thesis on the Mayan language. During the following busy year he finished his master's work and published his first novel, *Laughing Boy*. A romance about two Navajo lovers, *Laughing Boy* was an overwhelming success and won the 1929 Pulitzer Prize for fiction.

La Farge married Wanden Matthews in 1929 and began a lifelong devotion to Indian affairs. In 1933 he became President of the Association of American Indian Affairs, a group which championed the rights of native Americans. In 1937 he was divorced by his wife and two years later he married Consuelo Baca, whom he had met on a visit to Santa Fe. La Farge continued to write books of social history and science as well as fiction. His long novel of 1937, *The Enemy Gods*, offers a more realistic picture of Navajo life in modern America. During World War II he served as the chief historical officer in the U.S. Air Force. After the war he returned to his adopted home in Santa Fe, where as a local celebrity he wrote a newspaper column for the *New Mexican*. He also resumed his post as head of the Association of American Indian Affairs. In his later years he worked on several children's books. This New England son, who later in life nicknamed himself "Indian Man," died on August 2, 1963, in an Albuquerque hospital.

OLIVER LA FARGE
From "Main Line"
*Raw Material*
1945, pp. 202–10

As far as I can make out, the creative urge of writing or story-telling was there first, then it became absorbed in the refuge of day-dreams, but it still existed. Like so many other adolescents, the beginning of writing was in part imitative, in part arose from the discovery that writing compositions was a pleasure at times when I was able to handle the kind of subject I liked. My writing at school was imitative of many authors, mainly those with a flowery style, the subjects were as remote and imaginative as possible. When I got altogether too lush my father, who took all attempts at art seriously, toned me down. I wrote largely about pirates, vikings and Elizabethan seafaring, with some wistful stuff about Rhode Island and some attempts at fantasy à la Dunsany. It was kid stuff, just about like all the rest.

Then the Indians came into my life and my whole urge to flight found its direction. From the point of view of writing I think this was a lucky thing for at least it set me to trying to tell the truth, as far as I could learn it, about actual people. It also had the same appearance of reality that my whole study of Indians had, and a purposefulness which was real in fact. This enabled me entirely to disguise from myself the nature of what I was doing. ⟨. . .⟩

When the circumstances removed me from the Southwest to Central America, the subject of my love, the Navajos, became less real. The Navajo country, out of reach, became even more the promised land than it had been when I could go to it. I kept on studying the subject on the side, and compiled a pretty good thesis on it. I also kept on writing about it.

In the course of my study I had to read as much of the mythology of about forty tribes as I could unearth, which was a lot. I remember particularly the work of a Franciscan, Father Pettitot, who translated the rather drab legends of half a dozen northern Athabascan tribes word for word into French. It made remarkably hard sledding, but from time to time one ran across nuggets of pure gold. There was one passage describing how a Chippewyan stole back his wife, whom the Crees had captured, after she had been enslaved for more than a year.

'All that night,' the story ran, 'he moved back and forth on top of her. Yes, all night long he was marching on her. Why not?'

Much of the material I read was in literal translation, more than one might have hoped for in the free translations had been done by men with enough literary gift to render the character of the original. These texts interested me deeply, above all I was struck by the clarity, economy, and emphasis of the literal wording. Up to then I had been a great user of the periodic sentence, an addict of the flowery passage. When I started to write *Laughing Boy* I was soaked in Indian literature and deeply affected by the Navajo and Apache particularly. Very shortly after I started I translated a number of myths from the Jacalteca. As I got going in the novel I found to my astonishment that all my sentences came out short. My construction looked monotonous to me when I studied it, I was serious worried, and believed that I had fallen victim to a vice of style which would ruin the job. But still I rather liked the writing when I read it unanalytically, and besides, I found it impossible to write in any other way. I was well started in the story when Hemingway and Faulkner together burst upon me like my first view of the sun. Hemingway comforted me a good deal on the question of short sentences. The curious fact is that, to whatever extent my style in that book is modern of its period, the Indians did it.

*Laughing Boy* was written for myself alone as nearly as that is possible in an attempt at a work of art. All my friends were agreed that no book about Indians could ever be sold. It was a rare bit of luck that enabled me to place one Indian short story in *The Dial*. (I wish someone would endow such a magazine today, there is a great need for it, which *Story* definitely does not fill.) Negroes one could write about, Latin America perhaps, but Indians, absolutely not. I was pretty well persuaded of this. But I had the idea, and once conceived the idea carried with it the necessity that it be written. With that, too, was the emotion of longing and farewell to a beloved country which I might never see again. In this book I should pour out all my love. Self-expression? Perhaps, but indirectly through the expression of a beauty seen.

I worked on it in my spare time. In my spare time I wrote things that I hoped would sell, the indulgence of the novel was for afterwards. Having, in the course of some eight years, three times determined that I had thoroughly proven to myself that I could never be a writer, having formally given it up, and having gone right on writing, I determined to test the matter once and for all. I arranged to go on half-time at Tulane, working there five afternoons a week, giving myself the mornings and evenings free. This went on for five months. In that time (I kept careful track) I wrote one hundred and twenty thousand words, of which I sold exactly one thousand two hundred, for twelve dollars, also to *The Dial*. Several of the stories sold for high prices after I won the Pulitzer Prize, one to a magazine which had formerly rejected it. A number of them were reprinted and have gone into anthologies, one got an O. Henry Prize, which doesn't mean much. I mention this because it illustrates the extent to which a writer depends on reputation, as all artists do, and the timidity of editors, similar to that of the people who buy pictures.

On the side I wrote about half of *Laughing Boy*. I had a bad conscience about this as it was a work which could not further my purpose, but I was unable to let it alone. ⟨. . .⟩

No writer can form a valid opinion on his own work. I know only that I am dissatisfied with mine. Least of all can I judge *Laughing Boy*, for it was the product of a young man who I have ceased to be and at the same time it is so loaded with associations as to make it impossible for me to approach it impersonally. I have a certain dislike for it because it has been so popular whereas my other books have done only fairly well. I

grow sick of smiling fools who tell me, 'Oh, Mr. La Farge, I did so love your *Laughing Boy*, when are you going to give us another book?' Having written four other novels, a book of short stories and two non-fiction books, and being like all writers badly in need of more royalties, one can hardly avoid giving a short answer.

I know a woman whom I like for various reasons, but whom I should adore in any case simply because she prefers *Sparks Fly Upward*. I know a writer who was actually influenced by my style in another book. I prize such people. If anybody wants to seduce me into doing something for him, the most effective thing he could do would be to praise any book of mine other than that first success. Which is unfair to a perfectly honest novel, but a prejudice I can't help but feel. Other writers suffer from it, too.

That success set me free to return to the Southwest, and then began the process of education towards reality through my chosen medium of escape. My writing did not keep pace. My second novel was laid in Latin America, in an imaginary country, in the first half of the nineteenth century, which was making it about as remote as could be managed. The next dealt with privateers in the War of 1812. My Indian short stories mostly avoided what I was learning and continued to reconstruct the relatively untouched Indian country of *Laughing Boy* although a feeling of the disaster inherent in white contacts ran through them.

If I had stayed in New Orleans, or at least among artists, things might have developed quite differently. When I was still in the French Quarter I wrote a short story, not much good, which was almost straight reporting. At that time I saw the material for a novel in the life around me. I had not evolved a plot for it, but thought about the possibilities from time to time, liked them a lot, and thought that I should probably tackle the idea as soon as the decks were cleared of work in hand. I had no idea that this would be a big change, not merely in subject matter, but in the entire type of my work. I was near enough to freedom then for it merely to seem the handiest and most promising material.

Established in New York, I discarded the idea. It didn't appeal to me. Then, after several years, I decided one day to write a short story *against* Bohemia and the French Quarter. That, I decided, was the true interpretation of the material I had considered. I started out with that purpose in mind, laid out my story, and found it changing under me. At the same time the writing of it excited me much more than usual. What I produced was not autobiographical, but willy-nilly I set down honest observations on the life I had abandoned, I wrote, not against it, but passionately for it, and in clear, easily interpreted symbols I stated the flat truth about the choice I had made.

This was most disturbing. The logic of character and situation, I explained to myself, prevented me from turning the story the way I wanted it to go. I had stated a special case. The symbolism I flatly denied. As a man I succeeded in avoiding the implications of what, as a writer, I had been unable to help doing. Some day I should write the answering, 'true' story. From time to time I fiddled around with that intention, but somehow I could never cook up a convincing idea. Oh, well, it had been a youthful stage and I was concerned with Indians.

One day it occurred to me that I was in a rut. Analysis of my writings showed that I had one theme and one fundamental love story. I had rewritten the theme from every angle, the only new treatment I could see for the love story would be to set it up between homosexuals. The stories sold, the books made money. If I didn't change pretty soon all hope of growth, all hope of eventually achieving at least once the kind of work I had set out to do, was gone. The only thing to do was to change right now. This meant that the flow of money would stop. Editors had me ticketed for Indian stuff with a romantic turn to it, so had the public. I hardly knew what it felt like to write about white folks, and I intended to experiment. There would be no more thousand-dollar checks, at least for a while. The big money days would go for good, and I'd better make up my mind to it.

At the same time I saw that in my writing I had run away steadily from the present-day realities which occupied most of my thoughts in connection with Indians. For the first time I felt a desire to tackle those realities. I should write a counterpart to *Laughing Boy*, a real study of what his son would be up against today. I did, and I still think *The Enemy Gods* is my first non-escape writing though the critics don't agree with me.

But *The Enemy Gods* was still about Indians, it was still the thing observed rather than the thing experienced. Writing about white folks still came hard. Back at last in contact with myself, my education was falling into coherence inside me, but I had taken the most essential experiences of my life and walled them up behind a solid wall the very existence of which I had denied.

All my life I have been lucky, and of all my luck the greatest has been in the calibre of my friends. Now at a critical time a friend stepped in, a woman of unusual quality, great perception, and remorseless persistence. Finally she forced the word, 'Bop,' across my unwilling lips. I was thirty-six; I had not spoken that word since I left School. The central stone, the key, came out with a loud bop! and the wall began to crumble. The first decent writing I ever did about the important things known to me of my own knowledge was about little boys at school. Then, and only then, I ceased to be afraid, and then at last I slew the Groton Boy.

So in effect I'm beginning again, which is perhaps the real reason behind the various ones I perceive for writing this account. My last novel is in many ways a first novel. I'm curious to see what I'll think of it ten years from now. I'm even more curious to see where I'll go from here, providing there is any going at all from now on for a luxury profession such as mine. ⟨. . .⟩

You write. You spend your life in pursuit of something you will never catch. Καλός, ἀγαθός . . . the good, the beautiful, and the true. They are all one. I suppose a painter would choose the second word for the name of the perfect union of the three, a writer finds ultimate beauty and goodness in ultimate, absolute truth, a brilliance of which the human mind can catch no more than glimpses. It lies in your idea, in your intention. In the story you are about to write you see the gleam of one fragment of universal truth, you see the possibility of that beauty. And you write. And you haven't caught it. Perhaps later. Perhaps if I become more skillful and learn to shed my inadequate self more completely. Perhaps if I write enough books, enough stories, somewhere in one of them I shall actually lay hands on the absolute and have my moment of greatness. You don't really believe this, but you have seen something—not really seen it but caught a fugitive glimpse, and that is enough. You haven't heard it but you have an idea of what is meant by the music of the spheres and a longing has been set up in you which will never cease. You can never give up hunting for it nor will you ever be satisfied; though in the end your juices may dry up, your vision and your memory of vision be clouded, and another man than the one you used to be may become satisfied.

I suppose everyone must visualize his objective in his own way. The crystal comparison is the one I think of most, the completely clear, flashing crystal which is also, in different terms and under different conditions, the goal of science and of religion. The crystal hidden in a medicine bag. Inadequate, but then, no visualization or metaphor will serve. You simply know that it exists and that you are shooting at the North star with a popgun.

## CHARLES ALLEN
### "The Fiction of Oliver La Farge"
*Arizona Quarterly*, Winter 1945, pp. 74–81

Oliver La Farge has published five novels and one collection of short stories since 1929. Two of the novels, *Laughing Boy* and *The Enemy Gods*, and five of the twelve stories in *All the Young Men*, are about Navahos. It is as an interpreter of this largest of all Indian tribes within the boundaries of the United States that La Farge's reputation as a fiction writer rests at the present time. He is at his second best when writing of other Indian tribes, the Jicarilla Apache and the various Mexican tribes. His two novels on Anglo-Americans, *The Long Pennant* and *The Copper Pot*, and the stories which are dominantly about Anglos are relatively insignificant and will soon be forgotten.

The Anglo-American stories and novels are, however, interesting, and a brief analysis of them will serve to indicate some of the characteristics of La Farge as a fiction writer. *The Long Pennant* (1933) is a far better narrative than *The Copper Pot* (1942). The characters of the former work, New England seamen of the early nineteenth century, are vigorously sketched: the obvious traits of the Yankee mind are well projected—the respect for hard cash, the religious preoccupation, the wanderlust, the combination of sentimental humanitarianism and sharp ruthlessness. But despite the novel's regional interpretation, it is little more than a picaresque adventure tale, compounded of many of the stock ingredients—fast-moving action, sprightly dialogue, high suspense, and fightin', swearin', drinkin' men, who, when they are not fightin', swearin', drinkin' are pretty well occupied chasin' women. The characters are vividly set off, though they are not round, complex individuals. La Farge does not make us realize, as Conrad or Virginia Woolf do, that people, even the simplest, are complex with mystery and elusiveness. In a sense La Farge's people lack flesh and bones and spirit. If the novel has a certain weight and dignity, it comes from the regional background, the swift insight into the obvious aspects of the Yankee mind, and the sharp flashes of the external details of early nineteenth century New Orleans life.

The later novel, *The Copper Pot*, is in almost every way a mediocre performance. The setting is the French Quarter of New Orleans in the late 1930's. The novel is an episodic and loosely constructed narrative about the artistic struggles of some uninteresting writers and painters. The action is focused largely through the mind of Tom Hartshorn, a rather priggish New Englander from Chog's Cove, Rhode Island. As a character Tom is not sufficiently highlighted. One does not see him clearly, though the stream-of-thought technique gives one a great deal of information about him. Nor does one adequately see any of the other characters in the book. The reason for this, I believe, is that the author does not employ the stream-of-thought technique as skillfully as he does in *The Long Pennant*, where the characters, although thin, are forcefully activated. In *The Long Pennant*, he managed to stylize and concentrate his stream-of-thought, and at the same time to convince us of its reality. In *The Copper Pot* the presentation of the thinking-feeling process is probably more realistic as a description of how the mind actually works than is the presentation in *The Long Pennant*; but *The Copper Pot* is also more verbose, water logged with a loose, sprawling style—as loose and sprawling as thought itself. In the end the characters, who do reach towards complexity, are pallid and bloodless, insufficiently dramatized because of a stylistic failure. The novel is interesting mainly in that it illustrates one of La Farge's main preoccupations—that of the growing-up struggle, a struggle which is a main concern in every book that he has written.

More significant is *Sparks Fly Upward* (1931), a novel that also has its setting in the first half of the nineteenth century, this time in Mexico. The central figure, a young mestizo Rashti Indian, discovers his powers gradually as he is caught up into leadership of revolutionary liberal reform. The action is brisk, the setting exotic, the love story poignant—on one level, a minor masterpiece of slick construction and romantic appeal. Again the characterization is brilliant but thin, and again the regional coloring, authentic and strong, raises the story considerably above the level of the average adventure story. In addition, the novel gains power because of its social and philosophic implications, implications which are lacking or not clearly focused in the New England and New Orleans stories. For in *Sparks Fly Upward* La Farge shows a forthright understanding of the reactionary economic and religious forces that have always combined to exploit the Mexican Indian. In its most significant aspect, the novel is a dramatization of the conflict, as bitter today as it was in the nineteenth century, between the reactionary churchmen and landmen and the liberal peons and intellectuals. La Farge's sympathies with liberalism are intense but admirably restrained; he does not allow himself the luxury of indignant wrath that mars the majority of propaganda novels of this kind. (The indignation is not so admirably restrained in *Laughing Boy* and *The Enemy Gods*.)

*All the Young Men* (1933), the collection of twelve stories, is mostly about Indians—Mexican, Jicarilla Apache, and Navaho. And all but three of the stories are good. "No More Bohemia," a long story that was later reshaped to fit as the last section of *The Copper Pot*, fails in the same way that the novel does; "The Goddess Was Mortal" is marred by shaky characterization and by a trite, cheap ending; and "All the Young Men" is inadequately focused. Otherwise the volume compares favorably with *Sparks Fly Upward*. Both books show a great deal of accurate knowledge of Indian life; a sharp observation of the landscape; the ability to focus a scene and to carry the action along at an appropriate pace; a tendency toward strong but skeletonized characterization; a preoccupation with the growing-up process; and an intense but dignified expression of liberal sympathies. And both books unite in their assertion that there is a satisfying beauty in the Indian way of life, the equivalent of which the Indian cannot often discover in alien cultures—a point that is more obviously made in *Laughing Boy*, La Farge's first book.

*Laughing Boy* gained the Pulitzer Prize for 1929. It is, indeed, a prize novel, a piece of expert craftsmanship, in many ways his best novel. The various elements of style, characterization, philosophy, setting, and tone are so perfectly blended that no one of them is obtrusive. It is a masterpiece of balance and proportion—a masterpiece technically: there is a steady, fast-moving action; a concise, color-sparking style (La Farge never over burdens his work with unnecessary realistic detail); and, though there are a number of minor characters and a good deal of description of the Navaho way of life, the author

manages to keep the focus of reader interest on his main characters.

Yet I should not say that *Laughing Boy* is a great novel. It is not great because of a fault I have noted several times earlier—the fault of thin characterization. Though there is, more than in any of his other novels, a tight illusion of psychological inevitability, and though there is strength and sharpness of character outline, roundness, allusiveness, complexity are again absent. There is still not enough suggestion of the hidden and unfathomable personality, though there is more of the contradictory and unpredictable about Slim Girl and Laughing Boy than about any of the other characters that La Farge has created. They are hollow only in reference to the characters fashioned by better artists.

A writer, when selecting his main figures, is likely to indicate a preference for a particular kind of personality, though his minor creations may run the range of human types. La Farge is no exception: he has his typical male protagonist and his typical female protagonist. Slim Girl is his Woman—competent, patient, wise, shrewd, passionate, comely—in the end suggestive of a combination of the *femme fatale* and the eagle-eyed Amazon. This is an exaggeration, of course, for Slim Girl does not develop all of her heroic proportions until towards the end of the novel. From the beginning she is comely, passionate, competent, shrewd; she has to grow out of impatience into patience, from confusion into wisdom. Usually, however, La Farge's women have pretty well found themselves by the time the story begins and remain the Great Woman throughout. They tend to be static rather than dynamic characters.

The Man, on the other hand, is generally a growing; developing Man—a Growing-Up-Man. It takes Laughing Boy a long time to find himself, just as it takes Estevan in *Sparks Fly Upward*, or Myron in *The Enemy Gods*, a long time. They always, however, except for a good many minor characters, make the grade, turn out just as admirable and heroic as the Women. La Farge does not too obviously take sides in the battle of the sexes.

In the magnificent prologue to *The Enemy Gods* (1937), the War Gods, Child of the Waters, and Slayer of Enemy Gods (Nayeinezgani), decide, in the words of Nayeinezgani, to "'look closely at our people . . .'", to "'pay attention, not only to the Navajos but beyond them, to the sources of all that afflicts them.'" The War Gods may have considered the total scene as it existed for the Navaho between the early 1920's and the late 1930's, but La Farge certainly did not, though the novel is considerably more inclusive in its scope than *Laughing Boy* or the short stories. The narrative is told from the Navaho point of view, and the reader is thrown glimpses, but only glimpses, of the many difficulties that confront the Navaho. There is something of the fight to preserve the land against the greediness of the Whites, and against drought and over grazing; there is something of the fight to maintain their religion against the encroachments of Christianity; but there is far too little of the struggle to preserve Navaho customs and mores while at the same time gaining the White Man's knowledge and use of machinery, medicine, and agriculture; and there is also far too little about the Navaho's effort to eradicate his own ignorance, superstition, and outmoded customs. La Farge suggests that the Navaho is pretty generally winning his battles, not only because of his own integrity and strength, but because of powerful outside aid from such sources as the American Association on Indian Affairs and the enlightened Bureau of Indian Affairs that has been in power under Presidents Hoover and Roosevelt. I, too, am convinced that the Navaho is winning, but I cannot say that *The Enemy Gods* has done as much to convince me as it might have.

The main energy of the novel is focused on the growing-up experience of Myron Begay, a rather bright but priggish young man, whose life is almost ruined by the under-educated churchmen and laymen who direct his life for sixteen years in various government Indian schools. The situation that La Farge has chosen allows him a splendid opportunity to analyze the changing attitudes toward Indian education and to reveal the corrupt practices of the Christian missionaries who infest the large government schools. La Farge bitterly attacks the government's cruel practice, which was standard in the twenties and which is still practised to some extent, of kidnapping children and forcing them, hundreds of miles from their families, into dreary concentration camps, where every effort was (and is) made by under-paid and under-educated disciplinarians to eradicate all evidences of native culture. He shows us a little of the early 1930 attempts to reform the nonreservation government school—attempts such as the one at Santa Fé, where the Indian is encouraged to maintain certain aspects of his cultural heritage, and where he is given fairly decent physical and health facilities. He tells us nothing at all about the most recent experiment, the reservation dayschool, an attempt to educate without breaking up the pattern of family and tribal life.

*The Enemy Gods* reminds one immediately of *The Grapes of Wrath*, and a comparison of the two novels, both representative of their author's best work, will give us a fairly accurate measure of La Farge's relative importance as a novelist. Steinbeck presents with realism and power the situation of the Okie, and La Farge with realism and power the position of the Navaho. Steinbeck is intensely sympathetic with the Okie and bitterly attacks his unscrupulous exploitation, a point of view which La Farge expresses for the Navaho. Both authors are propagandists; and, though both are perfectly capable of objectifying their ideas dramatically, neither is content to rely on dramaturgy alone. They both feel compelled to reinforce their points by expository paragraphs that only imperfectly mesh with the narrative action. (La Farge does not use the expository essay chapter, however.) And there are other obvious comparisons that one can make—the reliance of both writers on the strong, flat character, for instance. But the points of difference are more significant than the elements of likeness for an understanding of La Farge's limitations. Steinbeck's story has an inexorable inevitability of action that is missing in La Farge's novel. And while Steinbeck introduces just as many, if not more, important secondary characters as La Farge, Steinbeck is capable of keeping his main characters more consistently in the spotlight than La Farge; this, of course, means that Steinbeck's dramatic power is considerably greater. But more important, Steinbeck has a warmer personality: a more robust humor, a more flexible style. La Farge, despite his flair for color and romance and his liberalism and keen understanding of people, always burdens his work with a strong tincture of New England frigidity, a point which is very noticeable in every novel or story that he has written. Despite the fact that *The Enemy Gods* is not as topical, that it treats of a more enduring social situation than *The Grapes of Wrath*, the latter novel is a superior piece of work.

From what little I have observed of the Navaho, and from what I gather from such excellent studies as Alexander and Dorothea Leighton's *Navaho Door* (1944), I should say that La Farge cannot be accused of seriously romanticizing his Indians. True, he does not indicate anything of the shocking evidences of disease and malnutrition that even the most casual observer notices on all sides as he travels through the Indian country; nor, though he mentions them, does he realistically stress the filth (unavoidable in a country of little rain), close air, and over crowding that marks many a Navaho hogan; but he is careful to emphasize that the Navaho society is made up of all types of people: there is the average amount of stupidness and brightness, the average number of criminals and saints. Most of his people, however, are neither stupid nor bright, neither criminals nor saints. They are just average human beings: pleasant, confused, and perhaps a little more mystical, generous, superstitious, and sensitive to beauty than the average Anglo.

One does sense, however, a kind of escapist philosophy underlying all of La Farge's Indian fiction. In *Laughing Boy* the author's philosophy would pretty clearly seem to be one of romantic sentimentalism—i.e., the good life is the uncontaminated primitive life. Most obviously this primitivism manifests itself in the fact that Laughing Boy and Slim Girl become self-reliant and heroic only after they isolate themselves from the impinging alien and "civilized" cultures. Less insistently, this is also the point of *The Enemy Gods* and several of the short stories. But one must hasten to emphasize that in all of his work since *Laughing Boy*, La Farge has indicated an increasing sympathy with the Indian's own realistic effort to adjust his outlook with the demands of the modern world. This is apparent in the short stories, more apparent in *The Enemy Gods*, and is an intensely stated thesis in his expositional survey of Indian culture titled *As Long as the Grass Shall Grow* (1940). In this volume the point is made time and again, though never very specifically, that Indian culture cannot remain a museum piece, a relic of a colorful, primitive past. Here La Farge almost accepts the Indian's own growing conviction that a dynamic, socially responsible Indian culture must rest on the working synthesis of the best that is to be found in the Anglo and Indian ways. Specifically such a synthesis would seem to imply a wholesale adoption of the White Man's practical science and a cultivation of the Navaho spiritual insights. As the Navaho is successfully working out such a synthesis, there can be little doubt that it is a wiser conception than either the romantic primitivism suggested in *Laughing Boy* or the equally sentimental "civilizing" theories of the Christian missionaries and other hard-boiled materialists.

In the end, the reader is likely to be more impressed with La Farge as a stimulating and lively interpreter of the southwestern Indian cultures than with La Farge as a rounded, completely satisfying artist. One's final impression is not of a balanced and intense combination of psychology, style, philosophy, dramatic action, and regional elements: the characterization is too weak, and the author's underlying philosophical outlook too limited to give the effect of artistic balance. What remains is a nice sense of construction, of dramatic action, and, perhaps overshadowing all else, a fine understanding of the Southwest landscape and of the Indian culture.

LAWRENCE CLARK POWELL
From "*Laughing Boy*: Oliver La Farge"
*Southwest Classics*
1974, pp. 222–28

*L*aughing Boy was published in November 1929. Its choice by the Literary Guild boosted it into best-selling orbit. Then in May of 1930 it won the Pulitzer Prize, in competition with books by Sinclair Lewis, Thomas Wolfe, and Ernest Hemingway. The judges included Mary Austin and Owen

Wister, two of the foremost writers on the West. How could it *not* have won?

There are reasons for its brilliant success. The author knew his subject, the Navajos and their land, and thus his book was sure and true. He had developed skill as a writer, by writing. What might have been a tract became lyrical from the love he felt for those desert people and their environment. His emotion was nostalgic. In words he wrote years later, "The book sprang from a combination of vivid memory, the sad sense of saying farewell, and the knowledge experienced in writing a thesis as part of the requirements for a master's degree."

"He believed," La Farge went on to recall of himself, "that he might never go to the American Southwest again, certainly would never again be free to soak himself in the Navajo Indians. Among them he had seen something that had moved him greatly and this was his way of recording it. As the young can do, he had made personal friendships, experienced moments of genuine contact among the Navajos, despite the barriers of language and culture, and these loopholes of insight were vastly widened by his studies."

How did success affect the young man not yet thirty years old? Both for better and worse. It brought La Farge to a lifework on behalf of the American Indians—a labor of social benefit rather than linguistic research. It brought him back to the Southwest, though not immediately. He was also assured of being able to publish everything he chose to submit. These were positive results.

On the negative side, the sudden financial success led La Farge to leave the French Quarter for New York, to marry on his social level, and to do what was expected of a La Farge— carry on the family tradition. "I was of the 4th generation of artists and they were all gentlemen," he lamented. "One was supposed to live up to them."

He came to experience the ancient conflict between the conventional and the creative, between New England and New Orleans, a closed society and the open Southwest. "I was particularly prone to aspirations toward conservative gentility which were actually alien to my make-up," La Farge wrote later in properly inflated language, "to live uptown in a presentable apartment, have friends out of the same drawer as myself, give dinners of six and eight deftly served, accompanied by the right wines, and to be asked to small, fashionable parties (white tie)—a death in life, which I eagerly embraced as soon as financial success enabled me to, and of which it took a series of disasters to cure me."

Mary Austin was not taken in. La Farge told the story on himself. When that blunt woman first met the author of the book on which she had helped confer the coveted Pulitzer, she took one look around that uptown apartment and exclaimed, "Well, I never expected to find *you* in a place like *this!*"

What were the other "disasters"? Marriage was one. Although they had two children, this was not enough to reconcile the widening differences between him and his wife. His drinking made for moodiness. The Depression robbed him of the security that would have come from his book's earnings. The genteel La Farges were not rich. To earn money to maintain his new standard of living meant that La Farge had to go on turning out romantic Indian stories for the slick paper magazines.

He sought to break the pattern by writing two novels with settings other than the Southwest. *Sparks Fly Upward*, laid in Central America, and *Long Pennant*, an adventure story of New England privateers in southern waters, were good books, but they did not earn the money his way of life required. He realized that the kind of writer he intended to be could not be

financially secure nor could flourish in a society environment. He came to know that he should not have left New Orleans.

Because of the popularity of *Laughing Boy* and his prestige as a La Farge, he was drawn into work on behalf of the Indians, first with a private organization and then on government assignment under John Collier, the Commissioner of Indian Affairs who came in with the Roosevelt New Deal. This work took him back to the Southwest, with the Hopis, the Navajos, and the Apaches. He went on to become president and eloquent spokesman of the Association on American Indian Affairs. In this capacity he worked until his death in 1963 at age sixty-one.

By his concern for Indian rights La Farge both found and lost his life. He became less of an artist and more of a man. Out of the disillusionment that ensued, particularly during the Eisenhower administration when the Indian programs were largely abandoned, he managed to write book after book. One of the most meaningful is composed of the text he contributed to a book of photographs by Helen M. Post called *As Long as the Grass Shall Grow*. In a revulsion from the romanticism of *Laughing Boy* he wrote the sombre stories of *All the Young Men* and in 1937 his next to last novel, *The Enemy Gods*, an indictment of the missionaries and government agencies that took the Navajo and Apache children away from their parents and confined them in prison-like schools. Even thus had Lummis reacted a generation earlier at Isleta.

Then the war came. Paradoxically from the destructive conflict that saw him become Chief Historian of the Air Transport Command, with a far-flung staff of two hundred fifty, La Farge derived creative strength and a new life. After serving in theaters of action the world around, he wrote the history of the Command called *The Eagle in the Egg*. Thus was inaugurated the Air Age in which we now live.

Yet without a happy second marriage in 1939, it is doubtful whether the challenge of the Indian work, followed by the responsibility of wartime service, would have been enough to maintain La Farge's belief in himself as a creative writer.

He met the woman who became his second wife at the Santa Fe Fiesta in 1936. They were married three years later. She was as truly of the Southwest as he was of New England. Half French and half Spanish-American, Consuelo Otille Baca came into La Farge's life at the time of his most need, as he was experiencing disillusionment and despair from the fortune that had turned him the wrong way. Her families, the Bacas and the Pendaries, were the lords of Rociada, a high valley in the Sangre de Cristos between Santa Fe and Taos. The death of her father, who had become Lieutenant Governor of New Mexico, and the collapse of the wool market in the Depression, had forced the sale of the domain and brought the Bacas to live in Santa Fe.

After their marriage and reunion after the war, Oliver and Consuelo made Santa Fe their home. In addition to his Indian work, he wrote stories, juveniles, a pictorial history of the Indians, and one more novel, *The Copper Pot*, in which he returned to the French Quarter and told of an artist who did *not* leave that creative milieu for a New York society marriage. Although good therapy for him to have written it, the novel remains undistinguished.

A better book is a group of essays toward an autobiography called *Raw Material*, written after the war on a Guggenheim Fellowship. Because of wartime restrictions on materials, the publisher gave it a wretched format. The scarcest and least known of La Farge's books, it is one of his best, an illuminating, self-searching, writer's testament.

Three peaks dominate the range of Oliver La Farge's

books—*Laughing Boy, Raw Material*, and one which might outlive them both: *Behind the Mountains*. As much a child of Oliver and Consuelo as their son, John Pendaries, it first appeared serially in the *New Yorker*, with which La Farge had a lucrative agreement whereby after the war that magazine had first call on his stories, sketches, and essays.

*Behind the Mountains* was Consuelo's story, told through her husband, of her enchanted childhood and girlhood on the Baca domain high in the Sangre de Cristos. Here in a few simple artless, artful exercises in the transmutation of one person's memories into another person's prose is the quintessence of northern New Mexico. The book has the same ambience of *Laughing Boy*, that classic of northern Arizona—romantic, lyrical, and redolent with the fragrance of piñon and juniper and sweat-stained leather, fashioned from the Southwest that La Farge had loved and lost, wooed and won again.

The last years in Santa Fe were his Indian Summer. He never wrote another novel. After his work for Indian rights there was no strength left for a major undertaking. Stories and reviews and his weekly column in the Santa Fe *New Mexican* were the most he could do. His newspaper contributions were collected posthumously by Winfield Townley Scott, another Rhode Islander who had moved to Santa Fe, in *The Man with the Calabash Pipe*. They are in turn serious and gay, angry and mellow, and always written with skill and grace.

I met Oliver La Farge only once, at a luncheon in Santa Fe. He was wearing much Indian jewelry in the Navajo manner. He was darkly handsome, and taciturn. Ignorant then of his feelings about it, I praised *Laughing Boy* which I had just reread. He stared at me.

A year before he died La Farge wrote a new foreword to a paperback edition of *Laughing Boy*. In it he looked back in sadness at the book that had determined his life. He saw the Navajos as a "powerful community equipped with a modern government and many other improvements, treated with great respect by the Senators and Congressmen from the two states in which most of them reside. They are an unhappy people, sullen towards all others, unfriendly, harassed by drunkenness, their leaders at once arrogant and touchy. Still, here and there among them you can still find the beauty, the religion, the sense of fun, you can still attend a ceremony at which no one is drunk. In the space of thirty years, however, the wholeness has gone, the people described in *Laughing Boy*, complete to itself, is gone."

"It would have completely staggered that beginning writer," he went on in elegiac vein to say about his vanished self, "to learn that after all these years his book would still be selling. He did not expect it to sell at all. It would have staggered and gratified him enormously could he have known then, in his time of early struggle, the days of aching hope and profound self-doubt, that young readers would still be liking it thirty years later. But there is no way to reach back and tell him that, and it probably is better that he did the thing for itself, because he had to, and for no other reason. That leaves the gratification to me, his successor, who am much older and much more in need of encouragement."

In the end his devotion to the Southwest shortened his life, as he wore himself out in work for the Association he headed. Travels to reservations as distant as Alaska, legislative hearings, voluminous reports, speeches, and reviews, combined to drain his diminishing strength. His last effort was to aid the Taos Indians in their efforts to recover the Blue Lake lands in the mountains above the pueblo, taken from them in 1906 and added to the Carson National Forest. Only two months before he died, La Farge went a last time to the pueblo, so ill that he had to take an oxygen tank to aid his breathing. He did not live to see the final victory. It came on December 15, 1970, seven and a half years after La Farge's death, when President Nixon signed the Congressional bill that gave the Taoseños trust title to their sacred lands.

Lieutenant-Colonel Oliver Hazard Perry La Farge, U.S.A. F.R., lies buried under one of the small identical headstones in the National Cemetery in Santa Fe. If you would seek an epitaph for him, go to *Laughing Boy*. You will find it there in Laughing Boy's words of love for Slim Girl:

"I have been down Old Age River in the log, with sheet-lightning and rainbows and soft rain, and the gods on either side to guide me. The Eagles have put lightning snakes and sunbeams and rainbows under me; they have carried me through the hole in the sky. I have been through the little crack in the rocks with Red God and seen the homes of the Butterflies and the Mountain Sheep and the Divine Ones. I have heard the Four Singers on the Four Mountains."

*In Beauty it is finished.*

# RING LARDNER

## 1885–1933

Ringgold Wilmer Lardner was born in Niles, Michigan, on March 6, 1885. The youngest son of wealthy parents, he received his early education at home. Lardner attended Niles High School, where the 6'2" teenager played football. His family suffered several financial setbacks around the time of his graduation in 1901, and he took a few odd jobs before entering Chicago's Armour Institute of Technology in 1902. Lardner flunked out after one semester and returned home. The following year he wrote the music and lyrics to a two-act entertainment, *Zanzibar*, performed by a group of local minstrels. After taking a bookkeeping job with the local gas company, Lardner fell into a newspaper job, covering mostly sporting events. The editor of the South Bend *Times*, whose offices were located about ten miles from Niles, had come to the Lardner home looking for Ring's older brother Rex, who was already an established writer at the South Bend *Tribune*. Ring knew that Rex was under contract so he asked to take the job at the *Times*. Subsequently his sports reporting in

South Bend led to a series of jobs with Chicago papers. By 1913 he was writing a daily column, "In the Wake of the News," for the Chicago *Tribune*. His columns became extremely popular and were noted for their dry humor and overblown style. Lardner married his longtime sweetheart, Ellis Abbott, in 1911.

Around 1914 Lardner began to publish humorous short stories in *The Saturday Evening Post*. His first collection, *You Know Me Al* (1916), featured stories about Jack Keefe, a semi-illiterate baseball player. These stories were marked by the baseball slang that characterized Lardner's newspaper columns. In 1919 Lardner moved his family, which now included four sons, to Greenwich, Connecticut. He began to write a column for the Bell Syndicate, titled "Weekly Letter." The Lardners soon moved to Great Neck, Long Island, where they became friendly with their neighbors, Zelda and Scott Fitzgerald. Lardner's career as a fiction writer began to take off with the publication of *How to Write Short Stories (With Samples)* in 1924. Lardner's earlier collections were reissued as he enjoyed both critical and financial success. He continued to satirize aspects of American life throughout his works; by his death he had authored over 120 stories. Lardner also worked on several Broadway productions, of which his collaboration with George S. Kaufman on *June Moon* (1929) was most successful.

In 1926 Lardner discovered he had tuberculosis. He moved out to East Hampton, Long Island. Despite his poor health he continued to write, mostly because of financial pressures. Heavy drinking led to further health problems, and on September 25, 1933, he died at the age of forty-eight.

His stories, it seems to me, are superbly adroit and amusing; no other contemporary American, sober or gay, writes better. But I doubt that they last: our grandchildren will wonder what they are about. It is not only, or even mainly, that the dialect that fills them will pass, though that fact is obviously a serious handicap in itself. It is principally that the people they depict will pass, that Lardner's Low Down Americans—his incomparable baseball players, pugs, song-writers, Elks, small-town Rotarians and golf caddies—are flitting figures of a transient civilization, and doomed to be as puzzling and soporific, in the year 2000, as ⟨Thomas⟩ Haliburton's Yankee clock peddler is to-day.

The fact—if I may assume it to be a fact—is certain not to be set against Lardner's account; on the contrary, it is, in its way, highly complimentary to him. For he has deliberately applied himself, not to the anatomizing of the general human soul, but to the meticulous histological study of a few salient individuals of his time and nation, and he has done it with such subtle and penetrating skill that one must belong to his time and nation to follow him. I doubt that anyone who is not familiar with professional ball players, intimately and at first hand, will ever comprehend the full merit of the amazing sketches in *You Know Me Al*; I doubt that anyone who has not given close and deliberate attention to the American vulgate will ever realize how magnificently Lardner handles it. He has had more imitators, I suppose, than any other living American writer, but has he any actual rivals? If so, I have yet to hear of them. They all try to write the speech of the streets as adeptly and as amusingly as he writes it, and they all fall short of him; the next best is miles and miles behind him. And they are all inferior in observation, in sense of character, in shrewdness and insight. His studies, to be sure, are never very profound; he makes no attempt to get at the primary springs of human motive; all his people share the same amiable stupidity, the same transparent vanity, the same shallow swinishness; they are all human Fords in bad repair, and alike at bottom. But if he thus confines himself to the surface, it yet remains a fact that his investigations on that surface are extraordinarily alert, ingenious and brilliant—that the character he finally sets before us, however roughly articulated as to bones, is so astoundingly realistic as to epidermis that the effect is indistinguishable from that of life itself. The old man in "The Golden Honeymoon" is not merely well done; he is perfect. And so is the girl in "Some Like Them Cold." And so, even, is the

idiotic Frank X. Farrell in "Alibi Ike"—an extravagant grotesque and yet quite real from glabella to calcaneus.

Lardner knows more about the management of the short story than all of its professors. His stories are built very carefully, and yet they seem to be wholly spontaneous, and even formless. He has grasped the primary fact that no conceivable ingenuity can save a story that fails to show a recognizable and interesting character; he knows that a good character sketch is always a good story, no matter what its structure. Perhaps he gets less attention than he ought to get, even among the anti-academic critics, because his people are all lowly boors. For your reviewer of books, like every other sort of American, is always vastly impressed by fashionable pretensions. He belongs to the white collar class of labor, and shares its prejudices. He praises F. Scott Fitzgerald's stories of country-club flappers eloquently, and overlooks Fitzgerald's other stories, most of which are much better. He can't rid himself of the feeling that Edith Wharton, whose people have butlers, is a better novelist than Willa Cather, whose people, in the main, dine in their kitchens. He lingers under the spell of Henry James, whose most humble character, at any rate of the later years, was at least an Englishman, and hence superior. Lardner, so to speak, hits such critics under the belt. He not only fills his stories with people who read the tabloids, say "Shake hands with my friend," and buy diamond rings on the instalment plan; he also shows them having a good time in the world, and quite devoid of inferiority complexes. They amuse him sardonically, but he does not pity them. A fatal error! The moron, perhaps, has a place in fiction, as in life, but he is not to be treated too easily and casually. It must be shown that he suffers tragically because he cannot abandon the plow to write poetry, or the sample-case to study for opera. Lardner is more realistic. If his typical hero has a secret sorrow it is that he is too old to take up osteopathy and too much in dread of his wife to venture into bootlegging.—H. L. MENCKEN, "Four Makers of Tales," *Prejudices: Fifth Series*, 1926, pp. 50–53

The special force of Ring Lardner's work springs from a single fact: he just doesn't like people. Except Swift, no writer has gone farther on hatred alone. I believe he hates himself; more certainly he hates his characters; and most clearly of all, his characters hate each other. Out of this integral triune repulsion is born his icy satiric power.

There is no mitigating soft streak in him as there is in the half-affectionate portraiture of Sinclair Lewis; and none of the amused complacency of H. L. Mencken. He can be utterly savage with his "puppets" because he is merciless with himself; his rage, a double-pointed sword, turns inward and outward at the same time. Ring Lardner has spent his life in the company of commercial ball-players, prize fighters, Great White Highwaymen, song-writers, wealthy Long Islanders, and upper-class players of bridge and golf. He hates and despises this unsavory assortment of Americans. Yet he has elected to remain in and of these worlds perhaps because any other American milieu seems equally contemptible to him. There is, he would aver, little choice in a democracy of baseness. But he is honest enough to realize that his associates are at best a *pis aller* from which he can take no unction to his soul. He has found nothing whatsoever in American life to which to cling. Other writers who reveal this masochist pattern in a less pure form are George S. Kaufman and F. Scott Fitzgerald. But neither of these is cursed with Lardner's intuitive knowledge of the great American swine, a razor-keen knowledge which he uses as an instrument of self-torture. Like all puritans of stature he is self-accusatory. Despite his apparent objectivity, the blackness of American middle-class life (he never deals with workers and only occasionally with petty clerks) has entered into his own soul. Read beneath the lines and you will see that everything he meets or touches drives him into a cold frenzy, leaving him without faith, hope, or charity.—CLIFTON FADIMAN, "Ring Lardner and the Triangle of Hate," *Nation*, March 22, 1933, p. 315

⟨. . .⟩ the conception of Jack Keefe grew in the fillers Lardner composed for his *Tribune* column, as well as in his own private correspondence where he assumed various dictional guises to amuse his friends. The step was a short one to "A Busher's Letters Home," the first of which was published in March 1914 in the *Saturday Evening Post*.

By using an ill-educated narrator supposedly writing letters, Lardner was able to impose a distinctive style upon his prose. The long monotonous, virtually unpunctuated sentences, and the misspellings emphasize rhythm, sound, and surface. Prose harmonics was beside the point. At the cost of eccentricity Lardner bought homogeneity. Using the rambling sentence and the strategically placed misspelling, he was able to approach a norm of colloquial prose more closely than anyone since Twain.

*You Know Me Al*, the collection of Jack Keefe letters published in 1916, is accordingly based on run-on sentences varied with sprawling compounds. The infrequently paragraphed prose flows on and on, rarely broken into short units. Rather than on punctuation, its sense depends upon syntactically forced hesitations and unsignalled shifts of subject. Lardner's prose observed a high degree of superficial specification, but its effect is pertinently akin to Gertrude Stein's monotonously revolving, slowly advancing style. Here is a single Lardner sentence:

> Well Al I guess you know by this time that I have worked against them 2 times since I wrote to you last time and I beat them both times and Mcgraw knows now what kind of a pitcher I am and I will tell you how I know because after the game yesterday he road down to the place we dressed at a long with me and all the way in the automobile he was after me to say I would go all the way a round the world and finely it come out that he wants I should go a long and pitch for his club and not pitch for the White Sox.

Like Gertrude Stein, Lardner eliminated most of the punctuation inside the sentences, thereby shifting the responsibility for rhetorical organization from the printer to the reader.

I says Well if we dont get there until febuery we wont have no time to train for the next season and he says You wont need to do no training because this trip will take all the weight off of you and every thing else you got.

Because the mind is obliged to establish sense pauses independently, it is attentive to every detail. Lardner quietly forces delicate adjustments along each line. One must, for example, account for the space between "every" and "thing" in the quotation above, just as one must compensate for the loss of an "a" in "You just stick round town." Even as Gertrude Stein wrote in *Tender Buttons*, "look a bout," so Lardner in *You Know Me Al*: "I would rather throw $45.00 a way then go on a trip a round the world." The variety of these subtle foilings of expectation is endless. If carefully attended, their cumulative effect forces new rhythms upon the prose. When Gertrude Stein obliged the reader to establish Sam not as the object of the verb but as the person addressed in " 'You know Sam,' Rose said very often to him," she was anticipating Lardner's commaless title, *You Know Me Al*, as well as technically doing what he did when he wrote, "because you are hog fat." The insistence that just to apprehend words and sentences the mind must work harder than it customarily did in reading standard prose has always been one of the stubborn positions of the colloquial style.—RICHARD BRIDGMAN, "Copies and Misfires," *The Colloquial Style in America*, 1966, pp. 147–49

The enlivening and almost fatal committal to the clever journalist's dateline began but also led him to something like a grammarian's delight in the follies of syntax. Aloof, but accepted easily by everyone, he was silent: he was listening. (It is interesting that he loved music and was noted for his perfect ear.) In a very short time his work as satirical wit and exact sportswriter became well known and highly paid. ⟨. . .⟩

About 1920, something veiled and sophisticated came into vernacular writing. It seems to me that in the older humorists both the talk and the characters celebrate their comic life. The fact that the characters are always jawing away extends their extravagance until as human beings they become proverbial fantasies. Lardner's originality—a little later taken over by Hemingway and others—lies in showing his characters dismantling themselves unconsciously in their flat, ignorant or nonsensical language. We are made to see the lines of their dumb but pleasant repetitions. The inadequacy and abuse of language (and spelling) are as revealing, in their way, as fullness is. To deal with dumbness is a game of skill and cunning in itself. The very ordinary American was exposed, but not by being earnestly denounced, as he was by Sinclair Lewis, for mindless greed, social climbing and for being an ugly barrel of pathetic or ugly received ideas. ⟨. . .⟩

Lardner's mastery of the offhand, the flat and the non sequitur gives him an irony that was the right medicine for a society notoriously given to the bland. He does not condescend. He understands how a game—whether it is baseball or haircutting—forms the speech and character of a man. The barber in "Haircut" is every barber in the world. Lardner also knows that our real lives come to the surface in our off moments. The tired-out characters going glumly to their room in "The Golden Honeymoon" are universal casualties in their innocent expectations and their hurt. What Lardner tells us is that it takes a lot of courage to be a helpless human being. That story also shows that only an observer and listener as acute as Lardner knows how to make things true by knowing what to leave out.—V. S. PRITCHETT, "The Man with the Perfect Ear," *NYTBR*, Aug. 21, 1977, p. 7

## VIRGINIA WOOLF
### From "American Fiction"

*Saturday Review*, August 1, 1925, pp. 1–2

Excursions into the literature of a foreign country much resemble our travels abroad. Sights that are taken for granted by the inhabitants seem to us astonishing; however well we seemed to know the language at home, it sounds differently on the lips of those who have spoken it from birth; and above all, in our desire to get at the heart of the country we seek out whatever it may be that is most unlike what we are used to, and declaring this to be the very essence of the French or American genius proceed to lavish upon it a credulous devotion, to build up upon it a structure of theory which may well amuse, annoy, or even momentarily enlighten those who are French or American by birth.

The English tourist in American literature wants above all things something different from what he has at home. For this reason the one American writer whom the English whole-heartedly admire is Walt Whitman. There, you will hear them say, is the real American undisguised. In the whole of English literature there is no figure which resembles his—among all our poetry none in the least comparable to *Leaves of Grass*. This very unlikeness becomes a merit, and leads us, as we steep ourselves in the refreshing unfamiliarity, to become less and less able to appreciate Emerson, Lowell, Hawthorne, who have had their counterparts among us and drew their culture from our books. The obsession, whether well or ill founded, fair or unfair in its results, persists at the present moment.

⟨. . .⟩ One thing is certain—whatever the American man may be, he is not English; whatever he may become, he will not become an Englishman.

For that is the first step in the process of being American—to be not English. The first step in the education of an American writer is to dismiss the whole army of English words which have marched so long under the command of dead English generals. He must tame and compel to his service the "little American words"; he must forget all that he learnt in the school of Fielding and Thackeray; he must learn to write as he talks to men in Chicago bar-rooms, to men in the factories of Indiana. That is the first step; but the next step is far more difficult. For having decided what he is not, he must proceed to discover what he is. This is the beginning of a stage of acute self-consciousness which manifests itself in writers otherwise poles asunder. Nothing, indeed, surprises the English tourist more than the prevalence of this self-consciousness and the bitterness, for the most part against England, with which it is accompanied. ⟨. . .⟩

In some such way as this, then, the English tourist makes his theory embrace both Mr. Anderson and Mr. Sinclair Lewis. Both suffer as novelists from being American; Mr. Anderson, because he must protest his pride; Mr. Lewis, because he must conceal his bitterness. Mr. Anderson's way is the less injurious to him as an artist, and his imagination is the more vigorous of the two. He has gained more than he has lost by being the spokesman of a new country, the worker in fresh clay. Mr. Lewis it would seem was meant by nature to take his place with Mr. Wells and Mr. Bennett, and had he been born in England would undoubtedly have proved himself the equal of these two famous men. Denied, however, the richness of an old civilisation—the swarm of ideas upon which the art of Mr. Wells has battened, the solidity of custom which has nourished the art of Mr. Bennett—he has been forced to criticise rather than to explore, and the object of his criticism—the civilisation of Zenith—was unfortunately too meagre to sustain him. Yet a

little reflection, and a comparison between Mr. Anderson and Mr. Lewis, put a different colour on our conclusion. Look at Americans as an American, see Mrs. Opal Emerson Mudge as she is herself, not as a type and symbol of America displayed for the amusement of the condescending Britisher, and then, we dimly suspect, Mrs. Mudge is no type, no scarecrow, no abstraction. Mrs. Mudge is—but it is not for an English writer to say what. He can only peep and peer between the chinks of the barrier and hazard the opinion that Mrs. Mudge and the Americans generally are, somehow, human beings into the bargain.

That suspicion suddenly becomes a certainty as we read the first pages of Mr. Ring Lardner's *You Know Me Al*, and the change is bewildering. Hitherto we have been kept at arm's length, reminded constantly of our superiority, of our inferiority, of the fact, anyhow, that we are alien blood and bone. But Mr. Lardner is not merely unaware that we differ; he is unaware that we exist. When a crack player is in the middle of an exciting game of baseball he does not stop to wonder whether the audience likes the colour of his hair. All his mind is on the game. So Mr. Lardner does not waste a moment when he writes in thinking whether he is using American slang or Shakespeare's English; whether he is remembering Fielding or forgetting Fielding; whether he is proud of being American or ashamed of not being Japanese; all his mind is on the story. Hence all our minds are on the story. Hence, incidentally, he writes the best prose that has come our way. Hence we feel at last freely admitted to the society of our fellows.

That this should be true of *You Know Me Al*, a story about baseball, a game which is not played in England, a story written often in a language which is not English, gives us pause. To what does he owe his success? Besides his unconsciousness and the additional power which he is thus free to devote to his art, Mr. Lardner has talents of a remarkable order. With extraordinary ease and aptitude, with the quickest strokes, the surest touch, the sharpest insight, he lets Jack Keefe the baseball player cut out his own outline, fill in his own depths, until the figure of the foolish, boastful, innocent athlete lives before us. As he babbles out his mind on paper there rise up friends, sweethearts, the scenery, town, and country—all surround him and make him up in his completeness. We gaze into the depths of a society which goes its ways intent on its own concerns. There, perhaps, is one of the elements of Mr. Lardner's success. He is not merely himself intent on his own game, but his characters are equally intent on theirs. It is no coincidence that the best of Mr. Lardner's stories are about games, for one may guess that Mr. Lardner's interest in games has solved one of the most difficult problems of the American writer; it has given him a clue, a centre, a meeting place for the divers activities of people whom a vast continent isolates, whom no tradition controls. Games give him what society gives his English brother. Whatever the precise reason, Mr. Lardner at any rate provides something unique in its kind, something indigenous to the soil, which the traveller may carry off as a trophy to prove to the incredulous that he has actually been to America and found it a foreign land. But the time has come when the tourist must reckon up his expenses and experiences, and attempt to cast up his account of the tour as a whole.

⟨. . .⟩ Obviously there are American writers who do not care a straw for English opinion or for English culture, and write very vigorously none the less—witness Mr. Lardner; there are Americans who have all the accomplishments of culture without a trace of its excess—witness Miss Willa Cather; there are Americans whose aim it is to write a book off their own bat and no one else's—witness Miss Fannie Hurst. But the shortest tour, the most superficial inspection, must impress him with what is of far greater importance—the fact that where the land itself is so different, and the society so different, the literature must needs differ, and differ more and more widely as time goes by, from those of other countries.

American literature will be influenced, no doubt, like all others, and the English influence may well predominate. But clearly the English tradition is already unable to cope with this vast land, these prairies, these cornfields, these lonely little groups of men and women scattered at immense distances from each other, these vast industrial cities with their skyscrapers and their night signs and their perfect organisation of machinery. It cannot extract their meaning and interpret their beauty. How could it be otherwise? The English tradition is formed upon a little country; its centre is an old house with many rooms each crammed with objects and crowded with people who know each other intimately, whose manners, thoughts, and speech are ruled all the time, if unconsciously, by the spirit of the past. But in America there is baseball instead of society; instead of the old landscape which has moved men to emotion for endless summers and springs, a new land, its tin cans, its prairies, its cornfields flung disorderly about like a mosaic of incongruous pieces waiting order at the artist's hands; while the people are equally diversified into fragments of many nationalities.

To describe, to unify, to make order out of all these severed parts, a new art is needed and the control of a new tradition. That both are in process of birth the language itself gives us proof. For the Americans are doing what the Elizabethans did—they are coining new words. They are instinctively making the language adapt itself to their needs. In England, save for the impetus given by the war, the word-coining power has lapsed; our writers vary the metres of their poetry, remodel the rhythms of prose, but one may search English fiction in vain for a single new word. It is significant that when we want to freshen our speech we borrow from America—poppycock, rambunctious, flipflop, booster, good-mixer—all the expressive ugly vigorous slang which creeps into use among us first in talk, later in writing, comes from across the Atlantic. Nor does it need much foresight to predict that when words are being made, a literature will be made out of them.

## JOHN BERRYMAN
### "The Case of Ring Lardner"
*The Freedom of the Poet*
1976, pp. 204–16

I t is a disconcerting feature of much American literary art that either it's so closely bound up with the world of popular entertainment that the boundaries between are not easy to fix, or else—as of poetry, say (Ogden Nash allowed as an exception)—it has no relation to that world at all. In France, England, other countries, there is both less reciprocity and more. A man liked Noël Coward seeks his level quicker, after initial hesitation (in a play like *The Vortex*), and though an artist like Cocteau may operate also as an entertainer, no doubt is raised, by him or by anyone else, about his *being* an artist. The arts are less glumly separated from the life of the more or less educated citizenry, and at the same time their status is clearer. Here, matters are more ambiguous. A thing like Norman Corwin's *On a Note of Triumph* is not only praised by Walter Winchell and sells at least fifty thousand copies; it is also hailed, with happy illiteracy, in *The New York Times Book Review* ("Even if he had written this one, five or ten years after V-E Day, its values would be the same. His writing has some of

the quality of universal truth") and woofed up by Carl Sandburg, an actual poet, as "vast . . . terrific . . . certainly one of the great all-time American poems." We might be in Palmer Stadium. Pictures fly around of Corwin, portentous, brooding like Beethoven, and—God's truth—his thoughtless concoction was declared to be "the Eroica of this historic year."

Now these windy views do not fail to occur, though they are less frequent, in London, Paris, and Rome; but they are not taken seriously there, except by the author and his cronies. Here almost everybody takes them seriously, until some fresher fantasy has supervened. Some of our artists take them seriously; Hemingway and Faulkner, two of the most ambitious writers living, describe themselves as hunters and farmers. Moreover, we impose our view on the world; Pearl Buck wins the Nobel Prize. Oscar Hammerstein 12th makes a bulkier literary figure than J. F. Powers. The situation is not new, either. It goes back nearly a century. Cooper, Poe, Hawthorne, Melville were men of letters, and we have had others. But for a long time we have also, in figure after figure, faced this double anomaly of the artist who pretends not to be one and the entertainer who pretends to the status of an artist (or has it pretended for him).

With a man of letters, criticism has only to address itself to the perplexing questions of whether he is any good, and where, and how good, and in what ways. Plainly, if you are obliged to decide, in the first place, whether your subject is an artist at all, criticism will be more difficult. The extreme uncertainty of our criticism of our own literature, which is to be attributed partly to senses of inferiority and dependence, vanity, and remorse therefor, must be due as well to a sneaking down-with-him attitude toward the self-confessed deliberate artist and a sneaking admiration for the guy who entertains us without undemocratic pretensions—this admiration then translating itself naturally into the hope that after all he may prove *also* to be the real literary thing.

I offer these desultory remarks as prelude to some consideration of a borderline character named Ring Lardner. Nobody over thirty-five will have to be told who he was, but I don't find that younger people read him any more, except in short-story courses, where they run into "Haircut" or "Champion," and in any case they will know nothing of his extra-literary personality, which was so engaging to the rest of us during the twenties and early thirties. An extra-literary personality is so important to an entertainer, though unimportant to art, that we might begin with it, assisted by Donald Elder's biography.[1] This is comparatively artless, and too long—Elder's reluctance to cut a letter, no matter how trivial, is positively Byzantine; but it is full, shrewd, and surprisingly candid for a work produced so soon after its subject's death, and under the continuous assistance of his surviving family. I shall be quarrying shamelessly for a bit.

The outline of the life is very much what one expected. Niles, Michigan, 1885, to years of baseball reporting in Chicago, to New York and general celebrity and then literary recognition; a wife and four sons; loads of dough, monumental boozing; fading reputation, broken health, the protracted decline that his friend F. Scott Fitzgerald imaged in the musician Abe North of *Tender Is the Night*; death in 1933 at forty-eight, not old, not young, apparently unfulfilled. An American pattern, in short. Nor will it surprise anyone to learn that this famous clown was a very gloomy guy indeed, suspicious as W. C. Fields, silent as a pharaoh. But the filling in of the outline takes us into what one would not have expected.

Was it in the cards that this man who elected to spend most of his life with athletes and show people and assorted idiots, who presented himself weekly to millions, in dialect, as a "wise boob," should have been the precocious, petted ninth of nine children born into a cultured family of long-established wealth? Each child had its own nursemaid, and the house had its own tennis court and baseball diamond. One foot was deformed from birth, corrected by a surgeon, and he wore a brace until he was eleven; Elder connects with this his irrational admiration for athletes. But he would not have gone to school anyway: his mother, whose rather wild, deeply religious personality appears to have been eight feet high (with his father Lardner was never close at all), taught the three youngest children, until a tutor did. He entered what we *amusingly* call high school at twelve, played football, was graduated at sixteen.

At this point the family fortune collapsed. He spent part of a year at the Armour Institute in Chicago headed toward engineering. Then for four years he did practically nothing, in Niles: amateur theatricals, the gas company. By a fluke, a job on the South Bend *Times*, two years; then he was lifted to Chicago. Here he worked on the *Inter-Ocean, Examiner*, and *Tribune*, accompanied the White Sox, became a sports expert, took over an established column, began to publish in *The Saturday Evening Post*, perfected his mask, made one of his two abortive trips to Europe (a place nonexistent for Lardner, who had no historic sense whatever, no interest in politics or society, no interest in ideas), and succeeded in forming no relation with the enthusiastic remodelling of both verse and prose then supposedly taking place in Chicago—being himself intensely conservative and provincial, as he was to the end, with no visible quarrel of any kind with Niles.

This was one trouble. It let him be courteous, generous, modest, fastidious, romantic, scrupulous, chivalrous, and proud; but it left him worrying, deadpan, restless, suffocated—and bored. He was one of the most heavily armoured men, and one of the most exposed, that even this country can ever have produced. That is, Lardner was wise; he never let anybody get close. So if somebody ripped his heart out, it was not a friend. All the lies told about him were by acquaintances and strangers. On the other hand, among the things he never recovered from were the Black Sox scandal of 1919 and his disappointment later in Jack Dempsey. When he moved East in the fall of 1919, it was not to write about sports but to do a syndicated weekly column about anything, by the "wise boob."

Nearly all of his best writing was still to come; not that it is bulky. But I should say that he went to pieces with great rapidity—at a pace dissolved into Elder's narrative—for already during 1922-4, when he and Fitzgerald were neighbors in Great Neck (they never saw each other much after), it was the younger man's sense that Lardner was "getting off"—doing his work conscientiously but not enjoying it. Fitzgerald badgered him to collect his stories, supplied the title *How to Write Short Stories*, badgered Scribner's to bring them out (with the incongruous aid of Sir James Barrie, this came about); some of his uninteresting earlier books were reissued; and all this probably cheered Lardner more than Elder (who is rather chary about Fitzgerald altogether) is eager to allow. Fitzgerald wanted Lardner to organize himself and undertake a large work; so did Edmund Wilson; these notations belong later in this article, but have to be mentioned because Lardner must have recognized in himself an entire incapacity for anything of the kind, and in his silent way suffered. He was doing a comic strip, an exasperated fake autobiography, all sorts of things. *The Love Nest* came out in 1926. Elder sees him this year at his height, making some $30,000, his column in 157 papers. The

consumption of bourbon is not recorded. He found he had tuberculosis.

Now comes a phase unpredictable or gruesome. He gave most of this up, and attacked Broadway. The ruling passion of Lardner's life was music. He had perfect pitch, and taught himself six instruments. The music that interested him was not what we call classical music or "serious" music, and was not jazz—as Elder says, he was somewhat behind the times; he was interested in *popular* music: popular songs and, for he was also stage-struck, musical shows. It is a peculiarity that all his life he often wrote intimate letters in a sort of parody verse, precisely the kind of thing he appears to mock in "The Maysville Minstrel"; he was strongly interested in what he thought of as poetry, though it goes without saying that he disliked all real poetry. Music, drama, and poetry came together for him, and for years he contributed lyrics to Ziegfeld's shows. He did *Elmer the Great* for George M. Cohan in 1928, and Cohan redid it. There were various unproduced scripts, and the "nonsense" playlets that I'll say something about later. At last in 1929, with George S. Kaufman, he had a hit in *June Moon*. He wrote a film script for $7,500 in four days. He only published some dozen songs, however, and in general all this aspect of his career was a failure. He was in and out of hospitals all the final years—Florida, Arizona, California, New York— not only with dipsomania but recurrent attacks of tuberculosis, a heart ailment, digestive disorders, probably pernicious anaemia. *Round Up*, collecting thirty-five stories, came out in 1929. There is no interesting fiction after 1926, but his humourous stuff remained sometimes astonishing, as "Large Coffee" (you can find this one in the Whites' *Subtreasury of American Humor*) and the parodies of "Night and Day" which I remember in *The New Yorker* and am glad to see that Elder quotes:

Night and day under the fleece of me
There's an Oh, such a flaming furneth burneth the
    grease of me.
Night and day under the bark of me
There's an Oh, such a mob of microbes making a
    park of me.

Anybody who can still hear the daffy croon of Tony Wons reciting will be glad to know the cheer that Lardner made up for him:

Tony Wons! Tony Twice!
Holy, jumping . . .

These last things appeared in the midst of an intensely bitter and earnest crusade that Lardner carried on against the stupidity and especially the pornography of the lyrics of popular songs; he was so pathologically squeamish—as he was throughout his life about dirty stories (though it's true that he hated funny stories of any kind, and never told them) and indeed about anything sexual—that he even had doubts about "Tea for Two." He was extremely pedantic, in this as in other things, and was only less stern against ill grammar than against innuendo. His final work was about a drunkard, sympathetically portrayed, in the toils of family constriction. It is not likely that it would have been any good; he always lost all his irony when he wrote for the stage, and his energy anyway by now was so low that it had taken him six months to write a twenty-page story.

It is impossible to read the account of Lardner's life without admiration for his courage and dignity, and sympathy for his misery. The question is whether in it—never mind his work yet—one can perceive the sense of *purposefulness* that is obvious and strong in the lives of, say, Dreiser and Fitzgerald (drunkards, too, and popular and acquaintances of Lardner), or the drive toward *expression* visible in them.

Purposefulness, I think, is just what one does not see; except for the desire to escape (from familial protection and suffocation, intolerable frustration, boredom), which took the forms of alcohol and silence. He was a boozer from way back; began as a kid and improved. Some of the legends seem to be true, such as that of his sixty-hour vigil in one chair at the Friars Club. Apparently, seldom quarrelsome, seldom tiresome, he held liquor very well. That was unfortunate; and it must be remembered medically that he was drinking during the most devoted years Prohibition liquor. He went on the wagon again and again, like the man who found it so easy to stop smoking that he had done it fifty times; he telephoned friends and explained what a heel he was; he tried a psychiatrist. But on the whole he was very deliberate and unashamed, and so stubborn while drinking that he once, taken to hospital, refused to have an injury treated there but repaired to a club before he let a doctor come. Monumental remorse, often referred to, darkens the last years—for talent drunk up. Self-punishment, self-loathing. It is grievous to read that during the final months, at home, in East Hampton, "Sometimes he was observed alone, with his face in his hands, sobbing." And he had no recourse whatever: no satisfaction in his achievement; no discernible belief or even religious sense, an overmastering hatred of humanity in general, and all its works; no freedom. "He awoke a certain feeling," Sherwood Anderson wrote of him as he was at his most successful and happiest. "You wanted him not to be hurt, perhaps to have some freedom he did not have."

I said no freedom, but actually he had the freedom (and pride and grief) of silence: a profound reticence, a refusal to be known or speak out. Thomas Hardy's poem "He Resolves to Say No More," written at the very end of his long, expressive life, gives wonderful voice to this genuine impulse of artists. But as a lifelong characteristic, which is what it was in Lardner, nothing could promise less for the production of interesting work. He suffered from a lifelong drive toward *in*expression. It is under this reservation that we have to look at what he got done.

There are varying accounts of Lardner's characters, the world they inhabit, what he thinks of them, and so on; Constance Rourke has several good pages on his method; critics have argued at length about whether his work is by really a humourist or a realist or a satirist or whatever. But let us be inductive, and examine the kind of story in which his characters occur. He is certainly best known now for his stories—the eleven given by Gilbert Seldes in *The Portable Ring Lardner* and a few others; so that we are bound to try to decide whether or not we agree with E. B. White that he was "not essentially a writer of fiction." I take "The Love Nest" more or less at random, as one of his most familiar, one written during the half dozen years (1921–6) when he was most effective in story writing, and one he liked enough himself to make the title story of a collection.

"The Love Nest" goes like this. A writer named Bartlett is doing a piece on Lou Gregg, president of Modern Pictures, and the great man takes him in a Rolls out to his mansion for overnight, "to see us just as we are": his wife, Celia, a former actress, and their three little girls. Gregg offers Bartlett a drink and is surprised when the butler tells him a barely opened bottle of bourbon is only half full; it's happened before; he blames the servants (but the reader doesn't). Celia entrances. Much "sweetheart"-ing between the loving couple, Celia refuses a drink ("Lou objects to me drinking whisky, and I don't like it much anyway"), Gregg remembers that he has to go out for the evening, two of the girls are brought down and

exhibited, Gregg takes them upstairs. Celia is to show Bartlett around what she calls "our love nest," but asks if he minds her having a drink instead, and has two. After dinner Gregg leaves. She has various drinks, wants to dance, explains that she is drunk half the time, married Gregg only out of ambition, would now "change places with the scum of the earth just to be free instead of a chattel, a *thing*." She goes to bed, Gregg returns, and the men retire. In the morning Celia sleeps late but calls downstairs, "Goodbye, sweetheart!"

What can we say about this story except that it is undeveloped and manages to be both trite and implausible? About Bartlett we learn nothing except that he is single and does not dance, and the mystery is why we learn even these things; as a writer he is not convincing—a man after a story would not so readily give up being shown around the place; he has no tone, never comments. Gregg is even more primitively presented and less convincing—he is boastful, and that is all; according to Celia he is cruel, but we are given no evidence of it. Celia is managed worst of all: she has got through half a bottle either the night before or today and yet shows no sign of it; and yet two drinks and perhaps a sneaked one or two and a cocktail make her absent-minded and red-faced at dinner (almost the only physical image in the story, put as follows: "Her face was red"). Her husband does not know she drinks, or he does (in fact he would). But he doesn't, or he wouldn't ask in front of Bartlett about the bottle (compare "no matter what he had on me, he'd never let the world know it"). But he must, from the dinner exhibition and "She's had a lot of headaches lately"—or his stupidity ought to be more impressively conveyed. The author desires to have his cake and eat it, too; he simply doesn't care about an impression of life. Lardner's friends and Elder make much of his conscientiousness. That must be as a journalist, chiefly, for what this story displays is gross carelessness, indifference.

Now for the medium. The story is written in dialogue, which has either no tone at all or is too strident to be convincing or has this tone: "I mean nobody would ever thought Celia Sayles would turn out to be a sit-by-the-fire. I mean she still likes a good time, but her home and kiddies come first. I mean her home and kiddies come first." Two paragraphs are exceptions to this law. One tells us about the red face. Here is the other:

> While the drinks were being prepared, he observed his hostess more closely and thought how much more charming she would be if she had used finesse in improving on nature. Her cheeks, her mouth, her eyes, and lashes had been, he guessed, far above the average in beauty before she had begun experimenting with them. And her experiments had been clumsy. She was handsome in spite of her efforts to be handsomer.

As I say, this is the only *writing*, so to speak, in the story, and it must be clear that the paragraph is equally feeble and pretentious, the sort of thing you'd strike out of an apprentice's story, besides having nothing characteristic about it and nothing resembling it elsewhere in the story. It is just a little Jamesian attempt (compare "My dear, you're looking very well for him—within the marked limits of your range") that failed.

Why was this story written, apart from a check from *Cosmopolitan*? It cannot have sprung from a wish to create, or even to report, life. For instance, if Celia is as afraid of her husband as she says she is, she would never dare confide in Bartlett, especially Bartlett, a writer; or, unprincipled, with a life with her husband obviously so unsatisfactory, she would head for Bartlett—the nervous taking up, only to put it aside, of her sex life (men's pawing her) is about as close as Lardner ever came—not close enough—to this subject. The story is a fake, pretending to deliver more both in narrative and in character than it can deliver, except insofar as it produces a journalistic effect of *exposure*. You think big producers have happy marriages?—Don't give me that. Lardner's stories convey a perpetual effect of going behind an appearance—perpetual, and cheap, because the appearance is not one that could have taken in an experienced man for five minutes: the revelation is to boobs. How shall we describe then the strength of the emotional impulse behind the story? I should say that it had roughly the force of what we used to call in the third form a gripe.

To compare such a writer to Swift (as people have done, and I will come back to this), even to take him seriously, may seem ridiculous. But we are dealing with a very considerable reputation, established now in the literary histories; and "The Love Nest" has nothing funny about it—we are thinking of him now just as a story writer; and, though perfectly characteristic, it is not one of his five best stories. It has the advantage for us, however, that it is not a baseball story. The notion of Lardner's having any permanent interest as a baseball writer has got to be abandoned. Fitzgerald wrote: "During those years, when most men of promise achieve an adult education, if only in the school of war, Ring moved in the company of a few dozen illiterates playing a boy's game. A boy's game, with no more possibilities in it than a boy could master, a game bounded by walls which kept out novelty or danger, change or adventure . . . A writer can spin on about his adventures after thirty, after forty, after fifty, but the criteria by which these adventures are weighed and valued are irrevocably settled at the age of twenty-five. However deeply Ring might cut into it, his cake had the diameter of Frank Chance's diamond." Surely there is something wrong with this view.

In the first place, I do not believe it philosophically, any more than I believe Yeats's pronouncement is true, that "A man's mind at twenty-one contains all the truths that he will ever find." Neither allows for the self-transformations that many men active emotionally and intellectually achieve during their thirties. In the second place, Fitzgerald's view is nonsense both in the light of the facts and of what Lardner did. Yogi Berra is a boy? Lardner wrote about big leaguers largely: not boys, men, in danger every second of demotion to the minors, or focuses of national attention. They *were* nowhere, and they *will be* nowhere. Here they are, in continuous crisis, dramatized in the key plays Lardner describes so well. Now take a man who had always a dim view of life, and trusted nothing: this precariousness makes a good subject. It is the subject in fact of his only really fine baseball story, "Harmony," one of his few affecting and well-constructed stories, the kind of dramatic depthwork he only two or three times attempted. His two best stories are not about baseball: "The Golden Honeymoon," a beautifully modulated thing about the persistence of rivalry and pettiness into an area where everything ought to be solved, and "Haircut," which deserves its fame, as the simpleminded and incredible "Champion" does not. His two other good stories, "Some Like Them Cold" and "I Can't Breathe," are not about baseball, either.

Much of the semi-novel *The Big Town* is still readable, though unimportant; and the ends of certain stories—"Anniversary," "Ex Parte," "Now and Then"—are good, corroborating Lardner's not altogether joking account of his method of composition ("I write three thousand words about nothing; that is a terrible struggle. Then I come to, and say to myself, 'I must get a punch in this.' I stop and figure out the punch, and then sail through to the finish"). But the five stories

are really what matter. It will be noticed that four of them are first-person, and the fifth a series of letters, and I think we must agree that White is right: Lardner was only in appearance a fiction writer. His gift was for mimicry, burlesque, parody. He had no invention, little imagination, a very limited sense of style, and almost no sense of structure. His best work is accidents of talent. He was a humourist of course; but only two of the five stories are at all funny, and he is not likely to keep on being known as a humourist. Humourists—except one very special kind I want to say something about in a moment—do not interest posterity as humourists unless they have also all sorts of more important gifts as well, such as Mark Twain had. Humour dies fast. Lardner was a realist, too, and interesting to his contemporaries as that, but this value has vanished already; after just thirty-odd years it is hard to imagine the initial effectiveness of *You Know Me Al*. As a satirist he is unimportant. There was not enough power of mind, and no imagination of a *different* past or future condition for the object satirized. A comparison with Swift makes one's critical sense reel.

But two things remain to be said. He *was* as bitter as Swift. There is no doubt about it. But so are countless denizens of Skid Row, and what does it matter to anyone except a social worker, a relative, a friend? Lardner had some power of expression, and it matters. He was fitted by disposition—God knows why—for investigations of Hell, like Andreyev's; and he couldn't make it. Besides the desire for silence, one must certainly suspect here also a failure of courage, selflessness, ambition. That's one thing.

The other is that he had a special gift for what looks like nonsense. You see this most clearly in his little plays, of which my own favorite has always been *Clemo Uti—"The Water Lilies."* Its cast is:

> Padre, a Priest.
> Sethso ⎱
> Gethso ⎰ both twins.
> Wayshatten, a shepherd's boy.
> Two Capitalists. (Note: The two Capitalists don't appear in this show.)
> Wama Tammisch, her daughter.
> Klema, a janitor's third daughter.
> Kevela, their mother, afterwards their aunt.

Scene for Act I: The Outskirts of a Parchesi Board. People are wondering what has become of the discs. They quit wondering and sit up and sing the following song:

> *What has become of the discs?*
> *What has become of the discs?*
> *We took them at our own risks,*
> *But what has become of the discs?*

Wama enters from an exclusive waffle parlor. She exits as if she had had waffles.

Acts II and III are thrown out "because nothing seemed to happen."

IV takes place in a silo. Two rats have got in there by mistake. One of them seems diseased. The other looks at him. They go out. Both Rats come in again and wait for a laugh. They don't get it, and go out. Wama enters from an off-stage barn. She is made up to represent the Homecoming of Cassanova. She has a fainting spell. She goes out.

*Kevela:* Where was you born?
*Padre:* In Adrian, Michigan.
*Kevela:* Yes, but I thought I was confessing to you.

Act V winds up: Two queels enter, overcome with water lilies. They both make fools of themselves. They don't seem to have any self-control. They quiver. They want to play the show over again, but it looks useless. SHADES.

Now there is genius here—"genius limited and yearning," as B. H. Haggin once said of Gershwin, but genius—which ought to have taken Lardner into even better and firmer and more confident studies of irrelation, which might have brought him into the small, fascinating company of the great fantasists Lear and Carroll, who were, in fact, he once confessed, his favorite humourists. Elder canvasses various critics' views of these playlets and plumps for Gilbert Seldes's that they are an "attack of sheer lunacy" and "had no purpose at all." But surely what they are about is the failure of communication in the modern world, and especially in the modern American world, which is all Lardner cared about. They remind one of Peter Fleming's remark that in Europe conversation is like tennis—you hit the ball to the other man and he hits it back—whereas in America everybody goes on hitting his own ball. They are the work of a man who found it only too easy to communicate at a superficial level and who refused to communicate at any deeper level. Besides irrelation, you need relation. The trouble is that to mock the intellect successfully you have to be right in there yourself. But Lardner's scorn and hatred for everything "highbrow" is one of his chief marks. Unfortunately, everything good in the end is highbrow. All the artists who have ever survived were intellectuals—sometimes intellectuals *also*, but intellectuals. The popular boys cannot understand this. When Shakespeare mocked Chapman and Raleigh and their school of intellectual art, he did it with a higher brow than theirs. Hemingway studied Turgenev and everyone else he thought useful. Lardner never studied anybody. One of the weirdest sentences in Elder's book is about "Dryden, who probably had a greater influence on his earlier career than any other writer." Of course, this is *Charlie* Dryden, a sportswriter.

The differences between entertainment and art have less to do with the audience and the writer's immediate intention than with his whole fundamental attitude toward doing what he does at all. Inverting the common notion, art for the artist we might oddly regard as a means, entertainment for the entertainer an end. Elder, who quotes approvingly from a piece by T. S. Matthews called "Lardner, Shakespeare and Chekhov," seems to have no idea of this, and I doubt if Lardner had: the notion of art is "a self-discipline rather than a self-expression," as Auden has put it. Of this crucial sense there is no trace, I believe, in Lardner's work. He was not interested, he found it hard enough to hang on, he wanted just to be let alone, and he got what he wanted. The few fine stories come like reluctant fugitives from a room almost perfectly soundproofed. His art did nothing *for* Lardner.

*Notes*

1. *Ring Lardner: A Biography* (Garden City, New York: Doubleday and Company, 1956).

## JONATHAN YARDLEY
### From *Ring: A Biography of Ring Lardner*
### 1977, pp. 4–5, 211–18, 389–93

#### *Frank Chance's Diamond*

For more than five years—from March, 1908, to June, 1913—Ring Lardner reported the daily events of major-league professional baseball. For many more years than that, baseball was at or very near the core of his existence. As a boy in Niles, Michigan, he played the game with his friends,

cheered the local heroes in their contests against neighboring towns, and counted down the days to the baseball excursions he would make once or twice a year with his father and his brother, Rex, to Chicago, ninety miles to the west. As a beginning reporter in South Bend, Indiana, he heightened his understanding of the game by covering the Central League, a minor league in which many outstanding players of the day refined their skills to major-league levels. Though he stopped covering baseball regularly in the summer of 1913, it was one of the subjects most frequently discussed in the daily column he wrote for the Chicago *Tribune* until 1919, and he covered almost every World Series until the mid-twenties. His first fiction, published in 1914, had a baseball setting, and he became a national celebrity because of the baseball stories collected under the title *You Know Me Al*. Eventually he wearied of the stupidity of so many of the game's fans, and after the integrity of the game was conclusively undermined by the Black Sox scandal of 1919 he turned, in disgust and sorrow, to other subjects. Yet he never lost his love for baseball as he had once known it, and in the last years of his life he remembered it with deep nostalgic longing.

He was, however, much more than a successful baseball "scribe." He was one of the most respected writers of the twenties, widely discussed and widely imitated. His short stories were read by millions, honored and anthologized, scrutinized and praised by critics. For a time, at least, his name was invariably listed alongside those of the other certifiably "important" writers of the period: Scott Fitzgerald, Ernest Hemingway, John Dos Passos, Thomas Wolfe, Sherwood Anderson. But it was always listed with reservations—with, in baseball's statistical language, an asterisk. And the asterisk was baseball itself. Fitzgerald, who was his devoted friend, summarized the problem in a tribute written shortly after Ring's death in September, 1933:

> The point of these paragraphs is that whatever Ring's achievement was it fell short of the achievement he was capable of, and this because of a cynical attitude toward his work. How far back did that attitude go—back to his youth in a Michigan village? Certainly back to his days with the Cubs. During those years, when most men of promise achieve an adult education, if only in the school of war, Ring moved in the company of a few dozen illiterates playing a boy's game. A boy's game, with no more possibilities in it than a boy could master, a game bounded by walls which kept out novelty or danger, change or adventure. This material, the observation of it under such circumstances, was the text of Ring's schooling during the most formative period of the mind. A writer can spin on about his adventures after thirty, after forty, after fifty, but the criteria by which these adventures are weighed and valued are irrevocably settled at the age of twenty-five. However deeply Ring might cut into it, his cake had the diameter of Frank Chance's diamond.

Fitzgerald's words were both kind and unkind, accurate and inaccurate, selfless and self-serving. He insisted on judging Ring by the standards he had set for himself, and as a consequence he was blind to Ring's ultimate accomplishments. ⟨. . .⟩

#### *In the Wake of the News*

The 1919 World Series should have been just another assignment for Ring—a nuisance, if anything, since the responsibility of covering it delayed preparations for his move East, and into the bargain it had been stretched from best of seven games to nine to accommodate wide public interest in the contest between the good-pitch, no-hit Reds and the good-everything White Sox. Ring did, on the other hand, have a couple of personal reasons for following the Series. One was that his old friend Kid Gleason, after years as a coach, finally had become a manager and, with the powerful White Sox team, had a chance to win a World Series.

⟨. . .⟩ The fix was in. Seven White Sox ballplayers—Shoeless Joe Jackson, Lefty Williams, Happy Felsch, Chick Gandil, Swede Risberg, Fred McMullin and Eddie Cicotte—had agreed to throw the Series in exchange for $100,000 to be paid by a syndicate headed by the New York gambler Arnold Rothstein; an eighth player, Buck Weaver, took no money but knew of the plot and did not report it. To prove that the fix was in, a signal had been agreed upon: Cicotte was to hit the first Cincinnati batter. He hit Morris Rath squarely in the back.

One wonders what Ring thought as he saw Rath lope to first. He knew that Cicotte had superb control; in pitching a league-leading 307 innings during the regular season, and in winning a league-leading twenty-nine games, he had walked only forty-nine men—yet here he had not merely walked but actually *hit* the first batter in the World Series. But Ring also knew that there had been strange talk in the Cincinnati air, that the odds had fluctuated wildly before the opening game, that big money was pouring in.

The final score was Cincinnati 9, Chicago 1. Cicotte lasted only three and two-thirds innings and gave up six runs. Knowledgeable baseball men, from Charlie Comiskey and Kid Gleason on down, knew that something was wrong. So did Ring. According to Donald Elder, Ring later told Arthur Jacks that he had confronted Cicotte in his hotel room after the game and asked him: "What was wrong? I was betting on you today." Cicotte—did he, in this moment, at last and with shattering impact realize what he had done?—gave Ring a lie and skirted the issue. But by now Ring knew for sure. The next day the White Sox lost, 4 to 2, with Lefty Williams giving the Reds the runs they needed; Williams, who had a 23–11 regular season record with a 2.64 earned-run average, would outdo himself as a tyro crook, losing all three of his Series starts with a 6.61 E.R.A.

What happened that night is the subject of as many different versions as there are accounts of the 1919 Series. In the circumstances, it seems wisest to accept the story as Ring told it. He was at a roadhouse in Bellevue, Kentucky, near Cincinnati, with three fellow journalists, Tiny Maxwell, Nick Flatley and his old friend from the Chicago *Tribune*, James Crusinberry. Together they wrote a new lyric for "I'm Forever Blowing Bubbles":

> I'm forever blowing ball games,
> Pretty ball games in the air.
> I come from Chi.,
> I hardly try,
> Just go to bat and fade and die.
> Fortune's coming my way,
> That's why I don't care.
> I'm forever blowing ball games,
> For the gamblers treat me fair.

The Reds won the Series—or, to be more accurate if unkind to the Reds, the White Sox lost it—in eight games. Cicotte lost two games, but, in what may have been a belated gesture of honor and defiance, beat the Reds once, 4 to 1. It is a measure of Joe Jackson's greatness that, not trying, he still batted .375 for the Series; this innocent, ignorant boy—this Jack Keefe—was the true tragic figure, his great talent ruined by the flaw of greed.

It would be nearly a year before what most baseball people already knew was confirmed as fact. According to Eliot Asinof's *Eight Men Out*, Ring and Jimmy Crusinberry were talking in a New York hotel room in July, 1920, when Kid Gleason called to tell them that Abe Attell, one of the fixers, was spilling the beans at Dinty Moore's restaurant and speakeasy. After they had heard Attell out, Crusinberry filed a story that Harvey Woodruff declined to print for reasons of potential libel. But the scandal was bound to emerge in full and on September 28, 1920, the eight Black Sox were indicted on charges of fixing the 1919 World Series—one week before the first game of the 1920 World Series. Eventually the indictments were dismissed on procedural grounds, but all eight players were barred from professional baseball for life. ⟨. . .⟩

Baseball ⟨. . .⟩ lost the best and most influential writer it ever had. To be sure, Ring covered every World Series save two until 1927, he continued to bet on games and he kept up his friendships in the baseball press. But there are more meaningful ways to measure the depth of his disenchantment. He never again wrote a Jack Keefe story. He wrote no baseball fiction of any sort until 1925, by which time he was writing almost entirely for money and was willing to do just about whatever the market wanted. Even when he did cover baseball games, he left no doubt in the stories he wrote that he was doing so purely out of duty; much of the material he wrote had nothing to do with the games he saw. As he wrote four months before his death: "My interest in the national pastime died a sudden death in the fall of 1919, when Kid Gleason saw his power-house White Sox lose a world's series to a club that was surprised to win even one game."

The degree to which the Black Sox Series affected Ring's outlook on larger questions is the subject of sharply divergent opinions. Some critics have argued that this corruption of a game he loved by the forces of rank materialism made Ring a bitter misanthrope. Others, finding less evidence of venom in his writing and personality, contend that the 1919 Series was merely the last step in a process of disillusionment that had begun years ago, that Ring was relatively unaffected and unsurprised by what happened.

The elusive truth may lean toward the latter view, but not much. It is clear, as by now has been made plain, that early in his "Wake" years Ring moved away from baseball as a central preoccupation both professionally and emotionally. By the fall of 1919 he was indisputably the foremost figure in the "aw nuts" school of sports writing, and his short stories had much to do with the gradual reduction of ballplayers from demigods to human beings in the eyes of their public. He was mature and worldly wise enough not to be sent into a psychological spin by a selfish misdeed perpetrated by a handful of men making a living playing a game.

But to say that Ring was unhurt by Eddie Cicotte's betrayal—for surely that is how he saw it—is to deny the most basic human feelings of friendship and trust. To say that the scandal was not a profoundly disillusioning act is to ignore the intimate association in Ring's mind of baseball and his youth. It is also to deny that he saw baseball as a small universe with its own inviolable order, an order which would endure no matter how venal or petty some of those who lived under it.

⟨. . .⟩ Among that evidence is a famous passage in Scott Fitzgerald's novel *The Great Gatsby*. The raw material for that novel was acquired by Fitzgerald from the fall of 1922 to the spring of 1924, when he was renting a house in Great Neck and seeing Ring frequently. They talked sports, probably many times, for Ring was an authority and Scott, in that enthusiastic way of his, a fan. They also talked under the influence of liquor much of the time, and liquor brought Ring out; as he had said to ⟨his wife⟩ Ellis a decade earlier, there were some things he just couldn't discuss when he was on the water wagon. That at some point or another they talked about the 1919 World Series and Ring's feelings about it seems not only probable but certain. That their conversation inspired Scott to use that Series as yet another symbol of corruption in a novel filled with such symbols certainly is within the realm of possibility:

> Roaring noon. In a well-fanned Forty-second Street cellar I met Gatsby for lunch. Blinking away the brightness of the street outside, my eyes picked him out obscurely in the anteroom, talking to another man.
>
> "Mr. Carraway, this is my friend Mr. Wolfsheim."
>
> A small, flat-nosed Jew raised his large head and regarded me with two fine growths of hair which luxuriated in either nostril. After a moment I discovered his tiny eyes in the half-darkness. . . .
>
> As he shook hands and turned away his tragic nose was trembling. I wondered if I had said anything to offend him.
>
> "He becomes very sentimental sometimes," explained Gatsby. "This is one of his sentimental days. He's quite a character around New York—a denizen of Broadway."
>
> "Who is he, anyhow, an actor?"
>
> "No."
>
> "A dentist?"
>
> "Meyer Wolfsheim? No, he's a gambler." Gatsby hesitated, then added coolly: "He's the man who fixed the World Series back in 1919."
>
> The idea staggered me. I remembered, of course, that the World Series had been fixed in 1919, but if I had thought of it at all I would have thought of it as a thing that merely *happened*, the end of some inevitable chain. It never occurred to me that one man could start to play with the faith of fifty million people—with the single-mindedness of a burglar blowing a safe.
>
> "How did he happen to do that?" I asked after a minute.
>
> "He just saw the opportunity."
>
> "Why isn't he in jail?"
>
> "They can't get him, old sport. He's a smart man."

### Epilogue

⟨. . .⟩ Ring's current critical reputation ⟨. . .⟩ is far less a matter of rejection than of inattention. Considering how widely admired he was during his lifetime and how greatly he influenced other, more definably "literary" writers, it is astonishing how little serious critical study his work has received—and how little of *that* has been of any particular quality. There are only eight titles listed as "Principal Works about Ring W. Lardner" in the Bruccoli-Layman bibliography, and three of those are unpublished dissertations; three of the rest are works of criticism, the best being Walton R. Patrick's undoctrinaire *Ring Lardner*, a volume in the Twayne series of critical studies. Of miscellaneous pieces of criticism and commentary, aside from the Virginia Woolf analysis published in 1925, there is not much beyond a first-rate review in the *New Statesman* by V. S. Pritchett of a 1959 British collection of Ring's stories, and a 1972 article in the *Journal of Popular Culture* by Leverett T. Smith, Jr., called "'The Diameter of Frank Chance's Diamond': Ring Lardner and Professional Sports."

The very title of that second article suggests one reason why Ring's work has yet to receive the searching critical examination that it deserves: much of it is directly or tangentially about sport, and even though sport has caught the fancy of some intellectuals for its metaphoric possibilities, it continues to remain somehow disreputable as a subject of serious scrutiny. Even that, however, does not get to the heart of the puzzlement and occasional disdain with which Ring is generally viewed in scholarly circles. The real explanation lies in three interrelated considerations: Ring was basically a journalist, he declined to take his work with undue seriousness, and he refused to do what literary people thought he should do.

Ring knew that "serious" people held journalism and popular fiction in contempt, and—quite apart from a natural tendency to shrug his shoulders and say, "What of it?"—his awareness of this almost certainly was one reason why he offered his work to readers in such a self-deprecatory way. Particularly after he moved over to Scribner's and into the limelight of critical attention, he developed a defensiveness about his work that helps explain the prefaces so vexing to Edmund Wilson and other reviewers. The prefaces were basically self-mocking in intent, but they also gave Ring a form of protection against critical rejection; he could always let them stand as proof enough that he, too, didn't take his work seriously. He was scarcely as ignorant as Hemingway represented him to be—as if Hemingway were any intellectual—but he did have the understandable reticence of a person of limited formal education whose work was being presented to readers who were, in his eyes, his intellectual superiors.

In point of fact he knew full well that what he had written was honorable and in its own way serious. This workmanlike attitude and indifference to high artistic accomplishment infuriated many of his admirers, none more than Scott Fitzgerald. In his obituary piece he said that "Ring's achievement . . . fell short of the achievement he was capable of, and this because of a cynical attitude toward his work." A year after Ring's death he was far harsher. In November, 1934, Max Perkins wrote him that "you are profligate with your material as Ring told you." Scott replied with an explosion of anger and self-justification:

> . . . [Ring] never knew anything about composition, except as it concerned the shorter forms; that is why he always needed advice from us as to how to organize his material; it was his greatest fault the fault of many men brought up in the school of journalism—while a novelist with his sempiternal sigh can cut a few breaths. It is a hell of a lot more difficult to build up a long groan than to develop a couple of short coughs!

It was a brutal assessment and, though not without its element of truth, an unfair one. Ring got an enormous amount of work done in his lifetime, enough of it of such quality that eventually he will be duly recognized. Basically he knew that. Basically he respected the work he had done.

Yet two things nagged at him, compounded the guilt and self-doubt into which he, too, often lapsed late in his life. One was that he had worked as hard as he could to fulfill his potential, and when he saw what he had created he felt cheated: his talent was too limited and so was what it produced. If he thought of himself in terms of the athletes whose accomplishments he measured, perhaps he saw himself as a Morris Rath or a Nap Rucker rather than a Ty Cobb or a Christy Mathewson—good enough, to be sure, and worthy of high respect, but when stretched to the limit, still not great.

The other was that although he did not want to write a novel and did not think it necessary to do so in order to prove himself, there nonetheless nagged in his mind the sense that he had shirked the ultimate challenge of the field into which he had somewhat accidentally fallen. Americans equate bigness with greatness, and all around him people were saying that he had to do something big if he wanted to be great. In truth, he probably did not care all that much about being great, but neither did he want to disappoint. He was a miniaturist to whom the world seemed to be shouting "Inflate! Inflate!" and he could not handle it.

Which is a great pity, because what he did do should command our respect and gratitude. To begin with, he told us how to write the way we talk. V. S. Pritchett has pointed out that the "specifically American contribution to literature" is "talk" and that it began with Ring: "Now," he wrote in his 1959 review, "mainly under the double influence of Joyce and Lardner's American successors—the stream of consciousness being married to the stream of garrulity—we begin to have a talking prose and are likely to have more." If Ring's ear was so keen that it permitted him to be facile, to avoid the struggles most writers must face, it was also the chief instrument of a revolution in American fiction.

Ring made people laugh, and he still does. Jack Keefe, that true American original, is a great comic character; so is the "wise boob," whether he takes the name of Joe Gullible or Tom Finch or Fred Gross—or Ring Lardner. The nonsense plays have lost none of their wild humor and never will, for they are timeless. Ring's humor is as American as his language: wisecracking, sardonic, earthy, self-mocking. He helped teach us not only to laugh at ourselves but to laugh at that which is unique in us, to delight in our very American-ness.

In doing that, he helped us to see ourselves. He was a writer of manners, and the manners he described were those of a society markedly different from that in the novels of Edith Wharton and Henry James. He wrote about the manners of the bleachers and the clubhouse, the mezzanine and the dressing room, the barbershop and the beauty parlor, the Pullman car and the touring car, the kitchen and the diner, the bridge table and the bowling alley. He watched us get rich, and he showed us how foolish we often looked as we threw our new money after idle and inane pleasures and possessions; if he had been truly bitter or misanthropic or hateful, he never would have succeeded in making us laugh at ourselves so heartily.

He wrote so perceptively and accurately about what he saw because he was a great journalist. This, in the end, is the singular accomplishment of his life. Ring came into the profession when it was held in far too much disdain even to be considered a "profession"; it was a line of work pursued by coarse people who had a coarse talent for putting words together in a speedy way. He was one of the very first people to bring creativity and felicity of style to the press. He set an example that was eagerly followed by younger writers. His aristocratic manner and confident bearing gave the lie to the argument that journalists were by their very nature guttersnipes. The quality of his writing and the doggedness with which he kept it so high proved that good prose and journalism were not mutually exclusive. So, too, he showed that in newspapers one could do serious work and be respected for it.

In assessing him, moreover, the work of his life must not be stressed at the expense of his life itself. Marc Connelly, in a letter to Ellis, got somewhere close to the point when he wrote ". . . behind all his fun, his bitter satire, his criticism and his pity, was a great dignity, the dignity of humanity. Everything Ring started to write had somewhere behind it a point of view essentially noble. His humor was the humor of protest, a demand, by implication, that mankind be something more than the idiocy he was exposing." He had a great heart, as Max Perkins knew:

> . . . Ring was not, strictly speaking, a great writer. The truth is he never regarded himself seriously as a writer. He always thought of himself as a newspaperman, anyhow. He had a sort of provincial scorn of literary people. If he had written much more, he would have been a great writer perhaps, but whatever it was that prevented him from writing more was the thing that prevented him from being a great writer. But he was a great man, and one of immense latent talent which got itself partly expressed. I guess Scott would think much the same way about it.

Scott did:

> . . . At no time did I feel that I had known him enough, or that anyone knew him—it was not the feeling that there was more stuff in him and that it should come out, it was rather a qualitative difference, it was rather as though, due to some inadequacy in one's self, one had not penetrated to something unsolved, new and unsaid. That is why one wishes that Ring had written down a larger proportion of what was in his mind and heart. It would have saved him longer for us, and that in itself would be something. But I would like to know what it was, and now I will go on wishing—what did Ring want, how did he want things to be, how did he think things were?
>
> A great and good American is dead. Let us not obscure him by the flowers, but walk up and look at that fine medallion, all torn by sorrows that perhaps we are not equipped to understand. Ring made no enemies, because he was kind, and to millions he gave release and delight.

# IRVING LAYTON

## 1912–

Irving Lazarovitch (he later legally changed his name to Layton) was born on March 12, 1912, in Neamtz, Rumania. His family emigrated to Canada in 1913. He was educated at Macdonald College, where he earned a B.Sc. degree in agriculture in 1939, and at McGill, where he received an M.A. in economics and political science in 1946. He served in the Canadian Army during the war; in 1946 he married Frances Sutherland, the first of four wives. After the war Layton taught high school in Montreal and also lectured at the city's Jewish Public Library. In 1949 he took his first college lectureship at George William University in Montreal. Today he teaches at the George William campus of what is now Concordia University, having previously spent eight years in Toronto at York University.

During his early years in Montreal Layton helped publish the poetry magazine *First Statement*. His first collection of poetry appeared in 1945 under the title *Here and Now*. He has published more than thirty volumes since, and is known as one of Canada's leading contemporary poets.

So what I've written—besides my joy in being alive to write about them—has been about this singular business of human evil; the tension between Hebrew and pagan, between the ideal and real. The disorder and glory of passion. The modern tragedy of the depersonalization of men and women. About a hideously commercial civilization spawning hideously deformed monstrosities. Modern women I see cast in the role of furies striving to castrate the male; their efforts aided by all the malignant forces of a technological civilization that has rendered the male's creative role of revelation superfluous—if not an industrial hazard and a nuisance. We're being feminized and proletarianized at one and the same time. This is the inglorious age of the mass-woman. Her tastes are dominant everywhere—in theatres, stores, art, fiction, houses, furniture—and these tastes are dainty and trivial. Dionysus is dead: his corpse seethes white-maggotty with social workers and analysts. Not who is winning the Cold War is the big issue confronting mankind, but this: Will the Poet, as a type, join the Priest, the Warrior, the Hero, and the Saint as melancholy museum pieces for the titillation of a universal babbitry? It could happen.—IRVING LAYTON, "Foreword" to *A Red Carpet for the Sun*, 1959

Having long ago discontinued the temptation to regulate his life by probabilities; having registered such diverse phenomena as the conferral of *both* an honorary Sheriffship (Texas) *and* an Order of Merit (England) on a man born in Mark Twain's lifetime beside Mark Twain's Mississippi; having agreed to go on breathing air through whose upper strata are distributed the separated atoms of a metal canister and a small dog; having accustomed his nerves to a civilization which has achieved comparable pitches of excitement over the Atlas and the hula hoop; having been trained to conduct his affairs as usual while expecting hourly the instantaneous fusion of numerous hydrogen atoms, the appearance of the Great Sea Serpent in Lake Michigan, or some other prognostic of Armageddon: the knowing citizen will restrain his surprise on learning that there is a poet at large in Canada.

Mr. Irving Layton, to fit him quickly into the curriculum, should be bracketed with, say, Charles Olson and Robert Creeley; it is normal that he should turn up under the Jonathan Williams imprint. Canada provides him with a situation, not a tradition. He belongs to the anti-academic wing (though he is alleged to teach for a living) of the American poetic generation, a little younger than Auden and Spender, whose right and

center fill the better-capitalized quarterlies with cat's-cradle Meditations and grey flannel Suites: the generation that succeeded and should have inherited the achievements of Pound, Eliot, and Williams but could never grasp what they were up to. Mr. Layton's disdain for this poetic right and center is implicit; he will have us perceive that, though a wag, he is no Winters' tail. "If I'm not mistaken," he assures us on the front flap of *A Laughter in the Mind*, "the book is my best to date" [He is not mistaken. Sheer practice has lifted him to steady distinction.] "There are more than a dozen beast-type sockdolagers included. . . . The trout are running, not walking, upstream, the lox are eating cream cheese, the bagels are a-flutter like gefüllte u.f.o's. So—from that home, home on the range, where the ear and the ant elope, play, I strum these split-level ranch-type pomes. . . . Sblood, Sir, I expect a damned good response!" He inhabits roughly that quarter that ignores Eliot as a conformist, delights in Pound chiefly for the fact that he was fired from the only academic job he ever had (1907; Crawfordsville, Indiana), and takes from Dr. Williams what it can use, the aggressive notation of raw particulars.

⟨. . .⟩ The poetic situation, or absence of a poetic situation, in Mr. Layton's country of domicile confers on him the rare privilege of freedom from received procedures (though it does not discourage a received irreverent stance), and he in turn has the exceedingly rare energy that can fill a void with its own strength. There are bards as catachrestic as he in the North American attic, who throw themselves aimlessly about or stand around inhibited by the absence of chairs, or indulge in shapeless pieces of horseplay. There are also lady poets crocheting antimacassars for the packing-cases. Mr. Layton meanwhile has had the sense to see that he must create the situations within which he performs:

> And I who gave my Kate a blackened eye
> Did to its vivid changing colours
> Make up an incredible musical scale;
> And now I balance on wooden stilts and dance
> And thereby sing to the loftiest casements.
> See with what polish I bow from the waist.
> Space for these stilts! More space or I fail!

It is into such fictions that Mr. Layton's imaginative energy flows; the writing is simply good enough, perhaps often hasty; hundreds of poems have improved it without basing it on principle. He does not mind figuring as cynic, clown, lecher, or benevolent Caliban, father, historian, or tavern wit; he senses, apparently, that the only way for him to function in such a milieu is to work out the implications of self-sufficient acts of the imagination. "The Widows" does this; so does "Laurentian Rhapsody"; so do "Parting," "Individualists," the remarkable "Cain," and other poems which the reader is advised to try for himself, even though that will entail his laying out the price of the book.—HUGH KENNER, "Beast-Type Sockdolagers," _Poetry_, Sept. 1959, pp. 413–18

Many Canadian readers in the Forties and Fifties were repelled by the crude invective and frank eroticism in Layton's work. Even in the Sixties most reviewers were so preoccupied with the sensational aspects of his poetry that they failed to give adequate attention to its other important elements. This is partly Layton's own fault. A prolific writer, he proved to be an indiscriminate editor. Most of his volumes to date have included an inordinate number of ephemeral and inflammatory pieces. Moreover, he has frequently indulged in prefatory essays intended, no doubt, to throw light on his poems. These Forewords, however, were written in such a shrill and provocative style that they served mainly as reviewer-bait and distracted many a reader from taking the poems seriously.

⟨. . .⟩ it is apparent that no matter what mask he assumes—satyr, prophet, tender husband, jealous lover, teacher, father, minstrel, clown—Layton has been preoccupied with certain constantly recurring themes: the celebration of life in terms of love and sex; the denunciation of evil and corruption; compassion for the weak, the aged, the crippled; contemplation of death and of the mutability of youth and beauty; and an anguished recognition of the sacrifice and pain incurred by the inexorable process of nature and history. To these early and sustained themes may be added his growing conviction concerning the redemptive power of imagination and the prophetic role of the poet in society. All of these themes were explicit in his poetry by the mid-Fifties; his progression since then has been marked by deeper probings of his experience in these terms. ⟨. . .⟩

The quality of passion is a valuable clue to Layton's vision of reality. He is profoundly convinced of the positive existence of evil as a force dominating the world. Man is always at the mercy of the inhuman forces of nature and of the irreversible processes of history; but far worse, man as a moral being has created his own hell on earth. That this evil which man has created grows daily more real and horrible is attested to by the cruelty, violence, and hatred rampant in the world. All men are doomed to suffer. Yet the struggle of each individual— while it lasts—can have dignity if it is accepted with passion and delight. A man can even transform his defeat into a personal triumph with redemptive value for his fellow sufferers by affirming his power to love and his joy in the gift of imagination.

Layton's own suffering rage and defiant exultation suffuse all his poetry, but they are perhaps most cryptically rendered in these prophetic lines from a poem which he wrote in mid-career:

> They dance best who dance with desire,
> Who lifting feet of fire from fire
> Weave before they lie down
> A red carpet for the sun.

—WYNNE FRANCIS, "Preface" to _Selected Poems_ by Irving Layton, 1969

Layton is probably our first important poet to pour out books, good, bad or indifferent, with an absolute conviction as to the significance of poetry and the power of the word. He creates and lives in his own myth, most validity in his role of poet in the poems themselves. There he becomes Orpheus, Adam, the dying and rising god, the living word through whom the identity of all nature's divided things is manifest. He is worshipped and praised, for through him the vision of the community of living things is ever created anew, life is justified and men may praise, not the god but the world.

At best, it is not in himself but in his office as poet, as instrument of the imagination, that Layton finds his authority. As such, it does not matter what sort of scribbler his particular audience may think him to be; he knows that the poet is not irrelevant or powerless, but central to their lives. As he says in "The Fertile Muck":

> . . . if in August joiners and bricklayers
>   are thick as flies around us
> building expensive bungalows for those
> who do not need them, unless they release
>   me roaring from their moth-proofed cupboards
> their buyers will have no joy, no ease.

It is he who can extend their rooms for them, enlarge their world. ⟨. . .⟩

It is the Dionysian poet Layton cultivates, and whose irregular footprints so horrify those whose rooms he would extend; and in a time of cultural disintegration, when the visible or articulate order is so largely diseased, it is the Dionysian imagination that we may need to cultivate, abandoning ourselves to Eros and the deepest springs of our desire. And that is itself no easy matter when we have been so bombarded by voices telling us what we ought to think we desire.—D. G. JONES, "Myth, Frye and Canadian Writers," _CL_, Winter 1973, pp. 12–18

⟨. . .⟩ it is style and form, various and capacious, depend for their success on what he himself has called the "imperial rhetoric" of poetry, a vivid, fluent line and passionate language that scorn the levelling "republican diction" of younger writers. In that opposition of the imperial and the republican, we can recognize the younger Layton's aligning of himself with the prophetic and visionary traditions of poetry. But now, that imperial voice lends itself not only to his early themes of celebration of desire, condemnation of evil, the tension between flux and form, but more particularly to a recognition of the historical and symbolic significance of the Jewish experience for our understanding of contemporary society and its values.

He is still ready at a moment's notice to sharpen an epigram on the edge of his hatred of philistines, to drag respectability out of the door with a few well-chosen quatrains of bawdy verse, to praise a whore or a beautiful woman, or for that matter, an ugly one, in sensuous loving lines. But alongside the celebrations of an aging and vital lover, something more disturbing moves through these later poems. Sometimes he speaks of this as the Jewish experience, and at other times as the enormous cruelty of modern man, his capacity for savagery, his "gentility." Layton has written:

> Today the disparity between rhetoric and experience
> has taken a form different from that of the forties, one
> which I find more sinister than the earlier one. It is
> also, I believe, at the root of the continuing gentility
> which afflicted this country for the better part of a
> century, if not since its very beginnings. I indicated
> in the prefaces I wrote for _Balls for a One-Armed
> Juggler_ and _The Shattered Plinths_ that the poetic
> rhetoric of our times has not attempted to assimilate
> the experience of Auschwitz, Belsen, and Gulag.
> This is true for the poets living in English-speaking
> countries, not true for poets in Poland, Czecho-
> slovakia, and Germany. I am, I think, the only poet in

any English-speaking country to have pointed this out. But this gentility is only part of a larger gentility that averts its courteous gaze from the cruelties and harrowing injustices Western Christendom has visited on Jews and still continues to do so. This gentility, it should be said, has consequences equally important and damaging both for Jew and gentile.

Challenging words. But then the younger Layton never promised us he would in an older year mellow. Darker now, often angrier, even misanthropic, he rages like an old prophet, and like an old prophet he strikes fire out of rock and calls together in those sparks visions of past, present, and future that we may know ourselves anew, as if for the first time.—ELI MANDEL, "Foreword" to *The Unwavering Eye*, 1955, pp. x–xi

---

## GEORGE WOODCOCK
### From "A Grab at Proteus"

*Canadian Literature*, Summer 1965, pp. 7–21

By a convincing exhibition of his ferocity as a ring-tailed roarer in the little zoo of Canandian letters, Layton has in fact successfully embarrassed most of the critics into a kind of numbed evasiveness. In the seven years since I have been editing *Canadian Literature*, while two or three reviewers have made brief forays with bows-and-arrows into the fringes of Layton territory, no critic has submitted a complete and satisfactory study of Layton as poet, mainly because no critic has so far relished the task of considering a body of work by a notoriously irascible writer which varies so remarkably from the atrocious to the excellent, and which shows a failure of self-evaluation as monstrous as that displayed by D. H. Lawrence, who in so many ways resembled, anticipated and influenced Layton. To grasp Layton is rather like trying to grasp Proteus. But Proteus was grasped, and so must Layton be, for behind the many disguises an exceptionally fine poet lurks in hiding. ⟨ . . . ⟩

I applaud Layton's desire to flout conformity and attack its supporters, and if this were all I would gladly stand shouting beside him. But I cannot see any necessary connection between rebellion of this kind and the vocation of the poet. That vocation, surely, is no more than to write poetry, and a good poet can even stand for insanity and darkness, as Yeats sometimes did, can even retreat into the darkness of literal insanity, and still continue his vocation. The social and moral rebel is something different, though the two may be and often are united. Layton takes it for granted that they *must* be united; this, to be necessarily paradoxical, is the classic romantic stance, and Layton, in upholding it, is a traditional wild man according to conventions laid down early in the nineteenth century. His essential neo-romanticism crops up in many other ways: in his "anti-literary" stance when his poems are as crammed with literary and classical tags and allusions as the prose of any despised man-of-letters; in his "anti-academic" attitude when, unlike many of his fellow writers in Canada, he is a university graduate who—as his poems about lectures and students show—has been lurking for years in the underbrush of the academic groves. It manifests itself also in the archaic images and phrases which embellish even Layton's most recent poems with an undeniable tinge of antique poeticism. In the final pages of the *Collected Poems* one finds him talking of

The shadowy swaying of trees
Like graceful nuns in a forbidden dance;
The yearning stillness of an ended night . . . ;

telling us of his meeting with a faun (predictably conceived to point up the evils of a conformist world); and ending the volume with lines that are heavy with nostalgic echoes from the past of English romanticism:

Meanwhile the green snake *crept upon the sky*
Huge, his *mailed coat glittering with stars that made*
*The night bright*, and blowing *thin wreaths of cloud*
*Athwart the moon*; and as *the weary man*
Stood up, coiled above his head, *transforming all*.

There is, of course, nothing intrinsically wrong in using again the phrases and images I have italicized; they belong to the accumulated stock-in-trade of poets in the same way as Shakespeare and Sheridan belong to the accumulated stock-in-trade of actors, and the way they are used is what matters most. But the fact that Layton not only acts but often writes as a latter-day romantic becomes important when we grapple with the relation between the two levels of his poetic activity.

The concept of the romantic poet provides, to begin, a justification for Layton's Saint Sebastian attitude. In fact, it is nothing more than a logical extension of the illogical idea of the poet as prophet; if the poet is really inspired, if it is really the gods (whatever they represent) who make him howl, then he is one of the chosen, against whom criticism or even competition is not merely an act of presumption but also something very near to religious persecution. Such an attitude cannot simply be waved away. Layton is talking with conviction and passion when he says that if the poet "offers his hand in friendship and love, he must expect someone will try to chop it off at the shoulder." He feels his isolation as a poet and a man deeply, so deeply that it has inspired not only such malicious attacks on his fellow poets as figure in the "Prologue to the Long Pea-Shooter"[1] but also such a powerful vision of the fate of the rebel in the world of conformity as "The Cage". More than that, this feeling plays its ultimate part in the compassionate self-identification with the destroyed innocents of the animal and human worlds which inspires those of his poems that touch nearest to greatness and which pleads pardon for his arrogance towards his peers.

But there is another side to the idea of poetic inspiration. If it is blasphemous for others to criticize what the poet has written in the fine fury of possession, may it not also be an act of *hubris* for the poet himself to reject or diminish the godly gift? The whole vision of the poet as prophet denies not only the function of the critic; more seriously, it deprives the poet of the self-critical faculty which in all artistic activity is the necessary and natural balance to the irrational forces of the creative impulse. Once a poet sees himself as a vehicle for anything outside him, whether he calls it God or the Muse or Truth or, in Layton's words, "sanity and light", he abdicates the power of rational choice, and it is only logical that he should cease to discriminate between his best and his worst works, that he should seriously publish, in the same retrospective collection, a poem like *The Predator*, where pity and anger magnificently coalesce in the final verses:

Ghost of small fox,
hear me, if you're hovering close
and watching this slow red trickle of your blood:
Man sets even
more terrible traps for his own kind.
Be at peace; your gnawed leg will be well-
revenged . . .

and a joking jingle, like *Diversion*, of a kind which any versifier might whip up at two for a dollar.

Whenever I'm angry with her
or hold up my hand to slap or hit,
my darling recites some lines I've writ.

The crafty puss! She thinks that she
diverts my anger by vanity,
when it's her heaving breasts that does it.

If the lines she recites are anything like these, the breasts of Mr. Layton's darling must put on a very spectacular exhibition!

But nothing is so simple where Proteus is involved. The problem of Layton's switchback career as a poet, which makes one's reaction to his *Collected Poems* take the form of a wildly dipping and climbing seismograph, cannot be solved merely by suggesting that he is deliberately unselective or incapable of selection. That might be argued for a poet whose successes, when they came, were obviously the product of deep irrational urges which rarely and unexpectedly broke into the dull cycle of an undistinguished existence and produced a masterpiece that astonished its creator; there have, very occasionally, been such writers, but Layton is not one of them. On the contrary, on reading the *Collected Poems*, one is left with the impression of having been in the company of a trained and versatile craftsman liable to sudden fits of contempt for his public, in which he tries to palm off on them fragments of worn-out fustian instead of lengths of silk.

Perhaps the matter can be made clearer by bringing in an illustration from another field of art, and comparing Layton with Picasso. There is a verse at the end of his poem, "Joseph K", which suggests that he will not find the comparison offensive.

Then let him rise like a hawk.
Fiercely. A blazing chorus
Be, or like a painting by Picasso
Drawing energy from its own contours.

Picasso, to my mind, connotes enormous energy, and a flexible craftsmanship which has enabled him to paint and draw in many styles, and to select and use ruthlessly from past forms of art anything that might suit his purposes. No modern painter has spread such magnificent confusion, by the display of his talents, among those academic critics who originally damned the post-impressionists with the argument that they knew neither how to draw nor to paint. At the same time, as the collection of second-line material enshrined in the museum at Antibes has shown, Picasso's very energy has led him to produce a great many minor works which a more fastidious artist would have discarded or kept as mere exercises. Finally, there has always been a touch of the clown about Picasso, as became very evident in at least one of the films in which he performed as the impresario of his own art. He enjoys mystifying his more naïve admirers, and many of his works must be regarded as mere *jeux d'esprit* carried out to amuse himself or fox his public. But it would be foolish to assume that because of this Picasso is nothing more than a mountebank.

In one sense at least Irving Layton cannot be compared with Picasso. Picasso was the moving spirit in a trend that revolutionized our views of art, and it is hard now to imagine what painting would have been like anywhere in the world if he had not lived. So far there is no evidence of any real revolution that Layton had led in poetry; his work at its best has its own originality, but it breaks into no really new territory, and his followers among the younger Canadian poets have so far shown neither the vigour nor the talents of their master. In other respects, however, the resemblances between Layton and Picasso are striking. Layton, too, is an artist of great energy—in terms of quantity alone a formidable producer. And, like Picasso, he combines the ability to work in a variety of styles and to borrow freely from the past with a craftsmanship which at its best is so good that one cannot possibly attribute his worst

productions to the mere inability to do better. A different explanation has to be found. ⟨ . . .⟩

In fine, Layton is a poet in the old romantic sense, *a Dichter*, flamboyant, rowdy, angry, tortured, tender, versatile, voluble, ready for the occasion as well as the inspiration, keeping his hand constantly in, and mingling personal griefs and joys with the themes and visions of human destiny. Lately a somewhat negative element seems to have entered his poems; he is conscious of time beginning to sap the sources of life, he adjusts reluctantly to his own aging, he dwells on the unhappier aspects of sex, suspicious of the infidelity of women, of the untrustworthiness of friends. He is obviously at a point of transition, but his vigour will carry him over this and other weirs. Whatever happens, we shall have to take Layton as he comes and wishes, the good and the bad together; but that is better than not having him at all. For my last feeling, after journeying through Asia with Layton in the form of his *Collected Poems*, was that of having been in the disturbing company of one of the men of my generation who will not be forgotten.

*Notes*

1. "But if you have the gifts of Reaney / You may help your verse by being zany, / Or write as bleakly at a pinch / As Livesay, Smith, and Robert Finch; / And be admired for a brand-new pot / If you're as empty as Marriott; / I'll say nothing about Dudek: / The rhyme's too easy—speck or wreck . . ."

## HUGH KENNER

### "Introduction"

### *The Selected Poems of Irving Layton*

### 1977, pp. 5–8

Irving Layton is Canada's most prolific as well as most celebrated poet, and in thirty years he has issued some thirty volumes, which lately have been running to eighty poems apiece. Some of his poems are better than others, and Canadians who have lived with him for decades seem to take his habit of bundling the day's irritations into a poem for granted, like mosquitoes and imperfectly bilingual postmen. Readers elsewhere, making his acquaintance in a winnowed compilation, may double their pleasure in his best by reflecting that if his less good is missing from this volume, still it exists and has had its uses.

For the ephemeral poems do serve to keep the poet limber, and strewn through a Layton book they have value for a reader too, providing the noise from which the sonorities crystallize, making the successful poems when they happen seem random miracles like (on a cooling planet) the genesis of life.

Which is how they are meant to seem, as though just dashed off. Perhaps they are, perhaps not. Their genre anyhow is Blake's, Whitman's, Lawrence's, Williams's: that of the seeming improvisation. An example:

#### DIVINITY

Were I a clumsy poet
I'd compare you to Helen;
Ransack the mythologies
Greek, Chinese, and Persian

For a goddess vehement
And slim; one with form as fair.
Yet find none. O, Love, you are
Lithe as a Jew peddler

> And full of grace. Such lightness
> Is in your step, instruments
> I keep for the beholder
> To prove you walk, not dance.
>
> Merely to touch you is fire
> In my head; my hair becomes
> A burning bush. When you speak,
> Like Moses I am dumb
>
> With marvelling, or like him
> I stutter with pride and fear:
> I hold, Love, divinity
> In my changed face and hair.

All of this says, I stammer with wonder. The first line seems unsure whether to stress *clumsy* or *poet*: I'm not a *clumsy* poet, the kind that contrives comparisons when there aren't any; or, I'm not a poet at all. I do without art. Either way, I'm simply uttering what words I can, and as early as line six you can tell I'm not counting syllables; as for "instruments" in the third stanza, that's a nonce-word to be going on with. (What instruments can he possibly have in mind? John Donne would have let us know.) So the poem enacts its own sincerity: you reduce me to doggerel, to bare halting talk. And yet—

And yet those quatrains are more than typographical: their second and fourth lines all rhyme slantwise, the way Yeats rhymes *stain* and *moon*, or *head* and *blood*. (This takes more of a poet's concentration than exact rhyming, because the words won't prompt one another the way *stain* does *slain*.) And in its fourth and fifth stanzas this poem that began by rejecting literary talk is fetching its fire and its dumbness from Sappho (the "Phainetai moi" which Catullus also imitated) while allowing us to notice only the burning bush from Exodus. (And the poet is both the burning bush and Moses, both godlike and the god's supplicant.) Do such things simply happen, when a poet is sufficiently rapt? That's what the poem would have us believe.

Layton's art is always to sound artless, and maybe he is but one needn't wholly believe it. His fine gift of Voltairean detachment (see "The Cockroach") seems like something you could keep up just by cocking your head the right way, though you'd be unlikely to manage such a detail as "All the lovely, meaningful things they had said to each other about cockroaches were forgotten." His parables drawn from the vulnerability of animals (see "Cain") have the transparency of folktales. His climaxes are apt to explode in one-syllable words (see for instance the much-quoted quatrain,

> They dance best who dance with desire,
> Who lifting feet of fire from fire
> Weave before they lie down
> A red carpet for the sun

from "For Mao Tse-Tung: A Meditation on Flies and Kings.") He can seem to be just tossing words at the page—

> . . . the anguished
> half-choked
> sputtering cry
> the circumscribed tide
> makes—its hiss
> and last sign—

> before it collapses
> on the white sand
> and dies

—and achieve the imitation of a spent wave's phantasmal sound that has taunted poets to emulate it since Homer's *polyphloisboio thalasse*. (Layton's lines are a detail from "Tide," a poem not collected here. There's plenty of first-class Layton outside this selection.)

What keeps all this going is prodigious physical energy and a blustery defiance of Canada, where Layton has lived since he was one year old (he was born, 1912, in Roumania). Canada (Wyndham Lewis's "sanctimonious icebox") is an easy country to defy, its satirizable institutions have so little fight—

> A dull people, without charm
> or ideas,
> settling into the clean empty look
> of a Mountie or dairy farmer
> as into a legacy

—and Layton being caustic about it is doing two-finger exercises; that one is called "From Colony to Nation." But he owes it much too that he's never pinned down: a sunlight like his harsh ironic mind, an urban bustle that doesn't *engulf* in New York's way or London's, an easy commerce with the undeveloped land where for lack of barbered distances you may as well look closely at snakes and frogs; most notably a milieu for the mind that doesn't help a poet develop his idiom but, remote from any workable poetic, doesn't jam his signals either. (In England, Eliot found, the language needs viewing with "animosity," so insidiously do its literary echoes wrest control away from the poet.)

Neither French nor British, Layton looks around him in Montreal with the eye of an exasperated alien (see "On Seeing the Statuettes of Ezekiel and Jeremiah in the Church of Notre Dame"). It was natural that he should have developed the poetic of the one-man show—*Balls for a One-Armed Juggler*, as the title of a 1963 collection has it. Each new poem, of hundreds on hundreds, tests out the performance anew. (One-armed jugglers need luck, and it only works sometimes.) Defining his expectations against those of the city's pervading religion, he hopes for little from man save cussedness, from woman save felicity, or from life save moments of lovely instinctual flowering. That its members might from time to time stumble into the momentary joy of being alive is the most he can find it in him to wish for the human race, bound as it is to a mortality it shares with flies and a disingenuous passion it shares with Hitler. The lover breaks free sometimes, and the poet when his poem works. Distrusting alike theophanies and meliorations, the poems hold out hope only for themselves: for rare transparencies accessible it may be only to poets and vicariously a little to the rest of us.

> Enough that we two can find
> A laughter in the mind
> For the interlocking grass
> The winds part as they pass;
> Or fallen on each other,
> Leaf and uprooted flower.

# STEPHEN LEACOCK

## 1869–1944

Stephen Butler Leacock was born in Swanmore, Hampshire, on December 30, 1869. The Leacock family emigrated to Canada in 1876, settling on a farm near Sutton, Ontario. The marriage of Leacock's parents was not particularly strong. His mother, Agnes Butler, who was the daughter of an Anglican clergyman, was considered to have married beneath her when she wedded Peter Leacock, son of a Roman Catholic family. Peter Leacock was a financial failure, who trailed after Canada's economic booms, generally arriving just in time to catch the busts. Stephen came to resent his father for his inability to provide for the family, and on one of Peter's infrequent visits home Stephen told his father never to return.

Leacock received his early education at home from a tutor, Harry Parks. At age thirteen he entered Upper Canada College in Toronto, where he became Head Boy. He began studies at the University of Toronto, but ran short of funds. Leacock was forced to take a teaching post at Uxbridge, where his former tutor, Harry Parks, was then principal. After a year of teaching modern languages, Leacock took a job at Upper Canada College, enabling him to continue his university studies at night. In 1891 Leacock received a B.A. from the University of Toronto. He continued to teach at Upper Canada College until 1899, when he read Thorstein Veblen's *The Theory of the Leisure Class*. Leacock immediately applied for admission to the University of Chicago, where Veblen was teaching, and moved there in 1900 with his wife Beatrix Hamilton. In 1903 he earned a Ph.D. in political economy and political science and therafter took a teaching job at McGill.

Leacock wrote a highly successful textbook, *Elements of Political Science* (1906), which was translated into nineteen languages. He continued his academic writings; in 1907 he traveled abroad delivering Rhodes Lectures on Imperial Development. By 1908 Leacock was established firmly at McGill as head of the Department of Economics. Although his critics often charged that his knowledge of economics was minimal, no one challenged his knowledge of political science or his ability to write. In 1910 Leacock published *Literary Lapses*, beginning a long, successful career as a humorist. Later works such as *Sunshine Sketches of a Little Town* (1912), *Arcadian Adventures with the Idle Rich* (1914), and *My Discovery of England* (1922) furthered Leacock's literary reputation. Leacock continued to write until his death on March 28, 1944. Four chapters of his unfinished autobiography, *The Boy I Left Behind Me*, were published posthumously in 1946.

I met him only once, during the 'thirties, when I was lecturing in Montreal and he gave me dinner. He was a chunky man, with a square face, rumpled grey hair, bristling eyebrows and moustache, and small deep-set twinkling eyes: a good physical type. I cannot remember a word of our talk but I know it was easy and companionable and that we laughed a lot. There was nothing of the poker-faced professional funny-man about him; his rather loud laugh rang out at his own jokes as well as at mine, as we swapped stories and passed the whisky; he was immediately and immensely likeable, as the affectionate memoir by his niece makes plain to us.

There can be little doubt that he saw himself as a teacher first, an educator with humorous writing as a lucrative hobby. Possibly his former students would accept this estimate of him. But it is certain that the rest of us, who can judge him only by the work he has left us, cannot accept it. To us he is a humorist—or nothing. He lives by what he did in his spare time for fun. Indeed, his serious academic writing seems to me quite surprisingly commonplace, lacking originality and the insight that might have been expected of such a lively mind, just run-of-the-mill professorial stuff, sufficiently responsible and conscientious but without distinction. It is when he puts aside the cap and gown, lights a pipe and fills a glass, and begins playing the fool that he achieves originality, insight, distinction. It is here too, and not in the lecture-room, that he becomes thoroughly and most refreshingly *Canadian*.

Canada should not only be proud of Stephen Leacock but also be specially grateful to him. The best of his humour does something very difficult to do—it expresses an essential Canadian quality. It is the humour of a nation that notoriously finds national self-expression not at all easy. The Canadian is often a baffled man because he feels different from his British kindred and his American neighbours, sharply refuses to be lumped together with either of them, yet cannot make plain this difference. But Leacock was doing it in his humour. Very adroitly he aimed at both British and American audiences, but he never identified himself with either: always, at least when he is at his best, he remains a Canadian. And when he is very good indeed—as he is, for example, in *Arcadian Adventures with the Idle Rich*—he achieves an outlook, manner, style, that typically British or American humorists would find it impossible to achieve. These belong to the man but they also belong to his nation.

The best of Leacock exists somewhere between—though at a slight angle from—the amiable nonsense of characteristic English humour (e.g. Wodehouse) and the hard cutting wit and almost vindictive satire of much American humour. Leacock wrote plenty of cheerful nonsense, and examples of it may be found in this volume, although I have been sparing in my choice of it. But the Leacock I enjoy and admire is a satirist of sorts: he is keenly aware of cant and humbug; his work has an edge to it. As a fairly typical instance, here is a passage from 'The Great Fight for Clean Government' chapter in *Arcadian Adventures with the Idle Rich*:

> Take, for example, the case of the press. At the inception of the League it had been supposed that such was the venality and corruption of the city newspapers that it would be necessary to buy one of

them. But the words 'clean government' had been no sooner uttered than it turned out that every one of the papers in the city was in favour of it—in fact, they had been working for it for years.

They vied with one another now in giving publicity to the idea. The *Plutorian Times* printed a dotted coupon on the corner of its front sheet with the words, 'Are you in favour of Clean Government? If so, send us ten cents with this coupon and your name and address.' The *Plutorian Citizen and Home Advocate* went even further. It printed a coupon which said, 'Are you out for a Clean City? If so, send us twenty-five cents to this office. We pledge ourselves to use it.'

The satire is evident; the edge is here; but clearly the passage as a whole is poised—after some skilful manipulation by the author—between sharply-edged satire on the one side and sheer absurdity on the other, being neither savage American wit nor entirely amiable English nonsense. It is a kind of humour that might be compared to summer lightning, suddenly illuminating the scene of our follies but not striking and blasting.

It is in fact the satirical humour of a very shrewd but essentially good-natured and eupeptic man, anything but an angry reformer. And two sorts of readers may find it unsatisfactory; namely, those who prefer humour to be the nonsense of dreamland, in the Wodehouse manner, and those who regard humour as a weapon with which to attack the world, in the Shavian style. But there are enough of us between these two extremes to provide Leacock with a large admiring audience. And I can assure those who are doubtful about offering their admiration that what this writer does at the height of his form, balanced between cutting satire and sheer absurdity, is very difficult to do successfully. The Leacock of the *Arcadian Adventures*, the best of the *Sunshine Sketches*, and the more ambitious funny pieces, is no mere Canadian professor having holiday fun, not just another contributor to the comic papers, but a unique national humorist with a manner and style all his own. While I for one am willing to admit that his slighter things, especially the literary burlesques, have had more success than they deserved to have, I cannot help feeling that this easy popularity has led to his best and most characteristic work being seriously undervalued. It is one of the weaknesses of contemporary criticism, perhaps because it is uncertain in its taste and judgment, that it makes little or no attempt to discover genuine merit behind the façade of easy popular reputations. It refuses to believe that where there is a great deal of gilt there may also be a little gold.—J. B. PRIESTLEY, "Editor's Introduction" to *The Bodley Head Leacock*, 1957, pp. 9–12

As a people bent on self-preservation, Canadians have had to forego two luxuries: that of forgetting themselves in gay abandon and that of losing their tempers in righteous wrath. Yet there is a kind of humour that combines full understanding of the contending forces with a wry recognition of one's ineffectiveness in controlling them—a humour in which one sees himself as others see him but without any admission that this outer man is a truer portrait than the inner—a humour based on the incongruity between the real and the ideal, in which the ideal is repeatedly thwarted by the real but never quite annihilated. Such humour is Canadian.

What Lister Sinclair calls our "calculated diffidence" would never draw attention to itself in humour by exuberant slapstick or by linguistic pranks in the form of explosive wisecracks—and there is little of either in Leacock. The Socratic irony of letting the giants destroy themselves by their own utterances is a standard device of Leacock—witness, for example, the self-destruction so wrought amongst university administrators and professors, high financiers, clean-government reformers, and church boardmen in his *Arcadian Adventures with the Idle Rich*. Here Leacock may be, in Priestley's phrase, "anything but an angry reformer", yet a reformer he unmistakably is. So also with the *Sunshine Sketches*. Both these books display neither the "amiable nonsense" of a Wodehouse nor the "hard cutting wit and almost vindictive satire of much American humour." Good-tempered restraint is less easy to detect than slashing attack, and is perhaps less colourful to watch, but it has its own unique value. Given Canada's "precarious" situation of inner and outer relationships, self-restraint means self-preservation. We cannot enforce change or reform with a scourge or bludgeon, because the tightrope we walk is no place for flailing arms. The Canadian satirical weapon is, of necessity, the scalpel of the cool surgeon or the quick flip of the judo expert.

In his recent biography of Leacock, Ralph L. Curry frequently refers to Leacock's "favorite character, the little man in the society too complex for him", who preserves "his dignity by continuing, in his ignorance, to act like a man". Wearing his American spectacles, Mr. Curry has misread Leacock, for the "little man" he describes is portrayed by various American humorists but not by Leacock. In the light of his own description, it is rather surprising that Mr. Curry cites "My Financial Career" as a good portrait of Leacock's "little man". The protagonist of this most famous of all Leacock's sketches is certainly not an innocent overwhelmed by an environment too complex for his understanding.

The truth is very simple: Leacock's "favorite character" was indeed a "little man" but he was a Canadian type, not an American; and "My Financial Career" *is* a good portrait of him but only when its Canadian subject is properly identified and described. In this sketch Leacock introduces us to a somewhat diffident young man who, he tells us, knows "beforehand" what is likely to happen but who nevertheless enters the bank undeterred by this knowledge. The young man has formed an ideal of saving his money and he considers the bank the best place to accomplish his purpose. He understands the essentials of banking, if not the details; he understands how he appears to others (confused, incompetent, helpless, etc.) and also *why* he appears so; he understands what he does wrong while he does it; and above all he understands himself thoroughly, past and present, both his inner self and his outer appearance. Far from preserving any "dignity" by "continuing in his ignorance, to act like a man", he is acutely handicapped by the very completeness of his knowledge. It is true that he cannot control his nervous reactions any more than he can change the atmosphere of the bank—the humour lies in just this ineffectiveness.

Throughout the sketch the humour sparkles from the changing facets of the young man's "identity", how others see him and how he sees himself, the incongruities between appearance and reality. Besides his own true identity there is mistaken identity, assumed identity, and apparent identity. For instance, the bankers mistake him at first for "one of Pinkerton's men", and then for "a son of Baron Rothschild or a young Gould"; later he himself tries to act or look like an insulted despositor or an irascible curmudgeon; and at the end he appears to the bankers as an utter fool. All the while his essential nature remains intact and unchanged, despite all the environmental entanglements. Unable to adjust his inner self to an environment too powerful for him, he retreats under a barrage of laughter. But consider the ending of the story.

Following the description of the roar of laughter he hears as the bank doors close behind him come two concluding sentences:

> Since then I bank no more. I keep my money in cash in my trousers pocket and my savings in silver dollars in a sock.

In short, this diffident young Canadian's initial intention of saving his money has been quite unaffected by what has happened to him in the bank. Wryly recognizing *once more* his inability to cope with the overpowering atmosphere of the banking world, he changes his method of money-saving to one which is free from external pressures and is entirely within his own control. In his own way this "little man" has solved his problem—a richly humorous one for the reader, to be sure, because of the incongruity between the ideal of his intention and the reality of his sock. ⟨. . .⟩

All through our history, the favourite intellectual game of Canadians has been to measure ourselves against the British on the one hand and the Americans on the other. We have tended to define what we are almost exclusively by detecting our differences from both. Consequently, if any people anywhere should be especially skilled in the comparative study of human beings considered as groups or types rather than as individuals, it should be us. And we should also be equipped to tell the world whatever insights into general human nature such processes provide. Now consider what Leacock says:

> Comparison is the very soul of humour. . . . It is the discovery of resemblance and the lack of it that builds up the contrasts, discrepancies and incongruities on which . . . humour depends.

As Leacock well knew, poetic imagery also springs from the perception of similarities and differences; but humour, not poetry, builds upon the resultant discrepancies and incongruities, particularly as applied to types of human nature and typical human behaviour. For generations, then, Canadians have cultivated the soil from which humour springs, and we therefore should not be surprised that out of Canada have come two great humorists to whom the world has given its approval. Men everywhere can detect and savour a special "tang" without caring about its special ingredients or even its origins.—R. E. WATTERS, "A Special Tang: Stephen Leacock's Canadian Humour," *CL*, Summer 1960, pp. 26–32

---

## ROBERTSON DAVIES
### From "Stephen Leacock"
*Our Living Tradition: Seven Canadians*
ed. Claude T. Bissell
1957, pp. 129–49

Let me begin by reminding you of some of the biographical details about him which are relevant to a critical discussion. He was born in the south of England, at Swanmoor in Hampshire on December 30, 1869—which was, he reminds us, exactly midway in the reign of Queen Victoria. The Leacock family had made a good deal of money in the Madeira wine trade, but at that time it was running short. In his unfinished autobiography he tells us that among his early memories were the graceful sailing-ships lying at anchor, and an old sailor who was a veteran of "the Great War"—which meant the wars against Napoleon. On both sides of his family he came of what is called "good stock"—undistinguished people, but of assured social position—gentry, indeed. I think it important to remember that Leacock came of small gentry stock, for in later life he seemed always to be hankering for the stability of their values, and at the same time rebelling against what he conceived to be the injustice of inherited privileges; it was one of the tensions which plagued him, and which made him a humorist. For humour—as opposed to the mere mechanical jokesmithing of television, and similar painfully contrived fun—is always a result of tension in the mind. (Something of the same tension was observable in his later revulsion against the classics, upon which, nevertheless, he continued to draw heavily—particularly in the writings of his last years.)

The family story was one common in the history of all the British dominions. Because there seemed little likelihood that Leacock's father would do well in England, it was assumed—on some curious principle of nineteenth-century British logic—that he must do well in Canada, and in 1876 he and his family took up residence on one of those God-forsaken farms which Canada provides especially for Englishmen who know nothing about farming. It was a few miles south of Lake Simcoe. Here Leacock remained from his sixth till his twelfth year. His mother, of whom he writes with affection, strove to maintain the family gentility, and when her sons had tried the local school, and quickly took on the habits and grammar of the local farmers, she engaged a tutor to educate them as she thought fitting. But when Leacock's father—of whom he writes without affection—succumbed to drink and failure, and ran away from his family, she sent her sons to Upper Canada College in Toronto. In time Stephen Leacock became head boy there, and showed a marked aptitude for academic work.

When his schooling was completed, he taught school himself, at first in country schools; then, in 1891, he returned to Upper Canada College as a junior master, at the salary of $700 a year, and remained there for eight years, during which time he was able to attend some classes at the University of Toronto and take a degree. He hated school-mastering. It would be easy at this point to say some agreeable things about the teaching profession, but I shall deny myself that luxury. Let us agree simply that teaching children is a fine profession for those who enjoy the company of children, and who are happiest among those whose minds are less well-stored than their own. Leacock was not a man of that stamp. It is significant that he greatly enjoyed his work as a university professor, and gave it up with regret.

I should like to repeat here a story told me by Professor Keith Hicks, of Trinity College, Toronto. When Leacock was a master at U.C.C., another junior master amused and annoyed the Common Room by his repeated complaints about his salary. At last he requested Leacock to draft a letter for him to the Board of Governors. When completed, it ran thus: "Gentlemen: Unless you can see your way clear to increasing my stipend immediately, I shall reluctantly be forced to"—and here the page was turned—"continue working for the same figure."

Leacock had been given a classical education at school, but he turned towards political science in his university work. In 1899, having borrowed some money for that purpose, he went to the University of Chicago, and took his degree as Doctor of Philosophy—that degree which, as he says, signifies that a man has been filled as full of knowledge as he can hold, and must henceforth slop over. In 1901 he joined the Department of Economics and Political Science at McGill, and in 1908 he was appointed professor of that subject, holding the Dow Chair until he was retired, much against his will, in 1936. He won a great reputation as a teacher.

Now here I must advance an opinion for which I take full

responsibility, though it is not my own. It was usual to refer to Leacock during his lifetime as an economist, and some people generously extended his reputation as a great humorist into his academic life, and declared that he was a great economist. It is on the same principle that the public often assumes that a man who is a great money-maker must also be a profound student of public affairs or an infallible prophet of the future. But I have sought the opinions of several eminent Canadian economists, some of them former colleagues of his, and they are in agreement on this: Leacock was not really an economist at all. In many Canadian universities Economics and Political Science are combined in a single department, following a Scottish tradition which can no longer be defended. It was so at McGill in Leacock's day, though it is so no longer. Leacock was expected to give some lectures on economics, and he did so. He was an inspiring and indeed a brilliant teacher. But when Leacock wrote on economics he wrote—and I quote one of my informants—"some damn fool things." (Of course the best teacher is not necessarily the man who has the most profound understanding of his subject. Canadian educators have for some years been propagating the theory that a command of the technique of teaching is vastly more important than a knowledge of the subject to be taught. Indeed, we are sometimes led to feel that knowledge is a positive handicap to a teacher.) Again, Leacock has been described to me as "an untrained layman" in the realm of economics, though the man who said so said also that his economic efforts were graced by excellent common sense. Whether this means that a truly professional approach to economics cannot be reconciled with common sense is outside the scope of this essay.

But though apparently no economist, Leacock was a good political scientist—careful in study, sound in argument and wise in judgment. However, it appears that his most important book on this subject, *Elements of Political Science*, is now outdated. Again, I quote from a professional economist:

> Though his economic writings ought never to have been written, they really are irrelevant to his academic career. He was a great teacher of the subjects he had mastered. He was an inspiration to all who came in contact with him. He was a thoroughly competent political scientist, though his greatness did not lie there. Yet he deserved his professional honours on professional grounds. He was not an economist and it is a great pity that in his declining years he wrote on economic subjects. I hope a sympathetic biographer will forget these latter works.

I have given a good deal of emphasis to this point, because I want to make it clear that Leacock's importance to Canada rests solely upon the body of his work as a humorist. Perhaps that seems self-evident to you. It did not seem so to him. He was proud of his writings on political science and economics. He appears to have been proud, also, of his books on Canadian history, though these are unoriginal in viewpoint, and do not seem to me to be written with much literary skill. He also had a good opinion as a literary critic, and on his work in this field I may presume to speak with some degree of expert knowledge.

He possessed some of the qualities of a critic—some of the rarest gifts to be found in that ambiguous and over-valued occupation—for he was a great enjoyer of literature, and he had splendid flashes of insight. Because he was himself a creative artist of uncommon abilities, he understood the toil of creation and the temptations of the creative life better than the parasite-critic whose only writings are fastened, leech-like, upon the body of another man's work. But he was inexcusably careless about matters of fact and detail; in his book on Dickens it is astonishing to find that he has not even troubled to verify the names of some of Dickens' characters. And he was extreme in his judgments: when he says that Dickens' works "represent the highest reach of the world's imaginative literature," we must smile, because we know that Leacock had not read extremely widely in English, not to speak of other languages which deserve some consideration when such broad claims are being made. When he says that Shakespeare was a man of "far lesser genius" than Dickens, it simply means that Leacock had a very poor ear for poetry—a fact which he makes plain in several other books, by quoting second-rate and third-rate verse as if it were of the first order. His book on Dickens contains enough good material for a first-class long essay, but it is a poor book.

There is an odd element in the Dickens book which suggests a strong strain of Victorianism in Leacock. He writes at length and with indignation about Dickens' estrangement from his wife, and professes not to understand how it came about. Yet unless he depended on secondary sources to a degree which was most unscholarly, he must have examined Dickens' will, and he must have noticed that the first legacy named in it is to the woman who was Dickens' mistress. If he knew that, why did he not refer to it in his book? Is the clue in a remark which he makes in the book itself that "Charles Dickens is not yet history, to be mauled about like Charles the Second or Charlemagne"? Or was Leacock really deluded about Dickens, and wrote what he believed to be the truth when he said "In him was nothing of the philanderer, the Lothario, the Don Juan"? Whatever the truth of the matter, it is important that we should remember that Leacock's character was formed before the modern vogue for easy self-revelation came into being. If we are to seek the truth about him, we shall have to read between the lines in his work, for we shall not find what we are looking for plainly set forth. In so doing we must remember that reading between the lines of anybody's work is an exceedingly delicate and tentative business.

Leacock was a writer all of his adult life. But his real career as a writer did not begin until his fortieth year, when he gathered up some amusing pieces which he had written for papers and magazines, and published them at his own expense, for distribution at news-stands. A copy of this now extremely rare publication fell into the hands of John Lane, the English publisher, who made Leacock an offer, and that was how *Literary Lapses* came to be published in 1910. It was a success, and was followed in 1911 by another volume of reprinted pieces, *Nonsense Novels*. Of the fifty-seven books which Leacock wrote, altogether the majority, and those which now survive, were humorous works. He made a great deal of money out of them. Indeed, one biographical article says—I do not know on what foundation—that Leacock made as much as $50,000 in a good year from his books. This seems a very great deal of money, and I think it is probably much exaggerated. But it is a fact that he achieved affluence through his writing, and would have been a rich man if he had not had a passion for investing in the stock market. We might naturally assume that a professor of economics would be an unusually shrewd investor; we would be quite wrong in making any such assumption. The temples of Wall Street, St. Catherine Street and Bay Street are built on the bones of professors with infallible systems for making a million. But during the years after forty, Leacock was in easy circumstances, and several times in his autobiographical writings he refers to this fact with pride. Any author who has tried to make money by writing will know how completely and utterly such pride was justified.

Recognition of his undoubted genius as a humorist came first in England, and quickly spread to the United States. It came much later in Canada, and when it came it was not marked by an ungovernable enthusiasm. It would be possible to offer many explanations for that state of affairs, but they would be somewhat unkind, and I shall touch on them lightly. In Leacock's heyday, which may be roughly placed between 1920 and 1935, we were not sufficiently sure of ourselves in this country to realize that a humorist may be a serious literary artist, like the man who writes books in a more sober vein. Indeed, we still retain much of that unsophisticated approach to literature which assumes that what makes easy reading must have been easy writing. We undoubtedly owe much to the earnestness and seriousness of purpose which marked our pioneer ancestors, but we may surely recognize now that there was a negative side to that condition of mind; Canada was settled, in the main, by people with a lower middle-class outlook, and a respect, rather than an affectionate familiarity, for the things of the mind. Worthy and staunch though they were, there was also a grim dreariness and meagreness of intellect about them which has shaped and darkened our educational system and which casts a damp blanket over our national spirits to this day. We can laugh, but we are a little ashamed of doing so, and we think less of the man who has moved us to mirth. We retain a sour Caledonian conviction that a man who sees life in humorous terms is necessarily a trifler. Leacock's life offers more than one example of this. I am told by a Torontonian who is in a position to know that, immediately after the First Great War, when Canada was much exercised on the Total Abstinence question, Leacock appeared in Massey Hall to give a lecture, in a state which left no one in doubt as to where *his* sympathies lay in the argument. Toronto was scandalized and Gundy, Leacock's Canadian publisher, said that for three years after this appearance not one copy of a book of Leacock's was sold there. In Canada we may know little about literature, but we are great experts on questions of Respectability.

It would be wearisome to dwell at length on what was said about Leacock by Canadian critics. One characteristic example will be enough. In the article on "Literature" in the *Encyclopaedia of Canada*, we read that "He is a kindly critic of the foibles and absurdities of humanity. He has created no outstanding character, being content to show up, with his ridiculous verbiage and boisterous fooling, the nonsense of common people about him." The tone, you will observe, is faintly patronizing. Certainly we are given no hint that a great man was at work.

It would be unjust if I failed to mention three notable exceptions to this general cool appraisal of Leacock in Canada. B. K. Sandwell knew his worth, and gave him his due. Pelham Edgar appreciated what he was, and has pointed out with cogency what he failed to be. And in the volume on Leacock in the "Makers of Canadian Literature" series, which Peter McArthur wrote in 1923, there is a remarkable appraisal of Leacock's value and also a suggestion of his potentiality which reads now like prophecy. I shall not quote fully, but I shall offer you a capsule of what McArthur says: in his view Leacock was already, at that time, being victimized by publishers and a public who could not get enough of the "ridiculous verbiage and boisterous fooling" to which Dr. Lorne Pierce refers, and was not developing as a literary artist; McArthur points out that his power of pathos is great, and that it lies in his power to be a literary artist—a novelist—of great scope. "As matters stand he is one of the truest interpreters of American and Canadian life that we have had; but by giving free play to all his powers he may finally win recognition as a broad and sympathetic

interpreter of life as a whole." That Leacock did not do so was his tragedy—and ours.

I have used the word tragedy, and I do not intend to retract it, but on the other hand I do not want to push it too hard. When a man fails to realize the finest that is in him, is it really a tragedy? When a potentially great comic writer fails to become a great novelist—such a novelist as Dickens or Mark Twain—we may certainly say that the literature of his country has sustained a heavy blow. If Leacock had developed into a genuine heavyweight novelist the course of Canadian literature during the past thirty years would have been very different. Peter McArthur thought he could do it in 1923; as we look back now over the whole body of his work we must agree with McArthur. There is in the best of Leacock a quality of sympathetic understanding, of delicacy as well as strength of perception, which suggests something far beyond the range of the man who could, in cold blood, produce a book with the flat-footed title *Funny Pieces* which he did in 1936, when he was 67 and the time for great developments had gone by.

The notion of Stephen Leacock simply as a funny fellow, who loved all mankind and passed his life in an atmosphere of easy laughter, varied with plunges into economics, must go. The notion that "ridiculous verbiage and boisterous fooling" were his special gifts, must go. There are in his books too many hints at darker things, too many swift and unmistakable descents towards melancholy, for us to be satisfied with this clownish portrait any longer. He was a man of unusual maturity of outlook, whose temperament disposed him to comment on the world as a humorist; at the top of his form he was a humorist of distinguished gifts, with a range and brilliance not often equalled. But the humour, though deep in grain, was not the essence of the man's spirit. That essence lay in the uncompromisingly adult quality of his mind, and the penetration of his glance. These were qualities which, if circumstances had been slightly different—if he had not been a humorist—might still have made him a writer of great novels, or even of tragedies. Why was it not so?

Here I approach difficult ground. Not the least of my difficulties is that I am strongly conscious of how deeply Leacock himself disliked criticism of the kind which I am about to attempt—the criticism which tries to read between the lines, which tries to throw light into dark places, which wants to open cabinets the subject has chosen to keep locked. My excuse must be the old one: great men do not belong wholly to themselves; everything that can be found out about them is of interest; their motives and their weaknesses are probed by those resurrection-men of literature, the critics. They are mauled about like Charles the Second or Charlemagne.

Leacock was proud of his huge output as a writer. He had a farmer's or a Canadian's high estimate of industry for its own sake. All his life long he got up at five o'clock in the morning, to work. He declared proudly in *Who's Who* that he published at least one book every year from 1906 to 1936. That his work became mechanical and stale, and that there was sometimes an hysterically forced note in his fun was less to him than that he wrote a funny book every year. He made ferocious fun of industrialists in *Arcadian Adventures with the Idle Rich* and *Moonbeams from the Larger Lunacy*, but he was just as much under the compulsion to work, to produce, as they were. Why did he do it?

Frankly, I think he did it to make money. He had what we may call an addicted public, like P. G. Wodehouse. There were very large numbers of people who bought every book he wrote and who read and re-read them. Such people are not critical readers; they are attracted to a writer by something special in his work, and they want that special thing repeated, over and over again. To such readers nothing is more baffling than a writer who insists on trying something new, who experiments or improves. Recently Mr. J. B. Priestley made an irritable protest when in Canada about being associated always and forever with *The Good Companions*—his first big success. Any author who is more than a hack or a society clown knows precisely how Mr. Priestley felt. To be judged by what you have left behind—that is bitter indeed. Yet Leacock seems to have embraced his chains, and gloried in ploughing the same field over and over again. I have said that I think he did it for money.

And why not, you may ask. Certainly, why not? Authors like money as well as anyone else. But authors are occasionally—not invariably—artists as well, and there are supposed to be some things which they prize even beyond money. The time must have come in Leacock's life—when he reached the age of fifty—when he had enough money, we would say.

Ah, but that is the nub of it! *We* would say it, sitting at ease in our seats of judgment, surveying his life, but would *he* have said it? Have you ever known an instance of a man who tasted the bitterness of poverty in his youth who ever felt that he had enough money in his maturity? I have known only one such instance in all my experience of rich men and he is so extraordinary as to be considered almost insane by his wealthy friends. Leacock had the wretchedness of that pioneer farm in his bones to the end; he remembered his mother's struggles to keep the ship afloat on her private income of eighty dollars a month, when he was a schoolboy. Sometimes, when he had grown old, he boasted of his affluence. But he never had enough money to set him free from the desire for more.

And that desire led him to accede to the urgencies of his publishers and of his faithful public to produce books in his familiar, well-worn vein until it was too late to do anything else. He wrote in his unfinished autobiography that poverty was one of the chief drawbacks to being a schoolteacher; he uses a phrase in this connection which sticks in the mind—he says that the teacher ought to be able to feel that he is "as good as anybody else," and he seems to associate this feeling principally with money. Scholarship, the respect paid to education (not that this has ever been a big factor in Canada), the pleasures of a well-stored mind—these things are as dross if a man has not enough money. Leacock, it seems to me, spent a great part of his life trying to show that he was "as good as anybody else." The trouble is, of course, that if you set out to prove that, and make money your standard, you have embraced a career of disappointment, for you will always find that, however much money you amass, there is somebody who has a little more, and who is therefore, by your own standard, better than you are. It is odd that an economist should have fallen into such a curious state of mind. Yet, when we read in the book on Dickens that "There is no man living who can overcome the prejudice of social disadvantages," we think of the genteel poverty of the farm on Lake Simcoe; we think of the poverty, not at all genteel, of student and schoolmastering days, and we can find it in our hearts to forgive much that was undertaken "to be as good as anybody."

I do not believe for an instant that a man of Leacock's stamp spent his life getting money simply in order to have. He wanted popularity, too. That solid audience, which bought every book, was very dear and reassuring to him. We know that he delighted, quite legitimately and rightly, in his popularity among his students. He was a man of many friendships, and apparently he could be a demanding and absorbing friend. Let me quote from a letter written to me by one who knew him:

He had an enormous gift for friendship. Almost a terrifying one, because he could consume a man. In one case, well known . . . he did. The man ceased to exist as an intellectual being after Stephen died. As a friend Stephen was too rich a diet, and too demanding for the frail. . . . I've mixed some metaphors there, but I hope my point comes through.

Leacock needed popularity, as Dickens needed it, not from simple vanity but because it was the very air on which he fed, the reassurance that he was truly the public figure he had so painstakingly built up.

Was Leacock aware that there was danger in his popularity, and in his yielding to popular demand that he repeat his effects? Yes, I think he was, for it is a strange characteristic of great men that they can anatomize the very ills which seem to be destroying them. When he wrote in his book on Dickens, "You encourage a comic man too much and he gets silly," and again that "Praise and appreciation, the very soil in which art best flourishes, may prompt too rank a growth," he certainly knew what was happening to himself. But in every man there are many men, and the underpaid young schoolmaster in Stephen Leacock, who did not feel that he was "as good as anybody else," needed that praise and that solid audience, and was not inclined to risk losing it by experiment—even if experiment meant artistic growth.

Did Leacock think of himself as an artist? Unquestionably he did. He may not have used that actual word, because it is a word which makes many people shy, but certainly he knew himself to be a man of extraordinary gifts as a writer, and he cultivated those gifts assiduously in the fashion he thought best. What is that if it is not being an artist? He took a step at which many an artist has baulked—he undertook to explain the secrets of his art in one of the most unhappy of his books—the one called *How to Write*. In it he attempts to guide the steps of the beginner, and it is not all bad—it was not possible for Leacock to write a book which was bad from start to finish. But the book is chiefly interesting for what it tells us about the writer—what he thought about himself and his work. In this book, by the way, his extraordinary talent for misquotation and misattribution reached its finest flights; it seems astonishing that his publishers would have allowed a book containing so many howlers to go forth under their imprint. Quite the most embarrassing chapters in it are the two in which he undertakes to tell his reader how to write humour.

Now Leacock could not more tell anybody how to write humour than Jove could tell them how to turn into a bull, or a swan, and for the same reason—it was his special gift, his godhead, not susceptible of analysis or explanation. Yet he could not resist giving advice on the subject, and he seized every opportunity to hold forth on the nature of humour; it was the only subject on which he was ever pompous or silly.

Only once, in the whole body of Leacock's work, have I found a passage about humour, or the writing of it, which is worthy of him. I determined when I undertook this study that I would not pad with quotations, but I hope that you will permit this one extended passage:

Once I might have taken my pen in hand to write about humour with the confident air of the acknowledged professional. But that time is past. Such claim as I had has been taken from me. In fact, I stand unmasked. An English reviewer writing in a literary journal, the very name of which is enough to put contradiction to sleep, has said of my writing, "What is there, after all, in Professor Leacock's humour but a rather ingenious mixture of hyperbole and myosis?"

The man was right. How he stumbled upon this trade secret, I do not know. But I am willing to admit, since the truth is out, that it has been my custom in preparing an article of a humorous nature, to go down to the cellar and mix up half a gallon of myosis with a pint of hyperbole. If I want to give the article a decidedly literary character, I find it well to put in about half a pint of paresis. The whole thing is amazingly simple.

Now there we have the authentic voice of Leacock, the magician who could turn the leaden words of a critical jackass into the pure gold of his own delightful fun. But in *How to Write* we are saddened by the spectacle of the same magician, so eager to be popular with his audience that he is even willing to explain how his tricks are done. (His best advice on writing remains that pungent comment: "Writing is no trouble: you just jot down ideas as they occur to you. The jotting is simplicity itself—it is the occurring which is difficult.")

Only an artist could write like Leacock at his best. And only a man who thought of himself consciously as an artist would have undertaken to explain how he did it. And only a man who yearned for popularity would have thought it desirable or wise to do so.

I have stressed his desire for popularity because I want to call your attention now to the extraordinarily successful public personality which Leacock created for himself. There may be some among you who remember that personality—the strikingly masculine impression created by the big figure with the big head and the rough mop of grey hair; the rugged face alight with intelligence and merriment, the twinkling eyes and the infectious laugh, the deep voice, which he used as skilfully as a fine actor—for Leacock was a fine actor, and perhaps the finest that Canada has ever produced. Do you really suppose that there was no calculation in the impression which he gave, in his expensive, though rumpled clothes, his dress tie usually untied, and his great watch-chain fastened to his waistcoat with a safety-pin? He was a great man; he looked and behaved like a great man; and he knew that he was doing so. Please do not suppose that I say these things in reproach: on the contrary, I say them in admiration. I, for one, have no use for a great man who creeps and crawls about the earth trying to be smaller than his natural size, for fear of giving offence to little men. But great men of Leacock's stamp know very well what they are doing. When I say that he created a public personality for himself I mean that he did so as naturally, and as inevitably, and at the same time as carefully as his great heroes and masters, Charles Dickens and Mark Twain.

The word which pursued Leacock on his lecture tours was "fun." It is a word which is a little out of favour at present, for this is not an age when fun is much understood or valued. In our day humour has become, as never before, a marketable commodity, created and sold by committees of industrious, ulcerous, clever but basically humourless men to the movies, the radio and television. We have this commercial humour, with its synthetic clangour of empty laughter from studio audiences. And we have brittle, egghead wit, so fast and wry and nervous that it is exhausting rather than refreshing in its effect. But of fun—fun in the sense that the Edwardians used the word—we have very little. Leacock was a master of fun. He convulsed his audiences by a flow of nonsense which seemed so wonderfully easy that nobody sought to analyse how it was created. In *My Discovery of England*, which I personally rank among his best books, he tells how he almost killed a man in an English audience with laughing. This account is only slightly exaggerated. People who went to Leacock's lectures laughed until they hurt themselves; they laughed until mildly disgrace-

ful personal misfortunes befell them. And Leacock laughed with them. He delighted in their laughter, and he gloried in his own power to provoke it. There was nothing of the dry humorist or the pawky joker about him. His humour was plenteous and bountiful. If at times it suggested the sledgehammer rather than the rapier, this was the negative side which cannot be dissociated from positive virtues. He was in the greatest tradition, not of wit, not of irony or sarcasm, but of the truest, deepest humour, the full and joyous recognition of the Comic Spirit at work in life.

This was the Leacock who was known to the public. Was there another? Of course there was, and anyone who reads his work with any degree of attention must be conscious, from time to time, that that other man is revealing himself. I myself was conscious of this duality long ago, when I had no thought of making any critical study of his work. The command of pathos of which Peter McArthur spoke is indeed great, but I think that there are times when the pathos and the melancholy enter his work unbidden. And if we think of the matter seriously for even a few minutes, do we not see that it must be so?

It is not Nature's way to extend a man's range far beyond the common endowment in one direction, and to make no corresponding and balancing extension in another. Great gifts carry with them great burdens. The notion of the clown who amuses the crowd while his heart is breaking is a vulgar cliché—but like many a vulger cliché it has become so because it is the fossilized remainder of a valid and universal observation. A man is not able to look deep into the heart of life and see the fun and the nonsense there, and be blind to everything else whatever. A man is not capable of being carried aloft on the most astonishing and gravity-defying flights of pure delight, without also plunging into the depths, the abysses of melancholy and suffering. Nature is mercilessly insistent on balance and her own kind of order in human personality. Because Stephen Leacock was uncommon in one direction, he had, of necessity, to be uncommon in another. Unusual sensitivity is not confined to one realm of feeling.

This is not a fancy theory which I have concocted to make myself seem wise. What I found in his work, I have been able to corroborate in his life. Again I quote from a letter from a man who knew him and whose powers of discernment are beyond the common:

> You ask about the possibility of Stephen being a melancholy person. There can be no doubt about that. He had a melancholy nature, and he endured personal sorrows which preyed upon him. I felt a distinction between the Stephen Leacock I knew as a flesh and blood person and the strange, admired, distant author. The person I knew was a strange, moody, even melancholy man, sometimes defensive among his professional colleagues and definitely short-tempered. He was prickly, quick to take offence, insecure—so the modern jargon has it but in his case, I suspect, correctly,—and on occasion damned offensive. He was also—this is not hearsay—broody and sometimes depressed and, at such times, bloody rude.

In this connection I wish to call your attention to a story which was a great favourite with Leacock. It crops up again and again in his work, when he wants to illustrate what a joke is. It will certainly be known to most of you, but in this discussion I think it has a special meaning. The story goes that, perhaps a hundred and fifty years ago, a melancholy, depressed, lacklustre individual presented himself in the consulting room of a great London physician, and asked for treatment for his immovable depression of spirits. The doctor examined him with care, and said at last, "My dear sir, there is nothing physically wrong with you, but you need cheering up. Now I suggest that you go to the theatre tonight and see the great clown, Grimaldi. He is funny beyond anything that you can imagine; he creates a whole world of amusement which will lift you quite out of yourself and leave you a better man. Come now, what do you say?" "Sir," replied the wretched patient, "I am Grimaldi."

Leacock loved that story. Many other humorists have loved it as well. They understand it better than other people.

Again and again in what he wrote about humour, Leacock stresses his belief that it should be kindly, that it should never wound, or call up any image which might give distress. He must have known that he was demanding the impossible, for humour is criticism of life, and criticism will always, at some time and in some quarter, beget resentment. The very fact of being a humorist is enough to set people against a man in certain circumstances. I recall to your minds the plight of P. G. Wodehouse, apparently the least offensive of humorists, and the darling of a million readers; yet, when he was in trouble—not really very serious trouble, as we now know—how the world turned on him! What he had done, or was supposed to have done, was made to seem twenty times worse because he was a humorist, a man who made his living by making a joke of life. Humour is not always innocent or kindly; it is a comment on life from a special point of view, and there will certainly be times when it will give sharp offence and be deeply resented—often to the astonishment of the humorist. But Leacock wanted, above all things, to be free from the charge of having wounded anyone. Was it because he was, deep within himself, aware of how deeply he might wound if he were not unfailingly vigilant?

The love of truth lies at the root of much humour. And at this point I beg leave to make a departure which may seem a curious one in a consideration of such a man as Leacock. There have been many books written about humour, which attempt to trace its sources, but none, I think, is so provocative of thought as *Wit and Its Relation to the Unconscious* by the late Sigmund Freud. It is not an easy book to read, for it suffers greatly by translation into English, and it is apt to overwhelm us with that ennui which seems to be inseparable from writings which attempt to explain why things are funny—including Leacock's own. But it makes two points which are, I think, of great importance in any study of Leacock. The first is that humour is a way of saying things which would be intolerable if they were said directly. "Out of my great sorrows I make my little songs," said Heinrich Heine: the humorist might say, with equal truth, "Out of my great disenchantments I make my little jokes."

You have all, I suppose, read Leacock's wonderful little piece called *Boarding-House Geometry?* You recall that "A single room is that which has no parts and no magnitude"? That "the clothes of a boarding-house bed, though produced ever so far both ways, will not meet"? That "a landlady can be reduced to her lowest terms by a series of propositions"? Well, my friends, read what the author of that had to say about the seventeen Toronto boarding-houses in which he spent his student days in *The Boy I Left Behind Me* and then judge if Leacock has not said the intolerable in the only permissible way.

The second of Dr. Freud's conclusions which has a bearing on Leacock's humour is his assertion—backed by demonstration and proof of a kind too extended to be gone into here—that the object of the humorist is to strip away,

momentarily, the heavy intellectual trappings of adult life, including so many things which we regard as virtues, and to set us free again in that happy condition which we enjoyed in the morning of life, when everything came to us freshly; when we did not have to make allowances for the limitations or misfortunes of others; when we did not have to be endlessly tender towards the feelings of others; when we dared to call a thing or a person stupid if they seemed stupid to us; when we lived gloriously from moment to moment, without thought for the past, or consideration for the future: when we were, indeed, as the lilies of the field. The humorist can restore us momentarily to that happy state. He pays a great price for his ability to do so, and our gratitude is by no means always forthcoming. But that is his special gift, and as the tragic writer rids us of what is petty and ignoble in our nature, the humorist rids us of much that is cautious, calculating and priggish. Both of them permit us, in blessed moments of revelation, to soar above the common level of our lives. Judged by this demanding Freudian concept of humour, Stephen Butler Leacock emerges as a great humorist, for at his best he achieves the two desired ends—speaking truth, and setting us free from common concerns—and his humour rises from a mind itself comprehensive, vigorous and well-stored beyond the common measure.

We have already referred to that element in life which philosophers call *enantiodromia* or "the regulating function of opposites"—meaning simply that nothing exists without its direct contrary. If Leacock was so dogmatic on the point that humour must never hurt may it not be because he knew, deep within himself, that the truth in which so much humour is rooted can be extremely painful when it is brought to light? Certainly he knew that this could be true of other humorists than himself; read what he has written about W. S. Gilbert for confirmation of that. And as he wrote so much that was true of himself when he seemed to be writing about Dickens, I think that he wrote some of the truth about himself when he was writing about Gilbert. Leacock had one early and striking experience of the way in which humour can hurt when, in 1912, he published what is widely regarded as his finest book, *Sunshine Sketches of a Little Town*.

This book is a minor masterpiece, and of all his books it is the one most likely to live. It was quickly recognized as a work of importance, and it was hailed everywhere in the English-speaking world—everywhere, that is to say, except in the Little Town itself. There it gave deep and lasting offence.

I well remember the first time I mentioned the book to a former citizen of Orillia; it was about 1928 and I was an enthusiastic schoolboy in the school where Leacock himself had been a pupil. I shall not soon forget the outpouring of bitterness and wounded pride which I provoked in the lady to whom I spoke. The book, I was told, was an unforgivable piece of bad taste, in which the writer had pilloried good, kind people who had never done him any harm. Leacock was a nasty, sly, sneering man who made fun of people behind their backs. He was not a gentleman. And much more to the same effect.

Death settles all scores, and Orillia now publicizes itself, somewhat aggressively, as "The Sunshine Town." But while he lived, Orillia never forgave Leacock. And he seems to have been very, very careful about giving offence in print again.

If we examine the book closely, we may see what the people of Orillia saw in it. It is a detailed portrait of an Ontario community which is not only extremely funny, but also ferocious and mordant. We are beguiled by the manner in which the book is written from giving too much attention to its matter. What it says, if we boil it down, is that the people of Mariposa were a self-important, gullible, only moderately honest collection of provincial folk; they cooked their election, they burned down a church to get the insurance, they exaggerated the most trivial incidents into magnificent feats of bravery; the sunshine in which the little town is bathed seems very often to be the glare of the clinician's lamp, and the author's pen is as sharp as the clinician's scalpel. There is love in the portrait, certainly, and indulgence for the folly of humankind. But what community has ever acclaimed a man because he showed it to be merely human? The deeper love in the book seems to be directed towards the writer's own youth, and it is made clear in the nostalgic chapters which begin and end the book that he has removed himself from Mariposa, and that any real, spiritual return is impossible, because the clock cannot be put back. We have, most of us, known Jeff Thorpe, and Judge Pepperleigh and his daughter, and Peter Pupkin, and Golgotha Gingham, and John Henry Bagshaw—but which of us would gladly admit that he was the original of one of these portraits? The humour is rooted in truth, but the truth is a very sharp knife when it is turned against our own breasts.

Leacock strove to make his humour kindly, after that. He never fully succeeded. The Old Adam which is deep in the heart of every real humorist could be heard chuckling from time to time.

Here again it would be impossible to refer to the comparison which was so often drawn, during his lifetime, between Leacock and Mark Twain. For the iron was in Mark Twain's soul, too, and there is a savagery in much of his fun which must startle any reader who has literary sensibility above the cabbage level.

But I do not see any resemblance between Leacock and Mark Twain which calls for special attention. As Leacock fell short of Mark Twain's level in his total achievement and perhaps in the scope of his genius, so he far outsoared Mark Twain in the adult quality of his mind. Mark Twain wasted a great deal of time in attempting to apply the standards of a frontiersman to things which could not be judged in that way. Leacock's affectation of frontier attitudes and habits of speech was nothing more than the intellectual fancy dress of a highly educated, sophisticated and mature being.

I have not forgotten that, quite a long time ago, I set out to give you, briefly, the facts of Leacock's life. In 1900 he married Miss Beatrix Hamilton, of Toronto. She died in 1925 of cancer. He had one son, born in 1915. Leacock himself died of cancer in Toronto on March 28, 1944, in his 75th year. (Because I have talked so much about money, and stressed the important place which I believe it played in Leacock's development, it is relevant to say here that, although his McGill salary never exceeded $6,000 per annum, and although he spent freely, speculated heavily and gave open-handedly, he left about $140,000. Neither a large sum nor yet an inconsiderable one.)

Leacock's reputation is in decline at present, and inevitably so; such declines always follow the death of a literary man, and he is happy indeed if the beginning of the decline does not anticipate his last hour. But when this melancholy, apparently inevitable period is over, he will emerge as one who, living among us, fought the solitary fight of the literary artist in a special state of loneliness, for in spite of the vast audience which admired him and waited for his work, he was lonely. He lived at a time—a time which is still not completely past— when Canada was ready to acknowledge that a poet or a novelist might be an artist, worthy of the somewhat suspicious and controlled regard which our country accords to artists, but when a humorist was obviously a clown.

Yet we must beware of blaming Canada because Leacock did not follow the pattern which became clear with the publication of *Sunshine Sketches*, and develop into a great comic novelist. The intellectual climate of the country was not congenial to such development, certainly, but we must recognize that great artists create intellectual climates, and only artists of lesser rank are distorted or diminished by them. His failure to take that road which once seemed to lie so splendidly open before him was his own, and its causes lay within his own heart. Was it because the easier road lay in writing "funny pieces, just to laugh at"? Certainly that course brought big money, widespread popularity and was taxing only upon his powers of industry. The acclaim and the money helped to salve those early wounds inflicted by poverty and the sense of not being as good as the next fellow. If there was a failure to realize the highest that lay in his power—and I think there was—that may have been at the root of it.

Nevertheless, we are in danger, when we presume to rebuke the great dead for what they failed to do, of overlooking what they did do. And if we are to appreciate Leacock for what he was, forgetting all recollections of childhood readings of his work, and dismissing the popular legend of the genial professor from our minds, we must read his books afresh, with a new measure of adult understanding. Certainly let us not neglect the four chapters of autobiography, called *The Boy I Left Behind Me*, which must rank among the finest things he ever wrote and the finest things written by Canadians. Read the earlier Leacock in the light of those frank, heartfelt and somewhat bitter chapters, and new treasures will be revealed to you.

I have now carried the task which I outlined at the beginning as far as lies in my power. I promised nothing new— only a different and I hope, revealing, arrangement of what is already known. What emerges from it? A man of great spirit, deeply troubled; a literary artist, who fought his destiny; a man whose achievement, at its highest, puts him at the very top of any list of our Canadian writers. A great countryman of ours: a man to thank God for.

## F. W. WATT

### "Critic or Entertainer? Stephen Leacock and the Growth of Materialism"

*Canadian Literature*, Summer 1960, pp. 33–42

At the turn of the century Canadian society was undergoing changes so drastic as to constitute a social revolution. The agrarian and industrial "boom" following the opening of the West brought the Canadian economy its first great period of material expansion, returned the social order to a state of flux, stimulated the speculative spirit and the accumulation of wealth, and encouraged a mood of political and commercial optimism. It was an era to which Canadian writers for the first time applied the term "materialistic". This is the era that gave birth to Stephen Leacock, Professor of Political Economy and Humorist, and, to an extent scarcely yet realized, stamped his work with its imprint.

It is the *Arcadian Adventures*, with its destructive satirical portrayal of a rampant plutocracy, that marks an extreme of social consciousness and the closest approach to sustained social criticism in Leacock's work. Nowhere else is it quite so simple a matter to see the objects of his condemnation and his standards of judgment; and nowhere else, at the same time, is the element of kindliness (which, as we shall see, he considered a necessary part of the highest form of humour) spread so thinly. Leacock's portrayal of the ethos of the plutocracy centres on the Mausoleum Club: "The Mausoleum Club stands on the quietest corner of the best residential street in the City. It is a Grecian building of white stone. About it are great elm trees with birds—the most expensive kind of birds—singing in the branches." The conjunction of childlike pastoral purity and simplicity and the artificial powers and splendours of the wealthy is an incongruity Leacock allows mainly to speak for itself:

> The sunlight flickers through the elm trees, illuminating expensive nursemaids wheeling valuable children in little perambulators. . . . Here you may see a little toddling princess in a rabbit suit who owns fifty distilleries in her own right. There, in a lacquered perambulator, sails past a little hooded head that controls from its cradle an entire New Jersey corporation. The United States is suing her as she sits, in a vain attempt to make her dissolve herself into constituent companies. . . . You may meet in the flickered sunlight any number of little princes and princesses far more real than the poor survivals of Europe. Incalculable infants wave their fifty dollar ivory rattles in an inarticulate greeting to one another. . . . And through it all the sunlight falls through the elm-trees, and the birds sing and motors hum, so that the whole world seen from the boulevard of Plutoria Avenue is the very pleasantest place imaginable.

The princes of the Old World and those of the New, the hum of the motors and the singing of the birds, small innocent children and giant soul-less capital enterprises, fifty dollar ivory rattles and elm-trees in the sunlight, all together in the same idyllic scene form an active complex of incongruities. In the next paragraph the complexity gives way momentarily to a direct and harsh contrast:

> If you were to mount to the roof of the Mausoleum Club itself on Plutoria Avenue you could almost see the slums from there. But why should you? And on the other hand, if you never went up on the roof, but only dined inside among the palm-trees, you would never know that the slums existed—which is much better.

It is significant that Leacock was typically less concerned with such overt contrasts between the palaces of the rich and the hovels of the poor than with incongruities within the life of the wealthy. He sought to explode that life's myths and belittle its attractions, rather than to attack its villainies. The wealthy exploiter in Leacock's portrayal attains none of the grandeur of evil. Thus, that "wizard of finance", Mr. Tomlinson, emerges from the darkness of his backwoods farm into the highest circles of plutocratic achievement despite his earnest attempts to avoid the greatness thrust upon him. Mere ignorance of the mysteries of finance fails him, and even his most determined violations of common sense business practice cannot make him the poor man he involuntarily left behind him. The cult of money-making is debased to the level of its newest idol, a simple, ignorant farmer whose allegedly gold-bearing farm has transformed him into "*Monsieur Tomlison, nouveau capitaine de la haute finance en Amerique*", as Paris called him, an unhappy man whose fortune grows no matter how he tries to lose it. The qualifications of the members of the Mausoleum Club appear in a changed light in their mistaken admiration for Mr. Tomlinson; they remain neither admirable, dangerous or evil, but merely objects of scepticism and ridicule.

In similar fashion when the spectre of labour unrest appears in Leacock's Arcadia, it is merely an opportunity for the wealthy to display their ludicrous self-centredness and inconsistency. "Just imagine, my dear," says one rich lady to another, "my chauffeur, when I was in Colorado, actually threatened to leave me merely because I wanted to reduce his wages. I think it's these wretched labour unions." The "wretched labour unions" threatened the very heart of Arcadia, the Mausoleum Club, by a strike of the catering staff at a moment which proved embarrassing for Mr. Fyshe, the successful financier: "Luxury!" he was exclaiming at the beginning of the sumptuous dinner scene set to trap the (non-existent) fortunes of the Duke of Dulham, "Luxury! . . . It is the curse of the age. The appalling growth of luxury, the piling up of money, the ease with which huge fortunes are made . . . these are the things that are going to ruin us." Mr. Fyshe's propensity for social revolutionary doctrine, however, did not survive the test:

> "Eh? What?" said Mr. Fyshe.
> The head waiter, his features stricken with inward agony, whispered again.
> "The infernal, damn scoundrels!" said Mr. Fyshe, starting back in his chair.
> "On strike! In this Club! It's an outrage!"

But the *Arcadian Adventures*, even though its thesis is modest and uncontentious, makes Stephen Leacock appear more of a socially purposeful satirist than he really was. His work as a whole is not contained within the level of that severe, obvious and well deserved criticism of the vices and follies of the over-privileged which is characteristic of the *Arcadian Adventures*. Nor is there more justification elsewhere for an attempt to define Leacock as a writer with serious interests in radical reform. On the contrary, Leacock looked upon himself as a humorist (that being for him the term of wider range) rather than a satirist, and freely confessed himself to be a Tory in politics. Like Lucullus Fyshe, Leacock could have claimed himself to be, on the basis of the *Arcadian Adventures*, something of a "revolutionary socialist". But in *The Unsolved Riddle of Social Justice* (1920), his most elaborate and explicit discussion of the politics and economics of contemporary society, he denied himself this possibility once and for all: the book is primarily a critique of radical idealism, an attack on the socialist answer to the "riddle of social justice". In 1907 Thorstein Veblen, whom Leacock had known during their post-graduate days at the University of Chicago, indicated his awareness of the fact that socialism for many serious exponents of radical ideas had passed out of the Utopian phase. "The socialism that inspires hope and fears today," Veblen wrote, "is the school of Marx. No one is seriously apprehensive of any other so-called socialistic movement, and no one is seriously concerned to criticise or refute the doctrines set forth by any other school of socialists."[1] Leacock himself ostensibly did not agree with or did not know this argument of his brilliant acquaintance. *The Unsolved Riddle* is concerned with refuting socialism as it is described in Edward Bellamy's *Looking Backward*; and in the fact that it repeats the task undertaken in Canada by Goldwin Smith a generation before, it suggests the course of thought (or lack of it) on such matters undergone by certain portions of the Canadian intelligentsia during these years. "The scheme of society outlined in '*Looking Backward*'," Leacock asserted, without alluding to other socialist writings, "may be examined as the most attractive and the most consistent outline of a socialist state that has, within the knowledge of the present writer, been put forward . . . No better starting point for the criticism of collectivist theories can be found than in a view of the basis on which is supposed to rest the halcyon life of Mr. Bellamy's charming commonwealth." "Nor was ever," he claimed, "a better presentation made of the essential program of socialism." Without undue difficulty Leacock succeeded in knocking down this idealist of a former era. Socialism, he concluded his analysis, would function admirably in a community of saints, but for ordinary human beings it would be unworkable. "With perfect citizens any government is good," he argued (apparently he was no more aware than the theorist he was criticizing that the public and private virtues, the motives of the individual and the organization of social relations, are never in a simple causal relationship). "In a population of angels a socialistic commonwealth would work to perfection. But until we have the angels we must keep the commonwealth waiting." The movement towards socialism, he warned, using the apocalyptic image that runs through the book, will lead "over the edge of the abyss beyond which is chaos."

Not only did Stephen Leacock differ with socialism, as he saw it, in regard to solving the problem of social justice, but, as one would expect, he differed in his analysis of the conditions which gave rise to socialism. He saw the same kind of inequalities and incongruities in the materialistic society of 1920 as did the radicals:

> Few persons can attain adult life without being profoundly impressed by the appalling inequalities of our human lot. Riches and poverty jostle one another upon our streets. The tattered outcast dozes on his bench while the chariot of the wealthy is drawn by. The palace is the neighbour of the slum. We are, in modern life, so used to this that we no longer see it.

But Leacock's emphasis was different. While socialists were crying out against the suffering of the underprivileged, Leacock counselled against what he assured the reader was a kind of sentimentality which might lead to unfortunate social consequences:

> An acquired indifference to the ills of others is the price at which we live. A certain dole of sympathy, a casual mite of personal relief is the mere drop that any one of us alone can cast into the vast ocean of human misery. Beyond that we must harden ourselves lest we too perish.
>
> We make fast the doors of our lighted houses against the indigent and the hungry. What else can we do? If we shelter *one* what is that? And if we try to shelter all, we ourselves are shelterless.

For Leacock the root of social evils lay not at all in the nature of the political or economic system, but entirely in the nature of man. Thus, the war of 1914–18 for Leacock was a demoralizing force because it gave cause for an outbreak of the old Adam: "A world that has known five years of fighting has lost its taste for the honest drudgery of work. Cincinnatus will not go back to his plow, or, at the best, stands sullenly between his plow-handles arguing for a higher wage." But Leacock's most important difference with the socialists was in regard to the concept of freedom. Leacock, in the tradition of nineteenth century Liberalism, maintained that in his society the individual, whatever his hardships, was a free agent; the socialists were arguing that political freedom was meaningless in the face of economic slavery. Leacock wrote:

> Yet all [men in our society] are free. This is the distinguishing mark of them as children of our era. They may work or stop. There is no compulsion from without. No man is a slave. Each has his 'natural liberty', and each in his degree, great or small, receives his allotted reward.

But although Leacock was conservative in his rejection of the blueprint state, and in his refusal to "sentimentalize" the lower levels of society, his awareness of the vices of modern industrial civilization did not allow him easily to become an uncritical spokesman for reactionary Toryism. In the *Unsolved Riddle*, while condemning socialism, he also condemned the nineteenth century doctrine of laissez-faire individualism. Fifteen years later in the midst of the Great Depression, his was a somewhat chastened and reformed individualism: "I believe," he wrote, "that the only possible basis for organized society is that of every man for himself—for himself and those near and dear to him. But on this basis must be put in operation a much more efficient and much more just social mechanism."

There was something remarkably anachronistic about Leacock's failure (though himself an economist) to understand those economic factors of the modern world which were making freedom and individualism in any simple sense impossible. In 1936 he complained:

> I cannot bear to think that the old independent farming is to go: that the breezy call of incense breathing morn is to be replaced by the time-clock of a regimented, socialized, super-mechanized land-factory. We must keep the farmers. If they cannot regulate the 'how much' of their production, let them, as they used to, raise all they damn can, and then fire it around everywhere—pelt one another with new-mown hay and sugar beets. But don't lets lose them.

If such gaiety and gusto seem a little remote from the actual conditions of farming and marketing in the mid-thirties, on the other hand Leacock had no illusions about rural life as such, despite such parables of its virtues triumphing over the decadence of the city as that of Mr. Tomlinson, "wizard of finance". Having been raised on an Ontario farm "during the hard times of Canadian farming", Leacock could claim as he did in the Preface to *Sunshine Sketches of a Little Town* that he had seen "enough of farming to speak exuberantly in political addresses of the joy of early rising and the deep sleep, both of body and intellect, that is induced by honest toil."

Leacock has been described (by Desmond Pacey) as a "country squire" upholding the "eighteenth century values: common sense, benevolence, moderation, good taste",[2] but he apparently believed there was nothing in his own age which approximated or even partially embodied these values. The mild eighteenth century satire of Addison and Steele, certainly, was based on the kind of positive faith in man and in society which Leacock frequently and explicitly renounced. Leacock's attitude was more akin to that of cynicism, the cynicism of Diogenes, for example, of whom it has been said:

> He would deface all the coinage current in the world. Every conventional stamp was false. The men stamped as generals and kings; the things stamped as honour and wisdom and happiness and riches; all were base metal with lying superscription.

Leacock's extensive dissertation, *Humor, Its Theory and Technique* (1935), reveals more about the author than perhaps any other of his works. Especially it throws light on the basic attitudes which led Leacock to squander his talents in a mass of books turned out for the Christmas book-trade, to use his humour sparingly as a weapon or a tool of criticism, and by and large to accept the social *status quo* despite his criticism of it, rather than to try to alter it. In that work there is, indeed, praise for the two "greatest" humorists, Charles Dickens and Mark Twain, because each in his own way "sought as a part of his work to uplift the world with laughter." There is also condemnation for those modern writers who merely aimed at pleasing the masses, the "ten-cent crowd":

> Please the public! That's the trouble today . . . with everything that is written to be printed or acted, everything drawn, sung, or depicted. Nothing can appear unless there is money in it . . . It is the ten-cent crowd that are needed if profits are to be made, not the plutocrats. Hence has been set up in our time an unconscious tyranny of the lower class. The snobbishness of the term may pass without apology in view of the truth of the fact . . . It is the wishes and likings of the mass which largely dictate what the rest of us shall see and hear.

But these remarks cannot be taken as support for a kind of humour which is devoted to immediate social or moral purposes. On the contrary, Leacock has just as little use for that type: "Much of our humour now—dare one say, especially in America?—is over-rapid, snarling, and ill-tempered. It is used to 'show things up', a vehicle of denunciation, not of pleasure." The satirical aspect of humour must always mind itself lest it become simply "mockery, a thing debased and degraded from what it might have been." Somewhere in the course of history, "mere vindictiveness parted company with humor, and became its hideous counterpart, mockery", but still "too much of the humor of all ages, and far too much of our own, partakes of it."

The highest humour, then, is such that it will uplift the world but nevertheless avoid denunciation and mockery. Leacock apparently sees this type in the portrayal of Mr. Pickwick, for example, who "walks through life conveying with him the contrast between life as it might be and life as it is." Humour of this kind depends on a clearly understood and firmly held pattern of values, manners, and presuppositions. The difficulty arises when one attempts to infer such a pattern from Leacock's own works. *Sunshine Sketches* holds out the best promise of such a pattern, and readers have professed to find it there. Leacock's Preface offered the lead, touching as it does at its conclusion tenderly on the "land of hope and sunshine where little towns spread their square streets and their trim maple trees beside placid lakes almost within echo of the primeval forest," and asserting the "affection" at the basis of its portrayal. Mariposa, the most peaceful and the most foolish of small towns, stands as an unconscious critique of the big city ways it tries to ape. Yet Mariposa itself does not contain a pattern or even hints of the good life, unless we choose to pitch our understanding at the level of the beguiling narrator. There is nothing admirable, nothing fine, nothing dignified, nothing sacred in Leacock's portrayal of the little town: all its coinage is defaced. The only virtues are its sunshine and its littleness, its failure to achieve the larger vices of modern industrial urbanism, hard as it tries to do so.

One is tempted to say that Mariposa's curiously nostalgic appeal lies not in its positive attractions but in its success in transforming great evils into small, its rendering innocuous if not innocent the worst aspects of our modern world. Much of Leacock's writing answers to the same formula. "In retrospect," Leacock claimed in his book on humour, "all our little activities are but as nothing, all that we do has in it a touch of the pathetic, and even our sins and wickedness and crime are easily pardoned in the realization of their futility." It is by this perspective that *Sunshine Sketches* charms the reader, by making the "real" pleasantly innocent, not by comparing it with the "ideal", the "might have been". We are perhaps to understand that humour "uplifts" the reader by bringing him to this Olympian height of contemplation. In Leacock's philosophy the ideal is illusory. On occasion he himself may have

looked back longingly at "the wholesome days of the eighties or nineties," or at the simple life of the farmer, but at other times he repudiated such attempts to escape the present:

> Each age sees the ones that preceded it through a mellow haze of retrospect; each looks back to the good old days of our fore-fathers . . . Each of us in life is a prisoner. We are set and bound in our confined lot. Outside, somewhere, is infinity. We seek to reach into it and the pictured past seems to afford us an outlet of escape.

But in the end, "Escape is barred."

Humour as Leacock conceived it lay at the heart of his philosophy, in fact *was* his philosophy:

> . . . humor in its highest meaning and its furthest reach . . . does not depend on verbal incongruities, or on tricks of sight and hearing. It finds its basis in the incongruity of life itself, the contrast between the fretting cares and the petty sorrows of the day and the long mystery of the tomorrow. Here laughter and tears become one, and humor becomes the contemplation and interpretation of our life. In this aspect the thought of the nineteenth century far excelled all that had preceded it. The very wistfulness of its new ignorance—contrasted with the barren certainty of bygone dogma—lends it something pathetic.

The allusion to nineteenth century agnosticism is by no means irrelevant. It is the doubt about man's ultimate significance that provides the basis for humour at its highest, for the universe itself is a kind of "joke" in which the trivial and futile aspirations of mankind are the crowning incongruity. Humour

> . . . represents an outlook upon life, a retrospect as it were, in which the fever and the fret of our earthly lot is contrasted with its shortcomings, its lost illusions and its inevitable end. The fiercest anger cools; the bitterest of hate sleeps in the churchyard and over it all there spread Time's ivy and Time's roses, preserving nothing but what is fair to look upon.

Presumably the best joke of all, conducive to the most tears and the most laughter combined, will be the apocalypse as Leacock describes it:

> Thus does life, if we look at it from sufficient distance, dissolve itself into 'humor'. Seen through an indefinite vista it ends in a smile. In this, if what the scientist tells us is true, it only offers a parallel to what must ultimately happen to the physical universe in which it exists. . . At some inconceivable distance in time . . . the universe ends, finishes; there is nothing left of it but nothingness. With it goes out in extinction all that was thought of as matter, and with that all the framework of time and space that held it, and the conscious life that matched it. All ends with a cancellation of forces and comes to nothing; and our universe ends thus with one vast, silent unappreciated joke.

For Stephen Leacock as cynic there was no "might have been" except in a wistful and illusory nostalgia, and even here his sense of the follies and shortcomings of men would not allow him to be blinded. It was easier for him, with his belief in the futility of man's petty actions to take his role of artist lightly, to observe the evils of his society without bitterness or indignation, accepting and defending the world as he found it, and to turn his irreverent humour on every aspect of experience and upon all manner of people and things. But perhaps after all he was less like Diogenes, who also credited the world with no virtue, yet who asked its princes nothing in return but that they "stand a little out of his light", than like that other cynic, Teles, who taught the doctrine of self-love and received money from the hands of rich patrons with words like these: "You give liberally and I take valiantly from you, neither grovelling nor

demeaning myself basely nor grumbling." For Stephen Leacock was a part of the prospering materialistic civilization of which he wrote; he was sometimes its critic, but always its entertainer.

*Notes*

1. I. Kipnis. *The American Socialist Movement*, p. 4.
2. Desmond Pacey. *Creative Writing in Canada*. p. 101.

# URSULA K. LE GUIN

## 1929–

Ursula Kroeber was born on October 21, 1929, in Berkeley, California, the youngest child of the eminent anthropologists Alfred and Theodora Kroeber. Raised in an atmosphere of constant intellectual exploration, the young Ursula read voraciously in world literature and myth. For a while during her childhood she read the pulp science fiction of the day, particularly admiring the work of "Lewis Padgett" (Henry Kuttner and C. L. Moore). However, she soon tired of the formulas of the genre and its reliance on technological gimmickry, and progressed to other sorts of fiction, such as the fantasies of Lord Dunsany, to which her father had introduced her. In 1947 she entered Radcliffe, graduating with an B.A. in 1951; an M.A. from Columbia in French and Italian Renaissance literature followed in 1952. That same year she won a Fulbright scholarship enabling her to study the works of the poet Jean Lemaire de Belges in France; while aboard the *Queen Mary* on the way, she met Charles Le Guin, a young history professor. They were married in Paris that December, and she returned to the United States with him without having completed the work towards her doctorate.

Throughout the 1950s, as the couple moved from place to place, Le Guin wrote poetry and fiction; a few poems and one short story appeared in little magazines, but it was not until a friend loaned her a 1960 issue of *The Magazine of Fantasy and Science Fiction* with a story by Cordwainer Smith in it that Le Guin came to realize that her future might lie in the SF genre. That it did was confirmed when, in 1962, Cele Goldsmith published Le Guin's short story "April in Paris" in the September 1962 issue of *Fantastic*. This first sale was followed by several more short stories in the SF magazines over the next few years, and Le Guin's first three published novels. In 1967 a publisher of children's books offered Le Guin complete freedom to write a fantasy for older children; the result was *A Wizard of Earthsea* (1968), which won the Boston Globe–Horn Book Award, and its sequels *The Tombs of Atuan* (1971) and *The Farthest Shore* (1972), the latter winning a National Book Award in children's literature. Meanwhile, in 1969 Le Guin published her fourth SF novel, *The Left Hand of Darkness*, a complex tale of an androgynous race, set in the same "Hainish" universe as were her first three books. This novel won her both the Hugo and the Nebula awards for that year, putting her in the front rank of SF writers where she has remained since. In 1971 she published *The Lathe of Heaven*, a novel of shifting, mutable realities which she has referred to as her "*hommage à* Philip K. Dick." 1974 saw the publication of *The Dispossessed*, perhaps her most famous work so far; her last novel set in the "Hainish" continuum to date, it contains strong utopian and dystopian elements, but subtly subverts both. Again winning both the Hugo and Nebula awards, Le Guin accepted the Hugo at the World Science Fiction Convention in Melbourne, Australia, in 1975, where she also delivered an impassioned speech exhorting the SF community to "tear down the ghetto walls."

Since then Le Guin, never comfortable with the limitations of artificial publishing categories, has published work that challenges and redefines the boundaries of her genres. Among her more recent work has been *Orsinian Tales* (1976), a cycle of short stories set in a mythical Central European country, and *Always Coming Home* (1985), a complex fiction of the lives and myths of a hunting-and-gathering culture in a Northern California several centuries after a nuclear war. Her short stories have been collected in two books so far: *The Wind's Twelve Quarters* (1975) and *The Compass Rose* (1982). In 1979 she published a collection of essays and criticism about science fiction and fantasy, *The Languages of the Night*.

Ursula K. Le Guin and her husband Charles live in Portland, Oregon, where he is a professor of history. They have two daughters and a son.

## DOUGLAS BARBOUR
*"The Lathe of Heaven: Taoist Dream"*
Algol, November 1973, pp. 22–24

Ever since Falk turned for help to "the Old Canon" in *City of Illusions*, the *Tao* has been one of the major foci of Ursula K. Le Guin's artistic vision. Nowhere is the *Tao* more central than in *The Lathe of Heaven*,[1] a novel that is practically a primer in Taoist thought. James Blish calls it an allegory, but points out that, unlike most allegories, "It is also a true novel. The people breathe and feel; and informing every word of it is the perception that history and psychology are allied processes, that every 'I' is in large part—though not entirely—an accretion of what has happened to it, good and bad alike; to undo history is to undo man."[2]

Such are the morals to be drawn from this work: lessons about ends and means; the dangers of living completely by the technological thrust to the future; how one should best follow the Way. Le Guin is "not very fond of moralistic tales, for they often lack charity"; she obviously prefers "to play with . . . ideas"[3] in her fictions. In *LH* many of the ideas are Taoist, many are speculations on dreaming, and the literary games she plays are very complex indeed.

All the chapters have epigraphs (and all the epigraphs are relevant): chapters 5 and 8 quote *Tao*, 18 and 5; chapters 1, 2, 3, 9, and 11 quote the *Chuang Tzu*. But however cogently epigraphs may comment on the story, they do not make up its body the way internal allusions can. The descriptions of George Orr, contrasting his sanity and balance with the overweaning power-madness of Haber, are often specifically Taoist, and their images carry a specific weight of meaning. Orr is an unconscious Taoist sage; he has never tried to become what he so obviously is: a man who quite unselfconsciously obeys the dictates of *Tao*, 5: "It is better to keep to the center." (Chan, 107) Orr, the 'middleman,' becomes important because he finds himself in a frightening situation: an outrageous objectification of Prospero's famous speech on dreams and worlds in *The Tempest*. As Blish says, Le Guin has invented "an entirely new para-psychological power" for Orr: his power of "effective dreaming." The whole novel pivots on his ability to quite literally change the world with his dreams. Orr's talent exists in *LH*; the narrative speculates what should be done with such power.

Orr's answer is simple: nothing. "Tao invariably takes no action, and yet there is nothing left undone." (*Tao*, 37, Chan, 166) In fact, Orr wants to rid himself of his power because, like it or not, he sometimes exercises it, and he *knows* that's not good. The psychologist Haber, a very different person, always seeks to know "what he should *do*" (9), and he has a very different answer. Even before he allows himself to believe that Orr really has the power to change reality, he sets about using that power (and thus using Orr) to create a better world "for the good of all." (149) Haber and Orr are totally opposed. Evaluation of that opposition is the moral heart of this novel, best expressed in the conversation about "purpose" on p. 81, which, with its neat turn on the fact that Orr knows nothing about the Eastern religions Haber taunts him with, thoroughly reveals the deep differences between the two men. Orr is *not* a *student* of Eastern mysticism: he is merely and completely himself. In this integrity lies his salvation, not in any theoretical knowledge he might possess. Nevertheless, his position is completely Taoistic and his comments on function are very reminiscent of Chuang Tzu's on usefulness (Watson, 59–63). Haber's further arguments with Orr (139–151) deepen

our understanding of the basic conflict, but the issue has long been clear.

*LH* is a complexly organized novel, told from the perspectives of Orr, Haber, and Heather Lelache (who is not always 'alive' in Orr's changing worlds). Ideas and their personal human embodiments are presented, and we respond both emotionally as well as intellectually to them. As the story is told in the third person, changes in character, such as Haber's increasing blindness concerning his own will to power, or Heather's change of character when Orr dreams her back as his "grey" wife, can be registered with oblique subtlety, the narrative proceeding from without as well as within them.

"In the *Lao Tzez* water, the infant, the female, the valley, and the uncarved block are used as models for a life according to Tao" (Chan, 13). These 'models' are used as images to describe Orr at various points in *LH* but nowhere more obviously than during Heather's realization that Orr is the man for her:

> It was more than dignity. Integrity? Wholeness? like a block of wood not carved.
> The infinite possibility, the unlimited and unqualified wholeness of being of the uncommitted, the nonacting, the uncarved being who, being nothing but himself, is everything.
> Briefly she saw him thus, and what struck her most, of that insight, was his strength. He was the strongest person she had ever known, because he could not be moved away from the center. And that was why she liked him. . . .
> Here, short, bloodshot, psychotic, and in hiding, here he was, her tower of strength.
> Life is the most incredible mess, Heather thought. You never can guess what's next. (96)

The last two paragraphs reveal the kind of sharp wit that plays throughout the novel, to my great delight at any rate. Vhan's comment on the uncarved block of *Tao*, 15 is relevant to her insight:

> It connotes simplicity, plainness, genuineness in spirit and heart, and similar qualities. . . . Significantly, simplicity does not mean blankness. As a state of mind it is characterized by care, openness, the balance of tranquility and activity, and other positive qualities. (Chan, 126)

These positive qualities are associated with Orr throughout the novel. Even his stutter (41, 43, etc.) is sage-like: "The greatest eloquence seems to stutter." (*Tao*, 45, Chan, 180) but there are complexities, for Orr lost the centre the time of his first major effective dream: when he dreamed the world back after it had ended! Under the influence of sleep-preventing drugs, and then under Haber's control, he loses more and more of his sense of equilibrium. Then the aliens (whom he dreamed into being!) offer him some help. In a very difficult passage (141–145) Orr *arrives* at the centre again, during a waking dream in which an alien offers him the following advice:

> "We also have been variously disturbed. Concepts cross in mist. Perception is difficult. Volcanoes emit fire. Help is offered: refusably. Snakebite serum is not prescribed for all. Before following directions leading in wrong directions, auxiliary forces[4] may be summoned, in immediate-following fashion: Er' perrehne!" (142)

If J. A. Hadfield is correct, dreams are a biological mechanism by which the subconscious, selecting materials from both the unconscious and conscious minds, attempts to solve one's problems.[5] The solution for Orr has something to do with getting by "with a little help / With a little help from my friends" (157) as the Beatles record suggests. Since "what came would be acceptable" (157) what comes is good: the return of Heather as his wife. The 'friends' could be his own dream-powers, acting freely since he no longer fears them.

The climax to the novel comes when Haber tries to dream effectively, and "the emptiness of Haber's being, the effective nightmare, radiating outward from the dreaming brain, undoes connections." (176) Orr, with a little help from his friends, turns Haber off. He loses everything, it seems, and he even comes to accept this. But Heather *is* there, black once more, to be won again. Orr, at the centre, waits patiently, and eventually she appears along the Way.

There are Taoist references to Haber too, always negative ones. For Haber doesn't "like to waste time on means, getting to the desired end was the thing." (20) He is a doer, a man of action, and *Tao*, 38 is a pertinent comment on his attitude. Haber's contempt for Orr, like his curt dismissal of a colleague's comments that Orr's placing on the psychology tests reveals his "holistic adjustments" (138), demonstrates his basic insensitivity. Haber talks all the time, and "he who speaks does not know," (*Tao*, 56, Chan, 199) "He seemed not to know the uses of silence." (165) The *Tao* is quite clear about such uses, and about the value of those who live by too much speech. The citizen's arrest (135) provides a frightening glimpse of Haber's HURAD-controlled world: it is the very evil government *Tao*, 57 and 58 rail against. Haber is, as the carved legend on the HURAD building indicates, a Utilitarian. That philosophy and Lao Tzu's are irremediably at odds, for Lao Tzu and Chuang Tzu will always seek non-action: they look at the world and "Let it be!" (Watson, 33) The Tao clearly indicates that the end and the means are one: the Way itself. Orr realizes this, and lives by it; Haber, a perfect product of "the Judaeo-Christian-Rationalist West," (81) cannot see it, and thus loses the Way, and the world, altogether. Moreover, and this is the point of the steady deterioration of the fabric of existence under Haber's guidance of Orr's "effective dreams," the greatest good for the greatest number ignores the individual and his sense of personal 'reality.' Not that everyone shouldn't have a chance at a good world, but one person's idea of that good world shouldn't be shoved down their throats. This is why Le Guin not only uses her narratives to suggest possible alternatives to the totally materialistic technological philosophy of the West, which Haber perfectly represents and which is forcing a single kind of 'reality' upon us all, but chooses the Tao to provide a metaphoric basis for the imaging forth of those alternatives. Tao has a human face, as most technology has not.

There is much more to this novel than mere presentation of basic Taoist philosophy, brilliant characterization and great wit, especially where the fiction seems to be commenting on its own changing 'reality,' and Le Guin's usual fine stylistic control, but there can be little doubt that Taoism is deeply embedded in it. Le Guin's very real achievement here is to have provided so much thought in such a highly readable and moving manner, gripping our imaginations with her tale of disintegrating 'realities' even as she explores the morality of a situation that can lead to such happenings. *The Lathe of Heaven* is first of all fiction of very high quality, and only secondarily a moral allegory of no little force.

*Notes*

1. (New York, 1971). I'm going to refer to it as *LH* in the body of this article. All page references will be to the hardcover edition published by Scribner's. Avon has recently published the paperback. There are two major works in Taoism: the *Tao* or *Lao Tzu*, and the *Chuang Tzu*. The editions I used are, Wing-tzit Chan (ed., trans.), *The Way of Lao-Tzu* (New York, 1963) and Burton

Watson (trans.), *Chuang Tzu: Basic Writings* (New York, 1964). All references will be to the chapter of the *Tao* and the page in Chan, or to the page in Watson.
2. "Books," *Fantasy and Science Fiction* (July, 1972), p. 63.
3. See her "Afterward," in *Again, Dangerous Visions*, ed. Harlan Ellison (New York, 1972), p. 108.
4. All the images in this speech fit into a careful pattern of imagery built up through the whole novel: they are *not* merely relevant *at this point*.
5. J. A. Hadfield, *Dreams & Nightmares* (Harmondsworth, 1966), pp. 65–128. Le Guin refers specifically to his theories in her "Afterward" in *Again, Dangerous Visions*.

## SAMUEL R. DELANY
From "To Read *The Dispossessed*"
*The Jewel-Hinged Jaw*
1977, pp. 243–49, 274–78, 297–308

### II

The opening paragraph of *The Dispossessed* begins (p. 1/1)[1]: "There was a wall. It did not look important." These two short sentences raise, shimmering about this wall, the ghosts of those to whom, indeed, it does not look important; these ghosts wait to be made manifest by a word. The third sentence reads: "It was built of uncut rocks roughly mortered." Were this book mundane fiction this sentence would be merely a pictorial descript. Because it is science fiction, however, the most important word in the sentence is "uncut." To specify the rocks of the wall are uncut suggests that somewhere else within the universe we shall be moving through there are walls of *cut* rock. The ghosts shimmer beside those shimmering walls as well: we are dealing with a society that probably has the technology to cut rock—though for this particular wall (possibly because it was built before the technology was available) the rocks are whole. The fourth sentence reads: "An adult could look right over it; even a child could climb it." Because I have learned my language the way I have, from the black colloquial speech into which I was born, from family and neighborhood variations on it, from school-time spent largely with the children of East Coast intellectuals, from the pulp developments of Sturgeon and Bester on the language of Chandler and Hammett, from the neo-Flaubeteans and Mallarmeans whose chief spokesmen were Stein and Pound ("The natural object is always the adequate symbol"—1913), and whose dicta filtered down through voices like John Ciardi's, Elizabeth Drew's, and a host of other popularizers to form the parameters around which my language in adolescence organised itself, I hear, embedded in that sentence, a different and simpler set of words: "An adult could look over it; a child could climb it." Without asking what *this* sentence means—for it is not part of the text under consideration—we can limit our examination of the sentence that does appear by asking only about those aspects of the meaning that differ from the simpler sentence it suggests. In terms of the difference, I hear in the sentence that actually appears a certain tone of voice, a tone that asks to be taken both as ingenuous and mature, that tries to side with the adult ("right") and condescends to the child ("even a child"); these hints of smugness and condescention betray an unsettling insecurity with its own stance. The sentence protests its position too much. Because, in language, what comes now revises and completes our experience of what came before, this insecurity shakes the till-now adequate mortaring of the three sentences previous; this fourth sentence inadvertently asks us to listen for the echoes of any ponderousness or pontification that may linger from the others.

The echoes are there.

The fifth sentence reads: "Where it crossed the roadway, instead of having a gate it degenerated into mere geometry, a line, an idea of a boundary." We note that the phrase "instead of having a gate it degenerated into mere geometry" is mere fatuousness. If there is an idea here, *degenerate, mere* and *geometry* in concert do not fix it. They bat at it like a kitten at a piece of loose thread. Both "a line, an idea of a boundary" and the next paragraph (that the readers may check for themselves) suggest the referent is more likely topology than geometry; but perhaps it is the gestalt persistence of forms, or subjective contour that is being invoked; or, from the rest of the scene, perhaps it is merely, "Gates are not needed to keep people out." At any rate, it is so muzzy and unclear one cannot really say from *this* sentence what the idea is. We read the next: "But the idea was real." Since ideas are, this statement of the obvious only draws our attention to the non-expression of the idea in the statement before. The next sentence reads: "It was important." Even if we do not take this as over-protestation, we experience here a dimming and dispersing of those ghosts (to whom the wall looked *un*important) our second sentence called up. "For seven generations there had been nothing more important in the world than that wall." The ghosts have vanished.

I feel cheated by their dispersal, even more than I do by the "degeneration into mere geometry." The only person to whom that wall would look unimportant is some Victorian traveler who, happening accidentally upon the scene, would have noticed hardly anything out of the ordinary—a presence, a voice, a literary convention completely at odds with the undertaking.

In summary, so much in this paragraph speaks of a maturity, a profundity which, when we try to gaze to its depths by careful reading, reveals only muddy water, that what seems to stand with any solidity when the rest is cleared is:

"There was a wall of roughly mortared, uncut rocks. An adult could look over it; a child could climb it. Where the road ran through, it had no gate. But for seven generations it had been the most important thing in that world."

For the rest, it is the 1975 equivalent of Van Vogtian babble. And that babble, in Le Guin as in Van Vogt, suggests a vast distrust of the image itself—for a stone wall with no gate ("The natural object . . ."—Pound) gives all the look of unimportance such a wall would need to justify to the reader the "But . . ." of our last sentence. Filling up the empty gateway with degenerate geometry, topology, or subjective contour only sabotages the imagistic enterprise.

Because the book is science fiction, and because in science fiction the technology is so important, we wonder why the author did not use one of the ghostly sister walls of *cut* rock to sound the implicit technological resonance in a major key. When the whole book is read, and we return to commence our second reading, the image evoked of the first generation of Annaresti, newly off the spaceship, piling up rocks around the to-be spaceport like so many New Hampshire farmers, seems closer to surrealism than science fiction without some historical elaboration—but this sort of questioning is impelled by the momentum lent from the sum of all that opening paragraph's other disasters. It is not really to our purpose.

What is to our purpose?

That many of the images in Le Guin's work, as in Van Vogt's, are astonishing and powerful. And the larger point one wants to make to the Le Guins, the Silverbergs, the Ellisons (and even the Malzbergs) of our field: if all that verbal baggage meant nothing, there would be no fault. But it does mean, and

what it means is overtly at odds with the image's heart. That is what identifies it as baggage.

The way I have learned my language impells me to make another point here. While it is fair to analyse current, written American in the way I just have, it is totally unreasonable to analyse in this way the language, say, of the mother of the author of *Lady into Fox*. And to be an American intellectual of a certain (pre-Magershack) age is to have read more English prose by Constance Garnett than probably any other single English writer except Dickens. Nevertheless, Garnett's language, both because it is translation and because it is translation *into* the language of another country at another historical moment, is not ours. But too frequently the locutions and verbal signifiers that recall Garnett or other translatorese are scattered through contemporary American as signs of a "European" or "Russian" profundity that the texts simply do not have. Or, if the signs are not from translatorese, they are the borrowed accoutrements of that Victorian traveler, used to counterfeit a Victorian breadth or grandeur. This is pathetic.

I hope it is clear that I am not saying we cannot read works in translation (or Victorian novels). We can get vast amounts of information, both denotative and connotative, about their intended texture, structure, and substance. We can get such information from a translation (or from a book written at another moment in the development of our own language and culture) *because* languages are structurally stable systems. We are not talking about what is lost in the translation from the language of another time or place. We are talking about what is gained by writing in our own.

### III

What works in this science fiction novel?

The weaving through various textual moments of the image "stone." Passive, it appears in walls; active, hurled, it kills a man on the Defense Crew; another wings Shevek's shoulder. Moments later Annares itself in a stone falling away on a view screen (to wound or wing what . . . ?). The fragment "But the rock will never hit . . ." (p. 6/5) among Shevek's muddled thoughts presages, eighteen pages later (p. 25/23), a younger Shevek's spontaneous discovery of Zeno's paradox. "Are we stones on Annares?" (p. 13/12) Shevek asks Dr. Kimoe at one point. The web of resonances the word weaves through the text gives a fine novelistic density.

The first chapter's image of time as an arrow (between "river" and "stone") develops into half the controlling metaphor by which we are given (popularized) Shevek's scientific theory during Vea's party, as well as those theories that speak ". . . only of the arrow of time—never of the circle of time," (p. 197/179). What works is that image's resolution in Chapter Eleven, when Shevek is with the Terran Ambassador Keng in the old River Castle in Rodarred, now the Terran Embassy. At one point, as he discusses with her his plan to broadcast his coveted theory to all:

Shevek got up and went over to the window, one of the long, horizontal slits of the tower. There was a niche in the wall below it, into which an archer would step up to look down and aim at assailants at the gate; if one did not take that step up one could see nothing from it but the sunwashed, slightly misty sky (p. 307/280).

What works is the way in which the discussion of the conflicting "Sequency" and "Simultaneity" theories of time reflect the macrostructure of the novel itself, with its ordered, pendulating chapters, crossing time and space which is, by semantic extension, the goal of Shevek's theory.

What works is the way, on Annares, a sign is charged with

sexuality: First, a film of the Urrasti women's "oiled, brown bellies" (p. 37/33) presented in a context of death (corpses of children, funeral pyres), transformed, in one Annaresti boy's discourse: "I don't care if I never see another picture of foul Urrasti cities and greasy Urrasti bodies," (p. 38/34). Pages later, the transformation moves through another stage with the first description of (the then unidentified) Takvar: "Her lips were greasy from eating fried cakes and there was a crumb on her chin," (p. 53/48). Nearly a hundred pages later, this sex/oil/grease/food transition moved a stage further, when Takvar acquires a name and a further description:

> She had the laugh of a person who liked to eat well, a round, childish gape. She was tall and rather thin with round arms and broad hips. She was not very pretty, her face was swarthy, intelligent, and cheerful. In her eyes there was a darkness, not the opacity of bright dark eyes but a quality of depth, almost like deep, black, fine ash, very soft (p. 157/143).

One could attack this paragraph just as we did the first. We will make do, however, merely with a mention that the whole discourse of "cute/pretty/beautiful," even applied in the negative, does more to subvert the image than support it. One suspects that those to whom Takvar "was not very pretty" are the same ghosts to whom the wall "did not look important." But it is the text itself, as we pointed out in our analysis of the first paragraph, that disperses these ghosts—which is why the phrases, sentences, and ideas that are put in to placate and appease them register as aesthetic failings, or at best as a residue from an unconscious struggle in the author that, while we appreciate it, is inappropriate to the story unless brought consciously forward. Nevertheless, the locus of the erotic from its inception in the text to this most believable resting place is very real; and it is subtly supported by all the book implies about Annaresti agriculture and eating habits. This aspect of the book is novelistically and, more, science fictionally fine.

What works? A simple mention, in a single sentence in Chapter One, of "scrub holum" and "moonthorn" as the names of plants glimpsed in the distance (p. 5/4). Then, practically at the book's midpoint, the one plant name unfolds into landscape: "He found her on the steep slope, sitting among the delicate bushes of moonthorn that grew like knots of lace over the mountainsides, its stiff, fragile branches silvery in the twilight. In a gap between eastern peaks a colorless luminosity of the sky heralded moonrise. The stream was noisy in the silence of the high, bare hills. There was no wind, no cloud. The air above the mountain was like amethyst . . ." (p. 158–144). Despite the awkward "a colorless luminosity of the sky" (the word is 'glow'), or the logically strained "noisy in the silence," this landscape is affecting. And when, in Chapter Ten, there is another, passing mention of "scrub holum," it has been charged not only by what we have learned of its technological use on Annares in frabric and fermentation, but has also been charged by its association with moonthorn which, because of *its* absence in the passage quoted, renders that scrub holum, mentioned later and alone, that much starker.

Moonlight glimmers again and again through the tale: the development of the image above forms part of the context that gives this moonlight its unique coloration, that fixes just what this moonlight can reveal.

Briefly, what works are those moments when the text conscientiously recalls itself (or lightly recalls another text, as when a passing explanation of why Shevek remains a vegetarian on Urras—"his stomach had its reasons . . ."—recalls Pascal's epigram), so that for an instant two textual moments are superimposed in the reader's mind, slightly out of register, not to create confusion but rather to function like the two views necessary for a stereoptical image. Bringing together their divergences, we glimpse the matter in all its resonant (or, with the Pascal, humerous) depth.

But there are other places where the text recalls itself to no particular purpose:

On Annares, Shevek's neighbor at the Institute, the mathematician Desar, speaks in a elliptic and "telegraphic" style—a personal eccentricity that presumably implies something about general language trends in Pravic. The Ioti speech of Shevek's Urrasti servant Efor, when it "slips back into the dialect of the city" also becomes elliptic and telegraphic (acquiring in the process some gross metaphors, such as "old sow" for "wife") in much the same way. There is nothing confusing between the two: one is on one world in one language, one is on another world in another language. Because the recall of the one by the other does not accomplish some clear point, however (that *all* demotic speech movement is toward the elliptic, perhaps?), the similarity registers as a lack of purpose and attention to verbal invention in fleshing out the language texture of the two speakers.

At another place, we anticipate a recall and get none: In the first chapter we learn the third person singular is the polite form of address in Ioti: "Is he sure he didn't get hurt?" (p. 6/5) Dr. Kimoe asks Shevek about his injured shoulder. (Informal address can presumably be rendered as second person: "you.") Once Shevek comes fully to his senses, however, this peculiarity of the language is absorbed by the implied translation and is never mentioned again. It could have added so much color to the subsequent portrait of the Urrasti if, in any number of the encounters that occur, we had seen precisely *where* the men (and women) of Urras switch from polite to informal address. ⟨. . .⟩

## VI

The problems of didacta in *The Dispossessed* raises itself on every level. Indeed, the main subject under this rubric—the philosophy of Odo (*Cf.* Greek *Odos* street or road; and the Japanese *Tao* path or way)—manages to put itself beyond discussion. To disapprove either of the philosophy as an ethical construct, or the way the ethical construct has been used to contour the aesthetic construct of the novel, is simply to declare oneself out of sympathy with the book. A critic who is seriously uncomfortable with either of these aspects had best look for another work to discuss.

The signs Le Guin repeatedly presents to call up the richness of Shevek's character are, one: an inner energy and enthusiasm, and, two: a composed and contained exterior. For me, they never quite integrate into a readerly experience of personality. What stands between them and prevents their inmixing are all Shevek's cool, crisp answers to the straw arguments posed by the Urrasti to the Odonian way. All these answers, which are finally what identify the arguments as straw, belong ultimately to the world of art where, to paraphrase Auden's *Calaban to the Audience*, great feelings loosen rather than tie the tongue. On highly politicized Annares, one might argue, the inhabitants seem to spend half their time talking politics and are therefore very comfortable in political discussions; moreover, half their arguments seem to be a running rehearsal of an argument with their own fictionalized vision of Urras; but that "Urras," as Le Guin so effectively points out *is* an Annaresti fiction. And the arguments that the Annaresti get a chance to practice are all with other more or less convinced Odonians. Those basic premises that a displaced Annaresti like Shevek would have to retrieve to answer not even the political arguments of the Urrasti but the basic assumptions that the Urrasti make without even broaching overt political discourse might take a bit more digging on Shevek's part than they seem to.

On Urras, Shevek is constantly having to face what strikes him as injustice, injustice of a kind he has never met before. In my own experience, such precise and ready answers to injustice come only with repeated exposure to the (many times repeated) injustice, with space between to contemplate, conjecture, and rehearse one's response. The condition of modern woman and man in the face of new outrage, *esprit d'escalier*, is unknown to Shevek.

For me it would have added much to Shevek's psychological texture if three or four times instead of having the quick and measured reply on his tongue, or the proper passage from Odo in his mind to bolster him up, he had kept his composure in bewildered consternation but later thought, with the same passion he brings to his other abstract considerations, of what he *might* have said.

Atro's description of the coming of the Hainish to Urras (p. 125/114) and his comparison of origin myths *is* witty *and* easily expressed. If presupposes, however, that he has said as much many times before to many Urrasti who have posed arguments similar to Shevek's. This is why his little speech works both as humor and as characterisation. (One only wishes Le Guin could have trusted the humor enough to make do, in the paragraph on Shevek's response, with "Shevek laughed," and omitted the lumbering and tautological "Atro's humor gave him pleasure," (p. 127/115) before going on to "But the old man was serious.") But even in an Annares chapter, when Shevek, age nineteen, encounters Sabul over the publication of his paper, we find such descriptions of the young physicist facing his older, hostile professor:

> His gentleness was uncompromising; because he would not compete for dominance he was indomitable (p. 103/94).

This would be barely acceptable as description of a serene, sixty year old, Faulknerian patriarch, secure with the confidence of class, money, and age. As a description of a nineteen year old physics major—however sure he is of his rightness—it is ludicrous; and its suggestion of absolute virtue, for either a sixty year old or a nineteen year old, throws one back to the worst of pulp diction and pulp psychology. Too many sentences like the above dampen the live charge in the details of Shevek's presentation that might actually interact to cast lights and shadows in the reader's mind.

Many of the novel's didactic interchanges concern the difference in treatment of women between Urras and Annares. "Where are the women?" Shevek asks a group of Urrasti physicists (p. 65/59)—presumably to provoke them, though it seems somewhat out of character.

Mini-speeches follow. And from there on Shevek seems to forget completely the political situation of women on Urras and what (given the author's meticulous care to keep the production space of Annares equally deployed between males and females) must be taken as women's conspicuous absence.

Again I am thrown back to experience: an English, schoolteacher friend of mine once decided to take his vacation in South Africa to visit a mathematician of his acquaintance at the university there. John is a moderate liberal in matters of race—not particularly revolutionary. (Revolutionaries simply do not visit South Africa; nor is this in any sense an analogue of the situation between Urras and Annares, because trade, emigration, and tourist traffic in both directions between England and South Africa is immense.) Nevertheless, John, like most Englishmen, is aware of the South African racial situation. When he came back from his vacation, he told me: "It's fascinating. In Jo'berg, you just don't *see* any blacks. Anywhere. And because you know they *are* there, you find yourself looking for them *all* the time—even in bars and stores where you'd be rather surprised to see blacks in London. Michael—my mathematician friend—and I were driving from the University to his place, which is in a suburb, and we had a minor smash-up with another car. By the time we had gotten out, there was a policeman there with his pad out, taking down names and numbers. The driver of the other car was Indian. And when the policeman demanded, 'Colour?' my heart began to thud and I grew terribly embarrassed, because I thought *now* I'd run up against it. Then Michael answered, 'Green,' and I realised the policeman was taking down the colours of our cars."

There is no way one can read a ninety percent population of exploited and oppressed blacks as an exact analogue of a fifty-two percent population of oppressed and exploited women. My recount of John's anecdote is simply to indicate various tendencies in the basic psychology of the traveler in politically alien space. To take John's anecdote momentarily as fiction, any didacta laid *over* this psychological structure ("I guess the racial situation there wasn't as bad as I thought," or "The racial tension in the air was *that* great; the situation is even worse than I'd suspected," or any of half a dozen other possible didactic conclusions with any of half a dozen possible relations to the socio-economic reality of Johanesburg) *become* character painting. But without the support of some valid psychological structure, the didacta alone would be fictively vacuous.

There is certainly no way that John's anecdote about the visible absence of blacks could be transferred to the planet Urras and made to fit the visible absence of women in the Ieu Eun University. Such one-to-one transfers usually make schematic, lifeless science fiction at the best of times: and *The Dispossessed* veers close enough to the schematic. Yet one can see a scene in which Shevek, knowing he is going to teach a segregated class (his first), steels himself not to rock the boat. One of the "students," however, is a privileged Urrasti wife or daughter who, interested in such things, has gotten special permission to observe a single class. When she comes up to speak to him after class—perhaps it is customary for the shaved, Urrasti women in such situations to wear male wigs—the other men in the class know all about her. But Shevek mistakes her for a man. When he discovers his mistake, he wonders what is happening to his own perceptions of sex while he is here on Urras. In short, one wants something of the folded-back-on-itself recomplication in the psychology of the political alien that John's anecdote conveys. And again, because such an incident on Urras would have had to be an interface, both Shevek's reality and the reality of the A-io culture would have registered as richer by it.

I do not wish to give the impression that science fiction must imitate the real in any simple and singular way. But the charge—of most presumptuously re-writing Le Guin's novel for her—that I have already laid myself open to several times now is one that I cannot see how to avoid in order to make the point paramount here: that point is merely the specifically science fictional version of the advice the poet Charles Olson once gave a fiction writing class at Black Mountain College: "Without necessarily imitating the real, we must keep our fictions *up to* the real." No matter how science fictional our entertainments (in both the active—and middle-voice sense of 'entertain'), they must approach the same order of structural complexity as our own conscious perceptions of the real. ⟨. . .⟩

### IX

Some people may wish to argue that the sum of all these fictive thinnesses (easiest to discuss in terms of differences with our own experience) can be deconstructed into a political template at odds with the surface form of Le Guin's apparent political sympathies. But that is beyond the scope of this treatment.

Shevek's brief homosexual affair is far more affecting than his traditional heterosexual one—not because it is unusual but because it involves Shevek in intellectual change (their initial political disagreements) and leads to action (the establishment of the new Syndicate) as well as emotional support. In the portrayal of the book's major heterosexual relation, all aspects of Takvar's personality or intellect that might cause conflict and thus promote intellectual change and growth in either her or Shevek have been relegated to the same mysterious space as Annaresti contraception methods. The heterosexual relation is merely supportive—and supportive, when all is said and done, of some of Shevek's least attractive characteristics. Some people may wish to argue that all this follows a tradition so old and so pervasive in western literature that it currently threatens to leach all interest from the precincts of fiction itself. Such an argument is also beyond our purpose.

Such deconstructions and such traditions are primarily statistical entities. To argue such positions rigorously would demand an analysis and comparison of many, many works in even greater detail than we have exercised here. And to make such larger criticisms, when all is said and done, is only to say that Le Guin's novel suffers from the same failings as practically every other contemporary, mundane novel (as well as most nineteenth century ones).

If these failings are highlighted in *The Dispossessed*, one general highlighting factor is the structural focus peculiar to science fiction; for these failings *are* structural tendencies that the overall textus of western fiction has, unfortunately, incorporated into itself. The second highlighting factor is that Le Guin has taken for her central subject much of the socio-economic material to which these structural tendencies, in mundane fiction, are a response. That she has found, in the alternating chapters, an aesthetic form that reflects the technological underpinnings of her tale is admirable. If, however, she had found a form that reflected the socio-economic underpinnings, which are even more central to it, she would have written one of the great novels of the past three hundred years.

I suspect I am at odds even with most sympathetic contemporary critics of s-f in my feeling that science fiction, precisely through the particular quality of inmixing unique to it and the rhetorical postures available to it, has the greatest chance of overcoming, first by individual efforts and finally as a genre, precisely these fictive problems. The steps we have made in this direction are certainly small. But when we have gone a great deal further, Le Guin's novel may well hold its place among the earliest such steps.

The critic criticises by constituting a difference with an implied or explicit set of experiences. Quite possibly the writer—and particularly the writer of science fiction—writes by constituting a difference with her own experience (a sort of *differance*), but all we are prepared to discuss here is that attendant analysis of those experiences which is, I would hazard from introspection, the more accessible part of the process. The science fictional restructuring in which one's own experiences are broken down and reassembled within the framework of a given fictive future presupposes a far greater amount of analysis in the creative act itself, whether conscious or unconscious, than in the act of creating a mundane fiction. Indeed, this analysis *is* the creative aspect of that emphasis on structure that has already been noted for the genre.

In this sense, Le Guin's successes are successes of analysis (as her failures of anaylsis) of her fictive subject. Because of the unique nature of the inmixing that is science fiction, these successes of analysis manifest themselves not as didacta, but as emotional densities, verbal life, and an underlying psychological recomplication in the material, all of which invests the text with life and energy. The failures of analysis manifest themselves as a discrepancy between those same fictive densities and the didactic presence that runs through the work—and that, indeed, any fictive work (but especially science fiction) can always be reduced to (if it is not overtly manifest in the text) if we choose to make such a reduction.

A writer of mundane fiction works with difference in the following way. The first *analytical* question must be: What is the easiest way to express my subject in fictive terms? With this as basis, the second analytical question is: But what is my subject *really* like? The difference between the two gives the text all its energy, life, and significance—whether it be in the discourse of the senses presented as foreground, or the discourse of psycho-social analysis presented as recit. In such a text, a discrepancy between what registers as felt and what registers as didactic is best handled by excising the didactic—from the sensibility and the text.

The writer of science fiction deals with difference in the following way. Again the first analytical question must be: What is the easiest way to express my subject in fictive terms? With this as basis, the second question becomes: What have I experienced, and in light of that experience, what *could* what I want to express be really like? The difference between the easiest expression and the actual text again lends the text its brio. But in the situation of the science fiction writer, a discrepancy between what registers as felt and what registers as didactic is best handled by integrating the didactic through a further exploration and analysis of one's own experiences: by dramatising the didactic points in a foreground in which is perceptible some structural syntagm that can be reduced to the required didactum—and as frequently several more besides.

The science fiction author most generally associated with the problem of didacta is, of course, Heinlein. With Heinlein, the argument runs: The didacta in Heinlein are frequently absurd and are bearable, if at all, only because of a certain rhetorical glibness. If the foreground vision and the didacta were integrated, the foreground vision would change in such a way that it would no doubt be insupportable even to the author. With Le Guin, the argument runs: The didacta are frequently admirable, but as frequently clumsily put. If the foreground vision and the didacta were integrated, the foreground vision would be far stronger, livelier, more interesting, and relevant. Both, in their underlying assumptions, though, are still the same argument.

The actual talk of "integration" that appears in much of the sympathetic criticism we have had on Le Guin's work to date seems to me to do the author a disservice. The "social integration" cited as one of *The Dispossessed's* accomplishments is too frequently a manifestation of its failures of analysis, of questions not asked. And the sign of it in the text are the lack of science fictional integration between the didacta and the novelistic foreground.

Though it is certainly not Le Guin's fault, I am afraid the "integration" being sought for by this criticism is a kind of critical nostalgia for signs of an older fictive naivete.

Certainly science fiction novels are reminiscent of older genres. The progress of the young hero in Van Vogt's *The Weapon Shops of Isher* from the provinces into the social machinations of the city recalls the plots of how many Balzac novels (even to the gambling incident in *Père Goriot*); and the deployment of the City of the Game and the various pastoral locations on Venus in *The Pawns of Null-A* creates a geo-fictive syntagm practically congruent with that of Paris, Combrey and Balbec in Proust's great novel. Indeed, the alternating chapters of *The Dispossessed* suggests nothing so much as a development on the form so favored by Proust's near-contemporary, Edgar Rice Burroughs, who employed a somewhat similar alternating chapter format in Tarzan novel after Tarzan novel. But the very fact that Van Vogt recalls Proust while Le Guin recalls Burroughs is to say that the interest of the observation is exhausted with its statement. What is reminiscent in science fiction of older forms is only of minimal interest—or at any rate it is of the same order of interest as those elements in Shakespeare's plays which recall the chronicles, tales, and older plays from which he took his plots: to keep critical porportion, the relation must be discussed in terms of difference rather than similarity.

Here is the place to note that this analysis of the writer's own experience must not be confused with the critical analysis of the science fiction text into recognizable syntagms and unusual signifiers spoken of in section VIII. The analysis of experience I speak of leaves no explicit signs *in* the text. Rather, it becomes with recombination and inmixing the text itself. Indeed, all the text can explicitly sign is its lack: and *one* such sign is the split between didacta and foreground. To repeat: the inmixing of syntagm and signifier is an essentially inadequate discourse to signify the process unique to science fiction discourse (a process not definable, only designatable) that allows that science fictional materia that is both analysis and language to transcend both ideology and autobiography.

Just over fifty years ago Lukács wrote: "The novel is the only art form where the artist's ethical position is *the* aesthetic problem." Very possibly in the same year, Wittgenstein recorded the observation in the notebook which was to become the basis for the *Tractatus*: "Ethics *is* aesthetics."

That science fiction novels *are* novels is to say Luckács's observation still applies. But to be fully aware that they *are* science fiction is to be aware of the extended range of aesthetic technique s-f has at its disposal to solve the problem.

If Le Guin is to move her work into the area so frequently cited for it, where its successes are notable in terms of its difference from the run of mundane fiction—a run that takes in the best with the worst—she must, first, galvanize her style. It does no good to tell an author, much of whose language sentence by sentence is pompous, ponderous, and leaden, that her writing is lucid, measured, and mature. The tones of voice that many of her sentences evoke belong, under control, within quotation marks in the dialogue of characters, or, if outside quotation marks, in their reported thoughts. They do not belong in the auctorial voice.

If this stylistic galvanizing occurs, the result, I suspect, will be that her language, besides becoming far cleaner, sharper, and more exact, will also become far more "science fiction-y"—that is, it will show many more of those magical combinations of words that, simple and uncluttered, are still the language by which we recognise the alien world.

In an interview with the Eugene Women's Press Le Guin has suggested one possible way to bring about the refocussing that must go along with this stylistic refinement:

In public situations when people ask me, Why do you write about men . . . I say, because I like to write about aliens. It's very flip; it's also true. I'm fascinated by this attempt to get into the Other. I'm terribly fond of my women, it's just that they are me. It's too close. Now maybe what I ought to do is try to write about a woman who isn't at all like me. I've never done it. I've really never done it.

One wants to jump for joy at this suggestion!—though one pauses right after jumping to proffer a reminder only applicable to science fiction: The mundane fiction writer need only analyse what she sees to glean the materia which, by whatever transformations, will become her art. The science fiction writer must analyse as well the way it is seen, and how and why it is seen in a particular way. This does not mean any deep and profound searching among the inner, mythic mysteries; only a clear vision of the economic, social and technological biases and influences which organize our individual responses to the world. It demands a clear vision of the web of psychological expectations and social benefits (precisely *who* benefits) that exist for *every* idea and attitude taken as part of the social syntagm. For this is the materia which, by whatever transformation (including those peculiar to science fiction), we render an art which must so frequently project women and men who not only see and experience new things, but see and experience them in new ways because their entire, fictive lives have been radically different from ours all along. In science fiction, unlike mundane fiction, there is no implicit limit on the distance from the self to the Other (be it woman, man, or alien) to contour the fictive reality. There is only the perspicacity of the analysis of the self and the self-surround into the materia out of which an image of that Other, the self-hood of that Other, and that Other's self-surround are structured. To address Le Guin's comment directly: in science fiction unlike mundane fiction, short of one's analytical limits, there *is* no limit on how different these Other women may be from the author; and *this* is the reason that, in science fiction, not to explore them seems such a fictive failing.

The writer, during the actual work on her own text, has privileged access to its signified and its signifiers. If the new signified created does not please, the writer is free, in the light of that so-important analysis, to expand, cut, excise and replace signifiers throughout the web of the text. And in science fiction, there is, practically speaking, a far greater number of replacement points, and certainly a far greater number of signifiers to choose replacements from. We have already pointed out how, in her treatment of Annares' ergotic space, Le Guin has taken the familiar syntagm we daily encounter in the proportions of women and men and replaced, as it were, some of the men with women. The in-mixing that occurs *is* the readerly experience of the Annaresti labor devision and the experience of its implications as they spread into other aspects of the society. A final point on the subject of didacta: once the didactic concern has been analyzed and integrated, this leaves the rhetoric of didacta free to point, emphasise, and underline what is *in* the foreground far more subtley and ironically; and leaves it, in general, an aesthetically more interesting tool.

## X

*The Dispossessed* has excited many readers. For the second time its author has taken both Hugo and Nebula awards for best science fiction novel of the year; and the bestowal of both fills me with pleasure. Some years ago at the University of Washington at Seattle I had the privilege of teaching for several days with Le Guin at the Clarion West S-F Writers' Workshop. She has one of those individual and amazing minds which, so fortunately, seems to be the hallmark of, rather than the exception among, our genre's practioners. The experience was, frankly, thrilling.

A study of a genre that includes only a description of books must be a limited one. Any full exploration must cover the impact of those books on readers and writers. That alone would assure Le Guin's novel a substantial place in any study of contemporary s-f; no derogation I might make here could deny it that place. And, as I hope I have indicated, there is much more to the book than those things that strike me as its flaws.

To be fair, it is as much the excitement as it is the excitement's object that has impelled me to this lengthy examination. I only hope that my method, by displaying its biases clearly, invites its own refutation. At least this is what I have tried for.

The nature of this excitement may be what makes it so easy to loose hold of one truth we must never mislay if we are to keep our analysis rigorous: The science fiction novel—*The Dispossessed*—is a structure of words; any discourse it raises is raised by its words.

I have already discussed one moment, between Shevek and Bedap, when two sentences, artfully ambiguous, have produced a striking synthesis with affective intelligence. There are many more such moments—most at places, be they finely or faultily written, where the language is doing something it can *only* do in science fiction.

We shall close our discussion of *The Dispossessed* with a look at several examples of uniquely science fictional language in the text.

We are with the old, Urrasti physicist Atro:

My eyes get so tired these days. I think that damnable magnifier-projector-thingy I have to use for reading has something wrong with it. It doesn't seem to project the words clearly any more (p. 128/116).

This recalls the type of language we discussed using the example of the Heinlein sentence—with the difference that this one works nowhere near as well. Why? The analogic commentary it suggests on the cliché of old people forgetting names of things and their self-deceptions about their failing eyesight is not sufficiently intruded on by the new signifier ("magnifier-projector-thingy") to re-form as any new structure we can respond to as insight. As well, the external structure of "magnifier-projector-thingy" does not particularly connect it with anything else mentioned of the Urrasti society/technology; it is not reinforced by anything; it does not reinforce. At best, it is merely cute.

On Annares, however, where (though an incident on Urras) we know that the populous are vegetarians who eat some fish (we have seen the fishbones left over at Shevek's party) and that fish breeding (and fish genetics) is a modern profession, we find a description of a snowfall at night:

"At each crossing the dim streetlight made a pool of silver, across which dry snow flurried like shoals of tiny fish chasing their shadows." (p. 144/131). This works not only as a striking visual description, which it might well do in mundane fiction; it also lends an equally striking sense of coherence to the whole apprehension of Annaresti culture and consciousness; such reflections of consciousness and culture occur, of course, in the metaphors of mundane fiction, but seldom with such pointed effect.

At another point we see Shevek with his infant daughter:

He would sit the baby on his knee and address wild cosmological lectures to her, explaining how time was actually space turned inside out, the chronon being thus the everted viscera of the quantam, and

distance one of the accidental properties of light (p. 220/200).

Besides portraying Shevek at his most believable and human, the sentence takes the signifiers of the book's major scientific themes and reduces them to a purely abstract and verbal dance, where they strike us as a tiny reflection of the whole object of our consideration, seen far off in a spherical mirror. By extension, it humanizes these scientific concerns for us to see that they have some aspects—if only the sounds of the words on an enthusiastic physicist's tongue—that can please a baby.

At another point, the entire cosmological conceit of the novel is used to inform a simile for sex between Shevek and Takvar after a long separation: They ". . . circled about the center of infinite pleasure . . . like planets circling blindly, quietly, in the flood of sunlight, about the common center of gravity . . ." (p. 283/258). The point here is not the overwriting, but the invocation of the two real planets in the real fictive universe of the novel.

In the last chapter, when Shevek is returning to Annares on the intersteller ship *Davenant*, neither of Urras nor Annares, we read:

Very late on the following shipnight, Shevek was in the *Davenant's* garden. The lights were out, there, and it was illuminated only by starlight. The air was quite cold. A night-blooming flower from some unimaginable world had opened among dark leaves and was sending out perfume with patient, unavailing sweetness to attract some unimaginable moth trillions of miles away, in a garden on a world circling another star . . . (p. 340/310).

This charming image is a metaphor that touches on every relationship in the novel: it speaks mutedly of biological force, spiritual desire, political ambition; as well, it signs the existence of an aesthetic neither Urrasti nor Annaresti, yet necessarily extant in the universe of the novel—necessary to hold a critical counter up to both worlds we have been examining.

One of the most striking moments of the book is the closing of Chapter Three. On Urras, alone in the Senior Faculty room of Ieu Eun University, Shevek, who has come to appreciate much of the surface opportunity available to him on this decadent world, muses on his situation. Outside the window, night is coming on. After his musings, we read:

The shadows moved about him, but he sat unmoving as Annares rose above the alien hills, at her full, mottled dun and bluish white, lambent. The light of his world filled his empty hands (p. 80/73).

Whether or not we find the diction a trifle strained, whether we find the dialogue the image sets up with the lietmotif of "empty hands" that symbolises the Odonian philosophy fortunate or unfortunate, this is still the purest of science fiction, made reasonable by the implicit technology of space travel and made affecting by the human situation it describes and compels. It charges with near electric scintillation half a dozen other images to come, from Takvar sitting among the moonthorn to Shevek in the moonlight through the window of his room on Annares. With the evocation of this most charged moonlight complete, the next chapter begins: "The westering sun . . ." which is breathtaking—for we are on another world (p. 81/74).

The orchestration of image here is simple and superb. The situation of those closing sentences is one that could only arise in science fiction: by extension, the only place we could find sentences doing *this* is in a science fiction novel—*this* science fiction novel.

Yes, there are other unsteady points in the book: given their comparative diets and general standard of living, we would expect the Annaresti after seven generations to be shorter than the Urrasti rather than taller; and the discussion of Annaresti jewelry in Abbanay which does so much to relieve the bleakness of our image of Annaresti aesthetic life might well have come in the first three, rather than the last three, chapters. But there are also many other strong points: as a scene, the boys playing at prison is superb; the way in which the author, by carefully dropped biographemes (to borrow a neologism from Barthes), makes long-dead Odo emerge so vividly is masterful. But at this point, to me the book feels read, absorbed, in both its weaknesses and its strengths. The ideas, associations, and memories it has called up in me feel well wrestled. That is a good place for a critic to stop. That is the best place for a reader to begin another rereading.

There is an ideal model of writing which holds that a novel should begin with a moment of epiphanised intensity and never loose this energy from beginning to end. Nostalgically, we remember our early readings of the great works in our science fiction canon—*More Than Human* or *The Stars My Destination*—as if they were exactly this. The model is, of course, illusory—if only because of the nature of writing itself. An image—such as the one discussed at the close of Chapter Three—is not only an image in a chain of images, it is a detonator dropped into a readerly imagination organised to a certain potential of response by previous effects and images—a response the new image releases. The efficacy of such images is as frequently measured by their inseparability from the rest of the text that prepares for them as it is measured by their own, inner energy: intrusion and inmixing are ubiquetous.

Something I feel science fiction as a genre is beginning to learn—and the general rise in critical sophistication within the field is as much responsible for it as it is an emblem of it—is that the competition in science fiction is not with the novels of the nineteenth century or even the mundane fiction of this second half of the twentieth. Because science fiction *is* a genre, and is experienced through resonances sets up in a vastly complex textus, contoured both negatively and positively by millions of words that include the finest of Sturgeon and the clumsiest of Capt. S. P. Meek, any attempt to write a science fiction novel generates an image of that book in some idealised way. The competition is with an author generated, idealised form of the science fiction novel itself.

At the resolution of incident and action (where we begin the overt reading of the political significance of a novel) whatever *The Dispossessed* does not happen to accomplish, the truth is that very little western fiction does. But if we keep asking the book to do these things, we are only saying back to it full voice things the text itself, from beginning to end, keeps whispering of. *The Dispossessed* whispers of these possibilities very strongly; and that is an aspect of its indubitable significance. Compared to *The Dispossessed*, much mundane fiction—much of the best mundane fiction—is simply silent.

*The Dispossessed* will excite young and generous readers—indeed, will excite any reader beginning to look at our world and us in it. And it will excite for a long time. The novel is orchestrated; it shows signs of intelligence on every page. And its real successes, as with every work of art, are unique to it.

Nevertheless, some of these excited readers who return to the book a handful of years later will find themselves disillusioned: what excited them, they will see, was the book's ambition more than its precise accomplishments. But hopefully—a year or so after that—they will reach another stage where they will be able to acknowledge that ambition for what it was

and value it; and know how important, in any changing society, such ambition is.

*Notes*

1. All page references are to *The Dispossessed* by Ursula K. Le Guin, Harper and Row, New York, 1974, followed by the page reference in the paperback edition, *The Dispossessed* by Ursula K. Le Guin, Avon Books, New York, 1975.

## JOHN FEKETE
### From "*The Dispossessed* and *Triton*: Act and System in Utopian Science Fiction"
*Science-Fiction Studies*, July 1979, pp. 131–35

In *The Dispossessed*, Le Guin presents two worlds: there is the planet Urras, with its three politically obsolete regions (the totalitarian State-socialist region, the totalitarian profiteering region, and the totalitarian underdeveloped region), and there is the moon Anarres (which, in Latin, means beyond or without things and which here indicates both the absence of property and consumerism, and also the presence of extreme scarcity). One of the most interesting ideological features of *The Dispossessed*—pointing up, I think, a problem in the philosophical culture of our day—is that Le Guin incisively anatomizes the *illusions* of rationalist social-historical thought, charts its traps, and then—at a different level—proceeds to fall into them. She shows, to begin with, that the culture of the anarcho-communist society on Anarres, notwithstanding its admirable beginnings in creative and humane institutional innovation, is caught in the traps of its historical inheritance. This historical inheritance, in becoming alienated, has produced corrosion and degeneracy.[1] After several generations, what remains on Anarres is what could be called a degenerate workers' culture, or a degenerate rebels' culture. First of all, with the legend of revolution there develops the illusion of a radical rupture between past and future, a rupture which separates Anarres from Urras and is supposed to have revealed the meaning of history. Such an image of rupture sums up a self-enclosed society in which the content of this rupture becomes a fixed standard used to correlate and measure all activities. That fixed standard, moreover, is provided specifically by Odonian ideology, which has been progressively devitalized and congealed into doctrine. Thirdly, the governing principles and interpretations that have been derived from and increasingly projected into this doctrine aim to establish the relationship of Anarresti society to its Urrasti past in the form of the determinate negation of this past. Since Urras is represented in the image of private property and exploitation, Anarres is organized as its opposite, as its negation, frozen into the double image of egalitarianism and communitarianism. Le Guin then shows that these have become, in their dogmatic forms, deeply problematic.

The justice and importance of challenging concrete social inequalities are becoming well established in our time; in the pursuit of humanity's regeneration, to advocate community in place of alienated fragmentation is at least of comparable value. Yet, looking around and ahead, it is possible to see that both these goals may also come to present new human problems. Ideological egalitarianism when put into dogmatic practice can produce an impoverishing denial of the entire world of culture and civilization; enforced equivalence can mean a disregard for quality in favor of abstract quantity in order to make dissimilar things commensurable. Thus every time that Shevek asserts his unique interests or his advanced talent, he is accused of egoizing instead of sharing. Inability, envy, and resentment can cut the world of human wealth down to a very limited scale. In the same way, the desire for harmonious communitarian society can only too easily translate into homogeneous socialization which is meant to produce commensurable experiences. All of these cultural distortions, as Le Guin recognizes with great insight, have deep roots in the major left-wing social and philosophical traditions, indeed, beyond those, in the very soil of "Western" intellectual and social development. On Anarres, the result is a stultifying and self-destructive decay of organic revolutionary culture into mechanical conventionality; the decay sediments bureaucratic walls that become internalized (and invisible) as a fear of freedom. The *caveat* addressed to contemporary radical politics or philosophy could not be more obvious.

Yet it cannot be said that Le Guin's response is really free from comparable distortions. She does not share the Anarresti mystique of history as rupture; she makes it very clear through Shevek that a *human* act is one that links past and future in the present, i.e. that the past and the future co-exist in the present as memory and intention. Yet it is arguable that Shevek's image of time, though it opens up the society to its past and future, remains problematic. Shevek, the physicist, dreams of a General Temporal Theory that would unite Sequency and Simultaneity, the diachronic and the synchronic, the syntagmatic and the paradigmatic, becoming and being, duration and creation, ethics and geometry, casual logic and parataxis, humanism and structuralism. His is a grand synthetic desire to correlate without tension all phenomena within a time-space continuum. Within its own conventions in the novel, this is the ultimate rationalist reconciliation. On Anarres, the social correlative of this cosmic quest is the city of Abbenay (Mind, in Pravic) where, we are told, "nothing was hidden."[2] On Anarres, total harmony and total transparency are the fictions behind Shevek's illusion that a healthy society would and could *coordinate* all it's individual peculiarities—or what Le Guin calls "cellular functions" (10: 267) to represent that contribution which social theorists from Saint Simon to Marx expected each person, according to ability, to make to society. This rationalist dream of unitary cohesion (total coordination) is a symptom of our culture's illness, deeply embedded in all of its most hopeful formulations. It is a profound paradox that unitary cohesion, this curious emblem of our consciousness, should be embraced by both advocates and opponents of modern social administration, to the point where utopia becomes totalitarian and totalitarianism wears a utopian face.

This problem of unitary cohesion impinges as well on the anthropological dimension of Le Guin's model, as indeed it does on most of the radical discussions of human nature. On Anarres, it becomes evident that the abolition of profiteering ownership has still left a power structure of mental cowardice objectified in public opinion. In addition to the political-economic key to the social process that is basic to the outlook and language of the Anarresti, Le Guin through Shevek adds an anthropological key: he discovers that a transformation of the personality is essential to restore initiative and dynamism. Shevek recognizes that the overbureaucratized normative structure of Anarresti society has produced stagnation and decay, and he seeks to generate free spaces, well beyond the latitude left by the abolition of private property. He wants free spaces for the recreation of the spontaneity/negativity/otherness/non-identity that such a society needs as internal control mechanisms for continued development and vitality. At the same time, Shevek's conception points to a permanently revolutionary culture which requires a human personality that *needs to be* the revolution, and that places freedom at the peak of its value hierarchy, reaching for the future with empty hands joined in mutual aid with the empty hands of brothers who are sharers, not owners, and are dependent on each other. In my view, this goal—a conventional radical goal, really—of a renewed culture of harmoniously correlated revolutionary personalities is highly problematic. At the limits of this conception, society is again enclosed in a circle, this time with reference to an anthropological centre that gives it symbolic unity. The empty-handed, permanently revolutionary personality becomes the aim, meaning, and measure of all things. It is true that, from Jesus to Nietzsche and Marcuse, the anthropological imperative to change the personality has constituted a powerful demand to complement the social imperatives of institutional change. Nonetheless, one also has to consider that a universalizing anthropology, even with the best of intentions, is still totalitarian: a vain attempt of the cognitive mind to embrace and leave its unified imprint on all phenomena.

One further feature of Le Guin's outlook is as problematic as it is symptomatic of a pervasive cultural attitude in our day. Opposed to the walls of conventionality that public opinion erects, Shevek declares that the real revolution is a solidarity without walls. As it happens, on Anarres, where this solidarity is yet to be consciously willed as a *goal for itself*, it already exists *in itself*, though it has been alienated into obedient cooperation and conformity. As the Odonian rebels from Urras were exported to the moon and plunked down empty-handed in the howling desert that is Anarres, solidarity as a *means* of survival was a given of the situation at the very origins of Anarresti society, and was to be tested in the face of extreme scarcity. Out of the struggle to survive in the face of extreme scarcity is born the "bond . . . beyond choice" (9: 24), the brotherhood that begins in shared pain. The empty hand image thus does double duty for Le Guin: it signifies both the valued social absence of private property and the valued social presence of an environmentally coerced interdependence of the propertyless for survival.

Arguably, from the point of view of libertarian social theory, neither usage of the empty hand is legitimate, though in the fiction they sustain each other. First, once it becomes evident that the abolition of property domination fails to remove power and alienation from the social terrain, the whole nature of social domination needs to be rethought and reimaged (by Shevek, Le Guin, or any of us), including the question of ownership, whose interpretation will change in the overall context. Second, though the overwhelming survival necessities that test the solidarity of the empty-handed colonists are immanent in their history, nevertheless this environmental fate is really the product of transcendent intervention by authorial sleight of hand. Le Guin *chooses* to establish this bleak adversity as the laboratory for the socio-political experiment she constructs. Le Guin's interest is in the moral drama that is to occur within this environment, and it may not be proper to question the fictional logic. But metafictional or metaesthetic challenges are in order, especially insofar as asceticism is now once again becoming widespread in our culture—from labor-intensive back-to-nature crusades, through conserver-society advocates, energy-shortage Cassandras, wage controls and service sector cutbacks, to all the varieties of residual Puritanism.

If the false egalitarianism of the Anarresti threatens to narrow human abundance, it may be that so too does Le Guin's fictive landscape. All the fine libertarian institutions on Anarres are condemned to the redistribution of poverty. Certainly the distribution of labor through the Divlab computer system precludes the flowering of the qualitative needs of personalities and of a plurality of lifestyles. The central determination of needs according to purposive rationality prevails over particular communicative needs, bonds, or desires. Oddly, Le Guin sees the function of environmental adversity only as providing the possibility of fulfillment and purpose to the worker and the possibility of solidarity to the community. She does not connect the material and cultural poverty on Anarres. Le Guin's interest is in the moral advance of people in the face of challenge. The one law that Shevek accepts is human evolution, which for him means a development toward morality. The anthropological transformation that consists of recognizing solidarity as an end in itself and not just a means of physical survival—an adoption of necessity as a virtue—is posed as a moral imperative.

I would say that it is arguable, on the contrary, that moral abundance, conceived as a goal for all individuals, is not attainable without material abundance. Only the exceptional individual like Shevek is likely to be able to appropriate the moral abundance of the human race by sheer will and insight. It can be added that the survival-dominated landscape removes *The Dispossessed*, in this respect, in spite of its many analogical connections, from having any extra-polative bearing on our own situation which at the moment hovers at, though it is prevented from reaching, the threshold of a post-scarcity society endowed with the material preconditions of freedom.[3] Many-sided individuals, rich in human capacities, as well as creative forms of solidarity, presuppose the conscious appropriation of an abundance of objective mediation carrying the wealth of the human species into intersubjective relations. In any case, this *is* our heritage; the imminence of physical success is one of the greatest achievements of our civilization, won with great aspirations and at great cost. It seems to me that today we live in an extraordinarily fraudulent period of economic rationalization when scarcity is manipulated for social control at the same time that our world is literally destroying itself in order to remain within the structures of scarcity. Even so, we have no authentic choice, when we *speculate* about our future, but to postulate a society of great physical power. Neither the negative sides of material advance under conditions of domination—the manipulation, disaster, and unfreedom to which instrumental reason lends itself—nor the pernicious ideology of scarcity and survival are sufficient grounds to impoverish our horizons.

In other words, a narrowing of the objective horizons, the incorporation of the power of scarcity and survival necessity into the very structure of the situation, mark Le Guin's ambiguous utopia as less hopeful than is commonly supposed. Ambiguity in *The Dispossessed* pivots around the possibilities of anthropological revolution to provide the species with an evolutionary bias toward individuality and revolution, in preference to the entropic security-adaptation fostered in the society through spontaneously self-bureaucratizing cultural despotism. Yet the book's logic, notwithstanding its open-ended, tentatively hopeful attitude, is itself limited, on account of its physical parameters. These physical limits are characteristic of the author's outlook and preoccupations (whether in *Rocannon's World*, *Planet of Exile*, *Left Hand of Darkness*, or *The Dispossessed*): scarcity or the powers of nature constitute the ineluctable barriers of adversity against which Le Guin constructs an essentially moral drama to test the possibilities of the human fabric in the face of evolutionary challenge.

Le Guin has tremendous, virtually ecstatic empathy with the ascendant claims of life (e.g. in "The New Atlantis") but also reticence in conceiving any imminent or non-catastrophic

transition to physical success. The consequence seems to be that, notwithstanding its conceptual strength and socio-ecological depth, *The Dispossessed* fails to open the doors onto a non-ascetic and rich transcendence of property domination. In focussing the dilemma that J. S. Mill had articulated a hundred years ago—that of the threat to evolutionary creativity from the pressures of increasing cultural homogeneity[4]—*The Dispossessed* fails in the end to bring into a really strategic dynamic tension the physical and the anthropological. It fails to provide a multiplicity of technical life-support systems for a diversity of subjectivity.

The choice of a scarcity and necessity-dominated environment instead predisposes the mapping of the fictional progression toward the less interesting range of problems flowing out of scarcity and having to do with distributive justice. The more interesting range of speculative questions, having to do with permanent revolution and the forms of freedom in a libertarian post-scarcity society, remain untouched. In the explicitly utopian context, there is a Le Guinian axis of pessimism, the romantic asceticism that is here translated into socio-economic and psycho-political detail. This tends to identify *The Dispossessed* as ultimately a less daring exploration of evolving metaphors for modelling the possibilities and impossibilities of the human situation than some of her other works, which have confronted instrumental rationalism and the powers of nature with more intensely evocative (if less extensively mimetic) resonance.

Yet it is important to note that Le Guin always opts for a fundamental feature of the enlightened secular *epistéme*: its devotion to the immanent powers and intentions of human rationality. If she errs, it is because Le Guin is so suspicious of technical reason that she prefers to experiment with sheer moral will in the face of a limiting objective environment.

*Notes*

1. Throughout this analysis, if in place of Anarres we read any radical movement or tradition—Marxism, for example—we will soon recognize that it is not only on the moon that comparable corruptions produce comparable decay.

2. *The Dispossessed* (NY: Avon, 1974), 4: 80. Further page references in the text are to this edition. The formulation "nothing was hidden" recalls the giddy vision of D-503, the mathematician protagonist of that brilliant anti-utopia entitled *We*, written in 1920 by the disillusioned Bolshevik Yevgeny Zamyatin (trans. Mirra Ginsburg, NY: Bantam, 1972) against the purveyors of unanimity and harmony. In that story, the rulers of the euclidian One State are proponents of what they describe as "mathematically infallible happiness" and they are determined to "integrate the grandiose cosmic equation" (1: 1), "to unbend the wild primitive curve and straighten it to a . . . straight line" (1: 2), even if they have to perform frontal lobotomy on the population to excise the imagination, which is identified as "the last barricade on [the] way to happiness" (31:•180). One day, D-503 sees a man's shadow on the pavement and, looking ahead to post-operative perfection, says: "And it seems to me—I am certain—that tomorrow there will be no shadows. No man, no object will cast a shadow. . . . The sun will shine through everything. . . ." (31: 183).

3. CF. Murry Bookchin, *Post-Scarcity Anarchism* (San Francisco, 1971). Bookchin argues that Marx's great contribution was to have drawn attention to the material preconditions of freedom; moreover, that freedom cannot be represented only as the absence of domination but must be concrete, precisely *rid* of the burdens of the struggle with necessity, rid of want and toil.

4. See Mill's 1859 essay *On Liberty*, which is devoted to an analysis of the new "social despotism" of the majority over the individual, in contrast with the earlier political problem of the tyranny of a minority over the majority. Mill takes the view that if social conformity is permitted to extinguish individuality, and thus genius, humanity will stagnate then degenerate.

KATHLEEN L. SPENCER
"Exiles and Envoys:
The SF of Ursula Le Guin"

*Foundation*, October 1980, pp. 32–42

There are nearly as many ways to describe the central theme of Ursula Le Guin's sf as there are critics of her work: "wholeness and duality . . . , the awareness that balance must be sought where light and dark meet and mix";[1] "the paradox of communication: (that) in order to communicate, it is necessary to recognize differences and to move toward an understanding of these differences";[2] "the movement of the hero toward oneness with other human creatures";[3] "the loneliness of the self, the impossibility of understanding the self except through its relationship with the other, and the human need to establish that relationship through reaching out to the other in love."[4] However their formulations differ, nearly all critics agree that Le Guin is fundamentally concerned with the essential human duality of self and other, and with the profound sense of isolation and separation that is such a troubling part of the modern condition.

But Le Guin's novels are not so much about isolation as they are about communication growing out of isolation. Again and again in her fiction, we watch the crisis of encounter between alien cultures, and again and again we see the slow start of communication and understanding because of the actions of one or two people who are able to bridge the gap. These pivotal figures—envoys and exiles, bridge-builders and translators—all have one characteristic in common: they encounter the alien culture as isolated individuals, separated from their own cultures by physical distance, by circumstance, or by temperament. Genly Ai in *The Left Hand of Darkness* is a Terran alone on the planet Gethen, far from home, friends, and familiar ways; his one real Gethenian friend turns out to be Estraven—the traitor, the exile, rejected by his own people because his vision runs too far ahead of theirs. Jakob Agat, the Alterran leader in *Planet of Exile*, sets himself apart from his own people when he falls in love with and marries a Tevaran girl—Rolery, the Summer-born, a woman isolated among her people by her out-of-season birth, twenty years out of phase with her natural mates. In *The Word for World Is Forest*, Lyubov the hilfer is scorned by his fellow Terrans as a "creechie lover" for treating Athsheans like humans rather than furry green monkies; Selver, his friend, is separated from the rest of his people by the terrible and powerful dreams which make him a god. And Falk in *City of Illusions* is separated from not one but two cultures—from that of his home world on Werel by the memory-blanking of the Shing, as well as the vast time differential of space travel; and from his adopted culture on Terra, at first by his physical difference from the people who take him in, and later and more completely by his restored memories as Ramarren. He is in himself a bridge between the cultures of Werel and Terra, part of both and different from both. The same is true of Shevek in *The Dispossessed*: he can serve as a link between Urras and Anarres because he shares something with both; yet, because of that very ability to share, he can never belong wholly to either. Despite his love of and loyalty to Anarres, he is not only envoy but exile, neither purely an Odonian nor purely a physicist, permanently between.

However, the isolation that Le Guin's central characters experience is of a special kind: they are isolated without being alienated. The alienated man, as Marx explains the term, experiences life passively, as one to whom things happen; further, he is cut off from his own essential nature and therefore from other men, for he cannot confront others if he cannot confront himself.[5] The alienated man sits, fearful and angry, in a tiny cage of his own construction, staring at his hands in his lap and waiting helplessly for what will happen next. None of Le Guin's central characters match this description. They do not see themselves as objects, or as powerless victims shoved around by monstrous impersonal forces over which they have no control (even when there is some truth to that view, as for George Orr in *The Lathe of Heaven* or Belle and Simon in "The New Atlantis"). They may choose to refrain from action like the Handdarata, but they are never merely passive in the deathlike unintentional way of the alienated. Though they may find themselves among strangers or rejected by their own people, they do not give up—they still strive to reach out, to make some kind of meaningful contact with someone. Even Osden, the bitter empath of "Vaster Than Empires and More Slow", who seems more alienated than any of her other major characters, succeeds in communicating with the sentient World 4470. And far from being alienated from themselves, though some characters know themselves better or are stronger than others, they all ultimately act out of a profound sense of their own beings.

Social anthropology has a term for this special kind of isolation, and a theory of social patterns which explains how these people function in society and why they are vital in the process of change. Anthropologist Victor Turner, a student of ritual processes and symbolic behaviour in human culture, describes people in this non-alienated form of isolation as *liminal* (from the Latin *limen*, threshold), a term he borrows and modifies from the work of Arnold van Gennep on rites of passage. An understanding of what Turner means by liminality and how it functions in society will bring a new clarity and coherence to the pattern in Le Guin's fiction of the solitary hero reaching out to the alien.

Turner conceives of social structure as a process, not static and permanent like an organization chart, but dynamic and temporal, a dialectic over time between what he calls *structure* and *anti-structure* (or *communitas*). As Turner explains, "Implicitly, or explicitly, in societies at all level of complexity, a contrast is posited between the notion of society as a differentiated, segmented system of structural positions . . . and society as a homogenous, undifferentiated *whole*." The first of these notions is structure, the second communitas. In structure,

> the units are statuses and roles, not concrete human individuals. The individual is segmentalized into roles which he plays . . . The second model, communitas, often appears culturally in the guise of an Edenic, paradisiacal, utopian, or millenial state of affairs, to the attainment of which religious or political action, personal or collective, should be directed. Society is pictured as a communitas of free and equal comrades—of total persons. "Societas" or "society" . . . is a process involving both social structure and communitas, separately and united in varying proportion.[6]

By structure, Turner does not mean the kind of negative concepts associated with the word during the social protests of the 60's and early 70's—structure as another word for The System, narrow, inflexible, dehumanizing. Structure, as Turner uses the term, is the modality of human interaction responsible for stability, continuity, predictability, the preservation and transmission of tradition and knowledge. It is the blueprint or skeleton of society which indicates how each of the parts relates to other parts and to the whole. Structure is what differentiates the role of the hand from that of the eye or knee, the role of the factory worker from that of the teacher or police officer, and explains how each part contributes to the proper functioning of the whole. Communitas, complementarily, is the modality of universal brotherhood and spiritual renewal, the affirmation of the connectedness of all human beings, of the familial bond of the species. Equally important, it is also the modality of change, innovation, modification of "the way we have always done things" to meet new circumstances—society's protection from dysfunctional rigidity in a changing world. In order to be viable, a culture must provide for expressions of both modalities: the two together make up a whole.

This intimate relationship between structure and communitas, tradition and change, analysis and integration, does not however, mean that representatives of the different modalities necessarily understand each other or the relationship. In fact, the opposite is often true. Structure is, after all, the norm, for it is responsible for the day-to-day functioning of the society. Since structure is inherently a conservative modality—that is its functions, to conserve—it is no surprise that those people who are satisfied members of the structure also tend to be conservative and suspicious of change. But facilitating change is one of the important functions of communitas, and to call for change is to criticize the status quo, implicitly. Thus, says Turner, "from the standpoint of structural man, he who is in communitas is an exile or a stranger, someone who, by his very existence, calls into question the whole normative order" (p. 268)—in other words, the enemy of the structure. Equally, those in communitas can easily perceive the structural man as the enemy of necessary change, resisting out of stupidity or selfishness. Remember the bitterness and ferocity of the conflict between the American middle class ("structural men") and the anti-war youth movement (a classic example of communitas), the one insisting on the necessity of a change, the other resisting change and the changers doggedly—structure and communitas passionately rejecting not only the opinions of the other modality but the society's very need for the other modality. But in the end, very slowly, the change occurred, became integrated into the structure itself, following the archetypal pattern of change.

So: recognizing that structure is the norm but that communitas is essential for the growth and survival of a culture, what produces this magical yeast of social innovation and renewal? Turner identifies three conditions as intimately associated with communitas: liminality, outsiderhood, and lowermost status. Liminality is a term Turner borrows from van Gennep's cross-cultural study of rites of passage, which identifies three phases of such rites; separation, margin (or *limen*, threshold), and reaggregation. During the liminal period, "the state of the ritual subject . . . becomes ambiguous, neither here nor there, betwixt and between all fixed points of classification" (p. 231). The ritual subject is no longer what he was—a child, for instance, in the initiation into adulthood—but not yet what he will become at the conclusion of the ritual—a man. He is *between*, statusless, outside the social structure, if only temporarily. It is a dangerous condition, liminality. "In this gap between ordered worlds, almost anything can happen. In this interim of 'liminalilty', the possibility exists of standing aside not only from one's social position but from all social positions and of *formulating a potentially unlimited series of alternative social arrangements*" (p. 13–14, emphasis added). Turner comments, "It is the analysis of culture into factors and their free recombination in any and every possible pattern, no matter how weird, that is most characteristic of liminality" (p. 255). No wonder, then,

that the liminal condition in traditional rituals is hedged around with taboos and restrictions: society needs protection from the power of the sacred anti-structure, from the ability of the liminary to take apart and reshuffle the elements of the culture.

But Turner, though he begins with van Gennep's definition of liminality, does not end with it. Arguing that there is a strong "affinity between the middle in sacred time (the *limen*) and the outside in sacred space," Turner extends the concept of liminality beyond its original application in rites of passage and includes in it the notions of "outsiderhood" and "lowermost status" so that the term now means "any condition outside, or on the peripheries of, everyday life" (p. 52–3). This concept includes, of course, the temporary set-apartness of ritual liminality, but it also now applies to people who are set apart more permanently, for whenever there is a social structure—a clearly defined set of statuses and roles and relationships—there will also be people who for one reason or another do not fit comfortably in it. Some fall outside the structure altogether—transients, for instance, or the insane. Some people are outside the structure in another way: priests, for example, are set aside from the normal activities of the larger society by the very nature of their role. Since their concern is not with the material world but with the spiritual one, they are uninvolved in most of the structure-determined activities of the culture.[7] Other such outsiders would include, in various cultures, "shamans, diviners, mediums, . . . those in monastic seclusion, hippies, hoboes, and gypsies" (p. 233).

In addition to the outsiders, there are people who fall between the cracks of the structure, their positions ambiguous and imperfectly described by any one social role. Turner calls them structurally "marginal," those

> who are simultaneously members . . . of two or more groups whose social definitions are distinct from, and often opposed to, one another . . . These would include migrant foreigners, second-generation Americans, persons of mixed ethnic origin, parvenus (upwardly mobile marginals), the déclassés (downwardly mobile marginals), migrants from country to city, and women in a changed, nontraditional role. (p. 233).

Marginal people, that is, have two or more conflicting identities and sets of rules governing social behaviour, a fact which makes fitting comfortably into either structure very difficult. Consider the child of a mother who is Italian-American Catholic and a father descended from Russian Jews: to which of these two very different groups does the child belong? Partial participation in several such groups makes it impossible to identify wholly with any one of them.

There is one more category of people strongly linked with liminality by virtue of their position in the social matrix: the structurally inferior, those of the lowest caste, who in religion and art "have often been assigned the symbolic function of representing humanity, without status qualifications or characteristics. Here the lowest represents the human total, the extreme case most fittingly portrays the whole" (p. 234).

People in all these categories—the outsiders, the marginals, the lowermost—because they are "outside, or on the peripheries of, everyday life," are, by Turner's definition, liminal. But this kind of liminality is different from the ritual liminality van Gennep described. For these individuals, unlike the ritual liminary, the condition is not necessarily temporary: it may be indefinite, or even permanent. Nor is it necessarily a group experience; it is often a solitary one—isolation rather than renewal. And yet these misfits and outcasts are vital to their cultures, because they, even more than the ritual liminary, are the potential sources of growth and change. They share the power of all liminaries to stand outside the system and formulate alternative arrangements, to fit new phenomena into established systems of knowledge, to modify the structure as no one within the structure can do. These are the figures Le Guin puts at the fulcrum in each of her works, at the balance point where the weight turns. They are the people who make resolution and reaggravation possible. More important, they are the ones who make communication possible. Through all her variations of plot and character, this one constant emerges: liminality is the essential precondition for communication between self and other. When characters fail, wholly or in part, to achieve that kind of communication, they fail because the liminal quality is absent or insufficient or one-sided.[8] When characters succeed, they succeed because, whatever their differences, they come to share the liminal condition enough to reach out and touch the alien other.

One of the most explicit expositions of this theme in Le Guin's work is to be found in "Nine Lives," a story about the difficulties of encountering the alien, the stranger. Pugh and Martin, who have been alone on a hostile planet for six months, are to be joined by a team of miners. They look forward to the reinforcements with eagerness, but also with some trepidation.

> It is hard to meet a stranger. Even the greatest extravert meeting even the meekest stranger knows a certain dread, though he may not know he knows it. Will he make a fool of me, wreck my image of myself invade me destroy me change me? Will he be different from me? Yes, that he will. There's the terrible thing: the strangeness of the stranger.[9]

If it is so frightening to meet a stranger who presumably has the same fears and vulnerabilities as oneself, meeting someone who lacks them is overpowering. The mining team turns out to be a ten-clone, Jon Chow, a physically superb genius multiplied by ten. The clones' relationship to each other is utterly intimate and yet taken for granted, since they have never been without it; it fills all their needs, physical, intellectual, emotional, even sexual. As a unit they are completely self-sufficient. Though the clones are unfailingly polite to Pugh and Martin, they are not really interested in them. As Pugh thinks to himself, "Why should they have sympathy? That's one of the things you give because you need it back."

Then nine of the ten clones are killed in a mining accident, and the sole survivor, Kaph, finds himself alone for the first time in his life, cut off from the automatic intimacy which had shielded him from the fear of—and the need for—the stranger. He is at first so completely unresponsive Martin is sure that he has gone crazy, and that Kaph hates them for not being his brothers, but Pugh disagrees.

> Maybe. But I think he's alone. He doesn't see us or hear us, that's the truth. He never had to see anyone else before. He never was alone before. He had himself to see, talk with, live with, nine other selves all his life. He doesn't know how you go it alone. He must learn. Give him time. (p. 123).

Kaph, with Pugh's help, does begin to learn, until at the end of the story he is able to see that Pugh and Martin love each other, proof that it is possible to love someone who is not oneself. More important, Kaph is finally able to see "the thing he had never seen before: saw him: Owen Pugh, the other, the stranger who held out his hand in the dark" (p. 131).

In a more complex form, the same situation exists in *The Left Hand of Darkness.*[10] Genly Ai, of course, is obviously liminal in one sense: as First Mobile of the Ekumen to Gethen, he has left his family long dead behind him, has left all others of his own kind to venture alone into a society unlike any other human society in the known universe. But he also still has a recognizable role in a coherent structure, even though on Gethen that structure exists primarily in his own head. He has been, in fact, *sent*, and he is following a set of guidelines, a pattern of behaviour laid down and followed by others in similar situations. And he could, if great need arose, use the ansible to call down assistance. He is not totally alone; and he is highly conscious of his status, even if that status is doubted by the Gethenians. Perhaps it is this tremendous connection with structure which blinds Ai at first to Estraven's liminality. Though as Prime Minister Estraven is a part of the power structure in Karhide, he also has a unique breadth of vision. Alone of his people, Estraven has the courage and the imagination to believe in what Ai, in a fit of self-alienation, calls his "preposterous" story, to respond to Ai's message and his mission. But Ai, still secure in his structure, misreads the enigmatic Karhider and fails to perceive his profound set-apartness. Once Estaven falls from power and becomes Estraven the Traitor, Estraven the exile in Orgoreyn, he becomes even more obviously liminal—displaced, despised, outcast, "the spectre at the feast," "a banished man living off his wits in a foreign land" (p. 122). Even Genly Ai is beginning to notice that there is something unusual about Estraven, but he does not yet understand or trust the Karhider, for in Orgoreyn Ai feels more firmly connected than ever to his status as Envoy, and closer to success than he had ever felt in Karhide. This blindness lasts until Ai finds himself a captive in the darkness on the way to an unknown place. Only when he is totally cut off from his structural function, from the security of his mental structure, past all hope of contacting his friends— only then does Ai become unconditionally liminal. His position is strikingly similar to Turner's description of the experience of the ritual initiand, who "is structurally if not physically invisible in terms of his culture's standard definitions and classifications. He has been divested of the outward attributes of structural position, set aside from the main arenas of social life in a seclusion lodge or camp, and reduced to an equality with his fellow intiands regardless of their pre-ritual status" (Turner, p. 231–2). This is precisely Ai's situation, naked, freezing, starving, huddled in the dark with a group of people whom he does not know, hidden from sight in the back of a truck on his way to a prison farm. Significantly, though the conditions for an experience of communitas are present in that grim truck, it does not occur.

> Kindness there was, and endurance, but in silence, always in silence. Jammed together in the sour darkness of our shared mortality, we bumped one another continually, jolted together, fell over one another, breathed our breaths mingling, laid the heat of our bodies together as a fire is laid—but remained strangers. (p. 170).

This absence of communitas becomes a compelling indictment of the Orgota system for it indicates that the system acts to alienate men from each other rather than to unify them. As Ai remarks,

> It was the second time I had been locked in the dark with the uncomplaining, unhopeful people of Orgo-reyn. I knew now the sign I had been given, my first night in this country. I had ignored that black cellar and gone looking for the substance of Orgoreyn above ground, in daylight. No wonder nothing had seemed real. (p. 167–8).

Nothing, that is, but the prison, which, unlike all the other buildings in Mishnory, "is exactly what it looks like and is called. It is a jail. It is not a front for something else, not a facade, not a pseudonym. It is real, the real thing, the thing behind the words" (p. 166). Thus at Pulefen Farm, the only kind of real thing in Orgoreyn, Ai finds himself totally liminal—out of touch with his friends, stateless, invisible, divested of the outward attributes of his structural position as alien and as envoy of the Ekumen; and he is dying. When he encounters Estraven again, following Estraven's successful rescue of him from the farm, he must do for the first time without any of those vestiges of structure and status which stood between them before, and with no strength to support barriers of fear and distrust. On the ice, Ai and Estraven are at last equal, and equally liminal, the alien envoy and the exiled traitor, journeying together across the ice into understanding, into love. The journey itself is liminal also: like the place within the Blizzard, the Gobrin Ice is "temporarily liminal and spatially marginal," a place of "no-place and no-time" that resists classification, in which "the major classifications and categories of the culture emerge within the integuments of myth, symbol, and ritual" (Turner, p. 258–9). In this episode at last the central images of the book converge: Tormer's Lay, the source of the title; the yin-yang symbol; the place where there are no shadows. The symbolic core of the novel is here, in these totally liminal surroundings at the top of the world. During the journey Estravan and Ai come finally to know each other, to know deeply and fully, "Gnosis, 'deep knowledge,' is highly characteristic of liminality," says Turner. "Men 'know' less or more as a function of the quality of their relationship with other men" (p. 258). In this liminal state, Ai comes to know Estraven, but more, he comes to understand the wisdom of the Ekumen in sending a solitary individual as the First Mobile to a planet. He had originally believed that his solitariness was for the sake of the Gethenians, so that they could not possibly feel threatened by him, a lone individual—"not an invasion but a mere messenger-boy" (p. 259). And that is at least partly true, perhaps. But there is more to it than that, Ai realizes. As he tells Estraven,

> Alone, I cannot change your world. But I can be changed by it. Alone, I must listen, as well as speak. Alone, the relationship I finally make, if I make one, is not impersonal and not only political: it is individual, it is personal, it is both more and less than political. Not We and They; not I and It; but I and Thou. (p. 259).

Thus for Genly Ali, as for John Kaph Chow, leaving structure behind is what makes possible true communication between self and other.

While in "Nine Lives" and *The Left Hand of Darkness* Le Guin focuses on communication between individuals, in *The Eye of the Heron*[11] she changes her scope a little to examine the relationship of two groups, the two interdependent but separated human communities on the planet Victoria. That the society of Victoria City, based on the cultural pattern of Latin America, represents structure while the society of Shantih (or Shanty-Town) represents communitas is made clear by the images Le Guin chooses for the groups.

The dominant concern of the City is the idea of prison, a fact whose explanation seems partly pragmatic and partly psychological. Pragmatically, the constant possibility of imprisonment can be used by the Bosses to keep the lower orders under control; but more importantly, in psychological terms throwing someone in jail can help a man forget that, Victoria being in origin a penal colony, his ancestors were criminals.

Even more strongly, the Bosses proudly describe themselves, as often as possible, as "free men," but their tone has more of bravado in it than conviction. Somehow, for the Bosses no less than the other inhabitants, the City seems to be a combination of fortress and prison, locking out the terrifying sea of empty wilderness around them, but also locking them inside. "It was to keep out . . . their fear that the roofs and walls of the City had been raised, it was fear that had drawn the streets so straight, and made the doors so narrow" (p. 196). But the physical walls are only part of it: the men of the City have built other, less visible walls around themselves. As Vera tells Luz.

> You're not inside the walls with [your father]! He doesn't protect you—you protect him. When the wind blows, it doesn't blow on him, but on the roof and walls of this city that his fathers built as a fortress against the unknown, a protection. And you're part of that city, part of his roofs and walls, his house, Casa Falco. So is his title, Senhor, Councillor, Boss. So are all his servants and his guards, all the men and women he can give orders to. They're all part of his house, the walls to keep the wind off him. (p. 137).

Luz herself is obsessed with the idea of rooms, small square, enclosed places. Her room is the only place in which she has any freedom at all, but it is "close, dirty: a prison cell" (p. 104). Since the men run everything in Victoria City, "there was no room left for the women, no City for the women. Nowhere, nowhere, but in their own rooms, alone" (p. 107). But even that freedom, limited as it is, is precarious and uncertain. "All life had to show her was a locked door and behind the locked door, no room" (p. 108). Her images of freedom are scarcely less enclosed. The garden at the heart of Casa Falco seems to her "like an inner room of the house, shut in, protected. But a room with the roof taken off. A room into which rain fell" (p. 137)—that is, an open place. To Luz, walking in the rain in this inner garden seems as close to freedom as she will ever get.

In marked contrast to these linear, enclosed, constricted images of the City, the dominant metaphor in Shantih is the circle, the center. This is appropriate, because Shantih, the home of the People of the Peace, is an example of what Turner calls "normative communitas," the social order which results when a group experiencing spontaneous communitas organizes itself into an ongoing community which tries to preserve the original sense of brotherhood and fellowship in its religious and ethical codes and the statues which guide its daily function.[12] Unlike the sterile static image of the City, the metaphor for Shantih is dynamic and living, the ringtree of Victoria, which begins life as a single seedling that produces "one single seed on a high central branch." While the branches wither, the seed grows, until one day it explodes, showering hundreds of seedlets in a perfect circle around the central stem. "Ten years later, and for a century or two after that, from twenty to sixty copper-leaved trees stood in a perfect ring about the long-vanished central stem. Branch and root, they stood apart, yet touching, forty ringtrees, one tree-ring" (p. 118)—like the people of Shantih, four thousand individuals standing in a circle of communitas, separate, yet touching.

In contrast to the huge square capital in the City, "the biggest building in the world," the meeting hall of Shantih is mostly in the open, in the center of an old circle of ringtrees. Here the people of Shantih gather to discuss community affairs, to find the sense of the meeting, "to find and keep the center, the strength of the group. A center there was, and [Lev felt himself] in it—was the center, himself, with . . . all the others." "It was as if he were not Lev alone, but Lev times a thousand—himself, but himself immensely increased, enlarged, a boundless self mingled with all the other selves, set free, as no man alone could ever be free" (p. 160). In contrast to the City, "the walls [of Shantih] were not visible but were very strong: companionship, cooperation, love; the close human circle" (p. 196). So endemic is the circle to Shantih thinking that they even apply it to their enemies, conceiving of the City men as "caught in [a] circle of violence" (p. 124). Between these two groups, the square and the circle, the prison and the tree-ring, conflict is almost inevitable, and resolution (short of total defeat of one side or the other) likely to be limited at best. What resolution there is in the story is generated through the actions of Luz Marina, who is the one person able to understand both groups and to interpret the situation and its possibilities accurately, because she alone is liminal in both the City and the Town.

As Lev says to her, "You never were like the other City girls, you didn't fit, you didn't belong. You belong here" (p. 159). But he is only partly right, and he knows it.

> For despite his insistence that she was one of them, she was not; she was . . . not like any woman he knew. She was different, alien to him . . . There was a silence in her, a silence that drew him, drew him aside, toward a different center. (p. 162).

> There was a strength in her that was not drawn from love or trust or community, did not rise from any source that should give strength, any source he recognized. He feared that strength, and craved it. (p. 164).

The dramatic climax of the story—the confrontation between Herman Macmilan's homemade army and the People of the Peace—arrives and passes, leaving Lev dead in its wake, Lev and seventeen other Townspeople as well as eight men of the city (including Macmilan himself, killed by Luz's father). Luz's father is under house arrest for murder and Luz is very much alone, "a traitor to the City and a stranger in the Town." Oh, the Townsfolk are her friends, "Vera, Southwind, Andre, all the other, all the gentle people, but they're not [her] people. Only Lev, only Lev was, and he couldn't stay, he wouldn't wait, he had to go climb his mountain, and put off life till later" (p. 190).

But because of her very isolation, she becomes a vital figure in the destiny of Shantih. Lev's dream of a new settlement for the People of the Peace where they could be free from the domination and exploitation of the Bosses takes root in Luz and a few others in the Town; but, bound by their own conventions and assumptions, the others—especially Andre—cannot make the break with what they see as the community, by which they mean both Victoria City and Shantih. It is Luz, the outsider, who shows them a door in the wall they have built around themselves. When Andre objects that leaving surreptitiously would be running away, Luz responds angrily,

> Running away! . . . You talk about choice and freedom—The world, the whole world is there for you to live in and be free, and that would be running away! From what? To what? Maybe we can't be free, maybe people always take themselves with themselves, but at least you can try. What was your Long March for? What makes you think it ever ended? (p. 192).

So for a small group of Shanty-Towners, including Luz, the Long March continues into the trackless wilderness to the south, where at last, just before snowfall, they find a lovely little valley, sheltered, well-provided with food and water; and Luz suggests to Andre that they turn their temporary stop into a permanent one. But Andre is suddenly doubtful.

"They say when you're lost, really lost, you always go in a circle," he said. "You come back to where you started from. Only you don't always recognize it."

"This isn't the City," Luz said. "Nor the Town."

"No. Not yet."

"Not ever," she said . . . "There is a new place, Andre. A beginning place."

"God willing."

"I don't know what God wants." She put out her free hand and scratched up a little of the damp, half-frozen earth, and squeezed it in her palm. "That's God," she said, opening her hand on the half-molded sphere of black dirt. "That's me. And you. And the others. And the mountains. We're all . . . it's all one circle." (p. 206–7, last ellipsis Le Guin's).

Luz at last has found her place, has come into the circle. Now that her liminality, with her ability to see new possibilities and break old patterns, is no longer needed, she is free to become a member of the community. Because of her, the little group has moved not in a circle back to the same old place, but in a spiral, to a new place, a new beginning. Even without Lev to lead her, she has found her own way into the center, from liminality to communitas, from communitas into the structure of the new community.

Liminality leading to communitas is the common theme of all these works, as it is of a preponderance of Le Guin's writing. Though the focus and emphasis may shift from work to work, the essential message remains the same: shared loneliness and mutual vulnerability—the fundamental human condition, if we can only admit it—is the only ground in which communication, friendship, love can flourish. Social anthropology can help us understand intellectually why this is so; Le Guin's fiction, sane, wise, and profoundly mature, helps our hearts to understand and accept it.

*Notes*

I am deeply indebted to James Bittner for his encouragement, advice and support, for his probing questions and bibliographical generosity, and for his acceptance of an earlier version of this paper for the Le Guin Panel at the 1979 Popular Culture Association Convention.

1. Douglas Barbour, "Wholeness and Balance in the Hainish Novels of Ursula K. Le Guin," *Science-Fiction Studies*, 1 (1974), 167, 172.

2. Donald F. Theall, "The Art of Social-Science Fiction: The Ambiguous Utopian Dialects of Ursula K. Le Guin," *Science-Fiction Studies*, 2 (1975), 263–4.

3. Rafail Nudelman, "An Approach to the Structure of Le Guin's SF," trans. Alan G. Myers, *Science-Fiction Studies*, 2 (1975), 215.

4. Thomas J. Remington, "A Touch of Difference, a Touch of Love: Theme in Three Stories by Ursula K. Le Guin," *Extrapolation*, 18 (Dec. 1976), 28.

5. Erich Fromm, *Marx's Concept of Man* (New York, 1961), 43–58.

6. Victor Turner, *Dramas, Fields and Metaphors: Symbolic Action in Human Society* (Ithaca, NY, 1974), 237–8.

7. As a member of a hierarchy, each priest is also a participant in his own structural set (the Church), but from the perspective of the larger society, all priests are by definition structural outsiders.

8. "The New Atlantis" is an exception to this. We are given strong hints throughout the story that some kind of ghostly and dreamlike communication is already occuring, especially in the powerful shared vision of sunlight on the white towers of Atlantis; but Belle (presumably) drowns before the Atlanteans finally emerge, leaving behind only her journal to speak for her. So in this case at least, full communication is prevented by circumstance rather than insufficient liminality.

9. Ursula K. Le Guin, "Nine Lives," in *The Wind's Twelve Quarters* (New York, 1975), 107.

10. *The Left Hand of Darkness* (New York, 1976). This edition includes a preface by Le Guin; older editions lacking the preface have a different pagination.

11. *The Eye of the Heron*, in *Millennial Women*, ed. Virginia Kidd (New York, 1978).

12. Turner, p. 169. Monastic orders are a good example of this. Given that Turner derives much of his data on communitas from pilgrimages, both historical and modern, the Long March at the root of Shantih's philosophical and political structure takes on added significance.

## ROZ KAVENEY
### From "Science Fiction in the 1970s"
*Foundation*, June 1981, pp. 16–18

S. F. in the 70s was dominated by Ursula Le Guin whose simultaneously conservative and progressive art and insights created the terms in which all others, including those writers in the genre whose gifts are arguably greater than hers, are likely to be judged. In her 1976 lecture at the ICA "Science Fiction and Mrs Brown" she called for work that would concern itself essentially with people, and during the decade that is to a large extent precisely what she got—even if the means used to portray characters and their aspirations were at times more radical than those she used and advocated, and if the person concretely portrayed at the heart of some novels was recognizably the author. (It was perhaps with this lecture and its influence in mind that John Crowley in his story "The Reason for the Visit" for Le Guin's *Interfaces* anthology portrays so vividly her idol Virginia Woolf.) In "psychomyths" like "The Ones who Walk away from Omelas" Le Guin uses the freedom of sf and fantasy tropes to dramatize in concrete and apposite ways various problems of morality, particularly of social morality. In *The Dispossessed*, its pendant "The Day Before the Revolution" and the historical novel about Romanticism set in an imaginary country, *Malafrena*, she portrays the mutual interaction of individuals and society with a vibrant realism that is only really possible when all the details of the environment have been made up from scratch by the author. There is no need to discuss her work at vast length—Le Guin studies have become something more than a cottage industry. What is important is the extent to which Le Guin has created the terms of critical discussion in her decade. I have suggested that the social and cultural climate caused readers to favour social novels and novels of character above work which examined new ways of feeling or thinking without much emphasis on what that feeling and thinking was actually for: Le Guin acted as a focus within the sf and fantasy genres by being so precisely and so excellently the sort of writer we were all looking for. Even work which has concentrated on expression of the writer's personality, on rhetorical political polemic, on games with literary modes or statements about the career of writing, has tended to do so by means which include at least lip service to the vivid portraiture and sense of deep moral artistic and social responsibility which characterized both the prescription and the practice of Ursula Le Guin.

While specifically rejecting as a useful form of fiction Socialist Realism, she wrote a fiction that was as close as any in the fiction of the period to explicit comment on current affairs, but always with a depth and seriousness that keeps her work fresher than much politically relevant sf is likely to remain. Where Haldeman's *Forever War* looks increasingly like a glamourized moan about the experience of combat, concentrating as it does on the angst involved in being shot at and the dislocation of coming home to a changed society, Le Guin's *The Word for World Is Forest* looks deeply at some of the real

issues involved for a civilized moral humanist in America's involvement in S.E. Asia—the undercurrent of racism in Western society, the vindictiveness it awakes in its victims, the impotence of the "good" western "liberal" to control the agression of his fellow citizens and the link via sadistic sexuality between racism and sexism. Davidson's real crime is to make the Athsheans over into his image: for all Selver's pious hopes that once he lays down his mission his people will be able to control their newfound aggression, an innocence has been lost. Davidson, Selver and Lyubov are credible individuals, but stand for something beyond themselves: Le Guin fulfils her own prescription for plausible portraiture, but her characters also act out roles in the social and moral, if not political, debate that gives her fiction its direction and intensity. Odo in "The Day Before the Revolution" is a set of mannerisms and perceptions and memories—we are made to see the world through her failing eyes and are thus forced to believe that she is in there to see it with us—but she also stands for the author's observation of the old, for the hope that one can attain old age retaining integrity and dignity, as a portrait of a generation of noble radicals in our world—rather than in the imaginary capitalism of Urras—and as promulgator of a set of ideas.

By giving that story the title she did, Le Guin cheatingly achieves a sense, a sense no less real because we have been tricked into it, of Odo's successful and dominant interaction with her world; if a story with that title is concerned so intensely with an individual, we are half-convinced of that individual's agency within society even before Le Guin has begun to demonstrate it. In *The Dispossessed* she makes use of the knowledge of her fictional universe which many readers already possess to give intensity to our belief that the work Shevek is doing is important and thereby in the importance of free enquiry even when in the short term it clashes with the demands of what approximates to a just society, Le Guin is quite as unscrupulous as Disch or Crowley when it comes to using the standard expectations of fiction in general and sf in particular to manipulate audience sympathy: she has artistic integrity which is by no means the same thing as always playing fair with her audience in the crude sense. She has the freedom of one who has understood the underlying message of modernism and adapted its precepts to her less obviously progressive artistic ends. She is aware that at a crucial level all fiction is a form of rhetoric, a construct rather than a description of objective truth—though it may *represent* truth—that in art if not in life achieved ends justify moderately dishonest rhetorical methods. She works in an art whose nature is deceit—it is when she comes closest to speaking directly about pacifism and the role of women in "The Eye of the Heron", when she is so involved that she forgets to be clever, that she comes closest to the conventional and the dull.

## WAYNE COGELL
### "The Absurdity of Sartre's Ontology: A Response by Ursula K. Le Guin"
*Philosophers Look at Science Fiction*
ed. Nicholas D. Smith
1982, pp. 144–51

"A Trip to the Head" is a short story by Ursula K. Le Guin that presents a *reductio ad absurdum* of the existential philosophy of Jean-Paul Sartre and much more.[1] I will only discuss the *reductio* in this paper.

Le Guin calls attention to three absurdities in Sartre's philosophy: first, the arbitrariness and lack of firm grounds in Sartre's account of human choice, which makes ethics meaningless; second, the exclusive emphasis on subjective time, which results in solipsism; and third, the emphasis on self-created essence, which makes significant interpersonal human relations impossible.

Sartre's philosophy as presented in *Being and Nothingness* has the following features: (1) a being-in-itself, which is given complete in essence and act; (2) a phenomenological approach, which results in the claim that all is given in the phenomenal appearances of things; (3) a being-for-itself, which is consciousness in process of projecting meanings on things and itself; and (4) a being-for-others, which is viewed as a direct threat to personal freedom. I will detail the features of Sartre's ontology and Le Guin's response to them.[2]

Sartre conceives of being-in-itself *(en soi)* as an absolute plenum with no potency and no real relations to anything else.[3] It is complete because its essence is given in its actual, particular existence, as exemplified by a table or a rock. The result is a finished continuum fully actualized and totally complete, lacking all power and potency. Such a view is similar to Heidegger's suggestion that there is a subhuman existence, a determinate being-on-hand *(Vorbandensein)* which is something finished and simply there. According to Sartre, beings-in-themselves, such as trees and fawns, are completely given with an essence that indicates what they are. They are complete in act and therefore cannot change or cause anything.

Sartre is, like other existentialists before him, primarily interested in the concrete data of experience as they actually appear.[4] He claims to follow a purely descriptive, phenomenological approach. Anxious to reject the Kantian conception of a noumenal thing-in-itself behind the phenomena, Sartre asserts that things appear only in perception and that perceptions associated with them exhaust all positive reality. The appearances of things are their reality. This identifies being with the succession of its finished appearances.

According to Sartre, a real thing whose existence is presented phenomenologically can never be exhausted by any concept invented by men. There will always be properties in excess of anything the concept may imply.

In *Nausea*, the diary entry for Wednesday 6:00 P.M. indicates "the world of explanations and reasons is not the world of existence."[5] The chestnut tree is not a "chestnut tree" since the latter fails, like any general label, to capture the superabundant overflowing of the reality to which it is lamely applied. The basic theme which Sartre develops is that the structures of consciousness are different than the structures of the objects of consciousness.

In contrast to being-in-itself and the phenomenal appearances of things, a human being is a being-for-itself *(pour soi)*.[6] Being-for-itself is a potential nothingness. As potential nothingness, it is characterized as having its existence precede its essence and as having the capacity of consciousness, which is the power of negation.

Unlike being-in-itself, human beings find that they exist but do not understand why. They are not born with meaning or purpose—this they must define for themselves; they must create their essence. They must also create their world; since the realm of being is a dense field without distinction, there is no determinate structure or finite difference. Except as those distinctions are made by the projects of the being-for-itself, the world is not intelligible. This potential to create the world applies also to the self and resides in the capacity of consciousness.

The capacity of consciousness is the power of negations, that is, the ability to conceive of things as they are not. If being-in-itself is fully in act, it cannot be deprived of anything it requires; it is complete within itself. Therefore, negation and privation have no ground in being, but must be referred to the negativity of human consciousness.

Perceptions, for example, are given to consciousness as complete and only as what they are: a tree is given as branch, leaf, etc. The ability to conceive of a given tree in early spring as not given, cut down, or as bearing fruit, is the human power of negation as a projection on the given. Human consciousness as the power of negation operates as a projection on being-in-itself and being-for-itself. When consciousness results in a projection, a new reality is created.

Another aspect of Sartre's ontology is "being-for-others" *(autrui)*.[7] The temporalized world of being-for-itself is an insulated world. Into the world of being-for-itself, the others make their appearance. The interrelation of personal selves is disclosed in shame. Through shame I discover simultaneously the other and an aspect of my being. I am ashamed of my self before the other. The other reveals myself to me.

I need the other, Sartre maintains, in order to realize fully all the structures of my being. Other people make me aware of myself; they make me see how what I am doing is to be described. They label me as stupid, clever, dishonest. Other people's descriptions of my acts modify my view of myself. For example, the realization that other people regard me as predictably unpunctual modifies my view of myself, since from my own point of view each instance of unpunctuality is just a matter of chance, just bad luck.

Another way in which the other is disclosed is through "the look."[8] According to Sartre, "the look" of the other erupts into my world, decentralizes and dissolves it and, by reference to his own projects, reconstitutes it and the freedom which I experience. The other is apprehended as one who is about to steal my world, suck me into the orbit of his concerns and reduce me to the mode of being-in-itself, to an object or thing.

Through *my* look I can seek to shatter the world of the other and divest him of his subjective freedom, the freedom to decide for himself his future. I seek to remove the other from my world and put him out of play, but this can never succeed. I encounter the other; I do not constitute him. The other remains, threatening to counterattack. Thus there results a constant cycle of mutual objectivization.

The upshot of all this is an irreconcilable conflict between the self and the other with a consequent breakdown of all communication. Alienation has the last word in Sartre's doctrine of inter-subjectivity. The search for a positive doctrine of community is not part of Sartre's philosophy. All forms of "being-with" find their common denominator in an alienating "being-for."

Sartre's account of the constitutive structure of human existence has the significant implication that man has no common nature or essence. He makes himself into what he is by the projects which he chooses. Man is condemned to freedom, although he desires to be a being-in-itself, complete in essence.

Human action, however, is not a mode of being, but rather a mode of negativity. It is always pursuing itself, but never achieving unity. Any choice, for example, is a flight into the future from the present. No sooner is it realized than it must be rejected to preserve the fluid negativity of being-for-itself. Human beings can never rest; personal nothingness, incompleteness, and freedom are their existential predicament.

How does Le Guin represent and respond to Sartre's existential theory of man?

In "A Trip to the Head"[9] Le Guin presents to the reader endless Sartrian absurdities to study. She has two characters who do not know their own names or identities; an island, England, which has sunk; arbitrary jumps in time of twenty to thirty years in order that Ralph's sexual appetite may be satisfied; a trip in a sewer pipe; the disappearance of The Other for no apparent reason; and Ralph's assertion that he is Lewis D. Charles (but alas, he has given the wrong name, just as Sartre has given a wrong description of things).

These actions are meaningless, silly, inconsequential, and absurd. Throughout her story Le Guin has, in contrast to Sartre's view, the natural, uniform movement of the world turning on its axis. Nature is there in the forest with "mild eyes" unaffected by these Sartrian absurd contingencies.

Le Guin's two characters (Blank and The Other) are set in an absurd world entangled with the three aspects of Sartre's ontology: a given world of a being-in-itself, a being-for-itself, and a being-for-others. The world is absurd.

> In Zambia men are rolling down hills inside barrels as training for space flight. Israel and Egypt have defoliated each other's deserts. The *Reader's Digest* has bought a controlling interest in the United States of America/General Mills combine. The population of the earth is increasing by thirty billion every Thursday. Mrs. Jacqueline Kennedy Onassis will marry Mao Tse-tung on Saturday in search of security, and Russian has contaminated Mars with breadmold.[10]

Le Guin concretely shows what Sartre's world would be like. She not only satirically displays Sartre's philosophy but asserts, through her use of literary devices, that his view is empirically inadequate.

Le Guin presents Blank as a character unaware of where he is or who he is. He recognizes that he has a body (being-in-itself) but he is "a blank, a cipher, an X." She says, "He had a body and all that, but he had no who." Because he has no common nature or essence, Blank must make himself. The Other suggests that he could take any name or label, like Disposable, but blank wants to know his real name. He faces the question squarely. "How can I say who I am when I can't say what I am?"

The Other suggests, "It's what you do that counts," and Blank immediately stands up and declares that he will exist and call himself "Ralph."

What follows is Blank's attempt at a Sartrian definition of himself. He is a Yankee landowner hopelessly, romantically in love with a Southern lady, Amanda, who does not understand what he desires when he says, "I never wanted anything but you, my white lily, my little rebel! I want you! I want you! Amanda! Say you will be my wife!" Suddenly there is a leap of twenty or thirty years and Ralph's desires are made clear to Amanda. Now Amanda is knees up, naked against a pecan tree; she and Blank couple and climax is achieved.

In response to Sartre's position Le Guin has shown one absurdity in his existential theory of man: the supposed arbitrariness and the lack of firm grounds for human choice. In trying to create myself by the projects which I choose, according to Sartre, whether I die for justice or drink at a bar is a matter of indifference.

The arbitrariness of Blank's choice to be Ralph is followed by an arbitrariness of location, time, and character. Blank's frustration is remedied with a sudden leap of twenty or thirty years. The lack of firm grounds for his choice is clearly illustrated by Le Guin. When Blank returns to the original setting with The Other, he is confused about his sex. "Am I a man?" inquires Blank. "And are you a woman?"

Another absurdity in Sartre's existential theory of man,

resulting from the lack of firm grounds for human choice, is that no account of human ethics is possible. Since man has no stable nature, since he possesses no constant tendencies, and since he is condemned to no rest, personal nothingness, and freedom, it does not make sense to provide changeless norms to which he must conform his conduct. In fact if Sartre is right, all regrets must be momentarily felt but not understood since they are not the result of anything in the person. Thus Le Guin has Blank feel sorry for sexually abusing The Other but immediately moves on to a new project.

Another absurdity results in Sartre's account of being-for-itself as consciousness because of his emphasis on subjective time. According to this doctrine, human consciousness temporalizes itself through an integral order of qualitative changes in which the past that I have been and the future project that I will be are integrated in the present consciousness of my becoming.

Le Guin shows the effect of Sartre's emphasis on subjective time when Blank declares, "I'm on some kind of trip." He is paddling his canoe against the current, uphill, enclosed in a concrete sewer pipe. It's hard work but his canoe keeps gliding forward upriver as the black shining water moves back down. He can't say anything; he has no idea of where he is or if he is moving forward or only hanging still.

It is a consequence of Sartre's emphasis on consciousness that man is caught in solipsism. What one knows is limited to the sewer pipe of his consciousness in which he glides, not knowing if he is moving forward or hanging still.

Le Guin does not totally disagree with this analysis of subjective time. What she regards as wrong is Sartre's disregard for the importance of world-time. For Le Guin, there is also a flux of world-time which is sweeping the stars, the planets, and a person's life in a single irreversible direction. In terms of Sartre's position, however, man is enclosed in his own stream of consciousness without any possible passage to the external world.

In "A Trip to the Head," Le Guin confronts the problem of the Other from the beginning of the story: "As Jean-Paul Sartre has said in his lovable way, Hell is other people." The Other is a threat to Blank's being but is needed to aid in his creation of his essence. The Other is willing to place any label on Blank.

From Blank's view The Other is used to prove his being in sexual intercourse, which he views as "having and acting in its intensest form." The Other tries to show that it matters which man and which woman are involved together with their particular, unique, characteristics. "For instance," The Other says, "what if Amanda was black?"

Finally, when Blank realizes that he is nothing, the Other suggests that he might as well be Jean-Paul Sartre. This suggestion drives Blank to a denial that results in his asserting that he is Lewis D. Charles, at which point The Other disappears. "Lewis D. Charles looked in the red eye of the west and the dark eye of the east. He shouted aloud, 'Come back! Please come back!'"

If Sartre's account of man is correct then, as Le Guin properly points out, to create oneself is to destroy the other, and each person is alone. Love, friendship, and devoted cooperation for common ends are exluded *a priori*. All of this Le Guin views as dubious.

The consequence of Sartre's philosophy is that all that is given in the phenomenal appearances of things is contingent. In the classical discussion of being, thinkability, necessity, contingency, meaning, truth, and that which is accidental intersect in the doctrine of essence. Also the traditional account states that the existence of things does not form part of their essence. The definition of man—"Man is a rational animal"—indicates what man essentially is, independent of whether such a creature exists. The doctrine maintains as unthinkable that something should be human without being rational. (There is one exception in the tradition: the concept of God who exists necessarily, his existence being his essence). Thus the essence of a thing is logically prior to its existence.

In Sartre's philosophy of man, however, one's existence precedes his essence. Existence is always something literally extra. Hence the existence of a person is always logically superfluous and never part of the concept we may apply to him. What is absurd in Sartre's philosophy is that everything human is superfluous, because it is meaningless and contingent. However that which is merely contingent and without necessity is for Le Guin absurd, not merely silly or meaningless.

In "A Trip to the Head" Le Guin has Blank discover "I am myself," which rings as self-validating as the Cartesian *cognito ergo sum*.

"He knew it as well as he knew his own name," Le Guin says ironically. He is tied to world-time: "There he was," she writes, "The forest was there, root and branch." The paradox, however, is that he got the wrong name because "He had gone at it all wrong, backwards."

For Le Guin the world is not absurd; there are natural grounds for human choice which are found in the full history of an individual integrated in the present world flux. But there may be things hidden from view, such as internal structures of nature with "mild eyes" the look back at human beings from the "darkness of the trees." Le Guin's position here seems to be that each existing thing has finite structures which limit and act as its ontological ground; it has potencies which are marked by an absence of realization. Things can pass, turn away, or cease to be, but without the recognition of each living thing's finite structures, the fact of physical change and any view of nature becomes unintelligible and absurd.

> Under the trees Blank forgot his name again at once. He also forgot what he was looking for. What was it he had lost? He went deeper and deeper into shadows, under leaves, eastward, in the forest where nameless tigers burned.[11]

Le Guin would have us return to nature (as do the fawn and Blank), to nature the way things really are, nameless but not absurd.

*Notes*

1. Ursula K. Le Guin, "A Trip to the Head," *The Wind's Twelve Quarters* (London: Victor Gollancz Ltd., 1976), pp. 173–80.
2. Jean-Paul Sartre, *Being and Nothingness*, translated by Hazel E. Barnes (New York: Washington Square Press, 1953).
3. Ibid., pp. 24–30.
4. Ibid., pp. 7–9.
5. Jean-Paul Sartre, *Nausea*, translated by Lloyd Alexander (Norfolk, Conn.: New Directions, 1959), p. 171.
6. Sartre, *Being and Nothingness*, pp. 119–55.
7. Ibid., pp. 301–401.
8. Ibid., pp. 340–401.
9. Le Guin, "A Trip to the Head," pp. 173–80.
10. Ibid., p. 174.
11. Ibid., pp. 179–80.

## SARAH LEFANU

*Foundation*, November 1983, pp. 101–4

In the preface to this volume of short stories written over the last ten years ⟨*The Compass Rose*⟩, Ursula Le Guin makes claims for them that are both grandiose and obscure. She starts by talking about a map on which, or near which, the stories take place. It is a map of the author's mind, she suggests, then abdicates responsibility by saying that one's mind is never one's own. What does that mean? That the formation of our minds is multi-factorial? Well, yes. One's mind is never one's own and "ever less so as one lives, learns, loses etc." That etc bothers me. Is the alliteration obligatory? One could perhaps continue with loves, lies, leans on or leaps.

She goes on to describe the map of the Compass Rose and how its four directions arise out of an "unspoken fifth direction, the center, the corolla of the rose." Unspoken? Le Guin herself has just spoken it. In the next paragraph this structure is jettisoned in favour of one with six directions, the four wind directions and Above and Below, the latter two being radial to the "center/self/here and now". These three apparently interchangeable states of being "may", we are told, "sacramentally contain the other six, and thus the Universe". Well, that's a bold statement, but I am no clearer about this map than I was at the beginning. Wait, though. The obscurity is explained in the next paragraph, for "as a guide to sailors" the book is not to be trusted. Dreary old weather-beaten sailors whose deeply unspiritual attitude to the world comes from their use of maps to get from point A to point B. Why is the book not to be trusted? Because it is perhaps "too sensitive" to local magnetic fields. Aha. Much is revealed in that little phrase. If one carps at the irritating portentousness of the preface, it is because one is obviously not open to a world "alive with symbol and meaning". If you fail to catch the underlying pattern then you must be a spiritual imbecile.

The stories are grouped under directions, NSEW, Nadir and Zenith, yet we are told that the reasons why they are so assigned are "not very serious". So why do it? murmurs a small voice. We are, however, generously given some hints as to relations between the first and last stories, for instance. Try to visualize these circling motions. I imagined a kind of horizontal spiral along which all the other stories in the book are placed; but how does that fit in with the multi-directional compass rose, not to mention their sacramental containment within the centre/self etc? Or do perhaps all the other stories somehow circle about the first and last? My suspicion is that this, too, is "not very serious"; what is important is the concept of circularity, which is, as we all know, philosophically right on, unlike nasty old rationalist linear-type logic. The advantage of circles is two-fold: there is no hierarchy within the circle itself, by its nature it connects to itself and, better, if you have more than one of them you can make them all into links in a chain. And there we have a holistic approach to the Universe. But perhaps the circling motions represent the six years that passed between the writing of the two stories, as it is well known that planet Earth moves in a circle (more or less but accuracy doesn't seem to be a priority here) round old Sol and thus we have our years. No-one, I think would deny that in a writer's work connections of one kind or another can usually be made. In this instance I don't think much useful light is shed on them by the author's own commentary.

The preface is only a page and a half long, but for those who don't like to be told how to interpret the text on which they're about to embark it is annoying in the extreme and in some cases might even lead to what could be described as a negative attitude. This is a great pity. Ursula Le Guin is generally considered to be a serious and skilful writer, and this collection of stories does not contradict that. Her skill in storytelling is, however, undermined when she lets the preachiness that is apparent in her preface enter into her fiction.

"The Pathways of Desire", for instance, starts well, with the depiction of a planet 31 light years from Earth inhabited by people who appear to live in a state of pre-cultural innocence. The lack of complexity, the almost boring simplicity of their lives create an uneasiness in the minds of the researchers from Earth that leads to the sinister discovery that the language of the Ndif is no less than a crude form of English—basic, uninflected and almost ludicrously transparent. How is this possible? No-one from Earth has ever visited this solar system. One of the researchers suddenly dies as the result of a knife wound incurred during a fight that seemed to be purely ritualistic. At this point the story has an eerie, disquieting feel to it; I was reminded of Harry Harrison's depiction of innocence corrupted by bungling Christianity in his short story "The Streets of Ashkalon". Yet while maintaining its effects right up to the resonant and horribly predictable climax, Le Guin then sacrifices the tension she has built up for a speculation on the nature of reality that retrospectively undermines the story—the planet is nothing but the dream of a fifteen year old boy on earth—and whose unoriginality is, if anything, emphasized by semi-mystical talk of infinites of universe and infinities of dreams. "We are the dreamer", is the line, "and the worlds will endure as long as our desire". This is soppy stuff compared to Harrison's spine-tingling finale.

Le Guin is good at landscapes, atmospheres, nature—although I found the description of extreme cold in "Sur", an interesting story about an all-female expedition to the South Pole in 1909, nowhere near as chilling as the famous journey across the ice-cap in *The Left Hand of Darkness*—but again, in "The Eye Altering", the power of her physical description is dissipated by a quasi-philosophical denouement: that beauty is relative, not absolute, and that one woman's meat can be, literally, another's poison. In this story the colonists from earth have to take metabolizing pills twice daily to break down the foreign proteins of the ugly dimly-lit planet that is now their home. The plot depends for its resolution on the assumption that a largish group of people will infallibly take their daily pills and, further, that adaptation to foreign protein can be achieved in one generation—both rather unlikely, it seemed to me.

Ursula Le Guin herself, I imagine, might not accept that a distinction can be drawn between the spiritual and the political, yet it seems to me that the stories that are more overtly political, that is, those that deal with the social control of individuals, with questions of state organization, repression and dissent, are more successful than the others. "The New Atlantis" offers a vision of the lost Atlantis as a symbol of hope and freedom in a rigidly authoritarian society in which the state controls its citizens' lives to such an extent that to be private is to be subversive. This is a passionately angry picture of totalitarianism, which is further developed in "The Diary of the Rose" (published a year later), a diary kept by a government psychoscopist whose relationship with one of her patients, or prisoners, forces her into questioning the work she does and the ruling ideology of Positive Thinking. Le Guin has a fine ear for the turns of speech that reveal vanity and self-deception, and she is skilful at depicting how petty tyranny flourishes in the endless corridors and countless offices of a bureaucratic state.

I must admit to a partiality for short stories that deal with the specific and an impatience with the extrapolation from them of weightier matters. "The First Report of the Ship-wrecked Foreigner to the Kadanh of Derb" is, specifically,

about methods of narration, and the Foreigner chooses to describe the particular, in this case the city of Venice, as a means of expressing the general. Yet there is a problem that follows predictably from the somewhat hectoring tone of the preface to the collection: it is that Ursula Le Guin or, in this case, the Foreigner, despite assertions to the contrary, will not let the particular speak for itself, but must spell out its links with the generality.

I enjoyed *The Compass Rose* as a collection without connections: it shows Le Guin ranging from the serious to the playful, and if some stories seemed completely obscure—in particular a couple about animals, which perhaps means I am guilty of speciesism—the majority are entertaining. As the charmingly loquacious hero says in "Schrödinger's Cat", "Many things are not worth doing, but almost anything is worth telling." Even for a spiritual imbecile there is enjoyment to be had in hearing these tales.

### C. N. MANLOVE
### "Conservatism in Fantasy: Ursula Le Guin"
#### *The Impulse of Fantasy Literature*
#### 1983, pp. 31–44

Most fantasies seek to conserve those things in which they take delight: indeed it is one of their weaknesses that they are tempted not to admit loss. Their frequent looking to the past is conservative in itself: and the order to which they look and seek to re-create is usually a medieval and hierarchic one, founded on the continuance of the *status quo*. Many of them portray the preservation of an existing state of things as their central subject. C.S. Lewis's *Perelandra* describes the maintenance of the innocence of a Venusian Adam and Eve, and his *The Lion, the Witch and the Wardrobe* portrays the recovery of the original condition of a land called Narnia through the Christ-like sacrifice of the lion Aslan. Tolkien's *The Lord of the Rings*, while admitting historical change, is concerned with the survival of being and individualism in Middle-earth, imaged in the destruction of the annihilating power of Sauron and the restoration of the rightful king to the throne of Gondor. E. Nesbit's fairy tales are conservative in that they often end with the return of parents or the recovery of an amulet or the restoration of a descendant to true inheritance. Charles Williams's novels portray the removal of a supernatural irruption which has itself illuminated the true character of reality. Many fantasies end in disenchantment and restoration of 'normality'. The *status quo* so preserved is no dead thing, but rather a living balance founded on continuous choice or on a delicately maintained frontier between the orders of nature and supernature. Conservatism and its concomitant balance are at the heart of the 'Earthsea' trilogy of Ursula Le Guin—*A Wizard of Earthsea* (1968), *The Tombs of Atuan* (1972) and *The Farthest Shore* (1973).

Balance is the condition of being Mrs Le Guin's fantastic world. When the apprentice mage[1] Ged, who is to be the hero of the trilogy, is at the school for wizards on the island of Roke, the Master Hand tells him,

'you must not change one thing, one pebble, one grain of sand, until you know what good and evil will follow on the act. The world is in balance, in Equilibrium. A wizard's power of Changing and of Summoning can shake the balance of the world. It is dangerous, that power. It is most perilous. It must follow knowledge, and serve need." (WE, p. 54; see also FS, pp. 43, 74–5)

It is this balance which in *A Wizard of Earthsea* Ged upsets when, in arrogant contest with another apprentice mage Jasper, he summons up a spirit of the dead, and in doing so looses into the world a hideous black shadow which almost rends him to death (*WE*, p. 71); it takes all the power of the Archmage Nemmerle of Roke to save Ged, banish the shadow from Roke and close up the hole that has been made between the realms of life and death. The rest of the book describes Ged's attempt to restore the balance he has destroyed; and when finally he catches up with the shadow, he does so after voyaging 'towards the very centre of that balance, towards the place where light and darkness meet', and also to where land and sea merge in a unity out of time (*WE*, pp. 174–5, 184–6). In *The Farthest Shore* the mage Cob refuses to die, refuses that which is the balance of life (*FS*, pp. 188–9), and in doing so upsets the balance of the whole world and all but drains the life from it.

This balance is no static thing, but is part of the mobile fabric of life. In *The Farthest Shore* Ged (if rather explicitly) tells his companion, Prince Arren, ' "Only what is mortal bears life, Arren. Only in death is there rebirth. The Balance is not a stillness. It is a movement—an eternal becoming" ' (*FS*, p. 145). The balance has to do with a dialectically conceived world, where everything works by contraries. ' "To light a candle is to cast a shadow" ', says the Master Hand (*WE*, p. 54). Only by accepting death can one continue to live: in the land of the dead Ged tells Cob, of King Erreth-Akbe, ' "Here is nothing, dust and shadows. There, he is the earth and sunlight, the leaves of trees, the eagle's flight. He is alive. And all who ever died, live; they are reborn, and have no end, nor will there ever be an end" ' (*FS*, p. 189). As the epigraph from '*The Creation of Éa*' in *A Wizard of Earthsea* puts it, 'Only in silence the word,/only in dark the light,/only in dying life:/bright the hawk's flight/on the empty sky' (see also *WE*, pp. 28, 179, 189). The very nature of the fantastic world, Earthsea, paints a dialectical relation of earth and sea. The archipelago is not quite a 'land', since it is in fragments on an ocean. Yet it is united in legend and history, and as the huddle of the known world about such a centre as Roke, which sends out wizards to all parts of the world to preserve it from harm: it demonstrates the dialectic of unity in multiplicity in that the peoples are often insular and ignorant, and yet part of the larger, if often warring, group.

This 'dialectical balance' can be seen in the form of *A Wizard of Earthsea*, which is artistically the most satisfying book of the trilogy. Although Ged and the theme of the shadow are the central concern, there are many other topics not directly connected with it. These include the account of Ged's early life and education on Gont and Roke (*WE*, pp. 13–61); his career as mage of Low Torning and his vain attempt to bring back the sick child of the fisherman Pechvarry from the lands of the dead (pp. 88–93); his saving of Low Torning from the threat of the dragons of Pendor (pp. 94–102); the attempt of the Lord Benderesk and the Lady Serret on Osskil to persuade him to loose the evil power of the Terrenon stone (pp. 118–32); and Ged's encounter with the exiled king and queen on the mid-ocean shoal (pp. 145–52). But for his having loosed the shadow, Ged himself says, he would have explored much more of the diversity of Earthsea (p. 176). Unity is thus played against by multiplicity; and yet the multiplicity has in it the seeds of unity. For Ged's education as mage gives him both power and temptation (*WE*, pp. 31–5); the attempt to save the dying child is another, if more charitable, kind of the presumption that led him to try to call up a spirit of the dead; his battle with the dragons and his resistance of the old dragon Yevau's blandishments demonstrate his courage and purity of

heart; his behaviour in rejecting the stone of the Terrenon further shows his learnt refusal to try to use evil for his own ends (an attempt which would have led to his doom (*WE*, p. 128); and his meeting with the old king and queen gives him one half of the Ring of Erreth-Akbe which is to be central to the plot of *The Tombs of Atuan*. In short, what is portrayed in all save the last of these episodes is a moral development which helps to make comprehensible Ged's change, after the Terrenon adventure, from letting himself be hunted by the shadow to doing the hunting himself.

And that switch, from 'Hunted' to 'Hunting' (the titles of different chapters) is another instance of the formal balance of the book: chapters 5, 6 and 7 cover his attempts to flee the shadow and the next and last three cover his pursuit of it; and each section is of almost identical length. Again, in the 'Hunted' section Ged is in a sense directionless, going anywhere in the hope of escaping the shadow; but, 'Hunting', he has an increasing sense of where to trace the shadow: and in the end there is a trans-temporal fusion of these opposites when Ged travels across an empty sea with a fixed direction in mind, and meets the shadow on a featureless sandbank, where 'He strode forward, away from the boat, but in no direction. There were no directions here, no north or south or east or west, only towards and away' (*WE*, p. 186).

The Earthsea books have a formal structure expressing the theme of balance. Where in the first and third books Ged is journeying over Earthsea, in the second, *The Tombs of Atuan*, he remains in one place throughout, the labyrinth of the dark powers on the island of Atuan in the Kargad lands on the northeast of Earthsea. In *A Wizard of Earthsea* his journeying ends in a traverse of the East Reach, and in *The Farthest Shore* of the West Reach. Much is made of the number nine. There are nine lore masters on Roke,[2] nine months from the time that Ged leaves Roke after bringing his shadow into the world until he finally defeats it, nine chapters describing his development as a mage from the point of his apprenticeship to the wizard Ogion in *A Wizard of Earthsea* and nine great runes on the Ring of Erreth-Akbe. The course Ged follows in the first book, from Gont, via Roke, Low Torning, Pendor, Osskil, Gont, the shoal on which he finds the strange old couple, and Iffish, to the rendezvous with his shadow on the mid-ocean sand beyond the last land of the East Reach, traces out a figure 9 over the map of Earthsea; and the significant places stopped at also total nine. In *The Farthest Shore* the form of Ged's journey is that of a nine upside-down and reversed—a 6, starting at Roke, moving south-east to Hort Town, south-west to Lorbanery, Obehol, Wellogy and the floating town of the raft-people, then north up the West Reach to the Dragons' Run and Selidor: and here again there are nine places visited. The great constellation under the star Gobardon which dominates the sky of the West Reach and is in the shape of the Rune of Ending, Agnen, is in the shape of a figure 9 and has nine stars. In this way two journeys of the first and last books are balanced: one winds up, as it were, while the other winds down. The number nine is traditionally associated with the completion or 'winding up' of a spell (compare *Macbeth*, I, iii, 35–7: 'Thrice to thine, and thrice to mine,/And thrice again, to make up nine./Peace! The charm's wound up'). In this case it is associated with the making of a maker of spells, a true mage, in terms both of education on Roke and of the spiritual journey of Ged thereafter. Under the influence of the reversed nine in *The Farthest Shore*, however, Ged's magical power is steadily unwound until at the end he leaves Roke as a mere man. Thus too Ged in the first book moves towards the East Reach, the direction of sunrise and beginnings, and in the last towards the West Reach and the sunset.

There is also a degree of formal balance at a thematic level. In the first book the concern is with a personal evil and a personal solution to it: Ged has loosed the dark shadow of his own arrogance (*WE*, p. 76), one which turns out in the end to have his own name; and the story describes how he learns the courage to face and hunt down this shadow, and thereby overcome his own evil nature. In *The Tombs of Atuan* the emphasis is both individual and social. The young priestess Arha (meaning 'The Eaten One') acquires throughout that growth of the self which will enable her to break free from her custodianship of the dark labyrinth which in one way figures the enclosed individual. But here that growth is stimulated and brought to fruition by outside agency in the form of Ged, who has symbolically penetrated the tunnels of the labyrinth in search of the other half of the Ring of Erreth-Akbe (and the uniting of the two halves of the Ring represents the marriage of Arha's will with Ged's). Similarly Ged himself could not have escaped from the labyrinth without the help of Arha. In *The Farthest Shore* the moral conflict of the first book has become wholly external, being between the heroic Ged (helped by Arren) and the depraved Cob; and the issue is now social and universal, for Cob is destroying the whole world.

At both an artistic and a thematic level the second book can be seen as a pivot or mid-point between the other two books. It seems fitting therefore that where the first and third books are centrifugal in character, involving long pursuits, with their object the banishing of beings out of the world, *The Tombs of Atuan* involves Ged's quest for a centre, the centre of the labyrinth, and the joining together of the long-divorced halves of the Ring of Erreth-Akbe; and at the end of the book Arha is 'reborn' into the world (*TA*, p. 144; see also p. 127).

The trilogy is also informed with the ethic of accepting[3] or of keeping things as they are, or allowing them to express their true being—that is, so long as they are goods. In *A Wizard of Earthsea* Ged eventually succeeds in taking to himself the shadow he has admitted into the world and in so doing makes himself whole (*WE*, pp. 187, 189); in *The Tombs of Atuan* he recovers the lost half of the Ring of Erreth-Akbe and gives Arha the life she should have; and in *The Farthest Shore* he gives Cob the death he is wrongly resisting, closes the breach made between life and death and restores being and vitality to Earthsea. The duty of all men as of mages is to preserve the Balance. Ged tells Arren:

> 'Do you see, Arren, how an act is not, as young men think, like a rock that one picks up and throws, and it hits or misses, and that's the end of it. When that rock is lifted the earth is lighter, the hand that bears it heavier. When it is thrown the circuits of the stars respond, and where it strikes or falls the universe is changed. On every act the balance of the whole depends. The winds and seas, the powers of water and earth and light, all that these do, and all that the beasts and green things do, is well done, and rightly done. All these act within the Equilibrium. From the hurricane and the great whale's sounding to the fall of a dry leaf and the gnat's flight, all they do is done within the balance of the whole. But we, insofar as we have power over the world and over one another, we must *learn* to do what the leaf and the whale and the wind do of their own nature. We must learn to keep the balance. Having intelligence, we must not act in ignorance. Having choice, we must not act without responsibility.' (*FS*, pp. 74–5)

In Mrs Le Guin's science fiction, by contrast, there is much more emphasis on alteration of the *status quo*. In *Planet of Exile* (1966) the last remnants of mankind are dying out on the distant planet they have made their home for six hundred years, and are able to survive only when they are forced into alliance and ultimate intermarriage with the humanoid hilfs of that planet under the assaults of an army of ravaging Gaal from the north. The ambassador Genly Ai in *The Left Hand of Darkness* (1969) eventually succeeds in bringing the backward planet Winter into the galactic federation of the Ekumen. *The Lathe of Heaven* (1971) describes a man who changes the world every time he dreams: normality is never fully restored. The scientist Shevek in *The Dispossessed* (1976) discovers an aspect of time which will revolutionise interstellar transport; and in his own way initiates by his very absence from it a revolution in the society of his own planet. The very fact that all three of Mrs Le Guin's fantasies are set in one place, Earthsea, where each of her science fiction novels creates a different world (and in *The Lathe of Heaven* our own is being fundamentally altered from chapter to chapter) is an index to the conservatism at the heart of the former.

Keeping things as they are means keeping them essentially as they always have been: the past is central. Yet only *essentially*, for each age alters the factors in the Balance, or sees different threats to it, or recovers more of the past than was previously known: it is, as it were, a case of tradition and the individual talent. The power of the mage is founded on his knowledge of the names of things in the Old Speech, the speech of Segoy when he created Earthsea, for those are the true names of things and have runic power over the creatures and objects they describe. Ged tells Arha:

> 'Knowing names is my job. My art. To weave the magic of a thing, you see, one must find its true name out. In my lands we keep our true names hidden all our lives long, from all but those whom we trust utterly; for there is great power, and great peril, in a name. Once, at the beginning of time, when Segoy raised the isles of Earthsea from the ocean deeps, all things bore their own true names. And all doing of magic, all wizardry, hangs still upon the knowledge—the relearning, the remembering—of that true and ancient language of the Making. There are spells to learn, of course, ways to use the words; and one must know the consequences too. But what a wizard spends his life at is finding out the names of things, and finding out how to find out the names of things.' (*TA*, pp. 119–20)

The task of the magician is therefore one of recovery.[4] But the past also exists in the present in the form of the dragons, who still speak in the Old Speech, in the lays and legends and sense of history that are part of the fabric of Earthsea society, and even at the level of the primordial memory—when Arren hears the Old Speech used by the dragon Orm Embar, 'he felt always that he was on the point of understanding, almost understanding: as if it were a language he had forgotten, not one he had never known' (*FS*, pp. 160–1). Yet while the past and the sense of it are at the heart of life in Earthsea, each generation may produce a new hero: the great figures of legend, Elfarran, the Grey Mage of Paln, Erreth-Akbe, are not greater than the mage Ged, who is a legend living in the present day of his world.

This reverence for the past may also be traced at the level of the indebtedness of Mrs Le Guin's fantasy to other works. The Earthsea trilogy, in common with most fantasy, owes much to literary tradition, and quite demonstratively. The concept of Earthsea, with the mapped journey, the nine wizard masters, the great Ring of Erreth-Akbe, the shadow, the sense of the past and precedent, the frequent reference to lay and legend, the emphasis on language and on magic as a craft, look back to Tolkien. The idea of the islands recalls C. S. Lewis's *Perelandra* (1943) or his *The Voyage of the* Dawn Treader (1952), or perhaps Book 2 of Spenser's *Faerie Queene*, or *The Odyssey*. The theme of the evil shadow is also central in George MacDonald's *Phantastes* (1858) and *Lilith* (1895): in *Phantastes* the shadow is similarly released by an act of arrogant disobedience, and in *Lilith* there is also a theme concerning one's true name. The bestial, taloned form that the shadow first takes as it clings to Ged's face and tears his flesh is highly reminiscent of the appearance and behaviour of some of the horrible creatures in M. R. James's stories, particularly those in 'The Treasure of Abbot Thomas', 'The Tractate Middoth' and 'Mr. Humphreys and his Inheritance'.[5] The land of the dead, with its lightless towns and silence, recalls Dante and more directly James Thomson's poem *The City of Dreadful Night*. Ged's voyages in frail boats in *A Wizard of Earthsea* strongly suggest the legendary voyage of St Brendan, and the society and beliefs described in *The Tombs of Atuan* almost certainly look back to C. S. Lewis's *Till We Have Faces* (1956). Thus, just as Earthsea is profoundly traditional in character, so too are the books about it. Yet out of this indebtedness to the past Ursula Le Guin has made work which is uniquely hers.

The workings of magic in the Earthsea trilogy also express the conservative ethic of the fantasy. The accent is on magic not changing the nature of the world, except in cases of real need: as has been seen the job of the mage is to preserve the Balance. The arts of Changing and Summoning, whereby a wizard may transform himself or call other beings to him, are to be handled with peculiar care. It is his prideful summoning of Elfarran from the dead that causes Ged all his pain and fear in *A Wizard of Earthsea*. It is possible to change things for a short time and still be able to retract the deed, as Ged turns himself briefly into a dragon at Pendor to destroy the offspring of Yevau (*WE*, p. 97) or into a hawk to escape the servants of the dark powers of the Terrenon on Osskil (*WE*, pp. 131–3): but any longer would have risked permanent transformation. One may use magic to right an imbalance, as Ged slays the young dragons of Pendor or closes the breach Cob has made between the worlds; or to heal the imbalance caused by disease, as he heals the people of the village in the West Hand (*WE*, pp. 158–9); or to thank as he does the village-woman in *The Tombs of Atuan* for her hospitality by healing the infected udders of her goats (*TA*, pp. 147–8); but it is arrogant and dangerous to attempt to do more. The Master Summoner on Roke teaches his pupils to use spells over wind and sea 'only at need, since to summon up such earthly forces is to change the earth of which they are a part. '"Rain on Roke may be drouth in Osskil," he said, "and a calm in the East Reach may be storm and ruin in the West, unless you know what you are about"' (*WE*, pp. 63–4). When in *The Farthest Shore* Arren asks Ged why he does not work marvels with his magic he is told: '"The first lesson on Roke, and the last, is *Do what is needful*. And no more!"' (*FS*, p. 142). The reader may recall Ged's own impatience at the refusal of his early tutor Ogion to do miracles (*WE*, pp. 27–30).

Certain limits are inherent in the working of magic. Many of the true names of things in the Old Speech have been lost: Kurremkarmerruk, the Master Namer of Roke, tells Ged, '"some have been lost over the ages, and some have been hidden, and some are known only to dragons and to the Old Powers of Earth, and some are known to no living creature; and no man could learn them all. For there is no end to that language"' (*WE*, p. 57). And as he goes on to say, magic can work only locally, because the nature of Earthsea is such that generalisations are impossible:

> 'The sea's name is *inien*, well and good. But what we call the Inmost Sea has its own name also in the Old Speech. Since no thing can have two true names, *inien* can mean only "all the sea except the Inmost Sea". And of course it does not mean even that, for there are seas and bays and straits beyond counting that bear names of their own. So if some Mage-Seamaster were mad enough to try to lay a spell of storm or calm over all the ocean, his spell must say not only that word *inien*, but the names of every stretch and bit and part of the sea through all the Archipelago and all the Outer Reaches and beyond to where names cease. Thus, that which gives us power to work magic, sets the limits of that power. A mage can control only what is near him, what he can name exactly and wholly. And this is well. If it were not so, the wickedness of the powerful or the folly of the wise would long ago have sought to change what cannot be changed, and Equilibrium would fail. The unbalanced sea would overwhelm the islands where we perilously dwell, and in the old silence all voices and all names would be lost.'

(The last sentence is reminiscent of Ulysses' speech on degree in Shakespeare's *Troilus and Cressida*, I, iii, and indeed of the whole Renaissance emphasis on nature and universal order.) And, as Ged tells Arren, magic can be local in another sense: '"Do you know the old saying, *Rules change in the Reaches?* Seamen use it, but it is a wizard's saying, and it means that wizardry itself depends on place. A true spell on Roke may be mere words on Iffish"' (*FS*, p. 80). A further limit on magic is that it can be exhausted or confined. The Archmage Nemmerle loses all his power—and his life—through his actions after Ged has let the shadow into the world. By naming Ged with his true name the shadow removes for the time his power of wizardry (*WE*, pp. 115–16). Cob drains the powers of mages from the world and it takes the final exhaustion of Ged's powers to remove the damage he has done. Ged has to defy fatigue and resist sleep in order to keep together the magically synthesised boat of flotsam and jetsam in which he pursues the shadow (*WE*, pp. 153–6); his fellow-mage Vetch wonders at Ged's powers in sustaining the magic wind that blows them both in their boat over the sea, where he 'felt his own power all weakened and astray' (*WE*, p. 184).

Magic is seen as part of, rather than opposed to, nature and 'normality'. A mage is born with his talent, just as another may be born a scholar or warrior. But, as with all talents, it has to be educated: the young mage is put to school to learn the lore of his craft. Thus Ged is found learning the skills of the Master Changer, the Master Namer, the Master Chanter, the Master Herbal, the Master Windkey, the Master Hand, the Master Summoner, the Master Patterner and the Master Doorkeeper, just as one might learn French or geometry or history, or do games (compare on the last *WE*, pp. 52–3). Primarily what the mage-scholar is bent on discovering is the inmost character of the things of nature (there is little technology in Earthsea)—the names of creatures, objects, forces, plants and places, their order, how to call them up, how to perform illusory and actual changes with them, the secrets of plants and animals, how to direct such forces as wind and tide, and above all how to respect and preserve the immanent metaphysical balance of nature. Indeed, knowledge of the essence of nature contained in the true names of things in the Old Speech is the most powerful key to magic. To do magic aright the mage must be in sympathy with nature. Ged comes to believe 'that the wise man is one who never sets himself apart from other living things, whether they have speech or not, and in later years he strove long to learn what can be learned, in silence, from the eyes of animals, the flight of birds, the great slow gestures of trees' (*WE*, p. 92). Thus magic becomes bound up with the created world, '"the weaving of spells is itself interwoven with the earth and the water, the winds, the fall of light, of the place where it is cast"' (*FS*, p. 80; see also pp. 41–2).

And, further to portray the magic as 'moderate', it is emphasised that some of the most difficult things in the world are done not only by magic but out of one's own nature. It is not only magic that enables Ged to defeat his shadow, but courage, integrity and insight; and his defeat of Cob also asks a deep love of the world and heroic self-sacrifice. The reader is told, too, of Ged's friend Vetch that, though he was a skilled mage, 'a greater, unlearned skill he possessed, which was the art of kindness' (*WE*, p. 52). Similarly, when Ged has to try to enter to the school of Roke and cannot step over the threshold, he finds that no magic will help him, but only the simple act of asking the Doorkeeper for help (*WE*, pp. 44, 83–4). Frequently the wizard has to depend on the help of ordinary man, as Ged needs Arha to escape from the Tombs of Atuan (*TA*, pp. 127, 128, 131), and as he could not have found Cob without the assistance of Arren (*FS*, pp. 102, 131, 147–8).

The Earthsea trilogy is in large part panegyric, a celebration of things as they are. Centrally of course, this is done through the theme of the Balance: but there are other modes. *The Farthest Shore* is specifically about the loss of identity caused by Cob in the world, and its recovery when he is given, in his death, the true self he has so long refused. During Cob's refusal all meaning and distinctiveness had been largely drained out of Earthsea. The witch on Lorbanery who has lost her power tells Ged and Arren, '"I lost all the things I knew, all the words and names . . . There is a hole in the world and the light is running out of it. And the words go with the light"' (*FS*, p. 92; see also p. 163). As mages all over the world forget their powers and lose their knowledge of the Old Speech, so eventually do some of the great wizards on Roke itself, the Summoner, the Changer and the Chanter (*FS*, pp. 148–54). The lustre goes from the famous blue dyes of Lorbanery (p. 88) and the dyers themselves have 'no lines and distinctions and colours clear in their heads' (p. 95). Arren himself loses faith in Ged and magery (pp. 107–8), coming to feel that

> reality was empty: without life, or warmth, or colour, or sound: without meaning. There were no heights or depths. All this lovely play of form and light and colour on the sea and in the eyes of men, was no more than that: a playing of illusions on the shallow void. (pp. 129–30)

But when at length free of the darkness caused by Cob, Arren can perceive the glory of the dragons' flight in the West Reach (pp. 155–6), and can see with Ged how the apparently unexciting island of Selidor is full of being in its streams and hills:

> 'In all the world, in all the worlds, in all the immensity of time, there is no other like each of those streams, rising cold out of the earth where no eye sees it, running through the sunlight and the darkness to the sea. Deep are the springs of being, deeper than life, than death . . .' (p. 174; see also pp. 174–5)

In all three books of the Earthsea trilogy evil is a nonentity, a shadow, not substance. The evil powers in *The Tombs of Atuan* are the Nameless Ones; Cob's evil reduces people to shadows of themselves and eventually brings them into the land of shadows. Magic is centrally concerned with the identities of 'things as they are' in that it depends on knowing their true names, which are the names of their original making. Throughout the trilogy the reader is invited to feel a simple delight in the natures of things—a delight which is certainly 'thematic' but springs from the author herself[6] and her own pleasure in creation, or 'making', as Tolkien put it: in a sense she is analogous to her own Segoy and the creative joy he had in making Earthsea. So great is Mrs Le Guin's power of realisation of all the different places visited in *A Wizard of Earthsea* that she can make the sketchiest details conjure up a whole. When Ged leaves Low Torning after saving it from the threat of the dragons of Pendor,

> He went in a row-boat with a couple of young fishermen of Low Torning, who wanted the honour of being his boatmen. Always as they rowed on among the craft that crowd the eastern channels of the Ninety Isles, under the windows and balconies of houses that lean out over the water, past the wharves of Nesh, the rainy pastures of Dromgan, the malodorous oil-sheds of Geath, word of his deed had gone ahead of him. (*WE*, p. 104)

Each island has its character: even the bleak shoal where the old royal couple live receives an unforgettable thumbnail portrait (*WE*, p. 149). The result is that the reader feels that in the less than two hundred pages of this book he has covered an enormous canvas of highly individualised people and places, far more than (arguably) is present in all the eleven hundred of Tolkien's *The Lord of the Rings*. And all this comes from the thoroughness with which the author has seen things; the unsentimental realism with which she has presented them;[7] the metaphoric mode whereby she has so mingled the fantastic and the real that they give life to one another;[8] the originality of her descriptions and the re-creative force of her style (for example, *WE*, p. 29 and pp. 22–3, 37); and running through it all a lonely impulse of delight in all that is and is made.

### Notes

References are to the Gollancz editions, published respectively in 1971, 1972 and 1973 (and in one omnibus volume in 1977), and cited hereafter as *WE*, *TA* and *FS*.

1. On the use of the word 'mage' rather than 'magician' in the trilogy, see T. A. Shippey, 'The Magic Art and the Evolution of Words: Ursula Le Guin's Earthsea Trilogy', *Mosaic*, x, 2 (Winter, 1977) 147–50.
2. And his mage-tutor Ogion tells Ged that '"Mastery is nine times patience"' (*WE*, p. 28).
3. On acceptance, see also *FS*, pp. 36, 130, 147.
4. Compare Tolkien on 'Recovery' as an essential feature of fantasy, in his *Tree and Leaf*, pp. 51–3.
5. Particularly reminiscent is that in the last: see *The Collected Ghost Stories of M. R. James* (Edward Arnold, 1942) pp. 355–6.
6. See also her 'Science Fiction and Mrs. Brown', in Peter Nicholls (ed.) *Science Fiction at Large* (Gollancz, 1976).
7. Compare Shippey, pp. 154–6, 157–8.
8. See e.g. *WE*, pp. 52–3 (magical and 'natural' boat-handling), 55–6 (magical hide-and-seek), 58–60 and 88 (on the pet otak and its hunting of mice in the grass). Typical is the compound of 'A mage's name is better hidden than a herring in the sea, better guarded than a dragon's den' (p. 83).

URSULA K. LE GUIN

STEPHEN LEACOCK

DENISE LEVERTOV

IRVING LAYTON

PHILIP LEVINE

SINCLAIR LEWIS

VACHEL LINDSAY

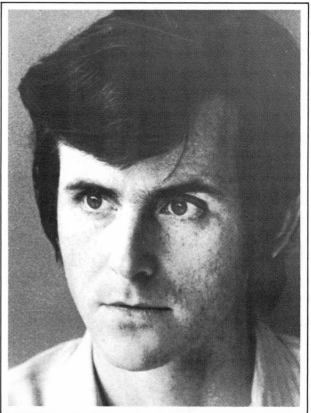

JOHN LOGAN

# DENISE LEVERTOV

## 1923–

Denise Levertov was born in Ilford, Essex, on October 24, 1923. Her mother was of Welsh descent and her father was an immigrant from Russia. On her mother's side she is a descendent of the mystic tailor and preacher Angel Jones of Mold, and on her father's side she is a descendant of Schneour Zalman, founder of the religious movement known as Habad Hasadism. Her father, Paul Philip Levertoff, a Jew by birth, was an Anglican priest who devoted his life to the unification of the Christian and Jewish faiths. Levertov was educated at home by her mother, Beatrice Spooner-Jones, who also was a writer. Her parents frequently read to her from both the English and Continental traditions. As a child she also seriously studied ballet for several years.

Levertov says she began to write when she was five years old. At age twelve she sent some of her poems to T. S. Eliot, who responded with a long letter offering advice and encouragement. When she was sixteen she met the poet and critic Herbert Read, who became her early mentor. Her first published poem, "Listening to Distant Guns," was printed in *Poetry Quarterly* in 1940. During the war she worked at St. Luke's Hospital, London, as a civilian nurse. Her first collection of poems appeared under the title *The Double Axe* in 1946. She married Mitchell Goodman, an American soldier and later a writer, and emigrated to the United States with her husband in 1948, settling in New York. There her only child, Nikolai, was born in 1949.

Levertov's second volume of poetry did not appear until 1956. *Here and Now* testifies to her immersion in American culture and adoption of American idioms. She became a naturalized citizen in 1956, and today considers herself an American. Levertov says that her extensive reading of William Carlos Williams upon her arrival helped her to adjust to her new cultural surroundings. Also important was contact with members of Charles Olson's Black Mountain school of poetry. Levertov's poetry is noted for its "organic form;" she has written in her collection of essays, *The Poet in the World* (1973), that "form is never more than a revelation of content." During the 1960s Levertov was active in the antiwar movement. She published several volumes of political poetry, including *To Stay Alive* (1970), a collection of her most moving war poems. During the early 1960s Levertov served as Poetry Editor of the *Nation*. She has also taught at several universities; from 1973 to 1979 she was on the faculty at Tufts. Recently she has been active in the anti-nuclear movement, while continuing to publish poetry. She presently resides in New York.

## General

For me, back of the idea of organic form is the concept that there is a form in all things (and in our experience) which the poet can discover and reveal. There are no doubt temperamental differences between poets who use prescribed forms and those who look for new ones—people who need a tight schedule to get anything done, and people who have to have a free hand—but the difference in their conception of "content" or "reality" is functionally more important. On the other hand is the idea that content, reality, experience, is essentially fluid and must be given form; on the other, this sense of seeking out inherent, though not immediately apparent, form. Gerard Manley Hopkins invented the word "inscape" to denote intrinsic form, the pattern of essential characteristics both in single objects and (what is more interesting) in objects in a state of relation to each other, and the word "instress" to denote the experiencing of the perception of inscape, the apperception of inscape. In thinking of the process of poetry as I know it, I extend the use of these words, which he seems to have used mainly in reference to sensory phenomena, to include intellectual and emotional experience as well; I would speak of the inscape of an experience (which might be composed of any and all of these elements, including the sensory) or of the inscape of a sequence or constellation of experiences.

A partial definition, then, of organic poetry might be that it is a method of apperception, i.e., of recognizing what we perceive, and is based on an intuition of an order, a form beyond forms, in which forms partake, and of which man's creative works are analogies, resemblances, natural allegories. Such poetry is exploratory.

How does one go about such a poetry? I think it's like this: first there must be an experience, a sequence or constellation of perceptions of sufficient interest, felt by the poet intensely enough to demand of him their equivalence in words: he is *brought to speech*. Suppose there's the sight of the sky through a dusty window, birds and clouds and bits of paper flying through the sky, the sound of music from his radio, feelings of anger and love and amusement roused by a letter just received, the memory of some long-past thought or event associated with what's seen or heard or felt, and an idea, a concept, he has been pondering, each qualifying the other; together with what he knows about history; and what he has been dreaming— whether or not he remembers it—working in him. This is only a rough outline of a possible moment in a life. But the condition of being a poet is that periodically such a cross section, or constellation, of experiences (in which one or another element may predominate) demands, or wakes in him this demand: the poem. The beginning of the fulfillment of this demand is to contemplate, to meditate; words which connote a state in which the heat of feeling warms the intellect. To contemplate comes from "*templum*, temple, a place, a space for observation, marked out by the augur." It means, not simply to observe, to regard, but to do these things in the presence of a god. And to meditate is "to keep the mind in a state of contemplation"; its synonym is "to muse," and to muse comes from a word meaning "to stand with open mouth"—not so comical if we think of "inspiration"—to breathe in.

So—as the poet stands openmouthed in the temple of life, contemplating his experience, there comes to him the first words of the poem: the words which are to be his way in to the poem, if there is to be a poem. The pressure of demand and the meditation on its elements culminate in a moment of vision, of crystallization, in which some inkling of the correspondence between those elements occurs; and it occurs as words. If he forces a beginning before this point, it won't work. These words sometimes remain the first, sometimes in the completed poem their eventual place may be elsewhere, or they may turn out to have been only forerunners, which fulfilled their function in bringing him to the words which are the actual beginning of the poem. It is faithful attention to the experience from the first moment of crystallization that allows those first or those forerunning words to rise to the surface: and with that same fidelity of attention the poet, from that moment of being let in to the possibility of the poem, must follow through, letting the experience lead him through the world of the poem, its unique inscape revealing itself as he goes.

During the writing of a poem the various elements of the poet's being are in communion with each other, and heightened. Ear and eye, intellect and passion, interrelate more subtly than at other times; and the "checking for accuracy," for precision of language, that must take place throughout the writing is not a matter of one element supervising the others but of intuitive interaction between all the elements involved.

In the same way, content and form are in a state of dynamic interaction; the understanding of whether an experience is a linear sequence or a constellation raying out from and into a central focus or axis, for instance, is discoverable only in the work, not before it.

Rhyme, chime, echo, reiteration: they not only serve to knit the elements of an experience but often are the very means, the sole means, by which the density of texture and the returning or circling of perception can be transmuted into language, apperceived. A may lead to E directly through B, C, and D: but if then there is the sharp remembrance or revisioning of A, this return must find its metric counterpart. It could do so by actual repetition of the words that spoke of A the first time (and if this return occurs more than once, one finds oneself with a refrain—not put there because one decided to write something with a refrain at the end of each stanza, but directly because of the demand of the content). Or it may be that since the return of A is now conditioned by the journey through B, C, and D, its words will not be a simple repetition but a variation . . . Again, if B and D are of a complementary nature, then their thought- or feeling-rhyme may find its corresponding word-rhyme. Corresponding images are a kind of nonaural rhyme. It usually happens that within the whole, that is between the point of crystallization that marks the beginning or onset of a poem and the point at which the intensity of contemplation has ceased, there are distinct units of awareness; and it is—for me anyway—these that indicate the duration of stanzas. Sometimes these units are of such equal duration that one gets a whole poem of, say, three-line stanzas, a regularity of pattern that looks, but is not, predetermined.

When my son was eight or nine I watched him make a crayon drawing of a tournament. He was not interested in the forms of such, but was grappling with the need to speak in graphic terms, to say, "And a great crowd of people were watching the jousting knights." There was a need to show the tiers of seats, all those people sitting in them. And out of the need arose a formal design that was beautiful—composed of the rows of shoulders and heads. It is in very much the same way that there can arise, out of fidelity to instress, a design that

is the form of the poem—both its total form, its length and pace and tone, and the form of its parts (e.g., the rhythmic relationships of syllables within the line, and of line to line; the sonic relationships of vowels and consonants; the recurrence of images, the play of associations, etc.). "Form follows function" (Louis Sullivan).

Frank Lloyd Wright in his autobiography wrote that the idea of organic architecture is that "the reality of the building lies in the space within it, to be lived in." And he quotes Coleridge: "Such as the life is, such is the form." (Emerson says in his essay "Poetry and Imagination," "Ask the fact for the form.") The *Oxford English Dictionary* quotes Huxley (Thomas, presumably) as stating that he used the word organic "almost as an equivalent for the word 'living.'"

In organic poetry the metric movement, the measure, is the direct expression of the movement of perception. And the sounds, acting together with the measure, are a kind of extended onomatopoeia—i.e., they imitate not the sounds of an experience (which may well be soundless, or to which sounds contribute only incidentally)—but the feeling of an experience, its emotional tone, its texture. The varying speed and gaite of different strands of perception within an experience (I think of strands of seaweed moving within a wave) result in counterpointed measures.

Thinking about how organic poetry differs from free verse, I wrote that "most free verse is failed organic poetry, that is, organic poetry from which the attention of the writer had been switched off too soon, before the intrinsic form of the experience had been revealed." But Robert Duncan pointed out to me that there is a "free verse" of which this is not true, because it is written not with any desire to seek a form, indeed perhaps with the longing to avoid form (if that were possible) and to express inchoate emotion as purely as possible. There is a contradiction here, however, because if, as I suppose, there is an inscape of emotion, of feeling, it is impossible to avoid presenting something of it if the rhythm or tone of the feeling is given voice in the poem. But perhaps the difference is this: that free verse isolates the "rightness" of each line or cadence—if it seems expressive, o.k., never mind the relation of it to the next; while in organic poetry the peculiar rhythms of the parts are in some degree modified, if necessary, in order to discover the rhythm of the whole.

But doesn't the character of the whole depend on, arise out of, the character of the parts? It does; but it is like painting from nature: suppose you absolutely imitate, on the palette, the separate colors of the various objects you are going to paint; yet when they are closely juxtaposed in the actual painting, you may have to lighten, darken, cloud, or sharpen each color in order to produce an effect equivalent to what you see in nature. Air, light, dust, shadow, and distance have to be taken into account.

Or one could put it this way: in organic poetry the form sense or "traffic sense," as Stefan Wolpe speaks of it, is ever present along with (yes, paradoxically) fidelity to the revelations of meditation. The form sense is a sort of Stanislavsky of the imagination: putting a chair two feet downstage there, thickening a knot of bystanders upstage left, getting this actor to raise his voice a little and that actress to enter more slowly; all in the interest of a total form he intuits. Or it is a sort of helicopter scout flying over the field of the poem, taking aerial photos and reporting on the state of the forest and its creatures—or over the sea to watch for the schools of herring and direct the fishing fleet toward them.

A manifestation of form sense is the sense the poet's ear has of some rhythmic norm peculiar to a particular poem, from which the individual lines depart and to which they return. I heard Henry Cowell tell that the drone in Indian music is known as the horizon note. Al Kresch, the painter, sent me a quotation from Emerson: "The health of the eye demands a horizon." This sense of the beat or pulse underlying the whole I think of as the horizon note of the poem. It interacts with the nuances or forces of feeling which determine emphasis on one word or another, and decides to a great extent what belongs to a given line. It relates the needs of that feeling-force which dominates the cadence to the needs of the surrounding parts and so to the whole.

Duncan also pointed to what is perhaps a variety of organic poetry: the poetry of linguistic impulse. It seems to me that the absorption in language itself, the awareness of the world of multiple meaning revealed in sound, word, syntax, and the entering into this world in the poem, is as much an experience or constellation of perceptions as the instress of nonverbal sensuous and psychic events. What might make the poet of linguistic impetus appear to be on another tack entirely is that the demands of his realization may seem in opposition to truth as we think of it; that is, in terms of sensual logic. But the apparent distortion of experience in such a poem for the sake of verbal effects is actually a precise adherence to truth, since the experience itself was a verbal one.

Form is never more than a *revelation* of content.

"The law—one perception must immediately and directly lead to a further perception." I've always taken this to mean, "no loading of the rifts with ore," because there are to be no rifts. Yet alongside this truth is another truth (that I've learned from Duncan more than from anyone else)—that there must be a place in the poem for rifts too—(never to be stuffed with imported ore). Great gaps between perception and perception which must be leapt across if they are to be crossed at all.

The X-factor, the magic, is when we come to those rifts and make those leaps. A religious devotion to the truth, to the splendor of the authentic, involves the writer in a process rewarding in itself; but when that devotion brings us to undreamed abysses and we find ourselves sailing slowly over them and landing on the other side—that's ecstasy.—DENISE LEVERTOV, "Some Notes on Organic Form" (1965), *The Poet in the World*, 1973, pp. 7–13

"Therefore dive deep," wrote Edward Young—author of the once so popular, later despised, *Night Thoughts*—"dive deep into thy bosom; learn the depths, extent, bias, and full fort of thy mind; contract full intimacy with the stranger within thee; excite and cherish every spark of intellectual light and heat, however smothered under former negligence, or scattered through the dull, dark mass of common thoughts; and collecting them into a body, let thy genius rise (if genius thou hast) as the sun from chaos; and if I then should say, like an Indian, Worship it (though too bold) yet should I say little more than my second rule enjoins, *viz.*, Reverence thyself."

What I have up to now been suggesting as the task of the poet may seem of an Emersonian idealism (though perhaps Emerson has been misread on this point) that refuses to look man's capacity for evil square in the eyes. Now as perhaps never before, when we are so acutely conscious of being ruled by evil men, and that in our time man's inhumanity to man has swollen to proportions of perhaps unexampled monstrosity, such a refusal would be no less than idiotic. Or I may seem to have been advocating a Nietzschean acceptance of man's power for evil, simply on the ground that it is among his possibilities. But Young's final injunction, in the passage just quoted, is what, for me, holds the clue to what must make the poet's humanity *humane*. "Reverence thyself" is necessarily an

aspect of Schweitzer's doctrine of Reverence for Life, the recognition of oneself as *life that wants to live* among other *forms of life that want to live*. This recognition is indissoluble, reciprocal, and dual. There can be no self-respect without respect for others, no love and reverence for others without love and reverence for oneself; and no recognition of others is possible without the imagination. The imagination of what it is to *be* those other forms of life that want to live is the only way to recognition; and it is that imaginative recognition that brings compassion to birth. Man's capacity for evil, then, is less a positive capacity, for all its horrendous activity, than a failure to develop man's most human function, the imagination, to its fullness, and consequently a failure to develop compassion.

But how is this relevant to the practice of the arts, and of poetry in particular? Reverence for life, if it is a necessary relationship to the world, must be so for all people, not only for poets. Yes; but it is the poet who has language in his care; the poet who more than others recognizes language also as a *form of life* and a common resource to be cherished and served as we should serve and cherish earth and its waters, animal and vegetable life, and each other. The would-be poet who looks on language merely as something to be used, as the bad farmer or the rapacious industrialist looks on the soil or on rivers merely as things to be used, will not discover a deep poetry; he will only, according to the degree of his skill, construct a counterfeit more or less acceptable—a subpoetry, at best efficiently representative of his thought or feeling—a reference, not an incarnation. And he will be contributing, even if not in any immediately apparent way, to the erosion of language, just as the irresponsible, irreverent farmer and industrialist erode the land and pollute the rivers. All of our common resources, tangible or intangible, need to be given to, not exclusively taken from. They require the care that arises from intellectual love—from an understanding of their perfections.

Moreover, the poet's love of language must, if language is to reward him with unlooked-for miracles, that is, with poetry, amount to a passion. The passion for the things of the world and the passion for naming them must be in him indistinguishable. I think that Wordsworth's intensity of feeling lay as much in his naming of the waterfall as in his physical apprehension of it, when he wrote:

> . . . The sounding cataract
> Haunted me like a passion. . . .

The poet's task is to hold in trust the knowledge that language, as Robert Duncan has declared, is not a set of counters to be manipulated, but a Power. And only in this knowledge does he arrive at music, at that quality of song within speech which is not the result of manipulations of euphonious parts but of an attention, at once to the organic relationships of experienced phenomena and to the latent harmony and counterpoint of language itself as it is identified with those phenomena. Writing poetry is a process of discovery, revealing *inherent* music, the music of correspondences, the music of inscape. It parallels what, in a person's life, is called individuation: not an isolation of intellectual awareness but an awareness involving the whole self, a *knowing* (as man and woman "know" one another), a touching, a "being in touch."

All the thinking I do about poetry leads me back, always, to Reverence for Life as the ground for poetic activity; because it seems the ground for Attention. This is not to put the cart before the horse: some sense of identity, at which we wonder; an innocent self-regard, which we see in infants and in the humblest forms of life; these come first, a center out of which Attention reaches. Without Attention—to the world outside us, to the voices within us—what poems could possibly come into existence? Attention is the exercise of Reverence for the "other forms of life that want to live." The progression seems clear to me: from Reverence for Life to Attention to Life, from Attention to Life to a highly developed Seeing and Hearing, from Seeing and Hearing (faculties almost indistinguishable for the poet) to the Discovery and Revelation of Form, from Form to Song.—DENISE LEVERTOV, "Origins of a Poem" (1968), *The Poet in the World*, 1973, pp. 52–55

## Works

In my opinion Denise Levertov ⟨in *Here and Now*⟩ is incomparably the best poet of what is getting to be known as the new avant-garde. This may sound to some, committed to the gospel of the professor poets—the first commandment of whose decalogue of reaction is: "The age of experiment is over"—like saying that she is very much better than her associates, Charles Olson, Robert Creeley, Allen Ginsberg, Cid Corman, Chris Berjknes, Gil Orlovitz and others who published in *Origin* and the *Black Mountain Review*. I don't believe these are bad poets—in fact, I think they are the best of their generation and the only hope for American poetry. It is just that Denise Levertov has several things they haven't got, at least yet.

In the first place, she is more civilized. One thing she has which they lack conspicuously is what Ezra Pound calls culture (which he himself is utterly without). She is securely humane in a way very few people are any more. This is not because she is English, of Welsh and Jewish parentage, although the fact that her father was a learned rabbi, a leading authority on the Kabbalah, who became an Anglo-Catholic priest, may have helped. She seems to have grown up in a household full of mildly Bohemian scholarship, freewheeling learning of the type Theodore Gaster made well known in his reminiscences of his own father (Rabbi Gaster and Paul Levertov were friends). Certainly this is a humanism older than the Renaissance, so well founded that it penetrates every bit of life. This is far from the humanism of Sigismondo Malatesta or even Henry Luce— it is more like Lao-tse. If it is really absorbed and manifest in an individual it becomes that rare thing, wisdom. I don't need to labor the point that there exist practically no wise poets nowadays and few for the last two hundred years.

This means that Denise Levertov knows more than her colleagues, far more than most; she is far sounder than Olson, whose learning suffers from the same sort of Frobenius-Lost Atlantis provincial oddity as Pound's. Many of them know practically nothing, not even French and algebra. Because it is humane, her knowledge is the result of doing what came naturally. She may have read Donne from her father's library at the age of ten—perhaps, like the Bible, for the dirty words. That is the way to read Donne. Cultured people do not discover him when they go to Harvard and use him to intimidate the yokels back home in St. Louis. This means too that she has an almost perfect ear. Reading her, especially hearing her read aloud, you feel she must have literally absorbed the rhythms of great poetry with her mother's milk. It is all so natural and so utterly removed from English 7649328 A—Forms and Techniques of English Verse (4 credits).

Nothing shows this better than the actual evolution of idiom and tone. During the years of the Second World War, Denise Levertov came up as one of the best and one of the most individual of the young English Neo-Romantics. Comfort, Woodcock, Gascoyne, Gardiner, Tambimuttu, Read, the whole "leadership" of the "movement" were quick to recognize her as something very special indeed. She was naturally "romantic." She didn't have to believe in it or belong to it as a movement. She was built that way. I said of her then that "in

poets like Denise Levertov this tendency (a sort of autumnal-evening *Wienerwald* melancholy) reaches its height in slow, pulsating rhythms, romantic melancholy and indefinable nostalgia. Once these qualities would have been considered blemishes. Today they are outstanding virtues. For the first time, *Schwärmerei* enters English verse." The only thing wrong with this statement in those days was that there weren't any "poets like Denise Levertov." She was unique. None followed her. The next crop, represented, say, by Heath-Stubbs, seem like muggy little Böcklins cut out of cardboard in comparison. It was as though for a moment in the October moonlight a girl's voice sang faintly across the Danube, "Knowest thou a land where the pomegranate blooms. . . ." And then she gave it all up. "Hospital nurse, land girl, charwoman, children's nurse, companion to an alcohol-ic . . ." Hitchhiking over France the year after the Second World War ended, she married a GI and came to the States. "She'll probably end up a professor's wife," said a friend in London in 1949, "pushing a pram in a supermarket."

Denise turned out to be made of tougher stuff . . . and the GI, himself a writer, was on the side of the angels. At first she fell under the influence of the Southern Colonels and the Country Gentlemen. It didn't last long. We were all horrified. "So and so is a lot like our Empson," said she to me. Said I to her, "'Ceptin' that he never seen a book until he went to school and his folks still got cotton seeds in they hair. And besides, you are a leader of the very generation of revolt against the impostures of Empson, Richards, Eliot and their sycophants." She allowed as how that was true. But nobody "influenced" her to turn away, pretty quick, from the smoking dogs and bicycling seals of the American academicians. It was her own good sense, the good sense of bona fide tradition and an infallible ear. W. H. Auden has spent years in America and never learned to use a single phrase of American slang without sounding like a British music-hall Yank comic and his verse has remained as British, as specifically "school," as Matthew Arnold. In no time at all Denise came to talk like a mildly internationalized young woman living in New York but alive to all the life of speech in the country. Her verse changed abruptly. It would be easy to say that it came under the influence of William Carlos Williams. It would be more true to say that it moved into the mainstream of twentieth-century poetry. She writes like Williams, a little, but she also writes "like" Salmon, or Reverdy, or Char—or Machado, or Louis Zukofsky, or Parker Tyler, or Patchen, or the early Lowenfels, or me. After all, as Shakespeare said, we are all civilized men. I think Miss Levertov is a better poet than Salmon, as Williams is a better poet than Reverdy. If all her work of the past ten years were collected, I suspect she would show as the equal of Char and as superior to all but a handful of American poets born in this century. Certainly she is better than any post-Second World War French poet—than Frenaud, or Cadou, or Becker, or Rousselot. Her only rival among the younger women in England is a poet once described by an older colleague as writing like an exquisitely well-bred lady's maid, and who hasn't been up to her early snuff in many years. The only trouble with *Here and Now* is that it is much too small a collection and it is a collection of her easiest verse.

The fact that Denise Levertov has had to wait so long for publication and now is able to publish so little is a shame to American publishers, who year after year put out the most meretricious, pompous, academic nonsense, which gets mere-tricious, pompous, academic reviews in the literary quarter-lies—and wins countless millions in Fellowships, Scholar-ships, Consultantships and Visiting Poetships. The official position is that people like Denise Levertov do not exist. Officialdom to the contrary, they very much do, and they will out-exist the jerry-built reputations of the *Vaticide Review* by many, many long years. Nothing could be harder, more irreducible, than these poems. Like the eggs and birds of Brancusi, they are bezoars shaped and polished in the vitals of a powerful creative sensibility. No seminar will break their creative wholeness, their presentational immediacy. No snob-bery will dissolve their intense personal integrity. However irrefrangible as objects of art, it is *that*, their personalism, that makes them such perfect poetic utterances. Denise may never have pushed a pram in a Cambridge, Massachusetts, super-market, but these are woman poems, wife poems, mother poems, differing only in quality of sensibility from thousands of other expressions of universal experience. Experience is not dodged, the sensibility is not defrauded—with any ambiguity, of seven types or seventy. One meets the other head on, without compromise. This, I was taught in school, many years ago in a better day, is what makes great poetry great. And the rhythms. The *Schwärmerei* and lassitude are gone. Their place has been taken by a kind of animal grace of the word, a pulse like the footfalls of a cat or the wingbeats of a gull. It is the intense aliveness of an alert domestic love—the wedding of form and content in poems which themselves celebrate a kind of perpetual wedding of two persons always realized as two responsible sensibilities. What more do you want of poetry? You can't ask much more. Certainly you seldom get a tenth as much.—KENNETH REXROTH, "Poets, Old and New," *Assays*, 1961, pp. 231–35

The healthfulness of ⟨William Carlos Williams's⟩ influence can be seen from the variety of the young poets who seem to have learnt from him: David Ignatow, Philip Levine, Denise Levertov, Robert Creeley, for example—each seems to owe something to Williams, but to owe it in the most open and grateful way, for he has helped them to realize their own very different poetic attitudes. It is unusual in Denise Levertov's ⟨*The Jacob's Ladder*⟩ to feel that she is borrowing his tone of voice: she is fully individual, even though her outlook is often very similar to his. It is relevant to quote her opening poem, "To the Reader":

> As you read, a white bear leisurely
> pees, dyeing the snow
> saffron,
>
> and as you read, many gods
> lie among lianas: eyes of obsidian
> are watching the generations of leaves,
>
> and as you read
> the sea is turning its dark pages,
> turning
> its dark pages.

If Williams is behind this poem, he is distantly so, and only as Jonson was behind Pope. One is at once aware of its "rightness," and the rightness is at least partly a matter of the delicate yet firm movement with which it progresses. It is like the movement of Williams at his best, yet, as I have said, Miss Levertov is far from a mere follower. The poem confidently and completely establishes the range of subject matter in the book that it prefaces. The first image is of the present: the bear's impulse is part of the natural process of life, which is beautiful because it is authentic, neither graceful nor awkward; the second image is of the past, continuing into the present in a special way; and the third laps the whole within the mystery of general tendencies. These things are to be "read," like the poems in the book; and conversely the poems are to be treated like things of the world, each distinct and unclassifiable. In

fact, in presenting us with particularities, Miss Levertov is constantly trying to break down categories and dismiss them from our minds: she implies that if we are to feel sympathy with the flux of life (such sympathy is the dominant emotion of the book) we must disregard the classifications into which we have come to divide the constituents of the world and regard each thing and process as special, unique. The purpose of her very metaphor is often to get rid of our preconceptions. New York City, for example, the background to many of the poems, becomes a kind of temple:

> The lights change: the avenue's
> endless nave echoes notes of
> liturgical red.

*The Jacob's Ladder* is a very distinguished book indeed, and the concluding thirteen poems from an earlier collection help to show up its virtues. She has abandoned the slightly tenuous fancifulness around which some of the early poems are organized, for a solid acceptance of the solid. It is not a glib acceptance, either, merely borrowed from the nineteenth-century romantics, but one which surely reflects (as any good poetry must) a manner of living, a personal discipline, in this case the discipline of tolerance. The book gives us confidence, of a sort that we can feel rather seldom, in the considerable and still expanding talent of a poet whose world is based on the world we share.—THOM GUNN, "Things, Voices, Minds," *YR*, Autumn 1962, pp. 129–30

What struck me first on reading *The Poet in the World*, which is a collection of Denise Levertov's prose writings about art, politics, and life in general,—what struck me first, and what still strikes me in my reconsideration of the book as I prepare to write this review, though now in a stronger, richer way, is the force of the author's good sense and practical wisdom. To many readers this may seem surprising. Levertov's base, both philo-sophical and temperamental, is in Neoplatonism, as I think is well known; certainly it has been more than evident in her poetry for twenty years. But unlike many writers who share this broad neoplatonic provenance, she never, or hardly ever, steps outside her role as a working poet aware of the practical and moral relationships between herself and her poetic materials: her experience, her life, her humanity. She keeps her mind on the reality of imaginative process. She rarely veers into mystical utterance for its own sake.

Recently I was reading Gilbert Sorrentino's *Splendide-Hôtel*. It is a discussion, in the form of an extended personal essay on motifs from Rimbaud and Williams, of the role of the poet in history and civilization. Sorrentino is a fine writer. His book is thoughtful, lucid, wide-ranging, witty, in many ways a work of originality and imagination; I read it with pleasure. But I was aware all the time that his view of the poet—namely, as a person apart, somehow special and superior, exempt from practicality in his vocation, and better qualified than others to deal with the real world (in effect by creating his own super- or anti-reality)—is both antiquated and dangerous. It was danger-ous when it was not antiquated, a century ago when it was the esthetic underground of the Victorian era, and it is equally dangerous, if not more, today. Many times, perhaps too many, I have argued this danger in the past, so I have no wish to revive the discussion here. And happily I need not, for Levertov has furnished the perfect answer to Sorrentino, and to a large extent from his own ground of feeling and ideas; I mean her essay entitled "The Poet in the World," the centerpiece of her book. It should be read by every poet in the country—in the world! Written from the working poet's point of view, out of Levertov's own active experience in the recent period of collaboration between poetry and politics, it has the immediacy and efficacy that my own more scholastic arguments, not to say tirades, doubtless lack.

Has Levertov solved the paradox of the poet as a specialist of sensibility in the practical human world? Not entirely. Her book contains many statements, and her poems many more, in which Sorrentino's view is at least implicit, and I suspect she could read *Splendide-Hôtel*, much of it anyway, without my degree of discomfort. Often she invokes The Poet in a role essentially vatic or ideally prophetic. Her affinity with Neoplatonism, from Plotinus to Swedenborg to Hopkins—a devious thread—is clear. My own base, which is not, whatever else it my be, Neoplatonism, makes me shy away from such statements. But always in her prose, and often in her poetry, there is this saving complementary strain, awareness of the poet as a craftsman engaged in a psychologically reasonable endeavor; ultimately her affinity is with makers more than seers, with Wordsworth and Rilke, Williams and Pound. The title of one of her essays gives it in a nutshell: "Line-Breaks, Stanza-Spaces, and the Inner Voice." Moreover, in her basic humaneness Levertov often realizes, reaches out to, and celebrates the poet in Everyman, at least *in posse*, thus incorporating a necessary disclaiming proviso among her attitudes. She does it best, I think, in the essay, cited above, that deals with sensibility as a moral and political instrument. The paradox remains, of course. It cannot be glossed over. Readers who are philosophically minded will be worried by it; some will be offended. But the point is that Levertov does not . . . well, I was going to say that she does not recognize it, but of course she does. Yet I think she does not *feel* it. She is not stopped by it, not boggled. She works through and beyond it, in her writing and in what we know of her life, conscious only of the wholeness of her vision. And she succeeds. She is practical.

This is the heart of the matter, I think. At any rate it is what I am interested in now: not the larger verities but her own work and the way her theoretical writing applies to her own work, particularly to her recent poetry. Undoubtedly her best known statement about poetry is the brief discussion of "organic form" that was originally published in *Poetry* in 1965, then reprinted a couple of times elsewhere before its appearance in her new book. It is a clear enough, and in some respects a conventional enough, statement; one hesitates to reduce it further than Levertov herself has already reduced it. But in essence it asserts that forms exist in reality as natural, or possibly more than natural, immanences, and that the poet perceives or intuits these forms through acts of meditation, which issue, once the perception has acquired a certain intensity, in the creation of verbal analogies; that is, poems. This is not simply the pathetic fallacy at work in a new way, because the analogy between poem and object is not superficial; there may be no resemblance whatever in exterior structures, textures, and styles. The resemblance is indwelling. Levertov refers to Hopkins and his invention of the word "inscape" to denote intrinsic, as distinct from apparent, form, and she extends this denotation to apply not only to objects but to all phenomena, including even the poet's thoughts, feelings, and dreams. She emphasizes the importance of the quality of meditation, speaking of it in basically religious language. Meditation is the genuine but selfless concentration of attention upon phenomena, the giving of oneself to phenomena, from which proceeds the recognition of inner form; it is, to use another of Hopkins' inventions, the disciplined or ascetic submission to "instress." And I must point out also, with equal emphasis, that although at times Levertov speaks of the poet as no more than an instrument of a larger "poetic power," and although more than once she implies that the poem as a verbal analogy may occur in part spontaneously in a sensibility which is thoroughly attuned to its object through a sufficient act of meditation, nevertheless she insists as well on the element of craft in the poetic process, the part played by verbal experiment and revision in bringing the poem into proper analogy to its phenomenal paradigm. The poem is a *made* object.

I don't say there aren't questions—risks, qualifications, paradoxes by the bucketful—and of course the entire complex is, as I have said, conventional, having appeared and reappeared at many times and in many places; yet Levertov's reformulation is very evidently her own, a personal vision, personal and practical; that is, *it comes from her practice*. One can't miss, either in her prose observations or in her poems, the way her understanding of what she is doing is instinctual at base, ingrained in her whole artistic personality. Look at her poems up to about 1968. They are what we call "lyric poems," mostly rather short; they fall into conventional categories: nature poems, erotic poems, poems on cultural and esthetic themes, and so on. Their style is remarkably consistent from first to last, changing only to improve, within its own limits, in matters of expressive flexibility, subtlety of cadence, integration of sonal and syntactic structures, and the like. But if the style is consistent the form is various, the *inner* form. From poem to poem each form is its own, each is the product of its own substance; not only that, each is the *inevitable* product—we sense it though we cannot demonstrate it—of its own substance. (She quotes Louis Sullivan approvingly: "Form follows function.") It has been customary to speak of the musicality of Levertov's poetry, and I have done so myself. But I think this is the wrong term. I doubt that she has been aware of music, e.g., as Pound was aware of it. But she has been deeply aware of formal consonance, of the harmony of inner form and vision; and certainly this, rather than the facility of artifice some critics have ascribed to her, is what lies at the root of her "musical" language.—HAYDEN CARRUTH, "Levertov," *HdR*, Autumn 1974, pp. 475–78

---

### RALPH J. MILLS, JR.
### From "Denise Levertov:
### The Poetry of the Immediate"
*Contemporary American Poetry*
#### 1965, pp. 177–96

We have considered in a previous chapter how the poetry of Robert Lowell moves into ⟨the⟩ area of the highly personal or confessional, though he comes from a very different corner of the literary map than does Denise Levertov or Robert Creeley or David Ignatow. The latter have steeped themselves for a long time in that tradition of modern writing whose pioneers are William Carlos Williams, Ezra Pound, and H. D.

Among her fellow-poets in this tradition, Denise Levertov stands out as one whose art, fresh and compelling, convinces us of her genuine rapport with the reality she presents as its core. Her poetry is frequently a tour through the familiar and the mundane until their unfamiliarity and otherworldliness suddenly strike us. Her imaginative gaze feasts on the small objects we usually treat as insignificant appendages to our lives, or pauses with affectionate interest on the seemingly trivial activities in which we spend so much of those lives. Thus she engages very naturally in a persistent investigation of the events of her own life—inner and outer—in the language of her own time and place, and completes that investigation in the forms emerging from what she discovers as it is translated into words. Miss Levertov shares the spirit of Martin Buber, for she always says "thou" to the persons, occasions, and objects she encounters; that is her imagination's essential humanizing gesture toward every aspect of existence.

As I have already indicated, Miss Levertov, along with a variety of other poets, departs sharply from the poetic and critical line passing down through Yeats, Eliot, Auden, and the critics who have developed aesthetic views from their initiative. In the introduction to his anthology *Contemporary American Poetry*, Donald Hall offers a good summary description of qualities emphasized by the poets working in the opposing tradition, with its foundation in the example of William Carlos Williams. "This poetry," Hall tells us, "is no mere restriction of one's vocabulary. It wants to use the language with the intimacy acquired in unrehearsed unliterary speech. But it has other characteristics which are not linguistic. It is a poetry of experiences more than of ideas. The experience is presented often without comment, and the words of the description must supply the emotion which the experience generates, without generalization or summary."

In allying herself with this movement, Miss Levertov had to grapple with prevailing literary modes and, finally, to discard them. A struggle of this sort, the purpose of which is to open a way for poetic development, normally makes or breaks a writer—that is, if he or she dares to undertake it, as many do not—and it is a real sign of Miss Levertov's abilities that she has returned victorious. But the effort to win a voice of one's own amounts to nothing or becomes artificial unless it has been prompted by the conditions of human experience itself, by all that is cast into the poet's field of vision in the course of living. Poetry, if it will earn its name, must never begin with experience at second hand, but with a steady eye on what surrounds us everywhere. As the French philosopher Jacques Maritain says in his *Art and Scholasticism*, "Our art does not derive from itself alone what it imparts to things; it spreads over them a secret which it first discovered in them, in their invisible substance or in their endless exchanges and correspondences." Miss Levertov has learned this lesson well, and it is identical to the one her art teaches us. The conclusion of her "Note on the Work of the Imagination" (*New Directions 17*, edited by James Laughlin) adds to the quotation from Maritain a consideration of this spiritual faculty which makes the poetic object possible; she writes, "What joy to be reminded . . . that the Imagination does not arise from the environment but has the power to create it!" ⟨. . .⟩

The change that takes place between her first and second books—in a decade that saw Miss Levertov leave England, travel in Europe, meet the American novelist Mitchell Goodman, marry him, and settle in this country—is remarkable and must have demanded no less than a complete renovation of her poetic values. But this revolution of the heart, the head, the senses, how worthwhile it all was! She was compelled to start from scratch, and that meant for Miss Levertov a confrontation of the happenings of her life. What she so shrewdly observed was that the ordinary is extraordinarily unusual:

> What a sweet smell rises
> when you lay the dust—
> bucket after bucket of water thrown
> on the yellow grass.
>     The water
> flashes
> each time you
> make it leap—
>         arching its glittering back.
> The sound of

> more water
> pouring into the pail
> almost quenches my thirst.
> Surely when flowers
> grow here, they'll not
> smell sweeter than this
>         wet ground, suddenly black.

Of course, as Kenneth Rexroth ⟨. . .⟩ noted, Miss Levertov came under novel influences in America that were quite unlike any English ones. He names as a chief influence the poet we have already mentioned, the writer whose lessons she must have learned well, though without sacrificing her own intentions and capacities. That poet is the late William Carlos Williams. It is likely that she also learned from Rexroth's own poetry and from the Imagists; in her moving tribute to H. D. entitled "Summer 1961," she records some of her debts to Williams, Pound, and H. D.:

> They have told us
> the road leads to the sea,
> and given
> the language into our hands.

Perhaps if we look at a brief but fairly representative poem by Williams to remind ourselves of certain qualities in his work we will be able to determine, by comparison with Miss Levertov's "Laying the Dust" above, some of their similarities. Williams' poem is called "Between Walls":

> the back wings
> of the
> hospital where
> nothing
> will grow lie
> cinders
> in which shine
> the broken
> pieces of a green
> bottle

Clearly, this poem has little relation to the kind of poetry in the ascendency during the first half of the twentieth century; the poetry of the French Symbolists has had no bearing on what we read in these lines. Again, if we try to apply the sort of exegesis to Williams' poetry—or to Miss Levertov's, for that matter—that is used on Eliot's or Rilke's or Valéry's, we shall miss the point and look foolish. Ingenious explication is beside the point here and will bury the meaning of both poems; we should do better to contemplate them as we would a painting. Williams' attraction to the *disjecta membra* of the physical world, particularly of the modern urban setting, set a firm precedent for Miss Levertov's own poetic venture. We should not forget, either, Williams' insistence that the moral responsibility of the American poet lies in using his native tongue "to represent what his mind perceives directly about him," because this endeavor is, to a degree, Miss Levertov's. Yet there is also a gradual inward turning in her latest poetry and an increasing preoccupation with parable, dream, and interior illumination that are foreign to Williams' imagination.

Williams was for years a champion of younger writers in the United States and, further, was a stalwart foe of the post-Symbolist literature of Yeats and Eliot, as well as an opponent of what he thought was an outworn tradition of English verse forms and meters. It is hardly by accident, then, that young poets, in search of a way past the official poetic idiom, looked to Williams' writings and his viewpoint for guidance. The rejection of conventional for organic form; the repudiation of established metrical patterns in favor of what Williams called "the variable foot"; the return to the spoken language, the

*American* spoken language—these are some of the most prominent results of the senior poet's influence. These younger poets likewise avoid in general the habit of making their work a repository of intellectual history, learning, and fragments of the European cultural heritage. I should like to call the poetry of Miss Levertov, and that of a number of her contemporaries, "poetry of the immediate."

My term requires some explanation. I do not mean by "the immediate" an art without craftsmanship, an art that fixes on the disorder of sheer impulse or emotional notation. Miss Levertov has never allowed her poetry to become even slightly vulnerable to that kind of charge—a glance at any one of her poems will prove it. Moreover, we need only cite the comment she supplies for Donald Allen's anthology *The New American Poetry 1945–1960*, where there is no mistaking her distaste for sloppy composition: "I long for poems," she writes, "of an inner harmony in utter contrast to the chaos in which they exist." Poetry must not be a shapeless replica of external things but an organically formed transfiguration of them in which the transfiguration, rather than poetic convention, dictates the form. What I call "the immediate," then, signifies the complex of relationships existing between the poet and the elements that are close at hand in her personal experience. The things, the happenings, the thoughts and dreams that are subjective events in themselves—everything that falls within the circumference of the poet's life as an individual—become the matter of poetry. The author's private circumstance is explored, its potentialities drawn out; but however far her speculations lead her, Miss Levertov never oversteps that circumference. Instead, she creates from within herself an attitude with which to face her environment, as in her poem "Something to Wear":

> To sit and sit like the cat
> and think my thoughts through—
> that might be a deep pleasure:
>
> to learn what news
> persistence might discover,
> and like a woman knitting
>
> make something from the
> skein unwinding, unwinding,
> something I could wear
>
> or something you could wear
> when at length I rose to meet you
> outside the quiet sitting-room
> (the room of thinking and knitting
> the rooms of cats and women)
> among the clamor of
>
> cars and people,
> the stars drumming and poems
> leaping from shattered windows.

This poems grows around the mind's self-reflective activity. While poems about poetry, the act of composition, or the mind contemplating its own powers and processes are common in the literary history of the past 170 years—Mallarmé and Wallace Stevens, for example, expended much of their artistic energy on these themes—Denise Levertov treats such matters in a more personal, autobiographical way than most previous poets have done. Mallarmé, in his famous sonnet, "La vierge, le vivace et le bel aujourd'hui," depicts the poet's failure of imagination through the remote but lovely symbolic image of a swan trapped in ice and earthbound:

> Un cygne d'autrefois se souvient que c'est lui
> Magnifique mais qui sans espoir se délivre
> Pour n'avoir pas chanté le région où vivre
> Quand du stérile hiver a resplendi l'ennui.

> (A swan of former times remembers it is he
> Magnificent but who without hope gives himself up
> For not having sung of the region where he should
>     have been
> When the boredom of sterile winter was resplen-
>     dent.)
>                         (Translation by Wallace Fowlie, from
>                                              *Mallarmé*, 1953.)

But however acutely the poet has felt the anguish of impotence in his art, he has removed those feelings from the sphere of his own life and incorporated them into the symbolic universe of his poetry. Stevens is less divided; indeed, his notebooks indicate that he wished to have his theory of the imagination become a cosmic view that could be shared by all men. Nonetheless, Stevens' poetry is generally impersonal and almost totally divorced from the important details of his existence as a man. Miss Levertov does not recognize such separations and refuses to hide her life from her imagination. Yet she may have learned from Stevens—as well as from her own thoughts or from other poets' work—that poetry can be involved in the mind's activity as an individual goes about his daily business of registering and interpreting and responding to surrounding reality. The poem "Something to Wear" describes in part the preparations the mind or self makes to encounter this reality ("the clamor of/cars and people . . .") and to elicit from it the substance of art and beauty ("the stars drumming and poems/leaping from shattered windows"). The contemplating self of the poem's beginning does not keep to solitude but, as in "Matins," vii, goes out to meet the world and come upon the stuff of poetry there:

> Marvelous Truth, confront us
> at every turn,
> in every guise, iron ball,
> egg, dark horse, shadow,
> cloud
> of breath on the air,
>
> dwell
> in our crowded hearts
> our steaming bathrooms, kitchens full of
> things to be done, the
> ordinary streets.
>
> Thrust close your smile
> that we know you, terrible joy.

Thus for Denise Levertov, as for certain other poets, it is proper, even imperative, for the literary enterprise to concentrate on assigning judgment and value, on finding the marvelous, within the particular range of personal observation and knowledge. If such writing is criticized for a lack of ambitious scope, one might reply that it compensates by a penetrating and scrupulous honesty, by a fundamental human resonance that is anything but restricted, and by a fidelity to the experience of contemporary life. Younger writers today, of almost every allegiance or group, have withdrawn their efforts from the elaboration of symbolic systems and mythologies; the *Cantos*, *The Waste Land*, *The Duino Elegies*, although they are still widely admired, apparently are looked upon as distant accomplishments. Now the poet believes he must use his art to define the space he inhabits as a person—if I may be permitted the figure—the space in which he exists, chooses and asserts value, loves and hates and dies. And so for Miss Levertov the poem is an instrument of personal measure, of tests and balances, estimating and preserving the valuable in the teeth of a public actuality that day by day magnifies its impersonality, falsity, and unreality. A poem such as "The Instant" rises out of personal experience and the depth of genuine emotion and significance attached to it by the author. As Miss Levertov's own testament the poem cannot be refuted or denied, for it stands well inside the space her poetic imagination circumscribes about her life as she lives it. Here is the complete poem, taken from her third book *Overland to the Islands* (1958); to cut it would be to destroy the form of an experience as she has realized it:

"We'll go out before breakfast, and get
some mushrooms," says my mother.

Early, early: the sun
risen, but hidden in mist
the square house left behind
sleeping, filled with sleepers;
up the dewy hill, quietly with baskets.
Mushrooms firm, cold;
    tussocks of dark grass, gleam of webs,
turf soft and cropped. Quiet and early. And no
        valley
no hills: clouds about our knees, tendrils
of cloud in our hair. Wet scrags
of wool caught in barbed wire, gorse
looming, without scent.
              Then ah! suddenly
the lifting of it, the mist rolls
  quickly away, and far, far—
"Look!" she grips me, "It is
      Eryri!
        It's Snowdon, fifty
miles away!"—the voice
a wave rising to Eryri,
falling.

      Snowdon, home
of eagles, resting place of
Merlin, core of Wales.
          Light
graces the mountainhead
for a lifetime's look, before the mist
          draws in again.

This poem is both an abbreviated narrative, dramatic in character (in this it resembles many poems by Robert Creeley, Paul Carroll, and others), and a spiritual adventure of a nearly ineffable sort. Within the tradition of post-Symbolist literature such a private illumination as the poet has here would be objectified into the order of a larger metaphorical universe— which is not to say that its value would be sacrificed, but that the value would be transmuted. But in the present poem the experience remains unchanged, is viewed in its own terms. Miss Levertov molds the event into art without abandoning the quality of direct utterance or leaving the domain of her life. The instant to which the poem's title refers is the moment of enlightenment that occurs when mist and clouds part to expose the far-off mountain peak shining in the early light of day and richly endowed with legendary meaning. Still, the poem retains its status as a poem of fact, so to speak, emerging from ordinary circumstances and immediate life, and returning there. We are acquainted with this kind of illumination in Blake or Rilke, though for them it confirms the basis of a whole mythological scheme: the world of things ablaze with the eternal Being they mirror. But to find any metaphysical revelation in Miss Levertov's art we must enter the precincts of the poet's own existence, for she justifies her art through that existence, as well as her existence through her artistic perception.

Miss Levertov's primary intention as a poet has not been the statement of visionary experiences but rather the dogged probing of all the routine business of life in search of what she calls "the authentic" in its rhythms and its details. ⟨. . .⟩

The quotidian reality we ignore or try to escape, Denise Levertov revels in, carves and hammers into lyric poems of precise beauty. As celebrations and rituals lifted from the midst of contemporary life in its actual concreteness, her poems are unsurpassed; they open to us aspects of object and situation that but for them we should never have known. And that is no mean achievement for any poet, though it is not the only one Miss Levertov can boast. Another side of her work has slowly asserted itself in two later books, *With Eyes at the Back of Our Heads* (1959) and *The Jacob's Ladder* (1961). I have already alluded to this visionary disposition in discussing "The Instant," but the subsequent pieces rely much more on dream, mystical imagery, and meditation than they do on external conditions that are suddenly transfigured. Some of these poems reflect on the sources of art and imagination and are developments in the line of "Something to Wear," though they find their materials in a deeper layer of consciousness. "The Goddess," "The Well," and "The Illustration," from *The Jacob's Ladder*, are excellent representatives of this category. Other poems press forward on a spiritual journey whose purpose is to uncover the nature of self and its destiny. Miss Levertov's father was a Russian Jew who later became an Anglican clergyman; something of this combination, plus her reading in Biblical, Hasidic, and other mystical writings, undoubtedly has had a decisive influence on these poems.

An example of her meditational poetry is the title poem "With Eyes at the Back of Our Heads"; here Miss Levertov brings to focus two planes of reality that seem to be distant but somehow border one another. The problem is how to get from the first into the second, and the poet addresses herself to it:

With eyes at the back of our heads
we see a mountain
not obstructed with woods but laced
here and there with feathery groves.

The doors before us in a façade
that perhaps has no house in back of it
are too narrow, and one is set too high
with no doorsill. The architect sees

the imperfect proposition and
turns eagerly to the knitter.
Set it to rights!
The knitter begins to knit.

For we want
to enter the house, if there is a house,
to pass through the doors at least
into whatever lies beyond them,

we want to enter the arms
of the knitted garment. As one
is re-formed, so the other,
in proportion.

When the doors widen
when the sleeves admit us
the way to the mountain will clear,
the mountain we see with
eyes at the back of our heads, mountain

green, mountain
cut of limestone, echoing
with hidden rivers, mountain
of short grass and subtle shadows.

Miss Levertov gives us here a parable of the inner life, a metaphorical presentation of spiritual pilgrimage in the individual. The heart of the poem appears paradoxical because the mountain, which is an image of paradisaical proportions, a depiction of the Great Good Place, is seen only within, by intuition (the "eyes at the back of our heads"), while the obstacles to be overcome and those to which we have to accommodate ourselves lie before us. Yet, as in Heraclitus and Eliot's *Four Quartets*, the way forward and the way back are one and the same. Thus movement ahead, with the alterations of the self it requires, will be completed in a reconciliation of the inner image of a desired goal with a personal condition of life. Perhaps what we are being told is, "The Kingdom of God is within you." In this, as in her other remarkable poems, Miss Levertov subtly points the way to see with our whole sight.

## RUDOLPH L. NELSON
From "Edge of the Transcendent:
The Poetry of Levertov and Duncan"
*Southwest Review*, Spring 1969, pp. 190–202

The metaphor of the threshold or border or boundary dividing realms of experience is common in the writings of ⟨Levertov and Duncan⟩. In fact, one could call it a dominating metaphor of their poetic imaginations. Duncan gives the figure its most explicit statement when he refers to the locus of the poet's attention at "the threshold that is called both *here-and-now* and *eternity*," where "identity is shared in resonance between the person and the cosmos." Less explicit but more evocative are references from his poems. In "The Song of the Borderguard," it is the poet who stands guard at "the beautiful boundaries of the empire"—"the borderlines of sense." In "The Structure of Rime VII," the poet is told: "The streams of the Earth seek passage through you, tree that you are, toward a foliage that breaks at the boundaries of known things." ⟨. . .⟩

In Levertov's work too we confront the image of the threshold or boundary. In his headnote to *Overland to the Islands*, Duncan placed Levertov's work in a sort of borderland: "that crossing of the inner and the outer reality, where we have our wholeness of feeling in the universe." That borderland becomes more readily identifiable as the same territory Duncan is exploring when we look at some of the relevant images in Levertov's poems. In the poem entitled "Threshold," a particular visual impression of form from the natural world excites the mind and raises the question of how that form can be captured in the pulsebeat of poetry. When she asks what stone hands turn "to uncover / feather of broken / oracle—" we become aware that the threshold leads to some sort of transcendental insight, a state which she labels "wonder." Much the same thought is expressed in "The Illustration," in which she speaks of learning "to affirm / Truth's light at strange turns of the mind's road, / wrong turns that lead / over the border into wonder." Another poem from *The Jacob's Ladder* refers to the gist of an insight "not quite caught, but filtered / through some outpost of dreaming sense." In an earlier poem, this borderland, identified as "the edge," is the source of the poem as true revelation, although it may not be the poem the poet expected to find there. And of course the Jacob's ladder image is borrowed from the Hasidic literature, where it represents a means of access between earth and heaven, the human and the divine. Even the colors on a brick wall, when properly perceived, can provide an entrance to the world of wonder: "archetype / of the world always a step / beyond the world, that can't / be looked for, only / as the eye wanders, / found." In the closest thing to a detailed statement of her poetics, "Some Notes on Organic Form," Levertov has referred to poetry as containing rifts, gaps between perceptions, which often span different realms of experience and understanding.

The X factor, the magic, is when we come upon those rifts and make those leaps. A religious devotion to the truth, to the splendor of the authentic, involves the writer in a process rewarding in itself; but when the devotion brings us to undreamed abysses and we find ourselves sailing slowly over them and landing on the other side—that's ecstasy.

This is one thing, then, that Denise Levertov and Robert Duncan have in common. For both of them, poetry is a dynamic means of exploration beyond what we already know into a realm of wonder or eternity which at this point we shall call transcendent. Whether Levertov's concept of the transcendent is the same as Duncan's is a key question. Clues to the answer may be found in the theories of organic form espoused by the two poets and practiced in their art.

The common denominator in all theories of organic form in poetry is the conviction that the form of a poem must emerge from the subject matter itself rather than from arbitrary predetermined structures and styles. Emerson's "ask the fact for the form" is usually cited as an authoritative precedent. With many contemporary poets, organic form simply means the freedom to be experimental in technique; it has no implications beyond style. With Duncan and Levertov, organic form goes much deeper; it has implications which can be called broadly theological. According to Levertov, organic form is "a method of apperception, i.e., of recognizing what we perceive, and is based on an intuition of an order, a form beyond forms, in which forms partake, and of which man's creative works are analogies, resemblances, natural allegories."

So far, this seems more philosophical, in a Platonic sense, then theological. But how is the poet to go about his task? A poem is demanded of him by the experience of a moment in life. To fulfil the demand, he contemplates, which means, says Levertov, "not simply to observe, to regard, but to do these things in the presence of a god." It demands an act of religious dedication to be able to see beneath the external characteristics and discern the form at the heart of creation. In "The Novices" a man and a boy go deep into the woods, "knowing some rite is to be performed." When they have shown their willingness to give themselves to nature in this way (much as Ike McCaslin did in Faulkner's *The Bear*), the gentle but awesome spirit of the forest appears and reveals his will—the rite was merely to enter the forest; now they are to look around them and see nature in a new way, "intricate branch and bark, / stars of moss and the old scars of dead men's saws." As the spirit recedes among the forms, "the twists and shadows they saw now, listening / to the hum of the world's wood." ⟨. . .⟩

Earlier I said that I was making no value judgment on simplicity and complexity. But now such a judgment must be made. We may grant that the world contains people who tend to simplify complex problems and people who counteract oversimplification by revealing the complexity of life—and that we need both kinds. We may grant that the history of human thought seems to be a pendulum swing between these tendencies. We may grant Thoreau's point in *Walden* (however overstated) that "it is a ridiculous demand which England and America make, that you shall speak so that they can understand you. Neither men nor toadstools grow so." And we may grant that Robert Duncan's complex vision is essentially mystical and ultimately ineffable. But when we contrast him with a poet whose poetic vision also crosses the threshold into transcendental wonder, who does not oversimplify the complexity of existence, but whose poetry, with all its profundity, must be classed for the most part as accessible to the understanding of the common reader, then I think we have grounds for concluding that Denise Levertov emerges as the superior poet.

The key to that superiority is that in the Levertov universe there is no radical discontinuity between the worlds of poetic vision and everyday reality. In her vision the threshold between eternity and the here and now does not seem to be so well-defined a boundary as it is in Duncan's. And while Duncan stresses the poet's transcendental vision almost exclusively, Levertov remains solidly anchored in the common life and enables the reader to see mystery within the here and now.

Ralph Mills, Jr., in a perceptive article ⟨. . .⟩ on Levertov's work, says that "she plumbs the depths of the proximate." "The quotidian reality we ignore or try to escape Denise Levertov revels in, carves and hammers into tight, precise lyrics." In doing so, "What she noticed so shrewdly was that the ordinary is extraordinarily mysterious." There are evidences all through Levertov's poetry that justify Mills's generalization. The title of one of her books is *Here and Now*. The title poem of *O Taste and See* begins: "The world is / not with us enough." In a poem entitled "Seems Like We Must Be Somewhere Else," she says, "If we're here let's be here now." In "The Goddess," she does not experience the Muse's power until she is thrown out of Lie Castle and tastes on her lips the mud of the ground outside. She quotes approvingly as a headnote to the poem "Joy" some words of Thoreau: "You must love the crust of the earth on which you dwell. You must be able to extract nutriment out of a sandheap. You must have so good an appetite as this, else you will live in vain." She finds metaphors from nature that reinforce this truth. The earth worm, "by passage / of himself / constructing," pays "homage to / earth, aerates / the ground of his living." As with the bee, "Beespittle, droppings, hairs / of beefur; all become honey," so in our lives the "honey of the human" emerges from the experiences of the common life. Borrowing a Joycean term, Robert Pack, writing in *Saturday Review* (Dec. 8, 1962), says that her best poems move "toward epiphanies, the intense rendering of a moment." He calls her poetry mystical and commends her for her freedom from the kind of self-consciousness that is prevalent in contemporary mysticism. The reason for this, he says, is that she begins not with dogma, but with perception. "Her sense of the invisible spirit of things is rooted in what she sees, and through precise description, through intimation and evocation, she leads the reader to the brink of mystery without trying to push him into the abyss."

Levertov, in her ability never to lose touch with the stuff of the common life even when her poetic vision leads her across the threshold into the realm of mystery, reminds one of Thoreau fishing at midnight on Walden Pond. Close to nature as he was, he found himself thinking transcendental thoughts. But then some horned pout would pull at his line. "It was very queer, especially in dark nights, when your thoughts had wandered to vast and cosmogonal themes in other spheres, to feel this faint jerk, which came to interrupt your dreams and link you to Nature again." Levertov keeps her own grip and ours firmly on the line. In searching out "the authentic," she even takes the poetic risk of making an observation "rising from the toilet seat." Even if she had not said this, we would have known intuitively that the poetic world of Denise Levertov contains toilet seats. We are not quite sure whether Robert Duncan's does or not. Levertov's Jacob's ladder from earth to heaven has solidly built steps with sharp angles that scrape the knees and console the groping feet. We are told to "taste and see" not only tangerines and weather, but "all that lives / to the imagination's tongue." And this includes the emotional experiences of life—grief, mercy—even our own deaths. It is Thoreau's "faint jerk" that is missing from Duncan's poetry. He

loses hold of the line that stretches from the private world of his mystical vision to the here and now.

One could argue that Denise Levertov's concept of the transcendent is not the same as Robert Duncan's. It could be maintained that although both of them operate at the threshold, in Duncan's poetic world the other side is clearly a divine realm, whereas the other side of Levertov's world is merely the dimension of mystery within the human. It is quite true that Duncan uses "God-talk" freely and equally true that Levertov tends to avoid the language of traditional transcendence. On the few occasions when she does use it, it is clear that she is not making conventional metaphysical statements. For example, when she quotes the subway poster slogan, "O taste and see," she adds that it obviously is intended to mean the Lord. But then she gives her own interpretation: "meaning / if anything all that lives / to the imagination's tongue," the full range of our human experiences.

In other words, if theological statements are to have any meaning at all, they must be understood in anthropological terms. Mills seems to take this tack in dealing with her poetry. While he acknowledges, in a poem like "The Instant," the presence of "a spiritual revelation of a nearly ineffable sort," he contrasts Levertov's handling of such an illumination with the way the tradition of post-Symbolist literature (by this he means Eliot, Pound, Yeats, Auden) would objectify it "into the order of a larger metaphorical universe." In Levertov's poetry, the experience stands alone, is viewed in its own terms. Then Mills likens her form of illumination to that of Blake and Rilke, "though with them it gives foundation to a whole mythological scheme."

Mills is correct, I think, in finally differentiating the Levertov vision from the Blakean. It is a distinction similar, though not identical, to the one I have been attempting to draw between Levertov and Duncan. But in correctly stressing Levertov's poetry of the immediate, Mills has not sufficiently clarified the dimensions of her "spiritual revelation."

I believe we are dealing with two different kinds of genuine transcendence here. Theologically, transcendence is much less of a problem for Duncan. Though it is certainly true that he does not "believe" in any orthodox creedal sense (he writes that "if Christ, heaven or hell are real, in the sense that Christian belief demands, then we are all damned"), he has no trouble whatsoever in the concept of the supernatural, making room in his world for fairies as well as Christs. He speaks in *Roots and Branches* of two returns of his mother's presence after her death. Levertov's calculated avoidance in her poetry of the language of traditional transcendence is evidence that she, much more than Duncan, is a product not only of the real world of immediate sights and sounds but of the equally real world of twentieth-century science, philosophy, and theology.

In her avoidance of "God-talk" which is less and less meaningful to the modern mind, while at the same time she steadfastly refuses to capitulate to a naturalistic view of the universe and probes into the wonder and mystery of existence, Denise Levertov has produced a body of poetry particularly congenial to the outlook of contemporary radical theology.

The recent popularizing of "death of God" theology obscures the fact that the traditional concept of a transcendent God has not been a viable option to many thoughtful people for a hundred years or more. The Altizers, Hamiltons, and Van Burens have simply called attention to the fact that such intellectual soul-searching has been going on within the province of theology itself. Without getting involved in any bizarre notions that a God who was once alive has somehow recently died, we can take seriously the redefinition of transcendence that has been going on as a result chiefly, though not exclusively, of the works of Paul Tillich and Dietrich Bonhoeffer. In *Honest to God*, John A. T. Robinson summarizes these insights:

> Statements about God are acknowledgements of the transcendent, unconditional element in all our relationships, and supremely in our relationships with other persons. Theological statements are indeed affirmations about human existence—but they are affirmations about the ultimate ground and depth of that existence.
>
> There are depths of revelation, intimations of eternity, judgements of the holy and the sacred, awarenesses of the unconditional, the numinous and the ecstatic, which cannot be explained in purely naturalistic categories without being reduced to something else. . . . The question of God is the question *whether this depth of being is a reality or an illusion*, not whether *a* Being exists beyond the bright blue sky, or anywhere else.

It is in this sense that Denise Levertov is a poet at the threshold of the transcendent. In the poem "Who Is at My Window?" a blind cuckoo sings a song of fear about the future. The poet responds: "I want to move deeper into today; / he keeps me from that work. / Today and eternity are nothing to him." Note that today and eternity are classed together, both being distinguished from the fear the bird directs toward the future. Clearly one reaches eternity by going deeper into today. Levertov often uses religious imagery to celebrate human life: a city "avenue's / endless nave echoes notes of / liturgical red." She sings a psalm praising the hair on man's body. When she gains insight into herself, the world stirs "with unheard litanies." Respect for the transcendent within the here and now involves not only the realization of the full dimensions of one's own humanity, a major theme in her poetry, but respect for the humanity of others. Her echoing of the biblical truth that "we are members one of another" takes on special impact, rising as it does from a consideration of the grotesque yet haunting figure of Adolf Eichmann on trial.

What then is the transcendent for Levertov? In "The Well" she stands on a bridge and in her mind's eye sees the Muse glide across the dark lake—"and I know / no interpretation of these mysteries." But her heart leaps in wonder as the doors of the world are opened to her. And like Thoreau, who saw the water of Walden Pond as connected underground with the sacred water of the Ganges, she looks into her river and realizes "that the humble / tributary of Roding is / one with Alpheus, the god who as a river / flowed through the salt sea to his love's well." This is as close as Levertov comes to defining the transcendent. God *is* mystery, the depths, wonder. That is all we know on earth and all we need to know. In "The Novices," the man and boy were enabled to see with new eyes when they enacted the rite of going deep into the woods. Our earlier discussion left out one important detail in the poem. Knowing that some rite was to be performed, before the spirit of the woods came to them, they found a chain running at an angle into the earth from an oaktree, "and they pit themselves to uproot it, / dogged and frightened, to pull the iron / out of the earth's heart." Then the wood-demon appeared and told them they need not perform any rite of obscure violence. They were not even to ask what the chain was. "Knowing there was mystery, they could go."

I began by referring to Levertov and Duncan as poets on the threshold of the transcendent. For Duncan the image can stand unchanged. It does not seem appropriate, however, to say that Levertov crosses the border into transcendence in a

horizontal sense, as if she were leaving the country of immediate experience for some special mystical realm. Rather, one might say, borrowing the Tillichian notion of depth, that Denise Levertov probes beneath the threshold of the here and now and finds the transcendent within the stuff of immediate experience.

## DIANA SURMAN
### From "Inside and Outside in the Poetry of Denise Levertov"
*Critical Quarterly*, Spring 1980, pp. 57–70

### I

'We awake in the same moment to ourselves and to things.' This sentence from Jacques Maritain was chosen by the Objectivist poet George Oppen as an epigraph to his book *The Materials*.[1] Its presence there accents a paradox central to some of the most interesting American writing today. 'Objectivism' is a term very loosely used at present, and I can think of no better way of giving it definition, than by recalling Louis Zukofsky's gloss on the word 'Objective' in the special number of *Poetry* Chicago he edited in 1930. First he takes a definition from Optics; 'An Objective—the lens bringing the rays from an object to a focus.' Then he offers its 'Use extended to poetry': 'Desire for that which is objectively perfect.'[2] The Objectivist movement initiated by Zukofsky in the thirties was a programmatic formulation of the poetic theory of Ezra Pound and the poetic practice of William Carlos Williams over the previous twenty years. In particular, it derived from Pound's effort, through the Imagist movement, to replace what he called 'the obscure reveries / Of the inward gaze' with a poetry concentrated on outward things. Hardness, edge, were the qualities that recommended the work of HD and Marianne Moore to him; he praised in their poems' [t]he arid clarity . . . of *le tempérament de l' Américaine*.[3]

Yet neither Pound nor Zukofsky was so ignorant as to emphasise the outward eye to the exclusion of what goes on inside the seeing mind. Indeed, Zukofsky claims that, among the Objectivists: 'Writing occurs which is the detail, not the mirage, of seeing, of thinking with the things as they exist. . . . Shapes suggest themselves, and the mind senses and receives awareness' (*Prepositions*, 20). It is implied here that the eye is the focal point in a two way process. This vivid commerce between inside and outside is a distinctive feature of the poets of the Black Mountain school, who have assimilated the discoveries of the Objectivists and their predecessors in the American *avant garde*. Consider Robert Creeley's

> I keep to myself such
> measures as I care for,
> daily the rocks
> accumulate position[4]

Here, interpenetration between the inner world of the poet and the outer world of objects, establishes a mode of writing which Denise Levertov has made hers also. ⟨. . .⟩

### IV

Denise Levertov's belief that one's inner discoveries should move hand in hand with one's outward perceptions has been the main impulse of her experiments in writing and her discussions of poetics. 'Some Notes on Organic Form', dated 1965, is one of her earliest published statements on a re-thought Romanticism. In it, she emphasises the concept that 'there *is* a form in all things (and in our experience) which the poet can discover and reveal'.[5]

This essentially Platonic version of the artist's task is perhaps the last thing that one would expect from a confessedly 'American, objectivist-influenced, pragmatic' writer. It leads Levertov to revive Hopkins' terms *inscape* and *instress*, and to add: 'In thinking of the process of poetry as I know it, I extend the use of these words, which he seems to have used mainly in reference to sensory phenomena, to include intellectual and emotional experience as well . . .' (*The Poet in the World*, 7). In another essay, she goes further than this, and argues that, just as 'the *being* of things has inscape' so too does the poet's own being, and that the act of transmitting to others the inscape of things, is also the act of awakening one's own being (*The Poet in the World*, 17).

It is by such steps that we arrive at that flow between inside and outside that Williams characterized as 'an interpenetration, both ways'. In the opening of *Paterson* Book II, 'Sunday in the park', Williams presents such interpenetration in overtly sexual terms; 'Dr. Paterson' is speaking:

Outside
            outside myself
                              there is a world,
he rumbled, subject to my incursions
—a world
            (to me) at rest,
                        which I approach
concretely—
            The scene's the Park
            upon the rock,
            female to the city
—upon whose body Paterson instructs his thoughts
(concretely)[6]

Here Paterson's role in relation to the rest of the world is obviously masculine: the objective world is 'subject' to him; some lines further on, he 'starts, possessive, through the trees'; yet within a page, he is describing himself as not merely possessive but 'passive-possessive', and he seems to present this as a proper condition for the poet.

There are, in Levertov's writings, an almost equal number of descriptions of the poetic process as a passive and so-to-say 'female' condition, as there are equations for a more aggressive and 'male' activity. She appears to have taken to heart Williams' advice, in a letter he wrote her, that a poet must be 'in essence a woman as well as a man'.[7] Indeed, she comments from her own experience, with unusual honesty: 'Perhaps I don't know myself very well, for at times I see myself as having boundless energy and a savage will, and at other times as someone easily tired and so impressionable as to be, like Keats, weighed down almost unbearably, by the identities around me . . .' (*The Poet in the World*, 216).

V

This combination of receptivity and creative energy appears to be essential not only to Denise Levertov's identity as a poet, but also to her sense of herself. In a comparatively recent poem, she records her delight at an interpretation of her name in its Hebrew meanings. D or Daleth means 'door'; hence we get:

entrance, exit,
way through of
giving and receiving
which are one[8]

'Giving and receiving' are capable of becoming 'one' in an American poetic which can incorporate somatic awareness— the body's sense of itself, as well as of the objects around it—in the disposition of words on the page.

Levertov has clearly cultivated such awareness at a subtle level. She speaks of *waiting* for the poem 'in that intense passivity, that passive intensity, that passionate patience that Keats named Negative Capability' (*The Poet in the World*, 29). Reading her poetry and prose we realize that she writes best from that state of restful alertness in which, Wordsworth claimed, 'we see into the heart of things'. Hence 'vision', 'inscape', 'revelation' are keywords in her criticism, and she frequently cites such writers as Coleridge, Emerson, Rilke, in trying to identify the special value of such insights to poetic composition. One such passage, from Carlyle, is worth quoting, as it seems to express her own experience: 'A musical thought is one spoken by a mind that has penetrated to the inmost heart of the thing; detected the inmost mystery of it, namely the melody that lies hidden in it; the inward harmony of coherence which is its soul, whereby it exists, and has a right to be, here in this world' ('Prospectus', *Sartor Resartus*; cited in *The Poet in the World*, 17). 'To write is to listen' says Levertov, on analogy with Picasso's 'To draw is to shut your eyes and sing' (*The Poet in the World*, 229). Carlyle, Picasso, Levertov, all imply that the value they seek in art is *inside* as well as *outside*, that the song is 'there' ready to be transcribed by him who hears it, that the composition exists already only to be seen by the artist. ⟨. . .⟩

VIII

In Levertov, as in Williams, there is no blurring of the edge between self and objects, but it is not a cutting edge: she is as free as he is of the *angst* that has dogged Romantic writers up to our own day. Hence the attitude with which she approaches the world is essentially one of wonder, of delight. Her poems bear out Williams's dictum that 'There is a long history in each one of us that comes as not only a reawakening but a repossession when confronted by this world'.[9]

For Levertov, writing is a way of recording such acts of 'reawakening', of 'repossession'; it is radiant with *recognition*:

That's it, [she exclaims in 'Matins']
that's joy, it's always
a recognition, the known
appearing fully itself, and
more itself than one knew[10]

The perpetual problem of a poetry of recognitions is that it may only rarely get beyond exclamation. This poem, for instance, is punctuated by ejaculations of 'the authentic!', and simply offers us fragments of experience that have struck the poet as in some way 'authentic'. Such criting remains obstinately Imagist, and lays itself open to the criticism of an early American review of Imagism, that: 'Poem after poem of this sort is full of the simple wonder of a child picking up pebbles on the beach . . .'[11] However, if we can accept such naïvete as, in itself, 'authentic', then we can begin to appreciate that it does not simply negate all our previous expectations of poetry, but offers a distinctively new mode.

IX

In order to describe this mode, I find myself falling back on Roman Jakobson's well-known distinction between the metaphoric and metonymic poles of discourse.[12] You will recall that Jakobson associates metaphor, the assertion of similarity, with poetry, and with Romantic modes of experience. Metaphor and simile record the Romantic poet's efforts to identify *likeness* in the world about him, to impose his meanings on it, to span the felt distance between subject and object. Metonymy, on the other hand, rests on *contiguity*; it is enough for things to be associated in space for them to be placed together in discourse. Thus Jakobson identifies metonymy as the pole towards which prose, and in particular the literature of Realism, tends.

We can see then that Henry James, who argues that: 'Life is all inclusion and confusion; art is all discrimination and selection', would be inclined to metaphor and symbolism, by Jakobson's definition; whereas Balzac, who expressed his intent to 'set forth in order the facts' is metonymic or Realist—if we may assume that, for him, the order in which the facts naturally occur is a sufficient order. Williams must undoubtedly be categorised with Balzac, since he overtly refuses the egotist's or artist's privilege of discrimination, in favour of transcription. 'What is there to select?' he asks, 'It *is* . . .'.[13]

Williams explicitly rejected metaphor and simile early in his poetic career. Here is a significant passage from the Prologue to *Kora in Hell* (1917):

> Although it is a quality of the imagination that it seeks to *place together* those things which have a common relationship, yet the coining of similes is a pastime of a very low order . . . Much more keen is that power which discovers in things those inimitable particles of dissimilarity to all other things which are the peculiar perfections of the thing in question . . . This *loose linking* of one thing with another has the effects of a destructive power little to be guessed at . . . All is confusion, yet it comes from a hidden desire for the dance.[14]

This is a charter for the metonymic writer. It lies behind all Williams' efforts to establish a new mode of writing, in the face of Eliot's tremendous success as a symbolist poet. Confronted by that success, he wrote in *Spring and All*: 'how easy to slip / into the old mode, how hard to cling / to the advance' (*Imaginations*, 103). The 'old mode' is the mode of symbolism, of metaphor; the 'advance', as Williams saw it, was the move beyond Romantic dualism into the metonymic mode.

The alternative to metaphor, in Williams' view, was a stress on particulars—hence the well-known slogan 'No ideas but in things'; and hence, too, the injunction of *Paterson* Book III:

> —of this, make it of *this*, this
> this, this, this, this.
>> (*Paterson*, 168)

Multiplicity, the listing of things without violating their particular existence, becomes a deliberate strategy, and is responsible for the shape of Williams' poems on the page. 'By the brokenness of his composition,' he wrote, 'the poet makes himself master of a certain weapon which he could possess himself of in no other way' (*Imaginations*, 16).

The first poem of *Spring and All* (in *Imaginations*) demonstrates this strategy in its local detail:

> All along the road the reddish
> purplish, forked, upstanding, twiggy
> stuff of bushes and small trees . . .

It stops short of personification even then 'sluggish / dazed spring approaches'; the poem continues:

> They enter the new world naked
> cold, uncertain of all
> save that they enter.
>> (*Imaginations*, 95)

The reader may extrapolate from these lines a metaphor for the immigrant's bleak prospect of America, or for the baby's arrival in the world, but he is not *entitled* to do so by the mode of the poem.

This is a major difficulty for English students coming to Williams from a training in reading Eliot's poetry or indeed any poetry in the European metaphoric tradition—and in that we

must include such writers as Wallace Stevens and Robert Frost. Because Williams is a metonymic poet, his work often seems, to the uninitiated, close to prose. His own development, indeed, involved a rejection of Keats's idiom in favour of the kind of Whitmanesque jottings that Allen Ginsberg has referred to as 'prose-seeds'.[15] Metonymy was the natural medium in which he could set down the contiguous pattern of his perceptions. Hence the necessity to his work, and to that of the writers who followed him, of typographic freedom, of open form, which allows the 'prose-seeds' to establish their own growth.

## X

This is the context of Levertov's belief that 'Form is never more than a *revelation* of content', and of her own poetic practice. In her writing, as in Williams', there is no *depth*, no measureable distance between what is said and what is meant. In this, both differ from the most well-intentioned of the Transcendentalists. Tony Tanner has pointed out the strain inherent in Thoreau's attempts to 'move from the surface detail to the Universal benevolent One which underlay it . . .', the evidence in his writing of 'an effort of penetration, a will to seduce the larger meaning out of the small particular'.[16]

Levertov seems, like Williams, to have achieved a concatenation of the 'surface detail' with the 'larger meaning'. Her poetry may be said to be *all surface*. I have attempted to show that this is not a matter of style alone, but of the poet's state of awareness. Thus she writes:

> . . . life is in me, a love for
> what happens, for
> the surfaces that are their own
> interior life[17]

In passages such as this, it seems to me that Williams' phrase 'passive-possessive' gets its full complement of meaning. Love is a precondition of Levertov's relaxed relationship with herself and with things. This persists in *The Sorrow Dance* at the very threshold of her poems against the Vietnam war. My last example, 'Joy', is from this volume. It has an epigraph from Thoreau, which robustly insists:

> You must love the crust of the earth
> on which you dwell. You must be
> able to extract nutriment out of a
> sandheap. You must have so good
> an appetite as this, else you will live
> in vain.

> Joy, the 'well . . . *joyfulness* of
> joy'—'many years
> I had not known it,' the woman of eighty
> said, 'only remembered, till now.'
> Traherne
> in dark fields.
>> On Tremont Street,
> on the Common, a raw dusk, Emerson
> 'glad to the brink of fear.'
>> It is objective,
> stands founded, a roofed gateway;
> we cloud-wander

> away from it, stumble
> again towards it not seeing it,

> enter cast-down, discover ourselves
> 'in joy' as 'in love.'[18]

In this poem, the very scraps of discourse are like the crusts from which Thoreau's nutriment must be extracted. Here the contiguity is not of things, but of 'prose-seeds', disparate recognitions. The poet allows them to lie, like found-objects, on the page, and to offer a sense of revelation analogous to her own.

It is in this sense that the poem *moves*: that is, it moves *us*, just as the original experience moved the poet. It also moves, as 'Overland to the Islands' moved, towards a final discovery. In Levertov's words 'the metric movement, the measure, is the direct expression of the movement of perception' (*The Poet in the World*, 11). Here the measure enacts the meaning as 'we / cloud-wander / away from it' and 'stumble again towards it'. The poem approaches its meaning in just such an oblique manner—via the words and experience of others, to a direct statement ('It is objective') which recalls the signal 'It quickens' of Williams' 'At the Ball Game'. Like Williams, Levertov seems intent on using the brokenness of things as a vehicle for wholeness, and she does indeed offer an analogy for this wholeness, close to the centre of the poem: 'stands founded, a roofed gateway'. Again, I restrain myself from the term 'metaphor', since it seems to me that the gateway is *there*, just as the experience is there, to be entered—an entry which is not simply into the full value of the world outside, but also the full value of the world within oneself. This is what the poem ultimately 'discovers' to us:

> and we discover ourselves
> 'in joy' as 'in love.'

## Notes

The first time a work is mentioned, details of publication are given in a note. In subsequent citations, titles and page references are given parenthetically in the text. The British editions of Denise Levertov's books, published by Jonathan Cape, are at present out of print.

1. Oppen, *The Materials* (New York: New Directions/San Francisco Review, 1962).

2. Zukofsky, 'An Objective' (1930); reprinted in *Prepositions* (London: Rapp and Carroll, 1967), 20.

3. Pound, 'A List of Books' (1918); reprinted in W. Cookson, ed., *Ezra Pound: Selected Prose 1909–65* (London: Faber & Faber, 1973), 394.

4. Creeley, *Poems 1950–65* (London: Calder and Boyars, 1966), 190.

5. Levertov, *The Poet in the World* (New York: New Directions, 1973), 7.

6. Williams, *Paterson* (New York: New Directions, 1963), 57.

7. Williams, letter of August 23, 1954; in 'Letters to Denise Levertov', *Stonybrook* 1/2, 1968: 163–4.

8. Levertov, 'To Kevin O'Leary, Wherever He Is', *Footprints* (New York: New Directions, 1972), 26.

9. *The Autobiography of William Carlos Williams* (New York: Random House, 1951), 19.

10. Levertov, *The Jacob's Ladder* (New York: New Directions, 1961), 73.

11. Lewis Worthington Smith, 'The New Naïveté' (*Atlantic Monthly*, 1916); cited by Glynn Hughes, *Imagism and the Imagists* (London: Oxford University Press, 1931), 67.

12. Jakobson, *Fundamentals of Language* (The Hague/Paris: Mouton, rev. edn. 1975), 90–6.

13. Williams, introduction to Byron Vazakas, *Transfigured Night* (New York: Macmillan, 1946), xi.

14. Williams, *Kora in Hell* (1917); reprinted in Webster Schott, ed., *Imaginations* (New York: New Directions, 1970), 18–20; my emphases.

15. Ginsberg, 'Notes for *Howl* and Other Poems' (1959); reprinted in Donald M. Allen, ed., *The New American Poetry* (New York/London: Grove Press/Evergreen Books, 1960), 414–15. See also *The Autobiography of William Carlos Williams* (see note 9), 53.

16. Tanner, 'Pigment and Ether: A Comment of the American Mind', *BAAS Bulletin* 7: 40–5 (1963).

17. Levertov, 'Entr'acte' from 'Staying Alive', *To Stay Alive* (New York: New Directions, 1971), 66.

18. Levertov, 'Joy', *The Sorrow Dance* (New York: New Directions, 1967), 33.

# PHILIP LEVINE

## 1928–

Philip Levine was born on January 10, 1928, in Detroit. His father, the son of Russian Jews who emigrated to America, was a business man; his mother was a bookseller. When he was fourteen Levine took the first of a number of factory jobs. During the early 1950s he worked on the assembly line at Ford and later at a railroad shipyard. He graduated with a B.A. from Detroit's Wayne State University in 1950; and in 1954 he earned his M.A. He also studied with Robert Lowell and John Berryman at the University of Iowa, where he received an M.F.A. in 1957. Levine did not want to serve in the Korean War and was able to get classified as 4F for mental instability, which he faked before the review board. He married Frances Artley, a gardener, in 1954; they now have three children. After his graduation from Iowa he started teaching at the California State University campus in Fresno, where he is now a professor of English.

*On the Edge*, Levine's first volume of poetry, was published in 1961. Like most of his poetry, this first volume contains several narrative verses depicting solitary individuals struggling against industrialism. Two themes of his early poetry are industrialism and the Spanish Civil War. As he continued to write and publish poetry, he developed a reputation as the poet of the blue-collar workers. Levine says his favorite poet is Whitman and he is considered by critics to be an independent voice unconnected with any specific school of poetry. In 1979 he won the American Book Award for Poetry after the publication of *Ashes*. The same year he also won the National Book Critics' Circle Prize in recognition of both *Ashes* and another book of poetry, *7 Years from Somewhere*. A collection of interviews, *Don't Ask*, was published in 1981. In collaboration with Ada Long, Levine edited and translated a volume of poems by Gloria Fuertes, which was published in 1984. Levine continues to write and teach in Fresno.

RALPH J. MILLS, JR.
"The True and Earthly Prayer: Philip Levine's Poetry"
*Cry of the Human:*
*Essays on Contemporary American Poetry*
1975, pp. 251–65

> We live
> the way we are
> (P.L., "The Sadness of Lemons")

The poetry of Philip Levine, from *On the Edge* (1963) to his two latest collections, *Red Dust* (1971) and *They Feed They Lion* (1972), has always displayed technical skill, a dexterous handling of both formal and, more recently, informal modes, and a command of the resources of diction and rhythm. Yet these aspects of technique seem in a way secondary, absorbed as they are by a central, driving intensity peculiar to this poet's approach. Such intensity leads him to a relentless searching through the events of his life and the lives of others, through the particulars of nature as these signify something about the processes of living, the states of existence, in order to arrive not at Eliot's transcendence, Roethke's "condition of joy," or Whitman's ideal of progress and brotherhood (though the sharing of suffering and the common ties of humanity are basic to Levine's attitude) but to the sort of awareness suggested by Yeats's phrase, "the desolation of reality": an unflinching acquaintance with the harsh facts of most men's situation which still confirms rather than denies its validity. If this is a difficult prospect, we must acknowledge how familiar it has become of late through the poems of Robert Lowell, David Ignatow, James Wright, Allen Ginsberg, and Galway Kinnell, to mention a few obvious names. In the writing of these poets, as in Levine's, the range of human sympathies, the frankness, perseverance, and sensitivity create of themselves an affirmative, life-sustaining balance to the bleak recognition of religious deprivation, war, social injustice, moral and spiritual confusion.

Levine's early poetry is taut, sharp, formal but gradually alters to accommodate his desire for greater freedom in line length and overall construction. A prominent theme of his first book is the reversal or defeat of expectations. Put another way, it motivates a struggle on the poet's part to view life stripped of the vestiges of illusory hope or promise, a type of hard spiritual conditioning which helps to engender his fundamental responsiveness to the dilemmas of the poor, embittered, failed lives of the "submerged population" (the late Frank O'Connor's term) in modern society, a responsiveness that accounts for much of both the energy and the deep humaneness of all his work. A firm grip on existence itself takes priority for Levine from the start, though with it necessarily comes an acceptance of pain and the admission that failure, defeat, and imperfection—but not surrender!—are unavoidable in men's affairs. The penetrating look he gives himself in "The Turning" from *On the Edge* points the direction he follows to maturity, which depends on the realization of flaws as well as the capacity to exist, to continue, made sturdier by this self-knowledge:

> . . . no more a child,
> Only a man,—one who has
> Looked upon his own nakedness
> Without shame, and in defeat
> Has seen nothing to bless.
> Touched once, like a plum, I turned
> Rotten in the meat, or like
> The plum blossom I never
> Saw, hard at the edges, burned

> At the first entrance of life,
> And so endured, unreckoned,
> Untaken, with nothing to give.
> The first Jew was God; the second
> Denied him; I am alive.

Committed to a fallen, unredeemable world, finding no metaphysical consolations, Levine embraces it with an ardor, anguish, and fury that are themselves religious emotions. In a brief comment on his work contributed to *Contemporary Poets of the English Language* (1970) he lists among his "obsessions" "Detroit" (where he was born, did factory labor, and studied), "the dying of America" (a recurrent theme in various guises), and "communion with others," which incorporates its predecessors as well as specifying what is for him a primary poetic impulse. Writing frequently of persons whose lives are distinct yet touch his own, he increases his consciousness and imaginative powers, and a chord of compassion and understanding reverberates within and beyond the boundaries of his poems. This is not to say that Levine puts himself out of the picture or chooses a mask of impersonality, but that his presence in a poem, whether overt or concealed, constitutes an enlargement of personality, a stepping out of the ego-bound "I" into the surrounding life. Paradoxically, he reaches inward, far into the recesses of the psyche, at the same time he reaches outward, thus fulfilling a pattern of movement Robert Bly has long advocated as essential to a modern poetry rich in imaginative potentialities.

Among the poems of Levine's initial volume, this self-extension appears most complete when he adopts the voices of different persons—the Sierra Kid, four French Army deserters in North Africa, the unnamed officer of "The Distant Winter"—to replace his own. Another sort of identification, of a crucial kind for the line of development his work pursues, occurs in the title poem "On the Edge," and also in "My Poets" and "Gangrene." In these instances he does not assume the role of another speaker but takes up the question of a poetic vocation and the destiny of poets in society today. In one shape or another, each of these poems really considers the problem of speechlessness, the lacerating irony of the mute poet imprisoned by circumstances which thwart or oppose his art, making its practice unlikely or impossible. So Levine sorts through the probabilities of his own future. The poet/speaker of "On the Edge" describes himself as the insane, alcoholic Poe of the twentieth century, born, as Levine was, "in 1928 in Michigan." This latter-day Poe plays the part of an observer who doesn't write, only watches the actions and prevarications of nameless people. In the last stanza he repeats a refusal of his art, though we are provided in its statement of alienation, perceptiveness, and silence with a poetry of angry eloquence:

> I did not write, for I am Edgar Poe,
> Edgar the mad one, silly, drunk, unwise,
> But Edgar waiting on the edge of laughter,
> And there is nothing that he does not know
> Whose page is blanker than the raining skies.

This abstention from writing, or persecution for telling the truth by means of it, occupies the other poems mentioned. Levine's effort here is to indicate the need for honest speech, the conditions which militate against it, and the frustrating atmosphere of separateness the poet faces. Thematically, the poem "Silent in America" from *Not This Pig* (1968), Levine's second collection, brings such matters to a critical climax and to a moment of transformation and decision. Though it is not the first poem in the book, dramatically speaking it should be thought of as a pivotal piece, for its procedure and resolution make possible what Levine is doing elsewhere in the same volume: breaking down those barriers which prevent him from entering areas of otherwise lost or unapprehended experience requisite to the poetry he wants to write. At the outset the poet announces his silence, which fashions for him a state of remoteness and solitude that border on anonymity. Watching ordinary things—a sprinkler wetting a lawn—stirs him toward utterance, but he stays quiet. A doctor's examination uncovers no defect. Details of nature engage him with the elusive tracery of their being; still, the animate *something* he notices in trees, water, and flowers defies his wish to name it, and thus his muteness persists. Locked in isolation, Levine now falls victim to inner torments, to his "squat demon,/my little Bobby," a splintered apparition of the self who plagues him with insatiable sexual demands. The poem develops rapidly toward hysteria and derangement until the poet bursts out with a negative cry of resistance. A section ensues in which he articulates the aims of his writing—to give voice to the varied experience of lost, unknown, or forgotten individuals he has met, speaking with and for them—but he is likewise forced to assent to the fact that each person remains finally impervious to total comprehension and communion. The following passage handsomely summarizes Levine's intentions and concerns:

> For a black man whose
> name I have forgotten who danced
>   all night at Chevy
>     Gear & Axle,
>   for that great stunned Pole
> who laughed when he called me Jew
>   Boy, for the ugly
>     who had no chance,
>   the beautiful in
> body, the used and the unused,
>   those who had courage
>     and those who quit—
> Rousek and Ficklin
> numbed by their own self-praise
>   who ate their own shit
>     in their own rage;
>   for these and myself
> whom I had loved and hated, I
>   had presumed to speak
>     in measure.
>
> The great night is half
> over, and the stage is dark;
>   all my energy,
>     all my care for
>   those I cannot touch
> runs on my breath like a sigh;
>   surely I have failed.
>     My own wife
>   and my children reach
> in their sleep for some sure sign,
>   but each has his life
>     private and sealed.

Levine's anxiety arises from the profoundly felt impulse to put his language, as poetry, in the service of others' lives, in addition to his own. The walls of privacy and individuality he cannot traverse cause him regret and a feeling of loss. Yet, just as surely, he *does* speak for others to the very limit of his abilities, not only here but also in the rest of this book, as well as in his subsequent poetry. If he is unable to appropriate the entirety of another life, like a second skin, it is still possible for him to go with others, moving to the rhythms of their existence and assimilating the details which his imagination requires. This kind of correspondence and kinship receives treatment in the closing section of the poem, where Levine meets a friend,

H., in a Los Angeles bar and talks with him. H. is perhaps a writer too; in any event, he is described as doing essentially what an artist does: he creates a world composed of half-real, observed figures and half-fictitious ones who fit in with their actual counterparts, and he lives with them in imagination and sympathy. In the tavern Levine senses the presence of a person of fabulous name, apparently a wholly fictive man, conjured by his mind, who imposes himself no less strongly on the poet's awareness and emotions because of that:

> Archimbault is here—
> I do not have to be drunk
>   to feel him come near,
> and he touches me with his
>   life, and I could cry,
> though I don't know who he is
>   or why I should care
> about the mad ones, imagined
>   and real, H. places
> in his cherished underground,
>   their wounded faces
> glowing in the half-light of
>   their last days alive,
>   as his glows here.

Whatever his self-questioning, Levine clearly cares, and his expressed wish in the next lines merges his own existence with that of such persons as fill the bar, until all seems to become part of poetry itself: "Let me have/the courage to live/as fictions live, proud, careless,/unwilling to die." So he would have his life speak itself as poems do, tenacious of their being. At the conclusion Levine and H. leave the bar and "enter the city." The poet urges his readers to join him, to blend into the mass of humanity thronging the streets in their restlessness, at last to go "beyond the false lights/of Pasadena/where the living are silent/in America." This invitation is as much a definition of his own poetic pursuits as it is a gesture by which the poet makes his reader a partner to what he sees. Levine will invade those areas of the unspoken life and lend them words.

Rich and complex though they usually are, the poems of Levine's first two collections are relatively direct, proceeding by certain logical, sequential, narrative, or other means which provide the reader with support and guidance. Levine never altogether abandons poems of this sort, but even in *Not This Pig* he begins to widen his fields of exploration to include experiences which manifest themselves in irrational, dream-like, fantastic, or visionary forms, doing so variously in such poems as "The Rats," "The Business Man of Alicante," "The Cartridges," "The One-Eyed King," "Animals Are Passing from Our Lives," "Baby Villon," "Waking an Angel," "The Second Angel," and "The Lost Angel." These pieces prepare the way for the surrealist atmosphere of *Red Dust*, the elliptical, disjunctive composition evident there, and further visible in portions of *They Feed They Lion*. Levine has cited the Spanish and Latin American poets Hernandez, Alberti, Neruda, and Vallejo, in addition to postwar Polish poetry, as having presented new possibilities available to him. The freedom, vigorousness, metaphorical and imagistic daring of these poets plainly has had a tonic effect on Levine's more recent writing, releasing him to new boldness and strength.

So, by any but a narrow or restrictive view, Levine's latest books must be judged extraordinarily successful, exhibiting an access of inventiveness and vision. In *Red Dust* the elements of experience move into different focus; they are less "distanced," talked about, or pointed to than rendered dramatically as the very substance of language and image in the poems. The general character of these poems is also freer, more intuitive, and thus occasionally more difficult, unyielding to logical analysis. From the beginning we find an openness in the structure of poems, in the sense that they are not brought to a tidy conclusion but often end in a startling, seemingly irrational—yet, on consideration, perfectly apt—statement. Here is the final section of "Clouds," a poem which gathers considerable momentum by associative leaping among apparently random details whose disconnectedness actually pulls together a grim portrait of the contemporary world. Over the shifting scenes and figures the aloof clouds travel, absorb, and spill out their rain, giving the poem coherence while at the same time implying a universal indifference to which the poet responds with vehemence in the striking lines at the close:

> You cut an apple in two pieces
> and ate them both. In the rain
> the door knocked and you dreamed it.
> On bad roads the poor walked under cardboard
>   boxes.
>
> The houses are angry because they're watched.
> A soldier wants to talk with God
> but his mouth fills with lost tags.
>
> The clouds have seen it all, in the dark
> they pass over the graves of the forgotten
> and they don't cry or whisper.
> They should be punished every morning,
> they should be bitten and boiled like spoons.

In poems of this sort the components are set down in combinations which resist or contradict ordinary rational expectations for them. The reader, thus perceptually thrown off balance, has the option either to give up or give in, and so to see and feel the particulars of experience fused in vivid, evocative ways. Gradually, the shifting shapes, the elisions and abrupt juxtapositions will disclose their significance, if the reader will only accept them on their own terms. As indicated previously, Levine's social and moral preoccupations retain their urgency, but, as in the work of the Spanish-speaking poets he admires, such interests tend at times to be integral with the immediate, elliptical, or surreal orderings of imagery and statement. Frequently now, the poems seek out specific details of landscape, cityscape, even vegetation and animal life, though these directly or obliquely correspond with aspects of human existence. Sensitivity to place—whether Detroit, California, or Spain (where Levine lived for two years recently)—the imagination exercised on what is perceived there, leads readily into poems of large expressive force. The figures inhabiting these pieces may be quite separate and distinct, with Levine himself only a transparent or invisible speaker (though, of course, an indirect commentator, sometimes a savage one), as in "The End of Your Life" or "Where We Live Now"; or they may involve the poet openly, as he tries to define himself and his life, or when he captures a moment's affective resonance, a mood charged with implications, of the kind we observe in "A Sleepless Night," "Told," "Holding On," and "Fist." In "Noon" he draws self and others together beautifully within the frame of a landscape:

> I bend to the ground
> to catch
> something whispered,
> urgent, drifting
> across the ditches.
> The heaviness of
> flies stuttering
> in orbit, dirt
> ripening, the sweat

> of eggs.
>         There are
> small streams
> the width of a thumb
> running in the villages
> of sheaves, whole
> ears of grain
> wakening on
> the stalks, a roof
> that breathes over
> my head.
>         Behind me
> the tracks creaking
> like a harness,
> an abandoned bicycle
> that cries and cries,
> a bottle of common
> wine that won't
> pour.
> At such times
> I expect the earth
> to pronounce. I say,
> "I have been waiting
> so long."
>         Up ahead
> a stand of eucalyptus
> guards the river,
> the river moving
> east, the heavy light
> sifts down driving
> the sparrows for
> cover, and the women
> bow as they slap
> the life out
> of sheets and pants
> and worn hands.

In this poem, as in many of Levine's newest, man's common attachments with earth, his relationship with objects, the hard, painful climate in which most lives are lived, are evoked through a skilled interweaving of images, the particulars of the world suddenly caught up to view, suffused with the "reek of the human," to borrow a phrase from Donald Davie. "How much earth is a man," Levine asks in another poem; his answer indicates an indissoluble, fateful bond: "a hand is planted/and the grave blooms upward/in sunlight and walks the roads." In the three angel poems from *Not This Pig*, which create a little sequence among themselves, the realm of transcendence, of the spiritual ideal, dissolves or collapses before the spectacle of flawed earthly reality. What aspects of the spiritual can become evident belong not to a hidden or remote sphere but radiate, if possible, from the ingredients of day-to-day mundane affairs. So, in Levine's work, life is circumscribed by the finality of death, but this inevitability is countenanced with toughness, stoicism, staying power. As he says of his fist in the final stanza of the poem bearing that title:

> It opens and is no longer.
> Bud of anger, kinked
> tendril of my life, here
> in the forged morning
> fill with anything—water,
> light, blood—but fill.

Between the poems of *Red Dust* and those of *They Feed They Lion* no alterations occur in Levine's attitude toward such matters; two poems, "The Space We Live" and "How Much Can It Hurt?", are even reprinted from the earlier book. In general, however, Levine employs less of the dense irrational or associative manner so prominent in *Red Dust*, though with no loss of concentrated force. The opening poems, "Renaming the Kings" and "The Cutting Edge," for instance, dramatize personal incidents in a direct, sequential way quite appropriate to the experiences. These pieces, along with several others, examine the poet's encounters in the midst of natural settings, with each occasion revealing some facet of a relation between the things of earth and a man—a relation sometimes assuring and harmonious, sometimes disturbing or painful. In "The Cutting Edge" a stone under water gashes the poet's foot; he casts it out of the stream and hobbles away. Later he returns, discovers it, and pauses to wonder before deciding what to do with it:

> I could take it home
> and plant it in a box;
> I could talk about
> what it did to me
> and what I did to it,
> or how in its element
> it lives like you or me.
> But it stops me, here
> on my open hand,
> by being a stone, and I send
> it flying over the heads
> of the fishing children,
> arching alone above
> the dialogue of reeds,
> falling and falling toward water,
> somewhere in water to strike
> a conversation of stone.

A very different type of "conversation" takes place in "To a Fish Head Found on the Beach Near Málaga," where Levine, walking alone, comes upon the ravaged body and head, hanging by its shred of bone, then confides his "loneliness," "fears," and torments to it. The result of his strange speech makes him sense the contours and characteristics of his own face and head, and, at last, "throw the fish head to the sea./Let it be fish once more." The poem's concluding lines assert the speaker's comprehension of the unalterable cyclicism of existence, the ironic necessity of destruction for renewal:

> I sniff my fingers
> and catch the burned essential oil
> seeping out of death. Out of the beginning,
> I hear, under the sea roar, the bone words
> of teeth tearing earth and sea,
> anointing the tongues with stone and sand,
> water eating fish, fish water,
> head eating head to let us be.

This volume also includes sequences of varying length, as well as groups of obviously connected poems. "Thistles," the longest of them, dedicated to the poet Goerge Oppen, is composed of discrete pieces each of which focuses on a singular occasion, perception, or ambiance of feeling. The same may be said for the shorter sequence, "Dark Rings." These poems are not bound tightly together, though the thistle appears in the first and last pieces of that sequence, and the "dark rings" refer not only to a specific detail in one poem but also to images in most and the mood of all of them. Yet their swift, free, occasionally abbreviated notation and arrangement give an impression of accuracy, deftness, and assurance in the handling of experience. The poems are full of nuances and overtones which linger on. One must place with these sequences most of the poems in the book's second section, dealing with Levine's Detroit life among the automotive workers and the abandoned, hopeless, silent figures we have

seen him desirous to know and to speak for. The angels return in this section in shifting but always earthly forms, evanescent protective spirits hovering about the poet, presences in his closet, or incarnate in someone of his acquaintance, as in the fourth poem of "The Angels of Detroit" group. Here "the angel Bernard," trapped and frustrated by the massive industrial system for which he labors and cannot escape, writing poems no one will read, aching for love, release, even death, awakens as always to find himself surrounded by the debris of manufacture, our values and lives rupturing from the shapes of steel and rubber in which we have conceived them:

> At the end of the mud road
> in the false dawn of the slag heap
> the hut of the angel Bernard.
> His brothers are factories and
> bowling teams, his mother is the
> power to blight, his father
> moves in all men like a threat,
> a closing of hands, an unkept
> promise to return.
>     We talk
> for years; everything we
> say comes to nothing. We drink
> bad beer and never lie. From
> his bed he pulls fists
> of poems and scatters them
> like snow. "Children are guilty,"
> he whispers, and the soft mouth
> puffs like a wound.
> He wants it all tonight.
> The long hard arms of a black woman,
> he wants tenderness, he wants
> the power to die in the
> chalice of God's tears.
> True dawn through the soaped window.
> The plastic storm-wrap swallows wind.
> '37 Chevie hoodless, black burst
> lung of inner tube, pot metal
> trees buckling under sheets.
> He cries to sleep.

Such a poem gives notice of the incredible strength, the economy and muscle with which Levine endows the majority of his poems. Two of the most amazing and powerful pieces, "Angel Butcher" and "They Feed They Lion," bring the book's second section to a climactic level of prophetic vision; the latter poem is dazzling in its syntactic, linguistic, and dramatic invention, its use of idiomatic effect. But both poems need to be read in their entirety and are too long for quotation here. It remains now simply to say for the purposes of this brief commentary that Levine's poetry, praiseworthy at the start, has developed by momentous strides in the past decade. His new poems make it impossible for him to be ignored or put aside. He stands out as one of the most solid and independent poets of his generation—one of the best poets, I think, anywhere at work in the language. It is time to begin listening.

> Can you hear me?
> the air says. I hold
> my breath and listen
> and a finger of dirt thaws,
> a river drains
> from a snow drop
> and rages down
> my cheeks, our father
> the wind hums
> a prayer through my mouth
> and answers in the oat,

and now the tight rows of seed
bow to the earth
and hold on and hold on.

## STEPHEN YENSER
"Bringing It Home"

*Parnassus: Poetry in Review*, Fall–Winter 1977, pp. 101–17

Auden once observed that every poem testifies to a rivalry between Ariel and Prospero. Ariel urges the poet to make "a verbal paradise, a timeless world of pure play" that affords some relief from the historical world with all its dilemmas and suffering. Prospero, concerned more with truth than with beauty, exhorts him to reveal life as it really is, to bring us face to face with "the problematic, the painful, the disorderly, the ugly" and thus to "free us from self-enchantment and deception." While any poem will owe something to each of these advocates, it is usually possible to decide whether a poem and occasionally whether a poet is "Ariel-dominated" or "Prospero-dominated." Few have listened as attentively to Prospero as Philip Levine. Ariel sometimes draws him aside, but Levine is too much a product of the fallen world to be comfortable for long in the realm of "pure play."

"If you want to die you will have to pay for it": Charon's caveat, as set down by Louis MacNeice, could be inscribed above the exit from the world of Levine's poems. Inhabited by exhausted blue-collar workers and derelicts, desperate young toughs, convicts, and bone-weary housewives, it is all bleared and smeared with toil and pain. Selections from Doré's *Inferno* illustrations might have accompanied the poems in Levine's most recent and grimly impressive volume. Here people wake to "the cold anger / of machines that have to eat"; there a harmless old bum gets a beating from the cops; near by, "Covered / with dust, rags over / their mouths," farm workers "go out in open trucks /to burn in the fields." For Levine, the plight of the man in "Waiting," convicted on the testimony of a lying witness and sweating out the ninth year of his sentence, merely exaggerates an all too common condition.

Since that condition is political, so is much of Levine's poetry, as he had to insist in a recent *Partisan Review*. His interviewer, admiring Levine's work and wanting to save it from itself, suggested that poems about lonely, depressed people who want to give up but find themselves enduring need not be political. Levine responded that "an accurate depiction of people's lives as they are actually lived" (Prospero's means precisely) must itself be "a political act" in our society. He continued:

> I mean, what are the sources of anger in a lot of the poems that I write and that a lot of people write? The sources of anger are frequently social, and they have to do with the fact that people's lives are frustrated, they're lied to, they're cheated, that there is no equitable handing out of the goods of this world. A lot of the rage that one encounters in contemporary poetry has to do with the political facts of our lives.

The American poets who might subscribe enthusiastically to that statement seem to me comparatively few—Allen Ginsberg, Imamu Amiri Baraka, and in certain moods Robert Bly, Galway Kinnell, Adrienne Rich, Robert Lowell—and none sounds much like Levine. When he speaks of "the agony of living" he is thinking chiefly of the life of the working class in a system in which "the people in power have no compassion." While his own compassionate skepticism saves him from being narrowly partisan, Levine is our notable heir to the radicalism

of the 1930s, a descendant of Henry Roth who has read Neruda and Vallejo closely.

He said in the same interview that he gets "ideas that encompass more than one poem at a time, that almost reach out to the idea of the whole thing" that he wants to write about in a book. Thus Buenaventura Durruti, the leader of the left wing of the anarchist movement during the Spanish Civil War, to whom Levine dedicates *The Names of the Lost*, stands at the center of this volume. My guess is that the cover photograph—of a line of men, faces half-shadowed, marching through a desert—pictures Durruti's column. Levine follows his dedication, in any case, with an epigraph—"*and the world he said is growing here in my heart this moment*"—that echoes Durruti's comments in an interview published in the Toronto *Star* in September, 1936. Since they help us to see Durruti as Levine does, they warrant fuller quotation here. The interviewer had just warned that a leftist victory might leave all of Spain in ruins, and Durruti replied:

> We have always lived in slums and holes in the wall. We will know how to accommodate ourselves for a time. For, you must not forget, we can also build. It is we who built these palaces and cities, here in Spain and America and everywhere else. We, the workers, we can build others to take their places. And better ones. We are not in the least afraid of ruins. We are going to inherit the earth. . . . We carry a new world, here, in our hearts. That world is growing this very moment.

He was to die soon in the defense of Madrid, perhaps shot by one of his own men, and within a few years Fascism had all but choked out that new growth everywhere in Spain.

Prospero counsels realism; Levine's epigraph is no declaration of faith. Seen in the light of many of these poems, it might even be read as a bitterly mocking epitaph, not only for Durruti and the *anarquistas* but also for the vision behind the movement. Levine recalls Durruti's vow in a derisive passage in "Gift for a Believer." In a friend's vision Durruti whispered that he would never forget his comrades "who died believing they carried / a new world there in their hearts"—but when Durruti died, "he forgot." Levine knows how lesser exigencies paralyze conviction: later in this poem he tells how he once swore never to forget an early, radicalizing experience at the Chevy plant, and yet eventually "the memory slept, and I bowed / my head so that I might live." If Durruti's faith survives today, he implies, it survives as tenuously as the wretched garden at the end of "Autumn Again," where "Down the oiled path of cans / and inner tubes in the field / by the river" a young mechanic struggles to keep his beans and herbs alive.

The garden recurs so often in *The Names of the Lost* that it becomes a unifying element closely related to the "*world growing here in my heart this moment*." The poet's wife almost always appears tending her plants ("New Season," "Autumn Again," "The Falling Sky," "Another Life," "My Son and I"), as though she embodied Durruti's spirit, or as though the growth he envisioned depended upon such steady, intense devotion. Levine's own detachment from the family garden reminds us that he has little faith in a new world, and the advent of the "New Season" seems to bear him out. While "the future grows / like a scar," the garden, so painstakingly cultivated each day, suffers at night the slow fury of the snails: "the rhododendrons shrivel / like paper under water, all / the small secret mouths are feeding / on the green heart of the plum." Surely Levine is playing those lines against the memory, continually imperiled, of Durruti's words. But of course—and from this qualification spring both the tension and the occasional self-righteousness in this book—Levine does finally remember. Nullifidian though he might be, he has his own plot, as the poems prove. His grafting of irony on to idealism is an attempt to develop a sustaining belief. As he says in "For the Poets of Chile," "Someone / must remember it over / and over, must bring / it all home and rinse / each crushed cell / in the waters of our lives."

The need to bring it all home, in both senses, shapes a number of these poems, including "For the Fallen," a moving elegy for Durruti, and "And the Trains Go On." In "For the Fallen" Levine remembers not only the Spanish Civil War but also his relationship to it, which he could not then have known, as a boy of eight. He first focuses on the burial of Durruti (Joaquin Ascaso was the President of the Council of Aragon, another anarchist leader) and then cuts to an image of himself, on the threshold of learning, less from history books than from the working people he grew up among, something about exploitation of labor:

> The comrades must have known
> it was over, and Joaquin
> Ascaso, staring at the earth
> that had opened so quickly
> for his brothers must
> have whispered *soon*.
> Soon the boy rose
> from his desk and went
> into the darkness
> congealing in cold parlours
> or in the weariness
> of old pistons, in the gasps
> of men and women asleep
> and dreaming as the bus
> stalls and starts on the way
> home from work.

Technically austere, as befits both the scene and Prospero's temperament, this passage is nonetheless subtly put together. The images in its narrow gauge lines flow as smoothly as in a film. Like much of his work, it calls up Eisenstein, some grainy black and white silent picture (for Levine's work is unusually chiaroscurist, his people rarely speak), the point of its montage unmistakably political. The covert analogy between the uneasy sleepers and the poorly running engine implies and implicates a society in which people with dreams but no power become worn parts in the machinery. As the boy rises from the desk, years pass; and with the unobtrusive shift in tense the past dissolves into the present, elegy into indictment. Levine sometimes considers Durruti's acts alms for oblivion, but he cannot forget their pertinence.

This volume's title, just near enough paradox to snag the attention, joins these barely reconcilable feelings. It derives from "And the Trains Go On," a highly concentrated meditative lyric which grows from memories of riding the rails with an unidentified companion some twenty-five years ago. Levine starts in the past tense, then shifts to present and future tenses in combination with images drawn from the Korean War to conjure the future, and finally modulates into a present tense that recovers the past. These taut lines get us from the second to the third phase:

> When I lie down at last to sleep
> inside a boxcar of coffins bound
> for the villages climbing north
> will I waken in a small station
> where women have come to claim
> what is left of glory? Or will
> I sleep until the silver bridge
> spanning the Mystic River jabs
> me awake, and I am back

> in a dirty work-shirt that says *Phil*,
> 24 years old, hungry and lost, on
> the run from a war no one can win?

In some contexts that river would seem too felicitously named to be true; here, coupled with the silver bridge that links past and future, the name is too obliquely accurate to have been invented. Quietly magical as that transition is, the poem's real achievement is its conclusion, where Levine and his friend come "back the long / tangled road that leads us home":

> Through Flat Rock going east
> picking up speed, the damp fields
> asleep in moonlight. You stand
> beside me, breathing the cold
> in silence. When you grip
> my arm hard and lean way out
> and shout out the holy names
> of the lost neither of us is scared
> and our tears mean nothing.

These lines bring the past incident rushing into the present, thus accomplishing in small one of the book's aims, and they image the movement into the future. Wearing his "dirty work-shirt," Levine seems already one of the lost whose names these poems shout into the darkness. Besides the men killed in Korea they include all of those whose lives have been wasted in futile political struggles—who have died in other wars, like Durruti, or who have been worn down by iniquitous systems, like Levine's Uncle Joe, or warped by them, like the black convicts. The tears "mean nothing," since they can change nothing, and that is what they mean.

The lost began to haunt Levine in *On the Edge* (1963), although he did not yet know they were to be his abiding subject. Looking at "An Abandoned Factory, Detroit," he lamented, in painfully mimetic, mechanically regular lines

> the loss of human power,
> Experienced and slow, the loss of years,
> The gradual decay of dignity.
> Men lived within these foundries, hour by hour;
> Nothing they forged outlived the rusted gears
> Which might have served to grind their eulogy.

This stanza might drug us into a sort of awareness; the first volume's more interesting poems, not all political, try to shock us into it. "Gangrene" does so as literally as possible. Beginning with a description of electrical and other tortures of political prisoners, packaged in fussy syllable stanzas, it then rounds on the reader, *ipso facto* "secretly thrilled by / the circus of excrement." "Think of the colossal brutality, cruelty and mendacity which is now allowed to spread itself over the civilized world. Do you really believe that a handful of unprincipled placehunters and corrupters of men would have succeeded in letting loose all this latent evil, if the millions of their followers were not also guilty?" So the more circumspect Freud in his self-vindication forty years earlier. For the American who might really believe himself innocent, Levine juxtaposes "Gangrene" with a searingly objective poem about a horse flayed alive by the bomb dropped on Hiroshima. In various ways, "L'Homme et la Bête," "Small Game," and "The Turning" serve the same end: Levine means to strip the reader of his own integument of moral pretension.

"Political facts" motivated many of the poems in *Not This Pig* (1968), but frequently Levine's animus took the form of satire on bourgeois conformity, viewed once more as the spiritually bankrupting price of admission to the system. The title "Barbie & Ken, Ken & Barbie" gives away that poem's game immediately. In "Obscure" Levine portrays a woman who lives in pathetic dread of never mothering "civic children" whose names would be "real" to her because she would be "reading them in the evening / during station breaks." In his advice "To a Child Trapped in a Barber Shop" he ridicules shibboleths that enshrine bourgeois values. "So don't drink / the Lucky Tiger, don't / fill up on grease," he warns, "because that makes it a lot worse, / that makes it a crime / against property and the state / and that costs time." Though he be a Jew, the child might find himself delivered the next morning into the hands of a teacher like the Miss Jennings of "Who Are You?", who will teach him to play " 'Here / Is the church, there the steeple.' " At best he might eventually withdraw, like the man in "Heaven," a rendering of the Ariel-dominated poet, who took to his room in a time of war to build a paradise for his "mad canary," complete with a "network of golden ladders." He was certain to be hunted down and "laid off"—"and it would do no good / to show how he had taken / clothespins and cardboard / and made each step safe."

"Heaven" is an eerie, softly-hued poem, but these others, although smooth enough—no, partly because so smooth seem thin and dated as old coins. The poem with the wonderfully skewed title, "Animals Are Passing from Our Lives," will always seem newly minted. A parable of the blinkered "progress" of the consumer society, it fascinates both because of its farming concept (how many poets would dream of adopting the point of view of the first little pig in the children's game?) and its execution of detail. Nothing could be more right, descriptively or politically, than the conjunction of "my massive buttocks slipping / like oiled parts with each light step" and the butcher's "pudgy white fingers / that shake out the intestines / like a hankie." Everyone will remember the last lines, where the pig senses that the boy driving him along believes

> that at any moment I'll fall
> on my side and drum my toes
> like a typewriter or squeal
> and shit like a new housewife
>
> discovering television,
> or that I'll turn like a beast
> cleverly to hook his teeth
> with my teeth. No. Not this pig.

What works so well, even to overcome the merely serviceable first simile and the confusingly extended last, is the flat refusal to act unpredictably. How better leave us to our own devices?

But such a poem is a tiny territory discovered and fully exploited at once, just as "Heaven" is an enchanting island to which one does not return. "The Midget" might stand for Levine's entrance into a country large and potentially productive as the Spain in which it is set. The poet is accosted, in a workers' bar in Barcelona once frequented by Durruti, by a midget who will not be bought off or discouraged by pleas to be left alone. As in a bad dream, the midget insists on intimacy, begs Levine to feel him where he is "big where it really counts," and finally crawls into his lap to sing drunken songs of "fabled Americas." The workers pay and leave, the odd couple are left alone, and now the poet sings lullabies to "this late-born freak / of the old world swelling my lap." Few poems deal as ruthlessly with our attempts to dissociate ourselves from the world's grief or dramatize as convincingly our utter moral defenselessness in the face of the claims of the poor and powerless. The heads of all our international conglomerates should be made to read it every night after saying their prayers.

Levine has never shaken that obstinate midget. His paradoxical image of potency was prophetic: from such narrow circumstances, whether in Spain or the United States, most of his finest poems have come. As early as "Silent in America" in

this second volume he could say that he "had presumed to speak" for the lost, for the laborers he had worked with in Detroit, and more generally "for the ugly / who had no chance, the beautiful in / body, the used and the unused, / those who had courage / and those who quit."

Levine's home turf is the urban setting, so it makes whimsical sense for *Not This Pig* to be dedicated in part to "the cities that are here, Detroit, Fresno, Barcelona." But often in *Red Dust* and throughout *Pili's Wall*, both published by small presses in 1971, Levine explored the rural areas of the country of the spirit that he had settled in. Two of the best poems in *Red Dust*, which now looks rather like a preparation for *They Feed They Lion* and must be slighted here, were reprinted in that later volume. None of *Pili's Wall*, a sequence of ten lyrics, has ever been reprinted, perhaps because the accompanying photos would pose a problem in a larger edition. Its limited printing is a pity, but one has to approve the decision not to publish the poems alone; for although they never refer to the wall's graffiti, reproduced in the photos, the two media come to seem inseparable. Levine never quite says so, but it seems that Pili, a "Spanish girlchild," chipped these figures into the wall. They are her poem at the same time that they inspire Levine's, which is also primitive, elliptical, out of perspective—and written in a tight free verse rather than the syllabics that predominate in the earlier volumes.

Through most of the sequence Levine assumes Pili's point of view, while she in turn merges with the elements of her small but inexhaustible world: a lost and frightened dog, a weary shepherd, even the wall itself, as in section VII, the germ of "They Feed They Lion":

> Out of saying No
> No to the barn swallow, No
> to the hurled stone
> No to the air
>
> out of *you can't*
> to the crying grain, *you won't*
> to the lost river
> of blackening ivy
>
> out of blind
> out of deaf, closed, still
>
> I stand and stand and stand into
> this wall.

While the syntax of this section owes an obvious debt to Whitman, the definition of self in terms of gritty negation is pure Levine. Again, the identifications at the heart of the sequence recall "There Was a Child Went Forth," but only Levine could so vitalize a wall that it could give a detailed, inventive account of its birth. In section IX we learn how the wall's "seed" gradually became a "fist / tightening into a turnip / with one hard eye" and then changed again, "broke the dried crust," and rose into the air, its "stiff . . . back humping," to stand in the morning "like a row of windless corn / never to be / eaten." The concluding negative, Levine's cachet, is more positive and specific than that in "Not This Pig." In this context of "The low houses of the poor" and a hardscrabble life the wall embodies the refusal of those who built it not to exist.

The force that drives the wall up also powers the rough beast in the ferocious, exhilarating title poem in *They Feed They Lion* (1972), but here the focus is once more on the city:

> Out of burlap bags, out of bearing butter,
> Out of black bean and wet slate bread,
> Out of the acids of rage, the candor of tar,
> Out of creosote, gasoline, drive shafts, wooden
>     dollies,
> They Lion grow.

The tremendous compression corresponds to the constraint of the energy Levine at once eulogizes and stands in awe of, like Michaelangelo's slaves, their bodies straining to free themselves from the marble. And like the sculptures, the poem catches moments at which raw material converts itself into raw power, and it too elicits a kinaesthetic response:

> From the sweet glues of the trotters
> Come the sweet kinks of the fist, from the full flower
> Of the hams the thorax of caves,
> From "Bow Down" come "Rise Up,"
> Come they Lion from the reeds of shovels,
> The grained arm that pulls the hands. . . .

Or perhaps we should take our cue from the black dialect it draws much of its strength from and think of it as a sort of apocalyptic jazz. In any case, Levine's Lion is plainly a later, fiercer version of his wall and an earlier, more joyful version of the world growing in the workers' hearts.

Someone is always asking whether the good political poem is possible in the United States today. An affirmative answer can only be concrete, and to confront the question with "They Feed They Lion" or "For the Fallen" (or Lowell's "For the Union Dead" or Kinnell's sixth poem in *The Book of Nightmares*) is to expose a pseudo-issue. Of course "They Feed They Lion" celebrates latent power at least as much as it condemns oppression, and its union of labor and nature (as in "caves," "reeds," and "grained") augurs something closer to the proverbial inheritance than to revolution, but it is not the less political on those accounts—though it might be the more visionary. If an accurate depiction of the lives of the undeservedly poor and luckless is a legitimate criterion (and I take "accurate depiction" to exclude sloganeering and stereotyping), this volume contains a host of other fine political poems. Here we have Luther, whose pregnant wife is delivering early and whose "old black Lincoln" (what else?) has broken down:

> Luther
> cocking his tattoo
> against the black rain and
> the rain of black luck, Luther
> pushing on toward
> the jewelled service station
> of free cokes
> and credit there ahead
> in a heaven of blue
> falling and nothing
> going to make him cry
> for nothing.
> ("Cry for Nothing")

Once again the negative—and how well Levine has listened to Luther's speech—amounts to an affirmation, as in its own small way the perfect placement of "falling" does. Or there is the Spanish stone cutter's thirty-six year old retarded daughter, making her "Salami" from an increasingly wondrous list of ingredients, ending with "dried cat heart, / cock claws." She is solid and undiscriminating as earth itself. Or there is the Cuban woman in "The Angels of Detroit," or Lemon in "Detroit Grease Shop Poem," or a half dozen others.

In spite of the harshness of the lives depicted, these poems are all laced with a certain delicacy, which in strange combination with repugnant subjects generates some of Levine's most original work. At one end of the spectrum is "¡Hola Miguelin!", a lovely lyric about a young Spanish neighbor just risen from love-making, which is all delicacy except for its last line's hint of a *frisson*. At the other end is "The Children's Crusade," an inscrutable tale in which a little girl who is an accomplice in the gruesome murder of her father

wears, very precisely, "silver ignition keys hooked in her / pierced ears." Somewhere between them is the astonishing "Angel Butcher." Set in a celestial abbatoir, it recounts a ritual execution by the speaker of a fellow angel, Christophe, who "wants to die / like a rabbit." After preliminary courtesies, Christophe is arranged as though for a portrait:

> I can
> feel my lungs flower as the
> swing begins. He smiles again
> with only one side of his mouth
> and looks down to the
> dark valley where the cities
> burn. When I hit
> him he comes apart like a
> perfect puzzle or an
> old flower.
> And my legs
> dance and twitch for hours.

As Christophe comes apart, Levine's puzzle completes itself, and we realize that one reason Christophe smiles with only one side of his mouth is that the other side is the butcher's (whose own legs "dance and twitch"). Another reason is Christophe's wry anticipation, for if "They Feed They Lion" is Levine's "Second Coming," "Angel Butcher" is his "Dialogue of Self and Soul," its "dark valley" being analogous to Yeats's ditch and its burning cities Levine's special object of love and hate.

But Yeats's Self praises life as he has known it, and to the extent that Levine does likewise his anger at its political facts must be affected. His discontent can afford only so much nostalgia. In *1933* (1974) Levine's emphasis shifted. As he said in the interview, this volume is "less aggressive" than its predecessor. It includes a number of his best realistic vignettes, but as its title hints, its wistfulness at least balances its rancor. When "Grandmother in Heaven" unpacks her market basket item by item, "with a little word for each, a curse / for the bad back and the black radish / and three quick spits for the pot," each plosive and stress serves a loving reminiscence. "Zaydee," about Levine's grandfather—crook, fruit vendor, stove factory worker, aging midwestern Autolycus who speaks like a god from a cloud of English Oval smoke—shapes the political facts of Levine's early life into a nearly Edenic world. "At the Fillmore" sketches a war-time romance at the dance hall, and neither the background presence of "the wards of the wounded" nor the appropriately stripped down tercets can subdue its lyricism. The woman dawdles in the ladies' room and feels her longing and tipsyness, "a warmth / like the flush of juice / up the pale stem / of the flower." It is enough to make you feel more strongly about efflorescence.

Yet Levine's nostalgia encourages the soft and the sentimental. Sometimes one cannot believe—or does not know how to believe—his claims, as when he says in "1933" (the year of his father's death) that "Once in childhood the stars held still all night / the moon swelled like a plum but white and silken." The standing still of the stars is patently symbolic and the image of the moon hardly calculated to substantiate the "Once." In "Once in May" he recalls that he stood "all afternoon under heaven / with water in my pockets / salt in my socks, naming / the grains of the sea." But it is no more clear what that too familiar "naming" might really mean than it is where else he might have stood on the beach. At such moments Prospero yields the floor to Ariel, but Ariel, flustered and out of practice, blurts out the first thing that comes into his head.

Nostalgia perhaps breeds another kind of self-indulgence in "Letters for the Dead," an ambitious elegiac poem 350 lines long which is crisply written, particular at every step, yet confusing as a whole. The problem is simply that it needs the fleshing out one often gets at readings. The relationships among its people remain stubbornly obscure, and the reader is so bedeviled by ambiguous second person pronouns that he can hardly tell how many people are involved. What is the purpose? I am not certain, but the vivid obscurity gives one an especially strong sense of being privy to an intensely personal transaction. For some readers the poem will prove the exceeding tolerance of Mill's definition of successful poetry as "feeling confessing itself to itself in moments of solitude." Yet one values just this quality of seeming "*overhead*" in Levine's recent political poems. They spurn what Mill called "eloquence"—"feeling pouring itself forth to other minds, courting their sympathy, or endeavoring to influence their belief, or move them to passion or to action." "And the Trains Go On" and "For the Fallen," far from having designs on us, allow us to eavesdrop on meditations. If occasional obscurity were the expense of the mode, it would be worth the price.

*The Names of the Lost* often reworks the political themes of *They Feed They Lion* in the elegiac manner of *1933*. The two meet in "Another Life," when Levine, who has earned the right if anyone has, asks "how many men, dying, passed me / the blood of their voices, the spittle / oiling their groans." This poem's lost person is a black man, Levine's age and like him born in Detroit, but "white haired" and "toothless" and a four-time loser now in Folsom, where Levine taught a writing course. The man rambles on about his prison terms and other things:

> about the poem he can write will follow
> me all the way home, try my chair,
> eat from my plate, take my voice
> until I'm the one walks all night
> in the rain, gets stopped by the cops
> at dawn, and with the sky reddening
> spread my arms and legs against the car
> and feel the gloved hand
> slide over my balls and pause
> and go on, leaving nothing.

The transition is flawless. If it is impossible to say whether the frisking is Levine's experience too or just the convict's, that seems to be the point.

At exactly this point one has to voice a reservation. The question—which threatens to raise itself even in the case of "I was the man, I suffered, I was there"—is whether the identification does not trivialize the experience it means to bring home, whether the technique has not subverted the subject. The final image means something for the convict that it cannot mean for Levine. He confronts the difficulty in "For the Fallen": "Look at your hands. They / are not scarred by / the cigarettes of the police." But then "For the Poets of Chile" opens with these lines:

> Today I called for you
> my death, like a cup
> of creamy milk I
> could drink in the cold dawn,
> I called you to come
> down soon.

Could any poem accommodate this passage? It might illustrate one problem with Mill's concept of poetry, which does not allow for the awareness of audience that can cut the grease of mawkishness that often films over conversations with the self. When Levine concludes with an image of the daughter of a slain political prisoner setting the breakfast table with "the tall glasses / for the milk" that she and her mother must drink each morning, the easy symmetry and the presumptuous equation betray whatever emotion has survived the opening lines.

Levine's rhetorical questions can also lead him to the brink of the bathetic. In "To My God in His Sickness" he asks: "Can the hands rebuild the rocks / can the tongue make air or water / can the blood flow back / into the twigs of the child." One imitates the rhetoric of Job's God at his own peril. These lines leave a faintly embarrassed impression of self-consciousness. Or take the passage in "Ask the Roses" where Levine demands: "Has anyone told the sea it must count / its tears and explain each one / has anyone told the blood / how long it must crust the sheets." Isn't this really a way of making witty images, a means of setting in motion a machine that can process, in the name of suffering, any material that comes to hand?

Still, such moments are rare in this volume. Besides "And the Trains Go On," "For the Fallen," and "Gift for a Believer," *The Names of the Lost* contains several other poems nearly as compelling, including "New Season," "My Son and I," "On the Murder of Lieutenant José Castillo by the Falangist Bravo Martinez, July 12, 1936," and "No One Remembers." A few others, such as "A Late Answer" and "Wednesday," are admirably done though more modest attempts. The latter begins unassumingly:

> I could say the day began
> behind the Sierras,
> in the orange grove the ladder
> that reaches partway
> to the stars grew
> a shadow and the fruit
> wet with mist put on
> its color and glowed
> like a globe of fire. . . .

There might be a touch of expediency in the sudden reduction of the grove to one orange, but the fusion of the rising sun and the fruit combines with the knowing overstatement about the ladder to work wonders. Even the line break after "grew" contributes its gram to the delicate balance between the sanguine will to action and the ironic recognition of limitation—or, to use the more dramatic terms of "They Feed They Lion," between "'Rise Up'" and "'Bow Down.'"

References to rising and falling run throughout this volume ("You," "Let It Begin," "Another Life," "Gift for a Believer," and "For the Fallen," for example), and the tension between the impulses they embody—parallel to that between remembering and forgetting—is at its very heart. A section of "For the Fallen," where Levine transports us to the cemetery in which Durruti is buried, will serve as synecdoche:

> You
> can go down on your knees
> and pray that the spirit
> of men and women come back
> and inhabit this failing flesh
> but if you listen well
> your heart will ask
> you to stand, under
> the fading sun or
> the rising moon, it
> doesn't matter, either
> alone or breathing as you
> do now the words
> of the fallen and the slow
> clouds of diesel exhaust.

Within the intricate local counterpointing, we might take as summarizing lines the two on "the fading sun" and "the rising moon," where the attribution of "rising" to the weaker "moon" nearly redresses the slight imbalance caused by the stronger position of that second adjective. In the sentence as a whole, the foreknowledge of the futility of rising up nearly frustrates the urge to do so. The standing must be accomplished, after all, within sight of "the fallen." And the "heart" (again one remembers Durruti's words) is saddled with the "failing flesh."

Not that bowing down is to be despised. On the contrary, the endurance it represents has often approximated heroism in Levine's work. The first poem in the first volume ends with a lone bird arrived too early in March who, "Frozen, holds on and sings"; in "The Way Down" in *They Feed They Lion* "the tight rows of seed / bow to the earth / and hold on and hold on"; and in "Gift for a Believer" Levine's wife "kneels / to the cold earth and we have bread." But it is no longer so clear to him that "From 'Bow Down' come 'Rise Up.'" "For the Fallen" and this book in general admit the near impossibility of that transition, either for the individual or society. Lacking the dynamism of "They Feed They Lion," "For the Fallen" might not be as immediately appealing, but it just might be more accurate, a poem Prospero could approve more quickly—as well as a harder one to write, or at least to be felt through, to have brought home.

If few others in this volume can stand with the prodigious poems in *They Feed They Lion*, we must remember that we do not have the right to expect such poems and can only be grateful when they appear. Perhaps not even Levine has the right to expect them. Randall Jarrell told us that a good poet is "someone who manages, in a lifetime of standing out in thunderstorms, to be struck by lightning five or six times." Levine has already been struck at least that many times, and Lord knows no one is more likely to continue standing out in thunderstorms.

## PHILIP LEVINE

### From an Interview by Calvin Bedient

#### *Don't Ask*

1981, pp. 97–107

*Bedient:* Do you have any thoughts on why there seems to be so little political commitment in American poetry—at least in the poetry that lasts?

*Levine:* There's some. I think there's too little, sure . . . I see it, of course, in Whitman. And I see it very powerfully in a lot of novelists: in Dreiser, Sherwood Anderson, Dos Passos at his best in *USA*; I see it in Anderson's and Dreiser's poetry, too—it's terrible poetry but it has political commitment. I see it in Patchen very much. I see it in some of Rexroth, some of his best poems. And then there was some during the Vietnam war. A lot of poets got political for a short time.

*Bedient:* Is there something defused, or diffuse, about the American political situation that discourages poets from taking a strong political stand in their poetry?

*Levine:* I think that's part of it. I think also that when you think about who's formed American poetry as it is now, you go back to, say, the Fugitives, you go back to Eliot, to Pound. The only politics they have are very conservative. Most of the poets are coming out of the universities too, and God knows they don't fool around with politics; I mean when they teach books they talk about structure and irony and things like that. And so I don't think people are encouraged to . . . and then we don't have to endure the kind of hell that a Latin American writer has to endure. We don't have to cope with censorship. The government here is much more efficient about the way it takes our money and takes our lives and our land and our water and our air. The Latin Americans are clumsy by comparison. They throw the poets in prison, they torture them, they break their hands, they shoot them. Here, they can write whatever they want. And all five thousand readers can read it and memorize it and it won't do a goddamn thing. They're not the kind of people who are going to go out and buy guns and shoot anybody. . . . We are so efficient that a poet can forget what poetry can do, it seems to me. I forgot what it can do for a long time.

*Bedient:* Are you writing political poetry now?

*Levine:* Yes. I have been for many years. I think there came a point where I came back to my original reasons for wanting to write. Probably around 1964. Although when I look at even my first book I see—I don't know if you know the poem "The Negatives" in my first book. It's about French deserters from the French Algerian army, and there's a guy in there, an American, who has come back to the United States from Algeria, and he feels "caught in a strange country for which no man would die." And I must have written that when I was thirty. So I was aware of why I started to write . . . but without readers it seems pointless to keep raging about politics. If you don't have readers you're not going to change anything. . . . I began writing poetry to do something with it, to effect some kind of moral change; but without readers I knew I couldn't do that. Meanwhile I was writing it and I enjoyed writing it, and I got better. And the most wonderful times in my life were when I was inspired writing poetry.

*Bedient:* Do you feel a strong kinship with certain other poets in your generation? Do you feel closer, perhaps, to some dead poets?

*Levine:* Yes, I think I feel closer to some dead poets. There are a couple of poets in my generation . . . I like a lot of them personally and I know them, some I like a great deal. And I like the work of many even though it isn't anything like mine . . . I'm glad they don't write like me; it would be very boring if everybody wrote like me. . . . There are certain poets who write poems that I wish I had written, because they're so beautiful. And they are about things that I'm concerned with. A few of Gary Snyder's poems strike me that way; a couple of Ginsberg's poems, a lot of Galway Kinnell's poems, of Jim Wright's, a lot of Denise Levertov's poems. . . . Some of the younger poets that I read—Laura Jensen, Louise Glück, Larry Levis, Michael Harper, Charles Wright: they don't write poems that I want to write, but I'm awfully glad that they're writing, because they write so goddamn well. But the poets that I derive from, none of them are my contemporaries, it seems to me.

*Bedient:* Would you name some names?

*Levine:* In an article I wrote for an anthology I was in, I talked about the influence of Bly and Rexroth, and I've always regretted that. At the time I thought it was true, but as the years have gone on I think that it's not true and I should have kept my mouth shut and waited to see. . . . I think a poet who has had an enormous influence on me is Robert Penn Warren, because I'm a narrative poet almost always, and he was a narrative poet; and I love the way he put narrative into his poetry. . . . Patchen was another, in his better poems. . . . They too were narrative, like "The Orange Bears." And there are poets of other countries that I feel great kinship with: Zbigniew Herbert and Czeslaw Milosz, the Polish poets. Some of the Spanish poets. . . . But there are other poets I learned a great deal from, because they just wrote so goddamn well that I studied the way they did it. Hardy was a poet like that. I love Hardy; I think he's a great poet. I love the way he puts a poem together when he's hitting it. Yeats—I don't think I could sit in a room with Yeats for five minutes without hitting him, but my God the poems are just extraordinary. . . . And Stevens is such a snob. Williams and Whitman I feel great kinship with.

*Bedient:* Whitman I expected you to name.

*Levine:* I forgot. He's my favorite poet.

*Bedient:* I hear an occasional line in your poetry that reminds me of Dylan Thomas.

*Levine:* I'm afraid I do too.

*Bedient:* And there's a launched quality to some of your lines that is like Thomas's—like those in "A Refusal to Mourn." . . . But there's less vibrato, less blur. . . . One thing you may have in common with Merwin and Kinnell is a certain orphic drive—though "orphic" doesn't really tell one much. Paul Zweig, in a review of *They Feed They Lion* in *Parnassus* (Fall/Winter, 1972), said that American poets have begun to create a language of revelation. And he sees you as engaged in this—what Rilke called building God through the labor of seeing. . . . Is revelation a term that. . . .

*Levine:* It doesn't distress me. I don't know if I'm trying to create a language. I've never really thought about that. In a curious way, I'm not much interested in language. In my ideal poem, no words are noticed. You look through them into a vision of . . . just see the people, the place. . . . Now obviously I'm never going to write my ideal poem, and maybe I'm talking about creating a language.

*Bedient:* You said in correspondence that you believe in romanticism—in all that bullshit. Are there aspects of romanticism that make you uneasy?

*Levine:* I don't think that there are aspects of romanticism that make me uneasy. I grew up at a time when the word *romantic* was a dirty word, when the romantic poets were being thrown out of the window, so that we could all worship John Donne, John Crowe Ransom, and poets of ahrny [irony], as Ransom used to say. But my favorite poet at that time was Keats, and I wasn't going to throw him out of the window for anybody.

I had the fortune or misfortune to spend one year of my life with Yvor Winters; and of course he wanted to heave all those guys out of the window in the worst goddamn way. For some dumb reason he picked me to come to Stanford on a writing grant; and when I got there he liked me personally, we got along pretty well; but he loathed my poetry. And that was a source of some satisfaction to me, because although I liked some of his poetry and I liked the way he had illuminated some Renaissance poetry, I wasn't really interested in the way he treated his contemporaries. And I wasn't interested in the poets he thought were gigantic in the twentieth century. I thought they were pretty puny, really. I remember once saying to him about Robert Frost, "You don't talk about a single one of his greatest poems. . . . You pick out his worst poems so that you can dismiss him. Is that fair?" And he said: "I wasn't trying to make him look good." Which was honest, but it told me where he was. He wasn't in the house of criticism that I felt was going to be useful to anybody. . . . He just scored a touchdown for neoclassicism or something. . . . So when I say "all that bullshit," I guess I'm sensitive to the fact that it has been written off as dreck. . . .

*Bedient:* Do you see yourself as being a poet who uses romanticism as a criticism of what we do to each other and what life does to us?

*Levine:* Yeah. The Keats for example that I loved was the Keats of the letters, not the poems, as much as I admire the odes. Because I think that he inherited a poetic tradition that was so puny that he could say, I would jump down Etna for any public good but I want to write beautiful poems. As though you couldn't perform a public good with poetry. And I think you can. . . . I mean, you think of all the misery that he saw and you read about it in his letters, and how little of it ever gets into his poetry. . . . He sits there for months while his brother Tom dies day by day of tuberculosis in what must have been one of the most polluted shitholes in the world, the London of the nineteenth century. And what does he get: "Here where

men sit and hear each other groan, . . . Where youth grows pale, and spectre-thin, and dies." Tom gets two lines. And that's it. Bingo. I mean, I couldn't let America take my brother and kill him at seventeen or eighteen, and just sit there and say, "Well, I have to write poems about Grecian urns." Shit, I mean I don't think I'd ever get over it. And I don't think Keats wanted to get over it. I don't think that he inherited as strong a tradition as I did. He didn't *have* Whitman.

When I say I'm a romantic poet, it seems to me that I feel the human is boundless, and that seems to me the essential fact of romanticism.

*Bedient:* In "On the Murder of José del Castillo" you refer at the end to a kind of romantic hold-all that is beyond mortality altogether, transcendental. And this seemed to me rare in your work, where the romanticism is mostly immanent. Did you feel, "This is a departure for me, I'm walking out on a plank"?

*Levine:* The poem originated in the ending. It just so happened that I was reading this book about José del Castillo and at the same time I was reading I had a very odd experience, which was a repetition of a youthful experience. I was driving on a Sunday morning and I turned on the radio and I heard a black preacher that I heard often when I was a kid. And this black preacher was talking in a way that was very familiar to me. And I got into the rhythm of what he was saying. . . . He was talking to people out there in the radio audience who couldn't be in the church because they were in one way or another hurt, sick, suffering. . . . And he was saying like, "Sally Benson, I know you're sick, I know you've had an operation. Hang on. We're praying for you." And then suddenly he said, "And you, Charles Something, old soldier, I know your wound. . . ." And then the problem became, How can I build a poem that will use this ending that I have in my head? . . . What I think I did was sit down and try to build a poem in which a man's death flows out from him. He dies, and his dying sort of goes out out out. And then what comes back is this prayer for him, back back back from the world. . . . That's what I saw as the structure that I had to create. I felt it was different from anything I'd ever done. I felt very excited about it. I mean, I went home and, man, I mean I was just, you know, flying, I knew I was going to get this son of a bitch.

*Bedient:* It's an exciting poem. It shares a quality that some of Robert Penn Warren's poems have: a kind of scattered sublimity, the scatteredness of sublimity. . . . Do you have any particular don'ts as a poet? What do you tell your students that they should try to avoid?

*Levine:* One don't is never to defend your poetry against anybody. . . . A lot of what you hear is stupid, but you should keep your mouth shut and listen; you might learn something . . . And I tell my students that. Defend your right to be a poet . . . but not your poetry, because you'll stop people from trying to tell the truth. That's one. The other is never to follow the idea that got you to sit down and write the poem if the poem seems to be going someplace else. It knows better than you do. I don't see myself as the captain of the ship, if you can say that writing a poem is like taking a voyage or something . . . I don't think I'm the captain; I think I'm down in the hold throwing coal into the thing, trying to stoke it. . . . But I'm not a cabbage, I have a mind, and when I see suddenly that I'm writing something that William Carlos Williams writes, or something that I've already written, I say, "Hey, come on." My biggest danger is that I'll imitate myself. And that's the thing I—my wife is very good on that. She's very quick to point that out. And she's very precise in telling, in the way she does it . . .

*Bedient:* Your poetry contains few abstract statements. Is this because you agree with Edmund Burke that a clear idea is a little idea?

*Levine:* I think part of it is that in a lot of poems (not my own) I'm aware of the fact that people create characters so that they can kill them and then make a point. And it seems to me that the people are more interesting than the point. And I don't want the characters in my poems giving up their lives so that a point can be made. . . . You know, abstract ideas are so monumental all the way from Plato to the present. They bore me. Philosophers bore me. I find them the most boring people I've ever come across in my life. I would much prefer spending, you know, an afternoon with a bunch of jockeys or car mechanics than with philosophers. I remember renting my house to a philosopher who let all the trees die. And when I got angry with him, because my wife planted those trees and loved them—seven trees he let die—he said, "I didn't think you were the kind of man who would care about something like that." And to me that was the voice of the philosopher—"something like that": a living thing.

*Bedient:* What question would you like an interviewer to ask you?

*Levine:* Are you happy you became a poet?

*Bedient:* Are you happy you became a poet?

*Levine:* Yes, very happy, and very surprised that I've gone as far as I've gone. . . . I had great ambitions but my hopes were small; and part of this was due to the fact that I came out of a situation where to say I'm a poet meant I'm nuts. . . . Yeah, I've liked my life in poetry for a number of other reasons, too. It's put me in touch with a lot of marvelous people that I've

had a chance to meet because I was a poet. And I know a lot of terrific young people. I keep meeting new people because I travel around and give readings. . . . I would never have become a teacher without being a poet, because I wasn't interested in scholarship. And I enjoy teaching . . .

*Bedient:* I want to ask you about the extreme contrast between what you call your buffoonery, the humor of your social personality, and the lyrical plangency of your poetry. Is the buffoonery a kind of defense for your vulnerability?

*Levine:* I don't really like wise men, or wise women for that matter. I don't like those wisdom machines telling people how they ought to live. Some of them are poets, and they go around telling people how they ought to live. So I want to make it clear that I don't know how other people ought to live. . . . And I make this very clear through the humor . . .

*Bedient:* What Ashbery has done is put the seriousness and buffoonery together in the poems.

*Levine:* Yeah. He said to me, "You probably think I'm frivolous." And I said, "No, John, I don't." And he insisted on it. And I insisted that I didn't feel that way. And then he said he liked my poetry a great deal but that I probably wouldn't believe it. And I said, "No, I believe it. I think it's pretty terrific myself. Why wouldn't I believe that you would like it?" And I said, "I like your poetry. I think you write with extraordinary brilliance." And Ashbery certainly is not a wisdom machine. I feel very sympathetic to him as a person. But there are a number of people who go around the country with a sort of program . . . they're gurus. And I'm not. I don't have the answer to anything, except, "Keep trying, kid, buddy, old man." Even though my poems are very serious, they're not answers.

# SINCLAIR LEWIS

## 1885–1951

Harry Sinclair Lewis was born in Sauk Centre, Minnesota, on February 7, 1885. His father, a country doctor, remarried in 1892, after the death of his first wife the previous year. At age thirteen Lewis attempted to run away from home and join the Spanish-American War forces as a drummer boy. His father caught him at a nearby railroad station and Lewis was forced to return to his quiet midwestern town. After his graduation Lewis spent a year at Oberlin Academy in Ohio, preparing to enter Yale the following year. In the fall of 1903 he arrived in New Haven, hoping to escape from the humdrum of small town U.S.A. The unpolished and unattractive Lewis was disappointed with what he found at Yale. Instead of creative and original thinkers, he found cold, over-cultured Eastern snobs. Although Lewis had a very successful academic career which include serving as editor of the literary magazine, his social life was negligible. Referred to by his classmates as either "Red" (he had red hair), or less kindly as "God-forbid," Lewis left Yale in 1906. He worked briefly as a janitor at Helicon Hall, Upton Sinclair's utopian colony in New Jersey. After holding a few more odd jobs, he returned to Yale and graduated in 1908.

The next years of his life were devoted to becoming a newspaperman. He worked in places as diverse as Waterloo, Iowa, and San Francisco. While in Carmel, California, Lewis met Jack London, to whom he sold several story ideas. By 1910 Lewis quit the world of journalism and moved to New York where he worked over the course of the next five years at various publishing jobs. His first serious novel, *Our Mr. Wrenn*, was published in 1914, the same year that he married Grace Hegger, a sophisticated New Yorker who worked as an editor at *Vogue*. Lewis's seventh novel, *Main Street* (1920), catapulted him into the national spotlight. The 1920s were his most productive years, during which he wrote *Babbitt* (1922), *Arrowsmith* (1925), *Elmer Gantry* (1927), and

*Dodsworth* (1929). Annoyed at not receiving the Pulitzer Prize for either *Main Street* or *Babbitt*, which he considered his best works, Lewis declined to accept the Pulitzer when it was awarded for *Arrowsmith* in 1926. His harsh satires of middle-class values and the conformity with which he believed Americans adhered to these values did not ingratiate him with many critics and readers. In 1930 Lewis was awarded the Nobel Prize for Literature, which he accepted, thus making him the first American to be so honored. The prize committee noted Lewis's unique insights into the American character and his hard-hitting, realistic style.

His fortunes declined sharply after receiving the Nobel Prize and his later years were marked by extreme unhappiness. Although he continued to write throughout the 1930s and 1940s, his works never achieved the success that his earlier works had enjoyed. His first marriage broke up in 1928 and a second marriage also ended in divorce in 1942. His appearance, which had always been of concern to him, worsened as a result of skin cancer which disfigured his face. His drinking also became an increasing problem in his later years. Lewis died on January 10, 1951, in a hospital in Rome. On the verge of a complete emotional collapse, he had spent his final days away from the family and friends he had alienated in recent years. His ashes were returned for burial in his hometown.

## Personal

Ben Stolberg, a close friend of his, brought Sinclair Lewis—"Red," as everybody called him—to the first Literary Rotary evening after his return from Sweden. The date was April 1, 1931. I think it was only our second party, and the group happened to be small that evening—about a dozen. We were all sitting about the vast round table in the corner, and had given our orders, when neat, round little Ben and tall, reedy, gangling Red entered.

Red had had cocktails somewhere else, and his eyes seemed to stick out of the narrow red face like a beetle's. He was forty-eight, and his red hair was graying above the large ears. His hands were long, slender, beautiful; the hands of an artist. His manner was intensely self-conscious, uncomfortable.

Ben introduced him around the table. Red knew Harry Hansen, Lewis Gannett, Henry Hazlitt, and Walter White and had heard of some of the others. His eyes stabbed into Hansen and Calverton.

I scarcely knew most of my fellow Rotarians, and was embarrassed when, as I was introduced to him, Red exclaimed, "Christ, Louis, you wrote a grand book!—*Dynamite*—just read it—jeez, a grand book!" He kept this up for half a minute or longer, holding my hand. I said, "Thank you," and saw the others smile at my embarrassment.

Red sat next to Ben, across the table from me. He ordered a wiener-schnitzel, which he hardly touched. He drank a seidel of beer.

The meal lasted about half an hour and everybody was uncomfortable. Red talked only to Ben and Lewis Gannett, and was almost antagonistic to all the rest, except me. There was very little conversation at the table, no joking or kidding, no telling of funny stories. Most of the men tried—vainly—to ignore Red. They did not dislike him, but were self-conscious before Ultimate Success in Literature in person.

Red kept looking at me; and when our eyes met, he winked. To Ben, who told me later, he mumbled, "I don't like this bunch. Louis is the only proletarian here. All the rest of you are highbrows."

He tried to talk to me, but it was next to impossible across the wide table. Scheffel Hall was a large, dinful place, with a small German orchestra playing a piece every five or ten minutes.

Embarrassed at being singled out by Lewis like this, I said, "Why don't you eat? Your schnitzel will get cold."

Red's face went into a grimace; he shook his head. "Say, Louis," he raised his voice when the orchestra stopped, "what

do you say we go to Detroit and Chicago, you and I. We'll tour the industrial Middle West."

"What for?" I asked.

"A trip," said Red. "I asked Ben to come with me, but he's a highbrow—doesn't want to come. What do you say?"

I said, "It's hard to talk here. Let's wait till we get out."

He nodded and, folding and unfolding his long arms and clasping and unclasping his long hands, he continued to mumble to Ben about not liking this bunch, to stare and wink at me, and to look the picture of self-conscious discomfort.

Red's gaze suddenly fixed itself on Calverton, who had lately written an article, "Sinclair Lewis—Babbitt," for *The Literary Review*, published in Paris. He looked at him for several minutes, then said sharply, "So I am Babbitt, am I?"

Calverton tried to laugh it off, unsuccessfully. He said something I could not hear. Red's eyes burned holes into him.

Thereupon Red turned to Harry Hansen, who was still on the *World*. "And you, Harry, what do you mean by printing in your 'Book Marks'—and on the day I return from Sweden, as if to greet me with it—that piece of gossip as to why I left Harcourt, Brace and went over to Doubleday, Doran?" He was referring to a brief item Hansen had published about a week before, explaining why America's first Nobel Prize winner in literature had changed publishers. The item had seemed harmless enough when I read it, but had evidently been salt on some raw spot in Red's makeup. He ripped·into Hansen, who replied calmly, trying to reason with him. Ben had his arm around Red's shoulder, saying, "Now, don't be a damn fool, Red." Lewis Gannett—typically of him—poured oil on the waters, saying to Red that now he was big news and all sorts of things would get into papers—even into his friends' columns; and by and by the storm subsided.

As we were all leaving, Red took me by the arm. "I don't like this bunch. Do you? Highbrows!"

"Most of them," I said, "I met just recently, and I really know only Ben, but some seem very nice fellows."

"Highbrows!" he repeated. "You come with me."

"Where?"

"We'll go somewhere."

I said: "I'm supposed to go with the group. We're having a sort of party. It's a monthly affair. Why don't you come with us?"

"No, no. . . . Highbrows! They think they know so much. Nothing worse than a highbrow. You come with me. I want to talk to you about taking a trip to Detroit and Chicago, Gary, Indiana, and places like that, and look at industrial conditions—workers, proletarians—not highbrows!" As I learned later, he had been thinking for some time of writing a labor novel and was working himself into a mood for the task. Hence his constant reference to "proletarians."

I spoke to Ben, who thought it would be all right with the group if I went with Red. I said I would rejoin them at Calverton's after Red got through with me.

Red wore a marvelous English overcoat and a fine hat, which made me sharply conscious of my shabby coat and cap. Third Avenue "L" trains rumbled above us.

"What do you say we go to Detroit tomorrow?"

"I don't know," I said, "this is a little sudden."

Red stopped in front of a tobacco store. "Wait a minute"—and went in to buy a package of cigarettes. He came out, smoking, and I found myself in a strange situation. Sometimes between his saying "Wait a minute" and his coming out of the cigar-store he had lost all interest in me and nearly ceased to be aware of my existence, although there I was, facing him, walking by his side.

I said something; he made no answer. We crossed the street and—still on Third Avenue—walked another block, at the end of which he became interested in a black tomcat perched atop a garbage-can that stood against the wall of a closed butcher shop. He stroked the animal, saying, "Kitty-kitty-kitty!"

I stood beside him and, disturbed by his manner during the last five minutes, I asked, "Do you like cats?" So far as I know he did not hear me.

The cat stretched himself, jumped off the can, and walked away, whereupon Red continued down Third Avenue, and I beside him, feeling more uncomfortable with every step. What had happened to him? Had I said or done something to offend him? Did he mind because I had hesitated to leave my party to come with him, or because I had not eagerly seized on his invitation to join him on his trip to Detroit? . . . I accompanied him for several more blocks, wondering what to do. He might never miss me if I suddenly stopped or turned about and let him go on alone. Should I ask him if anything was wrong? . . .

Then he noticed me by his side and, stopping, looked at me. He stuck out his slim, limp hand, which I took, and he said, "Well, good night."

"Good night!" I said.

We parted. I was confused, worried, amused. Rejoining the group at Calverton's, I told Ben what had happened. Ben thought I need not worry; Red was apt to do anything.

Two days later I learned from Ben and other sources that Lewis was going about in New York, boosting *Dynamite*. He called up the Viking Press, "raising hell" because my book was not advertised more extensively.—LOUIS ADAMIC, "'Red' Lewis," *My America*, 1938, pp. 97–99

Throughout the first three years of my total five years of London residence, Sinclair Lewis was to play a strange part and exert an inordinate influence. I had been back in London less than a month from my painful search for Irish "peace," when I received a cable from Ray Long telling me that the author of *Main Street* had just arrived in London and that I was to approach him at once and try to land his next novel for *Cosmopolitan*. I found that he was stopping "in chambers" at the comfortable old Georgian House at 10 Bury Street, near Piccadilly Circus, under the wise and friendly wing of Dungar, the unapproachable major-domo. I telephoned Lewis for an appointment. I was to come at four o'clock.

There was a friendly smile on his battle-scarred face when he met me at the door. He welcomed me profusely, and introduced me to a somewhat cross-bred European-Britisher named Beckhofer—later to be styled Beckhofer-Roberts—who was by way of being a writer-critic-friend-and-philosopher. We sat down and Lewis poured a tall drink. I was "Mr. Hunt" to him for a full ten minutes, and then I became "Frazier."

A little later he thundered: "Say! what in hell is your real name, anyway? You've surely got some other name besides Frazier. My name is Red."

"Friends and enemies call me Spike," I answered.

"Well, that's better. Let me get you a little drink, Spike."

That was all there was to it. We mixed like Scotch and soda. From that moment we were almost inseparables. When friends couldn't locate Red at his own diggings they would call up my house or office, and two-thirds of the time they'd run him down—or vice versa.

*Main Street* had shot Red to the very top of American authors. I always had a suspicion that the real reason he was so popular at this time with English craftsmen, and the British public generally, was because he had cracked down so frankly and brutally on the American small town. He painted just the sort of picture of the American scene and its crude intolerances that the average Britisher wanted to read. They welcomed him as one of their own kind—superior, a bit snooty, and extremely critical of inferior breeds.

But Red fooled them. He saw through their own sham and hypocrisy as easily as he could see through a freshly polished pane of glass. When great and near-great tried to patronize his own American self-criticism they were met by a stinging rebuff. Certainly he was not showing up the weakness and intolerance of his own land for the benefit of Englishmen.

The famous bohemian Savage Club asked Lewis to talk at one of their Saturday-night entertainments. Many distinguished American men of letters—Mark Twain, Bret Harte, Stephen Crane, Artemus Ward—had addressed the club and left behind them a tradition of friendly salute to "the mother country." Club members naturally expected honeyed phrases for English literature and hopes that some day America might catch up. Instead, Lewis charged them like Pancho Villa's irregular cavalry. He explained that he would like to write a *Main Street* about this self-satisfied and behind-the-times land. He had written *Main Street* for the good of America and not to make his country the misunderstood laughingstock of a people who were so placid and secure in their own ignorance that they seldom traveled or bothered to keep in touch with other people's points of view and accomplishments.

It left the good ale drinkers aghast. They had never heard such impertinence. But Red made them like it. He could switch moods as easily as an organ player could change the tremolo stops. In a way, he was not unlike the colored prize fighter who carried a horseshoe in his glove just for luck. Yet time and again I have seen him let one fly at some unsuspecting patronizer, when he was really aiming at himself. He was a many-sided genius, and when he caught himself aping his hosts in speech, thought, or intolerance he would strike out at them, when he was actually whipping himself back to his own amusing naturalness.

Largely through Red I was to be thrown feet first into a strange and talented group of literary, artistic, and newspaper radicals, who were principally Englishmen but had a healthy sprinkling of American expatriates. Many of them were to become tried and true, and friendships were to be cemented that neither time nor distance will ever break.

I had brought an American touring car to London that was to have a profound effect on the motor future of the British Isles. Certainly half of the then motor mechanics practiced up on it. It spent a large part of its life in garages and shops. There it would be tinkered with, taken apart, and generally used as a mechanical guinea pig. Even its demountable rims were an endless source of delight: mechanics would spring on them at the slightest provocation, and on cross-country trips, we would often be delayed from two to four hours while brawny but thick-witted workmen wrestled with those newfangled rims. Gas stations were only just beginning to be introduced into the stubborn land, and we invariably carried extra tins of fuel on our running boards. Petrol was sixty cents an imperial gallon, but even that did not keep us from galloping time and again from the southern coast of England to the mountains and lakes of Scotland.

Red went along on many of these trips. Gracie Lewis was not always in England when Red was there, but I vividly remember one rather long and leisurely trip that we all took together. Gentle and beloved Walter Fuller accompanied us as our guide and peacemaker. I had traveled most of the Continent in search of firsthand material for an "Is the World Going Dry?" magazine series. I wanted particularly to do the Glasgow slums on a drunken Saturday night, so we started north. Red and I kept a list of the roadside pubs we passed. Some of the names were a bit poetic: the Three Graces, the White Swan, the Seven Virgins, the Stag at Eve. As I recall it now the Red Lion won over the White Horse by a score of nineteen to seventeen. Coach and Horses was third and the Duke of Wellington fourth.

I am a little afraid that we pulled up at far too many of these inviting havens and that my investigation might just as well have been a little less personal and inclusive. Late each afternoon we would choose an attractive, old-fashioned inn, and settle down for the evening. After supper Red and I would find a quiet seat in the taproom and buy mugs of ale for the village squire, the doctor, the butcher, and whoever would sit and discuss affairs with us. More than one evening we would remain with the innkeeper and an old crony or two long after the pub had officially closed, and argue the war, the debts, and the next slaughter.

At supper we would always decide the hour we would meet for breakfast the following morning, so that we might all be ready to start at the same time. One morning, following a rather prolonged night session in the taproom, the five of us were on hand save only Red. Gracie, quite lovely to look upon, was among the first down, and confidently ordered the master's breakfast. On came the porridge and the blue milk. But no Red. Next came the rubber fish and the cold toast. But no Red. Last appeared the stage eggs and the Irish bacon. Still no Red.

In front of Red's empty chair there now spread a semicircle of stone-cold, unhappy-looking dishes, topped off by an uninspiring pot of tea, tepid enough by this time to bathe in. Of course we had no drinking water: only unlettered American tourists drank water at their meals.

Gracie was certain Red would appear at any moment. Finally through the open double-doors at the far end of the room strode the lean figure of the novelist. His thin red hair had not been combed and he had obviously completed his toilet on the way downstairs.

He barked a frosty good morning, and sat down. His slightly bloodshot eyes glared at the awful array of English cooking that confronted him. It would have made a far stouter man cringe.

"Miss!" he shouted at the bucktoothed waitress, half scaring her out of her hide. "Miss, get me some water, please."

No one spoke. There was a feeling of impending tragedy in the air. Red looked again at his breakfast and quickly turned his head. The rest of us were not exactly afraid of him but we thought it best to leave him to his own thoughts: he had been in a vast ale-buying mood the night before.

Red moved nervously in his chair. Our eyes were glued on the kitchen door. A full minute dragged by. Then when we had all but given up hope, the bucktoothed girl swung open the door and hurried toward our table. We drew a sigh of relief. The situation would be saved: Red would get his drink of nice cold water and then he'd feel better.

"Sorry to keep ya woitin', sor," she apologized, setting squarely in front of Red a pot of boiling hot water.

Red gave it one look. Then he half rose from his chair and threw out his long, lean arms in a gesture of despair. "My God, woman!" he screamed. "My God in Heaven! I want cold water. COLD WATER! C-O-L-D water!"

It was too much for us. We fairly exploded while Red only glared sullenly at the frightened girl. But we wouldn't be bullied. Finally a smile broke out on his thin lips. "Great God! What a country!" he swore. "I think they must boil their eggs in beer."

It was a Saturday afternoon when we reached Glasgow. That night Red and I wandered off to the slums. I had seen Chicago's red-light district and New York's Bowery, and I had watched men have the D.T.'s on the streets of Brisbane, Australia. I had seen opium dens in Shanghai and tequila and *aguardiente* bars in Mexico, but never had I seen anything to compare with this Scotch border town at the hour when the pubs closed for the week end. Men, women, and children were fighting in the dirty streets; gin-drinking charwomen were lying helpless in the gutters and alleys; a quarter of a great city was over-run with hundreds of poor, helpless, drunken wretches whose only sin was poverty, and who for a few hours were finding escape from their everlasting fears and their defeats by the only road they knew.

Finally Red stopped and raised his clenched fists to high heaven. Tears were streaming down his cheeks. "I can't stand it any more," he cried, "I can't stand it!"

All the way back to the hotel he cursed and raved. "God damn the society that will permit such poverty! God damn the religions that stand for such a putrid system! God damn 'em all!"

That was one side of this strange man, who seemed to spend half his time fighting his own intolerances and short-comings. In many ways he was a spoiled boy. He always had to be the center of the stage. He could brook no other hero. There was a strong streak of the actor in his make-up, too. Times without number I have seen him impersonate a little German professor of philosophy; again, with his head wrapped in a bath towel, he would become an Indian yogi; with a false mustache he would be the villain about to rape the village hired girl. And I shall never forget an evening at the home of the famed literary agent, Curtis Brown, when in blank verse Red improvised a complete saga of the winning of the West: the covered wagon trains, the start from Independence, the fording of the Platte, the Indian attack, the death of the baby, the wagon wheels grinding over the grave, the arrival in the rich lands of Oregon Territory. It was moving and beautiful. No one else in the world could extemporaneously have equaled it in drama and pathos. It was Lewis the artist, the imaginative American, exalted lover of his own land and its history. I was never so proud of him as I was at that moment.

It is difficult for me to stop writing about this extraordinary friend. I have always felt that the secret of his strange and diverse character lay hidden in his unhappy youth in the Minnesota town of Sauk Centre. The skinny, pimply-faced little Harry Lewis, brought up in stern old Doc Lewis's home by a kindly stepmother, had been a lonely, inadequate lad. He was backward at the rough-and-tumble games and sports of the tough boys of the town. He was a misfit. An old shoemaker was far more of a companion to him than were his schoolmates. With the aid of this odd codger and from books, the boy created a world of the imagination. Often even it was a bitter world, intolerant and cruel.—FRAZIER HUNT, "London Years," *One American and His Attempt at Education*, 1938, pp. 248–53

The first American to win the Nobel Prize for Literature, Sinclair Lewis, had one of the saddest lives I ever watched being lived. For at least half of his almost sixty-six years, we were friends, friends in that happy assurance that even though we saw each other seldom it was always as if we had stopped talking together only long enough to go out to the refrigerator to get some ice cubes. When I first knew him, he had what, for lack of a surer word, one must call faith: faith in a future of man's humanity to man; faith in the power of love; faith in hard work and in himself.

He lived to see his dream of becoming a great writer come true, only at the cost of the loss of his other faiths, even, I suspect, faith in the work that had always sustained him, for he was too honest a critic, too good an editor not to know that his last work was by no means his best. ⟨. . .⟩

Of all the man-woman relationships I have observed in a long life, I have never known a man more completely, utterly bewitched by a woman than Hal Lewis was by his Gracie. He literally adored her. She was for him the Venus of a summer night's star-spangled sky, which filled him with awe at both its beauty and its eternal remoteness. She was the first trillium of spring. She was to him the most beautiful, the most alluring, the most brilliant woman God had ever taken the trouble to shape, and, because she was his, he became a god, capable of anything. He wasn't maudlin about her, he was simply epically in love.

The night of her arrival was sacred to their reunion, but the next night he invited me and my beau to dinner to meet his incomparable "chum." What we expected to meet was an angel whose halo would blind us. Gracie, as she proved to be ineptly named, was by nature and practice, if not by birth, a duchess, with a veddy, veddy English accent, and a point of view apparently rubbed off from her association with one of the expensive women's magazines, where she had worked as a caption writer. She was half English, but when I met her brother, not long afterwards, he spoke with every R resounding, and he was as simple and American as Iowa corn.

One of the unforgettable shocks of my life was when she greeted us at the door with one of the most calculatedly deflating remarks I ever heard. Gracie's reaction to the days and nights of utter devotion that had gone into the transformation of an impersonal transient apartment into a spider web of entangling love, was—"O, did you see what Sinclair did? All those silly poems and presents. I told him the moment I realized what he had done that he shouldn't have spent his time so foolishly. Just wasted it. I was very cross with him."

Wrapped in that wet blanket, the four of us finally went on to dinner in a nearby neighborhood restaurant, where the table d'hôte was advertised as being very good. It was not a famous glamour spot, but after a month of living on heaven knows what rations, except for those evenings when he was plied with my mother's affectionate care, it was a potentially charming meal to Hal, as it was to us. My beau and I were happy that it *was* a neighborhood spot, and not too expensive. When the excellent soup came, Hal's dream girl took one delicate sip of it, pushed it away from her, and said, "I can't stand this place,

Sinclair," and got up. Thus ended our dinner party. Where we went to please Gracie is an utter blank in my mind.

Gracie, all of his friends knew long before he realized the truth about their marriage, was not what the doctor ordered. Or perhaps she was, for without her his gorgeous and bitter satires might not have been written. She taught him to see life with irony. It took time, though he repaid her by making her the wife of the disillusioned Dodsworth, as well as the starry-eyed heroine of *Main Street*. ⟨. . .⟩

Hal was unpredictable, sometimes pixyish, loving to play the bad little boy just to watch the results. I had casually mentioned to him when he was going to give a lecture for the building fund of Northwestern University that there was a rivalry between it and the University of Chicago. Hal had been paid, he told me, a thousand dollars for the talk, a practically unheard-of fee. The lecture was a sellout. Every seat in the vast Auditorium Theatre was filled, and the ovation that greeted the lanky author of *Main Street* was prolonged and clamorous. It was naturally expected that at some time the lecturer would pay some tribute to the great institution that was presenting him, and that he would point to its future growth. Hal talked delightfully and engagingly about how Chicago would always be his big city, not London or New York or Paris, because as a boy Chicago had seemed the center of the world to him. Then he began talking about Chicago's educational as well as cultural advantages, about its incomparable institution of learning. Suddenly the blood froze in my veins. He was talking about the University of Chicago. He never once mentioned Northwestern, and when he finished there was not enough applause to shake one small loose rafter.

Afterwards, when I told him I thought he ought to be ashamed, he said, "It served them right trying to bribe me to ballyhoo their campaign. I showed 'em. I'm incorruptible," and he laughed until he had to be slapped on the back to keep from choking. He deserved, of course, to be punched in his articulate jaw, and I got him away as quickly as possible lest he would be.

The highest accolade of the literary life is the Nobel Prize for Literature, and that honor was made even more sparkling for Sinclair Lewis because he was the first American to receive it—in 1930. When the news came over the *Tribune* wires that the Nobel had gone to my "big brother," I rushed a letter of congratulation to him. He rushed back a note that said, characteristically, "Dearest Fanny, a million thanks for your letter. Little did we think in the days when we used to hold hands on the shore of Lake Michigan that I would have anything like this inflicted on me. Golly, I've got to grow a red beard and be dignified, and the beard won't grow and I can't be dignified."

I judged from what he told me later that the Nobel Prize really was a shock to him. He and Dorothy Thompson were married then, but he was out of town when word of the award came to her over the ticker tape, some time in the middle of the night. She called him immediately, rousing him from a deep sleep to tell him the news, and, he said to me, "I thought she was guying me, so I told her what I thought about her for playing such a cheap joke on me and slammed down the receiver."

Soon after his return from Stockholm, where he had proof that it hadn't been a joke, I was in New York, and, curious, I asked him if the Nobel award itself looked like anything more than a check for thirty thousand dollars (which was its fiscal glamour at that time). "I'll show you," he said, and he began going through drawers, first in his desk, then in a tall secretary. "I haven't looked looked at the darn thing since I got back," he said, as he continued what proved to be a fruitless search. He called in his secretary, who had been with him fifteen years. "I've never seen it," was his helpful reply. Dorothy was out talking to a visiting prime minister, so she couldn't help in the search. Finally, by digging out every possible hiding place in the apartment, it was turned up. It was in a leather case about the size of a writing portfolio, its cover beautifully tooled with a replica of the New York skyline, and the citation itself was beautifully hand lettered. You can see it at Yale, if you're curious. He willed it to his alma mater, where he had gone a shy, gawky redhead from the Sauk Centre, Minnesota, high school.

The last time I saw Hal Lewis, he looked so nearly like a death's head that he saddened me, the way the ashes in a fireplace can make one sad for their having given out all the warmth that they were capable of sharing and were finally waiting only to be swept up. I never knew any man more capable of loving a woman, a career, or a world he wanted to make better for everyone than Sinclair Lewis when I first knew him, nor one who seemed, before he died, more like a shell one might find on a beach, empty of life, but echoing the sound of the sea in which it had once had its viable being if anyone took the trouble to listen.—FANNY BUTCHER, "Sinclair Lewis," *Many Lives—One Love*, 1972, pp. 383–98

## General

Tall, slim and well-barbered; his sandy hair sleeked down on either side of an immaculate parting; his clothes carefully pressed; two inches of shirt cuff showing; his shoes well-shined—Sinclair Lewis looks the personification of conventional elegance, as badly dressed as only the wearer of standardized fashions for men can be, when every trace of individuality, of personal taste, is lost in a resolutely orthodox combination of "what the well-dressed man is wearing." Sartorially he realizes the ideal of the supporters of nationally advertised products, "authentic styles for the better-dressed man," "designed to combat the rigors of hot weather, and in addition, to give that lasting dressy appearance," "suits in the New York manner, smart, cool-looking, and spirited," which "excel in smartness as well as service," "tailored in accordance with our own specification" and unexcelled "in patterns, styling, and fit." He looks the part of an aggressive, forward-looking, up-standing citizen, a sales promoter of ability, a key man and live wire, who works entirely on leads and full organization support, 80 per cent of whose annual business consists of repeat orders.

His appearance does not belie his activities, for Sinclair Lewis is the drummer of ideas, the sales executive of the new American literature. He has made the Revolt of the Younger Generation a paying proposition, operating an exclusive territory on a royalty basis, and presenting an unusual household specialty, burlesque made up to look like satire. Every home a prospect; its simplicity sells it. If you are interested in building a repeat business for the future, Mr. Sinclair Lewis can demonstrate his product; attractive book combinations that get orders; unlimited possibilities, with large royalties, selling a guaranteed product to an unlimited market, well prepared by extensive advertising. What are you hitting at? Have you read *Main Street* and *Babbitt*, or are you just drifting along with *Tarzan of the Apes* and *Flaming Youth*? Are you reading the books for which nature has specially fitted you— the books that make you feel SUPERIOR—or are you just plugging along at the novels which the movies suggest to you? If you feel that you have not the place in the civilized minority to which you are entitled, let our expert analyst tell you what

you would look like in Gopher Prairie. Get rid of that Main Street feeling.

There is pep and punch in this hustling, go-getting herald of a new era in American literature. As an academic admirer has said, "Everything that is candid, fresh, alert, clean, supple, active and darting, he likes," and he has "an inclination for purposeful young men who keep themselves fit." "This enterprising young man is notably hard-headed, a hard-worker, with a good workman's prejudice in favor of keeping himself and his tools in order. Mr. Sinclair Lewis's beauty is always tonic—never relaxing." Inevitably criticism of him sets out to be literary but almost subconsciously drops to the level and the *clichés* of the Male Help Wanted advertisements, the prospectuses of Correspondence Colleges and Physical Training Institutes. Criticism can deal only with what values are presented for its judgment. Sinclair Lewis inevitably suggests such compliments and appreciation as are due to his qualities as a clean-cut, energetic, attractive young business man of letters, with a line of goods that sell well, and a line of talk which captures the most unpromising "prospects." His literary technique is that of the follow-up letter, and his conversation has the charm of snappy salesmanship. He has "put over" something which is excellent parody and laughable burlesque, when taken in small doses, but which seems almost as good as authentic satire to customers bemused by his sales efficiency. It is no wonder that, while elevating him to the class of great satirists, his champions employ a language which, like his own, has none of the accents appropriate to the occasion. A Swift, a Flaubert, a Samuel Butler, are not congratulated on the exemplary practical virtues of their lives and teaching, their appeal is not measured in terms which might have validity in selecting an agent for Studebaker cars, or a bank clerk for promotion to the rank of tenth Assistant Vice-President. *Madame Bovary* was not written by a man who was crisp, darting, purposeful and fit, nor were hard-headedness and enterprise the traits which recommended Swift to the notice of his contemporaries. By their adjectives, ye shall know them, and those associated with Sinclair Lewis have little relation either to satire or to literature in general. He inspires the emotions peculiar to the kind of achievement at which he excels. His transparent honesty absolves him from the slightest suggestions of obtaining fame under false pretenses. He has put on the market a perfect substitute for the glad book, and has reaped the reward of pioneering enterprise. Have you a little Babbitt in your home?

His achievement, in the last analysis, is himself. In two lengthy self-portraits he explains his own success. His intentions are serious, and the rewards indicate how exactly the public recognized in him a man and a brother. It is the genius of salesmanship to be able to sell precisely the same article as the one it is to displace on the ground that the new one is different. It is the genius of Sinclair Lewis that he is able to combine the outlook of Carol Kennicott with the language and technique of his now famous realtor and boom the result as a satire on both. Old-fashioned manufacturers of marketable fiction are dismissed as popular entertainers, and derive whatever consolation they can from their perpetual presence at the head of best-selling lists, to offset the failure of the intellectuals to take them seriously. The author of *Main Street* shares their arithmetical glory, and his advertisements, like theirs, speak only of quantities sold and amounts of paper consumed in coping with the demand, but at the same time professors talk of his "significance," and disconsolate Liberals, always pathetically eager for an incongruous ally, hail him as another liberator breaking the shackles of conventionalism and commercialism from the limbs of the American People. The latter, with their accustomed flair, did not take long to realize that Sinclair Lewis was just gently "kidding" himself and their friends. This was no austere and superior highbrow, trying to ridicule the things they held sacred. He could burlesque as amusingly as Will Rogers, and as repetitiously, but there was more for the money—the speculators, too, always buy up the seats for the Follies, whereas his books were as readily procurable as any other nationally advertised commodity.

This, then, is "the significance of Sinclair Lewis," that he has burlesqued himself and "gotten away with it." He holds up the mirror to every face but that of the beholder, and by the supreme exercise of all the arts in the repertory of the energetic salesman, he has put over what the more timid would have deemed an unsalable product. He has done in literature what is done every day by the enterprising people whose advertisements emblazon the nightly heavens, and crowd even his own prose into a series of little segments concealed in the back pages of popular magazines. He has brought the civilized minority within the reach of all. He has persuaded the mob that it can appreciate satire, by taking the sting from its deadliest foe, for satire cannot rise above the level of the satirist. And so, this lithe, neat, well-groomed young American business man, on whose every garment and idea one can see the label that is a guarantee of authenticity, has come into his own, just like the hero of a success magazine story. He has carried the gospel of 100% Americanism into the effete countries of Europe and shown them what a live, two-fisted, literary he-man can do. In return, he has begun to take on a certain flavor of cosmopolitan experience, realizing the sweet uses to which a monocle may be put, and the charms of an established social hierarchy, where men are not merely men, but sometimes gentlemen. He has discovered, like so many of his countrymen, that it pays to advertise . . . Babbitt.—ERNEST BOYD, "Sinclair Lewis," *Portraits: Real and Imaginary*, 1924, pp. 183–88

One entering a moving-picture theater has to readjust oneself to new arrangements of brilliance and darkness. So, as we become accustomed to Lewis's glitter, we gradually sort out the elements of which it is composed. His world is at once oddly familiar and oddly grotesque; we recognize in these streets and names and cities—Gopher Prairie, Zenith, Dr. Pickersbaugh, Sharon Falconer, Will Kennicott—places and persons as customary as the evening paper; yet, set in the strange and fantastic lights of the author's mind, they dilate into enormous images until we rub our eyes and ask whether this is the United States or some Arabian Nights wherein men grow into genii as, before our eyes, Elmer Gantry swells into a preposterous travesty, and Babbitt's business day takes on the minute and interminable precision of a nightmare. This, we say, is our world, and yet it is not our world but an impossible parody of the known and familiar; for though the details are copied with a cruel and scientific precision, the proportions are those of faces seen in a close-up or on a billboard. There is in these books the nightmare quality of those engravings by Piranesi which used to haunt the opium-eater, in which endless ascending stairways led on to further stairs in an incessant and fatiguing acceleration of line.

For these fictions are enormous dilations of simple elements. Their central situations are those of short stories; time has no part in them; and when we compare them with novels like *Vanity Fair* or *War and Peace*, we find, for the most part, that they exhibit no development, no progress, no deterioration, but only an incessant repetition. At the end of seventy pages we have fathomed Elmer Gantry, we know the simple and hypocritical elements of which he is composed; but

the author is not content, and for thirty-one chapters he must repeat in ever-widening circles the original formula in which this travesty of a man is first presented. Though Carol Kennicott in the last chapter of *Main Street* wears eye-glasses and is the mother of two children, she is scarcely altered from the Carol Milford of page one. So Martin Arrowsmith, like the frog in the arithmetic problem, incessantly repeats the process of going forward a step and slipping back again; and at the end of 401 pages we know precisely what we guessed from the second section of the first chapter of *Babbitt*, namely, that the central figure is the unhappy victim of a certain environment which he will never surmount. Only Sam Dodsworth is fundamentally changed by this incessant bombardment of brilliant detail; and it is significant that of these novels *Dodsworth* alone is steeped in pity.

We probe deeper. We note as a fundamental postulate of this staccato style its well-nigh complete externality. The author's concern is to give names to things, to enumerate details, to describe surfaces; and if he feels that his characters stand in need of reflection, of calm, of poetry, he is himself without subjectivism, he has nothing lyrical, nothing drawn from within, to offer us. There is no tragedy and no humor in these books, but only satire, travesty, and pathos; even the admirable Gottlieb is pathetic, not tragic, and for the death of Leora Arrowsmith we have a passing sense of sorrow, but we feel no deep emotion. It is deeply significant that we remember nothing of external nature from these books, but only cities, towns, social contacts, and gregariousness. The country exists only that Gopher Prairie may be isolated, that Arrowsmith and Gantry may move incessantly across the map of the United States, that Dodsworth, returning from Europe, shall sum up his impressions of both continents by leaving out the landscape. And if Dodsworth tires of externality, his author never does; not all his satire hides Lewis's deep delight in describing the perfections of Babbitt's bathroom, the dull architecture of Main Street, Sharon Falconer's pulpit, and even the minor characters, who are absurd puppets seen from the outside.

As documents these books are brilliant and superb. As great novels they trouble the literary conscience. If we compare them to *Fathers and Sons* or *Crime and Punishment* or *Buddenbrooks*, they lack wisdom, beauty, and depth. It is instructive to read Lewis and then to read *The Old Wives' Tale*, a novel that likewise overflows with happily observed detail; we feel, however, that amidst his immense observations, Arnold Bennett himself is solid and quiet like the earth, whereas Lewis rushes incessantly from point to point and from method to method, now travestying American business English, now heaping up veracious detail about Zenith, now pitying his personages, now mocking their futility, now seeing life from their point of view, and now cruelly dissecting the very characters for whom, a moment ago, he asked sympathy. We do not know whether he is journalist or philosopher, muckraker or writer of comedy; he fatigues us with this perpetual change of rôle. He is, we are told, a satirist, but a great satirist like Thackeray or Swift lets us know in every moment how to take him. Lewis does not; the quiet art of their controlled and level style is beyond him, and if at times he approaches it, it is only in the next paragraph to burst into buffoonery.

And yet there remains something unexplained, huge, and memorable at the bottom. If he does not have the control, he has the energy of genius, and like Dickens breathes into his caricatures a wild vitality. Pickersbaugh in *Arrowsmith*, for example, like Micawber, resembles no human being that ever lived, and yet he exists and shares in the traits of men. As Chesterton said of Dickens that he does not so much present characters as create a mythology, so we may say of Lewis that he has created an American mythology whose Valhalla is the Reeves Building in Zenith, whose inhabitants are Babbitt and Carol Kennicott and (bad as in almost every respect the book is which he inhabits) Elmer Gantry. Lewis himself in *Dodsworth* uses Babbitt as a generic noun and recognizes his own divinity. Remembering that Conan Doyle created Sherlock Holmes, we see that one does not have to be a supreme artist to add to the mythology of fiction; that there is, outside the boundaries of great writing, a field in which these mythological creatures are born of the teeming imagination; and that Lewis resembles Dickens and Dumas more than he does Flaubert or Thackeray.

But there are others in these novels—thin caricatures, grotesque parodies like Sharon Turner, the staff of the McGurk Institute, and the distorted citizens of Gopher Prairie. Among them and among the mythological beings walk a few intensely human persons like Gottlieb in *Arrowsmith*, Will Kennicott, Dodsworth, and, for all the monotonous repetition of her simple formula, Mrs. Dodsworth. If *Main Street* is Carol's story, one finds oneself imagining what her husband thought of her; and it is significant of Lewis's bias that he has preferred to place Carol in the center of his novel. But perhaps he has not neglected Will Kennicott after all; Dodsworth is his later incarnation, who shakes himself free at last from his restless helpmate.

But while to create mythology is to be very great indeed, we regret that with all his gifts, Lewis lacks the gift of repose, of that pity and wisdom the need for which he so clearly recognizes. He writes of Main Street and Zenith because he is himself a citizen of this world, accepts its limitations, its confused feeling that something has been left out of life, its simple faith in a thing called Ideals. We compare his books with the serene art of Ellen Glasgow, for example, and it is like hearing a concert by a brass band and then hearing a concert by a symphony orchestra. None of Miss Glasgow's people is likely to pass into mythology; her star is too southern for Swedish telescopes to discover; her field is not the noisy externalities of America, but the quieter life of Virginia. Or rather her concern is with the life of the soul amidst the eternal problems of existence. Lewis's people do not have souls—he is troubled that they do not, yet he has not endowed them with souls, but only with a few vast and confused emotions. Alone of all his heroes Dodsworth approximates a central serenity, and in this fact there is hope. Unsurpassed in quick, sure, and amused drawing, Lewis has not yet developed the brooding mind of a painter; except for his latest novel, his books are those of an immense and clever adolescence, but there are indications of an increasing maturity which hint that he is far from being written out.—HOWARD MUMFORD JONES, "Mr. Lewis's America," *VQR*, July 1931, pp. 428–33

The entrance of Mr. Lewis upon the literary scene was so dramatic, and the stature which he attained in his six successful years was so great, that the public has not yet ceased being curious about what he has to say. But the very least critical part of the public knows that he has forsaken his promise and that the man who set out as the passionate observer of American life has now become one of its strangest phenomena; it knows that it has witnessed something dismaying when it sees a man who began with the knowledge that "it is a complex fate to be an American," acquire, with the increase of years, the belief that to be an American is a gay adventure.

It was not Mr. Lewis but Henry James who wrote the sentence about the complexity of the American fate. Perhaps there is something disproportionate and even priggish in the juxtaposition of the two names. Yet there is a specific point in the comparison beyond setting an American achievement beside an American failure. For Mr. Lewis's phantasies have this grace of maturity, without which we could dismiss entirely all his later work, that they are so curious about the moral life. In all the romancing, in all the boyish posturing, there is always some sense of what it means to be a disinterested man; indeed, this is Mr. Lewis's haunting theme: he gives his greatest measure of honor to the love of craft and technique, to creation or discovery, which, for him, always imply the good life. He likes to see his favorite people forced to some new frontier to free themselves from the morality of the crass and the dull. Like Ernest Hemingway, he has a love for the thing well done for its own sake, and to show the charms of professional devotion he has created his Gottlieb and his Arrowsmith, his Dodsworth, Ora Weagle, Ann Vickers and now Bethel Merriday. And it is here that Henry James comes in so patly, because he is in literature so much the sort of hero that Mr. Lewis, with a certain fresh vulgarity, loves to celebrate. James received but little honor from his nation, he never represented American literature to the world, and toward the end of his career he was never quite clear, when he read his publisher's statement, whether it was he or the publisher who owed the small amounts that appeared. The nature of his thought was such that it is—now—not surprising to find him spoken of (by Ezra Pound) as a "revolutionary" in morals; yet he was not really articulate about matters of morality but thought wholly as a craftsman, knowing that if one is a novelist one does not "deal" with morals except through novelistic arrangements. And James reminds us of the cause of Mr. Lewis's failure: it is that Mr. Lewis has little love and no respect for his own art; he lacks what he so admires in others, the delight in craft and the pleasure in forcing it to cope with difficult matter.

In his lecture, "The Lesson of Balzac," James remarked that "for the most part, these loose and easy producers, the great resounding improvisatori, have not, in general, ended by imposing themselves." Mr. Lewis, of course, is wholly the loose and easy producer and the question might arise whether his now depressing inadequacy does not arise from the novelistic method he uses. But, historically speaking, it is not at all certain that James is correct in his judgment; the improvisatori have impressed themselves enormously, and speaking critically, it is not easy to discriminate between the amounts of pleasure given, on the one hand, by the tight and careful work James especially admired, and, on the other hand, by the loose and easy productions; the quality of pleasure in each kind may be another matter, though even here we cannot, *a priori*, declare wholly in favor of the tight and difficult forms. James speaks of Balzac as standing "almost alone as an extemporizer achieving closeness and weight, and whom closeness and weight have preserved." If I understand rightly what James means by closeness and weight, I think they may be found as well in a rich abundance of matter as in the nice arrangement of a more limited material; one might venture the paradox, in despite of Mr. Eliot, that in the novel the spirit giveth life.

This defense of the "extemporizer" needs to be made in speaking of Sinclair Lewis because literary notions have changed rather importantly in the twenty years since he flamed across the sky with *Main Street*. A new generation is likely to believe that the roots of Mr. Lewis's fourteen years of failure are to be found in his six years of success—to believe, that is, that the failure lies in the method of improvisation, and so to dismiss the early work with the late. For the generation to which I refer has a conception of literature almost diametrically opposed to that of the advance-guard of two decades ago. It has built into its theory the closest critical thought, literary scholarship, new ideals of elegance, allusiveness and complication of form. One can admire this generation and yet feel a regret that it has become for our time the chief repository of literary seriousness: one can regret that the greater reading public, cut off as it is from this movement by reason of training and circumstance, is left to the sincere emptiness of the social novelists or to the swash of the "good story tellers," and it is hard not to feel that something better was happening to the public when it was being confronted, twenty years ago, with Sherwood Anderson, Dreiser and the Sinclair Lewis of *Main Street* and *Babbitt*. I think it would be a misfortune if, in the new preoccupation with the opposite of looseness and easiness, the improvisatorial style should be made to seem even less creditable than it has become in the hands of most of its practitioners.

For the improvisatorial style, from Defoe down, has always had its own function and its own poetry; in our own literature we can see its best success in Mark Twain; and to both Defoe and Mark Twain Mr. Lewis's own work has an affinity. We may grant that improvisation is not adequate to the complexity of some of the most interesting aspects of the American fate, and even grant, too, that when Mr. Lewis modifies the loose and easy chronicle of events with the devices of "construction," he gives us *Babbitt*, which is clearly his best book. Yet we can still see that between improvisation and improvisation there is a difference. In *Main Street*, in *Babbitt* (which, of course, is improvisatorial enough), in *Elmer Gantry* (often called a failure but really a considerable success in the genre of the rogue-novel), in *Arrowsmith* (which is absorbing despite its adoration of the high austerity of science) and even in *Dodsworth* (though to a lesser degree), the prose is quick, nervous, efficient, the details are all alive, the total effect is simple and—to use the adjective which will bring the best of Lewis into the line of the realistic English novelists—manly.
—LIONEL TRILLING, "Mr. Lewis Goes Soft," *KR*, Summer 1940, pp. 364–67

⟨. . .⟩ what is it about Lewis that strikes one today but how deeply he has always enjoyed people in America? What is it but the proud gusto and pleasure behind his caricatures that have always made them so funny—and so comfortable? Only a novelist fundamentally uncritical of American life could have brought so much zest to its mechanics; only a novelist anxious not to surmount the visible scene, but to give it back brilliantly, could have presented so vivid an image of what Americans are or believe themselves to be. It was the satire that always gave Lewis's books their design, but the life that streamed out of them impressed people most by giving them a final *happy* recognition. Lewis caught the vulgarity and the perpetual salesmanship, and caught it as effortlessly as he caught the sights and sounds, the exact sound of a Ford car being cranked on a summer morning in Zenith in 1922, the exact resemblance of Chum Frinkley to Eddie Guest and of Sharon Falconer to Aimée Semple McPherson. But he caught also, as almost no one did before him, the boyish helplessness of a Babbitt, the stammering romance of a Martin Arrowsmith on his first day at the McGurk Institute, the loneliness of a great Sam Dodsworth before all those Europeans in Paris. Even his novel on Fascism reminded Americans that when an exiled American Hitler like Buzz Windrip goes to Paris, he yearns only for Lucky Strikes and the smoking-car jokes of his pals. Even his assault on small-town ignorance and bigotry in *Main Street* suggested that if Carol Kennicott was heroically unhappy on Main Street, she was just a little silly with her passion for uplift.

Yes, and for all their sharp thrusts and irritable mutter-ings, his books also confirmed in Americans the legend of their democratic humility, the suspicion that every stuffed shirt conceals a quaking heart, and the need of an industrial magnate like Sam Dodsworth or a scientist like Martin Arrowsmith to translate the most momentous problems of his craft into the jargon of a manly American fellowship. Lewis's men are boys at heart, living in a world in which boys are perpetually stealing through their disguise as men, and glad to know that a certain boyishness in the native atmosphere will always sustain them. Businessmen, scientists, clergymen, newspapermen, they are forever surprised at their attainment of status and seek a happiness that will encourage them to believe that they are important. They are frontiersmen suddenly ushered into the modern inheritance, and can giggle at themselves, as John Jay Chapman did on his grand tour of Europe in the eighties, by remembering all the derisive ancestors who stand behind them—"Dear old Grandpa, with his old cotton socks; wouldn't he be proud if he could see me hee-hawing and chaw-chawing with Roman princes!" But if Lewis's natives are boys, the Europeans in his books—Max Gottlieb, Bruno Zechlin, Fran Dodsworth's cousins in Berlin—though they are usually crushed by the native barbarians, are older than the rocks on which they sit, older and wiser than life, the sage miracle men of some ancient world of light and beauty and culture. Old Gottlieb in *Arrowsmith*, for example, was not merely a European scientist; he was *the* European scientist, the very incarnation of that indescribable cultivation and fathomless European wisdom—a man on speaking terms with Leonardo, Brahms, and Nietzsche; a scientist whose classic work on immunology only seven men in all the world could understand; a cosmopolitan who advised—sneeringly—his students to read *Marius the Epicurean* for "laboratory calmness," and could prepare exotic little sandwiches for his grubby coworkers.

Martin Arrowsmith himself, be it remembered, had no such skills. In fact, it was not until he came to Chicago (that halfway station to Europe?), shedding the provincialisms of Wheatsylvania and even Zenith, that he heard Mischa Elman, saw a Russian play, and—"learned to flirt without childishness." The Europeans in Lewis's novels never flirted with childishness; they had all the learning of the world at their fingertips; and as Gottlieb, or Bruno Zechlin in *Elmer Gantry*, proved by their inevitable humiliation and fall, they were almost too good to live in the parched American wilderness. Here was only one American folklore legend that Lewis made his own, a legend based on a conviction of native inferiority and subservience to Europe; and nowhere did it show so clearly as in Sam Dodsworth's encounter with Europe, a Europe that was the negation of Gottlieb's, yet cut out of the same cloth—a Europe too charming, too learned, treacherous and sly. Henry James's favorite story of American innocence abroad came back here with a vengeance. Yet it is interesting to note that a character like Gottlieb succeeded so brilliantly because he was so sentimentally realized a type. Gottlieb suggested so abundantly for Lewis just what many Americans would have supposed a German-Jewish scientist in Winnemac to be that he lived, as it were, precisely because he was a stock figure; lived because in him banality had been raised to the rank of creation.

Lewis's characters have often been criticized as "types," and they are, partly because he memorialized some of them as such, gave people in George F. Babbitt what seemed the central portrait of a businessman. But what is really significant in his use of types is that his mind moved creatively in their channels. With his ability to approximate American opinion, his lightning adaptability to the prejudices, the fears, the very tonal mood, as it were, of the contemporary American moment, Lewis has always been able to invest his tintypes with a careless energy that other writers would not have been able to understand, much less share, since they did not work so close to the surface. Lewis restored life; he did not create it. Yet what that means is that for him the creative process lay in the brilliance of that restoration—the ability to restore one Picker-baugh, with his "he-males" and "she-males," out of the fledgling Pickerbaughs all over the American scene; the ability to set his villains or bores—Elmer Gantry, Chum Frinkley, especially Lowell Schmaltz—so to talking that though they were incredible, they attained a fantastic representative quality. It is doubtful, in fact, whether Lewis even wished to make Lowell Schmaltz credible in that long monologue, *The Man Who Knew Coolidge*. He wished only to hit him off perfectly, to make Lowell a kind of monstrous incarnate average, just as he wished to make Elmer Gantry an accumulative symbol of all the phoniness he hated in American life. With his lonely suffering rebels, however—Frank Shallard, Erik Valborg, Paul Reisling, Gottlieb and Zechlin—he attained not an average type but an average myth. For they are the protestants, the victims of the national life in which his other characters survive as a matter of course; and though Lewis admired them and suffered with them, the characters he gives them are just those which the artist-rebels, the men who are "different," would seem to possess by average standards.

Just as Lewis has always worked from type to type, embodying in them now the cruelty, now the sentimentality, now the high jinks, now the high-pressure salesmanship of one aspect of the national life after another, so he has always moved in his books from one topic to another, covering one sector of American life after another—the small town, Rotary, business, medicine, the smoking car, travel, religion, social work. More than any other American novelist since Frank Norris, he felt from the first the need to go from subject to subject that would lead him to cover the entire national scene. He knew that scene in all its range and could characteristically work up any subject; he had concentrated his whole ambition in the national life, and could hit the perfect moment again and again. In fact, like a sailor hitting ducks in a shooting gallery, Lewis gave the impression that he had only to level his aim, seize a new idea, a new flash of life in the American sector, and go after it. Yet this could work only up to a certain point, as the steady decline of his novels after *Dodsworth*, reaching a really abysmal low in *The Prodigal Parents*, has proved. For the ducks in the American shooting gallery soon stopped moving in convenient rotation. In a sense Lewis depended on an America in equilibrium, a young postwar America anxious to know itself, careless and indulgent to his friendly jokes against it, ambitious even to improve its provincial manners in the light of his criticism; but when that America lost its easy comfortable self-consciousness, Lewis's nervous mimicry merely brushed off against it.

It followed also from Lewis's whole conception of the novel that his brisk mimetic energy would become a trick repeating itself long after he had lost his sense of design and purpose. In some of the early brilliant descriptions in *Ann Vickers*, he seemed to be blocking out perfect scene after perfect scene that led to nothing; there is a forlorn flashiness about them that reveals Lewis running over his old technique even when he had little to say. In Lewis's first works his verve had always been able to light up an inconsequential book like *Elmer Gantry* with dozens of hilarious scenes, or, as in *The Man Who Knew Coolidge*, even to make one long monologue out of it; but now, with nothing more substantial to write about

than Barney Dolphin in *Ann Vickers*, Ora Weagle in *Work of Art*, or Fred Cornplow in *The Prodigal Parents*, he could keep on bringing in his "trick," his special gift and charm, while the books merely sagged. They were tired, evasively sentimental books, and full of a hard surface irritability and uncertainty. Even *It Can't Happen Here*, for all its attempt to cover the imaginary coming of Fascism to America, was not a really ambitious book and certainly not a careful and deeply imagined one. Responding to the public terror that filled the air out of Hitler Germany as he had responded to a certain public mood he had known so well in the twenties, Lewis could catch only the surface terror, the surface violence; and they erupted mechanically in his book. But he could not really imagine Fascism in America, he had not really tried to; he had tried to hit the bell in 1936 as he hit it in 1920 with *Main Street* and in 1922 with *Babbitt*, to sound off a surface alarm and strike the public consciousness.

What these later works also signified, however, was not only Lewis's growing carelessness and fatigue, but an irritable formal recognition of his relation to American life. Far from even attempting iconoclastic satire, he wrote these books as moralities for a new time; and his new heroes—Ora Weagle, the poetic hotelkeeper; Doremus Jessup, the amiable and cautious liberal; Fred Cornplow, the good solid husband and father betrayed by his erring children—were the final symbols of everything Lewis had always loved best. He had lampooned Babbittry easily enough; but when the Babbitts themselves were threatened, he rushed forward to defend them. From his own point of view, indeed, there were no Babbitts now, or at least nothing to lampoon in them—Fred Cornplow was the main-stay of the times and Doremus Jessup a representative Ameri-can hero.

Those who had missed Lewis's dependence from the first on the world Fred Cornplow represented, however, could only wonder at Lewis's sentimental tribute to him and his ugly caricature of those who mocked him. The thing didn't jibe; Lewis wasn't supposed to like Cornplow-Babbitt; and how could Doremus Jessup ever seem enough for him? Yet what was it but Doremus, with his fishing tackle and his wise little small-town editorials, that Lewis had ever known and loved? What was it but the Cornplows he had run after for twenty years, trying to catch the warts, the buffoonery up at the lodge on Wednesday nights, the pleasure of the open road on Sunday? The village rebels had all failed, and that was tragic; Gottlieb and Paul Reisling, Frank Shallard and Guy Pollack, had all gone down before meanness and ignorance and terror. But if the Fred Cornplows remained, they were not so bad after all; and Carol Kennicott really had been just a little silly. The village atheist ended his tirade, and sighed, and went on playing a friendly game of poker with the local deacons. —ALFRED KAZIN, "The New Realism: Sherwood Anderson and Sinclair Lewis," *On Native Grounds*, 1942, pp. 221–26

There are really no aristocrats in Lewis's work, nor is there, as in Dreiser, or Willa Cather, or Thomas Wolfe, any convincing middle-class aristocracy. Neither, on the opposite side of the social scale, does Lewis attempt to project a single working-class figure of any dimension; while in the entire body of work by this major critic of middle-class manners in the United States, from Carol Kennicott to Doremus Jessup, there is hardly an effective or even attractive social rebel. Actually, of course, this writer whose historical position is that of having established the 'classes' in American literature, deals only with the establishment of the middle class in American literature— with that 'bourgeois colony' which, up to 1917, as Lewis says in a curious historical inversion, 'was the only America,' or which, anyhow, after 1917, considered itself as the only America. It is interesting to notice the narrow social stratification of this purely middle-class cosmos of Lewis. There are no musicians, dancers, painters, poets, or sculptors of consequence in Lewis's work. The Ora Teagle of *Work of Art*, who is the only full-length study of a writer, and who does at least write one honest novel—a novel which is 'financially unnecessary,' and which convinces Ora of the futility of serious writing—is indeed Lewis's prototype of the artist in America. Furthermore, from the Raymond P. Wutherspoon of *Main Street* to the Lycurgus Watts of *Dodsworth*, are there any 'intellectuals' in Lewis's work who are not also by inference dilettanti or actual perverts—that is, when they are not 'radicals' and dangerous as rattlesnakes?

No, early and late, as I say, the only true hero of Lewis is the scientist. But in *Arrowsmith*, too, we saw not merely the inadequate nature of Lewis's 'scientific truth,' but also his failure to project that view of a native life and character which he had linked with this ideal. Right there was the very epitome of that petty, nagging, backbiting, provincial existence which the western scene seems to be identified with in Lewis's mind when it isn't a stereotype of the frontier or a ghastly vision of suburban standardization. So, too, the town of 'Catawba' in Lewis's novels, the up-state town of Winnemac which is intended to represent the best features of an older rural and democratic society, is actually a ghost town. . . . In the whole range of Lewis's work, where is there a view of life which could sustain a novelist's belief in life, or even in his own work? Perhaps this helps to explain the increasingly curious view that Lewis has taken of the eastern metropolis itself: the accumulating references to the bohemians and anarchists, the 'intellectual parasites' and 'one hundred per cent mongrels' who have becomes the typical inhabitants of the metropolis. ('Russian Jews in London clothes,' as Lewis tells us in *Dodsworth*, 'going to Italian restaurants with Greek waiters and African music. . . .')

In these tones of superstition, as well as in his earlier tones of naïve yearning, Lewis clearly shows his own lack of cultural roots or of any historical perspective. The country people and the city people of his tales are neither true country people nor true city people. Just as every extreme of Lewis's inner world has been eliminated, and the whole gamut of human feeling has been reduced to what you might call the medium-priced emotions, so, in his whole outward scene also, the true poles of his society have been removed—or, more accurately, perhaps, have never been established. As we have now seen, though, the central dramatic conflict of Lewis's work is precisely the conflict of these inadequate—or missing—extremes: of a specious aristocracy and an almost invisible working class; of a romantic socialism and a visionary capitalism; of Westerners who are trying above all to be Easterners and of Easterners who in spite of everything are exactly like Westerners. . . .

Yet, without these cultural roots or abiding human values—without a sense of either the flesh or of the mind—perpetually oscillating between such extremes, none of which are satisfactory, none of which are really imagined or felt, none of which are actually *there*, how can this writer do otherwise? Marked by a thin past and a narrow future, Lewis is indeed the Last Provincial of our letters: a provincial who wanders, homeless, between a barren and deteriorating hinterland and an increasingly appalling industrial order—a hinterland with which he feels no ties, an industrial order with which he cannot come to grips.

And it is interesting to realize just how little of the 'real' United States is in the work of a writer who is so full of its manners, habits, and idioms.

I mean, of course, the United States which is actually forming and determining Lewis's whole literary world: the U.S.A. of the Corporations and the Cartels, as well as of the factories, the mines, and the slums, which is the source and conditioning factor of Lewis's Middle-Class Empire and his Economic Man. If Lewis's work is in the literary tradition of Frank Norris, Theodore Dreiser, or Upton Sinclair, what a limited view it gives us, after all, of the North American continent, and with what a tender and tardy sort of 'realism'! The U.A.C. of *Dodsworth*—that Unit Automotive Corporation—is the true *Deus ex machina* of Lewis's world, but, showing as he did all its consequences at the dawn of the nineteen-twenties, it was only at the outset of the nineteen-thirties, at the point when the God of the Machine was Himself temporarily out of order, that Lewis allowed himself to take another look at it. Perhaps the most violent and brutal example of Lewis's social satire in the later twenties was directed, in *Elmer Gantry*, against rural life and evangelical religion. Just as Lewis has foreshortened the whole exterior scene of his people's activity, so he ignores the basic determinants of the life which surrounds them. The real institutions of finance-capitalism lie outside his world: a world of continuously worse results and no causes.

Thus the writer, who most clearly shows the effects of the new industrialism in the United States, least understands it, or has the least inclination to understand it. But in the clear pattern of Lewis's values—a pattern that is finally almost a spiritual blueprint in itself, without deviations or ambiguous areas—things can hardly turn out very differently. This is a literary world where the conflicts of 'Society' take precedence over the intimations of social conflict, where it is more important to *be* a middle-class aristocrat than to understand the nature of the middle-class rulers of America.

All through Lewis's work we may trace a curious transformation of that earlier and more intricate conflict of 'East' and 'West' which has marked the national letters. Perhaps never before has the familiar and uneasy artistic search for the cultivated and aristocratic 'eastern' life been so swiftly and surely transposed into the search for financial security and the material consequences of wealth. But what Lewis has done is to *bourgeoisize* this whole cultural conflict too; to make it completely middle-class, to remove both the upper and lower limits of this search—to reduce it all again to another formula where the 'East' simply means a little more money and the 'West' a little less money: where the Easterners are the people who have got the money, and the Westerners are the people who are going to get the money.

So Zenith is Lewis's true home, after all; Zenith, which is in itself an in-between world, a by-product of the cartels, a psychological suburb of the new money society in America which lives on financial sufferance as well as on the nationally advertised brands—this middle world of derived goods and derived values which is actually the whole world of Lewis's literary achievement. Perhaps we can now appreciate the fascination of hotel life for Lewis, from the Una Golden of *The Job* who found her salvation in running the White Line Chain to the Myron Teagle of *Work of Art* whose lifelong aspiration is to manage the Perfect Inn. To Zenith's Child, at any rate, a good hotel is all that home should be. . . .

Nor is it as difficult as it might seem for Lewis to move from the Zenith of 1920 to the New Zenith of 1940. The fact that the picture of George F. Babbitt's town was a fantasy of horror, a vision of the mechanized inferno—that Lewis neglected or ignored the residual resources of a democratic society as well as the natural human resistance to having human life stamped, labeled, and packaged—makes it so much easier, indeed, for the picture of Frederick William Cornplow's cosmos to become a fantasy of bliss. . . . Doesn't the artistic secret of this complete bourjoyce lie precisely in the fact that, just *because* Lewis's sense of reality is so limited, his fantasy life can be so varied, so flexible and so irresponsible—can move so easily from a ghastly notion of the future to a childlike notion of the past?—MAXWELL GEISMAR, "Sinclair Lewis: The Cosmic Bourjoyce," *The Last of the Provincials*, 1947, pp. 129–34

Lewis turned out 21 books—sufficient evidence that he wrote a lot of bilge. A man who wrote 21 masterpieces would be four or five ahead of William Shakespeare. But *Main Street, Babbitt, Arrowsmith, Elmer Gantry* and *Dodsworth* were social documents with a definite effect upon public opinion at the time; and they are likely to remain a permanent part of the social history of the United States. A man who has produced five novels that really meant something to his own generation is an extraordinary man indeed, one sure to be remembered for a long time.

The craftsmanship of these books is a matter of interest mainly to professors of English literature and to aspiring novelists. Lewis observed exactly, reported accurately, and checked, rechecked, compared and verified with the diligence of the dreariest German pedant who ever pursued a subjunctive through nine centuries and 900 volumes. But this was part of the mechanics of his trade. He worked hard. He worked harder than most of us can even conceive of working. But it wasn't industry that won him the Nobel prize. It wasn't industry that made him master of the American imagination for a decade or so.

The magic was an eloquence that arose from a source deeper than syntax and the rules of prosody. Because everyone recognized his own thoughts and his own words in the pages of Sinclair Lewis he was dubbed a realist, and some quirk of the literary mind holds that to be the antithesis of romanticist. But the terms are not exclusive. *Tom Sawyer* was realism. *David Harum* was realism. *Main Street* reported the idiosyncrasies of Gopher Prairie no more faithfully than those two books recorded the quirks and oddities of Missouri and upstate New York. But because they are placid and good-humored we list them in a different category.

Lewis was unhappy, and was indignant because he was unhappy. His indignation betrays his essential romanticism. If he had been a realist of the stripe of, say, Montaigne, he might have been just as unhappy, but he would not have been indignant about it, because he would have realized that happiness is impossible anyhow. But this admission is a psychological impossibility to a 100-percent American like Lewis. In the oldest state document issued by us as a nation we committed ourselves to "the pursuit of happiness," and pursue it we must, or repudiate our birthright.

Lewis proclaimed—and piled up mountains of evidence to prove—that Americans are unhappy largely by their own fault. Their stupidity renders them incapable of seeing in which direction true happiness lies. Their cowardice renders them incapable of grasping happiness when it is within their reach. Their blind greed sends them chasing after some will-o'-the-wisp that leads them into the mire. All this the average American must admit is very true. There was nothing in the assertion that came into collision with his most profound conviction, so he accepted Lewis as a prophet—of the order of Jeremiah, no doubt, but a prophet.

For he never fell into the heresy of denying that happiness exists *in posse*. On the contrary, in *Arrowsmith* he portrayed its attainment. Young Dr. Arrowsmith went after it the hard way,

to be sure, and the happiness of discovering what makes a man's liver do what it does is a stern, austere form of happiness that does not appeal to many of us. Nevertheless, it is conceivable; and even a Babbitt will readily grant that the happiness of a scientific mind is not necessarily that of a realtor. The point is that by the exercise of indomitable will power Arrowsmith pursued happiness and eventually overtook it. In the assumption that this is possible the book is American to the core.

This was the essence of the literary revolt of the twenties, of which Sinclair Lewis was one of the great chiefs. The whole crew denounced Americans furiously, and the public loved it, to the amazement of those who overlooked the fact that Amerians were being denounced, but not the American ideal. We were, in fact, unhappy, and to be told that it was our own fault was quite bearable; what would have been unbearable was to be told that there is no happiness, and that pursuit of it is utterly vain. If we are unhappy because we are stupid and blind, then to develop intelligence and vision is a way out—difficult, indeed, and a faint hope, but nevertheless possible and a hope.

In that they did not proclaim the impossibility and deny the hope the writers of the twenties remained well within the line of American literary tradition. Their thunderous assaults upon the frauds and imbecilities, the hypocrisies and quackeries of their time were reformist, not revolutionary; and the mood of America has been reformist most of the time since its beginning.

Where Sinclair Lewis will eventually stand in the hierarchy of American letters is not for this generation to decide, but there is no doubt that *Main Street, Babbitt* and, I think, *Arrowsmith* will survive, if only as *genre* pictures. It is my own belief that future generations will find in them a great deal more, but that may be a prejudiced view because I believe that the American philosophy of life is going to have a long run. We are not ready for quietism. We still believe that when something is wrong, something can be done about it; and a raucous voice bawling out the wrong is not yet to us mere sound and fury, but a trumpet blast summoning the mighty men of valor to stand to their arms.—GERALD W. JOHNSON, "Romance and Mr. Babbitt," *NR*, Jan. 29, 1951, pp. 14–15

Sinclair Lewis' first and last novels ⟨*Our Mr. Wrenn* and *World So Wide*⟩ neither of them among his happiest efforts and enclosing within their ragged brackets twenty other novels most of which are better, are curiously alike; indeed, toward the end of the first novel we find the phrase, echoed from Kipling, that supplies the title of the last, in which Kipling is acknowledged: "the world so wide." Both novels take as their theme that theme traditionally favored by our novelists, of the American innocent abroad, and while the two heroes are in some ways very different (one a nearly illiterate clerk, the other a successful architect), they are in some more basic ways than these, alike, and therefore the pattern of their experience is almost identical. There is something compulsive in this theme for Sinclair Lewis as for our other novelists, and the pattern, which is resolved by a vindication of our innocence, is no doubt now, as it was a hundred years ago, a portion of our folklore.

In each case, an accident frees the hero from the routines that give structure to his life, and he eagerly seeks the long-desired European experience. Each, without the embracing clichés of "the job," finds himself freed only to his own lonely emptiness. ". . . he was desolatingly free to wander in a world too bleakly, too intimidatingly wide". . . . "In Newlife [Colorado] . . . I was as lonely as I am here [Firenze]—only busier there." So for the later hero. The earlier, more desperately, "had no friend in all the hostile world" of London. However, each encounters a girl who seems at home in this hostile world, an American sophisticate, the first a bohemian painter, the second a scholar of the Renaissance; these women, familiar with Europe, are also half-corrupted by it, easily seduced by the false values that they associate with it. After a period in which the innocence of these heroes has been exposed to the dubious experience of these heroines, each hero turns to a sounder heroine, the undiluted American Miss with no intellectual or artistic nonsense about her. These fresher ladies are, again, basically alike, in spite of the superficial differences between the incredibly modest, hard-working girl of 1914 (employed by "Wanamacy"), and the incredibly brash career woman of 1950 who has a heart of modest gold under the layers of professional lacquer, a seeing eye under the mascara.

These novels are vastly imperfect, but it would be a mistake to call them simple. Each contains unresolved complexities that are not so peculiar to Lewis as they are to the American imagination itself. Europe is as fascinating to these heroes as it must be proved to be false. The yearning for a deeper experience than America offers is as strong in them as the loneliness that overcomes them when they are freed to that experience which they are then unable, in their wholesome naiveté, to utilize. There is in these novels an undercurrent of fear, fear of Europe itself: in *World So Wide*, Sam Dodsworth lectures the young hero at some length on the importance of not staying abroad too long lest he succumb to Europe; and in both novels Lewis, like Henry James, has his Osmonds and his Madame Merles, those Americans who have yielded up their native inheritance only to be vitiated by an alien tradition that they cannot make their own. Yet, curiously, it is the "Europeanized" women—silly Istra Nash of *Our Mr. Wrenn* and cool Dr. Olivia Lomond of *World So Wide*—the women whom the heroes must reject, who, nevertheless, communicate such higher values, intellectual and spiritual, as are implied by the total situation in each novel. The result is that when Mr. Wrenn turns to his simple American, Nelly Croubel, Lewis must necessarily write a satire on the limits of suburbia; and when Hayden Chart, in the last novel, turns to Roxanna Eldritch, Lewis must force his plot into sentimental melodrama to bring about the turn at all. These endings are hardly what one could call clear vindications of American values. We are left with the large, staring question: what *was* America to Sinclair Lewis?

⟨. . .⟩ It was, in the first place, as the novels tell us, too, an entity vast and formless that must be scolded into sense. Assuming this stance, Lewis needs the European reference, as the characters in his novels need it; and thus we have the famous Nobel Prize Address, delivered of course in Stockholm, called "The American Fear of Literature," and the almost equally famous letter to a purely native institution, declining the Pulitzer Prize on the ground that no institutionalized body could, without danger to the republic of letters, arrogate to itself the assumption of good judgment that such a reward implies. The Nobel speech is an impassioned diatribe against gentility in American literature (but made long after the victory was already won, as Lewis' own public reputation in 1930 demonstrates) and a plea for "a literature worthy of her vastness." The letter to the Pulitzer Committee is a rejection of any official body that might threaten to restrict such a literature.

This is the heart of the matter. What Lewis loved so passionately about America was its potentiality for and constant expression of a wide, casually human freedom, the individual life lived in honest and perhaps eccentric effort (all the better),

the social life lived in a spirit that first of all tolerates variety. And what he hated about America, what made him scold it, sometimes so shrilly, was everything that militated against such a free life: social timidity, economic system, intellectual rigidity, theological dogma, legal repression, class convention. These two, the individual impulse to freedom and the social impulse to restrict it, provide the bases of his plots. "If I seem to have criticized prairie villages, I have certainly criticized them no more than New York, or Paris, or the great universities." The point, perhaps, is that in his novels it was easier for him to dramatize the repressions than it was to dramatically affirm the freedoms, and therefore, even in such a character as Carol Kennicott of *Main Street*, there is a considerable ambiguity, as there is in the endings of the novels I have here discussed. The conflict is not so much between America and Europe as between the true America as Lewis saw it—that is, Americans true to themselves, and the false America, or Americans who submit to values not their own, not free. The result in the novels is often an apparent praise of provincialism, but the praise, in its impulse, is of something much larger. ⟨. . .⟩

There were grave defects in this imagination. Lewis himself reminds us, again and again, of his primary sentimentality. There are lapses in taste as in judgment. There is a deep pit of naiveté about human nature. There is that curious gift for seeming always a little old-fashioned that comes with the determination to be only bright and new. These are defects not unfamiliar in Americans in general. But above all there is another quality that we have almost forgotten to look for in him: there is a high and dedicated sense of justice that also has much to do with the making of Americans.—MARK SCHORER, "The World of Sinclair Lewis," *NR*, April 6, 1953, pp. 18–20

When Sinclair Lewis received the Nobel award in 1930, he ought to have shared it with H. L. Mencken. The latter, though no novelist, deserves a place here. His roaring success in the early Twenties, when he battered away at all the idols of the crowd, helped to clear the air. When Mencken is serious, he is nearly always bad; but as a kind of clown-critic, full of impudence and a rough sardonic wit and a vitality that keeps his earlier *Prejudices* still readable today, he was, and still is, good lively company. He was entirely destructive, caring at heart for nothing except a dream Germany born in Baltimore of string quartettes and beer. But destruction, especially of this noisy comic kind, breaking no heads or hearts with its bladders and custard pies, was what was needed. Chief of his clown-philosopher visions was one of America in the Twenties as an immense and almost free circus. (Mencken said President Harding cost him less than eighty cents a year: "Try to think of better sport for the money.") And it is really by way of Mencken's America-as-circus, and not by way of realism about the Middle West, that Sinclair Lewis appears. In the satirical-clown department, where social and literary criticism is represented by Mencken, Sinclair Lewis is in charge of the novel. Or it might be more accurate to say that the novel is in charge of him, compelling him to abandon realism for comic-cum-romantic fantasy. (We mean what we say here. Certainly for his earlier novels, Lewis, a good reporter, set to work like another Zola, filling notebooks with facts and observed details, and then shutting himself up with them, to write his novel. And it is when the method broke down, when the novel began writing itself, that he really created something.) He could not be a serious satirist because he did not possess any central fixed set of values and standards; he looks to Europe when he is in America, to America when he is in Europe, to Eastern America when he is in the West, to the West when he is in the East; as a man, and so as a writer, he was uncertain of the world and of himself, bewildered, confused, homeless and restless. (This is why, in *Work of Art*, he can take hotels so seriously.) He could not identify himself with any kind of life, was always the clever visiting journalist or the tourist. But only in his relation to the actual scene. His best work is raised high above journalism; sheer drive, applied to the mass of recorded detail, and a rare exuberance, bringing the unconscious into action, turn him into a genuine creator, not a conscious deliberate artist but a mythmaker. So his masterpiece, high above *Main Street*, is *Babbitt*, which is at once something less and something more than a novel, just as *Moby-Dick* and *Huckleberry Finn* are. This is a truly American creative imagination at work, uncontrolled and outrageous by European standards, just as America itself seems uncontrolled and outrageous; rushing, in *Babbitt*, from heights of satirical buffoonery, often clowning for its own sake, to quick shuddering glimpses of depths where terror and despair are lurking. The real Sinclair Lewis, the enduring writer, should not be looked for in *Martin Arrowsmith, Dodsworth, Ann Vickers*, but, apart from *Babbitt*, in *Elmer Gantry, The Man Who Knew Coolidge*, and some parts of *It Can't Happen Here*. He faded away, looking in his last years strangely empty, melancholy, spectral, because there was in him no creative and critical centre that could take over, once the necessary drive, energy, exuberance, were waning. But while they lasted, he was, as he remains, one of those creators who do not make works of art for the cultivated minority, but myths for the multitude. Even if criticism, quite mistakenly, should argue him out of literature, he will remain a figure in American history.—J. B. PRIESTLEY, "Between the Wars," *Literature and Western Man*, 1960, pp. 429–30

## Works

In an address made not long ago Mr. Kipling cited the curious fate of certain famous books which, surviving the conditions that produced them, have become to later generations something utterly different from what their authors designed, or their original readers believed, them to be. The classic examples are *The Merchant of Venice*, a rough-and-tumble Jew-baiting farce to Shakespeare's contemporaries, and *Don Quixote*, composed by Cervantes, and accepted by his public, as a gently humorous parody of the picaresque novel of the day; but Mr. Kipling found a still more striking instance in *Gulliver's Travels*, fiercest and most brutal of social satires when it was written, and now one of the favorites of the nursery.

Some such fate, in a much shorter interval, has befallen Mr. Sinclair Lewis's *Main Street*, that pioneering work which with a swing of the pen hacked away the sentimental vegetation from the American small town, and revealed Main Street as it is, with all its bareness in the midst of plenty. The novel was really epoch-making; but the epoch it made turned into something entirely different from what its author purposed. Mr. Lewis opened the eyes of the millions of dwellers in all the American Main Streets to the inner destitution of their lives, but by so doing apparently created in them not the desire to destroy Main Street but only to read more and more and ever more about it. The dwellers in Main Street proved themselves to be like the old ladies who send for the doctor every day for the pleasure of talking over their symptoms. They do not want to be cured; they want to be noticed.

It must not be regarded as diminishing Mr. Lewis's achievement to remind his readers that he was not the first discoverer of Main Street. Over thirty years ago, Robert Grant situated *Unleavened Bread* in the same thoroughfare; and so, a little later, did Frank Norris his *McTeague*, and Graham Phillips his *Susan Lenox*—and they were all, as it happens, not only "great American novels," but great novels. But they came before their time, their bitter taste frightened a public long nurtured on ice-cream soda and marshmallows, and a quick growth of oblivion was trained over the dreary nakedness of the scene they had exposed. It was necessary that a later pioneer should arise and clear this vegetation away again, and if Mr. Lewis had done no more than demolish the tottering stage-fictions of a lavender-scented New England, a chivalrous South, and a bronco-busting West he would have rendered a great service to American fiction. This having been accomplished, however, it is permissible to wonder whether, as a theme, Main Street—in a literary sense—has not received as much notice as its width and length will carry, or even more. The difficulty is that it is now established as a canon, a first principle in the laws of American fiction; and thence it will be difficult to dislodge it.

The term is of course used to typify something much more extended, geographically, than Mr. Lewis's famous thoroughfare. "Main Street" has come to signify the common mean of American life anywhere in its million cities and towns, its countless villages and immeasurable wildernesses. It stands for everything which does not rise above a very low average in culture, situation, or intrinsic human interest; and also for every style of depicting this dead level of existence, from the photographic to the pornographic—sometimes inclusively.—EDITH WHARTON, "The Great American Novel," YR, July 1927, pp. 647–49

The theory lately held in Greenwich Village that the merit and success of *Main Street* constituted a sort of double-headed accident, probably to be ascribed to a case of mistaken identity on the part of God—this theory blows up with a frightful roar toward the middle of *Babbitt*. The plain truth is, indeed, that *Babbitt* is at least twice as good a novel as *Main Street* was—that it avoids all the more obvious faults of that celebrated work, and shows a number of virtues that are quite new. It is better designed than *Main Street*; the action is more logical and coherent; there is more imagination in it and less bald journalism; above all, there is a better grip upon the characters. If Carol Kennicott, at one leap, became as real a figure to most literate Americans as Jane Addams or Nan Patterson; then George F. Babbitt should become as real as Jack Dempsey or Charlie Schwab. The fellow simply drips with human juices. Every one of his joints is movable in all directions. Real freckles are upon his neck and real sweat stands out upon his forehead. I have personally known him since my earliest days as a newspaper reporter, back in the last century. I have heard him make such speeches as Cicero never dreamed of at banquets of the Chamber of Commerce. I have seen him marching in parades. I have observed him advancing upon his Presbyterian tabernacle of a Sunday morning, his somewhat stoutish lady upon his arm. I have watched and heard him crank his Buick. I have noted the effect of alcohol upon him, both before and after Prohibition. And I have seen him, when some convention of Good Fellows was in town, at his innocent sports in the parlors of brothels, grandly ordering wine at $10 a round and bidding the professor play "White Wings."

To me his saga, as Sinclair Lewis has set it down, is fiction only by a sort of courtesy. All the usual fittings of the prose fable seem to be absent. There is no plot whatever, and very little of the hocus-pocus commonly called development of character. Babbitt simply grows two years older as the tale unfolds; otherwise he doesn't change at all—any more than you or I have changed since 1920. Every customary device of the novelist is absent. When Babbitt, revolting against the irksome happiness of his home, takes to a series of low affairs with manicure girls, grass-widows and ladies even more complaisant, nothing overt and melodramatic happens to him. He never meets his young son Teddy in a dubious cabaret; his wife never discovers incriminating correspondence in his pockets; no one tries to blackmail him; he is never present when a joint is raided. The worst punishment that falls upon him is that his old friends at the Athletic Club—cheats exactly like himself—gossip about him a bit. Even so, that gossip goes no further; Mrs. Babbitt does not hear it. When she accuses him of adultery, it is simply the formal accusation of a loving wife: she herself has absolutely no belief in it. Moreover, it does not cause Babbitt to break down, confess and promise to sin no more. Instead, he lies like a major-general, denounces his wife for her evil imagination, and returns forthwith to his carnalities. If, in the end, he abandons them, it is not because they torture his conscience, but because they seem likely to hurt his business. This prospect gives him pause, and the pause saves him. He is, beside, growing old. He is 48, and more than a little bald. A night out leaves his tongue coated in the morning. As the curtain falls upon him he is back upon the track of rectitude—a sound business man, a faithful Booster, an assiduous Elk, a trustworthy Presbyterian, a good husband, a loving father, a successful and unchallenged fraud.

Let me confess at once that this story has given me vast delight. I know the Babbitt type, I believe, as well as most; for twenty years I have devoted myself to the exploration of its peculiarities. Lewis depicts it with complete and absolute fidelity. There is irony in the picture; irony that is unflagging and unfailing, but nowhere is there any important departure from the essential truth. Babbitt has a great clownishness in him, but he never becomes a mere clown. In the midst of his most extravagant imbecilities he keeps both feet upon the ground. One not only sees him brilliantly; one also understands him; he is made plausible and natural. As an old professor of Babbittry I welcome him as an almost perfect specimen—a genuine museum piece. Every American city swarms with his brothers. They run things in the Republic, East, West, North, South. They are the originators and propagators of the national delusions—all, that is, save those which spring from the farms. They are the palladiums of 100 per cent Americanism; the apostles of the Harding politics; the guardians of the Only True Christianity. They constitute the Chambers of Commerce, the Rotary Clubs, the Kiwanis Clubs, the Watch and Ward Societies, the Men and Religion Forward Movements, the Y.M.C.A. directorates, the Good Citizen Leagues. They are the advertisers who determine what is to go into the American newspapers and what is to stay out. They are the Leading Citizens, the speakers at banquets, the profiteers, the corruptors of politics, the supporters of evangelical Christianity, the peers of the realm. Babbitt is their archetype. He is no worse than most, and no better; he is the average American of the ruling minority in this hundred and forty-sixth year of the Republic. He is America incarnate, exuberant and exquisite. Study him well and you will know better what is the matter with the land we live in than you would know after plowing through a thousand such volumes as Walter Lippmann's *Public Opinion*. What Lippmann tried to do as a professor, laboriously and without imagination, Lewis has here done as an artist with a few vivid strokes. It is a very fine piece of work indeed.

Nor is all its merit in the central figure. It is not Babbitt that shines forth most gaudily, but the whole complex of Babbittry, Babbittism, Babbittismus. In brief, Babbitt is seen as no more than a single member of the society he lives in—a matter far more difficult to handle, obviously, than any mere

character sketch. His every act is related to the phenomena of that society. It is not what he feels and aspires to that moves him primarily; it is what the folks about him will think of him. His politics is communal politics, mob politics, herd politics; his religion is a public rite wholly without subjective significance; his relations to his wife and his children are formalized and standardized; even his debaucheries are the orthodox debaucheries of a sound business man. The salient thing about him, in truth, is his complete lack of originality—and that is precisely the salient mark of every American of his class. What he feels and thinks is what it is currently proper to feel and think. Only once, during the two years that we have him under view, does he venture upon an idea that is even remotely original—and that time the heresy almost ruins him. The lesson, you may be sure, is not lost upon him. If he lives, he will not offend again. No thought will ever get a lodgment in his mind, even in the wildest deliriums following bootleg gin, that will offer offense to the pruderies of Vergil Gunch, president of the Boosters' Club, or to those of old Mr. Eathorne, president of the First State Bank, or to those of the Rev. Dr. John Jennison Drew, pastor of the Chatham Road Presbyterian Church, or to those of Prof. Pumphrey, head of the Zenith Business College, or even to those of Miss McGoun, the virtuous stenographer. He has been rolled through the mill. He emerges the very model and pattern of a forward-looking, right-thinking Americano.

As I say, this *Babbitt* gives me great delight. It is shrewdly devised; it is adeptly managed; it is well written. The details, as in *Main Street*, are extraordinarily vivid—the speech of Babbitt before the Zenith Real Estate Board, the meeting to consider ways and means of bulging the Chatham Road Sunday-school, the annual convention of the real-estate men, Babbitt's amour with the manicure-girl, the episode of Sir Gerald Doak, the warning visit when Babbitt is suspected of Liberalism, the New Thought meeting, the elopement of young Theodore Roosevelt Babbitt and Eunice Littlefield at the end. In all these scenes there is more than mere humour; there is searching truth. They reveal something; they mean something. I know of no American novel that more accurately presents the real America. It is a social document of a high order.—H. L. MENCKEN, "Portrait of an American Citizen" (1922), *H. L. Mencken's* Smart Set *Criticism*, ed. William H. Nolte, 1968, pp. 282–85

⟨. . .⟩ it is precisely by its hardness, its efficiency, its compactness that Mr. Lewis's work excels. Yet he also is an American, he also has devoted book after book to the description and elucidation of America. Far from being shelless, however, his books, one is inclined to say, are all shell; the only doubt is whether he has left any room for the snail. At any rate *Babbitt* completely refutes the theory that an American writer, writing about America, must necessarily lack the finish, the technique, the power to model and control his material which one might suppose to be the bequest of an old civilization to its artists. In all these respects, *Babbitt* is the equal of any novel written in English in the present century. The tourist therefore must make his choice between two alternatives. Either there is no profound difference between English and American writers, and their experience is so similar that it can be housed in the same form; or Mr. Lewis has modelled himself so closely upon the English—H. G. Wells is a very obvious master—that he has sacrificed his American characteristics in the process. But the art of reading would be simpler and less adventurous than it is if writers could be parcelled out in strips of green and blue. Study of Mr. Lewis more and more convinces us that the surface appearance of downright decision is deceptive; the outer composure hardly holds together the warring elements within; the colors have run.

For though *Babbitt* would appear as solid and authentic a portrait of the American business man as can well be painted, certain doubt runs across us and shakes our conviction. But, we may ask, where all is so masterly, self-assured and confident, what foothold can there be for doubt to lodge upon? To begin with we doubt Mr. Lewis himself: we doubt that is to say that he is nearly as sure of himself or of his subject as he would have us believe. For he, too, though in a way very different from Mr. (Sherwood) Anderson's way, is writing with one eye on Europe, a division of attention which the reader is quick to feel and resent. He too has the American self-consciousness though it is masterfully suppressed, and allowed only to utter itself once or twice in a sharp cry of bitterness ("Babbitt was as much amused by the antiquated provincialism as any proper Englishman by any American."). But the uneasiness is there. He has not identified himself with America; rather he has constituted himself the guide and interpreter between the Americans and the English, and, as he conducts his party of Europeans over the typical American city (of which he is a native) and shows them the typical American citizen (to whom he is related), he is equally divided between shame at what he has to show and anger at the Europeans for laughing at it. Zenith is a despicable place, but the English are even more despicable for despising it.

In such an atmosphere intimacy is impossible. All that a writer of Mr. Lewis's powers can do is to be unflinchingly accurate and more and more on his guard against giving himself away. Accordingly, never was so complete a model of a city made before. We turn on the taps and the water runs; we press a button and cigars are lit and beds warmed. But this glorification of machinery, this lust for "toothpastes, socks, tires, cameras, instantaneous hot water bottles . . . at first the signs, then the substitutes for joy and passion and wisdom" is only a device for putting off the evil day which Mr. Lewis sees looming ahead. However he may dread what people will think of him, he must give himself away. Babbitt must be proved to possess some share of truth and beauty, some character, some emotion of his own, or Babbitt will be nothing but an improved device for running motor cars, a convenient surface for the display of mechanical ingenuity. To make us care for Babbitt—that was his problem. With this end in view Mr. Lewis shamefacedly assures us that Babbitt has his dreams. Stout though he is, this elderly business man dreams of a fairy child waiting at a gate. "Her dear and tranquil hand caressed his cheek. He was gallant and wise and well-beloved; warm ivory were her arms, and beyond perilous moors the brave sea glittered." But that is not a dream; that is simply the protest of a man who has never dreamed in his life but is determined to prove that dreaming is as easy as shelling peas. Seas, fairies, moors? Well, he will have a little of each, and if that is not a dream, he seems to demand, jumping out of bed in a fury, then what is it? With sex relations and family affection he is much more at ease. Indeed it would be impossible to deny that if we put our ears to his shell, the foremost citizen in Zenith can be heard moving cumbrously but unmistakably within. One has moments of affection for him, moments of sympathy and even of desire that some miracle may happen, the rock be cleft asunder, and the living creature, with his capacity for fun, suffering, and happiness be set at liberty. But no; his movements are too sluggish; Babbitt will never escape; he will die in his prison bequeathing only the chance of escape to his son.
—Virginia Woolf, "American Fiction," SR, Aug. 1, 1925, p. 2

In a sense, it must be acknowledged, *Arrowsmith* stands apart from the bulk of Lewis's work. It is the only one of the novels in which the heroes deal in the more abstract reaches of higher science. Its major characters are more aloof, in labor, in intellectual temper, and in aim, from American civilization than are those of any other Lewis novel. At the opening of the story, a kinship is suggested between the searching mind of Martin Arrowsmith and the wanderings of a pioneer ancestor. But with modern America Arrowsmith can have no real communication: every attempt on his part, however well intentioned, to adapt himself to his American environment is represented as a betrayal of his mistress, Science.

This conception of science as a thing to itself, a seeking and a method that exist on their own rigorous and ultimate terms, suggests the hard intellectuality that Veblen assigned to the modern world and the clean modern aesthetic that Lewis Mumford has reported in *Technics and Civilization* and Sherwood Anderson in *Perhaps Women*. Like Veblen's scholars, Martin Arrowsmith and his mentor Max Gottlieb demand the right to an idle curiosity and to a pursuit of knowledge unencumbered by commercial or even humanitarian objectives, and Gottlieb wages quite a Veblenian war against university administration. The chaste aesthetic, the austere intellect of Anderson's and Veblen's twentieth-century civilization are called to mind again and again as the novel emphasizes the twin precisions of scientific labor: exactness in analysis, fineness in technique.

Gottlieb possesses a "flair of technique," a "sure rapidity which dignified the slightest movement of his hands"; and, executing some minute and subsidiary task, he lectures his students: "'. . . technique, gentlemen, is the beginning of all science.'" Gottlieb, we are told, has not published heavily, but his papers "were all exquisitely finished, all easily reduplicated and checked by the doubtfulest critics." He rejoices in "the exasperated carefulness" of Arrowsmith's investigations. Martin himself, in his maturity as a scientist,

> desired a perfection of technique in the quest for absolute and provable fact; he desired as greatly as any Pater to "burn with a hard gem-like flame," and he desired not to have ease and repute in the marketplace, but rather to keep free of those follies, lest they confuse him and make him soft.

But while Sinclair Lewis created a scientific realm that would square in many respects with the findings of Veblen and others, that realm comes closer to Veblen's community of scholars than to his broader civilization of machines and engineers. Gottlieb and Arrowsmith are most clearly not technicians, with a technician's concern for means and uses; these are the concerns of a physician, and Lewis was quite explicit in separating the work of the doctor from that of the scientist. As a physician, entangled in the practical urgencies of his profession and the compromises of commercial America, Arrowsmith almost loses himself; he regains his true direction only when he is sheltered within a research institute that is comparatively, though not absolutely, removed from utilitarian or commercial objectives.

Another distinction is even more telling. The machine, our other authors have insisted, is above all a dictator of pace; and the scientists of *Arrowsmith* seek a liberation from pace, the freedom to do slowly and speculatively the work that can be neither hastened nor timed. The labor of Lewis's scientist heroes is all founded in a careful patience, which is enjoined when Gottlieb advises his students to read Pater's *Marius the Epicurean*, that they might gain from it "'the calmness which is the secret of laboratory skill' "; or when he says of Americans that they are " 'impatient with the beautiful dullness of long labors' "; or when Arrowsmith prays for " 'unclouded eyes and freedom from haste,' " and the persistence to check through and destroy his own errors. If there is a similarity in structure between the quiet domain in which Arrowsmith moves and the machine-paced world of which Veblen wrote, it would be that the pace of Veblen's industrial society is an element in its complexity and in its exact synchronization of parts, and needs to be grasped with a precision as fine as that with which Arrowsmith analyzes the elements of his microscopic universe.

Yet however distinct Martin Arrowsmith and his fellow laborers may be from the homely middle-class Americans who people most of the Lewis novels, the values to which, in *Arrowsmith*, Lewis gave his assent seem to be in essence those that he would instinctively employ time and again in criticism or in praise of the American bourgeoisie—and throughout *Arrowsmith* these values are expressed with special clarity. For the strongest characters in Lewis's books, the Sam Dodsworths, possess a certain earthy solid competence, a clear-headedness about their job or their politics and a capacity for direct self-examination and self-confrontation; the weakest characters are incompetent and wordy. And how could the most flaccid qualities in American society be more distinctly identified than by their contrast to the craft of scientist as Lewis pictured it?

Here is work that can tolerate no incompetence, that calls for constant re-examination of its own findings, and that cannot cover up even its most minute imperfections by a well-chosen phrase. Measured against its purity, all men who are inexact or self-seeking or even decently mediocre stand sharply exposed: mercenary and social-climbing physicians, medical students who prefer rule-of-thumb to the rigors of accurate knowledge, imprecise and talkative uplifters. *Arrowsmith* therefore provides an even clearer statement than *Babbitt* of the case against Babbittry.—THOMAS REED WEST, "Sinclair Lewis: In Affirmation of Main Street," *Flesh of Steel*, 1977, pp. 122–25

⟨. . .⟩ Mr. Lewis is a very considerable person. He has mimetic genius to an extent that has hardly ever been transcended. *Babbitt* as a book was planless; its end arrived apparently because its author had come to the end of the writing-pad, or rather, one might suspect from its length, to the end of all writing-pads then on the market. But George Babbitt was a triumph of impersonation. It was a bit of character-exhibition comparable to Mr. Micawber; and if it be recalled to Mr. Lewis's disadvantage that Dickens invented a host of characters as vivid, it can also be recalled that never did Dickens make so complete an inventory of a human being as Mr. Lewis does in George Babbitt. We know the poor fatuous being in his standing up and his lying down. And so, too, we know Elmer Gantry, this snorting, cringing creature, this offspring of the hippopotamus and the skunk, between whose coarse lips the texts sound as if he were munching sappy vegetation, under whose coarse hands sex becomes a series of gross acts of the body ending in grosser acts of the spirit, such as deceit and cruelty. There are one or two conversations in the book—the scene where he refuses to marry a frightened child who pretends she is going to have his child, the scene where he rushes like a charging pachyderm on his moneyed and insipid bride—when one can hear in one's ears the alternate whine and snarl of the creature, its blind bellow, its canoodling softer tones. How exquisite, too, is his response to Mr. North, the vice-crusader, when that gentleman at last comes across with the long-sought invitation to speak on behalf of the National Association for the Purification of Art and the Press. "Do you suppose you could address the Detroit Y. M. C. A. on October 4?" "Well, it's my wife's birthday, and we've always made rather a holiday of it—we're proud of being an old-fashioned homey family—but I know Cleo wouldn't want that to stand in the way of my doing anything I can to further the Kingdom." How exquisite also are his notes for a sermon:

Love:
a rainbow
AM and PM star
from cradle to tomb
inspires art etc. music voice of love
slam atheists etc. who do not appreciate love.

Since Mr. Lewis has not lost this power of impersonation, since he has on certain pages exercised it even more successfully than he has ever done before, there must be some flaw in the central conception of the book which explains why the effect of the whole is tedious, and why he falls into these tricks of flat writing and lethargic handling of incidents. The sense of tedium must be the result of one's feeling that all these sermons and seductions are leading nowhere. The incompetence must be the result of the author's feeling that the enterprise on which he has embarked is not worth while. The trouble is that the book is not merely the life of a particular individual named Elmer Gantry, it is a satire on organized religion; and Mr. Lewis has neglected a very necessary condition which the satirist must fulfil before he starts working.

What that condition is has probably never been more neatly illustrated than by Yvonne Printemps in the vaudeville prelude of *L'Illusioniste*. She comes forth as the singer and dancer who practises under the *nom de guerre* of—is it Miss Hopkins or Miss Tompkins? It is ten years since I saw the play and I can remember only its essence. It is at any rate an English *nom de guerre*, for she is a second-rater and needs every adventitious aid she can find, and an English singer has an aroma of romance; since all the peoples of the world suspect that their neighbours have been endowed with an intenser life than themselves, and in peace are more alluring, as in war they are more hateful. Assuming this meagre personality, Yvonne Printemps gives a performance that is a satire on nearly all bad singing and dancing; on nearly all bad art of every kind. She cannot let her personality speak for itself. She has to point her youth and prettiness by assuming a baby beauty expression which is superimposed on the real expression into which her innate characteristics and her embarrassment at the present situation have moulded her young flesh, so that the result is confused and ineffective. She lifts up her little voice and it is strangled to a weak pretty pipe in her throat, because she has no clear idea of what sounds she wishes to produce. She importunes the audience, "Listen! Listen! I am being tender! Listen! Listen! In a minute I am going to be even more tender!" Even so her dancing creates no definite effect because she has not previously imagined a pattern woven through the air which she must follow, and her movements are retarded and qualified by this doubt of her enterprise.

Yvonne Printemps is able to do all this because she knows how not to do all this. She is an artist. She paints her personality not by assuming airs and graces, but by eliminating everything that is irrelevant to its effective characteristics. She has so clear a conception of what she wants to do before she does it that her voice and her movements flow in an unimpeded stream of grace towards their goal. Having known from the beginning that she was going to encounter certain crises in her theme, she is able to treat them with absolute justice, not dragging them on before their turn, not intervening between them and the audience by explanatory overemphasis.

It is because she has habitually practised perfection that she is able to anatomize imperfection and imitate it.

That is the first necessary condition which the satirist must fulfil. He must fully possess, at least in the world of the imagination, the quality the lack of which he is deriding in others.

Mr. Lewis does not fulfil that necessary condition of the satirist. He has not entered into imaginative possession of those qualities the lack of which he derides in others. He pillories Elmer Gantry and those who follow him because they are obviously misusing the force that makes men want to speak and to hear speech of religion; but he has no vision of the use they ought to be making of it. The passages in the book which present to one what Mr. Lewis regards as the proper attitude to religion are disconcertingly jejune—are disconcertingly on the same mental plane as Elmer Gantry. There is a St. Francis of Assisi type of good man who worries not at all about theology because of the comfort he can draw for himself and for others from God the Father. But he is perfunctorily described. One seems to hear a flushed and disorderly introduction, "Wancha to meet Father Pengilly. One of the best friens I have." . . . Mr. Lewis's enthusiasm over him is as glib and rootless and meaningless as the getting together of the salesmen of the Pequot Farm Implement Company, which he so masterfully records ("My name's Ad Locust—Jesus, think of it! The folks named me Adney. Can you beat that? Ain't that one hell of a name for a fellow that likes to get out with the boys and have a good time! But you can just call me Ad") and from which he so properly recoils. ⟨. . .⟩

The trouble is that Mr. Lewis is possessed by an idea that in order to combat Babbittry it is necessary to enter into argument with Babbitt; to disprove what he says; to reverse his opinions. This is a profound error which if persisted in would sterilize all radicalism. Babbitt receives pernicious ideas because he is arguing on a plane of thought where it is pretended that life is simpler and coarser than it is, so that our conclusions reached there can be valid in reality. Merely to contradict him is to take up another position in a futile world of fantasy. It is no effective repartee to prohibition to get drunk on Scotch. That is merely to match one crudity with another. But to educate one's perceptions in the direction of ecstasy by taking exactly the right amount of Napoleon brandy, that is an assertion of all that prohibition denies. In the practical world one may have to fight Babbitt when he does something foolish and tyrannous, and it may be the duty of the artist to turn journalist for a second or two and explain to the general public exactly what the silly old fool has been up to. But in the world of art, in the world of intellect, the artist must first raise himself above Babbitt by practising a finer and more complicated mode of thought and feeling. That Mr. Lewis has failed to do. Just as he ends by consorting with little Katie Jonas of the brickyards as an equal, so he approaches Elmer Gantry on his own level. The result of that is that this book will not start any great movement towards enhanced sensitiveness of life, which might make people reject fake religion. It will start a purely factual controversy as to whether parsons do in any large numbers get drunk and toy with their stenographers, which is really a matter of very little importance. Because hypocrisy stinks in the nostrils one is likely to rate it as a more powerful agent for destruction than it is. It is the creatures, with longings so largely and vaguely evil, that they cannot disappoint them by realizing them in the terms afforded by this wholesome world who make the dangerous opposition; as all those must realize who have heard the most famous vice-crusader preach and marked how he got more lustful pleasure out of saying the word "brothel" than any sinner ever got by going to one.

Why has Mr. Lewis produced a book that in spite of its humour, its research, its bravery, has not succeeded in being the satire he has the wit to plan? It is because he has not left himself enough energy to make that ultimate vigorous contraction of the muscles of the soul which is necessary for a work of genius. He has dissipated his forces in going about making the effect of a hand grenade, in throwing up his hat and cheering at floridities of existence that anybody over fourteen ought to take calmly. He has committed himself to pettiness by imitating the futile school of radicalism which finds no game too small and will on occasion waste powder and shot on a silly old woman in Iowa who announces her intention of reading the Bible for the three hundredth time in her life, as if Voltaire would have got anywhere if he had spent his emotions on the pietistic errors of washerwomen in Brittany. If he would sit still so that life could make any deep impression on him, if he would attach himself to the human tradition by occasionally reading a book which would set him a standard of profundity, he could give his genius a chance.—REBECCA WEST, "Sinclair Lewis Introduces Elmer Gantry" (1927), *The Strange Necessity*, 1928, pp. 298–308

I wonder if one could not start a literary journal that should be contributed to solely by the unspoiled readers of books, since, from the standpoint of the novelist, it seems wholly inappropriate that he should criticize the work of his brothers who are, also, inevitably his rivals! However, since the critics are usually too lordly to bother their heads about anything so humble as the inside problems of mere novel-writing, it is difficult to see who is to do that rather necessary job. The most, therefore, that one ought to permit oneself is a friendly hail across space, using the press as it were as a sort of broadcasting apparatus. Then, one may give forth an exposition!

I shall, thus, permit myself to say that I like *Dodsworth* much better than *Elmer Gantry* and that I like Mr. Dodsworth much better than Mr. Babbitt as being the more convincing, the more human and, I daresay, more "felt" by his creator. With an immense admiration for *Babbitt* as a book, I always had behind me the dim feeling that Mr. Babbitt himself was a little of a Robot, moved here and there by his creator in an unimaginably real projection of Main Streets—the landscape, as it were, being in the major chord. Humanly speaking (I am not here attempting literary criticism), this is a relatively wrong way to look at a landscape. The fact is, if you go to look at a landscape or to observe a country you won't much do so, your impressions being too self-conscious; whereas, if you live and are your normal self and, above all, suffer in any given environment, that environment will eat itself into your mind and come back to you in moments of emotion and you will be part of that environment and you will know it. It is because Mr. Dodsworth suffers and endures in odd places all over the European and semi-European world that both he, as a person, and the settings in which he suffers, as settings, seem to me to be very real. Perhaps that is only saying that *Dodsworth* is a poem which *Babbitt* isn't.

Indeed, the title might just as well have been "Europa, an Epic". For Mr. Lewis presents to you practically all of Europe that counts in our civilization, including New York which isn't America. He also poetizes these places so admirably through the emotions of the sympathetic Mr. Dodsworth that when you have finished the book you, too, will have suffered and had your own emotions in the rue de la Paix—genuine emotions and not limited to the fact that in a shoe-shop they tried to charge you one hundred and fifteen francs for paste shoebuckles instead of one hundred francs which is the price on the label. Indeed, I lately heard a lady say that Egypt was a rotten country because you could not get shredded wheat biscuits in Shepherd's Hotel, which was not true at that. I learn from another that Corsica is a bum island because the New York papers could not be had in an obscure mountain village, whereas it is a known fact that the birthplace of Napoleon might as well be sunk beneath the sea, but for American money.

That is the sociological value of *Dodsworth* and the benefit it may do to civilization. Indeed, I think it is safe to say that the superiority of Mr. Lewis as a sociological writer far in advance of others lies in the fact that he has a remarkable gift for rendering and the restraint which keeps him from pointing morals. Of course, his characters do indulge themselves in a great number of expository disquisitions but Mr. Lewis makes it sufficiently clear that he backs neither set of views when they do discourse. Thus, things remain very much as they were at the beginning and the final impression is one of a sort of solidarity of mankind from Altoona to the Adriatic and back.

That is a great achievement and I hope that *Dodsworth* will diffuse itself by the million on both sides of the Atlantic. It will do more to spread a knowledge of the world and its friendliness and freshness and attractions than a wilderness of Baedekers. Besides, it is a good novel, a good story. I found myself towards the end of the book really hoping that the hero might get his young woman—hoping against hope and turning to the last page to make sure. This is the real test—more particularly for a book that is going to do good: for it must be read for itself and the moral must sink in unperceived as do the morals that we draw from life itself. To that end, we must identify ourselves with the characters and live in the scenes.

I found myself, as I have said, hoping that Mr. Dodsworth might have his luck because, subconsciously, I regarded it as an omen that I might have mine; and that is to read a book as one read in the old good days before fifty or so winters and half a century or so of books had besieged these brows. That is the real, unconscious tribute and the real, true, friendly hail! —FORD MADOX FORD, *Bkm*, April 1929, pp. 191–92

You know, immediately, by the mere title ⟨of *It Can't Happen Here*⟩, what the book is about. The energy and vitality and up-to-dateness of the man have got into even his title now. A faint shudder will pass over a good many readers at these words in connection with a novel. I use them only because I can find none better. They are not good words for the purpose. But energy and vitality and up-to-dateness (in the sense I use them) are precisely the qualities which good English novels to-day ought to have and haven't. Above all up-to-dateness. It includes the others. No novelist to-day could be really up-to-date except he had energy and vitality. It doesn't work the other way about. Not a few American novelists have energy and vitality—Hemingway, Faulkner, Saroyan. But they go queer. Where English novelists are simply tired, and go soft, the Americans are fed up, and burst into pieces. Oh to HELL! say the Americans and fling themselves about accordingly. How too bogus! murmurs Evelyn Waugh; Brave new world! snickers Aldous Huxley.

But Sinclair Lewis is the big man of the American novel. He takes the big situation in the two hands of his imagination and grasps it hard. He doesn't try to escape it like his younger American contemporaries, into a world of gun-men and he-men; he doesn't toy curiously with its high-spots of hectic like Waugh, or indulge a weary intelligent pessimism like Huxley; still less is he like Priestley (with whom alone in England for sheer popularity he can be usefully compared) in playing up,

with an instinctive *expertise*, to most that is "wholesome" and rotten in his country. It would indeed be tempting to contrast these two men categorically, and say that Sinclair Lewis is out to shatter precisely that complacency in America which Priestley in England makes it his business to soothe until it purrs.

It's true enough to be worth saying; but it can't be more than half-true. American complacency and English complacency aren't of the same texture. Fundamentally, spiritually, scientifically, they are the same essences; but the manifestations are different. Not even a corresponding genius could batter and shatter our mighty English complacency one half so certainly as Sinclair Lewis pounds the American variety to fragments. There is what the English high-hat would call a certain crudity in the American situation which enabled Lewis to take hold of it. In England the surface is polished, and it's more difficult to get one's claws into it. But since we've got nobody who comes within a hundred miles of making the attempt, or even of seeing that it is necessary to make it, it's not for an Englishman to dwell on the comparison. Wells in the old days could have done it, and Wells in the old days might have wanted to do it. But he has always had a soft spot for minority dictatorships and hundred per cent efficiency. And anyway he's now hinting that there's no more work for a novelist—except scenario-writing.

If that nascent superstition of 1936 needs stifling, Sinclair Lewis's hands have done the work. It seems quite inconceivable to me that the real and effective substance of Sinclair Lewis's novel could be put across to the public on the screen. The satirical quotations from *Zero Hour*, by "Chief" Berzelius Windrip, with which every chapter is headed, are part of the book's flesh and blood. Lose them, and much of its essence is lost. Still more integral to it are the meditations of Doremus Jessup: without them, the book would be a shadow of itself. That does not mean that an effective film could not be based on the book; but it is doubtful whether any conceivable film of the sort would be more than a sensation. The novel is an experience; it is not merely an absorbing story, it is probably the wisest and most human, the most searching and suggestive piece of realistic political thinking that has been done in America or England for a dozen years.

The advent of Hitler (I should guess) set Lewis thinking; the sudden emergence of Huey Long kept him at it. Lewis, unlike the doctrinaire Marxists and "radicals," recognised that Fascism was a mass-movement—not of course a movement of those "masses" which exist (in a state of perpetual movement) in the imagination of enthusiastic revolutionaries; but the real masses of a modern industrialised and capitalist society, the masses that are summed up in the mass-man and whose mind is the mass-mind—the masses for whom the newspapers are written, the films produced, the advertisements designed, and the comic strips drawn. It didn't need Fascism to awaken Sinclair Lewis to the existence of this mass. He had known and studied and described it years before, in *Main Street* and *Babbitt*; one might almost say that he had made its existence and significance the main theme of his fiction.

Sinclair Lewis therefore was infinitely better prepared for the advent of Hitlerism than any of the political prophets or the Marxian economists. I should imagine that the spectacular rise of the Louisiana "Kingfish" was, in reality, no surprise to him. Hence comes the massive significance of his book; it grows out of all his previous work, and has all that work behind its impact. Lewis is not a novelist suddenly changed into a political propagandist. He is the pre-destined delineator of the social mass behind the popular dictatorship which is Fascism.

He has the knowledge of this mass in his bones; one might even, by a licence, say that he is the consciousness of the mass whose sinister potentialities he imaginatively explores. He knows the people who give Fascism its strength far better than the Fascists themselves.

The story is by now familiar to everyone who is likely to read these words. But there must be a word on Sinclair Lewis's conclusion. It is uttered by Doremus Jessup, ex-editor of the Fort Beulah *Daily Informer*, after months of barbarisation in the concentration camp. It arises from a meditation on the change in his Communist friend, Karl Pascal, who grows steadily more fanatical under duress.

> He was afraid that the world struggle to-day was not of Communism against Fascism, but of tolerance against the bigotry that was preached equally by Communism and Fascism. But he saw too that in America the struggle was befogged by the fact that the worst Fascists were they who disowned the word Fascism and preached enslavement to Capitalism under the style of Constitutional and Traditional Native American Liberty. For they were thieves not only of wages but of honour. To their purpose they could quote not only scripture but Jefferson.

> That Karl Pascal should be turning into a zealot, like most of his chiefs in the Communist Party, was grievous to Doremus because he had once simple-heartedly hoped that in the mass strength of Communism there might be an escape from cynical dictatorship. But he saw now that he must remain alone, a "Liberal," scorned by all the noisier prophets for refusing to be a willing cat for the busy monkeys of either side. But at worst, the Liberals, the Tolerant, might in the long run preserve some of the arts of civilisation, no matter which brand of tyranny should finally dominate the world.

> "More and more, as I think about history," he pondered, "I am convinced that everything that is worth while in the world has been accomplished by the free, inquiring, critical spirit, and that the preservation of this spirit is more important than any social system whatsoever. But the men of ritual and the men of barbarism are capable of shutting up the men of science and silencing them forever."

Oddly enough, that final sentence seems to belong to another book. It may possibly be true that the "men of ritual" are equal enemies with "the men of barbarism" to the free spirit. It does not emerge from Mr. Lewis's actual narrative, where he is careful to include Father Perefixe, the Canadian Roman Catholic priest, among the opponents of the tyranny who endure to the end. Even more striking is the curious limitation of "the free, inquiring, critical spirit" to "the men of science." Whether or not it is true that everything worth while in the world has been accomplished by that same spirit—and it is very easy to think of a number of good things, thirteenth-century Gothic included, that were not—it is perfectly certain that everything worth while in the world was not achieved by "the men of science." Nor are "men of science" conspicuously tolerant.

This is a queer twist given to the values heroically maintained by the humane Doremus. He is no man of science; he is just a decent and imaginative human being, as every man should strive, and may hope to be. What Doremus risks his life for, what he endures torture for, is not the freedom of science, but the freedom of men. The freedom of science is part of that freedom; from that freedom it derives. No doubt Mr. Lewis was horribly afraid of being sentimental—this Christian "love" of one's neighbour as oneself is not easy to talk about—but he

would have done better to make Doremus silent than allow him so to circumscribe and belittle the faith which inspires him.

But the problem—which it was none of Mr. Lewis's business as a novelist even to try to answer—for all members of democracies to-day, is how can the growth of this obscure thing be prevented. What Fascism is, is clear enough to any thinking man to-day. It is the deathly change that overtakes Democracy when it cannot, for lack of energy and courage and justice, move expansively forward to the realisation of that social justice which is implicit in the idea of Democracy. Since there is no evidence yet that any Democracy has that power to fulfil itself in Socialism, the possibility of Fascism is always before us. Until some one democratic country has actually pushed forward by the road of peace into the new socialistic order, Fascism must be a perpetual menace. Probably it is, at this actual moment, a greater menace in America than in England. Americans have considerably less respect for law than the English; they have developed a dangerous tolerance for the successful racketeer and gangster; their sense of public morality and civic responsibility is rather badly blunted. I do not think any responsible American, reading Sinclair Lewis's book, would say that the picture was seriously overdrawn. But the question: what is to be done? is not easy to answer; and no responsible Englishman would presume to answer it.

It is evident that Sinclair Lewis believes that the activities of the Communist Party, which is more active, more wealthy, more vocal, and richer in talent, than it is here, have not helped any; they tend rather to lessen that respect for the individual, and to weaken that instinctive repugnance to brutality, on which successful resistance to Fascism must ultimately depend. Once violence has been accepted as normal and legitimate, the most stubborn of the barriers against the mob-violence of Fascism has been broken down. Supposing the discrimination is really possible, the mass of men cannot discriminate between violence for a good end and violence for a bad one; and it cannot be expected that they should. Morality for the majority has to be simple. If you begin to break down the respect for the methods of peace, it is (I think) all up with Socialism under democracy. At all-in politics the other side will surely win; and the simple decent man will be bemused and unconvinced by revolutionary socialists who seem to claim a privilege of violence for themselves.

These are familiar considerations; the conclusion to be drawn from them is less familiar. There is only one firm basis for a radical movement in an advanced democracy—it is the old Christian, or Liberal, or humanist principle, of reverence for the individual. Undermine that basis, discredit that principle, and you are entered on the flowery path that leads to the everlasting bonfire. Yet it is equally certain that that old faith must be revivified; rescued from the contempt brought on it by a century of thug Capitalism waving its banner. Doremus Jessup, in Sinclair Lewis's parable, had to go through hell before the flame burned bright and true in him again. It is to avoid that bitterness that we must strain our energies. The problem in England and America is essentially the same—to rekindle the faith by imagination rather than tribulation. If this is possible, as I must believe, then Sinclair Lewis has done as much as any artist can do towards it. He has written a book which will be read and pondered by every American who is likely to be of service to the cause. If only we had a man in England who could do the same for us!—JOHN MIDDLETON MURRY, "The Hell It Can't," *Adelphi*, March 1936, pp. 322–27

This review of Sinclair Lewis's new novel—*Cass Timberlane*—is, I am afraid, going to be one of those articles in which the reviewer talks about himself, so if this irritates you, you might skip to the middle, where I really get to work on the book. Coming back a month ago to New York after visiting several countries of Europe, I found myself more alienated from the United States than I ever remembered to have been after any similar trip. This may have been due partly to the fact that in Europe I had constantly been thinking how much better off we were at home and had built up an ideal picture, and partly to the fact that making the trip by plane in two days from Naples to New York does not, if you are accustomed to the old-fashioned kind of travel, give you time to prepare yourself for the change from one continent to another. The old reflexes, conditioned by sea voyages, do not tell you that you are home again, and you feel that you are not really there, that the new place in which you seem to have alighted is some sort of simulacrum or mirage. In any case, it was almost like arriving in another foreign country. I noticed characteristics of the Americans of which I had not been aware when I left: they were much larger than Europeans, enormous; their faces seemed lacking in focus and their personalities devoid of flavor; and most of the things that they were doing seemed to me done in a boring way. I had looked forward to picking up my old interests and was baffled and disconcerted when I discovered that these no longer seemed interesting.

Then I saw that I had to make an adjustment quite different from the kind of adjustment that is involved in going abroad and learning one's way about. I already knew my way about at home, yet I could not find the values I had known, the values on which I depended; and I realized that what made the difference was that abroad you were always in the position of a spectator for whom the inhabitants were putting on a show. This show consists of their being foreigners and behaving in a foreign way, and it provides you with entertainment without your needing to do anything yourself. But at home you are no longer in the audience, you have to be one of the actors, and there will not be the old show unless you get back into your rôle. You have to contribute, yourself, to creating the interest and the value, and I was still in the state of mind of the passive looker-on. I had not begun working yet.

At this moment I read Sinclair Lewis, and I appreciated him in certain ways as I had never done before and as I perhaps should not otherwise have done. We have had Lewis around for so long, so consistently being himself, that he has become a familiar object, like Henry Ford or the Statue of Liberty, about which, if one has been living in America, one does not think very much. Up to his novel before this last one, I had not read him for years, and had heard little about him except routine complaints that he was repeating himself or going to pot. I did read his book before last, *Gideon Planish*, because I had heard it was about foundations and I had had enough experience of foundation workers to want to see Sinclair Lewis turned loose on them. *Gideon Planish* was an extremely funny caricature, and I saw that Lewis's writing had improved: he moved more swiftly, made his points with less effort, and had mastered a not common art of introducing colloquial American, with style, into literary prose. But I found in his new book, *Cass Timberlane*, some qualities that were new to me and that I had not expected. Lewis has returned to Minnesota to live and he has written about a small Middle Western city in a way that is quite distinct from anything in *Main Street* or *Babbitt*. These northern Middle Western cities, with their big lakes and their raw business buildings, their gloomy old houses of the eighties

that run to fancy windows and towers, and their people playing bridge and drinking cocktails, kept warm by a new oil furnace, in the midst of their terrific winters, have a peculiar impressiveness and pathos which is sometimes rather hard to account for in terms of their constituent elements but which, despite all the crassness and dullness, is inherent in the relation of the people to the country. This Lewis has got into his novel. Gopher Prairie, of *Main Street*, he hated; Zenith, of *Babbitt*, he ridiculed; but Grand Republic, Minnestoa, the scene of *Cass Timberlane*, has really been lived in and loved. And the book made me feel, when I read it, that I was back in touch with home again and made me realize that Sinclair Lewis, in spite of his notorious faults, is one of the people in the literary field who do create interest and value, that he has still gone on working at this when many others have broken down or quit, and that he is, in fact, at his best—what I never quite believed before—one of the national poets.

And what about the story itself? It is a story about a husband and wife and is very much the same sort of thing as such novels as H. G. Wells's *Marriage* and Arnold Bennett's *These Twain*, of the literary era in which Lewis grew up and to which he still more or less belongs. A judge in his early forties, a serious and upright man, falls in love with and succeeds in marrying a girl in her early twenties, pretty, clever, and rather perverse. They do all the usual things—there are clashes of taste and interest, quarrels and reconciliations, she has flirtations with other men and he makes her jealous scenes, she gives birth to a baby, which dies, and has a period of ill health and depression. When she recovers, he takes her to New York, and there she is unfaithful to him with an old friend turned city slicker. Back in middle-class Grand Republic, she decides that she will divorce the Judge and marry the other man, but when she goes to New York, she finds out that her lover has never taken her seriously. She falls ill; the Judge comes on and rescues her and takes her back to Grand Republic. She has learned to appreciate her husband and is prepared to like their neighbors better, and we assume that all will now go well.

What is new in Sinclair Lewis's picture is an attempt on the author's part to deal with a typical bright young woman of the forties, so different from the emancipated woman of the earlier decades of the century, the "Woman Who Did," that heroine who dared to get herself a job or be a social or political worker or desert her conventional husband for the unconventional man she loved. The new young girl wants to compete with the man without learning any trade, is rebellious against marriage but does not want a job, leaves her husband but does not stick to her lover. Lewis is trying to get hold of this type, and his perception of social phenomena is always alert and sharp; but the truth is that he does not like Jinny, is too old-fashioned, perhaps, to sympathize with her. He works hard to make her attractive, but her relentless cuteness and cleverness always sound off key and self-conscious. Does he know how obnoxious he has made her? At one point he remarks that if the Judge had not been so much in love, he might not have cared for her whimsicality; and we have an uncomfortable feeling that if the author changed his tone only a little, we should get one of his frank female caricatures, like the wife of Gideon Planish. Here is Jinny being cute in Florida: "Jinny eyed the crêpe myrtle, the roses, the obese wonder of a grapefruit growing, and looked at the Cass who had worked this magic for her. 'My Merlin!' she said." And here she is being clever on the subject of their going to New York: The Judge says, " 'We'll pick up New York and shake it.' 'Oh, but that headwaiter at the Marmoset Club, with eyes like a wet old dishrag, who looks at you just once and guesses exactly what your income is, and do you know any Astors.' 'Maybe we'd get to know a few Class B Astors, if we wanted to, which I doubt.' 'I'd love to know *lots* of Astors—big fat juicy ones, and little diamond-studded ones in sables!' . . . 'Jinny, you shall have all the Astors you want. Have Astors with your corn flakes.' 'And cream.' 'And extra cream, from the Ritz. God knows even a very rich Astor or Vanderbilt or Morgan, one nine feet tall with a robe made of securities, couldn't be more chilly than our local John William Prutts. Let's look their lodge over. I mean, before we actually decide whether I ever shall resign, I think we ought to go to New York and study it, to see whether, if we had a real home of our own there, we wouldn't enjoy the place.' 'And Cleo?' 'Naturally.'"

Cleo is an intolerable kitten, who goes all through the book and reflects the moods of their marriage.

The ending is absolutely Victorian. Lewis stacks the cards against Jinny by making her lover such a cold-hearted scoundrel—he has the currish name of Bradd Criley—as has hardly been seen in serious fiction for a century, and he has her develop diabetes so that she will become a chronic invalid. Scorned by her seducer and confined to her bed, she has no choice but to go home with the Judge, and Lewis evades the problem of finding out what such a girl would do if she were well and had pleasanter friends. He leaves her reading *Dombey & Son*, where, in the story of Edith Dombey and Carker, she must have found a singular parallel to the destiny which her creator has invented for her.

But with Judge Timberlane, Sinclair Lewis is much better. Here he has something he intimately knows, and the Judge in relation to his town is really thoroughly and admirably done. The most satisfactory section of the book is the early part, in which we see Timberlane, divorced from his first, worthless wife, living alone in his sombre house, hearing cases and dining with friends, working out chess problems at home, and discovering the birdlike young girl, living among the local Bohemia, whom he is passionate enough to pursue but not young enough or supple enough to meet on her own ground. The best and subtlest thing in the novel is the effect, on the Judge's behavior with his wife and his treacherous friend, of the conception of justice and individual rights to which he has trained himself in the law. Judge Timberlane, too, in his personal as well as in his official life, is creating interest and value for his less conscious and responsible neighbors.

These neighbors, the social organism of Grand Republic, are shown not only in relation to the Timberlanes but also by a series of brief histories, interspersed through the book, of the married lives of certain selected citizens. Some are funny, some are touching, some are implausible or superficial. But the general effect is successful. These sketches build up the community and serve to set the Timberlanes off. Nor can it nowadays be said of Lewis—as Sherwood Anderson used to do—that he does not see inside his characters and appreciate their human merits. He does not slight their commonness and ugliness any more than he did in *Main Street*, but Grand Republic, Minnesota, is a place in which one can imagine living, not, like Main Street, a circle of Hell.—EDMUND WILSON, "Salute to an Old Landmark: Sinclair Lewis," NY, Oct. 13, 1945, pp. 98–104

---

E. M. FORSTER
"Sinclair Lewis" (1929)
*Abinger Harvest*
1936, pp. 129–36

"I would like to see Gopher Prairie," says the heroine of Mr. Sinclair Lewis's *Main Street*, and her husband

promptly replies: "Trust me. Here she is. Brought some snapshots down to show you." That, in substance, is what Mr. Lewis has done himself. He has brought down some snapshots to show us and posterity. The collection is as vivid and stimulating as any writer who adopts this particular method can offer. Let us examine it; let us consider the method in general. And let us at once dismiss the notion that any fool can use a camera. Photography is a great gift, whether or not we rank it as an art. If we have not been to Gopher Prairie we cry: "So that's it!" on seeing the snap. If we have been we either cry: "How like it!" or "How perfectly disgraceful, not the least like it!" and in all three cases our vehemence shows that we are in the presence of something alive.

I have never been to Gopher Prairie, Nautilus, Zenith, or any of their big brothers and sisters, and my exclamations throughout are those of a non-American, and worthless as a comment on the facts. Nevertheless, I persist in exclaiming, for what Mr. Lewis has done for myself and thousands of others is to lodge a piece of a continent in our imagination. America, for many of us, used to mean a very large apron, covered with a pattern of lozenges, edged by a frill, and chastely suspended by a boundary tape round the ample waist of Canada. The frill, like the tape, we visualized slightly; on the New York side it puckered up into skyscrapers, on the farther side it was a blend of cinemas and cowboys, and more or less down the middle of the preposterous garment we discerned a pleat associated with the humour of Mark Twain. But the apron proper, the lozenges of pale pink and pale green—they meant nothing at all: they were only something through which railways went and dividends occasionally came from, and which had been arbitrarily spattered with familiar names, like a lunar landscape. As we murmured "Syracuse, Cairo, London even, Macon, Memphis, Rochester, Plymouth," the titles, so charged with meaning in their old settings, cancelled each other out in their new, and helped to make the apron more unreal. And then Sinclair Lewis strode along, developed his films, and stopped our havering. The lozenges lived. We saw that they were composed of mud, dust, grass, crops, shops, clubs, hotels, railway stations, churches, universities, etc., which were sufficiently like their familiar counterparts to be real, and sufficiently unlike them to be extremely exciting. We saw men and women who were not quite ourselves, but ourselves modified by new surroundings, and we heard them talk a language which we could usually, but not always, understand. We enjoyed at once the thrills of intimacy and discovery, and for that and much else we are grateful, and posterity will echo our gratitude. Whether he has "got" the Middle West, only the Middle West can say, but he has made thousands of people all over the globe alive to its existence, and anxious for further news. Ought a statue of him, camera in hand, to be erected in every little town? This, again, is a question for the Middle West.

Let us watch the camera at work:

In the flesh, Mrs. Opal Emerson Mudge fell somewhat short of a prophetic aspect. She was pony-built and plump, with the face of a haughty Pekinese, a button of a nose, and arms so short that, despite her most indignant endeavours, she could not clasp her hands in front of her as she sat on the platform waiting.

Angus Duer came by, disdainful as a greyhound, and pushing on white gloves (which are the whitest and the most superciliously white objects on earth) . . .

At the counter of the Greek Confectionary Parlour, while they [i.e., the local youths] ate dreadful messes of decayed bananas, acid cherries, whipped cream, and gelatinous ice cream, they screamed to one another: "Hey, lemme 'lone," "Quit dog-gone you, looka what you went and done, you almost spilled my glass swater," "Like hell I did," "Hey, gol darn your hide, don't you go sticking your coffin-nail in my i-scream."

She saw that his hands were not in keeping with a Hellenic face. They were thick, roughened with needle and hot iron and plough handle. Even in the shop he persisted in his finery. He wore a silk shirt, a topaz scarf, thin tan shoes.

The drain pipe was dripping, a dulcet and lively song: drippety-drip-drip-dribble; drippety-drip-drip-drip.

The method throughout is the photographic. Click, and the picture's ours. A less spontaneous or more fastidious writer would have tinkered at all of the above extracts, and ruined everything. The freshness and vigour would have gone, and nothing been put in their places. For all his knowingness about life, and commercially-travelled airs, Mr. Lewis is a novelist of the instinctive sort, he goes to his point direct. There is detachment, but not of the panoramic type: we are never lifted above the lozenges, Thomas Hardy fashion, to see the townlets seething beneath, never even given as wide a view as Arnold Bennett accords us of his Five Towns. It is rather the detachment of the close observer, of the man who stands half a dozen yards off his subject, or at any rate within easy speaking distance of it, and the absence of superiority and swank (which so pleasantly characterizes the books) is connected with this. Always in the same house or street as his characters, eating their foodstuffs, breathing their air, Mr. Lewis claims no special advantages; though frequently annoyed with them, he is never contemptuous, and though he can be ironic and even denunciatory, he has nothing of the aseptic awfulness of the seer. Neither for good nor evil is he lifted above his theme; he is neither a poet nor a preacher, but a fellow with a camera a few yards away.

Even a fellow with a camera has his favourite subjects, as we can see by looking through the Kodak-albums of our friends. One amateur prefers the family group, another bathing-scenes, another his own house taken from every possible point of view, another cows upon an alp, or kittens held upside down in the arms of a black-faced child. This tendency to choose one subject rather than another indicates the photographer's temperament. Nevertheless, his passion is for photography rather than for selection, a kitten will serve when no cows are present, and, if I interpret Mr. Lewis correctly, we must not lay too much stress on his attitude to life. He has an attitude; he is against dullness, heartiness and intolerance, a trinity of evils most closely entwined; he mistrusts Y.M.C.A. helpfulness and rotarian idealism; while as for a positive creed (if we can accept *Martin Arrowsmith* as an unaided confession of faith) he believes in scientific research. "So many men, Martin, have been kind and helpful, so few have added to knowledge," complains the old bacteriologist. One can safely class him with writers termed "advanced," with people who prefer truth to comfort, passion to stability, prevention to cure. But the classification lets what is most vital in him escape; his attitude, though it exists, does not dwell in the depths of his being. His likes and dislikes mean less to him than the quickness of his eye, and though he tends to snapshot muscular Christians when they are attacked with cramp, he would sooner snap them amid clouds of angels than not at all. His commentary on society is constant, coherent, sincere; yet the reader's eye follows the author's eye rather than his voice, and when Main Street is quitted it is not its narrowness, but its existence that remains as a permanent possession.

His method of book-building is unaffected and appropriate. In a sense (a very faint sense) his novels are tales of unrest. He takes a character who is not quite at ease in his or her surroundings, contrives episodes that urge this way or that, and a final issue of revolt or acquiescence. In his earlier work both character and episodes are clear-cut; in his later—but let us postpone for a moment the painful problem of a photographer's old age. Carol Endicott, the heroine of his first important book, is a perfect medium, and also a living being. Her walks down Main Street are overwhelming; we see the houses, we see her against them, and when the dinginess breaks and Erik Valborg arises with his gallant clothes and poet's face, we, too, are seduced, and feel that such a world might well be lost for love. Never again is Mr. Lewis to be so poignant or to arrange his simple impressions so nearly in the order of high tragedy; "I may not have fought the good fight, but I have kept the faith" are Carol's final words, and how completely are they justified by all she has suffered and done! Babbitt follows her—of grosser clay, and a native while she was an exile, but even Babbitt sees that there is something better in life than graft and goodfellowship, though he acquiesces in them at the close. Martin Arrowsmith succeeds where Carol and Babbitt failed, because he is built strongly and prepared to sacrifice a home, but, regarded as a medium, he is identical with them, he can register their doubts and difficulties. And the same is true of Elmer Gantry; his heavy feet are turned to acquiescence from the first, but he, too, has moments of uneasiness, and hypocrisy; religious eroticism and superstition can be focussed through him. And so with Samuel Dodsworth in *Dodsworth*. He reacts this way and that among the main streets of Europe, and many pictures of them can be taken before he decides that they will not do.

Now, in the earlier books this method was a complete success, but with *Elmer Gantry* doubts begin; the theme is interesting, but the snapshots less remarkable. And in *Dodsworth* doubt becomes dismay. Dodsworth is a decent citizen of Zenith who retires early and goes to Europe with his wife. She is cultivated and snobby—a *rechauffée* of the second Mrs. Arrowsmith, but served upon an enormous dish. She talks, talks, flirts, patronizes, talks, and he, humble and observant, gradually realizes her inadequacies, but all the time he talks, talks, talks. The talk is rhetoric, the slang tired, the pictures blurred. The English country church, palace at Venice, restaurant at Paris, journey in an aeroplane, Bernese Oberland, back in New York, the right sort of American tourist, the wrong sort, is there a right sort, is it wrong to think there is a right sort? . . . on the story trundles, unprofitably broadminded and with unlucky thematic parallels to Henry James. The method remains, but something has died. The following quotations will show us what:

> He found that in certain French bathrooms one can have hot water without waiting for a geyser. He found that he needn't have brought two dozen tubes of his favourite (and very smelly) toothpaste from America—one actually could buy toothpaste, corn-plaster, New York Sunday papers, Bromo-Seltzer, Lucky Strikes, safety razor blades, and ice cream almost as easily in Paris as in the United States; and a man he met in Luigi's bar insisted that if one quested earnestly enough he could find B.V.D.'s.

What has happened? What has changed the Greek Confectionery Parlour at Gopher Prairie, where every decaying banana mattered, to this spiritless general catalogue? The explanation is all too plain: photography is a pursuit for the young. So long as a writer has the freshness of youth on him, he can work the snap-shot method, but when it passes he has nothing to fall back upon. It is here that he differs from the artist. The artist has the power of retaining and digesting experiences, which, years later, he may bring forth in a different form; to the end of life he is accompanied by a secret store.

The artist may not be good. He may be very bad. He generally is. And it is not to celebrate him and to decry the photographer that I draw this distinction between them. But it does explain, I think, why quick spontaneous writers (the kind that give me more pleasure than any) are apt, when they lose their spontaneity, to have nothing left, and to be condemned by critics as superficial. They are not superficial, they are merely not artistic; they are members of a different profession, the photographic, and the historian of our future will cease to worry over this, will pick up the earlier and brighter volumes in which their genius is enshrined, and will find there not only that genius, but a record of our age.

Mr. Lewis is not our sole photographer. There is always Mr. H. G. Wells. They have just the same gift of hitting off a person or place in a few quick words; moreover, they share the same indifference to poetry, and pass much the same judgments on conduct. Consequently, one might have expected that their literary careers would be similar, that the authors of *Love and Mr. Lewisham* and *Main Street* would develop in the same way and at the same rate. They have diverged, and for an instructive reason. Wells is still kicking because photography was only one of his resources. When his early freshness wore off, he could bring into play his restless curiosity about the universe, and thus galvanize his later novels into life. In Mr. Lewis, curiosity about the universe has never been very strong. Only occasionally has he thought of the past, the future, international relationships, science, labour, the salvation or damnation of the globe. The people in the room and the houses across the street are what really interest him, and when the power to reproduce them sharply fails, he has nothing to do except to reproduce them dimly. If this view of his development is correct, the later stages of it are bound to be disappointing. However, there the early books are, done, safe, mankind's for ever; also, the longer one lives, the less important does "development" appear.

## JAMES BRANCH CABELL
### "Goblins in Winnemac"
*Some of Us: An Essay in Epitaphs*
1930, pp. 61–73

I perceive some merit in Sinclair Lewis, even though I fail to detect it upon the grounds usually advanced. People who ought to know a great deal better will tell you that Sinclair Lewis has portrayed many aspects of our American life. In fact, when *Babbitt* and *Main Street* were but lately included in the library presented to President Herbert C. Hoover, it was upon the tactless ground, as stated by one of the selectors, that "the reading of them will help a man to understand the temperament of the American people." I put aside the ineluctable inference—as being an over-blunt if unintentional criticism of our first British President's conduct in office,—and I remark merely that I do not think the statement itself is true.

I shall come back to that. Meanwhile, in whatsoever milieu, Mr. Lewis throughout the deceased 'twenties dealt incessantly with one single problem: whether or not it is better to do that which seems expected? As long ago as in the autumn of 1920, in *Main Street*, the question was raised whether Carol Kennicott should or should not conform to what Gopher

Prairie expected? The question was given perhaps its most nearly classic form in *Babbitt*, wherein the protagonist fidgets before this problem, of conforming or of not conforming, in connection with well-nigh all departments of life as it is led in Zenith the Zip City. Then Mr. Lewis turned to the especial variant of the same problem as it concerns the scientist, in *Arrowsmith*; in *Elmer Gantry* he brought the minister of the gospel face to face with this problem; and finally, in 1929, he confronted Sam Dodsworth with the problem (already touched upon in *Mantrap*) of conforming or of not conforming to that which seemed expected in—of all avocations—the pursuit of pleasure.

Very much as Ellen Glasgow has been haunted perpetually by the question, What should a woman do before the idiocy of male notions? so has Sinclair Lewis, I think, been beset for at least ten years by the kindred problem, What should a man do before the idiotic notions of other men? In brief, do the inhabitants of Zenith and Monarch and Sparta and Banjo Crossing, or of any other community in Winnemac, pay the more dearly for living as self-determining individuals or as conformists to their neighbors' communal follies?

Mr. Lewis does not ever answer that question outright: but he does very insistently compel his readers to cast about for an answer. Time and again Sinclair Lewis has exalted the bravery if not precisely the wisdom of individualism by the roundabout method of depicting the conformist. There is, he has discovered, a great deal of humbug and stupidity and viciousness going about masked as the correct thing to do in every walk of life as life speeds in Winnemac, the home of manly men and of womanly women and of other Regular Guys. And Mr. Lewis portrays with loving abhorrence superb monsters, now and then a bit suggestive of human beings, who make the very best (in an entirely utilitarian sense) of this humbug and of this stupidity and of this viciousness, to enhance their own moral standing and bank accounts.

I said, he portrays. Yet Sinclair Lewis is far too opulently gifted to have to plagiarize his manly men and his womanly women from the life about him. He has turned instead—compelled it may be by those freakish planets which ruled over the date of his birth,—to commemorate a more striking race. I perhaps can best explain my meaning by reminding you that upon 7 February 1812 was born at Portsmouth, in England, the discoverer of that gnome-like United States of America which, when young Martin Chuzzlewit visited it in 1842, was inhabited by Colonel Diver (of the *Rowdy Journal*) and Mr. Jefferson Brick and Major Cyrus Choke and Mr. Lafayette Kettle and the Honorable Elijah Pogram, and by yet other of the most remarkable goblins in the country,—a discomfortable country that clung with untirable lungs "to the Palladium of rational Liberty," in government of the people by the people. All these, we know, are superb and somewhat sinister grotesques which were not, as we likewise know, in 1842 or at any other instant, the least bit "true to life," but which none the less in 1930 continue exuberantly to live. I would remind you also that just seventy-three years after the birth of Charles Dickens, upon 7 February 1885, was born at Sauk Centre, in Minnesota, the portrayer of Almus Pickerbaugh and Vergil Gunch and Elmer Gantry and Chum Frink and scores of still other superb yet somewhat sinister grotesques. Their names alone, not altogether of this sunlit earth, but cacophonous and grating and darkly gnome-like, betray the origin which their conduct confirms. These are most plainly the elvish grandchildren, upon the distaff side, of that unhuman race encountered by Martin Chuzzlewit, Jr., during his exile to an uncanny land not ever again visited, I believe, by any other tourist until

Sinclair Lewis went a-wayfaring on faery seas and in 1920 discovered Winnemac.

I am far from suggesting that this shared birthday has made of Mr. Lewis our American Dickens. In fact, to describe any author whatsoever as "the American So-and-So" is the hall-mark of those whom an education beyond their mental means has but enabled to express their entire lack of ideas grammatically. Then, too, not even that kindred ever-present humorousness which flickers through the writings of both men, like incessant heat lightnings, should blind us to the fact that in fundamentals no writers differ more decisively.

In every book by Dickens the backbone of all is optimism and a fixed faith that by-and-by justice and candor will prevail. No reader of *Martin Chuzzlewit* believes for one paragraph that Martin and Mark Tapley may perhaps not win safely through the troll-haunted America to which they have been temporarily exiled. They are but taking part in a very old form of fairy tale, in which a particular room may not be entered by the human hero, or a magic broom be touched, or a pomegranate be tasted, except at the cost of his eternal slavery in goblin land. The goblins, that is, will get you if you don't watch out. They will get you if you enter the room they suggest or eat the pomegranates they offer you in profusion. But the firm of Chuzzlewit & Tapley, as we well know, travel in the cause of conventional righteousness: it follows, in Dickens' philosophy, as indeed it usually follows in actual life, that the pair will in due course be provided with monetary competence and acceptable brides. They will escape, in fine, from the goblins—just as in all fairy tales the heroes lightly escape, by the simple process of not conforming to that which the goblins urge them to do,—and somewhere in the neighborhood of the Blue Dragon Inn, near Salisbury, they will enter into a future of generally unalloyed bliss wherein will figure no Major Cyrus Choke and no Honorable Elijah Pogram.

The doctrine of Mr. Lewis would seem to run quite the other way. In book after book he has presented one or another individualist at least as truly heroic as ever was young Martin Chuzzlewit, and an individualist who, in opposing the solicitations of the elvish burghers of Winnemac, remains theoretically in the right, but who ends as a rule in material ruin and who ends always in defeat. I shall not labor this point, because Mr. Lewis himself does not make much of it. He does but indicate, by sketching lightly the career of a Frank Shallard or of a Max Gottleib, the truism that in Winnemac as elsewhere the opponent of any communal folly is in for a bad time of it. These adventurers find that the old recipe, of not conforming to that which the goblins urge them to do, is of no least avail to deliver them from the goblins of Winnemac. Instead, the Rev. Dr. Elmer Gantry and the Honorable Almus Pickerbaugh are with them to the very end, in some not unfriendly bewilderment as to why the poor mutt should have opposed the *mores* of Winnemac when he could so easily have made use of these fantasies to enhance his moral standing and his bank account.

This is a tragedy, I repeat, which Mr. Lewis does but indicate. His real interest turns otherwhither as though bewitched by the quaintness of the commonplace. It remains fascinated by the conformist and by the droll ways of his goblin flourishing (wherein timidity turns to sound money and lies become limousines) at the cost of intellectual and spiritual ruin. The individualist is lost in a world made over-safe for democracy; and the conformist becomes not worth saving. That is the doctrine which informs all the derisive apologues Sinclair Lewis has fetched out of Winnemac. That is, in one sense, the powder which speeds his every shot at our polity. In another sense it is the powder disguised in the succulent jam of his caricatures.

So it has been throughout the ten years since Mr. Lewis first toyed with his pet problem in Gopher Prairie. He then told us, with a mendacity which time and his later books have coöperated to expose, that Gopher Prairie was a small town in Minnesota. We all know now that Gopher Prairie—like Zenith and Monarch and Sparta and Banjo Crossing, and like every other place that Mr. Lewis has written about since 1920,—is a portion of the grotesque and yet always rather sinister, strange goblin land of Winnemac.

I delight in Winnemac and in all its citizenry: yet it is, as I have suggested, with very much the same pleasure I derive from Dickens. That pleasure is, to the one side, somewhat the pleasure I get from the "Mr. and Mrs." cartoons in the Sunday paper and from Amos and Andy over the radio, and (to the other side) from a great deal of Molière and Swift and Aristophanes and Lucian,—the pleasure, that is, of seeing a minim of reality exaggerated into Brobdingnagian incredibility. There is apparent in each that single grain of truth which has budded, through more or less skilled and patient gardening, into this gaudy efflorescence of the impossible. The seed explains the flowering: but it is the flowering which counts, and which charms. So when I hear Sinclair Lewis classed as a "realist," it is with something of the same wonderment in which I have heard that he lives, along with Messrs. Dreiser and Cabell and Anderson, in a never lifting atmosphere of despair and frustration. Each of these critical clichés has very often tempted me, I admit, toward just that quiet and ambiguous giving-out of a sedate "Well, well, we know," or of an "If we but list to speak," which the one Prince of Denmark to attain any international fame so justly reprobates.

All that, though, is extraneous, in addition to being only a matter of faith. If you can believe in the "realism" of Sinclair Lewis it will give you a great deal more of comfort than does any other "realism." For my part, I can but protest that I very heartily enjoy his books without any more believing in Almus Pickerbaugh and Elmer Gantry and the other hobgoblins as persons whom one may hope to encounter in our imperfect world than I can believe (after any such literal fashion) in Joe and Vi, or in Jefferson Brick and Colonel Diver, or, for that matter, in Bottom and Caliban.

Meanwhile if, as one hears freely nowadays, Sinclair Lewis is obsolescent, and his books are doomed, the trouble is not merely that the United States is due to lose one of its most interesting commonwealths, in the State of Winnemac. For one really wonders what in the world is to be done about George Follansbee Babbitt? Just eight years ago this Babbitt emigrated from 401 pages of a novel into the racial consciousness of mankind. He is one of those satisfying large symbols which at long intervals some author hits upon, and which promptly take on a life that is not confined to the books wherein they first figured. Babbitt is in train, I think, to become one of those myths which rove forever through the irrational Marches of Antan, and about which writers not yet born will weave their own pet stories as inevitably as writers will continue to concern themselves with Faust and Don Juan and the Brown God Pan.

None of us "new humanists" may kill Babbitt. Babbitt thrives not merely through the art of selling houses for more than the people of Zenith can afford to pay for them. He graces yet other sound business enterprises everywhere: his voice is heard in our legislative assemblies, nor is it silent in Wall Street: his matured opinions upon political matters have been known to issue even from the White House. He writes the most of our books: he reviews all of them. He shapes each law by which our lives are governed, and he instructs us too how to evade these laws: not even in death may we look to escape from Babbitt, for then to the one side of us shall sit Babbitt the physician and to the other side Babbitt the clergyman, each pottering over our last needs in that dark hour. The natural grief of our heirs and assigns he will forthwith capitalize in the form of a fat overcharge for our coffins: and about a year later, when once the grave has settled down cosily, then Babbitt will be engraving our tombstones with the most exalted sentiments of his own smug selecting. Babbitt cannot ever perish so long as all good Americans cling (in Colonel Diver's fine phrase) to the Palladium, in government of the people by the people, and the perturbed neighbors cling in self-protection to their sense of humor. There is something of Babbitt in every one of us.

Moreover, this Babbitt is no parvenu born only eight years ago. He had existed since time's youth; and Mr. Lewis did but serve as his literary sponsor in an oddly belated christening. George Follansbee Babbitt, as Walter Pater has phrased it, is older than the rocks he quarries into building material. For Babbitt, also, has trafficked for strange webs with Eastern merchants. His was the presence which rose so strangely beside the waters to further the commercial supremacy of Tyre, and Carthage, and Liverpool. Under the alias of Marco Polo, as was lately shown us, he has established satisfactory business relations with the Khan of Cathay; and as Cristoforo Colombo, he has looked for a paying traffic route into India. He has gone well-greaved against Troy, at the behest of the Greek draft laws; he has shouted "Crucify him!" in Jerusalem; he has burned Jews in Seville, and he has hanged witches in Salem, as conscientiously as he fetched back from his unwillingly attended Crusades only the syphilis. And all this, to that level head upon which all the ends of the world are come, all this has been to Babbitt, not quite as the sound of liars and brutes, but merely that which seemed expected of him, or of any other level-headed Regular Guy, in his then present circumstances.

### CESARE PAVESE
From "An American Novelist, Sinclair Lewis" (1930)
*American Literature: Essays and Opinions*
tr. Edwin Fussell
1970, pp. 6–29

The richness and the variety of Lewis' world reside in the innumerable attitudes with which he contemplates the spectacle of the daily human revolt against environment and self. And the spectacle makes him smile. In their insatiable timidity, men are comical. And the environment that oppresses them is both comical and grotesque. But sometimes, by virtue of a rebel who acts more seriously than the others or who reflects the common aspirations in a more universal way, the scene becomes tragic. Still, these outbursts of anguish are not the knowing contrivances of a contrapuntal novelist: sometimes, even (in *Elmer Gantry*), they destroy the harmony of the work. The author of *Babbitt* always begins with an amused and mocking tone. Usually he wants to make of all the characters a series of whimsical little men and women, slightly ridiculous, slightly sad. He does not want to have the naive air of taking such types seriously; but every so often it happens, and, in *Main Street*, in *The Job*, everywhere, he comes out with more heartfelt sentences, he contradicts himself, he believes, and he admires. For plainly he himself is the rebel described and all his character types are only the innumerable faces of his ego.

Thus it happens that he smiles and laughs, but always in the end caresses the victim with his sorrowful glance. For this reason, as we shall see, *Babbitt* turned out to be the masterpiece: in him, better than in any other character, Lewis fused the preposterous puppet with the human brother whom we must feel sorry for.

Sinclair Lewis is himself the rebel portrayed in the novels. The little man who suffocates and pants for air and doesn't even know what he wants or where he is going, or rather, continually discovers new avenues but argues and struggles with himself, perpetually in flight, is of course the figure of himself which we are permitted to glimpse between the lines. A curious phenomenon of his books illustrates this instability of his spirit: all the human types and backgrounds which in one place he ridicules he elsewhere delights in, he approves of them, he is moved by them. For example, the situation of the customary city dweller who is going to make an excursion to get close to nature—roughing it, as they say, living and laboring in the open air—occurs twice, at least, in two novels, *Bobbitt* and *Mantrap*. In the first, the attempt is viewed gaily, humorously, with typical Paul Riesling, half absorbed and half hysterical. In the second, the trip to Canada is a spiritual victory wherein Ralph Prescott has nothing comical about him, and he even manages, without becoming ridiculous, to wear the moccasins which would yield such comedy on the flabby feet of Babbitt. Gopher Prairie, the town that in *Main Street* Lewis excommunicated and described as not only grotesque but unbearable in its vulgarity, becomes in *Free Air* an interesting Western stopover where even the traveling salesmen are sympathetically treated. And the drinking that in *Arrowsmith* is practically acceptable in the emigrants of St. Hubert, who think they are now going home, is revolting in Eddie Schwirtz in *The Job*.

All these uncertainties of judgment which, in any case, ought to be gratefully accepted, since with them our author has multiplied the variety of his situations, are reflected in the last and most comprehensive uncertainty of all, that uncertainty through which Sinclair Lewis, the most knowing expert of slang and the American vernacular[1] now writing in the United States, and the first and most determined to derive from it artistic results, condemns, in effect, his own glory, making slang the characteristic of his most vulgar personages and calling attention to the fact: "slangy" and "backslapping" are the attributes of Schwirtz (*The Job*) and Schmaltz (*The Man Who Knew Coolidge*). But gradually this conventional judgment fades before the down-to-earth quality of the man's nature and origins, before his irresistible passion for the genuine and the powerful, and he ends in the creation of two superb figures, sturdy and full-blooded, sympathetic though theatrical, who are also, to return to our starting point, great drinkers: G. Sondelius (*Arrowsmith*) and Elmer Gantry ⟨. . .⟩

With *Main Street*, Lewis set out to show—polemically, fulminating against certain tyrannies imposed upon his youth—that reverse side of the picture of the Middle West that he has been painting ever since. *Main Street* is not badly written. The art of the novel is scrupulously observed. There is characterization, there is setting, there is unity, there are dramatic moments, there is even catharsis. And it brought fame to its author. Still, *Main Street* is boring. It is polemic. It is a long bill of particulars. It is a caricature without a smile. After reading the pages that describe all that moral meanness, we are willing to say: Yes, Sinclair Lewis is right. But Carol's torment, at which the author implacably hammers page after page, for four hundred and fifty pages, in the end tells us nothing further.

As for the things that are more entertaining, after a while

we notice that they have nothing to do with the center of the book. There are even characters or situations from the preceding books, Bjornstam, for example, the village atheist and socialist, alter ego of Bone Stillman of Joralemon in *The Trail of the Hawk*. Or (the usual irony) they are not that reverse side of the Middle West at which the author is supposed to be looking, but are instead portraits that in some way still represent and exalt their native land: they are, for example, reflections of the happy-go-lucky tramps, the vagabonds, of *Free Air* and *The Innocents*, Pinky from the former and Crook from the latter. The entire book resembles that stroll which Carol takes by herself, when she arrives at Gopher Prairie, along Main Street and side streets, where the author keeps slipping in tendentious descriptions and remarks on the houses and shops that are seen. The only interesting moment in Carol—after her first appearance, of course—is the change in her spirit following her encounter with Erik Valbord: if she can't succeed in reforming a city, she wants at least to refine a man. This is human, and so is the adventure of Fern Mullins, the scatterbrained young schoolmistress. But nothing else is poetry. It is, as I said, a bill of particulars. And it is boring.

Despite all this, *Main Street* marks a forward step for its author, an intellectual advance although an artistic failure. After it, Sinclair Lewis almost entirely forgets that world of youthful adventure that was so delightful to him, and with it the theoretical happy endings, the generous ideas, the idylls, and the socialistic tirades. He loses that slightly naive faith in existence that in all the novels prior to 1920 used to make him scatter abroad sayings about life, for the sheer fun of it, even when they were disenchanted. One might say that the extended cohabitation with his characters in the limbo of Gopher Prairie had revealed to him a tragedy of existence. His once indulgent smile will be henceforth laughter, sorrowful laughter, and the cheerful eccentrics will become painful grotesques. The imaginative adventures *(The Trail of the Hawk, Free Air)* are struck at the root: even the desire for them becomes ridiculous *(Babbitt)* or melancholy *(Arrowsmith)*. The self-reliant young women, cheerful and eager, who used to furnish happy endings to the idylls, now, like the already-mentioned Istra Nash, become unattainable, tortured even when simple; they die halfway through the story, or they go away, all of them desperate images of the author's relentless and henceforth tragic struggle for freedom.

Naturally, it is a great advance with respect to the breadth and resonance of a fictive world, this development suggested by *Main Street*. The characters become ampler and more numerous and more surely drawn. The plots become more exciting through lively contrast, where the Lewis irony still most subtly prevails, sadder now in tone. There remains, there is even increased, a single defect, as I have already said, the mania for undertaking in each novel the portrait of a social class with its background and the treatment of related problems. Of it is born a slight tedium of tone, quite different from that in *Main Street*, but no less wearying. In *Arrowsmith* everything is medicine, in *Elmer Gantry* everything is religion.

I have already said that *Babbitt* (1922) is Lewis' masterpiece because in it the most ridiculous puppet is seen with the most cheerfully hopeless eye possible. But it is inexact to say "puppet." Babbitt affects us precisely because he shows us how being an average man, a common man, a normal man, is like being a puppet. What reader of the novel, while reading it, has not every so often squirmed, asking himself how many times he himself has been a Babbitt?

And, I repeat, the book's greatness lies in the fact that Babbitt is restless, that Babbitt—in this respect more than ever

Babbitt—does not want to be a Babbitt, and that all his efforts fail, leaving him terribly resigned, terribly good-natured, and ready to begin again. At a certain point, every cliché, every glad-handing phrase, every gesture, every ridiculous scene— and the reader knows how full of them the book is—becomes a barb which we see stuck in Babbitt, and he doesn't notice, but from it his character emerges, tortured, quite stoic, and still without heroism, the most common—and thus the most extraordinary—martyr the world has ever seen.

It has been said that *Babbitt* is a great work because of its realism, that in it life is photographed, that to hear those big professional men and industrialists from the Middle West is like hearing a phonograph record of American vulgarity. That is not true, or at least it is not the whole truth. *Babbitt* is a paradoxical book. Yes, there is in it material collected by almost superhuman observation, but this is only raw material. In the book there is created a synthesis, a synthesis that is poetry, by means of which all the characters become functions of Babbitt, and by means of which all the characters speak realistically, since it is reality itself which will exasperate and clutch him again; but it is a realism so little realistic and instead so full of poetry that, if for a moment the figure of Babbitt is removed, we can see how all the fragments of that vaunted realism no longer of themselves say anything, how they no longer reflect any reality except (imperfectly) that of the missing hero.

So much for the work of art. As for history, we see in George F. Babbitt fused for the first time—the second time in Sam Dodsworth—two of Lewis' incompatible extremes: the sensitive and timid character, the dreamer, "our Mr. Wrenn," and the coarse and simpleminded Middle Westerner, Eddie Schwirtz. Thanks to a miracle of art, they coexist perfectly in Babbitt.

I don't want to summarize the book. Still, I will observe how this long story of escapes and defeats, until the end, the rebellion, the betrayal to Zenith, which concludes as unhappily as the other novels, has, in its almost journalistic treatment of a slice of life, a fascination that makes up for the possible defect of its lack of construction—in other words—as a novel. Here again, as several times already and other times still to come, Lewis follows a character through a certain period in his life, without organizing the whole into any obvious plot, but telling, as a newspaper reporter would, various adventures, unconnected with each other. Naturally, there is adventure and it is wholly intellectual—a flight, a rebellion, a discovery, a defeat—but the character so portrayed in the midst of daily life has the advantage of remaining more a type, presented to the mind, of being less tied to any particular events, of adapting himself more broadly to the readers' imagination. To see what I mean, think of what Mowgli is in the Jungle Books, in those disparate and isolated adventures that make up the chronicle of his life. He is a symbol that everyone likes to imagine. In the same way we may explain the extraordinary ease with which these types of Lewis' became a part of real life. And Babbitt, for the same reason as Don Quixote, is now better known as a type than as the creation of a poet.

This lust for symbolism may also be seen in the persistence of Zenith—Babbitt's city—in Lewis' world. It is unfortunate, since Zenith was made for Babbitt, as were all the characters and settings of the novel, and when Babbitt is removed they dry up and blow away. Thus in *Arrowsmith*, Lewis invents even the state in which Zenith is located, Winnemac, and gives its boundaries and conditions, and at a certain point Babbitt turns up in his setting, but now the reader is living with memories. Likewise in *Elmer Gantry*, in *The*

*Man Who Knew Coolidge*, in *Dodsworth*, Zenith is a symbol, the American city, as Gopher Prairie was the village; but Zenith is dead.

These novels of the second period, after *Main Street*, might even be called the Zenith novels, except for one, *Mantrap* (1926), which escapes the category. As for art, *Mantrap* contains Alverna, the first of the three magnificent women whom Sinclair Lewis creates in these last books. Alverna is an uncultivated Istra Nash. She is a manicurist whose husband takes her to Canada, where she is bored and runs away. The usual rebellion and an unexpecxted unhappy ending. All part friends, at last, but each by his own road. And it is still another idyll, of the earlier sort, this adventure all full of the joy of uncivilized life: a lawyer who in Canada becomes a man again, and there gets to know Joe Easter, the husband, a crude type characterized by courtesy and loyalty, and there he courts Alverna, who flirts in a heavenly fashion, and escapes in his company. ⟨. . .⟩

Taken as a whole, one thing is especially conspicuous in these novels by Lewis. The characters, and with them the author, are great provincial types. In every sense of the word, great. They begin as innocents. Those from the prairies go to be provincials in New York and those from New York go to be provincials in Europe. They end in dignity, but—charlatans or distinguished scientists or industrialists as they are—a room full of people in evening dress will always make them uneasy.

Still, it was such people—with whom the Middle West, the American heartland, perpetuates itself in art—that the national literature needed. It would carry me too far afield to tell how and with which writers this character was born. But, certainly, without its provincials a literature has no nerve. And the provincials and farmers include not only carefree Milt Daggett, full-blooded Elmer Gantry, and thoughtful Martin Arrowsmith, but the least expected types, like Sharon, who, before exercising control over crowds and playing the role of Cleopatra, was a stenographer at Utica (U.S.A.), and who has in her so much human energy that, out of the still hesitant Elmer Gantry from Paris, Kansas, she is able to make for a moment an impassioned and genuine lover and—without irony—a grandiose charlatan forever. Even the sad and right-minded Babbitt participates in this quality of the safe and sane province and, after all, even he, like Dodsworth, is a laborious creator of the race of people who have contributed to the richness of America. And Zenith, the ridiculous city, enlarged, is only the bustling village of the Midland, to which America—and even Sam lets us know it—owes so much.

The true provincial nature of Sinclair Lewis is shown in the use of slang and the vernacular. This kind of jargon and dialect, the national expression of America, is understood by him, loved, and finally made into poetry, resulting in the true creation of a language—the American vernacular: a thing of which there has been no example since the times when the neo-Latin peoples stabilized their virgin idioms in works of art and life. Before Lewis, American slang was local color or journalistic improvisation. Perhaps only O. Henry, that happy mad genius, used it in such a way as to compose a literary language. But in the others—Mark Twain, William Dean Howells, the greatest writers—the American vernacular is still too much in the condition of the Negro in the speeches of Jupiter ("The Gold Bug" of Edgar Poe): local color. In the authoritative works of H. L. Mencken,[2] one sees better than anywhere else the debt America owes Sinclair Lewis for this achievement, and Mencken was writing only at the time of *Main Street*, in 1920.

The ultimate foundation, therefore, of the poetry of

Sinclair Lewis, seems to me this powerful and happy world, this earthy spirit. Behind ironies and subtleties, behind problems and culture, our author has always remained the restless and versatile young man from Sauk Centre, Minnesota, who does not understand music, who does not understand (he says so himself) paintings, but who has dabbled in all the trades and who loves to tell his companions tales of his experiences—exuberant stories, even when tragic, stories of the region—where, in every one of them, there persists something of this people's open and healthy sense of life.

*Notes*

1. The difference between "slang" and colloquial American is well known: the former is practically a jargon, a pepper pot of grotesque metaphors and pungent expressions, a creation, in short, conscious, deliberate, and applauded except by the most cultivated, the purists; colloquial American, on the other hand, is simply the great body of the language spoken in the United States, different from English as phonetics and morphology, often as vocabulary, and nearly always as construction: the changed conditions of the English settlers, contacts with settlers from other peoples, natural evolution, and "slang" have contributed to its formation. Cf. Henry L. Mencken, *The American Language* (2d ed., New York, 1921).

2. Mencken, p. 270. Mencken isn't talking only about Lewis in this examination of the new language: he mentions Ring W. Lardner of Chicago, writer of "baseball" stories, Caroline Lockhart and John V. A. Weaver and Carl Sandburg, poets, but surely, above all these, among whom several have the air of being specialists or dilettantes—the same thing, in this case—rises Sinclair Lewis, who, with the importance of certain of his works, with the amplitude and assurance of his means, has definitively consecrated the American language as distinct from English, and as literary. I don't speak, naturally, of the new generation—the writers who began after the war—because these, beyond argument, write in the new language.

## GRANVILLE HICKS
### "Sinclair Lewis and the Good Life"
*English Journal*, April 1936, pp. 265–73

M any things may be said about Sinclair Lewis, and there are many points of view from which his work can be profitably examined. In this article I am treating him primarily as a moralist, as a man who wants to know what is the good life. His investigations are, of course, significant because of the qualities that make his novels effective, especially his understanding of human beings and his familiarity with America. But I am not here concerned with his literary talents as such, though I do not forget their importance.

Lewis's first four major novels seem to me to belong together and perhaps to be set apart from his later work. The ease with which *Main Street* and *Babbitt* may be coupled is obvious: one is a study of rebellion and the other a study of conformity. Carol Kennicott's chief virtue is her refusal to accept the standards of Gopher Prairie, and George F. Babbitt's principal fault is his submission to the standards of Zenith. Compare Carol's valedictory with Babbitt's. "I may not have fought the good fight," she says, "but I have kept the faith." Whereas Babbitt confesses to his son, "I've never done a single thing I've wanted in my whole life."

Lewis is so candid in exposing Carol's faults and so adroit in revealing Babbitt's virtues that rebellion comes to seem all that is right with the former and conformity all that is wrong with the latter. The tragedy of Babbitt's life is, of course, that he tried to rebel and failed. Lewis makes us realize, however, that the desire for rebellion is not peculiar to George F. Babbitt; dissatisfaction rankles in the hearts of Paul Riesling and Chum Frink, and perhaps it once stirred in Vergil Gunch. But these men have all surrendered, whereas Carol, not particularly intelligent and certainly not very successful, sticks to her guns.

It is no wonder that *Main Street* and *Babbitt* greatly encouraged the rebels and gave them effective ammunition in their struggle against the conformists. For Lewis was not the pioneer of revolt; his rôle was, rather, to consolidate the innumerable small gains of decades of warfare. The rebellion had been going on for a long time, and had steadily been gaining strength. By 1910 there was scarcely an author of any distinction who did not covet and deserve the name of rebel, and after the war, in the course of which conformity was made a patriotic and religious duty and the insistence upon it became sheer hysteria, the revolt burst out with new conviction and fresh fury. What Lewis did, in *Main Street* and *Babbitt*, was to unify the forces of rebellion and carry the war into the enemy's territory. He put the conformists upon the defensive.

We cannot take the time to trace the history of conformity and rebellion. All we need to know is that certain dogmas had developed among the solid middle-class people of the country, whether they lived in Gopher Prairie, Zenith, or New York City. Assent to these dogmas was demanded, and heretics were punished. The rebels sought the right not to believe the conformists' articles of faith. Their attitude varied from a sound experimentalism to a simple determination to be different at all costs, but it was almost always essentially negative.

Lewis, though he was in full sympathy with the rebellion, was aware of its negative character, and portrayed it in *Main Street* and *Babbitt*. Carol Kennicott never knows why she is rebelling; she is against the values of the conformists, but her own values are nebulous. Seneca Doane, the foil to George F. Babbitt, is courageous, is not provincial, is largely independent of public opinion; but one feels in him rather the absence of Babbitt's vices than the presence of positive virtues. Rebellion was good; Lewis had no doubt of that; but rebellion ought, he felt, to be for some higher end, for the sake of definite values. With this in mind, he wrote *Arrowsmith*.

In choosing to affirm the values of scientific research, Lewis ran little risk of disagreement. The modern mind respects the scientist's conception of integrity, even when it does not understand his conclusions. This is not merely because science is quantitative but also because it is so remote from the lives of most of us. In any other field, whatever Lewis chose to regard as integrity would have been condemned by many readers as either fanaticism or sheer wickedness. There can be little agreement, for example, as to what constitutes honesty in a labor leader or a college president. For Lewis' purpose as a novelist, the ending of the book was satisfactory, but not for his purposes as a moralist. When Lewis says that integrity involves sacrifice and is worth it, he is saying something that is relevant to any kind of life, but the concrete problems of application remain unsolved. No large number of persons can lead the good life in laboratories in the woods. What, we ask, and Lewis with us, is the practical equivalent?

What I have said is not a criticism of *Arrowsmith* as a novel; it is merely to make clear that Lewis had not advanced quite so far in his search for the good life as might at first be thought. If he had really come to a definite conclusion, he might not have written *Elmer Gantry*, for here he merely continues the researches into conformity he had begun in *Babbitt*. Babbitt is a conformist as a result, for the most part, of ignorance and indolence. Gantry is a conformist wholly for the sake of material advantage. It may be argued that, since Gantry is less typical, the study of his character throws less light on the moral problem involved, and certainly the very terms of his

investigation prevented Lewis from creating either a representative or a wholly credible person. Nevertheless, *Elmer Gantry*, defective as it is, rounds out the cycle: Carol, the naïve rebel; Babbitt, the likable conformist; Arrowsmith, the rebel for the sake of positive good; Gantry, the conformist for the sake of positive evil.

When he came to write *Dodsworth*, Lewis approached the problem on a different level. In the first four novels he had apparently accepted one of the common assumptions of the rebels—namely, that the good life and financial success are virtually incompatible. Arrowsmith deliberately rejects success, as George Babbitt and Elmer Gantry would understand it, for the sake of integrity. "The only failure is cheap success," says one of the characters in *Main Street*. The misfortunes of Frank Shallard are manifestly a greater triumph than Gantry's rise to eminence. But Sam Dodsworth, who is perhaps the most ardent of all Lewis' seekers for the good life, has made a million dollars manufacturing automobiles. It is true that Dodsworth has always felt and comes to admit that making money is not enough, but his industrial success is the foundation on which he proposes to build the good life, and he is quick to repudiate any suggestion that he ought to be ashamed of his past.

Although we must not exaggerate this change of emphasis, it seems to me that in *Dodsworth* Lewis' mind took a new turn. It should be remembered that when he wrote "The only failure is cheap success," he was in the process of rejecting the cheap success of *Saturday Evening Post* fame in order to write a novel that he believed could not sell. By the time he began *Dodsworth*, however, he had published four highly successful novels, in each of which he had said exactly what he thought. Success could be deserved; Sinclair Lewis had proved it. Moreover, he had grown increasingly impatient with the rebels as he saw how many of them failed to accomplish anything with the freedom for which they had cried. To the realization that some of the successful deserved to succeed he added the discovery that many of the failures deserved to fail.

In *Dodsworth* Lewis reached a number of interesting conclusions. Many of the rebels were maintaining that art was the only civilized occupation, that money was vulgar, and that the United States was wholly inferior to the countries of Europe. These dogmas, he realized, were quite as false as those of the conformists, and he proceeded to demonstrate this in *Dodsworth*. He showed that making things, such as motor cars, was socially useful and could be intellectually respectable. He showed that the dilettanti were very much preoccupied with money, and that an honest manufacturer could rise above financial considerations. He showed that the snobbish worship of Europe was just as provincial as the local pride of the inhabitants of Gopher Prairie. In short, he insisted that, though the Babbitts were bad, their enemies were not always good.

One feels that Lewis had made an advance, if only because he had achieved a more complex conception of his problem, but there is, nevertheless, a disturbing vagueness in *Dodsworth*. The hero, in the course of a discussion in Berlin, proposes the idea of an American aristocracy. Recalling that the book was dedicated to Edith Wharton, one wonders if Lewis did not intend the suggestion to be taken seriously. After all, *Dodsworth* was written during the boom period, when many tired radicals were expecting business men to work miracles. Lewis understood that rebellion, in Bernard Shaw's phrase, attracts those who are not good enough for the *status quo* as well as those who are too good for it. And often those who are too good are warped by the bitter fight against the massive majority. Lewis did not minimize the faults of the Sam

Dodsworths, but he was ready to wonder if they were not closer to aristocratic stature than any other group in America. Dodsworth himself, it is true, does not go much beyond the discovery that he is interested in something besides business and the determination to do something, not for the sake of making more money but in the spirit of *noblesse oblige.* Lewis was not drawing a diagram; he was simply making an experimental suggestion.

He did not continue his speculations on the subject of an American aristocracy, but he did continue to examine success and failure in their relation to conformity and rebellion and the good life and the bad. Neither *Ann Vickers* nor *Work of Art* seems to me of much importance, but both show Lewis retreating still further from the assumptions of the rebels. *Ann Vickers*, which parallels *Arrowsmith* in form, does not end with Ann taking up her abode in some wilderness to maintain her sociological integrity. Instead, the problems raised by her varied career in social work are brushed aside, and she ends in the arms of a man. Ann's behavior in love is intended, one supposes, to give pause to the feminist contingent of the rebel band, but more interesting, it seems to me, is the character of the man she loves. Judge Barney Dolphin is a regular fellow, not without taste, of course, but a man who accepts things— including bribes—as they are. One can almost imagine Lewis asking himself, "Who would such a fine woman as Ann Vickers fall in love with? Would it be a weak, narrow-minded, unsuccessful little rat of a rebel? No, it would be a man who did things, a man who knew his way round." Perhaps he even added—it is a chastening thought—"a man like me."

*Dodsworth* and *Ann Vickers* were supposed to correct some of the misapprehensions of the typical rebel; *Work of Art* was a deliberate slap in his face. But the amazing thing was that there was no face there. The reviewers were bewildered. For once Lewis' news-sense had failed him, and he had written a book about which there could be no controversy. The book maintained that running good hotels was better than writing bad poetry. Well, the reviewers asked in astonishment, who had ever denied it?

The truth is, of course, that it would have been a startling thing to say back in 1920. At that time, because it had been necessary to assert the value of the arts in the face of the derision of the business-ridden Babbitts, certain rebels, as we have seen, had fostered the dogma of the inherent superiority of any kind of artistic endeavor. But by 1934 such claims were rarely made and never listened to. Sinclair Lewis did not know this. It was apparent when he delivered his address in Stockholm on receiving the Nobel Prize that he was still fighting the old battle. He still felt it necessary to defend art against the Babbitts and the wowsers and the academicians. And because he took the rebellion seriously, he was preoccupied with the faults of some of the rebels.

The decline of the rebellion took place in two stages. First, during the years of Coolidge prosperity, there was the movement to proclaim, not the superiority, but the independence of art. Writers no longer worried—or pretended not to worry—about the absurdities of the Babbitts; they would create, and the Babbitts could be as Philistine as they pleased. Lewis and most of his generation were dismissed as old fashioned. And then, after the depression had set in, the second stage began. The rebels had originally revolted, for the most part, on personal, moral, and aesthetic grounds. After the depression, a personal revolt seemed unimportant. Historically the attack on the conformists had been necessary, but its achievements seemed almost meaningless in a world that was crumbling.

The rebellion had not solved the most serious problems of the individual because it had not solved the problems of society.

In 1934, then, when *Work of Art* appeared, not only had the Ora Weagles vanished, or at least been relegated to obscure holes; the issues of 1920 had vanished too. There were new issues and new alignments. The dissenters were calling themselves revolutionaries, not rebels, and they were arguing that by its very nature art did influence and should aim to influence the development of society. They maintained that, instead of merely trying to escape from the Babbitts, writers should consciously ally themselves with the proletariat. Of course, there were many artists and writers who did not agree with them, but the issues they raised were the issues that were being discussed.

The revolutionaries agreed with Lewis that it was ridiculous to put art on a pedestal, and their scorn of the Bohemians made his criticism seem gentle. But they had no patience with *Work of Art.* It seemed old fashioned, more so than *Main Street* or *Babbitt.* In *Main Street* Carol Kennicott does realize that "not individuals but institutions are the enemies." *Babbitt* shrewdly exposes the economic basis of conformity by showing how economic pressure brings the dissenter into line. But *Work of Art*, intended to show that craftsmanship is what counts, whether a man is running a hotel or writing poetry, almost completely ignores the extent to which the capitalist system makes craftsmanship impossible. Thus it juxtaposes an unreal conception of craftsmanship in the modern world with what we have already seen to be an unreal conception of art in the modern world.

In his latest novel Lewis has gone a long way toward justifying the revolutionary criticism of *Work of Art.* Until recently Lewis has assumed that the good life was possible under the existing economic order. At first it seemed to him that the great obstacle to the good life was conformity. Later he modified his views enough to want to see what was wrong with the rebels. But at every point he took the foundations of the good life for granted. Lewis has never been the kind of idealist who thinks a man can live the good life when he is starving, but he did pretty much ignore the fact that millions were living in poverty even in the days of prosperity, and in any case he felt that this problem was quite unrelated to the problem that interested him. Certainly it never occurred to him that millions who at the moment had the means for a good life might be robbed of them, and even the depression, to which younger writers were so sensitive, did not show him the precariousness of the foundations on which all his conclusions and aspirations were built. It took the rise of Fascism in Germany to make him realize that the values he vaguely called "civilized" could be wiped out. The rulers of our society, he was made to see, might, if their privileges and their power were menaced, deliberately organize the forces of intolerance and destroy every gain that emancipated individuals had made.

So he wrote *It Can't Happen Here.* Doremus Jessup, though perhaps the least completely individualized of all Lewis' heroes, embodies better than any other of his characters the qualities he admires. Jessup does well a minor but respectable job. He maintains his independence without losing his sanity. He has the common sense, the good taste, and the humor that Lewis so often finds lacking in rebels. He is neither a warped, fanatical hermit nor a good fellow at the mercy of his associates. He is a civilized human being, and he is precisely the kind of human being Fascism seeks to wipe out.

At one point in the book Doremus Jessup reflects: "The tyranny of this dictatorship isn't primarily the fault of Big Business, nor of the demagogues who do their dirty work. It's the fault of Doremus Jessup. Of all the conscientious, respectable, lazy-minded Doremus Jessups who have let the demagogues wriggle in, without fierce enough protest." On the one hand, this is encouraging, for it is an explicit statement of social responsibility. But, on the other hand, it sounds a little naïve, a little like a civil service reformer. To save the country from Fascism, something more than fierce protest is needed. In the long run, the only protection against Fascism is the building of a decent social order.

But at least Lewis is awake to the danger that the very possibility of the good life may be wiped out. At least he realizes that, under some circumstances, the only way in which one can serve individual virtue is to fight for social change. Whether he will go further than that remains to be seen. The revolutionary maintains that, because of the nature of society, the battle to maintain such liberties as we now have is doomed to defeat. We must have more or we will have less. Fascism is part of the sickness of capitalism, and that sickness cannot be cured. For Lewis to realize all this will involve a more drastic restatement of his problems than one finds, even in *It Can't Happen Here*, but it seems the only logical outcome to his search for the good life.

And at the same time this new novel, though in itself a good deal of a tract, gives reason to hope that Lewis will be restored to his eminence as a novelist. It may be that *Ann Vickers* and *Work of Art* were merely the incidental failures that one must expect from almost any artist. Or it may be that their defects directly resulted from Lewis' lack of contact with the central issues of American life. We have seen that *Main Street*, *Babbitt*, and *Arrowsmith* concerned a problem that was vital indeed in the days when they were written, and from that

particular problem they reached out to grapple with others, so that today, when we are less concerned with individualistic rebellion, they nevertheless have more than historical significance. Even *Dodsworth*, valid for the late twenties, those years that now seem almost as remote from us as the years before the war, is valid for us now, both as literature and as moral research, and we may reflect upon as well as enjoy the mystifications of the uprooted manufacturer. But *Ann Vickers* and *Work of Art*, though I should never think of condemning them *in toto*, seemed when they appeared and seem now to be full of strain and confusion, as if Lewis scarcely knew why he was selecting this incident or emphasizing that character.

If I am right, the fact that, with *It Can't Happen Here*, Sinclair Lewis has waded once more into the main stream may mean that we shall have another group of strong and memorable novels. I hope so, but I am not sure. He may turn back, just as, when recently he went to Vermont to observe the marble strike, he left after a few days, saying it was a perfectly ordinary strike, nothing to write about. This announcement hurt the strikers, who had expected much from his visit, and it damaged the strike, for local publicity suddenly dwindled. Lewis is a writer, and, if he finds nothing to write about, silence, he naturally maintains, is his privilege. But he is also an anti-Fascist. On seeing the marble company's deputies, he said, "Fascism in Vermont, by God! It can happen here!" but two days later he had forgotten this and was asserting the sacred right of the rebel individualist to run away when he is bored. Other rebel individualists have grown up—one thinks of André Gide, for example. Will Sinclair Lewis? On the answer to this question depends both the outcome of his search for the good life, and, I believe, his future as a novelist.

# VACHEL LINDSAY

## 1879–1931

Nicholas Vachel Lindsay was born on November 10, 1879, in Springfield, Illinois. His mother was an energetic civic reformer, an organizer of reading circles, amateur theatricals, and missionary and temperance societies; his father was a doctor. Lindsay's parents brought him up in their own Protestant fundamentalist faith, the Disciples of Christ; after he graduated from Springfield High School he entered Hiram College in Ohio, a school run by that denomination. His parents wanted him to become a doctor, but he felt unsuited to practice medicine and after three years left Hiram College with their blessings. From 1901 to 1905 he studied art, first at the Art Institute of Chicago and then at the New York School of Art, in the meantime writing poetry, teaching night classes at the YMCA, and meagerly supporting himself with a succession of dull jobs. His teacher Robert Henri advised him in 1905 that he seemed to have more aptitude for poetry than art, and Lindsay left school determined to support himself with his writing. Inspired, as he later said, both by the example set by the medieval troubadours and by that of Teddy Roosevelt, he had copies of two of his poems printed up. He peddled these directly to the public on the streets of Manhattan, and while he made very little money the response he received encouraged him in his next project. Lindsay set out on long walking tours of the rural United States, exchanging work and copies of his *Rhymes to Be Traded for Bread* for food and a place to sleep. The idea was successful, and he was able to travel for hundreds of miles in this fashion. He returned to live with his family in Springfield from 1908 to 1912; he wrote more poetry, published a series of pamphlets, and lectured on prohibition for the Anti-Saloon League of Illinois and on racial conflicts and stereotypes at his local YMCA. He also made one more walking tour, this time to California.

In 1912 Lindsay found himself with a national reputation when his *General William Booth Enters into Heaven and Other Poems* was published, and Harriet Monroe both printed and praised his work in *Poetry*. Lindsay's poems were a striking contrast to the compressed, erudite, understated work of the predominant Imagist school; his were wordy, colorful, and strongly rhythmic, written to be read aloud. This Lindsay did, spending years touring the country to give poetry readings. He called this "the higher vaudeville," an idea suggested by the way popular vaudeville shows and Chautauqua tours of the time combined entertainment with public education. Further collections of his poems include *The Congo and Other Poems* (1914), *The Golden Whales of California* (1920), and *Johnny Appleseed* (1922).

Lindsay's books of prose were written on a wide range of subjects; among them are *Adventures While Preaching the Gospel of Beauty* (1914), a collection of thoughts and descriptions from his walking tours; *The Art of the Moving Picture* (1915), one of the earliest attempts to construct a coherent theory of film; and *The Golden Book of Springfield* (1920), a utopian vision of Springfield, Illinois in 2018.

The years of poetry-reading tours badly eroded Lindsay's health and spirits, and when his mother died in 1922 he suffered a collapse. For a while he lived in Mississippi with a friend from his Hiram College days, and then the following year was poet-in-residence at Gulfport Junior College in Gulfport, Mississippi. He married Elizabeth Connor, a schoolteacher many years his junior, in 1925, and they moved to Spokane, Washington, her hometown. In the years that followed the couple had two children and Lindsay continued to write poetry, but he was often severely depressed. The family's move back to the Lindsay home in Springfield in 1929 did not halt his decline, and Lindsay died in his bed on December 5, 1931, after drinking a bottle of Lysol.

With an appreciation of these matters, one approaches his first important volume of poetry, *General William Booth Enters into Heaven and Other Poems*, with sympathetic understanding. Here one immediately encounters the curious blend of athletic exuberance, community pride and evangelism. Consider the first poem, which gives the book its title. Here is the apotheosis of a great social-religious movement; but it is not so much a tribute to the Salvation Army as it is a glorification of a spirit greater and far beyond it. From a technical standpoint, Lindsay's attempt to blend noise, novelty and an old ecstasy is highly successful—and almost fortuitous. The experiment of setting lofty lines and reverential sentiment to cheap and brassy music is daring and splendid; especially since, in its very tawdriness, the music of the verse gives back the flavor of those earnest and blatant gatherings. It is, in a more definitely revivalistic spirit, the first of those characteristic chants (with the germs of the "higher vaudeville") which Lindsay lifted to so individual a plane. Here is the first section:

*(Bass drum beaten loudly.)*

Booth led boldly with his big bass drum—
(Are you washed in the blood of the Lamb?)
The Saints smiled gravely and they said: "He's come."
(Are you washed in the blood of the Lamb?)
Walking lepers followed, rank on rank,
Lurching bravoes from the ditches dank,
Drabs from the alleyways and drug-fiends pale—
Minds still passion-ridden, soul-powers frail.
Vermin-eaten saints with mouldy breath,
Unwashed legions with the ways of Death—
(Are you washed in the blood of the Lamb?)

*(Banjos.)*

Every slum had sent its half-a-score
The round world over. (Booth had groaned for more.)
Every banner that the wide world flies
Bloomed with glory and transcendent dyes.
Big-voiced lasses made their banjos bang,
Tranced, fanatical they shrieked and sang:—
*"Are you washed in the blood of the Lamb?"*
Hallelujah! It was queer to see
Bull-necked convicts with that land make free!
Loons with trumpets blowed a blare, blare, blare
On, on upward through the golden air!
*(Are you washed in the blood of the Lamb?)*

And here is the rattling climax:

*(Grand chorus of all instruments. Tambourines to the foreground.)*

The hosts were sandalled, and the wings were fire!
(Are you washed in the blood of the Lamb?)
But their noise played havoc with the angel-choir.
(Are you washed in the blood of the Lamb?)
O, shout Salvation! It was good to see
Kings and princes by the Lamb set free.
The banjos rattled, and the tambourines
Jing-jing-jingled in the hands of Queens!

*(Reverently sung; no instruments.)*

And when Booth halted by the curb for prayer
He saw his Master through the flag-filled air.
Christ came gently with a robe and crown
For Booth the soldier, while the throng knelt down.
He saw King Jesus. They were face to face,
And he knelt a-weeping in that holy place.
*Are you washed in the blood of the Lamb?*

No more colorful and solemn noise has yet been heard in our living song. ⟨. . .⟩

It would be too much to expect the rest of the volume to live up to this amazing piece of work, and it does not. Lindsay the man is always a poet, but Lindsay the poet does not always write poetry. When he errs it is not, as one critic has pointed out, "on the side of the time-spirit"; when he fails it is not because he tries to express his age but because he expresses it badly. Frequently his verse rises from nothing more carefully constructed than a conviction, an anger, a crusade against the white-slave traffic or the corner saloon. Here his voice gets beyond his control; in his haste to deliver his message, he has no time to choose sharp and living words; he takes what comes first to hand—good, bad, indifferent—and hurries on, blurring the firm outline, losing the sense of leashed power without which no art-work can be ennobled. His aim is commendable but his volleys are erratic. In his anxiety to bang the bell, he sometimes shoots not only the target but the background to pieces.—LOUIS UNTERMEYER, "Vachel Lindsay," *The New Era in American Poetry*, 1919, pp. 72–75

Well, what is the net produce of the whole uproar? How much actual poetry have all these truculent rebels against *Stedman's Anthology* and *McGuffey's Sixth Reader* manufactured? I suppose I have read nearly all of it—a great deal of it, as a magazine editor, in manuscript—and yet, as I look back, my memory is lighted up by very few flashes of any lasting brilliance. ⟨. . .⟩

Lindsay? Alas, he has done his own burlesque. What was new in him, at the start, was an echo of the barbaric rhythms of the Jubilee Songs. But very soon the thing ceased to be a marvel, and of late his elephantine college yells have ceased to be amusing. His retirement to the chautauquas is self-criticism of uncommon penetration.

⟨. . .⟩ Many of the new poets, in truth, are ardent enemies of democracy; for example, Pound. Only one of them has ever actually sought to take his strophes to the vulgar. That one is Lindsay—and there is not the slightest doubt that the yokels welcomed him, not because they were interested in his poetry, but because it struck them as an amazing, and perhaps even a fascinatingly obscene thing, for a sane man to go about the country on any such bizarre and undemocratic business.
—H. L. MENCKEN, "The New Poetry Movement," *Prejudices: First Series*, 1919, pp. 86–92

He is, among recent American poets, the most impetuous enthusiast. Only he, among those recent American poets who are also important, has a record, which he avows, of membership in a more or less militant denomination, of admiration for foreign missionaries, of activities in the Young Men's Christian Association, of blows struck in behalf of the Anti-Saloon League. Other bards may see in prohibition a set of statutes against cakes and ale or an increase of tyranny deftly managed by clever lobbyists in the interests of a comfortable minority with stocks in its cellars; to Mr. Lindsay the prohibition movement is, or was, a gallant revolution against the sour and savage King Alcohol who has too long ruled the race. Others may see in Y.M.C.A. secretaries the least imaginative of those persons who believe that a Christian should be all things to all men, and may see in foreign missionaries the least imaginative of those persons who believe that God should be one thing to all men; to Mr. Lindsay such secretaries and missionaries are, or were, knights and paladins whose quarrels are just, whose conquests are beneficent, because they uphold and extend the healing hands of Christ. Others may see in the Campbellites an undistinguished, though aggressive, village sect with apostolic prejudices; to Mr. Lindsay the Disciples are the faithful legionaries of Alexander Campbell, the pioneer who proclaimed a millennium in the Western wilderness and set the feet of his companions and inheritors on the path which leads to a New Jerusalem.

Most of the poems in which Mr. Lindsay utters or hints at these opinions are early, and most of them are, as poems, trash. They are not, however, the whole story. They are merely items in his attempt to give his work a basis in the moods and in the rhythms of his native section. As a student of art in Chicago and in New York he was not entirely at home; he could not find a natural idiom to match his impulses. That idiom he eventually found in a language which expresses the mood of the local patriot in the rhythm of national vaudeville. He devised the terms "the new localism" and "the higher vaudeville" to give the authority of doctrine to his practice. Localism, of course, had long been one of the most potent forces in the country, particularly in Mr. Lindsay's Middle West. Town had striven with town to see which could sing its own praises loudest and so further its own aspirations by bringing in new inhabitants and larger business. The strife had encouraged all the natural tendencies toward optimism and complacency, and had developed the windy lingo of the booster until it had become perhaps the most customary oratory of the region. Here was something, Mr. Lindsay felt, to be translated into the worthier idiom of poetry. But he was a booster of a novel disposition. He wanted to see brought to his town of Springfield not more business but more beauty; not more inhabitants but more elevation of life. ⟨. . .⟩

If Mr. Lindsay's poetry is more original than his philosophy, so is it more valuable. Like all crusaders, he has difficulty in looking ahead to the end of the bright path he follows with such rapture. *The Golden Book of Springfield*, in which he sets forth his notion of what his native town may have become by 2018, is a Utopia of Katzenjammer. History serves him better than prophecy, as when he celebrates the fame of that John Chapman who as Johnny Appleseed is remembered for his gift of orchards to the Middle West. Indeed, Mr. Lindsay is at his best when he is engaged in promoting to poetry some figure or group of figures heretofore neglected by the poets: the Salvation Army, the motorists of the Santa Fe trail, the Springfield blacks, Alexander Campbell, John Chapman, John L. Sullivan, John P. Altgeld, the Bryan of 1896.

On these occasions the poet is not content to write history merely; he makes myths. His Alexander Campbell still rides his circuit, announcing the millennium and snatching back renegade souls to the faith; his John Chapman still roams the great valley, a backwoods St. Francis, with the seeds of civilization in his wallet. ⟨. . .⟩

And yet Vachel Lindsay is not the personage he was when he published *The Congo ⟨and Other Poems* (1914)⟩ in the same year with *Spoon River Anthology*. Both he and Edgar Lee Masters were deliberately going back to Greek models, the one to the chanted lyric, the other to the ironical epigram. Irony, however, won the day, helped by the presence in the times of a tumult through which nothing less cutting than the voice of irony could reach; and in the eight years since the appearance of the two books the tendency of American literature has been steadily toward irony, satire, criticism. To the drive for the new localism there has succeeded a revolt from the village, turning to ridicule the eloquence of the local patriot and laughing at the manners of the small community. To the confidence that much might be made for literature out of the noisier, rougher elements of the national life by the process of lifting them to richer, surer rhythms and giving them a sounder language, has succeeded the feeling, best voiced by H. L. Mencken, that such elements are menace, nuisance, or nonsense, and that the cause of the higher vaudeville, to be based upon them, is not worth fighting for. Some sense of this shift in the current literary mood must have been responsible, at least in part, for the loss of Mr. Lindsay of the full vigor with which he sang in those first hopeful days; for his inclination to turn away from creation to criticism and scholarship, from poetry to design.
—CARL VAN DOREN, "Salvation with Jazz," *Many Minds*, 1924, pp. 152–64

Vachel Lindsay was a Puritan in the personal sense; one might almost say in the political sense. He was even a Prohibitionist, and it is only fair to say that his orgiastic verse does demonstrate how very drunk a man can be without wine when he drinks the American air. Occasionally, even, a critic might be tempted to call it the American hot-air. For though Vachel Lindsay was a natural artist, and went right by the clue of the imagination, there are passages of his finest writing which would have been finer still if he had not lived in the land of the megaphone rather than the ivory horn; or if his traditions had not given him the choice of two trumpets—the brazen trumpet of publicity as well as the golden trumpet of poetry. He was himself a wholly simple, sincere, and therefore humble man; but the people around him did not believe in humility; no, not even when they practised it. But they did believe in go and gusto and the big noise; and to a certain extent Vachel Lindsay even at his best did practise that. I have myself a huge sympathy with his special gift for describing men banging their gongs to the glory of their gods; but it were vain to deny that in some ways their gods were not our gods.

⟨. . .⟩ Vachel Lindsay was something more than an American; he was (wildly as the term would be misunderstood) a Spanish-American. He was, spiritually speaking, a Californian. He did not get drunk only on the American air; he drank the air of a strange paradise, which is in some way set apart and unlike anything in the New World or the Old; a fairy sea, calmed as by a spell, that stretches far away into fantastical China and of which even the nearer coast is ruled by ghosts rather than by its modern rulers.—G. K. CHESTERTON, "On Vachel Lindsay" (1932), *All I Survey*, 1933, pp. 38–39

*The Art of the Moving Picture* is astonishing, as a work of analysis and vision. Over fifty years ago Lindsay saw the hunger that still obsesses the film enthusiast:

> I'm delighted to affirm that not only the *New Republic* constituency but the world of the college and the university where I moved at the time, while at a loss for policy, were not only willing but eager to take the films with seriousness.

As the present incumbent of the *New Republic* post, I can affirm all parts of the statement today, not least the desire for policy. All the eminent writers on film aesthetics from Lindsay and Bela Balazs to the present have contrasted the appetite for film with the absence of any reliable body of aesthetics—any canon from which one can at least depart. In my view, no film aesthetician has filled the gap nor—for reasons too complex to discuss here—is likely to fill it: I foresee no Aristotle of film; but Lindsay at least took the first strong step toward analysis.

Obviously, there is no merit in categories, as such. Lindsay was interested in opening up powers, in showing possibilities to film-makers, in showing possible demands and rewards to film-goers.

His three fundamental catgories—which he calls "foundation colors"—are Pictures of Action, of Intimacy, and of Splendor. They are still the foundation colors of film, sometimes subdivided and often blended, but still fundamental. He saw Action in the basic cinema manifestation of the chase, but he saw further that the Action film is a species of abstraction: as, for instance, "the gesture of the conventional policeman in contrast with the mannerism of the stereotyped preacher." The Intimate Picture, which today is probably our dominant mode, is not merely or not at all a work of greater realism, it proceeds *through* realism and naturalism toward an interiorism of "elusive personal gestures." The Splendor film he saw as "the total gesture of crowds", the film in which peoples, races, and history are the elements of drama.

Sculpture-in-motion, painting-in-motion, architecture-in-motion, are what he also calls these three types; but these are very much more than facile phrases. They are nuggets out of which he refines subtle perceptions. He also applies the traditional poetic categories to these film types: dramatic, lyric, epic. His point is to show continuity and advance: to show that the film is bound, conceptually and formally, to the past, but that it takes these concepts and forms into new dimensions. He is also quite patently propagandizing—giving (rightful) dignified affinities to an art that was being superciliously patronized by many of those who flocked to it.

The development of the book often tempts us to think of Lindsay as naive. All that talk of Fairy Splendor and Patriotic Splendor! More frequently, however, he pierces to the root or to the future. He understood the aesthetic fallacy that his friend Freeburg hammered in the first sentence of his own book: "It is

a common error to judge the photoplay by the standards of the stage drama and to condemn it because it cannot do exactly what the stage drama can do." Lindsay not only saw the special powers of the stage but the special provinces of film. *The Cabinet of Dr. Caligari* (the importance of which he recognized at once) "proves in a hundred new ways the resources of the film in making all the inanimate things which, on the spoken stage, cannot act at all the leading actors in the film."

His fascination with hieroglyphics, in connection with film, antedates Eisenstein's cognate fascination with the Japanese ideogram (in *Film Form*). Lindsay sees, in 1915, the revolution in human perception involved in the very existence of film. There is a clear prediction of McLuhan in: "Edison is the new Gutenberg. He has invented the new printing." Lindsay sees, in 1915, the quintessence of the *auteur* theory of film criticism, formulated some forty years later: "An artistic photoplay . . . is not a factory-made staple article, but the product of the creative force of one soul, the flowering of a spirit that has the habit of perpetually renewing itself."

He foresees film schools, film libraries and archives, documentaries, the use of film for instructional purposes. He foresees the need for an American tradition of serious film. He even foresees the sales film and TV commercial: "Some staple products will be made attractive by having film-actors show their uses."

He is certainly not free of false judgment and false prophecy. His animus against the musical accompaniment of silent films (he thought people should converse while watching pictures) is sheer quirk—and he is generous enough to quote a story against himself. His ideas on the sound-film—which, in crude form, is as old as the silent—are as unimaginative as most of the book is visionary. (His prejudices against sound and dialogue reflect his painterly education—a prejudice towards the eye alone that antedates some of the short-comings of the modern "visual" school of film criticism.) His drama analysis—dividing the theater into ancient, English, and Ibsenite traditions—is less simplifying than simplistic. His chapter on the screen as a possible substitute for the saloon can only be seen—with utmost charity—as the view of a man who worships Dionysus in his own way. And this catalogue of oddities is not complete.

But with all the oddities, the bad guesses, the exaggerations of prose and of judgment, the embarrassing touches of a much lesser Whitman, this book is a considerable marvel. Lindsay had a clear sense that a profound change was taking place, not only in cultural history but in all human histories—the external and also the most secret. He felt lucky to be alive at that moment.—STANLEY KAUFFMANN, "Introduction" to *The Art of the Moving Picture*, 1970, pp. xiv–xviii

Once you concede these two postulates to Lindsay, all the rest seems to follow, including such lofty Lindsay invocations as: "Love-town, Troy-town, Kalamazoo" and "Hail, all hail the popcorn stand." It follows that the Fundamentalist prophet, Alexander Campbell, should debate with the devil upon none other than "a picnic ground." It follows that real, tangible angels jostle Lindsay's circus-barkers and salesmen of soda pop. And certainly Lindsay has as much aesthetic right to stage a modern Trojan war, over love, between Osh Kosh and Kalamazoo as Homer between Greeks and Trojans. So far so good. But Lindsay often absurdly overstrains this aesthetic right, these old-world analogies. For example, he hails not an easily-hailed American *object* like, say, Washington's monument but the popcorn stand.

Lindsay's motive for choosing the popcorn stand is not unconscious crudeness but conscious provocation. In effect he is saying: "By broadening the boundaries of aestheticism to include such hitherto-inacceptable Americana, my poetry is deliberately provoking, and thereby re-educating, all you supercilious eastern-seaboard-conditioned readers or Europe-conditioned readers."

⟨. . .⟩ his use was determined by a blind instinct—a shrewdly blind instinct—for catching the very soul of spoken Americana. No one has ever equalled Lindsay's genius for manipulating the unconscious connotations of the colloquial, even though he perversely misused those connotations for the self-torturing purpose of provoking and then staring-down the ridicule of sophisticated audiences.

That willingness to provoke ridicule may produce his worst poems. Yet it is also the root of the moral courage producing his best poems, such as his elegy for Governor Altgeld of Illinois. Altgeld had defied a nineteenth-century kind of "McCarthyism" by his idealistic defense of slandered minorities. Political poetry, even courageous political poetry, is by itself merely a rhymed editorial, better written in prose, unless universalized beyond journalism and arid ideologies into the non-political realm of artistic beauty. Lindsay's Altgeld poem remains one of the great American elegies because it does achieve this humanizing process, transfiguring courage into lyric tenderness:

Sleep softly . . . eagle forgotten . . . under the
    stone . . .
The mocked and the scorned and the wounded, the
    lame and the poor
That should have remembered forever . . . re-
    member no more . . .
Sleep softly . . . eagle forgotten . . . under the
    stone,
Time has its way with you there, and the clay has its
    own . . .
To live in mankind is far more than to live in a
    name,
To live in mankind, far, far more . . . than to live
    in a name.

However, more frequently the heroes Lindsay's poetry presents as the American equivalent of old-world Galahads are not exactly Altgelds. For example, the subtitle of his actual poem "Galahad" reads: "Dedicated to all Crusaders against the International and Interstate Traffic in Young Girls." The subtitle of his poem "King Arthur's Men Have Come Again" was equally earnest and uplifting, namely: "Written while a field-worker in the Anti-Saloon League of Illinois." Of course, the moral heritage of rural Fundamentalism particularly objects to alcohol, along with "playing poker and taking naps."

These twin odes to the Anti-Vice Squad and the Anti-Saloon League are bad poems not because the evil they denounce is unserious but because their treatment of that evil sounds like a mock-heroic parody. To explain such bad writing in so good a poet, let us suggest the hypothesis that Lindsay's mentality included a demon of self-destruction, forever turning the preacher into the clown. ⟨. . .⟩

Thus considered, Lindsay's poetry is not mere clowning, whether intentional or unintentional, but—in his own reveal-ing phrase—"the higher vaudeville." The adjective "higher" makes all the difference; it means a medieval vaudeville, a messianic circus, a homespun midwest equivalent of the medieval fool-in-Christ.

In refusing to be apologetic toward the old world about America's own kind of creativity, Lindsay does have a valid point. In refusing to allow European legends, heroes, place-names a greater claim on glamor than American ones, he again does have a valid point. Likewise when he establishes the

American gift for finding loveliness in the exaggerated, the grotesque. But the self-sabotaging demon within him tends to push these valid points to extremes that strain even the most willing "suspension of disbelief."

When Lindsay fails to make us suspend our disbelief, the reason often is this: he is trying to link not two compatibles, such as prosaic object with prosaic rhetoric or fabulous object with fabulous rhetoric, but prosaic object with fabulous rhetoric. Modern university-trained readers of poetry react unsolemnly to: "Hail, all hail the popcorn stand." Why? Because of a gap I would define as: the Lindsay disproportion. The Lindsay disproportion is the gap between the heroic tone of the invocation and the smallness of the invoked object. But Lindsay's aim, rarely understood by modern readers, was to overcome that disproportion between tone and object by conjuring up a mystic grandeur to sanctify the smallness of American trivia. That mystic grandeur derived from his dream of America as a new world free from old-world frailty, free from original sin. His dream-America was infinitely perfectable, whatever its present faults.—PETER VIERECK, "Vachel Lindsay: The Dante of the Fundamentalists," A *Question of Quality: Popularity and Value in Modern Creative Writing*, ed. Louis Filler, 1976, pp. 126–30

---

## ANN MASSA
### "The Artistic Conscience of Vachel Lindsay"
*American Studies*, October 1968, pp. 239–52

*I*

Vachel Lindsay's description of himself as 'the "Casey At-the-Bat" of American poetry'[1] sums up his reputation during his lifetime (1879–1931) and today. Perhaps only half-a-dozen of his poems—'General William Booth Enters into Heaven', 'The Congo', 'Bryan, Bryan, Bryan, Bryan', for example—are regularly read; and the rest of his diverse literary output, from 1909 to 1931, of nine collections of poems (and a mid-way *Collected Poems*), five prose works, numerous short stories, articles and private periodical publications, remains virtually unknown.

Lindsay was one of fifty or so poets who were swift to send Harriet Monroe samples of their work when she was soliciting contributions for her new magazine *Poetry* in 1912. As a young man he had been torn between painting and poetry, and had moved uncertainly from Hiram College, Ohio (1897–1900), to art school in Chicago (1900–3), and to the New York School of Art (1903–8). In 1908 he decided for poetry, and returned home to Springfield, Illinois, where he wrote verses, printed them in broadsides and pamphlets, and gave them away on the streets of Springfield, and on cross-country tramping expeditions. He also bombarded the conventional magazine outlets with his poems; but by 1912 he had only placed one or two.

It was *Poetry*'s publication of 'General William Booth . . .' in January 1913 which sparked off Lindsay's meteoric rise to fame. He had based the poem on the cadences and tunes of 'The Blood of the Lamb', and had inserted marginal directions for recitation. Emotionally, the poem compressed intensity into simplicity. It was new poetry, and powerful poetry; and with the publication early in 1914 of 'The Congo', a more complex poem, but with the same characteristics of beat, colour, and original material originally expressed, Lindsay seemed to strike out a fresh trail for American verse. Eunice Tietjens' article on Lindsay in *The Little Review*, October 1914, typified critical enthusiasm. She described 'The Congo' as 'perilously near great poetry', and went on: 'It is not too much to say that many of us are watching Vachel Lindsay with the undisguised hope in our hearts that he may yet prove to be the "Great American Poet". '[2]

Lindsay quickly found, however, that the critics' and the public's enthusiasm was damningly confining; and that any of his writings which did not fall into the rhythmic and melodic mould of his early poems were treated as eccentricities and lamentable deviations. Books which ranged through an evaluation of a new art form (*The Art of the Moving Picture*, 1915), a prediction of an American sub-utopia in 2018 (*The Golden Book of Springfield*, 1920), socio-religious theory (*Adventures While Preaching the Gospel of Beauty*, 1914; *A Handy Guide for Beggars*, 1916), political speculation and historical comment (*The Litany of Washington Street*, 1929), lyrical and committed poetry (*Every Soul Is a Circus*, 1931), fell on deaf ears. Popular taste understandably preferred the stereotyped Lindsay, the flamboyant author and mesmeric performer of repetitive, syncopated chants; but it was less excusable that the majority of reviewers at best prejudged his books as a waste of talent, and at worst showed an inaccurate acquaintance with them. It was with justifiable annoyance that Lindsay commented:

> You call me a 'Troubadour';
> But I am an adventurer in hieroglyphics, buildings
>     and designs.[3]

What has been written about Lindsay since his death has done little to alter the narrow assessment of his importance. Edgar Lee Masters's critical biography, *Vachel Lindsay* (1935), which has been lackadaisically taken for authority, set the pattern of apology for Lindsay's writings outside poetry, a pattern followed by Eleanor Ruggles in the other major biography, *The West-Going Heart* (1959), with the additional motif of a killing kindness to his literary 'aberrations'. Lindsay might state that 'What I am lies between the lines of *The Golden Book of Springfield*';[4] Masters, after a few dismissive paragraphs on the book, concluded: 'Lindsay could not think straight in prose; a discussion of his poetry will prove vastly more fruitful.'[5]

Ultimately, Masters and Ruggles may prove to be right. A dozen good declamatory poems and a few delightful children's poems may be all that is worth salvaging from Lindsay's writings. But, before judgement is passed, his total output must be looked at afresh. Even if such a survey decided that no reassessment of Lindsay's literary merit was justified, it would be surprising if it did not conclude that the literary interest of Lindsay's work—its range of expression, its variety of themes, its ideological cohesion, its contemporaneity—has been underestimated; and that his place in the history of American literature needs redefinition.

The prelude to such a redefinition is the realization that literary excellence and conventional literary success were not Lindsay's aims. My intention in this article is to sketch the framework of beliefs, aims and attitudes within which he operated; a framework within which an *œuvre* of such substantial quantity and uneven quality makes sense. For Lindsay was a creative artist who, in his poetry, prose, drawings and career, was visibly and explicitly less interested in modes of expression than in the ideas he wished to express. He was a propagandist for a spiritually improved and physically planned America.

## II

Lindsay was convinced of the existence of a national *malaise*; and it was this conviction which diverted his artistic conscience into social channels. He was worried about amorality, conspicuous consumption, and urban eyesores. He was horrified by the perversion of electoral processes at city level,

and by scandals at Federal Government level. Darwinistic indifference to social and financial inequalities appalled him; so did the jungle that awaited immigrants. Dedicated materialism was gaining adherence, while traditional standards of religion and morality, to which he subscribed, were slipping.

He determined to stir up awareness of these alarming tendencies; and in the *War Bulletins* of 1909 (his privately printed monthly journal, which only ran to five issues) and in *The Golden Whales of California* (1919) he fulminated against the almighty dollar. To counteract American 'deviationism' he put together his gospel of (oecumenical) Religion, (moral) Beauty, and (socialistic) Equality; and through a series of poems on American history and myth—'Our Mother Pocahontas', 'In Praise of Johnny Appleseed', 'Old, Old, Old Andrew Jackson', 'Abraham Lincoln Walks at Midnight', 'Bryan, Bryan, Bryan, Bryan', 'The Eagle That Is Forgotten' (John Peter Altgeld), and 'Roosevelt'—he tried to establish an American entity. It is in such social contexts that the bulk of Lindsay's writings become comprehensible.

'The effort of my life'[6] and the crux of Lindsay's propaganda 'to build our young land right'[7] was his prose work *The Golden Book of Springfield* (1920), a cautionary description of the urban society that America seemed likely to evolve by 2018. Springfield, Illinois, a typical twenty-first-century city, showed little improvement in human terms. It was as full of race prejudice, political corruption and anti-intellectualism as Springfield, 1918, and as little characterized by sustained reform movements and citizens of integrity. Physically, the American city had changed; it was following Frank Lloyd Wright's urban blueprint for Broadacre City, the national unit which would merge city and country in such a way as to give the best of both worlds: ease and beauty. In a Wrightian 2018, jam-packed skyscrapers in overcrowded streets had been replaced by one or two surrounded by parks. A clean, quiet, functional elegance had refined an intrusive technology, and had made it possible to integrate the sectors of production and consumption.

Wright intended to create a 'city of Democracy',[8] an environmental harmony which would breed social harmony; for he saw the architect as the keeper of the social conscience. Lindsay, who signed himself a 'Rhymer and Designer', was, in his own way, planning American society; and his advocacy of Broadacre City stemmed not only from his aesthetic response to Wright's concept of a new beauty, but also from his concurrence with Wright's belief in the architect/artist/writer as a field worker for democracy. The two men apparently never met, though in the early years of the century both were in Chicago, where Wright lectured to, and Lindsay attended, Hull-House. Although the complete model of Broadacre City was not exhibited until 1934, Wright was publicizing the concept in articles, sketches and exhibits; and Lindsay was familiar with these, as he was with Wright's buildings in Chicago and Springfield. But, while Lindsay desired and described a Wrightian America, he did not positively predict a nation of Broadacre Cities. He merely saw the dual trend in America towards physical change and mental continuum, and argued as powerfully as he could for what he considered the right sort of change.

Lindsay moved in the ideological milieu of the reform impulse of the first two decades of the twentieth century. He had points of contact with the political theories of Herbert Croly, the economic panaceas of Henry George, the Social Gospel of Walter Rauschenbusch, and the muckraking activities of Henry Demarest Lloyd.[9] But his diagnosis of the national *malaise* was too grim for him to affiliate himself with men whose vision of a root evil, and whose advocacy of one-stroke remedies—the readjustment of constitutional checks and balances, a Single Tax, the municipal ownership of utilities, trustbusting—sprang from basic confidence in a just off-course, easily righted America. Lindsay was not so sanguine. He considered America's problems were as much the formidable problems of mentality as the soluble ones of institutional defects. For him the American Dream had become 'a middle-class aspiration built on a bog of toil-sodden minds'.[10]

In the 1920s his brand of pessimistic realism made him an even more alien figure. 'Arm yourself against the worst so that disappointment in humanity is impossible'[11] he had noted in his diary; and he had too few expectations to be disillusioned by the 1914–18 war, or by the Peace of Versailles (in his eyes it was a step forward that the idea of international government had been given top-level airing). As an internationalist he found it hard to condone American isolationism and crudely domestic Presidential criteria; as a conscientious practitioner of the kind of Christian morality that was preached in the Midwest Bible Belt[12] he could not come to terms with the decade's frenetic relaxation of taboos and its cultivation of materialism for its own sake.

But it was not solely in his capacity as an American citizen that Lindsay took it upon himself to criticize and protest; if the national need arose, the artist, as an individual with exceptional talents of perception and expression, had a duty to practise remedial art. Lindsay thus had a writer's concern with style and form; but the nature of his concern was idiosyncratic. He believed that a writer's duty was not to himself, but to his audience, which should be all-class and nation-wide. His artistic conscience told him to put matter and mass appeal before self-expression and aesthetics. Form was to follow the function of social utility.

### III

In 1915 in *The Art of the Moving Picture*, and again in the 1922 edition, Lindsay hailed the motion picture as the most important artistic event of his lifetime. Not only could it lure people in for entertainment, and proceed to please whilst insidiously educating; it was an art form, with an art form's power to regenerate and refine. He tried to imitate it by making his writing a deceptive art for the people.

This stance was as extreme as art for art's sake, and as open to disputation. The logic of Lindsay's theory placed severe limitations on subtleties of construction and vocabulary; obliqueness was at a premium when the common man was the envisaged audience. For, while Lindsay believed in a dormant equality of taste, the American masses he was writing for were at the stage when 'they love best neither the words that explain, nor the fancies that are fine, nor the voice that is articulate with well-chosen speech'. They only responded to emotional, raucous modes of expression, and 'words must be chosen accordingly'.[13]

It could be argued that Lindsay's disregard for traditional refinements of style, and for the Imagist experiments of the New Poetry, was less revolutionary and independent than it seemed. One of his talents was for the production of large, generous, rumbustious verse, which flowed along in spite of its imperfections, and without a great deal of stylistic reworking. A poet of emotion rather than one of intellectual discipline, he had a voracious appetite for recitation, both professionally (from 1913 to 1931) and in his leisure time at home. His conscientious response to duty, in fact, came easily, fulfilled his dramatic dimension, and involved genuine pleasure.

But talent and enjoyment did not guide his conscience; on the contrary, he almost failed to make the connexion. The

national literary circuit acclaimed the choruses in 'The Congo' of 'Boomlay, boomlay, boomlay, Boom', and 'Mumbo-Jumbo will hoo-doo you'; but Lindsay wondered whether he was writing poetry. After all, he admitted, 'one composes it not by listening to the inner voice and following the gleam, but by pounding the table and looking out of the window at electric signs'.[14] Even a prize from *Poetry* in 1913 for 'General William Booth . . .' did not still his doubts; it took the approval of William Butler Yeats to do that.

Lindsay and Yeats met at a dinner party given by Harriet Monroe for Yeats in Chicago in March 1914. Lindsay's recitation of 'The Congo' was the sensation of the evening, and impressed Yeats. In after-dinner conversation with Lindsay he preached the virtues of folk-culture, and told Lindsay that all that survived in America of the much-to-be-desired 'primitive singing of poetry' and the Greek lyric chant was American vaudeville and Vachel Lindsay. The *imprimatur* reconciled Lindsay to his achievement; a man whose artistic conscience was avowedly a social conscience was bound to develop what he came to call 'The Higher Vaudeville'.

Yeats commended to Lindsay the half-sung, half-spoken delivery of such vaudeville acts as Tambo and Bones dialogues, which had an apparent spontaneity, and a quick-fire, incantatory rhythm.[15] But when Lindsay went to vaudeville, he found the total medium had relevance for his propaganda. American vaudeville, which flourished from about 1875 to about 1930, was at the height of its popularity around 1914–15. In country areas touring vaudeville shows had attracted a cross-section of the population; and in the cities white-collar workers, ex-rural Americans, and immigrants with some degree of tenure made up the vaudeville audience. After the turn of the century, vaudeville promoters, capitalizing on the Social Gospel's relaxation of ecclesiastical strictures on entertainment, found it politic to replace the bawdy element of vaudeville with the mildly *risqué*; and, as touring vaudeville shows were gradually replaced by urban vaudeville theatres, a more sophisticated titillation evolved. Yet vaudeville did not merely pander to its public's predictable taste for fantasy and vulgarity, stunts and novelties, freaks and animals, broad humour and scanty costumes. The average vaudeville show regularly included moralizing playlets, dramatic monologues, and the occasional artist of calibre like Ethel Barrymore. Vaudeville got away with comedians who made German, Jewish, Irish and Italian Americans laugh at themselves, and think, however briefly, about the state of the nation. The vaudeville audience enjoyed Albert Chevalier without fully understanding his Cockney allusions; it enjoyed Yvette Guilbert's singing without knowing French: it could be mesmerized by art.

Lindsay enviously experienced this sizeable, mundane audience with an appetite for entertainment (and for a kind of knowledge), and with a capacity to be moved in spite of itself. He determined to imitate vaudeville's techniques, and to build up a recitation ritual which would mix the brash, the exquisite, the everyday, the exotic, the funny, the sentimental and the admonitory. If he could contrive a succession of swift, overwhelming moods, form and content would fuse in self-evident naturalness and rightness. This was why Lindsay became a one-man vaudeville show, willing to don fancy dress, to sing and dance, to use refrains and to repeat lines until they became as familiar as vaudeville fall-lines and catch-phrases. He occasionally achieved this within a single poem—'The Santa-Fé Trail' and 'The Ghosts of the Buffaloes', for example; but more often within a programme of contrasting poems: 'John L. Sullivan, The Strong Boy of Boston'; 'Why I Voted the Socialist Ticket', 'The Potatoes' Dance', and 'The Chinese Nightingale'.

To emphasize that his aim was more serious than vaudeville's, and to counteract its slapstick and revue connotations, Lindsay coined the phrase 'The Higher Vaudeville' to describe the poems he wrote in 'a sort of ragtime manner that deceives them [the American masses] into thinking they are at the vaudeville'. In spite of the rag-time manner he was 'trying to keep it to an art': it was a refined vaudeville, which sprang from his sensitive, critical response to American society, and his awareness of 'democracy [which] is itself a paradox'.[16] Any beauty the Higher Vaudeville might describe or create was as paradoxical as democracy. In 'Billboards and Galleons', for example, billboards were California's new symbols of promise and glamour; they were

> America's glories, flaming high,
> Festooned cartoons, an amazing mixture,
> Shabby, shoddy, perverse and twistical,
> Shamefully boastful,
> Slyly mystical.
>
> (p. 427.)

Lindsay's modification of vaudeville was apparent in his alternative phrase for the Higher Vaudeville, 'The Higher Irony'. 'The Kallyope Yell', for example, was 'part irony, part admiration, listing in metaphor the things that perplex and distract, thereby trying to conquer and assimilate'.[17] One might usefully coin a third term, Higher Chautauqua, to convey what Lindsay was trying to achieve in the Higher Vaudeville, and throughout his writings. The Chautauqua movement (1875–*c.* 1925), which carried on the popular educational traditions of the lyceums with correspondence courses and tours of eminent speakers ranging from Phineas Taylor Barnum to William Rainey Harper, was a uniquely effective way of communicating with the adult population. Chautauqua's aim was mass morality and mass education, McGuffey-style; and Chautauqua's realistic and successful technique was to insert entertainments—minstrels, opera singers, circus acts—among its educational items, or even to disguise education as entertainment. It was an object lesson, Lindsay thought, in the possibility and methodology of large-scale appeal. He pointed out the moral of Chautauqua to his fellow poets: 'From Boston to Los Angeles, we American versifiers, democratic poets, face the problems of our potential audiences of one million or one hundred million we have never conquered, but which the Chautauqua orator, like Bryan, in a tent . . . may reach any day.' He emphasized his conception of the creative artist as the man with the power to reach people and communicate a moral message by describing Bryan as 'from this standpoint . . . the one living American poet'. (This is hardly the place to argue Bryan's political morality!) Full poets in this social sense had to 'learn to make a few songs sturdy enough to endure the confusion of the Chautauqua in a tent, and strategic enough to outlast merciless newspaper scrutiny'.

Lindsay was probably the poet who came nearest his own hope that American poets would 'attempt the Chautauqua thing by devising some sort of rhymed oration of double structure, an oration, at the same time a lyric poem of the old school'.[18] 'Bryan, Bryan, Bryan, Bryan', for example, was *par excellence* a combination of lyricism and stump speech. It was a saga made tense and effective by the contrast between 'the ways of Tubal Cain' and the aspirations '. . . of prairie schooner children / Born beneath the stars / Beneath falling snows' [pp. 98, 101]. In 'General William Booth . . .'

> Big-voiced lasses made their banjos bang,
> Tranced, fanatical they shrieked and sang.

But Lindsay transformed their discordance and his tub-thumping into a perfectly attuned moment when

> The lame were straightened, withered limbs uncurled
> And blind eyes opened on a new, sweet world.
>
> (pp. 124–5.)

The Higher Vaudeville coincided with the pre-war heyday of Imagism, a movement which reflected precisely that dedication to form for form's sake, to the intrinsic worth of beautifully constructed, but comparatively unread and unheard poems, which Lindsay opposed. He scornfully called the imagists 'the Aesthetic Aristocracy',[19] who 'were singing on an island to one another while the people perish'.[20] Ezra Pound, *imagiste*, spoke for this school when he gleefully noted in July 1918 about the fourth volume of *The Little Review*: 'The response has been oligarchic; the plain man, in his gum overshoes, with his touching belief in W. J. Bryan, is not with us.' In the September issue, Lindsay was stung into an equally exaggerated, but telling response: 'I write for the good-hearted People of the Great Pure Republic.'[21]

IV

He might be writing for the people; but was he reaching them? Lindsay found himself in a quandary. He had the message—but had he found the medium? Higher Vaudeville recitations brought in a large audience, and reached a new set of hearers (and sometimes readers): the American *bourgeoisie*. But Lindsay gradually realized that audiences enjoyed and remembered 'The Kallyope Yell', for instance, because that poem revived memories of steam and circus, and not because he had made the calliope an image of bathetic democracy in the lines

> I am but the pioneer
> Voice of the Democracy;
> I am the gutter dream
> I am the golden dream
> Singing science, singing steam.
>
> (p. 122.)

As well as becoming dissatisfied with audience responses, Lindsay came to feel the difficulty of tying the Higher Vaudeville, a natural 'fun' medium, to serious topics; and he began to think of other media and other audiences. He was learning the hard way what Albert McLean noted about vaudeville, that 'cause and effect relationships were completely bypassed, the question of ultimate ends was never raised, and the problem of higher values could be submerged in waves of pathos and humor'.[22] But up to 1920 he continued to operate within the limitations of his audiences; the acclaim he received from 1913 to 1920, however narrowly based, was exhilarating, and must have seemed to him to augur well for the popularization of his ideas through literature. However, in 1920 the tide swung against him. The Higher Vaudeville was no longer a novelty, and his unfashionable artistic conscience would not allow him to project universal dilemmas in personal terms, as Hemingway and Fitzgerald did so successfully. And in 1920 his message in its most studied form, *The Golden Book of Springfield*, flopped. Ironically, its failure was partly due to the logic of Higher Chautauqua. Lindsay was still orienting himself to an all-class audience, and tempered his discussion of social and political trends with a linking fantasy-cum-story. The end-product was an incongruous mixture of the sane and the silly, which irritated serious readers, and bored the rest. Stylistically, the sentiment and rhetoric which he could control in poetry ran away with him in prose. Digressions and exaggerations spilled over one another. But what uncomfortably persistent critique would have been acceptable in 1920, except Mencken's unique brand? Lindsay had picked the wrong moment to be preoccupied with what Americans ought to be: hedonism was about to set in. Today, the sombre fascination of Lindsay's perceptions redeems the book; an ironic reversal of the stylistic success of the Higher Vaudeville. In neither case was the medium the message.

Lindsay hung on to his belief in equality of taste; but he concluded that mass potential was more deeply buried than he had imagined, and mass crassness more deeply rooted. He decided to concentrate on élite audiences, who might read his books, and respond to his schemes: on teachers, students, journalists, businessmen and local dignitaries. Higher Chautauqua techniques were not applicable to these audiences; and he approached them differently. He prepared the ground by sending out a circular letter, 'The kind of visit I like to make'. The letter adjured journalists to teach his verses 'by running them in the newspaper with paraphrases and local applications by the editor'; and made it clear that Lindsay expected the English teachers to have his books 'in the school library or the public library the month beforehand. I mean nothing whatever to an audience unfamiliar with my work . . . I want every member of my audience to have at least some knowledge of these books.'[23] When he lectured on one particular book, 'Dear reader, either bring the book or stay away!' [p. xxx]. At one time he made the half-serious suggestion that only those who could pass an examination on his books should be admitted to his recital/lectures.

Lindsay's attitude to his audience was barely recognizable as that of a creative writer seeking a hearing. He had come to think of himself as a teacher, and of his writings as textbooks. He had obviously become irritated and impatient, for he believed, however mistakenly, that he was offering a vital service to a public which would not avail itself of the service. An element of compensatory, personal arrogance was involved; but so was a generic, artistic arrogance; 'I have as much to say to the American people as Hoover or Hughes or Bryan and in as loud a voice . . . there is as much politics in them [his writings and lectures] . . . as in a speech by Bryan or Hoover or Hughes . . .'[24]

But, if arrogance had come to the surface of Lindsay's artistic nature, he retained humility. In 1910 he had written, illustrated and edited *The Village Magazine*, not so much a magazine as an anthology of his ideas, which he revised and reissued in 1920 and 1925. In his preface he wrote: 'The less you agree with it the more the perpetrator will be pleased. Do him the service to analyse your objections . . . He will welcome essays ten pages long. The editor wants your notion of a visible civilization.'[25] But it was not merely where content was concerned—in this case America's physical and social destiny—that he was open to correction. In 1920 he asked readers for criticism of *The Golden Book of Springfield* (even though it was his most cherished book) in '1. Spelling. 2. Punctuation. 3. Grammar. 4. Rhetoric. 5. Clearness. 6. Continuity. 7. Thought. 8. Practical utility of the book.' He even thought that 'if I am unable to write *The Golden Book of Springfield* as it should be written, maybe I can persuade Squire [J. C. Squire, a friend of Lindsay's, and at this time editor of the *London Mercury*] or some other to write it well and clearly and in a more directly stimulating fashion'. And, just as he had deferred to Bryan, so he called A. J. Armstrong, Professor of English at Baylor University, Waco, Texas, and Lindsay's tour organizer from 1918 to 1925, a greater poet than himself; not for any private poetry that Armstrong may have written, but became without his administrative ability there

would have been no sizeable audiences, and without sizeable audiences Lindsay did not feel justified in calling himself an exponent of that social art of communication, poetry.[26]

Of course, Lindsay's theories were partly Whitmanesque. He was advocating Whitman's 'sacerdotal literatuses', and his programme of culture for the practical life and the working man. But a comparison of the two helps to emphasize the more fundamental social commitment of Lindsay. Whitman called for great audiences if the democracy was to be great; but Lindsay painstakingly attempted to assemble and educate audiences. He consciously avoided a tortuous, Whitmanesque style which only the sophisticated could unravel, and sought for an informal idiom. In 1919, reviewing a book of American Expeditionary Force verse, *Yanks*, he commented that 'while we are reading it, it delivers us from Whitman, thank God. If you really want American poetry, I suggest that you forget Whitman a moment and read *Yanks*.'[27] The comment gives the precise measure of Lindsay's artistic conscience.

V

To his contemporaries Lindsay's work seemed stagnant and retrospective, though in content, if not in style, it was naggingly valid. In one sense, however, he was an anachronism: he was a precursor and practitioner of present-day 'pop art'. He affirmed that popular taste—'the human soul in action'[28]—was a neo-artistic perception; and he, as an artist, by acts of will, representation and reproduction, made this perception total art. Mass consensus had made Mary Pickford[29] a folk-culture queen; and Lindsay repeatedly celebrated her national visual impact in a way comparable to Andy Warhol's statement-painting 'Marilyn Monroe', which consists of repeated rows of her face. The American collage of popcorn and yellow cabs, 'Arrow-collar heroes' and the Star Spangled Banner preoccupied him as realistically and sentimentally as it does many pop artists. And, just as pop artists let others finish their creations, and have them mass-produced, Lindsay, with the same mixture of arrogance and humility, urged other people to adapt and rewrite his work—though he was too far ahead of his times to be taken at his word.[30]

Lindsay diverged from the main stream of pop art in that his aim was propaganda; pop artists tend to draw the line at comment. He was as much concerned to create as to accept popular culture, and he was interested in new media for the specific purposes of uplifting and educating the masses. Yet his enthusiastic support of the motion picture bears comparison with the pop-art theory of the interchangeability of words and pictures, and the communication potential of a nationally recognized alphabet of images. 'Edison is the new Gutenberg. He has invented the new printing',[31] Lindsay wrote; and he went so far as to try his own hand at a new word/picture art which he called 'hieroglyphics': an entirely public art, an easily identified currency of national symbols.[32] His nearest approximation of a successful hieroglyphic was the drawing of a lotus/rose to celebrate the East / West symbolism of the Panama Canal; a pacific symbolism that would have found one American dissenter in T.R.! Motion pictures were hieroglyphics of a more complex sort. They were sculpture-in-motion, painting-in-motion, architecture-in-motion and furniture-in-motion; they were the American people in its envisaged likeness; they were the pop artist's multi-evocative images.

H. L. Mencken wrote of Lindsay's career that 'the yokels welcomed him, not because they were interested in his poetry, but because it struck them as an amazing and perhaps even a fascinatingly obscene thing for a sane man to go about the country on such bizarre and undemocratic business'.[33] As usual, Mencken had a point amidst his hyperbole. Lindsay was implying not only mass deprivation, but temporary mass inferiority. He thus showed a certain lack of tact; and also, in failing to follow up the implications of the theory his conscience made him formulate, a lack of rationality. For instance, was abstract art necessarily selfish art? Did social insight always accompany creative ability? Was equality of taste desirable? Could any writer, without being an ideological weather-vane, consistently appeal to mass audiences which changed their tastes and *mores* in less than a generation?

Lindsay's failure to answer, perhaps even to pose, such questions made him react irrationally to his popularity with an audience which licked off the sugar coating, but left the rest of the pill. He had wanted to be like William Jennings Bryan—but resented being gaped at like a 'Bryan sensation' or 'like Tagore in his nightgown'. He felt he was being 'speculated in like pork'[34]—but wasn't he himself pushing a commodity—his gospel and his urban blueprint—and making certain assumptions about the market? He was paying the penalty of his illogic; he was reacting with heart rather than mind. But his confusion and irateness were measures of his ambitious, earnest socio-artistic conscience; and they were telling comments to his organization of himself as a writer.

*Notes*

1. *Indiana University Bookman*, 5 (1960), 41. Letter to Frederic Melcher, 10 June 1927.
2. Eunice Tietjens, 'Vachel Lindsay's books', *The Little Review*, 1 (Nov. 1914), 57.
3. Vachel Lindsay, *Every Soul Is a Circus* (New York, 1931), p. 110. The limitations of critical approval of Lindsay may be seen in, for example, Conrad Aiken, *A Reviewer's ABC*; Fred B. Millett, *Contemporary American Authors*; Louis Untermeyer, *Modern American Poetry*; Bruce Weirick, *From Whitman to Sandburg*; T. K. Whipple, *Spokesmen*. The works by Masters and Ruggles, cited below, sample journalistic reactions. Lindsay was most seriously treated by a variety of reviewers in the *New Republic*, for which he intermittently wrote movie criticisms.
4. A. J. Armstrong (ed.), 'Letters of Nicholas Vachel Lindsay to A. J. Armstrong'. *The Baylor Bulletin*, 43, iii (1940), 25.
5. E. L. Masters, *Vachel Lindsay* (New York, 1935), p. 385. No solely critical assessment of Lindsay has appeared. The most recent study, by Michael Yatron in *America's Literary Revolt* (New York, 1959), inaccurately treats Sandburg, Masters and Lindsay as city-hating populists. The most satisfactory book on Lindsay—Mark Harris, *City of Discontent* (Indianapolis, 1952)—conveys Lindsay's interest in social reform and cities; but its mixture of novel and biography makes it impossible for a non-specialist on Lindsay to distinguish fact from fiction.
6. Vachel Lindsay, *A Letter for Your Wicked Private Ear Only*, pamphlet (Springfield, 1920?), p. 6.
7. Vachel Lindsay, 'To Reformers in Despair', *Collected Poems* (New York, 1962), p. 335. All subsequent verse quotations are from this edition, and are paginated in the text.
8. See Frank Lloyd Wright, *When Democracy Builds* (New York, 1945), and *The Living City* (New York, 1958).
9. His familiarity with these men was apparent from his much-annotated library, as well as being sometimes implicit, and sometimes explicit, in his writings.
10. Vachel Lindsay, *The Art of the Moving Picture* (New York, 1922), p. 263.
11. Eleanor Ruggles, *The West-Going Heart* (New York, 1959), p. 261. She and Masters had privileged access to Lindsay's diaries.
12. Lindsay was brought up, and remained, a Campbellite, though he acquired oecumenical, supra-denominational loyalties.
13. Masters, op. cit. p. 66. At this early stage of culturization Lindsay thought uniform taste should be created; but he expected that ultimately the faculty of appreciation would show itself to be equally powered, but differently constructed and routed.
14. Ruggles, op. cit. p. 211.
15. For the stimulus of Yeats on Lindsay see Robert Nichols's

introduction of *General William Booth . . .* (London, 1919); for Lindsay's theory of recitation see his own introduction to *Every Soul Is a Circus* (New York, 1931).

16. Jessie B. Rittenhouse, *My House of Life* (Boston, 1934), p. 312 (a letter from Lindsay to Jessie Rittenhouse, 1916). Albert F. McLean, Jr., in a stimulating reappraisal of *American Vaudeville as Ritual* (University of Kentucky Press, 1965), argues that, in style and content, vaudeville was reaffirming the American dream of success, glamour and perpetual novelty; that it attracted an audience of 'New Folk'—city dwellers and immigrants; that it was a folk-culture, and both the creation and the instrument of Americanization. Such a view could be implied from Lindsay's work, though he wished to replace vaudeville's dream with his own. It was certainly his view of the motion picture (below, §V).
17. Vachel Lindsay, *A Letter for My Four Committees in Correspondence*, pamphlet (Springfield, 1916?), p. 4.
18. *A Letter for Your Wicked . . .* , p. 6.
19. *A Letter for My Four Committees . . .* , p. 6.
20. Rittenhouse, op. cit. p. 312.
21. *The Little Review*, 4 (July 1918), 54–5; 4 (September 1918), 6.
22. McLean, op. cit. p. 11. Lindsay also came to subscribe to the convention of prose for socio-political themes. *The Golden Book of Springfield* was disastrously distilled in 'Bob Taylor's Birthday' [pp. 410–22].
23. *The Kind of Visit I Like to Make*, broadside (Springfield, 1920).
24. Armstrong, op. cit. p. 69.
25. Vachel Lindsay, *The Village Magazine* (Springfield, 1910). Read on microfilm; no apparent pagination.
26. Armstrong, op. cit. pp. 30, 95.
27. *Poetry*, 13 (Oct. 1918–Mar. 1919), 329. See also Vachel Lindsay, 'Walt Whitman', *New Republic*, 27, no. 2 (Dec. 1923), 3–4.
28. *The Art of the Moving Picture*, p. 1.
29. Ibid., ch. III and passim; 'The Queen of My People', *New Republic*, 11, no. 2 (1917), 280. Gilbert Seldes, in *The Seven Lively Arts* and *The Great Audience*, cited and supported Lindsay's views.
30. American pop art, many-stranded, can only be tentatively characterized. I have drawn on Lucy Lippard, *Pop Art* (London, 1966). Readers can piece together their own collages from Lindsay's poems; mine was taken from 'The Santa-Fé Trail', 'Billboards and Galleons' and 'Dr Mohawk'.
31. *The Art of the Moving Picture*, p. 224.
32. His execution of hieroglyphics did not live up to his theory. For his theory see *The Art of the Moving Picture*, ch. XIII, and *Collected Poems*, pp. xvii–xlvii, 17–18; for his practice see *Going-to-the-Sun* (New York, 1923), *Going-to-the-Stars* (New York, 1926): 'interchangeable' pictures and text, from which he hoped the text would one day wither away.
33. H. L. Mencken, *Prejudices*, first series (New York, 1919), p. 94.
34. Armstrong, op. cit. p. 70.

## MARC CHÉNETIER
### From "Introduction"
### *The Letters of Vachel Lindsay*, ed. Marc Chénetier

1979, pp. xxiv–xx

Aug. 12, 1900. Do not despise letter writing. A circle of intellectual, worthy correspondents is a splendid field for the development of a wide sympathy, a training in the suppression of the ego, and good practice in English. When a man writes a letter, he should have a kindness in his heart, a rhetoric on his right hand, a dictionary on his left, and a skillful pen in his hand, and a forgiving correspondent in his mind's eye. (VACHEL LINDSAY, *"English" Notebook*. Courtesy of the University of Virginia Library.)

Most Americans and Europeans who specialize in American cultural studies will respond to Vachel Lindsay's name with the same associations: "The Congo," "General

William Booth Enters into Heaven," the Midwest, Edgar Lee Masters, Carl Sandburg, "an evangelist in rhyme," "a poet who jazzed poetry," and so forth. This traditional image is as limited as it is inaccurate.

Lindsay always wanted to be a painter; he studied for years in the Chicago Art Institute and was a student of William Chase and Robert Henri at the New York School of Art. He never renounced that preoccupation. His very vocabulary when speaking of his poetic achievements often partakes of the graphic artist's terminology. Practices and directions that seemingly contradict themselves in his life and works are united on aesthetic grounds. Some have considered him a belated fundamentalist; others, a dangerous radical; others again, a naive clown, a half-boiled uncouth militant of nostalgic Midwestern and populist causes, or, as Amy Lowell would have it, a "middle westerner of the middle class." Still others have thought him great only in what they liked, while they were miserable—or "impossible," to use T. S. Eliot's word—about elements they could not accept. What appeared dispersed, heterogeneous, and incoherent is, however, the active transcription of one unified vision of the world, in homothetic terms, on various fields. Lindsay, the world's first film critic, wrote *The Art of the Moving Picture* in 1915. D. W. Griffith was just beginning then; Sergei Eisenstein was ten years away. While Isadora Duncan revolutionized dancing and Pablo Picasso began—as John Dos Passos once wrote—"to rebuild the eye," Vachel Lindsay took up "Les Jeux Floraux" and invited people to dance his works in the frame of what he called "The Poem Games." The architects and landscapers of the turn of the century found in him a more than willing ear. Everything plastic fascinated Lindsay—a visionary who said in his notebooks, "My eyes are Imperial," who thought that "men see first."

For Lindsay, the different systems of signs were, at the same time, parallel and identical. Mostly they had the same origins and were, therefore, equal expressions of the world of ideas that his Platonist conscience envisaged. Thoughts were pictures in the air; pictures were given, sent by something above; the Logos found multiple channels to manifest itself, but it did not vary: The world was a message, and all systems of signification were attempts to re-create that world, to stem its flow toward the original Word. A keen eye, furthermore, enabled him to discern the similarities in shapes, and his formal approach confirmed his conviction that all signs were equal. His interest in calligraphy was based on its being placed at a philosophic crossroads. Ideas could be found again through forms created by gestures of the body; personality went to meet the truth of the universe by mere physical action. "Make the free flowing line the basis of your work and build upon it gradually all the other elements of composition you so little understand." To him, as to the Symbolists, every line or form was "the verb of an idea." Channeling ideas into forms found similar expression and explanation for Lindsay and, say, Alfred Kubin, Jan Toorop, or Maurice Denis. His intense study of forms, however, led him away from the strictly symbolistic apprehension of reality toward what, to some, are the distinctive marks of all truly modern art, a consciousness and an avowal of the semiotic character of all pictorial and poetic production.

If, with the Symbolists, Lindsay first thought artistic production consisted in "clothing the Idea with a sensible form," he soon became convinced that the interplay of forms themselves was significant enough. His research from then on oscillated between, on the one hand, the construction of a semiotic system that could fit and express both his personal reality and thought and the reality and culture of the land in which he lived and, on the other, a fascinated struggle with spontaneous forms, lines, and shapes that came to his mind. Guillaume Apollinaire, in 1907, wrote that "all plastic writings: the hieratic Egyptians, the refined Greeks, the voluptuous Cambodians, the productions of ancient Peruvians, the small statues of African Negroes proportioned to fit the passions that inspired them [can] interest an artist and help him develop his personality." That a poet should have taken such plastic examples tells of the accentuated convergence and mutual influence of the various arts of the period: Painting turned to a reflection on signs; poetry, to a study of plastic representation and spatial ordering of the linguistic message. Lindsay's own development of written signs into drawings that turned into the creative, inspirational source of his poems lay in the same ideological swath that was being cut all through Europe: somewhere between Wilhelm von Humboldt and René de Saussure, on the one hand, and Charles Blanc (whose "grammar of the drawing arts" came out in 1867) and Henri Matisse, on the other. Between the Impressionists, Malevitch, and Mondrian had begun the thaw of iconic signs that was to revolutionize the approach to signification. Vachel Lindsay was part of that movement, however far removed from it in space and culture and conscience. Codes began to be disrobed, the corporeal and sensual expressivity of forms irrupted onto the scene, gestures became recognized as constituents of systems, black and white struggled on canvases while form and content contracted a definitive wedding. Vachel Lindsay's interest in Paul Klee and Vasili Kandinski, his unintentionally acting in accordance with Giovanni Boldini's wild strokes, his own blend of what Charles Olson was to define in 1959 as "topos, typos and tropos" found a summary in his saying that "out of rhythm came words and form," in his fascination with patterns and movement, in his desire to prove that at the same time, rhythm can be rendered by words and the shapes of letters and forms can organize thought. The emergence of the visual as a new language and of language itself as texture, of canvases and poems as systems, found in Lindsay a somewhat untutored but enthusiastic supporter.

"We are sweeping into new times, in which the eye is invading the province of the ear and in which pictures are crowding all literature to the wall," Lindsay wrote in an unpublished manuscript on the cinema. Such a sentence gives an idea of the importance of Vachel Lindsay's theoretical and practical breakthrough, one that was on the direct line from Symbolism to modern art, one that may well be the missing link between artists of the late nineteenth century and such moderns as Jackson Pollock and Mark Tobey, between Imagism and today's research on the relations of illustrations to poetic texts, between the logocentric rule of nineteenth-century civilization and the media theories of Marshall McLuhan, nearly all of whose basic ideas Lindsay explored and expressed as early as 1915. "Edison is the new Gutenberg," he wrote. "He has invented the new printing."

A prophet in many important areas, Lindsay foresaw the use and power of the electronic media as "a real part of the community life"—of radio, of course, but also of television, and even the use of movies in such fields as advertising.

His study of Egyptian hieroglyphs began in earnest with his writing of *The Art of the Moving Picture*, one of the chapters of which is devoted to Egypt. The film as text and as writing is not divided from the film as pictures: Hieroglyphics organize pictures into a language, and so can the movies. Images dominate the modern psyche, and literacy is replaced by an all-out attack of pictures on the mind. Lest the mind become an "overgrown forest of unorganized pictures," some order must be found and people must learn to read images as they did letters. Light and forms prevail over oral and written language, and signs are the privileged way of access to national unity: "More and more hieroglyphics; more and more speed are making one nation of all the tribes and tongues under this government and really makes them a separate tribe."

His research was always aimed at reunifying a language gone wrong, at harmonizing expressive forms with the needs of the time. His poetry, derived from his art and film studies, consisted mainly in his attempt to elaborate, in his own verse, a system of "American Hieroglyphics." The main idea was to unify expression so that the country could take hold of itself once more, renew its mythology, revivify it, and reorganize the national unconscious. Such was the shamanic dimension of Lindsay's enterprise. His search was for a democratic art founded on the common recognition of signs capable of defining the national identity. The cultural nature of perception he clearly understood, and he tried to homogenize the people's references. American civilization had to ground itself in the education of the eye—in the storing of, and work on, a limited but expansible set of fundamental pictures that might sum up the American experience, fertilize reflection, allow new combinations, and reveal new vistas. Democracy could

only progress through the acquisition of the new language of images and signs, the mastering of the new visual tide flooding the country. Films, billboards, cartoons, advertisements, magazines, postcards, stills, illustrated books, photographs—all added to the more traditional units of visual expression: paintings, frescoes, architecture, gardening and landscaping, dance, pageants. The poet's task became largely to be the educator and mentor of the masses' visual and visionary abilities and tastes: "From the development of the average eye, cities akin to the beginning of Florence will be born among us as surely as Chaucer came, upon the first ripening of the English tongue, after Caedmon and Beowulf."

Poetry, art, the movies, American Hieroglyphics will have the same part to play; all will have to show the American people to the American people, using the most suitable means because, as Lindsay notes, "there is many a babe in the proletariat, not over four years old, that has had more picture enter its eye than it has had words enter its ear." In the last analysis, all of Lindsay's experience and reflections on his own art and that of others will have served but one great purpose: to help America define herself and thereby to improve democracy, "to bring the nobler side of the equality idea to the people who are so crassly equal. . . . Then the people's message will reach the people at last."

# JOHN LOGAN

## 1923–

John Logan was born in Red Oak, Iowa, on January 23, 1923. He studied biology at Coe College, receiving a B.A. in 1943. He earned an M.A. in English from the University of Iowa in 1949 and later undertook graduate work in philosophy at Georgetown. Logan married a librarian, Mary Minor, in 1945 and eventually fathered nine children.

Logan has taught at St. John's in Annapolis, Notre Dame, San Francisco State University, and at the State University of New York at Buffalo. He is a former poetry editor of *The Nation* and *The Critic* and he is the founding editor of *Choice*, a journal of poetry and graphics. He did not begin writing poetry until his late twenties when he was translating Rilke for his graduate studies. About the same time he also converted to Roman Catholicism. His first volume of poetry, *A Cycle for Mother Cabrini*, was published in 1955. Logan's poetry, which is often termed "confessional," relies on both religious sentiment and Freudian family psychology. Logan has written a fictional account of his childhood, *The House That Jack Built* (1974), and has published a collection of essays and interviews in *A Ballet for the Ear* (1983). He was the recipient of the 1982 Marshall Prize for two volumes of his poetry, *Only the Dreamer Can Change the Dream* (1981) and *The Bridge of Change: Poems 1974–1980* (1981). Today Logan is divorced and teaches at SUNY-Buffalo.

### Personal

In the summer of 1960, while working for The University of Chicago law library and stumbling toward a Master of Arts at the University, I needed to enroll in one course (any course) to qualify for comprehensive exams. I found one in the downtown center of the University: a poetry writing course with John Logan, whose name meant nothing to me. I had been writing bad, obscure, "experimental" poetry, but this was going to be my first chance to test my commitment. My idea of passing the test, at the time, was to write a lot. Which I did.

Then, John was teaching for Notre Dame, and riding the busses weekly the 95 miles between South Bend and Chicago. His second book, *Ghosts of the Heart*, was out, and he was writing the poems which would go into *Spring of the Thief*. He

carried a swollen briefcase, and claimed the ability to work aboard the busses. And in classes, he was nothing like any teacher I'd had before. For one thing, he wasn't embarrassed to speak of beauty, or of desire, or to treat the secret content of our badly-written poems seriously. I think most of us were used to thinking only of other people's psychologies, of the inner longings of everyone else. But John, with learning and generosity, convinced us that our poems (and, thus, the lives of the poets) could matter, and raised the level of our concerns. Moreover, when he read our poems aloud, he improved them into gorgeousness! One really wanted to please this man, as much as anyone ever wanted to please one's father. In my case, I never stopped wanting his approval. Like others, I wrote poems to or about him. Near the end of that course, we agreed we'd all write on one "subject." I suggested the circus, which was in town. A bad suggestion. On the basis of which many of us wrote so-so poems. John, however, brooded over it, and eventually completed "The Thirty-Three Ring Circus".

Later, at John's invitation, I joined a group with no academic affiliation: the Poetry Seminar. The group was filled with talented students of John's, including Dennis Schmitz, Bill Knott, Naomi Lazard, Roger Aplon, William Hunt, and many others. We'd meet (I think it was once a month) in the offices of Jordan Miller's Midwest Clipping Service, and talk over our poems with John.

John didn't speak much about technique. That wasn't his way. What he did, rather, was to find what our poems were really about, and to consider, in that light, the implications of what we'd said. And he loved song, and could find it in our mostly unmelodious poems. He encouraged us to read our poems aloud; he helped rid us of silly shame and fear (about our poems) so that we might look at the real shame and fear which was, more often than not, our subject. And always with an overwhelming sense of humanity, and in that singularly rich and tenderly suggestive language which was, and is, the distinctive resonance of the man and his poems. I sometimes think a poet's growth partly depends on his ridding himself of the sense of embarrassment. No one I know has ever helped young poets in this way as John has. It is only one reason, but an important one, I believe, why, whatever the look and feel of our own poems, those of us who studied with John regard him as an everlasting influence, and why the affection and admiration ex-students like myself feel for John keeps a special strength.—MARVIN BELL, "Logan's Teaching," *Voyages*, Spring 1971–Spring 1972, pp. 38–39

## Works

For John Logan the poet's task is to provide "metaphysical solace," to make poetry a weapon in the postmodern struggle Charles Olson has defined as the quest for "what is on the other side of despair." Logan has undergone many changes since the explicitly Catholic poetry of his first volume, *Cycle for Mother Cabrini*; yet, unlike Robert Lowell, whom he resembles in many ways, he struggles to maintain the form if not the content of his religious vision. Where Lowell's latest work narrows in scope and falls victim to a "pessimism of intelligence," Logan's tries to keep intelligence in the service of Lowell's "optimism of will" by meditating on the ways secular processes embody the imaginative forms celebrated by the religious vision. Resurrection, the religious concept most fundamental in his thought, becomes not God's transcendence of flesh into a new law but His lurking beneath the surface of the earth to be brought back to life by the loving attentions of a poetic consciousness. The world resurrected by such attention brings to people a kind of "secular grace"; experience is "revived and given a new life . . . so that there is a kind of resonant quality to it." Moreover, this grace enables the poem to create community, for it gives us not the poet's self but "ourselves", and gives us a vitalized world requesting our loving attention and participation for its completion.

In almost every interview he has given, Logan stresses the idea that "poetry is a secular form of religion" and refers to the following statement from the dust jacket of *Ghosts of the Heart*:

> A poet is a priest or necromancer of the baroque who dissolves by the incantations of his cadenced human breath the surface of the earth to show under it the covered terror, the warmth, the formal excitement and the gaudy color-burst of the sun. This is not a chemical function. It is a sacramental one, and John

Crowe Ransom is right to call poetry 'the secular form of piety.' 'Miraculism everywhere,' he says. . . . I now think poetry itself more religious than I used to do [when I was an explicitly Catholic poet]. There's another reason: I used to be more interested in the wound on the neck of the unicorn, but now I am more interested in the graceful, powerful unicorn underneath the wound. I have discovered that I was less afraid, and therefore (sadly) more prepared to find the ugly under the beautiful than I was to find the beautiful under the ugly. It's not really the skeleton in our closets that we fear, it's the god.

Yet these ideals are impotent without a dramatic context realizing their significance. Logan's ultimate task is to resurrect sentiment from sentimentality, and he achieves this by embodying in his work—both on the level of style and that of dramatic action—a continual struggle between the sufferings of fallen flesh and the forces allowing momentary transcendence of that condition.

The fall in Logan is essentially the fact of our bodies and their oppressive weight, a fact which allows numerous metaphysical and psychological overtones. The body, first of all, epitomizes man's limited powers: the body in its most reduced form is the utter inarticulateness of matter—the condition of the vegetable. Moreover, seen from the freedom of the imagination, it is the body which keeps us dependent on others, which makes us suffer the pains of flesh, and ultimately which steals our youth and our desires in its inexorable progress toward death, "I seek refuge from the elemental tears / for my heavy earthen body runs to grief / and I am apt to drown." The collocation of body, matter, and water recalls Joyce, as does Logan's recurrent linking of the body and matter with his ambivalence towards his mother. In Logan's case, the body in its urge to live literally displaced and destroyed his mother's; yet it still longs for the material support of her breast and continually runs the risk of engulfment as it seeks to fulfill its desires for peace. And an unexorcised mother, like the heavy body, keeps thrusting us back in time, locking us into a limited space and preventing us from gathering the full energies of the present. Finally, the body creates problems in terms of human communication. As Gabriel Marcel, one of Logan's favorite thinkers, puts it, our relation to our bodies is always problematic: we neither possess our bodies like a thing nor are we our bodies the way we are our thoughts and desires. Our bodies always mock our dreams of self-possession—we cannot even see our two eyes, and we thus need others to return us to ourselves. Yet how can we know others since we have for the most part only the presence of their bodies and the attempts these bodies make to articulate themselves? Nonetheless, Logan's Christian imagination works to convince himself and us that the fall is a fortunate one, "Blessed be sin if it teaches men shame." Given our fallen condition, we must renounce the easy temptation to consider ourselves Gods, creating and defining our world and take up "the burden of the tenderness," seeking to resurrect the fleshly needs into the burden of song. A God can only sing of himself, never of "ourselves," and community is for man the ultimate resurrected body.

"The Rescue" is the poem which most purely dramatizes these tensions in Logan's imagination. Not only does the poem enact a thematic resurrection from the despair of materiality through love but it also exemplifies one way that basic drama in Logan's work permeates his style as well:

> I doubt if you knew,
> my two friends,
> that day the tips
> of the boats' white wings

trembled over the capped,
brilliant lake
and fireboats at the regatta
rocketed their giant streams
blue and white and green
in the sun just off the shore,
that I was dying there

Young jets were play-
ing over the lake,
climbing and falling back
with a quick, metallic sheen
(weightless as I am
if I dream),
sound coming after the shine.
They rose and ran and
paused and almost touched
except for one
which seemed to hang back in the air
as if from fear.

I doubt if you know,
my two beloved friends—
you with the furious black beard
your classical head
bobbing bodiless above the waves
like some just appearing god
or you, brown, lean, your bright
face also of another kind
disembodied
when you walked upon your hands—

That as you reached for me
(both) and helped my graying bulk
up out of the lake
after I wandered out too far
and battered weak along the pier,
it was my self you hauled
back from my despair.

The drama of Logan's style might be figured in one of the many meanings in the title, *The Zigzag Walk*—the image of a drunk on his zigzag walk. The drunk treads a narrow line where the human body is continually threatened by two modes of inarticulateness—the first, a sheer aimless wandering whose analogue in speech is the drunk's endless half-meaningless discourse; and the second, the possibility he will lose his teetering balance and aimlessly fall into the sheer materiality of the unredeemed body. The linguistic analogue of this second state is a despairing silence or a literal-minded recording of facts. Yet Logan's drunk keeps trying to regain his balance, to explore the body in its most extreme demonic surrender to the fallen condition, and to possess that body in order to articulate it for a redeeming other drawn close in sympathy. "The Rescue" exemplifies primarily the first of these alternatives, but will also do for the second at this point. The speech seems always wandering off the main topic. Details of the scene or parenthetical notes seem to deny direct speech, but are regathered through the poem as a whole so that the details ultimately intensify and deepen the basic statement of grati-tude. The act of the two boys, in effect, transforms the world, at least for a moment, and that is the ultimate burden of the discourse. The first stanza begins as direct statement, yet breaks off the expected syntax and delays its very important conclusion ("I was dying there") in order to recall the details of the scene, details which contrast with and yet are set off in their clarity by the desperation of Logan's plight. The second stanza seems to digress even more—yet the moment of the literal parenthesis where the connections seem most strained provides the basic detail of weightlessness linked to dreaming which links the

subject of the stanza, the jets, to the boys and establishes the polar opposite of Logan's own condition. This contrast is, of course, what the boys give Logan in their rescue. The final stanzas then repeat and extend the rhetoric of the first. Now, though, it is not physical details that interrupt the statement but Logan's own associations awakened by the boys. Landscape leads to a sense of human presence, but rhetorically and thematically that presence is weightless, suspended, until the last two lines complete the opening clause and explain the redeeming act which justifies Logan's sense of their divinity. Moreover, those final lines preserve a touch of pathos: the gap between his weakness and their power is mirrored in his direct, sincere, yet wandering discourse. Both he and the poem are hauled back from a despair that seems almost inevitable.

It is important to recognize that the stylistic dynamic of "The Rescue" is not a tension between the Apollonian and the Dionysiac. What redeems and gathers meaning is not primarily form or style or any principle of order. And what is redeemed is weakness and matter, not collective energy or communal dream. The tension is Christian not classical, the model incarnational and not political. Style does play a part in the redeeming act—Logan's poems are often superbly crafted in their use of syllabics, of a couplet pattern of off-rhymes, and of verbal wit—but not as a surface phenomenon calling attention to itself. When James Dickey remarked that Logan's "technical abilities are relatively slight," he was in essence objecting to Logan's "prosaic way of writing." Without that prosaic texture, however, the poet approaches the condition of a God and needs no resurrection. He has transfigured the world into his own terms and not cut through the wound to the unicorn's beauty. Moreover, the poet able to transfigure his world into the artifice of language, the maker of autotelic objects has no need for the redeeming participation and love of the reader. The Christian God does not play with flesh, he enters it and suffers its pains before he works his resurrection—and the resurrection is incomplete without the Church as mystical union of partici-pants in the redeeming act.—CHARLES ALTIERI, "Poetry as Resurrection: John Logan's Structures of Metaphysical Sol-ace," *MPS*, 1973, pp. 193–98

*Interviewers:* How did you begin to write? Did you simply work out what you wanted to say, or did you depend a great deal on poetry that you had read?

*Logan:* Actually, one of the first two poems of mine that were published was based on reading—it was based on a text from the Roman author Pliny, from his *Natural History*. I had been reading that in connection with my work in biology classes at St. John's College, and was very much taken by one story that Pliny relates. It has to do with a very heroic man who is very dangerous and has killed a number of the enemy, but who can not be caught himself. When he is finally caught, they throw him to the ground and open his heart. They find his heart covered with hair. That strange quality of the hairy heart, in connection with the courage of the man, made me interested, and I wrote about it in my poem "A Pathological Case in Pliny."

*Interviewers:* Had you read many other poets whose style you learned from or tried to imitate?

*Logan:* No, not really, I had read a good deal of poetry, but I wasn't aware of influence outside of Rilke. I think in my third book, *Spring of the Thief*, there are a couple of poems that show his influence.

*Interviewers:* What do you think it was about Rilke that so attracted you?

*Logan:* It's his great gift of image and his own commit-ment to poetry. He has this marvellous group of letters published in a book called *Letters to a Young Poet*, in which he talks about the necessity of becoming one's own best critic and not continually taking one's work around to various people. One can always find somebody to approve it. It's a book I would recommend for all young students of poetry.

*Interviewers:* Some teachers of novice poets believe that in order to really become a poet you have to go through some sort of apprenticeship where you learn traditional forms. What do you do with your students?

*Logan:* There are two schools of thought on this. One of them, a traditional school, to which people like Milton and the contemporary Theodore Roethke belonged, encouraged writing in imitative forms at the beginning. But I have found with contemporary students that the big problem is to get them to believe in their own voice and to stop echoing other people. So I don't usually use strict forms at the beginning. I try to get them to write a good deal, and to find what is unique in themselves. But I have them read a lot. Then I believe in using forms somewhat later, in order to structure what one is doing once one is free of imitative material.

*Interviewers:* You've written a prose work, *The House That Jack Built*, which I've heard you refer to as a "fictionalized autobiography." We don't often hear those two words put together. Yet a lot of your poetry has an autobiographical "ring of truth" about it. Some people today might call it "confessional poetry." How does your life fit into your poems?

*Logan:* Very often it's not really, historically, "out of life," but the gift of the poet has to do with making it seem as though it were. The important thing is not whether it happened in the life of the poet, but whether it is somehow shared in the life of the reader. That's one of the reasons I don't like the notion of "confessional poetry." I don't really believe in it, because what one talks about is not primarily himself as a poet. If he has any power, he is talking about the reader too. So what is "confessed" is what is in the reader, in a sense—as much as what is in the author. An example might be my poem "Picnic." There never was, actually, such a girl as Ruth and a particular school picnic. I should perhaps not say that, because it disappoints people. It's a product of imagination. I of course went on a number of picnics, but "Picnic" is not about any particular happening.

*Interviewers:* And yet the moment of awakening you describe in "Picnic" is something that happens at one time or another to all of us.

*Logan:* Indeed.

*Interviewers:* Are you conscious of the reader as you write?

*Logan:* Oh, yes. The first audience is the listening part of yourself.

*Interviewers:* When do happenings in your life make for good poems?

*Logan:* Very often, it's an anxiety state, which one works through by writing through it. Poets have what I call the occupational hazard of poetry, which is that they don't know what's happened to them until they find the words to express it. Once you find the words, the experience is altered. If the poem works well, it brings what Dylan Thomas calls "a momentary peace," a temporary end to anxiety. This is something very much like what in religion is called "the state of grace." I think the natural equivalent of grace is the peace, or catharsis, to go back to the old term—refreshment of the inner spirit—that comes from art.

*Interviewers:* I've particularly enjoyed your poem "Shore Scene," and I wonder if we might use it to talk more

specifically about how your poems come into being. Could you read it for us?

*Logan:* Sure.

There were bees about. From the start I thought
The day was apt to hurt. There is a high
Hill of sand behind the sea and the kids
Were dropping from the top of it like schools
Of fish over falls, cracking skulls on skulls.
I knew the holiday was hot. I saw
The August sun teeming in the bodies
Logged along the beach and felt the yearning
In the brightly covered parts turning each
To each. For lunch I bit the olive meat:
A yellow jacket stung me on the tongue.
I knelt to spoon and suck the healing sea . . .
A little girl was digging up canals
With her toes, her arm hanging in a cast
As white as the belly of a dead fish
Whose dead eye looked at her with me, as she
Opened her grotesque system to the sea . . .
I walked away; now quietly I heard
A child moaning from a low mound of sand,
Abandoned by his friend. The child was tricked,
Trapped upon his knees in a shallow pit.
(The older ones will say you can get out.)
I dug him up. His legs would not unbend.
I lifted him and held him in my arms
As he wept. Oh I was gnarled as a witch
Or warlock by his naked weight, was slowed
In the sand to a thief's gait. When his strength
Flowed, he ran, and I rested by the sea . . .
A girl was there. I saw her drop her hair,
Let it fall from the doffed cap to her breasts
Tanned and swollen over wine red woolen.
A boy, his body blackened by the sun,
Rose out of the sand stripping down his limbs
With graceful hands. He took his gear and walked
Toward the girl in the brown hair and wine
And then past me; he brushed her with the soft,
Brilliant monster he lugged into the sea . . .
By this tide I raised a small cairn of stone
Light and smooth and clean, and cast the shadow
Of a stick in a perfect line along
The sand. My own shadow followed then, until
I felt the cold swirling at the groin.

*Interviewers:* What do you remember about its evolution—did it have many other versions? Where did the incident in it take place, if it took place at all?

*Logan:* Well, this one did take place. It happened that I was visiting with a couple of my children and a friend named Pat Sweeney (who later taught at Lone Mountain in San Francisco) and his young brother, Tim, in the sand dunes on Lake Michigan, I think the park that's called "Tower Hill." At any rate, I have difficulty sometimes in scenes with the sea and the sun. For one thing, I am very fair-skinned and I burn easily. I often don't enjoy myself as much as one would expect on an outing. But this day I was determined to enjoy myself. We unpacked the car; the kids went to this hill of sand, "The Tower," and were falling down. We made some peanut butter and jelly sandwiches, and the first thing I did was to bite into a sandwich and there was a bee in it! Actually, it was a yellow jacket, not a bee. It stung my tongue. It worried me a good deal, because I thought some people were very sensitive to yellow-jacket bites. I was expecting my mouth to swell up or swell shut or something.

Then I describe some scenes that took place on the beach that day: the girl building the canals which she then opens to let the lakewater in; the child who was tricked into being sanded into a pit. The last part of the poem—"My own shadow followed then, until / I felt the cold swirling at the groin"— reflects something about the anxiety of the scene, I suppose, but actually it describes the experience of slowly walking out into the water until the cold water reaches the level of the groin.

That's the literal basis of it. You always hope that there's more richness in the actual images and rhythms as they come out than in the literal story.

*Interviewers:* I take it, then, that what you've just said is an illustration of what you meant earlier when you talked about poems growing out of the poet's anxiety. Is the anxiety here the anxiety of a yellow-jacket bite, or do you think there's something more?

*Logan:* As I've said, a beach scene generally is an anxious one for me, partly because of the fear of sunburn, partly because of the Puritan inhibition about sensuality which is so present in a beach scene, and which I think it takes quite a while to get comfortable with—but not for people here in Hawaii who are so used to the constant scene. But when you have only a couple of months a year when you can visit the beach and see the lightly clad bodies, there's sometimes some anxiety associated with that.

*Interviewers:* How much after the incident was "Shore Scene" written?

*Logan:* Pretty shortly. I don't remember exactly.

*Interviewers:* Why did you think that this would be a good subject for a poem?

*Logan:* It seemed to me it had a kind of element of experience that could be shared. There's something archetypal about a beach experience, and about some of the details—the attraction of the boy trapped in the sand. I thought it had a number of details that would touch other people.

*Interviewers:* "Shore Scene" is constructed of ten-syllable lines. Why did you pick that particular form?

*Logan:* The syllabic form gives you a kind of minimum discipline for revising a line and for reaching ahead to discover new images. Of course, a ten-syllable line has been used in a lot of poetry—I don't use it anymore because it tends to break down too easily into iambic pentameter. That's now a sort of cliché rhythm in English poetry. But sometimes one notices that some of his best lines are in a certain number of syllables, and it seems to make sense to choose to write other lines with the same number, if you can.—JOHN LOGAN, Interview with Thomas Hilgers and Michael Molloy, *IR*, Spring–Summer 1980, pp. 221–26

---

## RICHARD HOWARD
### "John Logan"
### *Alone with America*
### 1969, pp. 307–17

John Logan was born in a place called Red Oak, Iowa, in 1923, was educated in Iowa City, has taught in South Bend, Indiana and more recently at the University of New York State at Buffalo. The poetry of this landlocked life has often ransacked literature and history for its pretexts, drawing resourcefully on quotations from Augustine, Virgil, biographies of Rimbaud, Christina Rossetti, Heine, retellings of Homer and observations from Pliny, Dr. Brill and a "sourcebook of Animal Biology." Imitations and epigraphs, versifyings and translations stiffen these poems, which for their length are formally dependent upon few enough means to keep them

erect in the reader's mind. Logan's invocation of Dante and of Botticelli, for example, is altogether inward, not a cry from the rooftops or even from the depths, but an assimilation of substance, as when the catgut stitches suturing a wound are absorbed into the tissues of the traumatized body—this poet is not concerned to derive from his apprenticeship to these creators of Christian formality any semblance of decorum as an Outward Sign. Hence his ardors of dedication, rewritings and apostrophes to *them*, not to their achievement. A further stiffener, often to the point of rigidity, is a recourse to Doctrine, the machinery of the Church which so often makes it hard for us to be sure what a poet would be if he were not part of a going concern larger than himself. The spirits said they had come to give Yeats "metaphors for poetry," and the Catholic Church has often afforded as much, though interested in doing so only, to be sure, as a by-product. One of the rewards of Logan's work is the sense that he must have struggled *against* dogma, must have appealed first to, then away from it (dogma being not the absence of thought but the end of thought), in order to *achieve* transfiguration, not yield to it. Anything else than such an engagement, such a grappling which is as much a flight from faith as a foundering within it, is indeed a succumbing, not an approach, of course, and when we read, in the dedication of Logan's third volume: "The Redemption has happened. The Holy Ghost is in Men. The art is to help men become what they really are," it is apparent, even before we expose ourselves to the poem's action upon us, that we are not in the hands of a mere pietist, that Logan is possessed by no theory but a thirst.

Tautologically enough, in the understanding of Christianity, for a man to become *what he really is* means that he does not become something else, does not undergo or initiate upon himself a metamorphosis, which is the central symbol of divine love as the understanding of Paganism conceived it. For Logan, a man initiates or undergoes a *transfiguration*, is made over only by becoming more intensely and ecstatically himself—becomes what he really is to the exclusion of accident and change. That is the lesson, for him, to be learned from the lives of the saints and the deaths of the martyrs, and to be rehearsed, dreadfully enough, in the very *realia* of his own existence, no less profound for being the more profane: "if some people find my subjects less religious now than they used to be, the reason is that I now think poetry itself more religious than I used to do . . . It's not really the skeleton in our closets that we fear, it's the god."

John Logan's most remarkable and happily most characteristic poems, then, will not be versified accounts of the torture and death of the British poet-martyr Southwell, or even Freudian *aperçus* into the overmothered life of a Heinrich Heine, individual and even indicative as the latter are:

> But his tough old mother stayed on
> And he never became
> The husband; he took to his marriage
> Couch interesting women,
> Remaining a curious virgin.
> In the last years of his life
> He wept at the pain of lust
> Stirred in his tree-like limbs
> Already dry. And he left
> Framing with paralyzed lips
> One more note to his mother.
> Only the ambiguous Dumas cried
> At the holy rite they danced when he died.

Logan's highest achievement, I think, the basis and perhaps the residue of all the other poems, are those—they are to be found in all of his books, more densely in the later ones—of confession, the kind of writing in which experience has not been mediated by knowledge, or at least by learning, and in which the risk, consequently, attendant on transfiguration is greatest precisely where it is run most egregiously—fastest. The autobiographical mode allows this poet to exploit to intense profit the confusion, if not the identity, of his beliefs in God and in the Oedipus Complex. Sometimes indeed I am not so sure about God, but the Western tradition of parricide and piety is certainly furthered here, whether acknowledged baldly ("Man's central difficulty is his old hell with his prick") or in the terms of violent metaphor:

> My mother died because
> I lived or so
> I always chose to believe . . .
> I watched at last for her
> Among our sacred
> Stones, for I was grown
> Before I found her tomb.
> Today I point to that:
> It's there my heavy mother
> Rots. Remember!
> . . . She suffers there the natural turns;
> Her nests on nests of flesh
> Are spelt to that irrational end,
> The surd and faithful Change. And stays
> To gain the faultless stuff reversed
> From the numbers' trace at the Lasting Trump.
> So here my mother lies. I do not
> Resurrect again her restless
> Ghost out of my grievous memory:
> She waits the quiet hunt of saints.
> Or the ignorance of citizens of hell . . .

This, by the way, is the poem that along with posterior attributions to Xenocrates, Richard Eberhart, T. S. Eliot and Alejandro Carrion, begins with epigraphs by Augustine and Dr. A. A. Brill's famous "Years ago I came to the conclusion that poetry too is nothing but an oral outlet." The Quest for Mom, Everyman's Children's Crusade, so to speak, is conducted and pursued in these poems through other biographies and into hagiography, as the "Cycle for Mother Cabrini" attests; yet as Freud insisted, always and only can be resolved in individual experience. Hence the apposite tone of "The Picnic," from which I quote only a glint at the center, an echo of the departure from Eden:

> Afterward we walked in the small cool creek
> Our shoes off, her skirt hitched, and she smiling,
> My pants rolled, and then we climbed up the high
> Side of Indian Gulley and looked
> Where we had been, our hands together again.
> It was then some bright thing came in my eyes,
> Starting at the back of them and flowing
> Suddenly through my head and down my arms
> And stomach and my bare legs that seemed not
> To stop in feet, not to feel the red earth
> Of the Gulley, as though we hung in a
> Touch of birds . . .

That is the articulation of a style, I think; that is a level of meaning: open, unarguable, ecstatic. I find it in the title poem of Logan's third book, *Spring of the Thief*, preeminently, and in perhaps a dozen disbosoming poems elsewhere. Not that Logan's other poems are a loss, or even a lessening, of necessity—just that they are so often something added to experience, not something made out of it, that they substitute for what they cannot enclose. By a paradox which is a commonplace of critical experience, the poems which involve the surface of recondite minds, of recorded lives, are for Logan an excuse for private (rather than personal) locution; after all,

the facts we have not discovered for ourselves are those we can—indeed, those we must—use as symbols. Whereas the poems committed to the often dreary processes of an Iowa boyhood and an Indiana surround—*they* are the poems of an exemplary publicity, personal but not private, not content with or confined to a merely surface report—indeed, like J. F. Powers' fiction, not competent to offer surfaces in any consistently attractive fashion—but condemned to deal with centers, surds, insights, illuminations witnessed in chosen, obsessive, *suffered* images.

John Logan's first brief book, *Cycle for Mother Cabrini*, was published in 1955. In it the poet initiated his series of versified abstracts from the lives of the holy and the modishly hellish. This is their strategy: an oblique title establishing the poet's intimacy with an alien world of discourse, furthered by a quotation in the epigraph, generally in a foreign tongue and untranslated. Then the body or at least the skeleton of the poem itself, usually in short lines and broken—splintered, actually, since this is never a discourse cut at the joints—into several stanzas and parts. Followed by further attributions of subject matter, as "after Athanasius; and after a painting by Morris Graves." There are poems commenting on or at least reporting a pathological case in Pliny and a *pensée* by La Mettrie, the latter full of Logan's peculiar rash learning (Plato, Diogenes, Descartes, Harvey, Boyle and Bacon of Verulam all brought forth) invariably exercised in the refutation of "a chemical function":

> . . . A few more wheels a few
> More springs than in
> Say your better animal?
> And with a closer heart
> To fill the brain with blood
> And start the delicate moral
> Hum in the anxious matter.
> Suppose I agree the soul is
> An engine, admit Descartes
> And the rest never saw
> Their pair of things—never,
> As you say, counted them;
> Then here's the ambiguity,
> And a further problem:
> You say you find an inner
> Force in bodies, and watch
> The smallest fiber turn
> Upon an inner rule.
> Now I don't see that this
> Is such a clear machine!
> In fact I think I wish it were.

This is like listening to one end of a telephone conversation whose significant sense depends on the words inaudible at the other. Yet if we do not know precisely what the familiar words drag after them into the poem ("their pair of things" refers, I guess, to the body and the soul as separate and separable entities), still we know vaguely what the weight of it feels like and, as in all these "commentary pieces," that seems enough to make a poem at one level (or remove) of listening. Logan himself puts it this way: "these poems try to disprove materialism by coming into existence; and that is the extent of their apostolate."

In the poem on Saint Augustine's sixteenth centenary, Logan comes closer to himself, to the experience he may appropriate, not merely cite:

> . . . The brass knobs
> On doors twist easily
> Spring back
> And I lift bread to mouth
> Without trouble, at the corner

Turn right sin is like this
Why sin is natural as blue is
But drags at joints
Unnaturally
Dries membranes with sand

Is most clinging most cold most
Crabbed of all the casual
Things. And you lost your mother
Just as you learned rejoicing
And before you studied

How not to grieve: your brilliant
Bastard Adeodatus
Died too . . .

The fear of being too perfectly understood, the fear that
banishes punctuation marks as it borrows puzzling material
from the context of biography, is mastered a little in one
astonishing poem of transfiguration in this book, "Grandfather's Railroad," which I give with punctuation adduced from
a prose version Logan published three years later in the
*Chicago Review*, part of an impressionist chronicle (by impressionist I mean that desperate skepticism which casts about
to find, but cannot find, a floor to the universe) of boyhood
called *The House That Jack Built*:

I think my grandfather knew
I'd never seen a negro
Before. I thought I saw

The shallow trough that cut
The field he showed me real
As a railroad, and reached

North for Kemling Store.
I could have seen the bright
And keen two rails where they

Grow so thin I could have
Run, vanishing where they did.
My grandfather told me

The old underground railroad
Wound through Montgomery
County; he pointed a fine

Haired finger and led
Across the dust-lit land
The believed negroes—gold,

Lithe and wild as the wind-
Burned wheatfield.
My grandfather didn't see

My pickanniny doll had three
Pigtails she shook like
Ribboned wings on wires

From the train windows. Fires
Shivered in our capturers' eyes.
Who cares! The cars of great

Black men roar past
Shadowing the field like clouds
Or giants that seem to slow

And stride as lean as trees
Against the north sky.

Here the world of the child, its unexplained terrors and
inexplicable tininess are really *enacted* in the verse; "I knew my
limbs sang on me sometimes," Logan acknowledges (and the
humility is really an assertion), his midwest vernacular strong
in another song of experience, "Pagan Saturday," and it is such
singing which makes him the religious poet he seeks to be
rather than the strained or anyway the strenuous devotions to
the saint celebrated in the cycle for which this first book is
named. Frances Xavier Cabrini, an Italian-born nun who
became the first Beata from the United States, was canonized

in 1950 by Pius XII, who named her the patron saint of
emigrants; in her grimy, unglamorous work founding schools,
orphanages and convents, hospitals and nurseries, across the
continent and even in Latin America until her death in 1917,
she looms for this poet as one of his company of "saints as
heroes of the will." It is because "Mother Cabrini" knows "our
schools / our stores our gods and business rules" that Logan says
he invokes her, and finds, visiting her body that is subject to the
laws of mortal decay, his peculiar comfort, rather like the
solace afforded by viewing Jocasta's corpse after she has been
embalmed:

I thank God Mother Cabrini's
Body is subject to laws
Of decay. To me it is
A disservice when flesh

Will not fall from bones
As God for His glory
Sometimes allows. I speak thus
For flesh is my failing:

That it shall rise again
Salvation. That it shall not
Conquer is my blind hope.
That it shall rise again

Commanding, is my fear.
That it shall rise changed
Is my faith. I think
I can love this saint

Who built highschools
And whose bones I came upon
Today . . .

This is closer to oratory, and then abruptly to natural utterance,
than the rest of Logan's cycle, which depends for its music, its
incantatory extension, on a single effect, that of the rhyme
concealed within the arbitrary line:

But Christ what do we do
That hate pain and can't
Pray and are not able
Not to sin; that stay
Contrite, until night: did you
Not die for us too?

In fact, as James Dickey has pointed out in one of the few
critical notices of Logan's work that signifies beyond the jacket
blurb, this poet's technical abilities are relatively slight, and
really begin and end with an uncommon capacity for coming
up with a strangely necessary and urgent observation and
setting it among others by means of ordinary, unemphatic but
rather breathless language "which makes his lines read something like a nervous onrushing prose." That is why we find, in
the same number of the *Chicago Review* that published *The
House that Jack Built*, Logan reviewing Edward Dahlberg as:

Sad with the melancholy of the young who yearn for
freedom from the curse of snakes—of Hippolytus
turned by the thought of Phaedra from his beloved
horse and bow. And sad with the other sadness of the
old who have failed to save their sons, the awful
agony of Laocoön seeing the ruin of his sons
. . . But nowhere the tenderness of the father
whose serpent is the instrument of his love, and his
sons the arrows of his quiver, his daughter the apple
of his eye.

And then find him in his second book, *Ghosts of the Heart*,
1960, versifying the passage into his own transfiguration of
experience, in the "Lines to His Son on Reaching Adolescence":

. . . But for both our sakes I ask you wrestle
Manfully against the ancient curse of snakes,
The bitter mystery of love, and learn to bear
The burden of the tenderness
That is hid in us. O you cannot
Spare yourself the sadness of Hippolytus
Whom the thought of Phaedra
Turned from his beloved horse and bow,
My son, the arrow of my quiver,
The apple of my eye, but you can save your father
The awful agony of Laocoön,
Who could not stop the ruin of his son.
And as I can, I will help you with my love.

This self-imitation, quarrying one's marble from one's own (already exhibited) bleached bones, is variously instructive, but most of all a lesson in what formal transactions and achievements we should *not* look for in Logan's verse and in his attitude toward versifying. In these long, incremental poems about the intensification of reality—the "starry pinnacle of the commonplace"—into an epiphany of being, the rhythms do not discover themselves in lines, or even in units cut from the lines "as the poet's mask is cut out of the flesh of his face—to amplify the light gestures of his soul"; rather Logan's verse is accessible—to him, to us—as mass, not as unity, so that his most successful poems are, like "The Picnic" in the second book and like the title poem in the third, *Spring of the Thief*, published in 1963, too long to illustrate favorably by quotation. If this is prose, though, if it is difficult to see the cause of the form (the appearance on the page) in this:

. . . but if I look the ice is gone from the lake
and the altered air
no longer fills with the small
terrible bodies of the snow.
Only once these late winter weeks
the dying flakes
fell instead as manna or as wedding rice
blooming in the light
about the bronze Christ
and the thieves. There these three
still hang, more than man-
sized and heavier than life
on a hill over the lake
where I walk
this Third Sunday of Lent.

—if this is prose, it wears, and not vainly, the poem's vestments, the apparel of priesthood. As Logan himself explains: "A poet is a priest or a necromancer of the baroque who dissolves by the incantations of his cadenced human breath the surface of earth to show under it the covered terror, the warmth, the formal excitement . . ." Cadenced human breath, call it, as an instrument to get at transfiguration. The energy of spiritual substance driving through endless labyrinths, the very corridors of the lungs, which occasionally coil into form. There is a strange innocence about this voice, for all its ecclesiastical knowingness and all its bookish insistence, the innocence of a man who does not say, like Jarrell's despairing Woman at the Washington Zoo, "Change me! change me!" but rather, "Make me Myself!" Besides the centripetal mode of confession he has come upon, the one I think most effective and convincing in his repertory:

I was born on a street named Joy
of which I remember nothing
but since I was a boy
I've looked for its lost turning.
Still I seem to hear my mother's cry
echo in the street of joy.

She was sick as Ruth for home
when I was born. My birth
took away my father's wife
and left me half
my life. Christ will my remorse
be less when my father's dead?
Or more . . .

—besides this guilt-ridden litany which manages never to sound like Robert Lowell even if it does so at times merely by not being very accomplished, Logan has two other means of approaching transfiguration: one is the historical commentary I have mentioned, which in *Spring of the Thief* he brings to a characteristic pitch of laceration, as in "The Experiment That Failed":

I have not written my poem
about the Pope and the two young men
the obscure muddle-headed muse
first sent when I first read
histories of the transfusion experiment.
And I do not know why,
except for the bitter fight
in me—about the fact
the boys died. (But so did he.)

. . .
What can I find out?
I don't even know what killed them.
Or him. And I do not want
to think it was the loss of the blood
of manhood. There is always more of that.
Besides, it is really feminine
to bleed and be afraid.
Well, what then?
The old one and the two young
men. Two fresh stones, or wells—
and the powerful untried pen.
What cut them down? . . .
Yet my mind keeps holding back
with its bloody axe of stone
another idea
nobody wants known:
that it was the hope of a fresh, transmuted life
for which the Pope
and the two sons died.

The other mode of access to transfiguration is the ecstatic identification of the poet's consciousness with objects, with landscape, with a weather intromitted into the self. Thus in his "Eight Poems on Portraits of the Foot," Logan comes right out with it:

It is the wish
for some genuine change other than our death
that lets us feel (with the fingers of mind)
how much the foot desires to be a hand

. . .
The man yearns toward his poem.

*The wish for some genuine change other than our death*, the transfiguration of life not in immortality but in the living of it—that is Logan's manfully shouldered burden and his quest: the body of this man's work *cries out* to be poems, and in that exploration, which is his own form of prayer, who can doubt he has already succeeded and will—over his towering argument as over his tottering art—prevail.

## ROBERT BLY
### "John Logan's Field of Force"
*Voyages*, Spring 1971–Spring 1972, pp. 29–36

### I

John Logan is one of the five or six finest poets to emerge in the United States in the last decades. He has won a position of considerable respect without the help of the major schools or their magazines. Most of the Black Mountain poets were unable to swallow a poetry that takes the Christian God seriously; the academics are unable to swallow a poetry both Christian and bristly, which looks wild and matted to them, like the head of a desert fanatic. In the title poem of *Spring of the Thief* Logan asks what is the new name, the winter name, of God—"where is his winter home?" He writes a poetry in which heavy, turgid sensuality, whirling like water in a ditch after a sudden rainstorm, is mingled with a luminous spiritual leaping, a desire that everything in the world shall shine from within, like the popular vision of an angel or a flying saucer. It differs profoundly, in kind, from most American poetry, in that the emotions in Logan's poems, and the subjects of them, matter. He remarks that perhaps "freshness is the changed name of God." "I bear him in the ocean of my blood/ and in the pulp of my enormous head. /He lives beneath the unkempt potter's grass of my belly and chest./ I feel his terrible, aged heart/ moving under mine. . . ."

We can feel in this quotation Logan's powerful phrasing— the words leave his hands bent permanently into their phrases and the phrases are bent so as to carry emotion better. He has a great gift for the phrase that carries deep emotion—and carries it somehow invisibly, in ways impossible to pin down. In his work, he shows himself again and again able to create a poem without the hectic surface which so many poets depend on to carry emotion. Instead he moves us simply by moving language.

> The partridge has some sadness or other
> knocking softly in his throat as a missing motor . . .

### II

It's not clear to me why his poems are able to move us, when so many other poems fail. Surely the extraordinary range of language has something to do with it—the shifts in tone keep our feelings alive as we read. Speaking of a workglove that was stiffened with white paint:

> It is the left glove, the hand of the Magus,
> of all who come late or by devious ways
> oblique to honor Christ.

There the language is dignified and elaborate. In "The Thirty-Three Ring Circus", a linked collection of tiny poems, the language is swift and sure, and resembles the simple language of Neruda in his *Odas Elementales*:

> The man who
> stands on one
> finger, on
> one edge of
> a ladder
> on one leg,
> on a ball,
> tentative
> as a soul.

Throughout the poem, the language changes abruptly and masterfully, alternating formal and street tones:

> An old, slop-hat, melancholy
> father, no Telemachus found,
> rushes weeping about the tent and ground.

> After the tent is down,
> the circus owner, having
> slept over, sets out
> in his red car, feeding
> his silver slug of a house
> over the waste he is lord of.

One of Logan's poems I love the most is "Eight Poems on Portraits of the Foot" (after some close-up photographs of human feet that Aaron Siskind did). The yearning everything alive feels to change into something still more alive is brought forward:

> It is the wish
> for some genuine change other than our death
> that lets us feel (with the fingers of mind)
> how much the foot desires to be a hand.

The language in this poem does not change mood so much as speed. Logan lets it hurtle forward, then suddenly slows it down. These changes too keep our feelings alive.

> The foot is more secret, more obscene,
> its beauty more difficultly won—
> is thick with skin and
> so is more ashamed than the hand.
> One nestled in the arched back of the other
> is like a lover
> trying to learn to love.
> A squid or a slug, hope still alive
> inside its mute flesh
> for the grace and speed of a fish.
> Sperm in the womb quickens to a man.
> The man yearns toward his poem.

The speed opens and closes like a heart-valve in slow motion.

### III

I feel in Logan's poems always that the language is being used to build something, rather than to reflect something. We can imagine phrases as a series of wood chunks which the speaker can pile on top of each other, to build castles, or to reach apples high on a tree, or we can imagine phrases as a series of pieces linked carefully on the horizontal, to make something calm like the surface of a pond. In the last decade, most poets feel that language should be surface-of-a-pond language. Hemingway began it in America—he presents a calm reflecting water-language, underneath which we are to imagine garfish, female alligators, despair-trolls, monster-emotions, that rise if the light above the water is turned off. David Ignatow writes this way, and succeeds just as often as Hemingway, that is, very often. The "New York Poets" or the St. Mark's school, write this way too, giving us the horizontal surface, though we are not so sure anymore that there are slashing emotion-creatures underneath. Maybe the pond is empty. W. S. Merwin used to build with his language, as in his whale poem, but for the last few books his language too has become the calm-pond-surface language, reserved, mysterious, able to catch moonlight, but too passive. If we drain the pond what we find is more water.

John Logan's language has never been passive, but always muscular and masculine, and he has always had a vision of language as something a man speaks to get off the earth, to cancel gravity temporarily. As he grows older, this element becomes stronger. No one alive has his fantastic power with adjectives. His sense for adjectives is really a love for the magnificence of the universe—there above us, which we can't quite reach. Here are his adjectives for a python in "The Zoo" from *Zigzag Walk*:

> The vicious, obvious and obscene
> greedy-eyed old python
> hauls itself along.

At times he builds slowly, laying down flight stairs upward,
then realizing what a hard time grandeur has on this planet,
suddenly pulls it all down in a second:

> Look
> even the great brown handsome official Kodiac
> bear
> has caramel in its hair.
> Twenty charming little tropical monkey kids
> jabber in the phony trees. The gibbon is unkempt.
> The yellow baboons bark, and they travel in groups.
> There, ugly and alone,
> awful and no longer young,
> is that ornery thing
> an orangutan.
> Disconsolate, contrite,
> red-haired widow who was once a wife
> you pace and turn, and turn and pace
> then sit on your repulsive ass
> and with a hairy hand
> and thumb delicately pinch an egg and
> kiss its juice deep into your head.
> Oh misery! Misery! You wretched bride.

At other times John Logan braids language, making a
whip that he hits himself with, or a jungle-vine rope with
which he lets himself down dangerous cliffs. Or in his greatest
poems he creates some sort of weaving, living, headed *thing*—
all muscle, weaving about in the air, swaying. Its motions are
curiously like the motions emotions make as they rise from the
unconscious, and we feel strange because we know these
motions: we have seen them at night since birth each time an
emotion rises toward a dream; and as in a dream, we have no
choice: we are moved.

What I have clumsily called the pond-surface-language is
able to reflect apples beautifully, and castles, and its development is a discovery, a triumph. But John Logan's creation of
this living swaying poem out of American language is a
discovery too, a great triumph.

### IV

If a man visualizes language as if it were a block of wood,
or a snake's body, that is, something with cubic space, one
implication is that he is not seeing it only from above, or
below, but also from the side—he is walking *around* it. Doing
that he becomes aware of the shape of a phrase but the shape of
a phrase is its sound. Mountains seen from far up look flattened
out, but if you are near them, they have jagged and powerful
shapes. Evidently each word has a different shape, if felt with
fingers of the throat.

Here is Logan, again in his new book *Zigzag Walk*,
writing a small poem on a Morris Graves painting:

> I'm the ugly, early
> Moor Swan of Morris Graves.
> I'm ungainly. I've got
> black splotches on my back.
> My neck's too long.
> When I am dead and gone
> think only of the beauty of my name.
> Moor Swan Moor Swan Moor Swan.

That's not a heavy poem, but it's very aware of the shape of the
phrase "Moor Swan." He says of Cummings that on the day of
his death

> like a young man again you cut down
> an aging, great New England oak.

Then he describes the stroke Cummings had later that
afternoon:

> Your back
> bent. You wrapped your lean,
> linen arms close around your life
> naked as before our birth,
> and began to weave away from earth
> uttering with a huge, awkward, torn cry
> the terrible, final poetry.

"Linen" is marvelous there, and the weaving away marvelous
too.

John Logan is one of the very few masters of sound we
now have alive, as the Russians have Voznesensky. Voznesensky's poetry, like Logan's, is basically a poetry of the body. I
think the reason Voznesensky's poems are so powerful in sound
is not because he is exploiting sound in the headway—as
Auden does sometimes—but because he is adapting the sounds
to express body-motions. His poems are rooted in the muscle
system and in the chest system, as Neruda's sound is rooted in
the stomach and intestinal system. A poem like Voznesensky's
"Goya" is made of body movements—a woman's body swinging from a rope, a war tongue moving—these movements have
found sound "embodiments."

So also in John Logan's work we see sound chosen by the
body-intelligence. He says of some Pacific rocks:

> A little way above and to the left, the gull
> folks form
> quiet lines of their own.
> They wait along the brilliant height,
> and then, when it's time,
> fling them—
> selves off into the wide
> arcs and dips of their angelic suicides.

We can find these embodiments in language of body movements everywhere in his poems; his new Hawaii poem is
brilliant in this respect. I'll quote two other examples from
older poems. He says of driftwood logs:

> Here the logs lie like lovers
> short by long, benign,
> nudging gently in the tide.

His lines about gorillas the Russians would like:

> Gorillas lope and glare and crash
> the glass in the Primate House.

The gorillas too have been pulled inside the body.

### V

In thinking of why John Logan's poems are moving, I
haven't even mentioned the most obvious reason—the marvelous openness in them, the way he talks directly of his
loneliness, his prayers, the decay of the body, his divorce and
his children, his disappointments or failures. This openness is
new to poetry of the last thirty years, and Allen Ginsberg and
James Wright in differing ways have done a lot to encourage it.
The so-called "Confessional Poets" have also. Yet something
mysterious is involved. We notice that sometimes a "confessional poet" confesses in a poem something more horrendous than anything Logan or Wright confesses and we are not
moved at all. Most underground newspaper poetry is not
moving either, though it's open. So openness is not poetry in
itself, unless something else—maybe body sound—is there.
Robert Lowell's recent *Notebooks* for example have almost no
sound in them at all, or rather, the sound they do have is
mental sound. The *Notebook* poems are full of mental sound,
but this mental sound doesn't link with the body processes, and
so it doesn't move us. Ben Belitt in his translations of Spanish

poets substitutes mental sounds for the body sounds that the Spanish poets have, and so the poem doesn't move us in English, though it is very moving in Spanish. Allen Ginsberg has some body sound, and a great deal of mental sound. His chanting is strengthening his body sound. But John Logan is suffering the anguish of the body. He is sensitive to its instinctual shifts, and the magnetic energies of the body-intelligence. He follows its paths in a zig-zag dance, like the heavy masted ship in the wind, or the capillaries moving sideways through the flesh.

He is one of the great masters in English of body sound, and, as we all know, that hints at a union of mind and body, of literary life and private life, of spirit and flesh, and though these worlds are always in danger of falling apart, yet, as Goran Sonnevi says in a poem "the powerful force field" "holds it together."

# JACK LONDON

## 1876–1916

Jack London was born in San Francisco on January 12, 1876, the only child of a spiritualist, Flora Wellman; his mother claimed that Jack's father was an itinerant astrologer, William Henry Chaney. Wellman married John London, a widower and father of two, in September 1876. John London gave his name to his wife's illegitimate child and it was not until his college days that Jack learned the truth about his birth. In later years London claimed that his favorite childhood book was Ouida's *Signa*, a story about an illegitimate peasant boy. As a child Jack was ignored by his mother and was all but raised by his stepsister Eliza. His stepfather was a devoted family man, but often could not work because of injuries suffered during the Civil War.

By the age of fourteen Jack was working eighteen-hour days at a cannery in Oakland. Frustrated with the low pay and poor working conditions, he bought a small sloop named the *Razzle Dazzle* and began pirating the commercial oyster beds. Known as "the Prince of the Oyster Beds," he briefly joined the California Fish Patrol after being caught by the government. In 1893 he signed on with the *Sophia Sutherland* and set sail for Asia. After his return he wrote "Story of a Typhoon off the Coast of Japan," which won him first prize and $25 in a San Francisco newspaper contest. In 1894 he set out with Kelly's Army, a group of militant unemployed workers determined to march to Washington. Eventually the group disbanded somewhere in the Midwest and London was arrested in Buffalo on charges of vagrancy. He described the wanderings of a tramp in *The Road* (1907). After serving his thirty-day sentence he decided to return to Oakland in order to finish his education. During his year as a nineteen-year-old high school student he joined the Socialist Party. In 1896 he passed the difficult entrance exam for the University of California and began his studies at Berkeley that fall. He lasted only one semester; this time he was off to the Klondike in search of gold.

His adventures in the tundra provided the impetus for his first successful works of fiction. Although he returned to California prematurely because of an attack of scurvy, he had seen enough in one year to write about the wilderness at length. By 1900 his stories were being published in national magazines to excellent reviews. His famous *The Call of the Wild* (1903) and *The Sea-Wolf* (1904) both sold well. During a visit to England he collected material about life in London's East End. These reflections on the ravages of industrialism were published in *The People of the Abyss* (1903). In 1904 he traveled to Asia to cover the Russo-Japanese War for the Hearst newspapers. His articles were tinged by ardent Anglo-Saxon bias, which today would be described as white supremacism. London ran for mayor of Oakland on the Socialist ticket in 1905. That same year he married Charmian Kittredge after divorcing Bessie Maddern, his wife of five years. Although he never had the son he longed for, he fathered two daughters by his first wife.

London was a prolific writer, authoring over 400 pieces of non-fiction, 200 short stories, and more than fifty books. Among his later works, *The Iron Heel* (1907), a dystopian novel containing premonitions of Fascism, and *John Barleycorn* (1913), a semi-autobiographical portrait of an alcoholic, are notable. His final years were marked by various unsuccessful projects of a non-literary nature; during this time, despite his doctors' warnings, he continued to drink heavily and consume his regular diet of raw meat and raw fish. He died on November 16, 1916.

GEORGE ORWELL
"Introduction"
*Love of Life and Other Stories*
1946

In her little book, *Memories of Lenin*, Nadezhda Krupskaya relates that when Lenin was in his last illness she used to read aloud to him in the evenings:

> Two days before his death I read to him in the evening a tale by Jack London, "Love of Life"—it is still lying on the table in his room. It was a very fine story. In a wilderness of ice, where no human being had set foot, a sick man, dying of hunger, is making for the harbour of a big river. His strength is giving out, he cannot walk but keeps slipping, and beside him there slides a wolf—also dying of hunger. There is a fight between them: the man wins. Half dead, half demented, he reaches his goal. That tale greatly pleased Ilyich (Lenin). Next day he asked me to read him more Jack London.

However, Krupskaya goes on, the next tale turned out to be "saturated with bourgeois morals," and "Ilyich smiled and dismissed it with a wave of his hand." These two pieces by Jack London were the last things that she read to him.

The story, "Love of Life", is even grimmer than Krupskaya suggests in her short summary of it, for it actually ends with the man eating the wolf, or at any rate biting into its throat hard enough to draw blood. That is the sort of theme towards which Jack London was irresistibly drawn, and this episode of Lenin's death bed readings is of itself not a bad criticism of London's work. He was a writer who excelled in describing cruelty, whose main theme, indeed, was the cruelty of Nature, or at any rate of contemporary life; he was also an extremely variable writer, much of whose work was produced hurriedly and at low pressure; and he had in him a strain of feeling which Krupskaya is probably right in calling "bourgeois"—at any rate, a strain which did not accord with his democratic and Socialist convictions.

During the last twenty years Jack London's short stories have been rather unaccountably forgotten—how thoroughly forgotten, one could gauge by the completeness with which they were out of print. So far as the big public went, he was remembered by various animal books, particularly *White Fang* and *The Call of the Wild*—books which appealed to the Anglo-Saxon sentimentality about animals—and after 1933 his reputation took an upward bound because of *The Iron Heel*, which had been written in 1907, and is in some sense a prophecy of Fascism. *The Iron Heel* is not a good book, and on the whole its predictions have not been borne out. Its dates and its geography are ridiculous, and London makes the mistake, which was usual at that time, of assuming that revolution would break out first in the highly industrialised countries. But on several points London was right where nearly all other prophets were wrong, and he was right because of just that strain in his nature that made him a good short-story writer and a doubtfully reliable Socialist.

London imagines a proletarian revolution breaking out in the United States and being crushed, or partially crushed, by a counter-offensive of the capitalist class; and, following on this, a long period during which society is ruled over by a small group of tyrants known as the Oligarchs, who are served by a kind of SS known as the Mercenaries. An underground struggle against dictatorship was the kind of thing that London could imagine, and he foresaw certain of the details with surprising accuracy; he foresaw, for instance, that peculiar horror of totalitarian society, the way in which suspected enemies of the régime *simply disappear*. But the book is chiefly notable for maintaining that capitalist society would not perish of its "contradictions", but that the possessing class would be able to form itself into a vast corporation and even evolve a sort of perverted Socialism, sacrificing many of its privileges in order to preserve its superior status. The passages in which London analyses the mentality of the Oligarchs are of great interest:

> They, as a class (writes the imaginary author of the book), believed that they alone maintained civilisation. It was their belief that, if they ever weakened, the great beast would engulf them and everything of beauty and joy and wonder and good in its cavernous and slime-dripping maw. Without them, anarchy would reign and humanity would drop backward into the primitive night out of which it had so painfully emerged. . . . In short, they alone, by their unremitting toil and self-sacrifice, stood between weak humanity and the all-devouring beast: and they believed it, firmly believed it.
>
> I cannot lay too great stress upon this high ethical righteousness of the whole Oligarch class. This has been the strength of the Iron Heel, and too many of the comrades have been slow or loath to realise it. Many of them have ascribed the strength of the Iron Heel to its system of reward and punishment. This is a mistake. Heaven and hell may be the prime factors of zeal in the religion of a fanatic; but for the great majority of the religious, heaven and hell are incidental to right and wrong. Love of the right, desire for the right, unhappiness with anything less than the right—in short, right conduct, is the prime factor of religion. And so with the Oligarchy. . . . The great driving force of the Oligarchs is the belief that they are doing right.

From these and similar passages it can be seen that London's understanding of the nature of a ruling class—that is, the characteristics which a ruling class must have if it is to survive—went very deep. According to the conventional left-wing view, the "capitalist" is simply a cynical scoundrel, without honour or courage, and intent only on filling his own pockets. London knew that that view is false. But why, one might justly ask, should this hurried, sensational, in some ways childish writer have understood that particular thing so much better than the majority of his fellow Socialists?

The answer is surely that London could foresee Fascism because he had a Fascist streak in himself: or at any rate a marked strain of brutality and an almost unconquerable preference for the strong man as against the weak man. He knew instinctively that the American businessmen would fight when their possessions were menaced, because in their place he would have fought himself. He was an adventurer and a man of action as few writers have ever been. Born into dire poverty, he had already escaped from it at sixteen, thanks to his commanding character and powerful physique: his early years were spent among oyster pirates, gold prospectors, tramps and prizefighters, and he was ready to admire toughness wherever he found it. On the other hand he never forgot the sordid miseries of his childhood, and he never faltered in his loyalty to the exploited classes. Much of his time was spent in working and lecturing for the Socialist movement, and when he was already a successful and famous man he could explore the worst depths of poverty in the London slums, passing himself off as an American sailor, and compile a book (*The People of the Abyss*) which still has sociological value. His outlook was democratic in the sense that he hated exploitation and hereditary privilege, and that he felt most at home in the company of people who worked with their hands: but his instinct lay towards acceptance of a "natural aristocracy" of strength, beauty and talent. Intellectually he knew, as one can see from various remarks in *The Iron Heel*, that Socialism ought to mean the meek inheriting the earth, but that was not what his temperament demanded. In much of his work one strain in his character simply kills the other off: he is at his best where they interact, as they do in certain of his short stories.

Jack London's great theme is the cruelty of Nature. Life is a savage struggle, and victory has nothing to do with justice. In the best of his short stories there is a startling lack of comment, a suspension of judgement, arising out of the fact that he both delights in the struggle and perceives its cruelty. Perhaps the best thing he ever wrote is "Just Meat". Two burglars have got away with a big haul of jewellery: each is intent on swindling the other out of his share, and they poison one another simultaneously with strychnine, the story ending with the two men dead on the floor. There is almost no comment, and certainly no "moral". As Jack London sees it, it is simply a fragment of life, the kind of thing that happens in the present-day world: nevertheless it is doubtful whether such a plot would occur to any writer who was not fascinated by cruelty. Or take a story like "The *Francis Spaight*". The starving crew of a waterlogged ship have decided to resort to cannibalism, and have just nerved themselves to begin when another ship heaves in sight. It is characteristic of Jack London that the second ship should appear after and not before the cabin boy's throat has been cut. A still more typical story is "A Piece of Steak". London's love of boxing and admiration for sheer physical strength, his perception of the meanness and cruelty of a competitive society, and at the same time his instinctive tendency to accept *vae victis* as a law of Nature, are all expressed here. An old prize-fighter is fighting his last battle: his opponent is a beginner, young and full of vigour, but without experience. The old man nearly wins, but in the end his ring-craft is no match for the youthful resilience of the other. Even when he has him at his mercy he is unable to strike the blow that would finish him, because he has been underfed for weeks before the fight and his muscles cannot make the necessary effort. He is left bitterly reflecting that if only he had had a good piece of steak on the day of the fight he would have won.

The old man's thoughts all run upon the theme: "Youth will be served". First you are young and strong, and you knock out older men and make money which you squander: then your strength wanes and in turn you are knocked out by younger men, and then you sink into poverty. This does in fact tell the story of the average boxer's life, and it would be a gross exaggeration to say that Jack London *approves* of the way in which men are used up like gladiators by a society which cannot even bother to feed them. The detail of the piece of steak—not strictly necessary, since the main point of the story is that the younger man is bound to win by virtue of his youth—rubs in the economic implication. And yet there is something in London that takes a kind of pleasure in the whole cruel process. It is not so much an approval of the harshness of Nature, as a mystical belief that Nature *is* like that. Nature is "red in tooth and claw". Perhaps fierceness is bad, but fierceness is the price of survival. The young slay the old, the strong slay the weak, by an inexorable law. Man fights against the elements or against his fellow man, and there is nothing except his own toughness to help him through. London would have said that he was merely describing life as it is actually

lived, and in his best stories he does so: still, the constant recurrence of the same theme—struggle, toughness, survival—shows which way his inclinations pointed.

London had been deeply influenced by the theory of the Survival of the Fittest. His book, *Before Adam*—an inaccurate but very readable story of prehistory, in which ape-man and early and late Palaeolithic men are all shown as existing simultaneously—is an attempt to popularise Darwin. Although Darwin's main thesis has not been shaken, there has been, during the past twenty or thirty years, a change in the interpretation put upon it by the average thinking man. In the late nineteenth century Darwinism was used as a justification for *laissez-faire* capitalism, for power politics and for the exploiting of subject peoples. Life was a free-for-all in which the fact of survival was proof of fitness to survive: this was a comforting thought for successful businessmen, and it also led naturally, though not very logically, to the notion of "superior" and "inferior" races. In our day we are less willing to apply biology to politics, partly because we have watched the Nazis do just that thing, with great thoroughness and with horrible results. But when London was writing, a crude version of Darwinism was widespread and must have been difficult to escape. He himself was even capable at times of succumbing to racial mysticism. He toyed for a while with a race theory similar to that of the Nazis, and throughout his work the cult of the "nordic" is fairly well marked. It ties up on the one hand with his admiration for prize-fighters, and on the other with his anthropomorphic view of animals: for there seems to be good reason for thinking that an exaggerated love of animals generally goes with a rather brutal attitude towards human beings. London was a Socialist with the instincts of a buccaneer and the education of a nineteenth-century materialist. In general the background of his stories is not industrial, nor even civilised. Most of them take place—and much of his own life was lived—on ranches or South Sea islands, in ships, in prison or in the wastes of the Arctic: places where a man is either alone and dependent on his own strength and cunning, or where life is naturally patriarchal.

Nevertheless, London did write from time to time about contemporary industrial society, and on the whole he was at his best when he did so. Apart from his short stories, there are *The People of the Abyss*, *The Road* (a brilliant little book describing London's youthful experiences as a tramp), and certain passages in *The Valley of the Moon*, which have the tumultuous history of American trade unionism as their background. Although the tug of his impulses was away from civilisation, London had read deeply in the literature of the Socialist movement, and his early life had taught him all he needed to know about urban poverty. He himself was working in a factory at the age of eleven, and without that experience behind him he could hardly have written such a story as "The Apostate". In this story, as in all his best work, London does not comment, but he does unquestionably aim at rousing pity and indignation. It is generally when he writes of more primitive scenes that his moral attitude becomes equivocal. Take, for instance, a story like "Make Westing". With whom do London's sympathies lie—with Captain Cullen or with George Dorety? One has the impression that if he were forced to make a choice he would side with the Captain, who commits two murders but does succeed in getting his ship round Cape Horn. On the other hand, in a story like "The Chinago", although it is told in the usual pitiless style, the "moral" is plain enough for anyone who wants to find it. London's better angel is his Socialist convictions, which come into play when he deals with such subjects as coloured exploitation, child labour or the treatment of criminals, but are hardly involved when he is writing about explorers or animals. It is probably for this reason that a high proportion of his better writings deal with urban life. In stories like "The Apostate", "Just Meat", "A Piece of Steak" and "Semper Idem", however cruel and sordid they may seem, something is keeping him on the rails and checking his natural urge towards the glorification of brutality. That "something" is his knowledge, theoretical as well as practical, of what industrial capitalism means in terms of human suffering.

Jack London is a very uneven writer. In his short and restless life he poured forth an immense quantity of work, setting himself to produce 1,000 words every day and generally achieving it. Even his best stories have the curious quality of being well told and yet not well written: they are told with admirable economy, with just the right incidents in just the right place, but the texture of the writing is poor, the phrases are worn and obvious, and the dialogue is erratic. His reputation has had its ups and downs, and for a long period he seems to have been much more admired in France and Germany than in the English-speaking countries. Even before the triumph of Hitler, which brought *The Iron Heel* out of its obscurity, he had a certain renown as a left-wing and "proletarian" writer—rather the same kind of renown as attaches to Robert Tressell, W. B. Traven or Upton Sinclair. He has also been attacked by Marxist writers for his "Fascist tendencies". These tendencies unquestionably existed in him, so much so that if one imagines him as living on into our own day, instead of dying in 1916, it is very hard to be sure where his political allegiance would have lain. One can imagine him in the Communist Party, one can imagine him falling a victim to Nazi racial theory, and one can imagine him the quixotic champion of some Trotskyist or Anarchist sect. But, as I have tried to make clear, if he had been a politically reliable person he would probably have left behind nothing of interest. Meanwhile his reputation rests mainly on *The Iron Heel*, and the excellence of his short stories has been almost forgotten. A dozen of the best of them are collected in this volume, and a few more are worth rescuing from the museum shelves and the second-hand boxes. It is to be hoped, too, that new editions of *The Road, The Jacket, Before Adam* and *The Valley of the Moon* will appear when paper becomes more plentiful. Much of Jack London's work is scamped and unconvincing, but he produced at least six volumes which deserve to stay in print, and that is not a bad achievement from a life of only forty-one years.

## DEMING BROWN
### From "Jack London and O. Henry"
*Soviet Attitudes toward American Writing*
1962, pp. 219–30

Until the 1950's, Jack London was by far the most popular American author in Soviet Russia. Over thirteen million copies of his works have been printed since the Revolution. Even today he continues as a popular classic, and it is probable that over the Soviet period as a whole he has been read more widely than any other non-Russian author.[1]

At the time of the Revolution, London had already been the favorite American writer in Russia for a number of years. He had been introduced shortly after the Revolution of 1905,[2] and by 1916 his vogue was described as "truly extraordinary."[3] In 1941, recalling London's influence on the pre-Revolutionary generation, the poet Ilya Selvinski wrote that "whoever has not passed through this view of life cannot be a real man. . . . This is the first cigar we smoke in our youth."[4] More solemnly, a critic contended that London had served the Russians as an antidote for the "gloom" and "despondency" of literature in the years just before World War I.[5]

Despite the curtailment of printing under War Communism, London's books continued to come out. Only in 1921, when almost all book production ceased, did a work of his fail to appear. With the revival of publishing in 1922, he quickly jumped to the leading position among Americans. The new burst of enthusiasm for London, however, was not all salutary. The best of his writing had already been translated before the Revolution, and by the middle twenties critics were protesting against the indiscriminate printing of everything he had signed.[6] His name had become a magic word among the enterprising publishers of the NEP, guaranteeing sure sales for even the trashiest of his potboilers. This overexuberance among the publishers explains in part the decline of interest in the author at the beginning of the next decade.[7]

The nature of London's appeal for Soviet Russians is clear. They deeply respect the elemental vigor of his writing, his hearty temperament, and his love of violence and brute force. Particularly fascinating are the primitive settings of many of his stories, in which man must pit his naked strength against the hostile forces of nature. In fact, the Russian taste for stories of hardy adventure in remote and uncivilized territories was cultivated largely through his works.[8] In the twenties critics even complained that his books had produced in the Russian mind a distorted image of America—a land of mysterious adventure instead of a country of industrialization and highly developed capitalist contradictions.

Less tangible, but equally charming for the Russians, is a quality which the critics have described variously as "love of life," "manliness," "a healthy attitude toward hardship," or "the will to live." London's ability to dramatize simple, fundamental virtues such as courage, perseverance, and strength of will is repeatedly extolled. It was natural for Soviet readers to identify themselves with this "singer of the strong man who struggles with and conquers nature."[9] In 1927 a critic explained the current enthusiasm for London by pointing out that the Russian people "themselves have had bitter experiences in life."[10] The virile mood of his writings probably harmonized with the feeling of limitless power and accomplishment through struggle which, by all accounts, millions of Russians were experiencing at the time.

Running through the whole body of Soviet commentary on London is a refrain of respect for his hardihood, expansive love for humanity, largeness of heart, forthrightness, and healthy aspiration. His strongest trait, the critics feel, is his optimism. Not a reasoned, philosophic position, but an emotion, a mood which dominates the action of his stories, this optimism springs from a feeling of human energy and power, and is based on faith in the strength of man. The bearers of this optimism are his heroes—cheerful, bold, purposeful fighters whose iron wills have been toughened in tense struggle. The potential hortative value of these heroes was great, for they exemplified traits which, theoretically, were being imbued in the new Soviet man himself. And there is evidence that London did provide Russians with a kind of inspiration. Here are excerpts from remarks made by three presumably typical Soviet readers, as quoted by a critic in 1933:

"London generates heroism in people, he writes about those who seek adventure in life."

"London's books give you energy. . . ."

"After every book of London you are cheerful for a long time, you have a thirst for movement, for activity."[11]

The fullest expression of admiration in this respect came in 1935, when the critic Nemerovskaya wrote: "London is strongest and brightest where he places man face to face with nature, where he reveals his physical power, increased a hundredfold by the exertion of his will and by the superiority of the human intelligence. Closeness to nature and the struggle with nature ennoble man, create their own special moral principles in the personal relationships of people and in the organization of the social collective. . . . A strong and active volition, and an inexhaustible thirst for life and a faith in victory over obstacles—this is the fundamental characteristic trait of London's heroes. . . ."[12] The critics' endorsement of London, however, has always been severely qualified. The defect most frequently mentioned is his all-pervasive individualism. His bold, aggressive heroes seek purely personal victories. They brave the Klondike and roam the seas solely in search of wealth or adventure. The heroes of *The Valley of the Moon* want only "independence, well-being, and cosiness,"[13] and Martin Eden is motivated by a "thirst to rise on the capitalist ladder."[14] Furthermore, they combat adversity single-handedly. While some of them display mitigating virtues of comradeship and self-sacrifice, most of them prefer a solitary to a collective struggle against their environment. London prefers sails to steamships. He writes a perpetual hymn to self-reliance, and while the heroes are fascinating on a purely emotional level, their rugged individualism militates against the idea of social cooperation.

Another aspect of London's heroes is even more disturbing, the critics feel, because it places the author squarely in the camp of social and political reaction. His typical hero is a "blond beast," an Anglo-Saxon morally and physically superior to the members of other races. Frequently this racial chauvinism is tied to a glorification of imperialism, for he sends his heroes on rapacious colonial adventures in which they subjugate and exploit primitive peoples. An apt summary of the critics' reaction is the remark of Startsev in 1938: "Indeed, all of Jack London is in this contradictory combination of hybrid elements: heroics, the pathos of struggle with nature and human bravery which are close to us, and bourgeois individualistic motives which are alien to us."[15]

Such estimates are typical of the Soviet period as a whole, for the critics have noted many paradoxes in the ideological makeup of London. The author consciously identified himself with the world proletariat, studied Marx, was a politically active Socialist, and wrote passionately about the class struggle. On the other hand, he squandered much of his talent in writing for the bourgeois market and was charmed by the capitalist fleshpots. His outlook on the class struggle was profoundly influenced by Nietzsche, whose individualism attracted him no less powerfully than the collectivism of Marx.

Contradictions such as these, however, could be tolerated by critics in the early and middle twenties, for the Soviet ideological mold had not yet hardened.[16] Some critics insisted that many of his writings were genuinely proletarian; others felt that he was little more than a mercenary of the bourgeoisie; and still others indulged in the temporary luxury of refraining altogether from ideological judgments. But the demand for definitive ideological analysis of established writers was growing, and the question of London was a particularly nagging one. His works were being read by precisely those broad Soviet masses who were supposed to be the true audience of a genuine writer of the people. However, Soviet theory already held that a writer who is popular with the proletariat is not necessarily "proletarian." Many opposing elements were present in his writing, but such complexity did not preclude Marxist classification.

A special inducement for establishing a consistent view was Lenin's own opinion of the American. As recorded by his widow, Lenin's reaction was the following: "Two days before his death I read to him in the evening a tale of Jack London, *Love of Life*—it is still lying on the table in his room. It was a very fine story. In a wilderness of ice, where no human being had set foot, a sick man, dying of hunger, is making for the harbour of a big river. His strength is giving out, he cannot walk but keeps slipping, and beside him there slides a wolf—also dying of hunger. There is a fight between them: the man wins. Half dead, half-demented, he reaches his goal. That tale greatly pleased Ilyich. Next day he asked me to read him more Jack London. But London's strong pieces of work are mixed with extraordinarily weak ones. The next tale happened to be of quite another type—saturated with bourgeois morals. Some captain promises the owner of a ship laden with corn to dispose of it at a good price; he sacrifices his life merely in order to keep his word. Ilyich smiled and dismissed it with a wave of his hand."[17] The critics have cited these episodes frequently—in each case an appeal to authority. But this authority had approved of one aspect of London and had disapproved of another, and it was still necessary to reconcile these views in terms of a single concept.

The year 1927 marks the turning point in interpretation of the man and his works. A completely damning article by an American, Joseph Freeman, appeared in Russian translation. Less a criticism of London's writing than of the man himself, this article described him as a complete political and moral bankrupt. He had begun as an honorable writer, and had ended by selling sexual novels to the Hearst press. He wrote for money and hated what he wrote. This was merely a symptom of his petty bourgeois nature. London's life had been a tragedy of internal paradoxes, since "everywhere we find in him contradictions between the word and the deed."[18] Later in that same year a Russian critic referred to London's "compromise."[19] From then on the critics agreed that he was *not* a proletarian writer, harbored no illusions regarding the "proletarian" content of his writing, and explained everything he had written in terms of his petty bourgeois ideology. Whether or not this indicates the establishment of a "line" on London, it seems evident that Soviet enthusiasm had indeed been disproportionately great in terms of his worth as a purveyor of Marxist values.

Adoption of the proposition that London was fundamentally oriented to the American petty bourgeoisie *in all that he wrote* finally enabled the critics to develop an elaborate rationale to explain his apparent ideological inconsistencies. Briefly, the analysis of London's ideology that has obtained in Soviet criticism for the past thirty years goes as follows: He was neither a proletarian nor an apologist for the bourgeoisie. Rather, he was a typical "petty bourgeois rebel," who vacillated between adoration of the standards of the dominant capitalist class and a longing for reorganization of society through socialism. According to the *Literary Encyclopedia* in 1932, he was a victim of the "unstable position" of his class: "The socialism of London is merely a 'promised land' for which those who would save themselves from the misfortunes of capitalism yearn, while still dedicating themselves to the individualism of the petty bourgeois milieu."[20] He sympathized with the proletariat, had some understanding of its psychology, and viewed social change as a process of class struggle. But his preoccupation with the strong individual and his fascination with the primitive "dog-eat-dog" element of economic and social conflict impelled him to portray the proletarian masses as an "abysmal brute," incapable of organized, decisive political action. Because he lacked faith in the strength and volition of the proletariat, his attitude toward the cardinal question of social revolution was defeatist.

An example of the change in interpretation is the critics' treatment of the novel, *The Iron Heel*. In 1925, the well-known Marxist critic Friche had cited the novel as evidence that a "healthy class instinct" had led London to revolutionary conclusions: ". . . compared with Sinclair, who believes in the possibility of peaceful installation of socialism . . . Jack London knows that the new society can be born only from the fire and blood of social revolution." His was "a laugh of triumph, in sympathy with the proletariat."[21] In that same year another critic, who contended that basically London was not a proletarian, nevertheless agreed that "such separate and relatively late works" as *The Iron Heel* could be considered proletarian.[22] By 1933, however, this was the prevailing opinion, as expressed by the critic Dinamov: "*The Iron Heel* is a continuous cry of despair, it is a retreat before the might of capitalism. . . . London, like Upton Sinclair now, tried to combine revolution with evolution . . . and it is clear that he could not understand the nature of revolution."[23]

In the past thirty years, Soviet criticism has adhered to the thesis that London was an ideologist of the petty bourgeoisie. As a rule, he concentrates either on characters who are being forced down from the petty bourgeoisie or on individuals who are trying to raise themselves up from the proletariat. Nearly all of them, however, are striving solely for personal independence. Their search can take any one of three forms: escape, compromise, or revolt. Those who seek escape leave the city and its frustrations in search of a simpler, more primitive existence, either on a farm or in the wilderness, where they undertake "imperialistic" adventures. Those who compromise seek economic independence by playing the game according to the rules of the existing order. Sometimes these heroes succeed, in which case the artistic results are considered deplorable. Others in this second group, however, either fail or, having attained wealth, become disillusioned with it. The third group of heroes—those who refuse either to escape or to compromise—is best exemplified by Ernest Everhard, the hero of *The Iron Heel*, a political leader militantly engaged in the class struggle. Finally, there is the semi-autobiographical hero, Martin Eden, who is torn between all three desires—escape, compromise, and revolt—and ends as a suicide. The *Great Soviet Encyclopedia* makes the following comment: "Idyllic or happy outcomes with London are presented most unconvincingly. On the other hand, the struggle, failure, and destruction of his favorite heroes are drawn with great brilliance."[24] The ability to show convincingly the failure of a hero in conflict with bourgeois society places London in the "main stream of American literature, the stream of petty bourgeois realism."[25] The paradox of this "petty bourgeois individualist" who is at the same time a socialist, is explained historically: "The unstable position of the American petty bourgeois of the end of the nineteenth and beginning of the twentieth centuries, the hopes of working one's way up in the world, which were generated by the rapid general ascent of capitalism in America, on the one hand, and the increasing engulfment of the petty bourgeoisie by big capital, its proletarianization, on the other hand—all this generated along with the idealization of personal success and power, along with the theory of inequality of people, along with the apologia of capitalism, also a certain inclination toward the perception of socialistic theory, the slogans of class struggle, and revolutionary reformation of capitalist society."[26]

After placing London in historical perspective, Soviet criticism became generally more lenient toward his ideological vagaries.[27] Typical was a remark made in 1941: "However naive and confused the social outlook of London may have been, he was subjectively honorable and his revolutionary convictions were deeply sincere. . . ."[28] Meanwhile, in the 1930's he remained a steady favorite, although the circulation of his books dropped to less than half of what it had been in the twenties. His stories of animals continued to fascinate young Soviet readers. (*White Fang* is his most popular book in Russia, and has been made into a movie.) And the critics, for all their ideological reservations, continued to admire his heroes. Dinamov, for example, felt that the stories of Alaska "teach firm comradely solidarity and give one a brisk zest for living."[29] In at least one instance, this kind of enthusiasm gave rise to wild excesses. One critic in 1937 was reported as feeling that the hero of *Smoke Bellew* was endowed with such qualities as socialists are made of. He is reported to have written that from such men as Smoke there emerge "people's heroes, fighters against social oppression, revolutionaries."[30] In response, another critic declared that Smoke in the role of a people's hero would be even funnier than one of O. Henry's cowboys would be as a "bearer of revolutionary morals."[31]

During World War II, London's works were singled out for publication when most other Americans were dropped, and he remained in favor even during the cold war. However, his reputation did not remain unscathed. As a Westerner, he was automatically suspect. In 1949, for example, a writer portrayed a Soviet wrestler as "deriving faith in his own strength, a burning desire to win, resolution in the struggle, sober courage in a difficult moment," from reading over and over a story of London. Two alert critics construed this as an act of kowtowing before the bourgeois West: "[The author] impudently asserts that the excellent Soviet wrestler was inspired to victory not by love of his Fatherland, but 'by the well-worn pages' of a book by Jack London."[32] Then, in 1951, a chance comparison of Boris Polevoi's *The Story of a Real Man* with London's *Love of Life* brought about a re-examination of the London hero. It was discovered that London's protagonist—deserted by his partner, dragging himself painfully across the ice, and locked in a savage death struggle with a hungry wolf—was fighting only for life itself, and that it had not occurred to the author to stipulate whether it was a capitalist or a socialist existence which the hero had in mind as he struggled! The fact remained that Lenin had liked the story. But a critic suggested that Lenin had probably valued it chiefly as an illustration of capitalist morality, in which comrades desert each other.[33] If this increasingly meticulous and absurd insistence on doctrinal purity in London should continue, Soviet critics may soon argue themselves into an ideological dead end.

The fact remains that in spite of his loss of ideological respectability in terms of current official doctrine, London continues to be published. Such novels as *Martin Eden* and *The Iron Heel* have recently been reissued in large editions, and the latter novel, which is actually a negative utopia, has been strongly promoted as a picture of contemporary America. This would suggest that London is now published as a critical realist, rather than as the creator of supercharged heroes.

*Notes*

1. "Publication of Fiction in the U.S.S.R.," *Soviet Literature*, No. 11 (1954), p. 209.

2. G. Lelevich, "Frants Yung. *Dzhek London kak poet rabochevo klassa*," *Pechat i revolyutsiya*, Nos. 5–6 (1925), p. 511.

3. Abraham Yarmolinsky, "The Russian View of American Literature," *The Bookman*, September (1916), p. 48.

4. Ilya Selvinski, "Obrazi Ameriki," *Internatsionalnaya literatura*, Nos. 9–10 (1941), p. 239.

5. V. Kirpotin, "Nashi simpatii k amerikanskoi literature," *Internatsionalnaya literatura*, Nos. 9–10 (1941), pp. 615–16.

6. Boris Anibal, "Dzhek London. *Igra*," *Novy mir*, No. 5 (1925), p. 156; L. Vasilevski, "Dzhek London. *Lunaya dolina*," *Zvezda*, No. 5 (1924), p. 279.

7. Lev Vaisenberg, "Perevodnaya literatura v Sovetskoi Rossii za desyat let," *Zvezda*, No. 6 (1928), pp. 110–22.

8. The critics considered London's influence to be responsible for the interest in James Oliver Curwood in the middle twenties. Curwood was soon found to be a pale imitation. R. Culle, "American writers and literature in Soviet Russia," *Russki golos*, November 6, 1927; Vaisenberg, op. cit., pp. 116 and 121.

9. Olga Nemerovskaya, "Sudba amerikanskoi novelly," *Literaturnaya uchyoba*, No. 5 (1935), p. 79.

10. Culle, op. cit.

11. S. Dinamov, "Zametki o Dzheke Londone," *30 dnei*, No. 9 (1933), pp. 53–54.

12. Nemerovskaya, "Sudba . . . ," op. cit., p. 80.

13. Vasilevski, op. cit., p. 279.

14. B. Pranskus, "Dzhek London," *Literaturnaya entsiklopediya*, Moscow, 1932, VI, 574.

15. A. Startsev, "K voprosu ob O. Genri," *Internatsionalnaya literatura*, Nos. 2–3 (1938), p. 353.

16. Prior to 1927, his faults were viewed as aberrations and not as organic deficiencies in his outlook. Thus, a reviewer in 1923 found many flaws in the novel *Hearts of Three*, but mildly concluded that "lovers of light and diverting reading will read it with great enthusiasm." (K. Loks, "Dzhek London. *Serdtsa tryokh*," *Pechat i revolyutsiya*, No. 6, 1923, p. 250.) Another found the novel "empty," but refrained from relating it to the rest of London's works. (Sergei Bobrov, "Novyie inostrantsi," *Krasnaya nov*, No. 6 [1923], p. 252.) In this same year a critic complained of the "banal images," "absence of powerful dramatic action," and "unskillful composition," of *The Iron Heel*, but merely added that the novel "does not belong among the author's best works." (L. Rozental, "Dzhek London. *Zheleznaya pyata*," *Pechat i revolyutsiya*, No. 5, 1923, p. 298.) A thoroughly scathing review of *The Valley of the Moon* in 1924 made no attempt to generalize about his total product. (Vasilevski, op. cit.) Also in 1924, *The War of the Classes* was criticized simply as the unfortunate attempt of an artist to write as a sociologist. (Ch., "Dzhek London. *Borba klassov*," *Zvezda*, No. 5, 1924, p. 283.) The tone of disappointment with an old friend, and of surprise at the extent of his error, continued in 1925. See Anibal, op. cit.; Sergei Obruchev, "Dzhek London. *Za kulisami tsirka*," *Pechat i revolyutsiya*, No. 4 (1925), p. 287; and Lelevich, op. cit.

17. Nadezhda K. Krupskaya, *Memories of Lenin*, New York, 1930, pp. 208–9.

18. Dzhozef Frimen, "Dzhek London kak revolyutsioner," *Na literaturnom postu*, No. 2 (1927), pp. 46–51.

19. V. Solski, "O. Genri," *Na literaturnom postu*, No. 7 (1927), p. 46.

20. Pranskus, op. cit., p. 577.

21. V. Friche, "Tri amerikantsa," *Novy mir*, No. 5 (1925), pp. 126–28. Apparently, Friche changed his mind in later years. The *Literary Encyclopedia* cites him as an authority for the opinion that London was *not* proletarian, and quotes him as having written, "London was heart and soul with an entirely different social milieu than the working class. . . ." Pranskus, op. cit., p. 578. The encyclopedia takes pains to specify that this opinion appeared in the third edition of Friche's *Ocherk razvitiya zapadnykh literatur* (1931), which may indicate that in the first two editions Friche expressed himself otherwise. His book *Ocherk razvitiya zapadno-yevropeiskoi literatury*, mentions London only in describing *The Iron Heel* as a "Utopian novel, which describes the coming socialist revolution in the United States." (p. 254) I have been unable to find a copy of any of the editions of *Ocherk razvitiya zapadnykh literatur*.

22. Lelevich, op. cit., pp. 511–13.

23. Dinamov, "Zametki . . . ," op. cit., p. 55.

24. "Dzhek London," *Bolshaya sovetskaya entsiklopediya*, Moscow, 1938, XXXVII, 397.

25. Pranskus, op. cit., p. 578.

26. Ibid., p. 576.

27. An exception was the critic Dinamov, who insisted bitterly that London's was the "ideology of a social traitor" ("Zametki . . . ," op. cit., p. 58), who had been "bought and corrupted." (S. Dinamov, "Smeshnoye i strashnoye u Marka Tvena," *Izvestiya*, April 21, 1935.)

28. G. Vainshtein, "Dzhek London (65 let so dnya rozhdeniya)," *Literaturnoye obozreniye*, No. 2 (1941), p. 83.

29. Dinamov, "Zametki . . . ," op. cit., p. 54.

30. As quoted in A. Startsev, "K voprosu ob O. Genri," op. cit., (1938), p. 353. The quotation is from an article of P. Balashov in *Literaturnoye obozreniye*, No. 21 (1937), which I have been unable to procure.

31. Ibid., p. 353.

32. From B. Ivanov and E. Rodikov, "Bourgeois Cosmopolitans in Sports Literature," *Komsomolskaya pravda*, March 6, 1949, as translated and condensed in *Current Digest of the Soviet Press*, April 5, 1949, pp. 55–56.

33. P. Skomorokhov, "Zhizn i literatura," *Znamya*, No. 5 (1951), pp. 158–61.

## RICHARD GID POWERS
### "Introduction"
### *The Science Fiction of Jack London*
#### 1975, pp. vii–xxiv

Jack London was an artist, a thinker and a rebel out of the lower depths of American society, out of the social and economic abyss where art, thought and rebellion were all but unknown, where the primal struggle for survival absorbed the energy, ambition and creativity that produced art and speculative thought in the more favored classes. For the young Jack London, writing promised an escape from this struggle, and he turned to scientific thought not from a need to solve problems growing out of his own condition and experiences, but as a source of ideas that could be put to literary use. In the peculiar relation between Jack London's life and his scientific interests there is a glimpse into the origin of the science fiction story as the response of the intellectual proletarian to life in an anti-traditional, technological and bureaucratic mass society.

The adventures of Jack London's youth are legendary; the deprivations that turned him into a romantic adventurer are less well-known. He was born in San Francisco in 1876 of poor parents, both of whom, as their son was later to do, sought romantic transcendence of their dreary conditions in a quest for power through occult thought. For the mother and father the magic was spiritualism and astrology, for the son it would be revolutionary socialism and scientific racism. The astrologer father disappeared before Jack was born; when Jack was eight months old his mother married John London, a migrant worker and farmer. The family moved five times during the first five years of the boy's life, and until he was nine years old Jack lived an isolated life on the truck farms and ranches of northern California where his father worked. The family suffered from a poverty that Jack London would later, after he had made himself an expert on the subject, certify as exceptional in its cruelty. When London was nine the family moved back to Oakland where, because of his stepfather's frequent unemployment, the boy had to deliver papers, packages and ice. When he was thirteen he quit school to work full time in a cannery for ten cents an hour, ten hours a day. For two years he slaved away in the cannery; at age fifteen, seeing little future in honest toil despite the encouragement of the Horatio Alger novels he was reading, he bought a boat with borrowed money and began to raid the private oyster beds in the Bay, quickly picking up a local reputation as a drinker, lover and brawler. Soon his renown as a thief was great enough for the Fish Patrol to hire him to round up his former comrades in crime. His taste for adventure whetted, he shipped off for Korea and Japan, and then in rapid succession he tramped the country first with Coxey's army and then as a free-lance hobo and chicken thief, served time in an upstate New York jail and hunted gold in the Klondike. Periodically he returned to his family in Oakland, where he found work in a jute mill, shoveled coal in a power station, managed to graduate from high school, joined the Socialist Labor Party, spent a semester at the university at Berkeley and, significantly, won a cash prize for a newspaper article about a typhoon he had sailed through off Japan. In 1898, a fully experienced man of twenty-two, he returned from the Klondike to find his family destitute and completely dependent upon him for support. For the short run he picked up odd jobs; for the future, remembering his success with the newspaper story, enjoying a local reputation as a storyteller and perhaps encouraged by a favorite story by Ouida about a peasant who achieved fame and fortune as a composer, he began to prepare himself to be a *popular* writer.

Even in these first steps in his career as an aspiring writer the hidden scars that London had suffered from his class origins were limiting and defining his art. Experience in full and gaudy profusion he had. Ambition and energy he never lacked—he immediately set himself a standard of a thousand words a day and rarely fell below it for the rest of his life. But there was one thing missing from his writer's equipment and for it he searched until he died. In his own words it was a "Philosophy of Life," some way to discover a connection and a direction in the materials and experiences he was trying to turn into art. For most writers this ability to find pattern in experience is furnished by their culture: it had been London's misfortune to belong to a class that was, in effect, without a culture either to adopt or reject. Keenly aware of his need, in 1903 he asked

> Without the strong central thread of a working philosophy, how can you make order out of chaos? how can your foresight and insight be clear? how can you have a quantitative and qualitative perception of the relative importance of every scrap of knowledge you possess? and without all this, how can you possibly be yourself? how can you have something fresh for the jaded care of the world?[1]

It was to remedy his cultural poverty that London began in 1898 to search for his "Philosophy of Life." He commenced a monumental effort to down in one gigantic draught all of modern thought, all that contemporary science had to say about man, society and nature. London had discussed socialism in boxcars and in the jail cell; he had given socialist lectures to working class audiences in Oakland. Now, where before he had taken his socialism from Edward Bellamy, he began to read Karl Marx and Friedrich Engels. In biology he read Charles Darwin, Thomas Huxley and Alfred Wallace, in anthropology Franz Boas and James Frazer. He read the economic theory of Adam Smith, Thomas Malthus, David Ricardo and John Stuart Mill; he pored over the philosophy of Aristotle, Edward Gibbon, Thomas Hobbes, John Locke, David Hume, G. W. F. Hegel, Immanuel Kant, G. W. von Leibnitz, Friedrich Nietzsche, Herbert Spencer and Ernst Haeckel. In particular he studied the racist socialist Benjamin Kidd and the mordant predictions of an emerging capitalist totalitarianism in W. J. Ghent's *Our Benevolent Feudalism* (1902).

London's writing was shaped by his frantic search through philosophy and science for a master formula for art. In the autobiographical *Martin Eden* (1909) London has one of his characters say "Martin's after career, not culture. It just happens that culture, in his case, is incidental to career." Lured by ambition, goaded by need, London pursued literary success with the ferocity of one of his loved and hated blond beasts. Some sort of culture as an orderly and self-consistent interpretation of experience was going to be necessary if he was going to be able to describe his experiences and imaginings forcefully and entertainingly in stories that would sell. Therefore he read widely but not well, his mind sailing before the storm of *fin de siècle* scientific thought without the rudder and keel that class interests furnished thinkers from the leisured strata of society. London's speculations were freed of the hobbles of class prejudice, but the price he paid for his freedom was gullibility: with the uncritical enthusiasm of the convert he adopted whatever newly-read and ill-digested book gave promise of integrating more of his experience than had his last reading. He was always an easy mark for intellectual quacks, for the hucksters of Spencerian scientism who filled the bookshelves at the turn of the century. The result was that he was never able to root his ideas in his emotions; he never deepened attitudes into personality; he left his own soul unexamined while he mapped out the minds of others, until his life (with its sea voyages, alcoholism, and money grubbing) took on the aspect of an obsessive flight from a self that he had never explored and that he had finally come to fear and abhor. Even when this self-alienating process was just beginning, he knew where it was taking him, but his need for an immediate formula was too great to allow him the luxury of careful thought and work. In 1902 he wrote: "Concerning myself, I am moving along very slowly, about $3000 in debt, working out a philosophy of life, or rather the details of a philosophy of life, and slowly getting a focus on things. . . . Between you and me, I wish I had never opened the books. That's where I was the fool."[2]

London spent his life looking for the quick artistic fix, the grand theory into which he could feed his experiences and out of which would come saleable stories—an automatic, streamlined process that he could then supervise without personal involvement or emotional cost. Of culture as a synthesis of personal and social values London had no idea. He never showed any understanding of his oft-paraded Marxism as the dialectical interplay between thought and deed; for him Marxism was—when he was interested in it—another philosophical formula, not a guide to action and understanding, but a substitute for them. London was a free thinker who raided the philosophies of Nietzsche, Spencer and Kidd as he had once raided the oyster beds of San Francisco Bay. What he read he wrote, what he stole he sold, without any of the ideas he used tincturing his system; his mind was a faculty divorced from his personality, a sponge that he regularly squeezed for the popular magazines.

London was an American proletarian from a class without self-awareness or consciousness, self-destructive and divided against itself. In his career he demonstrated what he sometimes argued in his socialist lectures: that capitalism had made cultural outcasts of its workers, cutting them off from tradition, condemning them to lives of isolated incidents, unconnected perceptions. The result was that London's writing, even at its best, was absolutely devoid of inwardness. His idea of characterization was to incorporate a speculative idea in human flesh and then to let it follow its logical but unsurprising development. For this reason he was at his worst when he tried to create realistic characters in familiar environments, at his best when he escaped into prehistory, into the future, into non-human species, or, in other words, into science fiction. In science fiction London's speculative fancies and his skill at turning the supposition "what if" into an engrossing story could be displayed to full advantage, without the essential shallowness of characterization destroying his credibility.

Jack London wrote stories of scientific speculation throughout his career. *Before Adam* (1906), *The Iron Heel* (1907) and *The Star Rover* (1915) are always described as his "science fiction" novels, while the tales in this volume, his "science fiction short stories," date from "A Relic of the Pliocene" (1901) at the beginning of his career to the posthumously-published "The Red One" (1918). In a certain sense, however, all of London's work was science fiction. London's stories were always fanciful rather than imaginative, speculative rather than introspective. He customarily explored a specific case as the logical implication of some theoretic assumption. Very rarely did he, as a serious artist, draw his generalization out of an examination of the specific case. All of his stories share the characteristic theme that man's life is dominated by natural laws, laws that man seeks to understand as London himself sought to understand them, but laws that he never totally comprehends, much less controls; he is forever balked by the unforeseen and unintended effects of his ingenuity.

Probably no story of London's is better known than "To Build a Fire" (1908), a justly celebrated tale that perfectly illustrates how London's method inevitably led him to explore the science fiction formula.

In "To Build a Fire" London's nameless tenderfoot in the Yukon

> was quick and alert in the things of life, but only in the things, and not in the significance. Fifty degrees below zero meant eighty-odd degrees of frost. Such a fact impressed him as being cold and uncomfortable, and that was all. It did not lead him to meditate upon his frailty as a creature of temperature, and upon man's frailty in general, able only to live within certain narrow limits of heat and cold; and from there it did not lead him to the conjectural field of immortality and man's place in the universe.

But for London a scientific fact *did* lead to conjecture upon "immortality and man's place in the universe." The tenderfoot breaks through the ice, soaking his feet which quickly begin to freeze. He must dry them at once or die. Rushing to a clump of trees he hurriedly throws together a fire and builds it up until its heat begins to warm him. The cold is held at bay and this "fact" seems to mean safety. But no: this same heat that is thawing his feet is also melting the snow in the boughs above the fire; the snow pours down, the fire is buried, extinguished. Now he is too cold to rebuild the fire successfully; his frozen fingers fail him, the chill creeps up his limbs; that "significance of things" of which he was unaware has killed him.

The taut and compelling structure of this story emerges naturally from London's exploration of the "significance" of the "fact." Because of the cold the tenderfoot must build the fire hurriedly. Because he must hurry he does not think to carry the kindling away from the trees. Because the fire is near the trees the snow melts and extinguishes the fire. His destiny, it is revealed, is a function of this chain of cause and effect, a chain whose further links are hidden from his gaze.

"To Build a Fire" is a scientific story in that London tried to think like a scientist in choosing his plot as a demonstration of natural laws and in then allowing the plot to unfold with the clarity of a scientific demonstration. But this was not the only way in which London exploited science in his stories: not only was science a realistic way for him to describe the probable; he also seized upon scientific ideas, particularly curious ones, to project his vision romantically into the realm of the improbable but conjecturally possible. In such cases he took scientific theories which had proven useful as descriptions of familiar reality and used them to carry the reader into the unfamiliar, transporting him from the present into the future. These stories are the ones which may be described as *science fiction*.

The ideas that London used in his science fiction stories were sometimes merely scientific curiosities. "Winged Blackmail" was one such slight effort; here London simply used the public's fascination with flying machines to give a new twist to a conventional story of crime and detection. The plot of "Winged Blackmail," in fact, was not even of London's own devising: it was one of the twenty-seven plots that London bought from the young Sinclair Lewis. "The Shadow and the Flash" (1903, reprinted in this volume), was another. In this case the scientific oddity was the ambiguous nature of color as light and as pigment. This puzzle led London, as it had H. G. Wells (to whose *The Invisible Man* [1897] "The Shadow and the Flash" is unmistakably indebted), to the subject of invisibility. In London's story, as in Wells', the characters' mastery over nature does not give them self-mastery over their own natures; on the contrary it permits their flawed personalities to develop without check or limit until finally their jealousy and hatred destroy them in a deathly embrace of opposites, light and dark. And yet, despite the similarities between London's story and Wells', one notes most of all the differences. For London science was here merely a plotting gimmick which did not touch, much less release, his imaginative powers, whereas the idea of invisibility led Wells to a profound exploration of what happens when intellectual powers develop without a parallel growth in moral and social responsibility. Because "The Shadow and the Flash" grew out of what for London was merely a superficial concern, its sentimentally anti-scientific conclusion carries little conviction: "As for me, I no longer care for chemical research, and science is a tabooed topic in my household. I have returned to my roses. Nature's colors are good enough for me." The story shows London at his worst, a hack writer performing for an audience he held in contempt.

A story like "The Shadow and the Flash," however, was exceptional. London's science fiction novels and the rest of his science fiction short stories derive from two scientific theories he relied upon to give order to his life and to make sense out of nature and society. These two theories were the doctrines of evolutionary racism and of revolutionary socialism.

It may seem bewildering today that so intelligent a man as London could have been committed to theories as totally opposed as these. It certainly was puzzling to London's socialist friends whose reproaches once drove London to shout at them in exasperation: "What the devil! I am first of all a white man and only then a socialist!" But in the late nineteenth century the two great intellectual syntheses were Darwin's and Marx's, and attempts to combine them into one overarching *summa* were not unusual. For instance, Etienne Lantier, Emile Zola's hero in *Germinal*, was ridiculed for attempting just such an intellectual integration. But if it was not rare to find these two intellectual traditions in combination, still London's acceptance of the racist and revolutionary varieties of each *was* peculiar.

All of London's science fiction stories show at least some trace of his interest in evolutionary racism and revolutionary socialism. Nevertheless it is possible to discuss each story as having a more direct dependence on either one theory or the other. His evolutionary racism produced two science fiction novels, *Before Adam* (1906), and *The Star Rover* (1915), and six of the stories in this edition: "A Relic of the Pliocene," "The Strength of the Strong," "The Scarlet Plague," "When the World Was Young," "The Unparalleled Invasion" and "The Red One." London's socialism led to the third science fiction novel, *The Iron Heel* (1907), as well as "The Minions of Midas," "The Dream of Debs," "Goliah" and "A Curious Fragment."

For many intellectuals and for most of the lay public in the last half of the nineteenth century the words Darwin and science were all but synonymous. Whether a reader studied Darwin in the original or in the works of the great popularizers of Darwin like Herbert Spencer, William Graham Sumner and Benjamin Kidd, or whether like London he read them both, the nineteenth century reader extracted from Darwinian theory an analytic tool that seemed to lay bare the inner meaning of all natural relationships, whether between the species, between the races or between individual human beings. Darwin's lay audience understood him to teach that all life was a competition for existence, a competition that led to progress by allowing only the fittest to survive. This doctrine, social Darwinism, was particularly attractive to the world-domineering white race; within that white race the dominant Anglo-Saxons embraced Darwinism most eagerly, and among the Anglo-Saxons its most fervent advocates were found among the ruling classes. Such was the intellectual hegemony of these ruling classes that social Darwinism, which might have seemed reassuring only to the winners of the social struggle, was accepted by the masses as well, who were the losers in the evolutionary competition. These masses were obliged to seek in the fantasies of popular entertainment victories in the Darwinian contests that they could not achieve in their ordinary lives.

Spokesmen for Anglo-Saxon racial superiority gained a wide audience during the last decades of the nineteenth century: William Z. Ripley's *The Races of Europe* (1899) was the most famous of such works. Ripley began by assuming white supremacy. His achievement was to flatter old-stock Americans by subdividing the white race into the superior Teutons (a class that included the Anglo-Saxons), the mediocre Alpines, and the inferior Mediterraneans. Ripley's book was no isolated phenomenon. Any book that offered arguments in favor of white supremacy or of Anglo-Saxon superiority or celebrated the civilizing mission of the colonialists was assured of an interested audience. The culmination of this tendency in popular science was Madison Grant's *The Passing of the Great Race* (1916) in which Grant warned that unless Anglo-Saxons took stern and rapid measures, they would be overwhelmed by the quicker-breeding inferior races. Anglo-Saxon superiority was a basic assumption not just of the popular audience—some of the most sophisticated thinkers in America identified American cultural traits with the racial characteristics of Anglo-Saxons. For instance, Herbert Baxter Adams, the founder of modern American historical research, argued in his *The Germanic Origins of New England Towns* (1882) that self-government was a racial trait of Anglo-Saxons, a political skill born in the prehistorical forests of Germany and carried into the modern world by their ancestors.

It was the Anglo-Saxon audience's acceptance of evolutionary racism and its fascination with the natural dramas that had produced the favored race to which it belonged that explain the popularity of stories set in pre-historic times when their caveman ancestors had first established their still persis-

tent racial superiority. Among the early caveman stories was Stanley Waterloo's *The Story of Ab* (1897), which London was accused of plagiarizing in *Before Adam* (1906). H. G. Wells wrote The "Grisly Folk" (1896) and A *Story of the Stone Age* (1897); even Arthur Conan Doyle had cavemen in *The Lost World* (1912). The caveman story was the popular form that exploited most directly the ancestor worship of the race-proud Anglo-Saxon. Drawing on the same source of interest were the jungle stories of Rudyard Kipling and Edgar Rice Burroughs and the sea and arctic stories of writers like London, in whose novel *The Star Rover* occurs a classic statement of the Anglo-Saxon race pride that attracted readers to stories about primitive origins of the race or ones set in primitive environments where that evolutionary superiority could be dramatized:

> I am all of my past, as every protagonist of the Mendelian law must agree. All of my previous selves have their voices, echoes, promptings, in me. My every mode of action, heat of passion, flicker of thought, is shaded, toned, infinitesimally shaded and toned by that vast array of other selves that preceded me and went into the making of me.[3]

The link between himself and the fossil world that evolutionary theory seemed to offer stirred London deeply. The result was a story like "When the World Was Young" (1910), the second (and only other) science fiction story of London's based on a plot purchased from Sinclair Lewis. This is a popular entertainment but it is also a coyly literary story, admitting its debt to Kipling's "'The Finest Story In the World'" and Stevenson's "Dr. Jekyll." The story relies heavily upon the sentimental convention where an unruly hero is tamed through good woman's love. But there is power in this tale because the evolutionary idea that had prompted it had importance, personal importance to London; for him evolution was more than an abstraction; evolutionary theory reassured him that despite the baleful effects of history, class and culture, he carried within him a primitive energy, a product of the storm and strife of the stone age, a secret self to which he—a barbarian in a business suit—could retreat from civilization, taking his reader with him. Caveman stories catered to racial insecurity as well as to race pride. In a world of monopolies, world markets, inherited wealth and closed frontiers, where was the hero of evolution, the Anglo-Saxon survivor, to see current proof of his fitness to survive his anxious and losing struggles with the layoff, the strike and the giant corporation? Such a reader could find his superiority dramatically demonstrated in London's stories, where London could take the reader into "a world of his own devising, a clean, beautiful, primitive world in which, he convinced himself, the fit, be they man or beast, could and would survive. . . . Because his readers, seeking refuge as eagerly as he from the complexity and defeats of modern life, clamored for more tales of victories on the frontier, further progress on this route to popularity became doubly attractive."[4]

While his escape into the primitive satisfied deep personal needs for London and his audience, he was too intelligent a man not to sense the absurdity of the escapism that he and his readers took so seriously. "A Relic of the Pliocene" (1901) was the ironic result; here London transforms a saga of the Arctic into a tall tale with the reader the gullible victim. "Listen," says London, "and you shall hear of a hunt such as might have happened in the youth of the world when cavemen rounded up the kill with hard axes of stone." London, like an old frontiersman telling a campfire story, plays on the need and desire of the tenderfoot, the civilized reader, to believe in adventure. The reader finds out too late that the real victim of the story is not the mammoth but himself, another tenderfoot who has let his thirst for adventure overcome his common sense.

There was a hidden side to primitivism, and that was a hatred of civilization, an almost pathological longing for a catastrophe that would sweep away civilization and restore the pre-Adamite ceremony of innocence—a will to believe that the future would be a restoration of a past that would eclipse the obscenities of the present. Mary Shelley's *The Last Man* (1826) was an early expression of this longing for catastrophe; later came Richard Jeffries' *After London* (1884), M. P. Shiel's *The Purple Cloud* (1900), George Allan England's *Darkness and Dawn* (1912), Alan Llewelyn's *The Strange Invaders* (1934), George Stewart's *Earth Abides* (1956), John Wyndham's *The Day of the Triffids* (1951), William Golding's *The Inheritors* (1955), and Walter M. Miller's *A Canticle for Leibowitz* (1959).[5] Jack London's "The Scarlet Plague" (1912) belongs to this primitivist subtradition, for behind the narrator's laments for the "lost! ah lost!" delights of civilization there is a solid sense of satisfaction that the civilization-destroying plague has occurred in imagination and might occur in reality; the story gives pleasure by suggesting that a future is scientifically possible where London and his readers can all be blond-beastly together again. As Chauffeur says, he (and perhaps London) "wouldn't trade back to the old time for anything." "The Scarlet Plague" is a rich story into which London wove the theme that he had explored fully in *The Iron Heel* (1907): the coming despotism of the capitalists and the revenge of the people of the abyss against their masters: "In the midst of our civilization, down in our slums and labor-ghettos, we had bred a race of barbarians, of savages, and now, in the time of our calamity, they had turned upon us like the wild beasts they were." Throughout the story there sounds a chant of exhilaration over the destruction of an unjust world that recalls Poe's stories of catastrophe, "The Masque of the Red Death" and "Hop-Frog."

The descent from the "paradise regained" imagery of "The Scarlet Plague" to the bloody-minded racial hatred of "The Unparalleled Invasion" (1910) is indeed precipitous, but the story grows out of the same *fin de siècle* scientific racism that produced London's more attractive science fiction tales of the primitive life. That the story could have been printed in a popular magazine (*McClure's*) is an index to the cultural environment that nurtured London's intellectual development. "The Unparalleled Invasion" belongs to the American tradition of the future war novel which, unlike the British variety that played upon the English fear of Europe, grew out of the "yellow peril" fears that were a near obsession in California during London's lifetime. The yellow peril took on a personal significance for London during the Russo-Japanese war when he had been shocked by the sight of Orientals guarding defeated Caucasian captives. There was no shortage of other future war-yellow peril literature around the turn of the century. The classic work was Homer Lea's *The Vale of Ignorance* (1909), which described a Japanese occupation of the United States, but many other writers urged awareness of the threat posed by the lesser races, the need for preparedness, and even—to use an inspired phrase of our own age— "preventive retaliation." London incorporated yellow peril ideology into several of his novels, notably *The Valley of the Moon* (1913; the heroine is named "Saxon"), and *The Mutiny on the Elsinore* (1914) where he draws upon Charles E. Woodruff's theory in *The Effects of Tropical Light on White Men* (1905) that perhaps climate will limit the spread of the white race to the temperate zone.[6]

"The Red One" (1918) was among the last stories London wrote before his death, and it is both his finest science fiction story and one of his best efforts in any genre. It is the story of a man at the end of his tether, and London may have meant it to be his own story—or at least we are encouraged to think so by the references to slave trading and delerium tremens, for London had slave-traded in the South Pacific himself, and the d.t.'s were not unfamiliar to him, particularly in his last days. "The Red One" was written when London's health was no better than Bassett's: alcoholic, fat, despondant, dependent upon drugs, isolated from family, friends, and political comrades, his financial affairs in terminal disarray, London must have wondered if the science and the socialism he had so long relied upon had not deflected him from more profound explorations of life and art. And so in this story London attempts an evocation of the pure mystery that neither faith nor formula can unravel, but only the fullness of time. Drawn by the closeness of death beyond confidence in his own prejudices and convictions, Bassett asks without prejudgement whether the creators of the sphere from outer space had "won brotherhood? Or had they learned that the law of love imposed the penalty of weakness and decay? Was strife, law? Was the rule of all the universe the pitiless rule of natural selection?" These were questions that London had once thought fully answered by his theories, but in his last days neither evolution nor socialism seemed to offer certain answers. Science fiction allowed him, as it had so many other writers, to gaze upon the blank sphere of the future as the ultimate arbiter that will determine which of the blind gropings of the present are pointless, and which are in fact harbingers of the ultimate form of things. This story, so suffused with the sense of death, was one of the few times London was able to transcend the scientific formulas that throughout his career limited his imagination even while they guided it.

"The Strength of the Strong" (1911) completes the group of science fiction stories that grew out of London's interest in evolutionary racism, and it can also serve to introduce the other principle dimension of London's scientific thought—his theory of revolutionary socialism. This caveman story is an allegory that slyly pays tribute to Kipling ("Lip-King") in its epigraph. A prehistoric parable, it recreates the race's discovery of group solidarity, and it is also an illustration in fiction of the theories proposed by the single most important influence on London's intellectual development, Benjamin Kidd. Kidd was an Anglo-Saxon supremacist who tried to portray socialism as the next stage in *Anglo-Saxon* history, a stage that would allow the Anglo-Saxon to manage the world for its own good. Kidd's reconciliation of racism and socialism made his ideas invaluable to London. "The Strength of the Strong" could have been written as a dramatization of one passage in Kidd's *Social Evolution* (1894):

> His [man's] first organized societies must have developed like any other advantage, under the sternest conditions of natural selection. In the flux and change of life the members of those groups of men which in favourable conditions first showed any tendency to social organization, became possessed of a great advantage over their fellows, and these societies grew up simply because they possessed elements of strength which led to the disappearance before them of other groups of men with which they came into competition. Such societies continued to flourish until they in their turn had to give way before other associations of men of higher social efficiency. This, we may venture to assert, is the simple history of a stage in human development over which much controversy has taken place.[7]

2290

But for Kidd not all races possessed this capacity for organization. Socialism was a development that lay within the capacities only of the Anglo-Saxons, and it had evolved "so as to give more strength to these certain, kindred races so that they may survive and inherit the earth to the extinction of the lesser, weaker races."[8]

London's subordination of socialism to racism—for which he found justification in Kidd—explains aberrations like his "black-birding" (slave-hunting) expeditions in the south seas on the Snark, his jingoistic approval of Woodrow Wilson's adventures in Mexico, and his famous repudiation of the Socialist Party in 1916 just before his morphine suicide. Furthermore, it may have been London's attempt to suppress this racist side of his socialism that accounts for the slightly disembodied, cerebral quality of his socialist novel, *The Iron Heel* (1907), and of his socialist science fiction tales. Of the two scientific theories he most relied on, London's imagination seems to have been stirred more strongly by evolutionary racism than by scientific socialism. Nevertheless, Jack London was one of the most famous socialists of his time; several of his socialist tracts are still read as revolutionary classics. He was active for years in the Socialist Labor Party, which he had joined in 1895; he ran for mayor of Oakland in 1905 on the Socialist ticket; he helped found the Intercollegiate Socialist Society in 1905; and he labored unselfishly and self-sacrificingly for socialism on the lecture tour and in the socialist press.

London was widely read in the Marxist classics, and yet the chief influences on his political thought were books from outside the socialist mainstream—books like Benjamin Kidd's. It is not just London's adaptation of scientific socialism into fiction that makes works like *The Iron Heel* science fiction: it is London's adoption of one particular futuristic mythology in his books—that of W. J. Ghent's *Our Benevolent Feudalism* (1902). Ghent's book provides a detailed description of the future in which capitalism has grown into a monolithic and terroristic system where the class distinction between owner and worker is formalized into a new form of chattel slavery. Whenever London wishes to describe the future in his science fiction stories or novels, he simply draws upon Ghent. *The Iron Heel* and "A Curious Fragment" (1908) derive directly from the Ghent mythos. While "A Curious Fragment" certainly is a science fiction story of the "dystopian" type, it also belongs to the American tradition of reform novels: London was an enthusiastic admirer of Stowe's *Uncle Tom's Cabin* (which led him to hail Sinclair's *The Jungle* (1906) as "The Uncle Tom's Cabin* of wage slavery")[9] and "A Curious Fragment" comes complete with a futuristic Sambo, Quimbo and even a soft-hearted Simon Legree, a character who was truly a reformer's villain for all seasons.

In "The Minions of Midas" (1901) and "Goliah" (1908) London develops two alternative visions of deliverance from the capitalist future—the first malevolent, the second benign. "The Minions of Midas," which appeared before *Our Benevolent Feudalism,* simply takes the socialist critique of capitalism and uses it to describe the coming reaction to oligarchy as the mechanical antithesis of it. Capitalism is "merely the successful lawlessness of the powerful, so that the same privilege of lawlessness may be claimed for the poor." "Minions of Midas" aims at turning the guilt of the capitalist into fear; it serves up the capitalist's nightmare stereotype of the proletariat and suggests that the nightmare is going to come true. It is science fiction as the straight-line projection of the fears of the present into the reality of the future. As such it foreshadows the paranoia of such writers as Charles Williams, G. K. Chester-

ton, and Ian Fleming, who also terrorized readers with vaguely-motivated international conspiracies of evil.

"Goliah," on the other hand, is socialist science fiction based on the Ghent mythos, which assumes that scientific innovation will alter the course of social development and perhaps even bring about the millenium. Both "The Minions of Midas" and "Goliah" are technocratic in that they attack inefficiency and irrationality as the primary sources of social evil. "Goliah" points in the direction of the benevolent scientific despotisms of Robert A. Heinlein ("Gulf" and *Stranger in a Strange Land,* 1961) and reveals the persistence of London's early affection for Edward Bellamy. The Messianic figure of Percival Stultz may have been intended to lend some Wizard of Oz whimsy to a serious tract, but his portrayal betrays London's essential lack of seriousness in this description of a scientific utopia. London could have had no great confidence in the likelihood or staying power of a social system that depends upon the abolition of human nature by an edict from on high, and the abolition of the class struggle by a similar edict. In fact, abolishing human nature is the one temptation science fiction writers must resist if they want to keep human readers interested in their stories. It was H. G. Wells' firm belief in the persistence of human virtues and vices amidst technological innovations that gave his stories such timeless interest.

The last story in this collection is London's "The Dream of Debs" (1909), a fine science fiction story as well as revolutionary tract in which for once London used an orthodox Marxist analysis to draw a picture of the future—a future that is not merely a projection of tendencies already present in his day, but is instead the outcome of as-yet-invisible forces that are the dialectical antithesis of the ones determining the reader's familiar existence. It is excellent science fiction that explores the social and human impact of a great scientific innovation, the development of proletarian class consciousness. As a work of propaganda it is one that socialist propagandists have never tired of reading, for it describes the future as the outcome of that very transformation of consciousness that is the goal of the revolutionary agitator.

Jack London's place in the history of science fiction is difficult to assess. He employed many of the classic devices of science fiction and explored many of the classic themes: prehistory, future war, apocalyptic catastrophe, scientific "dystopias," technocratic utopias. It cannot be said, however, that he contributed memorably to their development. His stories are most valuable for what they reveal about the relationship between science fiction and modern culture.

In assaying this relationship, a comparison of London with two of the classic writers of science fiction is illuminating. H. G. Wells' work, of course, is science fiction at its best. The difference between Wells' science fiction and London's is that Wells understood science as one who had *belonged* to scientific culture and not as a mere lay observer. Wells understood science as "what scientists do," as a process of inquiry growing out of social needs and subject to social scrutiny and not as a collection of "laws" offering occult power to initiated individuals and groups. Moreover Wells was *part* of a culture, no matter how ambiguous his relationship to it: "artist," "thinker," "rebel" all were recognized cultural roles in British society, whatever the class of those who filled them. More than that, the working class, no matter how brutalized, had a cultural identity within British society that it lacked in America. In short, Wells wrote as a member of society, a participant in culture and as a serious student of man: thus society, culture and man are ever the focus of his stories—and not that abstraction that London regarded as "science."

London, on the other hand, was an outcast member of an outcast class, a class without any well-defined or accepted role in American society other than that of hobo, drifter, bum. For London science was not culture or a part of culture: it was an abstract *substitute* for culture. London's work is filled with pain and sense of limitation growing out of this cultural isolation. He wrote of his initiation into publishing:

> . . . let me state that I had many liabilities and no assets, no income, several mouths to feed, and for landlady, a poor widow woman whose imperative necessities demanded that I should pay my rent with some degree of regularity. This was my economic situation when I buckled on the harness and went up against the magazines.
>
> Further, and to the point, I knew positively nothing about it. I lived in California, far from the great publishing centers. I did not know what an editor looked like. I did not know a soul, with the exception of my own, who had ever tried to write anything, much less tried to publish it. . . .
>
> I had no one to give me tips, no one's experience to profit by. . . . All my manuscripts came back. They continued to come back. The process seemed like the working of a soulless machine. I dropped the manuscript into the mail box. After the lapse of a certain approximate length of time, the manuscript was brought back to me by the postman. Accompanying it was a stereotyped rejection slip. A part of the machine, some cunning arrangement of cogs and cranks at the other end . . . had transferred the manuscript to another envelope, taken the stamps from the inside, and pasted them outside, and added the rejection slip.[10]

In London's sense of culture as a soulless machine and in his sense of isolation from it, he resembles no one so much as his unlikely countryman, Edgar Allan Poe, and in London's work as in Poe's there emerges the rage of the outsider against the culture that has excluded him. Therefore London's writing, like Poe's, seems to have been composed in a cultural vacuum. But where Poe made a virtue of his isolation by developing a personal mythos that allowed him full emotional and artistic expression, London turned to popular science. The result was at its best science fiction, at its worst pure escape into a substitute universe of self-gratification. A lonely life of individualistic speculation left him at the end as far outside any culture as he had been at the beginning. In *John Barleycorn* (1913) London summed up his career by saying

> I had read too much positive science and lived too much positive life. In the eagerness of youth I had made the ancient mistake of pursuing truth too relentlessly. I had torn her veils from her, and the sight was too terrible for me to stand. In brief, I lost my fine faiths in pretty much everything except humanity, and the humanity I retained faith in was a very stark humanity indeed.[11]

*Notes*

1. Jack London, "On the Writer's Philosophy of Life" (1903), quoted in Philip S. Foner, *Jack London, American Rebel* (New York, 1964), p. 33.
2. Jack London, letter (May 12, 1902), quoted in Joan London, *Jack London and His Times* (New York, 1939), p. 238.
3. Jack London, *The Star Rover* (New York, 1915), p. 253.
4. Joan London, pp. 252–53.
5. For a discussion of the future war genre, see I. F. Clarke, *Voices Prophesying War: 1763–1984* (London, 1965).
6. For Woodruff's influence, see John Higham, *Strangers in the Land* (New York, 1973), p. 360.
7. Benjamin Kidd, *Social Evolution* (New York, 1894), p. 42.
8. Jack London paraphrasing Kidd, in Joan London, p. 212.
9. Jack London, "The Jungle," in Foner, p. 524.
10. Jack London, "Getting into Print," in Foner, p. 32.
11. Jack London, *John Barleycorn*, quoted in Joan London, p. 237.

## CHARLES N. WATSON, JR.
### From "Revolution and Romance: *The Iron Heel*"
*The Novels of Jack London: A Reappraisal*
#### 1983, pp. 112–22

London built ⟨*The Iron Heel* (New York: Macmillan, 1908)⟩ out of a combination of his own experience and his reading in the literature of social conflict. But this material yields a rather different version of London's theme of the conflict between social order and anarchic individualism. The principle of order exists in two versions of society which, ironically, are ideological opponents: the conservative middle class of the early twentieth century and the utopian socialist Brotherhood of Man. Though ideologically antithetical, these societies are psychologically akin, for each represents a realization of stability. Their true antithesis is the spirit of revolution. To this spirit the present state of society is never good enough, while the future society is distant, possibly unattainable—at any rate too dull an affair to be of much interest.

At the heart of this novel, therefore, is the heady atmosphere of social upheaval, the loosing of violent anarchic forces, which are personified by the revolutionary leadership of Ernest Everhard. Yet it is crucial that London decided to present Ernest from an "outside" point of view—that is, from the perspective of one of the two stable societies, either that of the past or that of the future. In fact, through the framing device of the "found" manuscript, London's narrative method achieves both. Inside the frame Ernest is viewed from the perspective of Avis Cunningham, whose upper-middle-class attitudes cast her initially as Ernest's foil but who is soon converted to the spirit of revolution. Then from the outside, both Avis and Ernest are subjected to the comments of Anthony Meredith, the "editor" of Avis's manuscript, who views their revolutionary activities from his perspective seven centuries into the utopian future.

This narrative method is fundamentally well conceived, and its consequences, frequently ignored in the past, have been deservedly stressed by recent critics.[1] Yet the method is not wholly successful. The outer editorial frame works well enough, but the inner narrative is seriously flawed. To see why this is so, it is helpful to consider the novel as a *Bildungsroman*, a novel of development or education. As a didactic proletarian novel, it is something of a special case, because the education of its protagonist is a process of radicalization, of awakening to the realities of class conflict. To describe *The Iron Heel* in this way is to suggest that its protagonist is, after all, not Ernest Everhard but Avis Cunningham.[2]

Avis is at the center of the action from beginning to end, not only because she is the narrator but, more important, because her character—her very nature as a person—is at issue. It is true that Ernest is often in her thoughts, especially when he is engaged in a debate or speech, and to her he is a hero. His heroism, however, is always putative—always asserted by others but never dramatized. His only observable acts of courage occur when he speaks before hostile audiences at the Philomath Club and in the Congress. Yet we are seldom permitted to forget that his arguments serve to educate Avis even as they dramatize Ernest's talents as an "intellectual swashbuckler" (23). When he lectures the group of middle-class businessmen, for example, Avis too is listening and learning: "It was the first time I had ever heard Karl Marx's doctrine of surplus value elaborated, and Ernest had done it so simply that I, too, sat puzzled and dumfounded" (150). In the most impressive scenes of action—the investigation of Jackson's arm, the escape to the Sonoma hideaway, and the Chicago Commune—Ernest is not even present. He *seems* to dominate the novel because of the powers attributed to him by others, especially by the worshipful Avis; but aside from Avis and Bishop Morehouse, his words change no minds and persuade no one to act, unless it is to harden some in opposition. The small businessmen, seemingly overwhelmed by a parade of fact and theory, nevertheless fail to change their ways and are later crushed between the magnates and the workers. The Philomaths, effectively warned by Ernest's threats, are mobilized by Wickson into a more determined repressive force.

Furthermore, if Ernest is considered the protagonist, the novel must be said to suffer from a serious disunity. Through the early and middle chapters, Avis keeps Ernest before us; and with his tones of prophecy, he seems to be preparing the reader—even as he is preparing Avis, her father, and himself—for his assumption of the mantle of active heroism at the climax. But this expectation is disappointed. Ernest plays no role whatever in the Chicago scenes, materializing only at the end to escape with Avis. Paul Stein has recently argued that Everhard's disappearance at the crucial juncture is appropriate, because it "diminish[es] the centrality of the individual in history."[3] This may be good social theory, but it is not good narrative art. If Ernest is the true proletarian hero of this novel, then the ending is *Hamlet* without the prince.

The inner narrative, therefore, is the story of Avis. London may have identified himself emotionally with Everhard, just as he did with Wolf Larsen in *The Sea-Wolf*; but Avis is the narrator and true protagonist of her story as much as Humphrey Van Weyden is of his. Earle Labor has argued that the chief problem is Avis's narrative voice, that the novel sounds like "*1984* as it might have been penned by Elizabeth Barrett Browning."[4] To put Labor's point another way, *The Iron Heel* as narrated by Avis is what *The Sea-Wolf* would have been if it had been narrated by Maud Brewster. Humphrey Van Weyden, despite his occasional fatuities, is a more interesting and complex character than Maud, and the earlier novel gains from his conflict with Larsen. *The Iron Heel*, in turn, suffers from the lack of such psychological conflict. After their initial clash over Jackson's arm, Ernest and Avis are in perfect harmony, and the novel must depend on the cruder opposition between the selfless socialists and the villainous oligarchy. Despite editor Meredith's insistence that the story "vividly portray[s] the psychology of the persons that lived in that turbulent period" (x), such psychological penetration is precisely what the story lacks.

Accordingly, the characterization of Avis is most successful in the early chapters, when there is still some tension between her and Ernest. The initial situation is plausible and even promising: a genteel young woman is challenged to find out for herself how the other half lives—and, further, how she herself has unwittingly supported flagrant social injustice. Her pursuit of the dismaying truth about Jackson's arm grows more spirited as she becomes more disillusioned, and she might have become a modestly interesting character if, after her story was refused by the newspapers, she had gone on to publish it in *McClure's* and developed a muckraking career of her own. That, of course, would have been a different novel and not the one London wanted to write; but by having Avis marry

Everhard and become a revolutionary, he sacrifices her credibility almost completely. From that point on, her only plausible role is to retreat to the Sonoma refuge and await her reunion with her husband. She tells us that she is a secret agent for the revolution, but we never really see her functioning in that capacity. Although we do see her hiding under a pile of corpses in Chicago, her credibility as a revolutionary, or even as an innocent victim, is somewhat diminished by the fact that as soon as the enemy soldiers drag her out from under the gory heap, she begins primly "fixing up [her] hair . . . and pinning together [her] torn skirts" (334).

Thus the lines of Avis's character are fatally blurred by the incongruous roles she is asked to play, and her narrative voice accordingly drifts in and out of focus. At times she is barely present at all, as when she acts as the recording secretary for Ernest's polemics; and in the Chicago scenes her voice often disappears into the tough-minded reportage and overheated rhetoric of her husband—which is to say of Jack London himself—until a fainting spell or a torn skirt reminds us that the observer of all this carnage is indeed Avis. Elsewhere we are all too well aware that she is having a girlish fling at revolution. The change in her life is an "adventure, and the greatest of all, for it was love-adventure" (182). Her social conscience is on its honeymoon, her newfound radicalism inextricably bound up with her adoration of Ernest. No wonder she herself is so frequently struck by the unreality of her suddenly altered life, marveling that "I, little I, who had lived so placidly all my days in the quiet university town, found myself . . . drawn into the vortex of the great world-affairs" (163).

The gasping reference to "I, little I," is more than conventional modesty. However embarrassingly phrased, it represents a radical questioning of her identity. Later, in the Sonoma hideaway, that questioning becomes more explicit when her disguise—her "other self" (274) as (appropriately enough) a pampered daughter of the upper class—leads her to wonder which of her lives is real:

> At times it seemed impossible, either that I had ever lived a placid, peaceful life in a college town, or else that I had become a revolutionist inured to scenes of violence and death. One or the other could not be. One was real, the other was a dream, but which was which? Was this present life of a revolutionist, hiding in a hole, a nightmare? or was I a revolutionist who had somewhere, somehow, dreamed that in some former existence I had lived in Berkeley and never known of life more violent than teas and dances, debating societies, and lecture rooms? (278)

Credibility disintegrates here not because Avis has changed her old self into a new one; that is easier to believe than what London also asks us to accept: the existence of two Avises simultaneously—the fluttery young woman of the love adventure and the hardened revolutionary of the political drama. In one role she is unattractive, in the other unconvincing.

It is the former society girl, one should observe, who is the "author" of the repulsive description of the Chicago proletariat as "the refuse and scum of life." Ernest, in contrast, after his emergence from prison, has become more acceptable to her by adding "a certain nobility of refinement" (287) to his features. These social discriminations are most tellingly dramatized when, near the end of her Chicago ordeal, she encounters a wounded rebel—a "wretched slave," she calls him—tottering along the street: "One hand he held tightly against his side, and behind him he left a bloody trail. His eyes roved everywhere, and they were filled with apprehension and dread. Once he looked straight across at me, and in his face was all the dumb pathos of the wounded and hunted animal. He saw me, but there was no kinship between us, and with him, at least, no sympathy of understanding. . . . All he could hope for, all he sought, was some hole to crawl away in and hide like any animal" (344). The irony of this passage is clear. Having herself suffered nothing worse than a few bruises and a torn dress, Avis, in her self-pity, accuses this "wounded and hunted animal" of having no "sympathy of understanding" to offer *her.* Plainly the stare of nonrecognition, the denial of kinship, though she projects it onto him, is entirely her own. Her "strong class instincts" (5), which earlier were shocked by Ernest's bold sexual force, have never deserted her; and in this respect she is perilously close to the gentility of Ruth Morse, whom London was to characterize so devastatingly in his next novel, *Martin Eden.* Avis represents one more attempt by London to portray a heroine who is both genteel and spirited, but Avis wading in blood on the streets of Chicago is no more convincing than Maud Brewster slaughtering seals on Endeavor Island. Her identity remains as much of a mystery to the reader as it does to her.

In the face of such serious defects, it may seem unlikely that any defense of this novel can be made at all. Yet its power is undeniable, for London at times managed an effective combination of realism and the stylized, larger-than-life qualities of a didactic fable or heroic romance. On the one hand, he said that "from a pseudo-scientific standpoint" he considered the novel "plausible,"[5] a claim tallying with his rejection of many of the melodramatic absurdities and futuristic fantasies of Donnelly and Wells, supporting the impression that he wanted his action to seem a credible projection of events taking place only a few years in the future. This realistic dimension depends heavily on the interplay between Avis's point of view and that of the "editor," for Avis's glorification of her adventures in revolution and romance needs the detached, antiromantic comments of Anthony Meredith to bring it down to earth. Again and again this editorial irony deflates both her romantic flights and her vestiges of class-consciousness. At the outset Meredith prepares us to "smile . . . and forgive Avis Everhard for the heroic lines upon which she modelled her husband. We know to-day that he was not so colossal, and that he loomed among the events of his times less largely than the Manuscript would lead us to believe" (ix). When Avis refers to Ernest as a Nietzschean blond beast, the editor dismisses Nietzsche as a lunatic (6); and her pride in her father's "stout old *Mayflower* stock" is treated with gentle editorial scorn: "Descendants of these original colonists were for a while inordinately proud of their genealogy; but in time the blood became so widely diffused that it ran in the veins practically of all Americans" (177).

But the editorial frame accomplishes more than the deflation of Avis's romanticism. As recent critics have pointed out, it provides the entire inner narrative with an illusion of objective distance and historical inevitability, implying the dialectic of class conflict and the final synthesis of a socialist utopia. London only hints at the nature of that utopia and, unlike Bellamy, seems to have had little interest in describing its details. What interests him much more is the nature of the present conflict, and one of the most impressive aspects of *The Iron Heel* is his dramatization of the forms of intimidation and repression characteristic of the modern totalitarian state: Mr. Cunningham's forced resignation from the university, the suppression of his book, the clandestine seizure of his stock, the forgery and foreclosure of his mortgage, the threat of the asylum, and finally his sudden, unexplained disappearance.

Yet the Marxist critics have also been right in viewing the novel as a didactic fable, in which the characters are flat and the action romantically heightened because, as Trotsky put it,

"the form of [*The Iron Heel*] represents only an armor for social analysis and prognosis," its author being interested "not so much in the individual fate of his heroes as in the fate of mankind."[6] London himself took a similar line in his notes, observing that the scenes must be made "striking, to make up for absence of regular novel features." *The Iron Heel* is thus a proletarian fable in the form of a heroic romance, in which life among the dedicated revolutionaries is "lived on the heights, where the air was keen and sparkling, where the toil was for humanity, and where sordidness and selfishness never entered" (187). From this enlarged perspective, the novel is not only framed by the Marxist dialectic but also pervaded by the apocalyptic vision of Christianity and the naturalistic imagery of social Darwinism. All of these perspectives blend into a single teleological view of history, in which unregenerate primitive man moves through a period of transitional crisis to achieve a final secular paradise—a movement not unlike that of White Fang.

The Christian framework involves, for the individual capable of it, a transforming moment of inspired vision; for the society incapable of such a vision, a providential catastrophe and ultimately the regeneration of society through martyrdom. Images of spiritual rebirth pervade the narrative. At the beginning, Avis feels herself about to witness "a new and awful revelation" (60). In the midst of the Chicago violence, she feels "strangely exalted" (327), and her immersion in the pile of corpses is her "red baptism" (332). Ernest, too, is "transfigured" (79) by his righteous zeal, and under his tutelage Bishop Morehouse sees the light "as Saul saw his on the way to Damascus" (112).

But for those willfully blind to the new revelation, there remains only the cleansing force of catastrophe. In the Sonoma hideaway, the revolution "took on largely the character of religion" (250). The imminent disaster is signaled by the sudden emergence of "wild-eyed itinerant preachers" and the "religious frenzy" of "countless camp-meetings." It was, they claimed, "the beginning of the end of the world" (235). Chicago during the First Revolt is like the earth during the Flood, or like Sodom and Gomorrah destroyed by the wrath of God. As Avis's train approaches the city, the portents increase: "The sky had clouded, and the train rushed on like a sullen thunderbolt through the gray pall of advancing day" (314). Smoke and fire fill the air, and the surge of the maddened workers resembles an "awful river," a "rushing stream of human lava" (326, 327).[7]

Yet through this chaos shines the beacon of martyrdom. The bishop, harrowed by his "journey through hell," has turned consciously Christ-like and "is rushing on to his Gethsemane" (107). Befriending the poor and making his home a haven for prostitutes, he becomes in Avis's eyes "God's hero" (200), and he is last seen among the mangled corpses in Chicago, a martyr of the failed revolt. The bishop's death serves in turn to foreshadow the martyrdom of Ernest, who Avis believes may also be "destined for a cross" (61), and she later notes that "for man he gave his life" and, figuratively, was "crucified" (182). Ernest himself finds among the revolutionaries a spirit of "renunciation" and "martyrdom," envisioning the fulfillment of the future as "Christ's own Grail" (79).[8]

The biblical imagery is also present when Ernest speaks to the middle-class businessmen of the "antediluvian ways of your forefathers" (150). Obliquely, Ernest is prophesying the deluge that will wipe out the sinful capitalists forever. But in the same argument he also speaks of the "tide of evolution" that "flows on to socialism" (141). Unhappily for this metaphor, tides ebb as well as flow, but London's intention is to link the naturalistic image to the biblical and Marxist teleology in order to suggest progress toward some inevitable destiny. Another such naturalistic metaphor is that of organic growth, fruition, and decay. As the "editor" comments retrospectively, "Out of the decay of self-seeking capitalism, it was held, would arise that flower of the ages, the Brotherhood of Man. Instead of which . . . capitalism, rotten-ripe, sent forth that monstrous offshoot, the Oligarchy" (xii-xiii). In the ultimate fulfillment of this cycle, the flower of the socialist commonwealth will grow out of the fertilizing decay of a rotten capitalism.

A related metaphor, which London had employed a few months earlier in the primitive fantasy *Before Adam*, presents the rise of the oligarchy as an event in social evolution. As the "editor" asserts, "primitive communism, chattel slavery, serf slavery, and wage slavery were necessary stepping-stones in the evolution of society. But it were ridiculous to assert that the Iron Heel was a necessary stepping-stone. Rather, to-day, is it adjudged a step aside, or a step backward, to the social tyrannies that made the early world a hell" (xi-xii). In the same vein, Ernest views the "primitive" capitalists of the Philomath Club as "the caveman, in evening dress, snarling and snapping over a bone" (74). The catch-phrases of social Darwinism continually recur. In such a society the "big wolves ate the little wolves" (48); life is a "fang-and-claw social struggle" (126); it is "dog eat dog" (129). The "fiat of evolution," Ernest says, is "the word of God," which dictates that because primitive man was a "combative beast . . . he rose to primacy over all the animals" (132). Socialism, he insists, is "in line with evolution," and those who "prefer to play atavistic roles . . . are doomed to perish as all atavisms perish" (134).

By thus tying the immediate action to larger myths of cosmic process and purpose, London is following Zola's *Germinal*, where violent class conflict is set against the cyclical processes of nature: germination, growth, and fruition. Though London had read *Germinal* years earlier, a nearer influence may have been Frank Norris's *The Octopus* (1901), itself strongly influenced by *Germinal*. Despite his reservations about the "inordinate realism" of minute detail, London praised and quoted at length from the "broad canvas" and heightened rhetoric of Norris's description of the colossal power of the railroad and the primordial energy of the wheat.[9] Thus, even more than in *The Sea-Wolf*, he directs *The Iron Heel* toward the large effects of the romance, especially the flat characterizations embodying the abstract forces of virtue and villainy, which are thrown into violent conflict in the Armageddon of class warfare. When Avis finds among the socialists nothing but "unselfishness and high idealism" (100), or when Ernest speaks in the stylized platitudes of heroic romance ("To-morrow the Cause will rise again, strong with wisdom and discipline" [351]), we are meant to accept these violations of verisimilitude as appropriate to a didactic fable.[10]

Whether such allowances can in fact be made, however, is a question that will be answered differently by different readers. We can thank recent Marxist criticism for a clearer appreciation of the function of the double point of view and for a proper insistence that *The Iron Heel* cannot be judged solely by the criteria of the realistic novel. Yet these corrections do not dispose of the two inescapable flaws: the unconvincing characterization of Avis, and the absence of the hero at the climax. Ernest's martyrdom, which should have come at the height of the Chicago cataclysm, is instead displaced into the hazy future, where its impact is drastically diminished. Bluntly, if we are to take Ernest seriously, we need to see him die.[11]

With subtler art, with more careful novelistic construc-

tion, London might have turned a "minor revolutionary classic"[12] into a major one. Even the most sensitive of the Marxist critics descend at times to special pleading in their defense of a novel that London seems to have written too much out of his heart, too little out of his head. That disproportion is no doubt responsible for the most successful scenes, which depict a society's capacity for vindictive violence and injustice. Unfortunately, it is responsible also for the crippling flaws. In his next novel, *Martin Eden*, a proletarian hero would be presented with greater art.

*Notes*

1. See especially Nathaniel Teich, "Marxist Dialectics in Content, Form, Point of View: Structures in Jack London's *The Iron Heel*," *Modern Fiction Studies* 22 (1976), 85–99; Dorothy H. Roberts, "*The Iron Heel*: Socialism, Struggle, and Structure," *Jack London Newsletter* 9 (1976), 64–66; and Paul Stein, "Jack London's *The Iron Heel*: Art as Manifesto," *Studies in American Fiction* 6 (1978), 77–92.

2. The only ones to view Avis as protagonist (rather than merely as narrator) are H. Bruce Franklin, *Future Perfect: American Science Fiction of the Nineteenth Century*, rev. ed. (New York: Oxford Univ. Press, 1978), p. 229; and Jon Pankake, "The Broken Myths of Jack London: Civilization, Nature, and the Self in the Major Works," Ph.D. diss. Univ. of Minnesota 1975, pp. 128–30. Pankake precedes me in recognizing the importance of Avis's problem of identity, though both he and Franklin find her metamorphosis more convincing than I do.

3. Stein, "*The Iron Heel*: Art as Manifesto," p. 90.

4. Earle Labor, *Jack London* (New York: Twayne, 1974), p. 104.

5. Jack London to George P. Brett, 15 December 1906, *Letters from Jack London*, ed. King Hendricks and Irving Shepard (New York: Odyssey, 1965), p. 235.

6. Quoted in Joan London, *Jack London and His Times: An Unconventional Biography* (New York: Doubleday, 1939; rpt. Seattle: Univ. of Washington Press, 1968), p. 313. In his essay "The Question of the Maximum," as he speculated over whether the future would lead to socialism or to the advent of powerful industrial oligarchies, he considered the latter course "possible" but "not probable" (*War of the Classes*, New York: Macmillan, 1905, p. 193). Similarly, when the apparent pessimism of *The Iron Heel* was attacked by some of the more conservative socialists, London complained: "I *didn't* write the thing as a prophecy at all. I really don't think these things are going to happen in the United States. I believe the increasing socialist vote will prevent—hope for it, anyhow. But I will say that I sent out, in 'The Iron Heel,' a warning of what *might* happen if they don't look to their votes" (Charmian London, *The Book of Jack London*, New York: Century, 1921, II, 139). Here he seems to maintain that the novel is not so much a prophecy as a cautionary tale, a lurid romance aimed at rousing the indifferent and the faithful from their lethargy.

7. The apocalyptic imagery has been noted by David Ketterer, *New Worlds for Old: The Apocalyptic Imagination, Science Fiction, and American Literature* (Bloomington: Indiana Univ. Press, 1974), pp. 126–33; Jon Pankake, "The Broken Myths of Jack London," pp. 118–21; and D. Seed, "The Apocalyptic Structure of Jack London's *The Iron Heel*, *Jack London Newsletter* 13 (1980), 1–11. Jack London resorted to similar imagery after the outbreak of World War I, declaring that civilization was going through a "pentecostal cleansing that can only result in good for mankind" (Jack London to Perriton Maxwell, 28 August 1916, London Collection, Henry E. Huntington Library, San Marino, Calif.).

8. Images of crucifixion were commonplace in the literature of protest, the most famous one occurring in William Jennings Bryan's "cross of gold" speech. Similarly, in Edward Bellamy's *Looking Backward* (Boston: Houghton Mifflin, 1888), Julian West cries, "I have seen Humanity hanging on a cross!" (p. 326).

9. Rpt. in Walker, *Jack London: No Mentor But Myself: A Collection of Articles, Essays, Reviews, and Letters on Writing and Writers*, ed. Dale L. Walker (Port Washington, N.Y.: Kennikat, 1979), pp. 35–36.

10. For a more balanced characterization of the working class, see

London's Preface to *War of the Classes*, where he insists that socialism must deal "with what is, not what ought to be," and that "the material with which it deals is the 'clay of the common road,' the warm human, fallible and frail, sordid and petty, absurd and contradictory, even grotesque, and yet, withal, shot through with flashes and glimmerings of something finer and God-like, with here and there sweetnesses of service and unselfishness, desires for goodness, for renunciation and sacrifice, and with conscience, stern and awful, at times blazingly imperious, demanding the right" (pp. xvi-xvii).

11. London's notes reveal that at an early stage of his planning for the novel, he did intend such a focus on Ernest: "Very concrete, begin most likely with him—the leader of the people—his surroundings, his home, etc. etc.—At the end, dying, the word is brought him that the world war is afoot . . . and the final liberation comes." At some point London rejected this plan and decided to shift the focus to Avis, as is indicated by another set of notes: "She—first chapter—tells briefly of herself, date, place in life, father, etc. etc.—all with forerunning hints of her meeting with Ernest & the great part he was to play in her life, & the great change in it" (MS notes, Jack London collection, Henry E. Huntington Library, San Marino, Calif.).

12. Walter B. Rideout, *The Radical Novel in the United States*, 1900–1954 (Cambridge, Mass.: Harvard Univ. Press, 1954), p. 42.

# H. P. LOVECRAFT

## 1890–1937

Howard Phillips Lovecraft was born on August 20, 1890, in Providence, Rhode Island. When he was three his father suffered a paralytic attack, dying five years later. The boy's upbringing was left to his overprotective mother, his two aunts, and his grandfather, a wealthy industrialist. A precocious boy, Lovecraft was reading at two, writing poems and horror stories at seven, and learning Latin and Greek at eight.

The family's fortunes suffered a reversal in 1904, and Lovecraft and his mother were forced to move into smaller quarters in Providence. Distressed at the loss of his birthplace, the young Lovecraft immersed himself in intellectual pursuits. His formal education was sporadic due to chronic ill health, and in 1908 he apparently suffered a nervous breakdown which prevented him from enrolling at Brown University. The next five years were spent in relative hermitry, as Lovecraft continued to amass an impressive self-education in literature, science, and philosophy.

In 1914 Lovecraft joined the amateur journalism movement, plunging into the literary and political activities of the United Amateur Press Association and, later, the National Amateur Press Association. He produced thirteen issues of his own journal, *The Conservative* (1915–23), filling it with poems, essays, and commentary. Gradually, at the urgings of friends, Lovecraft recommenced the writing of horror tales: "The Tomb" (1917) is the first story of his mature period.

For years Lovecraft had no thought of publishing his work professionally. In 1923, however, he was urged to contribute to the fledgling pulp magazine *Weird Tales*. Over the next fifteen years, the bulk of his fiction appeared in the pages of that magazine. Still, Lovecraft's genteel upbringing rendered him persistently diffident about commercially marketing his writing, and several attempts by book publishers to issue his work between hard covers came to nothing.

In May 1921 Lovecraft's mother died; a few months later he met Sonia Greene (later Davis), a Russian Jew several years his senior. In 1924 they married, and Lovecraft moved to Brooklyn. Their marriage, however, was not a success; Lovecraft was unable to find a regular job, Sonia's health quickly gave way, and financial troubles forced her to seek a job in the Midwest, leaving Lovecraft alone in a city he had come to loathe for its noise, decadence, and "foreigners." He wrote few stories during this period, but did the bulk of work on his study *Supernatural Horror in Literature* (1927). In April 1926 he returned to Providence, essentially ending the marriage, and proceeded to write his greatest work—tales such as "The Call of Cthulhu" (1926), "The Colour out of Space" (1927), "The Whisperer in Darkness" (1930), *At the Mountains of Madness* (1931), and "The Shadow out of Time" (1934–35), as well as the sonnet cycle *Fungi from Yuggoth* (1929–30). He traveled widely on various antiquarian expeditions, and became a stunningly voluminous letter-writer, corresponding with fantasists such as August Derleth, Donald Wandrei, Clark Ashton Smith, Robert E. Howard, Frank Belknap Long, Robert Bloch, and many others.

By the 1930s Lovecraft, although still unknown to the literary world, had become a legend both in the realm of amateur journalism and among the budding community of modern fantasy writers and critics. He continued selling stories sporadically, supporting himself in penury by extensive ghost-writing. Upon his death in Providence on March 15, 1937, his friends set about rescuing his work from the oblivion of the fantasy pulps. In 1939 an omnibus of his tales, *The Outsider and Others*, was published by Derleth and Wandrei; many other volumes have followed.

Lovecraft's stories—especially a series of tales sometimes called the "Cthulhu Mythos" or "Lovecraft Mythos"—have exercised a tremendous influence upon subsequent fantasy writing. His copious essays and poetry have also been collected, and his *Selected Letters* (1965–76) have been published in five volumes.

## *Personal*

Lover of hills and fields and towns antique,
How hast thou wandered hence
On ways not found before,
Beyond the dawnward spires of Providence?
Hast thou gone forth to seek
Some older bourn than these—
Some Arkham of the prime and central wizardries?
Or, with familiar felidae,
Dost now some new and secret wood explore,
A little past the senses' farther wall—
Where spring and sunset charm the eternal path
From Earth to ether in dimensions nemoral?
Or has the Silver Key
Opened perchance for thee
Wonders and dreams and worlds ulterior?
Hast thou gone home to Ulthar or to Pnath?
Has the high king who reigns in dim Kadath
Called back his courtly, sage ambassador?
Or darkling Cthulhu sent
The Sign which makes thee now a councilor
Within that foundered fortress of the deep
Where the Old Ones stir in sleep,
Till mighty tremblors shake their slumbering continent?
Lo! in this little interim of days,
How far thy feet are sped
Upon the fabulous and mooted ways
Where walk the mythic dead!
For us the grief, for us the mystery. . . .
And yet thou art not gone
Nor given wholly unto dream and dust:
For, even upon
This lonely western hill of Averoigne
Thy flesh had never visited,
I meet some wise and sentient wraith of thee,
Some undeparting presence, gracious and august.
More luminous for thee the vernal grass,
More magically dark the Druid stone
And in the mind thou art for ever shown
As in a magic glass;
And from the spirit's page thy runes can never pass.

> —Clark Ashton Smith, "To Howard Phillips
> Lovecraft" (1937), *Selected Poems*, 1971, pp.
> 287–88

Let us go back almost exactly ten years before Lovecraft's death:

Belonging as I did to the lowest class of the downtrodden proletariat, I was obliged to go to menial labor in the morning, and so had to cut the session short about midnight. I left Howard sitting at my desk in the study, with the kitten curled up happily in his lap. The kitten, a part-Angora, was an unusually independent, self-centred, cold-blooded member of his tribe, but had yielded to Howard's blandishments in spite of the fact that it had been referred to as "a member of the *Felidae*." I give it the credit for having the prescience that for *that* night, at least, it could escape banishment to the basement.

About half-past six in the morning, before going down to breakfast, I poked my head in the study door. There sat Howard, in the same pose in which I had left him six hours before, eyes heavy but head unbowed, with the kitten apparently unmoved.

"Good Lord!" I exclaimed, "haven't you been to bed?"

"No," said Howard, "I didn't want to disturb kitty."

Now I am myself a cat-lover. There is one at this moment curled up on the pile of paper on the desk, and I must extract from under it the next sheet I use. And I will at any time share my last mouse with one. But I question if I would act as nursemaid for a perfectly healthy cat to the extent of sitting up all night with it. Sickness is another thing—the old lodge-brother stuff.

When you have had more or less intimate contact with a man for twenty years and over, it is an incident of this kind which will first pop into your head when he is mentioned. A man is remembered by his friends for the little things, not for his achievements. And, indeed, such a recollection is sure to give an inkling of character. This was much more than a demonstration of Lovecraft's fondness for cats, although that was genuine and deep-rooted. I have never known a cat to refuse to make friends with him except one, a very cold and haughty short-haired animal in Newburyport—an alley cat gone high-brow—having evidently attached itself to one of the old families which, like the city, has been finished and frozen into immobility forever, retaining only an overweening pride in ancestry. Incidentally, I may say that Howard's predilection for cats resulted in perhaps the only time he was ever worsted in argument—and of course it was by a woman. A bird-lover, a crusader for the cause and an authority on the subject, simply overwhelmed him. Of course where there are no arguments, but only sentiment, on your side, how can you argue?

But this incident of the kitten in my study gives a truer picture of Lovecraft than any he would willingly have conveyed. He considered it the part of a gentleman to possess poise, to keep a poker-face at all times, to show emotion at nothing, to treat all things calmly, to wear his heart anywhere but on his sleeve. ⟨. . .⟩

From Lovecraft's early years there has come to us but one story outside of what he himself occasionally told. The incident comes from one of the Lovecraft neighbors and of course occurred before he was stricken with the ailment which took him out of school. That section was then open fields, rather swampy here and there, with very few houses. One day this neighbor, Mrs. Winslow Church, noticed that someone had started a grass fire that had burned over quite an area and was approaching her property. She went out to investigate and found the little Lovecraft boy. She scolded him for setting such a big fire and maybe endangering other people's property. He said very positively, "I wasn't setting a *big* fire. I wanted to make a fire one foot by one foot." That is the little story in the words in which it came to me. It means little except that it shows a passion for exactitude (in keeping with him as we knew him later)—but it is a story of Lovecraft.

It is a significant fact that Howard suddenly became sick and was taken out of school and secluded at or about the time of his father's death. I shall always believe that it was his mother and not he that was sick—sick for fear of losing her sole remaining link to life and happiness. The result on the boy could only be to make him an invalid. ⟨. . .⟩

I doubt if there was ever a more widely loved man than Howard Phillips Lovecraft. The immense correspondence which he carried on was one reason. I frequently pointed out to him that this could be only a detriment to his literary work. He would acknowledge the fact and resolve to cut various correspondents off his list, or at least to shorten his letters to them. But a chance remark in a letter would start in motion a train of thought and the result would be a sizable manuscript. I have casually made some apparently harmless remark in the course of a letter, and in reply to a ten or twelve word observation have had the postman come staggering to the door bowed under the weight of a thesis of twenty or even thirty minutely written pages. All of his correspondents, like myself, enjoyed getting his letters, but some of us groaned to see how the man was using up his energy, and he had only so much, on these private letters, which, after all, amounted to very little, when he should have been working on such creative writing as would give him the place he deserved in literature. We wanted to see him world famous, and in a way he was, but we have also wanted to see him in a position where he could indulge all his fancies and have his aspirations fulfilled.

Lovecraft was so lenient toward the foibles and the literary efforts of his friends that he was not only forgiven but loved for his little idiosyncracies and for his many strong opinions on subjects that ordinarily are calculated to stir up argument or worse. He was the only contributor I ever had who was coddled and allowed to use English instead of American spelling. His "u" inserted here and there and his substitution of "s" for "z" in various words were adhered to in spite of protests from linotype and monotype operators, a class who are not trained in these days to the good old hand-compositors' rule to "follow copy if it goes out of the window." I have sent a proof back to the machine three times, and finally stood over the operator using terse Anglo-Saxon language until I got a "u" inserted in a word. All but the most ignorant and flag-waving Americans (and he encountered few such in his circles) forgave him his Anglomania and his cutting remarks concerning the Revolution, which he thought should never have happened. I cannot help thinking how actually fortunate it was, if Howard had to die in middle age, he should have had his last sickness in 1937 instead of in 1940. I doubt if any degree of philosophical detachment which he might try to attain would have prevented him from being torn asunder by the bombing of St. Paul's. And he would have made no attempt to reach an attitude of detachment. ⟨. . .⟩

It was a surprise to many when Lovecraft wholeheartedly embraced the New Deal. It should not have been. He was not, and it was impossible for him to be, a believer in democracy—"the glorification of the clodhopper," as someone has called it. (If you want to put "exploitation" instead of "glorification" in the above definition, it is all right with me—I am merely quoting.) The New Deal was a decided move toward what he could and did believe in—an aristocracy of intellect, the rule of the intellectuals, a paternalistic government, a dictatorship of the intelligentsia instead of a dictatorship of the proletariat. Its leaders had not emerged from the masses of the people, but by birth were of a class fitted to rule. Its leader was the Squire of Hyde Park, and its inner circle was what Franklin Adams ineptly but catchily called the "Brain Trust." It was incumbent upon the higher classes to rule and to take care of the masses. It was their duty to see that the lower classes were sheltered, fed, and given as much opportunity for literacy as was good for them. I doubt that if he had lived and seen the thing develop into a one-man dictatorship, he would have changed his mind except to differ in details. The suppression of minority parties and the final extinction of the untrammeled free speech which had been a feature of the American polity, would not have altered his basic attitude. He would not have considered it a trend in the wrong direction to see the fostering of a class consciousness and the sudden emergence of a proletariat for the first time in the history of this country. I am sure it would not have displeased him at all to witness the pitiful spectacle of a delegation from Congress (representatives of "The Peepul") cooling its heels in an anteroom while waiting for admission into the executive Presence to be informed what legislation it would be allowed to pass or what *fait accompli* it would be permitted to put its "O.K." on.

I am leaving myself wide open to the charge of calling Lovecraft a snob because I stress his feeling of class. I do not call him a snob, and to my way of thinking he was no snob; but if it is insisted that a very high idea of what is a gentleman, and what is class, and what is heredity, and what places one person fit to rule and another fit only to be ruled—if it is insisted that these constitute a snob, then he was a snob. But I do not consider him a snob. A snob is a low order of mentality in Lovecraft's class. Lovecraft was not of a low mental order. His mind raised him above snobbery. If he had gone to England, he would have found difficulty in fitting himself into that great snob class for which he had the most feeling. There have been snobs with brains, *vide* Bulwer-Lytton, but they are the exceptions. ⟨. . .⟩

I never decided exactly how much was pose and what was genuine in Lovecraft's various freaks, eccentricities, idiosyncracies and oddities. The same stands for his expressed beliefs. There was so much admitted pose that we were too prone to question the genuine. In the first place, being a gentleman in this day and age he was a freak, which was no pose. A genuine sense of humor was behind much of his posing. Being an incongruity in the modern setting pleased his sense of the ridiculous. Dubbing his friends by Latinized (or hog-latinized) forms of their names was a playful compliment to them. He would write, "Culinarius, why not try to drop down to Providence next week-end? Eddy inquired about you yesterday. We must see him and buy a book and make the old boy happy. He says he will keep open all night if necessary." "Culinarius" was concocted by one of the New York gang, but Lovecraft immediately adopted it for all familiar use. My own unfortunate name is of course plebeian, lacking in euphony, short, and far from sonorous. There was nothing of a pose about his Anglomania. His adherence to eighteenth century diction and Johnsonian phrases was not a pose at first but became one later. He would cheerfully admit the pose in many cases and would justify it by saying that it pleased him—which was reason enough.

I have never thought it proper to inquire closely into the religious (for want of knowing a better word) opinions of my friends. In fact, I haven't cared. But Lovecraft could on occasion be so aggressive in support of pure materialism that that very fact caused one to question. How a confirmed materialist could with solemnity aid in carrying out an expressed request and scatter the ashes of the mother of a friend under her favorite rose bushes is difficult to understand. The artistic temperament or a leaning toward paganism are definitely out as answers.—W. PAUL COOK, *In Memoriam: Howard Phillips Lovecraft*, 1941, pp. 2–18, 67–72

Long before H. P. and I were married he said to me in a letter when speaking of ⟨Samuel⟩ Loveman, "Loveman is a poet and a literary genius. I have never met him in person, but his letters indicate him to be a man of great learning and cultural background. The only discrepancy I find in him is that he is of the Semitic race, a Jew."

Then I replied that I was a little surprised at H. P.'s discrimination in this instance—that I thought H. P. to be above such a petty fallacy—and that perhaps our own friendship might find itself on the rocks under the circumstances, since I too am of the Hebrew people—but that surely, he, H. P., could not have been serious, that elegance of manner, cultural background, social experience and the truly artistic temperament, intellectuality and refinement surely do not choose any particular color, race or creed; that these attributes should be highly appreciated no matter where they may be found!

It was only after several such exchanges of letters that he put the "pianissimo" on his thoughts (perhaps) and curtailed his outbursts of discrimination. In fact, it was after this that our own correspondence became more frequent and more intimate until, as I then believed, H. P. became entirely rid of his prejudices in this direction, and that no more need have been said about them. However, for many months (perhaps for a year before we were married) I constantly reminded him of my own background affiliations with the Semitic race, giving him every opportunity to retract his proposal of marriage.

It was his prejudice against minorities, especially Jews, that prompted me to invite both H. P. and S. L. to spend some time in New York, so that if H. P. never met a Jew before, I was happy to know that for the first time he would meet two of them, both of whom were favorably cultured and enlightened, and that the favored of the race is not limited to this infinitesimal number.

Unfortunately, one often judges a whole people by the character of the first ones he meets. But H. P. assured me that he was quite "cured"; that since I was so well assimilated into the American way of life and the American scene he felt sure our marriage would be a success. But unfortunately (and here I must speak of something I never intended to have publicly known), whenever he would meet crowds of people—in the subway, or, at the noon hour, on the sidewalks in Broadway, or crowds, wherever he happened to find them, and these were usually the workers of minority races—he would become livid with anger and rage.

I would then tell him that I, too, disliked the ignorant, not only of my own race, but of his, too; that these underprivileged of all races and nations, they and their children, are what made America the great and strong country that it is—that I felt exceedingly sorry for them and that *we*, he and I, really ought to start some benevolent, artistic and intellectual cult, and take into our circle all who by dint of a desire to rise to cultural heights, regardless of race, creed or origin, would care to join us. At such times he would agree with me, but again, would almost lose his mind when he next came inadvertently among crowds.

If the truth must be known, it was *this* attitude toward minorities and his desire to escape them that prompted him back to Providence. Yet he did not wish to give me a legal separation. For nearly two years our almost daily exchanges of letters consisted of each assuring the other of real appreciation. On his part it was a case of "Oh, it isn't you, my dear, it is all the others." "You don't know how much I appreciate you!" etc. etc.

When I confessed at the outset that I was seven years his senior he said that nothing could please him better; that Mrs. Whitman was also older than Poe and that Poe might have met with better conditions and better fortune and circumstances had her parents approved and permitted the marriage.

The nomenclature of "Socrates and Xantippe" were originated by me because, as time marched on and our correspondence became more intimate, I either *saw* in Howard or endowed him with a Socratic wisdom and genius, so that in a jocular vein I subscribed myself as Xantippe.

It was *this* that I sensed in him and had hoped in time to humanize him further by encouraging him toward the wedded path of true love. I am afraid that my optimism and my excessive self-assurance misled me, and perhaps him, too. I had always admired great intellectuality perhaps more than anything else in the world (perhaps, too, because I lacked so much of it myself) and had hoped to lift H. P. out of his abysmal depths of loneliness and psychic complexes.

Notwithstanding his scores of correspondents and visitors he was an extremely lonely soul. In this respect he seemed to be abnormal, and like Pope's "Vice" at first I "shunned, then accepted, and then embraced". I had hoped (perhaps it was wish-thinking) that my "embrace" would make of him not only a great *genius* but also a lover and husband. While the genius developed and broke through its chrysalis, the lover and husband receded into the background until they became apparitions that finally vanished.

Yet regardless of this atrocious candor let me go on record as saying and meaning it, that aside from some of these unfortunate facts, Howard Phillips Lovecraft was a marvelous person. He was "as wise as a serpent and as gentle as a dove", where circumstances or the occasion prompted it; yet he was not of a calculative turn of mind, and never sought for the main chance.

Notwithstanding his desire to return to Rhode Island because of all that had happened to him in New York, I like to believe that his nature became more mellowed, and that his prejudices and discriminations toward minorities gradually diminished as he met men of other races, sects and creeds and found them to be normal, kindly folks with the same tastes, desires, aspirations, and foibles as himself.

And even though I am not his widow, I bow my head in sorrow and reverence at the untimely passing of a gentle soul and great genius. May the God in whom he so little believed rest his soul in peace.—Sonia H. Davis, *The Private Life of H. P. Lovecraft*, 1985, pp. 21–23

## General

Some former art attitudes—like sentimental romance, loud heroics, ethical didacticism, &c.—are so patently hollow as to be visibly absurd & non-usable from the start. Others, like those dependent on moods & feelings (pity, tragedy, personal affection, group loyalty &c.) which are still empirical conduct-factors though intellectually undermined, have an excellent chance of survival. Fantastic literature cannot be treated as a single unit, because it is a composite resting on widely divergent bases. I really agree that *Yog-Sothoth* is a basically immature conception, & unfitted for really serious literature. The fact is, I have never approached serious literature as yet. But I consider the use of actual folk-myths as even more childish than the use of new artificial myths, since in employing the former one is forced to retain many blatant puerilities & contradictions of experience which could be subtilised or smoothed over if the supernaturalism were modelled to order for the given case. The only permanently artistic use of Yog-Sothothery, I think, is in symbolic or associative phantasy of the frankly poetic type; in which fixed dream-patterns of the natural organism are given an embodiment & crystallisation. The reasonable permanence of this phase of poetic phantasy as a *possible* art form (whether or not favoured by current fashion) seems to me a highly strong probability. It will, however, demand ineffable adroitness—the vision of a Blackwood joined to the touch of a de la Mare—& is probably beyond my utmost powers of achievement. I hope to see material of this sort in time, though I hardly expect to produce anything even remotely approaching it myself. I am too saturated in the empty gestures & pseudo-moods of an archaic & vanished world to have any successful traffick with symbols of an expanded dream-reality. But there is another phase of cosmic phantasy (which may or may not include frank Yog-Sothothery) whose foundations appear to me as better grounded than these of ordinary oneiroscopy; personal limitation regarding the *sense of outsideness*. I refer to the aesthetic crystallisation of that burning & inextinguishable feeling of mixed wonder & oppression which the sensitive imagination experiences upon scaling itself & its restrictions against the vast & provocative abyss of the unknown. This has always been the chief emotion in my psychology; & whilst it obviously figures less in the psychology of the majority, it is clearly a well-defined & permanent factor from which very few sensitive persons are wholly free. Here we have a natural biological phenomenon so untouched & untouchable by intellectual disillusion that it is difficult to envisage its total death as a factor in the most serious art. Reason as we may, we cannot destroy a normal perception of the highly limited & fragmentary nature of our visible world of perception & experience as scaled against the outside abyss of unthinkable galaxies & unplumbed dimensions—an abyss wherein our solar system is the merest dot (by the same *local* principle that makes a sand-grain a dot as compared with the whole planet earth) *no matter what relativistic system we may use in conceiving the cosmos as a whole*—& this perception cannot fail to act potently upon the natural physical instinct of *pure curiosity*; an instinct just as basic & primitive, & as impossible of destruction by any philosophy whatsoever, as the parallel instincts of hunger, sex, ego-expansion, & fear. You grossly underestimate this physical instinct, which appears to be as undeveloped in you as superficial exhibitionism is in me; yet its potent reality is attested by the life-work of a Pliny, a Copernicus, a Newton, an Einstein, an Eddington, a Shapley, a Huxley, an Amundsen, a Scott, a Shackleton, a Byrd . . . but hell! what's the use? Who can tell a blind man what sight is? At any rate, the lure of the unknown abyss remains as potent as ever under any conceivable intellectual, aesthetic, or social order; & will crop out as a forbidden thing even in societies where the external ideal of altruistic collectivism reigns. In types where this urge cannot be gratified by actual research in pure science, or by the actual physical exploration of unknown parts of the earth, it is inevitable that a symbolic aesthetic outlet will be demanded. You can't dodge it—the condition must exist, under all phases of cosmic interpretation, as long as a sense-chained race of inquirers on a microscopic earth-dot are faced by the black, unfathomable gulph of the Outside, with its forever-unexplorable orbs & its virtually certain spinkling of utterly unknown life-forms. A great part of religion is merely a childish & diluted pseudo-gratification of this perpetual gnawing toward the ultimate illimitable void. Superadded to this simple curiosity is the galling sense of *intolerable restraint* which all sensitive people (except self-blinded earth-gazers like little Augie Derleth) feel as they survey their natural limitations in time & space as scaled against the freedoms & expansions & comprehensions & adventurous expectancies which the mind can formulate as abstract conceptions. Only a perfect clod can fail to discern these irritant feelings in the greater part of mankind—feelings so potent & imperious that, if denied symbolic outlets in aesthetics or religious fakery, they produce actual hallucinations of the supernatural, & drive half-responsible minds to the concoction of the most absurd hoaxes & the perpetuation of the most absurd specific myth-types. Don't let little Augie sidetrack you. The general revolt of the sensitive mind against the tyranny of corporeal enclosure, restricted sense-equipment, & the laws of force, space, & causation, is a far keener & bitterer & better-founded one than any of the silly revolts of long-haired poseurs against isolated & specific instances of cosmic inevitability. But of course it does not take the forms of personal petulance, because there is no convenient scape-goat to saddle the impersonal ill upon. Rather does it crop out as a pervasive sadness & unplaceable

impatience, manifested in a love of strange dreams & an amusing eagerness to be galled by the quack cosmic pretensions of the various religious circuses. Well—in our day the quack circuses are wearing pretty thin despite the premature senilities of fat Chesterbellocs & affected Waste Land Shantih-dwellers, & the nostalgic & unmotivated "overbeliefs" of elderly & childhood-crippled physicists. The time has come when the normal revolt against time, space, & matter must assume a form not overtly incompatible with what is known of reality—when it must be gratified by images forming *supplements* rather than *contradictions* of the visible & mensurable universe. And what, if not a form of *non-supernatural cosmic art*, is to pacify this sense of revolt—as well as gratify the cognate sense of curiosity? "Dunt esk", as they say in your decadent cosmopolis! No, young Belloc, you can't rule out a phase of human feeling & expression which springs from instincts wholly basic & physical. Cosmic phantasy *of some sort* is as assured of possible permanence (its status subject to caprices of fashion) as is the literature of struggle & eroticism.—H. P. LOVECRAFT, Letter to Frank Belknap Long (Feb. 27, 1931), *Selected Letters: 1929–1931*, eds. August Derleth, Donald Wandrei, 1971, pp. 293–96

Lovecraft is one of the few authors of whom I can honestly say that I have enjoyed every word of his stories. He wrote every word of his stories. He wrote every kind of prose—earning money as a ghost writer, to compose what he really wanted to write. His essays that I have seen are occasionally amusing. His study, *Supernatural Horror in Literature*, makes one feel he could have been a remarkable interpreter of Literature. And while his poetry seems to me mostly written "with his left hand," it includes that marvellous bacchanalian song (in "The Tomb") with the magnificent line,

> Better under the table than under the ground

which makes one think he might under some circumstances have been a fine poet. But it was a writer of weird fiction that he chose to be primarily, and that choice seems to me justified by what he wrote.

His gifts were unusual. He was a scientist at heart, and that gave him a love of clarity. But he was also a dreamer, and could command the record of his own dreams, so as to make his readers yield "to shadows and delusions here." But mere style and clarity and careful planning cannot make a writer outstanding. There must be a narrative power for the writer of stories to excel, and that narrative power was the greatest of Lovecraft's gifts. It could outbalance his one greatest weakness—as recognized by himself, a tendency to melodrama, to kill off a dozen victims where one would have served better. It could have outbalanced a dozen weaknesses he did not have.

From time to time he is compared to Poe. There is little basis and no necessity for comparison. He was a great appreciator, admirer, and even interpreter of Poe (his recognition of the central theme of the "House of Usher" as the possession of but one soul by brother, sister, and the house itself seems to have been as novel as it is obviously correct) and he shared to a large extent Poe's views of the purpose of literature and the attitude the artist should have toward the weird. Lovecraft says in "The Unnamable": "It is the province of the artist . . . to rouse strong emotion by action, ecstasy, and astonishment." Poe thought the creation of a mood the end—and by mood something rather like ecstasy is meant. Lovecraft said to Mr. E. Hoffmann Price, "But don't you shudder and ask, Can these things really be?" and Poe said to a friend he feared "demons take advantage of the darkness to carry people away—though I do not believe there are any demons." I do not think any better attitude or theory can be held by the writer of weird tales—one reads dozens of them in which the writer betrays his own incredulity, and it is always fatal to the artistic effect. The two writers had a similar attitude, and one that would work for them. The chief difference is hard to explain although it is easy to feel; Poe was more interested in method of thought, Lovecraft more in a record of ideas; yet Lovecraft tried to make his tales consistent with each other, while Poe could allow the devil to read human minds in one tale and not in another with insouciance. It is also notable that Poe, like most writers, was only occasionally interested in the weird, while Lovecraft confined himself to a single genre.—T. O. MABBOTT, "H. P. Lovecraft: An Appreciation," *Marginalia* by H. P. Lovecraft et al., ed. August Derleth, 1944, pp. 338–39

Lovecraft's real value as a creative artist is similar to that of the Edgar Allan Poe he so much admired and so often imitated. Lovecraft sets loose the boundaries of the imagination and allows for the exploration of other worlds, which may or may not be specifically "Lovecraftian" worlds. Those young writers who formed what was called the "Lovecraft Cult" after his premature death in 1937 took over the mythos and atmospheric effects which Lovecraft had perfected, but they failed miserably because they seldom went beyond the uncanny dimensions and expansive fantasies which Lovecraft himself had only begun to explore. It is as an opener of doors that Lovecraft remains significant, though he may sometimes open doors of a truly fearsome and morbid nature. ⟨. . .⟩

Although H. P. Lovecraft's view of an intimate contact with nature is a dark one, still in his own way he does restore much of that "profound emotional energy" which Jung describes as being lost in our modern world. Lovecraft recreates that dialogue of cosmic voices, as the characters in his stories are seized, in spite of themselves and their innate scientific skepticism, by forces which compel horrified obedience and primitive response. His appeal and his concern are with primal roots of human feeling—fear, disgust, wonder, awe—and with an epic backdrop of the fantastic and the dreadful which we find in ancient folk-chronicles such as *Beowulf*, which become in turn the source for a popular modern myth-cycle as mannered as that of Lovecraft, namely J. R. R. Tolkien's *Lord of the Rings*.

As the modern world and modern literature moved more and more into the ego, the completely solipsistic world of stream-of-consciousness, Lovecraft and others like him moved further and further away from that world into the dark, immense, and unknown regions which exist beyond, behind, or below that ego. And when Lovecraft explored consciousness itself, he did not stop at the delineation of merely personal motives and sensations; he went far beneath them into the archetypes and the images which had helped to shape, as well as to define, their substance. His two great themes both involve the Triumph of the Shadow. In one class of his stories, this triumph is the dominance of Jung's interior "shadow" of the collective unconscious, coming from deep inside the human self to overwhelm its conscious, "civilized," or "daylight" realm in a dark eclipse of atavism and violent instinct (as in the famous short tale, "The Rats in the Walls"). Other stories, which tend more toward science fiction than to psychological thrillers, detail the incursion of forces outside and beyond the self, raising the plight of the individual to a cosmic level, and subsequently questioning both man's place in the universe and his conception of his own destiny (as in the significant novella, "The Shadow out of Time"). Even these approaches, however, can be referred back to the tradition of the so-called "Gothic Novel," of which Lovecraft was so consciously a part, and especially one of its main spokesmen, Mrs. Ann Radcliffe, who

differentiated between the terms "terror" and "horror" by demonstrating that while terror "expanded" the soul to intimations of the sublime (Lovecraft's science fiction), horror "contracted the soul to a freezing-point of near-annihilation (Lovecraft's psychological chillers). At a time when such words as "outer-space" and "soul" have become current and when there is paradoxically a growing interest in witchcraft, ritual, magic, the demonic, and all forms of the occult, a "Lovecraft revival" should not be a totally unexpected phenomenon. —BARTON L. ST. ARMAND, "Facts in the Case of H. P. Lovecraft," *RIH*, Feb. 1972, pp. 6–8

H. P. Lovecraft was a "mechanistic materialist," in the philosophical sense of the words, totally devoid of any dualistic belief in religion or the supernatural. Possessing a bright scientific mind, already manifest in his childhood interest in chemistry and astronomy, he clearly perceived man's abysmal insignificance and meaninglessness in the vast mechanistic and purposeless cosmos, governed by blind, impersonal ("mindless") streams of force. A believer in the inexorable action of causality, he stated as early as 1921, in a letter to R. Kleiner: "Determinism—what you call Destiny—rules inexorably; though not exactly in the personal way you seem to fancy. We have no specific destiny against which we can fight—for the fighting would be as much a part of the destiny as the final end. The real fact is simply that every event in the cosmos is caused by the action of antecedent and circumjacent forces, so that whatever we do is unconsciously the inevitable product of Nature rather than of our own volition. If an act correspond with our wish, it is Nature that made the wish, and ensured its fulfillment."

Contrary to what is assumed by many, Lovecraft did not conceive the cosmos as basically inimical *or* beneficial to man. He stated in a letter to J. F. Morton, dated 30 October 1929: ". . . I am . . . an *indifferentist.* . . . I do not make the mistake of thinking that the resultant of the natural forces surrounding and governing organic life will have any connexion with the wishes or tastes of any part of that organic life-process . . . [The cosmos] doesn't give a damn one way or the other about the especial wants and ultimate welfare of mosquitoes, rats, lice, dogs, men, horses, pterodactyls, trees, fungi, dodos, or other forms of biological energy."

Lovecraft was pessimistic with respect to man's ability to cope with the realisation of his own meaninglessness and insignificance in an indifferent universe. The first paragraph of "The Call of Cthulhu" reflects his doubts about man's capacity to preserve his precarious sanity in a confrontation with bleak and unpalatable reality: it is only "the inability of the human mind to correlate all its contents" which prevents our mental disintegration when we come across dissociated bits of knowledge about our frightful position in the black seas of infinity that surround us. Notice that here Lovecraft is *not* deploring knowledge, but rather, *man's inability to cope with it.* Lovecraft's fiction, and in particular his pseudomythology (which I prefer to call the Yog-Sothoth Cycle of Myth, to differentiate it from the distorted version labelled "Cthulhu Mythos" by Derleth) was *not* a reaction *against* his austere and parsimonious materialistic philosophy, but instead formed the natural outgrowth of the same. Lovecraft wrote primarily to give himself "the satisfaction of visualising more clearly and detailedly and stably the vague, elusive, fragmentary impressions of wonder, beauty, and adventurous expectancy which [were] conveyed to [him] by certain sights . . . , ideas, occurrences, and images encountered in art and literature," as he stated in "Notes on Writing Weird Fiction," and chose weird stories "because they suit[ed his] inclinations best—one of [his] strongest and most persistent wishes [having been] to achieve momentarily the illusion of some strange suspension or violation of the galling limitations of time, space, and natural law which for ever imprison us and frustrate our curiosity about the infinite cosmic places beyond the radius of our sight and analysis." Inclined to write *weird fiction*, Lovecraft's rationalistic intellect could conceive no weirder or more bizarre happening than a dislocation of natural law—not ghosts, daemons, or the supernatural, but the suspension of the laws of Nature.

Predisposed to write imaginative fiction by temperament and environmental contingencies, Lovecraft became also aware of the fact that supernatural themes were rapidly losing their ability to envoke the emotion of fear needed to "create a convincing picture of shattered natural law or cosmic alienage and 'outsideness,'" at least among the more educated and sceptical readers. Consequently he turned to the unplumbed abysses of space and the unknown and unknowable spheres of alien dimensions (as well as to the tortuous depths of the unconscious) for the source of horror in his tales. As George T. Wetzel and Fritz Leiber have pointed out, he developed the concept of the "mechanistic supernatural," and was, in a sense, a "literary Copernicus," producing a body of *cosmocentred* fiction unlike most of the anthropocentred writings of his predecessors and, regrettably, of most of his successors. Being a materialist, Lovecraft created the materialistic tale of supernatural horror. Far from implying an unconscious rejection of his philosophy, it was highly consonant with the same—it was the only kind of fiction he could have written, in view of his intellectual genius, his *Weltanschauung*, and his aesthetic inclinations! ⟨. . .⟩

Lovecraft did not envision the various mythopoeic conceptions that were going to become integral parts of his *oeuvre* at the start of his writing career. Instead, the various elements involved in his pseudomythology gradually evolved and constantly changed during his lifetime. The Yog-Sothoth Cycle of Myth centres around a certain group of alien entities from "Outside"—from beyond the sphere of conscious human experience: the unplumbed abysses of space, other dimensions, other universes, and the nightmare depths of the unconscious. The main ones are Azathoth, Yog-Sothoth, Nyarlathotep, Cthulhu, and Shub-Niggurath, and these are known with the generic name of "Old Ones" (although it does *not* follow that they are related or belong to a similar "species"; with the possible exception of Cthulhu, each seems to be unique). These Old Ones *were*, *are*, and *will be*. They are *not* mere symbols of the power of evil, although they may appear to be inimical to man, in the same way that man would appear to be inimical to ants, should these get in his way. The Old Ones are above and beyond mankind—they transcend man, and care no more for him than he does for ants.

As the result of occasional and more or less fortuitous contacts between man and those forces from Outside which he could not control nor comprehend, cults, superstitions, legends, and books of forbidden lore (such as the *Necronomicon*) emerged. Several of Lovecraft's stories record the consequences of attempts to use such forbidden knowledge to meddle with the powers from Outside—man, essentially helpless and impotent in his encounters with the Unknown (although at first often unaware of the extent of his own helplessness), does not fare well. In the few instances in which he escapes annihilation or insanity, it is ironically due, not to his own efforts, but to some accident beyond his control (e.g. the second sinking of R'lyeh). And what could be more terrifying for man than the realisation of his own impotent insignificance face to face with the Unknown and the Unknowable?—DIRK W. MOSIG, "H. P. Lovecraft: Myth-Maker" (1976), *H. P. Lovecraft: Four Decades of Criticism*, ed. S. T. Joshi, 1980, pp. 105–7

## Works

Lovecraft's work has both great merits and great defects. He was an exceedingly cultivated and well-read man. His approach to literature and especially to weird fiction was that of a scholar as much as that of a creative artist.

Moreover his vast correspondence shows that he was a distinguished linguist and his scientific interest in language is clearly reflected by his writing. Lovecraft's tales strike us by their exceedingly rich vocabulary, verbal imagination and almost scientific research of the *mot propre*; and though his style is often somewhat artificial, it is clearly that of an author with a solid background of etymological learning.

No doubt the language he wrote was not the kind that would appeal to the customary public of horror fiction. This may to a certain extent explain his failure during lifetime while he wrote for popular magazines and his sudden revival when a more refined public began to take interest in his work. ⟨. . .⟩

Yet Lovecraft's greatest merit was also his greatest fault. He was too well read. In his critical study *Supernatural Horror in Literature* he displays an encyclopædic knowledge of supernatural fiction, and since he read that enormous amount of weird fiction with obvious pleasure he has been subjected to a corresponding series of influences. In fact he was influenced by so many authors that one is often at a loss to decide what is really Lovecraft and what some half-conscious memory of the books he has read. Some of the writers to whom he owes most are Poe, Machen, Bram Stoker, E. T. A. Hoffmann, H. G. Wells, Lord Dunsany, and perhaps William Hope Hodgson, but there are many more. ⟨. . .⟩

The fact remains that when Lovecraft adopted a motif which his forerunners had already used, he frequently handled it far better. His 'Call of Cthulhu' and other stories on the ancient gods rank high above Machen's 'The Novel of the Black Seal', 'The Shining Pyramid' or 'The White People'. His 'Shadow out of Time', a novel about strange trips through time and space, and the forced exchange of human bodies with those of the mysterious pre-human 'Great Race', is at once reminiscent of Wells' *The Time Machine* and of Machen's tales. It also contains many Poesque scenes. Yet, as a whole, the story is infinitely more poignant and convincing than either Wells' or Machen's works. The hero's final descent into the ruined capital of the 'Great Race', where he discovers his own manuscript written quadrillions of years ago, is one of the most perfect climaxes in the history of weird fiction.

It would be unjust to say that Lovecraft's inventive powers were limited to a better presentation of old themes. In 'The Call of Cthulhu' he created a whole mythology of his own which now and then appears in his other tales. Later some authors borrowed the Cthulhu mythology with Lovecraft's permission. It is a highly-evolved and completely renewed form of Machen's primitive idea. ⟨. . .⟩

It is difficult to interpret the symbolism of Lovecraft's tales. It lies between the unconscious choice of horrible symbols as we find it in Machen and Crawford, and the subtle intellectual perversity that makes Hartley's 'Travelling Grave' the greatest tale of its kind. Lovecraft deliberately plays on the reader's subconscious fears as well as on his conscious repulsion from the scenes he is compelled to witness. While Machen and Crawford involuntarily symbolised the problems that seem to have obsessed them, Lovecraft keeps a certain critical distance from his work and simply chooses the effect he wishes to produce. Moreover he was an avowed unbeliever in the supernatural, and considered that a pure materialist would be a better writer of supernatural tales than would someone who believed in occult powers.

It may be well to remark here that occult believers are probably less effective than materialists in delineating the spectral and the fantastic, since to them the phantom world is so commonplace a reality that they tend to refer to it with less awe, remoteness, and impressiveness than do those who see in it an absolute and stupendous violation of the natural order.

The way in which he was influenced by so many other writers makes it very difficult to decide which symbols found an echo in his own personality, which were used for subtly calculated effect, and which arose from a more or less distinct recollection of his reading.

As it is, the most dominant motif in Lovecraft's work is the nameless, ancestral horror lurking beneath the earth, or ready to invade us from the stars; the dethroned but still potent gods of old. The symbol is a very common one and is not bound to any particular complex. It therefore strikes and horrifies more readers than would any theme having a single subconscious origin. Probably C. G. Jung's theories on the collective subconscious give the only explanation of such symbols as 'great Cthulhu', 'the father Yog-Sothoth'. According to him they would symbolise very old hereditary fears. Edgar Dacqué, the famous German palæontologist and philosopher, whose theories are somewhat different from Dr. Jung's, would, strangely enough, point to a similar origin. While the latter believes in an exceedingly ancient but yet subconscious origin of certain collective fears and spiritual tendencies, Dacqué suggests an equally ancient but materially existent basis for these terrors in the distant past. Perhaps such tales as 'Pickman's Model' or 'The Call of Cthulhu' are, after all, more than the result of purely intellectual search for effect.

Even if there is a true symbolism in Lovecraft's tales it is his realistic descriptions of pure shameless horror that strike one as the dominant feature. If any writer was able to cram his tales with more loathsome physical abominations than Crawford and Machen it is Howard Phillips Lovecraft. He delights in detailed descriptions of rotting corpses in every imaginable state of decay, from initial corruption to what he has charmingly called a 'liquescent horror'. He has a particular predilection for fat, carnivorous, and, if possible, anthropophagous rats. His descriptions of hideous stenches and his onomatopœic reproductions of a madman's yowlings are something with which even 'Monk Lewis' did not disgrace fiction. I could well understand Mr. Blackwood, when he once told me that to him 'spiritual terror' seemed entirely absent from Lovecraft's tales; for if there is any, it is hidden under so much repulsive detail that the English master may well be excused for not noticing it. ⟨. . .⟩

It is strange how Lovecraft uses material details even if he is describing purely supernatural entities. He is unable to evoke the glorious spectral and half-material shapes we find in Blackwood's tales. A presence felt, rather than perceived by the senses, is beyond his inventive powers. It is characteristic that he does not even mention Oliver Onions and Robert Hichens in his critical study; he would not have been able to appreciate such masterpieces of subtly suggested terror as 'The Beckoning Fair One', or 'How Love Came to Professor Guildea'. Nor was he able to make use of Dr. James' indirect method of describing

an apparition, with metaphors chosen from reality, but devoid of words directly alluding to horror. He would never have begun a climax with 'It seems as if'. Lovecraft's monsters are usually ridiculous compounds of elephant feet and trunks, human faces, tentacles, gleaming eyes and bat wings, not to mention, of course, the indescribable fœtor that usually accompanies their presence. The reader is often amused rather than frightened by the author's extraordinary surgical talents. Wells' Dr. Moreau could hardly have done better.

'Oh, oh, my Gawd, that haff face—that haff face on top of it . . . that face with the red eyes an' crinkly albino hair, an' no chin, like the Whateleys . . . It was a octopus, centipede, spider kind o' thing, but they was a haff-shaped man's face on top of it, an' it looked like Wizard Whateley's, only it was yards an' yards acrost . . .'

Though often slightly too long, Lovecraft's tales are nearly always perfect in structure. Suspense increases from the first page until the well-placed climax at the end is reached; only his exaggerated display of horrible details sometimes threatens to tire the reader before the end. ⟨. . .⟩

One can reject or accept the whole group of pure horror tales, but one must admit that within the limits of the genre there exists a certain hierarchy of lesser and greater as in any other art. In my opinion, the pure tale of horror has the highest literary standing when it is no longer a mere outlet for neurotic tendencies but has become a sort of intellectual game. The objection may be made that a pronounced taste for horror always denotes a certain perversion. This cannot be denied, but the artistic result may be a conscious or unconscious creation. The author may, or may not, be aware of the symbolism he is using. His symbols may find no echo in his own subconscious; they may not be symbols at all, but merely skilfully calculated effects, as are some of Lovecraft's. This latter technique is usually a failure when applied to most types of short ghost story. The horror tale is different. A fully conscious approach to the theme is likely to leave the reader with a less painful impression than a shameless display of unconscious and mostly hideous neurotic tendencies. At least one does not feel the author to be hopelessly in the grip of psychic disease. His tales are not necessarily filled with the oppressive atmosphere of a lunatic asylum.—PETER PENZOLDT, "The Pure Tale of Horror," *The Supernatural in Fiction*, 1952, pp. 165–72

No commentator on Lovecraft has made more than a passing notice of his verse. The United Amateur Press Association, which channeled so much of his writing, was not strong on literary criticism, and in magazines of the horror story, verse had only an incidental place. In Lovecraft's complete work his verse remains secondary; it has less distinction than his best stories and it is presumably less interesting than his letters. Yet the evidence is that, particularly in his youth, Lovecraft's most concentrated attention was upon the writing of poetry; that at one time or another he thought of himself as primarily a poet— as his mother referred to him in her recorded conversations with the psychiatrist at Butler Hospital. There are two good reasons for making at least a brief survey of his verse. One is that all the work of any writer as curious as Lovecraft merits consideration. The other is that a few of his poems are in themselves rather good. ⟨. . .⟩

The bulk of the poems fall into one or the other of two manners of verse brought to perfection in Lovecraft's beloved eighteenth-century England. One is the neat, or as Keats called it, "the rocking-horse" couplet. This is emulated by Lovecraft in "Old Christmas" and "New England Fallen," and possibly carried on to Sir Walter Scott's narrative manner in "Psychopompos." The other is the more dulcet, bucolic or elegiac tone, usually in quatrains, as mastered by Thomas Gray and James Thomson. "Providence," "On a Grecian Colonnade in a Park," "Sunset," and "On a New England Village Seen by Moonlight" are Lovecraft poems in this manner. The first stanza of "Sunset" illustrates the literary influence flawlessly:

> The cloudless day is richer at its close;
>   A golden glory settles on the lea;
>   Soft, stealing shadows hint of cool repose
> To mellowing landscape, and to calming sea.

All these poems, indeed most of Lovecraft's, are "early poems"; that is, they were written before his thirtieth birthday—most of them probably between 1912 and 1920. They are quite dull, even at times unreadable. Their inspiration is literary and they never escape from or overcome the derivative tone. Their eighteenth-century mannerisms refuse transposition into the twentieth century. They are completely out of touch with Lovecraft's actual time as no vital poetry can ever be. And they are further damaged by the strong racial and social snobbery of Lovecraft's earlier years; what they say is frequently as restricted and eccentric as the manner in which it is said. In short, the quaintness and old-worldness, which in his horror stories became an attractive otherworldliness, remain wholly inefficient in his poetry.

This same criticism can be made of another group of his poems where the dominant influence is Poe. Some of these are "Astrophobos," "Despair," and "Nemesis"; and probably others, in mood and feeling if not so slavishly in meter. One sample, from "Nemesis," will do:

> Through the ghoul-guarded gateways of slumber,
>   Past the wan-mooned abysses of night,
> I have lived o'er my lives without number,
>   I have sounded all things with my sight;
> And I struggle and shriek ere the daybreak, being
>     driven to madness with fright.

Lovecraft never got beyond schoolboy imitation in this sort of thing.

One wonders what, if anything, Lovecraft made of the American poetry of his own era; and particularly because from 1912—when he was coming to maturity and writing much of his own verse—our poetry itself had come to a great new resurgence of individuality and vitality. His letters might show. The few I happen to have seen revealed an admiration for the poetry of Robert Hillyer, a very able traditionalist, but quick disdain and misunderstanding of T. S. Eliot, with whose principles of aristocracy, royalism, and classicism Lovecraft actually had much in common. I have no idea whether he was familiar with the poetry of Hart Crane, whom he knew slightly. Yet of course one can safely guess on the evidence of Lovecraft's general character and on that of his verse that his sympathies, wrapped in his eighteenth-century escape, remained profoundly apathetic to the "new" poetry of his time. Not only did Walt Whitman live and die in vain as far as Lovecraft was concerned, so even did John Keats and all the Romantics (save as decayed in Poe). Lovecraft had a fatal misconception of poetry as a living art. In his work he was anti-realistic and therefore anti-poetic.

Oddly enough, Lovecraft got away from this. Perhaps not oddly; for after all in his last decade and despite his eccentric life Lovecraft showed a much firmer sense of reality, a warmer sense of humor and of friendship. Emotionally he was more adult. A poem called "A Year Off," dated 1925, hints the first flicker of freshness in his verse. It is light, humorous, deftly done, an extravaganza of far travel which concludes with J. K. Huysmans' touch that the thoroughgoing and imaginative

anticipation is probably better than the actuality. But in its course it has verbal fun with its ideas: "To dally with the Dalai Lama" is a particularly fortunate moment.

Then, far more impressively, came the prolific spate of poetry between December 1929 and early January 1930. In three or four weeks Lovecraft wrote "Brick Row" and "The Messenger" and—these possibly within a week—the thirty-six sonnets, *Fungi from Yuggoth*. In general their style is simple and direct, the earlier poetic derivations sloughed off. The horror of his best stories is at last used with effective understatement in verse. "They took me slumming" is, for instance, a phrase from one of the *Fungi* sonnets that would have dynamited the artificialities of his earlier poems; and almost everywhere the language is equally alive, and the horror is all the sharper for being quiet-spoken.

Perhaps as wholly satisfactory as any poem he ever wrote is the separate sonnet, "The Messenger," which Lovecraft did as answer to Bertrand K. Hart's joyous threat to "send a monstrous visitor" to Lovecraft's doorstep at 3 A.M.

> The Thing, he said, would come that night at three
> From the old churchyard on the hill below;
> But crouching by an oak fire's wholesome glow,
> I tried to tell myself it could not be.
> Surely, I mused, it was a pleasantry
> Devised by one who did not truly know
> The Elder Sign, bequeathed from long ago,
> That sets the fumbling forms of darkness free.
>
> He had not meant it—no—but still I lit
> Another lamp as starry Leo climbed
> Out of the Seekonk, and a steeple chimed
> *Three*—and the firelight faded, bit by bit.
> Then at the door that cautious rattling came—
> And the mad truth devoured me like a flame!

The chilling warning of that firelight fading bit by bit and then the "cautious" rattling—these two lines are worth more than all the pages of eighteenth-century rubbish he wrote as poetry. And several of the sonnets in the *Fungi* sequence are about as keenly controlled. ⟨ . . .⟩

His best remains restricted. Unlike Robinson's, it touched no depths of human significance. Its terror, unlike *The Ancient Mariner's*, has no meaning beyond itself, beyond mere nightmare. To scare is a slim purpose in poetry. But when Lovecraft at last brought his undoubted talent for horror themes into unaffected verse he made his poetry an interesting if minor portion of his total work.—WINFIELD TOWNLEY SCOTT, "A Parenthesis on Lovecraft as Poet" (1945), *Exiles and Fabrications*, 1961, pp. 72–77

Lovecraft's eighteenth-century interests are demonstrated as much in "The Poe-et's Nightmare" as in anything he wrote. His use of blank verse is traditional, and his polished lines of heroic couplets reflect his reading of Dryden, Pope, Swift, and other satirists who were admired during the Augustan period. Dryden's *Mac Flecknoe* ("From dusty shops neglected authors come, Martyrs of pies . . .") is particularly interesting for comparison in subject and tone; Pope's satire on poets was influenced by it, and Lovecraft had probably read it as well. Whatever his direct influences, Lovecraft applies his couplets to a *genre* in which his models had excelled and, in so doing, constructs lines of concise wit rather than the mere rhymed prose of such narrative pieces as "Psychopompos."

"The Poe-et's Nightmare" is composed of two distinct parts differentiated by both subject and style: the blank verse narration of the nightmare and the couplet description of the poet, together making "A Fable" about the nature of Truth.

The contrast between the two parts of the poem tends to heighten the effect of each, the comedy of the would-be poet making the tone of the nightmare all the more awesome, and the seriousness of the horrible truth rendering the poet all the more foolish. But if the nightmare represents a shocking revelation, its threat is restrained by being set in the context of a "real" world which allows the humorous criticism of an absurd, unwritten Poe-et.

As the title of the poem would indicate, its protagonist is not simply a poet, but a *Poe-et*, connoting Poe's romantic influences. His name "Lucullus Languish," confirms this— "Lucullus" after the Roman general known for his practise of gastronomy, and "Languish" relating to the romantic image of the suffering poet as well as recalling Lydia Languish, the heroine of Sheridan's *The Rivals*. Lucullus, like Lydia, is a romantic of simple-minded display. They are both needlessly dramatic, stiltedly impractical, and absurdly foolish. Lydia plays at being the romantic languishing lover; Lucullus acts the role of the languishing poet. Both succeed only in causing trouble and disappointment for themselves.

Lucullus Languish's opposed identities—his actual existence as a grocer's clerk and his assumption of the romantic role—are continually played upon in the poem as conflicting desires toward food and poetry. It becomes evident that, whatever Lucullus' aspirations, his fondness for eating makes him more a gourmand than an artist. Perhaps he is a "student of the skies," but he is also a "connoisseur of rarebits and mince pies" (ll. 1–2). Perhaps he does search for poetic inspiration, but he does so by overeating ice-cream and cake. His resolution to "chant a poet's lay" is easily broken by the "imperious call" of the supper hour (ll. 36, 43). Though Lucullus yearns for art, he fulfills himself with food. His true interests are far more in sympathy with his trade than he is willing to admit.

Because Lucullus' desires for expression are superficial, his poetic activity is a series of futile romantic gestures. The odes and dirges which he drops about the shop are forms of passionate expression, yet they do not "strike the chord within his heart" (l. 9). His searching the sky at night gives him a cold rather than a poem. He is charmed with his discovery of Poe (the allusions in ll. 23–24 are to "The Raven" and "Ulalume") but this only inflates his enthusiasm without bettering his art. He names a favoured grove "Tempe," a sacred place, but it is nevertheless a stunted copse and its "limpid lakes" remain mud puddles (ll. 27–31).

His poetic and gastric activities have one characteristic in common, however. The Latin motto of this first part of the poem, "Luxus tumultus semper causa est" (Mental disturbance is always caused by excess), suggests that it may have been the excess of both Lucullus' romanticism and his eating that led to his nightmare. He sought to excite inspiration with "overdoses" of ice-cream and cake (l. 12), and it is just after such an orgy of consumption that his fancies are exercised in the experience of the nightmare which was meant as a warning to "those who dine not wisely, but too well" (l. 58). His excesses have evoked the Poe-em he dreamed of as well as, ironically, an admonition he never expected.

Lucullus had "vow'd with gloom to woo" his muse, and he is "swath'd in gloom" in his bloated sleep (ll. 22, 64). In his romantic affectation, he has cultivated a passion for gloom, bringing it with him to his grove (l. 35). When his nightmare brings his fancies to life and transforms his poses into reality, the first changes evidence a realisation of his gloom. The "crystal deeps" (l. 18) he searched before are, in his dream, a "soundless heav'n" filled with "daemoniac clouds" (ll. 73–74). The stunted thicket in a vacant lot (ll. 26–27) becomes an "insomnious grove/Whose black recesses never saw the sun" (ll. 77–78), associated not with a "wooded plain" (l. 29) but a moor (l. 76). The mud puddles of his grove become a pool "that none dares sound; a tarn of murky face" (l. 81). Lucullus' assumed character would now be played in earnest.

As his nightmare continues, he senses foul beings around him, though he neither sees nor hears them (ll. 108–18). Then, with a flash of lightning (cf. *Fungi from Yuggoth*, VI, 13–14), the area around him glows, revealing what seem to be daemonic begins, groping trees, "moving forms, and things not spoken of" (ll. 118–35). A fire-mist blots out his view, followed by "the hot, unfinished stuff of nascent worlds" (l. 142) and, in the matter of newborn worlds, the poet is reborn "free from the flesh" (l. 148) which had been restraining him, free from his gorging to pursue his Poe-etic hopes.

In his aethereal state, the poet sees the mist clear to "a feeble fleck/Of silver light" which is what "mortals call the boundless universe" (ll. 142–44). Surrounding this, "each as a tiny star,/Shone more creations, vaster than our own" (ll. 155–56). The universe is hardly of great significance, being a fleck surrounded by larger flecks, these together forming "but an atom in infinity" (l. 170). In "the surge of boundless being," the earth is less than unimportant.

With his new-found consciousness, the poet begins to survey the endless vision before him and to "know all things" (l. 182). What he discovers is an endless course of existence which complements his knowledge of the insignificance of the human realm, physically, with the knowledge that, temporally, it has even less importance. Earth is a "speck, born but a second, which must die/In one brief second more" (ll. 198–99).

Once he realises the microscopic insignificance of "that fragile earth;/That crude experiment; that cosmic sport" (ll. 199–200), he can only reflect bitterly on the "proud, aspiring race of mites" who, through ignorance, "vaunt themselves/As the chief works of Nature" (ll. 202–08). The inhabitants of the thinnest film on the smallest, most fleeting speck of dust believe themselves the purpose of nature! In this context, it is not difficult to understand how this "moral vermin" (cf. *Gulliver's Travels*, II, 6), this "morbid matter by itself call'd man" (ll. 202, 219), would be only one of many minor "fest'ring ailments of infinity" (l. 218).

But this vision is too horrible for Lucullus to bear. Sickened, he turns away, mocked by his aethereal guide for searching after truth only to find it repulsive. The poet is reminded that he had originally sought to:

> . . . meditate
> On things forbidden, and to pierce the veil
> Of seeming good and seeming beauteousness
> That covers o'er the tragedy of Truth.
> (ll. 232–35)

But he learns that such good and beauty, however unreal, serve to palliate the Terrible Truth, helping mankind to "forget his sorry lot . . . [by] raising Hope where Truth would crush it down" (ll. 236–37).

Then is given a sight yet beyond what he had experienced before: "a rift of purer sheen, a sight supernal,/Broader than all the void conceived by man" (ll. 246–47). Here even his guide becomes awed, but the touch of celestial rhythm provokes a soulful horror in Lucullus. Though urged to find the unutterable Truth, his soul flees in terror.

Lucullus, of course, awakes to vow "no more to feed on cake, or pie, or Poe" (l. 276), that is, that he will no longer overindulge himself either in eating or in romantic quests for Truth. His point of view changed, his gloom lifts, and he becomes contented and successful as a grocer's clerk. The poem ends with a warning to all those who seek the "spark celestial" to restrain themselves from being "overzealous for high fancies" lest they, too, experience the "unutterable thing."

By itself, the couplet part of the poem would be a light satire, but the sombre narration of the dream lends a gravity to the composition. Blank verse is traditionally the medium for "high" or prophetic statements, and Lovecraft's Latin captions identify the focus of the vision's meaning. The *Aletheia Phrikodes*, the Monstrous Truth, is that "*Omnia risus et omnia pulvis et omnia nihil*" ("All is laughter, all is dust, all is nothing"). Whatever forces are involved in the universe, the vision makes quite clear that Good and Beauty are concepts used by humanity to hide its own insignificance. He who probes beyond these values risks the loss of the peace of mind they provide. The face of Truth is monstrous and is not seen with impunity: Lucullus' soul flees in madness.

The philosophic stance of "The Poe-et's Nightmare" can be readily found in Lovecraft's other writings. In his letters he expresses a disgust of romanticism; the probability of mankind's meaninglessness is asserted in other letters, though he finds poetry and other such cultivations palliatives for the knowledge of this meaninglessness.

J. Vernon Shea quotes a letter in which Lovecraft states that he found the greatest merit in weird stories "which bring in sharp reminders of the vast unplumbed recesses of space that loom perpetually around our insignificant dust-grain," as does "The Poe-et's Nightmare." In his fiction, a parallel could be drawn between many of Lovecraft's searchers and Lucullus. Basil Elton in "The White Ship" reaches the land of Fancy but, unsatisfied, destroys his chance for happiness by searching for the land of Hope. "Arthur Jermyn" destroys himself after discovering the truth about his family. "The Outsider" discovers a type of hoplessness, and other searchers—in such stories as "The Call of Cthulhu" and "The Shadow over Innsmouth"—are destroyed by their desire for enlightenment.

"The Poe-et's Nightmare," then, is a Lovecraftian nightmare which, in its philosophical expression of a central Lovecraftian theme, stands as an emblem to Lovecraft's poetry and fiction.—R. BOEREM, "A Lovecraftian Nightmare" (1976), *H. P. Lovecraft: Four Decades of Criticism*, ed. S. T. Joshi, 1980, pp. 217–21

---

PAUL BUHLE

From "Dystopia as Utopia: Howard Phillips Lovecraft
and the Unknown Content
of American Horror Literature"

*Minnesota Review*, Spring 1976, pp. 121–28

Lovecraft was in the first instance a direct descendant of the local color of Mary Wilkins Freeman and other New England artists. Such traditions gave him a sense of self extending back centuries, with a defined aesthetic of village life and beauty that American Renaissance writers would easily have recognized. Indeed, his descriptions of regional architecture, particularly of his home town of Providence, Rhode Island, are among his most carefully developed prose. Like Hawthorne and Freeman, he also found there the locus of horror, for as he wrote in an early tale: "The true epicure of the terrible, to whom a new thrill of unutterable ghastliness is the chief end and justification of existence, esteems most of all the ancient, lonely farmhouses of backwoods New England; for there the dark elements of strength, solitude, grotesqueness,

and ignorance combine to form the perfection of the hideous" ("The Picture in the House"). And not only the backwoods, with their fables of incest and degeneration; Lovecraft saw the horrors of the New England centers of commerce as well. His ghouls travel through those tunnels actually found in Providence extending from mansions to the sea, for the secret transfer of slaves; he relocates Devil Worship in the opulent "Kingsport" (apparently Marblehead, Massachusetts), product of a corruption of the spirit always close to the Puritan hubris and perhaps the penalty for fostering capitalism (see "The Festival").

Lovecraft was the profound child of Poe, and one of the most serious scholars of that writer in a time when, in the High Culture of America, his reputation had gone into a decline.[1] Lovecraft's fictional god of horror was not the vengeful and moral Jehovah but his own invention, "Nyarlathotep," the "Crawling Chaos" felt "through this revolting graveyard of a universe [in] the muffled, maddening beating of drums, and . . . the monotonous whine of blasphemous flutes from inconceivable, unlighted chambers beyond Time." This gave a definite cosmic character to Poe's unification of the terrible and the beautiful, and was akin not so much to Poe's simple morbidity (like "The Pit and the Pendulum") as to his more "philosophical" horrors like the "House of Usher," "Masque of the Red Death," and his poems "Silence, a Fable" and "Shadow, a Parable." The Southern links to Lovecraft's own Rhode Island are also significant; its historic "Plantations" and its analogous decadence, more attuned to death than to life, its vivid architecture and cultural traditions a counterpoint to its wrecked and decaying class of Anglo-Saxon rulers.

Lovecraft built upon Poe's sepulchral foundation, adding the work of modern terror writers Arthur Machen and Lord Dunsany to give him more modern techniques and spirit. But like his fellow fantasists of the 1920's, he was also deeply affected by a scientific influence, or rather the impress of the great iconoclast of science, Charles Fort. In *The Book of the Damned* (1919), Fort had compiled phenomena beyond scientific explanation, the excluded elements of life that he described as "corpses, skeletons, mummies, twitching, tottering . . . damned alive . . . arm and arm with the spirit of anarchy . . . pale stenches and gaunt superstitions and mere shadows and lively malices."[2] This was a literary or imaginative interpretation of the indeterminacy of modern scientific discovery: unexplained disappearances (of Ambrose Bierce, among others), black rains, unnatural appearances of astral phenomena—for these Fort supplied his own poetic suggestions, like the secret movement of some great compensating force overruling man's blunders, moving through the Negative (as Poe had suggested) toward some unforeseeable reconciliation of forces. An immediate best-seller, *The Book of the Damned* influenced writers like George Allan England and allowed fantasists like Lovecraft to encompass modern psychology (as another quest into the unknown) while escaping its contemporary, reductionist interpretations of the unmysterious and unpoetic character of human existence. The change of professions of one of Lovecraft's protagonists, from economics to psychology, mirrors the larger literary mood of the period. But Lovecraft's hero finds not "answers" but new uncertainties which link the mental unknown to unfathomable cosmic forces, his mental "distortion" perceived by the outside world as madness, allowing his perception of a Reality beyond day-to-day existence ("The Shadow out of Time"). Thus Lovecraft restated Poe's message at a higher level by adding the literary implications of scientific relativity, and proclaimed "the essentially intellectual wonder of one who looks out upon the whirling, grotesque, and unfathomable reaches which engulf the entire world."[3] Of all the wonders, *Time* was the greatest. As his friends suggested, Lovecraft felt himself out of place in an apparently wonderless age, his protagonist and alter ego forming "chimerical notions about living in one age and casting one's mind all over eternity for knowledge of past and future ages" ("The Shadow out of Time"). The summation of these influences was an incorporation and simultaneous transcendence of the Romantic mood or (in the spirit of Hegel who viewed Romanticism as "self-transcending") its continuation by other means. Lovecraft was a life-long student of Romantic influences like the *Arabian Nights*, and of the great purveyors of Romantic themes as were Coleridge and De Quencey. He reached even further than they into the power of the Dream, since so many of his own tales were inspired by the horrific visions he had had since early childhood. He argued that "no first rate story can ever be written without the author's actually experiencing the moods and visions concerned in a sort of oneiroscopic way,"[4] while one of his early protagonists muses:

I have often wondered if the majority of mankind ever pause to reflect upon the occasionally titanic significance of dreams, and of the obscure world to which they belong. Whilst the greater number of our nocturnal visions are perhaps no more than faint and fantastic reflections of our waking experiences— Freud to the contrary with his puerile symbolism— there are still a certain remainder whose immundane and ethereal character permits of no ordinary interpretation, and whose vaguely exciting and disquieting effect suggests possible minute glimpses into a sphere of mental existence no less important than physical life, yet separated from that life by an all but impassable barrier. ("Beyond the Wall of Sleep")

Yet in the major literature of the nineteenth century, the Romantic had fallen victim to Lovecraft's *bête noir*, the "mannered" writing of Dickensian sentimentality and the didactic masters of Realism. The mainstreams of both Romanticism and Realism dealt with the objective world— Romanticism through emotion, Realism through reason—and thereby obviated the imagination capable of grouping "strange relations and associations among the objects of visible and invisible nature."[5] Mystery in the twentieth century had largely become pure mysticism—as in the poetry of T. S. Eliot which Lovecraft abjured as dead-ended—and Realism had become the reduction of the world to what his friend Clark Ashton Smith called the "Five senses and three dimensions [that] hardly scratch the hither surface of infinitude," only embellished with meaningless adventure.[6] Science had cut off even the nineteenth-century imaginative fiction of marvellous machines, transforming the emerging Science-Fiction (as Lovecraft saw two generations early) into what are essentially Space Westerns. What remained was an incorporation of the real and the fantastic, whereby imagination reached beyond the limits of truth. This was not a simple return to the supernatural of preindustrial cultures; it was rather, as Lovecraft scholar Matthew Onderdonk has written, the uplifting of these myths to the "supernormal," allowing the power of Romanticism to play upon subjective perception in new, more forceful and significant ways than ever before.[7] Because modern humanity so completely placed its faith in Science and Progress, its shadowy fears "Out of Space, Out of Time" materialised as things at once all-powerful and irrational, mindless or mad.

Lovecraft's true strength, then, lay in his ability to give the modern sense of indeterminacy a weird and poetic interpretation. What Man feared was not correctly speaking the "Unknown." Lovecraft's own most terrifying dreams were of being on the verge of rediscovering something terrible and arcane, what he once referred to as "the strange spires and steep roofs, vaguely suggesting some lost horizon which was once familiar to me."[8] It was the "unknown outside, clawing at the rim of the known," the more threatening because in another sense it was known already, that was the peak of spectral horror.[9] The hideous beings under the surface of human civilization's superficial conquest of Nature and of its own nature were ever poised to wipe out Man. But even worse than their standing threat was their very existence, and this *presence* drove their discoverers to insanity. Lovecraft says of one of his heroes that his studies of science and philosophy were an error since these "offer two equally tragic alternatives to the man of feeling and action; despair if he fail in his quest, and terrors unutterable and unimaginable if he succeed" ("From Beyond"). To uncover the Monsters was to co-exist with them always.

Generally in metaphor, but sometimes with a rare directness Lovecraft revealed the social content of this dread. At the close of his most famous early tale, "Dagon," a sailor pursued by monsters of "unhealthy antiquity" dreams fantastically of "a day when they may rise above the billows to drag down in their reeking talons the remnants of puny, war-exhausted mankind—of a day when the land shall sink, and the dark ocean floor shall ascend amidst universal pandemonium." Lovecraft looked forward to a time he also feared, when "people will gape at the legends which their old women and medicine men will weave about the ruins of concrete bridges, subways and building foundations."[10] At an historic moment when European intellectuals recognized and even embraced decay, while Americans rarely deigned to admit its presence in their own culture, Lovecraft lived and wrote from a sense of pastness in the fragments of the America he loved. His New England's promise had been eradicated after the Civil War by the invasion of heightened industrialism, the destruction of much of the old architecture, the immigration of new groups, and the adoption of European sophistications by the reigning intellectuals. The rest of America seemed likewise stricken, with only less tradition to resist the "commercial and industrial determinism" that he so despised.

The fear of race suicide was never far from the surface of Lovecraft's conceptions. He was an avowed racist for nearly all his life, not only suspecting but dreading all non-Yankees. He may as well have been writing his own sojourn in New York (the only lengthy absence from Providence in his life) when a narrator of one of his stories reflects:

My coming to New York was a mistake; for whereas I had looked for poignant wonder and inspiration in the teeming labyrinths of ancient streets . . . I had found instead only a sense of horror and oppression. . . . Garish daylight shewed only squalor and alienage and the noxious elephantiasis of climbing, spreading stones where the moon had hinted of loveliness and elder magic; and the throngs of people that seethed through the flume-like streets were squat, swarthy strangers with hardened faces and narrow eyes, shrewd strangers without dreams, without kinship to the old scenes about them, who could never mean aught to a blue-eyed man of the old folk. . . . ("He")

But to shrug off Lovecraft's racism as an atavism is inadequate; for horror was also fascination. He composed one of his most delicious tales (and his only one that dealt with women as a satanic force), "The Horror at Red Hook," from his life near that section of Brooklyn and his friends' description of it.

Another of his protagonists stares from his own College Hill in Providence down at the Federal Hill dwellings of Eastern and Southern European immigrants, lost in fascination about their apparently mysterious habits. Jews, Blacks, Poles, Syrians, the further removed from the Old New Englander the better—in many of his stories these were the means whereby horrible and marvellous Old Gods would return and give the existing civilization the destruction it had earned ("The Haunter of the Dark"). Like Spengler, who greatly influenced him for a time, Lovecraft saw the collapse of the Western way of life unflinchingly; unlike Spengler, he took a pleasure uncertain even in himself over that collapse and the rages of excess that the calamity would unloose. ⟨. . .⟩

In purely literary terms, the contributions of Lovecraft and his friends evoke the critical approach of a Lucács, who would seek to make the author's struggles the truest and most eloquent tale of all. For their time, the task was impossible to accomplish: to explain to an America in the midst of an industrial expansion and locked in the forms of nationalism—democratic and undemocratic—the illusory character of the entire project for the ultimate goal of human wisdom and happiness. And like their predecessor Poe, these writers were none too clear-minded about the cultural or political alternatives for society. Like the last of many an old radical impulse, their conceptions caused them to turn their backs on the present and future, able to express their vision only for a burning moment in the space of a tale, in a fragmentary line of a poem. A philological study, following Vico, might suggest that their use of words (as they believed themselves) had at its best moments the character of a universal myth, more on the order of ancient, oral poetry than of modern literary Realism and Experimentalism.

*Notes*

1. Thomas Ollive Mabbott, a Poe scholar, certifies that "H. P. Lovecraft must always be remembered as a Poe student of the highest rank." "Lovecraft as a Student of Poe," *Fresco* 8 (Spring 1958), 37.
2. Charles Fort, *Book of the Damned* (New York, 1941), 16.
3. Quoted by Barton St. Armand, "H. P. Lovecraft: New England Decadent," in *Caliban* 12 (1975), 136; see also Matthew Onderdonk, "Charon—in Reverse," *Fresco* 8 (Spring 1958), 48–50.
4. H. P. Lovecraft, *Selected Letters*, III (Sauk City, Wisconsin, 1971), 213.
5. "In Defense of Dagon," *Leaves* 2 (1938), 117 (original text January, 1921).
6. Smith to Lovecraft, n.d., H. P. Lovecraft Collection, John Hay Library, Brown University.
7. Matthew Onderdonk, "The Lord of R'lyeh," in G. Wetzel, ed., *Howard Phillips Lovecraft: Memoirs, Critiques, and Bibliographies* (North Tonawanda, New York, 1955), 29.
8. *Selected Letters*, III, 215.
9. *Selected Letters*, II (Sauk City, Wisconsin, 1968), 309.
10. Quoted by St. Armand in "H. P. Lovecraft: New England Decadent," 131.

## DONALD R. BURLESON
### "The Mythic Hero Archetype in 'The Dunwich Horror'"

*Lovecraft Studies*, Spring 1981, pp. 3–9

Lovecraft's "The Dunwich Horror" presents rich opportunity for mythic interpretation, and this critical approach reveals a great deal about the nature of the work. A casual reading of the story suggests simply that Henry Armitage, facing alien forces for which the reader is to feel repulsion, acts

heroically in vanquishing the horror. The story appears to have a kind of "good versus evil" flavour, recalling August Derleth's peculiar notion[1] that the Lovecraft Mythos parallels the Christian Mythos; such is one's impression if what one sees in "The Dunwich Horror" is a drama wherein the "good guys" rush in at the end to rout the "bad guys". A more thoughtful reading casts some doubt on the real significance of Armitage's victory. But, more importantly, a reading with attention to mythic or archetypal detail shews that in terms of the hero archetype, Lovecraft—consciously or otherwise—has in "The Dunwich Horror" fictionally underscored his personal view of man's insect-like position in the cosmos by presenting a mythic *inversion* of what a more casual, sub-mythic reading would suggest. Not only does Armitage fall decidedly short of the characteristics of the archetypal hero—these characteristics, indeed, one discerns only in Armitage's alien adversaries, Wilbur Whateley and his twin brother.

On the face of it, the story presents Armitage as a kind of hero in the popular sense; by his own quick and ingenious action and at great peril to himself, he meets the horror and puts it down by counter-sorcery. But there is textual evidence that his "victory" is a decidedly hollow one. Wilbur Whateley and his nameless brother are spawns of Yog-Sothoth, the old Wizard Whateley presumably having arranged a May-Eve mating with his half-wit daughter Lavinia. (Note that in Roman legend a Lavinia is given in marriage, by her father, Latinus, to a hero: the Trojan Aeneas.) There is no reason to suppose that the occurrence is, or will be, unique. The passage selected by Wilbur from the Latin *Necronomicon* says of the Old Ones: "By Their smell can men sometimes know Them near, but of Their semblance can no man know, *saving only in the features of those They have begotten on mankind*, and of those there are many sorts,"[2] suggesting that such begetting has occurred, or will occur, repeatedly; there will be other Lavinias, and other wizards like old Whateley to arrange such monstrous procreations. Armitage, in the end, tells the Dunwich farmers, "We have no business calling in such things from outside, and only very wicked people and very wicked cults ever try to" (*DH*, p. 202), suggesting that (as in "The Call of Cthulhu") there are cults devoted to alliance with the Old Ones. The *Necronomicon* sonorously prophesies their eventual success: "Man rules now where They ruled once; They shall soon rule where man rules now. After summer is winter, and after winter summer. They wait patient and potent, for here shall They reign again" (*DH*, p. 175). Thus Armitage has merely put down a local manifestation of a horror that can be repeated elsewhere, at other times, with more effect.

Indeed, if one is to look even for a temporary saviour of mankind in the Dunwich affair, the saviour would have to be the dog in the Miskatonic library, for this beast dispatches Wilbur before he and his brother can proceed with the grand design. (So much for the messianic vision in Lovecraft's world.) On his deathbed old Wizard Whateley has reminded Wilbur that "ef it busts quarters or gits aout afore ye opens to Yog-Sothoth, it's all over an' no use" (*DH*, p. 172), and it is Wilbur's failure to return that allows the brother's premature and thus relatively inconsequential release.

Armitage, further, does not bear any of the archetypal tags of the mythic hero. He merely enters the story, late in his life, at a point where his erudition is needed, acting to quell the Dunwich disturbance, and he represents the "hero" only in the sub-mythic sense; his brief quest, though courageous, is certainly not one of mythic proportions. There are plentiful signs of the true hero archetype in "The Dunwich Horror", but by a curious irony they belong wholly to Armitage's monstrous adversaries, who bear a remarkable number of the necessary traits.

These horrific entities may perhaps be seen as exemplifying what has been called the Twin Cycle of the hero myth, one of four myth cycles or categories to be found in the realm of hero mythology.[3] In the Twin hero myth, the twins operate as invincible heroes at first, but eventually succumb to an overreaching *hybris* and the resulting excesses of their own power. Clearly Wilbur and his brother find their end because of dreadfully ambitious plans, which obliquely at least may be seen as a kind of pridefulness—obliquely, because in the Lovecraft *oeuvre* it is in general doubtful practice to ascribe human emotions to such beings, though here the creatures are partly human and expressly have motives that from a purely human viewpoint could be seen as a species of *hybris*. In the Twin myth it is generally necessary, but difficult, to reunite the twins once they are separated; the narrative flow of "The Dunwich Horror" bears this out, in that Wilbur and his brother, separated by the quest for the *Necronomicon* and its vital formulae, must be—but are not—reunited by Wilbur's return from Arkham to Dunwich in time to prevent the brother's premature emergence so that they may carry on the planned sorcery in proper fashion.

But in the Twin Cycle the twins may be thought of *as a single entity*, and it is from this point of view that one may readily discern in Wilbur and his brother the main features of the mythic hero as given by what is called the "monomyth" underlying all hero mythology. The monomyth has eight stages: miraculous conception, initiation, withdrawal, quest, death, descent to the underworld, rebirth, and ascension.[4] It will be shewn that the Dunwich twins fit all eight stages remarkably well.

The first stage of the monomyth concerns miraculous conception (as in the virgin birth of Quetzalcoatl or Jesus, or the immaculate conception of Buddha, Lao-Tzu, or Horus); and the Dunwich story provides a classic example of this myth. Traditionally, a disguised god sires the hero; Yog-Sothoth, in May-Eve rites on Sentinel Hill, has sired the twins, though whether the father was disguised we do not know. Traditionally, the infant is threatened (as Dionysos by the Titans, Jesus by Herod) and must be hidden; Wilbur is shunned by villagers and threatened by dogs (with the recurrent mention of menacing dogs foreshadowing his demise), and while he "hides" by covering his partly monstrous body strategically with clothing, the brother is literally hidden in the Whateley farmhouse, a second womb that grows as he grows, and in which he is nurtured and allowed to attain enormous size.

The second stage of the monomyth concerns the childhood and initiation of the hero. In "The Dunwich Horror" Wilbur takes part, with his mother and grandfather, in unseen rites at May-Eve and All Hallows Eve on Sentinel Hill, and thus is initiated, as it were, into the cult of Yog-Sothoth, though the reader is told little of these rites. In fact, as Lord Raglan points out, we are typically told little or nothing of the mythic hero's childhood,[5] and in "The Dunwich Horror" after Wilbur's fourth year, the narration skips to his tenth year (*DH*, p. 170), and this skip must be assumed to involve a good deal of development in Wilbur. But we do see the extraordinary development during his first few years. In the childhood and initiation myth pattern, it is common for the hero to shew uncanny wisdom as a child—see Buddha and Jesus, for examples—and Wilbur's development is rapid not only physically, to parallel his brother's on a smaller scale, but mentally. He begins to talk at the age of eleven months, as clearly as a child of three or four years, and by nineteen months he is "a fluent and incredibly intelligent talker". By the age of four, Wilbur reads fluently and avidly, and has learned to

"chant in bizarre rhythms which [chill] the listener with a sense of unexplainable terror" (*DH*, pp. 168–69).

The hero monomyth's third stage has to do with the hero's preparation, meditation, and withdrawal. Typically, the hero withdraws to some secluded place, as Buddha to the Bodhi tree, Moses to his mountain, Jesus to the wilderness, Mohammed to his cave. Here again "The Dunwich Horror" fits the pattern. Wilbur's grandfather puts in order a room in the old farmhouse for him, with the rare and ancient books that have lain about the house in disarray—"for they're goin' to be all of his larnin'"—and Wilbur pores over them and undergoes catechism "through long, hushed afternoons" in preparation for his quest (*DH*, p. 168). The grandfather, in fact, clearly acts as the sort of "tutelary figure" often present in this type of hero myth, a guardian or mentor who offsets the hero's early inability to perform alone.[6] (Wilbur has, after all, learned to read even the Latin *Necronomicon* by the time he visits Arkham.) The grandfather also acts as a guardian to Wilbur's monstrous brother, hidden upstairs, who cannot thrive without the prodigious supply of cattle that the old man provides.

The fourth stage of the monomyth concerns trial and quest; the hero always embarks on some quest, as for example the quest of Gilgamesh for the plant of life, or Sir Gawain for the chapel of the Green Knight, or Percival for the Holy Grail. In "The Dunwich Horror" Wilbur, after his preparatory period of withdrawal with the grandfather and his books, sets out in an effort to obtain the complete Latin texts with which he can pursue his sorcery on behalf of Yog-Sothoth. This "little quest" for the *Necronomicon* in the face of difficult obstacles (Henry Armitage, the guard dog, general enmity) is embedded in the grander quest, that of "opening the gates" to Yog-Sothoth and loosing unthinkable horrors upon the world. In such hero myths, the hero typically seeks some sort of life renewal, and Wilbur's diary, deciphered by Armitage, shews a concern of this sort. Writing of his brother, he says, "The other face"—the human face with Lavinia's features, monstrously enlarged—"may wear off some." Extending this is cleared off and there are no earth beings on it. He that came with the Aklo Sabaoth said I may be transfigured, there being much of outside to work on" (*DH*, p. 189). Some of the sardonic comment of Lovecraft's narration shews through here, in that it is the human side of the twins' ancestry that Wilbur is ashamed of.

Stage five of the hero monomyth concerns the hero's death because of his quest, and Wilbur Whateley once more fits the mythic pattern. Traditionally, death often comes by dismemberment (see Osiris, Dionysos, Orpheus), and in keeping with this motif we find Wilbur, foiled in his quest for the unholy *Necronomicon*, torn to shreds by the guard dog. Traditionally in this type of myth the genitals are destroyed or lost, as with Osiris or Dionysos; in Wilbur's case they are not to be found at all, at least in terms of human anatomy: "Below the waist . . . it was the worst; for here all human resemblance left off and sheer phantasy began" (*DH*, p. 179).

The sixth stage is that of descent to the underworld, and this is suggested symbolically by the descent of Wilbur's brother into Cold Spring Glen, the "great sinister ravine". The ravine is described as a hellish place and is based on an actual ravine in North New Salem, Massachusetts, deep and ominous-looking indeed, which Lovecraft visited with H. Warner Munn in 1928 shortly before writing "The Dunwich Horror".[7] In the tale, Sally Sawyer says of the place, "I allus says Col' Spring Glen ain't no healthy nor decent place. The whippoorwills"—psychopomps of the underworld—"an' fireflies there never did act like they was creaters o' Gawd. . . ." (*DH*, p. 183), so that the symbolism of descent to the underworld is textually clear. In this sixth stage of the monomyth one traditionally also has the theme of the overcoming of the forces of death (see Heracles and Cerberus, for example), and Wilbur's death scene provides this connexion, in that at Wilbur's last breath, the guard dog howls lugubriously and bolts out a window; and the psychopomp whippoorwills, gathering outside to catch Wilbur's soul (traditionally, for a journey to the underworld), "rose and raced from sight, frantic at that which they had sought for prey" (*DH*, p. 180).

The seventh stage is that of resurrection and rebirth (Dionysos, Buddha, Adonis, Osiris, Jesus), and when Wilbur and his brother are considered as constituting one character, this character is symbolically reborn, for when Wilbur dies in the Miskatonic library and thus fails to return to Dunwich, the brother bursts forth from the Whateley farmhouse, his symbolic womb. In fact, the Yog-Sothoth spawn is even "reborn" in a stronger form when the brother comes forth from confinement. The notion of death and rebirth is further suggested symbolically by the brother's descent into and emergence from the ravine, much like the symbolic nature of Hamlet's leaping into and out of the grave.

The eighth and final stage of the hero monomyth is that which concerns ascension, apotheosis, and atonement. "The Dunwich Horror" fits the mythic pattern at least with regard to ascension and a kind of resolution. Wilbur's hideous brother, having left trails of destruction around the village, finally ascends Sentinel Hill with Armitage and his two colleagues in pursuit. The creature has ascended earlier, leaving a trail to and from the ravine, and in this respect perhaps he symbolically resembles Maud Bodkin's characterisation of the archetypal hero, who "stands poised between height and depth".[8] The brother, in keeping with Lord Raglan's description of the mythic hero, has done something like returning to his birthplace after a victory over adversaries; he has annihilated a number of the inhabitants of Dunwich, and returns to the great table-rock on Sentinel Hill, where he was not born, but conceived. Lord Raglan, in fact, also specifies that the archetypal hero often meets his end atop a hill.[9] The monster's end amounts to a "tragic" (from the Yog-Sothothian point of view) failure in the grand quest, but he is returned alive to the outer realm of Yog-Sothoth, the father. And it can be pointed out again that although the quest is not successful in this instance, the *Necronomicon* clearly prophesies that such a quest *will* one day be completed by the Old Ones and their terrestrial avatars, as a completion of a cosmic cycle not to be denied—"They wait patient and potent, for here shall They reign again."

This cosmic cyclicity and its mythic importance are underscored continually in the story by the cyclic fashion in which Lovecraft refers to time. We see repeated reference to such cyclically recurrent points in time as May Eve and All Hallows Eve; and "the Dunwich horror itself came between Lammas and the equinox of 1928" (*DH*, p. 177). The horror is thus linked to cosmic cycles of time that transcend, in their significance, mere calendar dates of human reckoning.

Similarly, "The Dunwich Horror" contains various other motifs and images suggesting the high appropriateness of a mythic interpretation, the interpretation that best shews what Lovecraft is doing with heroism in the story. The epigraph from Charles Lamb—"the archetypes are in us, and eternal" (*DH*, p. 160)—strongly suggests a mythic view; but there is internal support as well, in abundance. For example, there is the matter of the whippoorwills, psychopomps that try to capture the departing souls of the dying. Lovecraft's direct source of this

motif was an actual folktale told to him by his hosts during a stay in Wilbraham, Massachusetts just before he wrote "The Dunwich Horror".[10] But this local folklore itself parallels well the mythic tradition of the psychopomp, which was associated with the Greek god Hermes, guide of departed souls to the underworld; the traditional "herm" has often been given with a caduceus, a snake or two snakes twined around a staff, and interestingly Lovecraft gives us, in the opening descriptions of the Dunwich country, a view of the river Miskatonic (recalling the Styx?) whose line of "upper reaches has an oddly serpent-like suggestion as it winds close to the feet of the domed hills among which it rises" (*DH*, p. 161). In Egyptian lore Hermes was originally known as Thoth (of which the name Yog-Sothoth may also be echoic), the bird-headed god,[11] so that the use of whippoorwills as psychopomps is well in keeping with mythic tradition.

There is also the matter, again in the opening descriptions, of "queer circles of tall stone pillars" (*DH*, p. 161) crowning the hills around Dunwich. This motif recalls the circle or mandala of mythic-archetypal significance, symbolising the centre or the completion of the psyche,[12] as well as the cyclicity of cosmic events. In "The Dunwich Horror" the circles of pillars are associated with the sort of sorcery by which people like Wizard Whateley invoke the horrors of the Old Ones; thus the circles have more to do with the interests of monstrous beings than with the human players on the scene, and it is not without significance, symbolically, that physically the circles stand always above man. Consistently, Lovecraft's narration suggests the preëminence of the Old Ones—*their* completeness, *their* consummation in the cosmic cycle, *their* ultimate prevalence—over mankind. The story's descriptive imagery continually gives this same suggestion. We are warned, for example, in our introduction to the environs of Dunwich: "Gorges and ravines of problematical depth"—the work of untrammeled nature, the ubiquity of unfathomable mystery—"intersect the way, and the crude wooden bridges"—the efforts of man to deal with the forces of nature, to come to terms with the mystery—"always seem of dubious safety" (*DH*, p. 161).

Altogether, then, "The Dunwich Horror" in its mythic content presents a sardonically inverted view of the hero archetype as it traditionally applies to the interests of humankind. The character Armitage, for whom the casual reader presumably is to feel empathy, is a fictional prop whose "victory" is virtually meaningless in cosmic terms, and he is devoid of the features of the mythic hero. The monstrous twins, together, form a character for whom the casual reader is to feel loathing and antipathy, but who can be seen closely to fit the archetypal pattern of the hero in myth. To the extent that Lovecraft's Old Ones are symbolic of chaos—of the blindly indifferent forces of nature, the forces of an impersonal and purposeless cosmos—"The Dunwich Horror", by its association of the hero archetype with *these* forces, gives fictional articulation to a view that happens to correspond to Lovecraft's personal *Weltanschauung*: the view that man is but an evanescent mote in the universe of stars, a universe that neither blesses nor damns him, unless to be ignored is to be damned. It is, of course, only on the mythic level of interpretation that this sense of the story is fully evident. Seen in this way, "The Dunwich Horror" ceases to appear to be a "good versus evil" story that fits only awkwardly into the Lovecraft canon—it becomes a work centrally expressive of the vision underlying all of the Lovecraft Mythos.

*Notes*

1. August Derleth, "H. P. Lovecraft and His Work", in H. P. Lovecraft, *The Dunwich Horror and Others* (Sauk City: Arkham House, 1963), p. xiii.
2. Lovecraft, *The Dunwich Horror and Others*, p. 174. All further references to this work appear in the text, with denotation "*DH*".
3. Joseph L. Henderson, "Ancient Myths and Modern Man", in *Man and His Symbols*, ed. Carl G. Jung (New York: Dell Publishing Co., 1964), pp. 101–07. The other categories are termed the Trickster Cycle, the Hare Cycle, and the Red Horn Cycle, as characterised by Dr. Paul Radin from the example of Winnebago Indian myth.
4. Joseph Adams Leeming, *Mythology: The Voyage of the Hero* (Philadelphia: J. J. Lippincott, 1973), passim.
5. Lord Raglan, *The Hero: A Study in Tradition, Myth, and Drama* (New York: Oxford University Press, 1937), pp. 179–80.
6. Henderson, p. 101.
7. Donald R. Burleson, "Humour beneath Horror: Some Sources for 'The Dunwich Horror' and 'The Whisperer in Darkness'", *Lovecraft Studies*, 1, no. 2 (1980), 9.
8. Maud Bodkin, *Archetypal Patterns in Poetry* (London: Oxford University Press, 1963), p. 245. Maud Bodkin argues eloquently for the idea that Satan is a true hero figure in *Paradise Lost*. Perhaps we are only just beginning to understand the influence of Milton on Lovecraft, an influence of which Lovecraft himself may well not have been conscious.
9. Lord Raglan, p. 180.
10. Burleson, pp. 6–7.
11. Henderson, pp. 154–55.
12. Aniela Jaffé, "Symbolism in the Visual Arts", in *Man and His Symbols*, pp. 266–67.

## S. T. JOSHI

### From "Topical References in Lovecraft"

*Extrapolation*, Fall 1984, pp. 247–65

The myth that H. P. Lovecraft was completely detached from the political, social, literary, and philosophical movements of his day is one whose death has been anomalously slow, despite the volumes of comment on the contemporary scene found not merely in his letters but in his essays from so early as "The Crime of the Century" (1915). Lovecraft is in a way partially to blame for this state of affairs, since he not only liked to portray himself (more often than not with tongue in cheek) as an eighteenth-century gentleman with allegiance to the traditions of Republican Rome, but could write such a line as "I know always that I am an outsider; a stranger in this century and among those who are still men."[1] And while there can be no question of Lovecraft's sincere adherence to the standards of the past, there can equally be no doubt, as Robert Bloch wrote, "but that H. P. Lovecraft was very much alive in the Twentieth Century of Picasso, Proust, Joyce, Spengler, Einstein, and Adolf Hitler."[2]

Bloch himself, however, felt that Lovecraft's fiction was almost wholly—and quite consciously—devoid of reference to the political and social upheavals of the time. "Lovecraft ignores the post WWI Jazz Age in its entirety: Coolidge, Hoover, FDR, Lindbergh, Babe Ruth, Al Capone, Valentino, Mencken, and the prototypes of Babbitt have no existence in H. P. L.'s realm. It is difficult to believe that Howard Phillips Lovecraft was a literary contemporary of Ernest Hemingway."[3] This remark itself is not correct in its details, and I maintain that it may not even be entirely true in the general sense in which Bloch meant it. The fact is that there are many topical references in Lovecraft's fiction, and that these references—sometimes glancing, sometimes more or less central to the tale—are echoes of lengthier and more detailed remarks on modern literature, politics, and society as found in his letters and essays. ⟨. . .⟩

Some indications of the modernity (or, rather, contemporaneity) of Lovecraft's fiction can be derived from his reference to previous epochs. Hence there are frequent references to the Victorian age in the tales, and these occur in such a fashion as to tell us that that age is hopelessly outmoded and antiquated. Lovecraft here actually shares the outlook of his time in his rejection of nineteenth-century standards, although he claimed to do so simply so as to return to (what he felt were) the truer and more rationally based attitudes of the eighteenth century. This stance was, however, a little disingenuous, since part of the initiative for Lovecraft's condemnation of nineteenth-century values was his adoption of very advanced philosophical views from Nietzsche, Haeckel, T. H. Huxley, Spengler, Russell, and Santayana. Hence part of Lovecraft's condemnation of the "pathetic Puritanism" (*D*, 129) of Dr. Allan Halsey in "Herbert West—Reanimator" is in its adoption of "sins like . . . anti-Darwinism [and] anti-Nietzscheism." The Darwin controversy is, of course, still with us, amazing as it may seem; and it may be well to note that Nietzsche died only in 1900. The very remoteness of the Victorian age is hinted more directly in "The Silver Key" (1926), where Randolph Carter decides to refurnish his home "as it was in his early boyhood—purple panes, Victorian furniture, and all" (*MM*, 391). And note the description of Old Man Marsh in "The Shadow over Innsmouth," who "*still* [my italics] wore the frock-coated finery of the Edwardian era" (*DH*, 327).[4] This emphatically places the tale in at least the late 1920s, since the reign of Edward VII spanned the years 1901 to 1910.

I have elsewhere briefly discussed some elements of social satire found in Lovecraft's later tales, especially "The Mound," *At the Mountains of Madness*, and "The Shadow out of Time."[5] Some earlier examples of it may, however, be noted. We can hardly fail to note the acidity of Lovecraft's allusion to the "notably fat and especially offensive millionaire brewer" (*D*, 65) who has taken over Trevor Towers after the death of Kuranes in "Celephaïs"; this, certainly, is an instance where Lovecraft reveals his adherence to the aristocratic standards of a previous epoch. A similar sort of satire, more topical this time, is found in "The Moon-Bog" (1920), where it is said of Denys Barry: "For all his love of Ireland, America had not left him untouched, and he hated the beautiful wasted space [i. e., the bog] where peat might be cut and land opened up" (*D*, 92)—a reference which accidentally relates it to the theme of Dunsany's later novel, *The Curse of the Wise Woman* (1933). Here again it is precisely this "modern" stance of Barry's that leads directly to his doom. ⟨. . .⟩

Lovecraft's disapproval of the general radical trend of modern literature—particularly its abandonment of traditional form and its excessive dwelling on the day-to-day realities of life—comes out frequently in both early and late fiction. "Celephaïs" (1920) provides perhaps the first example, and pungent remarks are made about modern writers who "strove to strip from life its embroidered robes of myth, and to shew in naked ugliness the foul thing that is reality" (*D*, 60). The theme is refined in "Azathoth" (1922), where we find that "learning stripped earth of her mantle of beauty, and poets sang no more save of twisted phantoms seen with bleared and inward-looking eyes" (*D*, 335). This is actually not an inaccurate description of the subjectivity of modern poetry, although the remark was made just before Lovecraft read the most celebrated and revolutionary of modern poems, *The Waste Land* of T. S. Eliot.[6] Lovecraft seems to have read this almost immediately upon first publication (*The Dial*, November 1922), and jumped upon it in an editorial in *The Conservative* of March 1923. The parody "Waste Paper" probably dates to about this time, although its appearance in "the newspaper" (*SL*, IV.159)—presumably *The Providence Journal* or *The Providence Evening Bulletin*—has yet to be located. In any case, the most celebrated reference to Eliot in all Lovecraft is that mention at the end of *The Case of Charles Dexter Ward* where Willett, in the basement of Ward's bungalow, tries to calm himself by muttering the Lord's Prayer, "eventually trailing off into a mnemonic hodge-podge like the modernistic *Waste Land* of Mr. T. S. Eliot" (*MM*, 197). The very use of the word "Mr." implies a reference to a living contemporary. ⟨. . .⟩

It is, however, in the realms of science and philosophy that Lovecraft's tales gain their greatest sense of topicality; for, as his letters amply testify, Lovecraft kept closely abreast of the latest findings in astronomy, astrophysics, anthropology, and many other of the sciences, and was also very well read in contemporary philosophy. Bloch himself came to this conclusion when he wrote that the fundamental link between Poe and Lovecraft was "their mutual interest in science," and that this interest "softens the charge that the two writers were totally unaware of the actual world and unrealistic in their treatment of their times."[7] Bloch made no attempt to treat this topicality in detail, but we shall try to provide at least a few hints here. ⟨. . .⟩

References to modern psychology enter into only a few tales, but in a telling manner. It is interesting to note that both "Beyond the Wall of Sleep" (1919) and "From Beyond" (1920) were revised after initial publication to incorporate some rather snide references to Freud. In the former tale, as ⟨George T.⟩ Wetzel long ago pointed out, the cynical insertion "—Freud to the contrary with his puerile symbolism—" (*D*, 23) was added subsequent to the tale's appearance in *Pine Cones* (October 1919). Wetzel did not realise that a similar addition was made in "From Beyond": in the original manuscript the sentence "I laugh at the shallow endocrinologist, fellow-dupe and fellow-parvenu of the Freudian" (*D*, 69) is missing, and must have been added at some point preceding the tale's first appearance in *The Fantasy Fan* (June 1934). Can we perhaps date these insertions? They may theoretically have occurred quite early, for in June 1921 Lovecraft announces: "Dr. Sigmund Freud of Vienna, whose system of psycho-analysis I have begun to investigate, will probably prove the end of idealistic thought" (*SL*, I.134). Lovecraft was unfortunately mistaken in his prediction (just as he was wrong when he noted that "a mere knowledge of the approximate dimensions of the visible universe is enough to destroy forever the notion of a personal godhead" [*SL*, I.44], even though this knowledge seems to have had such an effect upon him), and no contradiction need be assumed between the tolerably favorable mentions of Freud in the letters and the rather sarcastic ones in the two tales in question: Lovecraft is merely criticizing Freud's single-minded attribution of all human impulses to the libido (a position which most modern Freudians have themselves abandoned), since, as he remarked, "I am inclined to accept the modifications of Adler, who in placing the ego above the eros makes a scientific return to the position which Nietzsche assumed for wholly philosophical reasons" (*SL*, I.136). The glancing reference to the "big three" of early twentieth-century psychology in "The Trap" (1931)—"Even the most prosaic scientists affirm, with Freud, Jung, and Adler, that the subconscious mind is most open to external impression in sleep"[8]—can be noted in brief.

It is, actually, somewhat curious that pure philosophers do not receive much notice in the fiction. We have observed the passing reference to "anti-Nietzscheism" in "Herbert West—Reanimator"; and in the same story Lovecraft notes that West believed "with Haeckel that all life is a chemical and physical process, and that the so-called 'soul' is a myth" (*D*, 124). Ernst Haeckel (1834–1919) was probably the greatest of the biologist-philosophers of the late nineteenth and early twentieth centuries, and the great apostle for materialistic monism in his time (although Santayana could note, as early as 1923, that "In natural philosophy I am a decided materialist—apparently the only one living";[9] certainly Santayana would have modified his remark if he could have read Lovecraft's trenchant essay, "Idealism and Materialism: A Reflection"!), and Lovecraft was greatly influenced by Haeckel's seminal volume, *The Riddle of the Universe* (English translation 1900), which he seems to have read in late 1919 or 1920 (*SL*, I.87, 141). But of other philosophers we find no mention.

Einstein, however, runs through Lovecraft's fiction like an elusive thread, although here, of course, we are treading the borderline between astrophysics and metaphysics (as, indeed, physics since Einstein has tended increasingly to do). The first—and very allusive—citation occurs so early as "Hypnos" (1922), where it is remarked that "one man with Oriental eyes has said that all time and space are relative, and men have laughed" (*D*, 161); this mention is actually anomalously early, for only in May 1923 does Lovecraft announce: "My cynicism and scepticism are increasing, and from an entirely new cause—the Einstein theory. . . . All is chance, accident, and ephemeral illusion—a fly may be greater than Arcturus, and Durfee Hill may surpass Mount Everest—assuming them to be removed from the present planet and differently environed in the continuum of space-time" (*SL*, I.231). Indeed, Lovecraft's remark here that "All the cosmos is a jest" is peculiarly reminiscent of what he had written a year before in "Hypnos": "The cosmos of our waking knowledge, born from such an universe as a bubble is born from the pipe of a jester, touches it only as such a bubble may touch its sardonic source when sucked back by the jester's whim" (*D*, 161).

I can only assume that Lovecraft heard generally of the Einstein theory in 1922, and read about it more detailedly in mid-1923. What could have been the source of his new information? It could not have been Bertrand Russell's *ABC of Relativity*, since that volume first appeared in 1925 (and Lovecraft did not seem to become acquainted with Russell's work until the late 1920s); and it certainly could not have been Einstein's own elucidations of his theory, since these require a prodigious knowledge of higher mathematics and physics far beyond anything Lovecraft ever attained. My guess (and it is only that) is that he read Garrett P. Serviss's popular account, *The Einstein Theory of Relativity*, which came out precisely in 1923. Lovecraft owned three of Serviss's books on astronomy,[10] and probably kept up on Serviss's other publications.

Whatever the source, Lovecraft's immediate reaction to Einstein is typical of that of many intellectuals; and indeed, it is precisely this sort of misunderstanding and false application of the theory of relativity that led many philosophers to reject the positivism of the later nineteenth century and to usher in a new age of idealism and mysticism. Lovecraft, of course, snapped out of his naïve perceptions of the Einstein theory quite early, and by 1929 was telling Frank Belknap Long: "If any mystic thinks that matter has lost its known properties because it's been found made of invisible energy, just let him read Einstein and try to apply his new conception by butting his head into a stone wall" (*SL*, II.267)—which is rather amusingly reminiscent of

Dr. Johnson's refutation of Berkeley. Lovecraft knew, however, that in the "nearer heavens" the "given area *isn't big enough* to let relativity get in its major effects"—hence he wisely warned Long: "Don't let the Einstein-twisters catch you here!" (*SL*, II.265). All this reveals a really admirable grasp of the Einstein theory and its integration into a positivist and even materialist scheme, at least partially similar to that produced by Russell and Santayana.

In any case, Einstein reappears in vivid fashion in "The Whisperer in Darkness" (1930), where the pseudo-Akeley boldly announced: " 'Do you know that Einstein is wrong, and that certain objects and forces *can* move with a velocity greater than that of light?' " (*DH*, 259). One wonders whether this remark was inspired by Frank Belknap Long's "The Hounds of Tindalos," where the protagonist notes: "What do we know of time, really? Einstein believes that it is relative, that it can be interpreted in terms of space, of *curved* space. But why must we stop there?" And compare pseudo-Akeley's statement—"With the proper aid I expect to go backward and forward in time" (*DH*, 259)—with the remark of Long's character: "With . . . the aid of my mathematical knowledge I believe that I can *go back through time*."[11] Lovecraft almost certainly read "The Hounds of Tindalos" in manuscript, and even if he did not he could have read it in its appearance in *Weird Tales* (March 1929) in time to use it in his own tale.

But the two most interesting citations of the Einstein theory—as well as other advances in modern physics—occur in two tales, "The Shunned House" and "The Dreams in the Witch House." The former is particularly interesting in that it reinterprets the traditional vampire legend in terms of modern physics. Note these passages:

> To say that we actually believed in vampires or werewolves would be a carelessly inclusive statement. Rather must it be said that we were not prepared to deny the possibility of certain unfamiliar and unclassified modifications of vital force and attenuated matter; existing very infrequently in three-dimensionsal space because of its more intimate connexion with other spatial units, yet close enough to the boundary of our own to furnish us occasional manifestations which we, for lack of a proper vantage-point, may never hope to understand. . . .
>
> Such a thing was surely not a physical or biochemical impossibility in the light of a newer science which includes the theories of relativity and intra-atomic action. One might easily imagine an alien nucleus of substance or energy, formless or otherwise, kept alive by imperceptible or immaterial subtractions from the life-force or bodily tissue and fluids of other and more palpably living things into which it penetrates and with whose fabric it sometimes completely merges itself. (*MM*, 237-38)

The overt mention of relativity is to be observed, and the mention of "intra-atomic action" presumably alludes to the quantum theory. What Lovecraft actually made of the quantum theory is not easy to deduce from the letters, where neither the theory itself nor Max Planck is mentioned at all frequently. Like the Einstein theory, Planck's findings were hailed by idealists as spelling the downfall of determinism and a *carte blanche* for all sorts of previously outmoded notions about the universe and man's relation to it. Lovecraft knew better, and by the time he assimilated the quantum theory he felt that it posed no real threat to determinism. "What most physicists take the quantum theory, at present, to mean, is *not that any cosmic uncertainty exists* as to which of several courses a given reaction will take; but that in certain instances *no conceivable*

*channel of information can ever tell human beings which course will be taken*" (*SL*, III.228).

Lovecraft thus seems to regard the "uncertainty" revealed by the quantum theory as epistemological and not ontological—i.e., it is simply our inability to predict the movement of sub-atomic particles which produces the "uncertainty," but the uncertainty does not inhere in Nature. This conclusion (although also adopted by Einstein, who made the celebrated remark that "God does not play dice with the cosmos") does not appear to be correct, since, in the words of Russell:

> In quantum theory, individual atomic occurrences are not determined by the equations; these suffice only to show that the possibilities form a discrete series, and that there are rules of determining how often each possibility will be realized in a large number of cases. There are reasons for believing that this absence of complete determinism is not due to any incompleteness in the theory, but is a genuine characteristic of small-scale occurrences. The regularity which is found in macroscopic phenomena is a statistical regularity. Phenomena involving large numbers of atoms remain deterministic, but what an individual atom may do in given circumstances is uncertain, not only because our knowledge is limited but because there are no physical laws giving a determinate result.[12]

Nevertheless, determinism as a philosophical position is by no means undermined, since "the crucial but so far unanswered question is whether there are processes by which random sub-atomic occurrences trigger larger scale neural processes and so introduce some randomness into them."[13] Hence Lovecraft's belief that "the future, though wholly determinate, is . . . essentially unknown" (*SL*, III.31)—where again the distinction is made between ontological determinism and human epistemological uncertainty—is still viable, although the case for determinism now tends to be based rather on psychological than metaphysical foundations.

The point of all these reflections is that Lovecraft could use the findings of modern physics to produce an "updated" or "modernized" version of such standard supernatural themes as the vampire in "The Shunned house." A similar transformation occurs in "The Dreams in the Witch house" (1932), where witchcraft and time travel are reinterpreted through Einstein. At the very beginning of the tale is a mention of "quantum physics" (*MM*, 249)—nowadays called "quantum mechanics"—and shortly after we are given a hint as to the possible sources of Keziah Mason's powers: " . . . some circumstance had more or less suddenly given a mediocre old woman of the seventeenth century an insight into mathematical depths perhaps beyond the utmost modern delvings of Planck, Heisenberg, Einstein, and de Sitter" (*MM*, 250). ⟨. . .⟩

Lovecraft, then, was not merely very much alive in the era of Hitler, T.S. Eliot, and Einstein (as his letters clearly prove), but he was not above making overt references to contemporary political, social, literary, and scientific movements in his fiction. It is certainly true that these references rarely occupy a larger or central place in his tales, and we have nothing akin to the minute descriptions of life in seventeenth- and eighteenth-century Providence forming the sub-narrative about Curwen in *The Case of Charles Dexter Ward*; but it is clear that Lovecraft assumes knowledge of the culture in which he was writing and makes few attempts to depict a consciously archaic environment or to write in an archaic idiom. Indeed, the belief that Lovecraft's work is "antiquated" either in theme or in style has been greatly exaggerated by critics. The very allusiveness of many of the references—note the mention of "the President" and not "President Harding" in "The Rats in the Walls"—signifies a shared body of information which Lovecraft expected of his reader. Even if Lovecraft intended his fiction to be, as with Thucydides, a "possession for all time," there can yet be no doubt but that it is firmly rooted in the culture of the inter-war years in America and Europe which Lovecraft observed so perceptively in his life and letters.

*Notes*

1. "The Outsider" (1921), in *The Dunwich Horror and Others* (Sauk City, Wis.: Arkham House, 1963), p. 59. Subsequent references to works by Lovecraft will be made parenthetically in the text with the following abbreviations: *DH = The Dunwich Horror and Others; MM = At the Mountains of Madness and Other Novels* (Arkham House, 1964); *D = Dagon and Other Macabre Tales* (Arkham House, 1965); *SL = Selected Letters* (Arkham House, 1965–76; 5 vols.).
2. "Out of the Ivory Tower," in Lovecraft's *The Shuttered Room and Other Pieces* (1959), p. 174.
3. "Poe and Lovecraft" (1972), rpt. in my *H. P. Lovecraft: Four Decades of Criticism* (Athens, Ohio: Ohio University Press, 1980), p. 159.
4. See my "Autobiography in Lovecraft," *Lovecraft Studies*, 1, no. 1 (Fall 1979), 17–18, for the hypothesis that this is a veiled reference to Oscar Wilde.
5. See my "Humour and Satire in Lovecraft" and "Lovecraft's Alien Civilisations: A Political Interpretation" (both forthcoming in *Crypt of Cthulhu*).
6. On this subject see now Peter Cannon, "Lovecraft and the Mainstream Literature of His Day," *Lovecraft Studies*, 2, no. 2 (Fall 1982), 27–28.
7. "Poe and Lovecraft" (see note 3), p. 159.
8. *Uncollected Prose and Poetry II* (West Warwick, R.I.: Necronomicon Press, 1980), p. 9.
9. Santayana, "Preface" to *Scepticism and Animal Faith* (1923). Lovecraft, of course, later read this volume.
10. See S. T. Joshi and Marc A. Michaud, comps., *Lovecraft's Library: A Catalogue* (West Warwick, R.I.: Necronomicon Press, 1980), #s 732–34. From one of these—*Astronomy with the Naked Eye* (New York and London: Harper, 1908), p. 152—Lovecraft derived the citation from Serviss at the close of "Beyond the Wall of Sleep."
11. "The Hounds of Tindalos," in August Derleth, ed., *Tales of the Cthulhu Mythos* (1969); rpt. in *Tales of the Cthulhu Mythos, Volume I* (New York: Ballantine, 1971), pp. 84–85.
12. *Human Knowledge: Its Scope and Limits* (New York: Simon and Schuster, 1948), pp. 23–24.
13. J. L. Mackie, *Ethics* (Harmondsworth: Penguin Books, 1977), p. 220.

## STEVEN J. MARICONDA
### "Notes on the Prose Realism of H. P. Lovecraft"

*Lovecraft Studies*, Spring 1985, pp. 3–11

The strength and coherence of H. P. Lovecraft's philosophy was such that it pervaded every branch of his literary output—essays, letters, poetry and fiction alike. It has often been noted that Lovecraft's infamous pantheon of "gods"—actually primal beings incomprehensible and indifferent to human beings—is a fictional reflection of his materialistic conception of a purposeless universe governed by a fixed and only partially knowable set of laws. For example, Lovecraft's conviction that "the cosmos is a mindless vortex; a seething ocean of blind forces"[1] is brilliantly symbolized by the "blind idiot god, Azathoth, Lord of All Things", who sprawls at the center of Ultimate Chaos "encircled by his flopping horde of mindless and amorphous dancers."[2] But if Lovecraft's outlook dictated his fiction's themes, it also implicitly influenced his stylistic approach; for the realistic narrative voice and detail found in his tales may likewise be traced to his philosophical stance. Lovecraft's rationalistic world-view eliminated the possibility of religion, since scientific evidence mitigated against the existence of God, and caused him to seek another imaginative outlet—one which supplemented rather than contradicted reality. This imaginative outlet was fantasy fiction. Fantasy fiction of a certain type only, however, would satisfy him; a type in which reality was first convincingly and accurately portrayed before the "supplementing" took place. The need for such portrayal was the primary force behind Lovecraft's prose realism.

The influences upon Lovecraft's rendering of this prose realism may be roughly classed into two groups. One group is those writers whom he more or less consciously took as models; horror authors such as Edgar Allan Poe and (to a lesser extent) Hawthorne, M. R. James, and Bierce, who had likewise anchored their tales in realistic detail. Poe left him a far broader legacy than the others mentioned; for Lovecraft's psychological realism, in which the terrible mental reaction of a character (usually the first-person narrator) to the horror is documented by the use of vocabulary and syntax, is derived from his early favorite.

The second influence is far more subtle, and one over which Lovecraft himself in some ways had very little control. Lovecraft's style was shaped by youthful influences exceedingly apt to its later role of fostering the believability of his narratives. His prose was a product primarily of his avid early reading of eighteenth-century essayists, historians, and scientists. These writers, employing vocabulary and syntax which seem pedantic to the modern reader, lent Lovecraft exactly the erudite tone and precision of style necessary for him to delineate realistic scenes with an authority and convincingness which instills in the reader a subtle sense of confidence. This sense of confidence leaves us especially vulnerable for the supernormal intrusion of horror at the end. The irony here is that Lovecraft's style was influenced by exactly the "right" writers for its later purpose.

So while Lovecraft willfully followed and expanded upon the approach of Poe and certain other "supernatural realists", the influence of the eighteenth-century prose stylists became an unconscious, inherent part of the fabric of Lovecraft's writing. It is the element which is constant in all Lovecraft's prose; be it letters, essays, or fiction. We will briefly return to these two influences later; first let us look more closely at the philosophic basis of Lovecraft's inclination towards prose realism in weird fiction.

Writing weird fiction gave Lovecraft an essential "imaginative refuge" from what he viewed as a directionless cosmos. He felt that

> objective phenomena—endless and predictable repetitions of the same old stuff over and over again—form only the very beginning of what is needed to keep [a] sense of significance, harmony, and personal adjustment to infinity satisfied. *All* sensitive men have to call in unreality in some form or other or go mad from ennui. That is why religion continues to hang on. . . . (SL III.139)

Lovecraft's objectivity, however, prevented him from embracing religion as the solution to his dilemma, since he saw religion as "insulting to the intellect in its outright denial of plain facts and objective probabilities" and as having "no foundation in reality" (SL III.139f.). Thus, left to his own devices by his unyielding rationalism, Lovecraft turned to that form of "unreality" to which he had been inclined since his youth: the creation of imaginative fiction. However, he found that this fiction, in order to be satisfying, had to be firmly rooted in the real world and must not contradict what we know to be true about it:

> I do *not* share the real mystic's *contempt* for facts and objective conditions, even though I fail to find them interesting and satisfying. *On the contrary*, I am forced to respect them highly, and allow for them in every system of imaginative refuge I formulate. . . . I get no kick at all from *postulating what isn't so*, as religionists and idealists do. . . . My big kick comes from *taking reality just as it is*—accepting all the limitations of the most orthodox science—and then permitting my symbolising faculty to *build outward* from the existing facts; rearing a structure of *indefinite promise and possibility* whose topless towers are in no cosmos or dimension penetrable by the contradicting power of the tyrannous and inexorable intellect. But the whole secret of the kick is *that I know damn well it isn't so* (SL III.140).

In concluding that the fantastic element of his fiction had to "*supplement*, rather than *contradict*, reality" (SL III.140), Lovecraft set himself the task of creating as realistic a background as possible for his tales. The degree of his success is attested to by our reaction to such tales as *At the Mountains of Madness*, where the central events of the story seem frighteningly plausible. Lovecraft laid the foundation for his best tales with a verisimilitude approaching that of the "true" school of literary realists. His dictum that "No avenue can lead us away from the immediate to the remote unless it really does begin at the immediate—and not any false, cheap, or conventional conception of the immediate" (SL III.195) echoes in the very convincingness of his best work, from "The Rats in the Walls" to "The Shadow out of Time".

Paramount among what I will term the conscious influences on Lovecraft's rendering of prose realism was his "God of Fiction", Edgar Allan Poe. Lovecraft lauded Poe for establishing "a new standard of realism in the annals of literary horror", and followed his example of "consummate craftsmanship"[3] by carefully researching and laying out the background for his tales. A good example of Poe's background realism is "The Gold Bug", with its descriptions not only of Sullivan's Island but of the intricacies of cryptography and etymology. Impressed with these tales as a child, Lovecraft doubtless followed Poe in his meticulous planning and emphasis on accurate description.

Poe also left Lovecraft a far more important legacy in the area of realism—that of psychological realism. In addition to carefully thought-out character motivation, Lovecraft learned from Poe the importance of documenting with his prose the mental effects of horror upon his characters. First-person narration is best suited to this, and was thus favored by Poe in such tales as "The Fall of the House of Usher" and "The Pit and the Pendulum". In these stories the emotional excitement of the narrator—and the frenzy of the style—grows as the horrible events of the tale unfold. This first-person viewpoint, its prose a finely tuned reflection of the narrator's psychic state, is found in nearly three-quarters of Lovecraft's original fiction as well.

Lovecraft has been roundly criticised for his use of subjective adjectives, which were his primary tool for documenting the state of mind of his characters. These critics evidently fail to agree with another of Lovecraft's explicitly stated guidelines for weird fiction:

> In relation to the central wonder, the characters should shew the same overwhelming emotion which similar characters would shew toward such a wonder in real life.[4]

Lovecraft's characters have good reason to become feverish and frantic at what they experience—for example, the realization of man's relative position in a cosmos dominated by vast life forms whom we cannot understand and to whom we are mere ants; or the discovery of an antediluvian city inhabited hundreds of millions of years ago by a race of well-nigh omnipotent cone-shaped beings who accidentally created mankind; or the uncovering of an undeniably prehistoric artifact written in one's own handwriting; or a descent into a twilit grotto whose sea of skeletons and other gruesome artifacts prove that for centuries one's progenitors had practiced cannibalism in a bizarre ritualistic cult. These things are indeed adequate justification for Lovecraft's use of subjective adjectives.

In the last-named example ("The Rats in the Walls") and in several other tales, Lovecraft felt that the horror was such that he had to go beyond simple subjective descriptions, and documented the total collapse of the narrator's sanity with a stream-of-consciousness flood of fragmentary phrases. The atmospheric tensity of these passages has rarely been equalled in horror fiction—even by Poe, from whom Lovecraft ultimately derived the principle. "The Tell-Tale Heart", for example, is a rather less extreme development of the same type of technique.

Lovecraft's quest for realistic backgrounds also contributed to his frequent use of New England, which he knew and loved so well, as a fictional setting; to the point where some critics have called him a local-colorist. For this we can thank not only Poe but, as Donald R. Burleson has shown, Nathaniel Hawthorne.[5] The scholarly antiquarianism of M. R. James, whom Lovecraft read at a rather later date, doubtless also reinforced the latter's tendency to include references to actual books (such as the cryptographic reference materials mentioned in "The Dunwich Horror") and other historical detail in his stories.

Beyond Lovecraft's obvious attention to detail, mixing of factual information with fantastic imagination, psychological accuracy, use of "local color", and so on, there is a more basic element which binds these things into a convincing whole: his writing style. Indeed, Lovecraft's prose is the very fabric of the realistic approach which his philosophical orientation impelled him to take with his fiction. For in Lovecraft's prose style lies the realism which we *perceive* but do not *observe* when we read his stories, to which we respond without being consciously aware of it. All readers of Lovecraft know the peculiar *tone* of his narration; the surety, the authoritative voice of his narrators as they recount their incredible tales. In reading we acquire a subtle trust in the narrator, as much for *how* he expresses things as for *what* he is expressing. The deliberate, erudite word choice and phrasing make the reader sense that the narrator is a man of caution and intelligence; this instills in the reader a certain respect for the events to follow. The message of Lovecraft's style is that the narrator's voice is the voice of sanity—even when that sanity is threatened by monstrous intrusions from "Outside".

The force behind the unique and subtle credibility of Lovecraft's narration is what S. T. Joshi has termed the "precision" of Lovecraft's writing style.[6] This precision is manifest in vocabulary and syntax alike, and serves to reflect both the objective and subjective reactions of the narrator. That the precision and authoritative tone ring true, in an almost subconscious manner, reflects the fact that these qualities are inherent to Lovecraft's style rather than some technique he adopted for use. Lovecraft's unique combination of vocabulary and syntax (or *ideolect*) was shaped, like anyone's, by the linguistic stimuli of his youth. The vast bulk of this stimuli consisted of volumes written in the eighteenth century which he found in his ancestral library. At about age six he "began to choose only such books as were very old—with the 'long s' ", and selected as his guide to composition Abner Alden's *The Reader* (1802), "which was in the 'long s', and reflected in all its completeness the Georgian rhetorical tradition of Addison, Pope, and Johnson" (SL II.107f.). Lovecraft himself noted the strength of these influences in his autobiography, "Some Notes on a Nonentity" (1933):

> I used to spend long hours in the attic poring over the long-s'd books banished from the library downstairs and unconsciously absorbing the style of Pope and Dr. Johnson as a natural mode of expression. This absorption was doubly strong because of the ill health which rendered school attendance rare and irregular.[7]

Lovecraft's style forever after bore the indelible stamp of these early studies. Louis T. Milic, in *Stylists on Style*, expresses this as follows:

> The child acquires language in uneven increments. He learns a great deal during the third year and again when he first goes to school. In general, however, the curve of language learning describes a downward trend. The more he has learned about his language, the less he is able to change. The longer he speaks or writes, the more fixed become the patterns in his active repertory. The older he gets, the less he can modify his style. . . . This progressive hardening or "set" of the style also helps explain why the writer seems so much at the mercy of his medium.[8]

Milic goes on to stress the inviolability of a writer's ideolect—and, by implication, the early linguistic influences which shape it:

> The writer's choice is not really free. As we have seen, his stylistic options are limited by the resources of his ideolect (his active repertory of lexicon and syntax) and by the way this ideolect functions below the surface of his consciousness. Thus, though a writer may state his stylistic preferences, cultivate rhetorical choices he considers effective, or even pattern his style upon models, the essence of his expression, that which is inescapably unique to him, is governed by factors over which he has little control.[9]

This passage has great implications on any assessment of Lovecraft's stylistic influences. It seems clear that the writers whom Lovecraft absorbed in his early years, primarily Johnson, Addison, Steele, and Gibbon[10] (and also Poe, to whom he became devoted at age eight), are those who shaped his prose style. We can, too, minimize the stylistic effect of Lord Dunsany (whom Lovecraft did not read until he was nearly thirty years old), Machen, et al., upon Lovecraft.

In general, we may say that the traits characteristic of the eighteenth-century writers central to Lovecraft's style are: "philosophick" vocabulary, parallelism, inverted syntax, chiasmus (an inverted symmetry among the elements of two parallel phrases), and antithesis.

Lovecraft's detractors have been quick to vilify his tendency to use "big words", rather than express himself as simply as possible. Yet this tendency, honestly inherited from his influences, did much to give Lovecraft's writing a subtle and very pervasive sense of authority. Referring to Samuel Johnson,

W. K. Wimsatt, Jr., describes the effect of the use of general or abstract words which have a scientific or philosophical flavor:

> There are certain words for delineating objects which may not denote these any more generically than other words denoting the same objects, but which suggest that the objects are to be thought of as a class rather than individuals; they emphasize by their tone the aspect under which the class is concerned and have little or no connotation of complete appearance or the physical accidentals which clothe individuals of the class. These terms speak as having been coined by men who knew more accurately than common men the precise aspect, or complex of aspects, that constitute the class, who named classes only after studying them with the advantage of vast preliminary erudition.[11]

Thus we find such words as the celebrated "rugose" and "squamous" sprinkled throughout Lovecraft's stories, and to good effect regarding the confidence we have in the narrator's intelligence and judgment. Wimsatt notes, too, that the same sort of impression is made upon the reader, by implication, by more basic word choices made by the writer—the use of "frequently", for example, in place of "often".

Also worth a second glance among Lovecraft's eighteenth-century-derived traits is a syntactical element of extreme frequency, and importance, in his prose. This is parallelism, the repetition of syntactically similar elements. A single sentence from "Hypnos" (1922) supplies several examples:

> And when he opened his immense, sunken, and wildly luminous eyes I knew he would be thenceforth my only friend—the only friend of one who had never had a friend before—for I saw that such eyes must have looked fully upon the grandeur and the terror of realms beyond normal consciousness and reality, realms which I had cherished in fancy, but vainly sought. (D 160)

On the simplest level of parallel, there are the words coupled with "and", which is very frequent in Lovecraft. These doubled words, which are a salient characteristic of Johnson's style as well, can be roughly divided into four classes.[12] They may describe:

§ exact range (i.e., "the grandeur and the terror");
§ illustrative range ("[his voice was] the music of deep viols and of crystalline spheres" [D 161]);
§ different aspects of an object ("low and damnably insistent whine" [D 165]); or
§ overlapping aspects of an object ("the strange and hideous thing" [D 165]).

The last two classes, especially, make for increased emphasis, and predominate in Lovecraft as well as in Johnson.[13] It is sometimes difficult among these four types, as in this example from "The Shunned House" (1924):

> He was at once a devil and a multitude, a charnel house and a pageant.[14]

Another type of parallelism important and frequent enough in Lovecraft to mention and evidently derived from this school of writing is anaphora, where the parallel elements begin with the same words or phrase. In the first-quoted sentence from "Hypnos", an example is the phrase beginning with the word "realms". This parallelism likewise makes for increased emphasis, as does the chiasmus centered on the words "only friend".

If in the last analysis Lovecraft had relatively little control over his ideolect, he was well aware of its natural erudition. In many tales he reinforced this characteristic of his writing by giving his narrators positions of responsibility and intelligence; thus the predominance of academics, writers, and men of science we find relating Lovecraft's fantastic narratives. Here (and in Lovecraft's third-person narration also) we get the impression that the storyteller is intelligent enough to be able to distinguish between fact and fallacy, and is not one to be frightened without cause. And when we watch as the narrator becomes more and more upset—sometimes to the point of breaking down entirely—we are most affected by these series of events.

Lovecraft also drew attention to the intelligence—and, by extension, the credibility—of his narrators by contrasting their exposition with that of (ostensibly) common people, and also individuals who have come in contact with outside forces and been utterly deranged as a result. An example of the first kind is found in "Cool Air" (1926):

> Anxious to stop the matter at its source, I hastened to the basement to tell the landlady; and was assured by her that the trouble would quickly be set right.
>
> "Doctair Muñoz," she cried as she rushed up the stairs ahead of me, "he have speel hees chemicals. . . . He nevair go out, only on roof, and my boy Esteban he breeng heem hees food and laundry and mediceens and chemicals. My Gawd, the sal-ammoniac that man use for to keep heem cool!"
>
> Mrs. Herrero disappeared up the staircase to the fourth floor, and I returned to my room. (DH 204)

Similarly, there is the narrator's clinical description of Joe Slater's attack in "Beyond the Wall of Sleep" (1919, and a pivotal tale in the development of Lovecraft's prose realism) which contrasts so strikingly with Slater's ravings:

> Rushing out into the snow, he had flung his arms aloft and commenced a series of leaps directly upward in the air; the while shouting his determination to reach some 'big, big cabin with brightness in the roof and walls and floor, and the loud queer music far away'. As two men of moderate size sought to restrain him, he had struggled with maniacal force and fury, screaming of his desire and need to find and kill a certain 'thing that shines and shakes and laughs'. At length, after temporarily felling one of his detainers with a sudden blow, he had flung himself upon the other in a daemonic ecstasy of blood-thirstiness, shrieking fiendishly that he would 'jump high in the air and burn his way through anything that stopped him'. (D 25)

These two passages seem almost grotesque in their contrast between the reserve and intellect of the narrator and the lack of control of the other characters; but this contrast does serve to reinforce Lovecraft's point: that the narrator is one of exceptional erudition and judgment, and whose word is to be trusted.

We can conclude that Lovecraft's desire for realism in his weird fiction had a large philosophical component. To him, an intellectually acceptable imaginative refuge had to be based solidly in objective fact. Religion did not meet this criterion, earning his disdain because of it. In setting out to create his own fictions, however, he did his utmost to show that their fantastic—though often theoretically possible—events took place in the world which our science knows.

In technique, for both physical and psychological realism, he found his primary model in his literary idol, Edgar Allen Poe. But a great deal of the effectiveness of his realism is derived from other, more unconscious sources, the eighteenth-century writers in whom he immersed himself all through his early life. These elements of philosophical thought, adopted technique, and unconscious influence form a very fortuitous combination. They are the basis of the realism which helps make Lovecraft's tales so credibly terrifying.

*Notes*

1. Lovecraft, *Selected Letters* (Sauk City, WI: Arkham House, 1965–76; 5 vols.), I, p. 156. Further references are in the text, abbreviated as SL.
2. Lovecraft, "The Haunter of the Dark" (1935), in *The Dunwich Horror and Others* (Sauk City, WI: Arkham House, 1963), p. 115. Further references to this volume are in the text, abbreviated as DH. Textual errors in the Arkham House editions of the fiction cited here have, where possible, been silently corrected from transcriptions provided by S. T. Joshi.
3. Lovecraft, *Supernatural Horror in Literature* (1927; final rev. 1936), in *Dagon and Other Macabre Tales* (Sauk City, WI: Arkham House, 1965), p. 375. Further references to this volume are in the text, abbreviated as D.
4. Lovecraft, "Notes on Writing Weird Fiction" (1934), in *Uncollected Prose and Poetry III* (West Warwick, RI: Necronomicon Press, 1982), p. 44.
5. Donald R. Burleson, *H. P. Lovecraft: A Critical Study* (Westport, CT: Greenwood Press, 1983), p. 218.
6. S. T. Joshi, *Reader's Guide to H. P. Lovecraft* (Mercer Island, WA: Starmont House, 1982), p. 62.
7. Lovecraft, in Jack L. Chalker, ed., *Mirage on Lovecraft: A Literary View* (Baltimore: Jack L. Chalker and Mark Owings, 1965), p. 4.
8. Louis T. Milic, *Stylists on Style* (New York: Scribner's, 1969), p. 8. That this passage rings true is also reflected in Lovecraft's astonishing ease in writing rhymed couplets, most impressively shown in the many surviving impromptu poetic book inscriptions and Christmas greetings to his friends. This ability was obviously derived from his very early exposure to poetry; cf. Lovecraft's reminiscences regarding his experiences at age two with the poetess Louise Imogen Guiney, who had him recite nursery rhymes, and also his unusually early fondness for Pope, Dryden, etc.
9. Ibid., p. 10.
10. Lovecraft conveniently identifies these authors as his primary eighteenth-century prose influences at SL I.11.
11. W. K. Wimsatt, Jr., *The Prose Style of Samuel Johnson* (New Haven: Yale University Press, 1963), p. 60.
12. Ibid., p. 20. Examples are from "Hypnos".
13. Ibid., p. 22.
14. Lovecraft, *At the Mountains of Madness and Other Novels* (Sauk City, WI: Arkham House, 1964), p. 244.

# AMY LOWELL

## 1874–1925

Amy Lowell was born on February 9, 1874, at her family's suburban estate in Brookline, Massachusetts. The youngest child of one of Boston's oldest and richest families, Amy was educated by governesses and later at several private schools for girls. Her family, which owned the cotton mills in Lowell and Lawrence, Massachusetts, lived in a brownstone mansion known as the Sevenels. Here the young Lowell read in the vast library collection and acquired a taste for literature. Constantly plagued by a glandular disorder, she was a chubby child and an obese adult. By the time of her mother's death in 1895 and her father's death five years later her older siblings were married and living elsewhere, so she inherited the Sevenels.

Lowell claimed that she decided to become a poet after seeing Eleonora Duse perform on stage in 1902. She spent ten years preparing her first volume of poetry, A *Dome of Many-Coloured Glass* (1912), which received generally poor reviews. The following year she met Ezra Pound in London and was inspired by his new brand of poetry. She quickly internalized Pound's influence and her second volume of poetry, *Sword Blades and Poppy Seeds* (1914), became extremely popular. Regarded by some as the herald of a new age in American poetry, Lowell was the *grande dame* of a circle that included Robert Frost and Edna St. Vincent Millay. She used her great wealth to help other young artists and became a prominent reviewer in several magazines. She also published several collections of essays on contemporary literature, including *Six French Poets* (1915) and *Tendencies in Modern American Poetry* (1917).

In 1912 Lowell met the actress Ada Dwyer Russell, who from 1914 to 1925 was her faithful companion. In 1918 Lowell underwent the first of four hernia operations as her health steadily declined. In 1925 she published a lengthy biography of John Keats. She died of a cerebral hemorrhage shortly thereafter on May 12, 1925, but Ada Russell helped see a final book of poetry, *What O'Clock*, through the presses. This posthumously published collection won the 1926 Pulitzer Prize.

In ⟨Men, Women and Ghosts⟩ the dramatic monologues in the section called "The Overgrown Pasture" are perhaps the most keenly alive of the stories in various forms which compose it. Their free-verse presentation of the harsh Yankee dialect, and of the hard, stript Yankee character, is poetry as crabbéd as a barbed-wire fence, but it attains at times a certain tragic dignity by expressing with fit harshness the psychology of lonely New England rural women hurt to the point of madness or violence by solitude, silence, lack of sympathy and love. It is a generation gone to seed which she gives us here, an "overgrown pasture" which the hardy souls have deserted, and in which only ghosts, thwarted and wistful of life, remain.

The rest of the book might be called "Decorations," for it is essentially a series—or, rather, several series—of decorative paintings. As becomes an artist in that kind, Miss Lowell has a really vital sense of color; and she keeps her planes intact, and holds her vivid tones to the key and the pattern. The only trouble is, she is tempted to become too much involved with her decorative scheme. Her form, whether it be rhyme royal or polyphonic prose, is in danger of becoming too formal, holding not only the characters of the story, but the poet herself, in too tight a mesh. In the "Figurines in Old Saxe" this may be sufficient for her purpose—a close eighteenth-century mesh, with gesticulated lovers moving back and forth to a delicately shadowed fate. Yet that purpose is not quite enough to give a living soul to the work of her hand. In "Pickthorn Manor" and "The Cremona Violin" one can scarcely observe the clever psychology, analyzing women's involuntary infidelities, because of a certain over-neatness in the design; and it is a great relief when the heroine of "Patterns" cuts the mesh with the sword of tragedy, and lifts the poem to a higher plane with her poignant cry, "What are patterns for!" "Patterns" is, indeed, not only the most effective of the "Figurines" in decorative

quality, but the most human and convincing as well. And one cannot leave this group without a word of praise for the old-Venice atmosphere, like tarnished gold, in "The City of Falling Leaves."

Similarly the "War Pictures"—such pieces in polyphonic prose as "Bombardment" and "Lead Soldiers"—are too consciously designed; one cannot forget the pattern, and it has not enough spontaneity and violence for the subject. It is only when the pattern exactly fits the theme that we get such an admirable dramatic *suite* as "Malmaison"—if one may borrow a musical term for this kind of choric movement, or such an adorable grotesque as "Red Slippers." These are both in polyphonic prose, a pattern which hardly lacks intricacy, but which in these cases does not obtrude itself.

The book ends with a group of grotesques, a mood in which Miss Lowell delights as deeply as any Chinese woodcarver. They range from the delicate attitudinizing of "The Dinner-party" to the fiercely jerky gesticulation of the Stravinsky imitations. The art in these is very deliberate, no doubt, but that is the way with the grotesque, always a deliberate, mocking exaggeration.

It is a relief to find a poet who is always an artist. Miss Lowell may have too much art at times, but that is much rarer than too little.—HARRIET MONROE, "A Decorative Colorist," *Poetry*, Jan. 1917, pp. 207–9

Today whatever light surrounds her name is largely the reflected light of other litarary figures of her time. Her histrionic presence gave an air of excitement to readers who for the first time had read the Symphonies of John Gould Fletcher, the early poems of H.D., the pastorals of Robert Frost, who had heard the lilt of Vachel Lindsay's Simon Legree, the unrhymed cadences of Sandburg and Edgar Lee Masters. All these were poets of greater promise and accomplishment than hers. Her distinction had no relevance to the writing of poetry;

it was clearly and cheerfully the public expression of a personality, a literary celebrity of its day.

Proof of how fragile, though voluminous, her verses were, may be found in *The Complete Poetical Works of Amy Lowell*, a six-hundred-page book, published in 1955. Nor is there much of Amy Lowell in it. The verse is the expression of extraverted activity and observation, most of it as clear as daily reports upon the weather, and as perishable as last year's almanac. Amy Lowell's nearest approach to a revelation of whatever she felt or thought is in her prose, her *Tendencies in Modern American Poetry*, her life of *John Keats*. D. H. Lawrence's remarks on one of her best books of verse, *Men, Women and Ghosts*, which opened with her well-known "Patterns," are as true today as when he wrote his letter to her in 1916:

> You see it [the book] is uttering pure sensation *without concepts*, which is what this futuristic art tries to do. One step further and it passes into *mere noises*, as the Italian *futurismo* poems have done, or mere jags and zig-zags, as the futuristic paintings. There it ceases to be art, and is pure accident, mindless . . . You might have called your book 'Rockets and Sighs.' It would have been better than *Men, Women & Ghosts*.

This was and still is as true as his warning to her, "Do write from your *real* self, Amy, don't make up things from the outside, it is so saddening."

For this very reason *The Collected Poetical Works of Amy Lowell*, and this in spite of its glimpses of gardens, flowers and rockets, is a sad book, a lifeless monument to ten years of industry in jotting observations down on paper.—HORACE GREGORY, " Preface as Epilogue," *Amy Lowell*, 1958, pp. 212–13

Unquestionably she was an outstanding influence "in the American art of her time," as Elizabeth Sergeant said. She cleared the path for her younger contemporaries like Marianne Moore (who was just beginning her career when Amy died); Wallace Stevens (whose poetry she was among the first to recognize); e. e. cummings (whose lower-case and other typographical tricks she criticized as affectations, but who was the first to point out that in content he was an Elizabethan lyrist); Archibald MacLeish; William Carlos Williams, with whom she disagreed but whom she admired; and Babette Deutsch and Louise Bogan, also just beginning. Moreover, her pioneering groundwork paved the way for a later generation of poets. Among the women Muriel Rukeyser, Denise Levertov, Elizabeth Bishop, the late Anne Sexton, May Swenson, and that tragic genius Sylvia Plath come to mind; among the men, Williams' disciple, Allen Ginsberg (though Amy would have decried his "obscenities" as she did Joyce's, she nevertheless led the way for the experimenters); James Dickey; Howard Moss; L. E. Sissman (whose "Mt. Auburn: 1945" narrative might have come from her storytelling poetry); and even, though he disclaims any but a distant relationship, the present-day poet of her family, Robert Lowell, with his powerful, raw realism. Of course, there were other significant influences: Eliot's *The Waste Land*, whether it moved Amy Lowell or not, changed the course of modern poetry. But if it had not been for Amy's initial campaign, modern freedom of expression in poetry, whatever its form or lack of it, might have taken much longer to evolve and may have, one might guess, evolved differently. Contemporary poetry, like contemporary music and painting, can take any turn its creator pleases—though one may reject this as a thing totally good in itself—and although no one writes Amy's polyphonic prose today, it was an important

milestone along the road.—JEAN GOULD, " 'In Excelsis,' " *Amy*, 1975, pp. 354–55

Shall I uncrumple this muchly crumpled thing?
(Wallace Stevens)

When Amy Lowell died in 1925, in mid-career and at the height of her powers, she was regarded by most literate persons as the foremost American poet. Her eminence was not due solely to the appeal of a picturesque and unique personality. It was based, first of all, on some of the most original and expressive poems to be found in recent American literature.

The poems concerned were expressive of a distinctive mode of thought with a novel perspective and approach to meaning. The approach was impressionistic, that which the mind can discover through direct observation and its powers of intuition. The perspective was novel in that it focused on objects in the immediate foreground of life: flowers, trees, sky, or a lightly sketched nude, "slim and without sandals"; and then, in the far distance, the faint outlinings of a limitless spiritual realm which was their source and meaning. What this perspective minimized was the "quotidian," the exigent middle ground of existence, the ordinary daily concerns in which most human lives are entirely absorbed. From the vantage point of her aristocratic grandeur, the solitude of her celibate life, and the demands of a probing intellect no other approach and perspective were possible. Without conscious choice or direction, Miss Lowell's nature and circumstances guided her along this path, away from ordinary routines of existence in favor of explorations of what Wallace Stevens has called "the indefinite, the impersonal, atmospheres and oceans and, above all, the principle of order."

The perusal of Amy Lowell's poetry has always shown that she was, in fact, preoccupied with "atmospheres and oceans." It is the principal complaint against her that she was chiefly attracted to the "shining shells" of things, that her real successes were in the depiction of the external world and that she failed to do justice to the emotions and inner experience of man. This is true in the sense I have suggested above. But it is not true to say that Miss Lowell's poems are skillful color photographs which leave the vital issues of life untouched. Detached from the middle distances in which we realize ourselves in exaggerated self-importance, Amy Lowell's penetrating gaze sought and found, not flowers and trees or spare-limbed nude, but the spiritual presences that these forms manifest to the sensitive eye and ear.

The "unseen faces of the gods" as the true object of the poet's quest is the theme of the verses by de Regnier that Miss Lowell chose as motto for *Sword Blades and Poppy Seed*, her first volume in the Imagistic manner. In this way she connects the two major stages of her work: the early poems, collected in *A Dome of Many-Coloured Glass*, which are mystical in subject matter and the poems of her artistic maturity in which her apprehensions are presented indirectly by means of visual images. Eschewing traditional bodies of religious belief or philosophic thought, Miss Lowell responded to her world impressionistically and so gave varied testimony to the Divinity she felt but could not either name or categorize.

That her need for exploration was great is proved by the vast bulk of her output. In the years between 1914 and 1922, when Wallace Stevens was accumulating the seventy-six poems that appeared in his first volume, Miss Lowell wrote eight thick books of verse (one of them still unpublished) totaling 322 poems. Many of these poems consisted of two or three lines, but others were of epic length and pretensions and they included work in nearly every variety of poetic expression, some of them very ill-suited to Miss Lowell's gifts. As one would expect, the quality of this work was as uneven as its quantity was great. Some of her narrative poems sink into arid verbalism. A large part of her published work consists of technical exercises, preparatory sketches for other poems, or descriptive matter without a true core of thought or feeling. Unrewarding as such poems may be, they were the necessary preliminaries to her moments of genuine inspiration and these were frequent enough to produce a large body of distinguished work. In the words of John Lowes, written shortly after the poet's death, "She has added new beauty to English poetry. How great that contribution is will first be clearly seen when time has winnowed and her enduring work is brought together in one rare and shining book."

⟨. . .⟩ With a few notable exceptions Imagist verse has always been treated as realistic sense impressions. I believe that this is to miss the real nature of the poetry and it is hopelessly inadequate as an explanation of the mesmerizing power of Amy Lowell's best work. Miss Lowell's mind was deeply colored by her life-long interest in the Orient as it was by her interest in European Impressionism, and these were two currents which fused in her consciousness to produce the masterful art of her middle and late periods. The purpose of this study is to foster appreciation of that art by analysis of its novel qualities and the meanings it contains.—GLENN RICHARD RUIHLEY, "Preface" to *The Thorn of a Rose*, 1975, pp. 9–12

## CONRAD AIKEN

### From "The Technique of Polyphonic Prose: Amy Lowell"

*Scepticisms*

1919, pp. 117–24

Miss Lowell asserts in her preface, ⟨to *Can Grande's Castle*⟩ that polyphonic prose is not an order of prose. Let us not quarrel with her on this point. The important questions are: first, its possible effectiveness as an art form; and second, its effectiveness as employed through the temperament of Miss Lowell. She says:

> Metrical verse has one set of laws, cadenced verse another, polyphonic prose can go from one to the other in the same poem with no sense of incongruity. Its only touchstone is the taste and feeling of its author. . . . Yet, like all other artistic forms, it has certain fundamental principles, and the chief of these is an insistence on the absolute adequacy of a passage to the thought it embodies. Taste is therefore its determining factor; taste and a rhythmic ear.

But all this is merely equivalent to saying that any expression of the artist is inevitably self-expression, as if one "threw the nerves in patterns on a screen." The real touchstone of a work of art is not, ultimately, the taste or feeling of the author (a singularly unreliable judge) but the degree to which it "gets across," (as they say of the drama) to, let us say, an intelligent audience.

And here one may properly question whether in their totality Miss Lowell's prose-poems quite "get across." They are brilliant, in the aesthetic sense; they are amazingly rich and frequently delightful in incident; they are unflaggingly visualized; they are, in a manner, triumphs of co-ordination. And yet, they do not quite come off. Why is this? Is it the fault of Miss Lowell or of the form? A little of each; and the reasons are many. Of the more obvious sort is the simple but deadly fact that without exception these four prose-poems are too long.

Not too long in an absolute sense, for that would be ridiculous, but too long, first, in relation to the amount and nature of the narrative element in them, and second, in relation to the manner, or style, in which they are written. Parallels are not easy to find; but one can perhaps not outrageously adduce Flaubert's *Herodias* and *Salammbô* as examples of success in what is very much the same, not form, but tone of art. Miss Lowell, like Flaubert, attempts a very vivid and heavily laden reconstruction of striking historical events. No item is too small to be recreated for its effect in producing a living and sensuous veridity. But there are two important differences. In Flaubert this living sensuousness is nearly always subordinated to the narrative, is indeed merely the background for it; whereas for Miss Lowell this sensuous reconstruction is perhaps the main intention. And furthermore, whereas Flaubert employed a prose of which the chief purpose was that it should be unobtrusively a vehicle, Miss Lowell employs a prose bristlingly self-conscious, of which an important purpose is stylistic and colouristic brilliance.

The defects that arise from these two differences are very serious. They combine to rob Miss Lowell of the fruits to which sheer adroitness of craftsmanship might otherwise have entitled her. Put briefly, these poems are over-descriptive. When one considers their length, the narrative element is much too slight; and not only that, it is too disjointed. Narrative description, even though able, is not enough. In "Sea-Blue and Blood-Red" Miss Lowell introduces a really narrative theme—narrative, that is, in the sense that it involves real *dramatis personae*, in the persons of Nelson and Lady Hamilton—and in consequence the reader's interest is a good deal better held. It would be still better held however if the protagonists had been conceived less as gaudily sheathed mannequins, gesticulating feverishly in a whirl of coloured lights and confetti, and more as human beings. It is intended to show them as puppets, of course, but that effect would hardly have been diminished by making them psychologically more appealing. In "Hedge Island," "Guns as Keys," and "Bronze Horses" the unifying themes are still more tenuous: the supersession of the stagecoach by the train, Commodore Perry's voyage to Japan, the travels of the four horses of San Marco. All of them are acute studies of societal change. One feels in all of them the impressiveness of the conception, but in the actual execution the impressiveness has partially escaped. One is, in fact, less often impressed than fatigued.

And this fatigue, as above intimated, is due not merely to the lack of humanly interesting narrative (as would be added by the introduction of a character or group of characters who should enlist our sympathies throughout) but also to the nature of the style which Miss Lowell uses. For here Miss Lowell, led astray by love of experiment, has made, in the opinion of the present reviewer, a series of fundamental errors. The style she has chosen to use, whether regarded with a view to rhythm or to colour-distribution, is essentially pointillistic. Now Miss Lowell should have known that the pointillistic style is, in literature, suited only to very brief movements. A short poem based on this method may be brilliantly successful; Miss Lowell has herself proved it. A long poem based on this method, even though sustainedly brilliant, and perhaps in direct ratio to its brilliance, almost inevitably becomes dull. In her preface Miss Lowell says that she has taken for the basis of her rhythm the long cadence of oratorical prose. In this however she is mistaken. She has an inveterate and profoundly temperamental and hence perhaps unalterable addiction to a short, ejaculatory, and abrupt style—a style indeed of which the most striking merits and defects are its vigorous curtness and its almost total lack of curve and grace. This is true of her work whether in metrical verse, free verse, or prose; it is as true of "The Cremona Violin" as of "The Bombardment." This style, obviously, is ideal for a moment of rapid action or extreme emotional intensity. But its effect when used *passim* is not only fatiguing, it is actually irritating. Its pace is too often out of all proportion to the pace of the action. One feels like a horse who is at the same time whipped up and reined in. The restlessness is perpetual, there is no hope of relaxation or ease, one longs in vain for a slowing down of the movement, an expansion of it into longer and more languid waves. One longs, too, for that delicious sublimation of tranquillity and pause which comes of a beautiful transition from the exclamatory to the contemplative, from the rigidly angular to the musically curved.

This misapplication of style to theme manifests itself as clearly on the narrowly aesthetic plane as on the rhythmic. Here again one sees a misuse of pointillism, for Miss Lowell splashes too much colour, uses colour and vivid image too unrestrainedly and too much at the same pitch of intensity. The result is that the rate of aesthetic fatigue on the reader's part is relatively rapid. So persistent is Miss Lowell's colouristic attitude, so nearly unvaried is her habit of presenting people, things, and events in terms of colour alone, that presently she has reduced one to a state of colour blindness. Image kills image, hue obliterates hue, on page erases another. And when this point has been reached one realizes that Miss Lowell's polyphonic prose has little else to offer. Its sole *raison d'être* is its vividness.

One wonders, indeed, whether Miss Lowell has not overestimated the possibilities of this form. It is precisely at those points where polyphonic prose is more self-conscious or artificial than ordinary prose—where it introduces an excess of rhyme, assonance, and alliteration—that it is most markedly inferior to it. Theory to the contrary, these shifts from prose to wingèd prose or verse are often so abrupt as to be incongruous and disturbing. But disturbance as an element in aesthetic attack should be subordinate, not dominant—the exception, not the rule. Miss Lowell's polyphonic prose is a perpetual furor of disturbance, both of thought and of style. Again, refrain should be sparely used, adroitly varied and concealed; and the counterpoint of thought, if it is not to become monotonous, must be a good deal subtler than it is, for instance, in "Bronze Horses." All these artifices are used to excess, and the upshot is a style of which the most salient characteristic is exuberance without charm. "Taste" and "rhythmic ear" too frequently fail. And one is merely amused when one encounters a passage like the following:

> Such a pounding, pummelling, pitching, pointing, piercing, pushing, pelting, poking, panting, punching, parrying, pulling, prodding, puking, piling, passing, you never did see.

It is hard to regard this as anything but tyronism.

## STANLEY K. COFFMAN, JR.
### From "Amygism"
*Imagism: A Chapter for the History of Modern Poetry*
1951, pp. 170–75

Amy Lowell carried the generalizing tendency to its logical extreme: Imagism under her guidance became so inclusive that it was less a specific doctrine than a platform designed to win the approval of almost anyone interested in honest, sincere poetic technique. This is not to say that she had no clearly definable theory; in some respects her thinking about the problems of modern poetry was more conscientious and better organized than Pound's or Aldington's, but several of her

conclusions are incompatible with those on which Imagism was originally based. She made some effort to keep within the bounds prescribed for the movement; but Imaginism never successfully modified certain of her convictions, and these convictions were simply not those of Hulme, Pound, or Aldington.

Her views on the language of poetry are a case in point. She condemned the use of inversions and of locutions inappropriate to the diction of natural, conversational prose; she also asserted the importance of the exact word. Her "exact word," however, was not the one which describes a thing as it is, but the one which most effectively communicates the writer's impression of it. In illustration, she quoted:

> Great heaps of shining glass
> Pricked out of the stubble
> By a full, high moon.[1]

Though she meant to emphasize the use of *glass* to convey the writer's impression of stones or pebbles in this picture, *pricked out* could also serve as an example. Again in "Venus Transiens," trying to give her impression of a Botticelli painting, she described his waves as *crinkled*. Like Hueffer's Impressionist, Miss Lowell aimed to "render," not merely to report, and while her theory of diction begins as Imagist, it trails off into Impressionism.

She placed no particular stress upon the "hardness" of good poetry; but her strictures upon subject matter approximate the doctrine of Aldington and Pound and offer a pair of terms which, though too general to be final, shed further light on the Imagist position.[2] One was *internality*, "the most marked quality in the poetry of the nineties." Whether or not the term accurately characterizes the poetic attitude of the nineties, Miss Lowell was quite certain of what it meant to her. She referred to the pathetic fallacy, the view of nature as important only for its reflection of the poet's mood, as of no interest apart from the individual; and she criticized this view for its assumption that man is the center of the universe, a criticism that is by now familiar enough.

In contrast, she saw modern poetry as characterized by externality or exteriority, by "a contemplation of nature unencumbered by the 'pathetic fallacy.'" Externality encourages an "interest in things for themselves and not because of the effect they have on oneself." She pointed, for example, to the modern artist's handling of colors, light, and shade, "with practically no insistence on the substances which produce them, be they men or houses or trees or water." A product of the sensible attitude which sees man in his proper, relatively insignificant place in the universe, externality would not seem to encourage introspection, though she was not willing wholly to exclude it from poetry. Her theory is of some importance because it again draws attention to the very broad but basic difference between the impersonal art of Hulme and Pound on the one hand and the subjective, egocentric art of Symbolism on the other. While not necessarily derived from Hulme, it is a clear, if generalized and unphilosophical, echo of the principles underlying his aesthetic.

But she also discussed poetry in the exact terms Hulme had hoped to do away with. She declared that poetry consists of two ingredients, the vision and the words. When the vision is slight, it calls *fancy* into play; when its force is stronger, it finds expression through the *imagination*; when it carries the poet before it, it has become *inspiration*. She even stated that the domanant quality of the modern idiom (in which she included Imagism) was suggestion, "the invoking of a place or a character rather than describing it, . . . the implying of something rather than the stating of it, implying it perhaps under a metaphor, perhaps in an even less obvious way."[3] By supporting this assertion with two examples from Fletcher's poetry, she brought her definition to what is approximately the position of the Symbolist. On one she commented: "The picture as given is quite clear and vivid. But the picture we see is not the poem, the real poem lies beyond, is only suggested." On the other: "This is at once Mr. Fletcher and Japan. It is brief and clear, and the suggestion never becomes statement, but floats, a nimbus, over the short, sharp lines."[4]

However, Miss Lowell, from her own statements, was not a Symbolist; she considered Symbolist poetry "beautiful," but saw in it too much "internality," too much of the poet's "inner self."[5] Although her "Patterns" is symbolism, its concrete, vivid images (the garden paths, the brocaded gown, the rigid stays) symbolizing the human patterns and conventions that cut across the natural desires of the individual, it is what one might call a symbolism of externality. The Symbolists sought to communicate an "internal" meaning and used the symbol, among other devices, to heighten the mystery of the inexpressible; Miss Lowell dealt with the expressible, or with a tension very simple in nature; her poem expresses a state of consciousness, but it is an elementary and uncomplicated one having and making no claim to reproduction of the quality of consciousness itself—and her symbols are turned in the direction of making the expressible more concrete.

If she was not a Symbolist, neither was she an Imagist. Her concept of the image was so vague as to be meaningless. It is true that she did not completely ignore the function of the image in poetry: she accepted Hulme as the original Imagist, and her preface to *Sword Blades* explains that in order to give the reader some poignant feeling he has had, the poet must find new images, old ones, like *daybreak*, having been so overworked that they have lost their pictorial effectiveness. She recognized that vividness, the throwing of "an inescapable picture" on the mind's eye, was one of the dominant qualities of modern poetry, and pointed out the way in which this tends to encourage a concentration of poetic effect and discourage what Pound called hanging the image "with festoons."[6] Like other moderns, she could create a brilliant visual image:

> Grass-blades push up between the cobblestones
> And catch the sun on their flat sides
> Shooting it back,
> Gold and emerald
> Into the eyes of passers-by.[7]

However, she seldom tried to use an image in metaphor or simile, and what efforts she made in this direction were not always successful. "Bullion" describes the poet's thoughts "chinking" against his ribs like "silver hail stones," and, even if the reader accepts the idea that the thoughts are those emanating from the heart and that they may therefore not illogically chink against the ribs, the connotations of *chinking* and *hailstones*, even silver ones, are not appropriate to the emotion with which the poet is concerned. At the same time, a more successful use of a metaphor should be pointed out. Seeking to transcribe her impression of a composition by Stravinsky, Miss Lowell translates the music first into the heavy, uneven clomp of wooden shoes on slippery cobblestones, then into the cacophonous rattle of bones, a grotesque sound—"Delirium flapping its thighbones."[8]

What has been implied by the discussion so far is clearly given away in her statements about the Imagist movement. The doctrine of the image, she said, "refers more to the manner of presentation than to the thing presented"; and she summarized the Imagist credo without reference to it:

> Simplicity and directness of speech; subtlety and beauty of rhythms; individualistic freedom of idea; clearness and vividness of presentation; and concentration. Not new principles, by any means . . . but fallen into desuetude.[9]

A symbolist without the philosophical attitude of Symbolism and an Imagist without the image, she carried to its extreme a tendency to generalize Imagist principles until they ignored the tenet which presumably gave the doctrine its individuality and its name.

*Notes*

1. *Tendencies in Modern American Poetry* (Boston and New York, 1931), 242.
2. For her use of these terms, see "The New Manner in Modern Poetry," *The New Republic*, Vol. VI, No. 70 (March 4, 1916), 124; *Six French Poets* (New York, 1916), 215; "A Consideration of Modern Poetry," *The North American Review*, Vol. CCV, No. 734 (January, 1917), 106.
3. "A Consideration of Modern Poetry," *The North American Review*, Vol. CCV, No. 734 (January, 1917), 103–104; *Tendencies in Modern American Poetry*, 247.
4. *Tendencies in Modern American Poetry*, 247, 341.
5. *Six French Poets*, 215.
6. "A Consideration of Modern Poetry," *The North American Review*, Vol. CCV, No. 734 (January, 1917), 105.
7. "The Traveling Bear," *Some Imagist Poets* (1915), 83.
8. "Stravinsky's Three Pieces, 'Grotesque' for String Quartet," *Some Imagist Poets* (1916), 88.
9. *Tendencies in Modern American Poetry*, 246–47.

## BARBARA UNGAR
### From "Imagism, Amy Lowell and the Haiku"
*Haiku in English*
#### 1978, pp. 18–20

In *Twenty-Four Hokku on a Modern Theme* Lowell demonstrates clearly her lack of any real understanding of haiku, but also how well she has adapted many of its techniques, such as brevity, precision, suggestion, and, to an extent, internal comparison. The "modern theme" she speaks of is one of unrequited love, oddly enough. Surely this is as ancient as they come: perhaps she means to signify her awareness that haiku are traditionally nature poems. The poem is comprised of twenty-four numbered stanzas of three lines each, with a syllable count close to 5, 7 and 5. They are linked subtly. Several of them are haiku, but most have captured little of the quality of the form. Fifteen of them contain a mention of flower, tree or bird—some reference to nature. But they are not used in haiku fashion: they make direct statements about the poet's feelings. For example, Stanza XI reads,

> Take it, this white rose.
> Stems of roses do not bleed;
> Your fingers are safe.

The poem makes no claim to objectivity: there is an obtrusive narrator throughout, and a very obtrusive receiver of the verses.

Two of the most successful, most haiku-like verses seem to use internal comparison:

> XVI.
>
> Last night it rained.
> Now, in the desolate dawn,
> Crying of blue jays.

> XXI.
>
> Turning from the page,
> Blind with a night of labor,
> I hear morning crows.

The two are similar in that they contrast the moment of morning with a long night; in both the cry of birds is used to signify morning. Both jays and crows are unpleasant birds with raucous cries, helping to make the ironic twist that the morning, usually a joyful moment, is in these cases "desolate," still entangled in the pain of the night before. To appreciate the verses fully, perhaps it is necessary to know that Lowell's health and eyesight failed her later in life, yet she kept working relentlessly. She often suffered all through the night using very high-powered reading lamps to complete the intense work schedule she set herself. Another attractive morning verse from this series is Stanza VI:

> This then is morning.
> Have you no comfort for me
> Cold-coloured flowers?

Once again she reverses a convention regarding a natural phenomenon, in this case flowers, which we usually think of as bright-colored and gay. Here because of her condition, the flowers are imbued with her hopelessness and become "cold-coloured." She seems to understand that the comfort she expects from the flowers, like their cold color, is given to them by herself, and so they cannot help her.

These examples are remarkably free of adjectives for Lowell: they are simple and therefore startling. Here she seems to have chanced upon good haiku: the fact that she did not understand the form is evidenced by her inclusion of such poems with other verses which are definitely not haiku under the title *Twenty-Four Hokku on a Modern Theme*. If my criticism of her poetry seems harsh, I hope that the reader will remember that I am not criticizing her poems for not being haiku, but simply trying to show why they are not. I do not mean to judge apples by oranges, but rather to distinguish between oranges and tangerines.

In her introduction to *Pictures from the Floating World* Lowell states her intention to capture the brevity, suggestion and natural setting of the "hokku"[1] without attempting any syllabic count patterned after the Japanese. A few of the poems in this collection do seem to achieve this effect.

### NUANCE

> Even the iris bends
> When a butterly lights upon it.

This poem is simple and delicate. It does not have great depth or reverberation, but it is not marred by overstatement or comment. Another short poem seems to have been inspired by a Japanese haiku, perhaps the one by Buson about a butterfly perched on a temple bell.

### PEACE

> Perched upon the muzzle of a cannon
> A yellow butterfly is slowly opening and shutting its
> wings.

Her title "Peace" and placing of the butterfly on a cannon seem a bit heavy-handed, but at least she makes no further comment, letting the image speak for itself. In poems such as these, where the image is clear and simple, where there is no narratorial intrusion, and where natural objects are used suggestively, Lowell comes closest to haiku.

To sum up, Lowell successfully adapted some technical elements of haiku, as set forth in the Imagist manifesto, but missed the deeper philosophical underpinnings of the form. It is not necessarily a question of Zen, but even the poems which most closely resemble haiku lack the direct, wordless leap to the inner nature of things. There is no inspiration, in Bashō's sense of the word. This misunderstanding of haiku led to its eventual dismissal by the Imagists as a non-serious form. John Gould Fletcher wrote, after his infatuation with haiku had passed, that "the relation of Chinese Classical poets to the Japanese *tanka* and *hokku* poets is, psychologically speaking, like the relation of full-grown and mature human figures to a group of rather small and temporarily attractive children."[2] This kind of attitude became more widespread and, with the advent of World War II, interest in haiku was lost completely, while the experiments of the Imagists were largely forgotten.

*Notes*

1. The Imagists used the term "hokku," which properly refers to the starting verse in a linked poem, in referring to haiku, an independent poem.
2. John Gould Fletcher, "The Orient and Contemporary Poetry," in *The Asian Legacy and American Life*, ed. Arthur C. Christy (New York: The John Day Co., 1945), p. 148.

# ROBERT LOWELL

## 1917–1977

Robert Traill Spence Lowell, Jr. was born in Boston on March 1, 1917. His distinguished New England family, whose American roots date back to the arrival of the *Mayflower* in 1620, includes several generals, judges, congressmen, and even two well-known poets, James Russell Lowell and Amy Lowell. Robert's father was a naval officer of only moderate means, and the poet's mother was dissatisfied with the family's reduced circumstances; nonetheless, they lived quite well, if not luxuriously. While attending St. Mark's, a Massachusetts boarding school, Lowell acquired the nickname "Cal," short for Caligula, which would stay with him for years. After St. Mark's he spent two unhappy years at Harvard, the traditional choice of the Lowells. At the suggestion of Ford Madox Ford he travelled to Tennessee to meet Allen Tate in the spring of 1937. He spent four months camped out in a tent on the Tate's front lawn listening to and learning from one of the leaders of the Fugitive School. By the end of the summer Tate had convinced the young Lowell to study with John Crowe Ransom at Kenyon. That fall he arrived in Gambier, Ohio and three years later graduated having majored in classics. At Kenyon he associated with fellow students Randall Jarrell and Peter Taylor, and contributed a few poems to the *Kenyon Review* which Ransom edited.

In 1940 Lowell converted to Roman Catholicism and married the novelist and Catholic convert Jean Stafford. He studied briefly at Louisiana State University with Cleanth Brooks and Robert Penn Warren before moving to New York in 1941 to work at Sheed & Ward, a radical Catholic publishing house. In 1943 Lowell wrote an open letter to President Roosevelt notifying him of his decision not to serve in the armed forces. During the early stages of the war Lowell had been supportive of U.S. efforts; in fact he even tried to enlist, but was rejected because of his poor eyesight. However, by 1943 his thoughts had changed as American bombers levelled German cities, killing thousands of civilians. He served five months of a one year prison sentence for his refusal to obey the draft. His first volume of poetry, *Land of Unlikeness* (1944), was published shortly after his release. About this time Lowell also was institutionalized for mental instability. This would be the first of several stays in asylums that often included electroshock therapy. Although his first volume of poetry attracted little attention, his second volume, *Lord Weary's Castle* (1946), received much critical acclaim and was awarded the 1947 Pulitzer Prize. At the age of thirty Lowell was considered a leading American poet.

As his first marriage began to break up, so too did his religious fervor wane. By the late 40s he had abandoned Catholicism and left Jean Stafford. He was divorced in 1948 and in the following year married Elizabeth Hardwick, a leftist critic who later was an editor at the *New York Review of Books*. Together they had one daughter, Harriet, who was born in 1957. Lowell continued to write during the 50s and taught at various universities. Among his students were W.D. Snodgrass, Anne Sexton, and Sylvia Plath. At the end of the decade he published an autobiographical collection of verse and prose passages, titled *Life Studies*, which won the 1960 National Book Award. Lowell's noted works from the early 60s include *Imitations* (1961), a co-winner of the Bollingen Translation Prize, and *The Old Glory* (1965), a collection of three short dramas, one of which won an Obie for best off-Broadway play. He was also active in protests against the Vietnam War, and had his refusal to attend a White House arts festival printed on the front page of the *New York Times*. This open letter to President Johnson was followed by Lowell's involvement in the massive march on the Pentagon two years later. Norman Mailer gives a famous account of Lowell's participation in the march in *The Armies of the Night*.

During his last years he continued to be productive, winning a second Pulitzer for *The Dolphin*. His second marriage ended in 1972; thereafter, he married the British novelist Caroline Blackwood. She had already given birth to Lowell's son Sheridan in 1971. On September 12, 1977 Lowell landed at New York's Kennedy Airport, presumably to see Elizabeth Hardwick. When he arrived at her Manhattan apartment the taxi driver that had picked him up at the airport found Lowell dead in the back seat of a heart attack. He was buried at the family cemetary in Dunbarton, New Hampshire.

Some of Mr. Lowell's poems are so good, ⟨. . .⟩ and all are so unusual that it makes reviewing ⟨*Land of Unlikeness*⟩ a pleasure. A "traditional" poet is one who uses the usual properties and images to say the usual things: Mr. Lowell, a really traditional poet, is sometimes able to exploit the resources of language and the world for the organization of a poem almost exactly as some of the poets of the seventeenth century were able to. His language is nouns and verbs and the necessary connectives—a few adjectives, next to no adverbs; its exceptional strength is not merely the strength of intensity, emotional and rhetorical, but the basic intrinsic strength of language itself. Often he knows (as almost no contemporary poets know except in theory) that language at its strongest is *not* language that remains at the highest emotional and textural intensity as long as one can force it to; that sensibility is like money—good only for what it can buy; that the whole is what the parts are for. He has never been fooled into the vulgar belief in the separation (opposition, even) of the "connotative" and "denotative" functions of language—a belief that reaches its most primitive level of absurdity in Winters's positively pre-Socratic view. Mr. Lowell's essential source is early Milton; obvious but unimportant sources for a few details are Hopkins ("You are their belle / And belly too . . . Celestial Hoyden") and Tate. *What* Mr. Lowell says could not have been said, guessed at, or tolerated before. His world is our world—political, economic, and murderous—cruelly insisted upon, with all our green and pale hopes gone, their places taken by a blind and bloody Heaven. (He has succeeded in making salvation seem as real, and almost as frightening, as damna-

tion.) In these poems the blood of the martyrs is the creed of the Church; his Christ (named as one names Madonnas) is the Christ of the Tabloids. When over this coiling darkness there is a grave, indistinct, and serene lightening of pity, one is more than usually moved. His world, his rhetoric, and his beliefs are joined in an iron unity of temperament; in a day when poets aspire to be irresistible forces, he is an immovable object.
—RANDALL JARRELL, "Poetry in War and Peace" (1945), *Kipling, Auden & Co.*, 1980, p. 132

Many of the people who reviewed *Lord Weary's Castle* felt that it was as much of an event as Auden's first book; no one younger than Auden has written better poetry than the best of Robert Lowell's, it seems to me. Anyone who reads contemporary poetry will read it; perhaps people will understand the poetry more easily, and find it more congenial, if they see what the poems have developed out of, how they are related to each other, and why they say what they say.

Underneath all these poems "there is one story and one story only"; when this essential theme or subject is understood, the unity of attitudes and judgments underlying the variety of the poems becomes startlingly explicit. The poems understand the world as a sort of conflict of opposites. In this struggle one opposite is that cake of custom in which all of us lie embedded like lungfish—the stasis or inertia of the stubborn self, the obstinate persistence in evil that is damnation. Into this realm of necessity the poems push everything that is closed, turned inward, incestuous, that blinds or binds: the Old Law, imperialism, militarism, capitalism, Calvinism, Authority, the Father, the "proper Bostonians," the rich who will "do everything for the poor except get off their backs." But struggling within this like leaven, falling to it like light, is everything that is free or open, that grows or is willing to change: here is the generosity or openness or willingness that is itself salvation; here is "accessibility to experience"; this is the realm of freedom, of the Grace that has replaced the Law, of the perfect liberator whom the poet calls Christ.

Consequently the poems can have two possible movements or organizations: they can move from what is closed to what is open, or from what is open to what is closed. The second of these organizations—which corresponds to an "unhappy ending"—is less common, though there are many good examples of it: "The Exile's Return," with its menacing *Voi ch'entrate* that transforms the exile's old home into a place where even hope must be abandoned; the harsh and extraordinary "Between the Porch and the Altar," with its four parts each ending in constriction and frustration, and its hero who cannot get free of his mother, her punishments, and her world even by dying, but who sees both life and death in terms of her, and thinks at the end that, sword in hand, the Lord "watches me for Mother, and will turn / The bier and baby-carriage where I burn."

But normally the poems move into liberation. Even death is seen as liberation, a widening into darkness: that old closed system Grandfather Arthur Winslow, dying of cancer in his adjusted bed, at the last is the child Arthur whom the swanboats once rode through the Public Garden, whom now "the ghost of risen Jesus walks the waves to run / Upon a trumpeting black swan / Beyond Charles River and the Acheron / Where the wide waters and their voyager are one." (Compare the endings of "The Drunken Fisherman" and "Dea Roma.") "The Death of the Sheriff" moves from closure—the "ordered darkness" of the homicidal sheriff, the "loved sightless smother" of the incestuous lovers, the "unsearchable quicksilver heart / Where spiders stare their eyes out at their own / Spitting and knotted likeness"—up into the open sky, to those "light wanderers" the planets, to the "thirsty Dipper on the arc of night." Just so the cold, blundering, iron confusion of "Christmas Eve under Hooker's Statue" ends in flowers, the wild fields, a Christ "once again turned wanderer and child." In "Rebellion" the son seals "an everlasting pact / With Dives to *contract* / The world that *spreads* in pain"; but at last he rebels against his father and his father's New England commercial theocracy, and "the word *spread* / When the clubbed flintlock broke my father's brain." The italicized words ought to demonstrate how explicitly, at times, these poems formulate the world in the terms that I have used. ⟨. . .⟩

Anyone who compares Mr. Lowell's earlier and later poems will see this movement from constriction to liberation as his work's ruling principle of growth. The grim, violent, sordid constriction of his earliest poems—most of them omitted from *Lord Weary's Castle*—seems to be temperamental, the Old Adam which the poet grew from and only partially transcends; and a good deal of what is excessive in the extraordinary rhetorical machine of a poem like "The Quaker Graveyard at Nantucket," which first traps and then wrings to pieces the helpless reader—who rather enjoys it—is gone from some of his later poems, or else dramatically justified and no longer excessive. "The Quaker Graveyard" is a baroque work, like *Paradise Lost*, but all the *extase* of baroque has disappeared—the coiling violence of its rhetoric, the harsh and stubborn intensity that accompanies all its verbs and verbals, the clustering stresses learned from accentual verse, come from a man contracting every muscle, grinding his teeth together till his shut eyes ache. Some of Mr. Lowell's later work moved, for a while, in the direction of the poem's quiet contrast-section,

"Walsingham"; the denunciatory prophetic tone disappeared, along with the savagely satiric effects that were one of the poet's weaknesses. Some of the later poems depend less on rhetorical description and more on dramatic speech; their wholes have escaped from the hypnotic bondage of the details. Often the elaborate stanzas have changed into a novel sort of dramatic or narrative couplet, run-on but with heavily stressed rhymes. A girl's nightmare, in the late "Katherine's Dream," is clear, open, and speech-like, compared to the poet's own descriptive meditation in an earlier work like "Christmas at Black Rock." ⟨. . .⟩

It is unusually difficult to say which are the best poems in *Lord Weary's Castle*: several are realized past changing, successes that vary only in scope and intensity—others are poems that almost any living poet would be pleased to have written. But certainly some of the best things in the book are "Colloquy in Black Rock," "Between the Porch and the Altar," the first of the two poems that compose "The Death of the Sheriff," and "Where the Rainbow Ends"; "The Quaker Graveyard at Nantucket" and "At the Indian Killer's Grave" have extremely good parts; some other moving, powerful, and unusual poems are "Death from Cancer," "The Exile's Return," "Mr. Edwards and the Spider," and "Mary Winslow"—and I hate to leave entirely unmentioned poems like "After the Surprising Conversions," "The Blind Leading the Blind," "The Drunken Fisherman," and "New Year's Day."

When I reviewed Mr. Lowell's first book I finished by saying, "Some of the best poems of the next years ought to be written by him." The appearance of *Lord Weary's Castle* makes me feel less like Adams or Leverrier than like a rain-maker who predicts rain and gets a flood which drowns everyone in the country. One or two of these poems, I think, will be read as long as men remember English.—RANDALL JARRELL, "From the Kingdom of Necessity" (1947), *Poetry and the Age* (1953), 1955, pp. 188–99

I am, and have been for some years, particularly interested in Robert Lowell's mind and work. He is now in Italy, and spent a week or more in Rome in the autumn, when I saw him almost every day. I think that he is a good deal like Rimbaud, or like what Rimbaud might have become if he had remained devoted to his poetic genius. There are dark and troubled depths in them both, with the same gift for lurid and mysterious images; but Lowell has had more tragic experiences and a more realistic background, strongly characterised. In these London articles ⟨in the *Times Literary Supplement*⟩ he is highly spoken of, and although he is not a person about whose future we can be entirely confident, it may well turn out to be brilliant. —GEORGE SANTAYANA, Letter to John Hall Wheelock (Jan. 30, 1951), *The Letters of George Santayana*, ed. Daniel Cory, 1955, pp. 406–7

In his new book ⟨*Mills of the Kavanaughs*⟩ Robert Lowell gives us six first-rate poems of which we may well be proud. As usual he has taken the rhyme-track for his effects. We shall now have rhyme again for a while, rhymes completely missing the incentive. The rhymes are necessary to Mr. Lowell. He must, to his mind, appear to surmount them.

An unwonted sense of tragedy coupled with a formal fixation of the line, together constitute the outstanding character of the title poem. It is as though, could he break through, he might surmount the disaster.

When he does, when he does under stress of emotion break through the monotony of the line, it never goes far, it is as though he had at last wakened to breathe freely again, you can feel the lines breathing, the poem rouses as though from a trance. Certainly Mr. Lowell gets his effects with admirable economy of means.

In this title poem, a dramatic narrative played out in a Maine village, Mr. Lowell appears to be restrained by the lines; he appears to *want* to break them. And when the break comes, tentatively, it is toward some happy recollection, the tragedy intervening when this is snatched away and the lines close in once more—as does the story: the woman playing solitaire in the garden by her husband's flag-draped grave. She dreams of the past, of the Abnaki Indians, the aborigines, and of how, lying prone in bed beside her husband, she was ravished in a dream.

Of the remaining five poems, "Her Dead Brother" is most succinct in the tragic mood that governs them all, while the lyric, "The Fat Man in the Mirror" (after Werfel) lifts the mood to what playfulness there is—as much as the mode permits: a tragic realization of time lost, peopled by "this pursey terror" that is "not I." The man is torn between a wish and a discipline. It is a violently sensual and innocent ego that without achievement (the poem) must end in nothing but despair.

Is the poet New England—or what otherwise is his heresy (of loves possessed only in dreams) that so bedevils him? At the precise moment of enjoyment she hears "My husband's Packard crunching up the drive." It is the poet's struggle to ride over the tragedy to a successful assertion—or is it his failure?—that gives the work its undoubted force.

Shall I say I prefer a poet of broader range of feeling? Is it when the restraints of the rhyme make the man restless and he drives through, elbows the restrictions out of the way that he becomes distinguished or when he fails?

It is to assert love, not to win it that the poem exists. If the poet is defeated it is then that he most triumphs, love is most proclaimed! the Abnakis are justified, their land repossessed in dreams. Kavanaugh, waking his wife from her passionate embraces, attempts to strangle her, that she, like Persephone, may die to be queen. He doesn't kill her, the tragedy lying elsewhere.

The tragedy is that the loss is poignantly felt, come what may: dream, sisterhood, sainthood—the violence in "Falling Asleep Over the *Aeneid*"; "Mother Maria Theresa"; "David and Bathsheba in the Public Garden," excellent work. What can one wish more?—WILLIAM CARLOS WILLIAMS, "In a Mood of Tragedy: *The Mills of the Kavanaughs*" (1951), *Selected Essays*, 1954, pp. 324–25

⟨*Life Studies*⟩ is a curious mixture, not only of the best and worst poems he has had in print, but of completely different kinds of writing. It is in four parts. The first consists of four poems both recognizably and unrecognizably in the "Lowell style." They read, in fact, like parodies. The familiar bumps and grinds communicate no passion, and the poems are like the work of a slavish and unimaginative disciple. The second part of the book consists of a fragment of autobiography, which is certainly superior to the average *New Yorker* account of childhood but inferior to the first chapter of Henry Adams. It is here, I suppose, because it provides a background to some of the poems that follow. The third and fourth sections contain the interesting departure in subject-matter and style which is so surprising. The attitude of most critics I have seen is: this is not what we are used to from Lowell, so let us play safe by saying that it *may* lead to great poetry. I'm not sure that they will "lead to" great poetry, but some of the poems are remarkably perceptive and fresh in themselves.

Obviously if his old manner had reached the state of bankruptcy indicated by the first poems in the book, he was right to change. What he has changed to is about as far from Lowellese as can be imagined. It is unassertive and relaxed—at times so relaxed that we feel the poem could do with a bit of tightening up. But oddly enough the virtues of these new poems are similar to those of the poets I have been discussing earlier in this review: he is modest, he is literal, he is even charming (and no one could have called the *old* Lowell charming). The new poems vary a great deal in quality, from the catalogues of trivial autobiographical details, rambling and without unity, to the very moving statements about his personal situation which we find in "Man and Wife".

> Tamed by *Miltown*, we lie on Mother's bed;
> the rising sun in war paint dyes us red;
> in broad daylight her gilded bed-posts shine,
> abandoned, almost Dionysian.

He speaks of the past, then returns to the present—

> Now twelve years later, you turn your back.
> Sleepless, you hold
> your pillow to your hollows like a child;
> your old-fashioned tirade—
> loving, rapid, merciless—
> breaks like the Atlantic Ocean on my head.

Partly what I admire here is the absence of vices: it is honest and clear, with little attempt at any rhetoric but the simplest; it risks—and sometimes falls into—flatness with its rather loose prosy style. And yet it does have a positive virtue, and so do such poems as "For Sale," "Home after Three Months Away," and "Skunk Hour." The virtue is that of describing a human experience so that it is recognizable and at the same time has a certain meaning. Perhaps the very flatness serves to convince us.—THOM GUNN, "Excellence and Variety," *YR*, Sept. 1959, pp. 304–5

I am not an authoritative critic of my own poems, except in the most pressing and urgent way. I have spent hundreds and hundreds of hours shaping, extending and changing hopeless or defective work. I lie on a bed staring, crossing out, writing in, crossing out what was written in, again and again, through days and weeks. Heavenly hours of absorption and idleness . . . intuition, intelligence, pursuing my ear that knows not what it says. In time, the fragmentary and scattered limbs become by a wild extended figure of speech, something living . . . a person.

I know roughly what I think are my better poems, and more roughly and imperfectly why I think they are; and roughly too, which are my worst and where they fail. I have an idea how my best fall short. To have to state all this systematically, and perhaps with controversial argument, would be a prison sentence to me. It would be an exposure. But which is one's good poem? Is it a translation? Can one write something that will sing on for years like the sirens, and not know it?

Reading other critics on me, as I have the pleasure of doing here, gives me the surprise of seeing my poems through eyes that are not mine. Younger, older . . . refreshingly different and perhaps keener eyes . . . mercifully through the eyes of another, for a poem changes with each inspection. Variability is its public existence. Yet variety has limits; no one could call *Macbeth* or my "Quaker Graveyard" hilarious minuets. That would take an insensately amusing theorist.

Politics? We live in the sunset of Capitalism. We have thundered nobly against its bad record all our years, yet we cling to its vestiges, not just out of greed and nostalgia, but for our intelligible survival. Is this what makes our art so contradictory, muddled and troubled? We are being proven in a sort of secular purgatory; there is no earthly paradise on the horizon. War, nuclear bombs, civil gangsterism, race, woman—the last has always been the writer's most unavoidable, though not only, subject, one we are too seriously engaged in to be fair, or . . . salvationists.

It seems our insoluble lives sometimes come clearer in writing. This happens rarely because most often skill and passion are lacking, and when these are not lacking it happens rarely because the goddess Fortuna grudgingly consents. It is easier to write good poems than inspired lines.

*Influences:* I assume this is a live subject. When I began to publish, I wrote literally under the rooftree of Allen Tate. When I imitated him, I believed I was imitating the muse of poetry. When I erred, I failed, or accidentally forced myself to be original. Later, I was drawn to William Carlos Williams and Elizabeth Bishop. I can't say how much I hope I learned. Yet I differed so in temperament and technical training (particularly with Williams) that nothing I wrote could easily be confused with their poems. How many poets I wish I could have copied, the Shakespeare of *The Winter's Tale*, the Wordsworth of the "Ruined Cottage," the Blake of "Truly my Satan . . .", the Pound of the best Pisan Cantos. Baudelaire? Hardy? Maybe I have. The large poet of the nineteenth century who attracts and repels us is Robert Browning. Who couldn't he use, Napoleon III, St. John, Cardinal Manning, Caliban? He set them in a thousand meters. Nor was his ear deficient—take the opening of "Andrea del Sarto," hundreds of lines of "Christmas Eve," all of the "Householder," most of "Mr. Sludge the Medium." And yet Browning's idiosyncratic robustness scratches us, and often his metrical acrobatics are too good. One wishes one could more often see him plain, or as he might have been rewritten by some master novelist, Samuel Butler or George Eliot, though not in her Italian phase. Yet perhaps Browning's poems will outlast much major fiction. Meanwhile he shames poets with the varied human beings he could scan, the generosity of his ventriloquism.

Looking over my *Selected Poems*, about thirty years of writing, my impression is that the thread that strings it together is my autobiography, it is a small-scale *Prelude*, written in many different styles and with digressions, yet a continuing story—still wayfaring. A story of what? Not the "growth of a poet's mind." Not a lesson and example to be handed to the student. Yet the mind must eventually age and grow, or the story would be a still-life, the pilgrimage of a zombi. My journey is always stumbling on the unforeseen and even unforeseeable. From year to year, things remembered from the past change almost more than the present.

Those mutilating years are often lenient of art . . . If only one's selected poems could keep their figure like Madame Bovary!

I haven't said what I wished to write in poems, the discordant things I've tried. It isn't possible, is it? When I was working on *Life Studies*, I found I had no language or meter that would allow me to approximate what I saw or remembered. Yet in prose I had already found what I wanted, the conventional style of autobiography and reminiscence. So I wrote my autobiographical poetry in a style I thought I had discovered in Flaubert, one that used images and ironic or amusing particulars. I did all kinds of tricks with meter and the avoidance of meter. When I didn't have to bang words into rhyme and count, I was more nakedly dependent on rhythm. After this in the *Union Dead*, I used the same style but with less amusement, and with more composition and stanza-structure. Each poem was meant to stand by itself. This stronger structure would probably have ruined *Life Studies*. Which would have lost its novelistic flow. Later on in *For the Union Dead*, free

verse subjects seemed to melt away, and I found myself back in strict meter, yet tried to avoid the symbols and heroics of my first books. After that I wrote a long sequence in Marvell's eight line four foot couplet stanza. God knows why, except that it seemed fit to handle national events. Indeed the stanza was a Godsent task that held me almost breathing couplets all one summer and deep into the next autumn. Shine compensated for the overcompression. For six years I wrote unrhymed blank verse sonnets. They had the eloquence at best of iambic pentameter, and often the structure and climaxes of sonnets, with one fraction of the fourteen lines balanced against the remaining fraction. Obscurity and confusion came when I tried to cram too much in the short space. Quite often I wasn't obscure or discontinuous. I had a chance such as I had never had before, or probably will again, to snatch up and verse the marvelous varieties of the moment. I think perfection (I mean outward coherence not inspiration) was never so difficult. Since then, I have been writing for the last three years in unrhymed free verse. At first I was so unused to this meter, it seemed like tree-climbing. It came back—gone now the sonnet's cramping and military beat. What I write almost always comes out of the pressure of some inner concern, temptation or obsessive puzzle. Surprisingly, quite important things may get said. But sometimes what is closest to the heart has no words but stereotypes. Stereotypes are usually true, but never art. Inspired lines from nowhere roam through my ears . . . to make or injure a poem. All my poems are written for catharsis; none can heal melancholia or arthritis.

I pray that my progress has been more than recoiling with satiation and disgust from one style to another, a series of rebuffs. I hope there has been increase of beauty, wisdom, tragedy, and all the blessings of this consuming chance.
—ROBERT LOWELL, "After Enjoying Six or Seven Essays on Me," *Salm*, Spring 1977, pp. 112–15

The power and scope of poetry depend upon individual poets, what they are prepared to expect from it and how they are prepared to let it happen or to make it happen in their lives. Robert Lowell was exemplary in his dedication and achievement, and if there was some disagreement and some disappointment among his readers about the direction his gift took in *Notebook* and its progeny, there was never any doubt about the integrity and passion with which he pursued his artistic ambitions. There was a nineteenth-century sturdiness about the career. He was a master, obstinate and conservative in his belief in the creative spirit, yet contrary and disruptive in his fidelity to his personal intuitions and experiences.

There was a stylistic drama being played out all through his work. There was perhaps a conflict between his love of literature and his sense of his times, between his predilection for the high rhetorical modes of poetry and the age's preference for the democratic and the demotic. When, for example, I talked to him about that last buoyant poem in *The Dolphin*, the one beginning 'My dolphin, you only guide me by surprise', he said, in a self-deprecatory way, 'Oh, set-piece, set-piece', as if its self-contained energy, its finish and lift-off, were old hat. He did not really believe that, I think, but at that moment he was standing up for life against art, implicitly defending the bulk and flux of the less finished work that constituted the whole sequence.

That fourteen-line stanza or blank sonnet which he used compulsively during the years after *Near the Ocean* was an attempt to get nearer the quick of life, to cage the minute. Yet Lowell was not essentially a poet of the present tense: he was a looker before and after, a maker, a plotter, closer to Ben Jonson than to D. H. Lawrence. The annotations of *Notebook* were always straining away from the speed and particularity of their occasions and pining for the condition of meditation. Was there a 'misalliance'—a word he uses forcefully in *Day by Day*—between the gift and the work it was harnessed to do? One is reluctant to say yes in face of the gigantic effort, the pile-up of magnificent things he brought off within the general plan, the honesty and daring with which he lived through private and public trauma in the late sixties and early seventies, and the boldness with which he wrote them out—but finally and reluctantly, yes is the answer.

One is all the surer of this on reading the best poems in *Day by Day*. Here he abandoned the arbitrary fourteen-line template to which he had been cutting his poetic cloth; the poems are in a variety of verse paragraphs and stanza forms, freed but not footless, following the movement of the voice, sometimes speaking formally, often intimately, occasionally garrulously. But the reader is kept in the company of flesh and blood. We are always being told something interesting or sorrowful even when the manner of the telling falls short of whatever we recognize to be his level best.

*Day by Day* might have been subtitled 'love songs in age', although this would not cover some of the more agonizing personal pieces, such as 'Visitors'—they arrived to take him to the mental institution: 'Where you are going, Professor, you won't need your Dante'—or the unrelenting poem about his mother called 'Unwanted', or the poem about his school days, 'St. Mark's, 1933', which has the coarse strength of a graffito. These and other poems crowd the book with specific autobiographical cries, yet I believe that the definitive poems are ones that conduct all his turbulence and love into a fiction or along the suggestions of an image—'Ulysses and Circe', for example, or the marvellous poem centred on Van Eyck's portrait of the Arnolfini Marriage and entitled simply 'Marriage':

> They are rivals in homeliness and love;
> her hand lies like china in his,
> her other hand
> is in touch with the head of her unborn child.
> They wait and pray,
> as if the airs of heaven
> that blew on them when they married
> were now a common visitation,
> not a miracle of lighting
> for the photographer's sacramental instant.

There is a received literary language shimmering behind that writing and its simplicity and amplitude recall Pound's dictum that the natural object is always the adequate symbol. The feeling, being a bloom off the things presented, does not have to be stated, or restated. Lowell here attains what he calls in 'Epilogue', another of the book's definitive poems, 'the grace of accuracy':

> Pray for the grace of accuracy
> Vermeer gave to the sun's illumination
> stealing like the tide across a map
> to his girl solid with yearning.
> We are poor passing facts
> warned by that to give
> each figure in the photograph
> his living name.

The intimation of mortality in that last cadence is typical of many other moments in the book when a sad, half-resigned autumnal note enters and nowhere with more typical riddling force than in the poem for his son Sheridan:

> Past fifty, we learn with surprise and a sense
> of suicidal absolution
> that what we intended and failed
> could never have happened—
> and must be done better.

Lowell's bravery was different from the bravery of John Berryman or Sylvia Plath, with whom his name has often been joined. They swam away powerfully into the dark swirls of the unconscious and the drift towards death, but Lowell resisted that, held fast to conscience and pushed deliberately towards self-mastery. His death makes us read this book with a new tenderness towards the fulfilments and sufferings of the life that lies behind it and with renewed gratitude for the art that he could not and would not separate from that life. It is not as braced and profiled as, say, *Life Studies*; rather the profile has turned to us, full face, close, kindly, anxious, testing—a husband's face, a father's, a child's, a patient's, above all a poet's.—SEAMUS HEANEY, "Full Face: Robert Lowell" (1978), *Preoccupations: Selected Prose 1968–1978*, 1980, pp. 221–24

---

## JOHN BERRYMAN
### From "Robert Lowell and Others" (1947)
### *The Freedom of the Poet*
#### 1976, pp. 286–92

In some very serious sense there is no competition either on Parnassus or on the hard way up there. Darley, that is, with *Nepenthe* and a lyric or so, is as good as Keats. Ransom was probably wrong both in theory and practice when he concluded an unfriendly study of *The Waste Land*, many years ago, with the remark that there was not room in the pantheon for both Wordsworth and Eliot, and he thought the prior occupant of the seat would dispute it stoutly; a position, no doubt abandoned since, which I recall to illustrate what can never receive illustration enough, namely, the difficulty and uncertainty of contemporary judgment. But there is another sense in which it is sometimes worth saying that work like Keats's demonstrates that work like Darley's doesn't even exist. You can find in Keats everything you can find in Darley, and you find it with transfigured power, and you find many other things as well. Whatever the devotion of a lesser poet, it may be put as the difference between the *occasional* and the *thematic*, between the making of a few fine poems and the conversion of a whole body of material. If the first is impressive, the second is oppressive as well, troubling, overwhelming. Now Robert Lowell (in *Lord Weary's Castle*) seems to me not only the most powerful poet who has appeared in England or America for some years, master of a freedom in the Catholic subject without peer since Hopkins, but also, in the terms of this distinction, a thematic poet. His work displays, in high degrees, passion, vista, burden. He looks

> Beyond Charles River to the Acheron
> Where the wide waters and their voyager are one

and when he addresses his Maker there is no device, the verse wheels and enlarges, the man really sounds like a prophet,

> Lord, from the lust and dust thy will destroys
> Raise an unblemished Adam, who will see
> The limbs of the tormented chestnut tree
> Tingle, and hear the March-winds lift and cry:
> "The Lord of Hosts will overshadow us."

Without first-rate qualities, ambition is nothing, a personal disease; but given these qualities, the difference is partly one of ambition. Hardy, for instance, had little and notwithstanding a long and reverent love for Hardy, I think Eliot was right when he observed on the occasion of Yeats's seventieth birthday that Hardy now appeared, what he always was, a minor poet. There is much human development over the sixty years between "Hap" and "He Resolves to Say No More," but little poetic development, nothing comparable to what Lowell has achieved in the two years between his first book and *Lord Weary's Castle*. I should say from the poems that this author's ambition is limitless. Whether he has yet written poems as good as Hardy's best this is no moment for judging, though I think the question will one day come up. What is clear just now is that we have before us a genuine, formidable, various, and active poet; as to which character I put in evidence "The Drunken Fisherman," "The Quaker Graveyard in Nantucket," "The Exile's Return," "At the Indian Killer's Grave," "After the Surprising Conversions," and parts of a dozen other poems.

Readers of the new book will find it very different from *Land of Unlikeness*, though it brings over ten poems from that book, heavily rewritten as a rule. The earlier poems writhed crunched spat against Satan, war, modern Boston, the Redcoats, Babel, Leviathan, Babylon, Sodom. The style was bold, coarse, surexcited, so close in some respects to its models—the Jacobean lyrists, early Milton (as Jarrell pointed out in a perceptive review), Allen Tate as a Roman and polemic writer, Yeats as a dynastic—that it was surprising that one had nevertheless a stormed impression of originality. Lowell avoided by instinct the chief religious influences that might have crushed him, Hopkins, and Eliot, as well as the influence (Auden) that has straitjacketed much talent among men just older than himself; but he began like Eliot and Auden with satire—as most ambitious writers in a society like ours apparently must do. Despite some continuing violence of style, however, and the persistence of sardonic detail, the general effect of *Lord Weary's Castle* is not satirical. It is dramatic, moral, elegiac; and the escape from satire represents a triumph for a talent not essentially satirical. Not only is there nothing here like the tosspot "Christ for Sale," but the whole uncontrolled ferocity of poems like it has disappeared. The best new poems, insofar as they reflect the same interests, develop less from that tone than from the trumpet and the sigh simultaneous in the extraordinary distich quoted in *Partisan Review* by Jarrell:

When the ruined farmer knocked out Abel's brains,
Our Father laid great cities on his soul . . .

I give the lines again because, though the poem they began has been discerningly scrapped, they announce a major theme. Such a writer's symbols are worth examination. I propose that we take seriously both the title and the illustration on the title page, of Cain's second crime (the murder and flight), and see what they come to. The precise cause of Cain's ruin has been lost, but the cause of Lord Weary's—the title comes from the ballad of *Lamkin*—is known: when his castle was finished he refused payment to his mason Lamkin and sailed away, whereupon Lamkin, helped by the false nurse, broke into the castle and destroyed his wife and babe. Lord Weary's castle is a house of ingratitude, failure of obligation, crime and punishment. Possibly Cain did not bring *enough* of his first fruits, or brought them grudgingly: "I canna pay you, Lamkin, / Unless I sell my land," which he will not do. Later, as the stabbed babe cries in death, Lamkin calls up to its mother, "He winna still, lady, / For a' his father's land"; and the wandering blood of Cain cannot repent. Besides frequent references to Cain, the stories may be deliberately juxtaposed in a sonnet based on Rilke's "Letzter Abend" ("Wearily by the broken altar, Abel," etc.; though *wearily* is taken from MacIntyre's translation, which other details of the poem repeat, it must have been retained for a reason). But of course the myths are suggestive not symmetrical. Thus, Cain's guilt rings through the war poems; the nurse is Eve, who, letting in the Devil, brought vengeance on Adam; but Lamkin, sometimes the Serpent who

murdered innocence (at the ballad's end he and the nurse are executed), mainly is the Lord, who enters with sharp sword the faithless house He built.

Therefore, most of the thematic poems occur in Hell or ante-Hell, the world "that spreads in pain," the rich house we use without paying for; which the defrauded One will enter suddenly. Already with the capitalist of an early poem, here revised into "Christmas Eve under Hooker's Statue," Lowell had begun to imagine characters moving about in it, but for the most part in the first book he simply abused it. By a shift toward the dramatic which is one of the large features of his development, he is now peopling it. (It is to be noted that Lowell is an *objective* poet; except as a Christian or a descendant he scarcely appears in his poems.) The most elaborate example is a dramatic sequence "Between the Porch and the Altar," at the end of which, with astonishing style, he damns the mother-fixed adulterous drunken protagonist,

the Day
Breaks with its lightning on the man of clay,
*Dies amara a valde*. Here the Lord
Is Lucifer in harness: hand on sword,
He watches me for Mother, and will turn
The bier and baby-carriage where I burn.

The Lord has often this aspect in these poems. If reproached with it, the poet might reply in the words of the Katherine of this poem: "The winter sun is pleasant, and it warms / My heart with love for others, but the swarms / Of penitents have dwindled"; or say that he had taken John Davidson's impressive advice, "Enlarge your Hell; preserve it in repair; / Only a splendid Hell keeps Heaven fair." Still one wonders whether he would have allowed the piercing, non-formulary salvation imagined by the Balzac of *Christ in Flanders*, and one is surprised that, with two poems based on writings by the prodigious Edwards, he passed over "Sinners in the Hands of an Angry God."

But the poems are rich with nonformulary life, and Lowell has other religious tones also.

John, Matthew, Luke and Mark,
Gospel me to the Garden, let me come
Where Mary twists the warlock with her flowers—
Her soul a bridal chamber fresh with flowers
And her whole body an ecstatic womb
As through the trellis peers the sudden Bridegroom.

He is weakest on the whole when near a substance-model, he seems to rely on the model as well as on himself, and his evergreen ingenuity gets too-free play; yet even the poems with immediate sources show, together with their defects, qualities thoroughly rare and valuable. (About a third of the new poems have direct literary or historical sources, transformed under his imagination.) His "Ghost," based on a beautiful elegy of Propertius (iv. 7) not touched by Pound, is not by some distance as fresh delicate firm as Pound's "Homage," but it will stand the comparison without looking idiotic—a sufficient compliment. Lowell is as individual; less energetic with more appearance of energy (that is, higher keyed—*beat*, to take an amusing detail, rendering equally *effugit* and *pelle*); more original in the respect that he is indifferent where Propertius is magnificent, best where nothing remarkable is happening in the Latin or he is inventing; more faithful, only transposing lines 49 ff. and 73 ff.; less flexible; much less witty; as capable as Pound of a dense memorable detail, "At cock-crow Charon checks us in his log." Some of these poems are "imitations" in the eighteenth-century sense, and despite their heightened tone should perhaps be judged by a special standard. More independent is the second Edwards piece, "After the Surprising

Conversions," which is written in that phoenix metre, heroic couplet, the best run-on couplets I have seen in a long time:

> In the latter part of May
> He cut his throat. And though the coroner
> Judged him delirious, soon a noisome stir
> Palsied the village. At Jehovah's nod
> Satan seemed more let loose amongst us: God
> Abandoned us to Satan . . . / We were undone.
> The breath of God had carried out a planned
> And sensible withdrawal from this land.

Set the simplicity and manliness of this poem beside the mysterious frenzy of "The Drunken Fisherman" or the drenched magnificence of "The Quaker Graveyard" and you will observe a talent whose ceiling is invisible.

But I don't wish to make a noise about Lowell, reviewers in other channels being equipped for this, and popularity in the modern American culture having proved for other authors not yet physically dead a blessing decidedly sinister. One certainly wants to see fine poems honoured and read; and "I say it deliberately and before God," Hopkins wrote to Bridges, "that fame, the being known, though in itself one of the most dangerous things to man, is nevertheless the true and appointed air, element, and setting of genius and its works." The secular dangers are to candour and development, perhaps to fellow feeling, considering the kind of honour a comics culture can confer; self-consciousness is the general reef. Luckily Lowell is so intense tough unreasonable that he will probably be safe. I will only make a historical remark. The author of a very interesting leading article recently in *The Times Literary Supplement*, taking *The Orators* as the key book of the thirties, mentions in his conclusion the fact that writers of the period, young and old, "preferred to precision of design and execution an approximate; a general feeling arose that careful finish was in some way base . . . the brilliant improvisation became a standard instead of an adventure." This is so just as scarcely to need illustration; you can see it best, after Auden's early books, in the beautiful work done by Delmore Schwartz at the decade's end in America—to name one line of corroboration, Blackmur hung his review of *In Dreams Begin Responsibilities* on the word "improvised." Of course Auden himself reacted at once (even in *Look, Stranger* regular forms predominate), as Eliot's 1920 volume, under the influence of Gautier, reacted against "Prufrock"; and there have not been wanting other signs. But Lowell's poetry is the most decisive testimony we have had, I think, of a new period, returning to the deliberate and the formal. In other respects, it is true, the break is incomplete. Our best work is still difficult, allusive, and more or less didactic in intention.

A few technical notes. Lowell uses very heavy rime, and thud metre, spondaic substitution being much commoner than any other; these characteristics alone permit him to indulge frequently and not cripplingly in the hard short runover that generally marks bad poets. He stops as a rule after the first, the seventh, or the ninth syllable. For instance, *each but one* of the nine lines quoted above from "Between the Porch and the Altar" shows caesura after the seventh syllable (the first begins, "and the day"). Perhaps only a master could keep in so narrow an area and make it interesting, but the mastery is as yet certainly very limited. Poets half his size are much more resourceful by way of movement. His ear is not infallible, and this may have something to do with refrain weakness; though repetition, a considerable element in his designs, he handles admirably (see a fine passage on p. 10). What we might call simultaneous repetition-with-variation, or the serious pun, he abounds in, and the examples sometimes sound better than

they are. Thus search guns "nick the slate roofs on the Holsterwall / Where torn-up tilestones crown the victor"; here *crown* is effective, if it is, against the implausibility of one meaning (invest, reward) and the infrequency of the other (fall on, finish off): one leg ought to be firmer. The same wish to crowd meaning is responsible for a good many of the slurred references of which Jarrell complained in the earlier poems, and these continue, now and then confusingly. Direct echoes are rare; "Fear with its fingered stopwatch" remembers Auden's "Fear gave his watch no look"—a later "Fear, / The yellow chirper, beaks its cage" is original and good. Considering the complication of his tradition, the book is notably fresh and consistent. Sonnets, for whatever reasons, tend to be inferior to other forms. The chief danger for a writer so dense is obviously turgidity, and in the sonnets it is least successfully avoided. Whether Lowell owes anything to a poet similarly "packed," Dylan Thomas, it is not easy to say, and so he cannot owe much; there is some common ground in diction for movement (lurch, blunder, lumber, sidle, heave, etc.) and an illimitable barrier in religious attitudes; like Thomas's early similarities to Hart Crane, whom he had not read, I set down to temperament and tradition such resemblance as there is. Finally, despite a good deal of international reference, perhaps inevitable now in the work of a sophisticated poet, and despite some objection I feel to the very obscure word "American," used chiefly as it is by canters and radio announcers, nevertheless it seems worthwhile saying that Lowell's poetry is deeply a local product.

## JOHN BAYLEY
### "Robert Lowell: The Poetry of Cancellation"

*London Magazine*, June 1966, pp. 76–85

> All that grave weight of America
> Cancelled! Like Greece and Rome
> The future in ruins!
>                    (Louis Simpson)

In attempting the appraisal of a modern poet the critic does well to remember Auden's reminder to his tribe—'X's work is more important than anything I can say about it'—but such a proviso leaves one still free to ask just how and why Robert Lowell's poetry is important. For where a living poet's status is concerned, the word is apt to be little more than the hand-out of a public relations man, retained by a society which supposes it must have 'important' poetry as it must have important breakthroughs in space travel and cybernetics.

And much of Lowell's early poetry lends itself to this public notion of importance, on the score of which Hugh Staples, who wrote the first critical study of Lowell, called 'The Quaker Graveyard in Nantucket' 'a major poem of sustained brilliance, which challenges comparison with the great elegies of the language'. Of this judgment one can only say, and with confidence, that it is not true. The critic has assumed a pretension and mistaken it for an achievement. Another book on Lowell,[1] which has just appeared, also assumes a real size and importance in the inflated verse of the early collections, and reverently sorts through the frenetically but meaninglessly cunning entanglements of its religious imagery. This is importance as the D. Phils have it. What in fact is extraordinary is that the poet who wrote so much resounding stuff could also have written the remarkable poems of the later volumes, which neither critic sees as contributing much to this phantasmal 'importance' of Lowell. It is on this point that criticism should concentrate.

The early poetry is a signal instance of what T. S. Eliot

called 'a poetry that is purely verbal, in that the whole poem will give us more of the same thing, an accumulation rather than a real development of thought and feeling'. It creates no world into which we can move, explore, discover. And the creation of such a world can be a real criterion of an important poetry, a world like that of Eliot himself—or Auden—a world which our own consciousness can inhabit and find out more about each time the poetry is re-read. But such a poet's world is necessarily a retrospective thing. When it has become fully visible to us, and livable in, it has already receded a little into the comfort of history. The poet himself may not have left it yet, but in a sense he is already in the past when we see how to live with him. It *may* be only a question of time before we see how to live with Lowell, but I doubt it. I think the real and radical importance of his best poems is of a different kind—a kind we can diagnose historically in *The Phoenix and the Turtle*, in a sonnet of Wyatt or a lyric of Blake, no less than in such a poet as Baudelaire—the importance of a poetry which does not create a world of its own in its age, but looks out.

Lowell's poetry looks out in an unexpected direction. It yearns towards non-existence. If a poetry can be said to have the death-wish, it has it. As his poetry has transformed itself it has perfected a capacity for self-extinction. The words of the early poems lie about helplessly, turgid and swollen: the words of the later ones achieve a crispness of cancellation, leaving behind them only a kind of acrid exhaust smell. A lot of *poets*, no doubt, have had a death-wish, but none have entailed it by method on their poetry—their poetry is on the contrary an insurance against the extinction they may personally seem to crave. The contingency, tedium, disgust enshrined in much modern poetry—Auden's suburb 'where helpless babies and telephones gabble untidy cries'; Eliot's 'their only monument the asphalt road and a thousand lost golf-balls'—these become in fact a monument, before which the poet's audience can stand in satisfaction and intimacy.

The cancellation, or alienation, so marked in Lowell's best poems severs this bond of intimacy, and in so doing emphasises how much we have come to expect it in modern writing. The writer alienated from society, the creator of madness, meaninglessness, the extreme situation—he is indeed a commonplace today, but the greater the alienation he describes the more uncomfortably close he comes to *us*, the reader, the more he depends on a personal relation with us. Like a drunk in a bar this author needs his finger in our buttonhole—the further off he is from the social and moral world the more urgent is his need to share his alienation with the reader. It is Lowell's achievement to have successfully alienated *the poem itself*, to have made it as unaware of us as the suicide caught by the camera flash. And this seems to me the real thing. It gives *Life Studies* and many of the later poems their quality of nicking the advanced edge of time, the moment that burns us before the unmeaning future and the numbed unordered past.

Professor Fiedler, in *Partisan Review*, has associated Lowell with Messrs Burroughs, Ginsberg, Maclure, etc., because, as he said, the young respond to the madness in him and associate it with the same drugged or alienated mental states celebrated by their other favourites. If indeed the young do so they are missing the point, which here means missing the style. The camaraderie of alienation is not essentially different from the camaraderie of surfing or stock-car racing: it has the same cosy clubbable quality; it is the fashion in common. For all that their subject is alienation and the states induced by drugs, the writings of Burroughs and the rest share the artless and rather pathetic cosiness of the campus magazine. And this

togetherness is not really very far from more conventional kinds of togetherness in American writing, that of the 'poetry workshop', of the neat, delicate, civilised shoal poetry in which recent American schools have excelled, and which we find in collections like the Faber *Five American Poets* and the Penguin *Contemporary American Poetry*.

Like the Tribe of Ben, or certain Japanese schools, these poets are not so much individuals as a way of life, and their poems a way of writing poetry suited to that way of life. Each poem is perfectly self-satisfied, which does not mean complacent. It creates a moment of being which is designed to last, and which appeals, in that ambition, to what we cherish as durable moments in our own mode of being. A poem by William Stafford, for instance, 'Travelling through the Dark', admirably creates such a weighty moment. The poet driving on a mountain road sees a dead deer, and alights to remove it in case it causes an accident. Finding it had been a female about to give birth, and that the foetus is still alive, he stands in indecision—a moment solicitously registered:

> I thought hard for us all—my only swerving—
> Then pushed her over the edge into the river.

It is the claim of this well-written poetry that it 'thinks hard for us all,—the phrase well suggests its outlook and method—but it does so with extreme self-consciousness. Though the poetry is in a sense so homogeneous, its method means that each poet attempts, almost embarrassingly, to establish his own individuality with the reader.[2]

And it is just this self-consciousness which is lacking in Lowell. Though his best poems seem constructed from the same sorts of material as theirs—moments in a considered life, life studies in fact—nothing in them is making this appeal to us. When Lowell says in 'Skunk Hour':

> I myself am hell
> Nobody's there . . .

we believe him, not because he is asserting it to us, but because this moment when we read does indeed seem the last moment before there is nobody there, not even the poem:

> One dark night,
> My Tudor Ford climbed the hill's skull,
> I watched for love cars. Lights turned down,
> they lay together, hull to hull,
> where the graveyard shelves on the town . . .
> My mind's not right.

The bald assertion, 'my mind's not right', seems neither less nor more than the fact. 'What use is my sense of humour?' asks Lowell in another of these poems. What indeed? But he is not asking us. Reliable old concepts like irony—bonds between poet and reader which sustain the poem on its journey into the reader's mind—fall flat on their faces here. So does the shared and knowing allusion. *One dark night* . . . yes, Lowell is no doubt recalling the first line of a famous poem by St John of the Cross, but the connection gives us none of the usual pleasure to make, since it seems to have given him none to select it. And for all that the lovers are subsumed into their cars, the human into the mechanical, there is no insistent and reassuring note of misanthropy. These are life studies in the sense that life is the thing that happens before death, no more than that. They could only have been written in America today, because they afford a peculiarly American style of cancellation, a refusal of all that America has stipulated, stood for, taken for granted. And stylistically the impressive thing is that this refusal, this cancellation, is not said by the poem but *is* the poem.

It is all the more singular because these poems appear, on the face of it, to build up a whole world of intimacy with Lowell and with his family and provenance, his father and mother, grandfather and grandmother, their incomes, estates, and social standing. We hear of the poet's own wife and child, job and friends. The ease with which these facts are related is itself remarkable, and indeed probably unique in American literature—it reminds us of the aristocratic simplicity of an earlier class of English memoirists, and of Tolstoy and Aksakov in Russia. It beguiled the first reviewers into enthusing over the poem's 'touching' and 'human' quality. But this was surely to miss the point. The point is that these simple intimate things—all involuntary, as it might be, with the common good of life—come before us here in a context of total alienation. Commander Lowell, like his son, is caught by the camera just before hitting the ground. And the facts of his life—how at the age of nineteen he was 'old man' of a gunboat on the Yangtse, and left Lafcadio Hearn's 'Glimpses of Unfamiliar Japan', a present from his mother, 'under an open pothole in a storm'—these facts do not come before us redolent with the Betjeman-ish charm and queer pathos of a family past; they are nothing but the facts. When Lowell tells us:

> Father's death was abrupt and unprotesting.
> His vision was still twenty-twenty.
> After a morning of anxious, repetitive smiling,
> his last words to mother were:
> 'I feel awful.'

he is not being smart. Smartness, like irony and humour, depends upon an eye kept on the reader that is here kept staringly on the object. It is almost frightening when Lowell makes a claim which in another poet would sound coy:

> 'My Grandfather found
> his grandchild's fogbound solitudes
> sweeter than human society.'

No doubt it was so. The word 'human' ambushes us with a glassy stare, seemingly unaware of its own charge of meaning. If it is loaded and pointed it contrives utterly to conceal the fact, and that is what one means by style in Lowell. If there *is* a moving quality in these poems—and in a muffled way there can be—it is that of a drama without an audience, even that of the poet himself. We have the intimation of a human life in a state of shock, remembering, like Wordsworth's Old Man, 'the importance of his theme'—or at least its human potentiality—'but feeling it no longer'.

Lowell has managed to freeze into the style of these poems the utter detachment of the mad, and he may be the first poet to have done this systematically. It might itself appear a characteristically modern achievement—certainly Clare, writing in the Northamptonshire County Asylum, was as aware as any other poet of the normal 'I and my audience' relation. But so, in many poems, is Lowell; and his sanity then makes one wonder about the rumour that American alienists sometimes actually *help* their patients to go mad, by way of therapy, as the LSD and morphia popularizers proclaim that we should. Perhaps alienation is the logical and coming response to the madness of modern society? For when Lowell is writing *about* himself and his state of mind, instead of compelling the poem to *be* it, he is not only a less good poet but—which makes the transition more painful—inferior in an area in which other modern poets have shown their most specific superiority. Yeats, for instance, can not only be openly rhetorical about himself but can combine, as Lowell cannot, the tone of open rhetoric with the confidence of intimacy. Lowell tries it in a poem which has often been admired, 'Night Sweat':

> My life's fever is soaking in night sweat—
> one life, one writing! But the downward glide
> and bias of existing wrings us dry—
> always inside me is the child who died,
> always inside me is his will to die—

That 'always inside me' couplet is strangely unconvincing, which does not of course mean that Lowell is not telling us the truth as he sees it, but that he cannot tell it in this way. It is mere bow-wow, mere gloss. Instead of extinguishing itself in one of Lowell's multiple acts of poetic suicide the poem lingers limply in the area of mere explanation.

'For the Union Dead' is an ambiguous poem, nearly very fine, but significantly not quite able to carry off the contrast between Lowell himself and the high title's imputation. Yet to take the intention of this title as just a smack at Allen Tate's 'Ode to the Confederate Dead' does not help at all, for satire—even oblique satire—is as little Lowell's *forte* as humour or ironic and Empsonian cosiness. 'What was said by Lincoln, boys, what did he perpend?' . . . no, such a suggestion won't do. Cancellation cannot be imputed: American history cannot be alienated like the poet's own world. Which amounts to saying that Lowell cannot speak on behalf of other people. He himself is as alienated from the dead, and from their hero Colonel Shaw, whom he attempts to celebrate in Whitman-esque lines:

> He rejoices in man's lovely,
> peculiar power to choose life and die

as he is from the 'giant finned cars' of modern America, its 'savage servility'. The tone of denunciation and nostalgia in the poem is not quite real, because these impulses claim an open relation to the traditional human world of value which Lowell's most effective poetry does not and cannot have. Lowell himself, one receives the impression, is a good man, who has the right views on Vietnam and the race problem, who is against sin. But about these things he can only be poetical.

## II

'The man really sounds like a prophet!' exclaimed John Berryman of Lowell's early poetry, apparently without irony. It was just the trouble. Lowell did, and on occasion still does *sound* like a prophet. The thunderous title of his second volume, *Lord Weary's Castle*, aided the effect. It recalls the Scottish ballad of *Lamkin*:

> O Lamkin was a mason good
> As ever built wi' stane.
> He has built Lord Weary's castle
> But payment got he nane.

'America', suggested Berryman, 'is Lord Weary's Castle, the rich house we use without paying for, which the defrauded one will enter suddenly.' It may well be so. But all the gravely incongruous weight of conscience implied—the puritan family's and the Catholic convert's—is mere water under the bridge. Lowell's most ambitious attempt to create a prophetic myth of the American past and present—'The Mills of the Kavanaughs'—is a complete and incoherent failure. He has written no open public prophecies, no *Waste Land* or 'Second Coming'. And one must emphasise again that the notion of him as 'important' in that way is quite misleading. He is not a prophet, but his best poems are in themselves prophetic indications of a state which may be becoming increasingly common in Anglo-American society, the state in which traditional 'feelings' are ceasing to exist, or to have their traditional status assumed—the state in which more and more people come to have knowledge of, even to desire, the symptoms of clinical alienation.

It is this state which Lowell catches, in himself and others. But the 'others' are in fact usually himself, for, as I have suggested, one cannot project madness. Lowell's attempts at a Browning-like seizure of Men and Women (something of a confidence trick in Browning himself) do not come off as creations of outside people but as images of states within the poet. The best are the shortest: 'Katherine's Dream' and the Jonathan Edwards poems extend the thing too far and risk the reader's disbelief in the actuality of the portrait. One of the most superlative is 'To speak of the Woe that is in Marriage':

. . . My hopped-up husband drops his home
    disputes
and hits the street to cruise for prostitutes,
free-lancing out along the razor's edge.
This screwball might kill his wife, then take the
    pledge.
Oh the monotonous meanness of his lust . . .
It's the injustice . . . he is so unjust—
whiskey-blind, swaggering home at five.
My only thought is how to keep alive.
What makes him tick? Each night now I tie
ten dollars and his car-key to my thigh . . .
Gored by the climacteric of his want,
He stalls above me like an elephant.

This is Lowell's style at his most brilliant: style and matter, as in the studies of his own life, are fused into one, wholly effective for the given fact, wholly extinguished where the fact ends. The lightning coherence and bite of the words cannot be and are not intended to be followed into the world of relation and probability (in the marital predicament she claims the lady would scarcely have chosen her thigh as a hiding-place?) but each word makes its precise electrical contact—*lance* and *razor* with *kill*, the seductive *thigh* with the desolating and comic sexual image of the last couplet—and then goes off with an almost audible click. This way of using words in poetry reminds us of Dryden, who never looks towards us, whose vocabulary is always perfect for its context and yet never goes on to create a livable world. That last couplet, with its powerfully Augustan image of the husband *stalling* like a car (we remember the amorous cars of 'Skunk Hour') at the beginning of the end of sexual desire, and *stalled* above his wife like an animal presence—one can almost imagine Dryden flourishing it off as a sample for his bookseller! The alienated aspect of Lowell's genius fits in oddly well with its professional side: in both there is no lingering, no hopeful glance in our direction, only the cancellation of the account when the job is done.

### III

The *Imitations* and the translation of *Phèdre* are done in this spirit, and Dryden would have approved Lowell's words in the preface to *Imitations*. 'I have tried to write live English and to do what my authors would have done if they were writing their poems now and in America.' The older poet who rewrote Virgil and Chaucer would also have been robustly different to the implications of the poems' *not* having been written now and in America. Lowell's success comes from the same assured and business-like confidence: he does not agonize, like most translators, over whether he is getting the precise *nuance*—he rewrites the thing in his own way. None the less, the impulse involved is a destructive one. By the time that Dryden, in *All for Love*, has finished with Cleopatra's barge there is nothing left of Shakespeare's creation. And Lowell exaggerates the mordant brutality of Baudelaire's 'Voyage à Cythère', and the brooding sleep march of Rilke's 'Orpheus', until there is nothing left but a number of insistent words and striking phrases. The implicit has become all too explicit. The destructive process, it is interesting to note, works best with Rimbaud, for it brings out that poet's odd and rather disconcerting extensibility and open-endedness. You *can* tack more

of the same on to Rimbaud—it merely deepens and emphasizes the *dérèglement* which led logically to silence and self-extinction, and which seems in accord with Lowell's own poetic temper.

But with Racine it is a different matter. Lowell tells us himself that he took the English restoration dramatists as his model here, and that he has tried to give Racine's lines 'speed and flare'. In this he has succeeded admirably. But again one cannot but feel the unspoken wish to pulverize the original, to convert it into mere energy as an engine converts its fuel. I take it that the triumph of Racine is somehow to have admitted the predestinate obsessions of lust, and the misery of monstrous longings, within the strict limits of a classic poetry; and that the miracle of the thing is its exhibited control. Venus is suggested in all the grossness of her power, but she is never allowed to disturb the Apollonian clarity of speech. In destroying this balance Lowell destroys dignity. 'Frothing with desire', his Phèdre is almost as energetically ludicrous a figure as the poisoned Nourmahal in Dryden's *Aurungzebe*. She calls on Hippolytus—in a phrase which mocks the simmering coolness of the Racinian confrontation,—for his 'sword's spasmodic final inch'; and converts the unearthly sorrow of Phèdre's statement about the youthful pair:

'Tous les jours se levaient clairs et sereins pour eux!'

into a chatty banality,

'For them each natural impulse was allowed
Each day was summer and without a cloud.'

Does it matter? Not really, for the adaptation is a success in its own right. But it makes one wonder what is Lowell's motive in this way of writing. The tormented confusion of his early poetry, which seemed bent on burying itself and everything else in 'the dark downward and vegetating kingdom', is still strangely apparent in the urge to obliterate 'all that grave weight', the poetic selfhood of the past. One might even suspect an unconscious irony in his statement that he is trying to rewrite these poems now and in America, where the latest film version of some classic reduces the celluloid of its predecessor to literal nothingness. As long ago as 'The Quaker Graveyard' Lowell treated *Moby-Dick* in this way, thrashing Melville to pieces in his own frenzy; and 'For the Union Dead' makes a not dissimilar use of the moving recollections of Colonel Shaw and his regiment by William and Henry James. Lowell's most recent enterprise, three lengthy playscripts based on three short American tales, belabours their slight, strange point until it has yielded up its last drop into obviousness. This is not imitation but execution. One might remember, too, that for all their occasional absurdities and mistranslations the 'imitations' of Pound had none of the destructive background of Lowell's. They carried on, as Eliot did in his poems, the American tradition of cherishing the European past, as fragments to shore against our ruins. Lowell seems to want to add its ruins to our own.

It is all the odder because his poems, at their best, understand so well how to be; and these Imitations are usually saying, and at some length, what their originals are. In them Lowell still seems to be attempting by other means the rhetorical and explanatory side of his poetry which is also its weakest side. However much he is expected to be in America he simply is not a poet of the 'big bow-wow'—he is a big poet who cannot write 'big' poems. Unquestionably his best poems to date are the most seemingly trivial ones, poems which find their precision and their weight in the slightest context; and when he moves us, as in such a poem as 'Man and Wife', he does so unexpectedly and as it were unmeaningfully, as Dryden does in his 'Epistle to Congreve'. In an age when destruction and madness oppress the poet, like every other citizen, Lowell has learnt not to write about these things but to take them on; and he has taken them on with brilliant success and logic in terms of a style which can perfectly *be* its own alienation, if it can be little else.

*Notes*

1. *The Poetic Themes of Robert Lowell*, by Jerome Mazzaro.
2. The doyen of this sort of forthcomingness was probably William Carlos Williams.

## JEROME MAZZARO
### "Lowell after *For the Union Dead*"

*Salmagundi*, Volume 1, Number 4 (1966–67), pp. 57–68

Although it is evident that Robert Lowell's most recent poetry has entered the contexts of a post-Christian world, it is still asking teleological questions. It still wishes to know what man's ultimate purpose is, and it still tends to effect its most jarring evocations by suggesting possible answers in the juxtapositions of immediate experience and historical perspectives. Moreover, since man's ultimate purpose is somehow related or relatable to his origins, it searches out these origins, aware that once the nature of the origins alters, so, too, does man's purpose. From these searches, Lowell's concepts of free will and meaningful action have evolved, and now, as the God-created universe and Christian experience of the early volumes fade into sentimentality and man no longer seeks in his actions to know, love, and serve God, the poetry becomes both the record and moral of their loss. In the most public poems, it shows man's struggle against first a scientific, evolutionary universe and then, in turn, a larger and perhaps more disarming overview of lost religious purpose. Here, as man's origins are nature and chance, his purpose, unhampered by Christian charity, is to extend his dominion over nature and chance so as to insure continued survival. In the more personal poems, where neither origins nor ends can be determined, absurdism is offered. Man finds himself consistently confronted with the circumstance that his experience of things is radically incongruent with the demands that his life have meaning. But the most persuasive force at work is the will of history, the future, working on the will of what from a Christian point of view is ungracious man. It is the irrational will which Arthur Schopenhauer portrayed as coming like supersensible soapbubbles and which man's reason works on to augment and give rationality. This will, which cares nothing for the individual, cherishes the form or species.

In many respects, the acceptance of this Schopenhauerian, post-Christian world with its rejection of the world as illusion and its investment of value in the ideal is prepared for in *For the Union Dead* (1964). Here Lowell first names the masks of the historical and philosophical perspectives which are to oppose on a time-possessed plane his formerly Christian ideal. Each of these masks is modelled after his own nickname Cal, lending a kind of whimsical congruence to both the elements of the juxtapositions. The personal experiences of one Cal evoke the larger perspectives of other historical "Cals." Lowell's choice for the most pervasive of these larger perspectives, the predetermined, damned "Cal," is John Calvin as viewed in his writings through the writings of Jonathan Edwards. He is ostensibly the sinner caught like the spider in the "hands of the Great God" or Josiah Hawley about to take his own life. Lowell chooses for its evolutionary counterpart, Caliban and Robert Browning, and for the absurd man, the perspective of the Roman Emperor Caligula and Albert Camus. The already established nature and function of the

dramatic monologue which Lowell likewise inherits from Browning and his own view of the synthetic nature of the poet's function permit him to speak either as himself or to shift into any of these historical voices with equal integrity and facility.

In *For the Union Dead*, his or his shifting voice reveals at various times the conditions which proclaim that modern man like the predetermined man of Calvinist theology is powerless and foredoomed. There are no worldly answers either to man's isolation or to his problem of suffering. Men die, one poem admits, and they are not happy. All acts of will, like events of physical nature, another insists, are subject to the laws of causation. Because of man's basically passive and mechanical will, a third remarks, once separate laws of man and nature reduce themselves into a single principle. Within the bounds of these combined perspectives, the volume's subject, untouched by grace, becomes the victim of historical determinism, relying upon imagination for the key to his origins and purposes and succumbing compulsively to the same cycles of rot and renewal which have undercut Lowell's once Christian ideal. This ideal, which in its contemplative state was identified with Bernard of Clairvaux and which in its active state, with founders of religious societies like Noah and Aeneas, was able once through grace to escape absorption into such compulsive historical cycles. Likewise, within the bounds of these perspectives, Lowell prepares his readers for the subsequent acceptance of the Schopenhauerian belief that "salvation is the victory over, and the annihilation of, the world, which is nothing; of life, which is suffering; and of the individual ego, which is an illusion."

Typical of the poems which establish these perspectives in the volume and which also point the direction of Lowell's most recent work is "The Neo-Classical Urn." The poem on one level recounts the seemingly senseless destruction of turtles by the young Lowell. The turtles are on a historical level kin of the straggler crab with purple spots which in Browning's "Caliban on Setebos; or, Natural Theology in the Island" Caliban threatens to maim by twisting off one pincer, and which in Lowell's "Florence" the ungracious, Florentine children do actually "throw strangling ashore." With them Lowell introduces for investigation the same Calvinistic determinism, the same interest in natural theology, and the same struggle for existence that Browning offers in his poem. Specifically, both poets seem bent on rejecting the idea of moral law as proposed by Charles Darwin in *The Origin of Species* (1859) and the belief of the American Transcendentalist Theodore Parker that at every stage of human development man has produced a theology to express the highest reaches of his spiritual life.

The protagonists of both the Lowell and Browning poems assume the poses of a Calvinistic God working his wrath and caprice upon the helpless world. Knowledge of this God each protagonist assumes by evidences provided in nature, and each expresses him in the humanized or anthropomorphized manner proposed by Parker. The nature over which each rules is Darwinian. In its continuing struggle for existence, only the most cleverly adapted plants and animals survive. They leave offspring, which inherit and in turn improve the genetic endowment they received from their forebears. In the slow changes in bodily form which become necessary for continued survival, they image man's origin as chance and nature and his purpose as survival. For both poets, who draw exaggerations of such images, neither Parker nor Darwin offers a theory so satisfying as Augustine's notion that one's knowledge of God comes from a memory which is different from man's memory of worldly objects or the traditional religious accounts of man's ultimate origin as a creation of God.

Nevertheless, as Browning ends his poems with the creation of an anti-Setebos in the Quiet, indicative of his own clear view of man's ultimate purpose, Lowell does not. Instead, his concluding picture of the boy hobbling "humpbacked through the grizzled grass" crystalizes failures both in the poem and in the volume to resolve finally the purposes morally and aesthetically to which the "Cal" masks are to be put. Lowell's own doubt about the validity of any answer to man's purpose results in a reluctance to create clearly distinct personal and non-personal actions. As a consequence, his historical perspective which normally measures his meaningful action comes crashing upon the world of personal experience and obscures both in an onrush of anguish. The meaning of the poem's actions along with the means to weigh such meaning floods out like matchstick houses caught in a real overflow. Added to this is a corresponding failure on aesthetic grounds to resolve the nature of his artistic vision. Lowell does not know whether the vision is to be like "Life Studies," lyrical, direct, and personal, or like the earlier volumes, epical, complex, and didactic. Throughout the volume, as his helpless, hapless subject is acted upon by force after force, the anguish of the immediate experience prevents a quick and conclusive withdrawal into non-personal perspectives. At the same time, in the lyrical poems like "Water" and "The Old Flame," he chooses to ignore the historical perspectives altogether and portrays in self-cancelling images the actions of life.

In the midst of Lowell's announced abandonment of contemplative poetry which appeared about the same time as the volume, both failures prove particularly unfortunate. Readers approached the book, despite the apparentness of its litany of doubt concerning man's purpose, and expected to find in it socio-political programs similar to, but more acceptable than those of Ezra Pound's active poetry. They were further encouraged in this by Lowell's real willingness to assume what Matthew Arnold called "the high destinies of poetry" and deal more and more with public issues in both his life and writing. This willingness, once backed by Christian conviction, prompted in the 1940's a refusal to be inducted into World War II because of America's policy of total bombing and the active poetry and socio-political attacks of *Land of Unlikeness* (1944). Now, backed by the possibility of similar convictions, it would lead eventually to his refusal in 1965 to take part in a White House Arts Festival because of America's involvement in Vietnam, to his newspaper protests against police brutality and his endorsements of artistic freedom, and possibly to a new active poetry based similarly on an Arnold belief that in the collapse of religion men must at least be true to one another. What readers found, however, was the delineation of man not as a doer but as some kind of elaborate receiver.

Robert Bly, for one, in his review of *For the Union Dead* in *The Sixties* (1966) reveals the results of such expectations. His review disregards almost entirely the integrity in Lowell's dealing with the teleological problems of his vision and launches an attack into his failure to form an acceptable, practicable socio-political program. Bly extends this failure generally to writers whom he groups about *The Partisan Review*: "The Partisan Review writers never broke through to any clear view of modern literature or politics. . . . Their insistence on the values of alienation, their academic notions of modernism, are dead, like fatigued metal. . . . Since the ideas behind the book are decrepit, Lowell has no choice but to glue the poems together with pointless excitement." The disappointment might have been less had Bly disregarded *The Partisan Review* altogether and proceeded along lines suggested

by Ralph Waldo Emerson's "Self-Reliance" that the failure to believe in one's values makes for a literature and a life whose excitements can only be pointless. He might have then seen that Lowell's current message to a post-Christian world is precisely the portrayal of fatigue, decrepitude, and pointless excitement.

Despite the influence of Schopenhauer in the poetry which has appeared since *For the Union Dead*, Lowell has still not come to any firm convictions about man's ultimate purpose. Action is still minimal. It occurs mainly as ruminations on received stimuli. However, technical changes have occurred to suggest Lowell's ability in the intervening period to come to grips with the substance of his vision so that the anguish which disrupted his rhythms and lines has disappeared and the personal and non-personal elements of his juxtapositions which tended to merge now remain distinct and effective. First, suggestive of the new mastery over their content, the poems generally follow a plan of run-on, octosyllabic couplets. Enjambment occurs strategically to keep the content from the completely resolved sense of a closed epigram. Second, and paralleling this sense of mastery, the language is hard and clear and object, rather than emotion-oriented. There are no longer lines as in "Myopia: a Night," where the impression, not the object takes precedence. Instead, there is a sense of detail which borders on what Mary McCarthy calls the woman writer's penchant for décor, but which here works well to evoke both the personal experience and its surroundings. In amassing this detail, balanced constructions are used, indicating again a sense of control. Finally, and perhaps most importantly, the tone managing the action is not involved, but detached. This permits for a better handling of the masks.

The means by which Lowell seems to come to grips with the substance of his vision and handle these tasks is twofold. First, having gained in the interval distance from his once Christian convictions, he is able now, for the purposes of his art, to sustain perspectives in which he does not necessarily believe. He is able to do so because in an age of overkill such perspectives evoke nightmare visions of a world either destroyed by continuing its wrong idea of a struggle for existence or else reduced to an equally destructive sado-masochism in the drive by its populations to prove their existences through their powers to inflict and endure pain. The real fears of both prospects in the absence of a constructive alternative contribute to Lowell's ability to make them visible, human alternatives rather than mental hypotheses. Moreover, he is able to strengthen his distance from them by adding to the outlines of the masks he formed elements which either so repulse his nature that they preclude his sympathy or so work to reinforce his initial antipathy that they provide complementary, supporting arguments.

For example, to the perspectives and theories of evolution which he develops in "The Neo-Classical Urn," he now adds the view of other evolutionists that not only man emerged from nature by chance, but also the earth emerged as well from some chance, cooled remnant of a cosmic explosion. In time, it, too, is threatened with extinction either by a second cosmic explosion or by the sun's burning itself out. In the prospect of such extinction, he complements the horror of a moral law based upon the fact of man's survival with allusions to the "survival of the fittest" notion of Herbert Spencer's *Principles of Biology* (1864), which rationalized most of England's will toward expansionism and America's turn-of-the-century cutthroat economic and social theories.

In support of his opposition to such brutal theories of man's origins and purposes, he turns to the work of Alfred Russel Wallace, who co-developed with Darwin the idea of evolution, but who later challenged the whole Darwinian position on man by insisting that artistic, mathematical, and musical abilities could not be explained on the basis of natural selection and the struggle for existence. Lowell seems also to gain support from the arguments of C. S. Lewis, who in *The Abolition of Man* (1947) propounds his objections to man's using his intelligence as a tool to turn everything into an extension of nature. Lewis sees in man's change from qualitative to quantitative values and in man's acknowledged ability to control quantity a will to extend control over more aspects of life much in the manner of the scientist's desire to control chance. He decries this drive to turn human engagement into disengaged problems.

Next, the effect in Lowell's poetry of this gained distance is a temporary acceptance of an ironic view of life similar to that which began his career. Then, the intensity of a Christian vision in a world of perverted Christianity on the verge of the Last Judgment turned the irony into a source for invective and satire. Now, as his protagonists lack the grace for meaningful action, the irony results in a picture of the combined futility and absurdity of weighing the minimal actions which man can muster against an irresolvable purpose. Time and again these actions turn into a mockery of the protagonist as Lowell ends his poem by evoking a Schopenhauerian future. This future, if it will not solve the problems of meaning raised, will at least distance them into some perspective that perhaps may overcome their pain as time is reputed to heal all wounds. Thus, what begin as basically personal and ontological poems evolve into seemingly didactic, impersonal observations which record simply the biding of time.

The movement to these final observations with their releases from the bondage of the present by the acceptance of this Schopenhauerian will recalls structurally the release or escape to God in the contemplative poems of Lowell's initial volumes. A similar pattern of vividly constructed scenes which start off the contemplation which, in turn, proceeds to annihilate and escape the scenes is established. However, whereas the pattern of this annihilation in the contemplative poems followed a progression of humility (self-knowledge) to love (knowledge of others) to contemplation (knowledge of God), the pattern now seems to flow from egoism (the impulse toward one's own good) to malice (the impulse toward others' woe) to compassion (the impulse toward others' well-being). This last impulse, under the guise of Christian charity, is probably Lowell's strongest link with the past.

The poems which define most clearly how the acceptance of this ironic vision affects both the struggle for existence and the masks named in poems like "The Neo-Classical Urn," are "Central Park," "Fourth of July in Maine," and "Waking Early Sunday Morning." All picture modern man caught up as the protagonist in a world variously described in geological terms as "a dying crust" and a "volcanic cone." This predetermined world is warmed by the red coal of the sun "until it cinders like the soul," presumably the soul described by Jonathan Edwards in "The Future Punishment of the Wicked Unavoidable and Intolerable" and paraphrased by Lowell in "Mr. Edwards and the Spider." In such a world the Bible is "chopped and crucified," and religion in its truest sense is something far off somewhere when "the universe was young." It is past resurrecting.

The problem of this world is how to curb the brute natural force of the struggle for existence without some means of compassion. Unchecked, the force may otherwise destroy man altogether either in the "small war on the heels of small war" which Lowell envisions at the end of "Waking Early Sunday Morning" or in man's having been made victim of its brute

force in "Central Park." Here he is imaged as having to beg "delinquents for his life" or else rely upon the clubs of equally brutal policemen behind "each flowering shrub." In a Heraclitean way, the brute force which society was created to control is triumphing over society as it gives way to an even greater brutality. This new brutality threatens in the conclusions of each poem to return man to a form of tribalism. The idea is similar to the second of three possibilities which Bertrand Russell draws in "The Future of Mankind" (1950). Russell feels that unless law governs the relations of nations by the end of this century, "a reversion to barbarism after a catastrophic diminution of the population of the globe" may well occur.

"Near the Ocean" concerns a second aspect of this post-Christian world. In it, Lowell enters the "New Carthage" of an absurd world similar to that which Edward Albee draws in *Who's Afraid of Virginia Woolf?* In its search for meaning, the poem outlines the marital "fun and games" of a husband who conceives of his wife as basically a monster whose love is at once both suffocating and devouring. Echoes of an archetypal pattern of thwarted male inconstancy emerge as the husband's fantasy dreams of direction (egoism) fail to coincide with his abilities to exercise this direction except by inflicting pain (malice). Thus, the poem projects a notion of love which insists that the psychological basis to most sex is not so much physical satisfaction as it is a will to power. What the protagonist sees is himself, first as an echo of Cellini's statue of Perseus in the Piazza della Signoria lifting the head of Medusa (his wife) to please the mob, and then, joined with her, as one of two children standing before a Terrible Mother, who on the basis of having given them succor makes her demands. In the continuation of such sado-masochistic dreams and actions, the husband concludes "nothing will age, nothing will last / or take corruption from the past."

The poem is, in fact, the latest variation on the continuing element of psychic individuation as a necessary adjunct to Lowell's preoccupation with teleology. His heroes, even in a post-Christian world, must encounter and subdue their imaginations' Terrible Mothers. Besides serving their reputed, necessary psychological need, these encounters work to provide the means by which the would-be hero may escape the lockstep of time. The pattern, established in *Land of Unlikeness*, first pitted the potential hero against the Biblical Whore of Babylon, whose subjection would give him knowledge so that he might in turn alter history's course which was then seen as "blood begetting blood." For her subjection, Lowell called upon Christian faith as both the weapon to slay the monster and the means of gaining the grace whereby history's lockstep would be broken. In *Lord Weary's Castle* (1946) and *The Mills of the Kavanaughs* (1951), the castrating Terrible Mother was variously portrayed as the constrictions of a perverse Christian tradition. Here Lowell called upon the founders of religious cultures, Noah and Aeneas, to act as liberators and to set into being the dialectic of liberation and constriction which characterizes this stage of Lowell's work. In *Life Studies* (1959), the evil mother became more identifiable with Lowell's own mother and the course of history from which man had to be set free, the destructive, terrible pipe dreams of the Winslow family. Here his failure to subconsciously subdue her led to the honoring of his first non-heroes and the despair which marked the volume's completion. Now the Terrible Mother has become his wife and their lies, the historical course which needs to be altered but which they cannot be freed from until "time, that buries us, lay bare." These lies which both tell each other and themselves prove their abilities to hurt and hence affect one another as well as provide the means to rationalize their basically irrational wills. Lowell would have done with such betrayals for their more charitable moments; but the failure to overcome these lies other than by the projection of a Schopenhauerian future leaves him egoless and committed even further to his continuing preoccupation with non-heroes.

"The Opposite House" speaks also of everything giving way to death. In this instance, Lowell traces the disappearance of a police station in a burst of flames. Before its destruction, like the empty churches of Philip Larkin's "Church Going," it had been abandoned to whatever sought to use it. Pigeons mainly fly in and out. With its destruction, the station, symbolic of social institutions which attempt to curb violence with violence, assumes the image of a catherine wheel lit at the end of a lawn party. The image is taken from T. S. Eliot's *Murder in the Cathedral* (1935), where it is among several proving man's passage "From unreality to unreality." Hopefully, here the station is to give way to a better world as the turtle-slow imagination of man churns onward more quickly than the moving squad-car to what must be new institutions and new unrealities. Out of the differing rates of the loss of these institutions and man's ability to construct others arises his sense of alienation. Eventually, as he loses touch with all social institutions, he feels imprisoned by them, and, since all people would soon find, by outdistancing the institutions proper to their development, a world filled with institutions they cannot relate to, anomie results. Thus arises man's need to strike through the social structures in Lowell's early poems or man's current need to accept not as a beneficial by-product of time's irresistible will. It is this second which Lowell celebrates in the closing line of the poem, for out of this principle of Death—the absolute of Existentialism—he is able to rationalize his being.

In concert, the poems reveal that man is somehow at odds with the structure of his world and ill-equipped to create permanent new structures without some sort of absolute purpose. On the basis of the purposes suggested by any of the perspectives left after Christianity, Lowell advocates a preservation of Christian charity or Schopenhauerian compassion as basic to all social reform since it establishes the spirit for law. On this spirit rather than on law or social institutions, Lowell bases his socio-politics. Thus, the few specific references which he makes to social and economic reform are principally to structures which have been outdistanced rather than to structures which should come into being. He does point out, for example, that somehow inequities have to do with "poverty and fear" in "Central Park," that the "poor" are still without rights in "Fourth of July in Maine," and that the industrialist still "goes down to the sea in ships" in "Waking Early Sunday Morning."

These references provide an additional, immediate, practicable, but limited clue to why a poet whose system of history is consistently cyclical may need to go into a negation of evolution and its basic open-ended progress. They are the catch-phrases current in American politics, which in the hands of President Lyndon B. Johnson does tend to see itself capable of possibly evolving into a Great Society, and which on that basis proposes a kind of cultural imperialism similar to that rationalized in nineteenth-century England on the bases of Darwin and Spencer. Peoples of primitive cultures, small societies lost on the world's margins seem destined again to be absorbed, regardless of their desires, into the benefits, gadgets, and politics of this Great Society by virtue of the Darwinian law of America's superior technology and consequently superior powers of survival.

The need to attack this political optimism has an equally important corollary in two other current trends which Lowell may see as contingent on the acceptance of an evolutionary

ontology. He may well be acting in opposition to the popularity of Pierre Teilhard de Chardin, who in books like *The Phenomenon of Man* (1959) proposes a kind of religious evolution that counteracts Lowell's picture of the demise of Christianity with an image of an evolving perfect Christianity. This concept is already under attack by theologians who question the concept of free will involved. There is likewise the popularity of literary figures such as Theodore Roethke and Dylan Thomas, who accept as good the single law of man and nature which is part of an evolutionary ontology and speak of a natural sympathy among all living things. The opening line of "Waking Early Sunday Morning" with its pun of "chinook-schnook" can easily be taken as an echo of Roethke's wish in "The Longing" to be "with the salmon," or the description of the salmon run in "First Meditation." In Lowell's vision, such sympathy is merely another sign of lost Christian purpose.

The main basis of Lowell's socio-political program, however, remains independent of these practical considerations. Ideally, it invests itself in a concept of politics which sees its end as identical with the end of man, now almost exclusively relegated to the problem of psychic individuation. As Lowell insists in his recurrent images of Terrible Mothers on the need for man individually to overcome restricting structures in order to provide the basis for his ego—however illusory, he manages to differ from most would-be social and religious reformers. The differences are pronounced. First, unlike most social reformers who see egoism as an end in itself, Lowell, like Schopenhauer, feels that this egoism must ultimately be surrendered for salvation. Second, he conceives of the clash then between man and social structures, much as the clash in the poem "Florence" between men and monsters, as a necessary part of the hero's development in that it provides the hero with a knowledge of the nature of evil. For this reason, he would have many structures remain. In this, he is probably closer to a tradition of writers which includes Herman Melville rather than one which includes Ralph Waldo Emerson, and closer still to a tradition of medieval carol writers who celebrated the Fall of man because it produced the glories of Christ's birth and death.

In an age when the unexamined life and the struggle for existence tend to threaten mankind with annihilation instead of survival and the controls which a Christian teleology once imposed upon brute force have disappeared, the importance of Lowell's continuing to probe man's purpose becomes clear. Regardless of their truths, upon the answers to such questions, the future pressing upon mankind will be rationalized and shaped. Thus, despite the paralysis of his characters who do little more than reminisce or indulge in self-pity, Lowell is able to continue according to the functions of the poet and of poetry outlined by Arnold in "The Study of Poetry" (1880), by not selecting any of the alternatives. Instead, he can be a moralist in a society where religion and science have been called into doubt by probing the ontological bases for law and order independent of any individual, prescribed purposes for man. Out of what he envisions as a basic human tendency toward self-awareness may come the awareness of others and the Schopenhauerian compassion for one's fellowman that will halt the mass destruction. Thus, although Lowell may no longer be able to see the true city of the religious mystic or even of the romantic, he can still tell the Vanity Fairs along the way. He may no longer be the conscientious objector crying out against the evils of war in *Land of Unlikeness* and *Lord Weary's Castle*, or the Arnoldian in "The Mills of the Kavanaughs" and *Life Studies* struggling with a belief in personal relationships which gives out in *For the Union Dead*. Nevertheless, he has still not lost faith with human concerns, nor with history, or rather faith with the inevitable will, which for him is now the reality of the future.

### HAYDEN CARRUTH
### From "A Meaning for Robert Lowell"
*Hudson Review*, Autumn 1967, pp. 432–47

I n each stage of his poetic evolution, Lowell has written a few poems that seem to me extremely fine, and he has also written poems that seem to me mannered, pointless, incomplete, and obscure. Indeed, try as I may—and I have tried again and again over the years—some of his poems, particularly his earliest and then again his latest, remain incomprehensible to me, as dark and profuse as a pot of Bostonian whistleberries. Moreover, I cannot escape the feeling that some of this obscurity has been purposely, even crassly laid on.[1] For me, this is the single largest detracting element in his work.

One point, however, I wish to make perfectly clear. Lowell's position of leadership seems to me not only to have been earned but to be altogether suitable. I say this on two counts. As a man, Lowell has given us more than enough evidence of his firmness and integrity—one thinks of his conscientious objection during the war and all that it entailed, his refusal to attend White House sociables, and many other such actions—to substantiate his moral fitness for the role. As a poet, he gives us this same integrity in art. When I read his poetry, however negative my response may be to its effect, I know I am in the presence of an artist *in extremis*, operating, I should say struggling, at the limits of sensibility and technique. This is a quality which we consider peculiarly American, a kind of hardrock Yankee pertinacity, and to me it is peculiarly attractive. Who was it that said he would fight it out on this line if it took all summer? An American military man, I believe. When I read Lowell's lines, I feel that he has fought it out upon them for years. This is tough and homely and American. It is admirable. It is what leads me to place Lowell alongside William Carlos Williams, rather than in the company of other older poets to whom he bears a closer superficial resemblance. It is also what leads me, in the perennial confrontation of artists and the rest of the world, to rest content under his leadership. If my standing behind him will add to the strength of his position, he may be sure I am there.

So much for preliminary considerations. The phases of Lowell's poetic evolution are so well-known that I need indicate them only briefly. We may dismiss his first book, *Land of Unlikeness*, which was published in a limited edition that few people have seen; Lowell himself effectively dismissed it when he republished its main poems, considerably revised, in *Lord Weary's Castle*, the book that established him with one shot as a leader of his generation. Written in the first flush of enthusiasm after his conversion to Catholicism, the poems were highly charged devotional lyrics mixed with autobiographical elements, presented in an elaborate formal dress: close rhymes, exact meters, a heavy reliance on couplets, and an equally heavy reliance on the rhetoric of allusion. It was a virtuoso performance. At its best, in perhaps a fourth of the poems, it showed a young poet writing with genuine spontaneity in the strict forms of the English metaphysical convention, while bringing to them his own distinct voice and idiosyncratic manner. In short, Lowell had done what everyone had been saying could not be done: he had invented a new style. In his next book, *The Mills of the Kavanaughs*, he stuck with it, but

most readers considered the book a falling-off, especially the long title poem. What this poem, a dramatic narrative in monologue, showed was that the ability to sustain narrative tension across the librations of discrete pentameter couplets is lost to us: the suspension bridge has replaced the viaduct.

Lowell waited eight years to publish his next book. Then, in 1959, he presented us with a change of appearance so radical that it seemed a reversal. The formal manner was gone; no pentameters, no rhymes, no ornate rhetoric. The book, called *Life Studies*, which more than recouped his reputation, gave us instead poems in open, loose measures, without rhyme, in a diction that seemed easy and almost insouciant. The heart of the book was a group of autobiographical poems so intensely candid that critics immediately called them "confessional"; an unfortunate choice of terms. It implied that Lowell was engaged in public breast-beating, a kind of refreshing new psycho-exotic pastime, or in a shallow exercise of "self-expression," long ago discredited; whereas in fact his aim was far more serious than that.

The following two collections of poems, *For the Union Dead* in 1964 and *Near the Ocean* this year, have continued to explore themes of autobiographical candor, but have gradually reverted toward formalism. Not the conventional formalism of *Lord Weary's Castle*, however. Now the meters, though basically iambic, are cast in rough lines of trimeter and tetrameter, punctuated with purposefully inexact rhymes. The diction is more extreme, more peculiar and concise, than in *Life Studies*, and the syntax has become progressively more taut, split up into smaller and smaller units. This has gone so far in the latest poems that one can scarcely find a complete sentence from stanza to stanza, but only phrases, expletives, stabs of meaning. The effect, although entirely different from the high style of *Lord Weary's Castle*, nevertheless brings us back to an obscurity and artifice that seem to denote another reversal; the simplicity of *Life Studies* has been jettisoned.

In effect, Lowell made, in *Life Studies*, a considerable leap into a new area of poetic experience, which he has been exploring, since then, through increasingly elaborate means. Why he did this, what was in his mind, are questions readers must try to answer if they would understand the actual meaning of Lowell's experiment.

I have said nothing about the translations, perhaps because they are a source of embarrassment to me. Over the years Lowell has made a good many, including a couple of long ones and a whole book of short ones, from many languages, called *Imitations*. When this book was published in 1961, I reviewed it enthusiastically. The density and tonicity of the best translations took hold of me and persuaded me that Lowell had reached far toward the intrinsic qualities of the original poems, especially in his Baudelaires. Since then, my friends who know Baudelaire better than I have informed me with cogency that this is not true, and that I had no business reviewing such a book in the first place. Well, they are right on both counts, as I have ruefully come to see. Aside from the intended alterations of sequence and literal meaning which Lowell acknowledges, there is, for instance, the way in which Baudelaire's charateristic elegance, deriving from the fluent, almost sinuous build-up of stanzas and longer passages, is fragmented and rigidified in Lowell's choppy phrasings. And there is the way, too, in which Baudelaire's post-romantic sense of beauty is both reduced and roughened in its passage through Lowell's anguish-ridden, New Englander's sensibility; the flowers of evil become merely evil flowers—a considerable difference when you stop to think about it. Lowell's detractors seize on these points, and others, as ammunition for their campaign, which is made easier by the evident inferiority, when judged against any standard, of some of the translations. The Villons are quite bad, the Rimbauds and Pasternaks barely passable. But I continue to feel that the best of the Baudelaires, Rilkes, and Montales are excellent Lowells indeed, and this is all he had claimed for them. He does not call them translations, but imitations. Perhaps he should have gone further and specified that what he was imitating was not the poetry of Baudelaire or Rilke or the rest, but the poetry of Lowell; perhaps he should have chosen another title, e.g., *Appropriations* or *Assimilations*. No matter; the point is that Lowell has made a perfectly legitimate effort to consolidate his own poetic view of reality by levying upon congenial authentications from other languages and cultures. The best of his translations go together with the best of *Life Studies* and *For the Union Dead* to comprise the nucleus of his mature work, the organic unity of which must be apprehended by those who wish to form reliable judgments.

Even at the most superficial level of technique, the prosodic level, Lowell's evolution, both his successes and his failures, offers a fascinating study to people who are interested in the disciplines of poetry. This is usually the case when important poets change styles. Consider Lowell's commonest prosodic device, the suspended or Hopkinsian upbeat produced by ending a line on the first syllable of a new unit of syntax, a phrase or sentence. He made it work well, not to say famously, in his early poems, but when he abandoned strict pentameters he had more trouble with it. How do you employ this very useful concept of metrical enjambment when your line-structure has been purposely unfixed? It is the old story: you can't have your cake and eat it too. Simple as it appears, this is a crucial problem, perhaps *the* crucial problem, of contemporary unmetered poetry, which different poets have met in many different ways. Some have adopted the practice of reading their poems with abrupt pauses at the end of each line, but this is an oral stratagem that seems to have little connection with the actual dynamics of the poem. Denise Levertov has gone further by developing her concept of "organic form," which appears, however, to be incompletely worked out at this stage.[2] Like her, Lowell has preferred to work on the page, i.e., within the poem's prosodic structure; but with indifferent success in many instances. Conceivably such a simple matter as this, which is nevertheless extremely important in terms of Lowell's natural style, lies behind his recent return to more exact, or more exacting, meters.

But that is a topic for another discussion. What I am interested in here is something prior to poetry. Before a man can create a poem he must create a poet. Considered from the limited perspective of artistry, this is the primal creative act.

Imagine Lowell seated at his work-table on some ordinary morning in 1950. *Lord Weary's Castle* has been out for four years; already its triumph is a burden. The poems in *The Mills of the Kavanaughs*, now at the press, have been finished for a year or more, and are beginning to slip into the past, to seem stale, remote, and incidental—like the verses of one's friends. Now I have no idea what Lowell would be doing in such circumstances, probably brooding and daydreaming like the rest of us, but for the moment let me ascribe to him a simple, orderly, godlike self-mastery that neither he nor you nor I nor Charles de Gaulle can claim in actuality. In 1950, given that marvelous perspicacity, he would have had to ask himself two questions. In essence, what is my theme? In general, what is my defect?

One does not ask these questions once and then go on to something else, one asks them over and over, as one asks all unanswerable questions. A serious poet moves progressively toward his essential theme, though he can never reach it, by means of exclusions, peeling away, from poem to poem, the inessential, working down to bedrock; and he examines every word he writes for clues to his defect. In the case of Lowell we cannot doubt that he works in such a state of constant tension and self-interrogation. Yet it seems clear to me, even so, that at some point around 1950 he must have asked these questions with special intentness. Nothing else can account for the change of poetic stance so strikingly evident in *Life Studies*.

What had Lowell set out to do in his first poems? He had set out explicitly, I think, though ingenuously, to build on the Donne-to-Hopkins tradition of devotional poetry in English, to write poems of faith. The evidence, in the poems themselves, is unmistakable. Consequently he had produced a rather large number of set pieces in a high style, such as the poems about Jonathan Edwards and other historical figures or events, affirming a public, devotional aspiration. This is what all young poets do, isn't it? They begin, or at least they try to begin, where the mature poets they admire left off. They do this in the compulsion of their literary zeal, in spite of the evident unfeasibility of it, owing to the irremediable disparity of experience. At the same time Lowell interspersed among his devotional pieces various autobiographical elements, usually disguised and highly wrought, set out in the same taut, allusive, difficult style as the rest, but genuine autobiography nevertheless. I think it must have become evident to him by 1950 that in spite of the very great but purely literary success of the devotional set pieces, these autobiographical poems were the more alive, the more interesting, and ultimately the more comprehensible.

Poems like "Mr. Edwards and the Spider" and "After the Surprising Conversions" are good specimens of their kind, but like all their kind they are sententious. That is to say, a large part of their meaning is a stable and predictable element of the general cultural situation, with which the poems are, so to speak, invested. (And under "meaning" I intend the entire affective and cognitive experience of the poem.) But the autobiographical poems or partly autobiographical poems, like "Mary Winslow" and "At the Indian Killer's Grave," work themselves out in their own terms, within their own language; and in spite of the high gloss of artifice that remains upon them, they speak with urgency.

All this is even more evident today, fifteen years later. The most prominent motifs of the poems in *Lord Weary's Castle* are the Christ, the Crucifix, and the Virgin; they are repeated on almost every page. Yet they remain inert. They are not personal realizations, they are not symbols, they are merely tokens (which perhaps, in the tradition Lowell had chosen, is all they can be). The personal motifs, on the other hand—personal guilt, personal death, personal time, personal violence and desire—are what carry the poet along, and they are connected, not with devotional aspirations, but with his experienced life. He returns to them again and again in poems about himself, about his mother and the Winslow family, and about his father, Commander Lowell. In *Life Studies* he simply relinquished one set of motifs, the former, and took up the other. The resulting augmentation of his poetic stature—his personal stature as creator within the domain of his poetic materials—was enormous.

As I say, Lowell cannot discover the precise specifications of his theme, which is lucky for him. If he were to do so, he would be clapped into silence instantly. Nor can we do it for him, which is equally lucky. All we can do is brood, as he does, over his lines and the shadows behind them, tracking down the motifs to see where they lead. In my own recent brooding I turn especially to two lines from the poem called "Night Sweat" in *For the Union Dead*:

> always inside me is the child who died,
> always inside me is his will to die . . .

Simple enough; explicit enough. They are one expression of the radical guilt which seems to lie at the base of Lowell's poetic nature. It is a guilt which took form like any other, leaving aside psychoanalytical factors: first from elements of generalized cultural guilt, in Lowell's case the New Englander's shame over the Indians and the Salem women, which has exercized an obviously powerful influence on his imagination; then from guilt that all men feel, with deep necessity, for the deaths of their own fathers; and finally from the horrendous events of contemporary history. But what is the punishment for the crimes that produce this pervading guilt? It is personal death. We all know this, from the first moment of our mortal recognition. Yet against this Lowell casts again and again his instinctive belief in the remission of sin, or rather his knowledge, his feeling, of his own undiminished innocence. Then what can our death be? What is our guilt? There is only one answer, outside of absurdity. Our death is our sin, for which we pay in advance through our guilt. Our death is a crime against every good principle in the universe: nature, God, the human heart. Yet we, the innocent, are the responsible ones—this is the idea Lowell cannot forego. We carry this crime, like a seed, within us. Our bodies are going to commit it, do what we will. They are going to carry out this murder, inexorably, while we stand by, helpless and aghast.

This is the ultimate Yankee metonymy, you might say. Puritan death as punishment for sin contracts, under the paradox of benign Transcendentalism, to death as sin. Naturally it is a theological monstrosity. It is impossible. Yet in the human and poetic sphere, it is a validity of staggering force.

Well, all this is highly conjectural, of course. There are scores of other, doubtless better ways to approach Lowell's theme, I'm sure. Yet I feel this progressive identification of sin, guilt, and death can be traced fairly directly from such poems as "At the Indian Killer's Grave" to "Night Sweat" and beyond. The two lines I have quoted strike close to it. They are literal. When Lowell says "inside" I think he means inside: he is carrying this sin-death around in him like a monstrous illegitimate pregnancy. I would almost bet that if he suffers the common nightmare of artists, the dream of male parturition, it is a dead thing that comes out (at which point, if he hasn't awakened, his dream may be suffused with bliss).

Meanwhile Lowell has his defect, for which he should give thanks. It permits him to relax into the mercy of technical self-criticism. Not that it is easy to deal with; quite the contrary. Like all fundamental defects, it is a function of his personality, and hence wears many faces. I call it the defect of pervasive extraneity; but it could have other names. One aspect of it was quite clear, however, in *Lord Weary's Castle*: the laid-on metaphysical obscurity. This was the fashion of poetry at the time, and Lowell accommodated himself to it easily and naturally; and without the least poetic infidelity. We must bear in mind in considering fashion that a fashion during the period of its ascendancy is not a fashion; it is merely what is right. In composing the poems of *Lord Weary's Castle*, Lowell had no sense, I'm certain, of doing anything but what was necessary. He had no sense of *doing* anything at all, except writing poetry as it is written. Nevertheless, the obscurity, like the ornate style and the use of inert figures from a general cultural conspectus, was clearly extraneous to his main themes and objectives, as he could see five or six years later, and he gave it up; this was his defect and he chopped off its head. But it sprang up elsewhere,

hydra-like. Other aspects of it were more difficult to see. For instance, in the title poem from *The Mills of the Kavanaughs*, he had shown his inability to sustain the long units of poetry, and at the same time his great talent for the short units: the line and phrase and isolated image. These are his forte. Lowell can rap out a single sharp line with extraordinary facility. The trouble is that these brilliant strokes may contribute nothing to the whole fabric and intention of a poem; they may be merely extraneous—pervasively extraneous because in spite of their irrelevance, they do sit within the total structure and they cannot be eradicated once the poem has acquired a certain degree of distinctness.

In a poem called "The Scream" from *For the Union Dead*, Lowell writes of the time when his mother gave up her mourning:

> One day she changed to purple,
> and left her mourning. At the fitting,
> the dressmaker crawled on the floor,
> eating pins, like Nebuchadnezzar
> on his knees eating grass.

We have all seen this, of course, a woman crawling on the floor, her mouth full of pins, to adjust another woman's hem, and so we are struck by the originality of Lowell's simile. It seems to me absolutely genuine; I have never encountered it before. Hence the pins and grass collapse together spontaneously in my mind like a perfect superimposition of images. I am charmed. Only when I stop to think do I realize that Nebuchadnezzar and what he stands for have only the remotest connection with this scene, and that the dressmaker herself is a figure of no importance in the poem. As an image, this is a brilliant extraneity: the defect at work.

And what shall we say about the appearance of the new book, its crass and confused ostentation? This is gross extraneity and nothing else.

In short, Lowell's defect is a temptation to mere appearance, to effects, trappings—to the extraneous. And it arises, I believe, from a discrete imagination, i.e., an imagination which works best in disjunctive snatches. I suppose some people would call it an analytic, rather than a synthetic, imagination. His problem as a poet during the past fifteen or twenty years has been to continue digging deeper toward his essential theme, while at the same turning, if it is possible, his defect into an advantage.

So far I have been writing about Lowell as if he were an isolated case, but the reverse is the truth. He is a poet of his time. The shift of focus in his poetry has been one part, a very small part, of a general shift in artistic values and intentions during the past quarter-century.

When was the last time in our western civilization that a writer at his work-table could look at a piece of writing and call it finished, self-enclosed and self-sustaining, autonomous—a work of art in the original sense? I'd say in poetry it must have been at the time of Pope, and in fiction, since the novel lags behind, perhaps as late as Flaubert or Turgenev; but actually no one could draw the lines so precisely. The change from one notion of art to another was very gradual. All we can say with certainty is that sometime during the nineteenth century—that changeful time!—the old idea of the enclosed work of art was dislocated in the minds of serious artists: Heine, Rimbaud, Strindberg. Such men began to see that art is always unfinished; and from this arose the concept of its a priori unfinishability, i.e., its limitlessness. For a time—quite a time—the two concepts ran side-by-side; many artists tried by various means to combine them. In the forepart of our century, for instance, we got the idea of the circularity of artistic structure, from which derived the work of art that was both limitless and enclosed: *The Waste Land* and *Finnegans Wake*. These were grandiose conceptions. They made art into something it had not been before, a world in itself.[3] They were helped along by the general collapse of values in the post-Nietzschean cultures of Europe. Some artists, despairing of their own painful nihilism, even tried to substitute for the reality of the world the anti-reality of art—or of style, the word, or whatever— believing that only by this means could they create a bearable plane upon which to enact human existence and build a consistent scheme of values. I am thinking of such men as Gottfried Benn, Céline, and Wyndham Lewis, or in a different way of Breton and the Surréalistes. Of course Hitler's war smashed all that, proving the ugliness and irresponsibility of it. Reality was reality after all. We came out of the war badly shaken, clinging to the idea of existential engagement. Henceforth, contrite as we were, we would be responsible and free, creative within the real world. Yet what could this mean in a reality over which we had no control, a reality in which we, the conscious element, possessed nothing but the lunatic knowledge of our own supererogation, to use Auden's terms? If anti-reality were denied us by our own responsibility, and if reality were denied us by our own alienation, what could we create? We decided—and to my mind the inevitability of it is beautiful—that what we could create was life. Human life.

It was not a retreat to anti-reality. In looking back we saw that, after Nietzsche, we had been living in a crisis of intellectual evolution, a terrible blockage and confusion; we had been absorbing what Jaspers calls "the preparing power of chaos." Now we were ready to go forward. Now, in freedom and responsibility, we began to see the meaning of what we had known all along, that a life is more than a bundle of determined experiential data. (For the biggest horror of our crisis had been the complex but empty enticements of Fruedian positivism.) A life is what we make it. In its authenticity it is our own interpretation and re-organization of experience, structured metaphorically. It is the result of successive imaginative acts—it is a work of art! By conversion, a work of art is life, *provided it be true to the experiential core.* Thus in a century artists had moved from an Arnoldian criticism of life to an Existential creation of life, and both the gains and the losses were immense.

The biggest loss perhaps was a large part of what we thought we had known about art. For now we saw in exactly what way art is limitless. It is limitless because it is free and responsible: it is a life. Its only end is the adventitious cutting off that comes when a heart bursts, or a sun. Still, the individual "piece" of art must be objective in some sense; it lies on the page, on the canvas. Practically speaking, what is a limitless object? It is a fragment; a random fragment; a fragment without intrinsic form, shading off in all directions into whatever lies beyond. And this is what our art has become in the past two decades: random, fragmentary, and open-ended.

Hence in literature any particular "work" is linear rather than circular in structure, extensible rather than terminal in intent, and at any given point inclusive rather than associative in substance; at least these are its tendencies. And it is autobiographical, that goes without saying. It is an act of self-creation by an artist within the tumult of experience.

This means that many of our ideas about art must be reexamined and possibly thrown out. I have in mind not our ideas of technique, derived from the separate arts, but our esthetic generalizations derived from all the arts. Such notions as harmony, dynamism, control, proportion, even style in its broadest sense. How do these criteria apply to a work which is not a work at all, conventionally considered, but a fragment? I do not say they do not apply; I say the applications must be radically re-determined.

As readers, where does this leave us? In a mere subjective muddle? Sometimes it seems so. For that matter, why should we read another person's poems at all? Our life is what concerns us, not his. Is he a better observer than we, a better imaginer, a better creator? Can his self-creation of his life assist us in ours, assuming a rough equivalence of human needs and capacities? Perhaps; but these too are subjective criteria. What then?

All I can say is that the most progressive criticism we have now *is* subjective, resolutely so and in just these ways. It asks what a poem can *do* for us. The reason we have so little of it is that we are unused to such methods and fearful of them, and we do not know upon what principles to organize them. Our critics are years behind our artists, still afraid of the personal, ideal, moral, and contingent. For strangely enough, these four qualities are just what we preserve in fragments but destroy in wholes. Working philosophers know this. In a grave correspondence to human limits, an apothegm is better philosophy than an organon.

Still, I see some evidence, here and there, that the critics are beginning to stir themselves.

What Lowell thinks of all this he hasn't said. He has written almost no criticism, and apparently does not intend to write any. I salute him! But at all events we know that he has been working for twenty years in the heart of the movement I have described, among eastern writers and artists. He has been associated with the painters who gave their work the unfortunate names of abstract expressionism and action painting, and with theatrical people who have used such concepts as the happening and non-acting acting; these being half-understood designations for the artist's life-constructing function, This has been Lowell's milieu. Of course he has shared it with many other writers; what I have been discussing in terms of Lowell's work is a shift or tightening of artistic intention which cuts across every line. And one thing more is certain. Whatever the rationale, or whether or not there is any rationale, we cannot read Lowell's autobiographical writing, from *Life Studies* to *Near the Ocean,* without seeing that we are in touch with a writer who is in fact making his life as he goes along, and with a degree of seriousness and determination and self-awareness that surpasses the artistic confidence of any previous generation. He has resolved to accept reality, all reality, and to take its fragments indiscriminately as they come, forging from them this indissoluble locus of metaphoric connections that is known as Robert Lowell. No wonder he is enthusiastic.

Hence we see that in his translations, and for that matter in all his work, Lowell's methods are distinct from those of Ezra Pound. This is a distinction we must be careful to draw, I think, because Pound's methods have become so much second-nature to us all that they blur our recognition of the principal fact about the two poets, viz. that the historical gulf separating them is enormous. Thus when Pound wrenches and distorts Propertius in the translations from the Elegies, or when he capsulates writing from many sources in the *Cantos,* he does so in the interest of a general program of cultural aggrandisement conducted from a base of personal security. There is no uncertainty of values in the *Cantos;* in this respect the poem is as old-fashioned as *Candide* or Boethius. Nor is there any uncertainty of poetic personality. The writer—"ego, scriptor"—is a steady and reliable, if sometimes rudimentary, presence. Pound's work, in effect, is an Arnoldian criticism of life on a very grand scale, which is only possible because the critic looks out from the secure bastion of his own personality founded on a stable scheme of values. Lowell, on the other hand, is a poetic ego without fixtures: in a sense neither being nor becoming, but a sequence of fragments, like the individual frames of a movie film, propelled and unified by its own creative drive. This does not mean that Lowell's work lacks values; his poems are as strenuously moral as anyone's. But his objective is not critical, nor even broadly cultural; it is personal; and the moral elements of his poetry are used, not as precepts, but as the hypotheses of an experimental venture in self-validation. In his autobiographical work, both translations and original poems, Lowell employs many of Pound's devices, perhaps most of them, but his ends are his own—and this makes all the difference. It means a radically different creative outlook, issuing in new poetic justifications and criteria.

And so I return to my starting-place; for I am sure everyone knows that the hypothetical reviewer with whom I began is really myself, and that all this speculation springs from the moment when my review copy of *Near the Ocean* arrived in the mail. I have already said that I do not like the sequence of autobiographical poems which forms the heart of this new book. Let me add to this three further points.

1. Why has Lowell moved progressively away from the simplicity of *Life Studies* toward a new formalism? Is it only a reversionary impulse? Is it an attempt to give greater objectivity to the random, fragmentary materials of his autobiography by reintroducing elements of fixative convention? Is it from a desire to make fuller use of his talent; i.e., to turn his defect to advantage by emphasizing prosody and syntax? No doubt all these reasons, and others, are at work. But the result is a too great concentration of effort upon the verbal surface—to my mind very unfortunate. We now have poems which are compositions of brilliant minutiae, like mosaics in which the separate tiles are so bright and glittering that we cannot see the design. A mosaic is fine, it is the model *par excellence* for poetry in our time, but if we are to see the pattern, the separate pieces must be clear and naturally arranged; and in the best mosaics the colors are subdued rather than gaudy.

2. In point of substance I ask, still in a firmly subjective mode: what are the most useful parts of autobiography? To my mind the most interesting of Lowell's poems are those from his present, concerning his wife, divorce, children, illness, etc., but these are few and small compared to the great number about his youth and childhood, his ancestors, his visits to the family graveyard. I detect a faint odor of degenerate Freudian sentimentalism. Have we not had enough of this, and more? We are interested in the man, the present, unfinished, lively being. If the term "confessional" is to be applied to Lowell's work, although I have said why I think it is inadequate, then I suggest he has not confessed enough. In particular one topic is lacking, unless I am mistaken: his conversion to the Church of Rome and his subsequent—should I say recusancy? I hardly know. He was in and then he was out, and the rest for us is a mystery. Surely this touches the man. And surely it touches many issues of our time: justice, probity, the individual and the mass, the role of love in society, even peace and war. In effect, I advocate a stiffening up of autobiographical substance, a colder and more realistic view. Let the rigor now reserved for verbal superficies be applied to the exact new content of experience.

3. But judgment fails. In this art it has not found its place. If I were to suggest one ultra-technical criterion still available to a poet in Lowell's circumstances, I would say: relevance. Be random, yes, fragmentary and open-ended—these are the

conditions of life—but scrutinize every component of your act of creation for its relevance. The advantage of random observation is not only in what comes but in what is let go. Avoid the extraneous like the plague. Lowell does not always manage it, and his defect is not the advantage it might be. His style, though more deeply in-wrought than before, is still too much like a shell, a carapace, an extraneity. We see again and again that the most difficult work of imagination is not when it soars in fantasy but when it plods in fact. And what a force of imagination has gone into these poems! A man's being, fought for, fragment by fragment, there on the page: this we can recognize. And we know that in such poetry the risk of failure is no longer a risk, but a surety. It must be taken, eaten. The very poem which seems most awkward to us may be the one that will wrench us away, finally, from the esthetic fixatives of the conventions of irresponsibility, and release us into responsible creation. If we read Lowell's new poems in the light of the problems he is facing, we will know that although we must, since we are human, judge them, our judgment is not something superior or separate, it is a part of his struggle, as his struggle is a part of ours. In this knowledge we may discover what we have been groping toward for centuries: not humility, which we don't need, nor magnanimity, which I hope we already have, but the competence of human freedom.

*Notes*

1. Lowell has admitted as much. See his *Paris Review* interview.
2. Miss Levertov assumes a base in Charles Olson's "projective verse," of course, but to my mind Olson's ideas are even more unfulfilled (and unfulfillable).
3. An extreme statement; in one sense art had always been a world apart. But in another the enclosed *and* limitless masterpieces of 1910–1940 did raise the possibility of an art that was not only distinct from "objective reality" but contradistinct; thus engendering a philosophical departure far more serious than the shallow Yellow-Book estheticism from which it partly sprang.

## HELEN VENDLER
### "A Difficult Grandeur" (1975)
### *Part of Nature, Part of Us*
#### 1980, pp. 125–36

In 1973 Robert Lowell, our greatest contemporary poet, published three volumes at once—*History, For Lizzie and Harriet*, and *The Dolphin*—and by that decisive self-presentation made us all once again confront his tumultuous and vexed career. The books were prudishly ignored by the National Book Award judges, who refused even to nominate the entirely new one, *The Dolphin*, for an award, but it later won the Pulitzer Prize for poetry, and reviews mirrored the mixed feelings reflected in the award-giving. *History* is a recasting, in chronological order and revised form, of the poems which appeared in *Notebook*; bracketing it are *For Lizzie and Harriet*, about Lowell's former wife and child, and *The Dolphin*, about his new wife and child. Personal history and the history of the race are Lowell's subjects, and the brutal force of the three books taken at once forced energetic postures of repudiation or championship from all his readers.

Lowell, though born of the Winslows, the Starks, and the Lowells, and perhaps our last intellectual New England poet, is nonetheless not a parochial Boston voice. The eccentricity of his life began, we may think, with his expulsion, for throwing stones, from the Boston Public Garden; it continued with his leaving Harvard for Kenyon College; it was marked by a conversion, though temporary, to Roman Catholicism, followed by imprisonment during World War II as a conscientious objector; it included successive periods of mental illness and successive marriages; and in its combination of reclusiveness and public action, it embodied its own contradictions. The books that issued from this life trace, at first obscurely and then candidly (some have said exhibitionistically), the contours of Lowell's experience, and offer us a poetry of difficult grandeur.

In Lowell, the "mill of the mind" (as Yeats called it) grinds a diverse grain with a stony force. Perhaps the first and only question put to us by its incessant activity is why the grim books that make up his collected works should give us, in any sense, pleasure. Lowell's dramatic power has an edge of malice and, in his tragic moments, cruelty. Both malice and cruelty are countered by a quietism that took its extreme form in the early portrait of the shrine of Our Lady of Walsingham in "The Quaker Graveyard at Nantucket"—the face of the statue "expressionless, expresses God." This quietism later took the form of an expressionless, if biting, historical impartiality. But behind cruelty, malice, and deadly observation lies a covert idealism, sometimes self-indulgent and knowingly sentimental, sometimes pure. His commonest fantasies are of "tyrannizers and the tyrannized," whether Jonathan Edwards terrifying his congregation, or Stalin executing his friends; in our putatively democratic America, Lowell speculates on the use and abuse of power and kingship.

His sonnets throw up nearly indigestible fragments of experience, unprefaced by explanation, unexplained by cause or result; sudden soliloquies of figures from Biblical times to contemporary history; translations; diary jottings; stately imitations of known forms; the whole litter and debris and detritus of a mind absorptive for fifty years. His free association, irritating at first, hovering always dangerously toward the point where unpleasure replaces pleasure, nonetheless becomes bearable, and then even deeply satisfying, on repeated rereading. And if Verdun or Thomas More or Frank Parker is not in our sphere of reference, we can slide off to poems on the march on Washington, or private walks, or Emerson, or a Cambridge blizzard, or New York taxi drivers. The presence of the familiar, and the genuineness of its note, act to assure the genuineness of the rest.

Lowell is one of our most learned and widely read poets, liking encyclopedic reference for its own sake. He tells us that when he was a boy, he "skulked in the attic, / and got two hundred French generals by name, / from A to V—from Augereau to Vandamme." Any one of the two hundred might put in an appearance in *History*, and other, more private allusions to a family past jostle the large and casual mention of historical figures. Lowell has a formidable genius for the details of life, those details which made *Life Studies* an unrivaled family history in verse, and which, filling the pages of *History*, constitute an unspeakably dense poetic or secondary world. It is a world where, even after the publication of *Life Studies*, the Lowell ancestors refuse to disappear:

They won't stay gone, and stare with triumphant
    torpor,
as if held in my fieldglasses' fog and enlargement.

Like some crowded Tiergarten, Lowell's poetry exhausts all species. Since everything is here, we cannot exactly define the poet as a selective collector; he is rather the curator of the world, and it is only in the tone of regard with which this curator presents his specimens, whether alive or fossilized, that we can catch his likeness. That tone, though fierce, is measured. For him, the monuments of culture are not, as they

were for Rilke, inexhaustible proof of the ecstatic potential of man; history has not for Lowell, as it had for Tennyson, a teleological shape; and family and home are not finally, as they are to Allen Ginsberg's monstrous piety, sacred. The disloyalty of Lowell-as-grandson in *Life Studies*, where we see him doodling moustaches on the last Russian Czar, plays a decisive role in Lowell's historical perspective. Though his poetry has been seen, with some truth in respect to the early books, as one rising out of disgust, preoccupied with the grotesque, and violent in its sensibility, these qualities are not its determining ones. He has learned, partly through the fitful tenderness first manifested in *Life Studies*, to tame the apocalyptic to the eternal dailiness of life. It is not that his Miltonic avidity for omnipotence has disappeared; but its direction has altered, and the temporal has obscured the prophetic. In fact, *History* and its companion volumes, with their tenderness toward the earth and its offerings, contain the first legitimate continuance of Shakespeare's sonnets since Keats, full of "Any clear thing that blinds us with surprise . . . wandering silences and bright trouvailles." The closing poem in *For Lizzie and Harriet* demands quotation in any writing about Lowell's sonnets. In it he puts transcendence all that demands aspiration, vengeance, order, justice, law, salvation—to rest, and chooses instead a Shakespearean recurrence:

Before the final coming to rest, comes the rest
of all transcendence in a mode of being, hushing
all becoming. I'm for and with myself in my otherness,
in the eternal return of earth's fairer children,
the lily, the rose, the sun on brick at dusk,
the loved, the lover, and their fear of life,
their unconquered flux, insensate oneness. . . .

"My breath," says Lowell, "is life, the rough, the smooth, the bright, the drear."

Into his infernal scenarios enter the odd domestications of the universe, like the turtle discovered on the road, kept in the bathtub, then in the sink, where he refuses to eat:

raw hamburger mossing in the watery stoppage,
the room drenched with musk like kerosene—
no one shaved, and only the turtle washed.
He was so beautiful when we flipped him over:
greens, reds, yellows, fringe of the faded savage,
the last Sioux, old and worn. . . .

Lowell and his wife take the turtle to the river, watch him "rush for water like rushing into marriage." The "uncontaminated joy" of the turtle finding his proper food and element at last transforms the river for Lowell:

lovely the flies that fed that sleazy surface,
a turtle looking back at us, and blinking.

The turtle has some of the staunchness of the skunks in "Skunk Hour" (from *Life Studies*), but in that poem the poet cannot share in the cheerful animal life; his "ill-spirit sob[s] in each blood cell." In the vistas of the sonnets, however, the human species performs generic acts, like the lizard:

The lizard rusty as a leaf rubbed rough
does nothing for days but puff his throat
on oxygen, and tongue up passing flies,
loves only identical rusty lizards panting:
harems worthy this lord of the universe—
each thing he does generic, and not the best.

In the sonnets, Lowell embodies his maxims in fine-drawn descriptions, and views himself as not distinct from the lizard: "I, fifty, humbled with the years' gold garbage, / dead laurel grizzling my back like spines of hay." He moves ahead, "drawn on by my unlimited desire, / like a bull with a ring in his nose, a chain in the ring." The cause of our will to direction is only language: If seals should suddenly learn to write, "Then all seals, preternatural like us, / would take direction, head north—their haven / green ice in a greenland never grass." "The fish, the shining fish, they go in circles, / not one of them will make it to the Pole— / this isn't the point though, this is not the point." The "horrifying mortmain of ephemera" becomes in another view our only night on stage, as Lowell says in his poem about his ten-year-old daughter:

> Spring moved to summer—the rude cold rain
> hurries the ambitious, flowers and youth. . . .
>
> Child of ten, three quarters animal,
> three years from Juliet, half Juliet,
> already ripened for the night on stage—
> beautiful petals, what shall we hope for . . . ?

If I quote such poems, it is because the inexhaustibility of the world, the eternal return of earth' fairer children, became Lowell's subject in the sonnets, expressed with full knowledge of the fragile in the inexhaustible. This poetry has no need of invitation or seduction to win us; it beckons by the comprehension of its atlas, historical and geographical, its representation of all we know.

It does not abandon its previous myths, but it subjects them to a relentless modernizing. Genesis is thrust into Darwinian time, as we see the beginning of the world:

> The virus crawling on its belly like a blot,
> an inch an aeon; the tyrannosaur,
> first carnivore to stand on his two feet,
> the neanderthal, first anthropoid to laugh—
> we lack staying power, though we will to live.
> Abel learned this falling among the jellied
> creepers and morning-glories of the saurian sunset.

Lowell believes equally in Abel and the dinosaurs; and he decides, in a bold throw of the dice, to give twentieth-century speeches to all his characters, even those lost in antiquity. So Clytemnestra becomes Lowell's mother, complaining about her husband:

> "After my marriage, I found myself in constant
> companionship with this almost stranger I found
> neither agreeable, interesting, nor admirable,
> though he was always kind and irresponsible."

Lowell himself appears as the young Orestes, in Clytemnestra's Christmas poem:

> "O Christmas tree, how green thy branches—our
>     features
> could only be the most conventional,
> the hardwood smile, the Persian rug's abstraction,
> the firelight dancing in the Christmas candles,
> my unusual offspring with his usual scowl,
> spelling the fifty feuding kings of Greece,
> with a red, blue and yellow pencil. . . . I
> am seasick with marital unhappiness—"

The compulsion to rewrite history, to afford privileged glimpses of the hidden moments of intimacy in public lives, to insert in the book of history the commentaries of poets— Horace, Du Bellay, Góngora, Heine, Baudelaire, Bécquer, Leopardi, Rilke, Rimbaud—to modernize relentlessly in laconic colloquialisms, to assume familiarity, to impute motive—all this rules more of *History* than perhaps it should.

Yet what fixes us in admiration of this poetry is the continual presence of Lowell himself. He is at the shore, has eaten lobster, watches his dying fire, and thinks how we still discover the dead fires of druidic Stone Age men and quasi-mythical Celtic kings:

> . . . The fires men build live after them,
> this night, this night, I elfking, I stonehands sit
> feeding the wildfire wildrose of the fire
> clouding the cottage window with my lust's
> alluring emptiness. I hear the moon
> simmer the mildew on a pile of shells,
> the fruits of my banquet . . . a boiled lobster,
> red shell and hollow foreclaw, cracked, sucked dry,
> flung on the ash-heap of a soggy carton—
> it eyes me, two pinhead, burnt-out popping eyes.

This is the quintessential beauty of the appalling exactly drawn. It stands in counterpoint to the equal beauty of the beautiful exactly drawn, in this "imitation" from Bécquer:

> The thick lemony honeysuckle,
> climbing from the earthroot to your window,
> will open more beautiful blossoms to the evening;
> but these . . . like dewdrops, trembling, shining,
>     falling,
> the tears of day—they'll not come back. . . .

The vignettes of history spoken in Lowell's voice strike even more sharply than the resurrected voices of history left to speak for themselves. Here are the Pilgrims in New England:

> The Puritan shone here,
> lord of self-inflicted desiccation,
> roaming for outlet through the virgin forest,
> stalking the less mechanically angered savage—
> the warpath to three wives and twenty children.

As *History* moves to the modern era, Lowell speaks to his contemporaries, the dead poets—Eliot, Pound, Schwartz, MacNeice, Frost, Williams, Jarrell, Roethke—and to the then still living Berryman. He speaks as well to the other admired dead, from F. O. Matthiessen to Harpo Marx to Che Guevara. Each is allowed a remark, an epigram, a moment of appearance, before the spurt of life dies out: "The passage from lower to upper middle age / is quicker than the sigh of a match in the water." Interspersed are other sighs of aging, this one adapted from a letter by Mary McCarthy:

> Exhaust and airconditioning klir in the city . . .
> The real motive for my trip is dentistry,
> a descending scale: long ago, I used to drive
> to New York to see a lover, next the analyst,
> an editor, then a lawyer . . . time's dwindling
>     choice.

It was not to be expected that Lowell should forsake his autobiographical vein, but it is tempered often, in *History*, with episodes of pure and detached observation, as an immortal eye, indifferent to its own decay, makes notations of the disordered wonders of the earth—the panorama, for instance, of Cambridge in a blizzard:

> Risen from the blindness of teaching to bright snow,
> everything mechanical stopped dead,
> taxis no-fares . . . *the wheels grow hot from*
>     *driving*—
> ice-eyelashes, in my spring coat; the subway
> too jammed and late to stop for passengers;
> snow-trekking the mile from subway end to air-
>     port . . .
> to all-flights-canceled, fighting queues congealed
> to telephones out of order, stamping buses,
> rich, stranded New Yorkers staring with the wild,
>     mild eyes
> of steers at the foreign subway—then the train home,
> jolting with stately grumbling.

Such a passage rests in the present, in the isolation of perfect registering of sense, and prevents the worse isolation of the mind withdrawn from sense:

> Sometimes, my mind is a rocked and dangerous bell;
> I climb the spiral stairs to my own music,
> each step more poignantly oracular,
> something inhuman always rising in me—

Lowell works, in his poems of sense, like those "star-nosed moles, [in] their catatonic tunnels / and earthworks . . . only in touch with what they touch."

There are morals that can be quoted or deduced from the poems in *History* and its companion volumes, but they are not what vivifies them. These poems live neither on ideology nor on logic—props thought to be the mainstays of an earlier Lowell; instead, they yield to the lawless free associations of the rocked and dangerous mind. The worst one can say of Lowell's later verse is that its connections are often at first sight baffling and its use of slang sometimes uncertain; but the awed formality of the early verse was a young man's evasion of his own language. Repudiating the "monotony of vision" inherent in unending attachment to the child he was, and yet knowing that child alive in himself till death, Lowell feels the thread of self as perpetual clue, while following the labyrinths of change, forcing works into shape, dismayed by the recalcitrance of words, wishing a real, not artificial, flame on the hearth:

> I want words meat-hooked from the living steer,
> but a cold flame of tinfoil licks the metal log,
> beautiful unchanging fire of childhood
> betraying a monotony of vision . . .
> Life by definition breeds on change,
> each season we scrap new cars and wars and women.
> But sometimes when I am ill or delicate,
> the pinched flame of my match turns unchanging
>     green,
> a cornstalk in green tails and seeded tassel . . .
> A nihilist has to live in the world as is,
> gazing the impassable summit to rubble.

Of all styles, description is the most difficult to describe. Lowell freed himself from his large early abstractions, even from the categories of the individual soul that once seemed so natural. Taking on history as a discipline, Lowell refuses to be less than the world is.

Have we had a nihilist poet before this later Robert Lowell? Not a nihilist who is a disappointed idealist, but a philosophical nihilist, incorporating within truth both instinctual hope and equable resignation? How Lowell came to this nihilism is not clear; political and marital discouragement, the weariness of twenty years of cyclical mania and depression, and repeated, inevitable hospitalization would suffice, even without the blighting of Lowell's own generation by insanity, suicide, and tragedy. But the weariness is allowed to remain weariness, tending toward but never reaching that death whose "sweetness none will ever taste." "Life, hope, they conquer death, generally, always."

The comparative lack of fertility in Lowell's two weaker volumes, *For the Union Dead* and *Near the Ocean*—after their exquisite predecessor, the original *Life Studies*—warned us that Lowell had to find a new impulse of energy or die as a poet. It seemed impossible that he should go beyond *Life Studies*, with its finely modulated satiric memoir, "91 Revere Street," and its subsequent collection of family portraits. Though there were many beautiful poems in *Life Studies*, it was Part IV of that book, with its quality of sporadic memoir from a son not detached enough to be all-forgiving, but old enough to permit himself detachment, that immediately gained Lowell a new fame, a fame as misplaced in the adjective "confessional" as it was, in itself, deserved. It was not the confessions that made *Life Studies* so memorable; it was rather the quality of memory indelibly imprinted, a brilliance of detail almost unconsciously preserved in a store of words perpetually refreshed.

In *Life Studies*, a deliberate sparseness of syntax enhanced minute details, as daguerrotype succeeded daguerrotype, rendering the furniture, the cuckoo clocks, the lamps with doily shades, the hot water bottle, the golf-cap, the ivory slide rule, the Pierce Arrow, the billiards-table, the decor "manly, comfortable, / overbearing, disproportioned." If we believed in the confessions, it was because we were made to believe in their ambience. And all the forceful particularity of *Life Studies* reappears in Lowell's sonnets.

It is astonishing that anyone confronted with Lowell's three volumes of sonnets should still be praising *Lord Weary's Castle* over *History*. And yet it is done, for example, by a fellow poet who accuses Lowell of "self-exploitation" in *History*: "One senses the life lived in order to provide material for poems; one sees with horror the cannibal-poet who dines off portions of his own body, and the bodies of his family." There are flaws in *History*, of course, since there are no flawless books of poetry, but flaws die of themselves, in silence, and need no criticism for their extinction. A poet's necessary conversion of experience into art can hardly be called cannibalism, and if the accusation that "the life is lived in order to provide material for poems" is to be convincing, it must be proved. Poems are Lowell's life as much as his life is; perhaps more.

> Conscience incurable
> convinces me I am not writing my life;
> life never assures which part of ourself is life.

Lowell is not at his best in describing the chaos of present relation; *Life Studies* benefited from the haze, the selective screens of memory, which refined the *dramatis personae* into effigies of themselves, sepulchral statues fixed in eternally characteristic positions. The slip and flow of changing personal give-and-take is apparently not yet available to Lowell, and that truth is more damaging to his later poetry than any moral criticism. The lapses in the three books of sonnets spring from two sources—the cruel brevity of a fourteen-line form used for encyclopedic material, and the attempt to write of immediate personal interchange. When we lack Lowell's penumbra of information about Rome or the Enlightenment or the Chicago Convention, we miss the point; wishing for intimacy in the personal sonnets, we find sometimes simply the rags and tatters of conversation. "I am learning to live in history," Lowell says in *For Lizzie and Harriet*, and adds his definition: "What is history? What you cannot touch." Once it is irremediably past, and only then, does life give itself to the epiphanies of Lowell's verse, without losing itself as plight, and without divesting itself of dailiness. The shame of wrongdoing, the bitterness of the wronged, the claims of fidelity and the claims of change, must in life clash to a standstill, but nothing in the art of poetry serves justice as justice might urge in life. The extreme power, even of an apparently unjust position, cannot be gainsaid when it occurs. Here is Lowell, for instance, on the eternal problem of the subjection of women: In youth they were swallows, beautiful, capricious, full of movement and gaiety; they asked to be domesticated, to be put into nests, to be fed; now, oppressed by the drudgery of life, they metamorphose into stinging wasps: What are they but prostitutes? I quote the earlier version, called "Das ewig Weibliche":

> Serfs with a finer body and tinier brain—
> who asks the swallows to do drudgery,
> clean, cook, peck up their ton of dust per diem?

Knock on their homes, they go up tight with fear,
farting about all morning past their young,
small as wasps fuming in their ash-leaf ball.
Nature lives off the life that comes to hand;
yet if we knew and softly felt their being,
wasp, bee and bird might live with us on air;
the boiling yellow-jacket in her sack
of zebra-stripe cut short above the knee
escape . . . the nerve-wrung creatures, wasp, bee
    and bird,
felons for life or keepers of the cell,
wives in their wooden cribs of seed and feed.

Whatever our judgment of the social view of the poem,
who can dismiss its powerful metamorphoses, its fuming wasps
and boiling yellow-jackets, its lethal conjunction of seed and
feed? Finally, the only test of a poem is that it be unforgettable,
the natural held in the grip of vision. We know Lowell's vision,
a powerful one that has forgone the comforts of nostalgia, of
religion, seemingly of politics. In the sterner poems, he even
forgoes love, though *The Dolphin* lingers in a forlorn hope for
that subject even yet. Love itself bows to the eternal phenomenon of recurrence and fate:

I too maneuvered on a guiding string
as I execute my written plot.
I feel how Hamlet, stuck with the Revenge Play
his father wrote him, went scatological
under this clotted London sky.

But even within the rigid confines of the plot, still declaiming
words fed by the prompter, the poet finds some liberties of
choice and action hovering in possibility: To waver is to be
counted among the living, he says, and "survival is talking on
the phone." While death becomes "an ingredient of [his]
being," he nonetheless watches, from night to morning, "the
black rose-leaves / return to inconstant greenness." Writing and
writing and writing, with an urgency showing no diminution,
Lowell places himself, myopic and abashed, below his former
epic assaults on heaven:

I watch a feverish huddle of shivering cows;
you sit making a fishspine from a chestnut leaf.
We are at our crossroads, we are astigmatic
and stop uncomfortable, we are humanly low.

Though this is not a comfortable poetry, it has the solace
of truth in its picture of the misery, sense of stoppage, and
perplexed desultoriness of middle age. "They told us," says
Lowell, remembering the old motto, "by harshness to win the
stars." That was, for a long time, his mode, the Luciferian
embattled ascent, accompanied by an orchestration of clashing
arms and wars in heaven. Now, making a net, as he says, to
catch like the Quaker fishermen all the fish in the sea of life
and history, even up to Leviathan, he works with no props but
the mood of the occasion, with no sure guide but the
inexplicable distinctiveness of personal taste. Foretelling the
mixed extinction and perpetuity of his own poetic accomplishment, Lowell hangs up his nets in perpetuity. They are the
equivocal nets woven and unraveled by a Penelope:

I've gladdened a lifetime
knotting, undoing a fishnet of tarred rope;
the net will hang on the wall when the fish are eaten,
nailed like illegible bronze on the futureless future.

The self-epitaph was premature, but not on that account false.
The subjects of these poems will eventually become extinct,
like all other natural species devoured by time, but the
indelible mark of their impression on a single sensibility
will remain, in Lowell's votive sculpture, bronzed to
imperishability.

## STEPHEN YENSER
### From "Introduction: Prospects"
*Circle to Circle: The Poetry of Robert Lowell*
### 1975, pp. 2–11

He must have had an aim of his own in mind when,
during an interview in 1961, he remarked admiringly
that T. S. Eliot "has done what he said Shakespeare had done:
all his poems are one poem, a form of continuity that has
grown and snowballed."[1] As Lowell's own oeuvre has grown, it
has become more and more apparent that he is emulating the
examples of Eliot and Shakespeare, that his poetry is developing in a steady, organic manner, so that it has not only that
unity which is bestowed by a distinctive sensibility, but also
something of that quality of aesthetic necessity which we expect
to find in individual works of art. Although his successive
volumes have hardly been predictable, they do seem in
retrospect indispensable parts of an evolving pattern; and if that
pattern is not without its irregularities, the poetry is not the less
an organic whole for that. To study Lowell's career to date, in
other words, is to discover the precision of the paradox in his
phrase "a form of continuity."

When Lowell's first volume, *Land of Unlikeness*, appeared in 1944, it was immediately noted for its prosodic
intricacies, its "wit," and above all its energetic, not to say
zealous, Roman Catholic tone and imagery. In light of its
author's subsequent work, however, this volume now seems
most remarkable for the attitude toward language that it
reveals, for this attitude not only encourages specific poetic
forms, particular sorts of ingenuity, and a peculiar perspective
on the religious subject matter, but also gives rise to the basic
method of the early poetry. That method, which is not fully
developed until Lowell's second volume, consists in the
exploitation, frequently at the expense of referential function,
of the symbolic dimension of the language, and the cultivation, frequently at the expense of orthodox religion, of a
dialectical structure in the poems.

Lowell's early work, that is to say, is closely associated with
one of the strongest of our modern traditions, which is
redefined and referred to in the second chapter as neo-
symbolism. With other poets in this tradition, several of whom
were his friends and mentors, Lowell shares a modus operandi
that is rooted in the assumption that a verbal symbol has an
ontological status, that—as Coleridge had it—words are
"living things."[2] Among the ramifications of this assumption in
its modern form are the implicit principles, explained in detail
in the second chapter, that a symbol in a poem contains *ab ovo*
the whole poem; that any particular symbol *is* its interactions
with other symbols; and that a poem is thus a dynamic
structure whose action constitutes its meaning. Lowell has
done little public criticism and less aesthetics, but in view of
the influences adduced and the structures disclosed in the
second chapter, one seems warranted in thinking that these
fairly common, although rarely explicit, principles of neo-
symbolism underlie his poetry. Certainly these principles help
to explain the organizations of individual poems in *Lord
Weary's Castle* (1946), as well as the structures of later volumes
and the development of the work as a whole.

In fact, it is in his second volume that Lowell, forecasting
a development in *Life Studies*, begins to extend his structural
principles beyond the boundaries of the poem. Some readers
have noticed that beneath the panoply of religious symbolism,
several of the poems in *Lord Weary's Castle* are very personal,[3]
while at least one critic has pointed out that the volume has a
discernible organization.[4] What remains to be said is that more

of the poems than have been considered so are concerned with the poet; that some allude specifically to his own work; and that this latent autobiography, in which the poet's experience is figured as a circle whose end is in its beginning, is the major unifying element in the book. At this juncture early in his career, even as Lowell is developing a poetry in which the symbols are organically interrelated, two other changes are taking place: he is beginning to see his poems in the same way that he sees his symbols, and he is starting to organize those poems into a narrative sequence that is itself symbolic.

The latter strategies are suspended in *The Mills of the Kavanaughs* (1951), where Lowell attempts to find a means of plotting individual longer poems. His means—a combination of dream-vision and mythological parallelism—is only partially successful as a method of organization because he treats its elements virtually as though they were more metaphors to be organized; that is, he modifies dream with vision and myth with myth, just as in the shorter poems he modifies image with image, and the result is complexity without a framework. R. P. Blackmur has commented, in another connection, on this weakness in most younger poets:

> What happens in young poets, in poets short of mastery of plot, is that they use the plots of elder poets as if they were, what they appeared to be when seen, actually integral to the poems instead of the mere integrating agent. In short, your young poet treats plot like a detail, as if it were one more tension in his substance.[5]

Perhaps the motivation for Lowell's treatment of plot as a detail in *The Mills of the Kavanaughs* is that he cannot accept the eschatological resolution that accompanies any one of his appropriated parallels, for such acceptance would keep his poems from doing what he says elsewhere they should do: "include a man's contradictions."[6] In any case, the form that his dialectic takes in the longer poems of this third volume is that of careful self-contradiction, the repeated assertion in various ways of contrary analogies until the variants have overlapped often enough that the originally opposed terms are hardly separable.

The development of a poem by means of mutually qualifying analogies is a direct outgrowth of the poetics of *Lord Weary's Castle*, for that poetics emphasized the process of the poem and the dependence of any symbol for its meaning upon its interaction with other symbols. Lowell has never abandoned these operational principles, but with *Life Studies* (1959) he does surrender the attempt to construct a single long poem on the basis of them, and at the same time he relinquishes his religious and mythological symbolism. He does not, however, give up the effort to escape the confines of the lyric. On the contrary, even as he returns to short poems, he seeks to unify an entire book.

That the unity of *Life Studies*, like that of most of Lowell's volumes, has provoked comparatively little discussion can probably be attributed to the beguiling insouciance of many of the individual poems. As the poetry expands beyond the limits of the lyric, the poems sometimes seem incomplete and less self-contained than before; and since Lowell does deal more directly with the world about him as he moves away from religion, it is not unreasonable to suppose that this seeming incompleteness reflects the immediacy and fragmentary quality of raw experience. It is as though the struggle between contraries or within the flux of experience that heretofore has been the substance of Lowell's method were now a single term in his dialectic, with form its opposite member. To put this another way, until *Life Studies* Lowell had taken it for granted

that form was a necessary part of the individual poem, a vehicle for the wars that the Powers waged; but now form itself seems almost to be viewed as a deity (of an ambivalent nature) that needs to be challenged. With the formal integrity of separate poems thus a debatable matter, it is easy to forget to look beyond these poems to the new larger structures—the sequence and the book—that Lowell has created. Nevertheless, the term "studies," in the sense of unfinished sketches or preliminary drafts, only describes the appearance of these poems to the casual eye; and that this careless, frequently "confessional" surface is part and parcel of the meticulous, dispassionate organizations of some individual poems is one of the points of the fourth chapter.

A more salient point is that this whole volume is carefully laid out, so that the sequences designated by Lowell not only cohere in themselves but also constitute a single long sequence. Developing a technique employed to some extent in his second volume, Lowell creates by use of motifs a situation in which poems act at a distance on one another. Collectively the poems form a context that helps to shape them individually. Moreover, this context, the book, has a definite organization, for—to appropriate one of C. Day Lewis's felicitous images—there is one main theme that winds through the book and is reflected as it goes from different angles by each of the sequences.[7] Since this theme is the "breaking up" of the culture, the structure of the volume contributes significantly to the complex counterpoint of order and disorder, for the view of a disintegrating world is itself highly integrated.

The motif is also an important unifying device in *Imitations* (1961), the work that has caused more critical controversy than any other single volume by Lowell. One of the sources of the controversy is the failure on both sides to recognize the nature of the volume and its unity. *Imitations* is primarily neither a collection of translations nor a collection of original poems based on others, but rather a carefully organized *book*, the thematic center of which is the continuity of life and art for the poet. In effect, Lowell exploits the analogy drawn by Renato Poggioli when he says that "like the original poet, the translator is a Narcissus who in this case chooses to contemplate his own likeness not in the spring of nature but in the pool of art."[8] The adjustment that might be made is that in this case the translator is also and primarily an original poet, so that instead of simply seeing himself in the works of others (and thereby making himself an artist), he could also view himself *qua* artist in those works (and thereby remake himself as artist). This is exactly what Lowell does, as he selects poets who not only possess sensibilities akin to his—as any translator would be likely to do—but who also comment, or can be made to comment, on the sort of poetry that he writes. *Imitations* is thus a reflection of the poet's life at the same time that it is an extension of that life.

This book is more than that, however, because it incorporates as both a thematic and a structural element the rationale behind the artist's life. The idea that one creates his life and gives it form in persistently returning to his calling in spite of the knowledge that lasting success is impossible is a recurrent theme in the poems that Lowell has selected. The very organization of the poems embodies this theme, for they constitute a narrative of the archetypal experience of the artist, the progression from commitment through frustration (paradoxically a revitalizing force) to renewed commitment. The structure of this book, like that of *Lord Weary's Castle* and like that of *For the Union Dead*, is thus essentially circular.

The structure of Lowell's fifth volume encourages another spatial metaphor, that of an inverted triangle, since its physical center is its psychological nadir; and this feature, as well as the others just touched upon, is also true of his sixth, *For the Union Dead* (1964). This volume turns on a dark night of the soul, occasioned chiefly by the persona's loss of contact with objective reality and eventuating in his rediscovery of self and thereby of the world about him. Just after the pivotal point, a poem significantly entitled "Myopia: a Night," Lowell seems to allude to a passage in the work of Henri Bergson, which has been glossed by Wylie Sypher in these pertinent terms:

> In his effort to "touch bottom," Bergson turns inward to contemplate how the self exists within the flow of time, how it endures behind or within change. . . . If the self is to be known, it must be intuited in the dim and quiet eddies streaming like quicksands far below the mechanism of the rational mind. . . .[9]

After just such an intuition in the middle of *For the Union Dead*, the poems take on a more affirmative tone and the way up in the second half of the volume balances the way down in the first half. Again a collection of poems has been arranged to embody an archetypal experience, and again the volume itself is a symbol that attempts to convert the experience of seeking form into form itself. At the same time that the poems constitute a search for self, the self is being constituted by the search. It is not just the word, as it was in Lowell's beginning, but also the volume that is a "living thing," with a movement that is its meaning.

From such a conjunction of process and product as the last two books mentioned exemplify, it is but a short step to the idea that the proper locus of form is not art but life, or even that aesthetic organization is a spurious reproduction of vital form. The gradual, devious, but undeniable movement that we have been summarizing—from the short, highly compressed lyric dealing ostensibly with religious absolutes, through the sequence of subtly organized poems surveying the poet's past, to the book comprising poems dependent to some degree upon one another for their form and embodying the experience of writing—can be viewed as a tracking of art back to its lair of life, where it might be found to have shed its disguise. To the extent that this aim is accomplished, of course, art loses its identity. If in his beginning the neo-symbolist threatens his own existence as artist by removing himself from the objective world, at this extreme he imperils it by integrating himself with that world. If from the last stage noted above the poet proceeds to the next, so that his books depend upon the actual world for their "form," he has partly undermined his own raison d'être.

One can only speculate whether thoughts such as these were in Lowell's mind after the publication of *For the Union Dead*, but they might have been one motivation for the return to formal verse in *Near the Ocean* (1967). If the ocean is the welter of circumstance that threatens to overwhelm the aesthetic form, Lowell was indeed near it, and the return to a strict prosody in this volume might be a means of reasserting the integrity of the poetry. Rhyme and metre are not, however, the only means by which Lowell establishes objective form in *Near the Ocean*. When first encountered, the vignettes and even the poems in the title sequence might seem to occupy arbitrarily assigned positions, and Hayden Carruth's summary of a trend in modern literature, inspired by a consideration of this book, might seem applicable:

> Hence in literature any particular "work" is linear rather than circular in structure, extensible rather than terminal in intent, and at any given point inclusive rather than associative in substance; at least these are its tendencies. And it is autobiographical,

that goes without saying. It is an act of self-creation by an artist within the tumult of experience.[10]

After some reflection, however, at least a few of Carruth's comments can serve as foils for, rather than descriptions of, this volume. While it is true that the individual poems in the title sequence and that sequence itself are "extensible" in the sense that they are not informed by a symmetry that imposes a beginning, middle, and end, it is also true that each of these poems and the group as a whole have a chronological progression and therefore acquire some of the irrevocability of position that hours of the day and days of the week have. Moreover, the volume as a whole describes a circular movement, for the chronological sequence in the present at the beginning of the book is balanced by a chronological sequence in the past at its conclusion, the inevitable implication being that the future is a repetition of the past, or that the future is to be found in the past. Borrowing a phrase used by Murray Krieger in another context, one might say that from this point of view the book's structure consists in "the circularizing of its linear movement."[11]

Carruth's comments on the autobiographical and self-creative aspects of this book seem entirely appropriate, on the other hand, not only to *Near the Ocean*, but also to the subsequent volumes, *Notebook 1967–68* (1969) and its revised and enlarged edition, *Notebook* (1970). These volumes undoubtedly make more concessions to the randomness and fragmentation of diaristic autobiography than any preceding book, and from the very title of each to its author's "Afterthought," they exist in the penumbra between flux and form. A notebook is perhaps the closest written analogue to raw experience, a largely unpredictable record of events and thoughts that might otherwise be lost in the shuffle of things, a repository for ephemera and inklings that might later be given more consideration, a higher polish. The dates in the title of the first edition drive home the point: this is art that goes hand in hand with its mortal and mortifying enemy. If experiences in time are not discrete entities, neither are the poems and sequences in these volumes, unless discreteness is defined only in terms of spatial limitation. If it is difficult to draw the line between experience and poetry in the first place, how much more difficult it must be to distinguish poem from poem. Lowell even insists upon the impossibility of such distinctions in his "Afterthought" in the first edition when he advises us that "the poems in this book are written as one poem." When he goes ahead to say that his plot "rolls with the seasons," he seems to have reached that point mentioned above at which the book becomes dependent upon the actual world for its form.

But, as Lowell himself suggests, there is again a circular movement through the *Notebooks*, and if the movement is modeled on the seasons, it is still a structural means. Indeed, the implications of the *Notebooks* are that the same principles underlie life and art, that there is a fructifying tension between flux and form in each realm, and perhaps even that art need be no less—or no more—than a reflection in small of this relationship as it exists in nature. In blurring these distinctions, however, Lowell weakens his aesthetic structures at almost every level. Surely such a recognition is at least partly responsible for the radical revision of his *Notebook*.

In the summer of 1973, Lowell published simultaneously three volumes of poetry, all written in the same fourteen-line blank verse form that he had used exclusively since 1967: *History*, a reworking of *Notebook*; *For Lizzie and Harriet*, a collection and revision of poems once scattered throughout *Notebook*; and *The Dolphin*, a new sequence. The two smaller volumes, dedicated respectively to the poet's second wife and their daughter and to his third wife, work the personal, journalistic vein that ran through *Notebook. History,* on the other hand, is a monumental structure built largely of what was quarried earlier. Perhaps still in progress, this volume promises or threatens to become Lowell's *Cantos,* or at least *His Toy, His Dream, His Rest.* It is structurally distinguished from these two works, however, as well as from its previous phases, by a chronological framework that shapes its dense reticulation of motifs, many of which derive from earlier volumes.

In fact, by including versions of poems from all of Lowell's preceding volumes (except the first, much of which was incorporated in the second), *History* testifies to and helps to establish a contextual relationship among all of these volumes that is comparable to the relationships among the poems within one of them. The book is a synecdoche for Lowell's work: what his poetry is to history, *History* is to his poetry. More than this, it is Lowell's most ambitious attempt to date to discover the whole of his life—which is to say its shape as well as much of its data—in a part of it.

If it still risks being lost, as one of its sections implies the *Cantos* risk being lost, "in the rockslide of history," *History* certainly better fits the conception of a book that is "one poem" than had either of the *Notebooks.* A troubling and troubled work, which takes chances that most of us did not even know could be taken, it nevertheless reassures us that Lowell has not lost touch with the formal desiderata of poetry, just as he has not lost touch with his earliest work. Perhaps there is little need to worry that he will ever do so. The principle that accounts for the nature of his development so far and betokens that of his future development also provides for the preservation of the shaping spirit. Lowell has stated this principle indirectly in the remark on Eliot quoted near the beginning of this introduction. More directly, in a statement that recalls that one and that the following chapters attempt to elucidate, he has said: "All your poems are in a sense one poem, and there's always the struggle of getting something that balances and comes out right, in which all the parts are good, and that has experience that you value."[12]

*Notes*

1. "The Art of Poetry III: An Interview [with Frederick Seidel]," *The Paris Review,* no. 25 (Winter–Spring 1961), p. 92. Lowell had in mind Eliot's comments on Shakespeare in "John Ford" (1932), in *Selected Essays* (London: Faber & Faber, 1951), pp. 193–204. Eliot argues that "what is 'the whole man' is not simply his greatest or maturest achievement, but the whole pattern formed by the sequence of plays; so that we may say confidently that the full meaning of any one of his plays is not in itself alone, but in that play in the order in which it was written, in its relation to all of Shakespeare's other plays, earlier and later: we must know all of Shakespeare's work in order to know any of it"; and that "the whole of Shakespeare's work is *one* poem, and it is the poetry of it in this sense, not the poetry of isolated lines and passages or the poetry of the single figures which he created, that matters most." For his extension of the argument, see "What Is Minor Poetry?" (1944), in *On Poetry and Poets* (1956; rpt. New York: Noonday, 1961).

2. S. T. Coleridge, *Unpublished Letters,* ed. E. L. Griggs (London: Constable, 1932), I, 256; quoted in Charles Feidelson, Jr., *Symbolism and American Literature* (Chicago and London: University of Chicago Press, Phoenix, 1953), p. 75. Chapter two below owes a great deal to Feidelson's book. See also M. H. Abrams's remarks on "Coleridge and the Aesthetics of Organicism," in *The Mirror and the Lamp: Romantic Theory and the Critical Tradition* (New York: Oxford University Press, 1953).

3. See esp. Hugh B. Staples, *Robert Lowell: The First Twenty Years* (New York: Farrar, Straus, 1962), pp. 38–39; and M. L. Rosenthal, *The New Poets* (New York: Oxford University Press, Galaxy, 1967), p. 71.

4. Irvin Ehrenpreis, "The Age of Lowell," in *American Poetry,* Stratford-on-Avon Series, 7, ed. Irvin Ehrenpreis (New York: St. Martin's Press, 1965), pp. 69–72.

5. "And Others," in *Form and Value in Modern Poetry* (New York: Doubleday Anchor, 1957), pp. 336–337.

6. Quoted in Stanley Kunitz, "Telling the Time," *Salmagundi,* 1, 4 (1966–67), 22.

7. *The Poetic Image* (London: Jonathan Cape, 1947), p. 50. Like Sypher's book, cited below, Day Lewis's has been a valuable but general reference.

8. "The Added Artificer," in *On Translation,* ed. Reuben Brower (1959; rpt. New York: Oxford University Press, Galaxy, 1966), p. 139.

9. *Loss of the Self in Modern Literature and Art* (New York: Random House, 1962), pp. 58–59. The dates of the two publications together with the similarity of the imagery make it seem that Lowell may have read Sypher's account.

10. "A Meaning of Robert Lowell," in *The American Literary Anthology 2,* ed. George Plimpton, et al. (New York: Random House, 1969), p. 72.

11. "*Ekphrasis* and the Still Movement of Poetry; or, *Laokoön* Revisited," in *Perspectives on Poetry,* ed. James L. Calderwood and Harold Toliver (New York: Oxford University Press, Galaxy, 1968), p. 324.

12. Lowell, "The Art of Poetry III," p. 72.

# MINA LOY

## 1882–1966

Mina Lowy (she later dropped the "w") was born in London on December 27, 1882. Raised among the middle class, she studied painting in London, Munich, and eventually Paris. While living in Paris she married another young English painter, Stephen Haweis, in 1904. Her works were exhibited in several Parisian salons; her future as an artist looked bright. She and her husband moved to Florence in 1907 and she began associating with the Futurists. Her husband left her as her interest turned towards poetry. By the time she arrived in New York in 1916 she already was a minor celebrity. Friends had submitted her avant-garde poetry to small American magazines, and her first poem, titled "Aphorisms on Futurism," appeared in Alfred Stieglitz's *Camera Work.*

Loy remained in New York until 1923, writing and publishing numerous poems. Conservative critics objected to her often explicit sexual themes and her unconventional use of punctuation. However, other critics compared her work favorably to the poetry of other young modernists like William Carlos Williams and Marianne Moore. When she returned to Paris in 1923 she found that a collection of her poems had been published under the misspelled title *Lunar Baedecker*. Gertrude Stein and Marcel Duchamp were among her many friends in Paris during the 1920s; by the end of the decade she had begun designing lampshades for a business backed by Peggy Guggenheim. Always reluctant to publish her work on her own, Loy's name disappeared from literary magazines as she devoted herself to other artistic endeavors.

Loy returned to New York in 1936 and became a naturalized citizen ten years later. In 1954 she retired to Aspen, Colorado, where she lived with her two daughters by a second marriage to Arthur Craven, the poet-boxer of Dada fame. Loy died in Aspen on September 25, 1966. Although her work had stopped appearing in magazines around 1925, Loy had continued to write throughout her lifetime. Some of her poetry was collected and published by Jonathan Williams in *Lunar Baedeker and Time-tables* (1958). Recently a volume of previously unpublished poetry, *The Last Lunar Baedeker* (1982), appeared along with several critical studies of her work.

During the war, another curious woman, exotic and beautiful, came to New York from foreign shores: the English Jewess, Mina Loy. Visiting the shrines of modern art and literature in Paris and Florence, and being accepted as a coeval in the maddest circles, Miss Loy, who is an artist as well as poet, imbibed the precepts of Apollinaire and Marinnetti and became a Futurist with all the earnestness and irony of a woman possessed and obsessed with the sum of human experience and disillusion. Her first poems appeared in Alfred Stieglitz's *Camera Work*, along with some of the earliest work of Gertrude Stein. Most of Mina Loy's later work, including a whole issue of her "Songs To Joannes," appeared in *Others*, and created a violent sensation. She has never published a book. Though *Others* was a private publication with a circulation of only a few hundred copies, the first number was hailed with public derision: it contained some of Miss Loy's "Love Songs." In an unsophisticated land, such sophistry, clinical frankness, sardonic conclusions, wedded to a madly elliptical style scornful of the regulation grammar, syntax and punctuation (page E. E. Cummings), horrified our gentry and drove our critics into furious despair. The nudity of emotion and thought roused the worst disturbance, and the utter nonchalance in revealing the secrets of sex was denounced as nothing less than lewd. It took a strong digestive apparatus to read Mina Loy. Unhappily for her, the average critic had been fed on treacle and soda water over too long a Puritanical term in the jails of our daily papers. I remember how some of the reviews puzzled, rather than injured her. She wondered what sort of a land she had come to and, wondering no longer, returned to the mountains and lakes of Italy. Here are the lines which opened the overture and released the pens of Billingsgate:

> Spawn of fantasies
> Sitting the appraisable
> Pig Cupid       his rosy snout
> Rooting erotic garbage . . .

To reduce eroticism to the sty was an outrage, and to do so without verbs, sentence structure, punctuation, even more offensive. And yet, behind the abnormally scornful style, the careful reader, reading many times, might have detected genuine emotions, feelings inspired by "something the shape of a man" whose "skin-sack" packed "all the completions of my infructuous impulses" and whose hair is "a God's door-mat" on the threshold of the mind. We, here in enlightened Manhattan, were simply unaccustomed to such passionate, clinical writing:

> We might have coupled
> In the bed-ridden monopoly of a moment
> Or broken flesh with one another
> At the profane communion table

> Where wine is spilled on promiscuous lips
> We might have given birth to a butterfly
> With the daily news
> Printed in blood on its wings.

Certain sacrilegious references to the love of the Holy Trinity, as compared with the love of manhood and womanhood sweeping the brood clean out, were too strong even for nonconformists. Had a man written these poems, the town might have viewed them with comparative comfort. But a woman wrote them, a woman who dressed like a lady and painted charming lamp-shades. It is difficult to appraise the work of Mina Loy in perspective. Though she was original, a number of eccentricities, some of which are conscious distortions of style, hamper one's full admiration. I am certain, in reviewing the glamorous years of the poetic civil war, that a few of her best poems will survive what I used to consider the still better poems of other members of the group. Some of my old enthusiasms have cooled in perspective, whereas doubts I held concerning Miss Loy have vanished. Though I printed the work she gave me almost in toto, much of it puzzled me at the time. I felt that she might have made a greater effort to communicate herself more clearly. She did not have to compromise with the reader, but with a stricter artistic conscience. If some of her work still looks haphazard, the best of it remains provocative and wears well in the proverbial test of time. —ALFRED KREYMBORG, "Originals and Eccentrics," *Our Singing Strength: An Outline of American Poetry 1620–1930*, 1929, pp. 488–90

---

## YVOR WINTERS
### "Mina Loy"
*Dial*, June 1926, pp. 496–99

Mr Sacheverell Sitwell once wrote a very long poem, two lines of which stay in my memory:

> My natural clumsiness was my only bar to progress
> Until I conquered it by calculation.

As I go through such of Miss Loy's poems as I possess, this seems to describe her. If she has not actually conquered the clumsiness which one can scarcely help feeling in her writings, she has, from time to time, overcome it; and these occasional advantages have resulted in momentous poems. Or perhaps it is not clumsiness, but the inherently unyielding quality of her material that causes this embarrassment. She moves like one walking through granite instead of air, and when she achieves a moment of beauty it strikes one cold.

More intent on the gutter and its horrors than any of the group with which she was allied, and more intensely cerebral, perhaps, than any save one of them, her work ordinarily presents that broken, unemotional, and occasionally witty observation of undeniable facts that one came to regard as the rather uninviting norm of Others poetry. (Let me hasten to explain that I do not wish to appear to disparage Others, but norms, which are useful only as definite places from which to escape. Others seems to me the most interesting single group manifestation that has yet occurred in American verse.) Her unsuccessful work is easier to imitate than that of any of the three other outstanding members of her set—Miss Moore, Dr Williams, and Mr Stevens—and beyond a doubt has been more imitated. Rhythmically, it is elementary, whereas the metres of Miss Moore and Dr Williams are infinitely varied and difficult, and those of Mr Stevens are at least infinitely subtle. Emotionally, Dr Williams is no farther from what one might regard as some sort of common denominator than Miss Loy, and he has covered—and opened to poetry—vastly more territory, so that the likelihood of his becoming the chief prophet of my own or some future generation is probably greater. Already, in fact, he is something of this nature, as the Dada movement has added to the principles that he has at one time or another stated, indicated, or practised, nothing save a few minor vices. Of all contemporary poets, he is, I should say, the closest in spirit to Miss Loy. Miss Moore, on the other hand, as a point of departure, is unthinkable—like Henry James, she is not a point of departure at all, but a terminus. Her works suggests nothing that she herself has not carried to its logical and utmost bounds. And Mr Stevens, with his ethereal perversity, inhabits a region upon which one feels it would be a pity to encroach.

And yet I think that few poets of my own generation would deny that these writers as a group are more sympathetic, as well as more encouraging, than either the Vorticists or the Mid-Americans. Their advantage over the professional backwoodsmen consists in part, perhaps, in superior intellectual equipment, but mainly, I suspect, in a larger portion of simple common-sense—they have refused from the very beginning to consider themselves in any way related to Shawnee Indians or potato-beetles, and have passed unscathed through a period of unlimited sentimentality. Their advantage over the Vorticists consists not so much in their having superior brains, but in their having used their own brains exclusively. Had their own brains been unequal to the task, this would have been but little advantage, as Mr Pound, Mr Eliot, and H.D. are formidable rivals, and, it seems to me, genuinely great poets, but the courage of the Others group appears, by this time, to have been pretty thoroughly justified. It was a hard-headed courage, and little repaid by adulation, and is nearly as admirable as its poetic outcome. One can find little in contemporary poetry of a similar sturdiness except in the work of Messrs Hardy and Robinson.

Of the four Mr Stevens and Miss Moore deserve the least compassion for their struggle, if compassion is to be meted out—one suspects that they always knew they could do it; and Dr Williams, hurling himself at the whole world with the passion of the former bantam-weight champion who bore his name, has achieved a blinding technique and magnificent prose and poetry by sheer excess of nervous power. And indeed compassion is scarcely the proper offering to bring Miss Loy—one feels timorous in bringing anything. She attacked the dirty commonplace with the doggedness of a weight-lifter. Nearly any one might have written her worst poems, and innumerable small fry have written poems as good. Her success, if the least dazzling of the four, is not the least impressive, and is by all odds the most astounding. Using an unexciting method, and

writing of the drabbest of material, she has written seven or eight of the most brilliant and unshakably solid satirical poems of our time, and at least two non-satirical pieces that possess for me a beauty that is unspeakably moving and profound. Satires like "The Black Virginity" and the piece on D'Annunzio need give little if any ground before the best of Pope or Dryden, and poems like "Der Blinde Junge" and the "Apology of Genius" need, in my judgement, yield ground to no one. And then there is the host of half-achieved but fascinating poems like "Lunar Baedecker." One cons them—with the author's pardon—as one might a rosary, and is thankful if the string doesn't break, but most of the beads are at the very least spectacular:

> Delirious Avenues
> lit
> with the chandelier souls
> of infusoria
> . . .
> Onyx-eyed Odalisques
> and ornithologists
> observe
> the flight
> of Eros obsolete

They are images that have frozen into epigrams. It is this movement from deadly stasis to stasis, slow and heavy, that, when unified and organized, gives to her poetry its ominous grandeur, like that of a stone idol become animate and horribly aware:

> Lepers of the moon . . .
> unknowing
> How perturbing lights
> our spirit
> on the passion of Man
> until you turn on us your smooth fool's faces
> like buttocks bared in aboriginal mockeries
> . . .
> In the raw caverns of the Increate
> we forge the dusk of Chaos
> to that imperious jewelry of the Universe
> —the Beautiful . . .

Such an apology is in itself a proof of genius—and of a genius that rises from a level of emotion and attitude which is as nearly common human territory as one can ever expect to find in a poet. Mr Rodker once said that she wrote of the SOUL (in four capital letters, unless my memory betrays me) but the word doesn't mean much, no matter how one spells it. One might substitute the *subconscious* (which Mr Rodker doubtless meant) but this word is nearly as frayed. Whatever tag one fastens to it, and regardless of what happens to her emotion in passing through her brain (which, being a good brain, is responsible for her being a good poet) one can scarcely help sensing at bottom a strange feeling for the most subterranean of human reactions, of a padding animal resentment, and of a laughter that is curiously physical. This habitation of some variety of common ground, although it may have no intrinsic aesthetic virtue, yet places her beside Dr Williams as one of the two living poets who have the most, perhaps, to offer the younger American writers—they present us with a solid foundation in place of Whitman's badly aligned corner-stones, a foundation which is likely to be employed, I suspect, for a generation or two, by the more talented writers of this country, or by a rather large part of them. This suggested development is not a call to salvation, nor even a dogmatic prediction, but simply a speculation. If it materializes, Emily Dickinson will have been its only forerunner.

KENNETH FIELDS
"The Poetry of Mina Loy"

*Southern Review,* Summer 1967, pp. 597–607

Mina Loy was a contemporary of Williams and Pound, and although she was born in England, her poems are an important part of the American free verse movement. She published her first poems in Alfred Stieglitz's *Camera Work,* and later appeared in *Little Review, Others, The Dial,* and other prominent American magazines. Like the work of most first-rate writers, her poems were controversial, but she was held in high regard by her contemporaries. In 1921, Pound writes to Marianne Moore: "Also, entre nooz: is there anyone in America except you, Bill and Mina Loy who can write anything of interest in verse?" *Lunar Baedecker* [sic], containing 31 poems, was published in 1923, and Jonathan Williams, in 1958, published *Lunar Baedeker and Time-tables,* unfortunately, on his small and little-known press. This book went out of print almost immediately, and today Mina Loy's poems are virtually unobtainable. One of the best poets of the period, she is now scarcely read, and her name appears only in the midst of semischolarly lists compiled by men more interested in history than in distinguished poets.

Everyone knows that the tens and twenties were a difficult period for writers, and the fragmentary and obscure details of Mina Loy's private life which emerge are anything but happy. Her attitude toward her experience and much of her poetic subject matter is one of detached irony of an unusual directness. "Mina Loy," recalls William Carlos Williams in his *Autobiography,*

> was very English, very skittish, an evasive, long-limbed woman too smart to involve herself . . .
> with any of us . . .

And from the questionnaire in the final issue of the *Little Review* (May 1929) we learn that she considered her weakest characteristic to be her "compassion," and her strongest, her "capacity for isolation." These answers tell us something about her poetry. She does not mean that her compassion is deficient; but rather, that compassion, inescapable and human, causes her so much pain that isolation seems a virtue. And we find both characteristics in her poems.

I have said that her attitude is one of detached irony of unusual directness. This may appear contradictory, but it is not. Let me illustrate what I mean by quoting the final lines of "Lunar Baedecker," in which she describes the moon ("Crystal concubine") in terms of its excessive use as a poetic property. The irony permits her to achieve objective distance, but the lines are impressive for their straightforwardness:

> Pocked with personification
> the fossil virgin of the skies
> waxes and wanes.

Such directness may be disconcerting to some, but it is the source of her power. At a time when "cerebral" was a pejorative term, Mina Loy was dealing with ideas. Pound's genius lay in other directions; his importance is his diversity: his mastery of various styles, his influence on the little magazines, and the fragments of a curious sort of scholarship. It may be that Williams, in a few poems only, surpasses Mina Loy stylistically, because of his extraordinary finish and precision, but the body of his work does not compare with her poems; his subjects are frequently trivial, and hers are not. And where Marianne Moore is clever and superficial, Mina Loy is profound; where Miss Moore is amusing, Miss Loy is bitterly satirical. The poets of this period tended toward a narrowness which was concerned

with the image, "the thing itself," and with the technical aspects of free verse. This sort of brilliant specialization is always beneficial for the sophistication of poetic style, but it may prevent the writer from dealing with broader and more permanent areas of human experience. Thus Williams, because of his scepticism, his desire for communication, and his personal limitations, narrowly restricts his subject in his best poems and presents the isolated object with great clarity. While Pound, who lacks nothing in depth of subject, breaks his material into intractable fragments, resulting in an incoherence of which Pound is most aware. And in the poems of H.D., who cultivates effects of rhythm and sound to a high degree, subject gives way to a monotonous and private ecstasy.

Mina Loy's intelligence enables her to deal with matters of more general concern than those of her contemporaries, while her sharp perceptions and style always render the experience unique. Frequently with great brevity, she handles many of the sentimental stereotypes which had been too easily accepted for some time; and this refusal to accept the merely conventional involves a rigorous examination of states of mind and feeling, and gives to her poems a very personal quality. Perhaps the most famous example of this sort of thing is, from "Love Songs I,"

> Pig Cupid     his rosy snout
> Rooting erotic garbage,

but a better example is the brief "Love Songs VI":

> Let Joy go solace-winged
> To flutter whom she may concern.

Miss Loy has written poems on D'Annunzio, Brancusi, Wyndham Lewis, and Joyce, and much of her subject matter involves a critique of many of the aesthetic commonplaces of the period and of the preceding "nineties." One of these commonplaces was the artist-as-clown, a notion which relegates art to the skillful pose and derives from an aesthetic such as Wilde's which declares that "All art is quite useless." It is art for art's sake, or art specialized to the point of excluding life. She may sympathize with the despair which is usually found behind the dandy's pose, but she satirizes the attitude which undermines artistic integrity. For style, if one takes the notion in its extreme sense, may become simply a game, and all art, a fraudulent discourse. Here are the opening lines from "Crab-Angel," which treats the subject:

> An atomic sprite
> perched on a polished
>     monster-stallion
> reigns over Ringling's     revolving
> trinity of circus attractions
> Something the contour
> of a captured crab
>     waving its useless pearly claws.

In "Lunar Baedecker," the moon at first emerges as a nineties effigy, the superficial artists "draped / in satirical draperies." The irony in phrases such as "posthumous parvenues" is consistent and cannot be summarized. Moreover, the figurative language of the poem controls several areas of experience, and a good deal of careful reading is required to keep them in mind. The language, for example, evokes, not only the sterile poetic commonplaces ("Eros obsolete"), but also the effete, superficially dazzling life of (presumably) New York of the period. Both aspects are brought into juxtaposition by very forceful imagery. I quote the entire poem:

> A silver Lucifer
> serves
> cocaine in cornucopia

To some somnambulists
of adolescent thighs
draped
in satirical draperies
Peris in livery
prepare
Lethe
for posthumous parvenues
Delirious avenues
lit
with the chandelier souls
of infusoria
from Pharoah's tombstones
lead
to mercurial doomsdays
Odious oasis
in furrowed phosphorous

the eye-white sky-light
white-light district
of lunar lusts

            Stellectric signs
"Wing shows on Starway"
"Zodiac carrousel"

Cyclones
of ecstatic dust
and ashes whirl
crusaders
from hallucinatory citadels
of shattered glass
into evacuate craters

A flock of dreams
browse on Necropolis

From the shores
of oval oceans
in the oxidized Orient

Onyx-eyed Odalisques
and ornithologists
observe
the flight
of Eros obsolete

And "Immortality"
mildews . . .
in the museums of the moon

"Nocturnal cyclops"
"Crystal concubine"

Pocked with personification
the fossil virgin of the skies
waxes and wanes.

The infusoria (lines 12–18) are marvelous. A certain species of these microscopic organisms is shaped something like a chandelier and, seen through a microscope, appears to be tremulously glowing with light. The image describes both the neon lights of Broadway ("Stellectric signs") and the stars of this "Lunar Baedecker"; it is a controlled vision of decay in which macrocosm and microcosm, the telescopic and the microscopic, are united. It is this compression by way of imagery which is peculiar to Mina Loy. It is her own special brilliance.

Mina Loy's versification is unsophisticated and sometimes awkward. Her line resembles neither the quick, nervous line of Williams and H.D., nor the smooth, longer line of Pound, sometimes Stevens, and John Gould Fletcher. Her most serious rhythmic deficiency is a lack of unity from beginning to end of many of her poems. In "Lunar Baedecker," for example, she stops and starts, moving from one subject to the next, the individual stanzas nearly becoming separable sections in

themselves. Her rhythms vary in speed, but the movement of most of her verse is slow; if it is uncomplicated, it is nevertheless unpretentious. What is most impressive about her verse, finally, is the incredible energy of her language—and her intelligence. The simple movement is often accentuated by the use of unusual and unexpected rhymes and effects of alliteration (for example, the first twelve lines); note the striking use of assonance in the following lines:

        Onyx-eyed Odalisques
        and ornithologists
        observe
        the flight
        of Eros obsolete

But these devices may be used excessively, and "Lunar Baedecker" comes short of her best work because of the awkwardness and obvious redundancy of lines such as 24–26 and 44–48.

"Apology of Genius" is better. The theme of the artist's isolation grew increasingly more common toward the end of the nineteenth century as a result of very narrow ideas about art and epistemology. Here, the experience is more universal. If poetry is a function of the intelligence, and if great poets are to be persons of genius, then their poems will be largely unintelligible to the majority of the people. I am not speaking about technical features only; many poets, I suspect, would be satisfied if the simple content of their poems were understood. This is not to say that great poems are obscure; but poetry, contrary to popular notions, is not for the enlightenment of the masses; it is available to those who possess the talent and the energy to acquire a rather specialized knowledge, and who, additionally, are willing to respect the mind of the poet of genius. Consequently, those who lack this respect are often the cause of unpleasantness for the poet; at best, his poems are misconstrued. But poets wish to have their poems understood, and the isolation, increasingly more modern as fewer ideas are commonly shared, is painful and desperate.

To the first number of *The Blind Man*, dedicated to the Independents, Mina Loy contributes a short note, evidently the transcript of a public address, on the subject of educating the public. "*The Public* likes to be jolly; *The Artist* is jolly and quite irresponsible. Art is *The Divine Joke*, and any *Public*, and any *Artist* can see a nice, easy, simple joke, such as the sun . . ." She presents ironically the split between the artist and the public and concludes the note:

So *The Public* and *The Artist* can meet at every point except the—for *The Artist*—vital one, that of pure, uneducated *seeing*. They like the same drinks, can fight in the same trenches, pretend to the same women; but never see the same thing ONCE.
    You might, at least, keep quiet while I am talking.

In "Apology of Genius," we get the public view of the artist ("Lepers of the moon" and "sacerdotal clowns") along with the poet's view, stated with the force which illustrates her genius:

unknowing
how perturbing lights
our spirit
on the passion of Man
until you turn on us your smooth fools' faces
like buttocks bared in aboriginal mockeries.

The procedure differs from that of a "compensatory ironist" such as Laforgue in this way: while Laforgue vacillates between the sentimental cliché and its hard-boiled reverse (this is essentially the method of Cummings), Mina Loy presents the double view while maintaining the integrity of her art. The result is an unsentimental poem of great irony and satiric force, in which the bitterness is stated in precise terms.

### APOLOGY OF GENIUS

Ostracized as we are with God—
    The watchers of the civilized wastes
    reverse their signals on our track

    Lepers of the moon
    all magically diseased
    we come among you
    innocent
    of our luminous sores

    unknowing
    how perturbing lights
    our spirit
    on the passion of Man
    until you turn on us your smooth fools' faces
    like buttocks bared in aboriginal mockeries

    We are the sacerdotal clowns
    who feed upon the wind and stars
    and pulverous pastures of poverty

    Our wills are formed
    by curious disciplines
    beyond your laws

    You may give birth to us
    or marry us
    the chances of your flesh
    are not our destiny

    The cuirass of the soul
    still shines
    And we are unaware
    if you confuse
    such brief
    corrosion with possession

    In the raw caverns of the Increate
    we forge the dusk of Chaos
    to that imperious jewelry of the Universe
    —the Beautiful

    While to your eyes
        A delicate crop
    of criminal mystic immortelles
    stands to the censor's scythe.

The use of "lights" as a verb in line 10 is at first ambiguous, but the writing everywhere else seems distinguished. Lines 28–31 are very powerful; the slow movement, with the repetition of vowel and consonant sounds in the heavily stressed words, gives peculiar force to the abstract statement. Lines 32–35 may seem a little grandiose, for they are an elaboration of an aesthetic commonplace of the *fin de siècle*. But the lines serve to set up the irony of the contrasting final lines, in which poetry, immortal art, becomes, "to your eyes," nothing more than a crop of "immortelles"—merely dried flowers.

"Der Blinde Junge" is, I think, her best poem (Jonathan Williams does not reprint it in his 1958 edition). There is no awkwardness here. The poem has a thematic and rhythmic coherence which many of her poems lack, and its conclusion is, for me, as moving as anything in the period. Here, she deals with another, more absolute sort of isolation, in which feeling, cut off from its object, becomes a "centripetal sentience" of unfulfilled craving, objective values having been lost which might accurately inform experience. The treatment of vision in religious terminology is another example of the density of her figurative language. The black lightning of war has desecrated the retinal altar of the young boy, the purposeless eremite. By

virtue of this compressed diction, she can keep before us the general and the particular situations at once, both of which are equally terrifying. The motive is World War I, and the blind youth is "Kriegsopfer," war's offering, of Bellona, the goddess of war. Though the poem may be an analogue for the bleakness of much of modern experience, and though Mina Loy is in sympathy with the blind anguish of the youth, her statement is more than the effusion of "concussive dark"; for the poem is written with great precision:

    The dam Bellona
    littered
    her eyeless offspring
    Kriegsopfer
    upon the pavements of Vienna

    Sparkling precipitate
    the spectral day
    involves
    the visionless obstacle
    this slow blind face
    pushing
    its virginal nonentity
    against the light

    Pure purposeless eremite
    of centripetal sentience

    Upon the carnose horologe of the ego
    the vibrant tendon index moves not

    since the black lightning desecrated
    the retinal altar

    Void and extinct
    this planet of the soul
    strains from the craving throat
    in static flight upslanting

    A downy youth's snout
    nozzling the sun
    drowned in dumfounded instinct

    Listen!
    illuminati of the coloured earth
    How this expressionless "thing"
    blows out damnation and concussive dark

    Upon a mouth-organ.

There is the suggestion of a tenuously restrained violence in "Der Blinde Junge" in regard to both diction and rhythm. The heavy stresses (ˋ) occur generally in an iambic environment (upón the pàvements óf Viènna) and account for the slow and deliberate movement of the poem. But in lines 16 and 17, in which the diction for a moment reaches a peak of abstraction and violence, the rhythm becomes much quicker and lighter. The lines contain rapid trochaic words of very short stress ("vibrant tendon index"). Line 17 runs over into a more heavily stressed line in which the rhythm is resumed. And the complexity of diction and rhythm in lines 27–30 concludes in the final short line ("Upon a mouth-organ") with stunning plainness, the movement of the passage nearly suggesting that furious music.

The purpose of this essay has been to acquaint the reader with a few facts about Mina Loy and to provide him with the texts of three of her poems. She is one of the great modern poets and, in spite of her faults, should be read in bulk. It will be slow work for the curious, carried out in rare book rooms and magazine files. But I know of no poetry in English which resembles hers; she is unique. This is the distinction, and, I suppose, the despair of the great.

ROBERT LOWELL

JACK LONDON

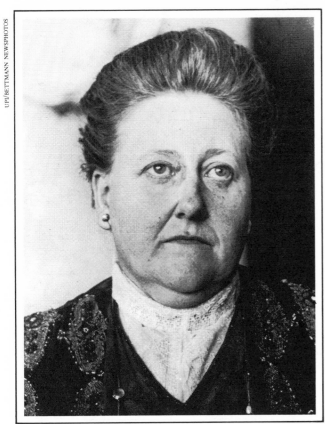

AMY LOWELL

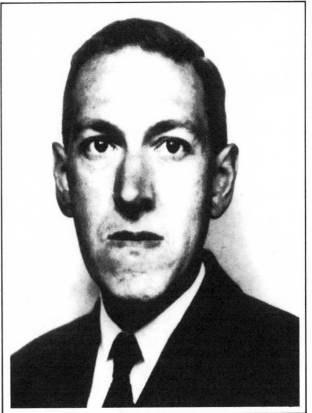

H. P. LOVECRAFT

MARY MCCARTHY

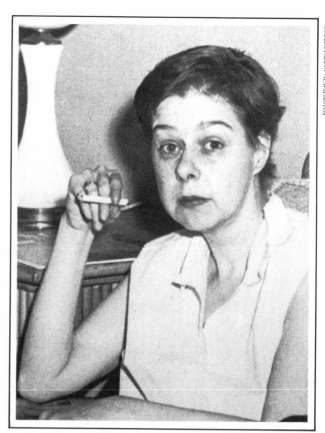

CARSON MCCULLERS

ARCHIBALD MACLEISH

ALISON LURIE

# ALISON LURIE

## 1926–

Alison Lurie was born in Chicago on September 3, 1926. She was raised in White Plains, New York, and attended Radcliffe, graduating with a B.A. in 1947. After working for one year in a New York publishing house, she married an English graduate student, Jonathan Peale Bishop, Jr. She gave birth to three sons and moved to Ithaca, New York, where her husband taught English at Cornell.

Since her childhood Lurie has been an avid reader and writer. After several unsuccessful attempts at publishing a novel, her memoir of V. R. Lang, a friend of Lurie's who helped found Boston's Poets' Theatre, was published privately in 1959. Her first published novel, *Love and Friendship* (1962), is marked by the acerbic wit and the open discussion of sexuality which characterizes her later works. In 1968 she joined the Cornell faculty, teaching creative writing and children's literature courses. *The War Between the Tates* (1974), a story about adultery among academics, brought Lurie widespread recognition. Her latest book, *Foreign Affairs* (1984), was awarded the 1985 Pulitzer Prize. Lurie is divorced and divides her time between her teaching job at Cornell, a vacation home in Key West, Florida, and a London flat.

The novels of Alison Lurie are almost enough to make one believe in the increasingly dubious notion that reading fiction is fun. Evidently free of tormenting scruples about such matters as point of view and form, they are full of high spirits and comic inventiveness, what E. M. Forster calls "bounce." In each of them the central character, a sophisticated upper-middle-class Eastern type, takes the tour of a particular scene—a small college campus in *Love and Friendship* (1962), Los Angeles in *The Nowhere City* (1965), a small-town spiritualists' group in *Imaginary Friends* (1967), and an artists' colony in *Real People*.

Because the title of Alison Lurie's first book is borrowed from Jane Austen, one feels even more than usually compelled to make the inevitable comparison. Like Jane Austen, she is funny, cruel, and clever; unlike Jane Austen, she does not have a perfectly lucid structural sense nor a faultless control of language—the prose takes an occasional perilous swoop down into the regions of the ladies' magazines—and her ironies do not ultimately have moral resonance, but remain largely a matter of surfaces. Like many women writers, she has a malicious sharpness of observation, a fastidious eye for the details of appearance, dress, and manner that identify a type. Unlike most ladies (and most men, too) she does not shift into high gear for sex, but manages to write about it as if it were just like anything else.

Her first novel, *Love and Friendship*, like all her books, is in the tradition of the English novel of manners, where the comic effects arise from the writer's sense of the excessive and inappropriate, from the violation of conventional norms of good manners and good sense. Emmy Turner, a big, beautiful, giggly ex-debutante, comes to a little New England college town with her husband, a stuffy young man with a passion for teaching an unusually sadistic brand of freshman English. Emmy is a perfect center of vision for a comic novel, so full of upper-class expectations that she is continually being astonished; seen through her eyes, the familiar personnel of the academic novel blossom into grotesques. The irony, however, operates on more than one level: while Emmy is cheerfully putting everyone down because of their funny clothes, dirty nails, and bad manners, she too is being made fun of for her naive snobbishness, and her placement in the center gives the novel a perfectly controlled perspective. The plot, Emmy's love affair with a young composer, involving lots of comic intrigue

and sylvan sex, is resolved in a peculiarly sour, disappointing, and lifelike way: Emmy's lover turns out to be a cad, while her husband develops the stodgy pathos of the cuckold; reverting to fundamentally conventional type, Emmy stays with her husband. The irony falls equally on everyone.

The second and third novels use this multifaceted irony in a more schematic and less successful way. In *The Nowhere City* a young Eastern academic couple, Paul and Katherine Cattleman, go West for a year among the freaks and frauds of Los Angeles. Paul makes the ultimate Hollywood scene with Glory Green, a starlet with silver-pink tresses and dyed-to-match pubic hair, while Katherine, an ethereal type who suffers from frigidity and sinusitis, gets defrosted by Glory's husband. The plot seems both haphazard and predictable, and the characters are familiar Hollywood grotesques out of Waugh and West. But Katherine is a good invention, and her neurasthenic perspective makes what might have been a simple satire into a collision of values from which no one emerges very well.

In *Imaginary Friends*, the most slickly written and unconvincing of the novels, two sociologists insinuate themselves into a group of religious fanatics who believe they are in contact with an extraterrestrial being, Ro, of the planet Varna, through the person of a schizoid teenager named Verena Roberts. The project ends with Verena cured of her delusions and one of the sociologists in a mental hospital convinced that *he* is Ro. The people in this novel are not really characterized at all; the novelist's observations of personality are reduced to the sociologist's shorthand: "White Protestant American middle-class middle-aged housewife, in a housedress and flowered apron." The characters are flattened-out freaks from an animated cartoon, funny but noticeably unreal.

Though *Imaginary Friends* is billed on the jacket flap as an attack on sociology, it can be read more plausibly as a kind of unconscious parody of Alison Lurie's earlier novels, an attack of bad conscience on the part of the novelist herself. All her protagonists are essentially like the two sociologists: sophisticated Easterners, they go out into the worlds of their novels like spies into enemy territory. Their norms of value, those of upper- or upper-middle-class life style, are used on other people to categorize rather than characterize them, sorting them out relentlessly into U and non-U. The novels are ultimately saved from the snobbery of their central characters by a reversal of the irony—thus Katherine Cattleman ends up bleached and tanned as any starlet, and the sociologists are loonier than their subjects—but this reversal takes place only at the end, after the novelist has done her worst and can afford to pull the rug out from under her character and herself. —ELIZABETH DALTON, "Life and Art," *Cmty*, Aug. 1969, p. 60

*Imaginary Friends*, Alison Lurie's third novel, tells of a group of Truth Seekers in Sophis, upstate New York, a sibyl named Verena Roberts who claims to receive messages from the spirit Ro in the planet Varna, and two sociologists, Tom McMann and Roger Zimmern, who are professionally interested in the effects of internal opposition on a small group. The sociologists join the Seekers to pursue the Project. After several adventures, Verena lights out for Albuquerque and McMann comes to the conclusion that he is Ro of Varna. Some of the adventures are funny, in a way, like the scene in which the Ur-Ro tells the Seekers to rid themselves of all organic material: but this is not a comic novel. Nor is it a serious social study. Miss Lurie takes it for granted that the Seekers are bogus and Verena's communications merely the result of sexual frustration. We are unlikely to waste much spirit on characters who are deemed to be adequately explained by suburban boredom. We are not concerned, because Miss Lurie is not concerned. When Henry James wrote *The Altar of the Dead* he was deeply engaged with George Stransom's belief in the presence of the dead. He did not assume that the belief was bogus, so he did not station Roger Zimmern to tell us that it was. Offered as a character, Verena suffers from the disability that Miss Lurie has starved her to death. She is nothing. In fact, Miss Lurie has gone out of her way to insist upon the restriction of interest. Inventing bogus characters, she entrusts them to Zimmern, who is good enough up to the point at which his intelligence fails and his conscience recedes. Everything that might have been interesting in the situation is blocked off, as if Miss Lurie, hesitating between seriousness and farce, settled for the trivial. Occasionally we are given an idea with a semblance of gravity: that sociologists get the data they deserve, that scholars love to play God, that research is mostly brain-washing. But these, however limited in their possibilities, are not given a chance, because Miss Lurie has already concluded that they are not worth the candle.

This is a matter of some moment, because Miss Lurie is an unusually gifted writer. There is a scene near the beginning of her second novel, *The Nowhere City*, a row between Glory Green, a Hollywood starlet, and her husband, the psychiatrist Isidore Einsam. This scene is brilliantly done, the dialogue impeccably accurate while it lasts. It does not go very far or very deep: Miss Lurie has a way of preventing development, lest we should begin to care. Her writing suggests that she herself is terrified of caring, and determined to find something to make caring archaic. It seems to be a condition of her powers that they are allowed to revel, provided they revel in triviality. If, reading her books, one insisted upon caring, the insistence would constitute a gaffe, like serious talk at a silly party, breaking decorum. So in reading *The Nowhere City* we are discouraged from caring what Paul Cattleman does to Ceci O'Connor, or how Katherine cures her sinus ailment. Similarly, it is ludicrous to think of that novel as a serious confrontation of East and West, Boston and L.A. Miss Lurie sets up an ostensible opposition precisely because it is nothing; or at least to ensure that, after her book, its nullity will be complete. The only established difference between Cambridge, Mass., and Westwood Village, as far as the novel is concerned, is that in the East women wear respectable clothes, in California sea-green velvet pants, ropes of beads, and high-heeled satin pumps. The action of the novel, such as it is, is to

get Katherine into Capri pants, bright yellow. This is achieved by first putting her to bed with Dr. Einsam.

What is remarkable in Miss Lurie's books is the evidence of high talent devoted to carefully prepared insignificance. She disowns gravity without voting for anything else. Indeed, in *Imaginary Friends*, she seems to have made a pact with the ordinary universe; she will take from its store anything she chooses, but on condition that everything, once chosen, is deemed to be trash. Choice makes it trash. The only difference between things chosen and things neglected is that the latter are trash already. "You're suffering from material clingings, that's your trouble," McMann says to the old-fashioned Zimmern. We easily fancy Miss Lurie saying this to the Art of the Novel. Her recourse is also McMann's: make Zimmern throw away his good clothes and don, instead, the shoddiest things he can find in J. C. Penney's. McMann knows they are shoddy. So does Zimmern. So does Miss Lurie.—DENIS DONOGHUE, "The Ordinary Universe," *NYRB*, Dec. 7, 1967, pp. 23–24

The first thing to be said about Alison Lurie's new novel, *The War Between the Tates*, is that it's a pleasure to read. This is no surprise. All her books hitherto have been a pleasure to read: witty, lucid, elegant and perceptive, her style is completely distinctive, completely assured. She never lets the reader down with a false word, let alone with a false paragraph or a false situation. She can be read with confidence. And yet what she writes—particularly in this novel—is by no means reassuring. The satisfaction of finding prose and character and incident so elegantly handled does not take the edge off her comments: it simply makes the intolerable tolerable.

This novel is about marriage and middle age: commonplace subjects, handled here as though for the first time. As in several of her other works, she has chosen a small, ingrown community for her setting, where a wife cannot go to a chemist to buy contraceptive jelly without the fear of gossip, where one cannot go to a party without meeting every man one has ever known, and all of them married. The community this time is the not very mysteriously named University of Corinth, and her embattled protagonists are Brian and Erica Tate, he a 46-year-old professor, expert in foreign politics, she a 40-year-old housewife, one-time beauty and part-time illustrator. Brian has been bullied into an affair by a student of his named Wendy, a savagely-drawn representative of modern youth, who dresses 'usually in Indian style, but—like his children when they were small—confusing the Eastern and Western varieties'. The Tate children, drawn with even more savagery, are two teenagers, who are revealed to their father on Hallowe'en in their true colours as the Fat Witch, Matilda, who listens endlessly to the Rolling Stones and dyes her hair pink, and The Plastic Man, Jeremy, who uses foul language, refuses to be helpful, and sits around at the age of 16 reading comics.

The family is at war: society is at war. As the war in South East Asia escalates, so does the civil war between the Tates. The analogies are carefully drawn, the metaphor continues through the book: family relationships are seen in terms of alliances, hostages, prisoners of war. The first whiff of gun-shot comes from the burning cookies that Erica forgets in her astonishment at her discovery that her ideal, handsome, responsible husband has been unfaithful: the final appalling truce takes place at a Peace Demonstration over Vietnam. Handled by anyone else, the comparisons might seem tasteless, an attempt to shore up a slight theme with heavy machinery, to dignify middle-class marital squabbles with a deeper significance. But there is little sense of this: the constant reminders of the real war of blood and napalm serve, it is true, to point out the triviality of the issues here—loss of one's social status, loss of one's children, loss of one's looks. But the domestic battle is nonetheless a real battle, no less terrible to its puny participants. Small though they are, they suffer. There is a fine sequence of moments in which Erica looks in mirrors to find her once slim, confident self, and finds increasingly 'an old woman's face, blank, white, creased . . .'. The terror with which Erica contemplates the transformation, the inevitability of having to live through 'the bad last part of my life', is superbly done. It would be unfair to quote the memorable lines of this novel's finely modulated conclusion, for they fall into their own place, but I can warn you that they stick in the mind with a classic ring.

There are, of course, plenty of lighter pleasures, not least that of watching Ms Lurie's analysis of the changing social scene. A cold observer, she notes every detail of culture and counter-culture: her use of the idiom of the young, so often embarrassing even as a comic effect when used by its elders, is here caught precisely and unsympathetically. At one point Matilda says to her mother as her mother sets off to a party, 'Hey, you look flaky,' and Erica (like this reader) is unable to tell whether the remark is a compliment, an insult, or simply a description. Revolting students and the Women's Liberation movement both get their share of attention: the way in which Erica is transformed from an aloof observer of the latter to an unwilling participant is done with finesse, and the movement emerges with more sympathy than almost anything else in the book, which is not saying much. Nobody, in this world of petty manoeuvres and skirmishes, is particularly admirable: nobody is particularly bad. The only character, oddly enough, who emerges with any real dignity is a one-time admirer of Erica, a man called Zed, once a philosopher, now owner of a mystic bookshop: hopeless, shabby, near-impotent, ridiculous (and the author is well able to make him look all these things), at least he is not out for himself. He is the Fool, walking dressed in rags into the void. Erica experiences a moment of temptation, when she thinks that she might follow him into the void, but she draws back 'with a laugh of fear, thin and hysterical, of someone who sees that she has almost stepped off the edge of a cliff'. Rational herself, Alison Lurie presents her so-called rational characters, her normal sane citizens, with such revealing insight that her Fool, a real non-combatant, a real pacifist, emerges almost as a victor. There are worse things to be than a fool.—MARGARET DRABBLE, "Family Battles," NS, June 21, 1974, pp. 893–94

Admirers of Alison Lurie's five previous novels will find much to enjoy in *Only Children*, for it shares with these comedies of manners—most specifically with *The War Between the Tates*—a quick, light, deft tone that brings to life, often in a paragraph or two, characters who might otherwise strike us as clichés. Here is, for instance, the Southern belle Honey Hubbard: "Ah was the cutest thing in Greensboro, if Ah do say so mahself. Ah was having the most fun you ever can imagine, right through the war. And after the boys came home it was even better. . . . And then, all of a sudden, Ah was twenty-six years old. . . . Geezus. It's just plain awful growing old." Though she is now 40, Honey manages, with the aid of makeup and a relentlessly childish manner, to pass for much younger; she not only charms the blustering, handsome Dan Zimmern (a would-be writer who has sold himself, and quite successfully, to an advertising agency), but she evokes, in her rather stodgy, unimaginative, "socialist" husband, fits of uncharacteristic rage.

That *Only Children* is really a novel of the 1970's set in the Depression years is clear from its concentration on issues that have become much-discussed lately: the role of women in and out of marriage; the nature of "love"; distorted male perceptions of women ("See, the women we know, they most of them grew up before the Eighteenth Amendment. They're usually pretty irrational, like children really, because that's how they were brought up to be. When they got the vote, and short skirts, and all that, it was too late for them. They might try to be like men, but they don't know what it means even"); equally distorted and cynical female perceptions of men (Honey is nice to men, her daughter Mary Ann thinks, "while they are there, but as soon as they go away she makes fun of them and says how poor and dumb and old they are. 'What else can you expect from a man?' she says, the exact same way she used to say, 'What else can you expect from a mutt?'"). Honey's mercenary, manipulative attitude is partly explained by the fact that she had wanted, as a girl, to study chemistry—but her father ridiculed her ambition.

Though set on a farm, *Only Children* is really a sort of drawing-room comedy. It is formally plotted: It begins and ends with the Hubbards in their old Franklin car, struggling in traffic; each chapter is laid out in a scrupulous workmanlike way, usually involving two characters who, chatting at first about incidental matters, become quite frank with each other (though their revelations—and no doubt this is part of Alison Lurie's satiric vision—bring them to no lasting changes in their lives). The Hubbards quarrel over the superficial issue of Bill's stodginess; the Zimmerns fail to quarrel, which is worse, for Celia—fading, near-anonymous, martyred Celia—is so intimidated (that is, so "in love") that she cannot define herself against Dan; Anna King, to whom "love is not very significant and a rather childish emotion, talks over the weekend with each of the characters and emerges as queenly. Or is she, perhaps, "kingly"?: "It's easy to be decent," Celia says of her, "when you don't care about anybody too much."

Nearly everybody puzzles over love, even the precocious Mary Ann, who thinks, "Love made you sicker than chicken pox or even mumps. It was no wonder Anna hated it as much as nasty medicine disguised with syrup. . . . The disease of love can make you act mean and even crazy. It is like, as near as she can understand it, as if you were very very hungry, practically starving, but there was only one single food in the whole wide world you could eat. For instance jello, and you could only even eat jello if this single person fed it to you spoonful by spoonful, like a baby in a high-chair." At the novel's conclusion no one appears to be much wiser except, perhaps, the troubled children. The Hubbards and the Zimmerns, though badly matched, will continue with their "successful" marriages.—JOYCE CAROL OATES, "Honey and Bill and Dan and Celia," NYTBR, April 22, 1979, pp. 7, 27

A large part of the appeal of Alison Lurie's *Only Children*, which takes place in 1935, is that Lurie gives us objects of the past that we can crave: gas-station-sign horses with wings, coolie hats, sundresses, Franklin cars. And she uses Thirties diction with such deftness that it becomes itself an object. People have "ants in their pants," and "one too many," and are "parlor Pinks." Dan Zimmern says his wife is "getting all worn out keeping up with my sex drive." Friends are described as being "good at figures," enemies are told to "go tell it to the Marines." Swimmers worry about waiting an hour after lunch to go into the water and parents worry that their children are "underweight for [their] height and age groups."

Alison Lurie's view of the world is always permeated with irony but she also satisfies our taste for past sweetness by a highly intelligent use of novelistic tactics—by setting her novel in the safely distant but remembrable past, and by making her central characters children. She has thus allowed herself to write in good faith about an innocence that readers may value, about a simplicity that they may not feel bound to disbelieve.

Lurie also sees that innocence of diction or of objects does not necessarily lead to innocence of behavior. Her novel takes place on a particularly hot Fourth of July weekend. There are two couples, the Zimmerns and the Hubbards, and their daughters, Lolly and Mary Ann, who go to visit Anna King, the unmarried headmistress of the daughters' progressive school. As the weekend goes on, everyone behaves badly, except Lolly who never behaves badly because she is too frightened and too absorbed in the life of her own mind.

Lurie is wonderful about the terrifying effect that adult bad behavior, drunken and sexual, has on children. When adults are children, children have to be adults, and that is dreadful for them. "Grown-ups were supposed to act grown up. When they didn't, it could be lovely fun for a while, like driving to the village store Thursday. But if they went on too long, it got sort of embarrassing and awful and even scary," Mary Ann tells us. ⟨. . .⟩

Because Lurie so often captures the landscape and the tone of childhood, when she slips the reader feels badly let down. I have trouble following Lurie when Mary Ann and Lolly indulge in flights of fancy. Mary Ann's dreamy moralizing fantasies are the least interesting thing about her, and it is no help that they occur at the beginning and very end of the book. Children probably do make up stories like Mary Ann's final one about people who wish for strawberry soda and peach ice cream to come out of the faucets, and who then nearly drown in it and have to be rescued by a flying dog. But the stories that children make up are sometimes not very interesting and it is precisely the excessively quotidian nature of their imagery—strawberry soda and peach ice cream coming out of water faucets—that can deaden their language.

Occasionally, I am troubled by the fact that Mary Ann and Lolly seem to be too old to have the thoughts they do. Would an eight-year-old say, "A mean bush hurt me," or refer to the creatures of her nightmares as "spookies"? Even if we grant the difference of eight-year-olds of 1935, who were indubitably children, and the eight-year-olds of today, who use deodorant and shave their legs, this diction sounds too young, particularly for Mary Ann, whom we have seen to be toughminded. In a novel in which diction is so important, such occasional lapses badly jar.

But diction is a vexing problem when one is writing about children. In *The Waves*, Virginia Woolf makes her children sound like little mandarins. "I should wear a fiery dress, a yellow dress, a fulvous dress to wear in the evening," says one of the little girls in that novel, when she is even younger than Mary Ann and Lolly. And James's Maisie often sounds like a short Madame Merle. When talking to her French doll she notes that "she could only pass on her lessons and study to produce on Lisette [the doll] the impression of having mysteries in her life, wondering the while whether she succeeded in the air of shading off, like her mother, into the unknowable."

We all know that in real life children don't talk as Woolf and James suggest in these passages, but we are convinced when we read them against the evidence of our common sense. Lurie is probably closer to mimicking the real texture of children's speech, but the effect is less successful than the obviously artificial constructions James and Woolf have made. Perhaps that is because good dialogue, even good interior monologue, does not resemble real speech very much; it resembles good dialogue in other novels.

On the other hand, the talk among the adults in *Only Children* is sharply revealing, usually damning. When the two men discuss the necessity of chasing women, the scientific Bill explains:

> "It's the result of natural selection. For thousands of years men who didn't chase after women had fewer descendants, or none. So eventually those genes died out."
>
> "Yeah, I get it," Dan said, pacing. "You mean if you love your wife, but you can't resist a beautiful babe, it's just heredity."

All this is particularly awful since it is Bill's wife who is the babe Dan can resist.

Sex is the snake in Lurie's garden; it divides the good parents from the bad. The good ones, Mary Ann's father Bill and Lolly's mother Celia, are morose and sexually put upon. The bad parents, Dan and Honey, think they are going to have a good time, but Dan is simply incompetent when he tries to seduce Honey, and Honey has been teasing Dan and knows it. As Lurie showed in *The War Between the Tates*, she is a fine observer of manners, not least when she is a comedienne of sexual failure. Here, however, she is doing something different from what she has already done successfully, and has tried to go deeper. This is the most interior of Lurie's novels, the most reflective, the most lyrical. Her decision to make children her central characters must have been a difficult step for a novelist of manners. For children do not define themselves by their manners—their manners are their parents'. When they are told to mind their manners, it is not their own manners that they have to mind.

But it should not be surprising that the novelist who once described selfish, lumpish adolescents is here being kind to younger children. There has always been a generosity to her comedy, and it has always centered itself around the importance of domestic life. Children are sentenced to live in the domestic world until they are old enough to escape it. In *Only Children*, Lurie makes it clear why they want to escape. Their safety there is temporary and uneven. The grown-ups aren't always in charge. Even during an innocent July weekend in 1935 they weren't. Perhaps they never were.—MARY GORDON, "What Mary Ann Knew," *NYRB*, June 14, 1979, pp. 31–32

Overheard in a suburban shopping center some eight or ten years ago, one middle-aged woman to another: "Marian, what a surprise to see you! I know I must look awful. Usually I'd be wearing pants, I wear pantsuits *constantly*, but today you've caught me in a skirt."

It's the kind of remark that sticks in your memory, mostly because it's so mysterious. Oh, the meaning is clear enough— "I'm not who I appear to be; I'm someone else, someone better"—but why did she feel a pantsuit would have proved it? What was it, exactly, that this woman perceived to be the message of a pantsuit?

In *The Language of Clothes*, novelist Alison Lurie takes a sharp-eyed look at a good many of the messages our clothes may give—or the messages we may imagine them to give, which is not necessarily the same thing. Dress, she says, is a form of communication that precedes even our hellos:

> Long before I am near enough to talk to you on the street, in a meeting, or at a party, you announce your sex, age and class to me through what you are wearing—and very possibly give me important information (or misinformation) as to your occupation, origin, personality, opinions, tastes, sexual desires and current mood. . . . By the time we meet and converse we have already spoken to each other in an older and more universal tongue.

She carries the metaphor of clothing as language almost straight through the book, from the "slang" of blue jeans to the "adjectives and adverbs" of accessories. A man who reflexively dons the same jacket or shoes no matter what the occasion suffers from a "stammer." A mature woman in girlish frills displays a "childish lisp"; an unzipped fly is a "lapse of the tongue," and mousy dress is the "drab, colorless equivalent of the inability to speak above a whisper." When an incompetent employee puts on one of those dress-for-success business suits, he is, in effect, lying. When a hospital patient is ordered into a johnnycoat, he is "struck dumb"—no longer allowed to express himself through clothing of his own choice.

In many respects, this book brings to mind the work of Erving Goffman—the sociologist who, in such books as *The Presentation of Self in Everyday Life*, interpreted the gestures and tiny formalities we'd hardly bothered to notice before, let alone analyze for hidden meanings. Like Goffman, Alison Lurie has a sometimes startlingly fresh way of looking at things, as if she'd only recently arrived from another planet. She points out that hats stand for the ideas within the heads they cover—that the sheik in Western-style suit and turban is telling us that mentally, if not physically, he remains unassimilated. We respect this message but not its reverse: a sheik in native robes and a bowler hat would be merely comical, with his implication that "though not physically at ease in our country, [he has his head] full of half-baked Western ideas." Carrying this thought to its logical conclusion, Alison Lurie suggests that American tourists might take note. Perhaps, in American dress and Mexican sombreros, they appear equally ridiculous to their hosts.

There are other bits of ingenuity. She holds that the 1960s custom of wearing parts of outdated military uniforms to peace demonstrations was meant to show that the wearer was not a coward—that he opposed not all wars but just the war in Vietnam. She unveils the irony of that Virginia Slims ad in which modern woman is liberated from the suffocating clothes of bygone days: liberated she may be, but she still teeters precariously on very high heels, and the ad copy still calls her "baby." And she analyzes the appeal of the Annie Hall look: the mannish, whimsical clothes imply that the wearer is a good sport, fun-loving, easygoing; but the outsized, dressing-up-in-Daddy's-suit bagginess conveys an air of "helpless cuteness, not one of authority; it invites the man to take charge, even when he is as incompetent himself as are the characters played by Woody Allen."

Also like Goffman, Alison Lurie derives many of her most inventive theories from an almost breathtaking literal-mindedness. The shoulder pads affected by women in the Depression, she says, signified the women's "willingness and ability to bear the burdens of the world by literally squaring their shoulders." Then there's the idea of inner layers of clothing representing the inner self while outer layers represent the outer self. A severely dressed woman in a frilly apron is informing her guests that "a serious career woman is only playing at cooking." An architect in a rustic cord suit wears beneath it a business shirt and tie to display his inner sense of practicality—"to reassure his clients that their buildings will not run over the cost estimate or fall down."

These theories work, for the most part. They may first astonish and amuse us, but then on second thought, we tend to agree. A few, however, seem *too* literal. The wide white stripes in a baseball uniform symbolize the wide spaces of inactively endured by the average player? The gangster's reversal of colors—black shirt and white tie—implies a reversal of traditional values? Well, maybe, but. . . .

There are other theories I'd quibble with, but mostly just for the fun of quibbling. It seems improbable that foreign teenagers wear Levis so that the "power and virtù" of America will rub off on them. More likely it's the casualness, the deliberate eschewal of elegance and political or parental restrictions, that they're hoping will rub off. Nor do I agree that our taboo against elderly women in youthful dress has anything to do with the message of sexuality persisting into old age. It's possible, instead, that youthful clothes simply accentuate age by means of contrast, making sags and wrinkles more obvious and therefore more garish—and none of us cares to see old age as garish, not so long as we're headed there ourselves.

Also, I believe that Alison Lurie is unduly charitable to fashion designers. It's not, she says, that they're manipulating us, but rather that they're trying to read us, to guess the message we wish to convey this year—in some cases, guessing wrongly, as with the maxiskirt they pushed in a period when everyone was idealizing youth. But the fact that the designers don't always succeed is no proof they don't *sometimes* succeed; and I remain as baffled as ever by our lemming-like rush to shorter hemlines, or flatter bodies, or whatever style seems subliminally implanted in our heads season by season.

On the meaning of color, this book is superb—all the more noticeably because there happens to be another book making the rounds these days that proposes each woman should find "her" colors and wear only those colors forever after. What that book almost totally fails to recognize is that color has more purposes than simply to flatter the wearer. It may also send messages of stability, raffishness, vulgarity, or honesty. Imagine, Alison Lurie suggests, a stockbroker greeting his customers in a shocking pink suit.

⟨. . .⟩ the only serious problem with this book is that it's too convincing. Once you've read it—again, as with Goffman's work—you'll be self-conscious to the point of paralysis. What shall I wear with my jeans today, anyhow? My blue chambray shirt? But that would make me one of those shrill-voiced writers in the "artists-are-workers-too" category. My Indian gauze? I'd be falsely expressing an interest in acupuncture, astrology, and Zen. Well, all right, my lace-trimmed Victorian blouse. But then, not only would I be giving a message of feminine helplessness, I'd be making my husband guilty of Vicarious Consumption.

Besides, there are the jeans themselves. They're Lees, and it says right here in this book that only freaks wear Lees.
—ANNE TYLER, "The Glass of Fashion," NR. Dec. 23, 1981, pp. 32–34

In *Foreign Affairs*, although Lurie leaves her American setting behind and ventures into the bowels of the British Museum and the drawing rooms of country estates, she carries along many of her old belongings. The two characters at the center of the story, Vinnie Miner and Fred Turner, are by now familiar types in her fiction: professors from Corinth University who are painfully aware of their own provincialism, but seemingly incapable of overcoming it. Vinnie is a jaded, unattractive middle-aged specialist in children's folklore with "no significant identity outside her career"; Fred, a dashing but priggish and dim-witted young colleague who is writing a book about John Gay and pining over his estranged wife, Roo (who has grown from the animal-loving child in *The War Between the Tates* into a defiantly feminist photographer). They are on leave to pursue projects in London of equally dubious scholarly merit, and to indulge in unrestrained Anglophilia.

Unexpectedly, however, sexual adventures beckon for both of them. In an effort to forget Roo, Fred impulsively takes up with a stunning British aristocrat and actress named Lady Rosemary Radley; and Vinnie, who is nursing her rage over a vicious reference in *The Atlantic* in her life's work as "a scholarly study of playground doggerel," is slowly won over, to her chagrin, by the man who sat next to her on the flight to London, a retired waste disposal engineer from Tulsa named Chuck Mumpson. As Vinnie is making her startling discovery of the true Chuck (he's a lovable—even witty—oaf, not a boorish one), Fred is slowly uncovering the sordid truth about Lady Rosemary (her refined Boucher-like features mask dissipation, just as his own Edwardian looks and manners disguise an empty soul). In the process each stumbles across the rotting underbelly of Britain's upper class, and both briefly reckon with their own neglected consciences.

There is potential here for the kind of sharp social satire Lurie excels in, and the novel contains flashes of her distinctive wit and style. But *Foreign Affairs*, like its two protagonists, is hampered by an inability to surmount its own pettiness. The plot is mechanical and cluttered with unpolished jottings on everything from tourist disorientation to the ways in which specialists in Vinnie's field relate to real children; and the characters are both overwrought and undeveloped. Even Lurie's keen ear for colloquial speech and her eye for revealing mannerisms frequently fail her: in characterizing Chuck and Rosemary, Lurie vacillates between joining Vinnie and Fred in their crude typecasting—Chuck talks in an exaggerated Western twang; Rosemary flutters and giggles and pouts—and taking them to task for it.

All of Lurie's novels are programmatic: like most comic writers she relies upon formal contrivances to heighten irony, to create startling juxtapositions, to make a larger point about the individual's accommodations to the demands of society. In *The War Between the Tates* Erica and Brian's marital battles were punctuated by a sonorous voice-over narration which compared them to the social and political upheavals accompanying the Vietnam War. In *Only Children* Lurie failed in her occasional attempts to blend the naïveté of two little girls with her own stinging cynicism. But Erica and Brian were energetically and realistically drawn; and Lolly and Mary Ann, if somewhat limited as narrators, brought a fresh glimpse into the old themes of marital boredom and infidelity. In both novels Lurie credibly evoked a chapter in American social history. Alas, in *Foreign Affairs* the characters are so unappealing and the contrivances of plot so labored that the ironies are leaden rather than leavening. And, its title notwithstanding, the only affairs she addresses here are carnal.

As for the lessons Lurie lays out, they are of the most rudimentary socio-psychological sort. Yet these two reputable professors are maddeningly slow learners. Fred, filled with self-love, can't find happiness until his obsession with what Lady Rosemary represents is replaced by a clear-eyed recognition of what she is. (Even his lovers assume the shape of academic equations in his mind: "She is small, soft, and fair; Roo large, sturdy, and dark. . . . In manner and speech Rosemary is graceful, melodious; Roo by comparison clumsy and loud—in fact, coarse. Just as, compared with England, America is large, naïve, noisy, crude, etc.") It is during a game of charades—what else?—that he has his first vague glimmerings that Rosemary is not quite the fragile English flower she seems. Suddenly she and her cultivated friends appear raucous, even depraved: Rosemary "is not only vulgarly made up and loaded with costume jewelry, but is wearing the lace butterfly nightgown in which, just a few hours ago. . . . He wants to protest, but makes himself laugh along with the rest; after all, it's only a game." Vinnie, for her part, filled with self-hate, must not only cease to see Chuck Mumpson as a source of revulsion and pity, but herself as well. "Vinnie doesn't want her

London friends to confuse her with Chuck, to think of her as after all rather simple, vulgar, and amusing—a typical American." In the end, of course, it becomes clear to Fred that Lady Rosemary, far from representing "the best of England," actually embodies the destructive self-indulgence of a decadent class society; and to Vinnie that Chuck, who reminds her of all that's shameful and ugly in America, in fact personifies American openness and stolid decency.

Still, simplicities and stereotypes aside, Lurie is as deft as ever when she turns to the mortifications of romance. She is an uncannily accurate observer of the ambivalent emotions that enter into unconventional sexual alliances, and when she abandons her gimmicky plot devices and moral posturing, *Foreign Affairs* is funny, touching, and even suspenseful. As Fred's affair with Lady Rosemary is being consumed in horror (the final revelation scene is a weirdly appropriate combination of Hitchcock suspense and Lurie humor), Vinnie's affair with Chuck is being consummated in a moment of poignant farce. This odd couple is finally brought together thanks to a suitably ludicrous matchmaker: Chuck's plastic fold-up raincoat.

At last, a character with integrity. This homely garment not only has a perverse charm of its own, it also helps to transform Vinnie, the perpetually peevish man-hating snob, into a flustered, touchingly vulnerable woman. When Vinnie and Chuck first bump into each other in London, she disdainfully notes that he is wearing "a semi-transparent greenish plastic raincoat of the most repellent American sort," and registers it as an emblem of his personality: coarse, tasteless. Yet the raincoat comes to show Vinnie more about her own shortcomings than it does about Chuck's. Her hatred of it festers over the weeks, and she turns on it in furious embarrassment after Chuck's first bumbling embrace in her tiny kitchen, in which he knocks a bowl of watercress and avocado soup over them both: "If he only had a decent raincoat instead of that awful transparent plastic thing—she gives it a nasty look as it hangs in the hall—then he could wear that while his clothes dried, or even go home in it." In several quick scenes the raincoat explains Vinnie's social pretensions and fragile dignity; and in the scenes that follow, it gives credence to the evolution of her contempt for Chuck into tolerance, affection, and—most remarkably of all—hearty sexual appetite.

In *Foreign Affairs* Lurie shows once again that she is a farsighted observer of human fallibilities, but an odd kind of moralist. Hers is a particularly brutal form of mockery: she forces her character into compromising positions and then denies them any real escape. The end of the novel superficially follows the traditional comic pattern—the characters are sent back home; the social order resumes—but Lurie doesn't think much of spiritual regeneration. In the departure lounge at Heathrow, Fred begins to berate himself for behaving like a cad toward Roo (who has forgiven him) and Rosemary (who has not), and to reflect on his shattering experiences in London. "Well, if he's learned one thing this year, it's that everyone is vulnerable, no matter how strong and independent they look. . . . Fred feels worse about himself than he has ever felt in his adult life." Even this elementary insight, however, is quickly supplanted: "he is, after all, a young, well-educated, good-looking American, an assistant professor in a major university; and he is on his way home to a beautiful woman who loves him." Vinnie, whose affair has ended no less disastrously, is courageous enough to confess to her gossipy British friend Edwin, who makes a slighting remark about Chuck, that she loved him. "Something has changed, she thinks. She isn't the same person she was; she has loved and been loved." An hour later she's telling herself, "It's not her nature, not her fate to be loved . . . her fate is to be always single, unloved, alone."

Of course, neither Fred nor Vinnie has essentially changed at all; he is still impossibly obtuse, she has reverted to whining self-pity. This elaborate novel is more of an exercise in verbal and structural ingenuity than it is a full-fledged comedy or melodrama. The snugness has become oppressive, and the secrets Lurie invites us to share, no longer enticing, are for the most part trivial, sordid, and sad.—DOROTHY WICKENDEN, "Love in London," NR, Oct. 8, 1984, pp. 35–36

# MARY McCARTHY

## 1912–

The first of four children, Mary McCarthy was born in Seattle on June 21, 1912. Her father was the son of wealthy Minneapolis Irish Catholics and her mother was the daughter of a prominent Episcopalian lawyer from Seattle and his Jewish wife. McCarthy's mother converted to Roman Catholicism and her children were raised in the faith of her husband. Mary's idyllic childhood came to an abrupt end in 1918 with the deaths of her parents. In the course of moving the family from Seattle back to her father's home in Minneapolis, both parents died of influenza within one day of each other. The next five years are remembered by McCarthy as being a period of emotional hardships inflicted by unfeeling guardians. Eventually in 1923 her maternal grandfather brought her back to Washington where she attended school. At Tacoma's Episcopalian boarding school, the Annie Wright Seminary, McCarthy was an excellent student, showing special interest in Latin. After her graduation in 1929 she spent the summer taking acting lessons at the Cornish School in Seattle. In the fall of 1929 she entered Vassar and graduated with a B.A. four years later.

During the summer of 1933 she married an actor, Harold Johnsrud, whom she had met in Seattle. The first of four marriages, it ended three years later in divorce. During the 1930s McCarthy reviewed books for *The New Republic* and *The Nation*, establishing a reputation as a tough and demanding critic. Later she wrote theatre reviews for the *Partisan Review* and became associated with New York's anti-Stalinist literary forces. Her second husband, the critic Edmund Wilson, suggested that she try her hand at fiction writing. Her first story, "Cruel and Barbarous Treatment," appeared in the *Southern Review* in 1939. Three years later a collection of loosely related semi-autobiographical stories was published under the title *The Company She Keeps* (1942). More strictly autobiographical, *Memories of a Catholic Girlhood* (1957) reveals the nature of McCarthy's turbulent and sad childhood. *The Group* (1963), which chronicled the lives of eight Vassar women for the seven years following their graduation, was a best seller and earned McCarthy a national reputation. Her other works include two art history books, *Venice Observed* (1956) and *The Stones of Florence* (1959), and two vehement criticisms of U.S. involvement in Indochina, *Vietnam* (1967) and *Hanoi* (1968). She is also a noted drama critic and in 1956 published a collection of her essays on theatre, *Sights and Spectacles: 1937–1956*.

Today McCarthy lives in Paris with her fourth husband, James Raymond West. They have been living abroad since 1960, although they usually spend part of the summer at their house in Maine. In 1984 McCarthy was awarded the National Medal for Literature as well as the Edward MacDowell Medal.

Mary McCarthy! "'The Man in the Brooks Brothers Shirt'! That's my Bible!" I once heard a young woman exclaim. No doubt the famous short story is rightly understood as a sort of parable representing many a young girl's transgressions, even if it does not concern itself with the steps in the sinner's rehabilitation. It would be hard to think of any writer in America more interesting and unusual than Mary McCarthy. Obviously she wants to be noticed, indeed to be spectacular; and she works toward that end with what one can only call a sort of trance-like seriousness. There is something puritanical and perplexing in her lack of relaxation, her utter refusal to give an inch of the ground of her own opinion. She *cannot conform*, cannot often like what even her peers like. She is a very odd woman, and perhaps oddest of all in this stirring sense of the importance of her own intellectual formulations. Very few women writers can resist the temptation of feminine sensibility; it is there to be used, as a crutch, and the reliance upon it is expected and generally admired. Mary McCarthy's work, from the first brilliant *The Company She Keeps* down to her latest collection of essays, *On the Contrary: Articles of Belief 1946–1961*, is not like that of anyone else and certainly not like that of other women. ⟨. . .⟩

Plot and dramatic sense are weak in Mary McCarthy's fiction. Taste and accuracy are sometimes substitutions. What people eat, wear, and read are of enormous importance. The reader follows the parade of tastes and preferences with a good deal of honest excitement and suspense, wondering if he can guess the morals of the kind of person who would cover a meat loaf with Campbell's tomato soup. He participates in a mysterious drama of consumption, in which goods are the keys to salvation. Taste is also used as the surest indication of character. "There were pieces of sculpture by Archipenko and

Harold Cash, and the head of a beautiful Egyptian Queen, Neferteete." Accuracy, unusual situations documented with extreme care, mean for the reader a special sort of recognition. The story "Dottie Makes an Honest Woman of Herself" is about contraception in the way, for instance, Frank Norris's *The Octopus* is about wheat. "Dottie did not mind the pelvic examination or the fitting. Her bad moment came when she was learning how to insert the pessary herself. Though she was usually good with her hands and well-coordinated . . . As she was trying to fold the pessary, the slippery thing, all covered with jelly, jumped out of her grasp and shot across the room and hit the sterilizer. Dottie could have died." This story, *memorable* to put it mildly, could not have been written by anyone except Mary McCarthy. Reading it over again, the suggestion came involuntarily to mind that perhaps it was meant as a parody of the excesses of naturalistic fiction, a parody, too, of the brute, prosaic sexual details in, for instance, a writer like John O'Hara. There is an air of imparting information—like whaling in Melville or, more accurately, the examination of dope addiction in Gelber's play, *The Connection*. This aspect of *information* brings to memory the later story by Philip Roth in which a college girl suggests she knows all about contraception because she has read Mary McCarthy.

In a writer of this kind there is an urgent sense of the uses to which a vivid personal nature may be put by a writer's literary talent. There is very often an easily recognized element of autobiography and it is in autobiography that Mary McCarthy excels—that is, of course, if one uses the word in its loosest and largest sense. *The Company She Keeps* and *Memories of a Catholic Girlhood* are richer, more beautiful, and aesthetically more satisfying than, say, *A Charmed Life* or *The Groves of Academe*. The condition that made *The Oasis* somewhat stillborn was that it was more biography than autobiography. In autobiography, self-exposure and self-justification are the same thing. It is this contradiction that gives the form its dramatic tension. To take a very extreme case, it is only natural that critics who find importance in the writings of the Marquis de Sade will feel that the man himself is not without certain claims on our sympathy and acceptance. In Mary McCarthy's case, the daring of the self-assertion, the brashness of the correcting tendency (think of the titles *Cast a Cold Eye* and *On the Contrary*) fill us with a nervous admiration and even with the thrill of the exploit. Literature, in her practice, has the elation of an adventure—and of course that elation mitigates and makes aesthetically acceptable to our senses the strictness of her judgments.—Elizabeth Hardwick, "Mary McCarthy" (1961), *A View of My Own*, 1962, pp. 33–38

The famous acidulousness of Mary McCarthy's fiction is something else, for she is essentially a brilliant culture critic, with the critic's irritable sense of mental independence, who stolidly taught herself to write fiction as a way of putting into relief one woman's unassimilability. There is always one theme in Mary McCarthy's fictions: none of these awful people is going to catch *me*. The heroine is always distinctly right, and gives herself all possible marks for taste, integrity and indomitability. Other people are somehow material to be written up. This heroine began in the Forties as the bohemian girl in a world of men she would do anything with except respect; she went on with undeviating sharpness to discuss academic types in *The Groves of Academe*, old radicals and ex-utopians in "The Oasis," Cape Cod residents in *A Charmed Life*, college girls of the Thirties in *The Group*, America and Americans at large in *Birds of America*.

This most recent book is less in the form of a novel than Mary McCarthy's other books, for the protagonist is for the

most part a young American student in Paris, Peter Levi, rather than his celebrated musician mother, Rosamund Brown, and we are steadily told what Peter thinks. His mother, though she soon disappears from the book, is more directly active a figure in her few scenes, and what *she* thinks is that America has gone to hell in the form of frozen foods. Rosamund Brown is a lovely sweet artist woman who wants to cook in her New England kitchen with the same access to real food that her mother had in Marietta, Ohio. The theme is that Nature Is Dead. What is interesting about this, and more than a little touching, is that though the evidence as a novel given for this is paltry, and everybody in the book except mother and son is, as usual, contemptible, Mary McCarthy as a polemicist at last rises to a point beyond the heroine's intense self-approval. Nature *is* dead now for most Americans, and it is interesting that so stark a traditionalist should have appeared in Mary McCarthy to say so.—Alfred Kazin, "Cassandras," *Bright Book of Life*, 1973, pp. 188–89

The dilemma of the woman writer in the second half of the twentieth century—struggling against convention to tell her own truth, and faced with male critics' contempt for it, and female critics' suspicion of it—is dramatized in the case of Mary McCarthy and *The Group*. Published in 1963, *The Group* is a subversive novel about women's roles and marriage, a deliberate exposure of the fantasy of the educated American woman's freedom. As McCarthy described it, the novel is about the failure of the idea of "progress in the feminine sphere." Nothing—not education, not politics, not technology, not sex—can jolt these somnolent young women, these sleeping beauties, from their Vassar tower, into dynamic growth. They are empty at the core, because they have never been free to experience themselves without the screen of male authority: cook books, sex books, child-rearing books, merge in their minds with their Vassar lectures, as infallible guides to the conduct of life.

In 1963 this message—McCarthy even makes the happiest woman in the book a lesbian—was not one America wished to recognize. While the book became a best-seller because of its allegedly sexy passages (sex from the woman's point of view seemed especially titillating and risqué) and because women readers responded to its underlying anger and accuracy, the male intellectuals hastened to attack this "trivial lady-writer's book" (Norman Podhoretz). John W. Aldridge thunderously banished McCarthy from the intellectual kingdom in an essay entitled "Princess among the Trolls." Now, he announced triumphantly, the masquerade was over. She was no great thinker; she gave herself airs; she felt superior to men; in fact, she hated men. *The Group*, according to Aldridge, was a kind of wish-fulfillment for her, enabling her to act out her self-deluding fantasies of intellectual dominance. "It is probably not surprising," he says wearily, "that Miss McCarthy's militant egotism should ultimately take the form of militant feminism and find its most satisfactory expression in the sexual contest between the brute male and the morally and intellectually superior female."

Norman Mailer, as one might guess, went wild. In a long essay called "The Case against McCarthy," he ranted against the detail of *The Group*, seeing in it what he calls the "profound materiality of women." In a classical Freudian analysis of his own metaphors and obsessions, Mailer describes this detail as the "cold lava of anality, which becomes the truest part of her group, her glop, her impacted mass." With sensitive critics like these, and best-sellerdom to boot, *The Group* virtually destroyed Mary McCarthy's literary and intellectual reputation. By the time Hollywood got hold of it, Pauline Kael reports in "The Making of *The Group*," McCarthy herself was regarded as "poison . . . she's competitive"; the book was interpreted as proof that higher education made women aggressive and neurotic.

Yet there is great irony in McCarthy's fall as a "militant feminist," for the chorus of women's voices in her fiction creates a veritable symphony of female self-hatred. McCarthy is only merciless with her own sex; it is to the women in her narratives that she directs her most relentless mockery. In her famous short story "The Man in the Brooks Brothers Shirt," the Babbitty man on the train emerges with considerable dignity and integrity, despite his crude middle-class tastes; it is the autobiographical arty heroine who is stripped of all self-respect and pretension. Similarly, in *The Group*, the female characters internalize all their aggressions against men. John Aldridge managed to find Amazons triumphant, but in truth, Kay, Noreen, Priss, and the rest pour their anger and frustration into bitchiness with each other, self-doubt, self-sacrifice, depression, madness, and suicide. They do not confront their men, much less defeat them.

Pauline Kael was more perceptive when she said that McCarthy's satire was an effort to protect herself against the horrible image of the castrating woman by "betraying other women. And of course women who are good writers succeed in betrayal but fail to save themselves." Since *The Group*, we have heard no more about women from McCarthy. Her subsequent books, a report from Vietnam, and a recent novel, *Birds of America*, narrated by an expatriate college boy obsessed with ecology, have found more favor.—ELAINE SHOWALTER, "Killing the Angel in the House," *AnR*, 1973, pp. 345–47

---

## MARY McCARTHY

### From an Interview by Elisabeth Niebuhr

*Paris Review*, Winter–Spring 1962, pp. 86–94

*McCarthy*: There may be something wrong with ⟨A *Charmed Life*⟩, I don't know. But it was always supposed to have a fairy tale element in it. New Leeds is *haunted*! Therefore nobody should be surprised if something unexpected happens, or something catastrophic, for the place is also pregnant with catastrophe. But it may be that the treatment in between was too realistic, so that the reader was led to expect a realistic continuation of everything going on in a rather moderate way. It was, to some extent, a symbolic story. The novel is supposed to be about doubt. All the characters in different ways represent doubt, whether it is philosophical or ontological doubt as in the case of the strange painter who questions everything—"Why don't I murder my grandmother?" and so on. Or the girl's rather nineteenth-century self-doubt, doubt of the truth, of what she perceives. In any case, everyone is supposed to represent one or another form of doubt. When the girl finally admits to herself that she's pregnant, and also recognizes that she must do something about it, in other words, that she has to put up a real stake—and she does put up a real stake—at that moment she becomes mortal. All the other characters are immortal. They have dozens of terrible accidents, and they're all crippled in one way or another, and yet they have this marvelous power of survival. All those drunks and human odds and ends. Anyway, the girl makes the decision—which from the point of view of conventional morality is a wicked decision—to have an abortion, to kill life. Once she makes this decision, she becomes mortal, and doesn't belong to the charmed circle any more. As soon as

she makes it, she gets killed—to get killed is simply a symbol of the fact that she's mortal. ⟨. . .⟩

*Niebuhr*: ⟨Have you⟩ thought of this distinction between "mortal" and "immortal" in relation to characters in other of your novels besides A *Charmed Life?*

*McCarthy*: I didn't think of this distinction until just recently, and not in connection with myself. It's just at this very moment—*now* talking with you—that I'm thinking of it in connection with myself. I would say that it is a law that applies to *all* novels: that the comic characters are *figé*, are immortal, and that the hero or heroine exists in time, because the hero or heroine is always in some sense equipped with purpose.

The man in *The Groves of Academe*. Well, he's immortal, yes. He is a comic villain, and villains too always—I think—partake in this comic immortality. I *think* so. I'm not sure that you couldn't find an example, though, of a villain it wasn't true of. In Dickens again. In the late novels, somebody like Bradley Headstone, the schoolmaster, he's a mixed case. He's certainly not a villain in the sense of, say, the villain in *Little Dorritt*, who belongs to the old-fashioned melodramatic immortal type of villain. Headstone is really half a hero, Steerforth is half a hero, and therefore they don't conform to this.

This all came to me last year, this distinction, when I was thinking about the novel. Not my novel: *The Novel*.

But maybe that's really part of the trouble I'm having with *my* novel! These girls are all essentially comic figures, and it's awfully hard to make anything happen to them. Maybe this is really the trouble! Maybe I'm going to find out something in this interview! That the whole problem is *time*! I mean for me, in this novel. The passage of time, to show development. I think maybe my trouble is that these girls are comic figures, and that therefore they really can't develop! You see what I mean? They're not all so terribly comic, but most of them are.

How're they ever going to progress through the twenty years between the inauguration of Roosevelt and the inauguration of Eisenhower? This has been the great problem, and here I haven't had a form for it. I mean, all I know is that they're supposed to be middle-aged at the end.

Yes, I think maybe that *is* the trouble. One possibility would be . . . I've been introducing them one by one, chapter by chapter. They all appear at the beginning, you know, like the beginning of an opera, or a musical comedy. And then I take them one by one, chapter by chapter. I have been bringing each one on a little later on in time. But perhaps I can make bigger and bigger jumps so that you could meet, say, the last one when she is already middle-aged. You see what I mean. Maybe this would solve the problem. One five years later, another eight years later, and so on. I could manage the time problem that way. This has been very fruitful! Thank you!

*Niebuhr*: I want to ask you about the problem of time in the novel. You have written that a novel's action cannot take place in the future. But you have said that the action described in *The Oasis* all takes place in the future.

*McCarthy*: *The Oasis* is not a novel. I don't classify it as such. It was terribly criticized, you know, on that ground; people objected, said it wasn't a novel. But I never meant it to be. It's a *conte*, a *conte philosophique*.

*Niebuhr*: And A *Charmed Life* you say has fairy tale elements.

*McCarthy*: I'm not sure any of my books are novels. Maybe none of them are. Something happens in my writing—I don't mean it to—a sort of distortion, a sort of writing on the bias, seeing things with a sort of swerve and swoop. A *Charmed Life*, for instance. You know, at the beginning I make a sort of inventory of all the town characters, just telling who they are.

Now I did this with the intention of describing, well, this nice ordinary old-fashioned New England town. But it ended up differently. Something is distorted, the description takes on a sort of extravagance—I don't know exactly how it happens. I know I don't mean it to happen.

*Niebuhr:* You say in one of your articles that perhaps the fault lies simply in the material which the modern world affords, that it itself lacks—

*McCarthy:* Credibility? Yes. It's a difficulty I think all modern writers have.

*Niebuhr:* Other than the problem of arrangement of time, are there other specific technical difficulties about the novel you find yourself particularly concerned with?

*McCarthy:* Well, the whole question of the point of view which tortures everybody. It's the problem that everybody's been up against since Joyce, if not before. Of course James really began it, and Flaubert even. You find it as early as *Madame Bovary*. The problem of the point of view, and the voice: *style indirect libre*—the author's voice, by a kind of ventriloquism, disappearing in and completely limited by the voices of his characters. What it has meant is the complete banishment of the author. I would like to restore the author! I haven't tried yet, but I'd like to try after this book, which is as far as I can go in ventriloquism. I would like to try to restore the author. Because you find that if you obey this Jamesian injunction of "Dramatize, dramatize," and especially if you deal with comic characters, as in my case, there is so much you can't say because you're limited by these mentalities. It's just that a certain kind of intelligence—I'm not only speaking of myself, but of anybody, Saul Bellow, for example—is more or less absent from the novel, and has to be, in accordance with these laws which the novel has made for itself. I think one reason that everyone—at least I—welcomed *Doctor Zhivago* was that you had the author in the form of the hero. And this beautiful tenor voice, the hero's voice and the author's—this marvelous voice, and this clear sound of intelligence. The Russians have never gone through the whole development of the novel you find in Joyce, Faulkner, et cetera, so that Pasternak was slightly unaware of the problem! But I think this technical development has become absolutely killing to the novel. ⟨. . .⟩

*Niebuhr:* In reading the Florence book, I remember being very moved by the passage where you talk of Brunelleschi, about his "absolute integrity and essence," that solidity of his, both real and ideal. When you write about Brunelleschi, you write about this sureness, this "being-itself," and yet as a novelist—in *The Company She Keeps* for instance—you speak of something so very different, and you take almost as a theme this fragmented unplaceability of the human personality.

*McCarthy:* But I was very young then. I think I'm really not interested in the quest for the self any more. Oh, I suppose everyone continues to be interested in the quest for the self, but what you feel when you're older, I think, is that—how to express this—that you really must *make* the self. It's absolutely useless to look for it, you won't find it, but it's possible in some sense to make it. I don't mean in the sense of making a mask, a Yeatsian mask. But you finally begin in some sense to make and to choose the self you want.

*Niebuhr:* Can you write novels about that?

*McCarthy:* I never have. I never have, I've never even thought of it. That is, I've never thought of writing a developmental novel in which a self of some kind is discovered or is made, is forged, as they say. No. I suppose in a sense I don't know any more today than I did in 1941 about what my identity is. But I've stopped looking for it. I must say, I believe

much more in truth now than I did. I do believe in the solidity of truth much more. Yes. I believe there is a truth, and that it's knowable.

## GORDON O. TAYLOR

### From "Cast a Cold 'I': Mary McCarthy on Vietnam"

*Journal of American Studies*, April 1975, pp. 103–6

### I

'There is always one theme in Mary McCarthy's fictions', writes Alfred Kazin in *Bright Book of Life*: 'none of these awful people is going to catch *me*. The heroine is always distinctly right, and gives herself all possible marks for taste, integrity and indomitability. Other people are somehow material to be written up.'[1] Whether or not one accepts this as fair, one *is* inclined to agree that a pattern of identification exists between the novelist and her fictional heroines. A reader of McCarthy's *non*-fiction is also often struck, particularly of late, by the extent to which self-portrayal can become central to her treatment of a subject. The inward play of her imaginative response is frequently as much the substance as the servant of her outwardly avowed literary purpose, or the onward momentum of her narrative line. The intellectual, aesthetic or moral assurance of her self-characterization exerts defining pressure on her materials, be they those of the critic or the polemicist, the autobiographer or the reporter. This pressure of personality indeed relates more than it distinguishes, sometimes even fuses, these various literary roles, along with a number of their respective techniques.

This seems particularly true of *Vietnam* (1967), *Hanoi* (1968) and *Medina* (1972),[2] McCarthy's short books about the American presence in South Vietnam, the impact of the war on the North and the psychic as well as legal aftermath in America of the killing at My Lai. Materials originally written for magazine publication,[3] each set of articles reworked and enlarged into pamphlet form before the next set was composed, constitute a rather fragmented basis for generalization concerning a writer's methods and effects. Yet read as a continuous sequence (the author herself has come to view them as one) these volumes convey a coherent narrative of experience absorbed as much as observed by McCarthy, and of her shaping personality correspondingly shaped. The circumference of her attention progressively contracts (as her titles suggest) from the abstract illusions underlying American involvement in Vietnam, to a more geographically and humanly specific consideration of the view from Hanoi, finally finding in Captain Medina a 'juncture-point' of the war's contradictions, more accessible to the novelist's than to the professional reporter's eye. So, too, one's sense of McCarthy's personal investment in her accounts progressively intensifies.

'Facts', those she accepts as given at the outset and reaffirms at the end, together with those she discovers or revises along the way, gradually become internalized, their secure possession by the reader increasingly a matter of McCarthy's *self*-possession. The 'integrity' of the novelist-heroine impugned by Kazin is in these works to be understood as a process through which the author-protagonist integrates the factuality of her material with her sense of herself, strives to complete herself in relation to it. This process, moreover, depends for rhetorical and moral persuasiveness on McCarthy's willingness to risk through self-questioning that safe certainty which Kazin suggests is an *un*questioned premise of her fictional self-projections. She *is* in these books, whatever the case in her novels, 'caught' in situations in which her *own* 'awfulness' or innocence eventually becomes a central issue, one determinant among many of the 'truthfulness' of her reportage. In order to 'write up' others she must, in the literary situation evolving around her here, write up herself.

## II

'I confess that when I went to Vietnam . . . I was looking for material damaging to the American interest', she states in the opening sentence of *Vietnam*. It is hardly an apology, despite the confessional note, though its tense allows for shadings between the anticipated and the directly observed facts. McCarthy's own 'interest' as a writer at the outset is to document further an existing case against the war, the prosecution of which case indeed concerns her throughout all three books.

From the start, however, there are signs of more subtle problems and possibilities involving self-representation. Personal pronouns gradually become charged, stress-points in a structure through which McCarthy begins to negotiate the issue of her own Americanness in relation to American acts or attitudes she is attacking. This web of self-reference is further complicated as it expands by the developing relationship between author and reader, a relationship with its own points of presumed contact or tension. 'I' and 'you', 'we' and 'they'—the problematical quality as well as the grammatical necessity of such designations emerges early as a condition of McCarthy's probing of relations between her subjective resources and her objective aims. Early suggestions also arise of a mind deflected inward by, as well as reacting outward to, its encounters; of involuntary as well as deliberate forays into the personal past for perspective on the national present. As she grows accustomed to the 'sight and sound of . . . massed American might' in Saigon, an earlier notebook entry registering her initial shock at the open display of power loses its meaning for her, 'as when a fragment of a dream, written down on waking, becomes indecipherable'. So also, but in reverse, 'buried fragments of . . . personal history' start to work their way—like bits of shrapnel through flesh—towards the surface of her text, blending with the impressions which summon them, and which they help to decipher.

Though 'the mind cannot excavate what Saigon must have been like "before"' the overwhelming American presence, McCarthy's mind does attempt, and her prose begin to express the energy of the effort, to penetrate the past so as to grasp the present. At times she wishes to explode by the force of her disgust the Americanized surface, verbal strategy appropriate to a cultural impact as violent as any bomb-crater. At times it is a matter of 'excavating' an imaginative truth by careful siftings of immediate observation through memory or association, the strategy now an 'archaeological' procedure of patient verbal brushwork. Sometimes, too, an alternative image floats mirage-like beyond the actual scene, as when she sees in Hué, an imperial capital, the 'dignified and melancholy' face of an older Vietnam, sudden fragment of her dreaming on what has been destroyed. Or, having observed that 'war, a cheap form of mass tourism, opens the mind to business opportunities', as when her own mind opens 'as if on a movie screen' to a scene of fast-buck real-estate development, Manifest Destiny and the California Dream revived and reconverging on Saigon.

Such self-investments in her subject-matter are intermittent in *Vietnam*, prospects rather than resources fully exploited. They illuminate from the edges, rather than the core, arguments which finally focus more abstractly on the paradox of American powerlessness to leave a situation predicated on American power. But even some of McCarthy's conventional argumentation, given these bursts of participatory energy, reflects the growth of a persona within the assertion of a

viewpoint. The misuse of language by military and political figures, deliberately distorting or unwittingly revealing the truth, is a recurrent theme. But each instance of linguistic mutilation she cites, while it contributes to her case, seems also to irritate her own mental and moral tissues, to provoke her towards personal confrontation and thus to stimulate one's sense of her personal voice. So too the listless boredom of Saigon, even in the midst of frantic profiteering, serves McCarthy's polemic purpose as an index of the war's venality and the emptiness of its professed aims. Yet such evidence of incuriosity—and 'in this half of the century Americans have become very incurious', like deadened language both cause and effect of our paralysis of Vietnam?—seems beyond its argumentative function to abrade her own curiosity, to incite questions spilling over the banks of her specific case. Abhorring the vacuums in the mental and moral life around her, McCarthy's personality begins naturally enough to fill those vacancies, there to gain new purchase, literary-technical as well as intellectual, on questions of increasing personal urgency.

Thus, oddly yet significantly, *Vietnam* culminates in a question put by an emergent self just *before* a final chapter, 'Solutions', argues the impossibility of solutions without some break in the pathology of official attitudes. McCarthy notes that repeating certain acts (*i.e.*, bombing strikes) with foreknowledge of their consequences (*i.e.*, civilian casualties) while denying those consequences (*i.e.*, by first denying they occurred and then terming them 'accidents') suggests 'an extreme and dangerous dissociation of the personality'. Then she asks, 'Is that what is happening with the Americans in Vietnam?' The personality of Captain Medina, registering at close range in McCarthy's imagination, eventually affords a point of interpretive leverage as to just how dangerous to American moral sanity, let alone the physical well-being of Vietnamese peasants, such dissociation might be. Here at the end of *Vietnam*, however, 'Solutions' can only restate, not explore, the problem. In *Hanoi*, by contrast, the questionings of a more prominent self are from the first more central to the shape, tone and pace of the discussion, borne inward by the pressure of personal implications: 'Quite a few of the questions one does not, as an American liberal, want to put in Hanoi are addressed to oneself.'

*Notes*

1. Alfred Kazin, *Bright Book of Life: American Novelists and Storytellers from Hemingway to Mailer* (Boston: Little, Brown, 1973), p. 188.
2. All published in New York by Harcourt, Brace; all quotations are from these editions. These texts have recently been re-issued, together with a new essay dealing further with the circumstances of their composition, as *The Seventeenth Degree* (New York: Harcourt, Brace, Jovanovich, 1974).
3. Portions of *Vietnam* and *Hanoi* first appeared in *The New York Review of Books*; excerpts from *Medina* first appeared in *The New Yorker*.

## WENDY MARTIN

### From "The Satire and Moral Vision of Mary McCarthy"

*Comic Relief: Humor in Contemporary American Literature*, ed. Sarah Blacher Cohen

1978, pp. 201–6

In "The Woman Writer and the Novel," written in 1922, H. L. Mencken asserts that women novelists have been hindered by a "lingering ladyism—a childish prudery inherited from their mothers." Women will succeed in the novel as they "gradually throw off inhibitions that have hitherto cobwebbed their minds."[1] In *The Group*, McCarthy certainly succeeds in shredding inhibitions when she writes about sex, birth control, and childbirth. In *Cast a Cold Eye*, she succeeds in "killing the angel in the house" as she discusses the private lives of her heroines from their college days to their lives as young matrons, wives, and mothers. *The Group* is the novel which Mencken forecasts will be written by the woman of the future: "If I live to the year 1950, I expect to see a novel by a woman that will describe a typical marriage under Christianity, from the woman's standpoint. . . . That novel, I venture to predict will be a cuckoo. . . . It will seem harsh, but it will be true. And, being true, it will be a good novel. There can be no good one that is not true."[2]

In addition to exploring taboo subjects and presenting a view of the other side of patriarchy—a view of the world behind dominant men—the novel deflates romantic illusions based on the mythology of love as a benevolent force, and exposes the limitations and absurdities of bourgeois individualism. The novel enraged reviewers who dismissed it as trivial or bitchy. But it is Norman Mailer who complained most bitterly, insisting that McCarthy is insufficiently daring: "She simply is not a good enough woman to write a major novel. . . . She suffers from a lack of reach. She chooses not to come close enough to the horror of the closet . . . nice girls live on the thin, juiceless crust of the horror beneath"[3] Yet, *The Group* contains the essentials of life; it begins with a wedding and ends with a funeral. In the course of the novel, free love, adultery, cruelty, divorce, insanity are confronted squarely—the horror beneath social surfaces *is* exposed, and McCarthy's courage to examine these issues gives the novel its power. *The Group* is the pivotal point in McCarthy's career: in this work, she successfully fuses private lives with political issues.

In general, McCarthy's writing evolves from personal subjects, such as her childhood memories, to public events, such as the Vietnam war and the Watergate trials. But when her whole work is viewed in its totality, a distinction between private and public cannot be made—what happens to individuals happens to social groups, as well as to nations. *Birds of America* (1965), dedicated to Hannah Arendt, is a novel about the difficulty and dangers of allowing an idea to dominate perceptions so that it obscures the diversity and variety of nature and impairs the capacity for virtue and vice. It is also a satire about the rape of nature by technological society. Peter Levi and his mother attempt to ignore or sidestep the mushrooming standardization, mechanization, plastification of their world. They move to a New England seacoast town where he watches birds and she plays the clavichord and cooks Fanny Farmer dishes which are at least one hundred years old. Although their reactionary responses are frequently absurd, not a day goes by that they aren't forced to confront the fact that their world is shrinking. Loss pervades the novel: The great horned owl disappears; the library-benefit cake sale no longer offers "potato salads and chicken pot pies and clam pies. Rice, salad, lobster salad, macaroni salad . . . baked beans and home-made ice cream. Peppermint . . . Boston brown bread. Oatmeal bread. Date bread"; instead, commercial ice cream and hot dogs are sold.[4] There are no longer flowers in the gardens; Peter muses, "Old Mother Nature seemed to have taken the pill" (p. 80), while Mrs. Levi remembers: "Those old New England gardens could be marvelous. . . . Old-fashioned roses. White double narcissus and poppies that bloomed every year on Memorial Day. Spicebush, lemon

lilies, a kind of Persian lilac that smelled of Necco Wafers. . . . Beauty Bush . . . sensitive plant . . . heliotrope and verbena and pinks. Hollyhocks. . . . A great deal of honeysuckle, privet and box. Sundials, arbors, trellises, an occasional gazebo" (p. 77). At every turn, the variety of life is diminished as people narrow their existences for the sake of convenience. Nature is no longer appreciated, and Peter and his mother are anachronisms.

In *The Mask of State: Watergate Portraits* (1973), the corrective impulse in the form of social satire is a necessary and healthy response to greed and corruption in public life. Viewing national politics with the same discerning judgment she uses in *Memories of a Catholic Girlhood*, she untangles the threads of a national scandal just as she puzzled through the confused memories of her childhood. Instead of satiric portraits of Uncle Myers, the Man in the Brooks Brothers Shirt, the Yale Intellectual, Mr. Sheen, or Mulcahy, there are biting descriptions of Maurice Stans, Jeb Magruder, Mitchell, Haldeman, Ehrlichman, John Dean, and Gordon Liddy. Again, McCarthy uses the technique of correlating moral qualities with physical appearance, and the Watergate Group is ridiculed for being as self-indulgent, arrogant, domineering as any of their fictional counterparts in Mary McCarthy's rogues' gallery; "With his white fluffy celebrity sideburns, small well-cut features, smart suit accessorized with tie-clasp and cuff links bearing the presidential seal, Maurice Stans resembled a successful actor, a combination of Claude Rains in *Caesar and Cleopatra* and Claude Dauphin."[5] Mitchell is described as "sour, old, rancid, terse," and the portrait of Ehrlichman vividly recalls her description of the ape-like Uncle Myers: "Everything about his features and body movements is canted, tilted, slanting, sloping, askew. The arms swing loosely; the left hand with a big seal ring, like a brass knuckle, moves in a sweeping gesture. The broad head is too round—pygmyish" (pp. 94–95).

These men are self-important, bombastic, and pompous, and McCarthy's portraits of them as unthinking beasts expose them to public ridicule. Stripping away illusions of their reliability and competence as public leaders, her satire does not remedy the underlying pathology of their lives, but it does reveal the effects of their distorted values on a nation.

Like the satire of her eighteenth-century counterpart, Jane Austen, McCarthy's writing judges as well as chronicles a complex social and economic reality, exposing the pretensions of men and the illusions of women in patriarchal society. Finally, McCarthy's work substantiates the effort of the modern woman to erode the encrusted traditions which prevent her from being heard. She is our contemporary Ann Hutchinson, who looks her judges in the eye and refuses to let them tamper with her reality.

*Notes*

1. H. L. Mencken, "The Woman Writer and the Novel," *Prejudices: Third Series* (New York: Knopf, 1922), p. 103.
2. Ibid., p. 104.
3. Norman Mailer, "The Case against McCarthy: A Review of *The Group*," in *Cannibals and Christians* (New York: Dial Press, 1966), p. 82.
4. Mary McCarthy, *Birds of America* (New York: Harcourt Brace Jovanovich, 1965), p. 74. All other references to the work are cited in the text.
5. Mary McCarthy, *The Mask of State: Watergate Portraits* (New York: Harcourt Brace Jovanovich, 1973), pp. 9–10. All other references to the work are cited in the text.

ROSALIE HEWITT
"A 'Home Address for the Self':
Mary McCarthy's Autobiographical Journey"
*Journal of Narrative Technique*, Spring 1982, pp. 95–104

The relation between autobiography and fiction has long provided the basis for literary experimentation and for subsequent literary debate, certainly since the eighteenth century with such autobiographical fictions as *Moll Flanders*, *Pamela*, and *Tristram Shandy*, and since the nineteenth century with such fictional autobiographies as *Confessions of an English Opium-Eater*, "The Custom-House" section of *The Scarlet Letter*, and *Life on the Mississippi*. The literary artist's fascination with these self-conscious mergers of the real and the fictional is still reflected in a substantial body of modern and contemporary American literature, most recently in such works as Kurt Vonnegut's *Palm Sunday*, Truman Capote's *Music for Chameleons*, William Styron's *Sophie's Choice*, and Lillian Hellman's *Maybe*, and in the more distant past in Ernest Hemingway's *A Moveable Feast*, Richard Wright's *Black Boy*, Norman Mailer's *Armies of the Night*, and Sylvia Plath's *The Bell Jar*. But despite the consensus that these writers, as well as many, many others, are intrigued, sometimes haunted, by the psychological and philosophical implications of their "facts in fictions" and their "fictions in fact," we, as readers and critics, still have not yet fully articulated the specific narrative effects that these various autobiographical works achieve. Particularly of interest to our understanding of the communicated self of the writer are the shifting narrative voices and stances that occur within the work. Perhaps because of the very dynamic nature of the autobiographical mode itself—the self is always in the process of change or growth—or perhaps because of the blurred distinctions between facts and fictions in these auto-biographical hybrids, we have been hesitant to make justifiable and plausible connections between the real self and the narrating self or selves explicit or implicit in the literary work. In essence, we need to explore in more depth what exactly each writer is saying about self when the choice of mode is not clearly either autobiography or fiction but a mysterious, yet intentional, combination of both.

The phrase "fact in fiction" is one that Mary McCarthy made famous in her now classic essay on the novel, and it is through her own "facts in fiction" and "fictions in fact" that we may see ways in which the writer conveys a concept of self in literary forms that rely heavily on the autobiographical mode—usually signaled by the identification of the author or speaker with the narrator or central figure of a narrative text—but, nevertheless, unite, in a variety of ways, the fictional with the real. Between 1942 and 1957 Mary McCarthy published three works—*The Company She Keeps* (1942), *Cast a Cold Eye* (1950), *Memories of a Catholic Girlhood* (1957)—that combined the fictional with an autobiographical reality, all three relying essentially upon the raw material of McCarthy's early childhood through her high school and college years, of her early writing career, of her first three marriages, and up to a time when she was firmly established as an important writer of the American scene.[1]

The complexity of the McCarthy self and her intentions towards the self as revealed in these three works is vividly signified in Paul de Man's statement in *Blindness and Insight* about the challenges of literary studies:

> In the study of literature the question of the self appears in a bewildering network of often contradictory relationships among a plurality of subjects.

> . . . From the start, we have at least four possible and distinct types of self: the self that judges, the self that reads, the self that writes, and the self that reads itself. The question of finding the common level on which all these selves meet and thus of establishing the unity of a literary consciousness stands at the beginning of the main methodological difficulties that plague literary studies.[2]

Here de Man is speaking of the literary consciousness of a detached literary critic, but in McCarthy's work, as in much twentieth century autobiographical literature, the literary consciousness is one aspect, often a major aspect, of both the author self and the self that is being narratively depicted. Thus, the McCarthy self that emerges from these three works is not simply the self who has experienced, but the literary self who judges, reads, writes, then reads itself. And if we examine each work within the context of the publishing history of all the works, we can see a very definite pattern of the McCarthy "self" and the McCarthy "self-concept" emerging; we shall find that each text offers its own fictional/autobiographical signals and secrets, that each text becomes a richer, denser exploration of the McCarthy identity when examined within the context of the others.

*Company*, *Cast*, and *Memories* not only share a similar autobiographical foundation but all three are also similar in format: each work consists of a series of "chapters," each chapter having been published earlier as an isolated piece in a mass-circulated periodical. *The Company She Keeps* was labeled a novel by the publisher, later called a novel by McCarthy herself in an interview, and was reviewed primarily as a novel, although some reviewers referred to the six "chapters" as "stories," others using the more neutral term "episodes." In 1950 *Cast a Cold Eye* was published with the acknowledgment page referring to the individual "chapters" as "stories"; the Table of Contents consists of two divisions: Part I with four "stories," Part II with three "stories," these three to appear later in changed form in *Memories of a Catholic Girlhood*. Most reviewers referred to *Cast* as either a collection or a book of "short stories." In 1957 *Memories* was published without any formal classification on the title page; the copyright page calls the divisions "chapters." Mary McCarthy, however, begins the book with an essay "To the Reader" in which she establishes in the first sentence the authentic autobiographical nature of the book: "These memories of mine have been collected slowly, over a period of years" (*Memories*, p. 3). Here McCarthy is referring to the seven chapters which, like the "stories" of *Company and Cast*, appeared first as isolated pieces. None of the *Memories* chapters appearing primarily in *The New Yorker* from 1946 to 1957 was designated with any classification; only the title was given, and *The New Yorker* pieces were placed after "The Talk of the Town," a placement traditionally reserved for short fiction.

As we shall see, the publication data and history of these texts are extremely important for an understanding of the author's intentions and the readers' responses, for the texts of the "chapters" in each collection although changing very little linguistically (with one exception) from periodical to book have been very dynamic texts rhetorically. These texts are a prime example of what Barbara Herrnstein Smith is referring to when she argues that the identity of a text, including the generic properties, "cannot always or necessarily be established by any surface inspection or even deep analysis of the text itself, and, in fact, that the same text may change its identity not only *in* time but at *any* time under different circumstances."[3] Smith's statement may be further applied to McCarthy's three collections: although the collections remain static in terms of linguistic surface structure, their publishing and reading history have re-created them rhetorically.

And this re-creation has to a large extent been initiated by the author, by Mary McCarthy herself who has changed or modified her public autobiographical identity by the very decisions she has made about publication. The self she conveys in her isolated pieces in periodicals is not the same self that will emerge when these pieces are placed in a collection, and the identity of the self in the collections will be partially defined in terms of any additional materials—such as forewords or epilogues—she chooses to add. The literary consciousness of Mary McCarthy thus gains complexity because not only is the self within the original "episodes" self-conscious literarily but the self who is putting these "episodes" together in a collection and explaining this collection is displaying a literary consciousness that has to be squared in some way with the self of the originals.

*The Company She Keeps* begins with a foreword by Mary McCarthy, the first of two reading, also judging, selves that appear in the three collections. The "Foreword," of course, was written for the publications of *Company*, a work referred to by publishers and reviewers as a "novel." But in the "Foreword" McCarthy clearly wants the "novel" to be read as an autobiographical journey—a desire that was not communicated and could not have been communicated explicitly when the "episodes" first appeared separately. And McCarthy identifies herself in the "Foreword" with the reader, both of whom are to accompany the heroine back over her life's "itinerary" as the heroine searches for her lost identity. McCarthy closes with a statement that is an implicit controlling device to force the reader into a perspective similar to the one she herself has when she confronts the various personalities of the heroine in the "episodes" of *Company*: "For the search is not conclusive: there is no deciding which of these personalities is the 'real' one; the home address of the self, like that of the soul, is not to be found in the Book" (*Company*, p. 7). But McCarthy now is not only identifying with the reader but also with the heroine, for the third person emphasis in this last sentence merges the self of the heroine with McCarthy's own self who is the person who knows whether the self is really to be found in the book.

The "episodes" of *Company* indeed suggest, both in narrative technique and in thematic content, that the heroine is not a very integrated self, although in the last episode of "Ghostly Father, I Confess" there is a more direct movement toward self-understanding and wholeness of self. But again McCarthy uses the "Foreword" to tell the reader how to read, this time directions not for a philosophical reading, but for a technical reading—instructions on how to confront the linguistic signals, particularly the pronouns that establish point of view. As a reader, McCarthy says she revisits "points of view . . . the intimate 'she,' the affectionate, diminutive 'you,' the thin, abstract, autobiographical 'I'" and is moved to ask, as she imagines her reader will too, "Can all this be the same person?" (*Company*, p. 7). One thing McCarthy is doing here is trying to establish indirectly a rationale for calling this series of "stories"/"episodes" a "novel," but she is also less indirectly pondering the nature of the self and its contradictions and inconsistencies. That the self of the heroine is connected in McCarthy's mind with her own self and that she intended the heroine to be a fictional representation of her own self is implicitly signaled in the foreword and in the text itself, but these connections will not become explicitly apparent until some years after the 1942 publication.

Before we move to the extratextual autobiographical conclusions, let us examine the text itself and the points of view

as McCarthy has suggested. The first narrative in *Company* is "Cruel and Barbarous Treatment," a narrative related by an omniscient narrator in the third person, using "she" to refer to the heroine. No proper names are given in the narrative. The pronoun references as well as other references do not clearly establish the author McCarthy with the "she"; most readers would initially draw the conclusion that the narrative was fiction. The next narrative "Rogue's Gallery" shifts point of view to the "I," the heroine who, given McCarthy's instructions, we must equate with the unnamed "she" of "Treatment" even though other references do not necessarily establish that bond. "Gallery," however, focuses on a character study of the heroine's employer and only becomes autobiographical through the mirror of biography. It is in "Gallery," some distance into the narrative, that we are given the name of the heroine, "Miss Sargent," spoken by the employer, the first name "Margaret" appearing near the end. The next narrative "The Man in the Brooks Brothers Suit" again moves to third person, but this time center of consciousness, the "she" central. The "she" is very much a participant in the action, becoming infamous to McCarthy readers as the young wife who allowed herself to be seduced by a salesman on a cross-country train. Although the heroine's name is not mentioned in this narrative, and although the heroine and the author McCarthy are clearly separate, there is a sympathy built up between author and heroine and then transferred to the reader (much like the James-Strether-reader relationship in *The Ambassadors*.) In the next narrative "The Genial Host" the heroine becomes the "you," to be identified both with the narrator and the participant, but the identity established is one of type rather than individuality, a type representative of the "Trotskyite, bohemian intellectual." The next narrative "The Portrait of the Intellectual as a Yale Man" is identical to "The Genial Host" in its emphasis on type but it returns to the omniscient point of view of the first narrative, with the heroine a minor character who exists primarily in terms of her usefulness to the "Yale man." The last narrative "Ghostly Father, I Confess" is most autobiographical in mode; the internal identity of the heroine becomes defined by her development of a consciousness of self as she remembers past experiences. The point of view is center of consciousness moving to the "I" of interior monologue, the context a session between the heroine and her psychoanalyst. Here, for the first time in the narratives, the heroine refers to herself as "Meg," thinking of herself as an entity that can be named even though her sense of self is still, like the shifts of point of view in *Company*, one of unintegration.

When Meg tries to establish a sense of identity by returning to the past, recalling in some detail incidents that had long been suppressed, she is also creating for the first time her own autobiography, but it is a private, nonarticulated autobiography. The fact that some of the details of Meg's memories— the death of her mother in the flu epidemic, her being punished by her aunt for winning a literary prize, her loss of faith—again reappear in Mary McCarthy's avowed autobiography, *Memories of a Catholic Girlhood*, might prompt later readers to speculate that the double disguise in *Company* (Mary McCarthy's creation of a fictional heroine who cannot publicly articulate her past) testifies to McCarthy's own inability at that time to confront her own past directly. Yet, to read *Company* as it was intended, as fiction, there is, as the McCarthy of the "Foreword" would desire, a kind of coherence established by the heroine's search for self even if there are contradictions, inconsistencies, incoherences in the identity of self (this search for self would have not emerged during the reading of these narratives in periodical publication).

As readers of *Company*, we may also perceive the many selves as defined by de Man reflected in the heroine. Margaret Sargent reads the world, she judges the world and herself in the world, she writes (both in her occupational role as writer and in her metaphorical role as composer of the biographical narratives), and she reads herself (most consciously in the last narrative). And these same selves may be reflected in the author McCarthy as she writes, then reads and judges, and writes again. Yet to take the narrative texts alone, separate from the "Foreword," there is no linguistic evidence for concluding that McCarthy intends her self, her "real" self as intellectual, as bohemian, as wife, as writer, as divorcee, etc., to be directly identified with the heroine. And most of McCarthy's contemporary readers (at the time of publication) would not make any autobiographical connections. Only McCarthy's family, closest friends, and co-workers would have legitimately read the narratives as autobiographical fiction. However, as McCarthy becomes more famous, as she begins to write more overt autobiography, as she speaks in interviews of the connections between episodes of *Company* and her own life, new readers and former readers will read *Company* differently than it was read in 1942. But, though readers will read it as autobiographical fiction, it is still to be read as *fiction*. For McCarthy invented a character and invented a fictional world—the Meg Sargent figure is not to be equated with the real McCarthy self. In other words, McCarthy is not yet ready to write autobiography. The metaphor of search, of quest that McCarthy uses in the "Foreword" is revealing, for there isn't yet a "Mary McCarthy" to write the direct autobiography of self. There is only the Mary McCarthy who creates Margaret Sargent, both without a home address.

By the time *Cast a Cold Eye* was published in 1950 Mary McCarthy had published several autobiographical pieces in various periodicals, three of these pieces then included in the *Cast* collection. As mentioned earlier, all the narratives in *Cast* are called "stories" on the acknowledgment page; however, the division into two Parts, Part II containing all the autobiographical pieces, indicates that McCarthy the author and the publisher wished to make some distinction by having the two groupings. There are also textual clues, although some ambiguous, that the last three pieces were intended as "real" autobiography. Each of these "stories" is narrated in the first person by an "I" who is looking back on her childhood and on particular persons in that childhood—her grandmother ("Yonder Peasant, Who Is He?"), her grandfather ("The Blackguard"), her former classmates ("C.Y.E."). There are a few clues to indicate that the narrating "I" is the same person in all three: the reference to the "Protestant grandfather" appears in more than one narrative; the use of the first name "Mary" in more than one; the setting of the Sacred Heart Convent in more than one; but these references would not in themselves establish the "I" as Mary McCarthy, the author, and certainly not when the narratives were read separately in the periodicals.

There are, however, two significant direct clues to the real autobiographical nature of the narratives. In "Yonder Peasant" the "I" emphasizes the form: ". . . I am writing a memoir and not a work of fiction . . ." (*Cast*, p. 163); this clue alone does not establish the narrator as nonfictional, that is, as Mary McCarthy, but in "The Blackguard," at the very end, the narrator recalls a statement made by the Mother Superior: ". . . Mary McCarthy did not resemble Lord Byron . . ." (*Cast*, p. 196). With this reference and the cumulative effect of the others I have mentioned, the narrator is established as Mary

McCarthy herself and the form as autobiography. If readers of *Cast* in 1950 would be reading it after having read *Company*, they would also be interpreting *Company* differently than they had earlier, for now certain references—death of parents, a Catholic girlhood spent with an aunt, the midwestern upbringing, etc.—which the two collections have in common would connect the two heroines and thus enrich, or deepen, the sense of the McCarthy self that is now explicitly emerging.

As far as Mary McCarthy's authorial intentions are concerned, the formal characteristics of *Cast* indicate something different from the fiction of *Company*, a movement toward autobiography but still not relinquishing the fictional disguises that obscure the autobiography (for instance, the inclusion of the three pieces in a collection including narratives that are explicitly fictional). The distance between the Mary McCarthy author self and the narrating "I" of *Cast* is not as great as the distance between the author self and Margaret Sargent, but the distance is still there. In *Cast*, the "I" is so concealed as to its identity with Mary McCarthy herself, it is as if McCarthy the author were saying: "These narratives are about me, but don't really focus on me, and if you want to take them as fiction, O.K., no disservice to the work or to me will take place if you do." The kind of autobiography McCarthy is writing here is what Alfred Kazin calls "autobiography as fiction." These narratives in *Cast a Cold Eye* have, to use Kazin's words, "no purpose other than to tell a story, to create the effect of a story, which above all asks . . . to be read for its value as a narrative."[4] And by communicating this message, McCarthy is also saying that she is still ambivalent about autobiography as a form to explore and reveal her sense of self.

This ambivalent self is not at all apparent in the narrative stance that McCarthy takes in the 1957 *Memories of a Catholic Girlhood*. *Memories* includes the three narratives of *Cast a Cold Eye* ("C.Y.E." is drastically revised, almost unrecognizable in "Names") along with five other narratives that had previously appeared separately in periodicals, primarily *The New Yorker*. In *Memories*, McCarthy is so adamant about, so confident of her identity and its revelation in undisguised autobiography, she prefaces the work with a "To the Reader" section which unquestionably establishes her autobiographical intentions, and then even goes beyond that to include an epilogue to each of the chapters (except the last, which is commented upon in the prologue) indicating the distinctions between fiction and autobiography in the original chapters, the effect of which is to establish the preface and epilogues as indisputable autobiography.

Here Mary McCarthy assumes the "double persona" that we associate with the genre of autobiography, a point of view clearly distinguished from the points of view of fiction. (Barbara Herrnstein Smith's argument would again apply here for this point of view in autobiography is often more a rhetorical one established by the communicated intention of the author—as, for instance, the signature on the title page— than a linguistically identifiable distinction.[5]) This "double persona in *Memories* is Mary McCarthy, a real person, as narrator but also acting within her narrative as protagonist.[6] *But* then McCarthy doubles the "double persona" for in the preface and the epilogues we have a narrator, Mary McCarthy, who is distanced in time from the Mary McCarthy narrator of the original chapters, and a protagonist, Mary McCarthy, who is recast because of the narrator's re-evaluation of the original protagonist.

The complexity of *Memories* and the resultant brilliance of the book—thematically, stylistically, structurally—derives in large part from the number of selves that are present and inextricably intertwined. And Mary McCarthy now is ready to acknowledge these several selves with varying perspectives, selves that are often contradictory, ambivalent, insecure, but now, paradoxically, one integrated self. McCarthy is now so willing to reveal herself to the world and so secure about that revelation that she begins the "To the Reader" section with an admonishment to those readers who had taken these memories in their original periodical presentation as fiction: "Can it be that the public takes for granted that anything written by a professional writer is *eo ipso* untrue?" (*Memories*, p. 3). Of course McCarthy is being a bit coy here; she is not accepting her own responsibility in this matter, that, indeed, with the earlier presentations, she herself was contributing to the disguising of self; that her readers, even perhaps her friends, might see those narratives as more fictional than autobiographical, in form as well as in true-value, should have been of no great surprise. Later her distress is self-directed as she acknowledges her attempts to distinguish fact from fiction: ". . . there are cases where I am not sure myself whether I am making something up . . ." (*Memories*, p. 4); "About the butterfly episode, I must make a more serious correction or at least express a doubt about [factual accuracy] . . . the most likely thing, I fear, is that I fused two memories. Mea Culpa" (*Memories*, p. 83); "There are some semi-fictional touches . . ." (*Memories*, p. 164). Nevertheless, the very fact that McCarthy expresses her doubts, her "fictional touches," her faulty memory does support even more her testimony of the truth of self that the whole of *Memories* is to convey. Her method is a very significant part of her autobiographical revelation.

Mary McCarthy's analysis of the process by which she arrives at the truth also contributes to the literary consciousness that is very much a part of the self of *Memories*. That she now wishes to acknowledge her "fictions" will help to assure her readers of the sincerity of her attempt to create her real self but her process also reveals that she cannot escape, nor does she wish to escape, that part of self that is a creator, a writer. This literary consciousness also, interestingly, contributes to the intellectual detachment that McCarthy wants to convey as part of her real self. This detachment will manifest itself in McCarthy's presentation of self as refracted from the portraits of her family, friends, and teachers. Emily Dickenson's dictum "Tell it slant" often seems to be McCarthy's autobiographical stance, particularly evident in the final haunting portrait of her Jewish grandmother, "Ask Me No Questions," a narrative that when read in isolation would probably be perceived as biography, but when it comes at the end of *Memories*, it also becomes an evocation of the vulnerability of the McCarthy self. In *Memories*, McCarthy creates several paradoxes, not the least of which is that through the subtleties and indirections of her literary methods she has released herself to the full exposure of autobiography. In *Memories* she has found her home address.

Mary McCarthy implicitly conveys this view herself when she relates in her *Paris Review* interview of 1961 that she is no longer, as she was in *The Company She Keeps*, in quest of the self. She knows that

> . . . you really must *make* the self. It's absolutely useless to look for it, but it's possible in some sense to make. . . . you finally begin in some sense to make and choose the self you want. . . . I suppose in a sense I don't know any more today than I did in 1941 about what my identity is. But I've stopped looking

for it. I must say, I believe much more in truth now than I did. I do believe in the solidity of truth much more. Yes. I believe there is a truth, and that it's knowable.[7]

So if the truth of *Memories* is reflected in the complexity of the multiple reading selves, judging selves, and writing selves of Mary McCarthy, both the truth and the complexity are deepened if we place *Memories* within the historical context of *The Company She Keeps* and *Cast a Cold Eye*, each contributing in its own way to the dynamic making of the McCarthy self. For if *Memories* records the being, it is *Company* and *Cast* that record the becoming.[8] Somewhat echoing Mary McCarthy's metaphor, Alfred Kazin uses the phrase "to make a home for oneself, on paper . . ." to express the need that is fulfilled by autobiography; it is a need not only to tell the truth, but also the desire to find the "line, pattern, the form" that will articulate that truth.[9]

In trying to summarize the significance of Mary McCarthy's autobiographical journey, and what it can convey to us about the relationship between fiction and autobiography, we might agree that in the fictional *Company* there is autobiography and in the autobiographical *Memories* there is fiction. Yet in fiction, no matter how autobiographical, the author is not asserting any historical self outside the fiction. The Margaret Sargent of *The Company She Keeps* exists only in the fictional world that Mary McCarthy created. The author of fiction is denying history. But in autobiography, and in *Memories*, with all of its fictions, the author is asserting a self, a sense of self, and exposing self to history and to historical judgment.

*Notes*

1. Mary McCarthy, *The Company She Keeps* (New York: Simon and Schuster, 1942); *Cast a Cold Eye* (New York: Harcourt, Brace, 1950); *Memories of a Catholic Girlhood* (New York: Harcourt, Brace, 1957). All subsequent references to these editions will be placed within the text, and each title will usually be shortened to the first main word: *Company*, *Cast*, and *Memories*.
2. Paul de Man, *Blindness and Insight* (Oxford: Oxford Univ. Press, 1971), p. 39.
3. Barbara Herrnstein Smith, *On the Margins of Discourse: The Relation of Literature to Language* (Chicago: Univ. of Chicago Press, 1978), p. 81.
4. Alfred Kazin, "Autobiography as Narrative," in *To the Young Writer*, ed. A. L. Bader (Ann Arbor: Univ. of Michigan Press, 1965), p. 183.
5. Smith, p. 81, states that the identity of a text changes because of what she terms "linguistic *function*" which is largely defined by some combination of the author's "*purpose or intention*" and the reader's "*value, attitude, or response.*"
6. The term "double persona" and the definition is from William L. Howarth, "Some Principles of Autobiography," *New Literary History*, 5, no. 2 (1974), p. 365.
7. Mary McCarthy, Interview with Elisabeth Niebuhr, *Writers at Work: The Paris Review Interviews*, Second Series, ed. George Plimpton (New York: Penguin Books, 1979), p. 315.
8. Patricia Meyer Spacks in *Imagining a Self: Autobiography and Novel in Eighteenth-Century England* (Cambridge, Mass.: Harvard Univ. Press, 1976), p. 6, distinguishes between autobiography and fiction in that in fiction the characters' "becoming, more than their being, compels our attention." The emphasis on "being," however, in autobiography does not deny the fact that the creating self is dynamic, is growing/changing/becoming during the very act of defining being.
9. Alfred Kazin, "The Self as History: Reflections on Autobiography," in *Telling Lives: The Biographer's Art*, ed. Marc Pachter (Washington, D.C.: New Republic Books, 1979), p. 89.

# CARSON McCULLERS

## 1917–1967

Lula Carson Smith was born on February 19, 1917, in Columbus, Georgia. As an adolescent she studied music intensively with her teacher Mary Tucker. In 1934 she left Columbus for New York, hoping to continue her studies at Juilliard. Shortly after her arrival in New York her tuition money was "lost" by a roommate who was holding the cash for Carson. She took a series of day jobs and at nights she studied writing at Columbia. In 1937 she married a fellow Southerner, Reeves McCullers, and the two eventually moved to New York.

While at Columbia McCullers studied with Whit Burnett, influential editor of *Story* magazine. Her first work of fiction, a semi-autobiographical story titled "Wunderkind," was published in *Story* in 1936. Her first novel, *The Heart Is a Lonely Hunter* (1940), received favorable reviews. Both she and Reeves were bisexual and the emotional strain of their various sexual relationships became too much. In 1940 she moved into February House, Brooklyn Heights' famed literary enclave whose residents included Auden, Isherwood, MacNeice, and later Dali and Nin. She divorced her husband in 1942 and stayed in Brooklyn until 1945, spending some of her summers at the Yaddo Colony, a writers' retreat in Saratoga, New York. In 1945 she moved with Reeves, whom she had remarried that year, into a house in Nyack, New York, which she had purchased for her mother and sister.

McCullers continued to write throughout the 1940s, publishing *The Ballad of the Sad Café* in 1943 and *The Member of the Wedding* in 1946. In less than six years she wrote four novels, each of which sold over a half million copies. At the suggestion of Tennessee Williams she dramatized *The Member of the Wedding*, which had a long successful Broadway run beginning in 1950. For her efforts on this play she was awarded the New York Drama Critics Circle and Donaldson prizes for best play of 1950. An untreated childhood case of rheumatic fever later brought about severe health problems for McCullers. In 1947 she suffered a debilitating stroke which left her partially blind and paralyzed on her left side. She made an unsuccessful suicide attempt in 1948. However, five years later her husband committed suicide in Paris as it seemed that their marriage would again end in divorce. The death of her mother in 1955 sent McCullers into a prolonged state of grief which was complicated by further medical problems, including breast cancer, a fractured hip, and several bouts of pneumonia.

In her final years McCullers wrote *The Square Root of Wonderful* (1957), which did not fare well with Broadway critics, and a last novel, *Clock without Hands* (1961). In 1963 Edward Albee dramatized her *Ballad of the Sad Café*. On September 29, 1967, she died after suffering a stroke.

## Personal

Many people have asked me why I like writing for the theatre. I wrote *The Member of the Wedding* first as a book and it took me five years. Once the novel was finished I had that happy, depleted feeling a writer has after finishing a long stretch of work. I had no notion at the time that I would dramatize it. Then Tennessee Williams wrote me about the book and asked me if I would come and spend the summer with him on Nantucket and I accepted the invitation.

During that sea-summer lit with the glow of a new friendship (we had not met before and had known each other only through our work) he suggested I do *The Member of the Wedding* as a play.

I was hesitant at first, knowing nothing about the theatre. I had seen only about ten plays in my life, including high school *Hamlets* and *Vagabond Kings*, but the visual and dramatic aspects of the novel I had written compelled me. Tennessee borrowed a typewriter for me and we settled down to the same dining table. He was working on *Summer and Smoke* while I began the play version of *The Member of the Wedding*. We would work from ten to two and then go to the beach on sunny days or read poetry aloud when it rained. Tennessee and I have spent many ocean-summers since and our friendship is a continuing joy and inspiration to me.

Despite forecasts of disaster the vitality and truth of the play, magnificently produced and performed was immediately appreciated. My own financial problems were solved and, most important, I fell in love with the theatre. The play was a new and radiant creative experience to me.

When people ask why I write for the theatre I can only counter with another question. Why does anyone write at all? I suppose a writer writes out of some inward compulsion to transform his own experience (much of it is unconscious) into the universal and symbolical. The themes the artist chooses are always deeply personal. I suppose my central theme is the theme of spiritual isolation. Certainly I have always felt alone. In addition to being lonely, a writer is also amorphous. A writer soon discovers he has no single identity but lives the lives of all the people he creates and his weathers are independent of the actual day around him. I live with the people I create and it has always made my essential loneliness less keen.

In *The Square Root of Wonderful* I recognize many of the compulsions that made me write this play. My husband wanted to be a writer and his failure in that was one of the disappointments that led to his death. When I started *The Square Root of Wonderful* my mother was very ill and after a few months she died. I wanted to re-create my mother—to remember her tranquil beauty and sense of joy in life. So, unconsciously, the life-death theme of *The Square Root of Wonderful* emerged.

Present-day audiences have been accustomed to plays that have a single emotional direction. If it's a modern tragedy the overtones of tragedy are undisturbed by the comedy of the every day. In the modern comedy such themes as death and failure are so subordinated that they are almost inexistent. Yet audiences do respond to tragi-comedy when the absurd and painful truths of life are combined in a single line.

I was aware of the risk in alternating comic and tragic scenes, aware that it confuses the same audience who can respond readily to a single situation with both laughter and tears. This is mostly true in the theatre; a reader of novels is more emotionally flexible because he has the time to reflect before he is pushed on to the next action.

Writing a play can be among the most satisfying experiences of an author's life. If he is lucky, the production, with the constellation of artists involved, can heighten and give the fullest dimension to the script and the audience serves to intensify the experience and to make the author feel yes, that's it. That's just what I had in mind—and more. The author is rarely so lucky. There are pressures of the theatre—the deadlines, the last-minute decisions and changes that are nerve-breaking for a writer. For the theatre is a most pragmatical art, and if a scene does not work it has to be altered.

I have learned this in my work in the theatre: the author must work alone until the intentions of his play are fulfilled—until the play is as finished as the author can make it. Once a play is in rehearsal, a playwright must write under unaccustomed pressure, and alas, what he had in mind is often compromised. This may be due to the actors, the producer, the director—the whole prism of the theatrical production.

And so begins a transmutation that sometimes to the author's dismay ends in the play being almost unrecognizable to the creator.

That is why of the five or six evolutions this play went through I prefer to publish the one which follows. It is the last one I wrote before the production was set in motion and is the most nearly the truth of what I want to say in *The Square Root of Wonderful*.

Many novelists have been attracted to the theatre—Fitzgerald, Wolfe, James and Joyce. Perhaps this is because of the loneliness of a writer's life—the unaccustomed joy of participating creatively with others is marvelous to a writer. It is rare that a writer is equally skilled as a novelist and a playwright. I don't want to open this can of beans, but I would say simply that the writer is compelled to write, and the form is determined by some veiled inward need that perhaps the writer himself does not fully understand.—CARSON MCCULLERS, "A Personal Preface" to *The Square Root of Wonderful*, 1958, pp. vii–x

Of all the characters in the work of Carson McCullers, the one who seemed to her family and friends most like the author herself was Frankie Addams: the vulnerable, exasperating and endearing adolescent of *The Member of the Wedding* who was looking for the "we of me." However, Carson once said that she was or became in the process of writing all the characters in her work. This is probably true of most real writers who often with pain draw from their unconscious what the rest of us would just as soon keep hidden from ourselves and others. So accept the fact that Carson was not only Frankie Addams but J. T. Malone, Miss Amelia and Captain Penderton; but familiarity with the work that she was able to finish would be only a partial clue to who and what she was. This was not simply because she had not finished what she had to say, but that she was the artist, and as she often quoted, "Nothing human is alien to me."

Before her death, I would have said that I knew Carson better than anyone did—that I knew her very well indeed. This would have been the truth as I saw it at the time, and at times I am still tempted to think that I knew her the best. After all, I knew her for forty-five years and lived with her off and on for much of that time. We shared the same heritage, the same parents, the same brother, the same room that looked out on the same holly tree and Japanese magnolia, and for the first twelve years of my life, the same mahogany bed. But we were sisters—sometimes intimate friends, sometimes enemies and at times strangers.

I remember very well the day that she told me—she did not ask me—that she had appointed me co-executor of her literary estate. I was annoyed. Unable to acknowledge her constant closeness to death, I resented her trying to force me to face it. Carson was there when I was born and would be there when I died. She had lived through enough close calls to prove to me that she was indestructible. ⟨. . .⟩

I might like to think I knew Carson better than anyone did. But Tennessee Williams on his first meeting with her caught the real spirit of Carson and the Carson I like to remember. ⟨. . .⟩ He wrote:

I should like to mention my first meeting with Carson McCullers. It occurred during the summer that I thought I was dying. I was performing a great many acts of piety that summer. I had rented a rather lop-sided frame house on the island of Nantucket and had filled it with a remarkably random assortment of creatures animal and human. There was a young gentleman of Mexican-Indian extraction who was an angel of goodness except when he had a drink. The trouble was that he usually had a drink. Then there was a young lady studying for the opera and another young lady who painted various bits of refuse washed up by the sea. I remember they gave a rather cold and wet odor to the upper floor of the house where she arranged her still-lifes which she called arrangements. If the weather had been consistently bright and warm these arrangements would not have been so hard to take. But the weather was unrelentingly bleak so that the exceedingly dank climate of the arrangements did little to dispell my reflections upon things morbid. One night there was a great wind-storm. Promptly as if they had been waiting all year to make this gesture, every window on the North side of the house crashed in, and we were at the mercy of the elements. The young lady who painted the wet arrangements, the opera singer and the naturally-good-humored Mexican all were driven South to that side of the house where I was attempting to write a play that involved the Angel of Eternity. At that time a pregnant cat came into the building and gave birth to five or six kittens on the bed in our downstairs guest-room. It was about this time, immediately after the wind-storm and the invasion of cats, that Carson McCullers arrived to pay me a visit on the island, in response to the first fan-letter that I had ever written to a writer, written after I had read her latest book, *The Member of the Wedding*.

The same morning that Carson arrived the two other female visitors, if my memory serves me accurately, took their departure, the one with her portfolio of arias and the other with several cases of moist canvases and wet arrangements, neither of them thanking me too convincingly for the hospitality of the house and as they departed, casting glances of veiled compassion upon the brand new arrival.

Carson was not dismayed by the state of the house. She had been in odd places before. She took an immediate fancy to the elated young Mexican and displayed considerable fondness for the cats and insisted that she would be comfortable in the downstairs bedroom where they were boarding. Almost immediately the summer weather improved. The sun came out with an air of permanence, the wind shifted to the South and it was suddenly warm enough for bathing. At the same time, almost immediately after Carson and the sun appeared on the island, I relinquished the romantic notion that I was a dying artist. My various psychosomatic symptoms were forgotten. There was warmth and light in the house, the odor of good cooking and the nearly-forgotten sight of clean dishes and silver. Also there was some coherent talk for a change. Long evening conversations over hot rum and tea, the reading of poetry aloud, bicycle rides and wanderings along moonlit dunes, and one night there was a marvelous display of the Aurora Borealis, great quivering sheets of white radiance sweeping over the island and the ghostly white fishermen's houses and fences. That night and that mysterious phenomenon of the sky will be always associated in my mind with the discovery of our friendship, or rather, more precisely, with the spirit of this new found friend, who seemed as curiously and beautifully unworldly as that night itself . . .

—MARGARITA G. SMITH, "Introduction" to *The Mortgaged Heart*, 1971, xi–xix

## Works

### THE HEART IS A LONELY HUNTER

No matter what the age of its author, *The Heart Is a Lonely Hunter* would be a remarkable book. When one reads that Carson McCullers is a girl of 22 it becomes more than that. Maturity does not cover the quality of her work. It is something beyond that, something more akin to the vocation of pain to which a great poet is born. Reading her, one feels this girl is wrapped in knowledge which has roots beyond the span of her life and her experience. How else can she so surely plumb the hearts of characters as strange and, under the force of her creative shaping, as real as she presents—two deaf mutes, a ranting, rebellious drunkard, a Negro torn from his faith and lost in his frustrated dream of equality, a restaurant owner bewildered by his emotions, a girl of 13 caught between the world of people and the world of shadows.

From the opening page, brilliant in its establishment of mood, character and suspense, the book takes hold of the reader. "In the town there were two mutes, and they were always together," Miss McCullers begins, and at once this unique novel swings into action. One of these mutes was the fat, greasy, ungainly Greek, Spiros Antonapoulos, who worked in his cousin's fruit store and made candy for him; the other was John Singer, who was employed as an engraver in a jewelry store. They lived together in two rooms, bound to each other by the physical handicap which made them alien in a world of normal people.

With a touch reminiscent of Faulkner but peculiarly her own, Miss McCullers describes their strange relationship, the fat Greek, greedy for food, petulant, mentally irresponsible, dominating the slender, gentle Singer. When the public habits of Antonapoulos become such that he is a menace to public decency, his cousin has him put away in an institution for the insane and John Singer is left alone, lost and stranded among people who talk.

Exiled from the home he and the Greek had made for

each other, Singer takes a room in the Kellys' boarding house and arranges to have all his meals in Biff Brannon's New York Café. The few things he needs to get over to people he writes in careful script on cards he carries with him. Accustomed to living in a world of silence, he neither expects nor wants companionship of those who live in a world of sound. Deepest in his heart is the yearning for the departed Antonapoulos.

With stinging subtlety, Miss McCullers builds up the growing importance of Singer in the lives of the people who come to know him. So excellent is her portrayal, so fine her balance of the imagined against the real, that there are times when the reader himself is bemused by the silence and the smile of the mute. In developing Singer as the fountainhead of understanding and wisdom, she plunges into the heart of human desolation, into the pain of the ineffectuality of words as a bridge between people. Sitting silently in Biff Brannon's restaurant, lost in his dreams of the two rooms where Antonapoulos had cooked, smiling vaguely as he plans his vacation visit to the incarcerated Greek, Singer becomes a symbol of godliness. Saying nothing, it is assumed he knows everything. His smile is gentle, built of his own loneliness and because he cannot defend himself against the spate of words forced upon him, he listens with eyes fixed sympathetically upon moving lips.

To Biff Brannon, lost in a world of emotional fears, Jake Blount is a crazy drunkard who uses his education to rant against the inequality between the rich and the poor. To Singer, Blount is a strange, unkempt creature who talks continuously of things Singer doesn't fully understand. But Singer listens or seems to and his smile is gentle. For Biff himself, Singer has the fascination of the unknowable.

To his daughter, Portia, cook at the poverty-stricken Kelly boarding house, Dr. Benedict Mady Copeland is a man who has strayed from the fold of the true church and will suffer for it in spite of his aid to the sick. To Singer he is the colored physician who talks passionately about the subjugation of his race. To her family Mick Kelly is a good kid who takes care of her younger brothers and goes off by herself when she is free of them. To Singer she is the little girl who comes to his room to talk about her dreams of music, who pours herself out to the man who sits and smiles and nods as he reads her lips. To all of them, through no fault or virtue of his own, except that of simplicity and kindliness, Singer becomes the one creature in their lives who can give them peace and understanding.

With powerful strokes Miss McCullers paints the details of the lives of these people and those they touch. She is squeamish neither of word nor incident and her canvas is alive with the realities of their existence, more often savage and violent than tender. Her imagination is rich and fearless; she has an astounding perception of humanity which goes with equal certainty into the daily life of a drunken social rebel like Jake Blount and into the dreams of the music-hungry, lonely Mick Kelly. The effect is strangely that of a Van Gogh painting peopled by Faulkner figures. That it is the degenerate Spiros Antonapoulos, greedy for sweets and vicious in an infantile way, who actually dominates the lives of the characters through his influence on John Singer, serves to heighten the terrific force of her story.

Carson McCullers is a full-fledged novelist whatever her age. She writes with a sweep and certainty that are overwhelming. *The Heart Is a Lonely Hunter* is a first novel. One anticipates the second with something like fear. So high is the standard she has set. It doesn't seem possible that she can reach it again.—ROSE FELD, "A Remarkable First Novel of Lonely Lives," *NYTBR*, June 16, 1940, p. 6

That *The Heart Is a Lonely Hunter* is to be interpreted on more than one level of meaning is undeniable. Carson McCullers herself has called her first novel a "parable in modern form"; and, while reviewers do not take very seriously her statement as to the meaning of this parable, practically every one realizes the importance of symbolism in the book. One critic even went so far as to write that "Carson McCullers is ultimately the artist functioning at the very loftiest symbolic level. . . ."

If, then, *The Heart Is a Lonely Hunter* is symbolic, what exactly is the symbolic intent? Mrs. McCullers has called it "the story of Fascism," presenting "the spiritual rather than the political side of that phenomenon," but this interpretation is not shared by many of her readers. Most see the theme as that of human loneliness and the individual's attempts to break through the barriers separating him from other human souls. This is certainly the major theme of the novel and of the corpus of Mrs. McCullers's work. But in *The Heart Is a Lonely Hunter* there is, it seems to me, an ironic religious allegory employed to reinforce the author's concept of the discreteness of human beings, not just from each other, but from God Himself. I call it an allegory because I find an almost continuous presentation of this religious thesis throughout, developing and growing through the narrative, as well as in "accidental" (in the Spenserian sense) symbols which serve to highlight this thesis. The anonymous reviewer in *Time* suggested, without full development, something of this religious allegory when he said, "The book is . . . a study in the relationship of human Christs and semi-Christs to a suffering world. . . ." And the sacrilege of the irony implicit in Mrs. McCullers's idea seemingly frightened another reviewer into asking tentatively if she is symbolizing something larger than is apparent.

The religious pattern in the novel involves a kind of pyramidal relationship of six people, though the quartet who form the base are unaware of either the existence or the importance of the one at the apex. These characters, going from apex to base, are Antonapoulos, the spoiled, self-centered Greek mute; John Singer, also a mute and rather an ascetic; Mick Kelly, the twelve-year-old girl who hears music in what she calls her "inside room"; Jake Blount, a half-mad anarchist; the Negro Dr. Copeland, who struggles for his race; and Biff Brannon, the impotent and frustrated cafe proprietor. The last four find their God-image in Singer, who, unknown to them, finds his in the Greek.

The figure of Singer is central. Yet in the opening sections of the novel, before Singer meets his four "visitors," the reader sees him in a position of dependence upon Antonapoulos, with whom he shares a small apartment. When the two walk, "The one who steered the way was an obese and dreamy Greek." Alone together, they find happiness; but it is Singer who does the "talking" in sign-language, with the Greek signaling only an occasional " 'Holy Jesus,' or 'God,' or 'Darling Mary,' " and stuffing himself with food and drink. "Singer never knew just how much his friend understood of all the things he told him. But it did not matter." He must tell them. His whole existence is wrapped up in the hedonistic, childish, whimsical Greek, and when the latter is to be sent away to a lunatic asylum, Singer is in a frenzy. His hands are busy telling Antonapoulos all he must say, "all the thoughts that had ever been in his mind and heart, but there was not time." The Greek listens drowsily, leaving Singer ignorant of the success or failure of his attempt at communication.

Once the Greek is gone, Singer is desolate, changing his lodgings, walking restlessly. Now he keeps his hands hidden in his pockets; his means of intimate communication is never used with his "visitors." Finally exhaustion sets in, "and there

was a look about him of deep calm. In his face there came to be a brooding peace that is seen most often in the faces of the very sorrowful or the very wise." Throughout the rest of the book, unknown to the others, he lives only for his visits to the asylum, where he is greeted indifferently by Antonapoulos, who evinces interest only in his friend's expensive gifts. Only in the presence of the Greek does Singer reveal his hands and bare the secrets of his heart. Just before the final visit Mrs. McCullers tells what Antonapoulos has meant to Singer:

> Behind each waking moment there had always been his friend. And this submerged communion with Antonapoulos had grown and changed as though they were together in the flesh. Sometimes he thought of Antonapoulos with awe and self-abasement, sometimes with pride—always with love unchecked by criticism, freed of will. When he dreamed at night the face of his friend was always before him, massive and wise and gentle. And in his waking thoughts they were eternally united.

It does not appear to me that Mrs. McCullers is trying to suggest an unnatural sexual relationship. Rather it is that Singer endows the Greek with Godlike qualities of understanding and finds solace through the confessional and through the serving of his God. Once the Greek's nod to a nurse "seemed one of benediction rather than a simple nod of thanks"; and Singer's dream of the Greek definitely attributes to him Godlike qualities. This dream passage is filled with both phrases and imagery of a religious nature. In the dream, yellow lanterns illumine dimly

> a dark flight of stone steps. Antonapoulos kneeled at the top of these steps. He was naked and he fumbled with something that he held above his head and gazed at as though in prayer. He himself [Singer] knelt halfway down the steps. He was naked and cold and he could not take his eyes from Antonapoulos and the thing he held above him.

Behind singer and on the ground kneel the four others, and "he felt their eyes on him. And behind them there were uncounted crowds of kneeling people in the darkness." Singer's hands are windmills, and he is fascinated by "the unknown thing that Antonapoulos held." Suddenly there is an upheaval of crashing steps, and Singer falls downward. Here, really, the religious allegory is presented microcosmically.

This religious theme is made more evident in the relationships Singer has with Mick, Jake, Dr. Copeland, and Biff. At first sight of the mute, each is drawn inexplicably to him. All seem to share Biff's feeling about him.

> The fellow was downright uncanny. People felt themselves watching him even before they knew that there was anything different about him. His eyes made a person think he heard things nobody else had ever heard, that he knew things no one had ever guessed before. He did not seem quite human.

And to Singer's room in the Kellys' boarding house goes each of the four to talk to him, to unburden innermost thoughts and hatreds and aspirations. His brooding serenity and his silent nod send each away with a feeling of assurance, of blessing, even.

When Jake, the anarchist, goes off with Singer after their first meeting and Biff has been pondering the strange attraction of the mute, it is surely not mere coincidence that Biff overhears his wife preparing as her Sunday School lesson the passage in which Jesus calls Simon and Andrew to be fishers of men: "And when they had found Him, they said unto Him, 'All men seek for Thee.' "

To Mick, Singer "was like some kind of a great teacher, only because he was mute he could not teach." She sees him, too, as "what she used to imagine God was," and she rehearses a group of words "just as she would speak them to Mister Singer: 'Lord forgiveth me, for I knoweth not what I do.'"

And with the others it is the same, though Biff maintains a little detachment and occasionally wonders just how much of what they say Singer really understands.

Aside from these four relationships, Mrs. McCullers underlines Singer as the God-image repeatedly. She more than once refers to his "Jewish face," but never states definitely that he is Semitic. In fact, she has the Jews calling him a Jew, the merchants declaring him wealthy, the textile workers thinking him a C. I. O. organizer, and a lone Turk vowing that Singer is a fellow countryman. Each sees in Singer what he wants to see. Later a Negro woman declares that Singer knows "the way of spirits come back from the dead." Also he is repeatedly giving water and wine and food to his visitors. Often as they talk he sits and moves chessmen on a board. And, if one may go slightly Freudian, this Father-God image is heightened by the fact that Singer works in a jewelry store. Mrs. McCullers's father was a jeweler.

The irony of this allegory and these symbols is, of course, that man makes God in the image of his desire. For Mrs. McCullers's Antonapoulos-God and Singer-God can neither understand their suppliants nor really communicate with them. In an unmailed letter to the Greek (for Antonapoulos cannot read) Singer reveals his bewilderment as to what his visitors seek and find in him. Of Jake Blount he says, "He thinks he and I have a secret together but I do not know what it is"; of Mick, "She likes music. I wish I knew what it is she hears. She knows I am deaf but she thinks I know about music"; of Dr. Copelend, "This black man frightens me sometimes. His eyes are hot and bright. . . . He has many books. However, he does not own any mystery books." Singer's only reading is mystery books. Biff he passes off with the comment: "he is not just like the others. He has a very black beard so that he has to shave twice daily. . . . He watches." Unlike the others, Biff seems to him to have nothing he hates or loves excessively. But Biff does have something; and Singer is not quite sure what it is the others hate and love. Later he admits to himself that "He had agreed with each of them in turn, though what it was they wanted him to sanction he did not know." We have seen that Antonapoulos did not understand Singer, as Singer was sure that he did. The muteness, then, engenders mystery, but behind the mystery lies misunderstanding—or nothing.

So Singer, on whom the other four leaned, was even more dependent than they. For when the Greek died, Singer shot himself, leaving his personal affairs in a terrible mess. When God is dead, life is over for Singer. But when their God dies, Mick and Jake and Biff and the Doctor are only changed, left baseless for a while. For each, life goes on—a different life, but life. Mick, her music a bitter memory, clerks at Woolworth's; Jake goes blundering off to preach his diatribes against capitalism elsewhere; Biff phlegmatically watches the customers in his New York Cafe and yearns for children to mother; old, sick, and broken, the Doctor alone seems defeated, and he is carried off to the country leaving the struggle for his people unfinished. But even he has the fortitude to wait for death. Without God, then, life goes on, but something—a touch of glory, a feeling of communion with an all-encompassing understanding—has gone from it.

Perhaps there is also a larger symbolic framework to this allegory of the personal relationship between the individual and his self-created god. Antonapoulos is Greek; Singer has a "Jewish face." Like the gods of classical antiquity, of paganism, Antonapoulos is whimsical, selfish, scandalous, sensual, and at the same time capable of seeming wise, of bringing consolation and reassurance to his devotee. Singer, like the Christian deity, is ascetic, reflective, withdrawn, and yet intimate. For a while the two share the same dwelling, with the Greek as the dominating spirit. Then the Greek is thrown into the discard, discredited as it were by the label of lunacy; and Singer, alone but always aware of his own dependence on the past, assumes the mantle of divinity. Then, perhaps Mrs. McCullers is saying, with the destruction of the pagan past the Christian myth derived from it collapses.

At any rate, here is the religious allegory which seems to underlie and to reinforce the theme of loneliness in *The Heart Is a Lonely Hunter*. It is not an intricately perfected allegory, and often its symbolism is fuzzy. But it does seem apparent that the author has written an iconoclastic religious novel, ambitious, sensitive, vivid, and underlaid with the rebellion against tradition not unexpected in a precocious young woman of twenty-two.—FRANK DURHAM, "God and No God In *The Heart Is a Lonely Hunter*," SAQ, Fall 1957, pp. 494–99

Reflections appear in Carson McCullers' fiction. In *The Heart Is a Lonely Hunter* each character ⟨. . .⟩ is a double—Biff, Mick, Blount, and Copeland are broken images of one another. Each is concerned with himself, unconsciously refusing to notice another person. As John B. Vickery writes: there is "a sense of terror aroused by the tragic fact that those who are seeking salvation through companions with whom they might create a community are in fact incapable of recognizing their fellows."

This central situation is reinforced by various images of fragmentation. On the first page we note that Singer and Antonapoulos, although linked arm in arm, are incomplete images of each other. The Greek has half-closed eyelids, a stupid smile. Singer, on the other hand, has "quick, intelligent" eyes. The two are in love, but the love implies cruel fragmentation. Their situation reflects the other relationships in the novel; it "mirrors as well as creates the larger scene in which the characters operate." This is immediately evident in the Biff-Alice relationship. Alice likes lying in bed; she enjoys religion; she knows how a business should be run. Biff is completely opposite. Again the relationship is fragmented, but this very fact reflects the mutes' relationship.

Distortion is evident in physical description. There are many things about Blount "that seemed contrary. His head was very large and well-shaped, but his neck was soft and slender as a boy's. The mustache looked false, as if it had been stuck on for a costume party and would fall if he talked too fast." Biff looks at Mick and sees a "gangling, towheaded youngster, a girl of about twelve. . . . She [is] dressed in khaki shorts, a blue shirt, and tennis shoes—so that at first glance she [is] like a very young boy." Later Biff thinks that in every person there is "some special physical part kept always guarded"—the body itself is fragmented. Biff thinks that for Singer it is the hands; for Mick, her tender breasts; for Alice, her hair; and for himself, his genitals. Jake at one point looks in the mirror and sees "the same caricature of himself he had noticed so many times before." Already deformed, he seems even more so. Copeland's body fights his mind: his tuberculosis destroys his strong true purpose. The distortion is effectively presented in terms of sex by Biff: often old men acquire high voices and "mincing" walk; old women get "rough and deep voices" and grow dark mustaches. He himself wishes he could be a mother; after Alice dies, he uses her lemon rinse. The human being is a freak.—IRVING MALIN, "Self-Love," *New American Gothic*, 1962, pp. 24–25

## THE BALLAD OF THE SAD CAFÉ

It is a feeling of intense loneliness, Stephen Spender has written, which gives all great American literature something in common, and this feeling finds expression in its recurrent theme: "the great misunderstood primal energy of creative art, transformed into the inebriate . . . the feeling ox . . . the lost child."

Spender's insight seemed to me a particularly acute one when I first read it. Surely one is haunted by loneliness and longing in Hemingway, in Fitzgerald, in Faulkner. When I was reading the collected novels and stories of Carson McCullers, his observation struck me with new force. Here is a young American talent of the very first order, and one leaves her work with an almost terrifying sense of the tragic aloneness of man. The symbol for this aloneness is always, as Spender has said, the sensitive, the dumb, the suffering, the lost child. In reading the work of Mrs. McCullers, we become aware of being in the presence of a great tragic spirit, and we ourselves become possessed of a great pity and fear.

This apprehension of loneliness, this pity and fear, is constant in Carson McCullers' work. The present volume, in addition to the title story ⟨*The Ballad of the Sad Café*⟩, contains her three novels, *The Heart Is a Lonely Hunter*, *Reflections in a Golden Eye*, and *The Member of the Wedding*, and six of her short stories. Through them all we move from one level of tragedy and terror to another: Miss Amelia, the fearsome and cross-eyed, hopelessly in love with an almost diabolical hunchback; Madame Zilensky, the musician, living vicariously through the pathological lie; the deaf-mute, finding his voice only through another mute; the inarticulate soldier, keeping secret vigil by the bed of a woman to whom he can never speak; all these and others probe depths of man's misery, depths to which few writers ever gain access. The art of Carson McCullers has been called "Gothic." Perhaps it is—superficially. Certainly her day-to-day world, her little Southern towns, are haunted by far more masterful horrors than were ever conjured up in the dreary castles of a Horace Walpole. It seems to me, however, that the "Gothic" label misses the essential point. Because Carson McCullers is ultimately the artist functioning at the very loftiest symbolic level, and if one must look for labels I should prefer to call her work "metaphysical." Behind the strange and horrible in her world there are played out the most sombre tragedies of the human spirit; her mutes, her hunchbacks, speak of complexities and frustrations which are so native in man that they can only be recognized, perhaps, in the shock which comes from seeing them dressed in the robes of the grotesque. They pass us on the street every day but we only notice them when they drag a foot as they go by.

At the very opening of the title story, the face of Miss Amelia, the proprietor of the "Sad Café," is described as a face ". . . like the terrible dim faces known in dreams . . . sexless and white, with two gray crossed eyes which are turned inwards so sharply that they seem to be exchanging with each other one long and secret gaze of grief." This description, remarkable for its metaphysical fusion of horror and compassion, might serve as a symbol of Carson McCullers' art. And this fusion, I would say, represents an achievement equalled by few other contemporary American writers.—WILLIAM P. CLANCY, *Com*, June 15, 1951, p. 218

Clearly Carson McCullers is primarily interested in the drama that is enacted within the soul of the lover and which finds its source in the painful discovery of the self as a sharply defined and limited ego. The very act of loving implies a desire for some vital and immediate contact and hence a separation. As Berenice explains to Frankie Addams, one becomes conscious of the fact that "'me is me and you is you and he is he. We each one of us somehow caught all by ourself.'" The feeling of being trapped within one's own identity and unable to form a meaningful relationship with others leads to the idea of uniqueness and ultimately of freakishness. In its simplest form, this is apparent in the actual physical deformities of Amelia Evans and Cousin Lymon in *The Ballad of the Sad Café*. In subsequent books the freakishness is attributed to the characters either by the observers who see in Blount, for example, something deformed even though "when you looked at him closely each part of him was normal and as it ought to be" or by the characters themselves who, like Frankie, imagine and fear their own abnormality.

Moved by his desire to break out of his isolation, to communicate and share his thoughts and experience, to become part of another person, a group, or the world, the lover finds only a new and more intense loneliness. As Miss McCullers phrases it, the lover and the beloved "come from different countries." The equality of these two worlds is presented through a series of interlocking contrasts between dream and reality and between child and adult. With respect to the latter, the central figure is the adolescent whose journey from child to adult awakens him from the dream of a life to which one is freely admitted and in which one can experience a feeling of belonging to the adult world in which life is an irrevocable commitment and in which the imaginative idylls survive only in disconnected memories recurring at infrequent and unpredictable intervals. Both Mick Kelley and Frankie Addams envision the party and the wedding as the means and the symbol of their inclusion in the adult world. But these very events which stand for group conviviality and family cohesion only reinforce the bitter fact of their own exclusion.

With respect to the contrast between dream and reality, the central figure is the lover. He may indeed see his beloved "as clearly as anyone else—but that does not affect the evolution of his love one whit." The rational vision of the mind learns to coexist and even to yield to the imaginative delusions of the heart. Thus Singer takes a practical attitude to his friend's, Antonapoulos', eccentricities while still believing him to be wise, profound, and loving beyond all men. Concomitantly, he himself is transformed into a Christlike figure of compassion and understanding by all who know him. Dream and reality are juxtaposed not simply for the sake of irony but as a poignant illustration of man's need to seek, to love, and to dream. His frustration and suffering are inherent in the lover-beloved dichotomy, but his measure as man is taken by his continuing belief in the possibility of love, both personal and universal. The vision of all men forming "one loving family on the earth" forms the bridge between God's promise and man's faith. As such it is the necessary root of man's existence.

The archetypal pattern of love is presented in its clearest and simplest form in *The Ballad of the Sad Café*. For each of the three main characters is successively lover and beloved. Each, then, is in turn a slave and a tyrant, depending on whether he is loving or being loved. The refusal or inability of the characters to synchronize their changes of heart produces the interlocking romantic triangles which constitute the plot, while the grotesque comedy arises out of their each in turn conforming to a role they contemptuously rejected in another.

Chronologically Marvin Macy is the first to be subjected to the metamorphosis of love. Without rhyme or reason, this man, handsome and virile though insolent and wild in nature, falls passionately in love with Amelia Evans of the Amazonian figure and crossed eyes. In the process he is transformed into a love-sick calf, shorn of his masculine pride and inherent violence. As the villagers watch with malicious delight, he is unceremoniously ejected from the marriage bed and finally from the house itself. By refusing to accept him into her home and life, to call him by name, or even to speak of him save "with a terrible and spiteful bitterness," Amelia preserves her physical and emotional inviolateness. Thus Marvin's love simply reinforces her in her chosen isolation and complete self-sufficiency.

She herself, however, is not invulnerable. That passion which she incongruously awakened in Marvin is evoked in her by a pompous little hunchback. Cousin Lymon becomes the focus of her life, providing her with a whole new world and whole new set of relationships. For to her he is simultaneously the lover-husband she has rejected and the child she will never have. Furthermore, through him she establishes a precarious contact with the rest of the village insofar as the cafe, formed for Lymon's entertainment, becomes a meeting place for all who seek "fellowship, the satisfactions of the belly, and a certain gaiety and grace of behavior." But even as she escapes from that constricting loneliness of which Cousin Lymon makes her aware, she loses her cherished independence. As in the case of Marvin, by loving she herself creates the beloved tyrant who eventually repudiates and destroys her.

Although Lymon, unlike Marvin, is courted and does not court, yet in his first meeting with Amelia he too begs wordlessly, like a child, for her compassion. It is only later when this compassion has deepened into a grotesque love that he assumes his place as master and invites Marvin to stay in Amelia's house. Only when he becomes imbued with the masculinity which Marvin has regained in the world outside the town is he capable of straightforward self-assertion. Indeed he himself becomes a psychic projection of Marvin, and by stealing Amelia's love, he amply redresses the latter's failure. But if the hunchback comes to love the power resident in that violence of which Marvin is the symbol, he, nevertheless, began as the child of Amelia's heart. In relation to her he is a homuncular incubus, the product of a nightmare marriage and the dark, secret perversion of her own soul. And it is only with the flight of the hunchback and the victorious Marvin, who wins revenge by publicly humiliating her, that she grasps the solitary nature of love and accepts its suffering. It is this awareness which constitutes the first stage in the agon of experience which is human love.—JOHN B. VICKERY, "Carson McCullers: A Map of Love," *CoL*, Winter 1960, pp. 16–18

It is interesting that the last and the most successful of Mrs. McCullers' works, *Reflections in a Golden Eye* and *The Ballad of the Sad Café*, 1951—the story was published in magazine form in 1943—should strike us as a variation on the same fictional genre. There is a statement by Frank O'Connor which serves to clarify the genre, and serves also to put both works in a nice relation to the tradition of the novel. "If Jane Austen were writing *Pride and Prejudice* in the modern way," O'Connor says in *The Mirror in the Roadway*, "the hero would never need to reveal his arrogance by all those subtle touches which Jane Austen analyzed. He would have been satisfied with a peacock on the lawn, and Elizabeth Bennett would have ultimately wrung its neck. . . . The main thing is that the character would be represented by an image corresponding to the author's view of his principal obsession or the author's view of his part in a poetic phantasmagoria. Either way, his character and role are determined, and his part in the story is more metaphorical than real." The characters of *The Ballad of the*

*Sad Café* are both metaphors and grotesques (grotesques almost in Anderson's sense); the plot moves in the familiar pattern of a whirligig spinning out the impossible intricacies of love and pain; and the style, unconscious of its power, transforms this eccentric tale into something as universal as the old ballads about love and dread, madness and revenge.

The decayed house of Miss Amelia, its porch half-painted, its shuttered windows boarded, appears in the first scene of the story and in its last. The house, edifice to love betrayed, to loneliness irrevocable, stands in a small, dreary Southern town. The winters are short and raw, the summers white with glare and fiery hot. From behind its shutters, the strange face of Miss Amelia occasionally peers, a face "sexless and white, with two gray crossed eyes which are turned inward so sharply that they seem to be exchanging with each other one long secret gaze of grief." Firmly and with a sense of finality the narrative unfolds in retrospect before it comes to pause once again, at the end, on the same scene; the gothic touches never seem out of place, so strong is the feeling of mystery and doom. The story itself is simple. Miss Amelia, a powerful blunderbuss of a person, more than six feet tall, owns the only store in town. At the age of nineteen, she is courted by a strong, darkly handsome loom-fixer, Marvin Macy, with an "evil reputation"—he is supposed to carry around the dried, salted ear of a man he killed in a razor fight. Under the spell of love, Macy reforms temporarily, and Miss Amelia marries him in her slow, absent way. But the marriage, which is never consummated, lasts only a few days; Miss Amelia, despite all of Macy's pitiful protestations, beats him out of bed, and subsequently out of house, after despoiling him of his possessions. Macy vanishes to lead a violent criminal life in other counties. Some years after, Lymon, the hunchback, appears at the doorstep of Miss Amelia, a tried and forlorn figure, seeking shelter, timidly claiming the rights of a dubious kinship. Lymon touches a hidden chord in Miss Amelia's character, touches in her a formless instinct, neither wholly feminine nor altogether maternal. She takes him in; he becomes Cousin Lymon; and the miraculous transformation in her life, of which the new café is evidence, induces a comparable transformation in the town. For Miss Amelia had ceased to be alone and ceased to find herself the beloved: she has suddenly become the lover, with all the pain, perplexity, and uncertain joy which attend that condition. Cousin Lymon thrives on her affections; alternately sour and saucy, mischievous and coy, he soon becomes the natural center of the café. But quick as Lymon is to respond in his egocentric fashion to any external interest, and much though he may be pampered by Amelia, he must secretly wilt, as Mrs. McCullers would have it, until *he* can find an object for *his* love.

The object is ironically provided by the sinister return of Macy, recently out of the penitentiary and bent on vengeance. The hunchback becomes immediately, outrageously, attached to Macy; he follows him around like a crippled mongrel, wiggling his ears, a figure of humble and obscene subjugation. And so the wheel has come full circle. Macy can torture Miss Amelia through the hunchback almost at will. The tension rises to an intolerable pitch, the showdown is preordained. The showdown is a marvelous and frightening scene, a grim wrestling match between the tigerish Macy and the virginal Amazon, Miss Amelia. It takes place by tacit consent on Ground Hog Day in the café, is witnessed by the whole town, and presided over by Lymon who stands watch on the counter, an unholy trophy of man's eternal struggle with Evil, with Death itself, which is the negation of Love. And just as Amelia is about to win the day, Lymon alights screaming and clawing on her back, to give the victory, after all, to Macy. The intruding *alazon* is not confuted or expelled: he triumphs. Lymon and Macy go off together after wrecking the café, wrecking the town really, and wrecking Amelia. Miss Amelia immures herself, the town resumes its sleep of death. "There is absolutely nothing to do in the town. Walk around the millpond, stand kicking at a rotten stump, figure out what you can do with the old wagon wheel by the side of the road near the church. The soul rots with boredom. You might as well go down to the Forks Falls Highway and listen to the chain gang." Yes, the chain gang. It is the envoy of the ballad, its hidden refrain: "The voices are dark in the golden glare, the music intricately blended, both somber and joyful. . . . It is music that causes the heart to broaden and the listener to grow cold with ecstasy and fright. . . ." Unlike Pascal who saw in the image of a chain gang looking at each other sorrowfully and without hope a parable of the human condition, Mrs. McCullers manages to summon for once, in the song of "twelve mortal men," the indestructible joy of endurance and transcendent pain.

The novelette sets a standard of performance for Mrs. McCullers and gives authority to a certain gothic vision, at once quaint and elemental, stark and involuted, which writers like Truman Capote and Tennessee Williams have been inclined to explore. What the novelette does not set forth is a new conception of the irrefragable conflict between the selfhood of man and the otherness of reality, between private need and communal fulfillment. Hints of man's buried life, here as elsewhere in Mrs. McCullers' work, flash darkly to the surface. There is Miss Amelia's whiskey, for instance, which has the power to reveal the secret truth in a man's heart, and which goes a long way toward creating the convivial fellowship of the café, creating the sense of pride and openness and ceremony: "There, for a few hours at least, the deep bitter knowing that you are not worth much in this world could be laid low." But good whiskey alone is not enough; the broad sense of community in the café springs from a more personal source—Miss Amelia's love for the hunchback. It is a love, of course, that remains wholly desexualized; as the town puts it, there is no "conjunction of the flesh" between Amelia and Lymon. For love, it seems, must remain beyond sexual reach, untainted by casual gratification or instinctive need.

Few readers will insist that Mrs. McCullers' image of love should be touched by the Corneillian attributes of reasonableness and high-soulfulness—the age requires another image, less rational, perhaps, and more grotesque. But many readers will regret that no one in the novelette seems to have full access to his experience, to have any ultimate or even provisional understanding of it. In a sense, the work denies the possibility of *recognition*, and avoids, therefore, the fictional equivalent of tragedy, a feature symptomatic of an age in which experience seems, more than ever, unyielding to human intelligence. Moreover, when love specifies the only contact between the hero and his world, heroism itself becomes not merely a call to isolation as in tragedy, but also an inducement to surrender all volition. Without volition no external field for our interests or our actions can ever be defined. The wages of alienation are always compounded. Irony prevails. It is the envoy, the style of anonymous celebration and immitigable sadness, that raises the work to the condition of a haunting performance. The style of pretended ballad reticence and naïveté, of folk motifs and stark tragedy, of augurs and foreshadowing, of incremental repetition and telescoped action—the enfabled style seems to incarnate the very spirit of story-telling whose medium is language in and for itself.—IHAB HASSAN, "Carson McCullers: The Aesthetics of Love and Pain," *Radical Innocence*, 1961, pp. 223–27

## THE MEMBER OF THE WEDDING

In *The Member of the Wedding*, 1946, Carson McCullers exhibits the kind of formal unity which her first novel lacks. There is also a smarting sense of life in the work, a profound sense of change, and a quality of intense groping which the behavior of the central characters seeks continually to incarnate. The story is primarily that of Frankie Addams, a motherless, twelve-year-old girl engaged in a romance with the world. The agonies of growth, the search for identity, the paradoxical desire to escape, to experience, to belong, suddenly converge on Frankie on the occasion of her brother's wedding which becomes the intolerable symbol of all her longings and the focus of her perverse misunderstanding of the adult world.

Like Mick Kelly, Frankie is first of all animated by the desire to escape: escape boredom, escape her adolescent self, escape the South itself. Her life, like the dream she relates to a fortune teller, is a door slowly opening on nowhere. "You going, but you don't know where. That don't make no sense to me," Berenice, the Negro cook, expostulates. Yet Frankie dimly knows what she is escaping *from*. It is partly the familiar scene of lazy buzzards, rotten gray shacks, and lonesome cotton fields she watches on her bitter return from the wedding. (Snow throughout the story acquires the romantic reference of the Far Away—and it may be of interest to note here that Mrs. McCullers has confessed she never saw snow until she came to New York at the age of seventeen.) It is also the accident of her identity that Berenice recognizes as inescapable: "We all of us somehow caught," Berenice says. "We born this way or that way and don't know why. But we caught anyway. . . . And maybe we wants to widen and bust free. But no matter what we do we still caught." And when John Henry, Frankie's six-year-old cousin, asks in his child's voice, "Why?" Berenice can only answer, "Because I am black. . . . Because I am colored. Everybody is caught one way or another." Frankie, however, cannot reconcile herself to the condition of "being caught." She is still propelled *toward* experience, still obsessed by images of the "spinning world" which riddle the novel in response to her romantic imagination, to her need of giving substance to her dreams. Images of the "world," the same that in *Antony and Cleopatra* betrayed the expense of love, betoken here the promise of initiation. Yet it is characteristic of initiation in the contemporary world that its course must be oblique and its rewards ambivalent. Mrs. McCullers' treatment of the traditional theme of sexual initiation is to the point. The sexual impulse, as we might expect, is diffused through the novel; it acts as a faint, persistent scratching on Frankie's consciousness; and it is never really understood. Nowhere do we perceive Frankie's insight into sexual experience or confront the action which gives form to that insight. This is not to say that sexual initiation is the central theme of the novel. It is not. The point is simply that initiation no longer requires the commitment of action, the definition of choice, or the confirmation of self-knowledge. Frankie's dominant mode of coming to terms with the world is *feeling*, and her prime mode of acquiring experience is *dreaming*. She dreams of participating in the war as a Marine, of traveling round the world with the bridal pair; she likes to pretend that she is a Mexican or a Hollywood star. Against the wiles of her fantasies, even earthy Berenice is powerless. But the animating center of the novel, the unifying force in Frankie's character, is of course her wish to *belong*. "She belonged to no club and was a member of nothing in the world." If she dreams inordinately, it is because her dreams confirm her in the illusion that she is enlarging her experience at the same time that she is communing with the world at large. Thus, the blood she wants to donate to the Red

Cross is not simply a modest token of heroism; it would flow "in the veins of Australians and Fighting French and Chinese, all over the world, and it would be as though she were close kin to all these people." The urgent need to belong comes to focus in the ritual of the wedding. Frankie, in search of "we-hood," says of her brother and his bride, "they are the we of me"; and Berenice, with her customary shrewdness, quickly sees that Frankie has "fallen in love" with the wedding, that in fact, she is determined to walk down the aisle between the bridal pair. But after the wedding, what then? "We will have thousands of friends, thousands and thousands and thousands of friends. We will belong to so many clubs that we can't even keep track of all of them," Frankie gloats. If the novel accords to the idea of the wedding so much significance, it is because the ceremony happens to satisfy all of Frankie's needs in that particular August of her life.

Formally the novel is divided into three parts, each taking its character from the role Frankie assumes. We see her first as Frankie Addams, the tomboy, bored and restive. "Until the April of that year, and all the years of her life before, she had been like other people." Her actual world is defined by the kitchen which she shares with Berenice and John Henry. "The three of them sat at the kitchen table, saying the same things over and over, so that by August the words began to rhyme with each other and sound strange." The transformations begin when Frankie suddenly decides to become a member of the wedding: her heart divides like two wings. In the next section of the novel we see Frankie as the new, exotic personalilty, F. Jasmine, who is all pride and anticipation. Her flirtation with a soldier, her lengthy conversations with Berenice on the subject of love, her lone wanderings through the town, reflect the mood of willfulness which is the prelude to disenchantment. It is in the last part of the novel that disenchantment—what else?—sets in. Mrs. McCullers beautifully disposes of the wedding itself in a few lines and devotes the rest of the book to convert the initial bitterness of, not Frankie or F. Jasmine, but Frances now, to a final affirmation of youth's resilience. Frances, entitled at last to her full name, outgrows the humiliation of her first defeat. Unlike Mick Kelly, she moves beyond the acrid feeling that the world has cheated her. And with the heedlessness of youth she takes up new friends and other illusions, remotely conscious of the death of John Henry and the separation from Berenice. There is change; there is really no knowledge or confirmation. Guilt and anxiety are equally forgotten, only pathos remains. As the identity of Frankie changes from part to part, so do her images of "the spinning world," now fractured, now whole; and the seasons, keeping richly in step, change from spring to fall. The mode is often the mode of poetry as is the mood:

> After the plain gray winter the March winds banged on the windows, and clouds were shirred and white on the blue sky. April that year came sudden and still, and the green of the trees was a wild bright green.

> In June the trees were bright dizzy green, but late the leaves darkened, and the town turned black and shrunken under the glare of the sun. . . . At last the summer was like a green sick dream, or like a silent crazy jungle under glass.

> It was the time of golden weather and Shasta daisies and the butterflies. The air was chilled, and day after day the sky was a clearer green blue, but filled with light, the color of a shallow wave.

The style of the novel presents the blossoming of human feelings no less aptly than it presents the varying moods of nature. But it is a style of confession, or rather manifestation, sensitive to the sudden epiphanies of daily life. It is not dramatic despite the inimitable tang and humor of its dialogue, and despite the plasticity of character which allowed the novel to be made into a successful play.

What drama the novel contains, it draws from the juxtaposition of three characters to one another—not from their interactions. Thus is Frankie caught between the violated innocence of John Henry and the viable experience of Berenice. Berenice is indeed the rock on which the novel rests. She calls to mind both Portia and Brannon, and calls forth a quality of existence as wholesome as our daily bread and as enduring. To all of Frankie's wild dreams, she stands as a silent modifier—for she is too wise to rebuke. With three husbands behind her and a fourth in the offing, she speaks as one who has known love and experienced loneliness. Her understanding of life is as tragic as Frankie's misunderstanding is pathetic. Without her, the tortured sensitivity of Frankie—a sensitivity, after all, which has no correlative but the wistfulness of puberty—would seem pointless and contrived. But between innocence and experience only illusions can lie. And the illusions of Frankie disguise the hopes of all mankind even if her destiny falls short of what our moment fully requires.
—IHAB HASSAN, "Carson McCullers: The Aesthetics of Love and Pain," *Radical Innocence*, 1961, pp. 219–23

## CLOCK WITHOUT HANDS

Although it exhibits Mrs. McCullers' best qualities, *Clock without Hands* is not her best work. Her gifts of understanding, tenderness and humor are evident once more; her love for her characters vitalizes even those whose actions are destructive. There is none of the cold irony which she used to show up the characters of *Reflections in a Golden Eye*. Mrs. McCullers is most herself as the novelist of inward experience, but in *Clock without Hands* she attempts to add another dimension by making her characters stand for the whole South. It is a mistake. The private and the symbolic roles are not fused; the individual and the representative do not merge. The result for the reader is confusion arising from what seems to have been Mrs. McCullers' uncertainty about her objective. There is also a looseness of structure which weakens the novel and which apparently came of her attempt to make it a far bigger book than she finally published.

A novelist who begins, "Death is always the same, but each man dies in his own way," must expect to remind her readers of the famous first sentence of *Anna Karenina*. The expectation of a novel of scope is reinforced when it becomes apparent that each of the chief characters has a symbolic role; nothing less than the entire Southern dilemma is to be represented through the tangled private histories of a restricted group in a small city. Mrs. McCullers allows the Supreme Court decision on integration of schools to reach the bedside of a dying man who has sunk beyond any concern with news, in a scene which makes sense only if the large implications are a chief intention. *Clock Without Hands* does not live up to the intention, for the implications of the action undercut the symbolic roles assigned the chief characters.

The title is itself ambiguous. J. T. Malone, the druggist of Milan, Georgia, is under sentence of death from leukemia, a man confusedly watching his time run out on a clock without hands. But when in that last scene Malone's old friend Judge Clane bursts into the sickroom with news of the decision, the reader catches the suggestion that the Court's "all deliberate speed" is also to be measured by a clock without hands. Behind this scene and the other references to the clock there is the implied warning "It is later than you think," the legend which Baudelaire is supposed to have affixed to his own handless clock in the anecdote which possibly suggested Mrs. McCullers' title.

Besides Malone and Judge Clane, there are two other characters of importance: Jester Clane, the Judge's grandson, and Sherman Pew, a Negro. Both are eighteen. Their connections with Judge Clane provide once more the contrast of youth with age which deepens the pathos of many scenes in *The Heart Is a Lonely Hunter* and *The Member of the Wedding*. They also, in a friendship which holds them in close conflict, repeat the baffling experience which Mrs. McCullers envisions for all friends and all lovers: isolation without hope of communication, within the bonds of an affection that is onerous to the loved one and frustrating to the lover.

The symbolic roles which were to have given *Clock without Hands* its forceful social reference detract from the effectiveness of the novel on the level of immediate, inward experience where Mrs. McCullers' powers are greatest. Besides, the symbolic action is questionable. J. T. Malone represents the conscience of the South, and at a crucial moment he recoils from violence. His quiet death in bed, however, has doubtful implications for the collective conscience for which he stands. Judge Clane, with all his demagoguery and his delusions, is made the embodiment of the Old South. He is obvious as a type and symbol, but one feels uneasy. Granted that Mrs. McCullers uses him to express contradictions of attitude amounting to bankruptcy of ideas in a class, the Judge as a man is a grotesque. If, on the other hand, he is to be accepted as a pitiable old man whose curse through life has been a combination of sentimentality and invincible stupidity in all human relations, the burden of his symbolic role is too great.

As representatives, the younger characters appear to no better advantage. Jester Clane is forcefully identified as one of the "men of good will" who may redeem their society, but in his symbolic role he is not only ineffectual in aiding his friend (he cannot even persuade Sherman to escape murder), he is incapable of retribution when the wretched human condition of the murderer is brought home to him. Sherman Pew is the rebellious Negro whose accumulated humiliations and frustrations drive him to the senseless cruelty of hanging Jester's dog, and to the open defiance of renting a house in the white section of town. He is isolated by hatred and self-contempt for all men, and his gestures become equally compulsive and self-destructive. More even than the others he is unacceptable as the symbol Mrs. McCullers has tried to make him, for he is an Outsider rather than the representative of a social class.

The crux of the difficulty is most apparent in the portrayals of Sherman Pew and Jester Clane, and it comes of Mrs. McCullers' being sensitively penetrating when she deals with the inner life but fumbling and uncertain when she attempts a social paradigm. She makes the boys live; she feels their adolescent longings and frustrations; she portrays a friendship that is another degree of the love relation defined in *The Ballad of the Sad Café*. But what she does with these two whose fates have been entwined from before their birth has no typical social relevance. Mrs. McCullers comprehends the human rather than the social condition, as was apparent from her earliest work. For all its social reference, *The Heart Is a Lonely Hunter* was a definition of the fatality of man's estate, and Biff Brannon's moment of illumination was his glimpse of the human struggle and the endless passage of humanity through time. The similar glimpse of the human perspective in *Clock without Hands* comes after the discovery of self which

both Sherman and Jester undergo, at the moment when Jester has taken Sherman's murderer up in an airplane, intending to kill him in the crash which will follow his own suicide. But he comes to understand the man's pitiable condition, and in his revulsion against further violence sees the earth from above, at such height that the earth assumes order and the details of man's humiliation cannot be seen. This order is foreign to the heart; to love, one must come closer. At the nearer approach of the plane's descent above the town, men again become visible, but they seem to move mechanically among haphazard miseries. Not to see their eyes becomes finally intolerable. One long look into a pair of human eyes, even the eyes of the enemy, means more than the whole earth from a great distance. Like Baudelaire, who could see "the hour of Eternity" in the handless clock of his mistress' eyes, Jester in the terrified eyes of Sammy Lank finds the vision which ends his odyssey of passion, friendship, love, and revenge, and it denies relevance to the uneasy symbolism which has been tacked onto his experience.

Besides failing to achieve the dimensions which Mrs. McCullers intended, the novel is structurally weak. Mrs. McCullers has customarily restricted the scope of her fictions, and she limits her cast in *Clock without Hands*. But there is no central character with whom all the others feel the sole relation they all experience, as with the deaf-mute Singer in *The Heart Is a Lonely Hunter*. There is no tight pattern of antipathies such as enmeshed the men, the women, and the horse in *Reflections in a Golden Eye*. No single character such as Frankie Addams of *The Member of the Wedding* exists to give the novel a viewpoint. In her latest novel, Mrs. McCullers begins with Malone and the Judge, neglects this relation to concentrate on the Judge, Jester, and Sherman, and returns to it to put a period to the action. Malone is removed almost from significance in the lives of the others.

His significance for the novel is at the level where Mrs. McCullers excels: the depth of conscious being which exists below the hope of communication, where the self, however vaguely apprehended, is forever alone. Her penetration to this essential privacy is made possible by Mrs. McCullers' compassion, which goes as far beyond sympathy as understanding exceeds observation. Here she touches the characters of *Clock without Hands* with the tenderness she has shown even the grotesques in all her work save *Reflections in a Golden Eye*, in which the fantastic, jewel-like eye of Anacleto's peacock feather reflects coldly the ironies of troubled lives. Compassionate identification which reveals how Malone, the Judge, Jester and Sherman all grope toward a sense of identity is too far removed from awkward political symbolism for easy reconciliation; the distance explains the defects of the novel, the looseness of plot, and the failure of *Clock without Hands* to rank with Mrs. McCullers' best work. This same distance, however, justifies praise of Mrs. McCullers' best qualities, which appear even in the disappointing attempt to merge individual and typical roles for a timely social commentary.

The year of Malone's dying sets the period of the novel's action, but Malone is essentially cut off from men from the beginning, and he slips down rungs of despair past fear, rebellion, hope and acceptance into indifference. Except for the occasion when he protests against the plan to murder Sherman Pew, his last months of life touch others only tangentially. His inward life, however, is a leading motif in the counterpoint of Mrs. McCullers' real subject: the self, and its experience of love, frustration, and the isolation of defeat.
—DONALD EMERSON, "The Ambiguities of *Clock without Hands*," *Col*, Fall 1962, pp. 16–19

## CARSON McCULLERS
### "The Flowering Dream: Notes on Writing"
*Esquire*, December 1959, pp. 162–64

When I was a child of about four, I was walking with my nurse past a convent. For once, the convent doors were open. And I saw the children eating ice-cream cones, playing on iron swings, and I watched, fascinated. I wanted to go in, but my nurse said no, I was not Catholic. The next day, the gate was shut. But, year by year, I thought of what was going on, of this wonderful party, where I was shut out. I wanted to climb the wall, but it was too little. I beat on the wall once, and I knew all the time that there was a marvelous party going on, but I couldn't get in.

Spiritual isolation is the basis of most of my themes. My first book was concerned with this, almost entirely, and all of my books since, in one way or another. Love, and especially love of a person who is incapable of returning or receiving it, is at the heart of my selection of grotesque figures to write about—people whose physical incapacity is a symbol of their spiritual incapacity to love or receive love—their spiritual isolation.

To understand a work, it is important for the artist to be emotionally right on dead center; to see, to know, to experience the things he is writing about. Long before Harold Clurman, who, bless his heart, directed *The Member of the Wedding*, I think I had directed every fly and gnat in that room years ago.

The dimensions of a work of art are seldom realized by the author until the work is accomplished. It is like a flowering dream. Ideas grow, budding silently, and there are a thousand illuminations coming day by day as the work progresses. A seed grows in writing as in nature. The seed of the idea is developed by both labor and the unconscious, and the struggle that goes on between them.

I understand only particles. I understand the characters, but the novel itself is not in focus. The focus comes at random moments which no one can understand, least of all the author. For me, they usually follow great effort. To me, these illuminations are the grace of labor. All of my work has happened this way. It is at once the hazard and the beauty that a writer has to depend on such illuminations. After months of confusion and labor, when the idea has flowered, the collusion is Divine. It always comes from the subconscious and cannot be controlled. For a whole year I worked on *The Heart Is a Lonely Hunter* without understanding it at all. Each character was talking to a central character, but why, I didn't know. I'd almost decided that the book was no novel, that I should chop it up into short stories. But I could feel the mutilation in my body when I had that idea, and I was in despair. I had been working for five hours and I went outside. Suddenly, as I walked across a road, it occurred to me that Harry Minowitz, the character all the other characters were talking to, was a different man, a deaf mute, and immediately the name was changed to John Singer. The whole focus of the novel was fixed and I was for the first time committed with my whole soul to *The Heart Is a Lonely Hunter.*

What to know and what not to know? John Brown, from the American Embassy, was here to visit, and he pointed his long forefinger and said, "I admire you, Carson, for your ignorance." I said, "Why?" He asked, "When was the Battle of Hastings, and what was it about? When was the Battle of Waterloo, and what was that about?" I said, "John, I don't think I care much." He said, "That's what I mean. You don't clutter your mind with the facts of life."

When I was nearly finished with *The Heart Is a Lonely Hunter*, my husband mentioned that there was a convention of deaf mutes in a town near-by and he assumed that I would want to go and observe them. I told him that it was the last thing I wanted to do because I already had made my conception of deaf mutes and didn't want it to be disturbed. I presume James Joyce had the same attitude when he lived abroad and never visited his home again, feeling his Dublin was fixed forever—which it is.

A writer's main asset is intuition; too many facts impede intuition. A writer needs to know so many things, but there are so many things he doesn't need to know—he needs to know human things even if they aren't "wholesome," as they call it.

Every day, I read the New York *Daily News*, and very soberly. It is interesting to know the name of the lover's lane where the stabbing took place, and the circumstances which the *New York Times* never reports. In that unsolved murder in Staten Island, it is interesting to know that the doctor and his wife, when they were stabbed, were wearing Mormon night-gowns, three-quarter length. Lizzie Borden's breakfast, on the sweltering summer day she killed her father, was mutton soup. Always details provoke more ideas than any generality could furnish. When Christ was pierced in His *left* side, it is more moving and evocative than if He were just pierced.

One cannot explain accusations of morbidity. A writer can only say he writes from the seed which flowers later in the subconscious. Nature is not abnormal, only lifelessness is abnormal. Anything that pulses and moves and walks around the room, no matter what thing it is doing, is natural and human to a writer. The fact that John Singer, in *The Heart Is a Lonely Hunter*, is a deaf-and-dumb man is a symbol, and the fact that Captain Penderton, in *Reflections in a Golden Eye*, is homosexual, is also a symbol, of handicap and impotence. The deaf mute, Singer, is a symbol of infirmity, and he loves a person who is incapable of receiving his love. Symbols suggest the story and theme and incident, and they are so interwoven that one cannot understand consciously where the suggestion begins. I become the characters I write about. I am so immersed in them that their motives are my own. When I write about a thief, I become one; when I write about Captain Penderton, I become a homosexual man; when I write about a deaf mute, I become dumb during the time of the story. I become the characters I write about and I bless the Latin poet Terence who said, "Nothing human is alien to me."

When I wrote the stage version of *The Member of the Wedding*, I was at the time paralyzed, and my outward situation was miserable indeed; but when I finished that script, I wrote to a friend of mine, "Oh, how wonderful it is to be a writer, I have never been so happy. . . ."

When work does not go well, no life is more miserable than that of a writer. But when it does go well, when the illumination has focused a work so that it goes limpidly and flows, there is no gladness like it.

Why does one write? Truly it is financially the most ill-rewarded occupation in the world. My lawyer has figured out how much I made from the book *The Member of the Wedding*, and it is, over the five years I worked on it, twenty-eight cents a day. Then the irony is, the play *The Member of the Wedding* had made so much money that I've had to give eighty per cent to the government—which I'm happy, or at least *have* to be happy, to do.

It must be that one writes from some subconscious need for communication, for self-expression. Writing is a wandering, dreaming occupation. The intellect is submerged beneath the unconscious—the thinking mind is best controlled by the imagination. Yet writing is not utterly amorphous and unintellectual. Some of the best novels and prose are as exact as a telephone number, but few prose writers can achieve this because of the refinement of passion and poetry that is necessary. I don't like the word prose; it's too prosaic. Good prose should be fused with the light of poetry; prose should be like poetry, poetry should made sense like prose.

I like to think of Anne Frank and her immense communication, which was the communication not only of a twelve-year-old child, but a communication of conscience and courage.

Here truly there was isolation, but physical rather than spiritual isolation. Several years ago, Anne Frank's father made an appointment to see me at the Hotel Continental in Paris. We talked together and he asked me if I would dramatize the diary of his daughter. He also gave me the book, which I had not yet read. But as I was reading the book, I was so upset that I broke out in a rash on my hands and feet, and I had to tell him that under the circumstances I could not do the play.

Paradox is a clue to communication, for what is *not* often leads to the awareness of what *is*. Nietzsche once wrote to Cosima Wagner, "If only three people could understand me." Cosima understood him and years later a man called Adolf Hitler built a whole philosophical system around a misunderstanding of Nietzsche. It is paradoxical that a great philosopher like Nietzsche and a great musician like Richard Wagner could have contributed so much to the world's suffering in this century. Partial understanding for an ignorant person is a warped and subjective understanding, and it was with this type of understanding that the philosophy of Nietzsche and the creations of Richard Wagner were the mainstay of Hitler's emotional appeal to the German people. He was able to juggle great ideas into the despair of his time, which we must remember was a real despair.

When someone asks me who has influenced my work, I point to O'Neill, the Russians, Faulkner, Flaubert. *Madame Bovary* seems to be written with divine economy. It is one of the most painfully written novels, and one of the most painfully considered, of any age. *Madame Bovary* is a composite of the realistic voice of Flaubert's century, of the realism versus the romantic mind of his times. In its lucidity and faultless grace, it seems to have flown straight from Flaubert's pen without an interruption in thought. For the first time, he was dealing with his truth as a writer.

It is only with imagination and reality that you get to know the things a novel requires. Reality alone has never been that important to me. A teacher once said that one should write about one's own back yard; and by this, I suppose, she meant one should write about the things that one knows most intimately. But what is more intimate than one's own imagination? The imagination combines memory with insight, combines reality with the dream.

People ask me why I don't go back to the South more often. But the South is a very emotional experience for me, fraught with all the memories of my childhood. When I go back South I always get into arguments, so that a visit to Columbus in Georgia is a stirring up of love and antagonism. The locale of my books might always be Southern, and the South always my homeland. I love the voices of Negroes—like brown rivers. I feel that in the short trips when I do go to the South, in my own memory and in the newspaper articles, I still have my own reality.

Many authors find it hard to write about new environments that they did not know in childhood. The voices reheard from childhood have a truer pitch. And the foliage—the trees of childhood—are remembered more exactly. When I work from within a different locale from the South, I have to wonder what time the flowers are in bloom—and what flowers? I hardly let characters speak unless they are Southern. Wolfe wrote brilliantly of Brooklyn, but more brilliantly of the Southern cadence and ways of speech. This is particularly true of Southern writers because it is not only their speech and the foliage, but their entire culture—which makes it a homeland within a homeland. No matter what the politics, the degree or non-degree of liberalism in a Southern writer, he is still bound to this peculiar regionalism of language and voices and foliage and memory.

Few Southern writers are truly cosmopolitan. When Faulkner writes about the R.A.F. and France, he is somehow not convincing—while I'm convinced in almost every line about Yoknapatawpha County. Indeed, to me *The Sound and the Fury* is probably the greatest American novel. It has an authenticity, a grandeur and, most of all, a tenderness that stems from the combination of reality and the dream that is the divine collusion.

Hemingway, on the contrary, is the most cosmopolitan of all the American writers. He is at home in Paris, in Spain, in America, the Indian stories of his childhood. Perhaps it is his style, which is a delivery, a beautifully worked out form of expression. As expert as Hemingway is at producing and convincing the reader of his various outlooks, emotionally he is a wanderer. In Hemingway's style some things are masked in the emotional content of his work. If I prefer Faulkner to Hemingway, it's because I am more touched by the familiar—the writing that reminds me of my own childhood and sets a standard for a remembering of the language. Hemingway seems to me to use language as a style of writing.

The writer by nature of his profession is a dreamer and a conscious dreamer. How, without love and the intuition that comes from love, can a human being place himself in the situation of another human being? He must imagine, and imagination takes humility, love, and great courage. How can you create a character without love and the struggle that goes with love?

For many years I have been working on a novel called *Clock without Hands*, and will probably finish it in about two more years. My books take a long time. This novel is in process day by day of being focused. As a writer, I've always worked very hard. But as a writer, I've also known that hard work is not enough. In the process of hard work, there must come an illumination, a divine spark that puts the work into focus and balance.

When I asked Tennessee Williams how he first thought of *The Glass Menagerie*, he said it was suggested by a glass curtain he saw at the house of one of his grandfather's parishioners. From then on it became what he called a memory play. How the recollection of that glass curtain fitted into the memories of his boyhood, neither he nor I could understand, but then the unconscious is not easily understood.

How does creation begin in any art? As Tennessee wrote *The Glass Menagerie* as a memory play, I wrote "Wunderkind" when I was seventeen years old, and it was a memory, although not the reality of the memory—it was a foreshortening of that memory. It was about a young music student. I didn't write about my real music teacher—I wrote about the music we studied together because I thought it was truer. The imagination is truer than the reality.

The passionate, individual love—the old Tristan-Isolde love, the Eros love—is inferior to the love of God, to fellowship, to the love of Agape—the Greek god of the feast, the God of brotherly love—and of man. This is what I tried to show in *The Ballad of the Sad Café* in the strange love of Miss Amelia for the little hunchback, Cousin Lymon.

The writer's work is predicated not only on his personality but by the region in which he was born. I wonder sometimes if what they call the "Gothic" school of Southern writing, in which the grotesque is paralleled with the sublime, is not due largely to the cheapness of human life in the South. The Russians are like the Southern writers in that respect. In my childhood, the South was almost a feudal society. But the South is complicated by the racial problem more severely than the Russian society. To many a poor Southerner, the only pride that he has is the fact that he is white, and when one's self-pride is so pitiably debased, how can one learn to love? Above all, love is the main generator of all good writing. Love, passion, compassion are all welded together.

In any communication, a thing says to one person quite a different thing from what it says to another, but writing, in essence, is communication; and communication is the only access to love—to love, to conscience, to nature, to God, and to the dream. For myself, the further I go into my own work and the more I read of those I love, the more aware I am of the dream and the logic of God, which indeed is a Divine collusion.

## FRANK BALDANZA
### From "Plato in Dixie"
*Georgia Review*, Summer 1958, pp. 151–62

Aside from the towering figure of William Faulkner, some of the most popular writers in the current Southern literary renaissance bear a resemblance to each other that is astonishing. It would be as difficult, for example, to attribute one typical unidentified short story of the school to Eudora Welty, Carson McCullers, Flannery O'Connor, or Truman Capote as it would be to say if one particular cubist canvas of a certain period belonged to Braque or Picasso. There are many possible explanations for such a situation: obviously the literature grows out of an isolated, provincial culture with distinctive values, racial strains, customs, food, and climate; and a literary historian might point to traditions of folk-lore, local color, and humor, in which the South is particularly rich. Although such traditions account for a good deal, neither of these explanations justifies the type or quality of the similarities. Particularly in the cases of Truman Capote and Carson McCullers, the resemblances are so pervasive and unique that we need to look further.

What these two authors share, along with Eudora Welty in varying degrees, is a nearly morbid preoccupation with sublunar imperfection. They most typically treat characters whose spiritual loneliness is paralleled by a defect of the senses (blindness, muteness, or deafness), by a physical defect (paralysis, lameness, and hunched backs), or by a more complex disorder—gynandromorphy, dipsomania, egregious eccentricity, feeble-mindedness, insanity, a dwarfed body, or unnatural precosity in children and adolescents. None of their major characters is ever under any circumstances happily married, and the large majority never marry at all. The loneliness and imperfection of their states are permanent because the heart, they seem to feel, is indeed a lonely hunter.

The novels and stories of this school are parables on the nature of love. They share with Plato's *Symposium* and *Phaedrus* in particular that curious tone of purely and abso-

lutely spiritual love which grows out of a diffused and circumambient atmosphere of sexuality that never clearly manifests itself. A mysterious young man pities a deaf-mute wife in a railroad station and gives her a glittering key that reconciles her to her deaf-mute husband who already selfishly hoards a similar key; or a lonely and defeated girl in New York maintains a joyous relation with a drunken tramp in the automat; or a psychotic army wife passes the early morning hours with the Filipino houseboy, watching Japanese paper flowers expand in water. The identification is spiritual: it is remarkably intense because the physical and mental defects have driven away all possibility of normal intercourse, and when spiritual love blossoms, it is miraculous. The adolescent protagonists are extremely contemplative, introspective creatures who muse through private dream worlds, called "the inside room" in *The Heart Is a Lonely Hunter* and "the other room" in *Other Voices, Other Rooms*.

But it is in the manner as well as in the matter that the resemblance occurs. Often the reader is impressed in these stories with a sense of insubstantiality in the characters; they do not have the weight and texture that we ordinarily associate with fictional representations. Now one of the most obvious reasons is that the concomitant elements of grotesquerie and fantasy do not sort easily with everyday reality and some of the weight and specificity of reference to ordinary reality must thus be sacrificed. Another consequence of this manner we have mentioned is the insistent drive toward allegory or at least some form of symbolic reference which we feel impelled to seek out in any fairy story or fantastic tale. If the work of art does not refer to the real situation as we experience it, we expect at any rate a reference at second or third or fourth remove, and we necessarily attempt to wrest the materials the author gives us into some kind of symbolic semblance to that reality.

I should like to suggest that the common denominator that most adequately accounts for these resemblances is the appearance in many of these books of distinctly Platonic theories of love. In addition to these specific theories, many of the preconceptions and assumptions of the writers agree, accidentally or not, with Platonic distinctions. Whether or not this Platonism stems from a social or cultural tradition is a bit beyond our scope here, although the South is certainly hospitable, throughout its history, to romantic idealism; Latin and Greek classics were the staple of much ante-bellum education, and Vice President Alexander Hamilton Stephens chose the Platonic "colloquy" as the form for his *Constitutional View of the War Between the States*. In addition, the post-bellum history of defeat, poverty, and injustice was borne stoically with a proud and high-minded consciousness of the spiritual rectitude of their cause, which made Southerners bank heavily on invisible rewards and intangible values.

Platonism as a general force in European and American culture is a mystic philosophy that emphasizes the primacy of spiritual experience and absolute spiritual values over the weaker and less reliable evidence of the senses and their correlative dependence on the changeable physical world and its phenomena. It is dichotomizing in method (the whole Socratic dialectic takes false dichotomy as its motive force) and makes great use of parables, similitudes, and allegories in its teachings. Thus far, it is nearly identical with Christianity, to be sure. But it often appeals to figures like Shelley who have rejected traditional Christianity with all its iconography and dogma and moralizing and who find themselves more at home in a philosophy that, while it resembles Christianity in its essentials, places a higher value on generalized notions of Beauty, Truth, and Goodness, without dictating, as the local preacher often does, that dancing is a specifically evil manifestation. In short, it retains the primacy of spiritual value along with a broad premissive latitude of individual behavior. And particularly in its doctrines of love, formulated to take into account the pederastic institutions of Athenian life, it has the appeal of an erotico-religious philosophy. Platonism is also, of course, the more esoteric system of Ideas, and a body of specific epistemological and ethical doctrines which are embodied in a memorable series of famous literary dialogues. In the long run, it might easily be seen as a mystic grab-bag (especially when one takes Neo-Platonic elaboration into account) out of which anyone can fish up whatever it pleases him to seek.

I submit, however, that if one finds that a specific group of authors goes along with the elements of Platonism that are identical with those of Christianity, and that if this group employs the dichotomy and the allegorical parable as primary manners of exposition, and that if, in addition, one finds specific references to recognizably Platonic epistemological and spiritual doctrines, one has then presented sufficient evidence to at least speculate on a clearly Platonic basis for the literature involved. I am not, let me repeat, interested in narrowly insisting that Carson McCullers and Truman Capote are exclusively, primarily, or even consciously dependent on Platonic models or doctrines for the large body of their work; I am merely suggesting that they are what James A. Notopoulos calls "natural" Platonists, persons who are impelled by their natures to a similar interpretation of reality; and that in addition, there are traces here and there of what the same critic calls "direct" and "indirect" influence, either from reading the dialogues or from a cultural tradition that has already assimilated these concepts; and, thirdly, that the culture of the modern South, conscious of defeat and disgrace and poverty, finds such an idealism congenial. As J. A. K. Thomson remarks, "This belief that behind the world of sight and sound there is another, unseen by mortal eyes but more true and more real, giving in fact to the objects of sense what truth and reality they may have, is the central doctrine of Platonism. Whoever shares that conviction is consciously or unconsciously a Platonist."

The flamboyant "decadence" of this school which presents its truth through the experience of dwarfs, circus freaks, paralytics, deaf-mutes, "drivin' women" with moustaches and beards, dipsomaniacs, and idiots has become enough of a national byword to be the subject of burlesque in smart Broadway reviews; but on the philosophical level, the defects of the characters serve symbolically to represent the worthlessness of the material realm. As suggested earlier, the triumph of love in these persons' lives is the more precious and miraculous precisely because it flourishes in spite of seemingly insuperable barriers. And love, in one manifestation or another—in a large number of the cases, it is "Platonic love" both in the sophisticated and vulgar senses of the term—is the central theme.

This is most evident, perhaps, in Carson McCullers' story "A Tree . A Rock . A Cloud," where both the general Platonic flavor and a specific Platonic doctrine are illustrated at one time. In a tawdry all-night cafe, an old tramp with a big nose and faded orange hair stops a young newsboy with the opening remark, " 'I love you.' " He then proceeds to reveal to the twelve-year-old the "science of love" which he has learned painfully and slowly over a period of twelve years; but since he began the process at the age of fifty-one, he represents the ripe wisdom of a lifetime of experience which Plato so wholeheartedly respects. As is the case with most mystics, and particularly with this railroad engineer turned tramp, no words

were adequate to the stages of mystic revelation, so he expresses himself often crudely and ludicrously. At fifty-one he met a woman whose love made his experience coalesce into a unity and a wholeness he had never before thought possible. Thus when she ran away after a year of marriage, he sought her desperately, recalled her longingly, and then plunged into five years of debauchery. Finally one spring the great spiritual revelation occurred when he realized, with a great swelling of peace, that love is a ladder but that most men mistakenly try to begin at the top rung by loving a woman. One must begin with " 'A Tree . A Rock . A Cloud.' " He began with a goldfish, and when he learned to love it, he

> graduated from one thing to another. . . . And now I am a master. Son, I can love anything. No longer do I have to think about it even. I see a street full of people and a beautiful light comes in me. I watch a bird in the sky. Or I meet a traveler on the road. Everything, son. And anybody. All strangers and all loved! . . .

This "science of love" is a bald summary, of course, of the "single science, which is the science of beauty everywhere" of the *Symposium*, but played, as it were, a whole octave lower. In his description, Socrates quotes Diotima as saying

> 'And the true order of going, or being led by another, to the things of love, is to begin from the beauties of earth and mount upwards for the sake of that other beauty, using these as steps only, and from one going on to two, and from two to all fair forms, and from fair forms to fair practices, and from fair practices to fair notions, until from fair notions he arrives at the notion of absolute beauty, and at last knows what the essence of beauty is.'

Thus for Socrates individual human beauty is the lowest rung on the ladder, whereas Carson McCullers' beer-soaked tramp culminates at the love of a woman, exactly where Socrates takes up the progression. Now this difference, hardly important in itself, nevertheless suggests that perhaps many of the Platonic melodies as they appear in this school may be "played one octave lower."

But to return to the story, there are other insistent features to be disposed of. In the first place, there is no particularly dramatic incident in the story, and all the obvious opportunities for vivid conflict (the wife's going off with another man, and the like) are markedly played down. Miss McCullers carefully concentrates the reader's attention on the man's revelation to the boy (and one thinks of Socrates' session with the slave boy on the Pythagorean theorem) by a series of questions that make of the boy a typical Socratic stooge who must give the predetermined answers to further the progress of the dialogue. But the really central drama occurs in the boy's perplexity (exactly as with the boy in the diner in Hemingway's "The Killers") after the tramp has left.

Throughout the dialogue, Leo, the proprietor of the cafe, has addressed humiliating and cruel remarks to the tramp. We suppose, along with the boy, that he is a superior person who will provide a cynical but true explanation of the tramp's behavior. But after the tramp's departure with a final admonition " 'Remember. . . . Remember I love you,' " the newsboy himself becomes the Socratic gadfly and proceeds to quiz Leo; the latter denies that the man is either a drunkard, a dope addict, or a maniac. Now we see in Leo's obvious embarrassment that Plato's allegory of the cave stands behind the story too. The tramp was a true philosopher who had been vouchsafed escape from the cave of the bondage of the senses; he had seen the sun of spiritual reality, and when he returned to the cave to tell of the sun he had seen, men were simply embarrassed at his divine fervor. The capstone is the closing sentence, which the newsboy intends as an equivocal remark, but one that fits well with our Platonic interpretation: "'He sure has done a lot of traveling.'"

Two of these themes are also monotonously reiterated in the other works of these two authors—the concept of the cafe, of a place or a context that is congenial for conversations and confidences (like the spot beneath the plane-tree in *Phaedrus*); and the theme of love as an absolute, abstract force that overrides all barriers of age, sex, time, and distance and that manifests itself in an endless variety of ways.

In fact, the concept of place is fundamental to the latter one of love. The whole society of these novels is a microcosm. The clearly defined hierarchy of Southern society gives cohesion to this world, while its local, economic, and climatic isolation give it color and character. For example, in both Miss McCullers' and Mr. Capote's books, having seen either the sea or snow is a personal distinction of considerable weight. Obviously within such a society values tend to be more clearly realized and the novelist has a ready-made system against which to construct his own little world. Thus the group that cluster around Mr. Singer in *The Heart Is a Lonely Hunter*, the group in the kitchen in *Member of the Wedding*, the inhabitants of the cafe in *The Ballad of the Sad Café*, the army families on the post in *Reflections in a Golden Eye*, the household at Skully's Landing in *Other Voices, Other Rooms*, and the group in the tree-house in *The Grass Harp* function philosophically as symposia or, to some degree, as utopias, a projection of one selected group of persons against the matrix of society. There is little overt strife involved between the society as a whole and the little group, except in the smouldering resentments of *The Heart Is a Lonely Hunter* and in the pitched battle between townspeople and tree-people in *The Grass Harp*. These are the only two novels that could be said to deal with inherently social phenomena; in most of the examples, the microcosm is an arbitrary means of limiting the situation in order to focus intensively on the philosophical problem of love.

*The Heart Is a Lonely Hunter*, Miss McCullers' first novel, is less representative in method, since it attempts to reconcile formally the allegorical parable with the "timely," realistic tradition of naturalism. However, Biff Brannon's New York Cafe is a center for meetings and all-night consultations; out of the conversations initiated there, Mick Kelly, Jake Blount, Dr. Copeland, and Biff himself all come to love Mr. Singer, the deaf-mute to whom they confide their fears and hopes in his pleasant room. He is a defective confessor, though, since he does not entirely understand their eager, intense, and sometimes violent confidences. In turn, he lavishes an intensely passionate love on Spiros Antonapoulos, another deaf-mute, who, aside from being insane, is a greedy and voracious gourmand who hardly appreciates Mr. Singer's enthusiastic sign-language conversations. All the love is wasted in a sense, as it is in most of her novels, since it is never even understood, much less reciprocated. Biff's nearly motherly devotion to Mick remains entirely repressed; on Antonapoulos' death, Mr. Singer shoots himself; but the most frantically frustrated are Dr. Copeland and Jake Blount, both of whom are constantly rejected and reviled for their burning need to help others on a large social scale. Blount, in fact, is a kind of debased Socrates, not too different from the one presented us in *Barefoot in Athens*, a radical social reformer who needs to preach the truth in the streets. All the characters are driven by a need for fulfillment that consistently expresses itself as an epistemological dilemma: once they have found the truth, they are harassed by a need to find an adequate technique to communicate it to others. Again, this curious blend of erotic and epistemological needs strikingly recalls the peculiar flavor of many of a Platonic dialogue.

The theme of frustration, with fewer of the naturalistic trappings and a reduced number of characters, dominates *Reflections in a Golden Eye*, a short account of a multiple shooting at a Southern army fort. Captain Penderton and his neighbor's wife, Mrs. Langdon, are sensitive, intelligent psychotics plagued by the animalistic drives of both their spouses, Mrs. Penderton and Major Langdon, who have long been lovers. The excessive intelligence of the first pair is balanced on one side by Anacleto, the balletomane Filipino houseboy of the Langdons, and on the other hand, the avowedly feeble-minded tendencies in the second pair are balanced by Private Ellgee Williams, who is an even more crystal-pure idiot than Faulkner's Popeye. The balance is perfect when we observe that Mrs. Langdon is very profoundly devoted to Anacleto, while the Captain pursues Private Williams with an obsessive and confused mania. The clear structural division of the theme into animalistic love and spiritual love strikingly recalls, of course, the myth of the two pairs of horses pulling the chariot of the soul in *Phaedrus*.

Now in this myth, as in most of his other pronouncements on the subject in *Symposium*, *The Republic*, and other dialogues, Socrates specifically exalts the spiritual aspect of love, and while he never overlooks the physical aspect, he invariably sees it as a deterrent and a distraction, a vitiating tendency within the experience which needs to be resisted wholeheartedly. Carson McCullers, too, invariably focuses on the spiritual—and, in a sense, the asexual—relation, without, however, ignoring or denying the patently sexual basis from which the experience stems. This is the curiously disturbing synthesis of ideas which gives her writing the haunting flavor that one finds so hard to isolate in analysis. In this book, the heartily sensual relation of Mrs. Penderton and Major Langdon receives hardly more than passing mention, whereas the relations of Mrs. Langdon and the houseboy and Captain Penderton and Private Williams (the latter carried on exclusively by means of significant glances) are delicately and poetically explored.

But it is only with *The Member of the Wedding* that Miss McCullers hits her full stride. Here the perplexed spiritual odyssey of Frankie Addams is largely presented by means of three characters in the kitchen, Frankie, her cousin John Henry, and Berenice Sadie Brown, the one-eyed Negro cook whose spiritual vision is the more intense for her physical handicap. Frankie herself is twelve, at the dawn of puberty, an age and a spiritual condition that somehow fascinated Greeks from Homer through Plato. Her erstwhile playmates have rejected her, and in this portentous summer Frankie comes to lonely realizations about love and being. She vaguely feels she has passed through a phase (marked by the distinction between the "old Frankie" and the new F. Jasmine Addams) and the fresh awareness of her condition makes her want to become a "member" of her brother's wedding, and through participation with the couple in a series of gaudy imagined honeymoon adventures, she will become a "member of the world." The symbolic cohesion of this imagined group is represented thus:

> She was an *I* person who had to walk around and do things by herself. All other people had a *we* to claim, all other except her. When Berenice said *we*, she meant Honey and Big Mama, her lodge, or her church. The *we* of her father was the store. All members of clubs have a *we* to belong to and talk about. The soldiers in the army can say *we*, and even

the criminals on chain-gangs. But the old Frankie had no *we* to claim, unless it would be the terrible summer *we* of her and John Henry and Berenice—and that was the last *we* in the world she wanted. Now all this was suddenly over with and changed. There was her brother and the bride, and it was as though when first she saw them something she had known inside of her: *They are the we of me.*

The aura of physical passion is represented by the drunken soldier with whom F. Jasmine becomes innocently involved on the eve of the wedding; her perilously close escape from seduction crystallizes later into a vague awareness of the meaning of desire, and almost as in revulsion against the knowledge, she finds a new friend, Mary Littlejohn, to whom she becomes strongly attached.

The articulation of the truths about love and being which form the core of the book comes out of a long twilit kitchen seminar, punctuated by the sounds of rats in the walls and the distant tuning of a piano, and culminating in tears on the parts of all three participants. Berenice reviews in her song-like chant her own erotic history, a direct duplication of the essentials of Aristophanes' speech in *Symposium*, but this time the theme is played in reverse, rather than "one octave lower" as in "A Tree . A Rock . A Cloud." It will be remembered that Aristophanes maintains that at one time each human being was a double creature with two heads, four arms and legs, and the like; and that Zeus, in a moment of fury, punished mankind by splitting each creature in two; Aristophanes interprets the frenzied search of humans for love simply as a pursuit of one's own other half-soul; as a consequence, obviously, success and failure in love are dependent on whether or not one actually finds the other half of his own soul in the beloved. Thus love is synonymous, almost mathematically, with wholeness. Berenice extols her ecstatic first marriage to Ludie Freeman as a transfiguring experience. After his death, however, repeated attempts to duplicate the relation failed; she took up with Jamie Beale because his thumb resembled Ludie's, and with Henry Johnson because he had come into possession of Ludie's coat, and so on for a whole series of husbands. She drives the lesson home to F. Jasmine thus: "'It applies to everybody and it is a warning. . . . Why don't you see what I was doing?' asked Berenice. 'I loved Ludie and he was the first man I loved. Therefore, I had to go and copy myself forever afterward. What I did was to marry off little pieces of Ludie whenever I come across them. It was just my misfortune they all turned out to be the wrong pieces. My intention was to repeat me and Ludie.'"

She was reversing the Platonic theory by continuing the search after Ludie's death because supposedly once she had found the other half of her soul in Ludie, there would be no second chance, short of his reincarnation. But Berenice is very wise in the ways of love, and knows all about its power and its variety: "'I have knew mens to fall in love with girls so ugly that you wonder if their eyes is straight. I have seen some of the most peculiar weddings anybody could conjecture. Once I knew a boy with his whole face burned off so that—!'" After a bite of cornbread, she continues: "'I have knew womens to love veritable Satans and thank Jesus when they put their split hooves over the threshold. I have knew boys to take it into their heads to fall in love with other boys.'" But the aim of her whole exposition is the exclamation that despite all her experience, she has never known someone to fall in love with a wedding. She soberly warns F. Jasmine against the obsession. However, Berenice's commitment to sensual love puts her in a category of lesser beings, and the real concern of the tale is with F. Jasmine's spiritual discoveries about love and being. She

realizes that she is no longer the child who was hustled out of a movie for hooting at a showing of *Camille*, and now actually participates as an equal in the kitchen discussion of love. Berenice's warning about the troubles ahead for F. Jasmine may be well founded, to be sure, but it is the experience of people like her, Carson McCullers means to say, that embodies the most exquisite values.

What Frankie learns, and what Berenice knows only very fleetingly, is a nearly mystical conviction of "connections" with all sorts of random people seen casually on the street—precisely what Walt Whitman feels on the Brooklyn ferry and what Virginia Woolf's Mrs. Dalloway feels in her meanderings on London streets. In Platonic terminology, she had begun to experience love as an absolute. She can now exclaim with the tramp in the short story "'All strangers and all loved!'"

Her latest novel, *The Ballad of the Sad Café*, culminates the trend initiated with *Reflections in a Golden Eye*. The number of characters is even more reduced, the tale is shorter, and the insistent push toward allegorizing fantasy is realized in a form that seems to do for Miss McCullers all that she means for it to do. All the distracting profusion of naturalistic observation and social inclusiveness of *The Heart Is a Lonely Hunter* has been cut away, and every detail of the matrix of scene blends into the overall design of the meaning. The book is a short and powerful exemplum on the impossibility of being loved.

The book hauntingly recalls the theme of *Phaedrus*, wherein Socrates disabuses his young friend of his adulation for the tricky sophist Lysias. The latter had proved by a series of rhetorical feints that it is preferable to give oneself to a non-lover than to a lover; Socrates, in a series of brilliant ironical flourishes, proves the same thesis by different arguments simply to show he can do it, and then reverses himself in order to demonstrate his abiding contention that only a highly ethically inspired kind of spiritual love is really worthy of acceptance.

Now we have seen throughout all her books that Miss McCullers is preoccupied, too, with spiritual love, and that particularly in *Reflections in a Golden Eye*, she exalts it at the expense of sensual love. However, throughout these works the reader is disturbed by what we called the "waste of love" in our analysis of her first novel. Thus although she concerns herself almost exclusively with spiritual love, she lacks Plato's whole ethical buttressing, and also, necessarily, his direct (and fairly simple-minded) assumption of the rewards for persevering in this kind of love. Mr. Singer shoots himself in desperation, Jake Blount flees town as a hobo murderer, Dr. Copeland sinks into the last stages of tuberculosis, Mrs. Langdon maims herself horribly, Captain Penderton shoots Private Williams and himself, and so go the spiritual lovers. This is why I used the term "sublunar" at the opening of this essay: although Miss McCullers follows Plato in his essential distinctions about the nature of love, she confines her attention to a sublunar experiential sphere in which any kind of punishment-and-reward ethics (which Socrates couches in his reincarnation theory) is impossible. We saw too that typically Platonic themes were often played one octave lower or in reverse.

This is most strikingly demonstrated in *The Ballad of the Sad Café*, which is a kind of one-way circle of love much like Sartre's *Huis Clos*. The handsome Marvin Macy, foiled in his passionate love for the masculine Miss Amelia, returns to town years later to steal from her—for purely cynical motives—the love of the hunch-backed dwarf, Cousin Lymon. Each deeply loved the other, but in no case could the beloved reciprocate the feelings of the lover. It is almost as if the author were going

Socrates one better: not only are the attentions of the non-lover and the sensual lover unworthy, she says, but the attentions of the spiritual lover are invariably unwelcome, and he is bound to come to grief too.

We saw earlier that F. Jasmine Addams envied even the chain gang for its cohesion and sense of membership. Miss McCullers returns to this idea in the hauntingly bitter epilogue

to this novel, "The Twelve Mortal Men." Some readers object that this short description of the songs of a laboring gang is unrelated to the rest of the novel; in reality, it is the togetherness of the gang that is presented as the only alternative to the senseless waste of pursuing love. We simply have our choice between one kind of adversity and another, and suffering emerges as the one constant.

# CLAUDE MCKAY

## 1889–1948

Claude McKay was born in Sunny Ville, Jamaica, in 1889; the exact date of birth is uncertain. After being apprenticed to a wheelwright in Kingston, he emigrated to the U.S. in 1912 and studied agriculture at Tuskegee Institute and at Kansas State University. He abandoned his studies in 1914 and moved to Harlem, where he became a leading radical poet. Before coming to America McKay had published a collection of poetry entitled *Songs of Jamaica* (1912). While in Harlem he frequently wrote under the pseudonym Eli Edwards, a name derived from that of his wife, Eulalie Imelda Edwards. This marriage ended in 1914 after only six months, but McKay's wife subsequently gave birth to a daughter whom he never saw.

"If We Must Die," perhaps his best-known poem, was published in Max Eastman's magazine *The Liberator* in 1919. This stirring call to arms was written after the race riots that followed the end of World War I. McKay lived in London from 1919 to 1921 and, during this time, first read Marx. In 1922 he made a "magic pilgrimage" to the U.S.S.R. where he was warmly welcomed by the Communist leaders. His interest in Marxism seems to have been based on his perception of its calls for a return to agrarian values and for racial equality. However, McKay never joined the Party, and by the 1930s he had completely renounced all association with Communism.

From 1923 to 1934 McKay lived overseas, having left the United States because of his alienation from the black intelligentsia and from the leaders of the Harlem Renaissance. In Paris he came to feel that racial barriers separated him from the "lost generation"; he subsequently moved to Marseilles and later to Morocco. In Marseilles he wrote his first two novels, *Home to Harlem* (1928) and *Banjo* (1929). On its publication, *Home to Harlem* became the most popular novel ever written by a black author.

Returning to the U.S. in 1934, McKay worked briefly as a laborer in a welfare camp. In 1937 he wrote *A Long Way from Home*, an account of his life since first coming to America. In 1944 he was baptized into the Roman Catholic Church. He died in Chicago on May 22, 1948.

*Home to Harlem* is a book to invoke pity and terror, which is the function of tragedy, and to that extent—that very great extent—it is beautiful. It is hard to convey to the reader the impression this novel leaves upon the mind, just as it is hard to convey the impression that a blues-song leaves upon the mind. One reads, one hears and the heart is touched.

Out of his individual pain, Claude McKay, the poet, has fashioned his lyrics; and out of his impersonal sorrow he has written a fine novel. *Home to Harlem* is a story involving the lives led by the lost generations of colored folk in the teeming Negro metropolis of One Hundred and Tenth Street, New York. It is a story not of the successful Negroes who have done well in the trades and professions and have built themselves homes, sent their children to school, and engaged in civil and social pursuits of a sober and respectable nature: it is the story of the serving class—longshoremen and roustabouts, house-maids and Pullman porters, waiters and wash-room attendants, cooks and scullery-maids, "dime-snatchers", and all those who compensate for defeat in life in a white man's world by a savage intensity among themselves at night.

*Home to Harlem* is not a novel in the conventional sense. The only conflict in the mind of Jake, the hero, is as to whether

he will keep on working at whatever insecure, underpaid drudgery he can find to do on the docks, in the stoke-hole of a steamer and in dining-cars or turn his handsome body and good looks into the shameful asset of a "sweet-man", kept in luxury on the earnings of a woman. The only conflict of wills engaged in by the hero is when he takes a girl away from his former buddy, and anger and hate flare into being, with drawn gun and open razor. When the book closes and he is going away to Chicago with the girl to start life anew, he is the same wondering, indecisive being he was in the beginning, who "preferred the white folks' hatred to their friendly contempt" and found a sinister satisfaction in the fact that the white man is too effete to know the sensual pleasures of the blacks. ⟨. . .⟩

The language of *Home to Harlem*, whether Mr. McKay is setting forth dialogue in a perfect transcription of Negro slang and dialect or is telling his story in the Negro idiom, is a constant joy. A big black buck "lazied" down the street; another chap is "sissified"; Aunt Hattie remarks concerning some imported liquor offered her, "Ef youse always so eye-filling drinking it, it might ginger up mah bones some", and a sadistic yellow-brown girl inciting her new lover to attack her former lover cries "Hit him, Obadiah! Hit him I tell you. Beat his mug up foh him, beat his mug and bleed his mouf! Bleed his mouf! Two-faced yaller nigger, you does ebery low-down thing, but you nevah done a lick of work in you lifetime. Show him, Obadiah. Beat his face and bleed his mouf".

Mr. McKay is not at all solicitous toward his reader. He makes no case, he pleads no cause, he asks no extenuation, and he doesn't explain his idiomatic phrases. There is no glossary at the end of the book as there was to Carl Van Venchten's *Nigger Heaven*; and the unsophisticated happily will read whole pages of this novel depicting the utmost moral degradation without ever knowing what it is about. And this is just as well. —BURTON RASCOE, "The Seamy Side," *Bkm*, April 1928, pp. 183–84

In *Harlem Shadows* fierce emotions are expressed directly. While classical forms are adopted, most notably the sonnet, the effect is to heighten rather than to mitigate the intensity of expression. The love poems are erotic and rapturous; those longing for Jamaica and the countryside, unabashedly nostalgic; portrayals of the city, pungent; and poems dealing with racial prejudice, furious.

By New York City and Harlem McKay was alternately fascinated and repelled, as he had been during his first experience as a constable by Spanish Town, Jamaica. "Flame Heart" demonstrates that McKay was not fully used to life in an industrial city. As other immigrants committed to a new life in America still longed for their old countries, so McKay could never forget the green hills of his youth:

> So much have I forgotten in ten years,
> So much in ten brief years! I have forgot
> What time the purple apples come to juice,
> And what month brings the shy forget-me-not.
> I have forgotten the special, startling season
> Of the pimento's flowering and fruiting.
> What time of year the ground doves brown the fields
> And fill the noonday with their curious fluting.
> I have forgotten much, but still remember
> The poinsettia's red, blood-red in warm December. . . .

While McKay enjoyed the liveliness of Harlem, he saw, too, its commercialism and destructiveness. The poem "Harlem Shadows" reminds one both of McKay's earlier "Country Girl," and of Blake's "London."

> I hear the halting footsteps of a lass
> In Negro Harlem when the night lets fall
> Its veil. I see the shapes of girls who pass
> To bend and barter at desire's call. . . .
>
> Through the long night . . .
> The dusky, half-clad girls of tired feet
> Are trudging, thinly shod, from street to street.
>
> Ah, stern harsh world, that in the wretched way
> Of poverty, dishonor and disgrace,
> Has pushed the timid little feet of clay,
> The sacred brown feet of my fallen race!
> Ah, heart of me, the weary, weary feet
> In Harlem wandering from street to street.

Unlike Countee Cullen, McKay had no inhibitions about recognizing and condemning racial prejudice. In response to everyday personal encounters with racial discrimination, the sort Cullen rarely spoke of publicly, McKay wrote four bitterly defiant sonnets. "Into the furnace let me go alone," he declares in "Baptism." "Stay you without in terror of the heat . . . / I will come out, back to your world of tears, / A stronger soul within a finer frame." The individuality of this protest, however moving, weakens its relevance to Negro America as a whole. McKay seems almost to accept the terrible status quo

rather than search for ways in which it might be changed. Whatever the white world does to me, he seems to be saying, it cannot crush my own strong individual spirit.

Similarly, in "The White City," McKay asserts that while "I brood upon my hate, . . . without flinch / I bear it nobly." The trains, the wharves, and the dens of the city are "sweet like wanton loves because I hate." And, in "America," McKay declares that despite prejudice, his defiance and strength, bolstered by the very vigor of America, will permit him to profit:

> Although she feeds me bread of bitterness,
> And sinks into my throat her tiger's tooth,
> Stealing my breath of life, I will confess
> I love this cultured hell that tests my youth!

One poem of McKay's does propose an answer, though a desperate one, for Negro-Americans. Written in response to the race riots of 1919, "If We Must Die" is McKay's best known work.

> If we must die, let it not be like hogs
> Hunted and penned in an inglorious spot,
> While round us bark the mad and hungry dogs,
> Making their mock at our accursed lot.
> If we must die, O let us nobly die,
> So that our precious blood may not be shed
> In vain; then even the monsters we defy
> Shall be constrained to honor us though dead!
> O Kinsmen! we must meet the common foe!
> Though far outnumbered let us show us brave,
> And for their thousand blows deal one death-blow!
> What though before us lies the open grave?
> Like men we'll face the murderous, cowardly pack,
> Pressed to the wall, dying, but fighting back!

This powerful sonnet, terse and dramatic, was reprinted in nearly every leading Negro magazine and newspaper. Decrying it as evidence of the danger of Negro radicalism, Senator Henry Cabot Lodge had it inserted into the *Congressional Record*. Twenty years later, when Britain feared an imminent German invasion, Winston Churchill read the poem to the House of Commons. While Churchill probably was quite unaware of the race or radicalism of the author, his interpretation seems to have been the closest to McKay's.

The poem, as McKay later commented, was meant to be universally applicable to those cornered and desperate before a superior foe. It was written to apply to an extreme situation; such desperate fighting need be resorted to only when "the mad and hungry dogs" are at one's very heels, as McKay felt was the case in 1919. Hence it is wrong to interpret this poem, as did Senator Lodge and many Negroes, as a call to arms directed to all Negroes. Quiet defiance and personal integrity, McKay seems to have felt, would suffice for the Negro in all but the most desperate situations. It is worth noting that McKay spoke in a soft, lilting West Indian accent. His own reading of "If We Must Die," recorded in 1944, sounds almost casual compared to the way Churchill must have delivered it to the House of Commons.

Most striking about *Harlem Shadows* is the impact it must have had upon its white and Negro readers in the early 'twenties. Of those who recorded their impressions, Heywood Broun, Max Eastman, and James Weldon Johnson all were congratulatory. Many others must have been quite surprised. Not only was a Negro writing adeptly in classical verse forms, but a Negro was expressing his anger in words, as the rioters of 1919 had in actions.—STEPHEN H. BRONZ, *Roots of Negro Racial Consciousness in the 1920's*, 1964, pp. 72–75

⟨*A Long Way from Home*⟩ is unique in one aspect. Other accounts by prominent black men of their encounter with

America have been written by those who were born and bred in the United States. Claude McKay was one of the more talented individuals in the stream of immigrants from the British West Indies who have been seeking their fortune in the United States since the turn of the century. They were refugees from a poverty exacerbated by overpopulation, and from a social system in which British settlers and their mixed-blood descendants had kept most blacks in a subordinate position. During the twenties and thirties West Indians played an active role in the hectic politics of Harlem, a phenomenon that has been analyzed with insight and perception (and also some bias) by Harold Cruse in *The Crisis of the Negro Intellectual.* ⟨. . .⟩

Throughout a span of thirty years McKay had written poetry about the Jamaica he never ceased to love—of "Bananas ripe and green, and ginger-root," of ". . . dewy dawns and mystical blue skies," and of how ". . . hungry for the old, familiar ways, / I turned aside and bowed my head and wept." But in the period following the publication of *A Long Way from Home* his poetry reveals a sense of deep, sometimes bitter, alienation. Gone is the proud, defiant, resilient spirit of an earlier poem:

> Although she feeds me bread of bitterness,
> And sinks into my throat her tiger's tooth,
> Stealing my breath of life, I will confess
> I love this cultured hell that tests my youth!

Now, in his late fifties, sick in body and emotionally tired, watching a second World War erupt, he writes of America as "You whited sepulcher . . . worm-infested, rotten through within," fighting Germans and Japanese "While fifteen million Negroes on their knees / Pray for salvation from the Fascist yoke / Of these United States."

At the same time that McKay was questioning a government that fought fascism abroad but not at home, he was also reflecting about the goals worthy of struggle and about his own life. In "The Negro's Friend," for instance, he expresses an anti-integrationist view that would have had little popularity at the beginning of the civil-rights movement.

> Must fifteen million blacks be gratified,
> That one of them can enter as a guest,
> A fine white house—the rest of them denied
> A place of decent sojourn and a rest?
> Oh, Segregation is not the whole sin,
> The Negroes need salvation from within.

Yet by 1965 this had become the dominant mood within the black communities of the United States. ⟨. . .⟩

Claude McKay was concerned over the tendency of educated elites of African descent throughout the black world to pull away from the masses. Today, with new occupational opportunities and a relaxation of caste pressures throughout the country in commercial establishments and schools, and in some areas of social participation, this tendency may be accelerated. Only the tenacity of the pattern of residential segregation has slowed it down. At the cultural level as well as the level of social action, the quest for both "identity" and "black power" becomes complicated by cross-pulls toward "integration" and "black solidarity." McKay was not a racist in reverse, nor did he hate white people, as individuals, yet his observations on the need for racial solidarity are uncompromising.—St. Clair Drake, "Introduction" to *A Long Way from Home*, 1970, pp. ix–xx

The character Jake in McKay's immensely popular *Home to Harlem* typified the popular image during the 1920s of the primitive-exotic black man whose life-style was uninhibited by a repressive civilization. McKay continued to be intrigued with the figure in his other two novels, *Banjo* (1929) and *Banana*

*Bottom* (1933), and in his collection of short fiction, *Gingertown* (1932). Indeed, he was still singing the praises of the "natural man" in his controversial nonfiction account of Harlem in 1940. Throughout the period McKay persisted in his belief that Afro-American intellectuals had been educated by the white man away from the simple and natural enjoyment of life which was the African heritage of the black masses. Though related to Carter Woodson's concept of miseducation, McKay's approach was definitely not bourgeois. McKay was as much a black nationalist as Woodson or Du Bois—although he was loath to admit it—but his black nationalism was more genuinely directed toward the glorification of the black masses. ⟨. . .⟩

McKay's novels are crudely Manichean: the totally sterile and repressive white civilization versus the idealized fruitful existence of the black man in his natural state. *Banana Bottom* was praised by many critics because of its realism, because McKay, at times, portrayed low life realistically. But he never really dealt with the misery of low life. Just as Jake and Banjo were ideal types of the primitive-exotic, the pastoral life described in *Banana Bottom* was nostalgically ideal.

It is significant that all of McKay's major fiction was written while he was living either in Europe or in Morocco. Perhaps this accounts for his softening of the harsher aspects of reality. After nearly ten years of living the bohemian life abroad, he was out of touch with the violence and excruciating poverty that filled the lives of black men in the United States of the depression era. His celebration of black primitivism looked back into the "liberated" 1920s, but it simply was not relevant to the pressing reality of the 1930s.—James O. Young, "Black Reality and Beyond," *Black Writers of the Thirties*, 1973, pp. 213–17

---

## ROBERT BONE
### From "Claude McKay"
*Down Home: A History
of Afro-American Short Fiction*
1975, pp. 159–71

At the climax of D. H. Lawrence's novel, *The Plumed Serpent*, Kate prepares to merge, physically and psychologically, with Ramón, and through him, with the prehistoric consciousness of ancient Mexico. Contemplating her surrender, she imagines a time

> When great plains stretched away to the oceans, like Atlantis and the lost continents of Polynesia, so that seas were only great lakes, and the soft, dark-eyed people of that world could walk around the globe. Then there was a mysterious, hot-blooded, soft-footed humanity with a strange civilization of its own. Till the glaciers melted, and drove the peoples to the high places, like the lofty plateaus of Mexico; separated them into cut-off nations.[1]

This myth of separation and reunion, which is central to the art of D. H. Lawrence, captivated the imagination of Claude McKay.[2] For McKay shared with Lawrence, the great primitivist of twentieth-century letters, a fascination with "the world before the Flood, before the mental-spiritual world came into being."[3] Throughout his career, McKay yearns for that state of Perfect Oneness before the Flood: before, as a child, he was separated from his mother; before, as a youth, he was separated from Jamaica; and before, as a black man in a white man's world, he was separated from himself. He looks in vain for spiritual wholeness in what he comes to call "the pagan isms," but finds it ultimately in the bosom of the Roman Church.

Claude McKay's spiritual journey carries him from oneness to multiplicity and back again. The quest for experience is the basis of his personal peregrinations (recorded in *A Long Way from Home*), his poems of a vagabondage, and his picaresque novels, *Home to Harlem* and *Banjo*. Experience, however, leads to chaos and division in the soul, caused not only by the white man's contumely, but the curse of intellect, which sunders men and women from their primitive emotions. Recoiling from racial insult and abuse, and the complexities of consciousness as well, McKay turns for solace to the simple and harmonious strains of pastoral. The fruits of his revulsion from occidental civilization are the novel, *Banana Bottom*, and the book of stories, *Gingertown*. 〈. . .〉

McKay's literary career may be divided into four phases. The first, or provincial phase, encompasses his first two books of verse, *Songs of Jamaica* (1912) and *Constab Ballads* (1912). The second, or picaresque phase, includes a book of poems, *Harlem Shadows* (1922), and two novels, *Home to Harlem* (1928) and *Banjo* (1929). The third, or pastoral phase, consists of a book of stories, *Gingertown* (1932) and a novel, *Banana Bottom* (1933). The fourth, or retrospective phase, includes an autobiography, *A Long Way from Home* (1937), and a sociological study, *Harlem: Negro Metropolis* (1940).

The stories of *Gingertown* mark a transition from the picaresque to the pastoral phase. The first six tales are concerned with Harlem life. They express McKay's ambivalent feelings toward the black metropolis which, despite its glamor and excitement, he comes to regard as a whited sepulcher. The last six represent the recoil of McKay's imagination from the polluted centers of occidental civilization. Four are set in Jamaica, one on the Marseilles waterfront, and one in North Africa. Their esthetic mode is pastoral; they celebrate the values of simplicity, community, harmony with nature, reconciliation with one's fellow man, and freedom from political or sexual repression.

The two halves of the book were written at different times and under strikingly different circumstances. The Harlem tales were written in France between 1923 and 1926. In the spring of 1926 Louise Bryant, the widow of John Reed and a friend from *Liberator* days, showed the stories to Harper & Brothers, who agreed to publish a collection in the near future. Meanwhile McKay had acquired a Paris agent who urged him rather to attempt an episodic novel of Harlem life, based on the characters of the short stories. The result was *Home to Harlem* (1928), which Harper substituted for the stories. Four of the latter were published in various journals from 1927 to 1931.[4] Subsequently they appeared in the Harlem section of *Gingertown*.

The second half of the collection was written in North Africa in 1930–1931. McKay had left Europe to escape "the white hound of Civilization."[5] He had gone completely native in Morocco, whose landscape, people, and exotic customs reminded him of his Jamaican homeland. In the spring of 1931 he settled in Tangier to work on *Gingertown*. He was joined by an Afro-American woman of bohemian inclinations who was in flight from the stuffiness of bourgeois Harlem. After an idyllic "honeymoon" they quarreled, and she returned to Paris and her white lover. Wounded and resentful, McKay retreated to the mountains of Spanish Morocco, where he completed *Gingertown* and *Banana Bottom*.

This disastrous love affair compounded McKay's bitterness and increased his alienation from occidental values. The figure of his paramour, torn between her black and white lovers, became in his imagination an emblem of the Negro soul, torn between two hostile cultures and antagonistic ways of life.[6] At the same time, his withdrawal to the mountains awakened memories of his Jamaican childhood. In surroundings reminiscent of his native village he made a valiant effort to repossess his peasant heritage. The pastoral impulse which inspired his early poems now became the source of McKay's most enduring fiction.

The Harlem tales of *Gingertown* are concerned with the cultural dilemma of blacks who are compelled to function in a white man's world. These tales reflect McKay's experience as an immigrant to the United States from the West Indies. They express his shock and dismay at being transplanted from a country which is 90 percent black to one where the opposite ratio obtains. The tension that results between the self and its environment, leading in turn to a divisiveness within the self, is McKay's essential theme. He is concerned not so much with the humiliations and inconveniences of segregation as with the breach they open in the black man's soul.

The classic formulation of the black American's dilemma was made by W. E. B. DuBois in *The Souls of Black Folk* (1903): "One ever feels his twoness—an American, a Negro: two souls, two thoughts, two unreconciled strivings; two warring ideals in one dark body, whose dogged strength alone keeps it from being torn asunder."[7] McKay was introduced to *The Souls of Black Folk* by a white English teacher at Kansas State. He recalls in his autobiography that "The book shook me like an earthquake."[8] On the evidence of his Harlem tales, it was this passage concerning the black man's double consciousness that produced the seismic tremors in his soul.

The protagonists of McKay's Harlem stories are men or women divided against themselves. Trying to escape their blackness, and the penalties imposed upon it by the white world, they expose themselves to psychological disaster. They may experience a brief moment of happiness while in pursuit of white ideals, but invariably it proves to be illusory. Sooner or later some racial trauma intervenes to remind them that the barriers of caste are insurmountable. What holds these tales together is the fantasy of playing white. McKay is trying to exorcise a certain kind of psychological infatuation.[9]

The dangers and temptations of "white fever" are the focal point of these tales. Thus Bess of "Brownskin Blues" mutilates herself in a misguided effort to lighten her complexion. The heroine of "Mattie and Her Sweetman" is vulnerable to social and sexual humiliation by virtue of her passion for "yellow boys." Angie Dove of "Near-White" suffers a disastrous love affair with a white man symbolically named John West. The first half of *Gingertown*, in short, is part of a now familiar literature of extrication, whose aim is to liberate the blacks from psychological enslavement to a false cultural ideal.[10]

Unfortunately the literary quality of McKay's Harlem stories is not high. These early tales, after all, were his first experiments with prose fiction. Their awkwardness of style, which is especially pronounced in the dialogue, suggests that the former poet, in shifting his major emphasis to prose, has not yet mastered his new medium. The widely anthologized "Truant" is hardly free of this defect, but by virtue of its summary position it merits more extensive treatment than the rest. This story, which concludes the Harlem section of *Gingertown*, illustrates McKay's dilemma as he tries to dramatize his disenchantment with the urban scene through the inappropriate conventions of the picaresque.

As the story opens, the hero and his wife are watching a vaudeville show from the "Nigger Heaven" of a Broadway theater. The curtain discloses a domestic scene in which a troupe of Irish actors personifies the happy family of American popular culture. The initial impact of the scene is idyllic, but its ultimate effect is ironic, for the Merry Mulligans possess the warmth, cohesiveness, and cultural integrity conspicuously lacking in the life of the black protagonist.[11] The note of harmony on which the story opens thus serves as an ironic commentary on the disintegrating marriage of the two main characters.

Barclay Oram is an autobiographical creation closely related to the figure of Ray in *Home to Harlem* and *Banjo*. In a long flashback we learn that he has emigrated from the West Indies in pursuit of his dream of attending a Negro university. At Howard he meets and marries Rhoda, an Afro-American girl of middle-class background and assimilationist outlook. As the tale unfolds, Rhoda emerges as a kind of enchantress who holds her man in thrall to the false values of an artificial civilization. Nor does fatherhood relieve Barclay's feeling of entrapment, for he envisions his daughter marrying a railroad waiter like himself and raising children "to carry on the great tradition of black servitude."

As the present action of the tale begins, Barclay is rousted out of bed at an early hour, in order to report for work on the Pennsylvania Railroad. It is a disastrous trip, and during the layover in Washington he gets drunk, thereby missing the return run. Savoring his truancy, he is not at all disturbed when he is laid off for ten days. Rhoda, however, reproaches him for irresponsibility, and her rebuke precipitates a crisis which is resolved by Barclay's desertion of his wife and child. Through the metaphor of truancy, McKay depicts the black man as a dropout from the Western world, a *pícaro* who is condemned to a life of eternal wandering.

The trouble with "Truant" is a radical divergency of form and content. In his expansionist phase (Jamaica to New York), McKay gravitates instinctively toward the devices and conventions of the picaresque. The phase of recoil, however (New York to Jamaica), cannot be expressed through the same medium. The picaresque is a suitable instrument for the *celebration* of Harlem life (as in *Home to Harlem*), but it cannot be adapted to the theme of urban disenchantment. Pastoral is the appropriate vehicle for the expression of anti-urban sentiments. At this point in his career, McKay has made the emotional transition from expansion to recoil, but has not yet grasped its formal implications. He will do so in his stories of Jamaican peasant life.

Structurally speaking, "Truant" is the hinge of *Gingertown*. The last of the Harlem tales, it provides a logical transition to the counterstatement. For if "Truant" is a myth of disaffiliation, the Jamaican tales are parables of pastoral refreshment and renewal. As McKay's imagination turns from Harlem to Jamaica, a corresponding shift in tone occurs. Feelings of revulsion for the Western world are replaced by a vast affection for the Caribbean island and its people. The source of this tenderness is McKay's memory of his mother. Her presence hovers over the Jamaican tales, imbuing them with a tone of tranquillity and inner peace.

To describe the latter half of *Gingertown* as McKay's "Jamaican tales" is only an approximation. Two of the weaker stories, "Nigger Lover" and "Little Sheik," have Mediterranean rather than Caribbean settings. A third, "When I Pounded the Pavement," is not in fact a story, but an autobiographical account of McKay's experience in the Kingston constabulary. The three remaining tales, which constitute the core of *Gingertown*, are set in the Jamaican highlands.

"Crazy Mary" is an undistinguished piece, but "The Agricultural Show" and "The Strange Burial of Sue" are McKay's best stories.

"The Agricultural Show" is a pure specimen of Renaissance pastoral. The central characters are Bennie, an impressionable schoolboy, and his brother Matthew, the village pharmacist. Matthew, who is something of a local booster, undertakes to organize a country fair. There will be prizes for livestock and farm products, handicrafts and the domestic arts. Games and competitions will be held; band concerts and political speeches given; and the Governor himself will address the assembled multitudes. The fair is a communal ritual in which all segments of society participate, and during which all petty barriers of caste or class are momentarily surmounted.

Matthew plays the role of mediator, who orchestrates and harmonizes the great event. Under his direction, lowlander and highlander mingle for a day; Baptist, Methodist, and Anglican rub elbows; village, town, and city folk are represented; black, white, and all shades in between take part. United in a common venture, the peasantry, gentry, and aristocracy transcend their traditional roles. Among the surging throngs, artificial distinctions of rank and status give way to a natural camaraderie, while on the speakers' platform a symbolic reconciliation of the classes and races is effected. The sign and seal of this communal harmony, and a scene that Bennie never will forget, is the presentation of his mother to the Governor.

To a modern sensibility, unacquainted with the pastoral tradition, "The Agricultural Show" will seem a sentimental fantasy. When the lion lies down with the lamb, our cynical century believes, only the lion gets up. We will mistake the author's purpose, however, if we read the story as a realistic social commentary. It is rather a poetic vision, an expression of an inner need. McKay's Jamaican pastoral, with its images of racial harmony and social peace, is an objective correlative of the inner harmony that he so desperately seeks. Split and shredded by his contact with the Western world, he returns in his imagination to Jamaica in order to reconstitute his soul.

What follows is a process of reduction. Tormented by his doubleness, McKay endeavors to achieve a psychic unity by exorcising his Western self. From the complexities of Negro experience in America, he turns to the simplicities of Jamaican peasant life. Intellectuality, which he has come to regard as a burden, is renounced in favor of instinct and emotion. The oneness of spirit that he craves necessitates a stripping away of the false veneer of white civilization and a closer accommodation to his primitive sources. The alien culture must be repudiated, and especially in its oppressive sexual forms. Such are the themes of McKay's most impressive story, "The Strange Burial of Sue."

The plot turns on a sexual triangle involving the title character, her husband, and an adolescent boy. Sue Turner is a peasant woman of free-loving ways, who is nonetheless universally respected and admired in her community. A hardworking field hand, volunteer nurse, and befriender of pregnant village girls, she conducts her private life in such a way as to threaten neither Turner nor the village wives. Her husband is a steady man, amiable, phlegmatic, and totally lacking the proprietary attitude toward sex: "One day an indiscreet relative was trying to broad-hint Turner about Sue's doings, and Turner remarked that he felt proud having a wife that was admired of other men (181).[12]

Burskin is a shy and awkward youth, still a virgin at the outset of his liaison with Sue. After a passionate affair of several months' duration, she jilts him for a glamorous adventurer recently returned from Panama. Jealous and importunate, Burskin makes a scene at the local grogshop which precipitates a public scandal. Turner, who has thus far been a model of patience and forbearance, now feels compelled to undertake a legal action against the youth who has abused his generosity. Before the case can come to trial, however, it is rendered moot by the sudden death of Sue, perhaps brought on (the facts are never clear) by an unsuccessful effort to abort Burskin's child.

The story gains a new dimension with the introduction of the brown-skinned village parson. A self-righteous busybody, he sees fit at one point to protect the public morals by expelling Sue from church. He represents, in short, the intrusion of Anglo-Saxon values on a world more African than European. Two rival codes of conduct, or concepts of goodness, are thus at issue in the tale. The permissive sexual code of the black peasantry, inherited from slavery times if not from Africa, is weighed against the missionary morals of the Baptist seminarian. As in *Banana Bottom*, McKay employs the metaphor of sexuality to dramatize the sharp divergencies of culture, lifestyle, and moral outlook that separate the colonizer from the colonized.

In "The Strange Burial of Sue," the folk community rallies in defense of its immemorial customs. On the occasion of Sue's funeral, the whole mountain range turns out in tribute to her popularity. The parson makes the error, in his graveside sermon, of denouncing Sue as a backslider and a sinner. Outraged, Turner drives him off and invites the people to bear witness to his wife's goodness. In effect the folk community defrocks the village parson, rejecting him as the emissary of an alien culture. In defiant tribute to her passion—a value cherished by the black peasants—Turner plants two flaming dragon's bloods on his wife's grave.

Claude McKay's Jamaican pastorals, written in North Africa from 1930 to 1933, mark the outer limits of his flight from the West. The flight was doomed, as we can see in retrospect, because the fugitive was fleeing from himself. Within a year or two of the publication of *Gingertown* and *Banana Bottom*, McKay was back in the United States. In 1940 his last book appeared, a sympathetic portrait of urban life entitled *Harlem: Negro Metropolis*. His pastoral phase therefore must be seen as one polarity in a larger pattern of vacillation and ambivalence. It was a passing phase, expressive of a deep revulsion from the Western world, but incapable of sustaining an integrated moral vision.

McKay achieved his larger vision through conversion to the Catholic faith. Within its unifying framework, the intolerable tensions of duality could be resolved. The reductive strategy employed in the Jamaican pastorals did not prove permanently viable because it entailed a mutilation of the self. What was called for, McKay was later to discover, was not a mutilation but a synthesis. The oneness that he sought in a symbolic fusion with Jamaican peasant life he ultimately found in Roman Catholicism, which combined the simple faith and venerable customs of a peasant culture with the forms and rituals of a highly sophisticated and emphatically Western religion.

*Notes*

1. D. H. Lawrence, *The Plumed Serpent* (London, William Heinemann, 1926), p. 443.
2. In his autobiography, *A Long Way from Home* (New York: Lee Furman, 1937), McKay acknowledges that "D. H. Lawrence was the modern writer I preferred above any" (p. 247).
3. *The Plumed Serpent*, p. 444. For a dramatization of these ideas in McKay's fiction, see the contrast between Jake and Ray in *Home to Harlem* and *Banjo*.
4. "Highball" appeared in *Opportunity*, May/June 1927; "Truant" in *Europe* (Paris), 15 Mars, 1928; "Mattie and Her Sweetman" in *This Quarter* (Paris), Fall 1929; and "Near-White" in *Europe*, 15 Juin, 1931.
5. *A Long Way from Home*, p. 304. For the background of McKay's pastoral phase see Part Six of his autobiography, "The Idylls of Africa," pp. 295 ff.
6. See the character of Bita in *Banana Bottom* (New York: Harper & Brothers, 1933).
7. W. E. B. DuBois, *The Souls of Black Folk* (New York: Fawcett, 1961), p. 3.
8. *A Long Way from Home*, p. 110.
9. I am indebted for some of these ideas to Sister Mary Conroy, "The Vagabond Motif in the Writings of Claude McKay," *Negro American Literature Forum*, 5, 1 (Spring 1971), pp. 15–23.
10. LeRoi Jones is the chief prophet of extrication in our own time.
11. For McKay's empathy with the Irish and his envy of Irish nationalism, see "How Black Sees Red and Green," *Liberator* (June 1921), pp. 17, 20–21.
12. Page numbers are from Wayne Cooper, ed., *The Passion of Claude McKay* (New York: Schocken Books, 1973), where this story can most conveniently be found.

# Archibald MacLeish

## 1892–1982

Archibald MacLeish was born in Glencoe, Illinois, on May, 7, 1892. The son of a well-to-do family, MacLeish was a young man of wide-ranging interests whose pursuits included theatre, law, teaching, journalism, football, government, foreign affairs, and most importantly poetry. He received his early education at Hotchkiss and in the fall of 1911 entered Yale, where he later edited the literary magazine and was elected Class Poet at his graduation in 1915. After his first year at Harvard Law School he married Ada Taylor Hitchcock in the summer of 1916. From 1917 to 1918 he served with the U.S. Army in France, rising from private to captain during his enlistment. While in France *Tower of Ivory* (1917), his first volume of poetry, was published in the U.S. He graduated from law school with honors in 1919 and briefly taught constitutional and international law at Harvard. In 1920 he joined the Boston law firm of Choate, Hall & Stewart. Three years later he declined an offer to become a partner in the firm and instead traveled with his wife and children to Paris.

While abroad Ada MacLeish pursued her career as a concert soprano while her husband studied French and Oriental poetry in addition to teaching himself Italian. While in Paris he continued to write poetry much in the style of his contemporaries, Eliot, Pound, and Yeats. Unlike the other American artists living in Paris, with many of whom they were friendly, the MacLeishes did not consider themselves expatriates; although they traveled extensively throughout Europe (and even made a trip to Persia), they spent part of each summer in the United States. They returned home in 1928 to a farmhouse they had purchased in Conway, Massachusetts. The Berkshire farm was MacLeish's home for the next fifty-five years.

In 1929 Henry Luce, a friend from the poet's Yale days, offered MacLeish a position on the editorial board of his new business magazine *Fortune*. His work schedule was extremely flexible, allowing him ample time to remain home and write poetry. In 1932 he published a long poem based on a trip he had made to Mexico during which he followed the route of Cortés. This poem, titled *Conquistador*, won the 1933 Pulitzer Prize for Poetry. MacLeish continued working for *Fortune* until he joined the Roosevelt Administration in 1939, serving first as the Librarian of Congress and later as an Assistant Secretary of State. Throughout the 1930s MacLeish warned that the rising tide of fascism would have dire consequences in America. In 1940 he wrote *The Irresponsibles*, in which he criticized American scholars and writers for not working more forcefully to combat dangerous political developments in Europe.

After the war he served briefly as the chairman of the American delegation to UNESCO. From 1949 to 1962 he was the Boylston Professor of Rhetoric and Oratory at Harvard. MacLeish was a prolific poet whose literary work spans six decades. His *Collected Poems, 1917–1952* received unusual recognition, winning a National Book Award as well as the Pulitzer and Bollingen Poetry Prizes. Throughout his career he also wrote several dramas, of which *J.B.* (1958), first directed by Elia Kazan, was by far the most successful. After his retirement in 1962 MacLeish continued to write on important political issues. He died on April 20, 1982.

## ROBERT PENN WARREN
### From "Twelve Poets"

*American Review*, May 1934, pp. 213–18

There is a great similarity between MacLeish's early and late work. He has extended his technical resources, but not as far as might have been predicted from one whose first published work showed such facility; and he has written a poem, *Conquistador*, on more ambitious scale than any that preceded it. But his poetry, from first to last, shows the same kind of excellence, though in differing degree, and the same limitation.

From first to last there has been a certain imprecision of theme in MacLeish's poetry. Despite an increasing flexibility in technique, this imprecision has persisted from the early lyrics through *Conquistador*. Most of the lyrics present mere mood, a nostalgia, a melancholy, a weariness, a fatalism, which poetically is realized only in a series of appropriate images drawn from the processes of nature, the wind, the movement of water, the wax and wane of the moon. The poet is sensitive to these things and records the stimuli that have affected him, but he has exhibited little power to dominate them, to organize them as communication for anything more than the simple mood. The formula for most of the lyrics is a deft catalogue of these stimuli in conjunction with the single question, the single, almost inarticulate, cry: *Remember. Why should I weep for this? I remember the past time. Where shall we sleep, O night-bewildered birds? Why do you listen, trees? A stir, a sigh. What is it we cannot recall?* Rhetorical tags such as these appear as an almost constant mannerism for the conclusion of his verses: they are in incantation for the undigested mystery.

It is by the ejaculation, the question, frequently not substantiated in the context and circumstance which the poet has presented in his catalogue of physical nature or scarcely related event, that he attempts to give dramatic focus to the material, to define the theme itself. MacLeish is generally the artist of the simple, broad, uncontradictory effect. His poetry is a study in shading, not a study in resolution. In fact, his poetry

is carefully purged of all opposing stresses; it is singularly undramatic. It is poetry of the single impulse, which requires no resolution. This implies a certain formlessness, a defect in logic. If the theme is vague (not *difficult*), there can be no suspense or progression; there can be little more than the incidental excitement of the poetic perceptions, at creating which MacLeish is adept. He accumulates a set of images and statements which provide this incidental excitement (in any given poem an excitement of precisely the same unmixed order from image to image or statement to statement), but without any considerable architectural capacity. For practical example, let the reader try the experiment of shifting the order of a fair number of lines or stanzas, excepting the last in each instance, of the following pieces: "Cinema of a Man", "Le Secret Humain", "Memory Green", "Broken Promise", "Before March", "Salute", "Cook County", "Way Station", "Land's End", "Reproach to Dead Poets", "Epistle to Be Left in the Earth", or "American Letter". I do not mean to imply that these are bad poems, for they are successful in different degrees; but I do believe that even violent derangements of order will not greatly jeopardize the kind of success they possess. This may indicate why their effect is usually diffuse, vague, and general; and why MacLeish's work, if it is to be thoroughly enjoyed, must be approached in a very special temper. It engages the reader's capacity on one plane only.

MacLeish's more ambitious pieces are probably the most instructive examples of his weakness in construction. The "Hamlet" depends almost absolutely on the Shakespearean reference for any sense of progression or organization; it is, finally, a sort of versified marginalia, a commentary, brilliantly executed at times, which interprets the play as a special symbol. But the commentary breaks down precisely at the point where, for the purpose in hand, it should be most effective: the second half of section 13, and section 14. And it is in those parts that the poem loses contact with the play, and becomes more purely MacLeish's own poem. *Conquistador* is, in one sense, a poem within a poem within a poem. The action proper is sustained in the pathos of the recollection of Bernal Diaz, and that, in turn, is defined by MacLeish himself; that is, the narrative is read in the light of Bernal Diaz's Preface, and that in the light of MacLeish's own Prologue. The final effect is of something twice refracted. What, apparently, engaged the imagination of the poet was not the narrative or epic, but the lyric quality . . . the tone of reverie, the pathos of the big deeds swallowed in time. The poem is not regularly narrative at all; the narrative in the end is but a mechanism of reference for a simple lyric effect, but a mechanism so extended that the lyric effect loses force, a force not sufficiently redefined by the conclusion of the poem. But the narrative also serves a more immediate purpose: its long progress is sustained by the richness of MacLeish's physical perceptions, not by the movement of action, which itself is frequently submerged. The defect in structural and dramatic sense which impairs the lyrics impairs even more drastically *Conquistador*. This means, I suppose, that MacLeish failed in his primary effort in the poem; it does not mean, however, that the poem did not deserve the Pulitzer award, an award which came with surprising acumen after the selection the previous year of George Dillon's girlish suavities.

In one poem MacLeish has said, "a poem should not mean but be". This is perfectly true, in one sense: the artist constructs a work which is self-contained, which does not demand external reference for its justification, in which idea is vindicated in terms of perception. Again he has asked: "Is it just to demand of us also to bear arms?" But the alternatives, as he puts them, are not necessary. The external reference of idea is propaganda; that is, the poet bears arms. The option, the choice MacLeish has taken, is a poetry in which idea is reduced to the minimum, even as a structural element. Temperamentally, he is very close to the Imagists, being preoccupied with the play of objective nature. Frequently this preoccupation does not even take the form of metaphor, that is, a background for reference; it is, rather, enumeration for its own sake, embedded, as it were, in a matrix of mood.

The positive streak of anti-intellectualism in MacLeish's work is healthy in so far as it recognizes the root of poetic sensibility in perception of physical nature; but limited in so far as it does not recognize any complexities in human nature or experience that are worth any great trouble on the poet's part to differentiate. This streak of anti-intellectualism appears in much of MacLeish's later work as a kind of primitivism. The abortive mythologies which began to take shape in the volume *New Found Land* are, in short, an apologia for the poet's own preoccupation:

> These men do not speak: they have seen
> Shapes solid and real, live things.

Again, in "Frescoes for Mr. Rockefeller's City" the western lands were all "price" to the railroad speculators:

> . . . they never looked at it:
> why should they look at the land: they were Empire
>        Builders:
> it was all in the bid and the asked and the ink on their
>        books. . . .

And that, in a way, is the theme of *Conquistador* as well. Diaz "looked" at the land and the looking was what claimed the poet's interest. Further, the satirical aspects of MacLeish's poetry represent a satire directed against the people who take an abstract definition of the world. Morgan or Marx, it is all the same. He says:

> It may be that the earth and the men remain . . .
> There is too much sun on the lids of my eyes to be
>        listening.

The text for much of MacLeish's work, with certain obvious qualifications, might well be this sentence from Whitman:

"Nature (the only complete actual poem) existing calmly in the divine scheme, containing all, content, careless of the criticisms of a day, of these endless and windy chatterers."

MacLeish, like Wordsworth, has sought to immerse himself in nature, although, unlike Wordsworth, he has not maintained that one impulse from a vernal wood or the Great Plains or Lake Michigan instructs in regard to moral evil or good. Perhaps MacLeish is less fortunate than Wordsworth, who found in the philosophy of Hartley something to give a framework, and a certain variety, to his characteristic preoccupation. Both have the same strength and the same limitation: they have sought to keep fresh the poetic impulse by maintaining a constant connection with the richness of nature, and they have suffered because they were not able to dominate the richness of nature, to make it expressive. Both have been obsessed with the difficult relation of idea to the concrete materials of their art. Both have written much poetry about poetry, which, probably, is not the final business of the poet. I confess, however, that I had rather read MacLeish's *Poems, 1924–1933* than Wordsworth's *Prelude*; and I am prepared to accept whatever damnation that involves.

## ARTHUR MIZENER
### "The Poetry of Archibald MacLeish"
*Sewanee Review*, October–December 1938, pp. 501–19

The career of Archibald MacLeish has the appearance of having been a tortured series of unconnected allegiances. It is, after all, a long way from what Horace Gregory once called "the four-year illusion of supremacy at Yale" to the interest which lies behind "Pole Star for This Year". It seems even longer when one stops to consider that it leads through the terrible and wonderful days of the exiles when the pages of *transition* were being filled with manifestoes on "The Revolution of the Word"; when Harry Crosby and Hemingway were drunk in the streets of Saragossa and "their mouths are hard they say *que cosa*". MacLeish ("a few years older, but still affiliated with this present generation") had not left Paris when Cowley, Josephson and the rest began issuing their blasts against the exiles (though still in the pages of *transition*), impressed by the fact that

> 'Tis said all poetry must and can
> Resolve the ways of God to Man.
> And yet when Ford or Morgan raise their face
> Poets paddle off to some french watering place.[1]

It seems an even longer way when one remembers that it leads through the period when the exiles all returned, all but a few who died quietly away in the neighborhood of the rue de Fleurus or gradually got more interested in Major Douglas than in poetry. This was the period when the poets briefly discovered the romance of the pioneer Middle West, of "Tenochtitlan", of the Civil War and the pre-War-between-the-States South. Finally, this long way leads through the battle of the books, that curious scholastic debate about literature and propaganda which is only now dying out. Through that battle MacLeish fought valiantly for the Poet against the Propagandist, only to find in the end, not that the others were right and he wrong, but that these two words did not stand for real people at all; he did not find that "Background with Revolutionaries" was false, but that the poet was responsible for more of the uses of his poetry than he had imagined; and this discovery made it impossible for him not to accept these responsibilities, without running the danger of ceasing to be a poet altogether.

There does not, certainly, seem to be much order in such a career. Yet the order is there, and the appearance of confusion is the result of concentrating on the part of MacLeish's poetry about which he has always been least concerned, sometimes, perhaps, too little concerned for his own peace of mind. That consistency can probably be most simply illustrated from two articles separated by twenty years. The first was an editorial written by MacLeish as Chairman of the *Yale Literary Magazine* entitled "For Reformers Only." The argument of this editorial seems a curious one today, concerned as it is with the challenge to Yale and the other "older and poorer" eastern universities of the great western educational "plants" (Nebraska is instanced) which "are solving the problems of practical education"; and some of the battle plans proposed seem a little too heroic, as even their author realized. For having advocated that Yale ignore the "practical" side of education, which was found to include economics, journalism, history and the drama, and become a "classical seminary", he observed that "certain members of the Corporation would undoubtedly indulge prejudices, however unreasonable, against the destruction of the new laboratories. . . ." The point of the editorial is, however, not the argument, but MacLeish's insistence that what was of value at Yale was "the life of the College . . . the source which differentiates Yale from the universities whose first presidents are not as yet grandsires." Out of the atmosphere of the college, "of ivy and elm, of dreams and aspirations" came the power to create intellectual background and develop imagination. "We can," he said, warming to his conclusion, "preserve this priceless gift only by accepting the world we see here on the Campus . . . idealizing it if need be, but never cheapening it, never brightening our old mahogany with new enamel. . . . The phrase 'Old Yale' is more than the minor chord of sentiment. It is the reminder of our past, the explanation of our present and the necessity of our future. *In hoc signo vinces*."

If one separate out of this faith the unconscious snobbery which confuses the ability to use a tradition intelligently with having presidents who died in 1707 and make due allowance for the author's age and the 1890's air which he had acquired by living in the very tradition he was defending, there remains the essential MacLeish. There remains, that is, a man passionately devoted to the "creation of background and the development of the imagination", believing that without the one "a man is a barbarian; without the other he is a machine." Strip this essay of the means proposed and it comes down to a statement that for the author the education that counts most is the training of the responses to the thing seen or the idea, and these responses are ultimately a matter of what, for want of a more precise term, we call the emotions. In the early and simplified form of this conviction, MacLeish scorns not only "the 'science' of business management" which he was to scorn in the Yale he looked at again twenty years later, but also history, economics and drama. We may object—as will he—to the beliefs which seemed to him then the logical intellectual formulation for his sense that the most important aspect of consciousness was the apprehension of the simple, sensuous and passionate qualities of "the flowing away of the world". The point is not, however, and never has been with MacLeish, the intellectual formulation. The point is that the whole argument of this editorial springs from just that sense of the importance of the simple, sensuous and passionate.

The second article which illustrates this underlying consistency is an essay on "New-Yale" which MacLeish wrote for *Fortune* in 1934.[2] It is based on exactly the same feeling. Its author is, however, twenty years older, a far more complex and more sophisticated person. The measure of that difference is the substitution for "The phrase 'Old Yale' is more than the minor chord of sentiment" of the simple title: "New-Yale." But the same fundamental feelings are there, and some of the more superficial; they can be seen curiously mixed when MacLeish writes of "the most moving memories of a Yale graduate before the War": "he will remember the campus on one of those early spring nights when the raw taste of the harbor hung just under the smell of the new grass in the flukes of air. . . . He will remember the ironic ceremonies of the fence oration when that piece of much publicized realty was bequeathed by the sophomore class to the freshman class and by the freshman class, with equal irony, received". MacLeish himself gave the fence oration for the sophomore class in 1913.

But for all the greater complexity and precision of responses, and for all the sophistication of twenty years' intellectual development, the standard by which MacLeish judges the new Yale is the standard by which he judged it in 1915: How much better is Yale equipped, not to train people in "useful knowledge" nor to bring up what he called in 1915 "the decorous candidates for membership in the exclusive clubs of New York and Philadelphia" (the phrase becomes in 1934 "the vulgar manners of Park Avenue"), but to provide people an opportunity to develop attitudes which will make it possible for them to react like adults to what they know and what they will find after college. And his judgment of the physical alteration of the Yale campus is based on the same fundamental attitude which made him find a virtue in the "ivy and elm" of Old Yale, a virtue which no amount of Nebraska money could reproduce:

> As of the spring of the year 1934, therefore, the educational contribution of the Harkness Yale may be put down as quite precisely nothing. . . . Its novelty is the novelty of its buildings and the altered life they impose. And its creators are the creators of its brick and stone and steel . . . in the end, colleges, library, gymnasium and Gothic all come down to one thing only. And that one thing is the $60,000,000 which put them up . . . its measure is a measure accurately expressed in sums of cash. And sums of cash so allocated as to prefer the physical expansion of the university to its intellectual life.

In the very process of learning what this new Yale was, MacLeish was seeking to understand qualities rather than statistics:

> What is relevant is the quality, the *feel of the new institution*. . . . The quality of the new Yale, architecturally and physically considered, is the quality of the decade which produced the skyscrapers of New York, erected the great houses of the California litoral and installed the gilded plumbing of the banlieu of Oyster Bay.

He sees a hope for education in his sense of the term in the greater personal contact between scholar and student which should result if the university develops what he thinks is the logical corollary to the college plan: the tutorial system. But even that, he would like to believe, will be more the product of "the educational revolution which dates from 1916" (MacLeish was graduated in 1915) than of the new Yale. For to the MacLeish who found the "ivy and elm" of Old Yale so vital a part of its educational equipment this imposing physical expansion represents just that process of "brightening its old mahogany with new enamel" against which he had protested in 1915.

At either end, then, of this twenty-year period one finds MacLeish with the same purpose, the same fundamental standard and the same means of approaching the external world. This underlying consistency is the result of his having sought always for himself the quality of his experience ("[the poet] can satisfy the needs of his nature only by laboring to fix in some artificial substance of sounds and signs a moment, an aspect, of the flowing away of the world"); of his having judged others by the strength and completeness of the response they made to the ideas they professed to believe in ("unless we can not only perceive, but also *feel*, the race of men to be more important than one man, we are merely fighting back against the water"); and of his having measured institutions by their ability to provide an opportunity for the cultivation of these responses.

Always the thing MacLeish has clung to as most real, as the thing he could trust, has been his apprehension of the quality of things, of their nature, not as a concept, as a unit in a logical intellectual structure, but as a felt experience. "The condition of any writer's success as an intelligence is the refusal to think as everyone about him thinks and the ceaseless effort to arrive at personal perceptions." This way sometimes seems, however, extraordinarily difficult in our world:

So then there is no speech that can resolve
Their texture to clear thought and enter them.
The Virgin of Chartres whose bleaching bones still
          wear
The sapphires of her glory knew a word— . . .
And there were words in Rome once and one time
Words at Eleusis.
          Now there are no words
Nor names to name them and they will not speak
But grope against his groping touch and throw
The long unmeaning shadow of themselves
Across his shadow and resist his sense.

Nevertheless, using a name as a device for putting things in categories, even at its best, is no alternative; for "poetry, like any other art, can only reach its highest level in a universe of which man is the center. In a human world. And the world centered about man was destroyed by the impulses which produced the world explicable by science":

          He can count
Oceans in atoms and weigh out the air
In multiples of one and subdivide
Light to its numbers.
          If they will not speak
Let them be silent in their particles.
Let them be dead and he will lie among
Their dust and cipher them. . . .

And so, since "the poet . . . must always attack his world factually and physically, not abstractly, not in intellectual concepts", MacLeish comes back to what seems most real to him and to the only way he knows to communicate even a part of that reality.

Thus a system of beliefs, a dogma, a logical structure of concepts, has never been adopted by him for its own sake; its self-consistency or its consistency with its fellows or its predecessors has always been for him a secondary consideration. He has adopted it or rejected it accordingly as it served or failed to serve the slowly but steadily expanding wisdom of his emotions. For the ideas have been the by-product of a growth in sensibility. That growth has been slow but continuous (at least since 1923), and it has been accompanied by a steady search for the set of ideas which would make sense of, which would focus most sharply, the sensuous and emotional values which he has always felt strongly and which, as he has developed, have become clearer to him.

MacLeish's development as a poet cannot, then, be understood by tracing the sequence of his philosophic allegiances, because such development as he has shown has been a matter of growth in the range, complexity, and precision of his responses and in his awareness of the exact nature of these responses. This development is the only one that matters to him and the only one that ought to matter to his critics. It was because almost everything but that seemed to interest his critics that he wrote, in the Foreword to *Poems* in 1933: "My development as a poet is of no interest to me and of even less interest, I should suppose, to anyone else." Taken literally, as Conrad Aiken pointed out in a fine review in the *New Republic*, that statement simply cannot be accepted. There is, indeed, less possibility of that statement's being true for MacLeish than for most poets, for MacLeish's poetry concerns itself extensively, not merely with the attempt to communicate his responses to things, but with the far more difficult task of tracing the growth of those responses. MacLeish's remark was not, of course, consciously or unconsciously, intended to be taken literally; it was intended to indicate that the significant grouping of his poems was not the chronological one, but the very skillful arrangement according to subject, in the widest sense of the word, used in *Poems*; this arrangement frequently ignores chronology. For example, the "Land's End" group of poems, all dealing with the same theme, range all the way from 1924 to 1930. The remark thus indicates that what matters *to MacLeish* in his poetry is not to be learned by taking the poems chronologically, abstracting from their "ideas", and then trying to "explain" the sequence thus obtained.

The key poem in the growth of MacLeish's sensibility up to the present is "The Hamlet of A. MacLeish". There for the first time he managed to state with some exactness the quality of the central response to life itself which is either (both metaphors are inexact) the core or the sum of all his other responses to the details of experience:

Night after night I lie like this listening.
Night after night I cannot sleep. I wake
Knowing something, thinking something has
          happened.
I have this feeling a great deal. I have
Sadness often. At night I have this feeling.
Waking I feel this pain as though I knew
Something not to be thought of, something
          unbearable.
I feel this pain at night as though some
Terrible thing had happened. . . .
Much of the time I do not think anything;
Much of the time I do not even notice.
And then speaking, closing a door, I see
Strangely as though I almost saw now, some
Shape of things I have always seen, the sun
White on a house and the windows open and
          swallows
In and out of the wallpaper, the moon's face
Faint by day in a mirror; I see some
Changed thing that is telling, something that almost
Tells—and this pain then, then this pain. And no
Words, only these shapes of things that seem
Ways of knowing what it is I am knowing.[3]

This central feeling of pain, this sense of the inadequacy to their professions of human attitudes and of the inexplicable instability of the present, this despair, is the common denominator which runs through all his responses, unifying them. It can unify, in a wonderful poem like "You, Andrew Marvell", such apparently disparate elements as the personal life, civilization and nature itself:

And here face downward in the sun
To feel how swift how secretly
The shadow of the night comes on.

But it can be seen everywhere also in the less ambitious poems where MacLeish is trying to realize for the reader his responses to the details of his experience. You will find it, for example, in an emotionally characteristic and beautifully precise poem like "The End of the World":

Quite unexpectedly as Vasserot
The armless ambidexterian was lighting
A match between his great and second toe
And Ralph the lion was engaged in biting
The neck of Madam Sossman while the drum
Pointed, and Teeny was about to cough
In waltz-time swinging Jocko by the thumb—
Quite unexpectedly the top blew off:
And there, there overhead, there, there, hung over
Those thousands of white faces, those dazed eyes,
There in the starless dark the poise, the hover,
There with vast wings across the canceled skies,
There in the sudden blackness the black pall
Of nothing, nothing, nothing—nothing at all.

You will find it also in the fine close of "Yacht for Sale":

My youth is
Made fast
To the dock
At Marseilles
Rotting away
With a chain to her mast . . .
It's easy to see
She was frail in the knee
And too sharp in the bow—
You can see now.

And you will find it in any of the group beginning with "Land's End" in *Poems*. All these poems, then, are peripheral to this central feeling; they are quite inexplicable unless they are seen in the larger context of which this feeling is the core. That is, incidentally, why everyone, with the possible exception of Malcolm Cowley, was talking so irrelevantly in the controversy over "Frescoes".

The fact that MacLeish feels this way may be "explained" in the terminology of other modes of apprehension. One may, if it serves his purposes, "explain" that MacLeish was brought up in a dying culture, possessing rich and familiar traditions which were naturally attractive to him, but with a set of fundamental beliefs which are not adequate vehicles, in our time, for any sensitive person's responses. That the fragmentary beginnings of new cultures around us are as crude and unpolished by long usage and constant loving handling as a new haft which has not "fitted the palms of many". And one may add that T. S. Eliot taught poetry a diction and a way of communicating the frustration of a man born between these two particular worlds,[4] and thus made possible, or at least much easier, the complete expression of the individual variant on this theme.[5]

Against such an explanation MacLeish has rebelled constantly:

Why must I
Say I suffer? . . . or write out these words
. . . . for solemn lettered fools
To judge if I said neatly what I said?—

And he has frequently spoken with considerable feeling against the critiquins, those "sterile little pedants whom contemporary criticism has bred". It was in this mood that he wrote his fine saying about the defensive position to which poetry has been driven by the doctrinaire Marxists, a "position no less danger-

ous because it is also ridiculous. The lady treed by a sow is not the less in peril because the sow is an object of derision."

The intellectual abstraction from life of this critical method has always seemed to him a business of throwing overboard the cargo in order to save the ship. Everything that really matters to MacLeish is left out, for however much this method explains, it explains nothing away: the feeling is still there with its pain, for all that this learned explanation seems to ignore it. The futility of substituting this "explanation" for his statement is vividly present to him; and, since he feels with such passion, the uses of their intellectual aspect are not always apparent to him. When the uses of this aspect of things are not apparent to him, he does not see it as a complement to his way, but as the attempt to substitute for his careful poem an idea stripped of all its emotional connotations. So seen, of course, the intellectual explanation is an incredible piece of stupidity.

And sometimes the expounders of the intellectual aspect of things, blind in their turn, are trying to substitute their explanation. The rather silly *New Masses* review of *Poems* is a good example; as one reads its confident flippancies about its own irrelevant paraphrases of the poems, one realizes afresh the solid good sense of MacLeish's remark that, so far as the poetry as such is concerned, "interpretation is almost always vain. We can never, for example, know anything worth knowing about the *Chanson de Roland*. But we can . . . endow it with the apparent vivacity of our own recognition. We can save it from becoming an acknowledged historical fact in the haze back of the last horseman. And the same thing is true in a measure of the works of living writers." The incompleteness of that view depends on the fact that poetry itself has other uses than its purely poetic ones, important as those are. But it is perhaps as well that a poet should not concern himself with these other uses.

There must of course, even in the poet's view, be ideas, beliefs firmly held; but the essence of beliefs is the way they are held. It is the feeling deeply about them that matters; for ideas are not of value in themselves; they are valuable only as the bearers of feeling. Hence a real belief is "not to be had for a word or a week's wishing"; it is impossible for a belief so gained to be made emotionally a part of one.

This clear realization of the necessity for living up to one's ideas emotionally has led MacLeish, in a kind of desperation, to value deeply his own beliefs. This may seem paradoxical, but it is the fact that once an idea has come to life for him because he has oriented it to his feeling, it comes to have a kind of symbolic value for him and the process of shifting his ideas, of establishing a new symbol, produces a struggle which involves his whole personality. The thing which has kept him going has been his humility, his absolute refusal to allow any pride or any opinion to stand between him and the evidence his talent for feeling offers to his observation.

It is for this reason that MacLeish's career, considered in terms of the ideas he has held, has the appearance of being a series of unconnected allegiances. Its consistency depends on the realization that he has sought always for a more complete consciousness of the feeling which he is beginning to define in "The Hamlet of A. MacLeish"—not some approximation of it—and for the verbal correlative which would communicate that feeling. This search, its motive being what it is, has frequently created myths; made, that is, out of the ideas which for the time being were the intellectual residences of this central feeling, a kind of religious symbol. One can follow this mytho-poetic process from the beginning. In 1915 the old Yale atmosphere of "ivy and elm, of dreams and aspirations" was a part of his myth. Most of the rest of it, as one can see easily by reading his poems and short stories in the *Yale Literary Magazine*, was not his at all, but was composed of the views and values of Robert Louis Stevenson, seasoned with a touch of Masefield and the pre-Raphaelites. And this myth is just visible in 1934 when he noticed generously "the young professors and instructors [at Yale] who are fired with a vital purpose" and imagined to himself an intellectual renaissance at Yale coming as a revulsion to the "new Yale". This renaissance may have occurred, for the reasons MacLeish suggests or for other reasons. That is not the point; the point is that for MacLeish the idea of this renaissance became an emotional symbol, a factual home for the positive feeling by which he measured the "new Yale" and found it wanting.

One can see this same process going on in his attitude toward the war. He remembers his own experiences on the Marne and his feelings about his friends; he remembers, above all, Kenneth being shot down over Schoore in 1918

> I had not slept for knowing
> He too, dead, was a stranger in that land
> And felt beneath the earth in the wind's flowing
> A tightening of roots and would not understand,
> Remembering lake winds in Illinois,
> That strange wind.

Thus there were feelings for him attached to the idea of the War as an heroic and brave adventure such that he rebelled against the dispassionate historical analysis of it which he dubbed The Second World War. The First World War was the War as those who took part in it had felt it to be as they took part in it. Many of them died feeling that way; and "Is it perhaps conceivable that the measure of vanity in a man's death is to be found not afterwards in a history which to him has no existence, but presently in the circumstances in which his death is met?" Feeling so, he wrote to those who had died in the war about those living today:

> As for the gents they have joined the American Legion:
>
> Belts and a brass band and the ladies' auxiliaries:
> The Californians march in the OD silk:
>
> We are all acting again like civilized beings:
> People mention it at tea . . .
>
> You can rest now in the rain in the Belgian meadow—
> Now that it's all explained away and forgotten:
> Now that the earth is hard and the wood rots:
>
> Now that you are dead . . .

That First World War had a value for him out of all proportion to its historical validity, and no amount of cold reason about economic causes or passionate shouting about the horrors of war, calculated to disgust people with it, could make him want to forget that First World War.[6]

When Malcolm Cowley, writing, at least at first, with sympathy and understanding, suggested that this symbol did not serve for all one felt, since there were the dead of the next war to be thought of, and suggested that we put over the graves of those who died in the last war: *they died bravely, they died in vain*; when this occurred, one could see MacLeish beginning to move toward another symbol which would make place for both his feeling about the First World War and Cowley's concern for the result of the War, which MacLeish felt too:

> Obviously, standing here upon the little heap which time forever pushes up to give a better perspective of the past—obviously you and I, alive in the year 1933 and looking back—obviously we can say in your fine phrase: "they died bravely, they died in vain." The history of the post-war world proves they died in vain.

But one can also realize, reading his "Lines for an Interment" and his fine letter which I have just quoted, what profound feelings had to be detached from the old symbol before this change was possible. Indeed, it was three years before that new symbol was established and in "Speech to those who say Comrade" the comradeship of the old soldiers remembering "Their twentieth year and the metal odor of danger" became a part of that larger brotherhood which is "the rich and the rarest giving of life and the most valued" and which includes now also

> The puddlers
> Scorched by the same flame in the same foundries:
> Those who have spit on the same boards with the
> blood in it;
> Ridden the same rivers with green logs:
> Fought the police in the parks of the same cities:
> Grinned for the same blows: the same flogging: . . .
> Those that have hidden and hunted and all such—
> Fought together: labored together: they carry the
> Common look like a card and they pass touching.

The bitterest public quarrel of MacLeish's career was the result of his opponent's—and indeed his own—failure to realize the function in his poetry of these mytho-poetic symbols. The symbol in that case was America, and one must go back a little to see how it caused misunderstanding. MacLeish had never lost the memory of the America he had known as a child and as a young man, the America which is so remembered in "The Farm", and "Eleven". That other America which bulked so large in the eyes of the exiles, an America debauched by industrialism, with no roots down in the soil, with no traditions, appears in his poetry around 1928 with such poems as "& Forty-Second Street", "Critical Observations" and "Aeterna Poetae Memoria". It was this feeling and feelings like it which drove so many American poets abroad in these years. They were trying to go some place where industrialism had not completely destroyed civilization, where there were still traditions and "peoples". This feeling was never dominant in MacLeish's poetry, but its presence is plain. Soon, however, he turned once more to the America which had seemed valuable to him, and finally in "American Letter", the merging of this feeling for America with the feeling for a land far off begins. On the one hand

> America is West and the wind blowing.
> America is a great word and the snow,
> A way, a white bird, the rain falling,
> A shining thing in the mind and the gull's call;

on the other,

> A land far off, alien, smelling of palm-trees
> And the yellow gorse at noon in the long calms.

The merging, however, has just begun, the emotional problem only just been faced:

> This our land, this is our ancient ground—
> The raw earth, the mixed bloods and the strangers,
> The different eyes, the wind, and the heart's change.
> These we will not leave though the old call us.
> This is our country-earth, our blood, our kind.
> Here we will live our years till the earth blind us—
> The wind blows from the east. The leaves fall.
> Far off in the pines a jay rises.
> The wind smells of haze and the wild ripe apples.
> I think of the masts at Cette and the sweet rain.

Around this kernel of remembered feelings and new apprehensions there began gradually to accrete other feelings; gradually the feelings of the exile began to blend with the new feelings. Prominent among these new feelings was a sense of the greater importance of the common man, of the simple folk who actually do the work and have the experience at first hand:

> but I
> Fought in those battles! These were my own deeds!
> These names he writes of mouthing them out as a
>     man would
> Names in Herodotus—dead and their wars to read—
> These were my friends: these dead my com-
>     panions: . . .
> I: poor: blind in the sun: I have seen
> With these eyes those battles: I saw Montezuma:
> I saw the armies of Mexico marching. . . .

This same feeling is strong in the "Wildwest" and "Burying ground by the ties" sections of "Frescoes". For it is in "Frescoes" that the new symbol first achieves complete expression; and it is "Frescoes" which produced the quarrel.

The first fresco is of the figure of America:

> She lies on her left side her flank golden:
> Her hair is burned black with the strong sun:
> The scent of her hair is of rain in the dust on her
>     shoulders:
> She has brown breasts and the mouth of no other
>     country.

Then come "Wildwest", "Burying ground by the ties", and an attack on the artist who prefers the "land far off, alien", which had meant so much to MacLeish when he wrote "American Letter":

> He prefers a tidier stream with a terrace for trippers
>     and
> Cypresses mentioned in Horace or Henry James:
> He prefers a country where everything carries the
>     name of a
> Countess or real king or an actual palace or
> Something in Prose and the stock prices all in Italian.

This fresco is followed by the counterpart of the praise of the little folk, an ironic eulogy of the "Empire Builders":

> This is Mister Harriman making America:
> Mister-Harriman-is-buying-the-Union-Pacific-at-
>     Seventy:
> The Santa Fe is shining in his hair.

Then finally comes the satire on those others who do not share with the little folk their feeling for the reality of America, the dogmatic revolutionaries. Before considering this passage, it would be well to glance back over the feelings which can now be seen to have been gathered for MacLeish around the symbol of America. There is the feeling for "our country-earth, our blood, our kind", backed by MacLeish's love of the American country side; there is the populist feeling for democracy, with its sympathy for the forgotten man and its scorn of men who have too much money; there is the distrust of all those who do not understand the real America; of rich men, and revolutionaries, and foreigners; and there is the difficulty of reconciling himself to the fact that so much of America either lacks a tradition altogether or has an obviously faked one: "Neither a place it is nor a blood name."

From the beginning the "Niggers with narrow heels" and the "Bright Jews" had seemed to him one of the ironies of New York; and the emphasis on "family" and the mild, bridge-table anti-semitism of the upper middle classes must inevitably have been a part of his early environment, making him feel that the America he saw was a parody of the nation and race which ought to go to make a "people".

> Black white yellow and red and the fawn-colored
> Bastards all of them, slick in the wrist, gone

> Yank with a chewed cigar and a hat and a button,
> Talking those Inglish Spich with the both ends cut:
> And the New York Art and the real South African
>     Music
> (Written in Cincinnati by Irish Jews). . . .

By the time of "Frescoes" much of this exile feeling about America had been modified, but the feeling that revolutionaries, and perhaps particularly Jewish revolutionaries, did not understand the real America was still there, and their assurance that they did was a source of irritation to him. To him it appeared to be just one more attempt to substitute for a feeling an intellectual formulation:

> Dialectical hope
> And the kind of childish utopia
> Found in small boys' schools—
> Destiny written in Rules:
> Life as the Teacher left it. . . .

The mild anti-semitism which he brought with him from his past was just one more weapon of satire to be used against the schoolboy assurance of these people:

> Also Comrade Levine who writes of America
> Most instructively having in 'Seventy-four
> Crossed to the Hoboken side on the Barclay Street
>     Ferry.

Michael Gold, reviewing "Frescoes" in the *New Republic*, took the anti-semitism of this section for a fundamental attitude, and raised the cry of Fascism; one might as well call fascist all those mild and silly middle-class people who will not stay at a hotel frequented by Jews. That attitude is ugly and stupid, but it is not the product of a systematized racial cult, and to suppose so is to suppose that America is already fascist. MacLeish not meaning or perhaps not quite realizing that he was inclined to think, that all church-going and doctrinaire revolutionaries were likely to be Jews, saw Mr. Gold's review as "the hysteria with which the literary Marxist attacks and exterminates (as he believes) his literary enemies . . ." and finished his comment on the review[7] by stating precisely what he had intended by his satire: "Nothing which does not conform to the official dogmas will be endured [by literary Marxists] and any man who questions them, and certainly any man who makes fun of them, will be strung up to the nearest lamp post of Marxist invective." Because he knew how unimportant the anti-semitism was to the real point of the satire, and because he did not want his poem misunderstood again as Gold had misunderstood it, MacLeish quietly changed "Levine" to "Devine" when the "Frescoes" was republished in *Poems*. Perhaps, too, he was beginning to examine more closely that feeling of his about Jews and Niggers—not this Jew or that Nigger, but the idea of each as a group to which his traditional feeling was attached—and to realize that this unexamined feeling in him was emotionally illogical and, once one got beyond the poet's use of poetry, dangerous.

The use of this symbol of America with all its corollaries in MacLeish's poetry was exactly similar to the use of the First World War. The fact that MacLeish believed the symbolic "well known New York literary type" did not understand the America about which he felt so deeply, no more proves him anti-semitic than his emotional loyalty to the World War his brother died believing in proves him a lover of war. And the fate of those two symbols has been much the same. The comradeship of the war has been absorbed into the larger symbol of a greater brotherhood. And as more and more of the unconscious superstitions of his cultural background have disappeared from MacLeish's America, the focus of his attention has been less and less on those who mean well and sometimes are nonetheless ignorant and arrogant, and more and more on the common people whom, in their sometimes blundering way, these revolutionaries are trying to help too. "Not myself, my soul, my glycerine-dropping eyes, but these unknown and nameless men, anonymous under this sky, small in those valleys and far-off and forever there." The focus has been more and more on those who are addressed in "Speech to a crowd", and "Speech to those who say Comrade", and on what will help them:

> Liberty and pride and hope
> And every guide-mark of the mind
> That led our blindness once has vanished.
> This star will not. Love's star will not.

And on the possibilities of danger for them:

> The people invent their oppressors: they wish to
> believe in them.
> They wish to be free of their freedom: released from
> their liberty:—

Until now that shift is complete and in "Speech to Scholars" MacLeish identifies himself with them and calls on the scholars, both for their own sakes and for the sake of those who need their help, to "Arise! Enlist! Take arms and fight!"

I have dwelt on these last two symbols not only because they illustrate from MacLeish's later work the function of ideas in his poetry, but because they show clearly the change in MacLeish's emotions behind these symbols. This change has taken place in spite of the survival of many of the familiar attitudes, including, though it is less prominent, much of the central attitude of his earlier poetry, that sense of the frequent inadequacy of human emotions to human ideas, which is still present in poems like "Speech to those who say Comrade". This continuity of fundamental feeling, is one of the great rewards of MacLeish's approach to the world. His sensibility may develop—it has done so continuously up to the present—but there is never any sharp break. There is never the attempt to invent the feelings appropriate to a new idea, which is seen so frequently in people for whom the idea is more important than the attitude toward it, and which has been the cause of so much bad poetry. There is an organic and continuing relationship in MacLeish's poetry because he has so very rarely been false to what he felt, no matter what the cost. And the cost has sometimes been considerable. MacLeish knows well that "the creative intelligence . . . requires a transparence of mind, a naked sensitiveness, which puts it outside the protection of the stoic arm." Yet to present the poem embodying this naked sensitiveness to the kind of criticism MacLeish has frequently met, knowing that he has deliberately cleared the poem of all hedges and dodges, is no easy thing to do.

But the change, the development, which may be followed by studying the career of these two symbols, has been considerable. It indicates, I think, that the time is approaching, if it is not already here, when MacLeish will be faced by the necessity of a new definition of his central feeling similar to the new definition stated in "The Hamlet of A. MacLeish". For the cumulative effect of this gradual but steady change in MacLeish's feelings is such as to have shifted their center. The readjustment which began with his return to America appears to be approaching or to have reached a temporary completion. If that guess be correct, then we may look for a poem which will do for MacLeish's present attitude what "The Hamlet of A. MacLeish" did for his attitude in 1928, and what, on a smaller scale, "Frescoes" did for his attitude in 1933. Unless, and there is evidence for this, one chooses to believe that this kind of

definition does not come until MacLeish has begun to advance beyond the attitude dealt with in the definition.

*Notes*

1. Or to Rapallo.
2. There is in the Yale Library the manuscript of an early version of this article. Since the published essay is more impersonal and its author's feelings are communicated by a pervasive irony which it is not easy to convey by short quotation, I have frequently resorted to the early version for my illustrations.
3. The significance of this key passage to "The Hamlet" is indicated by its early career. It began as "Memories of A——" (1926), and appeared, substantially as it stands, under the title of "Fragment of a Biography" in the first *American Caravan* (1927), before being finally incorporated into "The Hamlet".
4. The resemblance between MacLeish's position in our world and Matthew Arnold's position in his might be worth working out, not merely for historical reasons, but because they resemble each other as poets. Their resemblance as poets is suggested by the similarity of section five, particularly the middle passage, of "The Hamlet of A. MacLeish" to "Stanzas from the Grande Chartreuse"; or of "Land's End" to "Rugby Chapel". Indeed, the image of land's end, which is the central image for this group of poems, has much the same function in his poetry as the Dover Beach image has in Arnold's. It is almost as if MacLeish recognized that resemblance when, beginning to move away from the attitude of "The Hamlet", he wrote " 'Dover Beach'—a note to that poem."
5. The influence of Eliot's means, insofar as means are separable from ends, has left its mark on MacLeish as well as on his contemporaries. "The new generation," as he wrote in 1925, "is first and foremost Mr. Eliot. It is an introspective, self-conscious, sensitive, doubtful, deeply stirred generation, a deflected generation compelled to difficult utterance, a passionate generation afflicted with that *maladie du siècle*—'ne pas vouloir être dupe.'"
6. The importance of his brother Kenneth's death in determining the value for MacLeish of this version of the War is perhaps best indicated by the fact that "Lines for an Interment" (from which the above passage is taken) is a reworking, with a more general referent, of a poem published in the *Nation* four years earlier and entitled "October 14, 1928 / For K. MacL."
7. These remarks were made ostensibly as a general observation on "American intellectual Marxism", and it is only a deduction that MacLeish was thinking of Gold's review of "Frescoes" when he wrote them. The connection is so clear, however, as to leave little doubt of MacLeish's reference.

## CLEANTH BROOKS
### From "Frost, MacLeish, and Auden"
*Modern Poetry and the Tradition*
1939, pp. 116–20

The basic method and impulse of MacLeish's poetry, in fact, resembles that of Carl Sandburg. There are great differences to be sure. Certainly MacLeish's verse reveals a competence which makes any comparison of the two seem at first glance absurd. Yet there is a basic resemblance. And an examination of this common element may provide us with the most fruitful approach to MacLeish's poetry.

MacLeish, like Sandburg, deals in a detemporized past. His longer poems are rather consistently "histories" and the world which they reveal is timeless—with the emphasis, not like Sandburg's on a timeless present, but on a timeless past. Sandburg tends to be brash and topical, and he is obsessed with the immediacy of his point, namely, that the real past was the world of ourselves—the trivial, tawdry, and yet somehow glorious world that we know in common experience. MacLeish has more delicacy and restraint. His imagery is richer, his canvas broader, his control of rhythms far more profound.

Compare with "Four Preludes on Playthings of the Wind" MacLeish's "Men":

> Our history is grave noble and tragic
> We trusted the look of the sun on the green leaves
> We built our towns of stone with enduring ornaments
> We worked the hard flint for basins for water. . . .

The poem continues with a recitation of a miscellany of items typical of the life of men:

> We planted corn grapes apple-trees rhubarb . . .
> We believed in the promises made by the brows of women . . .
> We fought at the dikes in the bright sun for the pride of it . . .

to conclude with the lines,

> Many cities are gone and their channel broken
> We have lived a long time in this land and with honor.

The poem is typical of all men everywhere. It might be spoken by Assyrians or Greeks or modern Americans. It is a tribute to MacLeish's skill in the use of imagery that the items, though sharp and distinct, give no clue—do not date or locate (and therefore, in this case, limit) the poem.

The images, of course, do a great deal more than this. They establish and sustain a certain tone. The history has its dignity and its simple seriousness. Man's foolishness and knavery are an integral part of that history—

> We were drunk and lay with our fine dreams in the straw . . .

They need not be, and are not, glossed over. In turn, the frank and even casual mention of such items removes any tinge of vaingloriousness from the recital. The poem is thoroughly successful; but the technique of the poem (and it is typical of MacLeish) is stringently limited.

Consider the way in which the poem is built. The poem is made up of a series of parallel statements, apparently stacked together with no effort at subordination or order of any sort. The naïve parallelism is, of course, part of the artistic method: it sorts with the character of the men who speak, men who see no pattern in their history and who have no point to make but merely set forward, simply and seriously, the memorable items of that history.

Thoroughly parallel to this method of organization is the piling up of nouns and noun phrases in *Conquistador*:

> Palms ragged with sea-gust . . .
>         all careened with the
> Weed in the rusty chains and the keelsons splintered . . .
> Bleaching with sun and the . . .
>             nights in . . .
>                 elegant knees
>         like the
> Girls in Spain and the sand still hot from the sun and the
> Surf slow . . .
>         wind over . . .
>             palm-trees sweeping the . . .

Or consider the imagery in "The Epistle to Be Left in the Earth":

> The earth is round
>             there are springs under the orchards
> The loam cuts with a blunt knife
>             beware of
> Elms in thunder . . .

It is the kind of imagery that dominates long sections of the "Hamlet" and "The Pot of Earth," and is the staple of the "Land's End" poems.

This piling up of separate items of detail is often, on the level of direct evocation, extremely successful, and in many of the poems it is dramatically justified. An index of its potentialities is one means of arriving at the scope and limitations of the poet himself. For MacLeish is in one sense an Imagist—though he surpasses the poets conventionally known as Imagists at every point.

For example, the passage quoted above from *Conquistador*—and many other passages from that poem—makes the Imagists seem very thin indeed. Moreover, in *Conquistador* the structure of detail set upon detail, loosely held together with and's and then's, admirably suits the conditions of narration. The succession of images, each momentarily held and illuminated for an instant by the mind, represents very well the process of memory as the old soldier lives back over his campaign.

But the poem is essentially reverie, not drama; the final effect pathos, not tragedy.

The point of this observation is not to censure *Conquistador* for failing to be something which the poet did not attempt. The poem is what it is, and surely must be judged one of the finer accomplishments of modern American poetry. The point of the remark is to define more narrowly the terms in which the poem achieves its success.

MacLeish's poetry, in this poem and elsewhere, is essentially a poetry of the noun, not of the verb. His images, far more than those of the Imagists, do tend to become symbols; but the symbols are relatively static, lack dynamic quality. MacLeish's sensibility is rich but lacks principles. His poetry does not have the intricacy of idea necessary to the poetry of a poet like Yeats. One may sum up by saying that his poetry lacks dramatic tension.

This fact may explain why his successful poems so often deal with a primitive people going about the essential concerns of human life, and why the imagery stresses only those things which are the common denominator of all peoples. In such "histories," there are no meanings, no interpretations, apart from the fact that the histories are "grave noble and tragic." Or to make the application to *Conquistador*, there can be no meaning to the history of the conquest of Mexico apart from the meaning of the campaign to Bernal Diaz as a man.

The poet asks in the prologue to this poem:

> What are the dead to us in the world's wonder?
> Why (and again now) on their shadowy beaches
> Pouring before them the slow painful blood
> Do we return to force the truthful speech of them
> Shrieking like snipe along their gusty sand . . .

The lines are noble, but no truth is forced from the dead. The parallel to Odysseus is superficial: what Bernal brings back from Hades is a personal possession—not wisdom but memory. The poem in essence is lyric, and a very fine one it is, but it is not an epic of the conquest of Mexico.

## DAVID BULWER LUTYENS
### From "Archibald MacLeish:
### Poet of Philosophical Rationalism"
*The Creative Encounter*
1960, pp. 66–77

Archibald MacLeish, who has achieved eminence in public life as Assistant Secretary of State, Librarian of

Congress, Chairman and one of the founding members of U.N.E.S.C.O., is a figure of international renown, as well as a writer of rare intellectual distinction, critical acumen and profound philosophical speculation.

Yet, unfortunately for his reputation as a poet, especially among those critics who seek to found their aesthetic of modern poetry on a sharp distinction between the content, or subject-matter of verse, and the semantic aspects of a specific text, MacLeish, according to their standpoint, has been at times too inclined to sacrifice the verbal texture of his verse to the message he desired to convey, with a consequent impoverishment of his work's purely poetic quality.

At times, though the ideas he seeks to express may and, indeed, often do compel respectful attention for their intellectual acuteness, the language appears to fall short, in certain respects, of his own highest standards. This is especially true of his specifically political poetry: "America Was Promises", "Empire Builders", "Speech to the Detractors", "Declaration", "Oil Painting of the Artist as the Artist", "Background with Revolutionaries", "Music and Drum", "Liberty", "Speech to Those Who Say Comrade". Others could be cited, but these are his most significant political poems for the light they throw on American society and the comment they make on American politics. Yet, this should be qualified, for, in "The Spanish Lie", he has achieved a political poem that stands out from the others for its quality of fervent feeling, for a sincere and deep compassion that goes beyond the political, and achieves an all-human quality, power and range:

> The tears of Madrid, of Barcelona, Valencia—
> The tears were not answered . . .
>
> The tears are dry on the faces.
> The blood is dry on the sand.
> The tears were not answered: the blood was not
>     answered.
> This will be answered.[1]

A passionate indictment of cruelty, brute force and injustice charges these simple words with an austere dignity. MacLeish was not content with voicing the evil of modern times. He was concerned to find a practical answer, and believed that he had discovered one in the programme of widespread economic and social reforms, instituted by Roosevelt. And how hampering political convictions can be to a poet, MacLeish reveals in these lines from his poem, "Invocation to the Social Muse":

> . . . poets, Fräulein, are persons of
> Known vocation following troops: they must sleep
>     with
> Stragglers from either prince of both views.
> The rules permit them to further the business of
>     neither.[2]

The comment that these lines make is illuminating, and they state a needful truth about the art of poetry and the nature of a poet. Yet, judged purely on linguistic grounds, the absence of arresting images and the slackness of the rhythm, do not seem altogether adequate to the content they are intended to convey. Furthermore, much of MacLeish's political poetry derives from the thesis he seeks to establish; it has lost some of its relevance, now that certain of the political issues, which provoked these poems, have become a thing of the past. ⟨. . .⟩

Even more than Hart Crane, MacLeish has integrated the creative myths of poetry with modern science. For, while Crane was by nature a mystic, MacLeish, a philosophical rationalist, sees science as the most potent source for viable values in a world, where, as it seems to him, the ancient myths, the old philosophies, former tenets of religion have

been, to a large extent, discredited. This key notion of his poetry is expressed in these terse and memorable lines:

> A world was ended when the womb
> Where girl held God became the tomb
> Where God lies buried in a man:
> Boticelli's image neither speaks nor can
> To our kind. His star-guided stranger
> Teaches no longer, by the child, the manger,
> The meaning of the beckoning skies.[3]

The two last lines reveal a pungent use of the poetic device of ellipsis. He sees the function of modern poets as the creation of new myths to meet the characteristic problems of twentieth-century life and culture:

> Poets, deserted by the world before,
> Turn round into the actual air:
> Invent the age! Invent the metaphor![4]

Not only must the modern poet, according to MacLeish, create a metaphor for contemporary life and experience, it is for his contemporaries that he must write, for only so can he bring his vision into accordance with the formative patterns of modern being and existence. This notion is crystallised in—

> I speak to my own time,
> To no time after.[5]

These lines express a scheme of values that could have been expressed almost as well in prose as in verse, but this does not lessen their intellectual validity. To assert the existence of values in an age of chaos and upheaval despite the holocausts and cruelties that mark our epoch, which has witnessed the sunset of humanism: this is the desideratum for which MacLeish strives:

> Works of soul—
> Pilgrimages through the desert to the sacred boulder:
> Through the mid night to the stroke of one!
> Works of grace! Works of wonder!
> All this have we done and more—
> And seen—what have we not seen—[6]

While aware of the evil of modern times, the corruption of standards, MacLeish has continued to affirm the dignity of man.

In his effort to define the position of man in the modern world, MacLeish has turned to the archetypal Biblical drama, Job, the most inspired poem of the ancient Hebrews, which raises the timeless philosophical problem of the nature of pain and suffering.

Job, in the Old Testament, is a symbol for man, who is overwhelmed by elemental and undeserved catastrophe. Job yearns to come to terms with God, yet God presents himself to Job in the guise of a revengeful, unjust and persecuting Deity.

So, in this modern version of the ancient drama, "J.B.", the happy, prosperous man, who is on good terms with his neighbours, loses his children in a series of grisly accidents. He is reduced to total destitution. His neighbours, seeking to understand the reasons why a pillar of society should have been felled by what appears to them to have been the hand of an unkind Providence, seek to compel him to deny his independent mind, his morally responsible attitude. But "J.B." refuses to be driven to despair. The Divine and Satanic protagonists of the original Biblical drama are here represented by two down-at-heels actors of a travelling road company of players, Mr. Zuss (referring to Zeus) and Nickles (referring to "Old Nick"). They are at once Greek chorus and ironic witnesses to the doom of the just man in an unjust world. The crucial passage of *J.B.*, a notable exposition of MacLeish's humanism—is:

> . . . I'd rather suffer
> Every unspeakable suffering God sends,
> Knowing it was I that suffered,

I that acted, I that chose,
Than wash my hands with yours in that
Defiling innocence. Can we be men
And make an irresponsible ignorance
Responsible for everything. I will not
Listen to you.[7]

The ordinary rhythms of speech are here packed with meaning and drive home MacLeish's philosophical speculation. The austere language serves, at all points of the drama, to underline the dramatic situation. *J.B.* is an example of how modern poetic drama should be written: the poetry arises from the situation, and serves to define it. Thus, the poetry inheres in the situation, the situation is resolved into the poetry. ⟨. . .⟩

In view of MacLeish's belief that the poet is evading the creative and imaginative challenge of modern poetic expression if he turns back to old myths instead of evolving new myths to meet the new patterns of experience and characteristic problems of our age, his desire to re-interpret "Job" may seem, to a certain degree, inconsistent with his theory of the task of poets and the function of poetry in our age. But in *J.B.* MacLeish has completely transformed the original Biblical drama: in the Bible, Job is a passive sufferer; in MacLeish's drama, "J.B." is an effective protagonist, challenging all values that are not the outcome of human choice and decision. Whereas "Job" is concerned with "being", *J.B.* is concerned with "doing": this insistence on choice is both profoundly contemporary and deeply existential. Behind this demand for knowledge lies the unhitched, restless, questing, anxious, probing mind of modern man, which, within the American context, MacLeish identifies (in a passage already quoted) with the mind of the American immigrant:

The immigrant mind is an unhitched mind. It sees the world as possibility, not barrier. . . . It is a mind filled with the new found world, in love with living.

In *J.B.* MacLeish makes an ancient myth a metaphor for an age without fixed values, lacking in absolute and permanent certitudes. This ability to re-think an old myth in terms of modern experience is what makes it one of the more exciting experiments in verse-drama in recent times. So discerning a producer as Elia Kazan, whose own mind is a questing, dynamic one, produced *J.B.* in the autumn of 1958 on Broadway. In reading the version of the play that appeared on Broadway, one is struck by the extent to which its pace has been accelerated and its rhythm tautened. May this not be because Elia Kazan has seen in this play of MacLeish an attempt to "invent the myth" and "create the metaphor" for an age when men are as much in need as ever of viable values. One of the reasons why MacLeish's best poetry commands respect is that it is both essentially and intentionally involved in a situation at a certain moment in world history. This is why MacLeish fulfils in a trenchant modern way Shelley's celebrated, if somewhat highflown definition of poets:

Poets are the hierophants of an unapprehended inspiration; the mirrors of the gigantic shadow which futurity casts upon the present.[8]

Another drama of poetic value is MacLeish's one-act play, *This Music Crept by Me on the Water.* The title is an obvious reference to these lines from Shakespeare's *Tempest*:

Where should this music be? i' th' air or th' earth?
It sounds no more: and, sure, it waits upon
Some God o' th' island. Sitting on a bank,
Weeping again the king my father's wreck,
This music crept by me upon the waters,

Allaying both the fury and the passion
With its sweet air.

(Act I, Scene II.)

In this play, MacLeish draws a picture of sophisticated Americans, weary of the "fury" and the "passion" of modern civilisation. They yearn for a peace, an order and a simplicity they cannot find among the distractions of modern urbanised life and society. The central idea of the drama is expressed in:

We cling to the skirts of suffering,
Like children to their mothers—hold
The hand that hurts our hand for fear
We'll lose ourselves unless it hurts us!
Making a virtue of our cowardice:
Pretending that a sense of sin and shame
Is holier than the happiness we fumble.[9]

Here, as in *J.B.*, MacLeish asserts that, despite the anguish, conflicts and torments of existence, man remains undefeated so long as he refuses to despair. The play is set in one of the attractive islands of the Antilles, which, like the enchanted island of Shakespeare's last sunset play, *The Tempest*, is a metaphor for that condition of being and of life, when men come to terms with nature and with themselves. It is an affirmation of MacLeish's distinctive humanism.

In view of the consistency between MacLeish's humanism and his political convictions, why does his specifically political poetry seem less satisfying, on an aesthetic level, than his speculative and metaphysical poems, or his best dramas? Do politics automatically inhibit the range of a poet's imagination? To answer this question, it is interesting to compare the political poetry of MacLeish with the political poetry of other poets of the same epoch as directly concerned with politics as he: notably Auden, Stephen Spender and Cecil Day Lewis. Though as responsive as MacLeish to the appeal of political convictions and as eager as he to make their verse a vehicle for the expression of their political ethos, they none the less achieved a political poetry that does not invite the same sort of strictures as too many of MacLeish's political poems are all too liable to provoke. This may be because, while they were members of an articulate opposition, with a restrictive following, MacLeish, from being a poet of opposition, went on to become the poet laureate of the New Deal. Politically, MacLeish was luckier than Auden, Spender and Day Lewis; but this made his task as a poet harder.

Even more than Crane, who borrowed his imagery from science, but whose spirit was, fundamentally, more imbued with metaphysics than with science, MacLeish has identified his poetic and humanistic vision with the scientific world-view; seeking to derive some of his myths from scientific invention, technological progress. This emerges from a close examination of "Einstein", and "The Hamlet of Archibald MacLeish", as well as "Immortal Helix", "Verses for a Centennial" and "Epistle to be Left in the Earth". In MacLeish's cosmological scheme, man no longer occupies the centre of the stage. One poem which articulates this experience of depersonalisation is "The Revenant":

O too dull brain, O unperceiving nerves
That cannot sense what so torments my soul
But like torn trees, when deep Novembers roll
Tragic with mighty winds and vaulting curves
Of sorrowful vast sound and light that swerves
In blown and tossing eddies, branch and bole
Shudder and gesture with a grotesque dole,
A grief that misconceives the grief it serves.

O too dull brain—with some more subtle sense
I know him here within the lightless room

Reaching his hand, and my faint eyes
See only darkness and the night's expanse,
And horribly, within the listening gloom,
My voice comes back, still eager with surprise.[10]

This poem is evocative of a mood of nameless dread—
what Heidegger refers to as "an acute cognition of non-being".
Part of its effect comes from the fusion of abstraction with
sentiency, as in the line:

Tragic with mighty winds and vaulting curves.

There is a concentrated menace in the line:

I know him here within the lightless room—

a whole ghost story in one sentence. The poet imports into the
movement of the wind his sense of the frangible hold that he
has on experience; and he evokes a vorticist whorl of planets, of
reeling spaces in—

In blown and tossing eddies, branch and bole
Shudder and gesture with a grotesque dole.

But the effect of the whole passage depends upon the
nightmarish quality, the sheer horror of the last two lines.

Nothing could be more stark, or more ominous than those two
counter-balancing phrases—

And horribly . . . eager with surprise.

For all this, the mood evoked is too specific (too horrific even)
for it to achieve the universality of the finest poetry. It is the
communication of a private nightmare.

*Notes*

1. "The Spanish Lie", *Collected Poems, 1917–1952*, Houghton
   Mifflin & Co., Boston, 1952, p. 138.
2. "Invocation to the Social Muse", ibid., p. 94. *Collected Poems*,
   Boriswood, London, 1936, p. 166.
3. "Hypocrite Auteur", ibid., p. 174.
4. "Hypocrite Auteur", ibid., p. 174.
5. "Sentiments for a Dedication", ibid., pp. 83–5.
6. "The Sheep in the Ruins", ibid., p. 165.
7. *J.B.*, Secker and Warburg, 1959, p. 103.
8. From Shelley's *A Defense of Poetry*, from *Collected Works*, Moxon
   Son & Co., London, 1839, p. 14.
9. *This Music Crept by Me on the Water*, Botteghe Oscura, XI,
   Roma, 1953, p. 211.
10. "The Revenant", *Collected Poems*, p. 85.

# HUGH MACLENNAN

## 1907–

John Hugh MacLennan was born in Glace Bay, Nova Scotia, on March 20, 1907. The son of a
doctor of Scottish descent, MacLennan became interested in classics at an early age. He received a
B.A. from Dalhousie University in Halifax in 1928 and was subsequently a Rhodes scholar at Oriel
College, Oxford. A championship tennis player, MacLennan participated in college athletics and
traveled widely on the Continent during his four years at Oxford. After taking his B.A. in 1932 he
studied at Princeton, completing a Ph.D. dissertation on an ancient Egyptian town, Oxyrhynchus,
in 1935. The following year he married an American writer, Dorothy Duncan, and took a job at
Lower Canada College in Montreal, teaching history and classics.

His first attempts at novel writing resulted in complex plots and flat settings. At the suggestion
of his wife MacLennan grudgingly agreed to write a novel set in the place he knew best, Canada.
The result was the much acclaimed *Barometer Rising* (1941), which is based on his childhood
experiences in Nova Scotia and the deadly Halifax explosion of 1917. Although he originally tried
to avoid being pigeonholed as a "Canadian" writer, his second novel, *Two Solitudes* (1945), secured
MacLennan an unwanted reputation as Canada's literary spokesman. He left Lower Canada
College and devoted himself to writing full time, winning numerous Canadian awards. In 1951 he
began lecturing at McGill and at the decade's end published *The Watch That Ends the Night*, which
many critics consider his most powerful novel. Written during his wife's long illness which
eventually ended with her death in 1957, *The Watch That Ends the Night* recounts the emotional
trauma which results from an unusual love triangle.

MacLennan married Frances Aline Walker two years later and continued writing novels as well
as essays for several Montreal newspapers. His latest novel, *Voices in Time* (1980), is set in Montreal
some fifty years after a nuclear holocaust. Although his works have been criticized for their
didacticism, MacLennan stands in the forefront of Canadian literature. He retired from teaching in
1979 and now lives in North Hatley, Quebec.

When I was engaged in selecting the essays that later appeared
in the book *Thirty and Three* I found that a pattern in the
material I had written began to disclose itself. All the pieces I
had written for American magazines had lost much of their
original vitality over the lapse of time. They had all appeared in
handsome formats, accompanied by large and colourful pictures. They had been well received in the months of their
publication, and even in Canada a few of them had won some
praise. But already they have begun to wither away.

The reason for this was not hard to discover, once
sufficient time had passed. Those pieces written for American
magazines with big names and glossy pages were written for a
public which does not really exist, for a public which is no
more than an abstraction invented by politicians, journalists,
and the editors of mass-circulation periodicals. Those articles I
wrote, with much labour and the expense of time and nervous
stability, were designed to make a quick impact on a more or
less unknown quantity. They were carefully constructed and

scrupulously polished, and contained a great deal of exact information. They were also, in terms of financial returns, big money-makers. But they lacked the essential ingredient of literature, they lacked intimacy. They were bound to lack intimacy because the magazines in which they appeared had a mass circulation. As communications, they were words spoken into dead air confused with static, not necessarily because most of the readers were living in a foreign country, but because no one who writes for that many people living all over the place can possibly know who his listeners are.

A strange thing, this. The writer is one of the most solitary of workers, but when he sits at his desk he must feel that he is writing for friends if what he writes is to be good. If he pretends to write only for himself, he lies, or lets his pride deceive him. Only the diarist does that, and the diarist is not interesting to others unless he is a famous personality or his material scandalous. The professional prose writer cannot possibly write for himself alone. He must convince himself that a personal relationship exists between himself and individual members of his audience. He must think of those individuals as valuable personally, each a person whose soul is inviolate, whose intelligence must never be insulted with clichés or by the kind of propaganda-prose which grabs him by the throat. Unless a writer can be convinced that a decent intimacy exists between himself and those who read him, what he writes may have impact for a day, but it will be dead a week later.

Since rediscovering this truth, which was ancient in Homer's day, I have felt a lot better about the future of that activity which the critics call "Canadian" literature and handle with tongs. I don't feel alone any more, as the critics try to make you feel, stuck with the job of creating some literature all by myself. I know that Canadian readers are sharing the job with me, and that the state of our culture depends as much on them as it depends on those of us who write. I know that if I respect them they will do their part, and that the way to respect them is to write with them in mind and not to consider them as a roadblock between myself and the huge, lucrative market of the outside world. ⟨. . .⟩

None of us are ⟨Francis⟩ Bacons, nor is it likely that Canada will ever again produce a writer with the unique texture of Stephen Leacock. But these men have showed us the way to go. The way is not the one of the highbrow critic who feels ashamed because nobody in Canada writes like Joyce or Proust or with the attitude of Jean-Paul Sartre. The right way is the one which brings the writer and the reader together in a closer intimacy, and the writer cannot travel this road alone. The reader must go along with him, accepting or rejecting his vision according to whether or not he likes it, but accepting or rejecting it himself, without waiting to find out what the American judgment of the man is going to be. After many years I believe this to be true. The future of Canadian literature depends as much on the development of a great, independent audience as on the existence of great, independent writers, for the communication which is literature's essence requires them both.—HUGH MACLENNAN, "Prologue: The Writer and His Audience" (1954), *The Other Side of Hugh MacLennan*, ed. Elspeth Cameron, 1978, pp. 1–5

As Hermann Boeschenstein has recently pointed out, Hugh MacLennan is a highly versatile writer, conversant with a host of psychological problems and sociological questions, commanding a variety of devices and techniques. Yet, there is a family resemblance between his novels, and if *The Watch That Ends the Night* seems an epitome of its predecessors, this is due to the limited number of motives in which MacLennan's artistic vision crystallizes. The return of a man believed dead is

the mainspring of action in *Barometer Rising* and *The Watch That Ends the Night*. Adultery is made the vehicle of protest against a narrow-minded environment in *Two Solitudes*, and is an escape from personal difficulties in all the other novels. Leading characters either tend to drop the burdens of civilization and go off by themselves, or, in the manner of Thomas Wolfe's figures, have to go abroad before they recognize what their home-country means to them.

There is, however, one recurring cluster of motives that, more than any other, gives expression to the triadic structure of MacLennan's vision and lends itself to historical interpretation. The starting-point for MacLennan's novels is incomplete man and his stifled, unduly restricted life. Man, at this stage, is seen to be determined by his environment or by a traumatic shock suffered in early youth or during the war. In his best works MacLennan telescopes this fact, which has been treated at length in the modern novel, into the brief moment of a sudden catastrophe and views man as a child running away in fright. Thus, ten-year-old Roddie Wain flees from the scene of disaster; Alan MacNeil hides from his father; Jerome Martell escapes in his canoe from the lumber camp; and Marius Tallard is shocked into becoming an enemy of his father when he watches him commit adultery. The second stage of development is characterized by the "farewell-to-arms" mood (Hemingway's work is mentioned and discussed in three novels). Released from the pressures of his environment and having gone through an ordeal, man is lonely, disheartened, and homeless. This period is likewise dealt with as briefly as possible. George Stewart's five-year stay at Waterloo is, for instance, glossed over in a couple of pages. And in *The Precipice* it is not Steve Lassiter, whose disillusion is growing from day to day, but Lucy Cameron who is in the centre of attention. For what MacLennan is, above all, interested in is how man reaches the third stage where he accepts life as it is and is able to make a quiet affirmation. As Stewart says about the political situation in the thirties:

> . . . why waste time explaining the pattern? It is obvious now, and dozens of books have been written about it. Less obvious have been some of the attendant passions that went along with this neo-religious faith. Passion has a way of spilling over into all aspects of the human mind and feelings.

Early in his career, MacLennan took issue with the notion that historical processes are rigidly determined. In his literary criticism, he has charged such writers as Joyce, Faulkner, and Hemingway with reacting "in extreme and private fashion against the change in mental climate which differentiates our time from the past." The mature man is to MacLennan one who faces violence or a narrow environment squarely and does not permit himself to be defeated or cramped by it. In contrast to the children, Neil Macrae and the adult Jerome Martell testify to the capacity of grown-up human beings to pass through an ordeal and assume their responsibility to themselves and to society, whereas Dr. Ainslie learns how to integrate even terrible accidents and catastrophes with a belief in love and God.

MacLennan, then, does not take a tradition for granted. Though the body of experience incorporated in the so-called modern novel is not denied but is partly accepted as valid, MacLennan, as a contemporary writer, wrestles for a positive solution. In this respect, all of his novels are experiments, for few modern writers have dared to encompass, in one work, the movement from violence to such a full affirmation as made in Dr. Ainslie's statement:

Life was never so vivid as when it was in danger, nor was a human being ever so vitally himself as when he had passed through pain and emerged on the other side of it.

To see MacLennan's achievement in proper perspective, we have to admit, however, that he has benefited from his quarrels with the American novelists. First of all, his frontal assault on the complex of violence, by means of a stylized story, aligns him with the major American writers. Secondly, MacLennan has fallen back, in method, on the major American tradition. It is the romance, with its air of probability in the midst of improbability and its proximity to mythic and allegoric forms of order, which enables him to blend catastrophe and affirmation successfully. Thirdly, MacLennan is close to the American writers when he deals with the third stage. His affirmation in *Barometer Rising* and *Two Solitudes* seems to be a nationalistic variant of the collective humanism typical of many novels of the thirties, such as, for example Hemingway's *For Whom the Bell Tolls*.

Yet even when MacLennan seems consciously to echo Hemingway, he is characteristically different. Both he and Hemingway (*In Our Time*) see the effects of the First World War anticipated by Jerome's and Nick Adams' childhood experiences in the New Brunswick and Michigan woods, respectively. But while Nick retreats behind the Hemingway code of "You got to be tough", Jerome responds more fully as a human being of his age would: he is truly afraid of the murderer of his mother and flees.

I suggest, then, that MacLennan's successful works of fiction are influenced by, and a reaction against, the American tradition of novel writing. This conclusion is borne out by MacLennan's own statements, for in 1946 he said:

> . . . is it natural for Canadians to adhere to the decaying Renaissance culture of Europe, or to the American branch cycle? There can only be one answer. Canadians must write for the American market because it is the cultural pattern to which they naturally belong. It is their only avenue to a world audience. And yet by doing so, they must compete on equal terms with American writers.

Since he believed, however, that the American writers were aping the decadent experiments of European novelists, he demanded that "American literary critics should cease looking to Europe as a model," and thus repeated Emerson's famous thesis, "We have listened too long to the courtly muses of Europe."—PAUL GOETSCH, "Too Long to the Courtly Muses," *CL*, Autumn 1961, pp. 28–30

The reasons for MacLennan's reputation, and for his undoubted importance as a novelist, are to be found in the original way in which he has interpreted the Canadian scene to his fellow countrymen rather than in any originality of approach to the art of the novel itself. Indeed, if we are concerned with fictional technique, one of the most striking characteristics of *Barometer Rising* and MacLennan's later novels is their relative conservatism. They are unashamedly didactic; they rely heavily on environmental atmosphere and local colour; their characterization is over-simplified and moralistic in tone; their language is descriptive rather than evocative; and their action tends to be shaped externally by a Hardyesque use of circumstance and coincidence. What does distinguish them is MacLennan's combination of theme and symbol—his development of action built on a simple but powerful foundation of universal myth.

The myth is that of Odysseus translated into terms of modern living; the *Odyssey* itself was the product of a people in the process of becoming aware of itself, and, appropriately, the theme which MacLennan uses it to illumine is the growth of a Canadian national consciousness. Indeed, the most striking—and in some ways the most jarring—feature of MacLennan's books is the degree to which the national theme in its various aspects forms an imposed pattern, within which the lives of the characters tend to be worked out, rather than working themselves out. In *Barometer Rising* it is the leap into a sense of national identity which MacLennan sees emerging among Canadians during the First World War; in *Two Solitudes* (1945) it is the clash of English and French traditions; in *The Precipice* (1948) it is the impact of American social mores on the Canadian consciousness; in *Each Man's Son* (1951) it is the lingering power in Canada of the Calvinist conscience; in *The Watch That Ends the Night* (1959), MacLennan's most recent and massive novel, it is the dual influence—destructive and creative at once—of the social idealism of the Thirties. This predominance of the national theme is a factor that must be taken into account in any attempt to understand MacLennan's work, since it bears a close relationship to his most evident weaknesses as a novelist, and also since its progressive assimilation into a fictionally viable form runs parallel to his growth towards maturity as a writer.

The expression of the theme in terms of the constant mythical structure is evident already in MacLennan's first novel. The setting of *Barometer Rising* is Halifax during the First World War. The novel opens as a young man returns secretly to the Nova Scotian capital. As the action progresses, it is revealed that he is an officer, Neil MacRae, whom his uncle Geoffrey Wain, also the colonel of his battalion in France, has attempted to blame for the failure of an attack. By chance MacRae was bombed on the night before his court martial, given up for dead, but found by a relieving battalion and patched up without his real identity being discovered. Now he returns home, risking execution for cowardice, in the hope of collecting the evidence that will clear his name. Meanwhile, there still lives in Halifax the cousin, Penelope Wain, with whom he was in love before he went away to the wars; she, besides being a capable ship designer, is the daughter of Neil's enemy.

Wain and Penelope both learn of MacRae's presence in Halifax, and while the Colonel—who has been sent home in disgrace because of the unsuccessful attack—sets out to frustrate Neil's efforts and to get rid of him as quietly as possible, Penelope and a drunken but good-hearted M.O., Angus Murray, do their best to see that MacRae vindicates himself. But the situation reaches its climax, not through the efforts of the two parties, but through the great Halifax explosion of 1917, which overshadows the latter part of the novel. MacRae and Murray recover their self-respect by superhuman feats of endurance in relieving the victims, while Colonel Wain is providentially among the dead. Meanwhile, Alec MacKenzie, a primitive giant of a Cape Breton fisherman, gives on his deathbed the evidence that will clear Neil MacRae and enable him to marry Penelope and assume parenthood of the child which, unknown to Neil, she bore him while he was away in France.

The adaptation of the *Odyssey*, if it were not otherwise evident, is indicated not only in the heroine's name, but also in MacRae's remark in the final chapter: "Wise Penelope! That's what Odysseus said to his wife when he got home. I don't think he ever told her he loved her. He probably knew the words would sound too small." But MacLennan not merely establishes in *Barometer Rising* a Homeric plot of the wanderer returning to a mysteriously changed homeland. He also uses for the first time a group of symbolic characters that will recur in various permutations in his later novels: the returning wanderer, the waiting woman, the fatherless child, the wise doctor—sometimes transformed into the wise old man—and the primitive, violent, but essentially good giant. If we wish to seek a Homeric parallel, the quintet of Odysseus, Penelope, Telemachus, Mentor and Eumaeus seems obvious, though MacLennan is too good a writer to follow the pattern slavishly, and we shall see the relationships of these five basic characters changing from novel to novel until, in *The Watch That Ends the Night*, the wanderer, the wise doctor and the primitive giant are finally united in that super-Odysseus, Jerome Martell.—GEORGE WOODCOCK, "A Nation's Odyssey: The Novels of Hugh MacLennan" (1961), *Odysseus Ever Returning*, 1970, pp. 12–14

Over the years, through a steadily deepening analysis of the national scene, Hugh MacLennan has been exploring the meaning of Canadianism; each of his novels, in some manner, has been a variation on this theme. His long study of all aspects of the Canadian character has peculiarly fitted him for the writing of *The Watch That Ends the Night* in which he traces Canada's coming-of-age. More important, in this novel he has gone back to examine what he feels are the character-shaping protoforms of the Canadian identity as exemplified by the fur trader. In one magnificent chapter of *The Watch That Ends the Night* in which the boy Jerome escapes down the wilderness river in his canoe, Hugh MacLennan is giving us his version not only of the Canadian character, but of the Canadian myth.

The most rewarding, and probably the shortest, route into MacLennan's latest novels is through his essay "The People behind This Peculiar Nation." In this brief study MacLennan wrote that the fur trade has been as basic to the Canadian character as the sea has been to England's; that nations as well as children tend to forget the events of early years; that these events sink into and become part of the national subconscious. The true makers of Canada, he maintains, were not the Victorians whose ghastly statues surround the Parliament Buildings in Ottawa, but the voyageurs:

> They were desperate men, and the story of their fabulous river voyages has no counterpart south of the border. It has no counterpart anywhere in the world, and if anyone wants to know why Canada is subtly different in character from the United States, it is to those men and to this period that he should look. *(Northern Lights)*

If we accept the true myth as originating in either the historical or the religious background of a people and belonging to their collective subconscious, then it becomes clear that Hugh MacLennan is leading us, in this essay, toward his definition of the Canadian myth. In the significant section dealing with Jerome's childhood in *The Watch That Ends the Night*, MacLennan has consciously embodied in narrative form all the mythic elements of our early history that he had outlined in his essay.—DOROTHY FARMILOE, "Hugh MacLennan and the Canadian Myth," *Mosaic*, Spring 1969, pp. 1–2

Almost without exception, MacLennan's critics have related the psychology of growing up to the voyages of the young men. They see in them the heroes' search for identity and a concurrent implication of a country's effort to probe its own nature and to establish itself as a distinctive nation. Similarly, almost all the critics have linked these quests with mythology. ⟨Hugo⟩ McPherson calls Bruce Fraser a "Promethean intellectual" and attributes a "Promethean pattern" to Dr. Ainslie's conflict with God. He did not expand his observations, and it remained for ⟨George⟩ Woodcock to take the subject up at

length. In his account, however, Ulysses overthrows Prometheus as the central mythological figure.

> The deliberate adaptation of the *Odyssey* . . . is admitted by MacLennan not only in the name of the heroine, but also in Macrae's remark . . . "Wise Penelope! That's what Odysseus said to his wife when he got home. . . ." But MacLennan not merely established in *Barometer Rising* a Homeric plot. . . . He also uses for the first time a group of symbolic characters which will recur . . . in his later novels; the returning wanderer, the waiting woman, the fatherless child, the wise doctor . . . and the primitive, violent, but essentially good giant.

Despite MacLennan's disclaimer, critics have continued to set Ulysses up as the controlling mythological symbol of his fiction, even for *Each Man's Son* "where," according to Douglas Spettigue, "a new concentration and depth were achieved through dividing Ulysses into three, as it were. . . ." thus Archie, the old prize-fighter, becomes not only the symbol of a returning warrior, but a third part of a mythological trinity.

The difficulty arises from Ulysses' unsuitability as a symbol in this book as a whole, and generally throughout MacLennan's fiction, for Woodcock's thesis presents some problems when examined closely in the context of the novels. Aside from a caveat or two that a name and a classical reference scarcely constitute a key to MacLennan's mythology and that the comment "he uses for the first time" is self-evident in a first novel, MacLennan's references to the classics do make a good point of departure for an examination of Woodcock's interpretation.

Like the author's father, Dr. Murray, Captain Yardley, and Dr. Ainslie were Greek "scholars," and, like the author, Paul loved Greece and Homer. Besides, MacLennan has in several essays declared himself an admirer of the Oedipus plays. "The theme of *Oedipus Rex* is," he wrote in 1946, "applicable to all times and places. . . ." One might "make Oedipus a boss of an oil company"; and, in continuing praise, years later, he added that the play has a plot "of great dramatic intensity." Here he found a myth that would give him scope for his favourite topic, "a son long frustrated by a domineering father he both admired and disliked," and that would likewise fit his theme of the national search for identity. Other circumstances bear on the subject. MacLennan's are family rather than epic novels despite their debt to the classics. Ulysses was an old man bringing hopes of restoring the old order in a disordered society. Neil Macrae and the other wayfarers are young men bringing hopes of setting up a new order in a disordered society; MacLennan stood with youth on the ramparts of the generation gap until *Return of the Sphinx*, when he left his position to cross over to the middle-aged. Jerome does fit the Ulysses pattern, but not necessarily exclusive of the Oedipal, if the word is taken to include the plays about the king and not merely the complex named after him.

The parallels between those plays and *Barometer Rising* are striking. Both Oedipus and Neil have been abandoned to death, one by a father and the other by an uncle. Both suffer permanent injury as a result. Both are believed dead and both return incognito to solve riddles and to establish their own identities. The question of the right to power, as in *Oedipus Rex*, motivates much of the plot and introduces the implied conflict of colonialism and a rising nationalism. The remaining novels conform fairly closely to the same models—heroes with physical defects; the return of allegedly dead men; the separation from the father; the search for a father during which the son, by growing up, unconsciously destroys the father image and, like Oedipus, in trying simultaneously to find the reason for a resultant uncertainty, discovers himself. In MacLennan's later work the Oedipus complex gets a firmer hold on some of the characters, as Dr. Ainslie's role illustrates, revealed briefly but vividly in this moment:

> Mollie's face was naked. He saw its delicacy, its tenderness, its love . . . and there was something else he recognized, a last reserve of strength which she was calling upon. To oppose him—to oppose his father? He passed his hand over his eyes.

Along with this phase of the Oedipal, *Each Man's Son* introduces the dark background of the myth. As Oedipus solves the riddle of the sphinx, so Ainslie tries to solve the social problem of the mine, a monster that lay in wait, also, for the youth of Broughton, while within himself he fears that through sex he falls prey to a beast—part animal, part woman—that would destroy him.

*Return of the Sphinx* develops this theme at length. The riddle recurs. Alan Ainslie cannot solve it and thus subvert the irrational forces that would crush those values on which civilized society depends. The "sphinx returned" in ancient days when it is alleged (probably apocryphally) that Sophocles' son charged him with insanity; and thematically in *Oedipus at Colonus*, when the father and king falls victim to the instinctive aggressions of his sons in their thirst for power. *Return of the Sphinx*, a long plunge down into doubt from the heights MacLennan reached in *The Watch That Ends the Night*, reads as if he believes his world, also, to be engaged in social and cultural suicide.—ALEC LUCAS, "Types and Myth," *Hugh MacLennan*, 1970, pp. 46–48

> Some natural tears they dropped, but wiped them
>     soon;
> The world was all before them, where to choose
> Their place of rest
>
>               (John Milton, *Paradise Lost*, Book XII)

A poignant sense of loss and longing, present even in Hugh MacLennan's optimistic early novels, increasingly pervades his fiction, becoming the dominant note particularly of his latest work, *Return of the Sphinx*. Much of the action in his novels is sustained by the underlying myth of a paradise lost (associated with childhood and mother love, gardens and the sea, a lost innocence, graciousness, and happiness) and of a search in a fallen world for a new paradise. The myth, which has psychological, social, and political implications in the fiction, finds expression most clearly through MacLennan's portrayal of marriage and the family. And, since the novels are often narrated from the perspective of the hero, women characters become representative of a lost Edenic world and a more elusive promised land, in their identification with nostalgically remembered moments of childhood security or youthful romantic involvement, as well as with the more demanding adult love which replaces such moments.

Northrop Frye has suggested that the pastoral myth, the vision of an ideal world associated with childhood or with earlier social conditions, is particularly strong in Canadian literature, and D. G. Jones specifies that frequently in this literature it is a female figure who is associated with the idyllic, with childhood and the garden. Neither however applies this analysis to MacLennan's work. It is not surprising to find the Eden myth so important in MacLennan's fiction, a fiction concerned with endangered values of civilization, marked by a strong sense of history and the passing of time, filled with wanderers, and concerned with the analysis of a Canada composed of exiled Loyalists, Scots, and Frenchmen, and of *émigré* Englishmen who, according to MacLennan, talk of their country "as Adam probably talked of the Garden after he had been thrown out of it." The role of the happy family and happy marriage in evoking this lost Garden and the new promised land is striking.

There are of course other mythological underpinnings which have been pointed out in MacLennan's novels, in particular the Odysseus and Oedipus myths, but the Eden myth rivals these in importance, and can be seen, particularly in its association with marriage and the family, as subsuming or containing elements of these other myths. George Woodcock, who has emphasized the influence of *The Odyssey* on MacLennan's writing, identifies the wandering Odysseus and the faithful Penelope as among MacLennan's recurring symbolic figures. So Penny, Heather, Lucy, Mollie, Catherine, and (in a less literal sense) Margaret are all portrayed as patiently awaiting the return of an absent husband or lover often while courted by other suitors. At the same time, however, the Ithaca with Penelope at its centre from which the wanderer has been separated and to which he gratefully returns after difficult struggles can be contained within the more comprehensive myth of paradise lost and paradise regained. The imagery surrounding MacLennan's characters extends beyond the specific Odysseus story to evoke this more general sense of a lost Eden.

The same is true of the Oedipus myth. Alec Lucas has argued that Oedipus rather than Odysseus is the controlling mythological symbol of MacLennan's work, and a number of the women characters do contain at least vague traces of the Jocasta wife-mother figure sought by the usurping son. These include Kathleen Tallard for whom her stepson Marius feels a guilty attraction, Lucy Cameron from whom Lassiter seeks a female approval denied by his mother, Mollie MacNeil whom Dr. Ainslie desires when he confuses her image with his mother's, Marielle Jeannotte who attracts Daniel because she reminds him of his mother and to whom he makes love in his parents' bed, and Constance who both reawakens and eases Alan Ainslie's longing for his mother. Again though this symbolism can be seen as part of a larger scheme. As we shall see, the mother figure is an important component of a symbolic Eden, of a moment lost and sought for in the novels. In keeping with the orthodox Freudian interpretation of the Oedipus legend, however, MacLennan insists on a movement away from the mother toward the wife. (Some negative minor characters like Marius Tallard, Huntly McQueen, Carl Bratian, and young Daniel Ainslie are portrayed unfavourably as never able to break away from their idealized and symbolically dead mothers.) The Eden myth, then, which underlies the novels, is a somewhat heretical version of Genesis, in which the paradise lost, however nostalgically recalled and mourned, is necessarily lost in exchange for the knowledge of good and evil. It is a story of the Fall in which time itself is the serpent, the destroyer of Eden, and in which innocence must therefore realistically give way to maturity. Despite the charm of pastoral security, MacLennan reminds us, "Life [is] never so vivid as when it [is] in danger, nor [is] a human being ever so vitally himself as when he [has] passed through pain and emerged on the other side of it."—HELEN HOY, "'The Gates Closed on Us Then': The Paradise-Lost Motif in Hugh MacLennan's Fiction," *JCan*, Winter 1979–80, pp. 29–30

Hugh MacLennan's novels can be looked at both as investigations into the growth of a Canadian national consciousness and as conventional romances about Canadian life. As fictions only, MacLennan's novels are commonplace; as structured analyses of his country's character and identity, they are unique.

When we speak about the themes in a writer's work, we recognize his concern with ideas and beliefs, and that his work is, at least in part, a fictional realization of these beliefs. The author is trying to "say something," and what he says is less a by-product of his craft than an *a priori* necessity for it. The distortions of reality that take place have a purpose beyond that of plot or character development; there is an idea or ideas to be expressed, beliefs to be transmitted.

Thus, with Hugh MacLennan, the point of view comes first. He begins writing his novels with a definite hypothesis in mind, and the novel is both a test and a demonstration of that hypothesis. The distinction being made is that between allegory, fable or parable and other forms of the novel. Between the two types of literature the primacies are reversed. In ordinary fiction structured reality is the author's chief concern; in allegory or parable, a concept, expressed fictionally, dominates. This thematic overlay has often in the modern novel led to a dense, symbolic underlay, initially obscuring, and eventually clarifying, the author's stance on a wide range of sociopolitical concerns. MacLennan's novels are both schematized and highly thematic but, interestingly, they lack effective symbols. MacLennan himself has said, "I don't use symbols in my writing, at least not consciously. . . ." It is possible to find a symbolic structure in the novels, and, because of the clear schematizing, it is tempting to do so. If symbolism may be defined as an attempt to evoke rather than to describe, and a symbol as that which "represents without reproducing," then it is clear that it is not within this broad area of the symbol that MacLennan is working.

Ultimately, however, novels which are intended to be read for the nature of the perceptions they contain must possess something more than the purely realistic. This component need not (as in, for example, Margaret Laurence or Sheila Watson) be densely symbolic, nor need it be the almost pantheistic overlay found, for example, in Frederick Philip Grove. What exists in MacLennan's novels is rather a vague symbolic underlay that leaves the reader aware that certain of MacLennan's creations can be taken to explain specific facets of the Canadian historical, political or social makeup. Direct equivalences are never given. There are no gulls or fishnets, as in the salvation chapter of Laurence's *The Stone Angel*, no overall symbolic pattern, as in Watson's *The Double Hook* or Callaghan's *A Passion in Rome*. MacLennan is writing basically realistic fictions which are intended to categorize "types" of Canadian experience or personality, by typifying rather than by symbolizing. His work is George Orwell's farm without the animals; William Golding's island without the island being a fallen Eden. Referring to Edmund Wilson's comment on *Barometer Rising*—"the book is the work of a powerful poet who has mastered the material of the engineer"—Claude Bissell writes: "This is true, not only of the great descriptions in the MacLennan novels (and here Wilson has in mind the description of the Halifax explosion). It also says a good deal about the general working of the MacLennan imagination. In reading a MacLennan novel, one can almost see the beams being lifted into place, the windows and doors carefully adjusted, the external walls attached."

The tradition of the novel within which MacLennan is working is an old one. The symbolist movement of the late nineteenth and early twentieth century seems to have had small influence on him. He is closer to the early and mid-nineteenth century. Jane Austen, George Eliot and Tolstoi—in their concern with depicting a broad view of society, its classes, shades and colours—are much closer to MacLennan than are Henry James, Conrad or Joyce. Moreover, the great experi-

ments in technique which these and other writers performed, techniques which revolutionized the art of the novel, seem not to have affected MacLennan at all. The distortion of time, the investigation of the subconscious and its use as a point of view, the fragmentation of language, the always increasing emphasis on connotation instead of denotation, the liberation of sexual attitudes: none of these appears to any large degree in his work. Even MacLennan's use of autobiographical material is strictly conservative. There are characters in the novels that remind us (if we have read the essays) of real people in MacLennan's life, or even of MacLennan himself, and certainly the physical environment of his childhood is reproduced in his fiction. But he does not use autobiographical data in the way that many modern writers have, to build a mythology of existence out of individual experience, or to make personal experience *per se* the touchstone for the fictional investigation of reality.

In an essay entitled "Youth and the Modern Literature," MacLennan makes his sympathies clear:

> John Galsworthy is no longer popular with the critics and I suppose he is unfamiliar to most readers under forty. Yet I have never been able to believe that any Englishman in the past twenty years has written a novel as true and important as *The Forsyte Saga*. It may be old hat now, but it was a good hat in its time, and if it is not valuable as a work of art, it is indispensable to anyone who wants to know what England was like at the end of the nineteenth century.

Whether or not this is a short *apologia*, it aptly states the case for MacLennan's own work. It also establishes his critical standards: what counts is the accuracy of the social investigation, even if that investigation suffers as a "work of art." —ROGER LESLIE HYMEN, "Hugh MacLennan: His Art, His Society and His Critics," *QQ*, Winter 1975, pp. 515–17

---

## HUGO McPHERSON
### From "The Novels of Hugh MacLennan"

*Queen's Quarterly*, Summer 1953, pp. 186–98

Hugh MacLennan's novels have survived both a domestic enthusiasm and the criticism of the larger world of English letters. Bernard De Voto is "a profound admirer of the novels of Hugh MacLennan"; J. Donald Adams (of the *New York Times*) considers Hugh MacLennan "your best living novelist." The great popularity of the Czech translation of *Two Solitudes* affords an international comment upon MacLennan's broad appeal. Popular criticism, however, has concerned itself largely with MacLennan's handling of such problems as Puritanism and Canadian nationalism; it has tended to ignore his technique, and the relation to his increasingly complex themes.

*Barometer Rising* and *Two Solitudes*, the first novels, have an almost classical clarity and simplicity of structure. Each, on multiple levels, deals with the theme of self-realization or rebirth; in each, the personal conflict is significant finally, as an image of a larger, symbolic conflict of social forces or attitudes. By objectifying social forces in real, though *typical* characters, MacLennan creates a dramatic and realistic story whose meaning, in Melville's phrase, "rays out" as from a lighthouse, beyond the individual to the national or even the universal.

But in *The Precipice* and *Each Man's Son*, novels which examine the *psychical* as well as the social problems created by Puritanism, the allegorical or 'typical' technique breaks down. It becomes clear in these novels that the technique of symbolic characterization is not, without radical alteration, adequate for the representation of characters who are at once symbolic figures and unique psychological case studies. This is not, of course, to argue that a symbolic character cannot also be uniquely individual. The artist's problem is to find a means or *form* which makes possible a simultaneous representation of *both* the symbolic and the unique.

The problem of Hugh MacLennan's art, then, is formal. The symbolic structure which worked well in the treatment of social conflict stumbles over the concealed trip-wire of individual uniqueness in the later novels. This increasingly complex nature of MacLennan's artistic vision has not been fully supported by parallel developments in technique. The resulting dilemma will be examined in detail. ⟨. . .⟩

*Barometer Rising* owes its success in large part to the clearly delineated social framework within which its characters move. It gives expression not only to the conflicts of individuals and social groups, but also to a basic, archetypal pattern. Unlike John Steinbeck, with his often inept and muddled analogizing in *The Grapes of Wrath*, Mr. MacLennan has maintained a precise and exciting equivalence between his superficial action and his larger theme or themes.

In *Two Solitudes* (1945) his equivalence is again established and maintained. The structure which supports its personal themes of self-realization is a thesis-antithesis-synthesis pattern. Like the warring Titans, Captain Yardley and Athanase Tallard fail in their quest; but Paul Tallard and Heather Methuen, the second generation, achieve (symbolically) a synthesis.

Unlike *Barometer Rising*, *Two Solitudes* emphasizes the conflict of social groups. Each of the major characters symbolizes one aspect of this knotty social problem in a direct, one-to-one ratio: Marius is the French-Canadian nationalist; Janet is the British imperialist; Huntley McQueen is the thrifty, Scottish Calvinist; Father Beaubien is the chauvinistic Roman Catholic; Athanase Tallard and Captain Yardley are the French and English Canadians who try to share in both cultures; Kathleen Tallard is the Irish Catholic misfit. Among the young people, Daphne is the Canadian who attempts to forget the problem in an artifical cosmopolitanism; Paul and Heather are the French and English young people who, when cosmopolitanized, will fuse the diverse elements of Canadian society into a new and mature Canadianism.

The story is constructed in triad form: root position, the background of the French-English social struggle, focused upon Athanase Tallard and Captain Yardley, the men of good will who fail equally in their attempts to heal the schism in Canadian life; second position, the meeting and separation of Heather and Paul who, still tied by parochial attitudes, cannot establish a common meeting ground between French and English; third position, a 'return' of the now mature Heather and Paul culminating in a marriage symbolic of the union of opposed forces in Canada.

The symmetry of this plan equals that of *Barometer Rising*. Unfortunately, the inversions of the triad strike with diminishing force. Like Nathaniel Hawthorne in *The Marble Faun*, Mr. MacLennan became fascinated with the first demand of his theme, the establishing of the necessary background. Moreover, the career of Athanase Tallard, who dissipated his potential powers of statesmanship in loving too many women, proved to be worthy of a full-length novel in itself. After devoting 218 pages to Tallard and the struggle of the older generation, the author diminished the execution of Parts II and III to near-skeletal form. These sections (152 pages) have about them a forced and tentative air: they are thin in characterization; they are withered by arid narrative. Where

the problems of the first section are bodied forth in the dramatically ingratiating actions of Captain Yardley and the erratic flourishes of Athanase Tallard, the problems of intellectual-emotional growth treated in sections II and III too often present themselves in set-piece dialogues or long passages of baldly prosaic thought. Characters who were important, symbolically, in (I), are later dismissed casually; thus Kathleen, the Irish-Catholic misfit, loses her symbolic identity by retiring to the arms of an American businessman; Father Beaubien, now facing the major problem of a factory in his ancient parish, is silenced by an unexplained bishop's edict.

The story deteriorates dangerously when Paul Tallard's years of emancipation abroad are summarized in a few pages and Heather's years in cosmopolitan New York are condensed into a few letters. The literal-symbolic parallel almost disappears at one point, when a "poor-boy rich-girl" tension, rather than a conflict of racial backgrounds, appears to be the cause of Paul and Heather's separation. The final chapters rally as the triumph of the new culture, symbolized by the marriage of Paul and Heather, is presented to imperialist Janet as a *fait accompli*. Even this excellent scene, however, cannot compensate for a resolution that is largely verbal and theoretical.

The flaw of *Two Solitudes* is not merely thinness of execution. It is a failure to discover an adequate 'objective correlative' for the presentation of intellectual development. Twice in *Barometer Rising* Neil fell into didactic, unrealistic (and unnecessary) reverie. The 'objective correlatives' of the 'explosion' and rescue work had *already* expressed dramatically his inner conflict and its resolution. In the last parts of *Two Solitudes* this dramatic 'objective correlative' of the subjective situation is largely lacking; thought has vaulted beyond flesh into abstraction. This practice of 'telling about' important or even crucial mental events becomes more serious in *The Precipice* where self-conscious reverie and set-piece dialogue abound. The form of the early novels thus proves inadequate to the author's new *psychical* materials. ⟨. . .⟩

*Each Man's Son* (1951) reveals Hugh MacLennan's consciousness of the formal weaknesses of *The Precipice*. It is an attempt to move beyond the allegorical structure of *Barometer Rising* to a full-length portrait of a single individual surrounded by characters who define his society and objectify the forces at work within his personality. For Daniel Ainslie, Puritanism is a personal problem which, however confusedly, he works out for himself. His ultimate "escape" to England is, perhaps, MacLennan's admission that the Puritan problem cannot be solved in the social-symbolic manner of *Two Solitudes*.

The theme, the 'ancient curse' of Calvinist austerity, is explicitly stated in a Prologue. The background is a Scottish mining community on Cape Breton Island. Daniel Ainslie is a brilliant mine doctor whose need to give and receive love (to find a benevolent rather than a repressive faith) forces him to deny the God of Calvin and to seek an acceptable object for the great warmth which he feels within himself. Driven by this consuming need, he centers his affection upon Alan MacNeil, the son of a simple-minded prize fighter who is vainly attempting to establish a reputation in the United States. When Alan's mother finally wrests her son from Ainslie's benevolently possessive grasp, the doctor is desolated. In an introspective passage, ending in an epiphany that the reader does not quite understand, (again one feels the lack of an 'objective correlative') Ainslie's disillusion sets him free from the 'ancient curse.' But soon, as an indirect result of the Doctor's possessive love for Alan, violent death overtakes Mollie and Archie MacNeil. Ainslie takes charge of the orphaned Alan and, a "father" at last, he "escapes" from Cape Breton's narrowness to the emancipated world of England where his scientific talent can develop freely.

Though this synopsis seems simple, the story is filled with persons and incidents whose exact significance is puzzling. On the one hand, some of the characters are blurred relatives of the types of *Two Solitudes*: Louis Camire, the admirer of Mollie MacNeil, is an alien 'Socialist'; Mrs. MacCuish is a spectral arch-Calvinist; Mrs. Ainslie represents softened New England Calvinism. On the other hand, some of the characters seem significant as *psychological* symbols (a new and important structural innovation): Mollie and Mrs. Ainslie are both mother figures specifically related to Ainslie's memories of his own mother; Alan MacNeil is associated with Ainslie's boyhood; Dr. MacDonald, the founder of the hospital, is a father image—the man Ainslie might like to resemble or replace.

Other suggestions of a larger dimension of meaning tantalize and thwart the reader. The individual miners become comments upon the narrowness and futility of the Calvinist community; their daily descent into the bowels of the earth is linked, perhaps, with the Calvinist conception of man's depraved nature. Similarly, Archie MacNeil, who rejects "going down into the pits" for a life of "prize fighting", seems to represent the unregenerate lost in a godless world (the U.S.A.). Dr. Ainslie's sterilization of his wife, his denial of Mollie's maternal rights and his scorn of his mother's supposed weakness, all carry with them the sense of a sexual maladjustment springing from more complex roots than the simple Calvinist fear of sensuality. The whole Promethean pattern of Dr. Ainslie's conflict (his need to defy the God image, his need and inability to become a father himself, his desire to devote his talent to the good of mankind) suggests a psychological and even mythical meaning which transcends and invalidates the over-simple thesis of the 'ancient curse.'

But despite this wealth of suggestive character and incident, no clear light "rays out" beyond the surface gloss of *Each Man's Son*. A resonant, coherent *form* for the representation of mental conflict is still lacking. Moreover, the departure from 'type characterization' and tight, symbolic structure has not, in this novel, marked the accession of a structure which keeps physical action and stated theme in consistent, organic relation. In the closing chapters, for example, we learn that Dr. Ainslie has, obscurely, won his spiritual battle by conquering his 'son' obsession. But Mollie, perhaps through fear of losing her son, has accepted the amorous advances of Louis Camire. Archie MacNeil, arriving home, broken and disillusioned, discovers his wife in the arms of her lover. In the ensuing battle, witnessed by little Alan, both Mollie and Camire are killed. Archie dies of a blood clot on the brain. As a result of this violent homecoming, Dr. Ainslie is left to look after the young orphan whom he has so long loved.

Such dramatic elimination of all the obstacles to Dr. Ainslie's wishes provides an effectively startling *dénouement*. However, the relation of this speedy nemesis of three characters to the theme of the "ancient curse" is not clear. If, on the psychological level, these three deaths represented a symbolic exorcism of the traumatic forces at work in Dr. Ainslie's personality, they would be relevant; but there is no ambiguity (such as we find, for example, in the tragic events of Henry James' *The Author of Beltraffio* or *The Turn of the Screw*) suggestive of a psychological or symbolic dimension in the MacNeils' tragedy.

*Each Man's Son*, in relation to the body of Hugh MacLennan's fiction, must be considered as experimental and transitional. Without abandoning completely the form of the early novels, it reaches out a tentative, exploratory hand towards new forms and new ideas. One need only consider the widely contrasted works of Virginia Woolf and Franz Kafka to visualize the diverse areas which Mr. MacLennan is now attempting to synthesize. The magnitude of his undertaking commands our respect and admiration.

# NORMAN MAILER

## 1923–

Norman Mailer was born in Long Branch, New Jersey, on January 31, 1923. In 1927 he moved with his family to the Eastern Parkway section of Brooklyn, where he later attended Boys' High School. He entered Harvard in the fall of 1939, intending to study aeronautical engineering; and although four years later he did graduate with a degree in engineering, his primary interest had by then become literature. By the end of his sophomore year Mailer already had gained some reputation as a writer; this was furthered when *Story* magazine published his short story "The Greatest Thing in the World", which had won a writing competition sponsored by that magazine.

In 1944 he entered the U. S. Army, serving for eighteen months in the Pacific. After the war he attended the Sorbonne on the G.I. Bill. While he was studying in Europe his first novel, *The Naked and the Dead* (1948), was published in the United States. Partially drawing on his own military experience, it was praised by critics as the best novel written about the recent war, and made Mailer a literary celebrity overnight. He has continued to write since then, and in 1969 won the National Book Award and the Pulitzer Prize for non-fiction for *The Armies of the Night*, his account of the march on the Pentagon. In 1980 *The Executioner's Song*, Mailer's book on the life and execution of murderer Gary Gilmore, won the Pulitzer Prize for fiction. Other works which have received critical attention include *The Deer Park* (1955), *An American Dream* (1965), and *Why Are We in Vietnam?* (1967).

Although Mailer's narrative skills have earned him a significant position in contemporary American literature, the unusual events of his life have drawn as much, if not more, public attention. A founder of the *Village Voice*, he became associated with the subculture of Greenwich Village during the 1950s. In 1969 he ran for mayor of New York City on a secessionist ticket which advocated the formation of a fifty-first state comprised of the New York City metropolitan region. More startling than his political beliefs has been Mailer's association with violence. In 1960, after an all-night party at his downtown apartment, Mailer stabbed his second wife, Adele Morales, seriously wounding her. He spent seventeen days in Bellevue Hospital undergoing psychiatric examination; however, Morales refused to press charges, and he was released. In 1981 Mailer was involved in obtaining the release of Jack Henry Abbott from the Utah State Prison. Abbott had written a series of letters to Mailer on the topic of violence, which Mailer helped arrange to have published under the title *In the Belly of the Beast* (1981). Six weeks after his release Abbott killed a waiter in a New York restaurant, causing a storm of controversy which enveloped not only Mailer but also several other writers who had worked for Abbott's release from jail.

The father of eight children by six different wives, Mailer now lives in New York's Brooklyn Heights with his sixth wife, actress Norris Church. He has been working on a series of novels set in ancient Egypt, beginning with *Ancient Evenings* (1983). In 1984 he published a detective novel, *Tough Guys Don't Dance*.

## GORE VIDAL
### "Norman Mailer: The Angels Are White" (1960)
#### *Rocking the Boat*
1962, pp. 161–77

I first heard of Norman Mailer in the spring of 1948, just before *The Naked and the Dead* was published. He was living in Paris or had been living there and just gone home when I arrived in France, my mood curiously melancholic, no doubt because of the dubious fame I was enjoying with the publication of a third book, *The City and the Pillar*. At twenty-two I should have found a good deal more to please me than I did that spring and summer in the foreign cities. I do recall at one point Truman Capote telling me about *The Naked and the Dead* and its author; a recital which promptly aroused my competitive instincts . . . waning, let me say right off, and for reasons which are relevant to these notes. Yet at that time I remember thinking meanly: So somebody did it. Each previous war had had its big novel, yet so far there had been none for our war, though I knew that a dozen busy friends and acquaintances were grimly taking out tickets in the Grand War Novel Lottery. I had debated doing one myself and had (I still think) done something better: a small cool hard novel about men on the periphery of the action; it was called *Williwaw* and was written when I was nineteen and easily the cleverest young fox ever to know how to disguise his ignorance and make a virtue of his limitations. (What an attractive form the self-advertisement is: one could go on forever relighting one's image!) Not till I began that third book did I begin to get bored with playing safe.

I took to the field and have often wondered since, in the course of many excursions, defeats, alarums and ambushes, what it might have been like to have been a safe shrewd custodian of one's talent, playing from strength. I did not suspect then that the ambitious, rather cold-blooded young contemporary who had set out to write the big war novel and who had pulled it off would one day be in the same fix I was. Not safe. Not wise. Not admired. A fellow victim of the Great Golfer's Age, then no more than a murmur of things to come in the Golfer's murmurous heart.

My first reaction to *The Naked and the Dead* was: it's a fake. A clever, talented, admirably executed fake. I have not changed my opinion of the book since, though I have considerably changed my opinion of Mailer, as he himself has changed. Now I confess I have never read all of *The Naked and the Dead*. But I read a good deal of it. I recall a fine description of men carrying a dying man down a mountain. Yet every time I got going in the narrative I would find myself stopped cold by

a set of made-up, predictable characters taken, not from life, but from the same novels all of us had read, and informed by a naïveté which was at its worst when Mailer went into his Time-Machine and wrote those passages which resemble nothing so much as smudged carbons of an early Dos Passos work.

Sourly, from a distance, that year I watched the fame of Mailer quite surpass John Horne Burns and myself, as well as Truman Capote who had made his debut earlier the same year. I should explain for those who have come in late or were around then but inattentive that the O.K. List of writers in 1947 and 1948 was John Horne Burns, Calder Willingham and myself. Capote and Mailer were added in 1948. Willingham was soon dropped; then Burns (my own favorite) sank, and by 1949 in the aftermath of *The City and the Pillar* I too departed the O.K. List.

"I had the freak of luck to start high on the mountain, and go down sharp while others were passing me"—so Mailer wrote, describing the time after *Barbary Shore* when he unexpectedly joined the rest of us down on the plain. Now the descent, swift or slow, is not agreeable; but on the other hand it is not as tragic as Mailer seems to find it. To be demoralized by the withdrawal of public success (a process as painful in America as the withdrawal of a drug from an addict) is to grant too easily a victory to the society one has attempted to criticize, affect, change, reform. It is clearly unreasonable to expect to be cherished by those one assaults. It is also childish, in the deepest sense of being a child, ever to expect justice. There is none beneath our moon. One can only hope not to be destroyed entirely by injustice and, to put it cynically, one can very often flourish through an injustice obtaining in one's favor. What matters finally is not the world's judgment of oneself but one's own judgment of the world. Any writer who lacks this final arrogance will not survive very long, especially in America.

That wide graveyard of stillborn talents which contains so much of the brief ignoble history of American letters is a tribute to the power of a democracy to destroy its critics, brave fools and passionate men. If there is anything in Mailer's new book ⟨*Advertisements for Myself*⟩ which alarms me, it is his obsession with public success. He is running for President, as he puts it. Yet though his best and most interesting works have been unjustly attacked, he should realize that in this most inequitable of worlds his one worldly success was not a very good book, that *The Naked and the Dead* is redolent of "ambition" (in the Mary McCarthy sense of the word—pejorative, needless to say) and a young man's will to be noticed. Mailer himself nearly takes this view: "I may as well confess that by December 8th or 9th of 1941 . . . I was worrying darkly whether it would be more likely that a great war novel would be written about Europe or the Pacific." Ambition and the day coincided and a success was made. Yet it is much less real a book than Burns's *The Gallery*, or even some of the stories of Robert Lowry, works which had the virtue of being felt, possessed entirely by the men who made them, not created out of stern ambition and dogged competence. But, parenthetically, most war books are inadequate. War tends to be too much for any writer, especially one whose personality is already half obliterated by life in a democracy. Even the aristocrat Tolstoi, at a long remove in time, stretched his genius to the breaking point to encompass men and war and the thrust of history in a single vision. Ernest Hemingway in *A Farewell to Arms* did a few good descriptions, but his book, too, is a work of ambition, in which can be seen the beginning of the careful, artful, immaculate idiocy of tone that since has marked both his prose and his legend as he has declined into that sort of fame which, at moments I hope are weak, Mailer seems to crave.

But it is hard for American writers not to measure themselves according to the standards of their time and place. I recall a conversation with Stephen Spender when I lapsed, unconsciously, into the national preoccupation. Some writer had unexpectedly failed, not gone on, blown up. Spender said rather pointedly, "The difference in England is that they *want* us to be distinguished, to be good." We order things differently; although our example is contagious, for in recent years the popular British press has discovered writers in a way ours never has. Outside the gossip column and the book page no writer except Hemingway is ever mentioned as news in the American press, but let the most obscure young English novelist attack the Establishment and there are headlines in London. Mailer can denounce Eisenhower as much as he likes in *Dissent* but the readers of the *Daily News* will never know the name of Mailer, much less the quality of his anger. Publicity for the American writer is of the "personality" kind: a photograph in *Harper's Bazaar*, bland television appearances . . . the writer as minor movie star, and as unheeded.

Mailer and I finally met in 1954. I had just published my last, or perhaps I should say latest, novel, *Messiah*, and it had sunk quietly into oblivion in America. (If it were not for the continuing interest of Europe, especially England, a great many of our writers would not survive as well as they do their various seasons of neglect.) I liked Mailer, though I am afraid my first impression of him was somewhat guarded. I am suspicious of people who make speeches at me, and he is a born cocktail-party orator. I have not the slightest recollection of what we talked about. I do recall telling him that I admired *Barbary Shore*, and he was shrewd enough to observe that probably I had been driven to read it to see if it was really as bad as everyone thought. Which it was not. Of his three novels I find it the most interesting and the least diffuse, and quite literally memorable. It is hallucinatory writing of a kind Mailer tried, as far as I know, only that one time; and though I think his talents are essentially naturalistic, he does seem again in his new novel (judging from the advance samples he displays in *Advertisements for Myself*) to be trying for that revelation through willful distortion which he achieved in *Barbary Shore*. One is curious to see the result.

I have gone into the chronology of Mailer's days and mine because they run parallel, occasionally crossing, and because the book he has just published is, in effect, an autobiography covering more or less his entire career with particular attention to the days of the Golfer's dull terror. Mailer gives us his life and his work together, and therefore it is impossible to review

the book without attempting to make some estimate of both his character and the corpus of his work, the tension of his present and the shape of his future. Mailer is sly to get himself all this attention, but I must point out that it is a very dangerous move for an artist to expose himself so completely. Indeed, in other times it would have been fatal for an artist not yet full grown to show us his sores and wounds, his real and his illusory strength. Until very recently the artist was a magician who did his magic in public view but kept himself and his effects a matter of mystery. We know *now* of Flaubert's suffering, both emotional and aesthetic, during the days of his work, but it is hard to imagine what would have happened if the court which prosecuted *Madame Bovary* could have presented as evidence a volume of his letters. In effect, Mailer has anticipated his own posterity. He is giving us now the storms and the uncertainties, private and public, which he has undergone. He has armed the enemy and not entirely pleased his allies.

However, it may be possible to get away with this sort of thing today, for we live in the age of the confession. What Mailer has done is no different in kind from what those deranged and fallen actresses have accomplished in ghost-written memoirs where, with a shrewd eye on the comeback trail, they pathetically confess their sins to Demos, receiving for their tears the absolution of a culture obscenely interested in gossip. I suspect Mailer may create more interest in himself by having made this "clean breast of it" than he would have got by publishing a really distinguished novel. The audience no longer consumes novels, but it does devour personalities. Yet what happens after one is eaten? Is one regurgitated? Or does the audience move on to its next dinner of scandal and tears, its previous meal absorbed and forgotten?

Nevertheless, I am fairly certain that Mailer will survive everything. Despite a nice but small gift for self-destruction, he is uncommonly adroit, with an eye to the main chance (the writer who lacks this instinct is done for in America; excellence is not nearly enough). I noted with some amusement that, despite his air of candor, he makes no new enemies in this book. He scores off those who are lost to him anyway, thus proving that essentially the work is politic. His confessions, when not too disingenuous, are often engaging and always interesting, as he tries to record his confusions. For Mailer does not begin to know what he believes or is or wants. His drive seems to be toward power of a religio-political kind. He is a messiah without real hope of paradise on earth or in heaven, and with no precise mission except that dictated by his ever-changing temperament. I am not sure, finally, that he should be a novelist at all, or even a writer, despite formidable gifts. He is too much a demagogue; he swings from one position of cant to another with an intensity that is visceral rather than intellectual. He is all fragments and pieces. He appears to be looking for an identity, and often it seems that he believes crude celebrity will give it to him again. The author of *The Naked and the Dead*, though not the real Mailer, was at least an identifiable surrogate, and duly celebrated. But Mailer was quickly bored with the war-novelist role, and as soon as possible he moved honorably to a new position: radical politics, in the hope that through Marxist action he might better identify himself to us and to himself. But that failed him, too. Nor is the new Mailer, prophet of Hip and celebrator of sex and its connection with time, apt to interest him or us for very long.

I also noted at moments toward the end of this book that a reaction was setting in: Mailer started using military allusions. "Back in the Philippines, we . . ."—that sort of thing. And there were references to patrols, ambushes. It was startling. Most of our generation was in the war, usually ingloriously, yet

I have never heard a contemporary make any reference to it in a personal way. The war to most of us was a profound irrelevance; traumatic for some, perhaps, but for most no more than an interruption. When the 1959 Mailer reminds us that he was a rifleman on Luzon, I get embarrassed for him and hope he is not going back to his first attitude to get the attention he wants.

Now for the book itself. It is a collection of stories, essays, notes, newspaper columns and part of a play. It begins with his first story at Harvard and ends with part of his new novel. The play, which I read in an earlier version, could be remarkable onstage. But the best work in this volume is two short stories. "The Language of Men" tells of the problems of an army cook who has an abstract passion for excellence as well as a need for the approbation of the indifferent men who eat his food. His war with them and himself and his will to excel are beautifully shown and in many ways make one of the best stories of its kind I have read, certainly preferable to Hemingway's *The Old Man and the Sea*, which it resembles in theme. But where Hemingway was pretentious and external, Mailer is particular and works with gentle grace from within his characters. The other story, "The Patron Saint of Macdougal Alley," is a wildly funny portrait of an archetypal drifter, and I think it is of permanent value: we have had this sort of fool in every age (Catullus and Juvenal each dealt with him), but I have not seen him done quite so well in our day.

By and large, excepting "The White Negro," I did not like the essays and the newspaper columns. Mailer is forever shouting at us that he is about to tell us something we must know or has just told us something revelatory and we failed to hear him or that he will, God grant his poor abused brain and body just one more chance, get through to us so that we will *know*. Actually, when he does approach a point he shifts into a swelling, throbbing rhetoric which is not easy to read but usually has something to do with love and sex and the horror of our age and the connection which must be made between time and sex (the image this bit of rhetoric suggests to me is a limitless gray sea of time with a human phallus desperately poking at a corner of it). He is at his best (who is not?) when discussing his own works and days. The piece about getting *The Deer Park* published is especially good, and depressing for what it reveals about our society. But, finally, in every line he writes, despite the bombast, there is uncertainty: Who am I? What do I want? What am I saying? He is Thomas Wolfe but with a conscience. Wolfe's motive for writing was perfectly clear: he wanted fame; he wanted to taste the whole earth, to name all the rivers. Mailer has the same passion for fame but he has a good deal more sense of responsibility and he sees that the thing is always in danger of spinning down into meaningless-ness. Nothing is quite enough: art, sex, politics, drugs, God, mind. He is sure to get tired of Hip very soon. Sex will be a dead end for him, because sex is the one purely existential act. Sex is. There is nothing more to be done about it. Sex builds no roads, writes no novels, and sex certainly gives no meaning to anything in life but itself. I have often thought that much of D. H. Lawrence's self-lacerating hysteria toward the end of his life must have come out of some "blood knowledge" that the cruel priapic god was mad, bad and dangerous to know, and, finally, not even palliative to the universal strangeness.

Perhaps what has gone wrong in Mailer, and in many of our fellow clerks, is the sense that human beings to flourish must be possessed by one idea, a central meaning to which all experience can be related. To be, in Isaiah Berlin's bright metaphor, hedgehog rather than fox. Yet the human mind is not capable of this kind of exclusivity. We are none of us hedgehogs or foxes, but both simultaneously. The human mind is in continual flux, and personality is simply a sum of those attitudes which most often repeat themselves in recogniz-able actions. It is naïve and dangerous to try to impose on the human mind any system of thought which lays claim to finality. Very few first-rate writers have ever subordinated their own apprehension of a most protean reality to a man-made system of thought. Tolstoi's famous attempt in *War and Peace* nearly wrecked that beautiful work. Ultimately, not Christ, not Marx, not Freud, despite the pretensions of each, has the final word to say about the fact of being human. And those who take solemnly the words of other men as absolute are, in the deepest sense, maiming their own sensibilities and controverting the evidence of their own senses in a fashion which may be comforting to a terrified man but is disastrous for an artist.

One of the few sad results of the collapse of the Judeo-Christian ethical and religious systems has been the displace-ment of those who are absolutists by temperament and would in earlier times have been rabbis, priests, systematic philoso-phers. As the old Establishment of the West crumbles, the absolutists have turned to literature and the arts, and one by one the arts in the twentieth century have become hieratic. Serious literature has become religion, as Matthew Arnold foresaw. Those who once would have been fulfilled in Talmudic debate or suffered finely between the pull of Rome and the Church of England have turned to the writing of novels and, worse, to the criticism of novels. Now I am not sure that the novel, though it is many things, is particularly suited to didacticism. It is certainly putting an undesirable weight upon it to use it as a pretext for sermons or the resuscitation of antique religious myths. Works of fiction, at best, create not arguments but worlds, and a world by definition is an attitude toward a complex of experience, not a single argument or theme, syllogistically proposed. In the nineteenth century most of our critics (and many of our novelists) would have been writing books of sermons and quarreling over points of doctrine. With religion gone out of the intellectual world they now write solemnly and uneasily about novels; they are clearly impatient with the vulgar vitality of the better novels, and were it not that they had one another's books about books to analyze, I suspect many of them would despair and falter. The novelists don't seem very bright to the critics, while their commentaries seem irrelevant to the novelists. Yet each affects the other; and those writers who are unduly eager for fame and acceptance will write novels which they hope might interest "religious"-minded critics. The results range from the subliterary bleating of the Beats to Mailer's portentous cry which takes the form of: I am the way and the life ever after, crucify me, you hackers, for mine is a ritual death! Take my flesh and my blood, partake of me and *know* mysteries . . . ! And the curious thing is that they will crucify him; they will partake of his flesh; yet no mystery will be revealed. For the priests have created the gods, and they are all of them ritual harvest gods.

I was most struck by this remark of André Gide in the posthumous *Ainsi Soit-il:* "It is affectation that makes so many of today's writings, often even the best among them, unbear-able to me. The author takes on a tone that is not natural to him." Of course it is sometimes the work of a lifetime for an artist to discover who he is and it is true that a great deal of good art results from the trying on of masks, the affectation of a persona not one's own. But it seems to me that most of my contemporaries, including Mailer, are—as Gide suggests—

desperately trying to convince themselves and the audience that they are something they are not. There is even a certain embarrassment about writing novels at all. Telling stories does seem a silly occupation for one fully grown; yet to be a philosopher or a religious is not easy when one is making a novel. Also, in a society such as ours, where there is no moral, political or religious center, the temptation to fill the void is irresistible. There is the empty throne, so . . . *seize* the crown! Who would not be a king or high priest in such an age? And the writers, each in his own way, are preoccupied with power. Some hope to achieve place through good deportment. Universities are filled with poets and novelists conducting demure and careful lives in imitation of Eliot and Forster and those others who (through what *seems* to have been discretion) made it. Outside the universities one finds the buccaneers who mean to seize the crown by force, blunt Bolingbrokes to the Academy's gentle Richards.

Mailer is a Bolingbroke, a born usurper. He will raise an army anywhere, live off the country as best he can, helped by a devoted underground, even assisted at brief moments by rival claimants like myself. Yet when all is said, none of this is the way to live. And it is not a way (at least it makes the way harder) to create a literature that, no doubt quixotically, remains the interest of each of us. I suppose if it helps Hemingway to think of literature as a Golden Gloves Tournament with himself pounding Maupassant to the mat or fighting Stendhal to a draw, then no doubt the fantasy has been of some use. But there is also evidence that the preoccupation with power is a great waste of time. Mailer has had the honesty to confess that his own competitiveness has wasted him as he worries about reviewers and bad publicity and the seemingly spiteful successes of other novelists. Yet all the time he knows perfectly well that writers are not in competition with one another. The real enemy is the audience, which grows more and more indifferent to literature, an audience which can be reached only by phenomena, by superior pornographies or willfully meretricious accounts of the way we live now. No serious American novelist has ever had any real sense of audience. C. P. Snow made the point that he would, given a choice, prefer to be a writer in England to a writer in America because, for better or worse, the Establishment of his country would read him and know him as he knew them, as the Greek dramatists knew and were known by their city's audience. One cannot imagine the American President, any American President, reading a work by a serious contemporary American writer. This lack of response is to me at the center of Mailer's desperation. He is a public writer, not a private artist; he wants to influence those who are alive at this time, but they will not notice him even when he is good. So each time he speaks he must become more bold, more loud, put on brighter motley and shake more foolish bells. *Anything* to get their attention, and finally (and this could be his tragedy) so much energy is spent in getting the indifferent ear to listen that when the time comes for him to speak there may be not enough strength or creative imagination left him to say what he *knows*. Exhausted, he becomes like Louis Lambert in Balzac's curious novel of the visionary-artist who, having seen straight through to the heart of the mystery, dies mad, murmuring: "The angels are white."

Yet of all my contemporaries I retain the greatest affection for Mailer as a force and as an artist. He is a man whose faults, though many, add to rather than subtract from the sum of his natural achievement. There is more virtue in his failures than in most small, premeditated successes which, in Cynic's phrase, "debase currency." Mailer, in all that he does, whether he does it well or ill, is honorable, and that is the highest praise I can give any writer in this piping time.

## JAMES BALDWIN
### From "The Black Boy Looks at the White Boy"
#### *Esquire*, May 1961, pp. 102–6

> I walked and I walked
> Till I wore out my shoes.
> I can't walk so far, but
> Yonder come the blues.
> (Ma Rainey)

I first met Norman Mailer about five years ago, in Paris, at the home of Jean Malaquais. Let me bring in at once the theme that will repeat itself over and over throughout this love letter: I was then (and I have not changed much) a very tight, tense, lean, abnormally ambitious, abnormally intelligent, and hungry black cat. It is important that I admit that, at the time I met Norman, I was extremely worried about my career; and a writer who is worried about his career is also fighting for his life. I was approaching the end of a love affair, and I was not taking it very well. Norman and I are alike in this, that we both tend to suspect others of putting us down, and we strike before we're struck. Only, our styles are very different: I am a black boy from the Harlem streets, and Norman is a middle-class Jew. I am not dragging my personal history into this gratuitously, and I hope I do not need to say that no sneer is implied in the above description of Norman. But these are the facts and in my own relationship to Norman they are crucial facts.

Also, I have no right to talk about Norman without risking a distinctly chilling self-exposure. I take him very seriously, he is very dear to me. And I think I know something about his journey from my black boy's point of view because my own journey is not really so very different, and also because I have spent most of my life, after all, watching white people and outwitting them, so that I might survive. I think that I know something about the American masculinity which most men of my generation do not know because they have not been menaced by it in the way that I have been. It is still true, alas, that to be an American Negro male is also to be a kind of walking phallic symbol: which means that one pays, in one's own personality, for the sexual insecurity of others. The relationship, therefore, of a black boy to a white boy is a very complex thing.

There is a difference, though, between Norman and myself in that I think he still imagines that he has something to save, whereas I have never had anything to lose. Or, perhaps I ought to put it another way: the thing that most white people imagine that they can salvage from the storm of life is really, in sum, their innocence. It was this commodity precisely which I had to get rid of at once, literally, on pain of death. I am afraid that most of the white people I have ever known impressed me as being in the grip of a weird nostalgia, dreaming of a vanished state of security and order, against which dream, unfailingly and unconsciously, they tested and very often lost their lives. It is a terrible thing to say, but I am afraid that for a very long time the troubles of white people failed to impress me as being real trouble. They put me in mind of children crying because the breast has been taken away. Time and love have modified my tough-boy lack of charity, but the attitude sketched above was my first attitude and I am sure that there is a great deal of it left.

To proceed: two lean cats, one white and one black, met in a French living room. I had heard of him, he had heard of me. And here we were, suddenly, circling around each other.

We liked each other at once, but each was frightened that the other would pull rank. He could have pulled rank on me because he was more famous and had more money and also because he was white; but I could have pulled rank on him precisely because I was black and knew more about that periphery he so helplessly maligns in "The White Negro" than he could ever hope to know. Already, you see, we were trapped in our roles and our attitudes: the toughest kid on the block was meeting the toughest kid on the block. I think that both of us were pretty weary of this grueling and thankless role, I know that I am; but the roles that we construct are constructed because we feel that they will help us to survive and also, of course, because they fulfill something in our personalities; and one does not, therefore, cease playing a role simply because one has begun to understand it. All roles are dangerous. The world tends to trap and immobilize you in the role you play; and it is not always easy—in fact, it is always extremely hard—to maintain a kind of watchful, mocking distance between oneself as one appears to be and oneself as one actually is.

I think that Norman was working on *The Deer Park* at that time, or had just finished it, and Malaquais, who had translated *The Naked and the Dead* into French, did not like *The Deer Park*. I had not then read the book; if I had, I would have been astonished that Norman could have expected Malaquais to like it. What Norman was trying to do in *The Deer Park*, and quite apart, now, from whether or not he succeeded, could only—it seems to me—baffle and annoy a French intellectual who seemed to me essentially rationalistic. Norman has many qualities and faults, but I have never heard anyone accuse him of possessing this particular one. But Malaquais's opinion seemed to mean a great deal to him—this astonished me, too; and there was a running, good-natured but astringent argument between them, with Malaquais playing the role of the old lion and Norman playing the role of the powerful but clumsy cub. And, I must say, I think that each of them got a great deal of pleasure out of the other's performance. The night we met, we stayed up very late, and did a great deal of drinking and shouting. But beneath all the shouting and the posing and the mutual showing off, something very wonderful was happening. I was aware of a new and warm presence in my life, for I had met someone I wanted to know, who wanted to know me.

Norman and his wife, Adele, along with a Negro jazz musician friend, and myself, met fairly often during the few weeks that found us all in the same city. I think that Norman had come in from Spain, and he was shortly to return to the States; and it was not long after Norman's departure that I left Paris for Corsica. My memory of that time is both blurred and sharp, and, oddly enough, is principally of Norman—confident, boastful, exuberant, and loving—striding through the soft Paris nights like a gladiator. And I think, alas, that I envied him: his success, and his youth, and his love. And this meant that though Norman really wanted to know me, and though I really wanted to know him, I hung back, held fire, danced, and lied. I was not going to come crawling out of my ruined house, all bloody, no, baby, sing no sad songs for *me*. And the great gap between Norman's state and my own had a terrible effect on our relationship, for it inevitably connected, not to say collided, with that myth of the sexuality of Negroes which Norman, like so many others, refuses to give up. The sexual battleground, if I may call it that, is really the same for everyone; and I, at this point, was just about to be carried off the battleground on my shield, if anyone could find it; so how could I play, in any way whatever, the noble savage?

At the same time, my temperament and my experience in this country had led me to expect very little from most American whites, especially, horribly enough, my friends: so it did not seem worthwhile to challenge, in any real way, Norman's views of life on the periphery, or to put him down for them. I was weary, to tell the truth. I had tried, in the States, to convey something of what it felt like to be a Negro and no one had been able to listen: they wanted their romance. And, anyway, the really ghastly thing about trying to convey to a white man the reality of the Negro experience has nothing whatever to do with the fact of color, but has to do with this man's relationship to his own life. He will face in your life only what he is willing to face in his. Well, this means that one finds oneself tampering with the insides of a stranger, to no purpose, which one probably has no right to do, and I chickened out. And matters were not helped at all by the fact that the Negro jazz musicians, among whom we sometimes found ourselves, who really liked Norman, did not for an instant consider him as being even remotely "hip" and Norman did not know this and I could not tell him. He never broke through to them, at least not as far as I know; and they were far too "hip," if that is the word I want, even to consider breaking through to him. They thought he was a real sweet ofay cat, but a little frantic.

But we were far more cheerful than anything I've said might indicate, and none of the above seemed to matter very much at the time. Other things mattered, like walking and talking and drinking and eating, and the way Adele laughed, and the way Norman argued. He argued like a young man, he argued to win: and while I found him charming, he may have found me exasperating, for I kept moving back before that short, prodding forefinger. I couldn't submit my arguments, or my real questions, for I had too much to hide. Or so it seemed to me then. I submit, though I may be wrong, that I was then at the beginning of a terrifying adventure, not too unlike the conundrum which seems to menace Norman now.

"I had done a few things and earned a few pence"; but the things I had written were behind me, could not be written again, could not be repeated. I was also realizing that all that the world could give me as an artist, it had, in effect, already given. In the years that stretched before me, all that I could look forward to, in that way, were a few more prizes, or a lot more, and a little more, or a lot more money. And my private life had failed—had failed, had failed. One of the reasons I had fought so hard, after all, was to wrest from the world fame and money and love. And here I was, at thirty-two, finding my notoriety hard to bear, since its principal effect was to make me more lonely; money, it turned out, was exactly like sex, you thought of nothing else if you didn't have it and thought of other things if you did; and love, as far as I could see, was over.

⟨. . .⟩ In the most important areas of anybody's life, the will usually operates as a traitor. My own will was busily pointing out to me the most fantastically unreal alternatives to my pain, all of which I tried, all of which—luckily—failed. When, late in the evening or early in the morning, Norman and Adele returned to their hotel on the Quai Voltaire, I wandered through Paris, the underside of Paris, drinking, screwing, fighting—it's a wonder I wasn't killed. And then it was morning, I would somehow be home—usually, anyway—and the typewriter would be there, staring at me; and the manuscript of the new novel, which it seemed I would never be able to achieve, and from which clearly I was never going to be released, was scattered all over the floor.

That's the way it is. I think it is the most dangerous point in the life of any artist, his longest, most hideous turning; and especially for a man, an American man, whose principle is action and whose jewel is optimism, who must now accept what certainly then seems to be a gray passivity and an endless despair. It is the point at which many artists lose their minds, or commit suicide, or throw themselves into good works, or try to enter politics. For all of this is happening not only in the wilderness of the soul, but in the real world which accomplishes its seductions not by offering you opportunities to be wicked but by offering opportunities to be good, to be active and effective, to be admired and central and apparently loved.

Norman came on to America, and I went to Corsica. We wrote each other a few times. I confided to Norman that I was very apprehensive about the reception of *Giovanni's Room*, and he was good enough to write some very encouraging things about it when it came out. The critics had jumped on him with both their left feet when he published *The Deer Park*—which I still had not read—and this created a kind of bond, or strengthened the bond already existing between us. About a year and several overflowing wastebaskets later, I, too, returned to America, not vastly improved by having been out of it, but not knowing where else to go; and one day, while I was sitting dully in my house, Norman called me from Connecticut. A few people were going to be there—for the weekend—and he wanted me to come, too. We had not seen each other since Paris.

Well, I wanted to go, that is, I wanted to see Norman; but I did not want to see any people, and so the tone of my acceptance was not very enthusiastic. I realized that he felt this, but I did not know what to do about it. He gave me train schedules and hung up.

Getting to Connecticut would have been no hassle if I could have pulled myself together to get to the train. And I was sorry, as I meandered around my house and time flew and trains left, that I had not been more honest with Norman and told him exactly how I felt. But I had not known how to do this, or it had not really occurred to me to do it, especially not over the phone.

So there was another phone call, I forget who called whom, which went something like this:

N: Don't feel you have to. I'm not trying to bug you.

J: It's not that. It's just—

N: You don't really want to come, do you?

J: I don't really feel up to it.

N: I understand. I guess you just don't like the Connecticut gentry.

J: Well—don't you ever come to the city?

N: Sure. We'll see each other.

J: I hope so. I'd like to see you.

N: OK, till then.

And he hung up. I thought, I ought to write him a letter, but of course I did nothing of the sort. It was around this time I went south, I think; anyway, we did not see each other for a long time.

But I thought about him a great deal. The grapevine keeps all of us advised of the others' movements, so I knew when Norman left Connecticut for New York, heard that he had been present at this or that party and what he had said: usually something rude, often something penetrating, sometimes something so hilariously silly that it was difficult to believe he had been serious. (This was my reaction when I first heard his famous running-for-President remark. I dismissed it. I was wrong.) Or he had been seen in this or that Village spot, in which unfailingly there would be someone—out of spite, idleness, envy, exasperation, out of the bottomless, eerie, aimless hostility which characterizes almost every bar in New York, to speak only of bars—to put him down. I heard of a couple of fistfights, and, of course, I was always encountering people who hated his guts. These people always mildly

surprised me, and so did the news of his fights: it was hard for me to imagine that anyone could really dislike Norman, anyone that is, who had encountered him personally. I knew of one fight he had had, forced on him, apparently, by a blowhard Village type whom I considered rather pathetic. I didn't blame Norman for this fight, but I couldn't help wondering why he bothered to rise to such a shapeless challenge. It seemed simpler, as I was always telling myself, just to stay out of Village bars.

And people talked about Norman with a kind of avid glee, which I found very ugly. Pleasure made their saliva flow, they sprayed and all but drooled, and their eyes shone with that bloodlust which is the only real tribute the mediocre are capable of bringing to the extraordinary. Many of the people who claimed to be seeing Norman all the time impressed me as being, to tell the truth, pitifully far beneath him. But this is also true, alas, of much of my own entourage. The people who are in one's life or merely continually in one's presence reveal a great deal about one's needs and terrors. Also, one's hopes.

I was not, however, on the scene. I was on the road—not quite, I trust, in the sense that Kerouac's boys are; but I presented, certainly, a moving target. And I was reading Norman Mailer. Before I had met him, I had only read *The Naked and the Dead*, "The White Negro," and *Barbary Shore*—I think this is right, though it may be that I only read "The White Negro" later and confuse my reading of that piece with some of my discussions with Norman. Anyway, I could not, with the best will in the world, make any sense out of "The White Negro," and, in fact, it was hard for me to imagine that this essay had been written by the same man who wrote the novels. Both *The Naked and the Dead* and (for the most part) *Barbary Shore* are written in a lean, spare, muscular prose which accomplishes almost exactly what it sets out to do. Even *Barbary Shore*, which loses itself in its last half (and which deserves, by the way, far more serious treatment than it has received), never becomes as downright impenetrable as "The White Negro" does.

Now, much of this, I told myself, had to do with my resistance to the title, and with a kind of fury that so antique a vision of the blacks should, at this late hour, and in so many borrowed heirlooms, be stepping off the A train. But I was also baffled by the passion with which Norman appeared to be imitating so many people inferior to himself, i.e., Kerouac, and all the other Suzuki rhythm boys. From them, indeed, I expected nothing more than their pablum-clogged cries of *Kicks!* and *Holy!* It seemed very clear to me that their glorification of the orgasm was but a way of avoiding all of the terrors of life and love. But Norman knew better, had to know better. *The Naked and the Dead*, *Barbary Shore*, and *The Deer Park* proved it. In each of these novels, there is a toughness and subtlety of conception, and a sense of the danger and complexity of human relationships which one will search for in vain, not only in the work produced by the aforementioned coterie, but in most of the novels produced by Norman's contemporaries. What in the world, then, was he doing, slumming so outrageously, in such a dreary crowd?

For, exactly because he knew better, and in exactly the same way that no one can become more lewdly vicious than an imitation libertine, Norman felt compelled to carry their mystique further than they had, to be more "hip," or more "beat," to dominate, in fact, their dreaming field; and since this mystique depended on a total rejection of life, and insisted on the fulfillment of an infantile dream of love, the mystique could only be extended into violence. No one is more dangerous than he who imagines himself pure in heart: for his purity, by definition, is unassailable.

But *why* should it be necessary to borrow the Depression language of deprived Negroes, which eventually evolved into jive and bop talk, in order to justify such a grim system of delusions? Why malign the sorely menaced sexuality of Negroes in order to justify the white man's own sexual panic? Especially as, in Norman's case, and as indicated by his work, he has a very real sense of sexual responsibility, and, even, odd as it may sound to some, of sexual morality, and a genuine commitment to life. ⟨. . .⟩

"Man," said a Negro musician to me once, talking about Norman, "the only trouble with that cat is that he's white." This does not mean exactly what it says—or, rather, it *does* mean exactly what it says, and not what it might be taken to mean—and it is a very shrewd observation. What my friend meant was that to become a Negro man, let alone a Negro artist, one had to make oneself up as one went along. This had to be done in the not-at-all-metaphorical teeth of the world's determination to destroy you. The world had prepared no place for you, and if the world had its way, no place would ever exist. Now, this is true for everyone, but, in the case of a Negro, this truth is absolutely naked: if he deludes himself about it, he will die. This is not the way this truth presents itself to white men, who believe the world is theirs and who, albeit unconsciously, expect the world to help them in the achievement of their identity. But the world does not do this—for anyone; the world is not interested in anyone's identity. And, therefore, the anguish which can overtake a white man comes in the middle of his life, when he must make the almost inconceivable effort to divest himself of everything he has ever expected or believed, when he must take himself apart and put himself together again, walking out of the world, into limbo, or into what certainly looks like limbo. This cannot yet happen to any Negro of Norman's age, for the reason that his delusions and defenses are either absolutely impenetrable by this time, or he has failed to survive them. "I want to know how power works," Norman once said to me, "how it really works, in detail." Well, I know how power works, it has worked on me, and if I didn't know how power worked, I would be dead. And it goes without saying, perhaps, that I have simply never been able to afford myself any illusions concerning the manipulation of that power. My revenge, I decided very early, would be to achieve a power which outlasts kingdoms.

⟨. . .⟩ While I was out of the country, Norman published *Advertisements for Myself*, which presently crossed the ocean to the apartment of James Jones. Bill Styron was also in Paris at that time, and one evening the three of us sat in Jim's living room, reading aloud, in a kind of drunken, masochistic fascination, Norman's judgment of our personalities and our work. Actually, I came off best, I suppose; there was less about me, and it was less venomous. But the condescension infuriated me; also, to tell the truth, my feelings were hurt. I felt that if that was the way Norman felt about me, he should have told me so. He had said that I was incapable of saying "F—— you" to the reader. My first temptation was to send him a cablegram which would disabuse him of that notion, at least insofar as one reader was concerned. But then I thought, No, I would be cool about it, and fail to react as he so clearly wanted me to. Also, I must say, his judgment of myself seemed so wide of the mark and so childish that it was hard to stay angry. I wondered what in the world was going on in his mind. Did he really suppose that he had now become the builder and destroyer of reputations,

And of *my* reputation?

We met in the Actors' Studio one afternoon, after a performance of *The Deer Park*—which I deliberately arrived too late to see, since I really did not know how I was going to react to Norman, and didn't want to betray myself by clobbering his play. When the discussion ended, I stood, again on the edge of the crowd around him, waiting. Over someone's shoulder, our eyes met, and Norman smiled.

"We've got something to talk about," I told him.

"I figured that," he said, smiling.

We went to a bar, and sat opposite each other. I was relieved to discover that I was not angry, not even (as far as I could tell) at the bottom of my heart. But, "Why did you write those things about me?"

"Well, I'll tell you about that," he said—Norman has several accents, and I think this was his Texas one—"I sort of figured you had it coming to you."

"Why?"

"Well, I think there's some truth in it."

"Well, if you felt that way, why didn't you ever say so—to me?"

"Well, I figured if this was going to break up our friendship, something else would come along to break it up just as fast."

I couldn't disagree with that.

"You're the only one I kind of regret hitting so hard," he said, with a grin. "I think I—probably—wouldn't say it quite that way now."

With this, I had to be content. We sat for perhaps an hour, talking of other things, and, again, I was struck by his stance: leaning on the table, shoulders hunched, seeming, really, to roll like a boxer's, and his hands moving as though he were dealing with a sparring partner. And we were talking of physical courage, and the necessity of never letting another guy get the better of you.

I laughed. "Norman, I can't go through the world the way you do because I haven't got your shoulders."

He grinned, as though I were his pupil. "But you're a pretty tough little mother, too," he said, and referred to one of the grimmer of my Village misadventures, a misadventure which certainly proved that I had a dangerously sharp tongue, but which didn't really prove anything about my courage. Which, anyway, I had long ago given up trying to prove.

I did not see Norman again until Provincetown, just after his celebrated brush with the police there, which resulted, according to Norman, in making the climate of Provincetown as "mellow as Jello." The climate didn't seem very different to me—dull natives, dull tourists, malevolent policemen; I certainly, in any case, would never have dreamed of testing Norman's sanguine conclusion. But we had a great time, lying around the beach, and driving about, and we began to be closer than we had been for a long time.

It was during this Provincetown visit that I realized, for the first time, during a long exchange Norman and I had, in a kitchen, at someone else's party, that Norman was really fascinated by the nature of political power. But, though he said so, I did not really believe that he was fascinated by it as a possibility for himself. He was then doing the great piece on the Democratic convention which was published in *Esquire*, and I put his fascination down to that. I tend not to worry about writers as long as they are working—which is not as romantic as it may sound—and he seemed quite happy with his wife, his family, himself. I declined, naturally, to rise at dawn, as he apparently often did, to go running or swimming or boxing, but Norman seemed to get a great charge out of these admirable pursuits and didn't put me down too hard for my comparative decadence.

He and Adele and the two children took me to the plane one afternoon, the tiny plane which shuttles from Provincetown to Boston. It was a great day, clear and sunny, and that was the way I felt: for it seemed to me that we had all, at last, reestablished our old connection.

And then I heard that Norman was running for mayor, which I dismissed as a joke and refused to believe until it became hideously clear that it was not a joke at all. I was furious. I thought, You son of a bitch, you're copping out. You're one of the very few writers around who might really become a great writer, who might help to excavate the buried consciousness of this country, and you want to settle for being the lousy mayor of New York. *It's not your job.* And I don't at all mean to suggest that writers are not responsible to and for— in any case, always for—the social order. I don't, for that matter, even mean to suggest that Norman would have made a particularly bad mayor, though I confess that I simply cannot see him in this role. And there is probably some truth in the suggestion, put forward by Norman and others, that the shock value of having such a man in such an office, or merely running for such an office, would have had a salutary effect on the life of this city—particularly, I must say, as relates to our young people, who are certainly in desperate need of adults who love them and take them seriously, and whom they can respect. (Serious citizens may not respect Norman, but young people do, and do not respect the serious citizens; and their instincts are quite sound.)

But I do not feel that a writer's responsibility can be discharged in this way. I do not think, if one is a writer, that one escapes it by trying to become something else. One does *not* become something else: one becomes nothing. And what is crucial here is that the writer, however unwillingly, always, somewhere, knows this. There is no structure he can build strong enough to keep out this self-knowledge. What *has* happened, however, time and time again, is that the fantasy structure the writer builds in order to escape his central responsibility operates not as his fortress, but his prison, and he perishes within it. Or: the structure he has built becomes so stifling, so lonely, so false, and acquires such a violent and dangerous life of its own, that he can break out of it only by bringing the entire structure down. With a great crash, inevitably, and on his own head, and on the heads of those closest to him. It is like smashing the windows one second before one asphyxiates; it is like burning down the house in order, at last, to be free of it. ⟨. . .⟩

One can never really see into the heart, the mind, the soul of another. Norman is my very good friend, but perhaps I do not really understand him at all, and perhaps everything I have tried to suggest in the foregoing is false. I do not think so, but it may be. One thing, however, I am certain is *not* false, and that is simply the fact of his being a writer, and the incalculable potential he as a writer contains. His work, after all, is all that will be left when the newspapers are yellowed, all the gossip columnists silenced, and all the cocktail parties over, and when Norman and you and I are dead. I know that this point of view is not terribly fashionable these days, but I think we *do* have a responsibility, not only to ourselves and to our own time, but to those who are coming after us. (I refuse to believe that no one is coming after us.) And I suppose that this responsibility can only be discharged by dealing as truthfully as we know how with our present fortunes, these present days. So that my concern with Norman, finally, has to do with how deeply he has understood these last sad and stormy events. If he has understood them,

then he is richer and we are richer, too; if he has not understood them, we are all much poorer. For, though it clearly needs to be brought into focus, he has a real vision of ourselves as we are, and it cannot be too often repeated in this country now, that, where there is no vision, the people perish.

## TOM WOLFE
### "Son of *Crime and Punishment*, or:
### How to Go Eight Fast Rounds with the
### Heavyweight Champ—and Lose"
*Book Week*, March 14, 1965, pp. 1, 10, 12–13

Norman Mailer announced in the December 1963 issue of *Esquire*, in a column he had in there called "The Big Bite," that he was going to write a serialized novel under the old nineteenth-century pop magazine conditions, namely, in monthly installments, writing against a deadline every month. A lot of *pressure* and everything. Mailer worked the whole thing out with the editor of *Esquire*, Harold Hayes. The idea was to write the first chapter and then, after that went to press, he would write the second chapter; and after that one went to press, he would write the third one, and so on, through eight chapters, turning out one every thirty days, writing right up to the press time all the time.

The idea stirred up a lot of interest among literati and culturati in New York. For one thing—daring!—it was like *Dickens* or something. That comparison came up quite a bit— Dickens. It was going to be interesting to see if Mailer could voluntarily put himself inside the same kind of pressure cooker Dickens worked in and not merely endure but thrive on the pressure the way Dickens did. *Tour de force! Neo-Dickens! Courage under fire!* Actually, looking back on it, everybody should have figured out at the time that it really wasn't Dickens that Mailer had in mind. Any old epopt of the Harvard EngLit like Norman Mailer would consider Dickens a lightweight. The hell with Charles Dickens. The writer Mailer had in mind was a heavyweight, Dostoevski. I will try to show in a moment, in the scholarly fashion, how specifically he had Dostoevski in mind.

The other thing that stirred up a lot of interest in this prospect of Mailer's was his personal history. Mailer had not written a novel in practically ten years when he started on this serial. Seventeen years ago, in 1948, Mailer had published a highly praised first novel, *The Naked and the Dead*. Among the military novels of the period, I would say it ranked second only to James Jones's *From Here to Eternity*. Mailer published his second novel, *Barbary Shore*, in 1951. The critics really bombed it. Somebody called it "a 1984 for D train winos." The D train on New York's IND subway line runs all the way from 205th Street in the Bronx to Coney Island and is great for sleeping it off. Mailer published his third novel, *The Deer Park*, in 1955. The critics bushwhacked him again. They cut him up, they *tenderized* him.

Mailer stopped publishing novels at that point, although he did try to write one, a kind of windy one, judging from excerpts. Yet during the next ten years, from then to now, Mailer became a bigger public figure writing no novels at all than he had by writing them. He was on television all the time and wrote articles here and there. He hung around with prizefighters the way Hemingway hung around with bullfighters, and he tried pot and existentialism and Negroes and did a great deal of brooding over God, freedom and immortality and the rest of it. He had a lot of good roughhousing ego and anger and showmanship and could always get an audience, even among people who didn't want to listen. *Happy Chutzpah!*

In 1960 his life really began to pick up momentum. He started to write articles for *Esquire*, reportage, which were by far his best work since *The Naked and the Dead*. The first big one was on John Kennedy's nomination. Mailer, like Gore Vidal and James Michener, had gotten very much wrapped up in politics and gotten a mystic crush on Kennedy, much the way the stock liberals of another generation had fallen for the first American "left aristocrat," Franklin Roosevelt. Mailer announced on TV that he was going to run for mayor of New York.

He also committed a number of acts that firmly established him in the Wild Boy of Western Literature tradition. Holy Beasts! That wasn't why he committed them, but that was the upshot of it. First off, in June 1960, he was arrested in the boho resort of Provincetown, on Cape Cod, for getting drunk and hailing a police car with the cry "Taxi! Taxi!" because it had a light on top of it. His head was cracked open in a fracas at the station house, but he got some revenge on the police by acting as his own lawyer at the trial and giving the police a going-over on the stand. On November 14, 1960, he was arrested about 4 A.M. in Birdland, the Broadway jazz club, after an argument over a check. Six days later he stabbed his second wife, Adele, after a party in their apartment on Ninety-fourth Street. She refused to press charges, and he got off with a suspended sentence, but the case got a lot of mileage in the papers.

He was all over the papers again in 1961 when they pulled the curtain on him during a poetry reading at the Young Men's Hebrew Association because his poems were getting too gamey for even that liberal atmosphere. In 1962, more headlines—Mailer married Lady Jeanne Campbell, daughter of the Duke of Argyll and granddaughter of Lord Beaverbrook. Their courtship, their marriage, their breakup, their divorce in 1963, the old Juarez route—people were fascinated by all this and talked about it all the time. The pace kept picking up and picking up, even to the point where Mailer hired a hall, Carnegie Hall, in 1963 and got up on a podium and orated, read from his own works, preached, shouted, held colloquies with the audience, great stuff. He also started writing his *Esquire* column, "The Big Bite," which kind of flamed out—but then—brave bull!—he began his serial novel, *An American Dream*, in *Esquire's* January 1964 issue.

The story, as it unfolded, ran like this: Stephen Rojack, war hero, ex-congressman, author, professor, television star, and accomplished stud, is separated from his wife, Deborah, a forceful woman who has noble blood in her veins and an English accent. He loves her but he hates her, because she is all the time humiliating him. He visits her apartment one night, they exchange their usual venomous *mots*, he gets mad and strangles her to death. He throws her body out the window onto the East River Drive, where it causes a five-car pile-up. Brought to a halt by the whole mess is a car bearing Eddie Ganucci, the Mafia boss, and Cherry, nightclub singer and Mafia love slave. Rojack and Cherry fall in love more or less at first sight. Rojack claims his wife committed suicide right in front of his eyes. The bulk of the story concerns whether or not the police can pin the murder on Rojack and, more important, whether or not he is strong enough to withstand the various pressures the whole thing puts on him. The police put him through an ingenious interrogation, but he maintains his cool and is released for the time being. He turns to Cherry, takes up with her, and beats up her Negro ex-lover, one of America's great popular singers, Shago Martin. Rojack is now ready to face up to his dead wife's father, fabulously wealthy, powerful

Barney Oswald Kelly. They have a talk-out in Kelly's Waldorf Towers apartment and a climactic ordeal-by-courage.

The scramble to meet the deadlines in writing the serial was just as wild as Mailer himself had predicted it would be. Hayes, *Esquire's* editor, kept the layout forms open for Mailer's installments practically up to the morning of the day the presses had to run. A lot of roaring around, one understands, gasps, groans, desperation, but even in all that Mailer wasn't really doing things the Charles Dickens way. Dickens was rather cool about the whole process. Sometimes Dickens used to come down in the living room and write down there with four or five guests sitting around and talking with his wife. He would put his head up from time to time and interject a remark when something in the conversation caught his ear. That cool, hip Dickens. But Mailer wasn't even thinking about Dickens. He was going to take on Dostoevski.

Mailer has always been measuring himself against other writers. He has been saying, Is Jones, Willingham, Capote or Kerouac or whoever as good as me, long after most literati regarded Mailer as no longer even in the competition. In one essay, "The Other Talent in the Room," he managed to tell off most of the prominent novelists in the country as inferior men—weaklings mostly, no guts, no cool, can't drink, you know?—as well as artists. Well, here he had demolished all his contemporaries, and so now he had nothing but a few dead but durable giants to look to. Hemingway, with whom Mailer identifies quite a bit, had the same streak. Hemingway once announced that he had beaten Turgenev's brains out and there was only one champ left to take on, Tolstoi. Mailer has even stronger motives, personal ones, to look to Dostoevski.

Dostoevski, like Mailer, had a solid decade in his young manhood when he didn't write a thing. In 1849 Dostoevski was convicted as a revolutionary and sent to Siberia. He didn't return to St. Petersburg and start writing until 1859, at the age of thirty-eight. Mailer had a hiatus almost that long, 1954 to 1964. Nobody sent Mailer off anywhere, but the result was the same. There he was, forty-one years old, and hadn't written a novel since he was thirty-one. Anyway, Mailer knew something about Dostoevski's comeback that isn't popularly known, namely, that Dostoevski did it all, suddenly burst forth as the greatest writer in Russia, by writing serialized novels under monthly deadline pressure. Dostoevski's greatest works, *Crime and Punishment, The Gambler, The Idiot, The Possessed, The Brothers Karamazov*, first appeared in magazines, most of them in *Russky Vestnik*.

Dostoevski wrote Katkov, the editor of *Russky Vestnik*, offering him the first in this incredible streak of magazine fiction, *Crime and Punishment*, one September (1865), the same month of the year Mailer picked to offer *An American Dream* to Hayes at *Esquire*. I haven't talked to Mailer about this, but I wouldn't be surprised if he didn't decide to follow Dostoevski's example just that closely. He has a great vein of nineteenth-century superstition in him, a lot of voodoo about *cancer*, for example, the personal outlook of the kidney cells, incredible gothic theorizing. Mailer apparently has read Dostoevski's letters and diaries. In his prospectus for the serial project in the December 1963 *Esquire*, he cites a passage from Dostoevski's journals telling how he used to work all night long, in the lucid moments between attacks of epilepsy, in order to keep going and meet the deadlines.

Dostoevski's performance in 1866, the year *Crime and Punishment* started appearing in *Russky Vestnik*, was prodigious. The first installment appeared in January—the month of the year Mailer's serial began—and there were eight installments in all—the same as with Mailer. In the same year (1866)

Dostoevski also signed a contract to do a novel for another magazine by November 1. If he didn't make the deadline, he would suffer a heavy financial penalty, and the publisher, Stelovski, would get the right to publish all of Dostoevski's novels, in book form, past and future, without giving him anything. As of October 1 Dostoevski still had about one-fourth of *Crime and Punishment* to write and hadn't written a line of the novel for Stelovski. On October 4 he hired a stenographer—later he married her—and started dictating *The Gambler* right out of his head. He finished it on October 30, a forty-thousand-word novel that is considered his most perfect novel from a technical point of view. The next day he sat down and started dictating the last two installments of *Crime and Punishment* and was home safe on both novels.

All of this must have had a double appeal for Mailer. First of all, here was a man who made his comeback in a big way through the magazine serial. Second, he did it through a *roman à thèse*, a philosophical novel. Mailer has a terrible hang-up on the *roman à thèse*. The reason for the failure of both *Barbary Shore* and *The Deer Park* was chiefly their soggy tractlike nature. But *Crime and Punishment* was a *roman à thèse* that did make it, and *An American Dream*—well, there are a great many things in Mailer's book that resemble *Crime and Punishment* in plot, structure, theme and detail.

Mailer's book, like *Crime and Punishment*, concerns a sensitive young man who murders a woman, and the story in each case hinges on whether or not the hero is going to have the existential—to use a term Mailer likes—the existential willpower, the courage, to weather the storm that follows. In each case, the hero turns to a quasi-prostitute for emotional sustenance immediately after the crime—Raskolnikov turns to Sonia in *Crime and Punishment* and Rojack turns to Cherry in Mailer's book. In both cases the hero comes together with the girl as the result of a wreck in the street. In both cases the hero confesses his guilt to the girl as a pledge of faith. In both books he undergoes a long, intriguing interrogation by the authorities, in which the questioner seems to know he did it and is trying to trap him emotionally and verbally into confessing. In both cases it is technically, circumstantially, within the power of the hero to get out of the whole thing without admitting his guilt. Most curiously of all, Mailer, like Dostoevski, has chosen to add to the story a short, final chapter, called "Epilogue"—rather weak and pointless in each case—in which the hero goes off into some kind of wasteland. Raskolnikov is sent off to Siberia, even though the book has a very powerful and dramatic natural ending with the confession itself. Mailer has Rojack drive off into the Nevada desert.

Dostoevski is not a great deal more profound than Mailer, but Dostoevski always had the good fortune of never being able to make his ideas dominate his characters. Dostoevski is always starting out to have some characters express one of his ideas and very quickly the whole thing gets out of hand, Dostoevski gets wrapped up in the character rather than the idea, as in Marmeladov's saloon scene. Dostoevski resembled Dickens in this respect. Both seemed to have such powers of imagination that characters grew in concept during the very process of the writing, with all sorts of baroque and humorous curlicues of the psyche coming out. Mailer's trouble is that whenever he has a theory, which is pretty often, he always kills some poor son of a bitch in his book with it. In *An American Dream* he crushes his hero, Rojack, with too much thinking in the first fourteen and a half pages and kills him off for the rest of the novel.

At the outset we get a picture of this brave, talented, and highly placed man—hero, author, scholar, TV star, socialite,

sex maestro—who for some reason is in a hopeless funk, foundering, sinking down through a lot of rancid gothic metaphysics. One is reminded of a remark Turgenev made about Dostoevski's weakest novel, *Raw Youth*: "I took a glance into that chaos. God! What sour stuff—the stench of the sickroom, unprofitable gibberish, psychological excavation." By page 13 Rojack is out on somebody's apartment terrace thinking about jumping, and by then he is already so boring and logorrheic, one's impulse is to put the book down and say, Jump. Mailer was clearly trying to establish a Dostoevskian mood of the Troubled Genius in this passage. What he does mainly, however, is give one the feeling that here is some old gasbag who doesn't know when he is well off. Rojack, like all of Mailer's people, doesn't know how to laugh. He opens his mouth and—aaaagh—just brays in a kind of sterile Pentecostal frenzy. Mailer could still have salvaged Rojack, I suspect, if he had only written the novel in the third person instead of the first. Use of the first person leads Mailer to have his hero think himself into all sorts of puling funk holes all the time.

If I were editing *An American Dream*, I would cut out the first fourteen pages and about half of page 15, through the sentence that ends ". . . they were flinching as the wind rode by." That sentence is too nineteenth-century gothic anyway, all this business of the wind riding by. The wind doesn't do much riding in this era of meteorology, it just blows. I would start the book with the next sentence, "A familiar misery was on me." That's a little Poe-like, but it's all right. If the book starts right there, no background information needs to be added. The whole thing starts off fast from that point and we have a good little action story going. One big advantage is that now, in the scene where Rojack starts having words with his wife, which is a fine scene, actually, we can have some kind of sympathy for him, because his wife is obviously such an accomplished bitch. We can even sympathize with his choking her to death and we can pull for the poor guy to outwit the police. As the book is actually written, however, one's first impulse is to hope that Rojack *gets his*, too.

The next passage that has to go is pages 41 through 46, which describes perhaps the most ludicrous love scene in fiction. Rojack starts *thinking* again, that is the trouble. He gets this *theory* that after he murders his wife he has got to make love to her maid, Ruta, by alternating, rapidly, from conventional copulation to buggery, back and forth. He does so, and he is *thinking* all the time. It is all wrapped up with God, the Devil, and the Proper Orgasm, and even aside from certain quaint anatomical impossibilities, it is all told in some kind of great gothic Lake Country language of elegance. It sounds, actually, with all these gods, devils, and orgasms running around, like some Methodist minister who has discovered orgone theory and, with a supreme ecumenical thrust, has decided to embrace both John Wesley and Wilhelm Reich.

If we get rid of that scene, we are quickly back into a stretch of fine fast-paced action, almost like James M. Cain. The spell breaks in the last chapter, however, when Rojack starts thinking his head off again during the confrontation with Barney Oswald Kelly. The scene bogs down further in another difficulty of the book, unreal dialogue. Kelly has a lengthy speech in this chapter and keeps slipping into such rhetoric as, "I thought myself a competitive fellow, just consider—I had to be nearly as supersensational with sex as with *dinero*, and Bess and I gave each other some glorious good times in a row; up would climb the male ego; applause from Bess was accolade from Cleopatra; then swish! she'd vanish."

Aside from the coy expressions, such as *dinero*, all this doesn't . . . *parse*. One reason, perhaps, is that Mailer brings his big characters on one by one in this book like cameo parts in a play like *The Days and Nights of Beebee Fenstermaker.* They have just one big scene each, and so they have to start talking like maniacs right from the word go and ricochet around all over the place and tell their whole life stories while Rojack, who is *thinking* all the time, lards up the scene a little more.

Even so, once the first fourteen and a half pages of the book are out of the way, Mailer exhibits much of the best things he has going for him, his drive, his pace, his gift of narrative, his nervous excitement, things Cain and Raymond Chandler had, but not too many other American novelists. Using the serial form—ending each chapter cliff-hanger style—Mailer creates excellent suspense—in fact, in much of the book Mailer moves, probably unconsciously, in the direction of Cain and shows great promise. In the context of a Cain adventure, Mailer's gothic attitude toward sex—which Cain shares—a great deal of new-sentimental business about how making love to a broad is all mixed up with death and fate and how you can tell your fortune by the quality of the orgasm—all this is not embarrassing in the context of a Cain novel like *The Postman Always Rings Twice.*

Of course, Mailer cannot match Cain in writing dialogue, creating characters, setting up scenes or carrying characters through a long story. But he is keener than Cain in summoning up smells, especially effluvia. I think Norman Mailer can climb into the same ring as James M. Cain. He's got to learn some fundamentals, such as how to come out of his corner faster. But that can be picked up. A good solid Cain-style opening goes like this:

"They threw me off the hay truck about noon . . ."

## CHRISTOPHER LASCH
### From "The Anti-Intellectualism of the Intellectuals"
*The New Radicalism in America [1889–1963]: The Intellectual as a Social Type*
1965, pp. 334–49

### V

Mailer has steadily enlarged ⟨his definition of totalitarianism in America⟩—as he has enlarged so many things, the length of his sentences, the heat of his indignation, the scope of his literary ambitions—until it includes everything he finds in the slightest degree distasteful: pacifists, liberals, modern architecture, Hollywood, experimental theater, homosexuals, masturbation, David Riesman, beatniks, psychoanalysis, "minor" writers, book reviewers, fallout shelters, "the Establishment's defense of life," organized labor, mental health, motels, science, people who refuse to admit that bombs can be beautiful, people who drop bombs on other people, television, and cancer.

In order to understand Norman Mailer, it is first necessary to understand the sociology of literary success in America. English readers find Mailer baffling and outrageous partly because they do not understand the problem an American writer faces when he becomes a celebrity, the problem, apparently, being peculiar to America.[1] Many Americans are equally puzzled to find that literary success should be considered a problem. Consequently they dismiss the fear of it as an expression of the fashionable cult of "alienation." Sidney Hook, for example, cannot contain his impatience with writers who complain that success in America is worse than failure.

The hypothesis that mass culture and the popular arts—the Hollywood trap!—threaten the emergence of a significant culture of vitality and integrity because they constitute a perpetual invitation to a sell-out seems very far-fetched. Unless one is an incurable snob (I am old enough to remember intense discussions by otherwise intelligent people as to whether the cinema is an art), the forms of mass culture and the popular arts should serve as a challenge to do something with them. There are "sell-outs" of course but there are two parties to every "sell-out." The writer who "sells out" to Hollywood or the slicks cannot absolve himself of responsibility on the ground that he wouldn't be able to live as plushily as if he did. Why should he? I shall be accused of saying that I am sentencing artists and writers to starvation. But if scholars can live Renan's life of "genteel poverty" and do important work so can those who don't go to Hollywood.[2]

The problem, however, is not that writers are tempted to sell out, although it must be admitted that many people talk as if it were. The problem is only incidentally one of money; much more important is the impact of success, even an unsought success, on the writer's view of himself and his work. Success tempts him to become a public "personality," and if he gives in to the temptation, he soon discovers that it is easier to sell his personality than his ideas. His eccentricities, his foibles, his "image," in short, constitute an invaluable asset in the literary marketplace; he can trade off his "name" much as movie stars and baseball players make a profitable business of publicly endorsing other people's products. His name, moreover—at a somewhat higher level of aspiration—guarantees him a hearing; whatever he says or does, as long as the magic lasts, is automatically news. But the price, if he chooses to play this game, is that the writer has to stay in character, has to play the part that he has made for himself; for if he deviates from it, his public is no longer interested. In the same way Hollywood actors, under the "star system," are expected to play the same part over and over, their marketability depending on their predictability. But whereas the star is largely the creation of his press agents, the writer creates his part for himself and then proceeds not only to act it but, worse, to believe in it. At length he loses his real self and takes on a synthetic self, which he then proceeds to write about as if it were his real one. Ernest Hemingway is a notable example of the lengths to which this process of re-identification can lead. Lillian Ross's famous profile of Hemingway shows him acting out, down to the last detail of his private life, the public image of himself. Even his conversation, a mixture of sporting-world slang, assorted unintelligible grunts, and Indian language, had become a parody of the famous Hemingway style.[3] Nature imitates art; but when the art is the art of public relations, the results, for a serious writer, are likely to be disastrous.

Norman Mailer had the bad luck to achieve success with his very first book. *The Naked and the Dead* was an immediate best-seller. Mailer was twenty-five, living in Paris.

> Naturally, I was blasted a considerable distance away from dead center by the size of its success, and I spent the next few years trying to gobble up the experiences of a victorious man when I was still no man at all, and had no real gift for enjoying life. Such a gift usually comes from a series of small victories artfully achieved; my experience had consisted of many small defeats, a few victories, and one explosion. So success furnished me great energy, but I wasted most of it in the gears of old habit, and had experience

which was overheated, brilliant, anxious, gauche, grim—even, I suspect—killing. My farewell to an average man's experience was too abrupt; never again would I know, in the dreary way one usually knows such things, what it was like to work at a dull job, or take orders from a man one hated. If I had had a career of that in the army, it now was done—there was nothing left in the first twenty-four years of my life to write about; one way or another, my life seemed to have been mined and melted into the long reaches of the book. And so I was prominent and empty, and I had to begin life again; from now on, people who knew me would never be able to react to me as a person whom they liked or disliked in small ways, *for myself alone* (the inevitable phrase of all tear-filled confessions); no, I was a node in a new electronic landscape of celebrity, personality and status.[4]

Among other things, Mailer's unexpected triumph, at the very outset of his career, rendered him cruelly dependent on the opinion of reviewers, whose praise had assured the success of *The Naked and the Dead*. The result was that when the reviewers with one voice consigned his next work, *Barbary Shore*, to the ash-heap of literary reputation—Anthony West in *The New Yorker* said it was a book of "monolithic flawless badness"—Mailer was oppressed with a sense of failure out of all proportion to the actual defects of the book.[5] He not only read the reviews, he compulsively returned to them again and again, and when he compiled *Advertisements for Myself*, in 1959, he printed long excerpts from them, as he printed all the other derogatory comments on himself that, over the years, he had carefully saved. Already obsessed with the dream of becoming a "major writer," he was driven more and more to define his goal in terms of popular and critical acclaim; in terms, that is, of celebrity itself.[6] Unable to wrench himself out of the self-contained community, the endless convolutions of the literary circuit, into which his early success had cast him, he suffered even social snubs as if they were artistic disasters, brooding over them intently. He began his third book, *The Deer Park*, with the deliberate intention of writing another best-seller. "Six or seven years of breathing that literary air" had taught him that "a writer stayed alive in the circuits of such hatred only if he were unappreciated enough to be adored by a clique, or was so overbought by the public that he excited some defenseless nerve in the snob."

> I knew if *The Deer Park* was a powerful best seller (the magical figure had become one hundred thousand copies for me) that I would then have won. I would be the first serious writer of my generation to have a best seller twice, and so it would not matter what was said about the book. Half of publishing might call it cheap, dirty, sensational, second-rate, and so forth and so forth, but it would be a weak rage and could not hurt, for the literary world suffers a spot of the national taint—a serious writer is certain to be considered major if he is also a best seller; in fact, most readers are never convinced of his value until his books do well.[7]

*The Deer Park* "did well," but it did not sell 100,000 copies. It sold half that many. "Poised for an enormous sale or a failure," Mailer found that "a middling success was cruel to take." "Like a starved revolutionary in a garret, I had compounded out of need and fever and vision and fear nothing less than a madman's confidence in the identity of my being and the wants of all others, and it was a new dull load to lift and to bear, this knowledge that I had no magic so great as to hasten

the time of the apocalypse, but that instead I would be open like all others to the attritions of half-success and small failure."[8] But instead of profiting from this self-knowledge—a self-knowledge which characterizes so much of the autobiographical writing in *Advertisements* but which exerts so little influence on Mailer's progress as a writer—he turned to a new undertaking more grandiose than ever, an undertaking destined to fail, it would seem, before it was fairly begun. He now proposed to write a long novel, a major novel on which his claims as a major writer would rest once and for all, a novel so big, so shocking, so outrageously true to life, that it would not even be printable in America but would have to circulate, like *Tropic of Cancer* and *Ulysses*, as "an outlaw of the underground." It would take ten years to write and would have, when it appeared, "a deep explosion of effect."[9] But the magnitude of this enterprise, together with the advance publicity which Mailer lavished upon it, was self-defeating. Instead of writing "the long novel," Mailer wrote *The Presidential Papers* and then, with the excuse that he needed money, turned to another potboiler, *The American Dream*, which he sold as a serial to *Esquire* as "proof against the advertisements I had devoted to myself, against the enemies I had made, and even against the expectations of those who were ready to like my work most." In a recent interview, Mailer claims to have given up his ambition to be a "great writer" in favor of the more modest ambition to be "a professional writer—and one of the best professional writers in the country." Yet he still talks of "that big novel." He says it will be 3,000 pages long.[10]

Meanwhile Mailer had acquired a public personality which he proceeded to exploit in the most obvious imaginable way by writing a series of advertisements for himself, the first of which were published under that title and the rest of which made up *The Presidential Papers* of 1963. In freely admitting his wish to promote his reputation, Mailer may actually have avoided some of the psychic dangers of that kind of publicity. It is yet not clear how fully Mailer himself believes in the myth of Mailer. It is reassuring to find that the best writing in *Advertisements* is the purely autobiographical writing. On the other hand, all that one learns of his private life—if it is any longer possible to distinguish between his private and his public life—suggests that Mailer increasingly acts as he believes his public expects him to act. *The Presidential Papers* consists of set pieces, of which Mailer is at once the reporter and the central character, and they show him to be acting very much *in* character as well: instructing Kennedy in his role as a charismatic leader, instructing Mrs. Kennedy in her role as a leader of the national taste, crashing the press conference after the Patterson-Liston fight. "I'm pulling this caper for a reason," Mailer tells Liston. "I know a way to build the next fight from a $200,000 dog in Miami to a $2,000,000 gate in New York."[11] His terms of reference confirm one's impression that Mailer's values have become indistinguishable from those of the entertainment world which he hates but from the embrace of which he seems unable to free himself. Success, for the American writer, is a carnival mirror in which he sees not himself but a cruel distortion of himself, without, however, being able any longer to tell them apart.

But there is another side to the matter. Mailer is not only a writer, he is a political and cultural radical bent on bringing about "a revolution in the consciousness of our time."[12] As such he is recognizably descended, for all his seeming eccentricity, from the line of Randolph Bourne and Lincoln Steffens. Like them, he has conducted his life as if it were an experiment. He has tried to plot the course of his career very deliberately, in order to achieve a certain end: the promotion of his own reputation, but also the promotion, in a somewhat old-fashioned sense, of the public happiness. His personal and his political ambitions run together, and it is hard to sort them out. His determination to write best-sellers, for instance, reflects his misdirected ambition to be a "major" writer, but it also reflects a legitimate unwillingness to settle for a limited readership of avant-garde intellectuals. Likewise his ambition to put himself at the center of the political stage expresses more than unrestrained egotism; it also expresses a desire to avoid the typical fate of radical intellectuals, that of political irrelevance. Mailer had a taste of that in 1948, when he worked for Henry Wallace's Progressive Party, and his revulsion was intensified by a personal humiliation which attended the occasion of his leaving the party in 1949. Invited to speak at a "peace conference" at the Waldorf-Astoria, Mailer disappointed his audience by saying (as he remembered afterward) that "only socialism could save the world, and America was not close to that, and Russia was not close, and people should not believe in countries and patriotism anyway, and peace conferences like this gave the idea that one could, and so were wrong." The feeling that he was "betraying" those who had come to hear him drove him close to tears, "and to avoid that disaster, I screwed up my face into a snarl, feeling like a miserable and undeserving rat, and then some flash bulbs went off," and the picture of his embarrassment and degradation became a matter of public record.[13]

After the Wallace campaign, Mailer made no further ventures into political sectarianism. Instead he attempted, as Lincoln Steffens had attempted, to play the part of a devil's advocate, "court wit," or "jester"; that is, he attempted to speak for the "underground" in the very citadel of the "establishment."[14] Like Steffens, Mailer regards himself as an "outlaw," and he shares Steffens's suspicion that successful men are also outlaws in disguise. Thus he describes Kennedy as "an outlaw's sheriff . . . one sheriff who could have been an outlaw himself," and in directing a series of open letters to Kennedy, Mailer was consciously addressing him, as Steffens had addressed the "big bad men" of his time, as "one crook to another."[15] The difference between them is that Mailer is far more deeply involved in the world of the establishment than Steffens was ever involved in the world of the big bad men. Not that Mailer has had any more influence over national policy. He claims to have assured Kennedy's election by writing of him as an "existential hero," but Kennedy did not show his gratitude, once in office, by following Mailer's advice. Mailer had no discernible influence on the Kennedy administration; but he nevertheless came much closer to sharing its values than Steffens came to sharing the values of the "good people" of his day. To be sure, Steffens, like Mailer, worshipped success, but he was sufficiently critical of his own motives not to pursue it for himself; the proof of which is that he survived twenty years of literary neglect and capped them by writing, not a gigantic monument to his own ambition such as Mailer has planned for himself, but the *Autobiography*, a work that owes its charm in large part to its being so utterly unpretentious. Mailer, on the other hand, is far too committed to the culture he claims to despise to be an effective critic of it, either from without or from within. He is not so much a devil's advocate as a man who has found it convenient to play the part of a devil's advocate, precisely because that is the part which his public expects him to play. "In America," he has written, "few people will trust you unless you are irreverent"; but the truth is that people trust you most when you merely *seem* to be irreverent.[16]

The fact is that Mailer's brand of cultural radicalism, a compound of Marx and Freud, has long since lost its capacity to shock. It is not that Marx and Freud themselves are no longer shocking or that a radical critique of American society cannot be fashioned out of their ideas. Herbert Marcuse, a radical thinker who makes no great show of his radicalism, has done that, and what is even more unusual, he has added some ideas of his own.[17] In some circles, however, Marxism and psychoanalysis have become clichés just because they have been associated for so long with the kind of self-conscious and mannered rebellion typified by Norman Mailer; and as clichés, they are so little shocking that it is necessary for Mailer himself constantly to try to go beyond them, to make more and more strident assertions of his nonconformity, and finally to throw his own person, in attitudes of rude and outrageous defiance, into the struggle, in the hope of making some ultimate proof of his revolutionary sincerity. But the deeper his involvement in the game of shocking for the sake of shock, the more innocuous is the impact of Mailer's rebellion. The wider the net of his indignation, the more his strictures come to resemble those interminable attacks on American "conformity" that were so popular in the 1950's. The deeper he digs in his probing for the sexual roots of social disorder, the shallower his observations become. He can write in all seriousness, and not only write but admiringly quote the sentence in another context: "The orgasm is anathema to the liberal mind because it is the inescapable existential moment."[18] *The White Negro*, which Mailer regards as the most daring of his writings and which the editors of *Dissent* published with great fanfare, is a rehearsal of old clichés about Negro sexuality; a reassertion, James Baldwin called it, of "the myth of the sexuality of Negroes which Norman Mailer, like so many others, refuses to give up."[19] In his more reflective moods, Mailer can still talk effectively, as when, confronted with Baldwin's observation, he amended his thesis by saying that "*any* submerged class is going to be more accustomed to sexuality than a leisure class."[20] But reflective moods, on the whole, are missing from Mailer's latest work. In the same breath he goes on to say that Negroes are more sexual than whites because they "come from Africa" and "tropical people are usually more sexual," and that in any case Baldwin in attacking *The White Negro* is "being totalitarian."[21] Mailer's increasingly indiscriminate use of the word "totalitarianism" indicates what has gone wrong with his social and political analysis. Reaching for terms of ultimate condemnation, his voice becomes indistinguishable from the voice of those cultural critics for whom the quality of television or the design of the latest automobiles is a burning political issue. Mailer himself says of television: "Every time one sees a bad television show, one is watching the nation get ready for the day when a Hitler will come."[22]

It is not surprising that so much of Mailer's radicalism approximates the liberalism of the New Frontier. Take away the talk of "existentialism" and Mailer's praise of Kennedy sounds a great deal like Richard Rovere's. If Kennedy eventually disappointed him, it was because Mailer, like the liberals, expected Kennedy and his wife to set in motion the long-awaited "revolution in the consciousness of our time." The fact that Kennedy "was young, that he was physically handsome, and that his wife was attractive," convinced Mailer in 1960 that his accession to the Presidency would be "an existential event."[23] Under Eisenhower, "the best minds and bravest impulses" had been "alienated" from "the faltering history which was made"; under Kennedy they might return to the seat of power."[24] Kennedy as President might be "capable of giving direction to the time, able to encourage a nation," as other existential heroes had done, "to discover the deepest colors of its character."[25] Naturally Mailer was disappointed; the nature of his expectations left him very little choice.

A hopeless undertaking from the start, Mailer's ambition to make of himself "some sort of center about which all that had been lost must now rally" was flawed by the terms in which the ambition was conceived, flawed by the old confusion of politics and culture.[26] The political results of his efforts were negligible, and the literary consequences, judging from his recent writing, were disastrous. His attempts to enrich the cultural life of the nation ended by impoverishing his own art. All that remained was the receding vision of "the big book," but "when I sit down," Mailer confessed at the end of *Advertisements*, "when I sit down, soon after this book is done, to pick up again on my novel, I do not know if I can do it, for if the first sixty pages are not at all bad, I may still have wasted too much of myself, and if I have—what a loss." Still a young man—he was thirty-six—Mailer, like Randolph Bourne, mourned the loss of youth. "How poor to go to death with no more than the notes of good intention."[27]

## VI

With Norman Mailer, the body of ideas and assumptions which I have called the new radicalism achieved some kind of final and definitive statement. The confusion of power and art, the effort to liberate the social and psychological "underground" by means of political action, the fevered pursuit of experience, the conception of life as an experiment, the intellectual's identification of himself with the outcasts of society—these things could be carried no further without carrying them to absurdity. Perhaps Mailer had carried them past that point already.

Mailer was not, of course, a representative man of his time in the strictest sense of the term. Even in New York literary circles, he was an eccentric; men such as Irving Howe, the editor of *Dissent*, and Norman Podhoretz, the editor of *Commentary*, were probably more typical products of that milieu. Yet these men, more modest than Mailer in their ambitions and more restrained in their manner of expression, nevertheless shared many of Mailer's opinions, and their writings showed also the effects, on the one hand, of the "sense of comradeship and solidarity," and on the other, of the "feeling of beleaguered hostility" toward the rest of society, that have accompanied the emergence of the intellectuals as a social class.[28]

⟨. . .⟩ The idiosyncratic is sometimes more revealing than the normal (which in any case, where the history of ideas is concerned, is exceedingly hard to define), the extremes are sometimes more revealing than the middle-of-the-road—providing, of course, that one remembers precisely that they are extremes. As Richard Gilman said of Mailer, in reviewing *The Presidential Papers*, "Mailer was engaged in defining the President's existence by his own, as in some case, we all were. But we were at a much lower and more innocent level of the game, we had not institutionalized ourselves into an alternative to the President or into his counterpart, and we lacked a mystique and a vehicle for imposing it."[29] If it is important to understand that "we were at a much lower and more innocent level of the game," it is also important to recognize, in the first place, that we were playing it at all—to recognize, that is, that the megalomanic fantasies of omnipotence which stand forth so sharply in the careers of men like Norman Mailer and Colonel House exist, in more muted form, in all of us, as the ambitions of Colonel House, for instance, were mirrored, in colors more subdued, in Lincoln Colcord.

I have argued that these fantasies of omnipotence, together with their concomitant fears of hostility and persecu-tion, spring from the isolation of American intellectuals, as a class, from the main currents of American life. I have argued further that it was their sense of isolation which drove intellectuals to identify themselves with what Benjamin Ginzburg called the "practical sweep of American life." William James once compared the "tough-minded" to the hard-bitten men of the mining frontier, the "tender-minded" to the "tenderfoot" New Englanders, overrefined and effete. "Their mutual reaction," he said, "is very much like that that takes place when Bostonian tourists mingle with a population like that of Cripple Creek."[30] A Bostonian himself, who nevertheless strove to be "toughminded" in his philosophy, James captured, in this image, the anxiety, the secret self-contempt, which runs through so much of the history of the twentieth-century intellectual. From James to Norman Mailer, different as they are in so many obvious respects, there is a curious line of descent. Half a century after James delivered his first lecture on pragmatism, Norman Mailer forced himself into the thick of the Patterson-Liston fight—another Bostonian tourist in the guise of a "Rocky Mountain tough."

## Notes

1. Beyond this, it is difficult for Englishmen to understand or sympathize with the desperation which underlies American radicalism—the sense of futility, in a gigantic country in which political debate is dominated by the organs of mass communica-tion and in which public opinion, misinformed and even deliberately misled, seems at once powerless, when it is a question of persuading government to pursue more liberal policies, and omnipotent, when it is a question of compelling it to pursue policies even more illiberal than the ones it wants to pursue (as in the case of Cuba)—the sense of sheer futility, in such a country, which afflicts those who seek to check the suicidal impulse the American people seem bent on pursuing.
    For a particularly clear illustration of this paradoxical contrast between European optimism and American despair, see George Lichtheim's review of Herbert Marcuse's *One-Dimensional Man* (*New York Review of Books*, II [Feb. 20, 1964], pp. 16–19) and the correspondence which followed between Lichtheim and some American students who took him to task for not understanding why it was necessary for any serious American scholar to think "negatively" about contemporary politics.
2. Hook: "From Alienation to Critical Integrity," *The Intellectuals*, p. 530.
3. Lillian Ross: *Profile of Hemingway* (New York: Simon and Schuster; 1961).
4. Norman Mailer: *Advertisements for Myself* (New York: G. P. Putnam's Sons; 1959), p. 92.
5. Ibid., p. 105.
6. "Before I was seventeen I had formed the desire to be a major writer." (Ibid., p. 27.)
7. Ibid., p. 241.
8. Ibid., p. 247.
9. Ibid., p. 477.
10. *Observer* [London], April 26, 1964.
11. Norman Mailer: *The Presidential Papers* (New York: G. P. Putnam's Sons; 1963), p. 265.
12. *Advertisements*, p. 17. Cf. Steffens: "Before I die, I believe I can help to bring about an essential change in the American mind."
13. *Advertisements*, p. 410.
14. *Papers*, pp. 1, 8.
15. *The Presidential Papers* (London: André Deutsch; 1964), n.p. [first page of unpaginated introduction written for English edition].
16. Ibid.
17. See Herbert Marcuse: *Eros and Civilization* (Boston: Beacon Press; 1955); and *One-Dimensional Man* (London: Routledge & Kegan Paul; 1964).
18. *Papers* (Putnam's), p. 198.
19. Ibid., p. 146.
20. Ibid. It must be admitted, moreover, that Baldwin himself comes close to endorsing the myth of superior Negro sexuality. In *The*

*Fire Next Time* (New York: Dial Press; 1963), pp. 56–7, he accused white Americans of being "terrified of sensuality," adding somewhat defensively: "The word 'sensual' is not intended to bring to mind quivering dusky maidens or priapic studs." I understand that in Baldwin's new play, *Blues for Mister Charlie*, the same idea is asserted in a much cruder form, without qualifications.

21. *Papers*, pp. 146–7.
22. Ibid., p. 134.
23. Ibid., p. 26.
24. Ibid., p. 43.
25. Ibid., p. 42.
26. Ibid., p. 81. "He is asking from politics . . . what it cannot give," writes Richard Gilman; "we may speak of the art of politics but political procedures and truth are not the precedures and truth of art. A president is not 'supposed to enrich the real life of his people,' he is supposed to protect and preserve it, enrichment being precisely the function of the artist." ("Why Mailer Wants to Be President," *New Republic*, CL [Feb. 8, 1964], p. 23.)
27. *Advertisements*, p. 477.
28. Renata Adler: "Polemic and the New Reviewers," *New Yorker*, XL (July 4, 1964), p. 64 (a review of Howe's *A World More Attractive* and Podhoretz's *Doings and Undoings*).
29. "Why Mailer Wants to Be President," p. 19.
30. William James: *Pragmatism and Four Essays from The Meaning of Truth* (Cleveland: Meridian Books; 1961), pp. 22–3.

## JONATHAN RABAN
### "Huck Mailer and the Widow Millett"

*New Statesman*, September 3, 1971, pp. 303–4

'She was the best girl I ever see, and had the most sand,' said Huck Finn of Mary Jane, and American fiction's best girls have been required to have sand ever since. Women in the American novel come in two sizes: bible-reading, piano-playing drags like Aunt Polly, and dashing tomboys, always good for a bit of fun in a sleeping bag between fishing trips, like Lady Brett Ashley and the rest of Hemingway's monstrous crew of flat-chested, knockabout lovelies. If girls are any good, they're your buddies—rather odd chaps, somewhat lacking in *cojones*, but touchingly endowed with tear-ducts and comforting mammaries. Most of them, though, are wives and mothers; prim guardians of culture, spoil-sports, Delilahs. Leslie Fiedler, in *The Return of the Vanishing American*, neatly glosses the myth of American womanhood:

> Women and Indians make for us a second, home-grown definition of what we consider the Real West, the West of the West, as it were; a place to which white male Americans flee from their own women into the arms of Indian males, but which those White women, in their inexorable advance from coast to coast, destroy.

But Fiedler, as usual, overstates the homosexual component of the myth. As John Smith found, there were Indian ladies too, like Pocahontas; and with the low franc and high dollar, together with the cheap boat to Europe, a whole continent of girls who wouldn't treat you like your auntie was opened up. When Henry Miller goes adventuring into the dark and forbidden places, the secret grottoes of nature are to be found, not in wigwams, but in the underbellies of Parisian whores. And after Mailer's own Stephen Rojack, hero of *An American Dream*, has strangled his posh American wife (whom he met on a double date with John F. Kennedy) and shoved her out of a hotel window, he gets back to the jungle in the arms of Ruta, the German maid. Ruta, indeed, turns out to be a veritable Natty Bumppo of the bed, with a peasant's flair for the sporting life. Woman, in the mythology, is a creature of earth, a natural centaur; it is only American women who have abandoned

nature for a precarious and censorious culture, who have transformed themselves, in an offence against natural law, into a grim regiment of suburban bitches.

In this context, Mailer's patriarchal rebuttal ⟨in *The Prisoner of Sex*⟩ of the Women's Lib case strikes with the limp force of saloon bar philosophy. Women, if one reads Mailer between the lines, are our last natural asset. Like green belts, the tribes of the Upper Amazon, and the one remaining prairie where the buffalo roam, women are in danger of extinction by technology, and are in urgent need of conservation. In the writings of Kate Millett, Valerie Solanis, Ti-Grace Atkinson and the other liberationists, Mailer detects the lineaments of a race of unsexed technogynes. He contrives to sound like a cross between a heavy Jewish father and Mr Norman St John Stevas as he contemplates the tide of industrial pollution into which the sisters of Women's Lib are spitefully hurling themselves. The chemistry of birth control represents the first incursion of science upon the mystery of the womb, closely followed by the dreadful physics of the curette abortion:

> The Work of The Aristocrat had first to be demolished. His vaults, His buttresses, His heavenly arch, yes, cess and riddance to the days of the honest abortion when the fingernails of the surgeon were filthy and the heart of a woman went screaming through a cave as steel scraped at the place where she touched the beyond. 'Shit, no,' said the ladies. 'Suck the fucker out.'

Even Swift would have found this particular irony hard to manage. What would Mailer prefer? Knitting needles and magical spells over menses? It would certainly seem so. For, like so many gloomy conservatives, convinced that we're on the brink of Armageddon, Mailer finds the mere fact of technology so disgusting that he can profess an unfeigned nostalgia for any horror, provided it's untainted by machinery. The technological metaphor becomes a sure-fire trigger in the rhetoric of revulsion. 'This view,' he writes of Anne Koedt's article, 'The Myth of the Vaginal Orgasm,' 'left a man confronting the clitoris like a twitch before the switch of a dynamo.' One only has to remember Henry Adams at the Great Exhibition to recall a time when that simile would have had precisely the reverse effect to the one Mailer intends.

But Mailer is in on the oldest of all American literary acts; he is playing God's messenger, defending nature against the unholy engines of Man's devising. The Aquarian third person, resurrected in *The Prisoner of Sex* as 'the PW' ('The Prizewinner' and 'The Prisoner of Wedlock'), is used as the prophets of the Old Testament used it, as an instrument of majestic bombast. As the PW never tires of reminding us, he talks most easily in paradoxes—God's own figure of speech, containing as it does the twin sides of a dualistic universe. And the PW's paradoxes, which make the book sound as if it was written in stage Welsh, are contrasted, greatly to their own advantage, with the rigid technical prose of the Liberationists. His most telling attack on Kate Millett comes when he has a go at her style, which is

> suggestive of a night-school lawyer who sips Metrecal to keep his figure, and thereby is so full of isolated proteins, factory vitamins, reconstituted cyclamates, and artificial flavours that one has to pore over the passages like a business contract.

The curse of the machine has polluted the very vocabulary and grammar of the American woman; like Thoreau miserably watching the coming of the railroad in the 19th century, Mailer's dreams are disturbed by the mechanical thunder of the Liberationists. The machine, as its enemies have always warned, enforces a glum democracy of the mediocre. And Mailer, as press relations man for a god he calls The Aristocrat, is no friend to democracy:

> Millett . . . had all the technological power of the century in her veins, she was the point of advance for those intellectual forces vastly larger than herself which might look to the liberation of women as the first weapon in the ongoing incarceration of the romantic idea of men—the prose of future prisons was in her tongue, for she saw the difference between men and women as non-essential—excesses of emotion to be conditioned out. So the power of her argument would be greatest for those who wished to live in the modest middles of the poisoned city. She was a way of life for young singles, a species of city-technique.

The remarkable thing about this passage is the way it snowballs, gathering all sorts of muddy issues as it goes: technology, pollution, democracy, cities, 'techniques'—all the shibboleths of the modern conservative are stuck hopefully on to the person of Kate Millett, in the presumed hope that some of them, at least, will stay there. And just behind the flood of abuse—which is delivered with such obvious relish that it turns into the sound of a man merely enjoying himself making a loud noise—lies that dusty American daydream of an organic society, of a craft community living a village life of elaborate hierarchies and home-grown vegetables. But Mailer's mayoral campaign on just this issue rang much more truly than this catch-as-catch-can rhetorical promiscuity. Being on God's side demands more than a synthetic pastiche of His wrath.

For despite all his homework on the Women's Lib manifestos, Mailer never manages to drag the debate out from the essentially 19th-century, mythical commonplaces in which it is phrased. Kate Millett and Aunt Polly are sisters under the skin. Just as Huck yearns for the paradoxes of magic, for the mysterious life of the river and the territory, so Mailer, in his fury, blames the women for the urban, technological dystopia of contemporary America:

> The Widow Douglas, she took me for her son, and allowed she would civilize me; but it was rough living in the house all the time, considering how dismal regular and decent the widow was in all her ways . . .

There *are* girls with sand, but somehow you never land up living with them; the raft goes on, Aunt Polly and the Widow turn up at the end of the journey, and the territory still beckons. What is important is to keep the dream still burning, the poignant *if only* of almost all classic American writing. And this is just what *The Prisoner of Sex* seems to be doing; it whips itself up to a verbal orgasm over the Lost Woman of America, the unreclaimable, unreachable girl with as much sand and mystery as the white whale itself. The book ends with an extraordinary grammatical conceit, an act of literal syntactical penetration, as Mailer tries to lay this all-womb dreamwoman between the sheets of language:

> Finally, he would agree with everything they asked but to quit the womb, for finally a day had to come when women shattered the pearl of their love for pristine and feminine will and found the man, yes that man in the million who could become the point of the seed which would give an egg back to nature, and let the woman return with a babe who came from the root of God's desire to go all the way, wherever was that way. And who was not to know that God was not the greatest lover of them all? The idiocy was to assume that the oyster and the clam

knew more than the trees and the grass. (Unless dear God was black and half-Jewish and a woman, and small and mean as mother-wit. We will never know until we take the trip. And so saying realized he had been able to end a portentous piece in the soft sweet flesh of parentheses.)

It has the heroic pathos of Huck and Captain Ahab, except that the writing has gone groggy. Like Twain, Mailer finishes with the trip still to come—a trip which the whole of the rest of the book leads us to believe is doomed. We're left only with the image of a tousle-haired rascal snapping petulantly at the womenfolk who surround him and dreaming vainly of the receding frontier. The pose of the patriarch, of the man of God, or the Great Conservationist, is a deceptive ploy; it fails to hide one of the most familiar of all American postures, that of the urchin with a distant gleam in his eye.

## RICHARD POIRIER
### From "Norman Mailer: A Self-Creation"
*Atlantic*, October 1972, pp. 78–82

One characteristic of the very ambitious writer is that he becomes a theoretician of his own work. In being so, he manages to set the terms for the criticism later written about him.

Criticism has not been conspicuously successful in dealing with this phenomenon. Faced with explanatory language, critics, like most other people, set about gratefully to understand rather than to question it. They do not want to imagine situations where all the words are in motion, where the proffered abstractions or analytical fixtures are as problematic as the material they seem to explain, where nothing is stabilized, nothing a standard by which to measure the mobility of anything else. If few will accept, even fewer will set out to create such fluidity in works where the author has tried to prevent it. To do so is to challenge the sufficiency of the very terms on which the author or the work depends for order and focus. And yet such skepticism, it seems to me, is absolutely essential to criticism.

Norman Mailer is a recent and extreme example of a writer who has tried to be the literary historian of his own work, and who in the process has tended to usurp the interpretive, even quite often the evaluative, function of criticism. His self-explanations and assessments are abundant to a fault. He gives so much that one gift is not evidently more important than another, and like an overgenerous lover he finally induces almost a lethargy of gratitude. A man who offers more than anyone wants is in danger of being taken for granted, even of being resented for forestalling what the reader would like to give of himself. Mailer, especially in his most recent work, leads our reading, organizes our impressions, assails us with interpretations of himself that prevent all but the stoutest reader from responding at his own pace, or with free enthusiasm to things that are on the periphery of Mailer's organizational formulas. It is all but impossible to have a peaceful or casual relationship to his writing. Even after the most obedient attention, the reader is seldom rewarded with any sense of achieved calm. Probably the reason is that Mailer himself is continually agitated and dissatisfied, and that he is always redoing what he has done by his subsequent commentaries on it.

Mailer's writings are best considered as one large work. However thematically repetitious, it is a work which constantly comes alive with extraordinary accumulations of intensity and brilliance. It is nonetheless a chaotic mixture that awaits some larger redemptive effort; so that despite *The Armies of the Night* and *Why Are We in Vietnam?*, Mailer now is like Melville without *Moby-Dick*, George Eliot without *Middlemarch*, Mark Twain without *Huckleberry Finn*. The present dangers are that he is applying to new issues and circumstances methods that he has already worked to exhaustion and, even more, that his achieved self-explanation has come to precede him to experience. In treating the moon shot, the Ali-Frazier fight, or Women's Liberation, he seems locked into a system that one hoped he could have transcended.

And yet it is, of course, Mailer himself who created this hope. By sitting so frequently in self-judgment upon his past he is always implicitly proposing for himself some fresh start in the future. If one gets impatient with his habitual mannerisms—the dualisms and the mixtures of styles that are meant to catch the contentions at work in the whole culture—part. of the reason is that they represent the souring of what once was a fresh start. The now too familiar methods that portend a crisis in his career were invented to save him from an earlier, probably more threatening one. They saved him from becoming a mere literary writer, one whose acceptance of the protective cover of moribund literary manners all but alienated him from the vital changes in his society. He is still relying on the persona of the perpetually embattled writer that he began to create in the pieces, particularly the prefatory comments, collected in *Advertisements for Myself* in 1959. The degree to which this persona was invented for literary purposes and the degree to which it is a necessity of his life is doubtless a mystery even to Mailer.

Mailer lost his voice by the discovery, after three novels, that he really did not have one. Out of this condition—which usually dissuades would-be writers and silences many who have written—he then made his literary fortune. His writing began to take form from the very instability of his voice, which means the instability of the self as well; it took its form from a species of debate or dialogue or "war" among the possible and competing voices that were alive within him. Not having fashioned *a* self, not having become *a* man by the usual process of accumulation, selection, and disposal of personal experiences, but having instead displaced the self by a mostly learned literary manner, he had the personal courage and fortitude, when this project failed, to release all the trapped, unfinished, stunted, disorganized selves that remained alive in him; and he did so, wisely in his particular case, without the help of a psychoanalyst to sort them out, put them in order, kill some in order to feed others. His mature style supports the claim, made in *The Armies of the Night*, that "he carried different ages within him like different models of his experience: parts of him were eighty-one years old, fifty-seven, forty-eight, thirty-six, nineteen, et cetera."

When he remarked in a *Paris Review* interview that he had learned most, technically, from E. M. Forster, he really meant that he had learned something about the possible versions of a given personality. Forster apparently helped confirm his inclination not to think any longer of a personality, including his own, as if it were of a piece. Reading *The Longest Journey* taught him that "personality was more fluid, more dramatic and startling, more inexact than I thought. I was brought up on the idea that when you wrote a novel you tried to build a character who could be handled and walked around like a piece of sculpture" (*Cannibals and Christians*). This lesson is at least as moral as it is technical, especially when he connects it with the realization that "a novel written in the third person was now impossible for me for many years." As a

matter of fact it never did prove possible, except in his first novel, in parts of *The Deer Park* which lapse from first to third person, and in some of his journalism, where he invents third-person equivalents to "I." Mailer himself is aware of the reasons for this difficulty: "In some funny way Forster gave my notion of personality a sufficient shock that I could not manage to write in the third person. Forster, after all, had a developed view of the world. I did not. I think I must have felt at that time as if I would never be able to write in the third person until I developed a coherent view of the world. I don't know that I've been able to altogether."

Before *Advertisements for Myself*, the effort to summon up "a coherent view of the world" was made at the expense of those elements in him which apparently disrupted or confused his sense of high literary mission, specifically of that personal past he associated with being a "nice" Jewish boy from Brooklyn. In *The Naked and the Dead*, his only way of handling analagous material belonging to his characters is through the mechanics of the Time Machine, through flash-backs tangential to the ongoing action and often tediously disruptive of it; in *Barbary Shore* he circumvents the problem by making his hero-narrator an amnesiac; in *The Deer Park* he is an orphan.

Mailer's difficulty in locating a developed view of the world is essentially a difficulty in locating a self, and while this is not necessarily a problem of literary technique, it becomes one as soon as Mailer, or any writer, tries to give his identity to the narrative voice or the point of view in any particular work. Mailer's special distinction, as his comments on Forster will attest, is that he sets out to "confuse" problems of literary technique with personal problems of life. This "confusion" is responsible for much of his diversity of effect, his capacity to appropriate the styles of others, first to learn and then to teach the reader what is most inward about them. These are the gratifying consequences to be found in his writings after about 1957, the time of "The White Negro."

Mailer's peculiar brand of existentialism finds its meaning within the personal-literary problem I am describing, and it should be investigated, it seems to me, not as an idea so much as a way of coping with a complex of personal-literary problems. It is a desperate effort at personal salvation, a way of situating himself and his career vitally in the passage of time. The simultaneities of past, present, and future that his brand of existentialism proposes are essentially a convenience to him in his writing, not something that his writing sufficiently explores or defends. The convenience is that he is able to coordinate the different aspects or "ages" of himself without feeling it necessary to reconstitute any one of them. His economies, omissions, even blind spots, are made to seem like philosophical choices rather than merely arbitrary ones, and the advantage, especially to his reportage, is enormous. With this in mind we can grasp the importance for him of a formula he developed in his essay, "The Political Economy of Time." Having said that "form is the physical equivalent of memory," he goes on to make a distinction between memory and an event: "An event consists not only of forces which are opposed to one another but also of forces which have no relation to the event. Whereas memory has a tendency to retain only the opposition and the context." Under this dispensation, there is no obligation to the past except as one chooses to reconstruct it. The past is that part of the self that one recognizes in the present as belonging to a dimension of time other than the future. Meanwhile, yet another self is being formed in the present, but this self will not be recognizable until the present has also become the past, until the self has moved on to a future and decided again to discover what has survived of its past. Form, that is, is the destiny that awaits any present event or experience.

The process has still further complications in the present. The very act in time of creating form, even of a sentence, runs the gamut of oppositions and circumstances. In the creation of a form, that is, one encounters not merely the self who acted in the past but the self who is acting at the typewriter. And then? The completed form awaits a future when it is to be reassessed in yet another form which is self-criticism. It is no wonder that Mailer's favorite image of form is a spiral.

Within the involutions, and the evolutions, I am describing, there is some room even for the Mailer he had learned to distrust—the blob, the nice boy, the modest fellow—room, too, for the literary young man of the first three novels. What is overlooked in the inevitable discussion of the alleged ego-tripping in Mailer's writing is that these more "modest" selves are often at work in the sounds and turns of his sentences—questioning the assertive, the heroic, the outrageous self. Modest Mailer emerges from the style as a rather shrewd, sometimes bewildered, charming, often ineffectual, and even downright clumsy fellow. It would, of course, be a sucker's game to think that this is the real Mailer, more sincere and more true than the manic egocentrist. Each is an agent for the effective pose of the other, and in fact the stylistic gestures of modesty and recantation are probably more calculated than any of the others. They get Mailer off the hook for propositions he makes but wants, in a pinch, to rescind or modify. He is like a lawyer determined that his listeners entertain possibilities even if they are to be ruled out of order.

Perhaps it is possible now to consider what might be called Mailer's amnesia. Once he decided to become a writer, once he thought of the career of writing as his future, all of his present became his past. All the past, everything that existed before that point, was consigned to literary oblivion; he had not lived through it with the expectation that it was to be a part of the only future he was to know, his future as a writer. It is hard to imagine a more purely, more instinctively literary mind than his, to the degree even that it treats what is presently going on as if it were already memory, as if the present were always in some sense retrospective.

Given this special involvement with time, it is understandable that most of Mailer's experience is teleological and guilt-ridden, all of it infinitely subject to expansions and linkages of association and opposition. It is also understandable why he should have the sexual attitudes that have become increasingly pronounced and biased in his writings. Putting the matter perhaps too bluntly, the connection between writing and time is the same as the connection between fucking and creation, and I would not assume necessarily that the sexual sequence dictated the literary one. In all likelihood it works the other way round, or perhaps both sequences claim equal jurisdiction to the same psychic structure. Fucking takes place in the present; the orgasm is of the present, but it looks forward in two ways, assuming that it freely and fully engages the body: to greater future orgasms—equivalent to the writing that will give birth to the Big Novel—and to the chance that this orgasm has initiated the creation of a child whose shape will emerge in the future—equivalent to any book that is the intended consequence of some present or local involvement. The present is always awaiting the future as a time when one can get to know and recognize the shape of what one has done in the past.

This means simply that no experience in Mailer is ever free, ever disconnected, ever unlinked. Everyone, and that includes the reader, is always made a "prisoner" in his work because it is impossible for him to imagine sex or any other human act which is not in the throes of dialectic. So great is his emphasis on the necessity to life of dialectical oppositions that after some acquaintance with his work it is easy to guess what his attitudes will be on any given subject. As an example, his comments on the relations of whites and Negroes in 1959, in the "Sixth Advertisement for Myself," are nearly identical with what he is to say more than a decade later about the relations of another repressed group to a superior group, women to men, in *The Prisoner of Sex*. "The comedy is that the white loathes the idea of the Negro attaining equality in the classroom," he writes, "because the white feels that the Negro already enjoys sensual superiority. So the white unconsciously feels that the balance has been kept, that the old arrangement was fair. The Negro had his sexual supremacy and the white had his white supremacy." Similarly, he argues in *The Prisoner of Sex* that the male desire for dominance is the desire not for tyranny but for equality. In their relation to time, to history, whether it be in writing or in other forms of action, all men, as Mailer sees them, are to a degree like Lawrence, for whom dominance "was the indispensable elevator which would raise his phallus to that height from which it might seek transcendence . . . some ecstasy where he could lose his ego for a moment." Women, Mailer assures us, already have this sense of transcendence, traveling as they do "through the same variety of space" occupied by men but "in full possession of a mysterious space within." No wonder women are already "on the edge of the divide" to which men like Mailer can arrive only after great struggle and where they must struggle still harder to maintain their equilibrium. "Women, like men, were human beings," he further assures us, "but they were a step, or a stage, or a move, or a leap nearer the creation of existence."

The usefulness of such contentions to the conduct of life is, with no joke intended, where we find it, but the habit of mind, in this and in other crucial instances, is what primarily interests me. Mailer's resolute practice is to locate a feeling of repression where there would for others be evidence only of the power of the oppressor, to find in the apparent majority the characteristics of a minority, and to cultivate in himself what might be called the minority within.

Like all his other theories, Mailer's theories about the relations between the sexes reveal his intuitive taste for "war," for the conflict by which one at last delineates the true form of oneself and of others. "War" is only an occasion, however, for his effort to discover the minority element within any person, constituency, or force which might be engaged in a "war." And it is this minority element which has the most beneficially corrosive effect upon form, forcing it to dispense with its merely acquired or protective or decorative attributes. It might be more accurate to say, in dealing with this very slippery subject, that "war" provides the context within which any creative minority pressure can assert itself formatively within society, the self, or a book.

This feature of Mailer is more complicated than one might infer from the sometimes simplified dichotomies in which he indulges. The minority element is not equivalent, that is, to one side in the "war," in the dualisms or oppositions found everywhere in his work. The minority is not God or the Devil, Black or white, woman or man. Rather it is that element in each which has somehow been repressed or stifled by conformity to system—including systematic dialectical opposition—or by fear of some power, like death, which is altogether larger than the ostensible, necessarily more manageable opponent apparently assigned by history. The minority element in men or Blacks or God is the result of their inward sense of inferiority which the outward or visible opposition from women or whites or the Devil did not of itself necessarily create. Blacks do not feel inferior to whites so much as to the psychotic brilliance created and, at once, thwarted within them by the accident of white oppression; whites do not feel superior to Blacks but inwardly terrified at the possibility that in any open sexual competition they would prove inferior. Behind each of his dualisms, Mailer's imagination searches out, sometimes with a harried ingenuity, the minority incentive that in turn gives dialectical energy to the dualism.

For Mailer, a masculine nature that denies the minority claims within it of feminine feeling—which is how he might account for a masculinized sensibility like Kate Millett's—chills the imagination, prevents it from encompassing even such admission of feminine inclination, or the need of masculine support, as D.J., in *Why Are We in Vietnam?*, might have had to make in order to recall his desires for Tex. That is why Mailer, at the appropriate point, has to imagine these desires for him and for the book, even if it means that the book doesn't become "crystallized." Mailer's commitment to dialectics means that he includes materials which threaten the symmetry of any possible form. His is the art of not arriving. In this case and throughout his work, dialectics is equivalent to imagination, and imagination evolves from his acceptance in himself of a feminine nature. It is probable that he associates being a writer with being a woman, and his remark in *The Prisoner of Sex* about Henry Miller and Kate Millett, even to the feminization of the males he alludes to ("dances," "curves") is a telling instance: "His work dances on the line of his dialectic. But Millett hates every evidence of the dialectic. She has a mind like a flatiron, which is to say a totally masculine mind. A hard-hat has more curves in his head." If writing, creativity, a personal style as opposed to an imposed one, could all be associated with femininity, then Mailer's selection of subjects, like war, boxing, politics, moon shots, and his own brawling activities, about which he writes with boyishly self-approving apology, can be taken as counterbalancing attempts to affirm his masculinity.

In some such way it is possible to understand a central contradiction in him: there is on one hand the marvelously fastidious stylist, a writer almost precious in his care for phrasing and cadence, and, on the other and seemingly at odds, the boisterous, the vulgar actor. More often than not his style will sound like Faulkner or James, like Proust or Lawrence, even while he is pushing Papa Hemingway as a model and precursor. As recently as *Cannibals and Christians*, he misreads Lawrence out of what I would guess is an anxiety to appear tougher than he really is, which means that Lawrence must be made less so. Lawrence, he there claims, is so sentimental about lovers that he misses their desire to "destroy one another; lovers change one another; lovers resist the change that each gives to the other." This is, of course, not what Lawrence misses. It is what he insists on. Not Lawrence but Mailer is deficient in imagining such relationships between a man and a woman. When the sexes meet in Mailer's novels, it is either for frantic sexual experiences or for conferences about manners and role-playing that never significantly modify either one. When he tries to get beyond this, as in *An American Dream*, he surrounds the relationship with portents and circumstances that prevent it from ever becoming more than an alliance for some mutual escape to an imagined ordinariness never to be achieved. Perhaps the reason for this is that the conflicts that might bring about a change in the relationships between men and women actually take place only *within* the nature of all the men in his works, within his own nature. Mailer is finally the most androgynous of writers. Perhaps that is why, of what are now eighteen books, only five are novels, a form where some developed relationship between the sexes is generally called for, and the rest, except for a quite good volume of poems entitled *Deaths for the Ladies (and Other Disasters)* and the scripts for his play *The Deer Park* and his film *Maidstone*, is a species of self-reporting.

And yet for all the self-reporting, what do we know about him? Very little. Nothing to do with his childhood, his schooling; very little about his love affairs, not much more about his friends or his wives. Though there are bits of incidental intelligence about drinking and drugs in *Advertisements for Myself* and about his fourth marriage in *The Armies of the Night* and *Of a Fire on the Moon*, and though we learn in *The Prisoner of Sex* that for part of one summer he kept house for six children before an old love, who was to become the mother of a seventh, arrived to rescue him, most of what we get from this presumably self-centered, egotistic, and self-revealing writer are anecdotes about his public performances. Even these prove to be not confessions so much as self-creations after the event, presentations of a self he makes up for his own as much as for the reader's inspection.

## JOSEPH EPSTEIN
### "Mailer Hits Bottom"
#### *Commentary*, July 1983, pp. 62–68

On page 421 of Norman Mailer's new novel, *Ancient Evenings*, my eyeballs glazed like a franchise doughnut, I came across the following line, spoken by the Pharaoh Ptah-nem-hotep to Menenhetet II, the character who for the most part narrates this more-than-700-page book: "To tell too little is becoming your sin." That caught my attention, as did, earlier, this line: "'Yes,' said my great-grandfather, 'and I have observed that most of those who are so fortunate as to have been given the great member of a god often show an uncontrollable lack of patience.'" Long before that moment I had thought to throw this small tombstone of a novel against the wall—patience, let me speak plainly, never having been my long suit. But I forbore, and instead, in the all-too-brief intervals among the multiple acts of buggery and other sexual permutations that festoon the novel's pages, allowed my mind to formulate reverse blurbs: "Insomnia sufferers, your cure is at hand." "Gives the argument for censorship a whole new lease on life." "Extremely repulsive, utterly loathsome."

My pleasure in *Ancient Evenings* was not, then, unbounded. Yet when a talented writer writes a truly wretched book—and I believe *Ancient Evenings* to be wretched in a big-time way—all sorts of interesting questions arise. First among them is, why did he do it? This might be followed by, how could he have lost his self-critical bearings so completely? What in the intellectual environment of the day encouraged him on his crash course? When did his wagon jump the track in the first place? And, finally, was there something in his general line of thought that made artistic disaster inevitable?

Many would deny the chief premise behind these questions—that is, that Norman Mailer is a talented writer. Certainly he has written more that is bloated, foolish, and simply junky than any other serious writer of our time. He has specialized in making a public buffoon of himself, and acted in ways that reveal a deeper strain of self-deception than is usually permitted a man who stakes out for himself the claim to being a major novelist. Writing empty books, running for mayor of New York City, and performing other clownish antics, aiding in the parole of a killer who, once out of prison, soon killed again, and generally leading a public life best fitted for the People section of *Time* magazine—Norman Mailer must have plenty to occupy his thoughts on modern evenings in Brooklyn Heights.

Still, when he is working well, Norman Mailer has impressive gifts. I was sharply reminded of this while reading *The Executioner's Song* (1979), his lengthy account of the life and execution of the murderer Gary Gilmore. In that book Mailer reveals himself as a man of enormous sympathy—and the best kind of sympathy, imaginative sympathy, the sympathy that a writer shows for the people he writes about by being able to enter into and successfully convey their interior lives. Again and again in *The Executioner's Song*—a book not without its flaws, which I shall get to presently—Mailer displays this power of getting inside the minds of people whose circumstances in life are so very different from his own: the arthritic mother of a killer, a successful Mormon lawyer, a police squealer. Mailer can portray the chaos in the life of a nineteen-year-old girl, unmarried, with two children, and no prospects of any kind—and make you believe in her, feel for her, wish her life were not so hopeless as you know it will be.

But if expenditure of imaginative sympathy has always been one of the great things that novelists do, it is not what Norman Mailer is famous for. He is famous instead for creating his own literary persona, that of an autobiographical journalist more than a novelist, a kibitzer known for pushing himself to the center of the stage, above all a personal voice, savvy, logorrheic, always and endlessly self-dramatizing. Here is a sampler from *Advertisements for Myself* (1959):

> Like many another vain, empty, and bullying body of our time, I have been running for President these last ten years in the privacy of my mind, and it occurs to me that I am less close now than when I began. Defeat has left my nature divided, my sense of time is eccentric, and I contain within myself the bitter exhaustions of an old man, and the cocky arguments of a bright boy. So I am everything but my proper age of thirty-six, and anger has brought me to the edge of the brutal. In sitting down to write a sermon for this collection, I find arrogance in much of my mood. It cannot be helped. The sour truth is that I am imprisoned with a perception which will settle for nothing less than making a revolution in the consciousness of our time. Whether rightly or wrongly, it is then obvious that I would go so far as to think it is my present and future work which will have the deepest influence of any work being done by an American novelist in these years.

Today this style seems pretentious in the extreme, feverish, self-parodying—"the edge of the brutal," "sour truth," "imprisoned within a perception"—yet it did not seem so then. It seemed then, in fact, rather seductive; it found many inferior imitators, among them not a few overheated academics. For a time, critics tended to praise Norman Mailer in quite Maileresque terms. In reviewing *The Armies of the Night*, Mailer's account of a 1967 anti-Vietnam war march on the Pentagon, Richard Gilman, in the *New Republic*, wrote:

> All the rough force of his imagination, his brilliant gifts of observation, his ravishing if often calculating honesty, his daring and his chutzpah are able to flourish on the steady ground of a newly coherent subject . . . history and personality confront each other with a new sense of liberation.

A new sense of liberation—the admiration for Norman Mailer during the late 1960's and the early 1970's certainly owed a good deal to that. But let us return briefly to the passage from *Advertisements for Myself* and check it for prophetic accuracy. Mailer was quite wrong about his influence as a novelist. Apart from two not very distinguished works, *An American Dream* (1964) and *Why Are We in Vietnam?* (1967), Mailer ceased writing novels. Instead he wrote an ample amount of journalism to which he would append the word novel in subtitles. *The Armies of the Night*, for example, carries the subtitle "History as a Novel, The Novel as History," and, later, *The Executioner's Song* is subtitled "A True Life Novel." It was not Norman Mailer the novelist, then, but Norman Mailer the journalist and public figure who did help make, in his phrase, something akin to "a revolution in the consciousness of our time." That does not seem to me in question. What is in question is the nature, or quality, of that revolution.

Along with Paul Goodman, Norman O. Brown, and a number of lesser figures—flacks, really—Mailer was one of the key men responsible for releasing the Dionysian strain in American life. To be sure, they had help from pot and other drugs, from the new sexual freedom, from rock music, and from the Vietnam war. Mailer was the premier journalist of this era. Whatever he wrote about—John F. Kennedy, the anti-war movement, our national political conventions—he pumped up with his self-dramatizations. Wherever Norman Mailer was, to hear Norman Mailer tell it, there was "the existential moment." He often referred to himself, in his own writings, in the third person, the better to mock yet also to push himself forward. A characteristic passage: "Yes, Mailer had an egotism of curious disproportions. With the possible exception of John F. Kennedy, there had not been a President of the United States nor even a candidate since the Second World War whom Mailer secretly considered more suitable than himself. . . ."

Yet he could on occasion shoot off observations of real power. In his coverage of the 1968 Democratic convention in Chicago he provided a portrait of Hubert Humphrey that could make anyone who cared for Humphrey wince at its deadly, and devastating, accuracy. There is a very moving moment in Mailer's *The Armies of the Night* where he describes the radical hippie contingent before the Pentagon exchanging stares with the young military policemen, each group seeing in the other its fantasies of the devil. No, had Mailer been less talented he could not have brought off what he did.

Nevertheless, read today his journalistic books all seem terribly overcooked—almost comically so. Crossing the line of MP's at the Pentagon in *The Armies of the Night*, Mailer has himself exclaim:

> "I won't go back. If you don't arrest me, I'm going on to the Pentagon," and knew he meant it, some absolute certainty had come to him, and then two of them leaped on him at once in the cold clammy murderous fury of all cops at the existential moment of their making their bust—all cops who secretly expect to be struck at that instant for all their sins— and a supervising force came to his voice and he roared, to his own distant pleasure in new achievement and new authority—"Take your hands off me, can't you see? I'm not resisting arrest."

And so on, into the dark night of the syntactical soul. A point that is worth making about this is that Mailer could not have been in danger for a moment. Someone unknown, someone without fame or funds, might have risked a blow over the head, but not a famous writer. There are, after all, existential moments and existential moments.

Feverish times get feverish writing, and this Norman Mailer through the 1960's was able to supply by the yard. Yet even before the tumult of the 60's, Mailer was a writer who seemed to flourish in tumult. His first novel, *The Naked and the Dead* (1948), was published when he was twenty-five, and though it was a great commercial success, it was also very much a young man's book—meant to be daring in its political views, its brave use (for the day) of blue language, its portrayal of low life. Right from the start Mailer had set up shop as an *enfant terrible*. Now sixty years old, he seems ever after to have been locked into the role. Thirty-five years as an *enfant terrible* leaves one a *vieux terrible*, which is a much more tiresome, not to say tiring, role to play.

Part of the terribleness of this particular *enfant* has been his penchant for literary violence. In much of Mailer's work some form of fascism, political or spiritual, looms as the great American danger, yet Mailer himself is almost invariably more fascinated than repelled by it. An incarnation of this fascist spirit appears in *The Naked and the Dead*, in the character of Sergeant Croft, a man whose very being is violent. The identification between Mailer and Croft is very strong, as Kenneth S. Lynn has recently remarked in these pages (in a review of *Mailer: A Biography* by Hilary Mills, March 1983), and as Croft only comes alive through the opportunity for violence, so does Mailer's prose come most alive in describing Croft.

In time, violence began taking an ideological turn in Norman Mailer's writing. Nowhere did this become more clear than in an infamous essay he wrote in 1957 entitled "The White Negro." The essay acquired its infamy because in it Mailer, in the course of explaining the phenomenon of a type of the social outlaw known as the hipster, appeared to condone murder. The offending passage, which came armored in parentheses, is the following:

> (It can of course be suggested that it takes little courage for two strong eighteen-year-old hoodlums, let us say, to beat in the brains of a candy-store keeper, and indeed the act—even by the logic of the psychopath—is not likely to prove very therapeutic, for the victim is not an immediate equal. Still, courage of a sort is necessary, for one murders not only a weak fifty-year-old man but an institution as well, one violates private property, one enters into a new relation with the police and introduces a dangerous element into one's life. The hoodlum is therefore daring the unknown, and so no matter how brutal the act, it is not altogether cowardly.)

So far as I know, Norman Mailer has never apologized for this passage, or for any part of this essay. It is scarcely likely that he could have done so, for "The White Negro" has running through it the blueprint for Norman Mailer's own artistic career. For this reason it is worth briefly summarizing.

Behind the essay are the assumptions that, what with its concentration camps and atomic bombs, ours has been a particularly murderous century. In American life, according to Mailer, the great enemy is conformity, which is, in ways never really explained, subtly totalitarian. Much Maileresque exaggeration now comes into play: "A stench of fear has come out of every pore of American life, and we suffer from a collective failure of nerve." Nor is there any shortage of dubious statement: "A totalitarian society makes enormous demands on the courage of men, and a partially totalitarian society makes even greater demands, for the general anxiety is greater" (tell it to Solzhenitsyn). "The shits," Mailer announces, "are killing us."

Onto the scene comes the hipster, or, as Mailer once refers to him, "the American existentialist." He is a great disrupter—part psychopath, but one who seems in some way to have generalized his psychopathology sufficiently to know that his true enemy is a society that perpetually threatens to deaden his instinctual life. It is only through great risk, through living in the present, through engaging death, that the hipster maintains his poise and his authority:

> It is this knowledge which provides the curious community of feeling in the world of the hipster, a muted cool religious revival to be sure, but the element which is exciting, disturbing, nightmarish perhaps, is that incompatibles have come to bed, the inner life and the violent life, the orgy and the dream of love, the desire to murder and the desire to create, a dialectical conception of existence with a lust for power, a dark, romantic, and yet undeniably dynamic view of existence for it sees every man and woman as moving individually through each moment of life forward into growth or backward into death.

Mailer remarks that, at a modest estimate, there are ten million Americans who are more or less psychopathic, yet "probably not more than one hundred thousand men and women who consciously see themselves as hipsters, but their importance is that they are an elite with the potential ruthlessness of an elite, and a language most adolescents can understand instinctively, for the hipster's intense view of existence matches their experience and their desires to rebel."

It is one thing to understand the psychopathology of the hipster; another to sympathize with it. Mailer sympathizes with it—completely. How could it be otherwise when, though he never says so outright, he nonetheless clearly sees himself as the artistic arm of the hipster enterprise? The following passages from "The White Negro," meant to apply to the hipster, make much more sense when understood as expressing the underlying assumptions of Norman Mailer's own career as a writer:

> Given its emphasis on complexity, Hip abdicates from any conventional moral responsibility because it would argue that the results of our actions are unforeseeable, and so we cannot know if we do good or bad.

> What is consequent therefore is the divorce of man from his values, the liberation of the self from the Super-Ego of society. The only Hip morality . . . is to do what one feels whenever and wherever it is possible, and—this is how the war of the Hip and the Square begins—to be engaged in one primal battle: to open the limits of the possible for oneself, and for oneself alone, because that is one's need.

> . . . it takes literal faith in the creative possibilities of the human being to envisage acts of violence as the catharsis which prepares growth.

> A time of violence, new hysteria, confusion, and rebellion will then be likely to replace the time of conformity.

In Mailer's view, as man and as artist, you either move forward or you die—and as for man and artist, so for society. Such a view allies Mailer thoroughly with the notion that art must always be about the business of transcending previously established boundaries; it must smash icons, loosen the hold of settled morals, everywhere shatter complacency. The artist is most useful when he is most disruptive. As a writer, Mailer sees himself as destructive for the public good.

Fairly early in his career Mailer took for his model Ernest Hemingway. In prose style and in the general texture of their minds no two writers are more unlike, but what Mailer acquired from Hemingway, along with a lot of cheap boxing metaphors to describe his artistic career, was the notion of the novelist as perpetually in competition, both with his peers and with the writers of the past. ("So, mark you. Every American writer who takes himself to be both major and *macho* must sooner or later give a *faena* which borrows from the self-love of a Hemingway style.") But he also took the notion that a major writer must also be a major public personality. ("Let any of you decide for yourselves how silly would be A *Farewell to Arms* or, better, *Death in the Afternoon*, if it had been written by a man who was five-four, had acne, wore glasses, spoke in a shrill voice, and was a physical coward.") Hemingway, it must be said, was much better at this than Mailer. While Norman Mailer has indeed managed to become a major public personality, the personality he has over the years projected has not been one of cool courage ("grace under pressure," in the old Hemingway formulation) but instead one of chaos and confusion—of a somewhat muddled man straining to seem spiritually larger than he is.

From Hemingway, too, Mailer seems to have absorbed the additional notion that writing, no less than life itself, entails taking terrible risks. Of course the idea that the best life is the life lived dangerously does not begin in the mind and work of Ernest Hemingway. "Believe me!" noted Nietzsche, "The secret of reaping the greatest fruitfulness and the greatest enjoyment from life is to live dangerously." And early in *Ancient Evenings* Mailer has his chief character announce: "In its true exchange, one cannot gain a great deal unless one is willing to dare losing all. That is how the loveliest plunder is found." But the notion that *writing* is a dangerous activity beautifully suits Mailer's sense of self-dramatization.

Such, then, has been the bulky baggage of ideas that Norman Mailer has dragged through his career: the artist must transcend all previous boundaries; he must be a disturber of the peace; he must regularly be making fresh breakthroughs; he must establish a public celebrity that will lend added luster to his work; he must see himself in perpetual competition with all other writers, in a kind of artistic-intellectual Mr. Universe contest; and, finally, he must recognize—and through his writing realize—that the life of the artist is fundamentally a most dangerous life, filled with risk and daring and the search for unknown treasure, a form of deep-sea diving of the mind.

Whatever the intrinsic merit of these notions—and I, for one, do not think there is much merit in them—they are dangerous above all to writers. Among other things, one cannot sustain a long literary career on them. It is noteworthy in this connection that those writers who *(mutatis mutandis)* did seem to work under such assumptions died, perhaps mercifully, young: Byron, Baudelaire, Rimbaud. Those who live long lives—Henry Miller comes to mind—become *vieux terribles*. A strong argument could be made that these same notions have done serious damage to Norman Mailer's own literary career. Not once but twice he has undergone a decade-long hiatus between novels. This probably should not surprise; after all, to shock, to break through, to live dangerously—a man cannot figure to do this year in and year out.

At the end of his first ten-year hiatus Mailer produced a novel entitled *An American Dream* (1965). He produced it, moreover, under extraordinary conditions. He wrote it in eight installments, for *Esquire*, under the pressure of magazine deadlines—the way, as the author himself modestly pointed out, Dostoevsky and Dickens wrote many of their novels. But Dostoevsky, but Dickens, *An American Dream* is not. It is instead a Maileresque fantasy with a hero, one Stephen Richards Rojack, who is the kind of man Mailer no doubt imagines himself to be. Along with being the "one intellectual in America's history with a Distinguished Service Cross," Rojack is a former U.S. Congressman, a television celebrity, a professor of existentialist psychology, author of *The Psychology of the Hangman*, a better than middling boxer, and a sack-artist of Olympian caliber. For intellectual provender, *An American Dream* offers a murder, a buggery, and a good deal of chatter about the CIA and the Mafia. Its message, put into the mind of Rojack, who goes off scot free after killing his wife, is this: "Comfortless was my religion, anxiety of anxiety, for I believed God was not love but courage. Love came only as a reward."

Mailer has taken his share of critical bumps over a long career, but at the same time there has also been a steady claque of admirers, always ready to justify, to find a deeper significance, to stand in articulate awe of his shoddiest work. Thus of even so puerile a novel as *An American Dream*, one claqueur, the critic Richard Poirier, could—and did—write that this novel showed "that there is clear indication that if he [Mailer] so chose he could write any kind of novel that literature has made available to us." Poirier went on: "What he wants to do, however, is something altogether more daring. He wants to show that the world of the demonic, the supernatural, the mad is not simply the reverse side of the world that sets the normal standards by which these other conditions are defined as abnormal. Instead he wants to suggest that these worlds are simultaneous, coextensive."

Ah, we sleep deep tonight. Criticism stands guard.

No one can ever accuse Norman Mailer of being lazy. His problem, as a writer, has never been that of getting his bottom in his chair and his chair up to the desk; rather it has been getting out of his chair—of stopping. In 1967 Mailer published *Why Are We in Vietnam?*, a novel which was not directly about Vietnam but rather about Texans in Alaska hunting bears from helicopters and chewing up the landscape with powerful weapons. He lavished his prose upon political conventions, heavyweight fights, Marilyn Monroe, graffiti, astronauts, the new feminism. He became first a celebrity, then a celebrity bore. It became very easy to cease reading Norman Mailer, to cease taking him seriously.

When *The Executioner's Song* appeared in 1979, I felt that undergoing exploratory surgery was a more pleasant prospect than reading this more-than-1,000-page book. I was wrong. True, *The Executioner's Song* would not suffer for being cut by a few hundred pages, but it is nonetheless a remarkable book. It tells those of us of the middle classes, who get most of our information about American life from books, newspapers, and television, something about which we are likely to know very little: the not-quite-rooted white lower-middle-classes of the Western states who tend to live on time-payments and food stamps, off six-packs and fast food, in trailers or cinder-block homes and motel-like apartments. And it tells us about it extremely well—entering into it, as I have said, with an imaginative sympathy that greatly enlarges our understanding.

This is the milieu of Gary Gilmore, the killer who in Utah refused to appeal his death sentence, which was eventually carried out in January 1977. Gilmore was then thirty-five and had spent eighteen of his last twenty-two years in jails. Out of jail a very short while, he murdered, twice, both murders connected with robberies. To one of his victims Gilmore claims to have said: "Your money, son, *and* your life." He then shot him, point blank, in the back of the head. He slaughtered his second victim in the same manner. In *The Executioner's Song*, Mailer recounts these murders and the events leading up to them and those following after them, going back into the life of Gary Gilmore, of his girlfriend, of his and her relatives, jailers, cellmates, prosecuting and defense attorneys, and everyone else connected with Gilmore. It is an extraordinary work of journalism—so extraordinary that it becomes, in my view, literature.

Mailer's method in this book is close to what in fiction used to pass under the label of naturalism. The author intrudes as little as possible; his task is to show how environment affects character and character leads out into destiny, from which emerges, when it is effectively done, a picture of man in society, or at least a segment of society. Mailer's writing in *The Executioner's Song* is artfully unadorned; it is a plain controlled prose served up in short paragraphs:

> It came down on Nicole what an expression like "horrible loss" really meant. It was throwing away the most valuable thing in your life. It was knowing you had to live next to something larger than your own life. In this case, it was knowing that Gary was going to die.
>
> She began to think there was not even a minute when she stopped loving him, not for a minute. Not a minute of her day in which the guy was not in her mind. That she liked. She liked what was inside her. But it was spooky. She would take in a breath and recognize that she was falling more and more in love with a guy who was going to be dead.

But Mailer is really telling two stories here. Along with the story of Gary Gilmore's life and death he is also telling the story—the distinctly and wretchedly contemporary story—of the elaborate negotiations involved in the "literary rights" to Gilmore's life. This story centers on a journalist named Lawrence Schiller, a former *Life* photographer, whose specialty it has become to purchase, organize and sell off the literary rights of the lives of the notorious. Schiller had acquired the rights to Lenny Bruce's story from Bruce's widow, he had acquired the rights to Susan Atkin's life (in the Charles Manson case), he was the man who secured the last interview with Jack Ruby, and now he had moved in on the Gary Gilmore story. The mechanics of Schiller's operation are fascinating—selling off an interview with Gilmore to *Playboy*, a few photographs to this or that scandal sheet, something to the newsweeklies, bits and pieces to the European press, interviews with family members to ABC. Schiller himself is an interesting character, a man highly sensitive to being called scavenger and worse. Mailer treats him most gingerly but goes into his dealings with the utmost thoroughness. Well, almost utmost thoroughness. The only deal he does not mention is that which Schiller must have cut with Norman Mailer that made possible the writing of *The Executioner's Song.*

*The Executioner's Song* is additionally interesting because of the light it throws both on the past and on the future of Norman Mailer's career. Gary Gilmore was declared by the state of Utah to be technically and hence legally a psychopath, rather than a psychotic, and his psychopathology very tidily fits the definition of the psychopath-hipster in Mailer's "The White Negro."

In that essay, as I have noted, Mailer remarks that no one has yet projected himself into "essential sympathy" with the psychopath. This Mailer does in *The Executioner's Song.* The projection, indeed the identification, of Mailer with Gary Gilmore, though it does not ruin the book, is nonetheless very great. Gilmore, at times, comes off as the very type of the artist. His parole officer, in Mailer's words, thinks, "They were about the same age, but Gilmore . . . looked much older. On the other hand, if you put up a profile of what an artist of thirty-five might look like, Gilmore could fit that physical profile." Gary Gilmore actually turns out to have been quite a good draughtsman. He was a prison autodidact; one of his favorite

novels was J. P. Donleavy's *The Ginger Man*. He did not like television. He was fearless. (His final words to his executioners were, "Let's do it.") He was, in several respects, many things that Norman Mailer, at least in his theoretical writings, would seem to wish the artist, Norman Mailer, to be—except, of course, dead.

But what saves *The Executioner's Song* is that it does not include any of Norman Mailer's theorizing. It is descriptive, naturalistic in the mode of James T. Farrell and John Dos Passos—writers Mailer much admired when he was a young man. Mailer's talent, in my view, lies in this mode. That may seem like a put-down but is not intended as one. The methods of modernism, with very few exceptions, have not been successful in the novel. Although *The Executioner's Song* is not a novel, it is the best of Norman Mailer's books, the one that seems most likely to be readable ten or twenty years from now. Mailer, to repeat, is best when he is descriptive, when his imaginative sympathies are engaged. He is at his worst when he is being Norman Mailer, the modern thinker. He is, that is to say, a serious writer except when he is thinking, and the trouble is that over his long career he has been thinking a very great deal.

In *Ancient Evenings*, unfortunately, Mailer is thinking nearly full-time. Although his new novel is set in the 12th and 13th centuries B.C.E., for the most part in the reigns of the Egyptian Pharaohs Ramses II and Ramses IX, Mailer is mostly concerned with his standard obsessions—ambition, sex, telepathy. To which one can now add reincarnation, though this came up in *The Executioner's Song*, where time and again Gary Gilmore remarks that in his current life he feels he is paying for the sins of an earlier life and time and again he remarks upon his confidence in yet another life to come. Mailer, too, has come to believe "that we're not here just one time, and I don't have any highly organized theology behind that—it's just a passing conviction that keeps returning."

*Ancient Evenings* is chiefly about the four lives of one Menenhetet I, who has been thrice reincarnated and who during his first life was charioteer to the great Pharaoh Ramses II, and later governor of his harem and guard of his two queens. The greater part of *Ancient Evenings* is taken up with this Menenhetet I recounting his life under Ramses II, and doing so for Pharaoh Ramses IX on the long night of the festival known as the Night of the Pig, when one may tell the Pharaoh unpleasant truths. The narration gets complicated, for sometimes Menenhetet tells his own stories, at other times we learn about things through his great-grandson, Menenhetet II, who has gifts of telepathy and who, through these gifts, tells us what other people in the novel are thinking.

The architecture of *Ancient Evenings* is highly elaborate. The novel begins in a tomb, where the spirits of Menenhetet I and Menenhetet II first encounter each other. After forcing the spirit of his great-grandson to perform fellatio upon him—are you still with me?—he informs him (and us), lengthily, about the theogony of the Egyptian gods: Ra, Amon, Maat, Osiris, Isis, Set, Horus, and, as a baseball announcer in my town has it, "all that gang." Mailer has obviously swotted up the subject of ancient Egypt for this novel, studied *The Book of the Dead*, stuffed himself with such facts as are available on Egyptian methods of embalming, on religious ritual, on daily life. He has tossed into the stew a belief in telepathy and reincarnation, in neither of which Egyptians of the ancient world quite believed, and added ornate sets of his own devising. I do not know enough about Egypt to judge whether he has got this material down correctly—though it is comforting to note that at the court of Ramses IX they use the word "hopefully" quite as ungrammatically as do so many American undergraduates and television journalists—but I do know that as a subject, ancient Egypt presents certain very real problems.

The first of these problems is that reincarnation can wreak havoc on the fundamentals of plotting. One of the nice things about death, for a novelist, is that it brings plots to a close. But under reincarnation, if you die, that is only the beginning—your troubles have only started. It is worth noting that Menenhetet talks almost solely about his first life. If he had gone into similar detail concerning his second, third, and fourth lives, Mailer would have had on his hands a novel well in excess of 2,000 pages.

No one, surely, can have wished *Ancient Evenings* longer than it is now. Even among the novel's admirers, you can hear, in the midst of their praise, the groans of fatigue this book has brought on. Thus Walter Clemons, in *Vanity Fair:* "Whatever you decide about it, and I warn you it can be hard going. . . ." Thus Brigitte Weeks, in the Washington *Post:* "But it is not easy to stay afloat in a flood, and despite all the glitter and the magic, the imaginative gymnastics, this reader, at least, sometimes felt as if she were going under for the third time." Thus Peter S. Prescott, in *Newsweek:* "Stupefying the book may be. . . ." Thus Harold Bloom, in the *New York Review of Books:* ". . . if you read *Ancient Evenings* for the story, you will hang yourself."

Part of the problem is Mailer's Egyptology. If he has learned about some bit of Egyptian lore or craft, not wishing to be wasteful, he lays it on us. He will stop, for example, to expatiate on Egyptian methods of rock cutting. Too often the novel reads like something devised by Mel Brooks's Two Thousand Year Old Man—though he'd have to be three thousand years old—but without the jokes. Not that some of these items aren't finely done. Mailer's account of the battle of Kadesh is splendid; and so is his account of the embalming of Menenhetet II, as the spirit of the man being embalmed details it. Yet *Ancient Evenings* is finally a novel altogether without pace. As Menenhetet I explains the gods to Rama-Nefru, the Pharaoh Ramses II's second queen, he notes, "A haze was over my eyes." Friend, I thought, you are not alone.

Mailer has said that his novel is about magic and that it reflects his interest in the very rich. But the real subjects, once again for Mailer, are power and sex, and apart from the battle of Kadesh, all the big moments in the book have to do with sex. It is a sign of the deep poverty of Norman Mailer's imagination that the only climax he can imagine in any human relationship is really just that—a sexual climax. Everything in this novel builds up to someone penetrating someone else in one orifice or another, usually with a good deal of humiliation involved for one of the parties, a sense of triumph for the other. Tender feelings rarely come into play; love, never.

Sex, its contemplation or enactment, must take up more than half of *Ancient Evenings*. Without it the novel would not even be a bad *National Geographic* article. Since no one else has pointed it out, may I be the first to announce that the sex in *Ancient Evenings* is extremely repulsive? Mailer has wrought a courtly language for this novel, which he combines with a certain (as he imagines it) antiquity of phrasing, so that orgasms are described as "coming-forth"; so that, preparatory to buggering a thief, Menenhetet II notes, "No door could have withstood my horn"; so that Menenhetet remarks of his mother, "The fresh seed of my father was the finest lotion she had ever found for her face"; so that Nefertiri, first queen to Ramses II, says to Menenhetet I, "I will make love to you tonight with all three of My mouths." And here is Ramses II having at Menenhetet I:

I heard a clangor in my head equal to the great door of a temple knocked open by the blow of a log carried forward at a run by ten good men, it was with the force of ten good men that He took me up my bowels, and I lay with my face on the stony soil of the cave while a bat screamed overhead.

Buggery and sodomistic rape seem to be the central sexual experiences of *Ancient Evenings*. With the bracing humorlessness of modern criticism, Peter S. Prescott, in *Newsweek*, notes: "Mailer, we know from past novels, has thought long and hard about anal rape, but here he outdoes himself." While Harold Bloom, in the *New York Review*, chimes in: "In *Ancient Evenings* [Mailer] has emancipated himself, and seems to be verging upon a new metaphysic, in which heterosexual buggery might be the true norm." (The true norm? Can this be true, Norm?) The connection between buggery and excrement is not shirked in this loathsome book in which excrement is intended to have magical, even divine, properties. "Certainly," says Menenhetet I, "I came to the sad conclusion that excrement was as much a part of magic as blood or fire, an elixir of dying Gods and rotting spirits desperate to regain the life they were about to lose." There is much more of this kind of blather about, as Menenhetet II puts it early in the novel, "the sinuosities of shit." So much of it, in fact, that another admirer of the novel, George Stade, wrote in the *New Republic*: "If you do not buy [Mailer's] notions of magic and the unconscious, of course, you will simply feel that Mailer and his novel are full of shit." To answer a two-clause sentence in two parts: I don't, and therefore I do.

Why would Mailer write a novel so empty, so inert, so pretentious? Breaking through again, I fear. But breaking through to what—and why does he have to go all the way back to ancient Egypt to do it? Apart from the Cecil B. De Mille sets, the chit-chat about the significance of feces, and an untested recipe for successful reincarnation (impregnate a woman at the exact moment one is dying), *Ancient Evenings* is, for Norman Mailer, pretty much business as usual. I think he wrote an empty, inert, pretentious novel because, given the theories to which he is hostage, it is no longer possible for him to write a good novel.

Not that this has stopped critics from finding deep significance in *Ancient Evenings*. Professor Stade reads the book as "an on-and-off metaphor for the repressed unconscious." Mr. Prescott sees the book's "message (if it has one) . . . to be that the concentration of power at the top of the pyramid unhinges all stability: to rule all is to fear everyone." But the most ingenious reading comes from Harold Bloom, author of *A Map of Misreading*, who holds that "Mailer too wishes us to learn how to live, in an America where he sees our bodies and spirits as becoming increasingly artificial, even 'plastic' as he has often remarked." Professor Bloom, also the author of *The Anxiety of Influence*, finds Ernest Hemingway in *Ancient Evenings*, for he reads Hemingway into the character of Ramses II and Mailer himself into that of Menenhetet I, adding that "to have been bumbuggered by one's precursor is a sublime new variant on the sorrows of literary influence." Clearly, a critic's work is never done.

But then, in our era, neither is a novelist's. Since the publication of *Ancient Evenings*, Norman Mailer has been promoting his novel with furious energy. Through an endless round of interviews and a general media blitz, Mailer, with the aid of certain critics and reviewers, has pushed very hard to make his new novel seem important—so much so that one realizes that not long ago a new novel by Norman Mailer would have seemed an important literary event in its own right. Now it seems merely another media event—one more yelp in the contemporary racket—a novel that needs all the outside help it can get. "If it's no good," Mailer has said of this novel in

more than one place, "I'm no good." That may be putting the case more starkly than is necessary, but then, one suddenly begins to think, perhaps it is true. Could a good writer have written so foul a book?

# CLARENCE MAJOR

## 1936–

Clarence Major was born in Atlanta, Georgia, on December 31, 1936. After his parents' divorce he moved to Chicago with his mother and later studied at the Art Institute of Chicago. He abandoned his art studies and served in the U.S. Air Force for two years. After his discharge he worked in a steel factory in Omaha. During this same period he also began working for the *Coercion Review*, launching his fruitful literary career. He moved to New York and became associated with the Harlem Education Program at the New Lincoln School. In 1965 he published a collection of poetry called *Love Poems of a Black Man*. Although he has continued to write poetry, he is best known for his novels, *All-Night Visitors* (1969), *NO* (1973), *Reflex and Bone Structure* (1975), and *Emergency Exit* (1979).

Major was a columnist for the *American Poetry Review* and has edited several anthologies of black literature. He is also an accomplished lexicographer, responsible for *The Dictionary of American Slang* (1970). During the 1970s he held teaching posts at several universities and by the end of the decade he had earned a Ph.D. from the Union for Experimenting Colleges and Universities in Ohio. Married and divorced three times, he has been teaching at the University of Colorado in Boulder since 1977.

## Personal

*Interviewer:* In your essay, "A Black Criterion," you call for black writers to break away from Westernized literary strictures. Do you think of *All-Night Visitors* as being an example of a "non-Western" novel?

*Major:* I've changed since writing that essay in 1967. I now find repulsive the idea of calling for black writers to do anything other than what they each choose to do. A lot of blacks grew up in the United States and became writers. They are different because of the racial climate and because of this country's history, but they still are part of this common American experience. They may speak black English and use Afro-American slang, and eat black-eyed peas and corn bread, yet they are not African. And certainly they are not Chinese. So what do we have? We are Americans. We work in English; it may be black English, but at its roots, it's English. This does not mean that there are not several very unique black writers. If you look at Cecil Brown, Al Young, William Demby, Ron Fair, and Charles Wright, you'll see how original the contemporary black fictionist really is. But as far as some kind of all-encompassing black aesthetic is concerned, I don't think black writers can be thrown together like that into some kind of formula. Black writers today should write whatever they want to write and in any way they choose to write it. No style or subject should be alien to them. We have to get away from this rigid notion that there are certain topics and methods reserved for black writers. I'm against all that. I'm against coercion from blacks and from whites.

*Interviewer:* Then you did not intend that your first novel be seen as working against a Western idea of what the novel should be?

*Major:* No. *All-Night Visitors* was not a non-Western novel. I was struggling against a lot of Western concepts when I wrote it, but it is still an *American* novel. I once said that it was

not a Christian novel. Christianity is something with which I have been at war almost all my life. When I was a kid I believed the things I was told about God and the Devil. I think that in the West, Christianity's great attraction is that it offers life after death. It's something that people can lose themselves in because they can say that everything is going to be all right. Eastern religions don't have that built-in escape, nor do they have the tremendous self-hatred that's at the center of Christianity. These feelings about Christianity are in my work because I agonized with these things in my own experience of growing up, these problems of good and evil and sex. I think that's why there's so much sex in *All-Night Visitors*. Here was a man who could express himself only in this one natural way because he had absolutely nothing else. Christianity's view toward sex exists because of the great self-hatred that's so embedded in Christian teaching. Look at Saint Paul's doctrine of Original Sin. I can see it in everything around us: sex is something that's nasty and something to hide. *All-Night Visitors* was a novel I had to write in order to come to terms with my own body. I also wanted to deal with the other body functions. In *NO* I was trying to exploit all the most sacred taboos in this culture, not just sexual taboos, but those related to the private functions of the body, and that's where they all seem to center. ⟨. . .⟩

*Interviewer:* One recurring concern in both novels is that of the "self." One way of looking at your characters is that they lack a sense of who they are and they must discover that. But seen in the way I think you intend it to be, the self is really a non-existent thing, or something that is in a constant state of becoming. Moses in *NO*, for instance, *is* all the things that happen to him and all the ways that people look at him. In this sense, one cannot say that his problem is that he doesn't know who he is. The point is that he isn't one thing, but many. Is the self something that is created, rather than found, or uncovered?

*Major:* The notion of self in *NO* is dealt with in a

superficial way. The narrator says at various times that he thinks the idea of a self is ridiculous. He's called by many names. This might be a clue to just how artificial or shifting this whole business of self becomes. (The search for freedom is another artificial thing in the novel. That's deliberately artificial. There's no such thing as freedom, in the sense in which it's used in that novel.) At one point he's called Nicodemus, which is something out of Negro folklore. And he's called C. C. Rider.

*Interviewer:* And at times "the Boy."

*Major:* Right. And Ladykiller, the Inspector, and June Bug. And there's a play on Nat Turner; the narrator is called Nat Turnips. And, of course, the name he usually goes by is Moses. Did you get the sense that there were two Moses?

*Interviewer:* Yes. One is the narrator and the other is the father figure.

*Major:* One is definitely the father image. And although it wouldn't be the wisest thing to do, you could substitute "God" for "father." It wouldn't be too far off either. . . . But to get back to your question about the notion of self. I was trying to show all the shifting elements of the so-called self. One way I did it was by giving the narrator all these names. The other Moses, of course, is not concerned with problems of who he is. He's a doer, he's a hard-hitting, physical type; the narrator is more reflective and spiritual. The father is really the "ladykiller."

*Interviewer:* Yes, literally.

*Major:* He's a sort of pimp, and he's a hustler. He's deadly and yet he's gentle. I tried to make his character difficult to penetrate.

*Interviewer:* I wanted to ask you about the bullfight scene at the end of the novel in relation to this question of the self. Does it suggest something along the lines of the Hemingway idea of the moment of truth?

*Major:* I hope that it's not that corny, but it may be.

*Interviewer:* What is it that happens there? Must he have this encounter witih death before he can be free of these terrible things in his past?

*Major:* He must come to terms with an ultimate act. He has to have that look into the endless horror of things in order to get beyond the whole petty business of worrying about it.

*Interviewer:* I wonder why you did not write *NO* as a naturalistic novel. In some ways it is merely a story of a boy growing up.

*Major:* Why do you think that he is young?

*Interviewer:* I assumed that he was now looking back on the things that happened to him as a boy.

*Major:* Right. That's what I was trying to do. I was trying not only to construct a chronological story but one that was psychologically unrestricted by time. You notice that there are elements from the 1920s, the 1930s, and the 1940s. And there are qualities out of the 1970s and the space age. I was trying to bring all of this together and blend it into a kind of consciousness that was not restricted. I wanted a landscape in language that would give me the freedom to do this. I felt that this freedom could not be achieved in a naturalistic novel.

*Interviewer:* Yes. You would not have had the range you needed. You move through all different states of mind and ages. The narrator not only sees the action and events of the story the way a child would, but also as a grown man reflecting on and shaping those experiences.

*Major:* You also probably noticed that I was grabbing at every useful reference that I could get my hands on: magic, mysticism, Judeo-Christian religion, philosophy, witchcraft, American superstition and folklore, black terminology, and black slang. But I didn't start out with any conscious notion of doing that; it just developed in a very organic way. It was only after I finished the first draft that I saw what I wanted to do. When I got that finished I started making out elaborate charts with the names of the characters, personality sketches, and their possible ages. I worked hard at inventing names that would really work with the characters, names like Grady Flower, Lucy Nasteylip, Grew . . . and B.B.—a name little black boys in the South are often given.

*Interviewer:* There are many Southern elements in the novel. At times I was reminded of Faulkner.

*Major:* It's very definitely a Southern novel. I tried to capture the flavor of the South as I remember it. There was also a subdued treatment of the relationship between the country and the city, but it wasn't fully developed in the novel. The paradox of the country and the city is very deep in me because I know both. I was born in the city, but shortly after that I lived in the country. It's been that way on and off ever since. ⟨. . .⟩

*Interviewer:* You and I have talked before about the relationship between your poetry and fiction. What do you see as the relationship between the two?

*Major:* Much of my poetry is purely fictional. I sincerely believe good poetry should be fictional. I work hard to make all my poems work as fiction. My newest book of poems which hasn't been published yet, *The Syncopated Cakewalk*, is pure fiction. I think that it was Carson McCullers who said that poetry should be more like fiction and that fiction should be more like poetry. I am working very deliberately to break down what I think are the false distinctions between poetry and fiction.

*Interviewer:* Is there an essential difference, though, that still exists? Does it have to do with the use of language or with the fact that fiction is still narrative in nature?

*Major:* No, I don't see the difference. But I am really in a state of transition with all of this. It is rather difficult for me to abstract theories about what this means and where I'm going with it.

*Interviewer:* I know that you attended the Art Institute in Chicago for a while. Has painting affected your writing in any way?

*Major:* The Art Institute experience has often been misunderstood. It didn't involve any academic classes. I was there on a fellowship to sketch and paint. I learned a lot in those days, but mainly on my own, upstairs in the gallery and in the library. I was very serious about painting. I almost painted my mother out of house and home actually. We nearly ran out of space, but my mother always encouraged me to paint. She wanted me to become a painter. I think my experience with painting, the way that I learned to see the physical world of lines, color, and composition, definitely influenced my writing.

*Interviewer:* Can you describe your work habits?

*Major:* They change all the time because they depend on the thing I'm doing. If I'm writing a group of short stories, I might work exclusively on one each day. If I'm writing a series of poems I might do one or two a day.

*Interviewer:* How much revision do you do?

*Major:* I revise endlessly. Even after publication. I am not one of those writers who sees publication as a cut-off point.

*Interviewer:* Eli in *All-Night Visitors* says something very interesting and I wonder whether or not it describes your reasons for writing: "the universe is not *ordered*, therefore I am simply pricking the shape of a particular construct, a form, in it."

*Major:* I don't know. I suppose writing comes from the

need to shape one's experience and ideas. Maybe it assures us a future and a past. We try to drive away our fears and uncertainties and explain the mystery of life and the world.
—CLARENCE MAJOR, Interview by John O'Brien, *Interviews with Black Writers*, ed. John O'Brien, 1973, pp. 128–39

## Works

### POETRY

There is no indication in *Swallow the Lake* of the order in which the poems were written, but from internal evidence they seem to be reprinted in reverse chronology. Those at the end of the book are well made anecdotal poems that are skillful but not remarkable. Major himself seems to have been dissatisfied with this limited achievement, for in a poem with a higher emotional pitch, called "The Revered Black Woman," he writes:

> Teach me my emotional shallowness.
> Teach me my message, only you know.
> From your black breasts. Melodies of hurt.
> Tender ache, afro-blue, afro you.

What Major wants is to be able to write poems that relate his talents as a writer to his condition as a black citizen of the United States. So much of his experience seems irrelevant, and the rest is hard to express: "feelings I could not / put into words—into themselves—into people." Later in the same poem he speaks of "ideas I could not break nor form." Major's poems often betray the struggle he is going through and document his attempt to make a resonant statement. He does not want to be just another Black protest poet, a rôle unworthy of his talent. And so he experiments; and as often as not he fails. The lines of his verse are disjointed; he plays with shapes and punctuation: at this point his work is tentative. But it should be understood that this struggle is being carried on at an advanced level, and that it is brought on by a dissatisfaction with simple formulae. That is what makes *Swallow the Lake* an interesting book.—FRANK MACSHANE, "A Range of Six," *Poetry*, Aug. 1971, pp. 297–98

The influence of poetry on prose writing has been a vital factor in the evolution of what is called "experimental" fiction in this century. Techniques used by the modernist poets, in Europe and America, have been carried into modern novels on both continents. Without some exposure to the works of Ezra Pound, William Carlos Williams, and Robert Creeley, it would be nearly impossible for a reader of modern fiction to penetrate works by such disparate writers as Richard Brautigan, Donald Barthelme, Ishmael Reed, or Clarence Major.

The more committed a writer is to finding an aesthetic reality, the more likely he or she is to be a poet, or influenced by poetry; Clarence Major, writing both poetry and prose, is a fine example of an American writer who is passionately committed to the aesthetics of language. His poems, viewed as pure form, demonstrate a tireless quest for the right word.

Poetry, like most art forms, has the possibility of being supracultural. That is, questions of breath, line breaks, rhythm, and sound are as pressing for one writer as for the next. They are not questions of economics or even education, a fact which separates the twentieth century from the one before. The mysterious truth that great art arises from any cultural source is also one that separated American from European early on. The American quest for the authentic, as opposed to the traditional, voice was always in direct conflict with elitist expectations.

That true poetry is supracultural in both source and intention is an important fact to know. Much contemporary poetry delivers itself in flat rhetorical tones, substituting an attitude for music. The authentic poet is obsessed primarily with language, and secondarily with its meaning. The pursuit of a rhythmic code, which evokes a memory of the present, belongs to such a poet—and so belongs to Major, for he is a language man, each of whose poems is an experiment in sound and intensity.

> IS NATURAL, TAKES ME IN
>          my sense
> of my       self, a
>      black self
> unshocking to
> Mexican eyes the
>             innermost coat
> of the form, the perception
>         is gentle
>         is
> natural, takes me in
>       so
>          beautifully so
> sensibly

A poem like this one, from the collection *Symptoms & Madness* (New York: Corinth Books, 1971), is meant to be seen rather than heard, for the music in this case is visual. The placement of words on the page, the use of spaces, is calculated to reveal both an image (word-picture) and the emotional shape of the image. I like this poem a lot myself, first because it is familiar enough in structure to certain poets I admire—Williams in particular—to be quickly accessible, and second because it is stating, with extraordinary grace and simplicity, a hard-won realization about history and self-consciousness. Like a miracle, Major dramatizes the moment at which the persona realizes he is not strange, though in a strange land, and the form—spaces as expressions of awe—springs directly to the content and is right.

*Symptoms & Madness* is mostly composed of visual, rather than oral, poetry, to my eye. That is, the language is moved around in accordance with a silent and subjective thought process. All this has something to do with a sense of time: acceleration and meaning. The significance of any thought is retroactive, and Major's poetry works to latch memory and meaning together at the same speed time uses to kill us with. Either the reader "gets it" or doesn't. The audience is not Major's concern.

Association in poetry is like humor in society. The authentic poet understands that his words and images will resonate with association for some people, and not for others, so he does not concern himself with "a wide audience." The false poet often assumes the appearance of the common voice, a wolf dressing as a wolf. Or, conversely, he may react to his overconsciousness of audience by imitating the voices of accepted poets and thereby project a diction which is not natural to himself. Major, with his unequivocal devotion to the magic of language, avoids both dishonors by a know-what-I-am-and-be-it attitude. There is no pretension in these lines from "1919" in *The Cotton Club* (Detroit: Broadside Press, 1972):

> was born the year
> my mother, not my mother
> this lady steps sweet
> little steps, old black
> stepping shoes, she stops.
> right out into. the
> street, shakes hands, she
> is so proud, this
> year . . .

Poems like "1919" and others in the same collection demonstrate a shift in step, measure, and intent away from the earlier poems. The narrative voice of the poet is no longer so introspective, but comes through more in the way of a storyteller. The rhythms are counterpointed stresses interior to the line; a music comes through which is eccentric and closer to modern jazz than blues. An intricate dance step, which becomes true style, is achieved in Major's most recent collection of poems, *The Syncopated Cakewalk* (New York: Barlenmir House, 1974). Not only the style but also the content of these recent poems is different from those before. The timing is slower, history closer; the poems sound wonderful aloud. ⟨. . .⟩

Major's early work, by a leap of the imagination, can be seen geometrically as a star, or asterisk. The center is hot, the edges are myriad and take off into many directions. In the more recent work, the geometrical vision is that of a cross—vertical and horizontal and austere. He views other people as a series of details (horizontal); their history, or the cakewalk, is horizontal too. But all these figures must pass through a central point, himself, the poet; and so a moral viewpoint which is vertical emerges. The presence of the writer is here, as witness. Morality is one symptom of sanity. The narrator, as witness, serves justice by seeing all sides of a matter.

Major's language, achieved by long struggle, is original and should be useful to anyone honestly concerned with modern poetic diction. He has created a kind of code. What is not stated is what the poem is about. But that's a secret. It is said that a poem should not seem, but be. The modern poem does not so much "be" as imply, by the use of sound and tone. Major's poetry has tone. And tone is what you hear when someone speaks to you, far more closely than the sense of the words. Tone, in poetry, is achieved by line length, spacing, commas, periods, etc., rather than by a choice of words.

In the main, Major's poetry is never free of the tone of pain. Never sentimental, nor empty of humor, the poetry is still singed, burning. Those moments of pure delight encountered and transcribed by Creeley or Williams are not found in Major's work. And it is way down there, at that level of tone and mood, that the individual poet's voice remains linked to his history. While it is true that good art bests class, race, and economics, the effects of those three are still the tools used in the construction of good art. The absence of a historical memory is what accounts for the vacuity of much contemporary work. Without historical memory, questions of good and evil, guilt, and responsibility are meaningless.

Major, with his facility for poetic language, and his personal history, could have exploited both by fusing them into a slick and popular expression. What is honorable about his work is the unusual task it assumes, of welding a complex modern diction to a constant historical consciousness. There are not many writers, black or white, engaged in this struggle, and it must be lonely.—FANNY HOWE, "Clarence Major: Poet and Language Man," *BALF*, Summer 1979, pp. 68–69

## NOVELS

A sure thing about Clarence Major's first novel, *All-Night Visitors*, is that a lot of us, particularly the soul sisters, do or will not like it, and will not think too highly of Clarence Major for writing it. This will be because Eli Bolton, the central character in *All-Night Visitors*, is an aimless cockhound whose scores are mostly with white chicks and he describes all of his sex-based relationships with vivid detail in the first 60 pages. Understandably, the novel might not be finished by some who pick it up. Still, I believe there are reasons why Major, editor of

*The New Black Poetry*, has offered us what appears to be a stud novel; I believe his reasons are literary and social.

Eli, an orphan, is a veteran of the Nam. He is a numbed soul brother but not because of the Nam experience. He observes the world carefully and is hip to what's happening around him; he can dig the Muslim thing, and flavors his sex-vocab with Swahili. His story, a first-person-present narrative, is a wandering, outward-whirling vortex of flashbacks, dreams, smells, and commentary on his own precocious sensibility. The present tense brilliantly projects the author's poetic imagination as do the numerous metaphors which are skillfully handled.

Eli hustles through his limbo with intentions to hold an honest job. He works one gig at The Other Side Hotel of one-nighters; later he is a soda-jerk at Goldburg's drug-counter. Three white chicks and two soul sisters fall in and out of Eli's range of need and circumstance. There is Tammy, the unsophisticated impulsive liar from the Midwest; the restless Cathy, a prolonged love-object; Eunice, Eli's willowy sophisticated New England angel; Anita, a boss soul momma and love-object; and Clara, a daughter of Eli's foster parents. The novel is constructed so that the two Black women and what they mean to Eli are described nearest the center; at the end, Eli's three white object/angels also spin away from his grasp.

As we weave through Eli's tangled story, we find that the main plot involves Jimmy Sheraton, a white ex-comic turned drunkard nuisance, and his death. The derelict, who claims that a Black "Momma" raised him, is booted out of Goldburg's by Brogan, the store's bad Black assistant-manager. Eventually he decided to follow Eli home, bugging him on the subway. Preferring to avoid letting his irritation get the best of him, Eli walks swiftly to his pad. Stopping the youth near his destination, Sheraton is attacked by three young soul brothers who assume the responsibility of protecting members of the Black community; Sheraton's death is a "beef-kill."

At heart, Eli is a hedonist, motivated only by an unquenchable desire to T.C.B. He is ensnared by apathy and harassed by the proximity of circumstance. He will not neglect or forsake his rod; in fact, in the presence of women it is truly a fetish. Eli possesses a clinical curiosity. Sheraton's death, the brutal killing of the warden's pup at the orphanage, and the rape-killing of a Vietnamese child find Eli in a front-row seat, massaged by the medium. By the end of his narrative he will have acted in such a manner that even he doesn't fully realize the degree to which his actions permit him to break out of his malaise. First, he offers a confession of being witness to the "beef-kill" in order to save the three soul brothers from the chair. Gazing at the nape of one youth's neck as he is led from the interrogation room, Eli muses: "The view of an early defeat *or* the beginning of a kind of human victory?" His second redemptive deed comes with the offering of his living accommodations to a non-English speaking pregnant Puerto-Rican mother of seven whose husband has ousted them from their own upstairs apartment. This is effective dramatic irony; we will realize immediately the significance of these actions before Eli does.

*All-Night Visitors*, as a novel of a young Black man's psychic travels, contains some very believable people besides the narrator himself. Whether the characters are objects of Eli's passion and/or are structural props, they hold our interest because Eli's keen eye brings out their personalities with candor. Even when, in the novel's structure, they appear to come and go as phantoms, they are adequately developed. As a stylist Major has been influenced by Henry Miller and Anais Nin; his delivery is poetic and the finished product has his own earthy touch. In the fashion of Ishmael Reed, Major exploits the possibilities of surreal comedy and the ludicrous for momentary effect. In descriptive content, the sex scenes are reminiscent of the writings of John Cleland and de Sade—though no writer today needs these people as models. The orgiastic scene with the foxy Anita is described with brilliant sibilance.

Despite the fact that lengthy sex scenes seem a standard or a necessity for the "acceptable" contemporary American novel, the success or failure of *All-Night Visitors* will ultimately lie with what it represents as a novel by a Black American writer. Most of us agree that white America's current psycho-sexual fixation represents part of its demise. The fact to consider is Major's intent in starting out on this rubbish heap with his first novel. If we give *All-Night Visitors* an absolute condemnation it would contradict a casually accepted image (both in and outside of art) of the walking Black phallus, an image Eli doesn't mind fulfilling; this image has been assumed at times because it is what white America thinks of the Black man in the first place. But in Major's novel we do watch an apathetic Black man take his first steps toward maturity—social (community) responsibility. Eli Bolton is a numbed individual; sex is his only meaningful outlet. Eli, too, is not by himself. *All-Night Visitors* depicts a libidinous urge. But its character is headed in a worthwhile direction; he begins to live up to his honorable name when he *acts* in a manner that will attest to his selfless responsibility to reach out for others.

Clarence Major has the novelist's talent; but since he is contributing to contemporary Afro-American literature, his craft should be high-lighted by a central character who is able to carry the aesthetic motion of the story on a more active social level. Major already shows signs of being able to handle the psychological drama. The Afro novel today must project meaningful social concepts and spiritual values into the bloodstream of Black America, and this can be done and done well, with all the possibilities of style and message taken into account. In order to tell his story, in order to get the message across, Major gives us both what we want and don't want—his decision to do so is the artist's prerogative and his energy/vision is involved in the telling of truths. (What would have been the significance of John Coltrane, for example, if he had given the people the music they would have preferred to hear?) It is my guess that Clarence Major sees beyond this novel to the real needs of the Black community as those needs can be expressed and illustrated through fiction. Soul Brother Eli Bolton represents the living problem of apathy, and as both a wanderer of the psyche and a sexual waystation, his initial steps toward self-transformation were inevitable and justify his honesty. —RON WELBURN, *ND*, Dec. 1969, pp. 85–87

*NO* is a nightmare about a young man who is losing his wife. Moses Westby's nightmare centers on the childhood experiences that rendered him incapable of satisfying his wife sexually.

In a cryptic style full of oddly indented paragraphs, varying sized print and italics, we learn of the protagonist's first sexual encounter with his babysitter, of his second with a neighbor's daughter and his third with a thin black boy who hated girls. We also learn of the trauma associated with his learning to hold his bowels, which comes soon before the trauma caused by the racism that sets narrow limits on his bleak childhood in the rural South.

When the code is broken, we discover a life twisted by castration and mutilation fears, and a mind filled with images of feces, blood, urine, racism, sex organs and death. All the characters are imprisoned by these images. In fact, we learn little else about them. They act out strange, sometimes macabre, dramas. They either torture Westby or they fornicate with him; sometimes the two acts are indistinguishable.

The strength of the novel is not in the story line (which may take four or five readings to follow) but in the shocking images. These images sit like window displays in a shop that sells absolutely nothing except sex paraphernalia. This is a probing, honest book, which, among other things, proves that European Protestants are not the only men on earth pursued by Calvinistic demons.—GEORGE DAVIS, *NYTBR*, July 1, 1973, pp. 22–23

## SHORT STORIES

Although to date the greatest strength of Clarence Major's achievement seems to lie in the novel—especially in *Reflex and Bone Structure*—, his short fiction is valuable in its own right and deserves wide reading and critical discussion. The stories complement the longer fictions in their range and interests, their explorations of new subject matter, forms, and implications, and their suggestion of a writer deeply involved both with his craft and the age. As with the novels so with the stories: There is an unevenness which lets the critic say that some of the pieces are stronger than others. Such a judgment is no doubt inevitable for any writer, but in Major's case it reflects more than anything else his commitment to innovation and experimentation in each of the short fictions. With such writers as Raymond Federman, Steve Katz, James Purdy, Ronald Sukenick, and others, Major stands clearly on the fictive frontier. And with all these he pays a price for his engagement of the new and untried. No more than readers and literary critics can he tell us where he is going and what new discoveries he will make—that is the health and beauty of the kind of journey he is on. My guess is that, interesting and significant as the completed writings are, his best work lies ahead. In the meantime his fiction challenges us to articulate a criticism adequate to its special force and sense of presence rather than attempt to retreat behind traditional strictures and expectations.

⟨. . .⟩ For Major and a number of other writers now on the scene, traditional fiction fails to become its own reality because it is so largely a creature of a literalist mimetic on the one hand and the more or less uncritical voice of philosophical and cultural "meanings," values, and tropisms on the other. Both pressures must be resisted if the "deconstruction" process of the new fiction (and of other art forms) is to generate the kind of authenticity and autonomy under discussion. In ⟨his⟩ stories ⟨. . .⟩ we find differing levels of perspective brought to bear; but even in the fictions which move toward low mimetic surfaces, we realize that much more is going on—and it is this more which matters. Within the story itself we typically find that Major defies, breaks apart, or ignores the aesthetic of teleology, in which all "parts" point toward, imply, or subsist in an Aristotelian end or "whole." Rather than a concern for the "form" courted so strenuously by modernist writers and critics, we see that this fictionist works with "process," with open forms, with the inconclusive, and with the interplay of formal and non-formal tensions.

When he is at his best Major helps us to see that fiction created within an aesthetic of fluidity and denial of "closure" and verbal freedom can generate an excitement and awareness of great value; that the rigidities of plot, characterization, and illusioned depth can be softened and, finally, dropped in favor of new and valid rhythms. Spaces and times need no longer conform to the abstract demands either of plot or symbolic urgency, for example, but can be free to float in their own energies. Similarly what the textbooks sometimes still call "authorial intrusion" need not be construed as a felony or even a misdemeanor but rather as another manifestation of verbal energy and in fact as no "intrusion" at all. If some of the stories seem difficult or even incoherent to readers, it is because they are attempting to read by means of categories applicable to older fictional contexts but inadequate to the highly elliptical and at times improvisational way of Major's fiction. His way and that of other postmodern writers can help us realize all over again that the activity of "reading" is a highly conditioned one, too often a matter of the learned response rather than an engagement of the free and open mind. Thus, time spent with the fictions can be both a trip into the richness and surprise of words and their relationships and a way of redefining the self. In place of the hermetic quality with its correlative webbing of internally sustained ironies and symbols that one associates with modernist writing, the reader of Major's fiction finds that he must himself take part in the creation of the work and that in doing so he experiences a pleasurable liberation quite removed from the kind of response elicited by older fiction. In place of the glimpse into archetypal profundities often claimed—and justly so—for the latter, the reader of the new fiction experiences the relatively "informal" release of the creative and perhaps a sense of collaboration—communion even—with the writer. Because these are affirming and positive responses they may suggest, at least to whatever remains of the New Critical rear guard, that Major's work is shallow and lacking in seriousness. Such a view deserves no reply although it is worth saying that we desperately *need* the affirmative in the arts and the culture generally. And in any case Major shows us the grimness and horror of modern civilization to the point that he is hardly an escapist.

⟨. . .⟩ Together with such novels as *All-Night Visitors*, *NO*, and *Reflex and Bone Structure* the short fiction provides a body of work of great impressiveness and interest. In both the longer works and the stories Clarence Major shows us how fiction may bring its strengths to bear on the confusions and compromises of American culture while at the same time preserving its integrity as an art form and its right to break through the conventions of the academy in order to create new and potent rhythms, shapes, and perceptions. The stories are "experimental" in two important senses of the term: In the first place they demonstrate how fragile and provincial many of our sacrosanct aesthetic norms were/are; in the second place they move beyond parody and "deconstruction" to create new modes and new fictional life. Importantly also the stories reveal a writer who is as sensitive to the claims of his craft as he is willing to try new forms on new subject matters. In the stronger stories, especially, we find a subtle concern for the right phrase and a sensitivity for spaces and silences which only a craftsman can have. Finally, it should be said that the sheer energy and range of the stories point again to the healthy and growing nature of prose fiction. Each story is unique; each is itself; each is a challenge to both the old and the new. Taken together the short fictions rival even the richness and strength of *Reflex and Bone Structure*.—DOUG BOLLING, "A Reading of Clarence Major's Short Fiction," *BALF*, Summer 1979, pp. 51–56

# BERNARD MALAMUD

## 1914–1986

Bernard Malamud was born in Brooklyn, New York, on April 26, 1914. The son of Jewish immigrants, he received his early education at Erasmus Hall High School in Brooklyn. He later studied at the City College of New York, earning a B.A. in 1936, and at Columbia, where in 1942 he completed a master's thesis on the reception of Hardy's poetry in America. He worked briefly in Washington at the Bureau of the Census before returning to New York to write during the days and teach school in the evenings. In 1945 he moved to Greenwich Village with his new wife Ann de Chiara. Four years later he took a teaching job at Oregon State College in Corvallis, where he was allowed to teach only introductory classes because the upper-level literature courses were reserved for teachers with Ph.D's. He left Oregon in 1961 for Bennington College in Vermont, where he continued to teach, except for a two-year visiting lectureship at Harvard during the mid-1960s.

Around 1950 his short stories first began to appear in national magazines. His first novel, *The Natural* (1952), was well received by the critics. Malamud came to national attention with the publication of his first collection of short stories, *The Magic Barrel* (1958), which won the 1959 National Book Award. His most acclaimed work to date, *The Fixer* (1966), won both the 1967 Pulitzer Prize and the 1967 National Book Award. The novel is based on the historical events surrounding the 1913 trial of Mendel Beiless, a Russian Jew who was accused of the ritual murder of a Christian child. Along with Saul Bellow and Philip Roth, Malamud often is credited with bringing about the increased interest in Jewish-American fiction which has characterized the American literary scene since World War II.

Bernard Malamud died in New York on March 18, 1986.

## *Personal*

Late during the summer of 1949, Bernard Malamud, age 35 and a lifelong New Yorker, arrived in the Pacific Northwest to take a teaching position as an instructor in the English Department at Oregon State College. He was greeted at the train station in Albany, Oregon, by the Director of Composition at the small technologically and agriculturally oriented land-grant institution who drove the new instructor the few miles to Corvallis, a quiet community of about 10,000 in the heart of Oregon's farm-filled Willamette Valley.

As a New Yorker, Malamud had attended City College of New York and Columbia University where he received the B.A. and M.A. degrees and had taught English for nearly ten years at two area high schools. He had done some writing of his own and had published short stories in *American Prefaces*, *Threshold*, and the Washington *Post*. But in Corvallis, there seemed only time for the four sections of freshman English he would teach in a conservative and inflexible composition program which stressed, according to Department guidelines, "the writing of short expository themes, and the study of those elements of grammar, punctuation, spelling, and diction which are prerequisites to the writing of effective expository prose in any professional field." Under the watchful eye of the same composition director who was his first Corvallis acquaintance, Malamud endured the ordeals of group writing examinations, grading technical reports, and filing his themes in the Department "theme room."

Teaching four sections of composition every academic term is itself enough to dull the spirit. Doing so over a long period of time in a rigid, traditional program is almost unendurable. Faculty members who have taught in such programs quickly lose their vitality and even their equilibrium. But not so Bernard Malamud. For, while teaching four sections of composition a term and doing a good job of it, Malamud found time to write two important novels *(The Natural* and *The Assistant)* and the very fine volume of short stories, *The Magic Barrel*, for which he was awarded the National Book Award in 1959.

By the middle 1950's Malamud had become a novelist of some reputation, except in the administrative offices of the Oregon State English Department. Though he was promoted to assistant professor in 1954 and to associate professor in 1959, he was given large doses of composition classes to teach with only an occasional introductory literature course to break the monotony. Finally, in the spring of 1961, Malamud left Oregon State. He had come to Corvallis an unknown writer. He left a national figure, a novelist of genuine accomplishment in a time when few writers were successful in understanding, describing, and making plausible the bizarre facts of contemporary life.

*The Fiction of Bernard Malamud* was the third in a continuing series of conferences on major figures in modern American literature sponsored by the Department of English at Oregon State. It brought to the campus a group of notable scholars to talk about Malamud's craft and the importance of his fiction. ⟨. . .⟩ The Oregon State symposium and this volume are then the University's tribute to one of America's most important contemporary novelists and to the most distinguished faculty member ever to teach in its English Department. In the process, as Leslie Fiedler notes so well, we have transformed a man some among us once regarded as a "loveable misfit" or a "pain-in-the-ass" into a "cultural monument."—RICHARD ASTRO, "Preface" to *The Fiction of Bernard Malamud*, eds. Richard Astro, Jackson Benson, 1977, pp. 5–7

## General

Only those too perverse or fuzzy-headed to recognize cultural facts now refuse to acknowledge the existence of a Jewish Movement in contemporary American writing, and especially the writing of fiction. Saul Bellow, its brightest luminary, has been at work for more than thirty years. Bernard Malamud, a less spectacular but no less durable writer, began in the early 1950's. Even Philip Roth, just yesterday a child prodigy, has been around for better than ten years. In terms of simple longevity, then, the Jewish-American novel is more than a vogue. And with three such writers as Bellow, Malamud, and Roth, all versatile and consistently productive, it seems unlikely to fizzle out. As yet no signs appear of self-imitation, sure clue of a movement's degeneration. There is also an entire second string of writers of varying ages and abilities, Leslie Fiedler, Herbert Gold, Bruce Jay Friedman, to name but three. Not to speak of the Popular Front: e.g., Herman Wouk, Leon Uris, Jerome Weidman. Even those not aligned with the Movement, Norman Mailer and J. D. Salinger, contribute to it indirectly with an occasional half-Jewish hero and secularized Jewish *schmerz*.

⟨. . .⟩ the dominant and recurrent theme of the Jewish Movement, a theme which unifies its various members however different in method, is the theme of suffering. Furthermore, although such European-Jewish novels as André Schwartz-Bart's *The Last of the Just*, Elie Wiesel's *Night*, and Piotr Rawicz's *Blood from the Sky* treat the same theme with the unsurpassed authority of those who survived the annihilation, their work does not comprise a movement. We cannot bear their nihilistic suggestion that the suffering produced naught; or worse, that the European Jews collaborated in their own slaughter. Our writers, just far enough away from the holocaust to feel its heat but not be scorched, retain a little optimism, a little affirmation. With us, the suffering is meaningful. It can even be redemptive, stirring up a faint hope for the goodness of man after all. Jewish heroes may be *shlemiels* or *shlimazels* but unlike the major trend of much other contemporary fiction which depicts man as joke, cripple, or cipher, the Jewish-American writer continues to emphasize the fundamental worth of life and the possibility of humanity. Yet he does not retreat into the safe orthodoxy of formal religion. His affirmation is tough, qualified, secular. He is religious in that he portrays man as more than matter, but he is not pious.

I have been speaking about that abstraction "The Jewish Writer," but all along I have really been thinking about Bernard Malamud. Bellow may be flashier and more intellectually impressive, Roth may be subtler, shrewder, and funnier, but Malamud is to my taste the most solid, the most consistently fulfilled, and—I might as well get this chauvinism right out into the open—the most *Jewish*. What I mean is that Malamud best represents the phenomenon of the Jewish Movement; not only is he one of its founders and major practitioners, he is probably its best single exemplar. In Malamud's work we most clearly perceive just those characteristics which define the entire Movement.

First and foremost, there is the theme of meaningful suffering, which in Malamud also implies the quest for moral resolution and self-realization. But the theme of suffering cannot alone sustain either a movement or a writer's career. We can take just so much bad news. Malamud's writing, like that of the Movement at large, is also richly comic. Paradoxically, the comedy is at once a mode of expression of the suffering and a way of easing it. With the Jew humor is an escape valve for dangerous pressures, a manner of letting out things too painful to be kept in. (Could it be that one of the reasons we have able black writers like Ellison and Baldwin but not a Black Movement, is the prevailing solemnity of these writers?) Finally, the Jewish writer speaks in a distinctive literary voice. With Bellow and at about the same time, Malamud invented and perfected a fresh literary idiom, a "Jewish style." This style consists of much more than the importation of Yiddish words and phrases into English, or a mere broken Yiddish-English dialect, long the staple of popular works presenting lovable silly Jewish stereotypes *(Abie's Irish Rose)*. Rather, it is a significant development and expansion of the American colloquial style, established as a vital literary medium by Mark Twain. The Jewish style is for the first time in our literary history a voice that conveys ethnic characteristics, a special sort of sensibility, and the quality of a foreign language, yet remains familiar and eloquent to non-Jews. Although dialects and dialect styles tend to be reductive, rendering their speakers either funny or absurd, Malamud's style can evoke either tragic dignity or comic foolishness, or, miraculously, both at once.—SHELDON NORMAN GREBSTEIN, "Bernard Malamud and the Jewish Movement," *Contemporary American-Jewish Literature*, ed. Irving Malin, 1973, pp. 175–79

## Works

### THE NATURAL

The fact that a book touches something deep in us is no guarantee that it will be a good book; but the trouble with serious contemporary fiction in general is its neglect of the ordinary nerves which continue to be the most sensitive ones. Bad art has been allowed to monopolize the thunderbolts which once belonged as a matter of course to writers who knew better what to do with them. When a film about the Marines, no matter how stupid it may be, ends with "The Halls of Montezuma" throbbing in the background as John Wayne and company go forward staunchly to defend the Good, everyone feels a chill stealing up his spine. Whether or not this is a valuable chill depends on how the writer uses it; like all forms of power, a knowledge of what to appeal to in the reader can be used or abused. But it would be difficult to guess from high-brow modern fiction or criticism, with their constant emphasis on knowledge and ideas, that intelligent people are capable of responding to fire-engines, anthems, soldiers, or baseball players at all.

Consequently, the appearance of an intelligent novelist who finds it possible to say something about a popular—"mass"—phenomenon through the medium of a popular literary form is a very healthy sign. Bernard Malamud's *The Natural* is the first serious novel we have had (after Ring Lardner's *You Know Me Al*) about a baseball player. "Serious" means simply that the book appeals to a wider range of emotions and ideas than those which hang on winning or losing the game. But the fact that *The Natural* at the same time preserves and revitalizes so much of the "traditional" baseball story is the best thing about it. Mr. Malamud brings back the cocksure rookie who finally beats his way up, convinces the skeptics, transforms the team single-handed from a last-place club into a pennant contender, and breaks a few records while he's at it. In the absence of the European concern with class, this type of hero is one of our substitutes for the Young Man from the Provinces, and he interests us as Julien Sorel and Rastignac would, even if they were not characters in great novels. Plenty of the sheer melodrama of baseball turns up in *The Natural* too. The novel abounds in last-minute home runs that save the day, three-and-two pitches, agonizing play-offs, etc. etc.

Nevertheless, though Mr. Malamud has written an exciting baseball story which throws new light on responses we usually take for granted, he does not succeed in achieving that synthesis of the popular and the serious at which he aims.

> The third ball slithered at the batter like a meteor, the flame swallowing itself. He lifted his club to crush it into a universe of sparks but the heavy wood dragged, and though he willed to destroy the sound he heard a gong bong and realized with sadness that the ball he had expected to hit had long since been part of the past.

The incident being described is a contest between a young pitcher on his way up to the major leagues and a great hitter on his way down. Mr. Malamud is fully aware of the possibilities of a battle between the generations. But he does not let us see them directly; instead he turns on his eloquence to let us know that he knows that something primitive and elemental is going on here, a struggle of cosmic grandeur between two superhuman warriors. The effect of such prose is rather to interfere with his intention than to reinforce it. At his best moments, he allows the qualities he perceives in baseball to speak for themselves, as in the fine scene at the end of the book where a first-rate pitcher, overcome by the tension of a play-off game, faints while facing the greatest batter in the league, and for once Mr. Malamud's prose stays tight and clear, giving the force of his story a fair chance to communicate itself fully. Unhappily, however, the passage quoted above is Mr. Malamud's more characteristic note.

This defect we find cropping up in different ways all through *The Natural*. Mr. Malamud suggests that baseball is the American way of providing for needs which our culture generally refuses to satisfy. The heroic, nobility and endurance, a battle in which no one loses but somebody wins—such needs have nowhere else to go for nourishment except the local ball park. But the ball park in itself is not enough for the writer. Having offered us in Roy Hobbs a typical baseball-story hero, Mr. Malamud associates him with an era in which heroes were a good deal more at home than they are now. *The Natural* is loaded with Homeric parallels and suggestions of myth—overloaded in fact. Roy uses a bat that flashes golden in the sun (the wood comes from a tree struck by lightning—the weapon forged by Hephaestus); in a slump he is made to seem like Achilles brooding in his tent; the fainting pitcher mentioned above reminds us of Hector running from Achilles; and there is even a Thersites railing from the bleachers at the Achilles in left field.

All this amounts to a commendable effort to say that baseball is much more important than it seems to be. Using Homer, however, is not only too easy a way to do it, but also a misconception of what intelligence and seriousness of purpose demand from a writer. It is, I think, the same misconception which is responsible for Mr. Malamud's readiness to slip from a vigorous and sharp prose style into vague poeticality whenever his "meaning" collides with his narrative. The habit of symbolizing everything, from baseball bats to men and women, and of multiplying allusions to the point where they begin to crowd out reality altogether, is one of the more unfortunate legacies bequeathed by Joyce and Eliot to contemporary writers. And because this by now worn-out "advanced" convention has bred an indifference to simple realities and ordinary experience in our fiction, it is necessary that criticism, while encouraging the enterprise represented by *The Natural*, should carefully point out where and why it has failed.

Mr. Malamud is truer to the inherent purpose of his book when he finds the elements of myth, not in ancient Greece, but in the real history of baseball: Roy's team, the New York Knights, have the old Brooklyn Dodgers in them, complete with a Babe Herman kind of outfielder; Roy, like Lou Gehrig in a famous incident, hits a home run after promising a kid in a hospital that he would; several of the fans are based on well-known Ebbets Field characters, among them Hilda Chester with her cow bell. But the best instance of an intelligent reliance on the actual mythos of baseball is in the last scene of the novel, where Mr. Malamud comes very close to the synthesis we are looking for.

Though Roy is supposed to be a typical hero, he does something that neither Achilles nor a character in a John R. Tunis story could conceivably do—he accepts a bribe. The measure of Mr. Malamud's ability to get at our ordinary responses to baseball as soon as he forgets to be eloquent and erudite lies in the very real pain we experience as Roy throws the play-off game; when a kid outside the stadium pleads with him to "Say it ain't so!" he voices perfectly our protest and our misery. Mr. Malamud, of course, did not invent the little boy. The incident supposedly happened to Shoeless Joe Jackson after it was revealed that the Chicago White Sox had thrown the 1919 World Series with the Cincinnati Reds, and it has all the earmarks of true legend. The anguished little kid catches up the despair of a great many people whose whole world looked as if it might topple merely because a group of professional athletes turned out to be dishonest.

Why the despair? Mr. Malamud has the answer when he makes one of his characters explain that she hates to see a hero fail because "there are so few of them." Indeed there are few of them, even fewer today than there ever were. And the reason for this is not, I think, that we are a lesser age than any other, but that we are a more wary one. The sins of King David never compelled the ancient Hebrews to cut him down to size, nor did Achilles' childishness prevent the Greeks from seeing him as a hero. According to the thesis of Joseph Wood Krutch (in *The Modern Temper*) our suspicion of heroes is ascribable to the decline of Christianity and the work of Darwin and Freud. But today I think there is a simpler explanation to hand. The last twenty years have offered terrifying evidence that while modern man is by no means incapable of believing in heroes—indeed he may even be more prone to hero-worship than the Elizabethans ever were—hero-worship can have catastrophic effects. It is not for nothing that the art of debunking has been developed to perfection in America; as if to reassure ourselves that we don't have to go overboard the moment an idol is set up in the square, we commission some newspaper to publish a photograph of its clay feet.

Of course, we pay for these precautions by seeing ourselves mostly in relation to what is ordinary about our great men, rarely to what is extraordinary. But the need for heroes to define and direct our aspirations persists, and perhaps it is a good thing that we should satisfy it in a less dangerous area than politics. The essence of a hero is that he must embody convincingly the ideals of his culture, and he must do so not in fiction but in life where something important—it doesn't really matter what—is felt to be at stake. Baseball players seem to be the only public figures who have succeeded in filling the bill, and for this reason the game is probably the one public institution that has been spared by the debunkers, even by those most cynical of men, the sports reporters. (In *The Natural* those who are engaged in trying to pull the hero down are all figures of evil.) The players are given the highest public respect, at the price of behaving as no one else is expected to behave—not even a candidate for the vice-presidency. For example, it would never occur to a baseball fan that Pete Reiser was a sucker for ruining his career by playing too hard; that he did so is considered his fate and his glory.

The game, in short, holds up to the children in this country—and to their parents—the most concrete evidence that fierce competition is no justification for breaking the rules; that extraordinary effort for which you don't necessarily get time-and-a-half is still both desirable and mandatory, and that honesty is not a mere figment of a Sunday school teacher's imagination. Which is only to say what Mr. Malamud has

perceived: that baseball, at least as an educational institution, has much in common with epic and tragedy. But this is not all. Baseball gives people the chance to engage their feelings without fear of being cheated, and so they respond, naturally enough, with a gratitude that is almost fanatic. A regime of the most rigorous codes and controls has been sanctioned in the major leagues to make sure that Joe Jackson's little boy never emerges out of legend into fact again; the results have justified the precautions: and no player for thirty years now has been caught taking a bribe.

Morally, baseball is what we all would love politics to be—a beautiful abstraction whose clarity is unspoiled by the contradictions that bog us down in life. Oversimplified but true within its limits, the game doesn't so much teach us about life as enforce the beliefs without which living is a hopeless business. So if we are wondering what ever happened to the groundlings who sat through four and a half hours of Shakespeare and then came back for more, perhaps the place to look is not only in the local movie theater but in the bleachers during a Sunday doubleheader.

Having discovered a hero, then, Mr. Malamud goes on to try to rediscover the literary genre in which the hero once flourished—tragedy. But here again he is none too successful. We have already seen the consequences of Mr. Malamud's uncritical acceptance of the bad habits of ambitious modern fiction. Here his failure throws light on the limitations and dangers of an impulse to do something serious with worn-out *popular* conventions.

To write tragedy you need not only a sense of the heroic (shared by the writer and his audience), but an idea of Fate as well. Mr. Malamud makes overtures both to the conception of Fate as the doom drawn upon the hero's head by his great pride, and to that Shakespearean sense of Fate which Bradley described as a conspiracy of character and circumstance. Twice Roy Hobbs boasts that he will be "the greatest there ever was in the game," and twice disaster follows—the first time in the shape of a crazy young girl ("certainly a snappy goddess") who goes around shooting boastful athletes with silver bullets as if to remind them that human beings are really ghosts. But this is merely a warning; Roy survives the silver bullet, though wasting fifteen precious years before he can come up to the major leagues and do what he has to do (i.e., be "the greatest there ever was in the game"). He has ignored the warning, or rather he isn't intelligent enough to interpret the "snappy goddess" as a warning; like a mere baseball player unacquainted with Greek tragedy, Roy looks upon the shooting as a terrible stroke of bad luck which will and power can overcome (the sense we get of Roy's tremendous, all-encompassing will is a genuine achievement of Mr. Malamud's art, and the best means he employs to give whatever depth there is to Roy's heroism). Final destruction must come to him just at the dizzy pinnacle of success.

In spite of the careful attempts to reinforce the idea of Fate through the cosmic imagery which dominates the book, and through the constant stress on the superstitions which surround baseball, the idea remains too abstract to be effective: the connection between Roy's pride and his disasters comes out only as a weak suggestion, and would go completely unnoticed without the support of Greek tragedy in the background.

Moreover, convincing though Roy is, he remains far too simple a figure to be interesting as well. Mr. Malamud sees nothing in him but will and appetite—the third Platonic horse, Reason, is missing altogether (in street clothes, Roy "loses the quality of a warrior" and looks "like any big muscled mechanic or bartender on his night off"). We are all sick to death of the intellectual hero, but the answer is not to deprive your hero of even the slightest trace of mind—we have had more than enough of that tendency too. And in the end it is Roy's simplicity that destroys the tragic dimension of the novel. Though Mr. Malamud would like us to think that his hero's defect is a classic case of *hubris*, his failure to make the sense of pride concrete in any way is a tip-off that he no more believes in the tragedy of pride than we do. Apart from will, the only other quality of Roy's character that comes alive in the book is appetite. Appetite, nothing more, is Roy's tragic flaw; so long as his will remains in the service of his genius as a ballplayer (i.e., the hero part of him), Roy is safe; but the minute it gets behind his appetite either for food or for sex, the circumstances which destroy him come flying in the door.

Like his lust for home runs, Roy's yen for food and sex is of epic proportions. Early in the book, he falls in love with a girl named Memo, who is carrying the torch for a dead outfielder. Memo has a touch of Niobe in her constitution, as well as a strong flavor of Penelope, but neither of these delicate ingredients can disguise the tang of the gun-moll. Mr. Malamud uses her to point up the opposition between Roy's unenlightened appetites and the hero in him, but she looks for all that as if she would be much more at home in a James M. Cain novel. And then there is Iris Lemon, a grandmother before her time (another symbol: The Mother squared, we might say), who suddenly decides that she is in love with Roy because he too has suffered.

The truth is that Mr. Malamud's impulse to do something with popular conventions has betrayed him into choosing the wrong ones. The cheap and gaudy treatments of women and sex that are the hallmark of so much contemporary fiction cannot be transmuted simply by making them into symbols; there must be life and grace in the conventions to begin with if the serious writer is to find something valuable to draw out of them. For lack of this, and because of other artistic flaws and misconceptions, *The Natural* remains a loose mixture of clichés (both of the high- and the low-brow variety) with the authentic.

It would be a great pity if Mr. Malamud were to allow himself to go on chasing phantoms, for we badly need a writer who realizes that the "high-brow" "low-brow" distinction in American culture has done great harm on all sides. Many of us still have to learn that though we may not all be high-brows, there is always more of the low-brow in us than we are willing to admit or able to expel; nor is it desirable that we should expel it even if we could. Our response to baseball is not different in kind from our response to Dostoevsky or to the stock-in-trade of our lives. Until we learn this, we shall continue to fail to be affected by either in the way that counts.—NORMAN PODHORETZ, "Achilles in Left Field," *Cmty*, March 1953, pp. 321–26

The book was first published by Harcourt, Brace in 1952 and is, I should guess, out of print. I cannot even remember reading a notice of it at the time; and I did not see it at all until a month or two ago when I came across it in a cheap paper edition by Dell. There is on the cover an enthusiastic plug by Alfred Kazin (I trust it was as enthusiastic as it is made to sound with the aid of three dots) and a complimentary phrase from the *New York Times*; but I have no sense of the book's having made an *impression*. I, at any rate, was completely unprepared for the pleasure it gave me.

There are two things I think it strategic to say about it to begin with. First, that I have not found so much simple joy, so much sense of zest and rewarding nuttiness and humor, in anything I've read for a long time; and second, that the book has the distinction of being immune to misrepresentation by any jacket the publisher chose to dress it in. It is, that is to say, in certain ways a vulgar and disreputable book, really about sex and baseball as the cover of the paper edition unsubtly suggests. One of the library journals made the point that this is an especially likely book for men who do not think of themselves as readers, meaning, I suppose, that it is disarmingly unliterary. This is an absurd contention in one sense, but quite right in another.

If "literary" implies an almost principled avoidance of invention (and I think we have just about reached this point), then this book is something else than "literature." Our younger writers, whether naturalists or Jamesian impressionists or conventional symbolists, have come to despise narrative ingenuity as something naïve or primitive, well lost for the sake of documentation or sensibility or allegory. Harried into choosing between the Dreiserian or Jamesian academics, many of our young novelists end up performing ritual acts of piety when they believe they are in fact achieving verisimilitude or expressing insights. Academy answers academy and permits each side to believe it has left outmoded convention and achieved "truth" or "form." Dullness has become so expected a part of seriousness in literature that we are likely to suspect the writer who does not proffer it among his credentials. But Mr. Malamud is neither naturalist nor impressionist, and he is not even dull; his fancy, confined neither to the limitations of the sensitive observer nor the narrow world of "real experience," manipulates the details of his fable in the interests of surprise and delight.

The epigraph of his book might well have been that melancholy popular phrase, "He could of been a hero!" It is about heroism that the story turns: the obligations of the heroic and its uses. For Roy Hobbs, the protagonist, the problem is the proper and pious use of his gift, that natural (or magical) talent which has its meaning only in its free exercise, the gratuitous, poetic act. For the fans, which is to say for *us*, the problem is our relationship to the hero and the question of whether he can survive our bribes and adulation, make the singular, representative act which alone can fulfill us, before we corrupt him into our own sterile image. For in truth, we need almost as desperately to hate and destroy the hero as to love and live by him; our self-hatred is projected as ferociously onto the representative figure as our reverence before our own possibilities. To say that in our world (the world of the Judge who pays for the defeat of the team he owns and the depraved dwarf in the stands ready to hoot down with his automobile horn defeated excellence) the hero fails is scarcely necessary.

Mr. Malamud finds in baseball the inevitable arena in which to play out our own version of this drama: part ritual and part commerce and part child's game, bounded by stupidity and corruption and sung only in the clichés of the sports writers, there yet survives in its midst a desecrated but indestructible dream of glory. The ball team of *The Natural* is real, its slumps, its fans, the absurd psychologist who comes to hypnotize the players, their charms and spells; and being real, it is comic. The details are the details of something which remains stubbornly a fact for all of its abstract meaning, not of a contrived device which functions only for the sake of that meaning.

Having said this, I dare confess at last that behind the literal fable, there is the presence of a legend, of the Grail Legend. Mr. Malamud reaches out with one hand to Ring

Lardner and with the other to Jessie Weston. If this is outrageous, it is the sort of outrage I enjoy. Why none of the critics have noticed the influence of Miss Weston, whom Eliot has made almost a platitude of critical approach, I don't know; but they have not, though the hero, slain once with a silver bullet and miraculously resurrected, returns in a time of drought to a disease-ridden team called the Knights, presided over by a manager called Pop Fisher, etc., etc. I have thought it wise to save this modest revelation for the end of my comments, fearing to misrepresent the achievement of Mr. Malamud's book. The use of myth and symbol as a *machine* (an artificial and external device to lend the semblance of metaphysical depth to a half-imagined story) has become a convention and a bore.

The weariest sort of journals for aspiring hacks run these days articles headed, "Symbolism Can Save *Your* Story," and we should all be aware that we have had too many books (even ambitious and moving ones) in which the function of the myth is to save the book—to do the work of imagination, invention and coherence. But the point is, of course, quite the opposite; and we have had all too few books that have attempted to save the myth, to revivify an ancient insight without which we cannot fully live. Mr. Malamud has in *The Natural* found, not imposed, an archetype in the life we presently live; in his book the modern instance and the remembered myth are equally felt, equally realized and equally appropriate to our predicament. It is this which gives to his work special authority and special richness; for he has not felt obliged to choose between the richness of imagined detail and that of symbolic relevance. He is out of the trap! It is for this reason that I have been moved to ignore the small failures of technique and consistency in his book and to say quite simply, "Hurrah!" There is no real way to pay for the pleasure a work of art gives us; but one can at least record that pleasure and his gratitude.—LESLIE FIEDLER, "Malamud: The Commonplace as Absurd," *No! in Thunder: Essays on Myth and Literature*, 1960, pp. 103–5

## THE ASSISTANT

Bernard Malamud's second novel has been getting extremely friendly reviews, for he is a talented writer, has a particularly intense sympathy for his Jewish material, and—what doesn't always accompany sympathy—an utterly objective ear for the harsh and plaintive American Yiddish speech. But none of the reviews that I have seen has suggested that Malamud's seemingly modest and "warm" little tale about a Jewish grocer in Brooklyn and his Italian assistant is really a hymn to a symbolic Jew as he is confronted by a hostile, baffled, and finally envious Gentile. And it is because I think that Malamud's book tries for so much more, in symbol, than what he actually gives us as fiction that I find myself regretfully dissenting from the other reviews.

Like most second-generation American Jewish novelists, Malamud's problem is to form a creative synthesis out of the Yiddish world of his childhood and his natural sophistication and heretical training as a modern writer. As one can see in his highly surrealistic baseball novel, *The Natural*, and in his eery *Partisan Review* story of a Jewish marriage broker, "The Magic Barrel," Malamud is naturally a fantasist of the ordinary, the commonplace, the average. He writes, a little, the way Chagall paints—except that the natural course of Malamud's imagination is to seek not the open and the lyrical but symbols of the highly involuted personal life of Jews. He loves what he himself calls "violins and candles" in the sky, old-clothes-men who masquerade something sinister yet unnamable; he has a natural

sense for the humdrum transposed to the extreme, of the symbolic and the highly colored. He tends to the bizarre, the contorted, the verge of things that makes you shiver, not laugh. Although his dialogue in *The Assistant* is marvelously faithful to Yiddish-American, he makes you think not that Jews really talk this way but how violent, fear-fraught, always on the edge, Jewish talk can be. In the superb *The Magic Barrel* Malamud really caught the accents of the hallucinated, the visionary, and the bizarre that belong to a people whose images are as much of the next world, and of other worlds, as they are of this one.

Now the trouble with *The Assistant*, from my point of view, is that Malamud's natural taste for abstraction, his gift for symbolic representation, has gone to make up a morality story which is essentially a glorification of the Jew as Jew. My objection is that his understandable allegiance to this theme has been made the overriding motive of the book despite the fact that Malamud's talent is inherently too subtle to serve what I would call an emotional motive. Malamud is an extremely sympathetic and feeling writer, and I don't mean to suggest that he is a surrealist pure; his hold on reality is too strong, and he is, as I admiringly feel about him, very "Jewish," very much of this world. But in "The Magic Barrel" his sympathy with suffering and his deliberately distorted perspective—that sense of "magic" which seems to me the strongest element in his work—worked to represent things that could not be moralized; the character of the marriage broker was revealed entirely by technique, rendered exclusively by the use of incongruities rarely employed to describe Jewish life. The final effect was "strange" and true—there was nothing left over to paraphrase, to moralize.

In *The Assistant*, however, just the opposite is true. For what he is getting at in the life of the Jewish grocer, Morris Bober, is precisely what, after Bober's death, a rabbi—who never knew him—can say over his coffin:

"Yes, Morris Bober was to me a true Jew because he lived in the Jewish experience, which he remembered, and with the Jewish heart. Maybe not to our formal tradition . . . but he was true to the spirit of our life—to want for others that which he wants also for himself. . . . For such reasons he was a Jew. What more does our sweet God ask his poor people?"

Morris Bober is a Jew in exile, exiled even from most of his own formal traditions: in short, he is *the* Jew. But he opens his grocery at six each morning, groaning, in order to give a Polish woman a three-cent roll. When the Irish detective's bummer son, Ward Minogue, holds up Morris, Minogue curses him as a "Jew liar." When, in a fit of conscience, Frank Alpine, the other robber, forces himself on Morris as an "assistant," insists on working for spending money, he explains to Morris that "I always liked Jews." And watching Morris's miserable existence reveal itself all day long in the shabby little grocery, Frank reflects—"What kind of a man did you have to be to be shut yourself up in an overgrown coffin and never once during the day, so help you, outside of going for your Jewish newspaper, poke your head out of the door for a snootful of air? The answer wasn't very hard to say—you had to be a Jew. They were born prisoners." When Frank, increasingly moved by Morris's virtuous and threadbare existence, decides to confess his part in the robbery, it turns out that originally it was *because* Morris was a Jew that Ward Minogue planned to rob him, "so Frank agreed to go with him."

But as for Morris Bober himself—"he was Morris Bober and could be nobody more fortunate. With that name you had no sure sense of property, as if it were in your blood and history not to possess, or if by some miracle to own something, to do so on the verge of loss." He is *the* Jew in everything and to everyone. His grocery is devouring him; his wife, Ida, who never gives him a moment's tenderness, but loves him harshly, cries bitterly when she sees her daughter kissing the *goy*: "Why do I cry? I cry for the world. I cry for my life that it went away wasted. I cry for you." His unmarried daughter, Helen, is twenty-three and getting anxious, but she will not compromise in her demand for love. So that into this Jewish circle, this archetype family, the dark outsider, Frank Alpine, the "assistant," comes as another symbol. And the whole story turns on the fact that he learns from Morris not, as the jacket delicately puts it, "the beauty of morality," but the beauty of the Jews. Morris recounts his life to the assistant during the many dull stretches in the store, tells him how he ran away from the Czar's conscription to America. When Frank asks Morris what it is to be a Jew and taunts him with not obeying the dietary laws, Morris answers him—"Nobody will tell me that I am not Jewish because I put in my mouth once in a while, when my tongue is dry, a piece of ham. But they will tell me, and I will believe them, if I forget the Law. This means to do what is right, to be honest, to be good. . . . For everybody should be the best, not only for you or me. We ain't animals. This is why we need the Law. This is what a Jew believes." Frank persists: "But tell me why it is that the Jews suffer so damn much, Morris? It seems to me that they like to suffer, don't they. . . . What do you suffer for, Morris?" "I suffer for you."

At the end of the story, Helen is raped by Ward Minogue, and Frank, after rescuing her, forgets himself and hysterically forces himself upon her, too: to which symbol Helen replies by naming it. She calls him "Dog—uncircumcised dog!" Frank can expiate his guilt only by taking Morris's place, after Morris dies from the effects of shoveling snow from in front of his store so that people can pass. The point of the novel is made at the end: Morris has been cheated by his fellow Jews as well as robbed and assaulted by Ward Minogue. But Frank himself becomes Morris Bober, sends Helen to N.Y.U., and on the last page, is circumcised and converted to Judaism. The point, as he says, is not merely that for the Jews "Suffering is like a piece of goods. I bet the Jews could make a suit of [it]. . . ." but "The funny thing is that there are more of them [Jews] around than anybody knows about."

All these sentiments are unexceptionable, but the novel as constituted doesn't bear them out. The detail, while marvelously faithful, is always too clear in outline, the moral is too pointed, to convince me. And touching and utterly authentic as Morris is, there is a peculiarly unemphasized quality about him, as if Malamud were writing entirely from memory, were trying to get a beloved figure right rather than to create, with the needed sharp edges, the character demanded by the imagination. Bober himself remains too generalized a Jew, as Frank Alpine is too shadowy and unvisualized the Gentile, to make their symbolic relationship simply felt.

Where Malamud's very real talent comes through best in this book, it seems to me, is in figures of suffering—his natural element—who are not average but extreme figures. Malamud is the poet of the desperately clownish, not of the good who shall inherit the earth—and this unusual gift of his comes through in two wonderful little portraits of Jews. One is of Breitbart, a bankrupt, deserted by his wife, who took to peddling. "He bought electric bulbs at wholesale and carried two cartons of them slung, with clothesline rope, over his shoulder. Every day, in his crooked shoes, he walked miles, looking into stores and calling out in a mournful voice, 'Lights for sale,'" The other is of a professional arsonist, "a skinny man in an old hat and a dark overcoat down to his ankles. His nose was long, throat gaunt, and he wore a wisp of red beard on his bony chin." The "scarecrow" comes in saying "a gut shabos," though "shabos" is a day away and looking around the Bober grocery, remarks, "It smells here like an open grave." He wets his lips and whispers, "Insurinks you got—fire insurinks?" and taking out a piece of "celluloy," shows how he does his work. "Magic," he hoarsely announced. "No ashes. This is why we use celluloy, not paper, not rags." The word "magic" naturally occurs in Malamud's best work—or when he is at his best. And then, as befits a writer who has lived "in the Jewish experience," it serves to clarify and intensify our sense of what that experience really is.—ALFRED KAZIN, "Fantasist of the Ordinary," *Cmty*, July 1957, pp. 89–92

In his second novel, Bernard Malamud has turned away from the rich playfulness, the free use of myth and magic which made of his first book, *The Natural*, so welcome a sport in the dim world of contemporary fiction. It is impossible, I think, to appreciate the kind of discipline and self-denial which motivates the muted style of *The Assistant* without a knowledge of the earlier work, and a consequent awareness that Malamud is doing what he does because he *chooses* to, not because he lacks the fancy to conceive anything else or the invention to accomplish it.

He is playing a dangerous game in *The Assistant* all the same; and in the earlier portion of the book, his resolve to treat gray lives grayly, to render dull conversations dully, threatens to succeed only too well. The material he deals with seems at first depressingly familiar: we have read before of the lives of poor Jews, proprietors of groceries and candy stores, just as we have encountered before Jewish writers, plagued by an ideal of imitative form and impelled, in the face of their material, to give us not the poetry of banal lives but their banality.

Long before we have reached the end of the book, however, we realize that, though muted, the poetry is never denied and that Malamud's theme remains here what it was in the more extravagant *The Natural*: the Absurd—here specifically the absurdity of existence in its most commonplace forms. It is odd how the subdued tone, the show of "realism" in Malamud take us in, as life itself takes us in, with its routine surfaces. We tend to accept on the level of mere realistic observation and reporting an account, say, of a young man wedged perilously in a dumbwaiter shaft watching the daughter of the man he has robbed but loves strip for a shower; or the description of the same young man crouched in guilt and fear and hunger in the basement of a store, feeding frantically and in secret on stolen bottles of milk.

A slight shift in emphasis, a slight heightening of tone—and we would be face to face with some quasi-surrealist image of the Underground Man, not unlike, perhaps, the hallucinatory opening of Ralph Ellison's *Invisible Man*. But Malamud has chosen to create the least melodramatic of all possible versions of the Absurd: a vision of the commonplace as absurd. One is reminded by his ambition and achievement of Saul Bellow, especially in *The Victim*, and back, through Bellow, of Daniel Fuchs, author of *Homage to Blenholt*.

One is even tempted to say, on such grounds, that Malamud has with this book entered into the main Jewish-American tradition in the novel, taking up the frustrated experiments of writers like Fuchs or Nathanael West, ignored in the thirties in favor of "the proletarian novel," and overshadowed by the inflated reputations of Steinbeck and Dos Passos and Farrell. In a strange way, Malamud's novel *is* a belated novel of the thirties. It is not, I think, definitely located in time; but one imagines its events as happening in the dispirited years of the Depression. Only in that context does the struggle of the poor Jew, Morris Bober, to keep his store open achieve a proper sense of desperation, or the desire of his daughter Helen to go to college touch a full note of pathos.

But how different *The Assistant* is from any novel *written* in the thirties! The kind of politics which informed the "proletarian novel" is, of course, quite gone, as is the note of hysteria, the apocalyptic shrillness which characterizes all novels of the period, whatever their politics. Not even the humor of West or Fuchs is present, neither the half-mad belly laugh nor the self-deprecatory giggle by which such writers came to terms with terror and desolation. Indeed, Malamud's book is willfully, almost perversely humorless, even as it is apolitical. Helen Bober and her Jewish boy friends may talk the same stilted, hyperurban speech (indeed Malamud is masterful at reproducing it) as that of Arthur Kober's "Dear Bella" and her beaus; but here *it is no joke.*

Just as Malamud will not permit us the luxury of righteous indignation and political protest before the prospect of an honest man incapable of earning a living or a warmhearted girl cut off from the possibilities of love—so he will not let us snicker or guffaw at their plight either. He compels us to contemplate the absurdity of their situations—and that of Frank Alpine, the Gentile who alternately robs and aids them—with the pure response of *pity.* Beside this, politics and humor are revealed as rival opiates of the people: devices to prevent the confrontation of the full and terrible ridiculousness of human loneliness and desire, unsuccess and death. His is a book and a viewpoint essentially (questions of doctrine aside) *religious.*

The quite unpredictable, though distressingly up-to-date, absurdity of *The Assistant* belongs to the nature of its religiousness. We live in a time of an at least nominal revival of interest in religion, and the appearance of conversion stories surely surprises no one. *The Assistant,* however, is concerned with a conversion *to* Judaism—a theme by no means usual even at this moment of the ascendancy of Marjorie Morningstar. Marjorie, after all, is only confirmed in what Religious Emphasis Week speakers like to call "the faith of our fathers," and for her such subsidence means accommodation and "peace of mind." Malamud's Frank, on the other hand, is painfully impelled toward Judaism and accepts it as he accepts pain itself. After he has rescued Helen Bober from assault and more than half-raped her himself; after he has been cast out by Morris and has witnessed his quietly heroic death; after he has taken on himself the burden of the store which becomes in the novel scarcely distinguishable from the burden of life itself—Frank takes the final step. "One day in April," the book concludes in its characteristic low key, "Frank went to the hospital and had himself circumcized. . . . The pain enraged and inspired him. After Passover he became a Jew." As a happy ending, a springtime close for a story which begins in the chill of autumn, it is all quite ridiculous. Surely nothing is more conducive to titters and bad jokes than the notion of the circumcision of a grown man; and to *become* a Jew when it is hard enough to remain one—nothing could be more improbable.

At first glance, such a conclusion seems more sentimental than absurd; but it is saved from sentimentality by a further turn of the screw, a final note of the ridiculous. Frank becomes a Jew without knowing in any explicit way what a Jew is; and we are asked to accept his conversion knowing as little as he what he is converted to. What *is* the content of Jewishness as Malamud understands it? Easiest of all is to say what it is not: not an imaginary revived orthodoxy, not a literary man's neo-Hasidism out of Martin Buber by T. S. Eliot, not the rational "normative Judaism" of the Reformed. It is apparently nothing more than what an unlearned immigrant, who has not been in a synagogue in twenty years, but whom *everyone* would agree in calling a Jew, happens to live by.

Morris Bober is the book's exemplar of Judaism: a man who not only sells but eats pork, who knows scarcely anything of the Talmud, who can hardly answer when asked what a Jew is. Yet it is he, through the example of his life, who converts Frank Alpine, to whom being a Jew means practically taking on the responsibilities of Morris: his wife, his daughter, especially his accursed, ill-paying store. The nearest thing to an explicit definition of Morris' Jewishness is spoken by a rabbi called in after his death, a rabbi who has never known him and who improvises in broken English a eulogy on the basis of hearsay and the conventional lies one says in honor of the dead.

Yet in this speech, the novel reaches its climax of poetry and pity and truth. It must be read entire and in context for its full impact, though its sense can be resumed in a few excerpts:

> My dear friends, I never had the pleasure to meet this
> good grocery man that he now lays in his coffin. He
> lived in a neighborhood where I didn't come in.
> . . . He caught double pneumonia from shoveling
> snow in front of his place of business, so people could
> pass by on the sidewalk. . . . He was also a very
> hard worker, a man that never stopped working.
> . . . Fifteen, sixteen hours a day he was in the
> store, seven days a week, to make a living for his
> family. . . . This went on for twenty-two years in
> this store alone, day after day, except the few days
> when he was too sick. And for this reason that he
> worked so hard and bitter, in his house, on his table,
> was always something good to eat. So, besides
> honest, he was a good provider. . . .
> When a Jew dies, who asks if he is a Jew, we
> don't ask.

Is this, then, what Jewishness has become for us, our world—not at its worst but at its human best—"to take care of the store"? One is reminded of the oldest of Jewish jokes, of the dying man who blindly asks for all his family one by one, and when he discovers all are present, cries out, "Then who's taking care of the store?" Is this, after all, a joke not on the dying man, as we have always thought, but on *ourselves* who laugh at it? Is that ridiculous deathbed cry the cry of a *lamedvavnik,* one of the hidden just for whose sake the world is preserved? To believe it would be absurd.—LESLIE FIEDLER, "Malamud: The Commonplace as Absurd," *No! in Thunder: Essays on Myth and Literature,* 1960, pp. 106–10

*The Assistant,* presumably, is a love story, a domestic romance, a grocery store idyll of unwarranted poverty and harsh spiritual deprivation. It is a tale of loneliness, of lifelong frustrations and delicate, budding hopes. It is a "human" story albeit deeply ironic. For irony is indeed the key to Malamud's attitude toward man, to his estimate of him. The irony is not "dry," not scathing; it is best described by Earl Rovit when he says, "The affectionate insult and the wry self-deprecation are parts of the same ironic vision which values one's self and mankind as both less and more than they seem to be worth, at one and the same time." This is the ambivalence of vision which qualifies, sometimes even undercuts, the affirmative power of Malamud's fiction.

The world revealed by *The Assistant* is, materially

speaking, bleak; morally, it glows with a faint, constant light. Morris Bober and his wife, Ida, toil sixteen hours a day in a grocery store, barely eking out a living. They are well past middle age, and have given up their lives, their illusions, even the promise of a richer future which comes with education for their single daughter, Helen. The store, as we are told many times, is an open tomb. Twenty-one years are spent in it, and in the end Bober dies of double pneumonia, leaving his family penniless; he has to be buried in one of those huge anonymous cemeteries in Queens. America! "He had hoped for much in America and got little. And because of him Helen and Ida had less. He had defrauded them, he and the blood-sucking store." This is what Bober thinks as one of two men who hold up his store slugs him on the head, because he is a Jew, and Bober falls to the ground without a cry. An appropriate ending to his weary, profitless day. Others may have luck, like the affluent Karp who owns a liquor store across the street, or the Earls whose son, Nat, attends law school—and takes Helen's virginity. But the Bobers live on stolidly, honestly, in squalor and sickening destitution. They are, like the grocery "assistant," Frank Alpine, victims of circumstance. What, then, gives these characters the measure of spiritual freedom they still possess?

The nature of the characters themselves holds the answer. Morris Bober, to be sure, is another example of the *eiron*, the humble man. He is more. He has endurance, the power to accept suffering without yielding to the hebetude which years of pain induce. He is acquainted with the tragic qualities of life—"The world suffers. *He* felt every schmerz"—and he defines the Jew as a suffering man with a good heart, one who reconciles himself to agony, not because he wants to be agonized, as Frank suggests, but for the sake of the Law—the Hebraic ideal of virtue. Yet this is only one source of Bober's strength. His other source is charity, which in his case becomes nearly quixotic. Bober, though close to starvation himself, extends credit to his poor customers. He wakes up every day before dawn so that he may sell a three-cent roll to a Polish woman on her way to work. He takes in Frank Alpine, feeds him, and gives him an opportunity to redeem himself, though Frank begins by stealing the grocer's bread and milk. Nor can he bring himself, in the extremity of despair, to burn down his property in order to collect insurance. Inured to failure, Bober still strives to give suffering the dignity of men who may trust one another in their common woe. But Karp calls him a "schlimozel."

The central action of the novel, however, develops from Bober's relation to Frank Alpine, and from the latter's relation to Helen. Frank, as the title suggests, is probably the hero of the book. He, too, is an *eiron*, a collector of injustices—with a difference. The regeneration of Frank—his literal and symbolic conversion to the Jewish faith—is the true theme of the book. His regeneration, at best, is a strange and mixed thing. When Frank first appears, he is a wanderer, an anti-Semite, even a thief. Yet one of his idols is St. Francis, and his hardened face conceals a hungry soul. "With me one wrong thing leads to another and it ends in a trap. I want the moon so all I get is cheese," he tells Bober. The grocery store, which is Bober's grave, becomes a cave or haven for Alpine. It also becomes the dreary locus of his painful rebirth. Impelled by his gratitude to the grocer, and motivated by his guilt at having robbed him, with the aid of tough Ward Minogue, Frank puts all his energies into the store and ends by pumping some of his own obstinate life into the dying business. Meanwhile, he falls in love with Helen Bober.

From here on, ambiguities prevail. The racial prejudices of Frank are matched by those of Ida Bober, and to some extent, of her daughter Helen, against Gentiles. (The store improves, it is suggested, precisely because Frank is not a Jew.) Frank's gratitude to Morris does not prevent him from continuing to steal petty cash from the register—which he keeps account of and intends to return. Yet when Bober is incapacitated by sickness, Frank takes a night job, in addition to his grocery chores, and secretly puts his pay in the cash box. And his gnawing love for Helen, which she is slow to return, finally ends, ironically, with an act of near-rape as he rescues her from the clutches of Ward Minogue, only to force himself, right there and then in the park, at the very moment in their relationship when she is at last ready to surrender herself freely to him. "Dog," she cries "—uncircumcised dog!" Guilt, gratitude, love—perhaps even the hope of a life he could glimpse but never attain—combine to sustain Frank Alpine, Bober's strange, saintly, pilfering assistant, in his impossible struggle against poverty, against hopelessness itself.

> He wanted her but the facts made a terrible construction. They were Jews and he was not. If he started going out with Helen her mother would throw a double fit and Morris another. And Helen made him feel, from the way she carried herself, even when she seemed most lonely, that she had plans for something big in her life—nobody like F. Alpine. He had nothing, a backbreaking past, had committed a crime against her old man, and in spite of his touchy conscience, was stealing from him too. How complicated could impossible get?
>
> He saw only one way of squeezing through the stone knot; start by shoveling out the load he was carrying around in his mind. . . .
>
> So the confession had to come first. . . . He felt he had known this, in some frightful way, a long time before he went into the store, before he had met Minogue, or even come east; that he had really known all his life he would sometime, through throat blistered with shame, his eyes in the dirt, have to tell some poor son of a bitch that he was the one who had hurt or betrayed him. This thought had lived in him with claws; or like a thirst he could never spit out, a repulsive need to get out of his system all that had happened—for whatever had happened had happened wrong; to clean it out of his self and bring in a little peace, a little order; to change the beginning, beginning with the past that always stupendously stank up the now—to change his life before the smell of it suffocated him.

Purgation in humility, rebirth through love—this is Frank's inchoate purpose, the reason for his willing acceptance of a backbreaking burden others—Minogue, Karp—find easy to reject. Yet it is in consonance with the character of the novel that purgation and rebirth both should appear ironic, awkward, and inconclusive. Frank tells Bober about his complicity in the robbery only to discover that the latter already knows. Bober catches his assistant rifling his till just when Frank had resolved never to steal again. And Frank's attempt to make a clean breast of it all to Helen merely serves to confirm her revulsion. His dogged and desperate love expresses itself in the form of a physical outrage. The savior of the Bobers is, in a sense, their archenemy. (The symbolic inversion of this relation may be discovered in the burial scene in which Frank topples accidentally into Bober's open grave.) But enemies suffer too, according to their conscience. Frank Alpine, it seems, can only expend the last vestige of his money, energy, or hope in agonized silence, a prey to the ironies which rip and twist his purpose. In the end, the value of confession is to the soul that makes it. And even love is a kind of realized solitude. Like Frank, Helen goes her lonely way, carrying the broken dreams of the Bobers to some distant and uncompromising end.

It is obvious that if the world of *The Assistant* is not drained of values, it is nevertheless saturated with pain, flooded with contradictions. Its two major characters find their identity in humiliation, an extreme and quixotic sense of obligation. They are not tragic heroes but merely heroes of irony. They retreat before the ultimate tragic ordeal: the fullness of tragic awareness itself. This is a fact the form of the novel supports.

Time, we know, leaves the characters suspended in the void which their failures create; the hints of regeneration are barely audible. Morris Bober dies in bankruptcy; Helen continues at her dreary job, dreaming of a better life; Frank slaves at the store, trying to provide for the Bobers, send Helen to college, and win back her love. The fate of each remains less than what it could be in heroic tragedy, less even than what it usually amounts to in realistic fiction. Thus, for instance, does Helen evaluate the life of her father: "People liked him, but who can admire a man passing his life in such a store? He buried himself in it; he didn't have the imagination to know what he was missing. He made himself a victim. He could, with a little more courage, have been more than he was." And thus does Frank reflect upon his incessant labors: " 'Jesus,' he said 'why am I killing myself so? He gave himself many unhappy answers, the best being that while he was doing this he was doing nothing worse.' " Whatever awareness time brings to the characters, whatever qualified dignity it confers upon their failures, every act in the novel is whittled by irony, every motive is mixed with its opposite.

Because time cannot unravel the knotted relations of the characters—what could be more gnarled than the relation of Gentile to Jew, of savior, seducer, and thief to those upon whom he preys, those from whom he gains an identity—the point of view of *The Assistant* dissociates itself from the protagonists, veering toward one then the other in friendly detachment. The characters are simply there, and they criticize each other's behavior; the point of view encourages us to perceive how ludicrous pain can be, and how unhappy virtue. The subtle, incredible twists of the plot, the reversals and accidents which affect the fortunes of the Bobers, are finally envisioned in a moral as well as dramatic perspective which acknowledges no certainties except the fact of suffering. (It is appropriate that Morris Bober should be an unorthodox Jew, and that at his funeral the rabbi should say, "Yes, Morris Bober was to me a true Jew because he lived in the Jewish experience, and with the Jewish heart. . . . He suffered, he endured, but with hope.")

The achievement of Malamud's style, which survives his ironic play, lies in the author's capacity to convey both hope and agony in the rhythms of Yiddish speech.

> "I think I will shovel the snow," he told Ida at lunch-time.
> "Go better to sleep."
> "It ain't nice for the customers."
> "What customers—who needs them?"
> "People can't walk in such high snow," he argued.
> "Wait, tomorrow it will be melted."
> "It's Sunday, it don't look so nice for the goyim that they go to church."
> Her voice had an edge in it. "You want to catch pneumonia, Morris?"
> "It's spring," he murmured.

There is a Hemingway cleanness in this dialogue, a kind of humility and courage, but also a softness Hemingway never strove to communicate.

Morris, however, does catch pneumonia and die. Nor can the poetry of the style persuade us to forget that the search of Frank Alpine for an identity ends, in the last, brief paragraph of the novel, with the ritual of circumcision. The act is one of self-purification, of initiation too, in Frank's case, but it is also an act of self-repudiation, if not, as some may be tempted to say, of symbolic castration.—IHAB HASSAN, "The Qualified Encounter: Three Novels by Buechner, Malamud, and Ellison," *Radical Innocence*, 1961, pp. 162–68

## THE MAGIC BARREL

Although Bernard Malamud has been one of our most scrupulous and rewarding prose writers for a number of years, he never received wide, public recognition until the publication of his second novel, *The Assistant*, in 1957. Now that thirteen of his best short stories have been collected in *The Magic Barrel*, that recognition is certainly secure. Even book dealers and daily reviewers know his name, and I can think of few more obvious seals of approval. Of course, Malamud has not and likely will not ever get the hushed adulation of a Cozzens or the daffy notoriety of a Kerouac because he is as incapable of boring his readers into admiration as he is of capturing them with sophomoric phoniness. He owns both talent and discipline: properties that disqualify him from best sellership, easy contentment, and public office. Yet, in his own sober, dedicated, and humane way he has arrived. Since his arrival marks for all discerning readers the gain of a terse and unique sensibility manifesting itself in exciting and authentic literary terms, he deserves our fullest gratitude.

As every silver lining has its little cloud, however, so do certain conditions of Malamud's critical success beckon worry. He is, for example, frequently compared to Dostoevsky although his affinity in style and structure to Chekhov is far greater. Dim fuddlers like Granville Hicks and W. G. Rogers champion him—enough to dismay any artist. Herbert Gold and Leslie Fiedler laud him for his surrealistic use of myth without noting the extent of his removal from Tristan Tzara, André Breton, and all the little Henry Millers, or the fact that he has employed symbolic literary patterns only twice—in *The Natural* and "The Lady of the Lake." In both instances, the patterns have been derived from the Matter of Britain and have been superimposed upon rather than indigenous to the original materials.

More importantly, what these and other critics who have addressed themselves to his writing hold in common is an insistence upon his value as a Jewish writer. While it is true enough that Malamud is preoccupied with the figure of the Jew, it is equally true that to see him only as the portrayer of a single group or the pleader of a special case is to limit the largeness of his accomplishment. Alfred Kazin, free-associating in the May, 1958, issue of *The Reporter*, remarked the overeagerness of "minority" authors to "be freed of certain painful experiences through the ritualistic catharsis of modern symbolism." Aside from the clinical inaccuracy of a statement which confuses compulsion neurosis with catharsis, and in so doing completely misses the obsessional character of Malamud's vision, it is even more damaging in that it guesses about the writer's life instead of dealing with his work. Before a critic delivers himself of oracles on an author's motives, he had better examine his stories as closely as possible. The biographical problem of why something was said must wait on an accurate literary knowledge of what was said.

Now, the stories which make up *The Magic Barrel* do share and explore an archetypal pattern. Out of a world of dispossessed strangers, two characters, often an older person and a younger man, meet. The scene is stark and unpromising: a cheap and barren room in a rachitic tenement; a deserted city street under frozen powerlines; a run-down, beat-up grocery that smells like a graveyard. The physical background, in short, is as skeletal and yet as inescapable as the gutted ground of a concentration camp or the high, narrow barriers of a ghetto. Yet, once a cosmic accidentalism has crossed these two lives, the characters are transfixed in a long and agonizing moment. The irrelevant, chance meeting becomes the necessary relationship. The impossible demand becomes the imperative debt. Rosen, the hopelessly ill salesman in "Take Pity," is bound to offer both life and hope to the destitute widow Eva and her two children, Fega and Surale. In "The Bill," Willy Schlegel, a janitor dusty and gray from the ash cans of poverty and personal loss, is visited with an endless trial of shame because of his failure to pay his bill of eighty-three dollars and some cents to the proprietors of a "small, dark delicatessen . . . really a hole in the wall." And Lieb, the baker of one of Malamud's finest lyrics of despair, "The Loan," finds that his tear-sweetened loaves of bread have turned to "charred corpses," like so many bodies in the ovens of Birkenau, when he fails to give an old friend money for a grave stone for his wife.

The world which Bernard Malamud creates for us is a bitched-up, zero-at-the-bone world. His characters are poor past poverty; beaten past defeat. They drag their weary heels along cracked pavements that lead from one hell to another; indeed, the misery and bleakness of their surroundings and their journey are not only real in themselves, but are also the objective correlatives of their spiritual dilemma. Other writers may advertise the surface decorum of a society where money signifies decency and where wives are more properly pals than lovers. But Malamud will have none of this. No old lies, no hollow pretensions, no inflated oratory. Where Hemingway envisioned a botched civilization, Malamud envisions no civilization at all, only ghostly ruins where disinherited strangers pass in a feverish night.

This is not nihilism. To the contrary, Malamud's search is for value, and here he belongs squarely in the great line of moral realists which stretches from Hawthorne to Henry James, Stephen Crane, F. Scott Fitzgerald, and Hemingway himself. Hemingway's *nada* was never so much pure negation as assertion of the necessity for a value system in a day where conventional morals and manners had perished. The ethic he found for living when all else had gone to pot was what Edmund Wilson has so keenly termed "the principle of sportsmanship." Although Hemingway's heroes must suffer because they have a sharply defined code, they rise to a sort of grandeur in meeting betrayal and defeat on their own terms. Malamud's central characters also have an ethic, but their struggle is to discover it in themselves as well as to apply it. Hemingway's heroes must "feel good." Malamud's must do good.

And it is the wrenching difficulty of doing good when one is sick or aged or poor—and sometimes all three—which furnishes Malamud's characters with their spiritual crises. When Willy's wife suggests that he pay the Panessas, in "The Bill," he replies with frightening desperation: "What have I got that I can pay? With what? With the meat off my bones? With the ashes in my eyes. With the piss I mop up on the floors. With the cold in my lungs when I sleep." Nevertheless, Willy eventually recognizes the stringency of his obligation "because

after all what was credit but the fact that people were human beings, and if you were really a human being you gave credit to somebody else and he gave credit to you."

In these stories, the characters are forever laboring under the burden of debt. While the debt is frequently a literal one, it is always more than this. In a world of permanent depression where the moral terrain is uncharted, money becomes a counter for the measurement of good and evil. The tragedy of Willy and of Lieb, as of Fidelman in "The Last Mohican" and Rosen in "Take Pity," is that they cannot discharge the debts that would guarantee their humanity. Malamud's characters care compassionately, but when they are unwilling to bear the consequences of their caring they learn that the cost of material salvation is the expense of spiritual damnation. Rosen is tormented by the apparition of his failure even after death. Fidelman, lost in the moral ghetto of a triumphant but belated insight, must stand by as Susskind, his potential savior, flees through the streets of eternity.

Although human indebtedness, its circumstances and its complexity, is basic to Bernard Malamud's artistic preoccupation, not all of his characters are doomed. It is this capacity to envisage resurrection as well as self-crucifixion, along with the rare ability to love his characters who fail as much as those who succeed, that helps to make the world of *The Magic Barrel* (and *The Assistant*) so compellingly immediate and significant.

In "A Summer's Reading," George Stoyonovich, an ignorant neighborhood boy, is able to fulfill an inner imperative to attain knowledge and a sense of identity only after acknowledging his external obligation to an older man. In "The Mourners," old Kessler, once an egg candler, and his landlord, Gruber, have sinned against the past and poisoned the present; however, when they realize this and become mourners together, they are visited by a moment of fragrant and sunlit grace.

"Angel Levine," one of the most central stories in the Malamud canon, poses the problem of faith and salvation with sharp brilliance. Manischevitz, a tailor who has suffered excruciating losses, is now faced with the impending death of his wife, Fanny. Appears in his flat a Jewish Negro, Levine, who claims that he is on probation as a "bona fide angel of God . . . not to be confused with the members of any particular sect, order, or organization. . . ." If Manischevitz can believe, the condition of Levine's probation will be satisfied and Fanny will be spared. But herein lies the catch, for the tailor finds faith almost impossible.

"So if God sends to me an angel, why a black? Why not a white that there are so many of them?"

His doubt grows when he travels to Harlem in search of Levine and finds the Negro dancing in a shabby cabaret. Fanny is at death's door. Manischevitz visits a synagogue, but though he speaks to God he receives no reply. That afternoon in troubled sleep he envisions Levine preening tiny and fragile wings. The dream is not a surrealistic illumination; it is a Freudian confirmation. Manischevitz interprets the dream more directly and accurately than most of Malamud's critics. "This means," he tells himself, "that it is possible he could be an angel." The dream thus brings to light the belief which the tailor, beset by reverses and common-sense logic, has hidden from himself.

Once again he seeks out Levine. This time he wanders into a crude synagogue where four Negroes in skullcaps are pondering the riddle of the soul as immaterial substance. Although the Negroes are unable to resolve the apparent dichotomy of the theological axiom, they conclude with a triumphant hallelujah of faith. "Praise Lawd and utter loud His speechless name." "Blow de bugle till it bust the sky."

Heartened, Manischevitz limps across the street, finds Levine in the cabaret, and confesses to him his faith. This declaration saves both the Negro and the tailor, for when Manischevitz gets home his wife has recovered and is mopping the flat. "A wonderful thing, Fanny," he cries. "Believe me, there are Jews everywhere."

This, as well as any single line, conveys the essence of Malamud's vision and art. We, all of us, live in a world of loss, ghettos, and darkness. We are all of us strangers, scapegoats, refugees. Yet, if we can realize this, can realize that we owe still our human debt of humanity to others, that encroaching darkness may be stayed a little. The Jew is a typical figure in *The Magic Barrel* not because Malamud is exclusively interested in a given religion or race, but because the Jew is for him, as for all of us, a perduring symbol of him who would preserve the spirit despite his own absolute loneliness and defeat. Every man is a minority group of one. By his insistence upon the universality of such isolation, Malamud has given us not only an allegory of our common predicament, but also a clue to our redemption. To appreciate fully Bernard Malamud's contribution to contemporary letters we must understand that the body of his work forms a covenant of grace. We must understand, like Manischevitz, that although salvation may assume strange shapes in unlikely places, it is as simple and yet splendid as our deepest and most abiding impulse—as love itself.—ARTHUR FOFF, "Strangers Amid Ruins," NWR, Fall–Winter 1958, pp. 63–67

## A NEW LIFE

Bernard Malamud's *A New Life* is the first new novel of consistent excellence that I have found since I began regular reviewing, a lovely oasis after an interminable crawl through the hot sands. It is the story of S. Levin, a thirty-year-old failure, who leaves New York to be an English instructor at Cascadia College on the West Coast. The novel covers one year of rich experience, and at its end we see Levin, fired and disgraced, setting off for San Francisco with his booty: a second-hand Hudson, the wife of the chairman of his department, her two adopted children, and Levin's own child inside her.

*A New Life*, as a fable of redemption or rebirth, is accurately titled. "One always hopes that a new place will inspire change—in one's life," Levin says tentatively when he arrives in Cascadia. Later, "he felt like a man entering a new life and entered." At the height of his affair with Pauline Gilley, she says, "Oh, my darling, we must do something with our lives." When he despairs of her, he thinks of her as "the small town lady who talked of a new life but had been consistently afraid of it." When she determines to leave her husband, she says to Levin: "I want a better life. I want it with you."

The action of the novel is Levin's development into a kind of saint. To the outward eye, he is a typical *schlemiel*: he steps into cow pies, teaches with his fly open, makes the ruinous remark every time. But in truth he is a holy *schlemiel*, God's innocent, a Fool in Christ. Levin attains to sanctity (and I think that this represents a considerable advance for Malamud) not through denying and mortifying the flesh, as does the anchorite Frank Alpine in *The Assistant*, but through indulging the flesh, and his adultery is a holy adultery.

It begins in lust, and after his first adventure with Pauline in the forest, Levin thinks vulgarly: "his first married woman, sex uncomplicated in a bed of leaves, short hours, good pay."

The affair progresses, and Levin suddenly realizes: "The truth is I love Pauline Gilley." It then goes beyond love, or beyond what Levin understands as love, to the sacrificial acceptance of responsibility: feeling his love gone, he nevertheless accepts the burden of Pauline and her children. "Why take that load on yourself?" Pauline's husband Gerald challenges, itemizing the disadvantages, and Levin answers, in the true voice of a Malamud saint: "Because I can, you son of a bitch." It is a classic progress from *eros*, fleshly love, to *agape*, the spiritual love of one of God's creatures for another.

Malamud's vision of life in the novel redeems its ugliness and nastiness with humor, and redeems the humor with charity. Cascadia College is a dreadful place, narrow and mean, but it is also a terribly funny place where "there are no geniuses around to make you uncomfortable," fly-casting is taught for credit, and a textbook containing Hemingway's story "Ten Indians" is banned on the pretext that it might offend, "as degrading the American Indians." Gerald Gilley is a repulsive careerist, a golf-mad professor who is compiling a picture-book of American literature, but he is a comic masterpiece of a careerist, and Levin's ultimate understanding is that Gilley too is a suffering fellow human, and his final feeling for him is compassion.

Where the sex scenes in Malamud's earlier books were always interrupted at their climax, constituting a prolonged tease of the reader, or else were consummated under the aegis of death, producing an unlovely *liebestod* effect, here (although traces of the old bad habits remain) sex is funny, earthy, and sometimes beautiful. Before becoming involved with Pauline, Levin has had: an encounter with a waitress in a barn, ruined at the dramatic moment when a disappointed rival steals their clothes; a wrestle with an unmarried colleague on the floor of his office, broken off by Levin out of an obscure compassion; and a gay weekend with a student named Nadalee, resulting in her efforts to get her class grade raised from a C to a B. His involvement with Pauline is hardly more glamorous: he is disturbed by her flat chest; at one point in the affair he has excruciating muscle spasms in bed with her; at another point she is temporarily frigid, and he thinks bitterly, "Now we have truly come to adultery." At the novel's end, in one of the most wonderfully embarrassing scenes in modern fiction, Gerald warns Levin of Pauline's constipation and menstrual irregularities. Funny, awful, it nevertheless is love, and beauty, and value.

Levin's past, when it is finally confessed to Pauline, seems unnecessarily melodramatic: his father a thief, Harry the Goniff; his mother insane and a suicide; himself a gutter alcoholic. Levin's future, as we can picture it at the end of the novel, is less extreme: Pauline will develop breasts in pregnancy; Levin, with a new identity, will again have a first name; their life together will be responsible, hard-working, and devoted. If this is not joy, the top-gallant delight that Father Mapple's sermon promises the righteous in *Moby-Dick*, it is a happy ending nevertheless, and perhaps as much as our shabby modern world can promise anyone.

Malamud's technical mastery is impressive. His apparently episodic novel is tightly woven, mostly by means of foreshadowing. When the chairman of the department warns Levin against dating students or prowling among faculty wives, the weekend with Nadalee and the affair with Pauline are implicit in his warning, as though created by it ("Nay, I had not known sin, but by the law," says St. Paul, "for I had not known lust, except the law had said, Thou shalt not covet"). When Levin arrives in Cascadia, the Gilleys take him to their house for dinner, and Pauline spills the tunafish casserole in his lap;

when he has changed into a fresh pair of pants, the little boy wets on them. It is an uproarious scene, and announces Levin as the book's *schlemiel*, but it is also the annunciation of his future role as husband and father, victim and protector, of the woman and child who pour their love in his lap.

Some of *A New Life* is scandalously funny. C. D. Fabrikant, the department's scholar, is rarely seen except on horseback, and gallops off by way of punctuating his remarks. Levin first meets the dean carrying a bag of grapefruit, and as in an old silent movie, while they talk they scramble for the grapefruit after the dean has walked into a telephone pole, then scramble again when Levin walks into a tree. Like that of Malamud's best stories in *The Magic Barrel*, the humor is wild and surrealistic. The cold bare trip back to town with the waitress cursing Levin is nightmarish comedy, as is his later fruitless effort to expose a plagiarist, with the suspected plagiarist following him around and jeering.

At the height of his emotional disturbance, Levin walks into a bar, orders "Love," and when the bartender goes in search of the bottle, madly flees. When Levin goes to confront the wronged husband in his hotel room, Gerald greets him earnestly with: "Pardon the small room." In the terrible period when Levin has bravely given up Pauline, and is tormented by erotic dreams, Malamud writes:

> Amid such pleasures Mrs. Beaty's white cat fell in love with him, laying a broken-feathered bird at his door, fat headless robin. He asked the landlady to keep the cat out of the house but pussy in love was faithful, finding more ways in than he could block off, depositing another bloody-breasted bird. "Eat my heart," he cried and kicked the beast down the stairs. Ascending on three legs she delivered a mangled rat, then went into heat, her raucous cries sounding through the house.

Malamud's expressionist device, which he shares with several of the best writers of our time, is writing dreams, fantasies, and even similes as though they were literal realities. When he reads a theme of Nadalee's about swimming naked, "Though Levin's legs cramped after a too hasty immersion in cold water, he jumped in after her and spent most of the night swimming with Nadalee." When Gerald describes trout-fishing to Levin, his office becomes a mountain stream.

Malamud's work has some of the bitter comedy of Yiddish literature, some of the preoccupation with sin and redemption of Russian literature. It particularly resembles the work of that remarkable Soviet-Jewish writer, Isaac Babel, who combines both traditions, and combines them *within* the current of modern European literature. *A New Life*, in its progress from affair to bondage, may remind readers of *A Farewell to Arms*, but Malamud faces up to problems that Hemingway kills Catherine to evade. It has some of the grubby comedy of the British Angries, the compassion of Salinger, the moral earnestness of George P. Elliott. Yet this novel, like Malamud's work generally, remains unique, in its totality sharply unlike the work of anyone else.

Certainly there are flaws. *A New Life* is too slow getting started, and the book is half over before its action really begins. There are infelicities of style and syntax, although fewer than in the earlier books, and occasional weaknesses of diction, as when Malamud gets fancy and writes "dew" for "tears." Some of the plot, in which Levin becomes a candidate for chairman of the department and meets espionage with counter-espionage, is absurd, although Malamud saves himself at the worst point by writing a human and moving confrontation scene between Levin and the woman colleague who has just gone through his files.

In progressing from *The Natural* to *The Assistant* to *A New Life*, Malamud has achieved a new mature acceptance. Pauline is the Iris of *The Natural*, no longer scorned; Levin rakes leaves with the frenzy of Frank Alpine, but he has an insight into his nature and destiny that Frank never achieves. In a sense, Malamud has moved from the story of Samson, punished for the misuse of his powers, to Job, suffering because chosen to suffer, to Jesus, suffering voluntarily to redeem. If Malamud continues to find modern plots to embody his powerful redemptive themes, I know no limit to what he can accomplish.—STANLEY EDGAR HYMAN, "A New Life for a Good Man" (1961), *Standards: A Chronicle of Books for Our Time*, 1966, pp. 33–37

### THE FIXER

*The Fixer* represents for Malamud both a departure and a return to familiar territory. It picks up the major themes of *The Assistant*. The protagonist, Yakov Bok, seeks a new life; he is an unwilling Jew who does not believe in God and who wishes to enjoy the freedoms of Gentiles. Here the setting shifts from 1950s America to tsarist Russia, and the details of the plot loosely parallel those of an actual historical incident, the infamous Mendel Beiliss case.

This is the least complex of Malamud's novels and the plot the most straightforward. Yakov Bok, a Jewish handyman in prerevolutionary Russia, abandons his religious tradition and the hope that his childless wife will return to him, leaves his shtetl (native village) and settles in the city of Kiev, where he hides his identity in order to live and work illegally outside the Jewish ghetto. He is arrested and charged with murdering a Christian boy to use his blood in making Passover matzos. More than three-quarters of the novel is spent in portraying Bok's stubborn endurance through two and a half years in brutal pre-trial imprisonment; the novel ends as the trial is about to begin.

Bok is another of Malamud's poor Jews whose life seems to be an unending struggle to make ends meet. "If there's a mistake to make," he thinks, "I'll make it." Somewhat of a schlemiel, who is conscious of his role as loser, Yakov expects calamity and resolves to hold up under it. His speech and reflections are laced with wry Yiddish irony. Deserted by his wife who could bear him no children, barely able to earn enough at odd jobs to live on, Yakov nonetheless is unwilling to accept his status as born loser; thus he resolves to break out of the prison of the shtetl, "an island surrounded by Russia." Only his father-in-law, Shmuel—an old Jew who complains about the hardship of life but who remains faithful to God—is present to wish him well as he departs with his few belongings for Kiev. "Don't forget your God," Shmuel warns. "Who forgets who?" comes the bitter reply. Shmuel continues agitatedly, reminding Yakov that the Jews are surrounded by enemies and must stay under God's protection. "Remember, if he's not perfect, neither are we."

During the early portions of the novel, Malamud emphasizes the theme of denial of identity. Driving an old wagon pulled by a broken-down old nag with rotten teeth, Yakov begins a physical as well as a spiritual journey. The nag's erratic starting and stopping rouses Yakov's intense but feebly misdirected anger: "I'm a bitter man, you bastard horse." Later he beats the horse, thinking, "like an old Jew he looks." At the Dnieper River, Yakov trades the horse for a boat ride, and is ferried by a Charon-like boatman with a shaggy beard and bloodshot eye. Here for the first time Yakov hears of the widespread folk belief that fanatical Jews murder Christian boys as part of their cabalistic rites. Terrified by the hatred of his

Jew-baiting pilot, Yakov unobtrusively lets his bag of prayer implements (phylacteries and prayer shawl) slide into the icy water.

In Kiev, Yakov seeks to change his fortune. He rents a room in the Podol, the Jewish district, and looks for work. The Podol is already full of people searching for jobs that do not exist. So Yakov begins seeking employment outside the ghetto, hoping that he may have better luck among the Gentiles. In any case, he reasons, his chances could not be worse.

One night Yakov finds a drunken man lying unconscious in the snow—a fat, bald, prosperous-looking Russian who wears the Double Eagle emblem of the virulently anti-Semitic organization, Black Hundreds. In Good Samaritan fashion, Yakov rescues the man, who later rewards him with a job redecorating part of his house. Yakov's new benefactor, Lebedev, is a wealthy drunkard who speaks in pious platitudes and biblical phrases. Like Chaucer's nun (who is quoted in the novel's opening epigraph), Lebedev weeps over the death of a dog one moment and persecutes Jews the next. Yakov conceals his Jewishness and finally accepts a well-paying job as foreman in Lebedev's brickworks.

Yakov's new position forces him to live in an area of the city forbidden to Jews and, as a kind of overseer-policeman, to antagonize his coworkers. Thus, when the catalytic event occurs—the murder of a Christian boy and the discovery of his body mutilated by thirty-seven stab wounds—all the forces of potential destruction threaten to descend on Yakov's vulnerable head. According to an expert from the Kiev Anatomical Institute, the boy had had his blood drained, "possibly for religious purposes." Yakov's identity is revealed, and he is arrested for the crime. 〈. . .〉

During the rest of the novel, Yakov remains in prison while incriminating circumstantial evidence is found. Two previous incidents in particular are used against him, and both demonstrate the impossibility of escape from his own Jewish conscience. The first occurred when Lebedev's crippled daughter, Zina, made sexual advances to Yakov. After some hesitation, Yakov responded, partly out of pity for the girl, but could not bring himself to continue when he found that she was menstruating and hence, by Jewish law, was "unclean." Later, the angry and humiliated girl publicly accuses Yakov of assaulting her.

The second incident occurred when Yakov once again performed a simple act of human kindness. He found an old Jew one night who had been stoned by malicious boys and was lost and bleeding; Yakov bandaged his head and hid him for the rest of the night in his room. Later, after his arrest, the bloody shirt Yakov used for the bandage and the old man's bag of matzos are found in his room and used as evidence of Yakov's involvement in a conspiracy of Jewish fanatics who are said to use Christian blood in their cabalistic ceremonies.

Yakov's imprisonment introduces several new characters. The principal antagonist is prosecuting attorney Grubeshov, procurator of the Kiev superior court. He gathers evidence, real or imaginary, and combines it in novel ways, twisting reality to suit his own political bias. He continually tries to browbeat Yakov into "confessing." Working for Grubeshov is Father Anastasy of the Orthodox church, a self-proclaimed "specialist" on Judaism.

In a shocking scene, the investigators drag Yakov to the cave where the body was found. Father Anastasy recites a long "history of Jewish uses for Christian blood," and concludes by insisting that the existence of a fanatic Jewish bloodlust is revealed by the very frequency of the accusations against Jews. Yakov can only cry out in disbelief, "It's all a fairy tale, every

bit of it. Who could ever believe such a thing?" He cannot cope with the irrational forces around him. He is still convinced that if he could logically explain to his tormentors what kind of a person he is, he could convince them that he is incapable of such an act, and they would realize they have the wrong man.

Fortunately, not everyone is against Yakov. The investigating magistrate for Cases of Extraordinary Importance, B. A. Bibikov, is a humane and rational man who vows to help see that justice is done. While Yakov spends his first Passover in jail, Bibikov begins gathering evidence to clear him of the charge.

During the second part of the novel, after Yakov's arrest and imprisonment, Malamud focuses the major themes by weaving into the plot references to the philosophy of Spinoza. Somewhat implausibly, Yakov is represented as having developed a passion for reading the works of the great philosopher, alone at night in his cottage in the shtetl. He does not understand all the intricate twists of Spinoza's thought, but he does have an intuitive grasp of the major premises. In his initial interview with Bibikov, Yakov discovers that his learned counsel also has a fondness for Spinoza. Yakov explains that he admires Spinoza because he wanted to make himself free and independent by "thinking things through and connecting everything up." From Spinoza, Yakov learned the central condition of existence—"that life could be better than it is," and that the only way to improve the quality of life is for all men to strive for good will among men, to be reasonable, or else "what's bad gets worse."

Several weeks after the first meeting, Bibikov visits Yakov in his cell and tells him that the real murderer is the boy's mother, Marfa Golov, who is involved with a gang of thieves. Grubeshov, he says, also knows the identity of the real murderer, but finds it more expedient to accuse a Jew. The only hope of getting the truth out, Bibikov says, is by going to the press. "So that's how it is," sighs Yakov, "behind the world lies another world." Yakov had forgotten Spinoza's decree that there is no escape from involvement in the world. As Yakov himself said to Bibikov, "all things fit together underneath." Even false accusations fit into the larger scheme of things; lies remain until disproved. This conversation marks the beginning of Yakov's rational and meaningful resistance against his enemies, and it occurs just in time, for Bibikov is denounced and himself thrown into the solitary cell next to Yakov's. A few days later he hangs himself.

For all Grubeshov's cleverness at manipulating facts, he is unable to make a believable case out of the charge of ritual murder, and so he continually delays Yakov's indictment. For two and a half years Yakov is kept in solitary confinement. He is brutalized and dehumanized, experiencing beatings, hunger, poison, rats, numbing cold, insanity. Always there is worse to come. Twice a day he must submit himself to a humiliating search. Soon he is searched six times a day—and he is kept in chains the rest of the time.

Unexpectedly, Yakov is offered a way to escape his suffering. If he signs a confession, he can go free. He refuses because he knows that his confession will be used against the Jews. Yakov comes to realize that suffering is part of life, but a man can choose to make his suffering meaningful. Yakov chooses to suffer more so that others will suffer less. It is this awareness that leads Yakov to his greatest triumph. Grubeshov offers Yakov a new opportunity for freedom. The tsar has agreed to grant certain classes of criminals, including Yakov, amnesty. But Yakov does the unimaginable, he refuses—because he is to be pardoned as a criminal rather than freed as an innocent man. The gesture is absurd but magnificent, an affirmation of his personal dignity and moral integrity. This emotional high point of the novel inspires the reader at the same time that it defeats Yakov's enemies.

Finally the long-awaited indictment comes and with it a lawyer, Julius Ostrovsky, who informs Yakov of Shmuel's death, of the worldwide attention his case has received, and of the mounting evidence against Marfa Golov. Through Ostrovsky, Malamud explains how Yakov's case "relates underneath" to "the frustrations of recent Russian history." "I'm only one man, what do they want from me?" Yakov asks. Ostrovsky tells him that they only need one man to create an example of Jewish bloodlust. "You suffer for us all."

After Ostrovsky leaves, Yakov comes to the conclusion that "what happens to somebody starts a web of events outside the personal." He recalls that Ostrovsky told him that Russia suffers from much more than its anti-Semitism. "Those who persecute the innocent were themselves never free." In his sleep, Yakov dreams that Bibikov comes and tells him that "the purpose of freedom is to create it for others"; Yakov answers that something inside him has changed and he is not the same person he once was. A major irony of *The Fixer* is that Yakov Bok learns what freedom is by enduring a nearly intolerable imprisonment.

In the final pages of the novel, the miracle of Yakov's spiritual victory begins to emit a holy aura. When the deputy warden refuses to release Yakov to the soldiers who have come to escort him to his trial, the guard Kogin intervenes. Yakov is released, but Kogin is shot in the scuffle. He has sacrificed himself in order to insure that Yakov will finally receive justice.

The novel closes with Yakov riding in a carriage to his trial. The ending leaves the outcome of Yakov's case in doubt, but the verdict is really irrelevant to the main concerns of the novel, for Yakov has already achieved the understanding of freedom he envied in Spinoza. This point is underscored in the closing scene. A young Cossack rides as escort alongside the carriage that takes Yakov to his trial. Yakov envies him his youth, his good looks, his freedom. Suddenly, a bomb goes off and the Cossack's foot is blown away. "He looked in horror and anguish at Yakov as though to say, 'What has my foot got to do with it?'" The answer is that the youth is no more free than Yakov. All things connect underneath. Yakov has an inner freedom his oppressors lack. Malamud develops this paradox so powerfully that the memory of Yakov Bok is likely to inspire the reader long after he has finished reading the story.—SHELDON J. HERSHINOW, "Alienation and Aggression: *The Fixer*," *Bernard Malamud*, 1980, pp. 63–69

---

## MARCUS KLEIN
### "The Sadness of Goodness"
*After Alienation: American Novels in Mid-Century*
1962, pp. 280–93

*T*he *Assistant* insofar as it is naturalistic drama would seem to be such an attempt. A *New Life*, an academic picaresque composed directly, so Malamud has said, according to the influence of Stendhal,[1] is certainly a discipline, strenuous but comic, in real things. The "new life" his hero, S. Levin, seeks, is, it turns out, an alternative not merely to his past life. Levin sighs much in the novel about the encumbering presentness of his past, but that past, as he deals with it directly and briefly just once, is a vague history of drunkenness and a fairly tale of family horrors, in effect a non-life. The new life is life itself. And it is to be life with possibilities much more

extensive than those provided by Malamud's claustral grocery store.[2] Levin is set down in a place where, for one thing, nature is present—nature, Morris Bober had reflected, "gave nothing to a Jew." Moreover, this place will contain a community, a variety of private histories and domestic troubles, jobs, politics, a presence of American history, and, because the place is an academic community, it will provide as well for a clear encounter with large social forces and ideals. A *New Life* is oddly enough one of the few novels not journalism, of the mid-century, that contains specific speculations on Korea, the cold war, McCarthyism, Hiss and Chambers, loyalty oaths, the plight of liberalism, the definition and the duties of radicalism. Levin's speculations on these matters are not indeed analyses, but the materials are there as materials for his adventures, and it is the point of his adventures that he is to engage them, along with all the other present realities.

Near the beginning of the novel, Levin knows and he chooses to avoid the events and the meanings of current history. "America was," he says, "in the best sense of a bad term, un-American," and he is "content to be hidden amid forests and mountains in an unknown town in the Far West," and then, "Teaching was itself sanctuary—to be enclosed in a warm four-walled classroom." Toward the end of the novel, he commits himself to social leadership. In the same way, the novel moves Levin to a close engagement with nature, from New York City and an abstract, distant love of it. Levin's new life is a matter, indeed, as he repeatedly expresses his ambition, of coming out from his privacy, and virtually every pattern of events in the novel is designed to illustrate his coming out. Levin wears a beard, and at a certain point in the novel he shaves it off. He wears a hat and a raincoat and carries an umbrella, when none of the rugged Westerners do, and the progress of his consciousness, like Lear's, urges him to stripping in the wilderness. Levin learns to carry golf clubs, to rake leaves, to fire a furnace, to drive a car. He learns to distinguish friends and enemies. And he falls in love and learns how to have a family.

Levin is a young man from the capital, it happens, who in order to secure his initiation moves to the provinces. That would be the way of a contemporary American Julien Sorel. It is specifically to the Pacific Northwest that Levin goes, a place called Eastchester in the state of Cascadia,[3] where it might be expected that the American civilization could be discovered pure. Quite by the spirit of Stendhal, he is introduced there to manners and morals, passions, intrigues, hypocrisies, the workings of power, and the things of civilization, all of such a civilization as this is. The spirit is Stendhal's, as Malamud has said, but the facts are different ones. Quite like Julien Sorel's Paris, of the Bourbon Restoration, Eastchester is fallen into betrayal of the ideals of its own recent past, but the ideals are, or were, radical democracy, progress, and enlightenment, not empire and glory. And the circumstances of its past are different. In the spirit of Stendhal, Levin is introduced not to a surviving aristocracy, but to nature—nature, as Levin says on an occasion, is Eastchester's true history. And the social facts which this young-man-from-the-capital is in his new life to engage are those of a civilization no longer creative, but not sophisticated, either, and this is a civilization that has gone stale but that is without the certainties either of institutions or of social nuance upon which a Stendhal could depend.

The spirit is Stendhal's, but neither the problem nor the manner nor the voice could be. Remarkably, Malamud does discover a great deal and he does get it down on the page. For the first time in Malamud's fiction, the real things have a real and, more to the point, a continuous specificity. The physical descriptions are frequent, detailed, and exact. The place in which Levin finds himself makes demands. And there is a felt social organization available to him, re-created by a scrupulous, and a consistently ironic, attention to its manners. A *New Life* is indeed, one half of it at least, vivid social satire. But it is social satire in the manner and the voice—astonishingly, considering Malamud's dedication to a European literary tradition—not of Stendhal but Sinclair Lewis. But then inevitably. These are fallen democrats to whom Levin is to be given, whose society is not an institution complicated and refined by the ages but a relatively simple process of enthusiasm generated by loneliness. Their salience is their protective heartiness, and the literary apprehension which as a society they demand is caricature, just enough so that the hollowness may be heard. "People aren't too formal out this way," Levin is told as he arrives. "One of the things you'll notice about the West is its democracy," and his answer, tart and Yiddish, is "Very nice." And that, the hollowness of the democratic gesture, is just the demonstration to be made. Eastchester is not Gopher Prairie, of course. For one thing it contains Levin. But it would seem not to be far from Gopher Prairie, and in any event Malamud's procedures and perceptions are those of a somewhat harsher Sinclair Lewis.

So it is a completely amiable society that is to be seen, a society under an iron discipline of amiability. It is a society whose members nevertheless are in hot, fussy pursuit of petty ambitions. The imagination, the ideals, the sap have gone out of it. Its tone is a broad charade of its worthy past. The satire serves the purposes, since this is an academic novel, of an academic exposé, another exposé of the English Department, but the locale has larger uses. Because culture is this community's business, the past will be the more uncomfortably and the more tauntingly present. And this is a society whose members are all good guys, just a little on edge, open, sincerely devoted to harmlessness, pietistic about certain things, and, it will turn out by function of their organized effort toward triviality, altogether vicious. The basic materials are those of Gopher Prairie. Given them, the voice and the very inventions of specific character must be echoes of Sinclair Lewis. Levin's immediate superior and principal antagonist, Gerald Gilley, in their first talk talks boosterism:

> You're our twenty-first man, most we've ever had full-time in the department. . . . Professor Fairchild will meet you tomorrow afternoon at two. He's a fine gentleman and awfully considerate head of department, I'm sure you'll like him, Sy. He kept us going at full complement for years under tough budgetary conditions. Probably you've heard of his grammar text, *The Elements of Grammar?* God knows how many editions it's been through. The department's been growing again following the drop we took after the peak load of veterans, though we've still got plenty of them around. We put on three men last year and we plan another two or three, next. College registration is around forty-two hundred now, but we figure we'll double that before ten years. . . .
>
> We've been hearing from people from every state in the Union. For next year I already have a pile of applications half a foot high.

And in the next moment he talks cautionary self-exculpating Babbittry: "I like your enthusiasm, Sy, but I think you'll understand the situation better after you've been here a year or two. Frankly . . . Cascadia is a conservative state. . . ." And then, Gopher Prairie *redivivus*, the Department is "service-oriented." Professor Fairchild, the community ex-

emplar, resonates one-hundred per cent American clichés.[4] The community spirit has its opportunity in the college's football and basketball teams, and therefore they are a serious concern. The underground, as one should expect, consists of a couple of village atheists, one old and one young, both of whom confine themselves to cautious ironies. And even Malamud's heroine, Pauline Gilley, the wife whom Levin will steal from Gerald Gilly, emerges in the image of Carol Kennicott—she is a rangy girl vaguely dissatisfied with the narrowness and the restriction of the community, willing to take a chance, vaguely ambitious for something not very clear.

*A New Life*, Malamud predicted,[5] would be something new for his readers, and it is. The half of it that is social satire is, much of it, broadly funny. The fun is sometimes very good fun—Professor Fairchild, who will expire with the words "The mys-mystery—of the in-fin—in-fin—in-fin—In-fin-i-tive," in the beginning tells Levin an endless moralizing tale of his drunkard father who on his way to Moscow, Idaho, succumbed to drink and never got there, a tale that sounds like a biography by Tolstoy of W. C. Fields. And then the fun is sometimes corny—Levin meets on the road an old hayseed of a farmer who hands him a pair of pliers and asks Levin to pull his tooth: "Got an achin' tooth here at the back of my mouth. Could you give it a pull with these pliers?" And Levin declines. But fresh or corny, the fun is fabricated from perceptions not usual to Malamud. The perceptions are social and they are directed toward manners and they have breadth. It is here an American humor that, apparently, Malamud is after, to be discovered in a folk, in some Americans as they are in the first place typical, as they typically constitute a certain society, and then as they have just in back of them a certain folk tradition. This humor is far removed from the desperate uncertainties of the *shtetl*.

Levin's new life, then, is to be a serial engagement with the West, with nature, with a community, with some facts, current and traditional, of American history, with social forces, with American civilization and the American folk, all credibly realized. But then the fact is that though the real things are, at least in instances enough, really there, Levin never does come to the point of participating in them. More than that, Levin's adventures consist really of lengthy and private speculations leading to a series of fumbling and abortive attempts at engagement, followed by long retreats, culminating in a plunge into a situation which is meant to represent for Levin and for us a fullness of real life because it is unpleasant. The novel was to be written according to Stendhal, so Malamud said before he had written it, and it was to be, so Malamud also said, "a romantic love story, with warmth and richness."[6] The two intentions are not dissimilar. They meet in an intention toward engagement. And at the end of *A New Life* Levin does get the girl, all right, but in the end he no longer wants her, and at the end his love is neither romantic nor warm nor rich, but sternly dutiful. The story that Malamud tells in *A New Life* is at the end the old story: the real things propose not themselves but a moral imperative, and the hero plunges uncertainly after the things for lack of anything else. And what then is demonstrated is the extremity of the hero's attempt.

One half of *A New Life* is social satire and the other half is Levin, and the verve of the one is made uneasy by the melancholy of the other. Malamud does not accomplish for Levin the forward movement that will bring him progressively into the world, and that will, incidentally, bring the novel together. Levin's desire for a new life is in the first place merely desperate, an urge forced from the impossible dreamy loneliness of his past, a matter of discipline, and his true history is, so the evidence will come to suggest, his inevitable frustration.

One of the items of his desperation is his need not for lovers but simply for a friend or two, and some good part of his early adventuring in the novel is his searching for some casual friendship. Levin as he knocks on the doors of his various colleagues is in one instance after another rebuffed, but then more significant than his defeat is the fact that he is never in his search brought to any climactic confrontation. The matter simply tires itself out and is dropped, and what is dramatized, no matter what is intended, is a great weariness in Levin's searching and an inevitability of defeat.

What is dramatized in every other instance is a conviction of the inevitability of frustration, the consequence of which is inertia, against which by main force Levin stumbles and fumbles for engagement and discovery. Nature is a large part of the reality which Levin is to engage, and he does learn to perform some chores of gardening and such. Indeed he is moved to lyrical appreciation of natural beauties in such a way as perhaps only a boy from Manhattan might be. But the intimate connection, the real engagement, despite Malamud's forcing of a couple of moments, just never takes place.

The test is in those moments. Levin would seem to be derived in part from his namesake in *Anna Karenina*.[7] Like that Levin, he is provided in a set scene in an open clearing in a woods with opportunity for a redemptive insight. The scene in *Anna Karenina* apparently contains a special suggestiveness for Malamud. Frank Alpine was made to happen upon it in his reading and to be "moved at the deep change that came over Levin in the woods just after he had thought of hanging himself," and Frank had reflected that unlike Anna, at least Levin wanted to live. Malamud's Levin, on a spring day miraculously burst in the middle of January, in the middle of the novel, with some temerity enters a local woods to do some bird-watching. Bird-watching has consequences in Malamud's fiction, and here Levin meets and for the first time makes love to Pauline Gilley. This is an important scene, an anagnorisis. Levin has fumbled unhappily after other girls, but this is love. This forest, it happens, is a place where foresters are trained. And the moment, so Levin reflects, is marvelous. He has become at once a lover and Natty Bumppo. "In the open forest," he says to himself, "nothing less, what triumph!" He has discovered the promise of life.

Or that should be and would be the case except that the moment, brief as it is, is so qualified by ironies as to be contradicted. This time in nature is, first of all, a time out of nature—midwinter spring is its own season. The unusual weather for January indeed prompts Levin, as he sets out for the out-of-doors, to speculate with "a touch of habitual sadness" on "the relentless rhythm of nature," the eternal sameness which prevents human freedom. And whatever insight this day will offer, it will not offer nature as it is. Nature-as-it-is hovers near-by to cancel the illumination. Moreover, then, the promise of life, as it should be certified by Levin's love-making with Pauline, reneges on itself. Pauline, as her husband will much later tell Levin, is no bed of roses. And Levin finds out now that she is unfortunately flat-chested, a fact which, were Levin permitted to know Malamud's iconography, he would recognize as a symptom of failure at love.[8] In his passion clutching at her breasts, which is to say clutching after engagement with her, Levin seizes nothing. And then finally such joy and freedom as there is in this love-making is qualified by the secretive messiness of adultery it looks forward to. The sun shines brightly as he and Pauline leave the forest, but Levin opens an umbrella over their heads. And in the quick course of things the forest will shrink to a double bed in Levin's bachelor room.

The episode is forced—what Malamud asserts, he takes back. And then it is in its achievement the more suspicious because it should be redundant. The episode follows shortly upon another in which Levin, having suffered from a cold and from a long bout of dreary loneliness and from a recidivous thirst for alcohol, walks abroad to discover a magnificent Western sunset. He felt, so it is said, "like a man entering a new life and entered." But that is the abrupt end of that episode. In fact Levin's harmony in the woods is followed shortly by still another greeting from nature, occurring when he admits what he thinks he knows, that he is in love with Pauline Gilley.

> Above the tops of budding trees he watched the flaring, setting sun, wanting to abolish thought, afraid to probe the complexion of the next minute lest it erupt in his face a fact that would alter his existence. But nature—was it?—a bull aiming at a red flag (Levin's vulnerability, the old self's hunger) charged from behind and the Manhattan matador, rarely in control of any contest, felt himself lifted high and plummeted over violet hills toward an unmapped abyss. Through fields of stars he fell in love.

The experience does not, however, alter his existence. In the next moment, in the very next paragraph, he will retreat back into his habits of anxious speculation, the moment of his full engagement still before him, the reiteration necessary because the moment refuses finally to occur.

Levin reflects in the beginning, after some preliminary attempts at gardening, that "he had come too late to nature," and in fact all his efforts are conducted against a sense of something—whether or not his particular past—dragging him back. The Levin presented is a lonely, bearded Jew, locked in himself, desperate to get out, after great effort coming too late to everything. The best of an external reality that Malamud will allow him is one at second hand. So Levin buys a secondhand car, observing that "he had come too late to mechanics," as later he observes more largely, in the middle of his woodland adventure, that "he had come too late to the right place." He will reflect still later that he is no Chingachgook; wherever he had been, someone had been before. This new life after which he will finally plunge is forced from a sense of its opposite, and then if it isn't just the old life again to which Levin falls, it doesn't either contain anything entirely new. At the very end of the novel, Levin will drive off in his secondhand car with his secondhand wife and with the children she had in the first instance adopted. Pauline is pregnant with Levin's child, and that might be something new, but the child is only another possibility of the future, for which Malamud does not make himself responsible.

There is something secondhand and stale even in the objects of Levin's purely social commitment. There is no doubting the sincerity or the urgency of his idealism. "I worry," he says to one of his teaching colleagues, "I'm not teaching how to keep civilization from destroying itself," and if the statement is faintly pretentious, as Levin admits it is, it is also so blunt as to prove conviction.[9] And Levin's idealism should be of special usefulness to Cascadia College, which is "service-oriented," which (like, it is to be said, America) lost the liberal arts shortly after the First World War, which has lapsed into a viciously self-protective narrowness of political reaction, and which is on its way toward destroying the civilization by which it was nurtured. But Levin's passionate idealism accomplishes no revolution and it is impossible that it might, despite the fact that Levin actually does urge himself to the point of running for the position of head of the English Department, despite the fact that he actually does enter himself into such politics as there is. His idealism is a matter of his subscribing himself passionately to ideals—democracy, humanism, liberalism (and the liberal arts), radicalism, freedom, art, and intellect. The words are ever and easily at his lips. And splendid, and necessary, as his ideals are, they exist pure and at a tremendous distance from the social facts. Levin becomes aware of that distance, as apparently Malamud became aware at a certain point in the novel. Malamud presents Levin with, indeed, some particulars of social action. As Levin is a reform candidate, he urges upon the English Department: elimination of the Department's grammar text and also the examination in grammar, elimination of "censorship of responsibly selected texts," recommendation that every instructor teach a course in literature, and some other similar matters, all to an effect comparable to Trotsky lecturing at the local P.T.A.

Between Levin's ideals and the social facts there is tremendous distance and a total absence of social analysis. His ideals are not tested in the large social complication they require, and certainly they are not forged from social experience. Levin's ideals are the convenient instruments of his idealism, and what his idealism accomplishes, aside from elimination of the grammar text, is its own integrity. His idealism is not what it seems to be and should be, the way of his engagement with the new life out there. Confronted in his idealism by the facts, Levin is in fact apt to be foolish. So when he is told of a photograph of a man and woman swimming together naked, he refuses, quite with Malamud's assent, to believe that they were lovers, on high juridical grounds of reasonable doubt. There is in such idealism something not merely naive but also forced. It has no sensible commerce with the world, and what about Levin's idealism is effectively dramatized is its uncertain relevance to the real world.

But of course Levin will be a man who believes that ideals, as he says, "give a man his value if he stands for them," just as he will be a man for whom love is finally neither a joy nor an enrichment nor an emotional fulfillment, but a stern moral imperative. The world doesn't beckon to Levin. He and Malamud invent disciplines by which to secure an accommodation to what is only uncertainly there. So Levin's final plunge after Pauline is, as it must be, entirely dutiful, and merely desperate. After adventures in adultery, he no longer wants her. Moreover he has discovered reason to believe that she does not love him, but, instead, a previous lover whom he resembles. Then, in a final interview, her husband rubs Levin's nose, as it were, in Pauline, a woman who, as Gerald points out, was born dissatisfied, who is thrown off balance by almost anything, who is not a good housekeeper, who is unpunctual, who is afraid of growing old, and who suffers chronically from constipation and menstrual troubles. And the children Levin will inherit are not easy to live with either. He will love Pauline nevertheless because he can discover, so he tells her, no reason not to. He will love her without feeling, and on principle, and because, so he says to Gerald, he can. And off he then goes, with a car full of luggage, two children, one crying for its real daddy, the other, suffering eczema, covered with ointment, and his bride in a white dress.

Stendhal would have written a different ending, with irony less excruciating and a resolution more secure. At the end of *A New Life* nothing, no experience, has yet really happened, and the end is just a more extreme attempt by which Levin is to be got into life, under the rule of a stern discipline, and out of himself. But the record of Levin's failure is Malamud's startling strength. Malamud is not a Stendhal or a Balzac and—it is exactly his informing trouble—the world does

not tumble in upon him, and so he is forced to extremes to discover it. The strenuosity of such a hero as Levin is of the mood of Malamud's taut balance, elsewhere, on the edge of supernaturalism, and it is created in an apprehension of a world in which nothing certainly exists.

*Notes*

1. Bernard Malamud in an interview by Joseph Wershba, "Closeup," *New York Post Magazine*, September 14, 1958.
2. Levin's ambitions obviously parallel Frank Alpine's. Indeed it was Frank Alpine who first discovered for his ambitions the phrase "a new life."
3. Levin's locale has some relation, presumably, to Oregon State College in Corvallis, Oregon, where Malamud was a member of the faculty from 1949 until 1961.
4. The monger of pious clichés is a constant character in Malamud's fiction. Professor Fairchild's forebears are to be seen in the owner of the baseball team, Goodwill Banner, in *The Natural*, and in Julius Karp in *The Assistant*.
5. *New York Post Magazine* interview.
6. *New York Post Magazine* interview.
7. For a briefly extended comparison with *Anna Karenina* see Eugene Goodheart, "Fantasy and Reality," *Midstream*, VII (Autumn 1961), 102–105.
8. In a preceding episode Levin himself affirms, if he does not recognize, Malamud's pectoral iconography. A sexual encounter with a lady named Avis Fliss is frustrated because the lady, having suffered a fibroma, is sensitive in her breasts.
9. There is no doubting Levin's sincerity furthermore because he echoes Malamud's statement of his own purpose as a writer: "The purpose of the writer . . . is to keep civilization from destroying itself." *New York Post Magazine* interview.

### SANFORD PINSKER
From "The Schlemiel as Bungler:
Bernard Malamud's Ironic Heroes"
*The Schlemiel as Metaphor:*
*Studies in the Yiddish and American Jewish Novel*
1971, pp. 87–116

I f a writer like Isaac Bashevis Singer has to face the agonizing problem of re-creating a ghetto experience that, in some sense, had been all too short-lived, Bernard Malamud and a host of other postwar American Jewish writers had to discover the boundaries of a heritage that, for them, had hardly lived at all. Critic J. C. Levinson has pointed out that "after Buchenwald and Hiroshima, fiction can hardly remain the same, and in the most interesting of our postwar novelists, it has indeed changed."[1] For American Jewish writers, the problem of the Nazi holocausts was particularly acute; the prospect of confronting the six million dead—in either the terms of literary metaphor of the gut response of socio-religious feeling—seemed futile, almost as if the only appropriate reaction was a kind of numbed silence.

Curiously enough, though, the American Jewish writer—traditionally caught in the private difficulty of defining both his "Americanness" and his particular brand of "Jewishness"—now found himself called upon to be a spokesman at exactly the moment when he probably had no desire to speak at all. For a writer like Bernard Malamud, the Jew became a natural symbol for the postwar sensibility, the index of an age questing belief on one hand, but wrenched out of religious contexts on the other. Thus, the Jew emerged as "a type of metaphor . . . both for the tragic dimension of anyone's life and for a code of personal morality."[2]

But while subsequent literary history proved the validity of such statements, they always suggested that something akin to a literary plot had been abrew; the Malamuds and Bellows of the world somehow hatching up the whole thing in a lower East Side delicatessen. Writing in *Commentary* magazine, critic Robert Alter suggests that artistic failures can result

> when a writer assigns a set of abstract moral values to the representatives of a particular group, the connection thus insisted on may strike the reader as arbitrary, an artistic confusion of actualities and ideals.[3]

To be sure, the statement is provocative enough on its own terms, but even more so when one remembers that it was magazines like *Commentary* which, in effect, created the renaissance of American Jewish writing. Mr. Alter's charge could, of course, be brought to bear against more writers than Bernard Malamud, but it is Malamud whom we tend to think of first. His Jews always appear out of an offstage "nowhere," filled to the brim with suffering as if they had just changed clothes from a four-thousand-year trek across the desert. We are asked to accept—yea, even *believe*—that this is an a priori state of being, part of the author's *donnée* that is beyond question. And slowly what was once the thirties' concern with the "human condition" evolved into a fifties' fascination with a "Jewish" one.

But it is in this confusion between actualities and ideals that Malamud's peculiar tensions are created. The schlemiel may well have been a comic figure whose self-created failures became an index of socioeconomic limitation, but such a character is out of place in arenas of affluence and endless mobility. Marcus Klein sees the change as one from novels of alienation (i.e. works in which characters of sensibility "protect" themselves by systematically moving beyond the boundaries of the hostile society) to those of what he calls "accommodation."[4] Rather than, say, a Stephen Dedalus symbolically flapping his wings in the last line of Joyce's *Portrait of an Artist as a Young Man* and dreaming about a bohemian life in Paris, the contemporary American writer found himself in the city, in the System, in the affluence—and only vaguely unhappy about the situation.

At the same time that writers were learning how to accommodate, to preserve individuality beneath folds of gray flannel suiting, there was a growing concern about the larger moral issues which were attendant to the times. In some respects, the French Underground had it easier; their existential nausea was the result of a particular time and place. American counterparts, on the other hand, often got a double dose, but delayed some ten years and denied a setting in concrete experience. For American Jewish writers, the figure of the schlemiel became a way of dealing with these realities, although now he was more interested in moral transcendence than economic advancement. For Malamud, especially, the schlemiel was a moral bungler, a character whose estimate of the situation, coupled with an overriding desire for "commitment," invariably caused comic defeats of one sort or another.

The Malamud canon is filled with such schlemiels, from the early stories of *The Magic Barrel* to his most recent novel, *The Fixer*. I suspect the most damning thing one can say about Malamud's development is that he has done little more than rewrite "The Magic Barrel" for the past fifteen years. To be sure, a good many modern authors would welcome such "criticism," especially if they thought a repeat performance was possible.

For Malamud, the short story is more amenable to ambivalence, and in "The Magic Barrel" particularly, he achieved a nearly perfect blend of form and content. Con-

sidered as a whole, "The Magic Barrel" is an initiation story, although the exact dimensions of the "initiation" are hard to pin down. It opens innocently enough—"Not long ago there lived in uptown New York, in a small, almost meager room, though crowded with books, Leo Finkle, a rabbinical student in the Yeshiva University"—as if to answer the objections of critics who continually demand that American Jewish literature be more Jewish and less goyish, less like literature. But for all the kosher food and lower East Side *mame-loshen*, Jewishness is as much a literary illusion in "The Magic Barrel" as Negro dialects are in *Huck Finn*. Like most of Malamud's protagonists, Leo Finkle's problem is an inability to love, a failure to adequately relate his particular brand of isolation with the isolation of others. Finkle is initiated into "suffering" almost by accident. He "had been advised by an acquaintance that he might find it easier to win himself a congregation if he were married," and so Finkle opens himself to eros, shadchens (marriage brokers), and his fate as schlemiel. Initially at least, the rabbinical student is radically different from the mercuric matchmaker: Finkle represents the force of Law while Salzman stands for the power of Flesh. And yet, Salzman—for all his vulgarisms—betrays a "depth of sadness" which Finkle uses as a convenient mirror for his own.

The progress of the moral schlemiel nearly always involves identification with suffering and some strategy for taking on the burdens of others. In this sense the schlemiels of Malamud's canon bear a striking resemblance to the classical folk figure; both desire to change the essential condition of their lives, but each is inadequate to the task. Finkle's leitmotif is sympathetic suffering in much the same way that Salzman's is fish. Each of the "much-handled cards" in Salzman's magic barrel comes to represent a person whose aloneness is a counterpart of his own. To be sure, Salzman is more pimp than "commercial cupid"—regardless of Finkle's elaborate rationalizations about the honorable tradition of the shadchen. In fact, what Finkle really imagines is a world in which hundreds of cards—each one longing for marriage—are churned about and finally brought together by this indefatigable matchmaker. Finkle's schlemielhood is a function of his willingness to believe in such highly romantic visions and, moreover, to replace them as quickly as they go sour. Salzman, on the other hand, plays confidence man to the rabbinical student's sensitivity. All his marital candidates sound like used cars, perfectly suited to sales pitches like the following:

> Sophie P. Twenty-four years. Widow one year. No children. Education high school and two years college. Father promises eight thousand dollars. Has wonderful wholesale business. Also real estate. On the mother's side comes teachers, also one actor. Well known on Second Avenue.[5] [P. 196]

In this way, the juxtaposition of Finkle's hesitation about "buying" and Salzman's aggressive brand of "selling" create what might have been a purely comic situation. However, Finkle gradually begins to see Salzman's portfolio as a microcosm of the world's suffering and his shoulders as the proper place for it to rest. What breaks down, of course, are the very pillars of Finkle's world—the justifications of Tradition, the pragmatic need for a wife, the commonsense arguments for using a matchmaker, etc.

But if the "much-handled cards" of Salzman's portfolio make it clear that others suffer, his traumatic meeting with Lily Hirschorn makes it equally clear that he, too, has vital dimensions that are missing.

> Her probing questions irritated him into revealing— to himself more than her—the true nature of his

relationship to God, and from that it had come to
him, with shocking force, that apart from his parents,
he had never loved anyone. [P. 205]

In some sense, "The Magic Barrel" is a story of love—although
the word operates on both the levels of eros and agape. Finkle's
"learning," his ability to articulate about his own particular
deaths of the heart does not constitute his schlemielhood. Lily
Hirschorn—like the other cards in Salzman's magic barrel—
was simply another frantic figure yoo-hooing after a life that
had already passed her by. But if Finkle had been conned by
Salzman, so had Lily. She expected an Old Testament
prophet, a man "enamored with God," and instead she got a
man incapable of passion in either the physical or spiritual
sense of the word. In the Finkle-Salzman-Hirschorn triangle,
the end result is initiation; Finkle finds out what he is, and in
the context of the story this provides for a certain amount of felt
tension.

It is with the introduction of Stella, however, that Finkle
moves from moral initiate to moral bungler. Unlike the
portraits of the other women, Stella's dimestore picture
revealed that she "had *lived*, or wanted to—more than just
wanted, perhaps regretted how she had lived—had somehow
deeply suffered" (p. 209). Thus, in a world where "suffering" is
the standard for oneupsmanship, Stella emerges as the hands-
down winner. Lily Hirschorn may have wanted to live, Finkle
himself has the urge to try, but it is Stella who has actually been
there. And it is through the figure of Stella (her name
suggesting the ironic star which guides Finkle's destiny) that the
prospective rabbi hopes to "convert her to goodness, himself to
God." In this way, a new triangle is created with Finkle
representing a tortured attempt to achieve spiritual resurrection; Salzman (variously characterized as Pan, Cupid, or other
fertility figures) emerging as a kind of Yiddishized Creon while
Stella vacillates between the scarlet of her prostitution and the
whiteness of her purity.

It is the movement toward Stella which makes a schlemiel
out of Finkle, at least in the sense that his goal of spiritual
regeneration is incommensurate with his activity. In this
respect, Finkle's situation is a moral counterpart of traditional
Jewish stories in which a character aspires to financial success,
only to sow the seeds of his own destruction.

The concluding tableau crystallizes the matter of Finkle's
"salvation" and/or "destruction" without providing the luxury
of a clear reading direction. On one hand, Finkle runs toward
Stella seeking "in her, his own redemption" in ways which
make this passionate rabbinical student seem almost akin to the
biblical Hosea. On the other hand, however, Salzman is
always just "around the corner . . . chanting prayers for the
dead." Is the kaddish for Finkle? for Stella? or, perhaps, for
Salzman himself? In much of Malamud's early fiction, a kind
of ironic affirmation is an integral part of his aesthetic—almost
as if movements toward moral change were not enough, but
total regeneration was not possible.

*The Assistant* (1957) seems to be cut from the same bolt of
cloth (marked "Judaic suffering") that gave us the moral
qualms of a Leo Finkle. In this case, however, the patient
suffering of Morris Bober is a more genuine donnée than much
of the pain in "The Magic Barrel." I say "more genuine"
because Bober is neither the protagonist nor the moral filter of
this novel. His "suffering" merely *is* and it is the task of Frankie
Alpine, his assistant, to learn what such suffering means and
how it can apply to his own situation. To be sure, Frankie has
some rather curious notions about Judaism, but then again,
Bober may not be the best instructor. At one point in the novel
he claims to suffer "for the Law," although it is hard to see

exactly how Law—in the sense of *Halakha*—functions in
Morris's life. Instead, Bober is more often characterized as a
kind of secular *tsaddik*, a man who once "ran two blocks in the
snow to give back five cents a customer forgot." His cachet is in
his deeds—giving an early morning roll to the gray-haired (and
vaguely antisemitic) Poilisheh, extending endless credit to the
"drunk women," and even shoveling his sidewalks on Sunday
morning because "it don't look so nice for the goyim that go to
church."

And yet, the bulk of Bober's suffering was not a matter of
economic failure or even the fact that "in a store you were
entombed." Rather, it was the unspoken and often elusive
failures of fatherhood which continually torment Bober's
sensibility. In Malamud's world, people always seem out of
breath from carrying too many bundles, both physical and
psychological; when they finally do rest for a glass of tea, we
tend to believe their "sighs," to feel that such suffering is
justified.

> Breitbart, the bulb peddler, laid down his two
> enormous cartons of light bulbs and diffidently
> entered the back. "Go in," Morris urged. He boiled
> up some tea and served it in a thick glass, with a slice
> of lemon. The peddler eased himself into a chair,
> derby hat and coat on, and gulped the hot tea, his
> Adam's apple bobbing.
> "So how goes now?" asked the grocer.
> "Slow," shrugged Breitbart.
> Morris sighed. "How is your boy?"
> Breitbart nodded absently, then picked up the
> Jewish paper and read. After ten minutes he got up,
> scratched all over, lifted across his thin shoulders the
> two large cartons tied together with clothesline and
> left.
> Morris watched him go.
> The world suffers. *He* felt every schmerz.
> At lunchtime Ida came down. She had cleaned
> the whole house.
> Morris was standing before the faded couch,
> looking out of the rear window at the backyards. He
> had been thinking of Ephraim. [Pp. 6–7]

Jonathan Baumbach characterizes the novel as the intertwining
biography of surrogate fathers and surrogate sons. As he puts it,

> *The Assistant* has two central biographies: the life
> and death of Morris Bober, unwitting saint, and the
> guilt and retribution of Frank Alpine, saint-elect,
> the first life creating the pattern and possibility of the
> second. At the end, as if by metamorphosis, the
> young Italian thief replaces the old Jewish store-
> keeper, the reborn son replacing the father.[6]

In some respects, Bober's situation seems to be a variant of
Leopold Bloom's, although Ephraim is not Rudy, nor is
Frankie Alpine Stephen Dedalus. What seems similar, however, is the manner in which the respective "adoptions" take
place. Bober's suffering remains constant; it is a condition of his
life and the necessary result of Ephraim's death. Frankie, on
the other hand, vacillates between visions of absolute goodness
and the reality of compulsive evil. What he needs are standards
for moral excellence, of which the life of St. Francis is one and
the life of Morris Bober is another. About St. Francis, he says:
"For instance, he gave everything away that he owned, every
cent, all his clothes off his back. He enjoyed to be poor. He said
poverty was a queen and he loved her like a beautiful woman"
(p. 31). To be sure, he might have well been talking about
Bober, and as he grows into his role as "assistant," the
distinction between the two figures gradually blurs. However,
what Frankie really identifies with is a style of suffering,

confusing his own masochism with the martyrs from his Catholic sensibility and the Jewishness of his grocer boss. In this way, he becomes the moral schlemiel, the man whose estimate of the situation is as wrong-headed as his strategies for attaining moral perfection. What he desires, of course, is a kind of sainthood and his movements toward Bober's brand of Jewishness parallel Finkle's attraction to Stella. "Salvation" and/or "destruction" once again becomes the index of Malamud's ironic affirmation, the comic result of shlemielish behavior.

But Frankie does not immediately resemble the sort of schlemiel one remembers from Yiddish jokes nor does Bober's "suffering" seem totally ironic. There is a sense in *The Assistant* that at least a part of Malamud is playing it straight, believing in both Bober's essential goodness and Frankie's ability to learn from it. Things crystallize in the funeral scene, at the point where tensions begin to shift from the father/owner to his assistant/son. The Rabbi—unfamiliar with Bober and called in for the occasion—delivers the following eulogy at his graveside:

> My dear friends, I never had the pleasure to meet the good grocery man that he now lays in his coffin. He lived in a neighborhood where I didn't come in. Still and all I talked this morning to people that knew him and I am now sorry I didn't know him also . . . all told me the same, that Morris Bober, who passed away so untimely—he caught double pneumonia from shoveling snow in front of his place of business so people could pass by on the sidewalk—was a man who couldn't be more honest. . . . Helen, his dear daughter, remembers from when she was a small girl that her father ran two blocks in the snow to give back to a poor Italian lady a nickel she forgot on the counter. Who runs in wintertime without hat or coat, without rubbers to protect his feet, two blocks in the snow to give back five cents that a customer forgot? . . . He was also a very hard worker, a man that never stopped working. How many mornings he got up in the dark and dressed himself in the cold, I can't count. . . . So besides being honest he was a good provider.
>
> When a Jew dies, who asks if he is a Jew? He is a Jew, we don't ask. There are many ways to be a Jew. So if somebody comes to me and says, "Rabbi, shall we call such a man Jewish who lived and worked among the gentiles and sold them pig meat, trayfe, that we don't eat, and not once in twenty years comes inside a synagogue, is such a man a Jew, rabbi?" To him I will say, "Yes, Morris Bober was to me a true Jew because he lived in the Jewish experience, which he remembered and with the Jewish heart." [Pp. 228–29]

I suspect that Bober might well be considered a prize schlemiel by those prone to give the passage an ironic reading. The Rabbi asks, "Who runs in wintertime without a hat or coat?" and, for the hard-boiled among us, the answer must be "a *schlemiel!*" Bober cares about his customers, but the novel makes it clear that they continually desert him for fancier food and lower prices. At every point in the Rabbi's sermon the facts of the matter ironically undercut his well-meaning sentiment. Bober may have been "honest" (all the details suggest that he is a Hassidic saint, one of the Lamed Vov), but he was hardly a "good provider." His daughter reads *Don Quixote* and dreams of worlds beyond the confines of the grocery store, at the same time blaming Bober for spoiling her chances. His wife simply complains—about business, about Helen's boyfriends, and finally about Bober himself.

And then there is the sticky matter of Bober's "Jewishness." The Rabbi's words of consolation may have cheered a good many American Jews who share such a definition, but it hardly answers the question of Bober's "Jewishness" in the novel itself. For Bober, Jewishness seems to be inextricably bound with suffering, with a common humanity of which Jews—bound by the Law—seem to carry the greatest share. As I have mentioned before, whatever Bober might mean by the Law, it is clearly not talmudic Law that he has in mind. After all, "Nobody will tell me that I am not Jewish because I put in my mouth once in a while, when my tongue is dry, a piece of ham." For Bober, the issue really comes down to who has the "Jewish heart," and when Frankie asks why Jews "suffer so damned much," Bober can only reply:

> "They suffer because they are Jews."
>
> "That's what I [i.e. Frankie] mean, they suffer more than they have to."
>
> "If you live, you suffer. Some people suffer more, but not because they want. But I think if a Jew don't suffer for the Law, he will suffer for nothing."
>
> "What do you suffer for, Morris?" Frank said.
>
> "I suffer for you," Morris said calmly. [P. 125]

Part of Bober's "mystery"—particularly to a disciple like Frankie—is the ambivalent quality of Bober's instruction. If Bober has the Jewish heart already, how can it be transferred to someone else? For Frankie, the answer seems clear—Bober "suffered," and to be like him, one must also suffer. However, for all his apparent folly, for the personal goodness which he wasted and the unnecessary suffering he endured, Bober's life seems more a tragic commentary on the American Dream and the Traditions of Judaic suffering than an ironic joke about self-destruction. No matter how wrong-headed he might have been about his customers, his family or his friends, Bober's style had a certain amount of dignity, a certain bittersweet quality that made even his sighs seem justified and, more important, profoundly significant.

But the fate of his "assistant" is another matter. In Frankie's first outing after Bober's death, he quite literally makes a schlemiel out of himself.

> Then the diggers began to push in the loose earth around the grave and as it fell on the coffin the mourner wept aloud.
>
> Helen tossed in a rose.
>
> Frank, standing close to the edge of the grave, leaned forward to see where the flower fell. He lost his balance, and though flailing his arms, landed feet first on the coffin. [P. 231]

But the incident at the grave is only one of a long series of self-created accidents which spoil Frankie's chances. In an attempt to reverse his luck, to achieve the sort of moral perfection he desires, and most important of all, to emulate his grocer boss, Frankie converts to Judaism. However, it is a Judaism he does not understand and which cannot possibly sustain him. The situation is somewhat akin to Ike McCaslin's brand of learning in William Faulkner's "The Bear." Like Bober, Sam Fathers has intuitive wisdom about the woods that Ike patiently tries to discover. But with Sam Fathers dead and the woods slowly disappearing, the "wisdom" no longer seems to work. Frankie's case is even more complicated because there is a real question as to whether or not he understood Bober—much less his "Jewishness" or the value of his suffering.

For Frankie, conversion to Judaism suggests plot complications that exist beyond the novel itself. We accept the tableau at the conclusion of "The Magic Barrel" and even the multiple possibilities of Salzman's kaddish, as part and parcel of the short story, but it is a bit harder to know what to do with Frankie. Are we to presume that he will emulate Bober by taking over the grocery store and perhaps even marrying Helen? Will he be the one to supply the gray-haired Poilisheh with her six o'clock roll and the "drunken women" with endless credit? The novel concludes with Frankie circumcised and dragging "himself around with a pain between his legs," a pain which both "enraged and inspired him." However, unlike the suffering of his employer, Frankie's is a function of his penchant toward masochism. The old guilts must be punished and what better way than by circumcision? Implicit in the act are the complicated strands of sexual punishment (for his attempted rape of Helen), castration anxiety (for Bober as his Oedipal father), and religious conversion (for a Covenant he does not understand). But in his quest for moral perfection, Frankie Alpine emerges as more schlemiel than authentic Jew, more a victim of his desire for sainthood than actual "saint." At the end, he sees himself as a kind of St. Francis figure reaching into a garbage can to give Helen a wooden rose.

> He [i.e. St. Francis] tossed it into the air and it turned into a real flower that he caught in his hand. With a bow he gave it to Helen, who had just come out of the house. "Little sister, here is your little sister the rose." From him she took it, although it was with the love and best wishes of Frank Alpine [Pp. 245–46]

Finkle, too, had clutched flowers to his anxious breast and raced after Stella. And, in a similar way, Frank Alpine speeds toward a destiny (or destruction?) he does not fully understand, duping himself with the belief that he is no longer the "assistant" and that Bober's humanity will soon be his.

In *A New Life* (1961), Malamud continued with the progress of a moral schlemiel, but added more of the slapstick complication usually associated with the figure. After all, it is hard to see a novel like *The Assistant* as primarily "comic," at least in the sense that either Bober or Frankie emerge as primarily humorous figures. Perhaps there is something about the nature of grocery stores in Malamud's canon which not only restricts economic possibilities, but comic ones as well. With Pinye Salzman, for example, there was at least endless room to run around, but Bober and Frankie are literally stuck in the store. S. Levin, "formerly a drunkard," hails from the same sort of environment—what Philip Roth calls a "timeless depression and placeless lower East Side"—as the characters of *The Assistant*, until Malamud fairly throws him into both the American West and the groves of academe. That Levin should be a schlemiel is almost as much an a priori assumption in *A New Life* as Bober's suffering was in *The Assistant*. Unfortunately for Malamud, whatever gold may have been in those particular literary hills had already been well panned by the time Levin arrived, the "virgin land" idea having been exploited by one group of scholars while the anti-academic novel was being milked by another.

Although *A New Life* moves Malamud out of the city, its concerns are almost identical to those which provided tension in his earlier fiction. However, this time the focus is split between Levin's role as moral schlemiel and his initial appearance as capital-B Bungler. During the first few scenes of the novel, Levin is the schlemiel out West and newly arrived in academe—the economic scheming of his ghetto ancestors now turned toward the business of departmental tenure and perhaps even an eventual Ph.D. "Bearded, lonely," and looking around for a sign of welcome, Levin is the perfect candidate for the "accidents" which will befall him. In many respects, he is the rabbinical student from "The Magic Barrel" turned upside

down, the flip side of Finkle's brand of poignant aloneness. Met by Gerald Gilley, Director of Freshman Composition, Levin spends the evening in a series of outrageous "man who came to dinner" jokes—alternating, as the standard definition of the schlemiel would have it, between the one who "spills the soup" and the one who "gets spilt upon." Levin wastes little time establishing his credentials as that innocent victim of bad luck, the schlimmazzel.

> They sat down at the round table, for which he felt a surprising immediate affection. Pauline had forgotten the salad bowl and went in to get it. When she returned she served the casserole, standing. A child called from the kitchen. Distracted, she missed Levin's plate and dropped a hot gob of tuna fish and potato into his lap. [Pp. 9–10]

But Levin (alas) is denied even the luxuries of being a schlimmazzel. In a post-Freudian world, there are no accidents, or at least nothing is allowed to remain a mere "accident" for very long. And so Malamud begins a long series of pants jokes, each involving Levin as a comic figure and each involved with the element of farce so essential to the fabric of *A New Life*. Levin's trousers are, of course, ruined by the hot tuna and all the elements of a minor scene are present. Pauline suggests that Levin change into her husband's trousers (attention, Freudian critics!) and, after much argument, the situation seems resolved when Levin had "changed into Gilley's trousers in the bathroom."

With the new trousers, however, comes new *tsoriss*. Coaxed into telling the Gilley's youngest son a story,

> Levin, scratching a hot right ear, began: "There was once a fox with a long white beard—"
> Erik chuckled. In a minute he was laughing—to Levin's amazement—in shrieking peals. Levin snickered at his easy success, and as he did, felt something hot on his thigh. He rose in haste, holding the still wildly laughing child at arm's length as a jet of water shot out of the little penis that had slipped through his pajama fly. [P. 13]

Unfortunately, the total effect suffers from a kind of artistic diminishing returns, suggesting that what might work in a Laurel and Hardy movie or on the vaudeville stage may not always work in a novel. Robert Alter has suggested that

> the schlemiel, it should be said, lends himself much more readily to revelation in a short story than to development in a novel, perhaps because his comic victimhood invites the suddenness and externality of slapstick; when that technique is merely multiplied in being transferred to a novel—where we expect more subtlety and innerness, a more discursive and analytic treatment of character—the comedy becomes a little tedious.

But while Mr. Alter's point is certainly a valid one and helps to explain why *A New Life* is a less satisfactory piece of fiction than, say, a short story like "The Magic Barrel," there is also a sense in which Malamud's schlemiels move from situational humor to moral dilemma, the "comic victimhood" here depending a good deal more upon a frame of mind than the vicissitudes of an external world. In this sense, *A New Life* is an important novel, not because of its limited successes, but, rather, for the varied strands of its failure. To return a moment to Levin's bedraggled trousers, part of the progress of the schlemiel has to do with "great expectations" that are perpetually unfulfilled. For the first hundred pages or so, the prevailing temper of *A New Life* is one of ironic reversal, usually involving either Levin's career as teacher or lover—and always centering, finally, on the comic possibilities of his pants.

His night on the Northwestern town with Sadek is an excellent example. In a way, these two rather bizarre characters complement themselves—Levin, the former drunkard and high school English teacher from the impersonal East, and Sadek, a Syrian graduate student whom Levin describes as a

> fanatic about hygiene. The fumes of Lysol stank up the bathroom for a half hour after he had been in it; he [Sadek] rubbed everything he touched—before, not after—with his personal bottle. He was majoring in sanitary bacteriology and taking courses in rat control and the bacteriology of sewage. [P. 73]

Sadek's concern for the physical paralleled Levin's attention to the moral. To be sure, we see Sadek as excessive, a comic portrait that qualifies him as an actor in the farce of S. Levin's life. When they vie for the "hand" of the fair Laverne—Sadek dividing his time between seduction and frequent urination, while Levin sips his beer and dreams of love—ill luck seems to visit each of them. Sadek is apprehended for indecent exposure ("the toilet facilities of the tavern horrified him and he preferred not to do a major Lysol job there"), leaving the barmaid to Levin by default. Soon the would-be lovers are alone in a barn, each captivated by the uniqueness of their situation; Levin, the irrepressible romantic, observing that this was "my first barn" while Laverne reflects that she had "never done it with a guy with a beard." For Laverne the whole business is standard operating procedure, an effective foil to the ways in which Levin waxes poetic at the possibilities of love, the West and, of course, a new life: "In front of the cows, he thought. Now I belong to the ages" (p. 80).

And, in a sense, Levin does "belong to the ages," although not the ones he had in mind. He is the presumably "sensitive" young man out of an earlier tradition in American literature, the sort of boy who takes sexual initiation seriously because he knows (unconsciously of course) that this is the stuff out of which great literature is made. A more recent writer like James Jones (in, say, *Some Came Running*) might be intrigued by the possibility of unions between Spirit and Flesh. However, Malamud seems more interested in incongruity than resurrecting still another version of "pastoral." Rather than a protagonist plucked out of an American *Bildungsroman*, Levin is really the schlemiel—here in the guise of country bumpkin turned upside down until it is the farmer's daughter who seduces the city salesman.

> *Laverne:* "Why don't you take your pants off?"
> *Levin:* "It's cold here. Have you got a blanket to cover us?"
> *Laverne:* "No, just the one to lay on."
> *Levin:* "In that case I'll keep my jacket on."
> *Laverne:* "But take your pants off or they'll get crinkled. . . ."
> *Levin:* "Your breasts," he murmured, "smell like hay."
> *Laverne:* "I always wash well," she said.
> *Levin:* "I meant it as a compliment." [P. 81]

And if the traditional schlemiel is portrayed as the cuckold, Levin may well be a modern variant, the victim of comic *coitus interruptus*. Just at the moment when "Levin rose to his knees and was about to be in her," Sadek reappears, stealing their clothing and leaving the hapless Levin victimized in the very heart of the great Northwest. The incident may well be the result of ill luck, bad timing or what you will, but for Laverne, the fault is clearly his: " 'You sure are some fine flop,' she said acidly. 'It's what I get for picking you instead of waiting for the one with guts.' " Even when Levin surrenders his trousers to Laverne—this time suggesting more agape than eros—the

gesture is lost in a welter of comic complications. Laverne is hit by an empty beer can as they try to hitch a ride, and when they finally arrive at her porch, she "kicked his pants off the porch. 'No, you bastard, don't ever let me see you again in your whole goddam life. Don't think those whiskers on your face hide the fact that you ain't a man' " (p. 85).

But the misfortunes associated with Levin's trousers are not limited to his social life alone; they also play a prominent role in his academic career at Cascadia College. During his first class, "he carefully followed the mimeographed instruction sheet"—only to find that academic hours are longer than he had thought. With the fifteen items already covered, Levin "vaguely considered dismissing the class—what could he teach them the nervous first day—" when he happened to notice the boldface type at the bottom of the page:

N.B. DO *NOT* DISMISS YOUR CLASS BEFORE
THE END OF THE HOUR. G.G., DIR. COMP.
[P. 89]

The "bold-face type"—like the threats of a "black list" in Saul Bellow's *The Victim*—suggest the low-keyed, but constant threats of the modern condition. For Levin, Cascadia College is virtually his last chance—a matter too serious to risk by disregard of an official memorandum. I suppose conventional satire might feature a bumpkin too ignorant of the complexities to entertain such thoughts, his wide-eyed appraisal of the situation exposing folly in the manner of a Huck Finn or Lemuel Gulliver. However, academic satire usually contains some interesting shifts in perspective. In our best writers, there is always a curious tension between a feeling that the System has been taken over by incompetents and an equal desire for promotions in that very System. It is the difference between a novel like *Lucky Jim* and *Up the Down Staircase*—the former concerned with making faces at the college while you work for tenure by publishing scholarly articles, and the latter in which you emerge as the System's only sensitive soul with hardly any struggle at all. Levin shares qualities with the protagonists of both these novels, combining a penchant for accident that easily makes him an American counterpart of unlucky Jim Dixson with the hard-core idealism of Bel Kaufman's heroine. The recurring trousers, Levin's idealism about the profession, his twinges of paranoia and, most of all, his slapstick schlemiel-ism all combine to end his first class in high style. Surprised and somewhat heartened by the rapt attention of his new students, Levin—following the "bold-face type"—launched into the business of sentence diagram until only twelve minutes remained. At that point he "finally dropped grammar to say what was still on his mind"; I quote the scene *in toto*, letting Levin's comic victimhood speak for itself.

> . . . namely, welcome to Cascadia College. He was himself a stranger in the West but that didn't matter. By some miracle of movement and change, standing before them as their English instructor by virtue of appointment, Levin welcomed them from wherever they came: the Northwest states, California, and a few from beyond the Rockies, a thrilling representation to a man who had in all his life never been west of Jersey City. If they worked conscientiously in college, he said, they would come in time to a better understanding of who they were and what their lives might yield, education being revelation. At this they laughed, though he was not sure why. Still if they could be so good-humored early in the morning it was all right with him. . . . In his heart he thanked them, sensing he had created their welcome of him. They represented the America he had so often heard of, the fabulous friendly West. . . . "This is the life

for me," he admitted, and they broke into cheers, whistles, loud laughter. The bell rang and the class moved noisily into the hall, some nearly convulsed. As if inspired, Levin glanced down at his fly and it was, as it must be, all the way open. [Pp. 89–90]

There are, of course, other instances where Levin plays the slapstick schlemiel. In the mock seduction of Avis Fliss, Levin reenacts his abortive evening with Laverne as the scene shifts from pastoral barns to academic offices. Here, too, the comedy revolves around *coitus interruptus*, although this time Gilley adds a dash of paranoia to the proceedings. In the same spirit, Levin's accident-plagued ride to meet Nadalee at the motel suggests all the penchant for self-created failure that are traditional aspects of the schlemiel. And yet, the schlemiel of pratfall is far more at home on the vaudeville stage than in the confines of a novel. Levin's comic difficulties—the accidents seemingly earmarked for him and lurking around every corner—are established in the first hundred pages. Whereas a novel like Joseph Heller's *Catch-22* worked on a theory of reoccurring absurdity (Milo Minderbinder's mushrooming empire or the exploits of, say, Major Major Major Major), Malamud condenses for effect and then moves on to new thematic material. More than anything else, it is this failure to achieve a singleness of purpose which makes *A New Life* an artistic failure. The perennial bungler is more stereotype than character and when his role is split between that of naïve persona in an academic satire and moral Idealist in a corrupting world, the effect is a certain amount of distortion.

Levin's notebook gives perhaps the best clues as to the kinds of tensions which will ultimately become the focus of the novel—

One section of the notebook was for "insights," and a few pages in the middle detailed "plans." . . . Among Levin's "insights" were "the new life hangs on an old soul," and "I am one who creates his own peril." Also, "the danger of the times is the betrayal of man." [P. 58]

We have come to expect that Levin's notion of a "new life" based upon geographical change is destined to fail a priori. As Mark Goldman has pointed out, Levin is the "tenderfoot Easterner . . . (always invoking nature like a tenement Rousseau). Now he took in miles of countryside, a marvelous invention."[7] But whatever the "new life" might be or how ironic such slogans ultimately turn out, it hangs very definitely on an "old soul." It is almost as if Levin's notebook becomes a private place of understanding, often at odds with his public behavior or the clichés on which much of the novel seems to operate.

In a similar fashion, the element of academic satire has, I think, been misunderstood by a number of critics who were quick to point out that they were equally indignant about schools like Cascadia (and teachers like Gilley). After all, "The danger of the times *is* the betrayal of man" and it is not hard to see how this statement was interpreted as having something to do with the preservation of the liberal arts, the humanities, and most of all, English literature. Ruth Mandel, for example, sees Cascadia College in the following terms:

Here is a stereotyped, mediocre, service-oriented English department. The instructors are organization men of the worst kind, men who should know better, men educated in the humanities. The school is a Cascadian Madison Avenue, a school where the emphasis is on practical learning, prestige, school-board approval, and the well-rounded, shallow man who must be an athlete if he wishes to be accepted. The attack is devastating. Malamud's intensions are clear.[8]

But are they? If Levin is really to function as the traditional satiric persona, it seems odd that Malamud should fail to get his credentials straight. After all, S. Levin hardly comes "from a world of pastoral innocence," nor is he "the prophet come down from the hills to the cities of the plain; the gawky farmboy, shepherd or plowman come to the big city."[9] Rather, Levin ("formerly a drunkard") comes to this untainted (?) West from New York City, the very seat of Eastern corruption. He is, I suppose, a sort of reverse Nick Carraway who follows his dream of a liberal arts college westward—only to find, instead, freshman composition and departmental silliness. And yet, Levin often seems more like the Kurtz from Conrad's *Heart of Darkness* than the Carraway from Fitzgerald's *The Great Gatsby*. Far from being the innocent one who may see corruption and still refuse to understand it (Nick), Levin seems to be drawn into the evil System until he, too, becomes its victim. To be sure, Levin is virtually surrounded by academic absurdity: his chairman continually revises his *Elements of Composition*, 13th edition (which, naturally enough, is the required text of Levin's courses); another rewrites a dissertation on Laurence Sterne that no one will accept; still another cuts out pictures from old *Life* magazines for a proposed "picture" book of American literature. However, Levin is not paralyzed by what looks like the curious publish-or-perish character of Cascadia College; after all, he had some plans of his own.

(Levin) wondered if he could begin to collect material for a critical study of Melville's whale: "White Whale as Burden of Dark World," "Moby Dick as Closet Drama." . . . Levin began to read and make notes but gave up the whale when he discovered it in too many critical hats. He wrote down other possible titles for a short critical essay: "The Forest as Battleground of the Spirit in Some American Novels." "The Stranger as Fallen Angel in Western Fiction." "The American Ideal as Self-Created Tradition." Levin wrote, "The idea of America will always create freedom"; but it was impossible to prove faith. After considering "The Guilt-ridden Revolutionary of the Visionary American Ideal," he settled on "American Self-Criticism in Several Novels." Limiting himself, to start, to six books, Levin read and re-read them, making profuse notes. [P. 267]

The proposed articles—one has the awful feeling he has read them in some graduate seminar or other—serve a number of functions. First, they suggest the ironic dimensions of Levin's purity, a matter not nearly as important in the groves of academe as it will be in the regeneration of his moral fiber. After all, it is the "others" who have sold out, turning their talent from human concerns to more commercial ones—not Levin. His articles are filled to the brim with American guilt and Edenic innocence—all in the best traditions of Cotton Mather, Henry Adams, and the MLA. Levin may differ in degree, but not very much in kind. Of course, the titles are meant to be satiric, although I suspect that more than a few of Malamud's readers secretly thought that "The Stranger as Fallen Angel in Western Fiction" might not make a bad essay after all. My point is simply this: Levin's overriding concern is for moral preservation, both in the collective sense of America and in the individual sense of self. If his academic fantasies are those of a potential schlemiel, they must be seen in the larger context of Levin's moral structure. In a sense, the pettiness of Cascadia College is only a backdrop for Levin's more pressing concerns—his inability to love, his lack of commitment, his perennial death of the spirit.

However, it is in his last "insight"—"I am the one who creates his own peril"—that Levin unconsciously hints at the sort of self-knowledge traditionally associated with the figure of the schlemiel. It is the schlemiel, after all, who "creates his own peril" and Levin's "insight" is both an acceptable definition of the term and an accurate appraisal of his behavior thus far in the novel. Neither a "new life" in terms of geographical moves to a mythical West nor his romantic notions about the groves of academe can save Levin from himself. Whatever comic spirit derives from the incongruity of a Levin plunged into Nature, learning how to drive a car, or being initiated into the realities of Cascadia College fizzles out almost completely as he moves toward Pauline and the larger complications of the novel. For a time, it looks as if Levin will relive the legend of Leo Duffy. He arrived with a Duffy-like beard, began his career in Duffy's abandoned office and ended with Pauline. However, Malamud has more in mind for S. Levin than one more academic martyrdom. Whereas a Duffy commits suicide (the final "protest" and one that is sure to have "meaning"), Levin gradually switches roles from academic complainer and/or critic to moral bungler.

At one point in the novel, Levin tells Pauline about his first "awakening," his initial encounter with the new life.

> For two years I lived in self-hatred, willing to part with life. I won't tell you what I had come to. But one morning in somebody's filthy cellar, I awoke under burlap bags and saw my rotting shoes on a broken chair. They were lit in dim sunlight from a shaft or window. I stared at the chair, it looked like a painting, a thing with a value of its own. I squeezed what was left of my brain to understand why this should move me so deeply, why I was crying. Then I thought, Levin, if you were dead there would be no light on your shoes in this cellar. I came to believe what I had often wanted to, that life is holy. I then became a man of principle. [P. 201]

And it is from Levin's mushrooming sense of "principle" that his link to other characters in Malamud's canon is established. To be sure, his concerns take in the vast range of contemporary problems (unlike the more isolated concerns of, say, a Frankie Alpine), but the mechanism is very much the same. For Malamud, the important thing may not be that a Gilley or a Fabrikant are exposed, but rather that a Levin finally acts. However, moral action is almost always a qualified commodity in Malamud's world, more an occasion for ironic failures than spiritual successes. And if Levin's academic fantasies had a ring of moral urgency about them, consider the following slice of Levin's wishful thinking:

> He must *on principle* not be afraid. "The little you do may encourage the next man to do more. It doesn't take a violent revolution to change a policy or institution. All it takes is a good idea and a man with guts. Someone who knows that America's historically successful ideas have been liberal and radical, continuing revolt in the cause of freedom. 'Disaster occurs if a country finally abandons its radical creative past'—R. Chase. Don't be afraid of the mean-spirited. Remember that a man who scorns the idealist scorns the secret image of himself." [Levin's notebook: "Insights"] Don't be afraid of names. Your purpose as self-improved man is to help the human lot, notwithstanding universal peril, anxiety, continued betrayal of freedom and oppression of man. He would, as a teacher, do everything he could to help bring forth those gifted few who would do more than their teacher had taught, in the name of

democracy and humanity. (Whistles, cheers, prolonged applause.) The instructor took a bow at the urinal. [P. 230]

Meditations of this sort often occur in the john, as any disciple of either Norman O. Brown or Martin Luther would be quick to attest. However, Levin's fantasies have a rather elastic quality about them. They are able to expand until the savior of the Humanities in general and Cascadia College's English department in particular becomes the Christ-like savior of the entire world.

> He [Levin] healed the sick, crippled, blind, especially children. . . . He lived everywhere. Every country he came to was his own, a matter of understanding history. In Africa he grafted hands on the handless and gave bread and knowledge to the poor. In India he touched the untouchables. In America he opened the granaries and freed the slaves. [P. 273]

For Malamud, the giving of bread is a particularly important symbol. As I have suggested elsewhere, it encompasses such acts as Bober giving early morning rolls to the Poilisheh or a Yakov Bok (in *The Fixer*) giving matzoh to the wounded Hassid. During a symposium held at the University of Connecticut, Malamud kept stressing this connection, placing a strong emphasis on Levin's dream of giving bread and knowledge to the poor as evidence of both moral growth and the novel's "positive" ending. But the bread motif works in ways that are more subtle than mere fantasy. Much has already been written about the Protean character of S. Levin's name—from the ridiculously formal S. Levin to the more relaxed "Sam." Mark Goldman sees the line "Sam, they used to call me home" as particularly important because "their concluding words end the search for Levin, happily surrendering S. for Seymour, Sy for sigh, even Pauline's Lev for love, simply to identify with the real past." Evidently part of the contemporary critic's equipment is the ability to play name games with both ingenuity and endless patience. And while the shifting quality of "S. Levin" may not be nearly as challenging as, say, the possibilities of Moses Elkannah Herzog or almost any character from a Barth novel, I suspect the really crucial pun is centered on Levin's last name rather than the varieties of his first. As the "leven" of *A New Life* (a possibility Malamud would probably see as both silly and significant), he must come to terms with himself before there can be any bread. But the critics were inclined to disagree. They preferred to think of *A New Life* as a totally ironic (and not too terribly successful) piece of academic satire. They were annoyed that the novel ended with Levin forced to give up a college teaching career which had hardly even begun and his fantasies about doing even *more* "good" outside the profession did not help. The crux of the issue is freedom: in his imaginary articles, he muses that "the idea of America will always create freedom"; his fantasies at the john suggest that the betrayal of freedom is the very thing the self-improved man must combat; and finally, he rages to Gilley about Pauline's status as a "free agent." But, for Levin, "freedom" seems to be more entrapping than liberating. As Robert Alter puts it:

> Levin suffers the *schlemiel's* fate—ousted from the profession of his choice, burdened with a family he didn't bargain for and a woman he loves only as a matter of principle, rolling westward in his overheating jalopy toward a horizon full of pitfalls.

Perhaps this reluctance to see Levin leave the profession (as opposed to just Cascadia College) has something to do with the reasons Oregon State keeps asking Malamud back to lecture. For them, the reasons are purely pragmatic. To be sure, when the fictionized version of academic life in Corvalis was first published, it must have been painful reading indeed. However, in time, even *that* can be marketed, and I suspect that Oregon State has made much of the fact that Malamud once taught there. And, too, the mechanics of the situation also work on the most personal of levels. As the hard-boiled Jake Barnes might sneer, it is "pretty to think" that academic life can be better at some other school and Malamud's subsequent career at Bennington seems to suggest that it can. However, all of this says more about Levin's critics than Levin himself. He can accept Gilley's rather absurd condition that he never teach on the college level again because his ambitions are more oriented toward becoming a "savior" than a "professor."

As Levin abruptly exits from the profession, he rushes toward a salvation which, for all practical purposes, looks to be a surefire hell. At one point, Gilley gives Levin a dose of what Saul Bellow might call "reality instruction": "An older woman than yourself and not dependable, plus two adopted kids, no choice of yours, no job or promise of one and assorted headaches. Why take that load on yourself?" (p. 360). The lines might well have been Pinye Salzman's and the story, "The Magic Barrel." Like Salzman, Gilley has a talent for persuasion and his arguments are so sensible that Levin is reduced to the stature of schlemiel, his answer to Gilly's final question ("Because I can, you son of a bitch") suggesting his self-created victimhood. Like Finkle, it is Levin's zeal to affect a moral change, to create "a new life" that has unwittingly willed his destruction. And, like the final scene of "The Magic Barrel," the last lines of *A New Life* are packed with ambiguity.

> Two tin-hatted workmen with chain saws were in the maple tree in front of Humanities Hall, cutting it down limb by leafy limb, to make room for a heat tunnel. On the Student Union side of the street, Gilley was aiming a camera at the operation. When he saw Levin's Hudson approach he swung the camera around and snapped. As they drove by he tore a rectangle of paper from the back of the camera and waved it aloft. "Got your picture!" [Pp. 366–67]

On one hand, there is the terrifying "picture" of Levin's departure—the battered Hudson on the verge of breaking down and the human relationships inside very likely to follow suit— while, on the other hand, there is the "limb by leafy limb" destruction of both Nature and Humanity. Gilley may well have gotten one picture, but it is doubtful if he got the other. After all, "pictures" make up a large part of Gilley's sensibility: one thinks immediately of the "evidence" he collected against Leo Duffy and the stacks of *Life* magazines that make up his research. Perhaps all this concentration on visual media might please McCluhanites, but in the context of the novel Gilley's camera and his pictures suggest an unwillingness to demonstrate either human emotion (Duffy) or moral concern (Levin). His projected Picture Book of American Literature will be as much a failure as the sordid pictures of his personal life. Malamud once remarked that Gilley's last "picture" will leave a permanent impression on his mind "but I suspect it is more consistent to imagine his plotting to replace the *Elements* with his "pictorial history"—a situation that should not be too difficult at Cascadia.

*Notes*

1. J. C. Levinson, "Bellow's Dangling Men," *Critique*, 3 (Summer 1960), 3.
2. Theodore Solotaroff, "Bernard Malamud's Fiction: The Old Life and the New," *Commentary*, 33 (March 1962), 198.
3. Robert Alter, "Malamud as Jewish Writer," *Commentary*, 42 (September 1966), 71. Subsequent references to Mr. Alter are to this article.
4. Marcus Klein, *After Alienation* (New York, 1964), pp. 15–17.
5. All page references are included in the text. I have used the Farrar, Straus and Giroux editions of *The Magic Barrel*, *The Assistant*, *A New Life*, and *The Fixer*.
6. Jonathan Baumbach, *The Landscape of Nightmare* (New York, 1965), p. 111.
7. Mark Goldman, "Bernard Malamud's Comic Vision and the Theme of Identity," *Critique*, 7 (Winter 1964–65), 105. Subsequent references to Mr. Goldman are to this article.
8. Ruth Mandel, "Bernard Malamud's *The Assistant* and *A New Life*: Ironic Affirmation," *Critique*, 7 (Winter 1964–65), 117–18.
9. Alvin Kernan, *The Cankered Muse* (New Haven, 1959), p. 18.

# DAVID MAMET

## 1947–

David Mamet was born in Chicago on November 30, 1947. His family lived in the Jewish community of Chicago's South Side until the late 1950s when his parents were divorced and Mamet moved with his mother to a Chicago suburb. During the late 1960s he was enrolled at Goddard College, an experimental Vermont school. He also studied briefly at the Neighborhood Playhouse School of Theater in New York. After his graduation from Goddard in 1969 Mamet took an assortment of odd jobs, working at a cannery, a brick factory, a real estate agency, and a taxi cab company.

Originally he intended to pursue an acting career, but became interested in writing after composing a number of short skits which his friends used successfully in their classes. In 1973 he helped found the St. Nicholas Theater Company in Chicago and afterwards began an association with another Chicago playhouse, the Goodman Theater. His first plays, *Duck Variations* (1972) and *Sexual Perversity in Chicago* (1974), both enjoyed long runs in New York after initially opening in Chicago. *American Buffalo* (1975) earned Mamet a national reputation and was awarded the 1977 New York Drama Critics Circle Award for best American play. His most acclaimed work to date, *Glengarry Glen Ross* (1983), won both the 1984 New York Drama Critics Circle Award for best play and the 1984 Pulitzer Prize for drama. Critics have praised Mamet's dialogue which features working-class American idioms placed within a sparse linguistic framework. In addition to his theatrical efforts, Mamet also has worked on several movies. His screenplay for the 1982 film *The Verdict* was nominated for an Academy Award.

Mamet lives with his actress wife, Lindsay Crouse, and their daughter on a farm in Vermont. When not writing in his private cabin, he spends much of his time chopping wood and playing poker with friends.

## General

Mamet's biggest commercial success to date—A *Life in the Theater*—is at the same time his least characteristic play. Ordinarily he works from an oblique angle of vision, in flat tones. *Life* is all surface flamboyance, sight gags and gimmickry, lush language and posturing—in short, closer to a Feydeau farce than to the Beckett-like minimalism to which Mamet more typically aspires. The play is a duet between two actors—the older one a stereotypical ham, the younger a stereotypical Actors Studio grunter—and is structured as a series of alternating backstage and onstage "bits." At its best, *Life* is a mildly amusing diversion; at its more frequent worst, it is a tedious, offensively banal caricature of what daily life in the theater is actually like.

The sheer awkwardness of the play surprised me, since Mamet is the most technically proficient of the new writers. In *The Water Engine* he manages skillfully to juxtapose a 1930s radio play about an idealistic young inventor pursued by the evil forces of corporate greed with the insane chatter of a "Century of Progress" tour guide—and, in addition, intercuts ominous injunctions from a chain letter, which the actors take turns in reading out. Where the transitions in *Life* are amateurishly abrupt or nonexistent, in *The Water Engine* Mamet (aided by a brilliant young director, Steven Schachter) interweaves his triangulated tale with such dexterity that we're absorbed into the intricate shifts of time, place, and mood. Initially, that is. Once we catch on to the alternations in rhythm, the play's fascination rapidly evaporates. Schachter's stunning production—especially the marvelous simulation of radio sound effects—keeps us from lapsing into outright boredom. Eventually anger takes over instead—that so much is being put at the service of so little. Mamet has subtitled the play *An American Fable*. Well, yes—if you believe our culture (like our theater) is best seen as an allegory of emptiness.

Something more is going on in *American Buffalo*. Something to do with people. The play has three characters: Don, a man in his late forties who runs a junkshop; his crony, Teach, a middle-aged petty criminal; and Bob, a street punk in his early twenties, who runs indeterminate errands for Don and halfheartedly listens to his homilies about life ("What you got to do is keep clear who your friends are, and who treated you like what"). Like Babe and Innaurato, Mamet is attracted to the lumpen underside of contemporary life. Unlike Babe, he finds no lyrical profundities in it. Unlike Innaurato, he finds no resources for humor in it, grotesque or otherwise. He finds robots. And invents for them a suitable robot language. Sample dialogue:

> *Don*: I got him all spotted.
> *Pause*
> *Teach*: Who?
> *Bob*: Some guy.
> *Teach*: Yeah?
> *Bob*: Yeah.
> *Teach*: Where's he live?
> *Bob*: Around.
> *Teach*: Where? Near here?
> *Bob*: No.

> *Teach*: No?
> *Bob*: He lives on Lake Shore Drive.
> *Teach*: He does.
> *Bob*: Yeah.

They are preparing, you see, to steal a reputedly valuable coin collection. They never do. Why? Apparently—as the dialogue attests—because no one can get up the energy. They prefer to sit around and repeat each other's opaque nonstatements, for diversion occasionally converting declaration ("No") into query ("No?"). They also, now and then, languorously collide. We're never sure about what. And we soon cease to care. Perhaps Mamet had yet another fabulistic moral in mind. I refuse to guess at it. Two can play at his game.

It should be noted, however, that the game is a highly mannered one, full of falsity. If Mamet believes that by flattening his tone to a deadbeat monotony he has captured the authentic low-life rhythm, he should be encouraged to spend more time on the streets. If, as seems more likely, he believes that by emptying language of content and flair he will automatically uncover deeper subtexts, he ought to reread—it is clear he has read them once—the true masters of unspoken resonance, Beckett and Pinter. Silence *can* be eloquent speech, banal words can transmute into subtle metaphor—but only when the surrounding context has been properly prepared. When it has not been, we have self-consciousness and boredom. In both, *American Buffalo* abounds.—MARTIN DUBERMAN, "The Great Gray Way," *Harper's*, May 1978, pp. 86–87

The Theater ⟨. . .⟩ has its First Principles—principles which make our presentations honest, moral (and, coincidentally, moving, funny, and worth the time and money of the audience.)

Most of us are acquainted with these rules, which relegate everything in the production to the *idea* of the play, and cause all elements to adhere to and *express* that idea forcefully, fully, without desire for praise or fear of censure. But, at the first sign of discomfort we assure ourselves that principles of unity, simplicity, and honesty are well and good under normal circumstances, but we surely cannot be meant to apply them under the extraordinary pressures of actually working on a play.

We discard our first principles the moment they cause us unpleasantness—where they might send the author back for another draft, or the piece back for another week or month of rehearsal, or cause the director to work on a scene until it is *finished*, or cause a producer to say, "You know, on reflection this piece is garbage. I think it would be better for all concerned if we didn't put it on."

. . . yes, but we have seats to fill, we have to get on the next act, we have a deadline to meet.

If we act as if the Aristotelian Unities, the philosophy of Stanislavsky, or Brecht, or Shaw, were effete musings, and intended for some ideal theater, and not applicable to our own work, we are declining the responsibility for *creating* that ideal theater.

Every time an actor deviates from the through-line of a piece (that is, the First Principle of the piece) for whatever reason—to gain praise, or out of laziness, or because he hasn't taken the time to discover how that one difficult moment actually *expresses* the through-line—he creates in himself the habit of moral turpitude. And the *play*, which is a strict lesson in ethics, is given the lie.

Every time the author leaves in a piece of non-essential prose (beautiful though it may be) he weakens the structure of the play, and, again, the audience learns *this* lesson: no one is taking responsibility. Theater people are prepared to *espouse* a moral act, but not to *commit* it.

What is communicated to the audience when we deviate from first principles is a lesson in cowardice.

This lesson is of as great a magnitude as our subversion of the constitution by involvement in Vietnam, in Ford's pardon of Nixon, in the persecution of Larry Flynt, in the re-instatement of the death penalty. They are all lessons in cowardice, and each begets cowardice.

Alternatively, the theater affords an opportunity uniquely suited for communicating and inspiring ethical behavior: the audience is given the possibility of seeing live people on stage carrying out an action based on first principles (objectives) to its full conclusion.

The audience participates at a celebration of the idea that Intention A begets Result B. The audience imbibes that lesson as regards the given circumstances of the play, and they *also* receive the lesson as regards the standards of production, writing, acting, design, and direction.

If theatrical workers are seen *not* to have the courage of their convictions (which is to say, the courage to relegate every aspect of production to the laws of theatrical action, economy, and, specifically, the requirements of the super-objective of the play) the audience, once again, learns a lesson in moral cowardice, and we add to the burden of their lives. We add to their loneliness.

Each time we (in all aspects of production) relegate all we do to the necessity of bringing to life simply and completely the intention of the play, we give the audience an experience which enlightens and frees them: the experience of witnessing their fellow human beings saying, "Nothing will sway me, noting will divert me, nothing will dilute my intention of achieving what I have sworn to achieve." (In technical terms, "My Objective," in general terms, my "goal," my "desire," my "responsibility.")

The theatrical repetition of this lesson can and *will* in time, help teach that it is possible and *pleasant* to substitute action for inaction; courage for cowardice; humanity for selfishness.

If we hold to those first principles of action and beauty and economy which we know to be true, and hold to them in all things—choice of plays, actor-training, writing, advertising, promotion—we can *uniquely* speak to our fellow citizens.

In a morally bankrupt time we can help to change the habit of coercive and frightened action and substitute for it the habit of trust, self-reliance, and cooperation.

If we are true to our ideals, we can help to form an ideal society—a society based on and adhering to ethical first principles—not by *preaching* about it, but by *creating* it each night, in front of the audience—by showing how it works. In action.—DAVID MAMET, "First Principles," *Theater*, Summer–Fall 1981, pp. 51–52

## Works

*Sexual Perversity in Chicago* opens with a Pinteresque scene of mutual reinforcement: one character reassures another in the exchange between Bernie and Danny, as to the value and meaning of his recent enterprise:

*Bernie:* So okay, so I'm over at the Commonwealth, in the pancake house off the lobby, and I'm working on a stack of those raisin and nut jobs . . .
*Danny:* They're good.
*Bernie:* . . . and I'm reading the paper, and I'm reading, and I'm casing the pancake house, and the usual shot, am I right?
*Danny:* Right.
*Bernie:* So who walks in over to the cash register but this chick.
*Danny:* Right.
*Bernie:* Nineteen-, twenty-year-old chick . . .
*Danny:* Who we're talking about.
*Bernie:* . . . and she wants a pack of Viceroys.
*Danny:* I can believe that.
*Bernie:* Gets the smokes, and she does this number about how she forgot her purse up in her room.
*Danny:* Up in her room?
*Bernie:* Yeah.
*Danny:* Was she a pro?

The question of whether or not "she" was "a pro" takes pages more to answer, of course. But what is interesting is the way Mamet has organized these most banal of materials into a distinctly American version of Pinter's power plays of language. One character constantly defines himself as dependent, inferior, questioning, eager to learn—even going to the point of asking questions or making repetitions that merely continue the rhythm of the scene, allowing the other character to invent again ("Who we're talking about," "I can believe that"). The entire scene is in itself a handy introduction to Mamet's verbal techniques.

Another favorite Mamet device is introduced by means of a footnote: some dialogue is placed in parentheses, indicating "a slight change of outlook on the part of the speaker—perhaps a momentary change to a more introspective regard"; in all the plays in which this device appears, characters are given the opportunity to question their own motives, to create second levels of self-awareness, while yet holding "the floor." In other words, part of the dramatic opportunity afforded by the famous Pinter pauses, the chance to react or "do a take," is in Mamet given the speaker, and before the speech is concluded—in the process further advancing the invasion by stage direction of the former province of the director.

Mamet's use of humor is often a matter of two hard-edged personalities rubbing mannered toughnesses together. A man trying to pick up a woman in a library is told, "I'm a Lesbian," whereupon, after a slight pause, he asks, "As a physical preference, or from political beliefs?" "Did you miss me?" a girl who has been away with a man for two days asks her roommate: "No. Your plants died," is the reply. The gags, tongue-in-cheek pretensions that the characters can roll with any punch, also give a play like this an internal rhythm, an ability to work towards a blackout line, another scene. Or, reversing the process, a long story—such as the one about King Farouk—may end in a subject-closing banality: "An ancient land." Finally, a discussion in bed between Danny and Deborah, hilariously earthy, can end in a mention of love that rewards candor with another reversal:

*Danny:* . . . I love making love with you.
*Deborah:* I love making love with you. *(Pause.)*
*Danny:* I love you.
*Deborah:* Does it frighten you to say that?
*Danny:* Yes.
*Deborah:* It's only words. I don't think you should be frightened by words.

Particularly in the earlier plays, Mamet's humor has the propulsive energy of rim-shot burlesque jokes.

Yet *Sexual Perversity in Chicago* manages to make its pithy comments about love, "sexual perversity" at best, and do it by means of offbeat dramatic situationing; Joan and Deborah's talk about sex while they are constantly being distracted by the lunch they are enjoying is a case in point. The interplay of four lives ends, predictably, with the two men lying on the beach along the Lake—like Chicago itself—girl-hunting while discussing women around them in purely sexual terms; a lengthy coda somewhat at structural odds with what has gone before, it is also an indication of Mamet's ability to manipulate pacing for achieving an effect of pathos.—JOHN DITSKY, "'He Lets You See the Thought There': The Theatre of David Mamet," *KQ*, Fall 1980, pp. 26–28

Once again, like countless times before, it is the British that rescued our theatrical season. About the best our domestic playwrights could manage is *American Buffalo* by David Mamet, a rather disappointing work from the bright young author of *Sexual Perversity in Chicago* and *Duck Variations*. Here the thirty-one-year-old Mamet gets his first Broadway production, with a full-length play solidly directed by Ulu Grosbard and flawlessly acted by Robert Duvall, Kenneth Macmillan, and John Savage. Jules Fisher has searingly lighted Santo Loquasto's telling junk-shop set: enough extraordinary junk to provide a small museum with a show of both junk sculpture and the art of assemblage. Yet the play never takes us farther than from hither to yon.

The junk-shop owner and two other measly subcriminals are involved in microscopic squabbles and makings-up. The two elder ones plan to rob a coin collection but fail; there is a flare-up of violence in which part of the shop is demolished and the youngest man injured, and then comes some sort of final reconciliation. There may be drug addiction and homosexuality in the background, but this is not made clear. The two main elements are Mamet's apt use of the language of the illiterate or semiliterate, and an evocation of the state of mind of these petty crooks who see themselves as proper businessmen. The latter is supposed to make the play into a grand parable of capitalism and post-Watergate America, but the image is puny, uneventful, and uninvolving, which makes it hard if not impossible to go looking for deeper significance in it. As for the language (e.g., "My shop's fucked up. My whole fucking shop. You fucked my shop up!" "You mad at me?")—well, a good ear is only the foundation of dramaturgy, not its apogee; as for the poetry of scatology and obscenity, it has been of late, like the symbology of Watergate, milked rather dry.

Under close scrutiny, even Mamet's vaunted verbal mastery reveals a certain formulaic quality. "I *am* calm," protests one irate character; "I'm just upset." The same character will exclaim: "The cocksucker should be horse-whipped with a horsewhip!" Or he will explain his technique of breaking in: "If worst comes to worst, you kick in a fucking back door. What do you think this is—the Middle Ages?" Obvious redundancy and equally obvious unawareness that one means the opposite of what one said finally reduce themselves to mechanical devices that usurp other forms of character portrayal. Yet the critics were, for the most part, ecstatic: At last a playwright who uses plain language poetically, they all said, though some also complained of a lack of action. I think that when language is used truly poetically it becomes a legitimate kind of action; the sense of inaction here is proof that the language of *American Buffalo* is not all that poetic. Moreover, though I believe that gutter poetry is possible, it can't be something that fails to move us intellectually and emotionally, which I take to be the irreducible minimum of art. Instead of

moving in either sense of the word, the play just marks time with dumb, nasty, mildly funny verbalizations and petty gripes or flare-ups; gradually, it retreats deeper and deeper under the cover of a sheltering affectlessness.—JOHN SIMON, "Theater Chronicle," *HdR*, Summer 1977, pp. 259–60

The constancy of David Mamet's magnificently tuned ear for dialogue was evident in two short plays produced at the Yale Repertory Theatre. The first piece, *Dark Pony*, was no more than a curtain raiser. Fragile in its emotional nuances, *Dark Pony* gradually became a reassuring metaphor for life in the modern world.

Mamet's dialogue sounded like the comfortable, everyday chatter of a father and daughter, seated in the front seat of the family automobile, driving home on an often repeated trip. To pass time, the Father tells the story of the courageous Indian brave, Rain Boy, and his constant savior from harm, Dark Pony. The Daughter derives comfort from the story's familiarity, from the reassuring sound of her father's voice, and from the familiar road sounds which indicate that the car and its occupants are getting closer to the protection of home. Shortly after the climax of the story, when Rain Boy is saved from red-eyed, hungry wolves by the slashing hooves of Dark Pony, the Daughter says, complacently, "We're almost home."

The car in which the pair rides becomes a kind of mobile cocoon, carrying them through strange territories to the protection of home. The familiarity of the story, its predictable details and episodes, and its duration further insulates the pair from the world outside. The miraculous appearance of Dark Pony and the animal's protective ministrations to the adventurous Indian brave form a comforting myth for a threatening world.

The simplicity of this curtain-raiser was underscored by the staging at the Yale Rep. Downstage center was the car's bench seat. On either side of the stage were telephone poles, and the periphery of the stage was dark. The Father made the motions of driving. The Daughter sat with a blanket in her lap and a stuffed bunny in her hands. Complementing the simplicity of the staging and the truthful ring of the dialogue was the honesty of the playing of the two actors, Lindsay Crouse and Michael Higgins.

The second play, titled *Reunion*, was longer and more dynamic emotionally. A father, Bernie, waits for and then greets his daughter, Carol, whom he hasn't seen in 20 years. Tensions ebb and flow as two strangers search for points of emotional contact, each compelled to bare a few, small truths about their disparate and painfully lonely lives.

As with *Dark Pony*, not a great deal happens in *Reunion* beyond the definition and exploration of two very real characters. *Reunion*, although without metaphor, also explores loneliness, in this case arising from attachments broken by divorce. Carol says, "I come from a broken home, the most important institution in America." Inadvertently, she describes what "home" has become for many, and *Reunion* sympathetically explores some of the emotional consequences which result.

A spare set, consisting of the shabby table and chairs and the sink of Bernie's kitchen, lit starkly and without artifice, and the assured playing of the same two actors who appeared in *Dark Pony* were abetted by Walt Jones's direction. Jones has directed many of Yale's recent premieres sensitively and effectively. In *Reunion*, he let the actors develop their characterizations in an understated way and allowed them to take time to respond emotionally to the rambling conversation.—JOAN FLECKENSTEIN, *ETJ*, Oct. 1978, pp. 417–18

*The Water Engine* was originally written for radio, and for me it works best as a radio play. Mamet has defended the early stage productions as having resulted in "a third reality, a scenic truth, which dealt with radio not as an electronic convenience, but as an expression of our need to create and to communicate and to explain . . ." (note in Grove Press edition). But an intelligent listener of the radio performance is quick to see Mamet's point, while a viewer of the play keeps expecting the interplay between the two media to add up to something, when, in fact, it never does. On stage, the machinery of the play—the special-effects contraptions, the battery of microphones—threatens to distract attention from the meretricious verisimilitude of the action and to fix it on the mechanics of the production itself. It is in the transparency of that meretriciousness and in its ironic verisimilitude that the point of the play lies, however, and so neither should be obscured.

"Now we are characters within a dream of industry," intones a voice portentously between two scenes, "Within a dream of toil." The dream that drives *The Water Engine* is that of industrious Charles Lang, humble punchpress operator for Dietz and Federle and inventor of a machine that uses water as its only fuel. He wishes to patent and market his engine as a contribution to the millennium that Science is ushering in ("Things can work out if we will persevere"). The time is 1934, the place is Chicago, where the World's Fair ("The Century of Progress") is entering upon its second year, and the genre in which Lang's story is cast is busy radio melodrama. Big Business makes an early appearance, resolved to seize control of the machine; Lang is once saved from its clutches by the neighborhood candy-store owner and his young son Bernie (himself, of course, "another Steinmetz"); the scenes are frequently bridged by a voice describing the wonder-working providence behind a ubiquitous chain-letter ("Pass this letter on to three friends. Happiness and health will be yours"); the assurances of that voice ("All people are connected") ultimately persuade Lang to mail his blueprints to Bernie, thereby entrusting his dream to posterity. But all of this constitutes a fiction that is neither seamless nor chastely naïve; and the rents and stains in its fabric give us glimpses of a patently unmelodramatic world. Lang's hands are not as clean as they should be: like any Brecht hero at odds with the system, he has had, as a little man, to poach on that system, and his doing so leaves him open to attack ("I'd be arrested somewhere, wouldn't I?" he asks his persecutors. "For some two-dollar wrench I took from Dietz"). The "trust" that the chain-letter voice extols can be practiced by neither the kindly candy-store owner—who has always an eye on his cash-register—nor the chain-letter voice itself ("Make sure you send the letter on to someone who you trust will send the letter on. Do not send cash"). The newspaperman to whom Lang turns for help is hardly the stereotypical crusader: he seems more interested in arranging dates with his secretary and in padding out his puffs of American integrity ("Thank god I don't have to sign it") than in coming to the rescue of a crank. And justice is never served. Although the plans for the engine end up safely in Bernie's hands, Lang himself is killed. His murder is given ironically laconic coverage by the reporter to whom he had made his appeal; it in turn gives a grimly comic resonance to the final scene of the play, when the candy-store owner opens his newspaper, registers great shock, then awestruck, announces to Bernie that a "Free day" will be held at the Fair.

But it would be wrong to call *The Water Engine* merely an exercise in parody. Mamet is not only exposing the inadequacies and evasions of his form: he is suggesting why it found—and still finds—its hold. The representatives of the business interests in the play act and talk as Business acts and talks ("Quite simply, Mr. Lang, my people want the engine.

Will you entertain an offer for the right to patent the machine?"). The Forces of Evil are, in short, real. Real, too, is the source of their strength: a rhetoric that shamelessly legitimizes chicanery. Such legitimization breeds, as in *American Buffalo*, corruption at the heart of things, both verbal and political; it spawns a system in which business is mere thievery methodized. Thus the candy-store owner's close watch on his cash-drawer; thus Bernie's naïve admiration for the locomotive designer who, with a tap of a hammer, starts up a stalled engine, then shrewdly demands from the president of the railroad fifteen thousand dollars for *"knowing where to tap."* The corruption meets genuine ideological resistance in the play neither from Bernie nor from Lang—their technological-utopian idealism is itself the bad fruit of rhetoric—but from the reporter Dave Murray, contemptuous of the official pieties he deploys in filling up his daily column. Of course, as resistance, contempt is feeble. And we leave the play less impressed with the attitude than with the pervasiveness of the opposition.
—ROBERT STOREY, "The Making of David Mamet," *HC*, Oct. 1979, pp. 7–8

The most successful off-Broadway play of the first half of the season would seem to be David Mamet's *A Life in the Theater*. What hides behind the Stanislavskian title is a series of vignettes, showing the Falstaff-Hal type of relationship between a grand old ham of an actor now in his decline, and an ambitious young actor who, even while deferring and learning from him, is in the process of overtaking him and taking over. The action moves around various parts of a theater: the dressing rooms, the wings, the empty stage, even the stage with scenes from imaginary plays in progress and with sundry dirty tricks and mishaps punctuating the proceedings. What we get, in other words, is a compendium of theatrical lore, anecdotes, and back- (or front-) biting, all reduced to a series of duologues—or, if you prefer, Aretino's *Ragionamenti* translated from a literal brothel to a figurative one. For Mamet's view of the theater is here very much a worm's-eye view—even the mock plays are conceived as parodies of genres that have fallen into desuetude, which is somewhat like poking petty fun at David Belasco or R. C. Sherriff at this late date.

Certainly, some of Mamet's dialogue adroitly balances truth and mischievous distortion. At one point, the aging actor will say: "In our scene tonight, could you perhaps do less?" At another point, the younger one, catching his colleague staring at his reflection in the glass, says encouragingly: "Keep your back straight, John, the mirror is your friend—for a few years more." But, ultimately, two problems weigh down *A Life in the Theater*. One is that these are all anecdotes, quips, rivalries that can be hung on any theatrical stick figures, which is, in fact, what John and Robert are. Under the all too typical mockery, there are no human beings. True, this is intended as caricature, but even caricatures are first of somebody specific, and then invitations to laughter at the basic grotesquerie of faces. It is all very well for a character to be, say, *the* climbing young actor, provided he is also *a* climbing young actor, with some part of him ungeneralizable.

Secondly, I get tired of Mamet's eternal duologues. However many characters there may be in a Mamet play (and there never seem to be more than four), just about every scene is a twosome. It is as if a composer wrote nothing but duos for two instruments, which, however good, would finally make us cry out for fuller orchestrations. Gerald Gutierrez has directed competently, there is suggestive but unfussy scenery from John Lee Beatty (perhaps our leading minimalist set designer), and Robert Waldman's incidental music is helpful. Aside from a stage manager who says nothing, the cast consists of Peter Evans's well conceived, patently vacuous and sycophantic yet ambition-ridden Robert; and of Ellis Rabb's John, all ham and pineapple—or, at any rate, fruit. I am not sure whether this performance could not, with a little more restraint, have gained in pathos, which would have added a welcome further dimension.—JOHN SIMON, "Theater Chronicle," *HdR*, Spring 1978, pp. 154–55

*The Woods* is about a young man and woman who are in love. They have repaired to a quiet place in the country where the young man, Nick, spent a good part of his boyhood years with his now deceased parents. In their isolation and in the pauses between their bouts of lovemaking, Nick's character and that of Ruth, his companion, emerge. She is healthy, eager for experience, and far more intelligent or, at least, balanced than he. He is inarticulately troubled; he cannot locate the cause of his inner disturbances. His disaffection probably has to do with his childhood, but everything, it would seem, has to do with one's childhood. The easiest tag to apply to him is "neurotic," but what exactly does that mean?

He is abusive and apologetic—how tiresome his constant "I'm sorrys." He wants to be alone, he wants her to go away, he wants her to stay. His lovemaking is a kind of nervous impatience with himself. He requires solace from the nameless and wracking upset of his spirit. His confusion is disruptive of the relationship which he nevertheless pleads to preserve. Ruth, always more lucid, wants to break with him, but she recognizes in him a lost child adrift, and yields to her pity for him.

It is all literally "true to life"—which is exactly what troubles me. Innumerable love affairs everywhere may be similarly graphed, even to the point of the nervously inconsequential fragments of speech with which the lovers communicate. The play implies that, especially in the matter of love, we are all in the "woods." The phenomena of nature itself surround and wrap us in an impenetrable dark mystery, unresponsive to reasoned explanation.

This sentiment in itself may be banal, but that does not preclude its serving as material, even the essence, of sound drama. How many vital truths about life are there anyway? But the "realism" here dispels the larger dimension sought for. In language and behavior the characters are too concrete and superficially recognizable to take wing. We fail to learn anything beyond their immediate and unexceptional situation. They are not transfigured by any special insight, psychological or intuitive. The obvious symbolism—the maze of the lonely wooded landscape in which we find them—evokes nothing, and the realism is so commonplace that it makes the symbolism appear terribly "young."—HAROLD CLURMAN, "Theater," *Nation*, May 19, 1979, pp. 581–82

Ah, but Mamet, bless him, has written a play without a single soft spot, which once again allows you to believe that American playwriting, at its best, can hold its place with the finest in the world. Mamet's ear is uncanny. Nobody today has a more flawless gift for reproducing overheard colloquial speech. But Paddy Chayefsky had this too (so, indeed, does a tape recorder); what distinguishes Mamet's dialogue is the purpose to which it is put. Without a single tendentious line, without any polemical intention, without a trace of pity or sentiment, Mamet has launched an assault on the American way of making a living which is at the same time savage and compassionate, powerful and implicit, radical and stoical.

The first act of *Glengarry Glen Ross* consists of three short scenes in a seedy Chinese restaurant. The first of these—between the salesman, Shelley Levine, and the office manager, John Williamson—is materially similar to, yet significantly different from, the vaguely agitprop climactic scene in Miller's play where Willy gets fired by his boss, Howard. Levine is

aging, flagging, on his way out. What he needs from the bloodless Williamson is access to the prime leads so he can recover his past affluence and self-esteem. Williamson, his face cold with distaste, agrees to give him the leads providing Levine return 20 percent of his commission and $50 a lead, with $100 down. Levine accepts the deal but doesn't have the down payment. In a similar condition of helplessness, Willy Loman moaned "You can't eat an orange and throw the peel away"; Levine responds by pouring a flood of contemptuous invective on the head of his hated tormentor.

The second scene features another orange refusing the rubbish heap. Dave Moss, a bald dynamo, is discussing with another salesman, George Aaronow, the possibility of stealing the leads and selling them to a competitor—"Someone should rob the office . . . trash the joint, it looks like robbery." George half-listens until he realizes that Dave expects him to do the job. He is implicated now, an accessory before the fact. When George asks why he is doing this to him, Dave answers: "It's none of your fucking business," and then "Because you listened." In the third scene, the salesman Richard Roma lines up a potential mark, James Lingk, by engaging him in sexual small talk, then hauls out a brochure for Glengarry Highlands, a tract of land in Florida. This apparently insignificant action ends the act.

Written like obscene vaudeville riffs, these small Mamet mosaics become the basis for a large, ambitious narrative in which the pursuit of the leads assumes the magnitude of a quest for the Holy Grail. The second act setting is the real estate office. It has been thoroughly trashed; the leads have been stolen; a police detective is questioning the suspect salesmen. Both Levine and Roma have closed big deals, and they are exultant. But before the day is over, both men will lose their advantage. Levine's customers prove to be incorrigible eccentrics who sign worthless checks. And Roma's mark, Lingk, has come to cancel the sale by order of his wife who controls the checking account. Through a masquerade so inventive it almost establishes Roma as a Zen master in the art of conmanship, he manages to stall Lingk long enough to make cancellation impossible—only to have his con queered by the malignant Williamson. In the mayhem that follows, the true thief is exposed and apprehended (Mamet's only implausible plot tist), while Williamson regains his dominance over the beleaguered salesmen.

Those salesmen, however, for all their ruthlessness and competitiveness, have meanwhile managed to assume a kind of unexpected camaraderie, largely in opposition to such "fucking white bread" as Williamson. Except for him, Roma tells us, "Everyone in this office lives on his wits." But the race is becoming extinct. "It's not a world of men," reflects Shelley, "it's a world of bureaucrats, clock watchers, office holders—we're a dying breed." Dying they may be, but for Mamet this sleazy, smarmy race of losers still has a volatile energy, even an elegiac aura of heroism. The powerful tensions he has uncovered between the ethnic underclass and the WASP functionaries who administer its employment opportunities pick the scabs off a lot of ancient half-healed wounds.

The production comes from the Goodman Theater in Chicago and it is excellent. Gregory Mosher, Goodman's artistic director, has capitalized on his association with Mamet to create a forward momentum which is relentless, while deepening each of the performances. Robert Prosky as Levine maintains a manly resolve and courage in the midst of squeezed gray defeat; Joe Mantegna's Roma, with his patent leather hair, gold cufflinks, and pinkie ring, embodies the splendid vulgarity of a merchant of manipulation; James Tolkan is wired and taut as Moss; Mike Nussbaum plays

Aaronow like a forlorn beagle, his sad eyelids drooping over his perpetually woeful countenance; and J. T. Walsh is steely as the cold, handsome bureaucrat, Williamson, whose only physical defect is a spreading bureaucrat's bottom. Michael Merritt's sets are brilliantly rendered disaster areas, especially the cinder block office, and Nan Cibula's costumes provide an authentic polyester look for men with a weakness for terrible clothes.

Like *American Buffalo*, *Glengarry Glen Ross* is to my mind a genuine Mamet masterpiece, a play so precise in its realism that it transcends itself and takes on reverberant ethical meanings. It is biting, pungent, harrowing, and funny, showing life stripped of all idealistic pretenses and liberal pieties—a jungle populated with beasts of prey who nevertheless possess the single redeeming quality of friendship. It is a play that returns tragic joy to the theater—the kind of understanding O'Neill gave us in his last plays, facing painful truths with courage and thereby leavening profound pessimism with profound exhilaration. It is a play that shares the secret implicit in all fine works of dramatic art—that such truths are much more potent shown than told.—ROBERT BRUSTEIN, "Show and Tell," NR, May 7, 1984, pp. 28–29

### JACK V. BARBERA

#### From "Ethical Perversity in America: Some Observations on David Mamet's *American Buffalo*"

*Modern Drama*, September 1981, pp. 270–75

The setting of *American Buffalo* is Chicago, but in the text of the play the scene specified is "*Don's Resale Shop. A junkshop*," and the city is not mentioned.[1] There are telltale signs of locale however. The traveler from New York to Chicago still encounters verbal differences: "soda" becomes "pop," for example, and "bun" becomes "sweet roll." So a Manhattan audience attending *American Buffalo* knows Teach is not from the Big Apple when he vividly complains: "But to have that shithead turn, in one breath, every fucking sweet roll that I ever ate with them into *ground glass* . . . this hurts me, Don" (p. 11). And a Chicago audience, when it hears a passing reference to "Lake Shore Drive" (p. 40), knows the setting is, as it were, the neighborhood. A sophisticated Chicago audience also recognizes the allusion in the following bit of dialogue:

> *Teach*: (. . . *indicating objects on the counter*)
>       What're *these*?
> *Don*: Those?
> *Teach*: Yeah.
> *Don*: They're from 1933.
> *Teach*: From the thing?
> *Don*: Yeah.
>                 *Pause*
> *Teach*: They got that much of it around?
> *Don*: *Shit* yes. (It's not that long ago.) The thing, it ran two years, and they had (*I don't know*) all kinds of people every year they're buying everything that they can lay their hands on that they're going to take it back to Buffalo to give it, you know, to their aunt, and it mounts up. (pp. 17–18)

The "thing" that ran two years was the 1933 World's Fair held in Chicago in celebration of the city's 100th anniversary. Although it took place during the Great Depression, the Century of Progress Exposition was so popular it was held over for another year and attracted 100 million people.

Aside from the few specifically Chicago allusions in *American Buffalo*, Don's Resale Shop could be located in any number of large American cities. What is important is not

Chicago, but a particular kind of urban American subculture—urban because one does not imagine a character like Teach, his staccato manner, in rural Kansas, say, or Mississippi. And one is more likely to imagine a junkie like Bobby in an urban setting. But it is the characters' street language which is worth examining for a moment, because it has stirred controversy among the critics. Gordon Rogoff concluded that, "With friends like . . . [Mamet] words don't need enemies," and Brendan Gill wrote of the play's "tiresome small talk," which attempts "in vain to perform the office of eloquence. . . ." Jack Kroll, however, praised the "kind of verbal cubism" in which Mamet's characters speak, saying the playwright "is someone listen to . . . an American playwright who's a language playwright" and who is "the first playwright to create a formal and moral shape out of the undeleted expletives of our foulmouthed time."[2]

I find myself in tune with Kroll. In any assessment of *American Buffalo* Mamet's use of language must be regarded as an achievement. If the vocabulary of men such as Bobby, Teach and Donny is impoverished, Mamet's rendering of it reminds us that vocabulary is only one of the resources of language. Teach does have an eloquence when expressing his sense that he has been abused. Galled by Grace and Ruthie, he tells Don:

> Only (and I tell you this, Don). Only, and I'm not, I don't think, casting anything on anyone: from the mouth of a Southern bulldyke asshole ingrate of a vicious nowhere cunt can this trash come. (pp. 10–11)

This sentence, so politely diffident at first, lets fall its invective in a rain of hammering trochees. It is marvelous invective, more vivid than that in James Stephens's "A Glass of Beer," and ironic to boot, for in the most vulgar language Teach has denounced as "trash" Grace's sarcastic remark, "'Help yourself.'" Teach is constantly undercutting himself this way, as when he says, again referring to Grace and Ruthie, "The only way to teach these people is to kill them" (p. 11). In Act 2, Don does not want him to take a gun on a robbery, and Teach replies that of course the gun is not needed:

> Only that it makes me comfortable, okay? It helps me to relax. So, God forbid something inevitable occurs. . . . (p. 84)

The urban nature of the language in *American Buffalo* is a matter not just of its street vulgarity, or expressions such as "skin-pop" (p. 34) and "He takes me off my coin . . ." (p. 31), but also of an abbreviation characteristic of urban pace. One of my Mississippi students told me she had a job in Manhattan which required her to answer the telephone saying, "Hello, this is so-and-so of the such-and-such company." A typical caller responded, "I like your accent honey, but could you speed it up?" Teach telescopes "probably" into "Prolly" (p. 17), and utters such staccato sentences as: "He don't got the address the guy?" (p. 82), and, "I'm not the *hotel*, I stepped out for coffee, I'll be back one minute" (p. 54—in context one understands this as a conditional sentence: "[If] I'm not . . . [it means] I stepped . . ."). Such elliptic expression is a matter not of Mamet's invention, but of his ear for how some of us speak these days. On the Dick Cavett ETV show (Mamet appeared on November 29, 1979 and January 16, 1980), Mamet mentioned entering an elevator and hearing a woman say, "Lovely weather, aren't we?"

Besides the play's language, a second critical issue which has resulted in opposing assessments of *American Buffalo* is that of its content, or lack of it. Gill complained, in the review I have already mentioned, that the play provides the meager and familiar message "that life, rotten as it is, is all we have"

(p. 54). And in a review in *America*, Catharine Hughes found that what happens in the play "too often seems much ado about very little."³ Before I proceed with a defense of *American Buffalo* as being of intellectual interest, and as going beyond the "message" Gill found in it, a capsule of the plot seems in order.

In his late forties, Don Dubrow is conversing with the much younger Bob about a man Bob is supposed to watch. Four major motifs emerge from their conversation: friendship, looking out for oneself, business, and being knowledgeable. Teach enters Don's junkshop and, while Bob is getting coffee, learns of Don's plan to rob the man Bob has been watching. After the man spotted a buffalo-head nickel in Don's shop and purchased it for ninety dollars, Don concluded it must be worth much more and that the man must have another valuable coins. Teach talks Don into cutting him in on the robbery, and convinces him Bobby is too young and, as a junkie, too unreliable to be part of it. That night the plan goes awry and Teach, in anger and frustration, *"hits BOB viciously on the side of the head"* (p. 94). This unjust attack stirs Don against Teach, and restores the solicitude toward Bobby we noticed in Don at the start of the play. Even in this low-life ambiance, in effect, there is some decency. Though all three characters are losers, the friendship between Don and Bobby is something of worth.

It is in the relationships, tensions and contradictions in the patter of Don and Teach, concerning the motifs I mentioned, that the "content" of this play resides. Take the motif of business. Don tells Bobby that in business deals intentions are not good enough: "Action talks and bullshit walks" (p. 4). And a bit later he defines business as "common sense, experience, and talent" (p. 6). This soon turns into, "People taking *care* of themselves" (p. 7). But if business is looking out for oneself, what is the relation between business and friendship? In passing, Don and Bobby have been discussing a business deal between Fletch and Ruthie. It seems that Fletch purchased some pig iron from Ruthie and made such a profit on it that Ruthie felt cheated. Was it unfair of Fletch to profit so much from a friend? Don, who defends Fletch, saying, "That's what business *is*," and "there's business and there's friendship, Bobby . . .", goes on to say, "what you got to do is keep clear who your friends are, and who treated you like what" (p. 7). But that is clearly what Ruthie has done, and that is why she is angry with Fletch and feels he stole from her.⁴ Later we learn that when Don imagines the nickel he sold for ninety dollars must be worth much more, he feels *he* was robbed—so much for "That's what business *is*." Contradictions and elaborations on "business" continue through the play. A funny definition of free enterprise will stand as a last example:

Teach: You know what is free enterprise?
Don: No. What?
Teach: The freedom . . .
Don: . . . yeah?
Teach: Of the *Individual* . . .
Don: . . . yeah?
Teach: To Embark on Any Fucking Course that he sees fit.
Don: Uh-huh . . .
Teach: In order to secure his honest chance to make a profit. Am I so out of line on this?
Don: No. . . .
Teach: The country's *founded* on this, Don. You know this. (pp. 72–73)

Of course the individuals in this case see fit to embark on robbery. Part of Mamet's intent in *American Buffalo* is to expose the shoddiness of the American business ethic by having

his low-lives transparently voice it. He said as much in an interview with Richard Gottlieb:

"The play is about the American ethic of business," he said. "About how we excuse all sorts of great and small betrayals and ethical compromises called business. . . . There's really no difference between the *lumpenproletariat* and stockbrokers or corporate lawyers who are the lackeys of business," Mr. Mamet went on. "Part of the American myth is that a difference exists, that at a certain point vicious behavior becomes laudable."⁵

Mamet got the idea of an identical ethical perversity existing at both ends of the urban economic spectrum from Thorstein Veblen (1857–1929)—the American sociologist, economist, satirist, and sometime Chicagoan.⁶ In considering the relation between Veblen's thought and *American Buffalo*, one should start with Veblen's *Theory of the Leisure Class* (1899). His theory of the leisure class is related to his theory of business enterprise in that Veblen saw businessmen as involved with the pecuniary and predatory interests of ownership, rather than with the industrial and social interests of production. Teach is a good example of a Veblen "lower-class delinquent," and Veblen's ideas of emulation, and of the snob appeal of what is obsolete, are relevant to the play—the latter, especially, as it applies to collecting rare coins and World's Fair memorabilia.

That Mamet is justified in expecting an audience to accept his play's small-time criminals as representative of American businessmen is arguable. One way of understanding the play's title mainly applies to them as members of a marginal class of society. In a review of the play for the *Nation*, Harold Clurman wrote: "Look at the face of the coin, as reproduced on the show's playbill. The buffalo looks stunned, baffled, dejected, ready for slaughter. The animal is antiquated, and the would-be robbers are a mess. The combination is symbolic."⁷ Don and Teach and Bobby are as antiquated and out-of-it as the American buffalo or bison (successful American businessmen may or may not be ethical, but they are not marginal). We must admit that Don and Teach and Bobby are dumb. They are not even streetwise, though Don and Teach may think they are. Fletch probably is streetwise—consider the pig-iron deal, or the fact that he won at cards in the game in which Don and Teach lost. They admire and resent his success, and feel they have been cheated. They are envious of anyone who is knowledgeable and successful, such as the man who purchased the coin. Knowledge, an important motif in the play, is the key here. "One thing. Makes all the difference in the world," says Teach. And when Don asks, "What?", he replies, "Knowing what the fuck you're talking about. And it's so rare, Don. So rare" (p. 48). Of course Teach does not know what he is talking about, as we learn in the routines about which coins are valuable, where the man would keep his coins, how to get into his house, and what to do about a safe (pp. 45–50, 77–79).

This contradiction leads us to the other way of understanding the title, a way which applies to the characters as representatives of the business class as well as representatives of a class of urban marginal crooks. For "buffalo" read the slang verb "to intimidate." It is because he does not know anything that Teach must try to buffalo Don. And it is common for businessmen to buffalo the public: "The windfall profits tax will dry up America's oil," and "If you don't buy this laxative no one will love you." Fletch evidently can buffalo successfully; Standard Oil can; Teach cannot (aside from Don, who buys his line, "Send Bobby in and you'll wind up with a broken toaster"). But to buffalo is as American as to bake an apple pie. Notions of the American way—democracy and free enterprise—become corrupted when they enter the look-out-for-number-one rationalizations of crooks and unethical businessmen. Down-and-outs in a democracy may feel they have been cheated because "all men should be equal." Knowledge creates divisions among people, divisions of power and wealth, but such divisions can seem undemocratic, un-American. So robbing and cheating are attempts to restore justice. Or, "In America one is free to make a fortune for himself" turn into Teach's definition of free enterprise. My modest conclusion is that in satirizing such corrupt notions Mamet *has* written a play of intellectual content.

### Notes

1. David Mamet, *American Buffalo* (New York, 1977), unnumbered preliminary page. Subsequent quotations from the play are cited parenthetically in the text.
2. See Gordon Rogoff, "Theater: Albee and Mamet: The War of the Words," *Saturday Review*, 2 April 1977, p. 37; Brendan Gill, "No News from Lake Michigan," *The New Yorker*, 28 February 1977, p. 54; and Jack Kroll, "The Muzak Man," *Newsweek*, 28 February 1977, p. 79.
3. Catharine Hughes, review in *America*, 136 (1977), 364.
4. Don says Fletch bought the pig iron from Ruthie, but when Bob says Ruthie was mad because Fletch stole her pig iron he could be speaking literally. Later in the play Teach also says Fletch "stole some pig iron off Ruth," and Don replies, "I *heard* that . . ." (p. 75). Of course this does not *prove* Fletch stole the pig iron, but it does illustrate the teacher-student role-reversal Don undergoes when talking to Bob and Teach. Teach says in a matter-of-fact way that the man who purchased the nickel from Don "stole" it (p. 49). So much for his protestations about facts (p. 75)!
5. Richard Gottlieb, "The 'Engine' That Drives David Mamet," *New York Times*, 15 January 1978, Sec. 2, p. 4, col. 1–2.
6. Mamet referred to Veblen as his source in a letter to me, 6 June 1980.
7. Harold Clurman, "Theater," *Nation*, 12 March 1977, p. 313.

# WILLIAM MARCH
## W. E. M. Campbell

### 1893–1954

William Edward March Campbell was born in Mobile, Alabama, on September 18, 1893, and grew up in the poor sawmill country of western Florida and southern Alabama. At age fourteen he began working for a lumber company in Mobile, but longed to continue his education. He saved enough money to study at Valparaiso University in Indiana for one year. His money ran out in the summer of 1914 and he returned to Mobile where the following fall he entered the law school of the University of Alabama. By 1916 his savings had again been depleted and this time he ventured to New York where he worked as a law clerk. When America declared war on Germany March enlisted in the U.S. Marine Corps. During his tour on the front line in France he was wounded by flying shrapnel and was decorated several times for bravery. Although March escaped with few injuries, the horrors of war and his killing of a young German soldier in hand-to-hand combat left lasting impressions.

March returned to the U.S. a hero and joined the Waterman Steamship Corporation in Mobile. He quickly became Vice President in 1931. By this time he had published his first short story, "The Holly Wreath" (1929), in *Forum* magazine. Drawing from his war experiences March wrote his first novel, *Company K* (1933), which through the voices of 113 separate soldiers relates the brutality of combat. Deemed the "*Spoon River Anthology* of the trenches," this popular work was published just prior to March's departure for Europe. He managed offices in Hamburg and later in London for Waterman from 1932 to 1937. He returned to New York and resigned his executive post, taking with him a large amount of Waterman stock. In 1943 he published one of his best novels, *The Looking Glass*. March's ability to combine satire with symbolism and social commentary made this psychological study a success.

In 1947 March suffered an emotional breakdown. At first he thought he would never write again, but after leaving his New York apartment and settling in New Orleans he began to write again. His final works, *October Island* (1952) and *The Bad Seed* (1954), are among his best. *The Bad Seed* even made the best-seller list, the first in March's career. During his later years he befriended Manhattan art dealer Klaus Perls and March amassed one of the best private collections of modern French art in the U.S. Although contemporary critics compared his writing to Faulkner's, his reputation has suffered since his death on May 15, 1954.

Mr. March's Reedyville might very well be the same town as Mr. Faulkner's Jefferson. The same things happen and the same people live there. But March's idea is to catch on the wing some fleeting whiff of the essence distilled from the town and quickly set down on paper a brief record inspired by its impermanent and volatile fragrance—in the way that a poet conceives and writes a lyric. And his prose poems are well wrought.

March started out as a kind of Spoon River Anthologist of the war in his *Company K*; and even in his long novel, *Come In at the Door*, he harked back to his original method. His short stories in this very much worth-while collection ⟨*The Little Wife and Other Stories*⟩ are, although longer than the epitaphs and descriptions of the hundred-odd men of *Company K*, for the most part of the same order. His special gift as a storyteller is his faculty of catching on the wing some bit of penetration into human life, and creating about it a slight tale, a short narrative, an episode, a piece of realistic description, by way of elucidation.

These are superior stories; lacking the sensational qualities necessary for a journalistic success, they are sound to the core. Slight, they are not negligible. No one of them attains to major distinction; but all together they show the fine talent of an American artist who will go further. They prove that the brilliant *Company K* was no mere flash in the pan.

There are fourteen stories. "The Little Wife," which heads the volume, has achieved a place in anthologies and been commented on before. To the reviewer, it is the only story in the collection which is not quite convincing; and he would be willing to wager that Mr. March himself does not consider it his best tale. The idea is sound; and the conception is unusual and at the same time universal. The young man's wife has gone home to her parents in anticipation of the birth of their first child. He has arranged to get away from his job and be with her when the time comes. But he gets a telegram from her parents, a month ahead of time, to come at once. And on the train a second telegram is delivered to him. In terror he refuses to read it or to think about it. And on the long ride he engages several of the passengers in conversation, dilating on his new happiness in the birth of a fine son, boring every one with his detailed descriptions of his and Bessie's courtship and marriage, especially all the funny things that happened to them. The meaning is, of course, that he wants to keep her alive as long as possible, to deny the reality which he knows he is going to have to face. I do not believe it; I do not believe he would have torn up the second telegram without reading it.

But the Reedyville stories strike true at every swing. In "Mist on the Meadow," involving a simple hill-billy farmer who has lusty pride in his pigs and in his boy Tolly, "the beatenest" child ever, although Exa, his wife, slightly more worldly, is, though she loves her little idiot boy, ashamed of him before Preacher Hightower—in this tale of the country back of Reedyville you have a theme which is both familiar and fresh, and true all the way through. Brother Hightower performs the miracle of the Gadarene swine.

The soul of the little boy, heretofore happy while wallowing with the pigs when his mother did not chain him up, is reached by the preacher's verbosity and eloquence; the child breaks down and becomes human in childish tears and terror. "Po' little boy!" says the father. "If ere a man can show me where you're better off without your devils, I'll give that man a pretty."

"The Arrogant Shoat" is the life story of Rancey Catonhead. Rancey was just a young girl when she went to stay for a spell with her Aunt Lucy in Reedyville. But that visit was the climax of her life. At Aunt Lucy's and Uncle Henry's they had all sorts of fascinating, refined and genteel things. And Reedyville was a metropolis of never-ending fascination. There was a circus poster of a young woman in tights and spangles with her trained shoat, "The World's Most Intelligent Pig." And Rancey became fascinated by it. "I bet I could train a pig, too, iffen I put my mind to it, and iffen I had ere a pig to train," she thought. And to humor her, as a joke, Uncle Henry picked up a baby porker and made her a present of it. Rancey went home shortly afterward, taking her pig. The beast came to be as devoted and affectionate as a dog. And Rancey taught it to stand on its hind legs and do a waltz. She dreamed of a career in the circus, but Lem came along and Rancey forgot her ideal. She sold the pig to the butcher to get a wedding dress. She married and had many children. But, in the end, an old woman, dying with cancer and sustained by opiates, she came to declare: "I wish now I'd a-taken my shoat and run off to a circus, like I started to."

Two stories, "To the Rear" and "The American Diseur," are war stories of A. E. F., France and the front that, although longer, are reminiscent of the thumb-nail sketches in *Company K*. What's more, they are unusual and sound stories.

The best story in the book, to my way of thinking, is "George and Charlie," a Reedyville story but a universal tale, a little piece which has kinship, in its theme, with a whole great portion of world literature and which here, in Reedyville, is done on its little scale close to perfection. In connection with "George and Charlie" one would like to put a word in for "Happy Jack."

"Woolen Drawers" is a true bit of American comedy. Alice, from the cigar counter of a commercial hotel in Atlanta, surveyed her world with untroubled eye. Alice was neither tough nor simple, a practical girl who took the world as she found it. She went out with the traveling men who stopped at the hotel as a matter of course, but she sized them up first. She was both attractive and respectable. When Joe Cotton (Cotton by name and cotton by occupation) finally succeeded in dating her up, he gave her a good time and Alice went up to his room with him. Suddenly, in terror, she remembered she had put on her "woolens" that morning, feeling a cold coming on. Better death than the dishonor of being discovered in such undergarments; she used the defensive tactics of impregnable virtue. The result was that Joe Cotton was overcome and began to woo her in daily letters from the towns on his schedule. And that is how Alice married and settled down in Reedyville to a life of good works, where she became a leader in the Methodist Church and the secretary and most active force in the Reedyville "Temperance and Vice Society."

These are, to repeat, superior stories. They are slight on surface compared to the best American short stories being written (and they are to be compared with the best), but they have intelligence, depth and quality. And the prose is irreproachable. Mr. March is on the right track.—FRED T. MARSH, "The Fine Tales of William March," *NYTBR*, Feb. 17, 1935, p. 2

In *The Tallons* Mr. March deviates from his usual position of gentle irony and Chekhovian despair over life's problems, and attempts a tragedy on the grand scale. Two brothers, living on a farm in a small Alabama community, love the same girl. Andrew Tallon is idealistic, dependable, and physically repulsive (he has a harelip and a defect in his speech); Jim Tallon has all the contrasting qualities of thoughtlessness and physical charm. It is Jim, of course, who marries the girl; and when he brings her home to the Tallon farm, he insists that Andrew continue to live there. Andrew's presence, however, is a constant spur to his jealousy: there are violent quarrels and a general atmosphere of tension and hate. One night, after a particularly brutal scene, Andrew intervenes and kills his brother. With the assistance of Myrtle (Jim's widow), he is able successfully to conceal the crime; but his conscience gives him no peace—and he finally confesses. His love for his brother's wife is taken as the obvious motive for the crime; and he is convicted of murder in the first degree.

*The Tallons* has all the virtues of the realistic tradition: intelligence, honesty, detachment, and skill. It is upon these virtues, indeed, that Mr. March's reputation as a writer is based; and for such themes as have occupied him in the past— compassionate studies of "little men" pitted against some universal fate beyond their control or understanding—they are indispensable. Yet it is to be doubted whether they will suffice for such a study of the passions as the present book aims to portray. For the tragedy in *The Tallons* is the tragedy of individual wills: the fate which pursues and destroys the leading characters rises out of certain maladies peculiar to each— Myrtle's vanity, her savage desire to possess Jim at all costs, Jim's jealousy, Andrew's love for an inferior woman. And tragedy of this kind demands something more than mere discernment or a talent for narrative—be the author's eye ever so sure or his statements ever so convincing.

There must first of all be full-sized individuals; and while Andrew comes closest to satisfying us in this regard—he is plausible so long as the drama surrounding him remains familiar and unimpressive—as soon as he is posed against an event of startling proportions he stands revealed for the conventional figure that he is. But what is chiefly lacking in this tragedy is the tragic sense—that element of power which can take us beyond the act into the significance of the act: we feel at all times in the presence of craftsmanship rather than of power. There are times, too, when Mr. March's craftsmanship, expert though it generally is, tends rather to betray itself; when certain situations of prime importance to the plot appear to have been unduly forced. Jim's transformation from an easygoing, self-confident wastrel into a neurotically jealous husband—suspicious above all of his unattractive brother Andrew—is too sudden to be thoroughly credible. But neither these defects in composition nor the book's more serious weaknesses prevent it from being an extremely readable and for the most part honest piece of work.—HELEN NEVILLE, "Craftsmanship," *Nation*, Nov. 14, 1936, p. 582

It is about time someone "discovered" William March. True, there is a William March cult, but a man who has been writing for twelve years and has published six books that rank with the best American fiction being written should have something more than a cult and a quiet fame in the short-story anthologies. By now, March has explored his Alabama county almost as thoroughly as Faulkner has explored his Mississippi county, delved just as deeply into the recesses of the human personality, and come up with material fully as striking (if handled without Faulkner's somewhat excessive symbolism of horror).

*The Looking Glass*, March's fourth novel and his first since 1936, is almost impossible to summarize on the level of plot. It is concerned with the interrelated lives of the inhabitants of "Reedyville," including at least a dozen central characters and innumerable minor ones. There is Manny Nelloha, the boy obsessed with the fear that he is a Negro, who grows up to become a doctor, deliberately murders the girl he loves through a septic abortion, and spends the rest of his life in expiation; Honey Boutwell, the oversexed white girl who achieves international fame as a "Negro" singer of blues; Minnie McInnis McMinn, the small-town journalist who becomes a whopping success as a hack writer and radio personality; Virginia Owen, the Goodwife of Death, who spends her life preparing the dead for burial as a way of sending offerings to her husband, Death; and any number of others equally exotic.

Many of these characters are familiar from the other books, and all their obsessions are. March, in the great tradition, is centrally concerned with the theme of guilt and expiration: the idea, as he expresses it in the words of the Negro spiritual that is the epigraph for his best novel, that you can't go over, under, or around the Lord, but must come in the door, the "door" of sacrificial death or destruction. His first novel, *Company K*, was a bitter anti-war pattern of soldiers' reminiscences, its core (later amplified and reprinted as a short story) the wanton murder of German prisoners that made the nine men who participated in it themselves forever "prisoners," until one killed himself as Sacrificial King for them and brought the rest surcease. The next, *Come In at the Door*, was the study of a child who caused the death of a Negro friend and suffered lifelong tragedy until he found release in madness. March's third novel, *The Tallons*, was the almost classical story of a man who murdered his brother, took his brother's wife, and went inevitably through the tragic rituals of repentance, obsession, confession and execution. The two volumes of short stories, *The Little Wife* and *Some Like Them Short*, run to similar themes again and again.

In *The Looking Glass*, a more complex work than any of the others, March reduces this theme in scale and plays variations on it. The book's form is almost completely inchoate, as bad as Faulkner at his worst, with the story told backwards and forwards, the shifts in time and character almost haphazard, and the single small thread of continuity, a boy's attempt to borrow three dollars to pay a doctor, so trivial that it gets lost for chapters on end. What gives this seemingly formless book its high degree of organization is the imagery, which is as tight and carefully woven as a good symphony, and is impossible to do justice to within the brief space of a review. The central image of the book, the looking-glass itself, translates as "sacrificial death by immolation in ice" (as, for example, the twelve-year-old prodigy's suicide in a frozen pond), but it also partakes of such diverse characteristics as sex, blood, deformity, incest and the ultimate end of the world (a more terrible and final destruction, March says, than that by water, drought, fire or decay) and thus serves as a bridging device to unite all the scattered imagery in the book.

As in all the other books, March relies heavily on his favorite method, a kind of grisly irony that speaks out for good by flaunting evil. His stories are all magnificently turned exercises in irony, and the moral content of the novels frequently takes the form of outright parable (particularly in *Come In at the Door*, where a short, highly effective ironic parable is inserted after every few chapters.) What little direct social statement the books contain is either a wryly ironic presentation of the villain's case (as in a bitter story about peonage called "Runagate Niggers") or a cutting paradox that reverses the truth, like the comment on "passing" implicit in *The Looking Glass* when Honey Boutwell, the blues singer, begs a friend not to expose her as white and ruin her life.

*The Looking Glass* reiterates and amplifies the body of what might be called March's "philosophy," about as depressing a set of ideas as can be imagined. March seems to believe that all men must live in loneliness and isolation, their only possible communication "lies," but that the threads of their lives are nevertheless inseparably bound together. He tends to see all people as either mentally or psychologically deformed, and all relationships between them, particularly close family relationships, as only endless variants of sadism and masochism, hatred and answering love, murder and expiation. His books may be lower-keyed than Faulkner's, but they are quite as lively.

If there is any single clue to William March's preoccupations, it would seem to be a guilt obsession with his part in the last war. Whatever his preoccupations, he has been exorcising them on paper with consummate skill. *The Looking Glass*, although probably not so remarkable a novel as *Come In at the Door*, is remarkable enough, and contains spots that are better than anything March has done before. It is a pleasure to read a writer with a knowledge of his craft and so full an awareness of the material he is manipulating. William Faulkner had better look to his laurels.—STANLEY EDGAR HYMAN, "Alabama Faulkner," *NR*, Feb. 8, 1943, pp. 187–88

Though William March is a superb novelist and short story writer, it is some years since he brought out a new book. Twenty years ago his *Company K* was considered one of the best and most original novels of the First World War, and it remains fresh in the minds of many of its readers. His work is blessed with a style whose simplicity disguises its artistry. Though he has borrowed from no one, there is in *October Island* a tinge of the earlier Aldous Huxley's wit, the irony of Richard Hughes's *High Wind in Jamaica*, and the gentle satire of Norman Douglas's *South Wind*.

The story itself is fascinating and strange. In the 1890's the Reverend Samuel Barnfield and his wife, Irma, arrived on a mythical South Sea island as missionaries of a small but fervent sect known as the Church of the Gospel Prophets. The rawboned and aging pastor had been married to Irma for twenty-three years of sexless life. They were not aware that October Island was the seat of a prehistoric religion and a forgotten culture which was of the greatest interest to sociologists. There for uncounted ages the people had worshiped and sacrificed to the hermaphrodite god Rahabaat, born of the union of the sun and the moon, symbolized by the lofty twin volcanoes that from afar at sea resembled two recumbent and gigantic male and female figures. Nor did this strange and uncouth pair of missionaries know that their religion had promised that some day a virgin goddess would come to rule them.

Irma, many years younger than Samuel, had come from New Orleans. A vigorous, simple-minded, and unimaginative woman, she felt it her duty to convince the luxuriantly beautiful and quite amoral women of the island that they were sinful and their nakedness shameful. The natives listened to the thunderous rhythm of Samuel's sermons with exquisite politeness, though they ridiculed him in private. Irma was another matter; it was incredible and awesome to them that a married woman of fifty should be a virgin. She was also kindly and gentle, and when they discovered that she was unearthing the ancient and often obscenely carved stones which told the story of the islands' legendary past they began to revere this strange and uncouth visitor. She had found one young man with whom she could talk, the mate of a schooner and son of a native woman and a scientist who had long ago left the island. When he told her of the islanders' religion and of the fiery union of the sun and the moon which had created the earth and had given them their hermaphrodite god, she thought it was obscene nonsense. In her search for the sacred stones which she promptly threw into the craters of the volcanoes, Irma unearthed the legendary cup and spoon of the god. Her future as their virgin goddess was sealed. The fantastic conversion of the islanders to Samuel's harsh religion was due to Irma, though she was at the same time drawn to their pagan ceremonies, which she attended in a weird costume of white gauze, topped by a crown sparkling with Christmas tree ornaments. She gave up her vigorous attempts to clothe the girls and women in hideous mother-hubbards and surrendered the main purpose of her religion, the conviction of sin and the eternal punishment in the flames of hell.

When Samuel was stricken with a fatal illness, Irma took him home to the bleak house of his ancestors and buried him in a Vermont grave. She had so willed it; in fact, everything that Irma wished for in her practical mind came to pass. The sister she had left in New Orleans became a notorious prostitute, married a wealthy alcoholic, and left her a hundred thousand dollars. It enabled her to buy the schooner which had taken her to and from October Island and to present it to the only man who had ever stirred her emotionally, the mate of the vessel. And she was able to fulfil her promise to the islanders to come back to them. In her absence they had mourned her loss and had first sacrificed pigs disguised as babies, by throwing them daily into the volcano, and then when the god rejected them, their children. When Irma stepped ashore she was dressed in her weird flowing costume and accepted the frantic joy of these childless people with the calmness with which she had met all the incidents of her life.

The truth is that Irma is a hypocrite who is able to be both honest and dishonest, rational and fantastic, at the same time. In this witty and satirical novel Mr. March reveals a philosophy that would hardly be acceptable to Christian creeds. Irma's faith in herself produced a series of minor miracles. She received in the end the inexhaustible adoration she craved and the islanders were blessed with their virgin goddess and a new generation of children. *October Island* is destined to linger in the minds of its readers as a charming and wise fantasy. We have had little of this kind of enchantment in our recent literature.—HARRISON SMITH, "When Vermont Thaws in the South Seas," *SR*, Oct. 4, 1952, p. 34

Let it be said quickly: William March knows where human fears and secrets are buried. He announced it in *Company K*, a novel published twenty years ago and equaled only by Dos Passos' *Three Soldiers* as a sampling of men at war. He has proved it again and again in the other novels and short stories, all of them floored and walled in what Clifton Fadiman decided to call "psychological acumen." But nowhere is this gift better displayed than in *The Bad Seed*—the portrayal of a coldly evil, murderous child and what she does to both victims and family. In the author's hands this is adequate material for an absolutely first-class novel of moral bewilderments and responsibilities nearest the heart of our decade.

A spare, suggestable prose provides the right tool for delicate carving of mood, action, physical setting and the terrifying mother-child relationship which gives the novel its second theme. The child, the mother, the school mistresses, the neighbors and perverse minor figures of the comfortable southern town are related. One believes in their development and recognizes the inevitability of what happens to them.

As a study of the criminal mind *The Bad Seed* may draw some technical criticism from criminologists, psychiatrists and religious doctrinists. For one thing the reader is asked to agree that evil can be inherited. But as an impeccably written "suspense" novel with intellectual and emotional depths, this achievement defends itself.

"Some murderers, particularly the distinguished ones who were going to make great names for themselves, usually started in childhood; they showed their genius early, just as outstanding poets, mathematicians and musicians did."

Certainly Rhoda Penmark, age 8, did not look the part as she prepared for the school picnic: a tidy, precise, self-sufficient little girl with calculated charm for elderly apartment-house neighbors and a seeming affection for Christine, her flaxen-haired mother. Rhoda happened to be thinking hard about the school penmanship medal which classmate Claude Daigle had won. And when the picnic was over, Claude's body (minus medal) was found under a pier. Can Rhoda be involved in such a crime? Quick pictures of the dead boy's parents, three proud old ladies who own the school, a crazed janitor who serves as one-man Greek chorus, and Mr. and Mrs. Penmark themselves add a palpable quality to mounting tension. Then Rhoda is caught with medal and murder weapon and glibly explains present and previous crimes to her mother.

Shall the anguished mother expose or protect her child? Handled with compassion and artistic restraint, this dilemma occupies the second part of the book. And the tragedy of the actual solution is hastened when Christine finds that her own mother has been a notorious murderess. Too late to save the highly expendable janitor from Rhoda's wrath, Christine at last decides upon a heroic plan which ends in twisted failure. So great is the reader's involvement by now that his mind will speculate far beyond the final page.

All this with ephemeral irony and a touch of the wasp. It's pleasant to report that *The Bad Seed* scores a direct hit, either as exposition of a problem or as work of art. Venturing a prediction and a glance over the shoulder: no more satisfactory novel will be written in 1954 or has turned up in recent memory.—JAMES KELLY, "The Portrait of a Coldly Evil Child," *NYTBR*, April 11, 1954, pp. 4–5

### ALISTAIR COOKE
### "The World of William March"

*New Republic*, December 3, 1945, pp. 754–58

There is a special reputation reserved today for a sort of writer who in the nineteenth century might never have published his fantasies or who, if he had, would have seemed hardly concerned with literature. He is the writer who is instinctively unable to report the surface life of his time and whose natural element is what Gissing, I think it was, called "the dark underside" of human nature. It was the conventional assumption of the Victorians that the depths of human nature are tortured and unpleasant. They had pressing reasons to feel so, for the strict propriety of their public life could only be preserved at the cost of a rich private turmoil. Their writers whom we now tend to glorify were amazing oddities who were aware of this rich confusion and able to exploit it in various acceptable disguises: Melville interpreting the human absorption with the sea in terms of popular adventure; Lewis Carroll marketing a stark nightmare by calling it child's play; most of all, Dickens taking the curse off the unconscious by kidding it in exaggeration, an exaggeration that everybody deplored as crude, though he exaggerated traits that only he would have dared to recognize in life as quintessential. Those writers absorbed by the same depths, but unable to make as forceful a sleight of mind—Emily Dickinson and Manley Hopkins, say—did not publish, for they too must have thought their writing embarrassingly unlike what lay around in every drawing-room as "literature." Today, since there is a wider range of markets than ever before in literary history, they would be published, in odd places, and they would in their day share the kind of fame that is generally accorded William March.

His reputation is the rather bleak one of being a minor connoisseur of morbidity. The people who so rate him willingly describe him as a "distinguished" writer of short stories, as if to exorcise at little cost the harm his wider recognition might do to the comfort of more popular standards. His plots and people are no more morbid than those of Dickens, but Dickens waved the wand of his comic imagination so wildly, and so generously popped the candy of his sentimental sermons into the gaping mouths of the audience he had charmed, that his admirers were willingly blinded to the very raw material he was handling—the murders, seduction, sadism, the thievery, extortion, forgery, the drunkenness, child labor and ingrown virginity that were his meat. William March too is a preacher, but his sermons are not, like Dickens', meant to deny, by sentimental contradiction, the ruthlessness of his observation. They actually insist on underlining that observation and generalizing, sometimes weakly, from the vivid instance of the story.

This exegesis is sometimes provided by the author; often by the central character's recognizing, implausibly, the spring of his acts ("Album of Familiar Music," "Send In Your Answer," "I Broke My Back on a Rosebud"); occasionally, and at its most labored, by a character created for no other purpose than to demonstrate to the other characters (and so unsubtly to the reader) the psychological significance of the tale ("Dirty Emma," and the appalling Mrs. Kent, who succeeds in ruining "Not Worthy of a Wentworth," though not even she can suffocate the joyousness of "The Borax Bottle").

To the admirer of March, this is a serious technical flaw, souring the delicacy of his sympathy, taking too flourishing a bow for a satirical performance that is its own reward. But it gives his critics a handy reason to complain of the pathology of his material. Their objections surely go deeper, for Americans have responded without any such squeamishness to native writers who have a far more compulsive attraction to morbidity. The nineteenth century took with gusto to Poe and Bierce, and we do not resent, as such, the impotent heroes of Hemingway, the euphoric and embittered bums of Steinbeck and Saroyan, the flat, glib decadence of James M. Cain, or even the unrelieved psychopaths of Faulkner and Caldwell. Why, then, protest at March's girls in subways, park-bench sitters, nurses, middle-class husbands, shoe salesmen? It is precisely because we might easily be they, because he does not write about emotional disturbance as if it were rooted only in characters that may be instantly recognized as insane, or in milieus that may be accepted as genre. We can give ourselves without misgiving to Poe, for anything may be expected of ruined houses and opium addicts. We offer a wealth of liberal pity to Steinbeck's Okies, for book-readers are hardly likely to share their way of life. But almost anybody can be a father in a badly paid job, a husband with a nagging wife, a traveling salesman subject to bad news via Western Union. March is able quickly to enlist the sympathy of his readers in people as ordinary as themselves, and asks them to follow him when he proceeds to track down the secret springs of their behavior. Then the sudden fear that our own motives may lie as deep, and be as willfully irrational, is the cue for the unsure reader (especially for the intellectual) to deny his now angry identification, which might after all land him in some of the pitiable crises that confront so many of March's characters.

It is true that March has his share of the demonstrably insane (such a story as "Mist on the Meadow" might be right out of Poe). Yet his genius is best revealed, not in his studies of outright psychosis ("The Shoe Drummer" or "Cinderella's Slipper") but in his deep and tender understanding of what Erich Fromm has called "the pathology of the normal." And his art is so direct, so persuasive, and its symbols so familiar, that the reader unwittingly recognizes his own world and becomes gladly part of it, until the line between it and pathology is seen to be disturbingly thin. Not many men are grateful for being asked to consider a whole series of human tragedies where but for the grace of God, or the comforts of Mammon, go they. The audience for tragedy, when its subjects are contemporary, is greatly overestimated.

This echo of the Greek prescription for tragedy is not accidental. March's writing is classic in its undistracted realism, its bareness, its freedom from salable amenities. And this too may make it forbidding, for he is wholly free from certain fashionable vulgarities: from salaciousness, regionalism, humanitarianism. These current trappings are worth taking one at a time.

Colorful salaciousness. March has an extraordinarily unmodern acceptance of the sins of the flesh. One has the feeling with many modern writers that they are teasing themselves to attain in print an audacity, or a sensuous gallantry, they cannot come by in bed; From the evidence of the best-seller lists, this dissatisfaction must be alarmingly widespread, for to a reader whose appetites are enjoyed in kind, nothing is more tedious and delaying than adjectival descriptions of a rich meal, a daring seduction. March is concerned with the emotions that precede or surround the event. But he is a big boy, free from the itch to peek, devoid of the ambition of many fine writers who fantasize through their characters the conquests their dowdiness, their respectability or love of comfort will not permit them in life.

Evangelical regionalism. At least half of March's work is about the fictional town of Reedyville, which even a devoted reader might hardly discover is in Alabama. Few American writers are so unerringly accurate in the sense of their region— its folkways, vegetation, food, dialects, social equations—yet no writer is less "regional." Small-town life of the Deep South happens to be what he knows best, but Alabama is unlikely to crown him with laurel, for it becomes in his work a local habitation for many moods of the human spirit, and in his masterpiece, *The Looking Glass* (which I might gratuitously suggest is one of the half-dozen finest novels of our time), it is a microcosm of the universal. A Russian, or a Frenchman, or an Englishman, might in Reedyville recognize the spiritual anatomies of his neighbors, where Gopher Prairie or Cannery Row would appall or fascinate him.

Liberal humanitarianism, that is—the urge to be timely. March has been quite indifferent to contemporary idealism, so that it is almost a shock to read (in "Personal Letter") a contribution to anti-Nazi literature, written, by the way, in 1932. Only once does he return to a similar study of the mass defilement of the human personality, in a merciless satire on American radio ("Send In Your Answers"), and its tone is as unforgiving as the earlier study of Nazi character.

If his work had borrowed some of these familiar pigments, it would have been more pretentious, highly colored and impure. And his international reputation would have been more dashing. As it is, we have a prose style rather old-fashioned in its grave, consequential way, describing in unhurried serenity life as he has known it since the late eighteen nineties. Most of his characters, considered as historical types, appear to be Southerners of the years before and during the First World War (it may be his easy handling of the period vernacular, and his uncertain handling of later idiom, which reinforce this impression).

If I am right in thinking March to be living in advance of his permanent reputation, it cannot be because the life and manners of his characters are not of our day. They are behind it, and even in the period in which he is most at home he rarely gives the sense of "fixing" an era in the brilliantly photographic way that is second nature to O'Hara, Hemingway or Lewis. What he has is an austere power to express a sensibility truly modern in a contemporary setting stripped of the gadgets (the names, habits, speech) as well as the charm, of fashion.

We can come to a rough conclusion by pursuing the last and most chronic of the charges brought against his work by the professional critics. It is that he is too clinical, too obviously a psychiatric-textbook student. This is often true and, as I have suggested, he mars much of his best work by guiding the reader toward a doctrinaire view of character, or motive, where the observation of life is larger than any theory that would try to enclose it. Rather, he shares a perception of human character, a knowledge of why so many human relationships must end in unsought tragedy, with an age to which Freud is the pioneer moral naturalist; that is, with a modern age that is only just born, and a view of life by no means widely acceptable. For it is important to recognize that alongside his delineation of common sickness there goes a complementary awareness of health ("A Memorial to the Slain," "Woolen Drawers," the fresh delight of "The Borax Bottle," and the exquisite "She Talks Good Now"). If he attributes this emotional health often to social outcasts (the two Shakespearean whores in *The Looking Glass*) and illiterate Negroes (Lula in "She Talks Good Now"), it may be an excessive desire to see the blessings of irony in those whom the educated and the superior pity.

He can be protesting, and inept, and sometimes his satire is obvious. Yet his best work—at least half of ⟨his⟩ fifty-five stories and the whole of the incomparable *Looking Glass*— reflect the alternate play of two qualities that Anatole France perceived in fiction that is to be classic—pity and irony. There is little enough of it around for those of us who value this prescription to see in William March not so much an American classic as a classic modern, who happens to be an American, and who therefore—in a time when literary chauvinism keeps pace with the ferocious nationalism of world politics—is understandably the most underrated of all contemporary American writers of fiction.

# EDWIN MARKHAM

## 1852–1940

Charles Edward Anson Markham, later known as Edwin Markham, was born in Oregon City, Oregon, on April 23, 1852. His parents, who had left the Midwest in search of riches, were divorced shortly after his birth. Given the nickname Charley at birth, he moved with his mother to a farm in the Suisun hills of central California in the late 1850s. There he lived with his tempestuous mother until he left for Christian College in Santa Rosa, California. Markham's early career was as a schoolteacher and later as a school administrator. In 1875 he married Annie Cox, later to divorce her in 1884. In 1897 he married again, this time to a schoolteacher, Anna Catherine Murphy, who was also a writer.

Markham's literary fame rests on two volumes of poetry written around the turn of the century. The publication in the San Francisco *Examiner* of his long poem, "The Man with the Hoe" (1899), immediately thrust him into the national spotlight. This poem of social protest was inspired by the Millet painting of the same name. His second volume of verses, *Lincoln and Other Poems* (1901), was also well received. However, Markham's later works were generally considered overblown and not as powerful as his early protest poems. A friend of fellow Californian Ambrose Bierce, Markham may have inspired the character of Presley in the work of another California resident, Frank Norris.

    After his initial success Markham traveled across the country lecturing on poetry and social reform. He eventually settled with his wife on Staten Island, New York. An inspiring voice from the "Wild West," Markham died on March 7, 1940, at the age of eighty-seven.

"You are invited," said the invitation, "to participate with the Joint Committee of Literary Arts in a dinner in honour of Edwin Markham in recognition of his genius as a poet and his worth as a man."

    That seemed all right. So I acquired a ticket and noted the date of the dinner. In the interval I tried to recall what I knew about Edwin Markham and his very popular poem, "The Man with the Hoe." It was published nearly twenty years ago; it was suggested by Millet's painting; and it had the distinction of being the most quoted poem of the day. Innumerable newspapers published it; innumerable sermons were preached upon it; innumerable editorials were written on the questions with which the poem concludes—

> O masters, lords and rulers in all lands,
> How will the future reckon with this Man?
> How answer his brute question in that hour
> When whirlwinds of rebellion shake the world?

Strange to say the future reckoned with this Man by begging All Men to take up the hoe and help to feed the world. Neither Mr. Markham, nor anybody else, could foresee that with the pressure of the submarine menace in 1916 the Man with the Hoe would become a very important, a very necessary and much-admired person. In England everybody in their leisure hours wielded a hoe. It was unpatriotic not to do so. The present writer, clad in a costume as like to the garments worn by Millet's peasant as his scanty wardrobe permitted, hoed himself into a state that bordered upon ecstasy. He was doing his bit, not doing it surpassingly well, but he was helping to feed his native land; he was the new Man with the Hoe. And he murmured to himself the cheerful reply made twenty years ago by John Vance Cheney to Edwin Markham's sad "Man with the Hoe":

> Strength shall he have, the toiler, strength and grace,
> So fitted to his place.
> Tall as his toil. Nor does he toil unblest,
> Labor he has, and rest.

    I did not trouble to acquire the three editions of *The Man with the Hoe and Other Poems* at $2, at $1 and at 50 cents, because I was confident that the poem would be recited at the dinner; but I did reflect on popularity, and the extravagance of some literary judgments. I remembered a story, current at the time, that a well-known man had offered $5,000 to anybody who could produce a finer poem than "The Man with the Hoe," and in the advertisement pages of *The Shoes of Happiness and Other Poems*, by Edwin Markham, I read a series of "critical opinions." Well, not being a poet, I am not in the least envious, but I looked forward to the dinner with redoubled interest, eager to see if such extravagant praise had had any effect on the venerable poet. Here are a few of the "critical opinions."

    "The greatest poet of the century," Ella Wheeler Wilcox.

    "The Whole Yosemite—the thunder, the might, the majesty," Joaquin Miller.

    " 'The Man with the Hoe,' will be the battle cry of the next thousand years," Jay William Hudson.

    "A poem by Markham is a national event," Robert Underwood Johnson.

    "Excepting always my dear Whitcomb Riley, Edwin Markham is the first of the Americans," William Dean Howells.

    Can you wonder that my pulse beat high as the day of the dinner approached? Even though I do not write poetry, a Bookman's pride extends to all members of his craft, from the paternal poet to the pointed paragraphist, and I longed to see the man who wrote a poem that "will be the battle cry of the next thousand years." My hoe now stands in the umbrella stand in the little hall of my native home, from the oriel window of which may be seen the croquet lawn converted into a potato patch where

> Bound by the weight of centuries I leant
> Upon my hoe and gazed upon the ground,
> The emptiness of ages in my face,
> And on my back the burden of the world.

(The opening of "The Man with the Hoe" slightly altered.)

    Five hundred or so attended the dinner—mostly poets. It was heartening to see the guest of the evening greeted by his admirers, a kindly, wise, distinguished-looking man, in appearance something between Robert Browning and Walt Whitman. Of course there was more extravagance of praise. There always is on such occasions. The name of Shakespeare was used freely, but distinguished poets are accustomed to such flatteries, and they can do nothing but sit still and smile while they listen to the flattery. It was near midnight before the poet rose to reply and then something happened that endeared the author of "The Man with the Hoe" to me. In his speech, after a proper period of seriousness—greatest moment of my life, never to be forgotten, and so on—he side-tracked into reminiscences of delightful humour. A humorous poet! I could hardly believe my ears! He gave us a gay and sly account of his early years in Oregon and California, farming, blacksmithing, herding cattle and sheep, and so on, to newspaper writing, Christian sociology and poetry. The room rippled with laughter, and although midnight had struck we were quite willing that he should continue his autobiography to the present day, for a serious poet with an aura of humour is an infrequent experience.

    The next day I went to a club which has an excellent library and asked the librarian for Edwin Markham's poems. He looked blankly at me. The club did not possess a copy. "Such is fame," I murmured. "Is it some particular poem you want?" asked the librarian. "Yes, 'The Man with the Hoe.' " He retired, and presently returned staggering under the load of the largest book of poetry I have ever seen. It is called "The Home Book of Verse"; it contains 3,742 pages, which is necessary, as it enshrines poems from Spenser to the present day. When I have asked a carpenter if my bookshelves will stand the strain I shall certainly acquire this volume. It contains hidden in its 3,742 pages "The Man with the Hoe" and Cheney's "Reply," and Markham's "Lincoln," and "Auld Lang Syne," by Robert Burns, which I read that afternoon for the first time, although I have pretended to sing it on hundreds of occasions, and a little thing by Walt Whitman beginning "At the last, tenderly," and ending "Strong is your hold, O love!" that has been singing itself to me ever since.

That rich afternoon of poetry (it was Sunday and the library was empty) drinking from so many fountains placed Edwin Markham for me. He is a noble, dignified and beautiful singer of noble, dignified and beautiful themes, but he lacks magic. He could not have written

> that found a path
> Through the sad heart of Ruth, when, sick for home,
> She stood in tears amid the alien corn.

He is an author rather than a bard. You remember Macaulay's distinction between the two. But when I reached home that evening I read Markham's "Birthday Greeting to John Burroughs" and felt very grateful to him; and still more grateful when I read a quatrain which he calls

### OUTWITTED

> He drew a circle that shut me out—
> Heretic, rebel, a thing to flout.
> But love and I had the wit to win:
> We drew a circle that took him in.

There are folk who would rather have written that than most things.—C. LEWIS HIND, "Edwin Markham," *Authors and I*, 1921, pp. 195–200

Edwin Markham is the Blessed Damozel of American poetry. He is decent, flawless, virginal. He is an artist, a craftsman *sans reproche* but not *sans peur*.

Can you conceive of Mrs. Grundy astride Pegasus? No more than you could conceive of Lohengrin riding on the horn of Satan. Well, Edwin Markham has achieved the inconceivable. For he is really Mrs. Grundy riding Pegasus, the veritable Pegasus, for Edwin Markham is a real poet, sometimes a great poet, but always a poet.

Markham, with all his defects of platitudinous idealism, puritanical sex-prudence, sentimental metaphysics and dedication flap-doodle, is steeped in the ecstasy of eternals. There is a touch of crazy beauty in him, too. And he has caught the wild music of the Angel Israfel. But he is hopelessly of America, with its paste humanitarianism, its paste optimism, its paste culture.

He is productive but uncreative. He sticks to the old forms, the old metaphors, the old lilts, the old griefs, with suddenly a line or simile of mirific magic leaping forth from the page like a dazzling dragonfly out of a New England mince-pie. Many, many of his poems are the products of an Eddie Guest who has read Shelley—sheer rubbish. He is preoccupied with the dream of mediocre minds—Social Regeneration. His Muse is half the time on a soap-box. The poison of Jesus is in his blood and eats up the red corpuscles of unregenerate sin and lyrical *diablerie*. The syphilis of theology is in his veins. The pox of redemption disfigures his Endymion.

There is in Markham's poetry a gorgeous music—sometimes Miltonic, sometimes Swinburnian as in "The Crowning Hour":

> I saw you there with the sea-girls fleeing,
> And I followed you fast over rock and reef;
> And you sent a sea-fire into my being,
> The lure of the lyric grief.

And he has the magic of the great line:

> We are caught in the coils of a God's romances.

Or:

> A spider bars the road with filmy ropes
> Where once the feet of Carthage thundered by.

It is the fashion to make light of "The Man with the Hoe." Aside from its sentimentality, it is technically, to me, a great poem. There are vastness, power and passion in it. It is Markham on his soap-box, but his soap-box is a star.

Markham at seventy-four is a great big, back-slapping, bawling boy. He praises every one indiscriminately. The man, personally, is incapable of an evil thought, an evil act. He is the gushing, love-thy-neighbor Christian.

He hasn't the slightest doubt in his own mind that he is the greatest American poet, the Voice of the Age, the Light-bringer, the Anointed One. He used to pride himself on his resemblance to Victor Hugo; but I have never found in Markham any of Hugo's pomposity. And withal shrewd, for I doubt whether he would ever write a poem that did not have a market value.

Edwin Markham has proved that Demos and Prometheus are not enemies.—BENJAMIN DE CASSERES, "Five Portraits on Galvanized Iron," *AM*, Dec. 1926, pp. 398–99

Edwin Markham in his childhood unconsciously gave a good imitation of David. After the death of his father, his mother took the younger children from Oregon to California, and settled on a cattle range near the Coast Mountains. Here Edwin became a shepherd, and spent long happy days following the flocks and herds in the sunlight, and often slept under the stars.

The public school was open only three months in the year, but there happened to be a teacher who loved poetry, and it was this man who awakened in Edwin a passion for poetry which dominated his life. Later the young man became a school teacher himself, then Superintendent of schools in a little town in the Sierras. Here he happened to open a magazine that contained among the illustrations Millet's famous picture of the Man with the Hoe, the second inspiration of his life.

Edwin Markham was not a man of one poem; but it is certain, no matter what he himself thought of the whole range of his work, that this poem, "The Man with the Hoe," must always remain his masterpiece, because it had more influence than all the rest of his productions put together. As Browning said, we judge of the power of men by the length of the shadow they cast; and this poem threw a shadow across the whole world. It was not written impromptu, nor indeed even in a short time. He began it, worked on it at various places and at various times, and finished it near San Francisco in the Christmas vacation of 1899.

Had he spoken it over the radio, it could not have received more instant acclaim. The response of the world was immediate and tremendous. As a result he spent the rest of his happy life not only in writing, but in visiting every State in the Union, speaking to huge audiences and reading his works. On the occasion of the poet's eightieth birthday, widely celebrated, William Rose Benét made an accurate estimate of Edwin Markham's position in literature:

"Markham has retained unusual vigor, both in his personality and his writing. He has always been a dogmatic poet, but with a great liberality of spirit and an accomplished knowledge of versification. He has never surpassed his 'Hoe' and his 'Lincoln' poems. They were the work he was primarily born to do."—WILLIAM LYON PHELPS, "Edwin Markham," *Commemorative Tributes of the American Academy of Arts and Letters: 1905–1941*, 1942, pp. 406–7

Edwin Markham's "The Man with the Hoe" was surely the most celebrated item in the literature of protest on behalf of the agricultural laborer. If not a truly great poem, at least it is powerful in its impact, and its sympathies are hard to mistake:

> Bowed by the weight of centuries he leans
> Upon his hoe and gazes on the ground,
> The emptiness of ages in his face,
> And on his back the burden of the world.

Who made him dead to rapture and despair,
A thing that grieves not and that never hopes,
Stolid and stunned, a brother to the ox?
Who loosened and let down this brutal jaw?
Whose was the hand that slanted back this brow?
Whose breath blew out the light within this
    brain? . . .

O masters, lords and rulers in all lands . . .
How will you ever straighten up this shape. . . .
Make right the immemorial infamies,
Perfidious wrongs, immedicable woes? . . .
How will the Future reckon with this Man?
How answer his brute questions in that hour
When whirlwinds of rebellion shake the world?

Although he dealt with the farmer in stark and unflattering terms, Markham furnished in labor's cause a document of unmatched potency. But the farmer-poet, his sense of inferiority aroused by rural hardships and by the losing battle between farm and city, reacted not to Markham's espousal of the agrarian cause but to what he read as an insult:

How false the note of him who sings
That toiling hand lends sloping brow
But brutal minds behind the plow;
His soul may soar, but not on wings.

"'The man with the hoe,' but not 'a clod,'" one poet reprimanded him, while still another corrected, "Kin to the eagle, not brother to the ox." Thus, in ways both trivial and touching, did the intended recipients of Markham's sympathies shrug them off with petulant objections. Evidently conscious that his intentions had been misapprehended, Markham sought to clarify his message by offering in his next volume an obvious sequel to "The Man with the Hoe," called "The Sower" and based, like its predecessor, on a painting by Millet. Here he spoke of the farmer returning in the twilight "with hero step" and called him

. . . the stone rejected, yet the stone
Whereon is built metropolis and throne.
Out of his toil come all their pompous shows,
Their purple luxury and plush repose!

Yet by 1901 it was apparently too late; there were no retractions in the verse of those who had taken Markham to task. Even by pointing the finger at the farmer-hero, by taking his side against the city and the idle rich, he was unable to retrieve or mollify his intended audience.—ROBERT H. WALKER, "Progress and Protest," *The Poet and the Gilded Age*, 1963, pp. 70–71

---

## AMBROSE BIERCE
### "Edwin Markham's Poems" (1899)
### *Collected Works*, Volume 10
### 1911, pp. 137–48

I n Edwin Markham's book, *The Man with the Hoe and Other Poems*, many of the "other poems" are excellent, some are great. If asked to name the most poetic—not, if you please, the "loftiest" or most "purposeful"—I think I should choose "The Wharf of Dreams." I venture to quote it:

Strange wares are handled on the wharves of sleep;
    Shadows of shadows pass, and many a light
    Flashes a signal fire across the night;
Barges depart whose voiceless steersmen keep
Their way without a star upon the deep;
    And from lost ships, homing with ghostly crews,
    Come cries of incommunicable news,
While cargoes pile the piers a moon-white heap—

Budgets of dream-dust, merchandise of song,
Wreckage of hope and packs of ancient wrong,
Nepenthes gathered from a secret strand,
    Fardels of heartache, burdens of old sins,
    Luggage sent down from dim ancestral inns,
And bales of fantasy from No-Man's Land.

Really, one does not every year meet with a finer blending of imagination and fancy than this; and I know not where to put a finger on two better lines in recent work than these:

And from lost ships, homing with ghostly crews,
Come cries of incommunicable news.

The reader to whom these strange lines do not give an actual physical thrill may rightly boast himself impregnable to poetic emotion and indocible to the meaning of it.

Mr. Markham has said of Poetry—and said greatly:

She comes like the hush and beauty of the night,
    And sees too deep for laughter;
Her touch is a vibration and a light
    From worlds before and after.

But she comes not always so. Sometimes she comes with a burst of music, sometimes with a roll of thunder, a clash of weapons, a roar of winds or a beating of billow against the rock. Sometimes with a noise of revelry, and again with the wailing of a dirge. Like Nature, she "speaks a various language." Mr. Markham, no longer content, as once he seemed to be, with interpreting her fluting and warbling and "sweet jargoning," learned to heed her profounder notes, which stir the stones of the temple like the bass of a great organ.

In his "Ode to a Grecian Urn" Keats has supplied the greatest—almost the only truly great instance of a genuine poetic inspiration derived from art instead of nature. In his poems on pictures Mr. Markham shows an increasingly desperate determination to achieve success, coupled with a lessening ability to merit it. It is all very melancholy, the perversion of this man's high powers to the service of a foolish dream by artificial and impossible means. Each effort is more ineffectual than the one that went before. Unless he can be persuaded to desist—to cease interpreting art and again interpret nature, and turn also from the murmurs of "Labor" to the music of the spheres—the "surge and thunder" of the universe—the end of his good literary repute is in sight. He knows—does he know?—the bitter truth which he might have learned otherwise than by experience: that the plaudits of "industrial discontent," even when strengthened by scholars' commendations of a few great lines in the poem that evoked it, are not fame. He should know, and if he live long will know, that when one begins to be a "labor leader" one ceases to be a poet.

In saying to Mr. Markham, "Thou ailest here and here," Mrs. Atherton has shown herself better at diagnosis than he is himself in telling us what is the matter with the rich. "Why," she asks him, "waste a beautiful gift in groveling for popularity with the mob? . . . Striving to please the common mind has a fatal commonizing effect on the writing faculty." It is even so—nothing truer could be said, and Mr. Markham is the best proof of its truth. His early work, when he was known to only a small circle of admirers, was so good that I predicted for him the foremost place among contemporaneous American poets. He sang because he "could not choose but sing," and his singing grew greater and greater. Every year he took wider outlooks from "the peaks of song"—had already got well above the fools' paradise of flowers and song-birds and bees and women and had invaded the "thrilling region" of the cliff, the eagle and the cloud, whence one looks down upon man and out upon the world. Then he had the mischance to publish

"The Man with the Hoe," a poem with some noble lines, but an ignoble poem. In the first place, it is, in structure, stiff, inelastic, monotonous. One line is very like another. The cæsural pauses fall almost uniformly in the same places; the full stops always at the finals. Comparison of the versification with Milton's blank will reveal the difference of method in all its significance. It is a difference analogous to that between painting on ivory and painting on canvas—between the dead, flat tints of the one and the lively, changing ones due to inequalities of surface in the other. If it seem a little exacting to compare Mr. Markham's blank with that of the only poet who has ever mastered that medium in English, I can only say that the noble simplicity and elevation of Mr. Markham's work are such as hardly to justify his admeasurement by any standard lower than the highest that we have.

My chief objection relates to the sentiment of the piece, the thought that the work carries; for although thought is no part of the poetry conveying it, and, indeed, is almost altogether absent from some of the most precious pieces (lyrical, of course) in our language, no elevated composition has the right to be called great if the message that it delivers is neither true nor just. All poets, even the little ones, are feelers, for poetry is emotional; but all the great poets are thinkers as well. Their sympathies are as broad as the race, but they do not echo the peasant's philosophies of the workshop and the field. In Mr. Markham's poem the thought is that of the labor union—even to the workworn threat of rising against the wicked well-to-do and taking it out of their hides.

Who made him dead to rapture and despair,
A thing that grieves not and that never hopes,
Stolid and stunned, a brother to the ox?
Who loosened and let down this brutal jaw?
Whose was the hand that slanted back this brow?
Whose breath blew out the light within this brain?

One is somehow reminded by these lines of Coleridge's questions in the Chamouni hymn, and one is tempted to answer them the same way: God. "The Man with the Hoe" is not a product of the "masters, lords and rulers in all lands": they are not, and no class of men is, accountable for him, his limitations and his woes, which are not of those "that kings or laws can cause or cure." The "masters, lords and rulers" are as helpless "in the fell clutch of circumstance" as he—which Mr. Markham would be speedily made to understand if appointed Dictator. The notion that the sorrows of the humble are due to the selfishness of the great is "natural," and can be made poetical, but it is silly. As a literary conception it has not the vitality of a sick fish. It will not carry a poem of whatever excellence through two generations. That a man of Mr. Markham's splendid endowments should be chained to the body of this literary death is no less than a public calamity.

For his better work in poetry Mr. Markham merits all the praise that he has received for "The Man with the Hoe," and more. It is not likely that he is now under any illusion in the matter. He probably knows the real nature of his sudden flare of "popularity"; knows that to-morrow it will be "one with Nineveh and Tyre"; knows that its only service to him is to arrest attention of competent critics and scholars who would otherwise have overlooked him for a time. The "plaudits of the multitude" can not long be held by the poet, and are not worth holding. The multitude knows nothing of poetry and does not read it. The multitude will applaud you to-day, calumniate you to-morrow and thwack you athwart the mazzard the day after. He who builds upon the sea-sand of its favor holds possession by a precarious tenure; the wind veers and the wave

Lolls out his large tongue—
Licks the whole labor flat.

If the great have left the humble so wise that the philosophies of the factory and the plow-tail are true; if the sentiments and the taste of the mob are so just and elevated that its judgment of poetry is infallible and its approval a precious possession; if "the masses" have more than "a thin veneering of civilization," and are not in peace as fickle as the weather and in anger as cruel as the sea; if these victims of an absolutely universal oppression "in *all* lands" are deep, discriminating, artistic, liberal, magnanimous—in brief, wise and good—it is difficult to see what they have to complain about. Mr. Markham, at least, is forbidden to weep for them, for he is a lover of Marcus Aurelius, of Seneca, of Epictetus. These taught, and taught truly—one from the throne of an empire, one writing at a gold table, and one in the intervals of service as a slave—the supreme value of wisdom and goodness, the vanity of power and wealth, the triviality of privation, discomfort and pain. Mr. Markham is a disciple of Jesus Christ, who from the waysides and the fields taught that poverty is not only a duty, but indispensable to salvation. So my *argumentum ad hominem* runs thus: The objects of our poet's fierce invective and awful threats have suffered his *protégés* to remain rather better off than they are themselves—have appropriated and monopolized only what is not worth having. In view of this mitigating circumstance I feel justified in demanding in their behalf a lighter sentence. Let the portentous effigy of the French Revolution be forbidden to make faces at them.

I know of few literary phenomena more grotesque than some of those growing out of "The Man with the Hoe"—that sudden popularity being itself a thing which "goes neare to be fonny." Mr. Markham, whom for many years those of us who modestly think ourselves *illuminati* considered a great poet whose greatness full surely was a-ripening, wrote many things far and away superior to "The Man," but these brought him recognition from the judicious only, with which we would all have sworn that he was content. All at once he published a poem which, despite some of its splendid lines, is neither true in sentiment nor admirable in form—which is, in fact, addressed to peasant understandings and soured hearts. Instantly follow a blaze and thunder of notoriety, seen and heard over the entire continent; and even the coasts of Europe are "telling of the sound." Straightway before the astonished vision of his friends the author stands transfigured! The charming poet has become a demagogue, a "labor leader" spreading that gospel of hate known as "industrial brotherhood," a "walking delegate" diligently inciting a strike against God and clamoring for repeal of the laws of nature. Saddest of all, we find him conscientiously promoting his own vogue. He personally appears at meetings of cranks and incapables convened to shriek against the creed of law and order; speaks at meetings of sycophants eager to shine by his light; introduces lecturers to meetings of ninnies and femininnies convened to glorify themselves. When he is not waving the red flag of discontent and beating the big drum of revolution I presume he is resting—perched, St.-Simeon-Styliteswise, atop a lofty capital I, erected in the market place, diligently and rapturously contemplating his new identity. All of which is very sad to those of us who find it difficult to unlove him.

The trouble with Mr. Markham is that he has formed the habit of thinking of mankind as divided on the property line—as comprising only two classes, the rich and the poor. When a man has acquired that habit he is lost to sense and righteousness. Assassins sometimes reform, and with increasing education thieves renounce the error of theft to embrace the evangel of embezzlement; but a demagogue never gets again into shape unless he becomes wealthy. I hope Mr. Markham's fame will so promote his pecuniary interest that it will convert him from the conviction that his birth was significantly coincident in point of time with the Second Advent. Only one thing is more disagreeable than a man with a mission, namely a woman with a mission, and the superior objectionableness of the latter is largely due to her trick of inspiring the former.

Mr. Markham seems now to look upon himself as the savior of society; to believe with entire sincerity that in his light and leading mankind can be guided out of the wilderness of Self into the promised land of Altruria; that he can alter the immemorial conditions of human existence; that a new Heaven and a new Earth can be created by the power of his song. Most melancholy of all, the song has lost its power and its charm. Since he became the Laureate of Demagogy he has written little that is poetry: in the smug prosperity that he reviles in others, his great gift, "shrinks to its second cause and is no more." That in the great white light of inevitable disillusion he will recover and repossess it, giving us again the flowers and fruits of a noble imagination in which the dream of an impossible and discreditable hegemony has no part, I should be sorry to disbelieve.

## HORACE GREGORY AND MARYA ZATURENSKA
### From "Three Poets of the Sierras"
*A History of American Poetry 1900–1940*
1946, pp. 51–54

When Edwin Markham died at the age of eighty-eight, filled with his many years and uncounted honors, a few critics wondered if he remembered Ambrose Bierce's warning that "The Man with the Hoe" would eventually kill him. This was perhaps unfair to Markham's fame in the small town on Staten Island where he had made his home for forty years and where he died. Since the publication of "The Man with the Hoe" in the *San Francisco Examiner* of January 15, 1899, he had written five books of poems, was an editor of one of the most voluminous anthologies of "world poetry" ever published on the North American continent, had written several books of prose and many articles on social problems. These tended to solidify his reputation among members of The Poetry Society of America as well as with the president of Richmond Borough who in 1930 declared his birthday a holiday on Staten Island, at which hundreds of schoolchildren took part in a parade to Markham's home in Westerleigh and a pageant was held in his honor.

But to the majority of the American reading public, he was inevitably known as "the author of 'The Man with the Hoe'" and even his poem on Lincoln, which contained similar faults and virtues, never superseded the popularity of the earlier poem. To the younger generations of poets growing up during the first forty years of the present century, Markham was a picturesque, Whitman-bearded figure of the past, and if any of them read his books of verse, *The Man with the Hoe and Other Poems* (1899), *Lincoln, and Other Poems* (1901), *The Shoes of Happiness* (1914), *The Gates of Paradise* (1920), and *New Poems: Eighty Songs at 80* (1932), no influence of that reading can be discerned. Even when the poetry of social protest had gained momentum during the late 1920's and the mid-thirties, Markham never became more than an elderly figure in what is sometimes thought to be a simple and innocently flamboyant era, which included Christian Socialism, the fading memory of Joaquin Miller, pioneer activity and its enthusiasms, and Edward Bellamy's *Looking Backward*. Almost all of Markham's first forty-eight years were spent in California; and his work seemed to exist solely in an atmosphere that had made possible a faith in the natural goodness of man and the evolutionary triumph of democracy. If his work contained some few of the Byronic and naïve attitudes of Joaquin Miller, it was also distinguished by a greater restraint and modesty than anything that Miller wrote, and as Louis Untermeyer has remarked, it contained the rhetoric without the resonance of the elder poet's more exuberant moments.

Like Miller's, Markham's early childhood bore the marks of pioneer restlessness, hardiness, excitement, and privation; his family had moved westward from Michigan to Oregon, and at the age of five, Markham's boyhood career took a fresh start in California. The Markham legend includes a wide range of early activities; he was said to have been a sheep herder, farmer, blacksmith, and cowboy—but the most important influence upon his future life seems to have been the encouragement he received from a country schoolteacher, who recognized in Markham, then a boy of seventeen, the abilities that were to make him famous. It is significant that Markham himself became a teacher, and before he earned his fame as "the author of 'The Man with the Hoe,'" he was engaged as superintendent and principal of schools in California.

Though his childhood privations have been said to have provided a background for his interest in social problems, his general optimism readily cleared him of all tendencies toward bitterness. Violent methods for changing social conditions shocked him, and thinking of such possibilities, he wrote:

> I am neither an economist, nor a politician. In my writings I have only attempted to depict life as it appears to me. If they disclose there is something wrong, that is as much as can be expected from them. I am no back-seat driver. I leave the guidance of our political State to the men who have learned to direct it.

There can be no doubt of the essential goodwill contained in these remarks, nor of their honesty; and they explain why his personal qualities endeared his memory to many friends. The same atmosphere of goodwill and hopefulness enters his famous quatrain, with its triumphant title, "Outwitted":[1]

> He drew a circle that shut me out—
> Heretic, rebel, a thing to flout.
> But Love and I had the wit to win:
> We drew a circle that took him in!

The voice of the nineteenth-century Californian schoolteacher, who had read textbook anthologies of verse, may be found in his test for greatness in poetry: "Sublimity is the test. Very few poets have it—Homer, Aeschylus, Dante, Shakespeare, Victor Hugo—that's about all." But unfortunately, even the greatest names, particularly if they remain no more than and solely "great names" to the reader, are not always the best influences. It is sometimes to be feared that Markham read the best poets for the worst reasons. He took from them all the sublimity and rhetoric and ornamentation he could find, and to these elements he added a fondness for Miltonic blank verse, and in his latter years, an unguarded admiration for Edgar Allan Poe. When he forgot his own grim resolution that

> Life is a mission stern as fate,
>     And Song a dread apostolate.[2]

he turned to such attempted graces as

> Ah, once of old in some forgotten tongue
> Forgotten land, I was a shepherd boy,
> And you a Nereid, a wingèd joy.[3]

Here, as in his "Song of the Followers of Pan," he seemed to express, more than all else, a confused and boyish delight in finding scraps of knowledge floating through his mind.

His incorrigible optimism led the way through many varieties of verse and public affirmations. He seemed always willing to lend his name to anything that had the appearance of being a worthy cause. He celebrated the Russian Revolution in his best Miltonic manner (in a poem which was translated into Russian and greatly admired), and he appeared before a convention of pharmacists with the avowed purpose of creating sympathy for the drug addict. His poem, "Slaves of the Drug," was enthusiastically applauded and was reputed to have done much good. He also wrote an ode of welcome to Ramsay MacDonald and the British Labour Party when MacDonald visited the United States in 1929.

But throughout his campaigns for outmoded political figures and dimly realized social ideals, he kept his soul, as he once said, "as simple as a flower."

His remark concerning the welfare of his soul was by no means inappropriate; of the many featured contributors to the Hearst newpapers, Markham, like Art Young, the cartoonist, was among the few who retained a personal integrity. And it is in this setting and environment that the Populist sentiment of his poem, "The Man with the Hoe," still retains its brightest colors. Its language has the same character that earned for the young Arthur Brisbane the reputation for being the best editorial writer on Hearst's large staff. Although the sources of its inspiration have been credited by Markham himself to Jean François Millet's painting of the same title, its diction and imagery as well as its expert touches of journalistic craftsmanship bear a stronger relationship to whatever virtues might be found on the Hearst editorial page during the period when Hearst had found it profitable to champion the cause of the poor against the rich.

It was reputed that before Markham died his famous poem had earned for him the round sum of two hundred and fifty thousand dollars. Few Californians of the old mining days had struck so rich a mine, and Markham had an honest and almost humble faith in his good fortune. He once said to those who asked him for the secret of his success: "A chance stroke: I caught the eye and ear of the world."

*Notes*

1. From *Eighty Songs at 80*, Doubleday, Doran.
2. "The Poet" from *The Man with the Hoe*, Doubleday, Doran.
3. "Shepherd Boy and Nereid" from *The Man with the Hoe*, Doubleday, Doran.

# JOHN P. MARQUAND

## 1893–1960

John Phillips Marquand was born on November 10, 1893, in Wilmington, Delaware. Marquand's New England ancestors include two Massachusetts governors and the famous Transcendentalist writer Margaret Fuller. His father was a civil engineer who quit his profession in 1900 and invested his inheritance in the New York stock market. The comfortable surroundings of Marquand's childhood disappeared when the family fortune was lost in 1907. The young Marquand was forced to live with several great aunts at the family home near Newburyport, Massachusetts, while his father worked abroad. Family finances did not permit Marquand to enroll at one of New England's prestigious private schools, so instead he attended public high school in Newburyport. He was able to secure a science scholarship to Harvard, where he begrudgingly majored in chemistry. Unlike his ancestors he was not asked to join any Harvard clubs, although he did work for the *Lampoon*.

After his graduation in 1915 he worked for a Boston newspaper before traveling to France with the armed forces. He worked in New York at a newspaper and later at an advertisement agency during the early 1920s. His first novel, *The Unspeakable Gentleman* (1922), was published in the same year as his marriage to Christina Sedgwick, a member of another prominent New England family. During the next fifteen years he wrote numerous short stories and novels which were serialized in commercial magazines. In 1935 his famous character, Mr. Moto, a Japanese intelligence officer, appeared in *No Hero*. This novel was later made into a film, as were several other Mr. Moto novels.

Marquand was an enthusiastic world traveler and on a trip to China he began work on his first "serious" novel. *The Late George Apley* (1937), which he later dramatized with the help of George S. Kaufman, was awarded the 1938 Pulitzer Prize for fiction. The second and third books in this trilogy, *Wickford Point* (1939) and *H. M. Pulham, Esquire* (1941), continued the superb depiction of New England mannerisms which characterized the first novel. In the tradition of such American writers as Edith Wharton, Henry James, and Sinclair Lewis, Marquand's novels of social realism are best remembered for their careful dissection of American culture. He continued to write throughout the 1940s and 1950s, publishing the acclaimed *Point of No Return* in 1949.

During World War II he was a special consultant to the Secretary of War and served as a correspondent in the Pacific. Beginning in 1944 he sat on the editorial board of the Book-of-the-Month Club. Always concerned about money, Marquand enjoyed unusual financial security for a writer. The father of five children from two marriages, he divorced his first wife in 1935. A second, twenty-one-year marriage to a relative of the Rockefellers, Adelaide Hooker, also ended in divorce in 1958. He carried on a lifelong affair with Carol Brandt, wife of his close friend and literary agent Carl Brandt. At the age of sixty-six Marquand died on July 16, 1960, at his home on Kent's Island, Newburyport.

## Personal

When I was working my way through Harvard, I spent one summer as a family tutor in York Harbor, Maine, and early in my stay I remember having pointed out to me a small, wooden shack off by itself on a rocky promontory. "That's where John Marquand lives," I was told. "He is trying to write a novel." He had worked as a reporter and written copy for a big New York advertising agency before he felt ready to take the gamble of being a free lance. But you could tell from the looks of that little shack that whatever he was writing wasn't paying much. In the years that intervened between that summer and the publication of *The Late George Apley*, John P. Marquand supported himself by writing the Mr. Moto stories; they found increasing popularity in the *Saturday Evening Post*, and in time John rose to be one of the highest paid of its contributors, in company with Alice Duer Miller, Clarence Budington Kelland, and Mary Roberts Rinehart.

His in-laws, the Alexander Sedgwicks of Stockbridge, never quite approved of this connection: this was not literature with a capital L, and anything less was a subject for disparagement. They wore an air of polite apology for John, and I am sure that this galled him, as it would have any young writer who is supporting his family and gradually acquiring a professional competence, and that it stirred in him a fierce determination to break away from the short story field when the time was right for something more ambitious.

The break came in 1935. He had published novels before this, works of apprenticeship which had found few readers. As Japan stepped up its assaults on China, he realized that Mr. Moto's days of popularity were numbered. John's marriage had gone on the rocks, and he was unhappy and restive, which is a provocative mood for any satirist to be in. To the dismay of his literary agent, he ceased writing short fiction and began to experiment in a new medium. He wrote to accentuate the changes which had overtaken American society in his home state, Massachusetts, and in its capital, Boston. He wanted to catch to the very life the pompous mannerisms which characterized certain Boston clans in the Back Bay. For months he worked at this experiment, and when he had finished 40,000 words, needing encouragement, he sent the manuscript in its half-completed state to Brandt & Brandt in New York. The report he got back from his agent was wholly in the negative: no magazine would think of serializing such stuff; no publisher would touch it. Deeply troubled, John appealed to his friend and publisher, Alfred McIntyre:

> The last two months I have been working on a thing which I have often played with in the back of my mind, a satire on the life and letters of a Bostonian. I have now done some thirty or forty thousand words on it, and the other day showed it to a friend whose literary judgment I greatly respect, who feels it is a great pity for me to waste my time in going ahead with it. I suppose the most damning thing that can be said about the whole business is that I, personally, have enjoyed writing it, and think it is amusing, and think that it is a fairly accurate satire on Boston life. I certainly don't want to go ahead with the thing, however, if you don't think it holds any promise, and is not any good. Besides this, I do not, for purely artistic reasons, feel that the thing can be helped by any great changes such as injecting more plot, or by making the satire more marked. In other words, if it is not any good as it stands, I think I had better ditch it and turn my attention to something else. As this is the first time in a good many years that I have been in a position to write something which I really wanted

to write, I naturally feel bad about it. I know you will tell me frankly just how it strikes you, and its fate rests largely in your hands. Tell me quickly.

McIntyre did tell him quickly. He said, "John, I personally think it is swell. I can't tell you whether it will sell more than 2000 copies—it may be too highly specialized. But by all means, go ahead with it!" McIntyre's judgment was amply vindicated in 1938 when *The Late George Apley* was awarded the Pulitzer Prize and embarked on a sale which has not yet ended. *Apley* is not only a wonderful take-off on Boston—of the bird-watching in Milton, of the iron discipline in the summer cottage in Maine, of the fastidious economy of Beacon Street; it is also a beautifully sustained parody of a way of writing about Boston once widely practiced and, at the time of the book's appearance, still held locally in high regard. There were some in the Back Bay who accepted it quite literally as a biography and who appeared at the Boston Museum of Fine Arts on Sunday afternoons asking to be shown the "Apley Bronzes." Coming, as it did, after the gentility of Robert Grant's novels and the sugary romances with which Joseph C. Lincoln celebrated Cape Cod, *The Late George Apley* arrived with the shock of self-discovery.

It came to be fashionable to say that *Apley* was the best novel Marquand had ever written, and this, of course, was nonsense, for as a maturing satirist he was constantly seeking new directions and new targets in the works that followed. John himself used to tell the story of sitting beside Mr. Rantoul during lunch at the Somerset Club. Mr. Rantoul, who was deaf and only turned on his hearing aid when he wanted to be heard, said: "John, I have read your new book, and I don't like it. It isn't nearly up to your *Sorrell & Son*."

"Thank you, Mr. Rantoul," said John in that high quaver of his which hid laughter, "but I didn't write *Sorrell & Son*. Warwick Deeping did."

Mr. Rantoul turned off his hearing aid.

This, of course, was Boston's way of saying that they wished he would take his satire elsewhere, that his shafts came uncomfortably close to home.—EDWARD WEEKS, "John P. Marquand," *At*, Oct. 1960, pp. 74–75

## General

In attempting any estimate of John Marquand's writing, it is important to remember that with *Apley* he broke brilliantly into a new field of his own devising. In this novel he was writing about the older generation, the generation ahead of his, and it is undeniably easier to satirize one's grandparents and parents than it is to satirize one's contemporaries. In *Wickford Point*, which some regard as the most autobiographical of his novels, he is still devoted to the idiosyncrasies of the old, but there is also present his alter ego, the observer, Jim.

This story, with its comical and absolutely authentic mixture of high thinking and plain foolishness so attractively epitomized in the person of Great-aunt Sarah, has running through it a sort of gentle madness which I prize, for I can find it in no other of John's books. One of my happy memories of *Wickford*—and there are many—is the matter of the side door, which was supposed to be irretrievably closed and which had been left that way for years because nobody had bothered to deal with it, and how it was finally opened in a few moments of bored puttering by young Jim, who found that nothing more complicated than an old love letter had been wedged in at a crucial spot to keep it shut. There is loneliness and hurt and love (the love for Kent's Island, which eventually became his own home place) in *Wickford Point*, and somehow, in the fast, crisp prose of that book, I have the feeling that the author is speaking to me more intimately than in any other.

In *H. M. Pulham, Esquire*, Marquand devoted himself to a more conventional subject, the parochial Harvard frame of mind, but within this limitation, the irony is devastating. Harry Pulham has conformed at every stage of his career, from his boarding school to Harvard, from the final club to bond salesman, from financial consultant to his marriage with Kay, a marriage he can neither control nor quit. Step by step it is a story of conformity and of frustration—and of pathos too, for Pulham is as decent as he is defenseless.

Marquand was always more interested in men than in women, and the heroines in his books are usually given small scope. But in *Pulham* it is Kay, the wife, who supplies much of the comedy and the cruelty: the comedy when, after her capture of Harry, she arranges what is surely one of the oddest honeymoons in American letters. Off they go to a neighboring summer hotel, a hotel not unlike Wentworth-by-the-Sea, where in a matter of hours they are to be joined by her parents for the duration of their stay. The cruelty is in her infidelity with Bill King, a betrayal from which Pulham can only avert his eyes.

After completing his portraits of that professional Harvard alumnus, Bojo Brown, and the plaintive Pulham, Marquand widened his range, and with his remarkable power of assimilation he set out to satirize the foibles of the New Dealers in Washington (*B. F.'s Daughter*), of men in banking (*Point of No Return*), of those in the West Point fraternity (*Melville Goodwin, USA*), and of the ruthless, hard-driving businessman (*Sincerely, Willis Wayde*). He was so observant and had such an accurate inner ear for American idiom that it all came to seem deceptively easy. The critics, who are always suspicious of success, marked him down for this, just as earlier they had underestimated Somerset Maugham: storytelling as easy to read as this couldn't be that good.

The downgrading was unfair. It overlooks the credibility which Marquand brought to every line he wrote; it overlooks that fine blend of humor and skepticism which makes one laugh aloud as one reads; it overlooks John's almost infallible prescience. As a satirist, he was always two jumps ahead of the rest of the country. When he began the writing of *Point of No Return*, he correctly foresaw that many veterans would have no stomach for the jobs they returned to, and so his story of Charles Gray and the revulsion he feels at being caught in that Manhattan bank were a symbol of the rebellious self-examination going on privately everywhere.

I rank *Point of No Return* as one of the best and truest of his books, and having read it twice in manuscript, I know how carefully he checked the financial details with his friend Ed Streeter (who was a banker); of the many cuts, some of them sizable, which he made at the suggestion of Alfred McIntyre; and of the reading aloud and rewriting which made Charles Gray's disputes with Nancy, his wife, so natural and so disturbing.

Charles Gray, like Jim Calder in *Wickford Point*, is a man for whom the reader feels an increasing respect. This was rare in Marquand novels, for he never committed his liking wholeheartedly to anyone. More often, the leading character diminishes as the irony cuts him down. I remarked to John after reading *Sincerely, Willis Wayde* that Wayde had started out as a rather appealing young man, only to wind up as a truly disgusting individual. "That is certainly right," John replied, as if surprised himself at Wayde's excesses. "He turned out to be a real stinker, didn't he?"

John's loyalties were centered in Newburyport, and here his dearest family attachment was to his great-aunt Mary, the spinster sister of his grandfather Curzon. She was a person of great quality and independence; William Ellery Channing had proposed to her, and Whittier and Thomas Wentworth Higginson were her friends; she prided herself on coming from a family of shipowners, not ship captains; she served no liquor in her house, since it had once had a disastrous effect on an earlier Marquand; and until her death at the age of eighty-seven she maintained a regime, candlelit, handwritten, do-it-yourself, faithful to the disciplines she had been taught as a girl in the Federalist period. For John she epitomized the virtue and durability of a New England he loved and hated to see changed. Thus, it seems appropriate that he should give us such a generous and delightful view of his home town and of Aunt Mary (and, incidentally, of himself) in his posthumous volume, *Timothy Dexter Revisited*, which in its individual and discriminating reminiscence is the next thing to an autobiography. Three decades ago John wrote a short biography of "Lord" Timothy, the eccentric tanner who made his fortune by buying Continentals. In this amplification Dexter is still present, but the central story is the rise and decline of a colonial seaport.

Marquand's revaluation is somewhat at variance with the research of a team of social scientists, headed by W. Lloyd Warner, who descended on Newburyport twenty years ago with institutional funds. Their case study of the town, in that ponderous idiom social scientists use for shorthand, fills five volumes: they classified the town socially into "upper-upper, middle-upper, lower-upper; upper-middle, middle-middle, lower-middle; upper-lower, middle-lower, lower-lower," and in the process Mr. Warner told Marquand precisely where he belonged in this classification. John submitted to this pretentious pedagogy while it was in process, partly curious, partly skeptical; he paid his respects to social scientists with a nice caricature in *Point of No Return*, and now, in *Timothy Dexter Revisited*, the reverential irony with which he documents or ridicules Mr. Warner's theorizing is saucy reading.

A country is fortunate to have a writer of Marquand's magnetism to hold up the mirror to its extravagance and hypocrisy. He wrote as he felt, and in his own conversation he laid about him in talk that those who heard it will long remember. It was fun to watch him as he approached the verge of the preposterous: his pupils would enlarge, his lips seemed to curl in despair, his voice would rise in exasperation until, with a sudden sniff and an outthrust of both hands, he pushed the folly away from him and over the cliff. His soliloquies on the TV Westerns, which he could reproduce with sound effects, and even the commercials; his account of how his novels were emasculated when they were cut down to a third of their size for serialization; his description, point by point, of the abstract mural in the new Harvard house were convulsively funny and could have come only from a man who loved life and who relished the American way of doing things, even when it was at its zaniest.—EDWARD WEEKS, "John P. Marquand," *At*, Oct. 1960, pp. 75–76

Essentially Marquand has only one central character—the middle-aged New England gentleman (sometimes living in New York), who is under tremendous pressure to conform, from his inheritance, from his family, from the society in which he lives. In some books—in *So Little Time*, which is a study of America being sucked into Europe's wars for the second time within a generation, and in the novelette, *Repent in Haste* (1945), which deals with an unsuccessful "war marriage"—he is more topical than usual, but this consideration involves no change of method. In *Wickford Point*,

Jim Calder, who has no wife, finally breaks away from the victimizing relatives whose moral deterioration even surpasses their financial decline; this, however, is not typical. The usual fate of the Marquand hero is acquiescence. In *H. M. Pulham, Esquire*, the "suitable" wife not only fails to bring her husband happiness but comes very close to betraying him. Yet when he meets the New York girl, Marvin Myles, again, he realizes that he would have been no better off with her, for Marquand is as clear as Wolfe or Cabell that "We can't go back."

This is perhaps not quite true in *The Late George Apley*, which is by all means the most experimental in form among Mr. Marquand's books and technically quite the most brilliant. *Apley* takes the shape of a discreet "Life and Letters" of a solid Boston and Milton citizen, prepared by a typical Beacon Street memoirist for private circulation in an edition of fifteen copies. It is not news at this date that the novel sold considerably more than that: it must be, far and away, the most "successful" of all "literary" novels. George Gissing's *The Private Papers of Henry Ryecroft* is no doubt as famous a work but it certainly has not achieved anything like a comparable circulation. The satire is directed quite as much against Mr. Willing, the memoirist, as it is against George Apley himself, and Mr. Willing, unlike his subject, is set forth completely upon his own terms and left to condemn himself through the superficiality of his thinking and the limitations of his style. Marquand was never to trust the intelligence of his readers to quite the same extent again, and his later books are more conventional in form. Technically their outstanding quality is their use of the "flash back," which Marquand employs perhaps more extensively than any other novelist has ever ventured, though I think there is an element of artificiality about the structure in *Point of No Return*. He has an engaging way, too, of adding depth to his novels by offering a wholly inferential treatment of the more important themes while the foreground is occupied with trivialities, such as, for example, the very unpromising business of the class reunion upon which *H. M. Pulham, Esquire* opens. When Thomas Apley is in decline he suddenly remarks one day to his wife that he wonders whether it might not have been better after all "if George had married that little Irish girl." Mary Monahan was a Catholic, and she lived in South Boston; obviously it wouldn't have "done." Only, unfortunately, there was nothing else in life that George ever really wanted. When Thomas dies he leaves a million to Harvard to be used for the benefit of "deserving Protestant students" from the Milton area, and his son is compelled, upon the advice of his lawyers, to pay a considerable sum to a New York hussy who claims old Thomas as the father of her child, not, of course, because George believes the story but simply to protect his father's name from scandal. But in spite of all variations from book to book, the reader always knows where to "have" Mr. Marquand.
—EDWARD WAGENKNECHT, "Novelists of the 'Thirties," *Cavalcade of the American Novel*, 1952, pp. 441–43

A man, to Marquand, is a nexus of institutions, the half-unwilling, half-imaginary point at which Harvard, the Stock Exchange, and the Army intersect. He has one soldier say: "You're not in school any longer. Can't you forget it?" The other answers, *à la* Marquand: "Why should I? I'm always thinking about school"; and the first soldier reflects that war *is* like school, wonders whether "school and war do not go together." Marquand himself says in a speech: "Most people obviously believe that Harvard is the greatest and freest institution in the world," and finishes the speech with: "Let us not say it elsewhere, but perhaps we all are more fascinating and a little better than other people." This was said with a smile, and with a grain of irony, and to an audience a little

better for it than other people, an audience of Harvard men, but Marquand's heart was in what he said. He is in love with—or anyway, married to—the institutions of this world, and that is why he can observe them so carefully: he has, by now, all the grounds for the divorce he will never quite get, all the facts for the biography he will never quite write except in its authorized form; and when, in the end, he is laid away, by schoolfellows, he will be able to remember in detail everything that he is missing.

And how easily he might have missed it all! how easily America, with all its buffalo and Elks and Indians, might not have had any Oxford, any *Académie Française*, any *Almanach de Gotha* for Marquand to observe! If you reply, like James or Hawthorne, that America doesn't have them for Marquand or anybody else to observe, there is always the retort: "And what's wrong with Harvard and the National Academy of Arts and Letters and the Social Register?"—the retort, "And what's wrong with the Pentagon, the Senate, and General Motors?" No, the institutions are here for him to observe, and he is inside them observing: to Marquand there is something romantic, something miraculous, about both facts. As for the men whose shadows these institutions are—the men who make and break states, corporations, and academies—in Marquand's books they are a little gray, a little ghostly, except in so far as their organizations give them bone and hue.

But it *is* romantic, miraculous almost, that Marquand should be here, straight out of *The Age of Innocence*, to observe this new age of *adjusting to one's group*, and *sharing the experience of one's generation*, and getting divorced because the president of one's corporation doesn't approve of one's wife, and all the rest of it. Why doesn't General Motors give Marquand a few hundred thousand dollars, keep him around the office—the offices—for a year or two, and then let him write the great American novel, about General Motors? Of course, it would be the same novel he's always written, but that's all right too, isn't it?—what's good enough for the rest of the country is good enough for General Motors.

As a writer Marquand is somewhat short on talent, imagination, brute ability, but is long on care, observation, directed curiosity, and is longest of all on personal involvement, subjective compulsion. Most of his books, under their veneer of patiently observed objective detail, seem versions of the same subjective fable, one designed to say to him and also to us: "You were right to do as you did; or if not right, still, you had no choice; or if you had a choice, still, it's the choice all of us necessarily make wrong: life's life. If only—but it doesn't matter. And . . . and it was all so long ago." The fable is told in a series of flashbacks, of sighs as elegiac, nostalgic, and wistfully submissive—as mannered and unvarying—as a Puccini opera. These flashbacks are not optional technique, but compulsory content: because of them the hero never has to make, in close-up, a clear choice to kiss or kill—the choices are always obscured by the haze of the past, of rueful and lyric recollection.

At the proper distance of time everything looks inevitable: we do not judge, but feel about, what we did, and the possibility of doing or choosing differently seems naïve, one more of youth's illusions. A Marquand character says: "I was faced by one of those uncomfortable moments of illumination when life is clear and simple, and, consequently, grim." But usually, to a Marquand character, life is obscure and complicated, and, consequently, elegiac. Marquand characters—the "real" Marquand characters, those we think like Marquand—love nothing so much as saying: "No matter how you try, you can't really understand anything; no matter what you do, you can't really change anything." Marquand's coat of arms ought to have in the middle a man saying *It doesn't matter* because it matters so much that there is nothing else for him to say.

This "real" Marquand character is the hero of the books' persistent fable. A man a little different—and consequently a little on the outside—looks with half-superior, half-inferior understanding at those entirely un-different others who *are* the inside. This man has a chance to break out of it all and be a different failure: a female chance, generally, one as mesmeric and unreliable as life; and he refuses this chance, or accepts it only to regress, as soon as he gets a chance to be the same success the others are: a female chance, generally, as monotonous and inescapable as life. Lying alongside Eve's spare necessary shape, the man dreams of the Lilith he left—and, waking in the darkness, he sighs that he was right to leave her, and that life is life.

Browning said, "The sin I impute to each frustrate ghost / Is the unlit lamp and the ungirt loin"; we learn from Marquand that it wasn't a sin but a necessary evil. No wonder that our age and nation and species are grateful to him! Besides, there has always been something attractive about Marquand: we like somebody who succeeds with such bad conscience, and who seems to wish that he had had the nerve to be a failure or, better still, something to which the terms *success* and *failure* don't apply—as when Mallory said, about Everest: "Success is meaningless here." This small uneasy institution set down at the intersection of so many great ones, this little newsstand among the skyscrapers, looking up at them with a wistful accepting sigh—what if he *has* made as much money as some of them? It isn't money that is the legal tender of our dreams: the dreamer would trade all his royalty statements for one thaler of fairy gold. We leave Marquand with one of his own sighs: if only his good angel had been a person, and not an institution. . . .—RANDALL JARRELL, "'Very Graceful Are the Uses of Culture,'" *Harper's*, Nov. 1954, pp. 94–96

John P. Marquand engaged in the Balzacian task of drawing a picture of contemporary American society through a series of fictional biographies. We have a good tycoon, a bad tycoon, a general, a news commentator, a trust officer, a successful playwright, a Boston Brahmin of the old type and one of the new. Except for the Brahmins, the subjects are apt to be of middle class New England origin—often from a town called Clyde in Massachusetts—and their past hovers over their heads, even in the days of their triumph, like a miasma. They are never free of the sense of social distinctions bred into them in childhood. Afraid of condescending and afraid of being condescended to, they are haunted by the idea that they have not alighted on just the right rung of the social ladder. Into their make-up goes a strange mixture of ambition and humility, with some of the drive of the parvenu and some of the resignation of an old English servant. When I think of a Marquand novel I am apt to think of two characters, acquainted from boyhood, facing each other awkwardly over the gulf created by the success of one, as in *Women and Thomas Harrow*, when the local boy returns to buy the big house on the fashionable street and employs an old schoolmate to replant the garden.

"Hello, Jack," Tom Harrow said.

"Hello, Tom," Jack Dodd said. "You're looking good."

There must have been some sort of reverse explanation of why he was pleased that Jack Dodd should call him Tom. He could never be wholly at ease with Jack Dodd or with other of his contem-

poraries there in town, when he could deal with people in any other place in the world adroitly, affably, and without the slightest sense of strain.

It is not a coincidence that the finest novel of a writer so obsessed with the problem of class consciousness should be concerned with the past. The late George Apley's dates are 1866 to 1933, and he is born at the summit of a formidable Boston pyramid of classes which would have provided Trollope with as rich material as Barsetshire. We are shown the warping of Apley's character by the forces of property and position, we see him lose his early struggle for independence and the Irish girl whom he wants to marry, and we see him settle down at last in defeat to a life of bird watching, civic duties and the arid satisfaction of denouncing a new world. Yet for all his flag waving and for all his bitter prejudices, Apley remains a man of courage and a man of heart. His defeat is brought about by a wholly sincere veneration for the opposing forces. To have married Mary Monahan would have cost him the esteem of every human being whom he has been brought up to admire and disqualified him for the position of leadership that he believes it his duty to take up. The defeat of such a man holding to such a creed is not tragic, but it is pathetic, and pathos has a bigger place than tragedy in the study of manners.

*H. M. Pulham, Esquire* proves that the passing of a single generation has stripped the conflict of its pathos. Why should Harry Pulham (who might be Apley's son), a war hero, working in an advertising agency in New York, not marry Marvin Miles? His family might have frowned and criticized her dress and speech, but they would have come around soon enough. Such marriages were everyday affairs in the twenties, even in Boston. Pulham himself recognizes the change in the times when he assesses the social opportunities which his friend, Bill King, has passed up:

> Bill would actually have got on very well at Harvard, I think, if he had cared about trying. It was true that he did not have any connections, but if he had gone out for something besides the Dramatic Club, such as the Lampoon, or even the Crimson, and if he had bothered with the people to whom I had introduced him and who usually liked him, he would very possibly have made a Club.

We see what has happened. Bill King doesn't *want* a club, and Marvin Miles doesn't want Pulham. The shoe is now on the other foot. The trouble is that if Marvin doesn't want him, the reader isn't going to want him very much, either, for Marvin is a shrewd girl. Pulham's problem is not, like Apley's, that he is caught in the vise of a social system, but that he is totally lacking in humor and imagination. It is a bit difficult to sympathize with or even to believe in a decorated war hero who is afraid to ask the family butler for an extra glass and so disclose to the world below stairs that the woman he loves wants a drink before dinner.

After *Pulham* Marquand was permanently stuck with the problem of creating heroes who had to be strongly influenced by less and less influential environments and who at the same time would not strike his readers as Casper Milquetoasts. He solved it partially with the gentleman hero of the suburbs, a kind, earnest patient man of an absolute but rather wearisome integrity, a faithful husband and adoring father, who plods through a dull life in a sleepwalking fashion, prodded by a nervous, suspicious wife who has invested her emotional being in local standards of success and is terrified that her house of cards will fall if she allows her husband, even in joke, to question the least of her adopted values. Charles Gray in *Point of No Return* and Bob Tasmin in *B. F.'s Daughter* both fail with their first loves because they don't push hard enough, thus perhaps deserving the fate of being pushed about by their second. A few words uttered or held back might have turned the scales in Tasmin's relationship with Polly Fulton. Yet he moodily blames his ineptitude on his inheritance:

> I've always been a goddam gentleman, and I've always been afraid not to be one. Let's put it on my tombstone. That's my whole obituary.

In the later novels the function of each hero's elaborately described background becomes even fuzzier. What does that drugstore in Vermont have to do with Melville Goodwin's wanting to be a soldier? And how does Willis Wayde pick up the habit of sentimentalizing his motives and calling everything "lovely" in a bleak Yankee community like Clyde? Marquand seems to be tracing Willis' hunger for success to his family's move into the garden cottage on the great estate of the aristocratic Harcourts, a thoroughly Victorian situation. Bess Harcourt is as haughty as Pip's Estella, and poor Willis achieves his financial goal only to have her fling in his teeth a bitter Victorian epithet: "Get out of my way, Uriah Heep!" The moral seems to be that to such as Willis, the world of the fine old Harcourts, with its traditions of loyalty and integrity, will be forever closed. To such as Willis, yes. But why? Not because of his social ambition or even because of his business ruthlessness, but simply because of his drooling sanctimoniousness. If he had faced Bess Harcourt boldly, like a John O'Hara hero, and flung in *her* teeth that he was closing down the Harcourt mills because they didn't pay, she would have rewarded him as O'Hara ladies reward such heroes. What she really condemns him for (and who wouldn't?) is that he reads the Harvard Classics fifteen minutes a day and boasts about it.

My favorite of the novels, after *The Late George Apley*, is *Point of No Return*, perhaps because it dramatizes just the point that I have been trying to make, that the paralyzing effect of a class-conscious background is largely illusory. Charles Gray can only be liberated from Clyde by returning there and finding that Jessica Lovell is about to save herself from middle-aged spinsterhood by marrying Jackie Mason, who was born further down the social ladder than Charles himself. The poor old past is now revealed to him in all its smallness and sterility, as sad and foolish as Jessica's neurotic, deluded father who once told Charles that money made on the stock market was not the same as inherited money. So Charles goes back to New York and the Stuyvesant Bank, strengthened in the discovery that his youth was dominated by puppets, and finds that the promotion of which he has despaired has been assured him all along, that his rival for the bank vice-presidency has been as illusory as Clyde. His trip has had the effect of a psychoanalysis. But when the function of a character's background is only his misconception of it, the novel of manners has become a psychological novel.—LOUIS AUCHINCLOSS, "The Novel of Manners Today" (1960), *Reflections of a Jacobite*, 1961, pp. 142–48

## Works

*The Late George Apley* is sub-titled "A Novel in the Form of a Memoir," because it is the life and letters of a man who never lived in Boston and who never died there. These letters were compiled and the life was written by Mr. Apley's intimate friend, a Mr. Horatio Willing, who like Mr. Apley is a figment of the imagination. The same is true of all the lesser characters in the book. Mr. Apley's family, friends and enemies are in no sense individuals who have walked the streets of Boston or elsewhere in the flesh, and they are all concerned in adventures which never happened. This is as it should be, for there is nothing more glaringly inartistic than the sketch of an actual

person or the narration of an actual event in the pages of a novel, since neither can fit properly into the limited medium of print. The truth is, if fiction is to give a sense of reality, the writer must create characters and circumstances which would assume unbelievable distortions if they appeared outside the covers of a book. In short, it is my humble opinion that fiction, to give an illusion of fact, can never employ fact successfully. The *roman à clef*, I believe, is a species of literature that exists only in the critic's imagination.

Yet though there is nothing factual about the characters and events, I should be pleased if, when added together, they became the single reality of an attitude of mind. The mental approach of the late George Apley, which is in no sense confined to such a limited sphere as Boston, seems to me worthy of notice in a rapidly changing world. It is an attitude bred of security, the familiar viewpoint of generations of the *rentier* class. It is a phenomenon, observable in every civilization, and one which must exist whenever society assumes a stable pattern. I have tried to present a picture without analyzing my own reactions, but in conducting Mr. Apley through the trivialities of his years I confess I was startled to discover when I left him that he amounted to more than I had intended. Indeed, in many respects he seemed to approach the status of an apology for his class. I hope that other readers will agree with me in this and will share a little of my own surprise that Mr. Apley, as a human being, did the best he could; that he could not have done differently; that it was not his fault that he was an Apley.

Finally, it may be fair to warn the reader that the effusions of Mr. Willing and the letters to Mr. Apley must not be considered as literary models. In spite of all his pedantry and pretensions and pride at being called a purist, I have intended Mr. Willing to be a very unsound writer. It often amused me to make him rise to the heights of verbose elaboration, only to fall down hard on grammar and good usage. This habit of Mr. Willing's has been an annoyance to many readers, but I hope the device reveals his character. As for Mr. Apley and other members of his family, I had them write their letters hastily and informally, and so they exhibit many glaring faults. Mr. Apley was never a purist. There are many Bostonians like him in that respect.—JOHN P. MARQUAND, "Introduction" to *The Late George Apley*, 1940, pp. iii–iv

If the couple in T. S. Eliot's *Cocktail Party* represents the best the poet can say for middle-class life, then we may without apology offer George Apley to Eliot as an additional exhibit for his defense of aristocracy. Even in decay, Apley's class maintains the traditions of civilized behavior. Its members submit themselves to the influence of Harvard, of a few good novels, of art objects of a certain grace. It is culturally significant that the world of the late George Apley can still be reconstructed out of diaries, papers written for his club (if only annually), and letters of a Jamesian gentlemanliness and a pathos the more moving because it is so sublimely unaware of just how and why the world has passed the writer by.

George Apley emerges, despite Marquand's satirical intent, as a rather attractive figure, with a good deal more dignity and stamina than most contemporary fictional creations of any class. He does not belong, of course, to the great aristocratic tradition of a Churchill. He is quite a comedown even from his enterprising mercantile grandfather and his hard-headed industrialist father. But in an age which asks little of the spirit and is content with less, Apley is not without solid virtues.

A passionate writer could never cope with Apley; he could only rage at the absence of passion, the deliberate unthinking refusal to live in the senses or in the feelings. But Marquand, while he writes from an ironical height which comes close to being a point of despair, is sufficiently steeped in Apley's world to create it with a style that is its own image, its mild bare formal poetry. This is a world of the most modest pleasures, bird-watching and club meetings, of the most peculiar cultural gaps and lapses—yet of a generic aesthetic sense possessed, it would seem, by a whole class. It is a world which is absurd without ever departing seriously from good taste; in which Apley continues his collection of Chinese bronzes through boredom and distaste, with that persistence in the uninteresting which appears to be the major cultural talent of his class. Here wealth does not signify luxury; it is rather carried as a burden and a responsibility by men who make a fetish of discomfort, wearing starched collars and sitting in stiff chairs and refusing obstinately to cater to any spontaneous emotion.

"I have noticed," writes George Apley to his returning prodigal son, "that you are interested in certain social questions. Be sure to deal with these very lightly, if at all—better not at all. You must understand that the Berkeley Club and the Province Club are both havens of refuge where no one wishes to be emotionally disturbed." Troublesome subjects become "interesting topics for casual dinner-table conversation." The whole system of ritual in Boston Brahminism appears to be directed at deflecting emotional disturbances. Serenity is achieved through a resistance to change, through rites practiced scrupulously over years and generations. At this juncture, the decadent and the primitive meet, for if we want to locate a comparable set of inbred customs we have only to examine the anthropologists' Samoa or Bali. In Boston as in the South Sea Islands, ceremony wears down rough edges and by causing certain gestures to be repeated constantly, bestows grace upon them. Even the forms of daily expression take on an elegiac, timeless quality, expressed in Apley's complaint, "I don't know quite what will happen to us."

Marquand is not sure of his feelings toward Apley. The surface quality of the writing is dead-pan mockery: of Apley's obsessions and his occasional tries at literary criticism, of the Berkeley Club narrator's stilted and platitudinous and pretentiously ungrammatical style, of the ways in which self-interest dictates moral sentiments. But the satire is fundamentally gentle and we cannot be certain that Marquand does not share a number of Apley's sentiments . . . or that we do not ourselves. On the subject of progress, for example, Apley remarks (at an unusually felicitous moment) that "we have evolved a fine variety of flushing toilets, but not a very good world." Nor is he entirely unconvincing when he sees matters moving "too fast, far too fast." He was referring only to the subway connecting Boston with Cambridge and to the new dormitories at Harvard: he could not then envision the traffic of our big cities today, or the rooftop sprouts and the dank living-room roots of television.

In the end, Apley's tragedy is personal and universal, and beyond the range of the class terms in which it is expressed. It is true that Apley in his prime is no longer a free agent, that his immobility has been prepared for him by two generations of asceticism, accumulation of wealth, and repression of feeling. His life takes on its tragic aspect only because Apley is surreptitiously *aware* of the dead weight of tradition and respectability, and at rare moments of self-knowledge feels the impulse to break away. Twice he travels to Europe and each time Boston follows him. Once he was fascinated by an out-of-the-way road in a French village and wished, as he wrote a friend, "that I might be walking up to see something by myself and for myself, without guidance and without advice. I wonder will I walk up any road alone?"

Looking back later at his timid encounters with alien manners, however, he accounts them a waste of time: "Your own sort are the best friends." He had never really ventured into that other world except as one pokes a toe in a cold pool, but in Apley's adjustable memory, he can pretend to have dived bravely in and found the water muddy. As he grows older and his concerns become more rigid and more trivial—he writes his son at great length about the appearance of mice in the blanket chest—he is driven to insist, "I try to keep my mind open to new ideas." Almost uncannily, his letters exemplify the familiar ritual pattern of cultural indoctrination, muffled revolt, submission, and petrifaction. Bewildered and pathetic under the placid surface of good manners, George Apley completes the ordained arc of self-destruction.—NATHAN GLICK, "Marquand's Vanishing American Aristocracy," *Cmty*, May 1950, pp. 436–37

It is fair to claim that *Point of No Return* is the most philosophically ambitious of Marquand's novels. In the account of Charles Gray as much as in any of the works of Dos Passos or Dreiser there is a grim sense of the direction in which American society tended to move during the first four decades of the twentieth century. The central fact of the plot is the stock market crash of 1929, for that single event conditions the life and choices of every major character. Marquand was always strong in his handling of circumstantial details, and in no modern American novel does one get a sharper sense of the impingement of things, antagonistic, implacable, on private lives.

By now Marquand's great powers in the construction of character and the evocation of place function on a wider scale. The range of people from the business world becomes so extensive that it grows intimidating—the competitive and urbane Roger Blakesley, the aristocratic and sly Tony Beaton, Mr. Selig, whose credentials are not acceptable to the Stuyvesant Bank, the Zeus-like figure of Mr. Lovell, plotting financial tricks in his princely study, and the cautious Jackie Mason, who so desperately wants to succeed and who, appropriately, wins in marriage the aging and frustrated Jessica Lovell. The book shows the multiple ways in which commercial competition has become the chief operative force in American society, a force more doctrinaire and ultimately more perilous than any conventions of Boston brahmins or the indolence of the Brills. Charles Gray does not even possess the continuity, no matter how formalistic, which sustained Harry Pulham. "There was a curtain, translucent but not transparent," Charles is forced to conclude, "between the present and the past." No prior Marquand hero had ever found himself so isolated. At one point Charles compares living in the town of Clyde to "walking through spiderwebs without any spiders. . . ." It is natural that he should not see the adversaries who noiselessly trap him, for they no longer depend on the edicts of family, nor are they among the ghosts at the local historical museum. They wait, motionless and lethal, inside bank vaults.—GEORGE GREENE, "A Tunnel from Persepolis: The Legacy of John P. Marquand," *QQ*, Autumn 1966, pp. 351–52

The hero of John P. Marquand's new novel, *Women and Thomas Harrow*, is an American playwright and director of fifty-four who is unhappy with his third wife, unsure of his ability to turn out a new Broadway hit, and who lives in a fabulously costly old mansion in the small New England town where he grew up. He is charming and bright, a gentleman as well as a wit; he is as respectful of the traditions of the little old New England home town (once a famous seaport) as he is of the hard professionalism of the theater, and he would be as much at home in that town as he is in New York were it not for his uncomfortable sense of irony about his life, his mocking awareness of every situation as one which he might have written and directed himself.

It is the unforgotten bite of poverty and comparative social inferiority in his youth that helps to explain his sudden undoing. Ever since his unexpected first success in the 1920s with a sardonic play about a war hero's return, which enabled him to marry a local girl whose father was a failure, Tom Harrow's regular success in the theater has driven him to spread himself more and more recklessly. His first wife, Rhoda, who is obsessed with a desire for security, finally left him for real money when he was whooping it up in North Africa during the war; characteristically, he gave her an excessively generous settlement. His second wife, a hard, ambitious actress, still gets lavish alimony from him; his third, a duller woman than the first two, an unsuccessful actress who is getting stouter than she would like, feels imprisoned in the house which her husband keeps up only out of piety to the traditions that surrounded his youth. All these handsome gestures, these symbolic excesses and improvidences, led Tom to risk his investments with a costume musical comedy which failed. With his capital gone, his wife turns on him; his first wife, who had discovered that life with big money can be dull, offers to return both his original settlement on her, and herself. In a fit of despair, Tom barely saves himself from going over a cliff in his big new car and realizes that from now on he must go it alone.

Summarizing the story makes Tom Harrow sound more of a money writer than he is. The point about him is not that he is venal, but that he is used to success; not corrupt, and the very opposite of cheap, he is a writer with a definite public who has always written with professional self-respect and skill. The trouble with him is not that he is a grasping *individual*, like the self-betraying hero who used to figure in American novels about the vanity of success, but, one of many Americans who have done their best and have enjoyed the profits, he has been betrayed by life itself—by the mediocrity of the society in which he lives. Thomas Harrow reminds us of many Americans today. He suffers not from a lack of honor—the old-fashioned explanation of misery in a highly competitive society—but from a lack of differentiation in both his character and the America he lives with. It is no longer a tragedy of character that such heroes act out, but a world depressed by its own lack of expectation. Tom Harrow has done his best, but the America in which he lives has become increasingly inflationary and socially pretentious, and the disappointment and disgust that sensitive Americans feel about our failure as a civilization trouble him.

Everything Thomas Harrow has to look at is either, like his beautiful old house, too distant from contemporary experience to be meaningful or, like the overlarge and overcolored automobile in which he finally tries to die, an example of the submissiveness and vulgarity that the "juke-box civilization" of mid-twentieth-century America has come to. The house, built by local shipwrights, represents for Tom "a revolt and a craving for luxury which its builder had never known," while his present wife, Emily, is by his own admission perhaps not so shallow as she seems when she complains that he has absurdly sacrificed a comfortable bathroom to keep an old prayer closet. Tom Harrow has collected three-pronged forks, rattail spoons, pistol-handled knives, Crown Derby china, George the Second candlesticks, Chippendale tables, but recognizes that "he had in reality been travelling rapidly all his life over a shoddy road, decorated meretriciously . . . with plastic refreshment booths and over-night motels . . . places of temporary respite for temporary indulgence, but no more." When he walks down

the main street of the dear old town and passes the church where he was first married, he reads that the next sermon topic is "How happy are you inside?"; and when he steps into the beautiful and simple church, the Reverend Ernest W. Godfrey greets Tom as a fellow professional, describes the church as a psychological filling station for troubled souls, and reveals that he's been in "this game long enough to know that every single one of us has his own problem and his own method of motivation as well as his particular means of adjustment, and his own particular subconscious mind."

Thomas Harrow lives in the American world we all have to live in these days. When he reflects, in the dark night of his soul (the bank is calling in the stocks he put up as collateral), that "national life was approaching an average that expressed itself in gastronomical and in spiritual mediocrity, and he had always hated mediocrity. . . . They would all soon be engulfed in the wave of the commonplace," we agree that the essence of Tom Harrow's relation to women has been his concern with old-fashioned standards of aristocratic ease, gaiety, personal honor, which his wives have been too frightened or too hard to respect. These women symbolize the increasing spiritual imperfection, the anxious and external greediness, which to many observers has made the American woman seem unnatural. Tom Harrow, the parfit gentil knight, lavishes enormous marriage settlements on wives who have run off with millionaires and thinks wistfully of his old aunt Edith, who, like so many New England women of her generation, never married but "was able to understand nearly everything from the basis of almost no appreciable experience." Rhoda, his first wife, his true wife (in his old-fashioned way Tom Harrow reflects that no matter how many times you married, you truly married only once), was constantly worried because change made her feel insecure. Rhoda used to say: "Do you have a feeling that everything is beginning to move so fast that we'll have to run to keep up with it? . . . I like things so I know where they'll be tomorrow."

But isn't this Tom Harrow's feeling as well? Rhoda's fear of change took the form of greed; Emily's of dread that she would be left alone; Tom's takes the form of cultural piety of beautiful old houses in old seaports like Newburyport—where John P. Marquand and the heroes of so many of his novels grew up. The ruling and obsessive image in all of Marquand's novels is that of traveling the American road to the point of no return, to the hour when there is so little time. In this book the conception of life as loss has become the dramatic image of a successful and attractive American trying to kill himself in the chromium, long-finned, grotesquely colored car which incarnates all the showiness that he loathes. It is perhaps not the "shoddy" American road that troubles Tom Harrow so much as it is the mechanical defeat of life itself; it is not our great and confused America of the Eisenhower age, with its weapons that reach to the stars and its people—many of whom look as if all wisdom had been squeezed out of them by the strain of American life—that comes into play so much as it is the fact that people get old, and that when they get old enough, they die.

What bothers John P. Marquand, as it bothers Thomas Harrow, is the suspicion that as people get older in America, they do not get wiser; they just reminisce. No matter how much one may admire Marquand's social skill, his wit, his sense of tact, above all his cool honesty, one knows that a Marquand novel will sag into flashback as surely as a Shakespearean hero will spout blank verse. What is wrong with so much reminiscence—which in this case, despite all Marquand's charm and wit, makes a sad, soft, rather self-indulgent book out of *Women and Thomas Harrow*—is the fact that, among other faults, Marquand no longer bothers to find a very convincing or dramatically interesting frame for these flights into the past. The evening the Harrows are giving a dinner party, Tom tells Emily that they are busted; she denounces him; he gets thoroughly soaked on Martinis, champagne, brandy, Scotch; then, sitting up most of the night in an alcoholic haze of self-reference, he goes over the failure of his life. Technically, this makes a hole in the book only because there is so much formal separation between Tom Harrow in the present and the Tom Harrow he is remembering that we cannot believe very much in the strength of a character who is largely shown on the shady side of his life. The flashback is usually the structural center of a Marquand novel, but in previous books the past was shown as inaccessible—not, as it is symbolically in this book, unrelated. The symbol is that of the unconnection in Tom Harrow's own mind between past and present America; the American failure is always the inability to find the past or to learn from it: sure breeding ground for nostalgia.—ALFRED KAZIN, "John P. Marquand and the American Failure," *At,* Nov. 1958, pp. 152–54

---

### GRANVILLE HICKS
### From "Marquand of Newburyport"

*Harper's,* April 1950, pp. 103–8

#### II

T he upper-upper class in one of its purest forms—as it flourished in Boston between the Civil War and the New Deal—is the subject of *The Late George Apley.* The Apleys, it will be recalled, are an old New England family, respected rather than rich to begin with, then moderately prosperous as merchants, and finally well-to-do as manufacturers. The family has achieved real wealth and has firmly consolidated its social position in the two generations before George Apley's.

No apology need be made for the use of ⟨W. Lloyd⟩ Warner's terminology, for it fits. "In the upper-upper," he writes ⟨in *The Social Life of a Modern Community*⟩, "the children are definitely subordinated to the older group and their position is one of great subordination to the parental generation in comparison to that of the young generation within the families of classes beneath this group." That says, in a rather clumsy way, what *The Late George Apley* is about. It is, among other things, a very knowing study of the mechanisms by which a social class enforces its standards and achieves the conformity of its members.

If George Apley were a born conformist, there would be no drama; it is his ineffectual rebelliousness that gives the character its interest and the novel its pathos. But conform he does, and in time is pinned into position by that famous Boston device, the trust fund. It is in his attempt to find a function to match his position that he sometimes makes himself ridiculous and provides the opportunity for the more boisterous part of Marquand's satire.

Much of the second half of the novel is concerned with George Apley's efforts to keep his son John in line. Because of the first world war, John escapes for a time, and he distresses his father by marrying a divorced woman, but he has not strayed very far from the standards of his class, and in the end he returns to Boston and the Apley heritage. It was to John's generation, a generation over which it was more difficult to maintain class controls, that Marquand turned in his next novel but one, *H. M. Pulham, Esquire.* Harry Pulham is almost an exact contemporary of John Apley, and like John he escapes from Boston by way of the first world war. Unlike John

however, he does not marry the girl he falls in love with in New York, but is married to the girl his family has selected, and the book explores the cost of conformity, not only for Harry but also for his wife.

Between *The Late George Apley* and *H. M. Pulham, Esquire,* Marquand wrote *Wickford Point,* which, in spite of his denials, has always been regarded as a portrayal of his Newburyport cousins, the Hales.

It is the story of an upper-upper family that has gone downhill. Related to the intellectual aristocracy of nineteenth-century New England, maintained in tarnished elegance by a trust fund and the leniency of their creditors, the Brills go their erratic way, confident of their distinction, arrogant, indolent, and rapacious. Although Marquand, like his narrator, seems to find in some of the Brills a charm that is likely to elude the reader, he makes them out, on the whole, to be a pretty bad lot.

The character of the Brills emerges most clearly in their relations with persons who do not belong to their own class. The problem of relationships between members of different classes, and particularly the marital relationship, gives a novelist material for dramatic situations, just as it provides the sociologist with an opportunity for generalizations.

"Members of a class," Dr. Warner says, "tend to marry within their own order, but the values of the society permit marriage up and down." Marriage is, indeed, one of the principal ways in which social mobility operates. "In class, unlike caste," as Warner carefully puts it, "there are three possibilities of marriage instead of the one in caste. As Chart V demonstrates, a person may marry above, below, or evenly." Mr. Marquand has taken all these possibilities into account.

George Apley and Harry Pulham, against their own inclinations, marry evenly. Jeff Wilson, in *So Little Time,* has married into a class above his own. In earlier novels Marquand had introduced the Harvard boy from the wrong side of the tracks, and now he did a full-length portrait of him, with a Harvard the Apleys and Pulhams had never known in the background. Jeff is supporting his wife and their children according to his wife's standards by doctoring plays and movies instead of writing plays of his own. ("My wife had lived in a style to which I was not accustomed," Marquand once said, speaking of his first marriage. "And ever since then I've been over a barrel.") The novel is principally concerned with the mood of America just before Pearl Harbor, but everything is seen through the troubled eyes of a man who is paying a price for his social mobility.

In *B. F.'s Daughter* an unequal marriage is portrayed from the other side of the barrier. B. F.—Burton Fulton—is a man with a gift for making money who has landed in the lower-upper class without knowing how he got there. Polly, the daughter of the title, would naturally marry into the upper-uppers, thus confirming the family's social success. However, because she is her father's daughter, she wants to dominate the man she marries, and, not being able to dominate the upper-upper who is in love with her, she takes on one of Marquand's incompetent college professors. He, far from feeling any obligation to support Polly in her accustomed style, is quite willing to adopt that style for himself at her expense, but he compensates for his subordination by infidelity, and Polly regrets her choice.

The extraordinary thing about Marquand's handling of class relationships is his ability to suggest the elusiveness of class lines. Charles Gray, in *Point of No Return,* is not only characteristically American but perfectly sensible in his rejection of Malcolm Bryant's wordy generalizations. This scheme of Bryant's approximates only in the roughest way the social pattern that Charles has experienced. But in practice Charles knows that there *are* lines, even though they aren't quite where Bryant thinks they are, and are drawn with a delicacy Bryant could never perceive. Marquand knows this, too, and his awareness accounts for some of his happiest touches.

In terms of Dr. Warner's marital possibilities *Point of No Return* is the story of a man who might have married out of his class but didn't. Look at the structure of the novel. In Part I we see Charley Gray in 1947, a member of the lower-upper class in the New York-Westchester sector who is fighting tooth and nail to maintain his social position, spurred on by an ambitious wife. The question is whether Charles is going to become vice president of the bank in which he works, and it is a vital question to Charles and, even more, to Nancy. Then, by one of Marquand's more ingenious contrivances, we are back in Clyde in Charles's young manhood, when he was in love with Jessica Lovell, an upper-upper. The Grays were lower-upper, and precariously so, in spite of ancestors and connections, for Charley's father had a talent for losing money. We know that Charley isn't going to marry Jessica, who is in a position of "great subordination to the parental generation," and we know that he is going to marry Nancy, whom we have seen to be something of a nagger. It all happens: Mr. Lovell breaks the engagement; Charley leaves Clyde and goes to work in New York; he meets Nancy. But then it turns out that Nancy "really was a Spruce Street girl." (The Grays live on Spruce Street, in Clyde, not on the Lovells' upper-upper Johnson Street.) She is, in short, the right kind of wife for Charley, good for him in a way that Jessica could never have been. The Grays, we realize, are representative Americans, fighting their way upward together, doing their best in the world as they find it.

By means of this reversal, Marquand makes the reader—even this reader—care whether Charles Gray gets to be a vice president of the Stuyvesant Bank.

In *Point of No Return*, Marquand not only has a lot of fun with the sociologists; he beats them at their own game, for the chapters on Clyde tell us more about a well-integrated, reasonably autonomous community with a population under 20,000 than we are likely to learn from the Yankee City series. If, like Charley Gray, he scoffs at the sociologists' generalizations, he knows what he sees with his own eyes. If the social structure of Newburyport, to say nothing of New York City, is too complex and too subtly defined to be reduced to a diagram, it has its own kind of reality. Marquand's understanding of that reality is an important element in his success as a novelist of manners.

### III

Like most novelists of manners, Marquand is often satirical, though satire is less prominent in his work than some critics, probably misled by *The Late George Apley*, have assumed. He has satirized advertising agencies, the slick magazines, omniscient correspondents and commentators. He has polished off the country club set, the Fairfield County intelligentsia, the hangers-on of the New Deal, the soft professors. No one can do a better job with the small talk of the conjugal breakfast table or bedroom, and some of his funniest scenes, such as the account of the Pulham family's return from a summer in Maine—"I had always believed in assuming that a motor trip with the children would be pretty bad, but actually that trip was worse"—grow out of the trivia of domestic life.

As a rule, he aims at fair and not very difficult game. His great gift is for accurate reporting—his eye is as good as Sinclair Lewis's at its best, and his ear is more dependable than Lewis's ever was—and he achieves his finest results with only a slight

heightening of effect. He is not a crusader, has no great store of indignation, is likely to temper his roughest blast with pity.

Towards persons of established social position—the upper-uppers, as Warner would say—he has an attitude of amused respect. It is true that he hasn't much to say for the Brills in *Wickford Point*, but they are aristocrats gone to seed. For the Apleys, on the other hand, diverting as he finds their behavior on occasion, he has a warm regard—even for George and certainly for his father and uncle. As a person who knows the system and yet stands outside it, he can render the comedy in the shaping of a George Apley, but he has no desire to repudiate all the Apley standards.

If anything, Marquand has a bias in favor of upper-class values. Harry Pulham, with all his limitations, is obviously a better person, more honorable, more useful, happier, than Bill King, the Harvard boy from the wrong side of the tracks who becomes a successful advertising man. Bob Tasmin, the upper-class lawyer whom B. F.'s daughter almost married, turns out to be vastly more admirable than the middle-class college professor whom Polly does marry. And in *So Little Time*, Jeff Wilson, knowing that he is going to be a hack the rest of his life, looks up, not to some dramatist who has succeeded where he has failed, but to Minot Roberts, the first upper-upper he ever knew.

Born into one of the old Newburyport families and into a good deal of luxury, Marquand was headed for Groton, but his father lost heavily in the panic of 1907, and he went to Newburyport High School instead. (He lived with his Newburyport aunts while his father was working on the Panama Canal.) He did get to Harvard, but only by virtue of scholarships and with very little money in his pockets. He learned to make money with his typewriter, and, as he has observed, he needed to, since he was married to a Sedgwick. They were divorced in 1935, and two years later he married Adelaide Hooker, a connection of the Rockefellers.

All this may explain the ambivalence of his attitude towards the values of the upper class. He has never forgotten, however, that the values of the upper-uppers, like everyone else's, are subject to the corrosive influence of time. The Apleys must change or perish. Jeff Wilson, much as he admires Minot Roberts, knows that his type is "a little outmoded, a little dry and sterile." Even for a Bob Tasmin, the most Marquand can say is that his values may be as good as any we an find in this confused world. "We're like fish being moved from one aquarium to another," one of the characters in *B.F.'s Daughter* says. "We were in one body of water, and now we're in another, but everything is moving so fast I can't remember what it used to be like." Tasmin writes his wife from the Pacific theater of war: "We were all taught to expect something different—I don't know exactly what and I wish I did." Many of Marquand's characters are nostalgic for times and places in which values were fixed, but, as Harry and his wife say at the end of *H. M. Pulham, Esquire*, and as someone is always implying in Marquand's novels, "We can't go back."

It is because Marquand is so acutely conscious of the changes time brings not merely to people but also to their values that all of his major novels move back and forth between present and past. He is wonderfully adroit in the use of the flashback, and, especially in *H. M. Pulham, Esquire* and *Point of No Return*, has solved with great ingenuity the problem of bringing the past into the present. His sense of time is even more precise than his sense of place or his sense of class. He knows the past thirty-five years—on the social planes and in the places with which he is concerned—as unerringly as one of Mark Twain's pilots knew the Mississippi River. A serious anachronism in one of his books is almost unthinkable, not because he is a pedantic researcher but because his feeling for time approaches infallibility.

Marquand's heroes are always confused and usually conscious of their confusion. He once defined his typical hero as "the badgered American male—and that includes me—fighting for a little happiness and always crushed by the problems of his environment." The inclusion of himself is significant. Marquand has never pretended that he was any clearer on the problem of values than the people he is writing about. (That is why he cannot be in any fundamental sense a satirist.) He sees that the people who have clear-cut standards often make mistakes, but so do those who haven't, and the mistakes of the latter are often worse. There are a few fools in Marquand's novels, but there are no wise men.

In *Point of No Return* Marquand suggests that perhaps the only thing to do is to accept things as they are. Charles Gray says to Nancy, "We're part of a system where there's always someone waiting to kick you in the teeth in a nice way," and Nancy replies, "It's a rotten system." But what, Mr. Marquand asks, is better? Not anything, certainly, that Clyde might have offered. And are the Grays so badly off? They have each other, and, like most Marquand couples, get along together much better than appearances indicate. They have their children, their home, their social position. They have their fight for success, and, as it turns out, they have their victory. Marquand barely alludes to what the Grays would have if they lost the fight, but he does admit with complete candor that what they have won is an ample distance this side of Paradise. But, he asks again, is there anything better? If there is, he has not shown it in this novel or in any other.

### IV

Each of Marquand's six serious novels has been a best seller, and *Point of No Return* stood at the top of the list for month after month. Why? His books have none of the conventional attributes of the best seller—no sensational sex, no burning social issues, no harrowing adventures, no religious message. They deal with lawyers, stockbrokers, bankers, manufacturers, and writers. His heroes are not in the least heroic; they are badgered American males, often inarticulate and sometimes ineffectual. No murders take place, and the bedroom scenes are more often concerned with the bickerings of married couples than they are with the ecstasies of lovers. The people are everyday people, and they live in an everyday world, which Marquand describes in painstaking detail.

To say all this is not to suggest that Marquand is one of those writers who are obdurately indifferent to the demands of the reading public. He has always known what the customers want, and he still is ready to give it to them whenever he can. Since he does not choose to capitalize on the demand for sensational sex, he is quite willing to make the most of the demand for propriety: he cleans up the language of his characters, and he skirts situations that a bolder kind of realist would feel obliged to confront. If he cannot supply happy endings, he falls back on his worldliness and his literary skill to make resignation palatable. And if he has no solution to offer to his reader's problems, he knows how to make the reader feel that the lack of a solution is a mark of the reader's wisdom and his own.

These concessions, however, if that is what they should be called, do not measurably lessen the value of his work, nor do they explain its popularity. Obviously there must be a powerful demand for what Marquand gives—an intimate, detailed, credible account of the way in which the upper classes of the northeastern United States live. It is not enough to say that Marquand's readers have risen or hope to rise into the ranks of the prosperous and socially accepted. One has to take into account the revolution in social relationships and moral values that is, in one way or another, the theme of all Marquand's novels. As a result of this revolution, fewer and fewer people acquire clearly defined standards in childhood, and those who do are more and more likely to find their standards irrelevant. Increasingly our patterns of conduct are determined by observation of the way other people behave—often by vicarious observation, through movies, plays, and novels. There is not much help for us in the novels of Hemingway and Faulkner and Farrell, any more than there is in the cleavage-and-dagger romances, to which we turn for something else anyway, but there is a good deal of help in Marquand. Here we can discover what the values are for which there is a current market demand.

This hypothesis should not be regarded as disparaging to either Mr. Marquand or his readers. It is merely an attempt to explain why hundreds of thousands of people are intensely interested in novels that, according to most theories about the publishing business, ought to leave them cold. That other readers read Marquand for other reasons, that these readers find other values in him, ought not to need saying.

Moreover, it is precisely Marquand's human insight that makes him useful as a guide to behavior, if that is what he is. As I have been trying to say, he is a social novelist of great talent, and neither his slick past nor his successful present should blind us to that fact. It is true that he keeps close to the surface, in contrast to the more ambitious and more interesting of our younger writers, who plunge deeper and deeper into the mysteries of the human personality. On the surface, however, he has a mastery that is not to be underestimated.

The world that Marquand gives us in his novels is one in which the rules are enormously important, and yet one no sooner learns them than they change. It is a world in which there are few spectacular tragedies and a good deal of quiet desperation, in which there are few ecstasies but many little satisfactions. It is a world so full of confusion that only stupid people like Malcolm Bryant and Tom Brett and Walter Newcome believe they understand it, and they fool themselves only part of the time.

One may argue that Marquand has been all too ready to give in to confusion, to say that problems are insoluble, to abandon the search for better values than those that inhere in things as they are. Like most of his characters, though not the characters he most admires, he has been governed by the theory of the half-loaf, and he—and we—will never know whether or not he could have had a whole loaf if he had tried. Such reservations, however, may be left to time, that element whose power he has so often acknowledged. For his own era, he speaks with genuine authority, and he speaks to it, as his millions of readers demonstrate, with singular persuasiveness.

# DON MARQUIS

## 1878–1937

Don Marquis was born in Walnut, Illinois, on July 29, 1878. The son of a Calvinist physician, he left home in 1900 to begin a career in journalism. After working briefly for the Census Bureau he joined the staff of the *Washington Times* as a news reporter. He later worked in Philadelphia, Atlanta, and Cleveland before arriving in New York in 1912. While in Atlanta Marquis worked on Joel Chandler Harris's new publication, *Uncle Remus's Home Magazine*, writing book reviews and comic pieces. In Atlanta he also married Reina Melcher in 1909.

His first novel, *Danny's Own Story*, was published in 1912. This novel is in many ways reminiscent of *Huckleberry Finn* and Marquis himself often cited Twain as a major influence on his writings. He continued to write novels as well as his column for the *New York Evening Sun*, "The Sun Dial." In 1916 a philosophical cockroach named archy and an adventurous alley cat named mehitabel made their debut in "The Sun Dial." These two creatures delighted readers for years, and in the late 1920s and early 1930s three collections of the columns about them saw print. In addition to his newspaper and novel writing, Marquis also wrote several plays. The most successful of these, *The Old Soak* (1922), ran for 325 performances on Broadway.

Beginning with the death of his young son in 1921, his life was filled with personal tragedies. In 1923 his wife died, leaving Marquis to raise their daughter alone. He married the actress Marjorie Potts Vonnegut in 1926, and in 1930 moved to California for the sake of his daughter's health. Although his daughter died shortly after their arrival in 1931, Marquis decided to remain in Hollywood, where he worked as a screenwriter. With the death of his second wife in 1936, he returned to New York, where he died on December 29, 1937.

### E. B. WHITE
### From "introduction"
*the lives and times of archy and mehitabel*
#### 1950, pp. xviii–xxiv

The creation of Archy, whose communications were in free verse, was part inspiration, part desperation. It enabled Marquis to use short (sometimes very, very short) lines, which fill space rapidly, and at the same time it allowed his spirit to soar while viewing things from the under side, insect fashion. Even Archy's physical limitations (his inability to operate the shift key) relieved Marquis of the toilsome business of capital letters, apostrophes, and quotation marks, those small irritations that slow up all men who are hoping their spirit will soar in time to catch the edition. Typographically, the *vers libre* did away with the turned or runover line that every single-column practitioner suffers from. ⟨. . .⟩

The days of the Sun Dial were, as one gazes back on them, pleasantly preposterous times and Marquis was made for them, or they for him. *Vers libre* was in vogue, and tons of souped-up prose and other dribble poured from young free-verse artists who were suddenly experiencing a gorgeous release in the disorderly high-sounding tangle of non-metrical lines. Spiritualism had captured people's fancy also. Sir Arthur Conan Doyle was in close touch with the hereafter, and received frequent communications from the other side. Ectoplasm swirled around all our heads in those days. (It was great stuff, Archy pointed out, to mend broken furniture with.) Souls, at this period, were being transmigrated in Pythagorean fashion. It was the time of "swat the fly," dancing the shimmy, and speakeasies. Marquis imbibed freely of this carnival air, and it all turned up, somehow, in Archy's report. Thanks to Archy, Marquis was able to write rapidly and almost (but not quite) carelessly. In the very act of spoofing free verse, he was enjoying some of its obvious advantages. And he could always let the chips fall where they might, since the burden of

responsibility for his sentiments, prejudices, and opinions was neatly shifted to the roach and the cat. It was quite in character for them to write either beautifully or sourly, and Marquis turned it on and off the way an orchestra plays first hot, then sweet.

Archy and Mehitabel, between the two of them, performed the inestimable service of enabling their boss to be profound without sounding self-important, or even self-conscious. Between them, they were capable of taking any theme the boss threw them, and handling it. The piece called "the old trouper" is a good example of how smoothly the combination worked. Marquis, a devoted member of The Players, had undoubtedly had a bellyful of the lamentations of aging actors who mourned the passing of the great days of the theater. It is not hard to imagine him hastening from his club on Gramercy Park to his desk in the *Sun* office and finding, on examining Archy's report, that Mehitabel was inhabiting an old theater trunk with a tom who had given his life to the theater and who felt that actors today don't have it any more—"they don't have it here." (Paw on breast.) The conversation in the trunk is Marquis in full cry, ribbing his nostalgic old actors all in the most wildly fantastic terms, with the tomcat's grandfather (who trooped with Forrest) dropping from the fly gallery to play the beams. This is double-barreled writing, for the scene is funny in itself, with the disreputable cat and her platonic relationship with an old ham, and the implications are funny, with the author successfully winging a familiar type of bore. Double-barreled writing and, on George Herriman's part, double-barreled illustration. It seems to me Herriman deserves much credit for giving the right form and mien to these willful animals. They possess (as he drew them) the great soul. It would be hard to take Mehitabel if she were either more catlike or less. She is cat, yet not cat; and Archy's lineaments are unmistakably those of poet and pest.

Marquis moved easily from one form of composition to another. In ⟨*the life and times of archy and mehitabel*⟩ you will find prose in the guise of bad *vers libre*, poetry that is truly free verse, and rhymed verse. Whatever fiddle he plucked, he always produced a song. I think he was at his best in a piece like "warty bliggens," which has the jewel-like perfection of poetry and contains cosmic reverberations along with high comedy. Beautiful to read, beautiful to think about. But I am making Archy sound awfully dull, I guess. (Why is it that when you praise a poet, or a roach, he begins to sound well worth shunning?)

When I was helping edit an anthology of American humor some years ago, I recall that although we had no trouble deciding whether to include Don Marquis, we did have quite a time deciding where to work him in. The book had about a dozen sections; something by Marquis seemed to fit almost every one of them. He was parodist, historian, poet, clown, fable writer, satirist, reporter, and teller of tales. He had everything it takes, and more. We could have shut our eyes and dropped him in anywhere.

At bottom Don Marquis was a poet, and his life followed the precarious pattern of a poet's existence. He danced on bitter nights with Boreas, he ground out copy on drowsy afternoons when he felt no urge to write and in newspaper offices where he didn't want to be. After he had exhausted himself columning, he tried playwriting and made a pot of money (on *The Old Soak*) and then lost it all on another play (about the Crucifixion). He tried Hollywood and was utterly miserable and angry, and came away with a violent, unprintable poem in his pocket describing the place. In his domestic life he suffered one tragedy after another—the death of a young son, the death of his first wife, the death of his daughter, finally the death of his second wife. Then sickness and poverty. All these things happened in the space of a few years. He was never a robust man—usually had a puffy, overweight look and a gray complexion. He loved to drink, and was told by doctors that he mustn't. Some of the old tomcats at The Players remember the day when he came downstairs after a month on the wagon, ambled over to the bar, and announced: "I've conquered that god-damn will power of mine. Gimme a double scotch."

I think the new generation of newspaper readers is missing a lot that we used to have, and I am deeply sensible of what it meant to be a young man when Archy was at the top of his form and when Marquis was discussing the Almost Perfect State in the daily paper. Buying a paper then was quietly exciting, in a way that it has ceased to be.

Marquis was by temperament a city dweller, and both his little friends were of the city: the cockroach, most common of city bugs; the cat, most indigenous of city mammals. Both, too, were tavern habitués, as was their boss. Here were perfect transmigrations of an American soul, this dissolute feline who was a dancer and always the lady, *toujours gai*, and this troubled insect who was a poet—both seeking expression, both vainly trying to reconcile art and life, both finding always that one gets in the way of the other. Their employer, in one of his more sober moods, once put the whole matter in a couple of lines.

My heart has followed all my days
Something I cannot name . . .

Such is the lot of poets. Such was Marquis's lot. Such, probably, is the lot even of bad poets. But bad poets can't phrase it so simply.

## BERNARD DE VOTO
### From "Almost Toujours Gai"
*Harper's*, March 1950, pp. 50–52

T *he Almost Perfect State* ⟨. . .⟩ is the damnedest book, but which of Don's books isn't? You learn from it that the soul

comes just down to the midriff. You run into superbly angry outcries against man's nature and man's fate, usually with topspin and usually in the vernacular he had forged and burnished from the current slang. At least fifteen different ways of establishing the Almost Perfect State are explored in detail, but there are going to be no reformers in it for it is better to behead a man than to reform him, and the inhabitants are going to be equally divided between radicals and conservatives who will never work at either trade. At one point the Home Must Go but later on it has to come back again; and the same with the legal system: the State must have a lot of laws, for "The progress of humanity consists in the violation of laws," but on the other hand there are going to be very few, but anyone who wants to violate any of them will be free to do so but must "withdraw to a distance from his fellow men, so that the violation will not interfere with them," but also at any time a law may seem desirable anyone is free to make one up to fit. If a question of statecraft proves refractory, it may get summary treatment: "Economic problems that cannot otherwise be solved should be abolished." Or, just as likely, an Outcry from the Back of the Hall will protest something and there will be a "Response from the Platform: We don't know any more about it than you do." But ultimately the best guidance will come from the insane, and "Unless you have levity and wings you shall not enter into the Almost Perfect State," and "There will be in the Almost Perfect State a chance for everyone to go to hell. This is a promise." Dialogues so exquisite and cockeyed that partial quotation would spoil them are scattered through the text, and so are bits of Don's verse, played on every instrument from a violin to a kazoo. At intervals the way is cleared for another installment of his theory of history, that the decadence of peoples and the fall of nations can always be traced to baked beans. So the book carries an appendix which begins, "If you *will* eat beans, here is the way to prepare them." . . .

I wonder what books they read at Harvard now. ⟨. . .⟩

But Archy and Mehitabel have everything. All of them that has survived newsprint is in the book Mr. White has introduced, *the lives and times of archy and mehitabel*. I am not going to risk competing with Mr. White. I am glad that he explains the exigencies of time in relation to space in the newspaper business, and that he muses about a metropolitan press that does not manage to climb this high any more. There has never been anything like Archy or Mehitabel and there never will be. Don Marquis got all his rich and strange talent into a cockroach who had the literary urge because his soul was that of a *vers libre* poet, and a cat on her ninth life who had been Cleopatra and many other adventurous, unlucky dames but who was always a lady in spite of hell. Only fantasy was wide or versatile enough to contain him; his mind kept escaping through cracks in the sane, commonplace world out into dimensions that were loops and whorls and mazes of the unpredictable. And he would not stay put.

The world of these creatures was mainly after dark. Even the scrub-women had gone home, though not till they had scattered the roach-powder through which Archy had to pick his way all the time, just as he had to keep a wary eye on spiders, just as he had to be forever ready to leap inside the typewriter, for a gleam might come into even Mehitabel's eye and she had a deadly paw. The world of deserted office buildings and back alleys in from the river, lighted by a grisly moon that was usually frozen. You can sum it up with Mehitabel dancing all night to keep her blood moving because she had no place to sleep but reminding herself to

pick your guts with your frosty feet
they're the strings of a violin.

(The fundamental purpose of the Almost Perfect State was to get rid of loneliness.) As a superior roach Archy felt no great respect for the intelligence and ethics of bugs but he sided with them in regard to men, whom he had known, from a pharaoh who spent four thousand years with sand in his esophagus, right up to the boss. He put it,

the trouble with you
human beings is you are just plain wicked.

When the uprising of the insects came he would try to save the boss because

you have so many
points that are far
from being human.

His thought is spun of contempt and holy anger, down some dizzy slant of the mind where only he could keep his feet—happily, he had six. But this same world erupts with ribald, belly-shaking laughter, and through innumerable abductions that end with her slicing an eye out of her gentleman friend Mehitabel is toujours gai, and the Martian scientist who got a look at our planet

laughed himself to death crying out
goofus goofus goofus all the time.

He said that from the way it looked to him it would not possibly have any other name. Archy agreed with him. But Don was caught between Archy's judgment that

it takes all sorts of
people to make an
underworld

and the sympathy the parrot expressed for Shakespeare, whom he had known at the Mermaid, on learning that his plays were now well esteemed:

poor mutt little he would
care what poor bill wanted
was to be a poet.

You have to be as alert with this stuff as Archy in the roach-paste, for at any moment a thousand volts may hit you. I suppose there isn't any grave name for it. As Mr. White says, Don Marquis "was never quite certified by intellectuals and serious critics of belles-lettres." Simply, it was wonderful to read in those "pleasantly preposterous" days and reads better now. I have difficulty in remembering the names and books of a good many writers of that time who got the right certificates with red wax seal and dangling ribbons, and my inability is pretty widespread. But no one who ever read Don Marquis has forgotten him and on the publisher's word as of the end of 1949, the sale of *archy and mehitabel* remained "really astounding." That is a criterion to which Archy, along with Hermione and Fothergil Finch, was superior but it is an omen of good fortune for the young who are coming up. Nobody is going to write that way for them.

Let us avoid offense by calling it literature, which is a uniform substance that reacts dependably to standard tests, whereas Don Marquis is always slipping through your fingers. But the shelf his books stand on is not crowded. There is a small bulk of writing, winnowed out from the massive and rewarding, that people insist on reading for its own sake, regardless. They have always held it more precious than rubies and if it isn't literature, then literature be damned. There is no chart of the bay toward which the garbage scow is headed, but his fellow passengers will always find Don Marquis good to read. I'd say his books may be in the pilot house.

## EDWARD A. MARTIN
### From "A Puritan's Satanic Flight: Don Marquis, Archy, and Anarchy"
*Sewanee Review, Fall 1975, pp. 635–42*

The Archy and Mehitabel fables celebrate irrationality, which is a way of expressing hostility toward man and society. They reveal man's inadequacy before the terrors of both the known and unknown universes. They emphasize the foolishness of man's claim to superiority as a form of life. The fables are primarily vehicles for satire, and satire serves at least two purposes. There is specific topical satire, as in Archy's debunking of prohibition, free verse, and theories of evolution, or as in Mehitabel's eulogies on the bohemian life. The purpose implied by such writing would seem to be the reformation of a culture, as in a great tradition of puritan satire, beginning with Bunyan, Defoe, and even Swift. But there is also paradoxically more general, unspecified satire of the structure and values of that same culture. Marquis seeks, and asks his readers to share, relief and release from the demands made by his world for coherence, logic, progress, and allegiance, through his glorifying what is impulsive, anarchic, illogical, and disaffected. His best writing is generated out of the tension between his impulses toward puritanical reformation on the one hand and toward anarchic dissolution on the other.

Archy, the cockroach, who is biographer of Mehitabel, the alley cat, first appeared in the "Sun Dial" column of the *New York Evening Sun* in 1916. His creator took Archy and his other animal and insect friends and enemies to the *New York Tribune* in 1922; some of the verses appeared also in *Collier's*. The verses were collected in *Archy and Mehitabel* (1927), *Archy's Life of Mehitabel* (1933), and *Archy Does His Part* (1935). The three were reissued in one volume, *The Lives and Times of Archy and Mehitabel* (1950). The first and fourth of these volumes are still in print.

Archy has a dual nature, and he thereby reflects his creator's sense of the role of the artist. As an insect Archy is an upsetting nuisance; he threatens frequently to become an unsavory pest by drowning himself in mince pies, stews, and soups. As a poet he is both an articulate rational creature and, like his master, driven by an inner romantic intensity: "expression is the need of my soul." Archy "was once a vers libre bard." When he died, his "soul went into the body of a cockroach." As a result of this transmigration he finds that he has "a new outlook upon life," for he sees "things from the under side." Archy, we are told in the author's introductory explanation, expresses himself by laborious night-time typing sessions upon Don Marquis's typewriter. He jumps headfirst onto the keys, slowly and painfully tapping out his lower-case verses (he cannot work the shift key). The carriage return is also manipulated with great labor. When the inspiration has been literally pounded out of him, he crawls into a nest of discarded poems that clutter the floor and sleeps.

Marquis was continuing in the creation of Archy the ridicule of bohemian affectation that had been his primary purpose in his pieces and verses about Hermione. The same sort of ridicule is present in aspects of his depiction of Mehitabel, whose story Archy tells in bits and fragments. A manic lowbrow, slightly beat, somewhat faded, she is passionately committed to whatever is free and orgiastic: "there s a dance in the old dame yet." Usually her alliances with free-spirited tomcats are spoiled by the arrival of kittens. Mehitabel says she is "all maternal instinct," but kittens ruin her figure, and are inconveniences to her career as a modern dancer. She abandons her offspring quickly and ruthlessly. If Marquis was debunking an aspect of American culture that could produce emancipated ladies like Mehitabel, cruelly indifferent to the middle-class values of family life, he also reserved some admiration for her flagrant individualism. One of Mehitabel's favorite lovers is a highbrow and a poet, who sings of their times together:

> we would rather be rowdy and gaunt and free
> and dine on a diet of roach and rat
> than slaves to a tame society
> ours is the zest of the alley cat

Most of the early verses by Archy as bard of the animal and insect worlds concentrate on ridicule of artistic affectation. In one of the fables Archy overhears an argument between a spider and a fly. The fly argues that he should not be eaten, for he serves "a great purpose/in the world." He says he is a "vessel of righteousness" because he spreads diseases that kill people who have led wicked lives. The spider offers a higher argument. He says he serves "the gods of beauty" by creating "gossamer webs" that "float in the sun/like filaments of song"; he is

> . . . busy with the stuff
> of enchantment and the materials
> of fairyland my works
> transcend utility
> i am the artist
> a creator and a demi god.

There is an oblique satiric purpose in the poem: the creative imagination is seen as part of a world dominated by predatory instincts.

The world of Archy is struck through with the comic and the satiric; it is also a place of violence, terror, and sudden death. Archy is always in danger of annihilation. He is pursued by mice, and even by his friend Mehitabel, when she is moved by hunger or playfulness. On one occasion he is stepped upon, but his soul enters the body of another cockroach. When, bored with being a cockroach, he decides to try suicide (he hopes to transmigrate into a higher form of life), he discovers that killing himself is no easy matter. He jumps from the top of the Washington Monument but floats unharmed to the ground. He tries to hang himself with a thread, but again is too light; he just dangles. Violence also underlies the bohemianism of Mehitabel. She can be a savage antagonist when deceived by a lover; she thinks nothing of slashing off a lover's ear or clawing out a lover's eye.

Marquis ironically anthropomorphized the problem of survival in a world of predators in the fable called "the robin and the worm." A slow-witted angleworm is eaten by a robin before he can even "gather his/dissent into a wise crack." He finds that he is being digested:

> demons and fishhooks
> he exclaimed
> i am losing my personal
> identity as a worm
> my individuality
> is melting away from me.

As he is assimilated by the robin, he begins to "swoon into a/condition of belief," which is that "a/robin must live." A beetle, who has just preceded him into the robin's stomach, agrees with him:

> . . . is it not
> wonderful when one arrives
> at the place
> where he can give up his

> ambitions and resignedly
> nay even with gladness
> recognize that it is a far
> far better thing to be
> merged harmoniously
> in the cosmic all.

The robin, in his turn, is singing happily, singing praises to God and to his good digestion, when Mehitabel eats him. Mehitabel philosophizes:

> how beautiful is the universe
> when something digestible meets
> with an eager digestion
> how sweet the embrace
> when atom rushes to the arms
> of waiting atom
> and they dance together
> skimming with fairy feet
> along a tide of gastric juices
> oh feline cosmos you were
> made for cats.

This is light verse obviously and as such it is playful. Nevertheless it arises from an ironic sensibility that is defined on the one hand by impulses toward purification and renewal, and on the other by impulses toward disaffection and even apocalypse. The predatory instinct in Marquis's fables seems to be an objectification of his sense of original sin; it is both man's fate and paradoxically his glory: Marquis's creatures eat each other and die ecstatically. In his underlying seriousness there are echoes of the ironic visions with which such near-contemporaries as Yeats and Frost contemplated apocalypse in the years immediately following the first world war.

During the 1930s much of Archy's commentary was topical and aphoristic. The depression, and recovery schemes, proved a rich source of comic material. But the tone was very different from that in the wilder fables of the first fifteen years. Archy became simply a mouthpiece who spoke gentle irreverences in the manner of Will Rogers. He reported on his trips to Washington, he commented on recovery attempts, he held mock radio interviews on world affairs and current events, he climbed Mount Everest, he went flying, he deplored the waste of natural resources.

It was a time for reconstruction, not for debunking. Satire, it seemed, could entertain, but not radically criticize. Marquis made some unsuccessful attempts to introduce other animal and insect characters: there were Pete the Pup, Henry, another cockroach, and Lady Bug. None of them was the equal of Archy or of Mehitabel. The most notable character was Warty Bliggens, the toad who believed that the universe had been created for his pleasure and benefit. But he too was an early creation, and appeared only once. Archy, who in a sense as the biographer of Mehitabel was also her creator, remains the most enduring figure in the Archy and Mehitabel saga.

An undercurrent of hostility and disaffection formed the mainstream of Archy's character. As an insect and commentator on humanity, he was, of course, superior and hostile in his attitudes toward human hypocrisies and ideals. Most of all he hated false optimism, which was epitomized for him in the vapid chirping of crickets. He says, in "the cheerful cricket," "i hate one of these/grinning skipping smirking/senseless optimists worse/than i do a cynic or a/pessimist." In a much later poem entitled "the sad crickets," he decided that in spite of what "chas dickens believed" crickets sing a melancholy song:

> my love fell into a spiders web
> squeak squeak squeak
> and she screamed with pain as he
> crunched her bones into his
> bloody beak squeak squeak.

Archy's insect world was a world of violence, terror, and sudden death, which he describes with ecstatic intensity. And because the human world resembled his insect world, he viewed it with macabre humor and hostility. The essence of his hostility issued in an apocalyptic vision in which he declared:

> i shall
> eat everything
> all the world shall come at
> last to the multitudinous maws
> of insects
> a civilization perishes
> before the tireless teeth
> of little little germs
> ha ha i have thrown off the mask
> at last
> you thought i was only
> an archy
> but i am more than that
> i am anarchy.

He is both artist and predator. As artist expression is the need of his soul; with passionate intensity he creates order and form. As predator he is a nuisance and a pest who nibbles constantly at order and form in what is imagined as a total attrition and descent back into anarchy, a return to hell. Marquis similarly conceived of a dual role for himself as artist: a role as both poet and satirist, as both myth-maker and myth-destroyer. He was never comfortable with knowledge of this division in himself, yet the artist in him created a memorable image for one of the tensions of American life in the twentieth century.

Marquis was a son of the Puritans who rejected the religious, secular, and artistic authority of his time and sought either to purify or to destroy this authority. What he wanted was a kind of covenant of artistic grace for his own life and culture. He had a deep and frustrating sense of failure, a sense that he was not one of the elect, that he was the victim of something as pervasive as original sin. One of his responses was to glorify that awareness of damnation, and this is part of what produced Archy and Mehitabel. The images of Archy's world arise out of a tension between Marquis's sense of a need for purification set against his impulses toward anarchic destruction. Marquis, like many of his contemporaries, felt that the values of middle-class culture no longer made sense. His response was to create a fabulous world where hostility, violence, and the predatory instinct were the ordinary ingredients of existence, and thus were brought within a kind of tenuous artistic control. Marquis believed that mere anarchy was loosed upon the world. So he created and set loose an Archy of his own. He wanted to counteract the mereness, the absurdity of existence as he viewed it, through an ironic glorification of irrationality and of anarchy itself.

## DAN JAFFE
### "Archy Jumps Over the Moon"
*The Twenties: Fiction, Poetry, Drama*
ed. Warren French
1975, pp. 427–37

> archy leaps over the moon
> hey diddle diddle
> let mehitabel fiddle
> while archy leaps over the moon. . .

### Preface

I like to reread the poems of don marquis when the world seems too much with me, which is almost always directly after the 10 p.m. news. And although I am hardly profound then, having been pretty thoroughly worked over, I keep getting clear intimations that don marquis, or should I say archy, not only cheers me up but also has a lot to say. This has been the judgment made for more than 50 years by American readers despite the fact that courses in American literature, influential textbooks, and intellectual historians generally ignore don marquis and his friends. That's more than I'm willing to do for the following reasons:

Archy the cockroach has his own voice, fashioned out of the total language; he captures the American idiom but remains distinctly himself.

Archy is a compassionate realist. He faces the hardness of the world and still cares about the hurts of others.

Archy plays the game of poetry, making strengths out of limitations. Archy writes in lower case because he can't operate the capital lever. But his lower case turns, in addition to other things, into symbolic, class commentary.

Archy presents us with a wide range of concerns, locales, characters, and feelings.

Archy loves disguises. Only disguised could an American *epic* so full of cynicism, criticism of the culture, reminders of our pretentiousness and silliness not only be published in the commercial press but become widely successful.

Archy can dance to other people's music, mimic other people's gestures. Often his allusions, stylistic and referential, have ironic bite. How we love his satire and parody.

At times he even gets metaphysical.

Archy is the only cockroach I know who is a hero.

> i
> art for recoverys sake
>
> archy i have been trying to write
> to you for a long time but havent
> been able to find your address youre
> not listed in the phone book and
> neither is the new york evening sun
> or the herald tribune you may
> wonder why i thought about writing
> well its because the journalist you
> called boss put all your correspondance
> first in the papers then
> in a book and let us human beans know all
> about you and mehitabel some people
> would consider that a breach of confidence
> but i for one am glad because it made me
> one of your fans these days
> its awful hard to find a writer
> to read when youre sick and your stories
> about mehitabel the cat warty
> bliggens the toad your maxims your
> account of the heroic end of freddy the rat
> tragic full of pathos as it was
> brought me many hours of forgetting my aches and pains
> and the attendant philosophical uneasiness that
> comes when you lie in a bed too long
>
> ii
> down home style
>
> archy i guess theres not much
> chance youll get this letter i
> thought i would put it in a bottle
> and set it adrift in the main stream
> but a poet friend of mine says that goes
> right down the sewer these days
> so instead ill put it in a book
> the way don marquis did your jottings

youre probably wondering why since
im a human bean im not capitalizing
or putting in punctuation its much
easier for me to work the typewriter
than it was for you i dont
have to bounce up and down on my head
and lift weights in between times
to keep in sufficient shape to juggle words
its my egalitarian instincts thats why
i figure why shouldnt we be equals
considering your genius
and the lack
of periods and commas
is my signal to you
that im not some patronizing slummer
i always thought you had found
not only the quickest most expedient way
to send your message to the world but also
a style that was the direct reflection of
your philophical and class position
take away commas periods dashes and
capitals and the whole structure
comes tumbling down the
world is a typewriter and
in the beginning was
the word

### iii
### critics arent so bright

a critic i know says
he knows why im so hung up
on the writing of a cockroach
your enthusiasm says he
takes you right out of the
main stream there must be an answer
and hes sure he has it
in an earlier life dj says he
you must have been one too
and that explains why you like
to view life from the underside
so much why you enjoy the unrespectable
and hardly intellectual babble that don marquis
collected from the typewriter the morning
after all of which goes to show
that critics arent so bright archy
this one doesnt even know hes
accepted your whole transmigration
explanation of genius
so now how can he say
mehitabel the cat wasnt cleopatra
or archy a true vers libre bard
but what i really wonder is
what that critic was
in his earlier lives

### iv
### heehaw heehaw

one thing that the critic
never seems to understand
is that critics
seem just as useless to poets
as poets to critics
these days its getting harder
and harder to tell whose who
but archy i just want to know
why you waited to be a cockroach
before you dropped your poems on us

i mean you must have known
the abstract theys would put
you down no matter what
now if you could have roared or
trumpeted them out swashbuckled
across the landscape
instead of just leaving a trail of crumbs
ah the impact
but no matter what you say
this way they just laugh heehaw
point out the scurilous nature
of political discourse they heehaw
announce the anthropomorphical mess they
heehaw heehaw note the comic foibles of the day
they heehaw allude beyond their
heehaw heehaw and they just
heehaw so much heehaw they start to hurt
down in the belly
down near the essentials
which may be the point

### v
### backbiting

listen the other day i heard
some professorial types talking
about the world the university
capitol hill and tv
and i thought of you archy
because you said all the same
things in different words
and that so long ago
maybe poets are prophetic after all
its all a matter of perspective
said one regal looking dean
and even the writer in residence
agreed with that
but none of them rhymed very well
or really saw things from the under side

### vi
### sympathy

dear archy ive decided
not to feel sorry for you
and mehitabel any more
sure youve had your lumps
and some of them self willed
but you had your fun too
prancing around in the manner
of kipling and homer
and all sorts of others
you tickled and poked and
even sipped booze out of
saucers without ever going
to the hoosegow
and mehitabel always did
get around to yodel her
toujour gai toujour gai
which is more than i can
say for lots of folks i know
who stay kicked all their lives
i do not blame you archy
for your bitterness against mankind
but behind your hard words
theres always a soft joke
and i know archy the cockroach
would never bait a hook with a boy

vii
archys true colors

dear archy i was talking
with a speech teacher
the other day and he suddenly
says what happened to your voice
you dont sound like yourself
you sound like something that
came out of a book written by
a cockroach then he looked at
me as if he wanted to prescribe something
for my consonants and vowels
its all archys fault
i said and don marquis should bear
some of the blame but once they
get into you its hard to get them out
which i guess is why im writing
these notes in the way i am
well he said thats too bad
you could have been milton or
will shakespeare or even wallace
stevens they each had their own voices
i mean its all a matter of touchstones
all of which showed his bias

viii
MAKING IT IN THE BIG TIME

THE TIME HAS COME FOR ME TO SAY
IN THE MOST INSISTENT WAY
THAT ARCHY AND MEHITABEL
ARE REALLY PHILOSOPHICAL
THAT THEY'RE THE VICTIMS OF A PLOT
THAT SAYS NON HUMAN BEANS CAN NOT
ON THE WINGS OF POESY FLY
AND THAT IT'S UPPITY TO TRY
NO ONE SINCE AND NONE BEFORE
GAVE SUCH PROOF THE PRESS COULD SOAR
DESPITE THE BIAS OF THE HUMAN RACE
THEY BOTH DESERVE THE UPPER CASE

ix
telling them off

archy the other night
i heard a yodeling in the back yard
i thought mehitabel was with us
but it was just my critic acquaintance
fresh from a new triumph over literature
says he the epic spirit is dead
where is our homer now our
virgil who can speak with the voice of the age
that is ageless and grand
and then he twirled his phi beta chain
and scratched the protuberance of his vest
there are times archy to be tactful
and silent and let the insipidity
about us echo on the air
but i for one have never learned
such restraint i have declared war
on the critics who close the doors
of their anthologies on cockroaches
and who will not listen

archy you have ranged across
the landscape and through time
from barstool to city room
from alley to meeting hall from
pennsylvania station to mars
the green planet from olympus to
the oasis behind the radiator
and your lingo is ours in all our
stages for a cockroach youve got a
hell of a good ear you
are not only an american vers libre bard but
a veritable sam johnson who gives us the
words of shakespeare and bacon
along with toujour gai toujour gai
you never got stuck in a poetic diction archy
you just kept junketing
around from level to level like
mehitabel through her lives sipping
the cream and chewing fishheads
from the garbage can
such polyphony a lesson
for poetic runts who can only
play one instrument
a fellow named rod hereabouts
keeps beating the triangle with his head
more anon
    dj

x
justice at last

well archy i think ive figured out
why you have not announced yourself
recently through some new means
i know of course that by this
time youve probably transmigrated again
maybe youre our cat gatto but shes
certainly not letting on
anyway youve disappeared about
as completely as weldon kees off
the golden gate or hart crane
into the dark and thats sad
but not really surprising when
i think about the artists sensitive soul
oh its sad to be so ignored by
all the types who put the stamp
of approval and legitimacy on
things so what if people keep reading
those notes you wrote fifty years ago
its not enough archy you ought to
be in the canon of american lit
so sophomores could learn
about democratic vistas and
equality and the cockroach view of things
instead of henry adams
who i dont think
you would have got along with at all
but i wouldnt really grieve because
we will overcome and theyll have
to let you in after all because
readers insist

DAVID MAMET

BERNARD MALAMUD

CLARENCE MAJOR

NORMAN MAILER

John P. Marquand

H. L. Mencken

Don Marquis

Edgar Lee Masters

# Edgar Lee Masters

## c. 1869–1950

Edgar Lee Masters was born in Garnett, Kansas, probably on August 23, 1869 (or 1868, as suggested by some biographers). His mother was a bookish gentlewoman of New England stock and his father was a lawyer and politician of Virginian heritage. Masters grew up in Petersburg and Lewistown, both small towns in Illinois's Sangamon Valley. As a boy Masters was educated at the local public schools and worked part-time at area newspapers. He attended Knox College in Galesburg, Illinois, for a year before working for his father's law practice. Masters was admitted to the bar in 1891 and shortly thereafter moved to Chicago where he later established a successful practice with partner Clarence Darrow.

During his early years in Chicago Masters became involved in Populist politics and was especially attracted to the young William Jennings Bryan. Masters published articles on constitutional law as well as some anonymous poetry before his sudden fame in 1915. His friend William Marion Reedy of the St. Louis *Mirror* had given him a copy of J. W. Mackail's *Select Epigrams from the Greek Anthology*. The effect on Masters was enormous. Shortly thereafter he published *Spoon River Anthology* (1915), which was heralded as a major event in American literary history. This volume consisted of free verse epitaphs written in the form of short monologues. The 243 speeches, recited by the inhabitants of a village graveyard, provide a memorable account of life in a midwestern town.

After the success of *Spoon River Anthology* Masters gave up his law practice and moved to New York where he published a sequel, *The New Spoon River*, in 1924. By this time he had divorced his first wife, Helen Jenkins, and had married Ellen F. Coyne. His initial fame faded as his new poetry was described by critics as imitative and unoriginal. Later in life he wrote several biographies, including a sympathetic portrait of his friend Vachel Lindsay as well as accounts of Whitman and Twain. In 1931 he published *Lincoln, the Man*, in which he bitterly attacked his home state's most famous historical figure. Masters spent many of his last years living in relative obscurity at New York's Chelsea Hotel. Although he published numerous novels, plays, and biographies, he is today remembered for the breathtaking beauty of his poetic masterpiece, *Spoon River Anthology*. Masters died on March 5, 1950, in a hospital outside of Philadelphia.

## Personal

I first met Edgar Lee Masters in the summer of 1915: it was in Chicago, then the place of literary promise in America: Carl Sandburg, Sherwood Anderson, Vachel Lindsay were there, and Harriet Monroe had given literary energies focus by establishing a well-edited monthly devoted to poetry in that city. And there I was in Harriet Moody's drawing room, talking to one who had figured in the prophecies. He was Edgar Lee Masters.

He had friendly hazel eyes behind his glasses. He chuckled now and again. But there was an earnestness in his outlook that I respected. A humorous man—I don't mean a man who made jokes, but a man whose mind had play in it, who saw life, in the word that Burns gave us, as a variorum. We became friends; while I was in Chicago I visited his house and came to know him with some of his intimates. He was a practicing lawyer at the time: for myself I named him the Man of Lawe.

Shortly before had come the publication of *Spoon River Anthology*. I suppose a student of literature is bound to make a comparison between a new expression in letters and a former one of like, or nearly like, design. As I read the epitaphs of the prairie community I thought of the eighteenth-century poet's, George Crabbe's, records of a village. But there was, of course, an essential difference. Crabbe wrote histories. Masters wrote testaments. A clergyman going away from his registers did the first; a Man of Lawe exampled by the courtroom did the second. And it was by using the language of statement which was the language of a locality that Edgar Lee Masters made his impact. Here was something so far away from the urban that it

might be called parochial. Here was a poet for whom his country was rural with a history that was made by pioneers. But to say this is not to indicate the appealing thing that was and is in the *Anthology*. The appeal is in the presence of a community.

In a poem in *More People* the poet speaks of endurance as the support that enables him to face the darkness and the cold. The word recalls lines of another poet, the poet of *The City of Dreadful Night*:

> The strong to drink new strength of iron endurance,
> The weak new terrors; all, renewed assurance
> And confirmation of the old despair.

But Masters' endurance is not the endurance of the solitary. He is a man of attachments—attachments to places, to men and women, even to his country's future. For him the dead live because of the love they inspired:

> . . . as a star
> Can fade into the void and then
> Appear and shine, from realms afar
> He seems to pass me once again.

And in his Californian retreat Robinson Jeffers plants a tree for George Sterling and Edgar Lee Masters. It is to be remembered, that planting; it is out of time because Jeffers is so much of the spirit:

> I am still a witness thinking today about those trees,
> Thinking of Jeffers whose voice rides the mountain wind,
> Who is both Tiresias and Amphion,
> With eyes piercing through the land, the cities,
> With music that moves rocks and lifts them into walls.

Testaments are shown to us again in these poems published posthumously. His own are in certain of these. Edgar Lee Masters is a man of attachments—to persons, to the countryside in its immense variety, to what can be glimpsed of its future. "A democracy, even if I have to say a democracy of the graveyard," I said to myself when I compared Spoon River with the village of George Crabbe's histories. The spiritual foundations of a democracy are in the attachments that Edgar Lee Masters testifies to in ⟨his⟩ later poems.—PADRAIC COLUM, "Preface" to *The Harmony of Deeper Music* by Edgar Lee Masters, ed. Frank N. Robinson, 1976, pp. 11–12

### General

Some one once said that de Maupassant had cut down the giant oak Flaubert and made walking-sticks of it. So Edgar Lee Masters, in *The Spoon River Anthology*, has taken the vast panoramic canvas of Balzac and reduced it to exquisite vest-pocket etchings.

*The Spoon River Anthology* is one of the most original pieces of imaginative literature that I know of. Implacable ironist and realist, Masters, Prospero of a Middle Western graveyard, struck with the wand of creation upon the lidded skeletons of the dead and made them tell (as all things must out) their secrets to the world.

Yoricks, Hamlets and Ophelias, Hulots, Cousin Bettes and de Rastignacs, Quilps, Micawbers and Lady Deadlocks, Bovarys, Moreaus and Saint Anthonys, Raskolnikoffs, Karamazoffs and Bazaroffs, Romeos, Don Quixotes and Long John Silvers, Lorna Doones, Becky Sharps and Maud Mullers exist externally in flesh and blood wherever a thousand people live and weave and interweave their passions, dreams, loves and ambitions. They all live in Spoon River under the names that Masters has given them, and his great art consists in portraying their lives, their tragedies and comedies, and the vast inutility of it all, in the most condensed and vivid form conceivable.

The vulgar, uninteresting, commonplace being does not exist for the dramatist and the poet of high breed. He will sense drama, poetry, an epic, in three men surrounding a young girl who laps an ice-cream soda. The ironic imagination is the resurrection and the life. It glows and transfigures in all the splendor of its malign power in the Masters of the Anthology. After that his work lives in the reflected light of that first fresh burst of genius.

I would rather have been the author of *The Spoon River Anthology* than of any other book of American imaginative literature except Cabell's *Jurgen*. I do not know of any poetic fiction that gives me such an odor of reality, such a raw, rank taste of broken hearts and battered brains, such a sense of inexorable fatality. Masters does not describe; he creates, and his only ethic is the ethic of all great creators, pathos and irony, which are implicit in the pictures he evokes like overtones between his lines.

The formula of Masters is the formula of life itself. His creations rise from their graves as we rise out of the womb, tell their story, as we enact ours, and then return to their sleep, as we shall return to ours.

Ultimate judgment of all things planetary must be written, *In re*: Mankind against the Gods. Spoon River is the planet. The Author of Life must answer for His work to the Soul of Man. Masters holds a brief for Man, is an attorney, as it were, for the prosecution.

He is not a great poet in the narrow sense of the word. But he is a great poet if by great poet we mean one who sees the particular, the individual under the aspect of Eternity or Law. *The Spoon River Anthology* is our Comédie Humaine.

I met Masters many years after reading *The Spoon River Anthology*. It was in the Players Club and he wanted to ask me about the motion-picture possibilities of another one of his books. I could discern nothing in him, in our short talk, that was extraordinary. He was matter of fact and looked matter of fact. I did not mention that I had ever read his Anthology. It is curious how two creative natures, when they are brought together for the first time, examine each other, spar silently with one another, each fearing to hear an adverse judgment on his work. Artists are the greatest moral cowards, I think.

But I know of no man in English literature who has put so much in so little as Edgar Lee Masters has in *The Spoon River Anthology*.—BENJAMIN DE CASSERES, "Five Portraits on Galvanized Iron," *AM*, Dec. 1926, pp. 395–96

Masters had his roots in the America of Jeffersonian democracy, yet he liked to call himself a Hellenist. His effort in the *Spoon River Anthology* was to combine American provincialism with Greek universality. The germ of the book was the idea of telling the story of an American country town so as to make the story of the world. He found its prototype in the *Greek Anthology*, that superb collection of poems ranging from Simonides' stern epitaphs on those fallen in the Persian wars to the lyrics of tenth-century Byzantium. Masters' work has greater frankness, if it wants the other virtues of his models.

The town of Spoon River was a microcosm in which he saw the image of the small town of his boyhood as also of the metropolis he had come to know while practicing criminal law in Chicago. All manner of men and women speak from their graves in this community. Since wanderers from Poland, Germany, and even China were buried here, various nationalities, too, are represented, and nearly all these people are drawn with something of the savage candor, though never the wit, of Daumier's cartoons.

The book opens with a lyric echoing the cry that haunts the centuries. Masters' prelude lacks the music of those more venerable elegies, though his reiterated "All, all, are sleeping on the hill," has a mournful lyricism quite foreign to the prosaic phrases in which he presents the histories of the sleepers. But what sets this poem apart from its exemplars is that instead of lamenting great kings and dazzling ladies, or such masters of balladry as Robert Henryson, it recalls Ella, Kate, and Mag, Bert, Tom, and Charley, men who were burned to death in a mine or "killed in a brawl," women who "died in shameful childbirth," or "at the hands of a brute in a brothel." The governing emotion is not pity but bitter pain over the greed, the bigotry, the malice, of men. The memory of the Haymarket riots and their cruel consequences lives on in Spoon River as in Lindsay's poem to Altgeld, but these pages nowhere voice Lindsay's ready optimism. Repeatedly they remind one of Hobbes' description of the life of man in a state of nature: "solitary, poor, brutish, nasty and short." But the people who tell their stories here had lived in no jungle save that of industrial America.

Fairly typical in its grimness is the story of Adam Weirauch, who lost many friends fighting for Altgeld, and lost his slaughterhouse with the rise of the house of Armour. Weirauch entered politics and was elected to the legislature, but he sold his vote on a streetcar franchise and was caught. He ends up by asking whether it was Armour, Altgeld, or himself that ruined him. His unvarnished speech is more usual than the imaginative comment of Mrs. Kessler, who supported her family by taking in washing and learned people's secrets from their curtains, counterpanes, and shirts, felt that "The laundress, Life, knows all about it"; and never

Saw a dead face without thinking it looked
Like something washed and ironed.

These epitaphs do not hide any of the stains, the running
colors, the rents and patches, in the lives they record. Editor
Whedon, a lesser representative of the gentry on whom Ezra
Pound pours the vomit of his Fourteenth and Fifteenth
Cantos, lies in death

close by the river over the place
Where the sewage flows from the village,
And the empty cans and garbage are dumped,
And abortions are hidden.

Masters makes no attempt to conceal the sewage, the empty
cans, the garbage, the abortions. Not the shames of Spoon
River alone, but the shames of a nation are exposed. The brutal
actualities of the Spanish-American War as the soldiers in the
swamps knew them are related by a boy who went to uphold
"the honor of the flag." Near him rests a veteran of the Revolution, who endured the heartbreaking struggle of the frontier,
and whose last word is:

If Harry Wilmans who fought the Filipinos
Is to have a flag on his grave
Take it from mine!

The cruelties of an economic system based on exploitation, the meanness or stupidity of average minds, an inherent
weakness of body or spirit, had marred the lives of most of those
who came to lie in the Spoon River cemetery. Yet there is
Lucinda Matlock, who worked contentedly beside her husband
for seventy years, raising twelve children, and who cries out on
the "degenerate sons and daughters" of the younger generation:

Life is too strong for you—
It takes life to love life.

There is Fiddler Jones who ended up with forty acres,

ended up with a broken fiddle—
And a broken laugh, and a thousand memories,
And not a single regret.

There are the handful of men and women, among them not
only the astronomy teacher and the students of the Upanishads
(one of these "the village atheist"), but the piano tuner and the
gardener, whose minds have learned to soar and whose feet
walk the earth, rejoicing in it.

However they differ in their attitudes and the circumstances of their lives, the characters are not identifiable by their
speech. The cadences are monotonous and closer to prose than
to song. One exception is the epitaph of the poet, Thomas
Trevelyan. Yet the lyricism of the lines given to him is defeated
by his trite, conspicuously "poetic" language. More than the
rest of Masters' many volumes, this one escapes the weight of
his heavy rhetoric, but there is little relief from its flat diction.
It is only after reading the bulk of these stories that one hears an
overtone of compassionate objectivity that is the essence of the
book. It is the voice of old Gustav Richter, who worked all day
in his hothouses and in his sleep seemed to see his flowers
transplanted "To a larger garden of freer air," and there heard a
Presence, that walked between the boxes, noting what was
needful:

Dante, too much manure, perhaps.
Napoleon, leave him awhile yet.
Shelley, more soil, Shakespeare needs spraying—

It is the voice of the gardener and the voice of God. It is the
voice of Edgar Lee Masters observing the men and women of
Spoon River. The *Anthology* remains good realism because,
while exhibiting all the ugliness of life in a small American
town of the industrial age, it admits the beauties that may also
flourish there. Unique in the originality of its conception, it

pointed the way for later poets to execute thumbnail biographies in a stronger or subtler fashion.—BABETTE DEUTSCH,
"Farewell, Romance," *Poetry in Our Time*, 1952, pp. 45–49

The collection of short free-verse poems called *Spoon River
Anthology* written by Edgar Lee Masters, a Chicago lawyer,
was published in 1915 when he was forty-five years old; and it
shocked the American public so profoundly that it sold a great
number of copies. It became the first best seller of the 'poetic
Renaissance' which began in the Middle West with Masters,
Vachel Lindsay, Carl Sandburg and Harriet Monroe's oddly-
named *Poetry: A Magazine of Verse*; and the memories of its
sensational success have lasted so long that even today it is
regarded, when it is regarded at all, with deep suspicion,
though the reasons for the present suspicion are quite different
from what they were when the book boomed out first to the
hand-lifted horror of the giant parish press, the prairie pulpits,
the thin, baffled, sour officials of taste in the literary periodicals, and the innumerable societies of militant gentility. Now,
*Spoon River* is, I suppose, hardly read at all by the thousands of
university students who 'take' poetry in such enormous doses.
The poetry workshops attached to many universities and private
colleges leave him, I should think, untaught and alone, except
as a figure of minor historical interest, a cross, rhetorical, old
Bohemian lawyer rambling and ranting away in the bad past
about the conflict between materialism and idealism: a conflict
considered so old-fashioned that many of those in the poetry
workshops must imagine it to have been satisfactorily settled
long ago.

(In poetry workshops, by the way, would-be poets are
supposed to study the craft under some distinguished practitioner. Perhaps the original idea was to provide for apprentice
poets what a master's studio once did for apprentice painters.
But the master-painter used to paint all the time, and his
apprentices assisted him and were busy under his direction. A
master-poet, if he exists, is supposed, in these literary warrens,
to spend nearly all his time dealing with, and encouraging, the
imitations, safe experiments, doodlings and batchings of his
students, and to do his own stuff on the side. What a pity he
does not have the apprentice poets to help him with the duller
bits of his own work. There is a future in this, however ghastly.)

And the brash, antiseptic, forty-two-toothed, ardent,
crewcut collegiates, grimly pursuing the art of poetry with net,
notebook, poison bottle, pin and label, may be quite likely to
dismiss Edgar Lee Masters altogether because, in his lifetime,
he *was* so successful. I've noticed before, in the States, how
very many students devotedly read and devour masses of
modern poetry and insist, at the same time, that poetry
devotedly read and devoured by such numbers of people can't
be any good. Ezra Pound—for instance—can be appreciated
by only a very few, say armies of culture-vultures every day as
they drive through the *Cantos* with apparent ecstasy and
understanding. Masters was too successful to be honest, I've
heard it said: a rather touching remark, perhaps, to come from
an enlightened representative of a people notoriously not averse
to success in any way of life. But it was Masters' ironic honesty
that made *Spoon River* so popular among its denigrators.
Americans seem to enjoy being furious and indignant at being
kicked in their most sensitive places—and what more sensitive
a place than that great, dry backbone, the Middle West?

People bought and read *Spoon River*, when it first
appeared, for many reasons, few of which had anything to do
with the undoubted fact that it was poetry. Many people read it
in order to deny that it was true; many, discovering that in
essence it was, denied it even more loudly. One of the chief
reactions to these angry, sardonic, moving poems seemed to be:

'*Some* of the inhabitants of small towns in Illinois may indeed be narrow-minded and corrupt, fanatically joyless, respectable to the point of insanity, malevolent and malcontent, but not in the Illinois towns in which *we* live.' "East is East and West is West, but the Middle West is terrible," Louis Untermeyer once wrote, but he was a sophisticated cosmopolitan raconteur and man-of-smart-letters, and his opinion of the *Real America* could be taken as merely ignorant and facetious. (It is, I'm sure, significant that the most beautiful and exciting places in America are, without exception, all called untypical and un-American.) Masters, however, was a proper Middle-Westerner; he knew what he was writing about; and his detestation of the bitter and crippling puritanism in which he struggled and simmered up was nothing less than treacherous. 'He knows us too well, the liar,' was a common attitude.

I am very fond, myself, of the writers who came out of the Middle West round about the beginning of the First World War. All the stale literary guidebook phrases aside—the 'honest ruggedness,' the 'pioneering vitality,' the 'earthy humor,' the 'undying folk tradition,' etc.—the hick-town radicals and iconoclasts, the sports journalists, the contributors to *Reedy's Mirror*, the drinking, noisy Chicago preachers and atheists and ballad singers and shabby professional men, did bring something rough and good into a language that was dying on its feet; and not its own feet, either.

There is Vachel Lindsay: the semireligious revivalist; re-creator of railroad songs and sagas; the chronicler of Johnny Appleseed, the Blackfeet, the Pawnees, John Brown, John L. Sullivan, P. T. Barnum; the first poet to love the moving-pictures and see what they might become; who wrote about Blanche Sweet and Lillian Gish; who tried to live on pamphlets, *Rhymes to be Traded for Bread*, which he hawked around the country; who became a popular platform act; who killed himself in 1931. And Sherwood Anderson, whose book of stories, *Winesburg, Ohio*, is so near in place and spirit to *Spoon River*, but whose remembered vision of youth in that rich, remote, constricting, Main-Streeted desert is so much more detailed and more gentle, in spite of its terrors. And Carl Sandburg, born of Swedish immigrant parents, who, when he began to write about the packinghouses and factories of Chicago, did not see them as ephemeral features of an industrial nightmare but as living and undeniable facts of concrete, steel, flesh, and blood, who knew that the material of legend and song and ballad can never die so long as there are men working together. And, most of all, Edgar Lee Masters, jaundiced missionary, stubborn tub-thumper with a snarl and a flourish, acute in the particulars of ironic portraiture and lavish with high-blown abstractions, verbose, grotesquely concise, a man with a temper he wouldn't sell for a fortune.

In this sequence of poems, the dead of the town of Spoon River speak, from the graveyard on the Hill, their honest epitaphs. Or, rather, they speak as honestly as they can, having, while on earth, been defeated by their honesty and therefore grown bitter, or by their dishonesty and therefore grown suspicious of the motives of all others. In life, they had failed to make their peace with the world; now, in death, they are trying to make their peace with God in whom they might not even believe.

'Here lies the body of'—and then the name the monu-mental mason insignificantly engraved. Masters stopped at 'Here lies,' and then engraved his fierce, wounded, compas-sionate version of the skewbald truth. He was never deluded into thinking that the truth is simple and one-sided, that values are clearly defined; he knew that the true motives of men about their business on earth are complex and muddled, that man

moves in a mysterious way his blunders to perform, that the heart is not only a bloody pumping muscle but an old ball, too, of wet woolly fluff in the breast, a "foul rag-and-bone shop," in Yeats's phrase, a nest of errors, a terrible compulsion that lives by its hurt. And, what is more, he knew that people had poetry always, even if it wasn't always very good.

He wrote about the war between the sexes. The great gulf between men, that was created by the laws of men. The incompatibility of those who live their short lives together because of economic convenience, loneliness, the cavernous and ever-increasing distance from the first maternal grave, casual physical desire. Not that the reasons of economic convenience, or the assuaging of casual, though none the less urgent, lust are, in themselves, inconducive to a state of tranquility between two people lost; but who wants tranquility? Better burn than marry, if marriage puts the fire out.

He wrote about waste: how man wastes his vitality in the pursuit of cynical irrelevancies; and his aspirations through his allegiance to the bad laws, theologies, social institutions and discriminations, the injustices, greeds and fears, that have constantly and resentfully been reinforced by all those human beings of the past who also have suffered and died of them.

He wrote about the waste of man, but loudly, awkwardly, passionately revered the possibilities of greatness in what there was to waste.—DYLAN THOMAS, "Dylan Thomas on Edgar Lee Masters" (1955), *HB*, June 1963, pp. 68–69, 115

## Works

I could go into the matter of the prosody of the *Anthology* if I were writing a technical exposition. I could refer to the bald stark prose of the Bohn *Greek Anthology*, and then parallel it with rhythmical pieces like "Thomas Trevelyn," and "Isaiah Beethoven", and in this connection I could cite the fact that the Spooniad is in blank verse, quite conventional enough; and that the Epilogue is in rhymed lyrics. I could show that there are sixty-seven pieces which are both rhythmical and metrical; and that I invented a rhythmical pattern for such pieces as "Henry Tripp," which are distinctive of the book and expressive of the mood which created it. I could appeal to Aristotle's *Poetics*, which laid down the dictum that the difference between literature which imitates action and emotion, and literature which imitates nothing, like arguments and the like. I could as justification for the freedom I took, and the rebellion I asserted against technical groves and academicians, appeal to Goethe's instruction to use in poems alliteration, false rhymes and assonance, which in 1831 he said he would do if he were again young.

However, I did not know of Goethe's doctrines on that subject at the time. Nor did I know of Saint Beuve's words that "the greatest poet is not he who has done the best, but he who suggests the most," not he who writes the *Æneid*, but he who gives to the world that which most stimulates the reader's imagination, and excites him the most to poetize himself, which remote things like the *Æneid* cannot so much do. I could go into all this to repel the savage attacks that were made on the *Anthology* at the time and since to the effect that it was prose, and bald prose, that it was without harmony and beauty, that in a word it was not poetry at all. I shall do none of these things here; but I shall refer to some matters of substance before resuming the history of the *Anthology* and of myself during its composition.

There are two hundred and forty-four characters in the book, not counting those who figure in the Spooniad and the Epilogue. There are nineteen stories developed by interrelated portraits. Practically every ordinary human occupation is covered, except those of the barber, the miller, the cobbler, the tailor and the garage man (who would have been an anachronism) and all these were depicted later in the *New Spoon River*. What critics overlook when they call the *Anthology* Zoalesque, and by doing so mean to degrade it, is the fact that when the book was put together in its definitive order, which was not the order of publication in the *Mirror*, the fools, the drunkards, and the failures came first, the people of one-birth minds got second place, and the heroes and the enlightened spirits came last, a sort of Divine Comedy, which some critics were acute enough to point out at once.

The names I drew from both the Spoon river and the Sangamon river neighborhoods, combining first names here with surnames there, and taking some also from the constitutions and State papers of Illinois. Only in a few instances, such as those of Chase Henry, William H. Herndon and Anne Rutledge and two or three others, did I use anyone's name as a whole. I never heard of the Rev. Abner Peet; and the charge that I wantonly injured the feelings of a good man is false. In drawing the banker, Thomas Rhodes, I had in mind a Lewistown character who deserved all that I said about him, but the name Rhodes was never borne by anyone that I knew who played the mean part in life that Thomas Rhodes did.

As the Fall of 1914 came along, and as my memories of the Sangamon country and the Spoon river country became more translucent and imaginative under the influence of pale sunlight and falling leaves, I departed more and more from the wastrels and failures of life and turned more and more to gentle combinations of my imagination drawn from the lives of the faithful and tender-hearted souls whom I had known in my youth about Concord, and wherever in Spoon river they existed. As December came I was nearing exhaustion of body, what with my professional work and the great drains that the *Anthology* were making on my emotions. The flame had now become so intense that it could not be seen, by which I mean that the writing of the pieces did not seem to involve any effort whatever; and yet I should have known that I was being sapped rapidly. I had no auditory or visual experiences which were not the effect of actuality; but I did feel that somehow, by these months of exploring the souls of the dead, by this unlicensed revelation of their secrets, I had convoked about my head swarms of powers and beings who were watching me and protesting and yet inspiring me to go on.

I do not mean by this that I believed that I was so haunted; I only mean I had that sensation, as one in a lonely and eyrie room might suddenly feel that someone was in the next room spying upon him. Often, after writing, during which I became unconscious of the passing of time, and would suddenly realize that it was twilight, I would experience a sensation of lightness of body, as if I were about to float to the ceiling, or could drift out of the window without falling. Then I would go out of the room and catch up one of the children to get hold of reality again; or I would descend for a beer and a sandwich. These nights I was playing on the Victrola the Fifth Symphony of Beethoven, out of which came the poem "Isaiah Beethoven," and such epitaphs as "Aaron Hatfield," "Russell Kincaid," and "Elijah Browning".

I might have made the *Anthology* fuller and richer and longer at this time except for my professional distractions, and if I had not been begged to stop by some of my relatives, who said that the work was long enough. If I had not been at this time descending rapidly to a sick bed, I should have gone on despite every obstacle, and so long as the spirits swarmed. In that case, would I not have epitaphed James Rutledge, thereby introducing the miller into the list of characters, beside linking dramatically the days of the Declaration with the days of Lincoln? In that case, would I have missed Samuel Hill and John McNamar? Many times as a boy I passed John McNamar's house which was two miles from the Masters homestead, when my grandfather was taking me driving about the country. "Good morning John. How do you do, sir?" was my grandfather's courtly and benignant salutation. And there stood John McNamar, an old withered cow—John McNamar who had run away from Ann Rutledge! I have seen him dozens of times at his gate in front of his farm house.

Would I have missed Mentor Graham? Would I have missed John Calhoun, who appointed Lincoln his deputy surveyor at New Salem and later figured in the Lecompton Constitution, being then surveyor general of Kansas, and who died misunderstood and unhappy in the confusion with which the slavery agitation covered the intentions of good men? Would I have missed William G. Green, who was a railroad magnate of Petersburg, and involved in legal difficulties when my father entered upon his office there? Would I have failed to give a portrait of Peter Cartwright, who was entertained scores of times at the Masters homestead, who preached his last sermon in Petersburg in 1872 to an audience of which my father was a member—Peter Cartwright who, as a young man, was a card player and race-horse gambler, and then became a fighting parson, and the most stirring backwoods preacher of America?

In a word, I omitted many stories.—EDGAR LEE MASTERS, "The Genesis of *Spoon River*," AM, Jan. 1933, pp. 49–51

Everyone knows how to say that the great merit of Lee Masters is to have begun, in his country, the realistic, merciless description of provincial people, villagers, Puritans. The dates speak for themselves: *Spoon River*, 1915; *Winesburg, Ohio*, 1919; *My Ántonia* [1918] and *Main Street*, 1920. So Edgar Lee Masters holds the record. He is the father of contemporary literature. After which, we can go on to talk about other things. Now, leaving aside the fact that in America the village had passed through Hawthorne's crucible at least as early as 1846, it would seem to me a rather feeble title for the new writers, that of having for all originality called attention to their local environment, full of local problems, and then of having solved these problems in terms of local life. If we want to read about provincial life, there are already too many European writers who have dealt with it.

Where, then, *is* the interest of these books? The truth seems to me in the first place this: to take Edgar Lee Masters for an anti-Puritan, as so many wish to do, is to reduce him to a rather feeble muckraker. Problems of this sort are already boring enough in your own house. It is true that, as in all books, American or European, worth anything at all, there is in *Spoon River* an indigenous environment and experience, an appeal to ways of life and national types that will strike the eye of every modest moviegoer as old acquaintances. But this is only the book's honesty, its direct inspiration by life, its matter, and, as I said, all books of any merit more or less display this characteristic.

We must understand that, given this national background, the important achievement lies not in the assault on certain Puritan customs—an assault that in any case amounts to very little in the book—but in the really Puritanical energy with which, going well beyond the historical moment, the book confronts the problem of the meaning of existence and the problems of one's own behavior: the energy and the problems are essentially moral and of an almost biblical tone. If in the exploration some blow is struck at the Puritanical historical structure of the country, this may be very interesting to the Americans, who themselves observe this structure all around them and on top of them, but it means little to us, except insofar as the writer's genius has transformed what for the natives and the scholars is an obvious reference into a metaphor which is no longer a mere historical name but a new creation. And in order to do this, to succeed in this work of creation—which I think Masters in large part realized—it seems to me all too obvious to say that the writer had to love his environment, to take pleasure in his own characters, to feel them born in his spirit.

The animus of destructive caricature is extremely rare in Lee Masters. The passion of every one of the hundreds of souls buried at Spoon River becomes his passion, and quite literally the poet speaks to us through the mouth of every one. This ever-renewed exploration of the worth of existence *in articulo mortis* possesses such seriousness and candor that, even in the case of Lee Masters, we have to fall back on what is by now a commonplace in the history of American culture: in the fight against Puritanism are always found the greatest Puritans. ⟨. . .⟩

The importance of this book lies in the answer never definitively given, but forever renewed through each person, the conviction, sorrowfully felt on every page, that however satisfactory and final any solution of life may seem, there will always be other people who remain outside of it. Neither optimism nor pessimism is the answer, which rather depends on a spirit of inquiry continuously renewed. Like the dead souls in Dante, who are more alive than in life, the dead of Spoon River prolong in sepulchral form all their frustrations and their passions. But here the parallel ends, since Dante's dead have a universal system in which they are included, and none of the damned dreams of criticizing his lot, while those of Spoon River, even though dead, have found no answers, least of all those who say they have. This book of poems is quintessentially modern, in its spirit of inquiry, in the inadequacy of every formula, in its need at once individual and social. You find that a child's lament, dead of tetanus while playing, rises to the same cosmic importance as the ecstasy of a scholar who spent his life in adoration of heaven and earth. In an epilogue, there is a sort of Faustian miracle play, where the character of the devil who continues to create wretched lives, to foment quarrels, and to toy with his creatures, is opposed by the spectacle of life triumphant, of harmonious laws, a kind of Shelleyan hymn to the liberated world, and which concludes:

> Infinite Law,
> Infinite Life.

But this hardly concerns the voices of Spoon River. The problem of each of those dead souls remains forever the same, frozen on the stone of his graveyard testament.—CESARE PAVESE, "The *Spoon River Anthology*" (1930), *American Literature: Essays and Opinions*, tr. Edwin Fussell, 1970, pp. 41–47

The *Domesday Book* is a narrative poem in blank verse built around the death of Elenor Murray, whose body was found one morning by a rabbit hunter on the shore of the Illinois River near Starved Rock. Her death was later attributed by a coroner's jury to a physical condition known as syncope, but only after much evidence had been taken and many witnesses had been called to testify. Masters' method here, obviously similar to that of Browning's *The Ring and the Book* (though he vigorously denied using it as a model), was to sketch the biography of everyone remotely associated with Elenor Murray and then to let each person contribute what he could to the reconstruction through dramatic monologue of the dead girl's life. This plan

allowed the poet not only to continue on a somewhat larger scale the psychological analysis of the *Spoon River Anthology* but also to review a large segment of American life. Probably in this respect the coroner of the poem speaks for Masters and at the same time explains the poem's title:

> Why not a Domesday Book in which are shown
> A certain country's tenures spiritual?
> And if great William held great council once
> To make inquiry of the nation's wealth,
> Shall not I as a coroner in America,
> Inquiring of a woman's death, make record
> Of lives which have touched hers, what lives she touched;
> And how her death by surest logic touched
> This life or that, was cause of causes, proved
> The event that made events?

In the course of the narrative Masters introduces Elenor Murray's parents, her high-school teacher, various friends and lovers, a clergyman, a sheriff, associates in a French military hospital, and finally Barrett Bays, the last one to see the girl alive. From their various confessions the tragic story is pieced together and the final picture of the protagonist emerges, a girl who was eager, intelligent, restless, rebellious, determined to break the moral and social patterns which had been fixed for her, and perhaps in that very determination symbolic of a general iconoclasm. As Barrett Bays expresses it in the poem:

> This Elenor Murray was America;
> Corrupt, deceived, deceiving, self-deceived,
> Half-disciplined, half-lettered, crude and smart,
> Enslaved yet wanting freedom, brave and coarse,
> Cowardly, shabby, hypocritical,
> Generous, loving, noble, full of prayer,
> Scorning, embracing rituals, recreant
> To Christ so much professed; adventuresome;
> Curious, mediocre, venal, hungry
> For money, place, experience, restless, no
> Repose, restraint . . .

As a whole, the *Domesday Book* has interest and impact. Masters deftly fits the sections together and skilfully varies the evidence and the witnesses. Flashbacks reveal both Elenor Murray and her period, and the characters who impinge even momentarily on her life epitomize much of America. Nevertheless, Masters' preference for the poem on the score of originality and literary finish seems unwarranted. The monologues are longer than the Spoon River epitaphs and because they are self-confessions they lack incisiveness. Their effect is further weakened because of Masters' tendency to become the trial lawyer cross-examining witnesses rather than the psychologist probing into motives and deeds. Elenor Murray, wishing to burn her candle at both ends and motivated by a craving for self-satisfaction rather than by idealism, is a weak prototype of revolt against social conventions. Moreover, as in much of the poet's later verse, the style is rough and careless. Masters could use blank verse adroitly but here the lines often become turgid, and the scope of the narrative prevents the fine chiseling which won so many partisans for the *Spoon River Anthology*.—JOHN T. FLANAGAN, "The Spoon River Poet," SWR, Summer 1953, pp. 227–28

⟨A⟩ rural-urban duality characterizes much of *The Great Valley*. Often a character reflects favorably on his own agrarian past or on that of the pioneers in the Midwest, as in "Past and Present," "Memorabilia," and "Worlds Back of Worlds." In the last of these, the speaker meditates on the past: "The windmills, barns and houses swim / In a sphered ether, wheeling, dim." On the other hand, some of the more lengthy poems are about urban dwellers or urban values, and here we detect Masters' hostility. The subject of "The Typical American?" is described as "a cog-wheel in the filthy trade / Of justice courts, police, and graft in wine." Other lyrics in the same vein are "Having His Way" and "The Asp."

We see a similar hostility and sense of loss when Masters turns to the subject of religion. Christianity had a good beginning in its attempt to achieve spiritual fulfillment, but as time went on, Christians took what they wished from pagan learning and then attempted to stifle or change the remaining elements of paganism—as he points out in "The Apology of Demetrius." Thus, in Masters' mind repression and Christianity were always joined. In "Malachy Deagan" he speaks of the innocent diversions of a small town "before the Puritan rake / Combed through the city." He elsewhere examines ways in which churches try to force people to act contrary to their own inclinations ("The Mourner's Bench" and "The Church and the Hotel"). He even shows how a man might lose his life for a minor breach of the moral code (in "Steam Shovel Cut"): "They hung him up for a little beer / With a woman on his knees." Masters chose as his champion in this fight against religion "the great agnostic," Robert Ingersoll, one of the most noted—and denounced—residents of turn-of-the-century Illinois. In "Robert G. Ingersoll" he labelled him "a general in the war of ideas for freedom."

Why Masters felt free to use his verse in such a vituperative way is partially explained in three other groups of poems from *The Great Valley*. They are important because they foreshadow the direction his later verse would take. These are the poems about the failure of idealists, the success of cynics, and the necessity of national reform. In "The Search," the last poem in the volume, he tells of three romantics (Don Quixote, Hamlet, and Faust) whose idealism has led them to nothing, and all of Masters' other idealists, artists, and aspirant souls in the volume also fail. At one extreme we find a person unjustly punished—in "The Furies"—who speaks of "ambition that eludes, love never found" and "the memory of the dream." Likewise, a more modern romantic, in "Elizabeth to Monsieur D—," spends her life looking in vain for

> An altar for my genius, something true
> And near in flesh to triumph for, or brave
> The world of evil for.

Contrasted with these lyrics about fictive idealists who fail are two much more interesting poems about real men—successes, whom Masters saw as cynics: "Theodore Dreiser" and "John Cowper Powys." Both figures are characterized as shrewd men unafraid to speak openly about society's ills. Their success comes in great part from their pessimism. Powys is an "observer of men's involuted shells": "Scoffer with reverence, / visioned, quick to damn, / Yet laugh at, looking keenly through the sham." Dreiser is, in like fashion,

> Contemptuous, ironical, remote,
> Cloudy, irreverent, ferocious,
> Fearless, grim, compassionate, yet hateful. . . .

Given Masters' admiration for these two men, here characterized as scoffers and cynics, one wonders how much Masters' verse was influenced by his friendships.

That he was open to outside literary influences may be seen by his comments on the third area here under scrutiny, national reform. In "Come Republic," one of the better poems in the volume, he sounds like the mature Whitman in his attacks on the depravity of politics, religion, and society:

> Come! United States of America,
> And you one hundred million souls, O Republic,
> Throw out your chests, lift up your heads,
> And walk with a soldier's stride.

Masters seems, however, to have been convinced that the "greater republic" for which he was looking was not coming very fast. He could hardly hope for the nation's betterment when it was obvious that the integrity of his own "great valley" was declining. What he could not know was that he himself was shortly to experience a decline.—HERB RUSSELL, "After *Spoon River*: Masters' Poetic Development 1916–1919," *The Vision of This Land*, eds. John E. Hallusas, Dennis J. Reader, 1976, pp. 77–79

---

### STANLEY EDGAR HYMAN
"Truths from the Grave" (1963)
*The Critic's Credentials*
1978, pp. 91–96

Back in the days when poets had three names, in 1916, Edgar Lee Masters' *Spoon River Anthology* appeared, and scandalized the nation. I doubt that after almost half a century it will scandalize anyone. Yet it retains an odd sort of power despite its quaintness, like grandmother's pearl-handled revolver.

*Spoon River Anthology* consists of almost 250 epitaphs, all but two or three of them spoken by the deceased. Their composite picture of the Illinois town of Spoon River is thoroughly repulsive. Julia Miller married an old man to legitimize her unborn child, then took a fatal dose of morphine anyway. Nellie Clark, at eight, was raped by a 15-year-old boy, and the disgrace pursued her ever after and wrecked her life. Yee Bow was killed by a sneak punch from the minister's son. Oscar Hummel, drunk, was beaten to death by a fanatic prohibitionist. The amount of hidden crime would shame Singapore, and its quantity is equalled only by its nastiness.

The town's pervasive hypocrisy is worse than its crimes. From the epitaph of Daisy Fraser, the town whore, we learn that only she is honest in her whoredom: the newspaper editor takes bribes to suppress the instability of the bank; the judge is on the payroll of the railroad; the clergymen speak or keep silent as their masters command. Deacon Taylor is a prohibitionist and secret drinker who confesses that the true cause of his death was cirrhosis of the liver; and one after another all the hypocrites and whited sepulchres confess.

Unhappiness is endemic in Spoon River. "A bitter wind . . . stunted my petals," cries Serepta Mason. "Sex is the curse of life," says Margaret Fuller Slack, who might have been a great novelist if she had not had eight children. The cemetery is strewn with the wreckage of dreams and hopes. Only a handful of the dead are happy: a dedicated old maid schoolteacher, a blind mother of sighted children, a fiddler who had no worldly ambition, a loving old couple, a dancer whose final placid years were spent living in sin in Spoon River, a reader of Proudhon who murdered his rich aunt and got away with it, a man whose wife loves him and mourns him, several people who were inspired by knowing Lincoln, and a few others.

As poetry, *Spoon River Anthology* is wonderfully old-fashioned now and was wonderfully old-fashioned when it appeared. By 1916 Pound had published eight volumes of poems and translations, and Eliot had published most of the poems in *Prufrock and Other Observations*, but Masters was writing in an older tradition. He took that tradition to be that of the Greek Anthology, and his poems are full of references to Hades, Furies, Fates and other Grecian properties, but his true tradition is Browning, Whitman and the native ironies of Yankee gravestones.

The world of the poems is more remote from us than Mycenae. Wickedness is summed up by "I was drinking wine with a black-eyed cocotte" in Paris, or "I killed the son/Of the merchant prince, in Madam Lou's." A nickel then bought a supply of bacon, or was a proper tip for a waiter.

The style is fittingly archaic. "But thou grievest," Masters writes, or "Thou wert wise." Many of the poems end with exclamation points, and one ends with a little thicket of them:

> The loom stops short! The pattern's out!
> You're alone in the room! You have woven a shroud!
> And hate of it lays you in it!

The form is free verse. Sometimes it becomes almost metrical, falling into lines mostly anapaestic ("I know that he told that I snared his soul/With a snare which bled him to death") or mostly iambic ("'O, son who died in a cause unjust!/In the strife of freedom slain!'"), and sometimes it approximates rhyme ("Go out on Broadway and be run over,/They'll ship you back to Spoon River").

Masters' figures of speech are ponderous: labored similes ("She drained me like a fevered moon/That saps the spinning world") or interminable metaphors (Dippold the optician sees the afterlife as an eye examination, Joseph Dixon the tuner will be retuned by the great Tuner). In the much-anthologized "Petit, the Poet," Masters mocks the ticking of Petit's little iambics "While Homer and Whitman roared in the pines." There are several Homeric similes in the book, but I am afraid that despite his self-identification, Masters ticks irregularly more than he roars.

The touch is very unsure, and *Spoon River Anthology* is full of failures, many of them in endings. One poem ends with a true whimper: "Refusing medical aid." A good poem in which a tethered cow is a metaphor for the limited freedom of the will is ruined when the metaphoric cow pulls up its stake and gores the homespun philosopher to death. Masters overdoes everything. In a typical poem, he is not content with blind Justice; her eyes must suppurate under the bandages. The mock epic and play with which the book concludes are worse than the worst of the lyrics.

To balance these there are considerable successes. We encounter fine single lines ("Toothless, discarded, rural Don Juan") and fine similes ("While he wept like a freezing steer"). There is an eloquent impression of a rattlesnake ("A circle of filth, the color of ashes,/Or oak leaves bleached under layers of leaves") and a vivid mean description of a woman:

> She was some kind of a crying thing
> One takes in one's arms, and all at once
> It slimes your face with its running nose,
> And voids its essence all over you;
> Then bites your hand and springs away.
> And there you stand bleeding and smelling to
>          heaven!

Two of the poems seem to me, in their different fashions, completely successful. One is "Roscoe Purkapile," a slight comic poem about the ironies of marriage. The other is Masters' most famous poem, "Anne Rutledge," where his Lincoln worship somehow found its proper voice, the eloquence of understatement, and something that really does rival the spare beauty of the poems in the Greek Anthology was achieved.

The enormous popularity of *Spoon River Anthology* on its appearance warrants some discussion. One obvious explanation is *succès de scandale*—it was the sex-shocker, the *Peyton Place*, of its day. Knowing that childbirth would kill his wife, Henry Barker impregnated her out of hatred. The only feeling

Benjamin Pantier inspired in his wife was sexual disgust. Old Henry Bennett died of overexertion in the bed of his young wife. Hamilton Greene is really his father's child by the German maid, as her epitaph confesses, although his own epitaph blindly boasts his "valiant and honorable blood." There is even a touch of sodomy. We have not advanced that much further in half a century.

Another feature that would have attracted readers in 1916 is the book's sour socialism. Its pervasive fable is the easy fable of Populism: that the pioneers built the land by their labor and endurance but that it was all stolen from them by "the bank and the courthouse ring." "English Thornton" appeals to the descendants of the veterans of the Revolution and the Indian wars to rise up and battle the descendants of the profiteers and the thieves, to recover their inheritance. After Lincoln, Masters' heroes idolize Altgeld, Bryan and Henry George. Matching this Populist politics is the religious iconoclasm of the village atheist. "The reason I believe God crucified His Own Son," Wendell P. Bloyd explains, "is, because it sounds just like Him." Another hero is "Foe of the church with its charnel dankness."

The total effect of bitterness and frustration that *Spoon River Anthology* gives is greater than the sum of its poems. The dead really seem to be trying to tell us something about the quality of American life, something ugly yet essential to our knowledge. These are truths from the grave, thus *grave* truths. In his epitaph, the Town Marshall exults that Jack McGuire was not hanged for killing him, since he had first attacked McGuire. "In a dream," he says triumphantly, "I appeared to one of the twelve jurymen/And told him the whole secret story." But McGuire's epitaph on the next page explodes that inspirational account. McGuire really escaped hanging, he explains, because his lawyer made a crooked deal with the judge.

The most important factor in the appeal of the book, I believe, is that, as in *Winesburg, Ohio*, some larger vision of life shines through all the pettiness. The terms in which this is put are mostly inadequate. "I thirsted so for love!/I hungered so for life!" says the shade of the poetess Minerva Jones, raped by a bully and dead of an illegal abortion. Frank Drummer tried to memorize the Encyclopaedia Britannica. Mrs. Williams doesn't think Spoon River would have been any worse had its people "been given their freedom/To live and enjoy, change mates if they wished." Mrs. Charles Bliss pleads from her experience that divorce is far better for the children than a bad marriage. "Love of women," Ezra Bartlett argues, may lead one to the divine. Harmon Whitney has been wounded by his wife's "cold white bosom, treasonous, pure and hard." Edmund Pollard pleads boldly for hedonism and joy.

It is almost inarticulate, and much of it is silly, yet some suggestion of the good life, a richer and fuller life than Americans knew in 1916, is there. Masters never understood the reasons for his success in *Spoon River Anthology*, and he never attained it again. He is not a great writer, nor even a good one. But he confronted the spiritual poverty of his America— which is still our America—without blinking, whereas Sinclair Lewis in *Main Street* ultimately turned away, and Thornton Wilder in *Our Town* never looked at America at all, merely sat down to copy *Spoon River Anthology* in a sculpture of fudge.

ERNEST EARNEST

From "Spoon River Revisited"

*Western Humanities Review*, Winter 1967, pp. 59–65

I t is over fifty years since Edgar Lee Masters' *The Spoon River Anthology* first appeared in book form. It is safe to say that no other volume of poetry except *The Waste Land* (1922) made such an impact during the first quarter of this century. Since its first publication, seventy editions of *Spoon River* have followed; it has been translated into many languages.[1]

Now, when Eliot's reputation has far surpassed that of Masters, it may seem strange to mention them in the same breath, but this was not always the case. In 1915 Ezra Pound congratulating Harriet Monroe on the publication of *Prufrock* wrote that among contemporary poets Eliot and Masters, "are the best of the bilin."[2] Writing for *The Seven Arts* in 1917 Theodore Dreiser said that since Whitman, America had produced one poet, Edgar Lee Masters.[3] Van Wyck Brooks in 1918 spoke of the book's "immense and legitimate vogue," and Sinclair Lewis in his Nobel Prize speech of 1930 praised it as being "so utterly different from any other poetry ever published. . . ."[4] As late as 1948 Willard Thorp in *The Literary History of the United States* described *Spoon River* as "one of the most momentous in American literature.[5] During the fifteen years following its publication, almost every discussion of American poetry gave Masters a central place.

Many critics of the period, even while praising *Spoon River*, objected to its pessimistic tone; those hostile to it attacked it for indecency. In fact Mencken argued that its popularity "was chiefly due to the notion that it was improper."[6] At a time when the legitimacy of free verse was being much debated, a number of critics used the work as an example of prose masquerading as poetry.

However, the chief reason for the decline of the reputation of *Spoon River* may well have been the appearance of *The Waste Land* which, along with Eliot's critical writing, changed the direction of modern poetry. The pervasive influence of Whitman was displaced by the courtly muses of Europe; realism gave way to symbolism. William Carlos Williams speaking of the impact of *The Waste Land* on American poets said,

> It wiped out our world as if an atom bomb
> had been dropped on it and our brave
> sallies into the unknown were turned to
> dust. . . .
>
> I felt at once that it had set me
> back twenty years and I'm sure it did.
> Critically Eliot returned us to the class-
>     room. . . .
>
>     . . . if he had not turned away
> from the direct attack here, in the
> western dialect, we might have gone
> ahead much faster. . . .[7]

It is significant that Hart Crane's *The Bridge* (1930), originally conceived as a Whitmanesque poem, owes much of its technique to *The Waste Land*. After Eliot, poetry became learned, filled with literary allusion and abstruse symbols; its techniques became complex and sophisticated. Certainly today the repertorial, often flat, statements in *Spoon River* seem naive in an era nurtured on Eliot. Masters' rhythms lack the polish and intricacies we have learned to appreciate. Masters' structure has much of the do-it-yourself architecture of a midwestern baloon framed house; Eliot's has the borrowed luxury of Mrs. Jack Gardner's Fenway Court.

But in other ways these two disparate works have odd similarities—the most important being that each represents modern society as a wasteland. Both by means of a series of vignettes present a panoramic view of that society. Both Eliot and Masters contrast a more vital past with an enervated present. Thus Lucinda Matlock, a character based on Masters'

grandmother, after telling of her vigorous, happy life of ninety-six years, addresses the present generation as

> Degenerate sons and daughters
> Life is too strong for you—
> It takes life to love Life.

The photographer Rutherford McDowell contrasting the faces of the pioneers in the old ambrotypes with those of the present:

> Freely did my camera record their faces too,
> With so much of the old strength gone,
> And the old faith gone,
> And the old mastery of life gone,
> And the old courage gone
> Which labors and loves and suffers and sings
> Under the sun!

It is the sort of contrast which Eliot gives in a very different way between Cleopatra in her barge and the bored modern woman in the expensive boudoir; between Spenser's nymphs gathering flowers along the Thames and the modern nymphs who leave empty bottles, sandwich papers, silk handkerchiefs, cardboard boxes and cigarette ends.

Both poets might be accused of glamorizing a somewhat mythical past at the expense of the present. In Spenser's England there were certainly the equivalents of the modern untidy nymphs, and London pubs with characters like Lil, Doll Tearsheet, Pistol, and Mistress Quickly were contemporaries of Elizabeth and Essex. And among the women Masters knew or knew of were Jane Addams, Harriet Monroe, and Willa Cather—women as admirable as the rural Lucinda Matlock of an earlier generation.

The difference between the poets is one of technique. Masters' material is in the poem itself, whereas Eliot's is often outside the poem as witnessed by his own elaborate notes. For anyone familiar with Eliot's sources, his poetry is rich in connotation: the "Sweet Thames run softly till I end my song" brings to the reader whose mind is stored with pictures from the *Prothalamion* the idyllic atmosphere of the poem. On the other hand the symbolic significance of Thomas Rhodes' bank emerges from its impact on a variety of characters in *Spoon River*.

There is also an important difference in the uses of the past by the two poets. Eliot's is a mosaic past with fragments of Greek legend, Arthurian romance, Frazer's *Golden Bough*, Dante, Shakespeare, Spenser, Wagner, and many others. One of Eliot's avowed aims was to return literature and life to a tradition. But he specifically rejected the tradition of liberalism and Protestant pluralism in which he had been born. Instead he tried to create one based on classicism, royalism, and Anglo-Catholicism.[8] As Northrop Frye points out, "One cannot both accept a tradition and decide what it is to be."[9] Furthermore a tradition is not the same thing as a mosaic of traditions.

By contrast, Masters is very much a part of a tradition, the Jeffersonian tradition of free inquiry, humanitarianism, equalitarianism. Unlike Eliot's drawn from the library, Masters' was absorbed through his pores. The names that echo through the minds of his characters are Atgeld, Jefferson, Lincoln, Grant, Bryan; Valley Forge, Starved Rock, Missionary Ridge; there are memories of the hanged anarchists in Chicago, of war in the Philippines, of Lincoln speaking on the courthouse steps. ⟨. . .⟩

Of course what made *Spoon River* immediately popular was the shock of recognition. Here for the first time in America was the whole of a society which people recognized—not only that part of it reflected in writers of the genteel tradition. Like Chaucer's pilgrims, the 244 characters who speak their epitaphs represent almost every walk of life—from Daisy Frazer, the town prostitute, to Hortense Robbins, who had travelled everywhere, rented a house in Paris and entertained nobility; or from Chase Henry, the town drunkard, to Perry Zoll, the prominent scientist, or William H. Herndon, the law partner of Abraham Lincoln. The variety is far too great for even a partial list: there are scoundrels, lechers, idealists, scientists, politicians, village doctors, atheists and believers, frustrated women and fulfilled women. The individual epitaphs take on added meaning because of often complex interrelationships among the characters. Spoon River is a community, a microcosm, not a collection of individuals.

It is ironic that the early discussions of Masters emphasized the sexual element in *Spoon River*, for it is far less obsessed with sex than is *The Waste Land*. Only about 38 of the 244 epitaphs are primarily concerned with the sexual experiences of the speakers. In Masters' picture the sterility of modern society is not merely a matter of frustrated or loveless sex; it is a complex product of sexual, social, religious, economic, and political forces. *Spoon River* is essentially a picture of a society maimed by puritanism, materialism, narrow religion and hypocrisy. At times, however, an epitaph echoes Lear's cry against the gods. Thus Schofield Huxley, after telling of man's achievements, asks of God:

> How would you like to create a sun
> And the next day have worms
> Slipping in and out between your fingers?

There is at times a transcendental note, not the serenely optimistic one of Emerson, but the questioning one of Melville and Emily Dickinson. For instance Davis Matlock advises one to live "like a god, sure of immortal life, though you are in doubt," and

> If that doesn't make God proud of you
> Then God is nothing but gravitation,
> Or sleep is the golden goal.

Alfonso Churchill, who taught astronomy at Knox College,

> . . . preached the greatness of man,
> Who is none the less a part of the scheme of things
> For the distance of Spica or the Spiral Nebulae;
> Nor any the less a part of the question
> Of what the drama means.

The Village Atheist after reading the *Upanishads* experiences a sense of revelation:

> Listen to me, ye who live in the senses
> And think through the senses only:
> Immortality is not a gift,
> Immortality is an achievement;
> And only those who strive mightily
> Shall possess it.

Unfortunately for his later reputation Masters did not render this in Sanskrit.

Another element that is often overlooked in *Spoon River* is that despite its essentially realistic method it contains a considerable amount of symbolism. Just as Thoreau saw in a freight-car of torn sails "proof sheets which need no correcting" and telling "a story more legible and interesting now than if they should be wrought into paper and printed books," so Mrs. Kessler, the village laundress, reading the lives of the owners in the soiled and torn clothes brought to her, thinks that Life too is a laundress and that every face she saw in a coffin "looked like something washed and ironed." Abel Melveny, after buying every kind of farm machine that is known, and watching it rust away because he could not house it all and did not need it, saw it as a symbol of himself, "a good machine/The Life had never used."

This was of course the symbolic technique of Melville, who saw the monkey rope as the symbol of man's interdependence and the whale lines coiled about the men in the boat as analogous to the invisible forces that enmesh us all. It is also the method of Frost, who used such symbols as a farm wall, a tuft of flowers, or an apple harvest.

The advantage of the method is that it makes a more accessible poetry than one steeped in symbols derived from esoteric sources. Its dangers are flatness and literalness, as in Wordsworth's less successful poems. On the other hand this kind of poetry does not so easily overinflate an experience or an emotion by endowing it with some mythic significance. Not every gallant stand is a Thermopylae, not every downed airman an Icarus, nor every wanderer an Odysseus, every garage mechanic a Hephaestus. This method of Wordsworth, Frost, and Masters is less in danger of relying on the rehearsed response, the Pavlovian reaction to a borrowed line from Spenser or Donne, or a reference to Chartres or Knossos.

This is not to argue for any one school of poetry; rather it is to suggest a re-evaluation of Masters' achievement. The revolution in poetry since his time is similar to that which John W. Aldridge described in fiction.

> . . . the serious novel is no longer the vehicle of middlebrow ideas and middlebrow experience, as it pretty largely was back in the days of Dreiser and Anderson, Lewis, Fitzgerald, and Hemingway. . . .[10]

A symptom of this revolution is the fact that Frost never received the Nobel Prize. This change in critical—and publishing—values is of course largely responsible for the fact that the middlebrow or even the upper middlebrow no longer reads poetry after he gets out of college.

In addition to the changes in fashion there was also Masters' own decline represented by a rather dismal series of later volumes. The free verse of the brief epitaphs is not successful when used for longer narratives. Several factors make his style effective in *Spoon River*: its frequently colloquial language is suited to the speakers, as is the underplayed m; the brevity of the sketches precludes the kind of rambling which Wordsworth achieved in *The Excursion* (a poem which also records the lives of people in a village graveyard); the ironic view of life which pervades the work often saves it from banality; and the frequently effective aphoristic climax to so many of the epitaphs produces a firm structure.

As Louis Untermeyer demonstrated[11] by taking one of them and printing it as a prose passage without Masters' line divisions, the original structure is functional: it produces a kind of musical pattern. In a less eccentric manner it achieves some of the effects of Cummings' typography: the arrangement of the lives introduces a rhythm of its own. In *Spoon River* this rhythm is well suited to the meditative, reminiscent content of the epitaphs, usually ending with an aphoristic summing up. Very possibly it is a verse style unadapted to other purposes, but in *Spoon River* it was effective. However, even those critics who disliked the technique tended to agree that *Spoon River* had vitality. If it is not great poetry, it is certainly the stuff of poetry to a degree not always present in a lot of verse since its time. The dilemmas and emotions are those of real people; there is none of that tendency to overinflate the meaning of a fish, a red wheelbarrow, a dead groundhog, an ant, or a spider. *Spoon River* may lack intellectual or musical subtlety, but it has a robust, earthy quality that has been rare in the poetry since its time.

*Notes*

1. May Swenson, Collier edition, *The Spoon River Anthology* (New York, 1962) p. 1.
2. Harriet Monroe, *A Poet's Life* (New York, 1938) p. 368.
3. Theodore Dreiser, Volume I (1916–17) 282–83.
4. Van Wyck Brooks, *Letters and Leadership in America's Coming of Age* (New York, 1958) pp. 98–99.
5. Willard Thorp, "The New Poetry," *L.H.U.S.*, 1948, p. 1180.
6. H. L. Mencken, *Prejudices, First Series* (New York, 1919) p. 88.

7. *The Autobiography of William Carlos Williams* (New York, 1951) p. 176.
8. Eliot's Royalist politics are essentially French; his Anglican views as reflected in *The Idea of a Christian Society* are rather different from those of the Archbishop of Canterbury, and his classicism closer to Irving Babbitt than to Aristotle.
9. Northrop Frye, *T. S. Eliot* (Edinburgh, 1963) p. 99.
10. Quoted Stanley Kauffman, *Harper's*, November 1965, p. 256.
11. Louis Untermeyer, *The New Era in American Poetry* (New York, 1919) pp. 168–69.

# WILLIAM MAXWELL

## 1908–

William Maxwell was born in Lincoln, Illinois, on August 16, 1908. His mother died during the influenza epidemic that followed the end of World War I and his father, an insurance executive, soon remarried and moved the family to Chicago. Maxwell attended a Chicago high school and entered the University of Illinois in Urbana in 1926. He graduated in 1930 and received an M.A. from Harvard the following year. From 1931 to 1933 he taught at the University of Illinois, but left to work on his first novel, *Bright Center of Heaven* (1934). In 1936 he joined the staff of the *New Yorker*, working first in the art department and later as a fiction editor. Over the course of the past fifty years Maxwell has written numerous short stories and book reviews which have appeared in the pages of the *New Yorker*.

Aside from his magazine work he has written several novels. His second work, *They Came Like Swallows* (1937), offers a fictionalized account of a woman's death during the influenza outbreak which claimed the life of Maxwell's own mother. His third novel, *The Folded Leaf* (1945), also received commendable critical praise. His non-fiction writings include a history of his family's 250 years in America, *Ancestors* (1971). In 1980 he published *So Long, See You Tomorrow*, a combined personal memoir and fictional fantasy. His latest undertaking was a collection of Sylvia Townsend Warner's letters, many of which were written to Maxwell. He continues to live in New York with his wife of forty years, Emily Gilman Noyes. They have two daughters.

Treating with lightness and dexterity a number of subjects usually discussed only with the highest seriousness, of the sort commonly labeled "Social Problems," Mr. Maxwell in his first novel has put together an admirable satiric comedy, bittersweet in flavor, yet always humorous. *Bright Center of Heaven* exibits few of the weaknesses present in most recent efforts by American writers to achieve subtlety and a graciously detached viewpoint in dealing with human relationships. Nevertheless it is essentially original, and does not imitate the prevailing British and French conventions for such fiction. Even the most brilliant contemporary European work of this sort presents little that is more engaging than the best parts of this book.

The scatterbrained Mrs. West and her Wisconsin farm, her odd collection of guests, paying and otherwise, are specifically American in spite of the slightly fantastic atmosphere with which Mr. Maxwell gradually succeeds in surrounding them, and so are the serio-comic repercussions produced by the arrival of a negro friend of Mrs. West's, one Jefferson Carter. Thus the core of the plot has a peculiarly native quality for which the author is to be congratulated. Here are no accessories from Paris or the Riviera, no echoes of Chelsea or Bloomsbury. Besides this, the rest of Mr. Maxwell's material is sufficiently timeless and universal to be anyone's property, such themes as adolescent love, the musical temperament, and the servant problem supplementing his more novel central idea.

Technically, Mr. Maxwell has surprisingly little to learn. He shows remarkable skill in presenting his people and in making them understandable, and does not often overemphasize the tragic undercurrent which flows continually beneath his deliberately careless manner. On the other hand, his book is a little slow in starting, and his climax, in which the negro family arrives and upsets Mrs. West's already far from stable household, is too long delayed to be really effective. There is no particular reason why the writer of such a novel should pay great attention to narrative form, especially as he has confined the action within the limits of a single day; but there are a good many annoyingly loose ends left untied and unaccounted for at the close of these twelve hours. Exception taken for minor and comparatively unimportant abberations of this sort, it is possible to say that *Bright Center of Heaven* is a delightful and amusing satiric novel, and consequently also something of a rarity in this season.—THEODORE PURDY, JR., "American Comedy," *SR*, Sept. 15, 1934, pp. 109–10

Despite the fact that William Maxwell's *The Folded Leaf* is unusually easy and gratifying to read, it is a difficult book to write about. For it carves out such a seemingly minor literary task for itself—to tell the story of the friendship of two boys through high school and college—that one hesitates to burden it with the kind of "importance" to which the author is notably indifferent. And yet it not only goes about its work with a precise skill which is rare in current fiction but also manages to evoke very much larger meanings than appear on the surface. The source of this suggestiveness is, of course, its style. Style is latent content, and there is an uncommonly rich latent content beneath the modest explicit content of Mr. Maxwell's novel.

The prose of most current fiction is either excessively, and falsely, simple or prodigal without discipline, and in either category the only dimension added by style is likely to be the dimension of the author's ego. But *The Folded Leaf*, written with genuine simplicity, allows the author to stand in the most useful possible relationship to his material. In full control of his characters and situations but not merged with them, he is free to comment on their fates in his own person, so we have the advantage of his intellect as well as of his creativity; in the degree that he keeps his personality clear of his people, he achieves a true distinction of personality. Thus a scene of a high-school-fraternity initiation not only is reported for all its worth as narrative but also gives Mr. Maxwell the opportunity for a very pleasant essay on the anthropological occasion. Or often Mr. Maxwell will point out, lightly but sharply, the pattern of circumstance in which his characters have been caught. Obviously this commentative function is a very proper function of an author. All the great novelists of the past assumed it eagerly. But very few present-day writers have enough distance from their fictional material to permit it.

*The Folded Leaf* is divided into many small chapters, each of them concerned with a moment of significance in the lives of its characters, and Mr. Maxwell is at his best when these moments are physically seen. The initiation ceremony which I have mentioned is perhaps outstanding in the book, but there are any number of lesser scenes—in Spud and Lymie's college rooming-house, for instance, or at Spud's boxing work-outs, or at the college spring riot—which have an almost fragrant authenticity. Mr. Maxwell has a remarkable, if quiet, gift for observation; his record of Middle Western American life in the '20's adds up to a more important social document than he was perhaps conscious of. But in the last third of the novel, when, because the story must be brought to a climax and conclusion, Mr. Maxwell concerns himself with purely emotional developments, he becomes spare and even unconvincing. It is of course the scenerio of *The Folded Leaf* to bring Spud and Lymie to manhood at the end of the volume, but to assume, in a novel, that people are mature and competent simply because they have reached a point where maturity is asked of them is to contrive for fictional characters an outcome constantly denied people in reality. The resolution of *The Folded Leaf* is not only shadowy but fortuitous. I completely doubt the independence which Lymie is supposed to have found so suddenly, and I look to the future of Spud with an uneasiness which his author gives us no evidence that he shares.—Diana Trilling, *Nation*, April 21, 1945, pp. 466–67

William Maxwell has chosen an Illinois town in the year 1912 as setting for his fourth distinguished novel ⟨*Time Will Darken It*⟩. It is certain to induce many nostalgic sighs from mothers and fathers, and uncles and aunts, of the present war generation. And because Mr. Maxwell is sensitive and has sufficient restraint to recapture the tempo and mauve tints of those more tranquil days, even we, to whom that period can only be remotely appealing, cannot help but be caught up in the author's finely spun mood of nostalgia. If sometimes we feel the ironic tone in the book smothered, perhaps, by a too bittersweet ruefulness, Mr. Maxwell makes up for it by disclosing the poetry, the haunting sadness, and the myriad intimacies and subtle undertones which existed within the family circle when the horse-drawn surrey was still the fashionable conveyance of the day.

A novelist who is not content to show us the mere surface of urban lives, William Maxwell occasionaly penetrates right to the core of human motives, unearthing tragedy or its drab counterpart—that tragicomic passivity with which folk too

often will accept the harsh vicissitude of life. In a psychological novel we expect a deeper, more clinical probing into the frustrations and strained relationships between parents and children, husbands and wives, brothers and sisters; but here such treatment only manages to produce deeper and uglier rents in the quiet, painstakingly woven fabric of Mr. Maxwell's tale of yesterday.

With bold realistic strokes of a painter who has concentrated a little too much on the landscape—because all he really is interested in is examining the effect that time's landscape has on the set of arbitrary figures he has drawn on his canvas—Mr. Maxwell restores a picture that should be familiar to many of us who have lived in towns like Draperville, Illinois, or have ever tried to imagine what the inhabitants were like who once dwelt on one of our elm-shaded streets when the century was considerably younger. And if we shut our eyes, we can visualize Mr. Maxwell's characters almost with no trouble at all. There in that house in the foreground are the tall, dignified, polite young lawyer Austin King and his pregnant wife, Martha, and their four-year-old daughter, Abbey, while in the background Rachel, the Negro cook, hovers about the kitchen stove. Next door we can see the indomitable Mrs. Beach and her two cowed, spinsterly daughters, Lucy and Alice. Farther down the street live: shy May Caroline Link, waiting in vain for some high-school Lochinvar to sweep her off her feet, Doctor and Mrs. Danforth, and the Ellis family. These are the friends, antagonists, and neighbors of Austin and Martha King, who look out on a kinder, gentler age from their front-porch rockers, relaxing in the summer's evening heat, listening to the children playing games, and watching the lightning bugs blinking in the night air.

But suddenly as if a swarm of locusts or a flock of magpies had descended on this peaceful suburban scene, the Potters invade the privacy of Draperville's respectable homes. To Austin King, our well-meaning hero, the arrival of these foster relatives brings a realization of his own essential weakness in making decisions; above all, his inability to choose between the moonstruck, idealistic Nora Potter and his wife, whom he desperately loves but cannot reach. The Potters do not depart for their Mississippi plantation before they have thoroughly confused and disrupted the community, leaving in their wake injured prides, wounded hearts, and generally troubled minds, the memory of which only time will darken and soften.

Mr. Maxwell's novel will at least put an end to the impression that most American towns in the early part of the century were potential torture chambers, an impression which *King's Row* and novels of its sadistic genre left with us. William Maxwell is an entertaining and sympathetic chronicler who seeks to record the accurate, if not always the happiest, side of family history in his novels. Once again he reveals a strong flair for poetic imagery, for a well-turned, thoughtful phrase, which raises his writing from the pedestrian level of many of our novelists today.

The next time we open the family album, those old snapshots are going to appear less comic, they are going to take on a life and glow which we were not able to perceive so clearly before reading this book.—Richard McLaughlin, "Midwest Family Album, 1912," *SR*, Sept. 4, 1948, p. 9

Some years ago William Maxwell delivered at Smith College a lecture entitled "The Writer as Illusionist," in which he said: "In writing—in all writing but especially in narrative writing— you are continually being taken in. The reader, skeptical, experienced, with many demands on his time and many ways of enjoying his leisure, is asked to believe in people he knows don't exist, to be present at scenes that never occurred, to be amused or moved or instructed just as he would be in real life, only the life exists in somebody else's imagination. If, as Mr. T. S. Eliot says, humankind cannot bear very much reality, then that would account for their turning to the charlatans operating along the riverbank, to the fortune-teller, the phrenologist, the man selling spirit money, the storyteller. Or there may be a different explanation; it may be that what humankind cannot bear directly it can bear indirectly, from a safe distance."

In several novels, particularly *They Came Like Swallows* and *The Folded Leaf*, and in many short stories Maxwell has shown himself to be an adroit illusionist. His magic is of the quiet sort, even when, as in *The Folded Leaf*, he is working in the neighborhood of tragedy.

*The Chateau* is uncommonly quiet even for him, quiet, slow moving, and perhaps at times rather dull, but it casts its spell. It is the story of a young American couple in France in 1948. We are told only a little about them: Harold Rhodes is thirty-four, and works for an engraving firm; Barbara is a little younger. They have been married for three years and are saddened by their failure to have children. They have set out for France impulsively, without taking into account the difficulties of the postwar situation and with only a rudimentary knowledge of the language.

They have arranged to spend two weeks at a château near the Loire, and to this experience much of the novel is devoted. There are inconveniences and petty annoyances, partly because France has not fully recovered from the war, partly because the French are French. Harold and Barbara are often uneasy and sometimes downright miserable, but there are happy moments. They go to Paris for Bastille Day, returning to Beaumesnil for the balance of their fortnight. When they leave, they pay through the nose.

It is on their relationships with the people of the château that Maxwell concentrates. Both are friendly by nature, and Harold is unusually outgoing, but everywhere they find barriers and mysteries. Mme. Viénot, owner of the château, now befriends, now ignores, now exploits them. Elderly Mme. Straus-Muguet is attentive but puzzling. Most perplexing of all is Mme. Viénot's nephew, Eugène de Boisgaillard, who is warm and gay one minute and sullen and cold the next. No one behaves quite as they expect him to.

For the most part Maxwell tells all this in a straightforward, objective fashion, but now and then he pauses to explain a little about his young couple or to let us know what is going on in the minds of other characters. The magician steps out of his role, or at least pretends to, and though at first this startles us, he soon wins us over to his way of doing things.

The story continues. Eugene de Boisgaillard has invited the Rhodeses to stay in his apartment in Paris, and they do so, only to discover that he is an unpredictable and apparently an unwilling host. They see the sights, of course, and they again become involved with Mme. Straus-Muguet, who is as effusive and as incomprehensible as ever. They spend happy days in the South of France and then go to Italy and Austria, but we are told nothing about that, which is rather a blessing. Returning to Paris, for their last weeks in Europe, they again encounter some of the persons they have known in Beaumesnil. And finally the time comes for their departure.

This is the point at which the book could be expected to end, but Maxwell has written a kind of epilogue, which he calls "Some Explanations." This takes the form of a dialogue between a reader and the author. The reader wants to know what M. Viénot had been up to, why Eugène behaved as he did, what happened to various characters. The author answers these questions after a fashion, and goes on to tell how Barbara

and Harold revisited France five years later and to report to the readers that they eventually had a child. This supplement comes close to anticlimax, and yet one can see what Maxwell is trying to do: the explanation really explains nothing, for mystery lies behind mystery. "So strange, life is. Why people do not go around in a continual state of surprise is beyond me."

The American in Europe has long been one of the favorite themes of our writers, from Melville (in *Redburn*) and Hawthorne (in *The Marble Faun*) through Howells and Mark Twain and Henry James to Sinclair Lewis and Ernest Hemingway. And what could be more natural? This is one of the ways, one of the important ways, in which we learn what we are really like. Henry James found enough in the theme to occupy most of his writing career.

Maxwell has taken a critical moment in history, just as the great postwar invasion of American tourists was beginning. His Harold and Barbara are innocent Americans, nice Americans, quiet Americans; Harold thinks they are representative Americans, and one hopes and believes he is right. They fall in love with France—"the way Americans are always doing"—and Maxwell makes us feel their passion. France is easy to fall in love with, but the Rhodeses learn that the French are elusive. Part of the trouble is simply that they are Americans, and Americans just then seem too lucky to be likable. But there are also the difficulties that differences of custom and language have always created. "What it amounts to," Harold reflects, "is that you cannot be friends with somebody, no matter how much you like them, if it turns out that you don't really understand one another." There is also the fact, never forgotten, that communication between two human beings is rarely perfect, even between two as much in love as Harold and Barbara.

There will be differing opinions about the book. Some readers, with whom I sympathize, will find that the novel proper moves at too deliberate a pace; others will relish every word and wish there were more. To some the epilogue will seem too tricky a device; others, on whose side I stand, will hold that the artificiality is justified by the sense that is given of multiple meanings. Everyone will agree that Maxwell writes a firm, polished prose and that he is in every way a skilled illusionist, who, like all skilled illusionists, helps us to understand reality. The book belongs on a shelf that holds some of the most distinguished American fiction.—GRANVILLE HICKS, "A Quiet Sort of Magic," *SR*, March 18, 1961, p. 16

The stories in *Over by the River*, William Maxwell's new collection, have copyrights dating as far back as 1941—yet there is a remarkable sameness to the whole. Six of the twelve pieces take place in or near New York City, two in tourist's France, and the rest in that ancestral Midwestern town Maxwell has been peopling for decades. The title story—first and longest in the book—circumscribes his terrain. An upper middle-class family on Manhattan's East Side is haunted by the sense of death and disaster impinging—how suicide and drugs must be incorporated in the "Chinese scroll" that unfurls north from Gracie Square. In the last and less threatening piece, a Murray Hill housewife embroiders "The Thistle in Sweden" as a design on her living room curtains; the narrator observes, in the book's final phrase, "I think if it is true that we are all in the hand of God, what a capacious hand it must be."

The bulk of the work demonstrates such capacity: fathers reconcile with sons; pilgrims reach their Mecca—even if the price has been hiked in hotels on the way; fear and distrust are outlasted. Maxwell traces, as in one story's title, "The Patterns of Love." His characters are decent and striving to be better; his woods are full of thrushes and his chicken full of truffles.

Sometimes the author warns us against surfeit: "The snapshots show nothing but joy. Year after year of it." Telling of such empty superfluity, his voice edges up to despair; the wood-thrush is most deeply desired in its absence.

There is scant violence or impassioned action here: sex is linked to procreation, madness to a relative's demise. The suicide mentioned above is that of someone's cook, and a neighbor wonders whether she—a large woman—had had trouble scaling the park's protective bars. A cry for "Help" may be imaginary, and the reader wonders—together with the haunted protagonist, at story's end—"if something happened."

The answer is yes. There are ghosts enough in these middle-class households to keep any audience on edge. A flying squirrel steals Mildred Gellert's supper, and a snake may lurk beneath her porch; an artistically fashioned scarecrow seems to have its own inherent malevolence: "The chain is not as strong as it seems: The beaded profière fell down. All by itself. For no reason." Even bicycles are subject to assault: one gets stolen by a contemporary junkie and one gets wrecked, in 1922. In none of these instances, however, is physical injury sustained. And the cumulative effect of these pages is that of humanity's triumph; "The French Scarecrow" is deflated and the mugger shooed on down the stairs by a devoted maid.

Sometimes this effect can cloy: the tone shifts from benign to condescending. "There were places he would never see, experiences of the first importance that he would never have. He might die without ever having heard a nightingale." Or Maxwell's omniscience seems inappropriate; the "Young Francis Whitehead" who is the protagonist of one story appears as a character in "Haller's Second Home." Francis is in the army and at a great remove, but we are told that "He didn't really need a number to distinguish him from other soldiers, because he was the only one who could tell, in the dark, that the crease in the middle of the sheet he was lying on was not in the exact center of the bed." An elegant perception elegantly phrased, this nonetheless seems to me to call attention to itself and not the character described. Francis would need no number to identify himself, nor would the other soldiers use such detailing for identity—the authorial overview intrudes stage-center here.

Largely, however, such intrusions are welcome and Maxwell's characteristic asides seem apt. "The key to age is patience, and the key to patience is unfortunately age, which cannot be hurried, which takes time (in which to be disappointed); and time is measured by what happens; and what happens is printed (some of it) in the evening paper."

Such colloquial inclusiveness is one hallmark of his style. Maxwell moves from specific detail to the abstract assertion deftly, and his sense of time is supple throughout. The two stories set in France shift from the remembered and splendid occasion to the tawdry present; the whole continuous history of "The Thistles in Sweden" is present tense. Strangely, the author's persona seems least at home in what are his "hometown" stories; the elegiac mode appears a touch too pat.

But to complain about these stories is to cavil—they are never less than competent, and often the language is eloquent. "There is another secret that cannot be kept from me because, with her head in a frame made by my head, arms and shoulder, I know when she weeps." Or, in the last sentence of "The Pilgrimage," when he treats the quotidian with a reverence that renders it, near-comically, sacred: "A few minutes later, some more people emerged from the movie theatre, and some more, and some more, and then a great crowd came streaming out and, walking gravely, like people taking part in a religious procession, fanned out across the open square."

What his characters miss—preparing for bed, they ignore this spectacle—the author describes to us; what we might miss he stresses and provides. There is nothing wrong with consistency, if one's work is consistently fine—and the sameness of William Maxwell's oeuvre should be a thing to honor, not ignore. That the author of *They Came Like Swallows* and *The Folded Leaf* can still regale and inform us is a gift.—NICHOLAS DELBANCO, "In God's Capacious Hand," *NYTBR*, Oct. 16, 1977, p. 44

*So Long, See You Tomorrow* is a rare truth-telling fiction. Grave, moving, and wise, it presents a vision of life as a tragic order in which passion is fate, choice is illusion, and innocence and guilt have little meaning and no moral relation to suffering. There is no cure for this suffering, since its cause seems to be life, but there is an implied mitigation. This is the retrospective activity of the sympathetic imagination, which cannot change the facts of another's life, but can make their meaning present and in this way create a feeling of solidarity between oneself and others. This activity of the imagination is precious; it is not too much to call it the humanist's version of prayer. But it cannot make everything present, for some situations are so bad as to be unimaginable.

Consider this situation. The time is 1922; the place is Logan County, Illinois. Your name is Cletus Smith. You are a farm boy. And you have had a series of blows. Your father has killed his best friend, a man who had been like a second father to you. But that isn't all because your father has killed himself, too. (It is you who identify his shotgun at the inquest; it is easy to recognize since it is the same make as your bicycle.) And that is not all of it, either, because the man your father killed also was your mother's lover, and without him she is, as she says, "the most miserable woman in the world." But still that is not the worst because you have moved to Chicago where nobody remembers your father but where nobody knows you either; and in the corridor of the big Chicago high school you have been snubbed by the one friend you did have back in Logan County. How must you feel at that moment?

That question will always haunt the boy who snubbed you in the corridor, and when he is an old man and full of a lifetime's regret, he will write about you in a book, and of your grief at that time he will say: "In the face of deprivation so great, what is the use of asking him to go on being the boy he was. He might as well start life over as some other boy instead." That is as near as he will come to imagining how you felt. But his book will end with the hope that you weren't destroyed, in the mind and the feelings, by all that happened to you.

In the course of his narrative William Maxwell keeps coming back to the tragedy of Cletus Smith. But along the way he sketches in the sorrows of the minor characters who make up the world around the boy (his dog is one of them). And of course he includes the linked tragedies of the boy's father, who just wanted his wife to love him; of Lloyd Wilson, his father's best friend, whom she did love; and of his mother, who couldn't help the way she felt. The moral focus of the story, however, is on the narrator himself: his grief over the early death of his mother, his envy and anger over his father's second marriage, and his guilt for shunning the unfortunate Cletus—this tangle of emotion makes him the strongest presence in the novel. We accept his story as that of William Maxwell himself, and his book not as a fiction but as a memoir, a sincere offering for that snub 50 years ago. This sense of moral authenticity is the supreme illusion in fiction; something we experience only with the great masters of realism: Flaubert, Tolstoy, Chekhov. Like them, William Maxwell reduces life to its tragic essence without portentousness, that stylistic insistence on the terrible.

This is a short novel but only a quantitative theory of art would regard it as slight.—JACK BEATTY, NR, Jan. 26, 1980, pp. 39–40

---

## BRENDAN GILL
### "The Past Regained"
*New Yorker*, August 21, 1971, pp. 88–91

In this country, we have made a tradition of mocking tradition, which is to say that we have been uneasy about it and have come to terms with it disingenuously, if at all. They order this matter better in France, and, indeed, everywhere in Europe. Over there, to be curious about one's antecedents is not necessarily a form of self-aggrandizement; the family tree can be frolicked in, squirrel-fashion, or even dozed in and hung from, possum-fashion, without one's appearing to have embraced the exquisite folly of ancestor worship. Genealogy is held to be an interesting branch of knowledge and not simply a snobbish one. Moreover, to the extent that it opens innumerable doors upon the past, genealogy invites one to roam at will through a landscape that, as it grows every day more familiar and bizarre, gives bolder and bolder hints of who it is one has it in him to become; uncannily, one begins to take energy and direction from what had seemed at first but a great necropolis, stretching from horizon to horizon. Astonishing how pungent it is and how well pleased one is to breathe it, the dust of one's dead! European writers have always known how to savor this cannibal fragrance. One thinks of Yeats, who from earliest youth doted upon his ancestors and gathered courage and inspiration from them. Figuratively as well as literally, they were the making of him, and he never tired of celebrating in verse the manliness of what he called the "old fathers" and their notable estrangement from the marketplace. Country parsons, scholars, hunting and fishing masters of obscure demesnes in the green fastness of Ireland, they mattered not so much as a pinch in the scales of history, but their scion saw them as heroic: gentry wedded to the land and yet totally unlike the blunted peasant, locked in exhausting intercourse with it, or the meagre, moneymaking men in towns, ravishers of it at second and third hand. If to our eye Yeats is a far braver figure than his forebears, this may be because he looked back over his shoulder toward all those mingled Pollexfens, Middletons, and Butlers, and, striving to equal them, exceeded them. It was no mere literary conceit when, at the age of forty-eight, he apologized to their ghosts for having failed to beget more than books; it happened that he was ready to become an ancestor before he was ready to become a father, and in good time (for one of the things the past teaches is that there is nearly always time enough to do whatever we *really* want to do) he became both.

American writers have tended to reflect our national skepticism of pedigrees. Even an Adams, speaking of his distinguished lineage, manages to strike a note of sourness, and it is by an irony equally sour that the childless Washington is hailed as the father of his country. As for the rest of us, we may hesitate to ferret out family archives only in part because we fear to be thought to be putting on airs; we also fear, and with reason, that what we uncover in the course of our researches will prove to be of a spiritual and intellectual poverty so dire that we will hasten to tie up and put away the brittle pages, to let the heavy lid of the trunkful of sought-for souvenirs. For what have our writers of poetry and fiction wigwagged to us over the heads of their contemporaries but that the American past has often been an intolerable burden to totter under, not because there was so much of it but because there was so little, and that little so harsh, so thin, so mean, so unnourishing? No use looking back, they seem to say, except in revulsion. The family is what cannot feed you and yet will not let you go; to escape it is to make good. The authentic American voice has always been that of Frost's Yankee farmer saying, "Home is the place where, when you go there, they have to take you in." And there have been few to protest, along with the farmer's wife, "I should have called it something you somehow haven't to deserve." Only a hired man would come home to die; a proper man would die in a ditch, alone.

But now, as late in our history as 1971, something extraordinary has happened—a book has been written, perhaps the first of its kind, in which all our received ideas about tradition and the past and the family are quietly, charmingly, and with an unchallengeable self-confidence turned upside down and inside out and made to look very strange and yet very appealing in their new postures and skins. The pioneering book is by the novelist William Maxwell, and it is his first work of nonfiction. With perfect accuracy and with a no less perfect equanimity he calls it *Ancestors*. It is worth pausing to note that in Bowker's latest edition of *Books in Print* there is but one work that bears this title, and it is, as one might surmise, not by an American but by an Englishman. As if unaware that he is taking terrible chances with the expectations of readers brought up on the parched and lonely contrarieties of Dickinson, Jewett, Masters, Lewis, Anderson, and the like, Mr. Maxwell rummages about among two or three centuries of parents, grandparents, great-grandparents, and great-great-grandparents, and finds himself at peace with them and with his admiration for them. He writes about them at once truly and tenderly, though there is often little enough that is tender about *them*; the Maxwells were of Scottish Presbyterian descent, and even when they are sanguine such folk are dour. Having been born into this world to assist God by demonstrating His wisdom in choosing them, they owed it to Him to work and pray and beget and live as long as possible and then die, on their deathbeds perhaps still fiercely disputing the merits of infant baptism; earth was no laughing matter, and neither was eternity.

The accuracy of the title of *Ancestors* is not diminished if one points out that the author could almost as easily have called his book "Me Among Mine." For, with the much admired mischievous sleight of hand of his novels (in which it is nothing for him to saw people neatly in two and cause potted lilies to leap from a furled silk handkerchief), Mr. Maxwell has contrived to outwit the difficulty that most autobiographers face when they pretend to have been thrust against their will onto the stage at the very moment that they are making a leg at the audience. Not for him a tiresome display of false modesty; what is he writing his book for except to render himself visible? And knowable? He assumes his place in the spotlight as a matter of course, and with the audacious suavity of an expert magician continuously directs our attention elsewhere. Elsewhere is not, we may be sure, where the important action is to be looked for, and if we are diligent and alert what we are told about past Maxwells won't be a patch on what we deduce about the present one. How easy he makes his feats of autobiographical prestidigitation seem! Observe how, amused and unselfconscious, he begins one chapter at stage center: "I have always liked my name. This may be because the people I was surrounded with as a child. When they used my name, or my brother's, or for that matter one another's, it was almost always with affection, which somehow rubbed off on the name itself." Or, seeming to march briskly offstage in order to leave it available to his father: "I'm sure they didn't ride in a sleeping car—it would have cost too much. And that they brought something to stay their hunger: thick meat sandwiches. Pickles. Pie. And cake. And that my father had a great deal to say, for he was the youngest and it was the first time in his life that he had enjoyed his father's undivided attention all through a day and a night." Or, finally, as if from the wings, himself nearly obliterated: "Robert Maxwell and Mary Edie had fifteen children, of whom my great-grandfather, also named Robert, was the eleventh. They were all born between 1794 and 1818, which means that for twenty-five years there was always a baby in the house." How does the magician persuade us to follow with pleasure the complex interweavings of those long-loosened lives? What is the trick by which he holds us fast? Ah, yes! ". . . there was always a baby in the house." The magician is not as far offstage as we had supposed.

The author's most successful feat of deception is this: that at a certain, scarcely detectable point in his narrative the ancestors of *Ancestors* are made to slip away and we are left in the presence of a little boy who, all nakedly and touchingly, is about to lose his beloved mother by death, who is to suffer the ignominy of adolescence in a desolate household, and who is to spend years learning that the contest of love and suspicion between father and son can never be won by either and is not to be ended even after death. "It is not true that the dead desert the living. They go away for a very short time, and then they come back and stay as long as they are needed. But sooner or later a time comes when they are in the way; their presence is, for one reason or another, an embarrassment; there is no place for them in the lives of those they once meant everything to. Then they go away for good." That passage concerns the author's mother; the last glimpse we are given of the father before he dies, at eighty, implies that the author is not—at least, not yet—ready to make the passage concern the father as well:

> When I was in my forties, and married, and living in Westchester County, my father and my stepmother came for a visit. It was October, and cool enough for a fire in the fireplace. Before dinner I made a round of drinks, and my father and I sat on either side of the fire, talking, with our glasses on the floor beside us, and suddenly a suspicion crossed my mind, for the first time. I don't know why it took me so long to ask this question or why it never occurred to my father to tell me without my having to ask. I picked up the poker and rearranged the logs and then, leaning back said, "Am I like your father?" and he said, rather crossly, "Of course."

We are all more or less uneasily descendants, and we are all imminently ancestral. In the enemy country between those states stands the family tree. Mr. Maxwell has made the startling discovery that it is worth taking shelter in. We are lucky to have been allowed to join him under all those folded leaves.

# H. L. MENCKEN

## 1880–1950

Henry Louis Mencken was born in Baltimore on September 12, 1880. Both his father, who was a successful businessman, and his mother, with whom he was especially close, were of German ancestry. Mencken graduated as valedictorian from the Baltimore Polytechnic Institute in 1896. Instead of going to college or pursuing the career he wanted in journalism, Mencken was forced to work for his father's manufacturing business. After his father's sudden death in 1899 he joined the editorial staff of the Baltimore *Morning Herald*, beginning a long, successful career as a journalist. Mencken moved from news reporting to drama criticism and by 1905 he was the managing editor of the paper. In 1906 he began working for the Baltimore *Sunpapers* and in 1911 he started writing his famous column, "The Free Lance."

His first important book, *George Bernard Shaw: His Plays*, appeared in 1905. *The Philosophy of Friedrich Nietzsche* followed in 1908, earning Mencken a reputation as a leading purveyor of European culture for the American reading public. In 1908 he also began working with George Jean Nathan on the sophisticated magazine *Smart Set*. Later the two critics founded *American Mercury*, an important journal during the 1920s and early 1930s. Mencken's politics were an unusual blend of Social Darwinism with his own personal reading of Nietzsche. An outspoken writer, he was forced to relinquish his newspaper columns during the two world wars because of his pro-German sentiments. In fact, in 1915 Mencken defended the actions of the German submarine that had torpedoed the *Lusitania*. Later in his career he vehemently opposed Roosevelt and the New Dealers, thereby lessening his own popularity.

He published several important collections of critical essays, including *A Book of Prefaces* (1917), which contains his famous essay on the history of the control Puritan values have exercised over American literary tastes. His *In Defense of Women* (1918) caused much controversy; in it Mencken tried to show that women are more intelligent than men. From 1919 to 1927 he also published a series of books titled *Prejudices*, which contain essays on American life, politics, art, and religion. Perhaps his most influential and popular book was *The American Language*. First published in 1919, the work underwent numerous revisions throughout Mencken's lifetime. His contrasting of the American language to what he called "English English" is insightful as well as entertaining.

Mencken wrote a series of autobiographies chronicling different periods in his life. He lived in his family home in Baltimore until his marriage to Sara Haardt in 1930. After his wife's death in 1935 he moved back to the family home where he lived until his own death on January 29, 1950.

Mr. Mencken gives the impression of an able mind so harried and irritated by the philistinism of American life that it has not been able to attain its full power. These more carefully worked-over critical essays ⟨A Book of Prefaces⟩ are, on the whole, less interesting and provocative than the irresponsible comment he gives us in his magazine. How is it that so robust a hater of uplift and puritanism becomes so fanatical a crusader himself? One is forced to call Mr. Mencken a moralist, for with him appraisement has constantly to stop while he tilts against philistine critics and outrageous puritans. In order to show how good a writer is, he must first show how deplorably fatuous, malicious or ignorant are all those who dislike him. Such a proof is undoubtedly the first impulse of any mind that cares deeply about artistic values. But Mr. Mencken too often permits it to be his last, and wastes away into a desert of invective. Yet he has all the raw material of the good critic—moral freedom, a passion for ideas and for literary beauty, vigor and pungency of phrase, considerable reference and knowledge. Why have these intellectual qualities and possessions been worked up only so partially into the finished attitude of criticism? Has he not let himself be the victim of that paralyzing Demos against which he so justly rages? As you follow his strident paragraphs, you become a little sorry that there is not more of a contrast in tone between his illumination of the brave, the free and the beautiful, and the peevish complaints of the superannuated critics of the old school. When are we going to get anything critically curative done for our generation, if our critical rebels are to spend their lives cutting off hydra-heads of American stodginess?

Mr. Mencken's moralism infects the essay on Conrad perhaps the least. With considerable effort the critic shakes himself loose from the clutches of his puritan enemies and sets Conrad very justly in relation to his time. "What he sees and describes in his books," Mr. Mencken says, "is not merely this man's aspiration or that woman's destiny, but the overwhelming sweep and devastation of universal forces, the great central drama that is at the heart of all other dramas, the tragic struggles of the soul of man under the gross stupidity and obscene joking of the gods." He likes Dreiser for the same reason, because "he puts into his novels a touch of the eternal Weltschmerz. They get below the drama that is of the moment and reveal the greater drama that is without end." Mr. Mencken discusses Dreiser with admirable balance, and his essay is important because it criticizes him more harshly and more searchingly than many of us dare to do when we are defending him against the outrageous puritan. The essay on Huneker is perhaps the most entertaining. If "to be a civilized man in America is measurably less difficult, despite the war, than it used to be, say, in 1890" (when Mr. Mencken, by the way, was ten years old), it is to Mr. Huneker's gallant excitement that part of the credit is due.

Dreiser and Huneker Mr. Mencken uses with the utmost lustiness, as Samson used the jaw-bone, to slay a thousand Philistines, and his zeal mounts to a closing essay on Puritanism as a Literary Force, which employs all the Menckenian artillery. Here Mr. Mencken, as the moralist contra moralism, runs amuck. It is an exposure that should stir our blood, but it is so heavily documented and so stern in its conviction of the brooding curtain of bigotry that hangs over our land, that its effect must be to throw paralyzing terror into every American mind that henceforth dares to think of not being a prude. Mr. Mencken wants to liberate, but any one who took his huge concern seriously would never dare challenge in any form that engine of puritanism which derives its energy from the history and soul of the American people. Mr. Mencken is much in earnest. His interview rises above the tone of scornful exaggeration. But his despair seems a little forced. I cannot see that the younger writers—particularly the verse-writers—are conscious of living under any such cultural terrorism as he describes. Mr. Mencken admits that the puritan proscription is irrational and incalculable in its operation. Surely as long as there are magazines and publishers—as there are in increasing numbers—who will issue vigorous and candid work, comstockery in art must be seen as an annoying but not dominating force. Mr. Mencken queerly shows himself as editor, bowing meekly under the puritan proscription, acting as censor of "a long list of such things by American authors, well-devised, well-imagined, well-executed, respectable as human documents and as works of art—but never to be printed in mine or any other American magazine." But what is this but to act as busy ally to that very comstockery he denounces? If the Menckens are not going to run the risk, in the name of freedom, they are scarcely justified in trying to infect us with their own caution.

The perspective is false that sees this persecution as peculiar to America. Was not Lemonnier prosecuted in Paris? Did not Baudelaire, Flaubert, Zola suffer? Did not Zola's publisher in England die in prison? Has not D. H. Lawrence's latest novel been suppressed in England before it had even a chance to be prosecuted here? It is England not America that has an official censorship of plays. Comstockery is not so much a function of American culture as it is of the current moralism of our general middle-class civilization. The attack must be, as Nietzsche made it, on that moralism rather than on its symptoms. But Mr. Mencken is not particularly happy in his understanding of Nietzsche. He wrote the book from which a majority of the Americans who know about Nietzsche seem to have gotten their ideas. How crude a summary it is may be seen by comparing it with the recent study of Nietzsche by another American, W. M. Salter. One wishes Mr. Mencken had spent more time in understanding the depth and subtleties of Nietzsche, and less on shuddering at puritanism as a literary force, and on discovering how the public libraries and newspapers reviewers are treating Theodore Dreiser.

Mr. Mencken's mode of critical attack thus plays into the hands of the philistines, demoralizes the artist, and demoralizes his own critical power. Why cannot Demos be left alone for a while to its commercial magazines and its mawkish novels? All good writing is produced in serene unconsciousness of what Demos desires or demands. It cannot be created at all if the artist worries about what Demos will think of him or do to him. The artist writes for that imagined audience of perfect comprehenders. The critic must judge for that audience too.
—RANDOLPH BOURNE, "H. L. Mencken," NR, Nov. 24, 1917, pp. 102–3

H. L. Mencken once called himself a liaison officer between the American intelligentsia and European ideas, but he is something much more impassioned than that. He is a sort of heathen missionary zealously endeavoring to convert the barbarian Christians away from the false gods of Humility and Restraint, and his method is the method of the popular evangelist who expounds the Sermon on the Mount in the vocabulary of slang. Like Billy Sunday he preaches in his shirt-sleeves and any furniture about the platform is in danger of a smashing. The only essential difference is that Mr. Mencken knows what he is talking about. When he has finished, Nietzsche is still recognizably Nietzsche, while as much cannot be said for Mr. Sunday's Christ.

This also Mr. Mencken has in common with the popular preacher: his real genius is for denunciation. Words and phrases of gorgeous contempt like "boob-bumper," "spy-hunter," "emotion-pumper," and "propaganda-monger" flow readily from his pen, and a sort of immoral indignation is his specialty. Above all else, he is generally surer of what he doesn't want than of what he does. Let any man attack "the boobery" with sufficient violence, be it in the cause of naturalism, of aestheticism, of the aristocracy, or, as in the case of E. W. Howe, of mere common sense, and that man is Mr. Mencken's friend, for he is far too much interested in the slaying of Philistines to care whose jaw-bone it is done with. Thus he can welcome the naturalism of Theodore Dreiser because it outrages the populace, and he can welcome Edwin Muir's denunciation of naturalism because that denunciation does not proceed upon an ethical basis.—JOSEPH WOOD KRUTCH, "Antichrist and the Five Apostles," *Nation*, Dec. 21, 1921, p. 733

The incomparable Mencken will, I fear, meet the fate of Aristides. He will be exiled because one is tired of hearing his praises sung. In at least three contemporary novels he is mentioned as though he were dead as Voltaire and as secure as Shaw with what he would term "a polite bow". His style is imitated by four-fifths of the younger critics—moreover he has demolished his enemies and set up his own gods in the literary supplements.

Of the essays in the new book ⟨*Prejudices: Second Series*⟩ the best is the autopsy on the still damp bones of Roosevelt. In the hands of Mencken Roosevelt becomes almost a figure of Greek tragedy; more, he becomes alive and loses some of that stuffiness that of late has become attached to all 100% Americans. Not only is the essay most illuminating but its style is a return to Mencken's best manner, the style of *Prefaces*, with the soft pedal on his amazing chord of adjectives and a tendency to invent new similes instead of refurbishing his amusing but somewhat overworked old ones.

Except for the section on American aristocracy there is little new in the first essay "The National Letters": an abundance of wit and a dozen ideas that within the past year and under his own deft hand have become bromides. The Knights of Pythias, Right Thinkers, On Building Universities, Methodists, as well as the corps of journeyman critics and popular novelists come in for their usual bumping, this varied with unexpected tolerance toward *The Saturday Evening Post* and even a half grudging mention of Booth Tarkington. Better than any of this comment, valid and vastly entertaining as it is, would be a second Book of Prefaces say on Edith Wharton, Cabell, Woodrow Wilson—and Mencken himself. But the section of the essay devoted to the Cultural Background rises to brilliant analysis. Here again he is thinking slowly, he is on comparatively fresh ground, he brings the force of his clarity and invention to bear on the subject—passes beyond his function as a critic of the arts and becomes a reversed Cato of a civilization.

In "The Sahara of Bozart" the dam breaks, devastating Georgia, Carolina, Mississippi, and Company. The first trickle of this overflow appeared in the preface to *The American Credo*; here it reaches such a state of invective that one pictures all the region south of Mason-Dixon to be peopled by moron Catilines. The ending is gentle—too gentle, the gentleness of ennui.

To continue in the grand manner of a catalogue: "The Divine Afflatus" deals with the question of inspiration and the lack of it, an old and sad problem to the man who has done creative work. "Examination of a Popular Virtue" runs to eight pages of whimsical excellence—a consideration of ingratitude decided at length with absurd but mellow justice. "Exeunt Omnes", which concerns the menace of death, I choose to compare with a previous "Discussion" of the same subject in *A Book of Burlesques*. The comparison is only in that the former piece, which I am told Mencken fatuously considers one of his best, is a hacked out, glued together bit of foolery, as good, say, as an early essay of Mark Twain's, while this "Exeunt Omnes", which follows it by several years, is smooth, brilliant, apparently jointless. To my best recollection it is the most microscopical examination of this particular mote on the sun that I have ever come across.

Follows a four paragraph exposition of the platitude that much music loving is an affectation and further paragraphs depreciating opera as a form. As to the "Music of Tomorrow" the present reviewer's ignorance must keep him silent, but in "Tempo di Valse" Mencken, the modern, becomes Victorian by insisting that what people are tired of is more exciting than what they have just learned to do. If his idea of modern dancing is derived from watching men who learned it circa thirty-five, toiling interminably around the jostled four square feet of a cabaret, he is justified; but I see no reason why the "Bouncing Shimmee" efficiently performed is not as amusing and as graceful and certainly as difficult as any waltz ever attempted. The section continues with the condemnation of a musician named Hadley, an ingenious attempt to preserve a portrait of Dreiser, and a satisfactory devastation of the acting profession.

In "The Cult of Hope" he defends his and "Dr. Nathan's" attitude toward constructive criticism—most entertainingly—but the next section "The Dry Millennium", patchworked from the Ripetizione Generale, consists of general repetitions of theses in his previous books. "An Appendix on a Tender Theme" contains his more recent speculations on women, eked out with passages from *The Smart Set*.

An excellent book! Like Max Beerbohm, Mencken's work is inevitably distinguished. But now and then one wonders—granted that, solidly, book by book, he has built up a literary reputation most to be envied of any American, granted also that he has done more for the national letters than any man alive, one is yet inclined to regret a success so complete. What will he do now? The very writers to the press about the blue Sabbath hurl the bricks of the buildings he has demolished into the still smoking ruins. He is, say, forty; how of the next twenty years? Will he find new gods to dethrone, some eternal "yokelry" still callous enough to pose as intelligenzia before the Menckenian pen fingers? Or will he strut among the ruins, a man beaten by his own success, as futile, in the end, as one of those Conrad characters that so tremendously enthrall him? —F. SCOTT FITZGERALD, "The Baltimore Antichrist," *Bkm*, March 1921, pp. 79–81

⟨. . .⟩ in back of the Cultivated Superman there stalks the Frontier Rebel: notice also Mencken's stress on the absolute liberty of the individual. 'I believe that any invasion of it is immensely dangerous to the common weal—especially when that invasion is alleged to have a moral purpose. No conceivable moral purpose is higher than the right of the citizen to think whatever he pleases to think, and to carry on his private life without interference by others'. Yet, just as Mencken defends the sanctity of the domestic hearth, without, however, stressing the human relationships or family life or, in short, the domesticity that goes along with the domestic hearth, so his notion of liberty lacks the usual attributes of human liberty.

Very often it approaches the liberty of that solitary urban citizen whom we saw speeding through a diseased American hinterland in his steel-encased Pullman. Or it is the liberty of this writer, fully cognizant, as we have seen, of the condition of the less-privileged citizens in the Republic, and of the pathological social impulses which spring out of and flourish in this condition: it is his liberty to suggest, as he did, the establishment of 'brass bands and bull fights' as a solution. It is the liberty of this total individualist to express himself to the utmost in order to 'compel the attention and respect of his equals, to lord it over his inferiors.' It is a liberty, nourished on the precepts of pure self-survival, that often yearns for authority and even dictatorial authority in the case of these inferiors; a liberty that, while it has steadily increased the limits of its own demands, has just as steadily delimited the areas of its general social applicability. . . . It is interesting to notice the change in Mencken's own attitude here. While earlier he had described the great emancipators of the human mind as 'gay fellows who heaved dead cats into sanctuaries and then went roistering down the highways of the world,' his later definition was less jolly:

> The free man is one who has won a small and precarious territory from the great mob of his inferiors, and is prepared and ready to defend it and make it support him. All around him are enemies, and where he stands there is no friend. He can hope for little help from other men of his own kind, for they have battles of their own to fight. He has made of himself a sort of god in his little world, and he must face the responsibilities of a god, and the dreadful loneliness.

It was true, as Mencken added, that Jefferson himself had said that blood was the natural manure of liberty—but would Jefferson have recognized this new concept of liberty, at once so bloody and so bloodless? For this is a sense of human freedom which is so precarious as to seem almost paranoiac, and so absolute as to be icy.

In a similar manner the corollary of the Menckenian quest for absolute freedom—the search for an absolute truth—leads the contemporary philosopher into some strange détours. Here, too, is a writer who realizes the change in American life since the Civil War period, and accepts as a historical truism the scramble for power of the new industrial barons upon the foundations of the older republic, and acknowledges the dominant materialism of his own century: an economic penetration that colors the last remnants of the Puritan conscience and extends to the last reaches of the rural hinterland. Yet his earlier indignation has centered on the Puritans, and his later bile is concentrated—in the face of an increasing and almost total industrialization—on a 'benighted peasantry.' Here is a writer who records all the elements of a steadily sharpening economic conflict. And he resorts (in a nation which represents the blending of racial stocks to a point where an attempt at racial distinction becomes almost ludicrous) to an almost mythological racial conflict: to a struggle between the non-existent Anglo-Saxons and the imaginary Aliens.

To such a pass, then, has his quest for liberty and truth brought H. L. Mencken: to an almost absolute inversion of liberty and truth. This is the net result of the newest New Freedom, the end of the road for the curious new American of the nineteen-twenties: this pure Menckenian individualist whose right to think whatever he pleases leads him only to think about what is pleasing to himself. Here the 'western spaciousness' of Mark Twain, an early idol, and one with whom, in the variety of humor and the instinct for language, Mencken had much in common, has shriveled down. It approaches, instead, the eastern spaciousness of a Cal Tinney: the hard sense of the frontier has become rigid. There are echoes in Mencken of still earlier American figures. There is the Emersonian stress on self-reliance, on the courage to stand apart, to question, to dissent—these older national traits that are particularly valuable in the increasingly standardized American context which Mencken himself has recorded. Yet the transcendental strain has changed in Mencken's work: the self-reliance has turned into isolation, the caustic doubt into bitter negation, the delicate bond between the individual and his society into a barricade. The American preacher, who in the eighteen-thirties saved his own soul from the Calvinist fire, now, in the nineteen-twenties, condemns his brother's soul to the bottomless pools of finance-capitalism.

So, again, the Menckenian accents of wrath and rebuke are familiar. In these tones spoke the great preachers of the past to their flocks: thus spoke Zarathustra II, however demented. But to whom, for whom, does the Shepherd of the Smart Set speak? Here is a very special case of moral indignation without a morality: a Jonathan Edwards of Nihilism. And what a panorama of misdirected moral energies is spread before us! What spectacular forays on Home Cooking and on Prohibition, on Comstockery and on the Mann Act, or at best, and with some equivocation, on the Klan—on all the offshoots, if not the odds and ends, of a disturbed society! What passionate defenses of bootleggers or beauticians! What eloquence, again, is expended on the welfare of the arts, and what a minimum of concern is manifested for the true welfare of the people that produce these arts! Never directed against its true object, the writer's indignation bubbles over everywhere, and, lacking a central focus, the whole perspective of his American critique is distorted until it becomes a child's view of history. If Mencken's is a last voice from an American age of innocence (an innocence that was never quite so guileless as it seemed), it is now an innocence that is both tortured and devious.

For Mencken's account of the prevailing social arrangement in the United States was not projected by a radical critic of it, but, on the contrary, by a staunch believer in it, and the more clearly he saw its effects, the more blindly he seemed to cling to it.—MAXWELL GEISMAR, "H. L. Mencken: On the Dock," *The Last of the Provincials*, 1947, pp. 50–54

---

### EDMUND WILSON
#### "H. L. Mencken"

*New Republic, June 1, 1921, pp. 10–13*

#### I

A man has withdrawn from the tumult of American life into the seclusion of a house in Baltimore. He is unmarried and has surrounded himself with three thousand books. From this point of vantage he watches the twentieth century with detached and ironic dismay. A not ungenial materialist, he reflects that all human activities are, after all, mainly physical in origin: inspiration is a function of metabolism; death is an acidosis; love is a biological phenomenon; idealism is insanity. But the body is capable of much enjoyment; why worry about its obvious supremacy? As long as there is Chicken à la Maryland and plenty of liquor from the boot-leggers, as long as it is possible to read Conrad and hear Bach and Beethoven occasionally, why should a man of

aristocratic temperament be particularly disturbed about anything? Let the capitalist exploit the wage-slave and the wage-
slave blow up the capitalist; let political charlatans and
scoundrels pick the pockets of the Republic; let the women run
the men to ground and the men break their hearts for the
women; let the people go off to the wars and destroy each other
by the billion. They can never rob Mencken of his sleep nor
spoil a single dinner for him. Outside, it is all a question of
Christianity and democracy, but Mencken does not believe in
either, so why should he take part in the brawl? What has he to
do with the mob except to be diverted by its idiocy? He may
occasionally attend a political convention to gratify a "taste for
the obscene" or entertain his speculative mind by predicting
the next catastrophe, but, on the whole, the prodigious din and
activity and confusion of the nation roars along without
touching him particularly; it is all to him "but as the sound of
lyres and flutes." . . .

Something like this is the comic portrait which Mr.
Mencken has painted of himself; he has even pretended that it
is the character in which he prefers to be accepted. But there is,
behind this comic mask, a critic, an evangelist and an artist;
there is a mind of extraordinary vigor and a temperament of
extraordinary interest, and neither of these has ever yet been
examined as seriously as it should have been. Mencken has
been left far too much to the rhapsodies of his disciples and the
haughty sneers of his opponents. Indeed, he has assumed such
an importance as an influence in American thought that it is
high time someone subjected him to a drastic full-length
analysis. The present writer has only space for the briefest of
suggestions.

## II

The striking things about Mencken's mind are its ruthlessness and its rigidity. It has all the courage in the world in a
country where courage is rare. He has even had the fearlessness
to avoid the respectable and the wholesome, those two devils
which so often betray in the end even the most intelligent of
Americans. He fought outspokenly against optimism, Puritanism and democratic ineptitude, at a time when they had but
few foes. It is well to remember, now that these qualities have
become stock reproaches among the intelligentsia, that it was
Mencken who began the crusade against them at a lonely and
disregarded post and that we owe to him much of the disfavor
into which they have recently fallen,—and also that it was
Mencken who first championed the kind of American literary
activity of which we have now become proudest. But the
activity of his mind is curiously cramped by its extreme
inflexibility. In the first place, as a critic, he is not what is
called "sympathetic." His criticisms deal but little with people
from their own pont of view: he simply brings the other man's
statements and reactions to the bar of his own dogma and,
having judged them by that measure, proceeds to accept or
reject them. Though one of the fairest of critics, he is one of
the least pliant.

In the second place, in spite of his scepticism and his
frequent exhortations to hold one's opinions lightly, he himself
has been conspicuous for seizing upon simple dogmas and
sticking to them with fierce tenacity. When he is arguing his
case against democracy or Christianity, he reminds one rather
of Bishop Manning or Dr. Straton than of Renan or Anatole
France. The true sceptics like Renan or France see both the
truth and weakness of every case; they put themselves in the
place of people who believe differently from themselves and
finally come to sympathize with them,—almost, to accept their
point of view. But Mencken, once having got his teeth into an
idea, can never be induced to drop it, and will only shake his

head and growl when somebody tries to tempt him with
something else.

Thus, in 1908, when he published his admirable book on
Nietzsche, he had reached a certain set of conclusions upon
society and ethics. Humanity, he had come to believe, is
divided into two classes: the masters and the slaves. The
masters are able and courageous men who do whatever they
like and are not restrained by any scruples save those that
promote their own interest; the slaves are a race of wretched
underlings, stupid, superstitious and untrustworthy, who have
no rights and no raison d'être except to be exploited by the
masters. To talk of equality and fraternity is the most fatuous of
nonsense: there is as much difference in kind between the
masters and the slaves as there is between men and animals.

Therefore, Christianity is false because it asserts that all
souls are worth saving and democracy is a mistake because it
emancipates the slaves and tries to make them the masters. It is
absurd to try to correct the evolutionary process which would
allow the fittest to survive and the weaklings and fools to go
under. "I am," Mr. Mencken has said, "against the under dog
every time." But things are getting more and more democratic
and consequently worse and worse. What we need is an
englightened aristocracy to take charge of society. But there has
never been any such aristocracy and we are certainly not going
to produce one. In the meantime, one can but curse the mob
and die at one's post.

I have not space here to criticize these views—to ask, for
instance, when he says he thinks the strong should be allowed
to survive at the expense of the weak, whether he means the
strong like Jack Johnson or the strong like Nietzsche and
Beethoven. I must assume that the confusion of thought is
apparent to the reader and go on to point out that Mencken has
been upholding these theories without modification since 1908
at least. He has cherished them through the European war and
through the industrial war that has followed it. (Quite recently
they have led him into the absurdity of asserting that it would
have been a good thing for America if the war had continued
longer, because this would have stamped out "hundreds of
thousands of the relatively unfit." The men who were left at the
end of the war in the French and German armies, were, he
adds, "very superior men.") And, in consequence, it seems to
me that he has cut himself off in an intellectual cul-de-sac.

He has much to say to America that is of the first
usefulness and importance: he has no peer in the brilliance and
effectiveness of his onslaught upon political ignorance and
corruption, upon Y. M. C. A.'ism and popular morality, upon
the cheapness and sordidness of current ideals. But, though the
moral strength which gives him courage is drawn partly from
his Nietzschean principles, these principles so close his
horizon as to render his social criticism rather sterile. In the
matters of politics and society he can do nothing but denounce.
He has taken up a position in which it is impossible that any
development should please him. He detests the present state of
affairs, but he disbelieves in liberalism and radicalism, and any
change in their directions would presumably only make him
detest the world more. He really hates repression and injustice,
but has long ago repudiated the idea of human rights to
freedom and justice and he consequently cannot come out as
their champion.

There have, however, been a few signs of late that he feels
his old house is too small: in his recent discussion of Mr.
Chafee's book on free speech he reached a peak of righteous
indignation at which he has scarcely been seen before. "In
those two years," he cried, "all the laborious work of a century
and a half—toward the free and honest administration of fair
laws, the dealing of plain justice between man and man, the

protection of the weak and helpless, the safeguarding of free assemblage and free speech—was ruthlessly undone." This is obviously in direct contradiction to the faith he has previously professed. What has one who is "against the under dog every time" to do with "the protection of the weak and helpless"? He has told us again and again that we should let the weak and helpless perish.

The truth is that in the last few years Mencken has entered so far into the national intellectual life that it has become impossible for him to maintain his old opinions quite intact: he has begun to worry and hope with the American people in the throes of their democratic experiment. I know that this is a terrible statement; it is as if one should say that the Pope has begun to worry and hope with the western world in its attempt to shake off creed; but I honestly believe it is true. This phenomenon seemed to make its appearance towards the last page of *The American Language*; and if it does not come to bulk yet larger we shall have one of our strongest men still fighting with one hand tied behind his back.

### III

So much for the critic: but what of the evangelist and artist? For Mencken, in spite of all his professions of realistic resignation, is actually a militant idealist. Most Americans—even of fine standards—have long ago resigned themselves to the cheapness and ugliness of America, but Mencken has never resigned himself. He has never ceased to regard his native country with wounded and outraged eyes. The shabby politics, the childish books, the factories turning out wooden nut-megs have never lost their power to offend him. At this late date, he is, I suppose, almost the only man in the country who still expects American novelists to be artists and American politicians gentlemen.

And his expression of his resentment is by no means temperate or aloof. It is righteous indignation of the most violent sort. His denunciations are as ferocious as those of Tertullian or Billy Sunday. It is in purpose rather than in method that he differs from these great divines. (See especially his excommunication of the professors in the essay on "The National Letters.") In his exhortations to disobey the rules of the current American morality he has shown himself as noisy and as bitter as any other Puritan preacher.

And this brings us to what is perhaps, after all, the most important thing about Mencken, the thing which gives him his enormous importance in American literature today: it is the fact that here we have a genuine artist and man of first-rate education and intelligence who is thoroughly familiar with, even thoroughly saturated with, the common life. The rule has been heretofore for men of superior intelligence, like Henry Adams and Henry James, to shrink so far from the common life that, in a country where there was practically nothing else, they had almost no material to work on, and for men who were part of the general society, like Mark Twain, to be handicapped by Philistinism and illiteracy; but in the case of Mencken we have Puritanism and American manners in a position to criticize itself. For in his attitude toward all the things with which Puritanism is supposed to deal Mencken is thoroughly American and thoroughly Puritan. If he were what he exhorts us to be in regard to the amenities and the pleasures he would never rage so much about them. His sermons would be unintelligible, I should think, to a Frenchman or an Italian. Nobody but a man steeped in Puritanism could have so much to say about love and yet never convey any idea of its beauties or delights; poor Aphrodite, usually identified in his pages with the whore and the bawdy-house, wears as unalluring a face as she does in the utterances of any Y. M. C. A. lecturer; no one else would confine himself to a harsh abuse, on principle, of

the people who have outlawed love. Nobody else would express his enthusiasm for the innocent pleasures of alcohol in such a way that it sounded less like a eulogy than like an angry defiance. He is an unmistakable product of Puritan training and environment. Horace or Anatole France, who really represent the sort of civilization which Mencken admires, would never be so acutely conscious of the problems of love and art and wine; they would take them easily for granted and enjoy them as a matter of course. But Mencken, who was born an American, with the truculent argumentative mind of the Puritan, can never enjoy them as a matter of course, as even some Americans can do, but must call down all the dark thunders of logic to defend them, like any Milton or Luther.

And he is saturated with the thought and aspect of modern commercial America. He is, we feel, in spite of everything, in the long run most at home there: are we not told that once, when walking in Paris in the spring, he was annoyed by the absence of a first-class drug-store? Instead of taking refuge among remote literatures, like Mr. Cabell and Mr. Pound, he makes his poetry of the democratic life which absorbs and infuriates him. He takes the slang of the common man and makes fine prose of it. He has studied the habits and ideas and language of the common run of his countrymen with a close first-hand observation and an unflagging interest. And he has succeeded in doing with the common life what nobody else has done,—(at least with any authentic stamp of literary distinction): he has taken it in all its coarseness and angularity and compelled it to dance a ballet, in which the Odd Fellow, the stockbroker, the Y. M. C. A. Secretary, the Knight of Pythias, the academic critic, the Methodist evangelical, the lecturer at Chautauquas, the charlatan politician, the Vice Crusader, the Department of Justice, the star-spangled army officer,—and the man who reveres all these, with all his properties and settings: the derby hat, the cheap cigar, the shaving soap advertisement, the popular novel, the cuspidor, the stein of prohibition beer, the drug-store, the patent medicine, the American Legion button,—join hands and perform, to the strains of a sombre but ribald music, which ranges from genial boisterousness to morose and cynical brooding.

Take the following passage, for example, from a sort of prose poem:

> Pale druggists of remote towns of of the hog and cotton belt, endlessly wrapping up Peruna . . . Women hidden away in the damp kitchens of unpainted houses along the railroad tracks, frying tough beefsteaks . . . Lime and cement dealers being initiated into the Knights of Pythias, The Redmen or the Woodmen of the World . . . Watchmen at lonely railroad crossings in Iowa, hoping that they'll be able to get off to hear the United Brethren Evangelist preach . . . Ticket-choppers in the Subway, breathing sweat in its gaseous form . . . Family doctors in poor neighborhoods faithfully relying upon the therapeutics taught in their Eclectic Medical College in 1884 . . . Farmers plowing sterile fields behind sad meditative horses, both suffering from the bites of insects . . . Greeks tending all-night coffee joints in the suburban wilderness where the trolley cars stop . . . Grocery clerks stealing prunes and gin-gernsnaps and trying to make assignatioins with soapy servant girls . . . Women confined for the ninth or tenth time, wondering hopelessly what it is all about . . . Methodiest preachers retired after forty years of service in the trenches of God, upon pensions of $600 a year . . . Wives and daughters of Middle Western country bankers marooned in Los Angeles, going tremblingly to swami séances in dark

smelly rooms . . . Chauffeurs in huge fur coats waiting outside theatres filled with folks applauding Robert Edeson and Jane Cowl . . . Decayed and hopeless men writing editorials at midnight for leading papers in Mississippi, Arkansas and Alabama . . .

One recalls the enumeration of another set of visions:

The pure contralto sings in the organ loft,
The carpenter dresses his plank, the tongue of his foreplane whistles its wild ascending lisp,
The married and unmarried children ride home to their Thanksgiving dinner,
The pilot seizes the kingpin he heaves down with a strong arm,
The mate stands braced in the whale boat, lance and harpoon are ready,
The duck shooter walks by silent and cautious stretches,
The deacons are ordained with cross'd bands at the altar,
The spinning girl retreats and advances with the hum of the big wheel.
The farmer stops by the bars as he walks on a First day loaf and looks at the oats and rye . . .
The young fellow drives the express-wagon (I love him, though I do not know him)
The half-breed straps on his light boots to compete in the race,
The Wolverine helps set traps on the creek that helps fill the Huron,
The clean haired Yankee girl works with her sewing machine or in the factory or mill,
The Missourian crosses the plains toting his wares and his cattle . . .

This was the day before yesterday, and Mencken is today. Is not Mencken's gloomy catalogue as much the poetry of modern America as Walt Whitman's was of the early Republic? When the States were fresh and new and their people were hardy pioneers, we had a great poet, from whose pages the youth and wonder of that world can reach us forever: and now that the air is soured with industry and those pioneers have become respectable citizens dwelling in hideously ugly towns and devoted to sordid ideals, we have had a great satirist to arouse us against the tragic spectacle we have become. For Mencken is the civilized consciousness of modern America, its learning, its intelligence and its taste, realizing the grossness of its manners and mind and crying out in horror and chagrin.

## CARL VAN DOREN
### "Smartness and Light:
## H. L. Mencken: A Gadfly for Democracy"
*Century*, March 1923, pp. 791–96

The democratic dogma has had its critics in America ever since the priests and magistrates of the first colonies began to note the restive currents which stirred among their people. Critics of the same temper roared at the Revolution, and lost. During the probationary years of the republic there were Federalists, and then Whigs, and eventually Republicans, to say nothing of Bourbons of different varieties from time to time. Most of these skeptic voices have been merely political, but not all. Poe, for instance, was a poet, concerned with art and beauty, and a critic who spread death among the idols of popular taste. H. L. Mencken is a wit, concerned less with art or beauty than with the manners of his nation, who aims his wrath at the very heart of democracy, announces that the

system is no less a nuisance than a failure, and proclaims the empire of excellence. Like Poe, he uses every critical method except that of mercy, and, like Poe, he wins applause at every death he deals. He could not win this if there were not an alert minority which delights in the victories of criticism over commonplace.

*II*

Mr. Mencken, at whom academic circles still cock a frigid or a timid eye, grows steadily more significant. Before the war, of which he says that he neither advised nor approved it, he was a useful conduit leading to the republic from Shaw and Nietzsche and Ibsen. The war played into his hands, it begins to look, as into those of hardly any other literary American. Heretofore, to change the figure, he had been but an intern in the hospital of his American kind, satisfied with an occasional run in the ambulance, an occasional appendix to cut out, an occasional skull to help trepan. Now he was suddenly invited to apply diagnosis, surgery, or the lethal chamber in such a range of cases as no native satirist had ever been allowed to practise on. He found hundreds of politicians palsied with incompetence, thousands of journalists and educators and preachers flatulent with prophecy, millions of patriots dropsical with sentimentalism. He found idealists who had delusions of grandeur, scholars who suffered from obsessions of hatred, business men who had been shellshocked out of all self-control, women whose long-repressed instincts burst into frenzies of cruelty. He found, what seemed to him the source and cause of all these maladies, the plain people turned into a vast standard mass, now dumb and snuffling like a flock of sheep, now loud and savage like a pack of wolves. All the folly which overwhelmed him had, to his eyes, the symptoms of having risen from the body of democracy. No wonder, given his conception of life, that he should have laid aside his scalpel and have taken to the jolly bludgeon as the only tool he needed. No wonder, given the consequences of the madness he observed, that he should finally have declared the worst result of the war to be the fact that so many Americans survived it.

The wonder is, rather, that Mr. Mencken should have waked so many echoes among his countrymen. No other contemporary critic is so well known in the colleges. No other is so influential among the latest generation of boys and girls of letters. Substantial citizens and sound students who cannot agree with a half or a quarter of what he says, nevertheless delight in the burly way in which he says it and find themselves agreeing with more than they thought they could. He has endowed the decade with a whole glossary of words which breathe contempt for its imbecilities. It is in part because his voice is the least uncertain of all the critic voices that he is so clearly heard; but it is also in part because there was among Americans already a strong vein of discontent with democracy which needed only to be tapped to send forth gushers of criticism and ridicule. Idealism and optimism had been orthodox too long for their own health; suspicion had been gathering under the surface of the national temper. The war, by straining idealism to the point of reaction and optimism to the point of collapse, had considerably discredited both of them. The young and the irresponsible, looking at the mess the mature and the responsible had made of human life on the planet, lost what respect they had and broke out of bounds. Irreverence for institutions and ribald laughter for respectability and a hard directness of speech succeeded the older modes. And when the dispersed thousands who felt this new spirit cast about for a spokesman, they rapidly realized that in Mr. Mencken the hour had found its man.

### III

What first attracted them was pretty certainly his impudence, as it attracts most readers to him at first. He is as brash as a sophomore is supposed to be. He has never heard of a head too sacred to be smitten. That something is taboo merely makes him want to try it once. He walks briskly into shrines and takes a cheerful turn through cemeteries. Here is what Mr. Mencken says of Lincoln's Gettysburg Address, before which hardly an American has ever ventured to lift his voice unless he lifted it to a hymn:

"It is eloquence brought to a pellucid and almost childlike perfection—the highest emotion reduced to one graceful and irresistible gesture. . . . But let us not forget that it is oratory, not logic; beauty, not sense. . . . The doctrine is simply this: that the Union soldiers who died at Gettysburg sacrificed their lives to the cause of self-determination—'that government of the people, by the people, for the people,' should not perish from the earth. It is difficult to imagine anything more untrue. The Union soldiers in that battle actually fought against self-determination; it was the Confederates who fought for the right of their people to govern themselves. . . . The Confederates went into the battle an absolutely free people; they came out with their freedom subject to the supervision and vote of the rest of the country— and for nearly twenty years that vote was so effective that they enjoyed scarcely any freedom at all. Am I the first American to note the fundamental nonsensicality of the Gettysburg address? If so, I plead my aesthetic joy in it in amelioration of the sacrilege."

His final sentence is, it may be said, much the kind of impudence which led this critic in an earlier book to call an archbishop "a Christian ecclesiastic of a rank superior to that attained by Christ." Both comments at least reveal a keen pleasure in the saying of sharp things. But in the whole comment upon Lincoln there is a larger sagacity which grows upon Mr. Mencken as he widens his inquiries and leaves mere witticism behind him. Those whom he first attracts by his impudence he holds by his sagacity. He may play upon the saxophone with the gesticulations of jazz, but he knows many important harmonies and he constantly brings them into his performance. Regarding theology, politics, philosophy, law, medicine, art, business, morals, character, language, he has said some of the shrewdest things in his American generation. Not all are new, not all are true, but they proceed from a singularly powerful intelligence expressing itself in a singularly untrammeled speech. It happens to be a tory intelligence, impatient of whatever is untried, unimpressed by the bombastic, the heroic, the altruistic, scornful of the unsophisticated; an intelligence which holds that the vast majority of men are supine; that those who are not supine are foolish; that those who are not foolish are knavish; and that the few who have brains or virtues must stand together or they will be smothered in the mass. It happens also to be radical intelligence, cutting away excrescences of verbiage, challenging sluggish habits of thought, daring to drive through morasses of emotion to the solid ground of sense beyond, carrying the guidon of reason into desperate breeches. Tory or radical, this intelligence has a reach and thrust which make it noticeable, no matter of what persuasion its observers may at any moment be.

Such an intelligence, however, unaided by other qualities, could never have got Mr. Mencken his audience. Instead of being astringent, as his doctrine might have made him, he is amazingly full of the sap of life and comedy. Not since Poe has an American critic taken such a fling or enjoyed it more. The

motive of criticism, he maintains, "is not the motive of the pedagogue, but the motive of the artist. It is no more and no less than the simple desire to function freely and beautifully, to give outward and objective form to ideas that bubble inwardly and have a fascinating lure in them, to get rid of them dramatically and make an articulate noise in the world. . . . It is the pressing yearning of every man who has ideas in him to empty them upon the world, to hammer them into plausible and ingratiating shapes, to compel the attention and respect of his equals, to lord it over his inferiors." Yet even this exciting conception of the art of criticism had to be joined with a particular endowment if Mr. Mencken was to be the personage he is. That endowment is gusto, and gusto he possesses in a degree which no one of his contemporaries can rival. In a decade of which too many of the critics have dyspepsia, Mr. Mencken, as he might say, "goes the whole hog."

There comes to mind a curious parallel with Whitman, drunk with joy in the huge spectacle of his continent filled with his countrymen. Sitting in New York or Camden, he sent his imagination out over the land, across all its mountains and prairies, along all its rivers, into all its cities, among all its citizens at their occupations. He accepted all, he rejected nothing, because his affection was great enough to embrace the entire republic. His long panoramas, his crowded categories, are evidence that he gloated over the details of American life as a lover gloats over the charms of his mistress or a mother over the merits of her baby. So, in his different fashion, Mr. Mencken gloats over the follies of the republic. But is his fashion so different from Whitman's as it appears at first glance? His intellectual position compels him to see a side which Whitman overlooked. What to Whitman seemed a splendid turbulence, to Mr. Mencken seems a headless swirl. What to Whitman seemed a noble cohesiveness, seems to Mr. Mencken a herd-like conventionality. What to Whitman seemed a hopeful newness, seems to Mr. Mencken a hopeless rawness. Yet the satirist no less than the poet revels in the gaudy spectacle. "The United States, to my eye," Mr. Mencken explicitly says, "is incomparably the greatest show on earth. It is a show which avoids diligently all the kinds of clowning which tire me most quickly—for example, royal ceremonials, the tedious hocus-pocus of *haute politique*, the taking of politics seriously—and lays chief stress upon the kinds which delight me unceasingly—for example, the ribald combats of demagogues, the exquisitely ingenious operations of master rogues, the pursuit of witches and heretics, the desperate struggles of inferior men to claw their way into Heaven. We have clowns in constant practice among us who are as far above the clowns of any other great state as a Jack Dempsey is above a paralytic—and not a few dozens or score of them, but whole droves and herds. Human enterprises which, in all other Christian countries, are resigned despairingly to an incurable dullness—things that seem devoid of exhilarating amusement by their very nature—are here lifted to such vast heights of buffoonery that contemplating them strains the midriff almost to breaking."

### IV

Is Mr. Mencken, then, an enemy of his people? "Here I stand," he contends, "unshaken and undespairing, a loyal and devoted Americano, even a chauvinist, paying taxes without complaint, obeying all laws that are physiologically obeyable, accepting all the searching duties and responsibilities of citizenship unprotestingly, investing the sparse usufructs of my miserable toil in the obligations of the nation, avoiding all commerce with men sworn to overthrow the government, contributing my mite toward the glory of the national arts and science, spurning all lures (and even all invitations) to go out and stay out . . . here am I, contentedly and even smugly basking beneath the Stars and Stripes, a better citizen, I daresay, and certainly a less murmurous and exigent one, than thousands who put the Hon. Warren Gamaliel Harding beside Friedrich Barbarossa and Charlemagne, and hold the Supreme Court to be directly inspired by the Holy Spirit, and belong ardently to every Rotary Club, Ku Klux Klan, and Anti-Saloon League, and choke with emotion when the band plays the 'Star-Spangled Banner,' and believe with the faith of little children that one of Our Boys, taken at random, could dispose in a fair fight of ten Englishmen, twenty Germans, thirty Frogs, forty Wops, fifty Japs, or a hundred Bolsheviki." Whitman, with whatever other tones or arguments, never exhibited his essential Americanism more convincingly. Have Americans no speech but praise? Have they no song but rhapsody?

The truth of the matter is, Mr. Mencken is one of the most American things we have. Both his art and his success spring from the gusto which draws him to the comic aspects of the life around him—draws him with as great an eagerness as if he accepted all he saw and acclaimed it. To read him, even while dissenting from his doctrine on every page, is to gasp and whoop with recognition. Thus, for instance, he illustrates "Eminence," without a word of commentary: "The leading Methodist layman of Pottawattamie county, Iowa. . . . The man who won the limerick contest conducted by the Tooms-boro, Ga., *Banner*. . . . The President of the Johann Sebastian Bach *Bauverein* of Highlandtown, Md. . . . The girl who sold the most Liberty Bonds in Duquesne, Pa. . . . The man who owns the best bull in Coosa County, Ala. . . . The oldest subscriber to the Raleigh, N. C., *News and Observer*. . . . The author of the ode read at the unveiling of the monument to General Robert E. Lee at Valdosta, Ga. . . . The old lady in Wahoo, Neb., who has read the Bible 38 times. . . . The professor of chemistry, Greek, rhetoric, and piano at the Texas Christian University, Fort Worth Tex. . . . The leading dramatic critic of Pittsburgh. . . . The night watchman in Penn Yan, N. Y., who once shook hands with Chester A. Arthur"—and on and on with Rabelaisian fecundity. Nothing petty, nothing absurd, nothing grotesque, nothing racy of the soil, seems to have escaped Mr. Mencken's terrible eye. Though he has not traveled very widely in the United States, he knows the map as well as any continental drummer. Though he has taken only a journalist's hand in actual politics, he is virtually the first to hoot at any new political asininity. As if with a hundred newspapers and a hundred clubs for his whispering-gallery, he appears to have heard every secret and every scandal. Nor does he content himself with random citation of what he hits upon. He hoards them and makes treatises. With George Jean Nathan, his dapper David, this rugged Jonathan has collected nearly a thousand vulgar beliefs in *An American Credo*; by himself he has composed a large first and a huge second edition of *The American Language*. He has, in short, the range of a journalist, the verve of a comic poet, the patience of a savant. Among American humorists no one but Mark Twain has had more "body" to his art than Mr. Mencken.

### V

Poe, Whitman, Mark Twain—are they unexpected companions for an editor of the *Smart Set*? Perhaps; and yet Mr. Mencken, laying aside to some extent the waggish elements in his constitution, begins to have the stature of an important man of letters. Unlike Poe, he has in him nothing of the poet and he has written nonsense about poetry. Unlike Whitman, he has not deeply studied the common man at first hand and he dismisses such persons with the insolence of a city wit. Unlike Mark Twain, he despises the miserable race of man without, like Mark Twain, also pitying it. What Mr. Mencken most conspicuously lacks, indeed, is the mood of pity, an emotion which the greatest satirists have all exhibited now or then. Even Swift, as indisposed to forgive a fool as Mr. Mencken is, occasionally let fall a glance of compassion upon folly. This is the particular penalty of smartness: though it may have plenty of light, it fears, even for a moment, to be sweet. Embarrassed in the presence of nothing else, it is embarrassed in the presence of ungirt emotions. Far from suffering fools gladly, it finds it difficult to overlook the dash of folly which appears in enthusiasm and heroism. Any habitual addiction to smartness makes almost impossible that highest quality of the mind, magnanimity. Mr. Mencken is but rarely magnanimous. It seems significant that he, passionately devoted as he is to music, so often misses the finer tones of eloquence when, as in poetry or prophecy, they are attended by expressed ideas which his reason challenges. Unless he can take his music "straight," he suspects it. The virtue of his quality of suspicion is that it helps him to see through things; its vice is that it frequently keeps him from seeing round them.

At the same time, however, Mr. Mencken is an utter stranger to parsimonious or ungenerous impulses. No one takes a trouncing more cheerfully than he; no one holds out a quicker hand of encouragement to any promising beginner in literature or scholarship. The stupidity against which he wages his hilarious war is the stupidity which, unaware of its defects, has first sought to shackle the children of light. It is chiefly at sight of such attempts that his indignation rises and that he rushes forth armed with a bagpipe, a slapstick, a shillalah, a pitchfork, a butcher's cleaver, a Browning rifle, a lusty arm, and an undaunted heart. What fun, then! Seeing that the feast of fools has still its uses, he elects himself boy-bishop, gathers a horde of revelers about him, and burlesques the universe. Of course he profanes the mysteries, but the laughter with which he does it and the laughter which he arouses among the by-standers have the effect of clearing the packed atmosphere. When the saturnalia ends, sense settles down again with renewed authority. If it is a service to Mr. Mencken's country for him to be so often right in his quarrels and to bring down with his merry bullets so many giant imbecilities, even though with his barrage he not seldom slays some honest and charming idealism; so also it is a service to his country for him, even while he is vexing a few of the judicious with his excess of smartness, to enrich the nation with such a powerful stream of humor as no other American is now playing upon the times.

### IRVING BABBITT
#### From "The Critic and American Life"
##### *Forum*, February 1928, pp. 162–76

"The critic is first and last," says Mr. Mencken, "simply trying to express himself; he is trying to achieve thereby for his own inner ego the grateful feeling of a function performed, a tension relieved, a katharsis attained which Wagner achieved when he wrote *Die Walküre*, and a hen achieves every time she lays an egg." This creative self-expression, as practiced by himself and others, has, according to Mr. Mencken, led to a salutary stirring up of the stagnant pool of American letters: "To-day for the first time in years there is strife in American criticism. . . . Heretics lay on boldly and the professors are forced to make some defence. Often going further they attempt counter-attacks. Ears are bitten off, noses are bloodied. There are wallops both above and below the belt."

But it may be that criticism is something more than Mr. Mencken would have us believe, more in short than a squabble between Bohemians, each eager to capture the attention of the public for his brand of self-expression. To reduce criticism indeed to the satisfaction of a temperamental urge, to the uttering of one's gustos and disgustos (in Mr. Mencken's case chiefly the latter) is to run counter to the very etymology of the word which implies discrimination and judgment. The best one would anticipate from a writer like Mr. Mencken, possessing an unusual verbal virtuosity and at the same time temperamentally irresponsible, is superior intellectual vaudeville. One must grant him, however, certain genuine critical virtues—for example, a power of shrewd observation within rather narrow limits. Yet the total effect of his writing is nearer to intellectual vaudeville than to serious criticism.

The serious critic is more concerned with achieving a correct scale of values and so seeing things proportionately than with self-expression. His essential virtue is poise. The specific benefit he confers is to act as a moderating influence on the opposite insanities between which mankind in the lump is constantly tending to oscillate—oscillations that Luther compares to the reelings of a drunken peasant on horseback. The critic's survey of any particular situation may very well seem satirical. The complaint that Mr. Mencken is too uniformly disgruntled in his survey of the American situation rather misses the point. Behind the pleas for more constructiveness it is usually easy to detect the voice of the booster. A critic who did not get beyond a correct diagnosis of existing evils might be very helpful. If Mr. Mencken has fallen short of being such a diagnostician, the failure is due not to his excess of severity but to his lack of discrimination.

The standards with reference to which men have discriminated in the past have been largely traditional. The outstanding fact of the present period, on the other hand, has been the weakening of traditional standards. An emergency has arisen not unlike that with which Socrates sought to cope in ancient Athens. Anyone who is untraditional and seeks at the same time to be discriminating must almost necessarily own Socrates as his master. As is well known, Socrates sought above all to be discriminating in his use of general terms. The importance of the art of inductive defining that he devised may perhaps best be made clear by bringing together two sayings, one of Napoleon—"Imagination governs mankind"—and one of John Selden—"Syllables govern mankind." Before allowing one's imagination and finally one's conduct to be controlled by a general term, it would seem wise to submit it to a Socratic scrutiny.

It is, therefore, unfortunate that at a time like the present, which plainly calls for a Socrates, we should instead have got a Mencken. One may take as an example of Mr. Mencken's failure to discriminate adequately, his attitude toward the term that for several generations past has been governing the imagination of multitudes—democracy. His view of democracy is simply that of Rousseau turned upside down, and nothing, as has been remarked, resembles a hollow so much as a swelling. A distinction of which he has failed to recognize the importance is that between a direct or unlimited and a constitutional democracy. In the latter we probably have the best thing in the world. The former, on the other hand, as all thinkers of any penetration from Plato and Aristotle down have perceived, leads to the loss of liberty and finally to the rise of some form of despotism. The two conceptions of democracy involve not merely incompatible views of government but ultimately of human nature. The desire of the constitutional democrat for institutions that act as checks on the immediate will of the people implies a similar dualism in the individual— a higher self that acts restrictively on his ordinary and impulsive self. The partisan of unlimited democracy on the other hand is an idealist in the sense of that the term assumed in connection with the so-called romantic movement. His faith in the people is closely related to the doctrine of natural goodness proclaimed by the sentimentalists of the eighteenth century and itself marking an extreme recoil from the dogma of total depravity. The doctrine of natural goodness favors the free temperamental expansion that I have already noticed in speaking of the creative critic.

It is of the utmost importance, however, if one is to understand Mr. Mencken, to discriminate between two types of temperamentalist—the soft and sentimental type, who cherishes various "ideals," and the hard, or Nietzschean type, who piques himself on being realistic. As a matter of fact, if one sees in the escape from traditional controls merely an opportunity to live temperamentally, it would seem advantageous to pass promptly from the idealistic to the Nietzschean phase, sparing oneself as many as possible of the intermediary disillusions. It is at all events undeniable that the rise of Menckenism has been marked by a certain collapse of romantic idealism in the political field and elsewhere. The numerous disillusions that have supervened upon the War have provided a favoring atmosphere.

The symptoms of Menckenism are familiar: a certain hardness and smartness and disposition to rail at everything that, rightly or wrongly, is established and respected; a tendency to identify the real with what Mr. Mencken terms "the cold and clammy facts" and to assume that the only alternative to facing these facts is to fade away into sheer romantic unreality. These and similar traits are becoming so widely diffused that, whatever one's opinion of Mr. Mencken as a writer and thinker, one must grant him representativeness. He is a chief prophet at present of those who deem themselves emancipated but who are, according to Mr. Brownell, merely unbuttoned.

The crucial point in any case is one's attitude toward the principle of control. Those who stand for this principle in any form or degree are dismissed by the emancipated as reactionaries or, still graver reproach, as Puritans. Mr. Mencken would have us believe that the historical Puritan was not even sincere in his moral rigorism, but was given to "lamentable transactions with loose women and fiery jugs." This may serve as a sample of the assertions, picturesquely indiscriminate, by which a writer wins immediate notoriety at the expense of his permanent reputation. The facts about the Puritan happen to be complex and need to be dealt with very Socratically. It has been affirmed that the point of view of the Puritan was Stoical rather than truly Christian, and the affirmation is not wholly false. The present discussion of the relationship between Puritanism and the rise of capitalism with its glorification of the acquisitive life also has its justification. It is likewise a fact that the Puritan was from the outset unduly concerned with reforming others as well as himself, and this trait relates him to the humanitarian meddler or "wowser" of the present day, who is Mr. Mencken's pet aversion.

Yet it remains true that awe and reverence and humility are Christian virtues and that there was some survival of these virtues in the Puritan. For a representative Puritan like Jonathan Edwards they were inseparable from the illumination of grace, from what he terms "a divine and supernatural light." In the passage from the love and feat of God of an Edwards to the love and service of man professed by the humanitarian, something has plainly dropped out, something that is very near the centre. What has tended to disappear is the inner life with the special type of control it imposes. With the decline of this inner control there has been an increasing resort to outer control. Instead of the genuine Puritan we then have the humanitarian legalist who passes innumerable laws for the control of people who refuse to control themselves. The activity of our uplifters is scarcely suggestive of any "divine and supernatural light." Here is a discrimination of the first importance that has been obscured by the muddy thinking of our half-baked intelligentsia. One is thus kept from perceiving the real problem, which is to retain the inner life, even though one refuse to accept the theological nightmare with which the Puritan associated it. More is involved in the failure to solve this problem than the Puritan tradition. It is the failure of our contemporary life in general. Yet, unless some solution is reached by a full and free exercise of the critical spirit, one remains a mere modernist and not a thoroughgoing and complete modern; for the modern spirit and the critical spirit are in their essence one.

What happens, when one sets out to deal with questions of this order without sufficient depth of reflection and critical maturity, may be seen in Mr. Sinclair Lewis's last novel. He has been lured from art into the writing of a wild diatribe which, considered even as such, is largely beside the mark. If the Protestant Church is at present threatened with bankruptcy, it is not because it has produced an occasional Elmer Gantry. The true reproach it has incurred is that, in its drift toward modernism, it has lost its grip not merely on certain dogmas but, simultaneously, on the facts of human nature. It has failed above all to carry over in some modern and critical form the truth of a dogma that unfortunately receives much support from these facts—the dogma of original sin. At first sight Mr. Mencken would appear to have a conviction of evil—when, for example, he reduces democracy in its essential aspect to a "combat between jackals and jackasses"—that establishes at least one bond between him and the austere Christian.

The appearance, however, is deceptive. The Christian is conscious above all the "old Adam" in himself: hence his humility. The effect of Mr. Mencken's writing, on the other hand, is to produce pride rather than humility, a pride ultimately based on flattery. The reader, especially the young and callow reader, identifies himself imaginatively with Mr. Mencken and conceives of himself as a sort of morose and sardonic divinity surveying from some superior altitude an immeasurable expanse of "boobs." This attitude will not seem especially novel to anyone who has traced the modern movement. One is reminded in particular of Flaubert, who showed a diligence in collecting bourgeois imbecilities comparable to that displayed by Mr. Mencken in his *Americana*. Flaubert's discovery that one does not add to one's happiness in this way would no doubt be dismissed by Mr. Mencken as irrelevant, for he has told us that he does not believe in happiness. Another discovery of Flaubert's may seem to him more worthy of consideration. "By dint of railing at idiots," Flaubert reports, "one runs the risk of becoming idiotic oneself."

It may be that the only way to escape from the unduly complacent cynicism of Mr. Mencken and his school is to reaffirm once more the truths of the inner life. In that case it would seem desirable to disengage, so far as possible, the principle of control on which the inner life finally depends from mere creeds and traditions and assert it as a psychological fact; a fact, moreover, that is neither "cold" nor "clammy." The coldness and clamminess of much so-called realism arises from its failure to give this fact due recognition. A chief task, indeed, of the Socratic critic would be to rescue the noble term "realist" from its present degradation. A view of reality that overlooks the element in man that moves in an opposite direction from mere temperament, the specifically human factor in short, may prove to be singularly one-sided. Is the Puritan, John Milton, when he declares that "he who reigns within himself and rules passions, desires, and fears is more than a king," less real than Mr. Theodore Dreiser when he discourses in his peculiar dialect of "those rearranging chemisms upon which all the morality or immorality of the world is based?" ⟨. . .⟩

A genuinely critical survey would make manifest that the unsatisfactoriness of our creative effort is due to a lack of the standards that culture alone can supply. Our cultural crudity and insignificance can be traced in turn to the inadequacy of our education, especially our higher education. Mr. Mencken's attack on the "professors" is therefore largely justified; for if the professors were performing their function properly Mr. Mencken himself would not be possible. One must add in common justice that the professors themselves, or at least some of them, are becoming aware that all is not well with existing conditions. One could not ask anything more perspicacious than the following paragraph from a recent report of Committee G to the American Association of University Professors:

> American education has suffered from the domination, conscious or unconscious, direct or indirect, of political and sentimental, as well as educational, theories that are demonstrably false. If the views of some men are to prevail the intellectual life of the country is doomed; everybody except the sheer idiot is to go to college and pursue chiefly sociology, nature study, child study, and community service—and we shall have a society unique only in its mediocrity, ignorance and vulgarity. It will not do to dismiss lightly even so extreme a view as this; it is too indicative. Such influences are very strong, their pressure is constant; and if education has largely failed in America it has been due primarily to them.

In short, as a result of the encroachments of an equalitarian democracy, the standards of our higher education have suffered in two distinct particulars: first, as regards the quality of students; second, as regards the quality of the studies these students pursue.

⟨. . .⟩ our institutions of learning seem to be becoming more and more hotbeds of "idealism." Their failure, on the whole, to achieve standards as something quite distinct from ideals on the one hand, and standardization on the other, may prove a fact of sinister import for the future of American civilization. The warfare that is being waged at the present time by Mr. Sinclair Lewis and others against a standardized Philistinism continues in the main the protest that has been made for several generations past by the temperamentalists, hard or soft, against the mechanizing of life by the utilitarian. This protest has been, and is likely to continue to be, ineffectual. The fruitful opposite of the standardized Philistine is not the Bohemian, nor again the hard temperamentalist or superman, as Mr. Mencken conceives him, but the man of leisure. Leisure involves an inner effort with reference to standards that is opposed to the sheer expansion of temperament, as it is to every other form of sheer expansion.

Perhaps a reason why the standards of the humanist are less popular in this country than the ideals of the humanitarian is that these standards set bounds to the acquisitive life; whereas it seems possible to combine a perfect idealism with an orgy of unrestricted commercialism. It is well for us to try to realize how we appear to others in this matter. Our growing unpopularity abroad is due no doubt in part to envy of our material success, but it also arises from the proneness of the rest of the world to judge us, not by the way we feel about ourselves, but by our actual performance. If we are in our own eyes a nation of idealists, we are, according to our most recent French critic, M. André Siegfried,[1] a "nation of Pharisees." The European, Mr. Siegfried would have us believe, still has a concern for the higher values of civilization, whereas the American is prepared to sacrifice these values ruthlessly to mass production and material efficiency. ⟨. . .⟩

A proper discussion of Mr. Siegfried's position as well as of other issues I have been raising would transcend the limits of an article. My end has been accomplished if I have justified in some measure the statement with which I started as to the importance of cultivating a general critical intelligence. James Russell Lowell's dictum that before having an American literature we must have an American criticism was never truer than it is to-day. The obvious reply to those who call for more creation and less criticism is that one needs to be critical above all in examining what now passes for creation. A scrutiny of this kind would, I have tried to show, extend beyond the bounds of literature to various aspects of our national life and would converge finally on our higher education.

We cannot afford to accept as a substitute for this true criticism the self-expression of Mr. Mencken and his school, unless indeed we are to merit the comment that is, I am told, made on us by South Americans: "They are not a very serious people!" To be sure, the reader may reflect that I am myself a critic, or would-be critic. I can only express the hope that, in my magnifying of the critical function, I do not offer too close a parallel to the dancing-master in Molière who averred, it will be remembered, that "all the mistakes of men, the fatal reverses that fill the world's annals, the shortcomings of statesmen, and the blunders of great captains arise from not knowing how to dance."

*Notes*

1. See his volume *Les États-Unis d'aujourd'hui* (1927) translated under the title *America Comes of Age.*

## ALFRED KAZIN
### From "The Postwar Scene"
### *On Native Grounds*
### 1942, pp. 198–204

"*I had not thought*"—T. S. Eliot was writing in a poem of that same year entitled *The Waste Land*—"I had not thought death had undone so many." But it was precisely because the war had undone so much only to give new freedom to so many in America that Mencken, now master of the revels, was able to give that freedom the character of a harlequinade. Eliot himself, having established himself in London during these years, was becoming the exponent of a new traditionalism in a Europe where the decline of culture seemed to threaten the European idea itself. At home, however, Mencken's boisterous attack upon all the vaunted traditions seemed not indecent and irresponsible, but a service. At a time when the seriousness of a profound moralist like Paul Elmer More seemed utterly remote from anything the new writers understood; when an enemy of modern literature like Irving Babbitt could say nothing better of them than that they were the ill-begotten children of Rousseau; when a Stuart Sherman thought of Dreiser only as a "barbaric naturalist," and declaimed pompously that the Younger Generation was following "alien guides," that "Beauty has a heart full of service," Mencken seemed one of the few guides to a necessary culture and civilization. At any other time, it may be, Mencken would have been almost an affront; later, as he proved with all his familiar energy, he could be as tedious and inflexible an old fogy as any he had once demolished. But if Mencken had never lived, it would have taken a whole army of assorted philosophers, monologists, editors, and patrons of the new writing to make up for him. As it was, he not only rallied all the young writers together and imposed his skepticism upon the new generation, but also brought a new and uproarious gift for high comedy into a literature that had never been too quick to laugh. He was just the oracle the new literature had prepared for itself, the total of the wisdom it was ready to receive; and it was not entirely his fault if, at a time when the loudest noise made the brightest satire and the most boisterous prose recorded the most direct hits, Mencken proved that one could be "a civilizing influence" by writing like a clown.

Mencken belonged so resplendently to the twenties that it is sometimes fancied that he came in with them. The twenties came to him. Much as the thirties passed him by because he did not prove equal to them—was there ever an American writer who seemed to belong so squarely to one period of time?—he was in the prewar years a remotely satiric figure who propounded more than the times were prepared to understand. As a newspaperman from his earliest days, he was taught in the school of Huneker, Percival Pollard, and Vance Thompson, a school not so much of newspapermen as of the bright new esthetic of the nineties which found its shrines in Ibsen, Nietzsche, Wagner, and Shaw. Everything that has been characteristic of Mencken except the scholarly curiosity displayed in *The American Language* was learned in that school; there were times when the monotone of his rasping skepticism suggested that he had learned nothing else. There he absorbed and improved upon his facile style; there he picked up the learning—too often only the marks of learning—that marked the esthetic newspaperman of the period; a learning characterized by its flashing eagerness, its naïve addiction to tags and titles and appropriate quotations from the Latin or the German, its sharp wit and occasional penetration and theatrical superficiality.

What Mencken learned chiefly from the fin-de-siècle mind, however, was a superior contempt for the native culture and manners. The Huneker-Thompson type had all the opportunities of a cosmopolite, and none of the obligations—not even the common emotions, as it then seemed—of a citizen. America was home, unfortunately, but culture was everywhere else. As a newspaperman he was a spectator at the international show, privy to its secrets, appreciative of its color and gossip, and a participant in the gaiety of nations. As a writer he was a dilettante, and in his revolt against the provincial he believed himself a connoisseur. The sexual emancipation that was one of the main props of the renascence of the nineties gave him an added contempt for native American inhibitions; the greater resolution and intellectual distinction of European revolutionaries even provoked a final disgust with the plodding social reformers at home. But Mencken went far beyond Huneker in his contempt for social rebels. For him Marx was always the "philosopher out of the gutter," and Debs was "poor old Debs." Of others in his day one could say that they found Debs's rhetoric soggy because they had been dazzled by Shaw or moved by the nobility of Jean Jaurès; in the brilliance of the European revolutionary tradition, so characteristically European and so pleasingly intellectual, they had found the necessary excuse for their indifference to social problems at home. Mencken needed no excuse. There was a fatal want of generosity in his mind from the first, and his writing was finally corrupted by it.

The gay satire of the American scene that runs all through Mencken's first writings, and which is marked in his editing of the *Smart Set*, was a significantly theatrical revulsion against the American as a type. There was never in it the mark of that quarrel with something one loves that distinguished the best criticism before the war or the humanity and tenderness of postwar rebels like Anderson and Fitzgerald. Entering into critical journalism at a time when traditionalists and insurrectionists divided the field between them, Mencken began, almost experimentally, with a gay and mocking irresponsibility; and the irresponsibility worked so well that it entered into his constitutional habits as a writer. By 1919, when the *Prejudices* began to appear, this irresponsibility was no longer a trick; it was a facile and pyrotechnical dogmatism which persuaded Mencken himself as easily as it persuaded callow undergraduates in search of a cultural standard. He had no sound opposition; his most articulate opponents were village editors, clubwomen, Fundamentalists, or conservartive critics like Stuart Sherman, who called him "pro-German." The times demanded a certain violence of expression and exasperation, and Mencken's appreciation of his sudden notoriety satisfied that demand and encouraged it. If he had not written so brilliantly and recklessly, he would not have been fully understood; but there was no need at the time to know that many of his ideas were cynical improvisations designed to startle and shock. He was an irrepressible force, a stimulant, an introduction to wisdom; when he roared, it was enough to roar with him.

With gay confidence Mencken was thus able to say anything he liked, and he usually did. The American was a lumpish peasant, an oaf, a barbarian in the most elementary matters. His culture was a monstrosity, his manners absurd and indecent, his courage a fiction, his instincts generally revolting. His literature, at best second-rate but usually impossibly mediocre and pretentious, was riddled by impostors, snoopers, and poseurs, dictated to by fakers, criticized by nincompoops, and read chiefly by fools. If there had ever been anything good in it, it had been speedily throttled, since the one thing Americans feared above all else was truth; the worst of it was always ceremoniously glorified. The American was neither a tragic nor a humble figure; he was merely an object of amusement, a figure out of caricature whose struggles for culture were vain, whose heroes were absurd, and whose sufferings were mere drool. To put it gently, he was hopelessly bourgeois, provincial, hypocritical, cowardly, and stupid. Only the lowest representatives of the racial stocks of Europe had congregated to produce him. Everything he possessed was borrowed from the worst of Europe; everything he aped defiled the best of it.

In his own way Mencken thus illustrated perfectly the passage from the America of Randolph Bourne to the postwar America in which he glittered; but it was not entirely his doing. For if he capitalized on the twenties as the period of the Great Silliness, with its profligacy, its vice-snooping in literature, its oil scandals and shady politics, the decade made good use of him. It raised him from a newspaper Petrouchka to the dignity of a social critic; his mockery was prophecy, his very delivery— and what a delivery it was!—became a fashion, and his scorn was almost a benediction. By prodigious skill he managed to insult everyone except his readers. He flattered them by kindling a sense of disgust; his ferocious attacks on Babbittry implied that his readers were all Superior Citizens; his very recklessness was intoxicating. When he proclaimed, with his grand flourish, that all Anglo-Saxons were cowards, his readers were delighted. When he pronounced the Civil War a third-rate war, because no more than 200,000 soldiers had been killed in it, he was believed. When he snickered that Americans drank the beverages of French peasants,[1] played in mah-jong the game of Chinese coolies, wore on state occasions the garb of English clerks, had a melodic taste for the music of African Negroes, and ate in alligator pears the food of Costa Rican billy goats, he was applauded deliriously.

Under such a stimulus Mencken's craving to say the unexpected, as Louis Kronenberger put it, proved stronger than his integrity against saying what was untrue. What he believed and what his readers wanted to be told were soon indistinguishable; his work became series of circus tricks, a perpetual search for some new object of middle-class culture to belabor and some new habit or caprice of *Homo Americanus* to ridicule. There were no longer divergent American types and patterns; there was only a strange, fur-bearing, highly unpleasant animal entitled the American. Had the American once been a pioneer? "What lies beneath the boldness is not really an independent spirit, but merely a talent for crying with the pack." Were there American farmers in need? "No more grasping, selfish and dishonest Mammal, indeed, is known to students of the Anthropoidea." Did American workers seek higher wages? They were slaves, all of them; any fool could earn enough money in a country where writers grew prosperous by throwing a few pearls before swine. In a commonwealth of third-rate men only morons were ever hungry.

> The Anglo-Saxon of the great herd is, in many important respects, the least civilized of men and the least capable of true civilization. His political ideas are crude and shallow. He is almost wholly devoid of aesthetic feeling; he does not even make folklore or walk in the woods. The most elementary facts about the visible universe alarm him, and incite him to put them down.

Mencken's technique was simple: he inverted conventional prejudices. To a Protestant America, he proclaimed himself a Nietzschean; to a moral America, an atheist; to the Anti-Saloon League mind, a devotee of the fine art of drinking; to a provincial America, a citizen of the world. *His* sphere was that of scholarship, of good manners, and the European graces. It did not matter then that his scholarship, with the exception of his works on language, was as pedestrian as it was showy, or that the translator of Nietzsche and the great apostle of German culture was not a very trustworthy guide to German. Nor did it matter that his scorn for poetry was the manly bigotry of the locker room, or that his conception of the esthetic life, which saw in every great artist the cynicism of La Rochefoucauld, the devotion of Flaubert, the manners of a Hollywood duke, and the liberalism of Metternich, was monstrous in its frivolity and ignorance. Mencken was Civilization Incarnate. Every Babbitt read him gleefully and pronounced his neighbor a Babbitt. Every intellectual blushed for the idiocies of the Bible Belt, and thought Cabell's prose the height of elegance. Good citizens who had forgotten Bryan's significance in the days before he became the absurd figure at the monkey trial thought Mencken's ridicule of him the last word in political sophistication. Under the whip of Mencken's raillery people generally saw the world's folly in their Congressman, the world's wisdom in their scorn of him.

Fortunately, Mencken so parodied the best aspirations of criticism that his most egregious utterances seemed the work of a vigorous comic spirit. What could be more appropriate, in a day when Carol Kennicott dreamed of literary noblemen in velvet jackets and Hergesheimer's butlers came out of the *Almanach de Gotha*, than Mencken's call for an aristocracy? The *Uebermensch* sat on the white steps of Baltimore and invoked the spirits of Dante, Machiavelli, Voltaire, Beethoven, and General von Ludendorff, to come and make America inhabitable. It was to be a community of the rich, the witty, assorted magazine editors, George Jean Nathan, and those who could remember drinking at least one quart of genuine Pilsener. The arbiter elegantiarum was suddenly transformed into a Prussian Junker with a taste for Havelock Ellis. What could be more amusing than an "aristocratic" principle that was fully as provincial as the antics of the "booboisie" Mencken loved to bait, or as romantic and incoherent as Babbitt's search for the dream girl?

Occasionally, of course, Mencken was not amusing at all, and his loose tongue got in his way, as when he said of Altgeld that "his error consisted in taking the college yells of democracy seriously." And it was significant that one of the cruelest things he ever wrote, his essay on Bryan, was probably the most brilliant. But who in Mencken's heyday could seriously resent a writer who so joyously declared that there was no real poverty in the United States; or that public schools were a drag on the community; or "that the ignorant should be permitted to spawn *ad libitum* that there may be a steady supply of slaves"; or that war was an admirable institution, and capital punishment an edifying one?

Mencken's gaiety was the secret of his charm, and his charm was everything. He seemed so brilliantly alive, so superb a service toward the advancement of taste and civilization, that it would have been churlish to oppose him. In a young and growing modern literature which believed that the revolt against gentility was all, Mencken's scorn for the Henry Van Dykes and his long fight for Dreiser were extremely important. In a culture aching for emancipation from the Prohibition mind, from vulgarity and provincialism and conventionality, Mencken was a source of light and strength. What did it matter that he was an eccentric and willful critic who celebrated bad writers and cried down good ones simply because it suited his sense of fun to do so? What did it matter that he said as many false things about established writers simply because they were established as he could say true and urgent things about writers waiting to be heard? What did it matter that he was not always a sound guide to culture, that he frequently proved himself cheap and cruel, that his pronouncements on art and music and books were not always wise and witty, but frequently glib and malicious? He was the great cultural emancipator, the conqueror of Philistia, the prophet and leader of all those who had been given their emancipation and were now prepared to live by it.

Notes

1. In an essay written in collaboration with George Jean Nathan.

## VAN WYCK BROOKS
### "Mencken in Baltimore"
### *The Confident Years: 1885–1915*
### 1952, pp. 455–74

In Gertrude Stein's Baltimore, where Henry L. Mencken was a newspaperman, few readers had ever heard of the story "Melanctha" or those other stories about Lena and Anna, the German servant-girls who had also lived in the city where Poe lay buried. In fact, few readers anywhere knew Gertrude Stein in 1910, or Veblen, or Ellen Glasgow, or Theodore Dreiser. The reigning American talents in fiction were Winston Churchill, Booth Tarkington, Richard Harding Davis and James Lane Allen, and most of the authors, already at work and emerging one by one, who interested readers later were still obscure. The playwrights of whom one heard were Augustus Thomas and Clyde Fitch, while the splenetic Paul Elmer More spoke in a measure for a circle of critics who were generally indifferent or hostile to the march of mind. On a lower level but still esteemed by a legion of popularizers, Hamilton Wright Mabie discussed "great books" and "culture,"—the last attenuation of the Anglo-American Goethean line by way of Emerson, Arnold and James Russell Lowell. This essayist perfectly fulfilled Leo Stein's characterization of the writing that is "like the running of water down hill," for, possessing no tension whatsoever, it followed the grooves of popular thought, purveying an easy sweetness and an easier light.

While the first shoots of a more vigorous epoch were appearing now on every side, the prevailing tone of the moment was complacent and dull, and a few critics were lamenting already the sterility of the literary scene and the general flatness and tameness of American writers. John Curtis Underwood observed that Americans had become a machine-made people, conventionalized, standardized, commercialized in all walks of life, and he regretted with Percival Pollard that American writers wrote "down to the public" rather than "up to the art of literature." Percival Pollard was always asking, "What is wrong with American literature?"—in which one found scarcely an "ounce of style,"—for so many writers seemed to be "content with the easy and common phrase" and regarded their work quite simply as merchandise. It was true that Pollard, in *Their Day in Court*, wrote without any distinction himself,—both he and the "insurgent" Underwood were commonplace in style; and Underwood was so far at sea that he thought David Graham Phillips was a better writer than Henry James or Howells. But if Percival Pollard, in his own work, did little to quicken the scene, he delighted in audacity, wit and style in others, and, like Walter Blackburn Harte, the author of *Meditations in Motley*, he praised Ambrose Bierce as the "commanding figure" of the time. Like Harte, he wrote also on Oscar Wilde and others of the "glorious middle nineties" when "savoury pots were brewing," as Mencken said later, remembering how he had lain in wait for the sprightly magazine in which Pollard had appeared with James Huneker when he was a boy. Pollard had written *Masks and Minstrels of New Germany*, a subject that especially appealed to Mencken, and, as one of the survivors, with Vance Thompson and Huneker, of *M'lle New York*, he was a hero indeed for this Baltimore friend. He was "like a truth-seeker in the Baptist college of cardinals," said Mencken who met Ambrose Bierce through Pollard. But Huneker was the real enlivener for Mencken as for others, all-curious lover that he was of half a dozen arts, for his work was a running indictment of what he described as the "mean narrow spirit in our arts and letters." Almost as indifferent as Paul Elmer More to living American writers and artists,—for he was interested mainly in affairs of Europe,—Huneker made art seem, as Mencken said, a "magnificent adventure" and brought this spirit into American criticism. As Mencken continued, "he was apt to go chasing after strange birds and so miss seeing the elephants go by,"—he praised brilliantly coloured frauds, overlooking real talents; but "when his soul went adventuring among masterpieces . . . it went with vine-leaves in its hair."

Mencken, an offshoot of Huneker's circle with his own "assertive clang," had been writing for Baltimore newspapers since 1899, and when Pollard visited the town he planned with this half-German critic a joint translation of a number of German poems. When Pollard died in Baltimore, Bierce appeared from Washington and he and Mencken were thrown for a time together, two years before Bierce disappeared,—to "get the smell of my country," as he said, "out of my nose and my clothing,"—in Mexico. Bierce had toured the Civil War battlefields as if to retrieve an experience in which he and the country had felt they were truly alive, and his disgust with modern America and all things democratic was only equalled by his hatred of "yokels" and "louts." For Bierce all reformers were "anarchists" and all farmers were "peasants," and much of his choleric thought and feeling drifted into Mencken's mind, which was predisposed to this home-made aristocratism. "Our one genuine wit," as Mencken called Bierce,—forgetting Oliver Wendell Holmes, who was ninety-nine times wittier and much besides—undoubtedly influenced the man who was always girding at "peasants" and "hinds" and "the quacks who make laws at Washington." Mencken had something in common with Poe, who had also lived in Baltimore and detested the "rabble," the "canaille" and the "progress mongers," and he had found a philosophy in Nietzsche, the subject of his first important book,—the idol-smashing prophet of the "master-races." But Mencken's "boobus Americanus," the hero of an "Eden of clowns" which he also called "this glorious commonwealth of morons," together with his *Americana* and its national imbecilities were oddly reminiscent of the far less genial Bierce. His characterization of the American people as "that timorous, sniveling, poltroonish mob of serfs and goose-steppers" recalled *The Shadow of the Dial*. Mencken shared Bierce's peculiar cynicism.

Now Mencken had inherited, as he remarked, a "bias against the rabble" in his almost exclusively German Baltimore childhood, as the son of a German cigar-manufacturer who had married a German-American wife and who usually took him on Sundays to German beer-gardens. The family barber was a German too and so was the family farm-hand when the Menckens spent sufficient summers in the country to convince the boy that city life was "better," and Mencken had gone to a German school where they sang German *volkslieder* and the "pure American children" were regarded as "dunces." If Mencken was later inclined to regard most grown-up Americans as dunces too,—especially the "inferior" Anglo-Saxons,[1]—it was partly because of these impressions that he gathered as a boy, impressions that could scarcely have been dispelled when he briefly attended a Sunday school kept by the author of *What a Young Man Ought to Know.* He acquired early the bourgeois traits that made him a good citizen,

methodical, the most orderly of mortals, never late for trains, who never failed to appear in time for dinner, one who respected punctuality and solvency in others and who spent his life in one house in Baltimore. People lost in New York, he said, the sense of "abiding relationships" and the lares and penates that one found in this half-Southern city; and he liked what he described as the Baltimore "tradition of sound and comfortable living." Expressed in terms of a prosperous German cigar-manufacturer's house, this presupposed a contempt for the poor, for the shiftless and for workingmen who did not know their place, the peculiarly German contempt indeed that filled the mind of Nietzsche who regarded them as mere draught-animals to be used as tools. That Mencken should have been drawn to Nietzsche and his notion of the slave-proletariat,—a notion that was alien to Americans,—was preordained, as much as that he should have been drawn to Huneker if only as a lover of music who sketched for the piano ten or more sonatas. Mencken was a precocious composer of marches and waltzes. He was convinced, as a boy, for the rest, that life was essentially meaningless and that progress, democracy and religion were childish illusions, well summed up in the hullabaloo that amused him on street-corners when he stopped, looked and listened to the Salvation Army. Employed for a while in his father's factory, he went the rounds of cafés and saloons, taking orders for cigars and developing an epicure's palate; then, entering a newspaper-office, he became at eighteen a police reporter and was soon reviewing the theatre and music as well. He picked up the jargon and ways of thought of the city-room. When he came to compile his great work *The American Language*, Mencken was to know whereof he spoke.

Such was the "ruddy snub-nosed youth" with the "small-town roisterer's" air who called upon Theodore Dreiser in his New York office when this novelist, whom Mencken greatly admired, proposed him in 1908 as reviewer of books for the magazine *The Smart Set*. Dreiser had published in *The Delineator* some papers of Mencken's on medical themes and knew him as already a brilliant and forceful writer, one who suggested, in this personal encounter, "Anheuser's own brightest boy,"—as Dreiser said,—"out to see the town." Mencken had read *Sister Carrie* when it appeared in 1900, and Dreiser had impressed him as deeply even as Conrad; and this editor-in-chief of a Baltimore paper who was twenty-eight years old was in fact a voluminous writer in prose and in verse. It was true that Mencken had abandoned the verse in which he followed Kipling and some of the old French forms that were in vogue at the time, for he disliked all fanciful writing, he had no taste for fairy-tales and distrusted poetry as enervating and even as "nonsense." Mencken could see in *Alice in Wonderland* nothing but "feeble jocosity" and he had given up short-story writing, although he continued to write the burlesques that expressed his satirical feeling and his constant and ebullient sense of humour.

The satirical humorist in him had led him to devote his first book,—the first of all books on the subject,—to Bernard Shaw, though he had no sympathy with Shaw's socialistic doctrines; and meanwhile his discovery of *Huckleberry Finn*, which he reread every year, was the "most stupendous event," as he said, of his life. This led him further into the American language. On the whole, his positive mind delighted most in science, and, along with Macaulay, that "first-rate artist," T. H. Huxley was his model in style,—"the greatest virtuoso of plain English who has ever lived." But most of his intellectual gods, as he admitted, were German, from Beethoven to Hauptmann and Ibsen,"—"more German than Norwegian,"—and especially Nietzsche, who formed his mind more perhaps than anyone else and whose style, as he put it, was "almost comparable to Huxley's."

In a world in which democracy seemed to be triumphing everywhere and socialism was rising in every country, Nietzsche had become a cult with those who shared Paul Elmer More's disgust with the "canting unreason of equality and brotherhood." More wrote a little book on Nietzsche and W. M. Salter a larger book,—by general agreement the best American study,—while Nietzsche or his ideas appeared in various American novels and a crop of little Nietzsches sprang up in New York.[2] Among these were Benjamin De Casseres, who "danced with Nietzsche," as he said, describing himself as an "intellectual faun," whose "compass," as he also said, had a "thousand needles" and who was always "going in a thousand directions."[3] *The Encounter*, Anne Douglas Sedgwick's novel, was based on Nietzsche's actual life, while Stanford West in *The Man of Promise*, the novel by Willard Huntington Wright, devoted himself to spreading the doctrines of Nietzsche. As an author, Stanford West proclaimed the ideas of the "dancing philosopher,"[4]—which Wright expounded again in *What Nietzsche Taught*,—as Isadora Duncan proclaimed them in terms of her art. Jack London was one of many minds that were torn between Nietzsche and socialism, like the heroes of Max Eastman's *Venture* and Ernest Poole's *The Harbor*, both socialists who were diverted for a while by Nietzsche.[5] Mencken's *The Philosophy of Friedrich Nietzsche*, a book that appeared in 1908, the year in which he began his reviewing for *The Smart Set*, was a lucid presentation of this new group of ideas that were to serve him as touchstones in his work as a critic. Had not Nietzsche regarded himself as a Polish grandee set down among German shopkeepers by an unkind fate? Just so Mencken saw himself as a sort of German Junker whose lot it was to live with American peasants. As Nietzsche had constantly pointed out "what the Germans lack," so Mencken set out to "transvalue" American values,—another Dionysus in a pallidly Apollonian world, a hierophant of idol-smashing and "natural selection."

Mencken's great days were yet to come in the Dionysian twenties, the post-war decade of orgies that recalled *The Bacchae* when writers impersonated the nymphs and satyrs who had formed the train of the god of wine, dancing to the din of flutes and cymbals. The revels of the "jazz age" were in tune with the ideas that Mencken had been spreading in *The Smart Set* since 1908, in his monthly articles reviewing books, in his *Americana* and in other writings including *In Defence of Women*. He was associated with that other Nietzschean Willard Huntington Wright,—the "S. S. Van Dine" of the future,—and with George Jean Nathan, the reviewer of plays, another heir of the Huneker circle,—cosmopolitan minds that were bent on destroying "tradition." The "intelligently emotional" George Jean Nathan,—to apply to himself a phrase of his own,—an opener of the windows of America to the breezes of Europe, was an active apostle of the modern theatre of Hauptmann, Sudermann, Maeterlinck, Ibsen, whom Huneker and Emma Goldman were popularizing. An alert detector of "hokum" himself and as cynical as Cabell, a cockney for whom the country was for "yokels and cows," with a mind as urban as Huneker's or Mencken's, he was wholly an aesthete, unlike Mencken, and indifferent to economics, politics and religion. Mencken, on the other hand, was more interested in these, and in medicine, anthropology, biology, than he was in art, and almost more than in literature, aside from fiction; and he

directed his humorous-ferocious assaults at American life in virtually every aspect. At the outset of his career, he said, an ancient had advised him to make his criticism telling at any cost, to "knock somebody on the head every day" with a bladder on a string or, more usually, a "meat-axe." For the way to get rid of obstructive ideas was "not to walk softly before them but to attack them vigorously with clubs." So Mencken laid about him in a slashing style that was full of Nietzschean mannerisms.

Thus, with all the brasses sounding, the great Menckenian campaign began, like the coming of the circus in the springtime, with showers of epithets, attacks on democracy, the "universal murrain of Christendom," and shouts of defiance hurled at the "smuthounds" and the "shamans." According to Mencken, the United States was a "commonwealth of third-rate men" who were in full control of the state and the national standards,—Baptist mullahs scaring the peasantry, Methodist hinds of the "hookworm belt," theological buffoons and commercial brigands. The general average of intelligence, integrity and competence was so low that a man who knew his trade stood out as boldly as ever a wart stood out on a bald head, and the scene was a welter of knavery and swinishness, the operations of master rogues, the combats of demagogues, the pursuit of heretics and witches. It was the greatest show on earth, with Aimee MacPherson, for instance, "caressing the anthropoids with her lubricious coos," and with Orison Swett Marden as the national authority on the art of "getting on in the world as the only conceivable goal of human aspiration." Then there were the Elks and the undertakers who were initiated eighteen times and robed themselves to plant a fellow-joiner in garments that sparkled and flashed like the mouth of hell, who were entitled to bear seven swords, all jewelled, and hang their watch-chains with the busts of nine wild beasts. This race was as barbarous, Mencken said, as the Jugo-Slavs or the Mississippians with its "saccharine liberals," "right-thinkers" and "forward-lookers" and its professors, no longer from New England,—a region that he loved still less,—but now mostly from the land of "silos, revivals and saleratus." They "carried the smell of the dunghill into the academic groves." Nor could one forget the "uplifting vereins" and the countless American delusions and illusions, the notion that American literature was about to produce Walt Whitman's "new and greater literatus order" when it had no prodigies of the first class, few of the second and scarcely even more of the third or the fourth. This literature was colourless and inconsequential, timorously flaccid and amiably hollow, falteringly feeble and wanting in genuine gusto. It lacked salient personalities, intellectual audacity, aesthetic passion, it had an air of poverty and imitation, it evaded the serious problems of life and art; yet what was one to think of Paul Elmer More, who saw it as expiring with Longfellow and Donald G. Mitchell? More's "coroner's inquest criticism" infuriated Mencken, and he attacked the "crêpe-clad pundits, the bombastic word-mongers of the *Nation* school," although, like More, he too was an "incurable Tory." Was he not equally scornful of the "current sentimentalities," socialism, pacifism, deep-breathing and sex-hygiene? But, as he observed, Paul Elmer More preached the "gloomy gospel of tightness and restraint," while he was out to liberate and paganize the country. He seemed to agree with Nietzsche that "the one great intrinsic depravity" was the Christian religion, and his feeling that life, as he said, was "empty of significance" made it the more imperative to eat, drink and be merry.

Now there never could have been any doubt that Mencken played a decisive part in stabbing a flabby society wide awake, in shaking up the American spirit and rousing it out of its lethargy of optimistic fatuity and dull conventions. Mencken's astringent realism seared its adiposity, its provincial self-satisfaction and romantic moonshine, and, reintroducing acrimony into American criticism, he harrowed the ground for the literature and art of the future. As he said, all the benefits that he had ever got from critics had come from those who gave him a "hearty slating," for this led him to examine his ideas, shelve them when he found holes in them and set about hatching others that were better; and was he not right in saying that literature thrives best in an atmosphere of strife? Poe had introduced this three generations before at the dawn of the so-called American Renaissance, and what it really meant was that literary and aesthetic matters were felt to be worth the trouble of a *mêlée* and a combat. Mencken was hardly a literary critic, for his mind was devoid of the feminine traits this type must have in order to be effective. He was a social critic and a literary showman who had taken lessons from Macaulay, as well as from Nietzsche, Huneker and Bierce, and he fought with all his masculine force against the elements in American society that impeded the creative life and stifled its growth. A transatlantic Attila, with his own Teutonic fury, a coarse mind that had undertaken a literary spadesman's work, he accomplished a task that only a coarse mind could do. He was concerned with "numbers,"[6] the big Philistine public that blocked his way and that he attacked with his humour and his rude common sense,—the "Texas Taines," the "policemen of letters," the rural fundamentalists, the "Ku Klux Kritics" that battened in the solid South. In their fear of the new literature that he was fostering, the "cow-state John the Baptists" and their colleagues and supporters were as thoroughly American as the Knights of Pythias or chewing-gum, or Diamond Jim Brady, or Billy Sunday; and, defending what they called the sewage of the mental slums of Chicago and New York, he set the new realistic literature squarely on its feet. His campaign for Theodore Dreiser, a symbol of the rising Middle West, resulted in the general recognition of the other Western writers; and what did he not accomplish too in assaulting the "Sahara of the Bozart"[7] and insisting on a veritable Bismarckian *kulturkampf* there? It was largely thanks to Mencken that "Church" and "State" were separated there, in the sense in which these words meant much to writers,—the republic of letters shook off its clerical controls; and it was more than a coincidence that the birth of the new Southern literature followed the publication of Mencken's essay.[8]

It could scarcely have been questioned that the shifting of forces in American letters which led to the literary dominance of the West and the South,—that this striking phenomenon of the twenties owed much to Mencken, and long before the first world war he had roused the imagination of writers to a sense of the opportunities that America presented. For, along with his abuse, he conveyed a feeling of the "prodigal and gorgeous life of the country,"—a "circus" to which he awoke each morning with the "eager unflagging expectation of a Sunday school superintendent touring the Paris peep-shows." It was this that kept Mencken at home when the "expatriates" were leaving the country, filling every ship with a groaning cargo, issuing, as he put it, "their successive calls to the corn-fed intelligentsia to flee the shambles." He answered only with a few academic "Hear, Hears" and remained on the dock himself, "wrapped in the flag," for he was happy in a land of grotesques where one could visit Scopes trials and camp-meetings at which preachers denounced the reading of books. He delighted in the "cowtown hell-robbers," the "whoopers and snorters" of prohibition, the pious pornomaniacs listening to radio jazz and stealthily rising

and "shaking their fireproof legs," the hill-billy miracle-workers drinking poison and bitten by snakes and the "God-fearing professors laboriously striving to ram their dismal nonsense into the progeny of Babbitts." Mencken was a humorist, a more pungent successor of Artemus Ward, no longer the country showman but the man of the city, and he conveyed an infectious feeling of the spectacle of life in America as a monstrous county fair or museum of freaks. Then he had the pride of craftsmanship that betokened the genuine artist in words, and, "naturally monkish," for all his worldly cynicism, he had much, after all, in common with the professors. His work on *The American Language* showed this in time. He esteemed the man who devoted himself to a subject with hard diligence, the man who put poverty and a shelf of books above evenings of jazz or profiteering; and in all these and other ways he stimulated writers, especially those who appeared after the first world war. If, as he said, these younger writers had a "new-found elasticity," together with a "glowing delight in the spectacle before them,"—a vigorous naive self-consciousness and sense of aliveness,—it was partly owing to the influence of Mencken himself. He had seen an exhilarating prospect for American letters, as he put it in one of his essays, in the exhaustion of Europe.

Still later, after the jazz age passed, when he had become an institution, Mencken's limitations and faults were more generally apparent. It was evident that he had the vaguest of literary standards, that there were no fixed stars in his literary firmament such as sea-faring critics must have in order to sail. In music, with which he was more at home,—conventional as his taste there was, for he hated the "musical felonies" of Ravel and Stravinsky,—he never wavered in his devotion to the "lovely music of Haydn and Mozart" and even went so far as to call Beethoven "noble." This was a word he would never have connected with a writer, for he saw in Dante the "elaborate jocosity" of a satire on the "Christian hocus-pocus" and in *Romeo and Juliet* he found only "tinpot heroics." He called Greek tragedy an "unparalleled bore," he spoke of the "weakness for poetry" as "another hoary relic from the adolescence of the race," and, describing philosophy as "largely moonshine and wind-music," he referred to "metaphysics, which is to say, nonsense." He had no literary scale of values or he could scarcely have spoken of the "harsh Calvinistic fables of Hawthorne" or of Emerson as "an importer of stale German elixirs"; he could never have described Howells as a "placid conformist" because he was indifferent to the "surge of passion" or called Robert Frost a "Whittier without the whiskers." He was so undiscriminating that he spoke of Gertrude Atherton in the same breath with Sarah Orne Jewett, and "Prof. Dr. William James," when Mencken finished speaking of him, was virtually indistinguishable from Orison Swett Marden. He was apt enough when he referred to Veblen's "vast Kitchen-midden of discordant and raucous polysyllables," but this did not exhaust the subject of the "geyser of pishposh" even in the matter of style, and his dispraise of American critics lost much of its convincingness when he praised the third-rate Austrian Leon Kellner. Then what was one to say of the absence in him of the sentiment of reverence and the "shudder of awe,"—"humanity's highest faculty," as Goethe called it,—the recognition of certain realities of a spiritual kind upon which all human values are ultimately based? That Mencken really lacked this one saw in his treatment of Bernard Shaw, his early master and one of his early heroes, who became for him the "Ulster Polonius" in 1914, nine years after Shaw had been the subject of his first prose book. Mencken retained so little respect for the man he had admired so much that he said it was Shaw's life-work to "announce the obvious in terms of the scandalous." Mencken remained a child in this region of feeling. He related in his *Heathen Days* how, at thirty-five, in Rome, he had dodged into a crowd of pilgrims who were to be received by the Pope, and, running the risk of detection, obtained the Pope's blessing,—like a village boy squirming under a circus tent.

Mencken once observed himself that his "essential trouble" was that he was "devoid of what are called spiritual gifts." This was an actual trouble indeed, for without these "gifts" one lacks the scale, in the literary and human spheres alike, by which one distinguishes the ephemeral and the small from the great. Mencken's realistic note was admirable and useful, as one saw in his book, for instance, *In Defence of Women*,—women as the logical practical sex, aesthetically responsible, wary, discreet, in distinction from the vainglorious sex to which he belonged. He was as shrewd as Benjamin Franklin there and in other books, the *Treatise on Rights and Wrong* and the *Treatise on the Gods*,—in which he admitted the reality of a kind of "progress,"—but elsewhere his arid rationalism blended with a hedonism that was quite without spirituality and completely fatalistic. It was this tendency of his that blossomed in the jazz age in which so many writers were influenced by him, an age that also inherited the thinking of William Graham Sumner with his contempt for the idealism and "illusions" of the past. That life no longer had a purpose was the belief of millions then for whom the bootlegger became a national hero, and, while man was a "bad monkey" for many a scientific mind, others embraced the despair of Eliot's "waste land." Shakespeare's man, "glorious in reason, infinite in faculty," had been dethroned, and Melville's "man noble and sparkling,"—where now was he? He had been supplanted by Mencken's man, the "king dupe of the cosmos," the "yokel *par excellence*," the "booby." Much of Mencken's humour was based upon these denigrations of the "boob" man, "brother to the lowly ass," whose pretensions he delighted in undoing, and his disdain of democracy followed from this low view of human nature that struck the note of the fiction of the nineteen-twenties. If he saw democracy as "the art and science of running the circus from the monkey-cage," was it not precisely because he saw men as monkeys and because their continued existence in the world was therefore so inconsequential that one had no reason to assure and facilitate it? Inevitably, from this point of view, philanthropy, socialism, pacifism, like the notion of educability, were sentimental, while Mencken's opposition to birth-control was deadlier even than his attacks on most of the other aspects of the democratic process. He said the ignorant should be "permitted to spawn *ad libitum* that there may be a steady supply of slaves." For the rest, he was convinced that the war between the haves and the have-nots was an affair of "envy pure and simple."

With all his reactionary cynicism, Mencken was a liberator who opened paths for writers and made straight their way by turning many of their obstacles into laughing-stocks, but his campaign against democracy lost any glamour it might have had when Hitler murdered seven million Poles and Jews. While much that Mencken said was true, the inevitable answer was that all other forms of government had proved to be worse, that democracy, as Whitman put it, was the only safe system; and, when virtually every thinking German was only too happy to escape to America, Mencken's assaults on the country lost much of their force. Time broke the lance of the "literary uhlan," as the German-American societies had called him, and the critic who had said, "Most of the men I respect are foreigners," ceased to be a spokesman for the "mongrel and

inferior" Yankees. It was almost forgotten that he had performed a major work of criticism in giving the *coup de grâce* to the colonial tradition, while, by fully recognizing the new interracial point of view, he contributed to the nationalizing of American letters. More than anyone else perhaps, Mencken broke the way for writers who were descended from "foreign" stocks and who were not yet assured of their place in the sun, and it was he who signalized Chicago as a literary centre and praised the new writers who used the "American language." Howells had long since welcomed George Ade and many another, but Mencken, who hailed Theodore Dreiser, was foremost in hailing Ring Lardner and praising with discrimination writers of his type.[9]

As for the question of colonialism,—still a live issue in 1920,[10]—this was soon to be settled, thanks partly to him; and perhaps it could have been settled only by a critic of recent immigrant stock whose mind was entirely detached from the English tradition. Mencken's solution of the question was in certain ways unfortunate precisely because of this and all it implied, but he performed an invaluable work in helping to establish the interracial American literature of the future. Mencken had observed that the distrust of Dreiser was very largely racial,—he was felt to be sinister because he was not Anglo-Saxon; and it pleased him to point out how many of the new novelists and poets might be regarded as sinister for the same reason. But, he remarked, the "old easy domination of the 'Anglo-Saxon'" was rapidly passing,[11]—the nation was becoming "transnational," as Randolph Bourne put it,—and what was the use of attempting to restore, as Stuart P. Sherman wished to do, the Anglo-Saxon tradition in American letters?[12] Mencken was right in saying that this was a "demand for supine conformity," for, in fact, the *restoration* of this tradition was by no means the relevant or desirable thing. What was important was the *recognition* of it, the reëstablishing of a living relation between the future and the past, the sense of which, for a number of reasons, had been lost. Mencken was the last man to reëstablish this relation, for, having no inherited knowledge of the American past, he was even antagonistic to its main stream of feeling. He was "frankly against the Anglo-Saxon," and this led to a confusion he shared with others, especially during the first world war, when the issue of "colonialism" was confounded with the issue of "England." One could never tell how far "pro-German" American writers were opposed to colonialism because of this hostility to England. But to fight to "throw off the yoke of England's intellectual despotism,"—in the melodramatic phrase of Mencken's friend Wright,[13]—to settle this age-old question was a service to the country; and in order to exalt the new "foreign" strains in the American literary world it was natural enough to depreciate the Anglo-Saxon. The trouble was that Mencken carried this to impossible lengths, and he indulged in grotesque misstatements regarding New England, especially, that a serious critic should have been ashamed to utter. One wonders what the proud "founding fathers,"—or Governor Winthrop or William Byrd,—would have said to his remark about the first English settlers, that they were "the botched and unfit"; and what was anyone to say to his statement that "New England has never shown the slightest sign of a genuine enthusiasm for ideas"? In *Puritanism as a Literary Force*, he said that the literature of the years 1831–1861,—the times of Emerson, Melville, Thoreau and Hawthorne,—was the "work of women and admittedly second-rate men." It was by assertions of this kind that he "liquidated the American past," as certain of his admirers praised him for doing, and this was anything but a service to the country or its writers. But that one could impute these feats to him was a proof of the force of Mencken's mind, and one could leave the balance to be redressed by others.

### Notes

1. "Whenever the Anglo-Saxon, whether of the English or of the American variety, comes into sharp conflict with men of other stocks, he tends to be worsted . . . That this inferiority is real must be obvious to any impartial observer."—Mencken, *Prejudices: Fourth Series (The American Tradition)*.
2. Like the "crop of little Kierkegaards" for whom Leo Stein was looking at the end of the second world war.
3. Benjamin De Casseres called his philosophy an "erotic narcissism." In this a few critical perceptions were lost in a welter of exhibitionism and bad taste.

    Another of these "little Nietzsches" was Sadakichi Hartmann, the German-Japanese historian of American art, a Philadelphian, born in Japan, who studied in Munich and Berlin and wrote *Conversations with Walt Whitman*.

    One might also mention Charles Fort, the author of *The Book of the Damned*,—by which he meant the "excluded,"—a collection of surprising facts of nature recorded in scientific publications that science nevertheless refused officially to accept. De Casseres described Fort as a "Tyl Eulenspiegel perched on the windmill hurling whimsical questions at the professors, confronting them with facts from their own publications that do not 'fit in' with their dead reckonings." This "protest," as De Casseres called it, "against the popery of science" was a sort of forerunner of the popular *Believe It or Not*.
4. "West made no compromise . . . He was cold and unsentimental. He attacked ruthlessly the very structure on which modern education, morality and art were based. He insisted upon a natural aristocracy wherein there could be no concessions to the demands of illiteracy." In one of his papers this contemner of the "democratic idea" outlined "an aesthetic rationale for criticism wherein morality and ethics played no part. In still another paper, he analyzed modern moral institutions, denouncing them as the great enemies of all worthy aspiration . . . He censured the most sacred aspects of Western civilization, pointing out their deleterious effects upon the development of the aesthetic will."—Willard Huntington Wright, *The Man of Promise*.
5. In Max Eastman's *Venture*, Jo Hancock, who finally goes over to syndicalism, is fascinated for a while by the captain of industry Forbes whose gospel is Nietzsche's *Anti-Christ*. The hero of Ernest Poole's *The Harbor* is also captivated by the great engineer Dillon, his Nietzschean father-in-law.
6. See, e.g., in his essay on Dreiser, in *A Book of Prefaces*, the page-long table of statistics of the representation of Dreiser's novels in all the large town libraries in the country.
7. "Nearly the whole of Europe could be lost in that stupendous region of fat farms, shoddy cities and paralyzed cerebrums . . . You will not find a single Southern poet above the rank of a neighbourhood rhymester. Once you have counted James Branch Cabell . . . you will not find a single Southern prose-writer who can actually write . . . In that Gargantuan paradise of the fourth-rate there is not a single picture-gallery worth going into, or a single orchestra capable of playing the nine symphonies of Beethoven . . . In all these fields the South is an awe-inspiring blank."—H. L. Mencken, *Prejudices: Second Series (The Sahara of the Bozart)*.
8. See Vachel Lindsay's comment on "Mencken . . . the enemy with whom none of us agree" (in *Letters to A. J. Armstrong*): "A successful tour of Mencken through the South could be the beginning of a new Era for America, because it would set the pace for all the United States in free speech, the thing we abhor the most and the lack of which keeps us behind England all the time."
9. "What amused Mark [Twain] most profoundly was precisely whatever was most worthy of sober admiration—sound art, good manners, the aristocratic ideal—and he was typical of his time. The satirists of the present age, though they may be less accomplished workmen, are at all events more civilized men. What they make fun of is not what is dignified, or noble, or beautiful, but what is shoddy, and ignoble, and ugly."—Mencken, *Prejudices: Fourth Series*.
10. "The American social pusher keeps his eye on Mayfair; the American literatus dreams of recognition by the London weeklies; the American don is lifted to bliss by the imprimatur of Oxford or Cambridge; even the American statesman knows how to cringe to Downing Street."—Mencken, *Prejudices: Second Series* (1920).
11. "The fact is too obvious that the old easy domination of the 'Anglo-Saxon' is passing, that he must be up and doing if he would fasten his notions upon the generations to come . . . I am frankly against him and believe, as I have often made known, that he is doomed—that his opponents will turn out, in the long run, to be better men than he is."—Mencken, *Prejudices: Fifth Series*.
12. Stuart P. Sherman was ill-advised,—as no doubt he recognized in time,—in his invidious characterization of the "audience" of Mencken. He said this audience consisted of "children whose parents or grandparents brought their copper kettles from Russia, tilled the soil of Hungary, taught the Mosaic law in Poland, cut Irish turf, ground optical glass in Germany, dispensed Bavarian beer or fished for mackerel in the Skagerrak." But here Sherman was describing the audience of every American writer of the future, and was this not written in the stars of the American past? An "Anglo-Saxon" critic was certainly "doomed," as Mencken would have said, unless he was aware of this and all it implied, and unless he was able to present his tradition as fitting the Americans of the future instead of expecting them to fit his tradition.
13. Willard Huntington Wright, Mencken's fellow-Nietzschean, who was also pro-German in his sympathies in the first world war. This confusion of motives was evident in his *Misinforming a Nation* (1917), a critical examination of the *Encyclopædia Britannica*. Wright's ostensible motive was to combat the "intellectual colonization of America by England," the "insular judgments" and "venomous contempt" of British critics "for all things American." Written during the war, however, the book was substantially an act of war against British "bourgeois culture" and its "parochial egotism" in the fields of poetry, painting, music, philosophy, science, etc.

    Without doubt, a similar animus, unconscious perhaps, against England itself contributed to the making of Mencken's *The American Language*,—a book that one critic described as a "wedge to split asunder the two great English-speaking peoples."

## LOUIS D. RUBIN
### From "H. L. Mencken and the National Letters"

*Sewanee Review*, July–September 1966, pp. 728–34

When Mencken gets around to diagnosing the reasons for ⟨the⟩ national literary barrenness and superficiality, his prognosis is fairly close to one which a writer whom he was never able to understand had earlier put forth. Revisiting his native land in 1904, Henry James had found that its literature consisted for the most part of "a vast homegrown provision for entertainment, rapidly superseding any that may be borrowed or imported", prepared for a "public so placidly uncritical that the whitest thread of the descriptive stitch never makes it blink". Mencken echoed James's sentiments, adding some further complaints of his own. American literature, he declared, "habitually exhibits, not a man of delicate organization in revolt against the inexplicable tragedy of existence, but a man of low sensibilities and elemental desires yielding himself gladly to his environment, and so achieving what, under a third-rate civilization, passes for success. To get on: this is the aim. To weigh and reflect, to doubt and rebel: this is the thing to be avoided." What happens therefore is that the American artist who cannot swallow the American success story, whose viewpoint encompasses "the far more poignant and significant conflict between a salient individual and the harsh and meaningless fiats of destiny, the unintelligible mandates and vagaries of God", instinctively turns from American scenes and looks abroad for his models, and thus the better American writing "takes on a subtle but unmistakable air of foreignness". "The native author of any genuine force and originality," he says, "is almost invariably to be found to be under strong foreign influences, either English or Continental." This bohemianism in turn separates the writer from his culture, makes him an object of suspicion and distrust among his fellow-citizens, and creates what Mencken calls "the lonesome artist", neglected by his countrymen, attacked by the puritans in control of the national arts, and quite isolated in the American cultural wilderness.

This is a not altogether unfamiliar indictment; several years before Mencken, Van Wyck Brooks had said as much. What distinguishes Mencken from Brooks, I think, and makes him a considerably more important figure in our literary history, is his wholehearted commitment to the life of his own time. Where Brooks looked at American experience and found it deplorably distasteful, Mencken did not propose to approach it in such fashion. Here it is, he said in effect: now let our writers start dealing with it, and let our critics recognize that it exists. Brooks was, I think, every bit as idealistic and unworldly as the writers and critics he rebuked for their lack of vitality. He demanded nothing less than that our culture be changed entirely, so that we could have good writers. His famous division of American culture into Highbrow and Lowbrow wings was in essence a programmatic formulation: on the one side was effeteness, on the other vulgarity. Let us, he proposed, get rid of both, and in their place substitute the emancipated American artist—something not so different from the liberated American Scholar of Emerson.

It is hardly surprising that before too long Brooks was to be found attempting to set up a genteel tradition of his own—for the literature that came along to replace that existing when he composed *America's Coming of Age* was hardly free from either the devotion to craftsmanship he saw among the Highbrows or the acceptance of the reality of vulgarity that he detected in the Lowbrow attitudes. Brook's ideal was Emerson, and he subsequently devoted most of his life to proving that Emerson and his contemporaries were what American writers ought to be. Those who see in Brooks's later work a precipitous retreat from his earlier radicalism miss the fact that Brooks was never really sympathetic to modernism. His interests stopped at the Atlantic Ocean, and he held the line as surely as did Howells when Howells defended realism in its more smiling aspects only; Brooks was not greatly sympathetic with Joyce, Mann, Proust, Lawrence, Kafka—with, that is, many of the most vital currents of modern literary thought. He termed James an "immortal symbol"—of what he later decided was cultural treason. Calling though he did for less prudery and more bloodiness in American literature, he chose as his ideal exemplars Emerson, who defended these qualities theoretically but contained neither, and Whitman, who constantly invoked them but as spectator rather than participant.

By contrast, Mencken, though not I think as discriminating a critic as Brooks, went in for no such utopianism. He did not propose either to shore up the genteel tradition by making it less precious, or to infuse the dominant vulgarity of the day with more European spirituality. He wanted to get rid of the genteel tradition entirely, and to substitute more realistic and worldly-wise literary standards in its place. As for popular vulgarity, he entertained no hopes of ever reforming it. He wanted rather to have our writers admit its existence, as the European writers had been doing for some time. Nor was Mencken a chauvinist in literature; he read widely in the

European authors, and did not worry lest their version of reality corrupt American life. Like his favorite critic, George Huneker, his approach to the arts was aesthetic, not moralistic, and he saw the predominant moralistic approach of American literature as working to exclude much significant human experience from its spectrum. Mencken's long vendetta against puritanism in American life is well known. The reason for it is less well understood: he wanted our writers to deal with the significant phases of human experience, and any system which tabooed important aspects of that experience he considered unduly repressive. The Brooksian division of culture into Highbrow and Lowbrow, however much Mencken may have approved some of Brooks's bill of grievances, was utterly foreign to Mencken's way of viewing the matter; Mencken was an elitist all the way, in the sense that he considered literature as being properly written only for a cultural minority. The writers whom Brooks called Highbrows he considered timid souls. So-called Highbrow literature, he thought, wasn't nearly Highbrow enough; it didn't address itself to the best intelligences. As for preserving the tradition of Emerson and the classic American writers, Mencken was not very much interested. From time to time he invoked the spirit of Poe and Whitman (he rather preferred Poe), but his commitment and his allegiance were squarely with the moderns, and the past could look after itself.

Whatever one might now think of the ultimate merits of Mencken's basically anarchic position as compared with Brooks's dream of a revitalized tradition, it can hardly be disputed that Mencken's was the far more effective and useful approach for his time, so far as the immediate well-being of the serious American writer was concerned. To create an intellectual climate that would provide a hearing for a Dreiser and an O'Neill, not to speak of the host of better writers who came along after the first World War, far harder knocks were needed than Van Wyck Brooks was prepared or equipped to administer. The provincial narrowness of the American literary scene had to be expanded, and the complacent moralism that had made literature its bloodlessly virtuous handmaiden must be divested of power. Nowadays we are hardly prepared to concede that the great writers of the early twentieth century—Proust, Joyce, Eliot, Shaw, Dreiser, and so forth—are lacking in morality; Mencken's notion of good literature as being essentially amoral is not ours. But so long as morality was being conceived of exclusively in terms of the thin puritanism of the late genteel tradition, then most of what is worth reading in modern literature had perforce to seem not merely amoral but immoral, and Mencken's great virtue was that he refused to accept morality on any such impoverishing terms.

It ought to be pointed out that in one sense Mencken's adventurousness and his receptivity to modern literature was more a matter of theory than of practice; as a critic Mencken apparently possessed only a limited understanding of or sympathy with the kind of literature that he championed. Typically he was on much firmer ground while high-heartedly denouncing the second-rate moralistic writers of the dying genteel tradition than when discussing the books of the writers with whom he wanted to displace them. In poetry, for example, his tastes were quite conventional; writing about the new poetry of the 1910's, he declared that "there is no poet in the movement who had produced anything even remotely approaching the fine lyrics of Miss [Lizette Woodworth] Reese, Miss Teasdale and John McClure. . . ." With fiction he was more at home, but even there he showed no astounding critical insight; his strong praise of Dreiser is primarily for that writer's agnosticism, his lack of didacticism, his "wondering and half-terrified sort of representation of what passes understanding". Mencken's technique was essentially that of the Impressionist; he discussed the merits of works of literature by telling how he felt about them. He insisted that the act of literary criticism was an act of self-expression, and that the critic's rôle was essentially the same as the novelist's or the poet's: "the simple desire to function freely and beautifully, to give outward and objective form to ideas that bubble inwardly and have a fascinating lure in them, to get rid of them dramatically and make an articulate noise in the world."

Mencken's was not, obviously, a critical art involving fine discriminations of meaning, nor was it one of constructiveness. "I have described the disease. Let me say at once that I have no remedy to offer," he begins the concluding section of his essay on "The National Letters". And in another essay: "I cannot recall a case in which any suggestion offered by a constructive critic has helped me in the slightest, or even actively interested me. . . . constructive criticism irritates me. I do not object to being denounced, but I can't abide being schoolmastered, especially by men I regard as imbeciles." It has always seemed to me that Mencken's gradual retirement from the field of literary criticism during the 1920's, and his increasing involvement in social and political rather than literary commentary, is due primarily to the fact that Mencken was indeed not a so-called "constructive" critic, but an artist in destruction. In the 1900's and 1910's such a rôle suited his talents and the national need exactly; by the 1920's, however, the ruins of the genteel tradition had pretty much been cleared away, and the task that confronted the intelligent critic was no longer one of destruction so much as of discriminating recognition and evaluation. That was not Mencken's forte, and apparently he had the good sense to realize it; he was not vitally interested in evaulating Hemingway, Fitzgerald, Dos Passos, Eliot, Joyce, Proust, Mann, Kafka, and the other major writers who came into prominence after the first World War. This was a task for a man such as Edmund Wilson, who proceeded to perform it wonderfully well. In *Axel's Castle, The Triple Thinkers,* and *The Wound and the Bow,* as well as in his numerous magazine reviews, Wilson took on the job of training the reading public to read the literature of the day intelligently. One cannot imagine Mencken performing such a function.

Prejudiced as most of us are in favor of the builder rather than the destroyer, we sometimes tend therefore to undervalue Mencken's contribution. The party line on Mencken today appears to run something like this: He was an amusing but not very discerning champion of Dreiser and belaborer of puritans, whose work is interesting historically because he had considerable influence as a popular iconoclast during the 1920's, but has long since become very "dated", so that any lasting importance he possesses probably rests with his pioneering work in the American language—as (I echo one American literature professor's wording) "Baltimore's amateur philologist".

Such a verdict strikes me as being largely nonsense. No doubt *The American Language* and its several *Supplements* are important work for etymologists and other students of language lore and usage, but to say that H. L. Mencken's principal importance today must rest on his contributions to that highly specialized and peripheral branch of literary endeavor is to damn an exceedingly good writer with very faint praise. One frequently reads that Mencken's writing is "dated". Some of it without doubt is: much of his political journalism, for example, and book reviews of now-forgotten novels and studies. But Mencken at his best is no more "dated" than Boswell's *Life of Johnson* is dated. One need not, for example, know precisely who and what the late Nicholas Murray Butler was to savor Mencken's remark that "the president of Columbia, Nicholas Murray Butler, is a realist. Moreover, he is a member of the American Academy himself, elected as a wet to succeed Edgar Allan Poe." To be sure, the humor depends in part upon one's recognition of the term "wet" as Mencken used it, but even the most casual student of the 1920's would know that, and there seems little likelihood that future generations will lose interest in the folklore of the Jazz Age. Mencken's humor is no more spoiled by the presence within his prose of such references than the humor of Boswell's description of Samuel Johnson dining with John Wilkes is spoiled because the issues that divided Whig and Tory in the 1760's are no longer of general knowledge. What has happened to Mencken in that respect is that some of his wit is no longer available to a mass audience—something which is equally true of many of our best writers, and is hardly a disqualification of much importance. Is Samuel Pepys dated?

# WILLIAM MEREDITH

## 1919–

William Meredith was born in New York on January 9, 1919. Raised in Darien, Connecticut, he attended the Lenox School in Massachusetts. After graduating with a B.A. from Princeton in 1940, Meredith joined the *New York Times,* working as a copyboy and later as a reporter. In 1941 he enlisted in the armed forces and served as a pilot in the Pacific until 1946. He taught at Princeton and the University of Hawaii before returning to active duty in 1952 to fight in the Korean War. In 1955 he joined the English faculty at Connecticut College, where he taught until his retirement in 1984.

Meredith's career as a poet began in 1944 with the publication of *Love Letter from an Impossible Land* in the Yale Series of Younger Poets. Much of his early poetry draws upon his war experience as a navy pilot. A relatively slow writer, Meredith has published six volumes of poetry since 1944. Most notable are his two most recent books, *Hazard, the Painter* (1975) and *The Cheer* (1980). He has also published critical works on Shelley and translations of Apollinaire. During the 1950s he wrote an opera libretto; he now serves as vice-president of the American Choral Society.

From 1979 to 1980 he was the Consultant in Poetry to the Library of Congress and since 1964 he has been the chancellor of the Academy of American Poets. His many awards include the Harriet Monroe Memorial Prize in 1944, the Van Wyck Brooks Award in 1971, and the 1979 International Vaptsarov Prize in Sofia, Bulgaria. In 1984 he was awarded a $25,000 grant by the National Endowment for the Arts for his continuing contributions to American literature. Never married, he makes his home in Connecticut.

Believing in the marvelous mystery of the associative power of words, he emphasizes the necessity of being in a state of "unselfcentered attention" for that power to work. For him, he confesses: "This is apparently a rare state . . . because in the twenty-five years since the writing of ['A View of the Brookyn Bridge'] I have averaged about six poems a year." The choice of language, if an act requiring the suspension of the self can be called a choice, involves a readiness to receive, a social if not a convivial condition. And the form of a poem as well as its words must discover itself to him: "To this day I feel surer that I'm communicating with the poem if a prosodic pattern declares itself." In support of this way of working, he quotes Thom Gunn in a letter written in 1970: "The openness of the experience is brought into relation with the structures of the mind."

By ordering a poem's discovery according to the meditative process, "a structure of the mind" fruitful in its placing of an individual in a closer relationship to himself, to others, and to a world, elusive in its revelations of meaning, William Meredith has created a body of work remarkable not only for its craftsmanship but for its individuality of voice. I am not suggesting, of course, that Meredith consciously followed the practitioners of the art of meditation or those seventeenth-century poets whose work sprang from that habit of mind—though "influence hunters" might gleefully point to Meredith's poem "Airman's Virtue," an imitation of Herbert's "Virtue" (see Wendell Berry's "The Specialization of Poetry," in Reginald Gibbons, ed., *The Poet's Work*.) But I do suggest that this structure is especially effective in a poem that addresses a private secret in the light of its public significance. "Not yet a man given to prayer," as the poet describes himself in "The Open Sea," he is nonetheless a man of religious sensibility in his abiding need to make order out of mystery and to render himself responsible for the ordering act. The wary attentiveness of this approach to himself, to circumstances, and to his art, combined with a gracious awareness of his audience, compelled the emergence of a distinctive voice from some of the earliest poems, a feat Archibald MacLeish notes admiringly in his Foreword to *Love Letter from an Impossible Land* as "the way in which the literary vehicle (for it is nothing else) of the Princeton undergraduate turns into the live idiom of a poet's speech reaching for poetry."

In William Meredith's poetry there is an identifiable character, alive and informing, not that absence characteristic of the poet who speaks only of and to himself, who in Wendell Berry's words "can only describe the boundaries of an imprisoning and damning selfhood." The language of the tribe is more than "the vulgar energy of speech." It is the necessary means for the resolution of the tensions of a shared perplexity.—NEVA HERRINGTON, "The Language of the Tribe: William Meredith's Poetry," *SWR*, Winter 1982, pp. 16–17

*Interviewer:* Your poems tend to have a sly, angular way of going at a subject, approaching it from the side rather than directly. Would you say something about that?

*Meredith:* If it's so, it's the nature of the work that a poem is getting at something mysterious, which no amount of staring at straight-on has ever solved, something like death or love or treachery or beauty. And we keep doing this corner-of-the-eye thing. I remember when we were in training to be night fliers in the Navy, I learned, very strangely, that the rods of the eye perceive things at night in the corner of the eye that we can't see straight ahead. That's not a bad metaphor for the vision of art. You don't stare at the mystery, but you *can* see things out of the corner of your eye that you were supposed to see.

*Interviewer:* Do you think that writing a poem is a specific engagement of a mystery?

*Meredith:* I would say exactly that. It is the engagement of a mystery which has forced itself to the point where you feel honor-bound to see this mystery with the brilliance of a vision. Not to solve it, but to see it.

*Interviewer:* Does this relate to the statement in your poem "In Memory of Robert Frost," that Frost insisted on paying attention "until you at least told him an interesting lie."

*Meredith:* Well, he understood—and I'm afraid his biographer, Lawrence Thompson, does not understand—that at the higher reaches of our experience we don't know the things that we say, but we say that we do. That's the ultimate artistic lie. I tell you what I know today in a poem and I don't know it; in the first place it may not be true, and in the second place it may not be what I know tomorrow. Artistic truth is to declare, under torture, what the torturer does not want you to say, not what the torturer does want you to say. You try to tell the truth even though it's uncomfortable for everybody. When the hippies were talking about how the only two things you need to know about life is that you must love one another and not lie, they forgot to tell you that those are the only two really difficult things. We all know that's what we're supposed to do; it's much harder to love people than anybody ever tells you and it's much harder to tell the truth. Poets are professionally committed to telling the truth, and *how* do they tell the truth? They say something that isn't true. This is the slyness of art: if you tell enough lies, you're bound to say something true. I think my work is only as good as it is honest but as a data bank it's full of errors. ⟨. . .⟩

*Interviewer:* Although much of your work is concerned with moral purposes, it does not strike one as being blatantly religious. In fact, the speaker in most of your poems seems to offer the consolation of a well-honed agnosticism. But in a recent poem, "Partial Accounts," you write, "Growing older, I have tottered into the lists/ the religious, tilt." Is this incontrovertible evidence of a conversion?

*Meredith:* No, I would simply say I came out of the closet. My belief is a little clearer to me now and I feel that I ought not to hide it. You know that the best Christian writers don't talk about it as though they were trying to sell you a product. I think of Gerard Manley Hopkins. All the good criticism of Hopkins is written by agnostic Jews and brainwashed nuns who understand that the poetry is true and the truth is what will prevail as a religious example. I say that I'm careful not to practive Christianity conspicuously. But I want to pay attention through the medium of religion. I'm going to give a talk in chapel this month and my theme is going to be that the greatest imaginative accomplishment of the human imagination is atheism. It's the only thing that man has thought up creatively without the help of God. It's a short course but it's a very interesting one. It's sort of like concrete poetry; after you've gotten to the bottom of atheism, you don't have very much left. It's an experiment that has run its course. It is my feeling that all the other works of the imagination are derivatives of the creative imagination of a creator. I don't believe in being very doctrinaire and when I'm among the humanists in Bulgaria, what I say is "Indeed man isn't all the work of God. Indeed there is no reason that he need refer to God." But that's where I see it coming from.

*Interviewer:* Is it accurate to say that in recent years your work exhibits a greater willingness to speak to public subjects?

*Meredith:* I hope so. I think this had partly to do with my having to think of myself as a public servant again after twenty-five years of not being in public service. I considered myself a public servant when I was in the Navy. Afterwards, I wondered what a public servant does in the role of a poet. When I went to Washington as the poet to the Library of Congress I had a chance to see what could be done with a large audience. Thinking about what happened at the Library of Congress, the chain of artists that one follows there, you see that Americans do have some slight sense of the public function of the poet. It's nice that the Library of Congress has that. It's the branch of Congress that has literary opinions.

*Interviewer:* In poems like "Politics" and "Nixon's the One" (from *Hazard, The Painter*) and "On Jenkins' Hill" and "A Mild-Spoken Citizen Finally Writes to the White House" (from *The Cheer*), you develop an unusual civic stance for a contemporary poet, a kind of "poet as concerned citizen" approach to the political scene. Does that characterization seem accurate to you? And does this attitude signify a new kind of openness or political engagement in your work?

*Meredith:* I believe that it represents an openness that I've always felt and acted on but never found much way, before this, to talk about in poetry. The lyric poem is so often private. For example, my intention in writing "The Wreck of the Thresher" was to write a "public" poem about my feeling of disappointment in the hopes of the United Nations. When I was writing that poem (and I kept all the drafts of it because I wrote it as a sort of dialogue with my friend Charles Shane, who was here that summer without his wife, being the President of the College; I would leave the draft off for him in the morning and he would scribble notes on it and send it back), I remember seeing it change from a rather pretentious public statement to the very private statement it turned out to be. It occurred to me that this is simply a demonstration of what Auden said in *The Dyer's Hand*, that we don't trust a public voice in poetry today. I would say that my concern about politics is precisely the concern of a Joan Didion or a Denise Levertov but that my stance is very different, so it doesn't appear to be the same. There is a spectrum of political opinion and a spectrum of political involvement. I stand with regard to involvement where those two women stand, but in the political spectrum I'm much more Jeffersonian—I'm nearer the middle.

*Interviewer:* Your friend, the poet Muriel Rukeyser, had a great sense of the poet's social responsibility.

*Meredith:* Yes. I was never as clear about that as she is. I suppose I'm halfway between Muriel Rukeyser, whose every breath was socially responsible, and James Merrill, who pretends not to read the newspapers. Somewhere in the middle is where most artists belong. I sign a lot of things, I send a lot of funny dollars off. Every four years I have a kind of knee-jerk political life. But I can't compare myself to Muriel in that, except insofar as I pay attention to the things that need to be

done in the world. One doesn't miss Vietnam and El Salvador.—WILLIAM MEREDITH, Interview by Edward Hirsch, *PRev*, Spring 1985, pp. 40–41

## RICHARD M. LUDWIG
### "The Muted Lyrics of William Meredith"
*Princeton University Library Chronicle*, Autumn 1963, pp. 73–79

In his third and most recent volume of verse, William Meredith devotes a deft villanelle called "Trees in a Grove" to "five things put in mind by sycamores." First, he thinks of "a sad bald-headed man / In a pepper-and-salt tweed suit who knew the trees." In the second verse, he recalls

> I was seven the summer that I first got hold
> Of the white pied spicy word of sycamore,
> The age when children will incant new names.
> That night I dreamt I was a flying man
> And could escape the backyard of our suburb
> By saying sycamore, rise through the trees.

It may be pushing the dream too far to say that Meredith has turned it into reality, but to anyone reading his collected poems, particularly in chronological order, the thought may well occur. For it is clear that the war years spent as a Navy pilot left him with images and memories that have helped him escape his suburb and have permeated his poetry for almost two decades: the open sea, the authority of clouds, starlight, the sky as only a pilot can know it, the Aleutians, the carrier, the battlewagon, and the ubiquitous trees.

Meredith called his first collection of verse *Love Letter from an Impossible Land*. The last ten poems of this 1944 volume are quite naturally war poems. But unlike the war poetry of Randall Jarrell and Karl Shapiro—or even John Ciardi, who shared some of Meredith's reactions to flying—these are seldom bitter with the injustice of war. The familiar G. I. faces are not here, nor is the language harsh, not even colloquial. Instead Meredith observes from above, as it were, or as we would expect of a pilot. His poems are landscapes, of the mind as well as of the Aleutians, and as landscapes they turn on the visual image, outward to the "unsettled mountains" of this impossible land, to "streams of snow dancing in the moon at the summits" and "the wind creaking like a green floe," inward to the mind of the airman-poet, "rootless and needing a quick home." Like the young boy of seven, the airman still marvels at the power of flight. But the pleasures now are ambiguous as he flies "just above the always-griping sea / That bitches at the bitter rock the mountains throw to it." The remoteness of these islands, their solemn beauty, their "chill and stillness" have dampened his spirits, and yet he can acknowledge "they shake and change and finally enchant." Nowhere does their presence register so deeply as in the opening lines of his poem on a naval base in the Aleutians, "June: Dutch Harbor":

> In June, which is still June here, but once removed
> From other Junes, chill beardless high-voiced cousin
>     season,
> The turf slides grow to an emerald green.
> There between the white-and-black of the snow and
>     ash,
> Between the weak blue of the rare sky
> Or the milkwhite languid gestures of the fog,
> And the all-the-time wicked terminal sea,
> There, there, like patches of green neon,
> See it is June with the turf slides.

I have lingered over these early poems not to suggest that they are the best of his work, although "Love Letter" and

"Notes for an Elegy" belong in a collected Meredith, but to note that the stance he took as early as 1944 has proven to be right and natural for a man of his talents. These talents have been praised by fellow poets for many years. May Swenson felt that "he can occupy the sonnet so subtly that we hardly notice its familiar outline." James Merrill applauded the "intimate and urbane" tone in "poems that are elevated without arrogance or sacrifice to the sound of speech and delicate without fussiness." George Garrett admired the way in which Meredith joined toughness with the formal grace of the lyric. Dudley Fitts praised his "percipient force, [his] technical skill." What all these critics agree on is Meredith's absolute control of form, his confidence in his own taste, his wisdom in never pushing his talents to make poems out of *objets trouvés* or to generate false enthusiasms. In a dedicatory poem to an early mentor, Donald A. Stauffer, Meredith speaks of this scholar-critic's "indiscriminate delight / There in the sweet and obvious side of right." If I read him clearly (and I shall be the first to admit this poem's ambiguities could easily boomerang), Meredith himself is content to be on "the sweet and obvious side of right." From "Love Letter" to his most recently published poem, "Five Accounts of a Monogamous Man" (*Virginia Quarterley Review*, Summer, 1963), he has refused to shout, to strain, to experiment. The confines of traditional language and form are for him not obstacle but challenge. He attacks the beatnik poets who never learned discipline: "I read an impatient man / Who howls against his time, / Not angry enough to scan / Not fond enough to rhyme." He chides Léonie Adams because "she stuffs a poem full of special words, the way one does an orange encrusted with cloves." He praises Dan Hoffman for his "lucidity, which amounts to a careful and successful attention to the poem's rational exposition, . . . achieved at no expense to the intellectual or imaginative force. The diction and imagery are strong, oblique, and individual, but do not occasion any of the obscurity which we have come to allow as concomitant to those virtues." To insure himself against obscurity, he appends notes to both *Ships and Other Figures* (1948) and *The Open Sea* (1958), his second and third volumes, saying "I feel [these few notes] are valid in alleviating one quite unnecessary kind of obscurity, the kind that arises from a mere lack of special information." Meredith will be understood. In reviewing Elizabeth Drew's study of T. S. Eliot, he made his position clear: "The large body of criticism and explication which these poems have required and annexed to themselves tells against them as usable poems. In requiring such paraphernalia, Eliot's work is unlike both good art and good myth." Little wonder that his special heroes are Yeats, particularly the mature Yeats, Stephen Vincent Benét, and Robert Frost. A recent narrative poem, "Roots" (*Poetry*, January, 1962), shows clearly what he has learned from the New England poet. It has taken Meredith many years to come to this easy, colloquial diction within the pentameter line, the witty juxtaposition, the interior monologue. Needless to say, it is not typical of his work of the last decade. "Roots" and "Five Accounts of a Monogamous Man" may indicate new departures. It is too early to tell.

There are risks involved in this "calm style," as the young poet Thom Gunn warned him in a review of *The Open Sea*: "A poem should not be an exercise in small-talk that happens to scan: there is need for the calmest poet to be fiercely committed to his subject." Meredith is scholar enough to have taken this warning from Housman or Hardy or E. A. Robinson. In fact he imbeds this awareness obliquely in "An Account of a Visit to Hawaii."

> Mildness can enervate as well as heat.
> The soul must labor to reach paradise.
> Many are here detained in partial grace
> Or partial penalty, for want of force.

But force and fierceness are not synonymous. When Frost tells us that "strongly spent is synonymous with kept, "he is speaking not of fierceness but of "the way the will has to pitch into commitments deeper and deeper to a rounded conclusion." Meredith knows the commitments he must make to reach paradise or the rounded conclusion; and there is very little small talk along the way. When his poetry limps it is not for lack of force. Calm it may be, even mild, but it is never pallid. Reading in *The Open Sea* such poems as "Miniature" or "Starlight," "The Fear of Beasts" or "Falling Asleep by Firelight," or the lovely villanelle, "Notre Dame de Chartres," we encounter a deceptively easy surface. A re-reading reveals a poem that I can only call distilled. I do not mean rarefied. Detached, perhaps, the poetry "of a man who has put himself outside his subject so that he can comment on it calmly," as Thom Gunn suggests. But Meredith's particular achievement seems to me to lie in this very province. "There is no end to the / Deception of quiet things / And of quiet, everyday / People a lifetime brings," he writes in "The Chinese Banyan." His three volumes of verse are devoted to showing us "the deception of quiet things."

His subjects do not range widely, but they are deeply felt and keenly observed: a fish-vendor, a dead friend, godchildren, a bachelor awakening at morning, a Korean woman seated by a wall, crows at sunrise. His people are seldom named. Like the painter, he sees them posed, or at least caught at a moment in their lives, not involved in dramatic action. And he generally uses them as catalysts to contemplation, as he does the more common trees, sea, sky, firelight. His feeling for still-life may explain his enthusiasm for opera and the Kabuki-za Theater. He prefers people in ritual, stylized, static. The bachelor "takes a long view of toes in the bath-tub / And shaves a man whose destiny is mild." The fish-vendor's "feet shift in the brine / The thick fish threshing without resignation" while he sells his carp to "wives / With boiling dishes in their eyes." The Korean woman by the wall utters no sound. "Suffering has settled like a sly disguise / On her cheerful old face" and she "shifts the crate she sits on as the March / Wind mounts from the sea." A Korean couple, "the old woman and the old man / Who came a day's journey to see the airfield," are equally mute as they "Slide down the embankment of rubble / Like frisky children." Crows at sunrise are not in flight, not flecked with sun's gold, but are "badly adjusted; at sunrise these crows, / Neither attracted nor repelled, were vaguely cawing." At the Kabuki-za,

> This lady wobbles down the flowerway
> To show: one, she is leisurely and gay,
> And two, the play of all that gold brocade
> Over the human form (there is a maid
> To hold the weight up of her two gold sleeves),
> And three, what no one really quite believes
> Anymore, that she is a puppet anyway.

"Rus in Urbe" begins with a static image:

> In a city garden an espaliered tree
> Like Shiva, handling the brick south wall,
> Or better, like a Jesse Tree, holds big
> Real pears on each contrived square bough.

Even a convoy, in "Battle Problem," is seen as still-life:

> A company of vessels on the sea
> Running in darkness, like a company
> Of stars or touchless martyrs in the fields

> Above, or a wan school beneath its keels,
> Holds a discrete deployment.

If this urbanity is not to every reader's taste, Meredith would be the last to object. He has long ago taken sides in the split between "cooked" and "raw" verse, as Robert Lowell called it, or the poets of "the ivory tower" and the poets of "the streets," as Lawrence Ferlinghetti distinguished them. Espaliered verse, he might argue, can also bear real fruit. What is taken for catholicity in the formalist poet (detractors will point to the "contrived square bough") might only be concealing, at its worst, a fear of emotional explosions, at its best a devotion to what Coleridge called the architectonic faculty: the right details subtly organized into a coherent whole. Meredith will always sacrifice the flux of images and memories to their tight, even austere, control. If he seldom gives way to the dazzling moment (or at least seldom in his reader's presence), he develops his own kind of panache in graceful precision, immaculate diction, idea wedded exactly to form. "Rus in Urbe," we might call it, taking his own lines for elucidation:

> And in a tub, a yew turned like a top,
> Which might as easily have been a peacock
> Or half of a deer, in the unnatural kingdom
> Of topiary, where the will is done,
> Is lovely to the point you would not ask
> What would have been its genius, uncut?

All of which leaves the critic with little to do, except to register his approval or dissent. If it is the uncut yew he wants, Meredith assures him he will not find it in his muted lyrics. He has, in fact, anticipated his critics in the most beautiful sonnet he has published. He calls it "Sonnet on Rare Animals."

> Like a deer rat-tat before we reach the clearing
> I frighten what I brought you out to see,
> Telling you who are tired by now of hearing
> How there are five, how they take no fright of me.
> I tried to point out fins inside the reef
> Where the coral reef had turned the water dark;
> The bathers kept the beach in half-belief
> But would not swim and could not see the shark.
> I have alarmed on your behalf and others'
> Sauntering things galore.
> It is this way with verse and animals
> And love, that when you point you lose them all.
> Startled or on a signal, what is rare
> Is off before you have it anywhere.

Any poet who can write this well need listen only to his own voice. He knows without the help of critics what he can and cannot do. He has found his métier.

## HENRY TAYLOR

### From "In Charge of Morale in a Morbid Time: The Poetry of William Meredith"

*Hollins Critic*, February 1979, pp. 11–15

In 1970, Meredith published *Earth Walks: New and Selected Poems*. I have already suggested that he was too stingy in making his selections from the four previous books, though he makes a handsome apology for this in a foreword: "In making this selection from twenty-five years of work I have represented my early books scantily, as I have come to feel they represented me. Juvenile gifts apart, it takes time to find our real natures and purposes. But finally we have done so many things, good and bad, in character, that it is permissible to disown some of our other acts, at any rate the bad ones, as impersonations." He makes it clear in the next sentence, part of which is quoted earlier, that he is talking primarily about his

first two books, and it is hard to quarrel much with his selection from those. But the slimness of the selection as a whole should have the effect, intended or not, of sending the reader back to the early work, especially to *The Open Sea*, where among the thirty-three "disowned" poems there are several that reward continued attention.

But one turns with greatest interest, of course, to the fourteen new poems in *Earth Walk*, and one is struck first by the interesting variety of points of view. Poems spoken by fictional characters are not plentiful in Meredith's work, though on some occasions, as in "Five Accounts of a Monogamous Man," he has adopted, as Yeats often did, the device of applying third-person titles to first-person poems. *Earth Walk* opens with such a poem, "Winter Verse for His Sister," the speaker of which is not readily distinguishable from Meredith himself. Then in "Walter Jenks' Bath" the speaker is a young black boy thinking over what his teacher has said about the way atoms compose everything. The tension between the speaker's sophistication and that of the poet is first of all useful in setting the tone of the poem, the touching simplicity of the observations; but in the last six lines, what Walter Jenks says becomes larger in its grasp of things, so that in the final line, he seems to speak for the poet as well as for himself:

> And when I stop the atoms go on knocking,
> Even if I died the parts would go on spinning,
> Alone, like the far stars, not knowing it,
> Not knowing they are far apart, or running,
> Or minding the black distances between.
> This is me knowing, this is what I know.

That a child in the bathtub comes plausibly to thoughts like these is a tribute to the delicacy with which the tone is handled; the same delicacy sustains a rougher poem, "Effort at Speech," in which the speaker relates an encounter with a mugger. The speaker and the mugger wrestle briefly, the wallet parts "like a wishbone," the mugger flees with his ill-gotten half, and the speaker comes close to guilt at having retained the other half:

> *Next time don't wrangle, give the boy the money,*
> *Call across chasms what the world you know is.*
> *Luckless and lied to, how can a child master*
> > *human decorum?*
> *Next time a switch-blade, somewhere he is thinking,*
> *I should have killed him and took the lousy wallet.*
> Reading my cards he feels a surge of anger
> > blind as my shame.

The strength of the poet's control over these lines is felt in the prosody; this narrative of violence and guilt is cast in stanzas which come as close to Sapphics as idiomatic English can come. The classical echo puts a distance between the poet and the events described, but it also recalls the actual effort that real speech requires.

Colloquial language, contractions, and exclamations fall into regular stanzas in "Poem about Morning," a funny little lecture on waking up and facing the day. The suggestion of lecturing is made by casting the poem in the second person, though the "you" partakes of the speaker's experience, almost as if the speaker were addressing himself. And "Earth Walk" provides a final illustration of the experimentation with point of view which runs like a thread through these new poems. The title poem takes off from the phrase "moon walk," of course; it begins in the third person, as a man pulls off the highway and touches his seat belt. After the phrase "He thinks," the first stanza continues in the first person plural, as it describes our habit of travelling in straps and helmets. The second stanza is in the first person singular, but despite the stanza break, it all still follows from "He thinks." The man steps out of his car, parodying the careful steps of the men on the moon:

> I pick out small white stones. This is a safe walk.
> This turnpike is uninhabited. When I come back
> I'll meet a trooper with a soft, wide hat
> who will take away my Earth-rocks and debrief me.

The shift from third to first person, while it is perfectly within the bounds of narrative logic, still gives the poem a scope of observation that a single point of view might lack.

These new poems, with their restless personal pronouns, may now be seen as forerunners of Meredith's most recent book, *Hazard, the Painter* (1975). This collection of sixteen poems, seems to have been designed to provoke a number of reactions, not all of them charitable, and not all of them familiar to readers of Meredith's previous books. One notices pure surface: this is the most meticulous and beautiful job of book production which Knopf has so far given Meredith; the cover and typography seem to assert that the book amounts to more than its small bulk might suggest. Inside, there are poems comprising a "characterization," as Meredith calls it in a cagey note; he adds, "Resemblances between the life and character of Hazard and those of the author are not disclaimed but are much fewer than the author would like."

It comes to mind that in the work of William Meredith and John Berryman there are several references to their friendship; furthermore, as Meredith has acknowledged in public readings, a line in the first of the Hazard poems is taken from Berryman's conversation. The uncharitable speculation arises that Hazard is too closely akin to Berryman's Henry, in strategy if not in size and style. Clearly, though, Meredith cannot have conceived this book in any competitive way, as Lowell seems to have conceived his *Notebooks*; the very brevity of *Hazard* indicates that it is not useful to compare it with *The Dream Songs*, even though that book continues to loom as a distant forebear.

Hazard is a middle-aged painter with a wife and two children. For two years his subject has been a parachutist, but he is at the moment stalled in his work; various pressures— family, uneasy friendships with other painters, daydreams— take up more of his time than painting does. He has a fine eye for detail, and a wry sense of the absurd; lying at the beach, where "they use the clouds over & over / again, like the rented animals in *Aida*," Hazard nearly dozes as things impinge on his consciousness without order, making equal claims on his curiosity:

> The sand knocks like glass, struck by bare heels.
> He tries to remember snow noise.

> Would powder snow ping like that?
> But you don't lie with your ear to powder snow.
> Why doesn't the girl who takes care
> of the children, a Yale girl without flaw,
> know the difference between *lay* and *lie*?

The style of *Hazard* appears to be more casual, less concentrated, than anything Meredith has written before. One notices, for instance, that there is not a semicolon anywhere in these poems; instead, the independent clauses tumble along over their commas, contributing to the feeling of interior life, as in the second half of this stanza from "Politics," a poem about old liberals gathering to hear jazz for McGovern:

> Hazard desires his wife, the way people
> on the trains to the death-camps were seized
> by irrational lust. She is the youngest woman
> in the room, he would like to be in bed
> with her now, he would like to be president.

Gradually, as one rereads these poems, the accumulation of anecdote and detail provides the density that is missing from the style, and there arises the illusion of a life, a way of life, made difficult by a difficult time, but still enjoyable and cherished. "The culture is in late imperial decline," Hazard thinks in the line taken from Berryman; and in "Hazard's Optimism," considering his vision of the parachutist as he himself tries a parachute jump, Hazard concludes thus:

> They must have caught and spanked him
> like this when he first fell.
> He passes it along now, Hazard's vision.
> He is in charge of morale in a morbid time.
> He calls out to the sky, his voice
> the voice of an animal that makes not words
> but a happy incorrigible noise, not
> of this time.

The mask of Hazard gives Meredith, at least for the duration of this deceptively brief book, the freedom to work out of ways in which he might think he was becoming set. In the chattiness that contains more than it at first seems to, beneath the detailed surfaces, there is room here for satire as well as for a serious, loving exploration of a peculiar world.

But Hazard is not destined to take over Meredith's voice and life. He is an interesting character met along the way, and, having met him, Meredith is usefully diverted from his way. There are too few uncollected poems on which to base conclusions about apparent directions to come, except to note that in some recent "dialogue poems" responding to wittily chosen epigraphs, Meredith continues to find fresh ways of reminding us that there is joy in plucking at the hems of even the darkest mysteries.

# ADDITIONAL READING

### CHESTER HIMES

Boucher, Anthony. "Criminals at Large." *New York Times Book Review*, 7 February 1965, p. 43.

Fabre, Michael. "A Case of Rape." *Black World* 21 (March 1972): 39–48.

Himes, Chester. *The Quality of Hurt: The Autobiography of Chester Himes.* Volume I. Garden City, NY: Doubleday, 1973.

Lundquist, James. *Chester Himes.* New York: Ungar, 1976.

Nelson, Raymond. "Domestic Harlem: The Detective Fiction of Chester Himes." *Virginia Quarterly Review* 48 (1972): 260–76.

### DANIEL HOFFMAN

Aaron, Daniel. "Seven in One." *Commentary* 53 (May 1972): 98–101.

Cutler, Bruce. "A Long Reach, Strong Speech." *Poetry* 103 (1963–64): 387–93.

Dietrichson, Jan W. "The Criticism of Daniel Hoffman." *Edda* 74 (1974): 319–37.

Dorson, Richard M. "A Great Folk Hero, Perhaps." *Yale Review* 42 (1952–53): 298–99.

Levin, Harry. Review of *Poe Poe Poe Poe Poe Poe Poe.* *American Literature* 44 (1972): 488–89.

Meyer, Gerard Previn. "Nature's Various Vitality." *Saturday Review*, 9 October 1954, pp. 18–19.

Shaw, Robert B. "Poets in Midstream." *Poetry* 118 (1971): 231–32.

### JOHN HOLLANDER

Bloom, Harold. "Commentary." In *The Head of the Bed.* Boston: Godine, 1972, pp. 21–32.

Borroff, Marie. *Yale Review* 61 (1972): 90–93.

Howard, Richard. *Alone with America.* New York: Atheneum, 1969, pp. 200–231.

Lattimore, Richmond. *Hudson Review* 32 (1979): 443–44.

Martz, Louis L. *Yale Review* 65 (1976): 118–22.

### RICHARD HOWARD

Kalstone, David. "Untitled Subjects." *New York Times Book Review*, 14 April 1970, pp. 4, 22.

Martin, Robert K. "The Unconsummated Word." *Parnassus: Poetry in Review* 4 (1975): 109–15.

Ricks, Christopher. *New York Times Book Review*, 23 February 1975, p. 7.

Shaw, Robert B. "The Long and the Short of It." *Poetry* 119 (1972): 352–53.

Sloss, Henry. "'Clearing and Burning': An Essay on Richard Howard's Poetry." *Shenandoah* 28 (1977): 85–103.

### LANGSTON HUGHES

Bontemps, Arna. *Saturday Review*, 22 March 1947, pp. 12–13, 44.

Davis, Arthur P. "The Harlem of Langston Hughes' Poetry." *Phylon* 13 (1952): 276–83.

Dickinson, Donald C. *A Bio-Bibliography of Langston Hughes, 1902–1967.* Hamden, CT: Shoe String Press, 1967.

Emanuel, James A. *Langston Hughes.* New York: Twayne, 1967.

Meltzer, Milton. *Langston Hughes: A Biography.* New York: Crowell, 1968.

O'Daniel, Therman B., ed. *Langston Hughes: Black Genius.* New York: Morrow, 1971.

Wagner, Jean. *Black Poets of the United States.* Tr. Kenneth Douglas. Urbana: University of Illinois Press, 1973.

Waldron, Edward E. "The Blues Poetry of Langston Hughes." *Negro American Literature Forum* 5 (1971): 140–49.

### ZORA NEALE HURSTON

Bone, Robert. "Three Versions of Pastoral." In *Down Home: A History of Afro-American Short Fiction from Its Beginnings to the End of the Harlem Renaissance.* New York: Putnam, 1975, pp. 130–70.

Brown, Lloyd W. "Zora Neale Hurston and the Nature of Female Perception." *Obsidian* 4 (Winter 1978): 39–45.

Giles, James R. "The Significance of Time in Zora Neale Hurston's *Their Eyes Were Watching God.*" *Negro American Literature Forum* 6 (1972): 52–56.

Hemenway, Robert. *Zora Neale Hurston: A Literary Biography.* Urbana: University of Illinois Press, 1977.

Howard, Lillie P. *Zora Neale Hurston.* Boston: Twayne, 1980.

Hurst, Fannie. "Zora Hurston: A Personality Sketch." *Yale University Library Gazette* 35 (1961): 18.

Love, Theresa R. "Zora Neale Hurston's America." *Papers on Language and Literature* 12 (1976): 422–37.

Sherman, Beatrice. "Zora Hurston's Story." *New York Times Book Review*, 29 November 1942, p. 44.

Wall, Cheryl A. "Zora Neale Hurston: Changing Her Own Words." In *American Novelists Revisited: Essays in Feminist Criticism*, ed. Fritz Fleischmann. Boston: G. K. Hall, 1982, pp. 371–93.

Wallace, Margaret. "Real Negro People." *New York Times Book Review*, 6 May 1934, pp. 6–7.

### DAVID IGNATOW

Contoski, Victor. "Time and Money: The Poetry of David Ignatow." *University Review* 34 (1968): 211–13.

Martz, Louis. "Recent Poetry: Established Idiom." *Yale Review* 59 (1970): 551–53.

Mills, Ralph J. "Earth Hard: The Poetry of David Ignatow." *Boundary 2* (1974): 373–429.

———. "Introduction" to *The Notebooks of David Ignatow.* Chicago: Swallow Press, 1973.

Swados, Harvey. "David Ignatow: The Meshuganeh Lover." *American Poetry Review* 2 (1973): 35–36.

*Tennessee Poetry Journal* 3 (1970). Special David Ignatow issue.

Wakoski, Diane. "Working Poet." *New York Review of Books*, 30 December 1971, p. 26.

### WILLIAM INGE

Balch, Jack. "Anatomy of a Failure." *Theatre Arts* 44 (February 1960): 10–11.

Burgess, Charles E. "An American Experience: William Inge in St. Louis 1943–1949." *Papers on Language and Literature* 12 (1976): 438–68.

Dusenbery, Winifred L. "Personal Failure." In *The Theme of Loneliness in Modern American Drama.* Gainesville: University of Florida Press, 1960, pp. 8–17.

Gassner, John. "Low Men on a Totem Pole: William Inge and the Subtragic Muse." In *Theatre at the Crossroads.* New York: Holt, Rinehart & Winston, 1960, pp. 167–73.

Gibbs, Wolcott. "The Dream and the Dog." *New Yorker*, 25 February 1950, pp. 68–70.

———. "Inge, Ibsen, and Some Bright Children." *New Yorker*, 12 March 1955, pp. 62–68.

Shuman, R. Baird. *William Inge*. New York: Twayne, 1965.

### JOHN IRVING

Atlas, James. "John Irving's World." *New York Times Book Review*, 13 September 1981, pp. 1, 36–38.

Epstein, Joseph. "Why John Irving Is So Popular." *Commentary* 73 (June 1982): 59–63.

Haller, Scott. "John Irving's Bizarre World." *Saturday Review*, September 1981, pp. 30–34.

Hill, Jane Bowers. "John Irving's Aesthetics of Accessibility: Setting Free the Novel." *South Carolina Review* 16 (1983): 38–44.

McCaffrey, Larry. "An Interview with John Irving." *Contemporary Literature* 23 (1982): 1–18.

Priestley, Michael. "Structure in the Worlds of John Irving." *Critique* 23, No. 1 (1981): 82–96.

Towers, Robert. "Reservations." *New York Review of Books*, 5 November 1981, pp. 12–14.

### SHIRLEY JACKSON

Friedman, Lenemaja. *Shirley Jackson*. Boston: Twayne, 1975.

Hoffman, Steven K. "Individuation and Character Development in the Fiction of Shirley Jackson." *Hartford Studies in Literature* 8 (1976): 190–208.

Holzhauer, Jean. "Interpretation." *Commonweal*, 4 April 1958, pp. 20–21.

Kelly, Robert L. "Jackson's 'The Witch': A Satanic Gem." *English Journal* 60 (1971): 1204–8.

Lyons, John O. *The College Novel in America*. Carbondale: Southern Illinois University Press, 1962, pp. 62–67.

Nardacci, Michael Louis. "Theme, Character, and Technique in the Novels of Shirley Jackson." Ph.D. diss.: New York University, 1979.

Parks, John G. "Waiting for the End: Shirley Jackson's *The Sundial*." *Critique* 19, No. 3 (1978): 74–88.

Welch, Dennis M. "Manipulation in Shirley Jackson's 'Seven Types of Ambiguity.'" *Studies in Short Fiction* 18 (1981): 27–31.

### RANDALL JARRELL

Beck, Charlotte H. "Unicorn to Eland: The Rilkean Spirit in the Poetry of Randall Jarrell." *Southern Literary Journal* 12 (1979): 3–17.

Ferguson, Francis. "Randall Jarrell and the Flotations of Voice." *Georgia Review* 28 (1974): 423–39.

Ferguson, Suzanne. *The Poetry of Randall Jarrell*. Baton Rouge: Louisiana State University Press, 1971.

Ferguson, Suzanne, ed. *Critical Essays on Randall Jarrell*. Boston: G. K. Hall, 1983.

Graham, W. S., and Hayden Carruth. "Jarrell's *Losses*: A Controversy." *Poetry* 72 (1948): 302–11.

Hagenbüchle, Helen. *The Black Goddess: A Study of the Archetypal Feminine in the Poetry of Randall Jarrell*. Swiss Studies in English, No. 79. Bern: Francke Verlag, 1975.

Hoffman, F. J. "Randall Jarrell: Poet-Critic." *American Scholar* 52 (1982–83): 67–77.

Quinn, Sr. M. Bernetta. *The Metamorphic Tradition in Modern Poetry*. 2nd ed. New York: Gordian Press, 1966.

Updike, John. Review of *Fly by Night*. *New York Times Book Review*, 14 November 1976, pp. 25, 36.

Weisberg, Robert. "Randall Jarrell: The Integrity of His Poetry." *Centennial Review* 17 (1973): 237–56.

### ROBINSON JEFFERS

Bennett, Melba Berry. *The Stone Mason of Tor House: The Life and Work of Robinson Jeffers*. Los Angeles: Ward Ritchie Press, 1966.

Brophy, Robert J. *Robinson Jeffers: Myth, Ritual, and Symbol in His Narrative Poems*. Cleveland: Press of Case Western Reserve University, 1973.

Carpenter, Frederick I. *Robinson Jeffers*. New York: Twayne, 1962.

Coffin, Arthur B. *Robinson Jeffers: Poet of Inhumanism*. Madison: University of Wisconsin Press, 1971.

Gilbert, Rudolph. *Shine, Perishing Republic: Robinson Jeffers and the Tragic Sense in Modern Poetry*. Boston: Bruce Humphries, 1936.

Luytens, David Bulwer. "Robinson Jeffers: The 'Inhumanist' at Grips with the Dilemma of Values." In *The Creative Encounter*. London: Secker & Warburg, 1960, pp. 37–65.

Powell, Lawrence Clark. *Robinson Jeffers: The Man and His Work*. Pasadena: San Pasqual Press, 1940.

Squires, Radcliffe. *The Loyalties of Robinson Jeffers*. Ann Arbor: University of Michigan Press, 1956.

Sterling, George. *Robinson Jeffers: The Man and the Artist*. New York: Boni & Liveright, 1926.

Vardanis, Alex A. *The Critical Reputation of Robinson Jeffers: A Bibliographical Study*. Hamden, CT: Archon Books, 1972.

Zaller, Robert. *The Cliffs of Solitude: A Reading of Robinson Jeffers*. Cambridge: Cambridge University Press, 1983.

### JAMES JONES

Adams, Richard P. "A Second Look at *From Here to Eternity*." *College English* 17 (1955–56): 205–10.

Aldrich, Nelson W., Jr. "James Jones." In *Writers at Work: The Paris Review Interviews: Third Series*, ed. George Plimpton. New York: Viking Press, 1967, pp. 231–50.

Garrett, George. *James Jones*. San Diego: Harcourt Brace Jovanovich, 1984.

Geismar, Maxwell. "James Jones and the American War Novel." In *American Moderns*. New York: Hill & Wang, 1958, pp. 225–38.

Giles, James R. *James Jones*. Boston: Twayne, 1981.

Hopkins, John R. *James Jones: A Checklist*. Detroit: Gale Research, 1974.

Morris, Willie. *James Jones: A Friendship*. Garden City, NY: Doubleday, 1978.

Shaw, Irwin. "James Jones, 1921–1977." *New York Times Book Review*, 12 June 1977, pp. 3, 34–35.

Shepherd, Allen. "'A Deliberately Symbolic Little Novella': James Jones's *The Pistol*." *South Dakota Review* 10, No. 1 (Spring 1972): 111–19.

### JUNE JORDAN

Hentoff, Margot. "Kids Pull Up Your Socks!" *New York Review of Books*, 20 April 1972, pp. 13–15.

McHenry, Susan. "'. . . The Jumping into It.'" *Nation*, 11 April 1981, pp. 437–38.

Walker, Alice. Review of *Fannie Lou Hamer*. *New York Times Book Review*, 29 April 1973, p. 8.

Wilkinson, Brenda. Review of *Kimako's Story*. *New York Times Book Review*, 18 April 1982, p. 38.

## GEORGE S. KAUFMAN

Astor, Mary. *My Story: An Autobiography*. Garden City, NY: Doubleday, 1959.

Atherton, Gertrude. *Black Oxen*. New York: Boni and Liveright, 1923.

Atkinson, Brooks. *Broadway Scrapbook*. New York: Theatre Arts, 1947.

Chapman, John. "The Gloomy Dean of Broadway." *Saturday Evening Post*, 1 January, 1938.

Drennan, Robert E., ed. *The Algonquin Wits*. New York: Citadel, 1968.

Gordon, Max. *Max Gordon Presents*. New York: Bernard Geis, 1963.

Hart, Moss. *Act One*. New York: Random House, 1959.

Kaufman, Beatrice, and Joseph Hennessey, eds. *The Letters of Alexander Woollcott*. New York: Viking, 1944.

Marx, Groucho. *The Groucho Letters*. New York: Simon & Schuster, 1967.

## WILLIAM KENNEDY

Keates, Jonathan. "Spectator Sports." *Observer*, 11 November 1984, p. 24.

Kendall, Elaine. Review of *Ironweed*. *Los Angeles Times Book Review*, 26 December 1982, p. 1.

Mellors, John. "On the Game." *Listener*, 11 October 1984, p. 30.

Parrish, Michael E. "Immigration to an Ongoing Urbanity." *Los Angeles Times Book Review*, 29 January 1984, p. 2.

## X. J. KENNEDY

Boggs, Redd. "In a Green Shade." *Bête Noire* No. 19 (Spring 1970): 1–3.

McGann, Jerome. "Poetry and Truth." *Poetry* 117 (1970): 195–203.

Martz, Louis L. "Recent Poetry: The End of an Era." *Yale Review* 59 (1970): 252–67.

Ray, David. "Heroic, Mock-Heroic." *New York Times Book Review*, 24 November 1985, pp. 28–29.

Shapiro, David. "Into the Gloom." *Poetry* 128 (1976): 226–32.

## JACK KEROUAC

Corso, Gregory. "Books." *Kulchur* 3 (1961): 96–98.

Hipkiss, Robert A. "The American Hero Quest." In *Jack Kerouac: Prophet of the New Romanticism*. Lawrence: Regents Press of Kansas, 1976, pp. 15–40.

Jones, LeRoi. Letter. *Partisan Review* 25 (1958): 472–73.

Lindberg, Gary. "Faith on the Run." In *The Confidence Man in American Literature*. New York: Oxford University Press, 1982, pp. 266–70.

Moynahan, Julian. "Twenty Beat Years." *Listener*, 27 June 1968, pp. 841–42.

Podhoretz, Norman. Letter. *Partisan Review* 25 (1958): 476–79.

Rexroth, Kenneth. "San Francisco's Mature Bohemians." *Nation*, 23 February 1957, pp. 159–62.

Sheed, Wilfred. "Beat Down and Beatific." In *The Good Word and Other Words*. New York: Dutton, 1978, pp. 110–15.

Tytell, John. "Revisions of Kerouac." *Partisan Review* 40 (1973): 301–5.

Ungar, Barbara. "Jack Kerouac as Haiku Poet." In *Haiku in English*. Stanford, CA: Stanford Honors Essay in Humanities XXI, 1978, pp. 21–32.

Widmer, Kingsley. "The Beat in the Rise of the Populist Culture." In *The Fifties: Fiction, Poetry, Drama*, ed. Warren French. Deland, FL: Everett/Edwards, 1970, pp. 152–71.

## KEN KESEY

Boardman, Michael M. "*One Flew Over the Cuckoo's Nest*: Rhetoric and Vision." *Journal of Narrative Technique* 8 (1978): 171–83.

Carnes, Bruce. *Ken Kesey*. Boise: Boise State University, 1974.

Hoge, James O. "Psychedelic Stimulation and the Creative Imagination: The Case of Ken Kesey." *Southern Humanities Review* 6 (1972): 381–91.

Knapp, James F. "Tangled in the Language of the Past: Ken Kesey and Cultural Revolution." *Midwest Quarterly* 19 (1978): 398–413.

Leeds, Barry H. *Ken Kesey*. New York: Ungar, 1981.

Sullivan, Ruth. "Big Mama, Big Papa, and Little Sons in Ken Kesey's *One Flew Over the Cuckoo's Nest*." *Literature and Psychology* 25 (1975): 33–44.

Tanner, Stephen L. *Ken Kesey*. Boston: Twayne, 1983.

Wallace, Ronald. "What Laughter Can Do: Ken Kesey's *One Flew Over the Cuckoo's Nest*." In *The Last Laugh*. Columbia: University of Missouri Press, 1979.

Weixlmann, Joseph. "Ken Kesey: A Bibliography." *Western American Literature* 10 (1975): 219–31.

Zashin, Elliot M. "Political Theorist and Demiurge: The Rise and Fall of Ken Kesey." *Centennial Review* 17 (1973): 199–213.

## GALWAY KINNELL

Evans, Tania. "Galway Kinnell: An Appraisal." *Rackham Literary Journal* 4 (1973): 91–96.

Hobbs, John. "Galway Kinnell's 'The Bear': Dream and Technique." *Modern Poetry Studies* 5 (1974): 237–50.

Mills, Ralph J., Jr. "A Reading of Galway Kinnell." *Iowa Review* 1 (1970): 66–86, 102–22.

Taylor, Jane. "The Poetry of Galway Kinnell." *Perspective* 15 (1968): 189–200.

Thompson, William E. "Synergy in the Poetry of Galway Kinnell." *Gypsy Scholar* 1 (1974): 52–69.

Wagner, Linda. "'Spindrift': The World in a Seashell." *Concerning Poetry* 8 (Spring 1975): 5–9.

## CAROLYN KIZER

Cutler, Bruce. "What We Are, and Are Not." *Poetry* 108 (1966): 269–70.

Dickey, William. "Revelation and Homilies." *Poetry* 99 (1961): 128.

Enright, D. J. "Cats and Dogs." *New Statesman*, 31 August 1962, p. 626.

Hampel, Patricia. "Women Who Say What They Mean." *New York Times Book Review*, 25 November 1984, p. 36.

Lee, L. L., and Merrill Lewis, eds. *Women, Women Writers and the West*. Troy, NY: Whitson, 1980.

Montague, John. "Fluent Muse." *Spectator*, 29 June 1962, pp. 864–65.

## JOHN KNOWLES

Dirda, Michael. "Mining the Delderfield Vein." *Washington Post Book World*, 19 February 1978, p. E4.

Ellis, James. "John Knowles: *Indian Summer*." *Critique* 9, No. 2 (1967): 92–95.

———. "*A Separate Peace*: The Fall from Innocence." *English Journal* 53 (1964): 313–18.

Hicks, Granville. "Blandishments of Wealth." *Saturday Review*, 13 August 1966, pp. 23–24.

Witherington, Paul. "*A Separate Peace*: A Study in Structural Ambiguity." *English Journal* 54 (1965): 795–800.

Yardley, Jonathan. "A Novelist Groping." *New Republic*, 13 February 1971, pp. 27–28.

## KENNETH KOCH

Cohn, Ruby. "Poets at Play." In *Dialogue in American Drama.* Bloomington: Indiana University Press, 1971, pp. 310–13.

Featherstone, Joseph. "Teaching Writing." *New Republic,* 11 July 1970, pp. 11–14.

Gilbert, Sandra M. "Despairing at Styles." *Poetry* 127 (1976): 292–94.

Lehman, David. "When the Sun Tries to Go On." *Poetry* 114 (1969): 401–9.

Saroyan, Aram. Review of *The Art of Love. New York Times Book Review,* 28 September 1975, p. 10.

## JERZY KOSINSKI

Boyers, Robert. "Language and Reality in Kosinski's *Steps.*" *Centennial Review* 16 (1972): 41–61.

Bruss, Paul. "Part III: Kosinski." In *Victims: Textual Strategies in Recent American Fiction.* Lewisburg, PA: Bucknell University Press, 1981, pp. 167–227.

Cahill, Daniel J. "Jerzy Kosinski: Retreat from Violence." *Twentieth Century Literature* 18 (1972): 121–32.

Coale, Samuel. "The Cinematic Self of Jerzy Kosinski." *Modern Fiction Studies* 20 (1974): 359–70.

Corngold, Stanley. "Jerzy Kosinski's *The Painted Bird:* Language Lost and Regained." *Mosaic* 6 (1973): 153–67.

Klinkowitz, Jerome. "Insatiable Art and the Great American Quotidian." *Chicago Review* 25 (1973): 172–77.

Lavers, Norman. *Jerzy Kosinski.* Boston: Twayne, 1982.

## MAXINE KUMIN

Estess, Sybil P. "Past Halfway: *The Retrieval System,* by Maxine Kumin." *Iowa Review* 10 (1979): 99–109.

Fialkowski, Barbara. "Fields of Vision." *Shenandoah* 27 (1976): 104–11.

Hammond, Karla. "An Interview with Maxine Kumin." *Western Humanities Review* 33 (1979): 1–15.

Kumin, Maxine. "A Friendship Remembered." In J. D. McClatchey, ed. *Anne Sexton: The Artist and Her Critics.* Bloomington: Indiana University Press, 1978.

Meek, Martha George. "An Interview with Maxine Kumin." *Massachusetts Review* 16 (1975): 317–27.

Mills, Ralph, Jr. "In the Fields of Imagination." *Parnassus: Poetry in Review* 1 (1973): 211–24.

Oates, Joyce Carol. Review of *Up Country. New York Times Book Review,* 19 November 1972, p. 7.

Spacks, Patricia Meyer. "A Chronicle of Women." *Hudson Review* 25 (1972): 168–69.

## OLIVER LA FARGE

Bird, John. "The Future of Oliver La Farge." *Bookman* (New York) 72 (1930–31): 11–14.

Bunker, Robert. "Oliver La Farge: The Search for Self." *New Mexico Quarterly* 20 (1950): 211–24.

Gillis, Everett A. *Oliver La Farge.* Austin: Steck-Vaughn, 1967.

McNickle, D'Arcy. *Indian Man: A Life of Oliver La Farge.* Bloomington: Indiana University Press, 1971.

Pearce, T. M. *Oliver La Farge.* New York: Twayne, 1972.

Ricketson, Edith. "Oliver La Farge." *El Palacio* 71/72 (1964): 25.

Scott, Winfield Townley. "Introduction" to *The Man with the Calabash Pipe.* Boston: Houghton Mifflin, 1966, pp. xi–xxi.

## RING LARDNER

Bruccoli, Matthew J., and Richard Layman. *Ring Lardner: A Descriptive Bibliography.* Pittsburgh: University of Pittsburgh Press, 1976.

Caruthers, Clifford, ed. *Ring around Max: The Correspondence of Ring Lardner and Maxwell Perkins.* Dekalb: Northern Illinois University Press, 1973.

Geismar, Maxwell. "Ring Lardner: Like Something Was Going to Happen." In *Writers In Crisis: The American Novel, 1925–1940.* Boston: Houghton Mifflin, 1942, pp. 3–36.

———. *Ring Lardner and the Portrait of Folly.* New York: Crowell, 1972.

Schwartz, Delmore. "Ring Lardner: Highbrow in Hiding." *Reporter,* 9 August 1956, pp. 52–54.

Webb, Howard W. Jr. "The Meaning of Ring Lardner's Fiction: A Re-evaluation." *American Literature* 31 (1960): 434–45.

Wilson, Edmund. "Ring Lardner's American Characters." In *A Literary Chronicle: 1920–1950.* Garden City, NY: Doubleday, 1956, pp. 37–44.

## IRVING LAYTON

Dudek, Louis. "Layton on the Carpet." In *Selected Essays and Criticism.* Ottawa: Tecumseh Press, 1978, pp. 136–40.

Layton, Irving. "Foreward" to *The Swinging Flesh.* Toronto: McClelland & Stewart, 1961, pp. ix–xv.

Layton, Irving. "Foreword." *The Whole Bloody Bird.* Toronto: McClelland & Stewart, 1969, pp. 9–12.

Waterston, Elizabeth. "New-Found Eyes." *Canadian Literature* No. 52 (Spring 1972): 102–5.

Williams, William Carlos. "A Note on Layton." In *The Improved Binoculars* by Irving Layton. Highlands, NC: Jonathan Williams, 1956.

## STEPHEN LEACOCK

Berger, Carl. "The Other Mr. Leacock." *Canadian Literature* No. 55 (Winter 1973): 23–40.

Curry, Ralph L. *Stephen Leacock: Humorist and Humanist.* Garden City, NY: Doubleday, 1970.

Legate, David M. *Stephen Leacock: A Biography.* Toronto: Doubleday, 1970.

Lomer, Gerhard R. *Stephen Leacock: A Check-List and Index of His Writings.* Ottawa: National Library of Canada, 1954.

McArthur, Peter. *Stephen Leacock.* Toronto: Ryerson Press, 1923.

Mikes, George. "Stephen Leacock." In *Eight Humourists.* London: Allen Wingate, 1954, pp. 45–65.

## URSULA K. LE GUIN

Barbour, Douglas. "On Ursula K. Le Guin's *A Wizard of Earthsea.*" *Riverside Quarterly* 6 (1974): 119–23.

Bucknall, Barbara J. *Ursula K. Le Guin.* New York: Ungar, 1981.

Cogell, Elizabeth Cummins. *Ursula K. Le Guin: A Primary and Secondary Bibliography.* Boston: G. K. Hall, 1983.

DeBolt, Joe, ed. *Ursula K. Le Guin: Voyager to Inner Lands and Outer Space.* Port Washington, NY: Kennikat Press, 1979.

Kaufman, Jerry. "Haber Is Destroyed on the Lathe of Heaven." *Starling* No. 27 (January 1974): 35–40.

McCaffrey, Larry, and Sinda Gregory. "An Interview with Ursula K. Le Guin." *Missouri Review* 7, No. 2 (1984): 64–85.

Moylan, Tom. "Beyond Negation: The Critical Utopias of Ursula K. Le Guin and Samuel R. Delany." *Extrapolation* 21 (1980): 236–53.

Olander, Joseph D., and Martin Harry Greenberg, eds. *Ursula K. Le Guin.* New York: Taplinger, 1979.

Priest, Christopher, "Cool Dreamer." *Maya* No. 7 (1975): 19–23.

Watson, Ian. "Le Guin's *Lathe of Heaven* and the Role of Dick: The False Reality as Mediator." *Science-Fiction Studies* 2 (1975): 67–75.

Wood, Susan. "Discovering Worlds: The Fiction of Ursula K. Le Guin." In *Voices for the Future: Essays on Major Science Fiction Writers,* Volume 2, ed. Thomas D. Clareson. Bowling Green, OH: Bowling Green University Popular Press, 1979, pp. 154–79.

### DENISE LEVERTOV

Aiken, William. "Denise Levertov, Robert Duncan, and Allen Ginsberg: Modes of the Self in Projective Poetry." *Modern Poetry Studies* 10 (1981): 200–245.

Blaydes, Sophie B. "Metaphors of Life and Death in the Poetry of Denise Levertov and Sylvia Plath." *Dalhousie Review* 57 (1977): 494–506.

Carruth, Hayden. "An Informal Epic." *Poetry* 105 (1965): 259–61.

Duddy, Thomas A. "To Celebrate: A Reading of Denise Levertov." *Criticism* 10 (1968): 148–52.

DuPlessis, Rachel Blau. "The Critique of Consciousness and Myth in Levertov, Rich and Rukeyser." *Feminist Studies* 3 (1975): 199–221.

Gitzen, Julaian. "From Reverence to Attention: The Poetry of Denise Levertov." *Midwest Quarterly* 16 (1975): 328–41.

Harns, Victoria. "The Incorporative Consciousness: Levertov's Journey from Discretion to Unity." *Exploration* 4 (1979): 33–48.

Kennedy, X. J. "Fresh Patterns of Near Rhymes." *New York Times Book Review,* 29 April 1962, pp. 29–30.

Mottram, Eric. "The Limits of Self-Regard." *Parnassus: Poetry in Review* 1 (1975): 156–59.

Rexroth, Kenneth. "The Poetry of Denise Levertov." *Poetry* 91 (1957): 120–23.

Sutton, Walter. "A Conversation with Denise Levertov." *Minnesota Review* 5 (1965): 322–28.

Wagner, Linda. "Levertov and Rich: The Later Poems." *South Carolina Review* 11 (1979): 18–27.

Wagner, Linda Welshimer, ed. *Denise Levertov: In Her Own Province.* New York: New Directions, 1979.

### PHILIP LEVINE

Broughton, Irv. Interview with Philip Levine. *Western Humanities Review* 32 (1978): 139–63.

Molesworth, Charles. "The Burned Essential Oil: The Poetry of Philip Levine." *Hollins Critic,* December 1975, pp. 1–15.

Smith, Arthur. Interview with Philip Levine. *Stand* 17 (1976): 38–45.

### SINCLAIR LEWIS

Aaron, Daniel. "Sinclair Lewis: *Main Street.*" In *The American Novel,* ed. Wallace Stegner. New York: Basic Books, 1965.

Austin, Allen. "An Interview with Sinclair Lewis." *University Review* 24 (1958): 199–210.

Dooley, D. J. *The Art of Sinclair Lewis.* Lincoln: University of Nebraska Press, 1967.

Fleming, Robert E., and Esther Fleming. *Sinclair Lewis: A Reference Guide.* Boston: G. K. Hall, 1980.

Fyvel, T. R. "Martin Arrowsmith and His Habitat." *New Republic,* 18 July 1955, pp. 16–18.

Grebstein, Sheldon Norman. *Sinclair Lewis.* New York: Twayne, 1962.

Lewis, Grace Hegger. *With Love from Gracie: Sinclair Lewis 1912–1925.* New York: Harcourt, Brace, 1955.

Light, Martin. "H. G. Wells and Sinclair Lewis: Friendship, Literary Influence, and Letters." *English Literature in Transition* 5 (1962): 1–20.

Lundquist, James. *Sinclair Lewis.* New York: Ungar, 1973.

Miller, Perry. "The Incorruptible Sinclair Lewis." *Atlantic* 187 (April 1951): 30–34.

Millgate, Michael. *American Fiction: James to Cozzens.* Edinburgh: Oliver & Boyd, 1964.

O'Connor, Richard. *Sinclair Lewis.* New York: McGraw-Hill, 1971.

Schorer, Mark. *Sinclair Lewis: An American Life.* New York: McGraw-Hill, 1961.

Sheean, Vincent. *Dorothy and Red.* Boston: Houghton Mifflin, 1963.

Van Doren, Carl. *Sinclair Lewis: A Biographical Sketch.* Garden City, NY: Doubleday, Doran, 1933.

### VACHEL LINDSAY

Harris, Mark. *City of Discontent.* Indianapolis: Bobbs-Merrill, 1952.

Massa, Ann. *Vachel Lindsay: Fieldworker for the American Dream.* Bloomington: Indiana University Press, 1970.

Masters, Edgar Lee. *Vachel Lindsay, a Poet in America.* New York: Scribner's, 1935.

Sayre, Robert F. "Vachel Lindsay." In *Adventures, Rhymes & Designs* by Vachel Lindsay. New York: Eakins Press, 1968, pp. 7–41.

Wesling, Donald. "What the Canon Excludes: Lindsay and American Bardic." *Michigan Quarterly Review* 21 (1982): 479–85.

Yatron, Michael. "Vachel Lindsay." In *America's Literary Revolt.* New York: Philosophical Library, 1959, pp. 103–22.

### JOHN LOGAN

Carroll, Paul. "John Logan: Was Frau Heine a Monster? or 'Yung and Easily Freudened' in Dusseldorf and Hamburg and Berlin and Paris and New York City." *Minnesota Review* 8 (1968): 67–84.

Chaplin, William H. "Identity and Spirit in the Recent Poetry of John Logan." *American Poetry Review* 2 (May–June 1973): 19–24.

Isbell, Harold. "Growth and Change: John Logan's Poetry." *Modern Poetry Studies* 2 (1971): 213–23.

Mazzaro, Jerome. "Ventures into Evening: Self-Parody in the Poetry of John Logan." *Salmagundi* 2 (1968): 78–95.

### JACK LONDON

Barltrop, Robert. *Jack London: The Man, the Writer, the Rebel.* London: Pluto Press, 1976.

Geismar, Maxwell. "Jack London: The Short Cut." In *Rebels and Ancestors: The American Novel, 1890–1915.* Boston: Houghton Mifflin, 1953, pp. 139–216.

Lynn, Kenneth S. "Jack London: The Brain Merchant." In *The Dream of Success: A Study of the Modern American Imagination.* Boston: Little, Brown, 1955, pp. 75–118.

O'Connor, Richard. *Jack London: A Biography.* Boston: Little, Brown, 1964.

Stone, Irving. *Soldier on Horseback: The Biography of Jack London.* Boston: Houghton Mifflin, 1938.

Wagenknecht, Edward. "Towards Naturalism." In *Cavalcade of the American Novel.* New York: Henry Holt, 1952, pp. 204–29.

Woodbridge, Hensley C.; London, John; and George H. Tweney. *Jack London: A Bibliography.* Georgetown, CA: Talisman Press, 1966.

### H. P. LOVECRAFT

Bender, Barry L. "Xenophobia in the Life and Work of H. P. Lovecraft." *Lovecraft Studies* 1, No. 4 (Spring 1981): 22–38; 1, No. 5 (Fall 1981): 11–30.

Burleson, Donald R. *H. P. Lovecraft: A Critical Study.* Westport, CT: Greenwood Press, 1983.

de Camp, L. Sprague. *Lovecraft: A Biography.* Garden City, NY: Doubleday, 1975.

Derleth, August. *H. P. L.: A Memoir.* New York: Ben Abramson, 1945.

Faig, Kenneth W., Jr. *H. P. Lovecraft: His Life, His Work.* West Warwick, RI: Necronomicon Press, 1979.

Joshi, S. T. *H. P. Lovecraft.* Starmont Reader's Guide No. 13. Mercer Island, WA: Starmont House, 1982.

———. *H. P. Lovecraft and Lovecraft Criticism: An Annotated Bibliography.* Kent, OH: Kent State University Press, 1981.

Lévy, Maurice. *Lovecraft ou du fantastique.* Paris: Union Générale d'Éditions, 1972.

St. Armand, Barton L. *H. P. Lovecraft: New England Decadent.* Albuquerque, NM: Silver Scarab Press, 1979.

———. *The Roots of Horror in the Fiction of H. P. Lovecraft.* Elizabethtown, NY: Dragon Press, 1977.

Wetzel, George T., ed. *Howard Phillips Lovecraft: Memoirs, Critiques, and Bibliographies.* North Tonawanda, NY: SSR, 1955.

### AMY LOWELL

Damon, S. Foster. *Amy Lowell: A Chronicle.* Boston: Houghton Mifflin, 1935.

Faderman, Lillian. "Warding Off the Watch and Ward Society: Amy Lowell's Treatment of the Lesbian Theme." *Gay Books Bulletin* 1 (1979): 23–27.

Flint, F. Cudworth. *Amy Lowell.* Minneapolis: University of Minnesota Press, 1969.

Monroe, Harriet. Review of *Sword Blades and Poppy Seed. Poetry* 5 (1914): 136–38.

Overmyer, Janet. "Which Broken Pattern? A Note on Amy Lowell's 'Patterns.'" *Notes on Contemporary Literature* 1 (1971): 14–15.

Sprague, Rosemary. *Imaginary Gardens: A Study of Five American Poets.* Philadelphia: Chilton, 1969.

Tupper, James W. "The Poetry of Amy Lowell." *Sewanee Review* 28 (1970): 37–53.

Wood, Clement. *Amy Lowell.* New York: Harold Vinal, 1926.

### ROBERT LOWELL

Anzilotti, Rolando, ed. *Robert Lowell: A Tribute.* Pisa: Nistri-Lischi Editori, 1979.

Axelrod, Steven Gould, and Helen Deese. *Robert Lowell: A Reference Guide.* Boston: G. K. Hall, 1982.

Bell, Vereen M. *Robert Lowell: Nihilist as Hero.* Cambridge, MA: Harvard University Press, 1983.

Bly, Robert. "Not So Very Near the Ocean." *Michigan Quarterly Review* 7 (1968): 211–12.

Kalstone, David. *Five Temperaments: Elizabeth Bishop, Robert Lowell, James Merrill, Adrienne Rich, John Ashbery.* New York: Oxford University Press, 1977.

Mazzaro, Jerome. *The Poetic Themes of Robert Lowell.* Ann Arbor: University of Michigan Press, 1965.

Perloff, Marjorie. *The Art of Robert Lowell.* Ithaca, NY: Cornell University Press, 1973.

Poirier, Richard. "Our Truest Historian." *New York Herald Tribune Book Week,* 11 October 1964, pp. 1, 16.

Procopiow, Norman. "*Day by Day:* Lowell's Poetry of Imitation." *Ariel* 14 (1983): 127–45.

Raffel, Burton. "Robert Burton's *Imitations.*" *Translation Review* 5 (1980): 20–28.

Rudman, Mark. *Robert Lowell: An Introduction to the Poetry.* New York: Columbia University Press, 1983.

Saffiotti, Carol Lee. "Between History and Self: The Function of the Alexander Poems in Robert Lowell's *History.*" *Modern Poetry Studies* 10 (1981): 159–72.

Staples, Hugh B. *Robert Lowell: The First Twenty Years.* New York: Farrar, Straus & Cudahy, 1962.

### MINA LOY

Hunting, Constance. "The Morality of Mina Loy." *Sagetrieb* 2 (Spring 1983): 133–39.

Koudis, Virginia M. *Mina Loy: American Modernist Poet.* Baton Rouge: Louisiana State University Press, 1980.

Pound, Ezra. "A List of Books: 'Others.'" *Little Review* 4 (March 1918): 56–68.

### ALISON LURIE

Hollander, Anne. "Rags." *New York Review of Books,* 15 April 1982, pp. 38–40.

Hulbert, Ann. Review of *Only Children. New Republic,* 12 May 1979, pp. 37–38.

Jackson, David. "An Interview with Alison Lurie." *Shenandoah* 31, No. 4 (1980): 15–27.

Sanborn, Sara. Review of *The War Between the Tates. New York Times Book Review,* 28 July 1974, pp. 1–2.

Sissman, L. E. "Real and Unreal." *New Yorker,* 11 October 1969, pp. 199–200.

Treglown, Jeremy. "All in the Family." *New Statesman,* 20 April 1979, p. 563.

Unsigned. Review of *The War Between the Tates. Times Literary Supplement,* 21 June 1974, p. 657.

### MARY MCCARTHY

Auchincloss, Louis. *Pioneers and Caretakers: A Study of Nine American Women Novelists.* Minneapolis: University of Minnesota Press, 1965.

Balkian, Anna, and Charles Simmons, eds. *The Creative Present.* Garden City, NY: Doubleday, 1963.

Enright, D. J. *Conspirators and Poets.* London: Chatto & Windus, 1966.

Grumbach, Doris. *The Company She Kept.* New York: Coward-McCann, 1967.

Hardy, Willene Schaefer. *Mary McCarthy.* New York: Ungar, 1981.

Lifson, Martha R. "Allegory of the Secret: Mary McCarthy." *Biography* 4 (1981): 249–67.

McKenzie, Barbara. *Mary McCarthy.* New York: Twayne, 1966.

Mailer, Norman. *Cannibals and Christians.* New York: Dial Press, 1966.

Stock, Irvin. *Mary McCarthy.* Minneapolis: University of Minnesota Press, 1968.

### CARSON MCCULLERS

Auchincloss, Louis. "Carson McCullers." In *Pioneers and Caretakers: A Study of Nine American Women Novelists.* Minneapolis: University of Minnesota Press, 1965, pp. 161–69.

Dodd, Wayne D. "The Development of Theme through Symbol in the Novels of Carson McCullers." *Georgia Review* 17 (1958): 151–67.

Eisinger, Chester E. "Carson McCullers and the Failure of Dialogue." In *Fiction of the Forties*, ed. Chester E. Eisinger. Chicago: University of Chicago Press, 1963, pp. 243–58.

Evans, Oliver. *The Ballad of Carson McCullers: A Biography*. New York: Coward-McCann, 1966.

Gossett, Louise Y. "Dispossessed Love: Carson McCullers." In *Violence in Recent Southern Fiction*. Durham, NC: Duke University Press, 1965, pp. 159–77.

Griffith, Albert. "Carson McCullers' Myth of the Sad Cafe." *Georgia Review* 21 (1967): 45–56.

Hart, Jane. "Carson McCullers: Pilgrim of Loneliness." *Georgia Review* 11 (1957): 53–58.

Phillips, Robert S. "Carson McCullers, 1956–1964: A Selected Checklist." *Bulletin of Bibliography* 22 (1964): 113–16.

Presley, Delma Eugene. "Carson McCullers and the South." *Georgia Review* 28 (1974): 19–32.

Stewart, Stanley. "Carson McCullers, 1940–1956: A Selected Checklist." *Bulletin of Bibliography* 22 (1959): 182–86.

## CLAUDE MCKAY

Gayle, Addison Jr. *Claude McKay: The Black Poet at War*. Detroit: Broadside, 1972.

McLeod, Marian B. "Claude McKay's Russian Interpretation: *The Negroes in America*." *CLA Journal* 23 (1980): 336–51.

Pyne-Timothy, Helen. "Perceptions of the Black Woman in the Work of Claude McKay." *CLA Journal* 19 (1975): 152–64.

Singh, Amritjit. "Race and Sex." In *The Novels of the Harlem Renaissance*. University Park: Pennsylvania State University Press, 1976, pp. 41–69.

## ARCHIBALD MACLEISH

Benét, William Rose. "Round about Parnassus." *Saturday Review of Literature*, 29 July 1933, p. 21.

Blackmur, R. P. "A Modern Poet in Eden." *Poetry* 28 (1926): 339–42.

Dangerfield, George. "Archibald MacLeish: An Appreciation." *Bookman* (New York) 72 (1931): 493–96.

Eberhard, Richard. "The Pattern of MacLeish's Poetry." *New York Times Book Review*, 23 November, 1952, p. 15.

Falk, Signi Lenea. *Archibald MacLeish*. New York: Twayne, 1966.

Smith, Grover Cleveland. *Archibald MacLeish*. Minneapolis: University of Minnesota Press, 1971.

## HUGH MACLENNAN

Buitenhuis, Peter. *Hugh MacLennan*. Toronto: Forum House Press, 1969.

Cameron, Elspeth. *Hugh MacLennan: A Writer's Life*. Toronto: University of Toronto Press, 1981.

Cockburn, Robert H. *The Novels of Hugh MacLennan*. Montreal: Harvest House, 1969.

Goetsch, Paul, ed. *Hugh MacLennan*. Toronto: McGraw-Hill, Ryerson, 1973.

Jones, D. G. *Butterfly on Rock: A Study of Themes and Images in Canadian Literature*. Toronto: University of Toronto Press, 1970.

*Journal of Canadian Studies* 14, No. 4 (Winter 1979–80). Special Hugh MacLennan issue.

MacLulich, T. D. *Hugh MacLennan*. Boston: Twayne, 1983.

Morley, Particia A. *The Immoral Moralists: Hugh MacLennan and Leonard Cohen*. Toronto: Clarke, Irwin, 1976.

Tallman, Warren. "Wolf in the Snow: Part I." *Canadian Literature* No. 5 (Summer 1960): 7–20.

Wilson, Edmund. *O Canada: An American's Notes on Canadian Culture*. New York: Farrar, Straus & Giroux, 1964.

Woodcock, George. *Hugh MacLennan*. Toronto: Copp Clark, 1960.

## NORMAN MAILER

Abel, Lionel. "Murder and the Intellectuals: When Foul Looks Fair." *Commentary* 72 (November 1981): 64–68.

Adams, Laura. *Norman Mailer: A Comprehensive Bibliography*. Metuchen, NJ: Scarecrow Press, 1974.

Aldridge, John. "An Interview with Norman Mailer." *Partisan Review* 47 (1980): 174–82.

Bloom, Harold. "Norman in Egypt." *New York Review of Books*, 28 April 1983, pp. 3–5.

Dupee, F. W. "The American Norman Mailer." *Commentary* 29 (February 1960): 128–32.

Feeley, Gregory. Review of *Ancient Evenings*. *Foundation* 29 (November 1983): 93–95.

Fiedler, Leslie A. "Antic Mailer—Portrait of a Middle-Aged Artist." *The New Leader*, 25 January 1960, pp. 23–24.

Foster, Richard. "Mailer and the Fitzgerald Tradition." *Novel* 1 (1968): 219–30.

Howe, Irving. "A Quest for Peril." *Partisan Review* 27 (1960): 143–48.

Mailer, Norman. *Advertisements for Myself*. New York: G. P. Putnam's Sons, 1959.

Merrill, Robert. "Norman Mailer's Early Nonfiction: The Art of Self-Revelation." *Western Humanities Review* 28 (1974): 1–12.

Muste, John M. "Norman Mailer and John Dos Passos: The Question of Influence." *Modern Fiction Studies* 17 (1971): 361–74.

Page, Frank. "The Mailer Assignment." *Nation*, 26 February 1983, pp. 243–46.

Podhoretz, Norman. "Norman Mailer: The Embattled Vision." *Partisan Review* 26 (1959): 371–91.

Poirier, Richard. "The Minority Within." *Partisan Review* 39 (1972): 12–43.

Solotaroff, Robert. *Down Mailer's Way*. Urbana: University of Illinois Press, 1974.

Steiner, George. "Naked but Not Dead." *Encounter* 17 (December 1961): 67–70.

## CLARENCE MAJOR

Klinkowitz, Jerome. "Clarence Major's Superfiction." *Yardbird Reader* 4 (1975): 1–12.

———. "Reclaiming a (New) Black Experience: The Fiction of Clarence Major." *Oyez Review* 8 (Winter 1973): 86–90.

Lowenfels, Walter. "Black Poets." *New World Review* 37 (1969): 122.

McCaffrey, Larry, and Sinda Gregory. "Major's *Reflex and Bone Structure* and the Anti-Detective Tradition." *Black American Literature Forum* 19 (1979): 39–45.

Miller, Adam David. Review of *All-Night Visitors*. *Black Scholar* 2 (January 1971): 54–56.

## BERNARD MALAMUD

Alter, Iska. *The Good Man's Dilemma: Social Criticism in the Fiction of Bernard Malamud*. New York: AMS Press, 1981.

Avery, Evelyn Gross. *Rebels and Victims: The Fiction of Richard Wright and Bernard Malamud*. Port Washington, NY: Kennikat Press, 1979.

Ducharne, Robert. *Art and Idea in the Novels of Bernard Malamud*. The Hague: Mouton, 1974.

Field, Leslie A., and Joyce W. Field, ed. *Bernard Malamud and the Critics*. New York: New York University Press, 1970.

Kegan, Robert. *The Sweeter Welcome: Voices for a Vision of Affirmation, Bellow, Malamud, and Martin Buber*. Needham Heights, MA: Humanitas Press, 1976.

Kosofsky, Rita Nathalie. *Bernard Malamud: An Annotated Checklist*. Kent, OH: Kent State University Press, 1969.

Levy, Eric Peter. "Metaphysical Shock: A Study of the Novels of Bernard Malamud." Ph.D. diss.: Stanford University, 1975.

Meeter, Glen. *Bernard Malamud and Philip Roth: A Critical Essay*. Grand Rapids, MI: William B. Eerdmans, 1968.

Richman, Sidney, *Bernard Malamud*. New York: Twayne, 1967.

## DAVID MAMET

Gale, Steven H. "David Mamet: The Plays, 1972–1980." In *Essays on Contemporary American Drama*, ed. Hedwig Bock and Albert Wertheim. Munich: Max Hueber, 1981, pp. 207–23.

Hughes, Catharine. "New American Playwrights." *America*, 16 April 1977, pp. 363–64.

Miner, Michael D. "Grotesque Drama in the '70s." *Kansas Quarterly* 12 (Fall 1980): 99–109.

Sultanik, Aaron. "Death and David Mamet." *Midstream* 24 (May 1978): 56–57.

Vallely, Jean. "David Mamet Makes a Play for Hollywood." *Rolling Stone*, 3 April 1980, pp. 44–46.

## WILLIAM MARCH

Brody, Alter. "War as Collective Experience." *Nation*, 1 March 1933, pp. 238–39.

Du Bois, William. "Alabama Townsfolk." *New York Times Book Review*, 10 January 1943, pp. 4–5.

Kelley, Welbourn. "A Southern Boy's Life in a Dramatic Novel." *Saturday Review of Literature*, 24 February 1934, p. 505.

Marsh, Fred T. "Mr. March's Tales." *New York Times Book Review*, 26 March 1939, p. 7.

Miller, Merle. "An Off Offering." *Saturday Review*, 5 June 1954, pp. 33–34.

Strauss, Harold. "A Strange Triangle." *New York Times Book Review*, 25 October 1936, pp. 22–23.

## EDWIN MARKHAM

Filler, Louis. *The Unknown Edwin Markham*. Yellow Springs, OH: Antioch Press, 1966.

Fitch, George Hamlin. "Markham: The Poet of the American People." In *Great Spiritual Writers of America*. San Francisco: P. Elder, 1916, pp. 137–45.

M[acArthur], J[ames]. "Edwin Markham: The Author of 'The Man with the Hoe.'" *Bookman* (New York) 9 (1899): 441–45.

Miller, Joaquin. "Edwin Markham—His Life and His Verse." *New York Times Saturday Review*, 18 November 1899, p. 776.

Slade, Joseph W. "Edwin Markham, a Talented Failure: A Critical Biography." Ph.D. diss.: New York University, 1971.

Stidger, William L. *Edwin Markham*. New York: Abingdon Press, 1933.

## JOHN P. MARQUAND

Bell, Millicent. *Marquand: An American Life*. Boston: Little, Brown, 1979.

Birmingham, Stephen. *The Late John Marquand: A Biography*. Philadelphia: Lippincott, 1972.

Brady, Charles A. "John Phillips Marquand: Martini-Age Victorian." In *Fifty Years of the American Novel*, ed. Harold C. Gardiner. New York: Scribner's, 1952, pp. 107–34.

Butterfield, Roger. "John P. Marquand: America's Famous Novelist of Manners." *Life*, 31 July 1944, pp. 64–73.

Greene, George. "John Marquand: The Reluctant Prophet." *New England Review* 2 (1980): 614–24.

Gross, John J. *John P. Marquand*. New York: Twayne, 1963.

Gurko, Leo. "The High-Level Formula of J. P. Marquand." *American Scholar* 21 (1952): 443–53.

Hamburger, Philip. *J. P. Marquand Esquire: A Portrait in the Form of a Novel*. Boston: Houghton Mifflin, 1952.

Holman, C. Hugh. *John P. Marquand*. Minneapolis: University of Minnesota Press, 1965.

Milne, Gordon. "John P. Marquand." In *The Sense of Society*. Rutherford, NJ: Fairleigh Dickinson University Press, 1977, pp. 168–204.

## DON MARQUIS

Anthony, Edward. *O Rare Don Marquis: A Biography*. Garden City, NY: Doubleday, 1962.

Hasley, Louis. "Don Marquis: Ambivalent Humorist." *Prairie Schooner* 45 (1971): 59–73.

Hill, Hamlin L. "Archy and Uncle Remus: Don Marquis's Debt to Joel Chandler Harris." *Georgia Review* 60 (1961): 78–87.

Morley, Christopher. "Don Marquis." In *Shandygaff*. Garden City, NY: Doubleday, 1918, pp. 22–42.

Yates, Norris W. "The Many Masks of Don Marquis." In *The American Humorist: Conscience of the Twentieth Century*. Ames: Iowa State University Press, 1964, pp. 195–216.

## EDGAR LEE MASTERS

Flanagan, John T. *Edgar Lee Masters: The Spoon River Poet and His Critics*. Metuchen, NJ: Scarecrow Press, 1974.

———. "The Novels of Edgar Lee Masters." *South Atlantic Quarterly* 49 (1950): 82–95.

Hart, James. "The Sources of the Spoon: Edgar Lee Masters and the *Spoon River Anthology*." *Centennial Review* 24 (1980): 403–31.

Primeau, Ronald. *Beyond* Spoon River: *The Legacy of Edgar Lee Masters*. Austin: University of Texas Press, 1981.

Untermeyer, Louis. "Edgar Lee Masters." In *American Poetry since 1900*. New York: Henry Holt, 1923, pp. 111–32.

Yatron, Michael. *America's Literary Revolt*. New York: Philosophical Library, 1959, pp. 11–70.

## WILLIAM MAXWELL

Barry, Francis J. Review of *Ancestors*. *Commonweal*, 10 December 1971, pp. 262–63.

Bliven, Naomi. "Brief Encounter." *New Yorker*, 25 March 1961, pp. 161–63.

Gilman, Richard. "The Anti-Novel of a Trained, Cool-Tempered Sensibility." *Commonweal*, 1 April 1961, p. 50.

Hay, Sara Henderson. "The Magnetism of the Opposites." *Saturday Review*, 7 April 1945, p. 9.

Leiter, Robert A. "Simple Terms, Burning Words." *Commonweal*, 9 May 1980, pp. 283–84.

## H. L. MENCKEN

Boyd, Ernest. *H. L. Mencken*. New York: McBride, 1925.

Forgue, Guy Jean. *H. L. Mencken: L'Homme, l'oeuvre, l'influence*. Paris: Presses Universitaires de France, 1967.

Hicks, Granville. *The Great Tradition: An Interpretation of American Literature since the Civil War.* New York: Macmillan, 1933.

Hobsen, Fred C., Jr. *Serpent in Eden: H. L. Mencken and the South.* Chapel Hill: University of North Carolina Press, 1974.

May, Henry F. *The End of American Innocence: A Study of the First Years of Our Own Time, 1912–1917.* New York: Knopf, 1959.

Rascoe, Burton. "Fanfare." *Chicago Tribune,* November 11, 1917, p. 7.

———. "Notes for an Epitaph." *New York Evening Post,* March 4, 1922, p. 25.

Ruland, Richard. *The Rediscovery of American Literature: Premises of Critical Taste, 1900–1940.* Cambridge, MA: Harvard University Press, 1967.

Stenerson, Douglas C. "The 'Forgotten Man' of H. L. Mencken." *American Quarterly* 18 (1966): 686–96.

Wilson, Edmund. *Shores of Light: A Literary Chronicle of the Twenties and Thirties.* New York: Farrar, Straus, 1952.

## WILLIAM MEREDITH

Fitts, Dudley. "Meredith's Second Volume." *Poetry* 73 (1948–49): 111–16.

Howard, Richard. "All of a Piece and Clever and at Some Level, True." In *Alone with America.* Rev. ed. New York: Atheneum, 1980, pp. 372–85.

Fitz Gerald, Gregory, and Paul Ferguson. "The Frost Tradition: A Conversation with William Meredith." *Southwest Review* 57 (1972): 108–17.

MacLeish, Archibald. "Foreword" to *Love Letter from an Impossible Land* by William Meredith. New Haven: Yale University Press, 1944, pp. 9–10.

Rotella, Guy. *Three Contemporary Poets of New England: William Meredith, Philip Booth, and Peter Davison.* Boston: Twayne, 1983.

# ACKNOWLEDGMENTS

The Adelphi. JOHN MIDDLETON MURRY, "The Hell It Can't," Vol. 2, No. 6 (March 1936), copyright © 1936.

Algol. DOUGLAS BARBOUR, "The Lathe of Heaven: Taoist Dream," No. 21 (Nov. 1973), copyright © 1973.

America. JAMES FINN COTTER, July 25, 1981, copyright © 1981. PETER QUINN, March 17, 1984, copyright © 1984.

American Academy of Arts and Letters. WILLIAM LYON PHELPS, "Edwin Markham," Commemorative Tributes of the American Academy of Arts and Letters: 1905–1941, copyright © 1942 by the American Academy of Arts and Letters.

American Literature. HELEN E. NEBEKER, "'The Lottery': Symbolic Tour de Force," Vol. 46, No. 1 (March 1974), copyright © 1974.

American Mercury. BENJAMIN DE CASSERES, "Five Portraits on Galvanized Iron," Vol. 9, No. 4 (Dec. 1926), copyright © 1926. EDGAR LEE MASTERS, "The Genesis of Spoon River," Vol. 28, No. 1 (Jan. 1933), copyright © 1933.

American Poetry Review. PHILIP BOOTH, "Maxine Kumin's Survival," Nov.–Dec. 1978, copyright © 1978. JUNE JORDAN, "The Black Poet Speaks of Poetry," May–June 1974, copyright © 1974. ALFRED KAZIN, "The Esthetic of Humility," March–April 1974, copyright © 1974. J. D. MCCLATCHEY, "Speaking of Hollander," Sept.–Oct. 1982, copyright © 1982. STANLEY PLUMLEY, March–April 1976, copyright © 1976.

American Review. ROBERT PENN WARREN, "Twelve Poets," May 1934, copyright © 1934.

American Scholar. R. W. B. LEWIS, "Genius and Sheer Fudge," Vol. 41, No. 4 (Autumn 1972), copyright © 1972.

Antioch Review. ELAINE SHOWALTER, "Killing the Angel in the House: The Autonomy of Women Writers," Vol. 32, No. 3 (1973), copyright © 1973.

Archon Books. GLENN RICHARD RUIHLEY, "Preface" to The Thorn of a Rose: Amy Lowell Reconsidered, copyright © 1975 by Glenn Richard Ruihley.

Arizona Quarterly. CHARLES ALLEN, "The Fiction of Oliver La Farge," Vol. 1, No. 4 (Winter 1945), copyright © 1945. JAMES J. MCDONALD, "The Novels of John Knowles," Vol. 23, No. 4 (Winter 1967), copyright © 1967.

Arkham House Publishers, Inc. H. P. LOVECRAFT, Letter to Frank Belknap Long (Feb. 27, 1931), Selected Letters: 1929–1931, ed. August Derleth and Donald Wandrei, copyright © 1971 by August Derleth and Donald Wandrei. T. O. MABBOTT, "H. P. Lovecraft: An Appreciation," Marginalia by H. P. Lovecraft et al., ed. August Derleth, copyright © 1944 by August Derleth and Donald Wandrei. CLARK ASHTON SMITH, "To Howard Phillips Lovecraft," Selected Poems, copyright © 1971 by Mrs. Clark Ashton Smith.

Atheneum. RICHARD HOWARD, "Galway Kinnell," "Kenneth Koch," "John Logan," Alone with America, copyright © 1965, 1966, 1967, 1968, 1969 by Richard Howard. STANLEY EDGAR HYMAN, "Truths from the Grave," The Critic's Credentials, copyright © 1963, 1978 by Phoebe Pettingell. HOWARD TEICHMANN, "The Wit," George S. Kaufman: An Intimate Portrait, copyright © 1972.

The Atlantic. STOYAN CHRISTOWE, Oct. 1947, copyright © 1947 by The Atlantic Monthly Co. BENJAMIN DEMOTT, "Domesticated Madness," Oct. 1981, copyright © 1981 by The Atlantic Monthly Co. ALFRED KAZIN, "John P. Marquand and the American Failure," Nov. 1958, copyright © 1958 by The Atlantic Monthly Co. WILLIE MORRIS, "A Friendship: Remembering James Jones," June 1978, copyright © 1978 by The Atlantic Monthly Co. RICHARD POIRIER, "Norman Mailer: A Self-Creation," Oct. 1972, copyright © 1972 by The Atlantic Monthly Co. EDWARD WEEKS, "John P. Marquand," Oct. 1950, copyright © 1950 by The Atlantic Monthly Co.

Black American Literature Forum. DOUG BOLLING, "A Reading of Clarence Major's Short Fiction," Vol. 19, No. 2 (Summer 1979), copyright © 1979. FANNY HOWE, "Clarence Major: Poet and Language Man," Vol. 19, No. 2 (Summer 1979), copyright © 1979. ANN RAYSON, "Dust Tracks on a Road: Zora Neale Hurston

and the Form of Black Autobiography," Vol. 7, No. 2 (Summer 1973), copyright © 1973 by Indiana State University.

Black Mountain Review. JACK KEROUAC, "Essentials of Spontaneous Prose," Autumn 1957, copyright © 1957 by Black Mountain College.

Black Scholar. NTOZAKE SHANGE, March 1977, copyright © 1977. MILDRED THOMPSON, Jan. 1981, copyright © 1981.

Black World. JUNE JORDAN, "On Richard Wright and Zora Neale Hurston: Towards a Balancing of Love and Hatred," Vol. 23, No. 10 (Aug. 1974), copyright © 1974 by June Jordan. ELLEASE SOUTHERLAND, "Zora Neale Hurston: The Novelist-Anthropologist's Life/Works," Vol. 23, No. 10 (Aug. 1974), copyright © 1974 by Ellease Southerland.

The Bodley Head. J. B. PRIESTLEY, "Editor's Introduction" to The Bodley Head Leacock, copyright © 1957 by The Bodley Head.

Bookman (New York). BENJAMIN DE CASSERES, "Robinson Jeffers: Tragic Terror," Nov. 1927, copyright © 1927. F. SCOTT FITZGERALD, "The Baltimore Antichrist," March 1921, copyright © 1921. FORD MADOX FORD, April 1929, copyright © 1929. BURTON RASCOE, "The Seamy Side," April 1928, copyright © 1928.

Bowling Green University Popular Press. PETER VIERECK, "Vachel Lindsay: The Dante of the Fundamentalists," A Question of Quality: Popularity and Value in Modern Creative Writing, ed. Louis Filler, copyright © 1976 by Bowling Green University Popular Press.

Canadian Literature. PAUL GOETSCH, "Too Long to the Courtly Muses: Hugh MacLennan as a Contemporary Writer," No. 10 (Autumn 1961), copyright © 1961 by Canadian Literature. D. G. JONES, "Myth, Frye and Canadian Writers," No. 55 (Winter 1973), copyright © 1973 by Canadian Literature. F. W. WATT, "Critic or Entertainer? Stephen Leacock and the Growth of Materialism," No. 5 (Summer 1960), copyright © 1960 by Canadian Literature. R. E. WATTERS, "A Special Tang: Stephen Leacock's Canadian Humour," No. 5 (Summer 1960), copyright © 1960 by Canadian Literature. GEORGE WOODCOCK, "A Grab at Proteus," No. 25 (Summer 1965), copyright © 1965 by Canadian Literature.

Century Magazine. CARL VAN DOREN, "Smartness and Light," March 1923, copyright © 1923.

Chinese University Press. DOMINIC CHEUNG, "Carolyn Kizer and Her Chinese Imitations," China and the West: Comparative Literature Studies, ed. William Tay, Ying-hsiung Chou, and Heh-hsiang Yuan, copyright © 1980 by Chinese University of Hong Kong.

CLA Journal. ARTHUR P. DAVIS, "Langston Hughes: Cool Poet," June 1968, copyright © 1968. JAMES A. EMMANUEL, "The Literary Experiments of Langston Hughes," June 1968, copyright © 1968. BLYDEN JACKSON, "A Word about Simple," June 1968, copyright © 1968.

Cockatrice. REDD BOGGS, "Parnassus on Jets," No. 4 (Spring 1963), copyright © 1963 by Redd Boggs.

Columbia University Press. ONWUCHEKWA JEMIE, Langston Hughes: An Introduction of the Poetry, copyright © 1973, 1976 by Columbia University Press.

Commentary. ROBERT ALTER, "The Critic as Poet," Sept. 1975, copyright © 1975. ELIZABETH DALTON, "Life and Art," Aug. 1969, copyright © 1969. JOSEPH EPSTEIN, "Mailer Hits Bottom," July 1983, copyright © 1983. NATHAN GLICK, "Marquand's Vanishing American Aristocracy," May 1950, copyright © 1950. ALFRED KAZIN, "Fantasist of the Ordinary," July 1957, copyright © 1957. NORMAN PODHORETZ, "Achilles in Left Field," March 1953, copyright © 1953.

Commonweal. WILLIAM B. CLANCY, June 15, 1950, copyright © 1950. RICHARD HAYES, "A Question of Reality," March 14, 1958, copyright © 1958. SEYMOUR KRIM, "King of the Beats," Jan. 2, 1959, copyright © 1959.

Contemporary Literature. GLAUCO CAMBON, Spring-Summer 1962, copyright © 1962. DONALD EMERSON, "The Ambiguities of Clock without Hands," Fall 1962, copyright © 1962. JOHN B. VICKERY,

"Carson McCullers: A Map of Love," Winter 1960, copyright © 1960.

Cornell University Press. H. L. MENCKEN, "Portrait of an American Citizen," *H. L. Mencken's Smart Set Criticism*, ed. William H. Nolte, copyright © 1968 by Cornell University Press.

Coward-McCann. ALFRED KREYMBORG, "Originals and Eccentrics," *Our Singing Strength*, copyright © 1929 by Coward-McCann.

Critical Quarterly. DIANA SURMAN, "Inside and Outside in the Poetry of Denise Levertov," Vol. 22, No. 1 (Spring 1980), copyright © 1980.

Critique. SAMUEL COALE, "The Quest for the Elusive Self: The Fiction of Jerzy Kosinski," Vol. 14, No. 3 (1973), copyright © 1973.

Dial. YVOR WINTERS, "Mina Loy," Vol. 80, No. 6 (June 1926), copyright © 1926.

Dial Press. NORMAN MAILER, "Some Children of the Goddess," *Cannibals and Christians*, copyright © 1966 by Norman Mailer.

Dodd, Mead. G. K. CHESTERTON, "On Vachel Lindsay," *All I Survey*, copyright © 1933. JEAN GOULD, "'In Excelcis,'" *Amy: The World of Amy Lowell and the Imagist Movement*, copyright © 1975 by Jean Gould. ROBERT HEMENWAY, "Zora Neale Hurston and the Eatonville Anthropology," GEORGE E. KENT, "Patterns of the Harlem Renaissance," *The Harlem Renaissance Remembered*, ed. Arna Bontemps, copyright © 1972 by Arna Bontemps.

Doubleday & Co. ERNEST BOYD, "Sinclair Lewis," *Portraits: Real and Imaginary*, copyright © 1924. SCOTT MEREDITH, *George S. Kaufman and His Friends*, copyright © 1974. WINFIELD TOWNLEY SCOTT, "A Parenthesis on Lovecraft as Poet," *Exiles and Fabrications*, copyright © 1945 by Donald M. Grant and Thomas P. Hadley, copyright © 1961 by Winfield Townley Scott. REBECCA WEST, "Sinclair Lewis Introduces Elmer Gantry," *The Strange Necessity*, copyright © 1927 by *The New York Herald Tribune*, copyright © 1928 by Doubleday, Doran & Co., Inc. E. B. WHITE, "introduction" to *the lives and times of archy and mehitabel* by Don Marquis, copyright © 1950 by Doubleday & Co.

Dragon Press. SAMUEL R. DELANY, "To Read *The Dispossessed*," *The Jewel-Hinged Jaw*, copyright © 1977 by Samuel R. Delany.

Driftwind Press. W. PAUL COOK, *In Memoriam: Howard Phillips Lovecraft*, copyright © 1941.

E. P. Dutton Co. VAN WYCK BROOKS, "Mencken in Baltimore," *The Confident Years: 1885–1915*, copyright © 1952.

Educational Theatre Journal. JOAN FLECKENSTEIN, Vol. 30, No. 3 (Oct. 1978), copyright © 1978.

English Journal. GRANVILLE HICKS, "Sinclair Lewis and the Good Life," Vol. 25, No. 4 (April 1936), copyright © 1936.

Esquire. JAMES BALDWIN, "The Black Boy Looks at the White Boy," May 1961, copyright © 1961. CARSON MCCULLERS, "The Flowering Dream: Notes on Writing," Dec. 1959, copyright © 1959.

Everett/Edwards. DAN JAFFE, "Archy Jumps Over the Moon," *The Twenties: Fiction, Poetry, Drama*, ed. Warren French, copyright © 1975 by Warren French.

Explicator. ROBERT E. BJORK, Vol. 40, No. 2 (Winter 1982), copyright © 1982 by the Helen Dwight Reid Memorial Foundation. RONALD A. SHARP, Vol. 37, No. 3 (Spring 1979), copyright © 1979 by the Helen Dwight Reid Memorial Foundation.

Extrapolation. S. T. JOSHI, "Topical References in Lovecraft," Vol. 25, No. 3 (Fall 1984), copyright © 1984 by The Kent State University Press.

Farrar, Straus & Giroux. JOHN BERRYMAN, "Enslavement: Three American Fictions," "Robert Lowell and Others," *The Freedom of the Poet*, copyright © 1947, 1956 by John Berryman, copyright © 1976 by Kate Berryman. ELIZABETH HARDWICK, "Mary McCarthy," *A View of My Own: Essays in Literature and Society*, copyright © 1962. SEAMUS HEANEY, "Full Face: Robert Lowell," *Preoccupations*, copyright © 1980 by Seamus Heaney. RANDALL JARRELL, "From the Kingdom of Necessity," *Poetry and the Age*, copyright © 1953 by Randall Jarrell. RANDALL JARRELL, "Poetry in War and Peace," *Kipling, Auden & Co.*, copyright © 1945, 1980 by Mrs. Randall Jarrell. TOM WOLFE, "The Electric Suit," *The Electric Kool-Aid Acid Test*, copyright © 1968 by Tom Wolfe.

Forum. IRVING BABBITT, "The Critic and American Life," Feb. 1928, copyright © 1928.

Foundation. SARAH LEFANU, No. 29 (Nov. 1983), copyright © 1983. ROZ KAVENY, "Science Fiction in the 1970s," No. 22 (June 1981),

copyright © 1981. KATHLEEN L. SPENCER, "Exiles and Envoys: The SF of Ursula K. Le Guin," No. 20 (Oct. 1980), copyright © 1980.

Burt Franklin & Co. MARC CHÉNETIER, "Introduction" to *The Letters of Vachel Lindsay*, copyright © 1979 by Burt Franklin & Co., Inc.

Bernard Geis Associates. HARPO MARX, "No Use Talking," *Harpo Speaks!*, copyright © 1961.

Georgia Review. FRANK BALDANZA, "Plato in Dixie," Summer 1958, copyright © 1958 by the University of Georgia Press. DAVID BROMWICH, Fall 1975, copyright © 1975 by the University of Georgia Press. KATHRYN STRIPLING BYER, Spring 1973, copyright © 1973 by the University of Georgia Press. ALFRED CORN, Summer 1977, copyright © 1977 by the University of Georgia Press.

The Great Ideas Today. STEPHEN SPENDER, "Literature," 1965, copyright © 1965 by Encyclopaedia Britannica, Inc.

Gregg Press. RICHARD GID POWERS, "Introduction" to *The Science Fiction of Jack London*, copyright © 1975 by G. K. Hall & Co.

Grove Press. HORACE GREGORY, "Poet without Critics: A Note on Robinson Jeffers." *The Dying Gladiators and Other Essays*, copyright © 1955, 1961 by Horace Gregory.

Harcourt Brace Jovanovich. ST. CLAIR DRAKE, "Introduction" to *A Long Way from Home* by Claude McKay, copyright © 1970 by Harcourt, Brace & World. E. M. FORSTER, "Sinclair Lewis," *Abinger Harvest*, copyright © 1936 by E. M. Forster. HORACE GREGORY AND MARYA ZATURENSKA, "Three Poets of the Sierras," *A History of American Poetry 1900–1940*, copyright © 1942, 1944, 1946 by Harcourt, Brace & Co. GEORGE ORWELL, "Introduction" to *Love of Life and Other Stories* by Jack London, *Collected Essays, Journalism, and Letters of George Orwell*, Volume 4, ed. Sonia Orwell and Ian Angus, copyright © 1968 by Sonia Orwell. GERALD WEALES, "The New Pineros," *American Drama since World War II*, copyright © 1962 by Gerald Weales.

Harper & Row. LOUIS ADAMIC, "'Red' Lewis," *My America*, copyright © 1938 by Louis Adamic. FANNY BUTCHER, "Sinclair Lewis," *Many Lives—One Love*, copyright © 1972 by Fanny Butcher. J. B. PRIESTLEY, "Between the Wars," *Literature and Western Man*, copyright © 1960 by J. B. Priestley. TONY TANNER, "Edge City," *City of Words: American Fiction 1950–1970*, copyright © 1971 by Tony Tanner.

Harper's. BERNARD DE VOTO, "Almost Toujours Gai," March 1950, copyright © 1950. MARGARET DRABBLE, "Muck, Memory, and Imagination," July 1978, copyright © 1978. MARTIN DUBERMAN, "The Great Gray Way," May 1978, copyright © 1978. GRANVILLE HICKS, "Marquand of Newburyport," April 1950, copyright © 1950. IRVING HOWE, "From the Other Side of the Moon," March 1969, copyright © 1969. RANDALL JARRELL, "'Very Graceful Are the Uses of Culture,'" Nov. 1954, copyright © 1954.

Harper's Bazaar. DYLAN THOMAS, "Dylan Thomas on Edgar Lee Masters," No. 3019 (June 1963), copyright © 1963 by the Hearst Corporation.

Harvard University Press. HELEN VENDLER, "A Difficult Grandeur," *Part of Nature, Part of Us: Modern American Poets*, copyright © 1974 by Helen Vendler, copyright © 1980 by the President and Fellows of Harvard College.

Hermitage House. W. DAVID SIEVERS, "New Freudian Blood," *Freud on Broadway*, copyright © 1955 by W. David Sievers.

Hollins Critic. JOHN ALEXANDER ALLEN, "Another Country: The Poetry of Daniel Hoffman," Vol. 15, No. 4 (Oct. 1978), copyright © 1978 by Hollins College. ROBERT STOREY, "The Making of David Mamet," Vol. 16, No. 4 (Oct. 1979), copyright © 1979 by Hollins College. HENRY TAYLOR, "In Charge of Morale in a Morbid Time: The Poetry of William Meredith," Vol. 16, No. 1 (Feb. 1979), copyright © 1979 by Hollins College.

Holt, Rinehart & Winston. BABETTE DEUTSCH, "Farewell, Romance," *Poetry in Our Time*, copyright © 1952 by Henry Holt & Co., Inc. LOUIS UNTERMEYER, "Vachel Lindsay," *The New Era in American Poetry*, copyright © 1919 by Henry Holt & Co., Inc. EDWARD WAGENKNECHT, "Novelists of the 'Thirties," *Cavalcade of the American Novel*, copyright © 1952 by Holt, Rinehart & Winston.

Horizon Press. STANLEY EDGAR HYMAN, "A New Life for a Good Man," *Standards: A Chronicle of Books for Our Time*, copyright © 1966 by Stanley Edgar Hyman.

Houghton Mifflin Co. LOUIS AUCHINCLOSS, "The Novel of Manners Today," *Reflections of a Jacobite*, copyright © 1951, 1960, 1961 by Louis Auchincloss. BERNARD DUFFEY, "The Three Worlds of Jack Kerouac," *Recent American Fiction*, ed. Joseph J. Waldmeier, copyright © 1963 by Bernard Duffey. MAXWELL GEISMAR, "Sinclair Lewis: The Cosmic Bourjoyce," "H. L. Mencken: On the Dock," *The Last of the Provincials*, copyright © 1947 by Maxwell Geismar. OLIVER LA FARGE, "Main Line," *Raw Material*, copyright © 1942, 1943, 1944, 1945 by Oliver La Farge. CARSON MCCULLERS, "A Personal Preface," *The Square Root of Wonderful*, copyright © 1958 by Carson McCullers. MARGARITA G. SMITH, "Introduction" to *The Mortgaged Heart* by Carson McCullers, copyright © 1971.

Hudson Review. HAYDEN CARRUTH, "A Meaning of Robert Lowell," Autumn 1967, copyright © 1967 by Hudson Review, Inc. HAYDEN CARRUTH, Summer 1971, copyright © 1971 by Hudson Review, Inc. HAYDEN CARRUTH, "Levertov," Autumn 1974, copyright © 1974 by Hudson Review, Inc. DENIS DONOGHUE, "The Store of the Human," Winter 1965–66, copyright © 1966 by Hudson Review, Inc. DEAN FLOWER, Summer 1983, copyright © 1983 by Hudson Review, Inc. MARCUS KLEIN, "Imps from Bottles, Etc.," Winter 1958–59, copyright © 1959 by Hudson Review, Inc. WILLIAM H. PRITCHARD, "Youngsters, Middlesters, and Some Old Boys," Spring 1972, copyright © 1972 by Hudson Review, Inc. WILLIAM H. PRITCHARD, "Poetry Matters," Autumn 1973, copyright © 1973 by Hudson Review, Inc. WILLIAM H. PRITCHARD, "More Poetry Matters," Autumn 1976, copyright © 1976 by Hudson Review, Inc. JOHN SIMON, "Theater Chronicle," Summer 1977, copyright © 1977 by Hudson Review, Inc. JOHN SIMON, "Theatre Chronicle," Spring 1978, copyright © 1978 by Hudson Review, Inc.

Indiana University Press. SHELDON NORMAN GREBSTEIN, "Bernard Malamud and the Jewish Movement," *Contemporary American-Jewish Literature*, ed. Irvin Malin, copyright © 1973 by Indiana University Press.

Iowa Review. RUSSELL FOWLER, "Randall Jarrell's 'Eland': A Key to Motive and Technique in His Poetry," Vol. 5, No. 2 (Spring 1974), copyright © 1974 by the University of Iowa. JOHN LOGAN, Interview by Thomas Hilgers and Michael Molloy, Vol. 11, Nos. 2–3 (Spring-Summer 1980), copyright © 1980 by the University of Iowa.

Journal of American Studies. ANN MASSA, "The Artistic Conscience of Vachel Lindsay," Vol. 2, No. 2 (Oct. 1968), copyright © 1968. GORDON O. TAYLOR, "Cast a Cold 'I': Mary McCarthy on Vietnam," Vol. 9, No. 1 (April 1975), copyright © 1975.

Journal of Canadian Studies. HELEN HOY, "'The Gates Closed on Us Then': The Paradise-lost Motif in Hugh MacLennan's Fiction," Vol. 14, No. 4 (Winter 1979–80), copyright © 1980.

Journal of Narrative Technique. ROSALIE HEWITT, "A 'Home Address for the Self': Mary McCarthy's Autobiographical Journey," Vol. 12, No. 2 (Spring 1982), copyright © 1982.

Kansas Quarterly. JOHN DITSKY, "'He Lets You See the Thought There': The Theatre of David Mamet," Vo. 12, No. 4 (Fall 1980), copyright © 1980 by *Kansas Quarterly*.

Kenyon Review. HAROLD BLOOM, "The White Light of Trope: An Essay on John Hollander's *Spectral Emanation*," Winter 1979, copyright © 1979. LIONEL TRILLING, "Mr. Lewis Goes Soft," Summer 1940, copyright © 1940.

Alfred A. Knopf, Inc. CONRAD AIKEN, "The Technique of Polyphonic Prose: Amy Lowell," *Scepticisms*, copyright © 1919 by Alfred A. Knopf, Inc. LANGSTON HUGHES, "Harlem Literati," *The Big Sea*, copyright © 1940 by Langston Hughes. CHRISTOPHER LASCH, "The Anti-Intellectualism of the Intellectuals," *The New Radicalism in America*, copyright © 1965 by Christopher Lasch. H. L. MENCKEN, "The New Poetry Movement," *Prejudices: First Series*, copyright © 1919 by Alfred A. Knopf, Inc. H. L. MENCKEN, "Four Makers of Tales," *Prejudices: Fifth Series*, copyright © 1926 by Alfred A. Knopf, Inc. CARL VAN DOREN, "Salvation with Jazz," *Many Minds*, copyright © 1924 by Alfred A. Knopf, Inc.

John Lane. C. LEWIS HIND, "Edwin Markham," *Authors and I*, copyright © 1921.

Libra Books. STEPHEN H. BRONZ, *Roots of Negro Racial Consciousness in the 1920's*, copyright © 1964 by Stephen H. Bronz.

J. B. Lippincott Co. ZORA NEALE HURSTON, "Looking Things Over," *Dust Tracks on a Road*, copyright © 1942 by J. B. Lippincott Co., copyright renewed © 1970 by John C. Hurston. EDWARD MARGOLIES, "Race and Sex: the Novels of Chester Himes," *Native Sons*, copyright © 1968 by Edward Margolies.

Listener. TONY ASPLER, "Looking Tough," May 6, 1976, copyright © 1976 by the British Broadcasting Corporation.

Little, Brown. ALFRED KAZIN, "Cassandras," "The Decline of War: Mailer to Vonnegut," *Bright Book of Life*, copyright © 1971, 1973 by Alfred Kazin. GORE VIDAL, "Norman Mailer: The Angels Are White," *Rocking the Boat*, copyright © 1960, 1962 by Gore Vidal.

Liveright. CLARENCE MAJOR, Interview by John O'Brien, *Interviews with Black Writers*, ed. John O'Brien, copyright © 1973 by Liveright.

Livermore Publishing Corporation. STANLEY KAUFFMANN, "Introduction" to *The Art of the Moving Picture* by Vachel Lindsay, copyright © 1970 by Livermore Publishing Corporation.

London Magazine. JOHN BAYLEY, "Robert Lowell: The Poetry of Cancellation," Vol. 6, No. 3 (June 1966), copyright © 1966.

Louisiana State University Press. JAMES O. YOUNG, "Black Reality and Beyond," *Black Writers of the Thirties*, copyright © 1973 by Louisiana State University Press.

Lovecraft Studies. DONALD R. BURLESON, "The Mythic Hero Archetype in 'The Dunwich Horror,'" Vol. 1, No. 4 (Spring 1981), copyright © 1981 by Necronomicon Press. STEVEN J. MARICONDA, "Notes on the Prose Realism of H. P. Lovecraft," Vol. 4, No. 1 (Spring 1985), copyright © 1985 by Necronomicon Press.

Robert M. McBride & Co. JAMES BRANCH CABELL, "Goblins in Winnemac," *Some of Us: An Essay in Epitaphs*, copyright © 1930 by James Branch Cabell.

McClelland and Stewart. WYNNE FRANCIS, "Preface" to *Selected Poems* by Irving Layton, copyright © 1959 by Wynne Francis. ALEC LUCAS, "Type and Myth," *Hugh MacLennan*, copyright © 1970 by McClelland and Stewart. ELI MANDEL, "Foreword" to *The Unwavering Eye* by Irving Layton, copyright © 1975 by Eli Mandel. GEORGE WOODCOCK, "A Nation's Odyssey: The Novels of Hugh MacLennan," *Odysseus Returning: Essays on Canadian Writers and Writing*, copyright © 1970 by George Woodcock.

McGraw-Hill. ALLEN GINSBERG, "Kerouac," *Allen Verbatim*, copyright © 1974 by Allen Ginsberg.

Macmillan & Co. Ltd. C. N. MANLOVE, "Conservatism in Fantasy: Ursula K. Le Guin," *The Impulse of Fantasy Literature*, copyright © 1983 by C. N. Manlove.

Macmillan of Canada. HUGH MACLENNAN, "Prologue: The Writer and His Audience," *The Other Side of Hugh MacLennan: Selected Essays Old and New*, copyright © 1978 by Hugh MacLennan.

Minnesota Review. PAUL BUHLE, "Dystopia as Utopia: Howard Phillips Lovecraft and the Unknown Content of American Horror Literature," Spring 1976, copyright © 1976 by *The Minnesota Review*.

Modern Drama. JACK V. BARBERA, "Ethical Perversity in America: Some Observations on David Mamet's *American Buffalo*," Vol. 24, No. 3 (Sept. 1981), copyright © 1981 by the University of Toronto, Graduate Centre for Study of Drama.

Modern Fiction Studies. TERENCE MARTIN, "*One Flew Over the Cuckoo's Nest* and the High Cost of Living," Vol. 19, No. 1 (Spring 1973), copyright © 1973 by the Purdue Research Foundation. S. JAY WALKER, "Zora Neale Hurston's *Their Eyes Were Watching God*: Black Novel of Sexism," Vol. 20, No. 4 (Winter 1974–75), copyright © 1975 by the Purdue Research Foundation.

Modern Poetry Studies. CHARLES ALTIERI, "Poetry as Resurrection: John Logan's Structure of Metaphysical Solace," Vol. 3, No. 2 (Autumn 1973), copyright © 1973.

Mosaic. DORTHY FARMILOE, "Hugh MacLennan and the Canadian Myth," Vol. 2, No. 3 (Spring 1969), copyright © 1969.

Ms. ALICE WALKER, "In Search of Zora Neale Hurston," March 1975, copyright © 1975 by Ms. Magazine Corporation.

Nation. HAYDEN CARRUTH, "Melancholy Monument," July 7, 1969, copyright © 1969. HAROLD CLURMAN, "Theater," May 19, 1979, copyright © 1979. CLIFTON FADIMAN, "Ring Lardner and the Triangle of Hate," March 22, 1963, copyright © 1963. HANS

KONING, "Missions Impossible," Sept. 15, 1979, copyright © 1979. JOSEPH WOOD KRUTCH, "Antichrist and the Five Apostles," Dec. 21, 1921, copyright © 1921. JOSEPH WOOD KRUTCH, "Cold Cuts," Nov. 9, 1932, copyright © 1932. LUDWIG LEWISOHN, "Inferno," Feb. 27, 1924, copyright © 1924. GENE LYONS, "Something New in Theme Parks," Sept. 26, 1981, copyright © 1981. HELEN NEVILLE, "Craftsmanship," Nov. 14, 1936, copyright © 1936. HENRY TAYLOR, "Singing to Spite This Hunger," Feb. 2, 1970, copyright © 1970. DIANA TRILLING, "Fiction in Review," April 21, 1945, copyright © 1945.

Neale Publishing Co. AMBROSE BIERCE, "Edwin Markham's Poems," *Collected Works of Ambrose Bierce*, Volume 11, copyright © 1911 by Neale Publishing Co.

Necronomicon Press. SONIA H. DAVIS, *The Private Life of H. P. Lovecraft*, copyright © 1985 by Necronomicon Press.

Negro Digest. RON WELBURN, Vol. 19, No. 2 (Dec. 1969), copyright © 1969 by the Johnson Publishing Co., Inc.

Thomas Nelson. HORACE GREGORY, "Preface as Epilogue," *Amy Lowell: Portrait of the Poet in Her Time*, copyright © 1958.

Nelson-Hall. WAYNE COGELL, "The Absurdity of Sartre's Ontology: A Response by Ursula K. Le Guin," *Philosophers Look at Science Fiction*, ed. Nicholas D. Smith, copyright © 1982 by Nicholas D. Smith.

Peter Nevill. PETER PENZOLDT, "The Pure Tale of Horror," *The Supernatural in Fiction*, copyright © 1952 by Peter Penzoldt.

New Directions Publishing Corporation. HUGH KENNER, "Introduction" to *The Selected Poems of Irving Layton*, copyright © 1977 by New Directions Publishing Corporation. DENISE LEVERTOV, "Some Notes on Organic Form," "Origins of a Poem," *The Poet in the World*, copyright © 1965, 1968, 1973 by Denise Levertov. KENNETH REXROTH, "Poets, Old and New," *Assays*, copyright © 1961 by Kenneth Rexroth.

New England Quarterly. ALLEN GUTTMANN, Vol. 35, No. 1 (March 1962), copyright © 1962.

New Leader. JOSHUA GILDER, "Existential Cowboy Gone Astray," Nov. 19, 1979, copyright © 1979.

New Masses. RICHARD WRIGHT, "Between Laughter and Tears," Oct. 5, 1937, copyright © 1937 by New Masses Co.

New Republic. JACK BEATTY, Jan. 26, 1980, copyright © 1980 by The New Republic, Inc. JOHN BERRYMAN, "Matter and Manner," Nov. 2, 1953, copyright © 1953 by The New Republic, Inc. RANDOLPH BOURNE, "H. L. Mencken," Nov. 24, 1917, copyright © 1917 by The New Republic, Inc. ROBERT BRUSTEIN, "Show and Tell," May 7, 1984, copyright © 1984 by The New Republic, Inc. HAROLD CLURMAN, "A Good Play," March 13, 1950, copyright © 1950 by The New Republic, Inc. ALISTAIR COOKE, "The World of William March," Dec. 3, 1945, copyright © 1945 by The New Republic, Inc. DORIS GRUMBACH, "Fine Print," Nov. 9, 1974, copyright © 1974 by The New Republic, Inc. STANLEY EDGAR HYMAN, "Alabama Faulkner," Feb. 8, 1943, copyright © 1943 by The New Republic, Inc. JOSEPHINE JACOBSEN, "A Rich Fusion," April 16, 1974, copyright © 1974 by The New Republic, Inc. GERALD W. JOHNSON, "Romance and Mr. Babbitt," Jan, 29, 1951, copyright © 1951 by The New Republic, Inc. STANLEY KAUFFMANN, "Out of the Fires," Oct. 26, 1968, copyright © 1968 by The New Republic, Inc. W. T. LHAMON, JR., May 24, 1975, copyright © 1975 by The New Republic, Inc. WILLIAM MCPHERSON, Aug. 10 & 17, 1974, copyright © 1974 by The New Republic, Inc. WILLIAM H. PRITCHARD, "The Spirits of Albany," Feb. 14, 1983, copyright © 1983 by The New Republic, Inc. ISAAC ROSENFELD, "With the Best Intentions," Dec. 31, 1945, copyright © 1945 by The New Republic, Inc. MARK SCHORER, "The World of Sinclair Lewis," April 6, 1953, copyright © 1953 by The New Republic, Inc. HARVEY SWADOS, "What Is This World?," March 3, 1958, copyright © 1958 by The New Republic, Inc. ANNE TYLER, "Albany Warm-Up," Oct. 15, 1984, copyright © 1984 by The New Republic, Inc. ANNE TYLER, "The Glass of Fashion," Dec. 23, 1981, copyright © 1981 by The New Republic, Inc. REED WHITTEMORE, Aug. 2, 1969, copyright © 1969 by The New Republic, Inc. DOROTHY WICKENDEN, "Love in London," Oct. 8, 1984, copyright © 1984 by The New Republic, Inc. EDMUND WILSON, "H. L. Mencken," June 1, 1921, copyright © 1921 by The New Republic, Inc.

New Statesman. MARGARET DRABBLE, "Family Battles," June 21, 1974, copyright © 1975 by the Statesman & National Publishing Co. V. S. PRITCHETT, "The Beat Generation," Sept. 6, 1958, copyright © 1958 by the Statesman and Nation Publishing Co. JONATHAN RABAN, "Huck Miller and the Widow Millet," Sept. 3, 1971, copyright © 1971 by the Statesman and Nation Publishing Co.

New World Writing. ARTHUR FOFF, "Strangers amid Ruins," Fall-Winter 1958, copyright © 1958 by J. B. Lippincott Co.

New York Review of Books. DENIS DONOGHUE, "The Ordinary Universe," Dec. 7, 1967, copyright © 1967. F. W. DUPEE, "You're Welcome," Vol. 1, No. 2 (1963), copyright © 1963. MARY GORDON, "What Mary Ann Knew," June 14, 1979, copyright © 1979. ROBERT TOWERS, "Violent Places," March 31, 1983, copyright © 1983. MICHAEL WOOD, "Nothing Sacred," April 20, 1978, copyright © 1978.

New York Times Book Review. JOHN W. ALDRIDGE, "The Last James Jones," March 5, 1978, copyright © 1978 by The New York Times Co. JAMES BALDWIN, "Sermons and Blues," March 29, 1959, copyright © 1959 by The New York Times Co. JOSEPH WARREN BEACH, "The Dilemma of a Black Man in a White World," Dec. 2, 1945, copyright © 1945 by The New York Times Co. HAROLD BEAVER, "Snapshots and Artworks," March 18, 1984, copyright © 1984 by The New York Times Co. ROBERT COLES, "Teaching Old Folks an Art," April 10, 1977, copyright © 1977 by The New York Times Co. JOEL CONARROE, "Columnist Bites Newspaper," Sept. 30, 1984, copyright © 1984 by The New York Times Co. GEORGE DAVIS, July 1, 1973, copyright © 1973 by The New York Times Co. NICHOLAS DELBANCO, "In God's Capacious Hand," Oct. 16, 1977, copyright © 1977 by The New York Times Co. BABETTE DEUTSCH, "Waste Land of Harlem," May, 1951, copyright © 1951 by The New York Times Co. ROSE FELD, "A Remarkable First Novel of Lonely Lives," June 16, 1940, copyright © 1940 by The New York Times Co. THOMAS FLEMING, "A City and Its Machine," Jan. 1, 1984, copyright © 1984 by The New York Times Co. JOHN GARDNER, Dec. 23, 1973, copyright © 1973 by The New York Times Co. HENRY LOUIS GATES, JR., "A Negro Way of Saying," April 21, 1985, copyright © 1985 by The New York Times Co. JANET HARRIS, Feb. 11, 1973, copyright © 1973 by The New York Times Co. IHAB HASSAN, "Three Hermits on a Hill," Sept. 23, 1962, copyright © 1962 by The New York Times Co. JOHN HOLLANDER, Feb. 13, 1972, copyright © 1972 by The New York Times Co. JOHN IRVING, Interview by Thomas Williams, April 23, 1978, copyright © 1978 by The New York Times Co. JAMES KELLY, "The Portrait of a Coldly Evil Child," April 11, 1954, copyright © 1954 by The New York Times Co. STEPHEN KOCH, "The New York School of Poets: The Serious at Play," Feb. 11, 1968, copyright © 1968 by The New York Times Co. ROBERT LOWELL, "With Wild Dogmatism," Oct. 7, 1951, copyright © 1951 by The New York Times Co. FRED T. MARSH, "The Fine Tales of William March," Feb. 17, 1935, copyright © 1935 by The New York Times Co. JOYCE CAROL OATES, "Honey and Bill and Dan and Celia," April 22, 1979, copyright © 1979 by The New York Times Co. ALICIA OSTRIKER, "Memory and Attachment," Aug. 8, 1982, copyright © 1982 by The New York Times Co. DARRYL PINCKNEY, "Opinions and Poems," Aug. 9, 1981, copyright © 1981 by The New York Times Co. V. S. PRITCHETT, "The Man with the Perfect Ear," Aug. 21, 1977, copyright © 1977 by The New York Times Co. GEORGE STADE, "Life on the Lam," Jan. 23, 1983, copyright © 1983 by The New York Times Co. HELEN VENDLER, April 6, 1975, copyright © 1975 by The New York Times Co. HELEN VENDLER, "False Poets and Real Poets," Sept. 7, 1975, copyright © 1975 by The New York Times Co. PAUL ZWEIG, Oct. 17, 1971, copyright © 1971 by The New York Times Co.

New York University Press. WILLIAM MILES, "Isolation in Langston Hughes' *Soul Gone Home*," *Five Black Writers*, ed. Donald B. Gibson, copyright © 1970 by New York University Press.

New Yorker. BRENDAN GILL, "The Past Regained," Aug. 21, 1971, copyright © 1971. GEORGE S. KAUFMAN, "Annoy Kaufman, Jr.," Dec. 21, 1957, copyright © 1957. KENNETH TYNAN, "Roses and Thorns," Dec. 12, 1959, copyright © 1959. JOHN UPDIKE, "Bombs Made out of Leftovers," Sept. 25, 1971, copyright © 1971. EDMUND WILSON, "Salute to an Old Landmark: Sinclair

Lewis," Oct. 13, 1945, copyright © 1945. ALEXANDER WOOLL-COTT, "The Deep, Tangled Kaufman," May 18, 1929, copyright © 1929. UNSIGNED, "Talk of the Town," April 4, 1953, copyright © 1953.

Ohio University Press. R. BOEREM, "A Lovecraftian Nightmare," Dirk W. Mosig, "H. P. Lovecraft: Myth-Maker," *H. P. Lovecraft: Four Decades of Criticism*, ed. S. T. Joshi, copyright © 1976 by Dirk W. Mosig, copyright © 1980 by Ohio University Press.

Opportunity. COUNTEE CULLEN, "Poet on Poet," Feb. 1926, copyright © 1926.

Oregon State University. RICHARD ASTRO, "Preface" to *The Fiction of Bernard Malamud*, ed. Richard Astro and Jackson Benson, copyright © 1977.

Oxford University Press. RICHARD BRIDGMAN, "Copies and Misfires," *The Colloquial Style in America*, copyright © 1966 by Richard Bridgman.

Paris Review. MARY MCCARTHY, Interview by Elisabeth Niebuhr, No. 27 (Winter-Spring 1962), copyright © 1962 by *The Paris Review*. WILLIAM MEREDITH, Interview by Edward Hirsch, No. 95 (Spring 1985), copyright © 1985 by *The Paris Review*.

Parnassus: Poetry in Review. RICHARD LAVENSTEIN, "A Man with a Small Song," Fall-Winter 1975, copyright © 1975. STEPHEN YESNER, "Bringing It Home," Fall-Winter 1977, copyright © 1977.

Partisan Review. NORMAN PODHORETZ, "The Know-Nothing Bohemians," Vol. 25, No. 2 (Spring 1958), copyright © 1958. PHILIP STEVICK, "Voice and Vision," Vol. 41, No. 2 (1974), copyright © 1974.

Poetry. HAYDEN CARRUTH, Nov. 1958, copyright © 1958. TURNER CASSITY, Dec. 1963, copyright © 1963. TOM CLARK, "A Poetry Chronicle," May 1967, copyright © 1967. WILLIAM DICKEY, "Revelations and Homilies," Nov. 1961, copyright © 1961. WILLIAM HARMON, "Kumin and Kinnell (and Kilmer)," April 1983, copyright © 1983. THEODORE HOLMES, "Wit, Nature, and the Human Concern," Aug. 1962, copyright © 1962. RICHARD HOWARD, July 1965, copyright © 1965. RICHARD HOWARD, "Pursuits and Followings," Aug. 1972, copyright © 1972. HUGH KENNER, "Beast-Type Sockdolagers," Sept. 1959, copyright © 1959. JASCHA KESSLER, "Trial and Error," Feb. 1973, copyright © 1973. FRANK MCSHANE, "A Range of Six," Aug. 1971, copyright © 1971. HARRIET MONROE, "A Decorative Colorist," Jan. 1917, copyright © 1917. JOSEPH PARISI, "Coming to Terms," Sept. 1974, copyright © 1974. DELMORE SCHWARTZ, "The Enigma of Robinson Jeffers," Oct. 1939, copyright © 1939. DONALD SHEEHAN, "Numquam Minus Solus Quam Solus," Jan. 1971, copyright © 1971. YVOR WINTERS, "Robinson Jeffers," Feb. 1930, copyright © 1930.

Princeton University Library Chronicle. RICHARD M. LUDWIG, "The Muted Lyrics of William Meredith," Vol. 25, No. 1 (Autumn 1963), copyright © 1963 by Princeton University Library.

Princeton University Press. DEMING BROWN, "Jack London and O. Henry," *Soviet Attitudes toward American Writing*, copyright © 1962 by Princeton University Press. IHAB HASSAN, "Carson McCullers: The Aesthetics of Love and Pain," "Contemporary Scenes: The Victim with a Thousand Faces," "The Qualified Encounter: Three Novels by Beuchner, Malamud, and Ellison," *Radical Innocence*, copyright © 1961 by Princeton University Press.

G. P. Putnam's Sons. ROBERT BONE, "Claude McKay," *Down Home: A History of Afro-American Short Fiction*, copyright © 1975 by Robert Bone.

Queen's Quarterly. GEORGE GREENE, "A Tunnel from Persepolis: The Legacy of John P. Marquand," Vol. 73, No. 3 (Autumn 1966), copyright © 1966. ROGER LESLIE HYMAN, "Hugh MacLennan: His Art, His Society and His Critics," Vol. 82, No. 4 (Winter 1975), copyright © 1975. HUGO MCPHERSON, "The Novels of Hugh MacLennan," Vol. 60, No. 2 (Summer 1953), copyright © 1953.

Random House. ROBINSON JEFFERS, "Introduction" to *Roan Stallion, Tamar, and Other Poems*, copyright © 1935 by Robinson Jeffers. JOHN P. MARQUAND, "Introduction" to *The Late George Apley*, copyright © 1940 by The Modern Library, Inc. RALPH J. MILLS, JR., "Denise Levertov," *Contemporary American Poetry*, copyright © 1965 by Random House. WILLIAM CARLOS WILLIAMS, "In a Mood of Tragedy: *The Mills of the Kavanaughs*," *Selected Essays*,

copyright © 1951, 1954 by William Carlos Williams. JONATHAN YARDLEY, *Ring: A Biography of Ring Lardner*, copyright © 1977 by Jonathan Yardley.

Reporter. GEORGE STEINER, "The Lyre and the Pen," Feb. 16, 1961, copyright © 1961.

Reynal & Hitchcock. ALFRED KAZIN, "The New Realism: Sherwood Anderson and Sinclair Lewis," "The Postwar Scene," *On Native Grounds*, copyright © 1942 by Alfred Kazin.

Rhode Island History. BARTON L. ST. ARMAND, "Facts in the Case of H. P. Lovecraft," Vol. 31, No. 1 (Feb. 1972), copyright © 1972.

Salmagundi. ROBERT LOWELL, "After Enjoying Six or Seven Essays on Me," Spring 1977, copyright © 1977. JEROME MAZZARO, "Lowell after *For the Union Dead*," 1966–67, copyright © 1967. JEROME MAZZARO, "Circumscriptions: The Poetry of David Ignatow," Spring-Summer 1973, copyright © 1973.

Saturday Evening Post. STANLEY EDGAR HYMAN, "Shirley Jackson: 1919–1965," Dec. 18, 1965, copyright © 1965 by The Curtis Publishing Co.

Saturday Review. NED CALMER, "The Real Enemy Is Hard to Find," Feb. 24, 1951, copyright © 1951 by *Saturday Review*. MAXWELL GEISMAR, "Annals of Magic," Oct. 31, 1959, copyright © 1959 by *Saturday Review*. ALLEN GINSBERG, "The Great Rememberer," Dec. 2, 1972, copyright © 1972 by ALLEN GINSBERG. Doris Grumbach, "Fine Print: Perfect Pitch in Albany," April 29, 1978, copyright © 1978 by *Saturday Review*. GRANVILLE HICKS, "A Quiet Sort of Magic," March 18, 1961, copyright © 1961 by *Saturday Review*. EDWARD MARGOLIES, "America's Dark Pessimism," March 22, 1969, copyright © 1969 by *Saturday Review*. RICHARD MCLAUGHLIN, "Midwest Family Album, 1912," Sept. 4, 1948, copyright © 1948 by *Saturday Review*. THEODORE PURDY, JR., "American Comedy," Sept. 15, 1934, copyright © 1934 by *Saturday Review of Literature*. JOSEPH SLATKIN, "Wizards and New-Born Gods," Jan. 7, 1961, copyright © 1961 by *Saturday Review*. HARRISON SMITH, "When Vermont Thaws in the South Seas," Oct. 4, 1952, copyright © 1952 by *Saturday Review*. VIRGINIA WOOLF, "American Fiction," Aug. 1, 1925, copyright © 1925 by *Saturday Review of Literature*.

Science-Fiction Studies. JOHN FEKETE, "*The Dispossessed* and *Triton*: Act and System in Utopian Science Fiction," No. 18 (July 1979), copyright © 1979.

Charles Scribner's Sons. GEORGE SANTAYANA, Letter to John Hall Wheelock (Jan. 30, 1951), *The Letters of George Santayana*, ed. Daniel Cory, copyright © 1955 by Daniel Cory.

Secker & Warburg. DAVID BULWER LUTYENS, "Archibald MacLeish: Poet of Philosophical Rationalism," *The Creative Encounter*, copyright © 1960.

Sewanee Review. EDWARD A. MARTIN, "A Puritan's Satanic Flight: Don Marquis, Archy, and Anarchy," Vol. 83, No. 4 (Fall 1975), copyright © 1975. ARTHUR MIZENER, "The Poetry of Archibald MacLeish," Vol. 45, No. 4 (Oct.–Dec. 1938), copyright © 1938. LOUIS D. RUBIN, "H. L. Mencken and the National Letters," Vol. 74, No. 3 (July–Sept. 1966), copyright © 1966.

Shenandoah, M. L. ROSENTHAL, "Poetic Power—Free the Swan!," Vol. 24, No. 1 (Fall 1972), copyright © 1972.

Simon & Schuster. FRANKLIN PIERCE ADAMS, *The Diary of Our Own Samuel Pepys*, copyright © 1935. FRAZIER HUNT, "London Years," *One American and His Attempt at Education*, copyright © 1938 by Frazier Hunt. WALTER KERR, "As We Were: Conventional Theater," *The Theater in Spite of Itself*, copyright © 1963 by Walter Kerr.

South Atlantic Quarterly. FRANK DURHAM, "God and No God in *The Hearts Is a Lonely Hunter*," Vol. 56, No. 4 (Fall 1957), copyright © 1957. J. MEREDITH NEIL, "1955: The Beginnings of Our Own Times," Vol. 73, No. 4 (Autumn 1974), copyright © 1974.

Southern Illinois University Press. IRVING MALIN, "Self-Love," *New American Gothic*, copyright © 1962 by Southern Illinois University Press. SANFORD PINSKER, "The Schlemiel as Bungler: Bernard Malamud's Ironic Heroes," *The Schlemiel as Metaphor*, copyright © 1971 by Southern Illinois University Press. DARWIN T. TURNER, "Zora Neale Hurston: The Wandering Minstrel," *In a Minor Chord*, copyright © 1971 by Southern Illinois University Press. EDMOND L. VOLPE, "James Jones—Norman Mailer," *Contemporary American Novelists*, copyright © 1964 by Southern Illinois University Press.

Southern Review. KENNETH FIELDS, "The Poetry of Mina Loy," Vol. 3, No. 3 (Summer 1967), copyright © 1967.

Southwest Review. JOHN T. FLANAGAN, "The Spoon River Poet," Vol. 38, No. 3 (Summer 1953), copyright © 1953 by Southern Methodist University Press. NEVA HERRINGTON, "The Language of the Tribe: William Meredith's Poetry," Vol. 67, No. 1 (Winter 1982), copyright © 1982 by Southern Methodist University Press. RUDOLPH L. NELSON, "Edge of the Transcendent: The Poetry of Levertov and Duncan," Vol. 54, No. 2 (Spring 1969), copyright © 1969 by Southern Methodist University Press.

Spectator. PETER ACKROYD, "Mawkish Moments," Aug. 24, 1974, copyright © 1974. PETER ACKROYD, "Prurience," Feb. 11, 1978, copyright © 1978. BARRY COLE, "Short-Handed," Aug. 15, 1970, copyright © 1970. L. A. G. STRONG, "Fiction," Oct. 5, 1951, copyright © 1951.

Stanford University. BARBARA UNGAR, "Imagism, Amy Lowell and the Haiku," *Haiku in English*, copyright © 1978 by the Board of Trustees of Leland Stanford Junior University.

Stein & Day. LESLIE FIEDLER, "Malamud: The Commonplace as Absurd," *No! in Thunder: Essays on Myth and Literature*, copyright © 1960, 1971 by Leslie A. Fiedler.

Studies in Black Literature. LLOYD W. BROWN, "The Portrait of the Artist as a Black American in the Poetry of Langston Hughes," Winter 1974, copyright © 1974.

Studies in Short Fiction. JAY L. HALIO, "John Knowles's Short Novels," Vol. 1, No. 2 (Winter 1964), copyright © 1964. JOHN G. PARKS, "The Possibility of Evil: A Key to Shirley Jackson's Fiction," Vol. 15, No. 3 (Summer 1978), copyright © 1978. RONALD WEBER, "Narrative Methods in *A Separate Peace*," Vol. 3, No. 1 (Fall 1965), copyright © 1965.

Theater. DAVID MAMET, "First Principles," Vol. 12, No. 3 (Summer-Fall 1981), copyright © 1981 by Theater.

Times Literary Supplement. VALENTINE CUNNINGHAM, "Theoretical Thuggery," Aug. 20, 1976, copyright © 1976. PHILIP FRENCH, Oct. 5, 1985, copyright © 1984.

Frederick Ungar Publishing Co. SHELDON J. HERSHINOW, "Alienation and Aggression: *The Fixer*," *Bernard Malamud*, copyright © 1980 by Sheldon J. Hershinow.

University of California Press. CESARE PAVESE, "An American Novelist, Sinclair Lewis," "The *Spoon River Anthology*," *American Literature: Essays and Opinions*, tr. Edwin Fussell, copyright © 1970 by the Regends of the University of California. STEPHEN YENSER, "Introduction: Prospects," *Circle to Circle: The Poetry of Robert Lowell*, copyright © 1975 by the Regents of the University of California.

University of Chicago Press. CHESTER E. EISINGER, "The New Fiction," *Fiction of the Forties*, copyright © 1963 by Chester E. Eisinger.

University of Georgia Press. WILLIAM H. NOLTE, "Coda," *Rock and Hawk: Robinson Jeffers and the Romantic Agony*, copyright © 1978 by the University of Georgia Press.

University of Illinois Press. ROBERT HEMENWAY, "Introduction" to *Dust Tracks on a Road* by Zora Neale Hurston, copyright © 1984 by the Board of Trustees of the University of Illinois. WENDY MARTIN, "The Satire and Moral Vision of Mary McCarthy," *Comic Relief: Humor in Contemporary American Literature*, copyright © 1978 by the Board of Trustees of the University of Illinois. JEROME MAZZARO, "Between Two Worlds: Randall Jarrell," *Postmodern American Poetry*, copyright © 1980 by the Board of Trustees of the University of Illinois. RALPH J. MILLS, JR., "The True and Earthly Prayer: Philip Levine's Poetry," *Cry of the Human*, copyright © 1975 by the Board of Trustees of the University of Illinois. CARY NELSON, "Ecclesiastical Whitman: Galway Kinnell's *The Book of Nightmares*," *Our Last First Poets*, copyright © 1981 by the Board of Trustees of the University of Illinois.

University of Michigan Press. GALWAY KINNELL, Interview by A. Poulin, Jr., and Stan Sanvel Rubin, *Walking Down the Stairs: Selections from Interviews*, copyright © 1978 by The University of Michigan. PHILIP LEVINE, Interview by Calvin Bedient, *Don't Ask*, copyright © 1981 by The University of Michigan.

University of Missouri Press. CHARLES MOLESWORTH, " 'The Rank Flavor of Blood': The Poetry of Galway Kinnell," *The Fierce Embrace*, copyright © 1979 by the Curators of the University of Missouri. M. GILBERT PORTER, "The Ringing of Hank's Bell:

Standing Tall in Wakonda," *The Art of Grit: Ken Kesey's Fiction*, copyright © 1982 by the Curators of the University of Missouri.

University of North Carolina Press. CLEANTH BROOKS, "Frost, MacLeish, and Auden," *Modern Poetry and the Tradition*, copyright © 1939.

University of Oklahoma Press. STANLEY K. COFFMAN, JR., "Amygism," *Imagism: A Chapter for the History of Modern Poetry*, copyright © 1951 by the University of Oklahoma Press.

University of Pennsylvania Press. ROBERT H. WALKER, "Progress and Protest," *The Poet and the Gilded Age*, copyright © 1963 by The Trustees of the University of Pennsylvania.

University of Texas (Humanities Research Center). PADRAIC COLUM, "Preface" to *The Harmony of Deeper Music* by Edgar Lee Masters, ed. Frank N. Robinson, copyright © 1976 by Frank N. Robinson.

University of Toronto Press. ROBERTSON DAVIES, "Stephen Leacock," *Our Living Tradition: Seven Canadians*, ed. Claude T. Bissell, copyright © 1957 by the University of Toronto Press.

University of Washington Book Store. LOUIS ADAMIC, *Robinson Jeffers: A Portrait*, copyright © 1929 by Glenn Hughes.

University of Wisconsin Press. CHARLES N. WATSON, JR., "Revolution and Romance: *The Iron Heel*," *The Novels of Jack London: A Reappraisal*, copyright © 1983 by the Board of Regents of the University of Wisconsin System.

Vanderbilt University Press. THOMAS REED WEST, "Sinclair Lewis: In Affirmation of Main Street," *Flesh of Steel*, copyright © 1977 by Vanderbilt University Press.

Viking Penguin Inc. SHIRLEY JACKSON, "Biography of a Story," *Come Along with Me*, ed. Stanley Edgar Hyman, copyright © 1960 by Shirley Jackson, copyright © 1968 by Stanley Edgar Hyman.

Virginia Quarterly Review. HOWARD MUMFORD JONES, "Mr. Lewis's America," Vol. 7, No. 3 (July 1931), copyright © 1931.

Voyages. MARVIN BELL, "Logan's Teaching," Spring 1971-Spring 1972, copyright © 1972. ROBERT BLY, "John Logan's Field of Force," Spring 1971-Spring 1972, copyright © 1972.

Ward Ritchie Press. LAWRENCE CLARK POWELL, "*Laughing Boy*: Oliver La Farge," *Southwest Classics*, copyright © 1974 by Lawrence Clark Powell.

Washington Post Book World. RICHARD POIRIER, "Crossing Poetic Boundaries," Dec. 19, 1978, copyright © 1978 by The Washington Post. TOM WOLFE, "Son of *Crime and Punishment*, or, How to Go Eight Fast Rounds with the Heavyweight Champ—and Lose," March 14, 1965, copyright © 1965 by The Washington Post.

Western Humanities Review. ERNEST EARNEST, "Spoon River Revisited," Vol. 21, No. 1 (Winter 1967), copyright © 1967.

Western Illinois University. HERB RUSSELL, "After *Spoon River*: Masters' Poetic Development 1916–1919," *The Vision of This Land*, ed. John E. Hallwas and Dennis J. Reader, copyright © 1976 by Western Illinois University.

Jonathan Williams. IRVING LAYTON, "Foreword" to *A Red Carpet for the Sun*, copyright © 1959 by Irving Layton.

World Publishing Co. MARCUS KLEIN, "The Sadness of Goodness," *After Alienation: American Novels in Mid-Century*, copyright © 1962 by Marcus Klein.

Yale Review. DAVID J. GORDON, "Some Recent Novels: Styles of Martyrdom," Autumn 1968, copyright © 1968 by Yale University Press. THOM GUNN, "Outside Faction," June 1961, copyright © 1961 by Yale University Press. THOM GUNN, "Things, Voices, Minds," Sept. 1962, copyright © 1962 by Yale University Press. THOM GUNN, "Excellence and Variety," Sept. 1959, copyright © 1959 by Yale University Press. RANDALL JARRELL, Sept. 1955, copyright © 1955 by Yale University Press. LAURENCE LIEBERMAN, June 1968, copyright © 1968 by Yale University Press. J. D. MCCLATCHEY, Spring 1975, copyright © 1975 by Yale University Press. EDITH WHARTON, "The Great American Novel," July 1927, copyright © 1927 by Yale University Press.

Yale University Press. W. H. AUDEN, "Foreword" to *An Armada of Thirty Whales* by Daniel G. Hoffman, copyright © 1954 by Daniel G. Hoffman. W. H. AUDEN, "Foreword" to *A Crackling of Thorns* by John Hollander, copyright © 1958. ROBERT BONE, "Harlem Renaissance," "The Contemporary Negro Novel," "Aspects of the Rural Past," *The Negro Novel in America*, copyright © 1958 by Yale University. RAYMOND M. OLDERMAN, "The Grail Knight Arrives," *Beyond the Waste Land*, copyright © 1972 by Yale University.